CW00970443

The

~~English~~
Literature

Dinah Birch is Professor of English Literature, University of Liverpool. She has published widely on nineteenth-century literature, and has edited novels by Anthony Trollope, George Eliot, and Elizabeth Gaskell. Her books include *Ruskin's Myths* (1988), *Ruskin on Turner* (1990), and *Our Victorian Education* (2007).

Katy Hooper is Special Collections Librarian at the University of Liverpool Library and Assistant Editor for *The Oxford Companion to English Literature* Seventh Edition.

Margaret Drabble was born in Sheffield and educated at The Mount School, York, and Newnham College, Cambridge. Her numerous works include the novels *Jerusalem the Golden*, *The Needle's Eye*, *The Middle Ground*, and the trilogy of novels *The Radiant Way*, *A Natural Curiosity*, and *The Gates of Ivory*. She is married to the biographer Michael Holroyd and lives in London.

((( ))) SEE WEB LINKS

Many entries in this dictionary have recommended web links. When you see the above symbol at the end of an entry go to the dictionary's web page at www.oup.com/uk/reference/resources/englishliterature, click on **Web links** in the Resources section and locate the entry in the alphabetical list, then click straight through to the relevant websites.

Oxford Paperback Reference

The most authoritative and up-to-date reference books for both students and the general reader.

Accounting
Animal Behaviour
Archaeology
Architecture and Landscape Architecture
Art and Artists
Art Terms
Arthurian Literature and Legend
Astronomy
Battles
Bible
Biology
Biomedicine
British History
British Place-Names
Business and Management
Card Games
Chemistry
Christian Church
Classical Literature
Classical World
Computing
Construction, Surveying, and Civil Engineering
Contemporary World History
Cosmology
Countries of the World
Critical Theory
Dance
Dentistry
Earth Sciences
Ecology
Economics
Education
Encyclopedia
English Etymology
English Grammar
English Literature
English Surnames
Environment and Conservation
Euphemisms
Everyday Grammar
Film Studies*
Finance and Banking
First Names
Food and Nutrition
Foreign Words and Phrases
Forensic Science
Geography
Hinduism
Humorous Quotations
Idioms
Irish History
Islam

Kings and Queens of Britain
Law
Law Enforcement
Linguistics
Literary Terms
London Place-Names
Mathematics
Marketing
Mechanical Engineering*
Media and Communication
Medical
Medicinal Drugs
Modern and Contemporary Art
Modern Quotations
Modern Slang
Music
Musical Terms
Nursing
Opera Characters
Philosophy
Physics
Plant Sciences
Plays
Pocket Fowler's Modern English Usage
Political Quotations
Politics
Popes
Proverbs
Psychology
Quotations
Quotations by Subject
Rhymes
Rhyming Slang
Saints
Science
Scientific Quotations
Scottish History
Shakespeare
Slang
Social Work and Social Care*
Sociology
Sports Studies
Statistics
Superstitions
Synonyms and Antonyms
Theatre & Performance
Weather
Weights, Measures, and Units
World History
Word Origins
Zoology

forthcoming

Many of these titles are also available online at www.Oxfordreference.com

The Concise Oxford Companion to
English
Literature

FOURTH EDITION

Edited by DINAH BIRCH
and KATY HOOPER

Previous editions edited by
Margaret Drabble and Jenny Stringer

OXFORD
UNIVERSITY PRESS

OXFORD
UNIVERSITY PRESS

Great Clarendon Street, Oxford, OX2 6DP,
United Kingdom

Oxford University Press is a department of the University of Oxford.
It furthers the University's objective of excellence in research, scholarship,
and education by publishing worldwide. Oxford is a registered trade mark of
Oxford University Press in the UK and in certain other countries

© Margaret Drabble and Oxford University Press 2012

The moral rights of the author have been asserted

First issued as an Oxford University Press Paperback 1990
Second edition 2003
Third edition 2007
Fourth edition 2012

Impression: 1

British Library Cataloguing in Publication Data

Data available

Library of Congress Cataloging in Publication Data

The concise Oxford companion to English literature. – Fourth edition / edited by Dinah Birch and
Katy Hooper.
      pages cm – (Oxford paperback reference)
    Previous editions edited by Margaret Drabble and Jenny Stringer.
    "Based on the seventh edition of The Oxford Companion to English Literature (2009)"–Preface.
    ISBN 978-0-19-960821-8 (pbk.)
1. English literature–Encyclopedias. 2. English literature–Bio-bibliography–Encyclopedias.
3. English-speaking countries–Intellectual life–Encyclopedias. 4. English-speaking countries–In
literature–Encyclopedias. I. Birch, Dinah, editor of compilation. II. Hooper, Katy, editor of
compilation.
    PR19.D732 2012
    820.9'0003–dc23

                          2012004182

Printed in Great Britain on acid-free paper by
Clays Ltd, St Ives plc

ISBN 978-0-19-960821-8

Links to third party websites are provided by Oxford in good faith and
for information only. Oxford disclaims any responsibility for the materials
contained in any third party website referenced in this work.

Contents

Preface

This volume is based on the seventh edition of *The Oxford Companion to English Literature* (2009). Every entry retained has been revised, those on contemporary writers have been updated, and new entries have been added. We hope that this fourth edition of *The Concise Oxford Companion to English Literature* will continue to provide a lively and authoritative source of reference for general readers, scholars, students, and journalists looking for a guide to English literature in its broadest context.

Areas of literature which received enhanced coverage in the parent edition, including children's literature, black British writing, African American literature, postcolonial literature, science fiction, travel writing, and fantasy, have retained their expanded role, and there are new entries on nature writing and ecocriticism. Space has also been found for a small selection of contemporary writers not previously included, for example Lee Child and Nina Raine; for earlier writers in whose work recent research or translations have fostered a new interest, for example Mary Hays and Tove Jansson, and for themes and forms which have newly come to prominence, for example vampires in literature and manga. Internet links have been provided to guide readers to useful supplementary sources of information.

The editors would like to thank all the contributors to *The Oxford Companion to English Literature* whose work reappears in this volume in shortened form, and to acknowledge the thoughtful advice on young adult literature offered by Rowena Birch, Jenny Baines, and Gwen Baines. The editors alone are responsible for any differences between the material in this *Concise Companion* and that in its parent volume.

DINAH BIRCH
KATY HOOPER

Liverpool
October 2011

Contributors

The present volume is based on the work of all those listed below who wrote and revised entries for its parent volume, the seventh edition of the *Oxford Companion to English Literature*; we would like to thank them all by including their names here.

Associate Editors

Linda Anderson, Paul Baines, Chris Baldick, Elleke Boehmer, Mishtooni Bose, David Bradshaw, John Bull, J. B. Bullen, John Carey, Ian Christie, Neil Corcoran, Anthony Cross, Patrick Crotty, Jane E. Everson, Russell Goulbourne, Clive Griffin, Peter Kemp, Francis O'Gorman, Kimberley Reynolds, Isabel Rivers, David Seed, James Simpson, Angela Smith, John Strachan, Stanley Wells, Henry Woudhuysen, Tim Youngs.

Additional Contributors

Kirstie Blair, Roy Bridges, Guy Cuthbertson, Leigh Dale, Tom Earle, Jasper Griffin, Alexandra Harris, Katharine Hodgson, Peter Hunt, Alan Jones, W. Gareth Jones, N. H. Keeble, Jane Moore, David Norton, Peter Parker, Alasdair Pettinger, Deryn Rees-Jones, Nick Rennison, Christopher Rowe, Andy Sawyer, John Sloan, Eric Southworth, Carl Thompson, Sam Trainor, Norman Vance, Edward Welch, Richard White, Anne Whitehead, Michael H. Whitworth, Jane Wright.

Additional help was also gratefully received from: Rosinka Chaudhuri, Philip Davis, Matthew O. Grenby, Nigel Griffin, Daniel Hahn, Andrew Hamer, Faye Hammill, Philip Hensher, Rose Hepworth, Gordon McMullan, Robyn Marsack, Helen Moore, Dominic Moran, Peter Morey, Bernard O'Donoghue, Philip Pullman, Michael Rosen, and Greg Woods.

Abbreviations

anon.	anonymous	introd.	introduction, or introduced by
ASPR	Anglo-Saxon Poetic Records	KJB	King James Bible
b.	born	l., ll.	line, lines
BCP	*Book of Common Prayer*	MA	Master of Arts
Bk	Book	MBE	Member of the Order of the
c.	*circa*, about		British Empire
CB	Companion of the Bath	MC	Military Cross
CBE	Companion of the British Empire	MD	doctor of medicine
cf.	*confer,* compare	ME	Middle English
CH	Companion of Honour	MP	Member of Parliament
ch.	chapter	NT	New Testament
CIA	Central Intelligence Agency	OBE	Officer of the Order of the British
CT	*The Canterbury Tales*		Empire
d.	died	OE	Old English (Anglo-Saxon)
DBE	Dame Commander of the British	*OED*	*Oxford English Dictionary*
	Empire	OM	Order of Merit
DCL	Doctor of Civil Law	OS	Old Style dating, or calendar
DSO	Distinguished Service Order	OT	Old Testament
ed., eds	editor, or edited by, editors	p., pp.	page, pages
edn	edition	perf.	performed
EETS	Early English Text Society	pron.	pronounced
OS	Original Series	Pt	Part
ES	Extra Series	pub.	published
SS	Supplementary Series If no series	RA	Royal Academy of Arts
	is specified, the volume referred	RADA	Royal Academy of Dramatic Art
	to is in the Original Series	repr.	reprinted
enl.	enlarged	rev.	revised
est.	established	Revd	Reverend
FBI	Federal Bureau of Investigation	STS	Scottish Text Society
ff.	and following	*TLS*	*Times Literary Supplement*
fl.	*floruit*, flourished	trans.	translation, or translated by
FRS	Fellow of the Royal Society	vol., vols	volume, volumes
FRSL	Fellow of the Royal Society of		
	Literature		

Note to the Reader

The family names of real people are given in bold capital letters; the headwords of all other entries are in bold upper and lower case: italics for the titles of novels, plays, and other full-length works; roman in quotation marks for individual short stories, poems, essays; ordinary roman type for fictional characters, terms, places, and so on. Entries are in simple letter-by-letter alphabetical order, with spaces, hyphens, and the definite or indefinite article ignored. But where a work written in English has a title in a foreign language, the article conditions its alphabetical ordering: so 'L'Allegro' and 'La Belle Dame Sans Merci' are both listed under L. Names beginning with Mc or M' are ordered as though they were spelled Mac, St as though it were Saint, Dr as Doctor; but Mr and Mrs are ordered as they are spelled. An asterisk before a name, term, or title indicates that there is a separate entry for that subject. Modernized spelling has been preferred, for both titles of works and quotations.

Abbey Theatre, Dublin Opened on 27 December 1904 with a double bill of one-act plays, W. B. *Yeats's *On Baile's Strand* and *Spreading the News* by Lady *Gregory. The theatre rapidly became a focus of the *Irish Revival. In 1903 Annie *Horniman decided to provide a permanent Dublin home for the Irish National Theatre Society, an amateur company led by F. J. and W. G. Fay (which had Yeats for its president) and took over the disused theatre of the Mechanics' Institute in Abbey Street, together with the old city morgue next door, and converted them into the Abbey Theatre. The company, led by the Fays, with Sarah Allgood as principal actress, turned professional in 1906, with Yeats, Lady Gregory, and J. M. *Synge as directors, and in 1907 survived the riots provoked by Synge's The *Playboy of the Western World. The Fays left in 1908. In 1909 Lady Gregory, as patentee, withstood strong preproduction pressure from the lord lieutenant to withdraw *The Shewing-up of Blanco Posnet*, by G. B. Shaw. In 1910 Miss Horniman offered to sell the theatre, and Yeats and Lady Gregory became principal shareholders and managers. The early poetic dramas were gradually replaced by more naturalistic works, by Padraic *Colum, St John *Ervine, Lennox Robinson (1886–1958), Sean *O'Casey, and others. Robinson took over the management from Yeats in 1910 and became director in 1923. There were successful, if contentious, tours of Ireland, Britain, and the USA. After the First World War the Abbey's finances became perilous, although O'Casey's *The Shadow of a Gunman* (1923), *Juno and the Paycock* (1924), and *The Plough and the Stars* (1926) brought some respite. In 1925 the Abbey received a grant from the government of the new Irish Free State, thus becoming the first state-subsidized theatre in the English-speaking world. From the late 1930s more plays were performed in Irish, and actors were required to be bilingual. In 1951 the theatre was burned down, and the company played in the Queen's Theatre until the new Abbey opened in 1966, where the tradition of new writing by Brian *Friel, Tom *Murphy, and others continues to flourish.

Abbot, The A novel by Sir Walter *Scott, published 1820, a sequel to *The *Monastery*. This novel, set around the escape of *Mary Queen of Scots from Loch Leven, largely redeemed the relative failure of its predecessor. It is principally remembered today for the portrait of Mary herself, for attracting tourist trade to Loch Leven, and for being the first sequel novel in English, thus influencing the work of *Balzac, *Trollope, and many other 19th-century novelists.

ABELARD, Peter (1079–1142/4) A native of Brittany, a brilliant disputant and lecturer at the schools of Ste Geneviève and Notre-Dame in Paris, where *John of Salisbury was among his pupils. He was an advocate of rational theological enquiry, and his *Sic et Non* could be regarded as the first text in scholastic theology (*see* SCHOLASTICISM). He was primarily a dialectician rather than a theologian, though his theological views were condemned at Soissons (1121) and at Sens (1140), where he was vigorously opposed by St *Bernard. He became the tutor and then the lover of Héloïse, the niece of Fulbert, a canon of Notre-Dame in whose house he lodged. Their love ended in a tragic separation and a famous correspondence in the 1130s. Héloïse died in 1163 and was buried in Abelard's tomb. Pope's poem *'Eloisa to Abelard' was published in 1717.

ABERCROMBIE, Lascelles (1881–1938) Poet and critic, born in Cheshire. *Interludes and Poems* (1908) was followed by several further volumes of verse, including a collected edition in 1930 and *The Sale of St Thomas* (1931). Abercrombie contributed to *Georgian Poetry*, and to the four issues of *New Numbers* (1914), a journal he produced with his fellow 'Dymock Poets', Rupert *Brooke, John *Drinkwater, and W. W. *Gibson, who lived near the Gloucestershire village of Dymock.

ABISH, Walter (1931–) Novelist, poet, and university teacher, born in Vienna. His family fled the Nazis and Abish moved to the USA in 1957, taking American citizenship in 1960. Although his first publication, *Duel Site* (1970), was a collection of poetry, Abish is best known for his experimental, *postmodernist fiction. His first novel, *Alphabetical Africa* (1971), contains alphabetically incremental words, and *How German Is It* (1980) presents a montage of images of Germany. His more recent publications include *Double Vision* (2004), a memoir.

ABOULELA, Leila (1964–) Novelist who grew up in Khartoum and has lived in Egypt, Jakarta, Dubai, London, and Aberdeen. She focuses on religious identity in her novels *The Translator* (1999) and *Minaret* (2005). *Lyrics Alley* (2010) is set in 1950s Sudan. Her story 'The Museum', from the collection *Coloured Lights* (2001), won the Caine Prize for African writing.

Absalom and Achitophel An allegorical poem by John *Dryden, published 1681. A *mock-biblical satire based on 2 Samuel 13–19, portraying the intrigues of the earl of Shaftesbury and the ambition of the duke of Monmouth (1649–85) to replace James, duke of York (1633–1701; later James II) as Charles II's heir. Among public figures given biblical identities are Monmouth (Absalom), Shaftesbury (Achitophel), the duke of *Buckingham (Zimri), Charles II (David), Titus Oates (Corah), and Slingsby Bethel, sheriff of London (Shimei). In 1682 a second part appeared, mainly written by Nahum *Tate, but with 200 lines by Dryden attacking two literary and political enemies, Thomas *Shadwell as Og and Elkanah *Settle as Doeg.

ABSE, Dannie (Daniel) (1923–) Poet, novelist, playwright, and memoirist. His first volume of poetry, *After Every Green Thing* (1948), was followed by more than a dozen others, including *Poems, Golders Green* (1968) and *Running Late* (2006). *New Selected Poems* appeared in 2009. The title of *White Coat, Purple Coat*, a retrospective compilation from 1983, refers to Abse's dual career as physician (he worked as a chest specialist in London from 1954 to 1989) and poet. The most persistent dualism informing his precise, compassionate, and at times rueful verse concerns the relationship between his Welshness and his Jewishness ('I have two roots, that of Dafydd as well as David'). Abse's novels include *Ash on a Young Man's Sleeve* (1954) and *The Strange Case of Dr Simmonds and Dr Glas* (2002). *Goodbye, Twentieth Century* (2001) is the latest version of his autobiography. *The Presence*, a journal-memoir of his wife Joan,

appeared in 2007. His verse collection *Two for Joy* (2010) celebrates their marriage.

Absentee, The Novel by Maria *Edgeworth, first published 1812 in *Tales of Fashionable Life*. This story of (largely) Irish life was first written as a play, refused by Richard Brinsley *Sheridan, then turned into a novel. A swift, vivacious story, the greater part of which is in conversation, it begins with the extravagant London life of the absentee Irish landlord Lord Clonbrony and his ambitious, worldly wife. Their son Lord Colambre refuses to marry the heiress provided for him. A sensible young man, he gradually finds himself falling in love with his cousin Grace. Incognito, he visits the first of his father's estates, where he witnesses the dismissal, through a letter from Clonbrony, of the humane and honest agent Burke for not extorting sufficient income from the tenants. The next estate is managed by the brothers Garraghty. Here the castle is half ruined, the land is ill farmed, and the tenants are treated with callous indifference; but Clonbrony is satisfied because despite the Garraghtys' embezzlement money is forthcoming. Colambre returns to London and tells his father that he will himself pay off the debts, on condition that the Garraghtys are dismissed and the Clonbrony family returns to live on its Irish estates. After the sorting out of various troubles, he and Grace become engaged, his mother resigns herself to her return, and the family leave London to live in Ireland.

Absurd, Theatre of the A term coined by the theatre critic Martin Esslin to characterize the work of a number of European and American dramatists of the 1950s and early 1960s. As the name suggests, the function of such theatre is to give dramatic expression to the philosophical notion of the 'absurd', a notion that had received widespread diffusion following the publication of Albert *Camus's essay *Le Mythe de Sisyphe* in 1942. To define the world as absurd is to recognize its fundamentally mysterious nature, and this recognition is frequently associated with feelings of loss, purposelessness, and bewilderment. To such feelings, the Theatre of the Absurd gives ample expression, often leaving the observer baffled in the face of disjointed, meaningless, or repetitious dialogues, incomprehensible behaviour, and plots which deny all notion of logical or 'realistic' development. But the recognition of the absurdity of human existence also provided dramatists with a rich source of comedy, well illustrated in two early absurd plays, Eugène

Ionesco's *La Cantatrice chauve*, written in 1948 (*The Bald Prima Donna*, 1958), and Samuel *Beckett's En attendant Godot* (1952; trans. by the author, *Waiting for Godot*, 1954, subtitled 'A Tragicomedy in Two Acts'). The Theatre of the Absurd drew on popular traditions of entertainment, on mime, acrobatics, and circus clowning, and, by seeking to redefine the legitimate concerns of 'serious' theatre, extended the range of post-war drama. Dramatists associated with the Theatre of the Absurd include Arthur Adamov (1908–70), Edward *Albee, Beckett, Camus, Jean Genet, Ionesco (1912–94), Alfred Jarry (1873–1907), Harold *Pinter, and Boris Vian (1920–59). *See also* CRUELTY, THEATRE OF.

ACHEBE, Chinua (1930–) Writer, novelist, and poet, born and educated in Nigeria. At university he was invited to recognize his own people in such novels in English as Conrad's portrayal of the barbaric Africans in *'Heart of Darkness', leading him to a lifelong conviction that cultures must tell their own stories if they are to survive. Achebe published his first novel, *Things Fall Apart*, in 1958. He became the founding editor of the Heinemann African Writers Series in 1962 and of *Okike: An African Journal of New Writing*, in 1971. He was actively involved in politics during the Nigerian Civil War (Biafran War) of 1967–70 and has published widely on cultural, political, and social issues: *Morning Yet on Creation Day* (1975); *The Trouble with Nigeria* (1984); *Hopes and Impediments* (1988); *Home and Exile* (2000). The titles of Achebe's novels, *Things Fall Apart* and *No Longer at Ease*, are quotations, from poems by W. B. *Yeats and T. S. *Eliot. *Things Fall Apart* and *Arrow of God* (1964) imagine a precolonial Igboland which is evolving at its own pace, a complex society with legal, religious, and social structures which are unrecognized by the newly arrived colonial powers. Proverbial language is woven into the books, providing the modern reader with a dynamic rather than archaic insight into traditional life. *No Longer at Ease* (1960) engages with Nigeria's post-independence modernity, as does the coruscating satire of *A Man of the People* (1966). *Anthills of the Savannah* (1987), told in several narrative voices, pursues Achebe's bold, radical, and sardonic analysis of West African politics and corruption but concludes with a scene of female empowerment. Achebe was awarded the Gish Prize in 2010.

ACKER, Kathy (1947–97) Novelist, poet, and performance artist, who worked as a stripper and pornographic film actor. Influenced by William *Burroughs, the poetry of the *Black Mountain School, and the erotic writings of Georges *Bataille, she rejected plot and character in favour of fragments of autobiography, plagiarized material, and disconnected dreamlike sequences of explicit sexuality and violence. *Blood and Guts in High School* (1984) brought her a wide audience, and was followed by *Don Quixote* (1986), *Empire of the Senseless* (1988), and *In Memoriam to Identity* (1990). Later works include *My Mother: Demonology* (1995), *Pussy, King of the Pirates* (1995), and *Eurydice in the Underworld* (1997).

ACKERLEY, J. R. (Joe Randolph) (1896–1967) Gay writer. His play *The Prisoners of War* (1925) was based on his own experience as a prisoner of war. He was literary editor of the *Listener* (1935–59), where he encouraged W. H. *Auden and Stephen *Spender. *Hindoo Holiday* (1932) is based on his experiences as private secretary to the maharaja of Chhatarpurr; *My Dog Tulip* (1956) and his novel *We Think the World of You* (1960) describe his intense relationship with his Alsatian dog. *My Father and Myself* (1968) is an account of his discovery of his father's second family; see also *My Sister and Myself: The Diaries of J. R. Ackerley*, ed. Francis *King (1982). Winners of the Ackerley prize for autobiography, established in 1982, include Edward Blishen (1920–96) and Alan *Bennett.

ACKLAND, Rodney (1908–91) Playwright, born Nathan Ackland; his work was considered insufficiently frivolous by West End managements. He combined Chekhov's revolutionary dramatic technique with the robust native tradition of mixing tragedy with comedy; his best early plays—*Strange Orchestra* (performed 1931; pub. 1932), *After October* (1936)—inhabit a world which recalls the seedy bohemian gentility of the novels of Jean *Rhys. Other plays include *Birthday* (1934), *The Dark River* (pub. 1937; performed 1943), and *The Pink Room* (1952), a tragicomedy set in a seedy London club in 1945, which was revived at the *National Theatre in 1995 as *Absolute Hell* (performed 1987; pub. 1990).

ACKROYD, Peter (1949–) Novelist, biographer, poet, and reviewer, best known as a biographer and novelist whose work explores the continuities between those two genres. His lives of Ezra *Pound (1980), T. S. *Eliot (1984), Charles *Dickens (1990), William *Blake (1995), and Sir Thomas *More (1998) have been widely praised. In *The Last Testament of Oscar Wilde*

(1983) he has *Wilde himself looking back on his life from his last years in Paris. His novels question the nature of time and narrative and the distinction between invention and authenticity. *The Great Fire of London* (1982), based on Dickens's *Little Dorrit*, and later novels including *Hawksmoor* (1985) and *The House of Doctor Dee* (1993) mix historical retelling with present-day narratives. *Chatterton* (1987) displays his preoccupation with impersonation and history. London looms large in Ackroyd's fiction such as *Dan Leno and the Limehouse Golem* (1994), set in 1880 and centred on a series of grisly murders in the East End, and is itself the protagonist of *London: The Biography* (2000) and *Thames: Sacred City* (2007). *The English Ghost* (2010) has a countrywide focus.

ACTON, Sir Harold Mario Mitchell (1904–94) Writer and aesthete, the inspiration for the character of Anthony Blanche in Evelyn *Waugh's *Brideshead Revisited* (1945). He spent much of the 1930s in Beijing, teaching English at the university and translating Chinese poetry and plays. He wrote several volumes of modernist poetry, including *Aquarium* (1923) and *This Chaos* (1930); *The Soul's Gymnasium and Other Stories* (1982); a memoir of Nancy *Mitford (1970); and the autobiography *Memoirs of an Aesthete* (1948) and *More Memoirs of an Aesthete* (1970).

Acts and Monuments of these Latter and Perilous Days, Touching Matters of the Church Popularly known as the *Book of Martyrs*, by John *Foxe. It was first published in Latin at Basle 1559, printed in English in 1563, with woodcut illustrations, and in a revised and expanded form in 1570. This enormous work is a history of the Christian church from the earliest times, with special reference to the sufferings of the Christian martyrs of all ages, but more particularly of the Protestant martyrs of Mary's reign. The book is, in fact, a violent indictment of 'the persecutors of God's truth, commonly called papists'. The author is credulous in his acceptance of stories of martyrdom and partisan in their selection. The work, based on numerous histories and documents as well as oral testimony, is written in a simple, colloquial style and enlivened by vivid dialogues between the persecutors and their victims.

Acts of the Apostles *See* APOSTLES.

Adam *See* EDEN, GARDEN OF.

Adam Bede A novel by George *Eliot, published 1859. The action takes place at the close of the 18th century. Hetty Sorrel, pretty, vain, and self-centred, niece of the genial farmer Martin Poyser, is loved by Adam Bede, the village carpenter, but is deluded by the attentions of the thoughtless young squire, Arthur Donnithorne, and is seduced by him, in spite of Adam's efforts to save her. Arthur breaks off relations with her, and Hetty, broken-hearted, agrees to marry Adam. But before the marriage she discovers she is pregnant, flies from home to seek Arthur, fails to find him, and is arrested and convicted of infanticide. She is saved from the gallows at the last moment, her sentence commuted to transportation through Arthur's intervention. In prison she is comforted by her cousin Dinah Morris, a Methodist preacher, whose strong, serious, and calm nature is contrasted with Hetty's throughout the novel. In the last chapters, Adam discovers that Dinah loves him; his brother Seth, who had long and hopelessly loved Dinah, resigns her with a fine unselfishness.

ADAMOV, Arthur *See* ABSURD, THEATRE OF THE.

ADAMS, Douglas (1952–2001) Scriptwriter and novelist, whose *The Hitchhiker's Guide to the Galaxy* (1978) comedy radio series followed work on *Doctor Who*. Its success, charting the bemused Englishman Arthur Dent's adventures after the earth's demolition, resulted in a second series (1980), stage adaptations, records, computer games, five novels, and a film (2005). Adams's satire on bureaucracy and gift for character made him immensely popular. The unfinished *The Salmon of Doubt* was published in 2002.

ADAMS, Francis (1862–93) Novelist, poet, and journalist who travelled to Australia in 1884 for health reasons. *The Melbournians* (1892) is a novella describing social and political life in Australia and the emerging sense of national identity; *The Australians* (1893) collects articles and essays on similar themes. Adams returned to England in 1890, where he was to commit suicide. His posthumous novel, *A Child of the Age* (1894) is suffused with a *fin-de-siècle* melancholy.

ADAMS, Henry Brooks (1838–1918) American man of letters, and grandson and great-grandson of presidents of the United States. He edited the *North American Review* and published two novels, *Democracy* (1880, anonymously) and *Esther* (1884, as 'Frances Snow Compton'). His autobiography, *The*

Education of Henry Adams (1907), describes the multiplicity of the 20th-century mind.

ADAMS, Richard (1920-) Children's writer and novelist. He is best known for his highly successful fantasy *Watership Down* (1972), an anthropomorphic account of rabbit society.

ADAMS, Sarah Flower (1805-48) Poet, the daughter of a radical journalist, Benjamin Flower (1755–1829), and brought up a *Unitarian. She wrote a historical verse drama about martyrdom, *Vivia Perpetua* (1841), and *hymns, which include 'Nearer, my God, to thee' (*c.*1834)

adaptation Meaning the transfer of any work from one medium to another, became a major commercial activity during the 19th century, with popular novels regularly adapted for the stage as plays and operas. Walter *Scott's romances were dramatized from as early as 1816, when *Guy Mannering* made its debut at Covent Garden, while the novels of Edward *Bulwer-Lytton, *Dickens, and R. L. *Stevenson also enjoyed wide stage success, with the latter's *Dr Jekyll and Mr Hyde* playing on both sides of the Atlantic within months of its publication. These traditional translations have continued, alongside adaptation for cinema, later for radio and television, and most recently for computer games.

Early screen adaptations of popular works often drew on the stage versions, such as R. W. Paul's pioneering *Scrooge, or Marley's Ghost* (1901), and could assume the audience's familiarity with the story. Dickens and Shakespeare were among the most popular early film subjects, while many popular Victorian melodramas enjoyed a new lease of life, such as Ellen Wood's *East Lynne, filmed at least eight times before Theda Bara starred in a Fox version of 1916. Even a work considered the cornerstone of a new language of cinema, D. W. Griffith's controversial epic *The Birth of a Nation* (1915), was adapted from *The Clansman* (1905), a stage play based on a novel by Thomas *Dixon. Both Griffith and later Sergei Eisenstein would credit Dickens as the inspiration for such filmic techniques as the close-up and the flashback.

In the 1920s Oswald Stoll's 'Eminent British Authors' series of adaptations of best-sellers by the likes of Jeffery Farnoll, A. E. W. *Mason, Ethel Dell, and Baroness *Orczy became the mainstay of British cinema, as selling film rights became an important source of writers' income. Paradoxically, synchronized sound after 1929 meant that, while dialogue could be accurately reproduced, films were not necessarily more faithful to their sources. One outstanding British film-maker, Alfred *Hitchcock, understood the need to reinvent works for a different medium, claiming, 'I read a story once and, if I like the basic idea, I just forget all about the book and start to create cinema'. When William Wyler's *Wuthering Heights* (1939) was attacked for omitting half of the original, the critic Dilys Powell regretted a cinema 'still beset by people who bring the book with them'.

Radio, and later television, would offer new scope for much longer adaptations in their serial forms. In 1967, the BBC broadcast Galsworthy's *The *Forsyte Saga* as an unprecedented 26-part series. Fifteen years later, Granada produced an opulent eleven-part adaptation of Evelyn *Waugh's *Brideshead Revisited*, which became a new benchmark for scrupulous and evocative adaptation. Meanwhile, films are regularly 'novelized', adapted for the stage, and re-filmed; while films are now routinely accompanied by computer-game versions. 'Remediation' has been suggested by Jay Boulter and Richard Grusin in their book of the same title (2000) as an essential feature of how new media establish themselves.

ADCOCK, Fleur (1934-) Poet and translator, born in New Zealand, who settled in England in 1963. Her volumes of poetry include *The Eye of the Hurricane* (1964), *High Tide in the Garden* (1971), a translated selection of medieval Latin poems, *The Virgin and the Nightingale* (1983), *Time-Zones* (1991), *Looking Back* (1997), and *Dragon Talk* (2010). *Poems 1960–2000* appeared in 2000. Predominantly ironic and domestic in tone, her work suggests wider horizons through her evocations of travel and of varied landscapes, and in recent years she has written about public events (e.g. the fall of communism in Romania) and environmental issues. She edited the *Oxford Book of Contemporary New Zealand Poetry* (1983) and the *Faber Book of 20th Century Women's Poetry* in 1987.

ADDISON, Joseph (1672–1719) Essayist, educated at Charterhouse with Richard *Steele. In late 1704 he published *The Campaign*, a poem celebrating the victory at the battle of Blenheim. He was appointed under-secretary of state in 1705, and was elected to Parliament in 1708. In 1709 he went to Ireland as chief secretary to Lord Wharton, the lord lieutenant, losing office when the Whigs fell in 1710. He was a prominent member of the *Kit-Cat Club. From 1709 he contributed to Steele's *Tatler and joined him in the production of the *Spectator*. For this he wrote several important literary essays: on *Paradise Lost* (5 January to 3 May 1712), on Imagination (21 June to 3 July 1712) and on traditional ballads. In the tenth issue Addison declared, 'I shall be ambitious to have it said of me, that I have brought philosophy out of closets and libraries, schools and colleges, to dwell in clubs and assemblies, at tea-tables and coffee-houses.' He popularized the ideas of John *Locke, and introduced a polite decorum to essays of social comment. His *neo-classical tragedy *Cato* (1713) was a hit, but his opera *Rosamund* (1707) failed and his comedy *The Drummer* (1715) met with only modest success. He resumed political office in 1714, but retired in 1718. Addison was buried in Westminster Abbey; his works were edited by Thomas *Tickell (1721).

ADEBAYO, Diran (1968–) Novelist, born in London to Nigerian parents. His prize-winning first novel *Some Kind of Black* (1996) interrogates the fashionable use of blackness. *My Once upon a Time* (2000) is an inventive thriller set in London in the near future, fusing myth with metropolitan life.

Adeline Mowbray A cautionary satire by Amelia *Opie, published 1804, based on the unconventional life of Mary *Wollstonecraft, with whom the author was acquainted. Raised by an intellectual mother to think independently, Adeline refuses marriage to Glenmurray (modelled on William *Godwin), living with him as his sexual equal. In consequence, she loses her respectable friends, her stepfather attempts to seduce her, and her formerly enlightened mother disowns her. On her premature deathbed, Adeline is reunited with her mother, repenting her conduct and wishing she had been taught more by experience than theory.

ADICHIE,   Chimamanda   Ngozi (1977–) Novelist. She grew up in Nsukka, Nigeria. Her first novel, *Purple Hibiscus* (2003), is an exploration of a Nigerian family's tense but loving relationship. *Half of a Yellow Sun* (2006), set during the Nigerian Civil War, won the Orange Prize. *The Thing Around Your Neck* (2009) is a collection of short stories.

Adonais An elegy on the death of John *Keats, by P. B. *Shelley, published 1821. Composed in 55 Spenserian stanzas, the poem was inspired partly by the Greek elegies of *Bion and *Moschus (both of which Shelley had translated) and partly by Milton's *Lycidas. Keats is

lamented under the name of Adonais, the Greek god of beauty and fertility, together with other poets who had died young, such as Thomas *Chatterton, Philip *Sidney, and *Lucan.

Adonis *See* VENUS.

ADORNO, Theodor (1903–69) German social philosopher, musicologist, and cultural theorist. Because of his part-Jewish descent he was eventually obliged to leave Germany, settling in America before returning to a position at the Frankfurt Institute of Social Research in 1950. With Max Horkheimer (1895–1973) he published *Dialektik der Aufklärung* (1947: *Dialectic of Enlightenment*). His application of Marxist insights to music, literature, film, and popular culture has been highly influential in Germany, Britain, and America, and the collection of aphorisms *Minima Moralia* (1951) is regarded as a seminal text for Critical Theory.

Advancement of Learning, The A treatise by Francis *Bacon, published 1605, in which he sets out his ideas for the reform of knowledge. He denounces medieval scholasticism and Ciceronian rhetoric, arguing that by pursuing tenuous theological subtleties and mere verbosity they have deflected knowledge from 'the benefit and use of man'.

Adventures of Master F.J., The by George *Gascoigne. *See* F.J.

Adventures of Philip on his Way through the World, Showing Who Robbed Him, Who Helped Him, and Who Passed Him by, The The last complete novel of William Makepeace *Thackeray, serialized in the *Cornhill Magazine January 1861–August 1862, with illustrations by the author and Fred Walker. The story is told by Arthur Pendennis, now a middle-aged married man.

Æ Pseudonym of George William *Russell.

ÆLFRIC (*c*.950–*c*.1010) Benedictine monk, educated at Winchester (where he was a pupil of *Æthelwold) and the first abbot of Eynsham near Oxford. His chief works are the *Catholic Homilies* (990–95), largely drawn from the church *Fathers, which circulated widely, and the *Lives of the Saints*, also mostly translated from Latin. Other English works include his Latin *Grammar*, his *Colloquy*, and a series of translations and adaptations of the Old Testament. The greatest prose writer of his time, Aelfric is celebrated not only for his stylistic resourcefulness and varied subject matter, but also for his educational principles and the breadth of his learning as a product of the 10th-century Benedictine Revival in England.

Aeneid (written 29–19 BC) Epic in twelve books by *Virgil, reckoned the greatest poem in Latin literature. Key episodes are the fall of Troy, Aeneas's love affair with Dido, and the descent into the underworld. *Chaucer retold stories from the *Aeneid* in The *House of Fame*; and the poem underlies the epic aspirations of Milton's *Paradise Lost* and the *mock-epic grandeur of Pope's *Dunciad*.

AESCHYLUS (?525/4–456/5 BC) Greek trage-dian. Only seven of between 70 and 90 plays have survived: the early plays, *The Persians, Seven against Thebes,* and *The Suppliants*; the trilogy forming the *Oresteia* (*Agamemnon, Choephoroe, Eumenides*); and *Prometheus Bound* (which may not be his). In the 19th century, Lord *Byron's 'Prometheus' (1816) was followed by P. B. *Shelley's *Prometheus Unbound* (1820), S. T. *Coleridge's essay *On the Prometheus of Aeschylus* (1825), and a trans-lation of the play (1833) by Elizabeth Barrett *Browning. Several poets have translated the *Oresteia* in whole or in part, including Robert *Browning (*Agamemnon*, 1877), Louis *Mac-Neice (*Agamemnon*, 1936), Tony *Harrison (*Oresteia*, performed 1981), and Ted *Hughes (*Oresteia*, performed 1999). *See* EURIPIDES; POETICS, THE; PROMETHEUS; SOPHOCLES.

(⊕) SEE WEB LINKS

• Archive of Performances of Greek and Roman Drama

AESOP (6th century BC) Said to have been a Phrygian slave, traditionally the author of the collection of Greek fables which comes down to us in several late versions. Collections of *Erasmus' Latin edition were widely used in schools in the Renaissance. The fables have been frequently edited and adapted in English, for example by Roger *L'Estrange and Samuel *Richardson.

Aesthetic movement A cult of sensibility developed in the 1870s and 1880s, and influ-enced by the *Pre-Raphaelites, John *Ruskin, and Walter *Pater, in which art was separated from morality, and where form took precedence over content. Its female adherents often adopted anti-fashionable artistic dress. It was closely associated with Oscar *Wilde and was ridiculed by George *du Maurier in *Punch* and

in Gilbert and Sullivan's *Patience* (1881), etc. *See also* ART FOR ART'S SAKE.

ÆTHELWOLD, St (b. between 904 and 909, d. 984) Bishop of Winchester (963) after Edgar became king of England. He was an important figure too in the revival of learning, as his pupil *Ælfric testifies; most significantly, he translated the *Rule* of St Benedict (*c*.960), and wrote the *Regularis Concordia*, the code of the new English rule in the 10th-century revival.

Aethiopica A Greek romance by the 3rd-century AD Syrian Heliodorus of Emesa. The *Aethiopica* was first printed in 1534 and became widely known through Jacques Amyot's French translation (1547) and Thomas Underdowne's English version (*c*.1569). Its influence on later romances was considerable: *Tasso's *Jerusa-lem Delivered*, Sir Philip *Sidney's *Arcadia*, and John *Barclay's *Argenis*, are all indebted to it.

African American literature Writing or performed art produced by African slaves and their descendants in America. An early form was the slave narrative, where the author describes the gradual achievement of freedom against ex-traordinary odds, including draconian laws against slave literacy in some states (*see* SLAV-ERY, LITERATURE OF; EQUIANO, OLAUDAH; BROWN, WILLIAM WELLS; and DOUGLASS, FRE-DERICK). The publication in London of Phillis *Wheatley's *Poems on Various Subjects* in 1773 refuted the widely held belief that African Amer-icans could not produce their own literature. At the turn of the 20th century authors like W. E. B. *Du Bois and Booker T. *Washington examined in their prose the nature of race relations in the USA. Writers of the *Harlem Renaissance, like Langston *Hughes and Zora Neale *Hurston, drew on the vernacular tradition of spirituals, blues, and later jazz for their inspiration. This material formed a bedrock on which later wri-ters like Richard *Wright and Ralph *Ellison depended for their depictions of the violence in American life. Amiri *Baraka was a key figure in the mid-1960s *Black Arts Movement, whilst notable later 20th-century writers include Alice *Walker, Toni *Morrison (who won the *Nobel Prize for Literature in 1993) and Maya *Angelou, continuing the tradition of autobiographical memoir. African Americans have become im-portant presences in science fiction (Samuel Delany, Octavia *Butler), crime fiction (Walter Mosley), and historical fiction (Edward P. Jones (1951–)), among other genres.

Agamemnon of Aeschylus, The A translation by Robert *Browning, published 1877. It sparked debate because of its literalness, which Browning defended in his preface, including his spelling of Greek names ('Olumpos' for 'Olympus', etc.). The translation (or 'transcription', as Browning termed it) diverted from Matthew *Arnold's Hellenism by insisting on the alien nature of the ancient Greek original.

AGARD, John (1949-) Born in Guyana and now living in Britain: 'I didn't graduate | I immigrate'. A dynamic performance poet, he writes witty plays, poetry, and short stories for children and adults, widening access to Caribbean culture. *Weblines* (2000) includes poems about Ananse, the trickster spider of creation myths. *Alternative Anthem* (2009) contains his latest selected poems.

AGBABI, Patience (1965-) Performance poet, born to Nigerian parents in Britain. *Transformatrix* (2000) exemplifies her verbal and formal dexterity and dynamism. She writes, 'The written must be spoken. The chasm between page and stage must be healed.' Later books include *Bloodshot Monochrome* (2008).

Age of Innocence, The See WHARTON, EDITH.

Age of Reason, The By Thomas *Paine, published as a whole 1795; the first part appeared in 1793. The work was written in Paris at the height of the Terror, the second part during Paine's imprisonment when his own life was at risk. In it he states, 'I believe in one God, and no more', and proceeds to attack Christianity and the Bible. He concludes with a plea for religious tolerance.

Agnes Grey A one-volume novel by Anne *Brontë, published 1847. It is the story of a rector's daughter, the narrator, who takes service as a governess, first with the Bloomfield family, whose undisciplined children are described as 'tigers' cubs', and then with the Murrays, where the conduct of her eldest charge, Rosalie, a heartless coquette, is contrasted with her own dignified, stoical, and gentle behaviour. Rosalie marries ambitiously and unhappily, but Agnes is happily united with Mr Weston, the curate, the only one to have shown kindness in her days of servitude. The novel, which reflects Anne Brontë's Christianity and her views on education, is lightened by passages showing Agnes's warm response to the natural world.

Agrarians The name given to a group of writers from the Southern US states which included John Crowe *Ransom, Allen *Tate, and Robert Penn *Warren. They expressed their resistance to urbanization and the loss of tradition in their manifesto, the 1930 collection of essays *I'll Take my Stand*. Several of these writers subsequently retreated from their 1930 position.

Agravain, Sir In the Arthurian legends the second son of King Lot of Orkney and Arthur's sister Morgawse, the brother of *Gawain, Gareth, and Gaheris. He conspires against Launcelot and discloses to Arthur Launcelot's love for Guinevere.

AGRIPPA, Henricus Cornelius, of Nettesheim (1486–1535) Scholar and writer on the occult sciences. He wrote *De Occulta Philosophia Libri Tres* (1533) and *De Incertitudine & Vanitate Scientiarum* (1527), and argued against the persecution of witches and veneration of relics. He is mentioned in Mary *Shelley's *Frankenstein* and, briefly, in the first Harry *Potter book.

AHLBERG, Allan (1938-) and **Janet** (1944–94)   Admired husband-and-wife partnership who created many witty and inventive *picturebooks and series. These culminated in *The Jolly Postman* (1986). Janet Ahlberg's detailed illustrations are particularly effective in books steeped in nostalgic period images (*Peepo!*, 1981) and in portraits of contemporary society (*Starting School*, 1988).

AICKMAN, Robert See GHOST STORIES.

AIDOO, Ama Ata (1942-) Ghanaian dramatist, poet, novelist, and short story writer. In her novel *Our Sister Killjoy* (1979) an experimental fusion of prose and poetry in the narrative represents the protagonist's sceptical but compassionate recognition of her identity as an African. The oral tradition meets technological sophistication in her second novel, *Changes* (1991).

Aids to Reflection A religious and philosophical treatise by Samuel Taylor *Coleridge, published 1825. Intended primarily as a religious guide to young men and a work of biblical scholarship, it stresses the importance of Christianity as a 'personal revelation'. Another 'main object' was to develop further his famous distinction between Reason and Understanding, originally drawn from *Kant, as the source respectively of 'Moral' and 'Prudential' action. The massive and frequently chaotic footnotes contain much fascinating literary material, such as discussions of symbolism and metaphor.

AIKEN, Conrad Potter (1889–1973) American author, in the class of 1911 at Harvard university with T. S. *Eliot. His first volume of poetry, *Earth Triumphant* (1914), was followed by many others, including the Pulitzer Prize-winning *Selected Poems* (1930) and *Preludes for Memnon* (1931). His long poems, which he described as 'symphonies', show the somewhat diffused and diffuse influence of his *modernist contemporaries and friends. His novels, which show a debt to James *Joyce and Sigmund *Freud, and his own desire to explore 'the fragmented ego', include *Blue Voyage* (1927) and *A Heart for the Gods of Mexico* (1939), both concerned with actual and metaphorical journeys. *Ushant* (1952) is a psychological autobiography, with portraits of Malcolm *Lowry and of Eliot, who appears as 'Tsetse', an illustration of Aiken's fondness for pun and verbal invention. His short stories were collected in 1960, and his criticism, *A Reviewer's ABC*, in 1958. His *Selected Letters* were published in 1978. He is the father of Joan *Aiken.

AIKEN, Joan (1924–2004) Novelist and writer of children's books. She wrote 92 novels, including 27 for adults, many in *Gothic and fantastic modes. Her major series, beginning with *The Wolves of Willoughby Chase* (1962), is set in an imagined 19th century in which the Stuart kings are on the throne, and the Hanoverians are pretenders—and wolves have come through the channel tunnel. Aiken's vivacious heroine, Dido Twite, first appears in *Black Hearts in Battersea* (1964). She also had success with the 'Arabel and Mortimer' picture books (from 1972), illustrated by Quentin *Blake.

AIKIN, Anna Laetitia See BARBAULD, ANNA.

AIKIN, John (1747–1822) Physician, author, and Dissenter, and younger brother of Anna Laetitia *Barbauld, with whom he wrote the highly successful *Evenings at Home, or The Juvenile Budget Opened*, 6 vols (1792–6), for children. He was until 1806 literary editor of the *Monthly Magazine. In 1811 Aitkin became editor of the *Annual Register*.

AINSWORTH, William Harrison (1805–82) Novelist. His first successes were *Rookwood* (1834), romanticizing the career of Dick Turpin, and *Jack Sheppard* (1839), exalting the life of another highwayman. These 'Newgate' novels were satirized by W. M. *Thackeray in *Cathe-rine* (1839–40). From 1840 to 1842 he edited *Bentley's Miscellany*, then the *New Monthly Magazine*. He wrote 39 novels, chiefly historical; the Lancashire group, beginning with *The Lancashire Witches* (1848) and ending with *Mervyn Clitheroe* (1857), cover 400 years of northern history. Among the best known of the novels are *Jack Sheppard, Guy Fawkes* (1841), and *Old St Paul's* (1841).

aisling [lit. 'vision'; pronounced 'ashling'] A mode of lyrical poetry in late 17th- and 18th-century Irish in which the speaker encounters a *spéir-bhean* ('sky-woman'), a beautiful maiden representing Ireland; the poems dramatize the collapse of the Gaelic world under the Williamite dispensation. Aisling is recalled in 19th-century popular songs like 'The Colleen Rue', in W. B. *Yeats's 'Red Hanrahan's Song about Ireland', and in poems by Ciaran *Carson and Paul *Muldoon.

AKENSIDE, Mark (1721–70) Poet. His influential didactic poem *The *Pleasures of Imagination* (1744) was published by Robert *Dodsley on *Pope's advice. His *Odes on Several Subjects* (1745) marked an important shift in literary taste; other poems explore the scientific theories of the *Enlightenment. Akenside also wrote notable political satire in verse.

AKHMATOVA, Anna (1889–1966) Pseudonym of Anna Andreevna Gorenko, Russian poet. In 1911 she joined the Guild of Poets, the founders of Russian Acmeism, along with her husband Nikolai Gumilev and Osip *Mandelshtam. Her renowned early collections of poetry *Evening* (1912), *Rosary* (1914), *White Flock* (1917), *Plantain* (1921), and *Anno Domini MCMXXI* (1922) were deemed 'bourgeois' by the Soviet authorities. *From Six Books* appeared in 1940; *Requiem*, written secretly between 1935 and 1940, bearing witness to the Stalinist terror, was published in Munich in 1963. In August 1946 she was attacked by the Party during the post-war cultural freeze, along with the prose writer Mikhail Zoshchenko (1895–1958), and was expelled from the Union of Writers. Her literary rehabilitation began after the Soviet leader Khrushchev's 'secret speech' of February 1956. *The Complete Poems of Anna Akhmatova* appeared in 1992.

ALABASTER, William (1568–1640) Elizabethan theologian and Latin poet. His sonnets (first published in 1959) are among the earliest *metaphysical poems of devotion.

Alastor A visionary poem by P. B. *Shelley, published 1816. 'Alastor' is a transliteration from the Greek, meaning the 'evil spirit or demon of solitude', who pursues the Poet to his death because he will not be satisfied by domestic affections and 'human sympathy'.

Albany (**Albainn, Albin, Albania**) Ancient poetic name of Gaelic origin for the northern part of Britain.

ALBEE, Edward Franklin (1928-) American playwright, associated with the Theatre of the *Absurd, whose later explorations of sexual fantasy, frustration, and domestic anguish also recall the plays of Tennessee *Williams. His works include the macabre one-act satiric comedy *The American Dream* (1961); the more naturalistic marital tragicomedy of academe *Who's Afraid of Virginia Woolf?* (1962); *Tiny Alice* (1965), a fantasy of wealth and corruption; and *A Delicate Balance* (1966), a tragicomedy set in a hard-drinking domestic environment. Later plays include *All Over* (1971), *Seascape* (1975), *The Lady from Dubuque* (1980), *The Man Who Had Three Arms* (1982), *Marriage Play* (1986), and *Three Tall Women* (perf. Vienna 1992, New York 1994), the leading character of which was based on Albee's adoptive mother. Later works such as *The Goat* (2002) have included language games and word-play.

Albion An ancient name for Britain, perhaps derived from its white (Latin *albus*) cliffs. The author of *De Origine Gigantum* (1330s) claims that Albina, a Greek princess, populated the island with giant descendants (mentioned by *Geoffrey of Monmouth in *Historia Regum Britanniae*, I. 16) before Brutus renamed it. William *Blake uses Albion as a personification of England in such works as *Visions of the Daughters of Albion* (1793) and *Jerusalem*, adapting the presentation of England as a giant to his mythological purposes.

Albions England See WARNER, WILLIAM.

alcaics A verse form employing *quatrains with lines of 11, 11, 9, and 10 syllables. Named after the ancient Greek poet Alcaeus, the form was favoured by *Horace, and imitated in English by A. H. *Clough, A. C. *Swinburne, Alfred *Tennyson ('Milton: Experiments in Quantity'), W. H. *Auden, and Peter *Reading.

Alchemist, The A comedy by Ben *Jonson, performed by the King's Men 1610, printed 1612. Lovewit, during an epidemic of the plague, leaves his house in Blackfriars in London in charge of his servant Face, who sets up in business with Subtle, a fake alchemist, and Dol Common, a prostitute. They lure and fleece a variety of victims, including Sir Epicure Mammon, a voluptuous knight, Ananias and Tribulation Wholesome, fanatical Puritans, Dapper, a lawyer's clerk, Drugger, a tobacconist, and Kastril, a country bumpkin.

ALCOTT, Louisa May (1832-88) American author, daughter of educationalist and Transcendentalist Amos Bronson Alcott (1799-1888). She published sketches, stories, etc., to help support her impractical father and family, achieving fame and financial security with *Little Women* (1868-9), and its three sequels featuring Jo March.

ALCUIN (**Albinus:** English name **Ealhwine**) (c.735-804) Theologian, prolific man of letters, and the principal figure in the literary and educational programme of *Charlemagne in the 'Carolingian Renaissance'. He wrote liturgical, exegetical, hagiographical, philosophical, and polemical works, as well as numerous letters and poems in Latin, including an elegy on the destruction of Lindisfarne by the Danes. He adapted Tertullian's (b. c.150) words, 'What has Athens to do with Jerusalem?' in his famous question concerning heroic writing in monasteries: 'Quid Hinieldus cum Christo?' (Ingeld being a character in *Beowulf*).

ALDINGTON, Richard (1892-1962) Poet, novelist, and biographer, he married Hilda *Doolittle (known as H.D.) 1913 (separated 1919, dissolved 1938), and they worked as editors on the *imagist periodical the *Egoist. His poetry includes *Images 1910–1915*, *Images of War* (1919), and *A Fool i' the Forest* (1925), which shows an excessive debt to *The *Waste Land. Aldington achieved popular success with his first novel, *Death of a Hero* (1929, abridged; Paris, 1930, unexpurgated), based on his own war experiences (he joined up in 1916). It relates the life and death, in 1918, of George Winterbourne. The first two parts dwell on his youth and 'advanced' marriage, Part III is a horrifying description of life at the front in France. His biographies include *Portrait of a Genius, but...* (1950), a controversial life of D. H. *Lawrence, and his even more controversial biography of T. E. *Lawrence, *Lawrence of Arabia: A Biographical Enquiry* (1955). *Life for Life's Sake*, 1941 is an autobiography.

ALDISS, Brian W. (1925-) Novelist, poet, short story writer, and critic. He has long championed *science fiction as a literary genre, editing many anthologies and a history of the subject, *Billion Year Spree* (1973, revised, with David Wingrove, as *Trillion Year Spree*, 1986). His many works employing classic science fiction devices include *Non-Stop* (1958), *Hothouse*, (1962), and *Greybeard* (1964). *Report on Probability A* (1968), *Barefoot in the Head* (1969), and *The Malacia Tapestry* (1976) follow his association with the *New Wave of science fiction. *Frankenstein Unbound* (1973) pays tribute to his view of Mary *Shelley's work as 'the first novel of the Scientific Revolution'. The epic 'Helliconia' trilogy (1982–5) describes a planetary system in which seasons last for centuries, while *White Mars* (1999), written jointly with the mathematician Roger Penrose, explores utopian ideas. *Life in the West* (1980) and *Super-State* (2002) consider contemporary and near-future Europe. *Harm* (2007) engages with post-9/11 fears of terrorism. His short story 'Supertoys Last all Summer Long' was adapted by Stanley Kubrick for the film *A.I.: Artificial Intelligence* (2001).

ALEXANDER THE GREAT (356–323 BC) The most famous general in the classical world. Alexander was made the centre of a cluster of medieval legends, comparable to the cycles concerning *Charlemagne and King *Arthur. The chief romances concerning him are the great French *Roman d'Alexandre* of the 12th century and the English *King Alisaunder* of the early 14th century. The story of the rivalry of his two wives forms the subject of Nathaniel *Lee's tragedy *The *Rival Queens*.

ALEXANDER, C. F. (Cecil Frances) (1818–95) Irish hymn-writer and poet; her best-selling *Hymns for Little Children* (1848) included 'There is a green hill far away', 'Once in royal David's city', and 'All things bright and beautiful'.

alexandrine A verse line of twelve syllables, which in English takes the form of an iambic *hexameter, most commonly found as the last line of the Spenserian *stanza, sometimes too as a variant line among *pentameters, and more rarely as the *metre of a whole *sonnet, as in the opening sonnet of Philip *Sidney's *Astrophel and Stella*. The line was the dominant metre of French verse from the 16th century to the 19th, taking its name from medieval French poems about Alexander the Great.

ALFRED (the Great) (848/9–99) King of the West Saxons from 871 to his death, important for the revival of letters that he effected in his southern kingdom and as the instigator of a tradition of English prose translation. Whether he actually wrote or simply authorized the English works traditionally ascribed to him is now acknowledged to be a complex and unresolved issue.

ALGER, Horatio, Jr (1832–99) American novelist, whose prolific output, including *Ragged Dick* (1868) and *From Canal Boy to President* (1881), promoted the belief that success can be attained with courage and determination. The 1928 biography by Herbert R. Mayes is largely fictional, based on bogus material.

ALGREN, Nelson (1909–61) American novelist, writer of short stories, and journalist, best known for his descriptions of the dispossessed of Chicago. Algren's first novel, *Somebody in Boots* (1935), describes the homeless of the Depression. *Never Come Morning* (1942) grew out of Algren's reportage on boxing, but he achieved real fame with his account of the Chicago drugs sub-culture, *The Man with the Golden Arm* (1949). Algren constantly questioned American notions of prosperity and success, focusing in his fiction on the underdogs of the cities. He sub-titled *Who Lost an American?* (1963), a collection of travel essays, as *Being a Guide to the Seamier Sides of New York City, Inner London, Paris, Dublin, Barcelona, Seville, Almeria, Istanbul, Crete and Chicago, Illinois*.

ALI, Monica (1967–) Novelist, born in Bangladesh and raised in Bolton, Greater Manchester. Her debut novel, *Brick Lane* (2003), documents the experiences of a young woman from Bangladesh who moves, after an arranged marriage to an older man, to the Bangladeshi community of London's Tower Hamlets (members of which community denounced the novel and strongly opposed the filming of it). *In the Kitchen* (2009) is set amongst London's migrant community.

Alice's Adventures in Wonderland (1865) By 'Lewis Carroll' (*see* DODGSON, CHARLES). Possibly the most famous and most-analysed children's book, it was first written as a present for the young Alice Liddell in 1864 (facsimile, *Alice's Adventures Underground*, 1886) and expanded, with illustrations by *Tenniel. Alice's episodic journey through Wonderland involves characters who have become deeply embedded in English culture, notably the White Rabbit, the Cheshire Cat, the Mad Hatter, and the Mock Turtle, and contains parodies of the verse of Isaac *Watts, Jane *Taylor, Robert *Southey, and others. Commonly seen as a landmark *'nonsense' text, liberating children from didactic fiction, it has been interpreted as a complex political satire, a commentary on Victorian girlhood, and an exploration of death, sexuality, drugs, and nihilism. Carroll wrote an equally complex sequel, *Through the Looking-Glass and What Alice Found There* (1871), in which the dreaming Alice walks through the looking-glass where she finds that the pieces from her chess set are alive and inhabit a landscape modelled on a chess board. Many famous characters, passages, and incidents associated with Alice are found in *Looking-Glass* including Tweedledum and Tweedledee, Humpty Dumpty, the Walrus and the Carpenter, and 'Jabberwocky'. In performance the two books are often combined. In 1890 Carroll produced the shorter, sentimentalized *The Nursery 'Alice'* for younger readers. See Martin Gardner's *The Annotated Alice* (2000).

alienation effect A term (from the German *Verfremdungseffekt*) used to describe attempts by author or director to prevent the reader or audience from identifying with, trusting, or taking for granted what is happening in the text or on stage: such devices can include narrative interventions, disruptions of mood and sequence, and introduction of non-realistic effects. Bertolt *Brecht was the most celebrated exponent of the technique, and first treats of it in detail in his essay 'Alienation Effects in Chinese Acting' (1936), but it has been very widely adopted.

allegory A kind of narrative or description that carries partially veiled meanings behind its actions and cast of characters. George Orwell's fable *Animal Farm, in which dialogue between animals covertly echoes contemporary political conflicts, is a well-known modern example. Allegorical works can be understood as systematically extended *metaphors, typically employing personification of abstract qualities. Allegorical writing flourished especially in the later Middle Ages, in such works as *Piers Plowman and the morality play *Everyman; notable later works are Edmund Spenser's *The *Faerie Queene, John Bunyan's *The *Pilgrim's Progress, and John Dryden's political allegory *Absalom and Achitophel. Enigmatic suggestions of allegorical meaning are exploited teasingly in the novels and tales of Nathaniel *Hawthorne, Herman *Melville, T. F. *Powys, and Muriel *Spark, among others.

ALLEN, Grant (Charles Grant Blairfindie) (1848–99) Science writer and novelist. In 1873 he went to Queen's College, Jamaica, as profes-

sor of mental and moral philosophy, where his agnosticism and socialism led to the formulation of an evolutionary system of philosophy based on the works of Herbert *Spencer and Charles *Darwin. After his return to England in 1876 he published *The Colour-Sense* (1879), which won praise from Alfred Russel *Wallace, Darwin, and Thomas Henry *Huxley. His fiction includes *Strange Stories* (1884) and the best-selling *The Woman Who Did* (1895), intended as a protest against the subjection of women. Millicent Garrett Fawcett and other feminists condemned it, and Victoria Crosse published *The Woman Who Didn't* (1895) in response. Allen was also a pioneer in *science fiction, notably in his novel on time travel, *The British Barbarians* (1895), and in crime writing, creating an engaging anti-hero in his conman and master of disguise Colonel Clay (*An African Millionaire*, 1897).

ALLENDE, Isabel (1942–) Chilean writer born in Lima (Peru), an American citizen since 2003. She was encouraged by Pablo *Neruda to write fiction. *La casa de los espíritus* (1982: *The House of the Spirits*) was written in Venezuela after she fled Pinochet's 1973 military coup. A family saga exploring four generations of women, it incorporates her interests in Chilean politics and history from a feminist viewpoint; its style develops from *magical to brutal realism. *De amor y de sombra* (1984: *Of Love and Shadows*) and *Eva Luna* (1987) followed. *El plan infinito* (1991: *The Infinite Plan*) is a New Age novel set in California. Allende wrote movingly about the death of her daughter (*Paula*, 1994). Her prolific output includes historical romances, a memoir, and a trilogy for children. Her *Mi país inventado* (2003: *My Invented Country*) provides a good introduction to her work.

ALLESTREE, Richard (*fl.* 1617–43) *See* ALMANACS.

ALLESTREE, Richard (1619–81) *See* WHOLE DUTY OF MAN, THE.

All for Love, *or The World Well Lost* A tragedy by John *Dryden produced and published 1678. Written in blank verse in acknowledged imitation of *Shakespeare's *Antony and Cleopatra, it is Dryden's most performed and his best-known play. It concentrates on the last hours in the lives of its hero and heroine. In contrast to Shakespeare's play, it is an exemplary *neo-classical tragedy, notable for its elaborately formal presentation of character, action, and theme.

ALLINGHAM, Margery (1904–66) Short story writer, journalist, and novelist. She introduced her aristocratic and deceptively vacuous detective hero Albert Campion in *The Crime at Black Dudley* (1929). Campion, along with his manservant Lugg and Charlie Luke of Scotland Yard, reappeared in many of her best-known works including *Flowers for the Judge* (1936), *More Work for the Undertaker* (1949), *The Tiger in the Smoke* (1952), and *The Beckoning Lady* (1955). Atmospheric, intelligent, and observant, her works have maintained their popularity despite their strong period flavour. *See also* DETECTIVE FICTION.

ALLINGHAM, William (1824–89) Poet, diarist, and anthologist, born in Co. Donegal. His friends in the literary world included Coventry *Patmore, Thomas *Carlyle, D. G. *Rossetti, and Alfred *Tennyson. Allingham's diary, published in 1907, covers four decades and includes many accounts of Victorian literary culture.

All is True See HENRY VIII.

alliteration The repetition within the same phrase or line of similar consonantal sounds, most commonly at initial positions within neighbouring words or stressed syllables in poetry:

> Landscape-lover, lord of language.
> (Alfred *Tennyson)

Such effects were essential to the Old English and Middle English verse traditions that we refer to as *alliterative verse, in which vowel sounds could also be deemed to alliterate; but they subsequently became incidental or decorative devices. Alliteration may also be found in prose writing, especially in elaborately heightened styles such as that of John *Lyly.

alliterative prose A tradition of Old and Middle English prose elevated in style by the employment of some of the techniques of *alliterative verse. Its most distinguished exponents are *Ælfric and *Wulfstan in Old English, and the writers of the *Katherine Group in Middle English.

Alliterative Revival A collective term for the group of alliterative poems written in the second half of the 14th century in which *alliteration, which had been the formal basis of Old English poetry, was again used in poetry of the first importance (such as *Piers Plowman and Sir *Gawain and the Green Knight) as a serious alternative to the continental form, syllabic rhyming verse. As well as their common formal elements, many of the poems are linked by a serious interest in contemporary politics and ethics (*Wynnere and Wastour, Death and Liffe, The Parlement of the Three Ages, Piers Plowman).

alliterative verse The native Germanic tradition of English poetry and the standard form in Old English up to the 11th century, recurring in Middle English as a formal alternative to the syllable-counting, rhymed verse borrowed from French (*see* ALLITERATIVE REVIVAL). The Old English line was (normally) unrhymed, and made up of two distinct half-lines each of which contained two stressed syllables. The *alliteration was always on the first stress of the second half-line, which alliterated with either, or both, of the stresses in the first half-line; e.g.

> X   X   X
> Nāp nihtscūa, norþan snīwde
> (*The Seafarer, 31: The shade of night grew dark, it snowed from the north.)

In Middle English, the alliterative rules were much less strict, although the alliteration was often very dense:

> 'I have lyved in londe', quod I, 'My name is Longe Wille'. (*Piers Plowman B XV. 152)

Nothing after Middle English could categorically be said to be 'alliterative verse', despite its recurrent use as a device throughout English poetry, except perhaps for the rather self-conscious revival of the form in the 20th century by such poets as W. H. *Auden and Cecil *Day-Lewis.

ALLNUTT, Gillian (1949–) British poet. Allnutt was initially best known as a feminist poet; her recent preoccupations, though always philosophical, have become increasingly spiritual. The dramatized voices and accumulating imagery of Allnutt's later work constitute a refashioning of biblical language, reminiscent in their intensity not only of Christopher *Smart but of her contemporary Selima *Hill. Her collections include *Spitting the Pips Out* (1981); *Beginning the Avocado* (1987); *Nantucket and the Angel* (1997); *Lintel* (2001); and *How the Bicycle Shone: New and Selected Poems* (2007).

All Quiet on the Western Front See REMARQUE, ERICH.

All's Lost by Lust A tragedy by William *Rowley, acted *c.*1619, printed 1633. The story is taken from a legendary episode in Spanish history. The play remained popular throughout the 17th century, and was twice adapted during the Restoration. The story is also the subject of

W. S. *Landor's *Count Julian* (1812) and Robert *Southey's *Roderick* (1814).

All's Well That Ends Well A comedy by *Shakespeare, first printed in the first *folio of 1623. Like *Measure for Measure* it is often classified as a 'tragicomedy' or 'problem comedy'.

Its chief source is Boccaccio's *Decameron* (Day 3, Tale 9), which Shakespeare may have read either in the translation by William *Painter, or in the French version by Antoine le Maçon. Bertram, the young count of Roussillon, on the death of his father is summoned to the court of the king of France, leaving his mother and with her Helena, daughter of the famous physician Gerard de Narbonne. The king is sick of a disease said to be incurable. Helena, who loves Bertram, goes to Paris and effects his cure by means of a prescription left by her father. As a reward she is allowed to choose her husband and names Bertram, who unwillingly obeys the king's order to wed her. But under the influence of the braggart Paroles, he at once takes service with the duke of Florence, writing to Helena that until she can get the ring from his finger, and is with child by him, she may not call him husband. Helena, passing through Florence on a pilgrimage, finds Bertram courting Diana, the daughter of her hostess there. Disclosing herself as his wife to them, she obtains permission to replace Diana at a midnight assignation with Bertram, having that day caused him to be informed that Helena is dead. Thereby she obtains from Bertram his ring, and gives him one that the king had given her. Bertram returns to his mother's house, where the king is on a visit. The latter sees on Bertram's finger the ring that he had given Helena and demands an explanation on pain of death. Helena appears, explains what has happened, and claims that the conditions named in Bertram's letter have been fulfilled. Bertram, filled with remorse, accepts her as his wife.

All the Year Round See HOUSEHOLD WORDS.

almanacs were, technically, tables of astronomical and astrological events of the coming year, and as such had existed since antiquity; with the advent of printing they proliferated, and by the 17th century in England were the most popular literary form, containing a wide range of material, from farming notes to scurrilous verses and wild and colourful prophecies. They flourished particularly strongly from 1640 to 1700, when they engaged in political, social, and religious controversy. Well-known publishers and compilers of almanacs included Richard Allestree (active between 1617 and 1643); William *Lilly; John Gadbury (1627–1704); John Partridge (1644–1715); and Francis Moore (1657–1714?), the original *Old Moore. Almanacs declined in the more sceptical 18th century although Old Moore maintained vast popular sales. Old Moore and *Whitaker's Almanack* (*see* WHITAKER, JOSEPH) are still published annually.

ALMOND, David (1951–) Writer, best known for his children's books. These are set in the north-east of England, indebted to William *Blake, and incorporate *magic realist elements. Skellig (*Skellig*, 1998) is part tramp, part angel; in *Kit's Wilderness* (1999), the stories Kit writes inexplicably connect him to the past of the village to which he has moved. *My Dad's a Birdman* (2007), a book for younger readers, treats mental disorder and its consequences with a life-affirming playfulness, while *The Savage* (2008) is a dark exploration of death and renewal. *My Name is Mina* (2010), in journal form, is a prequel to *Skellig*.

A.L.O.E. (A Lady of England) Pen-name of Charlotte Maria Tucker (1821–93), writer and Indian missionary. Tucker's many novels were evangelical and didactic but entertaining. *Rambles of a Rat* (1857) is typical: it portrays the adventures of two likeable rats. Her writing encompassed anthropomorphic *allegories, *fables, and traditional Indian stories retold for British children and translated into Indian dialects.

alternate history A sub-genre of *science fiction which developed partly under the influence of historical 'counterfactuals' such as those collected by J. C. Squire in *If It had Happened Otherwise* (1931), partly through the 'many worlds' theory devised by the physicist Hugh Everett in 1957. Alternate histories often spring from a point of departure—the 'Jonbar point' after a world so named in Jack Williamson's *The Legion of Time* (1938) to (for example) reverse the outcomes of the American Civil War (Ward Moore) or the Second World War (Philip K. *Dick). Alternates also arise through technological development, as in *The Difference Engine* by William *Gibson and Bruce *Sterling. Kim Stanley Robinson's *The Years of Rice and Salt* removes Europe from world history while Christopher *Priest's *The Separation* blends historical and personal branching of time-tracks. Philip *Roth's *The Plot against America* (2004) imagines an alternate history in a 1940s USA shadowed by anti-Semitism.

ALTHER, Lisa (1944–) American novelist, short story writer, and magazine journalist, born in Tennessee. Her first novel *Kinflicks* (1976) humorously describes the escapades of a young woman negotiating the gender stereotypes of her time and was enthusiastically endorsed by Doris *Lessing. *Kinfolks* (2007) is an attempt by Alther to explore her family ancestry.

Alton Locke, Tailor and Poet An *Autobiography* A novel by Charles *Kingsley, published 1850. Alton Locke, son of a small London tradesman and educated by a widowed Baptist mother, is apprenticed to a tailor in whose sweatshop he experiences at first hand the miseries of the working classes and becomes imbued with the ideas of *Chartism. This section reuses material from Kingsley's pamphlet *Cheap Clothes and Nasty*, on abuses within the clothing industry. Despite its propagandist stridency, *Alton Locke* is a powerful social document, and had an impact similar to that of Benjamin *Disraeli's *Sybil* and Elizabeth *Gaskell's *Mary Barton*.

ALVAREZ, A. (Alfred) (1929–) Poet and critic. His works include *The Shaping Spirit* (1958), a study of modern poetry, and *The Savage God: A Study of Suicide* (1971), which contains an account of the death of Sylvia *Plath. He edited an influential anthology of verse, *The New Poetry* (1962, featuring work by John *Berryman, Robert *Lowell, and Ted *Hughes). His autobiography *Where Did It All Go Right?* appeared in 1999 and *New and Selected Poems* in 2002.

Amadis of Gaul (*Amadís de Gaula*) A Spanish or Portuguese romance, written in the form in which we have it by Garci Rodríguez de Montalvo in the second half of the 15th and printed early in the 16th century. The romance was translated into English by Anthony *Munday (*c.*1590–1619), and an abridged version by Robert *Southey appeared in 1803. *Amadis of Gaul* and *Palmerin of England* were two of the works excepted from the holocaust of romances of chivalry in *Don Quixote* (I. 6).

Amazing Marriage, The A novel by George *Meredith, published 1895, a vigorous exploration of the battle between the sexes. The character Gower Woodseer is based on Robert Louis *Stevenson.

Ambassadors, The A novel by Henry *James, published 1903, one of those in which James depicts the reaction of different American types to the European environment. Chadwick Newsome, the son of an overpowering Massachusetts widow, has been living in Paris and is reported to have entangled himself with a wicked woman. Mrs Newsome has decided to send out an ambassador to rescue Chad in the person of the elderly, amiable, guileless Lambert Strether. The story describes Strether's evolution in the congenial atmosphere of Paris, his desertion to the side of Chad and the bewitching comtesse de Vionnet, and his own mild flirtation with the pleasant cosmopolitan Maria Gostrey. An accident throws Strether unexpectedly into the company of Chad and Madame de Vionnet in circumstances which leave no doubt as to the nature of their real relations. Sadly disillusioned, but still insisting on the necessity of Chad's loyalty to Madame de Vionnet, Strether from a sense of duty turns his back on Paris.

AMBLER, Eric (1909–98) Writer of thrillers, *spy fiction, and screenplays. His many works of fiction include *The Dark Frontier* (1936), *Epitaph for a Spy* (1938), *The Mask of Dimitrios* (1939), *Journey into Fear* (1940), *The October Man* (1948), *The Schirmer Inheritance* (1953), *Passage of Arms* (1959), *Send No More Roses* (1977), and *The Care of Time* (1981). *Here Lies* (1985) is autobiographical, *The Story So Far* (1993), a collection of stories with reminiscences.

Amelia A novel by Henry *Fielding, published 1752 (for 1751). *Joseph Andrews* and *Tom Jones* end with the title characters about to embark on married life; in *Amelia* Captain and Mrs Booth have already enjoyed some years together, and the book is much concerned with tenderness and family happiness. Set in a London of pervasive squalor and violence, it opens in the court of Justice Thrasher, who throws the innocent Booth into Newgate because he cannot bribe his way out of trouble. In the filthy and corrupt prison Booth meets an old acquaintance, Miss Matthews, a courtesan who has the means to buy a clean cell which Booth guiltily shares with her. Colonel James, a distant connection, bails out Booth, and takes Miss Matthews as his mistress. Booth solicits an army commission, meanwhile wasting his half-pay on gambling: but even when Booth fails to return for her frugal but lovingly prepared meal of hashed mutton, Amelia does not upbraid him. Matters take a more sinister turn when 'My

Lord', a flamboyant and menacing character who is never named, plots, with James, to ensnare Amelia. The Booths' landlady (secretly My Lord's procuress) arranges for Amelia to be attended at an oratorio by My Lord in disguise. My Lord affably offers to acquire a command for Booth, and showers presents on Amelia's adored children. Amelia is invited to a masquerade, but is warned off by a fellow lodger, the learned widow Mrs Bennet, whom My Lord once seduced by similar means. After more dangers and complications, their protector, the good clergyman Dr Harrison, pays off Booth's debts. Amelia discovers that she is heiress to her mother's fortune, and the Booths retire to a prosperous country life.

American dream A phrase popularized by James Truslow Adams (1878–1949) in his 1931 study *The Epic of America*, which expressed the conviction that in America every individual had the opportunity for self-fulfilment regardless of their birth or position. The phrase is used ironically in Edward *Albee's *The American Dream* (1961) and Norman *Mailer's *An American Dream* (1965).

American Senator, The A novel by Anthony *Trollope, published 1877. Elias Gotobed, senator for the fictional state of Mickewa, comes to England on a fact-finding tour, and finds 'irrational and salutary' English manners and customs more than he can understand. In this quiet exposition of country life in and around the town of Dillsborough, two stories of courtship are highlighted. The first is a conventional Trollopean love-triangle, the second highlights Trollope's dislike of the Victorian marriage market.

AMIS, Sir Kingsley (1922–95) Novelist and poet. He achieved popular success with his first novel, *Lucky Jim* (1954), whose hero, lower-middle-class lecturer Jim Dixon, with his subversive attitudes, was hailed as an *'Angry Young Man'. Its setting in a provincial university was also indicative of a new development in fiction (*see* COOPER, WILLIAM; LARKIN, PHILIP; BRAINE, JOHN). *I Like It Here* (1958), a slight, xenophobic novel set in Portugal, displays his deliberate cultivation, for comic effect, of a prejudiced and philistine pose which was to harden into an increasingly conservative and hostile view of contemporary life and manners. He is best known for his satiric comedy (*One Fat Englishman*, 1963, set in America; *Ending up*, 1974, a savage study of old age; *Jake's Thing*, 1978, a dissertation on middle-aged impotence). The

Green Man (1969) is a novel of the supernatural, *The Riverside Villas Murder* (1973) an imitation of a classic *detective story, *The Alteration* (1976) an exercise in *alternate history. Amis's enthusiasm for Ian *Fleming's work expressed itself in *The James Bond Dossier* (1965) and *Colonel Sun* (1968), published under the pseudonym of Robert Markham. *The Old Devils* (1986) won the *Booker Prize. In *Difficulties with Girls* (1988), Patrick Standish and Jenny Bunn, from *Take a Girl Like You* (1960), reappear as a married couple. Amis's *Memoirs* appeared in 1991. His last novel was *The Biographer's Moustache* (1995). His *Collected Poems 1944–1979* appeared in 1979. (*See* MOVEMENT.)

AMIS, Martin (1949–) Novelist and journalist. His early novels—*The Rachel Papers* (1973), *Dead Babies* (1975), and *Success* (1978)—are knowing semi-satires of affluent young metropolitans awash in sexual cynicism, drink, drugs, snobbery, and greed. *Other People* (1981) showed a taste for technical experimentation which is also on view in *Time's Arrow* (1991), the story of a Nazi war criminal in which events are recounted backwards, and *Night Train* (1997), a pastiche version of American noir *detective fiction. *Money* (1984) is a scathing, scabrous comic novel that silhouettes rapacious monsters (especially its narrator, John Self) against a backdrop of 1980s New York and London, seen as hells of voracity and violence. *Einstein's Monsters* (1987, stories), shows his fascination with menace and the toxic shifting to the subject of nuclear threat, as does his apocalyptic horror-comedy, *London Fields* (1989). Later novels include *The Information* (1995), *Yellow Dog* (2003), and *The House of Meetings* (2006). His book about Stalin, *Koba the Dread* (2002), and his collection of stories and essays responding to the 9/11 attack on the World Trade Center, *The Second Plane* (2008), have generated controversy. His volumes of essays and journalism such as *Visiting Mrs Nabokov and Other Excursions* (1993) and *The War against Cliché* (2001) make clear his indebtedness to Vladimir *Nabokov and Saul *Bellow. His autobiography, *Experience* (2000), gives an account of his relationship with his father, Sir Kingsley *Amis. His novel *The Pregnant Widow* was published in 2010.

Amis and Amiloun A late 13th-century romance of 2,508 lines, adapted from an Anglo-Norman *lay, about the virtue of friendship. Amis and Amiloun are two noble foster-brothers, bound in friendship, which survives severe testing. William *Morris and Walter

*Pater (in *Studies in the History of the Renaissance*) tell the story as *Amis and Amile*.

Amoretti A series of 89 sonnets (sonnets 35 and 83 are identical) by Edmund *Spenser, which have been thought to illustrate the course of his courtship of Elizabeth Boyle. His marriage to her was celebrated in *Epithalamion*, which was printed following the *Amoretti* in 1595.

AMORY, Thomas (?1691–1788) Novelist. His *Memoirs of Several Ladies of Great Britain* (1755), was the only volume of a projected series to be published. In 1756 and 1766 Amory published a fantasy autobiography, *The Life and Opinions of *John Buncle, Esq.*

Amos Barton, The Sad Fortunes of the Rev See SCENES OF CLERICAL LIFE.

amphibrach In English verse, a trisyllabic metrical *foot in which the second syllable is stressed. *See* METRE.

Amphitryon A comedy by John *Dryden, produced and published 1690. Adapted from the comedies of *Plautus and *Molière, it represents the story of *Jupiter's seduction of Alcmena in the guise of her husband Amphitryon. He is aided by *Mercury, who is disguised as Amphitryon's slave Sosia. The cruel abuse of mortal love by the gods is in striking contrast to the play's uninhibited eroticism.

anachrony The narration of events outside their logical sequence, normally in retrospective 'flashback' (analepsis), less commonly by anticipatory 'flashforward' (*prolepsis).

anacoluthon A Greek term for a change of grammatical construction in mid-sentence, of a kind that leaves the initial construction unfinished, as with the Gentleman's announcement of Goneril's suicide in *King Lear* (V. iii. 199):

It came even from the heart of—O, she's dead!

ANACREON (6th century BC) A Greek lyric poet who is supposed to have written extensively on love and wine. Only a handful of complete poems survive, together with a number of fragments. A collection of Hellenistic poems, the *Anacreonta*, wrongly thought to be by him, were translated into English several times and much imitated from the 17th to the 19th centuries, for example by Ben *Jonson, Robert *Herrick, Richard *Lovelace, Abraham *Cowley, and Thomas *Moore.

Analytical Review (1788–99) An important literary and radical periodical, published by Joseph *Johnson, which was an early influence in encouraging the growth of *Romanticism. It included William *Gilpin's theories on the *picturesque, some of *Wordsworth's early poems, and work by William *Bowles, Robert *Southey, Charles *Lamb, and other young writers.

ANAND, Mulk Raj (1905–2004) Indian novelist writing in English. Anand made his name with the designedly proletarian novel *Untouchable* (1935), promoted by E. M. *Forster, which recounts a day in the life of street sweeper Bakha, roused to hopes of a casteless society by M. K. (Mahatma) Gandhi. More explicitly political novels include *Coolie* (1936) and a trilogy (*The Village*, 1939; *Across the Black Waters*, 1940; *The Sword and the Sickle*, 1942). The Indian colonial government proscribed his first three novels. The best known of Anand's later works is *Private Life of an Indian Prince* (1953).

anapaest A trisyllabic metrical unit (*foot) in which the first two syllables are unstressed and the last is stressed; or in Greek and Latin, where the first two are short and the last long. Anapaestic verse is rare in English, although it appears in modified form in the *limerick and in some jaunty songs ('With a hey, and a ho, and a hey-nonny-no'). Robert *Browning memorably exhibited its rhythmic effects in 'How they Brought the Good News from Ghent to Aix' (1845).

anaphora [Greek, 'carrying back'] The repetition of the same word or phrase in several successive clauses; for instance, 'Awake up, my glory; awake, lute and harp; I myself will awake right early' (Psalms 57: 9).

Anarchy, The Mask of See MASK OF ANARCHY.

Anatomy of Abuses, The See STUBBES, PHILIP.

Anatomy of Melancholy, The By Robert *Burton (1621, enlarged 1621–51). Ostensibly a treatise on abnormal psychology and its treatment, the *Anatomy* is written under the pseudonym of 'Democritus Junior' (*Democritus was 'the laughing philosopher') and its tone is, by turns, splenetic, satirical, mocking, self-mocking, confidential, scabrous, pessimistic, misanthropic, and tenderly humane. 'Melancholy', in Burton's usage, covers a vast range of obsessions, delusions, and mental malfunctions, including what is now called clinical depression. He concludes that the whole world is mad, including his readers and himself. The book is made up of a lengthy introduction and three 'partitions', the first on the nature, causes, and symptoms of melancholy, the second on its cure, and the third on two special forms—love melancholy and religious melancholy. It gave John *Keats the story for *'Lamia'.

Anchises *See* AENEID.

Ancient Mariner, The Rime of the A poem by Samuel Taylor *Coleridge, published 1798 in *Lyrical Ballads*. A revised version with marginal glosses was published in *Sibylline Leaves* (1817). An ancient mariner meets three gallants on their way to a marriage feast, and stops one of them in order to tell his story. His ship was drawn towards the South Pole by a storm. When the ship is surrounded by ice an albatross flies through the fog and is received with joy by the crew. The ice splits and the bird moves on with the ship; then, inexplicably, the mariner shoots it. After this act of cruelty a curse falls on the ship. She is driven north to the equator and is becalmed under burning sun in a rotting sea. The albatross is hung round the neck of the hated mariner. A skeleton ship approaches, on which Death and Life-in-Death are playing dice, and when it vanishes all the crew die except the mariner. Suddenly, watching the beauty of the watersnakes in the moonlight, he blesses them—and the albatross falls from his neck. The ship sails home and the mariner is saved, but for a penance he is condemned to travel from land to land and to teach by his example love and reverence for all God's creatures.

Ancrene Wisse A book of devotional and pastoral advice addressed to an initial audience of three anchoresses, regarded as the greatest prose work of the Early Middle English period. It has important linguistic and thematic connections with the group of texts known (from the subject of one of them) as the *Katherine Group.

ANDERSEN, Hans Christian (1805–75) Danish writer of *fairy stories, which first appeared in Danish from 1835 onwards, and in English in 1846. The four collections include such haunting tales as 'The Little Mermaid', 'The Snow Queen', 'The Ugly Duckling', 'The Red Shoes', and 'The Emperor's New Clothes'. They are deeply rooted in Danish folklore, but also shaped by Andersen's own psychological experiences and his at times morbidly acute sensitivity. Many of his narratives are wholly original, not least in their colloquial address and everyday settings; they shaped the modern literary fairy-tale. They were much admired by *Dickens.

ANDERSON, Sherwood (1876–1941) American writer, who made his name as a leading naturalistic writer with his third book, *Winesburg, Ohio* (1919), short stories illustrating life in a small town. Other collections, including *The Triumph of the Egg* (1921) and *Death in the Woods* (1933), also deal with the frustrations of contemporary life, as do his novels, which include *Poor White* (1920), *Dark Laughter* (1925), and the semi-autobiographical *Tar: A Midwest Childhood* (1926).

Andreas An Old English poem of 1,722 lines in the *Vercelli Book, based on a Latin version of the Greek Apocryphal *Acts of Andrew and Matthew amongst the Anthropophagi*. It was previously believed to be by *Cynewulf but is probably later, towards the end of the 9th century.

ANDREWES, Lancelot (1555–1626) Theologian and preacher. Admired by *James I, he headed the list of divines chosen to translate the Authorized Version of the *Bible, acting as general overseer of the project as well as leading the group responsible for Genesis to 2 Kings. He was a major influence in forming a distinctively Anglican theology, pitched between the extremes of *Puritanism and *Roman Catholicism. His sermons, in T. S. *Eliot's view, 'rank with the finest English prose of their time' (*For Lancelot Andrewes*, 1928). The opening of Eliot's 'Journey of the Magi' ('A cold coming we had of it') is drawn from Andrewes's *Sermon 15: Of the Nativitie*.

Anelida and Arcite An incomplete poem by *Chaucer in 357 lines. It is set, like 'The Knight's Tale' (*Canterbury Tales*, 1), in Theseus' Thebes and draws more on *Boccaccio's *Teseida* than on the sources it acknowledges, *Statius and Corinna. The simple story tells of the faithlessness of Arcite to Queen Anelida in 210 lines of *rhyme royal, as a preface to the elaborate *Compleynt* of Anelida in 140 lines of varying and accomplished metrical patterns.

Angel in the House, The A sequence of poems by Coventry *Patmore published in four parts, 1854–61. The work is a celebration of married love, with lyrical and reflective passages linked by a narrative of courtship and marriage. The title, largely thanks to Virginia *Woolf's 'Professions for Women' (1931), which spoke of the need for women writers to 'kill the Angel in the House', quickly established itself as shorthand, now much challenged, for a stereotype of Victorian womanhood.

ANGELOU, Maya (1928–) African American autobiographer and poet. *I Know Why the Caged Bird Sings* (1970), the most famous of her five volumes of autobiography, charts her harrowing childhood in Arkansas, her segregated education in Southern schools, and the beginning of her enduring relationship with literature. The other volumes, *Gather Together in my Name* (1974), *Singin' and Swingin' and Gettin' Merry like Christmas* (1976), *The Heart of a Woman* (1981), and *All God's Children Need Traveling Shoes* (1986), record her flamboyant career as a singer and dancer, her years in the Harlem Writers' Guild, and her role within the civil rights movement. *A Song Flung up to Heaven* (2004) engages with the assassinations of *Malcolm X and Martin Luther King (1929–68). Angelou's works of poetry include *Just Give Me a Cool Drink of Water 'fore I Diiie* (1971), *And Still I Rise* (1978), and *I Shall Not Be Moved* (1990).

Anglo-Indian literature (Indian literature in English). Produced both in India and across the vast Indian diaspora, Anglo-Indian literature represents one of the most innovative and dynamic fields of world writing in English today. It has its roots in the 19th century, in the work of poets such as Henry Derozio (1809–31), Michael Madhusudan Dutta (1824–1873), Toru Dutt (1856–77), Manmohan Ghose (1869–1924), and Sarojini Naidu (1879–1949). Both Dutta, pioneer of Bengali drama and sonnets, whose poems in English include *The Captive Lady* and *Visions of the Past* (1849), and Bankimchandra Chatterjee (1838–94), who wrote the first Indian novel in English, *Rajmohan's Wife* (1864), reverted to Bengali and are renowned as writers in that language, as is the poet Rabindranath *Tagore. In the late 20th century the reputation of the Indian novel in English came controversially to overshadow the vernacular literatures of the sub-continent, but the vernacular languages are heard in the rhythms and diction of reported speech, what the British Indian writer Salman *Rushdie calls 'chutnified' English.

Explanations for the vast success of Anglo-Indian literature include imperial nostalgia, the promotion of Indian writing as exotic, the impetus of globalization, and the ways in which the English language was used to manage the empire. Following independence in 1947, and despite moves to promote Hindi as the national language, English has been increasingly a uni-

fying medium and a mode of shaping Indian national identity, as reflected in the work of Rushdie, Mukul Kesavan and Vikram *Seth.

The two pioneers of the Indian novel in English are recognized to be the social realist Mulk Raj *Anand and the spiritual Raja Rao. Anand was influenced by James *Joyce and *Marx, the *Bloomsbury Group, and the teachings of Gandhi, followed by the comic social observationist R. K. *Narayan and the autobiographer Nirad *Chaudhuri. G. V. *Desani's *All About H. Hatterr* (1948) is a precursor to Rushdie's *magical realism.

Amongst writers of the independence generation are Nehru's niece Nayantara Sahgal (1927–) with her early memoir of the heady days of the Independence struggle, *Prison and Chocolate Cake* (1954); the autobiographer Ved *Mehta; Ruth Prawer *Jhabvala; and Anita *Desai. Trinidad-born V. S. *Naipaul's engagement with India, especially in his three nonfiction books, *An Area of Darkness* (1964), *A Wounded Civilization* (1977), and *India: A Million Mutinies Now* (1990), has been intense and controversial.

From the 1980s, a second literary generation includes Rushdie, its most influential member, and the women writers Gita Mehta (1943–), Githa Hariharan (1954–) and Sara Suleri. Technically Pakistani, *Ice-Candy Man* (1989), by Bapsi Sidhwa (1938–), is an outstanding response to Partition.

A number of different modes in the writing are evolving, including the stark realism of Rohinton *Mistry, the light, Austen-esque prose of Seth, the mordant social observation of Upamanyu *Chatterjee, the flamboyance of Vikram Chandra (1961–) (*Love and Longing in Bombay*, 1997), the multi-layered historical studies of Amitav *Ghosh (*In an Antique Land*, 1992); and the elliptical understatement of Amit *Chaudhuri.

A third generation is now becoming prominent, including Kiran *Desai, Manju Kapur, and the Keralan Arundhati *Roy with her ambitious, highly praised novel *The God of Small Things* (1997). Some writers of Indian descent, including Naipaul and Bharati Mukherjee, now reject the ethnicizing label of 'Indian writer'.

Anglo-Norman The dialect of Medieval French introduced into Britain following the Norman Conquest and spoken and written there until the end of the 14th century. It has had a marked influence on the vocabulary of modern English. One of the most prolific of Anglo-Norman writers was the Franciscan

Nicole Bozon (c.1280–1330), whose output included saints' lives, satires, and *Contes moralisés* (*see* FABLE). *Macaronic verse, both religious and secular, is another characteristic of Anglo-Norman writing.

Anglo-Saxon The Latin form of the word (*Anglo-Saxonicus*) applies originally to the people and language of the Saxon race who colonized the southern parts of Britain (as distinct from the northern parts colonized by the Angles), to distinguish them from continental Saxons. The word does not mean the combination of Angles and Saxons: i.e. the people and language of the whole of England. For the latter the term 'Old English' is more correct. The word became applied in the erroneous way very early; *Ælfric (c.1000) refers to the West Saxon he spoke as 'English'. So the 'correct' distinction, made by the *OED* and enforced by modern scholars (especially at Oxford), between 'Old English' and 'Anglo-Saxon' is a somewhat pedantic one; since the revival of such studies in the 16th century, 'Anglo-Saxon' has been used as the general term, without a sense of geographical distinction.

Anglo-Saxon Chronicles, The Early records in English of events in England from the beginning of the Christian era to 1154, surviving in seven manuscripts which C. Plummer arranged in four groups: the Parker Chronicle, named from Matthew *Parker; the Abingdon Chronicles; the Worcester Chronicle; and the Laud Chronicle, named from William *Laud, of which the most famous version is the *Peterborough Chronicle. The most important and fullest are the Parker and Laud chronicles. The most celebrated entries are those for 449 (the arrival of *Hengist and Horsa), for 755 (the notably taut narrative of *Cynewulf and Cyneheard), for 893 to 897 (Alfred's last series of Danish wars), and for the disastrous years of Stephen's reign at the end of the Peterborough Chronicle. A famous, distinctive feature is the occurrence of the poem on the battle of *Brunanburh (937). The organization of the Chronicles' records in a more orderly way has been attributed to *Alfred in the course of his literary ventures in the 890s.

Angria and **Gondal** Imaginary kingdoms invented by the *Brontë children.

Angry Young Men A journalistic catchphrase loosely applied to a number of British playwrights and novelists from the mid-1950s, including Kingsley *Amis, John *Osborne, Alan *Sillitoe, and Colin *Wilson, whose political views were radical or anarchic.

Animal Farm By George *Orwell, published 1945; a satire in beast fable form on revolutionary and post-revolutionary Russia (and, by extension, on all revolutions). The animals of Mr Jones's farm revolt against their human masters and expel them, the pigs becoming their egalitarian leaders. However, dominated by Napoleon, their chief, the pigs become corrupted by power and a new tyranny replaces the old. The ultimate commandment runs 'ALL ANIMALS ARE EQUAL BUT SOME ANIMALS ARE MORE EQUAL THAN OTHERS'. Napoleon, ruthless and cynical, represents Stalin, and Snowball, the idealist whom he drives away, Trotsky. Boxer, the noble carthorse, stands for the strength, simplicity, and good nature of the common man, but he ends up in the knacker's yard.

animal stories (for children), originating from fables and folklore, have been predominantly didactic from Dorothy Kilner's *The Life and Perambulations of a Mouse* (1783) to *Black Beauty* and Marshall Saunders's *Beautiful Joe* (1894). They can be naturalistic, as in Ernest Thompson Seton's *Wild Animals I Have Known* (1898) and Jack *London's *White Fang* (1906); political and symbolic (*The *Jungle Book*); or concerned with humans in disguise (*The *Wind in the Willows* and much of Beatrix *Potter's work). Modern examples include Richard *Adams's *Watership Down*, books by E. B. *White and Dick *King-Smith, pony books, and many commercial *series books.

animation Early film animation developed in both drawn and puppet forms, with the former initially making use of existing *comic-strip characters, before launching its own range of animal characters, ranging from Felix the Cat to Walt *Disney's Mickey Mouse (1928). Puppet animation developed strongly in Russia and Eastern Europe, with Wladyslaw Starewicz (1892–1965) an innovative creator of sophisticated *fables, and the Czech *Surrealist Jan Svankmajer (1934–), widely admired today for his savage parables and such subversive literary *adaptations as *Alice* (1988) and *Faust* (1994). The animated versions of much juvenile literature produced by Disney, ranging from the *fairy story *Snow White* and such novels as *Pinocchio* and *Bambi*, to Rudyard *Kipling's *Jungle Book* and *101 Dalmations* by Dodie *Smith, may have all but eclipsed their originals. Yet animation remains a potent ideological medium. Halas and Batchelor's animated *Animal Farm* (1954) modified Orwell's politics, with CIA encouragement; while today Aardman's

Wallace and Gromit have become wry emblems of English nostalgia.

Annals of the Parish A novel by John *Galt, published 1821, the source of the term 'utilitarian' adopted by John Stuart *Mill.

Anne of Green Gables First of nine books (1908–37) by L. M. *Montgomery featuring the enduringly popular red-headed orphan Anne Shirley, who is mistakenly sent to work for ageing brother and sister Matthew and Marilla Cuthbert (they want a boy to help on their farm). Despite many mishaps arising from her highly developed imagination fed by a taste for romantic literature, she wins their love. In later books Anne becomes a teacher and marries her childhood tormentor, Gilbert Blythe.

Annual Register, The An annual review of the 'History, Politicks, and Literature' of the past year, founded by Robert *Dodsley and Edmund *Burke; the first volume, covering 1758, appeared on 15 May 1759.

Annus Mirabilis (Year of Miracles) A poem by John *Dryden, published 1667. The year he celebrates is 1666, and the 'miracles' are Britain's victory in the Second Dutch War and the fire of London, miraculous because it was stopped before it destroyed the city.

ANSELM, St (c.1033–1109) A pupil of Lanfranc at the abbey of Bec in Normandy, whom he succeeded as prior of Bec, and as archbishop of Canterbury, in 1093. His most original works are the *Monologion*, its sequel the *Proslogion*, and *Cur Deus Homo*. The original title of the *Proslogion—Fides Quaerens Intellectum* ('faith seeking understanding')—encapsulates an intellectual method in which faith is subjected to meditative and logical examination. The book propounds the famous 'Ontological Argument': if God is defined as a Being than which no greater can be conceived, and such a Being can exist in the mind, then he must exist in reality, since what exists in the mind can be thought to exist in reality, which is greater than the mind. This argument was variously addressed by Aquinas, *Descartes, *Kant, and Bertrand *Russell.

ANSON, George, Baron Anson (1697–1762) Naval officer, administrator, and politician, who made his name circumnavigating the world in 1740–4. *A Voyage round the World by George Anson*, compiled by his chaplain Richard Walter, appeared in 1748. It was the source of William *Cowper's poem 'The *Castaway'.

anthem A form of Anglican church music sung antiphonally, i.e by two voices or choirs, and set to words from the *Bible; more generally, a song or hymn.

Anthology, The Greek (i.e. flower collection), a large number of epigrams (mostly short poems in elegiac couplets) by more than 300 Greek writers from the 4th century BC onwards, arranged in subjects in sixteen books; the subjects include Christian poems, sculpture, morality, homosexual love, and riddles. The anthology was put together in 10th-century Byzantium. A sixteenth book was assembled by the Byzantine monk Planudes c.1300; the Planudean anthology was published in 1494 and was widely read and imitated during the Renaissance.

anti-hero (or anti-heroine) An unheroic or inadequate *protagonist of a story or drama. Not to be confused with the villain or antagonist, the anti-heroic figure is an important type in the novel since *Cervantes and in some kinds of comic drama.

Anti-Jacobin, The, or *Weekly Examiner* (1797–8) A short-lived but remarkable journal founded by George Canning and a group of his friends, including George *Ellis and John *Frere, to combat the radical views supported by the *Monthly Magazine*, Coleridge's *Watchman*, and other *Jacobin influences.

Antiquary, The A novel by Walter *Scott, published 1816. The charm of the book, Scott's 'chief favourite among all his novels', lies in the character of Oldbuck, based, according to the author, on a friend of his boyhood, George Constable, but a recognizable portrait of Scott himself, and in the minor characters.

Antonio and Mellida A two-part play by John *Marston, printed 1602, probably acted two years earlier; it provided *Jonson with materials for his ridicule of Marston in *The *Poetaster*.

Antony and Cleopatra A tragedy by *Shakespeare probably written 1606, not printed until the first *folio of 1623. Its chief source is the *Life of Antony* by *Plutarch, as translated by Sir Thomas *North which Shakespeare followed extremely closely in places. Minor sources include plays by the countess of *Pembroke and Samuel *Daniel.

The play presents Mark Antony, the great soldier and noble prince, at Alexandria, enthralled by the beauty of the Egyptian queen *Cleopatra. Recalled to Rome by the death of his wife Fulvia and political developments, he tears himself from Cleopatra. His estrangement from Octavius Caesar is ended by his marriage to Octavia, Caesar's sister, provoking the intense jealousy of Cleopatra. But the reconciliation is short-lived, and Antony leaves Octavia and returns to Egypt. At the battle of Actium, the flight of the Egyptian squadron is followed by the retreat of Antony, pursued to Alexandria by Caesar. There, after a brief success, Antony is finally defeated. On the false report of Cleopatra's death, he falls upon his sword. He is carried to the monument where Cleopatra has taken refuge and dies in her arms. Cleopatra, fallen into Caesar's power but determined not to grace his triumph, takes her own life by the bite of an asp. *See also* ALL FOR LOVE.

aphorism A short pithy statement into which much thought or observation is compressed, e.g. 'he who praises everybody praises nobody' (Samuel *Johnson). Notable aphorists in English include Johnson, William *Blake (in *The *Marriage of Heaven and Hell*), and Oscar *Wilde. See John Gross (ed.), *The Oxford Book of Aphorisms* (1983).

Apocalypse [from a Greek verb meaning 'to disclose'] A 'revelation' or an 'unveiling', and the title given to the book of Revelation in the New Testament. The term 'apocalyptic literature' is used in a broader sense to describe prophetic writings generally, and especially those presenting visions of the end of the world: the category includes many of the works of William *Blake, of W. B. *Yeats (e.g. 'The Second Coming'), and the 'disaster' novels of J. G. *Ballard and other *science fiction writers. Frank *Kermode's *The Sense of an Ending* (1967) discusses apocalyptic narrative in terms of the Judaeo-Christian view of history as linear, i.e. as possessing a beginning, a middle in which narrator and reader exist, and a necessarily different ending. *See* NEW APOCALYPSE.

Apocrypha Books of Jewish origin in the Septuagint (Greek) version of the Old Testament which the Jews did not accept as part of the Hebrew canon of Scripture. *Jerome included them in the *Vulgate, with the name 'apocrypha' (i.e. non-canonical). At the *Reformation Protestants, unlike Catholics, excluded the Apocrypha from the canon. It forms a separate part of the Authorized Version (1611), in the order 1 and 2 Esdras, Tobit, Judith, the Rest of Esther, the Wisdom of Solomon, Ecclesiasticus, Baruch (with the Epistle of Jeremiah), the Song of the Three Holy Children, the History of Susanna, Bel and the Dragon, the Prayer of Manasses, and 1 and 2 Maccabees. Generally, 'apocrypha' and 'apocryphal' refer to non-canonical or inauthentic works or sayings.

Apollo (Phoebus) In classical mythology the most beautiful of the Olympian gods, son of Zeus (Roman *Jupiter) and Leto, and brother of Artemis (Roman Diana). He is identified by his bow and lyre: he is associated with the sun, archery, prophecy, music, and especially poetry, and hence is the leader of the *Muses and father of *Orpheus. He is prominent as Hector's supporter in the *Iliad* and is the subject of the Homeric *Hymn to Apollo*. In *Ovid's *Metamorphoses* he pursues the nymph Daphne and accidentally kills the boy he loves, Hyacinthus. In Milton's *Lycidas* and Keats's *Hyperion* he represents the poet's own artistic dedication. In *The Birth of Tragedy* (1872) the German philosopher Friedrich *Nietzsche contrasts Apollo with Dionysus as representatives of opposing principles within Greek culture. *See* DELPHIC ORACLE; NIOBE.

Apology for Poetry, An *See* DEFENCE OF POETRY, A.

aporia A rhetorical figure in which the speaker appears perplexed by indecision over some question or choice. *Hamlet's soliloquy 'To be or not to be . . .' is the best-known extended example.

aposiopesis A rhetorical device in which the speaker suddenly comes to a halt in mid-sentence, usually as if dumbstruck by powerful emotion.

apostles [meaning 'messengers'] Who spread the gospel in the New Testament. The term refers both to the disciples, the twelve followers of Jesus, notably Peter, and to later apostles, notably *Paul, who is often simply called the Apostle. The Acts of the Apostles narrates the early expansion of the church from Jerusalem to Rome. *See* BIBLE.

Apostles an intellectual society ('Cambridge Conversazione Society') formed in Cambridge University in 1820. During the 19th century members included Arthur Henry Hallam, Alfred *Tennyson, Monckton Milnes, and Richard Trevenix Trench, and in the early 20th century, the philosopher G. E. Moore (1873–1958), the economist Maynard Keynes (1883–1946), Lytton *Strachey, Bertrand *Russell, Leonard *Woolf, and E. M. *Forster. Arthur *Clough's *The Bothie* mulled over the society's faith in reasoned discussion.

apostrophe [Greek, 'to turn away'] A figure of speech in which the writer rhetorically addresses a dead or absent person or abstraction, e.g. 'Milton! thou shouldst be living at this hour' (William *Wordsworth, 'London, 1802').

Appius and Virginia (1) a tragedy printed in 1654 with a title-page ascription to John *Webster. It is now believed to be Webster's last play, dating from around 1627, and to have been written in collaboration with Thomas *Heywood, with Webster as the dominant partner. The plot is taken from the classical legend which forms one of the stories in William Painter's *Palace of Pleasure*. (2) a tragedy by John Dennis.

APULEIUS (*c.* AD 125–after 170) North African Roman poet, philosopher, and rhetorician, whose best-known work, the comic novel *Metamorphoses* or *The Golden Ass*, is the only complete work of Latin prose fiction to survive. The much-reprinted complete translation of 1566 by William Adlington, *The Golden Asse*, was known to William *Shakespeare. *Cupid and Psyche* is the most frequently retold of Apuleius' stories.

Arabia Deserta See DOUGHTY, CHARLES.

Arabian Nights Entertainments (*or A Thousand and One Nights*) A collection of Arabic stories, introduced in Europe through the French translation of Antoine Galland (1646–1715), whose version appeared between 1704 and 1717. An anonymous *'Grub Street' version appeared in English *c.*1708, and E. W. *Lane's bowdlerized version appeared in 1838–40. A more complete English translation was by John Payne (1842–1916); it appeared in a limited edition, published by the Villon Society 1882–4. This was followed by Sir Richard *Burton's eccentric and prurient version (1885–8), also published through a subscription society to avoid prosecution for obscenity. The first version for children was published by Elizabeth Newbery (d. 1821) *c.*1791 as *The Oriental Moralist or Beauties of the Arabian Nights Entertainments*; other juvenile editions include *Dalziel's Illustrated Arabian Nights Entertainment* (1863–5), with illustrations by John *Tenniel, John Everett *Millais, and others, and one by Andrew *Lang (1898). The best modern translation (only partial) is by Husain Haddawy (2 vols, 1990, 1995).

The *Nights* evolved slowly through oral transmission, but with a certain amount of written backing. A Persian collection called *Hazar Afsaneh* (*A Thousand Tales*) translated into Arabic *c.*AD 850 probably provided a nucleus and possibly even the frame story of Shahriyar and Sheherazade. The tales, which vary in kind, from heroic epics, fables, and pornographic stories to magic-adventure tales such as those about Sinbad and Aladdin, derive mainly from Persian, Arabic, and Indian sources. The collection continued to change, sometimes quite radically, as when large amounts of verse were added in medieval times, until the 19th century, when printed texts provided some stabilization.

There are many other large Arabic oral story collections, but the *Nights* has unequalled variety and verve. It captivated the European imagination, and contributed greatly to the vogue for *oriental tales in the 18th and early 19th centuries. Their influence continued through the 20th, and may be seen in the work of writers as diverse as John *Barth, Jorge *Borges, A. S. *Byatt, Angela *Carter, Pier Paolo Pasolini, and Salman *Rushdie, and in numerous films.

ARAGON, Louis (1897–1982) French poet, novelist, and political activist, one of the founding members of *Surrealism.

ARBUTHNOT, John (1667–1735) From 1705 to 1714 physician to Queen Anne. The *Scriblerus Club met in his rooms. Arbuthnot's *History of *John Bull* and his pamphlet *The Art of Political Lying* (both 1712) were high Tory satires. A serious poem, ΓΝΩΘΙ ΣΕΑΥΤΟΝ (*Know Thyself*) appeared in 1734; later that year Pope hastily assembled his *Epistle to Dr Arbuthnot*, turning a defence of satire into a tribute to his dying friend. Arbuthnot was a main author of the *Memoirs of *Martinus Scriblerus* (pub. 1741).

Arcadia A district in the central Peloponnese which, through *Virgil's *Eclogues*, became the traditional location of the idealized world of *pastoral. Virgil himself was aware of the clash between the genre's realistic and idealizing purposes. Renaissance writers knew nothing about the real Arcadia and idealized landscape dominates their work.

Arcadia A series of verse eclogues connected by prose narrative, published 1504 by Sannazar. The work was a link between the *pastorals of *Theocritus and *Virgil and those of Jorge de *Montemayor, Philip *Sidney, Edmund *Spenser, and later writers.

Arcadia, The A prose romance by Philip *Sidney, including poems and pastoral eclogues in a wide variety of verse forms. It exists in two versions: the first, completed by 1581, and much of it written at Wilton House, is known as the *Old Arcadia*. The second version, now known as the *New Arcadia*, was Sidney's radical revision, made about 1583–4 but never completed. This revised version was first printed, on its own, in 1590, with chapter divisions and summaries 'not of Sir *Philip Sidneis* dooing'. In 1593, and thereafter, books III–V of the *Old Arcadia* were added to the *New Arcadia* to make a complete-seeming but hybrid work. Until the 20th century, only the hybrid *Arcadia* was available to readers.

The *Old Arcadia* is in five 'Books or Acts', sometimes quasi-dramatic in use of dialogue, interspersed with a large number of poems and songs. The first four books are followed by pastoral eclogues on themes linked to or contrasted with the main narrative. The story is of the attempts of Arcadia's ruler, the foolish old duke Basilius, to prevent the fulfilment of an oracle by withdrawing to two rustic 'lodges' with his wife Gynecia and their daughters Pamela and Philoclea. Two young princes, the cousins Musidorus and Pyrocles, gain access to the retired court by disguising themselves as, respectively, a shepherd and an Amazon. A complicated series of intrigues ensues, with Basilius and Gynecia both falling in love with the disguised Pyrocles; Musidorus meanwhile becomes enmeshed with the family of Dametas, an ill-bred herdsman who has been made Pamela's guardian, his shrewish wife Miso, and their foolish daughter Mopsa. Pyrocles succeeds in seducing Philoclea, and Musidorus attempts to elope with Pamela and comes close to raping her, but their schemes go awry when Basilius appears to die of a potion believed by his wife to be an aphrodisiac, and Pyrocles and Philoclea are discovered in bed by Dametas. The climax of the narrative is a trial presided over by Euarchus, the just ruler of Macedon, who sentences Gynecia to be buried alive and Pyrocles and Musidorus to be executed. Euarchus does not recognize the young men as his own son and nephew, but even when their identities are revealed he asserts that 'If rightly I have judged, then rightly have I judged mine own children.' The day is saved, and all appears to end happily, by Basilius' awakening from what was only a sleeping potion. Among the minor characters Philisides, a melancholy gentleman-poet, is a version of Sidney himself.

No new poems were added in the *New Arcadia*, but the method of narration was made far more complex, both stylistically and thematically: the apparent pastoral comedy of the *Old Arcadia* gives way to heroic or epic and tragic writing.

The composite *Arcadia*, as printed from 1593 onwards, was a highly popular book throughout the 17th century. *Shakespeare based the Gloucester plot of *King Lear* on Sidney's story of 'the *Paphlagonian* unkinde king', and Samuel *Richardson took the name of his first heroine, Pamela, from Sidney's romance. Virginia *Woolf was an admirer of it.

ARCHER, William (1856–1924) Drama critic and translator. As an influential drama critic in London (*see* THEATRE CRITICISM), he did much to popularize Henrik *Ibsen in England. His translation of Ibsen's *Pillars of Society* became in 1880 the first Ibsen play to be produced in London; in 1889 the production of his translation of *A Doll's House* caused moral controversy. In 1890–1, Archer published his five-volume edition of Ibsen's prose dramas in translation (some with collaboration), in 1892 he and his brother produced a translation of *Peer Gynt*. The collected works of Ibsen appeared in 1906–7. In 1907, with Harley *Granville-Barker, he issued detailed proposals for a *National Theatre, and in 1919 he assisted with the establishment of the New Shakespeare Company at Stratford-upon-Avon. In *The Drama Old and New* (1923), he promoted the work of George Bernard *Shaw and John *Galsworthy, among others; his own play, *The Green Goddess*, was produced with great success in London in 1923.

archetype A primary symbol, action, setting, or character-type that is found repeatedly in myth, folklore, and literature. Religious mystics have at various times proposed that there is a universal symbolic language of dreams and visions; and in the 20th century this notion was encouraged by the speculative anthropology of J. G. *Frazer and the psychology of *Jung, who claimed that human beings shared a 'collective unconscious' for which archetypal images, whether in dreams or in imaginative literature, provided evidence. Archetypal criticism (*see also* MYTH CRITICISM) under Jung's influence has sought to trace the recurrence of such symbols and types as the Earth Mother, the Quest, the Paradisal Garden, and the Trickster. Maud Bodkin's *Archetypal Patterns in Poetry* (1934) was an early example. The wider significance of archetypes in literature was explored by Northrop *Frye.

Arden (1) a large Warwickshire forest often figuring in romance literature. In Drayton's *Poly-olbion* it extends from the Severn to the Trent (XIII. 16); (2) the forest in Shakespeare's *As You Like It*, often assumed to be identical with (1) but also suggesting the forest north-east of Bordeaux and the forest of Ardennes in present Belgium; (3) the surname of Shakespeare's mother Mary; (4) the distinguishing name of a series of scholarly editions of Shakespeare's plays initiated by W. J. Craig and R. H. Case in 1899; a third series was begun in 1995.

ARDEN, John (1930–2012) Playwright, who had his first professional production, at the *Royal Court, of The Waters of Babylon* (1957), a grotesque, satirical, sprawling play about a corrupt municipal lottery organized by a slum landlord. This was followed by *Live Like Pigs* (1958), dealing with social conflict and violence on a housing estate. *Serjeant Musgrave's Dance* (1959), set in a colliery town in the north of England in 1860–80, shows Musgrave, a deserter from the British army, attempting to exact revenge for the death of a colleague, but finding that violence breeds violence. Arden here mixes a rich, idiosyncratic, semi-historical prose with ballad and verse, as he does in *Armstrong's Last Goodnight* (1964), another fable about violence, set in the Border country in the 1530s. *The Workhouse Donkey* (1963) is a play about municipal corruption. Widely praised as one of the most innovatory dramatists of the 1960s, Arden fell out with the Royal Shakespeare Company, and *The Island of the Mighty* (1972) was the last of his plays to be performed by the British professional theatre. He and his wife Margaretta D'Arcy were already working with John *McGrath's 7:84 company and their later work became more directly socialist and concerned with the politics of Ireland where they were staged. *The Stealing Steps* is a collection of short stories published in 2003.

Arden of Faversham *The Lamentable and True Tragedy of Master Arden of Faversham in Kent, who was most wickedly murdered by the means of his disloyal and wanton wife* A play published anonymously in 1592 in a text that appears to be a memorial reconstruction. Ascribed to Shakespeare in a 1770 edition, it has hovered on the fringes of the Shakespeare canon. The plot derives from *Holinshed's account of an actual murder committed in February 1551. George *Lillo wrote a play on the same subject.

Areopagitica A tract championing freedom of the press by John *Milton, published in 1644. The title imitates the *Areopagiticus* of the Greek orator Isocrates (436–338 BC). Attempting (unsuccessfully) to persuade Parliament to repeal its licensing order of 14 June 1643, which effectively reinstated Stuart press censorship, Milton argues that readers should be free to choose between good and bad books, since good and evil are inseparable in the fallen world, and virtue lies in resisting evil, not being shielded from it. Truth is scattered, and can be recovered only by active search. However, he excludes *Roman Catholics from freedom to publish, regarding them as enemies of freedom themselves.

Arianism A Christian heresy named after the 4th-century Alexandrian priest Arius, who taught that the Son of God was not co-eternal with the Father but created by him and endowed with divine status. Arianism spread widely in the Roman Empire in the 4th century but died out by the end of the 5th. It revived among English radicals in the 16th century, and was held both secretly and publicly by a number of important writers and thinkers in the 17th and 18th centuries, including John *Milton, John *Locke, Isaac *Newton, Samuel Clarke, and Richard *Price. See UNITARIANISM.

Ariel (1) an airy spirit in William *Shakespeare's The *Tempest; (2) a rebel angel in Milton's *Paradise Lost* (VI. 371); (3) in Pope's *Rape of the Lock* (II. 53ff.) the chief of the sylphs.

Shakespeare's character (1) has inspired many later writers to identify the name 'Ariel' with poetic imagination. T. S. *Eliot called five Christmas poems (1927–54) 'Ariel poems', for instance, the first *Penguin paperback was Maurois's life of P. B. *Shelley called *Ariel* (1935), and there have been several literary journals with 'Ariel' as title. See also PLATH.

ARIOSTO, Ludovico (1474–1533) Italian poet and playwright, in the service of the Este family, whom he praised in his poem *Orlando furioso*, published in its final form in 1532, the greatest of Italian chivalric or romance epics. He also wrote Italian and Latin lyrics, satires in imitation of *Horace (known to Sir Thomas *Wyatt), and four comedies, modelled on ancient Roman comedy but set in the contemporary world, of which one, *I suppositi* (1509), came through to *Shakespeare's *The *Taming of the Shrew* via George Gascoigne's *Supposes*.

ARISTOPHANES (*c.*450/460–386 BC) Athenian comic playwright. His eleven surviving comedies are *The Acharnians*; *The Knights*; *The Clouds*; *The Peace*; *The Wasps*; *The Birds*; *The Frogs*; *Plutus*; *Lysistrata*; *Ecclesiazusae*; and *Thesmophoriazusae*. They represent the rumbustious Old Comedy, combining personal attacks, obscenities, parodies, songs, and hymns with ideas on poetry, politics, religion, the sexes. *Socrates is ridiculed in *Clouds*; *Euripides in *Thesmophoriazusae*. In *Frogs*, Euripides and *Aeschylus compete in the underworld to determine which poet can save Athens. Aristophanes' earlier plays, *Acharnians* and *Knights*, are savage attacks on Athenian warmongering; *Wasps* attacks the democracy's jury system. *Birds* is a fantasy of escape from war. *Lysistrata* and *Ecclesiazusae* ridicule notions about the equality of the sexes. In *Plato's *Symposium*, Aristophanes makes a lively and engaging speech on love. Aristophanes' influence on English drama can be seen in Ben *Jonson, Thomas *Middleton, and especially Henry *Fielding. Robert *Browning's poem *Aristophanes' Apology* has the dramatist defend the naturalness of comedy.

Aristophanes' Apology Including a Transcript from Euripides: Being the Last Adventure of Balaustion A long poem in blank verse by Robert *Browning, published 1875 as a sequel to *Balaustion's Adventure* (1871). The structure—a monologue containing the narrative of a dialogue and the reading of a play—explores the relation of poetic discourse to absolute values such as 'truth' or 'reality'.

ARISTOTLE (384–322 BC) Philosopher, born at Stagira in Macedon. Sent to Athens in 367, he studied under *Plato for twenty years. In 342 he was appointed by Philip II of Macedon as tutor to the future *Alexander the Great. Seven years later he returned to Athens, where he opened a school in the Lyceum, a grove outside the city; from its colonnades ('peripatoi'), where teaching took place, his school and its philosophical tradition later became known as the Peripatetic. His published works, including dialogues known to *Cicero, are lost; his extant works were probably written lectures. They cover logic, metaphysics, physics, zoology, psychology, ethics, politics, rhetoric, and poetics and demonstrate a strong commitment to the classification of empirical observations and the systematization of knowledge generally. Trans-

mitted through translations, they shaped the development of medieval thought first in the Arab world, then in the Latin West, where Aristotle came to be regarded as the source of all knowledge. His logical treatises won a central place in the curriculum during the 12th century. After a brief struggle his ethical, metaphysical, and scientific works were harmonized with Christianity and constituted the subject matter of higher education from the 13th to the 17th centuries. They shaped the thinking of Englishmen writing in Latin from *Grosseteste to *Herbert of Cherbury, but the 17th-century promoters of the new science saw Francis *Bacon as having overthrown Aristotle by his superior grasp of experimental observation and his method of induction. The humanists favoured the *Nicomachean Ethics* (identified by Edmund *Spenser as the source of the virtues in The *Faerie Queene*), *Politics*, and the *Poetics*, which contributed to the rise of *neo-classicism. *See* SCHOLASTICISM.

ARLEN, Michael (1895–1956) Novelist. He wrote a number of ornate and mannered novels of fashionable London life, but is chiefly remembered for his best-seller *The Green Hat* (1924).

Armadale A novel by Wilkie *Collins, published in 1866. This intricately plotted *sensation novel, Collins's longest, has two heroes, one fair, prosperous, and cheerful, the other penniless, dark, and disturbed. Both are named Allan Armadale, and both are infatuated with a compelling red-haired villainess, Lydia Gwilt. The complications stem from the previous generation, when the father of the dark Armadale murdered the father of the other. The dark Armadale, after a miserable childhood, adopts the name Ozias Midwinter, and meets the fair Armadale by chance. They become friends, but Armadale has a prophetic dream which convinces Midwinter that he is doomed to harm his friend. Lydia Gwilt, privy to the mystery surrounding them, marries Midwinter under his real name, becoming Mrs Armadale; her plan to murder Armadale and produce the marriage certificate in order to inherit his money is frustrated by Midwinter, and Lydia dies. The novel reflects Collins's characteristic interests in murder and detection, doubled identities, and the supernatural.

ARMAH, Ayi Kwei (1939–) Author, born in Ghana. His first novel, *The Beautyful Ones Are Not Yet Born* (1968), disconcerted readers by its savagely brilliant and witty attack on the corruption of independent Ghana. Baako in *Fragments* (1970) is a Been-to; he has been educated in Britain and is expected to return with material prosperity for his family. *Why Are We So Blest* (1972) asserts, from three different perspectives, that Africans 'have swallowed the wish for our destruction'. *Two Thousand Seasons* (1973), *The Healers* (1978), and *Osiris Rising* (1995) present an alternative position, focusing on healing through traditional story-telling and a revision of history.

Arminianism The doctrines of Jacobus Arminius (1560-1609), a Dutch Protestant theologian. In opposition to *Calvin's views, Arminius taught that Christ died for all, not only the elect, and that humans could choose whether or not to cooperate with divine grace. His doctrines spread rapidly; in England they were on the whole detested by Puritans but were embraced by both bishops and theological radicals, including John *Milton.

ARMITAGE, Simon (1963-) Poet and CBE. His first collection, *Zoom!* (1989), drew on his experience as a probation officer, and on the rhythms of Yorkshire vernacular, as well as on Frank *O'Hara and Paul *Muldoon. Its immediacy, wit, and originality brought him great critical and popular acclaim. *Book of Matches* (1993), *Dead Sea Poems* (1995), and *CloudCuckooLand* (1997) are more introspective. Recent collections include *Selected Poems* (2001), *Tyrannosaurus Rex Versus the Corduroy Kid* (2006), and *Seeing Stars* (2010). His novels include *The White Stuff* (2004). He has made versions of *Euripides, the *Odyssey*, and the medieval English poem *Sir *Gawain and the Green Knight* (2007), which employs a distinctively northern and contemporary demotic while scrupulously recreating the alliterative metres of the original. *Moon Country* (1996), a collaboration with Glyn *Maxwell, retraces the journey to Iceland made by W. H. *Auden and Louis *MacNeice in 1936.

ARMSTRONG, John (1709-79) London-based Scottish poet and physician, and friend of James *Thomson (who portrayed him in *The *Castle of Indolence*). He wrote a four-volume didactic poem *The Art of Preserving Health* (1744) and a satirical verse epistle, *Taste* (1753).

ARNE, Thomas (1710-78) Theatre composer. He produced a setting of Joseph *Addison's *Rosamond* (1733), and *masques, including an adaptation of *Milton's *Comus* (1738), and David *Mallet and James *Thomson's masque *Alfred* (1740), which added 'Rule Britannia' to the canon of English song. His many *Shakespeare settings include 'Where the bee sucks' and 'Fear no more the heat of the sun'.

ARNOLD, Matthew (1822-88) Poet and critic. His first volume of poems, *The Strayed Reveller, and Other Poems* (by 'A', 1849), contains sonnets written at Balliol College, Oxford, including 'Shakespeare'. In 1851 he became an inspector of schools, in which capacity he served for 35 years, travelling throughout England and observing at first hand the social conditions that prompted much of his later critical work. Part of 'Dover Beach' (1867) may date from his honeymoon (1851), which also inspired his 'Stanzas from the Grande Chartreuse' (1855). *Empedocles on Etna, and Other Poems* appeared, anonymously, in 1852, and in 1853 a volume of poems containing *'Sohrab and Rustum', 'The *Scholar-Gipsy', and 'Memorial Verses to Wordsworth' (who had been a friend of the Arnolds). Arnold's preface discusses the problems of writing poetry in an 'age wanting in moral grandeur'. He published *Poems, Second Series* (1855); *Merope, a Tragedy* (1858); and *New Poems*, (1867), but turned increasingly to prose, writing essays on literary, educational, and social topics which greatly influenced writers as diverse as Max Weber, T. S. *Eliot, F. R. *Leavis, and Raymond *Williams. His lectures on translating *Homer, with his definition of 'the grand style', were published in 1861 (*see* TRANSLATION); *Essays in Criticism (First Series)* in 1865 (*Second Series*, 1888); *On the Study of Celtic Literature* in 1867; *Culture and Anarchy* in 1869; *Friendship's Garland* in 1871; *Literature and Dogma*, a study of the interpretation of the Bible, in 1873. Arnold sharply criticized the provincialism, Philistinism, sectarianism, and *utilitarian materialism of English life and culture, and argued that England needed more intellectual curiosity, more ideas, and a more comparative, European outlook.

Artegal (Archgallo in Geoffrey) Legendary king of Britain, whose story is described in *Geoffrey of Monmouth's *Historia Regum Britanniae*, III. 17 and is the subject of William *Wordsworth's poem 'Artegal and Elidure'.

art for art's sake A phrase associated with the aesthetic doctrine that art is self-sufficient and need serve no moral or political purpose. The phrase *l'art pour l'art* became current in France in the first half of the 19th century and Théophile Gautier's formulation in his preface to *Mademoiselle de Maupin* (1835), which denied that art could or should be in any way useful, was admired by Walter *Pater, one of the leading influences on the English *'Aesthetic' movement of the 1880s. (*See* WILDE, OSCAR; DOWSON, ERNEST; JOHNSON, LIONEL; SYMONS, ARTHUR.) A. C. *Swinburne in his study *William Blake* (written between 1862 and 1867) championed the morality of 'art for art's sake' and Pater in his conclusion to *The Renaissance* (1873) spoke of 'the desire of beauty, the love of art for art's sake'.

Arthour and of Merlin, Of A later 13th-century non-alliterative romance in 9,938 lines of short rhyming couplets, a leisurely narrative of the life of Merlin, the upbringing and crowning of Arthur and his many battles.

Arthur, King The figure of King Arthur has probably some historical basis. He was probably a chieftain or general (*dux bellorum*) in the 5th or 6th century. The *Annales Cambriae* place the battle of Mount Badon, 'in which Arthur carried the cross of our Lord Jesus Christ on his shoulders', in 518, and the 'battle of Camlan, in which Arthur and Medraut fell' in 539. There is mention of him in certain ancient poems contained in the *Black Book of Carmarthen* and more especially in the ancient Welsh romance *Culhwch and Olwen*, where he figures with Kay, Bedevere, and *Gawain (Gwalchmei). According to the *Arthur* of the marquis of Bath's manuscript (1428: ed. F. J. Furnivall, EETS OS 2, 1864), he died in 542 after a reign of 22 years. He was said to be the father of *Mordred by his half-sister Morgawse; his sister was Anna. Guinevere was the daughter of Arthur's ally Leodegan. According to *Malory, the Grail was accomplished 454 years after the passing of Christ (i.e. in 487). The legend of the return of Arthur to rule Britain again is told by Malory and in the stanzaic *Le *Morte Arthur*. According to the alliterative *Morte Arthure*, he definitely died.

The Arthur of the cycle of legends first appears at length in the *Historia Regum Britanniae* of *Geoffrey of Monmouth. According to this, Arthur is the son of *Uther Pendragon and Ygaerne (*Igraine), wife of Gorlois of Cornwall, whom Uther wins through Merlin's magic. At the age of 15 he becomes king and, with his sword Caliburn (Excalibur), slays Childric, defeats the heathen, and conquers Scotland, Ireland, Iceland, and Orkney. He marries Guanhamara, a Roman lady, and holds his court at Caerleon on the Usk. He is summoned to pay tribute to the emperor Lucius of Rome, resists, and declares war. Guanhamara and the kingdom are left in the charge of Modred, his

nephew. Arthur slays the giant of St Michael's Mount. When about to enter Rome, he is warned that Modred has seized Guanhamara and the kingdom. He returns with Walwain, who is slain on landing; Modred retreats to Cornwall where, with all his knights, he is slain in a final battle. Arthur is mortally wounded and is borne to the island of *Avalon for the healing of his wounds, and Guanhamara becomes a nun. This version was developed by the 12th-century Norman writer *Wace; the Round Table is first mentioned by him as a device for the settlement of disputes over precedence; and Wace says that the wounded king is expected to return to rule the Britons again. Wace was the principal source of *Laʒamon's *Brut,* the first English version of the story which adds to both the magical and martial aspects: Arthur is borne off after the last battle at Camelford to Argante (Morgan le Fay) in Avalon in a magic boat. The story was very significantly developed in the French *'matter of Britain', by such writers as *Marie de France, *Chrétien de Troyes, and the authors of the 13th-century Vulgate prose cycles, and it became the centre of a mass of legends in several languages, most importantly German. Other characters—*Merlin, *Gawain, *Launcelot, and *Tristram—gradually became associated with Arthur, and he himself is the central character only in the narratives describing his early years and his final battle and death; in the intervening tales his court is merely the starting point for the adventures of various knights. The story of Arthur as given here is the basis of Malory's *Le *Morte Darthur* which was the most authoritative version of the legend in the English tradition. Malory's version gives great prominence to the exploits of the knights of the Round Table, the quest of the Holy Grail, the love of Launcelot and Guinevere, and the love of Tristram and Isoud. For other Arthurian writings, *see* TENNYSON, ALFRED; WILLIAM OF MALMESBURY; GLASTONBURY.

(⊕) SEE WEB LINKS

• The Arthuriana/Camelot Project Bibliographies

Arthur, Prince In Edmund *Spenser's *Faerie Queene* he symbolizes 'Magnificence', or Magnanimity, in the Aristotelian sense of the perfection of all the virtues.

Art of English Poesie, The *See* PUTTENHAM, GEORGE.

Art of English Poesy, Observations in the An attack on the use of rhyme in English poetry by Thomas *Campion, published in 1602, to which Samuel *Daniel replied in his *Defence of Rhyme*.

Art of Rhetoric, The See WILSON, THOMAS.

Ascent of F6, The A play by W. H. *Auden and Christopher *Isherwood published 1936, first performed 1937. The central character, Michael Ransom, 'scholar and man of action', succumbs to his mother's persuasions and leads a mountaineering expedition up F6, a mysterious and haunted peak on the borders of disputed colonial territory; all his men die en route and he himself dies as he achieves his mission, destroyed by his own self-knowledge, having rejected the possibility of evasion and the contemplative life. The Establishment figures are presented satirically, the figures of the mother and the comrades with more ambiguity; Ransom himself was in part modelled on T. E. *Lawrence, the Truly Strong Weak Man. The play is a parable about the nature of power, will, and leadership, with both political and Freudian implications, and may be seen to reflect the apprehension of and attraction towards the 'strong man' in the 1930s.

ASCHAM, Roger (1514/15–68) Scholar. In 1545 he published *Toxophilus*, a treatise on archery, in the form of a Ciceronian dialogue between Toxophilus (lover of shooting) and Philologus (lover of learning). He succeeded William Grindal as tutor to Princess Elizabeth, Prince Edward, and perhaps Lady Jane Grey in 1548, holding this post for under two years. In 1554 he became Latin secretary to Queen Mary, being tacitly permitted to continue in his *Protestantism, and he was renewed in this office under *Elizabeth I. His best-known work, *The Schoolmaster*, was published posthumously by his widow in 1570. Its three most distinctive features are: Ascham's dislike of corporal punishment; the Ciceronian technique of double translation, from Latin into English and back again; and his attitude to Italy. Although he valued Italian language and culture highly, Ascham felt that it was a dangerously corrupting country for English travellers. *The Schoolmaster* was an influence on Philip *Sidney's *Defence of Poetry*, as well as an important landmark in Renaissance educational theory. Ascham's English works are notable for their colloquial, personal style and for considerable economy of expression: they form an important bridge between the early Tudor writers and the Elizabethans.

ASHBERY, John (1927–) American poet. His first volume, *Song Trees*, was published in the Yale Younger Poets series edited by W. H. *Auden in 1956. His second collection, *The Tennis Court Oath* (1962), is his most radical, and has proved an important influence on the development of the American school of the 1970s which became known as 'The *Language Poets'. Ashbery achieved canonical status with the publication of his sixth volume, *Self-Portrait in a Convex Mirror* (1975). He was the first of the so-called *'New York Poets'—normally seen as comprising Frank *O'Hara, Kenneth Koch, and James *Schuyler—to achieve wide recognition. His poetry is characterized by its openness to the vagaries of consciousness, its wry, beguiling lyricism, and its innovative use of forms such as the pantoum (composed of four-line stanzas in which the second and fourth lines of each stanza serve as the first and third lines of the next) and the *sestina. The critic Harold *Bloom has declared him the most significant poet since Wallace *Stevens. His most recent collections are *A Worldly Country* (2007) and *Planisphere* (2009).

ASHFORD, Daisy (1881–1972) Born in Petersham, child-author of *The Young Visiters*, published in 1919 with an introduction by J. M *Barrie, who verified that she was genuine. An unwitting parody of *romantic fiction, it tells the adventures of Ethel Monticue and her admirer Mr Salteena. The BBC filmed it in 2003.

ASIMOV, Isaac (1920–92) American author credited with coining the term 'robotics' in a series of stories mostly published in *Astounding Science-Fiction* in the 1940s. Encouraged by the editor John W. Campbell, Asimov developed the sequence, collected as *I, Robot* (1950), as a series of moral puzzles with the 'three laws of robotics' offering enough ambiguity to suggest ethical dilemmas. In 1942, Asimov began a future history, collected as *Foundation* (1951), *Foundation and Empire* (1952), and *Second Foundation* (1953). *The Gods Themselves* (1972) won both *Hugo and Nebula awards in 1973. *Foundation's Edge* (1982) won a Hugo. Asimov's popular and distinctively humanistic stories made him, according to critic John *Clute, the default voice of 20th-century science fiction.

ASLAM, Nadeem (1966–) Novelist, born in Pakistan, whose painstakingly produced novels are *Season of the Rainbirds* (1993), *Maps for Lost Lovers* (2004), in which Aslam wanted each chapter to be like a Persian miniature, and *The Wasted Vigil* (2008).

assonance The repetition of similar vowel sounds in the stressed syllables (and sometimes too in those that follow) of neighbouring words:

> And round about the keel with faces pale
>   (Alfred *Tennyson)

It is distinct from full *rhyme in that while the vowel sounds correspond, the consonants do not.

ASTELL, Mary (1666–1731) Writer. *Letters Concerning the Love of God* (1695) was based on her correspondence with John *Norris. *A Serious Proposal to the Ladies for the Advancement of their True and Greatest Interest* (1694; part 2, 1697) sought to enhance women's situation and self-esteem through self-education. She proposed the establishment of a secular seminary for women who preferred intellectual pursuits to marriage. In *Some Reflections on Marriage* (1700) Astell argued that women who were not prepared to take the binding vows of obedience and subservience that marriage required of them should not marry (she herself remained unmarried). Astell's ideas on female education were publicized by Daniel *Defoe (*Essay upon Projects*, 1697) and absorbed into George *Berkeley's *Ladies Library* (1714). She was lampooned in the *Tatler* (nos. 32 and 63), but her influence on women writers was widespread.

Astraea Redux *See* DRYDEN, JOHN.

'Astrophel' A pastoral elegy, written by Edmund *Spenser *c.*1591-5 on the death of Philip *Sidney, and published in 1595 with *Colin Clouts Come Home Againe*. Spenser had previously lamented Sidney in 'The *Ruines of Time'. A. C. *Swinburne used the title for a volume of his poems in 1894.

Astrophel and Stella A sequence of 108 sonnets and 11 songs by Philip *Sidney, written *c.*1582. They plot the unhappy love of Astrophel ('star-lover') for Stella ('star'). As several authors make clear, e.g. 37, referring to one that 'Hath no misfortune, but that Rich she is', Stella is to be identified with Penelope Rich; but the exact nature of Sidney's real, rather than poetic, relationship with her cannot be known. Apart from snatching a kiss while she is asleep, Astrophel achieves nothing in the sequence, and the story breaks off—'That therewith my song is broken'—rather than being resolved. Poetically, however, the sonnets are an outstanding achievement, being written throughout in versions of the exacting Italian sonnet form, and displaying a striking range of tone, imagery, and metaphor. Among the best known is 31, 'With how sad steps, ô Moone, thou climb'st the skies' (Philip *Larkin's 'Sad Steps', published in his 1974 collection, *High Windows*, takes its title from the sonnet). There were two editions of *Astrophel and Stella* in 1591 which began a craze for sonnet sequences; from 1598 it was included in editions of *The *Arcadia*.

As You Like It A comedy by *Shakespeare, registered for publication 4 August 1600; probably written shortly before. It was first printed in the first *folio of 1623. Shakespeare's chief source was Thomas Lodge's *Rosalynde*, but Shakespeare's own additions include Jaques and the clown Touchstone, and the appearance of Hymen (V. iv), the first of his scenes to include a god, anticipating the late romances.

Frederick has usurped his brother the duke, who is living with his faithful followers in the forest of Ardenne (*see* ARDEN). Celia, Frederick's daughter, and Rosalind, the duke's daughter, living at Frederick's court, watch a wrestling match in which Orlando, son of Sir Rowland de Bois, defeats a powerful adversary. Rosalind and Orlando fall in love. Orlando has been driven from home by the cruelty of his elder brother Oliver, who became his guardian on his father's death. Frederick, learning that Orlando is the son of Sir Rowland, a friend of the exiled duke, banishes Rosalind from his court. Celia accompanies her. Rosalind assumes a countryman's dress and calls herself Ganymede; Celia passes as Aliena, his sister. They live in the forest of Ardenne, and fall in with Orlando, who has joined the banished duke. Ganymede encourages Orlando to pay suit to her as though she were his Rosalind. Oliver comes to the forest to kill Orlando, but is saved by him from a lioness, and is filled with remorse. He falls in love with Aliena, and their wedding is arranged for the next day. Ganymede undertakes to Orlando that she will by magic produce Rosalind at the same time to be married to him. When all are gathered to celebrate the double wedding, Celia and Rosalind shed their disguise and appear in their own characters. News is brought that Frederick, setting out to destroy his brother and his followers, has been converted by 'an old religious man' and has restored the dukedom.

Conversation rather than plot dominates this play, much of it provided by the reflections of Jaques and Touchstone, and by the large number of songs, more than in any of Shakespeare's other plays, including 'Under the greenwood tree' (which Thomas *Hardy used as the title for a novel) and 'Blow, blow, thou winter wind' (in II. v and II. vii respectively).

Atalanta in Calydon A poetic drama by A. C. *Swinburne, published 1865, which brought Swinburne fame and was highly praised for its successful imitation of Greek models (though the subject had not been treated by any Greek dramatist).

'Atheism, The Necessity of' A prose pamphlet by P. B. *Shelley and his friend Thomas Jefferson *Hogg, published anonymously at Oxford, 1811. Using the sceptical arguments of David *Hume and John *Locke, the authors—then both undergraduates—smartly demolish the grounds for a rational belief in the Deity. Shelley and Hogg were both expelled from the university for circulating the work to heads of colleges and to bishops, and for 'contumacy' (obstinate disobedience) in refusing to answer questions about it.

Atheist's Tragedy, The A tragedy by Cyril *Tourneur, printed 1611. D'Amville, the 'atheist', plans to marry his son to Castabella and, to effect this, he sends her betrothed Charlemont abroad on active service. Charlemont is supposed dead, but returns, and is advised by the ghost of his father (whom D'Amville has meanwhile murdered) to forgo revenge. In the end D'Amville accidentally dashes out his own brains when raising an axe to execute Charlemont, and Charlemont and Castabella are united. *See* REVENGE TRAGEDY.

Athelston A verse romance from the late 14th century, in 812 lines. It tells of the chance meeting in a forest of four messengers, one of whom, Athelston, becomes king of England. Of the other three, one becomes archbishop of Canterbury, pitting ecclesiastical against secular power; another becomes earl of Dover, plots against the king, and is executed; and the fourth becomes earl of Stone and the father of Athelston's successor.

ATHERTON, Gertrude Franklin Horn (1857–1948) American novelist. *Before the Gringo Came* (1894) and *The Californians* (1898) explore the history of her home state. *The Conqueror* (1902), is based on her research into the life of Alexander Hamilton (1755–1804), one of the Founding Fathers of America. Her autobiography *The Adventures of a Novelist* (1932) recalls her time in England and Germany. *Black Oxen* (1923, novel) describes a glandular rejuvenation treatment she had in Europe.

ATHILL, Diana (1917–) OBE. Novelist, editor, and memoirist. Her work as literary editor at André Deutsch, working with authors including John *Updike, V. S. *Naipaul, Norman *Mailer, and Jean *Rhys, is recalled in *Stet* (2000). Her selected memoirs *Life Class* (2009) brought together in one volume *Stet* and a selection of the frank personal memoirs for which she is best known, including *Somewhere Towards the End* (2008), about late old age. She has also written a collection of short stories, *An Unavoidable Delay* (1962) and a novel, *Don't Look at Me Like That* (1967).

ATKINSON, Kate (1951–) Novelist and short story writer. Her first novel, *Behind the Scenes at the Museum* (1995), a comedy of sibling rivalry and suppressed memory, is set largely in York during the 1950s but steps backwards in time to follow its central character's family history. *Human Croquet* (1997) and *Emotionally Weird* (2000) explore themes of identity and inheritance. Her latest novels feature the detective Jackson Brodie from *Case Histories* (2004) to *When Will There Be Good News?* (2008) and *Started Early, Took my Dog* (2010).

ATWOOD, Margaret (1939–) Canadian poet and novelist, who spent much of her early life in the northern Ontario and Quebec bush country. Her first volume of poetry, *The Circle Game*, appeared in 1966. Her first novel, *The Edible Woman* (1969), was followed by *Surfacing* (1972), *Lady Oracle* (1976), *Life before Man* (1979), and *Bodily Harm* (1981), all novels with political and feminist themes, and a controversial study of Canadian literature, *Survival* (1972). She has published books for children, and several collections of shorter fiction including *Dancing Girls* (1977), *Bluebeard's Egg and Other Stories* (1983), *Wilderness Tips* (1991), and *Good Bones* (1992). *The Handmaid's Tale* (1985) is a *dystopia set in the imaginary Republic of Gilead, where failing fertility results in the sexual enslavement of women for breeding purposes. *The Robber Bride* (1994) tells the story of three friends confronted by a disruptive *femme fatale* who they thought was dead. *Alias Grace* (1996), which revisits the ambiguous history of a 16-year-old Canadian housemaid, convicted of the murder of her employer and his housekeeper in 1843, was followed by *The Blind Assassin* (2000; *Booker Prize). *Oryx and Crake* (2003) contemplates a desolate future in a world ruined by misguided genetic manipulation, and reflects Atwood's long-standing interest in science and environmentalism. *The Penelopiad* (2005), a novella in which Penelope remembers the events of Homer's **Odyssey* was dramatized by the Royal Shakespeare Company (2007). *The Door* (2007) is a collection of poetry, *The Year of the Flood* (2009) her most recent novel. Atwood's own views on the writer's craft are represented in her *Negotiating with the Dead: A Writer on Writing* (2002).

aubade A song or lyric poem in any verse form or **metre in which the coming of dawn is lamented because it brings the pains of separation to a pair of lovers. The classic English example is John **Donne's 'The Sunne Rising'. Shakespeare's **Romeo and Juliet* III. v is an extended dramatic adaptation of the aubade convention.

AUBIN, Penelope (?1679–?1731) Novelist and translator. She wrote three patriotic poems (1707–8). Her seven popular novels, from *The Strange Adventures of the Count de Vinevil* (1721) to *The Life and Adventures of the Young Count Albertus* (1728), portrayed virtue under pressure from seduction and other threats in attractively exotic settings.

AUBREY, John (1626–97) Antiquary and biographer. His education at Trinity College, Oxford, was interrupted by the Civil War. In 1648 he was the first to discover the ruins of Avebury; in 1662 he was nominated one of the original fellows of the **Royal Society. His *Miscellanies* of stories and folklore were published in 1696, but he is chiefly remembered for his *Lives* of eminent people, much used (and in his view somewhat abused) by Anthony **Wood. He collected these over a period of years, depositing his manuscripts in the Ashmolean Museum in 1693. Early editions (1813, 1898) were edited to erase bawdy references. The *Lives* are a lively and heterogeneous mixture of anecdote, first-hand observation, folklore, and erudition, a valuable, open-minded, entertaining (if at times inaccurate) portrait of an age.

Aucassin and Nicolette An early 13th-century courtly story in northern French, composed in alternating prose and heptasyllabic (seven-syllabled) verse, about the forbidden love of Aucassin, son of the Christian Count Garins of Beaucaire, for Nicolette, a Saracen captive, their various adventures, and their eventual marriage. It deals playfully with the conventions of courtly love romances. First translated into English in 1786, *Aucassin and Nicolette* was the subject of an essay by Walter **Pater in *Studies in the History of the Renaissance* (1873) and two translations in 1887 by F. W. Bourdillon and Andrew **Lang. The most

recent translation is that by Glyn S. Burgess (1988). Charles **Causley's *The Ballad of Aucassin and Nicolette* is a play adaptation (performed 1978; pub. 1981).

AUCHINCLOSS, Louis (1917–2010) American novelist, historian, and essayist. He is widely regarded as the heir to Edith **Wharton. Auchincloss's chosen subject was the New York aristocracy, which he has depicted in novels like *Pursuit of the Prodigal* (1959) and *Portrait in Brownstone* (1962).

AUDEN, W. H. (Wystan Hugh) (1907–73) Poet. He began to be taken seriously as a poet while still at Christ Church, Oxford (1925–8), where he was much influenced by Anglo-Saxon and Middle English poetry, but also began to explore the means of preserving 'private spheres' (through poetry) in 'public chaos' which would become a hallmark of his work. Among his contemporaries were Louis **MacNeice, Cecil **Day-Lewis, and Stephen **Spender. (*See* PYLON SCHOOL.) After Oxford, Auden lived for a time in Berlin before returning to England in 1929; he continued to visit Germany regularly, staying with his friend and future collaborator Christopher **Isherwood. His *Poems* (1930) established him as the most talented voice of his generation. *The Orators* followed in 1932 and *Look Stranger!* in 1936. In 1932 he became associated with the Group Theatre of Rupert Doone (1903–66), which produced several of his plays (*The Dance of Death*, pub. 1933, performed 1934; and, with Isherwood, *The Dog beneath the Skin*, pub. 1935, performed 1936, *The **Ascent of F6*, pub. and performed in 1936, and *On the Frontier*, pub. and performed in 1938). All four owe something to the early plays of Bertolt **Brecht. Working from 1935 with the General Post Office film unit he became friendly with Benjamin **Britten, who set many of his poems to music and later used Auden's text for his opera *Paul Bunyan* (performed 1941). In 1935 the homosexual Auden married Erika Mann to provide her with a British passport and a means of escape from Nazi Germany; they never divorced. A visit to Iceland with MacNeice in 1936 produced their joint *Letters from Iceland* (1937); *Journey to a War* (1939, with Isherwood) records a journey to China. His poem 'Spain' (1937) followed his two-month visit there to support the Republicans. In January 1939 he and Isherwood left Europe for America (Auden became a US citizen in 1946) where he met Chester Kallman (1921–75), who became his lifelong companion. *Another Time* (1940), containing many of his most famous poems, was followed by *The Double Man* (1941, published in London as *New Year Letter*), a long transitional verse epistle describing the 'baffling crime' of 'two decades of hypocrisy', rejecting political simplifications, accepting man's essential solitude, and ending with a prayer for refuge and illumination for the 'muddled heart'. From this time Auden's poetry became increasingly Christian in tone, a transformation perhaps not unconnected with the death in 1941 of his devout Anglo-Catholic mother, to whom he dedicated *For the Time Being: A Christmas Oratorio* (1944). This was published with *The Sea and the Mirror*, a series of dramatic monologues inspired by *The *Tempest*. The Age of Anxiety: A Baroque Eclogue* (1948) is a long dramatic poem, set in New York, reflecting man's isolation.

Auden's absence during the war led to a poor reception of his works in England, but he was professor of poetry at Oxford from 1956 to 1961. His major later collections include *Nones* (1951, New York; 1952, London), *The Shield of Achilles* (1955), considered by many his best single volume; and *Homage to Clio* (1960), which includes a high proportion of light verse. Auden also wrote several libretti, notably for Igor *Stravinsky's *The Rake's Progress* (1951, with Kallman). *About the House* (1965, New York; 1966, London) contains a tender evocation of his life with Kallman at their summer home in Austria. Auden spent his final year in Oxford and died suddenly in Vienna on his way back to England. *Thank you, Fog* (1974) appeared posthumously, and his *Collected Poems* came out in 1991.

Auden's influence on succeeding poets is comparable in his era only with that of W. B. *Yeats and T. S. *Eliot. His progress from the engaged, didactic, satiric poems of his youth to the complexity of his later work offered a wide variety of models—the urbane, the pastoral, the lyrical, the erudite, the public, and the introspective mingle with great fluency. He was a master of verse form and accommodated traditional patterns to a fresh, easy, and contemporary language.

Augustan age A term derived from the period of literary eminence under the Roman emperor Augustus (27 BC–AD 14), during which *Virgil, *Horace, and *Ovid flourished. In English literature it is generally taken to refer to the early and mid-18th century. Augustan writers (such as Alexander *Pope, Joseph *Addison, Jonathan *Swift, and Richard *Steele) greatly admired their Roman counterparts, imitated their works, and themselves frequently drew parallels between the two ages. Oliver *Goldsmith, in *The Bee*, in an 'Account of the Augus-

tan Age of England' (1759), identifies it with the reign of Queen Anne, and the era of William *Congreve, Matthew *Prior, and Bolingbroke. *See also* NEO-CLASSICISM.

AUGUSTINE, St, of Hippo (354–430) Born at Tagaste in North Africa, he was trained as a rhetorician and abandoned the Christianity in which he had been brought up. He was a *Manichaean for some time, but was converted (387) after hearing the sermons of Ambrose, a scene vividly described in his *Confessions* (*c.*400), which contains a celebrated account of his early life. He became bishop of Hippo (395) and was engaged in constant theological controversy, combating Manichaeans, Donatists, and Pelagians. The most important of his numerous works is *De Civitate Dei* (416–22, *The City of God*), a treatise in vindication of Christianity. His principal tenet was the immediate efficacy of grace, and his theology remained an influence of profound importance in the Middle Ages, when it was often characterized as being an alternative orthodoxy to the Dominican system of Aquinas, and on 16th-century Protestant Reformers. His views on literature became standard in the Middle Ages, particularly as expressed in *De Doctrina Christiana* (*On Christian Doctrine*), and they have often been cited as an authority by 20th-century 'exegetical' critics of medieval literature, such as D. W. Robertson, who are sometimes called 'Augustinian critics'.

'Auld Lang Syne' A song whose words were contributed by Robert *Burns to the fifth volume of James Johnson's *Scots Musical Museum* (1787–1803). Based on what he called a 'glorious fragment', Burns's lyric reworks lines and phrases that have been traced to sources including Allan *Ramsay's *Scots Songs* (1720) and the Bannatyne Manuscript (1568). 'Auld Lang Syne' was matched to its now famous air by George Thomson (1757–1851) in the 1799 half-volume of his *Select Collection of Original Scottish Airs*.

Aulnoy, Marie-Catherine Le Jumel de Barneville, comtesse d' (*c.*1650–1705) French writer of historical fiction, notably *Hypolite, comte de Duglas* (1691), set in the England of Henry VIII, and *Contes des fées* (1697: *Fairy Tales*) which enjoyed considerable popularity in England: of the 62 French fairytales that appeared in English between 1691 and 1729, eighteen were by Aulnoy.

Aureng-Zebe A tragedy by John *Dryden, produced 1675, published 1676. The plot is remotely based on the contemporary events by which the Mogul Aureng-Zebe wrested the empire of India from his father and his brothers. The hero is a figure of exemplary rationality, virtue, and patience, whose stepmother lusts after him and whose father pursues the woman with whom Aureng-Zebe is himself in love. Apparently highly schematic in its organization, this last of Dryden's rhymed heroic plays evinces a deeply disturbing awareness of the anarchy and impotence which threaten every aspect of human life, emotional, moral, and political.

Aurora Leigh A poem over 11,000 lines long by Elizabeth Barrett *Browning, who described it as a 'novel in verse'. Orphaned as a girl, Aurora grows to be an independent woman and poet who believes artists have a responsibility to highlight and assess concerns of the present day. The poem explores social accountability in connection with religion, art, and class, and relationships between the sexes. Aurora rejects a clumsy proposal from her philanthropic cousin Romney, but later accepts him after he has learned to appreciate her social and artistic perspectives. In a melodramatic sub-plot, Marian Erle (a seamstress) is raped and moves to Paris, where Aurora follows, and helps raise her child. Thought scandalous by a few, the poem was a great success with contemporary readers.

AUSTEN, Jane (1775–1817) Novelist. Briefly tutored by a relative in Oxford, then in Southampton, she attended the Abbey House School, Reading (1785–6). As a child and young woman she read widely, including the novelists, Henry *Fielding, Lawrence *Sterne, Samuel *Richardson, and Fanny *Burney, and the poets, Sir Walter *Scott, William *Cowper, and, her particular favourite, George *Crabbe. Her life is notable for its lack of events; she did not marry, although she had several suitors. Any references there may have been to private intimacies or griefs were excised from Jane's letters by her sister Cassandra after the author's death, but the correspondence (1796–1817) retains flashes of sharp wit and occasional coarseness. Her correspondents include Cassandra, her friend Martha Lloyd, and her nieces and nephews, to whom she confided her views on the novel (to Anna Austen, 9 September 1814: '3 or 4 families in a Country Village is the very thing to work on'). In 1801, the family moved to Bath; in 1806, after Mr Austen's death, to Southampton; and in 1809 to Chawton. The novels were written between the activities of family life, and the last three (*Mansfield Park, *Emma, and *Persua-

sion) are known to have been written in the busy family parlour at Chawton.

Her juvenilia, written in her early teens, are already incisive and elegantly expressed: *Love and Freindship* (sic), A History of England, A Collection of Letters, and Lesley Castle. *Lady Susan* is also an early work. Of the major novels, *Sense and Sensibility* was published in 1811, *Pride and Prejudice* in 1813, Mansfield Park in 1814, Emma in 1816, *Northanger Abbey* and Persuasion posthumously in 1818. They were, however, begun or completed in a different order. The 1795–6 sketch Elinor and Marianne was rewritten in 1797–8 as Sense and Sensibility. Northanger Abbey (1798–9) was sold in 1803 to the publishers Crosby and Sons but not published. In 1809 Sense and Sensibility was again revised for publication, and First Impressions (1797) was recreated and renamed Pride and Prejudice.

Her unfinished novel, The *Watsons was abandoned in 1805 on her father's death. Mansfield Park was begun at Chawton in 1811, Emma in 1814, Persuasion in 1815; and in 1817, the year of her death, the unfinished *Sanditon.

The novels were generally well received from publication onwards; the prince regent kept a set in each of his residences, and Scott praised her work in the *Quarterly Review in 1815; he later wrote of 'that exquisite touch which renders ordinary commonplace things and characters interesting'. Charlotte *Brontë and Elizabeth Barrett *Browning, however, found her limited and a Jane Austen cult did not develop until after the publication of J. E. Austen Leigh's Memoir in 1870. Marilyn Butler's Jane Austen and the War of Ideas (1975) situates the writer's work, so often seen as literary escapism, in its social and political context.

AUSTER, Paul (1947–) American novelist, poet, playwright, and film-maker. His earliest one-act plays were influenced by Harold *Pinter and Samuel *Beckett, and his first novel, Squeeze Play, was a Chandleresque thriller published under the pseudonym 'Paul Benjamin'. He gained critical recognition with his New York Trilogy (City of Glass, 1985; Ghosts, 1986; and The Locked Room, 1987), which uses the conventions of the *detective novel to investigate urban isolation, identity, and language. In the Country of Last Things (1987) is a *dystopian fable, Moon Palace (1989) links a *picaresque plot to developments in American history. The Music of Chance (1991), an allegory of two men forced to build a wall, was filmed in 1993 by Philip Haas. In the early 1990s Auster adapted his own short tale, Auggie Wren's Christmas

Story, with the director Wayne Wang, and in 1995 they made films of two uncharacteristically optimistic stories of urban life, *Smoke* (with a script by Auster) and *Blue in the Face* (directed by Wang and Auster). Wang directed *The Centre of the World* (2001), from Auster's story about a couple in Las Vegas. In 2007 Auster wrote and directed *The Inner Life of Martin Frost*, about a fictitious writer; a screenplay of the same title features in his novel *The Book of Illusions* (2002). The *graphic novel adaptation of *City of Glass* was released for the PlayStation portable platform in 2010.

AUSTIN, Alfred (1835–1913) Poet; he published twenty volumes of verse between 1871 and 1908. In 1896 Austin was made *poet laureate, shortly afterwards publishing in *The *Times* an unfortunate ode celebrating the Jameson Raid. A waspish critic of his contemporaries, he was much derided and parodied as a poet. His *Autobiography* appeared in 1911.

autobiography has been recognized since the late 18th century as a distinct literary genre, with the first recorded uses of the term occurring around this time, but the history of the term has been bound up with ideological struggles about the status of the subject and the nature of authorship, including Paul *de Man's famous *post-structuralist challenge that there is no way of deciding what is truth and what fiction and that therefore autobiography, as distinct from fiction, does not really exist. The modern canon of autobiography looks back to the self-analysis of St Augustine (354–430) in his *Confessions*. The earliest known autobiography in English, *The Boke of Margery Kempe* (*c.*1420), recounts the visions of a mystic; John *Bunyan made an impassioned record of his spiritual awakening; and there was a strong relationship between autobiography and religion well into the 19th century, particularly among Nonconformists. Many early novels, including *Robinson Crusoe* (1719) and *Tristram Shandy* (1759–67), declared themselves to be autobiographies. In the greatest verse autobiography, *The *Prelude* (published 1850), William *Wordsworth traces the growth of his poetic imagination and accords this subject the status of epic. In the 20th century Virginia *Woolf turned to different autobiographical forms—*diary and *memoir—and experimented with ways of suggesting alternative feminine versions of selfhood which were fragmented or inchoate. Her draft memoir, 'Sketch of the Past', was one of many wartime autobiographies, including Henry *Green's *Pack my Bag* (1940) and Osbert *Sitwell's vast *Left Hand, Right Hand!* (1945–50). *Roland Barthes by Roland Barthes* (1975) drew out the implications for autobiography of 'the death of the author', eschewing chronology and development and encouraging readers to view it 'as if spoken by a character in a novel'. Autobiographies also can be forms of testimonial writing, Eva *Hoffman's *Lost in Translation* (1989), for instance, is an account of exile and the experience of being a second-generation Holocaust survivor. Recent autobiographies have documented the experience of terminal illness, making public what has usually remained intensely private. Both John Diamond's *Because Cowards Have Cancer* (1998) and Ruth Picardie's *Before I Say Goodbye* (1998) were newspaper columns before being published as books; Simon *Gray's *Coda* was published posthumously. Blake *Morrison in *When Did You Last See your Father?* (1993) and Lorna Sage in *Bad Blood* (2000) focused on the death of parents or difficult family circumstances. Autobiography is a best-selling genre from the hugely popular and much-denigrated 'misery memoir', through such publishing phenomena as Frank McCourt's *Angela's Ashes* (1996), to challenging experimental work. *See* BIOGRAPHY; LIFE-WRITING; DIARIES.

Avalon In Arthurian legends, one of the Celtic 'Isles of the Blest' to which Arthur is carried after his death. *Glastonbury has also been identified as the burial-place of Arthur and hence with Avalon.

AVELLANEDA, Alonso Fernández de *See* FERNÁNDEZ DE AVELLANEDA, ALONSO.

AVERROËS (Abū a'l-Walīd Muhammad bin Ahmad bin Rushd) (1126–98) A Muslim physician born at Córdoba in Spain (*Chaucer's Physician knows of him: *Canterbury Tales*, General Prologue, 433), and a philosopher, the author of a famous commentary on *Aristotle. He is placed in the limbo of the philosophers with *Avicenna by *Dante (*Inferno*, IV. 144). He is the inspiration for 'Latin Averroism' (1230 and afterwards), which regarded Aristotle as absolute in philosophy even when his view was not reconcilable with the absolute truth of Faith. He is of immense and lasting importance as the conveyor of Aristotle back into the Western tradition.

Avicenna (Abū-a 'Ali al-Husayn bin Sīna) (980–1037) A Persian physician (known to *Chaucer's Physician—*Canterbury Tales*, General Prologue, 432—and Pardoner—VI. 889) and philosopher, who made commentaries on *Aristotle and Galen. His views of love have been said to be influential on the ideas of *courtly love, and he was a major influence on the development of 13th-century *scholasticism. *Dante places him with *Averroës in the limbo of the philosophers (*Inferno*, IV. 143).

AWDRY, Revd W. (Wilbert) (1911–97). The 26 books about the railway on the island of Sodor, beginning with *The Three Railway Engines* (1945) and *Thomas the Tank Engine* (1946), supplemented by a further fourteen (1989–96) by Christopher Awdry, have been exhaustively marketed worldwide. The stories of Thomas, Gordon the express engine, the Fat Controller, and their companions evoke an idyllic England, but have class and gender overtones in the (female) carriages, the villainous diesels, and the (working-class) trucks.

Awkward Age, The A novel by Henry *James.

Awntyrs of Arthure at the Terne Wathelyne, The (*The Adventures of Arthur at the Tarn Wadling*, **in Cumberland**) Alliterative poem in 715 lines, surviving in five 15th-century manuscripts. While hunting, *Gawain and Gaynor (*Guinevere) see the apparition of Gaynor's mother rise from the lake. She asks that 30 trentals (sequences of 30 masses) be said for the relief of her suffering soul and attacks the vices of Gawain, Arthur, and the court, criticisms echoed in the second part of the poem, in which Sir Galeron of Galway (Galloway), demands the return of lands which Arthur had confiscated and given to Gawain. The lands are returned, and Gaynor has the masses said for her mother. The poem (in complex thirteen-line stanzas) confidently compresses many of the key elements of Arthurian romance, and its thoughtful ambivalence towards the materialism of Arthurian culture is similar to the detachment of *Sir *Gawain and the Green Knight*.

AYCKBOURN, Sir Alan (1939–) Playwright. His first London success, *Relatively Speaking* (1967), was followed by many others, including *Absurd Person Singular* (1973); *The Norman Conquests* (1974), a trilogy with elaborately overlapping action covering the same period of time and the same events from different points of view; *Absent Friends* (1975); and *Joking Apart* (1979). The plays are comedies of suburban and middle-class life, showing a keen sense of social nuance and of domestic misery and insensitivity, and displaying the virtuosity of Ayckbourn's stagecraft. Later plays include *Sisterly Feelings* (1980), *A Chorus of Disapproval* (1986), and *Women in Mind* (1986), showing an instinctive sympathy for women as victims. *Way Upstream* (1981) and *A Small Family Business* (1987) addressed the politics of the Thatcher era from a social democratic perspective. The claim that he is, after Shakespeare, the second most produced playwright in British theatrical history derives from the Arts Council's Cultural Trends report (1990). *Life of Riley* (2010), like the majority of his work, premiered at Scarborough.

Ayenbite of Inwit (*Prick of Conscience*) A devotional manual translated in 1340 by Dan Michel of Northgate, Canterbury, from an influential French moral treatise *Le Somme des vices et des vertues*.

Aymon, The Four Sons of A medieval French romance telling of *Charlemagne's struggle with these four noblemen, the eldest and most important of whom was Rinaldo. The English prose version of the romance derives from William *Caxton's printed version (1489–91), there being no surviving manuscript.

Ayrshire Legatees, The An *epistolary novel by John *Galt, published 1821, recording the impressions of the family of a Scottish minister, Dr Zachariah Pringle, on a visit to London. Their alternately naive and shrewd comments on travellers, the sophistications of the English capital, and the 'douce folk' back home gently satirize Regency manners and values.

AYTOUN, William Edmonstoune (1813–65) Poet. His ancestor Sir Robert Aytoun (1570–1638) is one of the supposed sources for *'Auld Lang Syne'. With Theodore *Martin the author of the parodic *'Bon Gaultier' Ballads (1845), he also published *Lays of the Scottish Cavaliers* (1849), extremely popular patriotic ballad-romances, based on stories of *Montrose, Dundee, and other Scottish heroes. His mock-tragedy *Firmilian, or The Student of Badajoz* (1854) parodied the poems of the *Spasmodic school. *Norman Sinclair* (1861) is a novel set in early 19th-century Scotland.

Baal A Canaanite god, strongly opposed by the prophets of Israel in the Old Testament (e.g. Elijah in 1 Kings 18).

Babbitt A 1922 novel by Sinclair *Lewis. 'Babbittry' became a term denoting middle-class conventionalism.

Babylon Middle Eastern empire to which the Jews were forcibly exiled, as described by the prophet Jeremiah. The Babylonian captivity is lamented in Psalm 137, 'By the rivers of Babylon'. In the Book of Revelation and St Augustine's *City of God* the earthly Babylon is the symbolic opposite of the heavenly *Jerusalem. Protestant writers often identified Catholic Rome with Babylon. *See* BIBLE.

BACON, Francis, First Baron Verulam and Viscount St Albans (1561–1626) Lord chancellor, politician, and philosopher; his mother, Lady Anne Cooke (c.1528–1610), was an exceptionally gifted scholar and translator in her own right. Bacon was tutored at Trinity College, Cambridge by the master, John Whitgift (1530–1604), subsequently archbishop of Canterbury. He spent from 1576 to 1579 with the queen's ambassador to France, Sir Amias Paulet (c.1532–88). In 1581 he became an MP (for Bossiney, Cornwall), but his boldness in the 1593 session in opposing the unusually heavy taxes that the queen wanted led to his being expelled from royal favour. His finances were precarious and he was arrested for debt in 1598. The queen severely tested his loyalty by appointing him one of the prosecutors of his former friend and patron the earl of *Essex, who was executed in 1601. With the accession of James I, Bacon rapidly achieved public office. Knighted in 1603, he was elevated to the House of Lords as Baron Verulam in 1618, and created Viscount St Albans in 1621. His systematic treatise on knowledge, *The *Advancement of Learning*, was published in 1605. But Bacon increasingly found that his carefully worked-out advice and counsel were ignored both by James and by the court favourite, the first duke of *Buckingham. Government officials under James depended for their livelihood on gifts from suitors and on selling their office, leading to a high degree of corruption. In 1621 a parliamentary group bent on reform, led by Sir Edward Coke (1552–1634) and Sir Lionel Cranfield (1575–1645), attacked the system of monopolies, where lucrative patents were allocated and enforced by illegal means. Bacon, who as head of the Court of Chancery had issued licences to patentees at the king's request, was impeached on 23 charges of corruption. His career was ruined: deprived of power, Bacon was vulnerable to Buckingham's greed, and was made to sell his birthplace, York House. Out of office, he devoted himself fully to writing, producing in quick succession *A History of the Life and Reign of King *Henry VII* (1622), the *De Dignitate & Augmentis Scientiarum* (1623, a Latin expansion of *The Advancement of Learning*), the *Essays* (1625), and the posthumously published *New Atlantis* (1627). Simultaneously a Protestant, humanist, or moderate Calvinist, as his posthumously published *Confession of Faith* (1641) shows, Bacon directed all his intellectual activities towards practical ends from which the whole of society would benefit. He outlined many schemes for reforming the laws, making them easier to understand and more coherent; he wanted the universities to widen their curriculum from the three traditional professions (theology, law, medicine) to take in the 'arts and sciences at large'; and he was ahead of his time in realizing that a continuous growth of knowledge was possible. Bacon's plan to reform the whole of natural philosophy (or science), outlined in the fragmentary *Instauratio Magna* (1620), of which the *Novum Organum* was the only more or less complete part, aimed to effect a new union between 'the mind and the universe', from which would spring a range of inventions to 'overcome the necessities and miseries of humanity'. He was regarded by succeeding generations as the instigator of the scientific revolution and the inventor of scientific method.

Bacon's writings inspired the founding of the *Royal Society in 1662, and had a considerable influence on Thomas *Hobbes, Robert Boyle, John *Locke, Daniel *Defoe, and many others. *See* SHAKESPEARE: AUTHORSHIP OF THE WORKS.

Badman, The Life and Death of Mr An allegory by John *Bunyan, published 1680. The allegory takes the form of a dialogue, in which Mr Wiseman relates the life of Mr Badman, recently deceased, and Mr Attentive comments on it. The story is entertaining as well as edifying and has a place in the evolution of the English novel.

BAEDEKER, Karl (1801–59) German editor and publisher of the famous series of *guidebooks, which introduced the star rating system for cultural sites, hotels, and restaurants. Under his son Fritz the business expanded, eclipsing the guides of John *Murray. Baedeker became synonymous with the flourishing tourist industry and shaped the experience of generations of tourists. Deliberate bombing assaults on British cultural sites in the Second World War were termed 'Baedeker raids'.

BAGE, Robert (1728/30–1801) Novelist. A radical by conviction, he was influenced by *Rousseau, and friendly with William *Godwin. *Hermsprong, or Man as He Is Not* (1796) is the best known of his six novels. Comic and satiric in tone, they were popular in spite of their *Jacobin leanings and were included in Anna Laetitia *Barbauld's 'British Novelists' and Walter *Scott's 'Ballantyne's Novelist's Library' series.

Bagford Ballads, The Illustrating the last years of the Stuarts' rule and the last years of the 17th century, published by the Ballad Society in 1878. They were assembled by John Bagford (1651–1716), originally a shoemaker, for Robert Harley, first earl of Oxford and later acquired by the duke of *Roxburghe.

BAGNOLD, Enid Algerine, Lady Jones (1889–1981) Novelist and playwright, she worked as nurse and ambulance driver during the First World War (see her *Diary without Dates*, 1917). The best known and commercially most successful of her novels was *National Velvet* (1935, filmed 1944 with Elizabeth Taylor as the girl who wins the Grand National). Of her plays, the most successful was *The Chalk Garden* (1955). Her *Autobiography* was published in 1969.

BAILEY, Nathan (d. 1742) Teacher and author of the *Universal Etymological English Dictionary* (1721, second volume 1727), a popular forerunner of Samuel *Johnson's *Dictionary*. Johnson used Bailey's illustrated *Dictionarium Britannicum* (1730) while compiling his work.

BAILEY, Paul (1937–) London-born actor turned writer. His novels include *At the Jerusalem* (1967); *Peter Smart's Confessions* (1977), which draws on Bailey's experiences in the theatre; *Old Soldiers* (1980), which displays an abiding fascination with London and the elderly; *Gabriel's Lament* (1986), which mixes tragedy with the comic-grotesque; and *Kitty and Virgil* (1998) and *Uncle Rudolf* (2002), which reflect a latter-day interest in Romania. Bailey's non-fiction includes *An English Madam* (1982), a biography of Cynthia Payne; *An Immaculate Mistake: Scenes from Childhood and Beyond* (1990); and the biographical triptych *Three Queer Lives* (2001).

BAILEY, Philip James (1816–1902) Poet, author of *Festus* (1839, enlarged 1845). The final edition of 1889, which exceeded 40,000 lines, incorporated the greater part of three volumes of poetry that had appeared in the interval (*The Angel World*, 1850; *The Mystic*, 1855; *Universal Hymn*, 1867). *Festus* is Bailey's version of the *Faust story; it was strongly influenced by *Goethe and John *Milton's *Paradise Lost*. Admired for its 'fire of imagination' (E. B. *Browning), it was a prominent representative of the so-called *Spasmodic school.

BAILLIE, Joanna (1762–1851) Scottish dramatist and poet. She achieved success in 1798 with her first volume of *Plays on the Passions*, in which each verse drama displays the effect of one particular passion. *Basil*, on the subject of love, and *De Montfort*, on hatred, were the most successful. She published a second volume (1802), *Miscellaneous Plays* (1804), and a third *Passions* volume (1812). Her tragedy *Constantine Paleologus, or The Last of the Caesars* (1804) was considered by John Stuart *Mill to be 'one of the best dramas of the last two centuries'. Her most successful play, *The Family Legend*, based on a bitter Scottish feud, was produced in 1810 with a prologue by Scott and an epilogue by Henry *Mackenzie. It established Baillie as a literary and social success, and her house in Hampstead became a meeting place for many of the literary figures of her time.

Bailly, Harry In Chaucer's *Canterbury Tales* the host of the Tabard Inn where the pilgrims meet in the General Prologue. He initiates the pilgrims' storytelling competition and serves as their goad and impromptu critic.

BAINBRIDGE, Dame Beryl (1934–2010) DBE, novelist. She began her career as an actress at the Liverpool Playhouse. Her first novels were little noticed, but in the 1970s a series of original and idiosyncratic works established her reputation. These include *Harriet Said* (1972), *The Bottle Factory Outing* (1974), and *Young Adolf* (1978). Short, laconic, and rich in black comedy, they deal with the lives of characters at once deeply ordinary and highly eccentric, in a world where violence and the absurd lurk beneath the daily routine of urban domesticity. The juxtaposition of the banal and the bizarre is also a feature of the dialogue, which shows a fine ear for the oddities of contemporary speech. Other novels include *Winter Garden* (1980), *Filthy Lucre* (1986), *An Awfully Big Adventure* (1989), and a series of *historical novels: *Watson's Apology* (1984) reconstructs a Victorian murder; *The Birthday Boys* (1991) follows Robert Falcon *Scott to the Antarctic; *Every Man for Himself* (1996) takes place on board the *Titanic*; *Master Georgie* (1998) is set during the Crimean War; and *According to Queeney* (2001) is a child's-eye view of Samuel *Johnson. *The Girl in the Polka Dot Dress* (2011) was published posthumously.

BAKHTIN, Mikhail Mikhailovich (1895–1975) Russian literary and cultural theorist. He developed his original theoretical approach in the 1920s and 1930s with a circle of collaborators including the Marxist scholars Valentin Voloshinov (1895–1936) and Pavel Medvedev (1892–1938). Between 1930 and 1960 he suffered periods of unemployment and internal exile. He returned to Moscow in 1969, where he enjoyed belated recognition and was finally able to see several works published. These included an extended version of *Problems of Dostoevsky's Poetics* (1963; trans. Caryl Emerson, 1984), originally published in 1929 just before his exile to Kazakhstan, *Rabelais and his World* (1965; trans. Helene Iswolsky, 1968), and essays, some of which were translated as *The Dialogic Imagination* (1981). Bakhtin's influence has been widespread in Western academic criticism since the late 1970s, partly because of his attractive notion of the *carnivalesque in his study of *Rabelais, but more for his concept of 'dialogism', in which language (and truth) are viewed as an open field of interactive utterances, and literature—especially the novel—is valued for keeping in play a variety of voices and languages.

BALDWIN, James (1924–87) African American writer, born in Harlem. He was helped by Richard *Wright. His first novel, *Go Tell It on the Mountain* (1953), set in Harlem, was followed by several on a more international scale, dealing with both homosexuality and the situation of African Americans; they include *Giovanni's Room* (1956), *Another Country* (1962), and *Just above my Head* (1979). He also wrote short stories, political and autobiographical essays, and plays. *The Fire Next Time* (1963) was a campaigning work for the American civil rights movement.

BALDWIN, William (d. in or before 1563) Printer and author. By 1552 he had written a carnivalesque satirical work *Beware the Cat* (pub. 1570), and *c*.1554 he initiated *A *Mirror for Magistrates*.

BALE, John (1495–1563) Author of religious plays, a catalogue of English writers, and numerous polemical and apocalyptic works promoting the Reformation. Of his 24 plays only five survive, the most notable being *King John*, performed in 1538, the first English historical play, forming a bridge between the *morality and the historical play proper.

'Balin and Balan' One of Tennyson's *Idylls of the King*, first published 1885. It is the story of two brothers who kill each other unwittingly, Balan mistaking for a demon the impassioned Balin, who is driven to frenzy by a conviction of Guinevere's adultery.

ballad A traditional song in which some popular story is graphically narrated in short stanzas, commonly in *quatrains of alternate four- and three-stress lines with the shorter lines only rhymed, as in *'Sir Patrick Spens'; or a narrative poem written imitatively in this popular style. The oldest example in F. J. Child's *English and Scottish Popular Ballads* (5 vols, 1882–98) is 'Judas' (*c*.1300), with an uncharacteristically religious theme; ballads more traditionally deal with the pagan supernatural (e.g. 'Tam Lin'), with tragic love (e.g. 'Barbara Allan'), or with historical or legendary events, e.g. the Border ballads, or the *Robin Hood ballads. Eighteenth-century interest in the form led to the researches and collections of Thomas *Percy (*Reliques*, 1765) and Joseph *Ritson, to the forgeries of Thomas *Chatterton and the adaptations of Robert *Burns, and to the deliberate antiquarian imitations of Thomas *Tickell ('Lucy and Colin'), Percy himself ('The Hermit of

Warkworth'), David *Mallet ('William and Margaret'), Oliver *Goldsmith ('The Hermit'), and others. Walter *Scott's *Minstrelsy of the Scottish Border* is a mixture of traditional ballads, adaptations, and imitations, whereas the *Lyrical Ballads* of William *Wordsworth and S. T. *Coleridge manifests, in poems like 'The Idiot Boy' and the *Rime of the *Ancient Mariner*, their own interpretation and development of balladry. The form has continued to inspire poets, from John *Keats (*'La Belle Dame sans Merci') to William *Morris, Oscar *Wilde, Thomas *Hardy, W. B. *Yeats, and Charles *Causley, and flourishes in a popular folk form as well as in a more literary guise.

(⊕) SEE WEB LINKS

- Bodleian Library Broadside Ballads
- English Broadside Ballad Archive

ballade A French lyric verse-form adapted into English by Geoffrey *Chaucer (e.g. in 'To Rosemounde'). In its standard form, it consists of three eight-line stanzas rhyming *ababbcbc*, each ending with the same line as refrain, and usually followed by a four-line envoy addressed to a prince. A. C. *Swinburne and others revived the English ballade in the late 19th century.

ballad opera An English theatrical and musical form, in which the action of the play (usually comic) is carried in spoken prose, punctuated by songs set to traditional or fashionable melodies, sung by the actors in character. The first ballad opera, *The *Beggar's Opera* (1728) by John Gay, was enormously successful and the ballad opera became the chief mode of opposition to the Italian opera imported by Handel and others; exotic kings and huge arias were exchanged for ordinary life and well-known tunes. Henry *Fielding made successful use of the form's satiric possibilities. But its vogue was short-lived and began to decline about 1735.

BALLANTYNE, James (1772–1833) and **John** (1774–1821) Respectively a printer and publisher, who set up the unsuccessful publishing and bookselling business of John Ballantyne and Co. with Walter *Scott in 1809. James had printed *Minstrelsy of the Scottish Border* in 1802, and continued to issue Scott's works, but was bankrupted by the crash of Constable and Co. in 1826 (*see* CONSTABLE, A.). Scott planned Ballantyne's Novelist's Library (1821–4) solely for John's financial benefit, but only one volume was published before the latter's death.

BALLANTYNE, R. M. (Robert Michael) (1825–94) Prolific Scottish writer of boys' adventure stories, remembered for *The *Coral Island* (1858), a *Robinsonnade which influenced Robert Louis Stevenson's *Treasure Island* and William Golding's *Lord of the Flies* (1954). *The Young Fur Traders* (1856) was based on his experiences in Canada with the Hudson's Bay Company, *Black Ivory* (1873) is set in Africa, and *Martin Rattler* (1858) in South America. Ballantyne's books are didactic, designed to teach readers about geography, natural history, religion, morality, and the responsibilities of empire. His heroes are plucky, courageous, morally sound British boys.

BALLARD, J. G. (James Graham) (1930–2009) English novelist and short story writer, the most prominent of the *'New Wave' science fiction writers of the 1960s. His first short story was published in 1956 in *New Worlds*, to which he continued to contribute during the influential editorship of Michael *Moorcock. His first novel, *The Drowned World* (1962), a 'catastrophe' novel in which the world turns into a vast swamp, was followed by *The Drought* (1965), in which he imagined post-apocalyptic landscapes and populated them with realistically observed, ultra-obsessive characters. *Crash* (1973; filmed 1996) was an outstanding, outrageous work on the eroticism of car accidents. His short stories were collected in *Complete Stories* (2001). In *Empire of the Sun* (1984, filmed 1988) he turned away from science fiction to draw on his own wartime experiences in a Japanese prison camp in China. Other novels include *The Venus Hunters* (1986), *The Day of Creation* (1987), *Running Wild* (1988), *The Kindness of Women* (1991), *Rushing to Paradise* (1994), a disturbing contemporary fable about eco-fanaticism, *Cocaine Nights* (1996), set in a high-security leisure-oriented Mediterranean resort complex, and *Kingdom Come* (2006), which explores the gated communities and designed Metro Centres of the coming century. *Miracles of Life* (2008) is an autobiography.

BALZAC, Honoré de (1799–1850) French novelist, author of the great series of 89 separately titled but interlocking stories and novels known collectively as *La Comédie humaine*, published in seventeen volumes between 1842 and 1847. In his 1845 prospectus Balzac presents *La Comédie humaine* as having the form of a pyramid: at the base are *Études de mœurs*, fictions describing contemporary society, subdivided into those dealing with private, provincial, and country life, Paris, military matters, and politics; above these are *Études philosophiques*, fictions considering the causes of social phenomena; and at the top are *Études analytiques*, fictions offering an analysis of the principles of life in society. Balzac is fascinated by the supernatural and the mysterious, the operation of the passions, the role of money in shaping personal and social relations, the determining effect of environment on the individual, and, conversely, by the various courses taken by energy and ambition in pursuit of social fulfilment. The best-known works in *La Comédie humaine* are *La Peau de chagrin* (1831: *The Wild Ass's Skin*), *Illusions perdues* (1837–43), *Le Médecin de campagne* (1833: *The Country Doctor*), *La Rabouilleuse* (1840: *The Black Sheep*), *La Cousine Bette* (1846), and *Le Cousin Pons* (1847). Balzac's influence has been immense, and his work is an essential reference point in the history of the European novel.

BAMBARA, Toni Cade (1939–95) African American novelist, short story writer, and documentary film-maker. She was active in the *Black Arts Movement and her short story collections, like *Gorilla, my Love* (1972), explore the importance of oral tradition. Her first novel, *The Salt Eaters* (1980), examines the role of activists within the community. *Deep Sightings and Rescue Missions* (1995) is a collection of essays and interviews.

BAMFORD, Samuel (1788–1872) Weaver, poet and, *Chartist activist. His *Passages in the Life of a Radical* (1840–4) gives a vivid first-hand description of the Peterloo massacre (1819): he was subsequently arrested and imprisoned for a year. His *Homely Rhymes, Poems and Reminiscences* (1839–41) collects some political poems, some pastoral, and a few written in dialect, many of them displaying considerable verve and energy. *Early Days* is an account of his childhood and of old Lancashire customs (1848–9).

BANDELE, Biyi (1967–) Born in Nigeria and now living in London. He has written plays, several novels including *Burma Boy* (2007), adaptations of novels for the stage, and scripts for radio and television. He has worked with the *Royal Court Theatre and the Royal Shakespeare Company.

BANDELLO, Matteo (1485–1561) Dominican friar, poet, and courtier, the best writer of Italian short stories in the 16th century. Geoffrey Fenton's *Certaine Tragicall Discourses* (1567) contains English versions of thirteen tales via the French translations by Belleforest. Painter's *Palace of Pleasure* includes 25 of Bandello's tales, nine translated from the Italian and sixteen from Belleforest. Bandello is the source of plots for many English plays, including *Romeo and Juliet*, *Much Ado About Nothing*, *Twelfth Night*, and The *Duchess of Malfi*.

BANIM, John (1798–1842) Irish Catholic novelist, dramatist, and poet. *Tales by the O'Hara Family*, depicting rural Irish society, were partly written with his brother Michael in self-conscious imitation of Walter *Scott and published in 1825, 1826, and 1827. Works mainly composed by John include *The Nowlans* (1833), a portrait of contemporary cabin life, and the historical novel *The Boyne Water* (1836). Michael Banim (1796–1874) claimed after his brother's death that he was himself responsible for thirteen of their 24 joint works, including *The Croppy* (1828) and *The Mayor of Windgap* (1835).

BANKS, Iain Menzies (1954–) Scottish novelist. He came to controversial prominence with his first novel, *The Wasp Factory* (1984), a macabre tale of teenage fantasies of death and destruction, narrated by 16-year-old Frank Cauldhame: it was condemned by some for its graphic violence but praised by others for its targeting of macho values. Succeeding novels, such as *Walking on Glass* (1985), *The Bridge* (1986), *Espedair Street* (1987), *Complicity* (1993), *A Song of Stone* (1997, a post-apocalyptic story set around an ancestral castle in the aftermath of a civil war), *Dead Air* (2002), and *The Steep Approach to Garbadale* (2007), fulfilled his promise as an inventive and often fiercely comic moralist. As Iain M. Banks he has also written *science fiction novels, many set in a hardedged utopian civilization known as the Culture, including *Consider Phlebas* (1987), *The Player of Games* (1988), *Feersum Endjinn* (1993), *Excession* (1996), *Look to Windward* (2000), *The Algebraist* (2004), and *Surface Detail* (2010). *The State of the Art* is a collection of short fiction, also published as by Iain M. Banks.

BANKS, Lynne Reid (1929–) London-born novelist and children's writer, whose first novel, *The L-Shaped Room* (1960), about Jane, a young girl, pregnant with an illegitimate child and living in a London bedsit, was a great success (film, 1962). Her other novels for adults include *An End to Running* (1962), *Children at the Gate* (1968), *The Backward Shadow* (1970), and *Two is Lonely* (1974). Her later books for children include a series about miniature toys that come alive, beginning with *The Indian in* *the Cupboard* (1981–98; the first book was filmed in 1995), and *One More River* (1973) and its sequel *Broken Bridge* (1994), set during the Six Day War of 1967 and reflecting her interest in Israel.

BANNERMAN, Helen *See* LITTLE BLACK SAMBO.

BANVILLE, John (1945–) Novelist. His fiction is characterized by an allusive, ironic style and a preoccupation with its own processes. The concluding novella of *Long Lankin* (1970, stories) was drawn on in Banville's first novel, *Nightspawn* (1971), whose narrator becomes a character in his own plot. The *'big house' novel *Birchwood* (1973) was followed by a trilogy of fictional portraits of famous scientists—*Doctor Copernicus* (1976), *Kepler* (1981), and *The Newton Letter* (1982)—in which the search for scientific certainty mirrors the quest for a persuasive artistic rendering of experience. *Mefisto* (1986) is the most explicitly Faustian of Banville's novels. *The Book of Evidence* (1989) introduced a second trilogy, completed by *Ghosts* (1993) and *Athena* (1994). Freddie Montgomery, the protagonist of all three works, is an aesthete and convicted murderer, obsessed with the issue of authenticity in the visual arts. *The Untouchable* (1997) is a deft transmutation of the *spy novel. *The Sea* (2005), a meditative novel about a man who returns to the marine setting of a childhood trauma after the death of his wife, won the *Man Booker Prize. His latest novel is *The Infinities* (2009). Banville publishes *detective fiction under the name Benjamin Black.

Baptists The title that in the 17th century superseded *Anabaptists* to designate those separatist Protestants who rejected infant baptism (*paedobaptism*) in favour of the baptism of adult believers (whence *anabaptists*, *rebaptizers*). General Baptists were Arminian in theology, Particular Baptists Calvinist. In England, the tradition derives from the Amsterdam congregation of John Smyth (?1570–1612), who in 1609 baptized himself (hence the sobriquet 'Se-Baptist') and then his church members, a number of whom in 1612 returned to England under Thomas Helwys (*c.*1550–*c.*1616) to establish the first English Baptist church. The Baptists' most notable literary figure is John *Bunyan.

BARAKA, Amiri (1934–) African American playwright, poet, and activist born as Everett LeRoi Jones. Throughout his career he has used his writing as an extended polemic against American racism. He was instrumental in founding the *Black Arts Movement in the 1960s. In that same decade he converted to Islam and changed his name. Like Ralph *Ellison, Baraka's work has been influenced by jazz musicians, and he has published a number of books on African American music. He has written novels (*The System of Dante's Hell*, 1965) and short stories, but his main emphasis has fallen on the theatre and poetry in performance. His best-known play is *Dutchman* (1964), about a confrontation between a naive black man and a calculating white woman. Baraka has constantly raised controversies, most famously in 2002 with his poem about the bombings of the New York Trade Centre the previous year: 'Somebody Blew Up America', where he raised questions about US government complicity.

BARBAULD, Anna Laetitia (1743–1825) Née Aikin, poet and editor. Her *Poems* appeared in 1773 and went though five editions by 1777. She published several popular volumes of prose for children with her brother John *Aikin, most notably the highly successful *Evenings at Home, or The Juvenile Budget Opened*, 6 vols (1792–6). After the suicide in 1808 of her mentally unstable husband, she threw herself into increased literary activity, editing *The British Novelists* in 50 volumes (1810). She was a friend of Hannah *More, Elizabeth *Montagu, and a circle of Dissenting radical intellectuals, and supported radical and philanthropic causes, notably Nonconformist liberties ('To Dr Priestley', 1792), and the abolition of the slave trade ('Epistle to William Wilberforce', 1791). Her stately *Juvenalian satire in heroic couplets, *Eighteen Hundred and Eleven* (1811), condemns the ongoing war with France and foretells the decline of Britain's 'Midas dream' of wealth and the rise of prosperity and culture in America. Distressed by the poem's reception, especially the venomous politically motivated review of John *Croker in the Tory *Quarterly Review*, Barbauld resolved not to publish any more poetry.

BARBELLION, W. N. P. Pseudonym of B. F. *Cummings.

BARBER, Mary (*c.*1685–1755) Poet. She was known to Mary *Delany and Jonathan *Swift, who used (according to Laetitia *Pilkington) to preside over the 'correction' of her verse. In the preface to her *Poems* (1734) she adopted a self-deprecatory pose as a woman writer; the poems themselves comment amusingly and poignantly on a wide range of social customs.

BARBOUR, John (c.1330–1395) Scottish poet. The only poem ascribed to him with certainty is *The Bruce*, written in over 13,000 lines of *octosyllabic couplets, which dates from 1375; it is a chivalric romance version of the deeds of King Robert the Bruce and his follower James Douglas, and it contains a celebrated, graphic account of the battle of Bannockburn.

Barchester Towers A novel by Anthony *Trollope, published 1857, the second in the *'Barsetshire' series. Archdeacon Grantly's hopes of succeeding his father as bishop of Barchester are dashed when an ineffectual evangelical, Dr Proudie, is set over him by a new Whig government. The novel is a record of the struggle for control of the diocese.

BARCLAY, Alexander (c.1484–1552) Poet, scholar, and preacher. He translated Brant's *Narrenschiff* into English verse as *The *Ship of Fools* (1509) and wrote his *Eclogues* at Ely (c.1513–14).

BARCLAY, John (1582–1621) Author of the extremely popular Latin romance *Argenis* (1621), which refers to real historical events and personages under a veil of allegory, and *Euphormionis Satyricon* (?1603–7), a satire on the Jesuits in the form of a *picaresque novel, also in Latin.

Bard, The A Pindaric *ode by Thomas *Gray, printed at Horace *Walpole's press in 1757. It is based on a tradition that Edward I suppressed the Welsh bards. From a crag the surviving bard curses the returning conqueror; the ghosts of dead comrades prophesy the fate of the Plantagenets, and the bard commits triumphant suicide.

bardic poetry A term used to describe the corpus of verse in standardized literary language, and in quatrains using strict syllabic metres, that dominated poetic production in Ireland and Gaelic Scotland from 1250 to 1650. The authors were members of poetic families and underwent rigorous training in the poetic schools that owed something both to the medieval monastic model and to the pre-Christian academies of the druids. In ancient Ireland *bard* was used to designate a lesser order of versifier than the true poet or seer, the *fili*. In Wales *bardd* came to mean 'poet'. The Romantic conception of the Celtic bard popularized by James

*Macpherson and Thomas *Gray has little historical authority.

BARHAM, Richard Harris (1788–1845) Churchman and poet. His *The Ingoldsby Legends; or Mirth and Marvels, by Thomas Ingoldsby Esquire* were first published from 1837 in *Bentley's Miscellany* and the *New Monthly Magazine*, and first collected in 1840. Their lively rhythms and inventive rhymes, comic and grotesque treatment of medieval legend, and quaint narratives made them immensely popular.

BARING, Maurice (1874–1945) Writer. Versatile, prolific, and successful, he is credited with having discovered Anton *Chekhov's work in Moscow and helping to introduce it to the West. His *Landmarks in Russian Literature* appeared in 1910. Of his various novels *C* (1924), *Cat's Cradle* (1925), *Daphne Adeane* (1926), and *The Coat without Seam* (1929) were very successful, and are still admired for their acute, intimate portrait of the period. His novella *The Lonely Lady of Dulwich* (1934) is highly regarded.

BARING-GOULD, Sabine (1834–1924) Devout clergyman, folk-song collector, and writer. In 1867 he defied family opposition to marry Grace Taylor, a mill girl, an experience described in his first novel *Through Fire and Flame* (1868). An extremely prolific writer, he wrote dozens of works on travel, religion, folklore, local legend, and folk song, composed various hymns (including 'Onward Christian soldiers' and 'Now the day is over'), and wrote more than 40 novels, of which the most powerful, *Mehalah* (1880), was compared by A. C. *Swinburne to *Wuthering Heights*.

BARKER, Clive (1952–) Writer, film-maker, and artist largely of *horror and *fantasy. From the stories in the *Books of Blood* (1984–5), several of which have been adapted as films or graphic novels, he has explored fantasy's veins of visionary grotesque, often, as in *Weaveworld* (1987), *The Great and Secret Show* (1989), imagining dark otherworlds parallel to ours. The 'Abarat' series (2002–8) is for children. *Hellraiser* (1987), based upon his novella 'The Hellbound Heart', is perhaps the most successful film adaptation of his works.

BARKER, George (1913–91) Poet. His first publication was *Thirty Preliminary Poems* (1933), which was followed by *Poems* (1935), *Calamiterror* (1937, a semi-political poem inspired by the Spanish Civil War), and *Lament*

and Triumph (1940). His relationship with Elizabeth *Smart is recorded in her prose poem *By Grand Central Station I Sat Down and Wept* (1945). His subsequent volumes include *Eros in Dogma* (1944) and *The True Confession of George Barker* (1950; augmented 1965). Barker's earlier work is characteristically rhetorical, unruly, and surreal; a *Neo-Romantic and a self-styled 'Augustinian anarchist', he has a marked penchant for puns, distortion, and abrupt changes of tone. His *True Confession*, written as he reached the age of 35, is autobiographical; its later stanzas, and works such as *Villa Stellar* (1978) and the long title poem of *Anno Domini* (1983), have a more sombre and questioning tone. A huge *Collected Poems* was published in 1987.

BARKER, Harley Granville- *See* GRANVILLE-BARKER, HARLEY.

BARKER, Howard (1946–) Playwright. He came to prominence with a series of scathing dramas about the injustices of society: these included *Stripwell* (1975), and two plays set in a nightmarish Britain of the future, *That Good between Us* (1977) and *The Hang of the Gaol* (1978). From *Victory* (1983), a wonderfully grotesque epic about the birth of capitalism in 17th-century England, his work, never wholly realistic, gradually became more darkly comic in tone, and less direct in its attack on Establishment targets: as witness *The Castle* (1985), *Seven Lears* (1989), and *Ten Dilemmas* (1992). He attacks the idea of a didactic theatre and insists that his audiences find their own meaning from what he has termed his 'Theatre of Catastrophe'.

BARKER, Jane (1652–1732) Poet and novelist. She converted to Catholicism and maintained strong *Jacobite links. Some early poems appeared, without authority, as *Poetical Recreations* (1688); subsequent verse, unpublishable because of its political content, was held in manuscript. Her fiction includes a heroic romance on Jacobite themes, *Exilius, or The Banished Roman* (1715), and a semi-autobiographical trilogy: *The Amours of Bosvil and Galesia* (1713), the innovative story of a spinster and author; *A Patch-Work Screen for the Ladies* (1723); and *The Lining of the Patch-Work Screen* (1726).

BARKER, Nicola (1966–) Novelist whose fiction, comic and surreal, explores the lives of wounded or hostile people, often in desolate settings. *Clear* (2004) is set in London at the time of David Blaine's four-day suspension over the capital in a transparent plastic box; *Darkmans* (2007) weaves together the lives of Edward IV's court jester and his biographer. *The Burley Cross Postbox Theft* (2010) is a comic epistolary novel.

BARKER, Pat (1943–) Novelist, whose early novels were: *Union Street* (1982), an episodic account of women in an impoverished northern community; *Blow your House Down* (1984), about prostitutes terrorized by a serial killer; and *Liza's England* (originally published as *The Century's Daughter*, 1986), in which a working-class woman relates her harsh life story to a sympathetic social worker. Barker achieved wider recognition with her First World War trilogy, beginning with *Regeneration* (1991). Based on an encounter at Craiglockhart War Hospital in 1917 between Siegfried *Sassoon and the psychologist and anthropologist William Rivers (1864–1922), it was followed by *The Eye in the Door* (1993) and *The Ghost Road* (1995, *Booker Prize). War remained important in *Another World* (1998), set in 1990s Newcastle, in the figure of a centenarian war veteran, Geordie; in *Double Vision* (2003), which focuses on a war photographer and a journalist who has witnessed atrocities in Sarajevo and Afghanistan; and in *Life Class* (2007), in which students and teachers from the Slade School of Art are confronted by the ethical and aesthetic challenges presented by the First World War.

Barkis In Charles *Dickens's *David Copperfield*, the carrier, who sent a message by David to Clara Peggotty that 'Barkis is willin''. The phrase has passed into the language.

Barlaam and Josaphat A medieval romance included in William *Caxton's *Golden Legend*, a Christianized version of the legend of Buddha.

BARLOW, Joel (1754–1812) American poet and diplomat, the author of *The Columbiad* (1787, originally published as *The Vision of Columbus* and revised and renamed in 1807), a lengthy patriotic epic in heroic couplets, and of the more enjoyable *mock epic *The Hasty-Pudding* (1796).

Barnaby Rudge A novel by Charles *Dickens published in 1841 as part of *Master Humphrey's Clock*. It is set at the period of the Gordon anti-popery riots of 1780, and Lord George Gordon himself appears as a character. Like the later *A *Tale of Two Cities*, it contains powerful evocations of mob violence, culminating in the sack of Newgate. Reuben Haredale, a country gentleman, has been murdered, and the murderer never discovered. His brother Geoffrey Haredale, a Roman Catholic, and the smooth villain Sir John Chester (who models himself on Lord Chesterfield) are enemies; Chester's son Edward is in love with Haredale's niece Emma, and the elders combine, despite their hatred, to thwart the match. The Gordon riots, secretly fomented by Chester, supervene. Haredale's house is burned and Emma carried off. Edward saves the lives of Haredale and Emma and wins Haredale's consent to his marriage. Haredale discovers the murderer of his brother, the steward Rudge, father of the half-witted Barnaby and the blackmailer of Barnaby's devoted mother Mrs Rudge. Rudge is hanged, Barnaby (who had been swept along as unwitting participant in the riots) is reprieved from the gallows at the last moment, and Chester is killed by Haredale in a duel.

The riots are vividly described, and the book which also displays Dickens's concern with the demoralizing effect of capital punishment in the characters of Dennis the Hangman and Hugh, the savage ostler who turns out to be Chester's son. The character of the coquettish Dolly Varden inspired songs, paintings, bonnets, and the 'Dolly Varden look' in ladies' clothes, fashionable for a while in the 1870s.

BARNARD, Lady Anne (1750–1825) Née Lindsay, Scottish writer, who in 1771 wrote 'Auld Robin Gray', a sentimental ballad of unsuitable marriage stoically endured. Published by David Herd in 1776, the ballad became immensely popular and Lady Anne kept its authorship secret until she wrote to Walter *Scott in 1823 after he had quoted it in *The *Pirate.

***Barnavelt** See OLDENBARNAVELT, SIR JOHN VAN.

BARNES, Barnabe (1568/9–1609) Poet and playwright. His sonnet sequence *Parthenophil and Parthenophe was published in 1593, and *A Divine Centurie of Spirituall Sonnets in 1595. In 1598 he was arraigned for attempting to poison the recorder of Berwick, but managed to escape sentence. He published *Foure Bookes of Offices in 1606, and in 1607 a Machiavellian drama, *The Divils Charter: A Tragaedie Conteining the Life and Death of Pope Alexander the Sixt,* said to have been performed before the king. It includes such melodramatic scenes as the murder of Lucrezia Borgia with poisoned face wash. Another play, *The Battle of Evesham,* is lost.

BARNES, Djuna Chappell (1892–1982) American writer and illustrator, whose works include *A Book* (1923), a volume of plays, poems, and stories; *Ryder* (1928, novel); *Ladies Almanack* (1928, privately printed in Paris), an erotic *pastiche of lesbian life; and *Nightwood* (1936, original text restored 1995), a novel originally published with a preface by T. S. *Eliot. It evokes, in highly wrought, high-coloured prose, a nightmare cosmopolitan world (chiefly located in Paris and New York) peopled by tormented and mutually tormenting characters, linked by the enigmatic doctor, priest of the secret brotherhood of the City of Darkness; it mingles elements of *fin-de-siècle* decadence with premonitions of the neo-Gothic. Her *Selected Works* appeared in 1962.

BARNES, Julian (1946–) Novelist and essayist, who worked as a lexicographer on the *OED* supplement (1969–72), then as a book and television reviewer. His first, semi-autobiographical novel, *Metroland* (1980), follows a London schoolboy from suburbia to student Paris in 1968, and back to marriage and domesticity in 1977. *Before She Met Me* (1982) deals with sexual jealousy, a recurrent theme in Barnes's fiction, which resurfaces prominently in his two dialogue novels, *Talking It Over* (1991) and its sequel, *Love, Etc.* (2000). *Flaubert's Parrot* (1984), which mixes fiction, biographical detection, and literary commentary, exemplifies the elegant eclecticism typifying much of his work, and his fascination with French literature and life (*Cross Channel*, 1996, is a volume of stories about Anglo-French relationships). His most virtuoso work of fiction, *A History of the World in 10½ Chapters* (1989), inventively links a wide diversity of stories and essays by shared themes of shipwreck and survival. He has also written a part-fantastic novel about a female aviator, *Staring at the Sun* (1986), which explores ageing (as do the stories in *The Lemon Table*, 2004); a satiric fable about Eastern Europe, *The Porcupine* (1992); a caustic *dystopia, *England, England* (1998); and a novel which fictionalizes Arthur Conan *Doyle's real-life investigation of criminal activities in a late 19th-century Staffordshire village, *Arthur & George* (2005). His translation of the notebook Alphonse Daudet kept while dying from syphilis, *In the Land of Pain*, appeared in 2002. *Nothing to be Frightened Of* (2008) is a family memoir and meditation on mortality. He is also the author of four crime novels under the pseudonym Dan Kavanagh, the name a homage to his wife Pat Kavanagh (1940–2008), a celebrated literary agent. *The Sense of an Ending* (2011) won the Man Booker prize.

BARNES, Peter (1931–2004) Playwright. His first real success came with *The Ruling Class* (1969), a bizarre farce exploring the mechanics of power. The follow-up, *Leonardo's Last Supper* (1969), weighs up the economic advantages of a dead *Leonardo da Vinci over a live one. The controversial *Laughter!* (1978) has a first half set in 16th-century tsarist Russia, and the second culminating in a sudden and terrifying shift into Auschwitz concentration camp. His use of *black humour was best seen in what was to be his last London production, *Red Noses* (1985), another disturbing 'misuse' of history.

BARNES, William (1801–86) Poet and schoolmaster, born near Sturminster Newton, Dorset. He learned Greek, Latin, and music, taught himself wood engraving, and studied French, Italian, Welsh, Hebrew, Hindustani, and other languages. He waged a lifelong campaign to rid English of classical and foreign influences, suggesting many 'Saxonized' alternatives, such as 'sun-print' for photograph and 'fall-time' for autumn. *Orra: A Lapland Tale* appeared in 1822 and his *Poems of Rural Life in the Dorset Dialect* in 1844; *Hwomely Rhymes* followed in 1859 and *Poems of Rural Life*, written in standard English, in 1868. His collected dialect poems appeared as *Poems of Rural Life in the Dorset Dialect* in 1879. As well as his volumes of poetry, Barnes wrote textbooks, a primer of Old English (*Se Gefylsta*, 1849), *Philological Grammar* (1854), a *Grammar . . . of the Dorset Dialect* (1863), and other works reflecting his interest in philology and local history.

According to his many admirers, who included Alfred *Tennyson, G. M. *Hopkins ('almost an admirer'), Thomas *Hardy, and Edmund *Gosse, Barnes was a lyric poet of the first rank and a vibrant force in regenerating poetic language through dialect. His poems evoke the Dorset landscape, country customs (as in 'Harvest Hwome' and 'Woodcom' Feast'), and happy childhood, although his few poems of grief, such as 'Woak Hill' and 'The Wind at the Door', written after the death of his wife, are among his most celebrated. He was interested in versification, prosody, and the techniques of verse (particularly in *alliteration), and the wide variety of his forms intrigued Hardy; his noun combinations ('heart-heaven', 'sun-sweep', and 'mind-sight') seem to foreshadow Hopkins. The dialect poems were written largely between 1834 and 1867; his standard English poems on either side of those dates. Hardy wrote an affectionate portrait in the *Athenaeum* on his death, and a poem, 'The Last Signal'.

BARNFIELD, Richard (1574–1620) Poet. He published *The Affectionate Shepherd* in 1594, *Cynthia: With Certain Sonnets* in 1595, and *The Encomion of Lady Pecunia* (the praise of money) in 1598. Two of his *Poems, in Divers Humours* (1598) appeared also in *The *Passionate Pilgrim* (1599) and were long attributed to William *Shakespeare. *The Affectionate Shepheard* is a pastoral (based on *Virgil's second eclogue) describing the homoerotic love of Daphnis for Ganymede, and includes a rather surprising digression on the 'indecencie of mens long haire'. The twenty sonnets in *Cynthia* are also addressed to Ganymede. Barnfield has the distinction of being the only Elizabethan poet other than Shakespeare known to have addressed love sonnets to a man.

baroque [from Portuguese *barroco*, Spanish *barrueco*, a rough or imperfect pearl] Originally a term of abuse applied to 17th-century Italian art and that of other countries, especially Germany, influenced by Italy. In a literary context the word baroque is loosely used to describe highly ornamented verse or prose, abounding in extravagant conceits; it is rarely used of English writers (with the exception of the Italianate Richard *Crashaw), but frequently applied to Giambattista *Marino and to Góngora (*see* GONGORISM).

BARRETT, Elizabeth *See* BROWNING, ELIZABETH BARRETT.

BARRIE, Sir J. M. (James Matthew) (1860–1937) Novelist and playwright. Baronet, OM. His *'Kailyard school' stories and novels drew on his mother's memories and were set in his Scottish birthplace, Kirriemuir (as 'Thrums'); they included *Auld Licht Idylls* (1888), *A Window in Thrums* (1889), and the highly successful *The Little Minister* (1891). His first play, *Richard Savage*, was performed in London in 1891. *Margaret Ogilvy* (1896) is an affectionate portrait of his mother; two self-revelatory books, *Sentimental Tommy* and *Tommy and Grizel* (both 1896), contain hints of *Peter Pan. His dramatic successes included *Quality Street* (1901; filmed 1927, 1937), *The Admirable Crichton* (filmed 1957; *see* CRICHTON, JAMES), *What Every Woman Knows* (1906; filmed 1915, 1921, 1924), and *Dear Brutus* (1917).

Barrie's creation 'Peter Pan' has become a literary immortal. The story sprang from Barrie's relationship with the sons of Arthur and Sylvia Llewellyn Davies, and appears in several forms. The idea of Peter Pan first emerged in the novel *The Little White Bird* (1902), the Peter Pan episodes being reprinted as *Peter Pan in Kensington Gardens* in 1906. The play was first produced, with spectacular special effects, in December 1904, and adapted as a novel, *Peter and Wendy*, in 1911. Barrie, and his complex relationship with the Llewellyn Davies family, is the subject of a BBC TV drama and biography by Andrew Birkin, a play by Alan Knee, and the film *Finding Neverland* (Marc Forster, 2004).

BARRY, Sebastian (1955–) Irish playwright, poet, and novelist. Barry's plays use lyrical, introspective language in place of overt dramatic conflict, and typically focus on the plight of people excluded from received narratives of Irishness. The protagonists of *Boss Grady's Boys* (1988) are rural bachelors, those of *Prayers of Sherkin* (1990) millenarians awaiting apocalypse on a remote island. *The Steward of Christendom* (1995) dramatizes the King Lear-like madness of a former officer of the pre-independence Dublin Metropolitan Police, while *Our Lady of Sligo* (1998) presents the last days of a middle-class woman dying of alcohol-induced cancer. *Andersen's English* (2010) examines Hans Christian *Andersen's visit to *Dickens in 1857. Concerned respectively with a policeman driven from Ireland during the War of Independence, a group of Royal Dublin Fusiliers in Flanders, and a contemporary centenarian who has spent her life in a soon to be shut mental institution, the novels *The Whereabouts of Eneas McNulty* (1998), *A Long Long Way* (2005), and *The Secret Scripture* (2008) extend and enrich Barry's challenge to historical myths.

Barry Lyndon See LUCK OF BARRY LYNDON, THE.

Barsetshire Novels By Anthony *Trollope. They include the following: *The *Warden, *Barchester Towers, *Doctor Thorne, *Framley Parsonage, The *Small House at Allington, and The *Last Chronicle of Barset. They depict middle-class domestic and ecclesiastical life in the fictional English county of Barsetshire.

BARSTOW, Stan (1928–2011) Novelist, the son of a miner. His first novel, *A Kind of Loving* (1960), is the first-person, present-tense narration of office-worker Vic Brown, trapped into marriage by his infatuation with small-minded Ingrid and harassed by his mother-in-law. It was followed by other vivid portrayals of Yorkshire life, including *Ask Me Tomorrow* (1962) and *Joby* (1964), which contributed to the development of the *regional novel associated with Alan *Sillitoe, Keith *Waterhouse (who adapted

A Kind of Loving for the screen), John *Braine, and others. Later novels include *Just You Wait and See* (1986), *Give Us This Day* (1989), and *Next of Kin* (1991). *In My Own Good Time* (2001) is an autobiography.

BARTH, John Simmons (1930–) American novelist, essayist, and short story writer. His 1967 essay 'The Literature of Exhaustion' argued that fiction was unable to keep up with the rapidly changing face of the post-war world, a position he modified in 1979 with 'The Literature of Replenishment'. His own work has tended towards *metafiction (*Giles Goat-Boy*, 1966), historical *pastiche (*The Sot-Weed Factor*, 1960), and academic parody (*Sabbatical*, 1992). *LETTERS* (1980) is a novel where both Barth and his own earlier characters appear. Barth has been drawn constantly to non-European story cycles, which have informed works like *The Tidewater Tales* (1987). His playful brand of *postmodernism—intrusive narrators, self-reflexive stories—suggests a body of work where means of representation form a major part of the subject. Two important essay collections are *The Friday Book* (1984) and *Further Fridays* (1995). *The Development* (2008) is a series of linked stories set in a gated community.

BARTHES, Roland (1915–80) French literary critic, essayist, and cultural theorist. His first book, *Le Degré zéro de l'écriture* (1953: *Writing Degree Zero*), is a response to Jean-Paul *Sartre on questions of literary style and political commitment. His witty articles on the workings of modern bourgeois ideology in all kinds of cultural product, from wrestling to popular magazines, were collected in *Mythologies* (1957), together with a more theoretical essay on the analysis of myths that is derived from Ferdinand de *Saussure. His commitment to *structuralism continued in *Éléments de sémiologie* (1965: *Elements of Semiology*), in his analysis of the codes of fashion writing in *Système de la mode* (1967: *The Fashion System*), and in essays proclaiming the 'death of the author'. As the scientific pretensions of structuralism came under assault from Jacques *Derrida and others, Barthes entered a phase of more personal and essayistic reflection in his book on Japan, *L'Empire des signes* (1970: *The Empire of Signs*), and in *S/Z* (1970), his influential study of *Balzac's *Sarrasine*. In these and later works of his 'post-structuralist' period, he emphasizes the multiple, open meanings of texts, and the *jouissance* (sexual bliss) of reading, notably in *Le

Plaisir du texte (1973: *The Pleasure of the Text*). The wistful and fragmentary late works *Roland Barthes par Roland Barthes* (1975), *Fragments d'un discours amoureux* (1977: *Fragments of a Lover's Discourse*), and *La Chambre claire* (1980: *Camera Lucida*) mix autobiography and aphorism in a manner remote from the certainties of the 1960s. His influence has been extensive, especially in his defence, partly inspired by Bertolt *Brecht, of *modernist experiment against the traditions of *realism.

Bartholomew Fair A comedy by Ben *Jonson, performed by the Lady Elizabeth's Men 1614, printed 1631.

The play is set at the fair which took place at Smithfield on 24 August, St Bartholomew's day, and follows the fortunes of its various visitors: Littlewit, a proctor, his wife Win-the-fight, his mother-in-law Dame Purecraft, and her mentor, the ranting Puritan Zeal-of-the-land Busy, who come to eat roast pig; the rich fool Bartholomew Cokes, Wasp, his angry servant, and Grace Wellborn, who is unwillingly engaged to Cokes; Justice Adam Overdo, who attends the fair in disguise in order to discover its 'enormities'; and two gallants, Quarlous and Winwife, who intend to jeer at the fair people. Many mishaps and misunderstandings ensue. The play ends with the performance of a puppet play written by Littlewit, in imitation of Marlowe's *Hero and Leander. Zeal-of-the-land Busy is defeated in a debate with a puppet about the morality of play-acting, and Overdo agrees to give up his censoriousness and invites everyone home to supper.

BARTLETT, Elizabeth (1924–2008) British poet. Her first collection, *A Lifetime of Dying*, was not published until 1979 and included poems written twenty years previously. Her hard-hitting depictions of the lonely, ill, and dispossessed offer a stark portrait of post-war Britain. Other titles include *Strange Territory* (1983); *The Czar is Dead* (1986); *Look No Face* (1991); *Two Women Dancing: New and Selected Poems* (1995); and more recently *Mrs Perkins and Oedipus* (2004).

BARTRAM, William (1739–1823) American Quaker naturalist and traveller, author of *Travels through North and South Carolina, Georgia, East and West Florida, the Cherokee Country, the Extensive Territories of the Moscogulges, or the Creek Confederacy, and the Country of the Chactaws* (1791), a travel book much admired by S. T. *Coleridge and William *Wordsworth,

who both drew on its descriptions of the natural wonders of the new world.

Basil (1852) The second novel of Wilkie *Collins, and an early example of the *sensation genre: a sombre exploration of sexual obsession. Basil, a serious young man of good family, becomes infatuated with a veiled woman he sees on an omnibus, Margaret Sherwin, the young daughter of a linen draper. They marry, but the marriage is kept secret and unconsummated for a year. When Margaret goes to a party with Robert Mannion, her father's confidential clerk, who has a sinister power over her, Basil follows. He sees them leave together and go to a dubious hotel. Listening through a partition wall, he realizes they are lovers. When Mannion leaves, Basil attacks him, leaving him horribly disfigured and blinded in one eye. Basil collapses in delirium, but later recovers. Mannion reveals that his father was hanged for forgery, and that Basil's father refused to help him. Margaret, visiting Mannion in hospital, contracts typhus and dies. Basil flees London; Mannion pursues him to Cornwall. In a clifftop confrontation Mannion falls to his death. The novel is remarkable for its violent and explicit representations of madness, jealousy, and sexuality.

BASILE, Giambattista (1566?–1632) Neapolitan courtier, poet, and writer of novelle; he is best known for *Lo cunto de li cunti* or *Pentamerone* (1634/6), a collection of tales in Neapolitan dialect structured on the model of the *Decameron. The work mixes folk tales, fables, and classical myths. Originally addressed to an elite, courtly audience, it later came to be viewed erroneously as a work of popular and children's literature. Individual tales provide the European source of many fairy stories including Cinderella, Puss-in-Boots, and Beauty and the Beast. *Perrault and the brothers *Grimm both drew on it.

Basilikon Doron See JAMES I AND VI.

BATAILLE, Georges (1897–1962) French writer and intellectual. His examination of the extremes of human existence and the margins of socially acceptable behaviour, and his radical analysis of the relationship between sex and death, made him an important touchstone for later thinkers such as Jacques *Derrida, Michel *Foucault, and Jacques *Lacan. He developed his ideas both in philosophical texts, including *La Part maudite* (3 vols, 1949; *The Accursed Share*), and in fictional works such as *Histoire de l'œil* (1928; *Story of the Eye*).

BATES, H. E. (Herbert Ernest) (1905–74) Novelist and short story writer. He was encouraged by Eve *Garnett to publish his first novel, *The Two Sisters* (1926). Other works include *The Fallow Land* (1932), *The Poacher* (1935), *A House of Women* (1936), and *My Uncle Silas* (1939); short stories published under the pseudonym 'Flying Officer X'; and *Fair Stood the Wind for France* (1944). Several novels (*The Darling Buds of May*, 1958; *A Breath of French Air*, 1959; *When the Green Woods Laugh*, 1960) featured the irrepressibly cheerful Larkin family. He also published three volumes of autobiography.

Bath, Wife of *See* CANTERBURY TALES, 6.

bathos [Greek, 'depth'] A descent from the sublime to the ridiculous in literary style or subject. The term originates from Alexander *Pope's satire *Peri Bathous, or The Art of Sinking in Poetry* (1727).

Batrachomyomachia, *or The Battle of the Frogs and Mice* A burlesque Greek epic (*c.*5th century BC), formerly attributed to *Homer. It describes in *mock-epic Homeric style a battle between mice and frogs in which Zeus and Athena join. Thomas *Parnell's version of the *Batrachomyomachia* attacking John Dennis and Lewis *Theobald appeared in 1717.

Battle of Alcazar, The A verse play by George *Peele, written *c.*1588/9, published 1594. It dramatizes the battle in 1578 between Sebastian, king of Portugal, and Abdelmelec, king of Morocco.

Battle of the Books, The (*A Full and True Account of the Battel Fought Last Friday, between the Antient and the Modern Books in St James's Library*) A prose satire by Jonathan *Swift, written 1697, when Swift was residing with Sir William *Temple, published 1704. Temple had written an essay on the comparative merits of 'Ancient and Modern Learning', which contained uncritical praise of the spurious *Epistles of Phalaris*; this drew the censure of William Wotton and Richard *Bentley. In Swift's treatment, the 'Battle' originates from a request by the moderns that the ancients shall evacuate the higher of the two peaks of Parnassus which they have hitherto occupied. The ancients, under the patronage of Pallas (Athena), are led by *Homer, *Pindar, Euclid, *Aristotle, and *Plato, with Temple commanding the allies; the moderns by John *Milton, John *Dryden, *Descartes, and Thomas *Hobbes, with the support of the malignant deity Criticism. Aristotle aims an arrow at Francis *Bacon but hits Descartes. Homer overthrows *Gondibert. *Virgil encounters his translator Dryden, in a helmet nine times too big. In general the ancients have the advantage, but the tale leaves the issue undecided.

BAUDELAIRE, Charles (1821–67) French poet, critic, translator, and essayist. *Les Fleurs du mal* (1857: *The Flowers of Evil*) represents a determined attempt to create order and beauty, notably by the discovery of hidden relations or 'correspondences', in a world which is largely perceived as ugly and oppressive. Baudelaire gave a detailed account of the effects of opium and hashish in *Les Paradis artificiels* (1860), which contains a commentary on the translated extracts from Thomas De Quincey's *Confessions of an English Opium Eater*. Baudelaire the poet has had a decisive influence on English verse: since 1890 there has been no decade without a major English translation, including versions by Edna St Vincent *Millay, Roy *Campbell, and Michael *Hamburger. The title story of Angela Carter's collection *Black Venus* (1985) describes Baudelaire from the point of view of his mistress, Jeanne Duval.

BAUDRILLARD, Jean (1929–2007) French philosopher, one of the principal theorists of *postmodernism. His pioneering work of the 1960s considers what he terms 'consumer society', exploring how human identity and relationships are mediated by a proliferating number of objects in the world. Later work dwells on the signs and meanings these objects produce, arguing that the contemporary world is saturated by 'simulacra', whose 'hyper-reality' appears to offer an escape from the banality of everyday life, but which in fact confront us with significant moral and ethical problems.

Baum, L. (Lyman) Frank (1856–1919) Writer, in collaboration with the illustrator William Wallace Denslow, of *Father Goose, his Book* (1899), and *The Wonderful *Wizard of Oz* (1900), which he adapted as a long-running musical.

BAWDEN, Nina (1925–) Née Mabey, CBE, novelist and children's writer. Her closely observed novels are almost equally divided between those for adults and those for children. Several, notably *Family Money* (1991), have been televised. Her highly regarded children's books include *The Peppermint Pig* (1976) and *Carrie's War* (1973, BBC 1974; 2003), based on her experiences of wartime evacuation. Non-fiction includes a memoir, *In my Own*

Time (1994), and *Dear Austen* (2005), addressed to her husband Austen Kark, who died in the Potter's Bar rail crash (2002).

BAXTER, James Keir (1926–72) New Zealand poet. He wrote prolifically, producing plays as well as poetry, survived a period of alcoholism, and in 1961 became a Roman Catholic. His early volumes (*Beyond the Palisade*, 1944; *Blow, Wind of Fruitfulness*, 1948; *The Fallen House*, 1953) dealt with themes of nature, place, colonial alienation, and guilt. In later work he expressed himself in a colloquial, hybridized, yet spiritual and questioning style, describing his own mission amongst the poor, and drawing on Christian imagery, small daily events, and the Maori language to create an intensely personal voice. Volumes include *Pig Island Letters* (1966), *Jerusalem Sonnets* (1970), and *Autumn Testament* (1972).

BAXTER, Richard (1615–91) A Presbyterian theologian who sided with Parliament and was a military chaplain during the Civil War. He was author of *The Saint's Everlasting Rest* (1650; the book that Mrs Glegg in George *Eliot's *The *Mill on the Floss* used to favour in a domestic crisis) and of *Call to the Unconverted* (1657), both of which played an important part in the evangelical tradition in England and America. Fined, imprisoned, and persecuted after the Act of Uniformity under both Charles II and James II for his Nonconformist preaching, he shared his sufferings with his young wife 'who cheerfully went with me into prison'. In her memory he wrote his moving *Breviate of the Life of Margaret Charlton* (1681). He was fined by the notoriously punitive Judge Jeffreys (1645–89) on the charge of libelling the Church in his *Paraphrase of the New Testament* (1685). His autobiography, *Reliquiae Baxterianae* (1696), gives a vivid portrait of the strife of the Interregnum and the Restoration, and he wrote several well-known hymns (e.g. 'Ye holy angels bright').

BAXTER, Stephen (1957–) Liverpool-born writer of epic *science fiction. From *Raft* (1991), he has published numerous novels and short stories, including *The Time Ships* (1995), a sequel to H. G. *Wells's *The Time Machine*, the 'Manifold' sequence (1999–2002), and the 'Destiny's Children' sequence (2003–6). Novels written in collaboration with Arthur C. *Clarke include *The Light of Other Days* (2000).

BAYLEY, John (1925–) Critic and memoirist. He married Iris *Murdoch in 1956, and after her diagnosis of Alzheimer's disease, wrote a book about her decline (*Iris: A Memoir for Iris Murdoch*, 1998). Further memoirs followed after her death in 1999.

Bay Psalm Book (1640) The first book printed in the American colonies. This metrical version of the *Psalms for the churches in Massachusetts was designed to replace that of *Sternhold and Hopkins. It was often reprinted and remained popular for over a hundred years.

BBC (British Broadcasting Corporation), Established by royal charter as a publicly owned corporation supported by licence fee in 1927. Its first, highly influential manager, John, later Lord, Reith (1889–1971) established the remit of informing, educating, and entertaining. Adding *television to its *radio output in 1936 (interrupted during the war), it has continued to innovate, while its role as a national institution, popularly known as 'Auntie' and 'the Beeb', has also led to recurrent controversies concerned with political bias. Issues of taste have periodically provoked national debate about changing values.

The BBC remains the world's largest commissioner and producer of creative work in serious and popular music, drama, short stories, and documentary programmes, with much of its output re-transmitted by other broadcasters around the world. From the 1940s onwards, many writers also worked as BBC producers and regular contributors, including George *Orwell, Louis *MacNeice, P. H. *Newby, Terence Tiller (1916–87), George *MacBeth, Anthony *Thwaite, Roy *Campbell, Derek *Mahon, Patric Dickinson (1914–94), Paul *Muldoon, and Nigel Williams (1948–). BBC producers were instrumental in commissioning new, often first plays from Samuel *Beckett, Caryl *Churchill, Joe *Orton, Harold *Pinter, John *Mortimer, Robert *Bolt, Giles Cooper (1918–66), Tom *Stoppard, Bill Naughton (1910–92), John *Arden, David Rudkin, Alun *Owen, James Saunders (1925–2004), and Alan *Plater. The tradition has continued with a new generation of dramatists, including Anthony Minghella (1954–2008), Martin *Crimp, Hanif *Kureishi, and Howard *Barker.

Apart from noted radio plays, original 'light entertainment' created for BBC radio includes *The Goon Show* (1951–60), Douglas *Adams's *The Hitchhiker's Guide to the Galaxy* (1978), and Sue *Townsend's *The Secret Diary of Adrian Mole* (1982), which have generated *adaptations in many media. BBC television comedy has a distinguished tradition including revue-style shows ranging from the satirical *That Was the Week That Was* (1962–3) to *Monty Python's*

Flying Circus (1969–74). Radio comedy continues to launch new performers and formats which often migrate to television. *See also* ADAPTATION; RADIO; TELEVISION.

(((●))) SEE WEB LINKS
• BBC television homepage
• BBC radio homepage

BEACH, Sylvia (1887–1962) American bookshop owner and publisher; owner from 1919 of the Shakespeare and Company bookshop and lending library on the Left Bank in Paris, meeting place for writers as diverse as James *Joyce, Ernest *Hemingway, André Gide, and Sherwood *Anderson. When Joyce could find no publisher for *Ulysses* after instalments of its serialization in the *Little Review* had been found obscene, she published it under the Shakespeare and Co. imprint in 1922, funding the enterprise through subscription.

Beach, The First novel of Alex Garland (b. London, 1970), published 1996 and filmed in 2000. A 'cult classic' provoking comparisons to William *Golding and Graham *Greene, it satirizes young international backpackers seeking authenticity in Thailand.

'Beachy Head' An unfinished poem in blank verse by Charlotte *Smith, published posthumously in *Beachy Head, and Other Poems* (1807), which combines sublime imagery and natural description with historical narratives of war and nationhood, alongside mournful meditation on the poet's personal unhappiness.

BEARDSLEY, Aubrey (1872–98) Illustrator and writer, notorious in the 1890s as the outstanding artist of *fin-de-siècle* decadence. His disturbingly erotic drawings develop rapidly from the murky sensuality of *Pre-Raphaelite medievalism to rococo wit and grace. Beardsley's most important illustrations are for Oscar *Wilde's *Salome* (1894), Alexander *Pope's *The Rape of the Lock* (1896), the *Lysistrata* of *Aristophanes (1896), and Ben *Jonson's *Volpone* (1898). He was art editor of the *Yellow Book* in 1894; the Wilde scandal led to his dismissal in 1895; he then became art editor to the *Savoy*. Beardsley's most significant achievement as a writer is *The Story of Venus and Tannhauser*, a charmingly rococo and highly cultivated erotic romance. An expurgated version entitled *Under the Hill* was published in the *Savoy*; an unexpurgated edition was privately printed in 1907; it contains a cruel caricature of Wilde.

Beat and Beat Generation 'Beat' was a term first used by the notorious hustler and drug addict Herbert Huncke (1916–96) to describe his own state of lawless drifting and social alienation. 'Beat' was quickly picked up by Jack *Kerouac as a triple entendre—an epithet that brought together a sense of being 'beaten' with the state of being 'beatific', as well as suggesting the pulse and 'beat' of music. The pioneers of the movement were Allen *Ginsberg, whose book *Howl* (1956) protested that America had seen 'the best minds of my generation destroyed by madness', and Kerouac, whose *On the Road* (1957) reinvented a mythic landscape of highways, bars, and male bonding. With other writers such as Gregory Corso (1930–2001) and William *Burroughs, the Beats developed an aesthetic based on the spontaneity of jazz, Buddhist mysticism, and the raw urgency of sex, in reaction against the perceived sterile conformity of post-war America.

Beatles, the A group of young musicians from Liverpool (George Harrison, John Lennon, Paul McCartney, and 'Ringo Starr'), whose songs and lifestyle, from 1962 until their breakup in 1970, attracted a vast following. Many of their lyrics (e.g. 'Penny Lane', 'Eleanor Rigby', 'She's Leaving Home') have been highly praised, and they had a considerable influence on the success of the *Liverpool poets and the underground poetry movement. Philip *Larkin described their work as 'an enchanting and intoxicating hybrid of Negro rock-and-roll with their own adolescent romanticism'. John Lennon was murdered in New York in 1980, and George Harrison died in 2001.

BEATRICE (?1266–1290) Identified by *Boccaccio as Bice, daughter of Folco Portinari of Florence, and wife of Simone de' Bardi. The principal subject of *Dante's *Vita nuova*, in which he claims to have fallen in love with her when she was 9. After her death Dante comes to a new understanding of her role in his life. Beatrice acts as Dante's guide in the *Divina Commedia*, from *Purgatorio* XXX to *Paradiso* XXX.

BEATTIE, James (1735–1803) Scottish poet and philosopher. His *Essay on the Nature and Immutability of Truth* (1770) was an attempt to refute David *Hume and George *Berkeley.*The Minstrel*, a poem in *Spenserian stanzas, traces 'the progress of a poetical Genius, born in a rude age, from the first dawning of fancy and reason', who finds his education in nature, in a manner that foreshadows Wordsworth's *Prelude*. Book I appeared in 1771, Book II in 1774.

Beauchamp's Career A novel by George *Meredith, published 1876. It deals with politics and the contemporary state of Britain after the Crimean War. The brilliant Renée was Meredith's favourite among all his women characters.

BEAUMONT, Francis (1584–1616) Dramatist. His most famous poem, on the Mermaid Tavern, is addressed to Ben *Jonson. The only play Beaumont is known to have written on his own, *The *Knight of the Burning Pestle* (1606/7), failed on its first appearance. Soon afterwards he began his celebrated collaboration with John *Fletcher. According to John *Aubrey they lived together 'on the Bankside, not far from the [Globe] play-house, both bachelors; lay together; had one wench in the house between them…the same clothes and cloak, etc.…'. The chronology of their work is uncertain, but at some point from 1608 to 1610 they began to write their four plays for the King's Men, including their greatest successes, *Philaster, A *King and No King*, and *The *Maid's Tragedy*. In 1613, Beaumont married an heiress, Ursula Isley, by whom he had two daughters; he also suffered a stroke and abandoned writing. He died in 1616 and was buried in Westminster Abbey.

BEAUMONT, Jeanne-Marie Leprince de *See* LEPRINCE DE BEAUMONT, JEANNE-MARIE.

BEAUVOIR, Simone de (1908–86) French writer, philosopher, feminist, and political activist. A lifelong companion of Jean-Paul *Sartre, her early novels, which were quickly translated into English, reflect the major preoccupations of *existentialism. Her highly influential analysis of women's oppression, *Le Deuxième Sexe* (1949; as *The Second Sex*, 1953 and 2009) paved the way for much modern *feminist criticism. Her four volumes of autobiography include *Mémoires d'une jeune fille rangée* (1958: *Memoirs of a Dutiful Daughter*) and *La Force de l'âge* (1960: *The Prime of Life*), the former translated into English by James *Kirkup in 1959. *Beloved Chicago Man: Letters to Nelson Algren 1947–64* (1997) collects her correspondence with her American lover, the writer Nelson *Algren. *See also* KRISTEVA.

Beaux' Stratagem, The George *Farquhar's final comedy, produced with great success in 1707. Aimwell and Archer, two spendthrifts, arrive at an inn at Lichfield, in search of adventure and money. To economize, Archer pretends to be Aimwell's servant. Dorinda, daughter of the wealthy Lady Bountiful, falls in love with Aimwell, who gets admission to her house by passing himself off as his elder brother Lord Aimwell. He is accompanied by Archer, who has formed a liaison with Mrs Sullen, the unhappy wife of Lady Bountiful's alcoholic son. The two men protect the women during an attack on the house. Overpowered by the trustfulness of Dorinda, Aimwell confesses the fraud. Mrs Sullen's brother brings news of Lord Aimwell's death and of Aimwell's accession to the title; Sullen agrees to the dissolution of his marriage, and Mrs Sullen is free to marry Archer.

BECKET, St Thomas (*c*.1120–1170) Archbishop of Canterbury under Henry II from 1162, assassinated on the king's orders in the cathedral on 29 December 1170. There was popular outrage. The king, officially at least, claimed that his orders had been misinterpreted. Becket's shrine at Canterbury became the most famous in Christendom as a place where miracles were performed, and it was the objective of *Chaucer's pilgrims 200 years later. The story of Becket has been the subject of plays by *Tennyson, T. S. *Eliot (*Murder in the Cathedral*), and Christopher *Fry; and by Jean Anouilh in French.

BECKETT, Samuel (1906–89) Author, born at Foxrock, Dublin, and greatly affected in childhood by the evangelical Protestantism of his mother. He taught briefly in Belfast before going to Paris as *lecteur d'anglais* at the École Normale Supérieure; there in 1928 he met James *Joyce, with whom he formed a lasting friendship. His first published work was an essay on Joyce (1929) and he assisted with the translation into French of the 'Anna Livia Plurabelle' section of *Finnegans Wake*. His first story, 'Assumption', appeared in *transition* (1929), and in 1930 he returned as lecturer to Trinity College, Dublin, resigning after four terms to embark on five unsettled, solitary years in Germany, France, Ireland, and London, before settling permanently in France. *More Pricks than Kicks* (1934, stories) was followed by several full-length novels, including *Murphy* (1938), a mordant evocation of London Irish life. Beckett emerged from his experience in the French Resistance during the Second World War as a francophone writer who had shed the slightly swaggering cleverness of his early work. His trilogy *Molloy* (1951); *Malone Meurt* (1951; Beckett's own English version, *Malone Dies*, 1958); and *L'Innommable* (1953; *The Unnamable*, 1960) was originally written in French, and all three novels are interior monologues, desolate, terminal, obsessional, irradiated with flashes of black humour: *Malone Dies* opens with the characteristic sentence 'I shall soon be quite dead at last in spite of all'. Beckett's highly distinctive, despairing, yet curiously exhilarating voice reached a large audience with the Paris performance in 1953 of *En attendant Godot* (pub. 1952; trans. as **Waiting for Godot*, 1955). Beckett became widely known as a playwright associated with the Theatre of the *Absurd, whose use of the stage and of dramatic narrative and symbolism revolutionized drama in England and influenced later playwrights, including Harold *Pinter, Athol *Fugard, and Tom *Stoppard. Subsequent stage plays include *Fin de partie* (first performed in French at the Royal Court, 1957; English version, *Endgame*, pub. 1958), a one-act drama of frustration, irascibility, and senility, featuring blind Hamm, his attendant Clov, and Hamm's parents, 'accursed progenitors' who spend the action in dustbins; *Krapp's Last Tape* (1958; pub. 1959), written for the Irish actor Patrick Magee, a monologue in which the shabby Krapp attempts to recapture the intensity of earlier days by listening to recordings of his own younger self; *Happy Days* (1961, pub. 1961), which portrays Winnie buried to her waist in a mound, but still attached to the carefully itemized contents of her handbag; *Come and Go* (1966; pub. 1967), a stark 'dramaticule' with three female characters and a text of 121 words; the even more minimal *Breath* (1969), a 30-second play consisting only of a pile of rubbish, a breath, and a cry; and *Not I* (1973; pub. 1973), a fragmented, disembodied monologue delivered by an actor of indeterminate sex of whom only the 'Mouth' is illuminated. Beckett has also written for television (*Eh Joe*, 1966) and, more frequently, for radio. His late prose fragments have excited considerable attention. He was awarded the *Nobel Prize in 1969.

BECKFORD, William (1760–1844) Author of the *oriental tale *Vathek. Indulging his passions for art, architecture, and music, he lavished his considerable fortune on the extravagant Fonthill Abbey and on continental travels, partly necessitated by homosexual scandal. His books of travels include *Dreams, Waking Thoughts and Incidents* (1783) and *Italy* (1834).

BEDDOES, Thomas Lovell (1803–49) Dramatist and poet, son of the physician, radical, and writer Dr Thomas Beddoes (1760–1808), who had been friend and doctor of *Coleridge, *Wordsworth, and *Southey. He published in 1821 *The Improvisatore* and in 1822 *The Brides' Tragedy*. His most important work, *Death's Jest-Book, or the Fool's Tragedy*, begun in 1825, was published after his death by suicide at Basle. It is in blank verse, heavily influenced by Elizabethan and Jacobean tragedy, and shows Beddoes's obsession with the macabre, the supernatural, and bodily decay. A. W. *Symons compared Beddoes to *Baudelaire and *Poe. He is now best known for his shorter pieces, such as 'Dream Pedlary' and the lyrics which appear in *Death's Jest-Book*

BEDE (Baeda, or 'The Venerable Bede') (*c.*673–735) A distinguished, influential scholar and prolific writer, in the charge of Benedict Biscop, abbot of Wearmouth, as a child. He went in 682 to Jarrow in the care of its first abbot, Ceolfrid, and spent most of his life there. Buried at Jarrow, his remains were moved to Durham during the first half of the 11th century. He was first called 'Venerabilis' during the 9th century. His *Historia Ecclesiastica Gentis Anglorum* (**Ecclesiastical History of the English People*) was finished in 731, by which time he had written nearly 40 works, including treatises, biblical commentaries, and homilies.

BEDE, Cuthbert Pseudonym of Edward *Bradley.

BEDFORD, Sybille (1911–2006) Author, encouraged to write by Aldous *Huxley, whose biography she would complete in two volumes (1973, 1974). Her 'biographical novel', *A Legacy* (1956), set largely in the years immediately preceding the First World War, is a witty, sophisticated tragicomedy whose vivid portrait of two ill-matched families—one from the Roman Catholic aristocracy, the other from the Jewish *haute bourgeoisie*—drew upon Bedford's own background. *A Favourite of the Gods* (1962) and the boldly lesbian *A Compass Error* (1968) were semi-autobiographical novels with echoes of Henry *James, while *Jigsaw* (1989) is based closely on her travels round the south of France with her mother. *Quicksands* (2005) is an evocative, seemingly frank, but elusive memoir.

Bedlam A corruption of Bethlehem, applied to the Hospital of St Mary of Bethlehem, just outside Bishopsgate, London. It was founded as a priory in 1247; in 1329 it is mentioned as 'an hospital', and in 1402 as a hospital for lunatics. From Bedlam are derived the expressions *Tom o' Bedlam and Bess o' Bedlam for wandering lunatics, or beggars posing as lunatics, and the hospital is referred to in plays by Thomas *Dekker, John *Ford, and Ben *Jonson.

Beelzebub The name of a demon or devil, derived from different biblical names. In the Old Testament, Baal-zebub is a false god (2 Kgs 1: 2-3), meaning in Hebrew 'lord of flies': in the New Testament, Beelzebub is 'prince of the devils' (Matt. 12: 24, Mark 3: 22) and associated with *Satan. He was seen in medieval and Renaissance times as Satan's second in command, a lurid figure in popular mythology and morality plays. He accompanies Lucifer in Marlowe's *Dr Faustus*; Milton gives the name to one of the fallen angels, next to Satan in power (*Paradise Lost*, I. 79) and William *Golding adopted one version of it for the title of his novel *Lord of the Flies*.

BEER, Patricia (1919-99) Poet and critic, the daughter of a railway clerk and a mother who was a member of the Plymouth Brethren, a background she describes vividly in *Mrs Beer's House* (1968). The legends and landscapes of the West Country form the background for many of her poems (collections include *The Loss of the Magyar*, 1959; *The Estuary*, 1971; *Driving West*, 1975; *Selected Poems*, 1980; *The Lie of the Land*, 1983), and *Moon's Ottery* (1978), a novel set in Elizabethan Devon. *Reader, I Married Him* (1974), a study of women characters in 19th-century fiction, was an early and influential example of the impact of feminism on academic criticism.

BEERBOHM, Sir Max (Henry Maximilian) (1872-1956) Drama critic, essayist, parodist, and caricaturist. His one completed novel, *Zuleika Dobson* (1911), is a fantasized distillation of the Oxford atmosphere of the 1890s. The audaciously entitled *The Works of Max Beerbohm* (1896) was followed by *More* (1899), *Yet Again* (1909), *And Even Now* (1920). *A Christmas Garland* (1912) expertly parodied the literary styles of Henry *James, H. G. *Wells, Rudyard *Kipling, and other contemporary writers. His best short stories were collected in *Seven Men* (1919). As an associate in the 1890s of Oscar *Wilde and Aubrey *Beardsley, the *Rhymers Club circle and members of the New English Art Club, Beerbohm was well placed to observe and comment upon avant-garde tendencies. The half-brother of the actor-manager Beerbohm Tree (1852-1917), Max was theatre critic of the *Saturday Review* from 1898 to 1910; he succeeded George Bernard *Shaw, who dubbed him 'the incomparable Max'. The dramatic criticism is collected in *Around Theatres* (1953) and *More Theatres* (1968). His caricatures, with witty captions, were as elegant and as individual as his literary

works; collections include *Caricatures of Twenty-Five Gentlemen* (1896), *The Poets' Corner* (1904), and *Rossetti and his Circle* (1922). In the 1930s he began a new career as broadcaster; his commentaries on England are collected in *Mainly on the Air* (1957).

Beggar's Bush, The A drama by John *Fletcher and Philip *Massinger, possibly with Francis *Beaumont; it was probably performed 1622, published 1647.

The play has been admired for its intricate plot, and for the realistic portrayal of its 'ragged regiment' of beggars, whose dialogue is enlivened by thieves' cant. *Coleridge, in his *Table Talk* (17 Feb. 1833), declared, 'I could read the *Beggar's Bush* from morning to night. How sylvan and sunshiny it is!' *Pepys said it was the first play in which he saw women act.

Beggar's Opera, The A *ballad opera by *John Gay, produced with enormous success in 1728. The play arose out of Jonathan *Swift's suggestion for 'a Newgate pastoral, among the whores and thieves there'. The plot is founded in part on the career of the thief-taker Jonathan Wild (bap. 1683, d. 1725), represented by the businessman Peachum, whose daughter Polly marries a gallant but promiscuous highwayman, Macheath; Peachum has him imprisoned in Newgate in order to claim reward money. Newgate is run by Peachum's partner in crime Lockit; Macheath persuades Lockit's daughter Lucy, another 'wife', to help him escape. Lucy attempts to poison Polly, but the squabble (alluding to a feud between operatic sopranos) ends when Macheath is recaptured. In the condemned hold, he drinks and sings to bolster his courage, but announces himself ready for execution when several more 'wives' turn up. He is saved by a comically arbitrary reprieve. The humour of the play consists in giving recognizably 'low' characters from the criminal world the 'high' language and self-regard of Italian opera and fashionable society; this functions satirically to suggest that politicians like Sir Robert Walpole (1676-1745) resemble criminal gangs. Bertolt *Brecht and Kurt Weill's *The Threepenny Opera* (1928) is a reworking of Gay's play.

BEHAN, Brendan (1923-64) Irish playwright, poet, songwriter, and memoirist. He was arrested in Liverpool in 1939 for IRA activities, and his subsequent period of incarceration is described in *Borstal Boy* (1958). His best-known plays are the anti-capital punishment *The Quare Fellow* (1954), and *The*

Hostage (1958), a sprawling tragicomedy about a British soldier kidnapped and held hostage in a Dublin brothel, which Behan spun with the help of Joan *Littlewood out of his sparer original play in Irish, *An Giall*.

BEHN, Aphra (1640–89) Playwright and novelist. She was employed in 1666 by Charles II as a spy in Antwerp in the Dutch war, but payment was not forthcoming and she was imprisoned for debt. On her release she began to write for her living. Her first play, *The Forced Marriage* (1670), was followed by some fourteen others, including her most popular, *The Rover* (in two parts, 1677–81), dealing with the adventures in Naples and Madrid of a band of English Cavaliers during the exile of Charles II; its hero, the libertine Willmore, was said to be based on *Rochester, though another model may have been her lover John Hoyle, lawyer and son of the regicide Thomas Hoyle. *The City Heiress* (1682) is a characteristic satiric comedy of London life and, like Thomas *Otway's *Venice Preserved*, contains a caricature of the first earl of Shaftesbury. *The Lucky Chance* (1686) explores one of her favourite themes, the ill consequences of arranged marriage. She also wrote poems and novels and edited a *Miscellany* (1685). Her best-remembered work is *Oroonoko, or The History of the Royal Slave* (*c*.1688), based on her visit to Surinam in 1663. Perhaps the earliest English philosophical novel, it deplores the slave trade and Christian hypocrisy, holding up for admiration the nobility and honour of its African hero. Despite her success she had to contend with accusations of plagiarism and lewdness, attracted in her view by her sex. But Virginia Woolf in *A *Room of one's Own* (1928) acclaimed her as the first English woman to earn her living by writing, 'with all the plebeian virtues of humour, vitality and courage'. She was buried, 'scandalously but rather appropriately' in Woolf's view, in Westminster Abbey.

Belial Adapted from a Hebrew word probably meaning 'wickedness', but in the Authorized Version of the *Bible it is retained untranslated, as a proper name (e. g. Deut. 13: 13, 1 Sam. 2: 12, 2 Cor. 6: 15), often in the phrase 'sons (or children) of Belial'. It has thus come to mean the spirit of evil personified, and is used from early times as a name for *Satan or one of the fiends, and by Milton (*Paradise Lost*, I. 490) as the name of one of the fallen angels. The phrase 'sons of Belial' was a republican term of odium for *Cavaliers in the English Revolution: Milton evokes them in the same passage (I. 501–2).

Believe as You List A tragedy by Philip *Massinger, acted 1631, not published until 1849. The original play was banned because it dealt with recent Spanish and Portuguese history. Massinger ingeniously transferred the story back to the safer days of the Roman Empire.

The play is a fine study of the recurring conflict between nationalism and imperialism; it was performed by the Royal Shakespeare Company in 2005 as *Believe What You Will*.

BELL, Clive (1881–1964) Art critic, educated at Cambridge where he came under the influence of the philosopher G. E. Moore (1873–1958) and met members of what was to be the *Bloomsbury Group. In 1907 he married Vanessa Stephen (*see* BELL, VANESSA). In 1910 he met Roger *Fry, whose views contributed to his own theory of 'Significant Form', outlined in *Art* (1914), which held that form, independent of content, was the most important element in a work of art. With Fry, he was a champion of the *Post-Impressionists. In *Civilization* (1928) he argued (with provocative and ironical undertones) that civilization, in itself artificial and characterized by tolerance, discrimination, reason, and humour, depended on the existence of a (not necessarily hereditary) leisured elite.

BELL, Currer, Ellis, and Acton Pseudonyms of Charlotte, Emily, and Anne *Brontë.

BELL, Gertrude (1868–1926) Travel writer and mountaineer. From 1905 she worked in the Middle East as an archaeologist, and from 1915 she worked for British military intelligence. Appointed oriental secretary to the British high commissioner in Iraq in 1917, she played an important role in the creation of an independent Iraqi state. In her popular works *Safar Nameh: Persian Pictures* (1894), *The Desert and the Sown* (1907), and *Amurath to Amurath* (1911), and in her *Letters* (1927) and diaries, she vividly conveyed Middle Eastern landscapes and personalities. An accomplished linguist in Arabic and Persian, she also published a translation of *Hāfiz.

BELL, Quentin (1910–96) Artist, art historian and biographer, son of Clive and Vanessa *Bell and nephew of Virginia *Woolf. He wrote a highly praised biography of Virginia Woolf (2 vols, 1972). He also wrote a memoir, *Bloomsbury Recalled* (1996), which was less about himself than his parents and friends.

BELL, Vanessa (1879–1961) Née Stephen, painter, and elder sister of Virginia *Woolf. Wife of Clive *Bell and mother of Quentin

*Bell. She had an open marriage and a number of affairs including one with Roger *Fry and another with the painter Duncan Grant (1885–1978) by whom she had a daughter, Angelica. From 1914, she, Grant, and Grant's homosexual lover David *Garnett shared a farmhouse, Charleston, near Firle, Sussex. As a central figure in the *Bloomsbury Group, she painted portraits of a number of the members including Virginia Woolf and designed dust-jackets for the Hogarth Press editions of Woolf's novels. Several of Woolf's female fictional characters show the influence of Bell, notably Katharine Hilbery in *Night and Day* (1919) and Lily Briscoe in *To the Lighthouse* (1927).

BELLAMY, Edward (1850–98) American novelist and political theorist, whose fame rests upon his popular *utopian novel *Looking Backward: 2000–1887* (1888). Its hero, Julian West, a young Bostonian, falls into a hypnotic sleep in 1887 and wakes in the year 2000 to find great social changes. Squalor and injustice have disappeared, private capitalism has been replaced by public, and everyone works for and is a member of the state. The moral, social, and cultural benefits of the new system are everywhere apparent. This work had an immense vogue and a Nationalist Party was formed to advocate its principles. Bellamy was widely read in Europe, and imitated by, among others, H. G. *Wells.

'Belle Dame sans Merci, La' *See* 'LA BELLE DAME SANS MERCI'.

BELLENDEN, John (John Ballantyne) (*fl.* 1533–48) Scottish poet, who translated *Boece's *Historia Gentis Scotorum* and the first five books of *Livy's *History of Rome* into Scots prose.

Bellerophon In Greek myth the heroic tamer of the winged horse Pegasus. His feats included killing the monster Chimera. He was thrown down from his mount because of his attempt to reach Olympus and became a blind wanderer on earth. Both Bellerophon and Pegasus, whose hoof struck the fount of Hippocrene from Mount Helicon, sacred to the *Muses, became associated with poetic ambition. John *Milton as narrator of *Paradise Lost* contrasts himself with Bellerophon (VII. 1–20).

Bell Jar, The A novel by Sylvia *Plath, published 1963 under the pseudonym of Victoria Lucas, and under her own name in 1966. Partly autobiographical, it describes how the narrator, Esther Greenwood, suffers a breakdown, undergoes electroconvulsive therapy,

attempts suicide, and finally emerges from her therapy. The novel is written in a taut, controlled, colloquial yet poetic prose, and takes an ironic view of social norms of success.

BELLOC, Hilaire (1870–1953) Anglo-French poet, critic, historian, novelist, travel writer, and Catholic apologist. His first publications were, in 1896, *The Bad Child's Book of Beasts* and *Verses and Sonnets*; other books of verse included *Cautionary Tales* (1907) and *Sonnets and Verse* (1923). His books attacking and satirizing Edwardian society (some with G. K. *Chesterton) include *Pongo and the Bull* (1910) and *The Servile State* (1912). He also wrote biographies such as *Danton* (1899), *Marie Antoinette* (1909), and *Charles II* (1939), and history books. *The Cruise of the 'Nona'* (1925) is probably the most intimate of his books. His most successful book of travel, *The Path to Rome* (1902), which was published with his own sketches and illustrations, is an account of a journey which he undertook, largely on foot, from the valley of the Moselle to Rome. *The Four Men: A Farrago* (1912), set in his beloved Sussex, also describes a walk. His novels include *Mr Clutterbuck's Election* (1908), *The Green Overcoat* (1912), and *Belinda* (1928), the author's favourite. See A. N. *Wilson, *Hilaire Belloc* (1984).

BELLOW, Saul (1915–2005) American novelist, born in Canada of Russian-Jewish parents, who moved to Chicago. This city is evoked in many of his works, including his first short novel *Dangling Man* (1944). *The Adventures of Augie March* (1953) also opens in Chicago and provides a lengthy, episodic, first-person account of Augie's progress from boyhood, moving to Mexico, then Paris. *Henderson the Rain King* (1959), designed on a grand and mythic scale, records American millionaire Gene Henderson's quest for revelation and spiritual power in Africa, where he becomes rainmaker and heir to a kingdom. *Herzog* (1964) reveals the inner life of a Jewish intellectual, Moses Herzog, driven to the verge of breakdown by his second wife's adultery with his close friend; he writes unsent letters about himself and civilization to the living and the dead. *The Dean's December* (1982) is a 'tale of two cities', Chicago and Bucharest. Bellow's last novel *Ravelstein* (2000) draws on his friendship with Allan Bloom (1930–92), portraying a professor of philosophy dying of Aids. Bellow's fiction constantly explores identity crises through reflective protagonists who meditate on the shortcomings of contemporary America. He also published a number of short story collections like *Him with his Foot in his*

Mouth (1984). *To Jerusalem and Back* (1976) is a memoir of a visit to Israel. He was awarded the *Nobel Prize for Literature in 1976.

Bells, The (1871) A dramatic adaptation by *Leopold Lewis (1828–90) of *Le Juif polonais* by Erckmann-Chatrian (Émile Erckmann, 1822–99 and Alexandre Chatrian, 1826–90), the story of a burgomaster haunted by the consciousness of an undiscovered murder that he has committed. It provided Henry *Irving with one of his most successful parts.

Bells and Pomegranates The covering title of a series of plays and collections of shorter dramatic poems by Robert *Browning, published 1841–6, comprising *Pippa Passes* (1841), *King Victor and King Charles* (1842), *Dramatic Lyrics* (1842), *The Return of the Druses* (1843), A *Blot in the 'Scutcheon* (1843), *Colombe's Birthday* (1844), *Dramatic Romances and Lyrics* (1845), and *Luria and A Soul's Tragedy* (1846). The title derives from the Bible (Exod. 28: 33–4, where it relates to the ornamentation and embroidery of the high priest's robe). The separate numbers were bound together and sold as a single volume after 1846.

Beloved A novel by Toni *Morrison (1987), set in 1873 in America. The narrative technique is deliberately non-linear and complex, the language richly poetic and suffused with biblical references. Sethe, a former slave, lives with her daughter Denver and the ghost of her dead baby girl. The book opens with the unexpected arrival of Paul D., one of the five men with whom Sethe had formerly been enslaved at Sweet Home, a Kentucky farm. An uncanny girl called Beloved comes to live with them who proves to be an incarnation of the daughter Sethe had murdered, in desperation, in order to prevent her being enslaved. The title word transcends its character, and becomes a symbol for all dead and suffering slaves. The book is dedicated to 'Sixty Million and more'. *See* SLAVERY.

Belphoebe In Edmund *Spenser's *Faerie Queene*, the chaste huntress, twin sister of Amoret; she partly symbolizes *Elizabeth I.

Belshazzar's feast The feast made by Belshazzar, the son of Nebuchadnezzar and the last king of *Babylon, at which his doom was foretold by a hand writing on the wall, as described in the Old Testament Book of *Daniel (ch. 5). Babylon fell to the Persians in 539 BC. Belshazzar is the subject of a drama by Henry Hart Milman, Robert *Landor's *The Impious Feast*, a

poem by Lord *Byron, and oratorios by Handel and William *Walton.

Belton Estate, The A novel by Anthony *Trollope, published 1866. It is characteristic of Trollope's many studies of courtship, with its emphasis on inheritance, divided loyalties, and restrictive social expectations.

BELY, Andrei (Boris Nikolaevich Bugaev) (1880–1934) Russian novelist, poet, and literary theorist, born in Moscow, who became a key figure in the Russian *symbolist movement. His most important novel is *Petersburg* (1913–16, trans. 1978), written in a rhythmical prose that at times approximates the rhythms of poetry. The appearance of its definitive version the same year as Joyce's *Ulysses* is a remarkable coincidence. Bely's four-part memoirs, *Diary of an Eccentric* (1922), *Reminiscences of Blok* (1923), *On the Border of Two Centuries* (1930), and *Between Two Revolutions* (1934), are widely regarded as Russia's finest autobiography.

BENET, Stephen Vincent (1898–1943) American poet. He is best known for his narrative poem of the Civil War, *John Brown's Body* (1928), and for some of the poems in *Ballads and Poems* (1931), including the popular 'American Names', with its resounding last line, 'Bury my heart at Wounded Knee'.

Ben-Hur: A Tale of the Christ A historical novel, published 1880, about the early days of Christianity by Lew (Lewis) Wallace (1827–1905), previously a general in the American Civil War. Already a successful stage *adaptation by 1900, it was first filmed in 1907, then as a major spectacle by MGM in 1925, opulently remade in 1959.

'Benito Cereno' (1856) A short story by Herman *Melville. A Gothic tale of white masters and implacable black revenge, it is set off the coast of Peru in 1799, where the amiable, condescendingly racist Yankee Captain Delano goes to the aid of a drifting slave ship. 'Benito Cereno' was dramatized by Robert *Lowell in 1967.

BENJAMIN, Walter (1892–1940) German critic and essayist, born in Berlin of a Jewish family. After failing to gain academic employment, he worked as a literary journalist, translator, and radio scriptwriter. Influenced by Marxist ideas, he became a friend of Bertolt *Brecht, whose dramatic methods he defended. Upon Hitler's seizure of power in 1933 he went into exile in Paris. The invasion of France in

1940 led him to seek refuge in the USA, but on attempting to enter neutral Spain he was stopped at the Spanish border, where he took his own life. Despite unusual elements of Jewish mysticism, his posthumously published essays on literature, criticism, modern culture, and the philosophy of history, in part edited by Theodor *Adorno, have exercised extensive influence on *Marxist cultural and literary theory. Notable collections are *Illuminationen* (1955: *Illuminations*, 1968, ed. Hannah Arendt which includes the essay on 'The Work of Art in the Age of Mechanical Reproduction'), and *Versuche über Brecht* (1966: *Understanding Brecht*, 1973). Portions of his unfinished studies in Paris have been translated as *Charles Baudelaire: A Lyric Poet in the Era of High Capitalism* (1973).

BENNETT, Alan (1934–) Dramatist and actor, born in Yorkshire. He made his name with the satirical review *Beyond the Fringe* (1960; pub. 1963, with Jonathan Miller and others); his other works, most of which are satirical comedies, include *Forty Years On* (1968), set in a public school, which has much fun at the expense of the *Bloomsbury Group, T. E. *Lawrence, and other fashionable cultural figures; *Getting on* (1971); and *Habeas Corpus* (1973). A more sombre work, *The Old Country* (1977), deals with the theme of exile through the life of an English spy in the Soviet Union as does one of his many television plays, *An Englishman Abroad* (broadcast 1983). Other works include *The Insurance Man* (1986); *Single Spies* (1988); *A Question of Attribution* (staged 1988, televised 1991), a brilliant treatment of the treachery of the spy and art historian Sir Anthony Blunt; *The Madness of George III* (1991); and *Talking Heads*, a series of six monologues originally written for television (1987). *Writing Home* (1994) is a collection of journal entries, reminiscences, and reviews, including his celebrated piece 'The Lady in the Van', on a female tramp who camped out in his garden. In 2004, he produced the very successful play, *The History Boys* (like *The Madness of George III* later made into a film) for the *National Theatre. *Untold Stories* (2005) is an autobiographical volume written after his diagnosis with cancer. *The Habit of Art* (perf. National Theatre, 2009) portrays the relationship between W. H. *Auden and Benjamin *Britten.

BENNETT, Arnold (1867–1931) Novelist, born in Burslem, Staffordshire. His first stories were published in the popular weekly magazine *Tit Bits* (1890) and the *Yellow Book* (1895). He wrote several successful plays, notably *Mile-stones* (1912, with the dramatist and novelist Edward Knoblock (1874–1945) but is best known for his novels and short stories set in the Potteries of his youth, a region he recreated as the 'Five Towns'. *Anna of the Five Towns* (1902) shows clearly the influence of the French realists whom he much admired. *The Old Wives' Tale* (1908) was followed by the Clayhanger series (*Clayhanger*, 1910; *Hilda Lessways*, 1911; *These Twain*, 1916; *The Roll Call*, 1918). The novels portray the Five Towns with an ironic but affectionate detachment, describing provincial life and culture in documentary detail, and creating many memorable characters. Bennett's concern for obscure and ordinary lives also manifests itself in the best novel of his later period, *Riceyman Steps* (1923), the story of a miserly second-hand bookseller. His entertaining lighter works include *The Grand Babylon Hotel* (1902), *The Card* (1911), and *Mr Prohack* (1922). His *Journal*, begun in 1896, modelled partly on that of the Goncourt brothers, was published in 1932–3, and offers a striking portrait both of the period and of his own highly disciplined working life. There is a biography by Margaret *Drabble (1974).

BENOÎT de Sainte-Maure A 12th-century trouvère patronized by Henry II of England, for whom he composed a verse history of the dukes of Normandy. His best-known work is the *Roman de Troie*, based on the writings of *Dares Phrygius and *Dictys Cretensis. The *Roman* was translated into Latin prose by *Guido delle Colonne, and thus served as a source on which many subsequent writers drew, including *Boccaccio, followed by *Chaucer.

BENSON, A. C. (Arthur Christopher) (1862–1925) author, brother of R. H. and E. F. *Benson. He published many volumes of biography, family reminiscences, reflection, criticism, including *The House of Quiet: An Autobiography* (1904) and had a facility for writing public odes, typified by his 'Land of hope and glory'. From 1897 until 1925 he kept a diary, amounting to five million words; extracts were published by Percy Lubbock in 1926, but the papers were locked away for 50 years. David Newsome makes use of them in his biography *On the Edge of Paradise: A. C. Benson, the Diarist* (1980), a work which reveals Benson's deeply depressive tendencies.

BENSON, E. F. (Edward Frederic) (1867–1940) Prolific and popular novelist, brother of R. H. and A. C. *Benson. His works include *Dodo* (1893, followed by other 'Dodo' novels) and

Queen Lucia (1920, the first of the irresistibly catty 'Mapp and Lucia' novels), and various volumes of reminiscences.

BENSON, Stella (1892–1933) Author, who worked for suffragist organizations before and during the First World War. In 1918 she travelled to the United States and worked in California before leaving for China, where in 1920 she met customs commissioner James O'Gorman Anderson. Their honeymoon journey by Ford across the United States is described in a book of travel pieces, *The Little World* (1925), which was followed by *Worlds within Worlds* (1928). Benson's numerous and critically neglected writings include eight novels, notably *The Far-Away Bride* (1930, published in Britain in 1931 as *Tobit Transplanted*); poetry; and the collections of short stories, *Hope against Hope* (1931) and *Christmas Formula* (1932). Her 42 volumes of diaries were published on microfilm in 2005.

BENTHAM, Jeremy (1748–1832) Social philosopher. He set himself to produce a simple, complete, and equitable legal system, rather than practise as a barrister. His ethical theory of Utility was propounded in *A Fragment on Government* (1776) and *An Introduction to the Principles of Morals and Legislation* (1789). 'It is the greatest happiness of the greatest number that is the measure of right and wrong.' Bentham believed it possible that the value of pains and pleasures as motives of action could be minutely calculated, giving scientific accuracy to legislation. Law and education must, by appropriate rewards and sanctions, induce the naturally self-interested individual to subordinate his own happiness to that of the community.

Chrestomathia, a series of papers on 'useful education', appeared in 1816. In 1823, with the assistance of James Mill, Bentham founded the *Westminster Review*, the organ of the philosophical radicals, which lasted until 1914. John Stuart *Mill, in his essay 'Bentham' in the review (1838), gives an interesting summary of Bentham's notorious hostility to imaginative literature, especially poetry. Bentham left his body to be dissected and his 'auto-icon', consisting of his skeleton dressed in his clothes, is on display at University College London.

BENTLEY, E. C. (Edmund Clerihew) (1875–1956) Author, a columnist on the *Daily News* and *Daily Telegraph*. As a schoolboy he invented the comical verse form named after him as the *clerihew, later exhibiting examples in *Biography for Beginners* (1905, illustrated by his schoolfriend, G. K *Chesterton), *More Biography* (1929), and *Baseless Biography* (1939), collected in *Clerihews Complete* (1951). His celebrated *detective novel *Trent's Last Case* (1913), intended as a spoof, heralded with its sprightly ingenuity the 'Golden Age' of that genre.

BENTLEY, Phyllis *See* REGIONAL NOVEL.

BENTLEY, Richard (1662–1742) Classical scholar. He made his reputation with his *Letter to Mill* (1691), a critical letter in Latin on the Greek dramatists, and the following year delivered the first Boyle Lectures on *The Folly and Unreasonableness of Atheism*, checking his science with Isaac *Newton. As keeper of the king's libraries, he engaged during 1697–9 in a famous controversy, during which he proved the *Epistles of Phalaris* to be spurious and queried the antiquity of *Aesop's fables. His most controversial editorial work was a bold revision of the text of *Horace (1711). Bentley's arbitrary revision of *Paradise Lost*, published in 1732 with over 800 suggested emendations, was based on the unlikely premiss that Milton had been ill served by an incompetent or malign amanuensis. He was caricatured in *The *Dunciad* (IV. 201 ff.) and elsewhere.

BENTLEY, Richard (1794–1871) Publisher, who included Thomas *Moore, both *Disraelis, and *Dickens among his authors. In 1830 he joined with Henry Colburn to found the firm of Colburn and Bentley, which in 1837 established *Bentley's Miscellany*. A cheap series of 'Standard Novels' in 127 volumes was also very successful. Bentley was succeeded by his son George Bentley (1825–95), whose authors included Wilkie *Collins and Mrs Henry (Ellen) *Wood.

Bentley's Miscellany (1837–69) A very successful periodical consisting of essays, stories, and poems, but mainly of fiction, begun by Richard *Bentley. Charles *Dickens was the first editor, and *Oliver Twist* appeared in its pages in 1837–8. John Hamilton *Reynolds, Theodore *Hook, William *Maginn, Harrison *Ainsworth, and later W. M. *Thackeray and Henry Wadsworth *Longfellow were among its contributors. George *Cruikshank and John Leech provided lively illustrations.

Beowulf An Old English poem of 3,182 lines, surviving in a 10th-century manuscript. The poem's date is unknown. The young Beowulf, a Geatish hero, fights and kills Grendel, a monster who has attacked Heorot, the hall of the

Danish king, Hrothgar. He then kills Grendel's mother, who has come to avenge her son. Fifty years later, when Beowulf has for a long time been king of the Geats, he fights a dragon which has attacked his people. He and the dragon are mortally wounded. The historical period of the poem's events can be dated in the 6th century, but much of the material of the poem is legendary and paralleled in Norse, Old English, and German literatures. A thread of tactful Christian commentary runs through the poem, distancing its readership from the heroic deeds and cultural assumptions of its characters even as it celebrates them. Remarkable for its resourceful diction, *Beowulf* is the most important poem in Old English and it is the first major poem in a European vernacular. Seamus *Heaney published a new translation in 1999. An animated film, *Beowulf*, loosely based on the poem, appeared in 2007.

Beppo: A Venetian Story A poem in *ottava rima* by Lord *Byron, published in 1818. Digressive, witty, and informal, it tells with great zest and style the story of a Venetian carnival, at which a lady's husband, Beppo, who has been absent for many years, returns in Turkish garb, and confronts her and her lover. Byron's praise of Italy's climate and women is offset by his lengthy satirical asides about English rain and English misses.

BERENSON, Bernard (1865–1959) Art historian, connoisseur, and philosopher. In 1887 he settled in Europe. In *Italian Painters of the Renaissance* (first published as separate essays, 1894–1907) he developed the theory that the 'tactile values' of a work of art, that is, its ability to communicate a sense of form, stimulated in the spectator a state of increased awareness of 'life enhancement'. His ideas influenced Roger *Fry's theories about the primacy of form, which, in turn, stimulated the development of literary formalism in Britain.

BERESFORD, J. D. (1873–1947) English writer. His *scientific romances are reminiscent of H. G. *Wells, of whom he wrote an early study (1915), as speculations on social and evolutionary change. *The Hampdenshire Wonder* (1911) tells of a mutant 'superman'.

BERGER, John (1926–) Novelist and art critic. He became well known as a broadcaster and journalist holding Marxist views, and has published novels, poems, and plays. His novels include *A Painter of our Time* (1958), *The Foot of Clive* (1962), *Corker's Freedom* (1964), *G* (*Booker Prize, 1972), *To the Wedding* (1995), and

From A to X (2008). His many works of nonfiction include *A Fortunate Man* (1967), the story of a country doctor. *Pig Earth* (1979), *Once in Europa* (stories, 1989), and *Lilac and Flag* (1991) form a trilogy. Other works include *Keeping a Rendezvous* (1992), a collection of essays and poems. One of his most influential texts has been *Ways of Seeing* (1972), which explores painting and commercial imagery in a context of cultural capitalism: it helped to popularize the concepts of Walter *Benjamin. See *Ways of Telling* (1986), a commentary by Geoff *Dyer.

BERGSON, Henri (1859–1941) French philosopher, awarded the *Nobel Prize for Literature in 1927. His major works, vividly written and accessible to the non-specialist reader, define his broad opposition to scientific materialism and positivism. His notion of the *élan vital*, or vital impulse, is conceived as directing the evolution of new forms and increasingly complex states of organization. He explored the aesthetics of comedy in *Le Rire: essai sur la signification du comique* (1900: *Laughter: An Essay on the Meaning of the Comic*).

BERKELEY, George (1685–1753) Irish philosopher. In 1713 he visited England, associating with Richard *Steele, Joseph *Addison, Alexander *Pope, John *Arbuthnot, and Swift, and contributed essays against freethinkers to the *Guardian*. His chief philosophical works are *An Essay towards a New Theory of Vision* (1709, 1710, 1732), *A Treatise Concerning the Principles of Human Knowledge* (1710, 1734), and *Three Dialogues between Hylas and Philonous* (1713, 1725, 1734). He defended his own philosophy in his dialogue *Alciphron* (1732, 1752) and *The Theory of Vision Vindicated and Explained* (1733). In 1734 he published *The Analyst*, criticizing Isaac *Newton's theory of fluxions; and in 1735–7 *The Querist*, dealing with questions of economic and social reform in Ireland. *Siris*, on the medical virtues of tar-water, appeared in 1744.

In his works on vision, Berkeley seeks to show the mind-dependence of the ideas derived from sight, and explains their 'arbitrary' though constant connection with the more primary ideas of touch by analogy with the way in which written words 'signify' speech. His philosophy is partly inspired by, and partly a reaction to, John *Locke's *Essay Concerning Human Understanding*. Samuel *Johnson famously claimed to have refuted Berkeley's idealism by kicking a large stone very hard, but Berkeley does not dispute the existence of matter so much as its status; its reality depends on perception. In *Alciphron*, Berkeley sees experience as functioning in the manner of a language, which to him implies a prior intelligence or design.

BERKENHEAD (Birkenhead), Sir John (1617–79) Pamphleteer and the principal editor and writer of the influential Royalist Oxford-based newsbook *Mercurius Aulicus* (1643–5), which was renowned for its cavalier insouciance and wit. His polite and satiric verse includes a mock-heroic piece called 'A Jolt', based on an incident when Oliver Cromwell was thrown from his coach in Hyde Park. He is notable as one of the first writers to make a career in journalism. *See* also NEWSPAPERS.

BERKOFF, Steven (1937–) Actor, director, playwright, born of immigrant Russian Jewish parentage in the East End of London. He formed the London Theatre Group in 1968 and caused a sensation with his adaptation of Franz *Kafka's *The Trial* (1969). He remained a vigorous maverick in the fringe theatre movement of the subsequent two decades, playing the leading role in his own productions of his own demotic verse plays *East* (1975), *Greek* (1979), *Decadence* (1981), and *West* (1983). His domestic fantasy *Kvetch* won the Best Comedy in the Evening Standard Awards in 1991. Success as a screen villain in Hollywood subsidizes his single-minded stage career, and a prolific writing output includes *I Am Hamlet* (1989) and his memoirs *Free Association* (1996). More recent work includes *Shopping in the Santa Monica Mall* (2000), *The Secret Love Life of Ophelia* (2001), and *Requiem for Ground Zero* (2002).

BERNARD, St (1090–1153) Abbot of the Cistercian foundation of Clairvaux at the age of 24 and one of the foremost figures of the 12th-century monastic Reformation. He preached the Second Crusade, and opposed the dialectical theological method of *Abelard. The characteristic quality of his thought was a lively and personal mysticism; he developed and preached 'the Cistercian Programme', a progression from carnal to spiritual love which, in its literary application, became one of the most important elements of medieval poetry from the *troubadours to *Dante. In his mysticism the stress is on God's grace, according to the Augustinian school, rather than on the deliberate achievement of man's contemplative efforts, which was the aspect emphasized by the *Neoplatonists and their followers in the prose mysticism of the 14th century.

BERNARDIN de Saint-Pierre, Jacques-Henri (1737–1814) French novelist and natural philosopher, a friend and follower of Jean-Jacques *Rousseau. His *Études de la nature* (1784: *Studies of Nature*) was a popular success; in the third edition (1788), he included *Paul et Virginie*. It tells the story of two children, who are brought up as brother and sister on the tropical island of Mauritius. The two mothers, refugees from social disgrace in France, accustom their childern to a simple existence free from social prejudice, religious superstition, or fear of authority. It ends in tragedy: Virginie is drowned. Paul and the two mothers die of shock and grief. Helen Maria *Williams, a friend of Bernardin's, translated the novel in 1796.

BERNERS (Barnes), Juliana (*fl.*1460) The alleged author of a treatise in verse on hunting contained in the *Book of St. Albans*, which was printed there in 1486. The treatise ends: 'Explicit Dame Julyans | Barnes in her boke of huntyng', but despite attestations to her existence by John *Bale and others, Juliana Berners has yet to be satisfactorily identified.

BERQUIN, Arnaud (1741–91) French writer of children's literature, best known for his collection of tales and dialogues *L'Ami des enfants* (1782–3: *The Children's Friend*), which was successfully adapted by Richard *Johnson as *The Looking-Glass for the Mind* (1787).

BERRY, James (1924–) OBE. Poet, born and educated in Jamaica, who came to London in 1948. An important figure in the field of multicultural education, he has edited various anthologies, including *Bluefoot Traveller: An Anthology of Westindian Poets in Britain* (1976), *Dance to a Different Drum* (1983, a Brixton Festival anthology), and *News for Babylon* (1984). His own collections include *Fractured Circles* (1979), *Lucy's Letter and Loving* (1982), *Chain of Days* (1985), *Hot Earth Cold Earth* (1995), *Rough Sketch Beginning* (1996), and *Windrush Songs* (2007). *When I Dance* (1988) is a volume of poems, songs, and 'work-sing' for children, mixing inner-city subject matter with rural Caribbean motifs. *A Thief in the Village* (1987), *Anancy Spiderman* (1988), *The Future-Telling Lady* (1991), and *A Nest Full of Stars* (2002) are some of his collections of stories for children, *Only One of Me* (2004) is a volume of selected poems for children. *See* JAZZ POETRY.

BERRYMAN, John (1914–72) American poet. Born John Smith, he took his stepfather's name after his father's suicide. Much of his poetry is anguished and confessional, exploring personal guilts and religious doubts, but it is also learned and often witty, and technically highly organized if idiosyncratic. His work includes *Poems* (1942), *The Dispossessed* (1948), and *Homage to Mistress Bradstreet* (1956), the last a complex biographical ode inspired by the first New England poet Anne *Bradstreet. *77 Dream Songs* (1964), with their imaginary and protean protagonist Henry, were completed by *His Toy, his Dream, his Rest* (1968), and together form his major work. He committed suicide in Minneapolis.

Bertram, *The Castle of St Aldobrand* A tragedy by Charles *Maturin, produced 1816. An entertaining if overwrought drama, centred on a *Byronic hero, it was the object of hostile criticism by S. T. *Coleridge in the *Biographia Literaria*.

BESANT, Sir Walter (1836–1901) Author, he collaborated with James Rice to produce several best-selling novels, including *Ready-Money Mortiboy* (1872), *The Golden Butterfly* (1876), and *The Chaplain of the Fleet* (1881). He was deeply interested in the life of the poor, especially in the East End of London, and the grim social conditions of industrial workers, and draws attention to these in *All Sorts and Conditions of Men* (1882) and *Children of Gibeon* (1886); he stimulated the foundation of the People's Palace, Mile End (1887), for intellectual improvement and rational amusement. In 1884 he founded the *Society of Authors, and became editor of the *Author* in 1890; he defined the financial position of authors in *The Pen and the Book* (1899). *A Survey of London* (1902–12) and his autobiography (1902) appeared posthumously.

BESTALL, Alfred *See* RUPERT BEAR.

BESTER, Alfred (1913–87) American author and scriptwriter; after publishing *science fiction stories in the early 1940s he spent several years writing comic book, radio, and television scripts before returning to science fiction with a baroque, fast-paced, cynical vision which made him one of the precursors of cyberpunk. *The Demolished Man* (1953), winner of the first *Hugo award for best science fiction novel, considers how murder might be committed where telepaths could uncover the thought before the deed. *Tiger! Tiger!* (1956) is the revenge of an outsider in a decadent world. *Golem*[100] (1980) is perhaps the best of his later novels.

bestiaries Medieval treatises derived from the Greek *Physiologus*, which was a collection of about 50 fabulous anecdotes from natural (mostly animal) history, followed by a 'moralization' of the anecdotes for a Christian purpose. The Greek original dates from some time between the 2nd and 4th centuries, and it was translated into many languages, most influentially Latin. In the 12th century additions began to be made to the Latin version from the popular encyclopedia of the Middle Ages, the *Etymologiae* of *Isidore of Seville. Those written in England in the 12th and 13th centuries were often richly illustrated with miniatures. The Old English poems 'The Panther' and 'The Whale' are isolated examples of the kind. Their method of moralization was influential on the relations between story and moral in many medieval texts, as well as being a popular source for such works as Sir Thomas *Browne's *Pseudodoxia Epidemica*.

(((())) SEE WEB LINKS
• Aberdeen Bestiary Project

BETJEMAN, Sir John (1906–84) Poet, educated at Magdalen College, Oxford, where he became friendly with W. H. *Auden and Louis *MacNeice. His first collection of verse, *Mount Zion*, appeared in 1931, followed by many other collections, including *Continual Dew: A Little Book of Bourgeois Verse* (1937), *New Bats in Old Belfries* (1945), *A Few Late Chrysanthemums* (1954), and his extremely successful *Collected Poems* (1958; expanded 1962). His blank-verse autobiography, *Summoned by Bells* (1960) covers his boyhood and life at Oxford. He was appointed *poet laureate in 1972. His poetry is predominantly witty, urbane, and satiric, a comedy of manners, place-names, and contemporary references. Many have commented, however, on the underlying melancholy, the chill of fear, the religion which dwells more on hope than faith. In the preface to *Old Lights for New Chancels* (1940) Betjeman writes of his 'topographical predilection' for 'suburbs and gaslights and Pont Street and Gothic Revival churches and mineral railways, provincial towns and garden cities', a predilection also displayed in his editing and writing of Shell Guides, some illustrated by his friend John Piper (1903–92), and various works on architecture, beginning with *Ghastly Good Taste* (1933). Hugo *Williams edited a selection of Betjeman's poetry in 2006.

Betrothed, The A novel by Walter *Scott, published 1825, the first of Scott's two *Tales of the Crusaders*. His publishers suspended publication while he embarked on *The *Talis-man*. The action of the novel takes place entirely on the Welsh Marches.

BETTERTON, Mary (c.1637-1712) The wife of Thomas *Betterton, the first notable actress on the English stage (until 1660 female parts were taken by men or boys). She was the first woman to act William *Shakespeare's great female characters, such as Lady Macbeth, Ophelia, and Juliet.

BETTERTON, Thomas (1635-1710) The greatest actor in the *Restoration. He joined Sir William *D'Avenant's company at Lincoln's Inn Fields, and was associated in the management of the Dorset Gardens Theatre from 1671. His dramas include *The Roman Virgin*, acted 1669, adapted from John *Webster's *Appius and Virginia*; *The Prophetess* (1690), an opera from *The Prophetess* of Francis *Beaumont and John *Fletcher; and *King Henry IV* (1700) from William *Shakespeare.

Beulah, Land of See Isaiah 62: 4. Derived from the Hebrew word for 'married', Beulah was traditionally equated with the erotic garden-paradise of the biblical Song of Solomon allegorized by Christians as the marriage of Christ and his church. In John *Bunyan's *Pilgrim's Progress* Beulah is a pastoral paradise of birdsong and eternal flowers. William *Blake associated Beulah with the third state of vision and sexual love. In **Milton* and *Jerusalem* Beulah is a shadowy, moony place of rest between Eternity and Ulro; the daughters of Beulah are the poet's muses. *See* BIBLE.

BEVINGTON, Louisa S. (1845-95) Poet and progressive thinker. She published several volumes of poetry, including *Key-Notes* (1876) and *Poems, Lyrics and Sonnets* (1882), which explore the nature of evolution, at times with a spare questioning lyricism. She also wrote and lectured on rationalism, religion, property, and evolutionary theory. Her last collection of poems, *Liberty Lyrics* (1895) expressed her radical political sympathies.

Bevis: The Story of a Boy A novel by Richard *Jefferies, published 1882. In this intense evocation of a country childhood, Jefferies draws on his own rural boyhood in Wiltshire.

Bevis of Hampton A popular verse romance from c.1324, derived from *Boeuve de Haumtone*, a 12th-century Anglo-Norman *chanson de geste*.

BEWICK, Thomas (1753-1828) Wood-engraver. He engraved blocks for John *Gay's *Fables* (1779), *Select Fables* (1784), *A General History of Quadrupeds* (1790), *Fables of Aesop* (1818), the poems of Oliver *Goldsmith and Thomas *Parnell (1795), and other books; his most celebrated and successful work was *A History of British Birds* (1797, 1804). His vignettes of country life were much admired by William *Wordsworth, Charlotte *Brontë, and Thomas *Carlyle. His *Memoir* (1862) is a vivid record of a north-country childhood and a craftsman's life.

Bhagavad-gītā A section of the *Mahā-bhārata*, the first section to be translated into English (by Charles Wilkins (1750-1836)), as *The Bhagvat-Geeta, or, Dialogues of Kreeshna and Arjoon* (1785). It has been influential in English translation on M. K. (Mahatma) Gandhi, the Theosophical movement, and the Bengal nationalist movement, amongst others.

Bible, the Collected holy texts of Judaism (the Old Testament, OT), and (with the New Testament, NT) of Christianity. The OT, written almost entirely in Hebrew, begins with the heart of the Hebrew Bible, the Torah or Law, the five books of *Moses (Genesis, Exodus, Leviticus, Numbers, Deuteronomy). Genesis tells of the seven days of God's creation, and the fall of Adam and Eve, tempted by a serpent in the garden of Eden. Cain kills his brother Abel, the first murder. Seeing the later wickedness of man, God sends a flood, but saves Noah and his family and pairs or sevens of all animals. The subsequent rainbow symbolizes God's promise that there will be no more such destruction. These early myths are followed with stories of the ancestral figures of the Israelites, including Abraham, Isaac, Jacob (and Esau), and Joseph and his eleven brothers. After the exodus from Egypt led by Moses, and the giving of the Law (Exodus to Deuteronomy), comes the conquest of the promised land, Canaan (Joshua). For a period the twelve tribes of Israel are ruled by judges, including Samson, whose secret, that he will lose his strength if his hair is cut, is wheedled out of him by Delilah (Judges). In the time of the prophet Samuel, the people demand a king, and are ruled first by Saul, a tragic figure who loses God's favour, then *David, then his son, Solomon, famed for his wisdom and builder of the Temple in *Jerusalem. The kingdom becomes divided, a northern kingdom, Israel, whose kings invariably fail to do what is right in the eyes of God, and a southern kingdom,

Judah, which includes Jerusalem, and has some righteous kings (1, 2 Samuel, 1, 2 Kings). Jerusalem is destroyed by the Babylonians and the people are exiled. The historical books end with the return to Jerusalem and the rebuilding of the Temple under Ezra and Nehemiah. The stories of faithful Ruth and of Queen Esther saving the people also come in this part of the OT.

The fall of Jerusalem and the exile are pivotal to the prophetic books, Isaiah to Malachi. As guardians of religious consciousness, the prophets observed the collective failure of the people and the two kingdoms to follow God and the Mosaic law, a failure often pictured in terms of sexual infidelity. They reported God's judgement on this failure or backsliding: the people and the nation would be destroyed. When that judgement was fulfilled, they began to offer consolation to the penitent people, envisioning spiritual redemption and leadership, and the coming of a Messiah or Saviour. With some uncertainties about the chronology, they divide into three groups. Amos, Hosea, first Isaiah (i.e. Isaiah 1–39), Micah, Habakkuk, Zephaniah, and Nahum are pre-exilic and emphasize sin and punishment. From the time of the exile come Jeremiah, Obadiah, Isaiah 40–55, Ezekiel, and, probably, Isaiah 56–66; they mix lament with promises of forgiveness. After the exile come several short books mixing hope and warning, Haggai, Zechariah 1–8, Malachi, Joel, and Zechariah 9–14. Jonah stands apart as a famous story about the duty of a prophet, and Daniel as the latest book of the OT, a combination of stories about the wisdom of Daniel and visions that reflect the situation of Israel prior to the 2nd-century BC restoration of the kingdom under the Maccabees.

In the Christian canon, which differs from the Jewish, books of wisdom (Job, Ecclesiastes, Proverbs) and poetry (Psalms and the Song of Solomon) come between the historical and the prophetic books. In Job poetic dialogues explore the problem of divine justice and human suffering, vividly expressed by the afflicted Job. Ecclesiastes is famous for its world-weary cynicism, 'vanity of vanities, all is vanity' (1: 2). The 150 psalms express faith and suffering in ways that have made them a perennial source of comfort. The poetic fragments of the Song of Solomon celebrate human love and, contrasting with the frequent use of images of infidelity in the prophets, are frequently read allegorically as expressing, for instance, Christ's love for the church (so interpreted in the King James Bible).

The Apocrypha follows the OT in the Protestant canon, but is now omitted from most Bibles because of the secondary status of its contents as uninspired writings. It includes alternative versions of OT books (e.g. 1, 2 Esdras), some fine stories such as Tobit, wisdom writings, notably the Wisdom of Solomon, and two histories of the Maccabean revolt against Syrian oppression.

Four Gospels begin the NT: Matthew, Mark, and Luke, known as the Synoptic Gospels because of the similarity of their viewpoint, and John. Each gives a version of Jesus' life replete with famous stories from the coming of the three wise men through healing miracles to the events which define his significance as the Christian Messiah: his triumphal entry into Jerusalem, the last supper, his trial, crucifixion, and resurrection. Jesus' teaching stresses God's love and forgiveness, and the need for the sinful individual to 'love the Lord thy God with all thy heart', and to 'love thy neighbour as thyself' (Matt. 22: 37, 39). Much of the teaching uses parables which range from brief similes for the kingdom of God to extended homely tales such as the Good Samaritan and the Prodigal Son (Luke 10, 15).

Acts relates the early spread of Christianity from the coming of the Holy Ghost to Jesus' followers shortly after the resurrection to just before the death of Paul. Then comes the second heart of the NT, the Pauline epistles (*see* PAUL, ST), together with shorter epistles by or attributed to other apostles; most of these latter are concerned with false teaching and belief and were for general circulation (hence James to Jude are known as the Catholic Epistles).

The final book, Revelation or Apocalypse, is a fantastic series of visions of the end time, concluding with the coming of the holy city of God, new Jerusalem. Its prophetic-apocalyptic mode goes back to Ezekiel and Daniel.

The OT Hebrew texts were early translated into other languages. Most important was the Greek Septuagint, so called because of the legend that it was made in 70 days by 70 inspired Jewish scholars. Begun some time in the 3rd century BC, it was the Bible of Greek-speaking Judaism and early Christianity; it remains the OT for the Orthodox Church. Because it is older than any surviving Hebrew manuscripts, it sometimes preserves older readings; it also has a more extensive canon, and is the prime source for the Apocrypha. When Latin became the dominant language, early Christians made Latin versions of both Testaments. These were superseded by *Jerome's Vulgate, which became the standard Bible of Christendom until the *Reformation, and remained standard for Roman Catholics. Protestants fought to give the people Bibles in their own vernacular, and they usually insisted on translating from the Hebrew and Greek texts rather than the Vulgate. Some translations became classics, and also strong influences on their own language, notably *Luther's German (NT 1522, completed 1534), and *Tyndale and *Coverdale's English, in the form of the King James Bible (*see* BIBLE, THE ENGLISH). See *The Cambridge History of the Bible* (1963–70); *The Oxford Companion to the Bible* (1993).

Bible, the English The principal *Bible of English religion and culture since the 17th century is the King James Bible (KJB) or Authorized Version (1611). Its language became not just the model for religious expression, but also an inescapable example of a predominantly Anglo-Saxon, simply constructed way of writing. Some of its sayings became so familiar that they are commonly used to enhance a piece of writing; some such as 'fall by the wayside' have become clichés. Writers have depended upon the familiarity of the KJB's language and the entire contents of the Bible as their most widely used source of allusion, story, and teaching.

Before the *Reformation, English writers and readers knew the Bible from the *Vulgate, a few paraphrases and translations such as those of *Cædmon, *Bede, and *Ælfric, and from adaptations such as the *Cursor Mundi* and *mystery plays. The earliest complete English translation was the *Lollard or *Wyclif Bible. Its earlier form (*c*.1382), a highly literal rendering of the Vulgate, was revised into somewhat more natural English (*c*.1388); these versions were widely circulated in manuscript but had little influence on the later translations.

What became the KJB began while vernacular Bible translation was forbidden. William *Tyndale, working directly from the original Greek and Hebrew, completed the New Testament (NT; 1526, rev. 1535), the Pentateuch (1530), and Joshua to 2 Chronicles (published posthumously in the Matthew Bible, 1537). His combination of everyday English and a nearly literal fidelity to the originals created English biblical style. Relying heavily on *Luther and Latin versions, Miles *Coverdale revised and completed Tyndale's work, producing the first complete printed English Bible in 1535. This became the basis of the English church's first official Bible, the Great Bible (1539–40), later revised as the Bishops' Bible (1568).

In Mary's reign exiled Protestants in Geneva produced what became the most popular English Bible for a century, the Geneva (or Breeches) Bible (1560). Usually better printed and cheaper than the official Bibles, it also ap-

pealed through its extensive annotations. In *Elizabeth I's reign Roman Catholics, now exiled in their turn, produced the Rheims–Douai Bible (NT 1582, Old Testament (OT) 1609–10).

At a conference in 1604 called by *James I to try to create religious uniformity, the Puritans complained of mistranslations in the Great Bible and suggested there should be a new translation. Probably, they hoped the Geneva Bible would be adopted, but James vehemently disliked the Geneva annotations. He ordered that a new revision, free of notes, should be made, based on the Bishops' Bible, but using Tyndale, Coverdale, the Matthew Bible, the Great Bible, and Geneva where they were truer to the original languages. Six companies of translators, two each at Oxford, Cambridge, and Westminster, revised their predecessors' work, intending not 'to make a new translation ...but to make a good one better, or out of many good ones one principal good one' (Preface). The result was a judicious combination of old work and new touches. Fidelity to the Hebrew and Greek originals was the chief aim.

Though quickly accepted by the learned as the most accurate translation into English, the KJB took 30 years to dominate the bible market, and longer to monopolize the English consciousness. After the 1760s it was generally acclaimed as fine, and, by many, as the greatest English literature. Popular affection and literary veneration grew as its scholarly reputation declined, eventually leading to the Revised Version (NT 1870, OT 1885), deliberately modelled on its style. This was never a literary success, but marked the start of increasingly frequent modern efforts either to improve the KJB while preserving a semblance of its style or to produce versions in contemporary language, such as the New English Bible (NT 1961, OT 1970). Many of these latter used literary advisers in a generally fruitless attempt to rival the literary success of the KJB.

biblical commentaries Works commenting on and interpreting the books of the *Bible have a long history and have had a powerful influence on literature and literary theory. *Paul in his epistles began the key process of interpreting events, persons, or things in the Old Testament as prefigurations or 'types' of corresponding events, persons, or things in the New Testament, a way of reading known as 'typology'. In the early Christian church, Origen in his commentaries emphasized *allegory as the key to interpretation, and developed a threefold meaning of Scripture, literal, moral, and allegorical. Later a fourfold meaning was developed—literal, allegorical, tropological (moral), and anagogical (concerned with eternity)—which was influential until the *Reformation. Important early commentators in Latin include *Jerome, Augustine, and *Bede. In the 18th and 19th centuries accessible commentaries in English, for example by Matthew Henry, Philip *Doddridge, and Thomas *Scott, were much reprinted and widely read in families.

BICKERSTAFF, Isaac (1733–?1808) Irish playwright, author of the successful 'comic opera' *Love in a Village* (1762), with music by Thomas *Arne. *The Maid of the Mill* (1765), with music by Samuel Arnold, was based on Samuel *Richardson's *Pamela*. *Lionel and Clarissa* (1768) had music by Charles Dibdin, who appeared blacked up in the role of Mungo in Bickerstaff's *The Padlock*, at David *Garrick's Drury Lane theatre; a comic success, the character was increasingly a focus for discontent about racial inequality. *The Hypocrite* (1769) was adapted from *Molière's *Tartuffe* via Colley *Cibber's *The Non-juror*.

BIERCE, Ambrose (1842–?1914) American writer. He served in the Civil War, 1861–5, and afterwards became a prominent journalist. He is best known for his short stories, realistic, sardonic, and strongly influenced by Edgar Allan *Poe. They were published in *Tales of Soldiers and Civilians* (1891), a title which was changed to *In the Midst of Life* (1892; rev. edn 1898).

Big Brother The head of the Party in George *Orwell's *Nineteen Eighty-Four* who never appears in person, but whose portrait, with the caption 'Big Brother is watching you', dominates every public space.

Biggles W. E. *Johns's national icon, Major James Bigglesworth, developed through 96 books for boys (from *The Camels are Coming*, 1932 to *Biggles Sees Too Much*, 1970) from sensitive First World War pioneer fighter pilot, into Second World War hero, finally becoming a post-war 'international air detective'. *See* WAR STORIES FOR CHILDREN.

'big house' fiction A genre of Irish fiction centred on the decline of a country house of the Anglo-Irish ascendancy. A comparative term drawn from the speech of landless Catholics, 'big' is inflected with hostility and irony. Maria *Edgeworth's *Castle Rackrent* introduced such staples of the mode as the improvidence of the gentry and the avarice of the middle classes. Later novels took on a political and historical dimension and paid more explicit attention to sectarian difference, incorporating responses to the Great Famine, the Land War, the Anglo-Irish War, and other disruptions. They include William *Carleton's *The Squanders of Castle Squander* (1852); Charles *Lever's *The Martins of Cro' Martin* (1856); *Somerville and Ross's *The Big House at Inver* (1925); Elizabeth *Bowen's *The Last September* (1929); J. G. *Farrell's *Troubles* (1970); John *Banville's *Birchwood* (1973); Molly *Keane's *Good Behaviour* (1981); William *Trevor's *Fools of Fortune* (1983); and works by Jennifer *Johnston. In George *Moore's *A Drama in Muslin* (1886) and Aidan *Higgins's *Langrishe, Go Down* (1966), the declining family is Catholic rather than Protestant. Bowen's *Bowen's Court* (1942) and David Thomson's *Woodbrook* (1974) are 'big house' memoirs. The motif also features in drama (Lennox Robinson's *The Big House*, 1926; W. B. *Yeats's *Purgatory*, 1939; Sean *O'Casey's *Purple Dust*, 1940; and Brian *Friel's *Aristocrats*, 1980) and poetry (Yeats's Coole Park poems; Richard *Murphy's 'The Woman of the House', 1959; John *Montague's 'Woodtown Manor', 1961; Louis *MacNeice's 'Soap Suds', 1963; Derek *Mahon's 'A Disused Shed in County Wexford', 1975; Paul *Muldoon's 'The Big House', 1977; Thomas *Kinsella's 'Tao and Unfitness at Inistiogue on the River Nore', 1978; and Seamus *Heaney's 'A Peacock's Feather', 1972/1987).

Bildungsroman The German term for an 'education-novel' (education being understood in a broad sense that includes self-formation or personal development); thus a significant subgenre of novel which relates the experiences of a youthful protagonist in meeting the challenges of adolescence and early adulthood. Such works, sometimes referred to in English as 'coming-of-age' novels, typically develop themes of innocence, self-knowledge, sexual awakening, and vocation. The most widely influential example was *Goethe's *Wilhelm Meisters Lehrjahre* (1795–6), known in England through Thomas *Carlyle's translation (*Wilhelm Meister's Apprenticeship*, 1824). English novels of this type include *Great Expectations*; and in the 20th century D. H. *Lawrence's *Sons and Lovers* (1913) and Rosamond *Lehmann's *Dusty Answer* (1927).

Billy Budd, Foretopman (written 1891; pub. 1924) A novella by Herman *Melville. Billy, 'the handsome sailor', wrongly accused by the satanic master-at-arms Claggart and unable to defend himself verbally because of a stammer, strikes Claggart dead. After being tried by the liberal Captain Vere, Billy is hanged, his last words being 'God bless Captain Vere!'

and he undergoes an apparently Christ-like apotheosis. Benjamin *Britten's *Billy Budd* (1951) sets the tale as an opera.

BINYON, Laurence (1869-1943) Author and art historian. His plays include *Attila* (1907) and *Arthur* (1923), the latter with music by *Elgar. His much-anthologized poem 'For the Fallen' ('They shall grow not old, as we that are left grow old') was set to music by Elgar in 1916. *Collected Poems* appeared in 1931.

Biographia Britannica Edited by William Oldys (1696-1761) and others and published in seven folio volumes (1747-66), was a collection of lives of the most eminent people in Great Britain and Ireland from the earliest times to the mid-18th century. It was indebted to the method of Pierre Bayle's *Dictionary* and Thomas *Birch's *General Dictionary*, and is the ancestor of the *Dictionary of National Biography*.

Biographia Literaria A work of philosophical autobiography and Romantic literary criticism, by S. T. *Coleridge, published 1817. Part I is broadly autobiographical, describing Coleridge's friendship with Robert *Southey and with the *Wordsworths at Stowey, and going on to trace his struggle with the 'dynamic philosophy' of *Kant, Fichte, and *Schelling in Germany. The narrative is gradually overwhelmed by Romantic metaphysics; ch. XIII contains his famous distinction between Fancy and Imagination. Part II is almost entirely critical, attacking Wordsworth's preface to the *Lyrical Ballads* and then marvellously vindicating the poetry itself. Coleridge concentrates on the psychology of the creative process, and propounds new theories of the origins of poetic language, metre, and form, as the interpenetration of 'passion and will' (chs XV-XVIII). Other chapters discuss the poetry of *Shakespeare, *Milton, Samuel *Daniel, George *Herbert, and others, as exemplary of true 'Imagination' and the 'language of real life'. The book gives some impression of Coleridge in full conversational flight.

biography A flourishing genre, with some 3,500 examples appearing each year, a range of experimental new methods, and lively debate about the nature of life-writing. The earliest biographies in England were written in Latin in the Middle Ages, largely to glorify saints (*see* HAGIOGRAPHY) or to commemorate and justify secular rulers. The Renaissance emphasis on man as an individual prompted a new approach and the first biography in English, Thomas *More's life of Richard III (*c*.1513), was a coruscating portrait with first-hand observations. Thomas North's 1579 translation of *Plutarch's paired character studies *Parallel Lives* particularly influenced Izaak *Walton, who wrote pious, affectionate, and artfully constructed lives of the poets John *Donne (1640) and George *Herbert (1670). The eccentric antiquary John *Aubrey gathered donnish scurrilities and courtly tattle in his *Brief Lives* (manuscript 1693, published 1813).

There were numerous biographical collections in the 18th century, such as the lives of criminals in the *Newgate Calendar* (five volumes, 1773) and Samuel *Johnson's The *Lives of the English Poets* (1779-81). The appeal that Johnson saw in the new form was set out in his essay 'On the Genius of Biography': 'No species of writing...can more certainly enchain the heart by irresistible interest, or more widely diffuse instruction to every diversity of condition...We are all prompted by the same motives, all deceived by the same fallacies, all animated by hope, obstructed by danger, entangled by desire, and seduced by pleasure.' James *Boswell, in his *The Life of Samuel Johnson* (1791), created a masterpiece of English biography, using vividly dramatized scenes (worked up from his *Journals*) within a meticulous chronological narrative. The imaginative tension between private and public lives would become a hallmark of modern life-writing. In the 19th century, many biographers saw themselves as dutiful celebrants paying homage to great lives, particularly where they were writing about a parent or friend, for example Hallam Tennyson writing on his father in *Alfred Lord Tennyson: A Memoir* (1897), John *Lockhart on his father-in-law Walter *Scott (1837-8), John *Forster on his friend Charles *Dickens (1872-4), and Anne Thackeray Ritchie on her father, the novelist W. M. *Thackeray, in *Chapters from Some Memoirs* (1894). The didactic portraits in Samuel Smiles's *Self-Help* (1859) also proved extremely popular. Elizabeth *Gaskell's *Life of Charlotte Brontë* (1857) aimed at new levels of openness, and J. A. *Froude caused a protracted scandal by exposing aspects of Thomas *Carlyle's domestic life. Froude's objective, sometimes iconoclastic biographical stance, was adopted uncompromisingly by Lytton *Strachey in his four elegant and mocking studies (with a satiric preface) in *Eminent Victorians* (1918)—of Cardinal Manning, Florence *Nightingale, Dr Thomas Arnold of Rugby, and General Gordon.

Edmund *Gosse followed a standard Victorian life of his father with a devastating reappraisal in *Father and Son* (1907). Other influential experiments include Virginia *Woolf's *Orlando*

(1928), a disguised life of Vita *Sackville-West through four centuries and a sex change, and *Flush* (1933), her life of Elizabeth Barrett Browning's dog. A. J. A. *Symons explored biography as detective story in *The Quest for Corvo* (1934). An embargo on biographical research brought by a living subject turned Ian *Hamilton's *In Search of J. D. Salinger* (1988) into a study of the ethics and psychology of life-writing itself. Julian *Barnes's *Flaubert's Parrot* (1984) was a postmodern parody of biographical misinterpretation, interweaving the figure of a pedantic, fictional biographer with illuminating scholarship. Peter *Ackroyd's *Dickens* (1990), which included fictional interludes, prompted the question of how far a biographer is necessarily a creative writer. Literary biography has returned to the comprehensive form of 'Life and Work' considered as a single dramatic and psychological unity. Outstanding among these are Richard *Ellmann's scholarly Irish trilogy, lives of W. B. *Yeats (1948), James *Joyce (1959), and Oscar *Wilde (1987), and Michael *Holroyd's portraits of Lytton Strachey (1967–8), Augustus *John (1974–5), and George Bernard *Shaw (1988–92). Roy Foster's biography of W. B. Yeats held to a chronological course on the basis that 'we do not, alas, live our lives in themes, but day by day', while Hermione *Lee's fine lives of Virginia Woolf (1996) and Edith *Wharton (2007) demonstrated the rich possibilities of a thematic approach. Other notable works include Richard *Holmes on P. B. *Shelley and S. T. *Coleridge, Hilary *Spurling on Ivy *Compton-Burnett (1974, 1984), Victoria *Glendinning on the adventures of Vita Sackville-West (1983), and Claire *Tomalin on Mary *Wollstonecraft (1974) and the 19th-century actress Dorothy Jordan (1994), and, on non-literary subjects, Martin Gilbert on Churchill, Jenny *Uglow's life of *Hogarth, and her 'group biography' *The Lunar Men* (2002). Recent biographies have also heeded Woolf's call for 'lives of the obscure'. Women are now far better represented in the magisterial *Oxford Dictionary of National Biography*, continuing the work of Leslie *Stephen, who launched the *Dictionary of National Biography* (1885–1890).

Early theoretical explorations of biography as a form were Woolf's lively essays on 'The New Biography' (1927) and 'The Art of Biography' (1939). Robert *Gittings, biographer of Keats and Hardy, defended the form in *The Nature of Biography* (1978); Richard Ellmann with mischievous wit in *Golden Codgers* (1976), which popularized Joyce's term 'biografiend'; and Leon Edel (biographer of Henry *James) in his *Writing Lives: Principia Biographica* (1984). Richard Holmes's seminal *Footsteps: Adventures of a Romantic Biographer* (1985) explored the overlap between biography and autobiography. Helpful recent discussions include David Ellis's *Literary Lives* (2000) and Hermione Lee's *Biography: A Very Short Introduction* (2009). The issues explored include: the ethics of 'invading' privacy; the ambiguity of the links between art and life; the questionable objectivity of such sources as *letters and *diaries; the distortions involved in 'plotting' a life as a continuous narrative; the role of empathy and psychological 'transference' between author and subject; and the vexed question of the 'celebrity' life. Many recent lives do not end with the death of the subject but go on to trace their various 'afterlives': the changes in reputation and the myths and apocrypha that grow up around a celebrated figure.

BION (*fl.c.*100 BC) A Greek pastoral poet. His best-known and only complete poem is his *Lament for Adonis*, which was imitated by *Ronsard and of which echoes can be found in Edmund *Spenser's *Astrophell* and William *Shakespeare's *Venus and Adonis*. John *Milton's *Lycidas* and P. B. *Shelley's *Adonais* draw directly from Bion's *Lament*.

BIRCH, Thomas (1705–66) Biographer and historian. He was the principal editor and author of *A General Dictionary, Historical and Critical*, 10 vols (1734–41); this is an expansion of Pierre Bayle's *Dictionary*, and a major source of new information about English figures, including poets, politicians, scientists, and theologians. His many publications include lives and editions of Robert Boyle, Catharine *Cockburn, John *Milton, and John *Tillotson.

BIRD, Isabella (1831–1904) Travel writer (also published as Isabella Bishop after her marriage). Her vivid accounts of her journeys—among them *A Lady's Life in the Rocky Mountains* (1879), *Unbeaten Tracks in Japan* (1880), *The Golden Chersonese* (1883), and *Travels in Persia and Kurdistan* (1891)—achieved both popular and critical success, and in 1892 she became the first female Fellow of the *Royal Geographical Society. She appears as a character and as a type of the intrepid Victorian woman in Caryl Churchill's *Top Girls*.

BIRRELL, Augustine (1850–1933) He made his name as an author with a volume of lightweight but witty essays, *Obiter Dicta* (1884), followed by a second volume *More Obiter Dicta* (1924) and books on *Hazlitt (1902) and *Marvell (1905). His son Francis

Birrell (1889–1935), journalist and dramatic critic, was associated with the *Bloomsbury Group.

BIRTWISTLE, Sir Harrison (1934–) Composer, he worked with Tony *Harrison on *Bow Down* (1977), based in part on Japanese *Nōh models. His theatre music includes scores for several *Shakespeare productions from *Hamlet* (1975) onwards. *Gawain* (1991), to a libretto by David *Harsent, is based on the medieval alliterative poem *Sir *Gawain and the Green Knight*.

BISHOP, Elizabeth (1911–79) American poet, educated at Vassar College, where she met Marianne *Moore, with whose work her own has much affinity. She later travelled widely, finally settling in Brazil; the titles of some of her volumes (*North and South*, 1946; *Questions of Travel*, 1965; *Geography III*, 1976) reflect her preoccupation with place and movement, and her verse is reticent, objective, spare yet colloquial. See Robert Giroux and Lloyd Schwartz (eds), *Elizabeth Bishop: Poems, Prose and Letters* (2008).

BISHOP, John Peale (1892–1944) American poet and story writer, educated at Princeton University with Edmund *Wilson and F. Scott *Fitzgerald. His *Collected Essays* and *Collected Poems* were published in 1948.

BISHOP, Michael (1945–) American author. *A Funeral for the Eyes of Fire* (1975) contains anthropological explorations of human–alien contact. *Brittle Innings* (1994) is an emotionally powerful updating of the *'Frankenstein' myth.

BLACK, William (1841–98) Scottish journalist and novelist, whose moralizing romances *A Daughter of Heth* (1871), *The Strange Adventures of a Phaeton* (1872), and *A Princess of Thule* (1873) achieved international success. Later novels include *Shandon Bells* (1883), and *Judith Shakespeare* (1884).

Black Arts Movement Founded in Harlem in the mid-1960s by Amiri *Baraka and promoted by Larry Neal (1937–81), the movement supported cultural separatism and the Black Power movement, and sought to devise a distinctive African American aesthetic. Drawing on African art forms, it aimed at a total cultural revolution. The movement was active until the mid-1970s.

***Black Beauty,** his Grooms and Companions: The Autobiography of a Horse. Translated from the Original Equine* (1877) by Anna Sewell (1820–78). It is a *'crossover' book, written 'to induce kindness, sympathy, and an understanding treatment of horses'. The 'innocent' eye of Black Beauty provides trenchant social comment made more powerful by the moving characterization of Beauty and his horse companions. Of these, Ginger's sad life featuring brutal treatment, hard and demeaning work, and ending in a cart on the way to the knacker's yard in particular has moved generations of readers. Sewell sold the copyright to Jarrold and Sons for £40; the book sold over 12,000 copies in its first year. It was promoted by the RSPCA, and pirated in the USA, where the American Humane Education Society gave away over two million copies between 1890 and 1910. It has been highly influential in the genre of *animal stories, and has been filmed at least eleven times. There is a life, *Dark Horse*, by A. E. Gavin (2004).

Black Book of Carmarthen, The A Welsh manuscript of the 13th century containing medieval Welsh poems in a variety of modes, including eight on legendary and *Arthurian themes, and a group of prophecies relating to *Merlin.

black British writing arguably denominates a political and cultural rather than a racial category. It became current in the late 60s and early 70s, at a moment of politicisation, but it is used retrospectively to refer back to the mass migration to Britain from its colonies and former colonies instigated by the Nationality Act of 1948. Though there were earlier writers who were both black and British, as they settled in Britain the Windrush generation of immigrants defined their own cultural and political position in relation to the pre-existing community and to other immigrant groups. Stuart Hall expresses it graphically: 'People like me who came to England in the 1950s have been here for centuries; symbolically, we have been here for centuries. I was coming home. I am the sugar at the bottom of the English cup of tea. *Black British writing as an assertive category arose among settlers of African, Asian and Caribbean descent who, in the face of racism and ostracism, collectively claimed their entitlement to belong in Britain. Black British writers' work in the 70s and early 80s often concerns the right to be treated as an equal citizen, as for example in Linton Kwesi *Johnson's 'Sonny's Lettah' and also locates them in specific neighbourhoods which are their homes, for example Jackie *Kay's Glasgow or Meera *Syal's Tollington in *Anita and Me* (1996), rather than in stopping posts on an unending diasporic journey. In

Kay's poem 'In My Country' the implicit question is: *'Where do you come from?* /"Here," I said. "Here. These parts."' Though many British writers dislike being labelled as black, including Kay herself, Caryl *Phillips and Fred *D'Aguiar, the category is likely to persist in the early 21st-century climate of racial and cultural tension and mistrust. The innovative narrative structures and idiosyncratic expression of many black British texts have altered metropolitan literary language as irreversibly as the encounter between the coloniser and the colonised.

Early black British writers The best-known early texts are slave narratives, in which former slaves who were freed and literate wrote their own stories. The earliest widely read text is *Letters* (1782) by Ignatius *Sancho, who corresponded with Laurence *Sterne among others on the subject of the abolition of slavery. Olaudah *Equiano's *The Interesting Narrative* (1789) was a best-seller, a description (perhaps partly fictitious) of his enslavement and eventual emancipation. His strategy was to demonstrate that he could deploy his educated opponents' weapons against them and articulate a sophisticated and rational argument against slavery. The anomaly is Mary *Prince's story which was dictated since she was illiterate; it anticipates the vitality of an oral tradition which characterises some later black British writing.

The Windrush Generation The *SS Empire Windrush* docked at Tilbury in June 1948, bringing the first major wave of immigrants from the West Indies. George *Lamming from Barbados and Sam *Selvon from Trinidad travelled to Britain on the same voyage in 1950. Lamming said: 'It was one of the ironies of history that here we were separated by imperialism—Jamaica from Barbados, Barbados from Trinidad and so on, but it was really at the metropole at London that we came together, so I first got to know Jamaica and Guyana and other territories at London.' Lamming and Kamau *Brathwaite from Barbados, Selvon, C. L. R. *James, and V. S. *Naipaul from Trinidad, Stuart Hall, James *Berry and Andrew *Salkey from Jamaica, and Wilson *Harris and Edgar Mettleholzer from Guyana all arrived in the 'mother country' with which they were familiar through their reading, hoping to get their work published and to become part of a lively literary scene. In Selvon's *The Lonely Londoners* (1956), the narrative voice as well as the dialogue uses a rhythmical but carefully constructed Caribbean dialect. While Moses, the narrator of *The Lonely Londoners*, is a restless settler in Britain, other black British writers focus on the disappointment of arrival and the impetus to keep moving. Brathwaite's *The Arrivants* (1973) traces the reiterated experience of rejection and disillusionment of slaves and their descendants and their eventual return from metropolitan centres to a compromised hope of home in the Caribbean. Naipaul's narrator in *The Mimic Men* (1967), Ralph Singh, analyses the dilemma of the hopeful arrivant. In a non-realistic mode, Wilson *Harris's work brings a mythical past into the present; his distinctively poetic and formally experimental fiction weaves together tropes of exploration and exploitation, combining modernist techniques with orality.

Civil Rights The Caribbean Arts Movement (1966–1973) was founded by the Trinidadian John La Rose, the Jamaican Andrew Salkey and the Barbadian Kamau Brathwaite. It drew on the work of revolutionary writers and activists in the American Civil Rights movement and was instrumental in the establishment of such magazines as *Race Today* (founded 1969) and of such publishing houses and outlets as La Rose's New Beacon, Jessica and Eric Huntley's Bogle L'Ouverture, Darcus Howe's Race Today Collective and Margaret Busby's Allison and Busby. They published such works of a frustrated and angry generation of black writers as Linton Kwesi Johnson's *Dread, Beat an' Blood* (1975). Buchi *Emecheta from Nigeria and Beryl Gilroy from Guyana gave a woman's perspective. Dub and protest poetry asserted the role of the performer on an urban stage; the work of such performance poets as Benjamin *Zephaniah, John *Agard and Grace *Nichols from Guyana, and Jean Binta *Breeze and Valerie *Bloom from Jamaica appeals to children and to a wide range of social groups.

1980s and 1990s Many black British writers established their centrality to British writing, publishing and literary awards. Salman *Rushdie and Ben *Okri both won the Booker Prize, while Rohinton *Mistry and Timothy *Mo were short-listed for it. Caryl Phillips won awards for *Cambridge* (1991) which tells the story of a slave taken to the Caribbean. Abdulrazak *Gurnah's novels interweave stories from East Africa and Europe, while David *Dabydeen's poem *Slave Song* (1984), Grace *Nichols' *I Is a Long-Memoried Woman* (1983) and Fred *D'Aguair's novel *Feeding the Ghosts* (1997) are all haunted by the Middle Passage. Joan *Riley's *The Unbelonging* (1985) traces a legacy of gendered brutality. Black British film-scripts such as Hanif *Kureishi's *My Beautiful Laundrette* (1986) and Meera Syal's *Bhaji on the Beach* (1993) were instrumental in shifting public consciousness of the cultural complexity of contemporary British life.

21st Century The younger generation of writers do not always write as migrants; most of them were born in Britain and have a regional identity: the poets Lemn *Sissay and Tariq Latif are Mancunians; Suhayl Saadi (1961–), a poet, dramatist and novelist, was born in Yorkshire and now lives in Glasgow; Meera Syal was born near Wolverhampton; Diran *Adebayo and Bernardine *Evaristo were both born in London. Sissay's poems are inscribed on buildings and streets in Manchester; his work is literally written into the landscape. Hari Kunzru's novels, *The Impressionist* (2002) and *Transmission* (2004), concern the fluidity of identity in the heyday of empire and in the current global economy. A regional and class identity is often expressed in the narrative voice or voices, as in Jackie *Kay's *Trumpet* (1998), Gautam Malkani's *Londonstani* (2006) or Donna Daley-Clarke's *Lazy Eye* (2005). They are less concerned with their ancestors' traumatic past than with the intractable present. Zadie *Smith in *White Teeth* (2000), Monica *Ali in *Brick Lane* (2003), and Andrea *Levy in *Small Island* (2004) tell British stories about the interwoven culture created by the country's colonial history.

Black Dwarf, The A novel by Walter *Scott, published 1816. The first of the *Tales of my Landlord* and published anonymously, the novel's most interesting feature today is Scott's treatment of deformity. At the time of writing, he was preoccupied by the possible influence of Lord *Byron's lameness (which Scott himself shared) on his character.

Blackfriars Theatre was built in the City of London within the boundaries of the old Dominican monastery lying between Ludgate Hill and the river. The first theatre on the site was adapted for performances by Richard Farrant in 1576; the second was bought and adapted by James *Burbage in 1596, but was handed over to the Children of the Chapel because of local opposition. It reverted to James's son Richard *Burbage in 1608. William *Shakespeare had a share in the new company that performed there. The building was demolished in 1655.

black humour A kind of humour which flourished from the late 1950s through to the 1970s in America, characterized by morbid, provocative treatment of subjects like death and disease. The typical unit of black humour narratives is the episode, and two of the best exemplars of this mode are Joseph *Heller's *Catch-22* (1961) and Stanley Kubrick's 1964 film *Dr Strangelove, or How I Learned to Stop Worrying and Love the Bomb*. The latter dramatizes a pathological sexual obsession with weaponry dominating the US military. Other practitioners include Terry *Southern, Kurt *Vonnegut, and Bruce Jay Friedman (1930–), who edited the anthology *Black Humour* in 1965.

BLACKMAN, Malorie (1962–) Writer of short stories, picture books, and *young adult fiction. Although her characters are often black, she rarely writes explicitly about race. *Hacker* (1992) is a thriller about IT; *Pig-Heart Boy* (1997, televised in 1999) deals with organ transplantation. *Noughts and Crosses* (2001, adapted as a play, *Royal Shakespeare Company, 2007) and its sequels *Knife Edge* (2004), *Checkmate* (2005), and *Double Cross* (2008) are set in an alternative world where race relations are reversed.

BLACKMORE, R. D. (Richard Doddridge) (1825–1900) Writer and fruit-farmer. His own marriage did not have the approval of his family, and barriers of religion and social class thwarting the union of lovers frequently figure in his fiction. His fame rests almost entirely on one of his novels, *Lorna Doone* (1869). He wrote thirteen other novels, with engaging descriptions of lovingly observed climate, wildlife, and vegetation.

Black Mountain poets A group of American poets associated with Black Mountain College, an experimental liberal arts college founded in 1933 near Asheville, North Carolina, which became in the early 1950s a centre of anti-academic poetic revolt. A leading figure was Charles Olson, rector of the college from 1951 to 1956, whose *Projective Verse* (1950) was a form of manifesto, laying much emphasis on the dynamic energy of the spoken word and phrase and attacking the domination of syntax, rhyme, and metre. His students and followers included Robert *Creeley, Robert Duncan (1919–88), and Denise *Levertov. The *Black Mountain Review* (1954–7; edited by Creeley) also published work by Allen *Ginsberg and Jack *Kerouac, thus heralding the *Beat Generation.

BLACKMUR, R. P. (Richard Palmer) (1904–65) American poet and critic, whose critical works, which include *The Expense of Greatness* (1940), *Language as Gesture* (1952), and *The Lion and the Honeycomb* (1955), link him with the *New Criticism; he was one of the early champions of the art of Wallace *Stevens.

BLACKWOOD, Algernon (1869–1951)- Journalist, short story writer, and novelist. His work included travel, adventure, humour, and pantheistic fantasies, but the stories for which he is chiefly remembered deal in the psychic and macabre. His second collection, *The Listener and Other Stories* (1907), contains 'The Willows', highly regarded by H. P. *Lovecraft for its cosmic awe. More than 30 books followed, including *Tales of the Uncanny and Supernatural* (1949).

BLACKWOOD, William (1776–1834) Scots publisher, founder of the firm of William Blackwood and Son, and of the highly successful *Blackwood's (Edinburgh) Magazine*. He early recognized the talent of John *Galt, whose *The *Ayrshire Legatees* he published, and of Susan *Ferrier.

Blackwood's Magazine (1817–1980) or 'the Maga', was an innovating monthly periodical founded by William *Blackwood as a Tory rival to the Whiggish *Edinburgh Review*. Beginning in April 1817 as the *Edinburgh Monthly Magazine*, it continued from October until December 1905 as *Blackwood's Edinburgh Magazine*; in January 1906 it became *Blackwood's Magazine*. The first editors were soon replaced by John Gibson *Lockhart, John *Wilson, and James *Hogg, who gave the 'Maga' its forceful partisan tone. Its notoriety was early established with the publication in 1817 of the so-called 'Chaldee MS', in which many leading Edinburgh figures were pilloried; and the long series of attacks on the *'Cockney School' of poetry, directed chiefly against Leigh *Hunt, John *Keats, and William *Hazlitt, to whom Blackwood had to pay damages. *Blackwood's* gave considerable support to William *Wordsworth, P. B. *Shelley, Thomas *De Quincey, Henry *Mackenzie, John *Galt, and Walter *Scott, and did much to foster an interest in German literature. The carnivalesque series of sketches *Noctes Ambrosianae* was highly popular.

BLAIR, Eric *See* ORWELL, GEORGE.

BLAIR, Hugh (1718–1800) Scottish preacher and Edinburgh professor of rhetoric and belles lettres. His literary circle included David *Hume, Alexander Carlyle, Adam *Smith, and (briefly) Robert *Burns. He incurred Samuel *Johnson's wrath for his defence of James *Macpherson in his *A Critical Dissertation on the Poems of Ossian* (1763).

BLAIR, Robert (1699–1746) Poet and Church of Scotland clergyman. His fame rests on *The Grave* (1743), a didactic poem of the *Graveyard School, consisting of 767 lines of *blank verse. It celebrates the horrors of death, the solitude of the tomb, the pains of bereavement, and the madness of suicide, and concludes on an orthodox Christian note some readers have found perfunctory. It has passages of considerable power and, like Edward *Young's *Night Thoughts*, was illustrated by William *Blake.

BLAKE, Quentin (1932–) MBE, Chevalier des Arts et des Lettres, artist. His many distinguished *picturebooks and pioneering *'crossover' books include *The Green Ship* (1997). His work is lively and often anarchic. Blake illustrated Roald *Dahl's children's books, and was the first children's laureate (1999–2001).

BLAKE, William (1757–1827) Engraver and visionary poet. He did not go to school, but was apprenticed to James Basire, engraver, and then became a student at the Royal Academy. From 1779 he was employed as an engraver by the bookseller Joseph *Johnson, and in 1780 met Henry *Fuseli and John *Flaxman, the latter a follower of Emanuel *Swedenborg, whose mysticism deeply influenced Blake. Flaxman introduced him to the progressive intellectual circle of the Revd A. S. Mathew and his wife (which included Anna Laetitia *Barbauld, Hannah *More, and Elizabeth *Montagu), and Mathew and Flaxman financed the publication of Blake's first volume, *Poetical Sketches* (1783). In 1784, with help from Mrs Mathew, he set up a print shop at 27 Broad Street, and at about the same period (although not for publication) wrote the satirical *An *Island in the Moon*. He engraved and published his *Songs of Innocence* in 1789, and also *The Book of Thel*, works which manifest the early phases of his highly distinctive mystic vision, and in which he embarks on the evolution of his personal mythology; years later (in *Jerusalem*) he was to state, through the character Los, 'I must Create a System, or be enslav'd by another Man's', words which have been taken by some to apply to his own need to escape from the fetters of 18th-century versification, as well as from the materialist philosophy (as he conceived it) of the *Enlightenment, and a Puritanical or repressive interpretation of Christianity. The ambiguity of *The Book of Thel* heralds the increasing complexity of his other works which include *Tiriel* (written 1789; pub. 1874), introducing the theme of the blind tyrannical father, 'the king of rotten wood, and of the bones of death', which reappears in different forms in many poems; *The *Marriage of Heaven and Hell* (engraved *c.*1790–3), his principal prose work, a book of paradoxical aphorisms;

and the revolutionary works *The French Revolution* (1791); *America: A Prophecy* (1793); and *Visions of the Daughters of Albion* (1793), in which he develops his attitude of revolt against authority, combining political fervour (he had met Thomas *Paine at Joseph Johnson's) and visionary ecstasy. By this time Blake had already established his poetic range; the long, flowing lines and violent energy of the verse combine with phrases of terse and aphoristic clarity and moments of great lyric tenderness. *Songs of Experience* (1794), which demonstrates his command of the lyric, includes 'Tyger! Tyger! burning bright', 'O Rose thou art sick', and other of his more accessible pieces.

Blake and his wife Catherine moved to Lambeth in 1790; he continued to evolve his mythology in *The Book of *Urizen* (1794); *Europe, a Prophecy* (1794); *The Song of Los* (1795); *The Book of Ahania* (1795); *The Book of Los* (1795); and *The *Four Zoas* (originally entitled *Vala*, written and revised 1797–1804). In 1800 he moved to Felpham, Sussex, working for his friend and patron William *Hayley, and on *Milton* (1804–8); in 1803 he was charged at Chichester with high treason for having 'uttered seditious and treasonable expressions, such as "'D——n the King, d——n all his subjects . . .'", but was acquitted. He returned to London, to work on *Milton* and *Jerusalem: The Emanation of the Giant Albion* (written and etched, 1804–20). In 1805 he was commissioned by Robert Cromek to produce a set of drawings for Robert *Blair's poem *The Grave*, but Cromek defaulted on the contract, and Blake earned neither the money nor the public esteem he had hoped for. This was symptomatic of the disappointment of his later years. Both his poetry and his art had failed to find a sympathetic audience, and a lifetime of hard work had brought him neither riches nor comfort. His last years were passed in obscurity, although he eventually began to attract the interest and admiration of younger artists. A commission in 1821 from the painter John Linnell produced his well-known illustrations for the Book of Job, published in 1826 (it was Linnell who introduced Blake to Samuel Palmer in 1824.) A late poem, 'The Everlasting Gospel', written about 1818, presents Blake's own version of Jesus, in a manner that recalls the paradoxes of *The Marriage of Heaven and Hell*, attacking the conventional 'Creeping Jesus', gentle, humble, and chaste, and stressing his rebellious nature.

At Blake's death, general opinion held that he had been, if gifted, insane; *Wordsworth's verdict, according to Henry Crabb *Robinson, was that 'There was no doubt that this poor man was

mad, but there is something in the madness of this man which interests me more than the sanity of Lord Byron and Walter Scott'. It was not until Alexander Gilchrist's biography of 1863 (completed after his death by his wife Anne *Gilchrist), that interest began to grow. This was followed by an appreciation by *Swinburne (1868) and by William Michael *Rossetti's edition of 1874, which added new poems to the canon and established his reputation, at least as a lyric poet; his rediscovered engravings considerably influenced the development of art nouveau. In 1893 Yeats, a devoted admirer, produced with E. J. Ellis a three-volume edition, with a memoir and an interpretation of the mythology, and the 20th century saw an enormous increase in interest. The bibliographical studies and editions of Geoffrey Keynes, culminating in *The Complete Writings of William Blake* (1966, 2nd edn), have added greatly to knowledge both of the man and his works. There have been many interpretative studies, relating his work to traditional Christianity, to the *Neoplatonic and Swedenborgian traditions, to Jungian *archetypes, and to *Freudian and *Marxist theory. Blake had a marked influence on the *Beat Generation and the English poets of the underground movement, hailed by both as liberator. There is a biography by Peter *Ackroyd (1995).

((◉)) **SEE WEB LINKS**
• The William Blake Archive.

BLAMIRE,   Susanna   (1747–94) Poet, daughter of a Cumberland farmer, whose verse was circulated among friends or pinned to trees, and sometimes published, in single sheets, anthologies, or magazines. It was collected as *The Poetical Works of Miss Susanna Blamire*, '*The Muse of Cumberland*' (1842). The poems range from Scots or Cumberland dialect songs, to personal lyrics, chatty epistles to friends, and the heroic couplets of 'Stoklewath, or The Cumbrian Village', a complex picture of rural life and her most substantial poem.

BLANCH, Lesley (1904–2007) Romantic biographer, orientalist, and travel writer, best known for her memorably entitled group biography *The Wilder Shores of Love* (1954). It tells the lives of four women 'enthralled by the Oriental legend': these include Isabel Burton, née Arundell (1831–96), wife of Sir Richard *Burton, and Frenchwoman Isabelle Eberhardt (1877–1904). *Pavilions of the Heart* (1974) is an anthology of various historic erotic venues.

Blanch also edited the memoirs of Harriette *Wilson as *The Game of Hearts* (1957).

blank verse Verse written in unrhymed lines of iambic *pentameter. It was first used by *Surrey c.1540, subsequently adopted for dramatic verse by Thomas *Sackville and Thomas Norton (1530/2–84) in *Gorboduc* (1561), and most powerfully developed by Christopher *Marlowe and William *Shakespeare. It remained a standard form in non-dramatic verse, notably in the hands of John *Milton, William *Wordsworth, and Alfred *Tennyson.

Blast A periodical of literature and art edited by Wyndham *Lewis, subtitled 'Review of the Great English Vortex' (*see* VORTICISM). Only two issues appeared, the first in June 1914, and the second, the 'War Number', in July 1915. Its contributors included Ezra *Pound, Ford Madox *Ford, T. S. *Eliot, Rebecca *West, Jessica Dismorr (1885–1939), and Helen Saunders (1885–1963).

⊕ SEE WEB LINKS
• Modernist Journals Project

Blatant Beast In Edmund *Spenser's *Faerie Queene*, Book VI, a monster, the personification of the calumnious voice of the world, begotten of Envy and Detraction.

blazon A heraldic term used to describe a catalogue of the different physical elements of a woman's beauty. The term is usually associated with poetry, as in Philip *Sidney's *Old Arcadia* poem 'What toong can her perfections tell' or William *Shakespeare's Sonnet 106, 'in the blazon of sweet beauty's best'.

Bleak House A novel by Charles *Dickens, published in monthly parts 1852-3. This dark and complex book combines a vigorous attack on the abuses of the old court of Chancery, the delays and costs of which brought misery and ruin on its suitors, with bitter satire on the callous neglect of the poor by the rich and powerful, and an intricate exploration of themes of hidden transgression, obsession, violence, and exposure. The plot centres on the fortunes of Richard Carstone, an irresolute youth, and his gentle cousin Ada Clare. They are wards of the court in the case of Jarndyce and Jarndyce, concerned with the distribution of an estate. The wards are taken to live with their kind elderly relative John Jarndyce. They fall in love and secretly marry. Richard, lured by the will-o'-the-wisp of the fortune that is to be his when the case is settled, sinks gradually to ruin and death, and the case of Jarndyce and Jarndyce comes suddenly to an end on the discovery that the costs have absorbed the whole estate in dispute.

When Ada goes to live with John Jarndyce she is accompanied by Esther Summerson, apparently an orphan, and the narrative is partly supposed to be written by her. Sir Leicester Dedlock is devotedly attached to his beautiful wife, Lady Dedlock, who hides a secret under her haughty exterior. Before her marriage she loved a Captain Hawdon and had a daughter by him, whom she believes dead. Hawdon is thought to have perished at sea. In fact the daughter is Esther Summerson, and Hawdon is now a penniless scrivener, or professional copyist. Lady Dedlock accidentally catches sight of his handwriting in a legal document, and its effect on her alerts the cunning lawyer Tulkinghorn to the existence of a mystery. Lady Dedlock's enquiries bring her, through the medium of the crossing-sweeper, Jo, a poverty-bitten and illiterate child, to the burial ground where her former lover's miserable career has just ended. Jo's unguarded revelation of this experience sets Tulkinghorn on the track, until he possesses all the facts and tells Lady Dedlock that he is going to expose her next day to her husband. That night Tulkinghorn is murdered. Bucket, the detective, presently reveals to the baronet what Tulkinghorn had discovered, and arrests a former French maid of Lady Dedlock, who has committed the murder. Lady Dedlock flies from the house in despair, and is found dead near the grave of her lover, in spite of the efforts of her husband and Esther to save her.

Much of the story is occupied with Esther's devotion to John Jarndyce; her acceptance of his offer of marriage from a sense of duty and gratitude, though she loves a young doctor, Woodcourt; Jarndyce's discovery of the state of her heart; and his surrender of her to Woodcourt.

Minor characters include Harold Skimpole (drawn from Leigh *Hunt); Mrs Jellyby, who sacrifices her family to her selfish addiction to professional philanthropy; Jo, the crossing-sweeper, who is chivvied by the police to his death; Krook, the 'chancellor' of the rag and bone department, who dies of spontaneous combustion; Miss Flite, the little lunatic lady who haunts the Chancery courts; and Jarndyce's friend, the irascible and generous Boythorn (drawn from Walter Savage *Landor).

BLEASDALE, Alan (1946-) Playwright, born in Liverpool. His stage plays include

Having a Ball (1981), a comedy set in a vasecto-my clinic, *Are You Lonesome Tonight?* (1985), about the singer Elvis Presley, and *On the Ledge* (*National Theatre, 1993), which is dramatically staged in a tower block with rioters below. His TV work includes *Boys from the Blackstuff* (1982), about a group of unemployed men in Liverpool, and *G.B.H.* (1991), a seven-part serial about corrupt left-wing local politics. His street-wise Liverpool lad Scully first emerged on *BBC Radio 4, then on TV in 1984.

'Blessed Damozel, The' A poem by D. G. *Rossetti. The first version appeared in the *Germ* (1850); many revised versions appeared sub-sequently. In this poem, inspired by *Dante, Rossetti described the blessed damozel leaning out from the ramparts of heaven, watching the worlds below and the souls mounting to God, and praying for union with her earthly lover in the shadow of the 'living mystic tree'. One of his ear-liest and most influential poems, it exemplified a *Pre-Raphaelite interest in medieval sacramental symbolism (she has three lilies in her hand, seven stars in her hair, a white rose in her robe) and was a powerful instance of Rossetti's representation—here in words—of variously eroticized women. He later painted the same subject.

BLIND, Mathilde (1841-96) German poet, born Mathilde Cohen; she took the name of her stepfather Karl Blind (1826-1907), who came to England in 1852 as a political refugee. Her upbringing led her to challenge religious and social orthodoxies: she translated D. F. *Strauss's *The Old Faith and the New* (1873), became involved in the women's movement and translated the journals of Marie Bashkirtseff from the French (1890). Her volumes of poetry show a keen sense of social concern and a posi-tivist outlook; they include *The Ascent of Man* (1889), which gives a vivid account of Darwinian evolution. She wrote a life of George *Eliot (1884).

Blind Harry *See* HARY'S WALLACE.

BLISH, James (1921-75) American author. His 'Cities in Flight' sequence (collected 1970) explores the theories of cyclic history of the historian and philosopher Oswald Spengler (1880-1936). *A Case of Conscience* (1958) con-siders the implications for religious belief of the discovery of apparently sinless aliens. *Doctor Mirabilis* (1964) is a historical novel featuring the 13th-century theologian/scientist Roger Bacon.

Blithedale Romance, The A novel by Nathaniel *Hawthorne, published 1852, based on Hawthorne's residence in 1841 at the *Tran-scendental utopian community at Brook Farm. It is narrated by a poet, Miles Coverdale (named after the 16th-century reformer and translator of the Bible Miles *Coverdale), who visits Blithe-dale Farm, near Boston, where he meets the queenly Zenobia (said to be based on Margaret *Fuller), the social reformer Hollingsworth, and the gentle Priscilla. Coverdale broods on the work of Charles Fourier, Thomas *Carlyle, and Ralph Waldo *Emerson, while the women fall in love with Hollingsworth; Zenobia is rejected and drowns herself, Hollingsworth marries Pris-cilla, and Coverdale remains a sceptical, solitary observer of mankind's aspirations and disap-pointments.

BLIXEN, Karen *See* DINESEN, ISAK.

BLOCH, Robert (1917-94) Chicago-born au-thor of *fantasy and *horror stories who, like his mentor H. P. *Lovecraft, published widely in *Weird Tales*. Other influences included Edgar Allan *Poe and 'Jack the Ripper'. *Psycho* (1959) was filmed successfully by Alfred *Hitchcock (1960).

BLOK, Aleksandr Aleksandrovich (1880-1921) Russian *symbolist poet, play-wright, and critic. Blok's powerful late work in-cludes the urban poetry of *The Terrible World* (1907-16), and *Native Land* (1907-16). Blok re-sponded to the Russian Revolution with his fa-mous poem of January 1918, 'The Twelve', which ends with the ambiguous image of Christ leading a band of Red Guards. After the revolu-tion he ceased to write poetry. His *Selected Poems* (trans. Jon *Stallworthy and Peter France) appeared in 2000.

BLONDEL De Nesle A French *trouvère of the late 12th century. Legend makes him a friend of *Richard Cœur de Lion: Richard, on his return from the Holy Land in 1192, was imprisoned in Austria. Blondel set out to find him and, sitting under a window of the castle where Richard was imprisoned, sang a song in French that he and the king had composed together; halfway through he paused, and Richard took up the song and completed it. Blondel returned to England and told of the king's whereabouts.

Bloodaxe Books Independent poetry press, founded 1978. Bloodaxe has become a major force in poetry publishing in Britain, with a large and diverse list of new and established English-language poets as well as European and international poetry in translation, which might otherwise fail to find a publisher in the United Kingdom. It has helped to establish the reputation of Simon *Armitage, Helen *Dunmore, Susan *Wicks, and Glyn *Maxwell. Other figures on its lists include Miroslav Holub, Tony *Harrison, and Nobel laureates Rabindranath *Tagore, Eugenio Montale, and Odysseus *Elytis, and a notably large number of modern women poets.

BLOOM, Harold (1930–) American critic, he specializes in the Romantic literary tradition, in opposition to T. S. *Eliot's classical critical orthodoxy. He is known for his ambitious reconsideration of poetic tradition in *The Anxiety of Influence* (1973) and *A Map of Misreading* (1975), which propose that major poets struggle against the suffocating weight of their predecessors, creating new poems by 'misreading' older ones through a complex series of rhetorical defence mechanisms. His *The Western Canon* (1994) defends the 'great' writers against egalitarian critical trends.

BLOOM, Valerie (1956–) A Jamaican performance poet, who often writes in Jamaican patois. *Surprising Joy*, a novel for children, was followed by *The Tribe*, a coming-of-age novel concerning the Spanish conquest of the Caribbean.

BLOOMFIELD, Robert (1766–1823) Poet, born in Suffolk; he worked as a farm labourer and then as a shoemaker in London, enduring extreme poverty. He is remembered chiefly as author of *The Farmer's Boy* (1800, ed. Capel Lofft, who portrayed the poet as a peasant prodigy in the manner of Robert *Burns), illustrated with engravings by Thomas *Bewick. The vogue for tales of rustic life led to immense sales, and translations into Italian and French.

Bloomsbury Group The name given to a relatively loose association of like-minded people rather than an organized body of opinion, it has possibly acquired more significance and solidity than it warrants. Centred at first on 46 Gordon Square, Bloomsbury, which became the home of the artist Vanessa *Bell and her sister Virginia *Woolf (both then unmarried) in 1904, the Group was to include, among others, Geoffrey Keynes (1887–1982), Leonard *Woolf, Lytton *Strachey, David *Garnett, Duncan Grant (1885–1978), E. M. *Forster, Clive *Bell, and Roger *Fry. Based on friendship, an acerbic anti-Victorianism, and a deep interest in the arts, it derived many of its attitudes from G. E. Moore's *Principia Ethica* (1903).

Blot in the 'Scutcheon, A A tragedy in blank verse by Robert *Browning, published in 1843 as no. V of *Bells and Pomegranates*. It was produced at Drury Lane in 1843, ran for three nights, and caused a final rift between Browning and William *Macready. The quarrel was instrumental in Browning's decision to write no more stage plays.

Blue Stockings An informal group of intelligent and sociable women, which flourished in London in the later 18th century, probably named after the worsted stockings worn to evening receptions by the impoverished Benjamin Stillingfleet (1702–71). Elizabeth Vesey began holding receptions for men and women of the fashionable and literary worlds in the 1750s; the other main hostesses were Elizabeth *Montagu, Elizabeth *Carter, Hester *Chapone, Mary *Delany, and Hannah *More. There were no cards, and no refreshment other than tea, coffee, or lemonade. Learned conversation was not be disfigured by pedantry; politics, scandal, and swearing were not allowed. Meetings were also held in the houses of Sir Joshua *Reynolds, Hester *Thrale, and many others; the most famous literary men in regular attendance were David *Garrick, Horace *Walpole, James *Boswell, and Samuel *Johnson. More's poem *Bas Bleu* (1786) celebrates the pleasures of the society.

(⊕) SEE WEB LINKS
• The Blue Stocking archive

BLUME, Judy (1938–) Popular American writer who helped establish the dominant fashion for demotic, first-person 'problem novels' for children and *young adults with, for example, *Are You There, God? It's Me, Margaret* (1970). *Forever* (1975) is still one of the most-banned books in the USA, for its unjudgemental and explicit depiction of teenage sexuality. Blume's adult novels, include *Wifey* (1978).

BLUNDEN, Edmund (1896–1974) Poet, born in London. The longest-serving poet of the First World War, he wrote the experience of the trenches into such poems as 'Third Ypres' and 'Report on Experience'; guilt at his own survival became an important theme in his later writing. *Undertones of War* (1928) is a prose account of the war, which describes the double destruction of man and nature in Flanders: his first *Collected Poems* appeared in 1930, followed by *Poems 1930–1940*. He also published an edition of the poems of John *Clare, whose work he rescued from obscurity, a collected edition of the work of Wilfred *Owen (1931), and an edition of the poems of the almost unknown Ivor *Gurney (1954).

BLUNT, Wilfrid Scawen (1840–1922) Poet, diplomat, traveller, anti-imperialist, and Arabist, who married Lord *Byron's granddaughter. His first volume of poetry, *Sonnets and Songs by Proteus* (1875, subsequently revised), passionately addresses various women. It was followed by several other volumes which include love lyrics, evocations of the Sussex countryside, and adaptations from the Arabic. He also wrote and agitated in support of Egyptian, Indian, and Irish independence, earning the support of G. B. *Shaw and a brief spell in an Irish prison. This inspired his sonnet sequence *In Vinculis* (1889). *My Diaries* appeared in two volumes, 1919–20.

BLYTHE, Ronald George (1922–) Author, born in Suffolk. Blythe is best known for *Akenfield: Portrait of an English Village* (1969), a study of an East Anglian village, evoked through a series of tape recordings of conversations with its inhabitants, linked by the author's own descriptions and interpretations. Blythe was also involved in *Akenfield*, a film directed by Sir Peter *Hall in 1974, and *Akenfield Revisited*, a BBC documentary first screened in 2004. Other works include *The View in Winter: Reflections on Old Age* (1979), *Talking about John Clare* (1999), and *A Writer's Day-Book* (2006).

BLYTON, Enid (1897–1968) London-born children's writer. She appears consistently amongst the world's top five most translated authors, according to UNESCO's Index Translationum, with sales exceeding six million copies annually. She wrote around 650 titles, her most successful series being 'The Famous Five' (21 volumes) and 'Noddy' (at least 23 volumes).

Boadicea (Bonduca) Corruptions of the name Boudicca, queen of the Iceni in the east of Britain. As described in *Tacitus' *Annals*, she led a revolt against the Romans but was defeated by Suetonius Paulinus in AD 61 and killed herself. She is the subject of a play by John *Fletcher and an ode by William *Cowper.

bob and wheel A metrical pattern used, for example, in *Sir *Gawain and the Green Knight*, at the end of the unrhymed strophes of the main narrative. The 'bob' is a short tag with one stress

and the following 'wheel' is a *quatrain of three-stressed lines rhyming *abab*:

And al waz holȝ in with, nobot an olde
cave Or a crevisse of an olde cragge, he couþe
    hit noȝt deme
wiþ spelle.
'We! Lorde,' quoþ þe gentyle knyȝt,
'Wheþer þis be þe grene chapelle?
Here myȝt aboute mydnyȝt
Þe dele his matynnes tell!'
                    (*Sir Gawain*, ll. 2182–8)

Here the words 'with spelle' form the 'bob', leading into the 'wheel' of the quatrain.

BOCCACCIO, Giovanni (1313–75) Italian writer and humanist. His formative years, from about 1325 until 1340, were spent in Naples. He returned to his birthplace, Florence, in 1340, and witnessed the ravages of the Black Death in 1348, described in the introduction to the first day of his best-known work, *The *Decameron*. He wrote a life of *Dante and was the first to deliver a course of public lectures on the text of the *Divina commedia* (1373–4), on which he also wrote a commentary. Boccaccio's chief works, apart from *The Decameron*, were: *Filocolo*, a prose romance embodying the story of *Floris and Blancheflour; *Filostrato*, a poem on the story of Troilus and Cressida; *Teseida*, a poem on the story of Theseus, Palamon, and Arcite, which was translated by *Chaucer in the 'Knight's Tale'; and *Fiammetta*, a psychological romance in prose, in which the woman herself recounts the various phases of her unhappy love. He also wrote a number of encyclopedic works in Latin which were widely read in England, including *De Casibus Virorum Illustrium*, the original source text of John *Lydgate's *The Fall of Princes*, which was also drawn upon by Chaucer, and for stories in *A *Mirror for Magistrates*. Boccaccio is an important figure in the history of literature, particularly of narrative fiction. Among the poets who found inspiration in his works were Chaucer, *Shakespeare, John *Dryden, John *Keats, Henry Wadsworth *Longfellow, and *Tennyson.

Boece (Boëthius), Hector (?1465–1536) Historian. His Latin history of Scotland to the accession of James III (1526) included many fabulous narratives, among others that of Macbeth and Duncan, which passed into *Holinshed's chronicles and thence to Shakespeare.

BOETHIUS, Anicius Manlius Severinus (*c.*480–524) philosopher, born at Rome and consul in 510, in favour with Theodoric the Great, Ostrogothic king of Italy, but later suspected of treason, imprisoned, and finally cruelly executed. In prison he wrote *De Consolatione Philosophiae* (*On the Consolation of Philosophy*), a dialogue between himself and Philosophy. This is his most celebrated work and one of the most translated works in history; there are notable English translations by *Alfred, *Chaucer (as *Boece*), and *Elizabeth I. It was translated into French by Jean de Meun, and was one of the most influential books of the Middle Ages. It is now generally believed that he was a Christian, though this is rarely explicit in the *Consolation*, whose philosophy is broadly *Neoplatonic. Its form is *'Menippean Satire', i.e. alternating prose and verse. The verse often incorporates a story told by *Ovid or *Horace, used to illustrate the philosophy being expounded—a relationship that itself influenced medieval moral narrative. Before the Middle Ages, Boethius was of most importance for his translations of and commentaries on *Aristotle, which provided the main part of what was known of Aristotle before the recovery of most of his writings from Arabic scholars in the 12th century.

BOIARDO, Matteo Maria (1441–94) Poet and courtier at the Este court in Ferrara. He was one of the finest lyric poets of the Quattrocento, but his reputation rests centrally on his chivalric epic, the unfinished *Orlando innamorato* subsequently continued by *Ariosto.

BOILEAU-DESPRÉAUX, Nicolas (1636–1711) French poet, satirist, and critic. A friend of *Molière, *La Fontaine, and *Racine, legislator and model for French *neo-classicism at its apogee, he achieved legendary status in his lifetime. His *Art poétique* (1674: *Art of Poetry*), in which he establishes canons of taste and defines principles of composition and criticism, achieved international currency. His *mock epic *Le Lutrin* (1674–83: *The Lectern*) was widely influential in England (see RAPE OF THE LOCK). John *Dryden, Alexander *Pope, and John *Oldham found in him a lesson in how to rework the Latin poets.

BOLAND, Eavan (1944–) Irish poet. She met fellow undergraduate poets Michael *Longley and Derek *Mahon at Trinity College, Dublin. Her first collection, *New Territory* (1967), was followed by *The War Horse* (1975). Her work took a strongly feminist turn in *In her Own Image* (1980) and *Night Feed* (1982), a trend continued in such later volumes as *The Journey* (1987) *Against Love Poetry* (2001), and *Domestic Violence* (2007). *Object Lessons* (1995) is a prose work reflecting on women, poetry, and the Irish literary tradition. Boland's verse, characteristically spare and condensed, draws on classical and Irish myth, on domestic life and maternal experience, and is informed by a strong visual sense.

BOLT, Robert Oxton (1924–95) Dramatist and screenwriter. His first West End success *Flowering Cherry* (pub. 1958) was followed by *The Tiger and the Horse* (1960; pub. 1961), reflecting Bolt's involvement with the campaign for nuclear disarmament, and *A Man for All Seasons* (1960; pub. 1960; filmed 1966), based on the life of Sir Thomas *More. *Vivat, Vivat Regina* (1970) was based on the conflict between *Elizabeth I and *Mary Queen of Scots. Bolt wrote the screenplays for David Lean's *Lawrence of Arabia* (1962), based on the exploits of T. E. *Lawrence, *Dr Zhivago* (1965), *Ryan's Daughter* (1970), and *The Mission* (1986, dir. Roland Joffé).

BOND, Edward (1934–) Playwright. His first play, *The Pope's Wedding*, was given a Sunday night performance at the *Royal Court in 1962, and in 1965 his grim portrait of urban violence, *Saved*, aroused much admiration as well as a ban from the Lord Chamberlain (*see* CENSORSHIP). Other provocative works followed, including *Early Morning* (1969); *Lear* (1971), a savage reworking of Shakespeare; *The Sea* (1973), a black country-house comedy; *The Fool* (1975), based on the life of John *Clare; *Restoration* (1981), a *Brechtian revolutionary historical drama with songs; and *Summer* (1982). Bond's theatre is an outspoken indictment of capitalist society and continues to arouse extreme responses from critics and audiences. At the *National Theatre in 1978, he had directed his own play *The Woman*, an excitingly innovative reworking of classical myth, and he was scheduled to co-direct his trilogy *The War Plays* for the Royal Shakespeare Company in 1985. He withdrew from the project, protesting at its treatment, and has never again allowed his work to be produced on the stages of the major subsidized theatres. However, there has been a regular stream of new plays, including *Jackets* (1989), *The Crime of the Twenty-First Century* (1999), and *Coffee* (2000).

Bond, James Originally the suave and ruthless hero of thrillers by Ian *Fleming, reborn as a screen icon in a series of increasingly spectacular, and sardonic, films that followed the success of

Dr No in 1962, starring Sean Connery. Later incarnations of '007, licensed to kill' have included Roger Moore, Timothy Dalton, Pierce Brosnan, and, since *Casino Royale* (2006), Daniel Craig.

Bondman, The A tragicomedy by Philip *Massinger with political implications, performed by the Lady Elizabeth's Men at the Cockpit and before Prince Charles at Whitehall in 1623, published 1624. One of the best of Massinger's tragicomedies, it is informed by his contempt for the arrogance of an effete aristocracy, perhaps reflecting Massinger's opinion of the Jacobean court.

Bonduca A tragedy by John *Fletcher, 1611–14, published 1647. The tragedy is based on the story of *Boadicea (Boudicca), as given by *Holinshed, but the principal character is her cousin, the wise and battle-hardened Caratach (*Caractacus), whose counsel to the impetuous Bonduca is disastrously ignored.

Bon Gaultier The pseudonym (taken from *Rabelais) under which W. E. *Aytoun and Theodore *Martin published *A Book of Ballads* (1845), a collection of parodies and light poems. Among the authors parodied are Alfred *Tennyson and, loosely, E. B. *Browning (in 'The Rhyme of Sir Lancelot Bogle').

Booker Prize for Fiction See MAN BOOKER PRIZE FOR FICTION, and APPENDIX 4.

book history (the history of the book) A rather imprecise label used to identify an interdisciplinary field of historical study, whose origins can conveniently be traced to the publication in France of Lucien Febvre and Henri Jean Martin's *L'Apparition du livre* (1958). The field gained wider recognition, however, with the appearance in 1979 of works by two American scholars: Elizabeth Eisenstein's *The Printing Press as an Agent of Change* and Robert Darnton's *The Business of Enlightenment: A Publishing History of the Encyclopédie*. During the 1980s the monumental *Histoire de l'édition française*, edited by Martin and Roger Chartier, initiated a series of national histories of the book. Although the field is commonly identified with the study of the book, its object is the history of written communication encompassing the production, publication, distribution, control, collection, conservation, reading, and uses of script and print in all media, including manuscripts, pamphlets, periodicals, newspapers, books, and electronic forms. In literary studies, it has insisted on the importance of material considerations in textual interpreta-

tion. Here book historians share some preoccupations with British Cultural Materialists like Raymond *Williams and American *New Historicists like Stephen Greenblatt, but their closest allies are the revisionist bibliographers and textual critics of the 1980s, notably Jerome McGann and D. F. McKenzie. Indeed, McKenzie's 'sociology of the text', first announced in the title of his Panizzi lectures in 1985 and intended there to point towards a radical transformation of Anglo-American bibliography, is often treated as a synonym for 'book history'.

Book of Martyrs, The See ACTS AND MONUMENTS.

Book of the Duchess, The A dream-poem in 1,334 lines by *Chaucer, written *c.*1369–72, in octosyllabic couplets. It is believed to be an allegorical lament on the death of Blanche of Lancaster, the first wife of John of Gaunt, who died in September 1368. The poem is one of Chaucer's earliest works, but it has great charm and accomplishment. It is founded on the French tradition of the dream as a vehicle for love poetry. 'A Complaynt of a Loveres Lyfe' by *Lydgate is based on it.

Bookseller, The See WHITAKER, JOSEPH.

Boom, the A term used loosely to refer to a group of Latin American authors who, in the late 1950s and 1960s, put fiction from the subcontinent on the international map. The principal writers are Julio *Cortázar (Argentina), the Mexican Carlos Fuentes (1928–), Gabriel *García Márquez (Colombia), and Mario *Vargas Llosa (Peru). An earlier generation of Latin American writers had already drawn inspiration from European and North American *modernist authors like William *Faulkner, James *Joyce, and Virginia *Woolf, adapting them creatively to their own context, but the Boom authors did so in a way that caught the imagination of a wide readership. Fuentes's novel *La muerte de Artemio Cruz* (1962: *The Death of Artemio Cruz*) and Vargas Llosa's *La ciudad y los perros* (1963: *The Time of the Hero*) and *La casa verde* (1966: *The Green House*) were experimentally realist works which drew upon Faulkner's narrative and structural techniques to depict the complexity and violence of, respectively, Mexico and Peru. Cortázar and García Márquez, while sometimes writing in a realist mode, incorporated fantasy (notably the *magical realism of García Márquez's *Cien años de soledad* (1967: *One Hundred Years of Solitude*) to create works that were at the same time ironic meditations on fiction. The Boom writers married experiment, which could make considerable demands upon their readers, with gripping storytelling, humour, and a political edge, rendering their works commercially successful.

BORGES, Jorge Luis (1899–1986) Argentine writer. He is best known for his short stories. Largely the fictionalized biographies of adventurers and criminals, the stories in *Historia universal de la infamia* (1935: *A Universal History of Infamy*) illustrate Borges's enduring preoccupation with the relationship of fiction, truth, and identity; with violence; and with the puzzles of *detective fiction. His two collections *Ficciones* (1944: *Fictions*) and *El aleph* (1949: *The Aleph*) are his most famous works, the publication of a selection entitled *Labyrinths* in Paris in 1953 establishing an international reputation. Many of his stories deal with the cyclical nature of time; they are themselves labyrinthine in form, and often dreamlike in their endlessly reflected facets of reality. Much of his fiction is humorous, drawing on an interest in philosophy and arcane knowledge, while parodying scholarly pedantry. Its metafictional nature and emphasis on the reader's role in forging meaning have made it attractive to many modern writers.

BORON, Robert de A 12th- to 13th-century French poet who composed *c.*1202 a trilogy (*Joseph d'Arimathie* in 3,514 lines; *Merlin*, a fragment of 502 lines; and *Perceval*) in which he developed the early history of the Holy *Grail in Britain, linking it with the *Arthurian tradition.

Borough, The A poem by George *Crabbe published 1810, in twenty-four 'letters', describing, with much penetration and detail, the life and characters of the church, the school, the professions, the surroundings, the workhouse, the prisons, the sea, and other aspects of the town of Aldeburgh, Suffolk. The work, defining a distinctive form of poetic realism, took eight years to complete. Two of the best-known tales, concerning *Peter Grimes and *Ellen Orford, were combined in *Britten's opera *Peter Grimes* (1945).

BORROW, George (1803–81) Travel writer; he spent several years travelling through Europe and learning languages (though there is some suggestion that he exaggerated his linguistic achievements and his travels). Between 1833 and 1840, as agent for the British and Foreign Bible Society, Borrow visited Russia, the Iberian Peninsula, and North Africa. *Wild Wales* (1862) is the most famous result of his later British

walking tours. His books, often characterized by a mixture of fact and fiction and by a fascination with outsiders and their language, also include: *The Zincali, or An Account of the Gypsies in Spain* (1841), *The Bible in Spain* (1843), **Lavengro* (1851), and *The *Romany Rye* (1857).

Borrowers, The (1952, filmed 1997) A children's novel by Mary *Norton, awarded the Carnegie Medal; it has four sequels, to *The Borrowers Avenged* (1982). The Borrowers are small people who live under floors and 'borrow' items from the 'human beans' to survive; even their names—Pod, Homily, Arrietty—are 'borrowed'. The series epitomizes the conflict between the rural past and the uncertain future characteristic of post-war British children's books, and is notable for the complex multiple frames of the narratives *Arrietty* (2011) is an animé version.

BOSTON, Lucy M. (Maria) (1892–1990) Lancashire-born author of six distinguished fantasy-realism novels for children, beginning with *The Children of Green Knowe* (1954). All are set in Boston's house, the ancient Manor at Hemingford Grey, Cambridgeshire, and illustrated by her son. Boston's books for adults include *The Guardians of the House* (1974).

Bostonians, The A novel by Henry *James, published 1886. Basil Ransom, a young lawyer, comes north from Mississippi and the humiliations of the Civil War to Boston, where he calls on his cousin Olive Chancellor and her widowed sister, the girlishly arch Mrs Luna. Olive, a wealthy chill feminist, introduces him to a reformist group (acidly portrayed by James). Selah Tarrant, a charlatan faith healer and showman, is presenting his daughter Verena as an 'inspirational' speaker. There follows a struggle for Verena between Ransom and Olive, who has schooled her as a suffragette, which Ransom ultimately wins.

BOSWELL, James (1740–95) Lawyer, diarist, and biographer. He met Samuel *Johnson on 16 May 1763 in London; he then went to Holland (where he met and courted Isabelle de Charrière) and on through Europe to Italy. His extraordinary persistence meant he met with *Rousseau and *Voltaire. On his return to Scotland he 'passed advocate' and was to practise there and in England for the rest of his life. His first substantial work, *An Account of Corsica* (1768), was followed in December of the same year by a book of edited essays 'in favour of the brave Corsicans'; he was to remain loyal to this cause, creating a sensation by his appearance at the Shakespeare Jubilee in 1769 in Corsican dress. Boswell visited London as frequently as possible, spending much time with Johnson, whose biography he already planned. They made their celebrated tour of Scotland and the Hebrides in 1773, in which year Boswell was elected a member of the Club. His last meeting with Johnson was in 1784; his *Journal of a Tour of the Hebrides* appeared in 1785 after Johnson's death. The rest of Boswell's life was devoted to an unsuccessful pursuit of a political career (he was recorder of Carlisle, 1788–90) and to the immense task of assembling materials for his life of Johnson, a labour in which he was encouraged by Edmond *Malone. *The Life of Samuel *Johnson LLD* appeared in 1791.

Bottom, Nick The weaver in Shakespeare's *A *Midsummer Night's Dream*. Whatever other associations it may have had, the name referred to the ball on which thread was wound. A *'droll' adapted from Shakespeare's play, *The Merry Conceited Humours of Bottom the Weaver*, was printed in 1661.

BOUCICAULT, Dion (originally Dion Boursiquot) (1820–90) Playwright. He achieved great success with his comedy *London Assurance* (1841), written under the pseudonym of Lee Morton. He subsequently wrote and adapted some 200 plays, including *The Corsican Brothers* (1852, from the French), *The Poor of New York* (1857), *The Colleen Bawn, or The Brides of Garryowen* (1860), *Arra-na-Pogue, or The Wicklow Wedding* (1864), and *The Shaughraun* (1874). He was responsible for important innovations, such as the introduction of a royalty from plays and copyright for dramatists in America. With the rise of realism and the emergence of Henrik *Ibsen and George Bernard *Shaw, his work fell out of fashion, but it influenced Sean *O'Casey, who praised his 'colour and stir'.

Boudicca *See* BOADICEA.

Bounty, The Mutiny and Piratical Seizure of H.M.S., By Sir John Barrow (1764–1848), published 1831. HMS *Bounty*, which had been sent to the South Sea Islands to collect breadfruit plants, left Tahiti on 4 April. On 28 April Fletcher Christian and others seized Lieutenant Bligh, the commander, and placed him with eighteen loyal members of the crew in an open boat, which they cast adrift. The boat eventually reached Timor and Bligh returned to Britain. Meanwhile the *Bounty* sailed east with 25 of the crew to Tahiti, where sixteen were put ashore. These men were later arrested and many of them were drowned when HMS

Pandora sank in August 1791. Fletcher Christian and eight of his companions, together with some Tahitians, went on and settled on Pitcairn Island. There they founded a colony, which was eventually taken under the protection of the British government. The events form part of Lord *Byron's poem 'The *Island' (1823), and of many books and films.

BOURDIEU, Pierre (1930–2002) French sociologist. His work investigates the mechanisms whereby social groups and classes vie for power at all levels of social activity, and highlights the role played by education and culture in this struggle. *Les Règles de l'art* (1992; *The Rules of Art*, trans. Susan Emanuel, 1996) considers the processes by which literary value and merit are established and challenged.

BOWDLER, Thomas (1754–1825) An Edinburgh doctor; his *Family Shakespeare* was published 1818. The role in the work of his sister Henrietta Maria Bowdler (1754–1830) is unclear. The Bowdlers' love and admiration of Shakespeare, demonstrated in the prefaces, were profound; but they believed that nothing 'can afford an excuse for profaneness or obscenity; and if these could be obliterated, the transcendent genius of the poet would undoubtedly shine with more unclouded lustre'. Profanity they found only a small problem; 'God' as an expletive is always replaced by 'Heaven', and other brief passages and exclamations cut. But they confessed to enormous trouble with the indecency scattered throughout the plays. Their method was to cut, not to substitute; they in fact added almost nothing except prepositions and conjunctions. But the cutting is severe. *Othello* they found 'unfortunately little suited to family reading', and recommended that it be transferred 'from the parlour to the cabinet'. Similar excisions were inflicted on Gibbon's *Decline and Fall*. Their work gave rise to the verb 'to bowdlerize', or expurgate.

BOWEN, Elizabeth (1899–1973) Novelist and short story writer. The family home in Co. Cork was the *'big house' she inherited in 1930 and described in *Bowen's Court* (1942). Bowen's skill in describing urban and rural landscapes and her sensitivity to changes of light and season—changes characteristically made emblematic of psychological and social fluidities—are distinguishing features of her prose. Her novels include *The Hotel* (1927), *The Last September* (1929), *The House in Paris* (1935), and *Eva Trout* (1969). The best known are probably *The Death of the Heart* (1938) and *The Heat of the*

Day (1949). The former focuses on the threat posed by the innocence of Portia, a 16-year-old orphan, to the precarious, sophisticated London lives of her half-brother and his wife; the latter centres on the tragic wartime love affair of Stella Rodney and Robert Kelway, and their reactions to the revelation that the latter is a spy. The war inspired many of Bowen's best short stories, including 'Mysterious Kôr' (1944); other stories subtly invoke the supernatural. Bowen writes mainly of the upper middle classes, but within her narrow social range her perceptions are acute; her works convey a powerful sense of period through their re-creations of detail and atmosphere.

Bowge of Courte, The An allegorical poem in seven-line stanzas by John *Skelton, satirizing court life (1480/1498). The word 'bowge' is a corrupt form of 'bouche', meaning court rations, from the French 'avoir bouche à cour', to have free board at the king's table.

BOWLES, Caroline Anne (1786–1854) Poet and prose writer. Left alone and impoverished at the age of 30, she sought advice about publication from Robert *Southey, thus beginning a correspondence (pub. 1880) and friendship lasting twenty years until their marriage in 1839 after the death of his first wife. Her blank verse autobiography, *The Birth-Day* (1836), was much admired by the *Wordsworth household, but her work also encompassed comedy, satire, and social protest. Southey acknowledged her superior poetic gift, but owing to her choice of anonymous publication her reputation was never consolidated in her lifetime. Her *Poetical Works* appeared posthumously in 1867.

BOWLES, Jane (1917–73) Née Auer, American writer, wife of Paul *Bowles, chiefly remembered for her short novel *Two Serious Ladies* (1943), an exotic, disjointed, staccato work about two contrasted lives. Her play *In the Summer House* (perf. 1953) was praised by Tennessee *Williams as 'elusive and gripping'. Her *Collected Works* were published in 1984: *Everything is Nice* (1989) adds some previously uncollected short fiction. The story of her obsessional and self-destructive life is told in *A Little Original Sin* (1981) by Millicent Dillon.

BOWLES, Paul (1910–99) American novelist, poet, composer, translator, and short story writer, who married Jane Auer (*see* BOWLES, J.) in 1938. In 1948 they went to Tangier, where they lived intermittently for the rest of their lives, and where they became familiar landmarks in the expatriate gay community, and points of call for many literary visitors in search of the exotic. His works, most of which are set in Morocco, include *The Sheltering Sky* (1949), 'an adventure story in which the adventures take place on two planes simultaneously: in the actual desert and in the inner desert of the spirit', *Let it Come Down* (1952), *The Spider's House* (1955), and *Up above the World* (1966).

BOWLES, William Lisle (1762–1850) Poet. His *Fourteen Sonnets Written Chiefly on Picturesque Spots during a Journey* (1789) was admired by Charles *Lamb, Robert *Southey, and S. T. *Coleridge. Lord *Byron, however, described him as 'the maudlin prince of mournful sonneteers', and was roused to further anger by Bowles's hostile edition of Pope (1806).

Box and Cox (1847) A *farce by John Maddison *Morton. Box is a journeyman printer, Cox a journeyman hatter. Mrs Bouncer, a lodging-house keeper, has let the same room to both, taking advantage of the fact that Box is out all night and Cox out all day to conceal from each the existence of the other. Discovery comes when Cox unexpectedly gets a holiday. Indignation follows, and complications connected with a widow to whom both have proposed marriage; and finally a general reconciliation. It was adapted as an operetta, *Cox and Box* (perf. 1867) by Francis Cowley Burnand (1836–1917).

BOYD, William (1952–) Novelist and screenwriter. *A Good Man in Africa* (1981, filmed 1994 with Boyd's screenplay) is a comic tale of diplomatic life in a minor West African posting. A collection of stories, *On the Yankee Station*, appeared in 1981 and was followed by *An Ice-Cream War* (1982), a serio-comic tale set in East Africa during the First World War. *Stars and Bars* (1984, filmed 1988 with Boyd's screenplay) and *The New Confessions* (1987) is the sadly comic autobiography of a self-styled genius. *Brazzaville Beach* (1990), set in Africa, explores human and animal violence. *The Blue Afternoon* (1993) is set in 1936. London is the setting for *Armadillo* (1998), *Any Human Heart* (2002), and *Ordinary Thunderstorms* (2009). *Restless* (2006) focuses on the role of spies and betrayal in the Second World War.

BOYLE, John, fifth earl of Orrery (1707–62) Biographer and writer of letters, a friend from the early 1730s of Jonathan *Swift and Alexander *Pope. His controversial *Remarks on the Life and Writings of Dr Jonathan Swift* (1751) gave a critical account of Swift's character, life, relations with Stella and Vanessa, and friendships with Pope, John *Gay, Patrick Delany, and Edward *Young.

BOYLE, Roger, first earl of Orrery (1621–79) Soldier and playwright. His works include *Parthenissa* (1654–65), the first English romance in the style of La Calprenède and Madeleine de *Scudéry; *English-Adventures by a Person of Honour* (1676), a source for Thomas *Otway's *The Orphan*; a *Treatise on the Art of War* (1677), and some rhymed tragedies, among them *Mustapha* (1665), based on de Scudéry's *Ibrahim* and the history of Richard Knolles.

Boz The pseudonym used by Charles *Dickens in his contributions to the *Morning Chronicle* and in the *Pickwick Papers*.

BRACEGIRDLE, Anne (?1673/4–1748) A leading *Restoration actress. William *Congreve, who was perhaps her lover, wrote Angelica in *Love for Love* and Millamant in *The Way of the World* for her.

BRACKETT, Leigh (1915–78) Screenwriter and novelist, born in Los Angeles, known for her adaptation of Raymond *Chandler's *The Big Sleep* (1946) and initial work on *Star Wars: The Empire Strikes Back* (1980), which drew upon her colourful *science fiction novels, such as *The Sword of Rhiannon* (1949).

BRADBURY, Sir Malcolm (1932–2000) Critic and novelist, instrumental in setting up an influential creative writing course at the University of East Anglia. His critical works include studies of Evelyn *Waugh (1962) and Saul *Bellow (1982). His first three novels are satirical *campus novels: *Eating People is Wrong* (1959), set in a redbrick university; *Stepping Westward* (1965), set in the Midwest of America; and *The History Man* (1975), set in the new plate-glass university of Watermouth. *Rates of Exchange* (1983) satirizes cultural exchange, and *Cuts: A Very Short Novel* (1987) satirizes Thatcherite Britain. In *To the Hermitage* (2000), the visit of the 18th-century philosopher Denis *Diderot to the court of *Catherine the Great is juxtaposed with a Bradbury-like novelist's comic misadventures in 20th-century St Petersburg.

BRADBURY, Ray (1920–) American *science fiction and *fantasy writer, playwright, and poet. Perhaps his best-known single work is *Fahrenheit 451* (1953), set in an authoritarian future state where reading is banned: fireman Montag is employed to burn books but rebels and makes a bid for freedom. It was filmed by François Truffaut (1966). The stories published as *The Martian Chronicles* (1950) include some of his most poetic work, suffused with ambiguity and nostalgia. A Gothic sense of the macabre is added to the stories in *The Illustrated Man* (1951) and *Dandelion Wine* (1957)—to which *Farewell Summer* (2006) is a sequel—and the novel *Something Wicked This Way Comes* (1962). His scripting of John Huston's film of *Moby Dick* (1956) inspired stories collected as *Green Shadows, White Whale* (1992).

BRADDON, Mary Elizabeth (1837–1915) Novelist and editor. She published several works, including *Garibaldi and Other Poems* (1861), before the appearance of the sensational and successful *Lady Audley's Secret* (1862, first serialized in *Robin Goodfellow* and *The Sixpenny Magazine*). The bigamous pretty blonde heroine, who deserts her child, attempts to murder her husband, and contemplates poisoning her second husband, shocked Margaret *Oliphant who credited Miss Braddon as 'the inventor of the fair-haired demon of modern fiction'. The novel has been dramatized, filmed, and translated and remained in print throughout the author's life. She published a further 74 inventive, vivid novels including the successful *Aurora Floyd* (1863) and *The Doctor's Wife* (1864; loosely based on Gustave *Flaubert's *Madame Bovary*).

BRADLEY, A. C. (Andrew Cecil) (1851–1935) Critic. His best-known works are *Shakespearean Tragedy* (1904) and *Oxford Lectures on Poetry* (1909). L. C. Knights in his essay 'How many children had Lady Macbeth?' (1933) mocked Bradley's 'detective interest' in plot and emphasis on 'character' as a detachable object of study.

BRADLEY, Edward (1827–89) Novelist using the pseudonym 'Cuthbert Bede'. The author of *The Adventures of Mr Verdant Green* (1853–7), a comic novel which traces the Oxford career of a gullible young undergraduate, fresh from Warwickshire, from his freshman days to graduation and marriage. It was reprinted in 1982 with an introduction by Anthony *Powell.

BRADLEY, Marion Zimmer (1930–99) American author, best known for her 'Darkover' *science fiction series in which a lost colony develops psychic powers indistinguishable from magic. Later episodes such as *The Heritage of Hastur* (1975) are much nearer to *fantasy, while Bradley's closer attention to feminism and gender politics becomes evident, especially in the *The Mists of Avalon* (1982) which retells the Arthurian legends from the viewpoint of *Morgan le Fay (here Morgaine).

BRADSTREET, Anne (*c*.1612–1672) American poet. She was born in England and emigrated in 1630. Her poems were published in London without her knowledge in 1650, under the title *The Tenth Muse Lately Sprung up in America*, and a posthumous second edition with her own corrections and additions was published in Boston (1678). She admired and was influenced by Francis *Quarles and Josuah Sylvester's translation of Du Bartas, and her work was highly praised in her own time. She has received much attention both as a woman writer and as the first poet of the New World. John *Berryman pays tribute to her in his *Homage to Mistress Bradstreet* (1956).

BRADWARDINE, Thomas (*c*.1300–1349) Oxford theologian appointed archbishop of Canterbury immediately before his death from plague in August 1349. His *De Causa Dei* reasserted the primacy of faith and divine grace in opposition to the rationalist sceptics (whom he characterized as New Pelagians) of the tradition of William of *Ockham and Robert *Holcot.

BRAGG, Melvyn (1939–) Novelist and broadcaster, appointed a Labour life peer in 1998. His twenty novels include *Without a City Wall* (1968), *The Silken Net* (1971), *The Maid of Buttermere* (1978), *A Time to Dance* (1990), and the powerful fictional sequence that began with *The Soldier's Return* (1999). Best known as a media personality, he was producer-presenter of the television arts programme the *South Bank Show* (1978–2010), and presented influential *radio discussion programmes, including *The Routes of English* and *In our Time*.

BRAINE, John (1922–86) Novelist. His first novel, *Room at the Top* (1957), set in a small Yorkshire town, was an instant success, and its hero, Joe Lampton, was hailed as a provincial *'Angry Young Man' of the 1950s. Lampton, a ruthless opportunist working at the town hall, seduces and marries the wealthy young Susan Browne, despite his love for an unhappily married older woman. *Life at the Top* (1962) continues the story of his success and disillusion. Braine's later novels express his increasing hostility to the radical views with which he was once identified.

Branwen *See* MABINOGION.

BRATHWAITE, Kamau (1930–) Poet and academic, born in Barbados; his volumes of poetry include *The Arrivants: A New World Trilogy* (1973), which consists of *Rights of Passage* (1967), *Masks* (1968), and *Islands* (1969). The poem explores the complex Caribbean heritage and search for identity, using (but not exclusively) vernacular rhythms and diction, what he calls 'nation language'; its references range from Afro-Caribbean religious beliefs to cricket matches at the Oval. *Mother Poem* (1977), *Sun Poem* (1982), and *X-Self* (1987) form a trilogy about Barbados, 'most English of West Indian islands'. *Born to Slow Horses* (2005) meditates on exile.

Brat Pack A phrase coined by the media to describe a group of young novelists from New York which emerged in the mid- to late 1980s. Also known as 'The Blank Generation', their fiction inhabits a youth culture of cocaine, nightclubs, Music Television (MTV), and hedonistic abandon. Bret Easton Ellis (1964–), in *Less than Zero* (1984, film 1987), and Jay McInerney (1955–), in *Bright Lights, Big City* (1984, screenplay and film 1988), heralded this new mood of fashionable disaffection. Written in hypnotically deadpan voices, they described lives that consisted of a cool surface bereft of substance. Their obsession with celebrity and vacuity reached apocalyptic proportions with Ellis's *American Psycho* (1991, film 2000), a novel in which the narrator, Patrick Bateman, blends into the persona of a serial killer.

BRAUTIGAN, Richard (1935–84) American novelist and short story writer associated particularly with the San Francisco counter-culture of the 1960s. His 1967 novel *Trout Fishing in America* set a keynote for his faux-naïf style. His works also show some influence from Zen Buddhism.

Brave New World A novel by Aldous *Huxley, published 1932; a dystopian fable about a world state in the 7th century AF (after Ford), where social stability is based on a scientific caste system. Human beings, graded from highest intellectuals to lowest manual workers, hatched from incubators and brought up in communal nurseries, learn by methodical conditioning to accept their social destiny. The action of the story develops round Bernard Marx, an unorthodox and therefore unhappy Alpha-Plus (something had presumably gone wrong with his antenatal treatment), who visits a New Mexican Reservation and brings a Savage back to London. The Savage is at first fascinated by the new world, but finally revolted, and his argument with Mustapha Mond, World Controller, demonstrates the incompatibility of individual freedom and a scientifically trouble-free society. In *Brave New World Revisited* (1958) Huxley reconsiders his prophecies, fearing that some of them were coming true sooner than he thought.

BRAWNE, Fanny (1800–65) The young woman with whom John *Keats fell in love in 1818. To what extent she returned or understood his passion for her (expressed in many of his letters and several poems) is not clear, but some kind of engagement took place, and after his death she wore mourning for him for several years. She married in 1833. His letters to her were published in 1878 and in the collected edition of 1937; hers to his sister, also called Fanny, were published in 1937.

BRAZIL, Angela (1868–1947) Writer for children, a formative influence on the development of modern girls' *school stories. She wrote 53 books from *The Fortunes of Philippa* (1906) to *The School on the Loch* (1946), and many short stories for annuals. Unlike most of her contemporaries, she did not write *series. Brazil favoured unidealized heroines and her books were criticized for their use of slang.

BRECHT, Bertolt (1898–1956) German dramatist and poet. His best-known work for the stage is the satirical *Die Dreigroschenoper* (1928: *The Threepenny Opera*) with music by Kurt Weill, an adaptation of *The *Beggar's Opera*. After the First World War he was closely associated with the Communist cause. In the 1930s he went into exile, and fled to the USA in 1941. Abandoning experiments with didactic agitprop, he wrote *Leben des Galilei* (*Life of Galileo*) and *Mutter Courage und ihre Kinder* (*Mother Courage and her Children*), set in the Thirty Years War (1618–48) in 1938–9. In the form of what Brecht termed Epic Theatre, these plays reject any empathetic identification with the characters and any theatrical illusion of reality, making extensive use of music, song, and verse, construction by 'loosely' connected scenes, and the *alienation effect. *Der gute Mensch von Sezuan* (1941–3: *The Good Woman of Setzuan*) and *Der kaukasische Kreidekreis* (1944: *The Caucasian Chalk Circle*) were both written in America. In 1948 he settled in East Berlin and was at last able to see his own works published in their final revised versions and staged in accordance with his theory, concisely formulated in *Kleines Organon für das Theater* (1949: *Short Organon*

for the Theatre). Brecht's theatre had a notable impact on several British playwrights of the second half of the 20th century including Edward *Bond, John *Arden, Howard *Brenton, and David *Hare.

BREEZE, Jean Binta (1957–) Born in Jamaica. She now lives in London, where she is a lecturer, performance poet, and joint editor of the *Critical Quarterly*. The first female *dub poet, she focuses on black women's experience in Kingston, Jamaica, and London.

BRENAN, Gerald (Edward Fitz-Gerald) (1894–1987) Writer, who lived in Spain from 1920, where he was visited by Dora *Carrington. His autobiography, *A Life of one's Own* (1962), records his friendships with members of the *Bloomsbury Group, and vividly describes his experiences in the First World War. *Personal Record 1920–1972* was published in 1974.

BRENDAN, St (*c.*484–578) or Brendan the Navigator. Irish monk, about whom there grew up a tradition of legendary voyages as a Christianized version of the Old Irish *immram* genre. Other examples include 'The Voyage of Bran' and 'The Voyage of Maeldune'. The Latin allegory *Navigatio Sancti Brandani* has been dated to as early as the eighth century. The legends of Brendan have been periodically revived, for example by Matthew *Arnold. They include the story of his encountering Judas exercising his annual privilege of cooling himself on a rock on Christmas night; and of his landing on a whale, mistaking it for an island, and lighting a fire on its back. Folk tradition credits Brendan with reaching America nearly a thousand years before Columbus. Brendan is cited in the poetry of both Louis *MacNeice and Seamus *Heaney.

BRENT-DYER, Elinor M. (May) (1894–1969) Writer for children. She wrote over 100 books for girls, including the 60 books in the popular 'Chalet School' series, from *The School at the Chalet* (1925) to *Prefects at the Chalet School* (1970), and the 'La Rochelle' series (1922–53). The exotic locations of the Chalet School, which moves from the Tyrol to the Channel Islands, to Wales, and to the Oberland, are matched by an acute understanding of girls' interests.

BRENTON, Howard (1942–) Playwright. An avowed socialist, Brenton combines jagged writing with raw, *Jacobean theatricality. His first full-scale *Royal Court play *Magnificence* (1973) was followed by a collaboration with David *Hare, *Brassneck* (1973), *The Churchill*

Play (1974), and four highly successful productions at the *National Theatre: *Weapons of Happiness* (1976); a new version of Bertolt *Brecht's *Galileo*; *The Romans in Britain* (1980), an allegory of the British army presence in Northern Ireland; and, again with Hare, *Pravda* (1985), a savage attack on the power politics of the tabloid press. *Moscow Gold* (1990) and *Berlin Bertie* (1992) moved Brenton's work into the new Europe. *Paul* (2005) was a controversial version of the life of St *Paul; *In Extremis* (2006) used the story of Eloise and *Abelard to consider the historical significance of the struggle between faith and reason. Brenton has also written thirteen characteristically Gothic episodes for the television series *Spooks*.

BRERETON, Jane (1685–1740) Poet. Separated from her husband, she lived at Wrexham and wrote verse to a circle of women friends, collected posthumously as *Poems on Several Occasions* (1744). She also published an imitation of *Horace (1716) and *Merlin: A Poem* (1735).

BRETON, Nicholas (1554/5–*c*.1626) Author of miscellaneous satirical, religious, romantic, and political writings in verse and prose. His stepfather was George *Gascoigne. Between 1575 and 1622 he published well over 50 books including: *The Will of Wit, Wit's Will, or Will's Wit* (*c*.1582); *Wit's Trenchmore* (a partly autobiographical dialogue on angling, 1597); *The Old Mad-Cap's New Gallimaufry* (1602); and *The Good and the Bad, or Descriptions of the Worthies and Unworthies of this Age* (1616). His best poetry is to be found among his short lyrics in *Englands Helicon* (1600) and in his volume of pastoral poetry *The Passionate Shepherd* (1604).

Breton lays In medieval English literature, are short stories in rhyme like those of *Marie de France. For examples, *see* ORFEO, SIR; DEGARÉ, SIR; Chaucer's 'The Franklin's Tale' (*see* CANTERBURY TALES, 12) and John *Gower's 'Tale of Rosiphelee' (*Confessio Amantis*, Bk IV).

Brewer's Dictionary of Phrase and Fable By the Revd Ebenezer Cobham Brewer (1810–97), first published 1870, regularly revised. It provides explanations and origins of the familiar and unfamiliar in English phrase and fable, including colloquial and proverbial phrases, embracing archaeology, history, religion, the arts, science, mythology, fictitious characters and titles.

BREYTENBACH, Breyten (1939–) South African poet, autobiographer, and essayist who writes in English and Afrikaans. In *True Confessions of an Albino Terrorist* (1984) he gives an account of his seven-year incarceration in maximum security prisons for political activism. His playful, angry, surreal prose eludes conventional categories.

Bride of Abydos, The A poem in irregular stanzas by Lord *Byron, one of his 'Turkish tales', published in December 1813: it sold 6,000 copies within a month. The beautiful Zuleika, daughter of the Pacha Giaffir, is destined to marry the rich, elderly Bey of Carasman, whom she has never seen. She confesses her grief to her beloved brother Selim, who reveals himself in magnificent pirate garb and declares he is not her brother but her cousin. Selim is killed and Zuleika dies of grief. In the first draft Zuleika and Selim were not cousins but half-brother and sister: a variation of the incest theme to which Byron was frequently drawn.

Bride of Lammermoor, The A novel by Walter *Scott, published 1819 in *Tales of my Landlord*, 3rd series.

'Bridge of Sighs, The' A poem by Thomas *Hood, published 1843, one of the most popular of his serious works. It is a compassionate elegy on the suicide by drowning of a 'fallen woman'.

BRIDGES, Robert (1844–1930) Poet. At Oxford University he met G. M. *Hopkins, and became his friend, adviser, and influential advocate of his poetry, later editing *The Poems of Gerard Manley Hopkins* (1918). Bridges's first book, *Poems*, was published in 1873, followed by *The Growth of Love*, a sonnet sequence (1876), *Prometheus the Firegiver* (1883), and *Eros and Psyche* (1885). Between 1895 and 1908 he wrote the words for four works by the composer Hubert Parry. He was greatly interested in musical settings, and edited the *Yattendon Hymnal*. His *Poetical Works* appeared in six volumes (1898–1905), and in one volume in 1912, and received great critical and popular acclaim. He was appointed *poet laureate in 1913. His highly successful anthology, *The Spirit of Man* (1916) included six poems by Hopkins, whose work was mostly still unpublished. *October and Other Poems* (1920) and *New Verse* (1925) were followed by *The Testament of Beauty* (1929), a long poem, in four books, on his spiritual philosophy, which he saw as the culmination of his work as a poet, and which sold extremely well. One of the founders of the Society for Pure English, he collaborated on tracts with his wife Monica as 'Matthew Barnes'.

BRIDIE, James (1888–1951) Pseudonym of Osborne Henry Mavor, Scottish dramatist. He served in the Royal Army Medical Corps in both world wars, becoming a full-time writer in 1938. Though he helped found the Glasgow Citizens' Theatre in 1943, Bridie wrote mainly for the London stage. His plays include *The Anatomist* (1930), *A Sleeping Clergyman* (1933), *Mr Bolfry* (1943), and *The Queen's Comedy* (1950).

BRIGGS, Raymond (1934–) London-born author-illustrator of children's books; best known for his comic-strip style employed in long-standing favourites *Father Christmas* (1973), *Fungus the Bogeyman* (1977), and *The Snowman* (1979). *When the Wind Blows* (1982) is a remarkable portrayal of the reality of nuclear war for an ordinary couple, Jim and Hilda, as they take refuge in their hopelessly inadequate home-made fallout shelter. *Ethel and Ernest* (1998) is a memoir of his parents in comic-strip form. Notable *picturebook illustrations include those for Elfrida Vipont's *The Elephant and the Bad Baby* (1969).

BRIN, David (1950–) Born Glendale, California; novelist with a Ph.D. in space science, active in promoting *science fiction for its engagement with the future. His second novel, *Startide Rising* (1983) won the *Hugo award. *Earth* (1990) explores social and environmental issues over the next fifty years.

BRINK, André Philippus (1935–) South African playwright, novelist, short story writer, and critic. He writes most of his novels in both English and Afrikaans and was snubbed during the era of apartheid by the Afrikaans literary community for his dissidence. His *Kennis van die aand* (1973), translated into English as *Looking on Darkness* (1974), was banned by the South African government; it tells the story of a coloured actor who works against apartheid by cultural means. After a passionate affair with a white woman, he is executed by the Security Police. Other novels include *An Instant in the Wind* (1976); *Rumours of Rain* (1978) and *A Dry White Season* (1979, filmed 1989), both of which explore the moral ambiguities of Afrikaner nationalism; *A Chain of Voices* (1982); *The Wall of the Plague* (1984); *States of Emergency* (1988); *An Act of Terror* (1991); and *On the Contrary* (1993), a *picaresque biography of an 18th-century adventurer, Estienne Barbier. Brink's post-apartheid novels include *The Other Side of Silence* (2002) and *The Blue Door* (2007), based on

what-if? choices. *A Fork in the Road* (2009) is a memoir.

BRISCOE, Sophia (*fl.*1771–8) Novelist, author of two epistolary novels: *Miss Melmoth, or The New Clarissa* (1771), and *The Fine Lady* (1772).

BRISLEY, Joyce Lankester (1896–1978) Writer-illustrator best known for her stories about Milly-Molly-Mandy (1928–67), first published in the *Christian Science Monitor* (1925). The stories describe the kindly Milly-Molly-Mandy's life in an idyllic village. The author's sister was Nina K. Brisley, designer of the first covers for *Brent-Dyer's Chalet School books.

Britannia by William Camden, first published in Latin (1586), the sixth (much-enlarged) edition appearing in 1607. It was translated in 1610 by Philemon *Holland; reprints continued in the 18th and 19th centuries. It is in effect a guidebook of the country, county by county, replete with archaeological, historical, physical, and other information.

Britannia's Pastorals See   BROWNE, WILLIAM.

Britomart The heroine of Book III of Edmund *Spenser's *Faerie Queene*. She is the most powerful of several types of *Elizabeth I in the poem.

BRITTAIN, Vera (1893–1970) Writer, pacifist, and feminist. Her university education at Oxford, opposed by her parents, was interrupted by the First World War. Her *autobiographical *Testament of Youth* (1933) is a moving account of her early struggles, her war experiences, and her grief at the loss of both her fiancé, Roland Leighton, and brother Edward during the war. She returned to Oxford after the war, where she formed a close friendship with Winifred *Holtby, recorded in *Testament of Friendship* (1940). *Testament of Experience* (1957) continues her autobiography whilst her diaries, *Chronicles of Youth* (1981), which she drew on in *Testament of Youth*, were published posthumously.

BRITTEN, Benjamin (1913–76) English composer. He collaborated with W. H. *Auden on *Our Hunting Fathers* (1936), an orchestral song cycle written in reaction to the Spanish Civil War, and his first opera, *Paul Bunyan* (1941). Britten returned to England from America in 1942 and registered as a conscientious objector, with his partner, the tenor Peter

Pears (1910–86). Pacifism underlies *The War Requiem* (1962), written for the dedication of the new cathedral at Coventry: the Latin Mass for the Dead is punctuated by settings for solo voice of poems by Wilfred *Owen. Britten's *Owen Wingrave* (1971), an opera for television based on Henry *James's story, is also on the theme of resistance to war.

In the *Serenade for Tenor, Horn and Strings* (1943), and the *Spring Symphony* (1949) Britten sets poems ranging from a medieval dirge through *Spenser, *Jonson, and *Herrick, to *Blake and *Tennyson. The darkly audacious opera *Peter Grimes* (1945) is based on poems from George *Crabbe's *The Borough*; *Billy Budd* (1951) on Herman *Melville's novella via E. M. *Forster's libretto. The chamber opera *The *Turn of the Screw* (1954), is derived from Henry James's story; the three *Parables for Church Performance* (1964–68), stylized pieces on the model of the *Nōh play, all have libretti by William *Plomer.

Broad Church A popular term especially current in the latter half of the 19th century for those in the Church of England who sought to interpret the creeds in a broad and liberal manner. The expression was used by Arthur Penrhyn Stanley in one of his sermons, about 1847, though the term appears to have originally been proposed by Arthur Hugh *Clough. The existence of the Broad Church school owes much to the influence of Thomas Arnold and Romantic philosophy as interpreted by S. T. *Coleridge, who earned the title of 'Father of the Broad Church Movement'. Other characteristic representatives of the school were Thomas *Hughes, Benjamin Jowett, Mark *Pattison, and most of the other writers for *Essays and Reviews*.

Broceliande A legendary region adjoining Brittany, in the Arthurian legends, home of *Merlin.

BRODBER, Erna (1940–) Novelist and academic, concerned with the untold stories of her native Jamaica. Her fiction, *Jane and Louisa Will Soon Come Home* (1980), *Myal* (1988), and *Louisiana* (1994), focuses on the spiritual power of the community, and particularly of women, to heal those isolated by the disruption caused by colonialism, slavery, gossip, and sectarianism. The characters' voices cover a range of vernaculars.

BRODSKY, Joseph (1940–96) Russian poet, born in Leningrad. His early poetic talent was recognized by Anna *Akhmatova. In 1964 he was tried for 'parasitism', and spent eighteen months in exile in northern Russia. He was exiled from the Soviet Union in 1972, and settled in the United States, where he held a number of university posts. His first volume of poetry in English, *Joseph Brodsky: Selected Poems* (1973), shows his distinctive kind of dry, meditative soliloquy and technical accomplishment. In *A Part of Speech* (1980) he collaborated with a range of distinguished translators including Derek *Walcott, Richard *Wilbur, and David McDuff (1945–). The award of the *Nobel Prize in 1987 coincided with the first legal publication of his poetry in Russia. *To Urania: Selected Poems 1965–1985* (1988) brings together translations of his earlier work with poems composed in English during his years of exile. *Collected Poems in English* (2000) is the most extensive single volume of Brodsky's poetry in translation. His collections of essays in English, *Less than One* (1986) and *On Grief and Reason* (1995) are made up of critical studies (Osip *Mandelshtam, W. H. *Auden, Thomas *Hardy, Rainer Maria Rilke, Robert *Frost), autobiographical sketches, and portraits of a number of his contemporaries, including Anna Akhmatova, Nadezhda *Mandelshtam, Auden, and *Spender. *Watermark* (1992) is an episodic account of his fascination with Venice.

Broken Heart, The A tragedy by John *Ford, written 1625/33, printed 1633. The scene is Sparta. Spartan values of courage and self-control dominate the action. The stately language and emblematic imagery make this one of the greatest of Caroline tragedies. It has had successful modern revivals.

BROME, Alexander (1620–66) A Royalist poet and friend of Izaak *Walton and Charles *Cotton. He wrote many attacks on the Rump Parliament, including a ballad entitled *Bum-Fodder: or Waste-Paper Proper to Wipe the Nation's Rump with* (?1660). He also translated *Horace, wrote songs, and was the author of one comedy, *The Cunning Lovers* (1654).

BROME, Richard (*c.*1590–1652/3) Servant or perhaps secretary to Ben *Jonson, and dramatist. His plays show the influence of Jonson and Thomas *Dekker. *The *Northern Lass*, his first extant play, was printed in 1632. *The Sparagus Garden*, a comedy of manners, was acted in 1635. *The City Wit* was printed in 1653. *A *Jovial Crew*, his best and latest play, was acted in 1641, often revived, and later turned into an operetta. Fifteen in all of his plays survive, including romantic dramas in the manner of John *Fletcher and Thomas *Middleton.

BRONTË, Anne (1820–49) Novelist and poet, sister of Charlotte and Emily *Brontë. She was educated largely at home, where, as the youngest of the motherless family, she may have fallen under the Wesleyan influence of her Aunt Branwell, who is thought to have encouraged her tendency to religious introspection. Emily and Anne invented the imaginary world of Gondal, the setting of many of their poems. Anne became a governess in 1839; her recollections of her experiences with the overindulged young children and the worldly older children of the two households she worked for are vividly portrayed in *Agnes Grey* (1847). The novel appeared under the pseudonym Acton Bell, as did a selection of her poems, published with those of her sisters, in 1846. Anne's poems show the influence of William *Cowper and John *Wesley. Her second novel, The *Tenant of Wildfell Hall* (1848), portrays in Arthur Huntingdon a violent, infantile, but sexually attractive drunkard clearly to some extent drawn from her brother Branwell. The novel may be read as a scathing indictment of sexual double standards enshrined in marriage law and the educational system. Anne died of tuberculosis at Scarborough, where she was buried.

BRONTË, Branwell (1817–48) Artist and writer, the brother of Charlotte, Emily, and Anne *Brontë. He collaborated with Charlotte in creating the imaginary world of *Angria. His ambitions as a painter and writer were frustrated and he took to drink and opium; he was dismissed from his railway post in 1842 for culpable negligence. In 1843 he joined Anne at Thorp Green Hall as tutor, but became emotionally involved with his employer's wife, Mrs Robinson. The affair ended disastrously, and he returned to Haworth in 1845, where his rapid decline and death caused much suffering to his family.

BRONTË, Charlotte (1816–55) Novelist and poet, daughter of Patrick Brontë, an Irishman, perpetual curate of Haworth, Yorkshire. Charlotte's mother died in 1821, leaving five daughters and a son to the care of their aunt, Elizabeth Branwell. Four of the daughters were sent to a Clergy Daughters' School at Cowan Bridge (portrayed as Lowood in *Jane Eyre*), which Charlotte believed to have hastened the death in 1825 of her two elder sisters and to have permanently impaired her own health. The surviving children pursued their education at home; they read widely, and became involved in a rich fantasy life that owes much to their admiration of Lord *Byron, Walter *Scott, The *Arabian Nights, the Tales of the Genii, and the engravings of John Martin. They began to write stories, to produce microscopic magazines in imitation of their favourite *Blackwood's Magazine, and Charlotte and Branwell collaborated in the increasingly elaborate invention of the imaginary kingdom of *Angria, Emily and Anne in the invention of Gondal. In 1831–2 Charlotte was at Miss Wooler's school at Roe Head, returning as a teacher in 1835–8, then working as a governess; in 1842 she and Emily went to study languages at the Pensionnat Heger in Brussels. Charlotte fell deeply in love with M. Constantin Heger, who failed to respond to the letters she wrote to him after her return to Haworth. In 1845 she 'discovered' the poems of Emily, and projected a joint publication; a volume entitled Poems by Currer, Ellis, and Acton Bell (the pseudonyms of Charlotte, Emily, and Anne) appeared in 1846. Charlotte's first novel, The *Professor, never found a publisher in her lifetime, but *Jane Eyre* was published in 1847 by Smith, Elder and achieved immediate success, arousing much speculation about its authorship. To quell the suspicion that the Bell pseudonyms concealed a single author, Charlotte and Anne visited Smith, Elder in July 1848 and made themselves known.

Charlotte was not able to enjoy her success as the death of Branwell, in September 1848 was followed by Emily's death in December, and Anne's the following summer. Through this tragic period she persevered with the composition of *Shirley*, (1849). The loneliness of her later years was alleviated by friendship with Elizabeth *Gaskell, whom she met in 1850 and who was to write her biography (1857). Villette, founded on her memories of Brussels, appeared in 1853. Although her identity was by this time well known in the literary world, she continued to publish as Currer Bell. In 1854 she married her father's curate, Arthur Bell Nicholls, but died a few months later of an illness probably associated with pregnancy. 'Emma', a fragment, was published in 1860 in the *Cornhill Magazine with an introduction by W. M. *Thackeray, and many of her juvenile works have subsequently been published. In her lifetime, Charlotte was the most admired of the Brontë sisters, although she was criticized for her alleged 'grossness' and emotionalism, considered particularly unbecoming in a clergyman's daughter. More widespread, however, was praise for her depth of feeling and her courageous realism, and her works continue to hold high popular and critical esteem.

BRONTË, Emily (1818–48) Novelist and poet, sister of Charlotte and Anne *Brontë. She briefly attended the school at Cowan Bridge with Charlotte in 1824-5, and was then educated largely at home, where she was particularly close to Anne, with whom she created the imaginary world of Gondal, the setting for many of her finest narrative and lyric poems. She was even more intensely attached than her sisters to the moorland scenery her work evokes so vividly. She was briefly a governess, probably in 1838, and in 1842 spent nine months in Brussels with Charlotte, studying French, German, and music. She returned on her aunt's death at the end of the year to Haworth, where she spent the rest of her life. In 1845 Charlotte 'discovered' Emily's poems, and the joint publication, *Poems, by Currer, Ellis and Acton Bell*, appeared in 1846. *Wuthering Heights* was written between October 1845 and June 1846, and published by T. C. Newby in December 1847. Unlike Charlotte's *Jane Eyre*, it met with more incomprehension than recognition, and it was only after Emily's death (of tuberculosis) that it became widely acknowledged as a masterpiece. Emily's response to her apparent lack of success, like so much in her character, remains enigmatic. The vein of violence, of stoicism, and of mysticism in her personality have given rise to many legends but few certainties. She is now established as one of the most original poets of the century, remembered for her lyrics (e.g. 'The night is darkening round me'), for her passionate invocations from the world of Gondal ('Remembrance', 'The Prisoner'), and her apparently more personal visionary moments ('No coward soul is mine').

BROOK, Peter (1925–) Theatre director. The most innovative director of post-war Britain and Europe, he has worked with the Royal Shakespeare Company and the *National Theatre, directing classics (memorably, *King Lear*, 1962, and *A Midsummer Night's Dream*, 1970) and modern plays, but is most celebrated internationally for his experimental work. Landmark productions include Peter *Weiss's *Marat/Sade* (1964), *The Ik* (1975, a multicultural drama of African famine based on an anthropological premiss), the *Mahābhārata* (1985; UK 1988), and *L'Homme qui* (1993), based on a work by Oliver Sacks. Working with the Paris-based company, the International Centre for Theatre Creation, travelling widely, and transcending conventional notions of text and theatrical space, he has been a powerful influence on 20th-century theatre, drawing inspiration from many sources. His travels to Iran in 1971 with

Ted *Hughes resulted in Hughes's play in an invented language, *Orghast*. His *The Empty Space* (1968) is a highly influential work. *Tierno Bokar* (2005), was based on the life of an African mystic, adapted by Marie-Hélène Estienne from the West African writer Amadou Hampaté Bâ's *The Life and Teaching of Tierno Bokar: The Sage of Bandiagara* (1957; rev. 1980); he returned to the same subject in *Eleven and Twelve* (2010). *Threads of Time* (1998) is a memoir. *See also* CRUELTY, THEATRE OF.

BROOKE, Charlotte (1740–93) Irish translator, daughter of Henry *Brooke. Her dual language *Reliques of Irish Poetry* (1789) renders an annotated selection of Gaelic poems into polite English verse, providing the most remarkable Irish contribution to the vogue for literary antiquarianism associated with Thomas *Percy in England and Allan *Ramsay in Scotland.

BROOKE, Emma Frances (1844–1926) Radical novelist, journalist, and poet. She published *Millicent: A Poem* (1881) as 'E. Fairfax Byrrne', writing as Brooke after 1887. Her polemical *New Woman novels include *A Superfluous Woman* (1894), which deals with the plight of young women who unknowingly marry men with venereal disease, and *Life the Accuser* (1896). An early member of the Fabian Society, she was also secretary to the Karl Marx Club, and joined the Fellowship of the New Life commune, before moving in the 1880s to a radical community in Kent.

BROOKE, Frances (1724–89) Novelist and dramatist. She conducted the periodical *The Old Maid* in 1755-6, then in 1760 published *Letters from Juliet Lady Catesby*, translated from Riccoboni. The pessimistic but highly successful epistolary novel *History of Lady Julia Mandeville* (1763) was followed by *The History of Emily Montague* (1769). *The Excursion* (1777) exposes the superficial nature of 'good breeding', it originally contained an attack on David *Garrick, motivated by his rejection of Brooke's tragedy *Virginia* (1756). *The Siege of Sinope* (1781) was more successful, as were two musical plays, *Rosina* (1783) and *Marian* (1788).

BROOKE, Henry (1703–83) Irish writer and playwright, a friend of Alexander *Pope. In 1735 he published *Universal Beauty*, a poem thought to have influenced Erasmus *Darwin's *The Botanic Garden*. Encouraged by David *Garrick, he wrote several plays, but his tragedy *Gustavus Vasa* (1739) was prohibited on the grounds that the villain resembled Sir Robert *Walpole. In 1765-70 he published his highly successful

The *Fool of Quality, and in 1774 another novel, *Juliet Grenville*, both of which are notable for their looseness of structure and for a sustained tone of high sensibility. Brooke was the father of Charlotte *Brooke.

BROOKE, Rupert (1887–1915) Poet. *Poems* (1911) was followed by contributions to the first two volumes of **Georgian Poetry*, which he had helped to conceive, and a stark one-act play, *Lithuania* (1912). In 1913, following a serious breakdown, he travelled in the USA, Canada, and the Pacific. In Tahiti, he had an affair with a local woman, and wrote 'Tiara Tahiti' and other poems, often thought to be among his best. In 1914 he served as a Royal Naval officer. His five 'War Sonnets', including 'The Soldier', appeared in *New Numbers* in 1914 and then posthumously in *1914 and Other Poems* (1915). Brooke was dispatched to the Dardanelles, but he died of blood poisoning on the way and was buried on Skyros in April 1915. His best-known poems are the war sonnets, the Tahiti poems, and especially 'The Old Vicarage, Grantchester'. A man of beauty and charm, Brooke had many friends, including Frances *Cornford, Henry *James, and Virginia *Woolf. *The Letters of Rupert Brooke* appeared in 1968, edited by Geoffrey Keynes, who also edited *The Poetical Works* (1946). *The Collected Poems*, with a memoir by his friend Edward Marsh, had appeared in 1918.

BROOKE-ROSE, Christine (1923–2012) Novelist and critic, born in Geneva, brought up bilingually in Brussels, London, and Liverpool. She is best known for her experimental novels, marked by bilingual neologisms, which have some affinity with the **nouveau roman*; these include *Out* (1964), *Such* (1966), *Between* (1968), and *Thru* (1975). *Amalgamemnon* (1984), about a university teacher who is made redundant, was followed by *Xorandor* (1986), which concerns twins who make contact with a 4,000-year-old being through computer technology, *Verbivore* (1990), and *textermination* (1991). *Remake* (1996) and *Life, End of* (2006) are autobiographical.

BROOKNER, Anita (1928–) Novelist and art historian. From *A Start in Life* (1981) her fiction has dealt with women whose lives have become something to be endured rather than enjoyed. *Hotel du Lac* (1984) won the *Booker Prize and was adapted for television by Christopher *Hampton in 1986. *Family and Friends* (1985), was a compact family saga; *Lewis Percy* (1989) the first of several novels featuring a male protagonist. Producing on average a novel every year, Brookner has confined herself to a distinctive type of heroine and a small but elegantly realized and instantly recognizable fictional milieu.

BROOKS, Cleanth (1906–94) American critic. His college textbook *Understanding Poetry* (with R. P. *Warren, 1938) helped to establish the methods of the *New Criticism in classrooms. His major works of poetic criticism, *Modern Poetry and the Tradition* (1939) and *The Well Wrought Urn* (1947), both regard irony and paradox as the typical virtues of poetry, in lucid developments from T. S. *Eliot's critical arguments. His later essays appeared in *The Hidden God* (1963) and *A Shaping Joy* (1971).

BROOKS, Gwendolyn (1917–2000) African American poet who began publishing poems in her teens and taught creative writing at a number of universities. At a writers' conference in 1967 she announced her rediscovery of her blackness and the first major work to demonstrate this change was *In the Mecca* (1968), which uses free verse and reflects continuing influence from blues music. She published one novel, *Maud Martha*, in 1953.

BROPHY, Brigid (1929–95) Novelist, writer, and campaigner. Her first novel, *Hackenfeller's Ape* (1953), concerned the attempt by a zoologist to prevent an ape being sent into space and marked an early interest in animal rights. Other novels include *Flesh* (1962); *The Finishing Touch* (1963), a pastiche of Ronald *Firbank set in a girls' school; *The Snow Ball* (1964); *In Transit* (1969); and the subversively satirical *Palace without Chairs* (1978). Among her works of non-fiction are two studies of Aubrey *Beardsley; and a biography of Firbank, *Prancing Novelist* (1973). She was a leading campaigner for Public Lending Right and founded the Writers' Action Group with Maureen *Duffy.

BROUGHAM, Henry Peter Baron Brougham and Vaux (1778–1868) Statesman, lawyer, and author, who rose to be lord chancellor. In literary history he is principally remembered as one of the founders, with Francis *Jeffrey and Sydney *Smith, of the **Edinburgh Review* in 1802. He is said to have been the author of the disparaging article on **Hours of Idleness* in the *Edinburgh Review* of January 1808, an article which provoked Lord *Byron into writing **English Bards and Scotch Reviewers*. Of the many squibs written on Brougham's character and activities, the most famous is the lampoon in Thomas Love *Peacock's *Crotchet Castle.

BROUGHTON, Rhoda (1840–1920) Novelist. Her many light, witty novels of country-house and town life, with their lively and articulate heroines, gained her a reputation for audacity. She began her career with the three- and two-decker novels that were still popular (*Not Wisely, but Too Well*, 1867; *Cometh up as a Flower*, 1867; *Nancy*, 1873), but was possibly more at home with the form of her later short, sharp, observant one-volume novels, which include *Mrs Bligh* (1892), *Dear Faustina* (1897), *Lavinia* (1902, which boldly presents an anti-Boer War hero, fond of old lace), and *A Waif's Progress* (1905). Despite the more conservative tone of her later fiction, she never lost her sense of the ridiculous, nor her compassion for women who find themselves helplessly hemmed in by social circumstances beyond their control.

BROWN, Charles Brockden (1771–1810) American novelist and editor, remembered for four *Gothic novels, *Wieland* (1798), *Arthur Mervyn* (1799), *Ormond* (1799), and *Edgar Huntly* (1799). Although obviously indebted to William *Godwin and Mary *Wollstonecraft, these were pioneer works which gave Gothic romance an American setting and combined fiction with historical fact. A precursor of Edgar Allan *Poe, Brown was admired in England, notably by Walter *Scott, John *Keats, and the *Shelleys.

BROWN, George Douglas (1869–1902) Scottish novelist; his novel *The House with the Green Shutters* (1901) bitterly repudiated the *'Kailyard' idyll of Scottish village life. It allies a realist narrative style to a self-consciously tragic structure in its portrayal of John Gourlay, a tyrannical businessman whose power over the inhabitants of Barbie comes to a catastrophic end as a result of his inability to adapt to change. Brown published *Love and a Sword*, a boys' adventure novel, under the pseudonym Kennedy King in 1899.

BROWN, George Mackay (1921–96) Scottish poet, novelist, playwright, and short story writer, born and brought up in Stromness, Orkney, where he remained almost the whole of his life. He was taught by Edwin *Muir. All his work springs from a deep local source and is rooted in Norse saga, island folklore, the cycles of rural life, and a deep Christian faith (he converted to Roman Catholicism in 1961). His volumes of poetry include *Loaves and Fishes* (1959), *The Year of the Whale* (1969), and *Following a Lark* (1996). His collections of short stories include *A Calendar of Love* (1967) and *Winter Tales* (1995). His first novel, *Greenvoe* (1972), was set on an imaginary northern island, Hellya, which becomes the site for a military project called Operation Black Star. The story describes the resulting destruction of the village of Greenvoe against the unchanging and self-renewing backdrop of nature. This was followed by *Magnus* (1973) and *Beside the Ocean of Time* 1994. Other works include *An Orkney Tapestry* (1969), a medley of prose and verse, and a posthumously published autobiography, *For the Islands I Sing* (1997).

BROWN, Dr John (1810–82) Scottish physician and essayist, most of whose writings are contained in his three volumes of *Horae Subsecivae* (1858–82), including *Marjorie Fleming* and the memorable dog story *Rab and his Friends*.

BROWN, T. E. (Thomas Edward) (1830–97) Manx poet. He published *Betsy Lee: A Foc's'le Yarn* (1873), *Foc's'le Yarns* (1881), and other books of verse, most of it in the Manx dialect, and dealing with Manx life. His narrative verses stirred some controversy with their swearing and unblushing accounts of prostitutes.

BROWN, William Wells (1814–84) African American writer and abolitionist, born a slave in Kentucky. In 1834 he escaped north where he worked on Lake Erie steamboats and helped other fugitives reach Canada. He became an abolitionist lecturer, and moved to Boston, where he published *Narrative of William Wells Brown, a Fugitive Slave* (1847). He is credited with writing the first African American travel book: *Three Years in Europe* (1852), novel: *Clotel* (1853); and play: *The Escape* (1858). His other works include *The Black Man: His Antecedents, his Genius, and his Achievements* (1863), and another volume of autobiography, *My Southern Home* (1880).

BROWNE, Charles Farrar *See* WARD, ARTEMUS.

BROWNE, Hablot Knight (1815–82) Under the pseudonym 'Phiz', he illustrated some of the works of Charles *Dickens, R. S. *Surtees, and F. E. *Smedley.

BROWNE, Sir Thomas (1605–82) Doctor and writer. He studied medicine at Montpellier and Padua, received a doctorate from Leiden, and settled in Norwich in about 1637 to practise medic[...] *Medici*—first published without [...] 1642— strives to reconcile scienc[...]. An authorized edition was pub[...]. It was placed on the papal in[...]bited books in 1645. *Pseudodox[...]* (1646), commonly known as V[...] a compendium of esoteric lea[...]. In the 1650s he wrote for friends the shorter tracts *Hydriotaphia, Urn Burial, The *Garden of Cyrus*, and *A Letter to a Friend* (published 1690). *Christian Morals*, said to be a continuation of *Religio Medici*, and *Certain Miscellany Tracts* were also published posthumously. Browne's admirers have included Thomas *De Quincey, S. T. *Coleridge, and Charles *Lamb, and, more recently, Herman *Melville (who was influenced by his style, and called him 'a cracked archangel'), W. G. *Sebald, and Jorge Luis *Borges.

BROWNE, William (?1590–1645) Poet. He published *Britannia's Pastorals* (Bks I and II, 1613, 1616), a narrative poem in couplets interspersed with lyrics; Book III, unfinished, remained in manuscript until 1852. He also contributed to *The Shepheard's Pipe* (1614) with George *Wither and others. Among various epitaphs he wrote the well-known lines on the dowager countess of *Pembroke, 'Underneath this sable hearse | Lies the subject of all verse'. His poetry has been praised for its sensuous richness and accurate observation of nature, and these qualities influenced John *Milton, who echoes him in *'L'Allegro' and *Lycidas, and John *Keats.

BROWNING, Elizabeth Barrett (1806–61) Poet, the eldest of twelve children of Edward Barrett Moulton Barrett, plantation owner, and his wife Mary. Her early works *The Battle of Marathon* (1820) and *An Essay on Mind* (1826) were privately printed at her father's expense. She became versed in the classics and in prosodic theory, and later published translations from ancient and Byzantine Greek poetry. Her *Prometheus Bound, Translated from the Greek of Aeschylus, and Miscellaneous Poems* (1833)—as the production of a self-educated young woman—prompted critical praise. Mary Russell *Mitford, whom Elizabeth first met in 1836, became an encouraging friend. In 1838, seriously ill, she was sent to Torquay where, two years later, her eldest brother Edward (known as 'Bro') was drowned, to her lifelong grief. The poems 'De Profundis' and 'Grief' record the pain of this period. She returned to London, still unwell, in 1841.

Her prolific creativity of 1841–4 culminated in *Poems* (1844), which confirmed her place as a significant poet. She was Alfred *Tennyson's rival for the laureateship of 1850. This publication also prompted Robert *Browning to write to her in 1845. Their courtship, from May 1845 until their marriage in September 1846, is recorded in their collected correspondence. The marriage was necessarily secret since Elizabeth's strong-minded father forbade his adult children to marry (on his discovery of the union he disinherited her) and the Brownings left England for Italy. Their only child, Robert Wiedemann Barrett Browning (known as Penini, or Pen), was born in Casa Guidi, their apartment in Florence, 1849. The *Sonnets from the Portuguese* (1850) bear eloquent witness to the conflicts and strength of her love for Browning, and were followed by *Casa Guidi Windows* (1851), on the theme of Italian liberation. Her principal work, *Aurora Leigh*, appeared in 1856.

Throughout her married life Elizabeth Barrett Browning's poetic reputation stood higher than Browning's in public opinion, though her progressive social ideas and audacious prosodic experiments were alarming for some. The highly political *Poems before Congress* (1860), which concluded with 'A Curse for a Nation', diminished her popularity; but *Last Poems*, issued posthumously in 1862, contained some of her best-known lyrics.

BROWNING, Robert (1812–89) Poet, the son of Robert Browning (d. 1866) and Sarah Anna Wiedemann (d. 1849), of German-Scottish descent. He received his education mainly in his father's large (6,000 vols) and eclectic library. The contrasting influences of his boyhood were those of his reading (particularly of P. B. *Shelley, Lord *Byron, and John *Keats) and an atmosphere of Nonconformist piety. His first published poem, *Pauline*, appeared anonymously in 1833 and attracted little notice. Browning travelled to Russia in 1834 and made his first trip to Italy in 1838. *Paracelsus* (1835) was a critical success, as a result of which Browning formed several important friendships, notably with John *Forster and William *Macready, who persuaded him to write for the stage; he also met Thomas *Carlyle, Charles *Dickens, and Alfred *Tennyson. In 1837 his play *Strafford* was produced at Covent Garden. The obscurity of his next published poem, *Sordello* (1840), led to a hostile reception which eclipsed his reputation for over twenty years. *Bells and Pomegranates* was completed by 1846. He began corresponding with Elizabeth Barrett (see BROWNING, E. B.) in January 1845 when, after returning from his second trip to Italy, he read and admired her 1844 *Poems*. They finally married and eloped to Italy in September 1846. They lived mainly in Italy until Elizabeth's death in 1861. They had one child, Robert Wiedemann Barrett Browning ('Pen', 1849–1913). In 1850 Browning published **Christmas-Eve and Easter-Day* and in 1855 the central work of his middle period, **Men and Women*, which, together with **Dramatis Personae* (1864), began to revive his reputation; the revival was completed by the success of *The *Ring and the Book* (1868–9). Meanwhile he had returned to England after Elizabeth's death. He was awarded an honorary fellowship by Balliol College, Oxford, whose master Benjamin Jowett was a close friend. The Browning Society was founded in 1881. Browning's publications after *The Ring and the Book* were: *Balaustion's Adventure* (1871), *Prince Hohenstiel-Schwangau* (1871), **Fifine at the Fair* (1872), **Red Cotton Night-Cap Country* (1873), **Aristophanes' Apology* (1875), *The *Inn Album* (1875), **Pacchiarotto . . . With Other Poems* (1876), *The *Agamemnon of Aeschylus* (1877), **La Saisiaz* and *The Two Poets of Croisic* (1878), **Dramatic Idyls* (1879), **Dramatic Idyls, Second Series* (1880), **Jocoseria* (1883), *Ferishtah's Fancies* (1884), **Parleying with Certain People of Importance in their Day* (1887), and *Asolando* (1889). Browning issued collections of his work in 1849, 1863, 1868, and 1888–9; he died in Venice and is buried in Westminster Abbey.

BROWNJOHN, Alan (1931–) Poet; he taught 1953–79 before becoming a full-time writer. He was a member of Philip Hobsbaum's **Group, and also has affiliations with the **Movement poets. He has published an early booklet of poems, *Travellers Alone* (1954), and volumes including *The Railings* (1961), *The Observation Car* (1990), *The Men around her Bed* (2004), and a *Collected Poems* in 2006. Brownjohn's poetry is characteristically good-humoured, ironic, and urbane. In Peter **Porter's phrase, it unites 'wit and civic responsibility' in a survey of contemporary social, domestic, and literary life. He has also written novels, children's books, and a study of Philip **Larkin.

BRUCE, Dorita Fairlie (1885–1970) Born Palos, Spain, educated at Clarence House, London. Bruce wrote popular girls' **school stories, notably nine 'Dimsie' books, from *The Senior Prefect* (1920; as *Dimsie Goes to School*, 1925) to *Dimsie Carries On* (1941).

BRUCE, James (1730–1794) Traveller and explorer, known as 'Abyssinian' Bruce. His five-volume *Travels to Discover the Source of the Nile* (1790) recounts an epic journey into Abyssinia (modern-day Ethiopia), undertaken between 1768 and 1772 with an Italian draughtsman named Luigi Balugani (who died during the expedition). On Bruce's return to Britain in 1774, his lurid and often self-glorifying reports of Abyssinian life were met with disbelief and ridicule; it was pointed out, by Samuel **Johnson among others, that the source of the Blue Nile had been discovered by Jesuit missionaries in the 17th century. *Travels*, intended to rebut these charges, only renewed the controversy, but many of his claims and scientific findings were corroborated in a posthumous second edition.

Bruce, The See BARBOUR, JOHN.

Brunanburh A poem in Old English (West Saxon dialect), included in four manuscripts of the **Anglo-Saxon Chronicles* under the year 937, dealing with the battle fought between the English (under Athelstan, the grandson of Alfred) and the Danes (under Olaf III Guthfrithson from Dublin, supported by Olaf's father-in-law, the Scots king Constantine II, and some Welsh). The site of the battle is currently unknown, but is thought to be somewhere on the west coast of England, between Chester and Dumfries. Bromborough on the Wirral peninsula is one suggested location. The poem is a triumphant celebration of the deeds of Athelstan and his brother and successor Edmund, in their defeat of the invaders. Alfred **Tennyson wrote a verse translation (*Ballads and Other Poems*, 1880).

Brut (Brutus) Legendary founder of the British race. **Geoffrey of Monmouth claims that Walter, archdeacon of Oxford, gave him an ancient book containing an account of the kings of Britain from Brutus to Cadwallader. Brutus was son of Sylvius, grandson of Ascanius, and great-grandson of Aeneas. Having killed his father, he brought a remnant of the Trojan race to England (uninhabited at the time 'except by a few giants'), landing at Totnes. He founded Troynovant or New Troy (later known as London) and was the progenitor of a line of British kings including Bladud, **Gorboduc, Ferrex and Porrex, **Lud, **Cymbeline, Coel, **Vortigern, and **Arthur. 'Brut' came to be used to mean 'chronicle of the Britons' in writings by Geoffrey of Monmouth's followers, such as the Norman poet **Wace, in his *Roman de Brut*, and the English **Laȝamon in the alliterative poem *Brut*.

Brut, The Prose A long English version, translated in the late 14th century, of the Anglo-Norman prose *Brut* which extends up to 1333. Over 180 copies are known, and the narrative was extended several times to take account of events between 1377 and 1461.

BRUTUS, Dennis (1924–2009) Poet. In radical opposition to apartheid he became president of the South African Non-Racial Olympic Committee which resulted in the exclusion of South Africa from international sport and his own imprisonment on Robben Island. He lived in the USA from 1971. His prison poems 'Letters to Martha' describe the self as its own labyrinth. His poetry records dogged resistance: *A Simple Lust* (1973), *Stubborn Hope* (1978), and *Leafdrift* (2005). *Poetry and Protest* (2005) collects interviews, poetry, and essays.

BRUTUS, Marcus Junius (*c.*85–42 BC) Roman republican, leader of the conspiracy to assassinate Julius *Caesar, and enemy of Marcus Antonius; after defeat at the battle of Philippi he committed suicide. He is included in *Plutarch's lives, and is the principal character in *Shakespeare's *Julius Caesar*. In *Dante's *Inferno* he is a monster of ingratitude.

BRYAN, Sir Francis (d. 1550) Poet and courtier, nephew of Lord Berners. A favourite of *Henry VIII's. His reputation was for telling the king the truth; distancing himself from his cousin Anne Boleyn, he earned the nickname 'the vicar of hell' from Thomas Cromwell. Bryan was a friend of Thomas *Wyatt, contributed to Richard *Tottel's *Miscellany* and his poetry was highly valued in his day, but is now, with the exception of a translation of Antonio de Guevara's *A Dispraise of the Life of a Courtier* (1548), almost entirely undiscoverable.

BRYHER (1894–1983) The pseudonym of Winifred Ellerman, novelist, poet, and patron of the arts. Bryher married twice, in 1921 and 1927, but by far her deepest relationship was with the poet Hilda *Doolittle (H.D.), whom she met in 1918 and to whom she remained devoted until H. D.'s death in 1961. Bryher published three autobiographical fictions, *Development* (1920), *Two Selves* (1923), and *West* (1925).

BRYSON, Bill (1951–) American travel writer. He moved to England in 1977 and is best known for his humorous, ambling narratives and irreverent social commentary, starting with *The Lost Continent: Travels in Small Town America* (1989). *Neither Here Nor There* (1991)

retraces a backpacking tour of Europe he made in his youth, and the hugely successful *Notes from a Small Island* (1995) recalls a valedictory trip around Britain before he returned to the United States. An Appalachian trek is the subject of *A Walk in the Woods* (1997) while *Notes from a Big Country* (1998) offers reflections on his homeland after twenty years abroad. Subsequent books include a memoir, *The Life and Times of the Thunderbolt Kid* (2006), and popular books on the English language (*Mother Tongue*, 1990; *Made in America*, 1994), science (*A Short History of Almost Everything*, 2004), and Shakespeare (2007).

BUCHAN, John, Baron Tweedsmuir (1875–1940) Author and publisher. While still at Oxford University he published a novel (*Sir Quixote of the Moors*, 1895) and a volume of essays (*Scholar Gipsies*, 1896). From the beginning he combined a literary career with a career in public life. He is remembered for his adventure stories, the first of which was *Prester John* (1910), set in Africa. Many of his other tales feature a recurring group of heroes (Richard Hannay, Sandy Arbuthnot, Peter Pienaar, Edward Leithen, etc.) and are set in Scotland, the Cotswolds, and South Africa. His last novel, *Sick Heart River* (1941) is set in the icy wastes of Canada, where he was governor general. The novels are packed with action, often involving elaborate cross-country chases; the characterization is simple, the landscapes are lovingly evoked. The most popular include *The Thirty-Nine Steps* (1915; filmed by Alfred *Hitchcock, 1935), *Greenmantle* (1916), and *Mr Standfast* (1919).

BUCHANAN, George (1506–82) Poet, humanist scholar, and historian, born in Scotland; he satirized the Franciscans, was condemned for heresy, and imprisoned at St Andrews. Escaping on the Continent, he became a professor at Bordeaux, where he wrote four Latin plays (*Baptistes*, *Medea*, *Jephthes*, and *Alcestis*) and taught *Montaigne. In 1547 he went to teach in the University of Coimbra, but was imprisoned by the Inquisition and tried for heresy. During this period he produced a celebrated Latin version of the Psalms. Released in 1552, he returned eventually to Scotland and professed himself a Protestant. He became a bitter enemy of *Mary Queen of Scots after the murder of Darnley, writing his *Detectio Maria Scotorum Regina* in 1571. He was tutor to *James VI and I during 1570–8. Buchanan's Latin poem *Sphaera* is an exposition of the Ptolemaic system against that of Copernicus; and his *Rerum*

Scoticarum Historia (1582), was long regarded as a standard authority. He wrote two vernacular works: *Ane Admonition*, and the *Chamaeleon*.

BUCHANAN, Robert Williams (1841–1901) Poet, essayist, novelist, and playwright, the son of a tailor who owned several socialist journals in Glasgow. Buchanan published many novels, poems, and plays, but is remembered now for his assaults on A. C. *Swinburne (whom he satirized in a poem 'The Session of the Poets' in the *Spectator* 1866) and on the *Pre-Raphaelites. He attacked D. G. *Rossetti in 'The Fleshly School of Poetry' in the *Contemporary Review* (1871) under the pseudonym 'Thomas Maitland'. After Rossetti's death, Buchanan altered his argument in an essay in *A Look Round Literature* (1887), in which he declared that Rossetti 'uses amatory forms and carnal images to express ideas which are purely and remotely spiritual'.

BÜCHNER, Georg (1813–37) German dramatist and radical. *Dantons Tod* (*The Death of Danton*), set in 1794 at the height of the Terror, was the only drama to be published in his lifetime (1835). Stephen *Spender collaborated on a version for the Group Theatre (1937), and a version by Howard *Brenton was performed at the National Theatre (1982). *Woyzeck* (pub. 1879), whose eponymous hero, a mentally unstable soldier, murders his common-law wife out of jealousy, was left unfinished at his death from typhus in Zurich. The play's innovative style anticipates features of both *naturalism and *Expressionism; it was also the basis of an opera by Alban Berg (*Wozzeck*, 1925).

BUCK, Pearl Sydenstricker (1892–1973) American novelist, playwright, and political commentator, who was educated and spent much of her early life in China. She is best known for her novel *The Good Earth* (1931), which describes the laborious rise to prosperity of a Chinese farmer. Buck championed the cause of cross-race adoptions and fervently opposed the Communist regime in China. She was awarded the Nobel Prize in 1938.

BUCKERIDGE, Anthony (1912–2004) Writer for children and teacher, remembered for his many humorous *school stories about the well-intentioned schoolboy Jennings and his friend Darbishire. Beginning in 1948 with *Jennings Learns the Ropes*, a radio play for the BBC's *Children's Hour*; numerous episodes followed until 1962. *Jennings goes to School* (1950) was the first of twenty-two Jennings books, all based on Buckeridge's observations of his pupils.

BUCKHURST, Lord *See* SACKVILLE, THOMAS.

Buckingham, duke of In Shakespeare's *Richard III*; he acts as Richard's ally in murdering Lord Hastings, but defects to Richmond after his master fails to reward him. The line 'Off with his head! So much for Buckingham' occurs in Colley *Cibber's adaptation (1700).

BUCKINGHAM, George Villiers, second duke of (1628–87) A prominent figure in the reign of Charles II, and the Zimri of John *Dryden's *Absalom and Achitophel*. His burlesque *The *Rehearsal*, was often performed in the 18th century with topical additions and substitutions. Famed for his debauchery and amorous adventures, the miserable death of 'this lord of useless thousands' in 'the worst inn's worst room' is described by Alexander *Pope in his *Epistle III* (*Epistles to Several Persons*). He also figures in Walter *Scott's *Peveril of the Peak*.

BUKOWSKI, Charles (1920–94) American poet, novelist, and screenwriter. His series of novels revolving around the semi-autobiographical persona of an uninhibited antisocial bachelor includes *Post Office* (1971) and *Women* (1978). Bukowski's writing tends to blur the boundary between poetry and prose, and he has been associated with the *Beat Generation.

BULGAKOV, Mikhail Afanasevich (1891–1940) Russian prose writer and dramatist. After the revolution he worked in Moscow as a journalist and wrote satirical and humorous stories and plays. By the late 1920s his plays were banned from the repertoire and his prose could not be published. His request to Stalin for permission to emigrate was answered with the offer of a post at the *Moscow Arts Theatre; in 1932 Stalin intervened again by ordering a revival of Bulgakov's play *The Days of the Turbins*. Thereafter the relationship between the writer and the state became a central theme in Bulgakov's writing. His major works include stories: 'The Fatal Eggs' (1924), 'The Heart of a Dog' (1925); novels: *The White Guard* (1924, a sympathetic portrait of a White Russian family in Kiev after the Revolution), *A Theatrical Novel* (*Black Snow*) (1936–7); and plays: *The Days of the Turbins* (1925–6), an adaptation of *The White Guard, Flight* (1926–8), *A Cabal of Hypocrites* (a play about *Molière) (1930–6). His masterpiece, *The Master and Margarita* (1928–40; pub. 1966–7; trans. 1992), is a Faustian tale of the devil's appearance in contemporary

Moscow and his relationship with a writer and his beloved, coupled with a narrative set in ancient Jerusalem in which Pilate condemns an innocent man to be crucified.

BULWER-LYTTON, Edward George Earle Lytton, first Baron Lytton (1803–73) Novelist, playwright, poet, editor, and MP whose versatile and prolific literary output financed his extravagant life as a man of fashion. His first success, *Pelham, or The Adventures of a Gentleman* (1828), was a lively novel of the *fashionable school, bearing some resemblance to Disraeli's recent *Vivian Grey. His *'Newgate' novels were more in the 'reforming' manner of William *Godwin, e.g. *Paul Clifford* (1830), about a philanthropic highwayman, and *Eugene Aram* (1832), about a repentant murderer. He also wrote popular *historical novels, including *The Last Days of Pompeii* (1834); tales of the occult, including *Zanoni* (1842) and *A Strange Story* (1862); and a *science fiction fantasy, *The *Coming Race* (1871). He was editor of the *New Monthly Magazine*, 1831–3, and wrote three plays, the romantic comedy *The Lady of Lyons, or Love and Pride* (perf. 1838), the historical play *Richelieu, or the Conspiracy* (perf. 1839), and the comedy *Money* (perf. 1840), all of which have been successfully revived. His published verse includes his earliest *Byronic tale, *Ismael* (1820); *The New Timon* (1846), an anonymous satirical poem in which he attacked Alfred *Tennyson as 'School-Miss Alfred'; and an epic, *King Arthur* (1848–9). Bulwer-Lytton made many enemies in his turbulent career, which was not helped by his disastrous marriage and separation from his wife Rosina in 1836 (*see* BULWER LYTTON, ROSINA, LADY); he was the frequent butt of *Fraser's Magazine*, of John *Lockhart, and of W. M. *Thackeray. Nevertheless he had powerful friends and admirers, including Benjamin *Disraeli and Charles *Dickens.

BULWER LYTTON, Rosina, Lady (1802–82) Novelist, born in Ireland. Her mother was a radical feminist, her father an alcoholic. Moving to London in her early twenties, she made friends with Letitia *Landon and Lady Caroline *Lamb, and in 1827 married Edward Bulwer, later *Bulwer-Lytton. Their stormy separation in 1836, after the birth of two children and his increasing unfaithfulness, permanently embittered her. Feeling acutely the powerlessness of a woman in her situation she turned to near-libellous publication, producing *Cheveley, or The Man of Honour* (1839), satirizing her husband's hypocrisy, followed by a string of equally spirited but less successful novels, as well as various public petitions and pamphlets. He retaliated by intimidating her publishers, withholding her allowance, denying her access to the children, and finally, in 1858, by having her forcibly committed to an asylum from which she was released only by public outcry. She published a memoir, *A Blighted Life*, in 1880. Her life was published in 1887 by Louisa Devey, incorporating material from *Letters of the Late Edward Bulwer, Lord Lytton, to his Wife*, ed. Louisa Devey (1884).

BUNIN, Ivan Alekseevich (1870–1953) Russian prose writer and poet. His popular early works include *The Village* (1910), *Sukhodol* (1912), and *The Gentleman from San Francisco* (1916). Totally opposed to the October Revolution of 1917, Bunin left Russia in 1918, eventually settling permanently in France. *The Accursed Days* (1935) is a diary of the post-revolutionary period, *The Life of Arsenev* (1930–9), an autobiographical novel. In 1933 Bunin became the first Russian to win the *Nobel Prize for Literature. His final volume of stories was *Dark Avenues* (1943). Bunin was a consistent opponent of *modernism, but remained aloof from other literary schools. He translated into Russian Lord *Byron's *Cain, *Manfred, and *Heaven and Earth*, Henry Wadsworth *Longfellow's *The Song of *Hiawatha*, and Alfred *Tennyson's *Lady Godiva*; *The Gentleman from San Francisco and Other Stories*, was translated by D. H. *Lawrence, S. S. Koteliansky, and Leonard *Woolf (1922).

BUNTING, Basil (1900–85) Poet, educated at Quaker schools (Ackworth and Leighton Park). Although he had been published abroad (*Redimiculum Matellarum*, Milan, 1930; *Poems*, Texas, 1950; *The Spoils*, 1951, *Poetry Chicago*) and had a considerable reputation among younger American poets as an important figure in the *modernist movement, he was virtually unknown in his own country until the appearance of his long, semi-autobiographical, and deeply Northumbrian poem *Brigflatts* (1966), named after the Quaker hamlet of Brigflatts. His *Collected Poems* (1978) includes translations ('Overdrafts') from Latin and Persian. *The Complete Poems*, edited by Richard Caddel, was published in 1994.

BUNYAN, John (1628–88) Preacher and writer of religious works, born at Elstow, near Bedford, the son of a brazier. He learned to read and write at the village school and was early set to his father's trade. He was drafted into the

Parliamentary army and was stationed at Newport Pagnell, 1644–6. In 1649 he married his first wife, who introduced him to two religious works, Dent's *Plain Man's Pathway to Heaven* and Bayly's *Practice of Piety*; these, the *Bible, the Prayer Book, and John *Foxe's *Acts and Monuments* were his principal reading matter. In 1653 he joined a Nonconformist church in Bedford, preached there, and came into conflict with the Quakers (*see* FRIENDS, SOCIETY OF), against whom he published his first writings, *Some Gospel Truths Opened* (1656) and *A Vindication* (1657). He married his second wife Elizabeth *c.*1659, his first having died *c.*1656 leaving four children. As an itinerant tinker who presented his Puritan mission as apostolic and placed the poor and simple above the mighty and learned, Bunyan was viewed by the Restoration authorities as a militant subversive. Arrested in November 1660 for preaching without a licence, he was derided at his trial as 'a pestilent fellow'. Bunyan spent most of the next twelve years in Bedford Jail. During the first half of this period he wrote nine books, including his spiritual autobiography, *Grace Abounding to the Chief of Sinners* (1666). After his release in 1672 he was appointed pastor at the same church, but was imprisoned again for a short period in 1677 during which he probably finished the first part of The *Pilgrim's Progress*, partly written during the latter years of the first imprisonment. The first part was published in 1678, and the second, together with the whole work, in 1684. His other principal works are *The Holy City* (1665), *A Confession of my Faith* (1672), *The Life and Death of Mr *Badman* (1680) and *The Holy War* (1682). Bunyan preached in many places, his down-to-earth, humorous, and impassioned style drawing crowds of hundreds, but was not further molested.

BURBAGE, James (*c.*1531–1597) Actor, father of Richard *Burbage. He was leader of the Earl of Leicester's Players by 1572. He leased land in Shoreditch (1576), on which he erected The Theatre, England's first major building specially intended for plays. The fabric was removed in December 1598 to the Bankside and set up as the *Globe Theatre. In 1596 he converted the *Blackfriars for the Lord Chamberlain's Men but they were not able to occupy it until 1608.

BURBAGE, Richard (?1567–1619) Actor, son of James *Burbage. He acted as a boy at The Theatre in Shoreditch and rose to be an actor of chief parts, 1595–1618, in plays by William *Shakespeare, Ben *Jonson, and Francis *Beaumont and John *Fletcher. He excelled in tragedy.

BURDEKIN, Katherine (1896–1963) Novelist. *Swastika Night* (1937), published under the pseudonym Murray Constantine, describes a future dominated by a victorious Nazi regime where the deification of Hitler and the brutal subjugation of women is slowly questioned when a young Englishman is given a book that reveals some of the truth. The influence on George *Orwell is clear. Other novels include *The Burning Ring* (1927) and the posthumously published *The End of This Day's Business* (1990).

BURGESS, Anthony (John Anthony Burgess Wilson) (1917–93) Novelist. His early career included years (1954–60) as an education officer in the colonial service in Malaya and Borneo. His first three novels, *Time for a Tiger* (1956), *The Enemy in the Blanket* (1958), and *Beds in the East* (1959), were published together as *The Malayan Trilogy* in 1972. *A Clockwork Orange* (1962, film dir. Stanley Kubrick, 1971), is a dystopian vision of 'ultra violence', high technology, and authoritarianism. Other works include a Rabelaisian sequence, brimming with pastiche, social satire, and linguistic panache, about a gross, fitfully inspired poet (*Inside Mr Enderby*, 1963, under the pseudonym 'Joseph Kell'; *Enderby Outside*, 1968; *The Clockwork Testament*, 1974; and *Enderby's Dark Lady*, 1984). *Earthly Powers* (1980), is a long, ambitious novel which combines real and fictitious characters to produce a panorama of the 20th century; *The Kingdom of the Wicked* (1985) is about early Christianity, and *Any Old Iron* (1989), a debunking of myths about military glory and racial purity. Burgess also published novels on *Shakespeare (*Nothing Like the Sun*, 1964) and Christopher *Marlowe (*A Dead Man in Deptford*, 1993); two volumes of 'Confessions', *Little Wilson and Big God* (1987) and *You've Had your Time* (1990); biographies of Shakespeare (1970), Ernest *Hemingway (1978), and D. H. *Lawrence (1985); an abundance of critical works (notably on James *Joyce), translations, books on language, screenplays, television scripts, and a torrent of reviews. His last, posthumous, novel, *Byrne* (1995), in the *ottava rima* form of *Byron's *Don Juan*, recounts the life of a philandering and pugnacious artist from a Lancashire Catholic working-class background strongly resembling Burgess's own.

BURGESS, Melvin (1954–) Controversial writer for children and young adults known for tackling topical issues, from animal rights to plastic surgery; best known for *Junk* (1996), about teenage runaways who become addicted to heroin and engage in stealing and prostitution, and two books about adolescent sexuality that became notorious, *Lady: My Life as a Bitch* (2001) and *Doing It* (2003, screened on US television as *Life as We Know It*, 2004–5). Burgess also writes film scripts and has retold the Icelandic *Volsund* *saga in *Bloodtide* (1999) and *Bloodsong* (2005).

'Burial of Sir John Moore, The' *See* WOLFE, CHARLES.

BURKE, Edmund (1729–97) Irish polemicist and politician. He moved to London in 1750, and made many lasting friendships with literary and artistic figures, including Samuel *Johnson (of whose Club he was a founding member), Oliver *Goldsmith, Joshua *Reynolds, David *Garrick, and the *Blue Stockings; he championed emerging writers such as Fanny *Burney and George *Crabbe. In 1757 he published *A Philosophical Enquiry into . . . the *Sublime and Beautiful*, and in 1759 started the *Annual Register*, to which he contributed until 1788. Other important publications include *Thoughts on the Cause of the Present Discontents* (1770), partly in relation to the Wilkes crisis and *Reflections on the Revolution in France* (1790). Burke's political life was devoted to several causes: the emancipation of the House of Commons from the control of George III and the 'King's friends'; the emancipation of the American colonies; the emancipation of Irish Catholics; the emancipation of India from the East India Company; and opposition to the Jacobinism of the French Revolution. For this last he was attacked by radicals, such as Thomas *Paine and William *Godwin, who considered he had betrayed his faith in political liberty. Goldsmith had described him in 1774 in a mock epitaph as one who 'born for the universe, narrowed his mind, | And to party gave up what was meant for mankind' (*Retaliation*). But *Wordsworth in The *Prelude saluted him as one who 'declares the vital power of social ties | Endeared by custom'. His prose was enormously admired by William *Hazlitt. Matthew *Arnold declared that 'almost alone in England, he brings thought to bear upon politics, he saturates politics with thought' (1864).

BURKE, Gregory (1968–) Scottish playwright, who shot to prominence with *Gagarin Way* (2001), a comic play about the rise and fall of the Soviet Empire, named after a road in west

Fife commemorating the first Russian astronaut. His *Black Watch*, on the history of the famous regiment, culminating in its deployment in Iraq, was the hit of the 2006 Edinburgh Festival. *Hoors* (2009) is a black comedy set in a time of recession.

BURKE, Kenneth (1897–1986) American literary theorist. He lived among artists in Greenwich Village, and acted as compositor for the first American printing of T. S. *Eliot's The *Waste Land. His early writings include a novel, a book of short stories, a literary essay, *Counter-Statement* (1931), and a theoretical work on systems of interpretation, *Permanence and Change* (1935). *The Philosophy of Literary Form* (1941) collects his critical essays of the 1930s. *A Grammar of Motives* (1945), *A Rhetoric of Motives* (1950), and the essays collected in *Language as Symbolic Action* (1966) are complex investigations into the workings of metaphor and other 'master-tropes', and propose a scheme of analysis by which formal features of texts can be understood in larger political and psychological terms. *See* NEW CRITICISM; PSYCHOANALYTIC CRITICISM; MARXIST LITERARY CRITICISM.

burlesque [from the Italian *burla*, ridicule, mockery] A literary composition or dramatic representation founded on the comical treatment of a serious subject or the caricature of the spirit of a serious work. Notable examples include Samuel Butler's *Hudibras* and James Joyce's *Ulysses*.

BURNET, Gilbert (1643–1715) A popular preacher, influenced by the *Cambridge Platonists, and a Whig. He refused four bishoprics before he was 29, and in 1674 was dismissed from the post of king's chaplain for his outspoken criticisms of Charles II. He became bishop of Salisbury in 1689. His account of the deathbed repentance of *Rochester, *Some Passages in the Life and Death of the Right Honourable John Wilmot Earl of Rochester*, appeared in 1680. His best-known work, *The History of my Own Times*, is a mixture of history, autobiography, and anecdote, and was published posthumously (2 vols, 1724, 1734).

BURNETT, Frances Hodgson (1849–1924) A writer of romances with fairy-tale roots, born in Manchester. She moved to the USA, where she produced hack-work to support her family until becoming internationally successful with *That Lass o' Lowrie's* (1877) and *Little Lord Fauntleroy* (1886, filmed 1914, 1921, 1936, and 1980). This book set a fashion for boys to be dressed in velvet suits with lace collars and long hair, endured by Compton *MacKenzie and A. A. *Milne, among others. Other lasting successes were *A Little Princess* (1905, filmed 1917, 1939, and 1995), developed from the novella *Sara Crewe* (1887), and *The Secret Garden* (1911), adapted by the BBC in 1975. *The One I Knew Best of All* (1893) is a memoir of her childhood.

BURNEY, Fanny (Frances, Mme d'Arblay) (1752–1840) Novelist and dramatist, daughter of the music historian Charles Burney (1726–1814), educated at home. She grew up in the midst of a London society which included Samuel *Johnson, Edmund *Burke, Sir Joshua *Reynolds, the *Thrales, the *Blue Stockings, and many members of the aristocracy. In 1778 she published *Evelina*, and the revelation of its authorship brought her immediate fame. She wrote, but suppressed, a satirical play, *The Witlings*; only *Edwy and Elgiva*, of her many other dramas, was performed in her lifetime. She published *Cecilia* in 1782, and in 1786 was appointed second keeper of the robes to Queen Charlotte. In 1793 she married Alexandre-Jean-Baptiste d'Arblay, a French officer in exile from the French Revolution. In 1796 she published *Camilla*. Her first three novels, which influenced Jane *Austen, depicted the entry into the social world of a young girl of beauty and understanding but no experience. Burney's last novel, *The *Wanderer* (1814), which reflected many darker kinds of 'female difficulties', was not a success. In 1832 she edited the *Memoirs* of her father. Burney was herself a prodigious writer of lively letters and journals. Her *Diary and Letters ... 1778–1840*, including a vivid account of her life at court, was published in 1842–6; her *Early Diary 1768–1778*, which includes attractive sketches of Johnson, David *Garrick, and many others, was published in 1889, with a modern edition by L. E. Troide appearing in 1988–94. Penelope *Fitzgerald in *The Blue Flower* makes use of Burney's description of surviving a mastectomy in September 1811.

'Burning Babe, The' *See* SOUTHWELL, ST ROBERT.

BURNS, Robert (1759–96) Scottish poet, one of seven children born to a cotter in Ayrshire. Though his formal schooling was intermittent, Robert received a good grounding in classic English authors from Shakespeare onwards, along with a reading knowledge of French and at least an elementary grasp of Latin and mathematics. Most of his time was taken up on the ailing farm as labourer and ploughman. His experience of poverty and injustice fuelled his egalitarian beliefs, and led to his involvement with the progressive New Light wing of the Church of Scotland and his enthusiasm for the French Revolution. After his father's death in 1784 he and his brother Gilbert continued to farm, now at Mossgiel in the parish of Mauchline, which is often mentioned in the poems he was beginning to write in some quantity. 'The *Cotter's Saturday Night', 'To a Mouse', 'The Twa Dogs', *'Holy Willie's Prayer', the Epistles to Lapraik, 'The *Holy Fair', and many other of his best-known poems belong to this period. In 1785 he met Jean Armour, whom he eventually married, but continued his long series of entanglements with women, many of whom are mentioned in his poems (for instance, Mary Campbell in 'To Mary in Heaven'), and with some of whom he fathered children.

When *Poems, Chiefly in the Scottish Dialect* was printed by John Wilson in Kilmarnock in 1786, Burns became an overnight celebrity. He found himself fêted by the literary and polite society of Edinburgh and was encouraged to write in the neo-classical and sentimental fashion of the day. Burns had, however, begun to transfer his creative energies from poetry to song writing, and from 1786 until his death he collected, amended, and otherwise created more than 200 songs remarkable for their subtlety and their variety of tone and feeling. Many of his best-known lyrics, such as 'A red, red rose', 'Ae fond kiss', *'Auld Lang Syne', 'It was a' for our richtfu' king', and *'Scots wha hae', were songs contributed gratis out of a sense of patriotic obligation to James Johnson's *Scots Musical Museum* and George Thomson's *Select Collection of Original Scottish Airs*.

In 1788 Burns finally married Jean Armour, and settled on a poor farm at Ellisland, near Dumfries. A year later he secured a post as an excise officer; in 1791 he moved to Dumfries, and published his last major poem, 'Tam o' Shanter'. His song for the Dumfries Volunteers, with whom he enlisted in 1795, has been interpreted variously as a repudiation of his earlier revolutionary ardour and as a radical's desperate dive for cover in the increasingly oppressive climate of the 1790s. He died of rheumatic heart disease in July 1796. The fierce political alertness of Burns's satires and songs is belied by the sentimentality of the Burns cult, and by the annual celebration of 'the Bard's' birthday in a tide of alcohol on 'Burns Night', 25 January.

BURNSIDE, John (1955–) Scottish poet and novelist. Such early collections of poetry as *The Hoop* (1988) and *Feast Days* (1992) fuse autobiography with an interest in landscape. A preoccupation with identity, memory, and the supernatural informs *The Myth of the Twin* (1994), in which the 'anima' is represented as inhabiting a parallel dimension to the self. Later volumes from *Light Trap* (2001) to *The Hunt in the Forest* (2009) and *Black Cat Bone* (2011) are increasingly philosophical in manner. Darker and more violent than his poetry, Burnside's fiction includes six novels, from *The Dumb House* (1997) to *The Glister* (2008), along with a collection of short stories, *Burning Elvis* (2000). *A Lie about my Father*, a sometimes harrowing memoir, appeared in 2006, with a sequel, *Waking up in Toytown*, in 2010.

BURROUGHS, Edgar Rice (1875–1950) American creator of adventure stories about John Clayton, Lord Greystoke, known as 'Tarzan', reared by great apes in the African jungle after his parents' death. *Tarzan of the Apes* was published in *All-Story* magazine (1912) and issued as a novel in 1914. The character rapidly entered popular mythology as the hero of many sequels, films, radio programmes, and comic strips, and is one of the iconic figures of 20th-century literature. Drawing upon Henry Rider *Haggard's lost-race romances, Burroughs invigorated popular *science fiction and *sword and sorcery.

BURROUGHS, John (1837–1921) American naturalist and essayist. Like Henry *Thoreau, his characteristic medium was the *nature essay. Burroughs also published *Whitman: A Study* (1896) and *John James Audubon* (1902), a biography.

BURROUGHS, William S. (Seward) (1914–97) American novelist, probably more famous for his life than his literature. His first novel, *Junkie* (1953), gave a semi-autobiographical account of his time as a drug addict. *The Naked Lunch* (1959) made him a *cause célèbre* through its graphic descriptions of sexual sadism, heroin abuse, and darkly satirical imaginings of a totalitarian state. Subsequent novels including *The Soft Machine* (1961), *The Wild Boys* (1971), and *Cities of the Red Night* (1981) focused on the nature of power and the dynamics of control. His belief that 'Language is a virus' led him, in collaboration with Brion Gysin, to employ the 'cut-up' technique—a process whereby words or sentences would be taken from any source and reassembled in a way that would *defamil-

iarize them. The random and anarchic were seen as modes of opposition to a predetermined universe. Although a homosexual, he married twice and accidentally shot his second wife Joan during the staging of a William Tell act. His unrepentant drug identity gave him an iconic status that would be used in such films as *Drugstore Cowboy* (1991) and by rock bands such as Nirvana and REM. Burroughs constantly experimented with different kinds of textual construction and frequently used 'routines' (a term taken from stand-up comedians) in his works, i.e. short, usually grotesque episodes. *See* BEAT AND BEAT GENERATION.

BURTON, Sir Richard Francis (1821–90) Prolific travel writer, ethnographer, co-founder of the racist Anthropological Society, linguist (he spoke 40 languages or dialects), and translator. He was expelled from Oxford, and joined the Indian army in 1842. In 1849 he left India and sensationally made the *hajj* to Mecca in disguise. His expedition to Africa with John *Speke discovered Lake Tanganyika in 1858. Other travels followed and a series of unsatisfactory consular appointments to Fernando Po, Brazil, Damascus, and Trieste, where he died. In addition to more than 40 volumes of travel, he produced books and articles on folklore, poetry, and translations from Arabic, Latin, and Portuguese. Burton is best remembered for his unexpurgated versions of the *Arabian Nights* (1885–8), *The Kama Sutra* (1883), *The Perfumed Garden* (1886, from the French), and other works of Arabian erotology. His interest in sexual behaviour and deviance (shared with his friends Richard Milnes and *Swinburne) and his frank ethnographical notes led him to risk prosecution for obscenity, and his more erotic works were published secretly or privately. On his death, his wife Isabel destroyed his papers and diaries, including his translation from the original Arabic of *The Perfumed Garden*, on which he had been working for fourteen years.

BURTON, Robert (1577–1640) The author of *The *Anatomy of Melancholy*.

Busie Body, The Comedy by Susannah *Centlivre, produced 1709. Sir George Airy and Miranda love one another, but her guardian, Sir Francis Gripe, intends to marry her himself. Airy and Miranda are eventually united, and Gripe's son Charles wins Isabinda, whom her father, Sir Jealous Traffic, intends to marry off to a Spanish merchant. The devices through which this end is accomplished are constantly interrupted by the well-meant but misdirected energies of Marplot, the 'busybody'.

BUSSY, Dorothy (1865–1960) Née Strachey, novelist, sister of the writer Lytton *Strachey and James Strachey (1887–1967), Sigmund *Freud's first English translator. Her only novel, *Olivia* (1949), draws on her experience as pupil and teacher at the Marie Souvestre school for girls. A friend of André Gide, she translated all his work into English.

Bussy D'Ambois A tragedy by George *Chapman, written for a boys' company, 1600–04, and later played by adults, published 1607. It was adapted by Thomas D'Urfey in 1693, and directed by Jonathan Miller at the Old Vic, London, in 1988. Chapman's most famous play, it was very popular in its day, and was revived at the Restoration, when *Dryden attacked it as 'a dwarfish thought, dressed up in gigantic words . . .' (1681).

Bussy D'Ambois (in real life, Louis de Bussyd'Ambois), insolent and courageous, is raised from poverty and introduced to the court of Henri III of France by the king's brother Monsieur, his protector. He quarrels with the king's courtiers, killing three, and even with the duc de Guise. He embarks on an affair with Tamyra, wife of Montsurry (Montsoreau). Monsieur, who also desires Tamyra, betrays Bussy to Montsurry, who forces Tamyra to lure Bussy into a trap. Overpowered, he dies defiantly on his feet. ('Here like a Roman statue I will stand | Till death hath made me marble.') Chapman's sequel is The *Revenge of Bussy D'Ambois.

The story is also told by Dumas *père* in *La Dame de Monsoreau* (1846).

BUTLER, Joseph (1692–1752) Moral philosopher. He was appointed bishop of Bristol in 1738, from which he was translated to Durham in 1750. His reputation stemmed from *Fifteen Sermons* (1726); while recognizing benevolence and a due degree of self-love as elements in virtuous conduct, he regards conscience as governing and limiting them by considerations, not of happiness or misery, but of right and wrong. His *Analogy of Religion* (1736) was an enormously influential defence of Christianity against *Deism, in which Butler argues that belief in immortality, revelation, and miracles is as reasonable as the beliefs upon which natural religion is founded. He had a strong impact in very different ways on David *Hume, J. H. *Newman, Matthew *Arnold, and W. E. *Gladstone.

BUTLER, Octavia (1947–2006) African American author born Pasadena, California, whose novels, such as the 'Xenogenesis' series (1987–89), frequently use concepts like genetic manipulation to explore race and gender issues. *Parable of the Talents* (1999) won a Nebula award as best *science fiction novel. Her most popular novel remains *Kindred* (1979) in which an African American woman time-travels back to the days of slavery.

BUTLER, Samuel ('Hudibras') (1613–80) Poet. By 1661 he was steward at Ludlow Castle to Richard Vaughan, earl of Carbery (1600?–86). The most significant event in an otherwise obscure life was the publication in 1663 of his *Hudibras*, which instantly became the most popular poem of its time. It was probably as a result of its success that he became secretary to the second duke of *Buckingham. In 1677 he was awarded an annual pension of £100 by Charles II, having apparently previously complained that, though a loyal satirist, he had been left to endure his old age in poverty. He wrote a number of shorter satirical poems, including 'The Elephant in the Moon', an attack on the *Royal Society, and a great many prose 'Characters'.

BUTLER, Samuel (1835–1902) The son of a clergyman and grandson of a bishop, but religious doubts prevented his ordination and in 1859 he went to New Zealand. *A First Year in Canterbury Settlement* (1863), compiled by his father from Samuel's letters, became the core of *Erewhon. He returned to England in 1864. In 1872 he published *Erewhon*, anonymously, which enjoyed a brilliant but brief success. *The Fair Haven* (1873), an elaborate and ironic attack on the Resurrection, brought him encouragement from Charles *Darwin and Leslie *Stephen. Between 1877 and 1890 Butler produced a series of works of scientific controversy, many of them directed against certain aspects of Darwinism, in particular Darwin's theory of natural selection. Butler's espousal of the cause of Lamarck and creative evolution won him the praise of George Bernard *Shaw in his preface to *Back to Methuselah* (1921); Shaw also praised Butler's outspoken views on religion and the 'importance of money' in his preface to *Major Barbara* (1907). Butler's *Alps and Sanctuaries of Piedmont and the Canton Ticino* (1881) was the first of several works on art and travel. In 1896 appeared his *The Life and Letters of Dr Samuel Butler*, his revered grandfather, who had been headmaster, bishop, and geographer. A long interest in *Homer led to his theory of the feminine authorship of the *Odyssey*. *The Authoress of the 'Odyssey'* appeared in 1897, and translations of the *Iliad* and the *Odyssey* into vigorous colloquial prose in 1898 and 1900. A quirky study, *Shakespeare's Sonnets Reconsidered*, appeared in 1899, and *Erewhon Revisited* in 1901. Butler's most revealing work was his semi-autobiographical novel *The *Way of All Flesh* (1903)

BUTOR, Michel (1926–) French writer. Butor's novels of the 1950s, including *L'Emploi du temps* (1956; *Passing Time*, 1960) and *La Modification* (1957; *Second Thoughts*, 1958), aligned him with the *nouveau roman*, thanks to their interrogation of traditional narrative modes: *La Modification* is narrated entirely in the second person. *L'Emploi du temps* is also notable for its evocation of Manchester. *Mobile* (1962; trans; 1963) deployed a montage of quotations in its depiction of the United States.

BUTTS, Mary (1890–1937) Novelist and writer. She contributed to the *Little Review* alongside T. S. *Eliot, Hilda *Doolittle (H.D.) and *Bryher (Winifred Ellerman), and in 1918 she married John *Rodker (they divorced in 1926). *Speed the Plough* (1923), a volume of short stories, was followed by two novels, *Ashe of Rings* (1925) and *Armed with Madness*, (1928), and *Imaginary Letters* (1928), illustrated by Jean Cocteau. In 1932 she made her home in Sennen Cove, Cornwall, and in 1934 she converted to Anglo-Catholicism. Her later works included the novel, *Death of Felicity Taverner* (1932), two volumes of short stories, *Several Occasions* (1932) and the posthumous *Last Stories* (1938), and her autobiography, *The Crystal Cabinet: My Childhood at Salterns* (1937; repr. 1988). Her books were neglected after her death, but they began to be republished in the 1980s, reviving her reputation.

BYATT, A. S. (Dame Antonia Susan) (1936–) Novelist and critic, educated at the Mount School, York, and Newnham College, Cambridge, sister of the novelist Margaret *Drabble. Her first novel, *Shadow of a Sun* (1964), describes a woman attempting to escape the shadow of her novelist father. *The Game* (1967) explores the relationship of two sisters, one an Oxford don, the other a popular novelist. *The Virgin in the Garden* (1978), set largely in the coronation year of 1953, is rich in allegorical allusions to (among others) Edmund *Spenser, Walter *Ralegh, and *Shakespeare, and provides a realistic and vivid portrait of provincial life in the 1950s. Frederica's story is continued in *Still Life* (1985), *Babel Tower* (1996), and *A Whistling Woman* (2002). Byatt's *Booker Prize-winning novel *Possession* (1990) concerns a group of

20th-century academics who reconstruct the relationship between two fictitious Victorian poets, and is notable for its pastiches of 19th-century literary style. *The Matisse Stories* (1993) is a sequence of three stories loosely linked to paintings by Henri Matisse (1869–1954). *The Djinn in the Nightingale's Eye* (1994) is a collection of original *fairy stories, including two previously published in *Possession*. Other works include *The Biographer's Tale* (2000), *Little Black Book of Stories* (2003), and *The Children's Book* (2009).

BYRD, William (?1540–1623) English composer; he gained the patronage of several Catholic nobles, and of *Elizabeth I, which shielded him from prosecution as a recusant. Elizabeth required Byrd to compose a consort song to her own text, *Look and Bow Down*, on the defeat of the Spanish Armada, and he wrote other works in her praise, including the *madrigal *This Sweet and Merry Month of May* (1590). He produced liturgical music for both Anglican and Catholic rites. His secular *Psalmes, Sonets and Songs* (1588) was one of the earliest books of English song. Among the authors he set were Philip *Sidney, Walter *Ralegh, Edward *Dyer, and Thomas Churchyard.

BYROM, John (1692–1763) Poet. He invented a popular system of shorthand or 'tychygraphy', and was elected a fellow of the *Royal Society in 1724. His *Private Journals and Literary Remains* (pub. 1854–7) include accounts of his friendship with William *Law. Byrom wrote the ambiguous toast beginning 'God bless the King! I mean the Faith's Defender'. His *Miscellaneous Poems* (1773) includes the hymn 'Christians, awake! Salute the happy morn'.

BYRON, George Gordon, sixth Baron (1788–1824) Poet, son of Captain John Byron and Catherine Gordon of Gight. Byron was born with a club-foot which (it is generally supposed) had a profound effect on his future temperament. Byron inherited the title in 1798, with the dilapidated Gothic Newstead Abbey. Staying at Newstead in 1802 he probably first met his half-sister, Augusta. In 1805 he went up to Cambridge, where he attended intermittently to his studies. His first published collection of poems, *Hours of Idleness*, appeared in 1807, and was bitterly attacked, probably by Henry *Brougham, in the *Edinburgh Review*. Byron avenged himself in 1809 with his satire *English Bards and Scotch Reviewers*. In 1808 he returned to Newstead, in 1809 took his seat in the House of Lords, then left for the first of his prolonged travels abroad. Between 1809 and 1811 he visited Portugal, Spain, Malta, Greece, and the Levant. In 1809 he began the poem that was to become *Childe Harold*; he swam the Hellespont; and he became fired with the wish that Greece should be freed from the Turks.

His first great literary triumph came with the publication of the first two cantos of *Childe Harold's Pilgrimage* in March 1812. He was lionized by aristocratic and literary London, survived a hectic love affair with Lady Caroline *Lamb, and became the constant companion of Augusta. In 1813 he wrote *The *Bride of Abydos* in a week, and *The *Corsair* in ten days: *The *Giaour* appeared in the same year. In 1814 Augusta gave birth to a daughter, who was generally supposed to be Byron's and was almost certainly so. After a long and hesitant courtship Byron married Annabella Milbanke in 1815. In the same year their daughter Ada was born, and Byron published *Hebrew Melodies*. But his debts were accumulating, and public horror at the rumours of his incest was rising. Annabella left him and a legal separation was eventually arranged.

Byron left England in 1816, never to return, and travelled to Geneva, where the *Shelleys and Claire *Clairmont had rented a villa. Here Byron wrote *The *Prisoner of Chillon*; Claire was by now his mistress. He wrote two acts of *Manfred*, Canto III of *Childe Harold*, and several shorter poems, but after four months left for Italy. His daughter by Claire, Allegra, was born in January 1817 in England. While living a riotous life in Venice in the same year, he wrote the third act of *Manfred*. While travelling to Rome he began the fourth and last canto of *Childe Harold*. He returned to Venice and there wrote *Beppo*, his first work in the ironic, colloquial style which was to lead him to *Don Juan*. Newstead Abbey was at last sold, and Byron was free of financial worries. In 1818 he wrote *Mazeppa*, and began *Don Juan*, the first two cantos of which were published in 1819 by John *Murray, reluctantly and anonymously. Byron met and became deeply attached to Teresa, Countess Guiccioli. They lived first in Venice, then he followed her and her household to Ravenna, where he wrote *The Prophecy of Dante*. In 1820 he wrote *Marino Faliero*, and became deeply involved with the cause of the Italian patriots. Teresa left her husband for Byron in 1821. In Ravenna and Pisa that year Byron became intensely interested in drama, and wrote *The *Two Foscari*, *Sardanapalus*, *Cain*, the unfinished *Heaven and Earth*, and the unfinished *The *Deformed Transformed*; he also wrote his brilliant

parody of *Southey, *The *Vision of Judgment*, and continued with *Don Juan*. The death in 1822 of his daughter Allegra, whom he had continually failed to visit, was a great grief to him. Byron left Pisa for Livorno, with Teresa and her family, where Leigh *Hunt joined them. Hunt and Byron cooperated in the production of the *Liberal magazine, publishing *The Vision of Judgment, Heaven and Earth*, and a translation from Luigi Pulci. In 1823 he wrote *The Age of Bronze*, a satirical poem on the Congress of Verona, and *The *Island*, but he had come to feel that action was more important than poetry. In January 1824, after various mishaps and escapes, he arrived at Missolonghi. He formed the 'Byron Brigade' and gave large sums of money, and great inspiration, to the insurgent Greeks, but before he saw any serious military action he died of fever in April. Memorial services were held all over Greece, but his body was refused by the deans of both Westminster and St Paul's.

Byron's poetry, although widely condemned on moral grounds, and frequently attacked by critics, was immensely popular in England and even more so abroad. Much of his poetry and drama exerted great influence on *Romanticism, and his legacy of inspiration in European poetry, music, the novel, opera, and painting has been immense. Bertrand *Russell wrote that 'As a myth his importance, especially on the continent, was enormous.' His *Byronic heroes, rejecting conventional morality, rebellious, proud, but often self-loathing, were influential in 19th-century English fiction, notably in Emily *Brontë's characterization of Heathcliff. Byron was also the leading figure, alongside William *Gifford and Thomas *Moore, in the flourishing satirical tradition of the late Georgian age.

He was an indefatigable writer of letters and journals, which provide a brilliantly vivid commentary both on his own life and on the times in which he lived. Moore's life appeared in 1830 (*Letters and Journals of Lord Byron, with Notices of his Life*, 2 vols).

BYRON, John (1723-86) As a midshipman on the *Wager*, one of the ships of George *Anson's squadron in his famous voyage, he was wrecked on an island off the coast of Chile in 1741. His 'Narrative' of the shipwreck, published in 1768, provided details for his grandson Lord *Byron's description of a wreck in *Don Juan*. Byron later led a circumnavigation of the globe, from 1764 to 1766, causing a sensation with his reports of Patagonian giants. An account of the voyage by John *Hawkesworth was published in 1773.

BYRON, Robert (1905–41) Travel writer, Byzantinist, and aesthete. His works include *The Station* (1928), an account of a visit to Mount Athos, and his classic study *The Road to Oxiana* (1937), a record in the form of diary jottings of a journey from Venice through the Middle East and Afghanistan to India in search of the origins of Islamic architecture and culture. Its admirers include Bruce *Chatwin and William *Dalrymple. Byron died when the ship on which he was travelling as a war correspondent was hit by a torpedo.

Byron, The Conspiracy and Tragedy of Charles, Duke of A two-part play by George *Chapman, written for the Boys of St Paul's, published in 1608. Its portrayal of the French provoked a protest from the French ambassador with a request that Chapman be imprisoned.

Byronic Characteristic of or resembling Lord *Byron or his poetry; in the words of Thomas *Macaulay, 'a man proud, moody, cynical, with defiance on his brow, and misery in his heart, a scorner of his kind, implacable in revenge, yet capable of deep and strong affection'.

CABLE, George Washington (1844–1925) American novelist and short story writer, best remembered for his portraits of Louisiana Creole life. The latter include his short story collection *Old Creole Days* (1879) and his novel *The Grandissimes* (1880). Cable, a pioneer of Southern Local Colour writing, wrote a number of works attacking Southern racism and became a close friend of Mark *Twain.

Cadenus and Vanessa Jonathan *Swift's longest poem, written probably around 1713 for Esther Vanhomrigh ('Vanessa'). Vanessa, Venus' favourite child, beautiful, rich, and intelligent, is immune to conventional social follies but falls in love with 'Cadenus', an anagram of 'Decanus', or dean (Swift). The poem delicately and wittily narrates in Swift's habitual octosyllabic couplets the inconclusive exchanges and emotional manoeuvrings of their unusual pupil–teacher romance. It appeared in 1726, three years after Vanhomrigh's death.

Cadmus In Greek myth, warriors sprang up and fought each other when Cadmus sowed the dragon's teeth; the survivors supposedly founded Thebes (see *Ovid, *Metamorphoses*, Bk 3). Cadmus is also associated with the introduction of the alphabet. John *Milton in *Areopagitica* compares books to the dragon's teeth, springing up as armed men.

CADWALLADER The last of the British kings of England, according to the various *Brut chronicles. He died in 689 according to *Geoffrey of Monmouth. After his day, which was characterized by plague and desolation, the British would be called Welsh (foreign) and the Saxons rule instead in England, until the time prophesied by *Merlin for the return of a British king.

CÆDMON (*fl.*670) Entered the monastery of Streaneshalch (Whitby) between 658 and 680, when already an elderly man. He is said by *Bede in his *Ecclesiastical History of the English People* to have been a herdsman who received the power of song in a vision and later put into English verse scriptural passages translated to him. The only work which can be attributed to him is the hymn which survives in several manuscripts of the *History* in various dialects.

CAESAR, Gaius Julius (100–44 BC) Roman politician and general. Victor in the factional struggles that destroyed the republic, and eventually dictator, he prepared the ground for six centuries of imperial rule: Octavian, later the emperor Augustus, was his heir. He wrote a lucid third-person account of his campaigns in his *Commentaries: On the Gallic War*, which includes his invasions of Britain, and *On the Civil War*, which opens with Caesar crossing the Rubicon with his army to invade Italy. During his Alexandrian campaign he began a love affair with *Cleopatra. He was assassinated on the Ides of March by a group of republican conspirators led by *Brutus. *Cicero is the principal contemporary source for the events of his lifetime; biographies were written later by *Plutarch and *Suetonius. Shakespeare's *Julius Caesar* and G. B. *Shaw's *Caesar and Cleopatra* are the most influential English retellings of his story. *On the Gallic War* was first translated into English by Arthur *Golding (1565), but for centuries the original Latin formed the basis of a classical education. *See* CATO; LUCAN.

caesura A pause within a line of verse, usually coinciding with a punctuated break between clauses or sentences. *Alliterative verse required a caesura at the middle of the line. The English *pentameter commonly displaces it to a position after the fourth or sixth syllable, but several other positions are permissible, and the caesura may not be employed at all.

CAIN, James Mallahan (1892–1977) American novelist, journalist, and screenwriter. One of the formative figures in the tradition of *hardboiled crime fiction, Cain is best remembered for his laconic first-person narratives like *The Postman Always Rings Twice* (1934), which was adapted for the cinema in 1946, directed by Carey Wilson. Cain insisted that his crime narratives were always motivated by a love story.

Cain: A Mystery A verse drama in three acts by Lord *Byron, published 1821. Cain, bewildered by the toil imposed on him by another's fault, and by the mystery of the 'evil' consequences of 'good' knowledge, is confronted by Lucifer, who teaches him to question the ways of God, the 'Omnipotent tyrant'. Cain expresses his doubts and fears to his sister-bride Adah and is reluctant to share his favoured brother Abel's sacrifice to Jehovah. In a fit of passion, revolted by the blood sacrifice and a God who could delight in such offerings, Cain strikes Abel and kills him, thus bringing into the world Death. Cursed by Eve, rejected by Adam, and marked on the brow by an angel of the Lord, Cain sets forth into exile with his wife and children, knowing that they will further the doom of mankind. This powerful enquiry into original sin, heredity, free will, and predestination caused intense indignation, and the publisher, John *Murray, was threatened with prosecution. Byron diplomatically denied that the views represented were his own.

CAINE, Hall (Sir Thomas Henry Hall) (1853–1931) novelist. In 1879 he lectured in Liverpool on D. G. *Rossetti, began a correspondence with him, and subsequently spent the last few months of Rossetti's life as his housemate: see Caine's Recollections of Dante Gabriel Rossetti (1882). He edited an anthology, Sonnets of Three Centuries (1882), in which all three *Rossettis, and William Bell *Scott were represented. He achieved spectacular success with a series of novels, many set in the Isle of Man, including The Deemster (1887), The Bondsman (1890), The Manxman (1894), The Christian (1897), The Eternal City (1901), The Prodigal Son (1904), and a pro-woman's rights novel, The Woman Thou Gavest Me (1913). The Woman of Knockaloe, his last novel, appeared in 1923.

CAIRD, Mona (1854–1932). A militant New Women writer who combined non-fictional feminist tracts that argued for equality in marriage (essays collected as The Morality of Marriage, 1897) with *New Woman fiction in which she interrogates the stifling effects of conventionality on women's lives. In The Daughters of Danaus (1894), the heroine leaves husband and family to study music. Other novels included The Wing of Azrael (1889), A Romance of the Moors (1891), and The Stones of Sacrifice (1915).

CALDECOTT, Randolph (1846–86) RA, author/illustrator, and painter. In 1878 the printer Edmund Evans commissioned The House that Jack Built, the first of sixteen *'toy books'.

Caleb Williams (Things as They Are, or The Adventures of Caleb Williams) A novel by William *Godwin, published 1794. This work is remarkable as an early example of the propagandist novel, as a novel of pursuit, crime, and detection, and as a psychological study. A provocative preface to the original edition was withdrawn.

It is related in the first person by its eponymous hero. The first part of the book deals with the misdeeds of Tyrrel, an arrogant and tyrannical country squire, who ruins a tenant on his estate, Hawkins, for refusing to yield to one of his whims. He comes into conflict with the idealistic and benevolent Falkland, a neighbouring squire, knocks him down in public, and is shortly after found murdered. Suspicion falls on Falkland but is diverted to Hawkins and his son, who are tried and executed. From this time Falkland becomes eccentric and solitary. Caleb Williams, the self-educated son of humble parents, is appointed his secretary, and convinces himself that Falkland is in fact Tyrrel's murderer. The remainder of the book concerns Falkland's unrelenting persecution of Williams despite his devotion to his employer and refusal to betray his secret. Williams is imprisoned on a false charge of robbing his employer, escapes, but is tracked by Falkland's agents until, in despair, he lays a charge of murder against Falkland, is confronted with him, and, although he has no proof to offer, through his generosity and sincerity wins from the murderer a confession of guilt. Godwin's original ending was radically different; in it Falkland maintains his innocence and Williams ends, nearly demented, in jail.

Caliban In Shakespeare's The *Tempest, is described in the *folio 'Names of the Actors' as 'a salvage [savage] and deformed slave'. Son of the witch Sycorax and the original possessor of Prospero's island, he is only semi-human, but has often been portrayed sympathetically in modern productions.

'Caliban upon Setebos' A poem by Robert *Browning, included in *Dramatis Personae.

Calisto y Melibea See CELESTINA.

CALLAGHAN, Morley (1903–90) Canadian novelist. His experiences in Paris in the 1920s are recorded in That Summer in Paris (1963), with portraits of Scott *Fitzgerald and other ex-patriate Americans. The works in his novel triptych: *Such is my Beloved* (1934); *They Shall Inherit the Earth* (1935); and *More Joy in Heaven* (1937) share a noticeably spare, simple prose and narrative style, and a religious concern with the redemption of the ordinary.

CALLIL, Carmen See VIRAGO PRESS.

CALLIMACHUS (c.310/305–c.240 BC) Perhaps the finest of Hellenistic poets and a scholar who worked in the Library at Alexandria. Of his many poems only six hymns, 60 epigrams, and a number of fragments survive. He was much admired by the Roman poets *Catullus, *Propertius, and *Ovid. A difficult author, Callimachus found few English readers until the 17th century. He was imitated by Mark *Akenside in his 'Hymn to the Naiads'. One of his epigrams served as a model for W. J. Cory's 'They told me Heraclitus . . .', and material of a mythological sort drawn from his hymns can be found in Alfred *Tennyson's *'Tiresias' and Robert *Bridges's *Prometheus the Firegiver*.

CALVERLEY, Charles Stuart (1831–84) Poet and translator (born Blayds, assumed Calverley from 1852). He became known under the initials C.S.C. as a writer of light verse, parodies, and translations: a serious translation of *Theocritus was issued in 1869; *Verses and Translations* appeared in 1862, *Fly Leaves* in 1872.

CALVIN, Jean (1509–64) French theologian and reformer. His name derives from Calvinus, the Latinized form of Cauvin. In 1536 he published the first edition of his *Institutio Christianae religionis* in Basle, and settled in Geneva. The *Institutio* was conceived as a defence of the Reformed Faith. It repudiated scholastic methods of argument in favour of deductions from biblical authority and the moral nature of man, and it advocated the doctrines of sin and grace—with the associated doctrine of predestination derived from St Paul—at the expense of salvation by works. Calvin was an unswerving opponent of the power of bishops, favouring the voice of independent congregations. His ideas had a major influence in 16th- and 17th-century England.

CALVINO, Italo (1923–85) Italian writer, whose first work, *Il sentiero dei nidi di ragno* (1947: *The Path to the Spiders' Nests*), on resistance against Fascism, is a leading example of neo-realism. His other works include the experimental narrative *Se una notte d'inverno un viaggiatore* (1979: *If on a Winter's Night a Traveller*) and the fantasy trilogy *I nostri antenati* (*Our Ancestors*): *Il visconte dimezzato* (1952: *The Cloven Viscount*); *Il barone rampante* (1957: *Baron in the Trees*), which plays with the 'reality' of Samuel *Richardson and Henry *Fielding; and *Il cavaliere inesistente* (1959: *The Non-existent Knight*), which draws ironically on Renaissance chivalrous epic. He was deeply interested in folklore and *fairy stories. From 1967 to 1979 he was resident in Paris where he came into contact with Roland *Barthes, George Perec, and the OuLiPo movement. *See* also MAGIC REALISM.

CAMARA LAYE (1928–80) Guinean novelist, noted in particular for *L'Enfant noir* (1953; *The Dark Child*—later *The African Child*—trans. James Kirkup, 1954), a largely autobiographical account of childhood and adolescence in Africa.

Cambridge Platonists A group of Anglican thinkers who had close connections with Cambridge University and tried to promote a rational form of Christianity in the tradition of Richard *Hooker and *Erasmus. The group included Benjamin Whichcote (1609–83), whose writings, mostly sermons and letters, were published posthumously and Whichcote's pupil John Smith (1618–52), who wrote *Select Discourses* (1660). Also Henry More (1614–87), whose early poetry in *Psychodia Platonica* (1642) has some remarkable passages and whose prose works are profound, complex, and demonstrate his conflicting attitudes. He attacked superstition but had himself a keen taste for the occult; he wanted to simplify religion so that all could understand it, but was bitterly opposed to the emotional fervour that had most appeal for the uneducated. Ralph Cudworth (1617–88), had a more lucid style and a more logical mind, and his major work, *The True Intellectual System of the Universe* (1678), must be regarded as the group's most detailed manifesto. Nathaniel Culverwell (d. 1651) is often included in the group, but his outlook differed from that of the rest, being more Calvinist and Aristotelian.

The aims of the group were to combat materialism, which was finding a forceful exponent in Thomas *Hobbes, and to reform religion by freeing it from fanaticism and controversy. Drawing inspiration from *Plato and *Plotinus, they maintained that Sense reveals only appearances, Reality consists in 'intelligible forms' which are 'not impressions printed on the soul without, but ideas vitally protended or actively exerted from within itself'. They held furthermore that Revelation, the Rational Order of the Universe, and human Reason were all in harmony, so that to search for Truth was to search for God. They rejected the Calvinist doctrine that human nature was deeply corrupt, capable of salvation only through the action of a Divine Grace granted to some and withheld from others, and saw Man as 'deiform', able to advance towards perfection through Reason and the imitation of Christ. Reason for the Cambridge Platonists was not just power of critical thought, but to function effectively had to result in virtuous behaviour. Truth and Goodness were inseparable.

These doctrines were presented in a rhetorical, quotation-laden, often long-winded late Renaissance manner which has masked their revolutionary character, but it is evident that they prepared the way for the *Deism of the 18th century. The odd fact that Cudworth's daughter was one of John *Locke's patrons was in a way symbolic.

Cambyses, King A tragedy (c.1568-9) by Thomas Preston, which illustrates the transition from the morality play to historical tragedy. It is founded on the story of Cambyses (king of Persia) in *Herodotus; its grandiloquence became proverbial and is referred to in 1 *Henry IV, II. V.

Camelot The seat of King Arthur's court, is said by Sir Thomas *Malory to be Winchester. It has variously been identified with Camelford in Cornwall or South Cadbury in Somerset, and John Leland says he found traces of Arthur in Queen's Camel in Somerset which (he says) was previously called Camelot.

CAMERON, Norman (1905-53) Poet. His poems were published in periodicals during the 1930s, principally in New Verse, and his first collection was The Winter House (1935). The Collected Poems of Norman Cameron appeared in 1957, with an introduction by Graves, and Collected Poems and Selected Translations in 1990. His poems are brief, lucid, and concentrated, built usually on a single image or parable.

CAMERON, Verney Lovett (1844-94) The first European to cross Africa from east to west; he recorded the exploit in Across Africa (2 vols, 1877). He also wrote a series of adventure stories in book form and in the Boy's Own Paper, often based on his own experiences.

Camilla, or A Picture of Youth A novel by Fanny *Burney (1796). At the centre lies the relationship between the lively and beautiful Camilla Tyrold and her eligible, but cool and judicious, suitor Edgar Mandlebert. The eventual marriage is delayed over five volumes by intrigues, contretemps, and misunderstandings, designed to exhibit the virtues and failings of Camilla's character or to illustrate similar difficulties in the lives of her sisters, and her exotic, selfish cousin Indiana Lynmere. It was dedicated to the queen and published for an unusually distinguished list of subscribers, which included Ann *Radcliffe, Hannah *More, and Jane *Austen.

CAMÕES, Luís de (c.1524-1580) In premodern times sometimes Camoens, Portuguese poet and dramatist, best known for his *epic Os Lusíadas (1572: The Lusiads). The work's principal inspiration is *Virgil, but Camões's erudition was wide-ranging and the poem became the model of the learned epic in early modern Europe. There have been some fifteen translations into English, including those by Sir Richard *Fanshawe in the 17th century and Sir Richard *Burton in the 19th.

Campaspe A prose comedy by John *Lyly, published 1584 as Alexander, Campaspe and Diogenes. The story of *Alexander the Great, Campaspe, his Theban captive, whom he loves, and Apelles, engaged to paint her portrait, whose love for Campaspe is returned, is told in *Pliny the Elder's Natural History, 35. 10.

CAMPBELL, Joseph (1879-1944) Irish poet, who published some of his works under his Irish name, Seosamh MacCathmhaoil. He supported the Republican cause in the Irish Civil War (1922-3), and was interned in Dublin. Many of his lyrics and ballads are based on legend and folklore; his collections include The Gilly of Christ (1907), The Mountainy Singer (1909), and Irishry (1913). Poems (1963) was edited by Austin *Clarke.

CAMPBELL, Ken (1941-) Actor, director, and writer. His interest in the bizarre and surreal resulted in co-founding the Science Fiction Theatre of Liverpool following his introduction to *science fiction by Brian *Aldiss. Illuminatus! (1976) was an epic romp through conspiracy theories lasting 8½ hours; The Warp (1980) lasted 22 hours. Other productions included adaptations of H. P. *Lovecraft's The Case of Charles Dexter Ward (1978) and Douglas *Adams's The Hitchhiker's Guide to the Galaxy (1979).

CAMPBELL, Ramsey (1946–) *Horror novelist and short story writer. His early published work, written in his teens, bears the stamp of H. P. *Lovecraft, but Campbell soon developed his own approach characterized by a sly and subtle undermining of his characters' perceptions of reality. *The Face That Must Die* (1979) shows a grimness intensified and counterpointed by the protagonist's puns—a technique used more subtly in *The Count of Eleven* (1991). Lovecraftian awe returns in *The Darkest Part of the Woods* (2003).

CAMPBELL, Roy (1901–57) Author, born in Durban, Natal. In 1924 he published, to great acclaim, *The Flaming Terrapin*, an exuberant allegorical narrative of the Flood. Returning to South Africa (1924–7), he founded with William *Plomer a satirical literary magazine, *Voorslag* ('Whiplash', 1926–7), to which Laurens van der Post contributed. Other works include *The Wayzgoose* (1928), a satire on South African life; *The Georgiad* (1931), a long, biting attack on the *Bloomsbury Group; *Mithraic Emblems* (1936); *Flowering Rifle* (1939), a noisily pro-Fascist work which brought him much opprobrium; and *Sons of the Mistral* (1941), a selection of his best poems. His first autobiography, *Broken Record* (1934), a swashbuckling narrative of adventure, had also revealed blatantly Fascist opinions; his second, *Light on a Dark Horse* (1951), helped propagate his reputation for showy self-promotion.

CAMPBELL, Thomas (1777–1844) Poet, son of a Glasgow merchant, and closely associated with the founding of the University of London in the late 1820s. He published *The *Pleasures of Hope* in 1799, *Gertrude of Wyoming* in 1809, *Theodric, and Other Poems* in 1824, and *The Pilgrim of Glencoe, and Other Poems* in 1842. He was very popular in his own day, in large part for his war songs, 'The Battle of Hohenlinden', 'The Battle of the Baltic', and 'Ye Mariners of England'; and for his ballads, such as 'Lord Ullin's Daughter'.

CAMPION, Thomas (1567–1620) Poet, musician, and theorist, and, in 1605, MD. Five songs by him were appended to the unauthorized *Astrophel and Stella* in 1591; in 1595 he published his Latin *Poemata*. *A Booke of Ayres* (1601) was a collaboration with Philip Rosseter. Campion's *Observations in the Art of English Poesie* (1602) defended classical metres against 'the vulgar and unarteficiall custome of riming'. Between about 1613 and 1617 Campion published four *Bookes of Ayres*, mostly settings of his own poems, and, with John Coprario, *Songs of Mourning* for Prince Henry (1613). In the early years of James I's reign he wrote a number of court masques.

campus novel A novel set on a university or polytechnic campus; usually written by novelists who are also (temporarily or permanently) academics; notable examples include Kingsley *Amis's *Lucky Jim* (1954), David *Lodge's *Changing Places* (1975), Malcolm *Bradbury's *The History Man* (1975), and Howard *Jacobson's *Coming from Behind* (1983).

CAMUS, Albert (1913–60) French novelist, playwright, and essayist, born in Algeria. His first novel *L'Étranger* (1942: *The Outsider*) and his essay *Le Mythe de Sisyphe* (1942) established him as a philosopher of the 'absurd' nature of the human condition. He distanced himself from the *existentialism of Jean-Paul *Sartre, but continued to explore the human condition in fiction (*La Peste*, 1947: *The Plague*), plays (*Caligula*, 1945; *Les Justes*, 1949; *see also* ABSURD, THEATRE OF THE), and stage adaptations, including William *Faulkner's *Requiem for a Nun* (1956).

Canaan Ancient region in the Near East, the land flowing with milk and honey promised to the Jews in the Old Testament, reached by crossing the river Jordan. In Puritan and evangelical literature, ranging from John *Bunyan to gospel songs, it represents eternal life, and the language of Canaan is that spoken by the godly. *See* BIBLE.

Candide A hugely successful philosophical tale by *Voltaire, published in 1759. Its innocent young hero, Candide, is much influenced by his tutor Pangloss, an incurable Optimist and a follower of *Leibniz who believes that 'all is for the best in the best of all possible worlds'. The grotesque misfortunes that befall all the characters provide witty satires of religion, politics, and philosophy.

canon A body of approved works, comprising either (i) writings genuinely considered to be those of a given author; or (ii) writings considered to represent the best standards of a given literary tradition.

'Canon's Yeoman's Tale, The' *See* CANTERBURY TALES, 22.

Canterbury Tales, The Geoffrey *Chaucer's most celebrated but unfinished work, extending to 17,000 lines in prose and verse of various metres (though the predominant form is the rhyming couplet). The General Prologue describes the meeting of 29 pilgrims in the Tabard Inn in Southwark. Detailed pen-pictures are given of 21 of them, perhaps corresponding to traditional lists of the orders of society, clerical and lay. The host (see BAILLY, HARRY) proposes that the pilgrims should shorten the road by telling four stories each, two on the way to Canterbury and two on the way back; he will accompany them and award a free supper on their return to the teller of the best story. The work is incomplete; only 23 pilgrims tell stories, and there are only 24 stories told altogether ('Chaucer', as pilgrim, tells two). In the scheme the stories are linked by narrative exchanges between the pilgrims and by prologues and epilogues to the tales. The final ordering of the stories is uncertain; the order that follows is that of the Ellesmere Manuscript, followed in *The Riverside Chaucer* (2008).

(1) 'The Knight's Tale', a shortened version of the *Teseida* of *Boccaccio, the story of the love of *Palamon and Arcite (told again in Shakespeare's *The *Two Noble Kinsmen*), prisoners of Theseus, king of Athens, for Emelye, sister of Hippolyta, queen of the Amazons, whom Theseus has married.

(2) 'The Miller's Tale', a ribald story of the deception, first of a husband (a carpenter) through the prediction of a second flood, and secondly of a lover who expects to kiss the lady's lips but kisses instead her 'nether ye [*eye*]'. He avenges himself on her lover for this humiliation with a red-hot ploughshare. The Tale has been said to be a parody of *courtly love.

(3) 'The Reeve's Tale' is a *fabliau about two clerks who are robbed by a miller of some of the meal which they take to his mill to be ground, and who take their vengeance by sleeping with the miller's wife and daughter. It is an obvious rejoinder to the miller's tale of the duping of a carpenter (the reeve, manager of an estate, had once been a carpenter).

(4) 'The Cook's Tale' of Perkyn Revelour breaks off after 58 lines. This is another ribald fabliau which ends with the introduction of a prostitute. *The Tale of *Gamelyn, not by Chaucer, is introduced for the cook in some manuscripts.

(5) 'The Man of Law's Tale' is the story of Custance, daughter of a Christian emperor of Rome, who marries the sultan of Syria on condition that he become a Christian and who is cast adrift in a boat because of the machinations of the sultan's jealous mother. It is a frequently told medieval story, paralleled by the romance *Emaré* and by John *Gower's Constance story in *Confessio Amantis*, II. 587ff. Chaucer's is based on a passage in the early 14th-century Anglo-Norman Chronicle by Nicholas *Trivet.

(6) 'The Wife of Bath's Tale' is preceded by an 856-line prologue in which the Wife condemns celibacy by describing her life with her five late husbands, in the course of which Chaucer draws widely on the medieval anti-feminist tradition, especially on Jean de Meun's *La Vieille* (the Duenna) in the *Roman de la Rose*. The Tale that follows is the story of 'the loathly lady' (paralleled by Gower's 'Tale of Florent' in *Confessio Amantis*, I. 1396ff.) in which a knight is asked to answer the question, 'what do women most desire?' The correct answer, 'sovereignty', is given to him by a hideous old witch on condition that he marry her; when he does she is restored to youth and beauty.

(7) 'The Friar's Tale' tells how a summoner (an official in an ecclesiastical court) meets the devil dressed as a yeoman and they agree to share out what they are given. They come upon a carter who curses his horse, commending it to the devil; the summoner asks the devil why he does not take the horse thus committed to him and the devil replies that it is because the commendation does not come from the heart. Later they visit an old woman from whom the summoner attempts to extort twelve pence, whereupon she commends *him* to the devil. The devil carries him off to hell because her curse was from the heart. The story is widely attested in popular tradition. It is clear that the friar tells it to enrage the pilgrim summoner, who interrupts the narrative and rejoins with a scurrilous and discreditable story about a friar.

(8) 'The Summoner's Tale' parodies contemporary theological disputes, telling of a greedy friar who undertakes to divide a deathbed legacy amongst his community; he receives a fart and has to devise an ingenious stratagem to divide it with perfect justice.

(9) 'The Clerk's Tale', which the poet tells us he took from *Petrarch, was translated into Latin by the latter from Boccaccio's Italian version in *The *Decameron* (Day 10, Tale 10). (Chaucer's version is rather more dependent on a French prose version than on Petrarch's Latin). The story tells of patient Griselda and her trials by her husband, the Marquis Walter.

(10) 'The Merchant's Tale', in which the merchant, prompted by the tale of Griselda's extreme obedience, tells his 'Tale' of January and May, the old husband with his young wife, and the problems with obedient fidelity involved in this relationship. January ignores the good advice of Justinus in favour of the time-serving opinion of Placebo and marries May. When he goes blind, she makes love to her suitor Damyan in a pear tree. Pluto mischievously restores January's sight at this point, but his consort, Proserpine, inspires May to explain that the

restoration of his sight was brought about by her activities in the pear tree and that this had been their purpose.

(11) 'The Squire's Tale', of Cambuscan, king of Tartary, to whom on his birthday an envoy from the king of Arabia brings magic gifts, including a ring for the king's daughter Canacee, which enables her to understand the language of birds. A female falcon tells Canacee the story of her own desertion by a tercelet (a male hawk). The tale is incomplete but it seems likely that Chaucer meant to finish it, judging from the fact that there is no suggestion that it is unfinished in the laudatory words of the franklin that follow it.

(12) 'The Franklin's Tale', of Dorigen, wife of Arveragus, who attempts to escape the attentions of her suitor, the squire Aurelius, by making her consent depend upon an impossible condition, that all the rocks on the coast of Brittany be removed. When this condition is realized by magic, the suitor, from a generous remorse, releases her from her promise. Chaucer states that the tale is taken from a *'Breton Lay', but if this is true, the original is lost. There are several parallels in medieval literature, of which the closest is Boccaccio's *Il filocolo*, Question 4.

(13) 'The Physician's Tale' tells of Virginia who, at her own request, is killed by her father to escape the designs of the corrupt judge Apius. The original source is *Livy's *History*, and this is what Chaucer cites, though his version seems to rely principally on the *Roman de la Rose*, ll. 5589–658, by Jean de Meun.

(14) 'The Pardoner's Tale' (a pardoner is a licensed seller of papal indulgences, promising remission of punishment for sins) follows a prologue in which he declares his own covetousness, and takes covetousness as its theme, relating it to other sins: drunkenness, gluttony, gambling, and swearing. Three rioters set out to find Death, who has killed their companion; a mysterious old man tells them they will find him under a particular tree, but when they get there they find instead a heap of gold. By aiming to cheat each other in possessing the gold they kill each other. The character of the pardoner in the prologue here is related to Faus-Semblant (False-Seeming) in Jean de Meun's part of the *Roman de la Rose*, ll. 11065–972.

(15) 'The Shipman's Tale'. There is a similar story in *The Decameron* (Day 8, Tale 1). The wife of a miserly merchant asks the loan of a hundred francs from a priest to buy finery. The priest borrows the sum from the merchant and hands it to the wife, and the wife grants him her favours. On the merchant's return from a jour-

ney the priest tells him that he has repaid the sum to the wife, who cannot deny receiving it.

(16) 'The Prioress's Tale' tells of the murder of a child by Jews because he sings a Marian hymn while passing through their quarter and of the discovery of his body because of its continued singing of the hymn after death. There are many parallels for the story.

(17) 'Chaucer's Tale of Sir Thopas' is a witty and elegant parody of the contemporary romance, both in its subject and in the insubstantiality of its *tail-rhyme form. Its targets include the heroes it catalogues (VII. 898–900): Horn Child, the legend of Ypotys, *Bevis of Hampton, *Guy of Warwick, the unidentified Pleyndamour, and *Libeaus Desconus.

(18) When the Host interrupts the tale of Sir Thopas, Chaucer moves to the opposite extreme with a heavy prose homily, 'The Tale of Melibeus'. This story of the impetuous Melibeus and his wise wife Prudence dates from Italy in the 1240s. Chaucer's immediate source was the 1336 version in French prose by Renaud de Louens.

(19) 'The Monk's Tale' is composed of a number of tragedies of persons fallen from high estate, taken from different authors and arranged on the model of Boccaccio's *De Casibus Virorum Illustrium*.

(20) 'The Nun's Priest's Tale' is related to the French cycle of Renart (*see* REYNARD THE FOX), telling of a fox that beguiled a cock by praising his father's singing and was in turn beguiled into losing him by pausing to boast at his victory. The mock-heroic story is full of rhetoric and exempla, and it is one of the most admired of the Tales. The famous ironic ending invites the reader to 'take the morality' of the Tale, in spite of its apparent lightness of substance, on the grounds that St Paul says that everything is written in order to teach us something.

(21) 'The Second Nun's Tale', in *rhymeroyal, is perhaps translated from the life of St Cecilia in *The *Golden Legend* of Jacobus de Voragine. It describes the miracles and martyrdom of the noble Roman maiden Cecilia and her husband Valerian.

(22) 'The Canon's Yeoman's Tale' is told by a character who joins the pilgrims at this late stage with his master, the dubious canon, whose alchemical skills the yeoman praises. The first 200 lines of the tale tell of the Alchemist's arcane practice and its futility, before proceeding to the tale proper, which tells of how an alchemical canon (who is *not* his master, he protests) tricks a priest out of £40 by pretending to teach him the art of making precious metals.

(23) 'The Manciple's Tale' is the fable of the tell-tale crow, told by many authors from *Ovid in *Metamorphoses* (2. 531–62) onwards. Phebus (Phoebus) has a crow which is white and can speak. It reveals to Phebus the infidelity of his wife and Phebus kills her in a rage. Then, in remorse, he plucks out the crow's white feathers, deprives it of speech, and throws it 'unto the devel', which is why crows are now black. A very similar version of the story is told in Gower's *Confessio Amantis* (III. 768–835), and there are other examples by Guillaume de *Machaut and in the *Ovide moralisé* (c.1324).

(24) 'The Parson's Tale' which concludes the work (and was no doubt meant to, despite the incompleteness of the *Tales*) is a long prose treatise, ostensibly on Penitence but dealing at most length with the *seven deadly sins. The two principal sources are Raymund de Pennaforte's *Summa* (1220s) for the sections on Penitence, and Guilielmus Peraldus' *Summa Vitiorum* (c.1250s) for the seven deadly sins. Most manuscripts have 'The Parson's Tale' leading straight into the closing 'Retraccions' in which Chaucer, or his narrator (the voice is uncertain), takes leave of his book. He asks forgiveness of God for his 'translacions and enditynges of worldly vanities', including 'The Tales of Caunterbury, thilke that sownen into [i.e. tend towards] synne'. But this rhetorical conclusion need not be read as a revocation of his work by the poet; following St Augustine's *Retractationes*, many medieval works end by distancing the writer from the non-spiritual elements in his work.

canto A subdivision of a long narrative or epic poem, employed in the works of Edmund *Spenser (the first to apply the term in English), Lord *Byron, Ezra *Pound, and many others.

Canute (Cnutr) A Dane who was king of England 1016–35. The legend of his failing to repel the sea is told by Holinshed, VII. xiii, after Henry of Huntingdon (who may have invented it) and Geffrei *Gaimar.

Canute, The Song of A famous early English poetic ballad fragment allegedly composed and sung by the king as he rowed past Ely, and recorded by a monk in the *Chronicles of Ely* in 1166.

Can You Forgive Her? A novel by Anthony *Trollope, published 1864–5, the first in the *Palliser series. Alice Vavasor, spirited and independent, is engaged to the 'paragon' John Grey, but irrationally rejects him in favour of her disreputable cousin George Vavasor. She extricates George from his financial and personal difficulties, and works to further his political ambitions. Nevertheless, George is ruined, and sets off for America, pausing only to make an attempt on the life of John Grey. Grey renews his courtship of Alice, who accepts him.

These difficulties are described alongside an account of the early married life of Lady Glencora Palliser, who, despite the virtues of her aristocratic husband Plantagenet, still loves the worthless Burgo Fitzgerald. She is tempted to elope with him, but is saved by the timely arrival of her husband, who takes her out of harm's way by embarking on a lengthy foreign tour, at the expense of his own political plans. His sacrifice results in an uneasy marital reconciliation.

The novel combines Trollope's interests in the dynamics of politics and courtship.

ČAPEK, Karel (1890–1938) Czech novelist and dramatist. The plays he wrote jointly with his brother Josef (1887–1945) include *The Insect Play* (1921), a satire on human society and totalitarianism. Čapek's best-known independent work was *R.U.R.* ('Rossum's Universal Robots') (1920, first English performance 1923). The concept of the robot (Czech 'robota', meaning drudgery) opened up a flexible vein of *science fiction, and added a word to the English language. Čapek also wrote *scientific romances, such as *War with the Newts* (1936); a trilogy of more realistic novels, *Hordubal*, *The Meteor*, and *An Ordinary Life* (1933–4); and travel books and essays, including *Letters from England* (1923).

CAPELL, Edward (1713–81) Shakespearian commentator. His edition of Shakespeare (1768) was the first to be based on complete and careful collations of all the old copies, and his arrangement of the lines has been influential. His *Commentary, Notes and Various Readings to Shakespeare*, begun in 1774, was published in 1783. Capell was responsible for the first full scholarly discussion of Shakespeare's sources, and for the first attempt to establish the relationship between the *folios and quartos.

CAPGRAVE, John (1393–1464) Augustinian friar. In addition to theological and historical works in Latin, he wrote in English lives of St Gilbert of Sempringham and St Catherine of Alexandria, and a small body of poetry. His most significant English work is his *Chronicle* of English history up to 1417, which is marked by simplicity and lucidity of style.

CAPOTE, Truman (1924–84) American author, whose work ranges from the light-hearted story of playgirl Holly Golightly in *Breakfast at*

Tiffany's (1958) to the grim investigation *In Cold Blood* (1966), a 'non-fiction novel' or work of *faction, in which Capote recreated the brutal multiple murder of a whole Kansas family by two ex-convicts, and traces the lives of the murderers to the moment of their execution. His unfinished novel *Answered Prayers* was published in 1985 and his previously lost first novel *Summer Crossing* in 2005.

CARACTACUS (*fl.*AD 50–1) Properly Caratacus, chief leader of the resistance to the Roman invasion of Britain in 43. He was taken a prisoner to Rome in 51, where according to *Tacitus his noble spirit so pleased the emperor Claudius that he freed him. He figures in John *Fletcher's *Bonduca* and William *Mason's *Caractacus*.

Cardenio A lost play, twice recorded as having been acted by the King's Men at court in 1613, and ascribed to Shakespeare and John *Fletcher in a bookseller's list of 1653. *Theobald in his successful tragicomedy *Double Falsehood* (1728) claimed to have 'revised and adapted' a play 'written originally by W. Shakespeare'. In 1770 a newspaper reported that 'the original manuscript' was 'treasured up in the Museum of Covent Garden playhouse'; the theatre, including its library, was destroyed by fire in 1808. Presumably Shakespeare's play, like Theobald's, was based on the story of Cardenio and Lucinda in *Don Quixote* (Pt 1, chs 24–8).

CARDINAL, Marie (1929–2001) French novelist. She is best known for her widely translated autobiographical novel, *Les Mots pour le dire* (1975: *The Words to Say It*), describing her childhood in Algeria, her difficult relationship with her mother, and the successful psychoanalysis that enabled her to become a writer.

Cardinal, The A tragedy by James *Shirley, acted 1641, printed 1652. This was the first play Shirley wrote for the King's Men, and both he and his contemporaries thought it his best. It is strongly reminiscent of *Jacobean tragedy, featuring a diabolical cardinal, masquers who turn out to be murderers, poison, and attempted rape.

Careless Husband, The A comedy by Colley *Cibber (1704). Sir Charles Easy neglects his wife and carries on an intrigue with her maid Edging and with Lady Graveairs. Discovering that his wife is aware of his infidelities, he is moved to reconciliation by her tolerance and virtue. In his dedication, Cibber claims that he has set out to avoid coarseness and to imitate the conversation of the polite world.

Caretaker, The A play by Harold *Pinter, performed and published in 1960. One of Pinter's characteristically enigmatic dramas, it is built on the interaction of three characters, the tramp Davies and the brothers Aston and Mick. Aston has rescued Davies from a brawl and brought him back to a junk-filled room, in which he offers Davies a bed and, eventually, an ill-defined post as caretaker. The characters reveal themselves in inconsequential dialogue and obsessional monologue. Davies is worried about his papers, the blacks, gas leaks, and getting to Sidcup; Aston reveals that he has suffered headaches ever since undergoing electric shock treatment for his 'complaint'; Mick, the youngest, is alternately bully, cajoler, and materialist visionary, with dreams of transforming the room into a fashionable penthouse. In the end both brothers turn on Davies and evict him.

CAREW, Thomas [pron. Carey] (1594/5–1640) Poet. His elegy for John *Donne was published with Donne's poems in 1633, his masque *Coelum Britannicum* (with settings by Inigo *Jones) was performed before the king in 1634, and his *Poems* appeared in 1640. He was a close friend of Sir John *Suckling and one of the best known of the *Cavalier poets; his works include many graceful, witty, and often cynical songs and lyrics, and several longer poems, including the erotic 'A Rapture', and 'To Saxham', a country-house poem in the genre of Ben *Jonson's 'To Penshurst', by whom, with Donne, he was much influenced.

CAREY, Peter (1943–) Australian novelist, who now holds dual American and Australian citizenship. His critical reputation was established with two volumes of short stories, *The Fat Man in History* (1974) and *War Crimes* (1979), and the novel *Bliss* (1981, filmed 1985). Carey's fascination with the relationship between storytelling and truth is indicated in titles like *30 Days in Sydney: A Wildly Distorted Account* (2001). He has successfully 'translated' Australian idiom and history for an international audience, witnessed by his *Booker Prize-winning novels *Oscar and Lucinda* (1988, film 1997) and *True History of the Kelly Gang* (2001). Other works include *Illywhacker* (1985), featuring 139-year-old narrator Herbert Badgery; *Jack Maggs* (1997), which reconfigures Charles *Dickens's *Great Expectations* from the point of view of the convict Magwitch; *Theft: A Love Story* (2006); *My Life as a Fake* (2004), on the Ern Malley hoax, in which poets James McAuley and Harold Stewart submitted pseudo-modernist poems to the journal *Angry Penguins* under the name of 'deceased garage mechanic' 'Ern Malley'; and *Parrot and Olivier in America* (2010).

CARLE, Eric (1929–) Prolific American author/illustrator. Carle uses collage, hand-painted papers, and die-cut pages as in *The Very Hungry Caterpillar* (1969), in which the Caterpillar 'eats' through pictures of food.

CARLETON, William (1794–1869) Novelist and story writer, born into an impoverished Irish-speaking Roman Catholic family in Tyrone. *Traits and Stories of the Irish Peasantry* (1830–3) appeared shortly after his conversion to Protestantism. Like much of Carleton's work, *Traits* mixes didactic, naturalistic, *Gothic, and melodramatic elements. *Fardorougha, the Miser* (1839) and *The Black Prophet* (1847), a bleak story of the potato famine, are perhaps the best known of his novels.

CARLYLE, Jane Baillie Welsh (1801–66) Letter writer. In 1821 she was introduced by her former tutor Edward Irving to Thomas *Carlyle, whom she married in 1826. Though much of her energy during her married life was devoted to the humouring and protection of a temperamental husband, she is remembered as one of the best letter writers in the English language, witty, caustic, and observant, and as a literary hostess who impressed all who met her. Her vast circle of friends, acquaintances, and correspondents included the Italian patriot Giuseppe Mazzini (1805–72), Robert *Browning, Alfred *Tennyson, John *Forster, and Geraldine *Jewsbury, but many of her best letters were written to her relatives in Edinburgh and Liverpool and, most notably, to Thomas himself, with whom she corresponded copiously during their temporary separations. Her subjects include personalities, travels, books, and, notably, her servants; she commented, 'I think, talk, and write about my servants as much as Geraldine [Jewsbury] does about her lovers.'

CARLYLE, Thomas (1795–1881) Historian, biographer, and essayist, born at Ecclefechan; his parents belonged to a Dissenting branch of the Presbyterian Church. The legacy of the *Scottish Enlightenment which Carlyle encountered at the University of Edinburgh led him away from his intention to join the ministry towards literary work, tutoring, and reviewing. He studied German literature and published his life of *Schiller (1825) and translations of *Goethe's *Wilhelm Meister's Apprenticeship* (1824) and *Wilhelm Meister's Travels* (1827). In 1826 he married Jane Welsh (*see* CARLYLE, JANE BAILLIE WELSH) and after two years in Edinburgh they moved for financial reasons to her farm at Craigenputtock, on the lonely moors of Nithsdale. 'Signs of the Times', an attack on *Utilitarianism, appeared in 1829 in the *Edinburgh Review*; *Sartor Resartus* followed in *Fraser's Magazine* in 1833–4, a highly idiosyncratic and personal work which showed his great debt to German philosophy and literature. In 1834 the Carlyles moved to Cheyne Row, Chelsea, where he worked on his *History of the *French Revolution* (1837); the manuscript of the first volume was accidentally used to light a fire while on loan to John Stuart *Mill, but with characteristic perseverance Carlyle rewrote it. The work established Carlyle's reputation, and he from this time onward strengthened the position that made him known as 'the Sage of Chelsea'. His series of lectures, *On *Heroes, Hero-Worship and the Heroic in History*, delivered in 1840 and published in 1841, attracted glittering and fashionable audiences, and taught him to distrust (and indeed to abandon) his own blend of 'prophecy and play-acting'. In *Chartism* (1839) and *Past and Present* (1843) Carlyle applied himself to what he called 'the Condition-of-England question', attacking both laissez-faire and the dangers of revolution it encouraged, castigating an economic and political climate where Cash Payment had become 'the sole nexus between man and man', and manifesting with more passion than consistency a sympathy with the industrial poor which heralded the new novels of social consciousness of the 1840s (*see* *GASKELL, ELIZABETH, and *DISRAELI, BENJAMIN). His evocation in *Past and Present* of medieval conditions provided a new perspective on machinery and craftsmanship that was pursued by John *Ruskin and William *Morris, but Carlyle, unlike some of his followers, turned increasingly away from democracy towards the kind of feudalism which he saw expressed in the rule of the 'Strong Just Man'. His 'Occasional Discourse on the Nigger Question' (1849) and *Latter-Day Pamphlets* (1850) express his anti-democratic views in an exaggerated form. His admiration for Cromwell was expressed in his edition of *Oliver Cromwell's Letters and Speeches* (2 vols, 1845), and for *Frederick the Great in his six-volume biography (1858–65). His life of his friend John *Sterling (with some remarkable reminiscences of S. T. *Coleridge), appeared in 1851.

Jane Carlyle died in 1866, a blow which he said 'shattered my whole existence into immeasurable ruin'. He gave her papers and letters in 1871, with ambiguous instructions, to his friend and disciple J. A. *Froude, who published them after Carlyle's death, in 1883; Froude also published Carlyle's *Reminiscences* (1881) and a four-volume biography (1882–4). These posthumous publications caused much controversy, largely by breaking the conventions of Victorian *biography (against which Carlyle had himself fulminated) to suggest marital discord and sexual inadequacy on Carlyle's part.

Carlyle's influence as social prophet and critic, and his prestige as historian, were enormous during his lifetime. In the 20th century his reputation waned, partly because his trust in authority and admiration of strong leaders were interpreted as foreshadowings of Fascism. His highly individualistic prose, which had always presented difficulties, became more obscure with the lapse of time; his violent exclamatory rhetoric, his italics and Teutonic coinages, and his eccentric archaisms and strange punctuation were already known by the late 1850s as 'Carlylese' (but many of his coinages have become accepted as part of the language).

Carmarthen See BLACK BOOK OF CARMARTHEN.

carnivalesque A term coined by the Russian critic Mikhail *Bakhtin to describe various manifestations of popular humour and cultural resistance to the restraints of official hierarchies. The institution of carnival itself provides a model for understanding some of the more playful effects of literature, principally in the novel and drama. According to this view, some kinds of literary *comedy are rooted in folk traditions of mockery directed at the church and other authorities.

CARPENTER, Edward (1844–1929) Socialist, poet, and anthologist, he became a fellow of Trinity Hall, Cambridge, and worked with F. D. Maurice. In 1874 he abandoned his fellowship and orders and moved north, settling at Millthorpe, near Chesterfield, where he pursued his own version of socialism and communal fellowship, inspired by *Thoreau, John *Ruskin, and William *Morris. His lifestyle and private middle-class revolt (expressed by sandals, vegetarianism, overt homosexuality, praise of manual labour and the working man) became an important symbol of liberation for many, including E. M. *Forster. His long poem *Towards Democracy* (1883–1902), inspired by Walt *Whitman and the *Bhagavad-gītā, expressed his millenarian sense of the cosmic consciousness and 'spiritual democracy', and of the march of humanity towards 'freedom and joy'. *My Days and Dreams* (1916) is an autobiography.

CARR, J. L. (James Joseph Lloyd) (1912–94) Novelist, children's writer, and independent publisher. His works include *A Season in Sinji* (1968, a cricket story); *How Steeple Sinderby Won the FA Cup* (1975); and *The Green Children of the Woods* (1976). *A Month in the Country* (1980; filmed 1987, with a screenplay by Simon *Gray) is set in the summer of 1920: the narrator Birkin, a war survivor, is engaged in restoring a wall painting in the village church at Oxgodby. *The Ballad of Pollock's Crossing* (1985), also set in the 1920s, takes a young Yorkshire schoolteacher to the American Midwest, where he challenges what was then the American orthodoxy of Indian history.

CARR, Marina (1964–) Dramatist. Carr's vivid and extreme plays typically adapt Greek prototypes to rural Irish settings, and deploy a theatrical dialect based on the speech of the Irish midlands. Her works include *Portia Coughlan* (1996), *Ariel* (2002)—a political satire based on the *Iphigeneia story—and the bleak, bitter *Woman and Scarecrow* (2006).

CARRINGTON, Dora (1893–1932) Painter, diarist, and letter writer. It was not until her extraordinarily vivid diaries and charmingly illustrated letters were posthumously edited for publication by David *Garnett (1970) that she became known to the general public. That book told the story of her mysterious and passionate love for the homosexual Lytton *Strachey, after whose death she committed suicide. Christopher *Hampton's film *Carrington* (1995) is based on Michael *Holroyd's life of Strachey.

CARROLL, Lewis Pseudonym of Charles Lutwidge *Dodgson.

CARSON, Ciaran (1948–) Irish poet, translator, novelist, and musician, born in Belfast. From *The Irish for No* (1987) onwards, his poetry uses complex, digressive narratives, influenced by Carson's Irish-speaking background and his knowledge of traditional music and story, to explore history, memory, and the layered maps of Belfast life from the 17th century to the post-1968 *Troubles. *Breaking News* (2003) offers a spiky commentary on the West's implication in Middle Eastern violence from the Crimean War to the present, while *For All We Know* (2008) is a cryptic, fugue-like sonnet sequence on the progress of a love affair. His latest collection is *On the Night Watch* (2009).

The vernacular flair that distinguishes Carson's poetry also informs his novels, including *Shamrock Tea* (2001), and his translations. His *Collected Poems* appeared in 2008.

CARSWELL, Catherine (1879–1946) Née Macfarlane, Scottish journalist, novelist, and biographer, born in Glasgow. She was dismissed from her job on the *Glasgow Herald* in 1915 for reviewing D. H. *Lawrence's The *Rainbow and with Lawrence's encouragement went on to complete her sexually frank autobiographical novel *Open the Door!* (1920). Her fictionalized *Life of Robert Burns* (1930) caused outrage in Scotland but is now considered a classic of literary biography.

CARTER, Angela (1940–92) Novelist and short story writer. Her work, imbued with a keen sense of the macabre and the wittily surreal, draws heavily on symbolism and themes derived from traditional fairy tales and folk myths. *The Magic Toyshop* (1967, filmed 1986), associated her with the tradition of *magic realism and was followed by *Several Perceptions* (1968). Succeeding novels—*Heroes and Villains* (1969), set in the aftermath of nuclear conflict, *Love* (1971), and *The Infernal Desire Machines of Dr Hoffman* (1972)—further displayed a fascination with neo-Gothic settings, often infused with a keen feminist sensibility. *The Passion of New Eve* (1977) was centrally concerned with feminist issues, as was a later cultural study, *The Sadeian Woman* (1979). *Nights at the Circus* (1984), about a female Victorian circus performer, Fevvers, who can fly, confirmed Carter's status as an outstanding literary fabulist, while her ability to evoke and adapt the darker resonances of traditional forms of *fantasy was brilliantly deployed in *The Bloody Chamber and Other Stories* (1979), which contains one of her best-known reworkings of traditional material, 'The Company of Wolves' (based on the story of Little Red Riding Hood), filmed in 1984. Her last novel, *Wise Children* (1991), was a rumbustious extravaganza, packed with Shakespearian analogies and allusions, about two theatrical dynasties. She translated the fairy tales of Charles *Perrault (1977) and produced a retelling of 'Sleeping Beauty' and other fairy-tales (1982). She also compiled *The Virago Book of Fairy Tales* (1990; 2nd vol., 1992); *Black Venus* (1985) is a collection of short stories. A selection of critical writings, *Expletives Deleted*, was published posthumously in 1992. A posthumous collection of stories and sketches, *American Ghosts and Old World Wonders*, appeared in 1993.

CARTER, Elizabeth (1717–1806) Scholar and poet; she learned Latin, Greek, and Hebrew with her brothers. With a persistence praised by Virginia *Woolf in *A *Room of one's Own*, she also acquired French, Italian, Spanish, German, Portuguese, and Arabic. She published volumes of poems in 1738 and 1762. Samuel Johnson, who thought very highly of her as a scholar, invited her to contribute to the *Rambler, (44 and 100). Her painstaking translation of *Epictetus (1758) gained her a European reputation. She chose independence rather than marriage, and was an energetic correspondent and member of the *Blue Stockings.

CARTER, Lin (1930–88) American novelist and editor. His own fiction pastiches Edgar Rice *Burroughs and Robert E. *Howard, but as editor and anthologist, reviving important figures like Lord *Dunsany and popularizing *Tolkien, his influence on modern *fantasy was immense.

CARTER, Martin (1927–97) Poet, born in Georgetown, Guyana. With his stirring and influential volume about political oppression, *Poems of Resistance* (1954), he established an international reputation. Other volumes include *Jail Me Quickly* (1964), *Poems of Succession* (1977), and *Poems of Affinity* (1980).

CARTLAND, Barbara *See* HISTORICAL FICTION.

CARTWRIGHT, Jim (1958–) Dramatist, born in Farnworth, the impoverished Lancashire town that inspired his first play, *Road* (1986), evoking a turbulent night in a run-down working-class community. Later plays include *The Rise and Fall of Little Voice* (1994, filmed 1998), about a mother's exploitation of her reclusive daughter's talent for mimicry; *I Licked a Slag's Deodorant* (1996); and *Hard Fruit* (2000). He wrote and directed *Johnny Shakespeare* (BBC, 2007).

CARTWRIGHT, Justin (1945–) Novelist and screenwriter, born in South Africa. His three novels featuring a journalist and filmmaker, Tim Curtiz—*Interior* (1988), *Look at It This Way* (1990), and *Masai Dreaming* (1993)—survey, often sardonically, manners and mores in Africa and Europe. *In Every Face I Meet* (1995) is set in London at the time of Nelson Mandela's release. *The Song Before It Is Sung* (2007) fictionalizes the relationship between Sir Isaiah Berlin (1909–97) and Adam von Trott (1909–44), the Prussian aristocrat involved in a plot to assassinate Hitler. *To Heaven by Water* explores the idea of transcendence, and *Other People's Money* (2010) is a thriller. *This Secret Garden* (2007) is a memoir of Oxford.

CARTWRIGHT, William (1611–43) Oxford scholar, preacher, poet, and dramatist, one of the 'sons' of Ben *Jonson. His most successful play, *The Royal Slave*, was performed before Charles I in 1636.

CARVER, Raymond (1939–88) American short story writer and poet. His first collection of poetry, *Near Klamath*, was published in 1968. This was followed by *Winter Insomnia* (1970) and *At Night the Salmon Move* (1976). Although he claimed that he would like to be remembered first as a poet, he became best known for his short stories. His first collection, *Will You Please Be Quiet, Please?* (1976) was followed by *What We Talk About When We Talk About Love* (1981), *Cathedral* (1983), and *Elephant* (1988). Like the stories of Richard Ford and Tobias *Wolff, with whom he shares the label of *'dirty realism', his work deals powerfully with unremarkable, glamourless small-town lives, described in pared-down, simple prose. Carver continued to write poetry through the 1980s, publishing *Where Water Comes Together with Other Water* (1985) and *Ultramarine* (1986), as well as *Fires* (1983), a volume which combined his poetry and short stories and a selection of his essays. His last collection of poetry, *A New Path to the Waterfall* (1989) was published posthumously, and a collected poems, *All of Us*, in 1996.

CARY, Elizabeth, Viscountess Falkland (1585–1639) Poet, playwright, and translator. A self-taught linguist, she had mastered five languages before marriage at 15 to Henry Cary, later Lord Falkland. Secretly embracing *Roman Catholicism, she separated from Falkland in 1625, was subsequently disinherited by her father, and died of consumption, in loneliness and want. She wrote hymns, poems, and translations from French, Spanish, Latin, and Hebrew, many of which are now lost, and *The Tragedy of Mariam* (1613), the first known play in English by a woman. The drama raises Mariam, the 'shrew' wife of Herod, to tragic status, and reflects Cary's own life. Her *History of Edward II* (c.1627) is the first English history play by a woman. Her daughter, a Benedictine nun, wrote her mother's biography.

CARY, Joyce (1888–1957) Novelist, born in Londonderry. After war service in Africa, he returned to England and devoted himself to writing. His early 'African' novels, *Aissa Saved* (1932), *An American Visitor* (1933), *The African Witch* (1936), and *Mister Johnson* (1939), show with shrewd sympathy the relations between Africans and their British administrators. His major work consists of two trilogies: *Herself Surprised* (1941), *To Be a Pilgrim* (1942), and *The Horse's Mouth* (1944), chiefly concerned with the life of the bohemian artist Gulley Jimson; and *Prisoner of Grace* (1952), *Except the Lord* (1953), and *Not Honour More* (1955), a study of politics. The major theme of the novels is the need for individual freedom and choice. Two further novels are studies of childhood: *Charley is my Darling* (1940) and the semi-autobiographical *A House of Children* (1941). Cary also wrote poetry, including *Marching Soldier* (1945) and *The Drunken Sailor* (1947); short stories, such as *Spring Song and Other Stories* (1960); and an unfinished novel with a religious theme, *The Captive and the Free* (1959).

CARY, Lucius See FALKLAND, LUCIUS.

CARY, Mary (b. c.1621) From 1651 known as Mary Rande. A Londoner during the English revolution, she was one of the most formidable intellectuals of the Fifth Monarchist movement, who constructed a systematic programme of radical social reform (including wage ceilings, postal service, and stamp tax) for the millennium, which she expected to begin in 1701. She maintained the equal right of women 'saints' to speak on public matters, and spoke for the poor and oppressed. Her most important works are *The Little Horn's Doom and Downfall* (1646), which predicts the fall of Charles I, the utopian *A New and More Exact Map* (1651), and *Twelve Proposals* (1653).

CASAUBON, Isaac (1559–1614) French classical scholar, born in Geneva of Huguenot refugee parents. From 1610 until his death he lived in London, receiving a pension from James I and becoming naturalized in 1611. Casaubon published critical editions and commentaries on the works of a number of ancient authors, chiefly Greek, including *Theophrastus (1592). He left a diary in Latin of his daily activities, the *Ephemerides*. There is a life of Casaubon by Mark *Pattison (1875).

Case is Altered, The An early comedy by Ben *Jonson, performed c.1597/8 by the boy actors of the Children of Blackfriars, printed 1609. Its main plot, involving complicated identity-swapping, draws on *Plautus' *The Captives*, and its farcical sub-plot derives from Plautus' *The Pot of Gold*.

'Castaway, The' A poem by William *Cowper, written 1799, published 1803, based on an incident from Captain *Anson's *Voyage round* *the World* (1748). Cowper depicts with sympathetic intensity the suffering of a seaman swept overboard to drown. Mr Ramsay in Virginia Woolf's *To the Lighthouse* is given to declaiming its closing lines.

CASTELVETRO, Ludovico (1505–71) Italian scholar and critic from Modena, best known for his commentary on Aristotle's *Poetics* (1570, 1576), which included a Greek text, an Italian translation, and a critical discussion. His views on the *unities, more rigid than Aristotle's own, had considerable influence on the development of neo-classical theory.

CASTIGLIONE, Baldassare (1478–1529) Italian courtier, diplomat, humanist, and author in a variety of genres. His best-known work is *Il libro del cortegiano* (1528), translated into English as *The Courtyer* (1561) by Sir Thomas *Hoby. The four books of this work purport to record a series of conversations at the court of Urbino in 1507. In the work Castiglione draws on the humanist dialogue form, handbooks for the education of princes, and the writings of *Cicero and *Quintilian. Each book centres on a particular theme: the qualities necessary for the ideal courtier (I); how to practise these qualities (II); the court lady (III); the relationship of courtier and prince (IV); the book concludes with a celebration by Pietro Bembo (1470–1547) of Neoplatonic ideas of love. *Il cortegiano* rapidly became extremely popular throughout Europe. For its influence in England see Henry Howard, earl of *Surrey, Sir Thomas *Wyatt, Philip *Sidney, Edmund *Spenser, and *Shakespeare; and later W. B. *Yeats.

Castle of Indolence, The A poem in *Spenserian stanzas by James *Thomson (1748). The first of the two cantos describes the castle of the wizard Indolence, into which he entices weary pilgrims who sink into torpor amidst luxurious ease. The inmates become diseased and languish in a dungeon. The second canto describes the conquest of the castle by the efficient and energetic Knight of Industry. *Wordsworth praised the poem's harmonious verse and pure diction.

Castle of Otranto, The Novel by Horace *Walpole (1764), published anonymously, with an elaborate preface describing the author as 'Onuphrio Muralto', a medieval Italian canon. Prince Manfred of Otranto has a devoted wife, Hippolita; a son, Conrad; and a daughter, Matilda. At his wedding to Isabella of Vicenza, Conrad is crushed by a vast, black-plumed helmet from the nearby statue of Alfonso the Good.

A bold young man in the crowd is accused of causing Conrad's death and imprisoned beneath the helmet. Manfred determines that he must have an heir and declares that he will divorce Hippolita and marry Isabella, who escapes through a gloomy vault with the assistance of the mysterious young man. Manfred is confronted by Friar Jerome, who gives Isabella sanctuary in his nearby monastery. The young man is discovered to be Theodore, the son of Jerome, now revealed as the count of Falconara. Theodore finds Isabella in an eerie forest cave, and wounds her father, Frederic, whom he mistakes for an enemy. At the castle Jerome confirms that Theodore's mother was the daughter of Alfonso. Manfred stabs a woman he believes to be Isabella, only to find he has killed his daughter. Distraught, he reveals that his grandfather poisoned Alfonso in order to gain Otranto. He and Hippolita retire to monastic penitence, and Isabella marries Theodore, the rightful prince. Subtitled 'A Gothic Story' in its second edition, the book established several key *Gothic conventions: ghosts, vaults, living statues, mysterious appearances, and a psychology of extreme emotion.

Castle of Perseverance, The A *morality play in 3,700 lines, dating from the first quarter of the 15th century, one of the group (the others are *Mankind and *Wisdom) known as Macro plays from their 18th-century owner. The earliest surviving complete morality, it is of interest as an exhaustive compendium of such morality features as a battle between vices and virtues, a mixture of allegorical (Backbiter) and diabolical (Belyal) figures, and the enactment of Death and Judgement; but it is also highly significant in the history of English theatre, largely because of a diagrammatic representation of the Castle-mound as 'Theatre in the Round' which its staging requires.

Castle Rackrent A novel by Maria *Edgeworth, published 1800. This work may be regarded as the first fully developed *historical novel and the first true *regional novel in English. Set 'Before the year 1782', the characters, the life of the country, and the speech are unmistakably Irish. It is narrated in his old age by the devoted Thady Quirk, steward to three generations of Rackrents. The rattling narrative begins with the wild life of the hard-drinking Sir Patrick, 'inventor of raspberry whisky', who lived before Thady's time. He was succeeded by the litigious and debt-ridden Sir Murtagh, a skinflint who died of a fury. His brother Sir Kit, who inherits, brings to the castle his unfortunate

English Jewish wife, who has 'never seen a peat-stack or a bog' and who, after many arguments over sausages, diamonds, and other matters, is shut up in the castle for seven years, until her gambling husband is killed in a duel. Meanwhile the cunning young lawyer Jason Quirk, Thady's son, is gathering more and more of the family's affairs into his hands. The next heir, Sir Condy, is an ardent, extravagant politician, who tosses a coin to decide whether to marry the rich Isabella Moneygawl or the pretty Judy M'Quirk. He marries Isabella and, keeping lavish open house in their tumbledown castle, they finally exhaust the last resources of the Rackrents. When the bailiffs arrive Isabella flees and Jason Quirk is found to own almost everything. The castle is sold and Condy amuses himself by feigning death at his own wake. When he eventually dies Isabella contests the property, but Jason emerges as a 'high gentleman with estates and a fortune'.

Miss Edgeworth wrote the book without her father's knowledge, and it is one of the few he did not 'edit'.

Catch-22 A comic, satirical, surreal, and apocalyptic novel by Joseph *Heller, originally entitled *Catch-18*, published in 1961, which describes the ordeals and exploits of a group of American airmen based on a small Mediterranean island during the Italian campaign of the Second World War, and in particular the reactions of Captain Yossarian, the protagonist. The title of the novel has passed into the language to describe a situation of deadlock, composed of two mutually exclusive sets of conditions. Heller conflates the war situation and the paranoia of McCarthy's America to produce an absurdist sequence of episodes which invert common-sense presumptions about reality.

catharsis A Greek word for 'purification' or 'purgation', which has long been a significant but much-debated concept in the theory of *tragedy, since Aristotle invoked it in his *Poetics*, where he writes that tragedy should succeed in 'arousing pity and fear in such a way as to accomplish a catharsis of such emotions'. Aristotle here seems to be responding to *Plato's view that poetic drama improperly fed the passions by a counter-suggestion that on the contrary it helped to cleanse and release them. The concept has been redefined by generations of critics, including Ludovico *Castelvetro, John *Milton, G. E. Lessing, Johann Wolfgang von *Goethe, and Arthur *Schopenhauer.

CATHER, Willa Sibert (1876–1947) American novelist. Her first book of poems was *April Twilights* (1903), followed by a book of short stories, *The Troll Garden* (1905). Her novels include *My Antonia* (1918), the story of an immigrant girl from Bohemia, settled in Nebraska, narrated by her childhood friend Jim Burden, *The Professor's House* (1925), which contrasts the middle-aged disillusion of Professor St Peter with his memories of his favourite student, and *Death Comes for the Archbishop* (1927), a historical novel based on the French Catholic mission of Father Latour, set in New Mexico. Her other works include two studies of the dangers and rewards of unconventionality: *My Mortal Enemy* (1926) and *Lucy Gayheart* (1935). The dual impulse towards exploration and cultivation, towards art and domesticity, towards excitement and safety, is a constant theme in Cather's work. She records her own debt to another pioneer, Sarah Orne *Jewett, in *Not under Forty* (1936).

Catherine A novel by W. M. *Thackeray, published serially in *Fraser's Magazine*, 1839–40. Thackeray took the outline of the story of the murderess Catherine Hayes from the *Newgate Calendar*, and deliberately made his novel as grim and sordid as possible, in reaction against the popular 'Newgate novels' of Edward *Bulwer-Lytton, Harrison *Ainsworth, and others.

CATHERINE II, the Great (Empress Ekaterina Alekseevna) (1729–96) Russian empress. She converted to Orthodoxy on her betrothal to Grand Duke Pavel Petrovich, who as Peter III acceded to the Russian throne in 1761. In June 1762 she was proclaimed empress in her own right after a palace coup. Her husband's subsequent murder (for Horace *Walpole, she was always 'Catherine Slay-Czar') and the succession of (increasingly young) favourites throughout her long reign were to bring a reputation for ruthlessness and sexual depravity. She promoted the westernizing policies of her predecessor *Peter I and established a society (1768) for the translation of classical and modern European works, which included novels by Henry *Fielding and Jonathan *Swift. Her many biographers include Mary *Hays (1760–1843).

Catiline A Roman tragedy by Ben *Jonson, performed 1611, based principally on *Sallust's *Catiline*. Like *Sejanus* it represents Jonson's wish to treat Roman history with scholarly accuracy, an aim that involved incorporating large portions of *Cicero's Orations in its text. Jonson called it a 'dramatic poem', and adopts the Senecan apparatus of an introductory ghost and a classical chorus. The plot portrays the events of the year 63 BC. Catiline, secretly encouraged by Caesar and Crassus, organizes a conspiracy to overthrow the existing government. Cicero summons the Senate and accuses Catiline, who leaves Rome and joins the army raised by his adherents at Faesulae, but falls in a decisive engagement with the government forces. The first performance was a notorious failure, as Jonson noted in an angrily defensive preface to the printed text.

Cato A tragedy by Joseph *Addison (1713). It deals with the death of *Cato the republican; the devotion of Juba, Cato's Numidian ally, to Cato's daughter Marcia, adds some emotional interest. Samuel *Johnson described it as 'rather a poem in dialogue than a drama', but in its day it was enormously successful, partly because of political claims made for it by opposing parties. Alexander *Pope wrote the prologue.

CATO, Marcus Porcius (95-46 BC) of Utica, statesman, otherwise known as Cato the younger to differentiate him from his great-grandfather. A Roman model of republican and *Stoic integrity, he committed suicide at Utica in Africa rather than surrender to Julius *Caesar. His daughter Porcia married Marcus *Brutus. He is included in *Plutarch's lives, is a hero of *Lucan's *Pharsalia*, and is the subject of Joseph *Addison's play *Cato*. His name is associated with liberty in Trenchard and Gordon's *Cato's Letters* (1720-23), widely read in revolutionary America.

CATULLUS, Gaius Valerius (*c.*84-*c.*54 BC) One of the most versatile of Roman poets, whose single verse collection, containing a mixture of 116 love poems, elegies, and satirical epigrams, ranges from the witty to the mournful and the delicate to the obscene. He was among the first to introduce into Latin the mannered style of the Hellenistic school, particularly *Callimachus. Many of his poems explore the extremes of his affair with Lesbia. His work remained virtually unknown during the Middle Ages, but after a manuscript of his poems had come to light at Verona in the 14th century interest multiplied dramatically. Individual poems (on kisses, sparrows, the death of his brother) as well as his themes and moods were much imitated. There are notable English examples by Thomas *Campion, Ben *Jonson, Robert *Herrick, Richard *Lovelace, Lord *Byron,

Leigh *Hunt, Walter Savage *Landor, Alfred *Tennyson, and Ezra *Pound, and a complete translation by C. H. *Sisson.

CAUSLEY, Charles (1917-2003) Poet, born in Launceston, Cornwall; Cornish topography and themes are central to his work. His first collection of verse, *Farewell, Aggie Weston* (1951), was followed by many others, including *Survivor's Leave* (1953), *Johnny Alleluia* (1961), *Secret Destinations* (1984), *A Field of Vision* (1988) and a *Collected Poems 1951-2000* (2000). He published highly successful collections of children's stories and anthologies of verse, and did not distinguish in his *Collected Poems* between work for adults and for children. His poetry is marked by a powerful simplicity of diction and rhythm, and shows the influence of popular songs and, notably, the ballad tradition. Innocence is a recurrent theme, and his admiration for John *Clare is the direct inspiration of several poems. Religious and seafaring images, often interwoven, are also characteristic. In many ways outside the poetic movement of his times, he was nevertheless hugely admired by such contemporaries as Philip *Larkin, Ted *Hughes, and Seamus *Heaney. He also published two verse plays, *The Gift of a Lamb* (1978) and *The Ballad of Aucassin and Nicolette* (1981, perf. 1978).

CAUTE, David (1936-) Novelist and historian. His first novel, *At Fever Pitch* (1959), was followed by many more which range in theme from *The Decline of the West* (1966), an epic of postcolonial power struggle, violent conflict, and race/sex relations, set in French West Africa, to *Veronica, or The Two Nations* (1989), a story spanning the post-war period of a boy's incestuous and damaging passion for his half-sister. *Fatima's Scarf* (1998) is a carefully researched novel set in the Yorkshire town of 'Bruddersfield' (a coinage borrowed from J. B. *Priestley) which explores the complex responses of the Muslim community in Britain and beyond to the publication of Salman *Rushdie's *Satanic Verses*, and the public debates surrounding the issue.

CAVAFY, Constantine (1863-1933) Greek poet, born in Alexandria. He published two privately printed pamphlets of verse, in 1904 and 1910, and later distributed his work to friends in broadsheets; his work achieved wider recognition largely through the influence of E. M. *Forster. Cavafy treats historical themes and characters (Julian the Apostate, Mark Antony, the fall of Constantinople) with great verve and originality, homosexual themes with frankness, and contemporary Alexandrian café life with realism and a strong sense of place.

CAVALCANTI, Guido (1260?-1300) Poet, a significant influence on the development of the *dolce stil nuovo and the early poetry of *Dante. Cavalcanti is the protagonist of Boccaccio's *Decameron* VI. 9. Dante Gabriel *Rossetti translated, and Ezra *Pound produced versions of, some of the poems.

Cavaliers A name given to supporters of Charles I in the Civil War, derived from the Italian for horseman or knight. 'Cavalier lyrics' is the term applied to lyrics by Thomas *Carew, Richard *Lovelace, John *Suckling, and Robert *Herrick, all of whom were influenced by Ben *Jonson.

CAVENDISH, George (1494–in or before 1562?) A gentleman of Thomas Wolsey's household, and author of a remarkable biography of the cardinal (*The Life and Death of Cardinal Wolsey*), in which he contrasts the magnificence of the cardinal's life with his subsequent disgrace, and indicates 'the wondrous mutability of vain honours . . . And the tickle trust to worldly princes'. First printed in 1641, it previously circulated in manuscript.

CAVENDISH, Margaret *See* NEWCASTLE, MARGARET CAVENDISH, DUCHESS OF.

CAXTON, William (1415/24–1492) The first English printer. After apprenticeship in London he worked for approximately 30 years in the Low Countries, where he translated the first book printed in English, the *Recuyell of the Histories of Troye*, and translated and printed *The Game and Playe of the Chesse*. The first major work published from his Westminster press was *The *Canterbury Tales* (*c.*1476). His version of *Malory was regarded as authoritative before the discovery of the Winchester Manuscript by W. F. Oakeshott (1934). Caxton's translations, calculated to appeal to Burgundian tastes among English readers, influenced the development of 15th-century prose style.

Cecilia, St Early Christian martyr and patron saint of music, celebrated in odes for St Cecilia's Day (22 November), written by John *Dryden and W. H. *Auden among others.

Cecilia *or Memoirs of an Heiress* (1782) Fanny *Burney's second novel. Cecilia Beverley inherits a large fortune on condition that her future husband takes her name. She lives with a succession of guardians: Harrel, a gambler, who, failing in his attempt to exploit his ward, kills himself; the vulgar and avaricious Briggs; and the Hon. Compton Delvile, a man of implacable family pride. Cecilia and his son Mortimer fall in love, but old Delvile is furious at the idea that his son should exchange his name for Cecilia's. The marriage is further thwarted by the apparently friendly Monckton, who hopes to win Cecilia and her fortune when his wife dies. Monckton's treachery is exposed; Cecilia, who has been driven to madness by her tribulations, marries Mortimer; old Delvile is reconciled to the match.

CELAN, Paul (1920–70) Pseudonym of Paul Anschel, poet, born in then Romania of a Jewish family, who wrote in German. Both his parents died in an extermination camp, and he was interned for two years in a Romanian labour camp. He settled in Paris in 1950 where he finally ended his life by suicide. His poems have been translated by Michael *Hamburger: see the selection *Poems* (1980) with an introduction by Hamburger; and more recently by Pierre Joris, John Felstiner, and Ian Fairley. His most celebrated poem *Todesfuge* (*Death Fugue*), which interweaves by means of quasi-musical motifs German and Jewish experience of a death camp, challenges Theodor *Adorno's famous remark on the barbarity of writing poetry after Auschwitz. John *Banville explores fictionally the meeting between Celan and Martin Heidegger in *Todtnauberg*, a radio play of 2006 commissioned by the BBC. *See* HOLOCAUST.

Celestina, *or The Tragi-Comedy of Calisto and Melibea* A Spanish novel in dialogue written by Fernando de Rojas. The first known edition appeared *c.*1499, in 16 acts, and a later version, in 1502, in 21 acts. The work has had several stage adaptations. A dark comedy of ambiguous moral intention, it marks an important development in the literary history of Spain and of Europe. Its characters are vividly depicted as deceitful and self-deceiving: Calisto, a young gentleman of birth and fortune; Melibea, a modest young lady; and Celestina, a cunning, greedy, and wise ex-prostitute who may also be a witch. An excellent and racy translation into English prose, *The Spanish Bawd*, was made by James Mabbe (1631). The early part of *Celestina* was translated into English verse by John Rastell, provided with a happy ending, and published, about 1525, as *A new commodye in englysh in maner of an enterlude*, better known as *An Interlude of Calisto and Melebea*.

Celtic literature Other than between Irish and Scottish Gaelic, there was little sense of common ground or purpose in the literature of the Celtic languages (Welsh, Cornish, Breton and the two major divisions of Gaelic) before the series of 'Celtic Revivals' that began in the 18th century and culminated with Matthew *Arnold and W. B. *Yeats. Common themes can nonetheless be seen in the writings collected by Kenneth Jackson in *A Celtic Miscellany* (1951) and in Arthurian materials that had expanded to a pan-European tradition. The postulation of a distinctively 'Celtic Note' in Arnold's *On the Study of Celtic Literature* (1866), following Ernest Renan, was widely challenged in the 20th century, not least on the basis of its stereotyping in the interest of imperial ideology.

Celtic Twilight, The A collection of stories by W. B. *Yeats, published 1893, illustrating the mystical belief of the Irish in the world of fairies, ghosts, and spirits. It has since become a generic phrase (slightly ironical) for the whole *Irish Revival in literature.

Cenci, The A verse tragedy by P. B. *Shelley, largely written at Livorno, in summer 1819, published 1819 and 1821 (performed in Paris 1891). The melodramatic plot is taken from the true story of Beatrice Cenci, who was tried and executed for the murder of her father, Count Francesco Cenci, at Rome in 1599. Shelley was attracted by the themes of incest and atheism: the play concentrates on the Iago-like evil of the count and the inner sufferings of Beatrice. Shelley claimed to have been influenced by the dramatic style of Calderón, but in fact the play is indebted to William *Shakespeare for much of its construction and language: Beatrice's great speech on the prospect of death, 'So young to go | Under the obscure, cold, rotting, wormy ground!' (V. 4), is based on Claudio's in *Measure for Measure* (III. i).

censorship In various forms has overshadowed English literature since the early 16th century, at first under statutory attempts to control the spread of printing through the monopoly of the *Stationers' Company, and subsequently through separate provisions for the official vetting of plays. Early censorship was directed chiefly against potentially heretical or seditious publications, and those satirizing public figures, as with the anonymous *Martin Marprelate pamphlets of 1588-9. The unpredictable dangers of public performance were addressed from 1581 by a licensing system in which new plays had to be presented for approval to the master of the *revels, a functionary in the lord chamberlain's office. A further Parliamentary

Act of 1606 provided for fines to be charged against actors using blasphemous oaths, a measure that led to the expurgation of older plays when revived. Control of printed material was increasingly evaded by anonymous *pamphleteering in the 17th century, and encountered protest from writers, notably in *Milton's unlicensed pamphlet *Areopagitica* (1644). Under Parliamentary rule, theatres were closed between 1642 and 1660, after which the lord chamberlain's department resumed stage licensing. Printed publications were again restricted by the Licensing Act of 1662, but Parliament declined to renew its powers in 1695, thereby opening the way to the emergence of the modern newspaper. Further controls on theatre were imposed in response to anti-government satires by John *Gay and Alexander *Pope: the Licensing Act of 1737 confined spoken drama (as distinct from musical theatre and mime) in London to the *Drury Lane, Covent Garden, and Haymarket theatres while giving new statutory powers to the lord chamberlain to censor plays before performance; these powers were later extended nationally by the Theatres Act of 1843. Unlicensed theatres found ways to circumvent such restrictions, while some playwrights resorted to the publication of unperformed *closet drama. In the 19th century, a succession of statutes attempted to control pornographic books and prints: the Vagrancy Act 1824, the Obscene Publications Act 1857, and the Customs Consolidation Act 1876; but literature was affected more by self-censorship practised by publishers and by the powerful *circulating libraries. From the 1890s, playwrights used private performances in theatre clubs as a means to circumvent censorship. In the early 20th century, Victorian legislation was misused to suppress works of literary value, notably D. H. *Lawrence's The *Rainbow and Radclyffe *Hall's The Well of Loneliness, and to confiscate imported copies of James *Joyce's *Ulysses. Protests from writers amid a public climate of liberalization led to a revised Obscene Publications Act (1959) which allowed literary merit as a defence: in a famous test case in 1960, *Penguin Books was acquitted of obscenity charges over its unexpurgated reprint of Lawrence's *Lady Chatterley's Lover. Soon after, the lord chamberlain's censorship of plays was abandoned (1968).

CENTLIVRE, Susanna (?1669–1723) Dramatist and poet. Her first play, *The Perjured Husband* (1700), appeared under the name Susanna Carroll, taken from her second husband. She wrote eighteen further plays, of which the most successful were *The Gamester* (1705), *The *Busie Body* (1709), *The Wonder: A Woman Keeps a Secret* (1714), and *A Bold Stroke for a Wife* (1718). She reviewed her career with irony in the poem *A Woman's Case* (1720).

Cent nouvelles nouvelles A collection of often licentious French tales about such characters as deceived husbands, wily wives, and cunning clerics, loosely modelled on Boccaccio's *Decameron*, and composed by an anonymous writer between 1456 and 1461 for Philip, duke of Burgundy. The tales are told by members of the Burgundian court, including the duke himself.

Certain Sonnets 32 sonnets and poems by Philip *Sidney first printed in editions of *The *Arcadia* (1598). The last two sonnets, incorrectly used by 19th-century editors to conclude *Astrophel and Stella*, are rejections of secular love.

CERVANTES SAAVEDRA, Miguel de (1547–1616) Spanish novelist and dramatist. His first attempt at fiction was a pastoral romance, *La Galatea* (1585), which was followed by his masterpiece, *Don Quixote*, of which the first part was dated 1605 (although probably published in 1604), the second 1615. He also wrote a number of plays (sixteen of which survive), a collection of highly accomplished short stories, *Novelas ejemplares* (1613: *Exemplary Stories*), and a tale of adventure, *Persiles y Sigismunda*, published posthumously in 1617. John *Fletcher drew largely on these last two for the plots of his plays.

CÉSAIRE, Aimé (1913–2008) Poet, dramatist, and politician born on the French Caribbean island of Martinique. With Léon Damas (1912–78) and Léopold Sédar *Senghor, he developed the Négritude movement, laying the foundation for *postcolonial literature and theory. His most influential work, *Cahier d'un retour au pays natal* (1939; *Return to my Native Land*, trans. Émile Snyder, 1968), is a passionate portrait of Martinique and an exhilarating call for the oppressed of colonialism to rise up against the status quo.

Chabot, The Tragedy of By George *Chapman, revised by John Shirley, written 1611–22, published 1639. The last of Chapman's plays on recent French history, it is based on *Les Recherches de la France* by Étienne Pasquier (1529–1615).

CHAMBERS, Aidan (1934–) Children's writer, critic, and publisher. The six *young adults' novels he describes as 'The Dance Sequence' are: *Breaktime* (1978); *Dance on my Grave* (1982), which explores homosexuality; *Now I Know* (1987); *The Toll Bridge* (1992); *Postcards from No-Man's Land* (1999, Carnegie Medal); and *This Is All: The Pillow Book of Cordelia Kenn* (2005). He co-founded Turton and Chambers to publish translated children's books.

CHAMBERS, Sir E. K. (Edmund Kerchever) (1866–1954) Shakespearian scholar and dramatic historian. His major works of dramatic history are *The Medieval Stage* (2 vols, 1903), *The Elizabethan Stage* (4 vols, 1923), and *William Shakespeare: A Study of Facts and Problems* (2 vols, 1930). As well as editions of all Shakespeare's plays for the Red Letter Shakespeare and an important lecture on 'The Disintegration of Shakespeare' (1924) his other works include *Arthur of Britain* (1927), a synthesis and reassessment based on available evidence.

CHAMBERS, Ephraim (?1680–1740) He published his *Cyclopaedia*, the first true English encyclopedia, in 1728. It had some influence on *Johnson's *Dictionary*.

CHAMBERS, Robert (1802–71) Scottish writer and publisher, who founded with his brother William the firm of W. and R. Chambers, Edinburgh. He established *Chambers's Journal* in 1832. His firm issued *Chambers's Encyclopaedia* (1st edn 1859–68). His anonymous *Vestiges of the Natural History of Creation* (1844) proposed a theory of biological evolution produced by the action of universal and progressive natural law and was immensely influential in popularizing an evolutionary view of nature. It appears to have had a particular impact upon Alfred *Tennyson.

CHAMBERS, R. W. (Raymond Wilson) (1874–1942) His scholarly interests extended from Old English to the Renaissance. His most celebrated works are studies of *Widsith* (1912) and *Beowulf* (1921); *On the Continuity of English Prose from Alfred to More* (1932); *Thomas More* (1935); and *Man's Unconquerable Mind* (1939), a collection of essays.

Chambers's Journal (originally *Chambers's Edinburgh Journal***)** One of the most popular of the 19th-century journals of literature, science, and the arts, founded by Robert *Chambers in 1832. It changed its name in 1854, and survived until 1938.

CHAMISSO, Adelbert von (1781–1838) German zoologist and poet, chiefly remembered for his story *Peter Schlemihls wundersame Geschichte* (1814: *The Strange Story of Peter Schlemihl*) whose hero sells his shadow to a devil figure, a mysterious man in a grey coat, and becomes an outcast. Thomas *Pynchon's *V* has a character who is called a Schlemihl.

CHAMOISEAU, Patrick (1953–) Novelist, playwright, and theoretician, born on the French Caribbean island of Martinique. Chamoiseau distanced himself from the previous generations of Aimé *Césaire and Édouard *Glissant by developing the notion of *créolité*, arguing that Caribbean identity is defined by plurality and hybridity. His novels, including *Texaco* (1992; trans., 1997), interweave French and *Creole and draw on local traditions of oral storytelling.

Champion, The A journal opposed to Sir Robert Walpole (1676–1745), written largely by Henry *Fielding, from 1739 to 1740.

Chances, The A play by John *Fletcher, written *c.*1617, printed 1647. The plot is based on one of *Cervantes's *Novelas ejemplares*. Popular after the Restoration, it was adapted by the second duke of *Buckingham (1682, directed by Laurence Olivier at Chichester in 1962), whose version was successfully adapted by David *Garrick.

CHANDLER, Raymond (1888–1959) American writer of thrillers and detective stories. His first novel, *The Big Sleep* (1939), introduced his detective narrator, cool, attractive, wisecracking, lonely tough guy Philip Marlowe, who owes something to Chandler's admiration for Dashiell *Hammett. Later works include *Farewell, my Lovely* (1940), *The High Window* (1942), *The Lady in the Lake* (1943), and *The Long Goodbye* (1953). All of his novels have been filmed and Chandler himself worked in Hollywood in the 1940s and 1950s, producing an original screenplay, *The Blue Dahlia* (1946). His work strongly influenced post-war crime writers like Ross Macdonald.

CHANG, Jung (1952–) Chinese-born writer, subsequently resident in London. Her popular and influential *Wild Swans: Three Daughters of China* (1992) traces the history of modern China through the life-stories of her grandmother, mother, and herself. Ten million copies have been sold. *Mao: The Unknown Story* (2005), co-written with her husband, the historian Jon Halliday, is a controversial biography of Mao Zedong.

Changeling, The A tragedy by Thomas *Middleton and William *Rowley, acted 1622, printed 1653. Beatrice, daughter of the governor of Alicante, is ordered by her father to marry Alonzo de Piracquo. She falls in love with Alsemero, and to avoid the marriage employs the villain De Flores, whom she detests but who loves her, to murder Alonzo. To her horror, De Flores claims sex with her as his reward. Beatrice is now to marry Alsemero. To conceal the fact that she is no longer a virgin, she persuades her maid Diaphanta to take her place on the wedding night; and to remove a dangerous witness, De Flores then kills the maid. The guilt of Beatrice and De Flores is revealed to Alsemero, and they are brought before the governor, whereupon they take their own lives. The title of the play comes from the sub-plot, in which Antonio disguises himself as a crazy changeling in order to get access to Isabella, wife of a madhouse keeper. The main plot is taken from John Reynolds's *God's Revenge against Murder* (1621).

CHANNING, William Ellery (1780–1842) American Unitarian clergyman, who exercised a marked influence on American intellectual life, and is considered a forerunner of the *Transcendental Club. His *Remarks on American Literature* (1830) calls for a literary Declaration of Independence. His nephew, also William Ellery Channing (1818–1901), poet and Transcendentalist, founded The *Dial with Ralph Waldo *Emerson in 1840, wrote the first biography of Henry *Thoreau (1841), and published the book-length poem *The Wanderer* (1871). Thoreau referred to Channing's poetic style as 'sublime-slipshod'.

Chanson de Roland See ROLAND; CHANSONS DE GESTE.

chansons de geste Epic poems in Old French, written mainly between the late 11th and the early 14th centuries, about the heroic deeds of broadly historical figures, usually drawn from the Carolingian era (*see* CHARLEMAGNE). Most of the surviving *chansons de geste* are anonymous, with the notable exceptions of *Aimeri de Narbonne* and *Girart de Vienne* from the late 12th century, which are attributed to Bertrand de Bar-sur-Aube. The representation of historical events in the *chansons de geste* offered the means of exploring the stresses within contemporary feudal society: in the *Chanson de Roland* (*see* ROLAND), which is the most translated of all Old French texts, we witness some of the strains caused by the impact of the Crusades. The only parallel English poems are those concerned with Charlemagne, such as the fragmentary Middle English *Song of Roland* (see FERUMBRAS, SIR; OTUEL, SIR).

Chanticleer The cock in **Reynard the Fox*, and in Chaucer's 'The Nun's Priest's Tale' (see CANTERBURY TALES, 20) as Chauntecleer.

chapbook A small illustrated pamphlet of ballads, folk tales, nursery rhymes, or popular romances such as **Bevis of Hampton* and **Guy of Warwick*, circulated cheaply in the provinces by pedlars and chapmen from the 17th to 19th centuries. Novels like **Robinson Crusoe* were often drastically abridged as chapbooks.

Chapel, Children of the See PAUL'S, CHILDREN OF.

CHAPLIN, Charlie (1889-1977) London-born actor and film-maker; Mack Sennett first filmed him in 1914, and he quickly became a noted attraction in a series of short comedies, playing a mischievous tramp-like character. His success enabled him to open his own Hollywood studio in 1921 and control every aspect of his subsequent work. Each Chaplin film became a global event, from *The Kid* (1921) and *The Gold Rush* (1925) to *The Circus* (1928) and *City Lights* (1931). He resisted the development of sound technologies, until his anti-fascist *The Great Dictator* (1940) demanded speech. In the McCarthy era, he was refused re-entry into the USA and moved to Switzerland. An *Autobiography* in 1964, together with David Robinson's definitive 1985 biography, were the basis of Richard Attenborough's faithful biographical film *Chaplin* (1992).

CHAPLIN, Sid See REGIONAL NOVEL.

CHAPMAN, George (?1559-1634) Author and translator. Chapman's earliest published works were non-dramatic poems and his completion of Marlowe's **Hero and Leander* (1598). He went on to write many plays, some of them lost. Eight comedies, mostly satirical and topical, survive: *The Blind Beggar of Alexandria* (1596; pub. 1598), *An Humorous Day's Mirth* (1597; pub. 1599), *All Fools* (1599; pub. 1605), *May-Day* (1601-2; pub. 1611), *Sir Giles Goosecap* (1602), *The *Gentleman Usher* (1602-3; pub. 1606), *The Widow's Tears* (1604; pub. 1612), and **Monsieur D'Olive* (1605; pub. 1606). He collaborated with **Jonson and John **Marston on a further comedy, **Eastward Ho*, in 1605, which

led to a short period of imprisonment for Jonson and Chapman because of its anti-Scottish satire.

The tragedies consist of two two-part plays, **Bussy D'Ambois* (1603-4; pub. 1607-8) and *The *Revenge of Bussy D'Ambois* (1610-11; pub. 1613), *The Conspiracy of Charles, Duke of *Byron* and *The Tragedy of Byron* (1607-8; pub. 1608), and one single play, *Caesar and Pompey* (1604; pub. 1631). *The Tragedy of Chabot* (1611-12; pub. 1639) appears to be a Chapman tragedy revised by James **Shirley. Chapman also collaborated with John **Fletcher, Jonson, and **Massinger in writing *The Bloody Brother* (c.1616; pub. 1639). His translations of the complete *Iliad* and **Odyssey* were published together in 1616 as *The Whole Works of Homer, Prince of Poets*; the work referred to in John **Keats's sonnet beginning 'Much have I travelled in the realms of gold'. Chapman is a serious, scrupulous, and intellectual writer, and was long the favourite candidate for the 'rival poet' referred to in Shakespeare's **Sonnets*.

CHAPMAN, John (1821-94) He published George **Eliot's translation of Strauss (1846), and the **Westminster Review*, which he edited continuously for 43 years until his death. His diaries for 1851 and 1860 survive and have been edited by G. S. Haight as *George Eliot and John Chapman, with Chapman's Diaries* (1940).

Chapman and Hall A publishing company founded in 1830 at 186 Strand, London, by Edward Chapman (1824-80) and William Hall (1801?-47). It owed much of its success to its early association with Charles **Dickens (**Pickwick Papers* having originated in a suggestion from Hall) and published many distinguished and popular authors, including Thomas **Carlyle, Charles **Kingsley, Elizabeth **Gaskell, and Anthony **Trollope. George **Meredith was for a time literary director.

CHAPONE, Hester (1727-1801) Née Mulso. She educated herself despite early discouragement and wrote her earliest dated poem 'To Peace. Written during the Late Rebellion. 1745' when only 18. In London she became a member of the **Blue Stockings, and knew Samuel **Johnson, who admired her poetry, particularly 'To Stella', a poem against love and in praise of the calm joys of friends. She married John Chapone in 1760, who unfortunately died in 1761; thereafter, she lived alone in London, publishing *Letter Written on the Improvement of the Mind* (1773) and *Miscellanies in Verse and Prose* (1775). Johnson invited her to contribute to the **Rambler*. Although 30 years younger, she was a particular friend of Samuel *Richardson, who called her 'little spit-fire' and with whom she discussed his female characters; Mary *Delany asserted that Hester Chapone was the model for one or two of Richardson's heroines. Her *Works* and *Posthumous Works* appeared in 1807.

Characters of Shakespeare's Plays

Essays by William *Hazlitt, published 1817. They comment not only upon Hamlet, Macbeth, and other protagonists, but also upon the distinctive qualities of each major drama, and more generally upon the 'magnanimity' of Shakespeare's imagination. Especially notable is the essay on *Coriolanus*, which considers the affinities between poetic imagination and political power.

character-writing Books of 'characters' were popular in the 17th century, and many were based, though some loosely, on Theophrastus, translated by Isaac *Casaubon in 1592 and by John Healey (printed 1616, but previously circulated). The first was published in 1608 by Joseph *Hall, followed by Thomas *Overbury in 1614, the *Satirical Essays, Characters and Others* of John Stephens in 1615, the *Certain Characters and Essays of Prison and Prisoners* (1618) by Geffray Minshull, John Earles's *Microcosmography* (1628), *Whimzies* (1631) by Richard Brathwaite, and others. The 'characters' gave generalized but detailed descriptions of the behaviour and appearance of a class or type; they were on the whole short, succinct, pointed, and less discursive than the essay, also a popular literary form of the period.

'Charge of the Light Brigade, The'

A poem by Alfred *Tennyson, first published in the *Examiner* in 1854 only weeks after the famous charge (25 October 1854) at Balaclava, near Sebastopol, during which, owing to a misunderstood order, 247 officers and men out of 637 were killed or wounded. The poem, drawing heavily on newspaper reportage, half-turned an error into a heroic affirmation.

CHARKE, Charlotte (1713–1760) Actress and cross-dresser, youngest daughter of Colley *Cibber. Educated in a manner 'sufficient for a son', she displayed an early fondness for masculine dress and pursuits such as shooting. She took to the stage, often in masculine roles, and in opposition to her implacable father. Her 'mad pranks' and varied career as waiter, pastrycook, farmer, and strolling player are vividly described in her *Narrative of the Life of Mrs Charlotte Charke* (1755).

CHARLEMAGNE (742–814) King of the Franks (768) and crowned by Pope Leo III as emperor of the West (800). He and his *Paladins are the subject of numerous *chansons de geste*, of which the *Chanson de Roland* is the most famous (*see* ROLAND). Of the three groups of French *chansons de geste* concerned with Charlemagne, only the first, the *geste du roi*, is represented in English, in such romances as *Otuel*, *Sir *Ferumbras*, and *The Sege of Melayne*. The tradition of learning Charlemagne established at his court (led by the Northumbrian *Alcuin) was copied a century later by King *Alfred.

CHARLES, duc d'Orléans (1394–1465) French poet. Captured at the battle of Agincourt in 1415, he was held prisoner in England until 1440, during which time he wrote poetry. On his return to France he established his court at Blois, where he cultivated poets and artists. He wrote numerous chansons, ballades, and *rondeaux, using the fixed forms as a means of striking self-exploration. A large number of English poems, many of which are versions of Charles's French lyrics, are also probably to be attributed to him.

CHARNAS, Suzy McKee (1939–) American author. *Walk to the End of the World* (1974), a *dystopia where women have been blamed for the collapse of civilization, was followed by *Motherlines* (1978) and *The Furies* (1994). *The Vampire Tapestry* presents the relationships between a vampire and the humans among whom he lives. Short fiction is collected in *Stagestruck Vampires* (2004).

Chartist movement A chiefly working-class political movement between 1837 and 1848, which arose as a result of the Reform Bill of 1832, which had excluded the working classes from political rights for lack of the necessary property qualification. Their six-point 'People's Charter' consisted of: Universal Suffrage, Vote by Ballot, Annually Elected Parliaments, Payment for Members of Parliament, Abolition of the Property Qualification, and Equal Electoral Districts. The movement was alluded to by novelists of the mid-19th century who were concerned with the *condition of England question, in particular Benjamin *Disraeli in *Sybil*, and Charles *Kingsley in *Alton Locke*; and also by Thomas *Carlyle in his essay 'Chartism'. Chartist writers, some of them writing in prison, included Samuel *Bamford; master bootmaker Thomas Cooper (1805–92), author of the lengthy and ambitious *The Purgatory of Suicides* (1853), a 'working man's epic' in Spenserian stanzas; Ebenezer *Elliott of Sheffield, the so-called 'Corn Law Rhymer'; Ernest Jones (1819–68/9?), author of an unfinished novel *De Brassier*; Thomas Martin Wheeler, author of *Sunshine and Shadow*, published in 37 parts in the Chartist periodical the *Northern Star* (1849–50); and textile worker Gerald Massey (1828–1907) whose *Original Poems and Chansons* appeared in 1847.

Chaste Maid in Cheapside, A By Thomas *Middleton, written 1613, printed 1630. The play centres on the attempt of the dissolute Sir Walter Whorehound to pass off his mistress as his niece and marry her to the foolish son of Yellowhammer, a rich goldsmith, while Whorehound himself is to marry Yellowhammer's daughter Moll. The first part of the plot succeeds, but the second fails. Moll and her resourceful young lover Touchwood finally succeed in evading their parents and marrying.

CHATEAUBRIAND, François-René, vicomte de (1768–1848) One of the major figures of early French Romanticism. He achieved celebrity with *Le Génie du Christianisme* (1802: *The Genius of Christianity*). From this work Chateaubriand extracted two fragments, inspired in part by his stay in America (1791), which he published separately: *Atala* (1801; trans. 1802) and *René* (1805; trans. 1813). Both had a wide and enthusiastic reception. *Mémoires d'outre-tombe* (1849–50: *Memoirs from Beyond the Grave*), his posthumously published autobiography, is now regarded as his most accomplished work. Between 1793 and 1800 Chateaubriand lived in exile in England.

CHATTERJEE, Upamanyu (1959–) Indian novelist, with Amitav *Ghosh and others part of a late 20th-century blossoming of Bengali writers in English. Drawing on his officer experience in the prestigious Indian Administrative Service, Chatterjee's first novel *English, August* (1988, filmed 1994), offers a comic-ironic portrait, informed by Hindu myth, of the ennui and self-disgust attendant upon this highly sought-after job. Other work includes the novels *The Last Burden* (1993) and its sequel *Way to Go* (2010).

CHATTERTON, Thomas (1752–70) In 1768 he published in *Felix Farley's Bristol Journey* a passage of pseudo-archaic prose, the original of which he claimed to have discovered in a chest in St Mary Redcliffe. This attracted the attention of local antiquaries, for whom he provided fake documents and pedigrees. He had already written some poems purporting to be the work of an imaginary 15th-century Bristol monk, Thomas Rowley, a friend of William Canynge, a Bristol merchant. He also fabricated their correspondence and other background documents. He offered some of the poems to James *Dodsley in December 1768; Dodsley had published Thomas *Percy's *Reliques*, greatly stimulating interest in early poetry. In March 1769 Chatterton sent Horace *Walpole a treatise on painting 'bie T. Rowleie', which Walpole briefly accepted as authentic. The only Rowleian piece published in Chatterton's life was 'Elinour and Juga', which appeared in May 1769. In April 1770 he went to London, writing home 'in high spirits', and claiming 'great encouragement' from publishers; four months later (still only 17 years old) he took a fatal overdose of arsenic, probably accidentally. The Rowleian 'An Excelente Balade of Charitie' was completed in London. The Rowley poems were published in 1777 by Thomas Tyrwhitt, with an appendix challenging their authenticity, which was further impugned by Thomas *Warton and Edmond *Malone. Chatterton's death, then treated as suicide, had a powerful effect on the *Romantic imagination; S. T. *Coleridge's first published poem was a 'Monody' on him, William *Wordsworth called him 'the marvellous Boy, The sleepless Soul that perished in his pride', John *Keats dedicated *Endymion to his memory, and he features prominently in P. B. *Shelley's *Adonais.

CHATWIN, Bruce (1940–89) Travel writer and novelist. His first book, *In Patagonia* (1977), an imaginative blend of fact and fiction, history, biography, anecdote, and geography, expanded the concept of *travel writing (though he disliked the label). *Patagonia Revisited* (1986) was written with Paul *Theroux. Other works include *The Viceroy of Ouidah* (1980), a fictionalized account of a real-life slave trader; *On the Black Hill* (1982), the story of reclusive twin brothers on the Welsh–English border; *The Songlines* (1987), linking Aboriginal stories of the land with Chatwin's theories of nomadism; and *Utz* (1988), a study of a collector of Meissen porcelain in Prague. A selection of miscellaneous writings, compiled before Chatwin's death from an Aids-related illness, was published posthumously as *What Am I Doing Here* (1989), and a further collection, *Anatomy of Restlessness* in 1996. *Photographs and Notebooks* (1993) was followed by *Winding Paths*, another volume of photographs, in 1999.

CHAUCER, Geoffrey (*c.*1340–1400) Poet, the son of John Chaucer, a London vintner.

Between *c.*1357 and 1360 he was a retainer in the household of Elizabeth, countess of Ulster, wife of Prince Lionel, afterwards duke of Clarence. In 1359 he was in France with Edward III's army, was taken prisoner, and ransomed. By 1366 he was married to Philippa, possibly the daughter of Sir Paon Roet of Hainault and the sister of John of Gaunt's third wife, Katherine Swynford. Philippa died in 1387 and Chaucer enjoyed Gaunt's patronage throughout his life. He held many positions at court, and in the king's service, and he travelled abroad on numerous diplomatic missions. As well as missions to France, he made a journey to Genoa and Florence in 1372–3, in the course of which he may have encountered the works of *Boccaccio, *Petrarch, and *Dante. In 1374 he was appointed controller of customs in the port of London and leased his house over Aldgate. He was knight of the shire for Kent in 1386. Between 1389 and 1391 he was clerk of the king's works. His last official position was that of deputy forester in the King's Forest at North Petherton in Somerset (1390s). He was buried at the entrance to the Chapel of St Benedict in Westminster Abbey, where a monument was erected to him in 1556: this was the origin of Poets' Corner. His writings develop from an early period of French influence (culminating in *The *Book of the Duchess*, *c.*1368–72), through his 'middle period' of both French and Italian influences (including *The *House of Fame* after 1374 and the mature Italian-influenced works, of which the most important is *Troilus and Criseyde*, complete by 1388), to the last period of most of *The *Canterbury Tales* and his short lyrics. His prose works include a translation of *The Consolation of Philosophy* by *Boethius (*Boece*) and *A Treatise on the Astrolabe*, written to 'little Lewis', probably the poet's son. There are portraits of Chaucer in the Ellesmere Manuscript (now in the Huntington Library); in the manuscript of *Troilus and Criseyde* in Corpus Christi College, Cambridge; and in Thomas *Hoccleve's *The Regement of Princes*, beside lines 4,995–6 (in several manuscripts: the best dates from Hoccleve's time, British Library Harley 4866).

CHAUDHURI, Amit (1962–) Indian writer in English, distinguished by his crystalline miniaturist style, born in Calcutta (Kolkata), where most of his fiction is set. His award-winning novels include *A Strange and Sublime Address* (1991), describing the gradual awakening to life of a young writer-to-be; *Afternoon Raag* (1993), narrated by an Oxford student remembering his earlier life in Bombay; *Freedom Song* (1998),

which follows the interconnected lives of three Bengali families in Calcutta; *A New World* (2000), which dwells on the daily lives of a man and his young son on vacation with his ageing parents in Calcutta in the aftermath of a bitter custody battle; and *The Immortals* (2009). *Real Time*, a book of short stories, appeared in 2002, and *D. H. Lawrence and 'Difference': Postcoloniality and the Poetry of the Present*, a poststructuralist study of D. H. *Lawrence, in 2003. He edited *The Picador Book of Modern Indian Literature* (2001). His poetry has been published in *St. Cyril Road and Other Poems* (2005). *See* ANGLO-INDIAN LITERATURE.

Cheap Repository Tracts A series of over one hundred entertaining moral tales, ballads, sermons, and Bible stories published by the Cheap Repository press (1795–8), many of which are by the *evangelical writer Hannah *More. Counter-revolutionary, they aim at teaching the poor to accept the authority of church, government, and social hierarchy but they can also be seen as morally radical in their concern with developing the religious and rational capacities of the lower classes, especially women. More (like Mary *Wollstonecraft) argued that a more rational system of education would allow women to take up their duties as responsible citizens.

CHEEVER, John (1912–82) American novelist, whose sophisticated, ironic novels and short stories satirize affluent suburban New England life. His novels include *The Wapshot Chronicle* (1957), *The Wapshot Scandal* (1964), *Bullet Park* (1969), and *Falconer* (1977). His daughter Susan Cheever has published novels, a memoir of her father (*Home before Dark*, 1985), and *American Bloomsbury* (2006), a biographical study of Louisa May *Alcott, Ralph Waldo *Emerson, and their contemporaries.

CHEKHOV, Anton Pavlovich (1860–1904) Russian dramatist and short story writer. The earliest examples of his mature stories are 'The Steppe' (1888) and 'A Boring Story' (1889). Other masterpieces followed: 'Ward Six' (1892), 'My Life' (1896), 'Ionych', and the trilogy 'The Man in a Case', 'Gooseberries', and 'About Love' (all 1898), 'The Lady with the Little Dog' (1899), 'Darling' (1899), and 'The Bishop' (1902). Chekhov's first successful full-length play was *Ivanov* (1888), but his status as a dramatist rests on his four late plays: *The Seagull* (1895), *Uncle Vanya* (1900), *Three Sisters* (1901), and *The Cherry Orchard* (1904). *The Seagull*, after a disastrous St Petersburg premiere, was triumphantly revived in the 1898 inaugural season of the *Moscow Arts Theatre. In 1901 Chekhov married the Art Theatre actress Olga Knipper (1868–1959). The first English productions of his plays were a staging of *The Seagull* in Glasgow in 1909 by George Calderon (1868–1915) and the Incorporated Stage Society's 1911 London production of *The Cherry Orchard*. E. M. *Forster, Virginia *Woolf, J. M. *Murry, and especially Katherine *Mansfield were among early admirers. Katherine Mansfield's stories are held to be the main channel through which his work influenced England, and her letters are full of expressions of her sympathy for him. G. B. *Shaw wrote *Heartbreak House* as a tribute to him. Chekhov's work is characterized by its subtle blending of naturalism and symbolism, dispassionate objectivity; and a sensitive combination of comedy, tragedy, and pathos. Since 1903 most of his work has been translated. The first major translation is that by Constance *Garnett, *The Tales of Tchehov* (1916–22) and *The Plays of Tchehov* (1923–4). The major modern translation is that by Ronald Hingley, *The Oxford Chekhov* (9 vols, 1964–80). An excellent modern version of the plays is by Michael *Frayn, *Plays* (1993).

Chemical Generation A term used to refer to a group of younger writers, predominantly Scottish, whose work displays a comfortable familiarity with 1990s youth culture: music, fashion, nightclubs, and drugs. Alan *Warner has sometimes been seen as a leader of the so-called 'Chemical Generation', along with Irvine *Welsh.

CHERRY-GARRARD, Apsley (1886–1959) Antarctic explorer. In 1910 he accompanied Robert Falcon *Scott to the Antarctic as assistant zoologist, editing the expedition's newspaper, the *South Polar Times*. He was in a support party for Scott's last race for the pole, and was one of those who discovered Scott's body ten months later. He wrote *The Worst Journey in the World* (1922), drawing on the diaries of Scott, Wilson, and Bowers, while convalescing from war injuries sustained in Flanders. It became a classic of Antarctic adventure.

CHESNUTT, Charles (1858–1932) African American novelist, short story writer, and political activist. A formative figure in the development of *African American literature, Chesnutt established himself with stories like 'The Goophered Grapevine' (1887), which describe black folk culture on the Southern plantations before the Civil War, followed by his collection of 'con-

jure stories' *The Conjure Woman* (1899), and three novels exploring the racial politics of the South: *The House behind the Cedars* (1900), *The Marrow of Tradition* (1901), and *The Colonel's Dream* (1905). *Post-Bellum—Pre-Harlem* (1931) is part autobiography, part reflections on how African American writing has evolved.

CHESTERTON, G. K. (Gilbert Keith) (1874–1936) Author, who made his name in journalism, taking a controversial, anti-imperial, pro-Boer line on the Boer War. His first published novel, *The Napoleon of Notting Hill* (1904), a fantasy of the future in which London is plunged into a strange mixture of medieval nostalgia and street warfare, displayed the full range of his political sympathies, glorifying the little man, revelling in the colour and romance of 'Merry England', and attacking big business, technology, and the monolithic state. His most accomplished novel, *The Man Who Was Thursday: A Nightmare* (1908), is an alarming but rollicking fantasy with a surreal anarchist background which attacks *fin-de-siècle* pessimism. His *detective Father Brown, an unassuming East Anglian Roman Catholic priest, first appears in *The Innocence of Father Brown* (1911); Chesterton himself became a Roman Catholic in 1922. His most characteristic poems tend to celebrate the Englishness of England, the nation of Beef and Beer, e.g. 'The Secret People' (1915) and 'The Rolling English Road' (1914). Chesterton's vigour, idiosyncrasies, optimism, puns, and paradoxes celebrate the oddity of life and the diversity of people and places with a peculiar and at times exhilarating zest.

CHESTRE, Thomas *See* SIR LAUNFAL.

CHETTLE, Henry (*c.*1560–1603/7) Printer, pamphleteer, and dramatist. He was for a time a partner with William Hoskins and John Danter in a printing business. Chettle may have had a hand in the compilation as well as in the printing of some literary works from the press, including the first quarto of *Romeo and Juliet* (1597); in 1596 he contributed prefatory letters to works by Thomas *Nashe and Anthony *Munday, identifying himself as being involved in their printing. Although in the satirical pamphlet *Kind-Heart's Dream* (?1593) he denied that *Greene's Groat's-worth of Wit* (1592), published after Robert *Greene's death, was his, there is strong evidence that it was in fact written by Chettle. By 1598 he was an established author of comedies for the stage and is listed in Philip *Henslowe's diary in association with 49 plays, 36 written in collaboration with authors such as John *Day, Thomas *Dekker, Thomas *Heywood, Ben *Jonson, Munday, and John *Webster, and thirteen on his own. Only a few of these collaborative plays were printed: these include two plays about Robert, earl of Huntingdon (1601), with Munday, *Patient Grissil* (1603) with Dekker and William Haughton, and *The Blind-Beggar of Bednal-Green* (1659) with Day. Chettle may well have had a considerable hand in the collaborative play of *Sir Thomas More*, which survives in manuscript. The only extant play for which he alone is known to be responsible is *The Tragedy of Hoffman* (*c.*1603), which was first printed 1631, but not then attributed to Chettle. He also published *England's Mourning Garment*, an elegy on *Elizabeth I, in 1603.

Chevy Chase, The Ballad of One of the oldest of the English ballads, included in Percy's *Reliques*; it probably dates in its primitive form from the 15th century. Its subject is the rivalry of the neighbouring families of Percy and Douglas, heightened by the national quarrel between England and Scotland. The two parties meet and fight, there is great slaughter on both sides, and both Percy and Douglas are killed (cf. *Otterbourne, The Battle of*). The ballad is quoted and discussed by Joseph *Addison, who admired its 'majestic simplicity' and compared it to Virgil, in the *Spectator* (nos 70 and 74, May 1711).

chiasmus A figure of speech by which the order of the words in the first of two parallel clauses is reversed in the second, e.g. 'He saved others; himself he cannot save.'

Chicano literature is the writing of Hispanic Americans, mainly of Mexican ancestry, which dates back to 1848, when parts of the south-west were annexed by the USA. The 1960s saw a renaissance in this area and the appropriation of the notion of Aztlan (originally denoting an Aztec homeland) to mean an ideal state of unification.

CHILD, Lee Pseudonym of Jim Grant (1954–), British-born author of the *detective novels featuring the ex-American Military Policeman Jack Reacher. The series began with *Killing Floor* (1997). Child emigrated to the USA in 1998. *The Enemy* (2004) is a prequel; *The Affair* (2011) is the 16th in the series. *Second Son* (2011) is a short story about Reacher's childhood, available as an e-book.

Childe Harold's Pilgrimage A poem in Spenserian stanzas by Lord *Byron, of which the first two cantos appeared in 1812, Canto III

in 1816, and Canto IV in 1818. The poem describes the travels, experiences, and reflections of a self-styled and self-exiled pilgrim, Childe Harold, whose wanderings correspond in many ways to Byron's own. Harold, a melancholy, defiant outcast, is the first of a series of histrionic *Byronic heroes: his character reappears, with little significant development, in *The *Corsair*, *Manfred*, and other works. The first two cantos describe how the wanderer, sated with his past life of sin and pleasure, finds distraction by travel: he journeys through Portugal, Spain, the Ionian Islands, and Albania. In Canto III, written six years later, the pilgrim travels to Belgium, the Rhine, the Alps, and Jura: Stanza XXI introduces his celebrated passage on the battle of Waterloo. In Canto IV, dedicated to his friend and travelling companion John *Hobhouse, he abandons the device of the pilgrim and speaks directly, in a long meditation on time and history, on Venice and *Petrarch, on Ferrara and *Tasso, on *Boccaccio and Florence, and on Rome. The poem enjoyed great success. After the publication of Cantos I and II in March 1812 Byron wrote, 'I awoke . . . and found myself famous.'

Childe Roland In an old Scottish ballad, a son of King Arthur. His sister, Burd Ellen, is carried away by the fairies to the castle of the king of Elfland. Aided by the instructions of Merlin, Childe Roland enters the castle and rescues his sister. 'Child Rowland to the dark tower came, His word was still "Fie, foh, and fum, I smell the blood of a British man"' (Shakespeare, *King Lear*, III. iv). J. O. *Halliwell (*Nursery Rhymes*) thinks that Shakespeare is quoting from two different compositions, the first line from a ballad on Roland, the second and third from the story of Jack the Giant-Killer.

'Childe Roland to the Dark Tower Came' A poem by Robert *Browning, published in *Men and Women* (1855). The title derives from a fragment of song recited by Edgar in *King Lear*. A knight-in-training crosses a nightmare landscape in search of the Dark Tower; he eventually reaches the Tower and blows his horn defiantly at its foot. The poem ends with the title phrase, and there is no indication of what happens next. The monologue is both satisfying as a Gothic dream narrative and disturbing as an impenetrable allegory—of life, of art, or of both. Browning refused to explain the poem, saying simply that it had come to him as a dream. 'Thamuris marching' in *Aristophanes' Apology* makes an intriguing comparison with this episode of an anti-romance.

CHILDERS, Erskine (1870–1922) London-born writer and political activist, he served in both the Boer War and the First World War. In 1921 he was appointed director of publicity for the Irish Republican Army, and in 1922 he was court-martialled and shot by a Free State firing squad. *The Riddle of the Sands* (1903) is often described as the first example of *spy fiction, a novel about two British yachtsmen sailing in the Baltic who discover German preparations for an invasion of England.

Children of the Chapel of Paul's *See* PAUL'S, CHILDREN OF.

children's literature From the sociological standpoint, what distinguishes children's literature from other literatures is its unique position in relation to the three institutions of publishing, education, and nurture. The publishing industry customarily marks its productions as being child specific and age specific. Education makes selections of appropriate children's literature and controls much of children's critical reading of books. The debates about child nurture in the mass media, including television, internet forums, and national newspapers, create an environment where certain kinds of books and ways of reading are thought to be suitable for different kinds of child or home.

From a literary standpoint, one of the key markers of children's literature has been the modified linguistic registers of its texts—sometimes expressed as 'the use of simplified language'. Thematically, certain topics have, in different times, been thought to be more or less appropriate: the subject of death was a central preoccupation of the stories and poems for children in late 17th-century England; in the 19th century, the political aspirations of empire were made quite explicit in juvenile literature (especially in boys' magazines). Structurally speaking, it has been thought that the resolution of stories should involve some kind of redemption, reconciliation, hope, or sense of homecoming (although this is less true of *young adult literature), and that the books should improve the child. There has also, however, been a powerful strain in children's literature that has mocked improvement, starting perhaps with Heinrich Hoffmann's satire of moralistic teaching *Struwwelpeter* (Germany 1845; England 1848) and taken up in a different way (celebration of mischief, mostly) by comics such as *The Beano*, established in 1938.

Children's literature also has some distinctive forms: *picturebooks, pop-ups, and *'mova-

bles', comics, annuals, and illustrated storybook anthologies or miscellanies; even *crossover books will have different cover designs for adult and children's versions. *Fantasy, *graphic fiction and *manga are categories that may blur the distinction. A child may relate to a book through a film, a TV programme, a computer game, a website, a radio programme, a music CD or download, a magazine article, toy, duvet cover, or any other piece of merchandising. Characters, such as *Winnie-the-Pooh (A. A. *Milne, 1926 and 1928), may now exist in several different formats and the original text may or may not be known to the child watching the TV programme or playing with the toy. In the case of Pooh, the *Disney representations may be recognized rather than the E.H. *Shepard illustrations. Children also create their own literature through their play, as recorded by Peter and Iona *Opie.

Clear examples of age-specific literature do not survive from the earliest literate societies, but an early medieval example is the 'Colloquy' of *Ælfric, a lively conversation in Latin between the teacher and his pupils designed as an aid to teach boys Latin. In the 17th century, a key moment came with the production in 1658 of *Orbis Sensualum Pictus* (*The Visible World in Pictures*) by the Protestant Czech educator Jan Komenský or Comenius. Each of its 151 little chapters (such as 'Aqua' (Water), 'Homo' (Man), or 'Mahometismus' (Mahometism)) is headed by a woodcut whilst underneath a set of words in Latin and German name parts of the picture and relate what Comenius regards as the facts. Didactic tales and poems for children were produced as part of the *Puritan tradition, in part as a reaction against the frivolities of the cheap *ballads which were seen as devil's work. Others wrote verses (like John *Bunyan's *A Book for Boys & Girls, or Country Rhymes for Children*, 1686) that told children how to observe, interpret, and love the world as God's creation. The 18th century produced the first literature for children that looked to entertain the child: the printer Mary *Cooper published *Tommy Thumb's Pretty Song Book* in two volumes (1744), of which only volume two survives. It is the earliest surviving example of a collection of *nursery rhymes. It includes versions of rhymes that have survived to this day, including 'London Bridge is falling down', 'Baa baa black sheep', 'Sing a song of sixpence'. In the same year, the publisher John *Newbery, influenced by John *Locke's thoughts on education, produced *A Little Pretty Pocket-Book, Intended for the Amusement of Little Master Tommy and Pretty Miss Polly with Two Letters from Jack the*

Giant Killer. Each letter of the alphabet has a rhyme and a moral and the book came with either a ball (for the boys) or a pincushion (for the girls). In the same decade, Sarah *Fielding produced what is thought of as the first full-length novel for children, *The Governess, or The Little Female Academy* (1749).

In the 19th century, the didactic strain of Christian children's literature produced by the *Religious Tract Society imitated the form and shape of street literature to produce illustrated moral tales for the same price. Authored poetry for children continued to focus on morally uplifting themes, but also incorporated fantasy and nonsense, as for example in William *Roscoe's *The Butterfly's Ball and the Grasshopper's Feast*, (1806). It is in this period that the traditions of oral storytelling and French aristocratic fairy-story writing combine to produce the child-specific, illustrated versions taken from such original collections as Charles *Perrault's *Les Contes de ma mère l'oye* (1697; *see* MOTHER GOOSE, and TRANSLATION FOR CHILDREN), the *Grimms' *Kinder und Hausmärchen*, and the more authored tales of E. T. A. *Hoffmann (1816) and Hans Christian *Andersen (1835).

Children's literature in the 20th century has become a diverse industry, flanked on one side by largely publicly funded education and on the other by the massive multinational publishing, distribution, film, TV, and merchandising companies. The importance of the market for children's books is evident in the prominence given to children's literature prizes, notably the Carnegie and Greenaway (see Appendix 4); the Costa prize includes a children's book category, which involves children in the selection and judging process, although Philip *Pullman's *The Amber Spyglass* is the only children's book to have been chosen as Book of the Year; since 1999, there has been a children's laureate (see Appendix 3).

There are many ways of making cross-sections of the field of children's literature, each offering a different perspective. In terms of gender, apart from some notable classics including those by Louisa May *Alcott and Laura Ingalls *Wilder, and some works by Frances Hodgson *Burnett, Edith *Nesbit, or Astrid Lindgren (1907–2002), the role of girls and women in children's books of most kinds used to be largely domestic, and secondary to males. Meanwhile, others claimed that children's books helped to construct masculinity by repeatedly casting boys as adventurers. On the race front, there was an outpouring of books, comics, and boys' magazines between 1880 and 1914 which represented almost anyone in the human race

other than people of northern European origin in the same way as working-class people, but also as childlike, cruel, and in need of chastisement or even, on occasions, summary execution. European white people were given implicitly or explicitly a mastering role at home and abroad.

The world of children's books has tried to change and a variety of books repositioning these roles have appeared. Sometimes this has been done through historical novels like Mildred D. Taylor's *Roll of Thunder, Hear my Cry* (1976), which explores the effects of racism in the American deep South during the Depression; sometimes through modern realism, as in the work of Jacqueline *Wilson or Benjamin *Zephaniah; sometimes with picture books, like Mary Hoffmann's *Amazing Grace* (1991), or Allan *Ahlberg's *Peepo* (1981).

The age-ranking of children's books has been identified as a feature specific to children's literature. At either end of this sequence there are books which are marketed, distributed, and consumed as Baby Books and books for Young Adults or Teens. The latter includes fiction which is largely adult in style but happens to focus on the lives of young people and children—rather in the way that J. D. *Salinger's *Catcher in the Rye* (1951), William *Golding's *Lord of the Flies* (1954), or Harper *Lee's *To Kill a Mocking-Bird* (1960) have done. Incidentally, Judy *Blume can be credited with having written the first novel produced by a children's publisher which had a girl and boy talking about their genitals and having sex (see *Forever* 1975).

There is reason to think of the *picturebook as one of children's literature's greatest inventions. It is a multiple approach, offering meanings through a variety of channels and in a variety of ways: print, sound (when read aloud), image, and, on occasions, touch. Maurice *Sendak single-handedly brought modern psychology into the picturebook with *Where the Wild Things Are* (1969).

Poetry for children has its own history, combining elements of the nursery rhyme, verse composed for children, including the *nonsense verse of Edward *Lear, and poems not originally composed solely for children but later adopted by publishers and educationists in their anthologies.

Lewis Carroll was a highly accomplished writer of narrative verse and parodies, mocking, in particular, the kinds of verses being given to children in Sunday Schools. The four best-known British writers of children's poetry prior to 1950 are Robert Louis *Stevenson, Hilaire *Belloc, A. A. Milne, and Walter *de la Mare.

Drama for children encompasses *pantomimes, J. M. *Barrie's *Peter Pan* (1904), often seen as the first children's play, *Punch and Judy, and such modern classics as dramatizations of Raymond *Briggs's *Snowman*. Clearly, the internet and the arrival of the electronic book have produced some major changes to what and how children will read in the future. Writers have become increasingly accessible to their readers through websites and chatrooms, although the recently relaunched *Puffin Post*, the magazine of Kaye Webb's Puffin Club, was encouraging such interaction from its foundation in 1967. New hybrids made up of moving photographic image, drawn image, computer-generated image, interactive game, linear text, music, sound effects, and *performance poetry or rap are likely to emerge over the next few years. Indications of this can be found anywhere from modern art installations to the children's pages of the BBC website.

(⊕) SEE WEB LINKS

• The Children's Literature Association

children's literature in translation
See TRANSLATION FOR CHILDREN.

Chimes, The A Christmas book by Charles *Dickens, published 1845. It is the story of a nightmare or vision in which Toby Veck, porter and runner of errands, under the influence of the goblins of the church bells and a dish of tripe, witnesses awful misfortunes befalling his daughter, a vision happily dissipated at the end.

Chips with Everything *See* WESKER, ARNOLD.

CHOPIN, Kate (1850–1904) Née O'Flaherty, American novelist and short story writer. She married Oscar Chopin, a *Creole, and went to live in New Orleans, Louisiana. Her husband died in 1882, leaving her with six children and his debts; she returned to her birthplace of St Louis, Missouri, and began to write, drawing on her memories of New Orleans and of Cane River. She was originally acclaimed as a 'local colourist', but has posthumously won recognition for *The Awakening* (1899), which tells the story of Edna Pontellier, married to a successful Creole business man, and leading a life of leisure. She commits adultery with one young man, while believing herself in love with another, and on the last page swims naked out to sea and presumably drowns. It was considered scandalous and morbid, and Chopin turned to poems, essays, and short stories.

CHRÉTIEN De Troyes (*fl.*1165–80) France's greatest writer of Arthurian *romance, the author of five major verse narratives in the second half of the 12th century, written in octosyllabic rhyming couplets and intended to be read aloud at court: *Erec and Enide* (*c.*1170); *Cligés* (*c.*1176); *Lancelot*, or *Le Chevalier de la charrette* (*c.*1177–81); *Yvain*, or *Le Chevalier au lion* (*c.*1177–81); and *Perceval* or *Le Conte du Graal* (1181–90), which he never completed. While generally supportive of chivalric values, he adopts in his poems a gently comic perspective on courtly conventions. He had an important influence on all subsequent Arthurian literature, including English, inspiring continuators, imitators, and adapters: the English romance *Iwain and Gawain* is a loose translation of his *Yvain*.

'Christabel' A poem by Samuel Taylor *Coleridge, published 1816. The poem is unfinished. The first part was written at Nether Stowey in 1797, the second at Keswick in 1800; Coleridge made plans for Part III but found himself unable to continue with it. It is a medieval romance of the supernatural, written in what is sometimes referred to as 'Christabel metre'—that is, in four-foot couplets, mostly iambic and *anapaestic, used with immense variety, so that the line length varies from seven syllables to eleven. Christabel, praying at night in a wood for her betrothed lover, discovers the fair Geraldine in distress and takes her to the castle of her father, Sir Leoline. Geraldine claims to be the daughter of Leoline's estranged friend Sir Roland of Vaux. She shares Christabel's chamber, and bewitches her as they lie in one another's arms. In the morning she meets Leoline, who vows reconciliation with her father and vengeance on the 'reptile souls' of her abductors. Christabel, who has seen Geraldine's true malignant serpentine nature, is at first silenced by the spell placed upon her, but manages to implore her father to send Geraldine away. Leoline, offended by his daughter's insult to a guest, turns from her to Geraldine. So the poem ends.

Christ and Satan An Old English poem of 729 lines in three sections, found in the *Junius Manuscript, once attributed to *Cædmon. The subjects of the three sections are: Satan's passionate and plangent lament for his fall from heaven; the *Harrowing of Hell; and the temptation of Christ by Satan.

Christian Morals *See* BROWNE, THOMAS.

Christian Year, The *See* KEBLE, JOHN.

CHRISTIE, Dame Agatha (1890–1976) Detective novelist. During the First World War she worked as a hospital dispenser, which gave her a knowledge of poisons invaluable when she started writing *detective fiction. Her first detective novel, *The Mysterious Affair at Styles* (1920), introduced Hercule Poirot, the Belgian detective who appeared in many subsequent novels (her other main detective being the elderly spinster Miss Marple). In the next 56 years she wrote 66 detective novels, among the best of which are *The Murder of Roger Ackroyd* (1926), *Murder on the Orient Express* (1934), *Death on the Nile* (1937), *Ten Little Niggers* (1939). She also wrote six novels under the pseudonym Mary Westmacott, two self-portraits (*Come Tell Me How You Live*, 1946; *An Autobiography*, 1977), and several plays, including *The Mousetrap;* this was first performed in London in 1952 and has run continuously since. Her prodigious international success seems due to her unrivalled and prolific ingenuity in contriving plots, sustaining suspense, and tantalizing and misdirecting the reader.

CHRISTINA of Markyate (c.1096–after 1145) Recluse and prioress of Markyate (Hertfordshire), the subject of a remarkable anonymous *Life*. When young she made a vow of virginity which she maintained even after a forced marriage. She was kept in confinement, but eventually escaped. In 1123, after the annulment of her marriage, she founded a community at Markyate, and made her monastic profession (c.1131).

CHRISTINE DE PISAN (c.1364–c.1431) French poet and scholar, born in Venice. She is best known for her feminist works, including the *Epistre au dieu d'amours* (1399: *Epistle to the God of Love*), an eloquent denunciation of the anti-feminist attitudes of Jean de Meun (*see* ROMAN DE LA ROSE), *La Cité des dames* (1404–5: *The City of Ladies*), in which she constructs an ideal city peopled by the great women of history and legend, and *Le Livre des trois vertus* (1405: *The Book of the Three Virtues*), which explores women's duties. A number of English translations of her work appeared in the late 15th and early 16th centuries.

Christmas Carol, A A Christmas book by Charles *Dickens, published 1843. Ebenezer Scrooge, a miserly old curmudgeon, receives on Christmas Eve a visit from the ghost of Marley, his late partner in business, and encounters a series of visions of the past, present, and future, including one of what his own death will

be like unless he mends his ways. He wakes up on Christmas morning a changed man. One of Dickens's most enduringly popular works, the book has been the subject of numerous adaptations on stage, screen, and television.

Christmas-Eve and Easter-Day A poem by Robert *Browning, published 1850. The poem is in two parts: 'Christmas-Eve', in narrative form, accepts that denominational religion is an imperfect medium for divine truth; 'Easter-Day', in dialogue form, examines the difficulties of holding to the Christian faith at all, and argues that the condition of doubt is essential to the existence of human faith.

Christ's Tears over Jerusalem A tract by Thomas *Nashe, published 1593. Nashe presents himself as a religious reformer and with his usual vigour, he analyses the vices and abuses of contemporary society.

chronicle play A type of drama popular in the 1590s and the early 17th century, depicting scenes from the life of a monarch or famous historical character. Examples are Shakespeare's *Henry V* and *Henry VIII*, the *Sir Thomas *More* play, and Thomas *Dekker and John *Webster's *Sir Thomas Wyatt.*

Chrononhotonthologos (1734) A burlesque of contemporary dramatic absurdities by the singer and dramatist Henry Carey (1687–1743) under the pseudonym 'Benjamin Bounce'. 'The Most Tragical Tragedy that ever was Tragediz'd by any Company of Tragedians', the play chronicled with joyous brevity the melodramatic fate of the eponymous king of Queerummania.

CHURCHILL, Caryl (1938–) Playwright. Most of her plays, predominantly radical and feminist in tone, have been performed at the *Royal Court Theatre: they include *Owners* (1972); *Light Shining in Buckinghamshire* (1976); *Cloud Nine* (1979); *Top Girls* (1982); *Serious Money* (1987); *Mad Forest* (1990), about the Romanian revolution; *The Skriker* (1994); *Blue Heart* (1997); and *This Is a Chair* (1997). *Far Away* (2001) is a darkly comic allegory about ethnic cleansing; *A Number* (2002) examines the implications of human genetic cloning; *Drunk Enough to Say I Love You?* (2006) is a savage critique of US foreign policy; and *Seven Jewish Children* (2009) a controversial ten-minute 'play for Gaza'.

CHURCHILL, Charles (1732–64) Poet and curate of St John's, Smith Square. His poverty was alleviated by the publication of *The *Rosciad* and *The Apology* (1761), which also brought him into the worldly circle of John Wilkes, for whom he edited the *North Briton* and whose opponents he attacked in verse. *The Prophecy of Famine* (1763) is a mock-pastoral satire on Lord Bute, John Home, and other Scots. Other targets were Tobias *Smollett (*The Author*, 1763) and William *Hogarth (*Epistle to William Hogarth*, 1763). *Gotham* (1764) jokingly installs Churchill as monarch of an ideal state. Churchill died at Boulogne on his way to visit Wilkes in France. His admirers included James *Boswell, despite Churchill's anti-Scottish prejudice and his attacks on Samuel *Johnson, and Lord *Byron.

Church of England Though there has been an organized church in England since the 4th century, the name refers to the institution established by law following Henry VIII's breach with Rome in 1532. The monarch became head of the church, the monasteries were dissolved and their wealth appropriated, and the authority of the papacy was repudiated. The church took its distinctive shape in the reign of Edward VI under the direction of Thomas *Cranmer, with its own liturgy, *The Book of *Common Prayer*; Articles of Religion (originally Forty-Two, the Thirty-Nine Articles received their final form in 1571); two books of Homilies (1547, 1571), i.e. sermons to be read in churches; and the Authorized Version of the *Bible (1611). Although Protestant in doctrine, the Church of England retained many Catholic features in its ceremonies and vestments and retained government by bishops, and it was regarded by Puritans as incompletely reformed. During the Civil War many of the distinctive features of the Church of England were abolished by Parliament, but the church was restored together with the monarchy in 1660. It remains the officially established Christian church in England. See PROTESTANTISM; PURITANISM; REFORMATION; ROMAN CATHOLICISM.

CIBBER, Colley (1671–1757) Actor and author. His first play, *Love's Last Shift* (1696), introduced Sir Novelty Fashion, a comic fop role later transformed into Lord Foppington in Sir John *Vanbrugh's sequel *The Relapse*; such figures were Cibber's speciality as an actor. He wrote the successful comedies *She Would and She Would Not* (1702), *The *Careless Husband* (1704), and *The Lady's Last Stake* (1707), and an enduring adaptation of Shakespeare's *Richard III* (1700). *The Non-juror* (1717), a comedy based on *Molière's *Tartuffe*, provoked a satirical pamphlet by Alexander *Pope. A loyal Whig, he was appointed poet laureate in 1730, to general derision. His disarmingly insouciant *An Apology for the Life of Mr Colley Cibber, Comedian* (1740) presents a vivid picture of the theatrical life of the time rather than autobiography as such: his infamous children Theophilus (1703–58) and Charlotte (*see* CHARKE) scarcely feature. The book was vengefully satirized by Henry *Fielding in *Shamela*; its brazen vanity gave Pope an excuse to install Cibber as the hero of the revised *Dunciad.

CICERO, Marcus Tullius (106–43 BC) Sometimes referred to as Tully, the supreme Latin orator and prose writer. He delivered his first speech in 81, and became praetor in 66, and consul in 63, at the earliest permitted age. As consul, he repressed the insurrection planned by *Catiline, executing his associates without trial. When civil war came, in 49, he reluctantly took Pompey's side. After Pompey's defeat Cicero was pardoned by Caesar, whose advances he rebuffed, and whose assassination he welcomed. At Mark Antony's insistence, Cicero was killed, and his severed head and hands were nailed to the Rostra (the orators' platform in the Roman Forum).

In the intervals of public life Cicero was a prolific writer. His works include a large number of speeches; treatises on rhetoric; collections of letters to Atticus and other friends; and philosophical dialogues on politics, ethics, epistemology, and religion. He was an important transmitter of Greek philosophy, especially *Stoicism, to Rome, and the creator of a Latin philosophical vocabulary. His influence on thought and expression from the Middle Ages to the 19th century was enormous. His rhetorical works, rediscovered in the 15th century, and his philosophical dialogues were essentials of humanist education. The long tradition of reading Cicero as an honorary Christian was challenged in the 18th century, particularly by David *Hume. See Robert *Harris's *Imperium* (2006), a lively fictionalized account of the early years of Cicero's career.

CID, the (*c.*1030–1099) The national hero of Spain in whose story history and myth are entangled. Born Rodrigo Díaz, and known in his lifetime as 'Cid Campeador' ('Seyd', lord; 'Campeador', champion), he rose to fame through military prowess. He was later banished and became a mercenary, fighting at times for Christians, at others for Moors. His principal feat was the capture in 1094 of Valencia from the Moors after a siege of nine months. In myth he has been transformed into a paragon of knightly and Christian virtue, and patriotic zeal. His achievements are narrated in the early 13th-century *Poema de mio Cid: Poem of the Cid* (the sole surviving full-length Spanish *epic poem, consisting of some 3,700 lines), in Spanish chronicles of the 14th century (translated by Robert *Southey, 1808), and in numerous ballads.

cinema became the dominant mass entertainment medium of the 20th century within a decade of the pioneering 'moving picture' displays in 1894–6 by Thomas Edison (1847–1931) in New York, Louis (1864–1948) and Auguste (1862–1954) Lumière in Paris, and Robert Paul (1869–1943) in London. Adaptations of literary and especially stage works soon appeared. Paul and Edison filmed single scenes from contemporary drama in 1896, while William *Shakespeare and Charles *Dickens were popular early sources. Tableaux from *King John* by the actor-manager Beerbohm Tree (1852–1917) were filmed in 1899 by Biograph and Paul produced a multi-scene *Scrooge*, based on a popular stage version of *A *Christmas Carol*, in 1901. Biblical subjects, especially the life of Christ, and traditional *fairy stories were also popular before 1910, providing opportunities for trick effects to represent miracles and magic. Georges Méliès (1861–1938) became the most famous producer of trick-based fantasies, including several loosely based on Jules *Verne's novels.

From around 1913, leading authors started to become involved in cinema, with a sophisticated Danish adaptation of Gerhart Hauptmann's *Atlantis* in 1913 and d'Annunzio lending his name to the ancient world spectacle *Cabiria* (1914). Arthur Conan *Doyle, Rudyard *Kipling, and Rider *Haggard enjoyed early screen success. Thomas *Dixon's lurid melodrama *The Clansman* provided the basis of Civil War epic *The Birth of a Nation* (1915) by D. W. Griffith (1875–1948), the success of which helped cement the global domination of American producers. Few authors managed to retain any control over the adaptation of their work— George Bernard *Shaw was an exception, refusing permission until the sound era—but many benefited from selling rights, especially to the Hollywood studios. Works by popular writers such as Dumas, Lew Wallace (1827–1905; *Ben-Hur*), Baroness *Orczy, Edgar *Wallace, and the Spanish novelist Vicente Blasco Ibáñez (1867–1928; *The Four Horsemen of the Apocalypse*) have been frequently re-filmed, making them classic in a new 'intermedial' sense.

While most writers since the mid-20th century have had some involvement with cinema, either working on scripts or having their works adapted, the relationship was traditionally considered fraught, with Scott *Fitzgerald the most celebrated of many supposed casualties of Hollywood. Graham *Greene pioneered a new relationship with cinema, writing such original screenplays as *The Third Man*, and scripting many of his own stories and novels, as Paul *Auster continues to do, while Harold *Pinter developed a respected parallel career scripting the works of others. More recently, playwrights such as Sam *Shepard, David *Mamet, Christopher *Hampton, and Stephen *Poliakoff have also become directors of their own films. *See* CHAPLIN; HITCHCOCK; WELLES.

(((iii))) **SEE WEB LINKS**
• The Internet Movie Database

Circe *See* ODYSSEY.

circulating libraries Commercial libraries from which books could be borrowed for a fee. Some booksellers lent books in this way in the 1660s, but the first regular example in Britain appears to have been Allan *Ramsay's, founded in Edinburgh about 1725. By 1800 some 200 were in operation. Such libraries stimulated the production of books, particularly of novels, though popular reading was often considered improper. *Mudie's Lending Library, opened in London in 1852, exercised a powerful censorship, and similar censorship was extended in the 20th century to writers such as H. G. *Wells and D. H. *Lawrence. The other large circulating libraries were those of the 19th-century bookselling firm W. H. Smith and Son, and 'Mrs Boot's Booklovers' Library', which was established by the Nottingham retail chemist Jesse Boot (1850–1931). By about 1970 circulating libraries had been replaced by local public libraries.

(((iii))) **SEE WEB LINKS**
• Library History Database of circulating libraries

citizen comedy An early 17th-century type of play, usually set in contemporary London and dealing with the common life of the middle classes, for example, Ben *Jonson's *Bartholomew Fair* and Thomas *Middleton's *A *Chaste Maid in Cheapside*.

Citizen of the World, The By Oliver *Goldsmith, a collection of letters purporting to be written by or to Lien Chi Altangi, a Chinese traveller in London. They appeared as *Chinese Letters* in John *Newbery's *Public Ledger* (1760–1), and were published in book form, with additions, in 1762. The letters comment with innocent surprise on the absurdities of English life and manners. The best-known characters are the 'Man in Black', a covert philanthropist, and 'Beau' Tibbs, an affected nonentity who claims acquaintance with the great.

City Heiress, The A comedy by Aphra *Behn produced in 1682, displaying Behn's Royalist sympathies.

City Madam, The A comedy by Philip *Massinger, acted 1632, printed 1658. The wife and daughters of London merchant Sir John Frugal have become proud and extravagant, and he decides to teach them a lesson. He pretends to retire to a monastery, leaving his property to his brother Luke, an ostensibly reformed wastrel. Luke treats the family, apprentices, and debtors with great harshness, but Sir John, and the two suitors his proud daughters have rejected, return disguised as Indians and expose his hypocrisy.

'City of Dreadful Night, The' *See* THOMSON, JAMES (1834–82).

'Civil Disobedience' *See* THOREAU, HENRY.

Civil Wars between the Two Houses of Lancaster and York, The An *epic poem in eight books by Samuel *Daniel. The first four books (published 1595) cover English history from the Conquest to Richard II, the remainder (1609) from the Wars of the Roses to Edward IV.

CLAIRMONT, Claire (1798–1879) Daughter of Mary Clairmont, William *Godwin's second wife. She accompanied Mary Wollstonecraft Godwin, her stepsister, on Mary's elopement with P. B. *Shelley, and in spite of pursuit remained with them on the Continent. She returned to London with the Shelleys in 1816, fell in love with Lord *Byron, and when he went to Switzerland induced the Shelleys to follow him with her. Byron's daughter Allegra was born to her in 1817. In 1818 Byron demanded the baby, offering to acknowledge and educate her. Strongly against her will, and against the advice of Shelley, Claire surrendered the child. Much to her distress, in 1821

Byron placed the child in a convent near Ravenna, where she died of a fever in the following year.

CLANCHY, Kate (1965–) Poet, born in Glasgow. Her first book *Slattern* (1995) was acclaimed for its melodious yet taut language, and acute observation, often drawn from her experience as a schoolteacher in the East End of London. It includes a series of love poems remarkable for their lucid description of female desire and hurt. In *Samarkand* (1999) she addresses a greater range of issues, using longer forms to explore masculine violence, national identity, fulfilment in love, grief, and the meaning of 'home'. *Newborn* (2004) is a sequence of poems exploring the delights and difficulties of pregnancy, birth, and caring for a baby. *What Is She Doing Here? A Refugee's Story* (2008) was renamed *Antigona and Me* in 2009.

Clandestine Marriage, The A comedy by George *Colman the elder and David *Garrick (1766). The play's blend of comic situation and warm sentiment was immediately and enduringly popular, despite a brief rift between the collaborators when Garrick declined the role of Ogleby.

CLANVOWE, Sir John (c.1341–c.1391) Diplomat and member of the king's household. Allegedly one of the *Lollard Knights, and author of the pacifist and puritanical work *The Two Ways*. He was a friend of *Chaucer, and he may also have been the author of *The Cuckoo and the Nightingale, or The Boke of Cupide*, an elegant debate-poem in 290 lines. *Wordsworth translated it, and it was viewed in the 19th century as 'one of the prettiest things in Medieval Literature'.

CLARE, John (1793–1864) Poet, the son of a labourer, born in Helpstone, Northamptonshire. In 1820 he married Martha Turner, having parted from his first love, Mary Joyce. His highly successful *Poems Descriptive of Rural Life and Scenery* was followed by *The Village Minstrel* (1821), *The *Shepherd's Calendar* (1827), and *The Rural Muse* (1835). In 1832 he left his native cottage for Northborough, only 4 miles away, but the move, to one so deeply attached to place, was disturbing, and reinforced the theme of loss in his work. In 1837 he was admitted as insane to an asylum in High Beach, Epping. He escaped in 1841, walking home to Northamptonshire in the delusion that he would there be reunited with Mary, to whom he thought himself married. He spent the rest of his life in Northampton General Asylum. The declining sales of his work may have contributed to his mental troubles, for by the 1830s the vogue for rural poetry and 'ploughman' poets such as Robert *Burns and Robert *Bloomfield was passing. Clare's best poetry demonstrates a complex sensibility and fine organization, and has been variously read as laments for lost love and talent, for the death of rural England, or for lost innocence.

CLARE, St (1194–1253) Founder of the first order of Franciscan nuns, also known as the Poor Clares.

Clarissa, *or The History of a Young Lady* An *epistolary novel by Samuel *Richardson, published 1748 (for 1747)–1749, in eight volumes. About one-third of the work (which is in all over a million words) consists of the letters of Clarissa to Anna Howe and of Lovelace to John Belford, but there are over twenty correspondents in all, displaying many points of view and variations in style. Lovelace, a dashing rake, is courting Clarissa's elder sister Arabella; when he transfers his affections to Clarissa her family decide she must marry the wealthy but repulsive Solmes. Lovelace, representing himself as her deliverer, persuades her to escape, under his protection, to London. He establishes her in a superior brothel, which she supposes to be respectable lodgings. She unwaveringly resists his advances and he is both enraged and attracted by her intransigence. She is fascinated by his charm and wit, but distrusts him and refuses his eventual proposals of marriage. Lovelace claims to believe her resistance is no more than prudery and that, once subdued, she will prove no more chaste than other women. To Clarissa chastity represents identity itself, and the climax of her tragedy comes when Lovelace, abetted by the women of the house, drugs and rapes her. Clarissa loses grip of her reason. She escapes, only to find herself trapped in a debtors' prison. She is rescued by Belford, a reformed character, who looks after her with affectionate care, and reports in his letters her long decline and Christian preparation for death. After her death her cousin, Colonel Morden, kills Lovelace, already overwhelmed by remorse, in a duel.

Despite its prolixity, the novel was resoundingly acclaimed for its emotional power, unprecedented psychological minuteness, and its (apparently) unmediated access to private thought.

CLARK, William *See* LEWIS, MERIWETHER.

CLARK-BEKEDEREMO, John Pepper (1935–) Nigerian poet and playwright; founder and editor of *The Horn,* which first published the work of Wole *Soyinka and Christopher *Okigbo. Clark-Bekederemo, influenced by modernist poets, reshaped English prosody to fit African experience in his poetry collections *A Reed in the Tide* (1965) and *Casualties* (1970).

CLARKE, Arthur C. (1917–2008) Prolific and popular writer of *science fiction. He was knighted in 2000. His great technical expertise in the realm of aeronautics and astronautics is manifested both in his fiction, which includes *Childhood's End* (1953), *The City and the Stars* (1956), and *Imperial Earth* (1975), in his many non-fiction works, and his script for Stanley Kubrick's *2001: A Space Odyssey* (film 1968, also adapted into a novel). He was a patron of the Science Fiction Foundation and funded the Arthur C. Clarke Award for best science fiction novel published in Britain.

CLARKE, Austin (1896–1974) Irish poet, verse dramatist, and broadcaster. While his early poetry is influenced by W. B. *Yeats and the *Celtic Twilight, it is informed by an unusually scholarly command of Gaelic sources. Much of his later work is satirical, attacking the collusion between church and state in mid-century Ireland. His subtle and complex versification is displayed in the ornate historical recreations of *Pilgrimage and Other Poems* (1929), the austerely confessional *Night and Morning* (1938), and in *Flight to Africa and Other Poems* (1963). Clarke was also greatly interested in verse drama. His *Collected Plays* were published in 1963 and his *Collected Poems* a few weeks after his death in 1974.

CLARKE, Charles Cowden- (1787–1877) The son of John *Keats's schoolmaster John Clarke, and a close friend of the poet. Keats's 'Epistle to Charles Cowden-Clarke' is full of affection and gratitude. With his wife Mary Victoria Cowden-Clarke he produced editions of Shakespeare, George *Herbert, and other poets. Also with his wife he wrote *Recollections of Writers* (1878), a lively and valuable collection of reminiscences of their close friends Keats, Charles *Lamb, Mary Lamb, Leigh *Hunt, Douglas *Jerrold, and Charles *Dickens.

CLARKE, Gillian (1937–) Welsh poet. Her main collections of verse are *Letter from a Far Country* (1982), *Letting in the Rumour* (1989), *The King of Britain's Daughter* (1993), *Five Fields* (1998), and *Making the Beds for the Dead* (2004). Her *Collected Poems* appeared in

1997. Clarke's work combines a sense of human implication in the cycle of the seasons with an awareness of Welsh history, language, and mythology. Sensuous and understated, her poems have a strong political dimension; their longstanding concern with issues of gender and ecology has been shadowed in recent work by apprehensions of post-9/11 global crisis. The title sequence of *A Recipe for Water* (2009) is dedicated to Sujata Bhatt.

CLARKE, John Cooper *See* PERFORMANCE POETRY.

CLARKE, Marcus (1846–81) Novelist, journalist, and dramatist, famed for the enduringly popular convict epic *For the Term of his Natural Life*. Clarke was friends with G. M. *Hopkins before emigrating to Victoria, Australia in 1867. *His Natural Life* was serialized in the *Australian Journal* (1870–72), published as a novel (1874), and under the longer title (after 1882). Protagonist 'Rufus Dawes'—Richard Devine—is wrongly transported to Tasmania, thence to the even more horrific Norfolk Island.

CLARKE, Susanna (1959–) Author of well-received *fantasy stories, and the novel *Jonathan Strange & Mr Norrell* (2004). Its wry precision and detailed evocation of English magic in an alternative 19th century made it a best-seller and *Hugo winner.

CLARKSON, Laurence (1615–67) A pamphleteer whose spiritual autobiography *The Lost Sheep Found* (1660) charts his progress through many religious affiliations; from his Church of England boyhood in Lancashire he became Anabaptist, Seeker, Ranter, and finally *Muggletonian, suffering imprisonment for his views. His tracts, written with originality, force, and feeling, shed an interesting light on the adventurous and speculative ideas of the age.

classicism, classic, and **classical** are terms used in several shifting and at times overlapping senses. A 'literary classic' is a work considered first-rate or excellent of its kind, and therefore fit to be used as a model or imitated; and this sense now applies as much to modern works and to those of a 'romantic' tendency as it does to the works of Greek and Roman ('classical') antiquity formerly known simply as 'the classics'. Similarly the term 'classical' itself has been applied to later literary periods: the 17th century, for instance, being regarded as the classical age of French and Spanish drama. Classicism denotes a particular commitment to and celebration of the lasting value of the Greek and Roman heritage, usually accompanied by or implying some disparagement of subsequent literary achievements and traditions. This critical position commonly favours such values as harmony, proportion, balance, decorum, and restraint, deploring the less regulated products of the vernacular modern literatures. While classicism is a critical position or unstated aesthetic preference, the applied imitation of Greek and Roman models in poetic and dramatic practice, along with the critical justification for such imitation, is more usually known as *neo-classicism, this being an important movement that flourished in England, and more powerfully in France, in the 17th and 18th centuries. The flourishing of *Romanticism in the first half of the 19th century, itself partly a revolt against neo-classical culture (although not usually against ancient poetry), provoked a more polemical phase of classicism led successively by Matthew *Arnold, the American critic Irving Babbitt (1865–1933), and T. S. *Eliot. It also promoted general discussion of the distinctions between opposed classical and romantic principles in literature, in which classical values are held to be those of order and respect for tradition, while the contrary romantic values are those of individualism, spontaneity, and inspiration.

CLAUDE LORRAIN (1600–82) Landscape painter from Lorraine, who worked mainly in Rome. Many 18th-century English travellers on the *Grand Tour were impressed by Claude's elegiac landscapes, and his compositions, were important to the theory of the *picturesque. Enthusiasts came to regard the Lake District as though it were a sequence of pictures by Claude and many carried a 'Claude glass', a blackened convex mirror which 'composed' the landscape into a view by Claude.

CLAUDIAN (Claudius Claudianus) (AD *c*.370–*c*.404) The last great classical Latin poet, court poet to the emperor Honorius in Rome; it is assumed that he remained a pagan. His short *epic *The Rape of Proserpina* influenced Edmund *Spenser's account of the garden of Proserpina (*Faerie Queene*, II. vii. 52) and was translated in 1617 by Leonard Digges (1588–1635). There was no complete English translation of his poems until 1817.

Claverings, The A novel by Anthony *Trollope, published 1867. It is characteristic of Trollope's interest in loyalty and temptation in courtship and marriage, complicated by questions of money and inheritance.

Cleanness (*or Purity*) An alliterative poem in 1,812 lines from the second half of the 14th century, the only manuscript of which is the famous Cotton Nero A. X which is also the sole manuscript of **Pearl*, **Patience*, and *Sir *Gawain and the Green Knight*. It deals with three subjects from the Scriptures and is hardly more than a vigorous paraphrase of them: the Flood, the destruction of Sodom and Gomorrah, and the fall of Belshazzar.

CLEAVER, Eldridge (1935–98) African American essayist and political activist born in Arkansas. He became a member of the Black Panther Party and his book of essays *Soul on Ice* (1967) became a key document for the **Black Arts Movement. His *Postprison Writings and Speeches* were collected in 1969 and *Soul on Fire* (1978) gives a memoir of his life in exile.

CLELAND, John (1710–89) Novelist. **Memoirs of a Woman of Pleasure*, completed while Cleland was imprisoned for debt and published 1748–9, made his publisher a fortune, but Cleland received only 20 guineas. Both men were convicted of publishing an obscene work, and Cleland produced an expurgated version. His later fiction includes *Memoirs of a Coxcomb* (1751), *The Surprises of Love* (1764), and *The Woman of Honour* (1768).

CLEMENS, S. L. *See* TWAIN, MARK.

CLEMO, Jack (Reginald John) (1916–94) Poet. He came to critical notice with his novel *Wilding Graft* (1948), which was admired by T. F. **Powys. His poetry includes *The Map of Clay* (1961), with an introduction by Charles **Causley; *The Echoing Tip* (1971), which evokes the tormented landscapes of the clay pits and expresses his own Calvinist faith; *The Bouncing Hills* (1983); *Selected Poems* (1988); and *Approach to Murano* (1992). He also wrote *The Shadowed Bed* (1986, novel), and two volumes of autobiography, *Confessions of a Rebel* (1949) and *The Marriage of a Rebel* (1980).

CLEOPATRA (69–30 BC) Queen of Egypt, famous as the lover of Julius **Caesar and Mark Antony. She committed suicide following the death of Antony to avoid humiliation by her conqueror Octavian (later the emperor Augustus). Her story was told by **Plutarch in his life of Marcus Antonius, and retold among others by **Shakespeare, John **Dryden in **All for Love*, Sarah **Fielding, and George Bernard **Shaw, who focuses unusually on her relationship with Caesar.

Cleopatra A tragedy in blank verse by Samuel **Daniel, published 1594. It is on the Senecan model, and deals with the story of Cleopatra after the death of Antony.

clerihew A humorous verse form invented by Edmund Clerihew **Bentley, consisting of two rhymed but metrically clumsy couplets, with the first line referring to a well-known person, e.g.

> Sir James Jeans
> Always says what he means;
> He is really perfectly serious
> About the Universe being Mysterious.

'Clerk's Tale, The' *See* CANTERBURY TALES, 9.

CLEVELAND, John (1613–58) Poet, an active Royalist in the Civil War. His poems took metaphysical wit to an extreme, and were highly popular (with 25 editions between 1647 and 1700). Samuel **Johnson admired his best-known satire 'The Rebel Scot' for the couplet 'Had Cain been Scot, God would have changed his doom | Not forced him wander, but confined him home'. But John **Dryden thought he offered merely 'common thoughts in abstruse words'. Twentieth-century interest in political satire revived his reputation.

CLIFFORD, Lady Anne countess of Pembroke, Dorset, and Montgomery (1590–1676) Diarist, sole surviving child of George, the third duke of Cumberland. She was tutored by Samuel **Daniel and acted in **masques at **James I's court. She fought a long battle to establish her right to the Clifford estates, commissioning a portrait triptych by Jan van Belcamp (now in Appleby Castle) to celebrate her victory in 1649. Her letters and diaries (1603–16) chronicle her campaign and her stormy marriages to the earl of Dorset (d. 1624) and Philip Herbert, earl of Pembroke (1584–1650). She also left a 'day book', an intimate record of her old age as matriarch, landowner, and sheriff in Westmorland. Vita **Sackville-West, herself debarred from the inheritance of Knole by her sex, edited *The Diary of Lady Anne Clifford* (1923).

CLIFFORD, Martin Pseudonym of Charles **Hamilton.

CLIVE, Caroline Archer (Mrs Clive) (1801–73) Poet and novelist, who wrote chiefly under the initial 'V'. Her first volume of poems, *IX Poems by V* (1840), attracted high praise, and her reputation was consolidated by her powerful novel *Paul Ferroll* (1855). The hero murders his wife, escapes suspicion, and marries his true love, who, after eighteen years of happy marriage, dies of shock when Paul Ferroll voluntarily confesses his crime in order to save innocent suspects. *Paul Ferroll*, with its challenges to morality, was a forerunner of the *sensation novel. *Why Paul Ferroll Killed his Wife* (1860) followed. The victim of a number of incapacitating accidents during her life, Clive was interested, like Dinah *Craik, in representing the consequences of infirmity: she was accidentally burned to death while writing in her library.

Clockwork Orange, A A novel by Anthony *Burgess, published in 1962. Set in the near future, Alex recounts his life from the age of 15 as leader of a gang of thugs to his emergence from State Jail 84F after a period of experimental aversion therapy, which has left him unable to enjoy his former pleasures of rape, assault, and listening to Beethoven while indulging in fantasies of crime. Written in what Alex calls 'nadsat', a highly inventive mix of Russian, neologisms, and archaisms, the novel conjures up a *dystopian world of youth violence and institutional manipulation in which Alex comes to see himself as a victim. The disturbingly brilliant film version by Stanley Kubrick (1971) omitted a final chapter in which Alex looks back at his youth, and provoked wide controversy. Amid claims that it had provoked copycat violence, Kubrick withdrew the film from distribution in Britain, and it did not reappear until 2000, after his death.

Cloister and the Hearth, The Charles *Reade's most celebrated novel, published 1861. The story is set in the 15th century. Gerard, the son of a trader in the Netherlands, is destined for the church, but falls in love with Margaret Brandt, whose father is an impoverished scholar suspected of sorcery. They become engaged, but family opposition prevents the marriage and forces him to leave the Netherlands. While he is in Italy Gerard hears of Margaret's death; not realizing the news is a trick, he throws himself into a desperate world of gambling, drinking, and women. Margaret meanwhile has given birth to his son. Eventually sickened by his life, Gerard takes his vows as a Dominican monk, and travels slowly back to the Netherlands. Because of his son he allows himself to return to her and is accepted as the vicar of Gouda. Their son, the end of the story indicates, is the future philosopher *Erasmus.

The novel was based on Reade's short story 'A Good Fight' (published in *Once a Week* in 1859),

in which the fight refers to the struggle against sexual feeling, a theme common in Reade's work. The novel arose from his discovery of the story of Erasmus' father.

closet drama A dramatic poem intended for reading in private rather than for staged performance, a closet in this sense being a private study. Notable examples in English include John *Milton's *Samson Agonistes*. Many writers turned to this form in the 18th and 19th centuries, faced with *censorship of public spoken drama, among them Lord *Byron (e.g. his *Manfred*) and P. B. *Shelley in his *Prometheus Unbound*.

Cloud-cuckoo-land (Nephelococcygia) An imaginary city built in the air in *The Birds* of *Aristophanes.

Cloud of Unknowing, The A mystical prose work, possibly from the north-east Midlands, dating from the late 14th century, and one of the most admired products of the Middle English mystical tradition. The author was presumably a priest, though no more certain identification of him has resulted from the many speculations about him. Other works have been plausibly attributed to him, including *The Book of Privy Counselling*, *The Epistle of Prayer*, and *Deonise Hid Divinite*.

CLOUGH, Arthur Hugh (1819–61) Poet. He became a fellow of Oriel College, Oxford, but resigned. In 1852–3 he spent several months in America, mostly working on his translation of *Plutarch's Lives* (pub. Boston, 1857), before returning to England to marry and become an examiner in the Education Office.

The Bothie of Tober-na-Vuolich (1848) is a poem in English hexameters about a student reading party in Scotland. Philip falls in love with Elspie, a peasant who represents 'work, mother earth, and the objects of living', and at the end of the poem the couple move to New Zealand.

Amours de voyage (mostly written 1849; pub. *Atlantic Monthly*, 1858) is similar in form, but *epistolary. *Dipsychus* (published posthumously, 1865), is a Faustian dialogue set in Venice. The best known of Clough's shorter poems, sharply contrasted, are 'Say not the struggle nought availeth' and the satirical 'The Latest Decalogue', both written early but published posthumously in *Poems* (1862), with a Memoir by Francis Turner *Palgrave. Clough's powerful conviction of the efficacy of doubt as a positive, productive condition has gradually been recognized by critics.

CLUNE, Frank (1893–1971) Australian writer, who left home at 15 to roam the world. He wrote his first autobiography, *Try Anything Once* (1933), in hospital. It recounted his adventures as a newsboy, bush labourer, US army deserter, seaman, bootlegger, Gallipoli veteran, vaudevillian, and mouse-trap salesman. An immediate success, it launched Clune as a best-selling author of another 58 books.

CLUTE, John (1940–) Canadian-born author and critic, resident in Britain since 1969. As reviewer and encyclopedist, co-editing *The Encyclopedia of Science Fiction* (2nd edn 1993, 3rd edn online 2011) and *The Encyclopedia of Fantasy* (1997), he is one of the most influential authorities on *science fiction and *fantasy. He has published the novels *The Disinheriting Party* (1977) and *Appleseed* (2001).

COBBETT, William (1763–1835) Author, the son of a farmer, and self-educated; he enlisted as a soldier and served in New Brunswick from 1784 to 1791. He brought an accusation of embezzlement against some of his former officers, and in 1792 retired, first to France then to America, to avoid prosecution. There he published in 1796 *The Life and Adventures of Peter Porcupine*, a provocatively pro-British work, and in 1801 his *Works*, critical of America. He returned to England in 1800, and became an anti-radical journalist, founding and writing the *Political Register* from 1802. Soon, however, as a result of what he observed, his views began to change, and from about 1804 he wrote in the radical interest, suffering two years' imprisonment for his attack on flogging in the army. He published Parliamentary Debates, afterwards taken over by Hansard, and *State Trials*. The reflections assembled in 1830 as *Rural Rides* began to appear in the *Political Register* from 1821. His *History of the Protestant 'Reformation' in England and Ireland* appeared in 1824; his *Advice to Young Men* in 1829. He became MP for Oldham in 1832. His prose style was commended by William *Hazlitt as 'plain, broad, downright English'.

COCKBURN, Alison (1713–94) Née Rutherford, Scots poet and songwriter, whose lively soirées brought together most of the literary talent of 18th-century Edinburgh. She was friendly with David *Hume, was admired by Robert *Burns, and was on close terms with the family of Walter *Scott, to whom she was distantly related. She wrote one of the well-known versions of 'The Flowers of the Forest'. *See* ELLIOT.

COCKBURN, Catharine (?1674–1749) Playwright and author, née Trotter. Her tragedy *Agnes de Castro* was performed at the Theatre Royal, Drury Lane, probably in 1695; her last play was performed in 1706. In 1702 she published an essay in defence of John *Locke, the first of several works on religion and philosophy, including one in defence of Samuel Clarke. Her prose works, letters, and occasional poems were edited, with her best-known play, *Fatal Friendship*, by Thomas Birch (1751).

Cock Lorell's Boat A popular verse satire of the early 16th century in which representatives of various trades take ship and sail through England. The captain of the boat is Cock Lorell, a tinker and probably a historical figure. It provides an interesting picture of contemporary low life.

Cockney School A term apparently first used in *Blackwood's Magazine* in October 1817, when John *Lockhart and his associates began a series of attacks 'On the Cockney School of Poetry'. Leigh *Hunt was the chief target, but William *Hazlitt and John *Keats were also objects of frequent derision. The Londoners, all of relatively humble origin, were contrasted with the great writers, all of whom 'have been men of some rank'. The virulence of the attacks, which described the writers as 'the vilest vermin' and of 'extreme moral depravity', was sustained over several years, and included an assault on Keats's *Endymion in 1818.

codex A manuscript with papyrus or parchment pages bound in book form in the ancient and medieval worlds. This crucial Roman invention replaced texts written on scrolls, which were far more difficult to search, and was the ancestor of the printed book.

COE, Jonathan (1961–) Novelist and biographer. His early novels, *The Accidental Woman* (1987), *A Touch of Love* (1989), and *The Dwarves of Death* (1990), are short, playful, and experimental. *What a Carve Up!* (1994), which takes its name from a blackly comic film of the 1960s, satirizes the rampant materialism of the 1980s by focusing on the morally repugnant Winshaw family. Coe's other novels are *The House of Sleep* (1997); *The Rotters' Club* (2001), which chronicles, with painfully funny precision, the coming of age of four Birmingham schoolboys in the 1970s; its sequel, *The Closed Circle* (2004), which tracks the progress of the characters through a further twenty-five years; *The Rain Before It Falls* (2007) and *The*

Terrible Privacy of Maxwell Sim (2010). *Like a Fiery Elephant* (2004) is a biography of B. S. *Johnson.

Coelebs in Search of a Wife A novel by Hannah *More, published 1809. The book, which was immensely successful, consists of a collection of sharp social sketches and moral precepts, informed by More's ardent evangelicalism. The episodes are strung together by the hero's search for a wife.

COETZEE, J. M. (John Maxwell) (1940–) Novelist and academic, born in Cape Town; in 2006 he took Australian citizenship. His fiction is self-reflexive, allusive, and disorienting. *Dusklands* (1974), contains two linked novellas, one concerning the American involvement in Vietnam, the other about an 18th-century Boer settler. *In the Heart of the Country* (1977) focuses on the meditations of an embittered Afrikaner woman. *Waiting for the Barbarians* (1980), a powerful allegory of oppression, was followed by the *Life and Times of Michael K* (1983, Booker Prize); *Foe* (1986) interacts with the world of *Robinson Crusoe*; *The Master of Petersburg* (1994) is set in 1896, and follows the exiled *Dostoevsky back to St Petersburg. *Disgrace* (1999, Booker Prize, the first writer to win it twice) is the painful story of a middle-aged professor of English in post-apartheid South Africa charged with sexual harassment who seeks refuge on his daughter's farm. The protagonist of *Slow Man* (2005) is visited by the title character of *Elizabeth Costelloe* (2003). *Boyhood* (1997) *Youth* (2002) and *Summertime* (2009) are fictionalised autobiography.

coffee houses were first introduced in the time of the Commonwealth; the first recorded in England was in Oxford in 1650 (mentioned by Anthony *Wood), and the first in London was in 1652, in St Michael's Alley, off Cornhill, at the Sign of Pasqua Rosee. They were much frequented in the 17th and 18th centuries for political and literary discussions, circulation of news, etc. Among the most celebrated coffee and chocolate houses were the Bedford (Covent Garden, a favourite with actors), Button's (Russell Street, Covent Garden, popular with Joseph *Addison and his circle), Slaughter's (St Martin's Lane, a favourite of William *Hogarth and other artists), White's (a chocolate house in St James's), and Will's (Bow Street, frequented by authors, wits, and gamblers, and particularly associated with John *Dryden). Their decline during the 18th century has been in part attributed to the increasing popularity of clubs.

Cold Comfort Farm (1932) The first novel of Stella Gibbons (1902–89), a witty and highly successful parody of a certain strain of doom-laden rural primitivism in English fiction. In passing, Gibbons makes fun of both Thomas *Hardy and D. H. *Lawrence, but her primary target is the fiction of Mary *Webb. Flora Poste goes to stay with distant relatives, the Starkadders, who are consumed by dark emotions and terrible intrigues. Flora sets out to apply common sense to their problems and to introduce them to the realities of the modern world.

COLERIDGE, Hartley (1796–1849) The eldest son of Samuel Taylor *Coleridge. He lost his Oxford fellowship for intemperance. He published *Poems, Songs and Sonnets* (1833), and *Biographia Borealis* (1833, unfinished; 1836 as *Worthies of Yorkshire and Lancashire*). He contributed to literary journals, and in 1840 published his edition, with brief biographies, of Philip *Massinger and John *Ford. His *Essays and Marginalia*, edited by his brother Derwent, were published posthumously in 1851. He is the subject of two important poems by his father, *'Frost at Midnight' and 'The Nightingale'.

COLERIDGE, Mary (1861–1907) Poet, the great-great-niece of S. T. *Coleridge. She published *Fancy's Following*, (1896) with the encouragement of Robert *Bridges, and *Fancy's Guerdon* (1897). Her first novel, a lively and fantastical romance, *The Seven Sleepers of Ephesus* (1893), was praised by R. L. *Stevenson but achieved little success; her second, *The King with Two Faces* (1897), a historical romance centring on Gustavus III of Sweden, was well received. In 1900 she published *Non Sequitur*, a collection of spirited and ironic essays.

COLERIDGE, Samuel Taylor (1772–1834) Poet, critic, and philosopher of *Romanticism. Youngest son of the vicar of Ottery St Mary, Devon, he was destined for the church. After his father's early death he went to Christ's Hospital school, London, where he attracted a circle of young admirers, including Leigh *Hunt and Charles *Lamb. At Jesus College, Cambridge (1792–4), a brilliant career in classics was diverted by French revolutionary politics, heavy drinking, and an unhappy love affair, which led Coleridge to enlist in desperation in the 15th Light Dragoons under the name of Comberbache. From 1794, his friendship with Robert *Southey led to their invention of *Pantisocracy, a scheme to set up a commune in America. Coleridge's first poetry, a series of sonnets to eminent radicals including William

*Godwin and Joseph *Priestley. was published in the **Morning Chronicle*. To finance Pantisocracy, he and Southey gave political lectures in Bristol and collaborated on a verse drama, *The *Fall of Robespierre* (1794); they also simultaneously courted and married two sisters, Sara and Edith Fricker. After quarrelling with Southey, Coleridge retired with Sara to a cottage at Clevedon, where their first son Hartley, named after the philosopher David *Hartley, was born (*see* COLERIDGE, HARTLEY). Here Coleridge edited a radical Christian journal, *The *Watchman*, and published *Poems on Various Subjects* (1796). He considered entering the Unitarian ministry (*see* UNITARIANISM).

In June 1797 Coleridge met *Wordsworth and his sister Dorothy. The intense friendship that sprang up between the three shaped their lives for many years and proved one of the most creative partnerships in English Romanticism. Between July 1797 and September 1798 they lived and worked intimately together; the Coleridges at Nether Stowey, Somerset, and the Wordsworths two miles away at Alfoxden, where they were visited by Lamb, William *Hazlitt, and others. Here Coleridge wrote a moving series of blank verse 'conversation' poems, addressed to his friends: 'Fears in Solitude', 'This Lime Tree Bower my Prison', 'The Nightingale', and *'Frost at Midnight'. He also composed his celebrated opium-vision *'Kubla Khan'. At Wordsworth's suggestion, Coleridge wrote *The Rime of the *Ancient Mariner*, and started three other ballads, including *'Christabel'. A selection from their work appeared as the **Lyrical Ballads* (1798), intended as an 'experiment' in English poetry, which, after a poor critical reception, achieved a revolution in literary taste and sensibility.

Disenchanted with political developments ('France: An Ode'), Coleridge now turned towards Germany, where he spent ten months (1798-9), partly in the company of the Wordsworths, studying *Kant, *Schiller, and *Schelling. Returned to London, he translated Schiller's verse play *Wallenstein*, wrote for the **Morning Post*, and first began to plan a great work on metaphysics. In 1800 he moved to the Lake District with the Wordsworths, but his marriage was increasingly unhappy and he had fallen disastrously in love with Wordsworth's future sister-in-law Sara Hutchinson, as recorded in 'Love' (1799) and other 'Asra' poems. His use of opium became a crippling addiction. Many of these difficulties are examined in the brilliant and emotional *'Dejection: An Ode' (1802). During these years he also began to compile his *Notebooks*, daily meditations on his life, writing, and dreams, which have proved among his most enduring and moving works. In 1804 Coleridge went abroad alone: he worked for two years as secretary to the governor of Malta, and later travelled through Sicily and Italy. In 1807 he separated from his wife and went to live with the Wordsworths and Sara Hutchinson at Coleorton, Leicestershire: here Wordsworth first read him 'The Poem to Coleridge' which became *The *Prelude*. In 1808, though ill, Coleridge began his series of Lectures on Poetry and Drama, which he continued sporadically over the next decade to audiences including John *Keats and Lord *Byron, and which as his *Shakespearean Criticism* introduced new concepts of 'organic' form and dramatic psychology. In 1809-10 he wrote and edited with Sara Hutchinson's help a second periodical, the **Friend*. The intellectual effort, combined with the struggle against opium, shattered his circle of friends: Sara left for Wales, Dorothy grew estranged, he quarrelled irrevocably with Wordsworth. Coleridge fled to London, where between 1811 and 1814 he was on the verge of suicide, sustained only by his friends the Morgans. His play **Remorse*, a melodrama of the Spanish Inquisition, was a critical success at Drury Lane (1813). After a physical and spiritual crisis in the winter of 1813-14, Coleridge rediscovered his Christian beliefs, admitted his opium addiction, submitted himself to a series of medical regimes, and began to write again. To this period belong the prose 'commentary' printed in the margins of the 'Mariner'; his essay 'on the Principles of Genial Criticism', adapted from Kant; and his **Biographia Literaria* (1817), a major work of poetic criticism, philosophy, and autobiography.

In the spring of 1816 Coleridge found permanent harbour in the household of Dr James Gillman. His by now almost legendary reputation among the younger Romantics was assured by *Christabel and Other Poems* (1816), which included for the first time 'Kubla Khan', and 'The Pains of Sleep'; it was published partly through Byron's influence. *Sibylline Leaves*, collected poems, was published in 1817 (expanded in 1828 and 1834); *Zapolya* in 1817. He became the centre of a new circle of young disciples: Thomas *Carlyle christened him 'the Sage of Highgate', and Lamb—who dedicated the **Essays of Elia* to him—described him as 'an Archangel a little damaged'.

His **Aids to Reflection* (1825) had a fruitful influence on John *Sterling, Charles *Kingsley, and the young Christian Socialists; while his *Church and State* (1830) was taken up by

Matthew *Arnold and John Henry *Newman. Coleridge's later works and unpublished lectures develop his critical ideas, concerning Imagination and Fancy; Reason and Understanding; Symbolism and Allegory; Organic and Mechanical Form; Culture and Civilization. The dialectical way he expresses them is one of his clearest debts to German Romantic philosophy. His final position is that of a Romantic conservative and Christian radical. He also wrote some haunting late poems, 'Youth and Age', 'Limbo', 'Work without Hope', and 'Constancy to an Ideal Object'. He died of heart failure. The last echoes of his inspired conversation were captured in *Table Talk* (1836).

Coleridge has been variously criticized as a political turncoat, a drug addict, a plagiarist, and a mystic humbug, whose wrecked career left nothing but a handful of magical early poems. But the importance of his highly imaginative criticism is now generally accepted, as is his position (with Wordsworth) as one of the two great progenitors of the English Romantic spirit. The modern editions of his *Letters* (6 vols, 1956-71), and his *Notebooks* (5 vols, 1957-2002) have been essential to the reassessment of his creative work.

COLERIDGE, Sara (1802-52) Daughter of Samuel Taylor *Coleridge, she grew up largely without her father in the company of Robert *Southey and his family and of the *Wordsworths. She edited and annotated her father's papers with such skill that much of her work still stands. *Pretty Lessons for Good Children* appeared in 1834, and in 1837 her long prose narrative 'Phantasmion'. The lively and engaging *Memoir and Letters*, published by her daughter in 1873, provides much information on the literary and personal lives of the Coleridges, the Wordsworths, and the Southeys. She appears, with Dora Wordsworth and Edith Southey, in Wordsworth's poem 'The Triad' (1828).

COLET, John (1467-1519) One of the principal Christian Humanists of his day in England. He lectured at Oxford on the New Testament from about 1495 to 1505, *Erasmus being in his audience. As dean of St Paul's (1505) he founded and endowed St Paul's School, writing for it a Latin grammar for which William *Lily, the first high master, wrote the syntax; later known as the Eton Latin Grammar, it became a standard school textbook. Although he was unwilling to publish in print, he was a famous preacher and lecturer; he has been seen as a precursor of the *Reformation. A friend of Erasmus and Thomas *More, he was a vitriolic and powerful opponent of *scholasticism, of ecclesiastical abuses, and of foreign wars.

Colin Clout The pastoral name adopted by Edmund *Spenser in The *Shepheardes Calender* and *Colin Clouts Come Home Againe*. Colin Clout is also the name of a rustic in John *Gay's The *Shepherd's Week*. See also COLLYN CLOUT.

Colin Clouts Come Home Againe An allegorical pastoral written by Edmund *Spenser on his return to Kilcolman after his visit to London of 1589-91, published 1595. The poem describes in allegorical form how Ralegh visited Spenser in Ireland and induced him to come to England 'his *Cynthia* to see'—i.e. the queen. The poet tells of the splendour of the queen and her court. Then follows a bitter attack on the court's envies and intrigues. The poem ends with a definition of true love and a tribute to Colin's proud mistress Rosalind.

COLLIER, Jane (1715-55) Satirist, a member of Samuel *Richardson's circle, offering advice on *Clarissa* and perhaps collaborating with her companion Sarah *Fielding on an experimental dialogue-novel, *The Cry* (1754). *An Essay on the Art of Ingeniously Tormenting* (1753) was a spoof conduct manual in the manner of Jonathan *Swift's *Directions to Servants*. It reappeared in six editions of 1804-11, and may have influenced Jane *Austen.

COLLIER, Jeremy (1650-1726) A clergyman who refused to swear the oath to William and Mary and was outlawed in 1696 for publicly absolving on the scaffold two of those found guilty of plotting to assassinate William III. He is chiefly remembered for his *Short View of the Immorality and Profaneness of the English Stage* (1698), in which he attacked John *Dryden, William *Wycherley, William *Congreve, Sir John *Vanbrugh, Thomas D'Urfey, and Thomas *Otway. Congreve and D'Urfey were prosecuted, Thomas *Betterton and Anne *Bracegirdle were fined, and several of the poets replied. Collier contributed towards the climate that produced the 'reformed' drama of Colley *Cibber and his successors. See RESTORATION.

COLLIER, John (1901-80) Poetry editor of *Time and Tide* during the 1920s and 1930s, but remembered as a novelist and writer of fantastic stories combining satire with the macabre and the supernatural. His best-known novel is *His Monkey Wife* (1930), describing the marriage between a repatriated explorer and his pet chimpanzee. In 1935 he moved to America and made his living as a Hollywood screenwriter. *The John Collier Reader* (1972) is an anthology of his major stories with an introduction by Anthony *Burgess.

COLLIER, John Payne (1789–1883) Antiquary; his *The History of English Dramatic Poetry to the Time of Shakespeare: And Annals of the Stage to the Restoration* (1831) contained valuable new documentary information but was contaminated with his own fabrications, the first of his insidious literary frauds. In 1840 he founded the Shakespeare Society for which he published many rare works including *The Memoirs of Edward Alleyn* (1841); as director of the Society many rare documents were made available to him on which he based his researches and forgeries. But it was his falsifications of the marginal corrections of the so-called Perkins Folio (a second *folio of Shakespeare's plays dated 1632, with a possibly forged signature of Thomas Perkins on its cover) that finally brought him discredit.

Doubt was cast on the nature and extent of Collier's frauds by D. Ganzel in a biography, *Fortune and Men's Eyes* (1982).

COLLIER, Mary (?1690–1762) Poet, taught to read by her parents. She earned a living by 'Washing, Brewing and such labour'. Her poem *The Woman's Labour: An Epistle to Mr. Stephen Duck* (1739) robustly defended the industry of rural women like herself against *Duck's aspersions in *The Thresher's Labour* (1730). Collier's *Poems on Several Occasions* (1762) was prefaced by 'Remarks of the Author's life, drawn by herself'.

COLLINS, Merle (1950–) Writer, born in the Caribbean. She left Grenada after the American invasion, completing her doctorate in London. She has published three collections of poetry, two novels, and a book of short stories. Her expression of resistance to any kind of colonialism is wittily idiomatic.

COLLINS, Wilkie (1824–89) Novelist, born in London. Though he never practised as a lawyer, his fascination with legal processes is evident throughout his fiction. His biography of his father (1848), was followed by the historical novel, *Antonina* (1850), and *Basil* (1852), which was admired by Charles *Dickens. The two writers became personal friends and occasional collaborators, and Collins's third novel, *Hide and Seek* (1854), is his most Dickensian work. In his four novels of the 1860s, *The *Woman in White*, *No Name* (1862), *Armadale*

(1866), and *The *Moonstone* (1868), Collins became a popular writer of intricately plotted stories of mystery, suspense, and crime, though his work continued to attract condemnation for sensationalism (*see* SENSATION, NOVEL OF). His portrayal of attractive but transgressive women such as Magdalen Vanstone in *No Name* and Lydia Gwilt in *Armadale*, was particularly attacked. Collins suffered from severe attacks of a rheumatic illness which caused him great pain, only relieved by the use of opium; he made use of the effects of opium in the plot of *The Moonstone*, following a particularly severe attack. It used to be considered that Collins's opium habit, and the loss of Dickens's constructive criticism after 1870, led to a decline in the quality of his writing. However his explorations of the darker side of Victorian society and his interest in abnormal physiology and psychology are now seen as innovative. His later 'novels with a purpose' include *Man and Wife* (1870), *The Law and the Lady* (1875), and his antivivisection novel *Heart and Science* (1883). Of the theatrical adaptations of his novels, *Man and Wife* and *The New Magdalen*, both produced in 1873, were the most successful. The only play for which he is now remembered is *The Frozen Deep* (1857). Collins's private life was as much a cause of scandal as his fiction. He never married, but from 1859 lived openly with Caroline Graves, a widow from a working-class background. In 1868 he began another liaison with Martha Rudd, the daughter of a farm labourer, who bore him two daughters and a son. Caroline Graves left Collins in 1868, but returned to him two years later, and remained with him for the rest of his life, though his relationship with Martha Rudd (known as Mrs Dawson) also continued until his death.

COLLINS, William (1721–59) Poet. Collins published his *Persian Eclogues* (1742) while an undergraduate at Oxford. His *Odes on Several Descriptive and Allegoric Subjects* (1746, dated 1747) includes his 'ode to Evening' and odes to Pity, Fear, and Simplicity (*see* ODE). His ode on the death of James Thomson appeared in 1749, and in 1750 he presented a draft of his *Ode on the Popular Superstitions of the Highlands* (published 1788) to John Home. Thereafter he suffered increasingly from depression, and wrote nothing. His poems were collected by John Langhorne in 1765.

COLLODI, Carlo (1826–90) Pen-name of Carlo Lorenzini, journalist, political activist, and author. He is best known for *Le avventure di Pinocchio* (1883: *The Adventures of*

Pinocchio). The first English translation appeared in 1892. The film by Walt *Disney (1940) sentimentalizes the original story.

Collyn Clout A poem by John *Skelton, satirizing ecclesiastical abuses (*c*.1521–2). See COLIN CLOUT.

COLMAN, George the elder (1732–94), Playwright and theatre manager. David *Garrick produced his comic afterpiece *Polly Honeycombe* in 1760 and his comedy *The Jealous Wife* in 1761. Colman and Garrick produced a theatrical newspaper, *The St. James's Chronicle*, as well as collaborating on *The *Clandestine Marriage* (1766). Colman managed Covent Garden Theatre, 1767–74, and the Haymarket, 1777–89. He produced adaptations of *Shakespeare and *Jonson, translated the comedies of *Terence into blank verse (1765), and edited Francis *Beaumont and John *Fletcher (1778).

COLMAN, George the younger (1762–1836), Son of George Colman the elder (1732–94). He made his name with the musical romantic comedy *Inkle and Yarico* in 1787, which was followed by other sentimental and humorous operettas. Among many other dramatic works, *The Iron Chest* of 1796 is a dramatization of *Caleb Williams* by William *Godwin. Colman's comedy of contemporary life, *The Heir-at-Law* (1797), became famous for the character of Dr Pangloss, a greedy, pompous pedant. *John Bull* (1803) contains a sketch of the supposed British character in Job Thornberry.

Colonel Jack, The History and Remarkable Life of Colonel Jacque, Commonly Call'd A novel by Daniel *Defoe (1722). The narrator, in some ways a masculine version of *Moll Flanders*, relates how he was abandoned by his parents and became (like Moll) a pickpocket. To abandon this risky profession, he enlists, but deserts to avoid serving in Flanders. He is kidnapped, sent (again like Moll) to Virginia, and sold to a planter. Promoted to the role of overseer, his 'humane' management of the slaves results in increased production and he is freed, to acquire much wealth as a planter in his own right. On his return to Britain he has a series of unfortunate matrimonial adventures, which culminate in penitent prosperity.

COLUM, Padraic (1881–1972) Irish poet, dramatist, and novelist, whose work brought a realistic corrective to the *Irish Revival's portrayal of rural life. He won the praise of Ezra *Pound and the friendship of James *Joyce. His first collection was *Wild Earth* (1907; expanded 1916); he emigrated to the USA in 1914. Colum was the author of 'She Moved through the Fair', perhaps the most famous Irish song of his time. With his wife Mary he wrote a memoir, *Our Friend James Joyce* (1958). His *Collected Poems* appeared in 1953.

COLUMBA, St (Columcille) (*c*.521–597) Born in north-west Ireland and the founder of the monasteries of Iona and Durrow. He went to Scotland in 563 and settled in Iona, from which the conversion of Scotland and Northumbria by the Celtic church proceeded. The book of his life and miracles was written by Adomnan of Iona.

COMBE, William (1741–1823) Author. He published a number of metrical satires, including *The Diaboliad* (1776) and many other works in prose and verse, including *The Devil upon Two Sticks in England* (1790) and *The Microcosm of London* (1808). He is particularly remembered for the verses that he wrote to accompany Thomas *Rowlandson's coloured plates and drawings of the adventures of 'Dr Syntax'. *The Tour of Dr Syntax in Search of the Picturesque*, a parody of the popular books of picturesque travels of the day, and particularly of the works of William *Gilpin, appeared in Rudolph Ackermann's *Poetical Magazine* in 1809, and in 1812 as a book which went into many editions. Dr Syntax is the grotesque figure of a clergyman and schoolmaster, who sets out during the holidays, on his old horse Grizzle, to 'make a tour and write it', and meets with a series of absurd misfortunes. The second and third tours followed (1820, 1821) and the three Tours were collected in 1826.

comedy is a capaciously varied dramatic genre with several recognized sub-genres, divided by George *Meredith and others between the 'low' forms reliant upon physical clowning (*farce, *pantomime, *burlesque) and the 'high comedy' of elegant wit and dramatic *irony (as in the 'comedy of manners' set in fashionable society, or the 'romantic comedy' involving the tribulations of young lovers). The broadest sense of the term extends beyond theatre to the comic effects produced by some kinds of narrative verse and of prose fiction, from the *fabliaux of *Chaucer to the novels and tales of P. G. *Wodehouse. In its principal dramatic sense, comedy is loosely defined as that kind of play in which, by contrast with *tragedy or *melodrama, the audience enjoys a relaxed superiority over the characters, and expects a happy and often festive conclusion to the action. The main line of English comedy derives from the Graeco-Roman 'New Comedy' of *Menander, *Plautus, and *Terence, which represents stock fictitious characters (misers, braggarts, young lovers) in amusing and happily concluded adventures. The *mystery plays and *interludes of the later Middle Ages include some farcical episodes, but are not held to be comedies. The first fully developed comedies in English date from the mid-16th century: *Ralph Roister Doister and *Gammer Gurton's Needle in verse, and *Supposes in prose. In the late 16th and early 17th centuries the leading English exponents were *Shakespeare, in such romantic comedies as A *Midsummer Night's Dream, *As You Like It, *Much Ado About Nothing, and *Twelfth Night, and Ben *Jonson in such plays as *Volpone and The *Alchemist, which employ *satire in his so-called 'comedy of humours'. After the reopening of the theatres in 1660, the wittily irreverent comedy of manners flourished in a phase now known as Restoration comedy, in the plays of William *Congreve, William *Wycherley, Sir George *Etherege, Sir John *Vanbrugh, Aphra *Behn, and George *Farquhar. The 18th century witnessed the rise of the more respectably subdued form known as 'sentimental' comedy, along with popular burlesques and pantomimes; Richard Brinsley *Sheridan's The *School for Scandal and Oliver Goldsmith's *She Stoops to Conquer are the classic comedies of that age. The 19th century is not noted for outstanding comedies until the advent of Oscar Wilde with The *Importance of Being Earnest and other plays. In the 20th century the major innovators were George Bernard *Shaw, with a new kind of intellectual comedy, and Noël *Coward in his elegantly structured comedies of manners; other notable examples are the suburban comedies of Alan *Ayckbourn, the black comedies of Joe *Orton, and the work of Samuel *Beckett and others associated with the Theatre of the *Absurd.

See also TRAGICOMEDY.

Comedy, The Divine See DIVINA COMMEDIA.

Comedy of Errors, The A comedy by *Shakespeare, acted at Gray's Inn 1594, first printed in the first *folio (1623), based mainly on *Plautus' Menaechmi.

Syracuse and Ephesus are enemies, and any Syracusan found in Ephesus is executed unless he can pay a ransom of 1,000 marks. Egeon, an old Syracusan merchant, has been arrested in Ephesus. He explains that he had identical twin sons, each named Antipholus, attended by two slaves called Dromio, also identical. Having in a shipwreck been separated, with the younger son and one Dromio, from his wife and the other son and slave, Egeon had never seen them since. The younger son (Antipholus of Syracuse) on reaching manhood went (with his Dromio) in search of his brother and mother and disappeared. After searching for five years, Egeon has now arrived in Ephesus.

The duke, moved by this tale, gives Egeon till evening to find his ransom. Now, the elder Antipholus (Antipholus of Ephesus), with his Dromio, has been living in Ephesus since the shipwreck and is married. Antipholus of Syracuse and the other Dromio have arrived there that very morning. Each twin is still identical with his brother, which gives rise to the comedy of errors. Antipholus of Syracuse is summoned home to dinner by Dromio of Ephesus; he is claimed as husband by Adriana, wife of Antipholus of Ephesus, who is kept out of his own house because he is supposed to be already inside. Antipholus of Syracuse falls in love with Luciana, his brother's wife's sister. Antipholus of Ephesus is confined as a lunatic, and Antipholus of Syracuse hides from his brother's jealous wife in a convent.

Evening comes and Egeon is led to execution. As the duke proceeds to the place of execution, Antipholus of Ephesus appeals to him for redress. Then the abbess of the convent presents Antipholus of Syracuse, also claiming redress. The simultaneous presence of the two brothers explains the misunderstandings. Egeon recovers his two sons and his liberty, and the abbess turns out to be his lost wife Emilia.

Comical Revenge, The, or Love in a Tub A comedy by Sir George *Etherege, acted 1664. The main plot, in heroic couplets, deals with the rivalry of Lord Beaufort and Colonel Bruce for the hand of Graciana. In the comic sub-plot, in prose, the libertine Sir Frederick Frolick's French valet Dufoy is confined in a tub, by his fellow servants, under the influence of opium. It was a great hit and often revived, though Samuel *Pepys, who saw it in 1666, thought it 'silly'.

comics, comic strips These flourished from the end of the 19th century with Ally Sloper's Half-Holiday (1884–1923) widely acknowledged as the publication that established the form, although comic strips had appeared earlier in papers such as The Graphic (1869–1932); Edwin John Brett's The Boys of England (1866–99); and Funny Folks (1874–94). Ally Sloper was a sharp, gin-drinking, working-class anti-hero, the first regular character in the comic world. The form flourished in such publications as *Comic Cuts* (1890–1953), *Chips* (1890–1953), *The Gem* (1907–39), and *The Magnet* (1908–40; *see* HAMILTON, CHARLES). They also featured in boys' adventure comics such as *Adventure* (1921–61), *Wizard* (1922–63), and *Hotspur* (1933–59), finding new life in the *Beano* (1938–) and *Dandy* (1937–), both still flourishing with many of their original characters. *Rainbow* (1914–56) was the first coloured comic designed exclusively for children. There was a sustained battle between the subversively entertaining and the morally improving: *Rupert Bear, in the *Daily Express*, was on the side of the angels, as was Dan Dare in the *Eagle*. The founding of *Eagle* in 1950 by Lancashire vicar Marcus Morris was directly prompted by the growing infiltration of American horror comics; the original series ended in 1969, but Dan Dare survives in *2000 AD*. The publishers' self-regulating Comic Book Code was introduced in 1954; recently its guidelines have regularly been transgressed. Some *picturebook makers, notably Raymond *Briggs, have drawn on the visual grammar of comic books. *See also* GRAPHIC NOVELS; MANGA.

Coming Race, The A novel by Edward *Bulwer-Lytton, published 1871. The narrator describes his visit to a subterranean race of superior beings that long ago took refuge, possibly from the biblical flood, in the depths of the earth. There they have evolved a highly sophisticated civilization, with the aid of a form of energy called Vril, which has great powers of destruction as well as great utility. Much of the novel is devoted to a satiric account of the narrator's own democratic society, of which he is initially proud, and to praise of the underground society, which has no war, no crime, and no inequality, and where women are stronger than men and free to choose their own mates. The sublime subterranean landscapes recall the paintings of John Martin, whose work Bulwer-Lytton much admired. A memory of this early and influential example of *science fiction lingers in the food brand 'Bovril', derived from 'Vril'.

commedia dell'arte A popular, unscripted form of comedy, which developed in Italy in the sixteenth century and flourished there until the 18th century; the name distinguishes it from literary, scripted *commedia erudita*. Some if not all the actors wore masks, and the names of certain characters became stereotypes, in particular the servants Harlequin, Pulcinella, and Colombine, and the ridiculous old man Pantaloon. In Italy *commedia dell'arte* was superseded by the theatrical reforms of Carlo Goldoni, but its influence continued in England in pantomime and puppet shows.

Common Prayer, The Book of The official service book of the *Church of England since the *Reformation, prescribing the structure of the Christian year, services for morning and evening prayer and for communion, matrimony, baptism, etc., and the texts of the *Bible to be read and *psalms to be sung throughout the year. It has had a huge impact on writers in English. The text evolved in stages. The first and second books of Edward VI (1549 and 1552) were largely compiled by Thomas *Cranmer, partly from earlier Latin service books. The wording of Cranmer's collects (short prayers spoken by the minister) and general prayers have entered the language, for example 'the devices and desires of our own hearts', 'whose service is perfect freedom', 'lighten our darkness'. The Prayer Book was revised under Elizabeth I (1559), reissued with minor changes under James I (1604), and a revised version was forced on the Scots in 1637 and then withdrawn. It was detested by the *Puritans, and in 1645 during the Civil War it was abolished. Under Charles II it was restored with further revisions (1662), and this has remained the official Prayer Book. A revised book agreed by the church was rejected by Parliament in 1928. Alternative forms in modernized language were then agreed: the Alternative Service Book (1980) has been replaced by the collection called Common Worship (2000), but without the official status of the 1662 Prayer Book. Supporters find modernized versions easy to understand; detractors regret the downgrading of the Prayer Book's literary qualities.

Commonwealth of Oceana, The (1656) A republican utopia by James *Harrington. Dedicated to Oliver Cromwell, it recommends a two-chamber system, elections ('through the suffrage of the people given by the ballot') that would replace one-third of the executive annually, and a redistribution of landed property by an agrarian law limiting land holdings. Other proposals include an elected *poet laureate and a National Theatre. 'Oceana' is England and the Archon, 'Olphaus Megalator', is Cromwell. Harrington expresses admiration for the republics of Greece and Rome, the Venetian republic, and *Machiavelli, 'the only politician of later ages'. He meant *Oceana* to be a reply to Thomas *Hobbes's *Leviathan*. David

*Hume described it as 'the only valuable model of a commonwealth that has yet been offered to the public'.

complaint A poetic form derived from the Latin *planctus*, bewailing the vicissitudes of life (as in Thomas *Hoccleve's *Complaint*) or addressed to a more particular end (such as *Chaucer's 'Complaint to his Purse'). The form is particularly common in poems up to the Renaissance; thereafter the terms *'elegy' and 'lament' were used.

Complaint of Buckingham, The A poem by Thomas *Sackville, contributed by him to the 1563 edition of A *Mirror for Magistrates*.

Compleat Angler, The, or The Contemplative Man's Recreation A discourse on fishing by Izaak *Walton, first published 1653, second, enlarged edition 1655, fifth edition with a continuation by Charles *Cotton, 1676. Piscator (a fisherman), Auceps (a fowler), and Venator (a hunter) debate during a fishing expedition along the river Lea. There are instructions for catching and cooking fish, also interludes of verse, angling anecdotes, moral reflections, and snatches of mythology and folklore. Walton's idyllic, deeply nostalgic celebration of his 'calm, quiet, innocent recreation' has become a classic, attracting readers not usually interested in fish or books, and is one of the most frequently reprinted texts in English literature.

COMPTON-BURNETT, Dame Ivy (1884–1969) Novelist. *Pastors and Masters* (1925), and other early works, such as *More Women Than Men* (1933), reveal an affinity with the brittle, deflationary wit and occasional satirical exuberance of Evelyn *Waugh and Anthony *Powell. But her highly condensed and abstracted novels, composed almost entirely in dialogue, were so unlike anyone else's that their impact was often compared to that of *Post-Impressionism in painting. They are generally set in the 1880–1914 period, in large, gloomy, dilapidated country houses full of servants, children, and dependent relatives, ruled by a more or less tyrannical parent or grandparent: hence the consistently high rate of domestic crime ranging from matricide, incest, and child abuse to bigamy and fraud. Dame Ivy held that 'nothing is so corrupting as power', and her isolated, inward-looking, self-contained, and heavily monitored households provided her with an ideal environment in which to examine the misuse of power together with the violence and misery that fol-

low. *A House and Its Head* (1935), *A Family and a Fortune* (1939), and *Manservant and Maidservant* (1947) are perhaps the most outstanding of Compton-Burnett's twenty novels.

COMTE, Auguste (1798–1857) French philosopher and positivist. In his principal works, *Cours de philosophie positive* (6 vols, (1830–42: *Lectures on Positive Philosophy*) and *Système de politique positive* (4 vols, (1851–4: *System of Positive Politics*) Comte argues that human knowledge passes through three successive phases: the theological, the metaphysical, and the positive. This was the 'Law of the Three States' and it applied to the historical progress of the mind and to the development of the individual mind alike. The positive or scientific state was the 'normal' or final state of humanity.

Comte intended to bring the science of social phenomena, sociology, into its final, positive, state and so lay the foundations of a social and political system proper to the age of industry, with a religion of Humanity. The influence of women on the feelings was to be foregrounded, in order to foster altruism, the basis of Comtean morality, expressed in the motto: 'Live for Others'.

Comte's principal English followers were Frederic Harrison, E. S. Beesly, J. H. Bridges, and Richard Congreve. The *Cours de philosophie positive* was condensed, with the author's approval, in English translation by Harriet *Martineau (2 vols, 1853); the *Système de politique positive* was translated by Harrison, Bridges, and others as *The System of Positive Polity* (4 vols, 1875–7). G. H. *Lewes provided an exposition of the leading ideas of the *Cours* in *Comte's Philosophy of the Sciences* (1853), and the fiction of his partner George *Eliot reflects Comte's influence. John Stuart *Mill gave a critical account of Comte's thought in *Auguste Comte and Positivism* (1865). *See also* POSITIVISM

Comus, *A Maske Presented at Ludlow Castle, 1634: on Michaelmasse Night, before the Right Honorable John Earl of Bridgewater, Lord President of Wales* By John *Milton, first printed, anonymously and untitled, 1637. Written at the suggestion of Milton's friend, the composer Henry *Lawes, to celebrate the earl of Bridgewater's elevation to the presidency of Wales and the Marches, it portrays the abduction and enchantment of Bridgewater's 15-year-old daughter Lady Alice by the evil sorcerer Comus, son of Bacchus and Circe, the failure of her brothers (aged 9 and 11) to rescue her, and her eventual release by Sabrina, goddess of the river Severn.

An Attendant Spirit, disguised as a shepherd, is sent from on high to protect the young aristocrats, and ensures that they are returned to Ludlow and presented to their parents at the end.

CONAN DOYLE See DOYLE, ARTHUR.

conceit An elaborate metaphor comparing two apparently dissimilar objects or emotions, often with an effect of shock or surprise. The *Petrarchan conceit, much imitated by Elizabethan sonneteers and both used and parodied by Shakespeare, usually evoked the qualities of the disdainful mistress and the devoted lover, often in highly exaggerated terms; the *metaphysical conceit, as used by John *Donne and his followers, applied wit and ingenuity to, in the words of Samuel *Johnson, 'a combination of dissimilar images, or discovery of occult resemblances in things apparently unlike', e.g. Donne's famous comparison of two lovers to a pair of compasses.

Conchubar (Conchobar) [pron. Conachoor] In the Ulster cycle of Irish mythology, king of Ulster. See also CUCHULAIN; DEIRDRE.

concrete poetry A term used to describe a kind of experimental poetry developed in the 1950s and flourishing in the 1960s, which dwells primarily on the visual aspects of the poem (although two other forms of Concrete poetry, the kinetic and the phonetic, have also been distinguished). Concrete poets experiment with typography, graphics, the 'ideogram concept', computer poems, collage, etc., and acknowledge influence from Dada, Hans Arp (1886–1966), Kurt Schwitters (1887–1948), Kazimir Malevich (1878–1935), and other visual artists. Ian Hamilton *Finlay expressed his own affinity with 17th-century *emblems and poems such as George *Herbert's 'Easter Wings', which use the shape as well as the sense of a poem to convey meaning. Edwin *Morgan has written a variety of concrete poems, which were criticized by some devotees of the form as being 'too verbal'. Mary Ellen Solt in 'A World Look at Concrete Poetry' (*Hispanic Arts*, 1/3–4, 1968) declares that 'the concrete poet seeks to relieve the poem of its centuries-old burden of ideas, symbolic reference, allusion and repetitious emotional content'. Others claim a less radical role, pointing to Herbert, William *Blake, Lewis Carroll (C. L. *Dodgson), Ezra *Pound's use of Chinese characters, and E. E. *Cummings as evidence of a long tradition of typographical experiment.

CONDELL, Henry See HEMINGES, JOHN.

condition of England A phrase coined by Thomas *Carlyle in the opening words of *Past and Present* (1843) to describe the social and political inequalities in what Benjamin *Disraeli, in *Sybil* (1845), was to term the 'Two Nations of England, the Rich and the Poor'. See also CHARTIST MOVEMENT; SOCIAL PROBLEM NOVEL.

CONDON, Richard (1915–96) American novelist, whose second novel, *The Manchurian Candidate* (1959 filmed 1962, 2004) remains his best-known work for its combination of brainwashing with a satire on Senator McCarthy. *Winter Kills* (1984) investigates the assassination of President Kennedy.

coney-catching See ROGUE LITERATURE.

Confessio Amantis See GOWER, JOHN.

confessional poetry A term principally applied to the self-revealing style of writing and use of intimate subject matter adopted and pioneered in America by Robert *Lowell (*Life Studies*, 1959): other writers in the tradition have included John *Berryman, Anne *Sexton, and Sylvia *Plath. A new wave of confessional writing in prose occurred in the 1980s and 1990s when a vogue for *autobiographical material, family history, and frank memoirs coincided in Britain with a new sense of male interest in domestic and psychological matters: this resulted in 'New Man' writing by Blake *Morrison, Nick *Hornby, and others. Lads' literature is a related and reactive variant of the phenomenon.

Confessions of a Justified Sinner See PRIVATE MEMOIRS AND CONFESSIONS OF A JUSTIFIED SINNER.

Confessions of an English Opium Eater By Thomas *De Quincey, published 1822 (enlarged version 1856). A study of De Quincey's opium addiction and its psychological effects tracing how childhood and youthful experiences are transformed, under the influence of opium, into symbolical and revealing dreams. The central experience for subsequent dream-formations was his childhood loss of his sister, duplicated by the disappearance of the 15-year-old prostitute Ann, who befriended him during his months of homeless near-starvation in London. The euphoric reveries of the early stages of his addiction and the appalling nightmares of the later stages are described in sonorous and haunting prose.

Confidence-Man, The A cryptic novel by Herman *Melville, published in 1857, which employs the term 'confidence-man', coined after a notorious 1849 case, to denote trickery and deception.

Congregationalism Otherwise known as Independency or Separatism, the system of church government based on the autonomy of individual 'gathered churches', with the right to choose their own pastors, outside the control of the established *Church of England. Independent churches grew in the late 16th century and were increasingly harassed in the early 17th, resulting in the emigration of some members to New England, where Congregationalism became the dominant religious and cultural force. The Independents, who were deeply unsympathetic to the *Presbyterian view of church government, were the victors in the Civil War. At the *Restoration they were persecuted, along with the Presbyterians, *Baptists, and *Quakers. Following the Act of Toleration of 1689, with the legal recognition of Protestant Dissent from the Church of England, the Congregationalists came to have an increasing impact on wider religious and literary culture. In the 18th century Congregationalism was heavily influenced by Calvinistic *Methodism, and increasingly at odds with rational Dissent and *Unitarianism. The most influential Congregationalist writer is undoubtedly Isaac *Watts.

See CHURCH OF ENGLAND; PROTESTANTISM; PURITANISM.

CONGREVE, William (1670-1729) Dramatist, a fellow student of Jonathan *Swift in Ireland. He achieved fame with his comedy *The Old Batchelour* (1693), written with some help from John *Dryden and Thomas *Southerne; other comedies followed: *The *Double Dealer* (1694), *Love for Love* (1695), and *The *Way of the World* (1700). In these plays Congreve studied the social pressures on love and marriage, demonstrating an amused tolerance for (male) sexual libertinism, and providing some sharply intelligent and witty female roles. His one tragedy, *The *Mourning Bride*, was produced in 1697. In 1698 he replied to the attack made on him in the *Short View* of Jeremy *Collier. After 1700 he wrote little for the stage, apart from an opera, *Semele*; he enjoyed the friendship of Swift, Richard *Steele, and Alexander *Pope, who dedicated his translation of the *Iliad* to him. He collected his own *Works* in 1710; his final poem, *Letter to Cobham* (1728), contained a meditative account of himself in retirement. *Voltaire visit-

ed him late in life. The actress Anne *Bracegirdle was a close female associate.

Coningsby A novel by Benjamin *Disraeli, published 1844. In the preface to the Hughenden edition of his novels in 1870 Disraeli declares that his ambition in the trilogy *Coningsby*-*Sybil*-*Tancred* was to describe the influence of the main political parties on the people, and to indicate how their condition might be improved; he chose the novel as the most effective means of influence on public opinion. *Coningsby* celebrates the new Tories of the 'Young England' set, and reflects their concern at the treatment of the poor and the injustice of the franchise.

The high-spirited Coningsby is orphaned, and sent to Eton College by his wealthy grandfather Lord Monmouth, who represents the old type of oppressive Tory aristocrat. There Coningsby saves the life of his friend Oswald Millbank, the son of a Lancashire manufacturer, detested by Monmouth. Coningsby develops political and social ideals far removed from those of his grandfather, and falls in love with Oswald's sister Edith. His behaviour so angers Monmouth that when the old man dies Coningsby finds he has been disinherited, and has to work in the Inns of Court. Gradually Millbank, who had been opposed to Coningsby's marriage to his daughter, realizes the young man's worth; he helps him to stand for Parliament and sees him returned. Edith and Coningsby are married and Coningsby's fortunes are restored.

CONQUEST, Robert (1917-) Poet, critic, and historian. He edited the important anthology *New Lines* (1956), widely seen as proselytizing on behalf of the new *Movement school of poets, which included Philip *Larkin, who was an admirer of Conquest's own poetry. Conquest's publications include *Poems* (1955), *Between Mars and Venus* (1962), and *Arias from a Love Opera* (1969); *New and Collected Poems* appeared in 1988. *Penultimata* in 2009.

Conquest of Granada by the Spaniards, The In two parts (Pt I produced in December 1670, Pt II in January 1671; both published 1672). A ten-act heroic extravaganza by John *Dryden, written in resounding rhyming couplets. The play was a huge box-office hit. As such it became the main target of the duke of *Buckingham's and others' burlesque in *The Rehearsal*, in which its high-blown verse and its larger-than-life hero were savagely satirized.

Conrad, Joseph (Józef Teodor Konrad Korzeniowski) (1857–1924) Novelist and short story writer, born of Polish parents in the Russian-dominated Ukraine. From an early age he longed to go to sea and in 1874 he went to Marseilles, embarked on a French vessel, and began his career as a sailor. In 1886 he became a British subject and a master mariner. In 1894, after twenty years at sea, he settled in England; a bequest from his uncle enabled him to devote himself to fiction, writing in English. His first novels, *Almayer's Folly* (1895) and *An Outcast of the Islands* (1896) are both set in the Malay archipelago; they were followed by *The Nigger of the 'Narcissus'* (1897) and **Lord Jim* (1900). The sea continued to supply the setting for most of his novels and short stories. His narrative technique is characterized by breaks in time-sequence and, in several works, a frame narrator, Marlow. His richly textured narrative prose sometimes bears traces of French idioms and Polish constructions.

He collaborated with Ford Madox *Ford on *The Inheritors* (1900) and *Romance* (1903), but disagreements brought their association to an end. *Typhoon* (1903) was followed by **Nostromo* (1904), an imaginative novel which explores one of Conrad's chief preoccupations—man's vulnerability and corruptibility. In the novella **'Heart of Darkness'* (1899 in *Blackwood's Magazine*; 1902 in *Youth*), Conrad had carried this issue to a terrifying conclusion. *The *Secret Agent* (1907) and *Under Western Eyes* (1911) are novels with political themes, the latter set in Switzerland and Russia and centred on the tragedy of a student caught up in the treachery and violence of revolution. Although warmly supported by Eve *Garnett, Conrad's work was generally ill received by critics and public, and he was plagued with money problems. It was only with *Chance* (1913) that Conrad achieved popular and financial success; the story combines the attractions of a sea background with the theme of romantic love and more female interest than is usual with Conrad. His other major works include *Youth* (1902), *The Mirror of the Sea* (1906), *Victory* (1915), *The Shadow-Line* (1917), *The Rescue* (1920), and *The Rover* (1923). Conrad's autobiography, *A Personal Record*, appeared in book form in 1912 and his unfinished novel *Suspense* was published in 1925.

By the time of his death, Conrad was well established as one of the leading *modernists; a decline of interest in the 1930s was followed by increasing scholarly and critical attention, pioneered in part by a study in 1941 by M. C. Bradbrook, and by an essay in the same year by F. R. *Leavis in **Scrutiny*.

Conscious Lovers, The Richard *Steele's last comedy, based on the *Andria* of *Terence, performed 1722. The play was a success and influenced the development of sentimental comedy in England.

CONSTABLE, Archibald (1774–1827) A Scottish publisher, who published most of Scott's early work. He established the highly successful **Edinburgh Review* in 1802, and bought the *Encyclopaedia Britannica* in 1812. Yet in 1826 he went bankrupt, heavily involving Scott in his debts. He was an enthusiast for the new concept of cheap books, and in 1827 established Constable's Miscellany, a series of volumes on literature, art, and science.

CONSTABLE, Henry (1562–1613) Poet and theological writer. He published *Diana*, a volume of sonnets, in 1592; it was republished in 1594 with additions by other poets. Some of his poems appeared in **Englands Helicon*.

CONSTANTINE, David (1944–) Poet and translator. *A Brightness to Cast Shadows* (1980) and *Watching for Dolphins* (1983) introduced a poet of rare lyric intensity. Learned but direct, Constantine offers a world lit by the supernatural, drawing on classical and Romantic traditions. The epic *Caspar Hauser* appeared in 1994, followed by *The Pelt of Wasps* (1998), *Something for the Ghosts* (2002), a *Collected Poems* (2004), and *Nine Fathom Deep* (2009). Constantine has also published short story collections and a novel. His translations include the *Selected Poems* of Friedrich Hölderlin (1996) and *Goethe's *Faust* (part I, 2004).

contact zone A term used by the North American literary theorist Mary Louise Pratt (1948–) to refer to spaces 'where cultures meet, clash and grapple with each other, often in contexts of highly asymmetrical relations of power'. The expression is intended to emphasize the range of ways in which people, usually from a position of disadvantage, imaginatively contest others' versions of themselves. The term is widely used by scholars interested in linguistic, religious, economic, sexual, and other exchanges in colonial and *postcolonial contexts.

COOK, David (1940–) Novelist, actor, and television playwright. *Albert's Memorial* (1972, novel), about the tragicomic friendship between widowed Mary and homosexual Paul, was followed by *Happy Endings* (1974) about the relationship between a 12-year-old boy and a schoolteacher. *Walter* (1978) is the story of a young man with severe learning difficulties trying to cope with the challenges of work, institutional life, and his mother's death: in the sequel *Winter Doves* (1979) Walter escapes to freedom with his friend June. Other works include *Sunrising* (1984), set in poverty-stricken rural England in the 1830s; *Missing Persons* (1986), on which the BBC series *Hetty Wainthrop Investigates* is based, and *Second Best* (1991), about a single man's attempt to adopt a 10-year-old boy. Cook's work displays a deep and humane sympathy with the disadvantaged. A TV adaptation of *Walter* with Ian McKellen in the title role was chosen to launch Channel 4 in 1982.

COOK, Eliza (1818–89) Poet, largely self-educated. Her first volume, *Lays of a Wild Harp* (1835), appeared when she was 17. Her most popular poem 'The Old Armchair' first appeared in 1837 in the *Weekly Dispatch*. Her poems were characterized by an unaffected domestic sentiment and sympathy with the poor and marginalized which appealed to a wide popular audience. She conducted *Eliza Cook's Journal* (1849–54), which supported programmes for social reform for women and the working classes. Her complete poetical works were published in 1870.

COOK, James (1728–79) Circumnavigator. The Admiralty entrusted him with three great voyages into the Pacific. The first (1768–71), on the *Endeavour*, was a high point of *Enlightenment science. John *Hawkesworth turned the journals of Cook and Joseph Banks, the botanist, into a narrative in 1773, achieving immense commercial success. Cook's own unpretentious journal was published in 1893.

His second voyage on the *Resolution* (1772–5) criss-crossed the South Pacific as far south as the Antarctic ice. In his final voyage (1776–80) he set out to find a North-West Passage, mapping the coast from Nootka Sound to the Bering Strait. Returning to Hawaii, he was killed by locals in February 1779. His later journals were published in 1777 and 1784. The published journals and tales that circulated informally promoted the ideas of the noble savage and a South Sea paradise. They provided source material for philosophy, for the new discipline of anthropology, and for literature, including S. T. *Coleridge's 'Ancient Mariner'.

COOKSON, Catherine (1906–98) Novelist, born in Jarrow. She was the illegitimate daughter of a domestic servant and tells the story of her own childhood in her memoir *Our Kate* (1969). Her outstandingly popular novels, often set in her native Tyneside, are romantic but also realistic, featuring strong and resourceful heroines: one of her most popular characters was 'Mary Ann', who featured in a long series.

'Cook's Tale, The' See CANTERBURY TALES, 4.

Coole Park Co. Galway, home of Lady *Gregory, famous as the headquarters of the *Irish Revival. Summer home of W. B. *Yeats for nearly twenty years, it was the subject of many of his poems, notably 'In the Seven Woods', 'Coole Park, 1929', and 'Coole Park and Ballylee, 1931'. Guests who carved their names on its famous autograph tree (a copper beech) included G. B. *Shaw, J. M. *Synge, W. B. Yeats, Jack B. Yeats, Augustus *John, G. W. *Russell (Æ), and Douglas *Hyde. The house, described by Lady Gregory in *Coole* (1931; enl. 1971), was pulled down in 1941.

COOLIDGE, Susan (1835–1905) Pen-name of Sarah Chauncy Woolsey, American children's writer of *family stories. Remembered for *What Katy Did* (1872) and its four sequels (1873; 1886; 1888; 1890) about Katy Carr, her family and friends. In the best-known first volume, impulsive, storytelling, tomboy Katy injures her back falling from a swing and is confined to bed where she attends 'the School of Pain' under the guidance of her invalid Cousin Helen, emerging as a feminine, domesticated young woman.

COOPER, James Fenimore (1789–1851) American novelist. His second book *The Spy* (1821), a stirring tale of the American Revolution, brought him into prominence. *The Pioneers* (1823) was the first of his best-known group of novels, *Leather-Stocking Tales*, called after the deerskin leggings of their hero, pioneer scout Natty Bumppo, who acted as intermediary between the Indian and European characters. The series continued with *The Last of the Mohicans* (1826), *The Prairie* (1827), *The Pathfinder* (1840), and *The Deerslayer* (1841). They give a vivid picture of American Indian and pioneer life, earning Cooper the description the 'American Walter *Scott'. From 1826 to 1833 Cooper travelled in Europe, and then published several highly critical accounts of European society, including *England, with Sketches of Society in the Metropolis* (1837); this was violently attacked in Britain, notably by John *Lockhart. Cooper was, however, also deeply critical of American democracy, and expressed his conservative opinions directly in *The American Democrat* (1838) and fictionally in *Homeward Bound and Home as Found* (both 1838). Mark *Twain humorously attacked his lack of verbal precision in 'Fenimore Cooper's Literary Offences' (1895).

COOPER, Mary (d. 1761) London-based printer 1742–61, who published three landmark books for children: *The Child's New Play-Thing* (1742), and two collections of nursery rhymes: *Tommy Thumb's Pretty Song Book* (vol. i, none survive, date unknown; vol. ii, c.1744) containing many still-famous verses.

COOPER, Susan (1935–) Children's writer and playwright. She moved to the USA from the UK in 1963. Her fantasy quintet, 'The Dark is Rising', beginning with *Over Sea, Under Stone* (1965), is based on *Arthurian and Celtic legends and the search by the 'Old Ones' for the *Grail and other symbols of 'the light'. *The Grey King* won the Newbery Medal (1975). Cooper has won awards for TV scripts; *Dreams and Wishes* (1996) is a key collection of essays.

COOPER, William (1910–2002) Pseudonym of Harry Summerfield Hoff, novelist. The Civil Service features in much of his work, as it does in that of his colleague C. P. *Snow. His most influential novel, *Scenes from Provincial Life* (1950), was hailed as seminal by writers of the 1950s, who also chose provincial, anarchic but ambitious, lower-middle-class heroes, and a low-key realist tone. It was followed by *Scenes from Married Life* (1961) and *Scenes from Metropolitan Life* (1982), originally written as the middle volume of the trilogy. *Scenes from Later Life* (1983), *Scenes from Early Life* (1990), and *Scenes from Death and Life* (1999) are sequels.

Cooper's Hill See DENHAM, SIR JOHN.

COOVER, Robert (1932–) American novelist. Like John *Barth, he has tended to avoid realism in favour of more experimental narrative forms. His first novel, *The Origin of the Brunists* (1966), describes how the survivor of a mining accident forms a religious cult; *The Public Burning* (1977) presents the execution of the Rosenbergs as a ludicrous national spectacle with walk-on parts by Richard Nixon and others. Coover was a co-founder of the Electronic Literature Association in 1999, a concern signalled by his 1992 essay 'The End of Books'. *Noir* (2010), a *'hard-boiled' detective story written in the second person, follows other titles drawn from Coover's interest in *cinema, including *A Night at the Movies* (1987), a collection of short stories. Coover's screenplay *After Lazarus* was published in 1980.

COPE, Wendy (1945–) OBE. Poet; she taught in London primary schools before becoming television columnist for the *Spectator* (1986–90). A gifted parodist, her first collection of poetry, *Making Cocoa for Kingsley Amis* (1986), was an instant popular success and established her as a skilfully subversive humorist, in the line of John *Betjeman. She employs traditional verse forms to satirical purpose, especially when directed at the sexual psychology of men, about which she can be both scathing and understanding, if always deflationary. Her relatively sparse output of original poetry includes *Serious Concerns* (1992) and *If I Don't Know* (2001). Her many other publications include two collections for children.

COPLAND, Robert See HIGH WAY TO THE SPITTLE HOUSE.

COPPARD, A. E. (Alfred Edgar) (1878–1957) Author of short stories and poetry. Admirers of his first collection of short stories, *Adam and Eve and Pinch Me* (1921) included Ford Madox *Ford. From his first book of verse, *Hips and Haws* (1922), he produced a book almost every year until the early 1950s. The first part of an autobiography, *It's Me, O Lord!*, was published posthumously in 1957. The deceptive simplicity of Coppard's stories conceals a widely admired technical skill; they display a deep sympathy for the oddity and misfit.

COPPE, Abiezer (1619–72) A Ranter, preacher, mystic, and pamphleteer, famed for his eccentric behaviour (he preached naked in the streets of London, denouncing the rich); his two *Fiery Flying Rolls* (1649) are charged with fervour and compassion, and are written in a highly original poetic prose. In 1650 these pamphlets were burned as blasphemous, by order of Parliament.

copyright The first definition of copyright as such in Britain was 'An Act for the encouragement of Learning, by vesting the copies of printed books in the authors or purchasers of such copies during the times therein mentioned' (1709), which stipulated that from 10 April 1710 an author of a printed book, or the publisher who had bought the rights, should have the right to publish that book for 21 years; for an unpublished book, the period was 14 years. Thereafter the right reverted to the author for a further 14 years. A few authors, such as Alexander *Pope, exploited the possibilities of this provision adroitly, but it was slow to affect authors' earnings. Publishers argued that the statute did not affect their 'perpetual' rights to property in classic authors such as *Shakespeare and *Milton, which had been bought and sold for generations. It was not until a landmark decision of 1774 that publishers lost this right. Since then the law has been continuously developed, on an international scale; the last major British revision was the Copyright, Designs and Patents Act 1988. Copyright is not infinite: broadly speaking, and with many variations, copyright in Europe and the USA lasts until 70 years after the author's death. In addition, the law provides for works to be used without permission in a range of special circumstances, including the quoting of limited extracts for purposes of criticism, review, research, or private study, or for teaching. The Copyright and Related Rights Regulations 2003 attempt to address the role of the internet and electronic transmission in copyright.

(((⊕))) SEE WEB LINKS

• Electronic Freedom Foundation—digital copyright advocates

Coral Island, The (1858) R. M. *Ballantyne's story for boys about how Ralph, Peterkin, and Jack take over a Pacific island, face hostile tribes and pirates, and eventually claim the territory for the queen. Admired by Robert Louis *Stevenson and William *Golding, it encapsulates the empire-building ethos of its period.

coranto or current of news, the name applied to periodical news-pamphlets issued between 1621 and 1641 (their publication was interrupted 1632-8) containing foreign intelligence taken from foreign papers. They were one of the earliest forms of English journalism, and were followed by newsbooks. *See* NEWSPAPERS.

CORBETT (Corbet), **Richard** (1582-1635) Poet. He became chaplain to James I and, later, bishop first of Oxford, then of Norwich. He was generous, witty, and eloquent, and his poetry—*Certain Elegant Poems* (1647) and *Poetica Stromata* (1648)—ranges from the entertaining traveller's story of 'Iter Boreale' and the ironical verses on 'The Distracted Puritan' to the charming little poem 'To his son, Vincent Corbet' on his third birthday.

CORELLI, Marie (1855-1924) Pseudonym of Mary Mackay, novelist. *A Romance of Two Worlds* (1886, novel) was followed by many more romantic melodramas, known for their inventive narrative fluency and exuberantly irrational theories on anything from morality to radioactive vibrations. She was immensely popular at the turn of the century, William *Gladstone and Oscar *Wilde being among her admirers, though scorned by critics. Her other novels include *Barabbas* (1893), *The Sorrows of Satan* (1895), *The Mighty Atom* (1896), *The Young Diana* (1918), and *The Secret Power* (1921). She was an influential figure in the development of the occult as a prevalent theme in the fiction of her day.

CORIAT, Thomas *See* CORYATE, THOMAS.

Coriolanus A play by Shakespeare first printed in the first *folio (1623). It was probably Shakespeare's last tragedy, written about 1608. Its main source is *North's version of *Plutarch's 'Life of Caius Martius Coriolanus'. The fable of the body's members rebelling against itself, told in the opening scene, was a popular Renaissance allegory of the state.

Caius Martius, a proud Roman general, fights with great courage in a war against the Volscians, and captures the town Corioli, receiving the surname Coriolanus. On his return it is proposed to make him consul, but his outspoken contempt of the Roman rabble makes him unpopular, and the tribunes of the people have no difficulty in securing his banishment. He goes to his old enemy the Volscian general Aufidius, is received with delight, and leads the Volscians against Rome to revenge himself. He reaches the walls of the city, and the Romans send old friends of Coriolanus to propose terms, but in vain. Finally his mother Volumnia, his meek wife Virgilia, her friend Valeria, and his son come to beg him to spare the city and he yields to the eloquence of his mother, suspecting that by so doing he has signed his own death warrant. He makes a treaty favourable to the Volscians, but Aufidius turns against him, accusing him of treachery, and with the help of fellow conspirators publicly kills him.

CORKERY, Daniel (1878-1964) Writer, and politician. The melancholy realism of his autobiographical novel *The Threshold of Quiet* (1917) and of the story collections *A Munster Twilight* (1916) and *The Stormy Hills* (1929) counters what he considered the misrepresentation of national life by the 'alien' Protestant elite who led the *Irish Revival.

CORMIER, Robert (1925-2000) The leading neo-realist writer for young adults in the USA. In *The Chocolate War* (1975) he subverted the *school story by having his brave protagonist be defeated and humiliated by corrupt boys and teachers. In *After the First Death* (1979) the teenage victims of a hijack are killed. Cormier felt that 'there are enough books with happy endings', and so tried 'to write warnings for what's waiting out there'. His later work, such as *Frenchtown Summer* (1999), was less controversial.

CORNEILLE, Pierre (1606–84) French dramatist. His tragicomedy *Le Cid* (1637; trans. John Rutter, 1637), inspired by Spanish drama (*see* CID, THE), caused such a scandal on account of its unconventionalities that he rewrote it and called it a tragedy. Other important plays include *Horace* (1640) and *Polyeucte* (1643). Corneille developed seventeenth-century tragedy into the form we recognize today: the desire to create an illusion of reality on stage was served, most notably, by the observation of the the *unities. Corneille also makes tragedy a site of intense psychological conflict. Corneille exerted a powerful influence on the English dramatists of the the *Restoration, particularly John *Dryden, thanks to important translations by Katherine *Philips and Charles *Cotton.

Cornelia A tragedy translated by Thomas *Kyd from a *Senecan play by Robert Garnier, published 1594; reissued in the following year as *Pompey the Great, His Fair Cornelia's Tragedy*. The play largely consists of Cornelia's lamentations for her misfortunes.

CORNFORD, Frances (1886–1960) Poet, born in Cambridge where she spent most of her life. She published several volumes of verse but is best known for her *triolet 'To a Fat Lady Seen from a Train', with its curiously memorable lines

'O why do you walk through the fields in gloves,
    Missing so much and so much?
O fat white woman whom nobody loves'.

Her *Collected Poems* appeared in 1954.

CORNFORD, John (1915–36) Poet and political activist, son of Frances *Cornford, said to have been the first Englishman to enlist against Franco in the Spanish Civil War, in 1936. He was killed in action in the same year. His poems had been published in various periodicals and were collected with miscellaneous prose pieces, mainly political, in *John Cornford: A Memoir*, ed. Pat Sloan (1938).

Cornhill Magazine (1860–1975) A literary periodical which began with William *Thackeray as editor and specialized in the serialization of novels. Anthony Trollope's *Framley Parsonage* was succeeded by the novels of, among others, Elizabeth *Gaskell, Wilkie *Collins, Charles *Reade, George *Eliot, and Thomas *Hardy. Many poems of Alfred *Tennyson, Robert *Browning, and Algernon *Swinburne first appeared in it, as well as work by John *Ruskin, George *Macdonald, and another of its editors, Leslie *Stephen. It ceased publication in 1975.

Corn Law Rhymer *See* ELLIOTT, EBENEZER.

CORNWALL, Barry (1787–1874) Pseudonym of Brian Waller Procter. Under his pseudonym he enjoyed great popular success, particularly as a writer of songs and lyrics. His works include *Dramatic Scenes, Marcian Collona* (1820), *Mirandola* (prod. by William *Macready, 1821), *English Songs* (1832), and biographies of Charles *Lamb and Edmund Kean. His daughter Adelaide Ann *Procter was also a writer.

Corridors of Power, The *See* SNOW, C. P.

Corsair, The A poem by Lord *Byron, published 1814. Conrad, a pirate chief, is warned that the Turkish pacha is preparing to descend upon his island. He takes leave of his beloved Medora, arrives at the pacha's rallying point, and introduces himself as a dervish escaped from the pirates. He is wounded and taken prisoner, but has rescued Gulnare, the chief slave in the pacha's harem, from imminent death. She falls in love with him, and brings him a dagger with which he may kill the pacha in his sleep. Conrad revolts from such an act, whereupon she kills the pacha and escapes with Conrad. When they arrive at the pirate island Conrad finds Medora dead from grief. Conrad disappears and is never heard of again: but *see* LARA.

CORSO, Gregory *See* BEAT AND BEAT GENERATION.

CORTÁZAR, Julio (1914–84) Argentine writer, a major figure in the Boom of Latin American literature. He is best known for his self-regarding, playful, and metaphysical novel *Rayuela* (1963: *Hopscotch*), in which the reader chooses the sequence in which to read its chapters, and whether to include a number of optional chapters (*see* INTERACTIVE FICTION).

CORVO, Baron *See* ROLFE, FREDERICK.

CORYATE, Thomas (?1577–1617) Travel writer. He travelled in 1608 through France,

Italy, Switzerland, Germany, and the Netherlands, mainly on foot. In 1611 he published a long narrative of his travels entitled *Coryats Crudities*. A shorter sequel, *Coryats Crambe*, was published later the same year. In 1612 he set out overland to India, travelling through Constantinople, Palestine, and Mesopotamia, and reaching Agra in 1616. Some of his letters from the East are included in a compilation called *Thomas Coriate Traveller for the English Wits: Greeting*. Coryate wrote in an extravagant and euphuistic style (*see* EUPHUES).

'Cotter's Saturday Night, The' A poem by Robert *Burns, published 1786. The domestic descriptions are in Scots, while the moralizing commentary is in English.

COTTLE, Joseph (1770–1853) A Bristol bookseller, who published the *Lyrical Ballads* and other work by *Wordsworth, *Coleridge, and Robert *Southey. He was the author of a poem, 'Malvern Hills', published 1798, and edited with Southey the works of Thomas *Chatterton in 1803.

COTTON, Charles (1630–87) Poet and translator. He wrote the dialogue between Piscator and Viator which forms the second part in the fifth edition of The *Compleat Angler* (1676), and published *Scarronides* (1664), a mock-heroic burlesque of *Virgil, and a burlesque of *Lucian (1665). His translation of *Montaigne, closer but less colourful than John *Florio's, appeared in 1685. His *topographical poem *The Wonders of the Peak* (1681) celebrates the beauties and curiosities of the Peak District. Cotton's love of his native landscapes is also expressed in many of his *Poems on Several Occasions* (1689). William *Wordsworth and S. T. *Coleridge both admired his work.

COTTON, Sir Robert Bruce (1571–1631) Antiquary and collector of manuscripts and coins. He gave the free use of his library to Francis *Bacon, William Camden, Walter *Ralegh, John *Selden, John Speed (?1552–1629), James *Ussher, and other scholars, and sent a gift of manuscripts to the Bodleian Library on its foundation. The Cottonian Library, largely composed of works rescued from the dissolved monasteries, was left to the nation by Sir John Cotton (1621–1701), grandson of Sir Robert; it suffered severely from fire in 1731. It was removed to the British Museum in 1753 and is now in the British Library. It includes the Lindisfarne Gospels and other splendid biblical manuscripts such as the Codex Purpureus, the manuscript of *Beowulf*, and the famous manuscript that includes *Pearl* and Sir *Gawain and the Green Knight*.

Country Wife, The (the title is an indecent pun) A comedy by William *Wycherley, published and probably first performed 1675. The two main characters are Horner, a libertine, who spreads the rumour that he is impotent, so as to get access to married women, and the innocent Margery Pinchwife, who comes to London with her jealous husband, and is seduced by Horner, to their mutual satisfaction. Its sexual explicitness created a scandal even in its own day, and from 1753 to 1924 it was considered too indecent for performance, being replaced by David *Garrick's cleaned-up version, *The Country Girl* (1766).

Courier An evening newspaper published in the early 19th century, under the management of Daniel Stuart. *Coleridge, *Wordsworth, Charles *Lamb, and Robert *Southey were among its occasional contributors, and John *Galt was at one time its editor.

courtesy literature As a distinct literary genre teaching courtiers and others good manners and morals, was imported into England through works such as *Castiglione's *Il cortegiano* (translated by Sir Thomas *Hoby in 1561). Henry Peacham's *The Compleat Gentleman* (1622) was one of the most popular native examples of this type of writing.

courtly love The term 'amour courtois' was popularized by the French scholar Gaston Paris (1839–1903) in 1883 in an essay on the *Lancelot* of *Chrétien de Troyes, to describe the conception of love developed by the *troubadours in the 12th century, which had become the central theme of lyric and epic poetry in France and Germany by 1200. Its relation of lover to adored lady is modelled on the dependence of feudal follower on his lord; the love itself was a religious passion, ennobling, ever unfulfilled, and ever increasing. A code of practice for courtly lovers, *De Arte Honeste Amandi* (*c*.1185), was written by Andreas Capellanus. The writing of this kind of poetry had spread to northern France and to the German *Minnesänger and epic by 1200; the most influential works in the 13th century were the *Roman de la Rose* (Guillaume de Lorris, *c*.1230, and Jean de Meun, *c*.1275), and the lyric poems of the *dolce stil nuovo in Italy; Guido Guinicelli, *Cavalcanti, and *Dante's *Vita nuova*. The influence of courtly love is found in many places in medieval and Renaissance English literature, such as in the Harley Lyrics (in London, British Library, MS 2253) and in some of *Chaucer's poetry.

Court of Love, The An early 15th-century allegorical poem in 1,442 lines of *rhyme royal, once doubtfully attributed to *Chaucer. It is in the tradition of the *Roman de la Rose*, describing the visit of the poet to the Court of Venus and the love scenes he saw portrayed there, ending with a May Day concert of birds when they sing descants on the opening words of psalms. It claims to be the work of 'Philogenet of Cambridge, clerk'.

Covenanters 17th-century Scottish *Presbyterians who supported the National Covenant (1638) to defend their religion, especially those extremists who fought violently against the re-imposition of bishops in the Church of Scotland after the Restoration. They are described from opposing viewpoints in Walter *Scott's *Old Mortality* and John *Galt's *Ringan Gilhaize*.

COVENTRY, Francis (1725–54) He wrote *The History of Pompey the Little: or The Life and Adventures of a Lap-Dog* (1751), a vividly comic satire based on the life of a dog 'born a.d. 1735 at Bologna in Italy, a Place famous for Lap-Dogs and Sausages'.

COVERDALE, Miles (1488–1568) Translator. He was ordained priest in 1514, and adopted Lutheran views. He translated at Antwerp, apparently in the pay of Jacob van Meteren, the *Bible and *Apocrypha from German and Latin versions with the aid of William *Tyndale's New Testament. His translation was first printed perhaps at Cologne; a modified version was issued in 1537. Coverdale also superintended the printing of the Great Bible of 1539 (*see* BIBLE, THE ENGLISH). He was bishop of Exeter in 1551–3, and was allowed to leave England in 1554 after Queen Mary's accession. He published his last book, *Letters of Saintes*, in 1564. If he was in fact (which has been questioned) the translator of the version of the Bible attributed to him, he is entitled to the credit for much of the noble language of the Authorized Version, and in particular for the Prayer Book version of the Psalter.

COWARD, Sir Noël (1899–1973) Actor, dramatist, lyricist, and composer. He achieved fame with *The Vortex* (1924), in which he himself appeared as Nicky Lancaster, a cocaine addict tormented by his mother's adulteries. His sophisticated and technically accomplished comedies include *Fallen Angels* (1925), *Hay Fever* (1925), *Private Lives* (1930, about two disastrous interconnected second marriages), *Design for Living* (New York, 1933; London, 1939, about a successful *ménage à trois*), *Blithe Spirit* (1941), and *Present Laughter* (1942). A more sentimental side of Coward was revealed in his patriotic works (*Cavalcade*, 1931) and wartime screenplays such as *Brief Encounter* (1944) and *This Happy Breed* (1942). After the war his plays were less well received, up to the 1963 revival of *Private Lives* at Hampstead Theatre. Coward published two volumes of autobiography, *Present Indicative* (1937) and *Future Indefinite* (1954). *The Noël Coward Diaries* (1982) are an entertaining fund of theatrical gossip.

COWLEY, Abraham (1618–67) Poet. His *Poetical Blossoms* (1633) includes 'Pyramus and Thisbe', a verse romance written when he was 10 years old, and 'Constantia and Philetus', written two years later. *Love's Riddle*, a pastoral drama, and *Naufragium Joculare*, a Latin comedy, appeared in 1638. On the outbreak of the Civil War Cowley left Cambridge for Oxford, where he wrote a satire, *The Puritan and the Papist* (1643), and a political epic, *The Civil War*, in the Royalist cause. Book I of *The Civil War* was published in 1679; the remainder of the work was presumed lost until discovered and edited in 1973. In 1644 he left Oxford for Paris, where he was at the court of Henrietta Maria. In 1654 he returned to England, apparently as a Royalist spy, and was imprisoned briefly in 1655. At the Restoration he was disappointed in his expectation of a reward for his services. He is buried in Westminster Abbey. His principal works include *The Mistress* (1647); 'Miscellanies', 'Davideis', and 'Pindaric Odes' (*see* ODE) in *Poems* (1656); *Ode, upon the Blessed Restoration* (1660); and *Verses on Several Occasions* (1663). His prose works, marked by grace and simplicity of style, include *A Proposition for the Advancement of Learning* (1661), and some 'Essays', notably one 'Of my Self'. Cowley's life was written by his friend Thomas Sprat and is prefixed to *The Works* (1668).

COWLEY, Hannah (1743–1809) Née Park-house, dramatist. Her comedies include *The Runaway* (1776), sent anonymously to David *Garrick who mounted it with great success in 1776, *The Belle's Stratagem* (1780), and *A Bold Stroke for a Wife* (1783). Cowley wrote two tragedies (one of them, *Albina*, provoking a bitter row with Hannah *More over alleged plagiarism), and corresponded in verse as 'Anna Matilda' with Robert Merry (*see* DELLA CRUSCANS).

COWPER, William (1731–1800) Poet, son of a rector. He was bullied as a schoolboy, suffered from severe depression, and attempted suicide. Thereafter he was subject to periods of acute melancholia, feeling himself cast out from God's mercy. In 1765 he became a boarder (in his own words, 'a sort of adopted son') in the home of the Reverend Morley Unwin at Huntingdon, and on Morley's death moved with Mary, his widow, to Olney. There he came under the influence of John *Newton, the evangelical curate, with whom he wrote *Olney Hymns* (published 1779); his contributions include 'God moves in a mysterious way' and 'Oh, for a closer walk with God'. Under social pressure he became engaged to Mrs Unwin, but in early 1773 suffered a period of intense depression, making further suicide attempts; he was so convinced of his complete exclusion from the Christian communion that he never prayed or entered a church again. Recovering through activities such as gardening, the keeping of pet hares, and carpentry, he wrote a series of moral satires in couplets which were published in 1782 with several shorter poems (including 'Verses Supposed to be Written by Alexander Selkirk'). *'John Gilpin', and *The *Task* (1785), were both on subjects suggested by a new friend, Lady Austen. They were published with 'Tirocinium', a vigorous attack on public schools. In 1786 he moved with Mrs Unwin to Weston Underwood, where he wrote various poems published after his death, including further poems promoting the abolition of the slave trade. His translation of *Homer into blank verse, published by subscription in 1791, was intended to rival the translation by Alexander *Pope. An attempt to edit the poems of John *Milton introduced him to William *Hayley, who secured Cowper a pension, and helped care for Mrs Unwin, who died in 1796. 'The *Castaway', written shortly before Cowper's own death, was a final expression of isolation and helplessness. Cowper's letters were published in 1803–4, alongside a sympathetic biography by Hayley; his 'Memoir' (c.1767) in 1816. The poems are often quoted by sympathetic characters in Jane *Austen's fiction. Robert *Southey's 15-volume edition (1835–7) made Cowper a Victorian classic.

CRABBE, George (1754–1832) Poet, born in Aldeburgh, Suffolk. He met Sarah Elmy (the 'Mira' of his poems and journals) while apprenticed to a doctor; in 1775, he published *Inebriety* a poem on the evils of drink. In 1780 he determined on a career in writing and went to London, where he was generously befriended by Edmund *Burke. *The Library* (1781), was published with his literary help. Burke introduced Crabbe to influential friends, and encouraged him to take orders. In 1781 he became curate at Aldeburgh. In 1783, after advice and revision from Burke and Samuel *Johnson, he published *The *Village*, a poem in heroic couplets which established his reputation, eschewing the conventions of the *pastoral, and painting instead a grim, detailed picture of rural poverty.

In 1785 he published a satirical poem on the contemporary press, *The Newspaper*. A long interval followed, during which he wrote and destroyed several unpublished novels. A volume published in 1807 contained his previous works, some new shorter poems, 'The *Parish Register' (which revealed his gift as a narrative poet), and another, atypical, narrative in 55 eight-line stanzas, 'Sir Eustace Grey', set in a madhouse. Alethea *Hayter relates the peculiarly vivid dream descriptions to Crabbe's opium-taking (on medical advice).

*The *Borough* (1810), a poem in 24 'letters' in which he illustrates the life of a country town (based on Aldeburgh), and which includes the tales of *'Peter Grimes' and *'Ellen Orford', was followed by *Tales in Verse* (1812). In 1814 Crabbe was appointed vicar of Trowbridge, and in 1819 published *Tales of the Hall*. He died in Trowbridge and much unpublished work was found, some of which was published in a collected edition in 1834; later discoveries appeared in *New Poems*, ed. A. Pollard (1960).

CRACE, Jim (1946–) Novelist. He worked in Botswana and the Sudan, and as a freelance journalist, before publishing his first book *Continent* in 1986. Set in an imaginary seventh continent, it established his characteristic fictional mode of bold excursions into fantasy combined with crisp precision of prose and concrete detail. Some of his novels such as *The Gift of Stones* (1988), *Signals of Distress* (1994), and *Quarantine* (1997), a reimagining of desert life in the 1st century, one of whose main characters is Christ, hark back to a semi-mythologized past. Others such as *Arcadia* (1992) and *The Pesthouse* (2007) portray *dystopian future worlds.

CRAIK, Dinah Maria (1826–87) Née Mulock, a prolific writer of novels, poems, children's books, fairy-tales, essays, and short stories. The death of her mother led her unstable father to abandon the family in 1845, and she turned to writing to earn a living. A novel, *The Ogilvies* (1846), was followed by *Olive* (1850), and nine further novels before *John Halifax, Gentleman* (1856), the great and prolonged success for which she is chiefly remembered. In 1857, she published *A Woman's Thoughts about Women*. Her short stories were collected under the title *Avillion* in 1853 and her *Collected Poems* appeared in 1881.

CRANE, Hart (1899–1932) American poet. He published two volumes of verse, *White Buildings* (1926) and *The Bridge* (1930), the latter an obscure but powerful work which explores the 'Myth of America', with many echoes of Walt *Whitman; its national symbols include Brooklyn Bridge itself, invoked in its Proem, and such historical and legendary characters as Columbus, *Rip Van Winkle, and Pocahontas, who, the poet explains, is the 'mythological nature-symbol chosen to represent the physical body of the continent, or the soul'. Crane was an alcoholic, and committed suicide by jumping from a steamer in the Caribbean after spending some time in Mexico. His *Complete Poems and Selected Letters and Prose* appeared in 1960, and his correspondence with Yvor *Winters in 1978.

CRANE, Stephen (1871–1900) American novelist, journalist, and short story writer. His first novel, *Maggie: A Girl of the Streets* (1893), was too grim to find a readership. His next work, *The Red Badge of Courage* (1895), a study of an inexperienced soldier (Henry Fleming) and his reactions to the ordeal of battle during the American Civil War, although based on no personal experience of war was hailed as a masterpiece of psychological realism, and Crane found himself working as a war reporter in Mexico, Cuba, and Greece. He settled in England in 1897, already ill with tuberculosis, and developed a close friendship with Joseph *Conrad (to whose work his own was compared as an example of literary *Impressionism). His collected works were published from 1969 to 1976.

Cranford A novel by Elizabeth *Gaskell, published serially in *Household Words*, 1851–3. *Cranford*, a series of linked sketches of life among the ladies of a quiet country village in the 1830s, is based on Knutsford in Cheshire where Elizabeth Gaskell spent her childhood. It centres on the formidable Miss Deborah Jenkyns and her gentle sister Miss Matty, daughters of the former rector. Drama is provided by the death of the genial Captain Brown, run over by a train when saving the life of a child, the panic caused in the village by rumours of burglars, the surprising marriage of the widowed Lady Glenmire with the vulgar Mr Hoggins, the village surgeon, the failure of a bank which ruins Miss Matty, and her rescue by the fortunate return

from India of her long-lost brother Peter. *Cranford* used to be valued chiefly for its loving portrayal of the old-fashioned customs and 'elegant economy' of a delicately observed group of middle-aged figures in a landscape; more recently, critical attention has turned to its subtle representations of the emotional and practical dynamics of women's lives.

CRANMER, Thomas (1489–1556) Archbishop of Canterbury. In 1529, he argued in support of *Henry VIII in his divorce from Catherine of Aragon, was appointed to the archbishopric in 1533, and maintained the king's claim to be the supreme head of the Church of England. He promoted the Bible in the vernacular; supervised the production of the first prayer book of Edward VI, 1549; prepared the revised prayer book of 1552; and drafted the 42 Articles of religion (afterwards reduced to 39) in the same year. To meet the need for suitable sermons, he contributed to and probably edited the first book of *Homilies* issued in 1547. In Queen Mary's reign he was imprisoned, condemned for heresy, and, in 1556, degraded from his ministry. He signed six documents admitting the pope's supremacy and the truth of all Roman Catholic doctrine except transubstantiation; he was burned at the stake, repudiating these admissions, on 21 March 1556 at Oxford, holding his right hand (which had written his recantation) steadily in the flames, that it might be the first burnt. His chief title to fame is that of being the principal author of the English liturgy. John *Foxe tells his story vividly in his *Acts and Monuments*.

CRASHAW, Richard (1612/13–49) Poet. He became a Catholic convert *c.*1645 and fled to Paris, where his friend Abraham *Cowley persuaded Queen Henrietta Maria to interest herself on his behalf. His principal work *Steps to the Temple* (1646; 2nd edn 1648) was a collection of religious poems influenced by Giambattista *Marino and the Spanish mystics. The secular section, the *Delights of the Muses*, contains 'Music's Duel', a paraphrase of the Latin of Strada, about a musical contest between a lute-player and a nightingale, and 'Wishes. To his (Supposed) Mistress' ('Who'er she be | That not impossible she'). His best-known poems are 'The Weeper', about Mary Magdalen, and those addressed to St *Teresa of Ávila. His baroque, Counter-Reformation sensuousness daringly challenges decorum.

CRAWFORD, Robert (1959–) Poet, critic, and anthologist. His first collection of poems,

A Scottish Assembly, appeared in 1990, along with *Sharwaggi*, a joint volume in *Scots with W. N. Herbert. Later books include *Masculinity* (1996), *The Tip of my Tongue* (2003), and *Full Volume* (2008). Crawford's good-humoured yet sharp poetry explores questions of national, cultural, and gender identity, while also celebrating the domestic and the personal with tenderness and speculative wit.

Creed, the Apostles', the Athanasian, the Nicene The creeds are fundamental statements of Christian doctrine, particularly the Trinity. Originally required of candidates for baptism, they came to be recited as part of the liturgy of Catholic and Protestant churches.

CREELEY, Robert (1926–2005) American poet and prose writer, and one of the *Black Mountain group; he edited (1954–7) the *Black Mountain Review*. His verse tends to use tighter metrical forms, to be more personal, less rhetorical than that of associates like Charles Olson, with whom he had an extended correspondence. His *Collected Poems* was published in 2006. Creeley also wrote a number of novels, including *The Gold Diggers* (1954/1965) and *The Island* (1963). His *Collected Prose* was published in 1984.

Creole is used as a noun or an adjective of both people and language. The word may derive from *criar*, 'to breed' in Spanish. In the West Indies it is used of people of African or European descent born or naturalized in the Caribbean. A creole language develops from pidgin, which is used between people with no common language and discards the inessentials of the original language. Creole languages were once associated with slavery and regarded as inferior but are now used in literature and the media, and are seen to have a particular cultural history and expressive vitality.

CRESSWELL, Helen (1934–2005) Prolific children's author. Her books often feature families, including the Bagthorpes (1978–2001) and the Lizzie Dripping books (1972–4; 1991). All her stories are wryly realistic. Cresswell successfully adapted Edith *Nesbit's and Enid *Blyton's books for television.

CRÈVECŒUR, Michel-Guillaume de (1735–1813) American prose writer, known as J. Hector St John de Crevecœur, born in France. He emigrated to Canada and took American citizenship in 1765. He settled in New York State, where he farmed, until the revolution obliged him to flee to Europe. His *Letters from an American Farmer* (pub. London, 1782), which describe rural life and customs, was much admired by the Romantics; the third essay, 'What is an American?', describes the nation idealistically as a cultural melting-pot and defines the American as a 'new man, who acts upon new principles'. D. H. *Lawrence commented on his role as myth-maker and described him as the 'emotional prototype' of the American (as distinct from Benjamin *Franklin, 'the real practical prototype').

CRICHTON, James ('The Admirable') (1560–82) Scottish polymath, poet, and adventurer, who served in the French army, travelled in Italy, and died in a brawl in Mantua. His colourful career is recounted by Sir Thomas *Urquhart and provides the subject of a historical novel by Harrison *Ainsworth. J. M. *Barrie's play *The Admirable Crichton* concerns a manservant marooned with his less gifted employers on a desert island.

CRICHTON, Michael (1942–2008) American novelist, film-maker, and creator of television series. Crichton published his first *science fiction novel, *The Andromeda Strain* (1969, filmed 1971), while still a medical student. This established a pattern of 'techno-thrillers', projecting current scientific knowledge into melodramatic fantasy, while often sounding a cautionary note. His subjects were often biological, from the virulent extraterrestrial disease of his first novel to the deadly self-reproducing nano-particles of *Prey* (2002) and a warning against genetic patenting in *Next* (2006). His best-known creations are the long-running hospital-based television series *ER* (1994–2009) and the screenplay for *Jurassic Park* (1993), which portrayed spectacular dinosaurs recreated from prehistoric DNA. *Rising Sun* (1994), apparently attacking Japanese business culture, and *State of Fear* (2004) questioning alarm over climate change, aroused controversy.

Cricket on the Hearth, The The third of Charles *Dickens's five Christmas Books, published 1846. John Peerybingle, carrier, and his younger wife, Dot, are a happy couple, although the venomous old Tackleton, who is about to marry the young May Fielding, throws suspicion on Dot's sincerity. This suspicion appears to be confirmed when an eccentric old stranger comes to live with the Peerybingles and is discovered by John, metamorphosed into a bright young man by the removal of his wig, in intimate conversation with Dot. By the fairy influence of the Cricket on the Hearth John is persuaded to pardon her offence, which he attributes to the incompatibility of their ages and temperaments. But there turns out to be no need for forgiveness, for the young man is an old friend, the lover of May Fielding, believed dead, who has turned up just in time to prevent her marrying Tackleton. Among the other characters are Caleb Plummer and his blind daughter Bertha, the toymakers; and Tilly Slowboy, the Peerybingles' loving and incompetent nanny. The book was a great popular success, with the highest sales figures of all Dickens's Christmas Books.

CRIMP, Martin (1965–) Playwright. He wrote fiction before being employed by the Orange Tree Theatre in south London, the venue for his early theatrical work, including *Dealing with Clair* (1988). *Attempts on her Life* was produced in 1997 at the *Royal Court, where he was writer in residence. The play abandons character identification and narrative continuity in favour of a series of short scenes that cause the audience to question what might be signified by the title. *Fewer Emergencies* (2005) was also produced at the Royal Court. He has also produced significant versions of *Ionesco's *The Chairs* (1997) for Theatre de Complicité, and *Rhinoceros* (2007).

Criterion (1922–39) An influential literary periodical launched as a quarterly and edited by T. S. *Eliot; *The *Waste Land* appeared in its first issue. It became the *New Criterion* in 1926, and in 1927, briefly, the *Monthly Criterion*, but then reverted to its original title. It included work by Ezra *Pound, William *Empson, W. H. *Auden, Stephen *Spender, Geoffrey *Grigson, etc.; it also introduced the work of Marcel *Proust, Paul *Valéry, Jean Cocteau, and other European writers.

Critic, The, or a Tragedy Rehearsed A comedy by Richard Brinsley *Sheridan, produced 1779. Modelled on Buckingham's The *Rehearsal, The Critic* is an exuberant burlesque of contemporary tragic drama. Mr Puff, an enterprising purveyor of literary wares and the author of a ludicrously bombastic and sentimental tragedy, 'The Spanish Armada', invites Dangle and Sneer, two inept theatre critics, and Sir Fretful Plagiary (a caricature of Richard *Cumberland) to a rehearsal of his play. The drama introduces Sir Walter *Ralegh and other historical figures alongside Tilburina, who complicates the plot with her love for Don Ferolo Whiskerandos, a Spanish prisoner. The rehearsal is comically plagued by the solemn discussions of the author and his guests as well as the queries and mistakes of prompters and stagehands. The play has also been taken as a covert satire on governmental passivity in the face of a resurgent Spanish invasion threat.

Critical Quarterly A literary review founded in 1959. From the beginning it published both criticism and creative writing. Latterly, under the editorship of Colin MacCabe, it has become oriented towards cultural studies more generally, including film and television, and literary theory. Contributors have included Philip *Larkin, Donald *Davie, D. J. *Enright, William *Empson, and Seamus *Heaney.

Critical Review A journal founded in 1756 to oppose the liberal *Monthly Review. Until 1763 it was edited by Tobias *Smollett. Apart from commentary on public affairs, it reviewed a wide range of books.

criticism, schools of See DECONSTRUCTION; ECOCRITICISM; FEMINIST CRITICISM; MARXIST LITERARY CRITICISM; MYTH CRITICISM; NARRATOLOGY; NEW CRITICISM; NEW HISTORICISM; POSTMODERNISM; PRACTICAL CRITICISM; PSYCHOANALYTIC CRITICISM; SOCIALIST REALISM; STRUCTURALISM. *See also* ARCHETYPE.

CROCKETT, S. R. See KAILYARD SCHOOL.

CROKER, John Wilson (1780–1857) Tory MP, secretary to the Admiralty, and a regular contributor to the *Quarterly Review, in which he made very plain his Tory and Anglican stance, even in his literary reviews, and for which he acted as an important link with circles of political power. Known for his bitter opposition to most of the younger writers of his day, he became notorious for his criticism of John Keats's *Endymion* in 1818. P. B. *Shelley (in his preface to *Adonais*) and Lord *Byron (in his jingle 'Who killed John Keats?') established the belief that Croker's review hastened the death of the poet. Yet Croker's views, although blinkered and ungenerous, were considerably more temperate than those of John *Lockhart in *Blackwood's Magazine. Croker's books include *An Intercepted Letter from Canton* (1804), a satire on Dublin society and a reliable edition of Boswell's *Life of Samuel *Johnson* (1831). He was a much-hated man, caricatured in three contemporary novels: Thomas Love Peacock's *Melincourt* (1817); Lady *Morgan's *Florence Macarthy* (1818); and Disraeli's *Coningsby* (1844); and was detested 'more than cold boiled veal' by his lifelong enemy Thomas *Macaulay. It appears that he was the originator of the political term 'Conservative', in the *Quarterly Review* in January 1830.

CROKER, Thomas Crofton (1798–1854) Irish antiquarian, probably the first collector to regard national and folk stories as examples of literary art. His *Researches in the South of Ireland* (1824), the very successful *Fairy Legends and Traditions in the South of Ireland* (1825–8), *Legends of the Lakes* (1829), and *Popular Songs of Ireland* (1839) provide a rich source of information on Irish folklore.

CROMPTON, Richmal (1890–1969) Creator of (Just) William. Crompton's 41 books for adults have been eclipsed by her *'William'* stories, the first of which was 'Rice-Mould' (1919) for *Home Magazine*. Until the 1940s, the stories, first collected in *Just William* (1922) were directed at adults; Crompton used the stories to satirize middle-class, middle England. Characteristic is 'Aunt Arabella in Charge' (*William the Pirate*, 1932) in which A. A. *Milne's Christopher Robin is mercilessly lampooned. The stories have been filmed and televised and gained new life through Martin Jarvis's radio adaptations.

CRONIN, A. J. (Archibald Joseph) (1896–1981) Novelist. He practised as a doctor before devoting himself, after the success of his first book, *Hatter's Castle* (1931), to an extremely successful career as a novelist whose works reached an even wider audience through film and television. His best-known novels are *The Stars Look Down* (1935) and *The Citadel* (1937).

CROSS, Gillian (1945–) Children's writer. Cross has produced over 40 books, from the televised comedy-thriller *The Demon Headmaster* (1982) to the challenging examination of families, fatherhood, and terrorism *Wolf* (1990, Carnegie Medal).

CROSSLEY-HOLLAND, Kevin (1941–) Poet, translator, and children's writer. His collections include *The Rain-Giver* (1972), *Time's Oriel* (1983), *Waterslain* (1986), *The Language of Yes* (1996), and *The Mountains of Norfolk* (2011). His *Selected Poems* was published in 2001. His translations include *The Battle of Maldon and Other Old English Poems* (1965), *Beowulf* (1968), *Storm and Other Old English Riddles* (1970), *The Exeter Book Riddles* (1978), and *The Old English Elegies* (1988). His work is imbued with the landscape and interwoven history and legend of East Anglia, where he has spent much of his life—its maltings, granaries, and woodlands, but most particularly the 'marsh, mud, creeks, shifting sand' of its coastline. His works for children, many based on East Anglian folk tales and Norse myths, include *Havelock the Dane* (1964), *The Wildman* (1976), and *Waterslain Angels* (2008). His prize-winning 'Arthur' trilogy opened with *The Seeing Stone* (2000) and closed with *King of the Middle March* (2003). He has also written libretti from his own works, notably with composer Nicola LeFanu (1947–).

crossover books A term that came to prominence in the 1990s, used to describe books such as J. K. *Rowling's 'Harry Potter' series and Philip Pullman's *His Dark Materials* trilogy, originally published for children but also successful with adults. The term is recent, the phenomenon is not: many 19th-century books, including those by G. A. *Henty and Frances Hodgson *Burnett, appealed to dual audiences. In the later 20th century, the popularity of fantasy blurred literary and audience distinctions; Richard *Adams's best-selling *Watership Down* (1972) was issued with different covers for adults and children, now a common feature of crossover books.

Crotchet Castle A satire by Thomas Love *Peacock, published 1831. The story assembles a group of theorists at a country house including Mr Skionar (who resembles Samuel Taylor *Coleridge), Mr MacQuedy (a Scottish economist), and Mr Chainmail (who wants to revive the Middle Ages). The Revd Dr Folliott, though more amiable and learned than Peacock's previous clerics, is mocked for his bigoted conservatism. The dinner-table conversations at Crotchet Castle turn on the clash between Folliott's Toryism and MacQuedy's progressivism. The guests take a journey by river and canal to Wales, reminiscent of a trip Peacock took up the Thames with P. B. *Shelley in 1815. Lady Clarinda is the most spirited and cynical of Peacock's heroines. The book ends with an assault by the mob on Mr Chainmail's 12th-century castle, an ironic comment on the more visionary schemes to solve the troubles of the age of reform.

CROWE, Catherine *See* GHOST STORIES.

CROWLEY, Aleister (1875–1947) Occultist and writer. Crowley dedicated himself to esoteric studies from 1897 and left Cambridge without taking a degree. He combined a wildly peripatetic existence (in Mexico, Asia, and elsewhere) with a regular stream of occultist publications (such as *The Book of Lies*, 1913) and reached the peak of his notoriety in 1923 when a newspaper denounced him as 'the wickedest man in the world' following the sensational publication of his *Diary of a Drug Fiend* (1922).

CROWLEY, John (1942-) American novelist, who began with *science fiction in novels like *Engine Summer* (1979) but whose *Little, Big* (1981) adapted the structure of Faerie constructed by 'Lewis Carroll' (*see* DODGSON, CHARLES) in *Sylvie and Bruno* (1889) to contemporary New York. John *Clute has called it a masterpiece of modern *fantasy. A later sequence, beginning with *Aegypt* (1987), develops the conceit of a 'secret history' of the world by drawing upon Giordano Bruno's Hermeticism.

CROWNE, John (?1640–?1703) Playwright. His first comedy, *The Country Wit* (1675), contained the character of Sir Mannerly Shallow, subsequently developed into *Sir Courtly Nice in the play of that name (1685). He wrote several other comedies, a court masque, *Calisto* (1675), and eleven tragedies, including the two-part rhymed *The Destruction of Jerusalem* (1677), *Thyestes* (1681), and *Caligula* (1698). The success of the tragedies is said to have owed much to expensive and elaborate scenery.

CRUDEN, Alexander (1701–70) Compiler of a concordance (an index of words and passages) of the King James *Bible, social campaigner, and reputed madman. He was incarcerated as a lunatic by the family of his first love who feared he had discovered her incestuous relationship with her brother. His experience of madhouses, related in *The London Citizen Exceedingly Injured* (1739), helped raise consciousness of their abuses.

The *Complete Concordance* (1737) included the Apocrypha and much miscellaneous but sometimes fanciful information now usually omitted (see e.g. 'serpent'). It became a standard reference work, as did his *Verbal Index to Milton's Paradise Lost* (1741).

Cruelty, Theatre of A phrase associated with French director Antonin Artaud, and introduced to Britain during the 1960s through the work of Peter *Brook and critic and director Charles Marowitz (1934-), who chose the name for their experimental theatre group in homage to Artaud: the most celebrated production of the movement was Brook's version of Peter *Weiss's *Marat/Sade*. The emphasis of this style of theatre was as much on gesture and movement as on text.

CRUIKSHANK, George (1792–1878) Illustrator and caricaturist. His vast amount of work

was largely in political caricature, but he illustrated many books, including *Sketches by Boz* in 1836, which began a long association with Charles *Dickens including the illustrations to *Oliver Twist* in 1837; and Harriet Beecher Stowe's *Uncle Tom's Cabin* in 1853.

Cry, the Beloved Country (1948) A novel by Alan Paton (1903–88), who was national president of the South African Liberal Party until it was declared illegal in 1968. The novel begins with the departure of the Reverend Stephen Kumalo from his impoverished homeland at Ndotasheni, Natal, for Johannesburg, in search of three members of his family including his son Absalom. Absalom has murdered the son of a white farmer, James Jarvis. Absalom is convicted and condemned to death, and Kumalo returns home with Absalom's pregnant wife. The novel ends with the reconciliation of Jarvis and Kumalo, and Jarvis's determination to rise above tragedy by helping the poor black community.

C.S.C. *See* CALVERLEY, CHARLES.

Cuala Press A private press founded in 1902 at Dundrum, Co. Dublin, by Elizabeth and Lily Yeats, sisters of W. B. *Yeats, to stimulate local crafts and employment. It was originally called the Dun Emer Press, changing its name in 1908, and it flourished as the Cuala Press until late 1946, publishing work by Yeats, J. M. *Synge, Oliver *Gogarty, Lady *Gregory, Ezra *Pound, and others. The press was revived by Anne and Michael Yeats, the children of W. B. Yeats, in 1969.

Cubism A movement in art pioneered by Pablo Picasso (1881–1973) and Georges Braque (1882–1963) between about 1907 and 1914. In its first phase, sometimes referred to as 'Analytic Cubism', forms were broken down for examination, and the multiple facets of objects splayed out as if seen from many points simultaneously. 'Synthetic Cubism', which emerged in 1912, involved a shift in emphasis from fragmentation to accumulation, with collage (or *papier collé*) becoming an important technique. Cubism was ground-breaking in its abandonment of fixed perspective and in its decisive move away from illusionistic representation, renegotiating the relationship between the three-dimensional world and the two-dimensional picture plane. It was also a radical investigation of the relationship between signs and their referents (*see* STRUCTURALISM). Using a limited vocabulary of objects (guitar, bottle, newspaper, pipe), Cubist artists explored the capacity for signs and referents to become interchangeable, or to generate further referents. It is partly for this reason that Cubism was closely allied to poetry, particularly to the work of *Mallarmé, *Rimbaud, and Apollinaire. Gertrude *Stein developed a form of Cubist prose, and her writing influenced, in turn, the development of Cubist painting.

Cuchulain [pron. Cuhoolin] Hero of the Ulster cycle of Irish mythology, the ward of Conchubar, king of Ulster. Among the feats which won him the love of many women was his single-handed defence of Ulster against Queen Medb (pron. Maeve) and her Connaughtmen. Some of the legends about him were translated by Lady *Gregory (*Cuchulain of Muirthemne*). He figures in James *Macpherson's Ossianic poems and in many of the poems and plays of W. B. *Yeats. Cuchulain has been adopted as an icon both by Irish nationalists and Ulster loyalists.

CUDWORTH, Ralph See CAMBRIDGE PLATONISTS.

CUGOANO, Ottobah (c.1757–?1803) Sold into slavery from present-day Ghana to the Caribbean. Freed, he settled in London, becoming active in abolitionist circles, meeting William *Blake, and collaborating with Olaudah *Equiano. His book *Thoughts and Sentiments on the Evils of Slavery* (1787) is a radical denunciation from a Christian perspective. See SLAVERY.

CULLEN, Countee (1903–46) African American poet, who was an important figure in the *Harlem Renaissance. His first collection, *Colour* (1925), celebrated blackness and a second, *The Black Christ* (1929), caused some controversy for its appropriation of Christian imagery.

cultural materialism See NEW HISTORICISM.

Culture and Anarchy A sequence of essays by Matthew *Arnold, published as a book in 1869. This work sets out Arnold's central arguments about the place in modern society of 'culture'. Arnold laments the aggressively partisan attitudes of the landed 'Barbarians', the lower-class 'Populace', and especially the 'Philistine' middle class, whose suspicion of state power, notably in the realm of education, he regards as dangerously self-defeating. He accuses the Philistines of blind complacency and of overemphasizing the value of 'Hebraism' (essentially Protestant moral vigilance) at the expense of the equally vital tradition of 'Hellenism' (the Renaissance and Enlightenment cultivation of beauty and truth for their own sakes).

CULVERWEL, Nathaniel See CAMBRIDGE PLATONISTS.

CUMBERLAND, Richard (1732–1811) Dramatist, grandson of Richard *Bentley. He wrote several comedies, of which *The *West Indian* and *The Jew* (1794) were the most successful, and *Memoirs* (1806). See also CRITIC.

CUMMINGS, Bruce Frederick (1889–1919) Diarist and biologist, who wrote a diary under the pseudonym of W. N. P. Barbellion, *The Journal of a Disappointed Man*. It was published in 1919 with an introduction by H. G. *Wells, who called it a 'specimen, carefully displayed and labelled' of 'recorded unhappiness'. He clearly intended publication, and modelled his work partly on the diary of Marie Bashkirtseff. The last entry was made on 21 October 1917, after which 'Barbellion's' death was recorded. In fact Cummings survived to see his own work published, and his *A Last Diary* (1920) covers the last two years of his life.

CUMMINGS, E. E. (Edward Estlin) (1894–1962) American poet. His first book, *The Enormous Room* (1922), an account of his three-month internment in a French detention camp in 1917, won him an immediate international reputation. *Tulips and Chimneys* (1923) was the first of twelve volumes of poetry. Strongly influenced by the English Romantic poets and Gertrude *Stein, the early poems attracted attention more for their experimental typography and technical skill than for their considerable lyric power; the frankness of his vocabulary and the sharpness of his satire also created some scandal. In *Eimi* (1933), a typographically difficult but enthralling journal of a trip to Russia, he broke in disillusion from his earlier socialist leanings, and thenceforth his work reflected his increasingly reactionary social and political views. His later lyrics, on the other hand, achieved a greater depth and simplicity. His other works include essays, plays, and *Tom* (1935), a satirical ballet based on Harriet Beecher Stowe's *Uncle Tom's Cabin*. His *Complete Poems: 1904–1962* was reissued in 1994.

CUNNINGHAM, Allan (1784–1842) Poet, born in Dumfriesshire. Cunningham profited from the vogue for *primitivism by disguising his poems as old Scottish songs, many of which were published by R. H. Cromek as *Remains of*

Nithsdale and Galloway Song (1810). He also published *Traditional Tales of the English and Scottish Peasantry* (1822); *The Songs of Scotland* (1825); and an edition of Burns (1834).

CUNNINGHAME GRAHAM, Robert Bontine (1852-1936) Adventurer, writer, and political radical. During a varied career Cunninghame Graham was a rancher in Argentina, a traveller, mainly in South America; and a socialist Liberal MP (1886-92). He published stories of Scotland, and travel books, including *Mogreb-el-Acksa* (1898), which inspired the play *Captain Brassbound's Conversion* by George Bernard *Shaw. *A Vanished Arcadia: Being Some Account of the Jesuits in Paraguay 1607- 1767* (1901) inspired the 1986 film *The Mission*.

Cupid Son of *Venus and winged god of love (Eros in Greek), whose arrows usually represent unsatisfied desire. Depictions in classical, medieval, and Renaissance literature vary from the naughty but dangerous child to the powerful divine force capable of transforming the human devotee. Philip *Sidney's *Astrophel and Stella* illustrates the first, Edmund *Spenser's *Colin Clout* the second. Cupid has continued to represent the power of erotic love in countless literary texts.

Cupid and Psyche The allegorical centrepiece of the *Golden Ass* of *Apuleius, in which the author blends a familiar folk tale with a Hellenistic epyllion (a short erotic epic). Psyche (meaning 'soul'), is beloved by *Cupid, who visits her nightly, but remains invisible, forbidding her to attempt to see him: one night she takes a lamp and looks at him as he sleeps, and agitated by his beauty lets fall a drop of hot oil on his shoulder. He departs in wrath, leaving her solitary and remorseful. Like the hero of the novel in which her tale is set, Psyche has forfeited her happiness through misplaced curiosity, and has to regain it through painful wanderings. Many elements of the story—the magic palace, the enchantress (Venus) to whom the hero (Cupid) is in thrall, the tasks the heroine has to perform, and the animals that aid her—belong to the world of the folk tale. Apuleius' story has been retold by many later writers, including William *Browne, Shackerley *Marmion, Mary *Tighe, William *Morris, Walter *Pater, and C. S. *Lewis. John *Keats's 'Ode to Psyche' owes a debt to it.

Curious Incident of the Dog in the Night-time, The (2003) *Crossover book by Mark *Haddon told as an account by 15-year-old Christopher Boone, who suffers from Asperger's Syndrome, of how he solves the mystery of who killed his neighbour's dog.

CURLL, Edmund (1683-1747) Bookseller notorious for instant biographies, seditious pamphlets, piracies, and pornography. In 1728 he was pilloried and fined for publishing the political *Memoirs* of John Ker and *Venus in the Cloister, or The Nun in her Smock*. He enraged Jonathan *Swift with his 'Key' to *A *Tale of a Tub* and unauthorized *Miscellanies*. Alexander *Pope ridiculed him in *The *Dunciad*. In 1735 Pope manoeuvred Curll into publishing an unauthorized edition of his letters, in order to promote an 'authentic' edition.

CURNOW, Allen (1911-2001) New Zealand poet and critic. From an early stage he was seen to be an important figure in the creation of a truly New Zealand poetry. His first significant book was *Not in Narrow Seas* (1939); his editing of *A Book of New Zealand Verse* (1945; rev. 1951) and then *The Penguin Book of New Zealand Verse* (1960) was both influential and controversial. A number of collected and selected volumes are drawn on in *Early Days Yet: New and Collected Poems 1941-1997* (1997), with a final volume *The Bells of St Babel's: Poems 1997- 2001* (2001).

Cursor Mundi A northern poem dating from *c.*1300, surviving in seven manuscripts of about 24,000 short lines, supplemented in most of them by another 6,000 or so lines of devotional material. The poem covers mankind's spiritual history from the Creation to the Last Judgement, divided into Seven Ages. It is derived from various late 12th-century Latin pseudo-histories made up of saints' lives, apocryphal legends, and biblical material.

CURTIS, Tony (1946-) Welsh poet, whose collections include *Album* (1974), *Taken for Pearls* (1993), *Heaven's Gate* (2001), and *Crossing Over* (2007). His celebrations of family life, golf, and the landscape of Pembrokeshire are increasingly shadowed by an awareness of war and macrocosmic misery.

CUSK, Rachel (1967-) Novelist and critic. *Saving Agnes* (1993) is an eloquent and witty account of the frustrations and disappointments of an insecure Oxford-educated young woman, and her efforts towards salvation. Widely acclaimed for their prose style and perceptive interpretation of domestic life, her subsequent novels include *The Temporary* (1995); *The Country Life* (1997), a bizarre comic novel about a woman who leaves London to become an au pair in the country; and *The Lucky Ones* (2003). *In the Fold* (2005) and *Arlington Park* (2006) are concerned with the dubious morality of the English middle class. *The Bradshaw Variations* (2009) examines the family lives of three brothers. *A Life's Work* (2001) is an unsentimental, often bleak memoir about becoming a mother.

Custom of the Country, The

A tragi-comedy by John *Fletcher and Philip *Massinger, composed between 1619 and 1622; derived from the *Persiles y Sigismunda* of *Cervantes. *Dryden thought it more bawdy than any Restoration play.

An adaptation by Nicholas Wright was performed by the Royal Shakespeare Company in 1983, and the play was given a staged reading at the *Globe Theatre in 1998.

Custom of the Country, The

A witty and satiric novel by Edith *Wharton, published in 1913, in which a beautiful, energetic, destructive, and ambitious American, Undine Spragg, works her way to wealth and power through a succession of marriages.

CUTHBERT, St

(*c.*635–687) Bishop of Lindisfarne. In 651, he entered the monastery of Melrose, of which he became prior. He later became prior of Lindisfarne, but received a vocation to the solitary life, and retired to the small island of Farne. In 684, at a synod held under St Theodore, archbishop of Canterbury, he was selected for the see of Lindisfarne in 684, but retired to Farne before his death on 20 March (his feast day) 687. His body, which was said to have remained for many years in a state of incorruption and was carried away by the monks when they were driven by the Danes from Lindisfarne, was finally buried in Durham Cathedral. An extended account of his life appears in *The *Ecclesiastical History of the English People* by *Bede.

CUTLER, Ivor

See PERFORMANCE POETRY.

cyborg

A term derived from 'cybernetic organism' to signify a fusion of human and machine. In *science fiction, this allows a rich range of explorations of the sense of uncanniness as we confront an Other. Deirdre, in C. L. Moore's 'No Woman Born' (1944), who has her brain inserted into a metal body, inspires unease because of her and her companions' questions about her identity. Is she still human? Is she female? Other fictions, such as Cordwainer Smith's 'Scanners Live in vain' (1950) and Frederik *Pohl's *Man Plus* (1976), explore the deliberate creation of cyborgs to cope with hostile environments such as space.

Cymbeline

A play by *Shakespeare, first published in the first *folio of 1623. It may have been written in 1610/11; Simon Forman saw a performance, perhaps at the *Globe, probably in April 1611. He refers to its heroine as Innogen. Its sources are *Holinshed, *A *Mirror for Magistrates*, and perhaps Boccaccio's *Decameron* (*see also* PHILASTER). Though included among the tragedies in the folio, it is now generally classified as a 'romance'. The play was much loved in the 19th century, however; *Tennyson died with a copy of it on the coverlet of his bed. G. B. *Shaw wrote an altered version of the long fifth act, published in 1938 under the title *Cymbeline Refinished*.

Innogen, daughter of Cymbeline, king of Britain, has secretly married Leonatus Posthumus, a 'poor but worthy gentleman'. The queen, Innogen's stepmother, determined that her clownish son Cloten shall marry Innogen, reveals the secret marriage to the king, who banishes Posthumus. In Rome Posthumus boasts of Innogen's virtue and makes a wager with Giacomo that if he can seduce Innogen he shall have a diamond ring that Innogen had given him. Giacomo is rejected by Innogen, but by hiding in her bedchamber he observes details of her room and her body which persuade Posthumus of her infidelity, and he receives the ring. Posthumus orders his servant Pisanio to kill Innogen; but Pisanio instead provides her with male disguise, sending a bloody cloth to Posthumus to convince him of her death. Under the name Fidele Innogen becomes a page to Belarius and Cymbeline's two lost sons, Guiderius and Arviragus, living in a cave in Wales. Fidele sickens and is found as dead by the brothers, who speak the dirge 'Fear no more the heat o'th'sun'. Left alone she revives, only to discover at her side Cloten's headless corpse, which she believes, because of his borrowed garments, to be that of her husband Posthumus. A Roman army invades Britain; Innogen falls into the hands of the general Lucius and becomes his page. The Britons defeat the Romans, thanks to the courage of Belarius and his two sons, aided by the disguised Posthumus. However, Posthumus, pretending to be a Roman, is subsequently taken prisoner. Lucius pleads with Cymbeline for the life of Fidele/Innogen: moved by something familiar in her appearance, he spares her life and grants her a favour. She asks that Giacomo be forced to tell how he came by the ring he wears. Posthumus, learning from this confession that his wife is innocent but believing her dead, is in despair till Innogen reveals herself. The king's joy at recovering his daughter is intensified when Belarius restores to him his two lost sons, and the scene ends in a general reconciliation. Tennyson described Posthumus' words to Innogen on being reconciled with her, 'Hang there like fruit, my soul, | Till the tree die!', as 'the tenderest lines in Shakespeare'.

CYNEWULF Probably a Northumbrian or Mercian poet of the 9th or early 10th century. Modern scholarship restricts attribution to him of four extant poems, all of which end with his signature in runes. They are *Juliana* (the life of a virgin martyr) and *Christ II* in the *Exeter Book (the last is a poem on the Ascension, placed between poems on the Incarnation and on the Last Judgement, the three together also often treated as a composite poem, *Christ*); and *The Fates of the Apostles* (of slightly more doubtful attribution than the others) and *Elene*, the story of the finding of the Cross by St Helena, the mother of the Roman emperor Constantine, in the *Vercelli Book.

Cynthia (1) a name for Artemis or Diana, from Mount Cynthus in Delos, where Artemis was born, and used poetically to denote the moon; (2) the name given by the Roman poet *Propertius to his mistress; (3) deriving from (1), a name used by Edmund *Spenser (in *Colin Clouts Come Home Againe), Walter *Ralegh, and others to denote *Elizabeth I as virgin moon goddess.

Cynthia's Revels An allegorical comedy by Ben *Jonson, performed 1600 by the Children of the Chapel at the *Blackfriars Theatre, printed 1601. The play satirizes court vices represented by characters with Greek names signifying their failings. They perform in *masques, devised by the wise poet Crites, in which each character impersonates his complementary virtue. As usual in plays acted by boys, who were also choristers, there are numerous songs, including 'Queen and huntress, chaste and fair', one of Jonson's most famous. *See* PAUL'S, CHILDREN OF.

Cypresse Grove, A *See* DRUMMOND OF HAWTHORNDEN.

CYRANO DE BERGERAC (1619–55) French soldier, dramatist, and novelist, author of the intellectually daring (and therefore posthumously published) *L'Autre Monde* (*The Other World*), which prefigures modern *science fiction. His colourful and controversial life is the subject of a highly successful play by Edmond Rostand.

DABYDEEN, David (1956–) Guyanese-born poet and novelist. Recurrent themes in Dabydeen's poetry include an exploration of slavery and indentureship, the cultural denigration and dislocation resulting from colonialism, and the power of language to redeem. *Slave Song* (1984) is notable for its innovative use of Guyanese rural *Creole; the poems are accompanied by a 'translation' and commentary in Standard English highlighting the cultural power relationships between the two forms of language. The long poem *Turner* (1994) takes the submerged African head in J. M. W. *Turner's painting *The Slave Ship* (1840) as its starting point. Dabydeen's first novel, *The Intended* (1991), refers to Joseph *Conrad's 'Heart of Darkness' and is set in multicultural south London, following the learning experiences of a clever Guyanese schoolboy; *Disappearance* (1993) is narrated by a West Indian engineer working in a Kentish village, and *The Counting House* (1996) is a migrants' story set in the 19th century. *A Harlot's Progress* (1999) imagines the life of the black boy in William *Hogarth's series of pictures; *Our Lady of Demerara* (2004) is a quest novel. *See* SLAVERY.

DACRE, Charlotte (?1782–1825) The pseudonym of Charlotte Byrne, née King, under which name she published erotically charged *Gothic fictions. Also a poet, writing as 'Rosa Matilda' for the *Morning Post*, she published *Hours of Solitude* (1805) as Charlotte Dacre. The poems reputedly influenced Lord *Byron's *Hours of Idleness* (1807), although he later satirized her in *English Bards and Scotch Reviewers* (1809). She also published in 1805 a notorious Gothic novel, *The Confessions of the Nun of St. Omer*, which was followed in 1806 by *Zofloya, or The Moor*, the fiction by which she is best known today.

dactyl A trisyllabic metrical *foot in which the first syllable only is stressed. The dactylic *hexameter was the line of Greek epic verse; but continuous dactylic *metre is rare in English: Alfred Tennyson's 'The *Charge of the Light Brigade' (1854) employs truncated dactylic *dimeters, Thomas *Hardy's 'The Voice' (1914) dactylic *tetrameters.

DAFYDD AP GWILYM (*c.*1315–*c.*1350) Welsh poet. He became a professional poet, travelling through Wales to give performances of his work, which marries European conventions (notably that of *courtly love) to indigenous modes. Dafydd perfected the seven-syllable *cywydd* metre that would dominate Welsh art poetry for centuries.

D'AGUIAR, Fred (1960–) London-born poet and novelist, brought up as a child in Guyana. He has written three volumes of poetry, *Mama Dot* (1985), which explores his early life in Guyana, *Airy Hall* (1989), and *British Subjects* (1993), which closely examines British and transcultural identity and contains a sequence called 'Frail Deposits', dedicated to Wilson *Harris, about a return trip to Guyana. His novels are *The Longest Memory* (1994), an intense, lyrical, brutal evocation of the life of Whitechapel, an 18th-century plantation slave in Virginia; *Dear Future* (1997), whose title refers to the letters its clairvoyant child protagonist writes to the future; and *Feeding the Ghosts* (1997), about the voyage of a slave ship returning from Africa, the captain of which throws his sick slaves overboard and is held to account by a survivor. The protagonist of *Bethany Bettany* (2003) is a 5-year-old girl whose mother hands her over to her dead father's family; she becomes a scapegoat for all their resentments. D'Aguiar's stage play *A Jamaican Airman Foresees his Death* was staged at the *Royal Court in 1995. *Bill of Rights* (1998) is a long poem on the theme of the 1978 Jonestown massacre/mass suicide in Guyana; *Bloodlines* (2000) is a narrative poem in rhyming verse about a black slave and her white lover. *Continental Shelf* (2009) contains elegies to those killed in the mass shooting at Virginia Tech

State University, where D'Aguiar is a professor. *See* SLAVERY.

DAHL, Roald (1916–1990) Short story writer, novelist, and children's writer, born of Norwegian parents in Llandaff, Wales. He describes his unhappy schooldays in the autobiographical *Boy* (1984). He established a reputation as a writer with a penchant for the macabre and the 'cruel tale': major collections include *Someone Like You* (USA 1953, UK 1954), *Kiss Kiss* (1960), and *Switch Back* (1974). Many of his stories were dramatized for television and republished as *Tales of the Unexpected* (1979). Dahl also wrote film scripts for Ian *Fleming's *You Only Live Twice* (1967) and *Chitty Chitty Bang Bang* (1968). In 1961 he published his first novel for children, *James and the Giant Peach* (UK 1967), followed by the phenomenally successful *Charlie and the Chocolate Factory* (1964, UK 1967). The book was filmed in 1971, in a version that Dahl disliked, as *Willie Wonka and the Chocolate Factory*, and again in 2005.

Dahl became the world's most successful children's writer in the 1970s and 1980s with books such as *The BFG* (1982) and *Matilda* (1988). His books have been widely criticized for misogyny (*The Witches*, 1983), racism (the 'oompa-loompas' in *Charlie and the Chocolate Factory*), and for violence and right-wing views. He benefited from a partnership with the illustrator Quentin *Blake.

DAHLBERG, Edward (1900–77) American writer. His early novels, including *Bottom Dogs* (1929), published with an introduction by D. H. *Lawrence, *From Flushing to Calvary* (1932), and *Those Who Perish* (1934) are proletarian fiction. *Do These Bones Live?* (1941) is an extended meditation on the American literary heritage of Edgar Allan *Poe and others.

Daily News Founded by Charles *Dickens in 1845 as a Liberal rival to the *Morning Chronicle*; the first issue appeared on 21 January 1846. John *Forster succeeded Dickens as editor. Among its notable contributors and members of staff were Harriet *Martineau, Andrew *Lang, George Bernard *Shaw, H. G. *Wells, Arnold *Bennett, and the eminent war correspondent Archibald Forbes (1839–1900). It became the *News Chronicle* in 1930, having absorbed the *Daily Chronicle*, and survived under this title until 1960.

Daisy Miller One of Henry *James's most popular stories, published 1879, dramatized by James (1883). Daisy Miller travels to Europe with her wealthy, commonplace mother, and in her innocence and audacity offends convention and seems to compromise her reputation. She dies in Rome of malaria. She is one of the most notable and charming of James's portrayals of 'the American girl'.

DALRYMPLE, William (1965–) Historian, travel writer, and journalist. Dalrymple's books, many of them on India, include *In Xanadu* (1989), *City of Djinns* (1993), *From the Holy Mountain* (1997), *The Age of Kali* (1998), *White Mughals* (2002), and *The Last Mughal* (2006). Characterized by their deep historical research and elegant prose, his works have placed him at the forefront of a new generation of British travel writers. His mature writings challenge Samuel P. Huntington's 'clash of civilizations' theory and the orthodoxies of the 'war on terror' by focusing on the history of coexistence of Islam and Christianity and on the productive but often forgotten exchanges between them. Dalrymple, who divides his time between Delhi and London, presented the BBC series 'Indian Journeys' (2002).

Damascus, road to *See* PAUL, ST.

Damon A shepherd singer in *Virgil's eighth *Eclogue*; a name adopted by poets for a rustic swain. Cf. *Epitaphium Damonis*, *Milton's Latin elegy on his friend Diodati.

DAMPIER, William (1652–1715) Buccaneer and explorer, who made three circumnavigations of the globe. His lively accounts of his adventures, particularly *A New Voyage round the World* (1697) and *A Voyage to New Holland* (1703, 1709), set the vogue for exploration narratives as entertainment and inspired fictional works. He participated in expeditions that marooned and rescued Alexander *Selkirk, the model for *Robinson Crusoe. His was the first extended description of Aboriginal Australians. While his scientific interest in plants and peoples was new, he displayed vestiges of older enthusiasms for 'marvels'.

Dance of Death (danse macabre, danse macabré) Gave expression to the sense especially prominent in the 15th century (perhaps as a consequence of the plague and the preaching of the mendicant friars) of the ubiquity of Death the leveller. The Dance appears to have first taken shape in France, as a mimed sermon in which figures typical of various orders of society were seized and hauled away each by its own corpse (not, as later, by the personification of Death). The earliest known painting of the Dance, accompanied by versified dialogues between living and dead, was made in 1424 in the cemetery of the Innocents in Paris.

DANE, Clemence (1888–1965) Pseudonym of Winifred Ashton, novelist and playwright. Her experiences as a teacher in a girls' school are reflected in her first novel, *Regiment of Women* (1917), which explores a lesbian relationship. Her first play, *A Bill of Divorcement* (1921), enjoyed a popular success never quite matched by her later plays, which include *Will Shakespeare* (1921), a blank verse drama, and *Wild Decembers* (1932), about the *Brontës.

DANGAREMBGA, Tsitsi (1959–) Film director and writer, born in Zimbabwe. Her novel *Nervous Conditions* (1988) challenges colonial and Shona patriarchy. Its opening line, 'I was not sorry when my brother died', defies the gendered role expected of the narrator, Tambudzai; she inherits her brother's education but it familiarizes her with a range of female nervous conditions. She recognizes that men control the traditional and the modernizing Rhodesian world. A second novel, *The Book of Not* (2006), continues Tambu's personal liberation struggle, which takes place during her country's violent guerrilla war.

Daniel An Old English poem of 764 lines, in the *Junius Manuscript. It paraphrases the Old Testament Book of Daniel.

Daniel, Book of *See* BIBLE.

DANIEL, Samuel (?1562–1619) Poet and historian, tutor to William Herbert, third earl of Pembroke (1580–1630), and later to Lady Anne *Clifford. In 1592 he published *Delia*, a collection of sonnets inspired by *Tasso and Philippe Desportes (1546–1606). Edmund *Spenser mentioned him by name in *Colin Clouts Come Home Againe*. Daniel's next work was *Cleopatra* (1594), a Senecan tragedy. *Musophilus: Containing a General Defence of Learning* appeared in 1599. In 1603 he published his verse 'Epistles' and *A Defence of Rhyme*, the latter being a reply to Thomas *Campion's *Observations in the Art of English Poesy*. His career as a court poet developed with his masques and plays, *The Vision of the Twelve Goddesses* (1604), *The Queen's Arcadia* (1606), *Tethys' Festival* (1610), and *Hymen's Triumph* (performed 1614, published 1615). His second tragedy, *Philotas*, performed in the autumn of 1604, was held—perhaps justly—to allude closely and sympathetically to the rebellion of the earl of *Essex in 1600. Daniel affixed an 'Apology' when the play was published in 1605. His weightiest work was his *Civil Wars*, a verse epic on the Wars of the Roses, published 1595–1609. In the *Romantic period, Charles *Lamb, William *Wordsworth, and S. T. *Coleridge were among those who read him appreciatively, the last finding his style and language as 'pure and manly' as Wordsworth's own.

Daniel Deronda George *Eliot's last novel, published 1876. Gwendolen Harleth, high-spirited, confident, and self-centred, marries Henleigh Grandcourt, an arrogant, selfish, and cold-hearted man of the world, for his money and his position, to save her mother, sisters, and herself from destitution, in spite of the fact that she knows of (and has indeed met) Lydia Glasher, who has had a long-standing affair with Grandcourt, and children by him. She suffers in consequence in terms of guilt and a sense of her husband's increasing power over her. In her misery she comes increasingly under the influence of the idealistic Daniel Deronda, who becomes her spiritual adviser. It is gradually revealed that he is not, as he had assumed, an illegitimate cousin of Grandcourt, but the son of a Jewish singer of international renown. This discovery strengthens his bonds with Mirah, a young Jewish singer whom he has saved from drowning, and her brother Mordecai, an intellectual Jewish nationalist. Gwendolen's husband is drowned at Genoa, in a manner that leaves her feeling partly guilty for his death; she confesses to Deronda, but discovers to her initial despair that he is to marry Mirah and devote himself to the Jewish cause. One of the themes of the novel is the nature of professional and artistic dedication, explored through Gwendolen's dilettante expectations, the musician Klesmer's seriousness and insistence on constant application, Mirah's acceptance of a hard-working but less than illustrious career, and the passionate and self-glorifying commitment of Deronda's mother, who sacrificed her own child to her success.

DANTE ALIGHIERI (1265–1321) Poet, born at Florence of a Guelf family. During the early period of his life he fell in love with the girl whom he celebrates under the name of *Beatrice in the *Vita nuova* and the *Divina commedia*. When she died, in 1290, Dante was grief-stricken and sought consolation in the study of philosophy. The *Vita nuova*, written in the period 1290–4, brings together 31 poems, most of them relating to his love for Beatrice. There is a translation by Dante Gabriel *Rossetti (1861).

DANZIGER, Nick (1958–) Photojournalist and travel writer, born in London. He went to school in Switzerland and studied at Chelsea Art School. *Danziger's Travels* (1987) records his overland journey to China, which involved crossing Afghanistan disguised as a mujahed during a Soviet offensive. Its sequel, *Danziger's Adventures* (1992), is a collection of shorter pieces. Jack *London was the inspiration for *Danziger's Britain* (1997), an investigation of poverty in the United Kingdom.

Daphnaïda An elegy by Edmund *Spenser closely modelled on Geoffrey *Chaucer's *Book of the Duchess*.

Daphnis and Chloe A Greek pastoral romance written by an otherwise unknown 'Longus' perhaps in the 2nd or 3rd centuries AD. Amyot's translation into French made it a popular text; Angel Day translated Amyot's version (1587), and George *Moore produced a modern version in 1924.

Dares Phrygius A Trojan priest mentioned in the *Iliad* (5. 9). He was supposed to have been the author of an account of the fall of Troy of which a Latin prose version is extant. This work, *De Excidio Troiae*, dating probably from the 5th century AD, provided, together with the complementary history of *Dictys Cretensis, the only detailed account of the Trojan War available in the medieval West.

Darkness at Noon A novel by Arthur *Koestler, published 1940, translated from German. It deals with the arrest, imprisonment, trial, and execution of N. S. Rubashov in an unnamed dictatorship over which 'No. 1' presides. Koestler describes Rubashov as 'a synthesis of the lives of a number of men who were victims of the so-called Moscow trials', and the novel did much to draw attention to the nature of Stalin's regime.

DARWIN, Charles (1809–82) Naturalist and author, grandson of Erasmus *Darwin. He embarked in 1831 with Robert Fitzroy as naturalist on the *Beagle*, bound for South America, returned in 1836, and published in 1839 his *Journal of Researches into the Geology and Natural History of the Various Countries Visited by H.M.S. Beagle*. His great work *On the *Origin of Species by Means of Natural Selection* appeared in 1859. Darwin had received from Alfred Russel *Wallace a sketch of his theory. Building upon the Uniformitarian geology of Charles Lyell (1797–1875), which supposed a very great antiquity for the earth and slow, regular change, Darwin argued for a natural, not divine, origin of species. In the competitive struggle for existence, creatures possessing advantageous mutations would be favoured, eventually evolving

into new species. In the 'survival of the fittest' (a phrase coined by Herbert *Spencer, but accepted by Darwin) organic descent was achieved by natural selection, by analogy with the artificial selection of the stockbreeder. Darwin, an agnostic, saw no higher moral or religious ends in evolution, only chance and necessity. His book gave rise to intense opposition, but found distinguished supporters in T. H. *Huxley, Lyell, and Sir Joseph Hooker (1817–1911); the reverberation of his ideas can be seen throughout the literature of the second half of the 19th century. In *The Descent of Man* (1871) Darwin discussed sexual selection, and argued that man too had evolved, from the higher primates. *The Life and Letters of Darwin* (1887–8) was edited by his son Francis Darwin.

(⊕) SEE WEB LINKS

• The Darwin Correspondence Project

DARWIN, Erasmus (1731–1802) Physician, natural philosopher, and poet. He embodied the botanical system of Linnaeus (whose works he translated) in *The Loves of the Plants* (1789). This became Part II of *The Botanic Garden* (1791), of which Part I was 'The Economy of Vegetation'. The poem, supplemented by notes on many scientific and industrial matters, expounds an embryonic theory of evolution. It was targeted by George Canning and John Hookham *Frere in 'The Loves of the Triangles', in the *Anti-Jacobin* in 1798. In his prose *Zoonomia* (1794–6), *Wordsworth's source for the story of Goody Blake, Darwin expounds the laws of organic life, normal and pathological, on evolutionary principles. Anna *Seward published *Memoirs* of him in 1804; the theories of his grandson Charles *Darwin owe some initial impetus to his grandfather's controversial views.

D'AVENANT, Sir William (1606–68) Playwright, poet, and theatre manager, rumoured to be the natural son of William *Shakespeare. In 1630–32 he was gravely ill with syphilis, a subject referred to in his own works and in the jests of others; his comic masterpiece *The *Wits*, was performed 1633, printed 1636. In 1638 he succeeded to Ben *Jonson's pension as unofficial *poet laureate, then actively supported Charles I in the Civil War and was knighted by him in 1643. In 1645 he visited Paris, and met Thomas *Hobbes, to whom he addressed his *Preface* (1650) to *Gondibert* (1651). He was imprisoned in the Tower in 1650–52, and is said to have been saved by John *Milton. With *The*

Siege of Rhodes (1656) he simultaneously evaded the ban on stage plays and produced one of the earliest English operas (but *see also* FLECKNOE, RICHARD). After the *Restoration he and Thomas *Killigrew the elder obtained patents from Charles II giving them the monopoly of acting in London. Among the innovations of the period were movable scenery and the use of actresses. In conjunction with John Dryden, D'Avenant adapted various of Shakespeare's plays to suit the taste of the day, among them *The *Tempest* (1667); he is satirized with John *Dryden in Buckingham's *The *Rehearsal*.

DAVENPORT, Guy (1927–2005) American writer, painter, and translator. His best-known essay collection is *The Geography of the Imagination* (1981), he also published several volumes of poetry, and translated *Sappho and others. But he became known mainly for his collections of short stories which deploy a wide range of verbal registers and narrative collage effects: *Tatlin!* (1974), *Da Vinci's Bicycle* (1979), and *Eclogues* (1981). Like Donald Barthelme, he was interested in the visual arts, including printing and book design, and he prepared a special edition of Canto CX for Ezra *Pound's 80th birthday. He experimented with typography and graphics in a number of his works.

DAVID *Bible poet and second king of Israel (reigned *c*.1010–*c*.970 BC). A figure of immense importance for Judaism and Christianity as the greatest king, creator of *Jerusalem as the capital of the nation, recipient of the covenant originally made with Abraham, and ancestor of Jesus, David has fascinated writers as a supremely noble and devastatingly human figure, and as an archetypal poet, 'the sweet psalmist of Israel' (2 Sam. 23: 1).

A youngest son and shepherd boy, he is anointed king by Samuel while Saul still reigns. His music soothes Saul's troubled spirit, and his skill with the sling overcomes the Philistine champion, Goliath. War between Saul and David ends when Saul and his son Jonathan die in battle with the Philistines. His lament for them is a high point of biblical poetry ('How are the mighty fallen!', 2 Sam. 1: 27). While he unites and strengthens the kingdom, his personal and family life disintegrates. The turning point is his adultery with Bathsheba, whose husband Uriah he has killed in battle.

He is traditionally the author of the *Psalms, many of which have been connected with incidents in his life. See 1 Samuel to 1 Kings 2, also 1 Chronicles 10–29.

David and Fair Bethsabe, The Love of King A play in blank verse by George *Peele, *c*.1581–94, printed 1599.

David Copperfield A novel by Charles *Dickens, published 1849–50. 'Of all my books,' wrote Dickens, 'I like this the best.' The most autobiographical of Dickens's novels, and much adapted, it was the first to be written as a first-person narrative, showing how the young David learns to govern 'the first mistaken impulse of the undisciplined heart'. David Copperfield is born at Blunderstone in Suffolk, soon after the death of his father. His mother, a gentle, weak woman, marries again, and the hypocritical cruelty of her second husband, Mr Murdstone, and his sister Jane Murdstone drives her to an early grave. Young Copperfield, who has proved recalcitrant, is sent to school, where he is bullied by the tyrannical headmaster Creakle, but makes two friends in the fascinating Steerforth and the good-humoured plodding Traddles. A period in London, where he lives a life of poverty and misery, is enlivened by his acquaintance with the impecunious Mr Micawber. He runs away and walks to Dover to throw himself on the mercy of his aunt Betsey Trotwood, an eccentric old lady. He is kindly received and given a new home, which he shares with an amiable lunatic, Mr Dick. Copperfield continues his education at Canterbury, living in the house of Miss Trotwood's lawyer, Mr Wickfield, whose daughter Agnes exerts a powerful influence on the rest of his life. He then enters Doctors' Commons, being articled to Mr Spenlow. Meanwhile, he renews his friendship with Steerforth and introduces him to the family of his old nurse, Clara Peggotty, married to *Barkis the carrier. The family consists of Mr Peggotty, a Yarmouth fisherman, his nephew Ham, and the latter's cousin Little Em'ly, whom Ham is about to marry. Mr Peggotty also shares his home with the widow Mrs Gummidge. Steerforth induces Em'ly to run away with him. Mr Peggotty sets out to find her, following her through many countries, and finally recovering her after she has been cast off by Steerforth. The latter's crime brings unhappiness to his mother and to her protégée Rosa Dartle, who loves Steerforth. The tragedy finds its culmination in the shipwreck and drowning of Steerforth, and the death of Ham in trying to save him.

Meanwhile Copperfield, blind to the affection of Agnes Wickfield, marries Dora Spenlow, a pretty empty-headed child, and becomes a celebrated author. Dora dies after a few years of married life and Copperfield, at first disconsolate, awakens to a growing appreciation and love of Agnes. Her father has fallen into the toils of a villainous and cunning clerk, Uriah Heep, who under the cloak of fawning humility has acquired complete control over him, reduced him to the verge of imbecility, and nearly ruined him. Uriah also aspires to marry Agnes. But his misdeeds are exposed by Micawber, employed as his clerk, with the assistance of Traddles, now a barrister. Uriah is sent to prison for life. Copperfield marries Agnes, and Mr Peggotty, with Em'ly and Mrs Gummidge, prospers in Australia, where Mr Micawber, relieved of his debts, appears finally as a respected colonial magistrate.

'Davideis' *See* COWLEY, ABRAHAM.

David Simple, The Adventures of, In Search of a Real Friend Novel by Sarah *Fielding (1744), described in the preface (by the author's brother, Henry *Fielding) as an exploration of 'the Mazes, Windings, and Labyrinths' of the heart.

DAVIDSON, John (1857–1909) Scottish poet, dramatist, and journalist. Davidson was a schoolmaster before moving to London, where he contributed to the *Yellow Book* and joined the *Rhymers Club. He became well known through *Fleet Street Eclogues* (1893) and *Ballads and Songs* (1894). His best-known monologue is the lively and satirical 'Thirty Bob a Week'. Between 1901 and 1908 he wrote a series of 'Testaments', expounding in verse his materialistic and rebellious philosophy, and an unfinished dramatic trilogy, *God and Mammon* (1907–8). His death by drowning was a suspected suicide. Davidson later influenced T. S. *Eliot, who admired his urban imagery, and Hugh *MacDiarmid.

DAVIDSON, Robyn (1950–) Australian travel writer. Davidson's first book, *Tracks* (1980), recounts her 1,700-mile journey across the desert interior of Australia. *Desert Places* (1996) describes a sojourn with Rajasthani nomads. *Ancestors* (1990) is a novel.

DAVIE, Donald (1922–95) Poet and critic, educated at Cambridge University, where he was influenced by the ethos of F. R. *Leavis and the Cambridge English school. His critical work *Purity of Diction in English Verse* (1952) expressed many of the anti-Romantic, anti-bohemian ideals of the *Movement and of his fellow contributors to *New Lines. His volumes of poetry include *Brides of Reason* (1955), *A Winter Talent* (1957), *Essex Poems* (1969), and

In the Stopping Train (1977); two volumes of collected poems appeared in 1972 (1950–70) and 1983 (1971–83). His poems are philosophical, speculative, and erudite, manifesting a mind that (in his own phrase) 'moves most easily and happily among abstractions', yet they also vividly evoke the various landscapes of his travels and academic appointments, from Ireland to California, from Essex to Italy, and show a marked rejection of the English provincialism which characterized some of his friends from the Movement. Davie adapted the *Pan Tadeusz* of Adam Mickiewicz in *The Forests of Lithuania* (1959). A further *Collected Poems* appeared in 2002.

DAVIES, Edward (Celtic Davies) (1756–1831) Antiquarian, poet, dramatist, and clergyman whose *Celtic Researches* (1804) and *The Mythology and Rites of the Celtic Druids* (1809) took issue with some of the wilder enthusiasms of Iolo Marganwg (Edward *Williams), though without questioning the fundamentals of his druidism.

DAVIES, Idris (1903–53) Welsh poet, who published two book-length sequences, *Gwalia Deserta* (1938) and *The Angry Summer* (1943), along with the miscellaneous *Tonypandy and Other Poems* (1945). Almost all his work is concerned with the plight of the industrial valleys of south Wales during and after the General Strike of 1926. It represents the most sustained British attempt to create a popularly accessible socialist poetry.

DAVIES, John (*c.*1564–1618) of Hereford, poet and writing-master. He published several volumes of verse, epitaphs, *epigrams, and so on, including *Microcosmos* (1603), *The Muses' Sacrifice*, containing the famous 'Picture of an Happy Man' (1612), and *Wit's Bedlam* (1617). Some of his epigrams, most of which are contained in *The Scourge of Folly* (1611), are valuable for their notices of Ben *Jonson, John *Fletcher, and other contemporary poets.

DAVIES, Sir John (1569–1626) Poet and lawyer. His *Orchestra, or A Poeme of Dauncing*, published in 1596, describes the attempts of the suitor Antinous to persuade Penelope to dance with him, giving a long account of the antiquity and universality of dancing. The *Hymnes of Astraea* and *Nosce Teipsum* both appeared in 1599: the latter, written in *quatrains, is a philosophical poem on the nature of man and the nature and immortality of the soul. His *Epigrammes* ('Middleborough' [?London], *c.*1599) and

Gullinge Sonnets (in manuscript) reflect his keen, satirical interest in the contemporary scene.

DAVIES, Rhys (1901–78) Prolific Welsh writer, whose novels include *The Withered Root* (1927), *Jubilee Blues* (1938), and *The Black Venus* (1944). The best of Davies's many short stories are admired for their Chekhovian objectivity and implicit homoeroticism.

DAVIES, Robertson (1913–95) Canadian novelist, playwright, and critic, born in Thamesville, Ontario (the fictional Deptford). Collections of his journalism include pieces published under the pseudonym Samuel Marchbanks; *The Diary of Samuel Marchbanks* (1947), *The Table Talk of Samuel Marchbanks* (1949), and *Samuel Marchbanks' Almanack* (1967); *A Voice from the Attic* (1960); *The Enthusiasms of Robertson Davies* (1979) and *The Well-Tempered Critic* (1981). Amongst the best of his full-length plays are *Fortune, my Foe* (1949), *At my Heart's Core* (1950), *A Jig for the Gypsy* (1954), *Hunting Stuart* (written in 1955; pub. 1972), and *General Confession* (written 1956; pub. 1972). His principal work as a novelist is contained in three extensive trilogies: the Salterton Trilogy—*Tempest-Tost* (1951), *Leaven of Malice* (1954), and *A Mixture of Frailties* (1958)—a sequence of urbane comedies of manners; the Deptford Trilogy, usually considered the best of the three—*Fifth Business* (1970), *The Manticore* (1972), and *World of Wonders* (1975); and the Cornish Trilogy—*The Rebel Angels* (1981), *What's Bred in the Bone* (1985), and *The Lyre of Orpheus* (1988). A collection of eighteen ghost stories was published as *High Spirits* in 1982. *The Cunning Man* (1995) follows the consequences of the death of a priest who collapses and dies while celebrating Holy Communion.

DAVIES, W. H. (William Henry) (1871–1940) Poet and autobiographer, born at Newport, Monmouthshire, Wales. He went as a young man to America, where he spent several poverty-stricken years. He lost a leg in an accident there, an experience recounted in a few laconic paragraphs in his *The Autobiography of a Super-Tramp*, published in 1908 with a preface by George Bernard *Shaw, after *The Soul's Destroyer and Other Poems* (1905). Davies's best-known poems, such as 'Leisure', record his child-like response to the natural world. In 1923 he married Helen, a girl much younger than himself, and he tells the story in *Young*

Emma, eventually published in 1980. *The Complete Poems* appeared in 1963.

DAVYS, Mary (1674–1732) Novelist, who moved from Dublin to London, York, and then Cambridge, where she opened a coffee shop. Her novels include the autobiographical travel story *The Fugitive* (1705, later expanded as *The Merry Wanderer*); *The Reform'd Coquet* (1724), whose sober hero disguises himself to protect the flighty heroine; *Familiar Letters* (1725), courtship exchanges with political commentary; and *The Accomplish'd Rake* (1727), a harshly satirical account of a 'modern fine gentleman'. One comedy, *The Northern Heiress* (1716), was performed; another, *The Self-Rival*, was published in her two-volume *Works* (1725).

DAY, John (*c.*1574–*c.*1640) Playwright; from 1598 to 1603 he wrote regularly for the Admiral's Men in collaboration with Henry *Chettle, Thomas *Dekker, and William Haughton (d. 1605). In 1607 he collaborated with George *Wilkins and William *Rowley on *The Travels of the Three English Brothers*, acted at the Red Bull. His best work, *The Parliament of Bees*, appeared perhaps in 1607, although the earliest extant copy is of 1641. It is an inventive dramatic allegory or masque, containing a series of 'characters' of different bees with their virtues and vices, and ending with Oberon's Star Chamber, where he judges the offenders, the wasp, the drone, and the humble bee.

DAY, Thomas (1748–89) Radical pamphleteer and author of the influential children's book *The History of Sandford and Merton* (3 vols, 1783–9), intended to illustrate the doctrine that people may be made good by reason and instruction. It consists of a series of episodes in which the rich and objectionable Tommy Merton is contrasted with the upright and tender-hearted Harry Sandford, a farmer's son; eventually Tommy is reformed. Day also wrote *The History of Little Jack* (1787), about a young wild boy suckled by goats. Day was a friend of the educational theorist Richard Edgeworth (*see* EDGEWORTH, MARIA).

DAY-LEWIS, Cecil (C. Day Lewis) (1904–72) Poet, born in Ireland. At university in Oxford he became friends with W. H. *Auden, with whom he edited *Oxford Poetry* (1927), Louis *MacNeice, and Stephen *Spender (they have been called the 'MacSpaunday' group, or the *Pylon School). He joined the Communist Party in 1936, and in 1937 edited a socialist symposium, *The Mind in Chains*, with contributions from Edward *Upward, Charles *Madge,

Rex *Warner, and others. These preoccupations are not reflected in his earliest verse (such as *Beechen Vigil*, 1925), but become apparent in *Transitional Poem* (1929), *From Feathers to Iron* (1931), and *The Magnetic Mountain* (1933), all of which have a strong revolutionary flavour. The poor reception of *Noah and the Waters* (1936), a verse morality play about the class struggle, may have encouraged him to turn to the more pastoral themes of his later years.

During the 1930s he also wrote *detective fiction, under the pseudonym of 'Nicholas Blake'. His first work in this genre, *A Question of Proof* (1935), introducing his Audenesque detective Nigel Strangeways, was followed by many others. *The Friendly Tree* (1936) was the first of three largely autobiographical novels. He moved to Devon in 1938; his collections *Overtures to Death* (1938) and *Poems in Wartime* (1940) reflect obvious political concerns. He published translations of Virgil's *Georgics* (1940), Paul *Valéry (1946), and Virgil again (*The *Aeneid*, 1952; *The Eclogues*, 1963), and collections of verse including *An Italian Visit* (1953), which records a journey with Rosamond *Lehmann. He was professor of poetry at Oxford from 1951 to 1956, the first poet of distinction to hold the post since Matthew *Arnold, although Day-Lewis's literary reputation does not now rival that of Auden or MacNeice. In 1968 he was appointed *poet laureate. His autobiography, *The Buried Day*, was published in 1960, and *The Complete Poems of C. Day-Lewis* in 1992.

DEANE, Seamus (1940–) Irish poet, scholar, and novelist, a contemporary of Seamus *Heaney at Queen's University, Belfast. His literary criticism includes *Celtic Revivals* (1985) and *Strange Country: Modernity and Nationhood in Irish Writing since 1790* (1997). He was the general editor of the *Field Day Anthology of Irish Writing 550–1988* (1991). In his poetry and in *Reading in the Dark* (1996), an autobiographical novel, Deane focuses on the political and social landscape of Northern Ireland, showing sectarian violence and enmities as a lethal undercurrent to the domestic world.

Death's Jest-Book See BEDDOES, THOMAS LOVELL.

de BERNIÈRES, Louis (1954–) Novelist, born in London. He worked in Colombia before publishing his trilogy, *The War of Don Emmanuel's Nether Parts* (1990), *Señor Vivo and the Coca Lord* (1991), and *The Troublesome Offspring of Cardinal Guzman* (1992), which mingles *magic realism with political satire. *Captain

Corelli's Mandolin (1994), the historical romance with which he achieved greatest success, takes place on the Greek island of Cephallonia during the Second World War. *Birds without Wings* (2004), which chronicles the destruction of an initially peaceful, mixed Christian and Muslim community, is set in Turkey during the First World War.

decadence Associated with the French decadent (renamed symbolist) movement of the 1880s, which included the poets Paul *Verlaine and Stéphane *Mallarmé and the novelist Joris-Karl Huysmans (*À rebours*, 1884), the concept was applied in the English *fin-de-siècle* to literature, art, and culture characterized by extreme *aestheticism and perversity in style or subject matter. The most characteristic decadent works in England are Oscar *Wilde's *The Picture of Dorian Gray* (1890) and *Salome* (1894); the poetry of Ernest *Dowson and Arthur *Symons; and the art of Aubrey *Beardsley. See also MODERNISM; SYMBOLISM.

Decameron, The Giovanni *Boccaccio's masterpiece, a collection of 100 tales told over a period of ten days (hence the title). The stories, which have many different sources, are contained within a frame narrative (cornice), an innovative feature. This relates how seven young women and three young men flee Florence during the Black Death and take refuge in the countryside, where they entertain themselves by telling these tales. *The Decameron* celebrates especially 'ingegno'—quick-wittedness, as the best instrument for success in all walks of life. The work had much influence on English literature, notably on *Chaucer; sixteen of the tales were incorporated in William Painter's *Palace of Pleasure*. John *Keats and *Tennyson both produced versions of individual tales.

de CAMP, L. Sprague (1907–2000) Fantasy author, born in New York. *Lest Darkness Fall* (1941) and *The Incompleat Enchanter* (1941), written with Fletcher Pratt, fused *fantasy with *alternate history. Among later novels were completions of stories by Robert E. *Howard, of whom he wrote a biography.

Decline and Fall First novel of Evelyn *Waugh, published to great acclaim in 1928. It follows the hapless career of Paul Pennyfeather, whose trousers are removed during a dining club's drunken rumpus but who is sent down from Scone College, Oxford, for 'indecent behaviour' all the same. He becomes a schoolmaster at Llanabba Castle, where he encounters, among others, the dubious, bigamous, and irrepressible Captain Grimes, and Beste-Chetwynde, a pupil whose glamorous mother Margot eventually carries him off to the dangerous delights of high society. They are about to be married when Paul is arrested and subsequently imprisoned for Margot's activities in the White Slave trade; however, Margot arranges his escape, and he returns, unknown but under his own name, to resume his studies at Scone.

Decline and Fall of the Roman Empire, The History of the By Edward *Gibbon, volume i of the first (quarto) edition published 1776, volumes ii and iii 1781, and the last three volumes 1788. This monumental work falls into three divisions: from the age of Trajan and the Antonines to the subversion of the Western Empire; from the reign of Justinian in the East to the establishment of the second or German Empire of the West, under *Charlemagne; from the revival of the Western Empire to the taking of Constantinople by the Turks. It thus covers a period of about thirteen centuries, and comprehends such vast subjects as the establishment of Christianity, the movements and settlements of the Teutonic tribes, the conquests of the Muslims, and the Crusades. It traces, overall, the connection of the ancient world with the modern. Gibbon's prose is cool, lucid, and enlivened by ironic wit, much of it controversially aimed at the early church and the credulity and barbarism that overwhelmed the noble Roman virtues he admired.

deconstruction An approach to the reading of literary and philosophical texts that casts doubt upon the possibility of finding in them a definitive meaning, and that traces instead the multiplication (or 'dissemination') of possible meanings. A deconstructive reading of a poem, for instance, will conclude not with the discovery of its essential meaning, but with an impasse ('aporia') at which there are no grounds for choosing between two radically incompatible interpretations. According to deconstruction, literary texts resist any process of interpretation that would fix their meanings, appearing to 'undo' themselves as we try to tie them up. The basis for this apparently perverse approach to reading lies in a certain view of the philosophy of language, and specifically of the status of writing, as developed since 1966 by the French philosopher Jacques *Derrida, and by his American followers at Yale and elsewhere, including Paul *de Man. On this view, derived from a critical reassessment of Ferdinand de *Saussure, meaning can never be fully 'present'

in language, but is always deferred endlessly—as when one may look up a word in a dictionary, only to be given other words, and so on ad infinitum. While speech gives the illusion of a fixed origin—the presence of the speaker—that can guarantee the meaning of an utterance, writing is more clearly unauthenticated and open to unlicensed interpretation. Derrida's alarmingly simplified account of the history of Western philosophy since *Plato proposes that the dominant metaphysical tradition, in its deep suspicion of writing, has repeatedly tried to erect a fixed point of reference (a 'transcendental signified' such as God, Reason, absolute truth, etc.) outside the promiscuous circulation of signifiers, one that could hold in place a determinate system of truths and meanings. The project of deconstruction, then, is not to destroy but to unpick or dismantle such illusory systems, often by showing how their major categories are unstable or contaminated by their supposed opposites. In philosophical terms, deconstruction is a form of relativist scepticism in the tradition of Friedrich *Nietzsche. Its literary implications are partly compatible with the *New Criticism's rejection of the *'intentional fallacy' or any notion of the author fixing a text's meanings, as they are with New Critical interest in paradox as a feature of poetry; but they go further in challenging the claims of any critical system to possess 'the meaning' of a literary (or any other) work. In some forms of deconstruction, notably that of de Man, literary texts are held to be more honest than other writings, because they openly delight in the instabilities of language and meaning, through their use of figurative language for instance. The deconstructive style of literary analysis commonly emphasizes this through puns and word-play of its own. *See also* STRUCTURALISM.

DEE, John (1527–1609) Mathematician and astrologer. He became a fellow of Trinity College, Cambridge, where the stage effects he introduced into a performance of *Aristophanes' *Peace* procured him his reputation of being a magician, which was confirmed by his erudition and practice of crystallomancy, alchemy, and astrology. He wrote *Monas Hieroglyphica* (1564); a preface to the first English translation of Euclid (1570); and *General and Rare Memorials Pertayning to the Perfect Arte of Navigation* (1577). A profoundly learned scholar and hermeticist, he was also a sham: his conversations with angels were published in 1659.

DEEPING, Warwick (1877–1950) Doctor and novelist. His novel *Sorrell and Son* (1925), inspired by his experiences in the First World War, tells the story of a wounded ex-officer who takes a menial job to pay for his son's private education, where he will not be exposed to 'class hatred' or 'the sneers of the new young working-class intellectuals'.

Deerbrook A novel by Harriet *Martineau, published in 1839; her only venture into domestic realism. It describes the experiences of two orphaned sisters, Hester and Margaret Ibbotson, who move to Deerbook from Birmingham. The malicious gossip and misunderstanding that permeate village life are vividly described, and the novel's exploration of changing social conditions for women, the rise of the professions, and the potential for happiness and unhappiness for both men and women in marriage look forward to the interests of Charlotte *Brontë, Elizabeth *Gaskell, and George *Eliot.

defamiliarization The process by which literary works unsettle readers' habitual ways of seeing the world. According to the literary theories of S. T. *Coleridge in *Biographia Literaria (1817), of P. B. *Shelley in *Defence of Poetry (1840), and of several modern *formalist critics, it is a distinctive feature of literature, especially poetry, that it tears away what Shelley called the 'veil of familiarity' from the world, making us look at it afresh. The concept of 'estrangement' (*ostranenie*) developed by the Russian theorist Viktor Shklovsky (1893–1984) has influenced modern restatements of the case.

Defence of Poetry, A An essay by Philip *Sidney written in 1579–80. Sidney's chief aim was probably to write an English vindication of literature to match the many recently written on the Continent. Two editions of the work appeared posthumously in 1595: one, published by William Ponsonby, bore the title *The Defence of Poesie* and the other, published by Henry Olney, *An Apologie for Poetrie*.

Sidney expounds the antiquity of poetry in all cultures. He demonstrates its superiority to philosophy or history as a means of teaching virtue. After defining and distinguishing the 'parts, kinds, or species' of poetry, vindicating each in turn, he digresses to England: he sees contemporary poetry as having reached a low ebb, with little to be admired since Geoffrey *Chaucer, but affirms with prophetic confidence that major poetry in every genre, including drama, can be written in the English language. *A Defence of Poetry* is remarkable for the lightness of Sidney's

style and the catholicity of his examples, often drawn from experience. The poetic qualities of the essay in themselves illustrate the power of imaginative writing.

'Defence of Poetry, A' An essay by P. B. *Shelley, written at Pisa 1821, first published 1840. It was begun as a light-hearted reply to his friend Thomas Love *Peacock's magazine article 'The *Four Ages of Poetry'. In vindicating the role of poetry in a progressive society, and defending the whole notion of imaginative literature and thinking (not just 'poetry') within an industrial culture, Shelley came to write his own poetic credo with passionate force and conviction. Against a background of classical and European literature, he discusses in some detail the nature of poetic thought and inspiration; the problems of translation; the value of erotic writing; the connections between poetry and politics; and the essentially *moral* nature of the imagination—an emphasis he drew from S. T. *Coleridge.

Throughout, Shelley associates poetry with social freedom and love. He argues that the 'poetry of life' provides the one sure response to the destructive, isolating, alienating, 'accumulating and calculating processes' of modern civilization. The essay frequently sharpens to epigrammatic point: 'the great instrument of moral good is the imagination'; 'the freedom of women produced the poetry of sexual love'; and the famous peroration, ending 'Poets are the unacknowledged legislators of the world'—which must be read in context and which echoes in part the argument of Imlac in Samuel *Johnson's *Rasselas.

DEFOE, Daniel (1660–1731) Author, born in London, the son of James Foe, a tallow chandler. He changed his name to Defoe from c.1695, after his first bankruptcy. He attended Morton's academy for Dissenters at Newington Green with a view to becoming a Dissenting minister, but by the time he married Mary Tuffley in 1683/4 he was established as a hosiery merchant in Cornhill. Defoe travelled in Europe, and he was absorbed by travel and *travel literature throughout his career. He took part in Monmouth's rebellion, and in 1688 joined the advancing forces of William III. His first important work was *An Essay upon Projects* (1697), followed by *The True-Born Englishman* (1701), an immensely popular satirical poem attacking the prejudice against a king of foreign birth. In *The Shortest Way with Dissenters* (1702), Defoe, himself a Dissenter, impersonated the kind of High Tory who demanded the savage suppression of Dissent; for this he was fined, imprisoned (May–November 1703), and pilloried. While in prison he wrote his *Hymn to the Pillory*, a mock-Pindaric ode which was sold in the streets to sympathetic crowds. Defoe was rescued by Robert Harley, who arranged for his release and employed him as a secret agent; between 1703 and 1714 Defoe travelled around the country, testing the political climate, especially in Scotland on the eve of the Union (1707). In 1704 Defoe began *The *Review*; anti-Jacobite pamphlets in 1712–13 led to his prosecution by the Whigs and to a brief imprisonment, and he started a new trade journal, *Mercator*, in place of the *Review*. Defoe produced some 250 books, pamphlets, and journals, almost all of them anonymously or pseudonymously, but he turned to fiction late in life: **Robinson Crusoe* and its sequel the *Farther Adventures* appeared in 1719. The next five years saw the appearance of several fictions: *Captain *Singleton* (1720); **Moll Flanders*, *A Journal of the *Plague Year*, and **Colonel Jack* (1722); **Roxana*, **Memoirs of a Cavalier*, and *A New Voyage round the World* (1724). His *Tour through the Whole Island of Great Britain*, a guidebook in three volumes (1724–6), is a vivid account of the state of the country. He died in hiding from creditors in Ropemaker's Alley, Moorfields, and was buried in Bunhill Fields cemetery. Defoe's influence on the evolution of the English novel was enormous, though he would not have recognized 'the novel' as a label for what he was writing. His background in trade and commerce colours his prose with realistic, material detail, and the fictions are characterized by overarching narrative schemes of redemption through energetic work, pragmatic accumulation, and intelligent opportunism.

de FOREST, John William (1826–1906) American author of military memoirs and novels. His own military service in the Civil War informs *Miss Ravenel's Conversion from Secession to Loyalty* (1867), an early piece of Civil War realism.

Deformed Transformed, The An unfinished poetic drama by Lord *Byron, written in 1822 and published in 1824. Arnold, a hunchback, is reviled and rejected by his mother for his deformity: he resolves on suicide, but is prevented by a stranger, who offers to change his shape. This version of the Faust legend is in part a meditation by Byron, born with a club-foot, on the inspirational effects of disfigurement: 'deformity is daring. | It is its essence to o'ertake mankind.'

Degaré, Sir A metrical romance in 1,073 lines of short couplets from the early 14th century in a south Midland dialect, one of the Middle English *Breton lays. Degaré, son of a princess of Brittany who has been raped by a knight, is abandoned in a forest with a purse of money, a letter of directions, and a pair of gloves which are to fit the lady that he is to marry. The poem recounts Degaré's prowess in the course of his searches for his parents. The lady that the gloves fit is, in the event, his own mother, who recognizes him with joy as her son immediately after their wedding ceremony and before its consummation. It has been suggested that the romance may be a medievalizing of *Oedipus, as *Sir *Orfeo* is of *Orpheus.

DEIGHTON, Len *See* SPY FICTION.

Deirdre The heroine of the tale of 'The Fate of the Sons of Usnach' (pron. 'Usna'), one of the 'Three Sorrowful Stories of Erin'. King *Conchubar destined her for his wife and had her brought up in solitude. But she accidentally saw and fell in love with Naoise (or Naisi; pron. 'Neesha'), the son of Usnach, who with his brothers carried her off to Scotland. They were lured back by Conchubar and treacherously slain, and Deirdre took her own life. See Lady *Gregory, *Cuchulain of Muirthemne*, and the dramas on Deirdre by G. W. *Russell (Æ), J. M. *Synge, and W. B. *Yeats.

Deism ('natural religion') The belief in a Supreme Being as the source of finite existence, with rejection of revelation and the supernatural doctrines of Christianity. The Deists, who came into prominence at the end of the 17th and during the 18th century, were much influenced by the views of Lord *Herbert of Cherbury, often known as 'the father of Deism'. They include Charles Blount (1654–93), John *Toland, Matthew Tindal (1657–1733), Anthony Collins, Thomas Chubb (1679–1747), and the third earl of *Shaftesbury. John *Locke, who rejected the label of Deist, nevertheless contributed significantly to the movement with his *Reasonableness of Christianity* (1695). One of the most cogent refutations was by Joseph *Butler.

'Dejection: An Ode' An autobiographical poem by Samuel Taylor *Coleridge, first published in the *Morning Post*, 1802. It describes the loss of his poetical powers, the dulling of his responses to Nature, the breakdown of his marriage, and the paralysing effect of metaphysics (or opium). Paradoxically, this is achieved in verse of great emotional intensity and metrical brilliance. *Wordsworth partly answered it in his *'Intimations of Immortality' ode.

DEKKER, Thomas (?1572–1632) He was born and mainly lived in London, and was repeatedly imprisoned for debt. He was engaged by Philip *Henslowe about 1595 to write plays (over 40 of which are now lost) in collaboration with Michael *Drayton, Ben *Jonson, John *Webster, and others.

The *Shoemakers' Holiday and *Old Fortunatus, comedies acted in 1599, were published in 1600. Having been ridiculed, jointly with John *Marston, by Jonson in his *Poetaster, he retorted in *Satiromastix, a play produced in 1601. His other principal plays are The *Honest Whore, (Part I, in collaboration with Thomas *Middleton, 1604; Part II, 1630); *Patient Grissil (1603), written in collaboration with Henry *Chettle and William Haughton (d. 1605); and The *Witch of Edmonton, written in collaboration with John *Ford and William *Rowley in 1621, first published 1658. He also collaborated with Webster in *Westward Ho (written 1604; pub. 1607) and *Northward Ho (written 1605; pub. 1607), with Middleton in The *Roaring Girl (written c.1605; pub. 1611), and with Massinger in The *Virgin Martyr (written 1620; pub. 1622). His tragicomedy Match Me in London, written 1604/5, was published in 1631. Dekker also wrote pageants, tracts, and pamphlets. His pamphlet The Wonderful Year (1603) is a poignant description of London during the plague of that year; it was used by Defoe for his Journal of the *Plague Year. News from Hell (1606) is an imitation of Thomas *Nashe; The *Gull's Horn-Book (1609) is a satirical book of manners with interesting information about theatres.

Dekker's work is remarkable for its vivid if romantic portrayal of London life, both domestic and commercial, for its sympathy with the oppressed, including animals tortured for man's amusement, and for its prevailing cheerfulness.

DELAFIELD, E. M. (1890–1943) The pen-name of Edmée Elizabeth Monica Dashwood, née de la Pasture (hence the nom de plume), novelist and journalist. She published over thirty novels, of which her most popular remains The Diary of a Provincial Lady (1930), a gentle satire of a middle-class country life; Thank Heaven Fasting (1932) is also noteworthy.

de la MARE, Walter (1873–1956) Author, born in Kent, and educated at St Paul's Cathedral Choir School. His Songs of Childhood appeared in 1902, under the name of Walter Ramal. The Listeners (1912) was his first successful book of poetry, and its eerie title poem is still widely remembered:

'Is there anybody there?' said the Traveller,
Knocking on the moonlit door;
And his horse in the silence champed the
    grasses
Of the forest's ferny floor.

With the story The Three Mulla-Mulgars (1910) and the poems of Peacock Pie (1913) he made his name as a children's writer. His work is frequently concerned with childhood, littleness, the outsider, and mystery, often with an undercurrent of melancholy. In his celebrated novel Memoirs of a Midget (1921), he describes the world of the minute Miss M. He was an accomplished author of shorter fiction, and his tales of the supernatural (including 'Seaton's Aunt' and 'All Hallows') are subtle and powerful examples of the genre (see GHOST STORIES). Come Hither (1923) was a widely admired anthology for children. The Collected Poems was published in 1979.

DELANEY, Shelagh (1939–2011) Playwright, known for A Taste of Honey, which she wrote when she was 17 after seeing Terence *Rattigan's play Variations on a Theme. It was presented by Joan *Littlewood in 1958, filmed in 1961, and was hailed as a landmark in the new school of *'kitchen sink' realism, a movement partly inspired by reaction against the drawing-room drama of Rattigan and Noël *Coward. Later work for cinema and television includes Charley Bubbles (1968) and Dance with a Stranger (1985).

DELANY, Mary (1700–88) Née Granville; she became a friend and correspondent of Jonathan *Swift, and married his friend Patrick Delany in 1743. She knew many literary figures, was a *Blue Stocking hostess, and a favourite at court, where she introduced Fanny *Burney. Her Autobiography and Correspondence (1861–2, 6 vols, ed. Lady Llanover) gives a spirited account of her literary and social life.

de la RAMÉE, Marie Louise See OUIDA.

DELEUZE, Gilles (1925–95) French philosopher whose thought is defined by movement, displacement, difference, and multiplicity, and has spread across a wide range of disciplines in the arts, humanities, and social sciences, from film studies to urban geography. His two-volume study of *cinema, L'Image-mouvement (1983: The Movement-Image) and L'Image-temps (1985: The Time-Image), which explores the changing way in which it represents space, movement, and time, has been particularly influential.

DELILLO, Don (1936–) American novelist, born and brought up in the Bronx, New York. Like Thomas *Pynchon, he employs black comedy and the language of science to deal with themes of paranoia and consumerism. His first book, *Americana* (1971), is a road novel in which a television executive attempts to impose meaning on his experiences by filming them. There are echoes of Jorge Luis *Borges and Laurence *Sterne in *Ratner's Star* (1976). *White Noise* (1984) is an environmental disaster story narrated by the professor of Hitler studies at a Midwestern university. His version of the Kennedy assassination, *Libra* (1988), focuses on the role of Lee Harvey Oswald in shaping the American psyche. Both *Mao II* (1991), a postmodern tale of celebrity, terrorism, and the behaviour of crowds, and *Underworld* (1997), a multi-layered secret history of the Cold War, examine the significance of spectacular events and media imagery in shaping the development of memory, history, and mass psychology. *Falling Man* (2007) ties its narrative to the destruction of the World Trade Center's twin towers in New York on 11 September 2001.

Della Cruscans A poetic coterie led by Robert Merry (1755–98), who lived in Florence from 1784 to 1787 as a member of the Della Crusca academy. With Hester *Thrale Piozzi and others he produced in 1785 a *Miscellany*, in which he signed his work 'Della Crusca'. In England, Merry began contributing salon verses to fashionable newspapers to which a number of pseudonymous poets replied, amongst them 'Anna Matilda' (Hannah *Cowley) and 'Laura Matilda' (Mary *Robinson). Their effusions were collected in the very successful *British Album* (1790), but William *Gifford's *The Baviad* (1791) was a savage satire on the Della Cruscans, followed by *The Maeviad* (1795).

DELONEY, Thomas (d. in or before 1600) Silk-weaver and writer. He wrote broadside ballads on popular subjects, including three on the defeat of the Armada in 1588. He is now best known for his four works of prose fiction, originally published between 1597 and 1600: *Jack of Newberie*; *The Gentle Craft* and *The Gentle Craft: The Second Part*; and *Thomas of Reading*. His fiction celebrates the virtues and self-advancement of hard-working craftsmen. *The Gentle Craft* includes the story of Simon Eyre, the shoemaker's apprentice who became lord mayor and founder of Leadenhall, which

was adapted by Thomas *Dekker in *The *Shoemakers' Holiday*.

Delphic oracle The most famous oracular seat of the god Apollo, who slew the monstrous Python there. Delphi, also called Pytho, is a striking site on the slopes of Mount Parnassus, traditionally the haunt of the Muses. The Pythia, a priestess, having purified herself in the Castalian spring, uttered the oracles in a trance; they were interpreted for those consulting the oracle by her prophet/priests. *Herodotus and, later, *Plutarch quote many Delphic oracles with respect. The gnomic motto 'Know yourself', carved on the walls of Apollo's temple, was thought characteristically Delphic. The oracle was closed by the Christian emperor Theodosius in AD 390.

de MAN, Paul (1919–83) American critic. His major works, *Blindness and Insight* (1971), *Allegories of Reading* (1979), and *The Rhetoric of Romanticism* (posthumous, 1984), examine the figurative nature of literary language and the gulf between language and meaning. He transformed academic analysis of literary *Romanticism by discarding the accepted view that Romantic poetry reconciles the human mind with nature; on the contrary, he argued, it reveals and laments the impossibility of such reconciliation. The leading American exponent of *deconstruction, he explored with notable rigour the ways in which literary works paradoxically undermine their apparent meanings. Posthumous works include *The Resistance to Theory* (1986).

DEMOCRITUS (b. *c.*460 BC) Greek philosopher; with his teacher Leucippus he founded ancient atomism. He was called the 'laughing philosopher' for his advocacy of 'cheerfulness' (*euthumia*); only fragments of his writings remain. The key to his atomism is that everything happens by necessity, probably interpreted in terms of forces of repulsion and attraction between atoms, themselves the absolutely uncuttable (*atoma*) building blocks of the world. Atomism was subsequently adopted by *Epicurus in the Hellenistic period, by *Lucretius in the Roman; then revived in the 17th century by the French philosopher Pierre Gassendi (1592–1655).

Demogorgon Supposedly the primeval god of classical myth, first named in late antiquity through a scribal error. He appears in *Boccaccio's *Genealogia Deorum*, Ariosto's *Orlando furioso*, Spenser's *Faerie Queene* (I. v. 22, IV. ii. 47), and Milton's *Paradise Lost* (II. 965). He is a prominent figure in P. B. *Shelley's *Prometheus Unbound*; his name may have attracted Shelley because it is supposedly compounded of 'demos' (people) and 'gorgo' (Gorgon, the name of three female monsters).

de MORGAN, William Frend (1839–1917)

Potter and novelist; he worked for a time in association with his friend William *Morris. At the age of 67 he embarked somewhat casually on the writing of fiction, his first and best novel, *Joseph Vance* (1906), proving to his astonishment a great success. His last two novels, *The Old Madhouse* (1919) and *The Old Man's Youth* (1921), left unfinished on his death, were skilfully completed by his widow, the artist Evelyn de Morgan.

DEMOSTHENES (384–322 BC)

Leading Athenian orator and politician who tried to unite the Greeks against the territorial ambitions of Philip II of Macedon. Sixty-one of his orations survive. He became a rhetorical and libertarian model both in antiquity and in the Renaissance and 18th century. His *Philippics* were imitated by *Cicero in his attacks on Mark Antony; *Plutarch paired his life with Cicero's; *Quintilian and *Longinus analysed his methods. Thomas *Wilson, who translated his *Philippics* (1570), said that they were 'most nedefull to be redde in these daungerous dayes, of all them that loue their countries libertie'.

DENHAM, Sir John (1615–69)

Poet. He is chiefly known for *Cooper's Hill* (piratically published 1642 and revised in later editions), an early and influential example of the *topographical poem, describing scenery around his home at Egham, Surrey. John *Dryden called it 'the exact standard of good writing'. He went mad after his 18-year-old second wife became the duke of York's mistress.

Denis Duval

W. M *Thackeray's last, unfinished, novel, published in the *Cornhill Magazine* 1864.

Deor

An Old English poem from the 9th or 10th century in the *Exeter Book, containing the refrain 'that passed; so can this'. Deor seems to be a minstrel who has fallen out of favour and consoles himself by considering the past misfortunes of others. It is one of the group of poems in the Exeter Book referred to as 'elegies', short poems whose theme is usually the transience and unreliability of the world, sometimes (though not in *Deor*) ending with a Christian consolation.

de QUINCEY, Thomas (1785–1859)

Journalist and author; he ran away from school in Manchester to the homeless wanderings in Wales and London which he was to describe in *Confessions of an English Opium Eater*. He later made the acquaintance of *Coleridge and *Wordsworth and settled at Grasmere. In 1804, while at Oxford, he had begun to take opium, and from 1812 he became an addict. In 1817 he married Margaret Simpson, and, having exhausted his private fortune, started to earn a living by journalism. *Confessions of an English Opium Eater*, by which he made his name, was published in 1822. For the next 30 years he earned a precarious living, mainly in Edinburgh, by tales, articles, and reviews, mostly in *Blackwood's Magazine* and *Tait's*, including *Klosterheim* (1832), *Recollections of the Lake Poets* (1834–9), and 'Sketches . . . from the Autobiography of an English Opium Eater' (1834–41, later entitled *Autobiographic Sketches*).

Since nearly all De Quincey's work was journalism, written under pressure to support his family, it is more remarkable for brilliant tours de force such as 'On the Knocking on the Gate in "Macbeth"', 'On Murder Considered as One of the Fine Arts', and 'The Revolt of the Tartars' than for sustained coherence. Eclectic learning, pungent black humour, and a stately but singular style distinguish his writing. His impressionistic reminiscences both of his own childhood and of his literary contemporaries are memorably vivid. His greatest, though never completed, achievement was his psychological study of the faculty of dreaming in 'Suspiria de Profundis' and 'The English Mail Coach', in which he traced—25 years before Freud was born—how childhood experiences and sufferings are crystallized in dreams into symbols which can form and educate the dreamer's personality, and can also give rise to poetry or 'impassioned prose', as De Quincey called his own climaxes of imagery.

DERRIDA, Jacques (1930–2004)

French philosopher, born to a Jewish family in Algiers, who studied in Paris at the École Normale Supérieure, where he taught from 1964 to 1984. He also held visiting professorships at several American universities. Following the publication in 1967 of *De la grammatologie* and *L'Écriture et la différence* (*Writing and Difference*), he exerted a huge influence upon literary theory as the founder of *deconstruction, a subtly and often playfully sceptical approach to the relations between language and meaning, which was adopted by Paul *de Man and others as a method for exploring problems of literary criticism. Among his later works are *Glas* (1974), on *Hegel and Genet; *La Carte postale* (1980: *The Post Card*), on *Freud and *Lacan; *Spectres de Marx* (1993); and a collection of eulogies, *Chaque Fois unique, la fin du monde* (2003: *Each Time Unique, the End of the World*).

DESAI, Anita (1937–) Indian-born novelist and short story writer; her father was of the Bengal elite, her mother German. Despite her sense of writing as an outsider to India though 'feeling Indian', Desai's elegant and lucid novels vividly evoke the atmosphere, society, and land-scapes of her native land, and are noted for their delicate portrayal of the inner lives of women. Her work includes *Fire on the Mountain* (1977), *Fasting, Feasting* (1999), and, possibly her finest novel, *Clear Light of Day* (1980), the story of a fragmenting family set within a nation in tur-moil. *Games at Twilight* (1978) and *Diamond Dust* (2000) are collections of short stories, and her writing for children includes the prize-winning *The Village by the Sea* (1982). *See also* POSTCOLONIAL LITERATURE; DESAI, KIRAN.

DESAI, Kiran (1971–) Indian novelist in En-glish, who has spent a significant part of her life in the USA. She is the daughter of the novelist Anita *Desai, whom she cites as among her strongest sources of inspiration. The self-professed follower of an aesthetic of 'messiness' and fragmentariness, rather than order and symmetry, Kiran Desai published her first novel, *Hullabaloo in the Guava Orchard*, a pas-tiche reworking of R. K. *Narayan's *The Guide*, to wide acclaim in 1998. She was the winner in 2006 of the Man Booker Prize that three times eluded her mother for her multi-layered second novel, a study in transnational migration and rootlessness, *The Inheritance of Loss* (2006).

DESANI, G. V. (Govindan Vishnoo-das) (1909–2000) Indian writer, born in Nair-obi, Kenya; he lived in Britain during the Second World War, where he became a regular lecturer and broadcaster. His prose poem *Hali* (1950) was published with a preface by E. M. *Forster, but he is known principally for his inventive avant-garde novel *All about H. Hatterr* (1948), in which Hatterr, son of a European merchant seaman and 'an Oriental, a Malay Peninsula-resident lady, a steady non-voyaging non-Chris-tian human', seeks wisdom from the seven sages of India. This was revised and republished in 1972 with an introduction by Anthony *Bur-gess. His hybrid and 'dazzling, puzzling, leaping prose' has been described by Salman *Rushdie (*Indian Writing, 1947–1977*, 1997) as 'the first

genuine effort to go beyond the Englishness of the English language' and has been an impor-tant influence on a range of *postcolonial wri-ters. *See* ANGLO-INDIAN LITERATURE.

DESCARTES, René (1596–1650) French philosopher and mathematician. His main works are: *Discours de la méthode* (1637), *Méd-itations philosophiques* (published in Latin in 1641, in French in 1647), *Principes de la philo-sophie* (published in Latin in 1644, in French in 1647), and *Les Passions de l'âme* (1649: *Passions of the Soul*). The influence of these on European thought has been considerable. Philosophically his starting point is the problem of certainty posed by *Montaigne's radical scepticism: in other words, the need for a method that estab-lishes reliable propositions. Rejecting the accu-mulated preconceptions of the past through a process of systematic doubt, he proposes to reconstruct the whole of philosophy on the basis of certain self-evident truths, including notably the existence of the self in conscious-ness, the famous 'cogito ergo sum' ('I think, therefore I am'). From this basis he attempts to deduce the existence of God as guarantor of the reliability of the perceptible world, and thus of its susceptibility to scientific analysis. As a mathematician, he considered mathematical reasoning to be applicable to the whole of sci-ence. Although his astronomical theories were demolished by Isaac *Newton, his reduction of matter to the quantifiable has remained funda-mental to science. In epistemology and ethics, his rigorous mind–body dualism has similarly been immensely influential.

Deserted Village, The Poem by Oliver *Goldsmith (1770), evoking the idyllic pastoral life of Auburn, 'loveliest village of the plain', in its former state of prosperous stability, now ruined; the poem deplores the growth of trade, the demand for luxuries, and the mercantile spirit which have ruthlessly depopulated such villages and driven 'a bold peasantry, their country's pride' to emigration. James *Boswell ascertained that the last four lines were contrib-uted by Samuel *Johnson. Goldsmith's idealized descriptions of a happy rural community pro-voked Crabbe's protest in *The *Village*.

Despair The most potent temptation to assail the Christian pilgrim; appears in Edmund *Spenser's *Faerie Queene*, I. ix, as an aged cav-ern-dweller whose call to suicide has a narcotic mellifluousness. Despair was understood to be the unforgivable 'sin against the Holy Ghost'. In John *Bunyan's *Pilgrim's Progress*, he appears as Giant Despair, resident of Doubting Castle, where he imprisons Christian and Hopeful. Great-heart kills him in Part II.

Desperate Remedies The first of Thomas *Hardy's published novels; appeared in 1871. The plot is influenced by the fashionable themes of the novel of *sensation.

detective fiction The classic English detective novel marries crime and a misdirection of the reader leading to a final denouement. The founding father of the genre was actually an American, Edgar Allan *Poe, whose three detective stories from the 1840s ('The Murders in the Rue Morgue', 'The Mystery of Marie Roget', and 'The Purloined Letter') strikingly anticipate many of its main features. English writers followed him in creating detectives on the model of the aloof and logical Auguste Dupin.

Around mid-century there were other fictional detectives, such as Charles Dickens's Inspector Bucket (*Bleak House, 1853) and Wilkie Collins's Sergeant Cuff (*The Moonstone*, 1868), who were apparently more homely and engaging, but Poe's model was followed by Conan *Doyle in his creation of Sherlock Holmes. Holmes and his comrade Dr Watson first appeared in A Study in Scarlet (1887) but the enormous popularity of the characters really began when the Strand Magazine started to publish Holmes short stories in 1891. Traces of the stereotypes of brilliant detective and dependable but dull-witted associate, initiated by Poe and carried on by Doyle, can be found in characters from Agatha *Christie's Hercule Poirot and Captain Hastings to Inspector Morse and Sergeant Lewis in the novels of Colin *Dexter (1930–). Conan Doyle's success, the huge sums a Holmes story commanded, and the large market offered by the magazines of the time attracted hordes of followers and imitators in the late Victorian and Edwardian periods. Some of the more memorable detectives include. Arthur *Morrison's Martin Hewitt also appeared in stories published in the Strand, Baroness *Orczy's Old Man in the Corner featured in several volumes of short stories, and G. K. *Chesterton's meek but insightful Roman Catholic priest Father Brown.

The so-called Golden Age is often said to have been inaugurated by Trent's Last Case (1913) by E. C. *Bentley but it was led by a quartet of women writers: Agatha Christie, Dorothy L. *Sayers, creator of the aristocratic Lord Peter Wimsey, Margery *Allingham, and Ngaio *Marsh. Christie in particular gave the public a stream of ingenious and satisfying puzzles whose solutions habitually left her readers feeling agreeably fooled. Other notable writers include R. Austin Freeman (1862–1943), the Anglophile American John Dickson Carr (1906–77), a specialist in so-called 'locked-room' mysteries, and Gladys Mitchell (1901–83).

After the Second World War the conventions and artifice of the Golden Age proved surprisingly resilient despite the challenge of the American *hardboiled fiction represented by Raymond *Chandler and Dashiell *Hammett. Allingham wrote many of her best novels, including her masterpiece The Tiger in the Smoke (1952), after the war. Christie continued to publish fiction into the 1970s, Marsh and Mitchell into the 1980s. Other writers, such as Edmund Crispin (1921–78), creator of the eccentric academic Gervase Fen, J. I. M. *Stewart (as Michael Innes), and Cecil *Day-Lewis (as Nicholas Blake) appeared to revitalize the traditional form, whilst others, such as Julian *Symons and Michael Gilbert (1912–2006) preferred to aim for greater realism, specializing in believable studies of the murderous mind or of everyday situations into which murder erupts.

In the late 1960s and 1970s, just as the Golden Age practitioners were coming to the ends of their careers, a new generation re-established the English detective novel: P. D. *James and Ruth *Rendell wrote novels in the whodunnit tradition, though neither would have anything to do with the Never-never-shire settings of some of the Golden Age writers. James's Inspector Dalgliesh, though, is a traditional outsider, a reputable poet, shy of emotional involvements, while Rendell can produce masterpieces of reader misdirection in the Christie tradition. Both writers' novels have been regularly adapted for television, and the success of these series, and of Dexter's Morse, has boosted the popularity of modern crime fiction as a whole.

Modern detective fiction strives to marry the whodunnit tradition with a realistic surface and treatment. Private detectives are the exception rather than the rule and many writers have pushed their British policemen in the direction of the tougher American police procedural genre. The scene of the crimes has also moved out of the fantasy England of the Golden Age novels and migrated to the regions. Pascoe and Dalziel, the police duo created by Reginald Hill (1936–2012), may operate in the entirely fictional Mid-Yorkshire force but the background against which Hill sets his increasingly ambitious narratives is recognizably the real county. Yorkshire also provides the backdrop for the fiction of Peter Robinson (1950–), creator of Inspector Banks. Scotland, and more specifically Edinburgh, is the setting for Ian *Rankin's maverick policeman Inspector Rebus in *Knots and Crosses* (1987), *Black and Blue* (1997), and *The Naming of the Dead* (2006). Many major British cites now have their own fictional detective: Nottingham plays a major role in the novels of John Harvey (1938–), Manchester in many of those by Val McDermid (1955–), and Portsmouth in the work of Graham Hurley (1946–). All these writers use their chosen milieu with a strong sense for the urban landscape and its moulding of people. Other British writers have chosen a foreign setting: Michael *Dibdin's Aurelio Zen novels take place in a variety of Italian cities from Venice to Naples; Alexander McCall Smith (1948–) has used Botswana to great effect in his No. 1 Ladies' Detective Agency series featuring the female investigator Precious Ramotswe.

The inner landscape of the criminal mind is studied by Ruth Rendell and her alter ego Barbara Vine (the pseudonym she created for a number of novels, beginning with *A Dark-Adapted Eye* in 1986), Minette Walters (1949–) in *The Ice House* (1992) and later novels, Frances Fyfield (1948–), and the journalists Nicci Gerrard (1958–) and Sean French (1959–), writing together under the pseudonym of Nicci French. Comedy crime fiction, popular since at least the 1920s, has been reinvented with a blacker hue by writers like Christopher Brookmyre (1968–) and Colin Bateman (1962–). Historical crime featured in the Brother Cadfael novels of Ellis Peters (1913–95) and many others have followed in their wake. The Falco novels of Lindsey Davis (1949–), which take place in ancient Rome, the Victorian-era fiction of Anne Perry (1938–), and the books of C. J. Sansom (1952–), set amidst the dangers of Henry VIII's court, are notable examples. P. C. Doherty (1946–), under his own name and many pseudonyms, including Paul Harding, Michael Clynes, and Anna Apostolou, has made a speciality of the Middle Ages but has also diversified into ancient Egypt and ancient Greece. True crimes have also featured as the basis for novels, for example *Arthur and George* (2005) by Julian *Barnes (who has also written detective fiction under the pseudonym Dan Kavanagh), which tells the story of Conan Doyle's investigation of the1903 Edalji case. The 1860 Constance Kent murder case has been treated fictionally (by Francis Henry *King) and by Kate Summerscale in *The Suspicions of Mr Whicher* (2008); it also informed contemporary works, including Wilkie *Collins's *The Moonstone* (1862) and *Lady Audley's Secret.*

The conventions of detective fiction have also been adopted by children's authors, and detective fiction for younger readers, including the 1928 novel *Emil and the Detectives* by Erich Kästner (1899–74), the title story of Richmal *Crompton's *William the Detective* (1935), *The Falcon's Malteser* (1986) by Anthony Horowitz (1956–), and Philip *Pullman's Sally Lockhart novels, has proved enduringly popular. Many of Enid *Blyton's tales feature her young protagonists in successful pursuit of criminals and spies. *See also* SENSATION.

(()) **SEE WEB LINKS**
• Crimeculture site on crime and detective fiction

deus ex machina [Latin for 'a god from the machine'] A god in Greek drama swung in by a crane to resolve a problem in the plot, especially in *Euripides; more generally an unexpected event or intervention in a narrative, introduced to resolve a difficult situation.

de VERE, Aubrey Thomas (1814–1902) Poet, born in Co. Limerick, Ireland, the son of Sir Aubrey de Vere (1788–1846, himself a poet). He came early under the influence of William *Wordsworth and S. T. *Coleridge and had many friends in the literary world. His voluminous works include *The Waldenses, or The Fall of Rora, with Other Poems* (1842); *English Misrule and Irish Misdeeds* (1848), which displays Irish sympathies, as do many of his works; and *Recollections* (1897).

de VERE, Edward *See* OXFORD, EDWARD VERE.

DEVEREUX, Robert *See* ESSEX, ROBERT DEVEREUX.

Devil Is an Ass, The A comedy by Ben *Jonson, acted by the King's Men 1616, printed 1631. Pug, a minor devil, is sent to London by Satan to try his hand at iniquity for a day, and becomes servant to Fitzdottrel, a foolish country squire, who is targeted by various cheats, including Meercraft, a 'projector', who lures him with a scheme for draining the fens, and two gallants Wittipol and Manly, who have designs on his wife. Her virtue wins them over, however, and they rescue Fitzdottrel from his entanglements. Pug, utterly outclassed by human wickedness, lands up in Newgate, and persuades Satan to take him back to hell.

'Devil's Thoughts, The' A satirical poem by Samuel Taylor *Coleridge and Robert *Southey, published 1799, describing the devil going walking and enjoying the sight of the vices of men. The poem was imitated by Lord *Byron in his 'Devil's Drive', and by P. B. *Shelley in his 'Devil's Walk'.

DEXTER, Colin (1930–) OBE. Writer of *detective fiction and creator of Chief Inspector Morse. From *Last Bus to Woodstock* (1975) to the last of the Inspector Morse novels, *The Remorseful Day* (1999), all his novels are based in and around Oxford. They have been successfully adapted for television (1987–2001).

Dial, The (1) (1840–44) The literary organ of the American Transcendental movement (*see* TRANSCENDENTAL CLUB), of which Margaret *Fuller was editor; she was succeeded by Ralph Waldo *Emerson. It contained contributions by Henry *Thoreau. (2) (1889–97) (nos 1–5) A literary and artistic periodical edited in London by Charles *Ricketts and Charles Shannon. The 'Dial Group' also included T. S. *Moore and Lucien Pissarro (1863–1944). (3) (1880–1929) A literary monthly founded in Chicago, which moved in 1918 to New York. In its last decade it was one of the most important international periodicals, publishing work by T. S. *Eliot, W. B. *Yeats, D. H. *Lawrence, Ezra *Pound, E. E. *Cummings, Conrad *Aiken, and many others.

Diana of the Crossways A novel by George *Meredith, published 1885. Diana is based on the writer Caroline *Norton, whose husband had tried to divorce her. After the family's protests Meredith included a note that the work 'is to be read as fiction'. The beautiful and impulsive Irish girl Diana Merion marries Mr Warwick. Her innocent indiscretions arouse his jealousy and he brings an action for divorce, citing Lord Dannisburgh (drawn from Melbourne), which he loses. Percy Dacier, a rising young politician, falls in love with Diana, but when she is about to live with him, the illness of her friend Lady Dunstane recalls her sense of duty and propriety. Dacier perseveres, but he discovers that an important political secret which he had confided to her has been passed to a London newspaper. He leaves in a fury and marries a young heiress. Diana's husband dies and she later marries her faithful adorer Thomas Redworth. Crossways, the name of Diana's house, reflects an emphasis on a historical turning point in marital and sexual politics.

DIAPER, William (1685–1717) Poet, born in Somerset, author of *Nereides, or Sea-Eclogues* (1712), in which the speakers are mermen and mermaids: He also wrote *Dryades* (1712) and a *topographical poem, 'Brent'. The poem describes vividly the damp Somerset levels, where rabbits took to the water with ducks, and all food allegedly tasted of frog.

diaries, diarists The tradition of diary-keeping in England seems to date from the 17th century. The motives of the earlier diarists are unknown, but an awareness that they were living in turbulent times may have inspired the most celebrated of diarists, Samuel *Pepys and John *Evelyn. *The Diary of Ralph Josselin, 1616–83*, ed. Alan Macfarlane (1976), gives an engaging portrait of the domestic life, illnesses, and religious attitudes of a clergyman-farmer in Essex. There are many Nonconformist diaries, including those of the ex-communicant Oliver Heywood (1630–1702), published in four volumes (1881–5), and the Presbyterian Peter Walkden (1684–1769). The *Journal* of John *Wesley is perhaps the finest example in this tradition. Jonathan *Swift's flirtatious letter-diary *Journal to Stella* (covering the years 1710–13) demonstrates the cross-fertilization of epistolary and diary-writing traditions. Explicit self-awareness emerges in the licentious *London Journal* of James *Boswell, written for his friend John Johnston, and unpublished until 1950. By the late 18th century diary-keeping was commonplace, and authors frequently intended publication, as did Fanny *Burney, whose first diary (1767) was addressed to Nobody 'since to Nobody can I be wholly unreserved'. Celebrity diaries made popular reading: Lord *Byron's friend Thomas *Moore instructed his executors to publish Byron's *Journal* (1818–41) to 'afford the means of making some provision for my wife and family'. The early 18th-century art world was documented in the diary of Benjamin *Haydon, whose last entry records his suicide, and literary life in the journals of Dorothy *Wordsworth, long valued for the light they shed on William, now justly feted for their intense evocation of landscape.

The flourishing tradition of political diaries began with the *Memoirs* (1821–60) of Charles *Greville, clerk to the Privy Council, which were criticized for indiscretion when published between 1874 and 1887. Twentieth-century diarists made a virtue of indiscretion, and have also benefited from post-Freudian self-analysis. The diaries of diplomat Harold *Nicolson, husband of Vita *Sackville-West, are as noteworthy for their colourful gossip as for their historical records.

Twentieth-century literary diarists, with widely contrasted styles and purposes, include Arnold *Bennett, Evelyn *Waugh, and Noël *Coward. Virginia *Woolf used her diary as an alternative space where she could experiment with different versions of her self and her writing in ways which would feed into her fiction; she also filled it with wicked portraits, much gossip, and incisive commentary on contemporary events. The late 20th-century vogue for sexual candour is exemplified in the *Diaries* (1986, ed. John Lahr) of the homosexual playwright Joe *Orton. Notable examples of the practice of writing diaries for virtually immediate publication include the *Diaries* (1993) of politician Alan Clark (1928–99) and *Peter *Hall's Diaries* (1983, ed. John Goodwin), while the playwright Simon *Gray's *Coda* (2008, published posthumously) was written after his terminal cancer diagnosis. Comic fictional diaries were popular in the 1880s, the most celebrated example being the *Grossmiths' *The Diary of a Nobody* (1892), and have recently been successfully revived with *The Secret Diary of Adrian Mole, aged 13¾* by Sue *Townsend (1982: originally created for the *BBC) and Helen *Fielding's *Bridget Jones's Diary* (1996).

Diarmid (Diarmait Ó Duibhne) A member of the Fianna (*see* FENIAN CYCLE) who elopes with *Grainne, wife of *Finn

Diary of a Nobody, The By George and Weedon *Grossmith, published 1892. Charles Pooter's diary covers fifteen months of his life in the early 1890s. His entries, describing the events of his life with his wife Carrie in Brickfield Terrace, Holloway, reveal in affectionate and comic detail the society of anxious gentility in which he lives. Pooter emerges as worthy, deferential, and acutely sensitive to minor humiliations. Text and illustrations reveal fascinating contemporary background, including details of clothes, the plaster antlers and splayed fans of the decor, the new fad for the bicycle, the fashion for imitations of Sir Henry *Irving, and the slang and popular songs of the time.

DIBDIN, Michael (1947–2007) Crime novelist. Before becoming a full-time writer, he taught English in Perugia, and much of his best work—such as his accomplished pastiche mystery *A Rich Full Death* (1986), and his eleven Aurelio Zen novels, from *Ratking* (1988) to *End Games* (2007)—is set in Italy. *The Last Sherlock Holmes Story* (1978) resurrected the London of

Jack the Ripper. *Dirty Tricks* (1991) is a blackly satiric comedy about Oxford. *The Dying of the Light* (1993) reworks the conventions of the country-house whodunit. *Dark Spectre* (1995) is a tense thriller with 'police procedural' features. Mordant wit, narrative verve, sardonic social and psychological penetration, trenchant pessimism, and vividly knowledgeable evocation of place distinguish all Dibdin's fiction. *See also* DETECTIVE FICTION.

DICK, Philip K. (Kindred) (1928–82) Writer of philosophical *science fiction who has had a profound influence on both science fiction and theories of *postmodernism. His early novel *Time out of Joint* (1959) explores consensus reality (the thought that reality is what exists, or what we can by consensus agree seems to exist), a question which troubled Dick through the *alternate history *The Man in the High Castle* (1962) and the *Gnostic *Ubik* (1969) to *Valis* (1981). *We Can Build You* (1972; written 1962; pub. in magazine form 1969), *The Simulacra* (1964), and especially *Do Androids Dream of Electric Sheep?* (1968; filmed as *Blade Runner* 1982) articulate ideas about authenticity later developed by the philosopher Jean *Baudrillard. Much of his science fiction, and the non-science fiction unpublished in his lifetime, is also a sympathetic depiction of 'ordinary' small-town people.

DICKENS, Charles (1812–70) Novelist, born in Portsmouth. His early boyhood, spent in Chatham, was happy, and he attended a competent private school. This was followed by a period of intense misery during which his father was imprisoned for debt in the Marshalsea and he himself (aged 12) worked in a blacking warehouse. These painful experiences inspired much of his fiction, notably the early chapters of *David Copperfield*. He then worked as an office boy, studied shorthand, and became reporter of debates in the Commons for the *Morning Chronicle*. He contributed to various periodicals the articles which were republished as *Sketches by Boz, Illustrative of Every-Day Life and Every-Day People* (1836–7) An approach from *Chapman and Hall led to the publication in twenty monthly numbers of *The Posthumous Papers of the Pickwick Club*, published in volume form in 1837 (*see* PICKWICK PAPERS). The series achieved immense popularity, and Dickens, with his young wife Catherine Hogarth, embarked on a promising future. On Christmas Day 1836 he met John *Forster, who became a lifelong friend, and his biographer.

In 1837 *Oliver Twist* began to appear in monthly numbers in *Bentley's Miscellany*, a new periodical of which Dickens was the first editor. It was followed by *Nicholas Nickleby*, also in monthly numbers. In 1840 Dickens launched a new weekly, called *Master Humphrey's Clock*, which carried instalments of the full-length novels *The *Old Curiosity Shop* (1840–41) and his long-deliberated *Barnaby Rudge* (1841). The novels proved so popular that the linking by 'Master Humphrey' was dropped. In 1842 he and his wife visited America, where he was rapturously received. His first impressions were favourable, but disillusion followed and his *American Notes* (1842) caused much offence in America, as did his portrayal of American stereotypes in *Martin Chuzzlewit* (1843–4). While in America he advocated international copyright and the abolition of slavery.

A *Christmas Carol* (1843) was the first of a series of Christmas books (*The *Chimes, The *Cricket on the Hearth, The Battle of Life*, and *The *Haunted Man*). In 1844 he paid a long visit to Italy, which produced 'Pictures from Italy' contributed to the *Daily News*, a new radical paper founded by Dickens in 1846. He began *Dombey and Son* (1848) during a visit to Switzerland in 1846. In 1850 he started the weekly periodical *Household Words*; in 1859 it was incorporated into *All the Year Round*, which he continued to edit until his death. In this he published much of his later writings. *David Copperfield* appeared in monthly numbers in 1849–50; *Bleak House* in 1852–3; and *A Child's History of England* appeared irregularly, 1851–3. *Hard Times* appeared in 1854, *Little Dorrit* in 1855–7, *A *Tale of Two Cities* in 1859, *Great Expectations* in 1860–61, and *Our Mutual Friend* in 1864–5.

During these years of intense productivity he also found time for his large family, for a vast circle of friends, and for philanthropic enterprises, at times combined with his passion for amateur theatricals; a fund-raising performance of Wilkie *Collins's *The Frozen Deep* in 1857 introduced him to the young actress Ellen Ternan. His admiration for her further strained his deteriorating relationship with his wife, and he and Catherine separated in 1858. He defied scandal, protested his own innocence, and continued to appear in public, distracting himself from domestic sorrow by throwing his restless energy into public readings of his own works. He revisited America in 1867–8, delivered a series of readings there, and on his return continued to tour the provinces. His 'Penny Readings', priced to admit the poor, are commemorated annually in Liverpool. Dickens died suddenly in 1870, leaving unfinished his last novel, *The *Mystery of Edwin Drood*.

Dickens captured the popular imagination as no other novelist had done and, despite murmurs against his sensationalism and sentimentality and his inability to portray women other than as innocents or grotesques, he was also held in high critical esteem, admired by contemporaries as varied as Queen *Victoria and *Dostoevsky. But it was not until the 20th century that he began to attract academic attention. Later criticism has tended to praise the complexity of the sombre late works at the expense of the high-spirited humour and genius for caricature traditionally labelled 'Dickensian'. A series of distinguished illustrators inseparably connected with his work, including Hablot K. *Browne ('Phiz'), John Leech, and George *Cruikshank, meant that he had a significant impact on the visual culture of the period. He collaborated with Wilkie Collins in various stories which appeared in *Household Words*.

DICKENS, Monica (1915–92) Novelist, great-granddaughter of Charles *Dickens. Her works of fiction included the best-selling *One Pair of Hands* (1939), based on her experiences as a cook and general servant, *One Pair of Feet* (1942), reflecting her years as a wartime nurse, and *My Turn to Make the Tea* (1951), which drew on her time as a reporter on a local newspaper. *No More Meadows* (1953) and *Kate and Emma* (1964) both arose from her involvement with the National Society for the Prevention of Cruelty to Children, while her work for the Samaritans (the first American branch of which she founded in 1974) produced *The Listeners* (1970).

DICKINSON, Emily (1830–86) American poet, born in Amherst, Massachusetts; during her early years she was lively, witty, and sociable, but from her mid-twenties she gradually withdrew into an inner world, eventually refusing to leave her home, although she maintained intimate correspondences with people she never saw face to face. Only seven poems out of nearly 2,000 are known to have been published during her lifetime, and those appeared anonymously and much edited. From c.1858 she assembled many of her poems in packets of 'fascicles', which were discovered after her death; a selection, arranged and edited by Mabel Loomis Todd and T. W. Higginson, appeared in 1890; eventually other editions and volumes of letters appeared, restoring her individual punctuation and presentation. Her work presents recurrent themes—a mystic apprehension of the natural world, a preoccupation with poetic vocation, fame, death, and immortality—and is expressed in a rhetoric and language of her own, cryptic, elliptical, and at times self-dramatizing and hyperbolic. Her imagery reflects an intense and painful inner struggle over many years; she refers to herself as 'the queen of Calvary', and her verse is full of allusions to volcanoes, shipwrecks, funerals, storms, imprisonments, and other manifestations of natural and human violence.

DICKINSON, Peter (1927-) British writer born in Northern Rhodesia (now Zambia), best known for his work for children, although he has published detective stories and *science fiction for adults, including the *alternate history *King and Joker* (1976). Achieving success with the 'Changes' trilogy (1968–71) and *The Blue Hawk* (1976), a *fantasy, Dickinson has also published novels such as *Tulku* (1979) and *AK* (1990) with historical or contemporary themes. *Eva* (1988) uses the device of a girl whose body is replaced by a chimpanzee's to explore issues from exploitation to evolution; theories about human evolution are also explored in *A Bone from a Dry Sea* (1992) and *The Kin* (1998).

diction The aspect of literary style determined by choice of vocabulary: for example, a recurrent adoption of archaic words, or a preference for words derived from Latin, or simply a marked avoidance of colloquial words, may characterize a given diction. For the controversy on artificial diction in English poetry, *see* POETIC DICTION.

dictionary In the late 16th century it became clear that the division between two levels of English, 'learned' or 'literary', as opposed to 'spoken' or 'popular', necessitated glossaries of the kind previously available for Greek, Latin, or French. Robert Cawdrey's *Table Alphabeticall . . . of Hard Usuall English Wordes* (1604), containing about 3,000 words, might be called the first English dictionary; Henry Cockeram's *English Dictionarie* (1623) translates hard words to easy as well as easy to hard. The first major English dictionary was Nathan *Bailey's *Universal Etymological English Dictionary* (1721), which had more entries than its famous successor by Samuel *Johnson (1755). Johnson's *Dictionary* was a great landmark in English lexicographical history; Johnson illustrates his words in practice, and attempts to indicate the connotations of words, as well as offering their exact meaning. The *Oxford English Dictionary* (1884–1928) is perhaps the greatest dictionary of

any modern language. The *OED* attempts to give a full history of the development of all English words since the 12th century, with full illustrative quotations, ordered according to the principal distinct senses of the word. *Roget's *Thesaurus*, in effect a dictionary of semantically linked words, first appeared in 1852. Noah *Webster's *American Dictionary of the English Language* (1828) has been controversial in its later revisions for its refusal to discriminate between 'good' and 'bad' English by identifying supposedly inferior categories of words, such as 'slang', or 'obscene'. Linguists now tend to use concordances based on vast digitized bodies of text ('corpora') as arbiters of meaning.

Dictionary of National Biography, The Designed and published by George *Smith, begun in 1882 with Sir Leslie *Stephen as editor. It included in its original form biographies of all national notables from earliest times to 1900. The work has been continued by the publishing of supplements at ten-year intervals. Stephen was succeeded in the editorship by Sir Sidney *Lee. In 1917 the *DNB* was transferred to *Oxford University Press. A complete revision, now known as the *Oxford Dictionary of National Biography* (*ODNB*), was published in 2004, edited by Colin Matthews and Brian Harrison. It is also available in an online version which is updated twice yearly.

Dictys Cretensis (of Crete) Supposed author of a diary of the Trojan War which exists in Latin. In the preface, written in the 4th century AD, Lucius Septimius claims that he translated the work from a Greek version prepared for Nero from a Phoenician original. Dictys claims to have been present at the siege of Troy. Like the narrative of *Dares Phrygius his diary is probably a fabrication, but the two were the chief sources of medieval Trojan legends.

Diddler, Jeremy The chief character in James Kenney's farce *Raising the Wind* (1803). Jeremy's habit of continually borrowing small sums which he does not pay back probably gave rise to the present sense of the verb 'diddle'—to cheat or deceive.

DIDEROT, Denis (1713–84) French philosopher and man of letters, a leading member of the *Enlightenment and from 1746 editor of the *Encyclopédie*. After translating the earl of Shaftesbury (1745), he maintained his interest in English culture, writing on Samuel *Richardson (1761), adapting Edward Moore's *The *Gamester*, and writing plays influenced by George *Lillo. He also wrote three remarkably 'modern' novels: *La Religieuse* (*The Nun*), *Le Neveu de Rameau* (*Rameau's Nephew*), and *Jacques le fataliste* (*Jacques the Fatalist*) which was influenced by Sterne's **Tristram Shandy* in its experimental form.

DIDION, Joan (1934–) American essayist and novelist. She is known for her uncompromising depictions of contemporary American society, in essay collections such as *Slouching towards Bethlehem* (1968), in which California of the 1960s comes to represent the decline in seriousness of the USA and the world; and *The White Album* (1979) and *Sentimental Journeys* (1993), where her laconic prose and sense of cultural despair are employed to scrutinize three American cities. She has published four novels which deal with the difficulties faced by women in a patriarchal society, including *Play It as It Lays* (1970) and *The Book of Common Prayer* (1977). Her moving memoir *The Year of Magical Thinking* (2005) documents her grief in the year following the sudden death of her husband and her daughter's illness.

Dido *See* AENEID.

Dido Queen of Carthage, The Tragedy of Published 1594 as written by Christopher **Marlowe and Thomas **Nashe. It is closely based on Virgil's **Aeneid* (Bks 1, 2, and 4), depicting Dido's failure to persuade Aeneas to stay with her in Carthage and her subsequent suicide.

DIDSBURY, Peter (1945–) British poet; closely associated with Douglas **Dunn and Sean **O'Brien in the 1970s, his work first appeared in Dunn's anthology *A Rumoured City* (1982), with a preface by Philip **Larkin. Didsbury's knowledgeable, eccentric, digressive, and often humorous voice is, however, more reminiscent of postmodernists such as John **Ashbery. His collections of poetry are *The Butchers of Hull* (1982), *The Classical Farm* (1987), *That Old Time Religion* (1994), and *Scenes from a Long Sleep: New and Collected Poems* (2003).

Digby Plays Three late **mystery plays from East Anglia, probably dating from the early 16th century, bearing the name or initials of Myles Blomefylde (1525–1603), in Digby MS 133. They are *Mary Magdalen*, *The Conversion of St Paul*, and *The Killing of the Children of Israel*.

dime novels The name for cheap (a dime is 10 cents), popular stories in America, the precursors of the modern paperback. The term, sometimes used for story magazines as well as novels, was first used in 1860 and thereafter was applied to series published in the late 19th and early 20th centuries.

(( )) **SEE WEB LINKS**

• Digitized Dime Novel and Story Paper Collection

dimeter A verse line with only two stressed syllables. *See also* METRE.

DINESEN, Isak (1885–1962) Pseudonym of Karen von Blixen-Finecke, née Karen Dinesen, short story writer and memoirist. *Seven Gothic Tales* (1934), densely woven stories which work through suggestion and metaphor rather than direct fantasy or horror, made her reputation. Her next book, *Out of Africa* (1937; filmed 1985), is her memoir of the seventeen years she spent in British East Africa, later Kenya, latterly her own. The memoir refers to a world that is lost and its tone is coloured by that and her personal losses; it also documents the redemptive power of nature, and her respect for African culture, however mediated through a colonial vision. She contracted syphilis from her husband after the first year of marriage; they were separated in 1921 and divorced in 1925. Dinesen met her lover, a big game hunter, during this period; his death in 1931 and the failure of her coffee plantation forced her return to Denmark. During the 1940s and 1950s she continued to develop the techniques of the storytelling tradition in tales such as 'Babette's Feast', of which a Danish film appeared in 1987. Though Danish, Blixen wrote her work first in English.

DIODORUS SICULUS (1st century BC) A Sicilian Greek historian, author of a universal history from the mythical past to 60 BC. Poggio Bracciolini's Latin translation of the first five books, which give an account of Egypt, Assyria, and early Greece, was published in 1472 and widely read in the 16th and 17th centuries. John **Skelton translated this version into English in the 1580s.

DIONYSIUS THE PSEUDO-AREOPAGITE (5th century AD) Greek author of an important collection of Neoplatonic mystical writings who attributed his work to the 1st-century Dionysius the Areopagite, converted by St **Paul at Athens (Acts 17: 34). His four treatises, *The Celestial Hierarchy*, *The Ecclesiastical Hierarchy*, *The Mystical Theology*, and *On the Divine Names*, were translated into Latin by **Scotus Eriugena and strongly influence the whole medieval mystical tradition. The 14th-century mystical prose work *Deonise Hid Divinite* is founded on him, as its name suggests, and John *Colet later drew on him for his lectures in Oxford 1497–8.

dirty realism The name given to a kind of American fiction of the 1970s and 1980s characterized by a sparse narrative style. Exemplars of this mode are Raymond *Carver, Richard Ford, and Tobias *Wolff.

DISKI, Jenny (1947–) Novelist and critic, born in London. After a difficult childhood, some of it spent in institutional care, she studied anthropology, a discipline which informs much of her fiction. Her first novel, *Nothing Natural* (1986), describes a single mother trapped in a sadomasochistic relationship, while *Rainforest* (1987) is an ecological drama partly set in Borneo. *Then Again* (1990), set in 14th-century Poland, and *The Dream Mistress* (1996) investigate sexual roles, extreme states of consciousness, and Jewish identity. *Only Human* (2000) and *After These Things* (2004) retell the biblical stories of Abraham and his family. *Skating to Antarctica* (1997), *Stranger on a Train* (2002), and *On Trying To Keep Still* (2006) are idiosyncratic travel books.

DISNEY, Walt (1901–66) American film producer, screenwriter, and entrepreneur, born in Chicago. A pioneer of animation films, his character Mickey Mouse first appeared in *Steamboat Willie* (1928) and Donald Duck in 1934. By the Second World War, Disney's cartoon characters had become household names. Walt Disney Productions, was responsible for further cartoons, educational films, and a TV show in the 1950s.

DISRAELI, Benjamin, first earl of Beaconsfield (1804–81) Politician, prime minister, and novelist, the oldest son of Isaac *D'Israeli. *Vivian Grey*, his extravagant first novel, was published anonymously in 1826, its success and notoriety encouraging him to provide a continuation in 1827. Between 1828 and 1831 he travelled in Spain and Italy, and he made much use of these journeys, and subsequent travels in Albania, the Levant, and Egypt, in future novels. In 1831 he published *The Young Duke*, with a dashingly Byronic hero, followed by *Contarini Fleming* (1832) and *Alroy* (1833), a highly coloured *oriental historical romance spiced with cabbalistic lore. In 1834, he published *The Revolutionary Epic*, his one serious attempt at poetry; and *A Year at Hartlebury*, an anonymous novel, written with his sister Sarah.

A Vindication of the English Constitution (containing ideas developed later in *Coningsby and *Sybil) followed in 1835; and the *Juniusinspired *Letters of Runnymede*, in 1836. Disraeli's experiences in high society are reflected in two novels published in 1837: *Henrietta Temple*, an exploration of young love, begun in 1834, during Disraeli's affair with Lady Henrietta Sykes, and *Venetia*, also a love story, set in the 18th century but drawn partly from the lives of P. B. *Shelley and Lord *Byron. Disraeli's parliamentary career (as MP for Maidstone) flourished, and for a while his political and literary interests worked together. The trilogy which is now most often remembered, *Coningsby* (1844), *Sybil* (1845), and *Tancred* (1847), was written to influence public opinion, and they may be regarded as the first truly political (*'condition of England') novels in English. They owe much to Blue Book enquiries of the day, and to personal observations made during a tour of the north of England in 1844. The first two, concerned with the conditions of the rural and urban poor, were particularly successful, and foreshadowed future social legislation. Disraeli published no more novels for more than twenty years, as his political career intensified, culminating in his appointment as prime minister, briefly in 1868, and then in 1874.

Lothair appeared in 1870, as did the first collected edition of the novels, with an illuminating preface by Disraeli. *Endymion* (1880), his last completed novel, for which he was offered the enormous sum of £10,000, was set in the period of his youth. He died without completing the intriguing *Falconet*, which attempted a satirical portrait of Gladstone. Politically astute, vigorous, and compassionate, Disraeli's novels reveal much of lasting significance about the literary and political culture of his day.

D'ISRAELI, Isaac (1766–1848) The father of Benjamin *Disraeli. *Curiosities of Literature* (1791–1834) was the first of several discursive and entertaining collections. In *The Literary Character* (1795), he attempts to identify the qualities of temperament common to creative writers. Lord *Byron's annotations and encouragement led to an expanded version of the book. *Calamities of Authors* followed in 1813, *Quarrels of Authors* in 1814.

dissociation of sensibility A phrase coined by T. S. *Eliot in his essay 'The Metaphysical Poets' (1921) to describe a separation of thought from feeling in English poetry since the mid-17th century. Whereas John *Donne and the other 'metaphysical' poets were capable of a 'direct sensuous apprehension of thought', Eliot argued, *Milton, John *Dryden, and their successors, especially the Victorian poets, suffered from a general malaise of 'the mind of England' in which thought and feeling were cultivated separately. The argument was not supported in convincing detail, and the causes of the supposed dissociation—religious, scientific, or political—never clearly identified; but Eliot's conception of English poetic history as a process of psychic and linguistic disintegration was endorsed by Ezra *Pound, F. R. *Leavis, and the American *New Critics.

Divina commedia The greatest work of *Dante, comprising the *Inferno*, the *Purgatorio*, and the *Paradiso*, in *terza rima* (lines of eleven syllables, arranged in groups of three and rhyming *ababcbcdc*).

The *Inferno* is a description of hell, conceived as a graduated conical funnel, to the successive circles of which the various categories of sinners are assigned. The *Purgatorio* is a description of Purgatory, a mountain rising in circular ledges, on which are the various groups of repentant sinners. At the top of the mountain is the earthly paradise, where Dante encounters *Beatrice. In his visit to hell and Purgatory, Dante has for guide the poet *Virgil, and there he sees and converses with his lost friends or former foes. The *Paradiso* is a vision of a world of beauty, light, and song, where the poet's guide is Beatrice. The poem is not only an exposition of the future life, but a work of moral instruction, full of symbolism and allusions based on Dante's wide knowledge of philosophy, astronomy, natural science, and history.

Dante's name first occurs in English in *Chaucer, and that of Beatrice in Philip *Sidney; Dante was read and admired in the 17th century by John *Milton, Jeremy *Taylor, and Sir Thomas *Browne, among others. The first acknowledged translation was by the artist Jonathan Richardson in 1719, a blank verse version of the famous Ugolino episode (*Inferno*, Canto XXXIII), which remained a favourite with translators, including Thomas *Gray; it was also the subject of one of William *Blake's illustrations. His reputation rose in the 19th century with the admiration of Lord *Byron, P. B. *Shelley, Thomas *Carlyle, and others, and with the enthusiasm of political refugees such as Ugo Foscolo and Gabriele Rossetti (1783–1854), father of Dante Gabriel *Rossetti. In the 20th century he profoundly influenced T. S. *Eliot, who particularly praised his universality, his 'visual imagination', and his power to make 'the spiritual visible'.

Among well-known translations are those of Henry Cary (1805–14, blank verse); Henry Wadsworth *Longfellow (1867, blank terzine, or stanzas of three lines); P. H. Wicksteed (1899, prose); H. F. Tozer (1904, prose); G. L. Bickersteth (1932–55, *terza rima*); Laurence *Binyon (1933–43, *terza rima*); J. D. Sinclair (1939–46, prose); Dorothy *Sayers (1949–62, *terza rima*); C. H. *Sisson (1980, unrhymed verse); and A. Mandelbaum (1980–84, unrhymed verse).

DIXON, Ella Hepworth (1857–1932) A prolific journalist, who briefly edited *The English-Woman*, she published collections of short comic sketches about finding a husband (*My Flirtations*, 1892), short stories (*One Doubtful Hour*, 1904), and a notable *New Woman novel, *The Story of a Modern Woman* (1894). Dealing with sexual double standards and the struggles of women in the literary market-place, it stresses the importance of solidarity between women in the modern world. The novel contains satirical portraits of the *Yellow Book circle and Oscar *Wilde. Dixon's autobiography, *As I Knew Them*, appeared in 1930.

DIXON, Thomas, Jr (1864–1946) American Baptist minister, playwright, and novelist, born in North Carolina. He grew up during Reconstruction and his father joined the Ku Klux Klan. Angered by the representation of Southerners in a dramatization of *Uncle Tom's Cabin*, he began writing novels, producing *The Leopard's Spots* (1902), *The Clansman* (1905), and *The Traitor* (1915). All celebrate the South before the Civil War, describe African Americans as racial inferiors, and present Reconstruction as a betrayal. The stage version of *The Clansman* became the basis of D. W. Griffith's 1915 film *The Birth of a Nation*. His 1916 novel *Fall of a Nation* continues the theme of national decline.

DOBELL, Sydney Thompson (1824–74) Poet. *The Roman* (1850) is a dramatic poem inspired by sympathy with oppressed Italy; *Balder* (1854) is one of the most extensive productions of the *Spasmodic school. Only the first part was completed. It describes the inner turmoil and aspirations of a young poet, who has taken his bride and baby daughter to live in 'a tower gloomy and ruinous' while he plans his great work. His search for the ultimate experience of death is rewarded by the death of his baby in mysterious circumstances; his wife Amy goes mad; and finally, unable to witness her sufferings, Balder kills her. Balder's destructive egoism so shocked readers that Dobell prefaced a second edition with an explanation, claiming that his hero was not held up for admiration, but as a warning. In 1855 Dobell published (jointly with Alexander *Smith) *Sonnets on the War* and in 1856 *England in Time of War*.

DOBSON, Henry Austin (1840–1921) Poet and essayist, an accomplished writer of light verse, with a particular fondness for French forms such as the *triolet and the *rondeau. Many of his poems evoke the courtly elegance of French society of the 18th century. His collections include *Vignettes in Rhyme* (1873), *Proverbs in Porcelain* (1877), and *At the Sign of the Lyre* (1885). He was a significant figure in the late Victorian reassessment of the 18th century and his works include biographies of William *Hogarth (1879), Richard *Steele (1886), Oliver *Goldsmith (1888), Horace *Walpole (1890), Samuel *Richardson (1902), and Fanny *Burney (1903). He also published three series of *Eighteenth Century Vignettes* (1892; 1894; 1896).

Doctor, The A miscellany by Robert *Southey, published 1834–47 (7 vols), chiefly renowned for containing the nursery story of 'Goldilocks and the Three Bears'.

Dr Doolittle (1920) The first in a series of books by Hugh *Lofting about a vet who can speak to animals. The doctor practises in the idyllic world of Puddleby-on-the-Marsh, and despite accusations of racism he and the animal characters, including Polynesia the parrot, Gub-Gub the pig, and the two-headed Pushmi-Pullyu, have remained popular. Rex Harrison (1967) and Eddie Murphy (1998) have starred in film versions.

Dr Faustus, The Tragical History of A drama in blank verse and prose by Christopher *Marlowe, published 1604 and, in a radically different version known as the 'B-text', 1616. The earliest known performance was in 1594. It is perhaps the first dramatization of the medieval legend of a man who sold his soul to the devil, and who became identified with a Dr Faustus, a necromancer of the 16th century. The legend appeared in the *Faustbuch*, first published at Frankfurt in 1587, and was translated into English as *The History of the Damnable Life and Deserved Death of Doctor John Faustus*. Marlowe's play follows this translation in the general outline of the story, though not in the conception of the principal character, who from a mere magician becomes a man thirsting

for infinite power, ambitious to be 'great Emperor of the world'.

Faustus, weary of the sciences, turns to magic and calls up Mephistopheles, making a compact to surrender his soul to the devil in return for 24 years of life; during these Mephistopheles shall attend on him and give him all he demands. Then follow a number of scenes in which the compact is executed, notable among them the calling up of Helen of Troy, where Faustus addresses Helen in the well-known line: 'Was this the face that launched a thousand ships...' Faustus's anguish as the hour for the surrender of his soul draws near is poignantly depicted. The play differs greatly from the *Faust* of *Goethe both in its end and in the conception of Faustus's character. It has been the most frequently performed of Marlowe's plays in modern times.

Dr Jekyll and Mr Hyde, The Strange Case of A short novel by Robert Louis *Stevenson, published 1886. Dr Jekyll, a physician, discovers a drug by means of which he can create for himself a personality that manifests all his base instincts. This persona, repulsive in appearance, he assumes from time to time and calls Mr Hyde, and in it he gives rein to his vicious impulses. It gradually gains the greater ascendancy, and commits a horrible murder. Jekyll now finds himself from time to time involuntarily transformed into Hyde, while the drug loses its efficacy in restoring his original form and character. On the point of discovery and arrest he takes his own life. The novel's vivid exploration of the duality of human nature made it an immediate and enduring success. Stage, film, and televison adaptations have been numerous, and the phrase 'Jekyll and Hyde' has entered the language as an expression of a divided personality.

DOCTOROW, E. L. (Edgar Laurence) (1931–) American novelist, who worked as a script reader for Columbia pictures. His first novel, *Welcome to the Hard Times* (1960), reworks the western as a semi-philosophical treatise. *The Book of Daniel* (1971) is a fictionalized account of the Rosenberg trial and has much in common with Robert *Coover's *The Public Burning* (1977). His most commercially successful novel, *Ragtime* (1975), blends real-life figures of the early 20th century with a cast of emblematic Jewish and African American characters. *Loon Lake* (1980), *World's Fair* (1985), and *Billy Bathgate* (1989) focus on the Great Depression and its aftermath; *The Waterworks* (1994) on life in 19th-century New York. Recent novels include *The March* (2005), describing Sherman's march to the sea (1864–5) in the American Civil War and *City of God* (2000). Doctorow's essays were published as *Creationists* (2006). *All the Time In the World* (2011) is a story collection.

Doctor Thorne A novel by Anthony *Trollope, published 1858, the third of the *'Barsetshire' series.

Doctor Who Iconic British *science fiction television series (originally for children, but with a strong adult following) which started in 1963, running until 1989. It was successfully revived in 2005. Its hero, known only as 'The Doctor', has adventures which take him through time and space. Gradually a back-story of sorts has emerged, with the device of 'regeneration' used every time the lead actor departs.

documentary film Emerged in Britain during the 1930s as a distinctive kind of non-fiction *cinema, inspired equally by the romantic ethnography of Robert Flaherty (1884–1951), by *Russian film-makers' montage techniques, and by the European avant-garde. John Grierson (1898–1972) gathered a group of young intellectuals, including Humphrey *Jennings, Basil Wright (1907–87), Edgar Anstey (1907–87), Len Lye (1901–80), and Harry Watt (1906–87), who, together with W. H. *Auden, Benjamin *Britten, and others, became known as the 'documentary movement', producing such imaginative sponsored films as *Night Mail*, *Housing Problems*, and *Song of Ceylon*. Enlightened commercial sponsorship gave many post-war film-makers their first opportunity to tackle social themes, while *television later became the major patron of documentary, with its distinctive unobtrusive filming style sometimes known as 'cinéma vérité' or 'fly on the wall'.

DODD, William (1729–77) A popular preacher and royal chaplain whose debts led him to forge a bond in the name of his former pupil, the fifth earl of Chesterfield. Despite the efforts of Samuel *Johnson and others to secure a reduced sentence, he was hanged. Johnson wrote a sermon, known as *The Convict's Address*, for Dodd to preach in Newgate. His writings include *The Beauties of Shakespeare* (1752) and *Thoughts in Prison* (1777).

DODDRIDGE, Philip (1702–51) *Congregational minister and celebrated academy tutor. His most influential publications were *The Rise and Progress of Religion in the Soul* (1745); *The Family Expositor, or A Paraphrase and Version*

of the New Testament (1739–56); a life of Colonel James Gardiner (1747), who figures in Walter Scott's *'Waverley*; and, posthumously, his *Hymns* (1755) and academy *Lectures* (1763).

DODGSON, Charles Lutwidge (1832–98) Celebrated under his pseudonym Lewis Carroll. He became a lecturer in mathematics at Christ Church, Oxford in 1855. His most famous work, *'Alice's Adventures in Wonderland* (1865), originated in a boat trip with the young daughters of H. G. Liddell, Lorina, Alice, and Edith; it was for Alice that he expanded an impromptu story into book form. *Through the Looking-Glass and What Alice Found There* followed in 1871: both volumes were illustrated by John *Tenniel. One reviewer attributed the success of these works to the fact that, unlike most children's books of the period, they had no moral and did not teach anything.

Dodgson's other works include *Phantasmagoria and Other Poems* (1869), *The Hunting of the Snark* (1876), and *Sylvie and Bruno* (1889, vol. ii, 1893). Dodgson was a keen amateur photographer, with a particular interest in photographing little girls, whose friendship he valued highly; he also took some striking portraits of *Tennyson's sons.

DODSLEY, Robert (1703–64) Publisher who began writing poems while a footman, including *Servitude* (1729) and *The Muse in Livery* (1732). In 1735 he set up as a bookseller (with Alexander *Pope's help) in Pall Mall. He wrote several plays, including *The Toyshop: A Dramatic Satire* (1735) and a musical afterpiece, *The Blind Beggar of Bethnal Green* (1741). He published major work by Pope, Samuel *Johnson, Edward *Young, Oliver *Goldsmith, Thomas *Gray, Mark *Akenside, and William *Shenstone. His *Select Collection of Old Plays* (12 vols, 1744) and *A Collection of Poems, by Several Hands* (1748–58) were important embodiments of, and influences on, mid-18th-century taste. He was the prime instigator of Johnson's *Dictionary*, and in 1758 founded *The *Annual Register*.

dolce stil novo Poetic style exemplified in the lyric poetry of *Dante's *Vita nuova* and that of fellow Florentine poets, especially *Cavalcanti. The phrase was coined by Dante in the *Divina commedia* (*Purgatorio* XXIV). The style emphasizes personal inspiration and experience of love, harmony between content and style, smoothness of diction and metre, and the praise of the lady as a heaven-sent being. This model for poetry particularly appealed to the *Pre-Raphaelites, who added their own interpretations and elaborations.

'Dolores' A poem in *anapaests by A. C. *Swinburne, included in *Poems and Ballads* (1866). One of his most notorious works, it addresses Dolores, 'Our Lady of Pain', in a profane hymn to perverse and cruel sensual delights. It clearly shows Swinburne's obsession with erotic pain and the image of a 'splendid and sterile' *femme fatale*

Dolorous Stroke The stroke dealt by Balyn to King Pellam in Book II of Malory's *Morte Darthur*. The story is the starting point of the anthropological investigation in J. L. Weston's *From Ritual to Romance* (1920).

Dombey and Son, *Dealings with the Firm of* A novel by Charles *Dickens, published 1847–8. When the story opens Mr Dombey, the frigid head of the shipping house of Dombey and Son, has just been presented with a son and heir, Paul, and his wife dies. The father's love and ambition are centred in the boy, an odd, delicate, prematurely old child, who is sent to Dr Blimber's school, under whose strenuous discipline he sickens and dies. His death moved the nation nearly as much as the death of Little Nell in *The *Old Curiosity Shop*. Dombey neglects his devoted daughter Florence, and the estrangement is increased by the death of Paul. Walter Gay, a good-hearted youth in Dombey's employment, falls in love with her, but is sent to the West Indies by Dombey, who disapproves of their relationship. He is shipwrecked and believed drowned. Dombey marries again—a proud and penniless young widow, Edith Granger—but his arrogant treatment drives her into the arms of his villainous manager Carker, with whom she flies to France. They are pursued, Carker meets Dombey in a railway station, falls in front of a train, and is killed. The effect of the railways on English life and the changing landscape is a dominant theme in the novel. The house of Dombey fails; Dombey has lost his fortune, his son, and his wife; Florence has been driven by ill treatment to fly from him, and has married Walter Gay, who has survived his shipwreck. Thoroughly humbled, Dombey lives in desolate solitude till Florence returns to him, and at last finds the way to his heart.

DONAGHY, Michael (1954–2004) American poet, born in New York, who lived for many years in London. His first collection was *Shibboleth* (1988). Musical themes are central to Donaghy's work, and in the sequence 'O'Ryan's Belt' (*Errata*, 1993) issues of identity underlie

the precarious survival of songs from forgotten musicians. His writing is also provocatively inhabited by a range of attention-seeking, buttonholing monologuists. *Dances Learned Last Night: Poems 1975–1995* appeared in 2000, and a posthumous volume, *Safest*, was published in 2005.

DONALDSON, Julia (1948–) MBE, Children's Laureate (2011–13), best known for her books for young children. *The Gruffalo* (1999, illustrated by Axel Scheffler), a best-selling *picturebook, has been adapted as an animated film for television and for the stage. *The Gruffalo's Child* (2004) is a sequel.

Don Juan According to a Spanish story apparently first dramatized by Tirso de Molina in *El burlador de Sevilla* (*The Seville Deceiver*), and subsequently by Molière in *Le Festin de pierre* (*Dom Juan, or The Stone Banquet*), and by Mozart in *Don Giovanni*, he was Don Juan Tenorio, of Seville. Having seduced an aristocratic lady, he is surprised by her father, whom he kills in a duel. Seeing a statue of the father erected over his tomb, Juan jestingly invites it to dine with him. The statue takes up the invitation, seizes Juan, and delivers the unrepentant rake to hell. Don Juan is the proverbial licentious, heartless, and, in some versions, impious seducer. This legendary figure has inspired countless reworkings in a variety of genres. Among them are plays by Thomas *Shadwell (*The Libertine*), Carlo Goldoni, Alexander *Pushkin, Henry de Montherlant, and George Bernard *Shaw (*Man and Superman*), as well as a poem by Lord *Byron. For Robert *Browning's Don Juan see *Fifine at the Fair*. Derek *Walcott's *The Joker of Seville* (1978) is an adaptation of *The Seville Deceiver* based on Roy *Campbell's blank verse translation.

Don Juan An unfinished epic satire in *ottava rima* by Lord *Byron, published 1819–24. Don Juan, a young gentleman of Seville, is sent abroad by his mother at the age of 16, in disgrace after an intrigue. His ship is wrecked and the passengers take to the long-boat. After many tribulations, Juan is cast up on a Greek island. He is restored to life by Haidée, the daughter of a Greek pirate, and the pair fall in love. The father, who is supposed dead, returns, finds the lovers together, and captures the fighting Juan, who is put in chains on one of the pirate's ships. He is then sold as a slave in Constantinople to the sultan's wife, who has fallen in love with him. He arouses her jealousy and is threatened with death, but escapes to the

Russian army, which is besieging Ismail. Because of his gallant conduct he is sent with dispatches to St Petersburg, where he attracts the favour of the empress Catherine, who sends him on a political mission to England. The last cantos (the 'English cantos') of the unfinished work are taken up with a satirical description of social conditions in England and with the love affairs of Juan. Don Juan himself is a charming, handsome young man, who delights in succumbing to the beautiful women he meets, but his character is little more than the connecting thread in a long social comedy. Despite critical outrage, the work became increasingly successful with the general public and was much admired by *Goethe, who translated a part of it. The outspoken wit and satire are especially directed at hypocrisy in all its forms, at social and sexual conventions, and at sentimentality. There are many attacks on the objects of Byron's scorn, among them *Southey, *Coleridge, *Wordsworth, and Wellington, Lord Londonderry.

DONNE, John (1572–1631) Poet and clergyman, related on his mother's side to Sir Thomas *More, born in London into a Catholic family. Educated at home by Catholic tutors, Donne went at the age of 11 to Hart Hall, Oxford (now Hertford College), popular with crypto-Catholics. Catholicism debarred him from taking a university degree and also from any public career. A portrait of 1592 bears a Spanish motto, *Antes muerto que mudado* (Sooner dead than changed), proclaiming his loyalty to Catholicism. However, in 1593 his younger brother Henry died in Newgate, having been arrested for harbouring a Catholic priest. This may have influenced Donne's decision to renounce the Catholic faith. *Satire III* may reflect this moment of crisis. He sailed as a gentleman volunteer with *Essex to sack Cadiz (1596) and with Walter *Ralegh to hunt the Spanish treasure ships off the Azores (1597). His poems 'The Storm' and 'The Calm' commemorate these voyages. On his return he became secretary to Sir Thomas Egerton (1540–1617), lord keeper of the great seal. He forfeited his chance of a civil career when late in 1601 he secretly married Lady Egerton's ward Ann More. He was dismissed from Egerton's service and briefly imprisoned. For fourteen years he tried to find employment, depending on the charity of his wife's relations and living with his ever-growing family in a cottage at Mitcham. In 1612 he moved to a London house owned by his patron, Sir Robert Drury (1575–1615); in honour of Sir Robert's dead child Elizabeth, he wrote his extravagant

Anniversaries. Other friends and patrons in these years were Lucy, countess of Bedford, for whom he probably wrote at least some of the Holy Sonnets, Magdalen Herbert (mother of George *Herbert), for whom he wrote *La Corona,* and Sir Robert Ker, Viscount Rochester. Despite Ker's good offices, *James I considered Donne unfit for confidential employment and urged him to enter the Church, which he did in 1615. Donne held several livings and the divinity readership at Lincoln's Inn. His wife died in 1617 at the age of 33, after giving birth to their twelfth child (the sonnet 'Since she whom I loved' commemorates her), and the following year Donne went as chaplain to the earl of Doncaster in his embassy to the German princes. His 'Hymn to Christ at the Author's Last Going into Germany', full of apprehension of death, was written before this journey. In 1621 he procured the deanery of St Paul's. One of the most celebrated preachers of his age, he died on 31 March 1631, having first, as his earliest biographer Izaak *Walton records, had his portrait drawn wearing his shroud and standing on a funeral urn, as if rising from the dead.

His earliest poems, the Satires and Love Elegies, belong to the 1590s. His unfinished satirical epic 'The Progress of the Soul' bears the date 1601, and some of his Holy Sonnets were probably written in 1609–11. His 'Songs and Sonnets' are, however, largely undatable. Donne's prose works include *Pseudo-Martyr* (1610), denigrating Catholics who had died for their faith, and *Ignatius his Conclave,* a scabrous satire on the Jesuits (1611). *Biathanatos,* the first English defence of suicide (to which Donne confessed he was tempted), could not be published until after his death. His *Essays in Divinity* (1651) were composed in preparation for his ordination and the *Devotions* (1624) were assembled in less than a month from notes made during a near-fatal fever. His sermons, edited by his son John, appeared after his death in three volumes, *LXXX Sermons* (1640), *Fifty Sermons* (1649), and *XXVI Sermons* (1660). His poems were collected by his son John and published in 1633 (2nd, enlarged, edn 1635). *See also* METAPHYSICAL POETS.

Don Quixote de la Mancha A comic romance by Miguel de *Cervantes, dated 1605, a second part appearing in 1615. Cervantes initially gave his work the form of a burlesque of the ballads and romances of chivalry (*see* AMADIS OF GAUL; PALMERIN OF ENGLAND), which were already beginning to lose their popularity. But he soon ceased to write mere burlesque, as the character of his hero developed and deepened, and his work acquired the richness and profundity that have made it one of the most popular classics ever written. Don Quixote, a poor gentleman of La Mancha, a man of gentle and amiable disposition and otherwise sane, has had his wits disordered by inordinate devotion to the tales of chivalry, and imagines himself called upon to roam the world in search of adventures on his old nag Rocinante, and clad in rusty armour, accompanied by a squire Sancho Panza, a curious mixture of shrewdness and credulity, whom he lures with the prospect of the governorship of the island of Barataria. Quixote seeks to conform to chivalric tradition by electing a beautiful damsel, one who in fact is a strapping peasant girl from a neighbouring village, to be the mistress of his heart. To him she is known as Dulcinea del Toboso, an honour of which she is entirely unaware. He is in absurd adventures, as in the famous episode (I. 8) when he tilts at windmills, imagining them to be giants. Finally one of his friends, Sansón Carrasco, in order to force him to return home, disguises himself as a knight, defeats Don Quixote in armed combat, and requires him to abstain for a year from chivalrous exploits. This period Don Quixote resolves to spend as a shepherd, living a pastoral life, but, falling sick on his return to his village, after a few days he dies. The plot also contains several lengthy digressions, including the 'Tale of *Inappropriate Curiosity'. After the appearance of the first part of *Don Quixote*, a continuation was issued by a writer who styled himself Alonso *Fernández de Avellaneda, a forgery with which Cervantes ironically engages in his own second part. The book was translated into English by Thomas Shelton (fl. 1598–1629) in 1612 and 1620, by John Phillips (1631–1706?), nephew of John *Milton, in 1687, and in the 18th century by at least Peter Motteux and Tobias *Smollett. John Rutherford's Penguin Classic version appeared in 2000. *Don Quixote's* underlying theme, the confrontation of illusion with reality, prefigures a topic that has been a staple of later fiction; its comic irony, multiple perspectives, and metafictional elements (e.g. its use of parody, its series of unreliable narrators, its characters' awareness of themselves as literary figures, and its general literary playfulness) have proved seminal.

Don Sebastian A tragicomedy by John *Dryden, produced 1689, published 1691. Dryden's first play after the (for him) disastrous Glorious Revolution, it is full of complicated political allusion. King Sebastian of Portugal, brave, pious, and a victim of foreign usurpation,

represents the deposed Catholic James II. His conqueror, the tyrant Muley Moloch, perhaps represents the new king, William, and is killed in a revolt. The comic sub-plot, involving the Mufti and Mustapha, ridicules James II's enemies, the Anglican clergy and the London mob.

DOOLITTLE, Hilda (1886–1961) American poet and novelist, who wrote as 'H.D.' In 1911 she followed her friend Ezra *Pound to Europe, where both became leading members of the *imagist movement. She married Richard *Aldington in 1913, but the marriage was not a success. She began a long-standing relationship with the writer *Bryher (Winifred Ellerman) in 1919. Her several volumes of poetry, from her first, *Sea Garden* (1916), to her last, the quasi-epic *Helen in Egypt* (1961), show a deep involvement with classical mythology, a mysticism in part influenced by her *Moravian ancestry, a sharp, spare use of natural imagery, and interesting experiments with *vers libre*. With Bryher she founded the film journal *Close Up* (1927–33) and made a number of experimental films including *Borderline* (1930). She also published several novels, including *Bid Me to Live* (1960), a *roman à clef* about her *Bloomsbury years, and *Tribute to Freud* (1965), an account of her analysis by Sigmund *Freud in 1933. Her *Collected Poems* were published in 1984 and a restored version of her memoir *The Gift* in 1998.

Doomsday Book (Domesday Book) 'The Book of the day of assessment'; the name since the 12th century of the record of the great inquest or survey of the lands of England made by order of William the Conqueror in 1086. It contains records of the ownership, area, and value of lands, and of the numbers of tenants, livestock, and so on.

Dorothea, St A Christian martyr who suffered in the persecution under Diocletian (*c*.304). Her story forms the subject of *The *Virgin Martyr* by Philip Massinger and Thomas Dekker, and an early poem by Gerald Manley *Hopkins.

DORSET, earl of *See* SACKVILLE, THOMAS.

DOS PASSOS, John Roderigo (1896–1970) American novelist. His first important novel, *Three Soldiers* (1921), which has war as its subject, was followed by many others, notably *Manhattan Transfer* (1925), a collective portrait in hundreds of fictional episodes of life in New York City, and *U.S.A.* (1938), a trilogy composed of *The 42nd Parallel* (1930), *1919* (1932), and *The Big Money* (1936). *U.S.A.* tries to capture the variety and multiplicity of American life in the first decades of the 20th century. In 1938 Jean-Paul *Sartre declared Dos Passos the 'greatest writer of our time'. He also wrote poetry, essays, travel writings, memoirs, and plays.

DOSTOEVSKY, Fedor Mikhailovich (1821–81) Russian prose writer. In April 1849 Dostoevsky was arrested and sent to the Omsk penal settlement for four years, during which he underwent a religious conversion, rejecting the progressive ideas of his early years, and replacing them by deep faith in the Russian Orthodox Church. After his return from Siberia in December 1859 he regained literary prominence with *Notes from the House of the Dead* (1860–61), a fictional portrayal of penal servitude, and the novel *The Insulted and the Injured* (1861) that refuted utopianism. His views on his travels in Western Europe are recorded in *Winter Notes on Summer Impressions* (1863), revealing his xenophobia and Russian chauvinism. In London, which he describes as 'Baal', centre of world capitalism, he saw the Crystal Palace of the 1862 World Exhibition, an image used to express the corruption of the modern scientific world in *Notes from Underground* and other works. Dostoevsky made further trips abroad throughout the 1860s. His reputation is based on the series of brilliant works which followed, *Notes from Underground* (1864), *Crime and Punishment* (1866), *The Idiot* (1868), *The Devils* (1872), *An Adolescent* (1875; also translated as *A Raw Youth*), and *The Brothers Karamazov* (1880). They reveal extraordinary powers of character analysis, and show Dostoevsky to be a significant and powerful thinker. Dostoevsky admired William *Shakespeare, Walter *Scott, Lord *Byron, and in particular Charles *Dickens, who had been known and translated in Russia since the 1830s. In his Omsk prison Dostoevsky read *The *Pickwick Papers* and *David Copperfield*. His letters and notebooks are full of references to Dickens, and they share an interest in the city, children, crime, and the suffering of the innocent. Many of Dostoevsky's novels appeared in English in the 1880s. Robert Louis *Stevenson was an early admirer, claiming in 1886 that *Crime and Punishment* was 'the greatest book I have read in ten years'. Its influence on *Dr Jekyll and Mr Hyde* (1886) is apparent. The main impact of Dostoevsky's work in England followed the appearance of Maurice *Baring's *Landmarks in Russian Literature* (1910), J. M. *Murry's *Fyodor Dostoevsky* (1916), and especially the translations by Constance *Garnett (1912–20).

Double Dealer, The A comedy by William *Congreve, produced 1693, published 1694. The Double Dealer is Maskwell, who is employed by the passionate and promiscuous Lady Touchwood to break off the match between Lord Touchwood's heir Mellefont and Cynthia. The action of the play takes place in Lord Touchwood's house in the three hours after dinner on the night before Mellefont and Cynthia's wedding day.

Double Marriage, The See MASSINGER, PHILIP.

DOUGHTY, Charles Montagu (1843–1926) Travel writer and poet, principally remembered for his remarkable record of *Travels in Arabia Deserta* 1888, carried out in 1876–8. The book was republished in 1921 with an introduction by T. E. *Lawrence, and widely read in Edward *Garnett's abridged version, *Wanderings in Arabia* (1908). It is notable for its extraordinary style: Doughty disapproved of 'Victorian prose', and mingled his own with Chaucerian and Elizabethan English, Latin, and Arabic. He wrote equally eccentric volumes of verse.

Douglas A romantic tragedy in blank verse by John *Home, based on the ballad 'Gill Morrice', and first performed in Edinburgh in 1756, where it outraged those who believed it improper for a clergyman to write for the stage. David *Hume and Adam *Smith supported it, the former saluting its improvement on 'the unhappy barbarism' of Shakespeare.

DOUGLAS, Lord Alfred (1870–1945) Poet, third son of the ninth marquess of Queensbury. He met Oscar *Wilde in 1891 and it was to him that Wilde addressed his letter from prison, *De Profundis*. Douglas translated Wilde's *Salome* from French to English (1894) and wrote various defensive accounts of his relationship with him, including *Oscar Wilde and Myself* (1914) and the less extreme *Oscar Wilde: A Summing up* (1940). He also published around twenty volumes of minor verse. His *Autobiography* appeared in 1929.

DOUGLAS, Gawin (Gavin) (*c*.1476–1522) Scottish poet and bishop of Dunkeld. He wrote an allegorical dream poem, *The Palice of Honour* (*c*.1501; pub. *c*.1535), dedicated to James IV, and a translation of the *Aeneid* (*Eneados*, 1513; printed 1553). He was one of the first to draw the distinction between *Scots and 'Inglis', and, unlike many of his contemporaries, wrote only in the vernacular. Ezra *Pound admired him and there is evidence that his version of Virgil was used by the earl of *Surrey and Thomas Sackville.

DOUGLAS, Keith (1920–44) Poet; the only volume published in his lifetime was *Selected Poems* (1943). He enlisted in 1940, was killed in Normandy in June 1944, and is inevitably remembered largely as a war poet, whose descriptions of wartime Cairo and desert fighting and whose contemplations of death ('Simplify me when I'm dead') show a rapidly maturing energy and simplicity of diction. *Alamein to Zem Zem* (1946) is a vivid experimental narrative of desert warfare. There are editions of Douglas's *Complete Poems* (1978), prose (1985), and letters (2000).

DOUGLASS, Frederick (Frederick Augustus Washington Bailey) (1818–95) Abolitionist, orator, editor, statesman, and autobiographer, born a slave in Maryland. He was sent to Baltimore, aged 12, where the wife of his owner taught him to read, and escaped from a later cruel owner in 1838. His autobiography, *Narrative of the Life of Frederick Douglass, an American Slave*, was published in 1845 to huge acclaim, and led to tours of Great Britain and Ireland. It is the most influential and significant account of a slave's life ever published. Douglass later began an anti-slavery newspaper, *The North Star*, advised President Lincoln during the American Civil War, and held several government offices. *See also* SLAVERY.

'Douglas Tragedy, The' A ballad included in Walter Scott's *Minstrelsy of the Scottish Border*, the story of the carrying off of Lady Margaret by Lord William Douglas. They are pursued by her father and seven brothers, who are killed in the ensuing fight. Douglas dies of his wounds and she does not survive him.

Dove Cottage Near the north-east shore of Grasmere, the home of William and Dorothy *Wordsworth (1799–1807), subsequently occupied by Thomas *De Quincey. It is now owned by the Dove Cottage Trust.

DOWIE, Ménie Muriel (1867–1945) Novelist and travel writer, who made her name with her travel book *A Girl in the Karpathians* (1891). *Women Adventurers* (1893) is a collection of essays. Her first novel, *Gallia* (1895), whose frank treatment of sexual relations established her as a leading *New Woman writer, was followed by *The Crook of the Bough* (1898) and *Love and his Mask* (1901). Her short stories, published in the *Yellow Book and *Chambers's Journal*, were collected as *Some Whims of Fate*

(1896), and her *Country Life* column was reprinted as *Things about our Neighbourhood* (1903). She withdrew from the literary scene after her scandalous divorce in January 1903.

DOWLAND, John (1563–1626) English composer and lutenist. He issued *The First Booke of Songes or Ayres of Fowre Partes with Tableture for the Lute* in 1597, the earliest and most popular book of its kind. A second (1600) and third (1603) book followed. A *Pilgrimes Solace* (1612), a fourth collection of songs, was more penitential in character. Richard *Barnfield's sonnet 'If music and sweet poetry agree' celebrates Dowland's success. Some of his song texts are by courtly amateurs like Sir Fulke *Greville or Sir Edward *Dyer, and there is an occasional poem by John *Donne or George *Peele. Most have texts by unknown authors, some perhaps by Dowland himself.

DOWSON, Ernest (1867–1900) Poet, who established himself in the London society of Aubrey *Beardsley, Richard *Le Gallienne, Oscar *Wilde, and their friends. He contributed poems to the *Yellow Book, the *Savoy, and the anthologies published by the *Rhymers Club, He was received into the Roman Catholic Church in 1891. His father was now suffering from advanced tuberculosis, and died (possibly by suicide) in 1894; within months his mother hanged herself. Dowson's stories *Dilemmas* appeared in 1895, the first of his two books of poetry, *Verses*, in 1896, and his second, *Decorations* (half of which consists of his experiments with 'prose poems'), in 1899. His one-act verse play *The Pierrot of the Minute* was published in 1897.

The poems group themselves chiefly into love poetry; devotional poems; poems of the natural world; and above all poems of ennui and world-weariness, such as 'Vitae Summa Brevis' ('They are not long, the days of wine and roses'), 'To One in Bedlam', and several translations and adaptations of *Verlaine. *See also* ART FOR ART'S SAKE.

DOYLE, Arthur Conan (1859–1930) Writer, the son of an artist and draughtsman, Charles Doyle, and nephew of the illustrator Richard Doyle. Educated at Stonyhurst and Edinburgh, he became a doctor and practised at Southsea, 1882–90. He is chiefly remembered for his widely celebrated creation of the subtle, hawk-eyed detective Sherlock *Holmes, whose brilliant solutions to a wide variety of crimes began in *A Study in Scarlet* (1887), continued through a long line of stories, chiefly in the *Strand Magazine*, and were collected in *The Adventures of Sherlock Holmes* (1892), *The Memoirs of Sherlock Holmes* (1894), *The Hound of the Baskervilles* (1902), and other works. His friend and foil, the stolid Dr Watson with whom he shares rooms in Baker Street, attends him throughout most of his adventures (*see* DETECTIVE FICTION). Doyle also wrote a long series of historical and other romances, which he believed to be superior to his 'Holmes' stories. Notable among them are *Micah Clarke* (1889), *The White Company* (1891), *The Exploits of Brigadier Gerard* (1896), the first of many 'Gerard' tales, *Rodney Stone* (1896), and *The Lost World* (1912). In 1902 Doyle wrote an influential pamphlet, 'The War in South Africa', which was much translated; and later many books on public themes, including a long history of the Flanders campaign in the First World War. His one-act play *Waterloo* provided Sir Henry *Irving in 1894 with one of his most successful parts. In 1926 Doyle published his *History of Spiritualism*, one of several books he wrote on the subject. His interest in fairies is a connection with the work of his uncle Richard Doyle, who illustrated many *fairy stories. See Andrew Lycett, *The Man Who Created Sherlock Holmes* (2007).

DOYLE, Roddy (1958–) Novelist, born in Dublin and educated at University College there, whose 'Barrytown trilogy' describes the adventures and misadventures of the Rabbitte family on Dublin's northside. In *The Commitments* (1987) Jimmy organizes a band to bring 'soul to the people'; in *The Snapper* (1990) his sister Sharon has an illegitimate baby; and in *The Van* (1991) Jimmy Sr struggles to survive unemployment and goes share in a chip van with his friend Bimbo. The dialogue is lively, contemporary, authentic, the scene setting minimal, and the large Rabbitte family portrayed with affection and sympathy. *Paddy Clarke Ha Ha Ha* (1993, *Booker Prize) vividly evokes the childhood world of a 10-year-old boy, whose life is overshadowed by the breakdown of his parents' marriage. *The Woman Who Walked into Doors* (1997) is the tough, sombre first-person narrative of an alcoholic mother of four, widowed when her violently abusive husband is shot by the Gardaí during an armed robbery. The emergence of the protagonist from alcoholism is chronicled in a sequel, *Paula Spencer* (2006). *A Star Called Henry* (1999) and *Oh, Play That Thing* (2004) trace the comic adventures of Henry Smart through a series of historical scenarios, including the Easter Rising in Dublin and the Jazz Age in Chicago. The stories

of *The Deportees* (2007) focus on immigration and multiculturalism in Celtic Tiger Ireland.

Drab Term used first by C. S. *Lewis in *English Literature in the Sixteenth Century* to denote poetry and prose of the later medieval period until the early Renaissance: 'a period in which, for good or ill, poetry has little richness either of sound or images'. Although Lewis claimed that he did not use the term disapprovingly, it has generally been employed to characterize Tudor works which are unappealing to a modern ear. Typically, 'Drab' poets preferred strongly rhythmical verse forms such as poulter's measure, making use of alliteration and of poetic 'fillers' such as 'eke', and employing few Latinate words. An example from *Tottel's Miscellany* illustrates these features:

'I know under the grene the serpent how he
　lurkes.
The hammer of the restles forge I wote eke how
　it wurkes.
I know and can by roate the tale that I would tel:
But oft the wordes come furth awrie of him that
　loueth wel.'

Yet many so-called 'Drab' writers, especially Sir Thomas *Wyatt and the earl of *Surrey, have been much admired. T. S. *Eliot admired the Tudor translators of *Seneca's plays, editing the *Tenne Tragedies* in 1927; and many other 'Drab' translations were of crucial importance for the later Renaissance in England, such as Sir Thomas *Hoby's version of *Castiglione's *Courtier* (1561) and Arthur *Golding's of *Ovid's *Metamorphoses* (1567).

DRABBLE, Dame Margaret (1939–) Novelist, born in Sheffield, and educated at the Mount School, York, and Newnham College, Cambridge. The novelist and critic A. S. *Byatt is her sister, and Drabble's first novel, *A Summer Birdcage* (1963), was a first-person account of the relationship between two young graduate sisters. It was followed by *The Garrick Year* (1964), which draws upon her brief career as an actor with the Royal Shakespeare Company. Her early novels deal primarily with the dilemma of educated young women caught by the conflicting claims of maternity, sexuality, and intellectual and economic aspiration. They include *The Millstone* (1965), the story of a young unmarried mother, which won the John Llewellyn Rhys Prize; *Jerusalem the Golden* (1968), about the social ambitions of a girl who comes to London from the north of England, which won the James Tait Black Memorial Prize; *The Needle's Eye* (1972), in which an heiress takes voluntary poverty upon herself (*Yorkshire Post*

Book Award); and *The Middle Ground* (1980), which tells the story of a journalist who comes to doubt her feminist creed. Later novels have a broader canvas, a more ironic relationship with traditional narration, and a wider interest in documenting social change: *The Ice Age* (1977) is a *condition of England novel that documents the effects of the oil crisis on social attitudes, while a trilogy of novels comprising *The Radiant Way* (1987), *A Natural Curiosity* (1989), and *The Gates of Ivory* (1991) follows the fortunes of three women friends through the social and political changes in Britain in the 1980s, moving in the third volume to war-torn Cambodia. *The Witch of Exmoor* (1996) is a mordant family chronicle inspired by a premiss borrowed from John Rawls (1921–2002), while *The Peppered Moth* (2004) traces a Yorkshire family through several generations. Later novels include *The Sea Lady* (2006), while her non-fiction includes *A Writer's Britain* (1979) and biographies of Arnold *Bennett (1974) and Angus *Wilson (1995). From 1979 to 2006 she was editor of *The Oxford Companion to English Literature*, seeing it through its 5th and 6th editions; she was awarded the DBE in 2008. She is married to the biographer Michael *Holroyd.

Dracula A novel by Bram *Stoker, published 1897, the most famous of all tales of vampirism. The story is told through the diaries of a young solicitor, Jonathan Harker, his fiancée Mina, her friend Lucy Westenra, and Dr John Seward, the superintendent of a large lunatic asylum at Purfleet, in Essex. It begins with Harker's journey to Count Dracula's eerie castle in Transylvania, in connection with the count's purchase of Carfax, an ancient estate adjoining Dr Seward's asylum. After horrifying experiences as an inmate of the castle, Jonathan makes his way to a ruined chapel, where he finds 50 great wooden boxes filled with earth recently dug from the graveyard of the Draculas, in one of which the un-dead count is lying, gorged with blood. These boxes are shipped to Whitby and thence to Carfax. Dracula disembarks at Whitby in the shape of a wolf, having dispatched the entire ship's crew en route, and proceeds to vampirize Lucy who, despite multiple blood transfusions and the occult precautions of Dr Seward's old teacher Professor Van Helsing, dies drained of blood but remains un-dead until staked through the heart. The rest of the book tells of the attempt to save Mina from Dracula's insidious advances and of the search for the boxes of earth, his only refuge between sunrise and sunset. All but one of these are neutralized with fragments of the Host. The last, with Dracula in it, is followed by Van Hel-

sing and the others back to Transylvania where, after a thrilling chase, the count is beheaded and stabbed through the heart, at which his body crumbles to dust.

The sinister but glamorous figure of Dracula has been the subject of many films, including F. W. Murnau's silent *Nosferatu* (1922) and Tod Browning's early talkie *Dracula* (1931). Stoker's novel, reflecting as it does contemporary thinking on the cultural role of women, sexuality, immigration, colonialism, and disease, has attracted much recent academic interest, while its prominence within popular culture is undiminished, and film, television, and stage adaptations continue to proliferate. *See* VAMPIRES.

Dramatic Idyls A volume of six poems, by Robert *Browning, published 1879. After the publication of a sequel (*see* DRAMATIC IDYLS, SECOND SERIES), the collection was called 'Dramatic Idyls, First Series'. The spelling 'Idyl' differentiated the poems from *Tennyson's 'Idylls'. The poems are among the finest of Browning's later period, particularly 'Ivàn Ivànovitch', a story based on a Russian folk tale of a woman who threw her children to the wolves in order to save her own life. The collection has a notable unity of tone, and focuses on human behaviour in conditions of extreme stress.

Dramatic Idyls, Second Series A volume of six poems by Robert *Browning, published 1880 and influenced by the success of the 1879 volume (*see* DRAMATIC IDYLS). Although the collection does not have the unity of the first series, it demonstrates Browning's continuing interest and vitality in the dramatic monologue form, notably in 'Clive'.

dramatic irony An effect produced by discrepancies between a character's misperception of his or her situation and the audience's fuller knowledge of that character's true destiny. *Macbeth* provides an example in Duncan's cheerful speech on arriving at Macbeth's castle, where his murder has already been planned. When found in a *tragedy, this is sometimes called 'tragic irony'. The device is also found in narrative works, as in the climactic eleventh chapter of Joseph Conrad's *The *Secret Agent*, when Verloc summons his wife for marital intimacy, unaware that she is murderously enraged upon discovering his complicity in her brother's death.

Dramatic Lyrics A collection of poems by Robert *Browning, published in 1842 as no. III of *Bells and Pomegranates*. Browning's publisher, Edward *Moxon, persuaded him to vary the format of the series, which had been intended to consist solely of plays. The collection included some of Browning's best-known poems, such as 'My Last Duchess', 'Porphyria's Lover', and 'The Pied Piper of Hamelin'.

dramatic monologue A poem presented as though spoken not by the poet but by a single imagined or historical person, usually to an imagined auditor: the speaker or 'persona' is thus dramatized, often ironically, through his or her own words. The early masters of this modern form in English are Robert *Browning (as in 'My Last Duchess', 1842, and 'Fra Lippo Lippi', 1855) and Alfred *Tennyson (as in *'Ulysses' and 'St Simeon Stylites', both 1842). From the 20th century the most celebrated example is T. S. Eliot's 'The Love Song of J. Alfred *Prufrock' (1917); poets of the later 20th century who favoured the form include Carol Ann *Duffy and Andrew *Motion. See Elizabeth A. Howe, *The Dramatic Monologue* (1996).

Dramatic Romances and Lyrics A collection of poems by Robert *Browning, published 1845 as no. VII of *Bells and Pomegranates*. Many of the poems were revised before publication in consultation with Elizabeth Barrett *Browning, whom Browning was courting at the time. The collection included some of Browning's best-known poems, such as 'How They Brought the Good News from Ghent to Aix', 'The Lost Leader', and 'The Flight of the Duchess'.

Dramatis Personae A collection of poems by Robert *Browning, published 1864. A few had been published previously, but most were new. They were marked by Browning's grief after the death of his wife (*see* BROWNING, ELIZABETH BARRETT) in 1861, and by his searching examination of the relation of human to divine love, especially as it concerns the nature of belief. A striking unity of theme and structure makes the collection an intermediate stage in Browning's development between *Men and Women* and *The *Ring and the Book*. Several of the poems are anthology favourites—notably 'Rabbi Ben Ezra' and 'Prospice'—but the heart of the collection is the long dramatic monologues such as 'A Death in the Desert', *'Caliban upon Setebos', and 'Mr Sludge, "the Medium"'.

DRAYCOTT, Jane (1954–) British poet, born in London; she studied English in London and Bristol. Strongly influenced by medieval dream poetry, she is also indebted to Gerard Manley Hopkins, whom she admires for 'his furious effort of expression, the choreography

of his rhythms and aural precision'. Draycott's acute awareness of sound sees her frequently using extended sentences in which meaning proliferates and echoes, allying her work with that of her contemporaries Medbh *McGuckian and Alice *Oswald. Her full-length collections include *Prince Rupert's Drop* (1999), *Tideway*, an illustrated poem about the Thames (2002), and *The Night Tree* (2004).

DRAYTON, Michael (1563–1631) Poet, born at Hartshill, in Warwickshire. His early life was spent in the service of Sir Henry Goodyer (1534–95), who introduced him to Lucy, countess of Bedford (1581–1627). His friends included John *Stow, William Camden, Ben *Jonson, William *Drummond, William *Browne, George *Wither, and possibly William *Shakespeare. He died in comparative poverty, but was buried in Westminster Abbey, where Lady Anne *Clifford paid for his monument. He was a prolific writer, and frequently revised and republished earlier works. His first publication, *The Harmony of the Church* (1591), comprised paraphrases from the Old Testament and Apocrypha. The nine *Spenserian pastorals of *Idea: The Shepherd's Garland* (1593) include praise of *Elizabeth I and a lament for the death of Sir Philip *Sidney. *Idea's Mirror* (1594), a 64-sonnet sequence, continued the pastorals' lovelorn theme. In its final version, entitled *Idea* (1619), it included the famous sonnet 'Since there's no help, come let us kiss and part'. His poems on legendary and historical figures began in about 1594 with *Piers Gaveston*, followed by *Matilda* (1594), an epic poem in rhyme royal, *Robert, Duke of Normandy* (1596), and *Mortimeriados* (1596), a long poem on the Wars of the Roses, later revised as *The Barons' Wars* (1603). *England's Heroical Epistles* (1597) was modelled on *Ovid's *Heroides*, consisting of twelve pairs of verse letters in heroic couplets exchanged by lovers from English history, such as Henry II and Fair *Rosamond, and Edward IV and Jane Shore. Another Ovidian poem was *Endimion and Phoebe* (1595), which acknowledges help Drayton received from Thomas *Lodge. *The Owl*, a satire, perhaps reflecting Drayton's failure to thrive at *James I's court, appeared in 1604, and *Odes* in 1606. This collection included 'To the Virginian Voyage' and 'To the Cambro-Britons and their Harp' and his 'Ballad of Agincourt', which opens with the lines 'Fair stood the wind for France | When we our sails advance'. He later wrote a narrative poem on the same subject, *The Battle of Agincourt* (1627), publishing in the same volume *The Miseries of Queen Margaret*, *Nimphidia*, *The*

Court of Faery, a wholly original and delightful epic of fairyland, and the interesting epistle to Henry Reynolds 'Of Poets and Poesie'. Drayton's largest project, the great topographical poem on England, **Poly-Olbion*, took many years and appeared in two parts, 1612 and 1622. Philip **Henslowe's diary shows that he also collaborated on plays but none has survived. His *Works* have been definitively edited in six volumes by J. W. Hebel, K. Tillotson, and B. H. Newdigate (1931–41; rev. 1961). See B. H. Newdigate, *Michael Drayton and his Circle* (1961); J. R. Brink, *Michael Drayton Revisited* (1990).

Dream of Gerontius, The *See* NEWMAN, JOHN HENRY.

Dream of John Ball, A A historical socialist fantasy by William **Morris, published in *Commonweal* (Nov. 1886–Jan. 1887, in volume form 1888). It takes the form of a dream in which the narrator is carried back to the time of the early stages of the Peasants' Revolt in 1381; he encounters the 'hedge-priest' John Ball, and in their final night-long dialogue Morris both satirizes the 19th-century present and offers hope for a future when men 'shall see things as they verily are' and rise in successful protest against their exploitation.

Dream of the Rood An Old English poem of 156 lines, found in the 10th-century **Vercelli Book, in three parts: a description of the poet's vision of the cross and the address to him by the cross describing the Crucifixion (paralleled in part by the Northumbrian runic inscriptions on the 8th-century **Ruthwell Cross in Dumfriesshire); a homiletic address to the dreamer by the cross; and a declaration of faith and confidence in heaven by the dreamer himself. There has been much argument about the coherence of the poem; it seems likely that, as it stands, it was composed in one piece, drawing on an earlier cross prosopopoeia related to the tradition of riddles in Old English and Latin. The poem is greatly admired for the devotional simplicity of its first, narrative section, and for the ingenious web of imagery upon which it is constructed. There are editions by B. Dickins and A. S. C. Ross (rev. 1963) and M. Swanton (1970).

DREISER, Theodore (1871–1945) American novelist, born in Indiana, the son of a Catholic German family, and brought up in semi-poverty. He left his family at the age of 15 for Chicago, and after various jobs became a journalist, meanwhile writing his first novel, *Sister Carrie* (1900), a powerful account of a young working girl's rise to the 'tinsel and shine' of worldly success. His supporter and friend H. L. **Mencken thought *Sister Carrie* a poorly balanced narrative and it was withheld from circulation by its publishers, who were apprehensive about Dreiser's frank and amoral treatment of Carrie's sexuality and ambition, and he continued work as a hack journalist until the greater success of *Jennie Gerhardt* (1911), again a novel of a working girl's betterment through liaisons. This was followed by the first parts of a trilogy about an unscrupulous business magnate, Frank Cowperwood (*The Financier*, 1912; *The Titan*, 1914; *The Stoic* was published posthumously in 1947). *The 'Genius'* (1915) is a study of an artist, with much autobiographical material. *An American Tragedy* (1925) is the story of Clyde Griffiths, son of unworldly, evangelist parents, who escapes from them to the life of a bell-boy in a Kansas City hotel; he moves to New York State to work in a collar factory, and when his girlfriend Roberta becomes pregnant he drowns her, possibly accidentally, and is tried and condemned to death; the narrative was based on an actual 1906 homicide. Dreiser's many other works include *Dreiser Looks at Russia* (1928, written after travels in Russia), *Tragic America* (1931), and *America Is Worth Saving* (1941), which express the growing faith in socialism that replaced the nihilistic naturalism and pessimism of his earlier works. Dreiser made unsuccessful attempts to break into the Hollywood film industry and became involved in a costly lawsuit against Paramount for their 1931 adaptation of *An American Tragedy*. See Jerome Loving's biography, *The Last Titan* (2005).

DRINKWATER, John (1882–1937) A prolific poet, dramatist, critic, and actor, born in Leytonstone, Essex. He attended Oxford High School and then worked as an office clerk before becoming an actor and co-founding, in 1907, the Pilgrim Players, which later became the Birmingham Repertory Theatre. He was the author of seventeen plays, including *Abraham Lincoln* (1918), *Oliver Cromwell* (1921), *Mary Stuart* (1921), and a successful comedy, *Bird in Hand* (1927). In 1903, he had also turned to poetry, and his work appeared in all five volumes of **Georgian Poetry*, and in the journal *New Numbers* (1914). His nine volumes of verse include *Swords and Ploughshares* (1915), *Olton Pools* (1916), *Tides* (1917), and *Summer Harvest* (1933). He also wrote stories and plays for children, and produced critical studies of, among others, Lord **Byron, Cromwell, William **Morris, Samuel **Pepys, **Shakespeare, and

A. C. *Swinburne. *Inheritance* (1931) and *Discovery* (1932) are two volumes of an unfinished autobiography.

drolls (droll-humours) In Commonwealth days when stage plays were forbidden, farces or comic scenes adapted from existing plays or invented by the actors, produced generally at fairs or in taverns. A few drolls, which are supposed to have been adapted and performed by an actor named Robert Cox, were published in 1655, but most were published after the Restoration by the bookseller and writer Francis Kirkman (1632–?1680) in *The Wits, or Sport upon Sport* (two parts, 1662, 1673). 'Bottom the Weaver', which was published separately in 1661, is described on the title page as having been 'often publicly acted by some of his majesty's comedians, and lately, privately, presented by several apprentices for their harmless recreation'. It is not known how many of the other drolls achieved performance.

DRUMMOND of Hawthornden, William (1585–1649) Poet, laird of Hawthornden, Midlothian. He was educated at Edinburgh University and studied law in Bourges and Paris. His European travels familiarized him with the work of poets in many languages, including Du Bartas, *Ronsard, *Tasso, and *Marino. His *Poems* (1616) mourn the death of his fiancée Mary Cunningham. *A Cypress Grove* (1623) counsels against fear of death. He also wrote satires and hymns, pamphlets and verses in support of Charles I, and a history of Scotland 1423–1524 (1655). He corresponded with Michael *Drayton, and in the winter of 1618/19 was visited by Ben *Jonson. His record of their Conversations is an unparalleled feast of literary gossip. The Hawthornden Prize, the oldest British literary prize (established in 1919), was named after Drummond of Hawthornden. See *Poetry and Prose*, ed. R. H. Macdonald (1976).

Drury Lane, London So called from the Drury family, who had a large house there from Tudor times. The Theatre Royal, Drury Lane, was originally a cockpit, converted into a theatre in the time of *James I. It was rebuilt by Thomas *Killigrew (1612–83), to whom Charles II granted a patent in 1662, again by Sir Christopher Wren in 1674, and again in 1812, when the reopening was celebrated in *Rejected Addresses*. Junius Brutus Booth (1796–1852), David *Garrick, Sarah Siddons, John Philip Kemble, and Edmund Kean are among the famous actors who have appeared there. In the 19th century it was the great house of Christmas pantomimes, and after the Second World War many successful American musicals were staged there, including *Oklahoma!* (1947) and *South Pacific* (1951), both by Rodgers and Hammerstein, and *My Fair Lady* (1958, adapted from G. B. Shaw's *Pygmalion).

DRYDEN, John (1631–1700) Poet and playwright, the eldest of fourteen children of Puritan landowning gentry. He processed at Cromwell's funeral with Andrew *Marvell and John *Milton. His *Heroic Stanzas* (1658) on Cromwell's death was followed by poems applauding Charles II's return: *Astraea Redux* and *To His Sacred Majesty*. Other poems were addressed to Sir Robert Howard, the earl of Clarendon, Walter Charleton, and the royal mistress Lady Castlemaine (bap. 1640, d. 1709). His *Annus Mirabilis* (1667), a spectacular poem commemorating the English defeat of the Dutch at sea and the fire of London, led to his appointment as *poet laureate (1668), but most of his early writing was for the stage and included several rhymed heroic plays, *The Indian Queen* (1664, *The Indian Emperor* (1665, on Montezuma), *Tyrannic Love* (1669), and *The Conquest of Granada* in two parts (1670). He also wrote comedies, *The Wild Gallant* (1663), *The Rival Ladies* (1664), *Sir Martin Mar-all* (1667, in collaboration with the duke of *Newcastle), *An Evening's Love* (1668), and a radical adaptation of *The *Tempest* (1667, with Sir William *D'Avenant). He was most original, however, with his tragicomedies, *Secret Love* (1667), *Marriage-à-la-Mode* (1672), *The Assignation* (1672), and a second *Shakespeare adaptation, *Troilus and Cressida* (1679). All these plays, together with the operatic adaptation of *Paradise Lost* (*The State of Innocence, and Fall of Man*, unperformed, pub. 1667), and the immensely successful *Oedipus* (1678, with Nathaniel *Lee), reveal Dryden's considerable interest in philosophical and political questions.

He was the first of the very few English authors who have published an influential body of literary criticism and of even fewer for whom criticism was an art. *Of Dramatick Poesy* (1668), was followed by *A Defence of an Essay* (1668), the preface to *An Evening's Love* (1671), *Of Heroic Plays* (1672), *Heads of an Answer* (to Thomas *Rymer, c.1677, pub. 1711), and *The Grounds of Criticism in Tragedy*, prefixed to *Troilus and Cressida* (1679). *Aureng-Zebe* (1675) was his best rhymed heroic play. The prologue, however, denounces rhyme in serious drama, and his next tragedy, *All for Love* (1678), based on Shakespeare's *Antony and

Cleopatra, was in blank verse. His eminence as critic and dramatist left him vulnerable to attack. He was represented as Bayes in *The *Rehearsal* (1671) by *Buckingham, and physically assaulted in 1679, possibly at the instigation of *Rochester. His principal opponent was Thomas *Shadwell, whom he ridiculed in *Mac Flecknoe* (c.1676, pub. 1682).

The constitutional crisis of the late 1670s and early 1680s saw Dryden's emergence as a formidable Tory polemicist. His contribution to the political debate included plays, especially *The *Spanish Friar* (1680), *The Duke of Guise* (1682, written with Lee), and *Albion and Albanius* (1685); his celebrated satires *Absalom and Achitophel* (1681), *The *Medal* (1682), and a number of lines for Nahum *Tate's *The Second Part of Absalom and Achitophel* (1682), as well as a host of partisan prologues and epilogues. In *Religio Laici* (1682) he offers a defence of the Anglican *via media*. However, following the accession of James II Dryden became a Catholic and wrote *The *Hind and the Panther* (1687) in support of his new co-religionists. *Threnodia Augustalis* (1685), on the death of Charles II, is a *Pindaric ode, as are *To the Pious Memory of Mrs Anne Killigrew* (1686), *A Song for Saint Cecilia's Day* (1687), 'An Ode, on the Death of Mr Henry Purcell' (1696), and *Alexander's Feast* (1697), which was later incorporated into *Fables, Ancient and Modern* (1700).

In 1689 he refused the oath of allegiance to the new government, lost his court offices and income, and returned to the theatre with *Don Sebastian* (1689), *Amphitryon* (1690), *Cleomenes* (1692), and *Love Triumphant* (1694). He then turned to the politically less compromising work of translation, his extraordinary sweep and versatility taking in small selections from *Theocritus and *Horace, and more substantial passages from *Homer, *Lucretius, *Persius, *Juvenal, *Ovid, *Boccaccio, and *Chaucer, as well as the whole of *Virgil. In many of these translations he made frequent but subtle allusions to his *Jacobite principles. He also returned to criticism, notably in 'A Discourse Concerning the Original and Progress of Satire' (1693). His culminating achievement as translator was *Fables, Ancient and Modern*, to which 'The Secular Masque' (1700) was a coda. He was buried in Westminster Abbey. (*See also* RESTORATION.)

dub, dub poetry Dub is an instrumental remix of a reggae recording, often involving reverberation, echo, and other electronic effects, used as a backing track for improvisation or 'toasting'. Dub poetry, which is often forth-

right in its political and social commentary, is performed over a dub backing track or using the rhythms of reggae music. Both forms developed in Jamaica and Britain in the 1970s. Though essentially designed for live performance, dub poetry has become increasingly available in printed form. Notable exponents include Linton Kwesi *Johnson and Benjamin *Zephaniah.

Du BELLAY, Joachim (c.1522–1560) French poet, a member of the *Pléiade. At the end of the 16th century, English translations of selections of Du Bellay's poetry included those by Sir Arthur *Gorges and Samuel *Daniel, and Edmund *Spenser's version of the *Antiquités* as *Ruines of Rome* appeared in the *Complaints* of 1591.

Dubliners A volume of short stories by James *Joyce, published in 1914. Focusing on life in Dublin, the stories follow a pattern of childhood, adolescence, maturity, and public life, culminating with the longest, 'The Dead', frequently described as 'the finest short story in English'. Joyce intended them to be a 'chapter of the moral history [of Ireland]', set them in Dublin 'because that city seemed to [him] the centre of paralysis', and wrote them in what he called 'a style of scrupulous meanness'. Because of Joyce's frankness and his insistence on publishing without deletion or alteration, he found himself in the first of what would be several battles with publishers who refused to print his work without excisions, as well as the focus of a brief campaign for freedom to publish (in the pages, for example, of *The *Egoist*).

Du BOIS, William Edward Burghardt (1868–1963) African American author, social reformer, and activist. *The Souls of Black Folk* (1903) is a collection of essays describing 'life within the Veil', which criticizes Booker T. *Washington for being insufficiently militant about black rights. He published his autobiography, *Dusk of Dawn*, in 1940; and a trilogy of novels about American racism: *The Black Flame* (1957), *Mansart Builds a School* (1959), and *Worlds of Colour* (1961). He became increasingly radical and anti-imperial during his long career, and in the year before his death moved to Ghana and became a citizen of that country.

Duchess of Malfi, The By John *Webster, written 1612/13, printed 1623. The story is taken from one of *Bandello's novelle, through Painter's *Palace of Pleasure*, and also shows the influence of Sidney's *Arcadia*.

The Duchess, a high-spirited and high-minded widow, reveals her love for the honest Antonio, steward at her court, and secretly marries him, despite the warnings of her brothers, Ferdinand, duke of Calabria, and the cardinal, and immediately after informing them that she has no intention of remarrying. Their resistance appears to be induced by consideration for their high blood, and by, as Ferdinand later asserts, a desire to inherit her property; there is also a strong suggestion of Ferdinand's repressed incestuous desire for her. The brothers place in her employment as a spy the cynical ex-galley-slave Bosola, who betrays her to them; she and Antonio flee and separate. She is captured, and subjected by Ferdinand and Bosola to fearful mental tortures, including the sight of the feigned corpse of her husband and the attendance of a group of madmen; finally she is strangled with two of her children and Cariola, her waiting-woman. Retribution overtakes the murderers: Ferdinand goes mad, imagining himself a wolf; the cardinal is killed by the now remorseful Bosola, and Bosola by Ferdinand. Bosola has already killed Antonio, mistaking him for the cardinal. The human tenderness of the scenes between the duchess, Antonio, and their children; the pride and dignity of the duchess in her suffering ('I am Duchess of Malfi still'); and individual lines such as the celebrated 'Cover her face: Mine eyes dazzle: she died young' have long been admired. There have been many revivals, emphasizing T. S. *Eliot's point that Webster's 'verse is essentially dramatic verse, written by a man with a very acute sense of the theatre' (1941).

DUCK, Stephen (1705-56) Farm labourer and poet, born in Wiltshire. Almost entirely self-educated, through reading the *Spectator and John *Milton, he took to writing verse. His poem *The Thresher's Labour* (1730) is a realistic portrayal of the unremitting toil of the labourer's life. Duck was taken up by several notable patrons, including Queen Caroline. In 1746 he took holy orders; ten years later he drowned himself in despair. His *Poems on Several Occasions* (1736) included a biography by Joseph *Spence.

Duenna, The Comic opera by Richard Brinsley *Sheridan, produced with great success in 1775. It incorporates many popular song tunes.

Duessa In Edmund *Spenser's *Faerie Queene*, the daughter of Deceit and Shame, Falsehood in general; in Book I she signifies, in particular, the Roman Catholic Church, and in V. ix, *Mary Queen of Scots.

DUFFY, Carol Ann (1955-) Poet, born in Glasgow. She graduated in philosophy from Li-

verpool University in 1977. Her debut collection, *Standing Female Nude* (1985), announced her interest in the *dramatic monologue, frequently using the voices of outsiders—the dispossessed, the insane, and those, especially women, ignored by history. Her interest in the speaking voice led her to the demotic and to a supple, distinctive grammar with frequent use of short sentences, italics, and slang. In *Selling Manhattan* (1987) her subtle rhythms marked by assonance and internal rhymes began to be used in more personal verse and in love poems as well as monologues. The themes of nostalgia, desire, loss, and memory, the search for 'first space and the right place', begun in that volume came to predominate in *The Other Country* (1990) and *Mean Time* (1993), which contain several much-anthologized love poems and lyrics. Her subsequent volumes *The World's Wife* (1999), *Feminine Gospels* (2002), and *Rapture* (2005) brought her critical acclaim and also a form of popularity beyond the usual reach of poets. All are also poetic sequences in which central preoccupations—marriage, women's experience, and the intensity of love and its ending—are reflected in different perspectives and varied forms. *The World's Wife*, in particular, which—extraordinarily for a volume of contemporary poetry—became a best-seller, employs the dramatic monologue of Duffy's earlier work in newly ironic and satiric modes: each poem is spoken in the 'voice' of the imagined female partner of one of the acclaimed men of history or mythology, usually to deflationary and sometimes to devastating effect. *New Selected Poems* appeared in 2004. In 2009, Duffy became the first woman to be appointed poet laureate. She is also the author of children's books, including *The Good Child's Guide to Rock N Roll* (2003), and a playwright.

DUFFY, Maureen (1933-) Writer of plays, poetry, and non-fiction, perhaps best known as a novelist. Her first novel, *That's How It Was* (1962), is a moving autobiographical account of her working-class childhood. It was followed by many others, some of which deal frankly with the subject of homosexuality, notably *The Microcosm* (1966), set in London's lesbian community. In *Love Child* (1971), which describes a woman's affair from her child's point of view, the gender of both the narrator and the lover is undisclosed. *Wounds* (1969), *Capital* (1975), and *Londoners* (1983) form a London trilogy, the last of them a sardonic but poignant view of the writer's lot in the contemporary bedsitter land of Earl's Court in which the sex of the narrator is again left intentionally ambiguous. Later novels include the science fiction *Gor

Saga (1981), which reflects her concern for animal rights, and *Illuminations* (1991), about a woman who translates the letters of an 8th-century nun. *Restitution* (1998) is a post-*Holocaust novel, set in England and Berlin, exploring themes of family guilt, genetic heritage, and existential freedom. Her poetry includes *The Venus Touch* (1971), *Evesong* (1975), *Memorials of the Quick and the Dead* (1979), and *Collected Poems 1949–84* (1985). Among her plays are *A Nightingale in Bloomsbury Square* (1974), about Virginia *Woolf, and a trilogy based on Greek myths: *Rites* (1969), *Solo* (1970), and *Old Tyme* (1970). Her works of non-fiction include biographies of Aphra *Behn (1977) and *Purcell (1994), and *The Erotic World of Faery* (1972).

DUHIG, Ian (1954–) Poet, born in London to émigré Irish Catholic parents, former worker with the homeless. Duhig is a learned, witty, and eclectic poet, versed in the Irish language and Irish history, drawn to the arcane and absurd, full of rococo allusion, conceit, and pastiche. *The Bradford Count* (1991) features monologues by David *Livingstone and a depressed medieval monk. *The Mersey Goldfish* (1995) was followed by *Nominies* (1998), an ambitious and emotionally complex collection, which includes ballads of destitution and history, as well as the blackly comic 'The Ballad of Freddie the Dolphin'. Some poems of *The Lammas Hireling* (2003) witness to a newly chastened directness. *The Speed of Dark* (2007) is based on a 14th-century French poem cycle.

DUJARDIN, Édouard *See* SYMBOLISM; STREAM OF CONSCIOUSNESS.

Duke of Milan, The A tragedy by Philip *Massinger, written *c.*1621, printed 1623, one of his earliest independent plays and a popular one. It is based on the story of Herod and Mariamne as told by *Josephus.

Duke's Children, The A novel by Anthony *Trollope, published 1880, the last in the *'Palliser' series. The novel combines political interests with Trollope's characteristic concern with the role of loyalty and inheritance in courtship. It also reflects his changing views of American culture, and of parent–child relationships.

DUMAS, Alexandre ('Dumas *père*') (1802–70) French novelist and playwright. A pioneer of the Romantic theatre in France, his plays include *Kean* (1836), about the colourful life of the actor Edmund Kean. But he is best known as a novelist. In 1844 he published both *Le Comte de Monte-Cristo* (*The Count of Monte-Cristo*), a masterpiece of mystery and adventure, and *Les Trois Mousquetaires* (*The Three Musketeers*), about the adventures of d'Artagnan, who comes from Gascony to Paris in the reign of Louis XIII to join the king's musketeers, and shares the exploits of three of them, Athos, Porthos, and Aramis; both works were translated into English almost immediately and have remained popular ever since. Dumas *père* continued d'Artagnan's adventures in *Vingt ans après* (1845: *Twenty Years Later*) and *Le Vicomte de Bragelonne* (1848–50). Dumas *père* also wrote numerous books of travel, 22 volumes of *Mémoires* (1852–5), several children's stories, and a *Grand Dictionnaire de cuisine* (1872).

Du MAURIER, Dame Daphne (1907–89) Novelist, born in London, the granddaughter of George *du Maurier. Her first novel, *The Loving Spirit* (1931), was an immediate success. Two more novels followed in quick succession, but it was her frank memoir of her father (*Gerald*, 1934) that encouraged her to develop her powerful narrative skill and evocation of atmosphere: the result was *Jamaica Inn* (1936). Married in 1932 to Major Frederick 'Boy' Browning, she was obliged to accompany him to Egypt, where she became desperately homesick, and this unhappy period produced *Rebecca* (1938), a study in jealousy based on her own feelings towards a former fiancée of her husband's. She wrote ten more novels, two plays, several collections of short stories, and three biographies, but *Rebecca* (turned into a film in 1940, as were seven more of her novels and stories, most notably *Hitchcock's *The Birds* (1963)) remained her finest work.

Du MAURIER, George (1834–96) Artist and writer, born in Paris, grandfather of the novelist Daphne *du Maurier. He contributed to *Punch* and other periodicals and illustrated editions of Elizabeth *Gaskell, George *Meredith, Thomas *Hardy, and Henry *James, among others. In 1865 he began to write humorous verse, including 'The History of the Jack Sprats', and a parody of William *Morris's ballads, 'The Legend of Camelot', with mock *Pre-Raphaelite illustrations. His first novel, *Peter Ibbetson* (1891), was followed by the vastly successful, *Trilby* (1894). *The Martian*, a story based on school life, appeared posthumously in 1897.

dumb show A piece of silent action or stage business, especially in the Elizabethan and Jacobean theatre, where speech is expected but not actually delivered. These shows, such as the one before the play scene in *Hamlet* or Revenge's in

The *Spanish Tragedy*, suggest by mime and symbolism what is shortly to take place and its meaning.

DUNBAR, William (?1460–1513/30) Prolific Scottish poet and priest, much of whose life remains obscure. In 1503, he wrote 'The Thrissill and the Rois', a political allegory in *rhyme royal, the Rose representing Margaret Tudor, who married James IV (the 'Thistle') in that year. In about 1507 he wrote 'The Goldyn Targe', the 'Lament for the Makaris', and 'The Tretis of the Tua Mariit Wemen and the Wedo', a visionary dialogue in which the three interlocutors relate their experiences of marriage, a satire on marriage reminiscent of Chaucer's Wife of Bath's prologue in the *Canterbury Tales. 'The Goldyn Targe' is a substantial allegory recalling *Chaucer and *Lydgate, in which the poet, appearing in a dream before the court of Venus, is wounded by the arrows of Beauty in spite of the shield ('targe') of Reason. The 'Lament for the Makaris' may, like the 'The Dance of the Sevin Deidly Synnis' (c.1507), relate to the tradition of the *Dance of Death. It is a powerful elegy for the transitoriness of things, with its refrain '*Timor mortis conturbat me*' ('the fear of Death disturbs me'), and in particular for the deaths of Dunbar's fellow poets (the 'makaris', or 'makers', are 'poets'), including Geoffrey *Chaucer, John *Gower, and Robert *Henryson. Dunbar's satirical energy and Rabelaisian humour are particularly well displayed in 'The *Flyting of Dunbar and Kennedie'. Some of his poems are preserved in the Asloan and Bannatyne manuscripts.

DUNCAN, Robert See BLACK MOUNTAIN POETS.

Dunciad, The A *mock-epic satire by Alexander *Pope. A three-book version was published anonymously in 1728; in 1729 Pope published *The Dunciad Variorum*, which added notes, indexes, and essays to the poem. In this material Pope simultaneously parodied the ponderous apparatus of scholarly editions and provided evidence to support his own position. The *New Dunciad*, a fourth book, was published in 1742, and a final complete version in 1743. The poem had its roots in the activities of the *Scriblerus Club, but the criticisms of Pope's edition of *Shakespeare contained in Lewis *Theobald's *Shakespeare Restored* (1726), and the coronation of George II in 1727, prompted Pope to finish and publish it. Theobald was the hero of the poem in its earlier form, but in the final version Colley *Cibber was enthroned in

his place. The satire is directed against 'Dulness' (characterized as a goddess in Swift's *Battle of the Books). In the course of the poem all the authors who had incurred Pope's enmity are pictured in humiliating situations that grotesquely parody epic conventions. In Book I, the hero, a struggling and incompetent writer, is carried off by the goddess and anointed king in the place of Laurence Eusden, the deceased poet laureate. In Book II, the coronation is celebrated by ceremonial games: a race between booksellers, including Edmund *Curll; a pissing contest (Curll again); a mud-diving exercise; and finally a test for the critics. In Book III the king is transported to the Elysian shades, where, under the guidance of Elkanah *Settle, he sees visions of the past and future triumphs of the empire of Dulness. In the last book these prophecies are brought to fruition; the sciences and universities are subjugated to Dulness, and the ancient empire of night and chaos (by allusion to *Paradise Lost) is restored. The poem was enormously controversial and generated much protest and vehement responses from those it attacked.

Dun Cow, Book of the The earliest extant vernacular Irish manuscript, of late 11th-century origin. Now fragmentary, it contains 37 texts, including tales of *Cuchulain, an Irish version of the *Historia Brittonum* (see NENNIUS), and an annotated version of *Amra Coluim Chille*, an early 7th-century elegy for St Columcille (*Columba).

DUNMORE, Helen (1952–) Poet, novelist, and children's writer, born in Yorkshire. Her poetry collections include *The Apple Fall* (1983), *The Sea Skater* (1986), *Short Days, Long Nights* (1991), and *Glad of These Times* (2007). Her first adult novel, *Zennor in Darkness* (1993), set in Cornwall in 1917, featured D. H. *Lawrence and his wife Frieda. It was followed by *Burning Bright* (1994), *A Spell of Winter* (1995), *Talking to the Dead* (1996), *Your Blue-Eyed Boy* (1998), and *With your Crooked Heart* (1999), all marked by richly textured writing and an eerie sense of place which matches their mysterious plots, often concerned with long-buried family secrets and betrayals. *The Siege* (2001), set against the backdrop of the siege of Leningrad, has a sequel in *The Betrayal* (2010). *Mourning Ruby* (2003) is an exploration of loss and grief; *House of Orphans* (2006) a historical novel set in Finland; and *Counting the Stars* (2008) recreates the obsessional love affair between the Roman poet *Catullus and his mistress Clodia. *Love of Fat Men* (1997) and *Ice Cream* (2000) are collections of short stories.

DUNN, Douglas (1942–) Scottish poet and critic, who worked in the Brynmor Jones Library at Hull under Philip *Larkin. Larkin's influence has been detected in the blackly humorous vignettes of working-class life in Dunn's first collection, *Terry Street* (1969). This was followed by *The Happier Life* (1972), *Love or Nothing* (1974), *Barbarians* (1979), and *St Kilda's Parliament* (1981). Dunn returned to Scotland in 1984 and published in 1985 the award-winning *Elegies*, on the death of his wife from cancer. Later works include *Northlight* (1988); *Dante's Drum-Kit* (1993); *The Donkey's Ears*, a narrative of the Russo-Japanese War in the *In Memoriam* stanza, *The Year's Afternoon* (both 2000); and *New Selected Poems 1964—2000* (2003). *Secret Villages* (1985) and *Boyfriends and Girlfriends* (1995) are volumes of short stories.

DUNN, Nell (1936–) Novelist and playwright, educated in a convent school, which she left at the age of 14. Her early novels, *Up the Junction* (1963; televised, 1965; filmed, 1968) and *Poor Cow* (1967; filmed, Ken Loach, 1968), showed a keen ear for working-class dialogue and an uninhibited approach to female sexuality. Other works include *My Silver Shoes* (1996), which continues the story of the heroine of *Poor Cow* in middle age. Dunn's best-known play, *Steaming* (1981), is a comedy with an all-female cast set in a Turkish bath; other dramatic works with a darker edge include *The Little Heroine* (1988) and *Sisters* (1994).

DUNSANY, Edward Plunkett, eighteenth Baron (1878–1957) London-born Anglo-Irish aristocrat. His first book of mythological tales, *The Gods of Pegana* (1905), and subsequent fantasies such as *The Book of Wonder* (1912) and *The King of Elfland's Daughter* (1924) were illustrated in *fin-de-siècle* style by S. H. Sime (1867–1941). Dunsany's first play, *The Glittering Gate*, was performed at the *Abbey Theatre in 1909; like many of his later plays it shows the influence of Maeterlinck. *If* was a success in London in 1921. The popular 'Jorkens' stories, beginning with *The Travel Tales of Mr Joseph Jorkens* (1931), show a talent for realism.

DUNS Scotus, John (*c.*1265–1308) The 'Doctor Subtilis', a Scottish Franciscan. He lectured on the *Sententiae* of Peter Lombard at Oxford, Paris, and Cambridge universities. His principal significance in the history of *scholasticism is that he drove the first wedge between theology and philosophy (a split which widened throughout the 14th century), with his emphasis on the separation between God as necessary Being from all contingent Beings, and the impossibility of arguing from the latter to the former. Although this emphasis, together with his associated Augustinian-Franciscan stress on faith and will rather than reason, distinguishes his thought from the synthesis of the Dominican Aquinas, like the latter he incorporated a good deal of *Aristotle into his metaphysics. He was much influenced too by Arabic philosophers, especially *Avicenna. He straddles the line between 13th-century system-building and 14th-century scepticism, and his work was an important influence on William of *Ockham among others. The word 'dunce', first in the sense of 'a maker of impossibly ingenious distinctions', derives from him; some of his formal metaphysical distinctions were referred to by G. M. *Hopkins in his development of a poetic psychology.

DUNSTAN, St (d. 988) Distinguished Benedictine monk and archbishop of Canterbury. He was a favourite with King Athelstan, but his piety made him unpopular at court. He was restored to favour by King Edmund, who appointed him abbot of Glastonbury (*c.*940–46). Supported by King Eadred (who succeeded in 946), he incurred the disfavour of his successor, King Eadwig, and retired to Flanders (956). Edgar recalled him and appointed him bishop of Worcester (957), bishop of London (959), and archbishop of Canterbury (960). Dunstan restored and reformed English monasteries and contributed to the integration of the Danes. He averted civil war by crowning Edward the Martyr (975), and foretold to King Ethelred the Unready the national calamities that would occur because of Edward's murder.

DURCAN, Paul (1944–) Irish poet, born in Dublin. Powered by parallelism, refrains, and startling transitions, his monologues are gleeful, painful, learned, and populist. Many of his poems are satires on the constriction of Irish life by prejudice and authority, often religious in origin. *The Berlin Wall Café* (1985) laments marital break-up. *Daddy, Daddy* (1990) and *The Laughter of Mothers* (2007) address tragicomic elegies and love poems to the poet's father and mother respectively, while commenting mordantly on the relationship of gender to nationality. Durcan's greatest originality lies in his gift for sceptical, humane fantasy ('The Haulier's Wife Meets Jesus on the Road near Moone'). *See A Snail in my Prime: New and Selected Poems* (1993); *The Art of Life* (2004).

DURHAM, Edith (1863–1944) Travel writer and anthropologist, who travelled in the

Balkans over two decades from the late 1890s. Her seven books on the region include *High Albania* (1909); she served on the Council of the Royal Anthropological Institute, but her pro-Albanian views attracted criticism.

DURRELL, Lawrence (1912–90) Poet, novelist, and travel writer, born in India. He was first recognized as a poet: his collections include *A Private Country* (1943), *Cities, Plains and People* (1946), and *The Tree of Idleness* (1955). His *Collected Poems* appeared in 1960. His first novel of interest, *The Black Book* (Paris, 1938; London, 1973) was influenced by Henry *Miller. Publication of *Justine* (1957), the first volume of his *Alexandria Quartet*, finally brought Durrell fame: *Balthazar* and *Mountolive* followed in 1958, and *Clea* in 1960. Set in Alexandria during the period just before the Second World War, the first three novels cover roughly the same period of time and the same events, with characters bound together in a web of political and sexual intrigue, while *Clea* advances the action in time. Durrell's later novels include *Tunc* (1968), *Nunquam* (1970), and the volumes known collectively as the *Avignon Quintet* (*Monsieur*, 1974, *Livia*, 1978, *Constance*, 1982, *Sebastian*, 1983, and *Quinx*, 1985). His best-known travel books are his three 'island' books, *Prospero's Cell* (1945), on Corfu; *Reflections on a Marine Venus* (1953), on Rhodes; and *Bitter Lemons* (1957), on Cyprus. Lawrence Durrell's brother, the zoologist Gerald Malcolm Durrell (1925–95), was also a writer, well known for his popular accounts of animal life and his own zoo on Jersey: titles include *The Overloaded Ark* (1953), *My Family and Other Animals* (1956), and *A Zoo in my Luggage* (1960).

DÜRRENMATT, Friedrich (1921–90) Swiss-German dramatist, novelist, and essayist. His dark comedies tend to parody the conventions of tragedy and have elements of the grotesque. His plays, though *Der Besuch der alten Dame* (1956: *The Visit*, 1958) and *Die Physiker* (1962: *The Physicists*, trans. James *Kirkup, 1963) are the best known, include adaptations of Shakespeare's *King John* (1968) and *Titus Andronicus* (1970). He explored the idea of using popular literary forms for serious purposes in his *detective fiction, which became well known in English through *The Judge and the Hangman* (1952: *Der Richter und sein Henker*, 1952), *Suspicion* (1954: *Der Verdacht*, 1953), and *The Pledge* (1959: *Das Versprechen*, 1958; filmed, 2001).

DYER, Sir Edward (1543–1607) Poet, one of the 'happy blessed Trinitie' with Philip

*Sidney and Sir Fulke *Greville. He was introduced at court by Robert Dudley, earl of Leicester, taking part in the queen's entertainment at Woodstock (1575). Few authentic poems have survived ('*My mind to me a kingdom is', is probably by the earl of *Oxford). One of the best of his surviving poems, 'The lowest trees have tops', was set by John *Dowland in 1603.

DYER, Geoff (1958–) Writer of fiction and non-fiction. His first, Brixton-based novel, *The Colour of Memory* (1989), was followed by *The Search* (1993), in which a man is asked to track down a woman's husband. *Paris Trance* (1998), Dyer's third novel, is set in the French capital. Dyer's enthusiasm for his chosen subjects is the link between his non-fiction works: *Ways of Telling* (1986), a critical study of the work of John *Berger, *But Beautiful: A Book about Jazz* (1991), *The Missing of the Somme* (1994), and *Out of Sheer Rage: In the Shadow of D. H. Lawrence* (1997).

DYER, John (1699–1757) Welsh poet, clergyman and farmer, born at Llanfynydd; his *topographical poem in tetrameter couplets, *Grongar Hill* (1726), describes the scenery along the river Tywi. Samuel *Johnson scorned his poem *The Fleece* (1757) for its prosaic subject: 'How can a man write poetically of serges and druggets?' But *Wordsworth admired it greatly, addressed a sonnet to Dyer, and in his notes to *The *Excursion* commented, 'He wrote at a time when machinery was first beginning to be introduced, and his benevolent heart prompted him to augur from it nothing but good.'

DYLAN, Bob (1941–) Born Robert Allen Zimmerman in Duluth, Minnesota, American singer-songwriter, influenced by the folk style of Woody *Guthrie, partly following the method of Pete Seeger (1919–). He gave concerts with Joan Baez (1941–) to support the civil rights movement, achieving fame with songs like 'Blowin' in the Wind'. In 1971 he published a *stream-of-consciousness novel, *Tarantula*, acted in Sam Peckinpah's film *Pat Garrett and Billy the Kid* (1973), and in 2004 brought out his autobiography, *Chronicles: Volume I*. In 2008, he was awarded a 'Special Citation' from the Pulitzer Board for 'his profound impact on popular music and American culture'.

dystopia a term coined to convey the opposite of Utopia. The dystopian mode, which projects an unpleasant or catastrophic future, is frequently used by *science fiction writers.

E

EAGLETON, Terry (1943–) Literary critic. Born in Salford to an Irish working-class family, he read English at Trinity College, Cambridge, where he was much influenced by Raymond *Williams. His first notable works were *Myths of Power* (on the *Brontës, 1975), *Marxism and Literary Criticism* (1976), and the ambitious theoretical work influenced by *structuralist Marxism, *Criticism and Ideology* (1976). His later work displays a new flexibility and lively wit, especially in parodic summaries of modern intellectual traditions, as in the widely admired *Literary Theory* (1983) and in *The Ideology of the Aesthetic* (1990). In his academic posts at Oxford (1992–2001), Manchester (2001–8), and Lancaster (2008–) his work has repeatedly satirized the assumptions of contemporary 'postmodern' thought, in *Ideology* (1991), *The Illusions of Postmodernism* (1996), and *After Theory* (2003). He has also published comic fiction (*Saints and Scholars*, 1987); drama (*Saint Oscar*, about Oscar *Wilde, 1989); a remarkable memoir, *The Gatekeeper* (2001); a range of critical studies of *Shakespeare, Samuel *Richardson, the theory of *tragedy, and Irish literature; and a philosophical essay, *The Meaning of Life* (2008).

Ealing Studios Produced a series of comedies, from *Hue and Cry* (1947) to *The Ladykillers* (1955), which have come to be regarded as expressing distinctive British post-war values, such as resentment of overbearing authority, community feeling, and an opportunism bordering on the anarchic or criminal. Other key 'Ealing comedies' include *Passport to Pimlico*, *Whisky Galore*, and *Kind Hearts and Coronets* (all 1949) and *The Lavender Hill Mob* (1951).

Early Irish lyric poetry A term that usually refers to the more epigrammatic among the poems produced in Old Irish after the introduction of the Roman alphabet by Christian missionaries in the 5th century AD. Many of the lyrics were written by monks in the margins of the illuminated manuscripts produced in Irish monasteries in Ireland, Britain, and Europe. Characteristically cast in syllabic *quatrains, they were the first European art poems to use rhyme, a feature that may have been borrowed from Latin hymns or from the marching songs of the later Roman Empire. The 'steelpen exactness' ascribed to the lyrics by Flann *O'Brien has been an ideal of English-language poets in Ireland from Austin *Clarke to Ciaran *Carson and Paul *Muldoon.

Earthly Paradise, The A poem by William *Morris, published 1868–70, consisting of a prologue and 24 tales, in Chaucerian metres. The prologue tells how a company of Norsemen, fleeing from the pestilence, set sail in search of the fabled Earthly Paradise 'across the western sea where none grow old'. They are disappointed in their quest and return after long wanderings, 'shrivelled, bent and grey', to a 'nameless city in a distant sea' where the ancient Greek gods are still worshipped. They are hospitably received and there spend their remaining years. Twice in each month they meet their hosts at a feast and a tale is told, alternately by one of the elders of the city and one of the wanderers. The tales of the former are on classical subjects (Atalanta, Perseus, the Apples of the Hesperides, etc.), those of the latter from Norse and other medieval subjects, including 'The Lovers of Gudrun', a version of the *Laxdaela saga*. Between the tales are interpolated lyrics describing the changing seasons, and the whole work is prefaced by an apology which contains some of Morris's best-known (and in a sense most misleading) lines, in which he describes himself as 'the idle singer of an empty day', 'born out of my due time'.

East Lynne A *sensation novel by Ellen *Wood (Mrs Henry Wood), published 1861. It tells the story of Isabel Vane, a refined lady who, finding herself unprotected in the world, marries Archibald Carlyle, a rising lawyer. Her marriage is unsatisfying, and she imagines that her husband loves a neighbour, Barbara Hare. In a moment of undisciplined passion, she runs away with Sir Francis Levison, an unscrupulous seducer, who abandons her and the child born from their illegitimate union. Having divorced Isabel, and mistakenly assumed her to have been killed in a railway accident, Archibald marries Barbara. Isabel, rendered unrecognizable by disfigurement resulting from the accident, returns to the household to act as a governess to her own children, to watch helplessly as her delicate son dies. Worn down by remorse and sorrow, she too dies, after being recognized and forgiven by her worthy but ponderous husband. The novel was a phenomenal best-seller, and was rapidly adapted for the popular stage, where it persisted for many years as staple of the repertoire (the line 'Dead! Dead! And never called me mother!' belongs to a stage version, not the novel).

Eastward Ho A comedy by George *Chapman, Ben *Jonson, and John *Marston, printed 1605, having been performed by the Children of the Revels at the Blackfriars. A passage derogatory to the Scots (III. iii) gave offence at court, and Chapman and Jonson were imprisoned, but released on the intercession of powerful friends. The play is particularly interesting for the light it throws on London life of the time. Like Thomas Dekker's *Shoemakers' Holiday, it gives a sympathetic picture of a tradesman.

The play has had successful modern revivals, especially by the Royal Shakespeare Company in 2002.

EBERHARDT, Isabelle (1877–1904) Author, born in Geneva, to an aristocratic German-Russian mother and the family tutor, an Armenian-born Orthodox priest turned anarchist. Eberhardt, who had been taught Arabic by her father, moved with her mother in 1897 to Algeria, where both converted to Islam. Eberhardt often travelled disguised as an Arab man, enjoying the greater freedom this gave her. She married an Arab soldier in 1901. English translations of her posthumously published collections of writings include *In the Shadow of Islam* (1993) and *The Passionate Nomad: The Diary of Isabelle Eberhardt* (1987). A volume of her short stories, *The Oblivion Seekers and Other Writings* (1975), was translated by Paul *Bowles.

Ecclesiastes See BIBLE.

Ecclesiastical History of the English People, The The most famous work by *Bede, complete by 731 and widely known. It is a five-book Latin history from the invasion of Julius *Caesar to an account of the state of the country in 731. Book I narrates Augustine's mission to England; Book II continues until the

conversion of the north; Book III ends with the Synod of Whitby; Book IV concludes with the death of *Cuthbert; and Book V takes events to 731. The *History*'s sources include patristic literature, Eusebius, Gregory of Tours, Gildas, and *Orosius, and it is characterized by a vivid and engaging narrative style. It was later translated into Old English.

ECKHARD, Johannes (?1260–1327) Known as 'Meister Eckhard', a German Dominican who is regarded as the founder of German mysticism and one of its greatest exponents.

eclogue A short *pastoral poem, usually in the form of a dialogue between shepherds, but sometimes a soliloquy. In Latin the term could denote any short poem, but it became associated especially with *Virgil's pastoral poems in imitation of *Theocritus, which he called *bucolica* but which have long been renamed the *Eclogues*. The classic English examples are the twelve eclogues of Edmund Spenser's *The *Shepheardes Calender.

Eclogues, The By Alexander *Barclay, written c.1513–14, interesting as the earliest English *pastorals, anticipating Edmund *Spenser. The five eclogues, printed between c.1518 and c.1530, are moral and satirical in character, dealing with such subjects as the evils of a court life and the happiness of the countryman's lot. They are modelled upon *Mantuan and the *Miseriae Curialium* of Piccolomini.

ECO, Umberto (1932–) Italian semiologist, novelist, and essayist. His critical works include: *Thema: omaggio a Joyce* (1958: *Themes: Homage to Joyce*, tape with music by Luciano Berio), *A Theory of Semiotics* (1975), and *Serendipities* (1998). His historical mystery novel *Il nome della rosa* (1981: *The Name of the Rose*), concerning a series of murders in a medieval monastery, was an international best-seller and was subsequently filmed with Sean Connery in the role of the 'detective', Brother William of Baskerville. His other novels are *Il pendolo di Foucault* (1988: *Foucault's Pendulum*), *L'isola del giorno prima* (1994: *The Island of the Day before*), *Baudolino* (2000), *La misteriosa fiamma della regina Loana* (2004: *The Mysterious Flame of Queen Loana*), and *Il cimitero di Praga* (2010: *The Cemetery of Prague*). His essays and journalistic pieces have been published in several collections including *Faith in Fakes* (1983) and *How to Travel with a Salmon and Other Essays* (1994). He has influenced the development of European semiotics (*see* SAUSSURE,

FERDINAND DE) and has a long-standing interest in aesthetics.

ecocriticism An area of literary criticism that appeared in the 1980s and 1990s, concerned with the relationship between literature and the natural world and with rediscovering and reinterpreting *'nature writings' such as those of H. D. *Thoreau in the light of environmentalist concerns. In the USA, it has prompted renewed interest in *Native American folklore and literature. The British critic Jonathan Bate has notably explored the English *Romantic tradition from this perspective in his *Romantic Ecology*, 1991 and *The Song of the Earth*, 2000.

(((🌐))) SEE WEB LINKS

• Association for the Study of Literature and Environment

Edda An Old Norse name of uncertain meaning given to a 13th-century poetic manual written by *Snorri Sturluson, known as the Prose, Younger, or Snorra Edda. The same name was applied in the 17th century to a manuscript collection of poems, the Poetic or Elder Edda. The Prose Edda is divided into a prologue and three parts: the 'Gylfaginning', or Deluding of Gylfi, a series of mythological stories in the form of a dialogue between one Gylfi and the Norse gods; the 'Skáldskaparmál', or Poetic Diction, in which Snorri illustrates the elaborate diction of *skaldic verse, retelling many myths and legends; and the 'Háttatal', or List of Metres, a long poem each strophe of which exemplifies a different Norse metre. Snorri's work is valuable for the stories it enshrines, the verses it has preserved, and Snorri's own gifts as a storyteller. The Poetic Edda was compiled in about 1270. The poems fall into two groups: heroic lays about legendary Germanic heroes and mythological lays, such as the Völsunga saga, a history of the Norse gods from creation to apocalypse, and the Hávamál, the words of the High One, Oðinn. W. H. *Auden wrote free translations of many Eddaic lays.

EDEN, Emily (1797–1869) Novelist, painter, and traveller; she accompanied her brother George to India when he was appointed governor general in 1835. *Up the Country* (1866) describes, through letters, her travels with her brother from Kolkata (Calcutta) to Shimla. Two posthumous volumes of letters have been published, *Letters from India* (1872) and a collection of her letters edited by her greatniece Violet Dickinson in 1919. Her novels *The Semi-detached House* (1859, anon.) and *The Semi-attached Couple* (1860, by 'E.E.') deal with fashionable society; their plots and characterization owe much to Jane *Austen and are a valuable record of the social life of the time.

Eden, garden of The mythical garden planted by God, as described in Genesis chs 2–3, containing the tree of life and the tree of knowledge of good and evil, and watered by four rivers. God puts Adam in the garden to keep it, and creates Eve from Adam's rib. In the story of the Fall, one of the most powerful myths of Western culture, God forbids them to eat of the tree of knowledge on pain of death; Eve, tempted by the serpent, eats the fruit, followed by Adam, so God expels them from the garden to endure labour and mortality. The yearning for the return to a prelapsarian Edenic state (i.e. Eden before the Fall) has parallels with the classical myth of the return of the Golden Age, the first of the *Four Ages. The fullest literary depiction of Eden is in John Milton's *Paradise Lost*.

EDGAR, David (1948–) Dramatist, born in Birmingham. *Destiny* (1976), a play about Fascism in British society, was produced by the Royal Shakespeare Company. He came to general prominence in 1980 with his hugely successful eight-hour adaptation of Dickens's *Nicholas Nickleby*. *Maydays* (1983), the first play by a contemporary dramatist to be staged by the RSC at the Barbican Theatre, dealt with the post-war decline of socialism. His work also includes *Entertaining Strangers* (1985), set in 19th-century Dorchester, on which he worked with community playwright Ann *Jellicoe; *That Summer* (1987), about the British miners' strike of 1985; and three plays about Eastern Europe around and after the time of the collapse of the Soviet Empire, *The Shape of the Table* (1990), *Pentecost* (1994), and *The Prisoner's Dilemma* (2001). He has also written for radio and television and in 1991 adapted Robert Louis *Stevenson's *The Strange Case of *Dr Jekyll and Mr Hyde* for the *National Theatre. *Albert Speer* (2000) is based on the life of Hitler's chief architect; *Playing with Fire* (2005) is concerned with racial tension in Britain.

EDGEWORTH, Maria (1768–1849) Novelist, the eldest daughter of the first wife of Richard Lovell Edgeworth (1744–1817), a wealthy Irish landlord. He was an eccentric, radical, and inventive man, deeply interested in the practical applications of science and in education. His influence on Maria was profound; he frequently 'edited' her work, managed her literary career, and imparted to her many of his own enthusiasms. They wrote together *Practical Education* (1798), a treatise which owes much to *Rousseau.

Maria Edgeworth's first publication was *Letters to Literary Ladies* (1795), a plea for women's education. Walter *Scott greatly admired her work, described her as 'the great Maria', and acknowledged his debt to her Irish novels in the preface to his 'Waverley' edition of 1829. Jane *Austen sent her a copy of *Emma*.

Edgeworth appears to have initiated, in her *Castle Rackrent*, both the first fully developed *regional novel and the first true historical novel in English (*see* HISTORICAL FICTION). Her writings fall into three groups: those based on Irish life (considered her finest), *Castle Rackrent* (1800) and The *Absentee* (first published in *Tales of Fashionable Life* in 1812) together with *Ormond* (1817); those depicting contemporary English society, such as *Belinda* (1801–2), commended by the heroine of *Northanger Abbey*, *Leonora* (1806), *Patronage* (1814), and *Helen* (1834); and her many popular lessons and stories for and about children, including The *Parent's Assistant* (1796–1800), *Moral Tales* (1801), *Popular Tales* (1804), and *Harry and Lucy Concluded* (1825).

Edinburgh Review (1802–1929) A quarterly periodical, established by Francis *Jeffrey, Sydney *Smith, and Henry *Brougham, and originally published by Archibald *Constable. It succeeded immediately in establishing a prestige and authority which (shared with the *Quarterly Review*) lasted for over a century. Thomas *Carlyle described it as 'a kind of Delphic oracle'. Under the influence of its first editor, Jeffrey, its politics became emphatically Whig. Jeffrey perceived the genius of John *Keats, but his veneration for 18th-century literature led him to notorious and scathing denouncements of William *Wordsworth, S. T. *Coleridge, and Robert *Southey as the 'Lake School'. Lord *Byron's satirical 'English Bards and Scotch Reviewers' (1809) was in part an attack on the *Edinburgh Review*, which had published Brougham's hostile response to *Hours of Idleness*.

EDRIC, Robert (pseudonym of **Gary Edric Armstrong**) (1956–) Novelist, born in Sheffield. He published *Winter Garden* (1985) and *A New Ice Age* (1986) under his own name. *Cradle Song* (2003), *Siren Song* (2004), and *Swan Song* (2005) comprise a present-day crime noir trilogy. Almost all his other works— among which *The Earth Made of Glass* (1994),

set in 17th-century East Anglia, *Elysium* (1995), set in 19th-century Tasmania, and *Gathering the Water* (2006), set in Victorian Yorkshire, particularly stand out—are *historical novels of remarkable power.

Edward II A tragedy in blank verse by *Marlowe probably first performed 1592, published 1594. It deals with the recall by Edward II, on his accession, of his lover, Piers Gaveston; the revolt of the barons and the capture and execution of Gaveston; the period during which Spenser (Hugh le Despenser) succeeded Gaveston as the king's favourite; the estrangement of Queen Isabella from her husband; her rebellion, supported by her lover Mortimer, against the king; the capture of the latter, his abdication of the crown, and his murder in Berkeley Castle. The play was an important influence on Shakespeare's *Richard II*. It has been frequently performed in modern times, and there is a film by Derek *Jarman.

Edward III, The Reign of King A historical play written entirely in verse, based mainly on Lord Berners's translation (1535) of *Froissart's *Chronicles*. Published anonymously in 1596, it could date from any time between 1588 and 1595. In recent times it has been attributed with increasing confidence, at least in part, to Shakespeare. The first two acts are concerned mainly with the dishonourable wooing of the countess of Salisbury by the king, who is finally brought to a sense of shame by her determination to kill herself if he persists. The rest is occupied with the French wars.

EDWARDS, Amelia B. *See* GHOST STORIES.

EDWARDS, Dic (1953–) Playwright, born in Cardiff. His first plays, *Late City Echo* (1981), about the firemen's strike, *At the End of the Bay* (1982), *Canned Goods* (1983), and *Looking for the World* (1986), were produced at the Sherman Theatre, Cardiff. In *Utah Blue* (1995), he brought his intensely poetic style to bear on the case of the murderer Gary Gilmore: 'Death came down the chimney at Christmas and death lit up the Christmas tree.' *Astrakhan (Winter)* was produced in 2005; *The Pimp* (prod. 2006) is about *Baudelaire.

EDWARDS, Dorothy (1914–1982) Writer for the BBC. Her autobiographical stories about 'My Naughty Little Sister' were broadcast on *Listen with Mother*, a radio programme she helped to devise, from 1950, first appearing in book form in 1952. Nine more books about the same character followed.

EDWARDS, Jonathan (1703–58) American minister and writer, born in Connecticut, philosopher and formidable preacher who provoked the religious revival in New England known as the 'Great Awakening'. He was for six years a missionary to the Native Americans. His principal philosophical work was *A Careful and Strict Enquiry into the Modern Prevailing Notions of . . . Freedom of Will* (1754), in which he attacked from a predestinarian standpoint the *Arminian view of liberty. His *Personal Narrative* (*c.*1740) describes his experience of conversion. His essay 'Images or Shadows of Divine Things' is an important statement of *Protestant typology.

EDWARDS, Monica (1912–98) Born in Belper, Derbyshire; she received little formal education. She is remembered for appealing pony stories, beginning with *Wish for a Pony* (1947), first in the linked Romney Marsh (1947–69) and Punchbowl Farm (1947–67) series.

EDWARDS, Richard (1525–66) Master of the Children of the Chapel Royal, 1561–6. He composed *Palamon and Arcite* (now lost) for Queen Elizabeth's entertainment at Oxford, 1566. Her Majesty was amused. *The Excellent Comedy of . . . Damon and Pithias* (performed at court and at Lincoln's Inn, 1564–5; printed 1571) is his only surviving play. He was the compiler of the *Paradise of Dainty Devices*, published posthumously (1576).

Edwin Drood, The Mystery of Charles *Dickens's final novel. Six of the planned twelve instalments were published in 1870, but Dickens died before completing the book. The fathers of Edwin Drood and Rosa Bud, both widowers, have before their deaths betrothed their young children to one another. The orphan Rosa has been brought up in Miss Twinkleton's school at Cloisterham (Rochester), where Edwin, also an orphan, has an uncle, John Jasper. It is understood that the two young people are to marry as soon as Edwin comes of age. Jasper, a sinister and hypocritical character, gives Rosa music lessons and loves her passionately, but inspires her with terror and disgust. Two more orphans appear, the twins Neville and Helena Landless. Neville and Edwin at once become enemies, and Jasper contrives a violent quarrel between them. On Edwin's last visit to Cloisterham before their marriage, Rosa and he break off the engagement. That same night Edwin disappears under suspicious circumstances suggesting that he has been murdered by Neville Landless,

a theory supported by Jasper. But Jasper is clearly dismayed when he learns that the engagement had been broken off before Edwin's disappearance, and this betrayal of himself is noted by Mr Grewgious, Rosa's eccentric, good-hearted guardian. Neville is arrested but, as the body of Edwin is not found, is released untried. The remainder of the text is occupied with the continued machinations of Jasper against Neville and his pursuit of Rosa, who in terror of him flies to her guardian in London; with the counter-moves prepared by Mr Grewgious; and with the proceedings of the mysterious Mr Datchery, directed against Jasper. Of the solution or catastrophe intended by the author no hint exists, beyond those which the fragment itself contains, and the statement as to the broad lines of the plot given by John *Forster. There have been many conjectures, turning mainly on two points: whether Edwin Drood had in fact been murdered or had miraculously survived; and the identity of Datchery. There have been several attempts at continuations, from *John Jasper's Secret* (1871–2) by H. Morford and others, to versions by Leon Garfield and C. Forsyte (contained in *The Decoding of Edwin Drood*) both 1980.

EGAN, Pierce, the elder (*c.*1772–1849) Novelist and sports journalist. He wrote the hugely successful *Life in London* (1820–21), illustrated by Robert and George *Cruikshank, which details the adventures of Corinthian Tom and his country cousin Jerry and is interesting for the light it throws on the manners of the Regency and for its ingenious use of slang. His son, also Pierce Egan (1814–80), was associated with him in several of his works, and wrote a number of novels.

EGERTON, George (1859–1945) Pseudonym of Mary Chavelita Dunne, short story writer, born in Australia and brought up in Ireland. Her first volume of short stories, *Keynotes* (1893), published by John Lane (1854–1925) with a cover by Aubrey *Beardsley, created something of a sensation with its echoes of Scandinavian realism and portraits of the *New Woman. Her later works include: *Discords* (1894), *The Wheel of God* (1898), and *Flies in Amber* (1905).

EGGERS, Dave (1970–) American writer, editor, and publisher His widely praised memoir *A Heartbreaking Work of Staggering Genius* (2000) was followed by the novels *You Shall Know our Velocity* (2002) and *What Is the What* (2006), and a collection of short stories,

How We Are Hungry (2004). In 1998 he founded McSweeney's publishing house, which produces a quarterly literary magazine. He co-wrote the screenplay for Spike's Jonze's film of *Where the Wild Things Are* (2009).

Egoist (1914–19) Originally the *New Freewoman: An Individualist Review*, founded by Harriet Shaw *Weaver and Dora *Marsden. It published articles on modern poetry and the arts, and from being a feminist paper became, under the influence of Ezra *Pound and others, a mouthpiece for the *imagist poets. Marsden and Weaver succeeded each other as nominal editors, with Richard *Aldington as assistant editor, followed by T. S. *Eliot. James *Joyce's *Portrait of the Artist as a Young Man* was published serially in the magazine in 1914–15.

(()) SEE WEB LINKS
• Modernist Journals Project

Egoist, The A novel by George *Meredith, published 1879. The Egoist is Sir Willoughby Patterne. Laetitia Dale, an intelligent young woman but past her first bloom, has loved him for many years, and his vanity has been flattered. But the dashing Constantia Durham is a greater prize, and she accepts his proposal, but then elopes with the officer Harry Oxford, bringing Willoughby his first bewildering humiliation. Soon he discovers the qualities he requires in Clara Middleton, the daughter of an elderly scholar (said to be a sketch of Meredith's first father-in-law, Thomas Love *Peacock). Clara, bewitched by Willoughby's, becomes engaged to him, but rapidly perceives his intention of directing and moulding her; her attempts to free herself from the engagement form the main theme of the book. Clara is meanwhile seeing more and more of Vernon Whitford, a poor and earnest young scholar (based on Leslie *Stephen). Crossjay, to whom Whitford is tutor, is finally the means of Clara's release, for he unintentionally overhears Willoughby seeking a way out of his humiliation by proposing to Laetitia Dale, a proposal which she, with sad dignity, refuses. Willoughby's persistence finally wins the reluctant Laetitia, and Clara marries Vernon Whitford. The sharply compressed dialogue of the last chapters is among Meredith's most brilliant.

egotistical sublime A phrase coined by John *Keats to describe his version of *Wordsworth's distinctive genius. Wordsworth possesses imaginative self-obsession, a 'devouring egotism', in contradistinction to *Shakespeare,

'who was the least of an egoist that it was possible to be'. *See* NEGATIVE CAPABILITY.

Eikon Basilike, *the Portraiture of His Sacred Majesty in his Solitudes and Sufferings* A book claimed to be by Dr John Gauden (1605–62), bishop of Worcester. Supposed to be the meditations of Charles I, it was published ten days after his execution, 30 January 1649, and appealed so strongly to popular sentiment that 47 editions of it were published. Parliament thought it necessary to issue a reply, John *Milton's *Eikonoklastes* (1649); 'Eikon Basilike' means 'royal image' and 'Eikonoklastes' 'image breaker'.

eisteddfod Originally a formal gathering of Welsh professional poets, the first of which may have been held in Cardigan in 1176, now a competitive festival covering a wide range of cultural practices. The structure and procedures of the modern bardic establishment, the *gorsedd*, were concocted in the late 18th century by Iolo Marganwg (Edward *Williams). The ceremony of chairing the winning poet became an integral part of the local, regional, and school eisteddfodau held throughout Wales since the 19th century, and of the national youth eisteddfod. The week-long National Eisteddfod, held annually in the first week of August, alternately in venues in north and south Wales, is the most important. Since the introduction of a 'Welshonly' rule in 1937 'the National' has become the most important cultural event in the calendar for Welsh speakers of all ages.

Elaine The name (variously spelt), in Malory's *Morte Darthur*, of several ladies whose identities sometimes overlap: (1) Elaine Le Blank, the daughter of Sir Bernard of Astolat and known as the Fair Maid of Astolat (*Tennyson's Shalott), who falls in love with Launcelot and dies for love of him (*see* LAUNCELOT OF THE LAKE); (2) Elayne the Fair or Sans Pere (Peerless), the daughter of King Pelles and the mother, by Launcelot, of *Galahad; (3) Elayne the sister of Morgawse and Morgan le Fay in the opening pages of Malory; (4) Elayne the wife of King Ban and mother of Launcelot; (5) Elayne the daughter of King Pellinore.

Elder Brother, The A drama by John *Fletcher, written *c*.1625, probably with Philip *Massinger, who completed it *c*.1635 (after Fletcher's death). The story was suggested in part by Sir Thomas *Overbury's Theophrastan 'character' of 'An Elder Brother' (1614).

ELDRIDGE, David (1973–) Playwright. His first play was *Serving it Up* (1996), followed by *Festen* (2004), his adaptation of the cult film, and *Incomplete and Random Acts of Kindness* (2005). In 2006, his *Market Boy* played at the *National Theatre in London, offering a savagely comic take on Margaret Thatcher's Britain and its consequences in the context of a London street market.

ELEANOR of Aquitaine (*c.*1122–1204) The granddaughter of the first troubadour whose work survives, Guilhem IX of Aquitaine, and inheritor of the kingdom of Aquitaine. She was married by Louis VII of France in 1137, and, on their divorce in 1152, remarried to Henry Plantagenet of Anjou, the future Henry II of England, to whom she bore eight children, including the future *Richard I (b. 1157) and, the youngest, the future King John (b. 1166). After the death of Henry II in 1189 she was regent of England in the absence of her son Richard until his death in 1199. She was an immensely influential patron of the arts, particularly in her patronage of the development of courtly poetry in Poitiers, a function carried on by her daughter with Louis, Marie de Champagne.

elegiac In the modern sense, characteristic of an *elegy, thus solemnly mournful. The *quatrain of iambic *pentameters rhyming *abab* is sometimes known as the elegiac stanza after its use by Thomas *Gray in his *Elegy Written in a Country Church-Yard*. Applied to ancient Greek verse, however, the term denotes a verse form employing *hexameters and pentameters paired as couplets.

Elegiac Sonnets Verses by Charlotte *Smith, published in several editions between 1784 and 1797. Poems of sensibility, they offer acute descriptions of nature and the poet's reaction to it. They were greatly admired by *Wordsworth.

elegy A formal poetic lament for the death of a friend, a fellow poet, or a public figure; or in a broader sense, a solemnly reflective poem. A third sense, derived from the Greek *elegiac couplet, survives in the naming by John *Donne of many of his poems as Elegies because written in couplet form. The modern mournful sense predominates from the 17th century, when Milton's *'Lycidas' (1638) established the most influential model of the fully elaborated English *pastoral elegy, a form attempted earlier by *Spenser in *'Astrophel' and later imitated by P. B *Shelley in *Adonais* (1821, on the death of *Keats) and by Matthew *Arnold

in *'Thyrsis' (1866, on the death of A. H. *Clough). In this form, the conventions derived from the Greek tradition of *Theocritus, *Moschus, and *Bion provide for a formal invocation of a Muse, the pretence that the poet and the person mourned are both shepherds, accusations of negligence against guardian nymphs, the plucking of flowers for the funeral bier, and signs of Nature herself grieving for the mourned one as for a favourite. The major 19th-century instance of Tennyson's *In Memoriam A.H.H.* (1850) is sometimes called an elegy but is better classed as a sequence of lyric lamentations on loss and the phases of grieving. The most admired English elegy of the 20th century is *Auden's 'In Memory of W. B. Yeats' (1939), which deliberately inverts or disappoints pastoral conventions. Douglas *Dunn's poetry collection *Elegies* (1985), like Christopher *Reid's *A Scattering* (2009), deals with his wife's death. In the second sense, there are numerous sombre poetic meditations on mortality and loss that have been referred to as elegies, beginning with those Old English poems known as the *Exeter Book Elegies (e.g. *The *Wanderer*, *The *Seafarer*), and including such later works as Arnold's 'Dover Beach' (1867); the best known among those entitled as elegies is Thomas *Gray's *Elegy Written in a Country Church-Yard* (1751).

Elegy Written in a Country Church-Yard Poem in quatrains by Thomas *Gray, published 1751, but begun earlier. The churchyard is identified with that of Stoke Poges, a village where Gray had family and where he was eventually buried. The poem situates the speaker alone in the churchyard at night, reflecting on the obscure destinies of the villagers who lie buried ('Full many a flower is born to blush unseen') but drawing comfort from the safety that obscurity granted them. The poem concludes by imagining a sympathetic but puzzled villager reacting to the death of the melancholy and unknown author.

Elene *See* CYNEWULF.

'Elephant in the Moon, The' *see* BUTLER, SAMUEL ('HUDIBRAS').

ELGAR, Sir Edward (1857–1934) English late Romantic composer. Amongst his settings of literary texts are: *The Dream of Gerontius* (1900), a lushly poignant setting of sections of John Henry *Newman's poem; *The Music Makers* (1912) an autobiographically inflected setting of Arthur *O'Shaughnessy's 'Ode'; *Fringes of the Fleet* (poems by Rudyard *Kipling); and *The Spirit of England* (1915–17,

Laurence *Binyon). His famous 'Land of hope and glory' sets words by A. C. *Benson).

Elia See ESSAYS OF ELIA.

ELIOT, George (1819–80) The pen-name of Mary Ann, later Marian, Evans, novelist, born in Warwickshire, educated at Mrs Wallington's school in Nuneaton, and the Misses Franklin's school in Coventry. Her early evangelicalism did not withstand the influence of Charles Bray, a freethinking Coventry manufacturer, but she remained strongly affected by religious concepts of love and duty. Her works contain many affectionate portraits of Dissenters and clergymen. She translated D. F. *Strauss's *Life of Jesus*, which appeared without her name in 1846. In 1850 she met John *Chapman, and became a contributor to the *Westminster Review*, then assistant editor in 1851. In 1854 she published a translation of Ludwig Feuerbach's *Essence of Christianity*; she endorsed his view that religious belief is an imaginative necessity for man and a projection of his interest in his own species, a heterodoxy of which the readers of her novels only gradually became aware. At about the same time she joined G. H. *Lewes in a union without marriage (he could not divorce his wife) that lasted until his death. 'The Sad Fortunes of the Rev. Amos Barton', the first of the *Scenes of Clerical Life*, appeared in *Blackwood's Magazine* in 1857, followed by 'Mr Gilfil's Love-Story' and 'Janet's Repentance'; these at once attracted readers for their domestic realism, pathos, and humour, and speculation about the identity of 'George Eliot'. *Adam Bede* (1859) was received with great enthusiasm and at once established her as a leading novelist. It was followed by The *Mill on the Floss* (1860); *Silas Marner* (1861); *Romola*, based on visits to Florence 1860–1, published in the *Cornhill Magazine* in 1862–3; and *Felix Holt, the Radical* (1866). Her dramatic poem The *Spanish Gypsy*, inspired by Tintoretto, appeared in 1868. *Middlemarch* was published in instalments in 1871–2 and *Daniel Deronda*, her last great novel, in 1874–6. Eliot was widely recognized as the greatest living English novelist, admired by readers as diverse as *Turgenev, Henry *James, and Queen *Victoria. In 1878 Lewes died. Her *Impressions of Theophrastus Such*, a collection of moral essays and character sketches, appeared in 1879, and in 1880 she married the 40-year-old John Walter Cross, whom she had met in Rome in 1869 and who had become her financial adviser. She died seven months later.

After her death her reputation declined somewhat: an obituary notice (1881) by Leslie *Stephen praised the 'charm' and autobiographical elements of the early works, but found the later novels painful and excessively reflective. Virginia *Woolf defended her in an essay (1919) which declared *Middlemarch* to be 'one of the few English novels written for grown-up people'. In the late 1940s a new generation of critics, led by F. R. *Leavis (*The Great Tradition*, 1948), introduced a new respect for and understanding of her mature works; Leavis concludes that she 'is not as transcendently great as Tolstoy, but she *is* great, and great in the same way'.

As well as the novels for which she is remembered, she wrote poems, and the novellas 'The Lifted Veil' (1859) and 'Brother Jacob' (1864). Her letters and journals were edited by Cross, 3 vols (1885).

ELIOT, T. S. (Thomas Stearns) (1888–1965) Poet, publisher, playwright, and critic, born at St Louis, Missouri. In 1914 he met Ezra *Pound, who encouraged him to settle in England; in June 1915 he married Vivien Haigh-Wood, and in the same month his poem 'The Love Song of J. Alfred Prufrock' appeared (also with Pound's encouragement) in *Poetry*. In 1917 Eliot began to work for Lloyds Bank; he was also assistant editor of the *Egoist*. His first volume of verse, *Prufrock and Other Observations* (1917), was followed by *Poems* (1919), handprinted by Leonard and Virginia *Woolf at the *Hogarth Press; the two volumes struck a new note in modern poetry, satiric, allusive, cosmopolitan, at times lyric and elegiac.

In 1922 Eliot founded a new quarterly, the *Criterion*; in the first issue appeared, with much éclat, The *Waste Land*, which established him decisively as the voice of a disillusioned generation.

In 1925 Eliot left Lloyds and became a director of Faber and Faber, where he built up a list of poets (including Ezra Pound, Herbert *Read, W. H. *Auden, Stephen *Spender, and George *Barker; see also FABER BOOK OF MODERN VERSE) which represented the mainstream of the modern movement in poetry in England.

In 1927 Eliot became a British subject and a member of the Anglican Church; his pilgrimage towards his own particular brand of High Anglicanism may be charted in his poetry through 'The Hollow Men' (1925), 'The Journey of the Magi' (1927), and 'Ash-Wednesday' (1930), to its culminating vision in *Four Quartets* (1935–42). His prose also shows the same movement; for example, the title essay of *For Lancelot

Andrewes (1928) praises tradition, prayer, and liturgy, and points away from 'personality' towards hierarchy and community, and in the preface to this collection he describes himself as a 'classicist in literature, a royalist in politics, and Anglo-Catholic in religion'. The same preoccupation with tradition continued to express itself in his critical works.

In the 1930s Eliot began his attempt to revive poetic drama. *Sweeney Agonistes* (1932), an 'Aristophanic fragment' which gives, in syncopated rhythms, a satiric impression of the sterility of proletarian life, was followed by a pageant play, *The Rock* (1934), *Murder in the Cathedral* (1935), *The Family Reunion* (1939), and three 'comedies': *The Cocktail Party* (1950), *The Confidential Clerk* (1954), and *The Elder Statesman* (1959). Eliot's classic book of verse for children, *Old Possum's Book of Practical Cats* (1939), which reveals the aspect of his character that claimed the influence of Edward *Lear, achieved a considerable stage success in a musical adaptation, *Cats*, in 1981.

In his combination of literary and social criticism, Eliot may be called the Matthew *Arnold of the 20th century. *The Sacred Wood* (1920), his first collection of criticism, contained several influential essays, including 'Hamlet and his Problems', in which he applied the phrase *'objective correlative' to poetic and dramatic creation. In his later criticism, including *The Use of Poetry and the Use of Criticism* (1933), *After Strange Gods* (1934), *The Idea of a Christian Society* (1939), and *Notes towards the Definition of Culture* (1948), Eliot turned increasingly to the relations of culture and society. He was awarded the *Nobel Prize for Literature and the OM in 1948.

In the 1980s and 1990s the idea of postmodernism was most readily established by criticizing the authoritarianism and conservatism of modernism, and Eliot, as the exemplary modernist poet, suffered. More specifically, Eliot's poetry and prose were criticized for their misogyny and anti-Semitism. There is a biography by Peter *Ackroyd (1984).

elision The suppression of a vowel sound or syllable in order to maintain metrical regularity, usually at the start of a word, as in 'Th'expense'; when found within a word (e.g. 'heav'n'), it is known as syncope.

Eliza, The Journal to By Laurence *Sterne, discovered 1851 and published 1904. The *Journal*, more correctly known as the *Bramine's Journal*, was kept April to July 1767. It documents with deliberate pathos Sterne's love for Mrs Elizabeth Draper. The first instalments of the *Journal*, sent to Eliza, were lost. The *Journal* is partly written under the persona of 'Yorick'.

ELIZABETH I (1533-1603) A daughter of *Henry VIII and Anne Boleyn, and queen of England from 1558 to 1603. She was celebrated by the greatest poets of her age, including Edmund *Spenser, Ralegh, Sir John *Davies, and *Shakespeare in his and John *Fletcher's *Henry VIII* and probably in *A *Midsummer Night's Dream*, under such names as *Cynthia, Diana, Astraea, and *Gloriana (with many allusions to her semi-mythological role as Virgin Queen), and has been the subject of innumerable plays, novels, romances, and biographies. She was famed for her ready wit and for the stirring eloquence called forth in, for example, her speech at Tilbury on the approach of the Spanish Armada, her various addresses to Parliament, such as her 'Golden Speech' in 1601, her numerous letters, and her prayers. She also wrote poetry, which was highly praised by her courtiers and by George *Puttenham, who used one of her few undisputed works ('The doubt of future foes', on the conspiracies of *Mary Queen of Scots) as an example of rhetoric in his *Art of English Poesy*.

'Ellen Orford' One of the tales in Crabbe's *The *Borough*. It tells the story of a courageous woman, who, after a neglected childhood, is seduced and abandoned. She appears in Benjamin *Britten's *Peter Grimes*.

ELLIOT, Jean (Jane) (1727-1805) Author of the most popular version of the old lament for the Scots killed in the battle of Flodden (1513), 'The Flowers of the Forest', beginning 'I've heard them lilting at our yowe-milking'. Written *c.*1763, published in 1769, and republished by David Herd in 1776, it is her only surviving work. Another version, was written by Alison *Cockburn.

ELLIOTT, Ebenezer (1781-1849) Poet. Born near Rotherham, Yorkshire, he is remembered as the 'Corn Law Rhymer'. In 1829 he published *The Village Patriarch*, in which Enoch Wray, an old blind mason, reflects on rural life and the bitter poverty brought about by cruelty and injustice. *Corn Law Rhymes* (1830) is a collection of plain poems which employ both satire and pathos in fiercely condemning the Bread Tax. His collected works were published in 1846.

ellipsis The leaving out from a sentence words necessary to express the sense completely.

ELLIS, Alice Thomas (1932–2005) Pseudonym of Anna Haycraft, novelist and editor; she was born in Liverpool, but grew up in Wales. She converted to Roman Catholicism at the age of 19 and was briefly a postulant in a Liverpool convent. Her novels include *The Sin Eater* (1977), *The Birds of the Air* (1980), and *The 27th Kingdom* (1982, shortlisted for the *Booker Prize). Set in a small Welsh rural community, *Unexplained Laughter* (1985) is characteristic in its wit, economy, elegance, and sense of the otherworldly. *The Clothes in the Wardrobe, The Skeleton in the Cupboard*, and *The Fly in the Ointment* (1987–90) form a trilogy. Her works of non-fiction include *A Welsh Childhood* (1990) and *Serpent on the Rock* (1994), a stout defence of Catholic orthodoxy.

ELLIS, George (1753–1815) One of the talented group who, with George Canning and John *Frere, founded and contributed to *The *Anti-Jacobin* in 1797. He contributed to the collection of Whig political satires, *Criticism on the Rolliad* (1784). His most important works were his translations and selections from Middle English verse: *Early English Poets* (1801) and *Specimens of Early English Romances in Metre* (1805).

ELLIS, Henry Havelock (1859–1939) Writer and sexologist, qualified as a physician. His literary pursuits included reviewing, translating, and editing the unexpurgated Mermaid Series of Elizabethan dramatists (1887–9). In 1884 he became an intimate friend of Olive *Schreiner, who shared his progressive ideas on sexuality, the subject with which he is most closely identified; other friends included Edward *Carpenter, Arthur *Symons, and the American advocate of birth control, Margaret Sanger (1879–1966). *Sexual Inversion* (1897), with J. A. *Symonds, the first in his influential and sexually liberating *Studies in the Psychology of Sex* (1897–1910), was the first serious study of homosexuality to be published in Britain. His many works included: *The New Spirit* (1890); *Affirmations* (1898); *The Dance of Life* (1923); and his autobiographical *My Life* (1939).

ELLISON, Ralph Waldo (c.1913–1994) African American novelist and essayist, mainly remembered for his novel *Invisible Man* (1952), which tells the story of a young African American travelling to New York from the South and trying to make his way there. The Surrealism of this novel owes a debt to Ellison's friend

Richard *Wright and makes complex use of Ellison's interest in jazz and blues. For some forty years Ellison worked intermittently on a second novel, which was finally assembled from his papers and published as *Juneteenth* in 1999. Ellison's *Collected Essays* appeared in 2003.

ELLMANN, Richard (1918–87) American scholar and biographer. His publications include *Yeats: The Man and the Mask* (1948, rev. 1979); several works on Joyce, including *James Joyce* (1959, rev. 1982), which made an influential contribution to new ideas about the art of *biography; and *Oscar Wilde* (1987, Pulitzer prize). He also edited the *New Oxford Book of American Verse* (1976).

ELLROY, James (1948–) American novelist and short story writer, born in Los Angeles. His mother was murdered in 1958, an event which Ellroy confronted in his memoir *My Dark Places* (1996). Ellroy's crime fiction is characterized by its rapid, complex plots and graphic violence. *Blood on the Moon* (1984), *Because the Night* (1984), and *Suicide Hill* (1985) make up a trilogy featuring the detective Lloyd Hopkins. *The Black Dahlia* (1987), which deals with a notorious 1947 murder, began a quartet of novels based in Los Angeles. *American Tabloid* (1995) was the first in a trilogy on the American underworld.

'Eloisa to Abelard' A heroic epistle by Alexander *Pope, published 1717, retelling the tragic love of Héloïse and *Abelard; in her Gothic seclusion of 'grots and caverns', Héloïse remains unable to renounce for God the memory of 'unholy joy'. The poem was regarded as one of Pope's most imaginative ventures.

ELSTOB, Elizabeth (1683–1756) Self-taught pioneer in Old English studies, sister of William Elstob (1673–1715), a fellow of University College, Oxford. She published *An English-Saxon Homily on the Birthday of St Gregory* (1709) and *The Rudiments of Grammar for the English-Saxon Tongue* (1715), the first Old English grammar in modern English. Impoverished by William's death, she abandoned her projects, setting up a school in Evesham, then becoming governess to the duchess of Portland's children. *See also* HICKES, GEORGE.

ELTON, Ben (1959–) English playwright, novelist, and scriptwriter. As a stand-up comedian and co-writer of television comedies such as *Blackadder* and *The Young Ones* he was one of the most influential figures of the 1980s, pioneering a style of articulate, politically acute comedy. His early novels were commercial rather than critical successes, but *Popcorn* (1996), an attack on Hollywood's glorification of violence, was widely acclaimed. Like its successor *Blast from the Past* (1998), it was subsequently a successful West End play. *Maybe Baby* (2000) is a film adaptation of Elton's novel *Inconceivable* (1999), on the trauma of infertility, written and directed by himself.

ELYOT, Kevin (1951-) Playwright, born in Birmingham. The first of his plays about modern homosexual love, loss, and betrayal was *Coming Clean* (1982), followed by *My Night with Reg* (1994) and *The Day I Stood Still* (1998). Other work includes versions of Ostrovsky's *Artists and Admirers* (1992) for the Royal Shakespeare Company, Wilkie *Collins's *The *Moonstone* (1996) for BBC television, and the plays *Mouth to Mouth* (2001), *Forty Winks* (2004), *And Then There Were None* (2005), *Clapham Junction* (2007, Channel 4), and *Christopher and His Kind* (2011, BBC2) on the life of Christopher *Isherwood.

ELYTIS, Odysseus (1911-96) Greek poet. He became associated with the so-called 'Thirties Generation' of poets, including George Seferis, who were much influenced by Paul Éluard and other members of the French *Surrealist movement. His most famous poem is *To Axion Esti* (1959; trans. 1974). The first complete collection of his poetry in English was published in 1997.

emblem book A genre of verbal-pictorial art which is particularly associated with the Renaissance. Important sources include the *Physiologus* and the epigrams of the *Greek *Anthology*.

The first emblem book, the *Emblematum Liber* of Andrea Alciati (1492-1550), was published in 1531. Each emblem consists of a motto, a symbolic picture, and an explanatory set of Latin verses called an epigram. All three parts of an emblem contribute to its meaning: e.g. Alciati's picture of a bee-hive in a helmet, together with the motto *Ex bello pax* and the explanatory epigram, means that the weapons of war may be turned into the works of peace. Writers often borrowed one another's pictures and wrote new verses which reinterpreted them. The earliest English emblem book to contain illustrations as well as verses was Geoffrey Whitney's (1548?-1600/01) *A Choice of Emblemes* (1586), which distinguished three categories: natural, historical, and moral. The 17th century produced many religious emblem books, of which the most famous English example was Francis *Quarles's *Emblems* (1635). George *Wither published *A Collection of Emblemes*, also illustrated (1634-5).

The poetry of some religious poets of the period, such as George *Herbert and Henry *Vaughan, is sometimes described as emblematic, though their books were not illustrated. John *Bunyan also wrote an emblem book without pictures, *A Book for Boys and Girls* (1686). By then the form had largely gone out of fashion; it enjoyed something of a revival in the Victorian period.

( ) SEE WEB LINKS

• University of Glasgow Emblem archive

Emblems A book of short devotional poems by Francis *Quarles, first published 1635; it was adapted from two Jesuit emblem books, *Typus Mundi* (1627) and Herman Hugo's *Pia Desideria*. The poems are each based on some scriptural text, and some in the form of dialogues (e.g. between Eve and the Serpent, between Jesus and the Soul, and between the Flesh and the Spirit).

EMECHETA, Buchi (1944-) Nigerian novelist and writer for children. She left her country at the age of 20 with four small children and moved to London. Her autobiographical novels, *In the Ditch* (1972) and its sequel, *Second-Class Citizen* (1974), were published in one volume as *Adah's Story* (1983); *Head above Water* (1986) is her autobiography. Succeeding novels, *The Bride Price* (1976), *The Slave Girl* (1977), and *The Joys of Motherhood* (1979), deal with the position of women in Nigerian society. *Double Yoke* and *Destination Biafra*, a fictional account of the Nigerian civil wars which draws on the experiences of family and friends, were both published in 1982. *Gwendolen* (1989) focuses on the subject of child abuse and cultural isolation; *The Rape of Shavi* (1983) and *The New Tribe* (2000) engage with the politics of diasporic experience.

EMERSON, Ralph Waldo (1803-82) American philosopher and poet. He studied theology, was ordained, and became a pastor in Boston, but resigned because he felt unable to believe in the sacrament of the Lord's Supper. In 1833 he visited England, where he met S. T. *Coleridge, William *Wordsworth, and Thomas *Carlyle; the latter became a lifelong friend and correspondent. On his return to America Emerson evolved the new quasi-religious concepts developed in the *Transcendental Club, which found written expression in his essay *Nature* (1836). Emerson became revered as a sage and his 1837 Harvard address, 'The American Scholar', urged America to assert its intellectual independence of Europe. *The *Dial*, founded in 1840, and edited by Emerson from 1842 to 1844, published many of his poems. His essays were published in two volumes in 1841 and 1844; the second contains 'The Poet', in which he declares: 'America is a poem in our eyes', a view given poetic expression by his devoted disciple Walt *Whitman. Emerson's lectures published as *Representative Men* (1850) owe something to Carlyle's concept of the Hero; his *English Traits* (1865), a perceptive study of the English national character, is based on his 1847 lecture tour. Emerson was actively engaged in the anti-slavery campaign, and wrote a moving tribute to his friend and follower Henry *Thoreau (1862).

Eminent Victorians (1918) A group biography by Lytton *Strachey, with chapters on Cardinal Henry Manning (1808–92), Florence *Nightingale, Dr Thomas Arnold of Rugby School, and General Charles Gordon (1833–85); also a critique of the Victorian age. Strachey's approach to biography is radically anti-heroic, seeing his subjects as locked within the assumptions and limitations of their age.

Emma A novel by Jane *Austen, begun 1814, published 1816. Emma, a clever, pretty, and self-satisfied young woman, is the daughter, and mistress of the house, of Mr Woodhouse, an amiable old fusspot. Her former governess and companion, Anne Taylor, has just left them to marry a neighbour, Mr Weston. Missing Miss Taylor's companionship, Emma takes under her wing Harriet Smith, a pretty, pliant girl of 17, the daughter of unknown parents. Emma sets to work on schemes for Harriet's advancement. She first prevents Harriet from accepting an offer of marriage from Robert Martin, an eligible young farmer, as being beneath her. This tampering greatly annoys Mr Knightley, Emma's unmarried brother-in-law, and one of the few people able to see that she has faults. Emma hopes to arrange a match between Harriet and Mr Elton, the young vicar, only to find that he aspires to her own hand. Frank Churchill, the son of Mr Weston by a former marriage, now comes to visit Highbury. Emma first supposes him in love with herself, but presently thinks that Harriet might attract him. Emma's encouragement is misunderstood by Harriet, who assumes it is directed, not at Frank Churchill, but at the great Mr Knightley himself, with whom Emma is half unwittingly in love. Emma then

suffers the double mortification of discovering, first, that Frank Churchill is already engaged; and second, that Harriet has hopes of supplanting her in Mr Knightley's affections. However, Knightley proposes to the humbled and repentant Emma, and Harriet is happily consoled with Robert Martin.

EMPEDOCLES (*c*.492–*c*.432 BC) Greek scientist, philosopher, and advocate of democracy. Only about 450 lines survive from his poem *On Nature*, which was an important model for *Lucretius. He was responsible for demonstrating the existence of air, and taught that the universe was in a state of unending change thanks to the contrary action of Love, which united the four elements, earth, air, fire, and water, and Strife, which drove them apart. Legends accumulated round his name: he was supposed to work miracles, and to have met his death plunging into the crater of Etna. The opposition of Love and Strife is an important principle in Edmund *Spenser's *Faerie Queene*, IV. The philosopher's death is the subject of Hölderlin's draft plays *The Death of Empedocles* (1797–1800), and Matthew *Arnold's poem *Empedocles on Etna* (1852).

Empedocles on Etna A dramatic poem by Matthew *Arnold, published anonymously 1852. Arnold portrays the philosopher *Empedocles, said to have committed suicide by throwing himself into the crater of Etna, on the verge of his last act: his physician friend Pausanias tries to cheer him. Empedocles expresses his intellectual doubts, dismissing the reassuring platitudes of religion and philosophy; man's yearning for joy, calm, and enlightenment is in itself no proof that these things exist or can be attained. He turns Pausanias away, grieves over his own 'dwindling faculty of joy', concludes that he is man no more, but 'a naked, eternally restless mind', and finally, in a kind of triumph, concluding that at least he has been ever honest in his doubts, hurls himself to his death.

EMPSON, Sir William (1906–84) Poet and critic. He studied mathematics at Cambridge, then English under I. A. *Richards. His *Seven Types of Ambiguity* (1930) is a widely admired and influential study of metaphor, verbal nuance, and multiple meanings in poetry. His criticism includes *Some Versions of Pastoral* (1935), *The Structure of Complex Words* (1951), and *Milton's God* (1961), the latter being notable for its attacks on Christianity as a sadistic cult of torture. Empson's technically brilliant poetry, collected in *Poems* (1935), *The Gathering Storm*

(1940), and the revised *Collected Poems* (1955), makes use of analytical argument and imagery drawn from modern physics and mathematics. Among several posthumously published volumes is *Using Biography* (1984), a spirited attack on the *New Criticism's neglect of the biographical element in literary interpretation.

Encounter A political, cultural, and literary review, founded in 1953, and originally edited by Stephen *Spender and Irving Kristol (1920–2009). It was the vehicle for Nancy *Mitford's celebrated formulation of the 'U' and 'Non-U' concept (1955), and C. P. *Snow pursued the *two cultures controversy in its pages (1959–60). It has also published poetry by Robert *Lowell, Sylvia *Plath, Theodore *Roethke, W. H. *Auden, Philip *Larkin, Kingsley *Amis, and others.

Encyclopédie, L' A dictionary of universal knowledge published between 1751 and 1772 in seventeen volumes of text and eleven volumes of plates. It was conceived originally as a translation of Ephraim *Chambers's *Cyclopedia*, but under the editorship of *Diderot and d'Alembert it aspired to provide an account of the current state of knowledge and to 'change the general way of thinking', embodying the ideas and aspirations of the *Enlightenment. Contributors included *Voltaire, Montesquieu, *Rousseau, Buffon, and Jacques Turgot (1727–81). Its attacks on superstition and credulity attracted the hostility of church and state, but the first edition had over 4,000 subscribers.

Endymion (Disraeli) The last of Benjamin *Disraeli's novels, published 1880. Set between *c.*1830 and the early 1850s, it vividly describes the political and social scene of that time, including the *Tractarians, railway mania, the *Chartists, and a satirical portrait of W. M. *Thackeray as St Barbe (in revenge for his *Codlingsby*).

Endymion (Keats) A poem in four books, by John *Keats, written 1817, published 1818. The poem tells the story of Endymion, who falls in love with Cynthia, the moon, and descends to the depths of the earth to find her. Its most famous line is its first, 'A thing of beauty is a joy forever'.

The work was violently attacked in the *Quarterly Review* and in *Blackwood's Magazine*, in which John *Lockhart attacked its 'calm, settled, imperturbable drivelling idiocy'.

Endymion, the Man in the Moon An allegorical prose play by John *Lyly, acted at court by Paul's Boys, 1588, published 1591.

ENGELS, Friedrich (1820–95) German philosopher, the son of a factory owner who supervised his father's business in Manchester. He wrote influential essays on the social and political conditions in Britain in the 1840s, including *The Condition of the Working Class in England* (1845), in which he praised Thomas *Carlyle as the only British writer to take account (in *Past and Present*, 1843) of the atrocious working conditions of the urban poor. Engels collaborated with Karl *Marx, whom he helped to support when the latter settled in London in 1849, in writing *The German Ideology* (1845–6, but not published until 1932), a critique of German philosophy as lacking in social application; the *Manifesto of the Communist Party* (1848); and their great work, *Das Kapital*, the third volume of which Engels completed after Marx's death (vols i–iii, 1867/84/94).

Englands Helicon A miscellany of lyrical and pastoral poetry of the Elizabethan age published in 1600, with additions in 1614, including pieces by Sir Philip *Sidney, Edmund *Spenser, Michael *Drayton, Robert *Greene, Thomas *Lodge, Walter *Ralegh, Christopher *Marlowe, George *Peele, Anthony *Munday, and others.

Englands Parnassus A collection of extracts from contemporary poets, by Robert Allott (*fl.* 1599–1600), published in 1600.

English Bards and Scotch Reviewers A satirical poem by Lord *Byron in heroic couplets, published 1809. Angered by Henry *Brougham's contemptuous criticism of his *Hours of Idleness* in the *Edinburgh Review*, Byron responded with this witty and spirited attack on Francis *Jeffrey, Robert *Southey, William *Wordsworth, S. T. *Coleridge, and Walter *Scott. He also poured patrician mockery on the 'doggrel' and 'childish prattle' of many of the minor poets (William *Bowles, Joseph *Cottle, and many others) of the Romantic movement, while upholding and defending those (e.g. William *Gifford, George *Crabbe) who continued to sustain the classical traditions of John *Dryden and Alexander *Pope. It is filled with woundingly memorable insults.

Englishman's Magazine (1831–3) An ambitious literary monthly, edited by Edward *Moxon. It published the work of the unknown young Alfred *Tennyson and vigorously supported William *Wordsworth and the *Cockney School, defending them against *Blackwood's*, the *Quarterly*, and similar journals. Unusually for the time, more than half the contributions were signed.

English Review A periodical founded in 1908 through the inspiration of a group of writers including Joseph *Conrad, H. G. *Wells, and Eve *Garnett, with the purpose, in the words of its first editor, Ford Madox *Ford (then Hueffer), of 'giving imaginative literature a chance in England'. Ford published work by established writers such as Arnold *Bennett, John *Galsworthy, Henry *James, and H. G. Wells, and by newcomers such as D. H. *Lawrence and Wyndham *Lewis, amongst others. The title merged with the *National Review* in 1937.

(((∙))) SEE WEB LINKS
• Modernist Journals Project

English Stage Company Founded in 1956 by George Devine (1910–66) to present modern plays and encourage new dramatists; its home was the *Royal Court Theatre, London. It established itself with the success of John *Osborne's *Look Back in Anger* (1956), and has produced important new work by Osborne, Arnold *Wesker, John *Arden, Edward *Bond, Christopher *Logue, David *Storey, Joe *Orton, Ann *Jellicoe, N. F. *Simpson, Samuel *Beckett, Christopher *Hampton, Heathcote Williams (1941–), David *Hare, E. A. Whitehead (1933–), Brian *Friel, Athol *Fugard, Mustapha Matura (1939–), Caryl *Churchill, Howard *Barker, Howard *Brenton, and others. *See* also KITCHEN SINK DRAMA.

English Traveller, The A romantic drama by Thomas *Heywood, written *c.*1624, printed 1633.

enjambment (enjambement) The continuation of the sense and grammatical construction of a verse line or couplet into the next without a punctuated pause, thus de-emphasizing the line-ending. The opposite effect, where the end of a line coincides with the end of a sentence or clause, is called end-stopping.

Enlightenment A term (originally the German *Aufklärung*) used to describe a scientific and rational ethos, including freedom from superstition and religious intolerance, observable in much of 18th-century Europe. The movement derives from thinkers such as John *Locke, the third earl of Shaftesbury, and Isaac *Newton. *Voltaire, *Rousseau, Condorcet, and Buffon were associated with the Enlightenment, as was one of its great monuments, *L'*Encyclopédie*. The *Encyclopaedia Britannica* was in part a product of the distinct intellectual movement sometimes described as the *Scottish Enlightenment, which featured such thinkers as Adam *Ferguson, David *Hume, and Adam *Smith. The American Declaration of Independence is in some senses a classic Enlightenment document. In his *Rights of Man* Thomas *Paine was much influenced by Enlightenment political ideals, and many other English writers echoed educational or egalitarian ideas associated with the movement, including William *Godwin, P. B. *Shelley, Erasmus *Darwin, Mark *Akenside, and the *Edgeworths. William *Blake subscribed to the political energies unleashed by the Enlightenment, but decried what he saw as the 'single vision' of Newtonian materialism; *Romanticism was in part a revolt against such pure rationality.

ENNIUS, Quintus (239–169BC) Known as the father of Roman poetry, author of *tragedies, *satires, and *epic. He introduced the *dactylic *hexameter and many Homeric devices to Latin poetry. His *Annales*, an epic poem in eighteen books, told the story of the expansion of Rome from the fall of Troy to the present. It was admired by and influenced later Roman poets, but only fragments totalling about 550 lines have survived.

Enoch Arden A narrative poem by *Tennyson, published 1864; the story was suggested by his friend Thomas *Woolner.

Enquiry Concerning Political Justice A philosophical treatise by William *Godwin, published February 1793, which established him as the chief proponent of British radicalism.

Enquiry into the Present State of Polite Learning, An Treatise by Oliver *Goldsmith, published 1759. It examines the causes of the decline of 'polite learning' from ancient times, through the Dark Ages, to its present state in Europe. He attributes the alleged decay in England to the low status of the writer, driven to hack-work for the booksellers through lack of *patronage; also to the lack of comic spirit among poets, the restrictive conditions of the theatre, and the malign detractions of critics. His attack on theatrical managers offended David *Garrick, and it was toned down for the second edition (1774).

ENRIGHT, Anne (1962–) Irish novelist and short story writer. Enright's sometimes surreal fictions bring a tart wit to their exploration of the dynamics of family life. Her novels *The Wig my Father Wore* (1995), *What Are You Like?* (2000), and *The Pleasure of Eliza Lynch* (2002) were followed by the Booker Prize-winning *The Gathering* (2007), a darkly comic excavation of the childhood secrets underlying the suicide of an alcoholic whose siblings assemble for his funeral. *Yesterday's Weather* (2009) includes many of Enright's stories from her earlier collections *The Portable Virgin* (1991) and *Taking Pictures* (2008). *Making Babies* (2004) is a wry autobiographical reflection on motherhood.

ENRIGHT, D. J. (Dennis Joseph) (1920–2002) Poet. He taught English literature for 25 years, mainly in the East; many of his poems are set in Japan, Egypt, Singapore, and Germany, and concern cultural differences and misunderstandings, themes which he also explored in his autobiographical *Memoirs of a Mendicant Professor* (1969). His verse collections include *The Laughing Hyena and Other Poems* (1953), *Bread rather than Blossoms* (1956), *Addictions* (1962), *Sad Ires* (1975), *A Faust Book* (1979; a sequence of poems on the *Faust legend), *Under the Circumstances* (1991), and *Old Men and Comets* (1993). He also published novels for children (*The Joke Shop*, 1976; *Wild Ghost Chase*, 1978; *Beyond Land's End*, 1979) and other prose works, including *The World of Dew: Aspects of Living in Japan* (1955), *Insufficient Poppy* (1960, a novel), and *Man Is an Onion* (1972, collected reviews and essays). His anthology *Poets of the 1950s* (1955) brought together many of the poets to appear in Robert *Conquest's *New Lines. His own work was predominantly detached and ironic in tone (although by no means impersonal) and wide-ranging in its subject matter. *Byblows: Uncollected Poems* (1996) was followed by *Collected Poems, 1948–1998* (1998).

Entail, The A novel by John *Galt, published 1823, a satire on the corrupting effects of greed. As a study in obsession the book is powerful, and it was admired by Lord *Byron.

Eōthen *See* KINGLAKE, ALEXANDER WILLIAM.

epic Originally a lengthy poem recounting in elevated style the exploits of a legendary hero or heroes, especially in battles or voyages. This is also known as a heroic poem. In modern times the term is sometimes extended to certain prose works, especially to large-scale historical novels. The major examples in English are John *Milton's *Paradise Lost, unusual in its biblical subject, and the Old English *Beowulf. Others include the *alliterative *Morte Arthure, while

John *Keats's *Hyperion is an unfinished attempt at an epic poem. English literature is somewhat richer in its tradition of *mock-epic poems (e.g. Alexander *Pope's *Dunciad, Lord *Byron's *Don Juan), which make fun of the classical epic conventions derived from *Homer and *Virgil.

🌐 **SEE WEB LINKS**
• Hyperepos—epic poetry resources

Epicene, or The Silent Woman A comedy by Ben *Jonson, acted by the Children of the Queen's Revels 1609–10, printed 1616. Morose, an old bachelor pathologically averse to noise, proposes to disinherit his nephew Sir Dauphine Eugenie, by marrying and producing children, provided he can find a silent woman. He marries Epicene, but after the wedding she turns into a loquacious shrew. Frantic, Morose accepts Dauphine's offer to rid him of Epicene for £500 a year and the reversion of his property—whereupon Dauphine pulls off Epicene's wig revealing that, unknown to everyone else, including the audience, she is a boy. John *Dryden thought this play the most perfectly plotted of all comedies.

epic simile An extended simile comparing one complex action with another, for example the charge of an army with the onset of storm clouds, elaborated at such length as to become digressive. Sometimes called a Homeric simile after its frequent use by *Homer, it was imitated by *Virgil and in English by *Milton.

EPICTETUS (mid-1st to 2nd century AD) *Stoic philosopher. He wrote nothing himself; his teachings were compiled in Greek by his disciple the historian Arrian as the *Discourses* and *Encheiridion* (Manual), or summary of his principles. Epictetus held health, pleasure, possessions to be of no account. Virtue alone mattered, and that resided in the will which should direct man to abstain and endure. The *Manual* was translated by John Healey (1610), and the complete works by Elizabeth *Carter (1758). *See* MARCUS AURELIUS ANTONINUS.

EPICURUS (341–270 BC) The founder of the school of philosophy that bears his name. Some fragments of his prolific writings survive, but his ideas are perhaps best studied in the *De Rerum Natura* of *Lucretius. Epicurus adopted the atomic theory of *Democritus but postulated an indeterminacy in the movement of his atoms which allowed him to believe in free will. In ethics he regarded the absence of pain—*ataraxia* or peace of mind—as the greatest good. Conventional moralists tended to describe him as a contemptible pleasure-seeker (hence the term 'epicure'), but his life had been marked by rigorous abstinence from greed, lust, and anger, a fact which made Sir Thomas *Browne defend his reputation (*Pseudodoxia*, VII. 17). Surviving texts by and about Epicurus were translated by Walter Charleton in *Epicurus's Morals* (1656).

epigram Originally an inscription, usually in verse, for example on a tomb; hence a short poem ending in a witty turn of thought; hence a pointed or antithetical saying.

Epigrams, The A collection of poems by Ben *Jonson, printed 1616, including 'Inviting a Friend to Supper', 'On my First Son', 'The Famous Voyage', and addresses to John *Donne and *James I.

epiphany Used in a Christian context to refer to the revelation of Christ to the Gentiles in the persons of the Magi (Matt. 2: 1–12), but adapted by James *Joyce in *Stephen Hero*, an early draft of *A *Portrait of the Artist as a Young Man*, where Stephen considers compiling 'a book of epiphanies'. By an epiphany he meant a sudden spiritual manifestation, whether in the vulgarity of speech or of gesture or in a memorable phase of the mind itself.' (ch. 25). In *Ulysses* Stephen Dedalus recalls his 'epiphanies on green live leaves, deeply deep'. There are similar moments in poems by W. B. *Yeats, such as 'Vacillation', and in Virginia *Woolf's *Mrs Dalloway* and *To the Lighthouse*. Forty epiphanies noted down by the young Joyce have been published in his *Poems and Shorter Writings* (1991).

Epipsychidion An autobiographical poem by P. B. *Shelley, published anonymously in 1821. Composed in couplets of breathless energy, the poem celebrates Shelley's lifelong search for the eternal image of Beauty, in the earthly form of his various wives, mistresses, and female friends: notably Harriet Westbrook, Mary *Shelley, Claire *Clairmont, and Emilia Viviani—to whom the work is addressed. Though drawing on the courtly love and planetary imagery of *Petrarch and *Dante, the work is passionately sexual as well as platonic: it ends with an invitation to Emilia to elope to 'an isle under Ionian skies, | Beautiful as a wreck of Paradise'. There is an attack on conventional marriage, 'the dreariest and longest journey', and praise of 'Free' or 'True' Love. The poem is partly also a study of the creative process itself. A close biographical reading reveals much sly humour.

Epistles, Pauline *See* PAUL, ST.

Epistles to Several Persons Four ethical poems addressed to friends by Alexander *Pope, published 1731–5; the collective title 'Moral Essays' was added later by Pope's editor William *Warburton. Epistle I (1734), addressed to Viscount Cobham, sets forth the difficulties in judging human character and finds the solution in the discovery of the 'ruling passion'. Epistle II (1735), addressed to 'a Lady' (Martha Blount), deals with the characters of women and includes a gallery of unstable noblewomen, disguised under code names, and affectionate praise for Martha's own perfections. Epistle III (1733), to Lord Bathurst, deals with the abuse of riches, arguing that neither the miser nor the prodigal derives happiness from them. Epistle IV (1731), to Lord Burlington, also discusses riches, giving instances of the tasteless use of wealth in architecture and gardening, and promoting the civic use of wealth.

epistolary novel A story written in the form of letters, or letters with journals, usually presented by an anonymous author masquerading as 'editor'. The first notable example in English, written entirely in epistolary form, was a translation by Roger L'Estrange from the French of the anonymous *Letters of a Portuguese Nun* (1678). In 1683 Aphra *Behn published *Love-Letters between a Nobleman and his Sister*, and many similar tales of illicit love followed. When Samuel *Richardson wrote *Pamela* (1741) he felt a duty to rescue the novel from a doubtful reputation. The immediacy of the epistolary form lends itself to intense subjective analysis, but also to charges of implausible absurdity (fully exploited by Henry Fielding in his parody, *Shamela*). Between the 1740s and about 1800, when the form chiefly flourished, it was employed not only by Richardson but by Tobias *Smollett, Robert *Bage, and Fanny *Burney, among many others. After 1800 the form fell into almost complete disuse. Among modern attempts at revival, William *Golding's *Rites of Passage* (1980) provides an interesting variation in the form of an epistolary journal.

'Epithalamion' A hymn by Edmund *Spenser, probably in celebration of his marriage with Elizabeth Boyle in 1594. The poem was printed with the *Amoretti* in 1595.

epithalamium (epithalamion) A poem celebrating a wedding, and conventionally sung on the bridal night. Examples include Edmund Spenser's *'Epithalamion', and poems by Philip *Sidney, Ben *Jonson, Andrew

*Marvell, John *Dryden, P. B *Shelley, and W. H. *Auden.

eponymous Name-giving; a term applied in literary contexts to a real or fictitious person whose name provides the title of a work. Thus Emma Woodhouse is the eponymous heroine of Jane Austen's novel *Emma*.

EQUIANO, Olaudah (1745–97) Writer of the most influential early slave narrative, *The Interesting Narrative of the Life of Olaudah Equiano, or Gustavus Vassa, the African, Written by Himself* (1789). Its elegant expression itself makes the case against assumptions about African savagery, and reveals the barbarism of the European slave trade. *See* SLAVERY.

ERASMUS, Desiderius (*c.*1467–1536) Dutch humanist. He came more than once to England, where he was welcomed by the scholars, Thomas *More, John *Colet, and William Grocyn, and was induced by St John *Fisher to lecture at Cambridge on Greek from 1511 to 1514. His principal works were a new edition of the Greek New Testament (1516), followed by Latin paraphrases (1517–24); *Encomium Moriae* (*The Praise of Folly*, 1511, a satire written at the suggestion of More, principally directed against theologians and church dignitaries); *Enchiridion Militis Christiani* (1503, a manual of simple piety according to the teaching of Jesus Christ, which was translated perhaps by William *Tyndale into English, and also into other languages); *Institutio Christiani Principis* (*Education of a Christian Prince*); the vivid and entertaining *Colloquia* and letters furnishing autobiographical details and pictures of contemporary life, which were drawn upon by Charles Reade in *The *Cloister and the Hearth* and by Walter Scott in *Anne of Geierstein*, and the *Adagia* (1500), a collection of Latin and Greek proverbs traced to their source with witty comments. His many editions and translations of the Bible, early Christian authors, and the classics revolutionized European literary culture. Erasmus prepared the way for the *Reformation, and at first sympathized with the movement. However, he refused to intervene either for or against Martin *Luther at the time of the Diet of Worms. He urged moderation, distanced himself from Luther's violence and extreme conclusions, and at a later stage (1524, in his tract on 'Free Will') entered into controversy with him.

ERDRICH, Louise (1954–) Native American novelist and poet, a member of the Anishi-naabe nation. Her first novel, *Love Medicine* (1984), set the keynote for her fiction, which incorporates Native American storytelling techniques through multiple narrators and time-jumps. *The Beet Queen* (1986) was attacked by Native writer Leslie Marmon Silko as being preoccupied with technique. Most of Erdrich's fiction, including *Last Report on the Miracle at Little No Horse* (2001), has been set in North Dakota, where she was brought up. *The Antelope Wife* (1998) is set in contemporary Minneapolis. *Shadow Tag* (2010), set in Minnesota, draws on her difficult marriage (with the poet Michael Dorris, (1945–97)). She has published a number of poems dealing with cultural conflict (e.g. *Jacklight*, 1984) and stories for younger readers.

Erewhon [pron. e-re-whon, an anagram of 'nowhere'] A satirical novel by Samuel *Butler, critical of socialism and Darwinism, published anonymously 1872. The narrator (whose name is revealed in *Erewhon Revisited* as Higgs) crosses a range of mountains and comes upon the undiscovered country of Erewhon. He is first thrown into jail, where he is helped by his beautiful girl jailer, Yram. On his release he is lodged with Mr Nosnibor (Robinson) and his family. In this society morality is equated with health and beauty, and crime with illness. The Unborn select their parents, who have to endure their selection. The Musical Banks produce a currency which is venerated but not used. The development of machinery, which had threatened to usurp human supremacy, had led to civil war and is now forbidden. The country is ruled by so-called philosophers and prophets, whom Higgs sees to be merely faddists and fanatics. Threatened with prosecution for contracting measles, Higgs announces that he will visit the air god and end the terrible drought; with Nosnibor's daughter Arowhena, he escapes in a balloon to England, where they marry.

Erewhon Revisited A sequel to *Erewhon, by Samuel *Butler, published 1901. John, the son of Higgs and Arowhena, is the writer of this account of his father's return to Erewhon. After twenty years Higgs finds that his ascent in the balloon has become that of a god, the Sunchild, in a sun-chariot, his conversation has become the basis of sacred texts, a temple has been built to him at Sunchildiston, and that the new religion is organized by two cynical exploiters, Professors Hanky and Panky. Once again Higgs's life is threatened, but again he escapes and, after further bewildered wanderings in Erewhon, returns, half unhinged, to England.

ERIGENA See SCOTUS ERIUGENA, JOHN.

ERNAUX, Annie (1940-) French writer whose autobiographical texts depict the radical changes affecting post-war French society, for example in *La Place* (1984: *A Man's Place*), the narrative of her estrangement from her working-class father. Ernaux draws on the work of the sociologist Pierre *Bourdieu.

ERVINE, St John (1883–1971) Playwright and novelist, born to deaf mute parents in Protestant east Belfast. Many of his early plays (including *Mixed Marriage*, 1911; *The Magnanimous Lover*, 1912; and *John Ferguson*, 1915) were performed at the *Abbey Theatre, and dealt with themes of religious conflict in Ulster. He later settled in England, where he achieved West End success with *The First Mrs Fraser* (1929) and other popular comedies.

eschatology In Christian writing the four last things, death, judgement, heaven, and hell.

Esmond See HISTORY OF HENRY ESMOND, ESQUIRE.

Essay Concerning Human Understanding A philosophical treatise on the nature of mind by John *Locke, published 1690. In Book I Locke rejects the doctrine of 'innate ideas', maintaining that all knowledge is based on experience. The objects of understanding are termed *ideas*, and Book II provides an account of the origins of our ideas in the observation of the 'qualities' of external objects or of the internal operations of the mind such as sensation or reflection. A number of simple ideas being constantly found to go together, the mind is led to suppose a substratum for them, and this we call *substance*, but we have no other idea of its nature. We are equally ignorant of spiritual substance, the substratum of the operations of the mind: we do not even know whether material and spiritual substance are the same or different. In Book III Locke discusses language. He holds that words have meaning insofar as they stand for ideas in the mind; distinguishing between 'real' and 'nominal' essence, he argues that terms for natural kinds (e.g. 'gold', 'horse') can express only nominal essences or sets of ideas; they cannot latch on to the real essences or hidden constitutions of the things themselves. Book IV defines knowledge as the perception of the agreement or disagreement of ideas. Knowledge in matters of real existence is limited to two certainties, of our own existence, by intuition, and of the existence of God, by demonstration. We have a lesser degree of certainty of the existence of finite beings outside us. If the mind perceives nothing but its own ideas, how can we know that they agree with the things themselves? Locke advances various arguments for the possibility of knowledge about real things, but points out that such knowledge is narrowly limited. Knowledge at once general and real must be, not of the relations of ideas to reality, but of ideas to each other, as in mathematics.

Essay on Criticism A didactic poem in heroic couplets by Alexander *Pope, published anonymously 1711. It provides a set of flexible rules for the humane conduct of criticism, and discusses the authority of ancient and modern writers on the subject.

Essay on Man A philosophical poem in heroic couplets by Alexander *Pope, published 1733–4. It consists of four epistles addressed to Bolingbroke. Its objective is to prove that the scheme of the universe is the best conceivable, in spite of appearances of evil, and that our failure to see the perfection of the whole is due to our limited vision. The epistles deal with man's relations to the universe, to himself as an individual, to society, and to happiness. Pope's assertion that 'Whatever is, is right' anticipates the motto of Pangloss in *Voltaire's *Candide*.

Essays, The By Francis *Bacon, first published in 1597, together with the 'Christian Meditations' and 'Of the Colours of Good and Evil'; it consisted of ten essays, in extremely bare style. The sentences were printed separately, marked with a paragraph sign, giving them the status of aphorisms—separate, succinct observations, drawn from experience in the realm of public life. The second edition (1612) contained 38 essays, in a more varied style, and on a wider range of topics. In this collection Bacon began to fill a gap he had drawn attention to in his *Advancement of Learning* (1605)—the lack of concrete knowledge of the different 'natures and dispositions' of human beings, and how they were affected by psychological and social factors. The final version, now called *Essays or Counsels, Civil and Moral* (1625), included 58 essays, treating both 'civil' or public life, and the behaviour of private individuals. Bacon's approach varies greatly from essay to essay, and within each essay the topic is regarded from several different viewpoints, juxtaposing systematic analysis with brilliant observations.

Essays and Reviews A controversial collection of essays on religious subjects from a

*Broad Church standpoint published in 1860. Among them were Mark *Pattison's 'Tendencies of Religious Thought in England 1688–1750' and Benjamin Jowett's 'On the Interpretation of Scripture'. The other essayists were the Revd H. B. Wilson (editor), Frederick Temple, Rowland Williams, Baden Powell, and C. W. Goodwin. A meeting of the bishops in 1861 denounced the book for its liberalism. The collection represented an important challenge to traditional biblical authority, all the more shocking to its first readers because it came from within the church.

Essays in Criticism The title of Matthew *Arnold's two major collections of literary essays, the first published in 1865, the second posthumously in 1888.

Essays of Elia, The Miscellaneous essays by Charles *Lamb, published in volume form (1823), and 1833 (The Last Essays of Elia). Lamb adopted the name Elia from a former Italian clerk at the South Sea House. The essays are not reliably autobiographical. The narrator is cast as a fanciful, old-fashioned character, 'a bundle of prejudices' with a strong liking for the whimsical, the quaint, and the eccentric. The tone is never didactic or seriously philosophical, and the more disturbing aspects of life are avoided. The style is very literary and carefully wrought, filled with archaisms and with echoes of Laurence *Sterne.

ESSEX, Robert Devereux, second earl of (1565–1601) Courtier and soldier, regarded as the natural successor to Philip *Sidney, whose widow he married in 1590. Despite a fierce rivalry with Walter *Ralegh during the 1580s, Essex was chosen for dispatch to Ireland in March 1599 to suppress Tyrone's rebellion. William *Shakespeare referred in *Henry V (V. Chorus 29–34) to the return of 'the General of our gracious Empress', but in fact Essex's return was sudden and ignominious. He made an abortive attempt at rebellion in the City of London in February 1601. On the eve of the revolt, Essex's supporters commissioned a special performance at the Globe Theatre by Shakespeare's company of what was probably his *Richard II. Essex was executed on 25 February, the episode casting a dark shadow over the last eighteen months of Elizabeth's reign.

Essex was a literary patron of some discernment, involved with, among others, Edmund *Spenser, Fulke *Greville, and George *Chapman, Essex himself wrote poems, of which a dozen or so have survived. Almost immediately after his death, his life became or was suspected of being the stuff of heroic and tragic writing in works such as Samuel *Daniel's Philotas (performed 1605). Lytton *Strachey's Elizabeth and Essex (1928) is a highly coloured and highly readable fictionalization.

Esther Waters A novel by George *Moore, published 1894. It is the story of the life of a religiously minded working-class girl, driven from home at 17 by a drunken stepfather. Employed by the Barfields at Woodview, she is seduced by a fellow servant and deserted. She has to leave her place, though kindly treated by Mrs Barfield. Then follows a tale of poverty, hardship, and humiliation: the lying-in hospital, service as wet-nurse, other miserable situations, even the workhouse, in the mother's brave struggle to rear her child. Her seducer reappears, marries her, and makes a good husband. But he suffers poor health and his public house is closed by the authorities. He dies, leaving his wife and son penniless. Finally Esther returns to Woodview, where she finds peace with Mrs Barfield, now a widow, living alone and impoverished in a corner of the old house. The book's sexually explicit scenes made it controversial, and circulating libraries (see MUDIE, CHARLES) would not stock it; nevertheless, it became Moore's most successful novel.

ETHEREGE (Etheredge), Sir George (1636–91/2) Playwright. In his first play, The *Comical Revenge, or Love in a Tub, performed in 1664, the serious parts are in rhymed couplets, but the lively, realistic comic parts, in prose, are often cited as showing William *Congreve and Oliver *Goldsmith the way to an English comedy of manners. In London he belonged to the circle of wits that included Sir Charles *Sedley and Sir John *Rochester. His second play, *She Would if She Could, was performed in 1668, and his best play, The *Man of Mode, or Sir Fopling Flutter, in which Dorimant is modelled on Rochester, was a tremendous hit in 1676. He died in Paris, a *Jacobite exile. His polished and fashionable comedies were savagely attacked as immoral and coarse by the more genteel generation of Sir Richard *Steele.

ethnographic allegory A form of *allegory identified by the influential anthropologist and cultural critic James Clifford (1945–), who argued that non-fictional writings which purport to offer accurate accounts of real places are 'inescapably allegorical'. In order to make sense of other cultures, ethnographers and travel writers tend to describe them in terms of myths or other explanatory schemes familiar to their readers. Perhaps the most enduring ethnographic allegories are those which invoke an idyllic paradise uncorrupted by civilization, or its opposite: a barbaric, violent world which has yet to receive its benefits. Allegories of salvage, which present themselves as attempts to document a dying race or culture or species before it disappears, have become increasingly common since the late 18th century.

Ettrick Shepherd A name given to James *Hogg.

Eugene Aram A novel by Edward *Bulwer-Lytton, published 1832. It is the story of a schoolmaster, driven to murderous crime by poverty, who is later tormented by remorse. The same subject suggested Thomas *Hood's poem 'The Dream of Eugene Aram'.

Eulenspiegel, Till A German peasant of the early 14th century whose jests and practical jokes form the subject of a collection of satirical tales; one of these incidents features in Chaucer's 'Summoner's Tale' (*see* CANTERBURY TALES, 8). There were early translations of the German tales into English, Czech, Danish, Flemish, French, Latin, Polish, and Swedish. In England Till was known as Owlglass; an abridged translation into English by William Copland was published as *A Merye Jest of a Man that Was Called Howleglas* (c.1555). Several references in Ben *Jonson and John Taylor assume a familiarity with Owlglass as prankster.

Euphues A prose romance by John *Lyly, of which the first part, *Euphues: The Anatomy of Wit*, was published in 1578, and the second, *Euphues and his England*, in 1580. Although very popular and regularly reprinted, their plots are very slender and really just a peg on which to hang the fashionable discourses, conversations, letters, mainly on the subject of love, and the witty language, which so appealed to contemporary readers.

Euphues is famous for its distinctive style, to which it has given the name 'euphuism'. Its principal characteristics are the heavy use of antithesis, which is pursued regardless of sense, and emphasized by alliteration and other devices; and of allusions to historical and mythological personages and to natural history drawn from such encyclopedic writers as *Plutarch, *Pliny, and *Erasmus. Walter *Scott satirized euphuism in the character of Sir Piercie Shafton in *The *Monastery* and Charles *Kingsley defended *Euphues* in **Westward Ho!*

Euphues' Golden Legacy See ROSALYNDE.

euphuism *See* EUPHUES.

EURIPIDES (c.480s–c.407/406 BC) Greek tragedian. Nineteen of c.90 plays survive, ten as a collection of selected plays with ancient commentaries: *Alcestis, Medea, Hippolytus, Andromache, Hecuba, The Trojan Women, The Phoenician Women, Orestes, The Bacchae,* and *Rhesus,* and nine others as part of what was probably a complete collection: *Helen, Electra, The Children of Heracles, Heracles, The Suppliant Women, Iphigenia in Aulis, Iphigenia in Tauris, Ion,* and *Cyclops.* The plays of Euripides are characterized by an ambivalent attitude towards religious myths, which he sometimes seems to deploy purely for their dramatic potential (*see* DEUS EX MACHINA). He is also unusually successful in his characterization of extreme emotion, particularly that of women.

Milton's **Samson Agonistes* was the first English tragedy to show his influence. John *Dryden praised his depiction of human behaviour, and P. B. *Shelley translated his satyr play *Cyclops.* William *Morris sentimentalized *Medea* in *The Life and Death of Jason* and *Alcestis* in *The *Earthly Paradise.* Robert *Browning's *Balaustion's Adventure* and **Aristophanes' Apology* contain striking interpretations respectively of *Alcestis* and *Heracles.* Many modern writers have drawn on Euripides' plots, for example T. S. *Eliot on *Alcestis* in *The Cocktail Party.* Wole *Soyinka has produced a notable version of *The Bacchae,* and elements of this story have appeared in many other works, including William *Golding's *Lord of the Flies. See* AESCHYLUS; POETICS; SOPHOCLES.

Europe: A *Prophecy* A poem by William *Blake, printed 1794 at Lambeth, in which he portrays the oppression of Albion during the 1,800-year sleep of Enitharmon, the female principle, and the approach of the French Revolution, symbolized by her son, the terrible Orc, the spirit of revolt.

Eurydice *See* ORPHEUS.

Eustace Diamonds, The A novel by Anthony *Trollope, published 1873, the third in the *'Palliser' series. The unscrupulous Lizzie Eustace marries for money and, when Sir Florian Eustace dies, she not only inherits the family estates, but pockets the family diamonds as well, despite the demands of the Eustace lawyers that they be returned. The novel, which was popular, was influenced by Wilkie *Collins's treatment of crime and detection.

Evangelical Revival, the A label loosely given to several mid-18th-century religious awakenings in England, Wales, Scotland, and the American colonies, characterized by irregular open-air and itinerant preaching, societies, meetings, hymn singing, conversions, the reading and writing of religious experiences, and the publishing and distribution of materials among members. Opponents dismissed such phenomena as 'enthusiasm'. Key figures include Jonathan *Edwards, (1714–73), George *Whitefield, and John and Charles *Wesley. Its main literary productions were accounts of revival, such as Edwards's *Faithful Narrative* (1737), spiritual biographies and autobiographies, letters, and hymns. *See also* METHODISM.

Evangelists, the Four The authors of the four Gospels, Matthew, Mark, Luke, and John. *See* BIBLE.

Evan Harrington A novel by George *Meredith, published 1861; a study of the nature of a gentleman, with autobiographical elements.

EVANS, Caradoc (1878–1945) Welsh writer, born David Evans, whose attacks on Nonconformist piety earned him the nickname 'best hated man in Wales'. Evans became a journalist in 1906, eventually acting as editor of *Cassell's Weekly* and *T.P.'s Weekly*. With their reductive parodies of Welsh syntax and idiom and their presentation of religion as a cover for greed and lust, the stories of *My People* (1915) caused a major controversy in Wales. *Nothing to Pay* (1930), a gloomy portrait of a miserly draper, is the most admired of his novels.

EVANS, Christopher (1951–) *science fiction author, who co-edited (with Robert Holdstock) anthologies of British science fiction in the late 1980s. *Aztec Century* (1993), is an *alternate history in which the Aztecs have conquered Britain.

EVANS, Margiad (Peggy Eileen Whistler) (1909–59) Novelist, short story writer, and poet, born in Uxbridge. She spent much of her life on the Welsh Marches, and the divided loyalties and latent violence of borders—between genders as well as territories—are explored in *Country Dance* (1932), her first novel. *Autobiography* (1943) is a compilation of essays and other writings, while *A Ray of Darkness* (1952) dispassionately describes the onset of epilepsy, a symptom of the brain tumour that would cause the author's early death. Her stories are collected in *The Old and the Young* (1948).

EVARISTO, Bernardine (1959–) Born in London of Nigerian and British parentage. Her novels include *Blonde Roots* (2008). Evaristo's work crosses national, historical, and generic boundaries: the Sudanese protagonist of her novel-in-verse *The Emperor's Babe* (2001), set in Londinium in 211, has an affair with the Roman emperor Septimius Serverus, himself an African. She also writes for the theatre and for radio, and collaborated with jazz musicians on the installation *Cityscapes* (2003).

Eve *See* EDEN, GARDEN OF.

Evelina or *A Young Lady's Entrance into the World* *Epistolary novel by Fanny *Burney, published anonymously 1778. Sir John Belmont, disappointed of the fortune he expected to receive with his wife, abandons her and their child Evelina, who is brought up by a guardian. Evelina is introduced into London society, where her failure to understand the social rules leads to many comic misunderstandings but Lord Orville, with whom she is in love, believes in her essential integrity. It is eventually discovered that Belmont's wife's nurse had passed her own child off as his daughter. Evelina is recognized as his heir, and marries Lord Orville. The novel enjoyed huge success and influenced Jane *Austen's fiction.

EVELYN, John (1620–1706) Diarist and founder member of the *Royal Society, he wrote on a range of topics that included theology, politics, horticulture, architecture, navigation, commerce, engraving, and cookery. Among his friends were Jeremy *Taylor and Samuel *Pepys. His *Fumifugium* (1661) was the first book on air pollution in London; *Sylva* (1664) was intended to encourage landowners to plant trees for the British navy. He is chiefly remembered for his *Diary*, first published in 1818 and in a full and authoritative edition by E. S. de Beer in 1955 (6 vols). It covers most of his life, describing his travels abroad, his contemporaries, disasters such as the plague and the fire of London, the rebuilding of St Paul's Cathedral, and court life, as well as reflecting his cultural and artistic interests, and is an invaluable record of the period. His manuscript biography of his friend Mary Bragge was first printed in 1847 as *The Life of Mrs Godolphin*. *See* DIARIES.

Evening's Love, An or The Mock Astrologer A comedy by John *Dryden, produced 1668, published 1671. Combining elements of Spanish intrigue comedy and fast-moving farce with sexually explicit language, it proved a great commercial success. The preface is among the most stimulating of Dryden's critical essays, defending drama as entertainment, and replying to charges of plagiarism.

'Eve of St Agnes, The' A narrative poem in Spenserian stanzas by John *Keats, written 1819, published 1820. Madeline has been told the legend that on St Agnes's Eve (January 20th) maidens may have visions of their lovers. Madeline's love, Porphyro, comes from a family hostile to her own, yet he contrives to steal into the house during a ball on St Agnes's Eve, and with the aid of old Angela is secreted in Madeline's room. When she wakes from dreams of him, aroused by his soft singing, she finds him by her bedside. Silently they escape from the house, and fly 'away into the storm'.

'Everlasting Gospel, The' See BLAKE, WILLIAM.

Everyman A popular morality play of c.1509–19, in 921 lines. Everyman is summoned by death and, in the last hour of his life, he discovers that his friends Fellowship, Kindred, Cousin, and Goods will not go with him. He is dependent on the support of Good Deeds whom he has previously neglected. It is the most admired of the English *morality plays and had a revival of popularity in the 20th century.

Every Man in His Humour A comedy by Ben *Jonson, performed by the Lord Chamberlain's Men 1598, with William *Shakespeare in the cast, printed 1601. In his folio of 1616 Jonson published an extensively revised version, with the setting changed from Florence to London, and the characters given English names, which make the play's class bias more apparent; the added prologue to the folio version gives an exposition of his dramatic theory.

Every Man out of His Humour A comedy by Ben *Jonson, acted by the Lord Chamberlain's Men at the newly built *Globe Theatre 1599, printed 1600. The play parades a variety of characters dominated by particular 'humours', or obsessive quirks of disposition: Macilente, a venomous malcontent; Carlo Buffone, a cynical jester; the submissive Deliro and his domineering wife Fallace; Fastidious Brisk,

an affected courtier devoted to fashion; Sordido, a miserly farmer, and his son Fungoso, who longs to be a courtier; Sogliardo, 'an essential clown, enamoured of the name of a gentleman'; and Puntarvolo, a self-important knight. By means of various episodes, each character is eventually driven 'out of his humour'. Two judicious onlookers oversee the action and provide a moral commentary. An opening debate includes an explanation of Jonson's theory of humours.

EWART, Gavin (1916–95) Poet; born in London. He contributed to Geoffrey *Grigson's New Verse when he was 17; his work include Poems and Songs (1939); Londoners (1964), and several volumes of light, comic, satiric, and erotic verse which shows the influence of W. H. *Auden. The Collected Ewart 1933–1980 (1980) was followed by Collected Poems 1980–1990 (1991). He was a master of the *limerick, the *clerihew, and the occasional verse.

EWING, Juliana Horatia (1841–85) Born in Yorkshire, writer of inventive and unsentimental tales for children, admired by Edith *Nesbit and Rudyard *Kipling. Most of her work first appeared in Aunt Judy's Magazine, edited by her mother, Margaret Gatty. Her many publications present events as seen through the eyes of a young child; the most enduring include Jackanapes (1879), a touching soldier-story illustrated by Randolph *Caldecott; A Flat Iron for a Farthing (1872); and Lob-Lie-by-the-Fire (1874).

Examiner, The (1) A Tory periodical started by Bolingbroke in August 1710; Jonathan *Swift took charge in October (nos 14–46), and was succeeded by Delarivier *Manley in 1711. It engaged in controversy with Richard *Steele's *Guardian and Joseph *Addison's Whig Examiner, and lasted, with interruptions, until 1716. (2) A reformist weekly periodical, established by John and Leigh *Hunt in 1808, closing in 1881. Under Hunt it supported the work of P. B. *Shelley, John *Keats, Charles *Lamb, and William *Hazlitt. It was often bitterly attacked by Tory journals such as the *Quarterly Review and *Blackwood's Magazine for its radical literary views and its disrespect towards the prince regent.

Excalibur A corrupt form of 'Caliburn' (the name used in *Geoffrey of Monmouth); King Arthur's sword, which he drew out of a stone when no one else could move it or which was given to him by the Lady of the Lake (*Malory, Bk I). Malory says that the name means 'cut-steel', but the Welsh form in the *Mabinogion* is related to the Irish *Caladbolg* (battlesword), a famous legendary sword. According to Malory, when Arthur was mortally wounded in the last battle, he ordered Sir Bedevere to throw Excalibur into the lake. A hand rose from the water, took the sword, and vanished.

Excursion, The A poem in nine books by William *Wordsworth, published 1814. This is the middle section of a projected three-part poem 'on man, on nature and on human life', of which this part alone was completed. The whole work was to have been entitled 'The Recluse', 'as having for its principal subject the sensations and opinions of a poet living in retirement'. It was planned in 1798, when Wordsworth was living near *Coleridge at Alfoxden. *The *Prelude* was originally intended to be the introduction to the first part of 'The Recluse'.

The poet, travelling with the Wanderer, a philosophic pedlar, meets the pessimistic Solitary, the source of whose despondency is found in his want of religious faith and lack of confidence in the virtue of man. He is reproved with gentle and persuasive argument. The Pastor is then introduced, who illustrates the harmonizing effects of virtue and religion through narratives of people interred in his churchyard. They visit the Pastor's house, and the Wanderer draws his general and philosophic conclusions from the discussions that have passed. The last two books deal in particular with the industrial expansion of the early part of the century, and the degradation that followed in its train. The poem ends with the Pastor's prayer that man may be given grace to conquer guilt and sin, and with praise for the beauty of the world about them. Book I contains 'The Story of Margaret' or 'The *Ruined Cottage', originally written as a separate poem. The poem was famously castigated in a review by Francis *Jeffrey which begins, forthrightly, 'This will never do'.

Exeter Book One of the most important manuscripts containing Old English poetry, given by Bishop Leofric (d. 1072) to Exeter Cathedral, where it still remains. It contains many of the most admired shorter poems, such as *The *Wanderer*, *The *Seafarer*, **Deor*, **Widsith*, *'The *Ruin'*, *''Wulf and Eadwacer'*, *The *Wife's Lament*, *The *Husband's Message*, and *Resignation*, as well as a famous collection of riddles and some longer poems of a religious nature, notably *Guthlac*, *Christ*, *The *Phoenix*, and *Cynewulf's *Juliana*.

existentialism A European philosophical tendency that flourished in the mid-20th century, although partly prefigured in the 19th by Søren *Kierkegaard and Friedrich *Nietzsche. It was not a school with an agreed doctrine, but a broad current with divergent atheist and Christian versions, Martin *Heidegger and Jean-Paul *Sartre leading the former camp, Gabriel Marcel the latter. It emphasized individual uniqueness, freedom, and responsibility in opposition to various forms of determinism, its name deriving from the principle that 'existence precedes essence': that is, human choices are not dictated by a determining essence or fixed human nature. The most influential literary exponents of this position were Sartre and Albert *Camus, whose impact can be felt especially in the early poems of Thom *Gunn and in the novels of Iris *Murdoch (who wrote a study of Sartre) and John *Fowles. Independently of such influences, the writings of W. H. *Auden from the 1940s onward echo idiosyncratically the themes of Christian existentialism.

Exodus A 590-line poem in Old English, based on the biblical story; it is contained in the *Junius Manuscript and may date from the 8th century. Once erroneously attributed to *Cædmon, it contains a vigorous description of the destruction of the Egyptians in the Red Sea.

Exodus See BIBLE.

Experience, Songs of See SONGS OF INNOCENCE.

Expressionism A term coined in the early 20th century to describe a movement in art, then in literature, the theatre, and the cinema, characterized by boldness, distortion, and forceful representation of the emotions. One of its earliest manifestations was in the group of German painters Die Brücke ('the Bridge'), formed in Dresden in 1905 and influenced by Vincent Van Gogh (1853–90) and Edvard Munch (1863–1944): a later group was Der blaue Reiter ('the Blue Rider', from the title of a painting by the Russian painter Wassily Kandinsky, 1866–1944), formed in 1911, which was more concerned with the evocative qualities of colour and pattern, unrelated to content. In the theatre the term has been associated with the works of Ernst *Toller, August *Strindberg, and Frank Wedekind. The epitome of Expressionism in German cinema was Robert Wiene's *The Cabinet of Dr Caligari* (1919). Expressionism flourished principally in Germany in the wake of a revival of interest in the writings of Friedrich

*Nietzsche and took little root in Britain, though Wyndham *Lewis and *Vorticism have some affinities with it, and traces of its influence can be found in the verse dramas of W. H. *Auden and Christopher *Isherwood.

EZEKIEL, Nissim (1924–2004) Poet, from an Indian Jewish family; also editor, art critic, lecturer, playwright, translator, and ironic social commentator. Ezekiel helped to create a fruitful literary and linguistic climate for a whole generation of Indian poets writing in English. The discipline, precision, and critical range of his work remain an enduring influence. His eight volumes of poetry include *A Time to Change* (1952), *The Unfinished Man* (1960), and *The Exact Name* (1965).

FABER, Michel (1960–) Novelist and short story writer; born in The Hague and brought up in Australia, he settled in Scotland in 1993. Faber's unsettling, frequently mischievous stories are collected in *Some Rain Must Fall* (1998), *The Fahrenheit Twins* (2005), and *The Apple: New Crimson Petal Stories* (2006). He has published two novellas, *The Hundred and Ninety-Nine Steps* (2001) and *The Courage Consort* (2004). *Under the Skin* (2000) is a novel about farming humans for alien consumption, and *The Crimson Petal and the White* (2002) a Victorian family saga centred on the life of Sugar, a prostitute. The *Fire Gospel* (2008) is inspired by the myth of *Prometheus.

Faber Book of Modern Verse, The An anthology published in 1936, edited by Michael *Roberts (at the request of T. S. *Eliot, then a director at Faber), which did much to establish the reputations of a rising generation, including W. H. *Auden, Louis *MacNeice, William *Empson, and Dylan *Thomas, and to create a lineage for the previous generation of modernists. In his introduction, Roberts traces the influences of Arthur Hugh *Clough, Gerard Manley *Hopkins (himself well represented), and the French *symbolists on modern poetry, defines the 'European' sensibility of such writers as Eliot, Ezra *Pound, and W. B. *Yeats, and offers a persuasive apologia for various aspects of *modernism which the reading public had resisted, identifying them as an apparent obscurity compounded of condensed metaphor, allusion, intricacy of ideas, and verbal play. See Janet Adam Smith, 'Mr Eliot's Proposal', *TLS*, 18 June 1976.

fable A term most commonly used in the sense of a short story devised to convey some useful moral or other didactic lesson about human manners and behaviour, but often carrying with it associations of the marvellous or the mythical, and frequently employing animals or inanimate objects as characters. *Aesop's fables and the *'Reynard the Fox' series were well known and imitated in Britain by *Chaucer, Robert *Henryson, and others, and *La Fontaine was imitated by John *Gay. *Mandeville's *The Fable of the Bees*, Jonathan Swift's *Gulliver's Travels*, and George Orwell's *Animal Farm* may be described as satirical fables.

Fables, Ancient and Modern By John *Dryden, published 1700. Verse paraphrases of tales by *Ovid, *Boccaccio, and Geoffrey *Chaucer are interspersed with poems of Dryden's own, and together with the preface, in itself one of the most important examples of Dryden's criticism, they compose themselves into an Ovidian and Catholic meditation on the place of nature, sex, and violence in the flux of history.

fabliau A short tale in verse, almost invariably in *octosyllabic couplets in French, mostly dealing with ordinary life from a comic point of view. The fabliau was an important element in French poetry in the 12th and 13th centuries. In English, it has come to be applied loosely to tales with a sexual element, such as *Chaucer's tales of the Miller, the Summoner, and the Pardoner in the *Canterbury Tales*.

faction A term coined *c.*1970 to describe fiction based on and mingled with fact, at first applied particularly to American works of fiction such as *In Cold Blood* (1966) by Truman *Capote and *The Armies of the Night* (1968) by Norman *Mailer. The genre has continued to flourish, as the *historical novel has gained new seriousness: works such as Thomas *Keneally's *Schindler's Ark* (1982; in USA as *Schindler's List*), based on documentary evidence, interviews, and research, may be classified as fiction or non-fiction. *See* GONZO JOURNALISM.

Faerie Queene, The The greatest work of Edmund *Spenser, of which the first three books were published 1590, and the second three 1596.

The general scheme of the work is proposed in the author's introductory letter addressed to Walter *Ralegh and dated '23. January. 1589' but the poem itself differs from the scheme. By the Faerie Queene the poet signifies Glory in the abstract and *Elizabeth I in particular (who also figures under the names of *Britomart, *Belphoebe, Mercilla, and *Gloriana). Twelve of her knights, the 'patrons' or examples of twelve different virtues, each undertake an adventure, on the twelve successive days of the queen's annual festival; an account of their origins was to have been given in the last of twelve books.

Of the six books Spenser published in his lifetime, the subjects are: I, the adventures of the Redcrosse Knight of Holiness (the Anglican Church), the protector of the virgin Una (truth, or the true religion), and the wiles of Archimago and Duessa; II, the adventures of Sir Guyon, the Knight of Temperance, his encounters with Pyrochles and Cymochles, his visit to the Cave of Mammon and the House of Temperance, and his destruction of Acrasia and her Bower of Bliss (Canto X of this book contains a chronicle of British rulers from *Brut to Elizabeth); III, the legend of Chastity, exemplified by Britomart and Belphoebe; IV, the legend of Triamond and Cambell, exemplifying Friendship, together with the story of Scudamour and Amoret; V, the adventures of Artegall, the Knight of Justice, in which allegorical reference is made to various historical events of the reign of Elizabeth I: the defeat of the Spaniards in the Netherlands, the recantation of Henry IV of France, the execution of *Mary Queen of Scots, and the administration of Ireland by Lord Grey de Wilton; VI, the adventures of Sir Calidore, exemplifying Courtesy. There is also a fragment on *Mutabilitie, being the sixth and seventh cantos of the legend of Constancie, which was to have formed the seventh book. This fragment, first published in 1609, contains a charming description of the seasons and the months.

Modelled to some extent on Ariosto's *Orlando furioso, The Faerie Queene is, with Philip Sidney's *Arcadia, one of the great achievements of Elizabethan literature. The poem's complex allegory (political, religious, moral, personal) is varied throughout, and its chief beauties lie in particular episodes and descriptions, such as those of the Cave of Mammon (Bk II), the marriage of Thames and Medway (Bk IV), or Calidore's vision of the Graces on Mount Acidale (Bk VI). The poem is written in the stanza invented by Spenser (and since used by James *Thomson, John *Keats, P. B. *Shelley, and Lord *Byron), in which a ninth line of twelve syllables (*alexandrine) is added to eight lines of ten syllables, rhyming *ababbcbcc*.

FAINLIGHT, Ruth (1931–) American poet and translator; now resident in England. From her first collection, *Cages* (1966), her distinctively cool, ironic, yet not dispassionate voice shows some affinity with the tone of Robert *Graves. Fainlight also knew Sylvia *Plath, and is the dedicatee of Plath's famous poem 'Elm'. Her later volumes include *To See the Matter Clearly* (1968), *The Region's Violence* (1973), *Poems* (1971, with her husband Alan *Sillitoe and Ted *Hughes), *Sibyls and Others* (1980), and *Sugar-Paper Blue* (1997). Her *New and Collected Poems* was published in 2010. Her topics are both domestic and global: she combines the personal and the austerely detached, and excels at the uncanny casual moment of recognition.

Fair Maid of Perth, The A novel by Walter *Scott, published 1828, the second of the *Chronicles of the Canongate*. Set at the end of the 14th century, it is chiefly remembered for its study of constitutional cowardice. The battle, and the sub-plot of the assassination of the king's heir, the duke of Rothesay, make this one of the most violent of Scott's novels.

Fair Maid of the West, The, or *A Girl Worth Gold* A comedy of adventure by Thomas *Heywood, in two parts, Part I *c.*1600, Part II *c.*1630, both printed 1631. The first part, a breezy and entertaining melodrama, opens with a vivid scene at Plymouth, where the earl of *Essex's expedition is about to sail for the Azores (1597); part II is less effective, with more extreme coincidences and incidents.

Fair Penitent, The Blank verse tragedy by Nicholas *Rowe, produced 1703, adapted from Philip *Massinger and Nathan *Field's *The *Fatal Dowry*. It held the stage into the 19th century. The character of Lothario has become proverbial, and was Samuel *Richardson's model for Lovelace in *Clarissa*.

Fair Quarrel, A A comedy by John *Middleton and William *Rowley, written 1614–16?, published 1617.

fairy stories Present in the oral tradition of all cultures, they were recognized as a distinct literary genre with the publication of the stories of Charles *Perrault. Many earlier literary works (including those of *Chaucer, *Boccaccio, *Malory, *Spenser, *Straparola, and Giambattista *Basile), had featured fairies and tales of the supernatural, but there was a new vogue for the written fairy-tale at the end of the 17th century. Many were published by women, e.g. Perrault's cousin Marie-Jeanne l'Héritier de Villandon (1664–1734; *Œuvres meslés*, 1695) and her friend Henriette-Julie de Castelnau, comtesse de Murat (1670–1716). Marie-Catherine

Le Jumel de Barneville, comtesse d'*Aulnoy's well-known tales featuring disguise, shape-changing, cross-dressing, and beast-husbands (*Les Contes des fées*, 1696) were quickly translated into English (some appearing in 1699; 3 vols, 1721-2) and remained popular well into the 19th century.

Translated story collections from other cultures, notably the *Arabian Nights*, reinforced the popularity of fairy stories. During the 18th century, fairy stories flourished, despite protests from some educationalists that they were unwholesome and immoral. During the 19th century, historians of folklore, notably the *Grimm brothers and Andrew *Lang, established the fairy story as a respectable subject for research; in the same period T. C. *Croker was making an important collection of Irish folk tales, and *Andersen's stories were appearing in Danish. Sir John Rhŷs collected stories in *Celtic Folklore, Welsh and Manx* (1901; repr. 1980); J. M. *Barrie's *Peter Pan* is one of the most enduring original stories with fairy characters.

The 20th century witnessed the rise of psychoanalytic, anthropological, feminist, and ideological studies of fairy stories, including by Sigmund Freud, Carl *Jung, and James *Frazer. Bruno Bettelheim's classic work *The Uses of Enchantment: The Power and Importance of Fairy Tales* (1978) argues that the stories offer children a valuable tool for psychological growth and adjustment. Key surveys of the genre include *The Ocean of Story* (1928) by Norman Penzer; Carol Ann *Duffy's *The Erotic World of Faery* (1972); and Marina *Warner's *From the Beast to the Blonde* (1994).

The late 20th century saw a revival of interest in the adult fairy-tale: A. S. *Byatt, Angela *Carter, Italo *Calvino, and Salman *Rushdie have all used the genre to remarkable effect.

Faithful Shepherdess, The
A pastoral tragicomedy in verse by John *Fletcher, written probably in 1607 or 1608, printed not later than 1610. The address to the reader includes a classic definition of tragicomedy.

FALKLAND, Lucius Cary,
second Viscount (1610-43) Politician and writer; he inherited the manor of Great Tew, Oxfordshire, in 1625, where he became the centre of a cultivated circle including George *Sandys, John Earle, Sidney *Godolphin, William Chillingworth, and Clarendon. Ben *Jonson, Sir John *Suckling, Abraham *Cowley, and Edmund *Waller all celebrated him in verse. He wrote verses and theological works including a *Discourse of Infallibility* (1646) defending reason in religion and opposing narrow dogmatism.

FALKNER, John Meade
(1858-1932) Novelist, antiquary, and topographical writer, born in Wiltshire. He compiled handbooks to *Oxfordshire* (1894) and *Berkshire* (1902), but is chiefly remembered for his three novels: *The Lost Stradivarius* (1895), a tale of the supernatural set largely in Oxford and Naples; *Moonfleet* (1898), a swift-moving historical romance involving smuggling; and *The Nebuly Coat* (1903), an antiquarian tale dealing with a church threatened by collapse. He also wrote poetry, a volume of which was published in 1933.

Fall
see BIBLE; EDEN, GARDEN OF.

Fall of Robespierre, The
A radical drama written in 1794 by Samuel Taylor *Coleridge, who wrote Act I, and Robert *Southey, who wrote Acts II and III.

FALLOWELL, Duncan
(1948-) London-born novelist and travel writer. His sexually frank works include the innovative, gay travel books *One Hot Summer in St Petersburg* (1994) and *Going as Far as I Can* (2008), which is set in New Zealand.

False One, The
A drama attributed to John *Fletcher, in which Philip *Massinger may also have had a share, performed 1621, printed 1647.

The play deals with the joint occupation of Egypt's throne by Ptolemy and his sister Cleopatra; the treacherous murder of Ptolemy by Septimius, 'the False One'; and Caesar's entanglement by the charms of Cleopatra.

Falstaff, Sir John
A character in Shakespeare's *1 and 2 *Henry IV* and The *Merry Wives of Windsor*. In the first play, Shakespeare seems originally to have named him after his historical original, the Wyclifite Sir John Oldcastle, but to have been compelled to change the name after the play had been performed but before it was printed, after protests from Oldcastle's descendants, the Lords Cobham.

His origins lie in the stock figure of the *Vice, together with some elements of the *miles gloriosus*, the 'boastful soldier' of Roman comedy. He is fat, witty, a lover of sack, and skilful at turning jokes on him to his own advantage— 'I am not only witty in myself, but the cause that wit is in other men' (*2 Henry IV*, I. ii). The Falstaff of *The Merry Wives of Windsor* is a different figure, whose attempts to mend his fortunes by wooing two citizens' wives simultaneously end in his discomfiture in Windsor Forest. It is this Falstaff who is the subject of at least nine operas, including *Vaughan Williams's Sir John in Love* (1929); Verdi's opera *Falstaff* (1893) draws on both the Henry plays and *The Merry Wives of Windsor*. Falstaff is also the hero of an exuberant novel (1976) of that name by Robert *Nye.

family stories A genre popular in children's publishing since the 19th century. Initially, as in Mary *Sherwood's *The History of the Fairchild Family* (1818), books depicted nuclear families where the father 'stood in place of God'. Charlotte *Yonge, a major exponent of the genre, influenced Louisa M. *Alcott and Edith *Nesbit. Subsequently families were not invariably depicted as secure or perfect; by the late 20th century, portrayals of dysfunctional families had become common, notably in the work of Jacqueline *Wilson, although the ideal of the family remains strong.

FANSHAWE, Anne, Lady (1625–80) Née Harrison, wife of Sir Richard *Fanshawe. She shared her husband's travels, and her affectionate *Memoirs*, written between 1674 and 1676, were first printed in 1829: 'whatever was real happiness, God gave it me in him.'

FANSHAWE, Sir Richard (1608–66) Poet, translator, diplomat, and Royalist, as was his wife Anne *Fanshawe, whom he married in 1644. His first published work was a translation of *Guarini's *Il pastor fido* (*The Faithful Shepherd*, 1647): a reissue the following year contained some of his own poems, including a delightful ode urging the pleasures of country living, some accomplished *Spenserian stanzas, and sonnets from the Spanish, translated with much elegance. A selection from *Horace (1652) was followed by the *Lusiads* of *Camões (1655), which he prepared in retirement during the Civil War.

fantasy fiction One of the most commercially successful literary genres of the later 20th century, but elements of the fantastic appear in much earlier works from *Beowulf onwards, including Sir *Gawain and the Green Knight, Malory's Le *Morte Darthur, Spenser's The *Faerie Queene, and Shakespeare. Fantasy fiction as a genre is, however, in some respects decisively modern. Readers in a period dominated by science and rationalism tended to accept the low rating given to fantasy and the fantastic by practitioners of the realistic novel, marginalizing fantasy into a form for satire, diversion, and above all for children, for example in the work

of George *MacDonald and Lewis *Carroll. Fantasy fiction, however, began to win a kind of autonomy as authors followed the late romances of William *Morris in creating imaginary otherworlds. Lord *Dunsany's fictions from *The Gods of Pegana* (1905, stories), and notably *The King of Elfland's Daughter* (1924) use indeterminate settings—at times set in a 'dreamworld' or on the borders of Faerie, they could also be set in earth's forgotten past or unknown future. All these locations, as used by later fantasy authors, liberate the reader from the constraints of the known while keeping a plausible inner coherence. The reader accepts the rules set up by the fiction, ignoring, or relishing, the contrast with everyday reality.

Fantasy fiction continued to be developed by individual writers such as E. R. Eddison or Mervyn *Peake, but fantasy fiction as genre began to create a readership for itself with the appearance of schools of writers, aware of each other's work.

The first of these was the group centred on *Weird Tales*, which included H. P. *Lovecraft, Robert E. *Howard, and Clark Ashton *Smith. Howard, perhaps, had the most generic influence, through his creation of the character Conan the Barbarian. *'Sword and sorcery' has remained prolific ever since, with Fritz Leiber (1910–92) and Michael *Moorcock among its most interesting exponents.

The other major early fantasy magazine was *Unknown* (1939–43, 39 issues), which related fantasy to the world of logic and science. 'Worlds where magic works' were created by Robert *Heinlein and in particular the 'Incomplete Enchanter' series of L. Sprague *de Camp and Fletcher Pratt.

The greatest influence within the fantasy genre, however, was J. R. R. *Tolkien. His first published fantasy, *The Hobbit* (1937), was for children, but its successor *The *Lord of the Rings* (1954–5, 3 vols) attracted a mass adult readership. Tolkien's knowledge of Old English and Old Norse recreated the world of Germanic folk tale as a consistent and coherent whole. To this he added creatures of his own invention, such as hobbits; a complete mythology, chronology, and cartography; and a compelling story. Later authors followed him in recognizing the need to create other worlds whose complexity outruns the immediate needs of plot. Among the most significant of his followers are Stephen R. Donaldson, David Eddings (1931–2009), and Robert Jordan.

Children's literature', or writing for young adults, such as Ursula K. *Le Guin's original 'Earthsea' sequence or the work of Diana

Wynne *Jones, has developed the genre as has the revival, by Angela *Carter, amongst others, of the traditional form of the *fairy-tale. Comic fantasy is best exemplified by the Discworld books of Terry *Pratchett. *The Colour of Magic* (1983) parodied generic fantasy, but the series went on to create a world of its own. The feedback effect of role-playing games based upon fantasy scenarios has resulted in the intensifying (but also the manipulation) of stereotypes. A more recent trend came and went as the *New Weird, but the fruitful collision of modes is more generally exemplified by the highly detailed work of China *Miéville.

Reasons for the popular appeal of fantasy fiction no doubt include discontent with everyday life, openly voiced in Le Guin's *The Beginning Place* (1980). Fantasy has, however, also shown itself ready to deal with questions of contemporary importance, in particular, the nature and origins of evil. T. H. *White declared that the theme of his Arthurian fantasy *The Once and Future King*, written for the most part between 1938 and 1941, was to find 'an antidote to war'. Fantasy fiction has shown itself capable of dealing with topics which seem outside the range of the traditional realist novel, and speaks for and to a contemporary mass audience whose taste it has itself created.

FANTHORPE, U. A. (Ursula Askham) (1929–2009) Poet, born in Kent. She taught English, then worked as a hospital receptionist before publishing her first volume, *Side Effects* (1978). Other collections include *Standing To* (1982), *Safe as Houses* (1996), *Queuing for the Sun* (2003), and *New and Collected Poems* (2010). Her poetry is lucid and accessible; her tone is both wry and lyrical, and her subject matter ranges from the classical to the historical and the domestic. She is also expert in the use of *dramatic monologue.

fanzines A term coined by *science fiction fan Russ Chauvenet in 1941 to describe the amateur magazines, published by fans for each other, in which much early bibliographical and critical discussion appeared.

FARAH, Nuruddin (1945–) Somali novelist. He says that 'I write because a theme has chosen me: the theme of Africa's upheaval and societal disorganisation. And I write in order to recover my missing half.' He spent over twenty years in exile from Somalia. *From a Crooked Rib* (1970) onwards, his characters reappear from book to book. *A Naked Needle* (1976) was followed by his first trilogy, *Variations on the Theme of an African Dictatorship: Sweet and Sour Milk* (1979); *Sardines* (1981); and *Close Sesame* (1983). His second, *Blood in the Sun, Maps* (1986), *Gifts* (1993), and *Secrets* (1998) was critically well received. Since *Territories* (2000) he has completed a new trilogy, *Links* (2005), *Knots* (2007), and *Crossbones* (2011).

farce A form of popular comedy with its distant roots in the improvisations which actors introduced into the text of medieval religious dramas (the word is derived from French *farce*, literally 'stuffing'). Later forms include the *interludes performed in the 15th and 16th centuries, the classical farce of *Molière, and 19th-century middle-class French farces, as practised by Georges Feydeau (1862–1921) and others. Full-length English farces of the 19th century include Morton's *Box and Cox, *Pinero's *The Magistrate* (1885), *The Schoolmistress* (1886), and *Dandy Dick* (1887), and Gilbert and Sullivan's comic operas. *Charley's Aunt* (1892) by Brandon Thomas (1856–1914) is still frequently performed. The term 'farce' is now generally used to cover a form of theatre which employs ridiculous situations, mistaken identities, split-second timing, and marital misadventures (hence the term 'bedroom farce'): later exponents include Ben Travers (1886–1980), whose celebrated 'Aldwych farces' included *A Cuckoo in the Nest* and *Rookery Nook*, both 1926; Ray Cooney (1932–); Alan *Ayckbourn, Michael *Frayn, Joe *Orton, and Tom *Stoppard. Dario Fo (1926–) is notable among those who have used the farce for serious political purposes. Television produced a new genre of serial and surreal farce in the Monty Python series and John Cleese's *Fawlty Towers*.

Far from the Madding Crowd A novel by Thomas *Hardy, published 1874. The title is a quotation from Gray's *Elegy Written in a Country Church-Yard*. The plot, which contrasts a patient and generous love with unscrupulous passion, was more complex and dramatic than anything Hardy had previously attempted, and the book earned wide and enduring popularity. The shepherd Gabriel Oak serves the young and spirited Bathsheba Everdene, owner of the farm, with unselfish devotion. The dashing Sergeant Troy loves one of Bathsheba's servants, Fanny Robin, but after a fatal misunderstanding deserts her, and she eventually dies in childbirth in the workhouse. Troy has meanwhile married Bathsheba, but soon begins to neglect and ill-treat her. When he hears of Fanny's death he disappears, and is thought to have been drowned. A neighbouring farmer, Boldwood, obsessed with Bathsheba, gives a party at which he pledges Bathsheba to marry him some time in the future. Troy reappears at the party and Boldwood shoots him. Boldwood is tried and pronounced insane. Gabriel and Bathsheba are at last married. Hardy made a stage version of the novel, produced by the Hardy Players in Dorchester in 1924.

FARJEON, Eleanor (1881–1965) London-born children's writer. *Nursery Rhymes of London Town* (1916) was followed by *Martin Pippin in the Apple Orchard* (1921; not originally intended for children), which established her reputation, and many volumes of poems, plays, fantasies, and stories. *A Nursery in the Nineties* (1935) contains reminiscences of her childhood. She was a close friend of and wrote about Edward *Thomas.

FARLEY, Paul (1965–) Poet and occasional radio dramatist, born in Liverpool. His first collection, *The Boy from the Chemist is Here to See You* (1998), was welcomed for its formal dexterity, evocation of place, and often deadpan humour. *The Ice Age* (2002) and *Tramp in Flames* (2006) evoke and transform vivid childhood memories against the backdrop of an increasingly dreamlike cityscape. His most recent volume is *The Atlantic Tunnel: Selected Poems* (2010). His study of the Liverpool film-maker Terence Davies (1945–) draws extensively on his own experience of growing up in the 1960s and 1970s.

FARQUHAR, George (1677–1707) Playwright, born in Londonderry. He had become an actor by 1696, but gave up the stage after accidentally wounding a fellow player. He moved to London and began writing comedies: *Love and a Bottle* (1698); *The Constant Couple* (1699); *Sir Harry Wildair*, its sequel (1701); *The Inconstant* (based on John *Fletcher's *The Wild Goose Chase*) and *The Twin Rivals* (1702); *The Stage Coach*, with Peter Motteux (1704); and after a brief military career, *The *Recruiting Officer* (1706) and *The *Beaux' Stratagem* (1707), staged just before he died in poverty. *The Adventures of Covent Garden* (1698) is a novella; *Love and Business* (1702), consists of letters and poems, including a self-portrait.

FARRAR, F. W. (Frederic William) (1831–1903) Philosopher and theologian. While a master at Harrow School, he published the enormously successful *Eric, or Little by Little* (1858), a partly autobiographical *school story about 12-year-old Eric Williams, who is bullied and corrupted at school despite the efforts of his noble friend Edwin Russell. Following Edwin's death, the dissipated boy runs away to sea where he is badly treated but morally saved. His reputation restored, he makes a good death. Farrar also wrote *Julian Home: A Tale of College Life* (1859) and *St Winifred's, or The World of School* (1862).

FARRELL, J. G. (James Gordon) (1935–79) Novelist, born in Liverpool. He contracted poliomyelitis in his first term at Oxford. He later travelled widely in America, Europe, and the East. His second novel, *The Lung* (1965), describes the experiences of a polio victim. His first substantial novel, *Troubles* (1970), is set in Ireland, in the decaying Majestic Hotel, just after the First World War, against a background of Sinn Fein violence. *The Siege of Krishnapur* (1973, *Booker Prize) deals with the events of the Indian Mutiny, in a characteristically ironic and comic vein. *The Singapore Grip* (1978), blending real and fictitious characters, describes the fall of Singapore to the Japanese. His last three novels all reflect a sense of the end of the empire and the stubborn, at times heroic, at times stupid, refusal of his characters to recognize the course of history. *The Hill Station* (1981) was left unfinished when Farrell was accidentally drowned.

FARRELL, James Thomas (1904–79) American naturalist novelist, best known in Britain for his trilogy about Studs Lonigan, a young Chicago Catholic of Irish descent; *Young Lonigan* (1932), *The Young Manhood of Studs Lonigan* (1934), and *Judgement Day* (1935).

Fascism Italian political movement and later political party, founded in 1919 in reaction to the post-war political settlement. It is principally associated with Benito Mussolini (1883–1945), who seized power in 1922. Though totalitarian in its aims and operations, at least until the alliance with Nazi Germany (1938) the regime did not consistently demand ideological conformity from the literary establishment. In its early years Fascism attracted the support of Filippo *Marinetti, Giuseppe *Ungaretti, and Luigi *Pirandello.

fashionable novel ('silver-fork school') A class of novel, popular *c.*1825–50, which held up for admiration the lives of the wealthy and fashionable. Theodore *Hook was one of the leaders of this popular school of writing. Edward *Bulwer-Lytton (whose own **Pelham* was a celebrated example) held that the genre was influential in the paradoxical sense that its effect was ultimately to expose 'the falsehood, the hypocrisy, the arrogant and vulgar insolence of patrician life'. M. W. Rosa, in *The Silver-Fork School* (1936), discusses the work of Susan *Ferrier, Thomas *Lister, Benjamin *Disraeli, Plumer *Ward, Catherine *Gore, and others, and argues that the school 'culminated in a single great book—*Vanity Fair*'.

FAST, Howard Melvin (1914–2003) American novelist, born in New York, who joined the Communist Party in 1944 and was jailed in 1950 for contempt of Congress. *Spartacus* (1951) features the Roman slave revolt. Fast renounced communism and in 1957 published his memoir on the Communist Party, *The Naked God*. Later novels, which included *The Crossing* (1971) and *The Immigrants* (1977), drew on his Ukrainian Jewish family background. He also published science fiction stories (*A Touch of Infinity*, 1973) and (as E. V. Cunningham) the Masao Masuto Mysteries (1967–84). *Being Red* (1990) is his autobiography.

Fatal Curiosity, The Blank verse tragedy by George *Lillo, successfully produced by Henry *Fielding in 1736. Old Wilmot, under stress of poverty and urged by his wife, murders a stranger who has deposited a casket with them, only to find the victim is his son, supposed lost in a shipwreck. The plot is archetypal and appears in many literatures; Lillo's version influenced the German 'fate-drama', and Albert *Camus used it in *Le Malentendu* (1945).

Fatal Dowry, The A tragedy by Philip *Massinger and Nathan *Field, acted *c*.1616–18, printed 1632. The play is based on one of the *controversiae* (or imaginary legal disputes) of Seneca the elder. Nicholas Rowe's *The *Fair Penitent* is founded on this play.

Fatal Marriage, The, or *The Innocent Adultery* A tragedy by Thomas *Southerne, performed 1694. Biron, having married Isabella, is reported killed. She marries Villeroy, but when Biron returns and is killed, kills herself. The play is founded on Aphra *Behn's novel *The Nun, or The Perjured Beauty* but, unlike Behn's heroine, Southerne's Isabella is portrayed as a helpless victim, 'born to suffer' and condemned by fate to 'a long line of woe'. The play was revived by David *Garrick in 1757.

Father and Son Memoir by Edmund *Gosse of his relationship with his father, Philip Henry Gosse, published in 1907. His mother died early and his father, a member of the Plymouth Brethren, was, though a noted naturalist, at odds with Darwin. The book documents Gosse's unhappy struggle as he gradually rejects his father's religious beliefs.

Fathers of the church The early Christian writers, a term usually applied to those of the first five centuries. Sometimes the Greek and Latin Fathers are distinguished, the former including Clement of Alexandria (*c*.150–*c*.215), the first to apply *Platonic philosophy to the exposition of Christianity, Origen, Athanasius (*c*.296–373), the scourge of *Arianism, Basil the Great (*c*.330–79), Gregory Nazianzen (329/30–398/90), and Chrysostom; the latter Tertullian (*c*.160–*c*.225), who was hostile to classical learning, Cyprian (d. 258), *Jerome, Ambrose (*c*.339–97), who introduced hymns into the Roman church, Augustine, *Gregory (Pope Gregory I), and *Bernard.

FAULKNER (originally **Falkner), William** (1897–1962) American novelist, born in Mississippi, where he spent most of his life, and on which he based 'Jefferson', the principal setting of several novels. Sherwood *Anderson encouraged him to write his first novel, *Soldier's Pay* (1926). Later novels include *Sartoris* (1929), the first of the series in which he describes the decline of the Compson and Sartoris families, representative of the Old South, and the rise of the crude and unscrupulous Snopes family. *The Sound and the Fury* (1929) is a narrative tour de force in which Faulkner views the decline of the South through several eyes, most remarkably those of Benjy Compson, a 33-year-old 'idiot'. *As I Lay Dying* (1930) demonstrates Faulkner's comic as well as his tragic vision. He made his name, however, with the more sensational work, *Sanctuary* (1931); *Light in August* (1932) and *Absalom, Absalom!* (1936) confirmed his reputation as one of the finest of modern novelists. Other important works include *The Hamlet* (1940), *Intruder in the Dust* (1948), and several volumes of short stories, collected in 1950. In the 1930s and 1940s he worked in Hollywood and collaborated with Howard Hawks on the adaptation of Ernest *Hemingway's novel *To Have and Have Not* (1944) as well as on *The Big Sleep* (1946). *Faulkner's MGM Screenplays* was published in 1982. He was awarded the *Nobel Prize in 1949.

FAULKS, Sebastian (1953–) Novelist and journalist, born in Berkshire. His hugely popular *Birdsong* (1993; stage adaptation 2009) recreates the world of sappers on the Western Front in the First World War; it forms part of a 'French trilogy', with *The Girl at the Lion d'Or* (1988), which encompasses French politics during the 1930s; and *Charlotte Gray* (1998), set in Nazi-occupied France. *On Green Dolphin Street* (2001) is set largely in America during the Cold War era, while *Human Traces* (2005), set in the 19th century, and *Engleby* (2007), set in the 1970s, explore mental illness. *Devil May Care* (2008) is a pastiche James Bond adventure novel. *A Week in December* (2009), set in London in the economic boom, was radically re-written as the banking system collapsed. *The Fatal Englishman: Three Short Lives* (1996) are biographical essays, linked by a common theme of the self-destructive impulse, of the painter Christopher Wood (1901–30), the pilot and author Richard Hillary (1919–43), and the journalist Jeremy Wolfenden (1934–65).

Faust The legend of the dissatisfied scholar who concludes a pact with the devil, which finally costs him his soul originated in 16th-century Germany and appears in a *chapbook of 1587. The story, possibly based on a historical figure, was used by Christopher *Marlowe in *Dr Faustus.* *Goethe's poetic drama *Faust* (Part I 1808, Part II 1832) marks a radical revision of the original theme; the pact takes the form of a wager, and at the end of *Part II*, with the hero 100 years old, *Mephistopheles fails to win his soul. The first English translations of *Faust, Part I* omitted 'offensive' matter, but in 1822 P. B. *Shelley's translations of the scenes concerned appeared in Leigh *Hunt's *The Liberal*. Lord *Byron's *Manfred* was influenced by Goethe's work, and in *Faust Part II* Byron figures as Euphorion, the doomed offspring of Faust and Helen of Troy. Later literary treatments of the legend include versions by Heinrich *Heine, Thomas Mann's novel *Doktor Faustus* (1948), and Robert *Nye's novel *Faust* (1980). In music, Charles Gounod's operatic treatment (*Faust*, 1859) is based on Goethe, and there is a modern rap version by the jazz violinist and composer Leroy Jenkins (1932–2007). It can be said that the notion of a 'Faustian Pact' has entered popular consciousness.

Faustus, Doctor *see* DR FAUSTUS.

Fawn, The *See* PARASITASTER.

FEAVER, Vicki (1943–) Poet, born in Nottingham. *Close Relatives* (1981) introduced Feaver's characteristic style: deceptively plain language enlivened by taut rhythms and suddenly enlarged by boldly imaginative metaphors. *The Handless Maiden* (1994) is more clearly feminist in theme, and more emphatic in its use of myth and biblical narrative, both as metaphor and in *dramatic monologues such as

'Circe' and the celebrated 'Judith'. *The Book of Blood* (2006) engages in forms of what has been called the 'domestic gothic', suggesting affinities with the work of Stevie *Smith; as in Smith, too, violence of various kinds is never far away.

FEDERMAN, Raymond (1928–2009) French-born American novelist and critic. His works often play on his name (penman, *l'homme de la plume*). As a child, Federman was hidden in a closet by his mother to avoid deportation to the concentration camps by the Nazis, a traumatic experience to which he gave expression in the trilingual volume *The Voice in the Closet* (1989). His *postmodern novels frequently experiment with typography, as in *Double or Nothing* (1971) and *Take It or Leave It* (1976). Other works include *My Body in Nine Parts* (2005), a prose self-anatomy; *Among the Beasts* (1967), a (bilingual) volume of poems; and *The Precipice & Other Catastrophes* (1999), collected plays. Federman was active in the *Fiction Collective and promoted experimental fiction in his edited collection *Surfiction* (1975; expanded 1981).

FEINSTEIN, Elaine (1930–) Poet, novelist, translator, and biographer, born in Bootle. Her volumes of poetry, from *In a Green Eye* (1966), include *Badlands* (1986), *Daylight* (1997), and *Gold* (2000). Her work is feminist, prominently preoccupied with European Jewish experience and family life, and influenced by American modernism. She has published biographies of Pushkin, Marina Tsvetaeva (whom she has translated), *Akhmatova, D. H. *Lawrence, and Ted *Hughes. *Collected Poems and Translations* appeared in 2003. Her novels, which, despite some experiment, are primarily realistic, include *The Circle* (1970), *Children of the Rose* (1975), *The Shadow Master* (1979), *Loving Brecht* (1992), and *The Russian Jerusalem* (2008).

Felix Holt, the Radical A novel by George *Eliot, published 1866. Set in 1832 in Loamshire, it vividly evokes the political ferment and corrupt electioneering tactics of the times. Harold Transome arrives home after many years in the East to inherit the family estate, and startles his family by standing as a Radical candidate. His political convictions are not incompatible with buying beer for the local workers to secure their support, and his character is strongly contrasted with that of Felix Holt, austere, idealistic, and passionate, who has chosen the life of an artisan, and aims to stir his fellow workers to a sense of their own worth and destiny. The heroine, Esther, who supposes herself to be the daughter of old Lyon, the Independent minister, has an innate love of refinement, and when Felix chastises her for her frivolity she gains a new consciousness, and gradually falls in love with him. A complex chain of events reveals that Esther is in fact the heir to the Transome estate; Harold woos her, from motives not entirely mercenary, and Esther is forced to choose between his worldly attractions, and poverty with Felix. She renounces her claim to the estate and chooses Felix. It is finally revealed to Harold (the reader having known from the beginning) that he is not his father's son, but the son of the hated lawyer Jermyn; the account of the years of suffering of the proud and lonely Mrs Transome, subjected in secrecy to a man she no longer respects, ever fearful of her son's discovery, befriended only by her faithful servant Denner, is often considered the most powerful feature of the novel.

FELL, Margaret (1614–1702) An early leader of the Society of *Friends, converted by George *Fox in 1652 during his stay at her home, Swarthmore, in Cumberland, which became the Friends' administrative centre. She was a powerful character and an organizer of genius, who coordinated the growing movement, wrote copiously on religious and political issues, interceded personally with Charles II on behalf of persecuted Friends, and suffered grievous imprisonments in the 1660s. She became the first to express the Friends' peace principles in 1660, and claimed full spiritual equality for women in *Women's Speaking Justified* (1666). After the death of her first husband, Judge Thomas Fell, she married Fox in 1669, but chiefly lived and travelled apart from him, continuing her radical activities into her eighties.

Female Quixote, The, or *The Adventures of Arabella* A novel by Charlotte *Lennox (1752). Arabella is a young, beautiful, and female version of *Cervantes's Quixote. Samuel *Richardson and Samuel *Johnson offered suggestions towards the writing of the novel, which was warmly reviewed by Henry *Fielding.

Female Tatler, The Light satirical periodical which began on 8 July 1709 under the editorship of 'Phoebe Crackenthorpe, a lady that knows everything', in rivalry with Richard *Steele's the *Tatler*. From issue 53 it was 'written by a society of ladies'; it closed in March 1710. The actual authorship is not known.

feminine rhyme *see* RHYME.

feminist criticism A modern tradition of commentary and polemic devoted to the analysis of women's literary work, and of their representation in literature. The beginnings of this movement are to be found in the journalism of Rebecca *West from about 1910. More influential as founding documents are the essays of Virginia *Woolf, notably *A Room of one's Own* (1929), and Simone de *Beauvoir's book *Le Deuxième Sexe* (1949; *The Second Sex*, 1953). The tradition was reborn amid the cultural ferment of the post-1968 period, especially in the United States. The misogynist attitudes of male critics and novelists were subjected to ironic scrutiny in Mary Ellmann's *Thinking about Women* (1968) and to iconoclastic rage in Kate Millett's *Sexual Politics* (1970). In the later 1970s woman-centred literary histories sought to trace an autonomous tradition of women's literature and to redeem neglected female authors. Influential examples of such work in America were Ellen Moers, *Literary Women* (1976), Elaine Showalter, *A Literature of their Own* (1977), and Sandra M. Gilbert and Susan Gubar, *The Madwoman in the Attic* (1979). By the 1980s, feminist criticism was becoming more differentiated: the mainstream of American feminist criticism eschewed 'male' literary theory and saw its own purpose as the affirmation of distinctly female 'experience' as reflected in writing; but black-feminist and lesbian-feminist critics objected that their own experiences were being overlooked. The value of 'experience' as a clue to women's writing was doubted by feminists allied to *Marxist criticism, *psychoanalytic criticism, and post-*structuralism especially but not exclusively in Britain and France. One such school, led by the French writers Julia *Kristeva, Hélène Cixous, and Luce *Irigaray, sought to define an *écriture féminine* on the basis of a psychological 'politics' of language itself: if language belongs not to women but to a masculine social order, the distinctive female literary strategy will be to subvert it. British feminist criticism, although drawing upon both American and French approaches, has usually been more historical and sociological. Feminist criticism has thus become a varied field of neglected debate rather than an agreed position. Its substantial achievements are evident in the re-evaluation of neglected women authors, in modern reprints and anthologies from feminist publishing houses such as the *Virago Press (1977) and the Women's Press (1978).

 SEE WEB LINKS

• Feminist theory site

Fenian cycle Also known as the Fionn cycle and the Ossianic cycle, a body of stories and verses featuring *Finn, son of Cumhal, and his band of 3rd-century hunter warriors, the Fianna (or Fenians). The early tales were set in Munster and Leinster; James *Macpherson's *Fingal appears to have been based on later Highland ballad versions.

FENN, Lady Eleanor (Ellenor) (1743–1813) Writing primarily as 'Mrs Teachwell' for the printer-publisher John Marshall, a popular, prolific, Norfolk-based writer best known for *Cobwebs to Catch Flies* (c.1873). Although childless, like many women writers of her day, she was interested in and experimented with new ways to instruct children.

FENN, George Manville (1831–1909) Born in London, and largely self-educated. He is remembered as a prolific writer of boys' adventure stories, often serialized in periodicals such as the *Boy's Own Paper*, beginning with *Hollowdell Grange* (1867). Fenn also wrote a biography of his friend G. A. *Henty (1907).

FENTON, James (1949–) Poet, essayist, and journalist, born in Lincoln. The main stylistic influence on his work is W. H. *Auden. His first collection, *Terminal Moraine* (1972), displayed an imagination hungry for stimulus of all kinds, from politics to anthropology and horticulture. *The Memory of War and Children in Exile: Poems 1968–1983* (1983) is similarly eclectic in its inspiration and exuberant in execution, although several pieces, grounded in his experiences as a reporter, display sombre authority in the contemplation of war and its aftermath: 'A German Requiem' is outstanding in its portrayal of post-war German 'forgetting'. *Manila Envelope* (1989) was published from the Philippines, where he was working as a correspondent: it expresses panic and desperation as nonsense verse. A collection of his reportage from Vietnam, Korea, and the Philippines, including his celebrated eyewitness account of the fall of Saigon, was also published in 1989 as *All the Wrong Places: Adrift in the Politics of Asia*. *Out of Danger* appeared in 1993, and his *Selected Poems* was published in 2006. He has also worked as a librettist, translator, and anthologist.

FERBER, Edna (1885–1968) American journalist, novelist and playwright, whose many works have been praised for their documentary realism. She served as a war correspondent in the Second World War. Several of her works were adapted for stage or screen; for example,

the novel *Show Boat* (1926) formed the basis for Jerome Kern's 1927 musical, and *Cimarron* (1930) was adapted by Louis Sarecky for his 1931 film. Several of her works deal with Oklahoma life, *Giant* (1952) with the rich of Texas.

Ferdinand Count Fathom, The Adventures of A novel by Tobias *Smollett, published 1753. In the 'Dedication' Smollett outlines his theory of the novel as 'a large diffused picture' dominated by a central figure surrounded by various groups and episodes.

FERGUSON, Adam (1723–1816) Philosopher, born in Perthshire; he was a member of the Select Society and co-founder of the *Royal Society of Edinburgh. In *The Morality of Stage-Plays Seriously Considered* (1757), he defended John *Home's *Douglas. An Essay on the History of Civil Society* (1767) was a pioneer work in political sociology; it contained a discussion 'Of the History of Literature', which argues that poetry is a more natural form of literary expression than prose, and that literature develops better during periods of social activity than in leisure and solitude.

FERGUSON, Sir Samuel (1810–86) Poet, antiquarian, and lawyer, born in Belfast, who was a key influence on the *Irish Revival. His many translations and works based on Gaelic legend include *Lays of the Western Gael* (1865); *Congal* (1872), an 'epic' poem on the last stand of Irish paganism against Christianity; the long narrative poem 'Conary'; and a retelling of the legend of *Deirdre (both 1880). He published a magisterial elegy on the nationalist leader Thomas Davis in 1845 and a striking dramatic monologue on the Phoenix Park murders ('At the Polo-Ground'). *Ogham Inscriptions in Ireland, Wales, and Scotland* (1887), is his most important antiquarian work.

FERGUSSON, Robert (1750–74) Scottish poet, born in Edinburgh. His early poems were imitations of William *Shenstone and other English authors. 'The Daft Days', one of the 35 *Scots works on which his reputation rests, appeared in Ruddiman's *Weekly Magazine* in January 1772. *Poems* (1773) was followed by the posthumous *Poems on Various Subjects* (1779), which inspired Robert *Burns to 'emulating vigour': 'Leith Races' foreshadows 'The *Holy Fair', while 'The Farmer's Ingle' provides a notably unsentimental prototype for 'The *Cotter's Saturday Night'. Fergusson vividly evokes the street life, taverns, and amusements of Edinburgh, and mocks the established literary world in his attacks on Henry *Mackenzie (in the English 'The Sow of Feeling') and Samuel *Johnson. In 1773 he developed manic-depressive symptoms, and he died shortly after his removal to Bedlam.

Ferishtah's Fancies A volume of poems by Robert *Browning, published 1884. Ferishtah is an imaginary Persian sage, and the volume was a significant contribution to the later Victorian interest in Islamic thought.

FERLINGHETTI, Lawrence (1919–) American *Beat poet. Although born in New York, he was the mainstay of the San Francisco Renaissance. In 1953 he co-founded City Lights Books (named after the Charlie *Chaplin film), a publishing house and bookstore that specialized in Beat poetry. He was arrested in 1956 for publishing Allen *Ginsberg's Howl and wrote a full account of the trial ('Horn on Howl') for the Evergreen Review (1957). His own work includes poetry collections such as A Coney Island of the Mind (1958) as well as two volumes of plays. Unlike many of his contemporaries he disapproved of the Beats' emphasis on the self and argued for a more directly political project with which they could be aligned. He was a fervent supporter of the Cuban Revolution and most famously composed the poem 'One Thousand Fearful Words for Fidel Castro' after his visit there in 1960. Love in the Days of Rage (City Lights, 2001) is a novel set in 1968 Paris. He described Americus I (2004) as 'part documentary, part public pillow-talk, part personal epic'.

FERMOR, Sir Patrick Leigh (1915–2011) Travel writer. In 1933 Fermor set off on foot for Constantinople, a journey recounted many years later in A Time of Gifts (1977) and Between the Woods and the Water (1985), the first two instalments of a projected trilogy. After leaving Constantinople, Fermor continued to live and travel in the Balkans and Greece. Disguised as a shepherd during the German occupation of Crete, he captured the commander of the German forces in Crete, an episode which became the basis of a film, Ill Met by Moonlight (1956). His first travel book, The Traveller's Tree (1950), and his novella, The Violins of Saint-Jacques (1953), are both set in the French Caribbean, whilst A Time to Keep Silence (1957) explores monastic life in Europe. Mani (1958) and Roumeli (1966) describe the southern Peloponnese and northern Greece. He has also published Three Letters from the Andes (1991), based on letters to his wife. Fermor's work combines infectious enthusiasm, a powerful sense of

place, and a highly informed historical imagination.

FERNÁNDEZ DE AVELLANEDA, Alonso The name assumed by the Spanish author of the spurious Part II of *Don Quixote, published in 1614. *Cervantes's own Part II appeared the following year, alluding ironically to Fernández de Avellaneda's sequel.

FERRERS, George see MIRROR FOR MAGISTRATES.

Ferrex and Porrex see GORBODUC.

FERRIER, Susan (1782–1854) Novelist, born in Edinburgh, the author of three widely read novels with largely Scottish settings: Marriage (1818), The *Inheritance (1824), and Destiny (1831). Her work combines a firmly moral didacticism with shrewd social observation. In later life she became increasingly religious and renounced her literary career.

Ferumbras (Firumbras), Sir A Middle English metrical romance of 10,540 short lines related to the French Charlemagne romances Fierabras and the Destruccion de Rome. It is one of the more artistic of the English romances of 'the *matter of France'. The story tells of the capture by Ferumbras, the son of the sultan of Babylon, of Rome and the Holy Relics, and of the conversion to Christianity of Ferumbras and his sister Floripas. The two become friends of Roland, Oliver, and Charlemagne, and Floripas marries Guy of Burgundy. The same story is told in The Sowdone of Babylon, a version from about 1400 of a lost French romance.

FEUCHTWANGER, Lion (1884–1958) German novelist and playwright. Born of a Jewish family in Berlin, he is best known as the author of Die hässliche Herzogin (1923: The Ugly Duchess) and Jud Süss (1925: Jew Süss). On Hitler's seizure of power he was expatriated and lived in France until interned by the Vichy government. Subsequently he escaped to the USA. Jew Süss, in a translation by Willa and Edwin *Muir (1927), was highly praised by Arnold *Bennett in his Evening Standard column, and became a best-seller. In 1924 he collaborated with Bertolt *Brecht on adaptations of Christopher *Marlowe's Edward II and Brecht's own drama Die Gesichte der Simone Machard (1943: The Visions of Simone Machard). Feuchtwanger appears as a character in Christopher *Hampton's play Tales from Hollywood (1983).

FICINO, Marsilio (1433–99) Italian humanist and philosopher, and a highly influential exponent of Platonism. He translated into Latin many important works of *Plato and the *Neoplatonists. His views influenced Johann Reuchlin and *Colet and were an inspiration to many English poets, including Philip *Sidney and John *Milton. *See* MEDICI.

Fiction Collective An independent American writers' collective, founded in 1973 by Jonathan Baumbach (1933–), Ronald *Sukenick, and others, whose purpose was to bypass commercial publishing restrictions by giving innovative and experimental novelists more control over the production of their works. Authors published included Russell Banks (1940–) and Gerald *Vizenor. In 1989 the press was reorganized and renamed Fiction Collective 2 (FC2).

FIEDLER, Leslie Aaron (1917–2003) American literary critic and novelist, best known for his 1960 study *Love and Death in the American Novel*, which argued that American fiction had a distinct *Gothic tradition (hence its obsession with death) and was incapable of dealing with adult sexuality. Fiedler opposed the *New Criticism, drawing instead on Sigmund Freud for his critical writings. Fiedler's first novel, *Nude Croquet* (1957), caused some controversy over its sexual content.

FIELD, Michael Poet and dramatist, pseudonym of Katharine Bradley (1846–1914) and her niece Edith Cooper (1862–1913). They attended University College, Bristol, together in the late 1870s, studying classics and philosophy, and adopted the name 'Michael Field' with the publication of *Callirrhoë; Fair Rosamund* (1884). They produced more than twenty volumes of verse drama and poetry, including *Long Ago* (1889), which retells the story of *Sappho, and *Sight and Song* (1892), which pairs their poems with paintings viewed on their frequent European travels.

FIELD, Nathan (1587–1619/20) Actor and dramatist; forced into service of the Children of the Chapel Royal, a theatre company; probably succeeded William *Shakespeare as actor and shareholder in the King's Men, *c.*1616. He wrote two comedies, *A Woman Is a Weathercock* (1609), which shows the influence of Ben *Jonson and includes a parody of a speech in *The *Spanish Tragedy*, and *Amends for Ladies* (1610). He is best known for his share of Massinger's *The *Fatal Dowry*.

FIELDING, Helen (1958–) Novelist, born in West Yorkshire. Her experiences as a television journalist and maker of documentaries in Africa for the charity Comic Relief inspired her first novel, *Cause Celeb* (1994). But it was *Bridget Jones's Diary* (1996), a lively 'chick lit' novel emerging from her columns in *The Independent* and the *Daily Telegraph* about the romantic misadventures of a 30-something 'singleton' and her friends in London, that brought her widespread readership (and spawned numerous imitations). *Bridget Jones: The Edge of Reason* (1999) continued both the story and Fielding's technique of underpinning her present-day comedy with situations and characters from Jane *Austen's fiction.

FIELDING, Henry (1707–54) Playwright, journalist, novelist, and lawyer, son of a colonel, born at Sharpham Park, Somerset, the house of his maternal grandfather. At Eton College he made lifelong friends of George *Lyttelton, who was to become a generous future patron, and of the future statesman William Pitt the elder. At 19 he attempted to elope with an heiress, but failing in this settled in London, earning his living as a dramatist. *Love in Several Masques* was successfully performed in 1728 at Drury Lane; between 1730 and 1737 he wrote some 25 dramas, mostly farces and satires, including *Tom Thumb* (published in a revised form the following year as *The Tragedy of Tragedies, or The Life and Death of Tom Thumb the Great*), a burlesque of the turgid tragedies of the day. In 1734 Fielding published *Don Quixote*, a tribute to *Cervantes, and married Charlotte Cradock, the model for Sophia in *Tom Jones* and for the heroine of *Amelia*. His improvidence led to long periods of poverty, from which he was periodically relieved by his friend Ralph Allen. In 1736 Fielding took over the management of the New Theatre, for the opening of which he wrote *Pasquin*, targeting various religious and political abuses. But *The Historical Register for 1736* was fiercer political satire than the government of Sir Robert Walpole (1676–1745) would tolerate, and the Licensing Act of 1737, introducing censorship by the lord chamberlain, ended Fielding's theatrical career. In 1739–40 he wrote most of the anti-Jacobite periodical the *Champion. In 1740 Samuel Richardson's *Pamela* enjoyed tremendous popular success; Fielding expressed his contempt in the parody *Shamela*. In 1742 the novel *Joseph Andrews*, also partly designed as a riposte to Richardson, brought him £185 11s. In 1743 Fielding published by subscription three volumes of *Miscellanies*, which included some essays, the Lucianic *A *Journey from this World to the Next*, and a ferocious satire, *The Life of *Jonathan Wild the Great*, in part directed at Walpole. In 1744 his wife died, and in 1747 he caused some scandal by marrying his wife's maid Mary Daniel. With the support of Lyttelton, he was appointed JP for Westminster in 1748 and at once joined battle with the 'trading justices' who imposed and embezzled fines. In 1749 *Tom Jones* was enthusiastically received by the general public, though Samuel *Richardson, Tobias *Smollett, and Samuel *Johnson criticized it heavily. In the same year Fielding's legal jurisdiction was extended to the whole county of Middlesex, and he was made chairman of the quarter sessions of Westminster. From his court in Bow Street he continued his struggle against corruption and lawlessness. *Amelia* (1751) sold the best of all his novels. He returned to journalism in 1752 with the *Covent-Garden Journal*, and published in 1753 an exhaustively detailed *Proposal for Making Effective Provision for the Poor*. In 1754, in hope of improving his health, he set off with his wife and daughter for Portugal, dying near Lisbon in October. The *Journal of a Voyage to Lisbon* (1755) describes the journey in unsparing detail.

Fielding characterized himself as 'the founder of a new province of writing'; his highly plotted 'comic epics in prose' interpret the lure of psychological intensity offered by Richardson's epistolary method as a delusive self-indulgence and instead link the emerging novel form with the humour of *Lucian, *Cervantes, and Jonathan *Swift.

FIELDING, Sarah (1710-68) Novelist, sister of Henry *Fielding. She published in 1744 her own best-known novel, *The Adventures of *David Simple*, a psychologically focused 'Moral Romance', with (in its second edition) a preface by her brother. *Familiar Letters between the Principal Characters in David Simple* followed in 1747, and in 1753 the sombre *Volume the Last*. Her *The Governess* (1749) was the first English school story written for children. She was almost certainly the author of *Remarks on Clarissa* (1749). With Jane *Collier she published *The Cry* (1754), an unusual dialogue between Portia (the Solo) representing integrity, and an audience (the Chorus) representing ignorant malice. The parallel of author against critic is implied throughout. Her other works include *The Lives of Cleopatra and Octavia* (1757); *The History of the Countess of Dellwyn* (1759); and the light-hearted epistolary novel *History of Ophelia* (1760). A successful translation of *Xenophon's *Memoirs of Socrates, with* the Defence of Socrates before his Judges appeared in 1762.

Fifine at the Fair A poem in alexandrine couplets by Robert *Browning, published 1872. The speaker is Don Juan, who is strolling with his wife Elvire near Pornic in Brittany, where a fair is being held. Attracted by the gypsy dancer Fifine, Don Juan discusses with Elvire the nature of his feelings, contrasting the ephemeral nature of desire with the dull permanence of love. This initial theme gives rise to a series of absorbing variations on the interconnected topics of knowledge, identity, and authenticity in life and art.

FIGES, Eva (1932-) Novelist and feminist, born in Berlin; she came to England in 1939, and during the 1960s belonged to a circle of 'experimental' writers which also included B. S. *Johnson, Alan Burns (1929-), and Ann Quin (1936-73). Her novels are poetic and fragmented, her preferred form the *interior monologue. They include *Winter Journey* (1967), *Days* (1974), *Waking* (1981), *Ghosts* (1988), *The Tree of Knowledge* (1990), a fictionalized biography of John *Milton's wife, and *Nelly's Version* (2002), an eerie study of amnesia. *Patriarchal Attitudes* (1970) and *Sex and Subterfuge: Women Writers to 1850* (1982) were influential works of *feminist social and literary criticism. Her memoirs *Tales of Innocence and Experience: An Exploration* (2004) and *Journey to Nowhere* (2008) recall her experiences as a refugee.

Film Society The Society enabled artists, intellectuals, and progressives in London to see a wide range of international cinema that was otherwise banned from exhibition by Britain's draconian film *censorship. Launched in 1925, with Roger *Fry, J. M. Keynes (1883-1946), George Bernard *Shaw, H. G. *Wells, and Virginia *Woolf among its founder members, the society showed predominantly German and *Russian films, but also included popular science and *animation in its wide-ranging programmes, which continued until the late 1930s.

Filostrato A poem in *ottava rima on the story of Troilus and Cressida, by *Boccaccio (1335), the source of Chaucer's *Troilus and Criseyde*.

FINE, Anne (1947-) OBE, FRSL, born in Leicester, award-winning writer for both older and younger children; the second children's laureate (2001-3). She has written over 50 books, beginning with *The Summer House Loon* (1978). Often comic, they feature pragmatic approaches to personal and social problems. *Goggle-Eyes* (1990, Carnegie Medal) and *Flour Babies* (1993, Carnegie Medal) were both adapted for television. *Madame Doubtfire* (1987) was filmed as *Mrs Doubtfire* with Robin Williams (1993). Fine's well-received adult novels include *Raking the Ashes* (2005).

Fingal, *an Ancient Epic Poem, in Six Books: Together with Several Other Poems, Composed by Ossian, the Son of Fingal. Translated from the Galic Language (1762) and Temora, an Ancient Epic Poem, in Eight Books (1763)* These extended narratives in poetic prose, which purported to be translated from ancient Gaelic epic originals, were largely the original work of James *Macpherson, though they were based loosely on *Fenian ballads current in his native Highlands. Macpherson transforms the legendary Irish hero *Finn or Fionn into the Scottish Fingal, ignores key episodes and characters in the original tales (including *Grainne, Finn's faithless wife, and her lover *Diarmid), and brings together Fingal and Cuthullin (the Irish *Cuchulain) who according to tradition were separated by more than two centuries. Morven, Fingal's kingdom in the north-west of Scotland, is Macpherson's invention. The enormous impact of Macpherson's work is indicated by the fact that even Edward *Gibbon took the trouble to discuss it, writing of 'the tenderness, the elegant genius of Ossian'. *Fingal* appealed to 18th-century ideas about *primitivism, the *sublime, and *sentiment.

FINLAY, Ian Hamilton (1925–2006) Scottish poet, graphic artist, and sculptor, born in the Bahamas and brought up in Scotland. A leading figure in the *concrete poetry movement, he published a series of handsome and innovative pamphlets, slim volumes, and postcard poems in association with his own Wild Hawthorn Press and other small presses. His creation of Little Sparta, a sculpture garden at Dunsyre, south of the Pentland Hills, is celebrated for its combinations of nature, word, image, and artefact, and its reconciliation of the classical with the modern. See *The Dancers Inherit the Party: Early Stories, Plays and Poems* (2004).

Finn (Fionn) The principal hero of the *Fenian cycle. Finn MacCoul has been thought a historical figure by some authorities, though most regard him as mythical. He was the son of Cumhal and father of *Oisín (Ossian), and is supposed to have lived in the 3rd century AD, a contemporary of King Cormac Mac Airt. The king appointed him chief of the Fianna, a military body composed of men of exceptional strength and prowess, of whose heroic or romantic deeds there are countless tales. Finn was chosen as their leader not for surpassing physical qualities, but on account of his wisdom, generosity, and truthfulness. He is said to have perished in a fight with mutinous Fenians in 283. *See also* DIARMID; FINGAL; GRAINNE.

Finnegans Wake The final, notoriously obscure, wondrously perplexing work of James *Joyce, laboured over for seventeen years and published in 1939. It defies synopsis and provokes exegesis in equal measure. Written in a unique style which makes abundant use of puns and portmanteau words (using at least 40 languages besides English) and a very wide range of allusion, it has yet to be fathomed and probably never will be. The central theme of the work is the cyclical pattern of history, of fall and resurrection, inspired by Giambattista Vico's *La scienza nuova*. This is presented in the story of Humphrey Chimpden Earwicker, a Dublin publican, and the book is apparently a dream-sequence representing the stream of his unconscious mind through the course of one night. Alongside its endless puzzles it contains passages of great lyrical beauty and much humour.

Finnsburh, The Fight at Known as 'The Finnsburh Fragment', to distinguish it from the 'Finnsburh Episode' in *Beowulf; a 48-line fragmentary poem in Old English dealing with part of the tragic tale of Finn and Hildeburh, a later part of which is sung by the *scôp* in *Beowulf,* ll. 1063–159.

FINZI, Gerald (1901–56) English composer, who made major choral settings of poems by Thomas *Traherne, Henry *Vaughan, and William *Wordsworth (*Intimations of Immortality*, 1950) and solo settings from John *Milton, William *Shakespeare, Christina *Rossetti, and Thomas *Hardy. He also publicized the work of Ivor *Gurney.

FIRBANK, Ronald (1886–1926) Novelist, born in London; he derived from his grandfather, a self-made railway contractor, an income which enabled him to pay for the publication of most of his own work. *Vainglory* appeared in 1915. This was followed by *Inclinations* (1916); *Caprice* (1917, the story of the spectacularly brief and dazzling theatrical career of the daughter of a rural dean); *Valmouth* (1919, set in a spa dominated by an erotic and manipulative black masseuse); *Santal* (1921, set in North Africa); and *The Flower beneath the Foot* (1923).

The first of his novels to be financed by a publisher was *Prancing Nigger* (1924), which appeared under that title in America, and under his own preferred title, *Sorrow in Sunlight*, in Britain; set in the West Indies, it describes the social aspirations and adventures of a black family, the Mouths. Posthumous publications include *Concerning the Eccentricities of Cardinal Pirelli* (1926) and *The New Rythum and Other Pieces* (1962). Dandy, aesthete, exotic, and homosexual, Firbank succeeded in creating a distinctive 'Firbankian' style, in both his life and works. His use of dialogue, his idiosyncratic ellipses, his highly coloured fantasies, and his intense concentration of language and image are now seen as truly innovative. Those who show traces of his influence include Evelyn *Waugh, Ivy *Compton-Burnett, William *Gerhardie, Anthony *Powell, and Muriel *Spark.

Fir Bolg Legendary early invaders of Ireland, according to tradition of an Iberian tribe, who were driven into Arran, Islay, and the Hebrides by the Milesians.

FIRDAUSĪ (Ferdosi), Abū l-Qāsim (*c.*940–1020) Persian poet and author of the *Shahnama* (*Shahnameh*), 'The Book of Kings', a vast epic of some 60,000 couplets, composed over a period of 35 years. The *Shahnama* is the earliest and still the most popular masterpiece of Persian literature. It recounts the history of the kings and heroes of Persia from legendary times down to and including the Sassanian period (226–651). Though every hemistich, or half-line of verse, has the same metre and the style is simple, Firdausī is adept at varying his phrasing to match the theme and mood of each episode. The *Shahnama* had a profound impact on wider Persian culture, some of the finest miniature paintings illuminating its major manuscripts.

There have been many partial translations into English from 1785 (by Joseph Champion) to the 21st century (by Dick Davis), almost all in abbreviated form. However, the epic is known to English readers principally through Matthew *Arnold's telling of one of its many vivid incidents, the story of *'Sohrab and Rustum'.

First Part of the Contention of the Two Famous Houses of York and Lancaster See HENRY VI.

FISHER, Roy (1930–) Poet and semi-professional jazz pianist, born in Birmingham. Pluralist in spirit and style, his poetry is notoriously difficult to pigeonhole. *City* (1961) combines burlesque, imagist, and lyrical poetry with paragraphs of prose varying from the documentary to the surreal; *Ten Interiors with Various Figures* (1966) is a sequence of hybrid verse and prose; *The Ship's Orchestra* (1967) is a *Cubist prose-poetry novella; *The Thing about Joe Sullivan: Poems 1971–1977* (1978) includes free verse sequences and lyrics which have invited comparisons to the *Black Mountain school and to *jazz poetry's syncopations and rhapsodic improvisations; *The Furnace* (1986) is a short epic that superimposes the industrial West Midlands onto the landscape of his new home in north Staffordshire; and *Birmingham River* (1994) foregrounds a voice-over (both a satire and a celebration) for a television documentary on the city. *Standard Midland* (2010) revisits the same terrains. His work includes numerous collaborations with visual artists, notably Tom *Phillips. *The Long and the Short of it: Poems 1955–2005* (2005) is the most comprehensive collection.

FISHER, St John (*c.*1469–1535) Theologian and martyr, he became chancellor of Cambridge university, and bishop of Rochester, 1504, and was president of Queens' College, Cambridge, 1505–8. He was a patron of *Erasmus. He wrote three treatises against the Lutheran Reformation and was committed to the Tower for refusing to swear to the Act of Succession. The pope did not improve his chances of escape from death by sending him a cardinal's hat while he was in prison. Fisher was deprived, attainted, and beheaded for refusing to acknowledge *Henry VIII as supreme head of the church. His English prose style showed a great advance, in point of rhetorical artifice and effect, on that of his predecessors. He was canonized in 1935.

FISHER, Vardis (1895–1968) American novelist born in Idaho, who wrote a series of historical novels about the Old West. These include *Tale of Valour: A Novel of the Lewis and Clarke Expedition* (1960) and *The Mothers: An American Saga of Courage* (1965), about the 1840s Donner party of migrants who resorted to cannibalism. *Children of God* (1939) draws on his Mormon upbringing. His twelve-volume Testament of Man series (1943–60) received a mixed reception.

FitzBoodle, George Savage One of W. M. *Thackeray's pseudonyms. As the narrator of the *FitzBoodle Papers*, published in *Fraser's Magazine* 1842–3, FitzBoodle, a bachelor clubman, tells the story of his own amorous misadventures.

FITZGERALD, Edward (1809–83) Poet and translator, born in Suffolk, where he spent most of his life. His quirky but engaging personality made him much beloved by many close friends, who included W. M. *Thackeray, Alfred and Frederick *Tennyson, and Thomas *Carlyle. His first published book (1849) was a biography of the Quaker poet Bernard Barton, followed by *Euphranor: A Dialogue on Youth* (1851), translations of plays by Calderón, *Aeschylus, and *Sophocles, a collection of aphorisms, and a selection of George *Crabbe's poetry. His only celebrated work is his free translation of The *Rubáiyát of Omar Khayyám* (1859). His other translations from Persian included Attar's *Bird Parliament* and Jami's *Salaman and Absal*. He was a prolific and delightful letter writer, whose anecdotes of his literary friends have been a gold mine to biographers. See his *Collected Letters* (1980).

FITZGERALD, F. Scott (Francis Scott Key) (1896–1940) American novelist and short story writer, born in Minnesota. His first novel, *This Side of Paradise* (1920), made him instantly famous; shortly after its publication he married the glamorous Zelda Sayre, and together they embarked on a life of high living, big spending, and party-going, seeing themselves as representative figures of the 'Jazz Age'. His stories chronicled the mood and manners of the times, including his fantasy of extravagance, 'The Diamond as Big as the Ritz'. *The Beautiful and Damned* (1922), a novel about a wealthy, doomed, and dissipated marriage, was followed by *The Great Gatsby* (1925), the story of shady, mysterious financier Jay Gatsby, who harbours a romantic and destructive passion for Daisy Buchanan. More short stories followed, and Zelda's only novel, *Save Me the Waltz*, appeared in 1932, but by this time she and Scott were suffering from mental breakdown and from the effects of their violent lives. *Tender is the Night* (1934, and later revised versions) records, through the story of American psychiatrist Dick Diver and his schizophrenic wife Nicole, his own sense of impending disaster. Fitzgerald's own 'crack-up' accelerated, as Zelda failed to recover: he died in Hollywood, of a heart attack, after working as a screenwriter, leaving his last novel, *The Last Tycoon* (originally *The Love of the Last Tycoon*), unfinished. It appeared in 1941, followed by a posthumous collection, *The Crack-Up* (1945).

FITZGERALD, Penelope (1916–2000) Novelist and biographer, born in Lincoln. Her first book was a biography of the *Pre-Raphaelite painter Edward Burne-Jones (1975), which was followed by two composite biographies, one of her father and his three brothers (1977), and one of the poet Charlotte *Mew and her circle (1984). Fitzgerald's first novel, *The Golden Child* (1977), written to divert her husband during his last illness, is a murder mystery involving an exhibition of Egyptian treasures in a London museum. *The Bookshop* (1978) is set in a fictional East Anglian town in the late 1950s. *Offshore* (1979, Booker Prize) is about life among a group of houseboat owners on the Thames during the 1960s. *Human Voices* (1980) is a story of the BBC during the Second World War and *At Freddie's* (1982) is set in a West End stage school. She had by this time 'finished writing about the things in my own life, which I wanted to write about'. *Innocence* (1986) takes place in 1950s Italy; *The Beginnings of Spring* (1988) is set in Moscow just before the start of the First World War; and *The Gate of Angels* (1990) is a love story set in Edwardian Cambridge. *The Blue Flower* (1996) recreates the life of the German Romantic poet Novalis (F. L. Hardenberg). *The Means of Escape* (2000) is a collection of short stories.

Fitzrovia A term which describes both the area north of Oxford Street in London's West End and its bohemian habitués between the mid-1920s and about 1950. Centred at first on the Fitzroy Tavern, on the corner of Charlotte Street, Fitzrovia, in the words of Augustus John (1878–1961), was 'the Artist's Quarter, its only rival being Chelsea' (*Finishing Touches*, 1964). Its focus then moved, according to Julian Maclaren-Ross (*Memoirs of the Forties*, 1965), to The Wheatsheaf. Dylan *Thomas, William *Empson, Wyndham *Lewis, George *Orwell, Roy *Campbell, and Patrick *Hamilton were all to a greater or lesser extent Fitzrovians.

F.J. *The Pleasant Fable of Ferdinando Jeronimi and Leonora de Valasco* Usually referred to, from its running title, as *The Adventures of Master F.J.*; a novella by George *Gascoigne, supposedly translated 'out of the Italian riding tales of *Bartello*', but probably his own invention. It exists in two versions: the first, printed in *A Hundreth Sundrie Flowres* (1573), is set in the north of England, is frankly erotic, and has every appearance of being a *roman à clef*; the second, printed in *The Posies of George Gascoigne* (1575), is more Italianate and has been to some extent expurgated.

Flashman The sadistic bully in *Tom Brown's Schooldays* by Thomas *Hughes, revived in a series of humorous novels by George MacDonald *Fraser. *See also* HISTORICAL FICTION.

FLAUBERT, Gustave (1821–80) French novelist, born in Rouen. His first novel, *Madame Bovary* (1857; English trans. 1886), the sardonic tragedy of life in provincial Normandy, is notable for its rigorous psychological development, its impersonal narrative method, its irony, and its highly worked style. Other works include *Salammbô* (1862), set in a meticulously researched Ancient Carthage; *L'Éducation sentimentale* (1869; English trans. 1898), with a backdrop of events in Paris between 1840 and 1851; *Trois Contes* (1877: *Un Cœur simple, La Légende de Saint-Julien l'Hospitalier, Hérodias*; English trans. 1903); *Tentation de Saint-Antoine* (1874; English trans. 1910), part poem, part prose narrative; and the unfinished and posthumously published *Bouvard et Pécuchet* (1881). Flaubert's published letters (4 vols, ed. J. Bruneau, 1973–98), make accessible his searching reflections on the art of fiction and the life of the novelist.

FLAXMAN, John (1755–1826) English neoclassical sculptor and draughtsman. His illustrations to the **Iliad* and the **Odyssey* (Alexander *Pope's translation, pub. 1793) won him an immense reputation throughout Europe. His illustrations to Dante's **Divina commedia* (1793), commissioned by Thomas *Hope, were praised by *Goethe (1799). Flaxman maintained a lifelong friendship with William *Blake.

FLECKER, James Elroy (1884–1915) Poet and playwright, of Jewish descent. At Trinity College, Oxford, he was influenced by the last flowering of the *Aesthetic movement. During a career in the consular service he produced several volumes of lyrical romantic verse, including *The Bridge of Fire* (1907), *Forty-Two Poems* (1911), and *The Golden Journey to Samarkand* (1913). He also published an experimental, highly individual novel, *The King of Alsander* (1914). The work for which he is possibly best remembered is a play, *Hassan* (1922). His other play, *Don Juan*, was published in 1925.

FLECKNOE, Richard (d. ?1678) A writer with an interest in experimental forms, many of whose works were published privately. His *Miscellanea* (1653) includes a defence of the stage (in his 'Discourse upon Languages') and a lament for the theatres silenced under the Commonwealth. His *Ariadne* (1654) is probably the first English opera, though the music (which he composed himself) is lost. His *Love's Dominion* (1654), a pastoral with songs, was acted after the Restoration under the title *Love's Kingdom*. Its reputation for insipidity, and Andrew *Marvell's earlier satire ('Flecknoe, an English priest at Rome', ?1645), suggested to John *Dryden his attack on Thomas *Shadwell, **Mac Flecknoe*.

FLEMING, Ian (1908–64) Journalist, thriller writer, and bibliophile. His first novel, *Casino Royale* (1953; filmed in James Bond series 2006), introduced the suave hero James *Bond, who subsequently appeared in a series of Cold War adventures with exotic settings, including *Live and Let Die* (1954), *Diamonds Are Forever* (1956), *From Russia with Love* (1957), *Goldfinger* (1959), and *On Her Majesty's Secret Service* (1963), which launched an even more popular film series with *Dr No* (1962). His children's story *Chitty Chitty Bang Bang* (1964, filmed 1968), became a spectacular stage musical in 2000. *See also* SPY FICTION.

FLEMING, Peter (1907–71) Journalist and travel writer, brother of Ian *Fleming, he is remembered largely for his travel books, which include *Brazilian Adventure* (1933); *One's Company* (1934), which followed a trip to China to report on the conflict between nationalists and communists; and *News from Tartary* (1936), an account of an overland journey from Peking (Beijing) to Kashmir.

Fleshly School of Poetry *See* ROSSETTI, DANTE GABRIEL; BUCHANAN, ROBERT WILLIAMS.

FLETCHER, Giles, the elder (1546–1611) Poet and diplomat. He was sent as envoy to Russia in 1588 and published *Of the Russe Common Wealth*, a pioneering account of Russian government, in 1591. His *Licia, or Poemes of Love* (1593) is notable both for being one of the first sonnet sequences to follow the publication of **Astrophel and Stella* (1591) and for having a dedication in which he sets out his belief that 'a man may write of love, and not be in love, as well as of husbandry, and not go to plough'. He was the uncle of John *Fletcher and father of Giles and Phineas *Fletcher.

FLETCHER, Giles, the younger (?1586–1623) Poet, younger son of Giles *Fletcher the elder. His best-known poem, *Christ's Victory, and Triumph in Heaven, and Earth, over, and after Death* (1610), is an allegorical work in four cantos dealing respectively with a dispute between Justice and Mercy, the Temptation, the Passion, and the Resurrection and Ascension. It influenced John *Milton's *Paradise Regained*.

FLETCHER, John (1579–1625) Playwright, nephew of Giles *Fletcher the elder and cousin of Giles *Fletcher the younger and Phineas *Fletcher. Little is known of his early life; about 1606 he began to write plays in collaboration with Francis *Beaumont, with whom he enjoyed a close personal and professional relationship. Before his death of the plague, he produced some fifteen plays with Beaumont, and around sixteen as sole author. He collaborated with Philip *Massinger, William *Rowley, Thomas *Middleton, Ben *Jonson, George *Chapman, and *Shakespeare. The chronology of his plays, and the extent of his collaborations, are exceedingly difficult to determine. Dates given below are mostly approximate dates of first performance.

The principal plays of which Fletcher was probably sole author are: *The *Faithful Shepherdess*, 1608–9; *The *Woman's Prize*, 1609–11; *Valentinian*, 1610–12; *Monsieur Thomas*, 1610–13; *Wit without Money*, 1614; *The Mad Lover*, 1616; *The *Chances*, 1617; *The *Loyal Subject*, 1618; *Women Pleased*, 1618; *The *Humorous Lieutenant*, 1619; *The *Wild Goose Chase*, 1620–21; *The Pilgrim*, 1621; *The Island Princess*, 1621; *A Wife for a Month*, 1624; *Rule a Wife and Have a Wife*, 1624.

Plays certainly or probably by Beaumont and Fletcher are: *Cupid's Revenge*, a tragedy based on material in the second book of Sidney's *Arcadia*, 1607–8, printed 1615; *Philaster*, 1608–9; *The Coxcomb*, 1608–10; *The Captain*, 1609–11; *Bonduca*, 1609–14; *The *Maid's Tragedy*, 1610; *A *King and No King*, 1611; *Four Plays in One*, c.1613 (possibly with collaboration from Nathan *Field); *The Scornful Lady*, 1613, printed 1616; *Thierry King of France*, 1613, printed 1621 (with Beaumont and Massinger); *The Honest Man's Fortune*, 1613, printed 1647; *The Knight of Malta*, 1618, printed 1647; *Love's Cure* (later rewritten by Massinger, printed 1647).

The following plays are probably by Fletcher and some other dramatists: *Love's Pilgrimage* and *The Double Marriage*, printed 1647; *Sir John Van *Oldenbarnavelt*, performed 1619; *The *Custom of the Country*, 1619; *The *False One*, 1621; *The Little French Lawyer*, 1621; *The Laws of Candy*, printed 1647; *The *Spanish Curate* and *The *Beggar's Bush*, both performed 1622. In all the above Fletcher certainly or probably collaborated with Massinger. The romantic drama *The *Lovers' Progress*, performed 1623, was later revised by Massinger. *The Maid in the Mill* was written by Fletcher and Rowley, 1623. *The *Elder Brother*, printed 1637, is thought to have been written by Fletcher and revised by Massinger. *The Fair Maid of the Inn*, 1626, was probably the result of a collaboration between Fletcher and Massinger. *The Nice Valour*, printed 1647, was probably by Fletcher and Middleton. *The Bloody Brother, or Rollo, Duke of Normandy* (performed c.1616) is by Fletcher, Jonson, Chapman, and Massinger. *The Noble Gentleman*, acted 1626, is probably by Fletcher, possibly with Beaumont or Rowley. Fletcher also collaborated with Shakespeare in *The *Two Noble Kinsmen*, *Henry VIII*, and the lost *Cardenio*.

FLETCHER, Phineas (1582–1650) Poet, elder son of Giles *Fletcher the elder. Like his brother Giles *Fletcher the younger, he was a poet of the Spenserian school. His parallel poems in Latin and English, *The Locusts, or Apollyonists* (1627), attack the Jesuits, and contain a diabolical conclave that may have influenced John *Milton. *The Purple Island* (1633) is an ingenious allegorical account of the human body and mind; *Piscatory Eclogues*, features fisher boys on the banks of the Cam. *Britain's Ida* (1628), published as Edmund *Spenser's, may be his.

FLINDERS, Matthew (1774–1814) Navigator and hydrographer (or ocean-mapper). He was 'induced to go to sea ... from reading *Robinson Crusoe*'. With George Bass he established that Van Diemen's Land was an island, publishing his careful surveys in 1801 and attracting the attention of Sir Joseph Banks. Charged with a well-equipped scientific expedition to systematically survey the coast of New Holland, he was first to circumnavigate the continent and largely completed its mapping; in 1804 he was first to suggest the name Australia for the continent. *A Voyage to Terra Australis*, completed under Banks's supervision, was published the day before he died.

Flodden (**Floddon**) **Field** The battle of Flodden, in Northumberland, fought on 9 September 1513, when Thomas Howard, earl of Surrey, on behalf of *Henry VIII (then in France), defeated James IV of Scotland, the latter being killed on the field along with some 10,000 of his followers. It was made the subject of poems, of rejoicing or lament, on both sides of the border. John *Skelton's 'Against the Scots' is a song of exultation of the English victory. The most popular version of the Scottish lament, 'The Flowers o' the Forest', is by Jean *Elliot: *see also* COCKBURN, ALISON. The battle is described in Walter *Scott's *Marmion*.

Flood *See* BIBLE.

FLORIO, John (c.1553–1626) Writer, translator, and teacher of languages, son of an Italian Protestant refugee. His collections of Italian–English dialogues, *First* and *Second Fruits*, were followed by an Italian dictionary, *A World of Words* (1598); it was revised as *Queen Anna's New World of Words* (1611). His translation from *Montaigne: *Essays or Moral, Politic and Military Discourses* (1603, 1613) displayed great resourcefulness and ingenuity in the process of translation; Shakespeare drew on Florio's version of Montaigne, in *The *Tempest* and elsewhere. Florio has been suggested as the earliest translator of the *Decameron.

Floris and Blancheflour A popular Middle English metrical romance in 1,083 lines from the first half of the 13th century, based on a 12th-century French original. Floris and Blancheflour are brought up together: he is the son of a Saracen king and she the daughter of a Christian lady who has been captured and brought to the king's court. They fall in love and Blancheflour is banished. Floris sets off to find her, equipped with a precious cup and a magic ring which prove instrumental in his finding her and their ultimate marriage by consent of the emir. The story, which has analogues in the *Arabian Nights* and other works, is the subject of *Boccaccio's *Filocolo.

Floure and the Leaf, The A 15th-century allegory in 595 lines of *rhyme royal, formerly attributed to Geoffrey *Chaucer. The followers of the flower and the leaf were the two parties in the mannered, courtly debates on love in the French poetry of writers such as Eustace Deschamps. It was modernized by John *Dryden in his *Fables Ancient and Modern*.

FLUDD, Robert (1574–1637) Fellow of the Royal College of Physicians. He entered the debate on the authenticity of the *Rosicrucian texts with his defence, *Apologia*, in 1616, and was deeply interested in Hermeticism and *Neoplatonism. His views on the universe as macrocosm–microcosm attracted much controversy; despite his own mystical views on the circulation of the blood, he was the first to defend William Harvey's *De Motu Cordis*. Hilary *Mantel's novel *Fludd* (1989) draws on Fludd's life.

flyting [from the Old English *flītan*, to quarrel or dispute] A verse contest in insults, practised in particular by the Scottish poets of the early 16th century but present in Old English and Old Norse literature. The most famous example is the 'Flyting of *Dunbar and Kennedie'.

focalization The technical term in modern *narratology for the adoption of a limited 'point of view' from which the events of a given story are witnessed, usually by a character within the fictional world. Unlike the 'omniscient' perspective of traditional stories, which in principle allows the narrator privileged insight into all characters' secret motives and the ability to recount simultaneous events in different places, a focalized narrative constrains its perspective within the limited awareness available to a particular witness, to whom the thoughts of other characters remain opaque. As seeing differs from telling, such a focalizing observer is not necessarily the narrator of the story, but may be a character in an account given by a third-person narrator: this method of using a 'centre of consciousness' within the fictional world is associated especially with Henry *James, but has been widely adopted by other novelists.

folios and quartos, Shakespearian Shakespeare's earliest published plays (like other early books) are referred to as folios or quartos according to the folding of the printed sheets and therefore the size of the book. Folios, being printed from sheets that have been folded once, are large and tall; quartos, printed from sheets folded twice, are smaller and squarer.

Of about 750 copies of the first folio printed between February 1622 and November 1623, some 230 survive in various states of preservation, 80 or so in the Folger Shakespeare Library. A second folio was issued in 1632, containing 'An Epitaph on … Shakespeare' by *Milton, his first published poem. A third folio was issued in 1663, whose second impression of 1664 contained *Pericles* and six apocryphal plays; the fourth and last folio was published in 1685. Thirty-six plays, eighteen printed for the first time, were arranged by *Hemings and Condell into sections of comedies, histories, and tragedies for the first folio. It contains the Droeshout portrait and a list of 'the Principal Actors in all these Plays', together with commendatory verses by contemporaries including Ben *Jonson.

During his lifetime eighteen of Shakespeare's plays were published in quartos, some of them with reprints, and *Othello* appeared in 1622. Following A. W. Pollard's analysis, it used to be thought that over half of those quartos were 'bad' ones, that is, that their texts are extremely corrupt as a result of their reconstruction from memory by a member, or members, of their cast. Some 'bad' quartos, for example *The First Part of the Contention* (1594) and *The True Tragedy of Richard Duke of York* (1595), were once thought of as source plays (for *2* and *3* *Henry VI*); similarly the quarto *The Taming of a Shrew* (1594) has been thought of as 'bad' and the folio text, *The *Taming of the Shrew*, as 'good'. In two cases, **Romeo and Juliet* (1597) and **Hamlet* (1603), 'good' second quartos were soon issued (in 1599 and 1604–5 respectively) to correct the 'bad' first quartos. The nature and number of these 'bad' (or 'short') quartos have been much disputed and theories about their origins have included the possibility that they derive from shorthand accounts taken down by members of the theatrical company or of the audience, that they represent authorial first drafts, and that they represent shortened or altered versions of the play made for various circumstances, such as provincial touring. It is increasingly thought that even 'bad' quartos may preserve authoritative theatrical readings.

Textual criticism and bibliography have largely been concerned with establishing relationships between the 'good' quartos (in some cases the 'bad' ones as well) and their versions in the first folio, to determine on which text an editor is to base his edition. In trying to establish this relationship scholars have mainly sought to determine the nature of the copy which the printers used. The chief types of copy which have been distinguished are: (1) 'foul papers', that is an original authorial draft, as in Q1 of *A *Midsummer Night's Dream* (1600); (2) a fair scribal copy, as in the folio text of *The *Tempest*; (3) a prompt copy from the theatre, as in the folio text of **As You Like It*; (4) a memorial text, as discussed above; and (5) a reconstructed text, that is one based on an early quarto but where some kind of manuscript copy has also been used, as in the case of the folio text of **Richard III*.

Stanley Wells, Gary Taylor, John Jowett, and William Montgomery, *William Shakespeare: A Textual Companion* (1987) provides a valuable introduction to the subject.

(⊕) SEE WEB LINKS
• The Shakespeare quartos archive

folk song A song or ballad, usually without identifiable author, handed down orally, evolving through the modifications of individual performers, often existing in different forms in different parts of the country. In the mid-18th century Thomas *Percy's fashionably edited collections of ballads stimulated interest in the music. The end of the 19th century saw an immense increase of activity in the collection, transcription, and publication of folk songs. The

Folk-Song Society was founded in 1898, and Cecil Sharp's Folk Dance Society followed in 1911; the two were amalgamated in 1932. The composers Percy Grainger, Gustav Holst, Ralph *Vaughan Williams, and George Butterworth all derived inspiration from folk song.

(⊕) SEE WEB LINKS
• English Folk Dance and Song Society Library

Fomorians The sea-giants of Gaelic mythology. They are represented as more ancient than the gods (the *Tuatha Dé Danann), and as having been ousted by them and destroyed at the battle of Moytura.

fool A character in English drama. The fool has a variety of origins, from the medieval court jester to the licensed clown of the Feast of Fools. He has numerous incarnations in Shakespeare: as the simpleton (the clown in *The *Winter's Tale*), the rogue (Autolycus, also in *The Winter's Tale*), and the wise court jester (the Fool in **King Lear*), licensed to speak freely, however satirically or disrespectfully. He is also related to the Arlecchino of the **commedia dell'arte*.

In Shakespeare's company the fools' parts were played by William *Kemp until his retirement *c.*1599; Kemp's name appeared in the place of the characters' in early printings of *Romeo and Juliet* and *Much Ado about Nothing*. The more complex parts of Feste in **Twelfth Night* and the Fool in *King Lear* were probably written for his replacement, Robert Armin.

Fool of Quality, The A novel in five volumes by Henry *Brooke, published in Dublin 1765–70 and in London 1766–70. The narrative follows the education, growth, and manhood of Harry Clinton, the Fool of Quality. The most important adult in his world is not his decadent father but his merchant uncle, Mr Clinton (sometimes Fenton), whose enlightened views on Harry's education (much influenced by *Rousseau's *Émile* and John *Locke's *On Education*) guide the boy's growth into a wise and generous adult. The book appealed greatly to John *Wesley and to Charles *Kingsley (who drew on it for his own novel *Yeast*).

foot A metrical unit of two, three, or (very rarely) four syllables. *See* METRE.

FOOTE, Samuel (1721–77) Actor and dramatist, with a talent for comic mimicry. In 1747 he produced *Diversions of the Morning*, a revue caricaturing several prominent actors. There followed a series of comic pieces and puppet shows, including *Taste* (1752), *The Minor* (1760), *The Patron* (1764), and *The Nabob* (1772), all satirizing contemporary personalities. Foote was embroiled in literary feuds with such writers as Henry *Fielding and Charles *Churchill, and other victims of his ruthless impersonations.

FORBES, Rosita (1890–1967) Traveller and writer. Her travel books include *The Secret of the Sahara: Kufara* (1921), which recounted her journey, disguised as a Muslim, across the Libyan desert with Egyptian explorer Ahmad Hassanein; *From Red Sea to Blue Nile* (1925); and *Conflict: Angora to Afghanistan* (1931). Forbes married Colonel Arthur Thomas McGrath in 1921 and visited the Yemen, again in disguise, in 1992. She published two volumes of autobiography, *Gypsy in the Sun* (1944) and *Appointment with Destiny* (1946).

FORD, Ford Madox (formerly Ford Hermann Hueffer) (1873–1939) Novelist and editor, grandson of the *Pre-Raphaelite painter Ford Madox Brown; he was deeply affected by his Pre-Raphaelite inheritance. His first published works were *fairy stories, beginning with *The Brown Owl* (1891). In 1894 he eloped with and married Elsie Martindale. In 1898 he met Joseph *Conrad and they collaborated in various works including the novels *The Inheritors* (1901) and *Romance* (1903); from 1901 their relationship deteriorated: During a diverse and productive literary career Ford published over 80 books, both fiction and non-fiction. He developed his own theory of 'Impressionism' in the novel and non-fictional prose, applied to great effect in *The Soul of London* (1905). In 1908 Ford embarked on two significant enterprises, an affair with the glamorous and emancipated novelist Violet *Hunt; and the founding of the *English Review*.

In 1915 Ford published what he himself regarded as his finest achievement, his 'one novel', *The *Good Soldier*, and in the same year enlisted in the army: he was invalided home from France in 1917 and changed his name from Hueffer to Ford in 1919. The war inspired his other major work of fiction, now known as *Parade's End* (or sometimes, after its hero, as the 'Tietjens' tetralogy), published in four parts between 1924 and 1928. In Paris in 1924 he founded the *Transatlantic Review*, in which he published work by Joyce, *Pound, Gertrude *Stein, E. E. *Cummings, and others. During his last years, which were spent in France and America, he published further novels, notably *The Rash Act* (1933), several volumes of autobiography and reminiscence (including *Return to Yesterday*, 1931, and *It Was the Nightingale*, 1933), and a volume of criticism, *The March of Literature* (1938). He died in Deauville. As an editor he has long been regarded as a highly influential figure whose devotion to literature and ready appreciation of originality and quality in others (*see* MODERNISM) did much to shape the course of 20th-century writing.

FORD, John (1586–after 1639) Playwright; he appears to have written all or a substantial part of around twenty plays, some of them lost. Between 1621 and 1625 he collaborated with Thomas *Dekker and others in at least five plays including *The *Witch of Edmonton*. After 1625 Ford probably worked alone. His chief plays are *The *Lover's Melancholy* (1629), *Love's Sacrifice* (1633), *'Tis Pity She's a Whore* (1633), *The *Broken Heart* (1633), *Perkin Warbeck* (1634), and *The Lady's Trial* (1639). Ford's plays are predominantly concerned with courage and endurance in suffering. He explores melancholy, torture, incest, delusion, but always seriously and objectively, through 'the distinct personal rhythm in blank verse which could be no one's but his alone' (T. S. *Eliot).

FORD, Mark (1962–) Poet and critic, editor of two anthologies of New York School poetry, *The New York Poets* (2004) and *The New York Poets II* (2005), and a book-length interview with John *Ashbery (2003). Two collections, *Landlocked* (1992) and *Soft Sift* (2001), entwine witty, erudite, emotionally complex discourses in self-conscious ways that recall Ashbery's work. His critical work includes *A Driftwood Altar: Essays and Reviews* (2005) and *Raymond Roussel and the Republic of Dreams* (2000).

FORD, Richard (1944–) American novelist and writer of short stories, born in Jackson, Mississippi. He is best known for his novel *The Sportswriter* (1986), followed by *Independence Day* (1995) and *The Lay of the Land* (2006). These novels, wistfully lyrical and sharply realistic by turns, tell the story of Frank Bascombe, novelist turned eponymous sportswriter, who by the second novel has quit his job and moved into the real-estate market. Ford's other work includes *The Ultimate Good Luck* (1981, novel), and the story collections *Rock Springs*

(1987) and *Women with Men* (1997), have been associated with *dirty realism.

FOREST, Antonia (1915–2003) Novelist, whose thirteen rich and complex novels (1948–82) combine elements of *school and *family novels and *historical fiction. All but one of her books feature the Marlow family, sometimes in the Elizabethan period, sometimes in the mid-20th century.

Forest, The A collection of miscellaneous short poems, odes, epistles, and songs, by Ben *Jonson, printed in the folio of 1616, including 'To Penshurst' and the songs 'Drink to me only with thine eyes' and, from *Volpone*, 'Come, my Celia, let us prove'.

FORESTER, C. S. (Cecil Scott) (1899–1966) Pseudonym of Cecil Lewis Troughton Smith, principally remembered for his seafaring novels set during the Napoleonic Wars. Horatio Hornblower is introduced in *The Happy Return* (1937). Forester's other works include *Brown on Resolution* (1929) and *The African Queen* (1935; filmed 1951, with a screenplay by James Agee).

formalism A term applied, usually pejoratively, to any creative performance in which technique or manner seems to have been cultivated at the expense of substance; or to critical approaches that disregard the subject matter of a work in favour of discussing its formal or stylistic features. More positively, formalism as a critical principle may be defended as a way of understanding art or literature primarily through its techniques rather than as a mere vehicle for personal expression or for moral and political doctrines. Formalism thus exists in continuous dispute with a range of biographical, social, and religious modes of criticism that show more interest in the 'message' of an art than in the medium. Just as in literary *modernism a 'formalist' emphasis on creative technical experiment is prominent, so in modern literary criticism formalism has been a powerful principle, notably in the *New Criticism of the mid-20th century. Outside the English-speaking world, the most important such critical tradition has been that of the *'Russian formalists'—a label applied to two groups of linguistic and literary scholars active in St Petersburg and Moscow in the period 1915–30, led by Roman Jakobson (1896–1982) and Viktor Shklovsky (1893–1984). They inaugurated a new 'scientific' approach to literature that focused upon the linguistic 'devices' and conventions—from metre to plot structure—by which literature distinguishes itself from ordinary uses of language.

They thus attempted to arrive at an objective account of 'literariness' through formal linguistic analysis, and of its principal effects through the concept of *defamiliarization. Stalin's suppression of intellectual life led to a recantation by Shklovsky in 1930, but Jakobson had earlier emigrated to Czechoslovakia, where he helped to found in 1926 the Prague Linguistic Circle, which became a major link between *Russian formalism and the emergence of the broader *structuralist movement. Meanwhile in Russia the arguments of the formalists had influenced, partly through strong disagreement, the work of *Bakhtin and his group. In the West, the work of Shklovsky and his associates, Boris Tomashevsky, Boris Eikhenbaum, and Vladimir Propp, was rediscovered in the 1960s; Propp's work in particular encouraged the development of *narratology.

FORREST, Leon (1937–97) African American novelist whose first three novels were edited by Toni *Morrison. *The Bloodworth Orphans* (1977) was respectfully received; *Divine Days* (1992) is akin to James *Joyce in its scale and brief time-span. Despite endorsements from Saul *Bellow and others, Forrest's work has only slowly been recognized, and has been criticized for its complexity.

FORREST-THOMSON, Veronica (1947–75) British poet and critic. Her doctoral thesis, 'Poetry as Knowledge: The Use of Science by Twentieth-Century Poets', was initially supervised by J. H. *Prynne. Her poetry was greatly influenced by William *Empson, Ludwig *Wittgenstein, Roland *Barthes, and other writers of the Tel Quel group in France. Collections include *Identi-Kit* (1967), *Language Games* (1971), and, posthumously, *On the Periphery* (1976). A revised *Collected Poems* was published in 2008.

Fors Clavigera: Letters to the Workmen and Labourers of Great Britain By John *Ruskin, issued monthly from January 1871 to March 1878, then at irregular intervals to 1884. *Fors Clavigera* was a sustained challenge, deliberate and serious, to the supporters of a capitalist economy. The obscurity of the title, and extraordinary diversity of subject matter, suggest how little he wished to ingratiate himself with the working classes. He analyses the letters of 'clerks, manufacturers and other' in the 'Notes and Correspondence' section as mercilessly as the writings and speeches of his more famous enemies; only the painter James *Whistler sued for libel. Ruskin's tactics were demonstrative rather than discursive. He delivers lessons in 'the principles and plans of political economy' by setting events from contemporary history and his own immediate experience against the nobler human possibilities expressed in literature and art. *Fors Clavigera*, which attracted a wide and disparate readership, became the mouthpiece of Ruskin's utopian Guild of St George.

FORSTER, E. M. (Edward Morgan) (1879–1970) Novelist, essayist, and short story writer. His happiest childhood years (1883–90) were spent at Rooksnest, Stevenage, a house he evokes in *Howards End*. In 1897 he went to King's College, Cambridge, where the atmosphere of free intellectual discussion, and a stress on the importance of personal relationships inspired partly by the philosopher G. E. Moore (1873–1958), was to have a profound influence on his work. In 1901 he was elected to the *Apostles and largely through them was later drawn into closer contact with *Bloomsbury. A year of travel provided rich material for his early novels, satirizing the attitudes of English tourists abroad, *Baedekers in hand. His first short story, 'The Story of a Panic' (1904) was followed by *Where Angels Fear to Tread* (1905). He tutored the children of Elizabeth *von Arnim in Germany, and, in 1906, became tutor to Syed Ross Masood (1889–1937), a striking and colourful Indian Muslim patriot. *The Longest Journey* (1907), and *A *Room with a View* (1908), were followed by *Howards End* (1910) which established Forster's reputation and *The Celestial Omnibus* (1911, stories). He visited India with Masood in 1912–13. In 1913, his visit to the home of Edward *Carpenter resulted in his writing *Maurice*, a novel with a homosexual theme which he circulated privately. He went to Alexandria in 1915 to work for the Red Cross, where he met the Greek poet C. P. *Cavafy, whose works, on his return to England in 1919, he helped to introduce. In 1921–2 he revisited India, working as personal secretary for the maharaja of the native state of Dewas Senior. *A *Passage to India* (1924), which he had begun before the war, was highly acclaimed. It was, as Forster feared, his last novel, and the remainder of his life was devoted to a wide range of literary activities; he took a firm stand against censorship, involving himself in the work of *PEN and the National Council for Civil Liberties. His Clark Lectures at Cambridge were printed as *Aspects of the Novel* (1927). F. R. *Leavis found the lectures 'intellectually null', but they were a popular success. *The Eternal Moment* (1928)

was a volume of pre-1914 short stories. In 1930 Forster met the policeman Bob Buckingham, with whom he was to enjoy a close and sustaining relationship for the rest of his life. Forster's other works include two biographies, *Goldsworthy Lowes Dickinson* (1934) and *Marianne Thornton* (1956); *Two Cheers for Democracy* (1951); *The Hill of Devi* (1953), a portrait of India through letters and commentary; and, with Eric Crozier (1914–94), the libretto for Benjamin *Britten's opera *Billy Budd*. He spent his last years in King's College, and was awarded the OM in 1969. *Maurice* was published posthumously in 1971, followed by *Albergo Empedocle and Other Writings* (1971); *The Life to Come and Other Stories* (1972); *Arctic Summer and Other Fiction* (1980); and *The Prince's Tale and Other Writings* (1999). Five of Forster's novels have been turned into successful feature films, notably by *Merchant-Ivory.

FORSTER, John (1812–76) Biographer, journalist, and historian. He was engaged in 1835 to Letitia *Landon, but married Eliza Colburn, the wealthy widow of the publisher Henry Colburn, in 1856. He was the literary associate and close friend of Leigh *Hunt, Charles *Lamb, Walter Savage *Landor, Edward *Bulwer-Lytton, and Charles *Dickens. From 1837 on he read in manuscript everything Dickens wrote. His popular literary biographies include *Life and Adventures of Oliver Goldsmith* (1848; rev. 2 vols, 1854), *Landor* (2 vols, 1869), *Dickens* (3 vols, 1872–4), and the first volume of a scholarly life of Jonathan *Swift (1875). He is recognized as the first professional biographer of 19th-century England.

FORSTER, Margaret (1938–) Novelist and biographer, born in Carlisle. Her first success was *Georgy Girl* (1965; film script with Peter *Nichols 1966), the story of an ordinary girl keen to sample the delights of the Swinging Sixties. *Mother Can You Hear Me?* (1979) is a sombre evocation of motherhood, portrayed through three generations of the same family; *Have the Men Had Enough?* (1989) a painful and angry account of old age and dementia. Forster's other fiction includes *Lady's Maid* (1990), *Mother's Boys* (1994), *The Memory Box* (1999), *Keeping the World Away* (2006), and *Over* (2007). Biographical works include lives of Elizabeth Barrett *Browning and Daphne *du Maurier. *Hidden Lives* (1995) and *Precious Lives* (1998) are poignant family memoirs. Forster is married to the author and journalist Hunter Davies (1936–).

Forsyte Saga, The A sequence of five texts by John *Galsworthy, first published in one volume in 1922. The saga comprises three novels, *The Man of Property* (1906), *In Chancery* (1920), and *To Let* (1921), and two interludes, 'Indian Summer of a Forsyte' (1918), and *Awakening* (1920), which together trace the declining fortunes of three generations of the Forsyte family. Among other things, Galsworthy lays bare the urbane brutality and blinding materialism which underpin the 'full plumage' of upper middle-class family life. *The Forsyte Saga* was serialized in 26 episodes for BBC television in 1967 and proved a phenomenal success.

FORSYTH, Frederick *See* SPY FICTION.

FORT, Charles (1847–1932) American journalist and author, whose collections of scientific anomalies including *The Book of the Damned* (1919) influenced numerous *science fiction writers with their iconoclastic scepticism and as sources of ideas. *The Outcast Manufacturers* (1906) is an underrated novel. 'Fortean' phenomena are events which seem to challenge the boundaries of accepted scientific knowledge, and the *Fortean Times* (founded as *The News* in 1973, and renamed in 1976) investigates such phenomena.

Fortnightly Review (1865–1934) An influential and respected literary periodical, monthly from November 1866. Almost all numbers ran a serialized novel; the first contained a chapter of Anthony *Trollope's *The Belton Estate* and a part of Walter Bagehot's *The English Constitution*. Positivist and anti-orthodox, the first editor, G. H. *Lewes, and his successor John Morley published work by *Thackeray, George *Eliot, Matthew *Arnold, T. H. *Huxley, George *Meredith, D. G. *Rossetti, Leslie *Stephen, Walter *Pater, and Thomas *Hardy, among others. The *Review* later published Henry *James, George *Gissing, Rudyard *Kipling, and H. G. *Wells. It survived from 1934 until 1954 as the *Fortnightly*, and was then incorporated in the *Contemporary Review*.

Fortunes of Nigel, The A novel by Walter *Scott, published 1822. The novel, set in 17th-century London, vividly portrays its historical characters, including King James VI and I, and draws on Scott's reading of Elizabethan and Jacobean dramatists for the vivid descriptions of Alsace.

FOUCAULT, Michel (1926–84) French philosopher, literary critic, and historian. His early work, notably *Folie et déraison: histoire de la folie à l'âge classique* (1961: *Madness and Civilization*), *Les Mots et les choses* (1966: *The Order of Things*), *L'Archéologie du savoir* (1969: *The Archaeology of Knowledge*), and *Surveiller et punir: naissance de la prison* (1975: *Discipline and Punish*), is devoted to the history of institutions (scientific, medical, penal, etc.) and the discourses on which their power is founded (*see* STRUCTURALISM). It expresses a libertarian distrust of the ways in which modern institutions regulate knowledge and submit people to the control of 'experts'. His later work includes a three-volume history of sexuality, left incomplete at his death: *La Volonté de savoir* (1976: *The Will to Knowledge*), which argues that sex became controlled by medical discourse in the 19th century, *L'Usage des plaisirs* and *Le Souci de soi* (both 1984: *The Use of Pleasure* and *The Care of the Self*). He had a strong influence on American historical and literary studies, notably *New Historicism and the work of Edward *Said.

Four Ages In *Ovid's *Metamorphoses*, history has declined inexorably from the perfect Golden Age through the Silver and Bronze Ages to the miserable Iron Age when Astraea, goddess of justice, leaves the earth. The return of Astraea and the recovery of the Golden Age is an important literary motif from *Virgil to John *Dryden.

'Four Ages of Poetry, The' A literary essay by Thomas Love *Peacock, published 1820. It makes ironic use of the argument advanced by 18th-century cultural historians such as Johann Winckelmann, that as society progresses, poetry deteriorates in inevitable stages. P. B. *Shelley's reply, A *Defence of Poetry, takes Peacock's charges seriously and rebuts them.

Four Quartets A poem in four parts by T. S. *Eliot, published as a whole in New York in 1943; it comprises 'Burnt Norton', 'The Dry Salvages', and 'Little Gidding', all previously published separately.

The four quartets represent the four seasons and the four elements, the imagery of the first centres on a Cotswold garden, that of the second round a Somerset village (from where Eliot's own ancestor had departed in 1669 for the New World), the third mingles the landscapes of Missouri and New England, the landscapes of Eliot's youth; and the fourth was inspired by the landscape and history surrounding St John's Church, Little Gidding, Cambridgeshire. But all are concerned with time past and time present: 'Little Gidding', for example, interweaves the wartime London of the Blitz with the England of *Julian of Norwich. These were the first of Eliot's poems to reach a wide public (they were seen as a unifying force in the war years), and they succeeded in communicating in modern idiom the fundamentals of Christian faith and experience.

Four Sons of Aymon *See* AYMON.

fourteener A verse line of fourteen syllables, usually in iambic *metre and so with seven stresses. Such lines were favoured by some English poets in the 15th and 16th centuries, and slightly later but more notably by George *Chapman in his translation of the *Iliad.

Four Zoas, The A symbolic poem by William *Blake, originally entitled *Vala*, written and revised 1795-1804, described by John Beer (*Blake's Humanism*, 1968) as 'a heroic attempt to write the first psychological epic'. It presents characters familiar from Blake's earlier symbolic works (Urizen, Los, Orc, and others), elaborating his cosmic mythology in a framework of a 'Dream of Nine Nights'; this framework was possibly suggested by Edward Young's *Night Thoughts*, which Blake was illustrating at the same period. The Four Zoas appear to represent the four human faculties, once united, but then at war with one another until the final radiant vision of joy and peace when the eyes of the Eternal Man 'behold the depths of wondrous worlds'.

FOWLER, Karen Joy (1950-) American novelist, who uses the contrast between *science fiction and realism to rich effect. *Sarah Canary* (1991) offers several interpretations of 'Sarah's' identity. *The Jane Austen Book Club* (2004) explores the relationships of members of a discussion group.

FOWLES, John (1926-2005) Novelist. His first novel, *The Collector* (1963), a psychological thriller, was followed by *The Magus* (1966; rev. 1977), in which reality and illusion become increasingly difficult to differentiate. *The French Lieutenant's Woman* (1969) takes place largely in Lyme Regis in 1867 and is notable for Fowles's extensive use of authorial commentary and for the alternative endings he provides. *Daniel Martin* (1977) is a long, semi-naturalistic, semi-experimental account of a screenwriter and his relationships; *Mantissa* (1982) is an erotic fantasy. Fowles's last novel to be published, *A Maggot* (1985), reworks a real-life 18th-century murder mystery. His non-fiction includes *The Aristos* (1965), an idiosyncratic exposition of his 'personal philosophy', and *The Tree* (1979), which explores the influence of the natural world on his life and on his writing. Two volumes of *Journals* have so far been published (2003 and 2006).

FOX, George (1624-91) Founder of the Society of *Friends, or Quakers. He had no formal schooling, but was apprenticed to a shoemaker and a shepherd, and left home in 1643 in search of enlightenment. A charismatic crowd-puller, he taught that the inner light of the Spirit, not ordination, gave both men and women the right to preach, and that the faithful might worship in the fields, not 'steeple-houses' (churches). He opposed violence, oath-taking, and marks of social rank such as titles and hat-doffing. For these views he was often imprisoned. His travels, mostly on foot, extended to Ireland, Barbados, New England, the Netherlands, and Germany, and included many spiritual enlightenments, such as his vision of souls coming to Christ on Pendle Hill in 1652. He married Margaret *Fell, a widow, in 1669. His *Journal*, revised by a committee under the superintendence of William *Penn and published in 1694, is one of the great visionary works of world literature.

FOXE, John (1516/17-87) Martyrologist; he became a fellow of Magdalen College, Oxford, but resigned his fellowship in 1545, being unwilling to conform to the statutes in religious matters. In 1554 he retired to the Continent, and issued at Strasbourg his *Commentarii Rerum in Ecclesia Gestarum* (the earliest version of what was to become his *Acts and Monuments*). He was employed at Basle as a proof-reader for Johann Oporinus, who published Foxe's allegorical verse drama *Christus Triumphans* (1556), and the new version of his Protestant martyrology *Rerum in Ecclesia Gestarum . . . Commentarii* (1559). On his return to England he was ordained priest by Grindal in 1560, and in 1564 joined John Day, the printer, who in 1563 had issued the English version of the *Rerum in Ecclesia Gestarum . . . Commentarii* as *Acts and Monuments*, popularly known as the *Book of Martyrs*. He preached his much-reprinted *Sermon of Christ Crucified* at Paul's Cross in 1570. His edition of Cranmer's canon laws *Reformatio Legum Ecclesiasticarum* appeared in 1571. Four editions of the *Acts and Monuments* (1563, 1570, 1576, and 1583) appeared in the author's lifetime; the 1641 edition contains a memoir of Foxe, attributed to his son Simeon.

FRAME, Janet Paterson (1924–2004) New Zealand writer, of Scottish parentage. Misdiagnosed as a schizophrenic, she spent several harrowing years undergoing treatment, an experience that coloured her work. Her first book, *The Lagoon* (1952, stories), was followed by *Owls Do Cry* (1957, novel, published in Britain in 1961), in which many circumstances of her life are mirrored. Other novels, which exhibit her gifts as a stylist, include *The Rainbirds* (1968) and *The Carpathians* (1988). She also published three volumes of autobiography—*To the Island* (1982), *An Angel at my Table* (1984), and *The Envoy from Mirror City* (1985)—which were made into a film by Jane Campion under the title of the second volume; the short story collections *The Reservoir and Other Stories* (1966) and *You Are Now Entering the Human Heart* (1983); and a volume of poetry, *The Pocket Mirror* (1967).

Framley Parsonage A novel by Anthony *Trollope, published in volume form 1861, fourth in the *'Barsetshire' series. Serialized in the newly founded *Cornhill Magazine* (January 1860–April 1861), the novel became Trollope's first popular success. Characters include Mark Robarts, an ambitious young clergyman, and the proud, impoverished curate Mr Crawley.

Francesca da Rimini *See* PAOLO AND FRANCESCA.

Francis (François) De Sales, St (1567–1622) Bishop of Geneva and spiritual writer, born in Savoy and educated in Paris and Padua. He was famed in his lifetime for converting Calvinists and ministering to the poor. His best-known works, *An Introduction to the Devout Life* and *Treatise on the Love of God*, were frequently translated into English.

FRANCIS of Assisi, St (Giovanni Francesco Bernardone) (1181/2–1226) A wealthy young man, he experienced a spiritual crisis, after which he lived in solitude and prayer, devoting himself to the relief of the poor, the sick, and lepers. He was joined by disciples for whom he drew up the first Rule of St Francis in 1209. The special emphases of his teaching were poverty and love of nature. Two years before his death, he is said to have discovered on his body the stigmata, the marks made by the nails of Christ's crucifixion. The *Fioretti de San Francisco* (*Little Flowers of St Francis*) is a 14th-century Italian narrative, partly legendary, of the doings of St Francis and his first disciples. He occurs with St Dominic, the founder of the Dominicans, in *Dante's *Paradiso*, XII.

FRANK, Anne (1929–45) Born in Germany; she fled to the Netherlands from Nazi persecution with her family in 1933. *The Diary of a Young Girl*, first published in English in 1952, describes Anne's life in hiding in Amsterdam during the German occupation. The family were betrayed in 1944 and Anne died in Bergen-Belsen concentration camp. The Diary is an important work in the literature of the *Holocaust, and there have been stage and screen adaptations.

Frankenstein, or The Modern Prometheus (1818) A *Gothic tale of terror by Mary *Shelley. In her preface she records that she, P. B. *Shelley, and Lord *Byron had spent the wet summer of 1816 in Switzerland reading German ghost stories; all three agreed to write tales of the supernatural, of which hers was the only one to be completed.

Technically an *epistolary novel, told through the letters of Walton, an English explorer in the Arctic, the tale relates the exploits of Frankenstein, an idealistic Genevan student of natural philosophy, who discovers the secret of imparting life to inanimate matter. Collecting bones from charnel-houses, he constructs the semblance of a human being and gives it life. The creature, endowed with supernatural strength and size and terrible in appearance, inspires loathing in whoever sees it. Lonely and miserable (and educated in human emotion by studies of *Goethe, *Plutarch, and *Paradise Lost), it turns upon its creator, and, failing to persuade him to provide a female counterpart, eventually murders his brother, his friend Clerval, and his bride Elizabeth. Frankenstein pursues it to the Arctic to destroy it, but dies in the pursuit, after relating his story to Walton. The monster declares that Frankenstein will be its last victim, and disappears to end its own life. Frequently filmed, the tale has been regarded as the origin of modern *science fiction, though it is also a version of the myth of the noble savage, portraying a nature essentially good corrupted by ill treatment. It is also remarkable for its description of nature, which owes much to the Shelleys' admiration for *Wordsworth, *Coleridge, and in particular *The Rime of the *Ancient Mariner*.

FRANKLIN, Benjamin (1706–90) Political writer and autobiographer, born in Boston, Massachusetts, largely self-educated. In 1724–5 he worked in a London printing house. After returning to Philadelphia, he set up his own press, from which he issued the *Pennsylvania Gazette*. He acquired a wide reputation by his occasional writings, especially *Poor Richard's*

Almanack (1733–58), the best known of American *almanacs. He was active as a public figure, founding the American Philosophical Society and the academy that became the University of Pennsylvania. In 1757 he travelled to England as agent for the colonies, where he mixed widely in intellectual society (his friends including Edmund *Burke, David *Hume, Adam *Smith, William Strahan, and Joseph *Priestley) and contributed to the controversies that caused the breach with England. He returned home in 1774 and, after helping to draft the Declaration of Independence, travelled to France as ambassador. Upon his return in 1785 he continued to be active in public affairs, and signed the Constitution as a member of the Federal Constitutional Convention. His *Autobiography* was published in England in 1793 (translated from the French), in America in 1818. Franklin's prose was much admired in England.

FRANKLIN, Sir John (1786–1847) Arctic explorer, and author of two *Narratives* (1823 and 1828) of voyages to the Polar Sea. His final voyage of discovery in *Erebus* and *Terror* in search of the North-West Passage began in 1845. After nothing was heard of his progress, numerous relief expeditions were sent out, including one organized by his widow. Through Inuit testimony and the discovery of artefacts and human remains, they established that all 129 members had died. Their fate, including claims of survival cannibalism, continues to exert a powerful fascination.

'Franklin's Tale, The' See CANTERBURY TALES, 12.

FRANZEN, Jonathan (1959–) American novelist who achieved critical and commercial success with his third novel, *The Corrections* (2001). *Freedom* (2010), another extensive family saga, with references to *Tolstoy, was preceded by *How to Be Alone* (2002), a collection of essays, and *The Discomfort Zone* (2006), a memoir.

FRASER, Lady Antonia (1932–) Née Pakenham, biographer, broadcaster, anthologist, and writer of mystery stories. She married Harold *Pinter in 1980; *Must You Go?* (2010) is a memoir of their life together. Her readable and scholarly biographies include lives of *Mary Queen of Scots (1969), Oliver Cromwell (1973), and *James I of England (1974). Her female detective Jemima Shore was introduced in *Quiet as a Nun* (1977). Amongst Fraser's other

books are *The Gunpowder Plot: Terror and Faith in 1605* (1997) and *Marie Antoinette: The Journey* (2001). She received a DBE in 2011.

FRASER, George MacDonald (1925–2008) Novelist and screenwriter, born in Carlisle; after joining the army in 1943, he served in Burma, the subject of his memoir, *Quartered Safe Out Here*, 1992. He also published *historical fiction such as *Black Ajax* (1997). But his most celebrated achievement is his sequence of rumbustiously satiric novels (and three stories published as *Flashman and the Tiger*, 1999) which debunk Victorian imperialism by chronicling the privately disreputable but publicly acclaimed military career of the cowardly bully Harry *Flashman, a character from Thomas Hughes's *Tom Brown's Schooldays*. From *Flashman* (1969) to *Flashman on the March* (2005), the novels combine meticulous historical research and a remarkable flair for capturing period slang combined with narrative gusto.

Fraser's Magazine (1830–82) A general and literary Tory journal, founded by William *Maginn and Hugh Fraser, which provided competition for *Blackwood's Magazine*. Among notable contributors were James *Hogg, S. T. *Coleridge, Robert *Southey, Thomas Love *Peacock, Thomas *Carlyle, Harrison *Ainsworth, W. M. *Thackeray, and John *Ruskin.

FRAYN, Michael (1933–) Novelist and playwright, his ten novels include *The Russian Interpreter* (1966), *Towards the End of the Morning* (1967, a comedy of Fleet Street life), *Headlong* (1999), and *Spies* (2002). His stage comedies include *Alphabetical Order* (1975), again with a background of journalism; *Donkeys' Years* (1976), based on a college reunion; *Noises Off* (1982), a farce of theatre life; and he has produced versions of virtually all of the plays of Anton *Chekhov. *Benefactors* (1984) a comedy, was followed by *Copenhagen* (1998), a tense, lucid drama about the unexplained meeting in 1941 in Occupied Denmark of German physicist Werner Heisenberg and his Danish mentor Niels Bohr, *Democracy* (2003), a play set in 1960s Berlin, and *Afterlife* (2008), which draws upon Hugo von *Hofmannsthal's 1911 play *Jedermann* (Everyman).

FRAZER, J. G. (Sir James George) (1854–1941) Scottish anthropologist and classical scholar. Fellow of Trinity College, Cambridge, from 1879, he was appointed to the first chair of Social Anthropology, at Liverpool, in 1907, but returned to Trinity in 1908. *The Golden Bough*

(1890; expanded in 12 vols, 1906–15) is a vast and enterprising comparative study of the beliefs and institutions of mankind, offering the thesis that man progresses from magical through religious to scientific thought. Its discussion of fertility rites, the sacrificial killing of kings, the dying god, and the scapegoat figure caught the literary imagination, and its most lasting influence may be seen in the works of D. H. *Lawrence, T. S. *Eliot, Ezra *Pound, and Naomi *Mitchison. Frazer's many other works include *Totemism and Exogamy* (1910) and *Folklore in the Old Testament* (1918).

FREDERIC, Harold (1856–98) American novelist and journalist, best known for his novel *The Damnation of Theron Ware* (1896; UK title *Illumination*). This centres on the treatment of a *Methodist minister and reflects the materialist priorities of Reconstruction in the period following the Civil War.

FREDERICK THE GREAT, of Prussia (1712–86) Ruled as king from 1740 until his death. He was an able administrator and military commander, as well as a man of considerable culture, and he greatly enhanced Prussian power. Frederick fostered strong links with the French Enlightenment, and he and *Voltaire were mutually admiring correspondents. He despised the German language, preferring both to speak and write in French. Several of his poems were published in London with great success. He was the subject of a biography by Thomas *Carlyle, entitled *The History of Frederick II of Prussia Called Frederick the Great* (6 vols, 1858–65), in which he is described as 'a questionable hero'.

free indirect style A way of narrating characters' thoughts or utterances that combines some of the features of third-person report with some features of first-person direct speech, allowing a flexible and sometimes ironic overlapping of internal and external perspectives. Free indirect style (a translation of French *style indirecte libre*) dispenses with tag-phrases ('she thought', etc.), and adopts the idiom of the character's own thoughts, including indicators of time and place, as *She'd leave here tomorrow*, rather than 'She decided to leave that place the next day'. The device was exploited by some 19th-century novelists such as Jane *Austen and Gustave *Flaubert, and has since been widely adopted.

FREEMAN, Mary Eleanor Wilkins (1852–1930) American novelist and short story writer, born in Randolph, Massachusetts. Like Sara Orne *Jewett, she produced local colour

fiction which describes the waning of *Puritanism, for example in her first collections *A Humble Romance* (1887) and *A New England Nun* (1891). *Goody Two-Shoes* (1883) is the best known of her short stories for children.

free verse A term loosely used from the early years of the 20th century to describe many forms of irregular, syllabic, or unrhymed verse, freed from the traditional demands of *metre; also known as *vers libre*. Some 19th-century poets, notably William *Blake and Walt *Whitman, practised kinds of free verse, but its widespread adoption was encouraged by Ezra *Pound and his *imagist associates, while their contemporaries T. S. *Eliot, D. H. *Lawrence, and Edith *Sitwell were also notable, and in their time controversial, for their free verse poems.

FRENCH, Marilyn (1929–2009) American novelist and feminist writer. *The Women's Room* (1977) was the first exploration of her central fictional theme: the institutionalized assumptions of male dominance which put women automatically at a disadvantage. French produced a number of attacks on sexism including *The War against Women* (1992) and *From Eve to Dawn: A History of Women in Three Volumes* (2002). *Beyond Power* (1985) is a collection of her essays. Her last novel, *The Love Children* (2009), is set in the American 1960s.

French Revolution, The: *A History* (1837) The historical work by which Thomas *Carlyle established his reputation. In three volumes ('The Bastille', 'The Constitution', and 'The Guillotine'), it opens with the death of Louis XV in 1774, covers the reign of Louis XVI, the period which included the assembly of the States General, the fall of the Bastille, the Constituent and Legislative Assemblies, the flight of the king to Varennes, the Convention, the trial and execution of the king and queen, the reign of terror, and the fall of Robespierre, and extends to 5 October 1795, when Bonaparte quelled the insurrection of the Vendémiaire, the title of the last chapter being 'The Whiff of Grapeshot'. A work of great descriptive power, it was admired by Charles *Dickens, and was in part the inspiration of *A *Tale of Two Cities*.

FRENCH-SHELDON, May (1847–1936) Travel writer and explorer, born in Pennsylvania. She was inspired by the example of her friend H. M. *Stanley to undertake a three-month trek to Mount Kilimanjaro (Tanzania). Her experiences and discoveries were recounted in *Sultan to Sultan: Adventures among the Masai and Other*

Tribes of East Africa (1892), which became a best-seller on both sides of the Atlantic. In 1903, she travelled to the Belgian Congo (Democratic Republic of Congo) at the behest of the campaigning newspaper editor W. T. *Stead. In later life she lectured widely in the USA, where her reputation as a female explorer made her a heroine to many women in the 1910s and 1920s.

FRENEAU, Philip Morin (1752-1832) The 'poet of the American Revolution', born in New York. He lived for a while (1775-8) in the West Indies, where he wrote poems inspired by the tropical atmosphere and landscape. In 1780, during the Revolutionary War, he was captured by the British, an experience which prompted the bitter satire of his poem *The British Prison-Ship* (1781). His first collection of verse, *Poems* (1786), was followed by various volumes of essays, poems, etc. His verse ranged from the satirical and patriotic to works such as 'The Wild Honey Suckle' (1786), a nature poem of delicacy and sensitivity which heralds *Romanticism.

FRERE, John Hookham (1769-1846) While at Eton Frere wrote a translation of *Brunanburh, and was one of the founders of *The Microcosm* periodical (1786-7). He contributed some accomplished satirical verse to *The *Anti-Jacobin*, including most of 'The Loves of the Triangles' (a parody of Erasmus *Darwin). He was one of the founders of the *Quarterly Review* in 1809. He is chiefly remembered as the inspirer of the style, stanza, and idiom of Lord *Byron's *Beppo* and *Don Juan*. In the Italian verses of Luigi Pulci he found a verse form and a colloquial voice which he felt could be adapted to English, and in 1817 he published the first two cantos of his mock epic *Prospectus and Specimen of an Intended National Work...by William and Robert Whistlecraft...Relating to King Arthur and his Round Table*. It gave *Byron what he wanted, and he describes *Beppo* as 'in or after the excellent manner of Mr Whistlecraft'. Frere also published lively metrical versions of *Aristophanes: *The Frogs* (1839) and *The Acharnians, The Knights*, and *The Birds* in 1840.

FREUD, Esther (1963-) Novelist, born in London, whose first novel, *Hideous Kinky* (1992, filmed 1998), draws on her experience as a child in Morocco with her hippie mother. (her father is the painter Lucian Freud). Her later novels similarly simple in style and

autobiographical in nature, include *Lucky Break* (2010).

FREUD, Sigmund (1856-1939) Born of Jewish parents at Freiberg in the present day Czech Republic, and famous as the founder of psychoanalysis. For most of his adult life he lived and worked in Vienna, but in 1938, following Nazi Germany's annexation of Austria, he fled and settled in London. His account of the dynamics of mental life evolved from his early study of clinical neuroses, and he developed his ideas in an extensive series of essays and volumes, from his famous work on dreams (1900) and the development of sexuality in children (1905) to late works applying his insights to questions of society and religion in the 1920s and 30s. Psychoanalytic ideas have had a profound and lasting effect on literature itself, on criticism, and on literary and cultural theory. Many of Freud's concepts, often in simplified form, have become commonly known— e.g. Oedipus complex, repression, the death instinct, penis envy, narcissism, 'Freudian' slips, phallic symbolism (about which he was sceptical), and his formulation of mental structure as a division between 'Id, the Ego, and the Superego'. The significance for both biographers and novelists of Freud's stress on the formative experiences of childhood is obvious, and in *Elizabeth and Essex* (1928) Lytton *Strachey produced what is possibly the first consciously Freud-oriented biography; its many successors include Leon Edel's life of Henry *James. Freud's works were made available in English by James Strachey, Lytton's brother, in the *Standard Edition of the Complete Psychological Works of Sigmund Freud* (24 vols, 1953-73; currently being revised). See PSYCHOANALYTIC CRITICISM.

'Friar's Tale, The' See CANTERBURY TALES, 7.

FRIEL, Brian (1929-) Irish playwright, born to a Catholic family in Omagh, Co. Tyrone. Friel began as a short story writer and his continuing interest in direct narration is reflected in the monologues in *Faith Healer* (1979) and *Molly Sweeney* (1994). In his first international success, *Philadelphia, Here I Come!* (1964), different actors play the protagonist's social and private selves. *The Freedom of the City* (1973), the much-revived *Translations* (1980), and *Making History* (1988) explore the gulf between experience and its public representation in explicitly political terms. *Dancing at Lughnasa* (1990) was filmed with Meryl Streep and

Michael Gambon in 1998. Friel has adapted works by *Chekhov and *Turgenev.

FRIEL, George (1910–75) Scottish novelist; his novels include *The Boy who Wanted Peace* (1964), *Grace and Miss Partridge* (1969), and the widely admired *Mr Alfred, MA* (1972). His short stories were collected in 1992 as *A Friend of Humanity*.

Friend A weekly periodical edited and largely written by Samuel Taylor *Coleridge in the Lake District, 1809–10. It was the first to publish early sections of Wordsworth's *Prelude*. In its final three-volume book form of 1818, Coleridge transformed it into a substantial series of interlinked essays 'to aid in the formation of fixed principles in politics, morals, and religion, with literary amusements interspersed'.

Friends, Society of (Quakers) A religious society founded in 1648–50 by George *Fox, distinguished by faith in the Inner Light, the spiritual equality of men and women, refusal of oaths, plain egalitarian dress, language, and manners, and antagonism to paid clergy and forms of worship. The movement was regarded as subversive by both the Protectorate and the restored monarchy, and heavily persecuted. Each member was also a minister, and the message was carried to the Netherlands, Rome, America, and Turkey. Margaret *Fell first declared the peace principle for which Friends are famous at the Restoration, when a quietist ethic succeeded the revolutionary phase. Quakerism encouraged literacy among people of all ranks. Six hundred and fifty Friends published 3,853 documents before 1700, 82 of the authors being women. The Society has pioneered social reform. The name 'Quakers' reflected the derisive public reaction to the 'quaking' convulsions of early Friends when seized by the power of the Inner Light. *See also* PENN, WILLIAM; NAYLER, JAMES.

Friendship's Garland (1871) A satirical collection of essays in letter form by Matthew *Arnold, originally printed in the *Pall Mall Gazette*. The principal imaginary correspondent is a Prussian, Arminius, Baron von Thunder-ten-Tronckh (a descendant of a character in Voltaire's *Candide*). Through him Arnold expresses his mockery of the English Philistine as represented by Bottles, a wealthy manufacturer; of narrow Liberal reform as represented by the 'deceased-wife's -sister' Act; of the *Daily Telegraph* and its naive patriotism, and of English foreign and educational policy. Arminius believes in the

application of 'Geist' or 'Intelligence', which the English persistently undervalue.

FROISSART, Jean (1337–after 1404) French chronicler and poet. His chronicles record the chivalric exploits of the nobles of England and France from 1325 to 1400. They were translated into English by John Bourchier (Lord Berners) in 1523–5. As author of lively personal *lais* and ballades he influenced *Chaucer.

FROST, Robert Lee (1874–1963) American poet, he moved at the age of 10 from San Francisco to the New England farm country of which his poetry was to be so deeply expressive. In 1912 he came to England, where he published his first volumes of poems, *A Boy's Will* (1913) and *North of Boston* (1914), which contains 'Mending Wall' and 'The Death of the Hired Man'; he met the *Georgian poets, and formed a close friendship with Edward *Thomas. Upon his return to New England in 1915 he settled in New Hampshire. His volumes include *Mountain Interval* (1916), which contains 'Birches' and 'The Road Not Taken'; *New Hampshire* (1923); *Collected Poems* (1930); *A Witness Tree* (1942); and *In the Clearing* (1962). He established himself as one of the most popular of 20th-century American poets, admired for the blend of colloquial and traditional in his verse. But beneath his country lore and wisdom lay a more troubled, combative, at times destructive spirit, both in his life and work, expressed in such poems as 'Fire and Ice' (1923) and 'Bereft' (1928). Frost recited his poem 'The Gift Outright' at the 1961 inauguration of President Kennedy.

'Frost at Midnight' A blank verse poem by Samuel Taylor *Coleridge written at Nether Stowey, Somerset, in February 1798. Addressed to his sleeping child Hartley *Coleridge, it meditates on the poet's own boyhood, and magically evokes the countryside, ending on a note of rare and thrilling happiness.

FROUDE, James Anthony (1818–94) Historian and biographer, fellow of Exeter College, Oxford. He became alienated from the *Oxford Movement, and increasingly found relations with organized religion untenable. His religious doubts and sexual frustrations led to a controversial autobiographical novel, *The Nemesis of Faith* (1849). Obliged to resign his fellowship, Froude left for London, where he edited *Fraser's Magazine* 1860–74. He fell under the influence of Thomas *Carlyle, and shared with him the desire to dramatize history through its significant actors. His *History of England from the Death of Cardinal Wolsey to the Defeat of the Spanish Armada* (12 vols, 1856–70) was a distinguished work of scholarship. He was the first to publicize and glorify the deeds of the Elizabethan seamen, a topic to which he returned in his Oxford lectures on *English Seamen in the Sixteenth Century* (1892–4; pub. 1895). All his books, including his collected essays, *Short Studies in Great Subjects* (4 vols, 1867–83) were highly successful. In his later years he attracted controversy, and his *Reminiscences* of Carlyle (1881) and his *Letters and Memorials* of Jane Welsh *Carlyle (1883), caused an uproar by exposing the failings of Carlyle's marriage. Many contemporary readers interpreted his frank approach as a betrayal of Carlyle's memory; nevertheless, his impact on the work of future biographers was considerable. In 1892 he accepted the Regius chair of modern history at Oxford.

FRY, Christopher (1907–2005) Playwright, born in Bristol. He made his name with works that were hailed in the late 1940s as a sign of a new renaissance of poetic drama; his mystical and religious plays, including *A Sleep of Prisoners* (1951), were frequently compared to those of T. S. *Eliot, though the theatre-going public tended to prefer the ebullient optimism and exuberant word-play of his comedies, e.g. *A Phoenix Too Frequent* (1946), *The Lady's Not for Burning* (1949), and *Venus Observed* (1950). *The Dark is Light Enough* (1954) was less successful; the vogue for poetic drama proved short-lived and *Curtmantle* (1962), about Thomas *Becket, struck critics as dated.

FRY, Roger (1866–1934) Art critic and painter, born in London of a Quaker family, educated at King's College, Cambridge, where he was a member of the *Apostles. He organized two highly influential and controversial exhibitions of *'Post-Impressionist' paintings (a term he coined himself) at the Grafton Galleries in 1910 and 1912, and his collected essays (*Vision and Design*, 1920; *Transformations*, 1926) were also instrumental in spreading enthusiasm for modern French painting. He was closely associated with the *Bloomsbury Group, and his biography was written by Virginia *Woolf (1940).

FRYE, Northrop (1912–91) Canadian critic, author of *Fearful Symmetry* (1947), an influential defence of William *Blake's allegorical system, and *Anatomy of Criticism* (1957), which redirected American literary theory away from

the 'close reading' of *New Criticism and towards the larger meanings of literary genres, modes, and archetypes. His early work did much to redeem the genre of *romance, the subject of *The Secular Scripture* (1976). His many other works include *The Great Code: The Bible and Literature* (1982). His emphasis on the deeper 'codes' or generic structures under the surface of literature foreshadowed the later turn to *structuralism in literary studies.

Fudge Family in Paris, The (1818) A satire by Thomas *Moore on the English in Paris after the restoration of the Bourbons. It takes the form of letters written by or to various members of the Fudge family when visiting France, and includes inane descriptions of Paris by the mindless Fudge children, and pompous, sycophantic letters from their father to the British foreign secretary, Castlereagh.

FUGARD, Athol (1932–) South African playwright. He moved in 1958 to Johannesburg, where he worked for some time as clerk to the Native Commissioner's Court, an experience which sharpened his awareness of racial tension and inequality, the subject of much of his drama. His plays include *The Blood Knot* (1961; pub. 1963); *Boesman and Lena* (1968; pub. 1969), a sombre work figuring a derelict middle-aged couple of Coloured migrant workers, whose presence as they set up their shelter on the open stage has a symbolic quality akin to that of the characters of Samuel *Beckett; *Sizwe Bansi is Dead* (1972; pub. 1974, written with John Kani and Winston Ntshona), based on the problems created by the pass laws; *A Lesson from Aloes* (1980; pub. 1981); and *'Master Harold'…and the Boys* (1982; pub. 1983). *The Island* (1973), co-written with Kani and Ntshona, was performed at the *National Theatre in 2000 by Kani and Ntshona in their original parts as two prisoners, partly for a generation no longer aware of the political significance of Robben Island. Later plays such as *Sorrows and Rejoicings* (2002) and *Exits and Entrances* (2004) are memory plays; his most recent play is *The Train Driver* (2010). *Tsotsi* (1980; filmed 2005, Academy Award) is Fugard's only novel. The plays often take place on an almost bare stage and depend on the mesmeric power of the dialogue.

Fulgens and Lucrece A late 15th-century *interlude by Henry Medwall (*fl.*1486), regarded as the earliest known purely secular play in English.

FULLER, John (1937–) Poet and novelist, son of Roy *Fuller. His first volume of poetry was *Fairground Music* (1961); others include *Cannibals and Missionaries* (1972), *The Illusionists* (1980), *Stones and Fires* (1996), and *Song and Dance* (2008). His poems are diverse in range and material, extending from lyrics to pastiche verse epistles, from sonnets to unrhymed monologues, from humoresques to grave meditations. In collaboration with James *Fenton he published a collection of comic poems, *Partingtime Hall*, in 1987. A *Collected Poems* appeared in 1996. His novels include *Flying to Nowhere* (1983), a fantasy about a 16th-century abbot who thinks he has discovered the seat of the soul, *The Burning Boys* (1989), and *A Skin Diary* (1997).

FULLER, Margaret (1810–50) American author and feminist, born in Massachusetts; she was a founder and editor (1840–2) of *The *Dial*, the literary organ of the *Transcendental Club. In 1839–44 she conducted a series of conversations or seminars for educated women in Boston. One of the products of these discussions was her influential feminist tract *Women in the Nineteenth Century* (1845), which argues that woman as a spiritual being should be liberated from male-imposed social restrictions. In 1846 she went to Europe and settled in Italy. Her *Memoirs* (1852) were edited by Ralph Waldo *Emerson, W. H. Channing, and J. F. Clarke. She is said to have suggested the character of the magnetic and passionate Zenobia in Nathaniel *Hawthorne's *The *Blithedale Romance*.

FULLER, Roy (1912–91) Poet and novelist, born near Oldham. During the 1930s he contributed to left-wing literary magazines, including *New Verse*, and his first volume, *Poems* (1939), shows the influence of W. H. *Auden and Stephen *Spender. *Collected Poems 1936–1961* (1962), with work from several previous volumes, forms a link between the poets of the 1930s and the poets of the *Movement, in its lucid, ironic, detached tone, and its formal accomplishment. His later volumes, which include *From the Joke Shop* (1975) and *The Reign of Sparrows* (1980), while displaying an equal interest in technique, frequently strike a more personal note, particularly in the many sardonic reflections on old age and the ageing process. Fuller also published several novels, including, notably, *Image of a Society* (1956), which is a portrait of personal and professional conflicts in a northern provincial building society, narrated in a low-key, naturalistic, yet ironic manner. He was professor of poetry at Oxford, 1968–73. He also published three volumes of memoirs, *Sou-venirs* (1980), *Vamp till Ready* (1982), and *Home and Dry* (1984).

FULLER, Thomas (1608–61) Clergyman and historian. After the Restoration he became 'chaplain in extraordinary' to the king. He published *The History of the Holy War* (i.e. of the Crusades) in 1639; *The *Holy State and the Profane State* in 1642; *Good Thoughts in Bad Times* in 1645 (followed by two sequels); *A Pisgah-Sight of Palestine*, a topographical and historical work, in 1650. His popular *The Church-History of Britain; with the History of the University of Cambridge* (1655), covers from the birth of Christ to the execution of Charles I. *The History of the Worthies of England* (1662) is his best-known and most characteristic work. His writings are marked by a lively and eccentric curiosity, by 'fantastic caprices' (Leslie *Stephen), and by a fondness for aphorisms.

Furies *See* ORESTEIA.

Fuseli, (Füssli), Henry (1741–1825) Swiss artist who later settled in London. Fuseli's works show the powerful attraction of Edmund *Burke's ideas of the *sublime. Fuseli drew his subjects from *Shakespeare, *Milton, *Dante, *Ossian, and other poets. He made brilliant contributions to John Boydell's Shakespeare Gallery, and his famous painting *The Nightmare* (1782) was known throughout Europe. A learned artist, Fuseli shone in literary and artistic society in London. William *Blake, a constant friend, engraved some of Fuseli's designs and Fuseli wrote the preface to Blake's edition of Robert *Blair's *The Grave*. Mary *Wollstonecraft suffered from an obsessive passion for Fuseli.

Futurism A 20th-century avant-garde movement in Italian art, literature, and music, founded by Filippo *Marinetti in 1909 in Paris. Its programme, outlined in the *Futurist Manifesto*, was to break with the past and its academic culture and to celebrate technology, dynamism, violence, and power. In language and in poetry it advocated the destruction of traditional syntax, metre, and punctuation in the name of the 'free word'. Roger *Fry gave the movement a cautious welcome, and their work had a strong influence on Wyndham *Lewis, T. E. *Hulme, Ezra *Pound, Ford Madox *Ford, and the British *Vorticist movement. The movement petered out during the 1930s after Marinetti's incorporation into Fascist academic culture. Vladimir Vladimirovich Maiakovsky (1893–1930) was a leading Russian *Futurist.

Fyge (later Egerton), Sarah (1670–1723) Poet, born in London; on the publication of her poem *The Female Advocate*, written in response to Robert Gould, her father sent her to live in the country with relatives. She was also married, reluctantly, to an attorney, who died *c.*1695. The deficiencies of her second marriage, to a clergyman, Thomas Egerton, were revealed in a scandalous and unsuccessful divorce case of 1703. *Poems on Several Occasions* (1703) contains several poems lamenting the conventions that bind women. Delarivier *Manley caricatured her tangled attachments in *The New Atalantis* (1709).

Gabriel One of the archangels, who foretold the birth of John the Baptist to Zacharias and of Jesus to Mary (Luke 1: 11–20, 26–38). In Islam he is Jibril, the angel who revealed the *Qur'ān* to Muhammad.

GADDIS, William (1922–98) American novelist, born in New York. The hero of *The Recognitions* (1955), Wyatt Gwyon, has abandoned his training as a priest to become a forger of Old Masters. The book offers an extended satirical meditation on the lack of authenticity in contemporary culture. *J.R.* (1975), about an 11-year-old stock-market dealer, is conducted entirely in fractured, frequently comic dialogue. *Carpenter's Gothic* (1985) and *A Frolic of his Own* (1994) both satirize America's obsession with litigation. The posthumous *Agape Agape* (2002) is the monologue of an elderly man meditating on value in art. *The Rush for Second Place* (2002) gathers Gaddis's uncollected pieces.

GAIMAN, Neil (1960–) *Science fiction and *fantasy author, born in Portchester, near Portsmouth. His fantasy novels, short stories, screenplays (including *Beowulf*, 2007), children's books, and comic book scripts consistently explore aspects of storytelling. The 'Sandman' comic book 'A Midsummer Night's Dream', based on *Shakespeare's play, won the World Fantasy Award for short fiction. After collaborating with Terry *Pratchett on *Good Omens* (1990) he published novels, such as *Neverwhere* (1996), *Stardust* (1999; filmed 2007), *American Gods* (2001), and *Coraline* (2002; filmed 2009); graphic novels, often in collaboration with the artist Dave McKean; and various collections of short stories. All are marked by an erudite sensitivity to the dark undercurrents of folklore and the potential for humour in fantasy and *horror. His *The Graveyard Book* (2008), a novel for children, won the 2009 Newbery Medal.

GAIMAR, Geffrei (*fl. c.*1136–7) Author of *L'Estoire des Engleis*, an Anglo-Norman romance history in octosyllabic rhymed couplets covering the period from the Anglo-Saxon set-tlements to the death of William Rufus. Gaimar was probably a secular clerk of Norman blood.

Galahad, Sir (The Haute Prince) In *Malory, the son (by enchantment) of *Launcelot and *Elaine, daughter of King Pelles. He is predestined by his immaculate purity to achieve the Siege Perilous (*see* ROUND TABLE) and the *Grail, after the vision of which he dies in ecstasy.

GALILEO Galilei (1564–1642) Italian astronomer and physicist, born in Pisa of a Florentine family. In 1604 he demonstrated that unequal weights drop with equal velocity, an observation apocryphally said to be based on the dropping of weights from the leaning Tower of Pisa. In 1609 he assembled a telescope on the basis of reports of such an instrument in the Netherlands, and so discovered the moons of Jupiter, the phases of Venus, the configuration of the moon, and the stars invisible to the naked eye, all of which were described in *Sidereus Nuncius* (1610: 'Starry Messenger'). His two principal works were *Dialogo sopra i due massimi sistemi del mondo* (1632), in which Copernicanism is shown to be superior to the Ptolemaic cosmology, and *Discorsi intorno a due nuove scienze* (1638). Galileo's publications led him into conflict with the Inquisition; in 1634 he was compelled to repudiate Copernican cosmology (the story of his muttering 'eppur si muove'—'yet it does move'—after his recantation is apocryphal). Milton records his meeting with Galileo in *Areopagitica*.

GALLAGHER, Stephen (1954–) Screenwriter, novelist, and television director known for suspense, supernatural dramas, and *science fiction (he wrote two series of *Doctor Who* in the early 1980s). He adapted his novel *Chimera* (1982) for television.

galliambics Verses written in imitation of a *metre used by *Callimachus in Greek and by *Catullus in Latin. Requiring lines of sixteen syllables or more with awkwardly paired stresses, it is unusually difficult to reproduce this metre in English. Alfred *Tennyson's 'Boädicea' (1864) is a rare attempt.

GALLOWAY, Janice (1956–) Scottish novelist and short story writer. *The Trick is to Keep Breathing* (1990), a typographically experimental study of mental breakdown on a bleak housing estate, was followed by *Foreign Parts* (1994) and *Clara* (2002), the latter an exploration of the life of the pianist Clara Wieck, wife of Robert Schumann. *Blood* (1991) and *Where You Find It* (1996) collect brief fictions which combine social observation with a dark sense of the uncanny. She has also written poems and a libretto on Mary *Shelley (*Monster*, 2002). *This is Not About Me* (2008) is a memoir.

GALSWORTHY, John (1867–1933) Novelist and dramatist, born at Kingston Hill, Surrey. His writing career followed a chance meeting with Joseph *Conrad in 1893. The Forsyte family made its first appearance in a story in *Man of Devon* (1901). His early work was published under the pseudonym John Sinjohn. *The Island Pharisees* (1904), published under his own name, revealed his abiding interest in the effects of poverty and the constraints of convention. The first of the Forsyte novels, *The Man of Property*, appeared in 1906, followed by *In Chancery* (1920) and *To Let* (1921), which, together with two interludes, appeared collectively as *The *Forsyte Saga* in 1922. The second part of the Forsyte chronicles, containing *The White Monkey* (1924), *The Silver Spoon* (1926), *Swan Song* (1928), and the two interludes 'A Silent Wooing' and 'Passers By', was published as *A Modern Comedy* in 1929. In 1931 Galsworthy followed the immense success of the Forsyte books with a further collection of stories, *On Forsyte Change*.

Galsworthy first play was *The Silver Box* (1906)—a play about theft in which he employed a favourite device of 'parallel' families, one rich and one poor. This was the first of a long line of plays on social and moral themes. *Strife* (1909), an examination of men and managers in industry, was followed by *Justice* (1910), part of Galsworthy's long campaign against the practice of solitary confinement. His later plays included *The Skin Game* (1920); *Loyalties* (1922); and *Old English* (1924). Posthumous publications included *Collected Poems* (1934) and the 1935 trilogy *The End of the Chapter* (*Maid in Waiting*, 1931; *Flowering Wilderness*, 1932 and *Over the River*, 1933), relating the family history of the Charwells, cousins of the younger Forsytes. Galsworthy was awarded the *Nobel Prize for Literature in 1932.

GALT, John (1779–1839) Scottish novelist, born in Irvine, Ayrshire. While travelling in Europe in 1809 he met Lord *Byron, of whom he published a biography in 1830. He founded the town of Guelph in Canada (nearby Galt is named after him). As a result of intrigues by his enemies he returned to England heavily in debt and moved back to Ayrshire in 1834. Galt wrote poetry, drama, historical fiction, biography, memoirs, and travel books, but is chiefly remembered for the studies of rural life in western Scotland he thought of as 'theoretical histories' rather than novels: *The *Ayrshire Legatees* (1821), *Annals of the Parish* (written 1813, published 1821), *The *Entail* (1823), *The *Provost* (1822), and *The Member* (1832).

GALTON, Sir Francis (1822–1911) Eugenicist and travel writer. He inaugurated the *Royal Geographical Society's 'Hints to Travellers' booklets, which, with his own *The Art of Travel* (1855), helped to popularize a serious approach to travel and recording information. Galton broke his connection with the RGS over its proposed admission of women as fellows.

Game at Chess, A A satirical comedy by Thomas *Middleton, produced 1624, when it was acted for a record run of nine performances at the Globe until suppressed by the authorities. Six different transcripts in manuscript survive.

It deals allegorically with the rivalry of England and Spain (the White House and the Black House) and the project of the 'Spanish Marriage' (1623), the failed plan for Prince Charles to marry the Spanish infanta in 1623. The play, reflecting the popular dislike of the Spanish match, was enthusiastically received, but gave great offence to the Spanish ambassador and to *James I.

Gamelyn, The Tale of A verse romance of the mid-14th century in 898 lines of couplets. It survives in 25 manuscripts, including some of *The *Canterbury Tales*, where it is usually assigned to the Cook, although there is no evidence that Chaucer himself intended to use it. Gamelyn is the youngest of three brothers whose father leaves them his property in equal shares, but whose eldest brother cheats him of his entitlement. It has affinities with *As You Like It* and the legends of *Robin Hood.

Gamester, The A comedy by John Shirley, acted 1633, printed 1637. This was one of Shirley's most popular plays, adapted (and sentimentalized) by Charles *Johnson in 1712 as *The Wife's Relief* and by *Garrick in 1758 as

The Gamesters. Its main plot is taken from the **Heptameron* of Marguerite of Navarre.

Wilding, the title character, tells his wife of his intention to make love to his ward, her relation Penelope, but is duped in a double bed-trick. *The Gamester* is also the title of a play by Susannah *Centlivre and of a tragedy by Edward *Moore.

Gammer Gurton's Needle The second English comedy in verse (the first being **Ralph Roister Doister*), published 1575, having been acted 1566, at Christ's College, Cambridge. Its authorship has been attributed either to John Still, fellow of Christ's College, or to William Stevenson, also a fellow of the college and one of its leading spirits in dramatic activities.

It is written in rhymed long doggerel, and deals farcically with the losing and finding of the needle used to mend the garments of Hodge, Gammer Gurton's man, who becomes acutely aware that the needle is in the seat of his breeches.

GARCÍA LORCA, Federico (1898–1936) Spanish poet and dramatist. Lorca's early prose and poetry is pervaded with intense erotic anxiety and anticlerical anger, and shows that by 1918 he was aware of being homosexual. *Libro de poemas* (1921, *Book of Poems*) was published in Madrid; *Canciones* (1927 *Songs*). and *Romancero gitano* (1928, *Gypsy Ballads*) followed, but in 1929, depressed, and by then within the orbit of *Surrealism, Lorca fled to New York. His work from that period included the anguished poems published posthumously as *Poeta en Nueva York* (1940: *Poet in New York*). Back in Spain, he shot to fame as a dramatist with the tragedies *Bodas de sangre* (*Blood Wedding*, performed 1933, trans. Ted *Hughes, 1996) and *Yerma* (performed 1934). His last play, *La casa de Bernarda Alba* (*The House of Bernarda Alba*), was completed just before the outbreak of the Spanish Civil War: it was published posthumously in 1945. He was murdered by the Fascists in August 1936.

GARCÍA MÁRQUEZ, Gabriel (1927/8–) Colombian novelist, a key figure in the *Boom. His first novel, *La hojarasca* (1955, *Leaf Storm*) introduces the isolated fictional town of Macondo, which became the setting for his exuberant, tragicomic novel of *magic realism, *Cien años de soledad* (1967: *One Hundred Years of Solitude*), written in Mexico and recounting the lives of several generations of the Buendía family. García Márquez's work is constantly experimental, from his realist novella *El coronel no*

tiene quien le escriba (1958: *No One Writes to the Colonel*) to the complex novel of dictatorship *El otoño del patriarca* (1975: *The Autumn of the Patriarch*), and the fictional investigation of a murder in *Crónica de una muerte anunciada* (1981: *Chronicle of a Death Foretold*). *El amor en los tiempos del cólera* (1985, *Love in the Time of Cholera*), is an examination of love, memory, and old age, in the form of a popular romance. His later work includes *El general en su laberinto* (1989: *The General in his Labyrinth*), a re-creation of Simón Bolívar's final days, *Del amor y otros demonios* (1994: *Of Love and Other Demons*), and *Memoria de mis putas tristes* (2004: *Memories of my Melancholy Whores*). His collections of stories include *Los funerales de la Mamá Grande* (1962: *Big Mama's Funeral*) and *Doce cuentos peregrinos* (1992: *Strange Pilgrims*). His work is influenced by writing in English, especially that of William *Faulkner, Ernest *Hemingway, James *Joyce, and Virginia *Woolf, while he has inspired writers like Salman *Rushdie and Angela *Carter. He was awarded the *Nobel Prize for Literature in 1982; *Vivir para contarla* (*Living to Tell the Tale*), the first volume of his autobiography, appeared in 2002.

GARDAM, Jane (1928–) Novelist and short story writer, born in Coatham, North Yorkshire. Some of her books are written for teenagers but have attracted adult readers as well. *Bilgewater* (1976) is a journey of enlightenment through the snares of adolescence, whose dangers Gardam portrays with extraordinary insight, as she does in *A Long Way from Verona* (1971), a comic novel set in wartime Yorkshire. Although Gardam's work, such as *The Queen of the Tambourine* (1991), is very English in feel, her first volume of stories for adults, *Black Faces, White Faces* (1975), is set in Jamaica, while *Old Filth* (2004) describes the long-term psychological effects on an unsuccessful international lawyer of being sent 'home' to England as a child by his Raj parents. *The Man in the Wooden Hat* (2011) revisits the story from his wife Elisabeth's, point of view Gardam's collections of stories include *The Sidmouth Letters* (1978) and *Showing the Flag* (1989).

Garden of Cyrus, The (1658) By Sir Thomas *Browne, the companion piece to **Hydriotaphia*; treats of the occurrence of the quincunx (∴) or lozenge and the number five in man-made objects, primarily the plantations of the ancients, and then their buildings, other artefacts, and customs, in plants, in animals, and in traditional philosophy and theology. He chooses his 'bye and barren theme' partly to please the dedicatee, an ardent horticulturist, partly because 'Paradise succeeds the Grave'. By intertwining many heterogeneous observations he playfully demonstrates his ability to elaborate and digress.

GARDNER, Erle Stanley (1889–1970) American writer of crime fiction,who began publishing crime and mystery stories in the 1920s. In 1933 he began his long-running series of 82 narratives of Perry Mason, a lawyer-cum-detective, which combined crime investigation with courtroom dramas. At first narrated in the *hardboiled style of the inter-war period, Gardner's novels later softened their tone and were adapted for the *Perry Mason* television series 1957–66.

GARDNER, John (1933–82) American novelist; his *Grendel* (1971) retells the story of *Beowulf through the monster's voice. *The Sunlight Dialogues* (1972) opposes different viewpoints of America; other works, such as *Mickelsson's Ghosts* (1982), use supernatural or fantastic images without wholeheartedly embracing them.

GARFIELD, Leon (1921–96) Author, born in Brighton. Garfield is an excellent but underestimated writer of what he called 'that old-fashioned thing, the family novel'—heavily atmospheric adventures set in the 18th and 19th centuries, owing something to *Smollett and *Dickens, notably in *Black Jack* (1968). His self-consciously inventive style is best seen in his series of novellas, *Garfield's Apprentices* (1976–8), and his adaptation of Greek myths (with Edward Blishen), *The God Beneath the Sea* (1970), awarded the Carnegie Medal. He wrote the scripts for *Shakespeare: The Animated Tales* (BBC, 1992–4).

Gargantua See RABELAIS, FRANÇOIS.

GARIOCH, Robert (1909–81) The pen-name of Robert Garioch Sutherland, Scottish poet, born in Edinburgh. He spent three years from 1942 as a prisoner of war in Italy and Germany, an experience recalled in the self-deprecating prose of *Two Men and a Blanket* (1975). Garioch is known principally for his *Scots poems. *Selected Poems* (1966) was his first full-scale collection. Later volumes include *The Big Music* (1971) and *Doktor Faust in Rose Street* (1973). His poetry is witty, satirical, and amusing, with an underlying pessimism. His many verse translations—of *Pindar, George *Buchanan, Belli, Apollinaire, and others—

made almost as notable a contribution to the 20th century's refurbishment of Scots as his original work.

Garland, (Hannibal) Hamlin (1860–1940) American novelist, born in West Salem, Wisconsin. *Main-Travelled Roads: Six Mississippi Valley Stories* (1891) established him as an important practitioner of realism. Garland published many novels and an autobiography, *A Son of the Middle Border* (1917). He also published studies of prairie life and of the Native Americans in his chosen region, winning the 1922 Pulitzer Prize for biography.

GARNER, Alan (1934–) OBE, born in Congleton, Cheshire, arguably the most distinguished writer for children of the 20th century. *The Weirdstone of Brisingamen* (1960) and *The Moon of Gomrath* (1963) are fantasies based on an eclectic mixture of Norse and Celtic mythology. His subsequent books have been marked by extensive scholarly study of folklore, language and dialect, anthropology, and other fields, typified by *The Owl Service* (1967), based on a tale from the fourth branch of *The *Mabinogion. *Red Shift* (1973), which involves three parallel stories (Roman soldiers in savage surroundings, a Civil War massacre, and a contemporary teenage romance), pushed at the boundaries of the children's book in terms of both its sometimes brutal content and its highly oblique and sophisticated style. *The Stone Book Quartet* (1976–8) is composed of intricate and stylistically intense novellas depicting the coming of age of boys in four generations of the Garner family. Their remarkable reconstruction of rural Cheshire is revisited in *Strandloper* (1996), a novel for adults based on a true story of transportation to Australia, and *Thursbitch* (2003), which, in the manner of *Red Shift*, involves linked stories from different eras.

Garner has published many retellings of British folktales; his essays and talks are collected in *The Voice that Thunders* (1997).

GARNETT, Constance (1861–1946) Née Black, translator from Russian. She married Edward *Garnett in 1889 and paid her first visit to Russia in 1893, when she met *Tolstoy. Her first translation, Goncharov's *A Common Story*, was published in 1894 and her career as a translator finished 71 volumes and 40 years later with *Turgenev's *Three Plays* (1934). She brought to the British public the major works of *Chekhov, *Dostoevsky, *Gogol, *Tolstoy, and Turgenev.

GARNETT, David (1892–1981) Novelist and critic, son of Constance and Edward *Garnett.

His first, award-winning, novel, *Lady into Fox* (1922) was followed by another fable, *A Man in the Zoo* (1924), about a thwarted lover who donates himself as a specimen of *Homo sapiens* for exhibition in the zoo. *The Sailor's Return* (1925) describes the conflict between a sailor, his black African wife, and the Dorset villagers among whom they settle. *Aspects of Love* (1955) was made into a successful musical by Andrew Lloyd Webber. Garnett also wrote a biography, *Pocahontas, or The Nonpareil of Virginia* (1933), the semi-fictional *Beany-Eye* (1935), and three volumes of autobiography, *The Golden Echo* (1953), *The Flowers of the Forest* (1955), and *The Familiar Faces* (1962).

GARNETT, Edward (1868–1937) Son of Richard *Garnett and husband of Constance *Garnett. He published several volumes, including novels, plays, and critical works, but is chiefly remembered as publisher's reader for several successive firms, the last of which was Jonathan Cape. In this role he encouraged and advised many of the most important writers of the period, amongst them Joseph *Conrad, D. H. *Lawrence, Dorothy *Richardson, E. M. *Forster, and W. H. *Hudson.

GARNETT, Eve (1900–91) Artist and children's writer. She illustrated Evelyn Sharp's *The London Child* (1927), which moved her to produce a book of drawings, '*Is it Well with the Child?*' (1938). *The Family from One End Street* (1937; Carnegie Medal), which attempted sympathetically to portray working-class characters (Mr Ruggles is a dustman, his wife a washerwoman), has been accused of being patronizing, but is perhaps better seen as ahead of its time. There are two sequels.

GARNETT, Richard (1835–1906) Superintendent of the British Museum Reading Room from 1875, a post from which he resigned in 1884 to become chief editor of the library's first printed catalogue. His publications include verse biographies, and editions, including *Relics of Shelley* (1862), but he is best remembered for his collection of pagan tales *The Twilight of the Gods* (1888), some of which originally appeared in the *Yellow Book*. He was the father Edward *Garnett.

GARRICK, David (1717–79) Actor and dramatist, born in Hereford. He accompanied Samuel *Johnson, briefly his tutor, to London. His mythological burlesque *Lethe* was performed at Drury Lane in 1740. He made a successful London debut as Richard III. He wrote farces, including *The Lying Valet* (1741), *Miss in her Teens* (1747), *A Peep behind the Curtain* (1767), and *Bon Ton, or High Life above Stairs* (1775), adapted and produced Shakespeare plays, and collaborated with George *Colman the elder in *The *Clandestine Marriage* (1766). In 1747 he became a partner in the management of Drury Lane. His last appearance was in 1776. In 1769 he organized a grand 'Shakespeare Jubilee' at Stratford-upon-Avon, but lost over £2,000 when heavy rain forced him to cancel most of the three-day event. He did however stage a dramatic procession of Shakespeare characters, *The Jubilee*, successfully. Garrick's brilliance as an actor was celebrated in Churchill's *Rosciad* (1761) and contemporaries responded warmly to his imaginative identifications with his characters.

GARTH, Sir Samuel (1660/61–1719) Physician and member of the *Kit-Cat Club. His *The Dispensary* (1699), a *mock-epic poem ridiculing the opposition of apothecaries to the establishment of a dispensary to offer discounted medical supplies to the poor, influenced his friend Alexander *Pope's *Rape of the Lock*. Garth wrote the epilogue to Joseph *Addison's *Cato*, and a *topographical poem, *Claremont* (1715), in the vein of *Windsor-Forest*.

GASCOIGNE, George (?1534/5–77) Soldier and poet, from a prominent Bedfordshire family. His poems and plays were initially published, supposedly without his authority, as *A Hundred Sundry Flowers* (1573); *The Posies of George Gascoigne* (1575) was his own corrected and augmented edition. This contained a variety of secular and devotional verse, including 'The Delectable History of Dan Bartholmew of Bath'; a verse account of his adventures in the Netherlands, 'The Fruits of War'; two plays written for performance at Gray's Inn in 1566, *Supposes*, a prose comedy based on *Ariosto's *I suppositi*, and *Jocasta*, a blank verse tragedy purportedly based on *Euripides*, but actually translated from Lodovico Dolce; a strange Chaucerian novella of sexual intrigue, *The Adventures of Master *F.J.*; and *Certain Notes of Instruction Concerning the Making of Verse or Rhyme in English*, a pithy and pioneering account of English versification. Gascoigne's other works include *The Glass of Government: A Tragical Comedy* (1575), *The Drum of Dooms Day* (1576), and *The *Steel Glass: A Satire* (1576). Gascoigne's achievement has been overshadowed by the later Elizabethan poets who followed in his path, such as Edmund *Spenser, Christopher *Marlowe, and Philip *Sidney; but he was an innovator in a wide variety of literary forms.

GASCOYNE, David (1916–2001) Poet and translator. He published *Roman Balcony* (1932), aged 16. *A Short Survey of Surrealism* (1935) established him as a champion of that movement and an English writer unusually aware of European literature. He translated many of the French Surrealists, and his own work shows the influence of writers such as Paul Éluard, Guillaume Apollinaire, and Tristan Tzara (1896–1963). *Man's Life Is his Meat* (1936), *Hölderlin's Madness* (1938), and *Night Thoughts* (BBC broadcast 1955, published 1956) were followed, after a long fallow period, by *Paris Journal 1937-39* (1979), *Selected Poems* (1994), and *Selected Verse Translations* (1996).

GASKELL, Elizabeth (Mrs Gaskell) (1810–65) Novelist. Born in London, she was brought up by her aunt in Knutsford, Cheshire (the original of 'Cranford' and of 'Hollingford' in **Wives and Daughters*). In 1832 she married William Gaskell, minister at the Cross Street Unitarian Chapel in Manchester; they had four daughters and a son who died in infancy. As a distraction from her sorrow at his death she wrote her first novel, **Mary Barton* (1848). It won the attention of Charles **Dickens, at whose invitation much of her work was first published in **Household Words* and *All the Year Round*. Her other full-length novels were **Cranford* (1853), **Ruth* (1853), **North and South* (1855), **Sylvia's Lovers* (1863), and **Wives and Daughters* (1866), which was left unfinished when Gaskell died suddenly of heart failure. She also wrote the first and most celebrated biography of Charlotte **Brontë—which caused a furore because it contained some allegedly libellous statements which had to be withdrawn—and many vivid short stories and novellas, including the fine *Cousin Phillis* (1864).

Gaskell was an active humanitarian, and in several of her novels she argued for the need for social reconciliation, for better understanding between employers and workers, between the respectable and the outcasts of society. She was a keen observer of human behaviour and speech, among both industrial workers in Manchester and farming and country-town communities, and a careful researcher of the background and technicalities of her novels. Her many friends included (besides Charlotte Brontë) John **Ruskin, the Carlyles, Charles **Kingsley, and Florence Nightingale (1820–1910). Her contemporaries classed her as a novelist with the Brontës and George **Eliot, but

although *Cranford* has always remained a favourite with the general reader her other novels were underrated in critical esteem for many years after her death.

GASS, William H. (1924–) American novelist and critic born in North Dakota. *Omensetter's Luck* (1966), a comparatively realist portrayal of Ohio life, was followed by *Willie Masters' Lonesome Wife* (1968), which combines experiments with photographs and typography. His later novels include *The Tunnel* (1995), written over 26 years, and *Middle C* (in progress, 2010).

GAUDEN, Dr John (1605–62) Reputed author of **Eikon Basilike*.

GAUDIER-BRZESKA, Henri (1891–1915) French sculptor and draughtsman, who came to London in 1910, where he became associated with avant-garde artists and writers. Some of his brilliantly accomplished pen and pencil line drawings were published in **Rhythm*. Gaudier, with Wyndham **Lewis and Ezra **Pound, founded the **Vorticist group in 1914, and contributed a Vorticist history of sculpture to the first issue of **Blast* which exalts the energy and intensity of primitive art and condemns the ideals of the Greeks and the Renaissance. Gaudier enlisted in the French army in 1914 and was killed in action. Pound republished several of his writings in *Gaudier-Brzeska: A Memoir* (1916).

GAVIN, Jamila (1941–) Indian-born writer for children Her books reflect her Anglo-Indian background, Britain's multicultural society, and her interest in history. The Surya Trilogy (1992-7) features partition; *Kamla and Kate* (1983) is about a mixed-race friendship; *Coram Boy* (2000, stage adaption 2005) depicts the 18th-century trade in orphans.

Gawain (Walwain), Sir The eldest of the four sons of King Lot of Orkney and Arthur's sister Morgawse. His wife, in some stories, was Dame Ragnell and their son was Ginglain, the Fair Unknown (**Libeaus Desconus). In the Arthurian legends he is prominent from the first 12th-century stories in which he is the leading knight, courageous, pure, and courteous. In later versions his excellence is surpassed by that of Launcelot. In **Geoffrey of Monmouth he is Arthur's ambassador to Rome; in **Malory he becomes at the end the bitter enemy of Launcelot, who has accidentally killed Gawain's beloved younger brothers Gaheris and Gareth, and also Agravain, who betrayed the affair between Launcelot and Guinevere. Gawain is killed when Arthur lands at Dover before the final battle with Mordred. The most celebrated single adventure of Gawain is the one described in *Sir *Gawain and the Green Knight*. In Malory his characterization varies according to the source being followed; he is a great and memorably conflicted character in the *Morte Arthur Saunz Guerdon* (the eighth of the eight *Works* ed. by Vinaver).

Gawain and the Green Knight, Sir A

greatly admired alliterative poem in the north-west Midlands dialect, believed to date from the second half of the 14th century, the only manuscript of which is the famous Cotton Nero A. X which is also the sole manuscript of *Pearl*, *Patience*, and *Cleanness*. It is in 2,530 lines in long-lined alliterative stanzas of varying length, each ending with a *'bob and wheel'. The poem is divided into four 'fitts', or narrative divisions:

Fitt 1: Arthur and his court are seated at a New Year's feast in Camelot waiting for a marvel when a huge green man enters, bearing an axe and a holly bough. He challenges a knight to cut off his head on condition that the knight agrees to have his own head cut off a year hence. Gawain accepts the challenge and cuts off the green knight's head; to the astonishment of all, the knight picks it up and rides away.

Fitt 2: A year later Gawain sets off to keep his side of the bargain. After riding through grim landscapes in wintry weather, Gawain comes upon a beautiful castle where he is graciously received. The lord of the castle, Bertilak de Hautedesert, makes an agreement with Gawain that each day he will hunt in the fields and Gawain in the castle; at the end of the day they will exchange spoils.

Fitt 3: For three consecutive days, the lord hunts and Gawain, famous for his skill and prowess in love, is amorously approached by the beautiful lady of the castle, who gives him one kiss on the first day, two on the second, and on the third day three kisses and a girdle which has magic properties that will save his life. Each evening Gawain exchanges the kisses with his host for the animals slain in the hunt; but on the third evening he keeps the girdle (thus breaking his bargain), to protect him in the imminent meeting with the green knight.

Fitt 4: Gawain is directed to the green knight's chapel where he kneels to receive his blow. Twice the knight feints at him, and the third time he makes a cut in Gawain's neck. Then he explains that he is Bertilak, and that the cut in Gawain's neck was sustained because of his infidelity in keeping the girdle. Gawain bitterly

curses his failing and the snares of women; but the green knight applauds him and, on Gawain's return to Camelot, Arthur's courtiers declare that they will all wear a green girdle for Gawain's sake. The poem's closing words, 'Hony Soyt Qui Mal Pence', may connect it with the founding of the Order of the Garter. Generally agreed to be one of the greatest and most enigmatic poems in Middle English, new translations into modern English have been made by the distinguished poets Simon *Armitage (2006) and Bernard *O'Donoghue (2007).

GAY, John (1685–1732) Poet and dramatist.

In 1708 he published, with Aaron *Hill's encouragement, a burlesque poem, *Wine*, and in 1711 an essay, *The Present State of Wit*. *Rural Sports* (1713) is a *georgic poem similar in some of its darker aspects to his friend Alexander *Pope's *Windsor-Forest*, and *The Fan* (1713) is reminiscent of the mock-heroic style of *The *Rape of the Lock*. The *Shepherd's Week* (1714) ridiculed the simplicity of the pastorals of Ambrose *Philips. Gay's satirical farce *The What D'ye Call It* was produced successfully in 1715. *Trivia*, an urban georgic poem, appeared in 1716. With Pope and John *Arbuthnot he wrote a controversial satirical comedy, *Three Hours after Marriage*, in 1717. His poem in *ottava rima* 'Mr Pope's Welcome from Greece', written *c.*1720 and first published in 1776, celebrated his friend's completion of the *Iliad* translation; it gives a vivid picture of the members of the *Scriblerus Club and of many other contemporary figures. The first series of his popular *Fables*, illustrated with plates, appeared in 1727, but great success came in 1728 with *The *Beggar's Opera* and its sequel *Polly*, which was banned from the stage but sold well on publication in 1729. He also wrote the libretti of Handel's *Acis and Galatea* (pub. 1732). He was buried in Westminster Abbey; his own epitaph was: 'Life is a jest, and all things show it; | I thought so once, and now I know it.' Various posthumous publications included a second series of more overtly political *Fables* (1738).

gay and lesbian literature A compara-

tively modern concept, although homosexual themes, occasionally explicit but more often coded, have been apparent in the literature of most cultures and countries almost from the outset, as in the Babylonian epic *Gilgamesh* (*c.*1700 BC). Although often bowdlerized by translators and editors, classical texts such as *Plato's *Symposium*, the Greek *Anthology*, and *Ovid's *Metamorphoses* provided models for later writers. *Shakespeare's *sonnets (1609), the first 126 of which are addressed to a young man, also caused editorial difficulties: John Benson (d. 1667) republished them in 1640, leaving out some sonnets altogether and regendering the pronouns of others. Other early texts, often drawing for their depiction of the various shades of male friendship upon *Theocritus' *Idylls* and the second of *Virgil's *Eclogues*, include Edmund Spenser's *Shepheardes Calender* (1579), Christopher Marlowe's *Edward II* (1594), and the poems of Richard *Barnfield.

With the exception of the fragmentary literary remains of *Sappho, lesbian writing lacks these strong classical precedents. Apart from extraordinary early figures like 'the English Sappho', Katherine *Philips, lesbian literature was born among the 'ephemera' in which women privately wrote down their affections for each other: letters, diaries, commonplace books. Among the most celebrated of these are the diaries of Eleanor Butler (?1739–1829) and Anne Lister (1791–1840).

The influence of bisexual libertines such as the earl of *Rochester (1647–80) and the marquis de Sade (1740–1814) looms over the Gothic novel, notably William Beckford's *Vathek* (1786) and Matthew Lewis's The *Monk* (1796), but homosexual literature proper dates from the late 19th century, expressing the newly pathologized concept of homosexuality as a lifelong condition. Although the trials of Oscar *Wilde caused an anti-homosexual backlash in literature, the ironic and melancholy poems about doomed youths in A. E. *Housman's A Shropshire Lad (1896) found a strong echo in the poetry of the First World War, notably that of Siegfried *Sassoon and Wilfred *Owen. Virginia Woolf's *Orlando* (1928) and the novels of Ronald *Firbank (1886–1926) effected a transition from 1890s decadence to camp modernism, but the difficulties of confronting contemporary homosexuality and lesbianism in a straightforward manner remained: E. M. *Forster felt unable to publish *Maurice*, written in 1913, 'until my death and England's', while Radclyffe *Hall's The Well of Loneliness (1928) was successfully prosecuted for obscenity. The mid-century produced much didactic, often apologetic fiction in which a central character was used to represent homosexual people in general. Many such novels ended in death, as Christopher *Isherwood noted while writing A Single Man (1964), which is arguably the first mainstream 'gay novel' Angus *Wilson did much to present homosexual characters as part of ordinary society, while writers such as Maureen *Duffy and Brigid *Brophy took a more oblique or experimental approach.

In poetry W. H. *Auden tended to omit third-person pronouns from his love lyrics, but younger poets such as Thom *Gunn were able to be more forthright. In the 1970s a new generation of writers emerged from the women's and gay liberation movements, notably Carol Anne *Duffy, and Mark Doty (1953–). Others include Edmund *White, Armistead *Maupin, Adam *Mars-Jones, Alan *Hollinghurst, Jeanette *Winterson, David Leavitt (1961–), and Sarah Waters (1966–). The widespread popularity in particular of Maupin's Tales of the City series and Waters's historical novels suggested gay and lesbian literature had finally merged with the mainstream, a notion confirmed when Hollinghurst's homosexually explicit The Line of Beauty won the Man *Booker Prize in 2004. Adrienne *Rich is amongst the proponents of 'queer theory', which, from the 1990s, broadened and complicated the binary oppositions of gay and lesbian studies.

gazetteer A geographical index or dictionary. The historian Laurence Echard (bap. 1672, d. 1730) wrote The Gazetteer's or Newsman's Interpreter; Being a Geographical Index (1693), intended for the use of 'gazetteers' or journalists.

GEE, Maggie (1948–) Novelist, born in Poole, Dorset. Her fiction, often formally innovative and experimental, has addressed social and political issues from racism to climate change and includes The Burning Book (1983), Grace (1988), Lost Children (1994), and The White Family (2002); My Cleaner (2005) and My Driver (2009) share many of the same characters.

Genesis See BIBLE.

Genesis An Old English poem of 2,396 lines in the *Junius Manuscript, previously attributed hypothetically to *Cædmon. Lines 235–851 are an interpolated section (usually called 'Genesis B') translated from a continental Saxon original which deals in a dramatic and vivid manner with the Fall of the Angels. There are also some echoes of this section in the early poems of W. H. *Auden.

Genesis and Exodus A Middle English poem in just over 4,000 lines of rhyming couplets, written about the middle of the 13th century in an east Midlands dialect, believed to originate in Norfolk. It relates scriptural history from the Creation to the death of Moses in popular form, based partly on the Bible but mostly, as in episodes such as the accidental killing of Cain, on the Historia Scholastica of Petrus Comestor.

Gentleman Dancing-Master, The A comedy by William *Wycherley, probably performed 1671, published 1673, loosely based on a play by Calderón de la Barca. Hippolita tricks her father Mr Formal by pretending her wooer, young Gerrard, is her dancing master, thus escaping marriage to the rich Frenchified fop Monsieur de Paris. There was a New York revival in 2005.

Gentleman's Journal A periodical edited by the Huguenot refugee Peter Anthony Motteux from 1692 to 1694, containing the news of the month and miscellaneous prose and poetry. It was the germ of the modern magazine (*see* PERIODICAL).

Gentleman's Magazine (1731–1914) A periodical founded by Edward Cave under the pseudonym 'Sylvanus Urban'. It constituted a 'monthly intelligencer', a well-illustrated digest of interesting news, essays, anecdotes, and information, and a record of publications, from the daily and weekly news-sheets and journals. Cave's appears to be the first use of the word 'magazine' to describe a journal. Soon original contributions had largely replaced news compilations and the magazine began to include serious works of criticism, essays, history, and poetry. Samuel *Johnson was a regular and influential contributor. His parliamentary reports evaded the official ban on such publications by claiming to emanate from 'Lilliput'. John *Nichols was editor from 1792 to 1826.

Gentleman Usher, The A tragicomedy by George *Chapman, probably acted *c.*1602–3, printed 1606. The play's name is taken from the usher, Bassiolo, a vain steward, possibly based on Malvolio in Shakespeare's **Twelfth Night*.

GEOFFREY DE VINSAUF (*fl.* *c.*1208–13) English author of *Poetria nova* ('The new poetics'), an influential medieval textbook; and most probably two prose treatises, *Documentum de Modo et Arte Dictandi et Versificandi* and *Summa de Coloribus Rhetoricis*. In 'The Nun's Priest's Tale' (**Canterbury Tales*, VII. 3347) *Chaucer's narrator comments on the skill displayed by Geoffrey in his apostrophizing of the Friday ('O Veneris lacrimosa dies!') on which Richard I died.

GEOFFREY OF MONMOUTH (Gaufridus Monemutensis) (d. 1154/5) Appointed bishop of St Asaph in 1151. In his greatly influential *Historia Regum Britanniae* ('History of the Kings of Britain', complete by 1139) he purports to give an account of the kings who dwelt in Britain since before the Incarnation of Christ, extending over a period of 1,900 years, from Brutus (*see* BRUT), the great-grandson of Aeneas, to Cadwallader, 'and especially of Arthur and the many others who succeeded him'. He drew on *Bede and *Nennius, on British traditions, and on a romantic imagination which has been deemed responsible for, among other things, the creation of Leir, the origin of **King Lear*. His work contributed substantially to the popularity of the Arthurian legends. The *Historia* was translated into Anglo-Norman by Geffrei *Gaimar and *Wace, and into English verse by *Laȝamon and by Robert of Gloucester; its translation into French was a major factor in the dissemination of Arthurian legends.

George Barnwell, The History of, or *The London Merchant* A prose tragedy by George *Lillo, produced 1731, based on a popular ballad. A young apprentice, Barnwell, is seduced by the heartless Sarah Millwood, who encourages him to rob his employer and murder his uncle. For this crime both are executed, he penitent and she defiant. The play was frequently performed as a moral warning to apprentices.

Georgian Poetry A series of five volumes of verse published between 1912 and 1922, planned by Rupert *Brooke, Harold Monro (1879–1932), who published it at his Poetry Bookshop, and Edward Marsh, the editor. The early volumes were widely influential and successful, bringing a fresh vision and manner into the tired poetry of the time. Writers represented in the first volume included Rupert *Brooke, W. H. *Davies, John *Masefield, D. H. *Lawrence, Walter *de la Mare, Lascelles *Abercrombie, Gordon Bottomley (1874–1948), and John *Drinkwater. Later volumes contained the work of Edmund *Blunden, Robert *Graves, Ralph *Hodgson, Isaac *Rosenberg, and Siegfried *Sassoon. Several poets objected to being identified as 'Georgian', and the term soon acquired a pejorative sense. Ezra *Pound, T. S. *Eliot, and the *Sitwells attacked the entire series.

Georgics, The (written 36–29 BC) *Virgil's substantial second poem, loosely modelled on *Hesiod's *Works and Days*. The poem is ostensibly a farmer's guide (the title means 'husbandry'). The first book tackles agriculture; the second, trees, especially the olive and grape; the third, cattle and horses; the fourth, beekeeping and honey. Virgil bases the appeal of rustic life on its frugal simplicity and the satisfactions of hard work. It is an aesthetic and moral vision, a nostalgic picture of what Italian country life might still have to offer, emphasizing the vital importance of peace, long banished by the horrors of civil war (1. 463–514). Incidental panegyrics stud the *Georgics*, and the third book opens with a glorification of Octavian (Augustus) and Rome (3. 1–48). Other notable passages describe the zones of the earth; the zodiac; the sinister omens at Caesar's murder; the unique excellence of Italy; and the tale of *Orpheus and Eurydice (4. 315–558). The poem was much admired and imitated in the 18th century, for example in *Windsor-Forest and *The *Seasons. There are important translations by John *Dryden and Cecil Day-Lewis.

GERAS, Adèle (1944–) Prolific novelist and poet for children and adults, born in Jerusalem. Her work spans genres, periods, and forms and includes several works about Jewish experience and folk tales, *school stories, and novelized retellings of *Homer and *Virgil.

GERHARDIE (originally Gerhardi), William Alexander (1895–1977) Novelist, born of English parents in St Petersburg, Russia. After the First World War he went to Worcester College, Oxford, where he wrote *Futility: A Novel on Russian Themes* (1922), and the first English book on Anton *Chekhov (1923). His second novel, *The Polyglots* (1925), is perhaps his best-known work, the bizarre narrative of a wildly egocentric young officer who on a military mission in the Far East comes into contact with a highly eccentric Belgian family, the Vanderflints; the intermingling of comedy and tragedy, of events of historical significance and the utmost human triviality, of Belgians, British, Russians, and Japanese, creates an oblique, lyrical, inconsequential world which is characteristic of Gerhardie. Other novels include *Pending Heaven* (1930), *Resurrection* (1934), and *Of Mortal Love* (1936). *Meet Yourself as You Really Are* (1936, written with Prince Leopold of Loewenstein) is an interesting early example of *hypertext: it consists of a questionnaire which leads along many different interactive paths to self-knowledge. Following his autobiography *Memoirs of a Polyglot* (1931), the historical study, *The Romanovs* (1940) was the last book he published during his lifetime.

Germ, *Thoughts towards Nature in Poetry, Literature and Art* (1 Jan.–30 April 1850) A periodical edited by W. M. *Rossetti, the organ of the *Pre-Raphaelite Brotherhood; the last two issues (of four) were renamed *Art and Poetry,* *Being Thoughts towards Nature*. It contained work by D. G. *Rossetti (including 'The *Blessed Damozel'), Christina *Rossetti, Coventry *Patmore, Ford Madox Brown (1821–93), William Bell *Scott, and others.

GERNSBACK, Hugo (1884–1967) Born Gernsbacher, American publisher and editor. Born in Luxembourg, Gernsback emigrated to the USA in 1904 to establish several businesses exploiting the new technology of radio, including the magazine *Modern Electrics*, in which he serialized his novel *Ralph 124C 41+* (1911–12), a utopian melodrama of what he was to call 'scientifiction'. In 1926, he launched *Amazing Stories*, the first English-language magazine dedicated to scientifiction (later *science fiction), which he promoted as a didactic and inspirational, even prophetic form, after the examples of Jules *Verne, Edgar Allan *Poe, and H. G. *Wells, all of whom were extensively reprinted in *Amazing*. 'Extravagant fiction today: cold fact tomorrow' was its slogan.

Gerontius, The Dream of See NEWMAN, JOHN HENRY.

Gertrude of Wyoming (1809) A poem by Thomas *Campbell, in Spenserian stanzas. This immensely popular poem centres on the destruction of Wyoming, Pennsylvania by a force of Indians under the Mohawk Brandt, and the death of Gertrude, the newly married wife of Sir Henry Waldegrave.

Gerusalemme liberata See JERUSALEM DELIVERED.

Gesta Romanorum A collection of stories, each with an attached moralization, in Latin, probably compiled in England in the late 13th century. The work's popularity is shown by the existence of 15th-century versions in many European languages and by its influence on later medieval writers such as *Boccaccio, *Chaucer, *Hoccleve, and *Lydgate.

GHOSH, Amitav (1956–) Indian author and academic; resident in New York. His novels include *The Shadow Lines* (1988), exploring the effect upon a family of the partition of Bengal, and *The Calcutta Chromosome* (1996), *science fiction which made early use of the World Wide Web as a tool for exploring a secret history involving early research into the malaria parasite. The ongoing Ibis trilogy (*Sea of Poppies* (2008); *River of Smoke* (2011)) is set at the time of the opium wars.

ghost stories The genre comprises short stories or, less commonly, novels or novellas that treat the power of the dead to return to the world of the living. Their ghosts take many forms, from the recognizably human to the fearfully alien. They may be insubstantial wraiths, or corporeal creatures with the ability to inflict physical harm. Or they may never reveal themselves at all, relying instead on an ability to infect and control the minds of the living, or to achieve their ends through inanimate objects—a pair of gloves, a car, even a saucepan.

Ghost stories are a comparatively recent phenomenon. Although the dead frequently rise again in classical and early modern literature—as in *Chaucer's 'Nun's Priest's Tale', when Chanticleer the cock tells how the ghost of a murdered man revealed the circumstances of his death to his sleeping companion—the literary ghost story represents the supernatural differently. Before the 19th century, the ghosts are less important than the information they reveal; and though they excite fear and wonder, their introduction is not designed to unsettle. In the literary ghost story, the ghost is central, and the arousal of fear is the story's primary purpose.

Literary ghost stories were largely a Victorian creation, part of a wider engagement with the unseen and the uncanny—like the enthusiasm for spiritualism—that challenged the prevailing forces of secularism and science. The author often posed as the detached reporter or recorder of events, as in *The Night-Side of Nature* (1848) by Catherine Crowe (1790–1876), a popular collection of tales and incidents claiming to be based on actual experiences.

The ghost story's immediate literary predecessors were the short stories and fragments common in English magazines during the late 18th and early 19th centuries, but Victorian ghost stories were quite different in character and intention from their Gothic forerunners. Where early *Gothic fiction had been largely unconcerned with either historical detail or present realities, Victorian writers of ghost stories usually set supernatural incidents in solid everyday settings, which made their violations of normality all the more convincing. There is a parallel with *sensation fiction, a literary vogue of the 1860s and 1870s, in which criminality lurks beneath the normality of domestic life.

An early example of a story which struck a new and distinctly anti-Gothic note was Walter *Scott's 'The Tapestried Chamber' (1828). The story takes place in a castle, but it is an English castle, set in a real English landscape in the recent past. Sheridan *Le Fanu, who created the strongest body of short fiction in the Victorian period, gave his most effective stories credible settings and characters and created ghosts that induced physical fear—like the famous spectral monkey in 'Green Tea' (1869). His first collection, *Ghost Stories and Tales of Mystery* (1851), began the Golden Age of the Victorian ghost story, which flourished in the pages of monthlies such as *Temple Bar*, *Tinsley's*, *Belgravia*, and *All the Year Round* (owned and edited by Charles *Dickens), helped by a boom in magazine publishing during the 1860s. Dickens himself was responsible for one of the most anthologized of all ghost stories, 'The Signalman' (1866), though his role as popularizer of Christmas and its association with the telling of ghost stories was of far greater importance. Many writers of magazine ghost stories were women, amongst them Amelia B. Edwards (1831–92), whose famous story 'The Phantom Coach' first appeared in *All the Year Round* in 1864; Mary Elizabeth *Braddon, author of 'The Cold Embrace' (1860) and 'Eveline's Visitant' (1867), both published in *Belgravia*; Rhoda *Broughton (*Tales for Christmas Eve*, 1873); and Mrs J. H. Riddell (1832–1906: *Weird Stories*, 1882). Through the 1890s and into the 20th century, writers such as 'Vernon *Lee' (*Hauntings*, 1890), Edith *Wharton (*Tales of Men and Ghosts*, 1910), Violet *Hunt (*Tales of the Uneasy*, 1911), Marjorie *Bowen (*Curious Happenings*, 1917), and May *Sinclair (*Uncanny Stories*, 1923), amongst others, contributed notably to the genre's development.

Le Fanu's heir, and the great exponent of the factualizing narrative, in which ancient objects and historical and bibliographical references are used to reinforce a sense of actuality and provide a conduit between past and present, was M. R. *James. His antiquarian ghost stories, from 'Canon Alberic's Scrap-Book' (1895) onwards, drew on his own formidable learning and were so convincing that some readers believed them to be factual accounts. The ingeniously plotted stories in his four collections, beginning with *Ghost Stories of an Antiquary* (1904), typically portrayed safe and ordered worlds invaded by terrifying agents of unappeasable supernatural malice. James's style was emulated by a number of younger contemporaries, including E. G. Swain (1861–1938: *The Stoneground Ghost Tales*, 1912), R. H. Malden (1879–1951: *Nine Ghosts*, 1943), and A. N. L. Munby (1913–74: *The Alabaster Hand*, 1949). Contemporary authors influenced by M. R. James include Ramsey *Campbell and Susan *Hill.

In *The *Turn of the Screw* (1898), Henry *James created a potent reinterpretation of Victorian conventions, which begins with a deliberately Dickensian evocation—ghost stories told round the fire at Christmas—but goes on to blur the boundary between subjective and objective phenomena. Similarly ambiguous stories include 'How Love Came to Professor Guildea' (in *Tongues of Conscience*, 1900) by Robert Hichens and 'The Beckoning Fair One' (in *Widdershins*, 1911) by Oliver Onions (1873–1961). Uncertainty also characterizes the ghost stories of Walter de la Mare (e.g. 'Out of the Deep', in *The Riddle*, 1923); more recently, the enigmatic stories of Robert Aickman (1914–81), in *Powers of Darkness* (1966), *Cold Hand in Mine* (1975), and other collections, fuse traditional elements of ghost fiction with oblique narrations concerned with 'the void behind the face of order'.

The 20th century was prolific in ghost stories. The first 30 years of the century saw the rise of specialist ghost story writers such as Algernon *Blackwood (*The Listener*, 1907); W. F. Harvey (1885–1937: *Midnight House*, 1910); E. F. *Benson (*The Room in the Tower*, 1912); A. M. Burrage (1889–1956: *Some Ghost Stories*, 1927); and H. Russell Wakefield (1888–1964: *They Return at Evening*, 1928) to satisfy what their contemporary Virginia Woolf called 'the strange human craving for the pleasure of feeling afraid'.

Giaour, The A best-selling poem by Lord *Byron; eight editions were published 1813. The story is of a female slave, Leila, who loves the Byronic Giaour (the term refers to an·infidel), and is in consequence bound and thrown in a sack into the sea by her Turkish lord, Hassan. The Giaour avenges her by killing Hassan, then in grief and remorse banishes himself to a monastery.

GIBBON, Edward (1737–94) Historian. He was a sickly child and his education at Westminster School and at Magdalen College, Oxford, was irregular and by his own account 'unprofitable'. He became a Catholic convert at the age of 16, and was sent to Lausanne by his father, where he was reconverted to Protestantism and returned to England in 1758. He published his *Essai sur l'étude de la littérature*, (1761; English trans. 1764) and left again for the Continent in 1763; it was in Italy, while 'musing amid the ruins of the Capitol', that he formed the plan of *The History of the *Decline and Fall of the Roman Empire*. He settled in London in 1772, and entered Parliament in 1774. In 1776 the first

volume of the *History* appeared and was generally favourably received, especially by figures in the *Scottish Enlightenment, but Gibbon's ruthlessly sceptical chapters on the growth of Christianity provoked much criticism, to which he replied in 1779 in *A Vindication of Some Passages in the XVth and XVIth Chapters*. The second and third volumes appeared in 1781; the last three volumes, written in Lausanne, in 1788. He returned to England and lived in the home of his friend the earl of Sheffield, who put together Gibbon's remarkable *Memoirs* from various drafts, publishing them in 1796 with his *Miscellaneous Works*.

GIBBON, Lewis Grassic (1901–35) The pen-name of James Leslie Mitchell, novelist, born near Auchterless, Aberdeenshire. He joined the Royal Army Service Corps in 1919 and was a clerk in the RAF from 1923 to 1929. His experience of travel with the forces resulted in *The Calends of Cairo* (1931), writtern under his own name, as were novels such as *Stained Radiance* (1930) and *Spartacus* (1933). He is now remembered principally for his trilogy *A Scots Quair*. Its constituent novels *Sunset Song* (1932), *Cloud Howe* (1933), and *Grey Granite* (1934) relate the life of Chris Guthrie from girlhood on her father's farm, through three marriages, the First World War, and the Depression, to her son's commitment to the Communist Party. All three were published under the name of Grassic Gibbon, taken from Mitchell's mother's maiden name, and are written in a powerful, idiosyncratic, and ingenious lyrical idiom which can be read as English by the general reader and as *Scots by the reader familiar with the old language and literature of the Lowlands; the plot abounds in lurid and violent incident. *Sunset Song* was hailed as the first really Scottish novel since John *Galt. An unfinished novel, *The Speak of the Mearns*, was published in 1982.

GIBBONS, Stella *See* COLD COMFORT FARM.

GIBBONS, Thomas (1720–85) Congregational minister and biographer, educated at dissenting academies in London. His most important works are his biography of Isaac *Watts (1780) and his edited collection of a wide range of women's lives, *Memoirs of Eminently Pious Women*, 2 vols (1777; considerably expanded in 1815), prefaced by an essay on the education of daughters.

GIBSON, W. W. (Wilfrid Wilson) (1878–1962) Poet, who contributed to *Georgian Poetry*. The four issues of *New Numbers* (1914) had featured Gibson and Rupert Brooke, along with Lascelles *Abercrombie and John *Drinkwater. Gibson's many volumes of verse often dealt with northern rural themes; his experiences in the First World War inspired several shorter, sharper battle pieces, such as 'Breakfast'. By *Collected Poems, 1905–25* (1926), his popularity was already waning.

GIBSON, William (1948–) American-Canadian writer. Gibson was one of the writers whose work began to be defined as cyberpunk in the early 1980s. He coined the term 'cyberspace' (for the 'virtual space' linking computer networks, or more loosely the World Wide Web) in his story 'Burning Chrome' (1982), later refining it in the influential novel *Neuromancer* (1984), popular among adopters of computer technology and theorists of postmodern culture. He co-wrote, with Bruce *Sterling, the *alternate history novel *The Difference Engine* (1990). Subsequent novels, such as *Pattern Recognition* (2003) and *Spook Country* (2007) have moved much closer to the shape of contemporary fiction. It has been said that Gibson's future has been in the same place, but the real world has travelled towards it.

GIFFORD, William (1756–1826) Satirist and editor. He published in 1791 and 1795 two satires, *The Baviad* and *The Maeviad*, the first directed against the *Della Cruscan school of poetry, and the second divided between the Della Cruscans and the contemporary drama. In 1797–8 he was editor of *The *Anti-Jacobin*, and in 1809 he was appointed the first editor of the *Quarterly Review*. His ultra-Toryism led him to attack some of the circle around Leigh *Hunt and the *'Cockney School'; he attacked William *Hazlitt personally and published John *Croker's virulent attack on Keats's *Endymion. He was an interventionist editor; among many instances, he wholly altered the warm tone of Charles *Lamb's essay on Wordsworth's *The *Excursion. He was satirized in turn by Hunt in *Ultra-Crepidarius* (1823) and was the subject of *ad hominem* attacks by Hazlitt in 'A Letter to William Gifford, Esq.' (1819) and *The *Spirit of the Age*. Gifford translated the satires of *Juvenal (1802) and of *Persius (1821), and edited the works of Philip *Massinger, Ben *Jonson, John *Ford, and James *Shirley.

GILBERT, Sir William Schwenck (1836–1911) Dramatist. In 1861 he began contributing regular columns of comic verse, with his own illustrations, to the magazine *Fun*; this was the beginning of the *Bab Ballads* (first col-

lected under this title in 1869). Here he sketched out his fantasy world, turning the odd into the ordinary, calling it 'Topsy-Turvydom', a phrase picked up in the title of Mike Leigh's film about Gilbert and *Sullivan, *Topsy-Turvy* (1999). The ballads were popular across a wide social range. His first drama was *Dulcamara* (1866), a burlesque based on Donizetti's opera *L'elisir d'amore*. *The Palace of Truth* (1870) is a poetical fantasy based on a novel by Madame de Genlis and influenced by the fairy work of James *Planché. *The Princess* (1870) a 'respectful perversion' of *Tennyson's poem, was followed by the successful verse play *Pygmalion and Galatea* (1871), *The Wicked World* (1873), and its burlesque version *The Happy Land* (1873), produced in collaboration with Gilbert Arthur À Beckett. Gilbert's strength was topical light verse, making clever use of rhyme and metre, and in 1869 he met Sullivan, whose talent for musical parody and pleasing melody was perfectly suited to Gilbert's verse. Their first collaboration was *Thespis* (1871), in which a group of actors usurp the places of the Olympian gods. In 1874 Gilbert met the impresario D'Oyly Carte, for whom he and Sullivan wrote *Trial by Jury* (1875). Carte built the Savoy Theatre in 1881, especially for the D'Oyly Carte company. The full series of light operas was: *Trial by Jury* (1875); *The Sorcerer* (1877); *HMS Pinafore* (1878), a huge success in America; *The Pirates of Penzance* (1879, New York; 1880, London); *Patience* (1881); *Iolanthe* (1882); *Princess Ida* (1884), a satire on female education suggested by Tennyson's *The *Princess; The Mikado* (1885), set in Japan; *Ruddigore* (1887), a mock melodrama; *The Yeomen of the Guard* (1888), their own favourite; *The Gondoliers* (1889); *Utopia, Limited* (1893), a highly political satire; and *The Grand Duke* (1896), the last and only unsuccessful Savoy opera. Gilbert continued writing plays and operas without Sullivan; among them the travesty of *Hamlet, Rosencrantz and Guildenstern* (1891), *Fallen Fairies* (1909), and *The Hooligans* (1911), his last play. Gilbert used the profits from his plays to build the Garrick Theatre.

Gil Blas *See* LESAGE, ALAIN-RENÉ.

GILCHRIST, Anne (1828–85) Née Burrows, the wife of Alexander Gilchrist (1828–61), author of a life of the then largely unrecognized William *Blake, on which he was working when he died. She finished it, and it was published in 1863; it made a considerable contribution to the awakening of interest in Blake's work in the late 19th century. Anne Gilchrist was friendly with the Carlyles, and with William Michael *Rossetti (also an admirer of Blake), who imparted to her his admiration for Walt *Whitman. She also wrote a life of Mary Lamb (1883).

GILDAS (*fl.* 5th–6th centuries AD) A British historian who wrote *De Excidio et Conquestu Britanniae* ('On the ruin and conquest of Britain'), a Latin account of the history of Britain followed by a castigation of contemporary rulers and priests. His account of the impact of the Anglo-Saxons was an influential source for historians from *Bede onwards.

gilded age, the The period of expansion and reconstruction in the USA after the American Civil War when much new wealth was created. The phrase was coined by Mark *Twain and Charles Dudley Warner (1829–1900) in their novel *The Gilded Age: A Tale of Today* (1873), which satirizes the cynical boosterism of the period.

GILFILLAN, George (1813–78) A Scottish Dissenting minister, literary critic, and editor, who for a brief period in the mid-19th century exercised considerable influence, particularly as the champion of the *Spasmodic school. He was befriended by Thomas *Carlyle, who found his prose 'full of fervour, and crude, gloomy fire—a kind of opium style'. His *A Gallery of Literary Portraits* ran to three series, 1845, 1850, 1854, with essays on the Spasmodics, Thomas *Macaulay, Carlyle, etc., and he also edited many volumes of minor British poets, with notes and memoirs.

GILMAN, Charlotte Perkins (1860–1935) American writer and feminist, born in Connecticut; niece of Harriet Beecher *Stowe. Gilman had only four years' schooling and was mostly self-taught. In 1884 she married Charles Walter Stetson and had one daughter. She suffered from post-partum depression; separation and divorce, socially frowned on, nevertheless saved her mental health. Her experience is recorded in her most famous short story, 'The Yellow Wallpaper' (1892), a disturbing first-person account of domestic entrapment, exacerbated by Dr Weir Mitchell's oppressive 'rest cure'. In Gilman's story, madness can be read as a reasonable response to intolerable treatment. Her treatises include *Women and Economics* (1898), *Concerning Children* (1900), and *The Home: Its Work and Influence* (1903). She edited her own magazine, *The Forerunner*, for seven years, in which she published her own fiction, including her utopian novel *Herland* (1911). Her autobiography, *The Living of Charlotte Perkins Gilman*, was published posthumously in 1935.

GILPIN, William (1724–1804) Clergyman and writer. Gilpin travelled extensively in Britain in his holidays and defined and popularized the notion of the *picturesque as a means of appreciating nature. His fashionable writings, beginning with *Observations on the River Wye* (1782), did much to form taste for the landscapes of *Romanticism in literature, art, gardening, and travel, helping to promote the Lake District and the Highlands as destinations for picturesque tourism. He expounded his theoretical principles in *Three Essays: On Picturesque Beauty; On Picturesque Travel; and On Sketching Landscape* (1792). He was parodied by William *Combe as 'Dr Syntax'.

GINSBERG, Allen (1926–97) American *Beat poet. He took the democratic spirit of Walt *Whitman and applied it to his own experiences of homosexuality and madness. Ginsberg's major poems *Howl* (1956) and *Kaddish* (1960) are composed according to the dictates of breath and are both declamatory laments for an America which has disowned marginalized figures like Trotskyites, Wobblies (i.e. Industrial Workers of the World, an international union), Hell's Angels, Junkies, Queers. His empathy for the outcast made him an ideal figurehead for the counter-culture of the 1960s and he wrote and campaigned tirelessly against the Vietnam War, in support of the drugs LSD and cannabis, and in defence of such contemporaries as Abbie Hoffman (1936–89), Timothy Leary (1920–96), and William *Burroughs. His later work, *Mind Breaths* (1978) and *Plutonium Ode and Other Poems* (1982), displays less of the urgency of his earlier work, yet still maintains a confessional tone wherein his most private concerns are addressed as a statement about the nation. Along with Ann Waldman (1945–) he founded the Jack Kerouac School of Disembodied Poetics at the Naropa Institute in Boulder, Colorado.

GINZBURG, Eugenia (Evgenia) (1904–77) Writer, born in Moscow to Jewish parents. Her memoir *Journey into the Whirlwind* (1967) documents her suffering and resilience during her long imprisonment (1937–55) under Stalin.

Gipsies Metamorphosed, The A masque by Ben *Jonson, performed before James I 1621, printed 1640. It is the most elaborate of his masques, and unusual in its assigning of principal parts to members of the court. The chief event is the telling of the king's fortune by the Gypsy captain, a part taken by the duke of Buckingham (1592–1628).

GIRALDUS CAMBRENSIS (Gerald of Wales) (?1146–*c.*1220/23) Writer and ecclesiastic, a native of Pembrokeshire. He studied at Paris and was archdeacon of Brecon, but his nomination for the see of St David's was twice rejected. His works include *Topographia Hibernica*, an account of the geography, fauna, marvels, and early history of Ireland; *Expugnatio Hibernica*, a narrative of the partial conquest of Ireland, 1169–85, *Itinerarium Cambriae*, a description of the topography of Wales; *Gemma Ecclesiastica*, a charge to the clergy of his district; *De Rebus a se Gestis*; and saints' lives.

Gismond of Salerne See TANCRED AND GISMUND.

GISSING, George Robert (1857–1903) Novelist, educated at Owens College (now the University of Manchester). Caught stealing from the college locker rooms to support a parentless girl, Nell Harrison, he was sentenced to one month's imprisonment. On his release, he went to America then, in 1877, returned to London, and married Nell. They were separated by 1882, and Nell, an alcoholic, died in 1888. Gissing wrote a series of novels with proletarian themes: *Workers in the Dawn* (1880), *The Unclassed* (1884; rev. 1895), *Demos* (1886), *Thyrza* (1887; rev. 1891), *The Nether World* (1889), *Isabel Clarendon* (1886), and *A Life's Morning* (1888). After a trip to Italy, he turned away from working-class subjects to write *The Emancipated* (1890; rev. 1893), **New Grub Street* (1891), his acknowledged classic, and *Born in Exile* (1892). In 1891, he entered into another unhappy marriage, with Edith Underwood, a stonemason's daughter. They had two sons, but parted in 1897, and in 1902 she was sent to an asylum. Gissing turned to the Woman Question in *The *Odd Women* (1893), **In the Year of Jubilee* (1894), and *The Whirlpool* (1897). Though never highly successful, he began to earn more money with *Denzil Quarrier* (1892), and a series of shorter one-volume novels: *Eve's Ransom, Sleeping Fires, The Paying Guest* (1895), and *The Town Traveller* (1898). George *Meredith had been an early supporter of Gissing's work; Gissing also met Thomas *Hardy and became friendly with W. H. *Hudson and H. G. *Wells. In 1898, Gissing met Gabrielle Fleury, with whom he fell in love. Unable to obtain a divorce, Gissing moved to France and to live with her. Subsequent works are the novels *The Crown of Life* (1899) and *Our Friend*

the Charlatan (1901); the travel book *By the Ionian Sea* (1901); an abridgement of John *Forster's *Life of Dickens* (1903); and a fictionalized version of his own memories and reflections, *The Private Papers of Henry Ryecroft* (1903). Gissing died of lung disease in the village of Ispoure in southern France. Posthumously published were *Veranilda* (1904), *Will Warburton* (1905), *The Immortal Dickens* (1925), *Notes on Social Democracy* (1968), and the short story collections *The House of Cobwebs* (1906), *The Sins of the Fathers* (1924), and *A Victim of Circumstances* (1927).

GITTINGS, Robert (1911–92) Poet and biographer, born in Portsmouth. *The Roman Road and Other Poems* (1932), was followed by several volumes of poems and plays, and a *Collected Poems* (1976). His biographical works include *John Keats* (1968) and a two-volume life of Thomas *Hardy (1975, 1978); and *The Nature of Biography* (1978). With his biographer wife Jo (Joan Grenville) Manton he wrote *Claire Clairmont and the Shelleys*, published posthumously in 1992.

GLADSTONE, William Ewart (1809–98) The great Liberal statesman, born in Liverpool, and educated at Oxford, where he distinguished himself as an orator. He is remembered in literary history for his *Studies on Homer and the Homeric Age* (1858), a subject further dealt with in his *Juventus Mundi* (1869) and *Homeric Synchronism* (1876). He firmly maintained his belief in a personal *Homer and 'a solid nucleus of fact in his account of the Trojan war', and, like Thomas Arnold and J. H. *Newman, sought to justify classical studies as the basis of a Christian education. *The Gladstone Diaries*, ed. M. R. D. Foot and H. C. G. Matthew, 14 vols (1968–94), shed new light on his complex personality, particularly his zeal for rescuing prostitutes. The diaries (which are for the most part restrained and factual) also illustrate Gladstone's literary tastes; he read his own verses, *Marmion, and *Lalla Rookh to his wife immediately after their marriage, was given to reading Tennyson's *The *Princess* and *Guinevere* to his rescue cases, and found Harrison *Ainsworth's *Jack Shepherd* 'dangerous' reading for the masses. His long and critical review of Mary *Ward's *Robert Elsmere* (1888) helped to ensure the book's enormous success.

GLANVILL, Joseph (1636–80) Clergyman and philosopher, rector of the abbey church in Bath. He attacked the scholastic philosophy in *The Vanity of Dogmatizing* (1661), a work that contains the story of 'The *Scholar-Gipsy'. He defended belief in the pre-existence of souls in *Lux Orientalis* (1662) and belief in witchcraft in *Saducismus Triumphatus* (1681).

Glastonbury In Somerset; its abbey was said to have been founded by Joseph of Arimathea, according to the *Grail legends. The abbey pre-dates the 10th century. *William of Malmesbury, in his *De Antiquitate Glastoniensis Ecclesiae* (*c*.1140), suggests that it may have been one of the first Christianized areas in England, founded by French monks. *Giraldus Cambrensis tells the story of the discovery there by the monks of the bodies of Arthur and Guinevere in the 1180s, confirming the story of 'a certain Breton poet' who, according to Henry II, said they were buried there. This led to the identification of Glastonbury with *Avalon. It has been suggested that Henry II arranged the finding of Arthur's body to scotch the tradition that he would eventually return.

GLENDINNING, Victoria (1937–) Née Seebohm, biographer and novelist author of *A Suppressed Cry* (1969), a portrait of her great-aunt Winnie Seebohm (1863–85), one of the first students to attend Newnham College, Cambridge, and her Quaker family: the research for this inspired her historical novel *Electricity* (1995). Other works include lives of Elizabeth *Bowen (1977), Edith *Sitwell (1981), Vita *Sackville-West (1983), Rebecca *West (1987), Anthony *Trollope (1992), Jonathan *Swift (1998), and Leonard *Woolf (2006). She was awarded a CBE in 1998.

GLISSANT, Édouard (1928–) Novelist, poet, playwright, and essayist born on the French Caribbean island of Martinique. Glissant is strongly critical of the notion of Négritude put forward by Aimé *Césaire and others. In *Discours antillais* (1981: *Caribbean Discourse*), he argues for a specifically Caribbean cultural identity, rather than a universal, and more abstract, black identity laying claim to African roots.

Globe Theatre The *Burbages' theatre on Bankside in Southwark, built in 1599. It was a large polygonal building, thatched, with the centre open to the sky. The thatch caught fire in 1613, when a theatrical cannon misfired as the king entered in *All is True* (*Henry VIII*), and the whole building was destroyed. It was rebuilt—tiled—in 1614 and demolished in 1644. Shakespeare had a share in the theatre and acted there. Shakespeare's Globe, which opened in 1996 close to the original site of the

Globe, includes a full-sized reconstruction of the theatre, built in oak using Elizabethan construction techniques, based on excavations carried out on Bankside: the driving force behind the building of this new theatre was the American actor-director Sam Wanamaker (1919–93).

Gloriana One of the names under which *Elizabeth I is figured in literature during her reign and particularly in Edmund *Spenser's *Faerie Queene*.

GLOVER, Richard (1712–85) Politician and poet. His blank verse epic *Leonidas* (9 books, 1737; 12 books, 1770) promoted the opposition to Sir Robert Walpole (1676–1745), and brought him fame. His ballad 'Admiral Hosier's Ghost' (1740) similarly undermined Walpole's policy towards Spain; the poem was included in Percy's *Reliques*. Glover also wrote *London, or The Progress of Commerce* (1739). At his death he left a play, *Jason* (1797); a 30-book epic, *The Athenaid* (1788); and *Memoirs* (1813) of his time as MP for Weymouth, 1761–85.

GLYN, Elinor (1864–1943) Née Sutherland, born on Jersey, author of many sensational romantic novels, of which the best known is *Three Weeks* (1907), a notorious success, which features illicit passion in Venice on a tiger skin. She and adaptations of her works achieved outrageous success in Hollywood in the 1920s.

Gnosticism [from the Greek 'gnosis', knowledge] A Christian heresy of the 2nd century AD. Gnostic teaching distinguished between a perfect and remote divine being and an imperfect demiurge who had created suffering. Gnosticism was long known only through hostile early Christian sources, but in 1945 key Gnostic texts, notably the Gospel of Thomas, were found at Nag Hammadi in Egypt.

Go-Between, The A novel by L. P. *Hartley (1953; film 1970).

'Goblin Market' A poem by Christina *Rossetti, published 1862. The fairy-tale plot, described in short, irregularly rhymed verses, concerns two sisters, Lizzie and Laura, tempted by goblins selling forbidden fruit. Laura yields, eats, and sickens, pining for more yet unable to hear the goblins' market-song. To save her sister, Lizzie braves their temptations while refusing to eat herself, reviving Laura by feeding her juices that the furious goblins smeared on Lizzie's skin. 'Goblin Market' has repeatedly been marketed for child readers, but late

20th-century readings also highlight its eroticism and interpret it in terms of religion, female sexuality, and commodity culture.

GODBER, John (1956–) Playwright and theatre manager, born in Yorkshire. His major breakthrough came with *Bouncers* (1983). His mixture of poeticized colloquial dialogue with physical theatre is best seen in *Up 'n' Under* (1984), in which a small cast enact an entire rugby match on stage. He has produced a stream of popular comedies for the Hull Truck Company, drawing from his own and the local community's interests: amongst these *Teechers* (1987) stands out. A prolific writer, he is, after Alan *Ayckbourn, the most frequently produced of his contemporaries.

GODDEN, Rumer (1907–98) Novelist and children's writer, who spent her childhood in India. Her novels include *Black Narcissus* (1939; filmed 1946), about life in a Himalayan convent; *The River* (1946; filmed 1951), set in India; and *The Greengage Summer* (1958; filmed 1961), about children discovering the sexual intensity of the adult world. In *The Doll's House* (1947), one doll attempts to kill another and a third dies attempting a rescue. *Miss Happiness and Miss Flower* (1961) and *The Diddakoi* (1972) display her interest in outsiders, while *Thursday's Children* (1984) is among several books featuring the world of dance. The autobiographical *Two under the Indian Sun* (1966) was written with her sister. She was appointed OBE in 1993.

Gododdin, Y Long poem about the history of Celtic Britons, or Brythons, which celebrates 300 Celtic warriors who were defeated at Catraeth (probably Catterick in Yorkshire) by much larger Anglo-Saxon forces. The poem, attributed to the survivor Aneirin, takes the form of a series of elegies, mostly for individual warriors, and tells how Mynyddawg Mwynfawr, king of the Gododdin people, assembled his force from various quarters of Britain and feasted them for a year at Din Eidyn (taken by most scholars to be Edinburgh) before setting off for Catraeth. The poem appears to have a temporal setting near the year 600, though the manuscript source dates from the 13th century.

GODOLPHIN, Sidney (1610–43) Poet and Royalist, a friend of Viscount *Falkland and described by Sir John *Suckling as 'little Sid'. He was killed at the battle of Chagford, Devon. His poems, not collected during his life, were edited by W. Dighton (1931).

GODWIN, William (1756–1836) Journalist, philosopher, and novelist. Educated at the Hoxton Dissenting Academy, he later became an atheist and political radical. His major work, *Enquiry Concerning Political Justice*, envisions a better society, founded in a belief that rational creatures can live in harmony without laws and institutions, including property laws and marriage.

In 1794 Godwin published the first of six psychological fictions, *Caleb Williams*, followed by *St Leon* (1799), a tale of domestic affections, featuring a portrait of Mary *Wollstonecraft, whom he had married in 1797; *Fleetwood* (1805); *Mandeville* (1817); *Cloudesley* (1830); and *Deloraine* (1833).

Wollstonecraft shared Godwin's faith in logic and rationality but opposed his atheism. Immediately following her death in 1797 (shortly after the birth of their daughter, the future Mary *Shelley) Godwin published his *Memoirs of the Author of a Vindication of the Rights of Woman* (1797), a loving and candid account of her life. His revelations of Wollstonecraft's love affairs and suicide attempts unintentionally scandalized the public. Godwin subsequently married Mary Jane Clairmont, whose daughter by her first marriage, Claire *Clairmont, bore a daughter, Allegra, to Lord *Byron.

GOETHE, Johann Wolfgang von (1749–1832) Germany's most celebrated poet, also a dramatist, novelist, and scientist. Born in Frankfurt am Main, he spent most of his life at the court of Weimar. His Italian journey (1786–8) marked a turning point in his life. In England Goethe initially gained a reputation as a dangerously immoral writer: his first novel, *Die Leiden des jungen Werthers* (1774: *The Sorrows of Young Werther*), caused outrage for its supposed defence of suicide. (*See* WERTHERISM.) Goethe's most celebrated work in England, the first part of *Faust* (1808), only compounded his reputation as a dangerously immoral and irreligious writer. (*See* FAUST.) The first translation of *Faust*, with the 'offensive' parts omitted, appeared in 1820. Lord *Byron, who was greatly admired by Goethe and returned the sentiment, relished the work's challenge to the timidity of prevailing taste, and P. B. *Shelley published a translation of the suppressed scenes in Leigh *Hunt's *The Liberal* in 1822. But Goethe's most influential advocate in the first half of the 19th century was Thomas *Carlyle, who translated two novels (*Wilhelm Meisters Lehrjahre* (1795–6) as *Wilhelm Meister's Apprenticeship* in 1824 and its sequel *Wilhelm Meisters Wanderjahre* (1821) as *Wilhelm Meister's Travels* in 1827) and in *Sartor Resartus*, went on to extol Goethe as 'the Wisest of our Time'. Carlyle's view of Goethe set the tone for his reception in England for much of the century. George Henry *Lewes's excellent biography (*The Life and Works of Goethe*, 1855) offers a fuller and more balanced view than Carlyle's, and Goethe was significant to many writers of the time, including *Tennyson, George *Eliot, and above all Matthew *Arnold. In his essay on Heinrich *Heine in *Essays in Criticism* (1865) Arnold lauds Goethe as a liberator of humanity and a 'dissolvent' of the 'old European order'. Although the many translations of *Faust Part I* during the course of the century are evidence of the work's continuing appeal, the *Faust, Part II* (1832) was relatively coolly received.

In the 20th century Goethe's influence and the urgency of what he had represented to the Victorians waned. Nevertheless, the 20th century saw important translations of his work, notably Louis *MacNeice's version of *Faust Part I* (1951) and W. H. *Auden's co-translation of *Italienische Reise* (*Italian Journey*, 1962). David *Constantine has translated *Die Wahlverwandtschaften* (*Elective Affinities*, 1999), and Faust I (2005).

Gogarty, Oliver St John (1878–1957) Dublin writer, surgeon, and wit, and in early manhood a friend of James *Joyce, who caricatured him in *Ulysses* as 'stately, plump Buck Mulligan'. He published several novels and volumes of verse and a notable book of reminiscences, *As I Went Down Sackville Street* (1937).

Gogmagog According to *Geoffrey of Monmouth, a twelve-foot member of the tribe of giants who occupied Britain before the coming of Brutus (*Brut). He attacked Brutus and killed many settlers. Brutus told the avenging Britons to spare Gogmagog so that he could wrestle with Brutus' ally Corineus (a companion of Antenor who joined Brutus at the Pillars of Hercules). Corineus defeated him, throwing him to his death at sea. See Edmund *Spenser, *Faerie Queene* (III. ix. 50).

GOGOL, Nikolai Vasilevich (1809–52) Russian prose writer and dramatist. His brilliant St Petersburg stories, 'Nevsky Prospekt' (1835), 'Notes of a Madman' (1835), 'The Portrait' (1835), 'The Nose' (1836), and 'The Greatcoat' (1842), are set in a mad city where nothing is what it seems. His 1836 play, *The Government Inspector*, is a savagely satirical picture of life in a provincial Russian town. The first part of his comic epic, *Dead Souls*, was published in 1842,

but in 1845, during a developing spiritual crisis, he burnt the drafts of the second part. After a pilgrimage to Jerusalem in 1848, he continued *Dead Souls*, but, in despair at his failure to imbue it with the intended moral content, he burnt the manuscript of Part II after adopting a regime of total fasting and prayer during Lent 1852. He died ten days later.

Golagros and Gawain A 15th-century Scottish poem of 1,362 lines in thirteen-line alliterative stanzas, first printed in 1508. It is loosely based on the French prose *Perceval* and concerns a journey made by Arthur and his knights to the Holy Land. There are two episodes, both demonstrating the courtesy of Gawain.

GOLD, Michael (1893–1967) American novelist, born in New York, whose Lower East Side was the setting for his novel *Jews without Money* (1930), which has become a classic of proletarian realism.

Golden Ass, The *See* APULEIUS.

Golden Bowl, The The last completed novel of Henry *James, published 1904. It describes a triangular love intrigue between an impoverished Italian prince, a rich American heiress, and her friend. The novel represents one of James's most sophisticated experiments with a limited point of view, and multiple symbolism in the golden bowl of the title.

Golden Grove, The *See* TAYLOR, JEREMY.

Golden Legend, The A medieval manual of ecclesiastical lore, including lives of saints, commentary on church services, and homilies for saints' days. A version in English of this compilation was published by *Caxton in 1483 and was often reprinted. One of its most important sources was the *Legenda Aurea* in Latin by Jacobus de Voragine (1230–98), an Italian Dominican friar who became archbishop of Genoa.

Golden Treasury *See* PALGRAVE, FRANCIS TURNER.

GOLDING, Arthur (1535/6–1606) Translator into English of Latin and French works, including *Ovid's *Metamorphoses* (1565, 1567) and *Caesar's *Gallic War* (1565). His translations are clear, faithful, and fluent; his popular and influential version in *fourteeners of *Ovid was known to William *Shakespeare.

GOLDING, Sir William (1911–93) Novelist, born in Cornwall. After naval service in the

Second World War he returned to teaching, and began writing in 1948. His acclaimed and highly influential first novel, *Lord of the Flies*, did not appear until 1954. *The Inheritors* (1955) portrays Neolithic man's extermination of his gentler ancestors. Later novels, also displaying Golding's concern with human corruption, include *Pincher Martin* (1956), *Free Fall* (1959), *The Spire* (1964), *The Pyramid* (1967), and *Darkness Visible* (1979). Golding's fiction (much influenced by the classical Greek literature he loved) concentrates on isolated individuals or small groups under extreme pressures and, from this, produces suspenseful fables of intense allegorical power. He also published *The Brass Butterfly* (1958, play), *The Scorpion God*, (1971, novellas), and the essay collections *The Hot Gates* (1965) and *A Moving Target* (1982). He was awarded the *Nobel Prize in 1983, and his novel *The Paper Men* (1984), about the pursuit of a world-famous English novelist by an American academic, reflects his discomfort at finding himself increasingly in the public eye. *Close Quarters* (1987) and *Fire down Below* (1989) complete his master-work, a trilogy (published as *To the Ends of the Earth*, 1991), begun with *Rites of Passage* (*Booker Prize) in 1980. Set on a decrepit ship sailing from England to Australia in Napoleonic times, it demonstrates his considerable talent for ironic comedy. *The Double Tongue* (1995), a novel of ancient Greece, was left in draft at his death.

GOLDSMITH, Oliver (?1728–74) Writer, son of an Anglo-Irish clergyman. He spent much of his childhood at Lissoy, Westmeath, and is thought to have drawn on his memories of it when writing *The *Deserted Village*. He was educated at Trinity College, Dublin, but, rejected for ordination, he studied medicine at Edinburgh. During 1755–6 he wandered about France, Switzerland, and Italy, reaching London destitute in 1756. He began a literary career as reviewer for Ralph Griffith's *Monthly Review*. His first substantial work was *An Enquiry into the Present State of Polite Learning in Europe* (1759). He wrote for Tobias *Smollett's *British Magazine*, and for John *Newbery's new *Public Ledger* he wrote his 'Chinese Letters', subsequently republished as *The *Citizen of the World*; he may also have written the nursery tale 'Goody Two-Shoes'. Around 1761 he met Samuel *Johnson, who remained his friend and champion, and in 1762 sold for him the (possibly unfinished) manuscript of *The *Vicar of Wakefield* to Newbery, thereby saving him from arrest for debt. Goldsmith wrote many biographies, compilations, translations, and abridge-

ments; his poem *The *Traveller* (1764) earned him more solid literary respect. Goldsmith's first comedy, *The *Good-Natur'd Man*, was rejected by David *Garrick but produced at Covent Garden in 1768; *She Stoops to Conquer* (1773) was a more spectacular success. Goldsmith's best-known poem, *The Deserted Village*, was published in 1770; his lighter verses include the unfinished *Retaliation* (1774) and the posthumously published *The Haunch of Venison* (1776), written to thank his patron Lord Clare for a gift of game. His eight-volume *History of the Earth and Animated Nature* (1774), also published posthumously, was adapted from Buffon, Linnaeus, and John Ray, among others, and inventively portrays 'tygers' in Canada, and squirrels migrating on bark boats in Lapland, fanning themselves along with their tails. Goldsmith never married, and his relationship with Mary Horneck, his 'Jessamy bride', remains mysterious. The 1801 *Miscellaneous Works* contain Percy's biographical memoir; other biographies include those by John *Forster (1848) and Ralph M. Wardle (1957).

GOLIARD, Goliardic *See* GOLIAS.

Golias (**Goliardus**) The mythical patron whose name is found attached in English manuscripts of the 12th and 13th centuries to Latin poems of a satirical and profane kind, the most famous of these being the so-called 'Apocalypse of Golias', for which no certain evidence of authorship can be claimed. The 'Goliards' are, it seems, to be linked with Golias, the biblical Goliath of Gath, the symbol of lawlessness and of evil, though the original derivation may have been from 'gula' (throat), on account of their supposed gluttony. The 'Goliardic' measure or 'Vagantenstrophe' appears to have passed from secular into religious verse.

GOLLANCZ, Sir Victor (1893–1967) Publisher; he founded his own firm in 1927, publishing writers including Ford Madox *Ford and George *Orwell, and in 1936 the *Left Book Club. He was well known for his progressive views, his resistance to *Fascism, his 'Save Europe Now' movement in 1945 to relieve starving Germany, and his opposition to capital punishment; these were reflected in his firm's publications.

Gondal *See* ANGRIA AND GONDAL.

Gondibert An uncompleted romantic *epic by Sir William *D'Avenant, published 1651, consisting of some 1,700 quatrains. It is a tale of chivalry, set in Lombardy; but the author declares himself bored with the poem before its complex plot is resolved.

Gongorism A Latinate diction and style introduced into Spanish literature in the 16th century by the poet Luis de Góngora y Argote (1561–1627), a style akin to Euphuism in England and Marinism in Italy (*see* EUPHUES; MARINO, GIAMBATTISTA).

gonzo journalism A phrase coined in 1970 about the work of Hunter S. *Thompson and subsequently applied to writing which combines fact and fiction, often in a flamboyant way. *See* FACTION.

Good Friday The annual commemoration of Jesus' crucifixion, two days before Easter Day, celebrating his resurrection. *See* BIBLE.

Good-Natur'd Man, The A comedy by Oliver *Goldsmith, produced 1768, on the theme of excessive generosity. Honeywood is an openhearted but credulous young man, who gives away to the importunate what he owes to his creditors; he is cured by the experience of being arrested for debt.

Good Soldier, The (1915) A novel by Ford Madox *Ford. Generally considered Ford's finest technical achievement, it consists of the first-person narration of American John Dowell (an archetypally unreliable narrator), who relates the history of relationships that begin in 1904, when he and his wife Florence meet Edward and Leonora Ashburnham in a hotel in Nauheim, Germany. The two couples form a foursome, and meet regularly. In August 1913 the Ashburnhams take their young ward Nancy Rufford to Nauheim with them, and Florence commits suicide. Later that year the Ashburnhams send Nancy to India (where she goes mad) and Edward also commits suicide. Subsequently, Dowell becomes Nancy's 'male sick nurse' and Leonora remarries. The substance of the novel lies, apparently, in Dowell's growing understanding of the intrigues that lay behind the orderly Edwardian façade both couples had presented to the world; the carefully plotted time-scheme (orchestrated round the fatal date of 4 August, Florence's wedding day and death day, but settled on by Ford well in advance of 4 August 1914, the date on which Britain declared war on Germany) introduces the 'facts' (that Edward and Florence had been lovers, that both Edward and Dowell were in love with Nancy and Nancy with Edward) in an apparent-

ly casual, haphazard way that lends plausibility to an essentially melodramatic tale.

Good Thoughts in Bad Times (1645) A collection of characteristically good-humoured reflections by Thomas *Fuller, published at Exeter during his service as chaplain to a Royalist army officer. It was followed by *Good Thoughts in Worse Times* (1647), and, at the Restoration, by *Mixed Contemplations in Better Times* (1660).

GOOGE, Barnabe (1540–94) Poet and translator, he published *Eclogues, Epitaphs, and Sonnets* (1563, and translations, including *Four Books of Husbandry* (1577). His eclogues are important as being, with Alexander *Barclay's, the earliest examples of pastorals in English.

Gorboduc, or *Ferrex and Porrex* One of the earliest of English tragedies, of which the first three acts are by Thomas Norton (1530/32–84) and the last two by Thomas *Sackville. It was acted in the Inner Temple Hall on Twelfth Night 1561. The play is constructed on the model of a Senecan tragedy, and the subject is taken from the legendary chronicles of Britain.

Gorboduc and Videna are king and queen, and Ferrex and Porrex are their two sons. The dukes of Cornwall, Albany, Logres, and Cumberland are the other chief characters. Ferrex and Porrex quarrel over the division of the kingdom. Ferrex is killed by Porrex, and Porrex is murdered in revenge by his mother. The duke of Albany tries to seize the kingdom and civil war breaks out. There is no action on the stage, the events being narrated in blank verse.

GORDIMER, Nadine (1923–) South African novelist and short story writer; her protests against apartheid were outspoken. Her collections of stories include *The Soft Voice of the Serpent* (1952), *Six Feet of the Country* (1956), *Friday's Footprint* (1960), *Livingstone's Companions* (1971), *Jump* (1991), and *Loot* (2003); her novels include *A Guest of Honour* (1970), in which an English colonial administrator returns to the newly independent African country from which he had been expelled for his sympathies with the black population; *The Conservationist*; *Burger's Daughter* (1979); and *July's People* (1981). Later novels include *A Sport of Nature* (1987); *My Son's Story* (1990); *None to Accompany Me* (1994), which appeared after the release of Nelson Mandela in 1990 and his election as president of South Africa in 1994; *The House Gun* (1998), which investigates a post-apartheid crime, with a black lawyer defending a white murderer; and *The Pickup*

(2001), which continues Gordimer's exploration of the legacy of mistrust in interracial relationships. *Get a Life* (2005) focuses on a new threat to South Africa, the exploitation of its fragile ecosystem. *The Essential Gesture* (1988) and *Writing and Being* (1997) are collections of essays.

GORDON, Lyndall (1941–) Academic and biographer. Her work includes *T. S. Eliot: An Imperfect Life* (1999); *Virginia Woolf: A Writer's Life* (1984); *Charlotte Bronte: A Passionate Life* (1994); *A Private Life of Henry James: Two Women and his Art* (1998); *Vindication: A Life of Mary Wollstonecraft* (2005); and *Lives Like Loaded Guns: Emily Dickinson and Her Family's Feuds* (2010). *Shared Lives* (1992) is her memoir of women's friendship in 1950s South Africa.

GORE, Catherine (Mrs Charles Gore) (1799–1861) A novelist of the *silver-fork school, who published about 70 novels between 1824 and 1862, many anonymously; they include *Mothers and Daughters* (1830), *Mrs Armytage, or Female Domination* (1836), *Cecil, or The Adventures of a Coxcomb* (1841), and *The Banker's Wife, or Court and City* (1843). She also wrote plays and short stories. Her lively novels were parodied by W. M. *Thackeray in 'Lords and Liveries', one of *Mr Punch's Prize Novelists.

GORGES, Sir Arthur (c.1557–1625) Courtier and poet, from 1580 a gentleman pensioner at court. His grief for the death of his young wife Douglas Howard was depicted by Edmund *Spenser in *Daphnaïda* (1591). Gorges's love poems, 'Vanities and Toys of Youth', remained in manuscript until edited with his other poems, including an elegy on Prince Henry, 'The Olympian Catastrophe' (1612), in 1953. Among his other works are a powerful rendering of *Lucan's epic *Pharsalia* (1614) into rhyming tetrameters; and a translation of Francis *Bacon's *Wisdom of the Ancients* (1619).

Gorgon *See* PERSEUS.

Gormenghast *See* PEAKE, MERVYN.

Gospels *See* BIBLE.

GOSSE, Sir Edmund William (1849–1928) Critic and man of letters, the son of Philip Henry Gosse (1810–88), eminent zoologist and member of the Plymouth Brethren of fundamentalist Christians, his relations with whom he describes (not always reliably) in *Father and Son* (1907). This is in Gosse's own words 'the record of a struggle between two temperaments, two consciences and almost two epochs', as well as a moving and amusing study of an individual childhood. Gosse saw himself as a poet and made early acquaintance with the *Pre-Raphaelites. *Swinburne became a close friend. When Gosse applied for the post of Clark lecturer at Cambridge in 1883, he was able to give *Tennyson, Robert *Browning, and Matthew *Arnold as referees. A great deal of his early critical work was devoted to Scandinavian literature and he was the first to introduce Henrik *Ibsen's name to England.

Gosse's books include lives of Thomas *Gray (1882), William *Congreve (1888), P. H. Gosse (1890), John *Donne (1899), Jeremy *Taylor (1904), Coventry *Patmore (1905), Ibsen (1907), and Swinburne (1917), as well as collections of poems and critical essays. His close friends included R. L. *Stevenson, Henry *James, and Thomas *Hardy. H. G. *Wells dubbed him the 'official British man of letters'.

GOSSON, Stephen (1554–1624) Author. His plays are not now extant, but were ranked by Francis *Meres among 'the best for pastorall'; however, he soon became a leader of the Puritan attacks on plays and players. His *School of Abuse* (1579) was dedicated to Philip *Sidney, as was a romance, *The Ephemerides of Phialo*, to which he appended *An Apology of 'The School of Abuse'* (both also 1579). The *School of Abuse* helped to stimulate Sidney to write his *Defence of Poetry*. Thomas *Lodge replied to Gosson in *A Defence of Stage Plays*, provoking Gosson's *Plays Confuted in Five Actions* (1582).

Gotham A village near Nottingham famed for its inhabitants' simplicity. The origins of the tradition are obscure, but there is a reference to it in the Towneley *mysteries, and related stories appeared in a collection, the *Merie Tales of the Mad Men of Gotam Gathered Together by A.B.*, of which a 1630 edition survives. Washington *Irving introduced the name as a sobriquet for New York (*Salmagundi*, 1807–8). Gotham was most readily recognized in the late 20th century as the skyscraper city of the exploits of the famous comic strip hero Batman, created in the 1930s by Bob Kane (d. 1998). *See also* CHURCHILL, CHARLES.

Gothic fiction A mode of narrative fiction dealing with supernatural or horrifying events and generally possessed of a claustrophobic air of oppression or evil. The literary tradition confusingly designated as 'Gothic' is a distinct modern development in which the characteristic theme is the stranglehold of the past upon the present, or the encroachment of the 'dark' ages of oppression upon the 'enlightened' modern era. This theme is embodied typically in enclosed and haunted settings such as castles, crypts, convents, or gloomy mansions, in images of ruin and decay, and in episodes of imprisonment, cruelty, and persecution. The first important experiment in the genre was Horace Walpole's The *Castle of Otranto (1764, subtitled A Gothic Story in the 2nd edn, 1765).

The three decades after 1790 saw a great vogue for Gothic novels, culminating in the appearance of Charles Maturin's *Melmoth the Wanderer (1820). The leading practitioner of the new genre was Ann *Radcliffe, whose major works were The Romance of the Forest (1791), The *Mysteries of Udolpho (1794), and The *Italian (1797). Udolpho in particular established the genre's central figure: that of the apprehensive heroine exploring a sinister building in which she is trapped by the aristocratic villain. Radcliffe's formula was followed by numerous clumsy plagiarists in the popular market for *chapbooks and 'shilling shockers'; the most striking of her more talented imitators is Matthew *Lewis, whose novel The *Monk (1796) cast aside Radcliffe's decorum in its sensational depictions of diabolism and incestuous rape.

The term 'Gothic' in this context means 'medieval', and by implication barbaric. In the late 18th century it was applied loosely to the centuries preceding the enlightened Protestant era that began with the Glorious Revolution of 1689. Radcliffe, Lewis, and Maturin set their novels in the Catholic countries of southern Europe in the 16th and 17th centuries, alarming their readers with tales of the Spanish Inquisition and of villainous, hypocritical monks and nuns, while drawing upon the imaginative liberties of greater English writers of the 'Gothic' age—principally *Shakespeare's use of ghosts and omens, and *Milton's portrait of Satan. Radcliffe in particular was careful to distance herself from vulgar belief in ghosts or supernatural marvels, by providing rational explanations for the apparitions and nocturnal groans that frighten her heroines.

Some of Radcliffe's contemporaries and immediate successors used more modern settings: William Godwin in *Caleb Williams (1794), his daughter Mary *Shelley in *Frankenstein, or The Modern Prometheus (1818), and the Scottish writer James Hogg in The *Private Memoirs and Confessions of a Justified Sinner (1824) all evoked powerful unease without employing medieval trappings. Although each of these three novels includes prominent prison scenes, the principal strength is the evocation of psychological torment, guilt, self-division, and paranoid delusion.

By the 1820s, the Gothic novel had given way to the more credible historical novels of Walter *Scott, its clichés by now provoking less terror than affectionate amusement, as in Jane Austen's parody *Northanger Abbey (1818). Some of the tales of terror published by *Blackwood's Magazine and its London rival the *New Monthly Magazine, however, retained the Gothic flavour in more concentrated forms, and John *Polidori's story 'The Vampyre' (1819) launched the powerful new Gothic sub-genre of *vampiric fiction, which commonly expresses middle-class suspicion of the decadent aristocracy. From these sources the first master of American Gothic writing, Edgar Allan *Poe, developed a more intensely hysterical style of short Gothic narrative, of which his story 'The Fall of the House of Usher' (1839) is the classic model. Since Poe's time, the strong tradition of American short story writing, from Nathaniel *Hawthorne to Joyce Carol *Oates, has frequently resorted to Gothic themes and conventions.

In English and Anglo-Irish fiction of the Victorian period, the Gothic influence is pervasive, from works by Edward *Bulwer-Lytton and Bram *Stoker to the novels of the *Brontë sisters: Charlotte Brontë's *Villette (1853) is a late example of the overtly anti-Catholic strain in this tradition. Charles *Dickens favoured such settings as prisons and gloomy houses, and cursed families and individuals who are paralysed by their pasts: the significantly named Dedlock family in *Bleak House (1852–3) and Miss Havisham in *Great Expectations (1860–61) are among the best-known examples. Somewhat closer to the spirit of the original Gothic novels are the so-called *sensation novels of the 1860s, notably Wilkie Collins's The *Woman in White (1860), and Sheridan Le Fanu's *Uncle Silas (1864), and ghost stories and tales of terror of Le Fanu, Elizabeth *Gaskell, and others. The last decades of the Victorian period witnessed a curious revival of Gothic writing by Irish- and Scottish-born authors in which the haunted house seemed to give way to the possessed body, as in Robert Louis Stevenson's The Strange Case of *Dr Jekyll and Mr Hyde (1886), Oscar *Wilde's The Picture of Dorian Gray (1890), and Stoker's vampire classic *Dracula (1897). At the turn of the century, more traditional Gothic settings and effects are found in such mystery stories as Henry James's The *Turn of the Screw (1898) and Arthur *Conan Doyle's The Hound of the Baskervilles (1902).

In the first part of the 20th century the Gothic tradition was continued principally by writers of ghost stories, such as M. R. *James and Algernon *Blackwood, and by *fantasy writers, of whom Mervyn *Peake is the most distinctive. William *Faulkner renews and transcends the Gothic genre in his preoccupation with the doomed land-owning dynasties of the American South. The English writer Daphne *du Maurier opened a new vein of popular Gothic romance with *Rebecca* (1938), which revived the motif of the defenceless heroine virtually imprisoned in the house of a secretive master figure.

In the later 20th century, the novels and stories of Angela *Carter, notably *The Magic Toyshop* (1967) and *The Bloody Chamber & Other Stories* (1979), showed how Gothic images of sexuality and domestic confinement could be used imaginatively to explore the concerns of contemporary feminism. Graham *Swift's *Waterland* (1983) and Toni Morrison's *Beloved* (1987) both encapsulate their larger tragic and historical themes within the convention of the dreadful family secret and the haunted house. American writers specializing in Gothic fiction at the end of the 20th century included the English-born novelist Patrick *McGrath, whose *The Grotesque* (1989) and later works display a mood of macabre humour, the hugely popular *horror writer Stephen *King, and the vampire romancer Anne *Rice, who also has a cult following associated with the 'Goth' youth subculture. *See* also GHOST STORIES.

Gothic Revival A revival of the Gothic style of architecture and design that began in the late 18th century with a new romantic interest in the medieval, and produced Horace *Walpole's Strawberry Hill and William *Beckford's Fonthill. This was followed in the 19th century by a more scholarly study of Gothic, expressed in the works of A. W. N. *Pugin and John *Ruskin. The widespread adoption of the Gothic style transformed English towns and cities.

GOUDGE, Elizabeth (1900–84) Born in Wells, Somerset; a prolific writer remembered for her works for children, especially *The Little White Horse* (1946), about Maria Merryweather who meets a unicorn. The book's combination of fantasy and reality is characteristic of Goudge's best work.

GOULD, Nat (Nathaniel) (1857–1919) Journalist and novelist; from 1884 he spent eleven years in Australia. Most of his vivid and extraordinarily popular novels (he published about 130) were concerned with horse racing. He also wrote two books of Australian life, *On and Off the Turf in Australia* (1895) and *Town and Bush* (1896).

GOWER, John (d. 1408) Poet, of a gentry family. He probably lived in Kent throughout the first half of his life; from 1398 to his death he lived at the priory of St Mary Overie in Southwark. He was married in 1398, and was blind by about 1400. He was a friend of Geoffrey *Chaucer and (jointly with Ralph Strode) the dedicatee of *Troilus and Criseyde* (see V. 1856).

Gower produced a considerable body of poetry in three languages. In French he wrote his *Cinkante Balades* (written in *Anglo-Norman and presented to Henry IV *c.*1400) and his first large-scale work, the *Mirour de l'omme*, an allegory written *c.*1376–9 in about 32,000 lines of octosyllabics in twelve-line stanzas, concerned with fallen man, his virtues and vices. *Vox Clamantis* (completed after 1381), an *apocalyptic poem of seven books in 10,265 lines of elegiac couplets, dealing with politics, kingship, and ecclesiastical abuses, and *Cronica Tripertita* (1399–1400), a critical account of the reign of Richard II, were written in Latin. In English Gower wrote 'In Praise of Peace' in 55 stanzas of *rhyme royal, as well as his principal work, the *Confessio Amantis*. This exists in three versions from the 1390s. In his revision of the *Confessio* (in the early 1390s, while Richard II was still on the throne) he removed the praises of King Richard at its conclusion and dedicated the final version to Henry of Lancaster (later Henry IV). The poem is over 33,000 lines long, containing 141 stories in octosyllabic couplets, handled with metrical sophistication and considerable skill. The framework of the poem is the confession of a lover, Amans, to Genius, a priest of Venus; the confessor helps to examine the lover's conscience and narrates exemplary stories of behaviour and fortune in love, organized under the headings of the *seven deadly sins and drawing widely on classical sources (most prominently *Ovid) and medieval romance. There are eight books: one for each sin, and one which gives an encyclopedic account of philosophy and morals. When the lover has been entirely forgiven of his sins and his grasp of the ethics of love is complete, the confessor tells him that he is too old for love and disappears. The lover sees the reason in this and returns home, a conclusion which has been seen as a comment on the inordinate extent of his apprenticeship in the self-perfecting of *courtly love. Several of the exemplary tales are paralleled by stories in *The *Canterbury Tales* and other works of Chaucer. 'Jason and Medea' (V. 3247–4222) and some of the shorter stories ('Narcissus', I. 2275–358; 'Canace and Machaire', III. 143–336; 'Rosiphilee', IV. 1245–446) are slight masterpieces of the classical narrative. Up to the 17th century almost every writer who praised Chaucer coupled his name with Gower's, and Gower speaks the prologue to William *Shakespeare's *Pericles, which is partly based on his 'Apollonius of Tyre' (Confessio Amantis, VIII. 271–2008).

Grace Abounding to the Chief of Sinners, or The Brief Relation of the Exceeding Mercy of God in Christ to his Poor Servant John Bunyan (1666) A Puritan conversion narrative by John *Bunyan, testifying to the focal events in his journey to assurance of salvation. Its pastoral purpose was to comfort his flock at Bedford during his imprisonment. The author bound himself to the Puritan 'plain style', for 'God did not play in convincing of me...I may not play in relating'. It tells of his joining the Bedford church, call to the ministry, and trials, and describes his anguished oscillation between suicidal despair and contrite reassurance, bearing witness to the volatile moods ('up and down twenty times in an hour') which typified Puritan experience. External events (military service in the Civil War, marriage, etc.) are subordinate to inner and spiritual events, as Bunyan struggles against the lure of church bells, the doctrines of the Ranters, Sabbath recreations, dancing, swearing, and blaspheming—even against envy of toads and dogs as being exempt from God's wrath.

GRAFFIGNY, Françoise d'Issembourg d'Happoncourt, Madame de (1695–1758) French novelist and playwright. Her epistolary novel Lettres d'une Péruvienne (1747: Letters from a Peruvian Princess), about a kidnapped Inca princess in Paris, quickly became a European best-seller; it was translated into English four times between 1748 and 1774.

GRAFTON, Richard (c.1511–1573) Chronicler and printer. As printer to Edward VI, Grafton produced the 1549 edition of the *Book of Common Prayer. Grafton's A Chronicle at Large (1568) was used by William *Shakespeare.

GRAHAM, Jorie (1950–) American poet, who grew up in Italy and France, returning to New York as a teenager to study film. The poems in her many collections, from Hybrids of Plants and of Ghosts (1980) up to her latest collection, Sea Change (2008), display an intense visual quality. The Dream of the Unified Field: Selected Poems 1974–1994 (1995) won the Pulitzer Prize in Poetry. In 1999, Graham became the first woman to be appointed Boylston

Professor in Rhetoric and Oratory at Harvard University, succeeding Seamus *Heaney.

GRAHAM, W. S. (William Sydney) (1918–86) Scottish poet, born and brought up at 1 Hope Street, Greenock (an address that deeply amused him); he settled in Cornwall in 1954. His early work in Cage without Grievance (1942), Seven Journeys (1944), and 2ND Poems (1945—the title is a punning dedication to his wife Nessie Dunsmuir) shows the influence of Dylan *Thomas. The White Threshold (1949), a breakthrough volume, makes use of marine images drawn from Graham's youth on the Clyde estuary. The long title poem of The Night-Fishing (1955) resourcefully deploys the metaphor of a herring fishing expedition to explore the poet's struggle with language and vocation. Malcolm Mooney's Land (1970) and Implements in their Places (1977) show Graham's characteristic preoccupation with solipsism, community, and communication. New Collected Poems was published in 2004.

GRAHAME, Kenneth (1859–1932) Author, born in Lasswade, Scotland; after his mother's death in 1864, he lived with his grandmother at Cookham Dene. Grahame contributed to the *Yellow Book, encouraged by W. E. *Henley, who published many of the essays which later appeared in Pagan Papers (1893). Six of the 'papers' describe the life of a family of five orphans, whose activities later appeared in The Golden Age (1895) and its continuation, Dream Days (1898). Their sharp, authentic vision of childhood and the shrewd observations of the narrator influenced writers such as Edith *Nesbit. The *Wind in the Willows, based partly on bedtime stories and letters to his son, owed some of its success to praise by Theodore Roosevelt, who recommended it to the publisher, Charles Scribner.

Grail, the Holy In Arthurian legend, a symbol of perfection sought by the knights of the *Round Table. In the latest development of the legend it is identified as the cup of the Last Supper in which Joseph of Arimathea caught the blood of the crucified Christ and which, in some versions, he brought to north Wales or Glastonbury at the end of his wanderings. The legend has a long history, drawing on Celtic elements as well as Middle Eastern ones, and it is most familiar in English in the version of Sir Thomas *Malory which is mostly an abridgement of the stories contained in three of the romances of the early 13th-century French prose 'Vulgate' cycle. The ten principal versions of the legend were written in a period of about 50 years, between 1180 and 1230. As well as Chrétien's *Perceval* or *Conte del Graal* and the Vulgate versions, there is a third major version in that period, the *Parzival* of Wolfram von Eschenbach (*c.*1205), which was the inspiration for Richard *Wagner's *Parsifal*. Von Eschenbach's and Chrétien's story, in which Perceval is the successful quester, may be regarded as related to the original and more 'authentic' Grail myth which later accumulated layers of Christian meaning until, by Malory's time, it was very far removed from its archetype.

In Malory's *Tale of the Sankgreal* (the sixth of Vinaver's eight *Works*) *Launcelot fathers *Galahad on *Elaine, the daughter of the Grail King Pelles. On the feast of Pentecost Galahad is brought to the Round Table and seated at the Siege Perilous; the Grail appears, accompanied by lightning, but the knights cannot see it. Led by *Gawain they set off in search of it. Launcelot fails in the quest, despite several glimpses, because of the sin of his amour with *Guinevere; Gawain gives up the quest. Three knights distinguished by great purity, Galahad, Bors, and Perceval, come to the castle of Corbenic where they have a vision of Christ and receive the Eucharist from him; they take the Grail from him and carry it to Sarras. Galahad dies in ecstasy; Perceval becomes a monk and dies two months later; Bors returns and reports their adventures in Camelot, in particular telling Launcelot of the eminence of his son Galahad.

The origins and motivation of the Grail have been explained in three principal ways: (1) as a Christian legend from the first, which altered only in detail through its history; (2) as a pagan fertility ritual related to the devastation and redemption of the land of King Pellam—a connection made briefly by Malory (*see* DOLOROUS STROKE); (3) as a Celtic story, already mythological in Irish, transmitted through Welsh (*see* MABINOGION) and Breton to the French romance tradition and gradually Christianized.

Grainne (Grania) In the legends relating to the Irish hero *Finn, the daughter of King Cormac. Finn sought to marry Grainne, but she fell in love with Finn's nephew Diarmid O'Duibhne (*see* DIARMID) and eloped with him. Finn finally causes the death of Diarmid.

GRAND, Sarah (1854–1943) The pseudonym of novelist Frances Elizabeth Bellenden McFall, née Clarke. She achieved sensational success with *The Heavenly Twins* (1893), which attacked sexual double standards in marriage and dealt frankly with the dangers of syphilis and the immorality of the Contagious Diseases Acts. The novel launched her on a public career as a *New Woman (a phrase she was said to have coined in 1894). *The Beth Book* (1897), a semi-autobiographical novel, describes with much spirit (and occasional lapses into melodramatic absurdity) the girlhood, disillusioning marriage, literary aspirations, and eventual independence of its heroine.

Grandison, Sir Charles, The History of An epistolary novel by Samuel *Richardson, published 1754; a portrait of a 'Good Man', to balance his female creations in *Pamela* and *Clarissa*, Sir Charles is an unlikely paragon of honour, wisdom, and virtue, suitable for a conduct manual. The beautiful Harriet attracts the unwelcome attentions of Sir Hargrave Pollexfen, a weakened version of *Clarissa*'s Lovelace. He has her abducted, and after the failure of a secret marriage ceremony she is carried off into the country. Sir Charles, hearing her cries, rescues her and they fall in love. He must, however, fulfil an obligation to go to Italy, where he has previously become involved with an Italian aristocrat, Clementina Porretta. Religious differences have kept them apart. Clementina's unhappiness has deranged her mind, and her parents, now prepared to accept any terms for the cure of their daughter, summon Sir Charles to Italy. As she recovers, however, Clementina reaffirms that she cannot marry a heretic (Protestant), and Sir Charles, released, returns to England to marry Harriet. The book was very popular, and Jane *Austen dramatized scenes from it for family performance.

Grand Tour Beginning as informal diplomatic training for Elizabethan courtiers, the Grand Tour reached its heyday in the mid-18th century: a leisurely journey of two or three years through Western Europe, during which the sons of the aristocracy completed a classical education, refined their manners, and learned the ways of the world before taking their place in society. The conventional route took the young traveller through Paris into Italy (the glories of ancient Rome were being excavated at Herculaneum and Pompeii), often returning via Switzerland, the Rhine, and the Low Countries. It served the social function of cementing the aristocracy within and across national borders. The tour was intended to combine pleasure and instruction: sexual adventures were as much anticipated as connoisseurship and sightseeing.

Tourists returned with artistic souvenirs and introduced to England a taste for the Palladian villa and the Claudian garden (*see* CLAUDE

LORRAIN). Some simply had their xenophobia confirmed. Many accounts of tours survive: journals and sketchbooks were expected outcomes of the educational purpose. Some, such as Joseph *Addison's *Remarks on Several Parts of Italy* (1705), took on features of the *guidebook. For the quality of writing, and a new subjectivity, the letters of Thomas *Gray and Horace *Walpole (on their tour in 1737–41) and accounts by James *Boswell, Edward *Gibbon, and William *Beckford stand out. Tobias *Smollett's *Travels through France and Italy* (1766) was a particularly cantankerous account, satirized in Laurence *Sterne's *Sentimental Journey* (1768).

By the 1760s fashionable 'macaronis' returning from Italy were increasingly lampooned by a more assertive and patriotic English taste. The Tour began to lose its cachet as middle-class travellers took part and more adventurous aristocrats were esteemed for less conventional travels. *Romanticism redirected the traveller's attention to the natural, the sublime, the unexpected, and the subjective response, though Grand Tourists themselves came to appreciate Alpine scenery and melancholy ruins. With continental travel opening up after 1815, and becoming easier with railways and package tours, the experience was very different, and the increasingly confident middle class found less that would improve them. However, in North America and Australasia the belief in the improving tour of Europe as necessary for the cultural elite lingered well into the 20th century.

GRANT, John (1949–) Pen-name of Paul Le Page Barnett, Scottish editor, novelist, and compiler of reference books. A prolific writer of *fantasy gamebooks in the early 1990s, he also wrote more ambitious works such as *Albion* (1991) and *The World* (1992). *The Far-Enough Window* (2002) is a witty, modern version of the Victorian fairy-tale.

Granta A Cambridge University undergraduate periodical started in 1889 and taking its title from an old name for the river Cam. An early editor was R. C. (Rudolph Chambers) Lehmann, later a regular writer for *Punch* and the father of the novelist Rosamond *Lehmann and the poet and publisher John *Lehmann. In the 1950s and 1960s, *Granta* was edited as a literary magazine devoted to publishing poetry and fiction by students at the university, including Michael *Frayn, Sylvia *Plath, and Ted *Hughes. After it was relaunched in 1979 as 'an international paperback magazine of contemporary fiction and cultural journalism', many highly acclaimed

writers, including Saul *Bellow, Angela *Carter, Peter *Carey, Raymond *Carver, Nadine *Gordimer, Milan *Kundera, Gabriel *García Márquez, Edmund *White, and Jeanette *Winterson contributed. In 1983, the magazine published a list of twenty 'Best of Young British Novelists'. Including Martin *Amis, Pat *Barker, Julian *Barnes, Kazuo *Ishiguro, Ian *McEwan, and Salman *Rushdie, the list proved to be remarkably prescient of future success, and *Granta* has twice (in 1993 and 2003) repeated the exercise of choosing such a list. The magazine also has a book publishing imprint named Granta Books.

GRANVILLE-BARKER, Harley (1877–1946) Playwright, theatre director, and critic. From 1904 to 1907 he directed with brilliant success at the *Royal Court Theatre, producing *Shakespeare, many classics, and the work of moderns (such as *Galsworthy, and his own *The Voysey Inheritance*, 1905), and above all establishing the reputation of George Bernard *Shaw. His own play *Waste* was banned in 1907 by the Lord Chamberlain. His 1912 productions of *The *Winter's Tale* and *Twelfth Night* revolutionized the presentation of Shakespeare. An apron stage, simple settings, an authentic text, and swift continuity of action were new to critics and public, but his 1914 production of *A *Midsummer Night's Dream* was generally acclaimed. After the war he retired from the stage (and hyphenated his name). In 1923 Granville-Barker began his Prefaces to Shakespeare, of which he eventually published five series between 1927 and 1947, covering ten plays. These intelligent studies broke new ground in presenting the producer's rather than the scholar's point of view.

graphic novels Term used to distinguish longer, more complex single works of sequential art conceived or developed as a unified work, from periodical comic books. The term was first popularized on the cover of *A Contract with God* (1978) by Will Eisner (1917–2005) and was used to reposition a new wave of more 'mature' comic writers in the 1980s, such as Alan *Moore and Dave Gibbons (1949–) in *Watchmen* (1987), or Neil *Gaiman in the 'Sandman' series, reprinted in album form, which aimed at the wider appeal of the French *bande dessinée* and Japanese *manga*. It was applied especially to more sophisticated works such as *Maus* (1991) by Art Spiegelman (1948–) or *The Tale of One Bad Rat* (1996) by Bryan Talbot (1952–), as well as the 'adult' work of Raymond *Briggs such as *Where the Wind Blows* (1982). For some it distinguishes books like these, or *Jimmy Corrigan* (2000) by Chris Ware (1967–), which won the *Guardian* First Book Award, from the more 'juvenile' market of superhero comic books. For others it is simply a marketing tool which includes album collections of the very same 'comic book' material.

GRASS, Günter (1927–) Prolific German novelist, essayist, and outspoken democratic socialist, born in Danzig, now Gdańsk in Poland. His long, often humorous, fantastic, and narratively and linguistically innovative novels, from *Die Blechtrommel* (1959: *The Tin Drum*), to *Im Krebsgang* (2002: *Crabwalk*), are concerned with the burden and the right remembering of Germany's past. After the award of the *Nobel Prize for Literature in 1999 he enjoyed the status of Germany's conscience. In consequence, his belated disclosure in his first volume of memoirs, *Beim Häuten der Zwiebel* (2006: *Peeling the Onion*), that his military service in the last months of the war had been in an SS regiment caused uproar. Attacked and vilified on all sides, he was defended by Salman *Rushdie, in whose defence Grass had spoken at the time of *The Satanic Verses* controversy in 1989.

GRAVES, Richard (1715–1804) Novelist, poet, and translator. His novel *The Spiritual Quixote, or The Summer's Ramble of Mr Geoffry Wildgoose* (1773) ran into several editions. Wildgoose, his head turned by religious controversy, abandons his estate to travel through the West Country and to the Peak District, challenging everywhere the 'enthusiasm' of new Methodists such as George *Whitefield, with ludicrous results. Graves's other novels include *Columella* (1779), based on the life of Shenstone; he published *Recollections of William Shenstone* in 1788.

GRAVES, Robert (1895–1985) Poet and novelist; he joined the army in 1914 and his first poetry appeared while he was serving in the First World War (*Over the Brazier*, 1916; *Fairies and Fusiliers*, 1917); his poems also appeared in *Georgian Poetry. In 1926, accompanied by his wife and a new acquaintance, Laura *Riding, he went briefly to Egypt as professor of literature. He was to live and work with Riding in Majorca, then Brittany, until 1939, publishing various works in collaboration with her, including *A Survey of Modernist Poetry* (1927). He was in England during the Second World War, then settled in Majorca in 1946 with his second wife, Beryl Hodge. Graves's output was prodigious; he wrote many volumes of poetry, essays, fiction, biography, and works for children, and published many free translations from various languages. He saw himself primarily as a poet. His powerful autobiography, *Goodbye to All That* (1929), which describes his unhappy schooldays and the horrors of the trenches, and gives a frank account of the breakdown of his first marriage, is an outstanding example of the new freedom and passionate disillusion of the post-war generation. Most of his novels have a historical basis; they include *I, Claudius* and *Claudius the God* (both 1934), narrated by the imaginatively and idiosyncratically conceived persona of the Emperor Claudius; *Antigua, Penny, Puce* (1936), a barbed tale of sibling rivalry; and the controversial *The Story of Marie Powell, Wife to Mr Milton* (1943). Notable amongst his non-fiction works is *The White Goddess: A Historical Grammar of Poetic Myth* (1948), which argues that true poets derive their gifts from the Muse, the primitive, matriarchal Moon Goddess, the female principle, now disastrously dispossessed by male values of reason and logic. This has influenced several subsequent poets, notably Ted *Hughes. Graves's often unorthodox interpretation of myth may also be seen in his *The Greek Myths* (1955), *The Hebrew Myths* (1963, with R. Patai), and other works. His *Collected Poems* (1955) confirmed a worldwide reputation; *The Complete Poems in One Volume* (2000) was edited by Beryl Graves and Dunstan Ward. Graves avoided identification with any school or movement, speaking increasingly with a highly individual yet ordered voice in which lucidity and intensity combine to a remarkable degree. His love poetry, some of his best-known and most distinctive work, is at once cynical and passionate, romantic and erotic, personal and universal.

graveyard poets Term applied to 18th-century poets who wrote melancholy, reflective works, often set in graveyards, on the theme of human mortality. Examples include Thomas *Parnell's 'Night-Piece on Death' (1721), Edward Young's *Night Thoughts (1742), Robert *Blair's *The Grave* (1743), and Thomas *Gray's *Elegy Written in a Country Church-Yard (1751).

GRAY, Alasdair (1934–) Scottish novelist, playwright, and painter, born in Glasgow. The dual narrative of his first novel, *Lanark: A Life in Four Books* (1981), which mirrors Glasgow with the nightmarish Unthank, established Gray as a leading figure in contemporary Scottish writing. It was followed by *Unlikely Stories, Mostly* (1983) and *1982, Janine* (1984). *Poor Things* (1992), a pastiche of the Victorian mystery novel, and *Old Men in Love* (2007), both employ multiple narratives and feature Gray himself in the role of semi-fictional editor. Gray's handsomely designed *Book of Prefaces* (2000) is a collection of introductory essays and verses by great English, Irish, Scottish, and American writers from the 7th century to the present, with glosses by the editor and a range of contemporary authors from Roger Scruton to Iain Crichton *Smith. Other works include the novellas *The Fall of Kelvin Walker* (1985) and *McGrotty and Ludmilla* (1990), *Something Leather* (1990), and *A History Maker* (1994), a futuristic tale set in the 23rd-century Scottish borders.

GRAY, Simon (1936–2008) Playwright, director, and novelist. He is best known for his plays about the problems and contradictions of middle-class and academic life, many of which show a clear debt to his Cambridge years: these include *Butley* (1971), *The Common Pursuit* (1984; the title an oblique tribute to F. R. *Leavis), and *Hidden Laughter* (1990). His novels include *Little Portia* (1967), inspired by his time as a language teacher in Cambridge, as was his play *Quartermaine's Terms* (1981). *Fat Chance* (1995) tells the disastrous story of the production and collapse of his play about espionage, *Cell Mates* (1995). *The Smoking Diaries* (2004) is a frank and comic account of his life. *Little Nell*, a play about *Dickens and his mistress Ellen Ternan, was produced in 2007.

GRAY, Thomas (1716–71) Poet, born in London, the son of a scrivener or professional scribe. He was educated at Eton College, with Horace *Walpole, whom he accompanied on a tour of France and Italy in 1739–41, but they quarrelled and returned home separately. In 1742 Gray moved to Cambridge, where he was to live, apart from travels and visits, for the rest of his life. *Ode on a Distant Prospect of Eton College* (1747) was the first of his works to appear in print. Reconciled with Walpole in 1745, the following year Gray showed him the beginning of his *Elegy Written in a Country Churchyard* (1751). In 1754 Gray finished his Pindaric ode, *The *Progress of Poesy*, and in 1757 a second Pindaric ode, *The *Bard*; both were published by Walpole in 1757, the first works printed by the Strawberry Hill Press. He was offered the laureateship on the death of Colley *Cibber, but declined. He turned to antiquarian studies and *'picturesque' travels in Scotland and the Lake District. New discoveries of Old Norse and Celtic poetry prompted Gray to pro-

duce various imitations, including 'The Fatal Sisters' and 'The Descent of Odin' (written 1761; pub. 1768). After his death, William *Mason constructed an edition of Gray's poems with accompanying 'Memoirs' out of Gray's papers, including his *Journal* of his visit to the Lakes. This was a model for *Boswell's *Life of Johnson*, but involved some falsification of the materials

SEE WEB LINKS
- Thomas Gray archive

Great Awakening A phrase initially used to describe the religious revival of the mid-18th century in the USA, most famously showing itself through the writings of Jonathan *Edwards.

Great Expectations A novel by Charles *Dickens, which first appeared in *All the Year Round* 1860–61, in volume form 1861. It describes the development of the character of the narrator, Philip Pirrip, commonly known as 'Pip', a village boy brought up by his tyrannical sister, the wife of the gentle blacksmith Joe Gargery. He is introduced to the house of Miss Havisham, who, half-crazed by the desertion of her lover on her bridal night, has brought up the girl Estella to use her beauty as a means of torturing men. Pip falls in love with Estella, and aspires to become a gentleman. Money and expectations of more wealth come to him from a mysterious source, which he believes to be Miss Havisham. He goes to London, and meanly abandons the devoted Joe Gargery. Misfortunes come upon him. His benefactor proves to be an escaped convict, Abel Magwitch, whom he, as a boy, had helped; his great expectations fade away and he is penniless. Estella marries his sulky enemy Bentley Drummle, by whom she is cruelly ill treated. Taught by adversity, Pip returns to Joe Gargery and honest labour, and is finally reunited with Estella, who has also learnt her lesson. Other notable characters in the book are Joe's uncle, the impudent old impostor Pumblechook; Jaggers, the skilful Old Bailey lawyer, and his good-hearted clerk Wemmick; and Pip's friend in London, Herbert Pocket. John *Forster's life of Dickens suggests that the author originally devised a less happy ending to the story, which he altered in deference to the advice of Edward *Bulwer-Lytton.

Greaves, Sir Launcelot, The Adventures of Novel by Tobias *Smollett, published 1762. Smollett's shortest novel, this was written in episodes (some of them while in prison for libel in 1760). Launcelot is handsome, learned, and good, but when the book opens he is unfortunately crazed by the loss of Aurelia; with his absurd cowardly squire Crabshaw, and his horse Bronzomarte, Launcelot undertakes a quixotic life of knight errantry, warring against the enemies of virtue and reason. After a terrible period in a madhouse, Launcelot recovers and Aurelia is at last restored to him. The imitation of *Cervantes works as a satiric device against the corrupt society Launcelot encounters; his 'reason' exposes social 'madness'.

GREEN, Henry (1905–73) Novelist, pseudonym of Henry Vincent Yorke. The first of his nine novels, *Blindness* (1926), had been written while he was still at school; his second, *Living* (1929), describes life on a factory floor in Birmingham, and is based on his own experiences; the novel vividly records working-class idiom. It also manifests the idiosyncrasies—dropped articles, sentences without verbs, a highly individual use of colloquial language—which contribute to his work's distinctive quality. *Party Going* (1939) has strong symbolic suggestions in an apparently trivial narrative. This was followed by his autobiographical *Pack my Bag: A Self-Portrait* (1940) and further novels: *Caught* (1943); *Loving* (1945), one of his most admired works, which describes life above and below stairs in an Irish country house during wartime (*see* 'BIG HOUSE' FICTION); *Back* (1946); *Concluding* (1948); *Nothing* (1950); and *Doting* (1952).

GREEN, Matthew (1697–1737) Poet. He appears to have had Quaker connections, and was employed at the Customs House; he left his manuscripts to his friend Richard *Glover. His posthumous poem *The Spleen* (1737) advises on melancholy and recommends in fluent octosyllabics a simple country life.

GREEN, Thomas Hill (1836–82) Fellow of Balliol 1866–78 (the first not to be ordained into the Church of England). Green's philosophical publications began with a criticism of *Locke, *Hume, and *Berkeley in the form of two very full introductions to a new edition of Hume's *Treatise of Human Nature*. Mary *Ward pays tribute to his persistent influence in her sympathetic portrait of him as Henry Grey in *Robert Elsmere* (1888); she describes him as one who held 'a special place in the hearts of men who can neither accept fairy tales, nor reconcile themselves to a world without faith'.

GREENAWAY, Kate (1846–1901) Writer for children, and artist; she wrote and illustrated children's books and magazines, designed Christmas cards, and exhibited pictures of attractive children playing picturesquely. Her reputation was established by *Under the Window* (1878), a collection of rhymes for children, which became an instant best-seller. She produced nine more of her own books (1880–89) and a series of almanacs (1883–95), and illustrated others' work including Robert *Browning's *The Pied Piper of Hamelin* (1888).

Greenaway's influence extends beyond her illustrations: her pictures of pretty children in old-fashioned clothes playing in idyllic gardens permeated culture, and there is an annual Kate Greenaway medal for illustration in a book for children. *See* also PICTUREBOOKS.

GREENAWAY, Peter (1942–) Filmmaker, who emerged as a creator of complex and enigmatic feature films with *The Draughtsman's Contract* (1982). *The Cook, the Thief, his Wife and her Lover* (1989) is a savage neo-Jacobean revenge drama; *Prospero's Books* (1991) is a phantasmagoric treatment of *The *Tempest*. Greenaway is prolific in many forms, including large-scale exhibitions and installations. He collaborated with the painter Tom *Phillips on *A TV Dante* (1989), presenting the first eight cantos of the *Inferno*. Running through his work is the mythic figure of Tulse Luper, ostensibly an ornithologist.

GREENE, Graham (1904–91) Novelist and playwright; he published a book of verse, *Babbling April* (1925), while he was still at Oxford University. He joined the Roman Catholic Church in 1926. His first three novels (1929–31), made little impression, but *Stamboul Train* (1932) sold well and was followed by many increasingly successful novels, short stories, books of reportage and travel, plays, children's books, etc. Greene describes his own early years in *A Sort of Life* (1971), which gives a vivid impression of a manic-depressive temperament tempted by deadly nightshade and Russian roulette, and a literary imagination nourished by influences as diverse as Stanley *Weyman, Marjorie *Bowen, and Robert *Browning.

His pursuit of danger (despite quieter interludes, e.g. as literary editor on the *Spectator and *Night and Day*) dominated much of his life and travels, as described in his second volume of autobiography, *Ways of Escape* (1980). His novels include *England Made Me* (1935); *The Power and the Glory* (1940); *The Heart of the Matter* (1948); *The End of the Affair* (1951; a wartime love affair with strong religious-supernatural touches modified by Greene himself in a later version); *The Quiet American* (1955, set in Vietnam); *A Burnt-out Case* (1961, set in a leper colony in the Congo); *The Honorary Consul* (1973, set in Argentina); and *The Human Factor* (1978, a secret service novel). Other works of fiction he classed as 'entertainments': these include *Brighton Rock* (1938, the first novel in which critics detected a strong Catholic message, introduces what was to be his central concept of 'the appalling strangeness of the mercy of God'); *The Confidential Agent* (1939); *Loser Takes All* (1955); and *Our Man in Havana* (1958). *The Third Man* (1950) was originally written as a screenplay and filmed (1949) by Carol Reed (1906–76; *see* EXPRESSIONISM). Greene's plays include *The Living Room* (1953), *The Potting Shed* (1957), and *The Complaisant Lover* (1959). He also published travel books, describing journeys in Liberia (*Journey without Maps*, 1936), Mexico (*The Lawless Roads*, 1939), and Africa (*In Search of a Character: Two African Journals*, 1961). His *Collected Essays* appeared in 1969. His range as a writer is wide, both geographically and in variations of tone, but his preoccupations with moral dilemma (personal, religious, and political), his attempts to distinguish 'good-or-evil' from 'right-or-wrong', and his persistent choice of 'seedy' (a word which he was to regret popularizing) locations give his work a highly distinctive and recognizable quality, while his skilful variations of popular forms (the thriller, the detective story) have brought him a rare combination of critical and popular admiration.

GREENE, Robert (1558–92) Author and playwright, born in Norwich. Although he liked to stress his university connections, his literary persona was that of a feckless drunkard, who abandoned his wife and children to throw himself on the mercies of tavern hostesses and whores; writing pamphlets and plays was supposedly a last resort when his credit failed. He probably died during a severe outbreak of plague. Greene was attacked at length by Gabriel *Harvey in *Four Letters* (1592) as the 'Ape of *Euphues' and 'Patriarch of shifters'; in the same year, Thomas *Nashe defended him in *Strange News*, acknowledging Greene to have been a drunkard and a debtor, but claiming that 'He inherited more virtues than vices.' Greene's 38 or so publications, progressing from moral dialogues to prose romances, romantic plays, and finally realistic accounts of underworld life, bear out Nashe's assertion that printers were only too glad 'to pay him dear for the very dregs of his wit'. The sententious moral tone of his works suggests that his

personal fecklessness and reported deathbed repentance may have been largely a pose.

Among the more attractive of his romances are the *Lylyan sequel *Euphues his Censure to Philautus* (1587); *Pandosto* and *Perimedes the Blacksmith* (1588); and *Menaphon* (1589). Among his 'repentance' pamphlets are *Greene's Mourning Garment, Greene's Never Too Late* (1590), and the attributed *Greene's Groat's-Worth of Wit* (1592). *Greene's Vision* (1592) is a fictionalized account of his deathbed repentance in which he receives advice from Geoffrey *Chaucer, John *Gower, and King Solomon. The low-life pamphlets include *A Notable Discovery of Coosenage* (1591) and three 'coney-catching' pamphlets in the same years 1591–2. His eight plays, all published posthumously, include *Orlando furioso* (1594), *Friar Bacon and Friar Bungay* (1594), and *James the Fourth* (1598)

Greene is renowned for his connections with William *Shakespeare. The attack on him in *Greene's Groat's-Worth of Wit* is the first reference to Shakespeare as a London dramatist; and his *Pandosto* provided Shakespeare with the source for *The Winter's Tale*. Greene probably provided a name and a model for the swaggering Nick Greene in Virginia *Woolf's *Orlando* (1928).

Greene's Groat's-Worth of Wit, *Bought with a Million of Repentance* (1592) A prose tract attributed to Robert *Greene, but edited and probably written by Henry *Chettle. The miser Gorinius dies, leaving the bulk of his large fortune to his elder son Lucanio, and only 'an old groat' to the younger, Roberto (i.e. the author's persona), 'wherewith I wish him to buy a groat's-worth of wit'. Roberto conspires with a courtesan to fleece his brother, but the courtesan betrays him, subsequently ruining Lucanio for her sole profit. The gradual degradation of Roberto is then narrated, and the tract ends with the curious 'Address' to his fellow playwrights Christopher *Marlowe, Thomas *Lodge, and George *Peele, urging them to spend their wits to better purpose than on the making of plays. It contains the well-known passage about the 'upstart crow, beautified with our feathers', the *'*Johannes Fac Totum*', who 'is in his own conceit the onely Shake-scene in a country', which probably refers to William *Shakespeare as a non-graduate dramatist newly arrived in London.

GREENLAW, Lavinia (1962–) Poet and novelist. Her first volume of poems, *Night Photograph* (1993), includes poems on scientific subjects whose combinations of precision and wonder are indebted to Elizabeth *Bishop. *A World Where News Travelled Slowly* (1997) and *Minsk* (2003) refine her characteristically taut style. More recent works include *Thoughts of a Night Sea* (photographs by Garry Fabian Miller; 2003), and the memoir *The Importance of Music to Girls* (2007). *Mary George of All-northover* (2001) and *An Irresponsible Age* (2006) are novels.

Green-sleeves The name of an inconstant lady who is the subject of a ballad; its earliest surviving complete form was published in 1584. The ballad, and the tune to which it was sung, became and remain very popular; both are mentioned by William *Shakespeare in *The Merry Wives of Windsor*, II. i and v. v.

GREENWELL, Dora (1821–82) Poet and essayist, who published seven volumes of poetry 1848–71, of which *Carmina Crucis* (1869), described by her as 'roadside songs with both joy and sorrow in them', was particularly admired. An evangelical Anglican who led a largely secluded life, her longer prose works were on religious subjects, but her essays covered a variety of social causes including women's education, child labour, and the education of the disabled. In this latter cause she edited a series of stories for children urging decent treatment for 'imbeciles'. She was a friend of Josephine Butler (1828–1906), met Elizabeth Barrett *Browning, and corresponded with Christina *Rossetti.

GREENWOOD, Walter (1903–74) Novelist and dramatist, born in Salford. He is chiefly remembered for his classic novel of life in a northern town during the Slump, *Love on the Dole* (1933; dramatized 1934; filmed 1941), into which he funnelled his own experience of poverty, deprivation, and unemployment. He wrote nine further novels, several plays, a book of short stories, and a volume of autobiography, *There Was a Time* (1967).

GREER, Germaine (1939–) Australian writer, journalist, and critic. Her first book, *The Female Eunuch* (1970), a classic of modern feminist argument, was followed by *The Obstacle Race* (1979), a discussion of the difficulties of women painters, and of their critical neglect; *Sex and Destiny* (1984); and *Slip-Shod Sibyls: Recognition, Rejection and the Woman Poet* (1995), a challenging view of women poets, known and little known, which does not spare what Greer sees as their failings as writers. *The Madwoman's Underclothes* (1986) is a collec-

tion of essays and occasional pieces (1968–85); *Daddy We Hardly Knew You* (1989) is a family memoir; *The Change* (1991) discusses the menopause; and *The Whole Woman* (1999) reconsiders the progress of feminism. There is an unauthorized biography by Christine Wallace (1997).

GREG, Sir Walter Wilson (1875–1959) Scholar and bibliographer, author of *A Bibliography of the English Printed Drama to the Restoration* (1939–59). In 1906 he founded, and was general editor of (1906–39), the Malone Society (named after Edmond *Malone). His edition of Philip *Henslowe's Diary and Papers (1904–8) is an outstanding example of his palaeographical abilities and his knowledge of Elizabethan theatrical history. Greg pioneered the New Bibliography, raising scholarly standards, and applying his skill in palaeography and textual criticism to editions of manuscript plays, notably *Sir Thomas *More* (1911). He published a remarkable parallel-text edition of '*Doctor Faustus*' 1604–1616 (1950), and important accounts of *The Editorial Problem in Shakespeare* (1942), *The Shakespeare First Folio* (1955), and *Some Aspects and Problems of London Publishing between 1550 and 1650* (1956).

GREGG, Percy (1836–89) Author and political journalist. *Across the Zodiac: The Story of a Wrecked Record* (1880) was one of the first novels to imagine a voyage to another planet by means of a spaceship. Its antigravity propulsion may have influenced H. G. *Wells's 'cavorite'. The Mars reached by the spaceship is an ambiguous *utopia, scientifically advanced, but socially menacing. *Interleaves* (1875) is a book of poetry: he published other poetry collections as Lionel H. Holdreth.

GREGORY, Augusta, Lady (1852–1932) Née Persse, born at Roxborough, Co. Galway; dramatist, folklorist, and literary patron. A leading figure in the *Irish Revival, she assisted W. B. *Yeats and Edward *Martyn in the foundation of the *Irish Literary Theatre, forerunner of the *Abbey Theatre, for which she became playwright, director, and patent holder. She helped popularize Irish legends with her translations *Cuchulain of Muirthemne* (1902) and *Gods and Fighting Men* (1904), and Irish folklore with *Poets and Dreamers* (1903), *A Book of Saints and Wonders* (1906; enl. 1907), and *Visions and Beliefs in the West of Ireland* (1920). Gregory's Gaelic-derived idiom (often called 'Kiltartanese') and knowledge of folklore were assets in her collaboration with Yeats on several plays including *Cathleen ni Houlihan* (1902), of which she wrote at least half, and *The Unicorn from the Stars* (1908). The best known of her many one-act plays are *Spreading the News* (1904) and *The Rising of the Moon* (1907). *Our Irish Theatre* (1913) is her partisan account of the Abbey's early years. Adapted versions of the sonnets she wrote during her 1882-3 affair with Wilfrid Scawen *Blunt were published by Blunt under his own name as 'A Woman's Sonnets' in 1892.

GREGORY I, St (Gregory the Great) (*c.*540–604) One of the greatest of the early popes (from 590), a reformer of monastic discipline and a prolific writer whose works include the *Cura Pastoralis* (*see* ALFRED), the *Dialogues*, and famous collections of letters and sermons. He sent Augustine of Canterbury to England. *Bede (*History*, II. i) writes that, seeing Anglo-Saxon boys for sale in the slave market at Rome, he remarked: 'Not *Angli* but *Angeli*, if they were Christians.' The story that he delivered the emperor Trajan from hell by his prayers, touched by his humility and justice, is mentioned by Aquinas, by *Dante, and by Langland (*Piers Plowman*, B XI. 140ff.).

GREGORY OF TOURS (*c.*540–594) Bishop of Tours, whose *Historia Francorum* is the chief authority for the early Merovingian period of French history. He places in 520 the raid against the Frisian territory of the Franks by a Scandinavian leader 'Chochilaicus' (in Latin) who has been identified with the Geatish king Hygelac in *Beowulf*; the raid is mentioned in *Beowulf* at lines 1207, 2357, 2503, and 2912. Gregory's identification provides the only historical corroboration for any character or event in the poem.

Grendel *See* BEOWULF.

GRENFELL, Julian (1888–1915) Poet, killed in the First World War. The day after his death, his poem 'Into Battle' appeared in *The *Times*; it has been much-anthologized.

GREVILLE, Charles Cavendish Fulke (1794–1865) Politician and diarist, for many years clerk to the Privy Council. From 1820 to 1860 he kept a detailed diary of his life in the inner circles of politics and power. He was the friend and trusted confidant of both Whigs and Tories, and includes in his work many lively portraits of friends and colleagues, such as the duke of Wellington and Lord Palmerston. His *Memoirs* were first edited and published in 1874–87. *See* DIARIES.

GREVILLE, Sir Fulke, first Baron Brooke (1554–1628) Courtier and writer, a close friend of Philip *Sidney. From the mid-1570s he was at court, in a succession of roles. In 1621 he was created Baron Brooke and granted Warwick Castle and Knowle Park by *James I. He was murdered by a servant, Ralph Heywood, who then killed himself. An elegy on Sidney was published in *The Phoenix Nest* (1593), but most of his writings were published posthumously in *Certain Learned and Elegant Works* (1633). They include a sonnet sequence *Caelica*. His two Senecan tragedies *Mustapha* (published 1609) and *Alaham* were written, in their earliest versions, before the fall of *Essex in February 1601, and are severe, moral studies of political power. His major prose work, *A Dedication to Sir Philip Sidney*, was probably begun in 1610. Greville was a compulsive reviser, however, and many works survive in variant versions. The printed version of the *Dedication* (1652, as *The Life of Sir Philip Sidney*) incorporates judgements of *Elizabeth I, whose biography he planned to write.

GRIEG, David (1969–) Scottish playwright. Grieg was brought to prominence by *Europe* (1994), a play exploring the aftermath of the collapse of the Soviet Union, set on an unlocated station at which no train ever stops. He has had more than thirty-five plays produced, including *The Cosmonaut's Last Message to the Woman He Once Loved in the Former Soviet Union* (1999), *San Diego* (2003), and *The American Pilot* (2005).

GRIFFIN, Gerald (1803–40) London-based Irish dramatist, novelist, and poet, born in Limerick. His best-known works are the novel *The Collegians* (1829), in which young Cregan, tempted by wealth and beauty, permits the murder of his humble country wife; and the song 'Aileen Aroon'. Dion *Boucicault's *The Colleen Bawn* is an adaptation of *The Collegians*.

GRIFFITH, Elizabeth (1727–93) Welsh actress and playwright. Her most successful plays were *The Double Mistake* (1766) and *The School for Rakes* (1769). She wrote several *epistolary novels, and published *A Series of Genuine Letters between Henry and Frances*, based on materials from her own courtship, in 1757.

GRIFFITH, George (1857–1906) Pen-name of George Chetwynd Griffith-Jones, *science fiction writer born in Plymouth. His popular magazine serials such as *The Angel of the Revolution* (1893) prefigured H. G. *Wells as stories of the apocalyptic future shaped by flight. *A Honeymoon in Space* (1900) imagined space travel.

Griffith Gaunt, *or Jealousy* A novel by Charles *Reade, published 1866. The story is set in the 18th century. The novel, based on a story by Wilkie *Collins, was unusually frank for its time and Reade was prosecuted in a case in which Charles *Dickens ('as a husband and father') refused to help him. Reade's interest lay clearly not only in the theme of jealousy, both male and female, but in the sexuality of the heroine, Kate, a spirited young Roman Catholic, who marries the less favoured of her suitors, Griffith Gaunt, then falls in love with her spiritual director, who is attacked by Gaunt. Gaunt bigamously marries Mercy Vint, but the novel ends with the reconciliation of Kate and Griffith, and the marriage of Mercy to Kate's first suitor.

GRIFFITHS, Ann (1776–1805) Née Thomas, Calvinistic Methodist hymn-writer from Montgomeryshire, whose 30 hymns are considered among the greatest religious poems in Welsh and whose life and work feature as an emblem of lost cultural integrity in the poetry of R. S. *Thomas.

GRIFFITHS, Trevor (1935–) Playwright, born in Manchester. His plays are all vitally concerned with socialist politics and history and, after an apprenticeship in the fringe, his *The Party* (1973) was staged at the *National Theatre. The play revisits the political events of May 1968 in Paris. He regards television as the most effective political medium, and his *Comedians* (1975) drew on the television series of that name to look at a group of aspiring comedians attending evening class. In 1971 he had provided the screenplay for Warren Beatty's *Reds*. In 1992, *The Gulf between Us* took a very critical stance on the Gulf War, and *Thatcher's Children* (1993) looked at the effects of Thatcherism on a generation born as Margaret Thatcher came into office.

GRIGSON, Geoffrey (1905–85) Poet, critic, and editor of the influential *New Verse* (1933–9), which he founded. His volumes of poetry include *Several Observations* (1939), *Under the Cliff* (1943), *The Isles of Scilly* (1946), *Collected Poems 1924–1962* (1963), *Angles and Circles* (1974), and *History of Him* (1980). Much of his work celebrates his native Cornwall, and his collections of essays, which contributed to his reputation as a fierce controversialist, include *The Harp of Aeolus* (1947) and *The Contrary View* (1974).

GRIMBALD (Grimbold), **St** (d. ?901) A monk of St Bertin at Saint-Omer, the details of whose life are uncertain. King *Alfred summoned him to England for the promotion of learning and acknowledges him as one of his teachers in the preface to the *Regula Pastoralis*. A *Life of Grimbald* survives in the *c.*1300 breviary of Hyde Abbey, Winchester.

GRIMM, Jacob Ludwig Carl (1785–1863) and **Wilhelm Carl** (1786–1859) German brothers who pioneered the study of German philology, law, mythology, and folklore. They are chiefly known in Britain for their collection of fairy-tales, *Kinder- und Hausmärchen* (1812–15), translated into English by Edgar Taylor with illustrations by George *Cruikshank in 1823 as *German Popular Stories*. The brothers regularly revised the collection (popularly known as 'Grimms' Fairy Tales') until 1858, increasingly directing them at children by removing bawdy material and inserting or intensifying Christian content. The pair also began the German etymological dictionary *Deutsches Wörterbuch*.

GRISHAM, John (1955–) Prolific American writer of legal thrillers, beginning with *A Time to Kill* (1988). *The Firm* (1991; filmed 1993) became a best-seller. Writing a novel every year, Grisham sold over 60 million books during the 1990s.

Groat's-Worth of Wit See GREENE'S GROAT'S-WORTH OF WIT.

GRONNIOSAW, Ukawsaw (*c.*1705–1775) Writer of the first account of an African being taken into slavery in English, *A Narrative of the Most Remarkable Particulars in the Life of James Albert Ukawsaw Gronniosaw, an African Prince Written by Himself* (1772). After his escape from slavery he lived in Colchester and Kidderminster. *See* SLAVERY.

GROSS, Philip (1952–) Poet and writer in a wide variety of genres, notably *young adult literature, with, as in *Going For Stone* (2002), elements of *horror. His latest poetry collection, *Off Road to Everywhere* (2010), was preceded by the prize-winning *The Water Table* (2009); *Changes of Address* (2001) collects the poems published from 1980 to 1998. His collaborations with artists in other media include *A Cast of Stones* (1996), meditations on Avebury and Stonehenge, with paintings by John Eaves and F. J. Kennedy, and works for the stage, including an opera and dance drama.

GROSSETESTE, Robert (*c*.1170–1253) Bishop of Lincoln and the first chancellor of Oxford University. He was the author of translations from the Greek, including *Aristotle's Ethics* and the works of Pseudo-Dionysius (*see* DIONYSIUS THE PSEUDO-AREOPAGITE). He was a prolific, influential figure in the development of the Augustinian philosophical tradition, and was largely responsible for the Oxford emphasis on the development of the natural sciences. Some of his writings tackle theological topics with originality; others develop his interest in experimental science, especially optics and mathematics. Influenced by the Platonic tradition in Arab philosophy, he developed his light-metaphysic in his work *De Luce*.

GROSSMITH, George (1847–1912) and **Weedon** (1852–1919) Brothers and authors of *The *Diary of a Nobody* (1892), which appeared in **Punch*, illustrated by Weedon. Its popularity with a wide range of readership was immediate, and has not faltered. *See* DIARIES.

GROTE, George (1794–1871) Historian, MP for the City of London, 1832–41. He took an active part in favour of the Reform movement. Radical and atheist, he was much influenced by James Mill (1773–1836) and *Utilitarianism. He retired from Parliament in order to devote himself to his famous *History of Greece* (eight volumes, 1846–56). It was for many years the standard work on the subject. Grote's other publications include studies of *Plato (1865) and *Aristotle (1872).

Group, the An informal association of writers, mostly poets, set up in London by Philip *Hobsbaum, with his then wife, poet Hannah Kelly, in 1955. A number of poems or a chapter of a novel (which had been previously distributed to other participants) would be read aloud by the author and discussed by all present. Members included Peter *Redgrove, Peter *Porter, Edward Lucie-Smith, and George *MacBeth. An anthology of the Group's writings, edited by Hobsbaum and Lucie-Smith, appeared in 1963 (*A Group Anthology*). When Hobsbaum moved to Belfast he established a similar group there in 1963, usually known now as the 'Belfast Group'. Members included Seamus *Heaney, Michael *Longley, and Paul *Muldoon. From 1966, when Hobsbaum went to Glasgow, meetings were organized by Heaney.

Grub Street According to Samuel *Johnson's *Dictionary*, 'originally the name of a street near Moorfields in London, much inhabited by writers of small histories, dictionaries, and temporary poems, whence any mean production is called *grubstreet'*. It ran north–south for a quarter of a mile through the insalubrious parish of St Giles Cripplegate. The name was changed in 1830 to Milton Street (in honour of a builder).

Grub Street Journal A satirical literary newspaper, which ran for 418 weekly issues, 8 January 1730 to 29 December 1737. *Pope (whose enemies were reviled as 'Knights of the Bathos') was suspected of having had a hand in it, but the connection has not been proved. Its targets included John *Henley's *Hyp-Doctor*, Lewis *Theobald, Colley *Cibber, and Edmund *Curll.

Gryll Grange The last satirical novel of Thomas Love *Peacock, serialized 1860, issued as a book 1861. Mr Falconer, idealist and classicist, lives in a tower attended by seven virgins, but is persuaded to join a convivial house party at Gryll Grange, where he woos and wins Morgana Gryll. As part of the Christmas festivities they act an Aristophanic play which parodies the competitive examinations newly introduced into the Civil Service: Hannibal, Richard Cœur de Lion, and Oliver Cromwell are all failed. Urbane and polished, *Gryll Grange* upholds civilization, harmony, and completeness against the rising prestige of technology and religious asceticism.

Guardian, The (1) A periodical started by Richard *Steele on 12 March 1713, ceasing 1 October 1713. Major contributors included Joseph *Addison, Eustace Budgell (1686–1737), George *Berkeley, and Alexander *Pope, whose attack on Ambrose *Philips is no. 40, and whose essay on gardens is no. 173. It was opposed politically by the Tory *Examiner* and was succeeded by the *Englishman*. (2) A national daily newspaper, generally thought to represent centre-left political views, originally published (1821–1959) as the **Manchester Guardian*.

GUARINI, Giovanni Battista (1538–1612) Italian playwright, author of the pastoral drama *Il pastor fido* (1589–1602), written in emulation of *Tasso's *Aminta*. It had a considerable vogue in England in the 17th century, where it was translated many times; notably by Sir Richard *Fanshawe in 1647 as *The Faithfull Shepherd*.

Gudrun (1) In the **Völsunga Saga* and in Morris's **Sigurd the Volsung*, daughter of the king of the Niblungs. (2) Heroine of the *Laxdaela saga* (*see* SAGA), who appears in Morris's version, 'The Lovers of Gudrun', in *The *Earthly Paradise*. (3) Gudrun Brangwen in D. H. Lawrence's *Women in Love*.

guidebooks Specialized works providing advice, recommendations, and instructions for travellers, associated with the rise of mass tourism in the mid-19th century. Earlier literature had provided impetus and determined itineraries for travel: religious texts for pilgrims; classical works for those on the *Grand Tour. The fifth book of the *Liber Sancti Jacobi*, a mid-12th-century pilgrim's guide to Santiago de Compostela, is often regarded as the first guidebook with its wide-ranging and opinionated advice. Mariana Starke (1761/2–1838) introduced a number modern guidebook conventions into *Letters from Italy* (1800), including suggested itineraries and a rating system of one, two, or three exclamation marks for paintings. Accommodating the surge in continental travel after 1815, a number of companies marketed uniform series of guidebooks: those of Karl *Baedeker and John *Murray became so well known that they served as synonyms for guidebook. The Murrays introduced the term 'handbook', and helped create the stereotype of the tourist with guidebook in hand, subservient to the star ratings by which they ticked off sights and decided their responses. The guidebook's practical purpose allowed other travel writing to become more self-consciously literary and personal, to allow full play to a *Romantic sensibility, and to disparage mass tourism.

Major 20th-century examples include the *Blue Guides* (1918 onwards) of James Muirhead (1853–1934) and his brother Findlay (1860–1935), which were particularly authoritative on art and architecture; the *Footprint* series, starting with South America (1924), and aimed at independent travellers with unusual destinations; and Fodor's, by the American Eugene Fodor (1905–91), updated yearly from 1936, with quirky comments on cultural difference. The more democratic American series—Arthur Frommer (1929–) began with *Europe on $5 a Day* (1957) and the Harvard students' *Let's Go* series followed in 1960—incorporated reader feedback. In the 1970s 'anti-tourist' tourist guides appeared, catering for the emerging backpacking phenomenon, including *Lonely Planet* (Melbourne) from 1973, and *Rough Guides* (London) from 1982. The internet has facilitated further interaction between guidebook content and reader comment, creating a sense of online community among travellers, but the convenient format and portability of the handbook ensures it remains popular.

GUIDO DELLE COLONNE A 13th-century Sicilian writer of Latin romances, influential author of the *Historia Destructionis Troiae*, which was in fact a prose version of a poem by *Benoît de Sainte-Maure. His romance was used as a source in poems attributed to John *Barbour and *Huchown, and by John *Lydgate in his *Troy Book*. The story of Troilus and Cressida, which Guido took from Benoît, was developed by *Boccaccio, *Chaucer, Robert *Henryson, and later *Shakespeare.

GUILLAUME DE LORRIS *SEE* ROMAN DE LA ROSE.

Guinevere The wife of King *Arthur in the Arthurian legend. The name figures in various forms: in *Geoffrey of Monmouth she is 'Guanhamara', of a noble Roman family, brought up in the household of Cador, duke of Cornwall. In the *Brut* of *Laȝamon she is 'Wenhaver', a relative of Cador; in *Sir *Gawain and the Green Knight* she is Wenore, Guenore, Gwenore, and Gaynor (the form also in *The *Awntyrs of Arthure*). The most widespread form of both her name and her story developed in the French tradition, in *Chrétien's *Lancelot* (1170s) and the related early 13th-century Prose *Lancelot* of the Vulgate cycle, where the queen Guenièvre is the lover of Lancelot, with disastrous consequences: Lancelot fails to achieve the *Grail, and in the final confrontation with Modred he arrives too late to save Arthur, finding that the queen has become a nun. This traces only the main tradition of Guinevere, from Chrétien to *Malory; there is also a more disreputable version of her as unfaithful and vengeful, reflected in such poems as *Sir Launfal*. But in this main tradition, the tragic love of Guinevere and Lancelot is one of the classics of *courtly love.

Gulliver's Travels A satire by Jonathan *Swift, published 1726 as *Travels into Several Remote Nations of the World 'By Lemuel Gulliver'*. It has a complex textual history. The idea of a satire in the form of a travel narrative probably emerged at the meetings of the *Scriblerus Club; in the *Memoirs of Scriblerus* the hero is described as visiting the same countries as Gulliver. In the first part, Gulliver, a surgeon on a merchant ship, relates his shipwreck on the island of Lilliput, the inhabitants of which are 6 inches high, everything on the island being on the scale of an inch to a foot compared with things as we know them. Because of this miniaturization, the pomp of the emperor, the civil feuds of the inhabitants, the war with their neighbours across the channel look ridiculous.

By implication, the English political parties and religious denominations are satirized in the implacable feuds between the wearers of high heels and low heels, and in the controversy about whether to break eggs at the big or small end. In the second part Gulliver is accidentally left ashore on Brobdingnag, where the inhabitants are as tall as steeples, and everything else is in proportion. Here the king, after enquiring into the manners, government, and learning of Europe, tells Gulliver that he 'cannot but conclude the bulk of your natives to be the most pernicious race of little odious vermin that nature ever suffered to crawl upon the surface of the earth'.

The third part (which was written last) is occupied with a visit to the flying island of Laputa, and its neighbouring continent and capital Lagado. Apart from some political animus in relation to England's treatment of Ireland, the satire is here directed against men of science (especially members of the *Royal Society), historians, and projectors, with special reference to the South Sea Company, which had generated a speculative economic bubble that had burst in 1720. In Laputa Gulliver finds the wise men so wrapped up in their speculations as to be complete fools in practical affairs. At Lagado he visits the Academy of Projectors, where professors are engaged in extracting sunshine from cucumbers and similar absurd enterprises. In the Island of Sorcerers he is enabled to call up the great men of old, and discovers, from their answers to his questions, the deceptions of history. The Struldbruggs, a race endowed with immortality, so far from finding this a mark of special status, are the most miserable of mankind. In the fourth part Swift describes the country of the Houyhnhnms, or horses endowed with reason; their rational, clean, and simple society is contrasted with the filthiness and brutality of the Yahoos, beasts in human shape whose human vices Gulliver is reluctantly forced to recognize. So alienated is he from his own species that when he finally returns home he recoils from his own family in disgust. *Gulliver's Travels* was an immediate if scandalous success and was read (according to Alexander *Pope and John *Gay) 'from the cabinet council to the nursery'.

Gull's Horn-Book, The (1609)   A satire on fops and gallants by Thomas *Dekker, which parodies the *courtesy books of the period. As a sociological document it reveals attitudes to leisure, luxury, and London's shifting population.

GUNN, Neil (1891–1973) Scottish novelist, short story writer, and playwright, born in Caithness. His first novel *The Grey Coast* (1926), short stories, and several of his plays contemplate Highland life in decline but *Morning Tide* (1931) introduces his characteristic sensuous lyricism, remarkable evocations of childhood and of the sea, and a hard-won confidence in humankind. *Sun Circle* (1933) and *Butcher's Broom* (1934) are historical novels. The modernist *Highland River* (1937) maps the life of its hero, Kenn, on to his experience of the river of his childhood. *The Silver Darlings* (1941) set in Caithness immediately after the Napoleonic Wars, synthesizes folk song, historical detail, acute psychological observation, and symphonic recurrences of almost supernatural experiences. *Young Art and Old Hector* (1942) explores the shared experience of a child and an old man. In *The Green Isle of the Great Deep* (1944) the duo return, but to a dystopian Celtic heaven. *The Silver Bough* (1948) and *The Well at the World's End* (1951) gently satirize those who wish to observe 'primitive communities'. The thriller *Bloodhunt* (1952) and the metaphysical *The Other Landscape* (1954) envisage rehabilitation after violence. *The Atom of Delight* (1956), Gunn's last book, analyses incidents in the first two decades of his life.

GUNN, Thom (1929–2004) Poet, born in Gravesend, a contemporary of Ted *Hughes at Cambridge. His first volume, *Fighting Terms* (1954), earned critical acclaim for combining vigorous contemporaneity with learned metrical verse. After Cambridge, he moved with his lifelong partner, Mike Kitay, to California; settled permanently in San Francisco in 1960. *The Sense of Movement* (1957) shows the distinct influence of Yvor *Winters, marrying Winters's rationalist precision to treatments of American pop culture (notably the motorcycle rebel). *My Sad Captains* (1961) is a consciously transitional volume: the first half reasserting Winters's 'technique of comprehension', the second introducing the more open syllabic style which would inform all of his subsequent work. *Moly* (1971) is predominantly the result of LSD experiences in the late 1960s; a seemingly counter-intuitive return to formal metrics. *Jack Straw's Castle* (1975) is based on a recurrent nightmare. *The Man with Night Sweats* (1992) is a frank and moving series about friends who were victims of AIDS, acknowledged as an exemplary poetic response to the epidemic. The *Collected Poems* (1993) contains all but the work of *Boss Cupid* (2000), his final volume of 'survivor' poems. His celebration of men of action (and violence), his gallery of heroes (ranging from Elvis Presley to Caravaggio), together with his rational, laconic, colloquial manner provide an interesting synthesis of the English *Movement and elements of American *Beat poetry.

GURDJIEFF, Georgei Ivanovitch (?1874–1949) Esoteric thinker and teacher. He claimed to have spent his youth travelling in Central Asia, India, and Tibet with a company of fellow seekers acquiring occult knowledge. In 1910 he appeared in St Petersburg practising as a healer with theosophical leanings, and in 1914 met his principal disciple, Peter Demianovich Ouspensky (1878–1947), who recorded his teaching in *In Search of the Miraculous* (1950). He moved to the Caucasus during the revolution, then via Constantinople and Berlin to France, where he set up the Institute for the Harmonious Development of Man at Fontainebleau, where Katherine *Mansfield died in 1923. His ideas influenced Aldous *Huxley (*After Many a Summer*, 1939, and *The Doors of Perception*, 1954) and Christopher *Isherwood. Alfred Orage, editor of the *New Age*, was a disciple, and followed him to Fontainebleau in 1922.

GURNAH, Abdulrazak (1948–) Novelist, critic, and academic, born in Zanzibar. His novels mostly engage with questions of cultural identity, betrayal, guilt, and displacement which affect both immigrants and the communities in which they settle, disturbing the view that ethnicity is peculiar to migrants. *Desertion* (2005) traces the transition within an East African coastal community from the colonial period to independence, and within a Muslim family from a claustrophobic but densely textured world to the narrator's arid experience in contemporary Britain.

GURNEY, Ivor (1890–1937) Poet and composer. In the First World War he served on the Western Front, from 1915 to 1917, and was gassed at Passchendaele. He published the volumes *Severn and Somme* (1917) and *War's Embers* (1919). His song settings include *Five Elizabethan Songs* (1920), the A. E. *Housman cycles, *Ludlow and Teme* and *The Western Playland* (1919), and six poems by Edward *Thomas, *Lights Out* (1918–25). After the war Gurney became increasingly unsettled, at times sleeping rough, and taking night walks back to his native Gloucestershire from London. He was committed to a mental institution in 1922, and spent the rest of his life in care, dying in the

City of London Mental Hospital. He had continued to write, producing altogether nearly 300 songs and 1,700 poems. Selections from the poetry were published by Edmund *Blunden (1954), and Leonard Clark (1973). P. J. *Kavanagh edited some 300 items as Gurney's *Collected Poems* (1982).

GUTENBERG, Johann (*c*.1400–1468) The inventor of printing with movable type. Born at Mainz, he learned printing skills in Strasbourg, where he lived from 1434. Returning to Mainz in 1444, he borrowed money from Johann Fust (*c*.1400–1466) in 1448, founding a press with him. Fust dissolved the partnership acrimoniously in 1455, taking possession of the equipment and stock. Books published up to 1455 cannot be assigned certainly to Gutenberg or Fust or Fust's son-in-law Peter Schöffer (*c*.1425–1503), but the 42-line Latin Bible (the 'Gutenberg Bible'), printed at Mainz in 1454, is usually attributed to Gutenberg.

GUTHRIE, Woody (Woodrow Wilson) (1912–67) American folk singer, born in Oklahoma. He travelled around the USA during the Depression, producing *Dust Bowl Ballads* in 1939. His autobiography *Bound for Glory* appeared in 1943. Despite failing health, Guthrie featured in the folk revival of the 1960s, influencing singers like Pete Seeger (1919–) and Bob *Dylan.

Guy Mannering A novel by Walter *Scott, published 1815, the second of the *Waverley* novels. The story, set in the 18th century, narrates the fortunes of Harry Bertram, son of the laird of Ellangowan in Dumfriesshire, who is kidnapped as a child and carried to the Netherlands, where he joins the army, and serves with distinction under Colonel Guy Mannering. Bertram's fortunes are eventually restored, partly due to the efforts of an old Gypsy, Meg Merrilies. The novel was hugely successful and went through eleven editions during Scott's lifetime.

Guy of Warwick Popular verse romance of about 1300, based on an Anglo-Norman original, occurring in four manuscripts ranging from 7,000 to 12,000 lines. Guy is the son of Siward, steward of Rohand, earl of Warwick. He performs many exploits in order to win the hand of the earl's daughter Fenice. The legend was versified by John *Lydgate (*c*.1450).

HABINGTON, William (1605–54) Poet and playwright. *Castara* (1634, anon.), a collection of love poems, celebrates his wife, Lucy Herbert. A later edition (1635) contained in addition some elegies on a friend, and the edition of 1640 a number of sacred poems. He also wrote a tragicomedy, *The Queen of Aragon* (1640).

HADDON, Mark (1962–) Novelist and poet, who achieved wide acclaim with his first adult novel, *The Curious Incident of the Dog in the Night-Time* (2003), a remarkable tour de force written from the point of view of a boy with Asperger's Syndrome. His second adult novel, *A Spot of Bother*, followed in 2006. A collection of poems, *The Talking Horse and the Sad Girl and the Village under the Sea*, appeared in 2005.

Hades The name given in classical mythology to both the god of the underworld (Roman Pluto), the husband of Persephone (Proserpina), and the underworld itself, guarded by the monstrous dog Cerberus. Odysseus' visit to the underworld (**Odyssey*, 11) is echoed in the Hades episode in **Ulysses*. The underworld to which Aeneas descends (**Aeneid*, 6) encompasses both the Elysian Fields of the blessed and Tartarus, the place of punishment. In the New Testament the Greek term Hades is usually translated as Hell, as in the story of Dives and Lazarus (Luke 16).

HADFIELD, Jen (1978–) Poet, whose poems reflect her travels in Canada and her domicile on the Shetland island of Burra. Combining startling metaphor with dialect and an inventively transgressive syntax, they explore the natural world, frequently from animal perspectives. A debut collection, *Almanacs* (2005), was followed by *Nigh-No-Place* (2008), which won the T. S. Eliot Prize.

HĀFIZ, Shams ad-dīn Muhammad of Shiraz (d. *c.*1390) Greatest of the Persian lyric poets. His poems, mainly lyrical odes (*ghazal*s), are collected together in his *Divan*. He sings of the sorrows of love, wine, and beauties of na-

ture, with a mystic tone and depth of language and feeling that make him unique. The poems are most commonly treated as mystical, less often as mundane, which points to a balance within them. However, any one single approach does less than justice to the poet's obvious joy in the subtle weaving of imagery and allusion in ways open to more than one interpretation.

Sir William **Jones was the first to translate one of Hāfiz's *ghazal*s into English, and since then there has been a plethora of translators, Gertrude **Bell (1897) and Richard **Le Gallienne (1905) being the best known. Arthur Arberry (1905–69) produced the most acute of the 20th-century interpretations (1947 and 1954). There is a new complete translation of the *ghazal*s by Peter Avery (2007). *See also* SAʿDĪ.

HAGGARD, Sir Henry Rider (1856–1925) Novelist; his first book, *Cetywayo and his White Neighbours* (1882), attacked the British policies in South Africa he observed as secretary to the governor of Natal. He achieved fame with his 34 novels of exotic adventure; the most celebrated of these—*King Solomon's Mines* (1886) and *She* (1887)—were set in Africa, and vividly convey the fascination he found in its landscape, wildlife, tribal society, and mysterious past. His worldwide readership included **Jung, who used *She* as a striking example of the anima concept, or the expression of a feminine inner personality. *The Days of my Life* (1926) is an autobiography.

hagiography Lives of the saints, sometimes including martyrology, lives of the martyrs. Originally written and collected by monks in the early and medieval churches, such collections of lives were also made of post-**Reformation saints, for example **Puritans and Quakers (*see* FRIENDS, SOCIETY OF). The term is often now used to condemn uncritical biography.

haiku A lyric verse form of Japanese origin, composed in unrhymed lines of five, seven, and five syllables (thus seventeen in all), and encapsulating a single impression of a natural scene or object at a particular season (e.g. by reference to blossom or melting snow). It arose in the 16th century and achieved classical expression in the work of Bashō (1644–94). At first the opening stanza in a sequence, the haiku became established as an independent form in the 19th century. Western poets of the early 20th century, notably the school of *imagism, admired its indirect evocation of feeling through natural images, and encouraged its now widespread use in English.

(⊕) SEE WEB LINKS

• American Haiku archives

HAKLUYT, Richard [pron. Haklit] (1552–1616) Geographer and travel writer who greatly influenced overseas enterprise and the development of English prose writing. From the 1580s he promoted colonial projects, especially in America, translating accounts of voyages and travels, writing about English enterprises, collecting existing accounts in English by others, and encouraging Elizabethan 'sea dogs' to write about their experiences. He produced some 25 travel works, including *Divers Voyages Touching the Discoverie of America* (1582), an edition of Peter Martyr's *De Orbe Novo* (1587), and *The Principall Navigations, Voiages and Discoveries of the English Nation* (1589, much enlarged, 1598–1600). Hakluyt popularized the exploits of men like Sir John Hawkins (1532–95), Sir Francis Drake, Sir Humphrey Gilbert (1537–83), and Martin Frobisher (1535–94). After his death, Hakluyt's papers came into the hands of Samuel *Purchas.

Hakluyt Society Named after Richard *Hakluyt and founded in 1846 to publish 'rare and valuable Voyages, Travels, and Geographical Records'. In practice, the edited texts are historical, emanating from any source, and if necessary translated into English. Henry Yule's *Cathay and the Way Thither* (1866) set a standard of scholarship the Society has striven to maintain in the subsequent volumes.

(⊕) SEE WEB LINKS

• Hakluyt Society website

HALE, Kathleen (1898–2000) OBE, Scottish writer and artist, remembered for her sixteen children's books about Orlando, a 'marmalade' cat, and his family, beginning with *Orlando's Camping Holiday* (1938). The stories were adapted for BBC Radio *Children's Hour*. There is an autobiography (1996).

HALEY, Alex (1921–92) African American writer, born in Ithaca, New York, co-author of *The Autobiography of Malcolm X* (1965). *Roots: The Saga of an American Family* (1976; TV miniseries, 1977) claimed to trace his ancestry to Kunta Kinte, who had been brought from Gambia to the province of Maryland in 1767, to be sold as a slave. He later admitted that passages had been taken from the novelist and anthropologist Harold Courlander (1908–96). *Queen: The Story of an American Family* (1993) investigated another part of Haley's family and was completed after his death.

half-rhyme *See* RHYME.

HALIBURTON, Thomas Chandler (1796–1865) Canadian writer and judge. His anonymous work, *The Clockmaker, or The Sayings and Doings of Samuel Slick, of Slickville* (1836; London, 1837), had a great vogue in England. Other works in the same series, including *The Attaché, or Sam Slick in England* (1843–4), were designed to stimulate political reform through the satirical observations of the character Sam Slick, a Yankee from Ohio. He spent the last years of his life in England.

HALIFAX, George Savile, marquess of (1633–95) Politician and writer, a powerful influence in the court of Charles II, known for the moderation and avoidance of extremes he advocates in his *Character of a Trimmer* (1688). He was an anti-Catholic, but he successfully opposed the Exclusion Bill of his uncle the earl of Shaftesbury, which would have debarred the future James II (a Catholic) from the throne. His *Letter to a Dissenter* dissuades Nonconformists (who, like Catholics, were excluded from public office) from the extreme step of throwing in their lot with James's court party. He is the 'Jotham' of John *Dryden's *Absalom and Achitophel*. His other works include *The Anatomy of an Equivalent* (1688), *A Lady's New Year's Gift, or Advice to a Daughter* (1688), and *A Character of King Charles II* (printed with *Political, Moral, and Miscellaneous Reflections* in 1750).

Hali Meihad 'Holy Maidenhood' A letter on virginity from the West Midlands, written *c.*1220s. It occurs in two manuscripts which also contain *Sawles Warde* and one or more members of the group of saints' lives known as the *Katherine Group. Its exaltation of virginity and hostility to marriage is extreme.

HALL, Edward (1497–1547) Author of a chronicle glorifying the House of Tudor entitled *The Union of the Two Noble and Illustre Families* of *Lancaster and York*. First published posthumously in 1548 by Richard *Grafton, it was prohibited by Queen Mary. Hall's *Chronicle* is interesting for the account it gives of the times of *Henry VIII and the vivid description of his court and of the Field of the Cloth of Gold. It was used by William *Shakespeare as a source in his early history plays.

HALL, Joseph (1574–1656) Anglican bishop, religious writer, and satirist. He was successively bishop of Exeter (1627) and Norwich (1641), but was ejected in 1643 when the Parliamentarians did away with bishops. His *Virgidemiarum* (1597, 1598), and a satirical description of London disguised as a travel narrative, *Mundus Alter et Idem* (1605?; trans. 1608) were not, as he claimed, the first English satires; Thomas *Lodge's *Fig for Momus* had appeared in 1593. Hall's *Characters of Virtues and Vices* (1608) is the first English example of Theophrastan *character-writing, and his *Three Centuries of Meditations* (1606–9), quarried from his sermons, offered a Protestant alternative to the influential Catholic mode of Ignatian meditation. His *Humble Remonstrance* (1640 and 1641), defending the rule of bishops, drew a reply from the syndicate of Puritan ministers who wrote under the acronym *Smectymnuus. Hall is famous for his plain, Senecan prose style.

HALL, Sir Peter (1930–) Director of plays, operas, and films. From 1955 to 1959 Hall ran the Arts Theatre in London, where he directed the British premiere of *Waiting for Godot* in 1955. He founded the Royal Shakespeare Company in 1960, laying great emphasis on intelligent verse speaking, and was director of the *National Theatre from 1973 to 1988. He then started his own theatre company, and in 2005 revived *Godot* as a touring production. He has applied the same classical rigour to Samuel *Beckett, Harold *Pinter, and Edward *Albee as to Stratford Shakespeare, where his joint production, with John Barton, of the history cycle *The Wars of the Roses* (1963) remains a modern landmark.

HALL, Radclyffe (1880–1943) Pseudonym of Marguerite Radclyffe-Hall, novelist and poet. Between 1906 and 1915 she published five volumes of verse, and she went on to write seven novels, from *The Forge* (1924) to *The Sixth Beatitude* (1936). Her restrained yet open treatment of lesbianism in *The Well of Loneliness* (1928) occasioned a trial for obscenity. It was banned and an appeal refused; it only became legally available in the UK in 1949.

HALLAM, Arthur Henry (1811–33) Scholar and critic, educated at Trinity College, Cambridge, where he became a close friend of Alfred *Tennyson and after his early death the subject of Tennyson's *In Memoriam* (1855). His *Remains*, edited by his father Henry Hallam in 1834, contain poetry, philosophy, and criticism.

HALLIWELL, James Orchard (later James Orchard Halliwell-Phillips, after his marriage to Henrietta, daughter of Sir Thomas Phillips) (1820–89), Shakespearian scholar. He entered Trinity College, Cambridge, in 1837 where he had unlimited access to the locked-up manuscripts. After seventeen volumes went missing, he transferred to Jesus College. He made important discoveries in the Stratford records, incorporating them into his biographical studies of Shakespeare. He published a *Life of William Shakespeare* (1848, etc.), *Observations on the Shakespearean Forgeries at Bridgewater House* (1853), on the John Payne *Collier controversy, *A Dictionary of Old English Plays* (1860), and *Outlines of the Life of Shakespeare* (1881–7). He edited the *Works* of Shakespeare (16 vols, 1853–65) and some 150 volumes, mainly of 17th-century literature; also *The Nursery Rhymes of England* (1842–6), a pioneering study which remained standard until that of the *Opies.

HALL-STEVENSON, John (1718–85) Writer. He owned the half-ruinous Skelton Castle, in Yorkshire, where he hosted a group of rakish literary friends, 'the Demoniacs', including Sterne. Laurence *Sterne, who may have based Eugenius in *Tristram Shandy* and *A *Sentimental Journey* on him. He published *Fables for Grown Gentlemen* (1761), *Crazy Tales* (1762), and other often bawdy verse. His *Works* (1795) include a frontispiece depicting his 'Crazy Castle'.

hamartia *See* POETICS.

HAMBURGER, Michael (1924–2007) Poet and translator, born in Berlin of a German family which emigrated to England in 1933. His volumes of poetry include *Flowering Cactus* (1950), *Weather and Season* (1963), which contains 'In a Cold Season', on the trial of the Nazi war criminal Adolf Eichmann, *Ownerless Earth* (1973), *Roots in the Air* (1991), *Late* (1997), and *Collected Poems 1941–1994* (1995). His many distinguished translations include versions of Hugo von *Hofmannsthal (1961), and the *Poems and Fragments* of Friedrich Hölderlin (1966). *A Mug's Game* (1983) is an autobiography.

HAMILTON, Anthony (Antoine) (c.1646–1720) Brother-in-law of the comte de Gramont (1621–1707). Hamilton wrote the *Mémoires de la vie du comte de Gramont*, published anonymously at Cologne in 1713, which are an important and entertaining source for the social history of the period. They were edited (in French) by Horace *Walpole and translated into English (with many errors) by Abel Boyer in 1714; this translation, revised and annotated by Walter *Scott, was reissued in 1811. The first part, dealing with Gramont's life on the Continent down to the time of his banishment from the French court, was probably dictated by Gramont to Hamilton. The second, relating to the English court, appears to be Hamilton's own work.

HAMILTON, Charles (1876–1961) Writer for children; he became the world's most prolific author of juvenile fiction, regularly writing in excess of 70,000 words a week. He wrote under many pen-names; best known were 'Frank Richards' of the *Magnet* (1908–40) and 'Martin Clifford' of the *Gem* (1907–39). The *Magnet* published his *school stories about Greyfriars School, whose pupils included Billy Bunter. George *Orwell, writing in *Horizon* (1939), objected to the snobbery, insularity, dated slang, and tedious style of this exclusively male world. See Hamilton's *The Autobiography of Frank Richards* (1952).

HAMILTON, Elizabeth (1756–1816) Novelist, born in Belfast, but domiciled mainly in Scotland. Her novels *Translations of the Letters of a Hindoo Rajah* (1796) and *Memoirs of Modern Philosophers* (1800) satirized contemporary radicals like William *Godwin. *The Cottagers of Glenburnie* (1808) portrays manners and economy in rural Scotland. Hamilton also wrote tracts on female education, and an autobiographical fragment.

HAMILTON, Ian (1938–2001) Poet, editor, biographer, and essayist. He published collections of poetry, *The Visit* (1970), *Returning* (1976), and *Fifty Poems* (1988); other works include *The Little Magazines* (1976); a life of Robert *Lowell (1983); and *In Search of J. D. Salinger* (1988), a compelling account of the difficulties he encountered in writing about his elusive subject, which he describes as 'a kind of *Quest for Corvo*, with *Salinger as quarry'. This investigation led to *Keepers of the Flame: Literary Estates and the Rise of Biography* (1992), in which he discusses historical, legal, and ethical questions associated with the growing interest in literary biography.

HAMILTON, Patrick (1904–62) Playwright and novelist. His plays include *Rope* (1929) and *Gas Light* (1939), both thrillers, and *The Duke in Darkness* (1943), a historical drama. His novels include *Craven House* (1926), the story of the inmates of a boarding house; the 'London trilogy' collected as *Twenty Thousand Streets under the Sky* (1935), which deals with the interlocking lives of a waiter, a prostitute, and a barmaid; *Hangover Square* (1941), a thriller set in Earls Court; and *The Slaves of Solitude* (1947), which centres on the wartime experiences of the quiet spinster Miss Roach. Hamilton's particular gift is for describing, in the words of J. B. *Priestley, 'a kind of No-Man's-Land of shabby hotels, dingy boarding-houses and all those saloon bars where the homeless can meet'. Hamilton's Marxism is expressed in his compassion for the hopelessness of his characters' lives.

Hamlet A tragedy by *Shakespeare, probably written by 1601. A short text probably reconstructed from memory by actors was published 1603 and a good text, almost twice as long, 1604–5. The *folio text (1623) adds passages not in the second quarto, and omits others. His chief non-dramatic source was *Saxo Grammaticus' narrative in his *Historiae Danicae*, as retold by Belleforest in his *Histoires tragiques*.

Old Hamlet, king of Denmark, is recently dead, and his brother Claudius is now king, having married his widow Gertrude. Young Hamlet, returning from university at Wittenberg, learns from his father's ghost that Claudius murdered him by pouring poison into his ear, and is commanded to avenge the murder without injuring Gertrude. Hamlet warns his friend Horatio and the guard Marcellus (who have also seen the apparition) that he intends to feign madness, and swears them to secrecy. Immediately after his famous speech of deliberation beginning 'To be, or not to be' (III. i) he rejects Ophelia, whom he has loved, while spied on by Claudius and Ophelia's father Polonius. He welcomes a troupe of visiting players, and arranges a performance of a play ('the Mousetrap') about fratricide, which Claudius breaks off when the player Lucianus appears to murder his uncle by pouring poison into his ear. Hamlet refrains from killing Claudius while he is at prayer, but stabs through the arras in his mother's closet, killing Polonius, before reproaching his mother for her affection for Claudius. Claudius sends Hamlet to England with sealed orders that he should be killed on arrival. Hamlet outwits him, however, returning to Denmark, having arranged the deaths of his old friends Rosencrantz and Guildenstern, who were his uncle's agents. During Hamlet's absence Ophelia has gone mad with grief from Hamlet's rejection of her and her father's death, and is found drowned. Her brother Laertes, having returned from France, is determined to avenge his sister's death. Hamlet and Laertes meet in the graveyard where Ophelia is to be buried, and fight in her grave. Claudius arranges a fencing match between Hamlet and Laertes, giving Laertes a poisoned foil; an exchange of weapons results in the deaths of both combatants. Gertrude drinks a poisoned cup intended for her son, and the dying Hamlet succeeds in killing Claudius. Fortinbras, prince of Norway, whose military heroism has been alluded to throughout the play, appears fresh from wars with Poland and gives Hamlet a military funeral. *See also* OBJECTIVE CORRELATIVE.

HAMMETT, Dashiell (1894–1961) American writer of *detective fiction, whose tough, realistic works (*Red Harvest*, 1929; *The Maltese Falcon*, 1930; *The Glass Key*, 1931; *The Thin Man*, 1932; etc.), based in part on his own experiences as a detective in San Francisco, created a vogue for *hardboiled heroes and seedy locales. Many of his stories were filmed, and he worked as a Hollywood screenwriter, before falling foul of the McCarthy witch-hunt and being imprisoned for 'un-American activities' in 1951. He was a long-standing companion of the playwright Lillian *Hellman (1905–84).

HAMMICK, Georgina (1939–) Novelist and short story writer. In her stories, *People for Lunch* (1987) and *Spoilt* (1992), and novels, *The Arizona Game* (1996) and *Green Man Running* (2002), she explores emotional terrain with acuity and an ironic wit which illuminates the dark corners of relationships. She is one of five poets in *A Poetry Quintet* (1976).

HAMPTON, Christopher (1946–) CBE, playwright, screenwriter, and translator. His first play, *When Did You Last See my Mother?* (1966), was followed by *Total Eclipse* (1968), based on the tormented relationship of Paul *Verlaine and Arthur *Rimbaud. The comedy *The Philanthropist* (1970) recalls *Molière's *Le Misanthrope*. *Savages* (1972) is a political and ecological drama set in the Amazon. *Treats* (1976) is a provoking study of sexual behaviour; *Tales from Hollywood* (1982) focuses on German literary refugees trying to survive in

Hollywood in the 1930s. Hampton has made many translations and stage and screen adaptations of works by Malcolm *Bradbury, George *Steiner, Joseph *Conrad, Graham *Greene, and Henrik *Ibsen. He adapted Laclos's *Les Liaisons dangereuses* (1985, stage; 1989, screen) and Ian *McEwan's *Atonement* for screen (2007). Most of his original work is marked by an ironic, good-humoured, and humane detachment.

Handlyng Synne By *Mannyng of Brunne, a treatise in octosyllabic couplets, begun in 1303 and based on the French *Manuel des pechez* by William of Wadington. It deals with sin under various headings: the Ten Commandments, the seven deadly sins, sacrilege, and the sacraments, culminating with penance. Each sin is illustrated by a story and the value of the work lies in Mannyng's narrative vigour.

Hand of Ethelberta, The A novel by Thomas *Hardy, published 1876. As the author suggests in his preface, this is 'a somewhat frivolous narrative'.

HANLEY, James (1901–85) Dublin-born novelist, short story writer, and playwright, brought up in Liverpool from 1908. He joined the merchant navy at the age of 12. His second novel, *Boy* (1931), about sexual violence on board a ship, was published by private subscription; the mass market edition in 1934 was prosecuted for obscenity. Hanley did not allow it to be republished during his lifetime. The lives of the Dublin poor were portrayed in *The Furys* (1935), *Secret Journey* (1936), and *Our Time Is Gone* (1940). His many other novels include *The Ocean* (1941), *Sailors' Song* (1943), *The Closed Harbour* (1952), and *A Woman in the Sky* (1973). His volumes of short stories include *Men in Darkness* (1931), *People Are Curious* (1938), and *A Walk in the Wilderness* (1950). *Broken Water* (1937) and *No Directions* (1943) are autobiographies.

hardboiled A term signifying a matter-of-fact, understated style of describing violence characteristic of American crime fiction since the 1920s. One of its earliest exemplars was Dashiell *Hammett and the term is also linked with *noir fiction.

Hard Cash: *A Matter of Fact Romance* A *sensation novel by Charles *Reade, published 1863 (published in serial form as *Very Hard Cash*). Reade's polemical and sometimes graphically violent novel attacks mid-Victorian Britain's poorly regulated asylum system through two main plot strands. The first concerns Alfred

Hardie, whose father Richard wrongfully incarcerates him in a lunatic asylum in order to conceal a banking fraud. He escapes only when a fellow inmate sets the institution on fire. A second plot involves genuine insanity. Reade concludes the novel with a request for information regarding the wrongful committal of sane persons—a request which eventually led to Rosina Bulwer-Lytton's *A Blighted Life* (1880).

hard science fiction A term describing a form of *science fiction in which scientific information and thinking is fundamental to the story and the aim is to be as accurate (or plausible) as possible. Encouraged by John W. Campbell, its exponents include Arthur C. *Clarke, Robert L. Forward, and Stephen *Baxter.

Hard Times A novel by Charles *Dickens, published 1854. Thomas Gradgrind, a citizen of Coketown, a northern industrial city (based on Dickens's impressions of Preston), is a misguided exponent of *utilitarianism, an 'eminently practical man', who believes in facts and statistics and brings up his children Louisa and Tom accordingly, ruthlessly suppressing the imaginative sides of their nature. He marries Louisa to Josiah Bounderby, a manufacturer 30 years older than herself. Louisa consents partly from the indifference and cynicism engendered by her father's treatment, partly from a desire to help her brother, who is employed by Bounderby and who is the only person she loves. James Harthouse, a young politician without heart or principles, comes to Coketown and, taking advantage of her unhappy life with Bounderby, attempts to seduce her. The better side of her nature is awakened by this experience, and at the crisis she flees for protection to her father, who in turn is awakened to the folly of his system. He shelters her from Bounderby and the couple are permanently separated. But Tom has robbed his employer's bank, and though he contrives for a time to throw suspicion on a blameless artisan, Stephen Blackpool, he is finally detected and hustled out of the country.

HARDY, Thomas (1840–1928) Novelist and poet, born near Dorchester in Dorset. At the age of 22 he went to London, where he worked for an architect, and lost his religious faith. He returned home in 1867, began his first (unpublished) novel, *The Poor Man and the Lady*, and probably fell in love with Tryphena Sparks, a relative aged 16. The success of *Far from the Madding Crowd* (1874) enabled him, in 1874, to give up architecture for writing, and to marry Emma Gifford, whom he had met in 1868. The marriage soon produced intolerable strains, but it also produced, after Emma's death in 1912, some of Hardy's most moving poems. Between 1874 and the publication of *Jude the Obscure* in 1895 Hardy wrote twelve other novels (see below), as well as many short stories and poems. During this time Hardy greatly enjoyed the admiration of London's literary and aristocratic society and complained of reviewers' views on his 'pessimism' and 'immorality' and the hostile reception of his last novels. He gave up the writing of fiction, which he had always regarded as inferior to poetry. In 1912 Emma died and in 1914 Hardy married Florence Dugdale. The underlying theme of many of the novels, the short poems, and the epic drama *The Dynasts* is the struggle of human beings against the indifferent force that rules the world. Hardy's sharp sense of the humorous and absurd finds expression largely in the presentation of the rustic characters in the novels.

Hardy's novels and short stories, according to his own classification, fall into three groups:

Novels of Character and Environment: *Under the Greenwood Tree* (1872); *Far from the Madding Crowd* (1874); *The Return of the Native* (1878); *The *Mayor of Casterbridge* (1886); *The *Woodlanders* (1887); *Wessex Tales* (1888); *Tess of the D'Urbervilles* (1891); *Life's Little Ironies* (1894); *Jude the Obscure* (1896, in the edition of the *Works* of that year).

Romances and Fantasies: *A *Pair of Blue Eyes* (1873); *The *Trumpet Major* (1880); *Two on a Tower* (1882); *A Group of Noble Dames* (1891); *The *Well-Beloved* (published serially 1892; revised and reissued 1897).

Novels of Ingenuity: *Desperate Remedies* (1891); *The *Hand of Ethelberta* (1876); *A Laodicean* (1881).

A Changed Man, The Waiting Supper, and Other Tales (1913) is a reprint of 'a dozen minor novels' belonging to the various groups.

Hardy published eight volumes of poetry: *Wessex Poems* (1898); *Poems of the Past and Present* (1902); *Time's Laughingstocks* (1909); *Satires of Circumstance* (1914); *Moments of Vision* (1917); *Late Lyrics and Earlier* (1922); *Human Shows* (1925); *Winter Words* (1928). The *Collected Poems* (1930), published posthumously, contain over 900 poems, 'Poems of 1912–13' in *Satires of Circumstance* are written in recollection of his first wife. Hardy disliked, to use his own words, the 'jewelled line' of poetry that did not, to his mind, follow the patterns of speech. He experimented with rhythms and verse forms, avoiding facile flow.

Hardy published over 40 short stories, most of which were collected in *Wessex Tales* (1888); *A

Group of Noble Dames (1891); *Life's Little Ironies* (1894); and *A Changed Man* (1913).

Hardy also wrote *The Dynasts* (3 vols, 1904–8) in blank verse and prose, and the poetic drama, *The Famous Tragedy of the Queen of Cornwall* (1923).

HARDYNG, John (*c.*1378–*c.*1464) Author of *The Chronicle of John Hardyng* in verse, written between the years 1440 and 1457. The *Chronicle* covers the period from Brutus (*see* BRUT) to 1437 and argues the claims of English kings (in the interests of Henry V and Henry VI) to over-lordship of Scotland. A second version revises the work in the Yorkist interest.

HARE, Sir David (1947–) Playwright and director, resident dramatist at the *Royal Court Theatre, 1970–71. *Slag* (1970), *The Great Exhibition* (1972), *Knuckle* (1974), and *Teeth 'n' Smiles* (1976) showed his keen eye for both the iniquities of social privilege and the contradic-tions of radical idealism. In *Plenty* (1978), Hare provides a metaphor of the economic and ideo-logical decline of post-war Britain through the experiences of Susan Traherne, a former courier in Occupied France. As an associate director at the *National Theatre, he directed *Pravda* (1985), a political satire concerning two national newspapers, co-written with Howard *Brenton, with whom he had previously collaborated on *Brassneck* (1973). Also at the National he staged his trilogy of plays on British institutions: *Racing Demon* (1990), about the Church of England; *Murmuring Judges* (1991) a critique of the Brit-ish criminal justice system; and *The Absence of War* (1993), about the Labour Party. *Amy's View* (1997) charts the antagonism between ageing actress Esme Allen and her daughter's partner, who represents the destructive 'Rise of the Media'. Hare appeared in his own account of a visit to Israel and Palestine, *Via Dolorosa* (1998). In 2003 and 2004 he acknowledged the growing strength of the docu-drama movement with his *The Permanent Way*, a devised piece question-ing Britain's railway system post-privatization, and *Stuff Happens*, in which Tony Blair and George Bush are shown as they move towards the decision to invade Iraq. *The Power of Yes* (2009) portrays Hare's own attempt to under-stand the financial crisis.

HARINGTON, James *See* HARRINGTON, JAMES.

HARINGTON, Sir John (1560–1612) Courtier, translator, and writer,godson of *Elizabeth I. Supposedly at the queen's com-mand, he translated *Ariosto's *Orlando furioso*

(1591), retaining the *ottava rima* of the original and providing *A Preface or rather Brief Apology of Poetry*, closely related to Philip Sidney's *De-fence of Poetry*. Harington's *A New Discourse of a Stale Subject, Called the Metamorphosis of Ajax* (1596), a proposal for the introduction of water closets, was an ill-judged bid for royal favour; together with other satires and epigrams it led to a period of exile from court. His letters and miscellaneous writings were collected in Henry Harington's *Nugae Antiquae* (1769–75).

Harlem Renaissance The flourishing of *African American literature and culture in the 1920s and 1930s, centred on the Harlem district of New York. Anthologies such as Alain Locke's *The *New Negro* (1925) helped promote a new ethnic pride; there was the first staging of a play by an African American on Broadway in 1925; landmark works of the decade included Jean *Toomer's *Cane* (1923). The new poets included Countee *Cullen and Langston *Hughes. James Weldon *Johnson and Zora Neale *Hurston also began their careers in this period.

Harley Lyrics A collection of 32 Middle English lyrics that have been collected with other material in Latin and French in the British Library manuscript Harley 2253, from Ludlow, Shropshire, dated to the 1340s. The collection preserves the only surviving versions of some secular poems, including 'Alysoun', 'Lenten ys come with love to toune', 'Blow, Northerne Wynd', 'Wynter wakeneth al my care', and 'The Man in the Moon'.

Harlot's Progress, The *See* HOGARTH, WILLIAM.

HARNETT, Cynthia (1893–1981) Writer and illustrator who is remembered for her six vivid and well-researched historical novels for children—*The Great House* (1949), *The Wool-Pack* (1951; winner of the *Carnegie Medal), *Ring out Bow Bells!* (1953), *Stars of Fortune* (1956), *The Load of Unicorn* (1959), and (with the illustrator Gareth Floyd) *The Writing on the Hearth* (1971).

Harper's Monthly Magazine Founded in 1850 by Harper & Brothers of New York, at first to reproduce in America the work of distinguished English contributors to serials like Charles *Dick-ens, W. M. *Thackeray, and Edward *Bulwer-Lytton. It subsequently became more American in character, publishing work by Herman *Melville, William Dean *Howells, Sarah Orne *Jewett, and others. From 1900 to 1925 it was known as *Harper's*

New Monthly Magazine, and subsequently as Harper's Magazine.

Harper's Weekly (1857–1916) An illustrated political and literary journal, published in New York, best known for its engravings and woodcuts. It serialized novels by Charles *Dickens, Elizabeth *Gaskell, and others, and later published work by Rudyard *Kipling, Henry *James, and Arthur Conan *Doyle.

Harrington (Harington), James (1611–77) Political philosopher, who wrote the great republican work The *Commonwealth of Oceana (1656). Harrington also wrote several tracts in defence of this work, and other political works expounding concepts including republicanism, the ballot, rotation of officers, and indirect election. In 1659 he founded the Rota, a *coffee-house academy which met for political discussion, the first of its kind in England. In 1661 he was arrested and imprisoned on a charge of treason, defended himself ably, and was later released. Harrington has never been considered a great stylist but his shrewd historical analysis and political projections have increasingly attracted attention.

HARRINGTON, Sir John See HARINGTON, SIR JOHN.

HARRIOT (Hariot), Thomas (1560/61–1621) Mathematician, astronomer, and polymath. He was employed by Sir Walter *Ralegh and went on the 1585–6 expedition to Virginia. His A Briefe and True Report of the New Found Land of Virginia (1588), an early example of an economic survey, was printed by *Hakluyt. It shows sympathetic understanding of the local Algonquian and, incidentally, promoted tobacco. His failure to publish and the probably unfair association of his name with atheism and necromancy spoilt his reputation.

HARRIS, 'Frank' (really James Thomas) (1856–1931) Author and editor. He edited the Evening News (1883–6), the *Fortnightly Review (1886–94), and, the *Saturday Review (1894–8), in which he published G. B. *Shaw (as a drama critic), H. G. *Wells, and Max *Beerbohm. As an editor he had great flair, but a scandalous reputation gathered round him, occasioned by his fight against Victorian prudery, by his decreasingly respectable role as editor (of such periodicals as the Candid Friend, Vanity Fair, and Hearth and Home), and by his sexually boastful, explicit (and unreliable) memoirs, My Life and Loves (4 vols, 1922–7). He also published The Bomb (1908), a novel

about socialist-anarchism; a play, Mr and Mrs Daventry (performed 1900; pub. 1956), based on a plot which he bought from his friend Oscar *Wilde; and lives of Shakespeare, (1909) Wilde (1918), and Shaw (1931). His one-time admirer and employee, Hugh Kingsmill, published a biography (1932).

HARRIS, Joel Chandler (1848–1908) American journalist and author, with a strong interest in the myths, customs, dialects, and idioms of black Americans, which he reproduced in his famous 'Uncle Remus' series, from Uncle Remus: His Songs and Sayings (1880) to Uncle Remus and the Little Boy (1910). Originally published in the Atlanta Constitution newspaper, these consist of trickster folk tales featuring a variety of animals, with cunning Brer Rabbit as hero, told by 'Uncle Remus', an elderly former slave, to a little boy and interspersed with comments on many other subjects.

HARRIS, Robert (1957–) Novelist and political journalist. His non-fiction books include Selling Hitler (1986), an account of the forged Hitler diaries. His successful fictional career began with Fatherland (1992), an *alternate history novel in which the Third Reich survives into the 1960s; Enigma (1995), set in Bletchley Park during the Second World War; and Archangel (1998), looking back from 1990s Russia to the terrors of the Stalin era. Pompeii (2003) is set against the eruption of Vesuvius in AD 79. His trilogy about Marcus Tullius *Cicero, including Imperium (2006) and Lustrum (2009; American title Conspirata) is due to be completed in 2012. Modern political novels include The Ghost (2007), on ghostwriting the memoirs of a recently retired British prime minister, which reflects his admiration for George *Orwell and Graham *Greene, and The Fear Index (2011).

HARRIS, Sir Wilson (1921–) Guyanese-born novelist, who came to England in 1959. His 'Guyana Quartet' consists of Palace of the Peacock (1960), The Far Journey of Oudin (1961), The Whole Armour (1962), and The Secret Ladder (1963). Later works include The Waiting Room (1967), The Age of the Rainmakers (1971), and The Tree of the Sun (1978). The Carnival trilogy consists of Carnival (1985), The Infinite Rehearsal (1987), and The Four Banks of the River of Space (1990). Jonestown (1996) describes the mass suicide of the followers of cult leader Jim Jones. It was followed by The Dark Jester (2001), The Mask of the Beggar (2003), and The Ghost of Memory (2006). His fiction is experimental in form, built on a complex, poetic structure, interweaving history, mythology, and the contemporary world. *See also* POSTCOLONIAL LITERATURE.

HARRISON, Tony (1937–) Poet, born and educated in Leeds. Memories of his working-class childhood and family life provide the material for much of his poetry. His volumes include *The Loiners* (1970), *Continuous* (1981), *A Cold Coming: Gulf War Poems* (1992), and *Under the Clock* (2005). There is a *Collected Poems* (2007). Among his 'theatre works' are versions of *Molière's The Misanthrope* (1973), *Racine's Phèdre* (*Phaedra Britannica*, 1975), the *Oresteia* (1981), and Victor *Hugo's The Prince's Play* (1996). *V* (1985; televised 1987), written during the miners' strike of 1984–5, was the first of his 'film poems'; others include *The Blasphemers' Banquet* (1989) and *The Shadow of Hiroshima* (1995). *Collected Poems* and *Collected Film Poetry* appeared in 2007. Harrison is renowned for his skilful adaptation of colloquial speech and impassioned commentary on public affairs.

Harrowing of Hell A semi-dramatic poem of 250 lines in octosyllabic couplets from about 1250, based on the legend (derived from the Apocryphal Gospel of Nicodemus) that Christ descended into hell to lead out the souls condemned there by Adam's sin. There are also versions in Old and Middle English prose, in *Piers Plowman*, and in the *mystery plays.

Harry Potter *See* POTTER, HARRY.

Harry Richmond, The Adventures of A novel by George *Meredith, published 1871. This began as 'an autobiographical study', particularly evident in the novel's consideration of the father–son relationship.

HARSENT, David (1942–) Poet. His volumes include *A Violent Country* (1969), *Dreams of the Dead* (1977), *Mister Punch* (1984), *News from the Front* (1993), *A Bird's Idea of Flight* (1998), *Marriage* (2002), and *Legion* (2005), and *Selected Poems 1969–2005* (2007). His early work is characteristically short-lined, imagistic, and melancholic; later work employs a longer line and experiments with versions of poetic sequence and of narrative. Harsent's knowledge of Bosnia underlies the sequence 'Legion', a desolating descant on modern warfare. Harsent has translated the work of the Bosnian poet Goran Simic. He also writes crime thrillers under a pseudonym, and has collaborated with Harrison *Birtwistle on the operas *Gawain*

(1991), based on the medieval poem *Sir *Gawain and the Green Knight*, and *The Minotaur* (2008).

HARTE, Bret (1836–1902) Author and poet. Notable among the short stories which made him famous were 'The Luck of Roaring Camp' (1868) and 'The Outcasts of Poker Flat', which were included in *The Luck of Roaring Camp and Other Sketches* (1870). His humorous-pathetic verse includes 'Plain Language from Truthful James' (1870), often referred to as 'The Heathen Chinee'. He collaborated briefly with Mark *Twain. After periods as American consul in Germany and at Glasgow he lived in England.

HARTLEY, David (1705–57) Philosopher and physician. In his *Observations on Man, his Frame, his Duty and his Expectations* (1749) he repudiated the view of the third earl of *Shaftesbury and Francis *Hutcheson that the 'moral sense' is instinctively innate in us, and attributed it rather to the tendency of ideas which have occurred together to recall one another. From this association of the ideas of pain and pleasure with certain actions, Hartley traces the evolution of the higher pleasures out of the lower, until the mind is carried to 'the pure love of God, as our highest and ultimate perfection'. The psychological doctrine was founded on an attempt to find Newtonian principles in the operation of the mind, notably in the theory of physical 'vibrations' or 'vibratiuncles' in the 'medullary substance' of the brain. This mechanistic theory of the processes of the imagination was popularized by Joseph *Priestley in *Lectures on Oratory and Criticism* (1777) and influenced the development of aesthetic theory up to the time of S. T. *Coleridge, who named his first son Hartley in honour of the philosopher.

HARTLEY, L. P. (Leslie Poles) (1895–1972) Novelist. His stories were published as *Night Fears* (1924) and *The Killing Bottle* (1932). *The Shrimp and the Anemone* (1944), *The Sixth Heaven* (1946), and *Eustace and Hilda* (1947) are a trilogy (known by the title of the third novel): the first volume is a powerfully evocative account of a childhood summer by the sea in Norfolk. Hartley's best-known novel is *The *Go-Between* (1953), narrated in the first person by an elderly man recalling in 1952 the events of the hot summer of 1900, when, staying with a school friend in a Norfolk country house for the holidays, he innocently carried letters between the friend's sister and the local farmer with whom she was having an affair. The novel's opening sentence, 'The past is a foreign country:

they do things differently there,' is often quoted. Hartley's other novels include *A Perfect Woman* (1955); *The Hireling* (1957); *The Brickfield* (1964); and *The Love-Adept* (1969).

HARVEY, Gabriel (1552/3–1631) Writer and scholar; as a fellow of Pembroke Hall, Cambridge, he became Edmund *Spenser's friend and probably his tutor. He figures as Hobbinol in Spenser's *The *Shepheardes Calender* (1579). In his exchange of *Letters* with Spenser (1580) he indicated the difficulties of writing English verse in classical metres, but also delivered his judgement of *The *Faerie Queene*, as it then existed, as '*Hobgoblin* run away with the Garland from Apollo'. Harvey's marginalia (comments written in the books he owned) record his wide-ranging interests in notes on rhetoric, mathematics and navigation, politics, astrology, medicine, his contemporaries, and literature, including references to William *Shakespeare and to his friends Philip *Sidney and Spenser.

HARVEY, Sir Paul (1869–1948) Scholar and diplomat, the compiler of *The Oxford Companion to English Literature* (1932), the first of the Oxford *Companions*, the idea for which originated in a suggestion from Kenneth Sisam at the *Oxford University Press in 1927–8; he wrote most of the entries himself. It was conceived as a reference book on the lines of *Brewer's *Dictionary of Phrase and Fable*, to contain English authors, plots of their works, and characters; foreign authors commonly quoted; legendary characters; a little classical background; and allusions, such as 'The Wise Men of Gotham'.

HARY'S *Wallace* A famous Scottish epic poem celebrating the deeds of Sir William *Wallace, written in the 1470s by Hary (Harry; *c.*1440–*c.*1492). The earliest extant version, now in the National Library of Scotland, was written in 1488 by John Ramsay, the scribe of John *Barbour's *The Bruce*. The poem consists of *c.*12,000 lines in heroic couplets. Wallace is presented throughout as a committed hero of great valour, in contrast to his English opponents. The rewriting of the poem in 1722, by William Hamilton of Gilbertfield, angered Robert *Burns.

Haunted Man and the Ghost's Bargain, The A Christmas book by Charles *Dickens, published 1848. Redlaw, a learned chemist, is haunted by memories of sorrow and injustice. He is visited by an evil spirit, who makes a bargain by which he will forget them, on condition that he communicates this power of oblivion to everyone he meets. He discovers with horror that forgetfulness blots out from his own life and the lives of those about him gratitude, repentance, compassion, and forbearance. He prays to be released from his bargain, which is effected by the influence of the angelic Milly Swidger.

Havelok the Dane, The Lay of A late 13th-century romance in 3,000 lines of rhyming octosyllables. There is an Anglo-Norman version, the anonymous *Lai d'Haveloc*, which resembles the 800-line account in Anglo-Norman at the beginning of Geffrei *Gaimar's *Lestoire des Engleis*. The dispossessed Havelok, prince of Denmark, marries Goldeboru, the dispossessed daughter of King Athelwold of England. Havelok is brought up by the fisherman Grim. At the end all three return to Denmark, defeat Havelok's usurping guardian Godard, and reclaim the throne. The story has parallels with events in English and Norwegian history, but most of its material and themes are legendary. The manuscript was discovered by accident in the Bodleian Library.

HAVERGAL, Frances Ridley (1836–79) Poet and hymn-writer, who spent much of her life with the poor. Her many published volumes were collected as *Poetical Works* (1884); her autobiography was issued in 1880. 'Take my life and let it be' remains her best-known hymn.

HAWES, Stephen (*c.*1474–*c.*1511) A poet in the tradition of *Chaucer and *Lydgate, groom of the chamber to Henry VII. His *Passetyme of Pleasure* was first printed by Wynkyn de *Worde, 1509. His *Example of Vertu*, an allegory of life spent in pursuit of purity, was printed by de Worde in 1512. Other works include *The Conversion of Swearers* and *The Comfort of Lovers*.

HAWKER, R. S. (Robert Stephen) (1803–75) Clergyman and poet, from 1834 vicar of Morwenstow in Cornwall; much of his poetry was inspired by Cornish landscape and legend. He was an isolated and eccentric figure, portrayed in Sabine *Baring-Gould's *The Vicar of Morwenstow* (1875) and in Piers Brendon's *Hawker of Morwenstow* (1975). He was the author of 'The Song of the Western Men', based on an old Cornish ballad, first published anonymously in 1825. He published part of a projected long blank verse Arthurian poem, *The Quest of the Sangraal* (1864), which has passages of visionary power attributed by some to his opium addiction.

HAWKESWORTH, John (1720–73) Schoolmaster and author. With Samuel *Johnson and Joseph *Warton, he successfully conducted the *Adventurer*, a bi-weekly successor to Johnson's *Rambler*, 1752–4. His highly successful *Almoran and Hamet* (1761) is an *oriental tale. Untrammelled by space or time, Almoran can change into any shape to pursue his strange, and often supernatural, adventures among magnificent heroes and base villains. Hawkesworth edited and annotated various journals, including those of James *Cook and the explorer Philip Carteret (1733–96), for his *Account of the Voyages . . . in the Southern Hemisphere* (1773).

HAWKINS, Sir Anthony Hope (1863–1933) Barrister and author. He gave up the law after the success of *The *Prisoner of Zenda* (1894), published under the pseudonym 'Anthony Hope', and its sequel, *Rupert of Hentzau* (1898).

HAWKINS, Sir John (1719–89) Lawyer and magistrate who devoted his life to music and literature. His edition of Izaak Walton's *Compleat Angler* (1760) was praised by his friend Samuel *Johnson. Hawkins wrote a detailed biography of Johnson (1787) and edited Johnson's works (15 vols, 1787–9).

HAWTHORNE, Nathaniel (1804–64) American novelist and short story writer,born at Salem, Massachusetts, where he began to write stories and sketches and published a novel, *Fanshawe* (1828), at his own expense. His stories were collected in *Twice-Told Tales* (1837) and later volumes, including *Mosses from an Old Manse* (1846) and *The Snow-Image and Other Twice-Told Tales* (1851). *A Wonder Book* (1852) and *Tanglewood Tales* (1853) are stories for children from Greek mythology. The *Blithedale Romance* (1852), a novel which conveys his mixed response to the *Transcendentalists, draws on his experience of the Brook Farm community in 1841. He married in 1842 and settled in Concord. The *Scarlet Letter* (1850), is a classic enquiry into the nature of American Puritanism and the New England conscience, and The *House of the Seven Gables* (1851) is a study in ancestral guilt and expiation. From 1853 to 1857 Hawthorne served as American consul at Liverpool; he then spent two years in Italy, which provided the setting and inspiration for *The Marble Faun* (1860); he spent his last years in Concord. *Our Old Home*, sketches of his life in England, appeared in 1863. Hawthorne has long been recognized as a moralist and allegorist much preoccupied with the mystery

of sin, the paradox of its occasionally regenerative power, and the compensation for unmerited suffering and crime.

HAY, J. MacDougall (1881–1919) Scottish preacher whose novel *Gillespie* (1914) brings an apocalyptic intensity to its portrayal of the impact of an entrepreneur on a rural community.

HAYDON, Benjamin Robert (1786–1846) Historical painter, best known for his posthumously published *Autobiography and Journals* (selections ed. Tom Taylor, 1853). He was a friend of John *Keats, William *Wordsworth, William *Hazlitt, Leigh *Hunt, Mary Russell *Mitford, and Elizabeth Barrett *Browning, and his vivid journals contain many interesting anecdotes and pen portraits of his contemporaries. His outrageous personality has interested many novelists, notably Charles *Dickens, who used him (combined with Leigh *Hunt) as the model for Harold Skimpole in *Bleak House*, and Aldous *Huxley, whose Casimir Lypiatt in *Antic Hay* is based on Haydon.

HAYLEY, William (1745–1820) A prolific poet, whose most ambitious works, *The Triumphs of Temper* (1781) and *The Triumphs of Music* (1804), were ridiculed by Lord *Byron as 'Forever feeble and for ever tame'. In 1805 his *Ballads on . . . Animals* was illustrated by William *Blake. He was a close friend of William *Cowper, whose *Life* he published in 1803. Robert *Southey commented that 'Everything about that man is good except his poetry.' He declined the laureateship in 1790.

HAYS, Mary (1759–1843) Novelist and feminist, friend of Mary *Wollstonecraft and correspondent of William *Godwin; she has been credited with encouraging the relationship which led to their marriage. She wrote for the radical publisher Joseph *Johnson's *Analytical Review* and for the *Monthly Magazine*. Her scandalously frank, partly autobiographical novel, *Memoirs of Emma Courtney* (1796), was followed by *The Victim of Prejudice* (1799) and the six-volume *Female Biographies* (1803). Her later work tended towards the conservative and didactic.

HAYTER, Alethea (1912–2006) Historian and biographer. Her writing includes *A Sultry Month* (1965), and *The Wreck of the Abergavenny* (2002), a study of the effect of catastrophe on other lives, including William *Wordsworth's, whose brother was captain.

HAYWOOD, Eliza (?1693–1756) Actress, playwright, and novelist. Her first novel, *Love in Excess* (1719), explored the complications of desire in a layered, complex narrative. *Fantomina* (1725) imagined the doomed sexual freedom of a masquerading woman. One of her novels libelled Martha Blount (1690–1762), and in revenge Alexander *Pope included a damaging portrait of Haywood in *The *Dunciad.* Haywood's later fictions were still contentious: *The Adventures of Eovaai* (1736) was a political satire, and *Anti-Pamela* (1741) satirized Samuel *Richardson's success. But *The History of Miss Betty Thoughtless*, a novel of female education and reform, had considerable influence. Haywood conducted a notable periodical, the *Female Spectator*, 1744–6.

HAZLITT, William (1778–1830) Critic, *theatre critic, and essayist, who grew up in Ireland, New England, and Shropshire. He attended the New Unitarian College at Hackney, London, absorbing *Enlightenment philosophy and radical politics. He refused to enter the ministry, hoping to become a philosopher or painter. The influences of S. T. *Coleridge, *Wordsworth, and Charles *Lamb turned him towards writing. Hazlitt's first books were philosophical studies: *An Essay on the Principles of Human Action* (1805), which disputes *Hobbes's account of self-interested motives, and a polemic against *Malthus, *A Reply to the Essay on Population* (1807). He moved to London and launched his career as a public lecturer, political journalist, and critic of painting, drama, and poetry, writing for the *Morning Chronicle*, for Leigh Hunt's *Examiner*, and for the *Edinburgh Review*. His *Characters of Shakespeare's Plays* and *The Round Table* (both 1817) were followed by a volume of theatre reviews, *A View of the English Stage*, *Lectures on the English Poets* (1818), *Lectures on the English Comic Writers* (1819), *Political Essays* (1819) including studies of Edmund *Burke. *Lectures Chiefly on the Dramatic Literature of the Age of Elizabeth* (1820), and *Table Talk* (1821–2).

Gripped by an obsessive infatuation with his landlord's daughter, Sarah Walker, he divorced his wife in 1822. *Liber Amoris* (1823), his confessional account of this episode, damaged his public reputation. After marrying Isabella Bridgewater in 1824 he wrote *The *Spirit of the Age* (1825) and *The *Plain Speaker* (1826). Posthumous works include *Literary Remains* (1836).

Hazlitt is now acknowledged as an original master of English prose in the 19th century and as a serious rival to Coleridge in the value of his critical writings. His prose style is variable, but always stamped with personality and passion. He revived the art of the essay, and brought new psychological and political insight into literary criticism. Devoted to the ideals of the French Revolution, he nonetheless grasped the imaginative force of conservatism; this tension between rational enlightenment and the power of 'genius' animates much of his work.

HAZZARD, Shirley (1931–) Australian novelist and short story writer. Her short story collections include *Cliffs of Fall* (1963) and *People in Glass Houses* (1967). *The Evening of the Holiday* (1966) and *The Bay of Noon* (1970) are novels exploring the fruitful theme of northern Europeans in Italy. Hazzard's dense, multi-layered survey of the post-war world *The Transit of Venus* (1980), follows the loves and careers of Australian sisters Caro and Grace, along with the British working-class astronomer Ted Tice, from post-war England through ensuing decades.

H.D. Initials used as pseudonym by Hilda *Doolittle.

HEAD, Bessie (1937–86) Writer, born in South Africa to a 'white' mother and 'black' father under apartheid classification; she lived as a refugee in Botswana, the setting of her major work, from the age of 26. *When Rain Clouds Gather* (1968) addresses the rural community's ability to survive economic hardship and the autocracy of their chief, while *Maru* (1971) and *A Question of Power* (1973) present a young woman's struggle against racism and sexism. Head's stories *The Collector of Treasures* (1977) develop the themes gleaned from interviews with villagers, which were published later as *Serowe: Village of the Rain Wind* (1981). *A Bewitched Crossroad* (1984) counters the European version of Botswana's past. *Tales of Tenderness and Power* (1989) and *A Woman Alone* (1990) collect additional stories and essays. *The Cardinals*, published posthumously (1993), was written in South Africa. Head envisions an Africa free of inherited and imported oppressions, hospitable to European thinking yet strongly enough informed with communal rural traditions to resist the social breakdown and materialism of postcolonial life.

Headlong Hall (1816) A satire by Thomas Love *Peacock, the first of the series of books in which Peacock adapts the Socratic dialogue as a tool for satirizing contemporary culture. Mr Foster the optimist, Mr Escot the pessimist, Mr Jenkinson the status-quo-ite, Dr Gaster, a gluttonous cleric, Mr Milestone, a landscape gardener, and many others gather at the Welsh country house of Squire Headlong to eat, drink, and discuss the arts. The debates of the philosophers enact the clash between the optimism of Condorcet and William *Godwin and the pessimism of *Malthus. *See also* PICTURESQUE.

HEANEY, Seamus (1939–) Irish poet, born in south Londonderry. The most prominent of the poets who emerged from Northern Ireland in the 1960s and 1970s, he moved to the Republic of Ireland in 1972. Heaney's early poetry in *Death of a Naturalist* (1966) is rooted in the farmland of his youth, and communicates a strong physical sense of environment. The more poignant and self-conscious lyrics of *Wintering Out* (1972) and *North* (1975) brood on the cultural and historical implications of words, exploring their use and history in the context of the unfolding crisis in Northern Ireland. The stately elegizing of *Field Work* (1979), the self-lacerating confessionalism of *Station Island* (1984), the cerebral parable spinning of *The Haw Lantern* (1987), the visionary meditations of *Seeing Things* (1991) and the formal plenitude and moral rigour of *The Spirit Level* (1996) exemplify a self-renewing energy that has evoked comparisons with W. B. *Yeats. *Electric Light* (2001), which includes translations and adaptations, and *elegies for Ted *Hughes, Joseph *Brodsky, and Zbigniew *Herbert, was followed by *District and Circle* (2006) and *Human Chain* (2010). Heaney's criticism argues for the relevance of poetry in an unjust world. Among Heaney's major translations are *Sweeney Astray* (1983), *Beowulf* (1999), and stage versions of *Philoctetes* (*The Cure at Troy*, 1990) and *Antigone* (2004). *Opened Ground* (1998) and *Finders Keepers* (2002) are compilations respectively of his poetry and criticism.

'Heart of Darkness' A tale by Joseph *Conrad, serialized in 1899 in *Blackwood's Magazine*, published in 1902. The story is recounted by the narrator, Marlow. Travelling in Africa to join a cargo boat, Marlow grows disgusted by what he sees of the greed of the ivory traders and their brutal exploitation of the natives. At a company station he hears of their most successful agent, Mr Kurtz, who is stationed in the very heart of the ivory country. Leaving the river, Marlow makes an arduous cross-country trek to join the steamboat which he will command on an ivory-collecting journey into the interior, but at the Central Station he finds that his boat has been mysteriously wrecked. He learns that Kurtz has dismissed his assistant and is seriously ill. It becomes clear that Marlow's arrival at the Inner Station is being deliberately delayed. With repairs finally completed Marlow sets off on the two-month journey towards Kurtz. The river passage through the heavy motionless forest fills Marlow with a growing sense of dread. Nearing its destination the boat is attacked by tribesmen and a helmsman is killed. At the Inner Station Marlow is met by a naive young Russian sailor who tells Marlow of Kurtz's brilliance and the semi-divine power he exercises over the natives. A row of severed heads on stakes round the hut give an intimation of the barbaric rites by which Kurtz has achieved his ascendancy. While Marlow attempts to get Kurtz back down the river Kurtz tries to justify his actions and his motives: he has seen into the very heart of things. But dying his last words are: 'The horror! The horror!' Marlow is left with two packages to deliver, Kurtz's report for the Society for Suppression of Savage Customs, and some letters for his girlfriend. Faced with the girl's grief Marlow tells her simply that Kurtz died with her name on his lips. The novel inspired Coppola's post-Vietnam film *Apocalypse Now* (1979). *See* POST-COLONIAL LITERATURE.

Heart of Midlothian, The A novel by Walter *Scott, published 1818 as the second series of *Tales of my Landlord*, loosely based on two historical events: the riots in Edinburgh, in which John Porteous, commander of the Edinburgh City Guard, was dragged from the Edinburgh Tolbooth ('the Heart of Midlothian') and hanged by a mob, and the story of Isobel Walker whose pardon for child murder, for which she had been sentenced to death, was obtained by her sister Helen, after walking to London. Scott had given a picture of the sterner, crueller side of strict *Presbyterianism two years earlier in *Old Mortality*; in this novel, its rigid tenets are seen through more compassionate eyes.

HEATH-STUBBS, John (1918–2006) Poet, educated at Worcester College for the Blind and Oxford, where his first published poems appeared in *Eight Oxford Poets* (1941). His inspiration came chiefly from ancient Greece, Rome, Alexandria, classical myth, Christian legend, and works of art and scholarship, and his poetry included translations from the 14th-century Persian poet *Hāfiz and Giacomo *Leopardi. He was also a poet of the contemporary megalopolis. His first volume was *Wounded Thammuz* (1942); others include *The Blue-Fly in his Head* (1962), *Artorius* (1972), a poem on Arthurian legend, *Sweet-Apple Earth* (1993),

Collected Poems 1943-1987 (1988), and *Pigs Might Fly* (2005). *Hindsights* (1993) is an autobiography.

HEAT-MOON, William Least (1939-) Travel writer,of English, Irish, and Native American (Osage Nation) ancestry, born William Trogdon in Kansas City. *Blue Highways: A Journey into America* (1982) recounts a 13,000-mile journey by van through rural areas and small towns; *PrairyErth (A Deep Map)* (1991) is a study of Chase County, Kansas; and *River Horse: The Logbook of a Boat across America* (1999) describes a four-month waterway journey from the east coast to the west.

Heaven and Earth A poetic drama by Lord *Byron, published in *The *Liberal*, 1822. Like its predecessor *Cain*, it is subtitled 'A Mystery', and questions God's choice to create only to destroy. The story, suggested by Genesis ch. 6, tells of the marriage of rebel angels and mortal women: Japhet, son of Noah, loves Anah, but she and her sister Aholibamah are carried away by their immortal lovers, the spirits Azaziel and Samiasa. The drama ends as the flood sweeps over the earth, and Japhet remains upon a rock as the Ark floats towards him.

Hebrew Melodies A collection of short poems by Lord *Byron, published 1815. Many are on scriptural subjects, but some are love songs and lyrics: the volume was published by Jewish composer Isaac Nathan (?1791-1864) who arranged some to traditional Hebrew melodies.

HECHT, Anthony (1923-2004) American poet, whose volumes include *The Hard Hours* (1967), *The Venetian Vespers* (1979), and *The Transparent Man* (1989). His combat experience in the Second World War fed into his poetry. *The Hidden Law* (1984) is a study of his friend W. H. *Auden. Many of his poems evoke an intense experience of Europe, in a restrained and poignant *confessional mode.

Hector *See* ILIAD.

HEGEL, Georg Wilhelm Friedrich (1770-1831) German philosopher. Endeavouring to overcome the Kantian dualism of nature and spirit, Hegel argues that all difference presupposes a unity, that a definite thought cannot be separated from its opposite, that the idea of fullness, for example, cannot be separated from that of emptiness, that they are identical in difference. Duality and unity are blended in consciousness and the boundaries between mind and matter set aside. Hegel's central idea is the dialectic of thesis–antithesis–synthesis, which he applied to the problem of historical evolution as represented by the *Weltgeist* or World Spirit. His dialectical method was adopted by political thinkers of both right and left, those who supported authoritarian rule in Prussia in the 19th century and those, like Ludwig Feuerbach, Karl *Marx, and Friedrich *Engels, who advocated reform and revolution. Hegel's view of history was significant for Walter *Pater, and he enjoyed a vogue in philosophical circles in England, particularly at Oxford, in the 1880s and 1890s.

HEGLEY, John (1953-) *Performance poet.

HEIDEGGER, Martin (1889-1976) German philosopher. Heidegger was primarily concerned with the question of being; in his formulation, he dealt with the question 'what is "is"?' Heidegger used the word *Dasein* to refer to specifically human modes of being; *Dasein* is, for him, self-conscious and involves not only Being but also the very Question of Being. In his most famous work *Sein und Zeit* (1927: *Being and Time*, 1962), he studies *Dasein* in relation to time, asking how Being deals with its temporality, including the fear of being 'thrown into Being'. Heidegger believed that Being can only be articulated through language; he defined as 'poetry' that language capable of doing this, language which is responsive to Being. His work arose as much out of literary as philosophical tradition, and although Heidegger's writing is often abstruse, and despite the backlash against him due to his sympathies—never unambiguously disavowed—with Nazism, his writings had enormous influence on 20th-century thought and literary theory. In *Todtnauberg* John *Banville explores fictionally the meeting between Paul *Celan, a victim of Nazism, and the philosopher. Heidegger was one of the founders (with Hans-Georg Gadamer) of *hermeneutic criticism, and a crucial influence for 20th-century *existentialism (especially Jean-Paul *Sartre). His work was a starting point for Jacques *Derrida's development of *deconstruction and also significant for the nascent 'ecopoetics'. A collection of his work on the nature of thought, language, and poetry has been translated as *Poetry, Language, Thought* (1971).

Heimskringla A series of short sagas making up a history of the kings of Norway from mythical times to the year 1177, written by *Snorri Sturluson. It has a bearing on English history, as it covers the reign of the Danish king

*Canute (Cnutr) and describes Viking expeditions to England. Its title is taken from its opening words, 'Kringla heimsins'—'orb of the world'.

HEINE, Heinrich (1797–1856) German poet, born of Jewish parents in Düsseldorf. His early lyric poetry, collected in the *Buch der Lieder* (1827: *Book of Songs*), is characterized by effusively romantic emotion combined with sharp self-mockery and deflating irony. His savage and witty attacks on German thought and literature brought him notoriety in Germany where his works were officially proscribed in 1835. George *Eliot wrote appreciative essays on his works. In *Essays in Criticism*, 1st series (1865), Matthew *Arnold acclaimed Heine as an embodiment of the modern spirit and as a force for liberation.

HEINLEIN, Robert Anson (1907–88) American *science fiction writer; his first story, 'Lifeline' (1939), was for *Astounding Science Fiction*, and he was one of the editor John W. Campbell's great successes. 'All You Zombies' (1959) is one of science fiction's most remarkable time-travel ideas. Many of his early stories linked into a loose 'future history', including the collection *The Past through Tomorrow* (1967). A series of successful children's science fiction novels in the 1950s was succeeded by *Starship Troopers* (1959), whose political libertarianism and support for the military made it controversial. *Stranger in a Strange Land* (1961) had a cult following in the mid-1960s. *Farnham's Freehold* (1964) and *The Moon is a Harsh Mistress* (1966) reflected his enthusiasm for the 'competent man', but an increasingly strident narrative voice emerged in novels such as '*The Number of the Beast*' (1980).

Heir of Redclyffe, The A novel by Charlotte *Yonge, published 1853. This novel, illustrating the contrast between real and apparent virtue, is the story of the cousins Guy and Philip Morville. Guy, the heir of a baronetcy and an ancient house, is hot-tempered but generous; Philip a much-admired prig. Guy's character, refined by Christian discipline, is eventually vindicated and he marries. On his honeymoon he finds Philip ill with fever; Guy nurses him, catches the fever, and dies, whereby the now repentant Philip inherits Redclyffe. A product of Yonge's devotion to Tractarian principles, *The Heir of Redclyffe* was extremely popular. Profits from the novel, donated to Bishop Selwyn of New Zealand, helped to finance a new missionary schooner, *The Southern Cross*.

He Knew He Was Right A novel by Anthony *Trollope, published 1869. The novel's strength lies in its exploration of the destructive power of sexual jealousy in the disintegrating marriage of Louis and Emily Trevelyan.

Helen of Troy Wife of Menelaus, king of Sparta, abducted by Paris, son of Priam, king of Troy; she was, as first told in the *Iliad*, the cause of the Trojan War, 'the face that launched a thousand ships' (*Dr Faustus*). She has come to epitomize variously love, beauty, and disastrous irresponsibility, in works from *Troilus and Cressida* to W. B. *Yeats's 'When Helen lived' and 'No second Troy'.

Heliand, The An Old Saxon paraphrase in alliterative verse of the New Testament, dating from the 9th century.

HELIODORUS *See* AETHIOPICA.

Hellas A lyrical drama by P. B. *Shelley, the last work to be published in his lifetime, 1822. Based in form on the *Persians* of *Aeschylus, it was inspired by news of the Greek War of Independence against the Turkish Empire.

The action, 'a series of lyric pictures', is set at Constantinople, where the Turkish Sultan Mahmud receives a number of messengers reporting the insurrection, and prophesying Greek victory. Shelley uses visionary figures—Christ, Mahomet, Ahasuerus the Wandering Jew, and the phantom of Mahomet II—to explore a cyclical philosophy of history. But the main interest lies in the choruses, composed like songs for opera, and concluding with the celebrated poem 'The world's great age begins anew'. Shelley's preface, his last great appeal for political liberty in Europe, remains a classic statement of English philhellenism: 'We are all Greeks.'

HELLER, Joseph (1923–99) American novelist. His experience as a bombardier in the air force during the Second World War resurfaced in his first novel, *Catch-22* (1961), a satire on the absurdity of war and McCarthyism which brought him instant fame and which has since become a classic of *black humour fiction. *Closing Time*, (1994) is a sequel. *Something Happened* (1974), is the domestic tragicomedy of a middle-aged New York executive, Bob Slocum, and *Good as Gold* (1979) a surreal and comic satire about Jewish New York and Washington politics. *God Knows* (1984), a monologue spoken by the biblical King *David, was followed by

Picture This (1988), on Rembrandt and *Aristotle. Heller published an autobiographical memoir, *Now and Then*, in 1998.

HELLMAN, Lillian (1905–84) American dramatist, screenwriter, librettist, and writer of memoirs. She was for many years the partner of Dashiell *Hammett, and with him was accused of 'un-American activities' during the McCarthy period. Her plays include *The Children's Hour* (1934), set in a girls' school, in which two teachers are accused by a malicious pupil of having a lesbian relationship, and lose the libel action they take against her grandmother; *The Little Foxes* (1939), a family melodrama set in 1900 in the deep South; and *Watch on the Rhine* (1941), an anti-Nazi war drama set near Washington. *Pentimento: A Book of Portraits* (1973) is an account of friendships with various people, including 'Julia', filmed as *Julia* (1977).

HÉLOÏSE *See* ABELARD, PETER.

HEMANS, Felicia (1793–1835) Née Browne, a prolific and popular poet, sometimes outselling even Lord *Byron. Her first volume, *Poems* (1808), published when she was 15, deals with subjects common in 18th-century women's verse—events in family life, apostrophes to genius, hope, and mirth, etc.—but also includes some political and patriotic poems, celebrating English military heroism. In 1812 she married Captain Hemans, an army veteran, from whom she lived apart from 1818, though they had five sons, whom she supported through her writing. *The Domestic Affections* (1812) links patriotism to a middle-class domestic ideology of empire and home. *Welsh Melodies* (1822) treats of local history, landscape, and legend; and *Records of Woman* (1828) evokes legendary, historical, and literary women. The volume is dedicated to Joanna *Baillie, a strong influence on Hemans, as was William *Wordsworth. Hemans made many translations from the Portuguese and published in 1818 *Translations from Camões and Other Poets*. Her best-known poem, 'Casabianca', beginning 'The boy stood on the burning deck', appeared in *The Forest Sanctuary* (2nd edn, 1829). Later works include *Songs of the Affections* (1830), *Hymns on the Works of Nature, for the Use of Children* (1833), *Songs and Hymns of Life* (1834), and *Poetical Remains* (1836).

HEMINGES (Heminge), John (1566–1630), and **CONDELL, Henry** (d. 1627) Fellow actors of Shakespeare and joint compilers of the first *folio of his plays (1623).

HEMINGWAY, Ernest (1899–1961) American short story writer and novelist; his journalism, an important source of income throughout his career, has been collected in *By-Line* (1967) and *Dateline: Toronto* (1985). He settled in Paris, where he met Ezra *Pound and Gertrude *Stein, described in *A Moveable Feast* (1964). Following their advice, he published *In Our Time* (1925), a *modernist sequence of vignettes alternating with stories. *The Sun Also Rises* (1926; in Britain, as *Fiesta*, 1927) catches the post-war mood of disillusion of the *Lost Generation. *A Farewell to Arms* (1929), the story of a love affair between an American lieutenant and an English nurse during the war on the Italian front, demonstrated a similar laconic and understated style. His collections of stories include *Men without Women* (1927) and *Winner Take Nothing* (1933). He celebrated bull fighting in *Death in the Afternoon* (1932) and big game hunting in *The Green Hills of Africa* (1935). He actively supported the Republicans during the Spanish Civil War, and *For Whom the Bell Tolls* (1940) is set against this background. In his later years he lived mostly in Cuba, where his passion for deep-sea fishing provided the setting for *The Old Man and the Sea* (1952), a parable-novella about man's struggle against nature. He shot himself in July 1961, having been seriously ill for some time. Posthumous publications include *The Dangerous Summer* (1985) and *The Garden of Eden* (1987).

hendecasyllabic Having eleven syllables to a verse line, as in a Latin *metre used by *Catullus and imitated in some poems by *Tennyson and by *Swinburne. The English iambic *pentameter, normally of ten syllables, becomes hendecasyllabic when it uses an extra syllable.

hendiadys [from the Greek words meaning 'one by means of two'] A figure of speech by which a single complex idea is expressed by two words joined by a conjunction, e.g. 'sound and fury' for 'furious sound'.

Hengist and **Horsa** The traditional leaders of the Jutes who, according to *Bede (*History*, I. 15), landed at Ebbsfleet in 449 and were given the Isle of Thanet by *Vortigern for a dwelling place.

HENLEY, W. E. (William Ernest) (1849–1903) Poet, critic, and journalist. He suffered from boyhood from tubercular arthritis and had a foot amputated; to save the other he went to Edinburgh in 1873 and placed himself under Joseph Lister's care. His 'Hospital Sketches', first published in the *Cornhill

Magazine in 1875, are a striking poetic record of this ordeal; as is his best-known poem, the defiant 'Invictus'. While in hospital he befriended Robert Louis *Stevenson. They collaborated on four unsuccessful plays in the 1880s and Stevenson acknowledged Henley as an inspiration for Long John Silver in *Treasure Island*. Henley's most important role was as a courageous and independent editor of the *Magazine of Art* (1881–6), the *Scottish* (later *National*) *Observer* (1888–94), and the *New Review* (1895–8); publishing work by Thomas *Hardy, Rudyard *Kipling, Stevenson, W. B. *Yeats, Henry *James, and H. G. *Wells, among others. His prolific literary output includes *A Book of Verses* (1888), *The Song of the Sword and Other Verses* (1892), *London Voluntaries* (1893), and *For England's Sake* (1900).

HENRI, Adrian (1932–2000) Poet and painter; he settled in Liverpool in 1957, and during the 1960s was known (with Roger *McGough and Brian *Patten) as one of the *'Liverpool poets'; from 1967 to 1970 he led the poetry/rock group 'Liverpool Scene'. His own collections of poetry include *Tonight at Noon* (1968), *City* (1969), *From the Loveless Motel* (1980), *Penny Arcade* (1983), and *Collected Poems 1967–1985* (1986).

Henry IV, King, *Parts 1* and *2* Historical plays by *Shakespeare, written and performed about 1597. Part 1 was printed in quarto 1598, Part 2 1600. The chief sources are the chronicles of Edward *Hall and *Holinshed, and Samuel *Daniel's historical poem *The *Civil Wars*. The contemporary popularity of the plays on the stage was attested by Leonard Digges, and they are still frequently performed.

The subject of Part 1 is the rebellion of the Percys, assisted by Douglas and in concert with Mortimer and Glyndŵr; and its defeat by the King and Prince Harry (or Hal), prince of Wales, at Shrewsbury (1403). *Falstaff (originally named Oldcastle) first appears in this play. The prince of Wales associates with him, and Poins, Bardolph, and Peto, in their disreputable life. Poins and the prince contrive that the others shall set on some travellers at Gadshill and rob them, and then be robbed by themselves. The plot succeeds, and leads to Falstaff's well-known fabrication to explain the loss of the booty, and his exposure. At the battle of Shrewsbury, Prince Harry kills Hotspur in single combat, and then discovers Falstaff feigning death. He mourns him with the words 'I could have better spared a better man.' After Harry's exit Falstaff resourcefully claims credit for having slain Hotspur.

Part 2 deals with the rebellion of Archbishop Scrope, Mowbray, and Hastings; while in the comic sub-plot the story of Falstaff's doings is continued, with those of the prince, Pistol, Poins, Mistress Quickly, and Doll Tearsheet. Falstaff, summoned to the army, falls in with Justices Shallow and Silence in the course of his recruiting, and borrows £1,000 from Shallow. Henry IV dies, reconciled to his son, and Falstaff hurries from Gloucestershire to London to greet the newly crowned king, who rejects him in the speech beginning 'I know thee not, old man. Fall to thy prayers', banishing him from his presence but allowing him 'competence of life'.

Henry V, King Historical play by *Shakespeare, written in the spring or summer of 1599. It was printed in 1600 from what may be a memorial reconstruction; the first *folio text (1623) is based on Shakespeare's own papers. Its chief sources are the chronicles of Edward *Hall and *Holinshed. The 1944 film version, with Laurence Olivier as Henry, was consciously patriotic; the 1989 film, directed by Kenneth Branagh, who also played Henry, presented a harsher and more questioning view of the play.

The play opens with the new King Henry astonishing clergy and courtiers by his piety and statecraft. The archbishop of Canterbury demonstrates, in the long 'Salic Law' speech, Henry's claim to the throne of France. The dauphin sends a mocking gift of tennis balls, in a reference to Henry's wild youth, giving the king an immediate pretext for invasion. Henry unmasks the three traitors, Scrope, Grey, and Cambridge, and sets out for France; he captures Harfleur, and achieves a resounding victory at Agincourt (1415), a battle for which he prepares his soldiers in the 'Crispin Crispian' speech. Comic relief is provided by the old tavern companions of *Falstaff, who have fallen on hard times, and by some of Henry's soldiers, especially the pedantic but courageous Welsh captain Fluellen. The new, patriotic, comic characters symbolically defeat the old when Fluellen compels the braggart Pistol to eat a leek (V. i). The last act is given to Henry's wooing of Katherine of France.

Henry VI, King, *Parts 1, 2,* and *3* Sections of a historical tetralogy (completed by *Richard III*) by *Shakespeare written between 1590 and the summer of 1592. Part 1 was not published until the first *folio (1623), but Part 2 was published anonymously in 1594 under the title 'The First Part of the Contention betwixt the Two Famous

Houses of York and Lancaster . . .', and Part 3 in 1595 as 'The True Tragedy of Richard Duke of York, and the Death of Good King Henry the Sixth'. Shakespeare's authorship of the plays was doubted throughout the 18th and 19th centuries; more recently some have argued that parts of the plays were written in collaboration, especially that most of the first act of *1 Henry VI* was by Thomas *Nashe. The plays' chief sources are the chronicles of Edward *Hall and *Holinshed.

Part 1, opening with the funeral of Henry V, deals with wars in France in which the gallant Talbot is a powerful leader on the English side, and the witchlike *Joan of Arc, 'La Pucelle', on the French. After a series of encounters Talbot, together with his valiant son John Talbot, is killed near Bordeaux. A crucial scene in the Temple Garden establishes the opposition of Plantagenet and York in the subsequent wars through the plucking of red and white roses. In the fifth act the earl of Suffolk arranges a marriage between the young Henry VI and *Margaret of Anjou, daughter of the king of Naples, vowing ominously to rule king, queen, and kingdom.

Part 2 shows Henry's marriage to Margaret. The giving of Anjou and Maine to her father as a price for her marriage angers Humphrey, duke of Gloucester, the lord protector; his wife Eleanor is banished as a witch (II. iii) and he is arrested on a charge of high treason, against the king's better judgement, and murdered. Suffolk is banished and, after a touching farewell to Queen Margaret, murdered by pirates on the Kent coast. Richard, duke of York, pretender to the throne, stirs up Jack Cade to rebellion. The final act concerns the battle of St Albans (1455), in which Somerset is killed, a victory for the Yorkists.

Part 3 opens with Henry's attempt to buy peace by making the duke of York his heir, thus disinheriting his son by Margaret. Margaret, enraged and eloquent, instigates the murder of the boy Rutland, York's youngest son, by Clifford, and the mock coronation and murder of York himself. Clifford is killed at the battle of Towton, which also includes a scene symbolic of the horrors of civil war in which a son who has killed his father encounters a father who has killed his son. Henry VI is captured and Edward (IV) declared king; he marries the dowerless widow Elizabeth Grey. Richard, duke of Gloucester (later Richard III), emerges as an ambitious schemer. Warwick, a powerful supporter of the Lancastrian side, is killed at Barnet by King Edward; the battle of Tewkesbury is a decisive victory for Edward, and Margaret's young son (also an Edward) is killed in cold blood by Edward, Richard, duke of Gloucester, and George, duke of Clarence. King Henry, imprisoned in the Tower, is murdered by Richard.

Henry VII, The History of the Reign of By Francis *Bacon, published in 1622. Bacon rejects in this work the medieval chronicle form and the idea of history as the theatre of God's providence. He follows *Machiavelli and Guicciardini in concentrating on political events, but fuses their focus on powerful individuals with *Tacitus' emphasis on underlying causes and motives.

HENRY VIII (1491–1547) King of England, from 1509. His book *A Defence of the Seven Sacraments*, directed against Martin *Luther's teaching, was printed in 1521 and presented to Pope Leo X, who conferred on Henry the title 'Defender of the Faith'. Henry was also an accomplished musician and poet, and several of his compositions survive, including 'Pastime with good company', 'Alas, what shall I do for love?', and 'O my heart and O my heart'. His lyrics deal with courtly and chivalric themes, with one known exception, the sacred composition 'Quam pulcra es'. Henry's private life has been the subject of numerous dramas and works of fiction, including a play by William *Shakespeare and John *Fletcher, and he is popularly remembered for his six wives, who were, successively, Catherine of Aragon (m. 1509), Anne Boleyn, mother of *Elizabeth I (m. 1533), Jane Seymour (m. 1536), Anne of Cleves (m. 1539), Catherine Howard (m. 1540), and Catherine Parr (m. 1543). His life was written by Lord *Herbert of Cherbury.

Henry VIII A historical drama originally acted as 'All is True'. *Shakespeare has been claimed as its sole author, but it is usually held that he was responsible for less than half of it, the remainder being written by John *Fletcher, whose hand in it was originally suggested by *Tennyson. On one of its earliest performances, in June 1613, the firing of cannon resulted in the burning down of the *Globe Theatre.

It deals with the fall and execution of the duke of Buckingham; the question of the royal divorce (vividly depicting the dignified resignation of Queen Katherine); the pride, fall, and death of Cardinal Wolsey; the advancement and coronation of Anne Boleyn; the triumph of Cranmer; and the christening of the Princess Elizabeth.

The chief sources of the play are *Holinshed's *Chronicles* and Foxe's *Acts and Monuments* (or *Book of Martyrs*).

HENRY, O. (1862–1910) Pseudonym of William Sydney Porter, American short story writer. He began to write short stories whilst imprisoned for embezzlement, and published the first of his many collections, *Cabbages and Kings*, in 1904.

HENRYSON, Robert (d. ?1490) Scottish poet. He belongs to a group known until recently, and misleadingly, as 'Scottish *Chaucerians'. Together with William *Dunbar, he is one of the most prominent of the 15th-century Scottish poets. His most important poems are *The *Testament of Cresseid*, a moralizing sequel to Chaucer's *Troilus and Criseyde* that narrates the fortunes of Cresseid after her betrayal of Troilus, and the *Morall Fabillis*, in which Henryson provocatively calls into question the relationship between beast fables and their ostensible morals. Henryson's poetry is notable for its ability to evoke pathos while acknowledging the intransigence of morality and mortality.

HENSHER, Philip (1965–) Novelist and journalist. His 1996 novel *Kitchen Venom* contains an early fictional portrayal of Prime Minister Margaret Thatcher. *The Mulberry Empire* (2002) is a *historical novel set largely in 19th-century Afghanistan. *The Northern Clemency* (2008) returns to England in the 1970s.

HENSLOWE, Philip (c.1557–1616) Theatre owner, manager and financier, he built the *Rose Theatre on Bankside in 1587. With his stepson-in-law Edward Alleyn he was involved in the affairs of several important companies of actors, notably the Lord Admiral's Men, and in the building of the Fortune and *Hope theatres. Most of the dramatists of the period, apart from Shakespeare, at some time wrote for his companies. His *Diary* (ed. R. A. Foakes and R. T. Rickert, 1961) contains a mass of information about theatrical life, and about dramatists and their methods of writing plays.

HENTY, G. A. (George Alfred) (1832–1902) Novelist and journalist, a war correspondent in the Crimea, Abyssinia, Ashanti, Spain, India, and in Paris during the Commune. He wrote several novels for adults, but achieved fame as the author of stories for boys, mainly based on military history. *Out in the Pampas* (1868) was followed by some 70 other books, sometimes at the rate of three or four a year, including *Under Drake's Flag* (1883), *With Clive in India* (1884), and *The Lion of St Mark's* (1889).

HENZE, Hans Werner (1926–) Prolific German composer with wide literary interests. Among Henze's many operas are two with libretti by W. H. *Auden and Chester Kallman, *Elegy for Young Lovers* (1961) and *The Bassarids* (1966); *Moralities* (1968) is a set of three scenic cantatas with texts by Auden after *Aesop. The large-scale stage work *We Come to the River*, described as 'actions for music' with a text by Edward *Bond, was written for the Royal Opera House, Covent Garden (1976).

Heptaméron, L' A collection in French of 72 tales of love (originally intended as 100, but unfinished) by Marguerite de Navarre (1492–1549), sister of King Francis I. The tales, which depict love as a serious and sometimes tragic passion, are linked by the fiction that the narrators are travellers detained in an inn by a flood. The name *Heptaméron*, or 'seven days', was first given to the collection in 1559, on the analogy of Boccaccio's *Decameron*.

Hera See JUNO.

HERACLITUS OF EPHESUS (fl. c.500 BC) Greek philosopher, commonly associated with the idea that 'everything is in flux'. 'Fluxing' afterwards became associated with weeping: hence Heraclitus becomes 'the weeping philosopher', as opposed to the 'laughing' *Democritus. More accurately he is 'obscure', preferring to express himself in aphorisms; more than 100 survive.

Her Benny A novel by the Methodist author Silas K. *Hocking, published in 1879. Set in Liverpool, it vividly describes the struggles of two street children to survive in the face of poverty and neglect. It proved enduringly popular, was translated into several languages, and sold a million copies in Hocking's lifetime. Anne Dalton's stage adaptation (1993) has been regularly revived.

HERBERT, Sir A. P. (Alan Patrick) (1890–1971) Writer and politician, His works include *The Secret Battle* (1919), a stirring account of the horrors of war; *A Book of Ballads* (1949); and *Independent Member* (1950), describing his experiences as MP for Oxford University (1935–50). Herbert campaigned for many causes, including reform in English spelling (in *What a Word*, 1935), improving authors' rights, and changes in the obscenity laws *The Water Gipsies*

(1930, novel) reflects his affection for the Thames.

HERBERT, Frank (1920–86) American *science fiction writer. *Dune* (1965; filmed 1984, dir. David Lynch) became one of the best-selling science fiction novels of the period, thanks in part to its detailed evocation of the ecology of the desert-planet Arrakis/Dune, which tapped into the growing concern for environmental issues. Several sequels followed, elaborating on its Messianic themes and political intrigues. *Whipping Star* (1970) and *Hellstrom's Hive* (1973) are also successful novels.

HERBERT, George (1593–1633) Poet, younger brother of Lord *Herbert of Cherbury, born in Montgomery into a prominent family; his mother was a patron of John *Donne. According to Izaak *Walton, Herbert sent his mother in 1610 a New Year's letter dedicating his poetic powers to God and enclosing two sonnets ('My God, where is that ancient heat towards thee?' and 'Sure, Lord, there is enough in thee to dry'). In 1616 he was elected a major fellow of Trinity College, Cambridge and in 1620 he became public orator at the university, a position that introduced him to men of influence at court. In 1624, and again in 1625, he represented Montgomery in Parliament. He was ordained deacon, probably before the end of 1624, and installed in 1626 as a canon of Lincoln Cathedral and prebendary of Leighton Bromswold in Huntingdonshire, near *Little Gidding, where Nicholas Ferrar, whom Herbert had known at Cambridge, had recently established a religious community. His mother died in 1627, and his *Memoriae Matris Sacrum* was published in the volume containing Donne's commemoration sermon. He became rector of Bemerton, near Salisbury, in April 1630, being ordained priest the following September. In his short priesthood he gained a reputation for humility, energy, and charity. He died of consumption shortly before his 40th birthday. When he realized he was dying he sent his English poems to his friend Ferrar with instructions to publish them, if he thought they might 'turn to the advantage of any dejected soul', and otherwise to burn them. *The Temple*, containing nearly all his surviving English poems, was published in 1633, *Outlandish Proverbs* (a collection of foreign proverbs in translation) in 1640, and Herbert's prose picture of the model country parson, *A Priest to the Temple*, in 1652, as part of *Herbert's Remains*. He told Ferrar that his poems represented 'a picture of the many spiritual conflicts that have passed betwixt God and my soul'. They were much admired in the 17th century, and thirteen editions of *The Temple* came out between 1633 and 1679. In the 18th century John *Wesley adapted some of his poems for hymns. S. T. Coleridge's appreciative notice in *Biographia Literaria* (1817) enhanced Herbert's revived reputation.

HERBERT, Mary *See* PEMBROKE, MARY HERBERT.

HERBERT, Zbigniew (1924–98) Polish poet and essayist, whose predominantly political poetry has appeared in English as *Selected Poems* (1968; repr. 1985, trans. Czesław *Miłosz and Peter Dale Scott) and *Collected Poems 1956–1998* (2007). His translated collections include *Report from the Besieged City* (1977, trans. 1985) and *The Epilogue of the Storm* (1998). His work is admired by Seamus *Heaney.

HERBERT of Cherbury, Edward, Lord (1582–1648) Elder brother of George *Herbert. His adventures are recounted by Herbert in his *Life*, a remarkable document, not least for its unabashed presentation of its author's martial valour, success with women, truthfulness, sweetness of breath, and other virtues. He aspired to a career in public service and in 1619 he became ambassador to France, on Buckingham's recommendation. His most famous philosophical work, *De Veritate*, (1624) was published in Paris. It postulates that religion is common to all men and that it can be reduced to five universal innate ideas: that there is a God; that he should be worshipped; that virtue and piety are essential to worship; that man should repent of his sins; and that there are rewards and punishments after this life. It gained him the title of father of English *Deism, and was widely read in the 17th century. Other works include *De Causis Errorum*, on logical fallacies, and *De Religione Laici* (both 1645); *De Religione Gentilium*, one of the earliest works of comparative theology, and his autobiography (begun in 1643). Herbert also wrote obscure and metrically contorted metaphysical poetry, evidently influenced by his friend Donne, and some tender and musical love lyrics (*see* METAPHYSICAL POETS).

Hercules (Greek Herakles) Mythical Greek hero and demigod. His twelve labours included cleansing the Augean stables, bringing back the apples of the Hesperides, and descending to the underworld to capture Cerberus. He came to represent both a Stoic hero and in Christian allegory a type of Christ.

HERDER, Johann Gottfried (1744–1803) German philosopher and critic. Inspired by Thomas *Percy's *Reliques*, he was an ardent collector of folk song, publishing two volumes of *Volkslieder* (1778–9). In this and in his admiration for James *Macpherson's *Ossian* and for *Shakespeare, about whom he wrote an enthusiastic essay in *Von deutscher Art und Kunst* (1773: *On German Art*), he exercised a profound influence on the young *Goethe.

Hergest, Red Book of See MABINOGION.

hermeneutics A term for the theory of interpretation, employed at first in biblical scholarship, but then also more generally in the humanities and social sciences. In modern literary theory and related fields, the term refers to a philosophical tradition, predominantly German, in which certain general problems of interpretation arise. It originates in the lectures of the theologian Friedrich Schleiermacher (1768–1834), who proposed that comprehension of the grammatical sense of a text was insufficient without a larger intuitive grasp of the author's intention. The philosopher Wilhelm Dilthey (1833–1911) later developed the implications of this idea, and formulated the problem of the 'hermeneutic circle': that we cannot understand any part of a text or of a historical period without understanding the whole, yet we cannot understand the whole without understanding its parts. His answer to the conundrum is that we reconcile part and whole through successively adjusted provisional understandings or intuitive projections. In the philosophical tradition of Martin *Heidegger and his followers, hermeneutics reaches far beyond mere interpretation, as 'understanding' is held to precede its objects. In modern literary theory, a return to hermeneutic problems is found in *Validity in Interpretation* (1967) by E. D. Hirsch (1928–) which distinguishes between a work's determinate 'meaning' and its variable 'significance', and in various alternatives to his view. An especially influential modern hermeneuticist was the French philosopher Paul Ricœur (1913–2005), who noted a distinction between the religious 'hermeneutics of the sacred', which seeks to restore an original meaning that has become obscured, and the modern 'hermeneutics of suspicion', which seeks (as in *Marx and *Freud) a concealed meaning behind misleading appearances.

Hermes See MERCURY.

Hermes Trismegistus The 'thrice great Hermes' of Milton's *'Il Penseroso', the name given by Neoplatonists and devotees of mysticism and alchemy to the Egyptian god Thoth, identified with the Greek god Hermes, and regarded as the author of all mystical doctrines. From the 3rd century onwards the name was applied to the author of various Neoplatonic writings, including *On the Divine Intelligence*. This work, translated by *Ficino (*c.*1490) into Latin and by John Everard (1650) into English, made a notable impact on 16th- and 17th-century writers, such as Thomas Vaughan, Sir Thomas *Browne, and the *Cambridge Platonists. In 1614 Isaac *Casaubon established that the Hermetic writings, far from being ancient, were actually later than *Plato, though many ignored his findings.

Hermsprong, *or Man as He Is Not* (1796) Robert *Bage's final and most popular novel. Hermsprong, who has been brought up among Native Americans (an indication of natural virtue), arrives in England via revolutionary France. Hermsprong's lack of social vices, and his radical views on the equality of women and the class divisions of society, produce many comic situations.

Hero and Leander The tragic story of Leander's love for Hero, the priestess of Aphrodite: he is drowned while swimming to her at night across the Hellespont, and she then in despair throws herself into the sea. This story has been the subject of poems by Christopher *Marlowe (completed by George *Chapman) and by Thomas *Hood, and of a burlesque by Thomas *Nashe in his *Lenten Stuff*.

HERODOTUS (5th century BC) Author of the earliest Greek history. He describes Egypt, Cyrene, and Babylon, apparently as an eyewitness. His main subject is the wars between the Greeks and the Barbarians (i.e. the Persians), but before reaching it he describes in detail the Persian empire, Egypt, Scythia, and the early history of Athens and Sparta. He was criticized for credulousness and fabulousness, even in ancient times, but his methods of research and verification constituted the first recognizable form of history in the modern sense. Indeed, the term 'historiē' or 'learning by enquiry', which is what he calls his work, has come to mean 'history' as we understand it.

Heroes, Hero-Worship and the Heroic in History, On A series of lectures on the role of heroes in history by Thomas *Carlyle, published 1841. Influenced by German thinking, particularly the work of the German philosopher Johann Gottlieb Fichte (1762–1814),

Carlyle establishes a version of history as 'the biography of great men'. Carlyle has six categories of hero—as Divinity, Prophet, Poet, Priest, Man of Letters, and King—and chooses as exemplars *Dante, William *Shakespeare, Martin *Luther, John *Knox, Samuel *Johnson, Jean-Jacques *Rousseau, Robert *Burns, Oliver Cromwell, and Napoleon Bonaparte (1769–1821).

heroic poetry Another term for *epic poetry.

heroic verse (heroic line) The *metre used in the heroic (i.e. *epic) poetry of a given language: in English since the 16th century the iambic *pentameter, in French the *alexandrine, in Italian the *hendecasyllabic line, in Greek and Latin the dactylic *hexameter.

HERRICK, Robert (1591–1674) Poet. Herrick's earliest datable poem was written about 1610 ('A Country Life: To his Brother M. Tho. Herrick'). 'To my dearest Sister M. Mercy Herrick' must also have been written before 1612. In 1613 he entered St John's College, Cambridge, as a fellow commoner, a status reserved for sons of wealthy families. In 1623 Herrick was ordained priest. He mixed with literary circles in London, particularly the group around Ben *Jonson. Friends included Phineas *Fletcher, William *Browne, John *Selden, Richard *Corbett, Mildmay Fane (second earl of Westmorland), and William and Henry *Lawes. He took up the living of Dean Prior, a village deep in the south Devon countryside, in September 1630. Initially repelled by rural life, he developed a feeling for folk customs and festivals like May Day and Harvest Home, which appealed partly because the Puritans tried to suppress them. An ardent loyalist, Herrick was ejected from his living by Parliament in 1647 and returned to London, where the following year his poems *Hesperides*, together with his religious poems *Noble Numbers*, were published. In 1660 he was reinstated at Dean Prior where he remained for the rest of his life. Herrick's secular poems are mostly exercises in miniature, very highly polished and employing meticulous displacements of syntax and word order so as to give diminutive, aesthetic grace to the great chaotic subjects—sex, transience, death—that obsess him. He is one of the finest English lyric poets.

HERSEY, John (1914–93) American novelist and journalist, whose report on the dropping of the first atomic bomb, *Hiroshima* (1946), has become a classic of modern reportage. His other works include *The Wall* (1950), a novel set in the Warsaw ghetto.

HERVEY, James (1714–58) became a Methodist when a student at Oxford, though his Calvinist beliefs later led to a breach with John *Wesley. His *Meditations and Contemplations* (1746–7) and *Theron and Aspasio* (1755), in which he attempted to combine the language of Puritan meditation with that of the *Spectator and Shaftesbury's *Moralists* and drew heavily on *Milton and Edward *Young, were extremely influential in the *Evangelical Revival and had enormous sales.

HERVEY, John, Baron Hervey of Ickworth (1696–1743) Whig courtier and poet. As vice-chamberlain (from 1730) he exercised great influence over Queen Caroline. He collaborated with Lady Mary Wortley *Montagu in response to attacks from Alexander *Pope, notably the 'Sporus' portrait of the *Epistle to Dr Arbuthnot*. Some of Hervey's poems appeared in Robert *Dodsley's *Collection of Poems by Several Hands* (1748–58). His carefully polished *Memoirs of the Reign of George II* give a vivid picture of the intrigues of court life.

HERZEN, Alexander (Aleksandr Ivanovich Gertsen) (1812–70) Russian revolutionary thinker and writer. Having settled in London in 1852, he established the first Free Russian Press (1853) and founded the influential *Bell* (1857–67). Smuggled into Russia, it advocated radical reform and emancipation of the serfs. *My Past and Thoughts* (1855–69), translated in six volumes by Constance *Garnett (1924–7) is his unfinished memoir.

HESIOD (*fl.*700 BC) One of the earliest Greek poets. The *Theogony* contains a very influential account of the origins of the world and the genealogy of the gods, for which the poet claims inspiration from the *Muses. *Works and Days* gives a picture of a farmer's life that was to serve *Virgil for a model in the *Georgics; hence George *Chapman entitled his translation *The Georgics of Hesiod*. The first complete English translation was published by Thomas Cooke (1703–56) in 1728; he was subsequently known as 'Hesiod' Cooke.

Hesperides *See* HERRICK, ROBERT.

HESSE, Hermann (1877–1962) German Swiss author of several mystical novels which attracted a revival of interest in Germany, Britain, and America in the 1960s–1970s. *Siddhartha* (1922) was later adopted as a New

Age cult book. *Der Steppenwolf* (1927) came into vogue with the cult of 'the outsider' initiated in part by Colin *Wilson. His books were banned in Germany in 1943.

hexameter In English, either (1) an iambic verse line with six stressed syllables (*see* METRE), as found in the final line of the Spenserian *stanza and sometimes as the basis of whole *sonnets (e.g. the opening sonnet of Philip Sidney's *Astrophel and Stella* sequence) or even of longer poems (e.g. Robert Browning, *Fifine at the Fair*), and commonly called an *alexandrine after the twelve-syllable French line; or (2) an imitative transposition into English stress patterns of the classical dactylic hexameter, which was the line of Greek and Latin *epic poetry among other forms. In Greek and Latin verse, the dactylic hexameter comprised five dactyls followed by a spondee or trochee, with possible substitution of a spondee for any of the first four dactyls. Several poets have attempted English imitations of this line, most notably A. H. *Clough in *The Bothie of Tober-na-Vuolich* (1848), and in the late 20th century Peter *Reading.

Hey for Honesty, Down with Knavery

A comedy attributed to Thomas *Randolph, printed 1651. The play is a free adaptation of *Aristophanes' *Plutus*, with allusions to current events and recent plays, including mentions of *Falstaff and *Hamlet's ghost.

HEYWOOD, John (?1497–?1580) Author. Under *Henry VIII he was a singer and player on the virginals. He was much favoured by Queen Mary. He published *interludes, substituting the human comedy of contemporary types for the instructive allegory of the *morality; but he used narrative and debate rather than plot and action. His principal works were *The Four PP* (first printed ?1544), *The Play of the Weather* (1533), in which Jupiter listens to conflicting opinions as to the kind of weather to be supplied, and *A Play of Love* (1534). He may also have been the author of *The Pardoner and the Friar* and *Johan Johan the Husband, Tyb his Wife and Sir John the Priest*. Heywood wrote a dialogue called *Witty and Witless*, collections of proverbs and epigrams, and a long satirical poem, *The Spider and the Fly* (1556).

HEYWOOD, Thomas (1573–1641) Dramatist and poet. He was writing and probably acting for Philip *Henslowe's Admiral's Men from 1596, and later became a leading dramatist of Queen Anne's and Lady Elizabeth's Men at the Red Bull and Cockpit theatres. He claimed to

have had at least a hand in over 200 plays, many of which are lost. His best plays are *A *Woman Killed with Kindness* (acted 1603; printed 1607), *The *Fair Maid of the West* (1601–2?; 1609?), and *The *English Traveller* (c.1604). His other chief plays were *The Four Prentices of London* (acted c.1600; printed 1615), ridiculed in Francis *Beaumont's *The *Knight of the Burning Pestle* (1607?); *Edward IV* (two parts, printed 1599); *The Rape of Lucrece* (printed 1608); *The Royal King and the Loyal Subject* (printed 1637), and *The Wise Woman of Hogsdon* (c.1604; printed 1638). *The Golden Age* and *The Brazen Age* (both printed 1611), *The Silver Age* (printed 1613), and *The Iron Age* (two parts, printed 1632) are a panoramic dramatization of classical mythology. His *An Apology for Actors* (c.1608; printed 1612) is the best Jacobean summary of traditional arguments in defence of the stage, and has some good anecdotes. He also translated *Sallust and published poems (including *The Hierarchy of the Blessed Angels*, 1635), translations, and pageants for seven lord mayor's shows.

Hiawatha, The Song of

American narrative poem in unrhymed trochaic *tetrameter (*see* METRE), by Henry Wadsworth *Longfellow, published 1855, reproducing Native American stories which centre in the life and death of Hiawatha. He marries Minnehaha ('laughing water'), and after various adventures departs for the Isles of the Blest to rule the kingdom of the Northwest Wind. Longfellow took his information from the ethnographer Henry Rowe Schoolcraft (1793–1864). The poem's incantatory metre and novel subject matter made it immensely popular, and attracted many parodies.

HICKES, George (1642–1715) The leader of the great generation of Anglo-Saxon scholars which included the *Elstobs, Humfrey Wanley, and Edmund Gibson (1669–1748). He published the first Anglo-Saxon grammar in 1689. The climax of his work was the monumental *Linguarum Veterum Septentrionalium Thesaurus*, or the 'Treasury of the Northern Tongues' (1703–5), a comparative grammar of Old English and the related Germanic tongues, produced through much collaboration.

HIGDEN, Ranulf (d. 1364) A Benedictine monk of St Werburgh's, Chester. His popular Latin prose *Polychronicon* is a universal history surviving in over 100 manuscripts, translated by *John of Trevisa in 1387 and printed by William *Caxton in 1482.

HIGGINS, Aidan (1927–) Novelist, born in Co. Kildare, and best known for *Langrishe, Go Down* (1966), an extension of the Irish *'big house' genre, which sets the decline of a once powerful family of Catholic landowners in the context of the larger European malaise of the 1930s. Other novels include *Balcony of Europe* (1972), and *Bornholm Night Ferry* (1983), a melancholy erotic variation on the *epistolary novel. His three autobiographies are collected in *A Bestiary* (2004).

HIGGINSON, Thomas Wentworth (1823–1911) American writer born in Cambridge, Massachusetts. Trained as a pastor, Higginson served in the Civil War and describes his experiences in *Army Life in a Black Regiment* (1870). He became Emily *Dickinson's correspondent and mentor, and published biographies of Margaret *Fuller, Henry Wadsworth *Longfellow, and James Greenleaf *Whittier. His works were collected as *The Magnificent Activist* (2000).

HIGHSMITH, Patricia (1921–95) American writer of crime fiction. Her stylish crime novels have a distinctively black humour: the best known, including *The Talented Mr Ripley* (1956), *Ripley under Ground* (1971), and *Ripley's Game* (1974), feature her amoral anti-hero, the leisure-loving amateur villain Tom Ripley, resident in France. *The Price of Salt*, a novel with a lesbian theme and a happy ending, was published pseudonymously (as Claire Morgan) in 1952, and, retitled *Carol* under her own name in 1990. Her last novel, *Small g: A Summer Idyll* (1995), was about a bohemian café in Zurich.

High Way to the Spittle House, The A tract printed and adapted from a French work by Robert Copland (*fl.* 1505–47), describing the beggars and other types of the poorer classes who visit St Bartholomew's Hospital in London. Taking the form of a dialogue between the author and the hospital's porter, it throws a vivid light on the poverty prevailing in the early 16th century.

HILL, Aaron (1685–1750) Poet, dramatist, and theatre manager. His varied output includes the libretto for Handel's *Rinaldo* (1711), the bi-weekly *Plain Dealer* (1724), and an influential theatrical periodical, *The Prompter* (1734–6). He was satirized by Alexander *Pope in *The *Dunciad, and responded in *The Progress of Wit* (1730). Samuel *Richardson promoted an edition of his *Works* (1753) to assist his daughters, Urania, Astrea, and Minerva.

HILL, Christopher (1912–2003) Marxist historian, who transformed the accepted view of the 17th century, seeing it as essentially the century of revolution. *The World Turned Upside Down: Radical Ideas during the English Revolution* (1972) provides a lively introduction to the prose of many of the lesser known and radical writers of the period, including Laurence *Clarkson, Abiezer *Coppe, William Walwyn, Gerrard *Winstanley, and the anonymous author of *Tyranipocrit Discovered*.

HILL, Sir Geoffrey (1932–) Poet. His first volume of poetry was *For the Unfallen* (1959), followed by *King Log* (1968), *Mercian Hymns* (1971), which consists of prose poems celebrating Offa, 'the presiding genius of the West Midlands', and *Tenebrae* (1978). His early works show the influence of William *Blake and A. E. *Housman. His long poem *The Mystery of the Charity of Charles Péguy* (1983) is a densely allusive meditation on the life, faith, and death of the French poet Péguy. Hill's *Collected Poems* was published in 1994. *Canaan* (1996), published after a long period of poetic silence, mulls over the political and religious history of England, and denounces what it takes to be the corruption of recent public life. Further poetic sequences include *The Triumph of Love* (1998), *The Orchards of Syon* (2002), *Without Title* (2006), and *Oraclau/Oracles* (2010). Hill's version of Henrik *Ibsen's *Brand* was produced at the *National Theatre in 1978.

HILL, Selima (1945–) Poet. Her first volume was *Saying Hello at the Station* (1984), and others include *The Accumulation of Small Acts of Kindness* (1989), a sequence charting a young woman's journey through mental breakdown and recovery, *Violet* (1997), *Bunny* (2001), *Red Roses* (2006), and *Fruitcake* (2009). Hill's singular poetic landscape invests the everyday with wild flights of imagination, often through her signature use of surreal, extended similes.

HILL, Susan (1942–) Novelist. Among her best-known novels are *I'm the King of the Castle* (1970), a dark investigation of childhood; *Strange Meeting* (1971), which drew upon the work of Wilfred *Owen and Siegfried *Sassoon; and *The Bird of Night* (1972). Hill's sensitivity to atmosphere and the physical environment is used to good effect in *The Woman in Black* (1983), a Victorian ghost story later adapted for a hugely successful stage play; *The Mist in the Mirror* (1992); *The Man in the Picture* (2007); and *The Small Hand* (2010). *Mrs de Winter*

(1993) is a sequel to Daphne du Maurier's *Rebecca*. Her short stories are collected in *The Albatross* (1971) and her radio plays in *The Cold Country* (1975). She also writes detective fiction.

HILTON, James (1900–54) Novelist and screenwriter. He was a prolific novelist, but is remembered principally for *Lost Horizon* (1933), set in the Tibetan lamasery of Shangri-La (the origin of this term) where the inmates enjoy extended youth, and *Good-bye Mr Chips* (1934), a novella about a schoolmaster. Both became successful films.

HILTON, Walter (*c.*1343–1396) Augustinian canon of Thurgarton, Nottinghamshire, the author of a prose work in two books, concerning prayer and contemplation, known as *The Scale of Perfection*, written in English and translated into Latin; and of *Mixed Life*, which considers how a lay person's devotional life might be regulated.

HIMES, Chester (1909–84) African American writer. He served a prison spell for armed robbery and in the 1950s moved permanently to Paris in the company of James *Baldwin and Richard *Wright. His first novel, *If He Hollers Let Him Go* (1945), depicts the life of a black shipyard worker during the Second World War, and in 1957 he began publishing a detective series with *A Rage in Harlem*. Himes's two autobiographies are *The Quality of Hurt* (1973) and *My Life of Absurdity* (1976).

Hind and the Panther, The A poem by John *Dryden, published 1687. Dryden became a Catholic in 1685, and the poem attempts to reconcile Anglican and Catholic political interests, while defending Catholic doctrine. The first part represents religious sects as different beasts, and in particular the Catholic Church and the Church of England as the Hind and the Panther. The second part explores arguments about church authority and transubstantiation, issues full of political as well as religious implications. The third part, constituting half the poem, recommends a political alliance between both Churches and the Crown against Whigs and Dissenters.

Hippolyta A queen of the Amazons given in marriage to *Theseus by *Hercules, who had conquered her and taken away her girdle, the achievement being one of his twelve labours. She had a son by Theseus called Hippolytus. According to another version she was slain by Hercules, and it was her sister Antiope who was

the wife of Theseus. She and Theseus frame the action in *Shakespeare's *A *Midsummer Night's Dream*.

His Dark Materials *fantasy *crossover trilogy (1995–2000) by Philip *Pullman. *Northern Lights* (1995; filmed as *The Golden Compass* 2007) was followed by *The Subtle Knife* (1997) and *The Amber Spyglass* (2000). The story, loosely based on *Paradise Lost*, is about Lyra Belacqua and Will Parry, who travel between worlds, unwittingly re-enacting the Christian Fall, thereby saving humans from an oppressive religious regime based on a defunct deity. In Lyra's world, each character is accompanied by a 'daemon', the soul manifested in animal form.

Historia Ecclesiastica Gentis Anglorum See ECCLESIASTICAL HISTORY OF THE ENGLISH PEOPLE.

historical fiction The origins of the British historical novel can be located in the medieval *romances of chivalry, but a convenient generic starting point is Horace Walpole's *The *Castle of Otranto* (1764), which patented many of the conventional devices of the *Gothic–historical tale. Walter *Scott's 25 Waverley novels (1814–32) established the historical novel as a dominant style of fiction. The variety of Scott's historical settings is remarkable, ranging from the early 'Scottish novels' (e.g. *Rob Roy*, 1817), through the English Middle Ages (*Ivanhoe*), medieval France (*Quentin Durward*, 1823), the Middle East of the Crusades (*The *Talisman*, 1825), and the Roman Empire (*Count Robert of Paris*, 1831).

For most of the Victorian period the historical novel was the most respected of fiction's genres. All the great Victorian novelists tried their hand at the form, from W. M. *Thackeray with *The *History of Henry Esmond* (1852) and Charles *Dickens with *A *Tale of Two Cities* (1859) to George *Eliot with *Romola*. The Victorians admired a number of historical novels which are rarely read today, including W. H. *Ainsworth's *Rookwood* (1834), Edward *Bulwer-Lytton's *The Last Days of Pompeii* (1834), Charles Reade's *The *Cloister and the Hearth* (1861), Charles *Kingsley's *Hereward the Wake* (1866), and R. D. *Blackmore's tale of 17th-century Devon, *Lorna Doone* (1869).

Robert Louis *Stevenson explored the genre's romantic potential with adventure tales such as *Kidnapped* (1886) and dark studies in psychology such as *The *Master of Ballantrae* (1889). Henry Rider *Haggard's large output of adventure novels included many with a historical setting, from *Eric Brighteyes* (1890), describing Viking raids and exploration) to *Montezuma's Daughter* (1893, last years of the Aztec Empire). The Education Act of 1870 helped to create a huge market in 'manly' historical yarns for boys, often with a strong imperialist tendency, notably supplied by G. A. *Henty.

Historical novelists of the first decades of the 20th century included Jeffrey Farnol (1878–1952), author of *The Broad Highway* (1910) and *The Amateur Gentleman* (1913), Rafael Sabatini (1875–1950), creator of Scaramouche and Captain Blood, Baroness *Orczy, author of *The Scarlet Pimpernel* (1905), and Georgette Heyer, who began publishing her 'Regency romances' in the 1920s. Drawing on the nautical-historical novel pioneered by Captain Frederick *Marryat, C. S. *Forester launched his Hornblower sequence (set in the Napoleonic Wars) in 1937. Mary *Renault's novels of ancient Greece, including *The King Must Die* (1958), *The Mask of Apollo* (1966), and *Fire from Heaven* (1969), provided vivid portraits of figures both from legend, like *Theseus, and from history, like *Alexander the Great.

New directions in historical fiction were indicated by John *Fowles's *The French Lieutenant's Woman* (1969). Henty's imperial world was revisited by J. G. *Farrell's serio-comic novels about British colonial rule, including *Troubles* (1970) and *The Siege of Krishnapur* (1973). George Macdonald *Fraser's Flashman series, from 1969, took the schoolboy villain of *Tom Brown's Schooldays* (1857), and invented a scandalous post-Rugby career for him.

More recent historical novels include the Sharpe books of Bernard Cornwell (1944–), set in the Napoleonic Wars ; the Tudor Boleyn family series of Philippa Gregory (1954–); the thrillers of Robert *Harris, set in ancient Rome; and *The Pillars of the Earth* (1989) by Ken Follett (1949–), the story of the building of a fictional medieval cathedral.

The commercial success of historical novels was boosted in the 1990s by a series of Booker Prize winners in the genre: A. S. *Byatt's *Possession* (1990), Barry *Unsworth's *Sacred Hunger* (1992), and Pat *Barker's *The Ghost Road* (1995). Peter *Ackroyd has resurrected the London of the past in *Hawksmoor* (1985) and *The House of Doctor Dee* (1993); Rose *Tremain's *Restoration* (1989) and *Music & Silence* (1999) are both set in the 17th century; Lawrence Norfolk's (1963–) *Lemprière's Dictionary* (1991) and *The Pope's Rhinoceros* (1996) mingle esoteric historical erudition with picaresque

narratives; Beryl *Bainbridge has written novels about Scott's Antarctic voyages (*Birthday Boys*, 1991), the Crimean War (*Master Georgie*, 1998), and Samuel *Johnson (*According to Queeney*, 2001); and Sarah *Waters (1966–) has built a reputation on novels set in the Victorian era, including *Tipping the Velvet* (1998) and *Fingersmith* (2002).

History of Henry Esmond, Esquire, The A historical novel by W. M. *Thackeray, set during the reign of Queen Anne, published 1852. Esmond, who tells his own story, mainly in the third person, is the (supposedly illegitimate) son of the third Viscount Castlewood, who dies at the battle of the Boyne. He lives at Castlewood House under the protection of the fourth viscount, his father's cousin, and his young wife Rachel. Rachel and her husband have two children, Frank, the heir, and Beatrix, a beautiful but wilful girl. Castlewood is killed in a duel. On his deathbed he reveals to Henry that he is in fact the legitimate heir, but Henry keeps silent for the sake of Rachel and her son. Beatrix and her brother Frank are ardent Jacobites, and Esmond plots with them to restore James Edward Stuart, the Old Pretender, to the throne. At the moment when he should be in London the Pretender is at Castlewood, 'dangling after Trix', and the plot fails. Esmond, disillusioned with Beatrix and the Jacobite cause, marries Rachel and they emigrate to Virginia. The later history of the family in America and England is told in *The *Virginians*.

Histriomastix See PRYNNE, WILLIAM.

HITCHCOCK, Sir Alfred Joseph (1899–1980) Film director. *The Lodger* (1927) established a reputation for creating high tension in everyday surroundings and drawing spectators into intense identification with ambiguous characters. Always technically ambitious, he converted an originally silent *Blackmail* (1929) into the British industry's first 'talkie'. He moved to Hollywood to make Daphne *du Maurier's *Rebecca* (1940) and was based there for the rest of his career. His more than 40 elaborate psychological thrillers defined an atmosphere still widely known as 'Hitchcockian', and several, including *Vertigo* (1958), are considered among the greatest of all films.

HOBAN, Russell (1925–2011) American *fantasy and *science fiction writer. In 1959 he wrote the first of over 50 children's books, the best known being *The Mouse and his Child* (1967). Hoban's fables for adults suggest the strategies of *magic realism in their bizarre but internally consistent worlds: *The Lion of Boaz-Jachin and Jachin-Boaz* (1973), draws on Sumerian mythology; *Turtle Diary* (1975; filmed 1985, screenplay by Harold *Pinter); *Riddley Walker* (1980), set in a post-nuclear holocaust society; *Pilgermann* (1983), set during the First Crusade of 1098; *Mr Rinyo-Clacton's Offer* (1998), a tale of damnation with echoes of the *Faust legend; and *Angelica Lost and Found* (2010), inhabited by characters from *Orlando Furioso*.

HOBBES, Thomas (1588–1679) Philosopher, in the service of the Cavendish (*see* NEWCASTLE) family, and mathematical tutor to the prince of Wales (later Charles II). He travelled on the Continent with pupils, meeting *Galileo, Pierre Gassendi (1592–1655), *Descartes, and the French mathematician Marin Mersenne (1588–1648), gaining a European presence and reputation.

As a philosopher Hobbes resembles Francis *Bacon in the utilitarian importance that he attaches to knowledge. Unlike Bacon, he regards science as essentially deductive, and takes geometry as the model of scientific method. He attached great importance to the definition of words and used rigorous definition to show that many popular ideas are nonsense (the idea of a 'free subject', for example). He was a materialist, regarding sensation as the basis of all knowledge and the motion of material particles as the cause of all sensation. Our appetites are our reactions to external motions, and are directed by self-preservation. Man is essentially selfish. What seem unselfish actions are motivated by the selfish wish to alleviate the pain of compassion. Being selfish, man, left to himself, would engage in perpetual conflict, and life would be 'solitary, poor, nasty, brutish and short'. To prevent this, Hobbes's political philosophy, expounded in *De Corpore Politico* (1650, originally *Elements of Law*), *De Cive* (Latin 1642, English 1651), and *Leviathan* (English 1651, definitive Latin text 1668), is in effect a defence of totalitarianism, asserting that the state must have absolute power, taking precedence over conscience and matters of faith and doctrine. Hobbes's philosophical works include *Human Nature* (1650), *De Corpore* (Latin 1655, English 1656), and *De Homine* (1658). He published the first English translation of *Thucydides in 1629, a translation of *Homer in quatrains (1674–5), and a sketch of the Civil Wars, *Behemoth, or The Long Parliament* (1680), which was suppressed. His prose, seemingly plain and direct, exhibits a masterly understanding of rhetoric, a weighted use of metaphor, and sustained irony, as in *Leviathan*,

chapter 47, which comes close to equating religion with a belief in fairies. On this and other grounds he was often branded an atheist.

Hobbit, The, or There and Back Again (1937) The first published excursion by *Tolkien into 'Middle Earth', an intricately realized other world. Hobbits are the bucolic residents of 'the Shire', based on the pastoral Midlands. The reluctant hero, Bilbo Baggins, is drawn into a quest for dragon's gold in wild lands by the magician Gandalf, in the course of which he acquires a magic ring which is central to Tolkien's epic, *The *Lord of the Rings*.

HOBHOUSE, John Cam (1786–1869) Friend and executor of Lord *Byron. His *Imitations and Translations from the Ancient and Modern Classics* (1809) contains nine poems by Byron, with whom he travelled in Europe; his *Journey through Albania* (1813) describes the same journey that appears in Byron's *Childe Harold*. He was an adviser to John *Murray, who published most of Byron's work, and he ensured that Byron's *Memoirs* were burnt immediately after the poet's death. His *Recollections of a Long Life* (1865) contains much material relating to Byron.

HOBSBAUM, Philip (1932–2005) Poet and critic. He was the founder of the *Group, first in London and later in Belfast, whose members at different times included Peter *Redgrove, Michael *Longley, and Seamus *Heaney. His books include *The Place's Fault* (1964) and *Women and Animals* (1972).

HOBY, Sir Thomas (1530–66) Translator of *Castiglione's *Il cortegiano*, as *The Courtier* (1561). It became immediately popular, being translated into Latin in 1577, and was an important influence on such writers as Edmund *Spenser, Ben *Jonson, and *Shakespeare.

HOCCLEVE (Occleve), Thomas (*c.*1367–1426) Apart from John *Lydgate the most significant named English poet of the 15th century. He was a clerk in the office of the privy seal and some of his poetry claims to be about his own life, as in 'La Male Regle de Thomas Hoccleve' (1405–6), the prologue to *The Regiment of Princes* (1411–12), and in two poems from the late sequence known as the *Series* (1420s): 'The Complaint' and 'The Dialogue with a Friend'. Hoccleve's poetry also includes translations from *Christine de Pisan and other French sources. Long regarded as a poor imitator of Geoffrey *Chaucer, whom he mentions with admiration, Hoccleve has recently been recognized as a significant contributor to the complex literary culture of his time.

HOCKING, Silas K. (Kitto) (1850–1935) Novelist and *Methodist minister, who wrote fifty books, including *For Light and Liberty* (1890), *A Son of Reuben* (1894), *For Such is Life* (1896), and *Who Shall Judge* (1910). Hocking's didactic but compassionate novels made him one of the most popular authors of his generation. His most enduringly celebrated book is *Her Benny* (1879), a story of street children set in Liverpool, which sold more than a million copies in his lifetime. He published an autobiography, *My Book of Memory*, in 1923.

HODGSON, Ralph (1871–1962) Poet, born in County Durham, but brought up in the south, where his lifelong love of the natural world took root. *The Last Blackbird* appeared in 1907, but his reputation was established by *Poems* (1917). Edward Marsh published some of his work in *Georgian Poetry*. *Collected Poems* was published in 1961.

HOFFMAN, Eva (1945–) Born in Poland to Jewish parents who survived the Holocaust in hiding in the Ukraine. She emigrated to Canada in 1958. Her works, including *Lost in Translation* (1989), *Exit into History* (1993), *Shtetl* (1997), and *After Such Knowledge* (2004), explore identity, memory, and dislocation.

HOFFMANN, Ernst Theodor Amadeus (1776–1822) German Romantic, musician, and writer. *Die Elixiere des Teufels* (1815–16: *The Devil's Elixir*) and the unfinished *Lebensansichten des Kater Murr* (1819–21: *The Life and Opinions of Murr the Cat*) are novels; shorter works, collected mainly in the *Fantasiestücke* (1814–15), *Nachtstücke* (1816–17), and *Die Serapionsbrüder* (1818–21), include *Der goldne Topf* (*The Golden Pot*) and *Der Sandmann* (*The Sandman*). Hoffmann's fiction is marked by extravagant and frequently macabre psychological fantasy. *Freud's essay *Das Unheimliche* (1919: *The Uncanny*) was among the first of many interpretations of *The Sandman*.

HOFMANNSTHAL, Hugo von (1874–1929) Austrian poet, dramatist, and essayist. His celebrated *Brief des Lord Chandos* (1902: *The Chandos Letter*), fictionally addressed to Francis *Bacon, expresses his sense of a crisis in language as inadequate to meaning or thought. Other works include *Das gerette Venedig* (1905), a version of Thomas *Otway's *Venice Preserved*; *König Ödipus* (1907); *Jedermann*

(1911: *Everyman*), a modernization of the old morality play; the wittily nostalgic comedy *Der Schwierige* (1921: *A Difficult Man*) and *Der Turm* (1925: *The Tower*), a tragedy, which completed his development towards the idea of literature as carrying a social and religious message. He wrote the libretti for six of Richard Strauss's operas, including *Der Rosenkavalier* (1911) and *Ariadne auf Naxos* (1912).

HOGARTH, William (1697–1764) British painter and engraver. In 1732 *The Harlot's Progress* introduced his 'modern moral subjects'; it was followed by *The Rake's Progress* (1733–5) and *Marriage à la Mode* (1743–5). This highly original and successful genre consisted of a series of paintings, popularized through engravings, which tell a story that is topical, erotic, spiced with contemporary portraits, and yet comments with humanity and passion on social and political vices and corruption. Hogarth's later engravings, the *Industry and Idleness* series (1747) and the prints *Beer Street* and *Gin Lane* (1750–51), are coarser, and their harsher morality is aimed at a mass market. Hogarth also published a work on aesthetics, *The Analysis of Beauty* (1753), in which he defined the serpentine 'line of beauty'.

Henry *Fielding, and later Tobias *Smollett, compared characters and scenes in their novels to the prints of Hogarth. Laurence *Sterne's *Tristram Shandy* (1759–67) shows the influence of Hogarth's aesthetics.

Hogarth Press Founded in 1917 by Leonard *Woolf and Virginia *Woolf at their home, Hogarth House, Richmond, Surrey, mainly as a hobby. Their earliest publications included Katherine *Mansfield's *Prelude* (1918), Virginia Woolf's *Kew Gardens* (1919), and T. S. *Eliot's *Poems* (1919). Their policy was to publish new and experimental work; they also published translations of Maxim Gorky, Anton *Chekhov, Lev *Tolstoy, Fedor *Dostoevsky, Ivan *Bunin, Rainer Maria Rilke, and Italo *Svevo. They introduced the work of Robinson *Jeffers, J. C. *Ransom, and E. A. *Robinson into England. In 1924 they moved to Tavistock Square, where John *Lehmann became assistant (1931–2), and then part-owner (1938–46). In 1947 Lehmann's share in the Press was bought by Chatto and Windus. Since 1987, the Hogarth Press has been an imprint of Random House.

HOGG, James (1770–1835) Scottish poet and novelist, 'the Ettrick Shepherd', born on a farm in the Ettrick Forest. Rising to the position of shepherd, he taught himself to read and write. *Scottish Pastorals* (1801) made little impact but in 1802 he met Walter *Scott while the latter was collecting songs for **Minstrelsy of the Scottish Border*. With Scott's backing, *The Mountain Bard* (1807), a collection of original ballads, was a success. Hogg made his name with *The *Queen's Wake* (1813). He was on the board of **Blackwood's Magazine*, to which he frequently contributed, notably to the 'Chaldee MS' and the **Noctes Ambrosianae*. His novels *The Three Perils of Man* (1822), *The Three Perils of Woman* (1823), and *The *Private Memoirs and Confessions of a Justified Sinner* (1824), were not highly regarded in his lifetime. Other works include *The Domestic Manners and Private Life of Sir Walter Scott* (1834), *Tales of the War of Montrose* (1835), and an edition of Robert *Burns (1834–5). His death elicited one of Wordsworth's last great poems, 'Extempore Effusion'.

HOGG, Thomas Jefferson (1792–1862) Educated at Oxford with P. B. *Shelley and sent down with him on the publication of their *'Necessity of Atheism'. He was one of the circle of Shelley, Thomas Love *Peacock, and other friends who about 1820 referred to themselves as 'The Athenians'. In 1832 he contributed reminiscences of Shelley at Oxford to the **New Monthly Magazine*, and these later formed a part of his *Life of Shelley* (1858). Peacock, in his *Memorials of Shelley*, felt obliged to question and revise many of Hogg's observations.

HOGGART, Richard (1918–) Scholar and writer, whose interest in literature, education, mass media, and working-class culture was expressed in his influential and partly autobiographical work *The Uses of Literacy* (1957), which became a founding text of cultural studies. His later works include *The Way we Live Now*, 1995, and three volumes of memoirs, *A Local Habitation* (1988), *A Sort of Clowning* (1990), and *An Imagined Life* (1992).

HOLCOT, Robert (c.1290–1349) Dominican scholar. Theologically, he was a follower of William of *Ockham at least in his insistence on human free will, opposing Thomas *Bradwardine. His prolific output included commentaries on Scripture and the *Moralitates Historiarum*, a series of stories that influenced the **Gesta Romanorum*.

HOLCROFT, Thomas (1745–1809) Successively stable-boy, shoemaker, actor, radical activist, and author. He was largely self-educated, a militant atheist, and believed fervently in man's capacity for self-improvement. His

Memoirs (edited and completed by his friend William *Hazlitt) contain reminiscences of Samuel *Foote and Charles *Macklin, and later accounts of radical associates such as William *Godwin and John Horne Tooke. He was acquitted in the treason trials of 1794, not least because of Godwin's pamphlet in support of the defendants, 'Cursory Strictures'. He wrote comic and sentimental plays, including *The Road to Ruin* (1792); his novels, *Anna St Ives* (1792) and *The Adventures of Hugh Trevor* (1794) were influenced by Godwin's radical philosophy. His play *Knave or Not?* (1798) had a hostile reception.

HOLINSHED, Raphael (c.1525–1580?) Historian, employed as a translator by Reyner *Wolfe, the printer and publisher. While working for him he planned the *Chronicles* (1577), which are known by his name, but were written and compiled by several people. They form the first authoritative vernacular and continuous account of the whole of English national history. The *History of England* was written by Holinshed himself. The *Description of England*, a vivid and humorous account of English towns, villages, crops, customs, etc. of the day, was written by William Harrison (1535–93). The *History and Description of Scotland* and the *History of Ireland* were translations or adaptations, and the *Description of Ireland* was the work of Richard Stanyhurst (1547–1618) and Edmund Campion. The *Chronicle* was reissued, with continuations, edited by John Hooker (alias Vowell; 1527–1601), in 1587, and politically offensive passages removed. This second edition was widely used by William *Shakespeare and by other dramatists.

HOLLAND, Philemon (1552–1637) Schoolmaster, celebrated for his vivid translations of *Livy (1600), *Pliny's *Natural History* (1601), *Plutarch's *Moralia* (1603), *Suetonius (1606), the 4th-century Roman historian Ammianus Marcellinus (1609), William Camden's **Britannia* (1610), and *Xenophon's *Cyropaedia* (1632).

HOLLINGHURST, Alan (1954–) Novelist, whose sexually explicit yet elegantly conceived and written work has done much to bring gay fiction into the mainstream. *The Swimming-Pool Library* (1988) is narrated by a young Oxford graduate, who saves the life of an octogenarian aristocrat and is subsequently asked to write his memoirs. Culturally allusive, the book explores with *Firbankian panache the dangers and pleasures of the homosexual world. The narrator of *The Folding Star* (1994) travels to an unnamed Belgian town (based on Bruges), where he develops a romantic and erotic obsession with one of his private pupils. The novel interweaves his memories of his youth with the story of a celebrated Belgian symbolist *fin-de-siècle* painter. *The Spell* (1998) describes the affairs of four gay men and their friends in London clubs and at drug-fuelled weekends in a beautifully evoked Dorset countryside. Hollinghurst's concern with the aesthetics of style and artifice achieves its fullest expression in *The Line of Beauty* (2004). Set in the Thatcherite 1980s, with Aids beginning to cut a swathe through the gay community, it is *Jamesian in both concept and style and tells the story of a comparative innocent caught up in the corrupting world of a Tory MP. *The Stranger's Child* (2011) is a *historical novel with an English country house setting.

Hollywood novel A term designating novels set in the American movie capital, which take the film business as their subject. Nathanael *West's *The Day of the Locust* (1939) is the most famous example.

HOLMES, Oliver Wendell (1809–94) American writer. His reflective essays, *Autocrat of the Breakfast-Table*, (1858) were followed by *The Professor at the Breakfast-Table* (1860), *The Poet at the Breakfast-Table* (1872), and *Over the Tea-Cups* (1891). His other works include novels: *Elsie Venner* (1861) deals with genetic inheritance; poems; memoirs of Ralph Waldo *Emerson and John Lothrop Motley (1814–77); and much light and occasional verse.

HOLMES, Richard (1945–) OBE, biographer. His first major biography, *Shelley: The Pursuit* (1974) was followed by the semi-autobiographical *Footsteps: Adventures of a Romantic Biographer* (1985), which broke new ground in its account of Holmes's personal experiences and travels in the course of pursuing, sometimes unsuccessfully, subjects who included Gérard de Nerval and R. L. *Stevenson, and *Sidetracks: Explorations of a Romantic Biographer* (2000). Other biographies include *Dr Johnson and Mr Savage* (1993); a two-volume biography of S. T. *Coleridge, *Early Visions* (1989); and *Darker Reflections* (1998); and *The Age of Wonder* (2008), exploring the influence of scientific discovery on the great Romantic writers.

HOLMES, Sherlock Famous fictional detective created by Arthur Conan *Doyle.

Holocaust, literature of the The racialized mass murder committed by the Nazis during the Second World War has been the subject of work ranging from diaries, testimonies, and memoirs, to fiction, poetry, and drama. *Diaries are often seen as most authentically concerned with the events they describe: both personal diaries, and diaries by self-styled archivists, such as Emmanuel Ringelblum's *Notes from the Warsaw Ghetto* (1958). Immediately after the war Holocaust writing was not popular; Elie Wiesel was unable to find a publisher for his long, Yiddish account of Auschwitz, *And the World Was Silent* (French trans. as *Night* 1958). However, Anne *Frank's *Diary of a Young Girl*, published in English in 1952, did much to increase public interest in the Holocaust, as did the trial of Adolf Eichmann in 1961. Sylvia *Plath, most notably in poems such as 'Daddy' and 'Lady Lazarus', was one of the first non-survivors to write about the Holocaust, to the chagrin of critics such as George *Steiner who saw these poems as enlisting an unprecedented tragedy to prop up personal angst. Others have seen her work, like that of Geoffrey *Hill and Randall *Jarrell, as the effort of a poet to represent a historicized subjectivity. Among the works written in the first decades after the war Primo *Levi's *If This Is a Man* (1960) is probably the best known, and his essays, particularly *The Drowned and the Saved* (1988), have contributed to his high reputation. Very quickly a tradition among survivor-writers arose for generic and narrative experimentation in order to represent the Holocaust: André Schwarz Bart's novel *The Last of the Just* (1960) draws upon Jewish tradition to represent Auschwitz in magic realist vein; while Piotr Rawicz's nightmarish black comedy *Blood from the Sky* (1964) describes life in hiding in Nazi-occupied Ukraine. Jiri Weil's allegorical novel *Life with a Star* (1989) renders the Nazi occupation of Prague without naming any of the different groups of protagonists; Jakov Lind's 1966 novel *Landscape in Concrete* is a Kafkaesque portrayal of a German soldier who 'only follows orders'; while Aharon Appelfeld's novels (*Badenheim 1939*, 1990; *To the Land of the Reeds*, 1994) are stylized accounts of the Holocaust years which imply but do not describe the facts of mass murder. Both Ida Fink (*A Scrap of Time*, 1989) and Louise Begley (*Wartime Lies*, 1991) have published fictionalized autobiographies of their experiences in hiding during the war. The work of non-Jewish survivors has also been characterized by formal and generic experimentation; such writers include Charlotte Delbo, a French political prisoner whose memoir *Auschwitz and After* (1995) considers the problem of memory and subjectivity, and Tadeusz Borowski, a Polish political prisoner whose blackly comic fictionalized vignettes in *This Way for the Gas, Ladies and Gentlemen* (1976) disconcertingly describe the life of a guard in Auschwitz. Such experimentation exists alongside a tradition of 'documentary fiction', in which the techniques of the novel are combined with eyewitness accounts or other historical material. Such works include Jean-François Steiner's *Treblinka* (1967) and Anatolii Kuznetsov's *Babi Yar: A Document in the Form of a Novel* (1970). This tendency not to trust outright invention continues even in works written more than 50 years after the Holocaust: Thomas *Keneally's *Schindler's Ark* (1982) is described as *'faction', while even novels which take the Holocaust simply as the trigger for fiction, such as William *Styron's *Sophie's Choice* (1979), Martin *Amis's *Time's Arrow* (1991), and D. M. *Thomas's *The White Hotel* (1981), all draw upon historical sources. Critical reactions to anything but the most scrupulously factual and respectful novels by non-survivors about the Holocaust have tended to be explosive—see for instance the response to Rolf Hochhuth's 1964 play *The Deputy*, about the role of Pope Pius XII in the Holocaust; by contrast, the poetic approach of Anne Michaels's prize-winning novel *Fugitive Pieces* (1996) was seen by many to be appropriate to its subject. Poetry has not been as popular a medium for representing the Holocaust, although the poetry of the survivor Paul *Celan is a striking exception. Celan's 'Death Fugue' (*The Poems of Paul Celan*, trans. Michael *Hamburger, 1988, 1994), is, alongside Nelly Sachs's 'O the chimneys' (*Selected Poems*, 1968), and Itzhak Katznelson's long poem *Song of the Murdered Jewish People* (1980), the best-known poetic treatment of the subject. As the Holocaust recedes further in time, the work of the generations after is growing in importance. The '1.5 generation', the child survivors, are represented by Georges Perec and Raymond *Federman, both highly experimental writers, the most celebrated work of the second generation is Art Spiegelman's *Maus* (1986, 1991) and a range of memoirs (Anne Karpf, *The War After*, 1996; Helen Epstein, *Where She Came From*, 1997; Eva *Hoffman, *After Such Knowledge*, 2004) and novels by Thane Rosenbaum and Melvin J. Bukiet. The best-known third-generation Holocaust novels are Joseph Skibell's *Blessing on the Moon* (1997) and Jonathan Safran Foer's *Everything Is Illuminated* (2002). The 'generation after' in Germany

is also concerned to address issues of memory arising out of the Holocaust; particularly notable here are the novels of W. G. *Sebald (*The Emigrants*, 1996; *Austerlitz*, 2001). Writing by and about other groups of victims has been far less extensive. In the case of the Gypsies, written records formed little part of their tradition (though see Alexander Ramati's documentary novel *And the Violins Stopped Playing*, 1989); and in the case of gay men, homosexuality remained illegal until the 1970s in Germany and Austria (see Heinz Heger's *The Men with the Pink Triangle*, 1980, and Martin Sherman's fictional 1979 play *Bent*, which takes the events of the Nazi persecution as an allegory for identity politics).

⊕ SEE WEB LINKS

- United States Holocaust Memorial Museum

HOLROYD, Sir Michael de Courcy Fraser (1935–) Author and biographer. His critical biography of Hugh Kingsmill, was followed by a two-volume life of Lytton *Strachey (*The Unknown Years*, 1967; *The Years of Achievement*, 1968), which greatly contributed to a revival of interest in the *Bloomsbury Group and to a new interest in the art of *biography, and incidentally achieved a remarkable recovery of the painter Dora *Carrington. Other works include a major two-volume biography of Augustus *John (1974, 1975); a four-volume biography of George Bernard *Shaw: *The Search for Love* (1988), *The Pursuit of Power* (1989), *The Lure of Fantasy* (1991), and *The Last Laugh* (1992); *A Strange Eventful History: The Dramatic Lives of Ellen Terry, Henry Irving and their Remarkable Families* (2008); and *A Book of Secrets: Illegitimate Daughters, Absent Fathers* (2010), a 'post-biographical' travel book centred on the Italian Villa Cimbrone and three women who visited it, including Violet Trefusis, lover of Vita *Sackville-West. In *Basil Street Blues* (1999), and *Mosaic* (2004, cast as a detective story) he turns his biographer's gaze on his own family and his younger self.

HOLTBY, Winifred (1898–1935) Novelist. She was an ardent feminist and a prolific journalist, and published several novels, the best known of which is her last, *South Riding*, published posthumously in 1936. Set in Yorkshire, it is at once the story of enterprising headmistress Sarah Burton and a portrait of a whole community. Her other novels include *Anderby Wold* (1923), *The Crowded Street* (1924), *The Land of*

Green Ginger (1927), and *Mandoa, Mandoa!* (1933). She also published several works of non-fiction, including the first book-length evaluation of Virginia *Woolf (1932). See Vera *Brittain, *Testament of Friendship* (1940).

'Holy Fair, The' A poem by Robert *Burns, published 1786, in which the poet humorously contrasts the conviviality of the folk assembled for a Mauchline prayer meeting with the puritanical exhortations of their spiritual leaders. The poem is the central text in a tradition of sardonic Scots celebrations of public festivity that stretches from 'Christis Kirk on the Green' and 'Peblis to the Play' through Robert *Fergusson's 'Leith Races' to 'Donegore Hill' by James Orr (1770–1816; *see* RHYMING WEAVERS) and Robert *Garioch's satire on the Edinburgh Festival, 'Embro to the Ploy'.

Holy Living *See* TAYLOR, JEREMY.

Holy State and the Profane State, The By Thomas *Fuller, published 1642, the most popular of his works during his life, a mixture of *character-writing, essays, and 30 short biographies; the characters include, for example, 'The Good Widow', 'The Good Merchant', and 'The True Gentleman'.

Holy War, The A Puritan prose allegory by John *Bunyan, published 1682.

'Holy Willie's Prayer' A *dramatic monologue by Robert *Burns, written in 1785 and circulated privately in the poet's lifetime, in which the Mauchline Kirk elder Willie Fisher (1737–1809) is overheard at his prayers, unwittingly revealing himself as a drunken and adulterous hypocrite.

HOME, John (1722–1808) Scottish playwright and clergyman, secretary to Lord Bute and tutor to the prince of Wales. His tragedy *Douglas* was performed to much acclaim at Edinburgh in 1756, and at Covent Garden in 1757. James *Macpherson produced his first 'translation' at his instigation in 1759 and Home remained a firm believer in the authenticity of 'Ossian'.

Homecoming, The A play by Harold *Pinter, performed and published 1965. A dark Freudian family drama, the play presents the return to his north London home and ostentatiously womanless family of Teddy, an academic, and his wife of six years, Ruth, once a photographic model. The patriarch, Mac, a butcher, is alternately violent and cringing in manner, and the other two sons, Lenny and Joey, in a very short time make sexual overtures to Ruth, who calmly accepts them; by the end of the play Teddy has decided to leave her with the family, who intend to establish her as a professional prostitute.

HOMER (supposedly 8th century BC) A biography was invented for 'Homer' in later antiquity, but in reality the name stands simply for the two great epic poems, the *Iliad* and the *Odyssey*. Nothing is known of the original singer/poet or poets, although it is assumed that some unknown individual must have given each poem a coherent shape and unity, from a mass of pre-literate heroic song. We do not know when or where the epics were first committed to writing. They are in an artificial dialect, containing elements from different periods and different dialects of Greek. These two epics were always regarded as the supreme creations of Greek literature, and their critical pre-eminence was confirmed in *Aristotle's *Poetics*. Traditionally Homer was blind, like the singer Demodocus in the *Odyssey*. The epics are set in the distant past, in the age of heroes, and specifically concern the legendary Trojan War, associated with the end of the Mycenaean age (13th century BC). Ptolemy II of Egypt (308–246 BC) collected manuscripts of the poems and assembled scholars in the Library of Alexandria, who set to work to produce an agreed and satisfactory text of Homer. The work done under him and his successors by scholars such as Aristarchus is the basis of our modern texts. Homer's reputation survived in the Middle Ages even in the Latin West where his works were unknown. Serious British interest in the poems began in the 17th century with George *Chapman's translation, the 'Chapman's Homer' of Keats's famous sonnet, and Thomas *Hobbes's version.

Homeric Hymns, The A collection of 33 ancient Greek hymns of unknown authorship, addressed to gods such as Demeter, *Apollo, Hermes, Aphrodite, and *Zeus, and a major source of myths relating to them. They were composed by various poets (not including *Homer) from the 8th to the 6th centuries BC. George *Chapman included his translation in *The Crown of All Homer's Works* (1624?). P. B. *Shelley translated seven of them and drew on the form for his 'Hymn to Intellectual Beauty'.

Homilies, Books of A title applied in the Church of England to two books of homilies (i.e. sermons), published 1547 and 1563, appointed to be read in the churches. The contents of the second Book of Homilies are listed in

Article 35 of the Thirty-Nine Articles in the Book of *Common Prayer.

HONE, William (1780–1842) Radical author and bookseller, who published numerous political satires, parodies, and pamphlets, many illustrated by George *Cruikshank. Their most notable collaborations are *The Political House that Jack Built* (1819), *The Queen's Matrimonial Ladder* (1819), *The Man in the Moon* (1820), and *A Slap at Slop* (1822).

Honest Whore, The A play by Thomas *Dekker in two parts, both written c.1604/5, of which the first was printed 1604, the second 1630. It appears from *Henslowe's diary that Thomas *Middleton collaborated in writing the first part.

In Part I Count Hippolito, meeting Bellafront, and discovering that she is a harlot, reproaches her bitterly for her way of life and converts her to honesty. She falls in love with Hippolito, who rejects her and marries Infelice, daughter of the duke of Milan. Bellafront marries Matheo, who had caused her downfall.

In Part II the converted Bellafront is the devoted wife of the worthless Matheo, who, to pay for his vices, is prepared to see her return to her old way of life. Hippolito, now falling in love with her, tries to seduce her. She stoutly resists, and is finally rescued by her father, Orlando Friscobaldo. The play's painful nature, strengthened by powerful scenes in Bedlam and Bridewell, is alleviated by the admirable character Orlando Friscobaldo, and by the comic subplot, dealing with the eccentricities of the patient husband Candido, the linen draper.

HOOD, Thomas (1799–1845) Poet and journalist. He edited various periodicals: *The Gem* (1829), the *Comic Annual* (1830), the *New Monthly Magazine* (1841–3), and *Hood's Magazine* (1843). He and John Hamilton *Reynolds published *Odes and Addresses to Great People* (1825), a series of satires and parodies which sold well. His humorous and satirical verse made use of his remarkable skill with puns. His serious poems include 'The *Song of the Shirt', which was immensely successful; 'The *Bridge of Sighs', about a suicide by drowning and 'The Dream of Eugene Aram', about a murder; 'The Last Man'; 'The Plea of the Midsummer Fairies' (which includes 'I remember, I remember, the house where I was born'); and shorter pieces, such as 'The Death-bed'.

HOOD, Thomas, the younger (1835–74) A talented humorous writer and artist, known as Tom Hood, the son of Thomas *Hood. *Captain Master's Children* (1865) was the most successful of his six novels; he became editor of *Fun* (1865) and founded *Tom Hood's Comic Annual* (1867). He wrote and illustrated many children's books; his collected verse, *Favourite Poems*, was published in 1877.

HOOK, Theodore Edward (1788–1841) Satirist, writer of light verse and dramas, and a prolific and popular novelist. He edited the Tory newspaper *John Bull* and contributed both acidulous invective and scurrilous satire. Imprisoned for debt in the 1820s, after his release he wrote 'silver-fork' or *'fashionable novels', including *Sayings and Doings* (1824–8), *Maxwell* (1830), *Gilbert Gurney* (1836), and *Gurney Married* (1838). As a former friend of the prince of Wales, Hook had known high society well, and his novels were read in large numbers by those aspiring to social fashion.

HOOKER, Richard (1554–1600) Theologian and philosopher. His fame rests on his great prose classic, *Of the *Laws of Ecclesiastical Politie*, a defence of the *Church of England as established in *Elizabeth I's reign. Books I–IV were published in 1593, Book V in 1597, Books VI and works were issued at Oxford in 1612–14. The influential biography by Izaac *Walton (1666) is delightful but often inaccurate.

HOPE, A. D. (Alec Derwent) (1907–2000) Australian poet. His first collection was *The Wandering Islands* (1955), but much of his work had already been published by this time. *Poems* (1960) was followed by *Collected Poems 1930–1965* (1966; rev. 1972). His work is technically accomplished, witty, and allusive, abounding in references to the Bible and classical mythology: he pays homage to Lord *Byron, S. T. *Coleridge, and W. B. *Yeats, among others.

HOPE, Anthony Pseudonym of Sir Anthony Hope *Hawkins (1863–1933).

HOPE, Christopher (1944–) South African-born poet, children's writer, short story writer, and novelist. His first volume of poetry, *Cape Drives* (1974), evokes the landscapes and racial tensions of South Africa: it was followed by a *A Separate Development* (1980, novel), the story of Harry Moto, a white teenage South African outsider who ends up in jail writing his memoirs, and *In the Country of the Black Pig* (1981, poems). Other titles include *Kruger's Alp* (1984), a historical satire about the aftermath of the Boer War; *Learning to Fly* (1990, short stories); *Serenity House* (1992), which deals with the legacy of the Holocaust; and *Me, the*

Moon and Elvis Presley (1997), a novel about post-apartheid problems. *My Mother's Lovers* (2006) has elements of thriller and autobiography.

HOPE, Thomas (*c.*1770–1831) Author of the popular novel *Anastasius* (1819), at first attributed to Lord *Byron. It tells, at considerable length, the story of a brave but unscrupulous Greek who travels in the Middle East and becomes involved in a variety of escapades. It is possible that the story influenced the later cantos of **Don Juan*.

Hope Theatre On Bankside, Southwark, built in 1613 by Philip *Henslowe as a bear-garden, with a movable stage on which plays could be performed. Jonson's **Bartholomew Fair* was acted there in 1614.

HOPKINS, Gerard Manley (1844–89) Poet and priest tutored at Balliol College, Oxford by Benjamin Jowett, T. H. *Green, and (very briefly) Walter Pater, among others. He developed a lasting friendship with Robert *Bridges. Hopkins's quest for security and religious certainty led him to convert to Roman Catholicism, with John Henry *Newman's guidance, in 1866. After Balliol he taught for a year at Newman's Oratory School, Birmingham and in 1868 he entered the Society of Jesus (Jesuits). Hopkins was strongly attracted to the strictness and self-suppression of Jesuit rule, but found conformity difficult. Believing that poetry and priesthood were irreconcilable, he burnt his poems on becoming a Jesuit (though he sent copies to Bridges for safe keeping) but continued to write and record his brilliantly detailed observations of nature in his journals. In response to a disaster at sea, he produced the innovative poem 'The *Wreck of the Deutschland' (1875): its rejection by the Jesuit periodical *The Month* ended his hopes for acceptance as a Jesuit poet. Following ordination in 1877, Hopkins had a peripatetic pastoral career, with eleven postings in eight years; in 1884 he was appointed to the chair of Greek and Latin at University College, Dublin. At this 'third remove' from homeland, family, and friends, he experienced desolation and anguish. He died of typhoid in June 1889.

Hopkins's earliest poems express a Keatsian sensuousness, a Ruskinian zest for natural detail, and a distinctive flair for aural and rhythmic effects. Oxford texts such as 'Heaven-Haven' and 'Easter Communion' trace his desire and need to convert. While studying for ordination, he spent three years in St Beuno's, North Wales, where he learned Welsh, and, inspired by 'God's grandeur' in Wales, he composed a remarkable series of experimental sonnets including 'The Wind-hover', 'Spring', and 'Pied Beauty'. Aesthetic and moral questions intensify in subsequent poems such as 'Henry Purcell' and 'Binsey Poplars'. Exiled in Dublin, he composed the 'terrible sonnets' such as 'Carrion Comfort', 'No worst, there is none', and 'Spelt from Sibyl's Leaves'; poems which have become classic representations of psychic despair and fragmentation. But he was also inspired to write further poems glorifying God and Nature, 'That Nature is a Heraclitean Fire' and 'To R.B.' In his journals and letters Hopkins developed highly personal theories of natural essence and expressiveness and of metre, and coined the terms 'inscape', 'instress', and *'sprung rhythm', respectively, to define them. 'Inscape' refers to 'the individual or essential quality of the thing' or 'individually-distinctive beauty of style'. 'Instress' is the force or energy which sustains an inscape; it originates in the Creator and is felt by the responsive perceiver (a concept claimed to relate to the theologian *Duns Scotus and his idea of *haecceitas*, or 'thisness', which Hopkins greatly admired). 'Sprung rhythm' is distinguished from regular or 'running rhythm' (with its regular metrical feet) because it involves writing and scanning by number of stresses rather than by counting syllables. Surviving prose writings, including journals, letters, and sermons, articulate Hopkins's profound responsiveness to nature and beauty, his acumen as a literary critic and theorist of prosody, his playful wit, devoted friendliness, and spiritual and theological insights. His correspondents included Coventry *Patmore and R. W. Dixon, one of his former teachers. He was also deeply influenced by the visual arts, keenly admiring the *Pre-Raphaelites.

Hopkins's poetic fame was posthumous and gradual. Bridges became the guardian of the manuscripts after his death. Doubting how the public would respond, he published a few poems in anthologies but delayed a full edition until 1918. It sold poorly, and it was not until the second edition in 1930, read and admired by F. R. *Leavis, W. H. *Auden, Stephen *Spender, and R. S. *Thomas, that Hopkins achieved recognition. T. S. *Eliot was persuaded to publish excerpts from the letters and notebooks in the *Criterion*, cementing Hopkins's reputation as a proto-modernist poet.

HOPKINSON, Nalo (1960–) Canadian author of *science fiction and *fantasy, born in Jamaica. *Brown Girl in the Ring* (1998) and

Midnight Robber (2000) draw upon the richness of Caribbean culture and its storytelling techniques.

HORACE (Quintus Horatius Flaccus) (65–8 BC) Roman poet. His father, an emancipated slave, gave him a good education and was remembered by Horace with gratitude (*Satires*, 1. 6). Ambitiously, he joined *Brutus' army; defeat meant the confiscation of his inherited property. A friend of *Virgil, he was taken up by *Maecenas, to whom he addressed several poems, and who gave him the Sabine farm much celebrated in the poems. In the 30s, Horace wrote *Satires* and *Epodes*. His greatest work is his lyric *Odes* (Books 1–3 23 BC, Book 4 8 BC), in the metres of such archaic Greek poets as Alcaeus, *Sappho, and *Anacreon. His verse *Epistles* allow readers to feel that they know Horace as a man. *The Art of Poetry* resonates with influential phrases: 'in medias res' (in the midst of things), 'ut pictura poesis' (as painting so poetry). English satire from Thomas *Wyatt to Alexander *Pope's *Imitations* derives much of its manner and aims from Horace. Rudyard *Kipling was a great admirer and composed a 'Fifth Book of Horace's Odes'. Notable translators include Christopher *Smart.

Horatian ode *See* ODE.

Horizon A literary magazine founded in 1939 by Cyril Connolly, Stephen *Spender, and Peter Watson, which ran from 1940 to 1950. It published works by George *Orwell, Auberon *Waugh, Laurie *Lee, W. H. *Auden, and Geoffrey *Grigson, amongst others.

HORNBY, Nick (1957–) Novelist and autobiographer. *Fever Pitch* (1992), his hugely successful memoir about his years as a supporter of Arsenal football club, opened the floodgates for a new genre of male *confessional writing. The comic novels, *High Fidelity* (1995) and *About a Boy* (1998; filmed 2002) both explored the emotional confusions and immaturity of a certain kind of white middle-class Englishman. The narrator of *How to Be Good* (2001), however, is a woman. A *Long Way Down* (2005) extracts poignant comedy from four characters who come together through failed attempts at suicide.

Horn Childe A northern verse romance from the period 1290–1340. The plot is similar to that of *King Horn. *Horn Childe* is probably the romance referred to in 'Sir Thopas' (*see* CANTERBURY TALES, 17).

HORNE, Richard Henry (Hengist) (1802–84) Poet and dramatist. He published *Orion* (1843), an allegorical epic, at a farthing 'to mark', he said archly, 'the public contempt into which epic poetry had fallen'. It was much praised by Thomas *Carlyle, G. H. *Lewes, and Edgar Allan *Poe; contemporary reviewers compared it with *Keats's *Hyperion* and *Endymion*. Horne wrote several blank verse tragedies, influenced by John *Webster, and adapted various plays for the stage. He contributed many articles to *Dickens's *Daily News* and *Household Words*, and in 1852, in the midst of the gold fever, went to Australia where he stayed until 1869. His adventures there are described in the autobiographical preface to his *Australian Facts and Prospects* (1859). From 1839 he corresponded with Elizabeth Barrett *Browning, who collaborated with him in his *A New Spirit of the Age* (1844).

HORNIMAN, Annie (1860–1937) Theatre patron and manager. She provided the financial assistance that allowed W. B. *Yeats and the Irish National Theatre Society to establish a permanent home in the *Abbey Theatre, Dublin, in 1904. She founded the Manchester Repertory Company at the Gaiety Theatre, Manchester, in 1908, where she was a pioneer supporter of the 'new drama' of Henrik *Ibsen and G. B. *Shaw.

HORNUNG, E. W. (Ernest William) (1866–1921) Novelist, the creator of Raffles, public-school man, gentleman burglar, and cricketer, who appeared in the best-selling thrillers *The Amateur Cracksman* (1899), *The Black Mask* (1901), *A Thief in the Night* (1905), and *Mr Justice Raffles* (1909), narrated by his admiring assistant Bunny. *See also* DETECTIVE FICTION.

HOROVITZ, Michael (1935–) Poet, performance artist, and editor, born in Frankfurt. He emigrated to England with his family as a child. He was one of the earliest British exponents of the counter-culture and *Beat Generation, editing important anthologies of new work for *New Departures* including *Children of Albion: Poetry of the 'Underground'* (1969), organizing the celebrated poetry festival at the Royal Albert Hall in June 1965, and encouraging many young poets, whose work appears in *Grandchildren of Albion* (1997).

horror The horror/*fantasy tradition goes back to the monster in *Beowulf* dating from the 10th century, and beyond to the bloody visions of *Sophocles (496–406 BC). More directly influential on the horror/fantasy fiction of the 20th century was *Romanticism and the *Gothic, in particular the richly iconic figure of the *vampire; and the macabre short stories of Edgar Allan *Poe. H. P. *Lovecraft is influential as a horror writer himself, and for his championing of writers like M. R. *James, Arthur *Machen, and Algernon *Blackwood. Robert *Aickman preferred to call his horror tales 'strange stories', but Ramsey *Campbell has never shied away from the term 'horror'. Stephen *King's *Danse Macabre* (1981) intelligently describes the various effects attainable in horror. In the USA, Peter Straub, Poppy Z. Brite (1967–), and British-born Clive *Barker produce notable work; in the UK, a new generation of horror writers which has grown up reading Campbell, Aickman, and M. John Harrison includes Joel Lane (1963–), Michael Marshall Smith (1965–), Mark Morris (1963–), Conrad Williams (1969–), Kim Newman (1959–), Christopher Fowler (1953–), and Graham Joyce (1954–). Anthologies such as Nicholas Royle's *Darklands* and *Darklands 2*, Stephen Jones and David Sutton's *Dark Terrors* series, and Ellen Datlow and Terri Windling's *The Year's Best Fantasy and Horror* have encouraged these new writers while continuing to support veterans such as John Burke (1922–), Basil Copper (1924–), and Ronald Chetwynd-Hayes (1919–2001). Of the popular genres, horror is arguably the one that runs closest to the literary mainstream and most interestingly subverts it. While much fiction categorized as horror touches on the fantastic or the supernatural, extremes of psychological or physical horror can be seen in more realistic genres, such as the fascination for stories of serial killers like the Hannibal Lector of Thomas Harris (1940–)

HOSPITAL, Janette Turner (1942–) Australian novelist and short story writer, whose works include *The Ivory Swing* (1982), *The Tiger in the Tiger Pit* (1983), *Borderline* (1985), *Charades* (1988), *The Last Magician* (1992), and *Oyster* (1996). The theme of dislocation—both cultural and emotional—is recurrent in her work, as is the damage wrought by secrecy, and the ways in which the past influences and can discolour the present. *Dislocations* (1986) and *Isobars* (1990) are collections of stories.

HOSSEINI, Khaled (1965–) Tajik novelist and doctor, born in Afghanistan; now an American citizen. *The Kite Runner* (2003; filmed 2007), which treats the recent history of Afghanistan and the experience of emigration to America through the events in the life of the young boy Amir and his father, was followed by *A Thousand Splendid Suns* (2007), the story of two Afghan women.

Hours of Idleness A collection of poems by Lord *Byron, published 1807. The first of Byron's works for general rather than private publication. The volume was bitterly attacked by Henry *Brougham in the *Edinburgh Review* as 'so much stagnant water'. Byron responded in *English Bards and Scotch Reviewers*.

HOUSEHOLD, Geoffrey (1900–88) Author of many successful adventure stories in the tradition of John *Buchan. The most characteristic (including, *Rogue Male*, 1939, and its sequel *Rogue Justice*, 1982) pit a sporting, well-bred, lonely adventurer against the forces of darkness in the modern world.

Household Words A weekly periodical started in 1850 by Charles *Dickens, and incorporated in 1859 into *All the Year Round*, which he edited until his death. Priced at twopence, it was aimed at a large audience, and achieved a weekly circulation of 40,000. Its contributors included Elizabeth *Gaskell, Charles *Reade, and Edward *Bulwer-Lytton. It established the reputation of Wilkie *Collins, and published poems by the young George *Meredith and Coventry *Patmore. Its attacks on the abuses of the day (poor sanitation, slums, factory accidents) were radical and persistent.

House of Fame, The An unfinished dream-poem by Geoffrey *Chaucer, possibly composed *c.*1374–*c.*1385. There are three books, in 2,158 lines; it is believed to be Chaucer's last poem in *octosyllabics.

After a sceptical prologue on dreams and the invocation to the god of sleep, Book I has its narrator fall asleep and dream that he is in a Temple of Glass where he sees depicted Aeneas and Dido (based on *Aeneid*, 4). At the end of Book I the poet sees an eagle who alights by him and is his guide through the House of Fame in Book II (initially suggested, perhaps, by *Fama*, Rumour, in *Aeneid*, 4. 173ff.). The eagle explains the arbitrary workings of Fame and the book ends with a vision of the world (ll. 896–1045). The eagle departs and at the beginning of Book III Chaucer enters the Palace of Fame (Rumour) where he sees the famous of both classical and biblical lore. Eolus, ruler of the winds, blows a trumpet to summon up the various celebrities who introduce themselves in categories reminiscent of the souls in Dante's *Divina commedia*, which Chaucer parodies throughout this poem. Towards the end comes a vision of bearers of false tidings: shipmen, pilgrims, pardoners, and messengers, whose confusion seems to be about to be resolved by the appearance of 'A man of gret auctorite...' when the poem ends. Poetic responses to the work were made by John *Lydgate (in *The Temple of Glas*), Gawin *Douglas, and John *Skelton.

'House of Life, The' A sequence of 101 sonnets by Dante Gabriel *Rossetti, published in *Poems* (1870) and *Ballads and Sonnets* (1881). They have been considered both a record of Rossetti's grief for his dead wife, and a commentary on his passion for William *Morris's wife Jane. Robert *Buchanan in 'The Fleshly School of Poetry' (1871) cited the work in his vehement attack on the perceived moral depravity of Rossetti's poetry.

House of the Seven Gables, The A novel by Nathaniel *Hawthorne, published 1851. It deals with the problem of hereditary guilt, unmerited misfortune, and unexpiated crime, through the story of the Pyncheon family, suffering from generation to generation from the curse of old Maule, the dispossessed owner of the Pyncheon property. An important part in the purging of this curse is played by a young daguerrotypist. The novel's semi-allegorical treatment of the theme of the 'transmitted vices of society' is characteristic of Hawthorne, and manifests his acute sensitivity about his own Puritan ancestry.

HOUSMAN, A. E. (Alfred Edward) (1859–1936) Poet and Classical scholar. Housman began to compose poetry in 1887, following the emigration to India and marriage of Moses Jackson, a contemporary at Oxford to whom he had formed a passionate attachment. In 1896 he published, at his own expense, *A Shropshire Lad*, a series of 63 spare and nostalgic verses, based largely on *ballad forms, and mainly set in a half-imaginary Shropshire, a 'land of lost content', and often addressed to, or spoken by, a farm-boy or a soldier. Many of the poems had been written in the early months of 1895, which happened to be the time of the Oscar *Wilde trial. Housman made the barest profit from the publication. During the First World War *A Shropshire Lad* became hugely popular. The 41 poems in *Last Poems* (1922) met with great acclaim. Housman's lecture 'The Name and Nature of Poetry' was published in 1933, followed by *More Poems* (1936), from work in the notebooks; Laurence *Housman's *A.E.H.* (1937), containing a further eighteen poems, and *Collected Poems* (1939). Housman is the principal

character in Tom *Stoppard's play *The Invention of Love* (1997).

HOUSMAN, Laurence (1865–1959) Writer and dramatist, brother of A. E. *Housman. He published many stories, for both children and adults, and wrote much on feminism and on socialist and pacifist themes. His work includes the somewhat derivative poems in *Green Arras* (1896) and *Spikenard* (1898); *An English-woman's Love-Letters* (1900), which enjoyed some notoriety and was widely parodied; and several successful novels, among them a political satire, *Trimblerigg* (1924), directed against David Lloyd George. His first play, *Bethlehem*, was performed in 1902. Some of his plays on controversial topics, such as *Pains and Penalties* (1911), were banned. *The Little Plays of St Francis* (1922), and further plays on St Francis and on St Clare, were well received. *Angels and Ministers* (1921) set in the court of Queen Victoria, were collected with further royal playlets into *Victoria Regina* (1934). When the lord chamberlain's ban on the impersonation of members of the royal family was lifted in 1937 the play enjoyed great success. *The Unexpected Years*, an autobiography, and *A.E.H.*, containing a valuable memoir of his brother, were published in 1937.

HOVE, Chenjerai (1956–) Born in Zimbabwe though now living in exile; he describes his country as 'a big wound'. His collections of poetry are *Up in Arms* (1982), *Red Hills of Home* (1985), *Rainbows in the Dust* (1998), and *Blind Moon* (2003). He writes in Shona, but is best known for his novels in English, *Shadows* (1991), *Ancestors* (1996), and the award-winning *Bones* (1988), exploring the role of women in the Zimbabwean liberation struggle.

HOWARD, Elizabeth Jane (1923–) CBE, novelist and short story writer; her third marriage, dissolved in 1983, was to Kingsley *Amis. Well crafted and strongly evocative of place and time, her novels of English middle-class life include *The Beautiful Visit* (1950), *After Julius* (1965), and *Getting It Right* (1982). *The Light Years* (1990), *Marking Time* (1991), *Confusion* (1993), and *Casting Off* (1995) form the saga of the Cazalet family from 1937 to the post-war period. *Mr Wrong* (1975) is a collection of her stories. Her many plays for television include an adaptation of *After Julius*. *Slipstream* (2002) is an autobiography.

HOWARD, Henry *See* SURREY, HENRY HOWARD.

HOWARD, Robert E. (1906-36) Prolific American author of stories of numerous genres (*fantasy, *horror, *historical, *western, and *detective fiction) for American 'pulp' magazines. He is best known for 'Conan the Barbarian', whose colourful adventures in a mythic past helped to define the sub-genre of *sword and sorcery.

Howards End *'Condition of England' novel by E. M. *Forster, published 1910, filmed by *Merchant-Ivory 1992. On the one hand are the Schlegel sisters, Margaret and Helen, and their brother Tibby, who care about ideas, civilized living, music, literature, and conversation with their friends; on the other, the Wilcoxes, Henry and his children Charles, Paul, and Evie, who are concerned with the business side of life and distrust emotions and imagination. Helen Schlegel is drawn to the Wilcox family, falls briefly in and out of love with Paul, and thereafter reacts away from them. Margaret becomes more deeply involved and acknowledges the debt of intellectuals to men of business like Henry. Eventually, she marries him, to the consternation of both families. Her marriage cracks but does not break. In the end, torn between her sister and her husband, she succeeds in bridging the mistrust that divides them. Howards End, where the story begins and ends, is the house that belonged to Henry Wilcox's first wife, and is a symbol of human dignity and endurance.

HOWELL, James (?1593-1666) Historian, political writer, and poet; he held diplomatic and administrative posts under Charles I and was imprisoned in the Fleet as a Royalist, 1643-51; at the *Restoration he became historiographer royal. Howell is chiefly remembered for his *Epistolae Ho-Elianae: Familiar Letters Domestic and Foreign* (1645-55), reprinted many times. These letters to correspondents, most of whom are imaginary, were written largely during his imprisonment; their intimate 'back-stairs' view of history had a lasting appeal, and W. M. *Thackeray wrote of them, 'Montaigne and Howell's *Letters* are my bedside books.'

HOWELLS, William Dean (1837-1920) American novelist; he was American consul at Venice, 1861-5, an experience reflected in his *Venetian Life* (1866) and *Italian Journeys* (1867). He was sub-editor of the *Atlantic Monthly*, 1866-71, and chief editor 1871-81, and was associate editor of *Harper's Magazine*, 1886-91, and also contributed many articles on literary subjects. He pioneered the promotion of realism in American fiction and, among his many novels, *The Rise of Silas Lapham* (1885) portrays the pursuit of commercial and social success and *A Hazard of New Fortunes* (1890) is a semi-autobiographical exposé of social hypocrisy. He also wrote dramas, critical works and memoirs.

HROTSVITHA (Roswitha) (*fl.* 10th century) A Benedictine abbess of Gandersheim in Saxony, who wrote plays loosely modelled on *Terence for the use of her convent, an example of the survival of classical influence in the Middle Ages.

HUBBARD, L. Ron (Lafayette Ronald) (1911-86) American author and founder of the Church of Scientology; he published widely in American pulp magazines, especially stories of *science fiction and *fantasy. After his success with the psychotherapy programme 'Dianetics', which became the Scientology religion, he abandoned fiction to return with *Battlefield Earth* (1982), and sequels.

hubris *See* POETICS.

HUCHOWN of the Awle Ryale (*fl.* 14th century) Apparently a northern alliterative poet mentioned by Andrew Wyntoun (*c.*1350-*c.*1423), *c.*1400, who claims that 'He made the gret Gest of Arthure | And the Anteris of Gawane, | The Epistill als of Suete Susane'. These poems have been tentatively identified as, respectively, the alliterative *Morte Arthure*, The *Awntyrs of Arthure*, and *The Pistyl of Susan*. Huchown has been identified with the Sir Hugh Eglinton mentioned in William *Dunbar's 'Lament for the Makaris' (l. 53).

Huckleberry Finn, (The) Adventures of A novel by Mark *Twain, published in 1884 as a sequel to *The Adventures of *Tom Sawyer* (1876). Narrated by Huck Finn, it describes the flight of Huck from well-meant attempts to 'sivilise' him, and from his feckless father, down the Mississippi where he eventually rejoins Tom Sawyer. He is accompanied by a runaway slave Jim, whose bid for freedom he supports, despite the inner promptings of a 'conscience' telling him he is stealing the rightful property of Jim's owner ('All right, then, I'll go to hell'). Huck's simplicity is used by Twain to reveal the absurdities of a family feud and the hypocrisies of shore society. His account has become a classic of vernacular narrative. The novel has continued to provoke controversy over its representation and designation of African Americans.

Hudibras A satire in three parts, each containing three cantos, written by Samuel *Butler (1613–80): part I (dated 1663, published December 1662), part II (dated 1664, published 1663), part III (1680). A revised version of parts I and II came out in 1674. Its narrative form is that of a mock romance, derived from *Don Quixote, in which a grotesque Presbyterian knight, Sir Hudibras, and his sectarian squire Ralpho set out on horseback and encounter a bear-baiting mob who, after a comic skirmish, imprison them in the stocks. In the second part a widow, whom Hudibras hopes to marry for the sake of her property, agrees to release them on condition that the knight undergoes a whipping for her sake. They visit Sidrophel, a charlatan posing as an astrologer, whom Hudibras assaults and leaves for dead. In Part III Hudibras returns to the widow and claims that he has fulfilled his promise to whip himself, but is interrupted by a gang which he mistakes for Sidrophel's supernatural agents. They cudgel him and force him to confess to his iniquities. He consults a lawyer, who advises him to write love letters to the widow in order to inveigle her in her replies. The second canto of Part III has no connection with the rest of the poem but includes an account of political enmities between the death of Oliver Cromwell and the restoration of Charles II. The loose narrative framework gives room for digressions which deal with academic pedantry, the theological differences between the Presbyterians and independent sectarians, Aristotelian logic, the Hermetic philosophy, the politics of the Civil War period, the ethics of oath-breaking, witchcraft, alchemy, astrology, and the nature of marriage. *Hudibras* is profoundly learned, but Butler treats all erudition with contempt. His most powerful satirical weapon is his style, the deliberately cumbersome octosyllabic metre and comic rhymes of which render absurd every subject to which they are applied.

Hudibrastic In the style of Samuel Butler's *Hudibras; in octosyllabic couplets and with comic rhymes.

HUDSON, W. H. (William Henry) (1841–1922) American novelist and *nature writer; he became a British subject in 1900. His first success was *The Naturalist in La Plata* (1892) praised by Alfred Russel *Wallace. It was followed by *Idle Days in Patagonia*, (1893) an engaging work of travel and natural lore; *Nature in Downland (1900); *Green Mansions* (1904,

novel); *A Shepherd's Life* (1910); *Adventures among Birds* (1913); and the joyful account of his boyhood, *Far Away and Long Ago* (1918). Hudson's collected works were published in 24 volumes in 1922–3.

HUGHES, Langston (1902–67) African American writer, a leading figure in the *Harlem Renaissance. Hughes applied blues and jazz techniques in his poetry from *The Weary Blues* (1926) onwards. Of his fiction, the most successful was the five volumes of Simple stories (1950–65), presenting Jesse B. Semple as the spokesman for urban black America. *The Big Sea* (1940) and *I Wonder as I Wander* (1956) are autobiographical. Hughes was a vigorous campaigner against racism and in the 1930s was drawn to the social promise of communism.

HUGHES, Richard Arthur Warren (1900–76) Writer of Welsh descent. His play *Danger* (1924) was the first original radio play commissioned by the *BBC; his first novel, *A High Wind in Jamaica* (1929), is an unsentimental story of a family of children sent from Jamaica to England and captured by pirates. After *In Hazard* (1938) Hughes published very little until *The Fox in the Attic* (1961), the first volume of a planned historical sequence charting the rise of Nazism. Opening just after the First World War, it mingles real and fictional characters, and ends with Hitler's Munich putsch of 1923. *The Wooden Shepherdess* (1973) followed, but the sequence was incomplete when Hughes died.

HUGHES, Shirley (1927–) OBE, prolific children's author-illustrator, born in West Kirby, Wirral. Initially a book illustrator, her first picture book, *Lucy and Tom's Day* (1961), established Hughes as the chronicler of suburban life for children, notably with her 'Alfie' series. *Dogger* (1977) and *Ella's Big Chance* (2004) were both awarded the Kate Greenaway Medal. She has published a non-fiction work: *A Brush with the Past 1900–1950* (2005), and an autobiography: *A Life in Drawing* (2002).

HUGHES, Ted (1930–98) Poet, born in west Yorkshire, educated at Pembroke College, Cambridge, where he met Sylvia *Plath, whom he married in 1956. His lifelong obsession with animals and his sense of the beauty and violence of the natural world appear in his first volume, *The Hawk in the Rain* (1957). This was followed by *Lupercal* (1960), *Wodwo* (1967), several books of children's verse, and *Poetry in the Making* (1967), a perennially popular book of essays, for children, on poetry. *Crow* (1970) introduced the central symbol of the crow, partly inspired by a meeting with the American artist Leonard Baskin. Hughes retells the legends of creation and birth through the dark vision of predatory, mocking, indestructible Crow. Other volumes include *Cave Birds* (1975), *Season Songs* (1976), and *Moortown* (1979). *Remains of Elmet* (1979), with photographs by Fay Godwin, celebrates the landscapes of his youth in the Calder valley, which he describes as 'the last ditch of Elmet, the last British kingdom to fall to the Angles'; *River* (1983), with photographs by Peter Keen, is a sequence of poems invoking riverside and river life. Together these volumes constitute arresting examples of the renewed vogue for *topographical poetry. Hughes's stress on the physical, animal, and subconscious is in marked contrast to the urbane tone of the *Movement, and his poetry, hailed as vital and original, has also been described as excessively violent. He was appointed *poet laureate in 1984. Later volumes include *Wolfwatching* (1989), *Rain-Charm for the Duchy and Other Laureate Poems* (1992), and *Birthday Letters* (1998), a sequence describing his relationship with Plath. The huge *Collected Poems*, edited by Paul Keegan, appeared in 2003. Prose works include *Shakespeare and the Goddess of Complete Being (1992)* and *Winter Pollen* (1995, criticism). *Selected Translations*, ed. Daniel Weissbort (2006) gathers examples of Hughes' work as a translator, ranging from Ovid and other ancient texts to contemporary European poetry. The *Letters* (2007) were edited by Christopher *Reid. *See also* RATTLE BAG, THE.

HUGHES, Thomas (1822–96) Novelist, author of the extraordinarily successful novel *Tom Brown's Schooldays* (1857, by 'An Old Boy'), which evokes the Rugby of his youth and his veneration for its headmaster, Dr Thomas Arnold. Hughes condemned, in the character of the tyrannical *Flashman, the bullying prevalent in public schools of the day, and advocated a form of what came to be known as 'muscular Christianity', which attempted to combine Christian principles with physical courage, self-reliance, love of sport, school loyalty, and patriotism, a mixture that had much impact on the public-school ethos. Its vigour did much to establish the *school story as a literary genre.

HUGH OF LINCOLN, LITTLE ST (?1246–55) A child supposed to have been crucified (27 August 1255) by a Jew named Copin or Jopin at Lincoln, after having been starved and tortured. A confession to this effect was extracted by John of Lexington. The body is said to have been discovered in a well and buried in the cathedral, and to have been the cause of several miracles. The story, often related with strong anti-Semitic overtones, is mentioned by Chaucer ('The Prioress's Tale', *see* CANTERBURY TALES, 16) and by Marlowe in *The *Jew of Malta*. See also the ballad of 'The Jew's Daughter' in Percy's *Reliques*.

HUGO, Victor-Marie (1802–85) Poet, novelist, and dramatist, the leading figure of the Romantic movement in France. Hugo's determinedly anti-classical plays include *Cromwell* (1827), the preface to which became a manifesto of the French Romantic movement. Hugo's novels, notably *Notre Dame de Paris* (1831) and *Les Misérables* (1862), were also hugely successful in France and in England.

Hugo award For achievement in *science fiction; named after Hugo *Gernsback, and presented at annual World Science Fiction Conventions.

HULME, T. E. (Thomas Ernest) (1883–1917) Poet, essayist, and (in his own phrase) 'philosophic amateur'. His reaction against *Romanticism and advocacy of the 'hard dry image' influenced *imagism. His essay 'Romanticism and Classicism' defines Romanticism as 'spilt religion', and predicts a new 'cheerful, dry and sophisticated' poetry; similarly, in the visual arts, he predicted the triumph of precise, abstract geometric form. Only six of his poems were published in his lifetime. Five of these, and essays on Henri *Bergson, were published in Alfred Orage's *New Age*. Hulme was killed in action during the First World War, and much of his work survived only in notebooks. The selection of his work edited by Herbert *Read, *Speculations* (1924), was influential; the *Collected Writings* (1994), clarifies the chronology. Hulme's double role as conservative and *modernist had considerable influence on the development of 20th-century taste; T. S. *Eliot described him in 1924 as 'classical, reactionary and revolutionary.'

HUMBOLDT, Alexander von (1769–1859) German explorer and scientist. The published results of his expedition to South America and Mexico (English translation, 1814–21) earned him an enormous celebrity—alluded to by Lord *Byron in *Don Juan*—and his work was a source of inspiration to both Charles *Darwin and Alfred Russel Wallace (1823–1913). *Kosmos* (1845–62), a description of the universe from celestial phenomena to the earth's biogeography, has claims to be the most important work of popular science ever published.

HUME, David (1711–76) Philosopher, born and educated in Edinburgh. He spent three years (1734–7) in private study in France, and in 1739 published anonymously his *Treatise of Human Nature*, a sceptical account of the workings of the mind, which sold poorly. His *Essays Moral and Political* (1741–2) was more popular. *A Letter from a Gentleman to his Friend in Edinburgh* (1745) includes Hume's defence of his *Treatise* when he contended unsuccessfully for the moral philosophy chair at Edinburgh, against the opposition of Francis *Hutcheson and William Wishart (c.1692–1753). He reworked his *Treatise* as *Philosophical Essays Concerning Human Understanding* (1748), better known under its 1756 title, *Enquiry Concerning Human Understanding*, and *Enquiry Concerning the Principles of Morals* (1751). In 1752 Hume published his *Political Discourses*, which made him famous on the Continent. The *History of Great Britain* (1754–62) was immensely popular in Britain and abroad, earning the praise of Edward *Gibbon and *Voltaire. *Four Dissertations*, dedicated to John Home, was published in 1757, after suppression of controversial essays on suicide and immortality. Hume brought *Rousseau to England, but Rousseau's suspicious nature led to a quarrel, Hume's account of which was published in 1766. James *Boswell visited Hume on his deathbed, hoping that his scepticism would crumble at the approach of death: it did not. Hume's religious views were highly contentious in their day, incurring the special wrath of Samuel *Johnson. Hume's *Dissertation* on 'The Natural History of Religion' (1757) further undermined orthodoxy by deriving religion from psychological processes; the *Dialogues Concerning Natural Religion* (1779) conclude merely 'that the cause or causes of order in the universe probably bear some remote analogy to human intelligence'. Hume's writings on politics and history show a strong interest in human character and motivation. Though a believer in civil liberties, and an opponent of 'divine right', he rejected the social contract theory of obligation as historically unrealistic; Hume favoured an explanation based on custom and convenience.

Humorous Lieutenant, The A comedy by John *Fletcher, acted c.1617–19.

humours Comedy of, a term applied especially to the type of comic drama written by Ben *Jonson, where a 'humour' is the embodiment in one of the characters of some dominating individual passion or propensity. The principal humours, whose balance was thought to determine a man's nature, were blood, phlegm, choler, and melancholy or black choler.

HUMPHREYS, Emyr (1919–) Welsh novelist and poet. His 23 novels include *Hear and Forgive* (1952), *A Toy Epic* (1958), *Outside the House of Baal* (1965), and a septet, running from *National Winner* (1971) to *Bonds of Attachment* (1991). Humphreys has described his work both as an attempt to 'show the Welsh condition as a microcosm of the human condition', and as an effort to create 'the Protestant novel'. *The Taliesen Tradition* (1983) meditates on the ways literature has influenced Welsh identity over the centuries. *Collected Poems* appeared in 1999.

Humphry Clinker, The Expedition of
*Epistolary novel by Tobias *Smollett (1771). It presents, in the words of Walter *Scott, 'the various effects produced upon different members of the same family by the same objects'. Nearly two-thirds of the letters are either from Matthew Bramble to his friend and doctor Lewis, or from Jery Melford (Bramble's nephew) to his Oxford friend Phillips. Others are from Bramble's sister Tabitha to her housekeeper; from Bramble's niece Lydia to her friend Letty; and from the comically semi-literate Winifred Jenkins, Tabitha's servant, to Molly, a maid at the hall. The narrative follows a journey from Wales to London, to Scotland and back again. On the journey to London, the destitute Humphry is engaged as a postilion; his Methodism outrages Bramble, but his female relations reconcile him to Humphry's simple sincerity. On the return journey from Scotland, their carriage overturns in a river, and Humphry rescues Bramble, whose natural son he is shortly afterwards proved to be. The novel ends with three marriages, which seal a general improvement in happiness and mutual understanding between the characters.

HUNT, John (1775–1848) The brother of Leigh *Hunt. He was a courageous and enterprising publisher who was prosecuted, threatened with legal actions, and fined many times. In 1808 he and his brother established the very successful *Examiner. In 1810 he started a quarterly, *The Reflector* (with Leigh as editor). In 1813 he and Leigh were both sentenced to two years' imprisonment in separate jails and fined £500 apiece for a libel on the prince regent. In 1815–17 John published those essays of his brother and of William *Hazlitt which were collected as The Round Table (1817). He was the publisher and Leigh the editor of the brilliant *Liberal, founded in 1822, in which Lord *Byron published The *Vision of Judgement and all the later cantos of *Don Juan (from Canto VI), which John *Murray had refused. The Literary Examiner, founded in 1823, was short-lived.

HUNT, Leigh (1784–1859) Writer, publisher, and editor, brother of John *Hunt. He wrote essays on a wide variety of subjects, many of which were published in his journals. He published Charles *Lamb's essays on William *Shakespeare and William *Hogarth in The Reflector (1810). While in jail for a libel in The Examiner on the prince regent he was allowed to continue to write and edit The Examiner, and to receive visits from friends, who included Lord *Byron, Thomas *Moore, the *Lambs, Jeremy *Bentham, James Mill, and Henry *Brougham. In 1816 he printed John *Keats's early sonnet 'O Solitude' in The Examiner, and began his vigorous and lifelong support of Keats, P. B. *Shelley, and the *Romantic poets; his name was linked with that of Keats and *Hazlitt in attacks on the so-called *Cockney School. His poem The *Story of Rimini (1816), dedicated to Byron, was followed by Hero and Leander and Bacchus and Ariadne (both 1819). In the *Indicator in 1821 he published Keats's *'La Belle Dame sans Merci'. The *Liberal, founded jointly with Byron, published works by Byron, Shelley, Hazlitt, Hunt, *Hogg, and others. Captain Sword and Captain Pen (1835) is an effective threnody on the horrors of war. His many other works include plays; Poetical Works and Imagination and Fancy, in which he usefully compares painting and poetry (both 1844); a lively Autobiography (1850), much admired by Thomas *Carlyle; Table Talk (1851); and a bowdlerized edition of *Beaumont and *Fletcher.

Hunt was a brave and outspoken radical during the Regency, and his gift for detecting talent, from Keats to *Tennyson, and his determined support for it, made him an invaluable editor. His sunny, optimistic nature is sketched in the early character of Skimpole in *Bleak House.

HUNT, Violet (1866–1942) Novelist and literary hostess, for some years the companion of Ford Madox *Ford. A flamboyant feminist, a supporter of women's suffrage, and a friend of H. G. *Wells, Henry *James, Rebecca *West, Ezra *Pound, Joseph *Conrad, Wyndham *Lewis, D. H. *Lawrence, amongst others. She published seventeen novels including The Maiden's Progress (1894), A Hard Woman (1895), The Human Interest (1899), and White Rose of Weary Leaf (1908), short stories, and an autobiography, The Flurried Years (1926).

HUNT, William Holman (1827–1910) Painter and founder member of the *Pre-Raphaelite Brotherhood. Many of his most famous paintings, such as The Scapegoat (1854) and The Light of the World (1851–3), have strong religious themes, though he also painted literary and historical subjects from William *Shakespeare, Alfred *Tennyson, John *Keats, and Edward *Bulwer-Lytton. His autobiographical Pre-Raphaelitism and the Pre-Raphaelite Brotherhood (1905) provided a full but biased history of the movement.

HURD, Richard (1720–1808) Clergyman and scholar, bishop successively of Lichfield and Worcester. He produced an edition of *Horace's Ars Poetica (1749) and Epistola ad Augustum (1751), including his 'Discourse Concerning Poetical Imitation'. Hurd's Letters on Chivalry and Romance (1762) was an important reassessment of Elizabethan literature: Hurd was sympathetic to *Spenser, arguing that the 'Gothic' was more poetic than the 'Grecian', and that *neo-classical rules were inappropriately applied to romances, which were composed on different but equally artistic principles.

HURSTON, Zora Neale (1891–1960) African American novelist, journalist, critic, and folklorist, born in Eatonville, Florida, the first incorporated all-black town in America. She was a prolific writer during the 1920s and 1930s, prominent in the *Harlem Renaissance: her works include Mules and Men (1935), a study of black American folklore in the South; the novel for which she is best known, Their Eyes Were Watching God (1937); plays, short stories, and Dust Tracks on a Road (1942), an autobiography. Alice *Walker and Toni *Morrison, amongst others, acknowledge their debt to her.

Husband's Message, The An Old English poem of 53 lines in the *Exeter Book, one of the group usually called 'elegies'. Its ostensible form is a message to a woman from her husband who has had to leave his own country because of a feud, telling her of his prosperity in another land and asking her to join him.

HUTCHESON, Francis (1694–1746) Irish Presbyterian clergyman and philosopher, who wrote a series of aesthetic, moral, and political essays for the Dublin and London press, in addition to two books, *An Inquiry into the Original of our Ideas of Beauty and Virtue* (1725) and *An Essay on the Nature and Conduct of the Passions and Affections with Illustrations on the Moral Sense* (1728). He was professor of moral philosophy at Glasgow from 1729 until his death. His *System of Moral Philosophy* (1755) inclued a biography by William Leechman. Hutcheson introduced the civic humanist tradition into higher education: he trained a generation of students, among them Adam *Smith, in the Whig philosophy of personal liberty and government restraint, and his progressive views were influential among Scots émigrés to America. In ethics he developed the ideas of the third earl of *Shaftesbury on the moral sense into a fully-fledged system. He saw a close relation between aesthetic and moral perception, by which we come to be aware of providentially designed order. Virtue is identical with benevolence insofar as it gives disinterested pleasure, that action being best which aims at the greatest happiness of the greatest number. This view anticipates *Utilitarianism.

HUTCHINSON, Lucy (1620–after 1675) Poet and biographer, wife of John Hutchinson (1615–64). She wrote *Memoirs of the Life of Colonel Hutchinson* (first published 1806) after her husband's death to preserve his memory for her children; it is a classic account of the state of the country at the outbreak of civil war and of the conflict in the vicinity of Nottingham, told from the point of view of the radical Puritan high gentry.

HUTCHINSON, R. C. (Ray Coryton) (1907–75) Novelist. His works include *The Unforgotten Prisoner* (1933), a powerful portrayal of revenge and conciliation in the aftermath of the First World War, seen partly through the sufferings of young Klaus, half English and half German, a victim of the conflicts of his parents and of his country; *Testament* (1938), set in Russia at the time of the revolution; *The Stepmother* (1955); and *Rising* (1976), a *historical novel set in South America.

HUXLEY, Aldous Leonard (1894–1963) Writer, grandson of T. H. *Huxley and brother of Julian Huxley. By 1919 he had already published three volumes of verse; a volume of stories, *Limbo* (1920), was followed by *Crome Yellow* (1921), a country-house satire which earned him a reputation for brilliance and cynicism. Other works include *Mortal Coils* (1922, stories), including 'The Gioconda Smile'); *Antic Hay* (1923), set mostly in post-war London's

nihilistic bohemia; *Those Barren Leaves* (1925); and *Point Counter Point* (1928), which includes a portrait of his friend D. H. *Lawrence. *Brave New World* (1932) attacked the utopian scientifically managed futures of H. G. *Wells and satirized mass culture. It was followed by *Eyeless in Gaza* (1936). Huxley left for California in 1937, partly to promote his new belief in absolute pacifism. His later works include novels: *After Many a Summer* (1939), *Ape and Essence* (1948), another, darker, *dystopia, and *Island* (1962), an optimistic utopia; essays, historical studies, travel works, and *The Devils of Loudon* (1952), a study in sexual hysteria. *The Doors of Perception* (1954) and *Heaven and Hell* (1956) describe his experiments with mescalin and LSD. *Brave New World Revisited* (1958) examines the original novel in the light of the evolution of the post-war world towards or away from his earlier prophecies.

HUXLEY, T. H. (Thomas Henry) (1825–95) Scientist. He was elected FRS in 1851, and in 1854 became professor of natural history at the Royal School of Mines. He wrote extensively on specialist subjects, but was also widely known and admired as a lecturer to lay audiences, often working men; he aimed to avoid 'technical dialect' and had a gift for explaining complicated scientific points in language that was generally intelligible. His views on religion, education, philosophy, and evolution, and on man's newly conceived place in the universe (e.g. in *Evidence as to Man's Place in Nature*, 1863, *Evolution and Ethics*, 1893, and other essays), had a profound impact on 19th-century thought. He was a friend of Charles *Darwin, and an influential though discriminating supporter of his theories. He coined the word 'agnostic' to describe his own philosophical position, which he expounded at the *Metaphysical Society and in the *Nineteenth Century*. His *Collected Essays* were published in 1893–4, his *Scientific Memoirs* in 1898–1903, and his *Life and Letters*, edited by his son Leonard, in 1900–03.

HYDE, Douglas (1860–1949) Irish writer, whose 1892 lecture on 'The Necessity of De-Anglicizing Ireland' provided an ideological blueprint for the *Irish Revival. Hyde became the first professor of Modern Irish at University College, Dublin, in 1909 and the first president of Ireland in 1938. His English translations in *Love Songs of Connacht* (1893) powerfully influenced the idioms of the Revival. In 1901 Hyde's *Casadh an tSúgáin* ('The Twisting of the Rope') became the first professionally produced play in Irish.

Hyde Park A comedy by James *Shirley, acted 1632, printed 1637. This comedy seems to have been written for the annual opening of the park, and it exploits the topical appeal of its subject.

Hydriotaphia (Urn Burial) By Sir Thomas *Browne, published with *The *Garden of Cyrus*, 1658. A sceptical meditation on human pomp in magnificent baroque prose, inspired by some burial urns excavated in Norfolk. It has been admired by many writers, including James *Joyce, Virginia *Woolf, and Jorge Luis *Borges.

Hymenaei A marriage masque by Ben *Jonson, performed at Whitehall on Twelfth Night 1606, and printed in that year.

hymns The Greek *hymnos* means a 'song of praise', honouring gods or heroes, and it is used in this sense by English poets such as P. B. *Shelley ('Hymn to Intellectual Beauty'). In the Christian tradition, hymns are songs of worship, sung by congregation and choir. They are often based on the Bible but, unlike canticles such as the 'Magnificat' or 'Nunc Dimittis', they are not settings of biblical texts. Hymn singing was revived in 16th-century Germany by the Lutherans, and some of the earliest English hymns were written for Dissenting churches: Isaac *Watts, an Independent minister, published *Hymns and Spiritual Songs* in 1707. Hymns were increasingly popular among evangelicals, as with Charles *Wesley's *Hymns and Sacred Poems* (1739), and *Olney Hymns* (1779), a collaboration between William *Cowper and John *Newton. Before 1820, only the singing of *psalms was permitted in the Church of England. After this date, there was a great revival of Anglican hymnody, leading to *Hymns Ancient and Modern* (1860), which included new compositions (by Cecil Frances *Alexander and John Henry *Newman) and translations from Latin hymns. In the *Yattendon Hymnal* (1899), edited by Robert *Bridges, and *The English Hymnal* (1906), edited by Sir Percy Dearmer (1867–1936) and *Vaughan Williams, folk melodies were frequently employed, as hymn singing was connected to ideas of Englishness.

Hymns Ancient and Modern A major collection of hymns for the Church of England, first published in 1860, ed. (Sir) Henry Baker (1821–77). The original inflection, revealing the influence of John Mason *Neale,

was *Tractarian. With the revised 1875 edition, the text's appeal was broadened. Subsequent editions have included *Hymns Ancient and Modern New Standard* (1983). Among many hymns established in the repertoire through the Victorian editions were Neale's 'Blessed city, heavenly Salem' ('Christ is made the sure foundation') and 'O come, O come Emmanuel' and Baker's 'O praise ye the Lord!' For generations of Anglican writers, texts from *Hymns Ancient and Modern* were a significant literary resource.

hypallage [from a Greek word meaning 'exchange'] A transference of epithet, as 'Sansfoy's dead dowry' for 'dead Sansfoy's dowry' (*Spenser).

hyperbole Exaggeration for rhetorical emphasis, as in the colloquial 'it took me ages to get here'. Hyperbolic expression is especially characteristic of inflated or bombastic styles of dramatic speech, as often in the plays of *Marlowe and *Shakespeare.

Hyperion: A Fragment and **The Fall of Hyperion** Fragments of epic poems by John Keats written 1818–19. *Hyperion* was published 1820, *The Fall of Hyperion* not until 1850.

In the first version, written as direct narrative, the fallen *Saturn, conquered by Jove, mourns the loss of his kingdom and debates with his fallen fellow Titans, in their craggy lair, how he may regain his kingdom. They conclude that only the magnificent Hyperion, who is still unfallen, will be able to help them. In Book III Apollo, god of music, poetry, and knowledge, speaks to the goddess Mnemosyne of his inexplicable anguish; then, at the moment of his deification, the fragment ends. In the second version, the poet is in a luxuriant garden, where he drinks an elixir, which induces a vision. He finds himself in a vast domed monument, then proceeds with pain and difficulty to climb the stair to the shrine of the priestess Moneta. Together they find the agonized fallen Saturn, and with Mnemosyne and Thea they speak to him of his pain and loss. In despair he leaves with Thea to comfort his fellow Titans, while the poet and Moneta watch the magnificent, but much troubled, Hyperion blaze into the west. Both poems have as their general theme the nature of poetry and the nature and development of the poet.

hypertext An interlinked group or network of texts, usually digital texts written and read on computers and connected through the activation of keywords that lead the reader from one block of text (lexia) to another. The term was coined by Theodor H. Nelson in 1965, with reference to the possibility of linking computerized texts and (as 'hypermedia') sounds and moving images too. It came also to be applied to the general realm of such textual connections, including, retrospectively, those of print culture too, both intratextual (indexes, contents tables, cross-references) and intertextual (citations, bibliographies, catalogues). Paperback 'gamebooks' for young readers, such as the *Fighting Fantasy* series, flourished in the 1980s: these were essentially hypertext stories in print. In 1987 Apple Computer released HyperCard, a hypertext reading and authoring programme included with every Apple Macintosh computer sold. The world community of hypertext readers and authors expanded rapidly, expanding still further with the growing use of the World Wide Web in the 1990s. The hypertext structure enabled by the standard HTML (hypertext mark-up language) feature of Web linkage came to be exploited by some American writers in the 1990s, bringing into being a distinctive body of electronic literature known as hypertext fiction or hyperfiction, in which the reader assembles the elements of the story by navigating among variously linked lexia. Among the best-known such works are Michael Joyce's (1945–) *Afternoon: A Story* (1990), Stuart Moulthrop's (1957–) *Victory Garden* (1992), Shelley Jackson's (1963–) *Patchwork Girl* (1995), and Mark Amerika's (1960–) *Grammatron* (1997). A common feature of these works is their self-conscious *metafictional play with the hypertext principle of connection itself, the new form becoming a thematic concern of the story. At the same time some academic literary theorists, notably George P. Landow in his book *Hypertext* (1992), along with established novelists such as Robert *Coover in his 1992 article 'The End of Books', saw the advent of hypertext in post-*structuralist terms as a liberation of readers from old cultural hierarchies and 'linear' determinism into unbounded participatory *intertextuality. Discussion of hypertext in the 1990s often displayed a utopian tendency to greet the multi-linearity and potential interactivity (*see* INTERACTIVE FICTION) of hypertext as the dawn of a more democratic literary millennium, despite an evidently persistent demand from most readers for immersion in continuous narratives produced by skilled storytellers. At the turn of the 21st century, increasingly sophisticated hypermedia programmes and computer games tended to eclipse this nascent literary tradition in favour of predominantly visual narratives. An evolution from written lexia to the use of visual elements is evident in, for example, *Grammatron* and in Talan Memmot's (1964–) innovative and characteristically metafictional *Lexia to Perplexia* (2000). See George P. Landow, *Hypertext 3.0* (2006).

 SEE WEB LINKS

• *Electronic Literature Collection* (2006)

iamb, iambic pentameter *See* METRE.

IBSEN, Henrik (1828–1906) Norwegian poet and dramatist, the founder of modern naturalistic drama. His first successes, *Brand* (1866) and *Peer Gynt* (1867), were 'dramatic poems', and established his reputation in Scandinavia, but it was over twenty years before the work of Edmund *Gosse and William *Archer (and later the support of Thomas *Hardy, William *James, G. B. *Shaw, and others) won him recognition as a major dramatist in England. Gosse's 1889 review of Ibsen's work in the *Fortnightly Review* was followed by a highly successful production of Archer's translation of *A Doll's House* (1889), a play which attacked the oppression of women in marriage. Shaw's *The Quintessence of Ibsen* (1891) championed Ibsen as a fearless moral pioneer. In the 1890s performances of both *Ghosts* (1881) and *Hedda Gabler* (1890) provoked public outrage. In 1900 the *Fortnightly Review* contained an enthusiastic review of *When We Dead Awaken* (1899) by the 18-year-old James *Joyce.

Ibsen's earlier plays (such as *Ghosts* and *An Enemy of the People*, 1882) were concerned largely with social and political themes, but the last six (*The Wild Duck*, 1885; *Rosmersholm*, 1886; *The Lady from the Sea*, 1888; *The Master Builder*, 1892; *Little Eyolf*, 1894; and *John Gabriel Borkman*, 1896) are more deeply concerned with the forces of the unconscious, and were greatly admired by *Freud. Ibsen created new attitudes to drama, and is credited with being the first major dramatist to write tragedy about ordinary people in prose. The quality of his dialogue, and his discarding of traditional theatrical effects, demanded a new style of performance. All his great prose dramas are now in the standard English-language repertoire, and the verse drama *Peer Gynt* is frequently revived.

Idea A sonnet sequence by Michael *Drayton, first published as *Idea's Mirror* in 1594, then much revised and expanded. It includes the famous Sonnet 61, 'since there's no help, come, let us kiss and part'.

'Idiot Boy, The' A poem by *Wordsworth, first published in *Lyrical Ballads* (1798). One of the most characteristic and controversial of the poet's early works, it takes as hero the idiot son of a poor countrywoman. The boy's description of a night-time journey, 'The cocks did crow to-whoo, to-whoo, And the sun did shine so cold', fittingly illustrate Wordsworth's intention of 'giving the charm of novelty to things of everyday'.

Idler, The A series of papers, mostly by Samuel *Johnson, published in the *Universal Chronicle, or Weekly Gazette*, 15 April 1758 to 5 April 1760. More lightweight and relaxed than those of the *Rambler, they include the well-known sketches of Dick Minim, the critic, of Mr Sober (Johnson himself), and Jack Whirler (John *Newbery the publisher). The title was later adopted for a monthly journal edited by Jerome K. *Jerome and Robert Barr, 1892–1911.

idylls *See* ECLOGUE.

Idylls of the King A series of twelve Arthurian poems by Alfred *Tennyson, written mostly between 1855 and 1874, but much revised. *'Morte d'Arthur', composed in 1833 after A. H. *Hallam's death, was incorporated into 'The Passing of Arthur'. In 1855–6 Tennyson began writing the first Idyll, to become 'Merlin and Vivien', which he followed with 'Enid', later divided into 'The Marriage of Geraint' and 'Geraint and Enid' The first four were published in 1859 as 'Enid', 'Vivien', 'Elaine', and 'Guinevere'. They were extremely successful, selling 10,000 copies in six weeks. In 1869 followed 'The Coming of Arthur', 'The Holy Grail', 'Pelleas and Ettarre', and 'The Passing of Arthur'. 'The Last Tournament' was published, with 'Gareth and Lynette', in 1872. 'Balin and Balan', written 1872–4, did not appear until 1885. The sequence as now printed first appeared in 1891.

The *Idylls* present the story of *Arthur, from his first meeting with Guinevere to the ruin of the realm in the 'last, dim, weird battle of the west'. The adultery of Guinevere and Lancelot may be a force that destroys the bright hopes of Camelot and the idealism of the Round Table, but both Victorian and subsequent critics have pointed out that the poem (almost despite itself) cannot sustain such blame.

IGNATIUS (Íñigo) LOYOLA, St (1491–1556) Born in the Basque country. He was wounded at the siege of Pamplona (1521), and thereafter devoted himself to religion. He studied at Paris, acquiring a circle of fellow students around whom he would build the Society of Jesus (Jesuits), which received papal authorization in 1540. Loyola's *Spiritual Exercises* (1548) is a manual of devotion and of rules for meditation and prayer.

Igraine Mother of *Arthur, conceived after *Uther Pendragon, disguised as her husband, lay with her.

Iliad A Greek epic poem traditionally by *Homer. It is set in the tenth year of the Trojan War, fought by the Achaeans under Agamemnon in order to recover *Helen, his brother Menelaus' wife. The Achaeans' best warrior, Achilles, refuses to fight out of rage with Agamemnon. When his great friend Patroclus is killed by the Trojan champion Hector, Achilles returns to battle and kills Hector beneath the walls of Troy. He then refuses to give up the body for burial, until old King Priam is brought through the night by the god Hermes, to beg for the body of his son. The death of Achilles and the fall of Troy are foreshadowed in the poem but not narrated. The heroes know that they cannot avoid what is destined by the gods. This heroic ethos is strongly challenged in *Paradise Lost. There are important 18th-century translations by Alexander *Pope and William *Cowper. See also ODYSSEY; LOGUE, CHRISTOPHER.

'Il Penseroso' A poem in rhymed octosyllabics by John *Milton, written ?1631, printed 1645; a companion piece to *'L'Allegro'. The title means 'the contemplative man'. The poem is an invocation to the goddess Melancholy, bidding her bring Peace, Quiet, Leisure, and Contemplation. It describes the pleasures of the studious, meditative life, of tragedy, epic poetry, and music. It had a considerable influence on the meditative *graveyard poems of the 18th century.

imagery A collective term for the references to perceptible things or actions found within a literary work, usually those evoked by *meta-phors and *similes; these are commonly assumed to involve mental pictures or 'images', but may also rely on other sense-impressions such as imagined sounds or flavours. Since the 1930s critical analysis of the recurrent imagery (e.g. horticultural, maritime, meteorological, culinary) found in a poem or play, and especially in the plays of *Shakespeare, has been used as a clue not only to the work's underlying theme but sometimes also to the author's typical preoccupations or mental universe.

Imaginary Conversations of Literary Men and Statesmen By Walter Savage *Landor, published 1824–9, followed by *Imaginary Conversations of Greeks and Romans*, published 1853. The conversations are between characters from classical times to the 19th century; some are dramatic, some idyllic, some satirical. There are some 150 dialogues. Their quality is somewhat uneven, for Landor's own passionate and often prejudiced views tend to obtrude.

imagism A movement of English and American poets, which flourished from around 1910 to 1917, partly derived from the *aesthetic philosophy of T. E. *Hulme. Contributors to its first anthology, *Des imagistes* (1914), edited by Ezra *Pound, included Richard *Aldington, Hilda *Doolittle (known as 'H.D.'), Ford Madox *Ford, Amy *Lowell, James *Joyce, Pound, and William Carlos *Williams. Some of D. H. *Lawrence's poems of this period may also be described as imagist. The characteristic products of the movement are more easily recognized than defined: they tend to be short, often close to Japanese forms, composed of short lines of musical cadence rather than metrical regularity, avoiding abstraction and treating the image with a hard, clear precision rather than with overt symbolic intent (Pound said that 'the natural object is always the adequate symbol'). Amy Lowell succeeded Pound as spokesperson of the group, and was responsible for several imagist anthologies.

Imitation of Christ See THOMAS À KEMPIS.

IMLAH, Mick (1956–2009) Scottish poet, editor of *Poetry Review* from 1983 to 1986. He published two collections, *Birthmarks* (1988) and *The Lost Leader* (2008), the latter an ambitious assembly of meditations and monologues on Scottish political and cultural history. He co-edited the *New Penguin Book of Scottish Verse* (2000) with Robert *Crawford.

IMLAY, Gilbert (1754–1828) American author; his *Topographical Description of the Western Territory of North America*, (1792) incorporates attacks on slavery. *The Emigrants* (1793) is an early frontier novel presenting utopian images of America. He met and began a liaison with Mary *Wollstonecraft in Paris in 1793.

Importance of Being Earnest, The: *A Trivial Comedy for Serious People* A play by Oscar *Wilde, first performed on 14 February 1895. It describes the courtships of two men-about-town, John Worthing (Jack) and Algernon Moncrieff (Algy). Jack becomes engaged to Algy's cousin, Gwendolen Fairfax, who believes Jack's name is Ernest; Algy is in love with Jack's ward, Cecily Cardew. Both young men lead double lives: in order to escape the country, Jack has invented a wicked brother Ernest whom he must visit in the city; Algy has created the sickly Bunbury, whose ill health requires a visit whenever he wishes to avoid engagements in town (particularly those with his formidable aunt Lady Bracknell). After many confusions of identity, during which we discover that Cecily's governess, Miss Prism, had once mislaid Jack as a baby in a handbag at Victoria Station, it is revealed that Jack and Algy are in fact brothers, and that Jack's name is indeed Ernest. All objections to both matches are thus overcome, and Gwendolen's desire to marry a man named Ernest is satisfied, so all ends happily.

Impressionism The name derisively given (from a painting by Monet called *Impression: soleil levant*) to the work of a group of French painters who held their first exhibition in 1874. Their aim was to render the effects of light on objects rather than the objects themselves. Claude Monet (1840–1926), Alfred Sisley (1839–99), and Camille Pissarro (1831–1903) carried out their ideals most completely. The term is used by transference in literature to indicate an emphasis on subjective impressions over objective facts. A theory of literary Impressionism was developed by Ford Madox *Ford in a 1913 essay and put into practice in his novel *The *Good Soldier* (1915).

Impressions of Theophrastus Such, The (1879) A volume of essays by George *Eliot, mostly character studies loosely based on the model of *Theophrastus.

imprimatur Official permission or licence for a book to be printed. During the reigns of Charles I and Charles II books had to be licensed before publication. This system (attacked by John Milton in *Areopagitica*) ended in 1695. *See* L'ESTRANGE, SIR ROGER.

Improvisatrice, The A long narrative poem by Letitia Elizabeth *Landon ('L.E.L.'), published 1824. Set in Italy, it recounts the doomed love of a beautiful young female minstrel and artist, whose tale is intermixed with narratives such as 'Sappho's Song', 'A Moorish Romance', 'The Hindoo Girl's Song', that call forth similar scenes of female suffering. This device allows the Improvisatrice's individual tale to become every woman's story, and the whole can be read as a lament for, but also a vindication of, erotic and passionate female love.

In a Glass Darkly A collection of five stories by Sheridan *Le Fanu, published 1872. They claim to be cases from the papers of 'Dr Martin Hesselius, the German Physician'—the first of a long line of psychic investigators in English literature. The best known are 'Green Tea', featuring a malignant monkey, and 'Carmilla', a powerful and much-anthologized tale of a female *vampire which antedates Bram Stoker's *Dracula* by 25 years and was adapted by Carl Dreyer in his film *Vampyr* (1932).

'Inappropriate Curiosity, The Tale of' An episode in *Don Quixote* (I. 33-5) set in Florence, which provided the plot of several English 17th-century dramas (e.g. Aphra *Behn, *The Amorous Prince*; Thomas *Southerne, *The Disappointment*; John Crowne (c.1641–1712), *The Married Beau*). Anselmo, having married the beautiful Camila, urges the reluctant Lotario to test her virtue. Camila's eventual seduction and its discovery leads to the death of Anselmo and, indirectly, that of Lotario, while Camila retires to a convent where she soon dies.

INCHBALD, Elizabeth (1753–1821) Née Simpson, a novelist, dramatist, and actress, chiefly remembered for her two prose romances, *A *Simple Story* (1791) and *Nature and Art* (1796), which display skill in character and narration and illustrate her faith in natural upbringing (*see* PRIMITIVISM); and her play *Lovers' Vows* (1798), the drama enacted by the Bertram family in Austen's *Mansfield Park*.

'Inchcape Rock, The' A ballad by Robert *Southey, written 1796–8, published 1802.

incunabula (**incunables**) Books printed before the 16th century, from the Latin word for 'swaddling clothes' or 'cradle', hence 'infancy'.

[⊕ SEE WEB LINKS]

• British Library incunable collection

Index Librorum Prohibitorum The list of books that Roman Catholics were forbidden to read. Rules for the formation of this list and of the related *Index Expurgatorius* (an authoritative specification of the passages to be expunged or altered in works Roman Catholics might otherwise read) were drawn up by the Council of Trent in 1564. Both indexes were abolished in 1966.

Indicator (1819–21) A literary periodical established and edited by Leigh *Hunt. It published the work of the young poets, including John Keats's *'La Belle Dame sans Merci'*, and introduced much foreign literature.

Inferno, of Dante *See* DIVINA COMMEDIA.

INGELOW, Jean (1820–97) Poet, who also published many stories for children (including *Mopsa the Fairy*, 1869), and adult prose fiction; her best-known poems are 'Divided', a poem of lost love, and 'The High Tide on the Coast of Lincolnshire, 1571', both in *Poems* (1863).

INGLIS, Esther (1571–1624) Huguenot scribe who worked in Scotland producing a large number of illustrated manuscripts which she presented to royal and aristocratic patrons. Her texts were largely compilations and translations, but included some original works of her own, as well as dedicatory poems. Some of her manuscripts took the form of miniature books and were supplied with embroidered bindings.

Ingoldsby Legends, The *See* BARHAM, R. H.

Inheritance, The A novel by Susan *Ferrier, published 1824. The novel relates, in an improbably complex but humorous plot, the fortunes of Gertrude St Clair, granddaughter of the earl of Rossville and heiress to his estate. Miss Pratt, a garrulous spinster, is a memorable character in this lively and vigorous novel.

inkhorn A term originating in the 16th century, applied to excessively literary, bookish, or pedantic language: *see* WILSON, THOMAS, for an example.

Inkle and Yarico A romantic musical comedy by George *Colman the younger, first staged 1787. The young Londoner Inkle, improbably saved from cannibals on a voyage to Barbados by the beautiful native girl Yarico, has to decide between fidelity to her and a wealthy marriage to Narcissa, the governor's daughter; he chooses the latter and is punished for his ingratitude. The plot is based on a story in *The *Spectator* (no. 11), which had been versified by Frances Thynne Seymour, the duchess of Somerset (1699–1754), as 'The Story of Inkle and Yarrico' (1738). *See* PRIMITIVISM.

Inklings An informal literary discussion group which met in Oxford from the 1930s to the 1960s, and read aloud their original compositions. The group's driving force was C. S. *Lewis, other members included J. R. R. *Tolkien, Charles *Williams, the philosopher Owen Barfield (1898–1997), and the scholar and theatre producer Nevill Coghill (1899–1980).

In Memoriam A.H.H. (1850) A poem by Alfred *Tennyson, written between 1833 and 1850 and published anonymously. The poem was written in memory of his friend Arthur Henry Hallam, who died aged 22. In stanzas of four octosyllabic lines rhyming *abba*, it is divided into 132 sections of varying length. Not a single elegy but a group of lyrics, it documents the changing moods of the author's bereavement, and expresses his anxieties about change, evolution, and immortality. The epilogue is a marriage song on the occasion of the wedding of Tennyson's youngest sister Cecilia to Edmund Lushington; Hallam had been engaged to another sister, Emily. A critical and popular success, it was widely regarded as a message of hope and an affirmation of faith. But T. S. *Eliot commented in 1936: 'It is not religious because of the quality of its faith, but because of the quality of its doubt. Its faith is a poor thing, but its doubt is a very intense experience. *In Memoriam* is a poem of despair, but of despair of a religious kind.'

Inn Album, The A poem of approximately 3,000 lines, in blank verse, by Robert *Browning, published 1875. Browning originally intended to write a play on the subject, but changed his mind to avoid competing with Alfred *Tennyson's forthcoming *Queen Mary*.

INNES, Michael The pseudonym of J. I. M. *Stewart.

Innisfail (Inishfallen) [from Irish *Inis fáil*] 'Island of destiny', a poetic name for Ireland.

Innocents Abroad, The A satirical account by Mark *Twain, published 1869 (in England, 1870, as *The New Pilgrim's Progress*), of a cruise on the *Quaker City* to the Mediterranean with a company of Americans in 1867.

inscape, instress *See* HOPKINS, GERARD MANLEY.

Intelligencer *See* L'ESTRANGE, SIR ROGER.

intentional fallacy A phrase coined by the American *New Critics W. K. Wimsatt, Jr (1907–75), and Monroe C. Beardsley (1915–85) in an essay of 1946 to describe the common assumption that an author's declared or assumed intention in writing a work is a proper basis for deciding upon the work's meaning or value. These critics argued that once a work is published, it has an objective status and that its meanings belong to the reading public.

interactive fiction A term encompassing a range of experimental approaches to fictional form and the writing process. Formal developments range from text-based role-playing games to *hypertext novels, and include material published in both print and electronic media. The defining feature of this work is that the author relinquishes to the reader a degree of control over the text, opening it to a range of readings. Notable examples include B. S. *Johnson's *The Unfortunates* (1969), which consisted of a box of 27 unbound sections, with only the beginning and end segments designated by the author, and Milorad Pavic's *Dictionary of the Kazars* (1988), a pastiche reference book in the form of three dictionaries representing separate cultural traditions, which enabled a linear reading, random consultation, or the tracing of themes and events across the texts. Developments in *hypertext, CD-ROM, and World Wide Web (WWW) technologies enabled further exploration of the relationship between author and reader. New forms of interactive authorship have been made possible by the development of the MOO—a computer-based technology (Multiple User Dungeons, Object-Oriented) enabling individual users to create imaginary spaces, roles, and personalities.

interior monologue An extended representation in prose or verse of a character's unspoken thoughts, memories, and impressions, rendered as if directly 'overheard' by the reader. The device is distinguished from the *dramatic monologue by the fact that the thoughts are unspoken. Many modern poems make use of this convention, and it is widely employed in modern fiction, notably in the deliberately incoherent '*stream-of-consciousness' style adopted by Dorothy *Richardson, James *Joyce, and others.

interludes Plays performed at court, in the halls of the nobles, at the Inns of Court, and in colleges, generally but not exclusively by professional actors, dealing with a short episode and involving a limited number of characters. Interludes were sometimes performed by villagers, as we know from 'Pyramus and Thisbe' in *A *Midsummer Night's Dream*. Their vogue was chiefly in the 15th and 16th centuries. They succeeded *morality plays in the history of drama, and are not always clearly distinguishable from them. The characters are still frequently allegorical, but the comic or farcical element is more prevalent, and they are shorter than the moralities. There are good examples by John *Heywood, John Rastell (*c.* 1475–1536), and Henry Medwall (d. 1502). The origin of the name is obscure.

intertextuality The sum of relationships between and among writings. This modern critical term, coined by Julia *Kristeva, usually covers the range of ways in which one 'text' may respond to, allude to, derive from, mimic, parody, or adapt another. The concept has been used in various ways under the influence of *structuralism and post-structuralism, often in reaction against the *New Criticism and its assumption that a literary work is a self-contained object. The idea that poems are made from other poems has been proclaimed by Northrop *Frye, Roland *Barthes, and Harold *Bloom, among others.

In the Year of Jubilee A novel by George *Gissing, published 1894, and in a censored American version 1895. The novel describes a group of young upper- and lower-middle-class people at the time of Queen Victoria's Golden Jubilee in 1887. Gissing's heavy irony condemns, but is resigned to, the emergent mass culture portrayed in the novel.

'Intimations of Immortality from Recollections of Early Childhood' The 'Great Ode' of William *Wordsworth, composed 1802–4/6, published 1807. It is Wordsworth's most profound and memorable exploration of the significance of the intensity of childhood experience of the natural world (which suggests to him a state of pre-existence), of its gradual fading into 'the light of common day', and of the consolations of maturity. The poem ends with a moving affirmation of the poet's faith in the powers of the philosophical mind and the human heart.

Invisible Man A surreal and claustrophobic novel by American writer Ralph *Ellison, published in 1952, which describes the experiences of a young African American in New York, drawing partly on Richard *Wright's *Native Son*.

Invisible Man, The A *scientific romance by H. G. *Wells, published 1897, about a scientist who fatally stumbles upon the secret of invisibility.

IONESCO *See* ABSURD, THEATRE OF.

Iphigeneia In Greek mythology the daughter of the royal couple Agamemnon and Clytemnestra. In one version of her story she was sacrificed by her father at Aulis, in order to appease the goddess Artemis and ensure that winds would take the Greek fleet to Troy; in another she was secretly saved by Artemis and became her priestess at Tauris. Different versions are told in the *Oresteia*, two plays by *Euripides, and *Racine's *Iphigénie*.

Ipomadon A Middle English romance, from the French of Hue de Rotelande (*c*.1190). There are three, independent English versions: one in prose; one in 8,890 lines of twelve-line, *tail-rhyme stanzas, thought to be from Yorkshire of the late 14th century; and a condensed version in rhyming couplets in a 15th-century manuscript.

IRELAND, John (*c*.1440–1495) Theologian. His surviving works include two books of his Commentary on the Sentences of Peter Lombard (1480s), a treatise *On Penance and Confession* (1484) in the Asloan Manuscript, and *The Meroure of Wyssdome* (completed 1490), a substantial treatise in Middle Scots in which he praises Geoffrey *Chaucer for his treatment of divine foreknowledge in *Troilus and Criseyde*.

IRELAND, William Henry (1777–1835) Remembered chiefly as a forger of Shakespeare manuscripts. He began at the age of 17, when he was working in a lawyer's office with easy access to old parchment, deeds, and antiquated forms of writing. An exhibition of his forgeries of poems and deeds, arranged in 1794 by his innocent and excited father, wholly deceived the general public. A facsimile edition was published in 1795, and other works, including the plays *Vortigern and Rowena* and *Henry II*, made their appearance. In 1796 Ireland admitted to the forgeries, and embarked on a more conventional literary career. He published

The Fisher Boy (1808), which, like Robert *Bloomfield's *Farmer's Boy*, satisfied the fashion for tales of rural life; *The Sailor Boy* (1809) and *Scribbleomania* (1815), satirical descriptions of his contemporaries.

Irene Samuel *Johnson's only play, a verse tragedy begun in 1736, and performed nine times (with David *Garrick's support) in 1749. The story, from Richard Knolles (*c*. 1550–1610), concerns Irene, a Greek slave loved by the emperor Mahomet.

IRIGARAY, Luce (1932–) Belgian feminist philosopher, psychoanalyst, and linguist. Having trained with Jacques *Lacan in the 1960s, Irigaray emerged as a trenchant critic of the Western philosophical tradition in general, and the dominant—and largely male-authored—psychoanalytic models of female sexuality in particular. Her work since the 1970s, including *Ce sexe qui n'en est pas un* (1977: *This Sex Which Is Not One*), has set out to articulate different ways of conceptualizing female sexuality, gender, and identity which foreground multiplicity and fluidity.

Irish Literary Theatre Founded by W. B. *Yeats, Lady *Gregory, and Edward *Martyn in 1899 to encourage Irish drama. It dissolved in acrimony after the departure of Martyn and the failure of the Yeats and George *Moore collaboration *Diarmuid and Grainne* in 1901.

Irish Revival A movement in Irish cultural nationalism which began in the last quarter of the 19th century and flourished until the 1920s. Among the books which fostered the revival were translations and retellings of Irish legend, folklore, and poetry, such as Samuel *Ferguson's *Lays of the Western Gael* (1865), and histories, such as Douglas *Hyde's *Literary History of Ireland* (1899). Repeated attempts to found a national theatre issued in the setting up of the *Abbey Theatre company. Plays by Yeats, J. M. *Synge, G. B. *Shaw, and Sean *O'Casey made the Abbey famous. Meanwhile the poetry of Yeats and the prose work of George *Moore, James *Joyce, and many others established the new literary stature of Irish writing.

IRVING, Sir Henry (1838–1905) Actor, originally John Henry Brodribb. He achieved fame as an actor for his performance in *The *Bells* (1871–2), and afterwards scored successes in a large number of Shakespearian and other parts, his impersonation of *Tennyson's Becket being one of his chief triumphs. His management of the Lyceum Theatre in association with

Ellen Terry, 1878–1902, was distinguished, and he revived popular interest in Shakespeare. His impact on theatrical production was profound; he established, for instance, the practice of darkening the auditorium in order to focus attention on the stage.

IRVING, John Winslow (1942–) American novelist. His serio-comic novels, which display great individuality of style and imagination, began with *Setting Free the Bears* (1968), about two young men on a motorcycle tour of Austria who plot to free all the animals in the Vienna Zoo. *The World According to Garp* (1978), the comic biography of a writer, was an international success. Later novels include *The Hotel New Hampshire* (1981), *The Cider House Rules* (1985 and screenplay, filmed 1999), *A Prayer for Owen Meany* (1989), *The Fourth Hand* (2001), and *Last Night in Twisted River* (2009), an overtly autobiographical work. *Trying to Save Piggy Sneed* (1993) is a collection of short stories.

IRVING, Washington (1783–1859) American writer. *Salmagundi* (1808), a series of whimsical and satirical essays and poems, was followed by his burlesque *A History of New York from the Beginning of the World to the End of the Dutch Dynasty*, by 'Diedrich Knickerbocker'. In 1815 he visited Britain, meeting Walter *Scott, John *Murray, and others. Encouraged by Scott, he published with great success *The Sketch Book* (1819–20), essays and tales under the pseudonym 'Geoffrey Crayon, Gent.', which contains picturesque sketches of English life and American adaptations of German folk tales (including *'Rip Van Winkle' and 'The Legend of *Sleepy Hollow'). Later works include *Bracebridge Hall* (1822), *Legends of the Alhambra* (1832), *The Crayon Miscellany* (1835), *Astoria* (1836; an account of John Jacob Astor's development of the fur trade), and his monumental five-volume life of George Washington (1855–9). He was acclaimed as the first American author to have achieved international fame.

'Isabella, or The Pot of Basil' A narrative poem by John *Keats, written 1818, published 1820.

The poem is based on a story in Boccaccio's *Decameron. The worldly, ambitious brothers of Isabella intend that she shall marry a nobleman. When they discover her love for the humble Lorenzo they lure him away, murder him, and bury his body in a forest. His ghost then appears to Isabella and tells her where he is buried. With the help of her old nurse she finds his body,

severs the head, and places it in a pot with a plant of basil over it. Her brothers, observing how she cherishes the plant, steal the pot, discover the mouldering head, and fly, conscience-stricken, into banishment. Pathetically Isabella mourns her loss, pines away, and dies.

Isaiah *See* BIBLE.

Iseult of the White Hands In Arthurian legend, daughter of the ruler of Brittany, with whom *Tristram falls in love and whom he marries after his banishment by King Mark. But Iseult of Brittany does not succeed in replacing *Iseult the Fair; in one version, when Tristram is dying, he sends for his first Iseult by ship; if she is on the ship on its return from Ireland it is to fly a white flag: if not a black one. The white flag is flown; but Iseult of the White Hands tells Tristram it is black, whereupon he dies.

Iseult the Fair Daughter of the king of Ireland in Arthurian legend. She is the lover of *Tristram (Tristan) who is sent by his uncle, King Mark of Cornwall, to bring her as his wife. This is the great classic of doomed love, since Tristram is the slayer of her uncle Marhaus and they are fated to fall in love by erroneously drinking a love potion meant for Mark and Iseult on their wedding night. A jealous Mark eventually murders Tristram.

ISHERWOOD, Christopher (1904–86) Writer; he met first W. H. *Auden and later Edward *Upward as a schoolboy. His first novels, *All the Conspirators* (1928) and *The Memorial* (1932), show the influence (as he acknowledged) of E. M. *Forster and Virginia *Woolf; his own voice is first most distinctly audible in *Mr Norris Changes Trains* (1935) and *Goodbye to Berlin* (1939), which reflect his experiences of living in Berlin, 1929–33 and give a vivid portrait of Germany on the eve of Hitler's rise to power. They were planned as part of a long novel, to be entitled *The Lost*, which was never written. The best known of the sketches, which make up *Goodbye to Berlin* is 'Sally Bowles' (published independently in 1937). Sally is a cabaret artist of more beauty, eccentricity, and wit than talent; her bohemian enterprises were successfully dramatized in 1951 by John Van Druten as *I Am a Camera*, turned into a stage musical in 1966 as *Cabaret*, and filmed (as *Cabaret*) in 1972. Isherwood travelled widely in Europe after leaving Berlin, went to China with Auden in 1938, and in 1939 went with him to America; Isherwood became an American citizen in 1946. During the 1930s he collaborated with Auden in the writing of *The Dog *beneath the Skin* (1935), *The *Ascent of F6* (1936), and several other works, and wrote the semi-autobiographical *Lions and Shadows* (1938). After settling near Hollywood, where he worked as a scriptwriter, he became interested in Hindu philosophy and Vedanta, influenced partly by Aldous *Huxley and Gerald Heard. He translated the **Bhagavad-gītā* (1944, with Swami Prabhavananda) and other Hindu classics. Novels written in America include *Prater Violet* (1945), about his experiences in Hollywood, *Down There on a Visit* (1962), and *A Single Man* (1964; film 2009), now regarded by many as his most important work of fiction; *Kathleen and Frank* (1971) is a memoir of his parents, and *Christopher and his Kind* (1977; BBC drama by Kevin *Elyot 2011) is a frank account of his homosexual life in the 1930s.

ISHIGURO, Kazuo (1954–) Japanese novelist, who studied creative writing on the postgraduate course run by Malcolm *Bradbury. His first three novels—*A Pale View of Hills* (1982), about a Japanese widow who has moved to England after the bombing of Nagasaki; *An Artist of the Floating World* (1986), in which a delicately skilled Japanese artist is coarsened by collusion with his country's militarism in the 1930s; and *The Remains of the Day* (1989, filmed *Merchant-Ivory 1993), a subtle portrait of a butler tainted by unquestioning service to a British aristocrat of Fascist sympathies—comprise a kind of trilogy about the disorientations caused by the Second World War. Each features a diffident narrator and they are much concerned with doubt. Ishiguro's next three novels are more experimental: *The Unconsoled* (1995) is a Kafkaesque story of a musician's disorienting experiences in a teasingly unidentified European country; *When We Were Orphans* (2000), in which a 1930s detective investigates his parents' disappearance in Shanghai, works surreal variations on the 'Golden Age' whodunnit genre (*see* DETECTIVE FICTION); *Never Let Me Go* (2005, filmed 2010) takes a *science fiction scenario and turns it into a haunting fable. Ishiguro has written two original screenplays, *The Saddest Music in the World* (2003) and *The White Countess* (2005).

ISIDORE OF SEVILLE (*c.*560–636) Archbishop of Seville and enormously influential through his *Etymologiae*, the earliest medieval encyclopedia in twenty books, which argues that the natures of things can be derived from their names. This work was an authority until at least the 14th century.

Island, The A poem by Lord *Byron, published 1823, based on the story of the mutiny on HMS *Bounty.

Island in the Moon, An An untitled burlesque fragment by William *Blake, written *c.*1784–5, first printed in 1907. It is a satirical portrait of scientific and cultural dilettantism and pretension, interspersed with songs (some of them bawdy).

Island of Dr Moreau, The A *scientific romance by H. G. *Wells, published 1896. It is an evolutionary fantasy about a shipwrecked naturalist who becomes involved in an experiment to 'humanize' animals by surgery. The theme was developed by Brian *Aldiss.

Isumbras, Sir Extremely popular verse romance in 804 lines of twelve-line *tail-rhyme stanzas, from the north-east Midlands, popular before 1320 and mentioned in **Cursor Mundi*. It is a variant on the story of St Eustace, of Eastern origin. Its moral theme of the man tried by fate is typical of 14th-century tail-rhyme romances.

Italian, The A novel by Ann *Radcliffe, published 1797, which is important in the development of *Gothic fiction. The romance between an Italian nobleman and his love, Ellena, is opposed by her mother, aided by the vicious monk Schedoni. A Satanic archetype, Schedoni's malevolent presence dominates the novel's powerful psychological and political symbolism.

Ithaca *See* ODYSSEY.

Ivanhoe A novel by Walter *Scott, published 1819. The story deals, somewhat anachronistically, with the antagonism in England between Saxon and Norman during the reign of Richard I. The hero, Wilfred of Ivanhoe, disowned by his father Cedric the Saxon because of his love for Cedric's ward, the lady Rowena, has joined King Richard on crusade; Prince John, taking advantage of the king's absence, endeavours to seize the throne himself.

The first of Scott's novels to deal with an English, rather than Scottish subject, *Ivanhoe* is also one of his best constructed. In Rebecca, the beautiful Jewess, he produced a heroine as virtuous and strong-minded as Jeanie Deans (**Heart of Midlothian*), but with all the graces which Jeanie lacked, and had the resolution to deprive her of the conventional happy ending. The novel was a great success, the first edition selling out within the week.

IYER, Pico (1957–) Travel writer, essayist, and novelist. Iyer, whose parents are Indian, grew up in England and California and spends much of his time in Japan; he has described himself as 'a multinational soul on a multinational globe'. Much of Iyer's writing concerns itself with travel in a globalized world. His books, which many believe have revitalized travel writing with a postmodern sensibility, include *Video Night in Kathmandu* (1988), *The Global Soul* (2000), and *The Open Road* (2008), on Iyer's conversations with the Dalai Lama.

JACKSON, Thomas (1783–1873) *Methodist minister and biographer. He wrote *The Lives of Early Methodist Preachers* (1837–8; 4th expanded edn, 1871–3); and his *Recollections of my Own Life and Times* (1873).

Jack Wilton, The Life of See UNFORTUNATE TRAVELLER.

Jacobean In literary terms, applies to writing of the period of *James I of England, who succeeded Elizabeth I in 1603: most commonly used of 'Jacobean tragedy'. *See* MIDDLETON, THOMAS; TOURNEUR, CYRIL; WEBSTER, JOHN; REVENGE TRAGEDY.

Jacobin Name given to the members of a political club established in 1789, in Paris, in the old convent of the Jacobins (French Dominican friars), to maintain extreme democratic and egalitarian principles. Applied also to sympathizers with their principles, and about 1800 became a nickname for any radical political reformer.

Jacobite Term used to describe supporters of James II of England (1633–1701), his son James (1688–1766), and Charles Edward Stuart (1720–88, 'Bonnie Prince Charlie'), especially after the Hanoverian accession of 1714. The most significant military 'risings' occurred in 1715 and 1745; the crushing of the latter at Culloden (1746) by troops under the duke of Cumberland (1721–65) ended Jacobite hopes. Alexander *Pope had some Jacobite sympathies, but was not an activist. The Jacobite defeat was lamented in many later songs, such as those of Carolina *Nairne, and depicted in novels such as *Waverley*.

JACOBS, Harriet (1813–97) African American writer, born into slavery in Edmonton, North Carolina. In 1835 she escaped and found employment for a time with the poet and editor N. P. Willis (1806–67). In 1861 she published *Incidents in the Life of a Slave Girl* under the pseudonym of Linda Brent. The narrative has since become a classic account of the sexual exploitation of female slaves. *See* SLAVERY.

JACOBSON, Dan (1929–) South African-born novelist and critic. His early novels were set in South Africa. Later novels include *The Confessions of Joseph Baisz* (1977) and *The Rape of Tamar* (1970), based on the biblical story. *Her Story* (1987) is set both in the future and at the time of the Crucifixion; *All for Love* (2005) is based on a royal scandal of the Hapsburg Empire. *Time and Time Again* (1985) and *Heshel's Kingdom* (1998) are autobiographical, the latter a quest for Jacobson's grandfather, a Lithuanian rabbi.

JACOBSON, Howard (1942–) Novelist. His first novel, *Coming from Behind* (1983), a *campus satire set in a Midlands polytechnic, was followed by *Peeping Tom* (1984), which similarly mixed erudite farce and erotic mishap. *Redback* (1987) shares an Australian setting with *In the Land of Oz* (1987, travel writing). Later novels, such as *The Making of Henry* (2004), *The Act of Love* (2008), and *The Mighty Walzer* (1999) have been more blackly comic explorations of the Jewish experience in Britain and of the battle between the sexes. *The Finkler Question* (2010), unusually for a comic novel, won the Man Booker prize.

Jacob's Room Third novel by Virginia *Woolf, published in 1922. It takes the form of a *Bildungsroman*, although the protagonist, Jacob Flanders, is viewed from a distance, and is an elegy for both Woolf's brother Thoby Stephen, who died in 1906, and the legions slaughtered in the First World War. It was the first of Woolf's novels to be published by the *Hogarth Press and makes full use of the freedoms such autonomy entailed.

JAGO, Richard (1715–81) Poet and clergyman. *Edge-Hill* (1767) is a *topographical poem in four books describing, with historical, moral, and scientific digressions, the views from that Warwickshire hill at morning, noon, afternoon, and evening. His collected *Poems*, with a biography, appeared in 1784.

JAKOBSON, Roman *See* FORMALISM; STRUCTURALISM.

JAMES I (1394–1437) King of Scotland. Held captive in England until 1406–24, at the same time as *Charles d'Orléans. In 1424 he married Lady Joan Beaufort, the granddaughter of John of Gaunt, who is the heroine of James's famous Boethian and semi-autobiographical poem *The *Kingis Quair. The account of his assassination at the hands of Sir Robert Graham was translated by John Shirley (*c.*1366–1456).

JAMES I (James VI of Scotland) (1566–1625) King of England 1603–25, and son of *Mary Queen of Scots. His belief in witchcraft, expounded in his *Demonology* (1597), may have influenced William *Shakespeare's *Macbeth. He is reputedly the author of *True Lawe of Free Monarchies* (1598), a reply to the argument of George *Buchanan that the king is elected by and responsible to the people. His *Basilikon Doron* (1599), precepts on the art of government, was addressed to his son, the future Charles I. He also wrote a polemic against tobacco-smoking (1604), theological works, poetry in Scots, Latin, and English, translations of Du Bartas and *Lucan, and a treatise on the rules for writing *Scots poetry. He was the target of the 1605 Gunpowder Plot.

JAMES, C. L. R. (Cyril Lionel Robert) (1901–89) Historian, novelist, Marxist theorist, and cricket enthusiast, born in Trinidad. His works include *Minty Alley* (1936), a realist novel describing the intrigues amongst the mixed-race lodgers in a West Indian boarding house; *The Black Jacobins* (1938), a study of the revolution led by Toussaint Louverture in Haiti; and *Beyond a Boundary* (1963), a memoir focusing on politics and cricket.

JAMES, George Payne Rainsford (1799–1860) Novelist and historical writer. He was appointed historiographer royal by William IV. Influenced by Walter *Scott he wrote numerous romantic novels, biographies, and popular historical works, including *Richelieu* (1829), *Darnley* (1830), and *Life of Edward the Black Prince* (1836). W. M. *Thackeray parodied him in his burlesque *Barbazure, by G. P. R. Jeames, Esq.*

JAMES, Henry (1843–1916) American novelist, younger brother of William *James. He settled in Europe in 1875. From 1865 he was a regular contributor of reviews and short stories (the *Complete Tales* were published in twelve volumes by Rupert Hart-Davis, 1962–4) to American periodicals and owed much to his friendship with William Dean *Howells. His early novels *Roderick Hudson* (1876), *The American* (1877), *Portrait of a Lady* (1881), and the novella *Daisy Miller* (1879) are concerned with the impact of the older civilization of Europe upon American travellers. In *The Tragic Muse* (1890), *The Spoils of Poynton* (1897), *What Maisie Knew* (1897), and *The Awkward Age* (1899) he analysed English character with extreme subtlety, verging at times on obscurity. *The *Turn of the Screw* (1898), an ambiguous narrative by a governess of the 'possession' of the two children in her charge, is the basis of a 1954 opera by Benjamin *Britten. In his last three great novels, *The *Wings of the Dove* (1902), *The *Ambassadors* (1903), and *The *Golden Bowl* (1904), he returned to the 'international' theme of the contrast of American and European character, expressing his narrative through nuanced prose geared to the perspectives of his main characters. His two unfinished novels, *The Ivory Tower* and *The Sense of the Past*, were published in 1917. For the revised New York Edition of his fiction, 26 vols (1907–17), James wrote a series of prefaces, published in 1934 as *The Art of the Novel*, edited by R. P. *Blackmur. In his critical essays James concentrated on the 19th-century novel, singling out George *Eliot and *Balzac ('the master of us all') for special praise. He also published several volumes of travel sketches (*Portraits of Places*, 1883; *A Little Tour in France*, 1884) and in *The American Scene* (1906) recorded the impressions produced on him by a visit to America after an absence of nearly twenty years. He wrote a number of plays, of which the few that were acted were not successful (*Complete Plays*, 1949). Nevertheless, James made attempts throughout his career to apply the techniques of the theatre in his fiction. For the English Men of Letters series he wrote a life of Nathaniel *Hawthorne (1879). *A Small Boy and Others* (1913), *Notes of a Son and a Brother* (1914), and *The Middle Years* (1917) were collected as his *Autobiography* in 1956. In 1915 James became a British subject, and in 1916 was awarded the Order of Merit. Leon Edel's five-volume biography (1953–72) takes a *Freudian approach.

JAMES, M. R. (Montague Rhodes) (1862–1936) Medievalist, palaeographer, and biblical scholar, born near Bury St Edmunds, successively provost of King's College, Cambridge, and Eton College. He edited works by Sheridan

*Le Fanu, and wrote distinguished *ghost stories, many with East Anglian settings, including 'Oh, Whistle, and I'll Come to You, my Lad'. *Ghost Stories of an Antiquary* (1904) was followed by *More Ghost Stories of an Antiquary* (1911), *A Thin Ghost and Others* (1919), *A Warning to the Curious* (1925), and his collected ghost stories in 1931.

JAMES, P. D. (Phyllis Dorothy) Baroness James of Holland Park, OBE (1920–) Crime writer, who worked with forensic investigations in the Home Office. Her first novel, *Cover her Face* (1962), introduced Adam Dalgleish, a police detective (and poet) who appears in most of her mystery novels from *A Mind to Murder* (1963) to *The Private Patient* (2008). A female private detective, Cordelia Gray, features in *An Unsuitable Job for a Woman* (1972) and *The Skull beneath the Skin* (1982). Often set on the coast of East Anglia or Dorset and in isolated or semi-closed communities, James's crime novels make sophisticated use of the conventions of 'Golden Age' *detective fiction.

She has also written a psychological thriller, *Innocent Blood* (1980), and a dystopian novel, *The Children of Men* (1992, filmed, with alterations, 2006). *Time to Be in Earnest* (1999) is an autobiography.

JAMES, William (1842–1910) American philosopher, the elder brother of Henry *James. He pioneered the study of psychology at Harvard University and numbered among his students W. E. *Du Bois and Gertrude *Stein. His views are embodied in his *Principles of Psychology* (1890), where he coined the expression *stream of consciousness. He opposed philosophical idealism, preferring empiricism, and took a pluralistic approach to the world, as demonstrated in *Varieties of Religious Experience* (1902) and *A Pluralistic Universe* (1909). His 1896 essay 'The Will to Believe' shifts religion away from the truth of beliefs to the psychology of the believer. James himself held to a belief in a larger spiritual universe and included psychic phenomena in his researches.

JAMESON, Anna Brownell (1794–1860) Writer, feminist, traveller. Born in Dublin, she began adult life as a governess. She became a close friend of the *Brownings, of Mary Russell *Mitford, and later of the Carlyles. She first attracted attention in 1826 with *A Lady's Diary* (later retitled *The Diary of an Ennuyée*), describing a visit to Italy. She produced many highly respected works of art history and criticism, biography, theology, history, travel,

social comment, and general essays, some of which exhibited a strong interest in the position and education of women. Her *Winter Studies and Summer Rambles* (1838), an account of her visit to Canada, is an important work in early Canadian literature. She is now chiefly remembered for *Characteristics of Women* (1832, later known as *Shakespeare's Heroines*), dedicated to the actress Fanny Kemble, and illustrated with her own etchings. *Shakespeare she saw as 'the Poet of Womankind'. She divides the 25 heroines of her book into four groups: the characters of intellect, such as Portia; those of passion and imagination, such as Viola; those of the affections, such as Desdemona; and those from history, such as Cleopatra and Lady Macbeth. In preparation Anna Jameson read Samuel *Johnson, William *Hazlitt, S. T. *Coleridge, Charles *Lamb, and other major critics, as well as relevant European and Greek drama, and thoroughly investigated the sources of the histories. Her interpretations were considered illuminating, and the work was received with considerable respect, Gerard Manley *Hopkins placing her among the most eminent of Shakespeare's critics.

JAMESON, Storm (1891–1986) Writer, born in Whitby, the daughter of a sea captain; her first novel, *The Pot Boils* (1919), was followed by many other works of fiction, including *Women against Men* (1933, stories), and the trilogy of *Company Parade* (1934), *Love in Winter* (1935), and *None Turn Back* (1936). She also published poems, essays, and biographies, and several volumes of autobiography, including *Journey from the North* (1969), describing her time during the Second World War as president of *PEN. Her second husband was Guy Chapman (1889–1972), remembered for his vivid personal account of trench warfare in France, *A Passionate Prodigality* (1933).

James the Fourth, The Scottish History of A play by Robert *Greene, published posthumously 1598. In spite of the title, this is a fictionalized romantic comedy, framed by the comments of Oberon, king of fairies.

JAMIE, Kathleen (1962–) Scottish poet and travel writer. The bulk of her early verse is collected in *Mr and Mrs Scotland Are Dead: Poems 1980–1994* (2002). Jamie's poetry is marked by a deepening lyricism and a slowly, almost reluctantly unfolding interest in Scottish themes and language. *Jizzen* (1999), a volume of interrelated poems broadly concerned with birth and childhood, includes a number of delicate lyrics in *Scots. The focus of *The Tree House* (2004) is on the natural world, apprehended in its quietness and vulnerability rather than its savagery. She has published two prose works, *The Golden Peak: Travels in North Pakistan* (1992; reissued as *Among Muslims*, 2002) and *Findings* (2005), a collection of autobiographical meditations on nature. *Waterlight* (2007) is the first selection of her poems to be published in the USA.

Jane Eyre A novel by Charlotte *Brontë, published 1847. The heroine, a penniless orphan, has been left to the care of her aunt Mrs Reed. Harsh treatment rouses her defiant spirit, and a passionate outbreak leads to her consignment to Lowood School (based on Brontë's own experience of the Clergy Daughters' School at Cowan Bridge). There she spends some miserable years, eventually becoming a teacher. She later obtains a post as governess at Thornfield Hall to Adèle, the ward of Mr Rochester, a *Byronic hero of grim aspect and sardonic temper. Rochester, despite Jane's plainness, is fascinated by her sharp wit and independence, and they fall in love. After much resistance she agrees to marry him, but on the eve of their wedding her wedding veil is torn by an intruder who Rochester assures her is a servant, Grace Poole, but who is the next day revealed to be his mad Creole wife Bertha, confined to the upper regions of the Hall for years, whose unseen presence has long disturbed Jane. The marriage ceremony is interrupted by Mrs Rochester's brother from the West Indies and, despite Rochester's full confession and pleadings with Jane to stay with him, she flees. After nearly perishing on the moors, she is taken in and cared for by the Revd St John Rivers and his two sisters. It emerges that they are her cousins, and that Jane has inherited money from an uncle; the legacy is equally divided between the four. Jane nearly consents to marry Rivers and share his missionary vocation in India, but is prevented by a telepathic appeal from Rochester. She returns to Thornfield Hall to find the building burned, and Rochester blinded and maimed from his attempt to save his wife from the flames. She marries him, and in the last chapter we learn that his sight is partially restored.

The novel's exceptional emotional and narrative power quickly made it a success, though, despite its strict adherence to conventional moral standards, it was considered by many to be unsuitable for young ladies. Additional scandal attended the publication of the second edition, which Charlotte dedicated to W. M. *Thackeray, unaware that he had a wife certified as insane. More recently its strong sexual undercurrents have led to *Freudian interpretations. Jean *Rhys's novel *Wide Sargasso Sea* (1966) is based on the first Mrs Rochester.

JANSSON, Tove (1914–2001) Finnish-born writer in Swedish and artist, creator of the Moomins. Their world, relationships, and adventures are the subject of eight novels, illustrated by Jansson, which have been translated into 35 languages: *The Moomins and the Great Flood* (1945, English trans. 2005), *Comet in Moominland* (1946, English trans. 1951), *Finn Family Moomintroll* (1948, English trans. 1950), *The Exploits of Moominpappa* (1950, English trans. 1952), *Moominsummer Madness* (1954, English trans. 1955), *Moominland Midwinter* (1957, English trans. 1958), *Moominpappa at Sea* (1965, English trans. 1966), and *Moominvalley in November* (1970, English trans. 1971). There are also Moomin comic strips (many originally written for the *London Evening News*), picture books, and stories. Jansson's collections of stories and novels for adults include *The Summer Book* (1972, English trans. 1975), and the newly translated *Fair Play* (1989, English trans. 2007), *The True Deceiver* (1982, trans. 2009), and *Travelling Light* (1987, trans. 2010).

JARMAN, Derek (1942–94) Painter, writer, and film-maker, who became a 'queer' activist following his own HIV diagnosis in 1986. Jarman's first feature film, *Sebastiane* (1976), with subtitled Latin dialogue and overt homosexuality, created a sensation, as did *Jubilee* (1977), a *dystopian punk view of contemporary England. Two Shakespeare films, *The *Tempest* (1979) and a dramatization of Shakespeare's *sonnets in *The Angelic Conversation* (1985), combined Jarman's literary interests with his acute sense of contemporary style, while *Caravaggio* (1986) and *Wittgenstein* (1993) portrayed the painter and the philosopher as gay heroes.

JARRELL, Randall (1914–65) American poet and critic, whose one novel, *Pictures from an Institution* (1954), satirizes life in a progressive women's college. His first volume of poetry was *Blood for a Stranger* (1942); his last, *The Lost World* (1966), was published with a memoir by Robert *Lowell. His critical writings on contemporary poetry were collected in *Poetry and the Age* (1953).

JARRY, Alfred *See* ABSURD, THEATRE OF THE.

Jaws A best-selling first novel by Peter Benchley, about a man-eating shark terrorizing an American seaside community; the 1975 film set a box-office record, making $100 million during its initial US release, and launching the modern summer 'blockbuster'. Mechanical sharks, daring marine photography, dramatic music, and fine performances, notably by Robert Shaw as an Ahab-like sailor (*see* MOBY-DICK), combined to make Steven Spielberg's film a modern classic, launching his career as the pre-eminent director of lucrative popular spectacle.

jazz poetry A genre presaged in the USA by Vachel Lindsay (1879–1931) with his incantatory ballads including 'General William Booth' (1913), 'The Congo' (1914), and *The Daniel Jazz* (1920) and by Langston *Hughes, who was probably the first to pitch his verse in conjunction with musicians in the late 1930s. The fusion was developed in the 1950s by Kenneth Patchen, Kenneth *Rexroth, Amiri *Baraka, and the poets of the American *Beat Generation; and in Britain from the mid-1950s to the 1980s by Christopher *Logue, Roy *Fisher, Michael *Horovitz, Pete Brown (1940–), Spike Hawkins (1942–), and others. Various permutations of primarily non-academic, often regional, entertainers and singer-songwriters have proliferated since, with the punk-rock, post-punk, and 'new wave' voices of John Cooper Clarke (b. 1949), Paul Weller (b. 1958) of the band The Jam, and the Rastafarian and reggae-cadenced contributions of Anglo-Jamaican poets such as James *Berry, E. K. *Brathwaite, Linton Kwesi *Johnson, and Benjamin *Zephaniah. *See* PERFORMANCE POETRY.

JEA, John (1773–1816) Born in West Africa and sold as a child, with his family, into slavery in New York. His autobiography *The Life, History, and Unparalleled Sufferings of John Jea, the African Preacher* (1811) describes his gradual conversion to Christianity, disastrous marriage, and missionary activity.

JEAN DE MEUN *See* ROMAN DE LA ROSE.

JEFFERIES, Richard (1848–87) Writer and naturalist. The books for which he is remembered combine his love of the natural world with a poetic apprehension and individuality of thought which blur the usual literary distinctions. *The Gamekeeper at Home: Sketches of Natural History and Rural Life* (1878) and *Hodge and his Masters* (1880) appear to have influenced Thomas *Hardy's article of 1883 on

'The Dorsetshire Labourer'. Jefferies relied greatly on 'field notebooks', where he entered his meticulous observations on the life of the countryside. In *Wild Life in a Southern County* (1879) the author, sitting on a Wiltshire down, observes in ever widening circles the fields, woods, animals, and human inhabitants below him. *Wood Magic* (1881), in which a solitary boy lives in a magical world of speaking wild animals, was followed in 1882 by *Bevis: The Story of a Boy*, an evocation of his country childhood. *The Story of my Heart*, tracing the growth of his unorthodox beliefs, caused a scandal on its publication in 1883. *After London* (1885) was a savage vision of the future. *The Open Air* (1885, essays) was much reprinted. Published in the year of his death, *Amaryllis at the Fair* (1887) contains in Iden an impressive portrait of Jefferies's father. Jefferies's early death was a result of long-standing tubercular illness. There is a life (1909) by Edward *Thomas.

JEFFERS, Robinson (1887–1962) American poet. The scenery of the Californian redwood and seashore inspires much of his works, and one of his dominant themes is what he called 'Inhumanism'—the insignificance of man, contrasted with the vast, merciless, enduring processes of nature and the animal kingdom; the hawk provides one of his most strikingly recurrent symbols. He made his name with *Tamar and Other Poems* (1924): the title poem is a tragic narrative of family passion and incest in a wild Californian setting. Later volumes, many of them of a similar pattern include *The Women at Point Sur* (1927). His popularity lapsed owing to his wartime espousal of an attitude of isolationism, expressed in 'The Eye'. He successfully adapted *Euripides' Medea* for the stage in 1947; his collected poems were published in 2001.

JEFFREY, Francis, Lord (1773–1850) Scottish judge and MP, who is remembered in a literary connection as the founder, with Sydney *Smith, of the *Edinburgh Review* in 1802, as its editor until 1829, and as a stern but judicious critic of the writers of his day. Often severe (he was challenged to a duel by Thomas *Moore), he nevertheless wrote appreciatively of many writers, including George *Crabbe, Walter *Scott, Lord *Byron, and, most notably, John *Keats, in whose *Poems* of 1820 he discerned genius. His critical blind spot was an inability to understand William *Wordsworth—his review of *The *Excursion* in 1814 begins: 'This will never do'—and this led to a series of attacks on 'a *sect* of poets' designated as 'The *Lake Poets'.

Jekyll and Hyde See DR JEKYLL and MR HYDE.

JELLICOE, Ann (1927–) Playwright and director; she made her name with the *English Stage Company's production of, *The Sport of my Mad Mother* (1958), an experimental drama about a London street gang. This was followed by *The Knack* (1962) and *Shelley* (1965). *The Reckoning* (1978), set in Lyme Regis and based on the 1685 Monmouth Rebellion, was one of her drama-documentaries performed by the local West Country community. A pioneer in community theatre, in 1985 she worked with David *Edgar on his community play *Entertaining Strangers* in Dorchester, and wrote *Community Plays: How to Put Them On* (1987).

JENKINS, Robin (1912–2005) Scottish novelist, whose many novels explore issues of morality and self-deception in the context of a materialistic understanding of society. His best-known works include *The Cone-Gatherers* (1955), *The Changeling* (1958), *A Very Scotch Affair* (1968), and *Fergus Lamont* (1979). *Some Kind of Grace* (1960) and the strongly anti-imperialist *The Holy Tree* (1969), set respectively in Afghanistan and Borneo, reflect his experience as a teacher and employee of the British Council in Asia.

JENNINGS, Elizabeth (1926–2001) Poet, whose early collections were *Poems* (1953), *A Way of Looking* (1955), and *A Sense of the World* (1958). She was somewhat arbitrarily associated with the *Movement, through Robert Conquest's inclusion of some of her work in *New Lines* (1956), but her later volumes of verse (e.g. *Recoveries*, 1964; *The Mind has Mountains*, 1966) are highly personal and confessional accounts of mental breakdown and hospital treatment, very far removed in tone from the laconic detachment of the more representative Movement poets. Her *Collected Poems* (1967) were revised and extended in 1987. Other volumes include *Lucidities* (1970) and *Moments of Grace* (1979), which manifest her quiet and sensitive control of, and openness towards, experiences of suffering, loneliness, friendship, and religious faith, *Celebrations and Elegies* (1982), *Extending the Territory* (1985), *Tributes* (1989), *Times and Seasons* (1992), and *Familiar Spirits* (1994).

JENNINGS, Humphrey (1907–50) Filmmaker, painter, and writer, widely considered the leading figure in British *documentary film of the 1930s and 1940s, also active in *Surrealism and co-founder with Charles *Madge in 1937 of *Mass Observation, the influence of which is apparent in his *Spare Time* (1939). Jennings's wartime films, *Listen to Britain* (1942), *Fires Were Started* (1943), and *A Diary for Timothy* (1945), combine stirring patriotism with a wry view of war's incongruity. His last films, *Dim Little Island* (1949) and *Family Portrait* (1950), reflected on Britain's post-war prospects before a fatal accident on location in Greece cut short his career. A collage text on the impact of the Industrial Revolution, *Pandaemonium*, appeared posthumously.

'Jenny' A poem by D. G. *Rossetti, first published 1870. It was among the poems buried with his wife Lizzie in 1862 and later exhumed. The speaker describes a night spent with a prostitute, golden-haired Jenny; as she sleeps, he meditates on her position as a fallen woman and implicitly on his own status as her client. Fallen women were favourite subjects with the *Pre-Raphaelites, as in Rossetti's painting *Found* and Holman *Hunt's *The Awakening Conscience*.

JENYNS, Soame (1704–87) MP, essayist, and poet, whose *Free Enquiry into the Nature and Origin of Evil* (1757) elicited a scathing attack from Samuel *Johnson in the *Literary Magazine*. Jenyns justified suffering as necessary within the 'scale of Being' and ignorance as the 'opiate' of the poor, recalling the moral philosophy of Alexander Pope's *Essay on Man*. Johnson attacked the facile optimism of these views.

jeremiad A prophetic warning or lament of a country's moral or social degradation, alluding to the biblical books of Jeremiah and Lamentations predicting and lamenting the fall of *Jerusalem to *Babylon.

JEROME, Jerome K. (Klapka) (1859–1927) Novelist, dramatist, and journalist. He achieved lasting fame with *Three Men in a Boat* (1889), the comic story of three young men and their dog who take a rowing holiday on the Thames, though *Three Men on the Bummel* (1900), describing a tour in Germany, was not a success. He also published essays, including *On the Stage—and Off* (1885) and *Idle Thoughts of an Idle Fellow* (1886); plays, including the well-received *The Passing of the Third Floor Back* (1908); and an autobiographical novel, *Paul Kelver* (1902).

JEROME, St (Hieronymus) (331/*c.*342–420) Church Father, and *Bible translator. From 386 to his death, he lived in Bethlehem, ruling the monastery, studying, and translating; he was the unsurpassed master of Latin among the *Fathers of the church.

Commissioned by Pope Damasus to make a new Latin translation of the Bible, he followed the Hebrew text for the Old Testament rather than the Septuagint Greek favoured by his contemporaries; his work became the *Vulgate or common translation, the official Bible of the Roman Catholic Church.

JERROLD, Douglas William (1803–57) Playwright, novelist, and journalist, who made his name in the theatre with *Black-Ey'd Susan* (1829), founded on John *Gay's ballad; other successful plays included *Fifteen Years of a Drunkard's Life* (1828), *The Rent Day* (1832), and *The Prisoner of War* (1842). He was associated with *Punch* from its beginnings and became a regular contributor, writing several serial works, including *Mrs Caudle's Curtain Lectures* (issued as a book in 1846), a comic series which greatly added to the journal's popularity. From 1845 he ran *Douglas Jerrold's Shilling Magazine* and from 1846 *Douglas Jerrold's Weekly Newspaper*. His studies of *Men of Character* (1838) were illustrated by W. M. *Thackeray.

Jerusalem Also known as Zion, Sion, Salem, the City of *David (a phrase also used for Bethlehem), and the Holy City; often thought of particularly as God's dwelling place, his 'holy hill of Zion' (Psalm 2: 6). As the site of the Jewish Temple, the passion and crucifixion of Jesus, and Muhammad's ascension to heaven, Jerusalem is the holy city of three religions, important both as a place and as a symbol. After Babylon had destroyed it (587/6 BC) and exiled the Jewish people, ideal visions of a new Jerusalem, together with a new heavens and a new earth, became a potent symbol of hope and promise (see e.g. Isaiah 65: 17–25, Revelation 21). Notable literary images of the new Jerusalem include 'the heavenly Jerusalem', the object of Christian's pilgrimage in Bunyan's *Pilgrim's Progress*, and Blake's *Jerusalem*.

Jerusalem: *The Emanation of the Giant Albion* A prophetic poem by William *Blake, written and etched 1804–20. (The poem beginning 'And did those feet . . .', commonly known as 'Jerusalem', appears at the beginning of Blake's *Milton*.) After a preface in which he defends his use of free verse ('Poetry Fetter'd Fetters the Human Race'), Blake proceeds to personify England as the fallen giant Albion, and to summon him to the 'awakening of Eternal Life'.

Jerusalem Delivered (Gerusalemme liberata) A poem by *Tasso, published without his consent 1580, in authorized form 1581.

The poem is an *epic of the First Crusade, with the addition of romantic and fabulous elements. The poem was translated into English in 1594 by Richard Carew (1555–1620), and in 1600 by Edward Fairfax as *Godfrey of Bulloigne*. Spenser's description of Acrasia's Bower of Bliss (*Faerie Queene*, II. xii) was modelled on the gardens of Armida, and the poem considerably influenced *Milton and others (see TASSO, TORQUATO).

Jessica's First Prayer A novel for children and newly literate readers by Hesba *Stretton, first published in *Sunday at Home* (1866). It tells the story of a neglected girl, one of the impoverished 'street arabs' for whose welfare Stretton campaigned vigorously, who is eventually rescued from poverty and adopted by a coffee-stall keeper. It sold two million copies in her lifetime. It was in part an attack on the hypocrisy of prosperous church and chapel congregations who ignored the plight of the poor, but its vivid descriptions of deprivation, and its optimistic conclusion, gave it a wide appeal. It was widely translated, and was for a while (by order of Tsar Alexander II) compulsory reading in all Russian schools.

jest book literature Collections of 'merry tales', 'quick answers', and 'pleasant conceits' popular throughout the 16th and 17th centuries and later. Their authorship was often ascribed to witty writers such as John *Skelton and George *Peele or to famous jesters such as John Scoggin and Robert Armin.

JEWETT, Sarah Orne (1849–1909) American novelist and short story writer. Her volumes include *Deephaven* (1877), *A Country Doctor* (1884), *A White Heron* (1886; short stories), and *The Country of the Pointed Firs* (1896). Her enduring reputation rests on her precise, realistic, subdued portraits of ordinary New England people and her sense of community and place.

Jew of Malta, The An ironical tragedy in blank verse by Christopher *Marlowe, performed about 1592, not published until 1633. The governor of Malta decides that the Jews of the island should pay the tribute demanded by Turkey. Barabas, a rich Jew who resists the edict, has his wealth impounded and his house turned into a nunnery. In revenge he embarks on an orgy of slaughter, killing his daughter Abigail's lover among others, and poisoning

Abigail. The prologue to the play is spoken by 'Machevil', and Barabas is one of the prototypes for unscrupulous *Machiavellian villains in later Elizabethan and Jacobean drama. His praise of gold and precious stones as 'Infinite riches in a little room' is often quoted. The play has been successfully revived in modern times.

JEWSBURY, Geraldine Endsor (1812–80) Novelist, journalist, and intimate friend of the Carlyles.. Besides contributing numerous articles and reviews to the *Athenaeum*, the *Westminster Review*, and other journals, she wrote six novels, including *Zöe* (1845), *The Half Sisters* (1848), and *Marian Withers* (1851), and two stories for children. The central subject of Jewsbury's forthright and often controversial fiction is the limitation—educational, financial, and emotional—of middle-class women's lives. Jewsbury destroyed all the letters to her from Jane Carlyle, except for one which was published in Mrs Annie Ireland's *Life of Jane Welsh Carlyle* (1891); it was the wish of both women that their letters be destroyed.

JEWSBURY, Maria Jane (1800–33) Poet, and sister of Geraldine *Jewsbury. In 1832 she married W. K. Fletcher, a chaplain with the East India Company. She published poetry and essays, contributed to the *Manchester Courier* and the *Athenaeum*, and was a close friend of the *Wordsworths. Her most remarkable work was perhaps the poem 'Oceanides', written on her voyage out to India, 1832–3, and published in twelve sections in *The Athenaeum*; the poem vividly celebrates the stages and changing moods of the voyage. She died of cholera not long after her arrival.

JHABVALA, Ruth Prawer (1927–) Novelist, born in Germany, the daughter of a Polish Jewish solicitor; she came to England in 1939 as a refugee. In 1951 she married a Parsi Indian architect, and subsequently lived for 24 years in India. Her novels *Esmond in India* (1958), *A New Dominion* (1973), and *Heat and Dust* (1975, *Booker Prize) reflect her mingled affection for and discomfort with her adopted country. She published volumes of short stories and wrote several original screenplays, including *Shakespeare-Wallah* (1965), and screen adaptations for Merchant-Ivory of E. M. Forster's *A *Room with a View* and *Howards End*, and novels by Henry *James and Kazuo *Ishiguro. In 1975 she moved to New York, where her novel *In Search of Love and Beauty* (1983) and numerous later works are set.

jig 'An afterpiece in the form of a brief farce which was sung and accompanied by dancing', popular in the Elizabethan and Jacobean theatre. Few survive, but there are numerous references to them in contemporary literature and both William *Kemp and Richard Tarlton performed them with great success.

JOAN OF ARC, St (1412–31) Jeanne d'Arc, or more correctly Jeanne Darc, as it was spelt in all contemporary documents, an illiterate girl who contributed powerfully to liberate France from the English in the reign of Charles VII. Inspired, she claimed, by the voices of Sts Michael, Catherine, and Margaret, her mission was a double one, to raise the siege of Orléans, and to conduct Charles to his coronation at Rheims. She accomplished these tasks and then wished to return home; but she yielded to the demands of the French patriots and was taken prisoner by the Burgundians, who handed her over to the English. But it was a French court of ecclesiastics (with the help of the Inquisition) who sentenced her as a heretic, and the English who burned her at Rouen. She was canonized in 1920. She appears in Shakespeare's *1 *Henry VI*, and is the subject of *Voltaire's *La Pucelle*, a tragedy by *Schiller, a poem by Robert *Southey, and a drama by Jean Anouilh. George Bernard *Shaw's play *Saint Joan* was successfully revived at the National Theatre in 2007.

Job *See* BIBLE.

Jocasta A tragedy in blank verse, translated from an Italian adaptation of the *Phoenissae* of *Euripides, by George *Gascoigne and Francis Kinwelmarshe, included in Gascoigne's *Posies* (1575).

Jocoseria A volume of ten poems of various lengths and metres by Robert *Browning, published 1883. The collection is consciously a miscellany. The volume contains the much-parodied lyric 'Wanting is—what?', an exquisite miniature on the notion of art as a form of desire.

JOHN, Augustus (1878–1961) OM, painter. His autobiography, *Chiaroscuro* (1952), contains many anecdotes about writers (including Oscar *Wilde, G. B. *Shaw, James *Joyce, and Wyndham *Lewis). Michael *Holroyd's two-volume biography (1974–5) suggests various fictitious characters who were partly based on John, including Struthers in D. H. *Lawrence's *Aaron's Rod*, Gulley Jimson in Joyce *Cary's *The*

Horse's Mouth, and the younger Strickland in Somerset *Maugham's *The Moon and Sixpence*.

JOHN, St *See* BIBLE; EVANGELISTS.

John Bull, The History of A collection of pamphlets by John *Arbuthnot, the first of which, *Law is a Bottomless Pit*, appeared on 6 March 1712. They characterized the War of Spanish Succession under coded satirical stories, designed to promote the peace negotiations of Robert Harley's administration. John Bull represents England: 'an honest plain-dealing fellow, choleric, bold, and of a very inconstant temper . . . very apt to quarrel with his best friends, especially if they pretend to govern him . . . a boon companion, loving his bottle and his diversion.'

John Buncle Esq., The Life and Opinions of A novel by Thomas *Amory (2 vols, 1756, 1766). The eccentric Buncle sets out on a journey through the magnificent landscapes of northern England. He comes upon small centres of civilized culture, encountering beautiful, learned women, seven of whom (with the intervention of successive deaths) he marries: Miss Spence, with 'the head of Aristotle, the heart of a primitive Christian, and the form of Venus de Medicis', is typical. The book otherwise consists of eloquent digressions on religious, scientific, and literary subjects.

'John Gilpin, The Diverting History of' Popular poem by William *Cowper, published anonymously in 1782 in the *Public Advertiser*, and reprinted in the same volume as *The *Task* (1785). Lady Austen told Cowper the story to amuse him, and he rapidly turned it into a ballad.

John Halifax, Gentleman A novel by Dinah *Craik published 1856. The story tells of the orphan John, who finds employment with the tanner Abel Fletcher. He is befriended by Abel's weakling son Phineas Fletcher (the name recalls the 17th-century poet Phineas *Fletcher), improves his position, and marries the book's heroine, Ursula March. John's status as 'gentleman' is earned not by birth and wealth but by his own Christian integrity and worth. The book's thoughtful analysis of the transfer of cultural and economic power from the aristocracy to the commercial middle classes made it immensely successful in both England and America. It was one of the first novels to give a heroic role to a tradesman, and helped to break down the suspicion of fiction among Nonconformist readers.

JOHN OF SALISBURY (late 1110s–1180) Churchman and humanist scholar; he studied at Paris under *Abelard. He was secretary to St Thomas *Becket, with whom he was exiled when he fell into disfavour with Henry II. He wrote a life of Becket and of St *Anselm. Ultimately he became bishop of Chartres in 1176. His principal works are the influential *Polycraticus* (or *De Nugis Curialium*), on the vanities of the court and miscellaneous questions on philosophy, and the *Metalogicon*, a defence of the seven liberal arts which conveys his respect for great authors and argues for the value of a liberal education.

JOHNS, 'Captain' W. E. (William Earl) (1893–1968) RAF bomber pilot in 1918, and author of 169 books. His fictional flying hero, *Biggles, was such a successful RAF recruiting device he was asked to produce a female equivalent—Joan Worralson (*Worrals of the WAAF*, 1941)—and Gimlet King (*King of the Commandos*, 1943) for the army.

JOHNSON, Amryl (1944–2001) Poet, born in Trinidad; she moved to Britain as a child. Renowned as a performance poet, her volumes include *Long Road to Nowhere* (1985), *Gorgons* (1992), and *Calling* (2000). *Sequins for a Ragged Hem* (1988) is a Caribbean travelogue.

JOHNSON, B. S. (Bryan Stanley) (1933–73) Novelist, poet, and film-maker. He published seven novels, each highly adventurous in form. *Travelling People* (1963) is a lightweight novel of comic misadventures, each chapter written in a different style; *Albert Angelo* (1964) vividly evokes the London of its era, and has holes cut through the pages to provide a 'flash-forward' to future events. *Trawl* (1967) and *The Unfortunates* (1969) are autobiographical pieces, the latter consisting of unbound sections presented in a box. (*See* INTERACTIVE FICTION.) *House Mother Normal* (1971), *Christie Malry's Own Double Entry* (1973), and *See the Old Lady Decently* (1975) continue his passionate crusade to break free of the confines of the neo-Dickensian novel. Johnson's work has an emotional candour and directness unusual in a so-called 'experimental' writer; the same qualities are to be found in his two volumes of poetry. He committed suicide at the age of 40. See *Like a Fiery Elephant* (2004), a biography by J. *Coe.

JOHNSON, Charles R. (Richard) (1948–) African American novelist. His first novel was *Faith and the Good Thing* (1974). In 1995 he aroused controversy by seeming to criticize Alice *Walker in his introduction to his

Oxherding Tale. He has written screenplays and his essays and articles were collected in *I Call Myself an Artist* (1999).

JOHNSON, Diane (1934–) American novelist and biographer. Her ironic and observant novels, many of which have a hint of thriller suspense, include *Fair Game* (1965), *The Shadow Knows* (1972), and *Persian Nights* (1987). *Le Divorce* (1997; filmed 2003), *Le Mariage* (2000), and *L'Affaire* (2003) are a trilogy of manners with a violent undertow, set in Paris. She co-wrote, with Stanley Kubrick (1928–99), the screenplay for *The Shining* (1980), and has also written an innovative feminist life of Mary Ellen Peacock (1821–61), wife of George *Meredith (*Lesser Lives*, 1972), and a life of Dashiell *Hammett (1983).

JOHNSON, James Weldon (1871–1938) African American writer and civil rights activist. In 1912 he published (anonymously) *The Autobiography of an Ex-Coloured Man*, describing the masked identity of a young African American in a white world. Johnson was a prominent figure in the *Harlem Renaissance, a productive poet, and a researcher into anthropology, publishing several collections of spirituals. He published an autobiography, *Along This Way*, in 1934.

JOHNSON, Joseph (1738–1809) A radical bookseller and publisher of St Paul's Churchyard, who encouraged and published many writers, including *Wordsworth (*Descriptive Sketches*, 1793), Anna Laetitia *Barbauld, William *Cowper, Erasmus *Darwin, and Mary *Wollstonecraft. From 1788 to 1799 he published the scientific and literary monthly the *Analytical Review*.

JOHNSON, Linton Kwesi (1952–) Poet, performer, and reggae artist; born in Jamaica, he came to England in 1963. His first books of poems, *Voices of the Living and the Dead* (1974) and *Dread Beat an' Blood* (1975), introduced his characteristic voice of disaffected dissent, with bleak and powerful lyrics. He coined the term *'dub poetry' to describe the way reggae DJs blend music and verse. Later work includes *Forces of Victory* (1979) with its influential 'Sonny's Lettah', condemning 'suspicion laws', *Bass Culture* (1980), *Inglan Is a Bitch* (1980), *Making History* (1984), and *Mi Revalueshanary Fren* (2002). His work (*Tings an' Times*, CD, 1991, and *More Time*, CD, 1998) continues to show a strong political commitment to the cause of black rights.

JOHNSON, Lionel Pigot (1867–1902) Poet, critic, and essayist. A perceptive supporter of Thomas *Hardy, his *The Art of Thomas Hardy* (1894) was among the first full-length studies to appear. His *Poems* appeared in 1895, *Ireland and Other Poems* in 1897, and *Post Liminium*, a posthumous collection of essays, in 1911. There is an account of his personality and decline into alcoholism in W. B. *Yeats's *Autobiographies*. *See* ART FOR ART'S SAKE.

JOHNSON, Pamela Hansford (1912–81), Critic and novelist. Her many works, from her first novel, *This Bed thy Centre* (1935), to her last, *The Bonfire* (1981), often evoke her upbringing in Clapham. In 1950 she married C. P. *Snow. She is most widely known for her 'Dorothy Merlin' trilogy, a satire on the pretensions of literary life, which consists of *The Unspeakable Skipton* (1959), *Night and Silence, Who is Here* (1962), and *Cork Street, Next to the Hatter's* (1965).

JOHNSON, Richard (*fl.*1592–1622) Author of *The Most Famous History of the Seven Champions of Christendome* (1596–7), a widely read chivalric romance, which influenced Edmund *Spenser; *The Nine Worthies of London* (1592); two collections of ballads (1612; 1620), the second of which refers to plays by *Shakespeare; *Tom a Lincoln*, an Arthurian romance (*c.*1599; earliest surviving edition 1631); and the *jest book *Pleasant Conceits of Old Hobson* (1607).

JOHNSON, Samuel (1709–84) Writer, born at Lichfield, son of a bookseller. He married Elizabeth Porter, a widow twenty years his senior, in 1735 and started a private school at Edial, near Lichfield. This was not a success; Johnson's lack of a degree and convulsive mannerisms hindered his prospects as a teacher, and in 1737 he set off with one of his few pupils, David *Garrick, to London. He began regular contributions to the *Gentleman's Magazine*, writing prefaces, essays, poems, Latin verses, biographies, and, most notably, his *Parliamentary Debates*, which were widely accepted as authentic speeches by the great politicians of the day. In 1738 he published his poem *London*, based in part on his friendship with the poet Richard *Savage; his *Life of Mr Richard Savage* (1744) is a vivid evocation of the pitfalls of *Grub Street. It was subsequently included in his *Lives of the English Poets*. His *Compleat Vindication of the Licensers of the Stage* (1739) was an ironic 'defence' of the Stage Licensing Act of 1737 by which the government of Robert Walpole (1676–1745) suppressed Henry

*Brooke's *Gustavus Vasa*. In 1743–4 he was employed, with William Oldys (1696–1761), on the *Harleian Miscellany*. His *Miscellaneous Observations on the Tragedy of Macbeth* (1745) brought him the praise of William *Warburton. In 1747 Johnson issued the 'Plan' of his Dictionary (*see* JOHNSON'S DICTIONARY), on which he had already started work at his new home in Gough Square; he dedicated the plan to the earl of Chesterfield. In 1749 he published *The *Vanity of Human Wishes*, the first work to bear his own name, and in the same year Garrick produced his tragedy **Irene*, which brought him almost £300. In 1750 he started the **Rambler*, a periodical written almost entirely by himself. His wife died in 1752, a loss which caused him intense and prolonged grief. From March 1753 to March 1754 Johnson contributed regularly to John *Hawkesworth's *Adventurer*. His *Dictionary* was published in 1755, after nine years of labour; it firmly established his reputation, and also brought him the Oxford degree he had failed to achieve earlier. He continued to write essays, reviews, and political articles for various periodicals, and during 1758–60 wrote the **Idler* papers. His only extended fiction was **Rasselas* (1759). In 1762 Johnson was relieved from hackwork by a Crown pension of £300 a year. The following year he met his biographer, James *Boswell, in the bookshop of his friend Thomas Davies.

By this point Johnson was one of the most eminent literary figures of his day, the centre of a circle of distinguished figures including Joshua *Reynolds, Edmund *Burke, and Oliver *Goldsmith. The Club was founded in 1764 to hold regular meetings of such men; later members included Garrick, Charles James Fox, and Boswell. Although Johnson himself was a fervent Tory, he was on intimate terms with several well-known Whigs, even managing, when Boswell engineered a meeting, to be civil to the radical John Wilkes. In 1765 he met the *Thrales, in whose town and country houses he found comfort and companionship, and his edition of Shakespeare was published. The value of Johnson's edition lies in the sanity and sensitivity of its notes; the preface is one of his finest works of critical prose. He returned to politics, this time on the government side, with four political pamphlets: *The False Alarm* (1770), against Wilkes; *Thoughts . . . Respecting Falkland's Islands* (1771); *The Patriot* (1774); and *Taxation No Tyranny* (1775), on the question of American taxation and representation: Johnson supported taxation as warmly as he opposed slavery. In 1773 he travelled with Boswell to Scotland and the Hebrides, a journey

recorded in his **Journey to the Western Islands of Scotland* (1775) and Boswell's *Journal of a Tour to the Hebrides* (1785). In 1777 he undertook, at the request of a number of booksellers, to write *The Lives of the English Poets*, the crowning work of his old age (1779–81). In 1784, saddened by his estrangement from Mrs Thrale, he died at his house in Bolt Court and was buried in Westminster Abbey.

Johnson's reputation rests not only on his works but also on Boswell's record of his powerful conversation, his eccentricities and opinionated outbursts (against Scots, Whigs, Americans, and actors), his interest in the supernatural, and many other aspects of his large personality. Johnson had no children, but accepted into his house many dependants, such as his wife's friend, the blind Anna Williams, and Robert Levet, an unlicensed, alcoholic doctor who worked with the poor and whose death in 1782 prompted Johnson's famous elegy 'On the Death of Dr Levet'. Johnson was always generous with literary support for other writers, including a surprising number of women writers (Charlotte *Lennox, Elizabeth *Carter, and Fanny *Burney among them). His profound but melancholy religious faith is revealed also in his *Prayers and Meditations* (1785). *Anecdotes of the Late Samuel Johnson*, by Mrs Piozzi, formerly Mrs Thrale, appeared in 1786, a year before Sir John Hawkins's biography (1787). *See also* JOHNSON, THE LIFE OF SAMUEL.

JOHNSON, Terry (1955–) Playwright and theatre director. *Insignificance* (1982), like much of his later work, is peopled with real characters: the play evokes a (fictional) meeting between Marilyn Monroe, Albert Einstein, Joe DiMaggio, and Senator McCarthy in a New York hotel room in 1953. *Unsuitable for Adults* (1984) was the first of his trilogy of plays examining the relationship between the British and their comic icons. In *Hysteria* (1993), Sigmund *Freud and Salvador Dali appear in a nightmarish reincarnation of a Freudian case history. Johnson continued his series on British comedy with *Dead Funny* (1994), and completed it in 1998 with *Cleo, Camping, Emmanuelle and Dick*, a behind-the-scenes look at the making of four 'Carry On' films. *Hitchcock Blonde* (2003) includes a re-creation of the shower scene from *Hitchcock's film *Psycho*; *Piano/Forte* (2006) retreats into domestic comedy.

Johnson, The Life of Samuel By James *Boswell, published in 1791, the most celebrated biography in the English language. Boswell informed *Johnson in 1772 of his intention to write his life, and had been collecting materials for this purpose as part of his journal since their first meeting in 1763. Boswell learned much from Johnson's own expertise in biography. His portrait is vivid and intimate, a 'Flemish picture' including letters, anecdotes, and much conversation, and full of trifling incidents as well as significant events. Boswell's skill in stage-managing encounters (as with John Wilkes adds greatly to the work's liveliness.

'Johnson's Dictionary' (*A Dictionary of the English Language*) By Samuel *Johnson, published 1755. In 1746 Johnson contracted with Robert *Dodsley and other booksellers to write an English dictionary, for a fee of £1,575. A 'Plan' and dedication to the earl of Chesterfield appeared in 1747. Johnson's object was to produce 'a dictionary by which the pronunciation of our language may be fixed, and its attainment facilitated; by which its purity may be preserved, its use ascertained, and its duration lengthened'. Working with six assistants, Johnson wrote definitions of over 40,000 words, illustrated with about 114,000 literary quotations from Philip *Sidney onwards. Five editions were published in his lifetime, and the work remained without rival until publication of *Oxford English Dictionary*.

JOHNSTON, Jennifer (1930–) Irish novelist, daughter of playwright Denis Johnston (1901–84). Her work employs a spare, delicate prose to explore Irish political divisions, focusing on relationships that promise to defy barriers of caste, class, and age but typically end in catastrophic surrender to historical imperatives. *The Gates* (1973) extends the elegiac tendencies of the '*big house' genre. *Shadows on our Skin* (1977) and *The Railway Station Man* (1984) probe the moral ambiguities of the violence of the Northern Irish *Troubles. Later work includes *The Invisible Worm* (1991), *Two Moons* (1998), and *Foolish Mortals* (2007).

JOHNSTONE, Charles (?1719–1800) Novelist. To supplement his legal practice in London he wrote *Chrysal, or The Adventures of a Guinea* (4 vols, 1760–65). 'Chrysal' is the spirit of gold in the guinea, whose progress from hand to hand, through six different countries, links a series of sharp satirical episodes. *The History of Arsaces, Prince of Betlis* (2 vols, 1774), is an *oriental tale which expresses covert sympathy with the American colonists in their struggle for independence.

JOLLEY, Elizabeth (1923–2007) Australian novelist, poet, and playwright, born in Birming-

ham. Her writing is characterized by a recurring sense of alienation and displacement, its source revealed in the semi-autobiographical trilogy *My Father's Moon* (1989), *Cabin Fever* (1990), and *George's Wife* (1993). Many of her earlier novels combine dark comedy, often centred on eccentricity and bizarre behaviour in characters who are invariably outsiders, with *Gothic plots and surprises.

Jonah *See* BIBLE.

Jonathan Wild the Great, The Life of Novel by Henry *Fielding, published as the third volume of his *Miscellanies*, 1743, following the eponymous hero's flamboyant criminal career to his death on the gallows. Like *The *Beggar's Opera*, the novel was loosely based on the notorious thief-taker Jonathan Wild (?1682–1725), but as with the play, it was really a satire: Wild is, with forceful irony, held up for admiration in his practice of the 'virtues' of hypocrisy, manipulation, and greed, and the figure of the Great Man among thieves and cheats is constantly compared with the Great Man in public life, with Sir Robert Walpole (1676–1745) (actually a subscriber to the *Miscellanies*) a particular target.

JONES, David (1895–1974) Poet and artist, strongly identified with Wales, although he lived there only from 1924 to 1927. He served in the trenches throughout the First World War, an experience significant for all his work. In 1921 he became a Roman Catholic and in 1922 began a long association with Eric Gill. The Welsh *Mabinogion, the 'matter of Britain', the Bible, and the Roman Catholic liturgy provide much of the material and the background for his poetry. *In Parenthesis* (1937) is an epic work of mixed poetry and prose on the subject of the war. *The Anathemata* (1952), a complex work of poetry and prose, part chronicle, part incantation, celebrates in richly allusive language the ancient 'matter of Britain'. *The Sleeping Lord and Other Fragments* (1974) is a collection of pieces of a projected work centred on the Crucifixion, the residue of which was published as *The Roman Quarry* (1981). *Wedding Poems*, written in 1940, appeared in 2002.

JONES, Diana Wynne (1934–2011) Writer of inventive, complex, and funny *fantasy books for children and adults, which display wide reading of canonical texts, myths, and legends: *The Homeward Bounders* (1981) uses the Prometheus legend; *Castle in the Air* (1990) draws on the *Arabian Nights*. Jones's books often involve multiple parallel worlds as in those about a magician known as the Chrestomanci, beginning with *Charmed Life* (1977); all celebrate the power of storytelling. *Howl's Moving Castle* (1986) was made into an anime film (Hayo Miyazaki, 2004); *House of Many Ways* (2008) is set in the same world.

JONES, Gayl (1949–) African American writer and critic. *Corregidora* (1975) *and Eva's Man* (1976) both treat domestic abuse. Her poetry and prose draw on the patterns of blues and jazz.

JONES, Glyn (1905–95) Welsh poet, short story writer, and novelist, born in Merthyr Tydfil, Glamorgan, the setting of much of his fiction. *The Blue Bed* (1937) and *The Water Music* (1944) contain his most influential stories. He drew on his experience of teaching in Cardiff primary schools in *The Dream of Jake Hopkins* (1944), a long poem for radio, and *The Learning Lark* (1960, novel). Other works include *The Island of Apples* (1965; rev. 1992); *The Dragon Has Two Tongues* (1968), a seminal account of Welsh writing in English; the anthology *Goodbye, What Were You?* (1994); *Collected Poems* (1996) and *Collected Stories* (1999).

JONES, Gwyn (1907–99) Welsh short story writer, novelist, anthologist, and Norse scholar. He founded the *Welsh Review* in 1939. His translation of the **Mabinogion* (with Thomas Jones) appeared in 1948. His longer works of fiction include *Times Like These* (1936), set in the Welsh valleys during the Depression, and the historical novels *A Garland of Bays* (1938) and *The Walk Home* (1962). He edited the *Oxford Book of Welsh Verse in English* (1977). *See Collected Stories* (1997).

JONES, Gwyneth (1952–) Children's writer, and author of *science fiction and *fantasy for adults. Her fiction for children, including the ghost story *King Death's Garden*, is published under the name Ann Halam. Her sense of the form and subject matter of science fiction is best seen in the 'Aleutian' trilogy beginning with *White Queen* (1991), whose imagined aliens demonstrate the fluidity of our ideas of identity and gender.

JONES, Henry Arthur (1851–1929) Playwright, who made his name in London with a melodrama, *The Silver King* (1882), written in collaboration with Henry Herman. A friend and contemporary of Arthur *Pinero, Jones was a prolific playwright, who did much to re-establish serious themes in the theatre, and fought for the abolition of censorship. His finest work included *The Case of Rebellious Susan* (1894), *The Liars* (1897), *Mrs Dane's Defence* (1900), and *The Lie* (1923).

JONES, Inigo (1573–1652) Architect, stage designer, painter, mathematician, and man of letters, whose depth of knowledge of Roman and Italian art and of Renaissance theory was new in England, and whose revolutionary buildings brought the classical style to Britain. In 1615 he became surveyor of the king's works; his most famous buildings are the Queen's House, Greenwich (1616–18 and 1629–35), and the Banqueting Hall, Whitehall (1619–22). Jones's career as a designer of *masques opened in 1605, and many of his drawings for costume and scenery survive. A stormy but fruitful collaboration with Ben *Jonson began with *The Masque of Blackness*, and lasted until 1630/31. Jones produced, with Thomas *Carew, *Coelum Britannicum* (1634), perhaps the most brilliant of later Caroline masques. Jones became one of the heroes of the Palladian movement, revered by Lord Burlington and Alexander *Pope. Many of his designs were published in two folio volumes, edited by William Kent (1727).

JONES, James (1921–77) American novelist who served in Hawaii during the Second World War and subsequently drew on this experience for his best-selling novel *From Here to Eternity* (1951).

JONES, Leroi *See* BARAKA, AMIRI.

JONES, Mary (d. 1778) Poet. Her ballad 'The Lass of the Hill' was a popular success in 1742. *Miscellanies in Prose and Verse* (1750) had a subscription list of about 1,400 people; when the volume went on public sale in 1752 it was very favourably reviewed in the **Monthly Review* by Ralph Griffiths (1720?–1803), who later invited her to become a reviewer, an exceptional offer for a woman writer. She declined gracefully. Her verse is witty, sociable, and self-mocking.

JONES, Russell Celyn (1955–) Welsh writer. His novels *Soldiers and Innocents* (1990), *Small Times* (1992), *An Interference of Light* (1995), and *The Eros Hunter* (1998) are notable for their pungent, laconic prose and rueful interrogation of masculine values, with a particular emphasis on fathers and sons. Of later work, *The Ninth Wave* (2009) is based on the **Mabinogion*'s **Pwyll*.

JONES, Sir William (1746–94) A distinguished orientalist and translator. Jones learned Arabic, Persian, and Sanskrit, and was a pioneer of comparative philology, publishing *Poems, Consisting Chiefly of Translations from the Asiatick Languages* (1772), *The Moâllakât* (1782), from Arabic, and *Sacontala, or The Fatal Ring: An Indian Drama* (1789). Jones had considerable influence on the oriental themes of Romantic poets such as *Byron, *Southey, and Thomas *Moore.

JONG, Erica (1942–) American novelist, who achieved fame with her first book, *Fear of Flying* (1973), a sequence of explicit sexual episodes delivered in a wisecracking style. Later novels include *Fanny* (1980), a pastiche *picaresque; she has also published poetry and essays. *Fear of Fifty* (1994) is a midlife memoir, and *Seducing the Demon* (2007) a series of reflections on the writer's life.

JONSON, Ben (Benjamin) (1572/3–1637) Dramatist, poet, scholar, and writer of court *masques. In 1597 he began to work for Philip *Henslowe's companies as player and playwright, and was imprisoned for his share in *The Isle of Dogs*, a 'very seditious and slanderous' satire now lost (*see* SWAN THEATRE). In 1598 he killed a fellow actor in a duel, but escaped hanging, being branded instead on his thumb as a felon. His first important play, *Every Man in His Humour*, with William *Shakespeare in the cast, was performed by the Lord Chamberlain's Company at the Curtain in 1598, and *Every Man out of His Humour* at the Globe in 1599. *Cynthia's Revels* (1600) and *Poetaster* (1600–1, attacking Thomas *Dekker and John *Marston) were performed by the Children of the Queen's Chapel, and his tragedy, *Sejanus*, at the Globe by Shakespeare's company, 1603. His first court masque, *The Masque of Blackness*, written to accommodate Queen Anne's desire to appear as a negress, was given on Twelfth Night, 1605. In that year he was imprisoned for his share in *Eastward Ho*, and gave evidence to the Privy Council concerning the Gunpowder Plot. His major plays are: *Volpone*, acted at both the Globe and at Oxford and Cambridge universities, 1605–6; *Epicene, or The Silent Woman*, 1609–10; *The *Alchemist*, 1610; and *Bartholomew Fair*, 1614. Though not formally appointed the first *poet laureate, the essentials of the position were conferred on Jonson in 1616, when a pension was granted to him by *James I. In the same year he published a folio edition of his *Works*. After *The *Devil Is an Ass* (1616), he abandoned the public stage for ten years, and his later plays, *The *Staple of News* (1626), *The *New Inn* (1629), *The *Magnetic Lady*

(1631), and *A *Tale of a Tub* (1633), show a relatively unsuccessful reliance on allegory and symbolism; John *Dryden called them his 'dotages'. From 1605 up to 1634 Jonson produced many masques for the court, with scenery by Inigo *Jones. He introduced the 'antimasque', an antithetical, usually disorderly, prelude to the main action which served to highlight by contrast the central theme of political and social harmony. There are examples of this in *The Masque of Queens* (1609), *Pleasure Reconciled to Virtue* (1618, which influenced John *Milton's *Comus), and *Neptune's Triumph for the Return of Albion* (1624). After *Chloridia* (1631), his collaboration with Jones ended with a famous quarrel. His non-dramatic verse includes his *epigrams (among them tender epitaphs on his first daughter, Mary, and first son, Benjamin) and *The *Forest*, printed in the folio of 1616. *The Underwood* and a translation of *Horace's *Ars Poetica* were printed in 1640. His chief prose works are *The English Grammar* and *Timber, or Discoveries*, printed in 1640.

During the reign of James I Jonson's literary prestige and influence were unrivalled. His friends included Shakespeare, whom he loved 'on this side idolatry', John *Donne, Francis *Bacon, George *Chapman, Francis *Beaumont, John *Fletcher, Sir Robert *Cotton, and John *Selden, and among the younger writers (who styled themselves the 'sons' or 'tribe of Ben') Richard *Brome, Thomas *Carew, William *Cartwright, Sir Kenelm Digby, Viscount *Falkland, Robert *Herrick, Thomas *Randolph, and John *Suckling. His chief patrons were the *Sidney family, the earl of Pembroke, Lucy, countess of Bedford, and the duke and duchess of Newcastle. He suffered a stroke in 1628, after which he was perhaps permanently bedridden until his death in August 1637. He was buried in Westminster Abbey, and celebrated in a collection of elegies entitled *Jonsonus Virbius* (1638). His reputation declined sharply from about 1700, as Shakespeare's, with whom he was inevitably compared, increased, but revived in the 20th century.

JORDAN, Neil (1950–) Irish novelist, film director, and screenwriter. After *Night in Tunisia* (1976, stories), and *The Past* (1979, novel), he wrote and directed *Angel* (1982), a poignant thriller set in troubled Northern Ireland. *The Company of Wolves* (1984), imaginatively adapted from Angela *Carter's story, led to the major success of *Mona Lisa* (1986). Sexual ambiguity is a feature of Jordan's most distinctive films, *The Crying Game* (1992) and *Breakfast on Pluto* (2005), the latter based on a novel by

Patrick *McCabe. Among many other films, his Graham *Greene adaptation *The End of the Affair* (1999) is notable. He has co-written the screenplay of Neil *Gaiman's *The Graveyard Book*.

JOSEPH, Jenny (1932–) Poet. *The Unlooked-for Season* (1960) was followed by *Rose in the Afternoon* (1974), which includes 'Warning: When I am an old woman I shall wear purple'. Other collections include *Persephone* (1980), which is a narrative in both poetry and prose, *Selected Poems* (1992), *Led by the Nose* (2002), a book on smells experienced by the gardener, and *Extreme of Things* (2006). She is also a writer of children's books.

Joseph Andrews, The History of the Adventures of, and of his Friend Mr Abraham Adams A novel by Henry *Fielding (1742). The title page proclaims that the story is told in the manner of *Cervantes, and in an important preface Fielding relates his innovative 'comic romance' to classical forms. His object is to defend what is good by displaying the Ridiculous, which arises from Affectation, and ultimately from Vanity and Hypocrisy. The work begins as a parody of Samuel Richardson's *Pamela*, with Joseph, in service with Sir Thomas and Lady Booby, as Pamela's brother and 'Mr B.' appearing as young Booby. Lady Booby makes amorous advances to Joseph, and when he rejects them he is dismissed. His old mentor, the vigorous but unworldly Parson Adams, and his beloved, the illiterate milkmaid Fanny, travel through the perilous hinterland of an England run by corrupt justices, vicious squires, hypocritical clergymen, and cheating innkeepers. Eventually they are given hospitality by Wilson, a country gentleman, whose life story clearly echoes much of Fielding's own experience. It is finally revealed that Joseph is the long-lost son of Wilson, and Fanny is Pamela's sister. Joseph and Fanny are married, and Adams is rewarded with a handsome living.

Joseph of Arimathea According to Matthew 27: 57–60, Joseph donated his own tomb for Christ's burial. For the legend of Joseph and the Grail, *see* GRAIL; GLASTONBURY. According to fable, St Philip sent twelve disciples, led by Joseph, into Britain to preach Christianity. They founded at Glastonbury the first primitive church, which developed into Glastonbury Abbey. Here Joseph was buried. Medieval treatments of his legend include Robert de *Boron's *Joseph d'Arimathie* and an English alliterative poem, ed. David Lawton (1983).

JOSEPHUS, Flavius (*c*.37–*c*.100) Jewish historian and Roman sympathizer who wrote in Greek for a Gentile audience. He obtained the favour of Vespasian by foretelling that he would one day become ruler of the Roman Empire. He was present at the siege and destruction of Jerusalem in 70, went to Rome with Titus, became a Roman citizen, and devoted himself to writing. His *History of the Jewish War* describes the Jews' struggle with Rome, much of it from his own experience. His *Jewish Antiquities* is a history of the Jews from the Creation down to the beginning of the revolt against Rome in 66; it includes a brief account of the death of Jesus which may have been added by a Christian author. There are English translations of his works by Thomas *Lodge, Sir Roger *L'Estrange, and William Whiston (1667–1752).

JOSIPOVICI, Gabriel (1940–) Novelist, playwright, and critic, born in Nice. His critical works include *The World and the Book* (1971), *The Lessons of Modernism* (1977), and an examination of the Bible, *The Book of God* (1988). His fiction is innovative and experimental, and includes *The Inventory* (1968); *Words* (1971); *Migrations* (1977); *Moo Park* (1994); *Now* (1998), which consists almost entirely of dialogue; *Goldberg: Variations* (2002); *Everything Passes* (2006); and *Heart's Wings* (2010).

Journey from This World to the Next, A Published in the second volume of *Miscellanies* by Henry *Fielding (1743). The tale purports to have been found in an almost indecipherable manuscript, left in an attic by someone now departed to the West Indies. The soul leaves the body in its lodgings in Cheapside and finds itself, guided by Mercury, in a stagecoach with other souls. At the door of Elysium the underworld judge Minos dictates who shall be permitted to enter; the generous and the honest are favoured, whatever their rank, while the cruel and hypocritical are rejected. In the Elysian Fields heroes and writers of antiquity converse animatedly with *Shakespeare, *Milton, *Dryden, *Addison, and Fielding's own *Tom Thumb. The spirit of Julian the Apostate appears and narrates his adventures in several guises: slave, Jew, courtier, statesman. The last section, Anne Boleyn's confessional story, is plausibly ascribed to Sarah *Fielding.

Journey to the Western Islands of Scotland, A By Samuel *Johnson, published January 1775. It is a personal narrative of the tour undertaken by James *Boswell and Johnson from August to November 1773 in Scotland and the Hebrides. Boswell gives an account of the journey in his *Journal of a Tour to the Hebrides* (1785). Johnson sets out his response to Scottish history, culture, and landscape, including current economic and political issues. On publication the book aroused the wrath of James *Macpherson because of its contemptuously sceptical comments on the authenticity of 'Ossian', and other Scots were offended by Johnson's uncompromising views of their country.

Jovial Crew, A, *or The Merry Beggars* A romantic comedy by Richard *Brome, produced 1641. Oldrents, a kindly country squire, is saddened by a Gypsy's prediction that his two daughters will be beggars. Springlove, an honest vagabond whom Oldrents has made his steward, is seized each spring with a desire to return to his wandering life. Oldrents's daughters decide to join him for a frolic, thus giving effect to the Gypsy's prediction, but all ends well. The play, Brome's masterpiece, is highly original in its picture of Oldrents's compassion for the poor and Springlove's longing for a vagabond life.

JOYCE, James (1882–1941) Writer, born in Dublin, and educated at Jesuit schools. A good linguist, in 1901 he wrote a letter of profound admiration in Dano-Norwegian to Henrik *Ibsen. Other early influences included Gerhart Hauptmann, *Dante, George *Moore, and W. B. *Yeats. Dissatisfied with the narrowness and bigotry of Ireland, as he saw it, Joyce went to Paris for a year in 1902, where he discovered the novel *Les Lauriers sont coupés* (1888) by Édouard Dujardin (1861–1949), which he was later to credit as the source of his own use of *interior monologue. He returned to Dublin in 1903 for his mother's death, stayed briefly in the Martello tower of *Ulysses with Oliver *Gogarty, then left Ireland more or less for good with Nora Barnacle (1884–1951). They lived at Trieste, then Zurich; after the war they settled in Paris. His first published work was a volume of verse, *Chamber Music* (1907), followed by *Dubliners* (1914), a volume of short stories published after great delays and difficulties. When the stories at last appeared they were greeted with enthusiasm by Ezra *Pound, in a review in The *Egoist. Harriet Shaw *Weaver, business manager and then editor of *The Egoist*, was a lifelong benefactress of Joyce. Joyce's play *Exiles* was published in 1918, staged unsuccessfully the same year in Munich, and first performed in London by the Stage Society in 1926. *A *Portrait of the Artist as a Young Man*, a largely autobiographical work, was published serially in *The Egoist*, 1914–15 (part of a first draft, *Stephen Hero*, appeared in

1944), and in one volume in 1916 (New York) and 1917 (London). With strong backing from Yeats and Pound, Joyce received a grant from the *Royal Literary Fund in 1915, and shortly after that a grant from the Civil List. But Joyce continued to struggle against poverty. Instalments of *Ulysses first appeared in the *Little Review* (March 1918–December 1920), and it was first published in its entirety in Paris on 2 February 1922, Joyce's 40th birthday. It was admired by T. S. *Eliot, Ernest *Hemingway, and Arnold *Bennett; but not by Virginia *Woolf. The first UK edition appeared in 1936. Another small volume of verse, *Pomes Penyeach*, was published in 1927, and his second great work, *Finnegans Wake*, extracts of which had already appeared as 'Work in Progress', was published in its complete form in 1939.

JOYCE, Patrick Weston (1827–1914) Irish antiquarian; his works include *Irish Names of Places* (1869–1913), *A Grammar of the Irish Language* (1878), *Old Celtic Romances* (1879, 1894, from which Alfred *Tennyson drew his 'Voyage of Maeldune'), and a *Social History of Ireland* (1903–20), all highly influential in the *Irish Revival.

Jude the Obscure A novel by Thomas *Hardy, originally printed in abridged and bowdlerized form in *Harper's New Monthly Magazine* (1894–5, as *Hearts Insurgent*), then in the 1895 edition of his works. In the author's words, it describes 'a deadly war waged between flesh and spirit'. Jude Fawley, a young Wessex villager of exceptional intellectual promise, is encouraged by the schoolmaster Phillotson. But he is trapped into marriage by the barmaid Arabella Donn, who shortly afterwards deserts him. He moves to Christminster (a version of Oxford), hoping one day to be admitted to the university. He meets his cousin, Sue Bridehead, a hypersensitive young woman who works in a shop selling ecclesiastical ornaments: they fall in love. Sue, in what appears to be a fit of desperate masochism, suddenly marries Phillotson. She is driven from him by physical revulsion, and flies to Jude; they begin to live together in Christminster, but do not consummate their love until Arabella reappears on the scene. Jude, who had been planning to enter the priesthood as a licentiate, as a substitute for his thwarted intellectual ambitions, is now doubly defeated. He and Sue become free to marry, but Sue shrinks from the step, partly because of her apprehension that a conventional union will destroy love, and partly from a superstitious fear that the Fawley family is doomed to marry unhappily: she compares the family to the house of Atreus, and Jude compares it to the house of Jeroboam, an interchange which reflects the theme of Hellenism and Hebraism prominent throughout the novel.

Under the pressure of poverty and social disapproval their relationship deteriorates, and tragedy overtakes them in the death of their children: the eldest, 'Old Father Time', son of Jude and Arabella, hangs the two babies and himself, leaving a note saying, 'Done because we are too menny.' In an agony of remorse and self-abasement, Sue returns to Phillotson and the church, and Jude, deeply shocked by her abandoning of her freethinking principles, begins drinking heavily and is tempted back by Arabella. He dies wretchedly.

The novel's provocative views on sexuality and marriage caused an uproar, and the *Pall Mall Gazette* set the tone by castigating it as 'dirt, drivel and damnation'. The hostile reception of the book was one of several reasons why Hardy wrote no more fiction.

Judith A 350-line poem in Old English, fragmentary at the beginning, found in the *Beowulf* manuscript. The poem corresponds to about the last quarter of the Apocryphal Book of Judith. It describes the banquet in the Assyrian camp, the bringing of Judith to the drunken Holofernes, her beheading of him and escape, and the defeat and flight of the Assyrians.

'Julian and Maddalo: A Conversation' A poem partly in dialogue form by P. B. *Shelley, published 1824. It is the most naturalistic of Shelley's long poems, deliberately opposed to the 'idealism' of his dramas.

Julian (Shelley) and Count Maddalo (Lord *Byron) ride and boat through 'bright Venice', discussing problems of free will, progress, and religious belief. They visit a 'Maniac', partly based on *Tasso and partly on Shelley himself, confined in elegant rooms in an island asylum. His presence deepens and darkens the terms of the debate: he provides 'the text of every heart'. A little child, based on Claire Clairmont's baby Allegra, is also introduced to show the powers of innocence and good. One of Shelley's most subtle studies of human affection and hopes, the poem is composed in fluent couplets, with marvellous evocations of the deserted Venetian lido and twinkling lagoon. It powerfully influenced Robert *Browning's *dramatic monologues.

JULIAN OF NORWICH (1342–after 1416) A recluse attached to the church of St Julian at Norwich. *Revelations of Divine Love* (the modern title) describes visions revealed to her during an illness in 1373 and her reflections on them. There is a Long version, written sometime after 1393, which incorporates revelations from 1388 and 1393. T. S. *Eliot quotes from her in 'Little Gidding' (*Four Quartets*): 'Sin is Behovely, but | All shall be well, and | All manner of thing shall be well.'

Julius Caesar A Roman tragedy by *Shakespeare, probably written and performed 1599, not printed until the first *folio (1623). Its major source is Thomas *North's translation of *Plutarch's *Lives*.

It begins with the events of the year 44 BC, after Caesar, already dictator, has returned to Rome from a successful campaign in Spain, amidst fears that he will allow himself to be crowned king. Distrust of Caesar's ambition gives rise to a conspiracy against him among Roman lovers of freedom, notably Cassius and Casca; they win Brutus to their cause. The conspirators murder Caesar in the senate house. Antony, Caesar's friend, stirs the people to fury against the conspirators by a skilful speech at Caesar's funeral. Octavius, nephew of Julius Caesar, Antony, and Lepidus, united as triumvirs, oppose the forces raised by Brutus and Cassius. The quarrel and reconciliation of Brutus and Cassius, with the news of the death of Portia, wife of Brutus, provide one of the finest scenes in the play (IV. iii). Brutus and Cassius are defeated at the battle of Philippi (42 BC), and kill themselves.

Jumpers A comedy by Tom *Stoppard performed and published 1972. The play's central character is a professor of moral philosophy, George Moore, who shares with the Cambridge philosopher G. E. Moore (1873–1958) not only his name but also his intuitionist ethics. The physical acrobatics of the jumpers of the title parallel the 'verbal gymnastics' of Moore's lengthy speeches, which are brilliantly witty parodies of academic philosophy.

JUNG, Carl Gustav (1875–1961) Swiss psychiatrist. Between 1907 and 1912 he worked in close collaboration with Freud but then broke with him to found his own school of 'Analytical Psychology'. Jung introduced into psychology the terms 'complex', 'collective unconscious', 'extrovert'–'introvert', *'archetype', and 'individuation'. Jung wrote extensively on topics far outside the normal field of psychology, and his influence has been commensurately wide, not least in the area of literary criticism, for example in the work of Northrop *Frye (1912–91), and the mythographer Joseph Campbell (1904–87). Alex Aronson's *Psyche and Symbol in Shakespeare* (1972) is an interpretation of Shakespearian drama in terms of Jungian psychology. Hermann *Hesse made use of Jung's concepts in his novels, and Jung himself wrote an essay on Joyce's *Ulysses*. Jung's work and ideas were of special importance to Ted *Hughes.

Jungle Book, The (1894), and **The Second Jungle Book** (1895) Fifteen stories by Rudyard *Kipling about India, seven featuring the feral boy, Mowgli, who is educated by Baloo the bear and Bagheera the panther in 'the law of the jungle'. The best-known non-Mowgli story may be 'Rikki-Tikki-Tavi', about the fight between a mongoose and cobras. 'Toomai of the Elephants' was filmed as *Elephant Boy* (1937), and the Mowgli stories were filmed as *The Jungle Book* in 1942 and 1994, and loosely adapted in the animated film by Disney (1967).

JUNIUS The pseudonymous author of a series of letters that appeared in the *Public Advertiser*, January 1769–January 1772, denouncing, with bitter scorn, the policies of the duke of Grafton, Lord North, and many other government figures, along with George III. Junius also took an active part on behalf of John Wilkes, and his arguments in favour of the freedom of the press and the liberties of the subject are of a classic Whig kind. The name is from the Roman republican hero Lucius Junius Brutus. The letters were much reprinted and attracted much attention, hostile and otherwise. An 'authorized' edition of the letters appeared in 1772. The identity of Junius has never been definitely established, but the most plausible candidate, on linguistic and political grounds, is Sir Philip Francis (1740–1818).

Junius Manuscript One of four major manuscripts containing Old English poetry, named after the editor Francis Junius who printed it at Amsterdam in 1655, calling it 'Cæd-

mon the monk's poetical paraphrase of Genesis, etc.' The biblical poetry in the manuscript (*Genesis A and B, *Exodus, *Daniel, and *Christ and Satan) continued to be associated with *Cædmon for some time, but it is unconnected with him.

Juno The principal Roman goddess (Hera in Greek), sister and wife of *Jupiter, and associated with marriage. In the *Aeneid* she is the great enemy of Aeneas and the Trojans.

Juno and the Paycock See O'CASEY, SEAN.

Jupiter (Zeus in Greek) Also called Jove, in Roman mythology king and father of the gods and brother and husband of *Juno. In the *Aeneid* he ensures that Aeneas fulfils his destiny as founder of the future city of Rome. His sexual encounters, often in disguise, with mortals of both sexes could be disastrous for them, as it was for Danaë, Leda, and Callisto; the youth Ganymede on the other hand became his cupbearer. His best-known human offspring was *Hercules, born to Alcmena. These stories, several of which are told in *Ovid's *Metamorphoses*, were often referred to in Renaissance literature, for example in Christopher *Marlowe's *Hero and Leander*.

JUVENAL (Decimus Iunius Iuvenalis) (*fl.* AD 100) The greatest Roman satiric poet, author of sixteen satires. Nothing definite is known about his life. The earlier Satires are unsurpassed in their expression of hatred and disgust; their caustic style is often contrasted with that of the urbane and witty Horace. Satire 3, translated by Samuel *Johnson as *London*, is a bitter tirade on the misery of being poor in Rome. Satire 10, also translated by Johnson, reveals with grim irony the vanity of human wishes. Other English imitators include Joseph *Hall and John *Oldham. John *Dryden edited and wrote in part a translation of Juvenal to which he prefixed his long discourse on satire.

KAFKA, Franz (1883-1924) German-speaking Jewish novelist, born in Prague. None of his three novels was completed to his satisfaction, and all were published posthumously: *Der Prozess* (1925: *The Trial*; filmed by Orson *Welles, 1963), *Das Schloss* (1926: *The Castle*), and the fragment *Amerika* (1927). Among the best-known short works are the stories 'Das Urteil' (1913: 'The Judgement'), 'Die Verwandlung' (1915: 'The Metamorphosis'), and 'In der Strafkolonie' (1919: 'In a Penal Colony'). Like the novels they display a tendency to fable and parable and explore themes of existential alienation and guilt. Much of his work was translated into English by Edwin and Willa *Muir, beginning with *The Trial* in 1930. W. H. *Auden declared Kafka 'the voice of the 20th century'. Those influenced by his work include writers as various as Milan *Kundera, Joseph *Heller, Vladimir *Nabokov, and *García Márquez. Kafka also left a large body of letters and diaries of exceptional interest for the insights they offer into his complex and tortured personality. The word 'Kafkaesque' has entered the language to signify a strange, baffling, nightmarish, or anxiety-ridden reality characteristic of that depicted in his work.

Kailyard school [from 'Kail-yard', cabbage patch] A term applied to a group of Scottish writers who exploited a sentimental and romantic image of small-town life in Scotland; the vogue lasted from the 1880s to the end of the 19th century. Leading exponents were J. M. *Barrie (in such books from his early career as *Auld Licht Idylls*, 1888, and *A Window in Thrums*, 1889), 'Ian Maclaren' (John Watson, 1850-1907), and S. R. Crockett (1859-1914). The Kailyard idyll was ferociously challenged by George Douglas *Brown's *The House with the Green Shutters* (1901) and J. MacDougall *Hay's *Gillespie* (1914).

Kama Sutra *See* BURTON, SIR RICHARD.

KANE, Sarah (1971-99) Playwright, whose first play, *Blasted* (1996), performed at the

*Royal Court, portrays events in a Leeds hotel room which suddenly explode into a European battleground of extreme violence. The play brought her overnight success and notoriety. *Phaedra's Love* (1997) was followed by *Cleansed* (1998), and *Crave* (1998), in which four unnamed characters create a series of interlinking dialogues on, amongst other things, sexual abuse and obsessional love. Her *4.48 Psychosis* was produced posthumously in 2000, following her death by suicide.

KANT, Immanuel (1724-1804) German idealist philosopher. His major contributions to philosophy began with *Critique of Pure Reason* (1781), followed by *Prolegomena to Any Future Metaphysics* (1783), *Fundamental Principles of the Metaphysic of Ethics* (1785), *Metaphysical Rudiments of Natural Philosophy* (1786), the second edition of the *Critique of Pure Reason* (1787), the *Critique of Practical Reason* (1788), and the *Critique of Judgement* (1790). His *Religion within the Boundaries of Pure Reason* (1793) called down on him government censure. His philosophy was subsequently developed and profoundly modified by Fichte, *Schelling, and *Hegel. S. T. *Coleridge made extensive use of his ideas in 'An Essay on Genial Criticism' (1814) and elsewhere. Kant also exercised a considerable influence on Thomas *Carlyle, though his reception of Kant's thought was a quirkily individual one.

Katherine Group The name given to five Middle English works of devotional prose found together in manuscript Bodley 34, dating from c.1190-1225: *Seinte Marherete*, *Seinte Iuliene*, *Seinte Katerine*, *Sawles Warde*, and *Hali Meidhad*. They are also associated with *Ancrene Wisse*: three of these texts appear with a version of it in a British Library manuscript. Their language, from a transitional period of English, is distinctive and interesting, and their style is lively and often colloquial, with vivid details of illustration. The three saints' lives are all concerned with heroic virgins who were frequently exalted in medieval writings:

St Catherine of Alexandria, St Juliana of Nicomedia (*see also* CYNEWULF), and St Margaret of Antioch, who were all believed to have suffered from the persecutions of Diocletian in the first decade of the 4th century.

KAVANAGH, Julia (1824–77) Novelist, born in Ireland, who spent much of her youth in France. After her father abandoned the family, Kavanagh supported herself and her mother Bridget (her lifelong companion) with her literary work, including the novels *Madeleine* (1848), *Nathalie* (1850), and *Adèle* (1858), and the biographical sketches, *French Women of Letters* (1862) and *English Women of Letters* (1863). *The Pearl Fountain* (1876) and *Forget-me-nots* (1878) are collections of stories, the former written with her mother. Kavanagh's popular and respected novels usually figure spirited and independent heroines. *Nathalie* has been identified as an influence on *Villette* by Charlotte Brontë, whom Kavanagh met in London in 1850.

KAVANAGH, P. J. (Patrick Joseph) (1931–) Poet and novelist. His volumes of poetry, from *One and One* (1960) include *Edward Thomas in Heaven* (1974), *An Enchantment* (1991), *Something About* (2004), and *Collected Poems* (1992). His novels include *A Happy Man* (1972), *Rebel for Good* (1980), and *Only by Mistake* (1986). *The Perfect Stranger* (1966) is a hauntingly memorable account of his life up to the sudden death of his first wife Sally, daughter of Rosamond *Lehmann, in 1958; *Finding Connections* (1990) is a travel autobiography.

KAVANAGH, Patrick (1905–67) Irish poet. His works include *Ploughman and Other Poems* (1936), *A Soul for Sale* (1947), *Tarry Flynn* (1948, a semi-autobiographical comic novel), and *Come Dance with Kitty Stobling* (1960). His best-known work is probably *The Great Hunger* (1942), a long cinematic poem contrasting the experience of its impoverished protagonist, Patrick Maguire with the idealizations of rural life in both the drama of *Abbey Theatre and the rhetoric of nationalist politicians. Kavanagh later repudiated the tragic pessimism of *The Great Hunger* in favour of the comic vision of his 1950s lyrics. A definitive *Collected Poems* appeared in 2004.

KAY, Jackie (1961–) Scottish poet, dramatist, and fiction writer. A version of her adoption at birth by Glaswegian parents is told in *The Adoption Papers* (1991), including the voice of the birth mother who remembers the absent Nigerian father. *Trumpet* (1998, novel) traces the revelation, after the death of the mixed race jazz musician Joss Moody, that 'he' was a woman, destabilizing racial and gender boundaries. *Why Don't You Stop Talking* (2002) and *Wish I Was Here* (2006) are collections of short stories. Her volumes of poetry, including *Other Lovers* (1993), *Off Colour* (1998), *Life Mask* (2005), *Darling* (2007), *Maw Broon Monologues* (2009), and *Red Dust Road* (2010), are witty and imaginatively empathetic. Her poetry and fiction for children includes the novel *Strawgirl* (2002).

KAYE-SMITH, Sheila (1887–1956) Novelist, whose *regional novels are precisely located, principally on the Kent-Sussex border, and include *Starbrace* (1909) and *Joanna Godden* (1921). The genre was satirized by Stella Gibbons in *Cold Comfort Farm* (1932).

KAZANTZAKIS, Nikos (1883–1957) Greek writer and philosopher, who studied in Paris under the philosopher Henri Bergson (1859–1941). Kazantzakis's prolific output includes essays, plays, poetry, novels, travel books, and translations. His massive *epic poem *The Odyssey: A Modern Sequel* (1938) offers contemporary reflections on the experiences of Odysseus; *The Last Temptation of Christ* (1951; filmed, Martin Scorsese, 1988) explores the humanity revealed in the ministry of Jesus. *Zorba the Greek* (1946; filmed 1964), Kazantzakis's best-known work, is the story of the friendship that develops between the uneducated but irrepressible Zorba, and the visiting writer and intellectual who employs him.

KEANE, Molly (1904–96) Novelist and playwright, born into a leisured Anglo-Irish world (her mother was the dialect poet 'Moira O'Neill'). At the age of 17 she wrote her first novel, choosing the pseudonym M. J. Farrell (after a public house) to hide her literary life from her sporting friends. Between 1928 and 1952 she published ten further novels, including *Devoted Ladies* (1934), *The Rising Tide* (1937), and *Two Days in Aragon* (1941). Her plays (written with John Perry, 1906–*c*.1994) include *Spring Meeting* (1938) and *Treasure Hunt* (1949). Chronicling the thrill of the chase, both sporting and sexual, her work is characterized by a detailed evocation of place. An underlying awareness of the cruelties, snobberies, and evasions of the decaying Anglo-Irish milieu is most notably articulated in *Good Behaviour* (1981), published under her own name. *Time after Time* (1983) and *Loving and Giving* (1988) followed.

KEATLEY, Charlotte (1960–) Playwright, best known for *My Mother Said I Never Should* (1987), a play that traces the changes in women's lives through four generations of the same family. The male family members never appear on stage, and the structure is non-chronological and non-linear.

KEATS, John (1795–1821) Poet, who began a translation of the *Aeneid* whilst still at school. His first efforts at writing poetry appear to date from 1814, and include an 'Imitation of Spenser'. In 1816 Keats was licensed to practise as an apothecary, but abandoned the profession for poetry; Keats's poems 'O Solitude' and 'On First Looking into Chapman's Homer' were published that year in Leigh *Hunt's *Examiner*. Keats's first volume of poems was published in March 1817, including 'I stood tiptoe', a precursor of *Endymion*, and 'Sleep and Poetry'; sales were meagre and it was attacked by John *Lockhart, who labelled Keats and his associates as members of the so-called *Cockney School, in *Blackwood's Magazine*. During the winter of 1817–18, Keats saw something of *Wordsworth and *Hazlitt, both of whom much influenced his thought and practice. *Endymion*, dedicated to Thomas *Chatterton, whom Keats greatly admired, was published in the spring of 1818. It was savagely reviewed by Lockhart in *Blackwood's* and in the *Quarterly Review*.

With his friend Charles Armitage Brown (1786–1842) Keats toured the Lakes, spent July and August in Scotland, and made a brief visit to Northern Ireland. He had travelled frequently in southern England but he had never before seen scenery of rugged grandeur. After his brother Tom's death in 1817, Keats moved into Brown's house in Hampstead, now known as Keats House. There he met Fanny *Brawne, with whom he fell deeply in love. September 1818 marked the beginning of what is sometimes referred to as his 'great year'; he began *Hyperion* in its first version, abandoning it a year later; he wrote, consecutively, *'The Eve of St Agnes', 'The Eve of St Mark', the 'Ode to Psyche', *'La Belle Dame sans Merci', *'Ode to a Nightingale', and probably at about the same time the *'Ode on a Grecian Urn', 'Ode on Melancholy', and 'Ode on Indolence'; *'Lamia Part I', 'Otho the Great' (in collaboration with Brown); the second version of *Hyperion*, called *The Fall of Hyperion*, *'To Autumn', and 'Lamia Part II'. During this year he became engaged to Fanny. In the winter of 1819 he began the unfinished 'The Cap and Bells', but he became increasingly ill with tuberculosis. His second volume of poems, *Lamia, Isabella, The Eve of St Agnes, and Other Poems*, was published in July 1820, and included, as well as the title poems, five odes, *Hyperion*, 'Fancy', and other works. The volume was generally well received, with criticism from *Blackwood's* much muted, but the sales were very slow. Shelley invited Keats to Italy and in September, after sorting out his copyrights and financial affairs, Keats set off with his friend Joseph Severn. They did not go to the Shelleys but settled in Rome, where Keats died in February 1821.

Keats has always been regarded as one of the principal figures in the *Romantic movement, and his stature as a poet has grown steadily through all changes of fashion. *Tennyson considered him the greatest poet of the 19th century, and Matthew *Arnold commended his 'intellectual and spiritual passion' for beauty. His letters, published in 1848 and 1878, have come to be regarded with almost the admiration given to his poetry. They include his central critical notions of the *egotistical sublime and *negative capability and were described by T. S. Eliot as 'certainly the most notable and most important ever written by any English poet'.

KEBLE, John (1792–1866) Churchman and poet; professor of poetry at Oxford, 1831–41. His sermon on national apostasy in 1833 was considered the start of the *Oxford Movement; he wrote nine of the *Tracts for the Times*. His immensely successful volume of sacred verse *The Christian Year*, published anonymously in 1827, was widely admired, not only by Tractarians, but also by *evangelical and *Broad Church readers; intended as a guide to devotion and a commentary on the *Book of *Common Prayer*, it shows the influence of George *Herbert and, in its feeling for the natural world, of William *Wordsworth. A second volume, *Lyra Innocentium*, followed in 1846. Charlotte Mary *Yonge was a pupil of his, and drew a vivid character sketch in *Musings over the Christian Year . . . with a Few Gleanings of Recollections of Keble* (1871). Keble College, Oxford, was founded in his memory in 1870.

KEILLER, Patrick (1950–) English filmmaker, he created a distinctive form of fictionalized *documentary in *London* (1994) and *Robinson in Space* (1997), which survey the changing face of, respectively, London and England, as seen by a jaundiced reincarnation of Daniel *Defoe's hero Robinson Crusoe.

Kells, Book of An 8th- to 9th-century manuscript of the Gospels, with prefaces, summaries, and canon tables. Written in the formal bookhand termed Irish majuscule, it has magnificent illustrations consisting of intricate patterns made up of abstract and animal forms. It was probably completed at Kells after the sack of Iona in 806. Collated by James *Ussher in 1621, it was presented to Trinity College, Dublin, after the *Restoration.

KELMAN, James (1946–) Novelist, short story writer, and dramatist, born in Glasgow, who left school at 15. The stories of *Not Not While the Giro* (1983) depict Scottish working-class life with terse humour and introduce the pared-back, multi-focal vernacular narrative style developed in the novels *The Busconductor Hines* (1984) and *A Chancer* (1985). *A Disaffection* (1989) offers a critique of the education system through its portrait of an alcoholic secondary teacher. *How Late It Was, How Late* (1994, *Booker Prize) caused outrage, both because of the novel's deployment of expletives and its sympathetic presentation of the alienation of its protagonist, an unemployed building worker and petty criminal. Other works include the stories in *Greyhound for Breakfast* (1987), *The Good Times* (1998), and *If It Is Your Life* (2010); *Hardie and Baird and Other Plays* (1991); and the novels *Translated Accounts* (2001), *You Have to Be Careful in the Land of the Free* (2004) (set respectively in an unnamed *dystopia and in America), and *Kieron Smith, Boy* (2008), which unsentimentally evokes the Glasgow of Kelman's childhood.

KEMP, Will (William) (c.1564–?1603) A comic actor and dancer, who acted in plays by *Shakespeare and Ben *Jonson. In 1599 he danced a morris dance from London to Norwich; his own account, *Kemp's Nine Days Wonder*, was published in 1600.

KEMPE, Margery (c.1373–c.1438) Mystic. She married John Kempe (c.1393) and had fourteen children, but abandoned conventional married life for religion, travelled throughout England, and went on pilgrimage to Jerusalem, Rome, Santiago de Compostela, and Wilsnack in Poland. The *Boke* that now bears her name was produced in collaboration with two scribes, and details her visions and social experiences, some aspects of which are explicitly authenticated by the scribe mediating the narrative. The *Boke* relates the reactions she provoked from various English clergy, resulting in a complex picture of religious life in England at this time.

KENDALL, May (1861–?1943) Satirist, poet, and essayist. She published a collection of satirical poems and essays entitled *That Very Mab*

(1885); a volume of poems, *Dreams to Sell* (1887); and a collection of stories, *Songs from Dreamland* (1894).

KENEALLY, Thomas (1935–) Australian novelist whose first novel was *The Place at Whitton* (1964). *Bring Larks and Heroes* (1967) and *Three Cheers for the Paraclete* (1968) both won the Miles Franklin Award. *The Survivor* (1969) and *A Dutiful Daughter* (1971) examine family relationships, the latter with an innovative second-person narrative. Historical themes unite *The Chant of Jimmie Blacksmith* (1972, filmed 1978); *Blood Red, Sister Rose* (1974), about *Joan of Arc; and *Confederates* (1979). War, notably the Second World War, recurs in novels ranging from *The Fear* (1965) to *The Widow and her Hero* (2007). Keneally's most celebrated work is *Schindler's Ark* (1982; *Schindler's List* in the USA and in Steven Spielberg's 1993 film), which tells of German industrialist Oskar Schindler, who risked his life to save Jews in Poland. Keneally's prolific later work includes the novels *The Playmaker* (1987), on a plan to stage George *Farquhar's *The Recruiting Officer* in a penal colony, which was itself adapted for stage by Timberlake *Wertenbaker as *Our Country's Good* (1988); *Woman of the Inner Sea* (1992); *A River Town* (1995), based on his grandfather's life; *The Tyrant's Novel* (2003), and the memoirs *Homebush Boy* (1995) and *Searching for Schindler* (2007). His travel writing includes *Now and in Time to Be: Ireland and the Irish* (1991), and *The Place Where Souls Are Born* (1992), on the American south-west.

Kenilworth A novel by Walter *Scott, published 1821. It celebrates the glories of the Elizabethan age and, despite many anachronisms, was very popular; published in the year of the coronation of George IV, the story of *Elizabeth I and her favourite Leicester and of the betrayal and murder of Leicester's wife Amy Robsart caught the national mood. *Shakespeare, *Spenser, and *Ralegh all appear, and the climax of the novel is the great pageant at Kenilworth in July 1575.

KENNEDY, A. L. (Alison Louise) (1965–) Scottish writer. Her bleak, pessimistic, but distinctive fiction includes both volumes of short stories, such as *Original Bliss* (1997), and novels like *So I Am Glad* (1995), *Everything You Need* (1999), and the well-received *Day* (2007).

KENNEDY, Walter (?1455–?1518) A Scottish poet from a powerful family, the rival (ostensibly, and probably in reality) of William *Dunbar in 'The *Flyting of Dunbar and

Kennedie' and mentioned by him in his 'Lament for the Makaris' as being on the point of death. The few poems by him that survive are in the Asloan and Bannatyne manuscripts and the Maitland Folio.

kenning A poetic compound made up of two or more nouns standing for another noun, occurring in ancient Germanic languages, notably Old Norse (Icelandic) and Old English. *Snorri Sturluson gives the authoritative discussion in his *Edda*. Strictly defined, it must be metaphorical, the poetic compound being literally distinct from its components. Thus, 'man' has been represented as 'tree-of-the-storm-of-Othinn': Othinn is god of battle and 'tree' (straight and upright) is a common element in 'person' kennings. 'Woman' is 'fir-tree-of-the-ember-of-the-wave': Gunnar throws the Nibelungs' treasure into the Rhine; the glowing ember in the water is gold, which this person (fir-tree) wears as decoration. Some Old English kennings are metonymic and thus not literally distinct: 'swan-road', 'whaleroad', and 'gannet's bath' (sea); 'voice-bearers' (people).

KERMODE, Sir Frank (1919–2010) Literary critic, he studied at the University of Liverpool, and served in the Royal Navy in the Second World War. He held a succession of academic posts resigning from his Professorship at Cambridge in 1982. His critical studies alternated between the English Renaissance—beginning with an edition of *The *Tempest* (1954)—and 20th-century literature, in which he has championed the works of Wallace *Stevens and Ford Madox *Ford. His most influential early books are *Romantic Image* (1957), which demonstrates continuities between late Romantic and early modernist uses of enigmatic symbols, and *The Sense of an Ending* (1967), which explores the ways in which narrative fiction makes sense of linear time. Through his editorship of the Fontana Modern Masters series of books on modern thinkers and his seminars on literary theory at University College London, he helped to inject fresh currents of European thought into literary studies in Britain. His later books include *The Classic* (1975), *The Genesis of Secrecy* (1979), *Essays on Fiction* (1983), *An Appetite for Poetry* (1989), *Shakespeare's Language* (2000), and a memoir, *Not Entitled* (1995). He was knighted in 1991.

KEROUAC, Jack (1922–69) American novelist, whose first novel, *The Town and the City* (1950), was written under the influence of Thomas *Wolfe. He achieved fame with *On the Road* (1957) where, thinly disguising himself as Sal Paradise, he describes his cross-county excursions with his friend Neal Cassady (1926–68; Dean Moriarty in the book). Written in a free-flowing confessional prose, the novel was composed on a continuous paper roll: see *On the Road: The Original Scroll* (2007), which restores deleted passages. The work became a classic of the *Beat movement. *The Dharma Bums* (1958) is based on his friendship with the poet Gary *Snyder. In his essays 'Essentials of Spontaneous Prose' (1953) and 'Belief & Technique for Modern Prose' (*Evergreen Review*, 1959), he outlined a philosophy of writing that refused all revision and was more akin to the free association and improvisation of jazz. He attempted to practise these principles in his poetry, including *Mexico City Blues* (1955). His later alcoholic decline alienated him from the group he helped to define.

KERR, Judith (1923–) Children's writer, born in Berlin; she fled to England via Switzerland and France in the 1930s. The story of her adjustment to life in Paris and London is told in the fictionalized autobiographical trilogy *Out of the Hitler Time* (1971–8), beginning with *When Hitler Stole Pink Rabbit*. Kerr is also known for her many picture books about Mog the cat and her family, and *The Tiger Who Came to Tea* (1968).

KESAVAN, Mukul See ANGLO-INDIAN LITERATURE.

KESEY, Ken (1935–2001) American novelist, who volunteered to participate in the CIA-backed MK-ULTRA programme of experimentation with LSD and other drugs at a Stanford hospital. This formed the basis for his first novel, *One Flew over the Cuckoo's Nest* (1962), which presents the mental ward of a hospital as a surreal form of prison. In 1964 Kesey joined with Neil Cassady (*see* KEROUAC, JACK) and other friends to travel round America in a school bus. These 'Merry Pranksters' are described in Tom *Wolfe's *The Electric Kool-Aid Acid Test* (1968). Kesey's later works include the miscellanies *Kesey's Garage Sale* (1972) and *Demon Box* (1986), as well as a screenplay, *The Further Inquiry* (1995).

KESSON, Jessie (1916–94) Née MacDonald, Scottish novelist and radio playwright, born in the Inverness workhouse and encouraged to write by Nan *Shepherd. Her work includes the novels *The White Bird Passes* (1958), *Glitter of Mica* (1963), and *Another Time, Another Place*

(1983, BBC film 1980); and *Where the Apple Ripens and Other Stories* (1985).

KEYES, Sidney (1922–43) Poet; he edited, with Michael Meyer (1921–2000), *Eight Oxford Poets* (1941), which contains some of his own work. His first collection was *The Iron Laurel* (1942). He joined the army that year; *The Cruel Solstice*, (1943, Hawthornden Prize, 1944) was published after his death in Tunisia on 29 April 1943. His *Collected Poems* (1945, rev. 1989) includes a memoir by Meyer.

Kidnapped and *Catriona* [Gaelic for Catherine and pronounced Catreena] A novel and its sequel by Robert Louis *Stevenson, published 1886 and 1893. The central incident in the story is the murder of Colin Campbell, the 'Red Fox' of Glenure, the king's factor on the forfeited estate of Ardshiel: this is a historical event. Young David Balfour, impoverished on the death of his father, goes for assistance to his uncle Ebenezer, a miserly villain who has illegally taken control of the Balfour estate. Having failed to murder David, Ebenezer has him kidnapped on a ship to be carried off to the Carolinas. On the voyage Alan Breck is picked up from a sinking boat. He is a *Jacobite who 'wearies for the heather and the deer'. The ship is wrecked on the coast of Mull, and David and Alan travel together. They witness the murder of Colin Campbell, and suspicion falls on them. After a perilous journey across the Highlands they escape across the Forth, and the novel ends with the defeat of Ebenezer and David's recovery of his inheritance. *Kidnapped* was a popular success, but *Catriona* was less well received. It is concerned with the unsuccessful attempt of David Balfour to secure the acquittal of James Stewart of the Glens, who is falsely accused, from political motives, of the murder of Colin Campbell; with the escape of Alan Breck to the Continent; and with David's love affair with Catriona Drummond, daughter of the renegade James More.

KIERKEGAARD, Søren Aabye (1813–55) Danish philosopher and theologian. Although he is now chiefly remembered as having initiated existentialist trends in modern philosophy (e.g. *Concluding Unscientific Postscript*, trans. W. Lowrie and D. F. Swenson, 1941), he also wrote on religious, psychological, or literary subjects (e.g. *The Concept of Dread* and *Fear and Trembling*, both trans. W. Lowrie, 1944). His satirical gifts are demonstrated in his essay on *The Present Age* (trans. A. Dru, 1962), reminiscent of Thomas *Carlyle's polemics. His insistence on personal decision, unmediated by artificial reasoning, lay at the root of his rejection of *Hegel. Some of Kierkegaard's most penetrating psychological observations occur in his descriptions of the 'leap of faith' and in his analyses of the state of 'dread' (*Angst*) which precedes and accompanies it. The emphasis on freedom as a condition which both fascinates and repels links his philosophical ideas and the doctrines of his existentialist successors. His ideas have influenced literary figures as diverse as W. H. *Auden, Franz *Kafka, Rainer Maria Rilke, and John *Updike. *See* EXISTENTIALISM.

KILLIGREW, Thomas, the elder (1612–83) Playwright and theatre manager. He was page to Charles I; groom of the bedchamber and a favourite companion of Charles II. With Sir William *D'Avenant he held the monopoly of acting in *Restoration London. He built a playhouse on the site of the present Theatre Royal Drury Lane, in 1663, and was master of the revels in 1679. His most popular play, *The Parson's Wedding*, a bawdy farcical comedy, was first performed 1640/41 and printed in 1664 with his other plays, which include *Thomaso, or The Wanderer* (in two parts), on which Aphra *Behn based her successful adaptation *The Rover*.

Killing No Murder A pamphlet ironically dedicated to Oliver Cromwell, which advocates his assassination. It was written by the Leveller Edward Sexby (d. 1658) and printed in 1657 in the Netherlands. The name on the title page is that of William Allen, who had been one of Cromwell's Ironsides.

KILNER, Dorothy (1755–1836) and **Mary Ann** (1753–1831) Sisters-in-law who wrote popular children's stories, often using an anthropomorphized animal or object as narrator, as in Dorothy's *Life and Perambulation of a Mouse* (c.1783) and Mary Ann's *The Adventures of a Pin-Cushion* (c.1780).

KILROY, Thomas (1934–) Irish playwright, whose plays include *Double Cross* (1986), a study of the mutually mirroring careers of two Irish Catholics, Brendan Bracken, Winston Churchill's wartime minister of information, and William Joyce, the Nazi propagandist ('Lord Haw-Haw'); *The Secret Fall of Constance Wilde* (1997); *The Shape of Metal* (2003); and resourceful Irish domestications of Anton Chekhov (*The Seagull*, 1981) and Henrik Ibsen (*Ghosts*, 1989). *The Big Chapel* (1971, novel) examines violent contention between liberal and conservative Catholics in post-Famine rural Kilkenny.

KILVERT, Francis (1840–79) Diarist, vicar of Bredwardine, Herefordshire, from 1877. He is remembered for his lively and humane diary (3 vols, 1938–40, ed. William *Plomer) kept with no thought of publication, from 1870 until his death. His wife, whom he married only five weeks before his death, destroyed large portions of it, but enough is left to provide a full portrait of the author and the remote and beautiful region of the Welsh borders where he lived and worked. Two encounters of great importance to him were with the niece of *Wordsworth, who told him that her uncle 'could not bear the act of writing', and with William *Barnes.

Kim A novel by Rudyard *Kipling, published 1901. Kimball O'Hara, the orphaned son of a sergeant in an Irish regiment, spends his childhood as a vagabond in Lahore, until he meets an old lama from Tibet and accompanies him in his travels. He falls into the hands of his father's old regiment, is adopted, and sent to school, resuming his wanderings in his holidays. Colonel Creighton of the Ethnological Survey notices his aptitude for secret service ('the Great Game'), and he embarks on the work under the directions of the native agent Hurree Babu. While still a boy he distinguishes himself by capturing the papers of a couple of Russian spies in the Himalayas. The book presents a vivid picture of India, its teeming populations and diverse religions, and the life of the bazaars and the road.

KINCAID, Jamaica (1949–) Novelist and short story writer, born Elaine Potter Richardson in Antigua. *At the Bottom of the River* (1983) is a volume of short stories; her novels include *Annie John* (1985), set in Antigua, which explores the fierce vicissitudes of a daughter's love for her mother and her homeland. *Lucy* (1990) about a girl leaving Antigua for America, and *The Autobiography of my Mother* (1996), a first-person narrative in which a woman looks back on her troubled life. *A Small Place* (1988) is a scintillatingly savage attack on Western tourism in Antigua. Non-fictional work includes *My Garden (Book)*, a series of meditations on gardening, and *Talk Stories* (2001), a collection of Kincaid's pieces for *New Yorker*'s 'Talk of the Town' (1978–83).

Kind Heart's Dream A pamphlet by Henry *Chettle, registered December 1592, noteworthy for its allusion to William *Shakespeare.

Kind of Loving, A A novel by Stan *Barstow.

KING, Francis Henry (1923–2011) Prolific novelist, short story writer, and critic, who published his first three novels while still an undergraduate. His work for the British Council, mainly in Italy, Greece, and Japan, provided settings for several of his novels, notably *The Dividing Stream* (1951), *The Firewalkers* (1956), and *The Custom House* (1961). His work is marked by cool, ironic detachment and a close analysis of human motivation, particularly in some of its less admirable aspects. *A Domestic Animal* (1970) was the subject of a libel action, itself turned to good fictional account in *The Action* (1978). Other compelling novels include *Act of Darkness* (1983), based on the Constance Kent murder case, but perhaps his finest achievements are his volumes of short stories, *The Brighton Belle* (1968) and *Hard Feelings* (1976). *Yesterday Came Suddenly* (1993) is an autobiography.

KING, Henry (1592–1669) Poet, of Chichester, and the friend of John *Donne and Izaak *Walton. He published poems sacred and profane, an unauthorized volume appearing in 1657. His best-known poem is 'An Exequy to his Matchless Never to be Forgotten Friend', written for his wife Anne.

KING, Stephen (1947–) American *horror and *fantasy writer, born in Maine, the location for much of his fiction. Initially, after *Carrie* (1974), he wrote as Richard Bachman—a clash of identities exploited in *The Dark Half* (1989). In *The Stand* (1978; as miniseries by Marvel Comics 2008–) he shows ordinary Americans in physical and metaphysical confrontation; other themes include relationships between writers and audiences (*Misery*, 1987), and childhood friendships ('The Body', 1982, filmed as *Stand by Me*, 1986). The final volumes of the 'Dark Tower' sequence (1982–2004; as miniseries by Marvel Comics 2007–), set in a world built from the myths of popular culture, are touched by reflections on a near-fatal accident in 1999. King has subsequently published some works solely in digital format, for example *The Plant* (2000, serialized online) and *Ur* (2009, for Amazon Kindle e-book reader).

KING, William (1663–1712) writer of burlesques, satires, and light verse, much of which was published anonymously. In his *Dialogues of the Dead* (1699) he joined Charles Boyle (1674–1731) in the attack on Richard *Bentley (*see* BATTLE OF THE BOOKS).

k

King Alisaunder An early 14th-century romance in 8,034 lines of short couplets, written in a lively verse and flexible metre. It is based on a legend according to which *Alexander the Great was not the son of Philip of Macedon but of the Egyptian king Nectanabus, who tricked Philip's wife by magic into sleeping with him. The poem relates the events of his life, including his perils and conquests in the Far East (describing the geography and wonders of those regions), and his death by poison.

King and No King, A A tragicomedy by Francis *Beaumont and John *Fletcher (probably largely by Beaumont), performed 1611, printed 1619; it was one of their most successful dramas.

Arbaces, king of Iberia, has defeated Tigranes, king of Armenia, in single combat, concluding a long war. The two kings subsequently both fall in love with Panthea, supposed sister of Arbaces. In the last act it is revealed that Arbaces is the son of Gobrias, the lord protector of the kingdom, and therefore 'no king', and he and Panthea, the true queen of Iberia, marry. Tigranes is reunited with his Armenian love, Spaconia. Comic relief throughout is provided by Bessus, a cowardly captain in Arbaces' army, reminiscent of Paroles in *All's Well That Ends Well.

King Horn An early surviving English verse romance in 1,545 lines, dating from the late 13th century. The story is substantially the same as that of the later *Horn Childe and the romance exemplifies many traditional motifs typical of the genre.

Kingis Quair, The ('The King's Book') A poem of 1,379 lines, arranged in 197 stanzas of 'lynis sevin', or *rhyme royal (so called because of its employment in this king's poem, but previously used in Chaucer's *Troilus and Criseyde and elsewhere). It is attributed to *James I of Scotland and may have been written about the time of his marriage (1424) to Lady Joan Beaufort, the poem's heroine. The poem survives in a single manuscript in the Bodleian Library. The author acknowledges the authority of both *Chaucer and *Gower. *Boethius' Consolation of Philosophy is also an important influence.

King John A historical drama written in a first version before 1536, by John *Bale.

King John, The Life and Death of A historical play by *Shakespeare, probably based on an anonymous play, The Troublesome Reign of John King of England (1591), though the latter may be a derivative rather than a source. Shakespeare's play was probably written about 1596. It was first printed in the *folio of 1623. The play, with some departures from historical accuracy, deals with events in King John's reign, principally with the tragedy of young Arthur, ending with the death of John at Swinstead Abbey. It is striking that it makes no mention of Magna Carta.

KINGLAKE, Alexander William (1809–91) Author of Eōthen: or Traces of Travel Brought Home from the East, published anonymously in 1844, an account of a journey undertaken in the Middle East some ten years earlier. It gives a lively description of his travels, recording his reactions to, for example, the desert, the Holy Land, an encounter with Lady Hester *Stanhope, and the plague in Cairo. The book was an instant success, but has been criticized for Kinglake's often sweeping dismissals of Middle Eastern culture. He later produced a history of the Crimean War (1863–87), having accompanied the British army to the Crimea in 1854.

King Lear A tragedy by *Shakespeare, dating from 1604–5, performed at court 1606. The quarto printed in 1608 (reprinted 1619) is now thought to have been badly printed from Shakespeare's original manuscript, and the text of the first *folio (1623) appears to represent a revision from a few years later. The play's sources include a chronicle play, King Leir (performed 1594, printed 1605), the Chronicles of *Holinshed, and A *Mirror for Magistrates. The Gloucester sub-plot derives from Sidney's *Arcadia.

Lear, king of Britain, a petulant and unwise old man, has three daughters: Goneril, wife of the duke of Albany; Regan, wife of the duke of Cornwall; and Cordelia, for whom the king of France and duke of Burgundy are suitors. Intending to divide his kingdom among his daughters according to their fondness for him, he demands professions of love from them. Goneril and Regan claim extravagant affection, and each receives one-third of the kingdom. Cordelia, disgusted with their hollow flattery, says she loves him according to her duty, neither more nor less. Infuriated, Lear divides her portion between his other daughters, with the condition that he shall be maintained by each daughter in turn, with 100 knights. Burgundy withdraws his suit for Cordelia, and the king of France accepts her without dowry. The earl of Kent, taking her part, is banished. Goneril and Regan reveal their heartless character, until, enraged, Lear rushes out of doors in a storm. The earl of Gloucester shows pity for the old king, and is suspected of being in league with the French, who have landed in England. His eyes are put out by Cornwall, who receives a death-wound in the struggle. Gloucester has been turned against his son Edgar by Edmund, Edgar's illegitimate brother. Edgar takes the disguise of a lunatic beggar (Tom o'Bedlam), and tends his father till the latter's death. Lear, whom rage and ill treatment have driven mad, is conveyed to Dover by the faithful Kent in disguise, where Cordelia receives him. Meanwhile Goneril and Regan have both turned their affections to Edmund. Embittered by this rivalry, Goneril poisons Regan, and takes her own life. The English forces under Edmund and Albany defeat the French, and Lear and Cordelia are imprisoned. Edmund is fatally wounded by Edgar in a duel; his last-minute reprieve for Lear and Cordelia comes too late to save Cordelia's life, and she is hanged. Lear dies from grief. Kent, Albany (who took no part in Goneril's cruel treatment of Lear), and Edgar are left to restore order, and Edgar accepts responsibility for the kingdom.

KINGSLEY, Charles (1819–75) Novelist and social reformer, rector of Eversley in Hampshire from 1844. His blank verse drama *The Saint's Tragedy*, (1848) treats the conflict between natural sexuality and asceticism, a persistent theme in his work. Influenced by Frederick Denison Maurice and the writings of Thomas *Carlyle, he was seriously interested in the movement for social reform, while condemning the violent policies of the *Chartists. He contributed, over the signature 'Parson Lot', to *Politics for the People* in 1848, and to its successor, *The Christian Socialist*, in 1850–51.

His novels *Yeast*, serialized in *Fraser's Magazine* in 1848, and published in book form in 1851, and *Alton Locke* (1850) are reforming novels, concerned with the sufferings of the working classes. *Hypatia, or New Foes with Old Faces*, published in *Fraser's* in 1851 and in book form in 1853, is set in 5th-century Alexandria; it exalts the Greek Neoplatonic philosopher Hypatia who was torn to pieces in AD 415 by a mob of infuriated Christians, and condemns the ignorant fanaticism of the Alexandrian monks. J. H. *Newman's *Callista* was written in part to correct its hostile portrait of the early church. *Westward Ho!* (1855), a patriotic response to the Crimean War, shocked some readers with its vehement anti-Catholicism and bloodthirsty narrative, but delighted more. *Two Years Ago* (1857) returns to the theme of social reform and *Hereward the Wake* (1866) is a historical novel based on the exploits of the legendary outlaw,

who attempts to save England from the Normans.

Other works include *The Heroes* (1856), in which he tells for young readers the stories of Perseus, Theseus, and the Argonauts, and *The *Water-Babies* (1863), also for the young. His songs and ballads, including 'The Sands of Dee', remained popular, and some of his lines, such as 'Be Good, sweet maid, and let who can be clever' (quoted in *Two Years Ago*) became proverbial. Kingsley became a respected public figure, but he remained the centre of controversy and had a notable confrontation with Newman, who responded with his *Apologia*, and was widely considered the victor of the exchange.

Kingsley was a keen sportsman who was tender to animals, a champion of the working man who despised black people, a muscular Christian who wrote much (like his friend Thomas *Hughes) of the virtues of 'manliness' and who nevertheless held an unusually explicit physical passion for his wife, an admirer of physical prowess who himself suffered from an acute stammer and occasional nervous breakdowns. His complex personality and vigorous fiction represent some of the central paradoxes of his age.

KINGSLEY, Henry (1830–76) Novelist, younger brother of Charles *Kingsley. From 1853 to 1858 he was in Australia, at the gold diggings and as a trooper in the Sydney Mounted Police, experiences which inspired two of his best novels, *Geoffry Hamlyn* (1859) and *The Hillyars and the Burtons* (1865). After his return to England he was editor of the *Edinburgh Daily Review*, and was its correspondent at the Franco-Prussian War.

Ravenshoe (1862), the best known of his 21 books, is a story of inheritance in a Roman Catholic family in Devon, and includes Crimean War scenes. Kingsley's strongest novels contain lively descriptions of landscape in England and Australia, engrossing accounts of storms and cyclones, attacks and alarms, and well-observed character sketches.

KINGSLEY, Mary Henrietta (1862–1900) Niece of Charles *Kingsley. Influenced by the ethnological work of her father, she made her first journey to West Africa in 1893, returning in 1894. *Travels in West Africa* (1897) is a lively account of her travels and ethnological researches, written in an engaging and witty style, including positive views of the people and landscape, and recommending to British rulers a closer understanding of African culture. *West African Studies* appeared in 1899.

KING-SMITH, Dick (1922-2011) Best-selling British author of *animal stories. His stories combine realism with anthropomorphism (his animals talk), celebrating animals' ingenuity and the nature of language. *The Sheep-Pig* (1983) was filmed as *Babe* (1995).

King Solomon's Mines A novel by Henry Rider *Haggard, published in 1885. It describes an expedition into uncharted regions of Africa, led by Sir Henry Curtis, who is hoping to find his brother, who was lost as he searched for the legendary mines of King Solomon. Captain John Good, the celebrated hunter Allan Quatermain, and a dignified black man, Umbopa, make up the rest of the party. Tightly constructed and vigorously written, the book became an instant best-seller, and has been filmed several times. It reveals complex thinking on issues of race, gender, adventure, and empire.

KINGSTON, Maxine Hong (1940-) Academic and writer, born in California to Chinese immigrant parents. Her book *The Woman Warrior: Memoir of a Girlhood among Ghosts* (1976) mixes memoir and storytelling and was followed by *China Men* (1980). Her book *The Fifth Book of Peace* (2003) reflects her lifelong commitment to pacifism. *I Love a Broad Margin to My Life* (2011) reflects on her earlier work; the title alludes to Henry David *Thoreau.

KINSELLA, Thomas (1928-) Irish poet and translator. Kinsella's grave, elegant work from *Another September* (1958) to *Nightwalker and Other Poems* (1968) was widely hailed as the most ambitious Irish poetry since the death of W. B. *Yeats. Under the influence of Jungian psychology and American poetry, notably that of Ezra *Pound, he produced a series of elaborately interconnected free verse meditations on origins, growth, memory, and decay, found in *New Poems 1973, One and Other Poems* (1979), and *Blood and Family* (1988). His translations include *The Táin* (1968) (*see* TÁIN-BÓ-CUAILNGE) and his dual language *An Duanaire: Poems of the Dispossessed* (1981, with Seán Ó Tuama). Kinsella's work subsequent to *Collected Poems* (2001) includes *Marginal Economy* (2006) and *Man of War* (2007).

KIPLING, Rudyard (1865-1936) Writer, born in Bombay (Mumbai), but brought to England in 1871; his unhappy separation from his parents is recalled in 'Baa, Baa, Black Sheep' (1888, story) and *The Light That Failed* (1890, novel). His attendance at the United Services College, Westward Ho! is depicted in his schoolboy tales *Stalky & Co.* (1899). From 1882 to 1889 Kipling worked as a journalist in India; many of his early poems and stories were originally published in newspapers or for the Indian Railway Library, and were later collected under various titles, including *Departmental Ditties* (1886), *Plain Tales from the Hills* (1888), *Soldiers Three* (1890), and *Wee Willie Winkie* (1890). In 1889 he came to London, where he achieved instant literary celebrity, aided by W. E. *Henley's publication in his *Scots Observer* of many of the poems later collected as *Barrack-Room Ballads* (1892). In 1892 he married Caroline Balestier, sister of his American agent Charles Balestier (1861-91); the Kiplings lived in Vermont until 1896, when they returned to England, settling finally at 'Bateman's' in Sussex in 1902. Widely regarded as unofficial poet laureate, Kipling refused many honours; in 1907 he was the first English writer to receive the *Nobel Prize.

Kipling's output was vast and varied. His early tales of the Raj, praised for their cynical realism, were compared to those of *Maupassant; his poetry of empire, for example 'Recessional', written for Jubilee Day 1897, was acclaimed for catching the mood of the moment, but he was increasingly accused of vulgarity and jingoism in *aesthetic and anti-imperialist circles. Kipling retained his popularity with the common soldier and reader, and his verse has added many phrases to the language (including 'the white man's burden'). His fluent versification has powerful echoes of *hymns and *ballads, and he was noted for his use of colloquial speech in both prose and verse. His most uncontroversial achievements are perhaps his tales for children (principally *The *Jungle Book*, 1894; *Just So Stories*, 1902; *Puck of Pook's Hill*, 1906; and *Rewards and Fairies*, 1910) and his picaresque novel of India *Kim. His autobiographical fragment *Something of Myself* was published in 1937.

KIRKUP, James (1918-2009) Poet, playwright, translator, and travel writer. His volumes of poetry include *A Correct Compassion* (1952), whose title poem celebrates the precision of a surgical operation, *The Descent into the Cave* (1957), *Paper Windows* (1968), *A Bewick Bestiary* (1971), and *Marsden Bay* (2008). In 1977 his poem 'The Love that Dares to Speak its Name' (which deals with the Roman centurion's homosexual fantasy about the dead Christ) became the subject of the first prosecution for blasphemous libel for over 50 years, and as a result the editor of *Gay News*, the periodical which published the poem, was fined and given a suspended prison sentence. Kirkup's

The Only Child (1957) is an evocative account of his working-class northern childhood; *A Poet Could Not But Be Gay*, 1991 and *Me All Over*, 1993 are very frank memoirs detailing his literary and homosexual adventures. He has also published many books on Japan, and translated works by Friedrich *Dürrenmatt, Henrik *Ibsen (with Christopher *Fry), Paul *Valéry, and others.

Kit-Cat Club Founded in the early 18th century by leading Whigs, and involving writers such as Richard *Steele, Joseph *Addison, William *Congreve, Sir Samuel *Garth, and Sir John *Vanbrugh. It originally met at the tavern kept by Christopher Cat, and subsequently at the publisher Jacob *Tonson's house at Barn Elms, where Sir Godfrey Kneller's portraits of the members were displayed.

kitchen sink drama A term applied in the late 1950s to the plays of writers such as Arnold *Wesker, Shelagh *Delaney, and John *Osborne, which portrayed working-class or lower-middle-class life, with an emphasis on domestic realism. Kenneth *Tynan was a principal advocate of this new group of writers.

KLEIST, Heinrich von (1777–1811) German poet, dramatist, essayist, and writer of novellas. Unrecognized in his lifetime, Kleist is best known in Britain for his dramas *Prinz Friedrich von Homburg* (1821), the play which inaugurated Manchester's Royal Exchange Theatre in 1976, and the comedy *Der zerbrochne Krug* (1811: *The Broken Jug*), versions of which have been made by John *Banville and Blake *Morrison. David *Constantine published an annotated translation of Kleist's best-known plays, stories, and essays as *Selected Writings* (1997). The essay *Über das Marionettentheater* (1810: *On Marionette Theatre*), made a profound impression on Philip *Pullman.

KLEMPERER, Victor (1881–1960) Born to a Jewish family, he kept a diary from 1933 (published 1995), in which he bore witness to the daily humiliation and terror of life for Jews in Nazi Germany.

Knickerbocker Magazine (1833–65) Founded in New York City, its contributors included James Fenimore *Cooper, Washington *Irving, and Henry Wadsworth *Longfellow.

KNIGHT, William Payne *See* PICTURESQUE.

Knight of the Burning Pestle, The A comedy now thought to be the unaided work of Francis *Beaumont, but formerly generally attributed to Beaumont and John *Fletcher; it was probably performed 1607–8, and was printed (anonymously) 1613. The most successful of Beaumont's plays, it is a high-spirited comedy of manners. It has clear echoes of *Don Quixote*, and satirizes the middle-class taste for improbable romances such as *Palmerin of England*, and fabulous and patriotic plays such as Thomas *Heywood's *The Four Prentices of London* and *The Travels of the Three English Brothers* by John *Day, William *Rowley, and George Wilkins.

It takes the form of a play-within-a-play: a grocer and his wife, members of an audience about to watch a drama called *The London Merchant*, interrupt the prologue to insist that their apprentice Rafe have a part. He therefore becomes a Grocer Errant, with a Burning Pestle portrayed on his shield, and undertakes various absurd adventures, including the release of patients held captive by a barber, Barbarossa. These are interspersed with the real plot, in which Jasper, a merchant's apprentice, woos, and after much opposition wins, his master's daughter Luce.

'Knight's Tale, The' *See* CANTERBURY TALES, 1.

KNOWLES, James Sheridan (1784–1862) Described by the *Edinburgh Review* in 1833 as 'the most successful dramatist of the day'. His *Virginius* was produced at Covent Garden in 1820; *Caius Gracchus* in 1823 (1815 Belfast); *William Tell* in 1825. His greatest success was *The Hunchback*, produced in 1832; *The Wife*, with prologue and epilogue by Charles *Lamb, followed in 1833, and in 1837 his highly successful *The Love Chase*. He was the recipient of many of the letters in William *Hazlitt's *Liber Amoris*.

KNOX, John (*c.*1514–1572) Scottish religious reformer. He began preaching for the reformed religion at St Andrews in 1547 and became chaplain to Edward VI in 1551. He left England in 1554 after the accession of Mary Tudor. He met *Calvin at Geneva, and was pastor of the English congregation at Frankfurt am Main, 1554–5. He lived in Geneva from 1556, finally returning home as leader of the reformers in 1559. In 1558 he published his *First Blast of the Trumpet against the Monstrous Regiment of Women* ('Regiment' having the older sense of 'rule, magisterial authority' and referring to the English reign of Mary Tudor and the Scottish regency of Mary of Guise). The *First Book of*

Discipline (1559), of which Knox was part-author, advocated a national system of education for Scotland ranging from a school in every parish to the three universities. His *Treatise on Predestination* was published in 1560. His *History of the Reformation in Scotland* (1587) contains a dramatic account of the return of Mary Queen of Scots to Scotland, of his interviews with her, and of his fierce denunciations from the pulpit of St Giles's Cathedral in Edinburgh.

KNOX, Ronald (1888–1957) Writer and Roman Catholic priest; *A Spiritual Aeneid* (1918) describes his conversion. Knox produced many theological works, published a new translation of the Bible (1945–9), and acquired a wide reputation as journalist and broadcaster. He also wrote six detective stories, including *The Viaduct Murder* (1926) and *Double Cross Purposes* (1937). *Let Dons Delight* (1939), a work for which he himself had a particular affection, uses a dream framework to describe, through conversations in an imaginary Oxford senior common room at 50-year intervals, the process of specialization and fragmentation that he saw as leading to the loss of a common culture.

KOESTLER, Arthur (1905–83) Writer, born in Budapest; in 1931 he joined the Communist Party (he left it in 1938) and travelled in the Soviet Union. He was imprisoned under Franco during the Spanish Civil War. After his release he came to England, and became a British citizen in 1948. His publications include *Spanish Testament* (1937); *Darkness at Noon* 1940; *Scum of the Earth* (1941), based on his experiences in a French concentration camp; *Arrival and Departure* (1943); *The Yogi and the Commissar* (1945); and *Thieves in the Night* (1946). His later work includes *The Ghost in the Machine* (1967), which reflected his growing interest in parapsychology, and two volumes of autobiography, *Arrow in the Blue* (1952) and *The Invisible Writing* (1954).

KORDA, Sir Alexander (Sándor László Kellner) (1893–1956) Film director and producer, he worked in Budapest 1914–19, then in Vienna and Berlin, before working in Hollywood from 1927 to 1930. Returning to Europe, Korda settled in London. *The Private Life of Henry VIII* (1933) set the pattern for Korda's shrewd populism as a producer. Spectacular adaptations of H. G. *Wells's *Things to Come* and *The Man Who Could Work Miracles* followed, together with three outings for Baroness *Orczy's Scarlet Pimpernel, and a cycle of 'imperial' films that included Edgar *Wallace's

Sanders of the River (1935) and A. E. W. *Mason's *The Four Feathers* (1939).

KOSINSKI, Jerzy (1933–91) Polish-American novelist, born Josek Lewinkopf in Łódż, who emigrated to America in 1957. His first novel, *The Painted Bird* (1965), was a surreal account of a young boy's experience of the Second World War, later charged with plagiarism. *Being There* (1971) was made into a film (1979) starring Peter Sellers. His essays are collected in *Passing By* (1992). He committed suicide in 1991.

'Kraken, The' A short poem by Alfred *Tennyson, published in *Poems, Chiefly Lyrical* (1830). It describes the mythical sea monster mentioned in Pontoppidan's *Natural History of Norway* (1755), sleeping in the depths of the sea 'his ancient, dreamless, uninvaded sleep', and waiting only to rise and die.

KRISTEVA, Julia (1941–) Bulgarian critical theorist, psychoanalyst, and writer. She moved to Paris in 1966, and quickly gravitated towards the research groups led by Roland *Barthes. She made a substantial contribution to contemporary thinking about the relationship between language, subjectivity, and desire. Her early essays, collected in *Séméiotiké: recherches pour une sémanalyse* (1969: *Desire in Language: A Semiotic Approach to Literature and Art*, 1980), brought the work of Mikhail *Bakhtin to the attention of a Western audience. Her engagement with *Lacanian psychoanalysis in works such as *La Révolution du langage poétique* (1974: *Revolution in Poetic Language*) influenced her account of *modernist writing, including that of James *Joyce, which traces its disruptiveness to the collision between the pre-linguistic libidinal energy of the individual, and the linguistic structures into which that energy must be channelled. In 1990, Kristeva published her first novel, *Les Samouraïs* (*The Samurai*), a portrait of the Parisian intelligentsia which can be seen as a response or sequel to *Les Mandarins*, Simone de *Beauvoir's account of the intellectual scene in Liberation Paris.

'Kubla Khan: A Vision in a Dream' A poem by Samuel Taylor *Coleridge, published 1816. In 1797, Coleridge took opium and fell asleep when reading a passage in *Purchas his Pilgrimage* (*see* PURCHAS, SAMUEL) relating to the Khan Kubla and the palace that he commanded to be built. He claimed that on awaking he was conscious of having composed in his sleep two or three hundred lines on this theme, and eagerly began to set down the lines that form this fragment. He was then unfortunately interrupted by 'a person...from Porlock', and, on returning to his task an hour later, found that almost the entire remainder of the poem had slipped from his memory. The poem consists of a series of potent visionary images, suggesting themes of eternity and change. Alph, the sacred river, flung up in a tremendous fountain, connects Khan's 'stately pleasure dome', great caverns, and the 'sunless sea'. Within the gardens of the pleasure dome are growth and sunlight and colour. There are hints of death and war, the vision of a damsel with a dulcimer, and of the frenzy of the poet who has drunk 'the milk of Paradise'. Coleridge thought the poem a 'psychological curiosity' and vigorously defended poetic images 'just on the vestibule[s] of Consciousness'.

KUNDERA, Milan (1929–) Czech novelist, who taught at the Institute for Advanced Cinematographic Studies in Prague. He lost his post after the Russian invasion in 1968, and in 1975 settled in Paris. His first novel was *Zert* (1967; *The Joke*, trans. 1969). His other novels include *The Farewell Party* (1972; trans. 1977) and *The Book of Laughter and Forgetting* (1979; French 1979; English 1980), a semi-fictional, semi-autobiographical evocation of the cultural, political, and sexual life of post-war Europe, seen partly through Kundera's own eyes, partly through those of several of the 'two or three new fictional characters baptized on earth every second'. Other novels include *Life is Elsewhere* (1973; French 1973; English 1986), and *The Unbearable Lightness of Being* (1985; French 1984; English 1985), a classic of *magic realism. *Laughable Loves* (1969; trans. 1974) is a collection of stories. From 1993, he has published in French rather than Czech. Recent fiction includes *La Lenteur* (1993; *Slowness*, 1995), *L'Identité* (1997; *Identity*, 1998), and *Ignorance* (2000; trans. 2002).

KUPPNER, Frank (1951–) Scottish poet, whose collections include *A Bad Day for the Sung Dynasty* (1984), *Ridiculous! Absurd! Disgusting!* (1989), and *A God's Breakfast* (2004). *A Concussed History of Scotland* (1990) and *Something Very Like Murder* (1994) are radically different exercises in prose.

KUREISHI, Hanif (1954–) CBE, playwright, novelist, and screenwriter. His screenplays include *My Beautiful Laundrette* (1986), *Sammy and Rosie Get Laid* (1987), *The Mother* (2003), and *Venus* (2006). His first novel, *The Buddha of Suburbia* (1990, adapted for television in 1993), is narrated by the bisexual Karim Amir, and offers a comic panorama of multicultural London life, with sex, party-going, and yoga. He wrote and directed the film *London Kills Me* (1991), set in west London. Other works include *The Black Album* (novel, 1995; adapted for stage, 2009), and *Love in a Blue Time* (short stories, 1997). The film *My Son the Fanatic* (1998), based on one of these stories, portrays the conflict between a liberal northern immigrant taxi-driver and his fundamentalist son. *Intimacy* (1998), a confessional novella narrated by a man who leaves his partner and sons, as Kureishi had done, was filmed by Patrice Chereau in 2001.

KYD (Kid), Thomas (1558–94) Dramatist, who wrote (now lost) plays for the Queen's Men, c.1583–5. He was associated with Christopher *Marlowe, whose 'atheistical' writings led to Kyd's suffering a period of torture and imprisonment in 1593. His *Spanish Tragedy* (c.1587) was published anonymously in 1592. The only work published under his name was a translation of Robert Garnier's *Cornelia* (1594), reissued in 1595 as *Pompey the Great, his Faire Cornelia's Tragedy. The First Part of Hieronimo* (printed 1605) is probably a *burlesque adaptation of a fore-piece to *The Spanish Tragedy*. Other works Kyd is likely to have written are a lost pre-Shakespearian play on the subject of Hamlet, *The Householder's Philosophy* (a prose translation from *Tasso), and *The Tragedy of Solyman and Perseda* (printed 1592).

'La Belle Dame sans Merci' A ballad by John *Keats, written 1819, published 1820, which describes a knight fatally enthralled by an elfin woman. It was much admired by the *Pre-Raphaelites, and William *Morris asserted that 'it was the germ from which all the poetry of his group had sprung'.

La Belle Dame sans mercy (1424) is the title of a poem by Alain Chartier; its translation into English (*c.*1526) was attributed at one time to *Chaucer, but is now thought to be the work of Sir Richard Ros.

LACAN, Jacques (1901–81) French psychoanalyst who reformulated *Freudian models of the unconscious and underlined the fundamental role played by language in the formation of human identity. For Lacan, humans are defined and driven principally by desire. He explores the consequences for the psyche when it is incorporated into the 'symbolic order', the pre-existing social structures which are mediated for the most part by language, and desire becomes subject to regulation as a result. Learning to speak is at once a necessity and a tragedy for Lacan, as it permits the socialization of the infant at the cost of an irredeemable sense of lack, which we try to mask by investing in the domain of the 'imaginary', a mis-recognition of the self as unified and stable. Lacan's rethinking of identity in terms of lack and instability has had a substantial impact on disciplines across the humanities and social sciences, including political science, film studies, and queer theory. However, it has also been subject to extensive critique, not least from feminist scholars such as Luce *Irigaray, who have taken issue with his account of female sexuality and desire.

Lady Audley's Secret A *sensation novel by Mary *Braddon, published in 1862. The beautiful but mysterious Lucy Graham is newly married to Sir Michael, after having worked as a governess. Sir Michael's nephew Robert Audley begins to suspect Lucy after the sudden and unexplained disappearance of his friend George Talboys, who has been searching for his wife Helen after returning from a long absence in Australia. His investigations reveal that Helen and Lucy are one and the same woman. Lady Audley's increasingly desperate and wholly unscrupulous struggles to avoid exposure and disgrace end with the revelation that, as she confesses, she is mad—this is her secret. She ends her life in a lunatic asylum. The racy and absorbing plot, and Lucy's defiantly unrepentant wickedness, fascinated the novel's first readers, and it became a best-seller.

Lady Chatterley's Lover Novel by D. H. *Lawrence (privately printed, Florence, 1928; expurgated version, 1932; full text, 1960). Constance Chatterley is married to Sir Clifford, who is confined to a wheelchair through injuries suffered in the First World War. She has a passionate love relationship with gamekeeper Oliver Mellors. She becomes pregnant, goes to Venice with her sister partly to obscure the baby's parentage, but returns and tells her husband the truth, spurred on by the knowledge that Mellors's estranged wife Bertha has been stirring scandal in an effort to reclaim him. The novel ends with the temporary separation of the lovers, as they hopefully await divorce and a new life together. Lawrence's frank descriptions of sex and his uncompromising use of four-letter words caused the book to be unpublishable until 1960, when *Penguin Books were prosecuted for obscenity and acquitted, a victory which had a profound effect on both writing and publishing in subsequent decades.

Lady of Pleasure, The A comedy by James *Shirley, acted 1635, printed 1637. The play's intrigue, fashionable conversation, focus on social deportment, and switch from amorality to a moral ending anticipate the *Restoration comedy of manners.

'Lady of Shalott, The' A poem by Alfred *Tennyson, published 1832, much revised for the 1842 *Poems*. An allegory of the artist's remoteness from human life, a contemplation of art's relationship with the real, of the 'femininity' of the poet, even of the political plight of handloom weavers, the poem has sustained a diversity of critical views. It was widely illustrated (e.g. by J. W. Waterhouse, 1849–1917), and set to music, during the Victorian period.

Lady of the Lake In the Arthurian legends, a rather shifting supernatural character. In *Malory she gives Arthur the sword Excalibur, but when she asks for the head of Balyn as payment, Balyn strikes off her head, for which deed he is banished from the court. Also called the Lady of the Lake (in Malory 'chief' lady, suggesting more than one) is Nimiane (Nymue and, probably by scribal misreading, Vivien), the wife of Pelleas, who loves Merlin, whom she tricks into revealing his magic arts and then imprisons in a tower of air in the forest of *Broceliande from which he never escapes. In Malory she is said to have accompanied the three queens who bore Arthur away by ship after his death. In Celtic origin she may derive from Morgan, the archetypal lake lady.

Lady of the Lake, The A poem in six cantos by Walter *Scott, published 1810. The action takes place chiefly on and around Loch Katrine in Perthshire, and involves the wooing of Ellen Douglas, the lady of the title and daughter of the outlawed Lord James of Douglas. The lively narrative evokes Highland scenery and manners, and contains various poetic interludes, including the coronach (Canto III) 'He is gone on the mountain' and the ballad (Canto IV) 'Alice Brand'.

Lady Susan A novel by Jane *Austen, written probably 1793–4, published 1871, from an untitled manuscript dated 1805. It is Jane Austen's only *epistolary novel, although her first version of *Sense and Sensibility, called *Elinor and Marianne*, was also in letter form.

The chief correspondents are the kindly Mrs Vernon and her mother Lady de Courcy, and the beautiful, unscrupulous Lady Susan, the widow of Mr Vernon's brother, and her London friend Mrs Johnson. The events occur mainly at Churchill, the country house of the Vernons.

LA FONTAINE, Jean de (1621–95) French poet, author of *Fables*, published in twelve books between 1668 and 1694. He draws in part on the familiar fables of *Aesop and Phaedrus, but also explores the limits of the genre; his thought-provoking little comedies, written in remarkably agile irregular verse, rarely offer up a simple lesson. Some of the *Fables* were translated as early as 1693 by John Dennis, followed by Bernard de *Mandeville's versions in

Aesop Dress'd (1704); in the 20th century, Marianne *Moore has made a distinguished complete translation (1954).

LAFORGUE, Jules (1860–87) French poet, prominent in the development of *vers libre*, author of *Les Complaintes* (1885: *Complaints*), *L'Imitation de Notre-Dame la Lune* (1886: *Imitation of Our Lady of the Moon*), and the posthumously published *Derniers Vers* (1890: *Final Verse*). He was an important influence on the early work of T. S. *Eliot, and on the poetry of Ezra *Pound (see *Canto CXVI*). Three of his poems were translated by Hart *Crane (1922).

Lake Poets, Lake School Terms applied to Samuel Taylor *Coleridge, Robert *Southey, William *Wordsworth, and sometimes to Thomas *De Quincey, who lived in the Lake District at the beginning of the 19th century. The expression 'Lake School' seems first to have appeared in the *Edinburgh Review. Lord *Byron, in the dedication to *Don Juan* (1819), refers slightingly to 'all the Lakers'. In his *Recollections of the Lake Poets* De Quincey denies the existence of any such 'school'.

Lallans *See* SCOTS.

Lalla Rookh A series of *oriental tales in verse connected by a story in prose, by Thomas *Moore, published 1817. The work enjoyed immense popularity, and went into twenty editions by 1840.

The frame story tells of the journey of Lalla Rookh ('Tulip Cheek'), the daughter of the emperor, from Delhi to Kashmir, to be married to the king of Bucharia. On the way she and her train are diverted by four verse tales told by Feramorz, a young Kashmiri poet, with whom she falls in love and who turns out, on her arrival, to be the king of Bucharia himself. A series of accidents on the way throws the pompous chamberlain Fadladeen into a bad temper, which he vents in pungent criticisms of the young man's verse, in the style of the *Edinburgh Review.

'L'Allegro' A poem in rhymed octosyllabics with a ten-line prelude by John *Milton, written ?1631, printed 1645. The Italian title means 'the cheerful man', and this idyll is an invocation to the goddess Mirth to allow the poet to live with her. It is a companion piece to *'Il Penseroso'.

LAMB, Lady Caroline (1785–1828) Gothic novelist, wife of William Lamb, afterwards second Viscount Melbourne. In 1812, shortly after her marriage, she became infatuated with Lord *Byron, and about the same time began to show signs of serious mental instability. Her first novel, *Glenarvon*, published anonymously in 1816 after Byron had broken with her, is a *Gothic extravaganza, in which she herself is cast as the dashing Calantha and Byron as the fated, fascinating Glenarvon. The novel was briefly a *succès de scandale*.

LAMB, Charles (1775–1834) Author and critic. He met S. T. *Coleridge at Christ's Hospital. After a few months at the South Sea House (*see* ESSAYS OF ELIA), he obtained at 17 an appointment in the East India House, where he remained until his retirement in 1825. For a short time in 1795–6 he was mentally deranged, and the threat of madness became a shadow on his life. In 1796 his sister Mary, in a fit of insanity, killed their mother. Lamb undertook the charge of his sister, who remained liable to periodic breakdowns, and she repaid him with great sympathy and affection.

Four sonnets of Lamb's appeared in 1796 in a volume of poems by Coleridge, who became a lifelong friend. *Blank Verse*, by Charles Lloyd and Charles Lamb, and the *Tale of Rosamund Gray and Old Blind Margaret*, was a melodramatic, sentimental village tragedy, both appeared in 1798. Lamb's plays *John Woodvil* (1802, at first called *Pride's Cure*) and *Mr H* (1806) were not successful. With his sister he wrote *Tales from Shakespear* (1807), designed to make the stories of Shakespeare's plays familiar to the young; and also *Mrs Leicester's School* (1809), a collection of original stories. *The Adventures of Ulysses* (1808) was an attempt to do for the *Odyssey* what he had done for Shakespeare. In 1808 Lamb published *Specimens of English Dramatic Poets Who Lived about the Time of Shakespeare*; he also wrote for Leigh *Hunt's *Reflector* and for the *Examiner*, and in 1814 contributed to the *Quarterly Review* an article (much altered by John *Gifford, the editor) on Wordsworth's The *Excursion*, commending the originality of Wordsworth's genius, as well as his high seriousness. From 1820 to 1823 Lamb was a regular contributor to the *London Magazine*, which published the first series of essays known as *Essays of Elia*, published in a collected volume in 1823. The second series was published in 1833. Of his poems the best known are 'The Old Familiar Faces'(1798), the lyrical ballad 'Hester' (1803), and an elegy 'On an Infant Dying as Soon as Born' (1827). *Album Verses* (1830) includes many other lyrics and sonnets.

As a literary critic, Lamb's sympathies were wide and his sensitivity acute; while careful always to approve moral worth he also enjoys 'an airing beyond the diocese of strict conscience', as into the then little read Jacobean or Restoration drama. He was a prolific letter writer of great charm, wit, and quality, and many of his observations on literature are scattered throughout the letters. His various homes were a meeting place for Coleridge, *Wordsworth, Leigh Hunt, William *Hazlitt, Robert *Southey, and others.

'Lamia' A narrative poem by John *Keats, written 1819, published 1820. The story was taken from Robert Burton's *Anatomy of Melancholy* and thence from Philostratus. Lamia, a sorceress, is transformed by Hermes from a serpent into a beautiful woman. She loves the young Corinthian Lycius, and he, spellbound by her beauty, falls in love with her. They retire to her secret palace in Corinth. Here, against Lamia's wishes, Lycius orders a magnificent bridal feast and summons his friends. Among them, though uninvited, comes his old guide and mentor, the sage Apollonius, who pierces Lamia's disguise and calls her by her name. Her beauty withers, with a frightful scream she vanishes, and Lycius dies in a frenzy of grief.

LAMMING, George William (1927–) Novelist and poet, born in Barbados. His first novel, *In the Castle of my Skin* (1953), tells of a boy's adolescence in a small village in Barbados, and of his growing awareness of the colonial situation. *The Emigrants* (1954) describes the arrival in Britain of a group of West Indians. *Of Age and Innocence* (1958) and *Season of Adventure* (1960) are set on the imaginary island of San Cristobal. *The Pleasures of Exile* (1960) is a collection of essays on Caribbean culture and politics. Later works include *Water with Berries* (1971) and *Natives of my Person* (1972).

LANCASTER, Sir Osbert (1908–96) Writer, artist, cartoonist, and theatre designer, whose many illustrated works gently mock the English way of life: he was particularly good at country-house and upper-class architecture and mannerisms, but also had a sharp eye for suburbia. Titles include *Pillar to Post* (1938) and *Homes Sweet Homes* (1939), and books based on Draynflete, the ancestral village of the Littlehampton family, which include *Draynflete Revealed* (1949) and *The Life and Times of Maudie Littlehampton* (1982).

LANDON, Letitia Elizabeth (1802–38) Prolific poet and novelist, whose poetry rivalled Felicia *Hemans's in popularity. She published under her initials 'L.E.L.'

She contributed poems to literary reviews including the *Literary Gazette* (becoming head reviewer in 1824), and supplied hundreds of love lyrics to gift books and annuals, including *The Keepsake* and *The Amulet*. She edited two such publications, *Fisher's Drawing Room Scrap Book* (1832–39) and *Heath's Book of Beauty* (1833), and from 1832 contributed poems and short stories to the *New Monthly Magazine*. The triple-deckers *Romance and Reality* (1831), *Francesca Carrera* (1834), and *Ethel Churchill* (1837) were 'silver-fork' or 'fashionable novels. Her first volume of verse, *The *Improvisatrice*, went through six editions in a year. Further volumes followed, including *The Troubadour* (1825), *The Golden Violet* (1826), *The Venetian Bracelet* (1829), *The Vow of the Peacock* (1835), a collection of children's stories, *Traits and Trials of Early Life* (1836), and a play, *The Triumph of Luca*, published posthumously.

Landon writes in a highly self-conscious, romantic vein about the suffering of the female lover and the female poet (the two themes merge in her work). Her unprotected position as a woman in the literary world gave rise to various vague scandals linking her name to William *Maginn and, less certainly, to Edward *Bulwer-Lytton, who appears with his wife Rosina in her novel *Romance and Reality* (1831). Such rumours caused her to break off her engagement to John *Forster.

LANDOR, Robert Eyres (1781–1869) Cleric and writer, youngest brother of Walter Savage *Landor. He wrote five tragedies including *The Count of Arezzi* (1823), which was attributed to Lord *Byron; a poem, *The Impious Feast* (1828); a fantastic prose story, *The Fawn of Sertorius* (1846); and *The Fountain of Arethusa* (1848), dialogues between two modern explorers and famous men of classical times, comparable with Walter Savage Landor's *Imaginary Conversations*.

LANDOR, Walter Savage (1775–1864) Poet and author, whose intractable temper involved him in trouble throughout his life. He published *Poems* (1795), *Gebir* (1798), an epic poem in seven books, *Poetry by the Author of Gebir* (1802) and *Simonidea* (1806). A dramatic tragedy, *Count Julian*, followed in 1812 but was never staged, and in the same year Landor's intemperate 'Commentary on the Memoirs of Mr Fox' had to be suppressed. He lived in Italy from 1815 until 1835, when he separated from his wife. *Imaginary Conversations of Literary Men and Statesmen* appeared 1824–9, followed by *Pericles and Aspasia*

(1836), *The *Pentameron* (1837), in which *Boccaccio and *Petrarch discuss the poetry of *Dante, and *Imaginary Conversations of Greeks and Romans* (1853). The trilogy *Andrea of Hungary, Giovanna of Naples*, and *Fra Rupert*, set in the 14th century, was published in 1839–40, and *The Hellenics*, a retelling in verse of various Greek myths, completed in 1847. His work was admired by Robert *Browning. Boythorn in Dickens's *Bleak House* is a genial caricature of Landor.

LANDSEER, Sir Edwin Henry (1802–73) Painter. A visit to Walter *Scott in 1824 introduced him to the landscapes of Scotland, which featured prominently in his work. He painted portraits, historical scenes (mostly from Scott), and some strange allegorical works, but is best remembered for his animal paintings, such as *The Monarch of the Glen* (1851).

LANE, Allen (1902–70) Publisher. With the foundation in 1935 of the *Penguin series, he became a pioneer in the paperback revolution in publishing.

LANE, Edward William (1801–1876) Arabic scholar. He published *An Account of the Manners and Customs of the Modern Egyptians* (1836) and an expurgated translation of *The Thousand and One Nights* (or *Arabian Nights Entertainments*, 1838–40). From 1843 to his death in 1876 he worked solely on his magnum opus, his *Arabic–English Lexicon*.

Lane's *A Description of Egypt*, which Murray had promised to publish in 1831, appeared in 2000.

LANE, John (1854–1925) *Fin-de-siècle* publisher who, with Charles Elkin Mathews, established the Bodley Head Press in 1887. Authors who appeared under its imprint included John *Davidson, Ernest *Dowson, Richard *Le Gallienne, John Addington *Symonds, and Oscar *Wilde. The firm gained a high reputation for the quality of its publications, and as publisher of the *Yellow Book* it became the centre of ferment in art and letters in the 1890s.

LANG, Andrew (1844–1912) Scottish folklorist, anthropologist, and one of the most prolific writers of his day. His many volumes of poetry (the *Collected Poems* (4 vols) appeared in 1923) and other works of belles-lettres are now largely forgotten, as are his melodramatic novels, which include *The Mark of Cain* (1886). He collaborated with H. Rider *Haggard in *The World's Desire* (1891) and with A. E. Mason in

Parson Kelly (1899). As a Greek scholar, Lang devoted himself largely to *Homer, contributing to prose versions of the **Odyssey* (1879) and the **Iliad* (1883). He wrote on the Homeric question, arguing with the unity of Homer. He also took part in the Baconian controversy (*see* SHA-KESPEARE: AUTHORSHIP OF THE WORKS), favouring Shakespearian authorship, in *Shakespeare, Bacon and the Great Unknown* (1912).

Lang also published *Custom and Myth* (1884) and other mythological works. Lang is remembered for his own *fairy stories, which include *The Gold of Fairnilee* (1888, drawing on Scottish history) and Prince Prigio (1889), set in the imaginary world of Pantouflia, and for his twelve collections of folk and fairy-tales, some in *translation. Each volume was named after a different colour, from *The Blue Fairy Book* (1889) to *The Lilac Fairy Book* (1910). He edited other collections including the **Arabian Nights* (1898); his *Tales of Troy and Greece* (1907) was long regarded as a children's classic.

LANGHAM (Laneham), Robert The name of the author of the printed letter describing some of the entertainments put on by the earl of Leicester for *Elizabeth I's visit to Kenilworth in 1575. William *Shakespeare may have remembered the shows in *A *Midsummer Night's Dream* (II. i. 148–68). The list of Captain Cox's books which 'Langham' gives is an important source for the titles of ballads, romances, and other popular contemporary literature.

LANGHORNE, John (1735–79) Clergyman and poet, rector of Blagdon, Somerset from 1766; author of the *oriental tale, *Solyman and Almena* (1762) and *Genius and Valour: A Scotch Pastoral* (1763), defending the Scots against Charles *Churchill's *Prophecy of Famine*. His poem *The Country Justice* (1774–7), reflecting his experiences as a justice of the peace (from 1772), was much admired by William *Wordsworth.

LANGLAND, William (*c.*1325–*c.*1390) The supposed author of **Piers Plowman*, about whose identity and life very little is known for certain. The poem in its various forms invites readers to think that 'Will', the dreamer ('Long Will' in the B-text), lived in London (Cornhill, more precisely, in the C-text), but that he had also lived in the Malvern district of the West Midlands.

Language Poets A movement beginning in the 1960s and continuing through the New York journal *L=A=N=G=U=A=G=E* (1978–82), whose practitioners foreground language and

the production of meaning in their works. Its members include Ron Silliman (1946–), Barrett Watten (1948–), and Charles Bernstein (1950–), the latter co-editing with Bruce Andrews (1948–) *The L=A=N=G=U=A=G=E Book* (1984). The movement draws partly on the practice of Gertrude *Stein.

⊕ **SEE WEB LINKS**
• Archive of early issues of L=A=N=G=U=A=G=E

LANIER (Lanyer), Emilia (1569–1645) Née Bassano, poet. Her collection of poems *Salve Deus Rex Judaeorum* (1611) includes 'The Description of Cookham', a country-house poem celebrating the patronage of Margaret Clifford, countess of Cumberland (1560–1616), and her daughter Anne *Clifford. A very early example of the genre, the poem may pre-date Ben *Jonson's 'To Penshurst'.

Laodicean, A A novel by Thomas *Hardy, published 1881; the Laodicean (i.e. a lukewarm or indecisive person) of the title is Paula Power; a vacillating young woman.

'Laon and Cythna' *See* REVOLT OF ISLAM.

Lara A poem by Lord *Byron, published 1814. Lara is in fact Conrad of The *Corsair returned to his domains in Spain accompanied by his page Kaled, who is his love, the slave Gulnare, in disguise. Lara lives, like other *Byronic heroes, aloof and alien, shrouded in mystery. He is, however, recognized as Conrad, and becomes involved in a feud in which he is finally killed, dying in the arms of Kaled.

LARDNER, Ring (1885–1933) American sports journalist and short story writer, born in Niles, Michigan. Lardner wrote a number of plays but is mainly remembered for his pioneering use of the vernacular in short story collections like *Gullible's Travels* (1917). He was a close friend of F. Scott *Fitzgerald and influenced the style of Ernest *Hemingway.

LARKIN, Philip (1922–85) Poet and novelist; he met Kingsley *Amis, who became a lifelong friend, and developed an interest in jazz at Oxford University. From 1943 he worked in various libraries before becoming librarian of the Brynmor Jones Library at Hull University. In his first book, *The North Ship* (1945), the poems were, by Larkin's own account, much influenced by W. B. *Yeats. *Jill* (1946), a novel, set in wartime Oxford, describes the undergraduate career of John Kemp, a working-class boy from Lancashire; 'Jill' is the fantasy sister he creates, who is transformed into a teasing reality. *A Girl in Winter* (1947), relates a day in the life of refugee librarian Katherine Lind, working in a drab English provincial town, with a lengthy flashback to an abortive adolescent romance with a penfriend. Larkin's own poetic voice (with a new allegiance to Thomas *Hardy) became distinct in *The Less Deceived* (1955), including the colloquial 'Toads'; his name was at this time associated with the *Movement, and his work appeared in *New Lines* (1956). *The Whitsun Weddings* (1964) adds satiric sociological commentary, and more stoic wit, manifested in 'Toads Revisited'. Many of the poems in *High Windows* (1974), notably 'The Old Fools', show a preoccupation with death and transience. Throughout his work, the adaptation of contemporary speech rhythms and vocabulary to an unobtrusive metrical elegance is highly distinctive. The controversial *Collected Poems* (1988, edited by Anthony *Thwaite) printed Larkin's published and unpublished poems in chronological order; a new version in 2003 reprinted the volumes as Larkin originally published them.

LA ROCHEFOUCAULD, François de Marsillac, duc de (1613–80) French courtier, soldier, and moralist, author of *Réflexions ou sentences et maximes morales* (1665), usually known as *Maximes*. By the fifth (1678) edition, the *Maximes* consisted of 504 brief reflections which range widely over human nature and society. The epigraph to the collection, 'Our virtues are mostly vices in disguise', expresses one of its leading themes; another is the discovery of the springs of people's actions in their vanity, self-interest, desire for praise, and readiness to deceive themselves. There were several English translations of the *Maximes* in the 17th and 18th centuries, including one by Aphra *Behn, *Reflections on Morality or Seneca Unmasqued* (1685).

La Saisiaz and **The Two Poets of Croisic** Two long poems by Robert *Browning, published 1878, the third and final such pairing in his work. *La Saisiaz* is a philosophical elegy prompted by the sudden death of a close friend of Browning's, with whom he had been holidaying in a chalet called 'La Saisiaz' near Geneva. *The Two Poets of Croisic* is lighter and more acerbic in tone than *La Saisiaz*. Its serious theme was the way in which art acts as a memorial for the dead.

LASKI, Marghanita (1915–88) Novelist, critic, and journalist. Her novels include *Little Boy Lost* (1949), *The Village* (1952), and *The Victorian Chaise Longue* (1953). She also wrote two books exploring mystical experiences, *Ecstasy* (1961) and *Everyday Ecstasy* (1980).

Last Chronicle of Barset, The A novel by Anthony *Trollope, published 1867, the last and one of the strongest of the *'Barsetshire' series. Josiah Crawley is accused of fraudulently acquiring a cheque for £20, and using it to pay off the debts resulting from his struggles to survive on his meagre curate's income. At the close of the novel the Crawley fortunes brighten. Mr Crawley is presented with the fatter living of St Ewold's, and the archdeacon finally removes his opposition to the marriage of loyal Grace Crawley and his son Major Grantly.

Last Days of Pompeii, The A historical novel by Edward Bulwer-*Lytton, published in 1834. It describes the events leading up to the destruction of the Roman city of Pompeii by the cataclysmic eruption of Mount Vesuvius in AD 79. Vivid and dramatic, the novel was adapted for the screen several times, most recently in a serialized version for television in 1984. *See also* QUO VADIS?

Last Man, The A novel by Mary *Shelley, published 1826. A *dystopia, it portrays a late 21st-century world where humanity is destroyed by a plague. It contains a thinly veiled portrait of Lord *Byron in the character of Lord Raymond and is sometimes seen, like *Frankenstein*, as a critique of the destructive potential within Romantic idealism.

Last of the Mohicans, The: *A Narrative of 1757* A novel by James Fenimore *Cooper, published in 1826.

LAUD, William (1573–1645) At Charles I's accession he was bishop of St David's, becoming archbishop of Canterbury in 1633. He encouraged the king's belief that he ruled by divine right, and, in his effort to impose uniformity on the Church of England, persecuted Puritans, Presbyterians, and sectarians, imposing harsh and humiliating punishments. In 1637 William *Prynne, John Bastwick (1593–1654), and Henry Burton (1578–1648) had their ears cut off and were branded on both cheeks for the crime of seditious libel. In the run-up to the Civil War he was accused of high treason and committed to the Tower. Tried and condemned in 1644, he was beheaded in January 1645. A few of his sermons were published in 1651, and a collected edition of his works in 1696–1700. A former chancellor of Oxford University, he gave some 1,300 manuscripts in eighteen different languages to the Bodleian Library.

Launcelot of the Lake, Sir The greatest and most romantic of the knights of the Round Table, father of *Galahad by *Elaine Sans Pere (daughter of King Pelles), and the lover of *Guinevere. He is a relatively late development in the English Arthurian tradition, not appearing at length before the 14th century, although the story of his love for Guinevere is the subject of *Chrétien de Troyes's *Lancelot* (*c.*1170s) and of the early 13th-century French prose 'Vulgate' *Lancelot*. His name refers to a tradition that he was abducted at birth and brought up by a lakelady, before being brought by a hermit to Arthur's court. Chrétien's romance *Lancelot*, or *Le Chevalier de la charrette*, is concerned exclusively with the love of Lancelot and Guinevere, presented faithfully as a *courtly love affair. The main elements of the Launcelot story are found in the three romances of the French prose cycle: *Lancelot*; the *Queste del Saint Graal*; and the *Mort Artu*. *Malory's treatment of Launcelot is closely based on this: Launcelot's love for the queen is central; it is strained by his relations with Elaine the Fair Maid of Astolat, whose death ends Guinevere's jealousy. Their love is betrayed by *Agravain; the lovers flee to Launcelot's castle of Joyous Gard and, after a siege, the queen is restored to Arthur. Launcelot withdraws to Brittany where he is pursued by Arthur and Gawain; in the ensuing clash Launcelot injures Gawain. Arthur returns to Dover to fight the usurping *Mordred and Gawain is killed. Launcelot comes back to help the king, but arrives too late for the final battle in Cornwall in which both Arthur and Mordred die. He finds that Guinevere has become a nun, so he becomes a priest. On his death he is carried to Joyous Gard where visions suggest that he is taken to heaven. He is very prominent in Malory who stresses the tragedy of his imperfection (his relationship with the queen) which prevents his full achievement of the *Grail.

LAURENCE, Margaret (1926–87) Canadian novelist and short story writer. Her huband's work as a civil engineer took them to live in Africa for five years. Her time there inspired *A Tree for Poverty* (1954), a translated selection of Somali poetry; *The Prophet's Camel Bell* (1963), a memoir of her life in Somaliland; her first novel, *This Side Jordan* (1960), set in Ghana; a collection of stories set in West Africa, *The Tomorrow-Tamer* (1963); and a critical work on contemporary Nigerian dramatists and novelists, *Long Drums and Cannons* (1968). In 1962 she moved to England and began the series of four books based on her home town of Neepawa, Manitoba, renamed Manawaka, for which she is now best known: *The Stone Angel* (1964); *A Jest of God* (1966), retitled *Now I Lay Me Down* for British publication, filmed as *Rachel, Rachel* (1968); *The Fire-Dwellers* (1969); and *The Diviners* (1974). *A Bird in the House* (1970), a collection of linked short stories, is also part of the Manawaka sequence. She returned to Canada in 1974. A draft of her memoirs, *Dance on the Earth*, edited by her daughter, was published in 1989.

Lavengro: *The Scholar, the Gypsy, the Priest* A veiled autobiography by George *Borrow, published in 1851. 'Lavengro' is a Romany term for 'wordsmith', and was a name given to Borrow in his youth by Ambrose Smith, who figures in the narrative as Lavengro's Gypsy friend Jasper Petulengro.

The work is presented as the story of Borrow's own restless life, though many of its elements are heavily romanticized. The hero's father is a soldier, and he follows him from post to post around Britain, striking up unconventional friendships. He becomes attached to a family of Gypsies, and meets tinkers, including the pugilistic Flaming Tinman, with whom he has a vividly described fight. Lavengro also develops an intellectual and literary life, and becomes expert in the comparative study of languages (though much of his scholarship is suspect). The book closes as Lavengro becomes involved with the Amazonian vagrant Belle Berners, a story which is resumed in *The *Romany Rye*.

LAVIN, Mary (1912–96) Short story writer and novelist, born in Massachusetts and brought up from the age of 9 in Ireland. Her first collection was *Tales from Bective Bridge* (1942), set in and around the village of Bective, Co. Meath. Subsequent collections include *The Long Ago* (1944), *The Becker Wives* (1946), *A Single Lady* (1951), and *The Shrine* (1977). Family relationships and domestic conflicts over class, religion, and property are recurrent issues, and are treated with irony and pathos. Some of Lavin's most memorable stories explore the psychology of widowhood through the character of Vera Traske. Her novels are *The House in Clewe Street* (1945), a three-generation family saga, and *Mary O'Grady* (1950). *A Likely Story* (1957) is a children's tale set in Bective.

LAW, William (1686–1761) Devotional writer. From 1711 to 1716 he was a fellow of

Emmanuel and curate at Haslingfield, Cambridgeshire, but lost his fellowship after refusing to take the oath of allegiance to George I. From 1723 to 1737 he lived with the family of Edward Gibbon at Putney, for part of this time as tutor to his son, father of Edward *Gibbon the historian. He is chiefly remembered for his devotional handbooks, *A Practical Treatise upon Christian Perfection* (1726) and especially *A Serious Call to a Devout and Holy Life* (1729). Their uncompromising message is enlivened with satirical portraits of the lives of the godless rich, contrasted with idealized ones such as Ouranius the country priest and Miranda the charitable gentlewoman. In 1740 Law returned to his Northamptonshire birthplace, King's Cliffe, with two companions, to live a life of charity, celibacy, prayer, reading, and writing. He had long been a student of *mysticism, and his detailed study of the works of Jacob Boehme is reflected in his most important later works, *The Spirit of Prayer* (1749–50) and *The Spirit of Love* (1752–4). The widespread influence of Law's writings was furthered by the many cheap abridgements published by his one-time disciple John *Wesley. *See* NONJURORS; BYROM, JOHN.

LAWES, Henry (1596–1662) and **William** (1602–1645) English composers. Henry became one of Charles I's musicians in 1631 and was widely recognized in his day as the most important songwriter after John *Dowland: his 433 songs include settings of Thomas *Carew (38), Edmund *Waller (16), Robert *Herrick (14), Sir John *Suckling, Richard *Lovelace, and Katherine *Philips. He arranged the original performance of his friend *Milton's *Comus*, contributing the songs. His brother William composed a large part of the music for John Shirley's *The *Triumph of Peace* (1634), and wrote incidental music for several of the masques of Ben *Jonson, Suckling, and Sir William *D'Avenant.

LAWLESS, Emily (1845–1913) Irish novelist, author of the historical novels *Hurrish* (1886) and *Grania* (1892); *With Essex in Ireland* (1890); *With the Wild Geese* (1902), a collection of austere poems; and a *Life of Maria Edgeworth* (1904).

LAWRENCE, D. H. (David Herbert) (1885–1930) Novelist and poet, born at Eastwood, Nottinghamshire, one of five children of a miner and an ex-schoolteacher. He grew up in poverty and was often ill as a child. His ill-suited parents quarrelled continually, and a passionate and deeply influential bond grew between Lawrence and his mother. With the help of a scholarship he attended Nottingham High School for three years, but at 15 was forced to give up his education, working for a short time as a clerk in a surgical goods factory before becoming a pupil-teacher. At this time he formed a close friendship with Jessie Chambers, a local farmer's daughter, the Miriam of *Sons and Lovers*. In 1906 he took up a scholarship at Nottingham University College to study for a teacher's certificate.

He was already writing poetry and short stories and he now began his first novel, *The White Peacock* (1911), which was followed by *The Trespasser* (1912). He taught for two years at an elementary school in Croydon, but after the death of his mother he became seriously ill and was advised to give up teaching. His first major novel, *Sons and Lovers* (1913), is an autobiographical account of these early years. In 1912 he met Frieda Weekley (née von Richthofen), wife of his old professor at Nottingham. They fell in love and eloped to Germany. They were always on the move, always short of money, and their life together was passionate and stormy. Lawrence spent the war years in England and began to form friendships in literary and intellectual circles: Aldous *Huxley, David *Garnett, Lady Ottoline *Morrell, J. M. *Murry, Katherine *Mansfield, Richard *Aldington, and Bertrand *Russell (with whom he was later to quarrel bitterly). His next novel, *The *Rainbow* (1915), was seized by the police and declared obscene. In 1919 he and Frieda left for Italy. He had finished his novel *Women in Love* in 1916 but was unable to find a publisher until 1920 in New York, and 1921 in London. In 1920 *The Lost Girl* (begun before the war) won the James Tait Black Memorial Prize, the only official honour he was to receive during his lifetime. *Aaron's Rod*, the first of several novels espousing strong male leaders, followed in 1922 and the same year he began his serious travels, to Ceylon and Australia (where he wrote *Kangaroo* (1923) and finally to America and Mexico, where he began work on *The Plumed Serpent* (1926) and wrote many short stories and poems. While on a visit to Old Mexico he fell desperately ill and was told that he was in an advanced state of tuberculosis. Frieda and Lawrence returned to Italy, settling finally near Florence at the Villa Mirenda, where he finished *Lady Chatterley's Lover*, his last novel. It was privately printed in Florence in 1928; more than 30 years would pass before unexpurgated editions appeared in the United States and England.

The outrage occasioned by Lawrence's work blinded many readers to its lasting value. He was a moralist, and believed that modern man was in danger of losing his ability to experience the quality of life. Passionately involved with his characters and the physical world of nature, he wrote of them with a fresh immediacy and vividness.

In his poems, written throughout his career, Lawrence wanted to be free of the weight of formalism but not, as he said, to 'dish up the fragments as a new substance'. At times uneven, his poetry always has the immediate and personal quality of his prose. His poetry was gathered in *Complete Poems* (3 vols, 1957). Other non-fiction works include *Movements in European History* (1921), *Psychoanalysis and the Unconscious* (1921), *Fantasia of the Unconscious* (1922), *Studies in Classic American Literature* (1923), and *Apocalypse* (1931).

LAWRENCE, George Alfred (1827–76) Novelist. His first and best-known novel, *Guy Livingstone* (1857), was a leading example of the 'muscular school', a revolt against the comparable but very much more high-minded 'muscular Christianity' of the time, embodied by Thomas *Hughes and Charles *Kingsley. It set a fashion not only in literature (*'Ouida' was a notable disciple) but even in the mode of dress and behaviour of the young men of the period. It was followed by *Sword and Gown* (1859) and *Border and Bastille* (1863), which describes Lawrence's attempts to join the Confederate forces during the American Civil War, and many others. His *Guy Livingstone* was parodied by Bret *Harte in his 'Guy Heaveystone'.

LAWRENCE, T. E. (Thomas Edward) (1888–1935) Soldier and writer. His daring exploits in the Middle East during the First World War won him the confidence and admiration of the Arabs, and later made him, as 'Lawrence of Arabia', a figure of myth. His subsequent career was marked by mental breakdown, self-accusation, and anxiety about his legend; he enlisted in the RAF in 1922 as an aircraft hand under the name of John Hume Ross, and a year later joined the tank corps as T. E. Shaw. He later returned to the RAF. *The Seven Pillars of Wisdom*, his account of the Arab Revolt, was printed for private circulation in 1926 (pub. 1935); a shortened version, *Revolt in the Desert*, was published in 1927. His account of life in the RAF, *The Mint* by '352087 A/c Ross', appeared posthumously in 1936 (USA) and 1955 (UK).

Laws of Ecclesiastical Politie, Of the
By Richard *Hooker, a philosophical and theological treatise in eight books (Books I–IV 1593, Book V 1597, Books VI and VIII 1648, Book VII 1662). The work is a defence, written in a dignified and harmonious prose, of the position of the *Church of England against the attacks of the Puritans. Books I–IV deal with first principles: the first, which has been the most influential, is a philosophical discussion of the origin and nature of law in general, as governing the universe and human society, and of the distinction between laws of a permanent and of a temporary character; the second, third, and fourth deal with the assertion of the Puritan party that Scripture is the sole guide in determining the actions of a Christian and the form of church polity, and that the Anglican Church is corrupted with popish rites and ceremonies. The later books deal with questions of worship and governance. The fifth is a defence of the *Book of *Common Prayer*. The last three books do not represent work prepared by Hooker for the press. According to Hooker's original scheme, the incomplete Book VI was to have dealt with *presbyterianism. Book VII is a defence of the role of bishops, and Book VIII explores the nature of the king's supreme authority. The *Laws* has been seen as the first major work on theology, philosophy, and political thought written in English. *See* PURITANISM.

lay A short lyric or narrative poem intended to be sung; originally applied specifically to the poems, usually dealing with matters of history or romantic adventure, which were sung by minstrels.

LAȜAMON (*fl.* 13th century) A priest of Areley Kings, Worcestershire. He wrote the *Brut*, a history of England from the legendary Brutus to *Cadwallader, drawing mostly on *Wace's French version of *Geoffrey of Monmouth's *Historia Regum Britanniae*. The *Brut* gives for the first time in English the story of Arthur and those of Lear, Cymbeline, and other figures prominent in later English literature. The poem is in 32,241 short lines and, though written in early Middle English, mainly observes the later Old English alliterative half-line with occasional rhyme. A transitional poem, it employs some of the epic formulas, such as eloquent similes, and other stylistic features of Old English.

Lay of the Last Minstrel, The A poem in six cantos by Walter *Scott, published in 1805.

Scott's first important original work, it is a metrical romance in irregular stanzas (much of it in rhymed octosyllabics) and tells a Border tale of feud and witchcraft and frustrated love set in the mid-16th century.

Lays of Ancient Rome A collection of poems by Thomas *Macaulay, published 1842, in which Macaulay takes episodes from Roman history (some from *Livy), including the defence of the bridge leading to Rome against the Tuscans ('Horatius'). Later editions included rousing poems from British history. 'Epitaph of a Jacobite', a touching lament by a follower of James II, was written in 1847, and was subsequently included with the *Lays*.

LAZARUS, Emma (1849–87) American poet, remembered for her 1883 poem 'The New Colossus'. Her poetry and other activities became more concerned with Judaism after she read George *Eliot's *Daniel Deronda*.

LEACOCK, Stephen Butler (1869–1944) Canadian humorist and political economist, born in England. He wrote biographies of Mark *Twain (1932) and Charles *Dickens (1933), but is best known for his many volumes of collected humorous essays and stories, including *Literary Lapses* (1910), *Nonsense Novels* (1911), and *Frenzied Fiction* (1918).

LEAPOR, Mary (1722–46) Poet, born in Northamptonshire, the daughter of a gardener. She was in early years discouraged from writing and 'overstudying'. Her domestic service in several houses is reflected in the comic 'country house' poem *Crumble Hall*. She produced a distinguished body of work which attracted the attention of Bridget Freemantle (1698–1779), a rector's daughter, who persuaded her to consider publication. Leapor died of measles before this plan was executed, but her *Poems upon Several Occasions* appeared in 1748 and 1751 with support from Samuel *Richardson and David *Garrick. Her work is predominantly satiric in tone, with sharply drawn and realized characters, but she also writes tellingly about her own position as a woman writer who runs the risk of being thought 'mighty proud' by her neighbours. Her verses 'Upon her Play Being Returned to her, Stained with Claret' elegantly demonstrate both her good humour and her sense of her own worth.

LEAR, Edward (1812–88) Artist, traveller, and writer. He worked as a zoological draughtsman until he came under the patronage of the earl of Derby, for whose grandchildren he wrote *A Book of Nonsense* (1845), with his own *limericks and illustrations. He travelled widely, and published accounts of Italy (1846), Albania and Illyria (1851), Calabria (1852), and Corsica (1870); he also visited and sketched Egypt, the Holy Land, Greece, and India. He settled in 1871 in San Remo. As a writer he is remembered for his *nonsense verses, with their linguistic fantasies and inventiveness and their occasional touches of underlying melancholy. Later nonsense volumes were *Nonsense Songs, Stories, Botany and Alphabets* (1871), which contains 'The Owl and the Pussy-Cat' and 'The Jumblies'; *More Nonsense, Pictures, Rhymes, Botany etc.* (1871); and *Laughable Lyrics* (1877), with the Dong, the Yonghy-Bonghy-Bò, and the Pobble who has no toes.

LEAR, King See KING LEAR.

LEAVIS, F. R. (Frank Raymond) (1895–1978) Critic. While a probationary Cambridge lecturer (1927–32) he married Queenie Roth (see LEAVIS, QUEENIE DOROTHY), co-founded the journal *Scrutiny*, and wrote his first major book, *New Bearings in English Poetry* (1932), which, under the critical influence of T. S. *Eliot, lamented the feebleness of most late Victorian verse and identified a recent recovery in the poetic vigour of Gerard Manley *Hopkins, Edward *Thomas, Eliot, Ezra *Pound, and W. B. *Yeats. He became a fellow of Downing College, where he taught until 1962, sending out many devoted students into the teaching profession as missionaries armed with his critical principles and cultural values. Among his early works, *For Continuity* (1933), *Culture and Environment* (1933, with Denys Thompson), followed by *Education and the University* (1943), stress the importance of creating within university English departments a discriminating intellectual elite whose task it would be to preserve the cultural continuity of English life and literature, a continuity he believed to be threatened by mass media, technology, and advertising. He soon became identified as a leading figure in a 'Cambridge school' of criticism, combining the 'close reading' of poetry advocated by I. A. *Richards with his own pessimistic diagnosis of modern cultural decline. His influential book *Revaluation* (1936) continued to reshape the main line of English poetry, tracing it through John *Donne and Alexander *Pope to Hopkins and Eliot, and aiming iconoclastic attacks at Edmund *Spenser, *Milton, and P. B. *Shelley. In *The Great Tradition* (1948) he pronounces the great English novelists to be Jane *Austen, George *Eliot, Henry *James, and

Joseph *Conrad, dismissing other major fiction (e.g. that of Henry *Fielding, Laurence *Sterne, Thomas *Hardy, and most of Charles *Dickens's work apart from *Hard Times) in notoriously summary fashion. In later years he reversed his position on Dickens (see Dickens the Novelist, with Q. D. Leavis, 1970), and increasingly abandoned his earlier devotion to T. S. Eliot in favour of the contrary influence of D. H. *Lawrence. His later essays appeared in The Common Pursuit (1952) and several subsequent collections. Throughout his career he cast himself as a persecuted outsider to the literary 'establishment', disparaged celebrated contemporary writers (e.g. the *Sitwells and Stephen *Spender) in offensively belittling terms, and engaged in bitter public disputes with rival critics. A notably ill-tempered public debate arose from his Two Cultures? The Significance of C. P. *Snow (1962).

LEAVIS, Queenie Dorothy (1906–81) Née Roth, scholar and critic. Her orthodox Jewish family repudiated her upon her marriage (1929) to F. R. *Leavis, a Gentile. Her Ph.D. thesis, supervised in part by I. A. *Richards, was published as Fiction and the Reading Public (1932), a pioneering study in the sociology of literature which examines the contemporary commercial market in fiction in historical perspective. She worked 1932–53 as an unofficial sub-editor for *Scrutiny while raising three children, also contributing many reviews and articles, notably on Jane *Austen. A strong influence upon her husband's work, she collaborated with him on Dickens the Novelist (1970). Her essays were reprinted posthumously in the three-volume Collected Essays (ed. G. Singh, 1983–9).

Le Carré, John (1931–) Pseudonym of David John Moore Cornwell. His earliest novels were conventional thrillers. The first, Call for the Dead (1961), introduced the mild-mannered secret agent George Smiley, who appears in many of his later books. The Spy Who Came in from the Cold (1963), a Cold War thriller inspired by the Berlin Wall, brought le Carré immediate fame. Its successors, including The Looking Glass War (1965), A Small Town in Germany (1968), Tinker, Tailor, Soldier, Spy (1974), Smiley's People (1980), The Little Drummer Girl (1983), The Russia House (1989), and The Night Manager (1993), confirmed his reputation as a storyteller who could combine elaborate plotting and realistic detail with a moral complexity unusual in the genre. Our Game (1995) is set in the aftermath of the break-up of the Soviet Union. Recent novels include The Constant Gardener (2001). The Mission Song (2006), and Our Kind of Traitor (2010).

Le CLÉZIO, Jean-Marie (1940–) French novelist, of French/Mauritian parentage. His novels, beginning with Le Procès-verbal (1963: The Interrogation) are increasingly preoccupied with the themes of travel, nature, colonialism, and dislocation: in Désert (1980), the heroine, Lalla, leaves her native shanty town in Morocco for Marseilles; in the semi-autobiographical Onitsha (1991: trans. 1997), set in 1948, the hero, Fintan, travels from France to Nigeria in search of his English father. Le Clézio was awarded the *Nobel Prize for Literature in 2008.

Lectures on the English Poets A critical work by William *Hazlitt, delivered as public lectures in 1818 and published that year. The series begins with *Chaucer and *Spenser, concluding with *Wordsworth and *Coleridge. By contrast with these *Lake Poets, *Shakespeare is praised for his lack of egotism, and immersion in his characters. This view influenced the poetics of *Keats, who attended the lectures.

LEDGWIDGE, Francis (1891–1917) Irish poet. He worked as a labourer and was befriended by Lord *Dunsany, who saw in his poems the promise of an authentic Irish rural voice, and wrote introductions for his three collections, Songs of the Field (1916), Songs of Peace (1917), and Last Songs (1918). He wrote 'Lament for Thomas McDonagh' (sic) and other elegies in Ebrington Barracks, Derry, for the executed poet-rebels of 1916.

LEE, Harper (1926–) American novelist, born in Alabama, a close friend of Truman *Capote. The 1960 Pulitzer Prize-winning novel To Kill a Mockingbird, which explores themes of racial injustice, courage, and childhood through the experiences of Scout Finch, a small-town tomboy, is Lee's only novel. Lee was awarded the Presidential Medal of Freedom in 2007.

LEE, Sir Henry (1533–1611) Master of the armoury and ranger of Woodstock. Lee was closely involved in much Elizabethan pageantry and, around 1570, probably initiated the annual celebration of the queen's accession day (17 November) with tilts and allegorical devices, involving speeches, poetry, and music: some of these are reflected in Philip *Sidney's revised *Arcadia. He played a part in the Woodstock entertainments of 1575 and 1592; on his own retirement as queen's champion in 1590 the poem, which Lee may have written himself, 'His golden locks, ¦ Time hath to silver turned', was sung. The event was commemorated by George *Peele in his *Polyhymnia.

LEE, Hermione (1948–) Critic and biographer. Her books include *The Novels of Virginia Woolf* (1977); *Elizabeth Bowen* (1981; rev. 1999); *Philip Roth* (1982); *Willa Cather: A Life Saved Up* (1989; rev. 2008); *Virginia Woolf* (1996); and *Edith Wharton* (2007). She has also published a collection of essays on biography and autobiography, *Body Parts: Essays on Life-Writing* (2005). *See* BIOGRAPHY.

LEE, Laurie (1914–97) Writer. His volumes of poetry (*The Sun my Monument*, 1944; *The Bloom of Candles*, 1947; *My Many-Coated Man*, 1955) show a sensuous apprehension of the natural world, as does his best-known work, the widely popular *Cider with Rosie* (1959), a highly evocative and nostalgic account of his country boyhood in a secluded Cotswold valley. It describes a vanished rural world of homemade wine, village school, church outings; Lee described himself as a chance witness of 'the end of a thousand years' life'. The 'Rosie' of the title is a village girl who 'baptized [him] with her cidrous kisses' behind a haycock. A second autobiographical volume, *As I Walked out One Midsummer Morning* (1969), describes his departure from Stroud, his walk to London, and his months in Spain on the eve of the Spanish Civil War. *A Moment of War* (1991) is a sequel.

LEE, Nathaniel (?1649–92) A failed actor turned playwright, whose tragedies, marked by extravagance and passion, include *Nero* (1675), *Sophonisba* and *Gloriana* (1676), all in rhymed heroic couplets; his best-known tragedy, *The *Rival Queens* (1677), in blank verse; *Theodosius* (1680); and one of his most serious dramas, *Lucius Junius Brutus*, which was banned for its anti-monarchical speeches after only three performances. He collaborated with John *Dryden in *Oedipus* (1679) and *The Duke of Guise* (1682). He lost his reason, was confined to Bedlam 1684–9, and died after a drinking bout.

LEE, Sir Sidney (1859–1926) Editor and biographer, born Solomon Lazarus Levi. He was a member of the editorial staff of *The *Dictionary of National Biography* from the beginning in 1882 and became joint editor in 1890 and sole editor from 1891. His publications include *Stratford-on-Avon from the Earliest Times to the Death of Shakespeare* (1885; new edn 1906), *Life of William Shakespeare* (1898; rev. edn 1925), which for many years was considered the standard biography, and *Principles of Biography* (1911).

LEE, Sophia (1750–1824) Daughter of an actor, who ran a private school in Bath with her sister Harriet Lee. She had some success as both dramatist and novelist. Her play *The Chapter of Accidents* (1780) was frequently staged; and her first novel, *The Recess* (1783–5), a form of early *historical novel, sold well and was translated into French. A long ballad, *The Hermit's Tale*, followed in 1787, and a verse tragedy, *Almeyda, Queen of Grenada* (1796). She contributed to her sister's *Canterbury Tales* (1798), and published an *epistolary autobiographical novel, *The Life of a Lover* (1804).

LEE, Vernon (1856–1935) Pseudonym of Violet Paget (derived from the name of her brother, Eugene *Lee-Hamilton). Influenced by Walter *Pater, and a contributor to the *Yellow Book*, she was the author of more than forty books and many essays. The subjects of her non-fiction include history, art, literary criticism, ethics, aesthetics, biography, and travel. Her tales of the supernatural include the enduringly popular *Hauntings* (1890).

LEE-HAMILTON, Eugene (1845–1907) Poet, novelist, and half-brother of Violet Paget (alias Vernon *Lee). He lived most of his life in Florence and, health permitting, hosted intellectual contemporaries including Edith *Wharton and Henry *James. Works such as *Imaginary Sonnets* (1888) and *The Sonnets of the Wingless Hours* (1894) demonstrate his skilful control of the sonnet form and use of dramatic impersonal voice.

Le FANU, Sheridan [pron. Léff-anew] (1814–73) Journalist, and writer of novels and tales of mystery and the supernatural. By 1840 he had published a dozen or so stories (including 'A Strange Event in the Life of Schalken the Painter', rated by M. R. *James as 'one of the best of Le Fanu's good things') in the *Dublin University Magazine*. From 1840 onwards he became increasingly involved in Irish journalism. His first two novels, *The Cock and Anchor* (1845) and *Torlogh O' Brien* (1847), were in the tradition of Walter *Scott and Harrison *Ainsworth. In 1861 he acquired the *Dublin University Magazine*, which began the serialization of *The House by the Churchyard*, followed by *Wylder's Hand* (issued in book form in 1864), *Uncle Silas* (1864), *Guy Deverell* (1865), *The Tenants of Malory* (1867), *A Lost Name* (1868), *The Wyvern Mystery* (1869), *Checkmate* (1871), *The Rose and the Key* (1871), and *Willing to Die* (1873). The story collection *In a Glass Darkly* appeared in 1872.

Le Fanu was one of the best-sellers of the 1860s–1880s; a subsequent period of 'unmitigated famelessness' ended with the publication in 1923 of *Madam Crowl's Ghost and Other Tales of Mystery*, edited by M. R. James, who considered that Le Fanu 'stands absolutely in the first rank as a writer of *ghost stories'. Le Fanu is now ranked with as the equal of Wilkie *Collins as a writer of mysteries.

Left Book Club Publishing venture founded in 1936 by Victor *Gollancz and others. Modelled on commercial book club lines, its educational aim was to resist the rise of Fascism and Nazism. In its heyday it had about 50,000 members. The vast majority of its publications were factual (though three novels and one play, *Waiting for Lefty* (1937), by Clifford *Odets, were included), and the best-known title today is George *Orwell's *The Road to Wigan Pier* (1937). The Club was dissolved in 1948.

Le GALLIENNE, Richard (1866–1947) Poet, novelist, and critic. His first volume, *My Ladies' Sonnets and Other 'Vain and Amatorious' Verses* (1887), was printed privately in Liverpool. In London from 1888, he became attached to the *fin-de-siècle* group which centred on Aubrey *Beardsley; he was an original member of the *Rhymers Club with W. B. *Yeats, Oscar *Wilde, and Lionel *Johnson. He contributed to the *Yellow Book* and throughout the 1890s wrote verse and literary criticism; he published several romantic novels, including *The Quest for the Golden Girl* (1896);. *The Romantic '90s* (1926) is an account of this period.

Legend of Good Women, The Written by Geoffrey *Chaucer and of uncertain date, based on works including *Ovid's *Heroides*, and *Boccaccio's *De Claris Mulieribus*. The prologue opens with some famous lines in praise of the daisy (conforming to the tradition of 'Marguerite' poems in French) and continues with the rebuking of the sleeping narrator by the god of love because of his previous dispraise of women (another commonplace convention). The narrator vows to make amends by composing this work in praise of women celebrated for their fidelity in love, as directed by the queen of love, Alceste. The unfinished poem contains nine stories of famous women: *Cleopatra, Thisbe, Dido, Hypsipyle and Medea, Lucrece, Ariadne, *Philomela, Phyllis, and Hypermnestra.

Legend of Montrose, A A novel by Walter *Scott, published 1819, in *Tales of my Landlord*, 3rd series. The novel is based on an episode in the earl of Montrose's campaign of 1644 to raise Scotland for Charles I against the Covenant forces of the marquis of Argyle.

Le GUIN, Ursula (1929–) American novelist and short story writer Her numerous works of *science fiction and *fantasy for both children and adults have been widely admired for their distinguished prose and their imaginative and thoughtful speculations. Her works include the 'Hainish' sequence, beginning with *Rocannon's World* (1966), *Planet of Exile* (1966), and *City of Illusions* (1967). *The Birthday of the World* (2002), and her other science fiction works are mostly set in the Hainish universe. The fantasy Earthsea sequence extends from *A Wizard of Earthsea* (1968) to *The Other Wind* (2001). *The Left Hand of Darkness* (1969), a *Hugo winner, imagines an androgynous species to consider issues of gender. *The Dispossessed* (1974) and *Always Coming Home* (1985) are thoughtful utopias. Other novels include *Malafrena* (1979) *The Beginning Place* (1980), and *Lavinia* (2008).

LEHMANN, John (1907–87) Poet, publisher, and editor, brother of Rosamond *Lehmann. Associated with the *Hogarth Press from 1931, he became managing editor in 1938. The press published his first book of poems, *A Garden Revisited* (1931). His *Collected Poems 1930–63* appeared in 1963. Lehmann is probably best known as the editor of *New Writing* (1936–41) and of the *London Magazine* (1954–61). He published three volumes of autobiography, *The Whispering Gallery* (1951), *I am my Brother* (1960), and *The Ample Proposition* (1966), and several volumes of reminiscence and biography, which include works on the *Sitwells (1968), the Woolfs, and Rupert *Brooke (1980).

LEHMANN, Rosamond Nina (1901–90) Novelist, sister of John *Lehmann; her first novel, *Dusty Answer* (1927), which describes a girl's awakening into womanhood, and its successor, *A Note in Music* (1930), dealing frankly with homosexuality, both created a stir. *Invitation to the Waltz* (1932) describes the impact on Olivia Curtis of her first dance; its sequel, *The Weather in the Streets* (1936), takes Olivia through a failed marriage, an adulterous love affair, and an abortion. *The Echoing Grove* (1953), a novel about the relationship of two sisters, was followed only after many years by *The Swan in the Evening: Fragments of an Inner Life* (1967). This short autobiography recalls her childhood, then describes the sudden death of her daughter in 1958 and her spiritual experiences which convince her of her daughter's survival after death.

LEIBNIZ, Gottfried Wilhelm (1646–1716) German philosopher and mathematician, one of the chief forces in the German *Enlightenment. As a philosopher he was inspired by René *Descartes, Benedict de *Spinoza, and Thomas *Hobbes, but broke away from Descartes's mechanical conception of the universe. Admitting that the interaction of spirit and matter is inexplicable, he assumed a 'pre-established harmony' between them. Voltaire satirized his 'optimism' in *Candide. His system is embodied in his *Théodicée* (1710) and *Monadologie* (1714), written in French.

LEIGH, Mike (1943–) Writer and stage and film director, who has evolved a unique way of working in extended periods of intense improvisation and collaboration with actors. His many plays now seem like a preparation for a prodigious output of television and feature films, although he returned to the stage in 2005 with *Two Thousand Years*, drawing on his Jewish background. His films range from the suburban repression of *Bleak Moments* (1971) to the inner-city anomie of *Meantime* (1983). *Abigail's Party* (1977), his best-known stage and television play, is a classic of social embarrassment. Particularly notable are *Life is Sweet* (1990), the provocative, Dostoevskian *Naked* (1993), and the richly poignant *Secrets and Lies* (1996); *Vera Drake* (2005) is a sympathetic portrayal of a 1950s backstreet abortionist. *Happy-Go-Lucky* (2008), a portrait of a primary school teacher, is an uncharacteristically sunny film. *Another Year* (2010) is unusual in portraying a happily married middle-aged couple. A collection of interviews was published in 2000.

Leinster, Book of An Irish manuscript of the 12th century, containing mythological, genealogical, and historical texts in prose and verse, including versions of *Táin-Bó-Cuailnge* and *The Fate of the Sons of Usnach* (*see* DEIRDRE).

L.E.L. Initials used as pseudonym by Letitia Elizabeth *Landon.

LEMON, Mark (1809–70) Founder, first joint editor, then editor of *Punch. Lemon wrote prolifically for the stage, and performed in Charles *Dickens's private theatricals. He collaborated with Dickens in *Mr Nightingale's Diary* (1851), a one-act farce with both authors in the cast. Lemon also wrote fairy-tales for children, and in his final years published several novels, of which *Falkner Lyle* (1866) was the most successful.

LENNOX, Charlotte (*c.*1730–1804) Née Ramsay, novelist and translator. Her first novel, the autobiographical *Life of Harriot Stuart, Written by Herself* (1750) was celebrated by Samuel *Johnson with a party and a huge apple pie. Her name was established by *The *Female Quixote* (1752), which was praised by Henry *Fielding. Her collection and translation of the sources of Shakespeare's plays appeared as *Shakespear Illustrated* (1752–3). *Henrietta* (1758), a novel concerned with female dependence, was dramatized as *The Sisters*, with an epilogue by Oliver *Goldsmith: it had one performance in 1769. David *Garrick produced her *Old City Manners* in 1775, with more success. She also translated many French texts; her poverty made her one of the early beneficiaries of the *Royal Literary Fund.

LEONARD, Elmore (1925–) American writer, who began his literary career writing *westerns. Many of his stories and novels became classic western films, including '3.10 to Yuma' (first filmed 1957, remade in 2007), and *Hombre* (1961; filmed 1966). As the market for westerns declined, he turned to crime writing, producing many titles including *City Primeval* (1980), *Glitz* (1985), *Freaky Deaky* (1988), *Get Shorty* (1990; filmed 1996), and *Rum Punch* (1992; filmed by Quentin Tarantino as *Jackie Brown* (1997). Admired for his terse dialogue, vividly observed locations, laconic wit, and short action scenes, he has been acclaimed as the heir to Dashiell *Hammett and Raymond *Chandler.

LEONARD, Tom (1944–) Scottish poet, essayist, and polemicist. Leonard's writings in prose and verse, sometimes with accompanying cartoons, focus on vernacular authenticity as a mode of resistance to hierarchies of power and aesthetic value. He is best known for the satirical poems in phonetically transcribed Glaswegian collected in *Intimate Voices: Selected Work 1965–1983* (1984). His anthology *Radical Renfrew* (1990) uncovers a rooted tradition of egalitarian poetry in the west of Scotland, while his formally innovative biography *Places of the Mind* (1993) pays homage to one of the greatest figures in that tradition, James *Thomson ('B.V.'). See *Access to the Silence: Poems and Posters 1984–2004* (2004).

LEONARDO DA VINCI (1452–1519) Florentine painter, sculptor, musician, scientist, and thinker. *The Last Supper* (*c.*1495) and the *Mona Lisa* (*c.*1503) are perhaps the two most celebrated pictures in the Western tradition.

In the 19th century the enigmatic charm of Leonardo's women mesmerized writers, and was powerfully evoked in a famous passage by Walter *Pater; his 'Lady Lisa' popularized the Fatal Woman whose development has been outlined by Mario Praz. Echoes of her fascination recur through Decadent poetry but she is parodied by Aldous *Huxley in 'The Gioconda Smile'.

leonine verse A form of Latin verse much used in the Middle Ages (for example in John *Gower's Latin poetry), consisting of hexameters, or alternate hexameters and pentameters, in which the last word rhymes with that preceding the caesura. The term is applied to English verse of which the middle and last syllables rhyme.

LEOPARDI, Giacomo (1798–1837) The greatest Italian Romantic poet. In his richly suggestive lyrics (*Canti*, 1831, 1845), he elaborated a Romantic poetics based on the tension between past and present, childhood innocence and adult awareness of insignificance, illusions and their loss. Both Ezra *Pound and Robert *Lowell produced versions of his poems.

LEPRINCE DE BEAUMONT, Jeanne-Marie (1711–80) French novelist and story writer, who emigrated to England c.1745. She published her influential four-volume *Magasin des enfants* in 1756, and her own English translation, *The Young Misses Magazine*, in 1757. The contents, in the form of conversations between a governess and her children, are both didactic and amusing; included in the text are two now-famous *fairy stories, 'Beauty and the Beast' and 'The Three Wishes', told specifically for young readers.

Lêr (Lir) In Gaelic mythology, the sea god, one of the *Tuatha Dé Danann; perhaps to be identified with the British sea god Llyr. He was the father of *Manannán.

LERMONTOV, Mikhail Iurevich (1814–41) Russian Romantic poet, novelist, and dramatist. Strongly influenced by Lord *Byron, Lermontov wrote lyric and narrative poetry on the themes of disillusionment, rebellion, and personal freedom. His verse melodrama, influenced by Alexandre Dumas (1802–70), *The Masquerade* (1836), was heavily censored, and published in full only in 1873, but his prose masterpiece, the novel *A Hero of our Time*, appeared in 1840, and has been much translated.

LESAGE, Alain-René (1668–1747) French novelist and playwright, best known as the author of two *picaresque novels: *Le Diable boiteux* (1707: *The Devil on Crutches*), a series of satirical sketches of contemporary society, and the enormously successful *Histoire de Gil Blas de Santillane* (1715–35). Translated by Tobias *Smollett in 1749, it can be considered with *Don Quixote* and *Rabelais, the greatest foreign influence on 18th-century English comic fiction. Lesage was also a prolific playwright, achieving greatest success with *Turcaret* (1709), a satire of an unscrupulous financier.

LESSING, Doris (1919–) Née Tayler, novelist and short story writer, born in Persia (Iran) and brought up in Southern Rhodesia (Zimbabwe). Her first published novel, *The Grass is Singing* (1950), is the story of the relationship between a white farmer's wife and her black servant. Her quintet *Children of Violence* (1952–69) is a *Bildungsroman*, tracing the history of Martha Quest from her childhood in Rhodesia, through post-war Britain, to an apocalyptic ending in 2000. *The Golden Notebook* (1962) was hailed as a landmark by the women's movement. Later novels, *Briefing for a Descent into Hell* (1971) and *Memoirs of a Survivor* (1975), enter the realm of 'inner space fiction', exploring mental illness and the breakdown of society. The sequence of five novels collectively entitled *Canopus in Argos: Archives* (1979–83) marks a complete break with traditional realism, describing the epic and mythic events of a fictional universe with a remarkable freedom of invention. In order to test the market for fiction by unknown writers, she submitted two far more conventional novels to her publishers under the pseudonym of Jane Somers. Initially rejected, *Diary of a Good Neighbour* (1983) and *If the Old Could* (1984) were eventually published and their authorship revealed. Other novels include *The Good Terrorist* (1985) and *The Cleft* (2007). Two evocative volumes of autobiography, *Under my Skin* (1994) and *Waiting in the Shade* (1997), cover Lessing's life up until 1962. Many other works of fiction and non-fiction, including the essays in *Time Bites* (2004) and *Collected Stories*, 2 vols (1978), display her concern with politics, with the changing destiny of women, with a fear of technological disaster, her love of cats and her interest in *Sufism and the works of Idries Shah. In 2007, to her evident surprise, she was awarded the *Nobel Prize for Literature and devoted her acceptance speech to the importance of books and her concern that the internet was resulting in 'a fragmenting culture', replacing the 'great store of literature' that once produced a truly international community of readers.

L'ESTRANGE, Sir Roger (1616–1704) Journalist and pamphleteer. After the *Restoration he was appointed surveyor of printing presses and licenser of the press. He issued the *News* and the *Intelligencer* (1663–6) which were ousted by the *London Gazette* of Henry *Muddiman; one of his earliest political pamphlets, was a reply to John *Milton, *No Blind Guides* (1660). In his periodical the *Observator* (1681–7) he attacked the Whigs, Titus Oates (1649–1705), and Dissenters in colloquial, forceful, and conversational prose. He was knighted by James II in 1685, but after the revolution was regarded by the Whigs as a grave threat to liberty, and was several times imprisoned.

letters and correspondence These are important autobiographical documents for both historians and literary critics. In the 16th and 17th centuries, letters were particularly associated with female writers and have provided a unique source of information about women's lives. Letters were written according to rhetorical exemplars such as *Erasmus' De Conscribendis Epistolis* (1522) and the *English Secretorie* (1586) by Angell Day (*fl.* 1563–95), but Renaissance manuals also introduced the concept of the 'familial' letter and encouraged improvisation. The conventions of letter writing allow writers to construct themselves in many ways according to the occasion and the recipient, while the practice of letter writing encouraged privacy, and a withdrawal into a separate space. In the 18th century the publication of letters began to confuse the letter's association with private space, even as epistolary novels such as Samuel *Richardson's *Pamela* and *Clarissa* drew on letters in order to explore their characters' interiority. Mary *Wollstonecraft in her *Letters Written during a Short Residence in Sweden, Norway and Denmark* (1798) turns the use of the letter round, using the conventional role of the female letter writer to make astute political and philosophical comments. John *Keats's letters, which T. S. *Eliot believed were 'certainly the most notable and most important ever written by any English poet', used the form as a vehicle for working out his aesthetics. For Elizabeth *Bishop, a frequent traveller, the letter had become an art form in itself.

LEVER, Charles (1806–72) Irish doctor who became a prolific and successful novelist, writing chiefly of military and Irish life. His first novels, *Harry Lorrequer* (1839), *Charles O' Malley* (1841), and *Jack Hinton the Guardsman* (1843), were extremely popular, and in 1842 he gave up medicine for the editorship of the *Dublin University Magazine*. *Tom Burke of Ours* (1844) and a *historical novel, *The Knight of Gwynne* (1847), were notable among the stream of his racy, anecdotal works. In 1845 he left Ireland and eventually settled in Italy. *The Martins of Cro' Martin* (1847) provides a spirited portrait of life in the west of Ireland, and *The Dodd Family Abroad* (1852–4) an account of an English family's vicissitudes on the Continent. Lever's later novels include *Sir Jasper Carew* (1855), *The Fortunes of Glencore* (1857), and *Lord Kilgobbin* (1872).

LEVERTOV, Denise (1923–97) British-American poet, who published the neo-Romantic *The Double Image* in 1947. In 1948 she moved to America where she became a central figure in the *Black Mountain group; she maintained her modernist aims in an unceasing flow of volumes from 1958 to 1996. Her search for the mystic and for 'organic form' led her to use free verse as she addressed family relationships, the natural world, and politics, notably the Vietnam War. *The Sorrow Dance* (1967) and *Selected Poems* (1986) contain some of her best work. Her prose includes *New & Selected Essays* (1992).

LEVI, Peter (1931–2000) Poet, translator, classical scholar, travel writer, and archaeologist; he was a Jesuit priest from 1964 to 1977, when he resigned the priesthood. His first volume of poetry was *The Gravel Ponds* (1960); a *Collected Poems 1955–1975* appeared in 1976. His poems mingle imagery and themes from classical antiquity, British history and prehistory, Christianity, and domestic life. A volume of autobiography, *The Flutes of Autumn* (1983), concludes with an eloquent tribute to David *Jones.

LEVI, Primo (1919–87) Italian chemist and writer of memoirs, fiction, essays, and poetry. In 1943 he was captured as a partisan and sent as a Jew to Auschwitz. His scientific training and self-effacing nature made him an observant and objective witness in *Se questo è un uomo* (1947: *If This is a Man*, 1960), his memoir of Auschwitz; *La tregua* (1963: *The Truce*, 1965), the story of his journey home; and the essays in *I sommersi e i salvati* (1986: *The Drowned and the Saved*, 1988). His 'chemist's autobiography', *Il sistema periodico* (1975: *The Periodic Table*, 1985), consolidated his international reputation. He took his own life on 11 April 1987. *See* HOLO-CAUST.

Leviathan, *or The Matter, Form, and Power of a Commonwealth, Ecclesiastical and Civil* A treatise of political philosophy by Thomas *Hobbes, published 1651, Latin text 1668. Hobbes works out his political philosophy from first principles. Men, he argues, are selfish by nature, and their judgements of what is good and evil are subjective, so their disputes cannot be settled by reference to any absolute values. Consequently the state of nature would be one of perpetual warfare, and man's life would be 'solitary, poor, nasty, brutish and short'. To prevent this Hobbes lays down certain 'Laws of Nature', which are not what we understand by natural laws, but rather agreements that must be reached to make social life possible. These are: that every man should seek peace, and should be contented with as much liberty towards other men as he would allow them towards himself. This amounts to a contract or covenant, and the obligation to perform covenants is the third Law of Nature. From this Hobbes develops the case for political absolutism. For to enforce these covenants it is necessary to establish a central power, and so all men must enter into a contract to confer their individual powers on one man, namely, a sovereign, whose powers are inalienable. This will transform a multitude into a commonwealth. Once such a contract has come into being, subjects cannot lawfully change the form of government, and since the sovereign represents all his subjects he cannot commit an injustice. Since the aim of the commonwealth is peace, it will be right for the sovereign to introduce censorship of the press and curtail freedom of speech if he thinks peace is threatened. The sovereign power is indivisible; it cannot for instance be divided between king and Parliament. Further, since there can be only one sovereign power, it will be inadmissible for a subject to obey his conscience, or his church. The church must be subordinate to the state. The obligation of subjects to obey the sovereign is understood, however, to last only so long as the power by which he is able to protect them.

LÉVI-STRAUSS, Claude (1908–2009) French anthropologist. His principal early works were the analysis of kinship systems in *Les Structures élémentaires de la parenté* (1949: *The Elementary Structures of Kinship*) and the auto-biographical travelogue *Tristes tropiques* (1955: *The Sad Tropics*). His major contributions to the analysis of myths appear in *Anthropologie structurale* (1958: *Structural Anthropology*), *Le Cru et le cuit* (1964: *The Raw and the Cooked*), and the four volumes of *Mythologiques* (1964–72). After Ferdinand de *Saussure, he was a chief exponent of *structuralism in the 'human sciences'.

LEVY, Amy (1861–89) Poet, essayist and novelist. Her collections are *Xantippe and Other Verse* (1881, of which the title poem is a dramatic monologue spoken by the allegedly shrewish wife of *Socrates), *A Minor Poet and Other Verse* (1884), and the posthumously published *A London Plane-Tree and Other Verse* (1889). Her novel *Reuben Sachs* (1888) tells the story of an Anglo-Jewish community, and was misrepresented by reviewers as an attack on Jewish identity. Levy's third novel, *Miss Meredith*, appeared in 1889, but, suffering from depression, she committed suicide later that year.

LEVY, Andrea (1956–) Born in London to Jamaican parents. Her novels *Every Light in the House Burnin'* (1994) and *Never Far from Nowhere* (1996) explore the experience of black British-born children in London. *Fruit of the Lemon* (1999) tells the story of a black Londoner who visits Jamaica. *Small Island* (2004) depicts the post-war wave of Caribbean immigration often called the 'Windrush generation' after the SS *Empire Windrush*, the ship that brought 492 Jamaican immigrants to England in June 1948. *The Long Song* (2010) is set in early 19th century Jamaica.

LEWES, George Henry (1817–78) A writer of extraordinarily varied interests and talents, the author of the first proselytizing article on *Hegel's aesthetics in England; a novel in imitation of *Goethe, *Ranthorpe* (1847); one of the first books in English on Auguste *Comte's positivist philosophy (1853); and a popular history of philosophy from Francis *Bacon to Comte (*Biographical History of Philosophy*, 1845–6). He is best known as the partner and supporter of George *Eliot. His life with George Eliot, dating from 1854, could not be regularized because he had condoned the adultery of his wife Agnes with Thornton Leigh Hunt. By the time he met George Eliot, he was estranged from Agnes, but could not divorce her.

Lewes's *Life of Goethe* (1855), which he researched with George Eliot's help in Weimar and Berlin in 1854–5, was a work of valuable scholarship. He turned his attention increasingly to science: his later works range from biological works like *Seaside Studies* (1858) and *The Physiology of Common Life* (1859) to his ambitious investigation of psychology, *Problems of Life and Mind* (1873–9), the last volume of which was completed by George Eliot after his death.

LEWIS, Alun (1915–44) Poet, born in Glamorgan. His first volume of poems, *Raiders' Dawn*, appeared in 1942, followed by a volume of stories, *The Last Inspection* (1943), most of which deal with army life in England. His most anthologized poem, 'All Day it has Rained' (published 1941), refers to Edward *Thomas. Many of Lewis's poems are concerned with isolation and death; Lewis died in Burma. Posthumously published collections include: *In the Green Tree* (1948, letters and stories); *Selected Poetry and Prose*, with a biographical introduction by Ian *Hamilton; and *Collected Poems* (1994); and *A Cypress Walk* (2006, letters).

LEWIS, C. S. (Clive Staples) (1898–1963) Belfast-born literary scholar, critic, and novelist. His critical works include *The Allegory of Love* (1936) and *English Literature in the Sixteenth Century* (1954). He is more widely known for his popular religious and moral writings, including *The Problem of Pain* (1940), *The Screwtape Letters* (1940), and *The Four Loves* (1960). *Out of the Silent Planet* (1938) is the first of three strongly Christian *science fiction novels, influenced by his friendship with J. R. R. *Tolkien and Charles *Williams.

In 1950 he began a series of seven 'Narnia' stories for children, beginning with *The Lion, the Witch, and the Wardrobe*. The alternative world of Narnia is populated by creatures from myths, legends, and sagas, the most important of these being Aslan the lion, a divinity modelled on Christ. The Chronicles have been filmed for television (1990) and cinema (2005) and turned into a computer game; *The Lion, the Witch, and the Wardrobe* is regularly staged.

Surprised by Joy (1955) is his spiritual autobiography; *A Grief Observed* (1961) records his four-year marriage, also the subject of a stage play and film, *Shadowlands* (1989), by William Nicholson. 'The *Inklings', a group of his friends, met for many years to talk and read aloud their compositions.

LEWIS, Cecil Day *See* DAY-LEWIS, CECIL.

LEWIS, Gwyneth (1959–) Bilingual Welsh poet. She has published five collections of poetry in Welsh, in addition to her English collections, including *Parables and Faxes* (1995), *Zero Gravity* (1998), *Keeping Mum* (2003), and

A Hospital Odyssey (2010). *Sunbathing in the Rain: A Cheerful Book on Depression* (2002) is a powerful account of her struggle with mental illness. The stories of *The Meat Tree* (2010) are based on the *Mabinogion.

LEWIS, M. G. (Matthew Gregory) (1775–1818) Remembered as the author of *The *Monk* (1796), a scandalous *Gothic novel. Lewis was greatly influenced by German Romanticism, and wrote numerous dramas in its more histrionic manner.

LEWIS, Meriwether (1774–1809) American explorer, personal secretary to President Thomas Jefferson (1743–1826). He led the Corps of Discovery expedition, which explored the area of the Louisiana Purchase (1804–6), with William Clark (1770–1838) as his second in command. The Lewis and Clark expedition covered more than 8,000 miles in its western journey from St Louis to the Pacific and back again, but failed in its quest for a direct water route to the Pacific. It studied and described more than 300 plant and animal species, the geology and mineralogy of the regions, and the Native Americans whose first contact with whites this was and several groups of whom provided invaluable support. Lewis's journals were published posthumously, and in a new thirteen-volume edition (2002, University of Nebraska Press). The expedition and its accounts stimulated American interest in the west and helped establish its dominance in the region over rival European interests.

LEWIS, Norman (1908–2003) Travel writer and novelist, whose many travel narratives recount journeys through Indo-China and Burma (*A Dragon Apparent*, 1951; *Golden Earth*, 1952), the Mediterranean, India, and Cuba, and combine vivid evocation of place, lively storytelling, and acute political analysis. His 1968 article in the *Sunday Times* 'Genocide in Brazil', exposed the near-extinction of the native population, and led to the creation of the charity Survival International. (See Christopher *Hampton's play *Savages*.) Lewis's novels include *The Day of the Fox* (1955), *The Volcanoes above Us* (1957), and *A Suitable Case for Corruption* (1984). *Jackdaw Cake* (1985, later revised as *I Came, I Saw*) and *The World, the World* (1996) are autobiographies.

LEWIS, Saunders (1893–1985) Welsh dramatist, poet, critic, literary historian, and cultural agitator, born in Wallasey (then Cheshire). In the scale and impact of his exertions, Lewis is a Welsh counterpart to W. B. *Yeats in Ireland

and Hugh *MacDiarmid in Scotland. In 1925 he co-founded the Welsh Nationalist Party (later Plaid Cymru). His nineteen plays include the (English) comedy *The Eve of St John* (1921), the austere poetic tragedy *Siwan* (1956), set in the Welsh Middle Ages, and *Brad* (1958), an acute exploration of the ethical dilemma of the participants in the 1944 plot against Hitler. *Monica* (1930) is the more admired of his two novels. Though he published fewer than 60 poems, Lewis is regarded as one of the greatest masters of Welsh metrics.

LEWIS, Sinclair (1885–1951) American novelist, who achieved his first success with *Main Street* in 1920. It describes with satirical realism the dullness of life in a small Midwestern town called Gopher Prairie. **Babbitt* (1922), is the story of George Babbitt, a prosperous and self-satisfied house agent in the Midwestern town of Zenith, who comes to doubt the conventions of middle-class society, but is eventually reabsorbed after a period of defiance and ostracism (hence the term 'babbittry') Other novels include *Arrowsmith* (1925); *Elmer Gantry* (1927), which takes a satiric view of Midwestern evangelism; and *Dodsworth* (1929). *It Can't Happen Here* (1935) speculatively describes the establishment of totalitarianism in the USA. Lewis was awarded the *Nobel Prize in 1930.

LEWIS, Wyndham (1882–1957) Novelist, critic, and artist. He was a leader of the *Vorticist movement and, with Ezra *Pound, edited *Blast* (1914, 1915); Lewis's own *little magazine, *The Enemy*, appeared in three book-length issues, 1927–9, written largely by himself (with poems by Laura *Riding and Roy *Campbell). His novels include the aggressively *modernist *Tarr* (1918; rev. 1928); *The Apes of God* (1930), an acerbic satire on London literary life; *The Revenge for Love* (1937); and *Self Condemned* (1957). His projected four-part work *The Human Age* (*The Childermass*, 1928; *Monstre Gai* and *Malign Fiesta*, both 1955) remained unfinished at his death. Essays and criticism include *Time and Western Man* (1927), *The Lion and the Fox: The Role of Hero in the Plays of Shakespeare* (1927), and *The Writer and the Absolute* (1952). *Blasting and Bombardiering* (1937) and *Rude Assignment* (1950) are autobiographies. Although his criticism of the increasing hollowness and mechanization of 20th-century civilization had affinities with the ideas of Ezra Pound, T. S. *Eliot, and D. H. *Lawrence, his savage satirical attacks on his contemporaries (particularly the *Bloomsbury Group) and his praise of the pre-Führer

Hitler (in *Hitler*, 1931) alienated him from many in the literary world, though his enthusiasm was repudiated in *The Hitler Cult* (1939) and the pro-Jewish *The Jews, Are they Human?* (1939). He is not to be confused with D. B. Wyndham Lewis (1891–1969), the biographer and journalist who also wrote as Beachcomber.

Li, Yiyun (1972–) Chinese American writer; she moved to the USA in 1996 and has applied for permanent residency. She is particularly known for her short stories, mostly set in contemporary China, which are collected in *A Thousand Years of Good Prayers* (2005; two stories filmed by Wayne Wang, 2007), and *Gold Boy, Emerald Girl* (2010); *The Vagrants* (2009) is a novel. Li acknowledges William *Trevor's influence on her writing.

Libeaus Desconus [a corruption of *le bel inconnu*, the fair unknown] A 14th-century romance in 2,232 lines of twelve-line, *tail-rhyme stanzas. Gingelein, the son of Gawain, asks Arthur for knighthood and, since his name is unknown, he is knighted as *Li Beaus Desconus*. The poem describes his adventures leading to his marriage with the Lady of Sinadoune, his kinship to Gawain revealed through his ability to rescue her from enchantment. In *Chaucer's 'Sir Thopas' the knight's name is given simply as 'Sir Lybeux' (see CANTERBURY TALES, 17). *Malory's tale of Gareth also has obvious affinities with the *bel inconnu* tradition.

Libelle of Englyshe Polycye, The ('The Little Book of English Policy') A political poem of about 2,250 lines written *c.*1436, in which the author urges his countrymen to regard the sea as the source of national strength, discusses commercial relations with other countries, and emphasizes the importance of retaining Ireland, Calais, and Wales. The poem was included by Richard *Hakluyt, and it has been doubtfully attributed to Adam Moleyns or Molyneaux (d. 1450), clerk of the king's council.

Liberal, The (1822–4) A magazine of four issues only but of great brilliance. Conceived by P. B. *Shelley, the plan was carried out after his death by Lord *Byron and Leigh *Hunt. Byron's *The *Vision of Judgement* first appeared in its pages, as did his *Heaven and Earth*, and much other work by Shelley, Hunt, William *Hazlitt, James *Hogg, and others.

Liber Amoris, or *The New Pygmalion* An autobiographical prose work by William *Hazlitt, published anonymously in 1823. It records in letters and dialogues the frenzied infatuation

Hazlitt conceived at the age of 43 for a 19-year-old girl, Sarah Walker, who eventually rejected him for another suitor. The fevered tone of the book, and its humiliating self-exposure, distressed Hazlitt's friends and gave ammunition to his various enemies, his anonymity having been seen through at once.

Liberty, On An essay by John Stuart *Mill, published 1859. In this hugely influential work, central to Victorian liberalism and continuously in print since its first publication, Mill attempts to define the proper relations between the individual and society. He argues that 'the sole end for which mankind are warranted, individually or collectively, in interfering with liberty of action of any of their number, is self-protection'. The individual is only answerable to society for conduct which affects others. 'Mankind are greater gainers by suffering each other to live as seems good to themselves, than by compelling each to live as seems good to the rest.'

libretto The Italian word for the 'little book' in which the text of an opera (or oratorio) was printed, and hence the text itself. In England, opera developed from stage plays and masques, such as The Siege of Rhodes, by the experienced playwright Sir William *D'Avenant, so libretti were normally, to begin with, play texts. Early English librettists include Nahum *Tate, author of the libretto for *Purcell's Dido and Aeneas; Thomas *Shadwell, whose Psyche (1675, with music by Matthew Locke) was adapted from *Molière, and John *Dryden, whose Albion and Albanius (1685) was set to music by Louis Grabu. After the formal establishment of Italian opera in Britain with the arrival of Handel, composers tended to set a text specially provided by a professional librettist. English libretti survived in the form of the *ballad operas which followed John Gay's The *Beggar's Opera, though these were in effect straight plays interspersed with music, and the many comic opera texts produced by Isaac *Bickerstaff in the 1760s and 1770s (set mainly by Thomas *Arne and Charles Dibdin). In the same vein is Richard Sheridan's The *Duenna (1775). In the 1870s the series of Gilbert and Sullivan operas foreshadowed popular musical collaborations between lyricists and composers such as Rogers and Hammerstein. In the 20th century, Gustav Holst and Michael Tippett wrote their own libretti. Thomas *Hardy, J. M. *Synge, A. P. *Herbert, Clifford Bax (1886-1962), J. B. *Priestley, and William *Plomer are among those writers who have provided texts for composers; W. H. *Auden, in his libretti for

Benjamin *Britten, Stravinsky, and Hans Werner *Henze, established himself as an important writer in the form. Peter Maxwell Davies and Harrison *Birtwistle have each worked closely with poets. James *Fenton contributed material to the libretto of the immensely successful musical adaptation of Victor *Hugo's Les Misérables (perf. UK 1985).

LICKBARROW, Isabella (1784-1847) Poet, born in Kendal. Her first volume, Poetical Effusions (1814), was published 'to assist the humble labours of herself and her orphan sisters'. William *Wordsworth features on the volume's subscription list (as do Thomas *De Quincey and Robert *Southey). Though sometimes melancholic, her tone lacks the air of despair evident in the work of her more famous predecessor Charlotte *Smith.

LIDDELL, Robert (1908-92) Novelist, travel writer, and critic. His fiction includes three novels which reflect the Mediterranean world he knew—Unreal City (1952, set in Alexandria towards the end of the Second World War), The Rivers of Babylon (1959), and An Object for a Walk (1966). His books on Greece reveal his sympathetic insight into the country's past and present; he also published a biography of the Greek Alexandrian poet *Cavafy (1974). In later life, he wrote of his friendship with novelists Elizabeth *Taylor and Ivy *Compton-Burnett in Elizabeth and Ivy (1986).

Life in London See EGAN, PIERCE.

Life of Charlotte Brontë, The The only biography written by Elizabeth *Gaskell, published in 1857. Gaskell, who first read and admired *Jane Eyre, met Charlotte *Brontë in 1850. Her biography makes her the heroine of a romantic story where she overcomes difficult circumstances through the force of her personality and finds happiness in her marriage to Arthur Nicholls. Gaskell made Brontë's life far more conventional than in fact it was, suppressing information about Brontë's love for Constantin Heger (1809-96), a married man who was Brontë's teacher in Brussels. The biography originally contained libellous material and had to be corrected and reissued.

life-writing A broad term for all forms of writing about lives, including *autobiography, *biography, memoirs, *diaries, and *letters, widely used since the 1970s. The inclusiveness of the term acknowledges the fluidity between genres, for instance, Richard *Holmes's Footsteps (1985) is an autobiographical discussion of biography, and Hermione *Lee's *Body Parts* (2005) is a series of essays about the problems of biography. The term also signals the expansion of self-reflection and reflection about lives beyond the literary mainstream and their use by groups, particularly women, working-class, gay, and black British writers, who felt themselves unrepresented within the canon. Sheila Rowbotham's *Woman's Consciousness, Man's World* (1973) begins with a personal journey which is also seen as a political one; Anne Oakley in *Taking it Like a Woman* (1984) assumes that in writing about her own life, she is also representing the common plight of women. Within education, particularly the social sciences, 'life-writing' was seen as empowering students, allowing them to use their own lives as a source of knowledge and to recognize themselves as subjects within their own worlds. Autobiography and biography were also seen as important forms for historians and offered new forms of social history from the perspective of subjects who had previously been 'hidden from history'. From the 1970s, oral history, the recording of eyewitness participants, also became important (*see* MASS OBSERVATION).

Light Shining in Buckinghamshire
The title of an anonymous pamphlet issued by the Levellers, a radical political movement, in 1648, attacking monarchy and calling for equality of property. It was used as the title of a play by Caryl *Churchill. *See* PAMPHLETEERING, ORIGINS OF.

LILBURNE, John (*c.*1614–1657) Pamphleteer, political agitator, and Quaker (from 1655). He was brought before the Star Chamber in 1638 for printing an unlicensed book, and imprisoned; *A Work of the Beast* (1638) gives an account of his barbarous treatment. He published pamphlets jointly with the Levellers Richard *Overton and William Walwyn.

'Lilli-Burlero Bullen-a-la!' An English approximation of the Irish *An Lile ba léir é, ba linn an lá* ('The Lily was clear, the day was ours'), a battle-cry attributed to the Irish Catholic insurgents of the 1641 rebellion. The phrase was used as the refrain of a satirical Williamite song, attributed to Thomas (later Lord) Wharton (1648–1715), on the appointment by James II of the Catholic earl of Tyrconnel as lord deputy of Ireland in 1687. The song is given in Thomas *Percy's *Reliques* and features in Orange Order parades up to the present. The employment (since 1955) of the tune as the signature of the BBC World Service's English-language news bulletin has been objected to on sectarian grounds, most notably by Robert *Graves.

LILLO, George (1691/3–1739) Playwright, author of *The History of *George Barnwell, or The London Merchant* (1731), based on a ballad story. His other plays include *The Christian Hero* (1735), and *The *Fatal Curiosity* (1736), produced by Henry *Fielding, who praised Lillo's work and personal ethos as evincing 'the Spirit of an old Roman, join'd to the Innocence of a primitive Christian'.

LILLY, William (1602–81) A noted astrologer, patronized by Elias Ashmole and by leading members of the Long Parliament. His *Christian Astrology* (1647) is the first comprehensive astrological textbook published in English rather than Latin. Its republication in 1985 is credited with bringing about the renaissance of astrology in Europe and America. He published hugely popular prophetic almanacs yearly from 1644 until his death. His prediction of Charles I's defeat at Naseby in June 1645 established his reputation as England's leading astrologer. His autobiography (*The History of my Life and Times,* ed. K. M. Briggs, 1974) gives a fascinating insight into the world of 17th-century professional magic, and contains accounts of talismanic magic, crystal-gazing, and the invocation of spirits. He was the model for Sidrophel in Butler's *Hudibras*. The case books recording his consultations survive among the Ashmole manuscripts in the Bodleian Library.

LILY, William (?1468–1522/3) Friend of John *Colet and Sir Thomas *More, grandfather of John *Lyly, and a leader of the revival of Greek studies in England. He contributed to the work known as *Lily's Grammar* (see the Latin lesson in William *Shakespeare's *The *Merry Wives of Windsor*, IV. i).

limerick A form of jingle, of which the first instances occur in *The History of Sixteen Wonderful Old Women* (1820) and *Anecdotes and Adventures of Fifteen Gentlemen* (*c.*1821), subsequently popularized by Edward *Lear in his *Book of Nonsense*. In the older form of limerick, as written by Lear, D. G. *Rossetti, and others, the first and last lines usually end with the same word, but in more recent examples, such as the following comment on George *Berkeley's philosophy by Ronald *Knox, and those written by W. H. *Auden, Gavin *Ewart, Ogden *Nash, Norman Douglas, Robert *Conquest, and others, a third rhyming word is supplied:

There once was a man who said: 'God
Must think it exceedingly odd
If he finds that this tree
Continues to be
When there's no one about in the Quad.'

LINACRE, Thomas (*c.*1460–1524) Physician
and classical scholar, MD of Padua, who became one of *Henry VIII's physicians. Later he
was tutor to Princess Mary, for whom he composed a Latin grammar, *Rudimenta Gramma-
tices* (1523?). He was largely instrumental in
founding the College of Physicians in 1518. In
addition to grammatical and medical works, he
translated from the Greek, mainly from Galen.
Linacre College, Oxford (founded 1962), takes
its name from Thomas Linacre.

LINDSAY, Lady Anne *See* BARNARD, LADY
ANNE.

LINDSAY, David (1876–1945) Scottish author born in London; best known for *Voyage to
Arcturus* (1920), in which the protagonist Ma-
skull embarks upon a visionary quest through a
series of alternative philosophies embodied in
the bizarre characters and landscapes of the
planet Tormance. The novel influenced C. S.
*Lewis's *Out of the Silent Planet* (1938) and Harold *Bloom's *The Flight to Lucifer* (1979); its
admirers include Philip *Pullman. Other works
include *The Haunted Woman* (1922). *The Violet
Apple* and *The Witch* (1975) were issued posthumously.

LINDSAY (Lyndsay), Sir David (*c.*1486–
1555) Scottish poet and Lyon king-of-arms,
and associated with the courts of both James
IV and James V. His first poem, 'The Dreme',
written *c.*1528 but not printed till after his death,
is an allegorical lament on the misgovernment
of the realm, followed by an exhortation to the
king. In 1530 he wrote the *Complaynt to the
King*, in octosyllabic couplets, commenting on
the improved social condition of the realm except as regards the church. The *Testament, and
Complaynt, of our Soverane Lordis Papyngo*
(finished 1530; printed 1538) combines advice
to the king, put in the mouth of his parrot, with a
warning to courtiers drawn from the examples
of Scottish history. Lindsay's distinguished, reformist morality play, *Ane *Pleasant Satyre of the
Thrie Estaitis*, was produced in Fife in 1552.
Other poems by Lindsay include *The Tragedie
of the Cardinale* (*c.*1547), *The Monarchie* (*Ane
Dialog betwix Experience and ane Courteour, off
the Miserabyll Estait of the Warld*) (1554), and

the *Historie of Squyer Meldrum* (first extant edition of 1582).

LINKLATER, Eric (1899–1974) Novelist,
playwright, and journalist. Born in Penarth,
Wales, he was brought up in Aberdeen. He
worked for two years in Bombay (Mumbai) as
assistant editor of the *Times of India* and then
briefly as an academic in Aberdeen, Cornell,
and Berkeley universities. His most popularly
successful novel, *Juan in America* (1931), genially satirizes Prohibition-era America, as *Private Angelo* (1946) does post-Mussolini Italy.
Magnus Merriman (1934), an ironic fictionalized treatment of his flirtation with Scottish
nationalism, contains a portrait of Hugh *Mac-
Diarmid ('Hugh Skene').

LINTON, Eliza Lynn (1822–98) Née Lynn,
novelist and journalist, born in Keswick. She
launched her London literary career with two
historical novels (*Azeth the Egyptian*, 1846;
Amymone, 1848), and also wrote for the *Morning Chronicle* (she was the first woman journalist in England to earn a fixed salary). Her third
novel, *Realities* (1851), was widely condemned
for its attack on conventional morality. She
wrote extensively for popular periodicals, including Charles *Dickens's *Household Words*
and later *All the Year Round*. Increasingly conservative, she became widely known for her
anti-feminist pieces in the *Saturday Review*,
collected as *The Girl of the Period* (1883), and
was a vehement critic of the *New Woman. She
published numerous successful novels of contemporary life, including *Rebel of the Family*
(1880). Her posthumously published memoir
My Literary Life (1899) contains a notably hostile portrait of George *Eliot.

LINTON, W. J. (1812–97) Wood-engraver,
radical polemicist, and poet. In 1858 he
married the novelist and journalist Eliza Lynn
(*see* LINTON, ELIZA LYNN); they separated in
1867. He worked as an engraver for several important literary projects, including Edward
*Moxon's edition of Alfred *Tennyson and
George *Eliot's *Romola*, and wrote about the
craft in *Masters of Wood Engraving* (1889) and
other works. His *Poems* appeared in 1895.

LINTOT, Barnaby Bernard (1675–
1736) Bookseller, a rival to Jacob *Tonson,
and publisher of several important works by
John *Gay, George *Farquhar, Richard *Steele,
Nicholas *Rowe, and especially Alexander
*Pope, including *The *Rape of the Lock* and
Windsor-Forest. He was the publisher for

Pope's translation of *Homer. Pope caricatured his corpulence in Book II of *The *Dunciad*.

LIPPARD, George (1822–54) American novelist, a close friend of Edgar Allan *Poe. He is remembered primarily for his sensational revelation of big-city vice in *The Monks of Monk Hall* (1844), also called *The Quaker City*. He acknowledged the influence of Charles Brockden *Brown on his writing.

Lir *See* LÊR.

Lisle Letters A collection of some 3,000 letters written to and from Arthur Plantagenet, Viscount Lisle (d. 1542; an illegitimate son of Edward IV), his family, and household, while he was lord deputy of Calais from 1533 to 1540. They give a vivid picture of the political and domestic life of the time.

Listener A BBC weekly magazine, of which the first number appeared on 16 January 1929, the last in 1991; it published reviews, broadcasts, essays, poetry, and so on. Its literary editor from 1935 to 1959, J. R. *Ackerley, attracted work from many distinguished writers. *The Music of What Happens: Poems from the Listener* (1981) contains work by Stevie *Smith, Philip *Larkin, Peter *Porter, Ted *Hughes, Seamus *Heaney, and others.

LISTER, Thomas Henry (1800–42) The first registrar-general of England and Wales. He was an accomplished novelist, much influenced by Jane *Austen, the names of whose characters he sometimes uses. *Granby* (1826), *Herbert Lacy* (1828), and *Arlington* (1832) describe with an ironic eye the aristocratic and upper-middle-class society of the time.

Literary Gazette (1817–62) Journal founded by Henry Colburn, with William Jerdan (1782–1869) as editor, which aimed at a very wide coverage of books, fine arts, and sciences. Early contributors, in the days of its greatest success, included George *Crabbe, Mary Russell *Mitford, Barry *Cornwall, and Letitia Elizabeth *Landon.

literati A term introduced into English in 1624 by Robert *Burton to refer to the literate class in China, and later applied to the writers and readers of fashionable literature in other communities, often by contrast with the practical scientists, or virtuosi. The term is now often used to identify those who frequented the literary clubs and leading bookshops of 18th-century Edinburgh; it is more narrowly applied to a group of professional men, mostly

lawyers and clergy, and supporters of the Moderate party in the Scottish Church, who deliberately cultivated an English writing style, both to make a cultural impact on London society and to cement the political union with England. They included the lawyers Henry Home (1696–1782) and James Monboddo, the philosophers David *Hume and Adam *Smith, and the clerical coterie of Hugh *Blair, Alexander Carlyle, Adam *Ferguson, John *Home, and William *Wilkie, several of whom were associated with the abortive first *Edinburgh Review*. Although their writings were primarily on history, philosophy, and the theory of criticism, many of them also supported the legalization and revival of the theatre, against strong Calvinist opposition. Hume in 1752 and James *Beattie in 1779 assisted the movement for stylistic 'improvement' by publishing collections of unacceptable 'Scotticisms'; and the actor-manager Thomas Sheridan (1719?–88) lectured to men's and women's classes on English elocution in 1761 under the auspices of the Select Society. *See* SCOTTISH ENLIGHTENMENT.

litotes A figure of speech in which an affirmative is expressed by the negative of the contrary, for example 'a citizen of no mean city', 'a not unhandsome man'; an ironical understatement.

Little Billee A humorous ballad of three sailors of Bristol, of whom Little Billee is the youngest. When provisions fail he narrowly escapes being eaten by the other two. *Thackeray wrote a version of the ballad. 'Little Billee' was the nickname of the hero of George Du Maurier's *Trilby*.

Little Black Sambo (1899) A best-selling picture book by Helen Bannerman (née Watson) (1862–1946), which became notorious as a supposed symbol of racism. Elizabeth Hay's *Sambo Sahib* (1981) details the controversy.

Little Dorrit A novel by Charles *Dickens, published in monthly parts, 1855–7. William Dorrit has been so long in the Marshalsea prison for debtors (where Dickens's own father was briefly imprisoned) that he has become the 'Father of the Marshalsea'. He has had the misfortune to be responsible for an uncompleted contract with the Circumlocution Office (a satirical portrait of government departments of the day, with their incompetent officials typified in the Barnacles). His lot is alleviated by the devotion of Amy, his youngest daughter, 'Little Dorrit', born in the Marshalsea, whose diminutive stature is compensated by her greatness of heart. Amy has a snobbish sister Fanny, a theatrical dancer, and a scapegrace brother, Tip. Old Dorrit and Amy are befriended by Arthur Clennam, the middle-aged hero, for whom Little Dorrit conceives a deep passion, at first unrequited. The unexpected discovery that William Dorrit is heir to a fortune raises the family to affluence. Except Little Dorrit, they become arrogant and purse-proud. Clennam, on the other hand, owing to an unfortunate speculation, is brought to the debtors' prison, and is found in the Marshalsea, sick and despairing, by Little Dorrit, who tenderly nurses him and consoles him. He learns the value of her love, but her fortune stands in the way of his asking her to marry him. The loss of it makes their union possible, on Clennam's release.

With this main theme is wound the thread of an elaborate mystery. Clennam has long suspected that his mother, a grimly puritanical paralysed woman, living in a gloomy house with a former attendant and present business partner, Flintwinch, has done some wrong to Little Dorrit. Through the agency of a stagy villain, Rigaud, alias Blandois, this is brought to light, and it becomes clear that Mrs Clennam is not Arthur's mother, and that her religious principles have not prevented her from suppressing a codicil in a will that benefited the Dorrit family.

Penetrating in its explorations of themes of imprisonment, hypocrisy, loyalty, and betrayal, *Little Dorrit* is now among the most widely admired of Dickens's novels.

Little Gidding A manor in Huntingdonshire where Nicholas Ferrar and his family established, 1625–46, a religious community of some 40 members, following a systematic rule of private devotion, public charity, and study. The house was visited by Charles I, Richard *Crashaw, and George *Herbert. Joseph *Shorthouse's novel *John Inglesant* (1881) portrays its life vividly. It was raided by Cromwell's soldiers in 1646, and the community dispersed. T. S. *Eliot celebrates it in 'Little Gidding', one of the *Four Quartets.

Little John Companion of *Robin Hood from early ballads and chronicles. A yeoman and archer, he figures in Walter Scott's *Ivanhoe.

little magazines A term used to describe minority literary and artistic periodicals, possibly derived from one of the better known of such publications, the *Little Review. Notable English 'little magazines' include the *London Magazine, New Verse, Poetry Review*, the *Review* and its successor the *New Review, *Stand, Agenda, Poetry and Audience, *PN Review, Areté, Printer's Devil*, and *Thumbscrew*.

(⊕) SEE WEB LINKS
• Modernist Journals Project

Little Review An American monthly magazine founded in Chicago in 1914 by Margaret Anderson. In 1916 it came under the influence of Ezra *Pound, who was foreign editor from 1917 to 1919; it published W. B. *Yeats, Wyndham *Lewis, T. S. *Eliot, Ford Madox *Ford, and, notably, from 1918, chapters of James *Joyce's *Ulysses. It later became a quarterly published from Paris (1924–9), edited principally by Jane Heap (1883–1964) and including work by Ernest *Hemingway, E. E. *Cummings, and Hart *Crane.

(⊕) SEE WEB LINKS
• Modernist Journals Project

Little Women (1868) By L. M. *Alcott, based on the author's New England childhood and concerning the lives of Meg, Jo, Amy, and Beth March and their 'Marmee', while their father is serving as a chaplain in the Civil War. One of the most popular of children's books, it has been filmed five times, and there have been many adaptations for television.

LITTLEWOOD, Joan (1914–2002) Director whose company, Theatre Workshop, had a strong influence on post-war British theatre. It evolved from Theatre Union, the left-wing touring company Littlewood created in 1936, and combined a radical social conscience with an exuberant musical style. Based at the Theatre Royal, Stratford East, from 1953, the company staged rare English and foreign classics, new works by Shelagh *Delaney and Brendan *Behan, and popular musicals by Lionel Bart. Littlewood's most celebrated production was *Oh, What a Lovely War!* (1963), a documentary satire counterpointing the grim statistics of First World War carnage with the affirmative popular songs of the period. *Joan's Book* (1994) is her idiosyncratic autobiography.

liturgy A formal act of worship or church service, as opposed to private devotion, involving a prescribed form of words and ceremonies spoken and performed by the priest and sometimes by the congregation. In Christian churches the Christian year forms the basis of the liturgy, and in some medieval churches

Latin liturgical drama based on stories from the life of Christ was enacted. Vernacular *mystery plays may have developed from these. The term was sometimes used as shorthand for the *Book of *Common Prayer*. Under Archbishop *Laud and again with the High Church revival in the 19th century, liturgy was particularly valued. It was deeply disliked by the *Puritans and their successors. Seventeenth-century poems on the passion of Christ, for example by Richard *Crashaw, or George *Herbert's 'The Sacrifice', owe a good deal to liturgical tradition, as does John *Keble's phenomenally successful *Christian Year* (1827). *See* PSALMS.

LIVELY, Dame Penelope (1933–) Novelist and children's writer. She began by writing novels for children, including *The Ghost of Thomas Kempe* (1973); her first adult novel, *The Road to Lichfield* (1977), was followed by *Treasures of Time* (1979). The intrusion of the past upon the present is a recurrent theme in her graceful, alert fiction. *Moon Tiger* (1987, Booker Prize) presents the recollections of a dying woman, from her childhood just after the First World War to the 1970s. *Pack of Cards* (1986) collects her short stories; *Oleander, Jacaranda* (1994) and *A House Unlocked* (2001) are autobiographies; *Making it up* (2005) an exercise in alternative autobiography.

Liverpool poets The name given to a group of three poets, Adrian *Henri, Roger *McGough, and Brian *Patten, who came together in the 1960s in the period of the Liverpool euphoria generated partly by the success of the *Beatles. They performed together, and published together in various periodicals and anthologies including *The Mersey Sound* (1967), *The Liverpool Scene* (1967), and *New Volume* (1983). The combined tone of their work was pop, urban, anti-academic, good-humoured, and vocal: poetry was conceived by them as a medium for public rather than private consumption, a *performance art.

Lives of the English Poets, The A work by Samuel *Johnson, originally entitled *Prefaces, Biographical and Critical, to the Works of the English Poets*, published 1779–81. Johnson was invited in 1777 by a deputation of London booksellers to provide biographical prefaces for an edition of the works of various English poets, from the period of John *Milton onwards, designed to rival cheap multi-volume collections published in Scotland. To the proposed selection Johnson added four minor poets (Sir Richard Blackmore, Isaac *Watts, John *Pomfret,

and Thomas Yalden (1671–1736), making 52 in all. When the work was completed the prefaces were issued separately as *The Lives of the Most Eminent English Poets*, 4 vols (1781). The *Lives* contain much interesting biographical matter, particularly where Johnson knew the poet concerned, as in the case of Richard *Savage; but they are not always accurate by modern standards. Johnson's criticism was fearlessly idiosyncratic and much of it was at once controversial, notably his hostility towards Milton's republicanism and the obscurity of Thomas *Gray's Odes, and his attacks on the earl of *Rochester and Jonathan *Swift; his critique of the metaphysical style in his account of Abraham *Cowley became notorious. But the work is also marked by a deep appreciation of the achievements of poets in their personal and historical situations, and remains a classic in the history of critical taste and judgement. *See also* BIOGRAPHY.

LIVINGSTONE, David (1813–73) Scottish explorer and missionary. He found settled missionary life uncongenial, and embarked upon a series of expeditions northwards. The discovery of Lake Ngami in 1849 was followed by encounters with the Makololo in the Zambesi Valley who, in effect, sponsored his epic crossing of the continent in 1853–6 including his visit to the Victoria Falls. *Missionary Travels and Researches* (1857) describes people and natural history in an expert but attractive way and makes clear Livingstone's serious moral purpose—to end the slave trade; it was followed by *Narrative of an Expedition to the Zambezi* (1865), based on an expedition to the interior from 1858 to 1863, which put Lake Malawi and other important features on the map. In 1866 he returned to Africa without European companions to report further on the slave trade and in the hope of solving the problem of the source of the Nile. His wanderings led to several relief expeditions but only Henry *Stanley reached him, in the famous encounter of October 1871. When he died in the swamps of Lake Bangweulu, his mummified remains were brought to the coast by his African companions and subsequently buried in Westminster Abbey. Horace Waller edited his *Last Journals* (1874), cementing the image of a modern saint and martyr dying to save Africa from the ravages of the slave trade.

LIVY (Titus Livius) (59 BC–?AD 17) Roman historian whose great work related the history of Rome from its beginnings to 9 BC. Of its

142 books only 35 have survived, the best known of which give us the legendary history of early Rome and the second Punic War. Most of what now survives was recovered by *Petrarch. *Machiavelli wrote *Discourses on Livy*, and Philemon *Holland translated Livy into English (1600). Livy's stories of Rome's beginnings became an essential part of classical education, and provided material for Painter's *Palace of Pleasure* (1566–7) and George *Pettie's similar work of 1576, for *Shakespeare's *Rape of Lucrece* (1594), and later for Thomas Babington *Macaulay's *Lays of Ancient Rome* (1842).

LLWYD, Morgan (1619–59) Puritan poet and preacher, whose *Llyfyr y Tri Aderyn* ('Book of Three Birds', 1653) is one of the classics of Welsh prose.

Llyr *See* MABINOGION.

LOCHHEAD, Liz (1947–) Scottish poet and dramatist, whose poems and plays employ a colloquially ironic idiom to explore such themes as the ambiguous role of women in working-class culture, historical responsibility, and the relationship between vocalization and cultural authority. Her plays include *Blood and Ice* (1982), based on the life of Mary *Shelley; a Scots adaptation of *Molière's *Tartuffe* (1985); *Mary Queen of Scots Got her Head Chopped Off* (1987); a version of the *Medea* of *Euripides (2000); and the romantic comedy *Good Things* (2006). Her mature poetry is collected in *The Colour of Black and White: Poems 1984–2003* (2003).

LOCKE, John (1632–1704) Philosopher. Locke's principal philosophical work is the *Essay Concerning Human Understanding* (1690), a work which led John Stuart *Mill to call him the 'unquestioned founder of the analytic philosophy of mind'. Always critical of 'enthusiasm', he was originally opposed to freedom of religion, and never supported Catholic emancipation; but later he defended the rights of the Dissenters on both moral and economic grounds. He published three *Letters* on Toleration between 1689 and 1692; a fourth was left unfinished at his death. His defence of simple biblical religion in *The Reasonableness of Christianity* (1695), without resort to creed or tradition, led to a charge of *Socinianism, which Locke replied to in two *Vindications* (1695, 1697). He was also involved in an extensive pamphlet war with Edward Stillingfleet (1696–8) over the alleged compatibility of his *Essay* with Socinianism and *Deism.

Locke's two *Treatises of Government* (1690) were designed to combat the theory of the divine right of kings. He finds the origin of the civil state in a contract. The 'legislative', or government, 'being only a fiduciary power to act for certain ends, there remains still in the people the supreme power to remove or alter the legislative when they find the legislative act contrary to the trust reposed in them'. Throughout, Locke in his theory of the 'Original Contract' opposes absolutism; the first *Treatise* is specifically an attack on Sir Robert Filmer's *Patriarcha*. Although Locke in his early manuscripts was closer to Thomas *Hobbes's authoritarianism and continues to share with Hobbes the view that civil obligations are founded in contract, he strongly rejected Hobbes's view that the sovereign is above the law and no party to the contract. He published a volume on education in 1693, and on the rate of interest and the value of money in 1692 and 1695. The first edition of his collected works appeared in 1714.

Locke's writings were very widely read: his *Thoughts Concerning Education*, concerned with practical advice on the upbringing of 'sons of gentlemen', were given to Samuel *Richardson's Pamela by Mr B—, and to his son by the earl of Chesterfield, and their influence is seen in Jean-Jacques *Rousseau's *Émile* (1762). His view of the child's mind as a *tabula rasa*, and his distinctions between wit and judgement, were the subject of much discussion in the *Augustan age. Perhaps his greatest literary influence was on Laurence *Sterne, who quotes him frequently in *Tristram Shandy*, and who was deeply interested in his theories of the random association of ideas, of the measuring of time, and the nature of sensation. *See also* RESTORATION.

LOCKER-LAMPSON, Frederick (1821–95) Poet and bibliophile, born Locker, whose light verse is, included in *London Lyrics* (1857), *Lyra Elegantiarum* (1867, and *Patchwork* (1879).

LOCKHART, John Gibson (1794–1854) Scottish critic one of the principal contributors to *Blackwood's Magazine*. In 1817 he began a long series of attacks on, in particular, Leigh *Hunt, John *Keats, and William *Hazlitt, castigating them as the low-born *'Cockney School of Poetry' and treating their work with great harshness. He did, however, support William *Wordsworth and S. T. *Coleridge. In 1818 he translated Friedrich von *Schlegel's *Geschichte der alten und neuen Literatur* as *Lectures on the History of Literature, Ancient and Modern*, and he contributed several important articles on German literature to *Blackwood*'s during the 1820s. From 1825 to 1853 he was editor of the *Quarterly Review*. His ferocity as a critic was reflected in his chosen nickname, 'The Scorpion'. He published a wide range of books: *Peter's Letters to his Kinsfolk* (1819), spirited sketches of life in Edinburgh and Glasgow; *Valerius* (1821), set in Rome under Trajan; *Some Passages in the Life of Adam Blair* (1822, novel); *Reginald Dalton* (1823), a popular romance; *Ancient Spanish Ballads* (1823, translations); and the biographical works *Life of Burns* (1828) and *Memoirs of the Life of Sir Walter Scott* (1837-8, his father-in-law)

Locksley Hall (1842) A poem in trochaics by Alfred *Tennyson, which consists of a monologue spoken by a disappointed lover. The narrator scorns the modern world of steamship and railway, and ends with an ambiguous acceptance of 'the ringing grooves of change'—a phrase that Tennyson wrote while under the temporary impression that the new railways ran in grooves, not on rails.

Locrine (**Logrin**) In *Geoffrey of Monmouth's *History* (II. 1-5), the eldest son of Brutus (*see* BRUT) and Ignoge. He rules over Loegria (*Logres), his inherited third of the kingdom. He abandoned his wife Gwendolen for Estrildis, later mother of his daughter Sabrina. A. C. *Swinburne wrote a play concerning him (*Locrine*, 1887).

Locrine, The Lamentable Tragedy of A play published in 1595, and included in the third Shakespeare *folio. The authorship is unknown. The play deals with the legend of *Locrine.

LODGE, David (1935-) Critic and novelist, who has done much to explain continental literary theory in Britain, while simultaneously expressing 'a modest affirmation of faith in the future of realistic fiction'. Critical books include *Language of Fiction* (1966), *Working with Structuralism* (1981), and *After Bakhtin* (1990). Many of his novels—*The British Museum is Falling Down* (1965), *Changing Places* (1975), *Small World* (1984), *Things . . .* (2001)—have academic settings. *Nice Work* (1988) is an elegant and entertaining 20th-century *condition of England novel, which throws together a post-structuralist feminist academic and a Midlands industrialist of unreconstructed views. *Author, Author* (2004) fictionalizes the events of Henry *James's middle years, particularly his ventures into play writing; *A Man of Parts* (2011) is based

on H. G. *Wells. Lodge's own plays include *The Writing Game* (1990) and *Home Truths* (1998, reworked as a novella, 1999). His 2008 novel, *Deaf Sentence*, addresses the trials of ageing.

LODGE, Thomas (1558-1625) Writer and doctor, who seems to have converted to Roman Catholicism *c*.1580. In 1579-80 he published an anonymous *Defence of Poetry*, a reply to Stephen *Gosson's *School of Abuse*, and in 1584 *An Alarum against Usurers* (dedicated to Philip *Sidney). Appended to it was a prose romance, *Forbonius and Prisceria*. *Scilla's Metamorphosis*, an Ovidian verse fable, was published in 1589. In 1585 and 1586 Lodge may have sailed on a privateering expedition to the Terceras and the Canaries; he said he wrote his best-known romance, *Rosalynde* (1590), 'hatched in the storms of the ocean, and feathered in the surges of many perilous seas'. *Phillis: Honoured with Pastoral Sonnets, Elegies, and Amorous Delights* (1593), includes many poems adapted from Italian and French models, to which was appended 'The Complaint of Elstred', the story of King *Locrine's unhappy mistress. His play *The Wounds of Civil War* (1594), about Marius and Sulla, had been performed by the Lord Admiral's Men; he also wrote *A Looking Glass for London and England* (1594), in collaboration with Robert *Greene. *A Fig for Momus* (1595), a miscellaneous collection of satirical poems, includes epistles addressed to Samuel Daniel and Michael *Drayton. In 1596, he published *Wit's Misery, and the World's Madness: Discovering the Devils Incarnate of this Age* and the romance, *A *Margarite of America*, written during a second voyage, under Thomas Cavendish (1560-92), while they were near the Magellan Straits. Lodge was incorporated MD at Oxford in 1602, and in the next year published *A Treatise of the Plague*. He translated *Josephus (1602) and Lucius Annaeus *Seneca (1614), and the commentary on Du Bartas (1621) by the French humanist Simon Goulart (1543-1628).

LOFTING, Hugh (1886-1947) As an Allied soldier in the First World War, Lofting was impressed by the animals' stoicism and the scanty care they received. His hero, *Dr Dolittle, created in illustrated letters sent home to his children, featured in fourteen books, including *The Voyages of Dr Dolittle* (1923, Newbury medal). Films based on the series were made in 1967 (Richard Fleischer) with Rex Harrison, and in 1998 (Betty Thomas) with Eddie Murphy.

Logic, Ratiocinative and Inductive, A System of A treatise by John Stuart *Mill, published 1843, revised and enlarged in the editions of 1850 and 1872. Mill's *Logic* argues that all knowledge is derived 'from experience, and all moral and intellectual qualities principally from the direction given to the associations'. In attributing to experience and association our belief in mathematical and physical laws, he came into conflict with the intuitional philosophers, giving his own explanation 'of that peculiar character of what are called necessary truths, which is adduced as proof that their evidence must come from a deeper source than experience'. This conflict is further developed in Mill's *Examination of Sir William Hamilton's Philosophy*.

Logres In *Geoffrey of Monmouth's History* (where it is called Loegria), the part of Brutus' kingdom assigned to his eldest son *Locrine, that is, England. It is the usual term for Arthur's kingdom in medieval romance from *Chrétien de Troyes onwards.

LOGUE, Christopher (1926–2011) Poet, playwright, and translator, he co-edited with Alexander Trocchi (1925–84) the influential magazine *Merlin* (1952–5) which published work by Samuel *Beckett, Jean Genet, and Pablo *Neruda. The *English Stage Company put on several of his plays, including the *Brechtian musical *The Lily White Boys* (1960, with Harry Cookson). He was a pioneer in the *jazz poetry movement, and experimented with publishing his poems as Verse Posters. His volumes of poetry include *Wand and Quartet* (1953), *New Numbers* (1969), *Ode to the Dodo: Poems from 1953–1978* (1981), and *Selected Poems* (1996). *Prince Charming*, (1999) is an autobiography. *Logue's Homer* (2001) collected his controversial, continuing versions of sections of *Homer's *Iliad*.

Lohengrin The son of *Perceval, first mentioned in the *Parzival* (*c.*1205) of Wolfram von Eschenbach, and in Wolfram's incomplete epic *Titurel*. His story is the subject of Richard *Wagner's opera (1850).

Lollards From Middle Dutch *lollaert*, 'mumbler', but also polemically associated with the Latin *lolium*, the tares of the parable in Matthew 13: 24–30. Commonly used since the 14th century to denote the followers of John *Wyclif. In the C-text of *Piers Plowman* the term is used in connection with both the idle (including delinquent friars) and those privileged with prophetic insight ('lunatyk lollares'); later examples suggest persistent imprecise usage, as in the

false accusations made against Margery *Kempe.

London A poem in heroic couplets by Samuel *Johnson, published anonymously by Robert *Dodsley in 1738, in imitation of the Third Satire of *Juvenal. The poem reflects with bitter irony on London's vices and affectations, on the oppression of the poor, and the corruption of Sir Robert *Walpole's administration.

LONDON, Jack (John Griffith) (1876–1916) American novelist, born in poverty in San Francisco. He vigorously attacked capitalism and exploitation, while maintaining some markedly chauvinist and racist attitudes. *The Son of the Wolf* (1900, stories) is based upon life in the far north, as is the book that brought him recognition, *The Call of the Wild* (1903), which tells the story of the dog Buck, who, after his master's death, returns to the primitive world to lead a wolf pack. *The People of the Abyss* (1903) is an emotive documentary based on the slums of London's East End. Other tales of struggle, travel, and adventure include *The Sea-Wolf* (1904), *White Fang* (1906), *South Sea Tales* (1911), and *Jerry of the South Seas* (1917). *The Iron Heel* (1908), a novel about the class struggle, prophesies a fascist revolution; *The Valley of the Moon* (1913) advocates a return to the land in an ideal community. The semi-autobiographical *Martin Eden* (1909) describes the struggles of a sailor and labourer to acquire education and to become a writer. *John Barleycorn* (1913) is a record of London's own struggle against alcohol. He also wrote socialist treatises, autobiographical essays, and journalism.

London Cuckolds, The A rollicking farce by Edward Ravenscroft (*fl.* 1671–97), first produced in 1681, annually revived on Lord Mayor's Day (9 November) for nearly a century, and adapted by Terry *Johnson (1998, National Theatre).

London Gazette See OXFORD GAZETTE.

London Labour and the London Poor See MAYHEW, HENRY.

London Library Founded in 1841 by Thomas *Carlyle, with the support of many literary figures, including William *Gladstone, George *Grote, and Henry Hallam. The manifesto deplored the lack of libraries in London; it opened on 3 May 1841, in two rooms in Pall Mall, with a stock of 3,000 volumes and with John George Cochrane (1761–1852) as its first librarian. Initial subscribers included Charles *Dickens,

Thomas *Macaulay, and William *Macready. It moved to its present premises in St James's Square in 1845.

London Magazine (1) A periodical which ran from 1732 to 1785, founded in opposition to the *Gentleman's Magazine*. (2) A magazine of great brilliance (1820–29), established under the editorship of John *Scott, who championed the work of the younger writers, including William *Wordsworth, Charles *Lamb, Thomas *De Quincey, John *Clare, Thomas *Hood, Thomas *Carlyle, and in particular the *'Cockney School' (John *Keats, Leigh *Hunt, and William *Hazlitt). Provoked into attacks on *Blackwood's Magazine, he was killed in a duel in 1821 by J. H. Christie, its representative, who was later acquitted of murder. John Taylor (1781–1864) took over the editorship, but his habit of editorial interference angered his writers, and many, including Lamb and Hazlitt, withdrew their work. (3) A monthly literary magazine founded in 1954 by John *Lehmann, and edited by him until 1961. Lehmann (*The Ample Proposition*, 1966) writes that he aimed to create 'the London magazine, and not the Magazine of Oxford, or Cambridge, or Redbrick', and to reach Samuel *Johnson's 'common reader'. He was succeeded as editor by Alan *Ross, who enlarged the magazine's range to cover other arts, including photography.

London Mercury A monthly literary periodical founded in 1919 by J. C. *Squire, who edited it along traditionalist lines until 1934, with contributors such as Walter *de la Mare, G. K. *Chesterton, Hilaire *Belloc, W. H. *Davies, and Edward Shanks (1892–1953). Modernist contributors, and those sympathetic to experiment, included Aldous *Huxley, D. H. *Lawrence, and Edgell *Rickword. In 1939 it was incorporated in *Life and Letters*.

London Prodigal, The A comedy published in 1605, attributed to Shakespeare in the title of the quarto edition of that year and included in the third and fourth *folios, but undoubtedly by some other, unidentified hand.

London Review of Books A literary and cultural review founded in 1979 and edited until 1992 by Karl Miller (1931–), professor of modern English literature at University College London, in conscious emulation of the *New York Review of Books* (founded 1963) in both design and editorial approach. It has published critical essays and articles, and poems and fiction, by many of the most prominent critics, and scholars, and writers of the day.

Loneliness of the Long Distance Runner, The A novella by Alan *Sillitoe.

LONGFELLOW, Henry Wadsworth (1807–82) American poet, a classmate of Nathaniel *Hawthorne. In 1836 he began his many influential years of teaching at Harvard; his wife had died the previous year whilst they were travelling in Europe.

His prose romance *Hyperion* (1839), a product of his bereavement, is the tale of a young man who seeks to forget sorrow in travel, a thread on which are hung philosophical discourses, poems, and legends. *Voices of the Night* (1839) includes his didactic pieces 'A Psalm of Life', 'Footsteps of Angels', and 'The Reaper and the Flowers'. *Ballads and Other Poems* (1841) contains 'The Wreck of the Hesperus' and 'The Village Blacksmith'. In 1842 Longfellow met Charles *Dickens in America, and visited him in London; on his voyage home he wrote *Poems on Slavery* (1842). By this time he was already one of the most widely read poets in America. Later volumes include *The Belfry of Bruges and Other Poems* (1847); *Evangeline* (1849) and *The Courtship of Miles Standish* (1858), both long narrative poems in hexameters; and *The Song of *Hiawatha* (1858). His creative life was tragically interrupted in 1861 by the death of his second wife, who was burned to death in a domestic accident. *Tales of a Wayside Inn* (1863, 1st series; with the rousing 'Paul Revere's Ride' and 'The Song of King Olaf') follows the form of the *Canterbury Tales*. Other 'Tales of a Wayside Inn' followed in 1872.

LONGINUS (1st century AD) Supposed author of an important but incomplete work on literary theory, known as 'Longinus *peri hypsous*' (*On the Sublime*). Longinus rejects the technicalities of rhetorical theory: sublimity is 'the reflection of greatness of soul', not to be achieved by mere stylistic devices, and inseparable from emotion. The first English translation was published in 1652 by John Hall (bap. 1627, d. 1656), but Longinus' influence in England, felt in such writers as John *Dryden, Alexander *Pope, and Joseph *Addison, dates from the French translation by Nicholas *Boileau (1674). *See* SUBLIME.

Longinus ('Longeus' in *Malory) The traditional name of the Roman soldier who pierced with his spear the side of Christ at the Crucifixion. The lance in the *Grail legend is sometimes identified as his spear, as by Malory.

LONGLEY, Edna (1940–) Née Broderick, poetry critic; she met her future husband Michael *Longley at Trinity College, Dublin. Daughter of a Scottish Presbyterian mother and an Irish Catholic father excommunicated for accepting the chair of mathematics at Trinity, she brings a subtly archipelagic imagination to bear on modern Irish and British poetry. Her work champions the aesthetic while insisting on the importance of the historical particularity out of which poems emerge.

LONGLEY, Michael (1939–) Irish poet, born to English parents in Belfast. With his wife Edna *Longley, he shares a devotion, manifest in his work, to Edward *Thomas and Louis *MacNeice. The formalist command of *No Continuing City* (1969) was increasingly tempered by colloquialism and an undercurrent of unnerving fantasy in subsequent volumes. Longley's work has been challenged by the post-1968 *Troubles: some of his most striking poems ('Wounds', 'The Linen Workers', 'The Butchers') explore the idea of home in relation to the despoliation of domesticity by political violence. Four collections from *Gorse Fires* (1991) to *Snow Water* (2004) bring an almost Japanese delicacy to their meditations on war, ageing, and the landscape of Co. Mayo. *Collected Poems* appeared in 2006.

LONGMAN, Thomas (1699–1755) Bookseller, founder of the family firm of publishers, and one of the consortium behind Samuel *Johnson's *Dictionary*. The firm was absorbed by Pearson in 1968, but the imprint survives as a publisher of educational books.

LONSDALE, Frederick (1881–1954) Playwright, born Lionel Frederick Leonard. His many successful, worldly, witty, and light-hearted drawing-room comedies include *Aren't We All?* (performed 1923), *The Last of Mrs Cheyney* (1925), and *On Approval* (1927).

Look Back in Anger A play by John *Osborne, first produced by the *English Stage Company at the Royal Court Theatre on 8 May 1956, published 1957. It proved a landmark in the history of the theatre, a focus for reaction against a previous generation (*see* KITCHEN SINK DRAMA), and a decisive contribution to the corporate image of the *Angry Young Man. The action takes place in a Midlands town, in the one-room flat of Jimmy and Alison Porter, and centres on their marital conflicts, which appear to arise largely from Jimmy's sense of their social incompatibility: he is a jazz-playing ex-student from a new university, working on a

market sweet stall, she is a colonel's daughter. He is by turns violent, sentimental, maudlin, self-pitying, and sadistic, and has a fine line in rhetoric. In the second act Alison's friend Helena attempts to rescue her from her disastrous marriage; Alison departs with her father, and Helena falls into Jimmy's arms. In the third act Alison returns, having lost the baby she was expecting, and she and Jimmy find a manner of reconciliation through humiliation and games-playing fantasy.

LORCA, Federico García *See* GARCÍA LORCA, FEDERICO.

Lord Jim A novel by Joseph *Conrad, published 1900. Jim is chief mate on board the *Patna*, an ill-manned ship carrying a party of pilgrims in Eastern waters. He is young, idealistic, and a dreamer of heroic deeds. When the *Patna* threatens to sink, the officers decide to save their own skins and escape in the few lifeboats; Jim despises them, but at the last moment, almost involuntarily, he joins them. The *Patna* does not sink and the pilgrims are rescued. What happens to Jim thereafter is related by an observer, Marlow. Jim, alone among the crew, remains to face the court of inquiry, disturbed at having abandoned his code of conduct. Condemned by the court, he tries to disappear, moving on whenever his past threatens to catch up with him. Through Marlow's intervention Jim is sent to a remote trading station in Patusan. His efforts create order and well-being in a previously chaotic community and he wins the respect and affection of the people: for them, he becomes Tuan Jim ('Lord' Jim). He has achieved some sense of peace, but the memory of his jump is still with him. When Gentleman Brown and his gang of thieves arrive to plunder the village Jim begs the chiefs to spare them, pledging his own life against their departure. But Brown behaves treacherously and a massacre takes place. Jim feels he has only one course of action; rejecting the idea of flight, he delivers himself up to Chief Doramin, whose son was a victim of the massacre. Doramin shoots him and Jim willingly accepts this honourable death.

Lord of the Flies (1954) A novel by William *Golding. An aeroplane carrying a party of schoolboys crashes on a desert island. The boys' attempts, led by Ralph and Piggy, to set up a democratically run society quickly fail and the savagery which in Golding's work underlies man's nature takes over. Terror rules under the dictator Jack, and two boys are killed; it is only with the arrival of a shocked rescue officer that a mask of civilization returns. It is a savage reply to the naive optimism of R. M. *Ballantyne's *The Coral Island*. *See also* BEELZEBUB.

Lord of the Rings, The (1954–5, 3 vols) J. R. R. *Tolkien's huge mythopoeic novel, which tells the story of the heroic and finally successful struggle to destroy a powerful ring forged by the evil Sauron; it sold a million copies in a 1965 pirated paperback edition in the United States and acquired cult status among 1960s hippies, to the author's dismay. It inspired the influential role-play game *Dungeons and Dragons* (1974) and many other games and memorabilia, before New Zealand film-maker Peter Jackson took charge of bringing Middle Earth to the screen in 1995. *The Fellowship of the Ring* (2001), *The Two Towers* (2002), and *Return of the King* (2003), combining live action with digital effects, achieved massive commercial success.

Lorna Doone (1869) A novel by R. D. *Blackmore, set in the later 17th century on Exmoor, Devon, where an outlawed family, the Doones, and their retainers terrorize the surrounding countryside. They murder a farmer, father of the novel's hero John Ridd, who is 12 when the story starts. He secretly discovers the child Lorna, who has been kidnapped by the Doones, and they grow to love each other. John Ridd becomes a giant in height and strength, and is involved in adventures with the highwayman Tom Faggus and rescues Lorna from the villainous Carver Doone during a superbly described blizzard. The Doones are eventually destroyed, Lorna turns out not to be a Doone but an heiress of noble family, and she and John are married; but Carver Doone shoots her at the altar. John avenges her, she recovers, and the story ends happily. The infamous Judge Jeffreys plays a part in the action, and John Ridd and Tom Faggus are also based on historical characters.

Lost Generation A phrase expressed by Gertrude *Stein to Ernest *Hemingway in his memoir *A Moveable Feast* (1964), describing the cynicism of American expatriates in Europe immediately after the First World War.

Lot King of Orkney in the Arthurian legends, the husband of Arthur's sister or half-sister *Morgawse. Their sons are *Gawain, *Agravain, Gareth, and Gaheris, as well as *Mordred in the earlier versions (before Arthur was made his unwitting, incestuous father).

Lothair (1870) A novel by Benjamin *Disraeli, published after his first term as prime minister. Like the hero of *Tancred*, Lothair is a young man in search of the truth. He is a wealthy nobleman, left, on his parents' death, in the joint guardianship of Lord Culloden, a member of the Scottish Kirk, and the brilliant cleric Grandison, who adopts the Catholic faith and becomes a cardinal. A deep interest in the merits of the Anglican and Catholic faiths, and their shared background in Judaism, pervades the book.

Memorable characters include the artist Mr Phoebus, modelled on Frederic Leighton, and Lord St Aldegonde, the aristocratic republican opposed to all privileges except those of dukes, and in favour of the equal division of all property except land. 'Lothair-mania' swept England, the USA, and Europe; a perfume, a racehorse, and a waltz were named after the hero. Although the book was poorly reviewed, the first edition sold out in two days and there were eight editions in 1870 alone.

LOVECRAFT, H. P. (Howard Phillips) (1890–1937) American writer; through his essay 'Supernatural Horror in Literature' (1927) and his own fiction in *Weird Tales* and elsewhere, he became the most influential figure in *horror fiction after Edgar Allan *Poe. Early stories were set in dreamworlds reminiscent of Lord *Dunsany. Others, such as 'The Colour out of Space' (1927) and the 'Cthulhu Mythos' tales, transform a strong sense of place into a cosmic awe and terror about what may intrude into it. Numerous collections include *The Call of Cthulhu* (1999).

Love for Love A comedy by William *Congreve, performed 1695. It was the first play put on in the new theatre in Lincoln's Inn Fields and was a huge success. The plot concerns the outwitting of curmudgeonly Sir Sampson Legend by his son Valentine, an extravagant but basically honourable young man.

Love in a Tub *See* COMICAL REVENGE.

LOVELACE, Richard (1618–57/8) Poet, courtier, and heir to great estates in Kent, who served in the Scottish expeditions of 1639. Having presented a 'Kentish Petition' to the House of Commons in 1642, he was thrown into the Gatehouse prison, where he is supposed to have written the song 'To Althea'. He rejoined Charles I in 1645, and served with the French king in 1646. According to Anthony *Wood, his betrothed Lucy Sacheverell married another on a false report of his death. He was imprisoned again in 1648 and in prison prepared for the press his *Lucasta: Epodes, Odes, Sonnets, Songs etc.*, which includes the lyric 'On going to the wars'. He died in extreme poverty. During the earlier part of the 18th century his work was entirely neglected, until Thomas *Percy reprinted two of his lyrics in his **Reliques* (1765), since when his reputation as a *Cavalier poet has steadily increased.

Lovel the Widower The story by W. M. *Thackeray, published in the **Cornhill Magazine*, 1860, with which he opened his new periodical.

'Lover's Complaint, A' A 47-stanza poem in *rhyme royal appended to William *Shakespeare's *sonnets (1609), in which a nameless young woman, weeping beside a river, tells how she was seduced and abandoned. In 2007 Brian Vickers attributed it to John *Davies of Hereford.

Lover's Melancholy, The A romantic comedy by John *Ford, printed 1629. The play contains a version of Strada's contest of the lute player and the nightingale, which is also dealt with by Richard *Crashaw.

The conventional plot is the framework for Ford's analysis of love melancholy, strongly influenced by Robert Burton's **Anatomy of Melancholy*. The recognition scene between the hero and heroine, Palador and Eroclea, contains some of Ford's finest poetry ('Minutes are numbered by the fall of sands, ¦ As by an hourglass').

Lovers' Progress, The A romantic drama by John *Fletcher, acted 1623, revised 1634 as *The Wandering Lovers* by Philip *Massinger, printed 1647.

Lovers' Vows A play by Elizabeth *Inchbald, adapted from *Das Kind der Liebe* by August von Kotzebue, acted 1798. The play is chiefly of interest because of the place it occupies in the story of Jane Austen's **Mansfield Park*.

Love's Labour's Lost A comedy by *Shakespeare, probably written and performed about 1595, printed in quarto 1598. No major sources for it have been identified. It has often been felt to contain topical references (*see* SCHOOL OF NIGHT).

The king of Navarre and three of his lords have sworn to keep away from woman and to live studying and fasting for three years. The arrival of the princess of France on an embassy, with her attendant ladies, obliges them 'of mere necessity' to disregard their vows. The king is soon in love with the princess, his lords with her ladies, and the courting proceeds amidst disguises and merriment, to which the other characters contribute: Don Adriano de Armado, the Spaniard, a master of extravagant language, Holofernes the schoolmaster, Dull the constable, Sir Nathaniel the curate, and Costard the clown. News of the death of the princess's father interrupts the wooing, and the ladies impose a year's ordeal on their lovers. The play ends with the songs of the cuckoo and the owl, 'When daisies pied and violets blue' and 'When icicles hang by the wall'.

Loves of the Angels, The A popular and controversial poem by Thomas *Moore, published 1823. The poem, founded on the *oriental tale of Harut and Marut and certain rabbinical fictions, describes the loves of three fallen angels for mortal women, and illustrates the decline of the soul from purity.

'Loves of the Triangles, The' A clever parody by George Canning and John Hookham *Frere in the **Anti-Jacobin* in 1798 of Erasmus *Darwin's *The Loves of the Plants*. Darwin good-humouredly acknowledged its skill.

Love's Sacrifice A tragedy by John *Ford, printed 1633. Less wide-ranging than **'Tis Pity She's a Whore*, the play's main theme is the folly of love, including the platonic love cult, fashionable at the Caroline court.

LOWELL, Amy (1874–1925) American poet, who took up *imagism and in 1913–14 visited England, where she met Ezra *Pound, D. H. *Lawrence, 'H.D.' (Hilda *Doolittle), and other writers, becoming so active in it herself that Pound spoke of 'Amy-gism'. Her volumes, which include *Sword Blades and Poppy Seed* (1914), *Men, Women and Ghosts* (1916), and *Can Grande's Castle* (1918), show her experiments in what she called 'polyphonic prose'. Two of her own favourite pieces, 'Lilacs' and 'Purple Grackles', were published in *What's O'Clock* (1925). She became well known as a public figure through her lectures and readings in America.

LOWELL, Robert (1917–77) American poet; at Kenyon College he became friendly with Randall *Jarrell and John Crowe *Ransom and encountered the *New Criticism methods of close textual analysis. In 1940 he married his first wife, the novelist Jean *Stafford, and became a fanatical convert to Roman Catholicism: his first volume of verse, *Land of Unlikeness* (1944), betrays the conflict of Catholicism and his Boston ancestry. He was jailed for six months during the Second World War as, in effect, a conscientious objector. He gained recognition with his second volume, *Lord Weary's Castle* (1946), and married his second wife, the writer Elizabeth Hardwick (1916–2007), in 1949. Later works include *The Mills of the Kavanaughs* (1951), *Life Studies* (1959), *For the Union Dead* (1964), and *Near the Ocean* (1967). He reached the height of his public fame during his opposition to the Vietnam War and support of Senator Eugene McCarthy, as his *Notebook 1967–1968* (1968) records; but his highly personal, confessional volume of poetry *The Dolphin* (1973) caused scandal with its revelations of marital anguish and discord. He married as his third wife the Irish writer Caroline Blackwood (1931–96) in 1973, but later returned to America, where he died: *Day by Day* was published just before his death.

LOWRY, Malcolm (1909–57) Novelist, born in Wallasey, near Liverpool. On leaving school, he went to sea, travelling to the Far East. In 1933 he published *Ultramarine*, a work indebted to *Blue Voyage* by his friend Conrad *Aiken, in whose autobiography *Ushant* (1952) he was to appear as Hambro. He travelled widely in Europe and the USA, settling in Mexico with his first wife Jan from 1936 to 1938; there he worked on *Under the Volcano*, his most important work, published 1947. His last years were spent in England, and he died 'by misadventure' in Sussex. He was a chronic alcoholic, as are many of his characters. His posthumous publications include *Hear Us O Lord from Heaven thy Dwelling Place* (1961), *Selected Poems*, ed. Earle Birney and M. B. Lowry (1962), *Dark as the Grave Wherein my Friend Is Laid* (1968), and *October Ferry to Gabriola* (1970).

LOY, Mina (1882–1966) Poet and artist, born Mina Gertrude Lowy in London. On moving to Italy in 1907 she became acquainted with F. T. *Marinetti and other *Futurists. The publication of her 'Love Songs' (in *Others*, 1915) caused, as William Carlos *Williams remarked, 'wild enthusiasm among free verse writers . . . and really quite a stir in the country at large'. Loy's work was noticed for its radical views and its innovative forms. Her *Lunar Baedecker*, a landmark in *modernist poetry, appeared in 1923; and her long autobiographical poem *Anglo-Mongrels and the Rose* between 1923 and 1925.

Loyal Subject, The A drama by John *Fletcher, acted 1618.

LUCAN (Marcus Annaeus Lucanus) (AD 39–65) Roman poet, born in Córdoba, Spain, and nephew of *Seneca. Favoured by Nero, then estranged from him, Lucan joined Piso's conspiracy to depose Nero and was forced on its discovery to kill himself. His various works are lost, except the unfinished epic *Pharsalia* or *Bellum Civile*, in ten books, on the civil war between Caesar and Pompey. Lucan's style, deliberately un-Virgilian, is dense, epigrammatic, and sombre. There are important translations by Arthur *Gorges, Thomas May, and Nicholas *Rowe.

LUCIAN (AD *c*.125–*c*.200) Of Samosata in Syria, rhetorician and writer of about 80 prose satires in Greek. Many of his works are dialogues where mythical or historical figures are placed in ridiculous situations, and the contrast between their traditional dignity and what they are made to say or do becomes a fruitful source of irony. Lucian was popular with the Renaissance humanists. The first influential selected translation into English, by Francis Hickes (1565/6–1631), was published in 1634, with additions by his son Thomas (1598/9–1634). John *Dryden's 'Life of Lucian' (actually a critical assessment) was published with a four-volume complete translation by many hands (1710–11). Lucian's *The True History* claimed to describe a visit to the moon and inspired a long series of imaginary voyages, including Jonathan *Swift's *Gulliver's Travels* (1726) and Samuel *Butler's *Erewhon* (1872).

LUCIE, Doug (1953–) British dramatist. His plays, from *John Clare's Mad Nuncle* (1975), have been widely admired for their sardonic portrayal of Britain in the 1980s, a place and period he sees as corrupt, acquisitive, and callous. Key plays include *Hard Feelings* (1982); *Progress* (1984); and *Fashion* (1987), about the world of advertising. With *Grace* (1993), the satiric attack switched to born-again religion. The melodramatic *Gaucho* (1994) is about a decent man who becomes a drugs smuggler, arms dealer, and international villain. Subsequent work includes *The Green Man* (2002) and *Pass It On* (2006), and plays and adaptations for radio.

Luck of Barry Lyndon, The A satirical *historical novel by W. M *Thackeray, published in *Fraser's Magazine* 1844, republished under the title *Memoirs of Barry Lyndon, Esq., Written by Himself* (1856). It is the *picaresque story of an Irish adventurer who unconsciously reveals his villainy while attempting self-justification.

The novel was filmed in 1975 by Stanley Kubrick.

Lucky Jim A novel by Kingsley *Amis.

Lucrece, The Rape of See RAPE OF LUCRECE.

Lucretia A legendary Roman heroine, whose story is told in *Livy's Book 1. She was raped by Sextus Tarquinius, son of Tarquinius Superbus, king of Rome, and after urging her father and husband to avenge her she stabbed herself. As a result Lucius Junius Brutus, the king's nephew, led the revolt which resulted in the expulsion of the Tarquins from Rome and the establishment of the republic. In later literature and painting Lucretia and Brutus (ancestor of Marcus *Brutus) became models respectively of female and republican virtue. See RAPE OF LUCRECE.

LUCRETIUS (Titus Lucretius Carus) (99/94–55/51 BC) Author of the Latin hexameter poem in six books *De Rerum Natura* ('On the Nature of the Universe'). Almost nothing is known about him. His poem versifies the philosophy of *Epicurus, which, it is argued, can rid the world of the evils of conventional religion and the superstition which inevitably accompanies it. The world is composed of atoms (*primordia*), falling forever through the void (*inane*), and by their interaction producing all things. This atomic theory, originated in the 5th century BC by Leucippus and *Democritus, is expounded with great energy and enthusiasm. Gods exist, but civilization is the achievement of human effort. There are notable translations (in whole or in part) by Lucy *Hutchinson, John *Evelyn, John *Dryden, Thomas Creech (1659–1700), and C. H. *Sisson. His supposed madness and suicide are the subject of a poem, 'Lucretius', by *Tennyson.

'Lucy poems' A group of poems by William *Wordsworth, most of which were written in Germany in the exceptionally cold winter of 1798–9. 'She dwelt among the untrodden ways' and 'Strange fits of passion have I known' were sent to S. T. *Coleridge in a letter, as was 'A slumber did my spirit seal'; 'Three years she grew in sun and shower' was written a little later, in the spring. All four were published in the *Lyrical Ballads* of 1800. A fifth poem, 'I travelled among unknown men', was sent in a letter in 1801 to Mary Hutchinson (later Wordsworth's wife), and published in 1807. The poems are remarkable for their lyric intensity and purity, and the identity of Lucy has aroused much speculation.

Lud A mythical king of Britain, according to *Geoffrey of Monmouth's *History* (I. 17). He renamed the capital Caerlud (Lud's city) from which derives the name London.

LUKE, St See BIBLE; EVANGELISTS.

Luria A tragedy in blank verse by Robert *Browning, published 1846, together with *A *Soul's Tragedy*, as no. VIII of *Bells and Pomegranates*. The plot concerns the fall of the noble-hearted Florentine commander Luria, a Moorish mercenary (Browning acknowledged the influence of *Othello*). The failure of political idealism, consummated and transcended by a heroic death, relates the play to Browning's earlier poem *Sordello*.

LURIE, Alison (1926–) American novelist and critic. Her sharply satiric and sociologically observant novels include *Love and Friendship* (1962), *Imaginary Friends* (1967), *The War between the Tates* (1974), and *Foreign Affairs* (1984). *The Truth about Lorin Jones* (1988) is a novel of biographical quest, *Women and Ghosts* (1994) is a collection of short stories, and *The Last Resort* (1998) is a benign comedy set in Key West, Florida, where Jenny Walker, the docile wife of an ageing eco-celebrity professor, finds herself happily involved in a lesbian affair: it reintroduces literary critic L. D. Zimmern, who first appeared in *Real People* (1969). *Truth and Consequences* (2005) is a campus novel dealing with the effects of chronic pain on relationships and the creative process.

LUTHER, Martin (1483–1546) German theologian and leader of the *Reformation in Germany. As an Augustinian monk he visited Rome in 1510, and his experience there of ecclesiastical venality influenced his future career. Famously nailing his *Theses* to the door of the church at Wittenberg in 1517, he attacked the principle of papal indulgences, and as a consequence was the subject of a papal ban pronounced at the Diet of Worms (1521). He left the monastic order and married, and devoted himself to forming the League of Protestantism. His translation of the Bible became an influence on the German language as profound as the Authorized Version on English. His popular hymn 'Ein' feste Burg' ('A fortress strong') has had many translators, including Thomas *Carlyle who devotes a chapter to Luther in *On *Heroes, Hero-Worship and the Heroic in History*. He is the subject of John *Osborne's play *Luther* (1961).

LUTTRELL, Henry (?1765–1851) Wit and member of the circle of political, literary, and artistic figures centred on Holland House. He was the author of clever and lively verses, including *Advice to Julia* (1820), admired by Lord *Byron.

Luve Ron ('the Love Song') Mystical love poem in 210 lines by the Franciscan Thomas de Hales, written probably in the second part of the 13th century. It describes to a young woman novice Christ's love and the joy of mystical union with him.

Lycidas (1638) A *pastoral elegy by John *Milton, it laments the death of Edward King (1612–37), who was at Christ's College, Cambridge, with Milton. Samuel *Johnson condemned it as 'easy, vulgar, and therefore disgusting', but more usually it is hailed as the greatest elegy in the language. The passage in which St Peter condemns the venal clergy records young Milton's opinion of the state of the Church under Archbishop *Laud.

LYDGATE, John (c.1370–1449/50) Poet, who spent nearly all his life in the monastery at Bury, Lancashire. He is one of the most prolific of English poets, with a corpus of well over 100,000 lines. Up to the 17th century, Lydgate was almost invariably coupled for praise with Geoffrey *Chaucer and John *Gower. Some of his most important shorter works include *The Complaint of the Black Knight* (modelled on Chaucer's *The *Book of the Duchess*); *The Temple of Glas* (indebted to *The *House of Fame*); and the allegorical *Reason and Sensuality*. His longer works are the *Troy Book* (1412–20), a 30,000-line translation of *Guido delle Colonne commissioned by Prince Henry (later Henry V); *The Siege of Thebes* (1420–22), a pseudo-'Canterbury Tale' translated from a French prose version of the *Roman de Thebes*; *The Pilgrimage of Man*, translated from Deguileville (1426–28), which comprises 24,000 lines of octosyllabic couplets; and *The Fall of Princes* (completed by 1438/9), a translation in 36,000 lines of a French version of *Boccaccio's *De Casibus Virorum Illustrium*.

LYLY, John (1554–1606) Writer and dramatist, the grandson of William *Lily. He was secretary to Edward de Vere, the earl of *Oxford, MP successively for Hindon, Aylesbury, and Appleby (1589–1601), and supported the cause of the bishops in the *Martin Marprelate controversy in a satirical pamphlet, *Pap with an Hatchet* (1589). The first part of his *Euphues: The Anatomy of Wit* appeared in 1578, and the second part, *Euphues and his England*, in 1580. Its distinctive style came to be known as 'Euphuism'. Among Lyly's plays, all of which were written for performance by boy actors to courtly audiences, are *Campaspe and Sapho and Phao (1584); *Endymion (1591); Gallathea and *Midas (1592); and Mother Bombie (1594). Although *Euphues* was his most popular and influential work in the Elizabethan period, his plays are now admired for their flexible use of dramatic prose and the elegant patterning of their construction.

LYNDSAY, David *See* LINDSAY, DAVID.

LYOTARD, Jean-François (1924–1998) French philosopher who emerged as one of the most prominent thinkers of *postmodernism, which he defines in *La Condition postmoderne* (1979) as a suspicion of the grand and totalizing narratives of progress dominating Western philosophical and political thinking since the *Enlightenment. In later work, including *Le Différend* (1983: *The Différend*), Lyotard went on to explore the challenge to ethics and justice posed by a rejection of grand narratives, and the universalism they articulate.

Lyra Apostolica A collection of sacred poems contributed originally to the *British Magazine* and reprinted in a separate volume in 1836. The poems, 179 in all, appeared anonymously. The six *Oxford Movement authors were J. W. Bowden (1798–1844), Richard Hurrell Froude, John *Keble, John Henry *Newman, Robert Wilberforce (1802–57), and Isaac *Williams.

lyric, lyric poetry A term usually applied to short poems expressive of a poet's thoughts or feelings; as a broad genre, it includes such forms as the *sonnet, *ode, and *elegy, along with many other varieties deriving from popular song. The term originally referred to a Greek song to be accompanied on the lyre, but later became associated with song-like poems uttered by a single speaker. In England lyric poems flourished in the Middle English period (in such manuscript collections as the *Harley Lyrics), and attained exceptional sophistication in the songbooks and plays of the Elizabethan age, then among such early 17th-century poets as John *Donne and Robert *Herrick. A further revival is seen in the late 18th and early 19th centuries (*see* ROMANTICISM) with the lyric verse of William *Wordsworth, P. B. *Shelley, John *Keats, and Alfred *Tennyson. In the period from the late 19th century to the mid-20th, notable lyric poets include A. E. *Housman, W. B. *Yeats, Thomas *Hardy, and W. H. *Auden.

Lyrical Ballads, with a Few Other Poems A collection of poems by William *Wordsworth and S. T. *Coleridge, of which the first edition appeared 1798, the second with new poems and a preface (known as the 1800 edition) January 1801, and a third in 1802. The book is a landmark of English *Romanticism. Coleridge's contributions to the first edition were *The Rime of the *Ancient Mariner*, 'The Foster-Mother's Tale', 'The Nightingale', and 'The Dungeon'; Wordsworth's included ballads and narratives such as 'The Thorn', 'The *Idiot Boy', and 'Simon Lee, the Old Huntsman', and more personal poems such as 'Lines Written in Early Spring' and 'Lines Written a Few Miles above *Tintern Abbey'. They appeared with a brief 'Advertisement' by Wordsworth, stating his theory of *poetic diction; his views were expanded in his important preface to the second edition, and again in 1802. The poems themselves, with their 'low' subjects and language and their alleged banality and repetitions, were much ridiculed. The second volume of the second edition added many of Wordsworth's most characteristic works, including the so-called *'Lucy poems', 'The Old Cumberland Beggar', and *'Michael: A Pastoral'.

LYTTELTON, George, first Baron Lyttelton (1709–73) Politician and writer, friend of Alexander *Pope, William *Shenstone, and Henry *Fielding. He was a notable literary patron and secured James *Thomson a pension; he was addressed in *The *Seasons* and contributed some lines to *The *Castle of Indolence*. His works include *Dialogues of the Dead* (1760) and a history of Henry II (1767–71). He was caricatured by Tobias *Smollett as Scragg in *Peregrine Pickle*; Samuel *Johnson's dismissive 'Life' of him incurred the lasting hostility of Elizabeth *Montagu, who had contributed the last three of the *Dialogues*.

LYTTON, Edward Earle Lytton Bulwer
See BULWER-LYTTON, EDWARD GEORGE EARLE LYTTON.

LYTTON, Edward Robert Bulwer, first earl of Lytton (1831–91) Poet, diplomat, and colonial administrator, son of Edward *Bulwer-Lytton. He published several volumes of verse, at first under the pseudonym 'Owen Meredith'. *Clytemnestra, The Earl's Return, The Artist and Other Poems* (1855) was followed by *The Wanderer* (1858); the Wanderer's mildly *Byronic and lyrical continental adventures had some success. His later volumes include *King Poppy: A Story without End*, a fanciful and lengthy blank verse allegory, circulated privately to his friends in 1875, revised over many years, and published in 1892. He published 'Last Words of a Sensitive Second-Rate Poet' in *Chronicles and Characters* (1868).

Mabinogion, The Strictly, the first four Welsh tales contained in the collection of Lady Charlotte Guest (1812–99), made in 1838–49. The four are preserved in two Welsh manuscripts: The White Book of Rhydderch (1300–25) and The Red Book of Hergest (1375–1425). The original common element of the four stories was probably the hero Pryderi; as they survive their subjects are (1) Pwyll, the father of Pryderi; (2) Branwen, the daughter of Llyr; (3) Manawyddan, the son of Llyr; (4) the death of Pryderi in battle with the nephews of Math who had cheated him. There is no mention of *Arthur in these four branches of the Mabinogion proper; but five of the other seven tales published by Guest from The Red Book of Hergest deal indirectly with him: *The Lady of the Fountain, Peredur, Gereint,* three romances from French originals; *Culhwch and Olwen;* and *The Dream of Rhonabwy.* The other two tales in Guest's collection are *The Dream of Macsen Wledig* and *Lludd and Llefelys.* David *Jones and Alan *Garner are two amongst many modern writers who have drawn on the legends.

macaronic verse A term originally applied to a kind of humorous Latin verse of the 16th and 17th centuries in which words from a modern language (more often French or German than English) would be included with deliberately incongruous Latin endings; thus a kind of dog-Latin burlesque. It is now more commonly applied to any poem into which lines, words, or phrases from other languages are frequently introduced, such as T. S. Eliot's *The *Waste Land.*

MACAULAY, Dame Rose (Emilie Rose Macaulay) (1881–1958) Author and journalist, whose novels include the boldly anti-war *Non-Combatants and Others* (1916), the satirical best-seller *Potterism* (1920), and *They Were Defeated* (1932), drawing on the life of Robert *Herrick. She published the travel books, *Fabled Shore* (1949) and *Pleasure of Ruins* (1953); and *Personal Pleasures* (1935, essays). *The World my Wilderness* (1950) and the idiosyncratic tragicomedy *The Towers of Trebizond* (1956) appeared after a decade in which she wrote no fiction, and her return to the Anglican faith.

MACAULAY, Thomas Babington (1800–59) Poet, politician, and historian, son of the philanthropic reformer Zachary Macaulay (1768–1838). His essay on John *Milton for the *Edinburgh Review* in August 1825 brought him instant fame, and for the next twenty years he wrote many articles on historical and literary topics for the *Review.* In 1830 he entered Parliament as a Whig and took an active part in the passing of the Reform Bill. But in 1834, in order to achieve financial independence, he took up a post on the Supreme Council of India. On his return in 1838 he began to write a detailed history of England from the revolution of 1688. He resumed his parliamentary career, but by now his literary fame was such that everything he published was a 'dazzling success', beginning in 1842 with *Lays of Ancient Rome.* His collected *Essays Critical and Historical* (1843) sold steadily down the century. His *History of England* (vols i–ii, 1849; vols iii–iv, 1855) was more restrained and deeply researched. The purpose of the *History* was defensive—to demonstrate that revolution on the continental model was unnecessary in England because of the statesmanlike precautions taken in 1688. He acknowledged a great debt to Walter *Scott, evident in his habit of exploring on the ground all the places in which his narrative was set. The *History,* with its descriptive power and narrative skill, was one of the best-sellers of the century; it brought him wealth and, in 1857, a peerage. He at first intended to take the *History* up to 1830, but when he died in 1859 he had only reached 1697. He was the subject of one of the strongest Victorian biographies, by his nephew Sir George Trevelyan (1876).

Macbeth A tragedy by *Shakespeare, probably written and first performed at the *Globe in 1606, but not printed until the first *folio (1623). The relatively short text has often been thought to contain non-Shakespearian material, probably by Thomas *Middleton. Two songs certainly by him (from *The *Witch*) were added to the play.

Macbeth and Banquo, generals of Duncan, king of Scotland, returning from a victorious campaign against rebels, encounter three witches, who prophesy that Macbeth shall be thane of Cawdor, and king hereafter, and that Banquo shall beget kings though he be none. Immediately afterwards comes the news that the king has created Macbeth thane of Cawdor. Motivated by the prophecy and urged on by Lady Macbeth, Macbeth murders Duncan, who is visiting his castle. Duncan's sons Malcolm and Donalbain escape, and Macbeth becomes king. To defeat the prophecy of the witches regarding Banquo, he causes Banquo to be murdered, but his son Fleance escapes. Haunted by the ghost of Banquo, Macbeth consults the witches, and is told to beware of Macduff, the thane of Fife; that none born of woman has power to harm Macbeth; and that he never will be vanquished till Birnam Wood shall come to Dunsinane. Learning that Macduff has joined Malcolm, who is gathering an army in England, he surprises the castle of Macduff and causes Lady Macduff and her children to be slaughtered. Lady Macbeth sleepwalks and dies. The army of Malcolm and Macduff attacks Macbeth; passing through Birnam Wood every man cuts a bough and under these 'leavy screens' marches on Dunsinane. Macduff, who was 'from his mother's womb | Untimely ripped', kills Macbeth. Malcolm becomes king of Scotland.

MACBETH, George (1932–92) Scottish poet, a member of the *Group, who in the 1960s was associated with the vogue for poetry in performance. His early work was experimental, and at times macabre and violent in its preoccupations; later collections show (in his own words) fewer 'comic and performance and experimental elements'. His books include *A Form of Words* (1954), *The Colour of Blood* (1967), and *Trespassing: Poems from Ireland* (1991). A *Selected Poems*, edited by Anthony *Thwaite, was published in 2002. He also published novels.

MCCABE, Patrick (1955–) Irish novelist. His novels include *Music on Clinton Street* (1986), which charts the encroachment of American culture on 1960s and 1970s rural Ireland; *The Dead School* (1995), an account of the ultimately catastrophic dissension between a conservative teacher and a younger colleague; *Breakfast on Pluto* (1998), in which the transvestite Patrick 'Pussy' Braden escapes to London only to become involved in prostitution and IRA

subversion; *Winterwood* (2006), and *The Stray Sod Country*. McCabe's macabre comedy of small town life has been called 'Bog Gothic', most memorably expressed in *The Butcher Boy* (1992), a horrifying story told in the voice of Francie Brady, an engaging but disturbed and ultimately homicidal boy living a life of neglect and compensatory fantasy.

MACCAIG, Norman (1910–96) Scottish poet, born Norman McCaig. After a false start as an exponent of the New Apocalypse, a group of poets influenced by neo-Romantic anarchism who took their name from the anthology *The New Apocalypse* (1939), he emerged with *Riding Lights* (1955) as an elegant formalist with a keen visual sense and an agile 'metaphysical' wit. From the 1960s he dispensed with regular forms and opted increasingly for short, unrhymed poems marked by an unusual blend of terseness and humour; many of his finest poems are elegies or meditations on the extinction of consciousness. A definitive *Poems* appeared in 2005.

MCCARTHY, Cormac (1933–) American novelist. His first novels were respectfully received, though with some reservations about his subjects: *Child of God* (1974) was based on an actual necrophilia case. His famous Border Trilogy—*All the Pretty Horses* (1992, filmed 2000), *The Crossing* (1994), *Cities of the Plain* (1998, filmed 2012)—was based on journey narratives, centring on young male protagonists, and set in southern Texas and Mexico. *No Country for Old Men* (2005, filmed 2007) dramatizes the workings of the drugs cartels in the same region and *The Road* (2006, filmed 2009) describes the travels of a father and son across a burnt American landscape.

MCCARTHY, Mary (1912–89) American writer, who used her college teaching experiences in her satirical *campus novel *The Groves of Academe* (1952), which describes the political persecutions of the McCarthy period. *The Group* (1963), a study of the lives and careers of eight Vassar girls, caused some stir when published in England because of its frank descriptions of the gynaeological detail of women's lives. She published two volumes of reportage, *Vietnam* (1967) and *Hanoi* (1968), protesting against American involvement in Vietnam, and an autobiography, *How I Grew* (1987). Her correspondence with Hannah Arendt was published in 1995.

MCCAUGHREAN, Geraldine (1951–) Prolific writer for children and adults. Her output includes numerous retellings of classic texts, among them Greek mythology (1992), Shakespeare's plays (1994), Bunyan's *Pilgrim's Progress* (1999), and *Cyrano* (2006). Her novels for younger readers are often set in the past, whether medieval England (*A Little Lower Than the Angels*, 1987) or ancient China (*The Kite Rider*, 2001). *Peter Pan in Scarlet* (2006) is a commissioned official sequel to *Peter Pan*. Adult fiction includes *Fires' Astonishment* (1990) and *The Ideal Wife* (1997).

MCCLURE, Michael (1932–) American poet, songwriter, essayist, and journalist, who participated in the *Beat movement. He subsequently gave poetry readings and performances during the 1960s hippy counter-culture. His 1965 play *The Beard*, about an imagined encounter between Billy the Kid and Jean Harlow, occasioned arrests for obscenity. His recent volumes include *Mysteriosos and other poems* (2010).

MCCOY, Horace (1897–1955) American novelist, who moved to Los Angeles during the Depression. This supplied the location for his *hardboiled novels, the most famous of which are *They Shoot Horses, Don't They?* (1936), about a dance marathon, and *Kiss Tomorrow Goodbye* (1948). McCoy was also a screenwriter in Hollywood.

MCCULLERS, Carson (1917–67) American novelist and short story writer, born in Georgia, where most of her works are set. Her best-known novel is *The Heart Is a Lonely Hunter* (1940), exploring her recurrent subject of isolation. Other works include *Reflections in a Golden Eye* (1941), *The Member of the Wedding* (1946; dramatized by the author, 1950), a collection, *The Ballad of the Sad Café* (1951), of which the title story was dramatized by Edward *Albee in 1963, and her unfinished autobiography, *Illumination and Night Glare* (1999). Her work has been linked to Southern *Gothic.

MACDIARMID, Hugh (1892–1978) Best known of the numerous pseudonyms of Christopher Murray Grieve, Scottish poet and cultural agitator, the prime instigator of the *Scottish Renaissance. MacDiarmid launched various literary and nationalist periodicals and became notorious for his iconoclastic 'Contemporary Scottish Studies' column in the *Scottish Educational Journal*. In 1928 he helped found the National Party of Scotland along with R. B. *Cunninghame Graham and Compton *Mackenzie. He moved to London in 1929, but after the break-up of his marriage and a period of

alcoholism he returned to Scotland and settled on the Shetland island of Whalsay in 1933 with Valda Trevlyn, a young Cornishwoman he had met in London, and their infant son. His incomplete *Collected Poems* of 1962 brought him belated recognition.

MacDiarmid's poetry is unusually various in kind as well as quality. The compressed *Scots lyrics of *Sangschaw* (1925) and *Penny Wheep* (1926) marry Expressionist techniques and a bleak modern cosmology to traditional Scottish tropes and idioms, while the tragicomic monologue *A Drunk Man Looks at the Thistle* (1926) combines ruthless satire of received versions of Scottishness with love lyrics and metaphysical speculations. *First Hymn to Lenin and Other Poems* (1931) foregrounds MacDiarmid's implacable communist politics. MacDiarmid dropped Scots in favour of English after 1933. *In Memoriam James Joyce* (1955) is one of the long, prosaic 'poems of fact' which he claimed provided a necessarily post-lyrical response to the complexities of modernity.

MCDONAGH, Martin (1970–) Playwright born in London to Irish parents. He came to prominence with *The Beauty Queen of Leenane* (1996), the first play of a trilogy set in Leenane, a remote small town in Connemara, and followed this with the Aran Trilogy, comprising *The Cripple of Inishmaan*, *The Lieutenant of Inishmore*, and *The Banshees of Inisheer* (1997–2001). The plays mix sardonic humour with dark, brooding meditations on life. Recent plays, including *The Pillowman* (2003) and *A Behanding in Spokane* (2010), have been set outside Ireland.

MACDONALD, Alexander (c.1695–c.1770) Scottish Gaelic poet, who composed under the pseudonym Alasdair MacMhaighistir Alasdair. *Ais-Eiridh na Sean Chánoin Albannaich* ('The Resurrection of the Ancient Scottish Language', 1751) was the first printed collection of secular verse in any variety of Gaelic. MacDonald draws on the classics and Scottish poetry in English and *Scots, as well as on Gaelic tradition. 'Birlinn Chlann Raghnaill' ('Clanranald's Galley') has been translated by Hugh *MacDiarmid (1935) and (in part) Iain Crichton *Smith (1977).

MACDONALD, George (1824–1905) Scottish writer for children and adults, whose novels *David Elginbrod* (1863) and *Robert Falconer* (1868) helped to found the *'Kailyard school' of fiction. His two allegorical fantasies for adults, *Phantastes* (1858) and *Lilith* (1895), were influenced by his study of Novalis and

E. T. A. *Hoffmann and, with his children's books, strongly influenced C. S. *Lewis, Frances Hodgson *Burnett, and Maurice *Sendak. MacDonald is primarily remembered for his fantasies for children, notably *At the Back of the North Wind* (1871) and *The Princess and the Goblin* (1872), both deeply symbolic, with elements of Christian mysticism.

MACDONALD, Sharman (1951–) Scottish playwright. She worked briefly for John *McGrath's 7:84 Company, before producing *When I was a Girl I Used to Scream and Shout* (1984) and *When We Were Women* (1988), exploring the relationship between a mother and daughter. *After Juliet* (1999, starring her daughter, Keira Knightley) and *Broken Hallelujah* (2006) were produced for the *National Theatre. She has also written BBC radio plays such as *Sea Urchins* and *Gladly my Cross Eyed Bear* (1999).

MCELROY, Colleen J. (1935–) African American poet and travel writer, born in St Louis, Missouri. Her poetry collections include *Queen of the Ebony Islands* (1984) and *What Madness Brought Me Here* (1990). The innovative *A Long Way from St Louie* (1997) offers travel memoirs, organized thematically rather than chronologically.

MCEWAN, Ian (1948–) Novelist and short story writer, the first graduate of the creative writing department established by Angus *Wilson and Malcolm *Bradbury at the University of East Anglia. His early books—the short story collections *First Love, Last Rites* (1975) and *In Between the Sheets* (1977), and two taut novels, *The Cement Garden* (1978; filmed 1993), a story of parentless siblings, and *The Comfort of Strangers* (1981; filmed 1990), a tale of sadomasochistic atrocity—show a fascination, often macabrely displayed, with the vulnerability of the immature. *The Child in Time* (1987), focusing on a couple whose young daughter is abducted, and *The Innocent* (1990; filmed 1993), set in Berlin during the early years of the Cold War, bring greater emotional depth and psychological complexity to the exploration of maturity and immaturity. *Black Dogs* (1992) contrasts religious and rationalist responses to evil in the wake of the Second World War. *Enduring Love* (1997; filmed 2004) traces the repercussions of a helium balloon accident. *Amsterdam* (1998, Booker Prize) is a black comedy about euthanasia. *Atonement* (2001; filmed 2007) is a masterly study of the dangers of the literary imagination. *Saturday* (2005; filmed 2008) takes place on the day of the 2003 mass demonstration in London against the impending war in Iraq. *On Chesil Beach* (2007) is a subtle and compelling short novel about a disastrous honeymoon night in 1962. *Solar* (2010) is a satirical comedy on the theme of climate change. McEwan has also written for television and film and collaborated with the composer Michael Berkeley.

Mac Flecknoe, or *A Satire upon the True-Blue-Protestant Poet, T. S.* A *mock-epic poem by John *Dryden, published 1682, and in a definitive edition, 1684. The outcome of a series of disagreements, personal, professional, and critical, between Dryden and Thomas *Shadwell, the poem represents the latter as heir to the kingdom of poetic dullness, currently governed by the minor writer Richard *Flecknoe. It brilliantly exploits the crudity of Shadwell's farces (notably *The Virtuoso*) and critical writings; while the range of its allusions to 17th-century theatre demonstrates the complexity of Dryden's critical thought and, since he satirizes his own work (notably *Tyrannic Love*) as well as Shadwell's, his humility towards the tradition in which he was working. *Mac Flecknoe* was a vital inspiration for Pope's *Dunciad*.

MCGAHERN, John (1934–2006) Irish novelist and short story writer. His richly symbolic short stories and his novels, from *The Barracks* (1963) through the acclaimed *Amongst Women* (1990) to *That They May Face the Rising Sun* (2001), focus on individuals trapped in situations over which they have little control but offer a panoramic view of post-independence Irish society. A startlingly Oedipal *Memoir* appeared in 2005.

MCGONAGALL, William (*c.*1830–1902) Scottish poet, actor, and handloom weaver, who possessed celebrity status in Scotland for his legendary public readings of his topical verse. His unintentionally hilarious poems, usually featuring gloom and disaster, were ridiculed but also gained him an enviable reputation as the world's worst poet.

MCGOUGH, Roger (1937–) OBE, poet and writer, born in Liverpool, a teacher before becoming a member of the music/poetry group the Scaffold (1963–73). Emphasis on *performance poetry became a hallmark of his style, and in 1967 he and the other *Liverpool poets, Brian *Patten and Adrian *Henri, published *The Mersey Sound*, followed by *The New Volume* (1983). His writing, including many volumes of poetry for both adults and children, as well as fiction and plays, is distinguished by high spirits, wit, and accessibility: works include *Watchwords* (1969, poems), *In the Glassroom* (1976, poems), and *The Great Smile Robbery* (1982, children's fiction). His *Collected Poems* (2003) was followed by a memoir, *Said and Done* (2005). McGough is also known as a radio presenter and for his translations of *Molière.

MCGRATH, John Peter (1935–2002) Playwright and director, whose first success was the play *Events while Guarding the Bofors Gun* (pub. 1966). He founded in 1971 the theatre group 7:84, through which he explored and expressed his belief in the possibility of a genuine working-class theatre, characterized by 'directness, comedy, music, emotion, variety, effect, immediacy', and often with a strong local or community interest (*A Good Night Out*, 1981). The group, which later divided into separate English and Scottish companies, presented plays by McGrath himself (including *The Cheviot, the Stag and the Black, Black Oil*, 1974; *Little Red Hen*, 1977; both dealing with Scottish politics) and by others, including John *Arden, Trevor *Griffiths, and Adrian *Mitchell. McGrath also wrote, directed, and produced extensively for film and television.

MCGRATH, Patrick (1950–) Novelist, who grew up in the grounds of Broadmoor, his father's workplace, surrounded by the criminally insane. His early fiction tended towards the bizarre: *Blood and Water* (1988); *The Grotesque* (1989) a morally serious parody of English *Gothic fiction; and *Spider* (1990). *Dr Haggard's Disease* (1993) and *Asylum* (1996) are both studies in romantic obsession. *Martha Peake* (2000) is *historical fiction, set in the dark underworlds of 18th-century London and America, *Port Mungo* (2004) the story of a turbulent relationship between two brilliant but dissolute artists, and *Trauma* (2008), a study of a New York psychiatrist.

MCGUCKIAN, Medbh (1950–) Née Maeve McCaughan, Irish poet. From *The Flower Master* (1982; rev. 1993), her first major collection, McGuckian's lyrical, beguiling, and slyly erotic poetry has delighted in flux. Many of her poems have a strongly intertextual character. An engagement with Irish history, from an oblique nationalist perspective, is notable in *Shelmalier* (1998), a series of elegiac meditations on the 1798 rebellion, *Drawing Ballerinas* (2001), and *Had I a Thousand Lives* (2003). Recent collections include *The Currach Requires No Harbours* (2006) and *My Love has Fared Inland* (2008).

MCGUINNESS, Frank (1953–) Irish playwright and poet, whose upbringing on the Irish border in the early years of the *Troubles may have been a crucial influence on McGuinness's presentation of communities isolated by conflict and violence. The vivid and angry *Factory Girls* (1982) deals with a group of women barricaded into a factory. *Observe the Sons of Ulster Marching towards the Somme* (1985) offers a Catholic writer's notably empathetic exploration of one of the key myths of Ulster Protestantism. The interest in sexual politics of these plays and of *Mary and Lizzie* (1989) and the Beirut-set *Someone Who'll Watch over Me* (1992) emerges as an explicit concern with issues surrounding gay identity in *Gates of Gold* (2002) and *Greta Garbo Came to Donegal* (2010).

MACHADO, Antonio (1875–1939) Spanish poet. His most famous collection, *Campos de Castilla* (1912: *Landscapes of Castile*), reflects on the poet's childhood in Seville, and the landscape of Castile. His poems have inspired numerous English versions, including *Castilian Ilexes* (1963) by the poet Charles *Tomlinson and the scholar Henry Gifford (1913–2003).

MACHAUT, Guillaume de (c.1300–77) French musician and poet. He was prominent in the development of the *ballade and the *rondeau, and his poetry influenced Chaucer, particularly in *The *Book of the Duchess*.

MACHEN, Arthur (1863–1947) Welsh *fantasy and *horror writer, deeply influenced by his lonely childhood, the Welsh landscape, and local folklore. He left for London in 1880, and his work as a cataloguer of occult books introduced him to secret sects and societies (he later joined the Order of the Golden Dawn of which W. B. *Yeats and Aleister *Crowley became members). He translated *L'*Heptaméron* (1886) and *The Memoirs of Casanova* (1894) and began writing mystic, supernatural tales of rural and urban life, including *The Great God Pan* (1894), *The Hill of Dreams* (1907), and *The Three Impostors* (1895). His short story 'The Bowmen' in the *Evening News* (Sept. 1914) was responsible for the legend of 'The Angels of Mons', said to have saved the retreating British forces. *Far off Things* (1922) and *Things Near and Far* (1923) are both autobiographical.

MACHIAVELLI, Niccolò (1469–1527) Political theorist, dramatist, and historian of Florence, and perhaps the most notorious Italian writer outside Italy. After holding various offices in the restored Florentine republic and discharging various missions abroad, he was exiled on suspicion of conspiracy on the return of the Medici in 1512, but was subsequently restored to some degree of favour. He turned his political experiences to advantage in his writings, including the *Discorsi sopra la prima deca di Tito Livio* (written 1516–17; printed in 1531: *Discourse on the First Ten Books of Titus Livius*) on republican government. His best-known work is *Il principe* (written 1513, pub. 1532: *The Prince*), in which Machiavelli teaches that the lessons of the past (of Roman history in particular) should be applied to the present, and that the acquisition and effective use of power may necessitate unethical methods not in themselves desirable. The first English translation of *The Prince* appeared in 1640, but it was well known throughout the previous century. It is repeatedly referred to in Elizabethan drama, and influenced the policy of Thomas Cromwell (?1485–1540), Robert Cecil (1563–1612), and the earl of Leicester. There is a sketch of Machiavelli's character in George *Eliot's *Romola*.

MCILVANNEY, William (1936–) Scottish novelist, poet, and journalist. *Docherty* (1975) draws on his own family history. McIlvanney's work balances literary allusiveness with a socialist desire to widen the readership of fiction. His three Inspector Jack Laidlaw novels (*Laidlaw*, 1977; *The Papers of Tony Veitch*, 1983; *Strange Loyalties*, 1991), set mainly in Glasgow, focus on the psychological, social, and political roots of crime. *The Big Man* (1985) is a parable of the break-up of working-class communities, while *The Kiln* (1996) continues the history of the Docherty family. *Weekend* (2006) is a variation on the *campus novel.

MACINNES, Colin (1914–76) Née McInnes, novelist was brought up partly in Australia, the setting of *June in her Spring* (1952). *City of Spades* (1957) and *Absolute Beginners* (1959) describe teenage and black immigrant culture, and the new bohemian underworld of Notting Hill, coffee bars, jazz clubs, drink, and homosexuality. MacInnes called himself an 'anarchist sympathizer' and defended several of the causes of the 1960s, including Black Power and the writers of *Oz. See also BLACK BRITISH WRITING.

MACINTYRE, Duncan Ban (Donnchadh Bàn Mac an t-Saoir) (*c*.1723–1812) Scottish Gaelic poet, influenced by Alexander *MacDonald. His long poem 'Moladh Beinn Dòbhrainn' ('The Praise of Ben Doran') has been translated by Hugh *MacDiarmid (1940) and I. C. *Smith (1969).

MACKAY, Shena (1944–) Novelist and short story writer, born in Edinburgh. *Toddler on the Run* and *Dust Falls on Eugene Schlumberger* (1964, novellas) were published together when she was only 19. Subsequent novels, *Music Upstairs* (1965), *Old Crow* (1967), and *An Advent Calendar* (1971), established her mastery of comic narratives in which bizarre sequences of events often flow from tiny accidents, and a profound sympathy for her characters' damaged lives is apparent beneath offhand ironies. After a long silence, her collection of stories *Babies in Rhinestones* appeared in 1983, followed by *A Bowl of Cherries* (1984) and *Redhill Rococo* (1986). *Dunedin* (1992) is partly set in New Zealand, but also provides a hellish vision of contemporary suburban London. *The Orchard on Fire* (1996), a dark tragicomedy about childhood friendship, was shortlisted for the *Booker Prize. *The Artist's Widow* (1998), a satire on modern artistic values, was followed by the more utopian *Heligoland* (2003). *The Atmospheric Railway* (2008) contains new and selected stories.

MCKENDRICK, Jamie (1955–) Poet and translator, born in Liverpool. *The Sirocco Room* (1991) and *The Kiosk on the Brink* (1993) are sardonic, anxious books whose promise is fulfilled in *The Marble Fly* (1997), *Ink Stone* (2003), and *Crocodiles and Obelisks* (2007), in which meditations on art and history mingle with bleak humour. McKendrick has developed a suggestive but economical idiom in which the ordinary sometimes warps into the uncanny. He has edited the *Faber Book of Twentieth-Century Italian Poems* (2004) and translated the poetry of Valerio Magrelli in *The Embrace* (2009).

MACKENZIE, Sir Compton (1883–1972) Author; a prolific writer in all genres, he is best remembered for his novels. The most notable include *Carnival* (1912); *Sinister Street* (2 vols, 1913–14), which presents in sexually frank terms a semi-autobiographical figure, Michael Fane, 'handicapped by a public school and university education'; *Vestal Fire* (1927); and *Extraordinary Women* (1928). Mackenzie published two volumes of war memoirs, *Gallipoli Memories* (1929) and *Greek Memories* (1932). His most ambitious work, *The Four Winds of Love* (1937–45), traces the life of John Ogilvie from the time of the Boer War to the emergence of Scottish nationalism in 1945. *Whisky Galore* (1947), a fictional account of an actual wreck of a ship loaded with whisky on the Scottish island of Eriskay, was made into a successful film. *Thin Ice*, a sombre novel of homosexual scandal, appeared in 1956, and in 1963–71 the ten 'Octaves' of *My Life and Times*.

MACKENZIE, Henry (1745–1831) Scottish novelist, playwright, essayist, and lawyer. His initially anonymous novel *The *Man of Feeling* (1771) went through many editions and was translated into several European languages. In 1773 he published *The Man of the World*, in which the protagonist is by contrast a villain; and in 1777 *Julia de Roubigné*, an *epistolary novel. Mackenzie was chairman of the committee that investigated James *Macpherson's 'Ossian'. *See* SENTIMENT.

MCKINLEY, Robin (1952–) American *fantasy author, now resident in Britain. Her fiction, often for children or young adults, includes *Beauty* (1978), recasting the traditional fairytale, and *The Blue Sword* (1982). *Water: Tales of Elemental Spirits* (2001) was co-written with her husband Peter *Dickinson.

MACKLIN (MacLaughlin), Charles (?1699–1797) Irish-born actor and playwright whose thoughtful playing of *Shylock, in 1741, brought a new standard of psychological realism to the stage. His most successful plays were the romantic comedies *Love à-la-Mode* (1759) and *The *Man of the World*, performed in 1781.

MACLAREN, Ian *See* KAILYARD SCHOOL.

MACLAVERTY, Bernard (1942–) Novelist and short story writer, born in Belfast. His collections of stories—*Secrets* (1977), *A Time to Dance* (1982), *The Great Profundo* (1987), *Walking the Dog* (1994), and *Matters of Life & Death* (2006)—and his novels explore damage done by parochialism and bigotry in Northern Ireland. *Lamb* (1980) portrays a Christian Brother rescuing an abused boy from a reformatory. *Cal* (1983) depicts a reluctant IRA man drawn into a doomed affair with the widow of one of his victims. In *Grace Notes* (1997), a composer who has escaped the turmoil of Ulster comes to terms with the tormented history of her birthplace through her music. *The Anatomy School* (2001) is an autobiographical-seeming account of a Catholic young man growing up in Belfast. His work for film includes adaptations of *Cal* (1984) and *Lamb* (1986), and an original screenplay, *Hostages* (1993).

MACLEAN, Sorley (Somhairle MacGill-Eain) (1911–96) Scottish Gaelic poet. *Dàin do Eimhir* ('Poems to Emer') is a sequence of 61 lyrics written in the late 1930s and published, in incomplete form, in 1943. *An Cuilithionn* ('The Cuillin'), a long poem apostrophizing Hugh *MacDiarmid, was abandoned unfinished in December 1939. His intricate, intensely musical poetry has been translated by I. C. *Smith (*Eimhir*, 1971), Seamus *Heaney (*Hallaig*, 2002), and (with misleading blandness) by the poet himself. See *O Choille gu Bearradh/From Wood to Ridge: Collected Poems* (1999).

MACLEISH, Archibald (1892–1982) American poet and dramatist; he was one of the American expatriates in Paris in the 1920s, and was strongly influenced by Ezra *Pound and T. S. *Eliot. His volumes of verse include *The Pot of Earth* (1924); *The Hamlet of A. MacLeish* (1928); *New Found Land* (1930); the narrative poem *Conquistador* (1932); and his *Collected Poems, 1917–1933* (1933). Among his verse dramas are *Panic* (1935), the anti-totalitarian *The Fall of the City* (1937), and the successfully staged *J.B.* (1958), an updating of the trials of Job.

MACLEOD, Fiona Pseudonym of William *Sharp.

Macmillan's Magazine A periodical founded in 1859, and edited successively by David *Masson (1859–68), George Grove (1868–83), John Morley (1883–5), and Mowbray Morris (1885–1907). It was one of the first magazines to use signed articles only. Contributors included Alfred *Tennyson, Thomas *Hughes, Thomas *Hardy, Margaret *Oliphant, Frederick Denison Maurice, and Henry *James.

MCMURTRY, Larry (1936–) American novelist and screenwriter, born in Texas, the setting for most of his fiction. His most famous novels are *The Last Picture Show* (1966) and *Lonesome Dove* (1985), about western cattle drives. His *Berrybender Narratives* (2002–4) concern a hunting expedition in the Old West. Among his screenplays, the adaptation of Annie *Proulx's *Brokeback Mountain* (2005) won McMurtry an Oscar.

MACNEICE, Louis (1907–63) Poet and writer, born in Belfast, who published a book of poems, *Blind Fireworks* (1929) while a student at Oxford and became known as a poet through his contributions to *New Verse* and his *Poems* (1935). *Letters from Iceland* (1937) was written in collaboration with W. H. *Auden. Subsequent volumes of poetry include *The Earth Compels* (1938); *Autumn Journal* (1939), a long personal and political meditation on the events leading up to the Munich Agreement of September 1938; *Plant and Phantom* (1941); *Springboard* (1944); *Holes in the Sky* (1948); *Autumn Sequel* (1954); and *The Burning Perch* (1963).

Suspicious of all rigid systems, whether political, religious, or philosophical, he worked to establish some pattern from life's flux, or the 'drunkenness of things being various' ('Snow'); his distinctive formal contribution was his deployment of assonance, internal rhymes, half-rhymes, and ballad-like repetitions. He was also renowned as an outstanding writer of radio documentaries and radio plays, including *Christopher Columbus* (1944) and *The Dark Tower* (1946). Other works include a fine verse translation of the *Agamemnon* (1936) and a translation of an abridged version of *Goethe's Faust* (1951); *Varieties of Parable* and a volume of autobiography, *The Strings are False*, both appeared posthumously in 1965. His reputation was revived by the publication of his *Collected Poems* (1966).

McPherson (MacPherson), **Conor** (1971–) Irish playwright and theatre and film director; his plays, sometimes marked by a *Gothic sense of the satanic and of the proximity of the dead to the living, explore themes of regret, anxiety, and self-delusion in the context of a rapidly modernizing Ireland. They include *This Lime Tree Bower* (1995), *The Weir* (1997), and *Shining City* (2004). *The Seafarer* (2006) was a major success on Broadway.

MACPHERSON, James (1736–96) Poet, born in Invertromie, Inverness-shire. In 1758 he published *The Highlander*, a heroic poem in six cantos. In 1759 he met John *Home, at whose insistence he translated his first 'Ossianic' ballad; encouraged by Home and Hugh *Blair he then produced *Fragments of Ancient Poetry, Collected in the Highlands of Scotland, and Translated from the Galic or Erse Language* (1760). Rumours that a Gaelic epic existed fuelled the contemporary passion for *primitivism; urged on by his admirers, Macpherson travelled round the Highlands and Islands collecting materials for *Fingal: An Ancient Epic Poem, in Six Books* (1762). It claimed to be Macpherson's faithful translation of an epic by Ossian, the son of *Finn (or, in this version, Fingal), dating from some vague but remote period of early Scottish history. A second epic, *Temora* (1763), soon followed. These works created a sensation; patriotic Scots praised them highly, and Ossian's fame spread to the Continent, but doubts of the poems' authenticity sprang up almost at once. Samuel *Johnson's

enquiries during his tour of Scotland and remarks published in his *Journey to the Western Islands* (1775) were highly critical. A committee appointed after Macpherson's death, chaired by Henry *Mackenzie, investigated the matter and reported in 1805 that Macpherson had liberally edited Gaelic poems and inserted passages of his own, a view supported by subsequent scholarship. The immense popularity of the poetry survived the exposure of its origins.

MACREADY, William Charles (1793–1873) Actor–manager, by 1819 an established rival of Edmund Kean. He was manager of both Covent Garden and Drury Lane theatres at various times, where he sought to improve standards of production and worked to restore Shakespeare's texts. In 1837 he appeared in *Strafford*, which Robert *Browning had written for him. His last performance was as Macbeth in 1851 and Alfred *Tennyson wrote a sonnet to mark the occasion.

Macro Plays Three *morality plays (*The *Castle of Perseverance*, *Mankind*, and *Wisdom*) named after their 18th-century owner, Cox Macro (1683–1767).

MADGE, Charles (1912–96) Poet and sociologist, whose left-wing sympathies were manifested in his poetry in *The Disappearing Castle*, (1937); *The Father Found* (1941); and, after a gap of 50 years, *Of Love, Time and Places* (1993). In 1937 with Humphrey Jennings and Tom Harrisson he founded *Mass Observation, a scheme which recruited hundreds of observers (including poets and novelists) to collect accurate sociological data about everyday life and popular culture. His first wife was the poet Kathleen *Raine.

Madoc A narrative poem by Robert *Southey, published 1805. The poem gave its title to *Madoc: A Mystery* (1990) by Paul *Muldoon.

madrigal Originally a short amatory lyric, but used in musical terminology to describe a type of song for several voices, to secular words, usually sung by amateurs, without instrumental accompaniment. The madrigal reached England from Europe but was not widely disseminated until *Musica Transalpina* (1588), an anthology of 57 Italian madrigals with English texts; four other such volumes appeared in England between 1588 and 1598, with 45 more by 1627. Major composers were Thomas *Morley, John Ward, Thomas *Weelkes, and John *Wilbye, followed by Orlando Gibbons (1612) and Thomas Tomkins (1622), after which the form, already challenged by the dominance of the lute song, largely died out.

Mad World, my Masters, A A comedy by Thomas *Middleton, written 1604–7, printed 1608.

MAECENAS (d. 8 BC) Wealthy friend of the emperor Augustus and patron of *Virgil, *Propertius, and particularly *Horace, to whom he gave his Sabine farm. His name has become the generic term for a generous patron of the arts.

Maeve (Medb) [pron. Mayv] In the Ulster cycle, queen of Connaught. *See* CUCHULAIN; TÁIN-BÓ-CUAILNGE.

magic realism A term used to describe a style of modern fiction in which the recognizably realistic mingles with the unexpected and the inexplicable, and in which elements of dream, fairy story, or mythology combine with the everyday, often in a mosaic or kaleidoscopic pattern of refraction and recurrence. It has been most commonly applied to works by Latin American authors such as *García Márquez, Alejo Carpentier (1904–80), and Isabel *Allende, and sometimes also to those of Günter *Grass, Italo *Calvino, Milan *Kundera, and other European writers. In the 1970s and 1980s it was adopted in Britain by several of the most original younger fiction writers, including, notably, Salman *Rushdie, Angela *Carter, and Emma *Tennant, who reached beyond the limits of fictional *realism in order to draw upon the imaginative resources of *fable, folk tale, or *Gothic romance.

MAGINN, William (1793–1842) Irish satirist and journalist, who wrote under various pseudonyms including 'Ensign Morgan O'Doherty'. He was a prolific contributor to *Blackwood's Magazine, notably to the *Noctes Ambrosianae. In 1830 he helped in the establishing of *Fraser's Magazine, in which 'Homeric Ballads' and 'A Gallery of Literary Characters', appeared. Maginn's wit and learning are evident in his parodies of Walter *Scott, S. T. *Coleridge, Thomas *Moore, Benjamin *Disraeli, Thomas *Carlyle, and many others. Maginn was the original of Captain Shandon in Thackeray's *Pendennis.

Magnetic Lady, The, or Humours Reconciled A comedy by Ben *Jonson, performed 1632, printed 1641. Between the acts there is an interlude of debate about the theatre between a boy actor and two sceptical youths, Probee and Damplay.

Magnificence A morality play (c.1519) by John *Skelton. Magnificence, symbolizing a generous prince, is ruined by mistaken liberality and bad counsellors, but restored by Good-Hope, Perseverance, and other similar figures.

Mahābhārata An ancient Hindu epic poem, written in Sanskrit, reputedly over 100,000 stanzas long, describing the war between two groups of cousins, the Pandavas and the Kauravas, unfolding and to some extent legitimizing the divine pre-existing order of the universe, or *dharma*. It dates in its earliest written forms to the 5th or 6th century BC, though it is presented as the creation of the god Vishnu. The characters of the *Mahābhārata*, unlike those of Greek mythology, seem surprisingly modern in their questioning of destiny and tradition, especially the central figure of Draupadi, wife to all five Pandava brothers. The work was introduced to an English-speaking readership through Charles Wilkins's 1785 translation of Krishna's rousing battlefield address to Arjuna. There have been numerous translations of sections of the poem, notably by Christopher *Isherwood and Swami Prabhavananda (1893–1976) (USA, 1944), and a stage adaptation (1985) by Peter *Brook. The *Mahābhārata* has exerted an important influence on *Anglo-Indian literature.

MAHFOUZ, Naguib (1911–2006) Egyptian author. His novels Midaq Alley (1947) and the trilogy Palace Walk (1956), Palace of Desire (1957), and Sugar Street (1957) depict life in the old quarters of Cairo. The first of his more allegorical and symbolic later novels, The Children of Gebelawi (1959), was banned in Egypt because of its controversial treatment of religion. Important later works include The Thief and the Dogs (1961), Autumn Quail (1962), Small Talk on the Nile (1966), Miramar (1967), The Harafish (1977), and The Journey of Ibn Fattouma (1983).

MAHON, Derek (1941–) Irish poet, born in Belfast. His work blends a stylistic insouciance owing something to W. H. *Auden and Louis *MacNeice with a Beckettian irony and despair. 'A Disused Shed in County Wexford' (from The Snow Party, 1975) is perhaps the most anthologized Irish poem of recent times. His collections include Lives (1972), The Hunt by Night (1982), The Hudson Letter (1995), The Yellow Book (1997), and Harbour Lights (2005).

MAHY, Margaret (1936–) Although a New Zealander, this highly respected, popular, and prolific writer for children and young adults has had a notable impact on readers, writers, and publishers in the UK, with seminal picture books such as *A Lion in the Meadow* (1969) and young adult novels including *The Changeover* (1984), all of which blur the boundaries between fantasy and reality in complex and satisfying ways.

Maid Marian Originally a female figure in traditional May Day pageants. From the 16th century, she appears as the companion of *Robin Hood, the association having probably been suggested by the fact that he was also represented in the pageants.

Maid Marian (1822) A medieval romance by Thomas Love *Peacock. It features *Robin Hood, *Maid Marian, Friar Tuck, and Prince John, while lampooning institutions such as the monarchy and the church in the post-Napoleonic era. The book was later adapted as a popular operetta.

Maid of Honour, The A tragicomedy by Philip *Massinger, acted about 1621–2, published 1632, based on a story by *Boccaccio.

Maid's Tragedy, The A tragedy by Francis *Beaumont and John *Fletcher, written ?1610, published 1619. Amintor, a gentleman of Rhodes, breaks his engagement to Aspatia at the king's request and she laments her loss in some of the finest verse in the play (II. ii); her lines 'And the trees about me, | Let them be dry and leafless; let the rocks | Groan with continual surges; and behind me | Make all a desolation. Look, look, wenches!' were used by T. S. *Eliot as an epigraph to 'Sweeney Erect'; the speech is also quoted by Emily *Eden in *The Semidetached House* (chapter 20). The last act of the play, in which Aspatia dies and Amintor takes his own life, was rewritten by Edmund *Waller, with a happy ending in which they survive and marry.

MAILER, Norman (1923–2007) American novelist and essayist; his naturalistic first novel *The Naked and the Dead* (1948), based on his experiences with the army in the Pacific, was followed by other novels, including *Barbary Shore* (1951), *The Deer Park* (1955), and *An American Dream* (1965). *Advertisements for Myself* (1959) mixes journalism, autobiography, political commentary, and fictional passages. *The Presidential Papers* (1963) and *The Armies of the Night* (1968) are his most famous works of political reportage. *The Executioner's Song* (1979) and his study of Lee Harvey Oswald (*Oswald's Story: An American Mystery*, 1995) use documentary methods. Mailer explores themes of power in *Ancient Evenings* (1983), set in ancient Egypt, *Harlot's Ghost* (1991), a portrait of the CIA, and *The Castle in the Forest* (2007), an account of Hitler's youth. *The Gospel According to the Son* (1997) is a first-person account of the life of Jesus and *The Spooky Art* (2003) collects Mailer's essays on the art of writing.

MAKIN, Bathsua (b. 1600, d. in or after 1675) Née Reginald, scholar, educationalist, and poet, and tutor to Princess Elizabeth, daughter of Charles I. Makin was described by the diarist Sir Simon D'Ewes (1602–50) as 'the greatest scholler, I thinke, of a woman in England'. Her *Essay to Revive the Ancient Education of Gentlewomen* (1673) insists that the whole 'encyclopaedia of learning' be opened to women. The moderation of her claims may have been linked with a wish to dissociate herself from the 1670 translation of Cornelius *Agrippa's inflammatory feminist *Female Preeminence: or The Dignity and Excellence of that Sex, above the Male* by Henry Care (1646/7–1688).

MALAMUD, Bernard (1914–86) American novelist, born in Brooklyn, who began publishing his short stories in the 1940s. His early novels *The Natural* (1952) and *The Assistant* (1957) were followed by *The Fixer* (1966), the story of a Jewish handyman in tsarist Russia just before the First World War, who is falsely accused of murder and turned into the scapegoat for anti-Semitic feeling in his neighbourhood. Other works include *A New Life* (1961), *The Tenants* (1971), *Dubin's Lives* (1979), and *God's Grace* (1982), a post-nuclear war narrative. Malamud's *Complete Stories* appeared in 1998.

MALCOLM X (1925–65) African American campaigner for civil rights, born Malcolm Little in Omaha, Nebraska, who chose X to erase his slave name. He collaborated with Alex *Haley in writing his autobiography and was shot in 1965 by political opponents.

Malcontent, The A tragicomedy by John *Marston, and generally considered his best play, published 1604 (with additions by John *Webster), written not earlier than 1602. The plot resembles that of *Measure for Measure, but the exposure of court corruption, lust, and greed is more harshly satiric.

Maldon, Battle of A 325-line poem in Old English, of uncertain date, incomplete at the beginning and the end, dealing with the battle fought in 991 at Maldon in Essex against Danish raiders. The Danes are drawn up by the river Pant (Blackwater), opposed by Byrhtnoth, ealdorman of Essex since 956, who rejects their demand for tribute. The poem's second half, in which Byrhtnoth's followers pledge their loyalty to their dead leader, is a powerful statement of fidelity and determination to avenge his death. The poem survives only in a transcript because the manuscript was destroyed in the 1731 fire at the Cotton Library (*see* COTTON, SIR ROBERT BRUCE).

MALLARMÉ, Stéphane (1842-98) French poet, leading figure in the *symbolist movement, and one of the heroes of *structuralism. His formidably dense verse has both lured and defied translators, beginning with Arthur *Symons.

MALLET (Malloch), David (?1705-65) Scottish writer, author of a philosophical poem, *The Excursion* (1728), tragedies including *Elvira* (1763), and a popular ghost ballad, 'William and Margaret'. He collaborated with James *Thomson in the masque *Alfred* (1740), wrote a *Life of Francis Bacon* (1740), and edited Bolingbroke's *Works* (5 vols, 1754).

MALLOCK, William Hurrell (1849-1923) Novelist, poet, and satirist. *The New Republic: or Culture, Faith and Philosophy in an English Country House* (1877) is a lively satire on English society and ideas, including a sympathetic portrait of John *Ruskin as Mr Herbert. Benjamin Jowett, Matthew *Arnold, Walter *Pater, T. H. *Huxley, and John Tyndall all appear under thin disguises. He also published poems, novels, and memoirs, including *A Human Document* (1892), the basis of the artist Tom *Phillips's collage *Humument*.

MALONE, Edmond (1741-1812) Scholar, the author of *An Attempt to Ascertain the Order in Which the Plays Attributed to Shakespeare Were Written* (1778), in George *Steevens's edition of *Shakespeare. His own edition of Shakespeare (10 vols, 1790) was followed by editions of Oliver *Goldsmith (1777), Joshua Reynolds (1797-8), and the prose works of John *Dryden (1800). He helped James *Boswell prepare the *Journal of a Tour to the Hebrides* (1785) and the *Life of Samuel *Johnson* (1791). He exposed the forgeries of Thomas *Chatterton in 1782 and William Henry *Ireland in 1796. His new edition of Shakespeare was completed and issued posthumously (21 vols, 1821) by James Boswell the younger.

MALORY, Sir Thomas (1415/18-1471) Author of *Le *Morte Darthur*, he was identified by Eugène Vinaver as Sir Thomas Malory of Newbold Revel, Warwickshire, made knight before 1442. The *Morte Darthur* was written in prison and Malory of Newbold Revel was charged with crimes of violence, theft, and rape after 1450. It was also proposed that Malory had been a hostage in France, because much of the work drew on a 'French book'.

MALOUF, David (1934-) Australian poet and novelist. His volumes of poetry include *Neighbours in a Thicket* (1974) and *First Things Last* (1980). *Selected Poems 1959-1989* appeared in 1994. *An Imaginary Life* (1978) is a lyrical prose meditation on the last years of the Roman poet *Ovid. His novels include the semi-autobiographical novel *Johnno* (1975), *Harland's Half Acre* (1984), *The Great World* (1990), *Remembering Babylon* (1993), *The Conversations at Curlow Creek* (1996), and *Ransom* (2009). His volumes of short stories, including *Antipodes* (1985) and *Every Move You Make* (2006), are collected in *The Complete Stories* (2007); *12 Edmondstone Street* (1985) is autobiographical.

MALTHUS, Thomas (1766-1834) Political economist. In 1798, provoked by William Godwin's *Enquiry Concerning Political Justice of 1793, Malthus published *An Essay on the Principle of Population*, in which he argued that population (growing geometrically) would soon increase beyond the means of subsistence (which grew only arithmetically), and that checks in the form of poverty, disease, and starvation were necessary. The *Essay* was heavily recast in a second edition of 1803 in which Malthus modified his conclusions, suggesting that the regulation of greed and sexual activity would act as more acceptable checks on population growth. His work was vigorously attacked by Godwin, William *Cobbett, William *Hazlitt, and others, but it exerted a powerful influence on social thought in the 19th century. Charles *Darwin declared in his *Life* that Malthus' *Essay* helped to point him towards his own theory of evolution.

MAMET, David (1947-) American playwright. His work is distinguished by its attention to the rhythms of blue-collar speech and the theme of how low-life criminality mirrors the world of big business, as in *American

Buffalo (1975) and *Glengarry Glen Ross* (1983). Often criticized for sexism, his work is unafraid to address crises in gender relations, as in *Sexual Perversity in Chicago* (1974), which satirizes the vacuity of male sexual bravado, and *Oleanna* (1992), a complex narrative of sexual harassment. He has written widely for the cinema, and has directed films of his own, including the highly acclaimed *House of Games* (1987). Other work includes a retelling of *Faustus* (2004); two novels, *The Village* (1994) and *The Old Religion* (1997); and *The Wicked Son: Anti-Semitism, Self-Hatred and the Jews* (2006).

Manannán The son of *Lêr, a highly popular god of the old Gaelic pantheon, the subject of many legends. The Isle of Man is said to take its name from him. There he has degenerated into a legendary giant, with three legs (seen revolving in the coat of arms of the island).

Manawyddan *See* MABINOGION.

Man Booker Prize for Fiction A prize founded (as the Booker-McConnell Prize for Fiction) in 1969, awarded annually to the best full-length novel published in the previous twelve months by an author from the Commonwealth or the Republic of Ireland writing in English. (See Appendix 4 (*d*) for list of winners) Originally financed by Booker wholesalers, and administered by the Book Trust, the prize was renamed the Man Booker in 2002 when the investment company Man Group plc became the chief sponsors. The administration was taken over by a newly registered charity, the Booker Prize Foundation. The prize, now worth £50,000, is considered by many to be the most prestigious of all British book prizes. In 1993, a so-called Booker of Bookers was awarded to Salman *Rushdie for his novel *Midnight's Children*, chosen as the best book to have won the prize in its first quarter of a century. In 2005, the Man Booker International Prize, a biennial award to a living writer of any nationality, intended to recognize his or her complete oeuvre, was established. The first recipient was the Albanian writer Ismail Kadare, followed by Chinua *Achebe, Alice *Munro, and Philip *Roth (2011). In 2008 the Lost Man Booker Prize was awarded to J. G. *Farrell's *Troubles* (1970), as rule changes in 1971 had excluded much of the previous year's fiction from eligibility for the prize.

Manchester Guardian Founded in 1821 as a weekly (daily from 1855); the principal Liberal paper outside London. Its title was changed to the *Guardian* in 1959; since 1961 it has been published from London. The paper has retained its liberal values.

Manchester School The name first applied by Benjamin *Disraeli to the political party, led by Richard Cobden (1804-65) and John Bright (1811-89), who advocated the principles of free trade. The 'Manchester School' of drama refers loosely to the playwrights associated with Miss *Horniman's Company of Actors at the Gaiety Theatre, Manchester, 1907-14, including Harold Brighouse (1882-1958), W. S. Houghton (1881-1913), and Allan Monkhouse (1858-1936).

'Manciple's Tale, The' *See* CANTERBURY TALES, 23.

MANDELSHTAM, Nadezhda (1899-1980) Writer; she shared the exile of her husband, Osip *Mandelshtam, under Stalin. After Osip's death in 1938 she lived on the run, having made it her mission to memorize and thus preserve his poetry. When she was eventually permitted to return to Moscow in 1964 she wrote and published her memoirs. The first volume, *Hope against Hope* (1970), details the last four harrowing years of her marriage whilst *Hope Abandoned* (1974) focuses on her own life as a widow; the volumes are the main source of information on her husband, and a powerful and harrowing description of the experience of 20th-century totalitarianism. The titles pun on the Russian word 'nadezhda' meaning hope.

MANDELSHTAM, Osip Emilevich (1891-1938) Russian poet. In 1911 he joined the Acmeist Guild of Poets with Anna *Akhmatova and Nikolai Gumilev, the poems of *Stone* (1913), are marked by Acmeist brevity and clarity. During the early 1920s Mandelshtam came under increasing attack for being 'out of step' with the new Soviet age. His first arrest, in 1934, resulted from his recitation of his famous poem denouncing Stalin. Prison was followed by a period of internal exile and attempted suicide. In 1938 he was sentenced to five years' hard labour; he died of a heart attack on the way to the camps. His collected works were first published abroad; the full range of his work became available in Russia for the first time in the 1990s. Mandelshtam is now regarded as one of the major poets of the 20th century.

MANDEVILLE, Bernard (1670-1733) Moral philosopher; he trained as a physician at

Leiden, settled in London, and published *A Treatise of the Hypochondriack and Hysterick Passions* (1711; enlarged edition, 1730). His other prose works include *The Virgin Unmasked* (1709, 1714), an odd mix of advice manual and political speculation; *Free Thoughts on Religion, the Church and National Happiness* (1720), a defence of *Deism and an attack on clericalism; and *An Enquiry into the Origin of Honour* (1732), on the social effects of self-esteem and self-love. *A Modest Defence of Public Stews* (1724), recommending governmental regulation of brothels, is often assumed to be his. In *The Fable of the Bees, or Private Vices, Public Benefits* (1714; enlarged 1723). Mandeville rejects the optimistic view of benevolent human nature put forward by Shaftesbury, and argues that the mutual help on which society thrives like a colony of bees is due to personal acquisitiveness and the love of luxury. Mandeville's writing was admired by Daniel *Defoe, but his ironic use of the language of 'vice' and 'virtue' was attacked by William *Law, John Dennis, Francis *Hutcheson, Isaac *Watts, and George *Berkeley.

MANDEVILLE, Sir John Ostensible author of the book of *Travels* translated into many European languages after its first appearance in France c.1357, which survives in 22 versions, including prose and metrical English versions. Claiming to be a guide, both geographical and ethical, for pilgrims to the Holy Land, it is really a compilation from authors including William of Boldensele, Friar Odoric of Pordenone, and *Vincent of Beauvais, combining geography and natural history with romance and marvels, and famously featuring a supposed encounter between 'Mandeville' and the sultan of Egypt, who offers some sharp criticisms of backsliding Christians. It was an important influence on English writers from *Chaucer to *Shakespeare.

Manfred A poetic drama by Lord *Byron, published 1817. Manfred, a Faustian figure, 'half-dust, half deity', lives alone in a castle in the Alps, tortured by guilt for 'some half-maddening sin'. He summons the spirits of the universe, who offer him everything except the oblivion he seeks. Eventually, overcoming his terror of death, he tries to hurl himself from an Alpine crag, but is dragged back by a hunter. He invokes the Witch of the Alps and reveals his sin—his incestuous love for his sister Astarte. He descends to the underworld, the Hall of Arimanes, and encounters a vision of Astarte, who promises him death on the morrow. Back in his castle an abbot begs him to repent, but he

cannot. He denies the power of the demons who summon him, and when they vanish he dies.

manga A Japanese genre of cartoons and comic books, notably longer than non-Japanese works in these genres, and particularly prevalent since the Second World War; animations in a similar style are called anime. Manga has a distinct visual style, its androgynous characters having large heads and exaggerated facial expressions. Shôjo manga is specifically written and marketed to a teenage girl audience; its fluid gender and identity boundaries give it an appeal similar to that of *young adult literature. Shônen manga, marketed to young boys, has more in common with superhero comics. In the 21st century the form has become outstandingly popular, and highly visible as a distinct category in libraries and bookshops. *See also* GRAPHIC NOVEL; COMICS.

MANGAN, James Clarence (1803–49) Irish poet. Some poems, such as 'Twenty Golden Years Ago' and 'The Nameless One', are querulously autobiographical, while others (e.g. 'Siberia') powerfully evoke famine and desolation. Mangan, who died of malnutrition, in destitution, has come to be seen as Ireland's greatest contributor to *Romanticism.

Manichaeism *See* GNOSTICISM.

Mankind A morality play in 914 lines from East Anglia, written c.1470–71, one of the group called *Macro Plays after their 18th-century owner (the others being *Wisdom and The *Castle of Perseverance). Its principal theme is Sloth (*Accidia*), and it provocatively juxtaposes exhortations to good Christian conduct with obscenity and topical satire.

MANLEY, Delarivier (c.1670–1724) Writer, whose colourful life included a bigamous marriage with her cousin John Manley and some years as mistress of the warden of the Fleet Prison, John Tilly. She wrote several plays and published many novels, including *The New Atalantis* (1709), a *roman à clef* which attacked various notable Whigs in sufficient detail for her to be arrested; the narrative of 'Delia' is autobiographical, as is *The Adventures of Rivella* (1714). In 1711 she succeeded Jonathan *Swift as editor of the Tory *Examiner* for a few numbers.

MANNING, Olivia (1908–80) Novelist. She married a British Council lecturer, R. D. Smith, in 1939 and travelled with him to Bucharest. From there they went to Greece, Egypt, and

Jerusalem, usually one step ahead of the Nazis, an experience which inspired *The Balkan Trilogy* (*The Great Fortune*, 1960; *The Spoilt City*, 1962; *Friends and Heroes*, 1965) and *The Levant Trilogy* (*The Danger Tree*, 1977; *The Battle Lost and Won*, 1978; *The Sum of Things*, 1980). This six-novel sequence mainly focuses on refugee civilians: it partly shifts its viewpoint in the second trilogy to a young British officer serving in the desert, and is a refreshingly tart portrait of a marriage.

MANNYNG, Robert (d. *c*.1338) Author of the verse *Chronicle of England* (finished 1338) and **Handlyng Synne*, an adaptation in octosyllabic couplets of the Anglo-Norman *Manuel des péchés*.

Man of Feeling, The A highly influential 'novel of *sentiment' by Henry *Mackenzie, published 1771. Supposedly found in a mutilated manuscript of unknown authorship, the story is fragmented, giving the effect of a series of brief, poignant episodes, with some humorous and ironic interludes. Harley, the man of feeling, travels to London and, though often cheated, demonstrates an unwavering benevolence and acute, tearful sensibility. He gives heartfelt but limited assistance to the downtrodden, reunites a prostitute with her father, rescues an old family friend, and returns home without achieving worldly success, dying as his beloved declares her love for him.

'Man of Law's Tale, The' *See* CANTERBURY TALES, 5.

Man of Mode, The A comedy by Sir George *Etherege, and a classic of the *Restoration period, first performed at court in 1676. Richard *Steele denounced its immorality and the cruelty of its sexual politics in the **Spectator*, 65, and John Dennis defended it. It has two interwoven plots. In one, rake and playboy Dorimant, who was modelled on John *Rochester, and first played by Thomas *Betterton, shakes off his mistress Mrs Loveit, seduces Belinda, and woos the heiress Harriet Woodvil. In the other Young Bellair outwits his father and marries Emilia. The fop Sir Fopling Flutter gives the play its title. It was revived in a modern-dress production by Nicholas Hytner at the *National Theatre in 2007.

Man of the World, The (1) A novel by Henry *Mackenzie, published 1773, with a villainous seducer as its hero, in contrast to his **Man of Feeling*. (2) A comedy by Charles *Macklin, performed 1781, adapted from his

The True Born Scotchman, performed in Dublin in 1764.

MANSFIELD, Katherine Pseudonym of Kathleen Mansfield Beauchamp (1888–1923), New Zealand-born writer, who settled in England in 1908: she never revisited her home country. In 1909 she became pregnant by a young musician, Garnet Trowell, married another man, George Bowden (they were divorced in 1918), but left her husband immediately after the ceremony and in time gave birth to a stillborn child in Bavaria, an experience that formed the background to her first collection of stories, *In a German Pension* (1911), most of which had been previously published in A. R. Orage's *New Age*. In 1911 she met J. M. *Murry, whom she was to marry in 1918; he was editing **Rhythm*, to which, and to its successor the *Blue Review*, she contributed stories, many based on her New Zealand childhood. In 1918 'Prelude' was published by the *Hogarth Press; Mansfield enjoyed a close, tense, admiring friendship with Virginia *Woolf. After the publication of *Bliss and Other Stories* (1920) she was increasingly recognized as an original and experimental writer, whose stories were the first in English to show the influence of Anton *Chekhov. *The Garden Party and Other Stories* (1922) was the third and last collection to be published in her lifetime. In that year she entered the institute at Fontainebleau, near Paris, run by G. I. *Gurdjieff, hoping to regain spiritual and physical health (her tuberculosis had been diagnosed in 1917); she died the following January. Two collections were published posthumously (*The Dove's Nest*, 1923; *Something Childish*, 1924) as well as extracts from her journal.

Mansfield Park A novel by Jane *Austen, begun 1811, published 1814. Sir Thomas Bertram of Mansfield Park, a stern but kind-hearted man, has two sons, Tom and Edmund, and two daughters, Maria and Julia. His wife, a charming, indolent woman, has two sisters: Mrs Norris, a near neighbour, who is spiteful and selfish, and Mrs Price, the wife of an impecunious officer of marines, with a large family of young children. To assist the Prices, Sir Thomas takes charge of their eldest daughter Fanny, a timid child of 9. In spite of her humble situation and the cruelty of Mrs Norris, Fanny becomes indispensable to the household. Her strength of character is shown when Sir Thomas leaves to take care of his plantations in Antigua, in the West Indies. Family discipline is considerably relaxed, forbidden private theatricals are mounted, and a flirtation begins between Maria Bertram, who is already engaged to marry Mr Rushworth, and Henry Crawford, the attractive, worldly brother-in-law of the parson of Mansfield. Against all this Fanny resolutely sets her face. Loving her cousin Edmund, she grieves to see him fascinated by the frivolous Mary Crawford, Henry's sister. Maria having become Mrs Rushworth, Henry turns his attention to Fanny, to his own and her astonishment falls in love with her, and proposes marriage. Fanny unhesitatingly rejects him, incurring the grave displeasure of Sir Thomas for what he regards as a piece of ungrateful perversity. During a visit paid by Fanny to her own home in Portsmouth matters come to a crisis. Henry, accidentally encountering Maria Rushworth again, runs away with her; and Julia elopes with a foolish and unsuitable suitor, Mr Yates. Mary Crawford's failure to condemn her brother's conduct, together with her aversion to marrying a clergyman (for Edmund has by now taken orders), opens Edmund's eyes to her true character. He turns for comfort to Fanny, falls in love, and they are married.

MANTEL, Hilary (1952–). CBE, novelist. She describes the disintegration of her Roman Catholic family in *Giving up the Ghost* (2003), a memoir complemented by *Learning to Talk* (2003, stories). Her first two novels, *Every Day is Mother's Day* (1985) and *Vacant Possession* (1986), were interlinked black comedies inspired by a job in social work. *A Place of Greater Safety* (1992) is set during the French Revolution. *A Change of Climate* (1994), about missionaries who had worked in Africa, is based on her life in Botswana with her geologist husband, from 1977. She and her husband later lived in Saudi Arabia, an experience which inspired her essay 'Last Months in Al Hamra', and her novel *Eight Months on Ghazzah Street* (1988). *Fludd* (1989), set in a northern village in the 1950s, concerns a mysterious figure who might be a force for good or evil. *An Experiment in Love* (1995), about the friendship between two girls through school and university, and *Beyond Black* (2005), set among psychics, have invited comparisons with Muriel *Spark. *The Giant O'Brien* (1998) viscerally recreates the 18th-century London world of surgeons and body-snatchers. *Wolf Hall* (2009) depicts the life of the statesman Thomas Cromwell (1485–1540).

MANTUAN (Mantuanus) (1448–1516) Johannes Baptista Spagnolo, a Carmelite of Mantua who wrote Latin *eclogues, which influ-enced the *pastoral poetry of Alexander *Barclay and Edmund *Spenser.

manuscript publication The circulation of works in manuscript continued long after the introduction of printing to England. In addition to controversial political and religious works, authors allowed their literary productions to circulate among their friends and to be published in multiple copies by scribes or scriveners for various reasons. These included a fear of the so-called stigma of print among women writers and among noble and aristocratic ones, a desire to evade censorship or punishment for libellous, seditious, heretical, or pornographic works, and a wish to limit personal writings to an immediate coterie or circle of friends. Among those authors whose work circulated widely in handwritten copies were Thomas *Wyatt and the earl of *Surrey, Philip *Sidney (especially his translation of the Psalms, completed and revised by Mary Sidney (1561–1621)), Sir John *Davies, John *Donne (especially the *Songs and Sonnets* at the Inns of Court), Ben *Jonson (especially his poems), Francis *Bacon, Walter *Ralegh, William Strode, Edmund *Waller, Katherine *Philips, and the earl of *Rochester.

All sorts of literary and non-literary works were copied, initially by an author and often by his or her friends, but the copying of texts was also undertaken by professional scribes. Ralph Crane (*fl.* 1589–1632) produced multiple manuscript copies of Thomas Middleton's politically scandalous *A *Game at Chess*; he also provided the manuscript copy from which other plays, including John *Webster's *The Duchess of Malfi* and plays by *Shakespeare in the first *folio, were first printed. The anonymous copyist known from his handwriting as the Feathery Scribe (*fl. c.*1625–40) made multiple copies of political, legal, and antiquarian works, perhaps at the rate of a penny-halfpenny per page. This sort of copying, probably organized by stationers who supplied paper, ink, and the works to be transcribed, seems sometimes to have taken place in scriptoria, whose distinctive products can be identified. Multiple copying was generally cheaper, quicker, and less subject to official attention than printing. The practice probably died out as a result of changes to *copyright law in the early 18th century. There are important studies of the subject by Harold Love, *Scribal Publication in Seventeenth-Century England* (1993), and Peter Beal, *In Praise of Scribes* (1998).

MAP, Walter (d. *c.*1209) From the Welsh borders; archdeacon of Oxford during the reign of Henry II, the author of a partly serious, partly satirical, and always entertaining miscellany entitled *De Nugis Curialium*, 'Courtiers' Trifles', which survives in a single Oxford manuscript. The collection, begun *c.*1181–2 but never formally completed, includes stories in different genres, history and satire, as well as a disquisition inspired by St *Jerome: the *Dissuasio Valerii ad Rufinum de Non Ducenda Uxore* referred to by Chaucer in the 'Prologue to the Wife of Bath's Tale' (*Canterbury Tales*, III. 671). Some *Goliardic poems have also been doubtfully attributed to Map.

MAPANJE, Jack (1944–) Malawian poet, detained without trial for nearly four years in his native Malawi in 1987. He has lived in Britain since his release. His first collection of poetry, *Of Chameleons and Gods* (1981), was banned in Malawi. *The Chattering Wagtails of Mikuyu Prison* (1993), *Skipping without Ropes* (1998), *The Last of the Sweet Bananas* (2004), and *The Beasts of Nalunga* (2007) trace the growth of an incarcerated poet's mind, with anger, wry wit, and compassion.

MARBER, Patrick (1964–) Playwright, who directed his first two plays, *Dealer's Choice* (1995) and *Closer* (1997) at the *National Theatre, and has successfully adapted *Molière's *Don Juan* as *Don Juan in Soho* (2006).

MARCUS AURELIUS ANTONINUS (AD 121–80) Roman emperor 161–80 and single-mindedly *Stoic philosopher, author of twelve books of personal 'meditations' written in Greek. The *Meditations* focus on practical ethics, death, and man's relationship to state (Rome) and cosmos. Antonio de Guevara published *Libro aureo del emperador Marco Aurelio* (1529), parts of which he falsely claimed to derive from Marcus; a French version of this was translated by John Berners as *The Golden Boke of Marcus Aurelius* (1535), and by Thomas *North as the *Diall of Princes* (1557).

MARECHERA, Dambudzo (1952–87) Controversial novelist, playwright, and poet, born in Zimbabwe. *The House of Hunger* (1978), a collection of short stories and *Black Sunlight* (1980, novel) flouted the realist conventions and nationalist preoccupations of most African fiction. Multiple genres are used in *Mindblast* (1984). *The Black Insider* (1990) and *Cemetery of Mind* (1992) appeared posthumously.

MARGARET OF ANJOU (1430–82) The 'she-wolf of France', daughter of Reignier (or René), king of Naples, who is a dominant character in Shakespeare's *1, 2, and 3 *Henry VI* and *Richard III*. In *1* and *2 Henry VI* she is the mistress of Suffolk, though married to Henry. In *3 Henry VI* she becomes more aggressive, with her mocking and murder of York, and in *Richard III* she is a powerful prophet of doom. When the plays are performed in sequence, as in John Barton's adaptation of the four plays as *The *Wars of the Roses* (1963), this becomes one of Shakespeare's most powerful female roles.

Margarite of America, A A prose romance by Thomas *Lodge published 1596, but written during his voyage to South America under Thomas Cavendish in 1591–3. It is notable for its variety of visual spectacle and pageantry, its highly patterned poems and songs, and the unsparing savagery of many of the incidents.

MARGUERITE OF NAVARRE *See* HEPTAMÉRON, L'.

Maria *See* WRONGS OF WOMAN.

'Mariana' (1830) and **'Mariana in the South'** (1832) Two poems by Alfred *Tennyson, suggested by Shakespeare's Mariana of 'the moated grange' in *Measure for Measure*. Both describe women waiting hopelessly for their lovers; the first inspired John Everett *Millais's painting of 1851, and the landscape of the second was drawn from Tennyson's journey with Arthur Henry *Hallam in 1832. Tennyson appears to have invented the stanza form.

MARIE DE FRANCE (*fl. c.*1180–89) A French poet resident in England, about whom little certain is known. She knew Latin and English. Three works have been attributed to her, most famously twelve *Lais*, a series of apparently Celtic stories told in Anglo-Norman couplets, some of which gave rise to versions in English (*see* BRETON LAYS). She wrote a collection of *Aesop's Fables which she called *Isopet* and which she says she translated from English.

MARINETTI, Filippo Tommaso (1876–1944) Italian dramatist, novelist, and poet, who launched *futurism in 1909.

MARINO, Giambattista (1569–1625) Neapolitan poet, best known for his *Adone* (1623), a long poem on the love of Venus and Adonis.

The term *marinismo* (or sometimes *secentismo*) denotes the flamboyant style of Marino and his 17th-century imitators, with its extravagant imagery, excessive ornamentation, and verbal conceits. Richard *Crashaw was profoundly influenced by Marino.

Marino Faliero, Doge of Venice A drama in blank verse by Lord *Byron, published 1821 and produced in the same year at Drury Lane, against its author's wishes. The play, based upon historical facts and inspired by Byron's 1816–17 period in Venice, is set in 1355. The elderly but vigorous Faliero was elected doge in 1354, and his conspiracy was also the subject of a tragedy by A. C. *Swinburne, 1885.

Marius the Epicurean A philosophical novel by Walter *Pater, published 1885. Pater describes the boyhood, education, and young manhood of Marius, a serious young Roman imbued with a 'morbid religious idealism'. With his friend Flavian (who, like so many of Pater's characters, dies young) he discovers the 'jewelled' delights of *Apuleius, in particular of the story of *Cupid and Psyche, then progresses through the philosophies of *Heraclitus, Aristippus, and *Marcus Aurelius to Christianity. He dies more or less a martyr to save a Christian friend. The work is a vehicle for Pater's own reflections on pagan and Christian art and religion. The book was a significant influence on the *Aesthetic movement, and was especially important to the development of the work of Oscar *Wilde.

Mark, King In Arthurian legend, the king of Cornwall and the husband of Isoud of Ireland, who is brought to Mark by her lover Tristram. *See* TRISTRAM AND ISOUD.

MARK, Jan (1943–2006) Best known as a writer of novels and short stories for children and young people. Her first book was *Thunder and Lightnings* (1976), about friendship between two boys who share a passion for aeroplanes. She moved between genres, constantly experimenting with forms and ideas, paying great attention to language and style, and never underestimating her readers.

MARK, St *See* BIBLE; EVANGELISTS.

MARKANDAYA, Kamala (1924–2004) British novelist, the first notable woman novelist in English from the Indian sub-continent. The impact of new economic and political forces on traditional Indian society is Markandaya's main theme in *Nectar in a Sieve* (1954), *A Silence of Desire* (1960), *Possession* (1963), *A Handful of Rice* (1966), and *The Coffer Dams* (1969). *The Nowhere Man* (1972) transports the clash of cultures to England, where Markandaya settled in the early 1960s. *Two Virgins* (1973) has a more experimental style. Her most ambitious novel, *The Golden Honeycomb* (1977), examines how the coming of Indian independence affected a native or princely state. The sensitive exploration of relations between Indians and Europeans is a hallmark of Markandaya's work, for example in *Pleasure City* (1982).

MARKHAM, E. A. (Edward Archibald) (1939–2008) Poet, editor, and fiction writer; he was born on Montserrat in the Caribbean and came to England in 1956. His volumes of poetry include *Human Rites* (1984), *Living in Disguise* (1986), *Towards the End of a Century* (1989), *Misapprehensions* (1995), and *A Rough Climate* (2002). His short story collections include *Something Unusual* (1986), *Ten Stories* (1994), *Taking the Drawing Room through Customs* (2002), *Meet Me in Mozambique* (2005), and *At Home with Miss Vanesa* (2006).

MARKHAM, Gervase (?1568–1637) Writer on country pursuits, the art of war, and horsemanship; he also wrote plays and poems. His chief work on country occupations, *A Way to Get Wealth* (1623), contains treatises on 'Cheap and Good Husbandry' (the management of domestic animals); 'Country Contentments' (hunting, hawking, fishing), with a section on the 'English Housewife' (cooking, dairying, physic); and agriculture and horticulture. Other works include a poem about Sir Richard Grenville (1595) and *The English Arcadia* (prose, 1607).

MARLOWE, Christopher (1564–93) Poet and playwright, atheistic and probably homosexual, and was probably employed as a government spy. In 1589 he was involved in a street fight in which the poet Thomas *Watson killed a man. Early in 1592 he was deported from the Netherlands for attempting to issue forged gold coins. On 30 May 1593 he was killed by one Ingram Frizer in a Deptford tavern after a quarrel over the bill.

The chronology of his writings is disputed. *The Tragedy of *Dido Queen of Carthage*, published in 1594, may have been written while he was still at Cambridge, possibly in collaboration with Thomas *Nashe. Part I of *Tamburlaine* was published in 1590. The next plays may have been *The *Jew of Malta*, not published until 1633, and *Edward II*, published in 1594.

The highly topical *Massacre at Paris*, which survives only in a fragmentary and undated text, and *Dr Faustus*, published 1604, may both belong to the last year of Marlowe's life. At various times he translated *Ovid's Amores*, published without date as *All Ovid's Elegies*, together with some of Sir John *Davies's 'Epigrams'; wrote two books of a humorously erotic narrative poem, *Hero and Leander*, which was completed by George *Chapman and published in 1598; made a fine blank verse rendering of *Lucan's First Book*, Book 1 of *Lucan's *Pharsalia*; and wrote the song 'Come live with me and be my love', published in The *Passionate Pilgrim* (1599) and *Englands Helicon* (1600), with a reply by Walter *Ralegh. In spite of his violent life Marlowe was an admired and highly influential figure. *Shakespeare's early histories are strongly influenced by Marlowe, and he paid tribute to him in *As You Like It* as the 'dead shepherd'.

Marmion: *A Tale of Flodden Field* A poem in six cantos by Walter *Scott, published in 1808. Marmion is a favourite of Henry VIII, proud and treacherous, who tires of one lover (a perjured nun, who is walled up alive in a scene of Gothic horror) and pursues another, the wealthy Lady Clare. There are stirring descriptions of the battle, during which Marmion is mortally wounded.

MARMION, Shackerley (1603–39) Playwright. He wrote three plays, *Holland's Leaguer* (1632), *A Fine Companion* (1633), and *The Antiquary*, which show the influence of Jonsonian comedy and his own interest in Platonic love.

Marprelate Controversy See MARTIN MARPRELATE.

MÁRQUEZ, Gabriel García See GARCÍA MÁRQUEZ, GABRIEL.

Marriage-à-la-Mode A tragicomedy by John *Dryden produced 1672, published 1673. The main plot concerns a usurper's discovery that his daughter and his (lawful) predecessor's son have fallen in love. The comic plot involves two friends and their pursuit respectively of the wife of the one and the betrothed of the other. The counterpointing of these contrasting plots is particularly striking, especially as each ends anticlimactically. The play contains some of Dryden's finest songs, and embodies the principles of comic writing outlined in his preface to *An *Evening's Love*.

Marriage of Heaven and Hell, The A prose work by William *Blake, etched c.1790–93, introduced by a short poem. It consists of a sequence of paradoxical aphorisms in which Blake turns conventional morality on its head, claiming that man does not consist of the duality of Soul=Reason and Body=Evil, but that 'Man has no Body distinct from his Soul...Energy is the only life, and is from the Body...Energy is Eternal Delight.' He proceeds to claim that *Milton's Satan was truly his Messiah, and that Milton 'was a true Poet and of the Devils party without knowing it', and to produce a series of 'Proverbs of Hell' ('Sooner murder an infant in its cradle than nurse unacted desires' being one of the most notorious), which also celebrate the holiness of the natural world. He then moves to a sequence of visionary encounters with angels and prophets, in the course of which he dismisses the writings of Emanuel *Swedenborg (whom he had greatly admired), accuses him of not having conversed sufficiently with Devils but only with Angels, and ends with an evocation of an Angel turned Devil. The aphorisms resemble the paradoxes of George Bernard *Shaw, who was much influenced by his doctrine of contraries; they were also adopted by the counter-culture movement of the 1960s.

MARRYAT, Captain Frederick (1792–1848) London-born author, naval captain, and FRS. His successful sea stories include *The Naval Officer, or Scenes and Adventures in the Life of Frank Mildmay* (1829, partly autobiographical), *Peter Simple* (1834), *Jacob Faithful* (1834), and *Mr *Midshipman Easy* (1836); they were followed by *Japhet in Search of a Father* (1836), about a foundling. He is chiefly remembered for his children's books: *Masterman Ready* (1841), *The Settlers in Canada* (1844), and *The Children of the New Forest* (1847), a historical novel about the adventures of the four Beverley children, orphaned during the Civil War, who learn the arts of survival from a poor forester.

MARSDEN, Dora (1882–1960) Editor and suffragette, she became a prominent member of Emmeline and Christabel Pankhurst's Women's Social and Political Union, but resigned in 1910. The next year, she co-founded the *Freewoman*, becoming its editor. Contributors included H. G. *Wells and Rebecca *West. The *Freewoman* was relaunched as the *New Freewoman* in 1913, and then as The *Egoist* in 1914. While she was editor, *The Egoist* began its serialization of James *Joyce's *A *Portrait of the Artist as a Young Man*.

MARSH, Dame Ngaio [pron. Ny-o] (1899–1982) New Zealand-born writer of *detective fiction. When young she worked as an actress and her interest in theatre is reflected in many of her novels. Her hero, Chief Detective Inspector Roderick Alleyn, first appears in *A Man Lay Dead* (1934); other titles include *Vintage Murder* (1937), *Surfeit of Lampreys* (1941), *Died in the Wool* (1945), and *Final Curtain* (1947).

MARSHALL, Paule (1929–) African American writer, whose first novel, *Brown Girl, Brownstones* (1959), describes the lives of Barbadian immigrants in New York. Her subsequent works include *The Chosen Place, The Timeless People* (1969), set in the Caribbean. *Triangular Road* (2009) is a memoir.

MARS-JONES, Adam (1954–) Writer and critic. His fiction includes two short story collections, *Lantern Lecture* (1981) and *Monopolies of Loss* (1992), which responds to the Aids epidemic, and a novel about an ailing gay man, *The Waters of Thirst* (1993). *Pilcrow* (2008) and *Cedilla* (2011) are the first parts of a projected four-volume sequence.

MARSTON, John (1576–1634) Poet and dramatist, who wrote satirical verse and plays for the new professional children's companies, playing at private indoor theatres. His *The Metamorphosis of Pygmalion's Image: And Certain Satires* and *The Scourge of Villainy* (both 1598) were published under the pseudonym Kinsayder, under which name he figures in *The Return from Parnassus* (*see* PARNASSUS PLAYS). Some of these satires were directed against literary rivals, including Bishop Joseph *Hall, and were burned by order of the archbishop of Canterbury in 1599. Marston's quarrel with Ben *Jonson resulted in his portrayal as Crispinus in *Poetaster*, but the two became friends again. His dramatic works were printed as follows: *The History of *Antonio and Mellida* (1602), of which *Antonio's Revenge* is the second part; *The *Malcontent* (1604), with additions by John *Webster; *Eastward Ho*, a comedy, written with Jonson and George *Chapman, and *The Dutch Courtesan* (both 1605), *The *Parasitaster, or The Fawn*, a comedy, and *Sophonisba*, a tragedy (both 1606); *What You Will* (1607), a comedy; and *The Insatiate Countess* (1613), a tragedy (possibly completed by William Barksted).

MARSTON, John Westland (1819–90) Dramatic poet and critic, who contributed to the *Athenaeum*, wrote several critical works, and more than a dozen plays, including the successful *The Patrician's Daughter*, performed at Drury Lane in 1842. His son Philip Bourke Marston (1850–87) published poems and short stories (*Collected Poems*, 1892). Their London home was a meeting place for many eminent friends in the theatrical and literary world, including Edmund Kean, William *Macready, Charles *Dickens, A. C. *Swinburne, and D. G. *Rossetti.

MARTEL, Yann (1963–) Canadian novelist and short story writer. He made his debut with a collection of experimental stories, *The Facts behind the Helsinki Roccamatios* (1993), and a fantastic and partly autobiographical novel, *Self* (1996). *The Life of Pi* (2001, Booker Prize) is a lively, ambitious fable about an Indian boy shipwrecked along with a Bengal tiger and other exotic animals; *Beatrice and Virgil* (2010) deals with the Holocaust.

MARTIAL (Marcus Valerius Martialis) (AD 38/41–101/4) Roman epigrammatist of Spanish origin. His 1,500 epigrams are usually direct addresses to individuals and include celebrations of friendship and the country life, flattery of the emperor Domitian, and satirical and often obscene portraits of the inhabitants of contemporary Rome. Martial was much imitated by 17th-century poets, notably Ben *Jonson, Robert *Herrick, and Abraham *Cowley. Translations include Thomas May's *Selected Epigrams* (1629) and Peter *Porter's *After Martial* (1972).

MARTIANUS CAPELLA (Marcian) (*fl.* 410–39) A North African writer, celebrated in the Middle Ages. He was the author of *De Nuptiis Philologiae et Mercurii* ('The Marriage of Mercury and Philology') in nine books of prose and verse. The first two deal with the wooing (in a wide, metaphorical sense) of Philology by Mercury, and the last seven are an allegorical encyclopedia of the seven liberal arts (consisting of grammar, rhetoric, and logic—the trivium; and arithmetic, geometry, astronomy, and music—the quadrivium). Marcian is referred to by Geoffrey *Chaucer in 'The Merchant's Tale' (*see* CANTERBURY TALES, 10) and in *The *House of Fame*. Richard *Mulcaster is still using Martianus' method in his allegorizing of Philology in *The First Part of the Elementarie* (1582).

MARTIN, Sir Theodore (1816–1909) Poet, biographer, and translator, who contributed, under the pseudonym *'Bon Gaultier', to *Tait's Magazine* and *Fraser's Magazine*, and collaborated with W. E. *Aytoun in the writing of the 'Bon Gaultier ballads', (1845). His other works include reminiscences of Queen *Victoria (*Queen Victoria as I Knew Her*, 1902).

Martin Chuzzlewit, The Life and Adventures of A novel by Charles *Dickens, published 1843-4; the last of Dickens's *picaresque tales. Martin, the hero, is the grandson of old Martin Chuzzlewit, a wealthy gentleman embittered by the greed of his family. The old man has reared Mary Graham, a young orphan, to look after him. Young Martin is in love with Mary; but the grandfather, perceiving his selfishness, repudiates him and gets him dismissed from his position as pupil to his cousin Mr Pecksniff, architect and arch-hypocrite. Martin, accompanied by the indomitably cheerful Mark Tapley as his servant, sails for America to seek his fortune. He goes as an architect to the fraudulent Eden Land Corporation, where he loses his money and nearly dies of fever (this part gave great offence in America). He then returns to England, his experiences having reformed his selfish attitudes. His grandfather has meanwhile established himself and Mary in Pecksniff's household and pretended to place himself under his direction, thus satisfying himself of Pecksniff's treachery. Pecksniff tries to bully Mary into marrying him. Old Martin exposes the hypocrite, restores his grandson to favour, and gives him Mary's hand.

A sub-plot concerns Jonas Chuzzlewit, the son of old Martin's brother, a character of extraordinary villainy. He murders his father (in intention if not in fact); marries Mercy Pecksniff and treats her brutally; murders the director of a bogus insurance company, by whom he has been deceived and blackmailed; is detected; and finally poisons himself.

MARTINEAU, Harriet (1802-76) Writer and journalist, deaf throughout her adult life. A devout Unitarian in youth, her first published work was *Devotional Exercises* (1823); she later repudiated her Unitarian faith, and indeed all religious belief. Between 1832 and 1834 she published a series of immensely successful didactic stories, *Illustrations of Political Economy*, revealing both her passion for social reform and the influence of Jeremy *Bentham and John Stuart *Mill. Her tales for Henry *Brougham's Society for the Diffusion of Useful Knowledge followed, and she became a literary celebrity, consulted by politicians on economic and social matters. In 1834 she travelled in America, and supported the abolitionists at some personal risk. *Society in America* appeared in 1837, and her first novel, *Deerbrook* in 1839. Her later works include *The Hour and the Man*, a fictional portrayal of Toussaint Louverture (1840); a book of children's stories, *The Playfellow* (1841); her

radical *History of the Thirty Years' Peace* (1849); the anti-theological *Laws of Man's Social Nature* (1851); and her translation and condensation of Auguste *Comte, *The Philosophy of Comte*, (1853). *An Autobiographical Memoir*, containing many observations on public and literary figures of her day, appeared posthumously.

Martin Marprelate The name assumed by the authors of a number of anonymous pamphlets (seven survive) issued in 1588-9 from a secret press, containing attacks in a mocking, rollicking style on the bishops, and defending the *Presbyterian system of discipline. They were stimulated by the attempts of Archbishop Whitgift (1530-1604) to impose uniformity in liturgical practice and to promote royal supremacy and the authority of the Articles.

The Marprelate tracts are among the best prose satires of the Elizabethan age. Their titles (in abbreviated form) are: *The Epistle, The Epitome, Mineral and Metaphysical Schoolpoints, Hay Any Work for Cooper* (a familiar street cry, here alluding to Thomas Cooper, bishop of Westminster (1517-94)), *Martin Junior, Martin Senior*, and *The Protestation*. As well as ballads, rhymes, and plays, they provoked replies from such noted writers as John *Lyly and Thomas *Nashe; Richard and Gabriel *Harvey later became involved in the controversy. Richard *Hooker's work eventually settled the matter for the church. Among the various suspected authors, the Welshman John Penry (1559-93) died in prison and the clergyman John Udall (1560-92/3) was executed. Their collaborator Job Throckmorton (1545-1601) denied his complicity at Penry's trial, and escaped punishment.

Martinus Scriblerus, Memoirs of the Extraordinary Life, Works and Discoveries of A prose satire, initiated by the *Scriblerus Club and written mainly by Alexander *Pope and John *Arbuthnot; it was printed in the second volume of Pope's prose works (1741). The story of Martinus' birth, christening, education, and travels offered many opportunities for burlesque on various forms of contemporary knowledge and study. The 'double mistress' episode, featuring a lawsuit about the sexual identity of conjoined twins, was often suppressed. Pope identified many of the notes and other mock-scholarly additions to *The Dunciad* as the work of Martinus Scriblerus, and other authors, such as Henry *Fielding, Richard Owen Cambridge (1717-1802), and George *Crabbe, used variants of the pseudonym.

MARTYN, Edward (1859–1923) Irish playwright, one of the founders of the *Irish Literary Theatre, and president of Sinn Fein from 1905 to 1908. His best-known plays are the *Ibsen-influenced *The Heather Field* and *Maeve* (1899), a drama of Anglo-Irish antagonism. He is caricatured as 'dear Edward' in his cousin George *Moore's *Hail and Farewell*.

MARVELL, Andrew (1621–78) Poet and politician. In 1637 he contributed Greek and Latin verses to a Cambridge volume congratulating Charles I on the birth of a daughter. Around 1639 Marvell may have come under the influence of Roman Catholic proselytizers: according to one story he went to London with them and was fetched back by his father, the Revd Andrew Marvell (*c.*1584–1641). In January 1641 his father was drowned while crossing the Humber, and soon after Marvell left Cambridge for London. Between 1643 and 1647 he travelled for four years in the Netherlands, France, Italy, and Spain, perhaps deliberately avoiding the Civil War (he said later that 'the cause was too good to have been fought for'). *An Elegy upon the Death of My Lord Francis Villiers* was published in 1648, and his poems to Richard *Lovelace ('his Noble Friend') and on the death of Lord Henry Hastings (1630–49) in 1649. In the early summer of 1650 he wrote 'An Horatian Ode upon Cromwell's Return from Ireland', and 'Tom May's Death'. From 1650 to 1652 Marvell tutored young Mary Fairfax, daughter of the Parliamentarian general, at Nun Appleton in Yorkshire, writing 'Upon Appleton House' and lyrics such as 'The Garden' and the Mower poems in the summer of 1651. In 1653 he wrote *The Character of Holland*, was appointed tutor to Cromwell's ward William Dutton, and moved to John Oxenbridge's house at Eton, where he wrote 'Bermudas'. In 1654 with 'The First Anniversary' (published 1655) he began his career as unofficial laureate to Oliver Cromwell, and was appointed in 1657 Latin secretary to the Council of State (a post previously occupied by his friend and sponsor John *Milton, now blind). He mourned Cromwell in 'Upon the Death of His Late Highness the Lord Protector' (1658) and took part in the funeral procession. The following year (January) he was elected MP for Hull. At the *Restoration his influence secured Milton's release from prison.

His satires against the earl of Clarendon were written and published in 1667. Later that year he composed his finest satire, 'Last Instructions to a Painter', attacking financial and sexual corruption at court and in Parliament, and took part in the impeachment of Clarendon. *The Rehearsal*

Transpros'd, a prose work advocating toleration for Dissenters appeared in 1672 (second part, 1673). Gilbert *Burnet called these 'the wittiest books that have appeared in this age', and Charles II apparently read them 'over and over again'. According to the report of government spies, Marvell (under the codename 'Mr Thomas') was during 1674 a member of a fifth column promoting Dutch interests in England, and in touch with Dutch secret agents. The second edition of *Paradise Lost* contained a commendatory poem by Marvell, and in his prose works he continued to wage war against arbitrary royal power. *Mr Smirk, or The Divine in Mode* and *A Short Historical Essay Concerning General Councils* (both 1676), and *An Account of the Growth of Popery and Arbitrary Government in England* (1677), were all Marvell's, though prudently published anonymously. The *London Gazette* offered a reward, in March 1678, for information about the author or printer of *An Account*. That August, however, Marvell died in his house in Great Russell Street from medical treatment prescribed for a fever. His *Miscellaneous Poems* appeared in 1681, printed from papers found in his rooms by his housekeeper Mary Palmer, who gave herself out to be his widow and signed the preface 'Mary Marvell'. This volume did not contain the satires (the authorship of some of which is still disputed): these appeared in *Poems on Affairs of State* (1689–97).

Famed in his day as patriot, satirist, and foe to tyranny, Marvell was virtually unknown as a lyric poet. It was not until after the First World War, with Sir Herbert Grierson's *Metaphysical Lyrics* and T. S. *Eliot's 'Andrew Marvell', that the modern high estimation of his poetry began to prevail. 'The Nymph Complaining for the Death of her Faun' and 'To his Coy Mistress') are amongst his best-known lyric poems.

MARX, Karl (1818–83) German philosopher, historian, political economist, and revolutionary activist. Born in Trier of Jewish descent, he became editor of the *Rheinische Zeitung* at Cologne in 1842, but the paper was suppressed by the censor. He moved to Paris where he met Friedrich *Engels. Expelled from Paris, he went to Brussels, but at the outbreak of the revolutionary movement of 1848 returned to Cologne, where, with Engels, he again conducted a newspaper, the *Neue Rheinische Zeitung*. His radical views caused him to be expelled, and he finally settled in London. His best-known works include *The Communist Manifesto* (with Engels, 1848) and *Das Kapital*, of which only the first volume was published in his lifetime (1867): two further unfinished volumes were edited by Engels and appeared after his death (1885 and 1894). His materialist view of history, with its emphasis on economic issues such as ownership of the means of production and the central importance of the conflict between social classes, as well as his dialectical methodology, adapted from *Hegel, have been especially influential. In the turbulent inter-war years of the 20th century many European literary figures, including Bertolt *Brecht and *García Lorca, as well as British poets such as the young W. H. *Auden, Stephen *Spender, and Cecil *Day-Lewis, found their understanding of the modern world coloured by Marx's ideas. For many literary critics Marx's ideas have been crucial to their understanding of literary texts and literary history (see MARXIST LITERARY CRITICISM).

Marxist literary criticism A critical tradition that approaches literature from the perspective of the 'historical materialism' developed by *Marx and *Engels; that is, as a changing form of material production that participates in and illuminates the processes of history. Marx and Engels tended to disparage socialist writers of a propagandist type, and suggested that art is not tied directly to phases of economic development but has a certain autonomy. These principles are upheld in 'classical' Marxism, by Georgi Plekhanov (1856–1918), Leon Trotsky (1879–1940), and Georg Lukács (1885–1971), against tendencies in more mechanistic applications of Marxism to reduce art to its economic circumstances or to dismiss the bourgeois cultural heritage in favour of some purely 'proletarian' art. Lukács eventually developed a consistent Marxist critical position that stressed the value of 19th-century *realism. In the Soviet Union under Stalin, the prescriptive policy of *Socialist Realism obstructed independent critical thinking, except in the then little-known *Bakhtin circle. The first significant Marxist criticism in the English-speaking world emerged within the doctrinaire constraints of Communist Party orthodoxy: Granville Hicks (1901–82) in the USA and the more imaginative Christopher Caudwell (Christopher St John Sprigg, 1907–37) in England assessed literature in terms of its usefulness as a weapon in the class struggle. The German Marxists Walter *Benjamin and Bertolt *Brecht provided more persuasive views of literature as a 'production' of new meanings rather than a mere reflection of history. In disagreement with Lukács, Brecht distrusted the 'illusionism' of realistic or naturalistic art, and claimed political value for his own kind of *modernist experiments. His influence was strong upon Roland *Barthes and other critics who brought about alliances among Marxist, *formalist, and post-*structuralist literary theory, usually of a kind that regards realism as inherently conservative. In the English-speaking world since 1968, the foremost Marxist critics have been Raymond *Williams, Terry *Eagleton, and Fredric Jameson (1934–). Eagleton and Jameson have both employed Marxist methods to illuminate general problems of literary theory and the phenomenon of *postmodernism. Since the 1930s, elements of Marxist theory have variously been combined with those of other critical schools such as *psychoanalytic criticism, *feminist criticism, structuralism, and *deconstruction.

(((●))) SEE WEB LINKS

• Links to early Marxist texts

Mary Barton: *A Tale of Manchester Life* Elizabeth *Gaskell's first novel, published 1848. The largely working-class cast of characters in this novel was then an innovation. The background of the story is Manchester in the 'hungry forties', and the acute misery of the unemployed mill-hands. Mary Barton is the daughter of the embittered John Barton, a trade unionist. She has attracted Henry Carson, son of one of the employers, and, flattered by his attentions and the hope of a grand marriage, has rejected her faithful admirer Jem Wilson, a young engineering worker. A group of workers, enraged by the failure of local mill-owners to take their suffering seriously, decide to kill Henry Carson. The lot falls on John Barton to do the deed. Suspicion falls on Jem Wilson when Carson is shot dead. Mary realizes her true love for Jem, and discovers that her father was the murderer. Her desperate efforts to save Jem without betraying her father are successful. John Barton finally confesses to the father of Henry Carson, is forgiven, and dies. Mary and Jem are married, and emigrate to Canada.

The book's views on industrial relations were attacked by both Tories and Manchester mill-owners, but it achieved a wide readership, and has become one of the best known of the *'condition of England' novels from the 1840s.

'Mary Morison' one of Robert *Burns's earliest surviving song lyrics, published 1786, possibly addressed to Alison Begbie.

Mary Poppins P. L. *Travers's magical Edwardian nanny, who first appeared in 1934 (*Mary Poppins*), then in seven sequels to 1988.

Where Travers's character has god-like powers, in the hugely successful Disney film (1964) and the London musical (2004), she is less mystic and egocentric.

MARY QUEEN OF SCOTS (Mary Stewart) (1542–87) Daughter of James V of Scotland and Mary of Guise; she married Francis II of France (1558), Lord Darnley (1565), and Bothwell (1567). Imprisoned by *Elizabeth I, she was beheaded on a charge of conspiring against her life. She figures as *Duessa in The *Faerie Queene, and in ballads with her four attendants, the *Queen's Maries. Works in which she appears include Walter *Scott's The Abbot; a tragedy by *Schiller (in which she and Elizabeth meet, as they did not in real life); James *Hogg's The Queen's Wake (1813); three plays by A. C. *Swinburne, and a novel by Maurice Hewlett (1861–1923). Her story has been dramatized by Robert *Bolt in Vivat! Vivat Regina! (1970) and Liz *Lochhead in Mary Queen of Scots Got her Head Chopped Off (1987).

masculine rhyme *See* RHYME.

MASEFIELD, John Edward (1878–1967) Poet, whose idyllic early childhood in Herefordshire was vital to his later work. At the age of 13 he was in training for the merchant navy. In 1894 Masefield sailed for Chile, suffered acutely from sea-sickness, and was returned home. He sailed again across the Atlantic, but at the age of 17 jumped ship in New York and became a vagrant in America. Back in England he began his prolific writing career, which included poetry, plays, novels, essays, children's stories, and, at the end of his life, memoirs. *Salt-Water Ballads* (1902) included ' I must to the seas again' (the line was altered to the more familiar 'I must go down to the seas again' for the musical setting by John *Ireland). *Ballads and Poems*, containing the poem 'Cargoes', appeared in 1910, followed by *The Everlasting Mercy* (1911), an account of the conversion of the rough Saul Kane; *The Widow in the Bye Street* (1912); and *Reynard the Fox* (1919) a rattling verse tale set in the rural world of Masefield's childhood. His *Collected Poems* (1923) sold in great numbers, as did the novels *Sard Harker* (1924), *Odtaa* (1926), *The Bird of Dawning* (1933), and his story for children *The Midnight Folk* (1927). In 1930 Masefield became *poet laureate, and in 1935 received the Order of Merit. His later works include the sea novels *Dead Ned* (1938) and *Live and Kicking Ned* (1939), and the autobiographical *So Long to Learn* (1952) and *Grace before Ploughing*

(1966), which describes his country childhood up to his mother's death n 1884.

Mask of Anarchy, The A poem of political protest by P. B. *Shelley, written in response to the 'Peterloo Massacre' at St Peter's Fields in Manchester in August 1819, published 1832.

Composed at speed and in anger, the poem uses the popular *ballad form with immense power and sometimes surreal effect. The 'mask' is a pageant, or masquerade, of British political leaders—Castlereagh (1769–1822), Eldon (1751–1838), Sidmouth (1757–1844)—whom Shelley blames not only for the killing of eleven people and injuries to around 500 others at a public demonstration for parliamentary reform, but also for the general conditions of harshness and oppression in England: what he calls the 'triumph of Anarchy' (compare The *Triumph of Life). Anarchy rides on a horse: 'He was pale even to the lips, | Like Death in the Apocalypse.' His bloody progress is only prevented by Hope, 'a Maniac maid', who throws herself under the trampling hooves. The poem ends with a celebration of freedom, and Shelley's historic appeal for non-violent mass political protest in a great assembly of working people: 'Rise like lions after slumber | In unvanquishable number.'

masks *See* MASQUES.

MASON, A. E. W. (Alfred Edward Woodley) (1865–1948) Failed actor turned successful novelist, best remembered for *The Four Feathers* (1902), the story of Harry Feversham's heroism in redeeming himself from the accusation of cowardice. There are several film adaptations, notably the 1939 version. His many other popular works include the series featuring Inspector Hanaud, which began with *At the Villa Rose* (1910).

MASON, William (1725–97) Poet and clergyman; he edited *The Poems of Mr Gray, to which are Prefixed Memoirs of his Life and Writings* (1775), the biographical portion of which was an important model for James Boswell's *Life of *Johnson*. Mason's own work includes the tragedies *Elfrida* (1751) and *Caractacus* (1759), the latter clearly influenced by Gray's interest in *primitivism, and *The English Garden* (4 books, 1771–81) expressing in blank verse his enthusiasm for the *picturesque style of landscape gardening.

masques (masks) Dramatic entertainments involving dances and disguises, in which the spectacular and musical elements predominated over plot and character. They were acted indoors by amateurs, and were designed to include their spectators in the action, sometimes simply by a concluding dance. As they were usually performed at court, many have political overtones. They were perhaps of Italian origin, but assumed a distinctive character in England in the 16th and 17th centuries. Many of the leading poets and dramatists, Samuel *Daniel, Thomas *Campion, George *Chapman, and Thomas *Middleton, wrote masques, and they reached their highest degree of elaboration at the court of *James I. Ben *Jonson was pre-eminent as a writer of masques for James, and introduced the 'antimasque' as a comic and grotesque foil to the main spectacle. The architect Inigo *Jones designed the machinery or decoration for some of them. Jonson's *The Sad Shepherd*, John *Milton's *A Mask*, better known as *Comus*, and other such works often called masques are closer to *pastoral dramas.

Massacre at Paris, The A play by Christopher *Marlowe written c.1592. The play deals with the massacre of Protestants in Paris on St Bartholomew's Day, 24 August 1572 (an event witnessed by Philip *Sidney). Its most memorable character is the Machiavellian duke of Guise. The massacre is depicted in a series of short episodes, a notable one being that in which the rhetorician *Ramus is killed after a verbal onslaught by the Guise on his emendations of Aristotle. The Guise himself is eventually murdered on the orders of Henry III. Leaping over seventeen years, the play concludes with the murder of Henry III and the succession of the (then) Protestant Henry of Navarre.

MASSIE, Allan (1938–) Scottish novelist, critic, and editor. One of the best historical novelists of his generation, his first novel, *Change and Decay in All Around I See* (1978), was a comedy of manners. His Imperial Trilogy, *Augustus* (1989), *Tiberius* (1990), and *Caesar* (1993), was extended with *Antony* (2009) and *Caligula* (2004), and a second historical sequence, starting with *An Evening of the World* (2001), begins in the Dark Ages. *King David* (1995) has a biblical theme, while *The Ragged Lion* (1994) recreates the life of Walter *Scott. *A Question of Loyalties* (1989) looks back to the Vichy regime in 1940s France, and *The Sins of the Father* (1991) is experimental in form and is set against the legacy of the Holocaust. *Surviving* (2009) is set in contemporary Rome.

MASSINGER, Philip (1583–1640) Poet and playwright. He became the chief collaborator of

John *Fletcher after the withdrawal of Francis *Beaumont, and on Fletcher's death in 1625 he became the principal dramatist of the King's Men.

He is known to have written or shared in the writing of 55 plays. Of these 22 are lost. Of the extant plays fifteen are of his sole composition, sixteen were written in collaboration with Fletcher, and two in collaboration with others: *The *Virgin Martyr* (with Thomas *Dekker) and *The *Fatal Dowry* (with Nathan *Field). He shared with Fletcher the writing of such plays as *The *Custom of the Country* (1619), *Sir John van *Oldenbarnavelt* (1619), *The Double Marriage* (1620), *The *Beggar's Bush* (1622), and *A Very Woman* (?1625) and with Fletcher and others collaborated in *The Bloody Brother* (c.1616). He wrote only two social comedies, *A *New Way to Pay Old Debts* and *The *City Madam*. *A New Way* was a mainstay of the English stage in the late 18th and early 19th centuries and has had modern revivals. Both comedies are inspired by Massinger's patrician contempt for the ambitions and affectations of the rising mercantile classes in the city. *The Guardian* (1633) and the feminist play *The Picture* (1629) are much more romantic comedies.

Massinger wrote several excellent tragedies. The early *Duke of Milan*, a tragedy of jealousy, was followed by *The *Roman Actor*, his favourite play. It makes remarkable use of plays-within-the-play, and reveals in the person of Paris his own prolonged difficulties with political censorship, which forced his complete rewriting of *Believe as You List*. His other plays include *The *Maid of Honour*, *The *Bondman*, *The Renegado*, and *The Great Duke of Florence* (acted 1627; printed 1636).

MASSINGHAM, H. J. (Harold John) (1888–1952) Nature writer and ruralist, son of journalist and editor H. W. Massingham. His many books reflecting his deep appreciation of the countryside include *Wold without End* (1932) and *The English Countryman* (1942).

Mass Observation A network of lay correspondents *formed in 1937 by the poet Charles *Madge and film-maker Humphrey *Jennings, with the anthropologist Tom Harrisson (1911–76). Conceived as an 'anthropology of ourselves', the movement provided valuable data on wartime morale and later consumer attitudes. Revived in 1981, its archive is held at the University of Sussex.

MASSON, David (1822–1907) Biographer, critic, journalist, a disciple of Thomas *Carlyle who became the founder and editor of *Macmillan's Magazine* (1859). He also wrote biographies of William *Drummond of Hawthornden (1873) and Thomas *De Quincey (1881) and edited the works of John *Milton, Oliver *Goldsmith, and De Quincey. His *Edinburgh Sketches and Memories* (1892), *Memories of London in the Forties* (1908), and *Memories of Two Cities* (1911) are accounts of mid-century literary circles.

Master Humphrey's Clock A weekly founded by Charles *Dickens in 1840, originally intended as a miscellany which would contain a continuous narrative (*The *Old Curiosity Shop*) linked by the reminiscences of the narrator, Master Humphrey. This device was soon dropped, as was the periodical's title after the publication in weekly numbers of *Barnaby Rudge* (1841).

Master of Ballantrae, The: *A Winter's Tale* A novel by Robert Louis *Stevenson, published 1889. A powerful study of fraternal jealousy, this is the story of the lifelong feud between the master of Ballantrae, violent, unscrupulous, elegant, and courageous, and his brother Henry, at the outset a quiet, dull, honest young man. The master joins Prince Charles Edward in the 1745 rebellion, disappears after Culloden, and is believed dead. After many adventures the master returns, with a price on his head, to find that Henry has appropriated his place and his intended bride. He embarks on a course of persecution, first in Scotland then in America, which brings both brothers to a melodramatic grave in the Adirondack Mountains. The extravagant action and the hints of the supernatural are rendered more plausible by the dour character of the narrator, the loyal Ephraim Mackellar.

MATHESON, Richard (1926–) American writer. The fusion of *science fiction and *horror in *I Am Legend* (1954), and the tension in stories like 'Duel' (1971) influenced Stephen *King.

MATHEWS, Harry (1930–) The only American member of OuLiPo. His early fictions, such as *The Conversions* (1962) and *Tlooth* (1966), offer eccentric narratives and sophisticated word-play. His recent novels, *Cigarettes* (1987) and *The Journalist* (1994), although equally inventive and bewildering, explore more recognizable American contexts. Mathews has also written a number of shorter, more obviously

experimental texts, such as 'Their Words, for You' (1977) which consists wholly of scrambled proverbs. Mathews's poetry (collected in *A Mid-Season Sky*, 1992) again employs rigid conventions as a means of embodying the surrealism of everyday life.

matter A term derived from French *matière* used to refer to medieval romances. It has its origins in the work of Jean Bodel (late 12th–early 13th century), a writer of *fabliaux* and *chansons de geste*. In his *Chanson de Saisnes*, 'matter of Rome' denotes romances based on stories from Greek and Roman mythology; 'matter of France' refers to Frankish events, specifically romances concerned with the emperor *Charlemagne and his circle; and 'matter of Britain' denotes Arthurian subject matter. These three categories are often used to denote a cycle of stories. Typical of the matter of Rome are stories about *Alexander the Great, a popular hero in the Middle Ages. The matter of France, which often celebrates conflicts between the Franks and the Saracens, includes *chansons de geste* that fall into subgroups: that is, narratives pertaining to Charlemagne himself, other knights, and rebels, respectively. The *Chanson de Roland* is one of the best-known narratives from the first group. The matter of Britain contains the *Brut foundation myth and the Arthurian chronicle tradition pioneered by *Geoffrey of Monmouth. Scholars have recently added the term 'matter of England' to refer to romances concerned with English heroes or localized in England (such as *King Horn, *Havelok the Dane, *Bevis of Hampton, and *Athelstan).

MATTHEW, St *See* BIBLE; EVANGELISTS.

MATTHIESSEN, Peter (1927–) Travel writer, novelist, and naturalist. His novels include *At Play in the Fields of the Lord* (1965; filmed 1991), the highly experimental *Far Tortuga* (1975), and *Killing Mr Watson* (1990; the Watson trilogy reworked as *Shadow Country*, 2008). His travel writings, including *The Cloud Forest* (1961), *The Snow Leopard* (1978), and *Sand Rivers* (1981), combine a strong environmentalist ethic and scientific rigour with a sense of spiritual reverence and self-enquiry that derives from Matthiessen's interest in Zen Buddhism.

MATURIN, Charles (1780–1824) Gothic novelist and dramatist. He published *The Fatal Revenge* (1807); *The Wild Irish Boy* (1808); and *The Milesian Chief* (1811). In 1816 his tragedy *Bertram* was successfully produced at Drury Lane, on the recommendation of

Walter *Scott and Lord *Byron. His most memorable work is *Melmoth the Wanderer* (1820).

Maud A poem by Alfred *Tennyson, published 1855; it is a monodrama in sections of different metres, in which the morbid narrator describes the progress of his emotions: first describing his father's death and his family's ruin, both contrived by the old lord of the Hall; then expressing his growing love for Maud, the old lord's daughter, and the scorn of her brother, who wishes her to marry a vapid 'new-made' lord. He secures a meeting with Maud, but they are interrupted and her brother is killed in the subsequent fight. He escapes abroad, goes mad; and finally reawakens to apparent hope in fighting in the Crimean War. There was much contemporary debate as to whether it was pro- or anti-war. Tennyson insisted that it was, first and foremost, *dramatic*. It was always his favourite poem to read aloud.

MAUGHAM, W. Somerset (1874–1965) CH, writer and playwright, trained as a doctor in London; his first novel, *Liza of Lambeth* (1897), drew on his experiences of slum life during this period. He achieved fame in 1907 with *Lady Frederick*, and in 1908 had four plays running in London. Primarily homosexual, he married in 1917 (dissolved 1929), but had met Gerald Haxton (1892–1944) in 1914; in 1916 they set off for the South Seas together and further travels to China, Asia, and Mexico followed.

Maugham wrote over 30 plays, including *Our Betters* (1917); *Home and Beauty* (1919); *The Circle* (1921); *East of Suez* (1922); *The Constant Wife* (1926), in which a woman takes revenge on her unfaithful husband and departs for Italy with an old admirer; *The Sacred Flame* (1928); and the anti-war drama *For Services Rendered* (1932). His best-known novel, *Of Human Bondage* (1915), describing the lonely boyhood of Philip Carey, burdened with a club foot (Maugham struggled with a severe stammer), was followed by *The Moon and Sixpence* (1919), *The Painted Veil* (1925; filmed 1934, 1957, and 2006), *Cakes and Ale* (1930), a comedy about the good-natured wife of a grand old man of letters, Edward Driffield, whom many took to be based on the recently deceased Thomas *Hardy, and *The Razor's Edge* (1944). *A Writer's Notebook* (1949) consists of extracts from notes which Maugham had kept from the age of 18.

Maugham also wrote many successful short stories: 'Rain', set in Samoa (*The Trembling of a Leaf*, 1921), tells of the conflict between a life-affirming prostitute, Sadie Thompson, and a repressed missionary, while 'The Alien Corn'

(*Six Stories in the First Person Singular*, 1931) is about a pianist who commits suicide when he realizes he will never transcend the second rate. Maugham claimed to take the view, expressed in his autobiography, *The Summing Up* (1938), that he stood 'in the very first row of the second-raters', an opinion which has been largely shared by critics.

MAUPASSANT, Guy de (1850–93) French short story writer and novelist, a member of the so-called 'groupe de Médan', supposedly influenced by Émile *Zola and *naturalism. He contributed *Boule de suif* to *Les Soirées de Médan*, tales narrating incidents from the Franco-Prussian War, intended to promote the ideals of the group. His collections include *La Maison Tellier* (1881, *Miss Harriet* (1884), *Le Horla* (1887), and *L'Inutile Beauté* (1890, and they earned for him a reputation as the 'French Chekhov', with translations appearing as early as 1887. His six novels, including *Une vie* (1883: *A Life*), *Bel-Ami* (1885), and *Pierre et Jean* (1888), have also been much translated.

MAUPIN, Armistead (1944–) American writer, best known for a sequence of six comic novels depicting alternative lifestyles in San Francisco, from *Tales of the City* (1978), to *Sure of You* (1989). Beginning life as a daily newspaper serial, this joyous *roman-fleuve* celebrates gay subcultures, chronicles the Aids epidemic, and has been adapted as a musical (2011). After *Maybe the Moon* (1992) and *The Night Listener* Maupin returned to the *Tales* series with *Michael Tolliver Lives* (2007) and *Mary Ann in Autumn* (2010).

MAWSON, Sir Douglas (1882–1958) Scientist and Antarctic explorer, whose family migrated to Australia in 1884. He rejected Robert *Scott's offer of a place in his ill-fated polar expedition, but organized his own Australasian Antarctic Expedition of 1911–14, scientifically the most valuable of all the early expeditions. Sledging in crevasse-infested George V Land, two companions were killed; his lone return trek, told in *The Home of the Blizzard* (1915), was an epic survival story.

MAX MÜLLER, Friedrich (1823–1900) Philologist and mythographer, son of the Romantic German poet Wilhelm Müller. He was commissioned by the East India Company to bring out an edition of the Sanskrit *Rigveda* (1849–73), and was acknowledged as a leading authority on Indian culture. He settled in Oxford in 1848, and was professor of comparative philology at Oxford from 1868 until his death. He devoted much attention to comparative mythology and the comparative study of religions; his views on solar mythology interested George *Eliot and John *Ruskin, amongst others.

MAXWELL, Gavin (1914–69) Writer, traveller, and conservationist. He is best remembered for *Ring of Bright Water* (1960), a poignant evocation of life on the remote Scottish coast and of his relationship with two semi-tame otters; his other works include travel writings and the autobiographical *The House of Elrig* (1965).

MAXWELL, Glyn (1962–) Poet and dramatist. His earliest collections are collected as *The Boys at Twilight* (2000). Many of the poems in *The Breakage* (1998) dwell on the First World War. His novel *Blue Burneau* (1994) is a political fantasy set on an imaginary island. He has written several verse dramas, encouraged by Derek *Walcott: three of them were published as *Gnyss the Magnificent* (1995). *Moon Country* (1996), written with Simon *Armitage, describes a journey to Iceland in the footsteps of W. H. *Auden and Louis *MacNeice. Recent work includes *Time's Fool: A Tale in Verse* (2000), *The Nerve* (2002), and *Hide Now* (2008), and many plays; *After Troy* premiered in March 2011.

MAYHEW, Henry (1812–87) Playwright, journalist, and social reformer. The first of his many plays and farces was *The Wandering Minstrel* (1834). In 1841 he was a co-founder and briefly a joint editor of **Punch*. He wrote many novels and stories, as well as books on science, religion, education, and travel, but he is chiefly remembered for the philanthropic journalism to which he turned at the end of the 1840s. His remarkable series of 82 articles, couched as lengthy 'letters', in the **Morning Chronicle* were published as *London Labour and the London Poor* (1851). His painstaking investigations into the plight of the poor revealed the extent to which starvation, disease, and transportation were daily horrors. He performed similar work on the subject of prisons. His plain but harrowing descriptions, often using the words of those he spoke with, did much to stir the public conscience towards reform.

MAYNE, William (1928–2010) The most distinctive stylist in British children's literature of the 20th century; Mayne produced over 100 books from *Follow the Footprints* (1954), including many subtle studies of family relationships, and distinguished fantasies such as *Earthfasts* (1967). *A Grass Rope* (1957) won the Carnegie Medal and *Low Tide* (1993) the Guardian

Award. His literary reputation was damaged by his imprisonment for sexual assaults on children in 2004.

MAYNE-REID, 'Captain' Thomas See REID, 'CAPTAIN' THOMAS MAYNE.

Mayor of Casterbridge, The: *A Story of Character* A tragic novel by Thomas *Hardy, published 1886. Michael Henchard, a hay-trusser, gets drunk at a fair and sells his wife and child for five guineas to a sailor, Newson. When sober again he takes a solemn vow not to touch alcohol for twenty years; he becomes rich, respected, and eventually the mayor of Casterbridge. After eighteen years his wife returns, supposing Newson dead, and is reunited with her husband. She brings with her her daughter Elizabeth-Jane, and Henchard is led to believe that she is his child, whereas she is in fact Newson's. Through a combination of unhappy circumstances, and the impulsive obstinacy of Henchard, troubles accumulate. He quarrels with his capable young assistant in his corn business, Donald Farfrae. Mrs Henchard dies and Henchard learns the truth about the girl. Farfrae marries Lucetta, whom Henchard had hoped to win. Soon Henchard's business is ruined, the story of the sale of his wife is revealed, and he takes again to heavy drinking. Farfrae now has Henchard's business, his house, and Lucetta, while Henchard works as a labourer in his yard. Eventually Farfrae becomes mayor. His stepdaughter is his only comfort, then Newson returns and claims her and after Lucetta's death Farfrae marries her. Henchard becomes lonelier and more desolate, and dies wretchedly in a hut on Egdon Heath.

Measure for Measure A tragicomedy by *Shakespeare, probably written in 1604, but not printed until the first *folio (1623). Its chief source is George *Whetstone's play *Promos and Cassandra*, itself based on a story in Cinzio's *Hecatommithi*. It has often been categorized as a 'problem play' because of its concern with sexual and political morality and the complexity of its plot and themes.

The duke of Vienna, on the pretext of a journey to Poland, hands over the government to his virtuous-seeming deputy Angelo, who enforces strict laws against sexual licence which for the past fourteen years had been neglected. Angelo immediately sentences to death Claudio, a young gentleman who has made Julietta pregnant. Claudio's sister Isabella, who is a novice in a sisterhood of nuns, pleads with Angelo for her brother's life. Angelo responds to her pleas by offering to spare Claudio's life if she will sleep with him. Isabella refuses, and will not be persuaded even by the desperate entreaties of Claudio in prison. The duke, disguised as a friar, has made a visit of spiritual comfort to Claudio, and now devises a way of saving his life. Isabella is to agree to a midnight assignation with Angelo, but her place is to be taken by Mariana, who was betrothed to Angelo and still loves him. This scheme is successful, but Angelo still proceeds with the order for Claudio's execution, though unknown to Isabella Claudio is saved by the substitution of the head of Ragozine, a pirate, who has died that night in the same prison. The duke lays by his disguise, simulates a return to Vienna, and pretends to disbelieve the complaints of Isabella and suit of Mariana, in favour of Angelo's hypocritical denial. When Angelo is forced to confess, both Mariana and Isabella plead for his life; Mariana is married to Angelo, and the duke proposes marriage to the novice Isabella. She makes no reply.

Medal, The A poem by John *Dryden, published 1682. The earl of Shaftesbury was acquitted of high treason in 1681, and a medal was struck to commemorate the event. Dryden's response includes savage attacks on Shaftesbury himself, the City, and the Commons. It predicts the constitutional instability which was to beset the country in the ensuing 30 years.

MEE, Sir Arthur (1875–1943) Writer and editor, remembered for the *Children's Encyclopedia*, which he conceived in 1919 and edited until his death. He also founded the *Children's Newspaper*, and wrote numerous instructional books and series about important figures and places.

MEHTA, Gita *See* ANGLO-INDIAN LITERATURE.

MEHTA, Ved Prakash (1934–) Indian writer and journalist (now an American citizen). His works include studies of Indian life and autobiographical and biographical memoirs, including *Face to Face* (1957), *Daddyji* (1972), *Mamaji* (1979), *Vedi* (1982), *The Ledge between the Streams* (1984), *Sound-Shadows of the New World* (1986), and *The Stolen Light* (1989)—a series now collectively entitled *Continents of Exile*. *Delinquent Chacha* (1966), a comic novel, satirizes Indians indigenized to English life.

meiosis An understatement, sometimes ironical or humorous and intended to emphasize the size, importance, and so on of what is belittled. Except in *litotes, which is a form of meiosis, the use of meiosis is chiefly colloquial (e.g. 'He's doing all right out of it'; 'That must be worth a few bob').

Meistersinger A title taken in the 15th century by certain professional German poet musicians. They were often respected master craftsmen in ordinary trades such as weaving and shoemaking. Their craft, and they themselves, were governed by an elaborate set of guild rules, affectionately depicted in Richard *Wagner's opera *Die Meistersinger von Nürnberg* (1868). Their work represents a phase in the development of bourgeois literature away from the courtly *Minnesang* (*see* MINNESÄNGER).

'Melibeus, The Tale of' *See* CANTERBURY TALES, 18.

Melincourt, *or Sir Oran Haut-ton* A satire by Thomas Love *Peacock, published 1817. One of the most ambitious of Peacock's books, with a novelistic plot, it concerns the abduction and threatened rape of a rich young heiress, Anthelia Melincourt. The plot, which is indebted to Richardson's *Clarissa* and to Thomas *Holcroft's *Memoirs: Anna St Ives*, has strong feminist implications. Anthelia is rescued by a humorous variant on the Noble Savage, Sir Oran Haut-ton, an orang-utan whom the hero, Mr Sylvan Forester, has educated to everything except speech, and for whom he has bought a seat in Parliament. His virtues show up the corruptions of 'advanced' society. Forester, whose idealist views resemble P. B. *Shelley's literary brand of radicalism, debates with Mr Fax, a Malthusian economist, such causes as rotten boroughs, paper currency, slavery, and the recent conservatism of the *Lake Poets. Provoked by an 1816 article by Robert *Southey in the *Quarterly Review*, Peacock censures Southey himself (Mr Feathernest), S. T. *Coleridge (Mr Mystic), William *Wordsworth (Mr Paperstamp), and William *Gifford, the editor of the *Quarterly* (Mr Vamp), as a group of political traitors.

Melmoth the Wanderer A novel by Charles *Maturin, published 1820, is a powerful *Gothic novel. Melmoth, who has sold his soul for the promise of prolonged life, offers relief from suffering to each of the characters, whose terrible stories succeed one another, if they will take over his bargain with the devil. After his trial Oscar *Wilde adopted the name Sebastian Melmoth.

melodrama A kind of sensational drama that flourished in the 19th century, noted for its simplified division of characters between the virtuous and the vicious and for its strong emotional impact in scenes of virtue in distress. Douglas *Jerrold's *Black-Ey'd Susan* (1829) and Dion *Boucicault's *The Colleen Bawn* (1860) are notable examples. This stage tradition had some influence upon 19th-century novels, especially those of Charles *Dickens, and on early 20th-century cinema.

MELVILLE, Herman (1819–91) American novelist and poet; after his father's business failure and death in 1832 Melville left school but read widely, devouring *Shakespeare, the King James *Bible, and 17th-century meditative writers such as Sir Thomas *Browne, as well as the numerous historical, anthropological, and technical works which he used to supplement his experiences when he wrote. After sailing as a 'boy' on a packet to Liverpool in 1839, Melville shipped in 1841 on the whaler *Acushnet* for the South Seas, where he jumped ship, joined the US navy, and finally returned three years later to begin writing. The fictionalized travel narrative of *Typee, or A Peep at Polynesian Life* (1846) was Melville's most popular book during his lifetime. Like most of his works, *Typee* was published first in Britain, for prestige and to guard against piracy. *Omoo: A Narrative of Adventures in the South Seas* (1847) was a well-received sequel.

Having married in 1847, and with a mother, sisters, and eventually four children to support, Melville wrote the realistic sea stories *Redburn: His First Voyage* (1849) and *White-Jacket, or The World in a Man-of-War* (1850), which he considered potboilers. Inspired by Nathaniel *Hawthorne, Melville changed his next sea tale into *Moby-Dick, or The Whale* (1851), a prose epic combining Shakespearian tragedy with encyclopedic sea lore. After the critical disaster of *Pierre, or The Ambiguities* (1852), a *Gothic romance and satire on the literary profession, Melville wrote anonymous magazine stories, among them 'Bartleby the Scrivener', and *'Benito Cereno', which were collected in *The Piazza Tales* (1856), and the historical novel *Israel Potter: His Fifty Years of Exile* (1855) about a neglected hero of the American Revolution. To recover from a breakdown he undertook a long journey to Europe and the Holy Land (depicted in the narrative poem *Clarel*, 1876). *The *Confidence-Man: His Masquerade* (1857), a mordantly nihilistic satire, was Melville's last novel. After unsuccessful lecture tours, he worked as customs officer in New York harbour,

where he wrote *Battle-Pieces and Aspects of the War* (1865), trenchant poems of disillusion with Civil War era America. Melville died virtually forgotten, with *Billy Budd, Foretopman* only being published in 1924. After long neglect, Melville's oeuvre is now recognized for its experiments in different genres and its exploration of metaphysical issues.

memoir-novel An early form of the novel, purporting to be true, and often including diaries and journals, but in fact largely or wholly fictitious. The author appears, if at all, merely as 'editor' of another's memoirs. Daniel *Defoe, with *Robinson Crusoe* (1719) and *Moll Flanders* (1722), was the first English master. *See* NOVEL.

Memoirs of a Cavalier A fictional military memoir generally ascribed to Daniel *Defoe, published 1724. The narrator, 'Col. Andrew Newport', travels in 1630 to Vienna, and accompanies the army of Ferdinand II, Holy Roman emperor, to the siege and sacking of Magdeburg. Under Gustavus Adolphus he participates in many battles of the Thirty Years War. Returning to England, he joins Charles I's army, first against the Scots, then against the forces of Parliament.

Memoirs of a Woman of Pleasure Often known as *Fanny Hill*, a novel by John *Cleland, published 1748–9. It was, completed while Cleland was confined for debt in the Fleet Prison. The story of Fanny's misfortunes, her descent into prostitution, and her eventual recovery to a happy marriage is recounted in a lively, breathless style, as a vehicle for Cleland's absorbed examination of sexual desire, in both men and women, in its many varieties and in minute but carefully euphemistic physiological detail. After being ruled obscene, the book was not published openly in Britain until the 1970s.

MENANDER (342/1–c.290 BC) Athenian dramatic poet of the 'Attic New Comedy', noted for his deft dialogue and psychologically perceptive characterization. Nearly a hundred titles are recorded. Papyrus discoveries—Menander was much read in Egypt—have restored one whole play, *Dyscolus* ('Mr Grumpy'), and substantial portions of *Epitrepontes* ('The Arbitration'), *Perikeiromene* ('He Cut her Hair off!'), *Sikyonius* ('The Man from Sicyon'), *Aspis* ('The Shield'), *Samia* ('The Girl from Samos'), and *Phasma* ('The Ghost'). His plays, popular classics in later antiquity, were fashionable in Rome, where *Plautus and *Terence translated and adapted some to Roman taste. *The *Importance of Being Earnest* is a last, brilliant, echo, complete with a lost-and-found baby. Another New Comedy staple, the *servus callidus*—the servant cleverer than his master—is still found in Mozart's Figaro and P. G. *Wodehouse's Jeeves.

Men and Women A collection of 51 poems by Robert *Browning, published in two volumes, 1855. The poems date from the period after Browning's marriage in 1846, and express a new-found energy and confidence. The poems show Browning's mind at its most multitudinous and eclectic, ranging over history, art, philosophy, and religion; they include many of his most celebrated dramatic monologues, such as 'Fra Lippo Lippi', 'Bishop Blougram's Apology', 'Andrea del Sarto', and 'Cleon'. The collection also includes 'Love among the Ruins', and the challenging *'"Childe Roland to the Dark Tower Came"'.

Menaphon A popular prose romance with *interludes of verse by Robert *Greene, published 1589. Thomas *Nashe's preface to the first edition offered a satirical survey of contemporary literature.

The convention of impenetrable disguise is taken to ridiculous lengths as the princess Sephestia, disguised as Samela, is wooed simultaneously by her father and her teenage son, while herself carrying on a love affair with her (disguised) husband.

MENCKEN, H. L. (Henry Louis) (1880–1956) American journalist and critic, who, through the pages of the *Smart Set* and the *American Mercury*, exercised a great influence on American taste, attacking its Puritanism and hypocrisy. He strongly supported American writers like Theodore *Dreiser and Sherwood *Anderson, and in 1919 published *The American Language*, documenting its vigour from multiethnic sources.

Menelaus See ILIAD.

Menippean satire A form of humorous writing, lighter and less censorious than satire proper, and characterized by miscellaneous erudition in the comical treatment of philosophical and otherwise intellectual topics. The term derives from the 3rd-century Greek philosopher Menippus, whose works were known and imitated by later Roman authors but did not survive. Notable works in English to which the term has been applied include Robert Burton's *Anatomy of Melancholy* (1621) and Lewis Carroll's *Alice's Adventures in Wonderland* (1865).

Men's Wives Three stories by W. M. *Thackeray, which appeared in *Fraser's Magazine*, 1843. Cynical and satirical, they are concerned with different kinds of unhappy marriage, and the exploitation of one partner by the other.

Mephistopheles A word of unknown origin, which appears first in the German *Faustbuch* of 1587 as 'Mephostophiles'. Mephistophilis is the name of the devil to whom Dr Faustus bargains away his soul in Christopher *Marlowe's tragedy. A 'Mephostophilus' is mentioned in *Shakespeare's *Merry Wives*. In Goethe's version of the legend Mephistopheles fails to win Faust's soul in the end. *See also* FAUST.

MERCER, David (1928–80) Playwright, who achieved recognition with his trilogy of television plays *Where the Difference Begins* (1961), *A Climate of Fear* (1962), and *The Birth of a Private Man* (1963), published together as *The Generations* in 1964. The trilogy is primarily concerned with problems of left-wing political commitment. His many subsequent works for stage, screen, and television include *A Suitable Case for Treatment* (TV 1962; published in *Three TV Comedies*, 1966; filmed as *Morgan*, 1965); *After Haggerty*, staged and published in 1970, which has as protagonist a Marxist theatre critic; and *Shooting the Chandelier* (TV 1977; pub. 1978). He was one of the first English playwrights to engage fully with television.

Merchant-Ivory A partnership between the Indian producer **Ismail Merchant** (1936–2005) and American director **James Ivory** (1928–), usually working with the German-born novelist Ruth Prawer *Jhabvala, which has been responsible for a distinguished series of literary *adaptations. *The Europeans* (1979) launched a series based on Henry *James and E. M. *Forster, including *The Bostonians, A Room with a View, Howard's End*, and *The Golden Bowl*. Other sources have included Jean *Rhys, for *Quartet* (1981), and Kazuo *Ishiguro, for *The Remains of the Day* (1993).

Merchant of Venice, The A comedy by *Shakespeare written 1596-7. It was printed in 1600, and this text was reprinted in the first *folio (1623). Its chief source is the first story of the fourth day in *Il pecorone*, Giovanni Fiorentino's collection of *novelle. Other sources include Anthony *Munday's *Zelauto* and the *Gesta Romanorum*.

Bassanio, a noble but poor Venetian, asks his loving friend Antonio, a rich merchant, for 3,000 ducats to enable him to prosecute fittingly his suit of the rich heiress Portia at Belmont. Antonio, whose money is all employed in foreign ventures, undertakes to borrow the sum from Shylock, a Jewish usurer, whom he has rebuked for his extortions. Shylock agrees to lend the money against a bond by which, if the sum is not repaid at the appointed day, Antonio shall forfeit a pound of his flesh. By her father's will Portia is to marry the suitor who selects, from three caskets (one of gold, one of silver, one of lead), the one which contains her portrait. Bassanio makes the right choice—the leaden casket—and is wedded to Portia, and his friend Graziano to her maid Nerissa. News comes that Antonio's ships have been wrecked, that the debt has not been repaid when due, and that Shylock claims his pound of flesh. The matter is brought before the duke. Portia disguises herself as an advocate, Balthasar, and Nerissa as her clerk, and they come to the court to defend Antonio, unknown to their husbands. Failing in her appeal to Shylock for mercy, Portia admits the validity of his claim, but warns him that his life is forfeit if he spills one drop of blood, since his bond entitles him to nothing but flesh. Pursuing her advantage, she argues that Shylock's life is forfeit for having conspired against the life of a Venetian citizen. The duke grants Shylock his life, but gives half his wealth to Antonio, half to the state. Antonio surrenders his claim if Shylock will turn Christian and make over his property on his death to his daughter Jessica, who has run away and married the Christian Lorenzo and been disinherited; Shylock agrees. Portia and Nerissa ask as rewards from Bassanio and Graziano the rings that their wives have given them, which they have promised never to part with. Reluctantly they give them up, and are reproached accordingly on their return home. The play ends with news of the safe arrival of Antonio's ships.

'Merchant's Tale, The' *See* CANTERBURY TALES, 10.

Mercury (Greek **Hermes**) Son of *Jupiter and messenger of the gods to men, characterized by his snake-entwined staff (the *caduceus*) and his winged hat and sandals.

MEREDITH, George (1828–1909) Novelist, who began his long literary career with 'Chillianwallah', a poem published in 1849. In the same year he married Mary Ellen Nicholls, the widowed daughter of Thomas Love *Peacock, and in 1851 paid for the publication of his own *Poems*, a volume he later disowned. *The Shaving of Shagpat* (1855), a series of *oriental

fantasies, was praised by the critics but did not sell well. In the same year he sat as the model for Henry Wallis's painting *The Death of Chatterton*. In 1857 his wife left him for Wallis. His first major novel, *The *Ordeal of Richard Feverel* (1859) sold poorly; its sexual frankness caused much scandal, and *Mudie's cancelled its order of 300 copies, but it brought praise in *The *Times* and the *Athenaeum*, as well as the friendship of Thomas *Carlyle and the *Pre-Raphaelites.

Meredith was now contributing to many periodicals, including the *Fortnightly Review*, in which *Evan Harrington* began to appear in 1860. *Modern Love* and *Poems of the Roadside* appeared in 1862 followed by *Emilia in England* (1864 retitled *Sandra Belloni* in 1886), and *Rhoda Fleming* (1865). *Vittoria*, a sequel to *Sandra Belloni*, began to appear in 1866, but was enlarged before its publication in book form in 1867. Few of these works brought much profit, but Meredith's reputation was growing steadily with the discerning public. *The Adventures of *Harry Richmond* (1871) was followed by a political novel, *Beauchamp's Career* (1876), and the novel for which he was chiefly celebrated, *The *Egoist* (1879). The only novel to meet with general popularity, though exhibiting the growing difficulty of Meredith's style, was *Diana of the Crossways*, which ran to three editions in 1885 alone. His three final novels were *One of our Conquerors* (1891) and *Lord Ormont and his Aminta* (1894), both studies of unhappy marriage, and *The *Amazing Marriage* (1895), his last novel and considered by some his most impenetrable. A collection of short stories, including the celebrated 'The Case of General Ople and Lady Camper', appeared in 1898. Among later volumes of verse were *Poems and Lyrics of the Joy of Earth* (1883), *Ballads . . . of Tragic Life* (1887), *A Reading of Earth* (1888), *A Reading of Life* (1901) and *Last Poems* (1909).

By the time he died Meredith had become a greatly revered man of letters, sought out by many younger poets and novelists, such as Henry *James, Thomas *Hardy, and Robert Louis *Stevenson. His reputation stood very high well into the 20th century, with his perceptive portrayal of women, his narrative skill, and his incisive dialogue receiving most praise; but the deliberate intricacy of much of his prose defeats many modern readers.

MERES, Francis (1565/6–1647) Author of *Palladis Tamia: Wit's Treasury* (1598). In it Meres reviewed 125 English writers from the time of Geoffrey *Chaucer to his own day, contrasting each English one with a similar Latin, Greek, or Italian author. Particularly notable are his list of twelve of William *Shakespeare's plays, including *Love's Labour's Won*, and of his 'sugared sonnets among his private friends', and his accounts of Robert *Greene's, George *Peele's, and Christopher *Marlowe's deaths.

Merlin A magician with analogues in several Celtic literatures, who most famously guides the destinies of *Arthur and his predecessor *Uther. His story is first set out by *Geoffrey of Monmouth in his *Vita Merlini* (c.1150), which draws on the story of Ambrosius as told by *Nennius. Merlin is born of a devil and a virtuous maiden and is named after his maternal grandfather. Although precocious and wilful, he is not malevolent as his father intended. He grows infatuated with Nimiane (Nimue or Vivien: *see* LADY OF THE LAKE), who imprisons him in a forest of air in Broceliande where he dies. He is also credited with a series of prophecies, as in Geoffrey of Monmouth's *Prophetiae Merlini*. Most famously, he predicts to *Vortigern the triumph of the Britons over the Saxons. In Geoffrey of Monmouth's *Historia Regum Britanniae*, Merlin aids Uther in the deceitful bed-trick by which he marries Igraine (Ygerna) and fathers Arthur. The Arthurian stories connected with him form a very important part of the whole tradition in French in the Middle Ages, particularly as transmitted by the (fragmentary) stories of Merlin by Robert de *Boron, the prose Vulgate *Merlin* and the *Suite du Merlin*. He also features prominently in the early tales of *Malory's *Morte Darthur*, and later in Alfred *Tennyson's 'Merlin and Vivien', one of his *Idylls of the King*.

MERRIL, Judith (1923–97) American-Canadian author, editor of *science fiction, and political activist. Her novel *Shadow on the Heart* (1950) and her story 'That Only a Mother' (1948), are responses to nuclear anxieties following the Second World War. Her 'Year's Best' anthologies (1957–68), gathered from non-genre sources, opened up new avenues. She influenced science fiction's *New Wave, introducing new British writers in the anthology *England Swings SF* (1968).

MERRIMAN, Brian (c.1749–1805) Irish-language poet, author of *Cúirt an Mheán Oíche* ('The Midnight Court'), a long satirical poem admired by W. B. *Yeats and translated by, among others, Ciaran *Carson, Seamus *Heaney

(incomplete, *The Midnight Verdict*, 1993), Thomas *Kinsella, and Frank *O'Connor.

MERRITT, A (Abraham) (1884–1943) American writer and journalist, born in New Jersey, whose novels (initially serialized) include *The Moon Pool* (1919) and *The Ship of Ishtar* (1926). Their supernatural and lost-race motifs, and Merritt's ornate style, made them influential works of pulp-magazine *fantasy, frequently reprinted.

MERRY, Robert (1755–98) English poet and dramatist; he became the centre of a poetic coterie (*see* DELLA CRUSCANS) which included Hannah *Cowley and Mary *Robinson. A supporter of the French Revolution, he published 'The Laurel of Liberty' (1790), one of the earliest works of English *Jacobinism and a poetic response to Edmund Burke's *Reflections on the Revolution in France* (1790). In the mid-1790s, he emigrated to the United States.

Merry Devil of Edmonton, The A romantic comedy of unknown authorship, acted by the King's Men before 1604. Based on real events and popular in its time, it was published anonymously six times between 1608 and 1656.

Merry Wives of Windsor, The A comedy by *Shakespeare; the tradition that it was written at the request of *Elizabeth I for a play showing *Falstaff in love is documented no earlier than 1702 (by John Dennis).

Falstaff, in need of cash, decides to make love to the wives of Ford and Page, two gentlemen living at Windsor, because they control their husbands' purses. Nim and Pistol, the discarded followers of Falstaff, warn the husbands. Falstaff sends identical love letters to Mistress Ford and Mistress Page, who contrive the knight's downfall. At a first assignation at Ford's house, they hide Falstaff in a basket when the husband arrives, cover him with foul linen, and have him tipped into a muddy ditch. At a second assignation, they disguise him as the 'fat woman of Brentford', in which character he is soundly beaten by Ford. The jealous husband having also been twice fooled, the plot is now revealed to him, and a final assignation is given to Falstaff in Windsor Forest at Herne's Oak, where he is plagued and pinched by mock fairies and finally seized and exposed by Ford and Page.

metafiction A kind of fiction that openly draws attention to its own fictional status.

Laurence *Sterne's *Tristram Shandy* (1759-67) is the classic English example, while a notable later exercise in this form is John *Fowles's novel *The French Lieutenant's Woman* (1969).

Metamorphoses See APULEIUS; OVID.

metaphor Description of one thing (or person, idea, feeling, action, etc.) in terms properly belonging to another, with the suggestion (rather than explicit likening, as in *simile) that they share some common quality, as in reference to a person as 'an angel' or to the act of 'devouring' a book. One of the most powerful of figurative expressions, it is also commonplace and in the case of so-called 'dead' metaphors (e.g. the 'branch' of a bank) may go almost unnoticed. Analysis of metaphors distinguishes a literal element (the 'tenor') from a figurative element (the 'vehicle'): in the hackneyed metaphor 'the ship of state', the state is the tenor, the ship the vehicle.

metaphysical poets Poets generally grouped under this label include John *Donne (who is regarded as founder of the 'school'), George *Herbert, Richard *Crashaw, Henry *Vaughan, Andrew *Marvell, and Thomas *Traherne, together with lesser figures like Edward Benlowes, Lord *Herbert of Cherbury, Henry *King, Abraham *Cowley, and John *Cleveland. The label was first used (disparagingly) by Samuel *Johnson in his 'Life of Cowley' (written in 1777), where he identifies them as a 'race of writers' who display their learning, use farfetched comparisons, and lack feeling, but earlier John *Dryden had complained that Donne 'affects the metaphysics', perplexing the minds of the fair sex with 'nice speculations of philosophy'. Earlier still William *Drummond censured poetic innovators who employed 'metaphysical ideas and scholastical quiddities'. The label is misleading, since none of these poets is seriously interested in metaphysics (except Herbert of Cherbury, and even he excludes the interest from his poetry). Further, they have in reality little in common: the features their work is generally taken to display are sustained dialectic, paradox, novelty, incongruity, 'muscular' rhythms, giving the effect of a 'speaking voice', and the use of elaborately extended metaphors, or 'conceits'. With the new taste for clarity and the impatience with figurative language that prevailed after the *Restoration, their reputation dwindled. Their much later revival was dramatic: indeed, the revaluation of metaphysical poetry, and the related downgrading of the *Romantics and John *Milton, was the

major feature of the rewriting of English literary history in the first half of the 20th century. Key documents in the revival were H. J. C. Grierson, *Metaphysical Lyrics and Poems of the Seventeenth Century* (1921), and T. S. *Eliot's essay 'Metaphysical Poets', which first appeared as a review of Grierson's collection (*TLS*, 20 Oct. 1921). According to Eliot these poets had the advantage of writing at a time when thought and feeling were closely fused, before the *'dissociation of sensibility' set in about the time of John Milton. Their virtues of difficulty and tough newness were felt to relate them closely to the modernists—Ezra *Pound, W. B. *Yeats, and Eliot himself.

Metaphysical Society Founded in 1869 by Sir James Knowles. It lasted until 1880 and brought together for discussion meetings most of the leaders of English thought of the period, of all shades of opinion, including T. H. *Huxley, John Tyndall, Henry Manning (1808-92), William *Gladstone, and Alfred *Tennyson.

Methodism From its origins in the 1730s, this religious movement in its Wesleyan form grew to nine million members worldwide by 1900. In the 18th century it had two main branches: the Calvinistic Methodism of the followers in Wales of Howell Harris and in England of George *Whitefield and the countess of Huntingdon, and the Arminian Methodism of the followers of the *Wesleys. Wesleyan Methodism was divided into local societies, preaching houses, and circuits, serviced by itinerant lay preachers, organized centrally by an annual conference, and directed by John Wesley. In its origins Methodism was a movement in the Church of England, but by the end of the 18th century both Calvinist and Arminian Methodists had separated from it, the former mostly to join *Congregationalists and *Baptists, the latter to set up the Methodist Church, which itself later split into separate bodies such as the Primitive Methodists. In the early 19th century the Welsh Calvinistic Methodists also formed a separate church. The various denominations had their own magazines and publishing outlets. *See* JACKSON, THOMAS.

metonymy A figure of speech which substitutes a quality or attribute of something for the thing itself, as *the fair* to mean 'the fair sex', *the deep* to mean 'the deep sea', *the bench* for the judiciary, or *Shakespeare* to mean the works of Shakespeare. In such examples, metonymy works by a kind of conventional abbreviation. A closely related figure is that of synecdoche, in which a part is substituted for the whole (*per head*, to mean 'per person'), or a whole is substituted for a part (*Pakistan*, to mean the Pakistani cricket team).

metre The more or less regular pattern formed by the sequence of syllables that make up lines of verse. Poems in which the sound patterns are not perceptibly formed from similar groupings of syllables are regarded as non-metrical, and thus placed in the category of *free verse. The largest body of traditional English verse, however, observes some form of metrical regularity. The particular forms of such regularity vary from one language to another: in ancient Greek and Latin, lines of verse were made from fixed numbers of 'feet', a foot being a combination of syllables regarded as either long or short; while in French and in Japanese what is measured is simply the number of syllables that make up the line, without distinctions of length or stress. These metrical systems are known as 'quantitative' and 'syllabic' respectively. Verse written in English almost always employs a different principle, one that relies on a distinction perceived between stressed (•) and unstressed (○) syllables. English verse lines are measured either principally or wholly by the number of stresses (i.e. stressed syllables) they are expected to contain. They may also observe further regularities in the total number of syllables, stressed or unstressed, that each line may include. The two major tendencies or traditions of English verse metre may be differentiated according to whether this inclusive syllable-count applies.

The older of the two dominant English metrical systems counts only the number of stresses in a line, so allowing variation in the number of unstressed syllables. This 'accentual metre' was the standard metrical principle of Old English verse, and was still vigorous in 14th-century literature, for example in the works of *Langland and in *Sir *Gawain and the Green Knight*. Following the example of *Chaucer, poets in English since that time have usually counted their syllables and thus departed to some degree from the pure accentual principle. Accentual verse has continued to flourish, however, in a wide range of popular songs, *hymns, *ballads, and *nursery rhymes, and in revivalist experiments such as that of Gerard Manley *Hopkins.

The second English metrical system is known as the 'accentual-syllabic', because it counts both the number of stresses and the total number of syllables in a line, thus restricting the use of unstressed syllables. So, in the standard line of post-Chaucerian English verse, the iambic pentameter, we expect to find ten syllables, of which five are stressed; in the perfectly regular version of this line, the unstressed and stressed syllables will alternate so as to conclude with a stress (○ • ○ • ○ • ○ • ○ •):

If Winter comes, can Spring be far behind?

Such a pattern is an expectation, not a rule, and accentual-syllabic verse of any sophistication requires variety in the placing both of the stressed syllables and of the pause (*caesura) within the line. Given the restriction that accentual-syllabic metres place upon the use of unstressed syllables, they fall into two basic kinds, known as duple and triple. By far the more commonly used are the duple metres, in which stressed syllables alternate with single unstressed syllables, as in the iambic metre illustrated above. In triple metres, pairs of unstressed syllables alternate with the stresses, as in *Hardy's dactylic tetrameter (• ○ ○ • ○ ○ • ○ ○ • ○ ○):

Woman much missed, how you call to me, call to me

The predominance of the duple metres in English gives the use of triple metres the appearance of being a special or even comical device, as in the anapaestic metre of the limerick (○ • ○ ○ • ○ ○ •):

There was an Old Man in a tree

Of the two duple metres, the iambic, in which unstressed syllables are heard to precede the stresses, is the standard. The less commonly used trochaic metre gives the impression that the stresses precede the unstressed syllables (• ○ • ○ • ○ • ○):

Ye whose hearts are fresh and simple

Trochaic metre is unusual in that its regular form, illustrated in the tetrameter by *Longfellow above, is quite rare by comparison with an irregular (truncated, or 'catalectic') version in which the final unstressed syllable is not used, allowing the line to end with a stress (• ○ • ○ • ○ •):

Tyger, tyger, burning bright.

The simplest description of the metre in a given line of verse is given by the number of stresses we expect it to include. In English, the two standard lines are the four-stress (tetrameter) and the five-stress (pentameter); in accentual-syllabic terms these standard lines may be described as octosyllabic and decasyllabic, if we take the use of duple metre for granted. The four-stress line is the older and the more persistent in all popular forms of verse and song, being easily compatible with the regularity of musical beats. It is also the natural line for accentual metres. The five-stress line has the effect of loosening or suppressing the assertive beat, and approximating itself to the rhythms of speech. Less frequently found as the regular basis of verse are the three-stress (trimeter) and two stress (dimeter) lines on the one hand, or the six-stress (*hexameter) and seven-stress (heptameter) lines on the other. Two-, three-, and six-stress lines find their usual place in verse forms that mix longer and shorter lines: the 'Burns stanza' employs dimeters for its fourth and sixth lines, the limerick for its third and fourth, while the Spenserian stanza has a hexameter as its final line.

The theory of metre, known as prosody or metrics, has been bedevilled by the survival of terminology and concepts derived from ancient Greek practice, despite the radical difference between Greek quantitative principles and English stress patterns. The ways in which stressed and unstressed syllables can be arranged in English verse have come to be named after the various kinds of Greek 'foot' they seem to resemble, when one mistranslates 'long syllable' as 'stressed syllable'. Many modern metricians regard the concept of the foot as a positive hindrance to the understanding of English metre and especially of accentual verse, but the names have stuck, and the analysis (scansion) of English lines as sequences of 'feet' is still attempted. Four principal kinds of metrical pattern in English are accordingly named after the *iamb* (○●), the *trochee* (● ○), the *anapaest* (○ ○ ●), and the *dactyl* (● ○ ○). Two other feet are sometimes invoked in scansion of English verse: the *spondee* (● ●) and the *pyrrhic* (○ ○); among several others that are of relevance to ancient Greek verse but only very rarely to English are the *amphibrach* (○ ● ○), the *amphimacer* (● ○ ●), and the *choriamb* (● ○ ○ ●).

Understanding the metrical effects of English verse requires some appreciation of the many variations that poets can play upon a regular metrical pattern. In the case of the iambic pentameter, especially, the scope for such variation is so wide that completely regular lines like P. B. *Shelley's 'If Winter comes, can Spring be far behind?' will be outnumbered by irregular versions. The principal variant upon the standard pentameter involves what is (in traditional foot-based scansion) known as 'initial trochaic inversion' because the line starts with a stress

but 'compensates' for this with an unstressed syllable (● ○ ○ ● ○ ○ ● ○ ●):

Far on the ringing plains of windy Troy

Similar inversions may be found in later positions in a line. Other permissible variations include the use of an unstressed syllable where a stress is expected, thus speeding up the line (e.g. ○ ● ○ ● ○ ● ○ ○ ○ ●):

A horse! a horse! My kingdom for a horse!

or the addition of an eleventh, unstressed syllable:

To be or not to be, that is the question

Metropolis (1927) Film by Fritz Lang (1890–1976). Its images of a *dystopian city and its humanoid robot echo throughout *science fiction.

MEW, Charlotte Mary (1869–1928) Poet and short story writer. Her short story 'Passed' appeared in the *Yellow Book* in 1894, but she became well known with her first volume of poetry, *The Farmer's Bride* (1915). Her second, *The Rambling Sailor*, appeared posthumously in 1929. Mew's themes of solitariness, guilt, unworthiness, and Catholicism have a peculiar sense of a personality under pressure; her meditations on sexual identity (including homosexual) are fraught. In life, her love for May *Sinclair was only one of a number of unsuccessful romances. She killed herself in 1928.

MEYNELL, Alice (1847–1922) née Thompson, poet and essayist whose first volume of poetry was *Preludes*, 1875; later volumes of verse included *Poems* (1893), *Later Poems* (1902), and *Last Poems* (1923); many of her most widely regarded poems deal with the theme of religious mystery. She is now also admired for her essays, introductions, and anthologies, which were freshly independent in approach and judgement. Her essays were collected under various titles, which include *The Rhythm of Life* (1893), *The Colour of Life* (1896), and *The Spirit of Place* (1899).

'Michael' A pastoral poem by William *Wordsworth, written and published 1800. A narrative in blank verse, it describes, with moving simplicity, the lonely life in Grasmere of the old shepherd Michael, his wife, and his beloved son Luke and their misfortunes.

Michael, St Archangel and victor in the war in heaven over the dragon *Satan and his host (Revelation 12).

MICHENER, James A. (Albert) (1907–97) American novelist, whose historical novels

(*Hawaii*, 1959; *The Source*, 1965; etc.) were the fruit of painstaking research. *The World is my Home* (1992) is an autobiographical memoir.

Midas A prose play by John *Lyly, published 1592, on the legend of Midas, king of Phrygia.

Middle Ages A conventional but contestable term designating a notional period from the Roman decadence (5th century AD) and the end of classical culture proper to its widespread revival during the 'Renaissance' (*c.*1500), although several European countries experienced 'renaissances' within this period, particularly given the growth of vernacular literatures in the 12th-14th centuries. The 'Middle Ages' have been associated with the development of the universities and the rise of *scholasticism in the 12th and 13th centuries. The earliest use yet discovered of 'Middle Age' in English is in John *Foxe's *Actes and Monuments* (1570); there are corresponding Latin terms from the 16th century, such as *medium aevum, media aetas*.

(⊕) SEE WEB LINKS
• The Labyrinth: resources for Medieval Studies

Middlemarch: *A Study of Provincial Life* A novel by George *Eliot, published 1871-2. The setting is the provincial town of Middlemarch, in the English Midlands, during the years of the agitation immediately preceding the first Parliamentary Reform Bill in 1832. The novel has a multiple plot, with several interlocking sets of characters. Dorothea Brooke, an ardent and idealistic young woman, under the care of her eccentric uncle, marries the elderly pedant Mr Casaubon, despite the doubts of her family and acquaintance. The marriage proves unhappy. Dorothea realizes during a disastrous honeymoon in Rome that Casaubon's scholarly plans to write a great work, a 'Key to all Mythologies', are doomed, as are her own aspirations to share in her husband's intellectual life, and her respect for him gradually turns to pity. She is sustained by the friendship of Casaubon's young cousin Will Ladislaw, a lively, light-hearted young man, detested by Casaubon, who begins to suspect that Dorothea's feelings for him are questionable. Shortly before he dies, with characteristic meanness, he adds a codicil to his will by which Dorothea loses her fortune if she marries Ladislaw.

Another storyline follows Fred and Rosamond Vincy, children of the mayor of Middlemarch; the extrovert Fred is in love with Mary Garth, but Mary will not accept Fred unless he rejects his father's ambition that he should enter the church, and proves himself responsible and self-sufficient. Rosamond, the town's beauty, sets herself to win the hand of Tertius Lydgate, the ambitious and high-minded young doctor. She succeeds, but the marriage is wrecked by her self-centred materialism. Lydgate, finding himself in debt, reluctantly borrows money from Mr Bulstrode, a religious hypocrite. Lydgate's career is ruined when he is implicated in the death of Raffles, an unwelcome visitor from Bulstrode's shady past. Only Dorothea, now widowed, continues to believe in him, but she is deeply shocked to find Ladislaw and Rosamond together in compromising circumstances. Rosamond reveals that Ladislaw has not betrayed his love for Dorothea, and Dorothea renounces her inheritance to marry him. Fred Vincy becomes a steady young man, and marries Mary Garth. Lydgate is condemned to a lucrative but unfulfilling practice as a fashionable doctor.

Throughout the narrative, George Eliot analyses and comments upon the social, intellectual, and political upheavals of the period, contrasting the staunch Tory attitudes of Dorothea's neighbours with the growing demand for Reform, espoused by Ladislaw, who becomes an 'ardent public man', and a member of Parliament, with Dorothea's support. The importance of marital loyalty is also a consistent theme.

George Eliot's reputation reached its height with *Middlemarch*.

MIDDLETON, Erasmus (bap. 1739, d. 1805) Church of England evangelical minister and biographer, expelled from St Edmund Hall, Oxford, in 1768 for *Methodist practices. His main publication is *Biographia Evangelica, or An Historical Account of the Lives and Deaths of the Most Eminent and Evangelical Authors or Preachers*, 4 vols (1779-86).

MIDDLETON, Stanley (1919-2009) Novelist, author of more than forty novels, mostly set in Nottingham, including *Terms of Reference* (1966), *Two Brothers* (1978), *Entry into Jerusalem* (1983), *Valley of Decision* (1985), *Against the Dark* (1998), *Love in the Provinces* (2002), and *Her Three Wise Men* (2008). *Holiday*, (1974, Booker Prize) is the story of a middle-aged man attempting to escape the pains of the present by returning to the seaside resort where he was happy as a child. Middleton remained committed to the social realism that prevailed when he began his career with *A Short Answer* (1958), and all his novels chronicle the family lives and domestic difficulties of his Mildlands characters.

MIDDLETON, Thomas (1580–1627) Poet and playwright. By 1603 he was writing for Philip *Henslowe, working with John *Webster, Thomas *Dekker, William *Rowley, Anthony *Munday, and others; much of his work of this period is lost. He collaborated with Dekker in the first part of *The *Honest Whore* (1604) and wrote many successful comedies of city life, including *The Family of Love* (with Dekker?, written 1602; pub. 1608), *The *Roaring Girl* (with Dekker, written 1604–8?; pub. 1611), *Michaelmas Term* (written 1604–6; pub. 1607), *A Trick to Catch the Old One* (written 1604–7; pub. 1608), *A *Mad World, my Masters* (written 1604–7; published 1608), *A *Chaste Maid in Cheapside* (written 1613; pub. 1630), and *The Mayor of Queenborough* (written 1615–20; pub. 1661). *A *Fair Quarrel*, a tragicomedy written with Rowley (*c.*1615–16; pub. 1617), discusses the ethics of duelling; *The Spanish Gipsy*, also with Rowley (and possibly John *Ford, written 1623; pub. 1625) is a romantic comedy based on two plots from *Cervantes. Other plays include *The *Witch* (written 1609–16; pub. 1778) and *Anything for a Quiet Life* (with Webster?, written? 1621); he probably revised Shakespeare's *Measure for Measure*, adapted *Macbeth, collaborated on *Timon of Athens*, and was responsible for *A *Yorkshire Tragedy* (*c.*1605).

A writer of great versatility, Middleton wrote many pageants and masques for city occasions, and was appointed city chronologer in 1620. His political satire *A *Game at Chess* (written 1624; pub. 1625) created a furore: it was described by T. S. *Eliot as 'a perfect piece of literary political art'. Middleton is now best known for his two great tragedies, *The *Changeling* (with Rowley, written 1622; pub. 1653) and *Women Beware Women* (written 1620–27; pub. 1657). Most scholars now also consider that *The *Revenger's Tragedy* (1607) is by Middleton.

Midshipman Easy, Mr A popular novel by Frederick *Marryat, published 1836. Jack Easy is brought up to believe that all men are equal, a notion which gives Jack many problems as a midshipman. But he is heir to a fortune and this, together with his cheerful honesty and the help of his Ashanti friend Mesty, help him through his adventures.

Midsummer Night's Dream, A A comedy by *Shakespeare, written probably *c.*1594–5; printed in quarto in 1600 and 1619; reprinted with changes. There is no single source, but Shakespeare drew, among other authors, on *Chaucer, Arthur *Golding's translation of *Ovid, and *Apuleius' *Golden Ass*.

Hermia refuses her father's command to marry Demetrius, because she loves Lysander, while Demetrius has formerly professed love for her friend Helena, and Helena loves Demetrius. Under the law of Athens, Theseus, the duke, gives Hermia four days in which to obey her father; else she must suffer death or enter a nunnery. Hermia and Lysander agree to leave Athens secretly in order to be married where the Athenian law cannot pursue them, and to meet in a wood a mile outside the city. Hermia tells Helena of the project, and the latter tells Demetrius. Demetrius pursues Hermia to the wood, and Helena Demetrius. This wood is the favourite haunt of the fairies.

Oberon and Titania, king and queen of the fairies, have quarrelled, because Titania refuses to give up to him a changeling Indian boy for a page. Oberon tells Robin Goodfellow (Puck), a mischievous sprite, to fetch him a certain magic flower, of which he will press the juice on Titania's eyes while she sleeps, so that she will fall in love with what she first sees when she wakes. Overhearing Demetrius in the wood reproaching Helena for following him, and wishing to reconcile them, Oberon orders Robin to place some of the love-juice on Demetrius' eyes, but so that Helena shall be near him when he does it. Robin, mistaking Lysander for Demetrius, applies the charm to him, and as Helena is the first person Lysander sees he at once woos her, enraging her because she thinks she is being mocked. Oberon, discovering Robin's mistake, now places some of the juice on Demetrius' eyes; he on waking also first sees Helena, so that both Lysander and Demetrius are now wooing her. The women quarrel, and the men go off to fight for Helena.

Meanwhile Oberon has placed the love-juice on Titania's eyelids. She wakes to find Bottom the weaver close by, wearing an ass's head (Bottom and a company of Athenian tradesmen are in the wood to rehearse a play for the duke's wedding, and Robin has put an ass's head on Bottom). Titania at once falls in love with him, and toys with his 'amiable cheeks' and 'fair large ears'. Oberon, finding them together, reproaches Titania for bestowing her love on an ass, and again demands the changeling boy, whom she in her confusion surrenders; whereupon Oberon releases her from the charm. Robin at Oberon's orders throws a thick fog about the human lovers, and brings them all together, unknown to one another, and they fall asleep. He applies a remedy to Lysander's eyes, so that when he awakes he returns to his former love. Theseus and Egeus appear on the scene, the runaways are forgiven, and the couples married. The play ends with the 'trage-dy' of 'Pyramus and Thisbe', comically acted by Bottom and his fellow tradesmen, to grace these weddings and that of Theseus and Hippolyta.

MIÈVILLE, China (1972–) Author of *fanta-sy fiction, whose second novel *Perdido Street Station* (2000) fuelled the hybrid energy of the *New Weird, attacking the conservatism of fan-tasy on both political and literary grounds. Short stories are collected in *Looking for Jake* (2005). Recent novels include *The City & the City* (2009).

Military Memoirs of Capt. George Carleton First published in 1728 as *The Memoirs of an English Officer*. It was once attrib-uted to Daniel *Defoe, and to Jonathan *Swift, but it is probably a genuine memoir. The narra-tive covers his service in the Dutch wars of the 1670s and in Spain from 1705 until his capture in 1708. His five years as a prisoner yield many observations on Spanish life.

MILL, John Stuart (1806–73) Philosopher and political economist, son of James Mill (1773–1836), philosopher. He formed the Utili-tarian Society and in 1825 edited Jeremy *Ben-tham's *Treatise upon Evidence*. In 1831 he met Harriet Taylor (1807–58), who was, in his view, the chief inspiration of his philosophy; they married in 1851, after her husband's death. His divergence from strict Benthamite doctrine is shown in his essays on 'Bentham' and 'Coler-idge' (1838, 1840, *London and Westminster Re-view*) whom he describes as 'the two great seminal minds of England in this age'; and, later, in *Utilitarianism* (1861). His works in-clude *System of Logic* (1843), *Principles of Politi-cal Economy* (1848), *On *Liberty* (1859), *Examination of Sir William Hamilton's Philoso-phy* and *Auguste Comte and Positivism* (1865), and *The Subjection of Women* (1869). His engaging *Autobiography* (1873) describes his intellectual and moral development; he was in-dependent MP for Westminster 1865–8.

MILLAIS, Sir John Everett (1829–96) Painter; a founder member of the *Pre-Raphaelite Brotherhood. His *Lorenzo and Isa-bella* (1848–9), from John *Keats's poem, is one of the earliest Pre-Raphaelite works. Millais made a distinguished contribution to the revival of book illustration in the 1860s, and illustrated several of Anthony *Trollope's novels with sharply observed scenes from contemporary Victorian life.

MILLAY, Edna St Vincent (1892–1950) American poet. *A Few Figs from Thistles* (1920), established her persona as a reckless, romantic, cynical, sexually frank *New Woman. She was the first woman to receive the Pulitzer Prize for poetry in 1923. Her *Collected Poems* were published in 1956. Her impact on a whole generation was recorded by Dorothy *Parker.

Millenium Hall, A Description of *uto-pian novel by Sarah *Scott, published in 1762 and much reprinted thereafter. Through inset stories within a frame narrative, it assembles a cast of women who have made or found them-selves independent of male control and have created a self-supporting philanthropic com-munity devoted to the protection of the weak and unfortunate.

MILLER, Arthur (1915–2005) American playwright. He made his name with *All my Sons* (1947), an *Ibsenesque drama about a manufacturer of defective aeroplane parts, and established himself as a leading dramatist with *Death of a Salesman* (1949), in which a travelling salesman, Willie Loman, is brought to disaster by accepting the false values of con-temporary society. *The Crucible* (1952) uses the Salem witchcraft trials of 1692 as a parable for McCarthyism in America in the 1950s. *A View from the Bridge* (1955) is a tragedy of family honour and revenge. *The Misfits* (1961) is a screenplay written for his then wife Marilyn Monroe. *After the Fall* (1964) presents the semi-autobiographical figure of Quentin, seek-ing to comprehend the meaning of his own past relationships, and *The Price* (1968) contrasts the lives and opinions of two long-estranged brothers. Other plays include *The American Clock* (1980), *Playing for Time* (1981), *The Last Yankee* (1993), *Broken Glass* (1994), and *Mr Peters' Connections* (1998). In his last play, *Fin-ishing the Picture* (2004), Miller returned to the subject of Monroe, exploring the troubled making of *The Misfits*. Miller published an auto-biography, *Timebends*, in 1987.

MILLER, Henry (1891–1980) American nov-elist and essayist; he left America for Paris in 1930, and his autobiographical novel *Tropic of Cancer* (Paris, 1934), a frank and lively account of an American artist's adventures in Paris, was published by the predecessor of the Olympia Press. Like many of Miller's works, it was banned in Britain and the USA for its sexual content. He was very influenced by *Surrealist writing and film, and experimented with Anaïs *Nin in composing dream narratives. *Tropic of Capricorn* (France 1939; USA 1962), a companion volume to the first 'Tropic', was followed by *The Colossus of Maroussi* (1941), about Greece, *The Air-Conditioned Nightmare* (1945), reflections on Miller's return to America, and the *Rosy Crucifixion* trilogy: *Sexus* (1949), *Plexus* (1953), and *Nexus* (1960). In 1944 he settled in California, and despite continuing attacks from censors, he gradually became accepted as a major figure in the fight for literary and personal freedom, and a spiritual sage who greatly influenced the *Beat Generation. Miller's phallic eroticism was attacked by Kate Millett and other feminists.

'Miller's Tale, The' *See* CANTERBURY TALES, 2.

Mill on the Floss, The A novel by George *Eliot, published 1860, the most autobiographical of Eliot's novels. Tom and Maggie Tulliver, the principal characters, are the children of the honest but ignorant Mr Tulliver, miller of Dorlcote Mill on the river Floss. Tom is good-hearted, but unimaginatively conventional. Maggie in contrast is highly strung, intelligent, emotional, and, as a child, rebellious. From this conflict of temperaments, and from Maggie's frustrated sense of purpose, spring much of her unhappiness and the ultimate tragedy. Her deep love of her brother is thwarted by his lack of understanding, and she turns to the clever and sympathetic Philip Wakem, who is the deformed son of a neighbouring lawyer, for companionship. Unfortunately lawyer Wakem is the object of Mr Tulliver's dislike, which develops into hatred when Tulliver is bankrupted as a result of litigation in which Wakem is on the other side. Tom, loyal to his father, discovers the secret friendship of Maggie and Philip, and forbids their meetings: Maggie reluctantly complies. After Mr Tulliver's death, Maggie visits her cousin Lucy Deane, who is to marry the handsome and agreeable Stephen Guest. Stephen is attracted by Maggie, and she by him. A boating expedition leads, partly by Stephen's design, partly by accident, to Maggie's being irremediably compromised; Stephen implores her to marry him, but she refuses. Her brother turns her out of the house, and she is ostracized. She takes refuge with the loyal friend of her childhood, the packman Bob Jakins. In the last chapter a flood descends upon the town, and Maggie courageously rescues Tom from the mill. There is a moment of recognition and reconciliation before the boat overturns, and both are drowned.

Mills and Boon A British publishing company founded in 1908 by **Gerald Mills**

and **Charles Boon**. Originally a publisher of general fiction (its early authors included P. G. *Wodehouse and Jack *London), its name has become synonymous with popular *romantic fiction. It launched the career of Georgette Heyer (1902–74) in the 1920s and, as the circulating libraries (*see* MUDIE, CHARLES) declined in the 1950s and paperback fiction became more popular, it published increasing quantities of light romances, doctor–nurse romances, and *historical fiction, selling not only in bookshops, but also in newsagents and, later, supermarkets. Acquired by the Canadian firm Harlequin in 1971, Mills and Boon continues to publish a range of romantic titles.

MILNE, A. A. (Alan Alexander) (1882–1956) A prolific essayist and light versifier, assistant editor of *Punch* (1906–14), and a popular playwright, with *Mr Pim Passes By* (1919; pub. 1921), *The Truth about Blaydes* (1921; pub. 1922), and *Toad of Toad Hall* (1929), a dramatization of part of Kenneth Grahame's *The *Wind in the Willows*. His novels include a notable detective story, *The Red House Mystery* (1922). Milne's books for children include two collections of poems, *When We Were Very Young* (1924) and *Now We Are Six* (1927), typifying the 'beautiful child' fashion of the day. *Winnie-the-Pooh* (1926) and *The House at Pooh Corner* (1928), featuring toy animals belonging to his son Christopher Robin, were illustrated by E. H. *Shepard. To his annoyance, these overshadowed the rest of his work.

MIŁOSZ, Czesław (1911–2004) Polish poet and translator, a leader of the Polish literary avant-garde in the 1930s, and prominent in the Resistance. His works include novels, volumes of essays, and *The Captive Mind* (1951), an apologia for his withdrawal from Poland (he settled in California). He was awarded the *Nobel Prize for Literature in 1980. *New and Collected Poems 1931–2001* was published in 2006. Miłosz's translations of modern Polish poets have been influential, and his own work has had great impact on, among others, Seamus *Heaney.

Milton A poem in two books by William *Blake, written and etched 1804–8, one of his most complex mythological works, prefaced by his well-known lines 'And did those feet in ancient time', commonly known as 'Jerusalem'. It uses the mythological and allegorical framework of his earlier poems and also develops Blake's own powerful and personal response to *Paradise Lost* and its author (*see* MARRIAGE OF HEAVEN AND HELL). Blake seems to suggest that he himself becomes permeated with the spirit of *Milton, who descends to earth in order to save Albion through the power of Imagination: the bizarre and the sublime mingle, as Blake describes the spirit of Milton entering his foot. In Milton's address to the Virgin Ololon, he proclaims his mission of regeneration—'To cast off the rotten rags of Memory by Inspiration | To cast off Bacon, Locke and Newton from Albion's covering'—and prophesies the purging away by Jesus of the 'sexual garments' which hide 'the human lineaments'. The final section is an apocalyptic vision, from which Blake returns to his 'mortal state' to hear the mounting lark.

MILTON, John (1608–74) Poet, the son of a scrivener (or professional copyist) and composer of music. He was educated at St Paul's School, where he became friendly with Charles Diodati, then at Christ's College, Cambridge, where he acquired the nickname 'the Lady of Christ's'. During his Cambridge period, while considering himself destined for the ministry, he began to write poetry, mostly in Latin. His first known attempt at English verse, 'On the Death of a Fair Infant', was probably written in 1628 on the death of his niece Anne Phillips. His first distinctively Miltonic work, 'On the Morning of Christ's Nativity', written at Christmas 1629, shows a baroque use of imagery and the love of resounding proper names apparent in his later work. His fragmentary 'The Passion' was probably written at Easter 1630, and *Arcades* probably in 1632. 'On Shakespeare', his two epitaphs for Thomas Hobson, the university carrier, and 'An Epitaph on the Marchioness of Winchester' belong to 1631. His twin poems, *'L'Allegro' and *'Il Penseroso', may have been written at Cambridge; on leaving Cambridge Milton embarked on an ambitious course of private study at his father's home in preparation for a future as a poet. His 'masque' *Comus*, published anonymously in 1637, was written, and performed at Ludlow, in 1634. In 1636 the Miltons moved to Horton, then in Buckinghamshire, where John pursued his studies in Greek, Latin, and Italian, devoting much time to the church *Fathers. In 1637 he wrote *Lycidas*, a pastoral elegy, which dwells on fears of premature death, unfulfilled ambition, and wasted dedication. From 1638 to 1639 Milton travelled abroad, and on his return established himself in London and became tutor to his nephews Edward and John *Phillips. His attentions were now diverted by historical events to many years of pamphleteering and political activity, and to a tireless defence of religious, civil, and domestic

liberties. In 1641 he published a series of five pamphlets against episcopacy, engaging in controversy with Bishops Joseph *Hall and James *Ussher. *The Reason of Church Government* (1642) was the first to which he put his name; it was followed in the same year by *An Apology against a Pamphlet . . . against *Smectymnuus*, which contains interesting autobiographical details. In July 1642 Milton married Mary Powell, daughter of Royalist parents; he was 33, she 17. Within six weeks he consented to her going home to her parents at Forest Hill, near Oxford, on condition that she returned by Michaelmas. She did not do so. Taking advantage of the breakdown in censorship, Milton published in 1643 *The Doctrine and Discipline of Divorce*. This pamphlet made him notorious, but he pursued his arguments in three more on the subject of divorce in 1644–5, including *Tetrachordon*. *Of Education*, addressed to his friend Samuel Hartlib, appeared in 1644, as did his defence of the liberty of the press, *Areopagitica*. During this period he became aware of his growing blindness; by 1652 he was to be totally blind. His wife rejoined him in 1645, and their first daughter Anne was born a year later: a second, Mary, in 1648 and Deborah in 1652. A son, John, born 1651, died in infancy.

After the execution of Charles I, Milton published *The Tenure of Kings and Magistrates* (1649), arguing in general terms that a people 'free by nature' had a right to depose and punish tyrants, and attacking the *Presbyterians, whose belief in church discipline and state authority posed in his view a growing threat to freedom. He was appointed Latin secretary to the newly formed Council of State. He replied officially to *Eikon Basilike* in *Eikonoklastes* (i.e. Image Breaker, 1649), and to Salmasius in *Pro Populo Anglicano Defensio* (1651: *A Defence of the English People*), a work which created a furore on the Continent; also to Du Moulin's *Clamor* in *Defensio Secunda* (1654), which contains some self-defensive autobiographical passages and reflections on his blindness. He was now assisted in his secretarial duties by Andrew *Marvell, amongst others. His first wife died in 1652, and in 1656 he married Katherine Woodcock, then aged 28, who died in 1658, having given birth to a daughter who survived only a few months. He retained his post as Latin secretary until the *Restoration, on the eve of which he boldly published *The Ready and Easy Way to Establish a Free Commonwealth* (1660). At the Restoration he went into hiding briefly, then was arrested, fined, and released: Sir William *D'Avenant and Marvell are said to have interceded on his behalf. He now returned to poetry and set about the composition of *Paradise Lost*. In 1663 he married his third wife, Elizabeth Minshull (who survived him by more than 50 years). *Paradise Lost* is said by John *Aubrey to have been finished in 1663, but the agreement for his copyright was not signed until 1667. *Paradise Regained* was published in 1671 with *Samson Agonistes*. In 1673 appeared a second edition of his *Poems*, originally published in 1645, including most of his minor verse. His *A Brief History of Moscovia*, drawn from the *Hakluyt and *Purchas collections, appeared posthumously in 1682.

The State Papers that he wrote as Latin secretary (discovered in 1743) are mostly concerned with the routine work of diplomacy, but include an interesting series of dispatches, 1655-8, on the subject of the expulsion and massacre of the Protestant Vaudois, also the subject of his sonnet, 'On the Late Massacre in Piedmont'. His theological treatise *De Doctrina Christiana*, based entirely on biblical citations, was first printed in 1825. It ridiculed the doctrine of the Trinity, justified polygamy as a Christian form of marriage, and argued that God was a material substance and that the soul died with the body. These unorthodoxies had made its publication during his lifetime impossible. His *Commonplace Book*, with interesting insights into his studies and plans for composition, came to light in 1874.

Milton died in 1674 and was buried beside his father in St Giles', Cripplegate. As a man he has been variously presented as sociable, good-natured, and increasingly serene, as a domestic tyrant who bullied his daughters, as a strict Puritan, a misogynist, a libertine, and as a radical heretic. As a writer, his towering stature was recognized early. Although appreciated as a master of polemical prose as well as of subtle lyric harmony, his reputation rests largely on *Paradise Lost*, which John *Dryden was describing by 1677 as 'one of the greatest, most noble and sublime poems which either this age or nation has produced'.

mimesis *See* POETICS.

Minerva Press A publishing house in Leadenhall Street, London, established in 1773 by William Lane (?1745-1814), using the name Minerva Press from 1790 until 1820. Lane created a network of *circulating libraries to distribute its output of mass-produced *sentimental and *Gothic fiction. Minerva published mainly female authors, including the Gothic novels recommended by Isabella Thorpe in Jane Austen's *Northanger Abbey*. Many works appeared anonymously, including some by Amelia *Opie, William *Godwin, Sydney Owenson (?1776-1859), and Jane *West.

Minnesänger *('minnesingers')* German lyric poets of the late 12th to the 14th centuries, so called because chivalric love (*Minne*) was the principal subject of their poetry. They were influenced by the Provençal troubadours and the northern French trouvères. The *Minnesang* flourished during the years 1180-1220, known as the *Blütezeit*, after which it began to decline and evolve into *Meistergesang*. Some of the greatest *Minnesänger*—Hartmann von Aue, Wolfram von Eschenbach, and Gottlieb von Strassburg—were also writers of epic. *See* COURTLY LOVE; MEISTERSINGER.

Minotaur The monstrous offspring of Pasiphaë's union with a bull sent from the sea by the god *Poseidon. He was kept in a labyrinth built by Daedalus for Minos, king of Crete and Pasiphaë's husband. Minos required the Athenians to send youths and maidens as tribute for the Minotaur to destroy. *Theseus with the help of Minos' daughter Ariadne slew the Minotaur and escaped from the labyrinth. The story symbolizes destructive passion in *Racine's *Phèdre* and Ted *Hughes's *Birthday Letters*. It is retold by Mary *Renault, and is the subject of an opera by Harrison *Birtwistle with libretto by David *Harsent.

Minstrelsy of the Scottish Border (2 vols, 1802; later expanded) A collection of *ballads compiled by Walter *Scott, divided into three sections: historical, romantic, and 'imitations'. *Minstrelsy* included works from the north-east of Scotland (notably *Sir Patrick Spens*, 1803 onwards). Scott had been collecting ballads since 1792 and was aided by John Leyden, James *Hogg, Robert Surtees, among others, and many old women, including Hogg's mother, who kept alive the oral traditions. The extent to which Scott altered and 'improved' the texts has been much discussed. Scott's intention in presenting the ballads was avowedly patriotic: 'By such efforts, feeble as they are, I may contribute somewhat to the history of my native country; the peculiar features of whose manners and character are daily melting and dissolving into those of her sister and ally.' The *Minstrelsy* contains many well-known ballads, including 'The *Douglas Tragedy', 'The Twa Corbies', and *The Wife of Usher's Well* (its first printing).

MIRRLEES, Hope (1887-1978) Novelist and poet. 'Paris: A Poem' was published by Leonard and Virginia *Woolf's Hogarth Press (1919). The republication in 1970 of her third novel *Lud-in-the-Mist* (1926), a dark fairy-tale, helped spark the modern *fantasy renaissance.

mirror (mirour) As a literary term, based on the medieval Latin use of the word 'speculum' (e.g. *Speculum Historiale* of *Vincent of Beauvais or *Speculum Meditantis* of John *Gower, translated into French as *Mirour de l'omme*) to mean a true reflection or description of a particular subject, hence compendium. Thus there are titles such as *Mirrour of the Blessed Lyf of Iesu Christ* by Nicholas Love, the *Mirrour of the World* (translated by William *Caxton from French), the *Mirror of Fools* (translation of the late 12th-century *Speculum Stultorum* by Nigel *Wireker), and, in the Renaissance, *A *Mirror for Magistrates*.

Mirror for Magistrates, A A work planned by George Ferrers (c.1510–1579), master of the king's pastimes in the reign of *Henry VIII, and William Baldwin (d. in or before 1563) of Oxford. In it various famous men and women, most of them characters in English history, recount their downfall in verse. The book was originally begun as a continuation of John *Lydgate's *The Fall of Princes*, itself based on *Boccaccio's *De Casibus*. After a suppressed edition (of 1554?) it first appeared in 1559, containing twenty tragedies by various authors. In the enlarged edition of 1563 Thomas *Sackville contributed the 'Induction' and the *Complaint of Buckingham*. Further enlarged editions were published up to 1609/10. John Higgins (c.1544–c.1602), compiler of the 1574–87 additions, added complaints by figures from early or mythical British history, such as Locrinus, Elstride, and Cordila, and from Roman history, such as Julius Caesar and Nero. The *Mirror* provided source material for many writers, including Edmund *Spenser, William *Shakespeare, Samuel *Daniel, and Michael *Drayton.

Misfortunes of Elphin, The A satirical romance by Thomas Love *Peacock, published 1829. It ingeniously blends Welsh Arthurian legend, in which Peacock was expert, and political debate. Elphin is king of Ceredigion in western Wales, but the bulk of his territory has been engulfed by the sea, owing to the incompetence of Seithenyn, drunk in charge of the embankment meant to keep out the waves. Seithenyn's celebrated drunken speech about the wall ('the parts that are rotten give elasticity to those that are sound'), imitating a speech made by George Canning in 1822, is perhaps Peacock's finest

political parody. The book also contains the 'War Song of Dinas Vawr', a sly comment on political opportunism, and a clever bardic contest in which the current Romantic fashion for escapist themes is gently mocked.

misrule, king, lord, or abbot of At the end of the 15th and beginning of the 16th centuries, an officer appointed at court to superintend the Christmas revels. At the Scottish court he was called the 'abbot of unreason'.

MISTRY, Rohinton (1952–) Indian writer, whose first book was *Tales from Firozsha Baag* (1987), a collection of linked short stories set among the Parsi residents of a Bombay apartment building. *Such a Long Journey* (1991) and *A Fine Balance* (1996) show history as a juggernaut sweeping aside ordinary people's lives. *Family Matters* (2002) deals with the financial and domestic burdens of a down-at-heel Parsi family in 1990s Bombay. The novel's characteristic Zoroastrian meditation on duty and the desire to pursue 'good thoughts, good words and good deeds' takes place against a backdrop of increasing communalism, leading to a denouement where the cost of personal and religious purism is vividly evoked.

MITCHELL, Adrian (1932–2008) Poet, novelist, and playwright. Associated with the pacifism, protest, and free verse forms of underground poetry, he has always been an accessible poet, a reputation to which his popular readings have contributed. His collections include *Out Loud* (1969), *Ride the Nightmare* (1971), *For Beauty Douglas* (1981), *Love Songs of World War II* (1989), *Greatest Hits* (1991), *Heart on the Left: Poems* 1953–1984 (1997), *All Shook Up* (2000) and *The Shadow Knows* (2004). His novels include *If You See Me Comin'* (1962) and *Wartime* (1973); his many plays and stage adaptations, making considerable use of songs and lyrics, include a version of Peter *Weiss's *Marat/Sade* (1966) and *Tyger* (1971), based on the life and work of William *Blake.

MITCHELL, David (1969–) Novelist, whose fiction—from his first novel, *Ghostwritten* (1999), onwards—has been distinguished by virtuoso use of pastiche and bravura intertwining of widely diverse storylines, narrative voices, and geographical and historical settings. *number9dream* (2001) and *Cloud Atlas* (2004), were shortlisted for the *Man Booker Prize, and in 2003 he was named among *Granta's Best of Young British Novelists. Mitchell recalls his childhood in *Black Swan Green*, (2006).

MITCHELL, Julian (1935–) Novelist, playwright, and screenwriter, whose novels include *Imaginary Toys* (1961), *The White Father* (1964, set in Africa), and the more experimental *The Undiscovered Country* (1968). Mitchell achieved West End success with *Half-Life* (1977) and *Another Country* (1981; pub. 1982; filmed 1984) which examines the pressures and conflicts that turned some of the young intellectuals of the 1930s towards Marxism, and made one of them a potential spy. Later plays include *Francis* (1983), based on the life of *Francis of Assisi, and *Consenting Adults* (2007), about the 1957 Wolfenden Report, which had recommended that 'homosexual behaviour between consenting adults in private should no longer be a criminal offence'. Screenplays include a study of Oscar *Wilde, played by Stephen Fry (1998); he also wrote stage adaptations of the novels of Ivy *Compton-Burnett and TV adaptations of Colin *Dexter's 'Inspector Morse' stories.

MITCHELL, Margaret (1900–49) American novelist; the best-selling novel *Gone with the Wind* (1936; filmed 1939) was the only fiction she published in her lifetime. Set in Georgia during the American Civil War, it is the story of headstrong Scarlett O'Hara, her three marriages, and her determination to keep her father's property of Tara at all costs, despite the vicissitudes of war and passion.

MITCHISON, Naomi (1897–1999) CBE, novelist, and author of more than 70 books, including *The Conquered* (1923), *The Corn King and the Spring Queen* (1931), a historical novel set in Greece and the eastern Mediterranean in 228–187 BC, *We have been Warned* (1935), *The Blood of the Martyrs* (1939), and *The Big House* (1950). Her non-fiction works, including three volumes of autobiography (*Small Talk*, 1973; *All Change Here*, 1975; *You May Well Ask*, 1979), reflect her commitment to many progressive political and social causes.

MITFORD, Jessica Lucy (1917–96) CBE, writer, journalist, and sister of Nancy *Mitford. Unlike her other sisters, Diana and Unity, who supported Hitler, she adopted left-wing views early in her life, and maintained a lifelong support of civil rights and other radical and sometimes unpopular causes. Her vivid and entertaining account of her early family life, *Hons and Rebels* (1960), was followed by many other works of polemic and biography, and by campaigning documentaries, ranging from *The American Way of Death* (1963), a spirited exposé

of the funeral industry, to *The American Way of Birth* (1992), attacking childbirth technology.

MITFORD, Mary Russell (1787–1855) Dramatist and writer, whose drama *Julian* was produced successfully at Covent Garden (1823), and was followed by the even more successful *Foscari* (1826) and *Rienzi* (1828). The series of sketches and stories which made up *Our Village* (1832) was followed by *Belford Regis* (1835), a portrait of Reading; *Country Stories* (1837); *Recollections of a Literary Life* (1852); and a novel, *Atherton, and Other Tales*, (1854). Her fluent letters to Charles *Lamb, Benjamin *Haydon, Richard Henry *Horne, John *Ruskin, Elizabeth Barrett *Browning, Walter Savage *Landor, and many others were published in a selection edited by A. G. L'Estrange (3 vols, 1870) and in a further selection edited by H. Chorley (2 vols 1872).

MITFORD, Nancy (1904–73) Novelist; *Wigs on the Green* (1935) satirizes the British Union of Fascists (of which her brother-in-law Oswald Mosley was leader). In her first popular success, *The Pursuit of Love* (1945), the sensible Fanny describes life with her six unruly Radlett cousins and their hapless parents, Aunt Sadie and irascible Uncle Matthew. That this eccentric family is based on Mitford's own is confirmed by her sister Jessica's autobiography *Hons and Rebels* (1960). *Love in a Cold Climate* (1949) is a sequel, and several characters reappear in *The Blessing* (1951) and *Don't Tell Alfred*, (1960). *Noblesse Oblige* (1956, with A. S. C. Ross *et al.*) was a characteristic Mitford 'tease', provoking a widespread debate on class distinctions ('U' and 'Non-U') in vocabulary. Her journalism, *A Talent to Annoy* (1986), and a volume of witty *Letters* (1993), including many to her close friend and literary mentor Evelyn *Waugh, were edited by Charlotte Mosley.

MO, Timothy (1950–) Novelist, born in Hong Kong. His first novel, *The Monkey King* (1978), set in Hong Kong's business community, was followed by *Sour Sweet* (1982; film adaptation, Ian *McEwan, 1988), about a Chinese family's move to London in the 1960s. Later works include *An Insular Possession* (1986), set during the 19th-century opium wars between Britain and China; *The Redundancy of Courage* (1991), the story of a young Chinese hotelier in East Timor whose life is transformed by violent events; and the Philippines-set *Brownout on Breadfruit Boulevard* (1995) and *Renegade or Halo2* (1999), both published under Mo's own imprint, Paddleless Press.

Moby-Dick, *or The Whale* (1851) Novel by Herman *Melville, first published in Britain, as *The Whale*. Its 135 chapters exhibit an extraordinary variety of styles, from sailors' slang to biblical prophecy and Shakespearian rant. Inspired by his friend Nathaniel *Hawthorne to say 'NO! in thunder' to Christianity, Melville fused his narrator Ishmael's search for knowledge with the tragic quest narrative of Captain Ahab seeking revenge on the white whale that has bitten off his leg. The whaler, *Pequod*, is a male microcosm of a crew drawn from many nations. Melville interrupts the narrative with factual data, tales, soliloquies, and meditations on the whale. After a fierce three-day chase Moby-Dick destroys the *Pequod*. Ishmael survives the vortex, buoyed up on the harpooner Queequeg's coffin. The novel is written in a dense and allusive style, packed with biblical and other symbolism.

mock biblical A rhetorical strategy in which scriptural quotations, narratives, or figures are used for satirical ends. Mock-biblical satire rarely attacks the Bible itself, but appropriating the Bible in parody to satirize the secular world has a special force because of the authoritative context of scriptural texts. John *Skelton's *Speke Parrot* (1552) is one of the earliest instances in English. During the *Reformation Lucas Cranach ('the elder'), with Martin *Luther, effectively deployed the mock biblical against Rome in satirical woodcuts. A cluster of writings surrounding the Popish Plot trials of 1679 and the Exclusion crisis of 1681—most notably John *Dryden's *Absalom and Achitophel* (1681)— propelled the mock biblical into the mainstream of partisan political writing. Jonathan Swift's *A *Tale of a Tub* (1704) boldly used a mock-biblical perspective from an Anglican point of view; Daniel *Defoe's *True-Born Englishman* (1701) and *Iure Divino* (1706) from a Dissenting angle; and Alexander *Pope's smutty parody of *Sternhold and Hopkins's metrical psalmody was published by Edmund *Curll as a 'Roman Catholick Version of the First Psalm'. Later 18th-century examples include Charles *Churchill's *Prophecy of Famine* (1763) and William Blake's *The *Marriage of Heaven and Hell* (1790–93) and *The Book of Los* (1793). The fashion for pseudo-biblical 'Chapters', 'Chronicles', 'Books', and 'Lessons' inspired by Robert *Dodsley's *Chronicle of the Kings of England* (1740) and Horace *Walpole's *Lessons for the Day* (1742) culminated in the publication of 'The Chaldee MS' (1817) in *Blackwood's Magazine*, to a storm of controversy. In the Romantic period, many of the most vibrant mock-biblical satires were found in the political prints of Thomas *Rowlandson, George *Cruikshank, and James Gillray (1756–1815).

mock epic (mock-heroic) A satirical form, usually a poem in heroic couplets, which presents low characters or trivial subjects in the lofty style of classical epic or heroic poems. It is similar in spirit and character to the *mock biblical. The disjunction between matter and manner (a petticoat likened to a warrior's shield, or a chamber pot regarded as a trophy) parodies the conventions of epic poetry and satirizes the people and events who appear to regard themselves in heroic light. Mock epic typically employs elevated *poetic diction, focuses on a single 'heroic' incident, and incorporates selected elements from the machinery of classical epic: invocation to the Muse; the challenge; battles; boasting from the hero; games and other tests of prowess; perilous journeys; *epic similes; prayers and sacrifices to gods and goddesses, and their subsequent intervention; the visit to the underworld; and the vision of future glories. Although the mock-epic satirical poem, which flourished in the later 17th and 18th centuries, portrayed real characters and events in contemporary and local settings, its literary ancestry may be traced back to classical antiquity. The pseudo-Homeric *Batrachomyomachia* ('Battle of the Frogs and Mice'), *Virgil's mock-heroic aggrandizing of the bees ('little Romans') in *Georgic* IV, and the pseudo-Virgilian *Culex* (in which a shepherd kills a gnat that has saved his life), though lacking any satirical design, supplied precedents. Later examples include Vida's *Scacchia Ludus* (1537); Tassoni's *Secchia rapita* (1622), Scarron's *Virgile travesti* (1648–52), and Charles *Cotton's creative adaptation, *Scarronides* (1664). *Boileau's *Le Lutrin* (1674, 1683), in which two ecclesiastical dignitaries fight over the placement of a lectern, was widely influential in England. Dryden's *Mac Flecknoe* (1682), a demolition of his rival Thomas *Shadwell, and Sir Samuel *Garth's *The Dispensary* (1699) are the most important mock-heroic poems between Boileau and Alexander *Pope, whose *Rape of the Lock* (1712, 1714) and *Dunciad* (1728, 1742–3) mark the high points of mock epic in English. Jonathan *Swift's *Battle of the Books*, though in prose, has some mock-epic features. After Pope, mock epic tended to abandon its epic machinery and learned allusion for more direct personal and political satire. Later examples include Paul Whitehead's *The Gymnasiad, or Boxing Match* (1744), R. O. Cambridge's *The Scribleriad* (1751), Christopher *Smart's *The

Hilliad (1753), Charles *Churchill's *Rosciad* (1761), Thomas *Chatterton's *Consuliad* (1770), and *The Lousiad* (1785 *et seq.*) of 'Peter Pindar' (John *Wolcot).

modernism resists neat definition, but is perhaps best understood as an epoch of radical cultural upheaval which flourished predominantly in Europe and the USA from, arguably, around the last quarter of the 19th century to, no less debatably, around the start of the Second World War. It is also the catch-all term for the remarkable variety of contending groups, movements, and schools in literature, art, and music that flourished in Europe in particular during this period, such as *Symbolism, *Impressionism, *Post-Impressionism, *Aestheticism, *decadence, fauvism, *Cubism, constructivism, *Expressionism, *imagism, *Vorticism, *Futurism, Dada, and *Surrealism. Collectively these movements represent modernist culture's uncompromising confrontation with and sense of severance from the conventions and tastes of both mass society and the governing elite and its determination to rebuild and renew the arts; the period is thus characterized by the issuing of manifestos, the proliferation of *'little magazines', and the rapid dissemination of avant-garde works and ideas.

Conversely, it was also a time in which mass modernity and its cutting-edge technologies, such as telephony, electricity and aviation, were seen by some modernists to presage the new and more heroic world they longed for. In addition, modernists took a keen interest in the parallel revolutions that were taking place in physics, psychology, anthropology, and so on, and wrote about the modern city with either contempt or awe.

In the United Kingdom and Ireland, the modernist period was predominantly an age of renewal in poetry and the novel (rather than drama). The modernist novel may be seen as a reaction against 19th-century conventions of representation and narrative omniscience and is often non-chronological, with experiments in time such as sudden jumps, temporal juxtapositions, simultaneity, or a concern with duration (making a great deal occur within a small amount of text, or stretching a small amount of action over a large textual space) in evidence. Instead of upholding the realist illusion, major modernist novelists, such as James *Joyce and Virginia *Woolf, break narrative frames or move from one level of narration to another without warning or foreground the reflexivity of their texts. Instead of plot events, there is an emphasis on characters' consciousness, memory, and

perception (from around 1900, the ideas of the philosopher Henri *Bergson and the psychoanalyst Sigmund *Freud began to infiltrate modernist writing). Works are often oriented around a centre or centres of consciousness and are characterized by the use of such techniques as *free indirect style and *interior monologue. Authority is often vested in strangely limited third-person or unreliable first-person narrators, or there are multiple, shifting narrators. Instead of using closure and the fulfilment of reader expectations, or following genre conventions and formulas, as in a Victorian novel, modernist novels often work towards open endings and they make free use of ellipses, ambiguity, and complexity.

In British and Irish literature, the beginning of modernism is associated with *fin-de-siècle* movements such as *naturalism, Symbolism, decadence, and Aestheticism. Together with the theories of Walter *Pater, the work of Charles *Baudelaire, Jules *Laforgue, and Stéphane *Mallarmé had a profound influence on the British and Irish poets of the 1890s, such as Oscar *Wilde, Ernest *Dowson, Arthur *Symons, Lionel *Johnson, and W. B. *Yeats. Henrik *Ibsen, Gustave *Flaubert, Joris-Karl Huysmans, and the Russians Ivan *Turgenev, Lev *Tolstoy, and Fedor *Dostoevsky, were important influences for such writers as Joyce, Woolf, D. H. *Lawrence, Ford Madox *Ford, Henry *James, and Joseph *Conrad (naturalized in 1886). In the late 1890s the novels of James and *'Heart of Darkness' (1899, 1902), by Conrad, signalled a new direction, becoming increasingly complex, dense, and ambiguous. In his 'late style', as it appears in *The *Wings of the Dove* (1902), *The *Ambassadors* (1903), and *The *Golden Bowl* (1904), James's writing is marked by convoluted, ultra-qualified sentences filled with parenthetical statements, self-interruptions, and indirection. Yet of the writers who began their careers in the late Victorian period, Conrad appears now to be the most roundedly modernist. His remarkable series of novels, *Heart of Darkness*, *Nostromo* (1904), *The *Secret Agent* (1907), and *Under Western Eyes* (1911), experiment with abrupt temporal and spatial shifts in the presentation of narrative information and employ a dense and shifting prose style characterized by ambiguity and repetition and by the use of multiple narrators and narrative frames. They are also engaged with key areas of *fin-de-siècle* anxiety: the corruption of imperialism and colonialism, urban chaos, political extremism, degeneration, and the inability to discover the truth. Joyce's career began with the deceptively rich naturalism of *Dubliners* (1914), but in *A*

Portrait of the Artist as a Young Man (1916) he started to experiment with interior monologue and free indirect discourse. *Ulysses* (1922) focuses on one day in the lives of two Dubliners, using a mixture of multiple narrators (including many different third-person narrative voices), interior monologue, *stream of consciousness, literary parodies, and numerous stylistic and technical changes. *Finnegans Wake* (1939) is a multilingual, multiple-punning, endlessly intertextual novel which some critics have seen as the zenith of modernism. Woolf's major novels, *Jacob's Room* (1922), *Mrs Dalloway* (1925), *To the Lighthouse* (1927), and The *Waves* (1931), are all markedly experimental in technique and narrative structure; other modernist novels include D. H. Lawrence's *Sons and Lovers* (1913), The *Rainbow* (1915), and *Women in Love* (1920); and *Tarr* (1918; 1928) by Wyndham *Lewis.

Modernist poetry followed a similarly iconoclastic agenda, overthrowing conventional forms and moving towards fragmentation, free verse, complex allusion and patterning, and personal discourse, often purposefully obscure. These effects are most evident in the poetry of T. S. *Eliot and Ezra *Pound, who, with W. B. Yeats, were the most important figures in British modernist poetry. Pound, who lived in London from 1908 to 1920, declared the start of imagism with his two-line poem 'In a Station of the Metro' and the publication of a group of poems by Hilda *Doolittle (H.D.) and Richard *Aldington. Pound's own poetry shifted from imitation of Robert *Browning and medieval forms, through imitation of Japanese poetic structures and the minimalist writing of imagism, to Vorticism, and, with the *Cantos* (on which he worked from 1915 to 1969), the epic poem. This extremely complex 'poem with history', almost 800 pages long, includes sections on Confucianism, 18th-century American history, Renaissance Italy, and elliptical personal memoirs. Making few concessions to the reader, it includes untranslated Chinese, Italian, Greek, Latin, French, and Provençal. T. S. Eliot published *Prufrock and Other Observations* in 1917, but his masterpiece is The *Waste Land* (1922), which would go on to capture the largest audience of any single modernist poem.

Although there were many continuities with modernism in the 1930s, notably in the work of Samuel *Beckett, Jean *Rhys, Malcolm *Lowry, Elizabeth *Bowen, and Flann *O'Brien, many of the writers of that decade set themselves apart from the earlier modernists by their involvement with left-wing causes and the fight against *Fascism and Nazism, including W. H. *Auden,

Cecil *Day-Lewis, Stephen *Spender, and Louis *MacNeice. When (if) the transition from modernism to *postmodernism began has been contested almost as hotly as when the transition from Victorianism to modernism occurred.

Modern Love A poem by George *Meredith, published 1862. An intense, innovative work of 50 verses, it is spoken by a narrator who painfully discovers the unreality of his ideas of women. The verses unfold the disillusionment of passionate married love giving place to discord, jealousy, and intense unhappiness, ending in the separation and wreck of two illassorted lives, and the death by poison of the wife, the 'Madam' who has given way to the narrator's mistress, the 'Lady'. The sequence only obliquely registers Meredith's own unhappy experience in his first marriage: the poems are extensive meditations on the imaginative and ethical implications of Darwinian evolution.

Modern Manners A satire in the manner of Alexander *Pope by Mary *Robinson, published 1793 under the pseudonym 'Horace Juvenal', criticizing contemporary fashionable life and literature.

Modern Painters By John *Ruskin (5 vols, 1843–60) began as a defence of contemporary landscape artists, especially J. M. W. *Turner. Ruskin's plan was to show his artists' 'Superiority in the Art of Landscape Painting to all the Ancient Masters Proved by Examples of the True, the Beautiful and the Intellectual'. Volume i deals with the true. Knowledge is to be attained not from the traditions of 17th-century landscape but from direct observation of the facts of nature.

In vol. ii the logical framework of ideas was rapidly constructed. Beauty is perceived by the 'theoretic', i.e. contemplative, faculty (as opposed to the aesthetic, which is sensual and base). It consists of the varied manifestations, in natural forms, of the attributes of God.

In the third and subsequent volumes the earlier systematic treatment gives way to a looser structure. A detailed analysis of mountain beauty takes up most of *Modern Painters* iv. Part of Turner's greatness lies in his representation of the gloom and glory of mountains.

In *Modern Painters* v Ruskin concludes his investigation of natural beauty. The volume reflects a new interest in myth. A history of *Invention Spiritual* from ancient Greece to the present ends in the defeat of man's spiritual and intellectual powers by the 'deathful selfishness' of modern Europe. Turner's greatness is finally revealed in his mythological paintings. The work had an enormous impact on the visual sensibility of the 19th century, and encouraged artists in the direction of a more accurate representation of the material world.

Modest Proposal, A, for Preventing the Children of Poor People in Ireland, from Being a Burden to their Parents or Country; and for Making Them Beneficial to the Publick (1729) A pamphlet by Jonathan *Swift in which an apparently well-meaning commentator suggests that the problem of Irish poverty would be solved by fattening the 'excess' children of the poor to feed the rich. 'A young healthy child, well nursed, is at a year old a most delicious, nourishing and wholesome food, whether stewed, roasted, baked or boiled, and I make no doubt that it will equally well serve in a fricassee or a ragout.' Swift imitates the style of the political economists of his time, and pursues the idea with a remorselessly sustained ironic logic.

MOIR, David Macbeth (1798–1851) Scottish doctor, who signed himself Δ, Delta, the author of Mansie Wauch, Tailor in Dalkeith (1828). This imaginary autobiography, in the manner of Moir's friend John *Galt, reveals a comically parochial view of the world, and satirizes the rising fashion for *autobiography.

MOLESWORTH, Mary Louisa (1839–1921) née Stewart. Molesworth initially wrote for both adults and children as 'Ennis Graham'. She is now remembered for fantasies such as The Cuckoo Clock (1877), which was influenced by George *MacDonald, works that blend fantasy and realism such as The Carved Lions (1895), and realistic, psychologically perceptive studies of childhood, typified by her first children's novel, Carrots: Just a Little Boy (1876).

MOLIÈRE (1622–73) Pseudonym of Jean-Baptiste Poquelin, French comic playwright and actor. He had a decisive influence on the evolution of French comedy by bringing together the 'high' comedy of *Corneille and the 'low' comedy of farce, particularly associated with the *commedia dell'arte. His major plays include L'Avare (1669: The Miser), Le Tartuffe (1664), Le Malade imaginaire (1673: The Imaginary Invalid), Le Bourgeois gentilhomme, (1660: The Bourgeois Gentleman), Don Juan (1665), and Le Misanthrope (1666) His influence on English *Restoration comedy exceeded that of Ben *Jonson: dramatists like William *D'Avenant, John *Dryden, William *Wycherley, John *Vanbrugh, and Thomas *Shadwell quarried his plays for

characters and situations. Modern translators and adapters of Molière include Ranjit Bolt (1959–), Christopher *Hampton, Tony *Harrison, and Roger *McGough.

Moll Flanders, The Fortunes and Misfortunes of the Famous A novel by Daniel *Defoe, published 1722. 'Moll Flanders' is the criminal alias of the narrator, whose real name is never revealed. The story purports to be the edited autobiography of a woman born in Newgate prison and abandoned as a child when her mother is convicted of theft. The story relates her seduction, her five subsequent marriages and other liaisons, and her visit to Virginia, where she finds her mother and discovers that she has unwittingly married her own brother. After leaving him and returning to England, she turns to crime to support herself. She becomes an extremely skilled pickpocket and shoplifter, but is eventually caught and transported to Virginia. She takes with her one of her former husbands, a highwayman. With the funds that each has amassed they set up as planters, and spend their last years in prosperity and ostensible penitence.

Moloch (Molech) The name of a Canaanite idol, to whom children were sacrificed as burnt offerings (Leviticus 18: 21 and 2 Kings 23: 10), represented by Milton (*Paradise Lost, I. 392) as one of the chief of the fallen angels; hence applied to an object to which horrible sacrifices are made.

MOMADAY, Navarre Scott (1934–) Native American writer, born on the Kiowa reservation in Oklahoma, whose second publication, House Made of Dawn (1968) played a key role in the resurgence of *Native American literature. His works include stories and poems (In the Presence of the Sun, 1992), Kiowa mythology (The Way to Rainy Mountain, 1996), and memoir (The Names, 1976). In the Bear's House (1999) is illustrated by his own paintings.

Monastery, The A novel by Walter *Scott, published 1820. The first of Scott's novels to be considered a failure, it had a successful sequel, The *Abbot (1820).

MONBIOT, George (1963–) Travel writer, journalist, and environmental campaigner. He is the author of three investigative travel narratives, Poisoned Arrows (1989), Amazon Watershed (1991), and No Man's Land (1994); and of works advocating political and environmental reform.

Money A comedy by Edward *Bulwer-Lytton, successfully produced in 1840.

Monk, The A *Gothic novel by Matthew *Lewis, published 1796. Ambrosio, the worthy superior of the Capuchins of Madrid, falls to the temptations of Matilda, a diabolical wanton who, disguised as a boy, has entered his monastery as a novice. Now utterly depraved, Ambrosio lusts after one of his penitents, pursues the girl with the help of magic and murder, rapes and finally kills her in an effort to escape detection. She is revealed to have been his sister. He is discovered, tortured by the Inquisition, and sentenced to death, finally compounding with the devil for escape from burning, only to be hurled by him to destruction and damnation. Although extravagant in its mixture of the supernatural, the terrible, and the indecent, the book contains scenes of great effect. It enjoyed considerable contemporary notoriety.

'Monk' Lewis The nickname of Matthew *Lewis, author of *The *Monk*.

'Monk's Tale, The' *See* CANTERBURY TALES, 19.

monody An *elegy or dirge presented as the utterance of a single speaker, as in Milton's *'Lycidas'. In ancient Greek usage, a monody was an *ode for a solo voice rather than a chorus.

MONRO, H. E. (Harold Edward) (1879–1932) Poet, chiefly remembered for his Poetry Bookshop which he founded in 1913 to publish poetry, to encourage its sale, and to promote poetry readings; and for publishing the series *Georgian Poetry*, edited by Edward Marsh. He founded and edited the *Poetry Review*; his *Collected Poems* (1933) has an introduction by T. S. *Eliot.

MONROE, Harriet *See* POETRY.

MONSARRAT, Nicholas (1910–79) Novelist, best remembered for his highly successful novel *The Cruel Sea* (1951), based on his wartime experiences at sea.

Monsieur D'Olive A comedy by George *Chapman, published 1606, acted a few years before.

MONTAGU, Basil (1770–1851) Writer and lawyer, the son of John, fourth earl of Sandwich, and his mistress Martha Ray, the singer. A friend of William *Wordsworth, S. T. *Coleridge, and William *Godwin, his young son, also

Basil Montagu, lived with Wordsworth during their West Country period, and inspired the poem 'Anecdote for Fathers'. Montagu's mock-heroic couplets, *Railroad Eclogues* (1846), describe the advent of the railways in rural England and the effects of speculation.

MONTAGU, Elizabeth (1720–1800) née Robinson, writer and literary hostess, a celebrated member of the *Blue Stockings. Her sister was the novelist Sarah *Scott. She helped many young authors, such as James *Beattie and Richard *Price, with hospitality, encouragement, and money. She wrote the first three of George Lyttelton's *Dialogues of the Dead* (1760) and *Essay on the Writings and Genius of Shakespeare* (1769), refuting the strictures of *Voltaire.

MONTAGU, Lady Mary Wortley (1689–1762) née Pierrepont, writer; she secretly married Edward Wortley Montagu, and accompanied him in 1716 when he went to Constantinople (now known as Istanbul) as ambassador. She was deeply interested in this unfamiliar territory and gained access to several areas from which men were excluded; her contemporary 'Turkish Letters' described many scenes previously unknown to Europeans, and explored her own ambivalent reactions to the Orient. On her return in 1718 she introduced the oriental practice of inoculation against smallpox. In 1716 Edmund *Curll piratically published three of her satirical *Court Eclogues* under the title *Court Poems*, leading to Alexander *Pope's infamous revenge by emetic, at one level a kind of gallant gesture. In later works he was to attack her under the name of 'Sappho' for her sexual incontinence and lack of cleanliness. In 1737–8 she wrote an anonymous periodical, the *Nonsense of Common-Sense* (ed. R. Halsband, 1947), and in 1739 left England and her husband to live for nearly 23 years in France and Italy. Her *Letters and Works*, ed. Lord Wharncliffe, appeared in 1837.

MONTAGUE, John (1929–) Irish poet, the first Ireland professor of poetry (1998–2001). His collections include *Poisoned Lands* (1961) and *The Rough Field* (1972), a long collage on the historical predicament of the Catholics of Ulster, and the love poetry of *Tides* (1970) and *The Great Cloak* (1978). With its unemphatic rhythms and spare use of rhyme, Montague's work absorbs the example of William Carlos *Williams, Robert *Creeley, and other poets of his native America. *A Ball of Fire* (2008) collects his fiction; *Company*, 2001 and *The Pear is Ripe*, 2007 are memoirs. See *Collected Poems* (1995).

MONTAIGNE, Michel de (1533–92) French moralist and author of the *Essais*. In the 16th century 'essais' meant 'tests' or 'trials'; it had no connotations of literary genre, and Montaigne is often regarded as the inventor of the modern 'essay'. Montaigne published the first two books of his *Essais* in 1580, and had them reprinted in a revised version in 1582; in 1588 he published an enlarged edition, containing the third book; and until his death he was working on a further, much-expanded edition, which was published posthumously in 1595. The individual chapters that make up the *Essais* cover a huge variety of topics: moral, historical, philosophical, political, and religious. They were first translated into English by John *Florio in 1603, whose version of Montaigne's 'Des cannibales' is quoted by Gonzago in Shakespeare's The *Tempest. Charles *Cotton's more accurate rendering (1685–6) remained popular until the late 19th century.

MONTEMAYOR, Jorge de (c.1519–1561) Portuguese poet and author who wrote mostly in Spanish. His principal work is *La Diana* (?1559), a prose pastoral interspersed with verses, which was extremely popular, was translated into several languages, and was influential in England. The English translation, *Diana*, was by Bartholomew Yonge (1598); the episode of Felix and Felismena in Yonge's version is almost certainly the direct source of much of the plot of Shakespeare's The *Two Gentlemen of Verona*. Two continuations were published: Alonso Pérez's *Segunda parte de la Diana*: *Second Part of Diana* (1563), which was condemned to the flames in *Don Quixote* (I. 6), and Gaspar Gil Polo's popular *Diana enamorada* (1564: *Enamoured Diana*); both were translated by Yonge.

MONTGOMERIE, Alexander (c.1543–1598) Scottish poet. He was outlawed for Catholic partisanship in 1597, the year of publication of his principal work, *The Cherry and the Slae*, a searching allegorical investigation of the relative merits of high ambition and lowly contentment.

MONTGOMERY, James (1772–1854) Poet, editor, and hymn-writer; as editor of the *Sheffield Iris* in the 1790s, he was twice imprisoned for publishing radical articles. He published *Prison Amusements* (1797), but made his name as a poet with *The Wanderer of Switzerland* (1806). He also published *The West Indies* (1809), *The World before the Flood*. *Greenland* (1819), and *The Pelican Island* (1827). His hymns include 'Angels from the realms of glory'.

MONTGOMERY, L. M. (Lucy Maud) (1874–1942) Canadian writer remembered for her series beginning with *Anne of Green Gables* (1908), set on Prince Edward Island. Emily, her other enduring heroine, also developed through a series, beginning with *Emily of New Moon* (1923). Both series are semi-autobiographical; Anne and Emily are complex, creative characters living on the margins of stunted worlds that they help to expand.

MONTGOMERY, Robert (1807–55) English poet and clergyman. He wrote on religious themes and also composed vitriolic social satire (*The Age Reviewed*, 1827). He was lampooned for his poetic pretensions in *Blackwood's Magazine* by John *Wilson and by Thomas *Macaulay in the *Edinburgh Review* for April 1830. Despite these critical attacks, Montgomery's work enjoyed wide popularity.

Monthly Magazine An influential radical publication founded in 1796 by Richard Phillips (1767–1840), a *Jacobin and a supporter of Thomas *Paine. Contributors included William *Godwin, Thomas *Malthus, William *Hazlitt, Robert *Southey, and William *Taylor. Its first editor was Dr John *Aikin; its last (in 1825) was John *Thelwall. The *Anti-Jacobin was founded, in part, to oppose the views of the *Monthly*.

Monthly Review A periodical founded by the bookseller Ralph Griffiths (?1720–1803) in June 1749, the first literary review designed to give an account of all publications above the level of *chapbook. It was liberal in outlook, by contrast with its main rival, the conservative *Critical Review*. It ceased publication in 1844.

MONTROSE, James Graham, fifth earl and first marquis of (1612–50) Royalist and general; remembered as a poet for a few songs and epigrams, printed in *Memoirs of Montrose and his Times* (2 vols, 1856) by Mark Napier (1798–1818), including lines said to have been written on his prison window the night before his execution in Edinburgh.

Moonstone, The A novel by Wilkie *Collins, published 1868. The moonstone, an enormous diamond originally stolen from an Indian shrine, is given to an English girl, Rachel Verinder, on her 18th birthday, but disappears the same night. Under suspicion of stealing it are Rosanna Spearman, a hunchbacked housemaid, formerly a thief; a troop of Indian jugglers; Franklin Blake, Rachel's cousin; and Rachel herself. A detective, Sergeant Cuff, is called in to solve the mystery, and is aided by the house steward Gabriel Betteredge, principal narrator of the story, but thwarted by Rachel's reticence and by the suicide of Rosanna. It is eventually discovered that Franklin Blake was seen by Rachel to take the diamond, that at the time he was sleepwalking under the influence of opium, that it was taken from him by Rachel's other suitor, Godfrey Ablewhite, a sanctimonious hypocrite, and finally secured (by the murder of Ablewhite) and returned to the forehead of the statue from which it was stolen by the Indian jugglers, who were its disguised guardians. Widely admired as an early detective novel, it has proved enduringly popular.

MOORCOCK, Michael (1939-) One of the most prominent of *science fiction's *New Wave when he edited *New Worlds* from 1964 to 1971. A prolific and versatile writer, his own works include the continuing 'Elric' fantasies, beginning 1963, themselves part of a much-revised meta-sequence in which various heroes are aspects of an 'Eternal Champion'. The 'Colonel Pyat' books, *Byzantium Endures* (1981), *The Laughter of Carthage* (1984), *Jerusalem Commands* (1992), and *The Vengeance of Rome* (2006), explore the development of *Fascism and the Jewish Holocaust through the unreliable memoirs of a self-deceiving Russian émigré. Other notable works include *Gloriana* (1978), *Mother London* (1988), and *King of the City* (2000).

MOORE, Alan (1953-) Comic-book writer, author of *Watchmen* (1986-7), *V for Vendetta* (1982-8), *From Hell* (1991-8), and *The League of Extraordinary Gentlemen* (1999-2000); stylistically and thematically challenging comic books later collected as *graphic novels.

MOORE, Brian (1921-99) Novelist, born and educated in Belfast; he subsequently moved to the USA. His first serious work under his own name was *Judith Hearne* (1955, filmed 1987 under its US title, *The Lonely Passion of Judith Hearne*). His subsequent works, many of which deal with transatlantic migrations, include *The Feast of Lupercal* (1957); *The Luck of Ginger Coffey* (1960); *I am Mary Dunne* (1968); *Catholics* (1972); and *The Mangan Inheritance* (1979, an American journalist in search of his Irish heritage and the poet J. C. *Mangan). Other works include *Lies of Silence* (1990), a novel of the *Troubles, and the *historical novels *The Black Robe* (1983), and *The Magician's Wife* (1997).

MOORE, Edward (1712-57) A linen draper turned author, who contributed to the *Gentleman's Magazine* and other periodicals, wrote some much-reprinted *Fables for the Female Sex* (1744) in imitation of John *Gay, and contributed to Robert *Dodsley's *Collection of Poems* (1748-58). His successful first comedy, *The Foundling* (1748), was followed by *Gil Blas* (1751), which took its plot from Tobias *Smollett's translation of *Lesage's *Gil Blas of Santillane* and the domestic prose tragedy, *The Gamester* (1753), an adaptation of Aaron *Hill's *The Fatal Extravagance* (1721).

MOORE, Francis *See* OLD MOORE.

MOORE, George (1852-1933) Irish novelist, whose first novel, *A Modern Lover* (1883), set in artistic bohemian society, was banned by the *circulating libraries, confirming Moore in his battle against prudery and censorship. It was followed by *A Mummer's Wife* (1885, set in the Potteries); *Esther Waters* (1894); *Evelyn Innes* (1898) and its sequel *Sister Teresa* (1901); *The Brook Kerith* (1916), which unfolds the interwoven lives of Christ, St Paul, and *Joseph of Arimathea; and *Heloïse and Abelard* (1921). *Confessions of a Young Man* (1888), *Memoirs of my Dead Life* (1906), and *Hail and Farewell* (3 vols, 1911-14) are all autobiographical; the last is an important though unreliable source for the history of the *Irish Revival. His Revivalist collections of stories, *The Untilled Field* (1903) and the novel *The Lake* (1905), were both influenced by *Turgenev. His collaboration with W. B. *Yeats in setting up the *Irish Literary Theatre ended in acrimony.

MOORE, John (1729-1802) Scottish surgeon, travel writer, and novelist; as tutor to the duke of Argyll from 1772, he travelled extensively in Europe and published in 1779 and 1781 highly successful accounts of his experiences there. His other works include his novels *Zeluco* (1786), a didactic portrait of a vicious man, which went through thirteen editions; *Edward* (1796), a less popular depiction of virtue; and *Mordaunt* (1800), an *epistolary novel.

MOORE, Marianne (1887-1972) American poet, editor of *The *Dial* from 1925 to 1929. Her *Selected Poems* (1935) has an introduction by T. S. *Eliot; other collections include *Poems* (1921), *Observations* (1924), *The Pangolin, and Other Verse* (1936), and *Collected Poems* (1951). Combining urbanity with sophistication, her poems are composed with a strong sense of visual effect; she influenced the work of the poet Elizabeth *Bishop.

MOORE, Thomas (1779–1852) Poet, song-writer, and biographer; in 1801 he published the mildly risqué *The Poetical Works of the Late Thomas Little. Epistles, Odes, and Other Poems* (1806) was attacked by Francis *Jeffrey in the *Edinburgh Review*. From 1808 to 1834 Moore continued to add to his patriotic and characteristically melancholy songs in *Irish Melodies*, which established him as the national bard of Ireland. He acquired a European reputation with *Lalla Rookh* (1817), followed by the satirical entertainment *The *Fudge Family in Paris* (1818) and the controversial poem *The *Loves of the Angels* (1823). In 1824 he was prevailed upon to permit the burning of Byron's *Memoirs*, which the poet had entrusted to him five years previously. Other works include biographies of Richard Brinsley *Sheridan, Byron, and the Irish revolutionary Lord Edward Fitzgerald (1763–98), *The Epicurean*, a novel about a Greek philosopher (1827) and *The Fudges in England*, a light satire on an Irish priest turned Protestant evangelist (1835).

MOORE, Thomas Sturge (1870–1944) Poet, wood-engraver, and illustrator, and brother of the philosopher G. E. Moore (1873–1958); he was a friend of Charles *Ricketts and the artist Charles Haslewood Shannon (1863–1937), and also of W. B. *Yeats, for whom he designed several books. *The Vinedresser and Other Poems* (1899) was followed by several other volumes, and by various verse dramas, including *Tragic Mothers: Medea, Niobe, Tyrfing* (1920).

MOORHOUSE, Geoffrey (1931–2009) Journalist and travel writer. His travel narratives include *The Fearful Void* (1974) and *Apples in the Snow: A Journey to Samarkand* (1990). His works on India include *Calcutta* (1971), *To the Frontier* (1984), and *Om: An Indian Pilgrimage* (1993).

MORAES, Dom (1938–2004) Prolific, widely travelled Indian poet and writer. His volumes of poetry include *A Beginning* (1957), *John Nobody* (1965), *Bedlam and Others* (1967), and an anthology of *Modern Hebrew Peace Poetry* (1998), co-translated with Aryeh Sivan; his autobiographical memoir *My Father's Son* (1968) was praised by Stephen *Spender.

morality plays Medieval allegorical plays (mostly 15th century) in which personified human qualities are acted and disputed. They developed into the *interludes, from which it is not always possible to distinguish them, and influenced the development of Elizabethan drama. Their revival in the 20th century was prompted by a new interest in more mannered, pageant-like theatre, such as the Japanese *Nōh theatre and the plays of W. B. *Yeats and Bertolt *Brecht. Among the most celebrated English examples are *Everyman; Ane *Pleasant Satyre of the Thrie Estaitis* by Sir David *Lindsay; *Magnificence* by John *Skelton; *King John* by John *Bale; *Mankind*; and *The *Castle of Perseverance*.

Moravians With its origins in pre-Reformation Bohemia, the Moravian Church developed in the 18th century in Germany as an offshoot of Lutheran Pietism. It had a marked impact on early *Methodism. In 1722 Moravian refugees settled on the estate of the German religious reformer Count Zinzendorf (1700–60) in Saxony, forming a religious community called Herrnhut. John *Wesley met Moravian missionaries on his voyage to Georgia in 1735–6 and visited Herrnhut in 1738, providing a very full account in his second *Journal*. The principal Moravian settlement in England, Fulneck, near Leeds, was founded in 1744. Moravians were required to write accounts of their religious experiences, and Moravian hymnody had its own distinctive language. Influential Moravians include the hymn-writers John Cennick (1718–55) and James *Montgomery.

Mordred (Modred) In Arthurian legends, the nephew of King *Arthur, the son of King Lot of Orkney and Arthur's sister *Morgawse or Morcades (sometimes Anna; *see* PENDRAGON). *Geoffrey of Monmouth makes him the son of Arthur and his sister by an illicit union; he is accordingly the brother or half-brother of *Gawain and his brothers. During Arthur's absence on a Roman war he seizes the queen and the kingdom. In the final battle in Cornwall he is slain by Arthur but deals the king his death-blow. He is alluded to as a traitor in the *Divina commedia* (*Inferno*, XXXII. 61–2).

MORE, Hannah (1745–1833) Writer and philanthropist. More came to London in 1774 and became friendly with David *Garrick, Edmund *Burke, Samuel *Johnson, Sir Joshua *Reynolds, Thomas *Percy, and Elizabeth *Montagu, whose *Blue Stocking salon she entered in 1775. Her poem *Bas Bleu* (written 1782; pub. 1784) vividly describes the conversational charm of Blue Stocking society. Her tragedy *Percy* was successfully produced by Garrick in

1777. She was much admired by Horace *Walpole, who printed her ballad *Bishop Bonner's Ghost* at his press at Strawberry Hill in 1781. Her paternalist concern for the poor appears in *Village Politics* (1793, in opposition to Thomas *Paine's *Rights of Man*), and *Cheap Repository Tracts* (1795–8 including *The Shepherd of Salisbury Plain*), which sold 2 million copies in four years and led to the formation of the *Religious Tract Society in 1799. More's *Strictures on the Modern System of Female Education* (2 vols, 1799) appealed to those who found Mary *Wollstonecraft's views too aggressively radical. *Coelebs in Search of a Wife* (1809, a novel, or fictionalized conduct manual) was a huge commercial success.

MORE, Henry *See* CAMBRIDGE PLATONISTS.

MORE, Sir Thomas (St Thomas More) (1478–1535) Humanist and martyr, who had a brilliantly successful legal career. He devoted his leisure to literature, becoming intimate with John *Colet, William *Lily, Thomas *Linacre, and, in 1499, *Erasmus. He entered Parliament in 1504. *Utopia* (1516) is his description (in Latin) of an imaginary island. He became master of requests and privy counsellor in 1517, being treated by *Henry VIII with exceptional courtesy during his residence at court. He completed his *Dialogue*, his first controversial book in English (directed mainly against William *Tyndale's writings), in 1528. He succeeded Thomas Wolsey (1470/71–1530) as lord chancellor in 1529, but resigned in 1532 and lived for some time in retirement.

Although willing to swear fidelity to the new Act of Succession, More refused to take any oath denying the pope's authority, or assume the justice of the king's divorce from Catherine of Aragon, 1534, and was committed to the Tower of London with John Fisher (c.1469–1535), bishop of Rochester. During the first days of his imprisonment he prepared a *Dialogue of Comfort against Tribulation* and treatises on Christ's passion. He was indicted of high treason, found guilty, and beheaded in 1535. His body was buried in St Peter's in the Tower and, according to Thomas Stapleton, (1535–98) his head exhibited on London Bridge, until it was purchased by his daughter, Margaret Roper (1505–44), and later buried with her.

More's English works (collected 1557) include his *Life of John Picus Earl of Mirandula* (printed by John Rastell, c.1510), his *History of Richard the Third* (printed imperfectly in Richard *Grafton's *Chronicle* 1543, used by Edward *Hall, and printed fully by William Rastell

(1508–65) in 1557), *The Supplication of Souls* (1529), *The Confutation of Tyndale's Answer* (1532), and *The Apology of Sir Thomas More* (1533). His Latin publications (collected 1563 onwards) include four of *Lucian's dialogues, epigrams, and controversial religious works. He was beatified by the Church of Rome in 1886, and canonized in 1935. Sympathetic portraits of More include Robert *Bolt's play *A Man for All Seasons* (1960, filmed, 1966) and the life by Peter *Ackroyd (1998); he is portrayed negatively in Hilary Mantel's *Wolf Hall* (2009).

More, Sir Thomas A play based on Edward *Hall's *Chronicle* and biographies of *More, surviving in an incomplete transcript with additions in various hands (British Library, Harley MS 7368) which was submitted to Sir Edmund Tilney, master of the revels, probably about 1593. The scribe, Anthony *Munday, is likely to have been at least part-author of the original play. Tilney required major changes before granting permission to perform. The revisions (which may date from 1593–4 or 1603–4) are in five different hands, probably including those of Henry *Chettle, Thomas *Heywood, Thomas *Dekker, and a playhouse scribe. The fifth ('Hand D') has been claimed, with strong support, as Shakespeare's. If so, this is his only surviving literary manuscript. A scene of three pages, it depicts More, as sheriff of London, pacifying apprentices in a May Day rebellion against foreigners. *More* was first printed in 1844; the first known professional performance was in London in 1954; it has been revived at the Nottingham Playhouse (1964, with Ian McKellen as More), and by the Royal Shakespeare Company (2005).

MORGAN, Charles Langbridge (1894–1958) Novelist and dramatist, and from 1926 to 1939 dramatic critic of *The *Times*. His novels include *The Fountain* (1932), *Sparkenbroke* (1936), *The Judge's Story* (1947), and *The River Line* (1949, dramatized 1952). The last is set against a background of the French Resistance; Morgan's status as a writer has been and remains significantly higher in France than in Britain.

MORGAN, Edwin (1920–2010) Scottish poet, playwright, translator, and critic, appointed 'Scots Makar' (national poet of Scotland) in 2004. Morgan's collections from *The Vision of Cathkin Braes* (1952) to *A Book of Lives* (2007) demonstrate an egalitarian spirit and an interest in the possibilities of science and technology. Sound poems and *concrete poems exist side by side with understated lyrics of homoerotic love and experimental deployments of traditional forms. He translated Montale, *Neruda, and many others into English, and *Shakespeare and Maiakovsky into Scots. *Essays* (1974) and *Crossing the Border* (1990) collect his subtle and wide-ranging criticism. See *Collected Poems* (1996); *Collected Translations* (1996).

MORGAN, Lady (*c.*1776–1859) Née Sydney Owenson, prolific and very popular Irish writer and socialite. *The Wild Irish Girl* (1806), central to the development of the national tale in Ireland, was imitated by Charles *Maturin in *The Wild Irish Boy* (1808). She was paid by her publisher £1,200 (a huge sum) for *Florence Macarthy* (1818), a serious novel on the subject of contemporary Ireland. Her travel studies, *France* (1817) and *Italy* (1821), were also highly successful. In *The Mohawks* (1822), jointly authored with her husband, the royal physician Sir Charles, she attacked her Tory opponents, notably in the *Quarterly* and *Blackwood's Magazine*.

MORGAN, William De See DE MORGAN, WILLIAM FREND.

Morgan le Fay Queen of *Avalon, the daughter of Arthur's mother Igerne and therefore his half-sister; she is derived from a figure in Welsh and Irish (the Morrigan) mythology. In *Malory she attempts to kill Arthur, but she is also the leader of the queens who carry him away to cure his wounds. In Sir *Gawain and the Green Knight* she is represented as the bitter enemy of *Guinevere. A related figure occurs in the *Orlando innamorato* and *Orlando furioso*, called 'Morgana' there and being a *Lady of the Lake. See MORGAWSE.

Morgawse (Morcades) Half-sister of Arthur, the wife of King Lot of Orkney, and mother of *Mordred, *Gawain, *Agravain, Gareth, and Gaheris. She seems to be in some ways identical in origin with *Morgan le Fay; in later versions Arthur sleeps with her in disguise, thus begetting Mordred. She is called 'Anna' in *Geoffrey of Monmouth, though Anna is otherwise attested as Arthur's full sister.

MORIER, James Justinian (1782–1849) Diplomat, novelist, and travel writer. His account of his travels with Sir Harford Jones's mission to Persia appeared in *A Journey through Persia, Armenia and Asia Minor to Constantinople in the Years 1808–1809* (1812); *A Second Journey through Persia* appeared in 1818. Morier published a number of *oriental romances including the popular *The Adventures of Hajji Baba of Ispahan* (1824) and its sequel, *The Adventures of Hajji Baba in England* (1828). In 1824 he was a founder member of the *Athenaeum*.

MORLEY, Henry (1822–94) Biographer and academic, who joined the staff of *Household Words* at Charles *Dickens's invitation, edited the *Examiner*, and became the first professor of English language and literature at University College London. He published biographies of Palissy the Potter (1852), Cardano (1854), and *Agrippa (1856), wrote *A First Sketch of English Literature* (1873) and eleven volumes of *English Writers* (1887–95), and edited cheap editions of English classics in Morley's Universal Library (1883–8) and Cassell's National Library (1886–92).

MORLEY, Lord, Henry Parker, tenth baron (1480/81–1556) Courtier to *Henry VIII and Queen Mary, who made translations from Latin and Italian, presenting them to his monarchs as New Year's gifts. The earliest was a translation of *Petrarch's *Trionfi*, made in the 1520s but not printed until *c.*1555. His first appearance in print, an *Exposition and Declaration* of Psalm 94 (1539), was really a defence of Henry's position as head of the Church of England. It was followed by his version of the first 46 lives from *Boccaccio's *De Claris Mulieribus* (1543).

MORLEY, Thomas (1557/8–1602) English composer, organist, and writer. He studied under William *Byrd, to whom he dedicated the important treatise *A Plaine and Easie Introduction to Practicall Musicke* (1597), the first work of its kind in the English language. Morley championed the Italian *madrigal, and actively developed its English counterpart. His first two publications, the *Canzonets, or Little Short Songs to Three Voyces* (1593) and the first book of *Madrigalls to Foure Voyces* (1594), contain the most original of his own work in this form. Morley was the moving spirit behind *Madrigales: The Triumphes of Oriana* (1601), a collection of madrigals for five and six voices by 23 English composers. His *First Book of Ayres . . . to the Lute* (1600) contains a setting of 'It was a lover and his lass' which is apparently the earliest Shakespeare setting to survive.

Morning Chronicle A Whig journal founded by the printer William Woodfall (1746–1803) in 1769. James Perry (1756–1821) became chief proprietor and editor in 1789. Its staff then included Richard Brinsley *Sheridan, Charles *Lamb, Thomas *Campbell, Sir James Mackintosh, Henry *Brougham, Thomas *Moore, and David Ricardo (1772–1823). Perry was succeeded by John Black (1783–1855), scholar, Scotsman, and friend of James Mill, father of John Stuart *Mill. Both Mills were among his contributors, Charles *Dickens was one of his reporters, and W. M. *Thackeray his art critic. The *Chronicle* closed in 1862.

Morning Post A London daily newspaper founded in 1772. Under the management of Daniel Stuart, Sir James Mackintosh and S. T. *Coleridge were enlisted in its service, and Robert *Southey, William *Wordsworth, and Andrew *Young were also contributors. It was amalgamated with the *Daily Telegraph* in 1937.

MORPURGO, Michael (1943–) OBE, children's laureate 2003–5, prolific children's writer. His *animal stories include *War Horse* (1982), an account of the First World War as experienced by a horse (staged by the National Theatre, 2007). *The War of Jenkins' Ear* (1993) is a *school story about new-boy Christopher, who thinks he is Christ on his Second Coming. *Private Peaceful* (2003), a *war story, criticizes the treatment of British soldiers in the First World War, and is a popular stage play.

MORRELL, Lady Ottoline (1873–1938) Literary hostess, who entertained a wide circle of literary and political celebrities at her Thursday evening gatherings at 44 Bedford Square, London from 1907, and continued her career as hostess and patron of the arts at Garsington Manor, Oxfordshire, between 1915 and 1927. Her friends and guests included Henry *James, Lytton *Strachey, Bertrand *Russell, Virginia *Woolf, T. S. *Eliot, W. B. *Yeats, D. H. *Lawrence, and Aldous *Huxley. She appears as a character in several works of fiction by her protégés, most memorably as Hermione Roddice in Lawrence's *Women in Love* and as Priscilla Wimbush in Huxley's *Crome Yellow* (1921). She was deeply hurt by both portraits. Her *Memoirs* (1963, 1974) were edited by Robert Gathorne-Hardy.

MORRIS, Jan (formerly James) (1926–) Travel writer, novelist, essayist, and popular historian, author of more than 50 books. As James, Morris travelled widely, working as a correspondent for *The Times* and for the *Manchester Guardian*. He established his reputation with his scoop on the 1953 ascent of Mount Everest. In 1972 Morris underwent surgery to complete her gender reassignment. *Conundrum* (1974) is an account of

her transsexuality. Of the many places Morris has written about, Oxford, Trieste, and Venice have especially influenced her. The 'Pax Britannica' trilogy (*Pax Britannica*, 1968; *Heaven's Command*, 1973; *Farewell the Trumpets*, 1978) is a sympathetic chronicle of the decay of British imperialism.

MORRIS, William (1834–96) Writer, artist, and socialist reformer; he was one of the originators of the *Oxford and Cambridge Magazine* (1856), to which he contributed poems, essays, and tales. *The Defence of Guenevere and Other Poems* (1858) includes poems notable for their medieval settings and their striking mixture of beauty and brutality. In 1859 he married Jane Burden (1839–1914), one of the most painted *Pre-Raphaelite 'stunners'; their home, Red House at Bexley, was an important landmark in domestic architecture. The failure to find suitable furniture for it led to the founding, together with D. G. *Rossetti, Edward Burne-Jones, Webb, Ford Madox Brown (1821–93), and others, of the firm of Morris, Marshall, Faulkner and Co.; its designs brought about a revolution in public taste. In the late 1860s Morris published *The Life and Death of Jason*, based on the legend of Jason and Medea, and *The *Earthly Paradise* (1868–70). In 1871 he moved to Kelmscott Manor and visited Iceland, which stimulated his interest in Icelandic heroic literature. His epic *Sigurd the Volsung* appeared in 1876; he also published translations from Icelandic with Eiríkr Magnússon. His later works, with the exception of two volumes of political poetry, were mainly in prose; the best known are A *Dream of John Ball* (1888) and *News from Nowhere* (1891), both utopian socialist fantasies. He also wrote historical romances set in the distant past of northern Europe, including *The House of the Wolfings* (1889), *The Roots of the Mountains* (1890), *The Story of the Glittering Plain* (1890), *The Wood beyond the World* (1894), and his last work, *The Sundering Flood* (1898). All were published by the *Kelmscott Press, which he had founded in 1890. Morris also translated numerous classical and medieval texts, including the *Aeneid* (1875) and the *Odyssey* (1887).

MORRISON, Arthur (1863–1945) Novelist, born in the East End of London, to working-class parents, whose *realist tales of East End life in London were first published in various magazines, and later collected as *Tales of Mean Streets* (1894). He is chiefly remembered for his novel *A Child of the Jago* (1896), which provoked a public debate about violence and the conditions of slum life in London.

MORRISON, Blake (1950–) Poet and novelist. He has published three volumes of poetry, *Dark Glasses* (1984), *The Ballad of the Yorkshire Ripper* (1987), and *Pendle Witches* (1996). A *Selected Poems* appeared in 1999. His non-fiction books include *And When Did You Last See your Father?* (1993), a candid memoir of his father and his responses to his death, which launched a genre of confessional autobiography; *As if* (1997), a response to the James Bulger murder trial; and *Things my Mother Never Told Me* (2002). He has also written three novels, critical studies of Seamus *Heaney (1982) and The *Movement and a book for children, *The Yellow House* (1987).

MORRISON, Toni (1931–) African American novelist, whose novels deal with the historical experiences of African Americans within a white social and cultural environment. *The Bluest Eye* (1970) recounts a year in the life of Pecola Breedlove, a victim of rape by her father. Succeeding novels included *Sula* (1974), the story of two young black girls, one of whom leaves the small Ohio community of their birth and returns ten years later; *Song of Solomon* (1977); and *Tar Baby* (1981). *Beloved* (1987) was set in the 19th century and is the story of a runaway slave who kills her daughter rather than see her brought up to slavery (*see* SLAVERY); *A Mercy* (2008) continues her exploration of the profound traumas of slavery. Her other work includes *Jazz* (1992), and a study of the significance of African Americans in American literature, *Playing in the Dark: Whiteness and the Literary Imagination* (1992). She was the first African American woman to be awarded the *Nobel Prize for Literature in 1993.

'Mortal Immortal, The' A short story by Mary *Shelley, published 1833. The story is narrated by the immortal Winzy, on his 323rd birthday. The student of the alchemist Cornelius Agrippa, he has discovered an 'Elixir of Immortality'.

***Morte Arthur, Le* (The Stanzaic *Morte Arthur)** A late 14th-century poem from the northwest Midlands in 3,834 lines of eight-line rhyming stanzas surviving in one manuscript, and an important source (directly or indirectly) for the sections in *Malory leading up to and dealing with the death of Arthur. The poem narrates Launcelot's love affairs with Guinevere and the Maid of Astolat, Arthur's last battles, and the king's being borne away to Avalon.

Morte Arthure A 14th-century alliterative poem in 4,346 long lines, adapted by *Malory for his story of Arthur and Lucius. Correspondences with the *Roman de Brut* by *Wace suggest that, directly or indirectly, this or *Laȝamon's *Brut* may have been the poet's principal source. The subject matter corresponds roughly to Malory's first, second, and eighth romances (in Vinaver's numbering): the early exploits of Arthur, his European ventures, and the final battle with Modred. Malory, however, adapted the *Morte* so as to procure a victory for Arthur early in his cycle of adventures, rather than allowing his continental exploits to lead to his defeat and death at home (*see also* MORTE ARTHUR) as they do in this poem. It is among the most important and powerful Middle English poems, influencing *The *Awntyrs of Arthur*, *Hary's *Wallace*, and other works.

'Morte d'Arthur' A poem by Alfred *Tennyson, written 1833–4, published 1842, subsequently incorporated in 'The Passing of Arthur' (1869), where it formed one of the *Idylls of the King*. Tennyson's first major Arthurian work, it describes the last moments of Arthur after the battle with Mordred's forces, and includes his elegy on the Round Table.

Morte Darthur, Le The title given to the cycle of Arthurian legends by Thomas *Malory, printed by William *Caxton in 1485, divided into 21 books. In 1934, W. F. Oakeshott discovered a manuscript dividing the work into eight parts, which was used by Vinaver as the basis of his new edition of Malory. Vinaver divides the cycle into eight *Works* which he views as separate romances: (1) The Book of King Arthur, based largely on the *Suite du Merlin* (*see* MERLIN); (2) The Tale of Arthur and Lucius, based principally on the Alliterative English *Morte Arthure*; (3) The Tale of Sir Launcelot du Lake, mostly from two sections of the Prose *Lancelot* in the Vulgate cycle; (4) Sir Gareth of Orkney, the precise source of which is not known; (5) Tristram de Lyones, thought to be a translation of part of a lost 13th-century prose *Tristan* in French; (6) The Quest of the Holy Grail, principally from the prose Vulgate *Queste del Saint Graal* (*see* GRAIL); (7) Launcelot and Guinevere; and (8) The Morte Darthur, both based to a considerable degree on the French Vulgate *Mort Artu*, and the English stanzaic *Le *Morte Arthur*. Although Vinaver's edition is now regarded as authoritative, the traditional view of Malory's work as a whole compounded of disparate parts (by analogy with the *Canterbury Tales* or cycles of *mystery plays) prevails.

MORTIMER, John Clifford (1923–2009) Novelist, barrister, and playwright, formerly married to novelist Penelope *Mortimer. Well known for his opposition to censorship and for his stories about an eccentric defence barrister, Horace Rumpole. Many of the stories, from *Rumpole of the Bailey* (1978) onwards, have been adapted for television. Other works of fiction include *Paradise Postponed* (1985), a comic saga of English life from 1945 to the 1980s, and its sequels, *Titmuss Regained* (1990) and *The Sound of Trumpets* (1998). His plays include *A Voyage round my Father* (1971), a powerful and poignant portrait of his blind barrister father. *Clinging to the Wreckage* (1982), *Murderers and Other Friends* (1994), and *The Summer of a Dormouse* (2000) are autobiographical.

MORTIMER, Penelope (1918–1999) Novelist whose works, with their emphasis on frankness about female experience, contributed to the development of the woman's novel in the 1960s. They include *The Pumpkin Eater* (1962; filmed 1964, script by Harold *Pinter), *My Friend Says It's Bulletproof* (1967, which tackled the taboo subject of breast cancer), *Long Distance* (1974), *The Handyman* (1983), and *About Time* (1979, autobiography).

Mortimer his Fall Fragments of a tragedy by Ben *Jonson, printed in 1640, concerning the earl of Mortimer, the murderer of Edward II. Only the Argument and the opening speeches survive.

MORTON, H. V. (Henry Vollam) (1892–1979) Travel writer and journalist. Appearing first as articles, *In Search of England* (1927) was an immediate success. Its focus on the countryside and historic towns contrasts with other influential inter-war travelogues that explore 'Englishness' such as those of J. B. *Priestley and George *Orwell. It was followed by a sequel, *The Call of England* (1928), books on Scotland (1929, 1933), Ireland (1930), Wales (1932), and several books of biblically inspired travel in the Middle East. In 1947 Morton emigrated to South Africa.

MORTON, John Maddison (1811–91) Playwright, son of the playwright Thomas *Morton, educated in France. The most successful of his *farces was *Box and Cox* (1847).

MORTON, Thomas (?1764–1838) Dramatist, the author of three successful comedies;

The Way to Get Married (1796), *A Cure for Heartache* (1797), and *Speed the Plough* (1798). The last features 'Mrs Grundy', a character representing the extreme of moral rigidity.

MOSCHUS (*fl. c.*150 BC) A *pastoral poet of Syracuse, author of a short *epic *Europa*, and traditionally linked with *Theocritus and *Bion. The anonymous *Lament for Bion* was long wrongly ascribed to Moschus. There are echoes of it in John *Milton's Latin *Epitaphium Damonis*, and in his *Lycidas*, P. B. *Shelley's *Adonais*, and Matthew *Arnold's *'Thyrsis'.

Moscow Arts Theatre Founded in 1898 by the actor and theatre director Konstantin Stanislavsky (1863–1938) and the playwright and theatre director Vladimir Nemirovich-Danchenko (1858–1943). It reformed several aspects of the theatre: the 'star system' was replaced by ensemble performance, artificial styles of acting gave way to a style based on psychological realism, and scenery, sound effects, and lighting were used to create an illusion of everyday reality on stage, and promoted the role of the director as the figure whose ideas provided a single, unifying vision for a production.

Anton *Chekhov's play *The Seagull* was successfully revived by the theatre two years after its first disastrous production in 1896, leading to the rehabilitation of Chekhov's reputation as a dramatist.

Harley *Granville-Barker met Stanislavsky in 1914 to discuss plans to recreate an original Moscow Arts Theatre production in London, but war and revolution intervened. After 1917 the theatre's repertoire and realistic acting style made it a target for attacks from the left, but the theatre was protected by the Bolshevik state. In 1932 it was renamed after the writer and dramatist Maxim Gorky. By the time of its first visit to Britain in 1958, the theatre had come under attack at home for being out of touch with contemporary audiences. Stanislavsky's theoretical writings on acting inspired the school of 'method acting' in the USA.

Moses Ancient Israelite leader and lawgiver in the *Bible; supposed author of the Pentateuch (the first five books of the Old Testament). Born an Israelite but found in the bulrushes and raised by Pharoah's daughter, he secured Pharoah's permission to lead the Israelites out of captivity through the ten plagues which culminated in the death of the firstborn, celebrated in the feast of the Passover (so named because the angel of death passed over the Israelites' houses). The exodus began with the crossing of the Red Sea, in which Pharoah's army drowned. The Israelites wandered forty years in the wilderness, saved from starvation by quails and manna, and given water when Moses struck the rock. God spoke directly to him from the burning bush and on Mount Sinai, where he dictated the Ten Commandments. See Exodus, Leviticus, Numbers, and Deuteronomy.

MOSLEY, Nicholas, third Baron Ravensdale (1923–) Novelist and biographer. His highly intellectual, experimental, and metaphysical novels include *Accident* (1964) *Impossible Object* (1968); *Natalie Natalia* (1971); and *Catastrophe Practice* (1979), a complex network of three plays with prefaces and a short novel, built on the mathematical 'catastrophe theory' of the 1970s, applied here to human relationships and identity. Later works include his much-praised panoramic novel *Hopeful Monsters* (1990), a life of Julian *Grenfell (1976, 1999) and a two-volume study of his father, *Rules of the Game: Sir Oswald and Lady Cynthia Mosley 1896–1933* (1982) and *Beyond the Pale: Sir Oswald Mosley 1933–1980* (1983).

Mosses from an Old Manse (1846) A collection of tales and sketches by Nathaniel *Hawthorne. The Old Manse itself is the author's home in Concord, Massachusetts.

Mother Goose Traditional name for a narrator of *nursery rhymes and *fairy stories. She entered the English language through the frontispiece of Charles *Perrault's tales in 1729; the name was taken up by children's publisher John *Newbery and others. She appeared as a comic, wise, or bawdy old crone, wearing a witch's hat above her hooked nose and sharp chin. Frequently she rides or is a goose, sporting bonnet and spectacles.

'Mother Hubberds Tale' ('Prosopopoia') A satire in rhymed couplets, by Edmund *Spenser, included in the volume of *Complaints* published in 1591. The ape and the fox, 'disliking of their evil | And hard estate', determine to seek their fortunes abroad, and assume the disguises first of an old soldier and his dog, then of a parish priest and his clerk, then of a courtier and his groom; their misdemeanours in these characters are recounted. Finally, they steal the lion's crown and sceptre and abuse the royal power, until Jove intervenes and exposes them. The poem is a satire on the abuses of the church and the evils of the court.

motion The name given to puppet plays in the 16th and 17th centuries. They originally dealt with scriptural subjects, but their scope was later extended. *Shakespeare in *The *Winter's Tale* (IV. iii) refers to a 'motion of the Prodigal Son', and there are references to 'motions' in Ben Jonson's *Bartholomew Fair, A *Tale of a Tub*, and *Every Man out of His Humour*.

MOTION, Sir Andrew (1952–) Poet and biographer, *poet laureate 1999–2009. His first collection, *The Pleasure Steamers* (1978), was mostly lyrical in character and showed the influence of Philip *Larkin. *Secret Narratives* (1983) contributed to the 'new narrative' poetry of the 1980s. *Dangerous Play* (1984) contains an autobiographical prose piece, 'Skating', which is concerned with the accident, coma, and death of his mother. Other volumes include *Love in a Life* (1991), *Salt Water* (1997), *Public Property* (2002), and *The Cinder Path* (2009). Motion's deepest literary affinity is probably with Edward *Thomas. Motion has also written biographies of Philip Larkin (1993) and John *Keats (1997), novels, including *The Pale Companion* (1989) and *The Invention of Dr. Cake* (2003), and a memoir of his childhood, *In the Blood* (2006). He founded the online *Poetry Archive of recordings of poets reciting their own work.

MOTTRAM, R. H. (Ralph Hale) (1883–1971) Writer, author of *The Spanish Farm Trilogy* (1927), based on his own experiences during the First World War. Set in northern France, it consists of *The Spanish Farm* (1924), *Sixty-Four, Ninety-Four* (1925), and *The Crime at Vanderlynden's* (1926).

Mourning Bride, The William *Congreve's only tragedy, produced 1697. It concerns the secret marriage of Almeria, daughter of Manuel, king of Granada, and Alphonso, prince of the enemy state of Valencia, and Manuel's unsuccessful attempt to part them. The play contains the lines 'Music has charms to soothe a savage breast', and 'Heaven has no rage, like love to hatred turned, | Nor hell a fury, like a woman scorned'.

movable books Picture books incorporating flaps, volvelles (movable dials), pop-up elements, or other devices that reveal hidden elements of a text, convert one image to another, or simulate action. Early examples include 18th-century harlequinades (adaptations of the *commedia dell'arte*); movable books came to prominence in the 19th century through publishers such as Dean and Son, Raphael Tuck, and Ernest Nister, and the German illustrator

Lothar Meggendorfer (1847–1925). Recent exponents are Robert Crowther and the American Robert Sabuda.

Movement, the A term coined by J. D. Scott, literary editor of the *Spectator*, in 1954 to describe a group of writers including Philip *Larkin, Donald *Davie, D. J. *Enright, John *Wain, Elizabeth *Jennings, and Robert *Conquest. Two anthologies (Enright's *Poets of the 1950s*, 1955, and Conquest's *New Lines*, 1956) illustrate the Movement's predominantly anti-romantic, witty, rational, sardonic tone; its fictional heroes (notably Larkin's John Kemp in *Jill*, and Kingsley *Amis's Dixon in *Lucky Jim*) tended to be lower-middle-class scholarship boys. Definitions of its aims tended to be negative, and by 1957 its members began to disown it.

MOXON, Edward (1801–58) A distinguished London publisher and bookseller, described by Leigh *Hunt as 'a bookseller among poets, and a poet among booksellers'. Various volumes of his poems were published between 1826 and 1835. He married the 'adopted' daughter of Charles *Lamb, Emma Isola. He published works by P. B. *Shelley, John *Clare, William *Wordsworth, S. T. *Coleridge, Lamb, Hunt, Robert *Browning, Coventry *Patmore, and Henry Wadsworth *Longfellow, as well as Alfred *Tennyson, whose close friend he became and whose work he continued to champion and publish until his death. In 1831 he established the *Englishman's Magazine*.

MOXON, Joseph (1627–91) Maker of globes and mathematical instruments, printer, and typefounder. He wrote *Mechanic Exercises, or The Doctrine of Handy-Works Applied to the Art of Printing* (1683–4; ed. H. Davis and H. Carter, 3rd edn 2003), the first manual of printing and typefounding, and probably the first English book to be published in serial parts.

'Mr Gilfil's Love-Story' See SCENES OF CLERICAL LIFE.

Mr Limberham, or *The Kind Keeper* A comedy by John *Dryden, produced 1679, published 1680. The play was banned by royal decree after three performances. Limberham, possibly based on the earl of Shaftesbury, is an impotent masochist, who is cuckolded by the oversexed hero Woodall. By implication the play attacks a sexually corrupt court, the blind hedonism of the nobility, and the hypocrisy of Dissenters.

Mr Scarborough's Family Anthony *Trollope's 45th novel, published in 1883 (Trollope died during its serialization).

Mrs Caudle's Curtain Lectures See JERROLD, DOUGLAS WILLIAM.

Mrs Dalloway Fourth novel by Virginia *Woolf, published 1925. The action is restricted to the events of one hot day in the middle of June 1923, punctuated by the chimes of Big Ben: one of the novel's key contrasts is between the oppressiveness of clock time and the unrestricted, time-defying freedom of the mind. It opens in Westminster as Clarissa Dalloway, wife of Richard Dalloway MP, sets off to buy flowers for her party that evening. Alive with the sights and sounds of the London scene yet interwoven with memories of Bourton, Clarissa's family home, where, aged 18, she refused to marry Peter Walsh, the narrative is handled with a technical confidence and bravura that herald a new phase in Woolf's mastery of the novel. Mrs Dalloway is seen through the eyes not just of Walsh, returned after five years in India, but, among others, her girlhood friend Sally Seton, her daughter Elizabeth, and her daughter's tutor Doris Kilman. Mrs Dalloway's experience is also contrasted with that of the shell-shocked Septimus Warren Smith, who commits suicide by hurling himself from a window; news of his death intrudes upon Clarissa's party, and the similarities between the two characters proliferate as the novel draws to a close.

Mrs Lirriper's Lodgings and **Mrs Lirriper's Legacy** Christmas stories by Charles *Dickens, which appeared in *All the Year Round*, 1863 and 1864.

Mucedorus, A Comedy of A play of uncertain authorship, published in 1598 with 'new additions' in the third edition, of 1610, which says that it was acted by the King's Men. The whole play and, less implausibly, the additions have sometimes been attributed to *Shakespeare.

Much Ado About Nothing A comedy by *Shakespeare, written probably 1598–9, first printed 1600. Its chief sources are a novella by Matteo *Bandello and an episode in Ariosto's *Orlando furioso*.

The prince of Aragon, with Claudio and Benedick in his suite, visits Leonato, duke of Messina, father of Hero and uncle of Beatrice. The witty Beatrice has a teasing relationship with the sworn bachelor Benedick. Beatrice and Benedick are each tricked into believing the other in love, and this brings about a genuine sympathy between them. Meanwhile Don John, the malcontented brother of the prince, thwarts Claudio's marriage by arranging for him to see Hero apparently wooed by his friend Borachio on her balcony—it is really her maidservant Margaret in disguise. Hero is publicly denounced by Claudio on her wedding day, falls into a swoon, and apparently dies. Benedick proves his love for Beatrice by challenging Claudio to a duel. The plot by Don John and Borachio is unmasked by the 'shallow fools' Dogberry and Verges, the local constables. Claudio promises to make Leonato amends for his daughter's death, and is asked to marry a cousin of Hero's; the veiled lady turns out to be Hero herself. Benedick asks to be married at the same time; Beatrice, 'upon great persuasion; and partly to save your life, for I was told you were in a consumption', agrees, and the play ends with a dance.

muckrakers Term coined by US president Theodore Roosevelt in 1906 to describe American writers attempting to expose abuses in commerce and politics. One of the most famous muckrakers was Upton *Sinclair.

MUDDIMAN, Henry (b. 1629) The most famous of the 17th-century journalists, who started the *Parliamentary Intelligencer* and *Mercurius Publicus* in 1659; his *newsletters in manuscript, sent twice a week to subscribers all over the kingdom, were an important political feature of the day. One of his principal rivals was Sir Roger *L'Estrange In 1665 he started the *Oxford Gazette* (the predecessor of the *London Gazette*), the court being then at Oxford on account of the plague. *See* GAZETTE; NEWSPAPERS.

MUDIE, Charles (1818–90) The founder of Mudie's Lending Library (1842–1937). Mudie played a large part in the rise of the three-volume novel. He embarked on a career as bookseller, stationer, and lender of books in Bloomsbury. The lending proved so successful that he opened premises in Oxford Street in 1852, where the business prospered, despite complaints about Mudie's moral scruples in selecting his stock, which amounted, some claimed, to a form of censorship. George *Moore was a particularly outspoken adversary, publishing *Literature at Nurse, or Circulating Morals* in 1885.

Muggletonians A sect founded c.1651 by Lodowicke Muggleton (1609–98), a tailor, and his cousin John Reeve (1608–58), who claimed to be the 'two witnesses' of Revelation 11: 3–6.

They denied the doctrine of the Trinity, and taught that matter was eternal and reason the creation of the devil.

MUHAMMAD (Mahomet) The founder of the Muslim religion. He was born at Mecca c.570, and, according to Muslim belief, he was called by the angel Gabriel c.610 to his role as a prophet. From time to time he imparted the revelations he received, and these became the *Qur'ān. After fierce opposition from the Meccans, he moved to Medina in 622 (the *hijra*). There he prospered both religiously, despite the opposition of local Jewish tribes, and on a secular level. After seven years of struggle Mecca surrendered, and by the time he died in 632 most of the Arabian peninsula had accepted his religious and political authority.

The first reasonably accurate, though unsympathetic, English account of Muhammad's life is in the *Preliminary Discourse* to the translation of the Qur'ān by George Sale (1697–1736), appearing in 1734. The next key assessment is that of Edward Gibbon (*Decline and Fall of the Roman Empire*, 1776–88, ch. L). In the 19th century, Thomas *Carlyle's lecture on Mahomet in *Heroes and Hero-Worship* (1840, lecture 2) had considerable vogue.

'Muiopotmos, or The Fate of the Butterflie' A mythological poem by Edmund *Spenser published among his *Complaints* (1591).

MUIR, Edwin (1887–1959) Poet, born in Orkney, where he spent his childhood. He started contributing to Alfred Orage's *New Age* in 1913. In 1919, he married Willa Anderson (*see* MUIR, WILLA); they moved to London, where Muir underwent a course of psychoanalysis which profoundly affected his writing. In 1921 the Muirs went to Prague, and remained in Europe for four years, a period that later produced their collaborative translations from the German (notably, 1939–40, of Franz *Kafka). *First Poems* (1925) was followed by collections including *Chorus of the Newly Dead* (1926), *The Labyrinth* (1949), and *Collected Poems, 1921–1951* (1952). Muir's poetry is mostly traditional in form, and much of his imagery is rooted in the landscapes of his childhood. A recurrent theme is the dream journey, and the narrative of the poet's own life lends itself naturally to the myth of an Eden threatened by various forms of catastrophe or expulsion. Muir also published three novels, critical works, including *Scott and Scotland* (1936), and an autobiography, *The*

Story and the Fable (1940, revised as *An Autobiography* 1954).

MUIR, Willa (1890–1970) Née Anderson, Scottish novelist, translator, and essayist; she was the senior partner in her collaborative translations, with her husband Edwin *Muir, of *Kafka and others. Her novels *Imagined Corners* (1931) and *Mrs Ritchie* (1933) are set in a fictionalized version of her birthplace Montrose ('Calderwick') and share a strong feminist awareness with her critical works *Women: An Inquiry* (1925) and *Mrs Grundy in Scotland* (1936). *Belonging* (1968) is an alternately rueful and tart memoir.

MULCASTER, Richard (1531/2–1611) Schoolmaster and writer the first headmaster of Merchant Taylors' School, London, where his pupils included Edmund *Spenser, Thomas *Kyd, Thomas *Lodge, and Lancelot *Andrewes. His books on education, *Positions* (1581), dedicated to *Elizabeth I, and *The Elementary* (1582) show his humanist interests and ideals, such as his suggestion that gentlewomen should be educated in school, though only up to the age of 13 or 14, and his stress on physical exercise, music, and vernacular literature, including the writing of English verse. He also published Latin and English verses on the queen's death (1603), and helped devise City shows and pageants.

MULDOON, Paul (1951–) Irish poet and librettist, whose precocious *New Weather* (1973) marked him out as a distinctive new voice: ironic, allusive, knowing. By the appearance of *Quoof* (1983) he had established himself as one of the most verbally inventive poets of the post-war period. Later volumes include *Madoc: A Mystery* (1990), inspired by the idealistic social philosophy of *Pantisocracy, as expounded by Samuel Taylor *Coleridge and Robert *Southey (author of the original *Madoc); *Hay* (1999); and *Horse Latitudes* (2006). *Maggot* (2010) is his thirtieth collection. See *Poems 1968–1998* (2001); *The End of the Poem: Oxford Lectures* (2006). He has also adapted Aristophanes' *The Birds* (1999) and translated *The Astrakhan Cloak* (1992) from the Irish of Nuala *Ní Dhomhnaill.

MULGRAVE, earl of *See* SHEFFIELD, JOHN.

MULOCK, Dinah Maria *See* CRAIK, DINAH MARIA.

Mum and the Sothsegger An incomplete alliterative poem (*c.*1409) of 1,751 lines, in a 15th-century British Library manuscript. Its idiom, range of concerns, dream vision, and wandering narrator clearly derive from William *Langland. Concerned with events in the early 15th century, it considers whether it is better to be Mum (as in 'keep mum') and to remain silent in evil days, or to speak unwelcome truths like the Sothsegger (Truth-teller).

mummers' play (St George play) A folk play evolved from the sword-dance, widespread through Britain. The play, in its characters and detailed action, varies in different localities, but the principal characters are St George (Sir George, King George, Prince George), the Turkish knight, Captain Slasher, and the Doctor. After a brief prologue, the fighting characters advance and introduce themselves, or are introduced, in boastful rhymes. A duel or several duels follow, and one or other of the combatants is killed. The Doctor then enters, and resuscitates the slain. Additional grotesque characters are then presented, and a collection is made. The central incident of the play is doubtless connected with the celebration of the death of the year and its resurrection in the spring. A celebrated description of mumming occurs in Book II, chs 4–6 of Thomas Hardy's *The *Return of the Native*.

MUNBY, Arthur Joseph (1828–1910) Poet, diarist, and lawyer. He published various volumes of verse, including *Verses New and Old* (1865) and *Relicta* (1909), but is remembered for his diaries and notebooks, used by Derek Hudson as the basis of his *Munby: Man of Two Worlds* (1972). These give an interesting picture of Victorian literary and social life; they also reveal Munby's obsession with working women and the story of his secret marriage to a domestic servant, Hannah Cullwick (1833–1909), which explain some of the allusions in his poems.

MUNDAY, Anthony (1560–1633) Hackwriter. He wrote or collaborated in a number of plays, and was ridiculed by Ben *Jonson as Antonio Balladino in *The *Case is Altered*. He probably wrote *John a Kent and John a Cumber* (*c.*1589–90, dealing with a conflict between two wizards); he collaborated in the writing of *Sir Thomas *More and in *The Downfall of Robert, Earl of Huntington* (printed 1601), followed by *The Death* of the same, dealing with the legend of *Robin Hood. Munday wrote ballads, which are lost, and as 'Shepheard Tonie' contributed several poems to *Englands Helicon* (1600). He also translated popular romances, including the *Palmerin* cycle (1581–1602), *Paladin of England* (1588), and *Amadis of Gaul* (?1590), and wrote City pageants from 1605.

MUNRO, Alice (1931–) Canadian short story writer, whose collections, *Dance of the Happy Shades* (1968), *Who Do You Think You Are?* (1978, published in Britain as *The Beggar Maid*), and *The Progress of Love* (1986), won the prestigious Canadian Governor General's Award. Her other collections include *Friends of my Youth*, *Lives of Girls and Women* (1973), *Open Secrets* (1994), *Hateship, Friendship, Courtship, Loveship, Marriage* (2001), *Runaway* (2004), *The View from Castle Rock* (2006), and *Too Much Happiness* (2009). Munro describes herself as writing about 'places where your roots are', in her case relatively poor, small-town southern Ontario. Her stories combine poetic intensity and economy with the surprising scope and depth of a novel.

MUNRO, H. H. (Hector Hugh) See SAKI.

MUNRO, Rona (1959–) Scottish playwright. *Iron* (2002), her most successful play, is about a mother and daughter attempting to forge a relationship, the former being imprisoned for the murder of her husband (and the daughter's father).

MURDOCH, Dame Iris (1919–99) Novelist and philosopher; her works on philosophy include *Sartre, Romantic Rationalist* (1953), *The Sovereignty of Good* (1970), and *Metaphysics as a Guide to Morals* (1992). In 1956 she married the literary critic John *Bayley, who later published two controversial books, *Iris* (1998, filmed 2001) and *Iris and the Friends* (1999), describing her final years as a victim of Alzheimer's disease. In an influential essay, 'Against Dryness' (*Encounter*, Jan. 1961), she distinguished between what she called 'crystalline' novels (tightly structured, self-contained fictions, making much use of myth, allegory, and symbol) and a more open and relaxed type of writing, exemplified by the great 19th-century English and Russian novels. Most of her 26 novels fall within the former category, including her first novel, the genially bohemian *Under the Net* (1954), and *A Severed Head* (1961; dramatized 1963 by J. B. *Priestley), an elegant satire wittily drawing on motifs from *Freud and Sir James *Frazer's *The Golden Bough*. *The Bell* (1958) is the most impressive of her more naturalistic novels.

MURPHY, Arthur (1727–1805) Playwright, born in Ireland. He was a close friend of Samuel *Johnson from 1754, and introduced Johnson to the *Thrales in 1765. Murphy wrote some twenty farces, comedies, and tragedies, including adaptations of *Molière and *Voltaire; his better-known pieces include *The Way to Keep Him* (1760), *Three Weeks after Marriage* (1764), and *Know your Own Mind* (1777).

MURPHY, Dervla (1931–) Irish cyclist and travel writer. She often told of receiving an atlas and a bicycle for her tenth birthday and deciding then to cycle to India. In 1963 she cycled solo from Dublin to Delhi, and described her sometimes hair-raising adventures in *Full Tilt* (1965), the first of more than twenty travel books. She travelled lightly, usually by bicycle, alone or with her young daughter born in 1968. Her books depict an intrepid but politically sensitive adventurer. She continued to cycle into her seventies, though, as in *Through Siberia by Accident* (2005), her plans sometimes went awry. *Wheels within Wheels* (1979) is an autobiography.

MURPHY, Richard (1927–) Irish poet. His poetry characteristically portrays the landscapes and seascapes of the west of Ireland; his publications include *Sailing to an Island* (1963) and the historical meditation *The Battle of Aughrim* (1968). Murphy's dry, classical, somewhat patrician style mediates powerful themes of social and sexual exclusion. His memoir *The Kick* (2003) includes vivid portraits of Theodore *Roethke, Ted *Hughes, Sylvia *Plath, and other writers. *Collected Poems* appeared in 2000.

MURPHY, Tom (1935–) Irish playwright, whose work marries the dominant naturalistic strain of Irish drama with the poetic impulse that had characterized the plays of the early *Abbey Theatre. *A Whistle in the Dark* (1961) ferociously exposes the violence of family life, while *A Crucial Week in the Life of a Grocer's Assistant* (1969) offers an angry portrait of the constrictions and hypocrisies of small-town Ireland. Later plays include the fantastical *The Morning after Optimism* (1971); the anticlerical *The Sanctuary Lamp* (1975); the exuberant *The Gigli Concert* (1983); *Bailegangaire* (1985), the most acclaimed of Murphy's 25 plays; and *The Last Days of a Reluctant Tyrant*.

MURRAY, Gilbert (1866–1957) Classical Greek scholar and translator. His translations of *Euripides into English verse were widely performed, and he imbued his influential interpretations of Greek literature with his own secular liberalism.

MURRAY, Sir James (1837-1915) Lexicographer, appointed editor of the *Oxford English Dictionary* in 1879. He laid down the lines on which the work was to be compiled, and persevered through many difficulties. There is a detailed account of the dictionary's composition in *Caught in the Web of Words* (1977) by his granddaughter K. M. E. Murray, which also gives a vivid portrait of his industry, his high moral standards and sense of responsibility, and his happy family life.

MURRAY, John (1778-1843) The son of John Murray I (1745-93), the founder of the publishing house, which continued in family hands until the early 21st century, when it was bought by Hodder Headline. The second John Murray was among those who began to substitute for the dying system of personal patronage his own encouragement and commercial expertise. With the help and encouragement of Walter *Scott he established the Tory *Quarterly Review* in 1809. He gave up the London agency of *Blackwood's Magazine* in protest at its attacks on the *Cockney School. His single most important author was Lord *Byron, although he was so apprehensive of the public reception of *Don Juan* that he published only the early cantos, without his imprint; the later cantos were published by John *Hunt, who also produced *The *Vision of Judgement*, which Murray had refused. Murray bought Byron's memoirs of 1818-21 from Thomas *Moore, and reluctantly consented to having them burned in his grate at Albemarle Street. His other authors included Jane *Austen, George *Crabbe, S. T. *Coleridge, Robert *Southey, Leigh *Hunt, and George *Borrow. The *Guide for Travellers on the Continent* (1820) by Mariana Starke (1761/2-1838) led to a long and profitable series of *guidebooks.

MURRAY, Les (1938-) Australian poet, whose first book of poems, *The Ilex Tree* (1965), was written in collaboration with Geoffrey Lehmann; In 1985 he moved to live permanently in Bunyah, near where he had grown up, having established himself as a distinctive poetic voice, and outspoken critic and editor. At the heart of Murray's poetry is a profound response, expressing itself through a rich visual imagination and meticulously crafted language, to the Australian bush, and to the ideals and values of the pioneer settlers. His many volumes of poems include *The Weatherboard Cathedral* (1969), *Poems against Economics* (1972), *Ethnic Radio* (1977), *The People's Otherworld* (1983), *The Idyll Wheel: Cycle of a Year at Bunyah* (1989), *Dog Fox Field* (1990), *Translations from the Natural World* (1992), *Subhuman Redneck Poems* (1996), *Poems the Size of Photographs* (2003), *The End of Symbol* (2004), and *Taller When Prone* (2010). His *Collected Poems: 1961-2002* (2002; 2006) is dedicated, like all of his work since 1983, to 'the glory of God'. Other works include two verse novels, *The Boys Who Stole the Funeral* (1980) and *Fredy Neptune* (1998); criticism, essays, and other writings collected in volumes from *The Peasant Mandarin* (1978) to *The Quality of Sprawl: Thoughts about Australia* (1999).

MURRY, John Middleton (1889-1957) Editor and critic; while still at Oxford he edited the *modernist periodical *Rhythm* (1911-13), through which he met his future wife Katherine *Mansfield. From 1919 to 1921 Murry was editor of the *Athenaeum*, in which he published an impressive range of writers, including Virginia *Woolf, T. S. *Eliot, and Paul *Valéry, and in which he attacked *Georgian poetry. In 1923, the year of his wife's death, he founded the *Adelphi*; although he was to marry again three times, he continued to dwell on her memory, editing her stories, letters, and journals. In addition to his many critical works he also wrote works of a semi-mystical nature, and became deeply interested in the concept of an ideal community and in pacifism; he remains an important figure in literary history. See his autobiography, *Between Two Worlds* (1935).

Musaeus (1) A legendary Greek poet, said to have been a pupil of *Orpheus. (2) A Greek poet, who perhaps lived about AD 500, the author of a poem on *Hero and Leander* which provided the groundwork for Christopher *Marlowe's poem of the same title. During the Renaissance the first, legendary Musaeus was sometimes assumed to have written what was in fact a late Greek poem. It was first translated into English, in 1645, by Sir Robert Stapylton (1607/9-1669).

Muses In Greek mythology there were nine Muses, daughters of Zeus and Memory, each patronizing a different art: Calliope (epic); Clio (history); Euterpe (music); Melpomene (tragedy); Terpsichore (dancing); Erato (lyric poetry); Polyhymnia (sacred poetry and rhetoric); Urania (astronomy); Thalia (comedy). They were associated with Mounts Helicon and Parnassus and the Pierian spring, and the god *Apollo was sometimes described as their leader. *Hesiod in the *Theogony* described himself as taught by them, and invocation of the Muse(s) to aid the poet, notably in *Homer and *Virgil, was a traditional formula of *epic. *In *Paradise Lost* Book VII John *Milton rejects Calliope for the Heavenly Muse Urania, identified with the Holy Spirit.

Muses Lookinge-Glasse, The A defence of the drama, in the form of a play, by Thomas *Randolph, printed 1638, in which Roscius persuades two doubting Puritans that drama may promote moral good.

'Mutabilitie Cantos' Name given to the fragmentary Book VII of Edmund *Spenser's *Faerie Queene*, consisting of two cantos only, first published with the 1609 folio edition of the poem. They describe the challenge of the Titaness Mutabilitie to the cosmic government of Jove. The goddess Nature vindicates Jove's rule, displaying its orderly beauty in a procession of Seasons and Months.

MYERS, Frederic William Henry (1843–1901) Poet, critic, and inspector of schools; his essay on George *Eliot, first published in the *Century Magazine* in 1881 (and reprinted in *Essays Classical and Modern*, 1883), describes the incident in which she spoke to him of '*God, Immortality, Duty*', and declared 'how inconceivable was the *first*, how unbelievable the *second*, and yet how peremptory and absolute the *third*'. Myers was a founder of the *Society for Psychical Research, and he was joint author (with Edmund Gurney and Frank Podmore) of *Phantasms of the Living* (1886), a two-volume work dealing largely with telepathy. He was also a member of the Theosophical Society.

MYERS, L. H. (Leopold Hamilton) (1881–1944) Novelist, son of F. W. H. *Myers. His novels are concerned with the problem of how human beings can live rightly in society if they exclude spirituality, which, to his mind, was an activity as natural as sex. Apart from *The Orissers* (1922), *The 'Clio'* (1925), and *Strange Glory* (1936), his novels are set in an imaginary 16th-century India: *The Near and the Far* (1929), *Prince Jali* (1931), *The Root and the Flower* (1935), and *The Pool of Vishnu* (1940); collected together under the title *The Near and the Far* in 1943. Myers committed suicide by taking an overdose of veronal while suffering from depression.

'My mind to me a kingdom is' The first line of a poem on contentment, originally printed in William *Byrd's *Psalms, Sonnets,*

and Songs (1588). Frequently referred to in the 16th and 17th centuries, it was often attributed to Edward *Dyer. It is more probably by the earl of *Oxford.

Mysteries of Udolpho, The A novel by Ann *Radcliffe, published 1794. The orphaned Emily St Aubert is carried off by her aunt's villainous husband Montoni to a remote castle in the Apennines, where her life, honour, and fortune are threatened and she is surrounded by apparently supernatural terrors. These are later explained as the result of human agency and Emily escapes, returns to France and, after further mysteries, is reunited with her lover Valancourt. The book was extremely popular, and plays an important part in Jane Austen's *Northanger Abbey*.

Mysterious Mother, The A *Gothic tragedy in blank verse by Horace *Walpole, printed at his press at Strawberry Hill in 1768. It deals with the remorse of a mother (the countess of Narbonne) for an act of incest committed many years before. The theme of incest shocked many of Walpole's readers but greatly interested Lord *Byron, who described the play as 'a tragedy of the highest order, and not a puling love-play'.

mystery plays A term conventionally used to denote biblical dramas popular in England from the 13th to the later 16th century. The term 'mystery', which is not contemporary, derives from the *mestier* (*métier* or trade) of their performers. 'Miracle plays', strictly, are enactments of the miracles performed by the saints, whereas the 'mysteries' enact the events of the *Bible from the Creation to the Ascension (and in some cases later). Their origin is much disputed; one of the earliest is the Anglo-Norman *Jeu d' Adam* (*see* ADAM), and there were cycles in many countries: France, Italy, Ireland, and Germany (surviving in the Oberammergau Passion Play). Though it is clear from their archives that many English towns had them, only three complete cycles survive—York, Chester, and Towneley (named after the owners of the manuscript)—as well as the N-town plays (so called because it is not known in which town they were performed). They are connected with the feast day of Corpus Christi (the Thursday after Trinity Sunday) which was first observed as a holy day in 1311. The various pageants were each assigned to a particular trade-guild, often with a humorous or macabre connection between the *métier* and the play: the York Shipwrights enact the story of Noah, for instance.

Their great popularity in England from the time of *Chaucer to *Shakespeare is attested by these writers, among others. Their end was no doubt mainly caused by *Reformation distaste for images and religious pageantry. As an early, popular form of theatre, they manifest energy, humour, resourceful stagecraft, and seriousness; their composers were anything but unlearned, as is clear from the group of six plays in the Towneley cycle assigned to a presumed author known as 'the Wakefield Master'. The latter's most celebrated play is the Second Shepherd's Play in which the Nativity is parodied by and collocated with a contemporary case of sheep stealing. It was not these plays so much as the moralities and *interludes which affected the development of Elizabethan drama. Benjamin *Britten's *Noye's Fludde*, and revivals of performances of the cycles, most notably at York, demonstrate continuing interest.

SEE WEB LINKS

• Luminarium: Middle English plays

mysticism In Christian thought this refers variously to attempts at union with or direct knowledge of God or Jesus achieved through contemplation, self-denial, visions, or trances. Medieval English mystics include Richard Rolle, *Julian of Norwich, Walter *Hilton, and Margery *Kempe. Despite *Protestant hostility to the assumptions of mysticism there has been much Protestant interest in *Roman Catholic mystics, such as *Thomas à Kempis, *Teresa of Avila, and St John of the Cross. There have been notable Protestant mystics, such as Jacob Boehme, who influenced William *Law, and Emanuel *Swedenborg, who impressed and then disgusted William *Blake. Mystical poets include W. B. *Yeats, T. S. *Eliot, and Geoffrey *Hill.

myth criticism An area of literary investigation and commentary that deals with the relations between 'myth'—in the positive sense of a traditional story—and literature, often drawing upon anthropology, psychology, and studies of folklore. Myth criticism is usually concerned to demonstrate that literary works draw upon a common reservoir of *archetypes or recurrent images, or that their narrative patterns repeat those of ancient myths or religious rituals, as in quests for sacred objects, or cycles of death and rebirth. Much *psychoanalytic criticism overlaps with myth criticism, not just in the tradition of Carl *Jung but in that of Sigmund *Freud, who interpreted literary texts as well as dreams and neurotic symptoms as echoes of the Oedipus myth. Notable works include *Archetypal Patterns in Poetry* (1934) by Maud Bodkin (1875–1967); *Quest for Myth* (1949) by Richard Chase (1914–62); Robert *Graves's *The White Goddess* (1948), W. H. *Auden's *The Enchafèd Flood* (1951), and C. L. Barber's *Shakespeare's Festive Comedy* (1959). A more elaborate theoretical foundation for myth criticism was proposed by Northrop *Frye in his *Anatomy of Criticism* (1957). This tradition of literary study came under repeated attack for dealing only with the 'contents' of literary works and ignoring all questions of language and style; and it declined in the 1960s as new theoretical agendas redefined the relations between anthropological and literary study (*see* STRUCTURALISM). Some of its concerns survive in the writings of the American critic Leslie *Fiedler and of the French anthropological philosopher René Girard (1923–).

mythography The compilation and interpretation of myths, drawn on especially in the Renaissance period by poets and painters. *Ovid's *Metamorphoses* was a very important source of knowledge of classical myth; the stories were often given allegorical meanings by later Christian interpreters. The major Renaissance Latin handbooks—*Boccaccio's *De Genealogia Deorum*, the *Mythologiae* by Natalis Comes (1520–82)—were well known to English poets such as Ben *Jonson. John Lemprière's *Classical Dictionary* was an important source for John *Keats, and the work of later mythographers like Friedrich *Max Müller, Andrew *Lang, Sir J. G. *Frazer, Carl *Jung, and Claude *Lévi-Strauss has been widely influential.

NABOKOV, Vladimir Vladimirovich
(1899–1977) Russian-born novelist, poet, and
literary scholar; his family left Russia for Germany in 1919. After studying at Trinity College,
Cambridge (1919–23), Nabokov lived in Berlin
(1923–37) and Paris (1937–40), writing mainly in
Russian, under the pseudonym 'Sirin'. His early
novels, like *Laughter in the Dark* (1932), tended
to be black comedies and reflect his constant
interest in the cinema. In 1940 he moved to the
USA; from then on all his novels were written in
English. The outstanding success of his novel
Lolita (Paris 1955; USA 1958) enabled him to
give up teaching and devote himself fully to
writing in Montreux, Switzerland. He wrote a
screenplay for Stanley Kubrick's film adaptation
of *Lolita*, which was not accepted. Two other
strong interests which influenced his fiction
were chess and lepidoptery (the study of butter-
flies and moths). Nabokov's reputation for linguistic and formal inventiveness led him into
controversy with his translation of Pushkin's
Eugene Onegin (1964); *Pale Fire* (1962) is a fictitious translation and commentary. A revised
version of his 1951 autobiography appeared
as *Speak, Memory* in 1967, and his lectures on
literature were published in four volumes
(1980–83).

NADEN, Constance (1858–89) Poet and
philosopher. Remembered for *A Modern Apostle* (1887), her witty and sceptical poems reflect
her radical views and incorporate commentary
on women's status, evolution, and social science.

NAIPAUL, Shiva (1945–85) Novelist and
travel writer, born in Trinidad, where his first
two novels, *Fireflies* (1970) and *The Chip-Chip
Gatherers* (1973), are set. *A Hot Country* (1983)
is set in Cuyama, a fictitious South American
state that much resembles Guyana. *North of
South* (1978) is an account of a journey through
Africa, and *Black and White* (1980) investigates
the mass suicide in Guyana instigated by Jim
Jones. *Beyond the Dragon's Mouth* (1984) consists of fictional and travel pieces. *An Unfinished*

Journey (1986) collects travel and personal
memoirs, including 'My Brother and I', an
essay on the author's relationship with his
elder brother V. S. *Naipaul.

**NAIPAUL, Sir V. S. (Vidiadhar Surajpra-
sad)** (1932–) Novelist and travel writer, born
in Trinidad, the brother of Shiva *Naipaul; his
first three books, *The Mystic Masseur* (1957), *The
Suffrage of Elvira* (1958), and *Miguel Street*
(short stories, 1959), are comedies about Trinidadian life. The tragicomic *A House for Mr Bis-
was* (1961), also set in Trinidad, portrays a man
(modelled on Naipaul's father) thwarted from
attaining independence. *Mr Stone and the
Knights Companion* (1963), Naipaul's only
novel located in London, was followed by *The
Mimic Men* (1967), narrated by a failed politician on a fictitious Caribbean island. After *A
Flag on the Island* (1967, stories) his work—
both fiction and reportage—becomes more
overtly political and pessimistic. *In a Free State*
(1971, *Booker Prize) explores problems of nationality and identity through linked narratives
about displaced characters. *Guerrillas* (1975)
depicts political and sexual violence in the Caribbean; *A Bend in the River* (1979) is an equally
horrifying portrait of emergent Africa. Naipaul's
predominantly gloomy view of postcolonial societies can also be seen in his travel and autobiographical books such as *The Middle Passage*
(1962) and *A Way in the World* (1994), about the
Caribbean; *An Area of Darkness* (1964) and
India: A Million Mutinies Now (1990), about
the sub-continent; *The Return of Eva Peron*
(1980), his account of Argentina; and *Among
the Believers: An Islamic Journey* (1981). His
recurrent themes of political violence, homelessness, and alienation have invited comparisons with Joseph *Conrad. Later works include
the novels *Half a Life* (2001) and *Magic Seeds*
(2004), and the controversial *A Writer's People*
(2007) on his literary influences. Naipaul was
knighted in 1990, and was awarded the *Nobel
Prize in 2001. *See* ANGLO-INDIAN LITERATURE;
POSTCOLONIAL LITERATURE.

NAIRNE, Carolina, Baroness (1766–1845) Née Oliphant, the author of many spirited and well-known *Jacobite songs, including 'Will ye no come back again?' and 'Charlie is my darling'; and of humorous and pathetic ballads. She concealed her authorship during her lifetime, and her poems were collected and published as *Lays from Strathearn* in 1846.

NARAYAN, R. K. **(Rasipuram Krishnaswami)** (1906–2001) Indian novelist writing in English In his first novel, *Swami and Friends* (1935), he created the imaginary small and microcosmic Indian town of Malgudi, which he was to map out and populate in several succeeding novels, including *The Bachelor of Arts* (1937), *The English Teacher* (1945), *Mr Sampath* (1949), *The Financial Expert* (1952), *The Guide* (1958: winner of the Sahitya Akademi Award), *The Vendor of Sweets* (1967), *The Painter of Signs* (1977), *A Tiger for Malgudi* (1983), and *The Grandmother's Tale and Other Stories* (1993). The characters in his fictional world are portrayed with a gentle irony as they struggle to accommodate tradition with Western attitudes inherited from the British. Graham *Greene compared the tragicomedy, pathos, and frequently disappointed aspirations of his characters to those of *Chekhov. A counterbalance to the fantastical and fabulist trend in Indian writing (represented by G. V. *Desani, Salman *Rushdie, and others), Narayan's work has consistently defied comparison. Characterizing his achievement, the renowned critic C. D. Narasimhaiah remarked that 'few writers have been more Indian'. Narayan's other publications include short stories (*An Astrologer's Day and Other Stories*, 1947; *Lawley Road*, 1956; *A Horse and Two Goats*, 1970; *Malgudi Days*, 1982) and a charming memoir, *My Days* (1975). *See* ANGLO-INDIAN LITERATURE.

Narnia *See* LEWIS, C. S.

narratology The term applied since 1969 to the formal analysis of narratives. Although in principle applicable to ancient theories of storytelling such as *Aristotle's, the term is applied to the modern tradition, of which *Morphology of the Folktale* (1928) by the Russian scholar Vladimir Propp (1895–1970) is taken to be the founding work. Narratology rests upon certain basic distinctions between what is narrated (e.g. events, characters, and settings of a story) and how it is narrated (e.g. by what kind of narrator, in what order, at what time). Propp's work on Russian folk tales proposed that there were no more than 31 basic elements or 'functions' common to all narratives, and that they always appeared in the same order. There is an English-speaking tradition of narratology, originating in the theory and practice of Henry *James, and codified in terms of narrative 'point of view' by his disciple Percy Lubbock in *The Craft of Fiction* (1921); other notable early contributions were E. M. *Forster's *Aspects of the Novel* (1927) and Edwin *Muir's *The Structure of the Novel* (1928). *The Rhetoric of Fiction* (1961) by Wayne C. Booth introduced important new distinctions such as those between the real author and the 'implied author' of a novel, and between reliable and unreliable narrators. The most comprehensive analyses of the various kinds of possible narrator and narrative order appear in the works of the French narratologist Gérard Genette (1930–), especially his *Figures III* (1972; partly translated as *Narrative Discourse*, 1980).

Narrenschiff *See* SHIP OF FOOLS.

NASH, Ogden (1902–71) American writer of sophisticated light verse, renowned for his puns, epigrams, elaborate rhymes, elaborate lack of rhymes, wildly asymmetrical lines, and other verbal fancies.

NASHE, Thomas (1567–*c.*1601) Writer; his first publications (both 1589) were a preface to Robert *Greene's *Menaphon*, surveying the follies of contemporary literature, and *The Anatomy of Absurdity*. His hatred of Puritanism drew him into the *Martin Marprelate controversy, but it is not clear which of the unascribed anti-Martinist pamphlets were his work. In 1592 he published the polemical works *Pierce Penniless his Supplication to the Devil* and *Strange News of the Intercepting Certain Letters* (in response to Gabriel *Harvey's attack on Greene). An offensive passage about London in *Christ's Tears over Jerusalem* (1593) led to his imprisonment. *The *Unfortunate Traveller* (1594) is described in the dedication as 'being a clean different vein from other my former courses of writing'. It is a mixture of *picaresque narrative, literary parody, and mock-historical fantasy. Nashe returned to satire with *Have with You to Saffron-Walden, or Gabriel Harvey's Hunt is up* (1596), to which Harvey replied; in 1599 John Whitgift (1530/31?–1604), archbishop of Canterbury, ordered the suppression of both writers' works. *Nashe's Lenten Stuff* (1599), a mock encomium of the red herring (or kipper), includes a burlesque version of the story of *Hero and Leander. *Summer's Last Will and Testament* was published in 1600, though it had probably been written in the plague year of 1592-3. Nashe had a share in Christopher *Marlowe's *Dido Queen of Carthage, and probably other plays, including 1 *Henry VI. He was amusingly satirized as 'Ingenioso', a Cambridge graduate who lost favour with his patrons and turned to satire, in the three *Parnassus Plays (1598-1606). Nashe was mourned by Ben *Jonson and, admired by Thomas *Dekker and Thomas *Middleton

NATION, Terry (1930-97) Television scriptwriter, best known for *Dr Who's adversaries, the 'daleks'. He also created Survivors (1975-7), where post-catastrophe anxieties of writers like John *Wyndham or George R. *Stewart were replayed for the 1970s, and Blake's Seven (1978-81).

National Anthem Various 17th-century tunes more or less resemble that of 'God Save the King'; the closest resemblance is that of a galliard composed by John Bull. The words appear to date from the 1680s, but no author is known. The first recorded public performance of 'God Save the King' took place at Drury Lane Theatre on 28 September 1745, during the alarm caused by the *Jacobite invasion, and was prepared from a version in Thesaurus Musicus, a song collection of 1744, by Thomas *Arne, composer of *'Rule, Britannia'. It soon became customary to greet the king with the song when he entered a place of public entertainment. It was sung at the coronation banquet of George IV, confirming its popular status as 'National Anthem'. Political parodies of the words include the 'New National Anthem' written by P. B. *Shelley in 1819 after the Peterloo massacre, and the 'People's Anthem' (1848) of Ebenezer *Elliott.

National Theatre A three-auditorium complex on London's South Bank devoted to the spectrum of world drama. Initially proposed by a London publisher, Effingham Wilson, in 1848, the idea of a National Theatre Company only became a living reality at the Old Vic in 1963 under the direction of Laurence Olivier. In 1976 it moved into its South Bank home, under the direction of Sir Peter *Hall, Sir Richard Eyre, Trevor Nunn, and Nicholas Hytner, its repertoire has ranged from *Aeschylus and *Sophocles to Bertolt *Brecht and Sean *O'Casey. It has achieved particular success with new plays including the David *Hare trilogy, charting the decline of British institutions under Thatcherism, The Madness of George III and The History Boys by Alan *Bennett, Arcadia by Tom *Stoppard, Closer by Patrick *Marber

and Nick Stafford's adaptation of Michael *Morpurgo's War Horse. It became officially known as the Royal National Theatre in October 1988.

Native American literature The body of work by indigenous American writers. In the writings of James Fenimore *Cooper, Mayne *Reid, and others, American Indians, as they were called, were usually depicted as picturesquely wild or part of the past history of America. Early converts to Christianity gave a voice to these groups. William Apess (1798-1839), for instance, produced one of the first autobiographies (A Son of the Forest, 1829) by a Native American. Later in the 19th century, the researches of the Smithsonian Institution and of anthropologists like Alfred L. Kroeber (1876-1960; the father of Ursula *Le Guin) began to record Native American cultural practices. Notable Native American writers include Louise *Erdrich, Leslie Marmon Silko (1948-), Navarre Scott *Momaday, and many others. Gerald *Vizenor is a leading theoretician of the semiotics of 'indianness'.

naturalism An international movement in prose fiction that flourished during the final third of the 19th century and the early years of the 20th; it achieved some influence also on the drama of the period. It developed the existing tradition of *realism in the direction of fully documented accuracy of representation of social and economic circumstances, with additional deterministic emphases on the supposed scientific 'laws' of human behaviour, understood to be governed by heredity and economic necessity. In France, Émile *Zola was the dominant practitioner of naturalism in prose fiction and the chief exponent of its doctrines. His novel Thérèse Raquin (1867), together with the Goncourt brothers' Germinie Lacerteux (1865), are considered as marking the beginnings of the movement. Other French writers who shared the ideas and aims of naturalism are Alphonse Daudet, Guy de *Maupassant, and, in his early fiction, Joris-Karl Huysmans. In the English-speaking world, some of the ambitions and effects of naturalism are to be found in novels of the 1890s and beyond, notably in George *Moore's Esther Waters (1894), Thomas Hardy's *Jude the Obscure (1895), Somerset *Maugham's Liza of Lambeth (1897), Frank *Norris's McTeague (1899), Theodore *Dreiser's Sister Carrie (1900), and Arnold *Bennett's Anna of the Five Towns (1902). In the theatre, the term was applied to some realistic works written under the influence of Henrik *Ibsen, for example the plays of Gerhart Hauptmann in Germany, but is more often used more generally in reference to the 'naturalistic', (i.e. faithfully lifelike) impressions made by certain acting styles and authentic stage furnishings or costumes.

nature writing The English tradition of nature writing is commonly dated back to Gilbert *White's *Natural History and Antiquities of Selborne* (1789), closely followed by John *Clare and Dorothy *Wordsworth. The genre includes fiction and non-fiction, poetry and prose, *diaries, memoirs, and journalism, especially essays, and overlaps with *travel writing in its detailed attention to place. It encompasses observations on the natural world, particularly animals and birds; evocations of particular landscapes, for example mountains, islands, and rivers, and specific localities; and explorations of man's relationship with the environment. Landmark texts on the natural world include: Henry *Williamson's *Tarka the Otter* (1927), T. H. *White's *The Goshawk* (1951), and Gavin *Maxwell's *Ring of Bright Water* (1960). J. A. Baker's elegiac *The Peregrine* (1967) followed the pioneer ecologist Rachel Carson's *Silent Spring* (1962), on the catastrophic environmental effects of pesticides. Notable texts on places and landscapes include: Richard *Jefferies' *Wild Life in a Southern County* (1879, Wiltshire), W. H. *Hudson's *Hampshire Days* (1903), Edward *Thomas's *The South Country* (1906, Sussex), *The Living Mountain* (1977) by Nan *Shepherd, on the Grampians, Jim Perrin's *Visions of Snowdonia* (1997), and more recently Adam Nicolson's *Sea Room* (2001), Alice Oswald's *Dart* (2002), and Philip Gross's *The Water Table* (2009). In the 21st century, a campaigning environmentalist stance, arising from close engagement with nature, has been evident in the work of both younger writers and their mentors, particularly Robert Macfarlane (*Mountains of the Mind*, 2003; *The Wild Places*, 2007) and Roger Deakin (*Waterlog*, 1999; *Wildwood*, 2007); Mark Cocker (*Birds Britannica*, 2005; *Crow Country*, 2007) and Richard Mabey (*Nature Cure*, 2005; *Weeds*, 2010). Kathleen *Jamie's *Findings* (2005, essays) eschews the manly adventure story aspect of some wilderness writing; the work has been compared to Gilbert White.

The American tradition of nature writing is particularly associated with the *Transcendentalists, Henry David *Thoreau and Ralph Waldo *Emerson, the conservationist John Muir (1838–1914), and more recently with *Native American literature. Notable texts and writers include: Robinson *Jeffers, Willa *Cather, Peter *Matthiessen (*Wildlife in America*, 1959), Annie Dillard, *Pilgrim at Tinker Creek* (1975, Pulitzer Prize), and Barry Lopez, *Arctic Dreams* (1986).

Nausicaa *See* ODYSSEY.

NAYLER, James (1616/17–60) A Quaker who had served in the Parliamentary army, converted by George *Fox in 1651. His eloquence and tenderness of heart won him many disciples, especially disaffected women, with whom he challenged Fox for the leadership. His entry into Bristol on a donkey in 1656 accompanied by followers shouting 'Hosannah' brought him before the House of Commons on a charge of blasphemy, for which he was cruelly punished and imprisoned in Bridewell. Though he had split the movement, his contrite release in 1659 brought reconciliation with Fox. He wrote pamphlets of striking beauty and depth, especially *Milk for Babes* (published 1661).

NEALE, J. M. (John Mason) (1818–66) Scholar and hymn-writer; his many hymns (some of them translations from Greek, medieval Latin, and Eastern sources) include 'O happy band of pilgrims', 'Art thou weary', and 'Jerusalem the Golden'. *Hymns Ancient and Modern* owes much to his inspiration.

Nedham (Needham), Marchamont (1620–78) Journalist, and chief author of *Mercurius Britanicus* (1643–6), the arch-enemy of the Royalist *Mercurius Aulicus* of Sir John *Berkenhead. In 1660, after some years of considerable power as editor of *Mercurius Politicus*, he fled to the Netherlands, obtained a pardon, and returned to England, where he practised medicine and continued to write pamphlets. He was also the author of verses and a translation of John *Selden's *Mare Clausum* (1652). *See also* NEWSPAPERS.

negative capability A phrase coined by John *Keats to describe his conception of the receptivity necessary to the process of poetic creativity, which draws on S. T. *Coleridge's formulation of 'Negative Belief' or 'willing suspension of disbelief'. In a letter to Benjamin Bailey (1791–1853; 22 Nov. 1817) Keats wrote, 'If a Sparrow come before my Window I take part in its existence and pick about the Gravel', and a month later (22 Dec. 1817) he wrote to his brothers George and Thomas defining his new concept: '*Negative Capability*, that is when man is capable of being in uncertainties, Mysteries, doubts, without any irritable reaching after fact and reason—'. Keats regarded Shakespeare as the prime example of negative capability, attributing to him the ability to identify completely with his characters, and to write about them with empathy and understanding; he contrasts this with the partisan approach of *Milton and the 'wordsworthian or egotistical sublime' (Letter to Richard Woodhouse (1788–1834); 27 Oct. 1818) of William *Wordsworth. However, he was ambivalent about his own attitude, and sometimes expressed admiration for the Miltonic approach.

NEILSON, Anthony (1967–) Scottish playwright, whose work includes *Normal: The Düsseldorf Ripper* (1991), *The Wonderful World of Dissocia* (2004), *Realism* (2006), and *God in Ruins* (2007). Neilson, whose uncompromising plays characteristically explore conditions of mental instability or social alienation, came to notice through his identification with the 'In-yer-face' drama linked with the *Royal Court Theatre of the 1990s.

NELSON, Robert (1656–1715) Devotional writer, *nonjuror, friend of John *Tillotson, and active early member of the *SPCK. His *Companion for the Festivals and Fasts of the Church of England* (1704), designed as an aid to the Book of *Common Prayer, and *Practice of True Devotion* (1708) were very popular until the mid-19th century.

NENNIUS (*fl. c.*770–810) Mistakenly believed, on the basis of a single revision, to be the author or reviser of the *Historia Brittonum*. He may have been a pupil of Elfoddw, bishop of Bangor (d. 809). Composed in Wales *c.*829–30, the *Historia* is a collection of materials on the history and geography of Britain, and claims to give an account of the historical *Arthur who led the Britons against the Saxons in twelve battles. It is one of the sources on which *Geoffrey of Monmouth drew for his *Historia Regum Britanniae*. A mixture of legend and history, it is characterized by pride in the Celtic people of Britain and interest in its topography.

neo-classicism In literature, the practice of imitating the great authors of Greek and Roman antiquity (notably its poets and dramatists) as a matter of aesthetic principle; and the acceptance of the critical precepts which emerged to guide that imitation.

Medieval writers had often used classical works for models, but *Petrarch in the 14th century was the first to do so because he considered it the only way to produce great literature. The *epic, *eclogue, *elegy, *ode, *satire, *tragedy, *comedy, and *epigram of ancient times all found imitators, first in Latin, then in the vernaculars. In the 16th century the previously neglected *Poetics of Aristotle was repeatedly edited, translated, and supplied with commentaries. *Castelvetro, author of the most influential of these (1570), and *Scaliger, author of the controversial *Poëtice* (1561), were amongst the theoreticians who imprisoned imitation within a rigid framework of rules, for which the flexibility of ancient practice offered little precedent. The observance of the dramatic *unities of time, place, and action won widespread support in 17th-century France. With the exception of Ben *Jonson, neo-classicism had little influence in England before the appearance of Boileau's *L'Art poétique* (1674), and of Thomas *Rymer's *Tragedies of the Last Age Considered* (1678), which influenced John *Dryden and other playwrights. Dryden's *All for Love* (1678) was a neo-classical version of Shakespeare's *Antony and Cleopatra*, while Joseph *Addison's *Cato* (1713) has been called the only correct neo-classical tragedy in English. At the same time the inescapable presence of *Shakespeare in English literary culture provided a stubborn obstacle to the domestication of French neo-classical principles. In the later 18th century neo-classicism was challenged by the alternative critical doctrine of the *sublime, as well as a patriotic revaluation of native *folk traditions and a *Romantic Hellenism which drew on Greek myth and landscape rather than cultural authority. *See also* AUGUSTAN AGE.

Neoplatonism A philosophical and religious system, combining Platonic ideas with Persian, Indian, and Egyptian theology, developed in Alexandria in the 3rd century AD by *Plotinus, an Egyptian philosopher whose *Enneads* were edited by Porphyry (*c.*233–309). He taught that there is a supreme 'One' transcending all human concepts, from which the universe emanated. Plotinus' successor Iamblichus (*c.*245–325) posited the existence of innumerable lesser gods, demons, and other superhumans, who could give knowledge of the future and influence events. Proclus (412–85) introduced an order of 'henads' between the One and the universe, whom he identified with the classical Greek gods. Transcendence of the material world, the soul's return to the One at death, and the belief that evil has no existence but is simply the absence of good are other features of Neoplatonic thought. Augustine's early attachment to Neoplatonism affected the development of Christianity, and in the Middle Ages Neoplatonic ideas also influenced Jewish cabbalists and Islamic and Sufi thinkers. From the 5th and 6th centuries Neoplatonism sometimes overlapped with *Gnosticism. In the Renaissance Neoplatonism was revived and variously refashioned by *Ficino, *Pico della Mirandola, *Agrippa, and *Paracelsus and tended to become associated with alchemy, Hermeticism, and magic. It influenced literature in a number of ways. The Neoplatonic theory that earthly love and beauty are images of spiritual absolutes, as expounded in Edmund *Spenser's *Hymns*, is common in love poetry. Prospero in The *Tempest is an example of a Neoplatonic magician who can raise spirits, and he had real-life counterparts in the 16th and 17th centuries. The Attendant Spirit or Daemon in Milton's *Comus* is Neoplatonic, as, on a humorous level, are the sylphs of The *Rape of the Lock*. The attempt to bring together all systems of belief that maintained the power of spirit over matter appears in Thomas Vaughan and in the writings of the *Cambridge Platonists.

Neo-Romanticism A movement in painting, literature, book illustration, film, and theatre from the late 1930s to the early 1950s. The term was first used in 1942 to designate figurative work by artists including Paul Nash (1889–1946), John Piper (1903–92), and Graham Sutherland (1903–80), who turned for inspiration to Samuel Palmer and J. M. W. *Turner, and to the landscape vision of the *Romantic poets. Characterized by the powerful evocation of place, and allegiance to a distinctively English tradition, Neo-Romanticism flourished during the Second World War. A younger generation of Neo-Romantics included Michael Ayrton, John Minton (1917–57), and John Craxton (1922–2009). Their work tended to be more explicitly melancholic, and more concerned with individual psychic states than with the representation of landscape. This later vein of Neo-Romanticism found literary expression in the writing of the New Apocalypse group, which included Dylan *Thomas and Norman *MacCaig.

Neptune (Greek Poseidon) In classical mythology the powerful god of the sea and brother of *Jupiter. In the *Iliad* he opposes the Trojans, but in the *Odyssey* he repeatedly thwarts the Greek Odysseus on his voyage home, and in *Aeneid* Book 1 he calms the sea after *Juno raises a storm to wreck the Trojan ships. His violent desire for Leander inadvertently drowns the young man in Christopher *Marlowe and George *Chapman's Hero and Leander.

NERUDA, Pablo (1904–73) Pen-name of the Chilean poet Ricardo Eliecer Neftalí Reyes Basoalto, the best-known 20th-century poet from Spanish America, Neruda was brought up in the southern Chilean town of Temuco. He travelled widely in the diplomatic service from 1927 to the early 1940s (in South-East Asia, Argentina, Spain, and Mexico), and supported the Spanish Republic during the Spanish Civil War. Having been appointed by the socialist president Salvador Allende (father of Isabel *Allende) as Chilean ambassador in Paris, he was awarded the *Nobel Prize for Literature in 1971. He died in Santiago de Chile shortly after Pinochet's coup. Neruda published over 40 volumes of poetry. His first major collection, *Veinte poemas de amor y una canción desesperada* (1924: *Twenty Love Poems and a Song of Despair*) draws upon *Romanticism and *Symbolism; it became the most popular collection of poetry ever written in Spanish. The first two volumes of his *Residencia en la tierra* (1933 and 1935: *Residence on Earth*) made him a leader of the avant-garde. His most ambitious collection was an alternative history of Latin America, his epic *Canto general* (1950: *General Song*), much of which he wrote on the run from the Chilean police and which consolidated his reputation. Subsequent volumes ranged from endearing odes dedicated to simple objects like an onion or a pair of winter socks, to propaganda, autobiographical verse, and short, intensely personal, and often amorous, lyrics.

NESBIT, E. (Edith) (1858–1924) Author, central to the development of 20th-century children's literature, both in her tone of address and her social ideas. She was closely associated with the Fabian Society, notably with George Bernard *Shaw. Her first book of poetry, *Lays and Legends* (1886), was admired by Algernon *Swinburne and Rider *Haggard. She produced hack-work to support her family, including retellings of *Shakespeare (1897). *The Story of the Treasure Seekers* (1899) was her first successful children's book; it was followed by *Five Children and It* (1902; adapted for BBC TV by Helen *Cresswell, 1991; filmed, 2004) and *The Railway Children* (1906); filmed, 1970; adapted for television, 1957, 1968, and 2000).

New Apocalypse A group of writers who flourished briefly as a group in the 1940s, united by a reaction against what they saw as the 'classicism' of W. H. *Auden. It was characterized by wild, turbulent, and at times surreal imagery. George *Barker, Vernon *Watkins, and Henry *Treece were associated with the movement.

New Atlantis, The An unfinished work by Francis *Bacon, posthumously published at the end of a volume containing his *Sylva Sylvarum, or A Natural History* (1627; some copies dated 1626). William Rawley (c.1558–1667), Bacon's chaplain and literary executor, called it a 'fable' devised to describe 'a college instituted for the interpreting of nature and the producing of great and marvellous works for the benefit of men, under the name of Salomon's House, or the College of the Six Days' Works'—alluding to the biblical account of the Creation. It begins with the narrative of a sea voyage in the Pacific, in which a ship gets blown off course into unknown waters near Peru, and lands on an island resembling the lost island of Atlantis, as described by *Plato in the *Timaeus* and *Critias*. The whole work expressed Bacon's forward-looking belief that scientific research could flourish only as a collective pursuit, and its vision had an inspiring effect in the mid-17th century, acknowledged by those associated with the *Royal Society such as Robert Hooke (1635–1703), Sir William Petty, John *Evelyn, Thomas Sprat, and Joseph *Glanvill.

NEWBERY, John (1713–67) Bookseller, a pioneer publisher of children's books. Oliver *Goldsmith, who contributed the papers later gathered as *The *Citizen of the World* to Newbery's *Public Ledger*, may have written the much-imitated 'Goody Two-Shoes' for Newbery; 'the philanthropic bookseller' in *The *Vicar of Wakefield* is based on the publisher.

NEWBY, Eric (1919–2006) Travel writer, the author of more than twenty books, of which the best known is *A Short Walk in the Hindu Kush* (1958). They stand in the comic tradition of A. W. *Kinglake, Robert *Byron, and Evelyn *Waugh, with Newby usually depicting himself as a bumbling Englishman abroad, always somewhat out of his depth. The tone is more sombre in *Love and War in the Apennines* (1971), probably Newby's best work, which recounts a period spent on the run as an escaped prisoner of war in Italy during the Second World War. He was made a CBE in 1994.

NEWBY, P. H. (Percy Howard) (1918–97) Novelist and broadcaster. His first two novels, *A Journey to the Interior* (1945) and *Agents and Witnesses* (1947), draw on his wartime experiences and broad knowledge of Egyptian society. Other works include *Something to Answer for* (1968), which won the first *Booker Prize, and *Feelings Have Changed* (1981).

NEWCASTLE, Margaret Cavendish, duchess of (1623–73) Writer, the second wife of William Cavendish, first duke of *Newcastle. Her *Poems and Fancies* (1653), which displays her interest in chemistry and natural philosophy, was followed by many other works, including plays, letters, and an affectionate, vivid, and informal biography of her husband (1667). She was praised (and influenced) by Thomas *Hobbes, and both Charles *Lamb and Virginia *Woolf wrote of her with sympathy. She was one of the first women to attend a meeting of the *Royal Society. Her *autobiography, *A True Relation of my Birth, Breeding and Life*, was appended to her collection of fictions, *Nature's Pictures* (1656). She regarded the female intelligence as distinguished by its fantastical quality, which she demonstrated by wearing outrageous fashions of her own devising.

NEWCASTLE, William Cavendish, first duke of (1592–1676) Husband of Margaret Cavendish, duchess of *Newcastle. He supported the king generously during the Civil War, and from 1644 lived abroad, often in much poverty, until the *Restoration. He was the author of several poems and plays, collaborating in the latter with James *Shirley, whose patron he was, and with John *Dryden and Thomas *Shadwell.

Newcomes, The A novel by W. M. *Thackeray, published 1853–5. Colonel Thomas Newcome is an unworldly soldier who has spent his career in India. His half-brothers Hobson and Brian are wealthy and pretentious. His son Clive loves Ethel, daughter of Sir Brian Newcome, but Ethel's ruthless brother Barnes and her grandmother Lady Kew want her to make a grand marriage. Though Ethel is independent-minded, she allows herself to become engaged first to her cousin Lord Kew, and then to the wealthy Lord Farintosh. Barnes's own disastrous marriage persuades her to remain single. Meanwhile Clive has been manoeuvred into marriage with a superficial girl, Rosey Mackenzie. Colonel Newcome's fortune is lost with the failure of a fraudulent bank, and the family is reduced to poverty. Rosey's discontented mother makes life so intolerable for the Colonel that he takes refuge in the Grey Friars almshouse, where he dies, in one of the most famously affecting scenes in Victorian fiction. Rosey also dies, and Thackeray allows the reader to assume that Clive and Ethel will marry. The novel is remarkable for its vituperative attacks on the cynicism and greed of the mid-Victorian marriage market.

New Criticism An important movement in American literary criticism in the period 1935–60, characterized by close attention to the verbal nuances of lyric poems, considered as self-sufficient objects detached from their biographical and historical origins. In reaction against the then dominant routines of academic literary history, the New Critics insisted that a poem should not be reduced to its paraphrased 'content', but understood in its own terms as a complex unity of verbal ironies, ambiguities, and paradoxes. They repudiated what they called the 'extrinsic' approaches to poetry—historical, psychological, or sociological—and cultivated an 'intrinsic' understanding of the actual 'words on the page'.

The early phase of the New Critical campaign was led by Southern poets and university teachers: J. C. *Ransom and his former student Allen *Tate, along with R. P. *Warren and Cleanth *Brooks, editors of the *Southern Review* (1935–42). The name applied to this movement comes from the title of Ransom's book *The New Criticism* (1941), which surveys the critical work of T. S. *Eliot, I. A. *Richards, and William *Empson in Britain, from which the New Critics clearly derived their inspiration. While Ransom and Tate formulated the theoretical principles, Brooks and Warren, notably in their textbook *Understanding Poetry* (1938), applied them to the teaching of literature in universities. More marginal contributions to the cause came from R. P. *Blackmur (*The Double Agent*, 1935) and Yvor *Winters (*Primitivism and Decadence*, 1937).

From 1939, when Ransom founded the *Kenyon Review* and Brooks published his *Modern Poetry and the Tradition*, the New Criticism made important headway in the universities; notably at Yale, where a second wave of New Critical theory was represented by *Theory of Literature* (1949) by René Wellek (1903–95) and Austin Warren (1899–1986), and by *The Verbal Icon* (1954) by W. K. Wimsatt (1907–75), with essays written by M. C. Beardsley (*see* INTENTIONAL FALLACY). The most celebrated work of 'applied' New Criticism was Brooks's *The Well Wrought Urn* (1947).

By the late 1950s, New Criticism had become an academic orthodoxy which younger critics found to be not only inapplicable to genres other than lyric poetry but narrow in its exclusion of social and historical dimensions of literature.

Newgate Calendar, The The title was originally used to signify a simple list of convicts in Newgate prison in London, but about 1773

appeared *The Newgate Calendar, or Malefactors Bloody Register*, a five-volume biographical compilation of notorious criminals from 1700 to that date. Similar large-scale anthologies of crime appeared in the next 50 years under varying titles, including *The Malefactor's Register, or The Newgate and Tyburn Calendar* (1779, much reprinted). Andrew Knapp and William Baldwin, attorneys-at-law, issued *Criminal Chronology* (1809), *The Newgate Calendar* (1824–6), and *The New Newgate Calendar* (1826). Plots derived from the Calendars appear in novels by Harrison *Ainsworth (*Jack Sheppard* and *Rookwood*), Edward *Bulwer-Lytton (*Pelham* and *Eugene Aram*), and William Godwin (*Caleb Williams*), and in Thomas *Hood's poem 'The Dream of Eugene Aram'. William Thackeray's *Catherine* and Charles Dickens's *Oliver Twist* also derived material from the Calendars.

Newgate novel *See* AINSWORTH, WILLIAM HARRISON.

New Grub Street A novel by George *Gissing, published 1891. It describes the jealousies and intrigues of the literary world of his time, and the effect of poverty on artistic endeavour. It contrasts the career of Jasper Milvain, the unscrupulous writer of reviews (who accepts the materialistic conditions of literary success), and Edwin Reardon, author of two fine works. Amy, Edwin's wife, leaves him in despair. Jasper marries Amy, the widow of Edwin, who was driven into an early grave by failure and the loss of his wife. The sombre story ends with Jasper's success, the triumph of self-advertisement over artistic integrity.

New Historicism A term applied to a trend in American academic literary studies in the 1980s that emphasized the historical nature of literary texts and at the same time (in contradistinction from 'old' historicisms) the 'textual' nature of history. As part of a wider reaction against purely formal or linguistic critical approaches such as the *New Criticism and *deconstruction, the New Historicists, led by Stephen Greenblatt (1943–), drew new connections between literary and non-literary texts, breaking down the familiar distinctions between a text and its historical 'background' as conceived in previous historical forms of criticism. Inspired by Michel *Foucault's concepts of discourse and power, they attempted to show in detail how literary works are entangled in the power relations of their time, not as secondary 'reflections' of any coherent world-view but as active participants in the continual remaking of meanings. New Historicism is less a system of interpretation than a set of shared assumptions about the relationship between literature and history, and an essayistic style that often develops general reflections from a startling historical or anthropological anecdote. Of Greenblatt's books, *Renaissance Self-Fashioning* (1980) and *Shakespearean Negotiations* (1988) are the exemplary models. While American New Historicism, following Foucault, tends to argue that literary dissent is harmlessly contained by 'power', the otherwise similar movement in Britain known as 'cultural materialism' parts company with it on this point, insisting that no ruling authority can neutralize every form of cultural subversion. The cultural materialists, such as Jonathan Dollimore, Catherine Belsey, and Alan Sinfield, are more closely aligned with *Marxist literary criticism, notably through the work of Raymond *Williams, and show a stronger interest in the adaptation, reproduction, and institutionalization of texts, especially those of Shakespeare.

New Inn, The, *or The Light Heart* A comedy by Ben *Jonson, performed in 1629 by the King's Men, printed 1631. Jonson records in his dedication that the play was hissed at its first performance, but it was successfully performed by the Royal Shakespeare Company in 1987.

New Journalism The title of a 1973 collection edited by Tom *Wolfe and E. W. Johnson, since used to describe a mode of journalism which incorporates first-person narration, gives prominence to the reporter, and uses other novelistic strategies. Practitioners of this mode include Truman *Capote, Norman *Mailer, Joan *Didion, and Hunter S. *Thompson. *See* GONZO JOURNALISM.

NEWLAND, Courttia (1973–) A dramatist and fiction writer of Caribbean heritage, who says, 'Telling untold stories keeps me alive.' His novels include *The Scholar* (1997) and *Snakeskin* (2002). His recent works are a novella, *The Dying Wish* (2006), and a short story collection, *Music for the Off-Key* (2006).

New Lines (1956) An anthology edited by Robert *Conquest, containing work by himself, Elizabeth *Jennings, John Holloway (1920–99), Philip *Larkin, Thom *Gunn, Kingsley *Amis, D. J. *Enright, Donald *Davie, and John *Wain, poets associated with the *Movement. In his introduction Conquest attacked obscure and over-metaphorical poetry, presenting the claims of 'rational structure and

comprehensible language'. *New Lines Volume II* (1963) added other poets including Anthony *Thwaite, Vernon *Scannell, and George *MacBeth.

NEWMAN, John Henry (1801–90) Theologian, cardinal, and writer. He became a fellow of Oriel College, Oxford, where he came in contact with John *Keble and Edward Pusey and later with Richard Hurrell Froude. He wrote much of the *Lyra Apostolica* while in Rome with Froude. In 1833 he resolved with William Palmer (1803–85), Froude, and A. P. Perceval (1799–1853) to fight for the doctrine of apostolic succession and the integrity of the Prayer Book, and began *Tracts for the Times* (*see* OXFORD MOVEMENT). He was moving slowly towards the Roman Catholic Church, and in 1841 his celebrated *Tract XC*, on the compatibility of the Articles with Catholic theology, roused great opposition and brought the Tractarians under official ban. In 1843 he resigned the living of St Mary's, and in 1845 he joined the Church of Rome. He went to Rome in 1846 and was ordained; on his return in 1847 he established the Oratory in Birmingham. His lectures and essays on university education appeared in various forms from 1852, and finally as *The Idea of a University Defined and Illustrated* (1873). In these he maintained that the duty of a university is instruction rather than research, and to train the mind rather than to diffuse useful knowledge. His *Apologia pro Vita Sua* (1864) appeared in answer to Charles *Kingsley, who had remarked in *Macmillan's Magazine* that Newman did not consider truth a necessary virtue. It is an exposition of his spiritual history, written with feeling, which displays his formidable powers of argument. His poem *The Dream of Gerontius* (later set to music by Edward *Elgar) appeared in the *Month* in 1865, and in book form in 1866; it is a vision of a soul leaving the body at death, and includes the hymn 'Praise to the Holiest in the height'. In 1870 he published *The Grammar of Assent*, an examination of the nature of belief. In 1879 Newman was created cardinal.

Newman's other writings include two novels, published anonymously, *Loss and Gain* (1848) and *Callista* (1856), many volumes of sermons, lectures, and lives of saints.

New Monthly Magazine (1814–84) A periodical co-founded by Henry Colburn and F. Schoberi, in opposition to the *Jacobin *Monthly Magazine*. Under Thomas *Campbell, editor from 1821, it became more literary in interest. Thomas Talfourd wrote well on William *Wordsworth, Charles *Lamb, John *Keats, and others; and among other distinguished editors were Edward *Bulwer-Lytton, Thomas *Hood, Theodore *Hook, and Harrison *Ainsworth.

New Negro Phrase in use from *c*.1895 onwards to describe the changing situation of African Americans, especially as re-examined by themselves. The *Harlem Renaissance was also known as the New Negro Movement.

News Chronicle See DAILY NEWS.

newsletters A term specially applied to the manuscript records of parliamentary and court news, sent twice a week to subscribers from the London office of Henry *Muddiman in the second half of the 17th century.

newspapers, origins of The direct ancestors of newspapers devoted to English news were the Dutch *corantos, newsbooks dealing with foreign events. The first to appear in English was a single-sheet publication, *The New Tydings out of Italie Are Not Yet Com* (Amsterdam, 2 Dec. 1620), followed by a second number, *Corrant out of Italy, Germany &c* (Amsterdam, 23 Dec. 1620), printed by Joris Veseler for Dutch map-engraver Pieter van der Keere. The first English weekly of home news appeared in November 1641 (*Heads of Severall Proceedings in This Present Parliament*), shortly followed by various other publications, for example Samuel Pecke's *A Perfect Diurnall*, Richard Colling's *Kingdomes Weekly Intelligencer*, Sir John *Berkenhead's *Mercurius Aulicus* edited from the Royalist headquarters in Oxford, *Mercurius Civicus*, which was the first to be illustrated with woodcuts, and, perhaps the most popular, *Mercurius Britanicus*, edited by Thomas Audley and the most professional journalist of the period, Marchamont *Nedham. Decreasingly efficient censorship and the stirring political climate stimulated demand for news, and by 1645 fourteen papers were on sale in English in London, including John Dillingham's *Moderate Intelligencer*. In 1647 appeared the pro-Royalist *Mercurius Pragmaticus*, edited by Nedham, John *Cleveland, and the minor poet Samuel Sheppard (*c*.1624–?1655); in 1648 the *Moderate*, edited by chief censor Gilbert Mabbott, became the first paper consistently to preach a radical programme. This period of rapid journalistic expansion also saw the birth of many unlicensed, short-lived, and counterfeit newsbooks, as well as the publication of literally thousands of pamphlets (*see* PAMPHLETEERING). The thirst for information introduced many new readers

to familiarity with the printed word and created a new class of professional journalist. This vigorous proliferation came to a sudden end in September 1649 when Parliament passed a stringent printing law with heavy fines which effectively silenced all the licensed weeklies, while authorizing two new papers, one to deal with army news, the other with news from Westminster. This left Nedham with a virtual monopoly of information in his official *Mercurius Politicus* and its close relation the *Publik Intelligencer* (1650–60): Nedham, having offended various shades of political opinion, fled to the Netherlands in 1660. His place was taken by Henry *Muddiman, who started his career as spokesman for the revived monarchy in 1659 with the *Parliamentary Intelligencer*, later *Kingdomes Intelligencer*. In 1665 he founded the *Oxford Gazette*, the first real newspaper. See L'ESTRANGE, SIR ROGER.

NEWTON, Sir Isaac (1642–1727) Scientist; he became Lucasian professor of mathematics at Cambridge in 1669, master of the mint in 1696, and president of the *Royal Society in 1703. His major scientific works were *Philosophiae Naturalis Principia Mathematica* (1687), *Opticks* (1704), and *Arithmetica Universalis* (1707). Newtonianism was the dominant philosophy of the *Enlightenment, influencing all fields of science, and finding its way into the poetry of Alexander *Pope, James *Thomson, and Edward *Young. Modern scholarship has not seriously affected his stature in the fields of mathematics, dynamics, celestial mechanics, astronomy, optics, natural philosophy, or cosmology. Newton was however attacked by Jonathan *Swift, and more fundamental opposition to Newtonian materialism came from *Goethe and William *Blake. Newton had in fact written more than two million words on alchemy; he was as steeped in the hermetic tradition as the mystical romantics, and the extent of his dedication to theology, biblical chronology, prophecy, and alchemy is now more fully appreciated. In these latter spheres, Newton is close in spirit to the *Cambridge Platonists.

NEWTON, John (1725–1807) Evangelical clergyman and former slave trader. His autobiography, *An Authentic Narrative* (1764), gives a vivid picture of his ordeals at sea and the beginning of his evangelical conversion. He became curate of Olney, Buckinghamshire, in 1764 and with William *Cowper wrote *Olney Hymns* (1779), his most famous contribution being 'Amazing grace'. See also HYMNS.

New Wave science fiction Term (almost certainly echoing the late 1950s 'new wave' of French cinema) given to the *science fiction (or *speculative fiction) published under the editorship of Michael *Moorcock in *New Worlds* magazine (1964–71). More generally applied to the work of Moorcock and others, including Brian *Aldiss, J. G. *Ballard, Harlan Ellison, Thomas M. Disch, John *Sladek, Samuel R. Delany, and Judith *Merril, who were dissatisfied with the standards and subject matter of contemporary science fiction. Moorcock and Ballard's championing of William *Burroughs emphasized experimentation, taboo-breaking, and wider literary ambitions. 'New Wave' writing faded in the early 1970s, but had a lasting impact on science fiction.

New Way to Pay Old Debts, A A comedy by Philip *Massinger, acted probably in 1625–6, published 1633. The play deals with the downfall of Sir Giles Overreach, a character based in part on the notorious extortioner Sir Giles Mompesson (1584–?1651).

New Weird Term given to an amorphous literary movement focusing on *horror and *speculative fiction, dating (broadly speaking) from the 1990s; less a school than a way of describing very different writers united only in avoiding the conventional. China *Miéville's preference for 'weird' rather than 'science' or 'fantasy' fiction to describe his work suggests the hybridity harking back to H. P. *Lovecraft, or Arthur *Machen. Michael Cisco (1970–) suggests that New Weird might simply be seen as a refusal to accept the boundaries between *general* and *genre* literature, noting the mention of writers like *Borges, *Calvino, and Angela *Carter among its 'practitioners'.

New Woman fiction A term used to describe late 19th-century writings which foreground the ideas and actions of the 'New Woman', a phrase said to have been coined by *Ouida when responding to Sarah *Grand's article 'The New Aspects of the Woman Question', 1894. Grand's own novels, like *The Heavenly Twins* (1893) and *The Beth Book* (1897), include many elements associated with this movement: attacks on sexual double standards; demands for better employment and educational opportunities for women; frankness about matters like venereal disease, contraception, and sex education; and questioning of traditional attitudes towards marriage and woman's place in the family and in relation to motherhood. The first example of the genre is probably Olive *Schreiner's *Story of an African Farm* (1883). Other significant contributors include Emma Francis *Brooke, Mona *Caird, Ella Hepworth *Dixon, George *Egerton, and Ménie Muriel *Dowie. Male writers who addressed similar themes include Henrik *Ibsen, George *Gissing, and Thomas *Hardy. Grant *Allen, Margaret *Oliphant, and Eliza Lynn *Linton were notably unsympathetic.

New Yorker An American weekly magazine founded in 1925 by Harold Ross (1892–1951). Famed for its humour. writers and cartoonists associated with it include James *Thurber, Ogden *Nash, S. J. Perelman (1904–79), and John *Updike. It has also published distinguished articles of reportage, including, notably, 'Hiroshima' by John *Hersey, which occupied an entire issue in 1946.

New York School Phrase attached to a group of artists, poets, and less commonly musicians active in New York from the 1950s onwards. The New York poets, including John *Ashbery, Kenneth Koch (1925–2002), Frank *O'Hara, and James *Schuyler, moved away from a *confessional style, experimenting with light, visual, and urban subjects partly influenced by *Surrealism.

NGUGI WA THIONG'O (1938–) Kenyan writer who changed his name from James Ngugi when he stopped writing in English and began publishing in Gikuyu. Both decisions were motivated by his belief that writing in the language of the colonizer alienated Africans from their own culture. His essays on postcolonial politics have been as influential as his fiction and plays: *Homecoming* (1972); *Writers in Politics* (1981); *Barrel of a Pen* (1983); *Decolonising the Mind* (1986); *Moving the Centre* (1993); *Penpoints, Gunpoints, and Dreams* (1998). His play in Gikuyu, translated as *I Will Marry When I Want* and co-written with Ngugi wa Mirii as a literacy project, was performed by a peasant cast to huge audiences in 1977; its licence was withdrawn and Ngugi was detained for a year. *Detained: A Writer's Prison Diary* (1981) is a scathing attack on neocolonialism. Ngugi went into exile in 1982. His novels include *The River Between* (1965), set around 1930; *Weep Not, Child* (1964), set during the State of Emergency occasioned by the Mau Mau uprising; and *A Grain of Wheat* (1967), which deploys dislocating shifts in perspective to enact for the reader the fragmentation of Kenyan society at the moment of independence. *Petals of Blood* (1977), a modernist version of crime fiction, depicts a community's attempt to realize the dream of national identity in opposition to global capitalism. *Devil on the Cross* (1982), *Matigari* (1987), and *Wizard of the Crow* (2006) engage directly with Gikuyu orality. *Dreams in a Time of War* (2010) is a memoir.

Nibelungenlied A Middle High German epic poem of the early 13th century of unknown authorship. Its story is found in primitive shape in both forms of the *Edda where it is substantially the same as that told by William *Morris in *Sigurd the Volsung*. The story in the *Nibelungenlied* is set in the contemporary world of chivalry and differs in detail. Siegfried, son of Siegmund and Sieglind, king and queen of the Netherlands, having got possession of the Nibelung hoard, rides to woo Kriemhild, a Burgundian princess, sister of Gunther, Gernot, and Giselher. Hagen, their grim retainer, later treacherously kills Siegfried at a hunt. Kriemhild later marries Etzel (Attila), king of the Huns, and in order to avenge her husband and secure the hoard, which her brothers have seized and sunk in the Rhine, persuades them to visit Etzel's court. The poem, which recounts the death of all the major figures, is pervaded with a powerful sense of inevitable tragedy. *Der Ring des Nibelungen* is Richard *Wagner's version.

Nicholas Nickleby A novel by Charles *Dickens, published 1838–9. Nicholas, a high-spirited boy of 19, his mother, and his gentle sister Kate are left penniless on the death of his father. They appeal to his callous and grasping uncle, Ralph Nickleby, of whom Nicholas makes an enemy by his independent bearing. Nicholas is sent to work at Dotheboys Hall, where Wackford Squeers starves and maltreats 40 urchins under pretence of education. His special cruelty is expended on the half-witted Smike, left on his hands and employed as a drudge. The infuriated Nicholas thrashes Squeers and escapes with Smike. He supports himself and Smike as an actor in the company of Vincent Crummles; he then enters the service of the benevolent Cheeryble brothers. Meanwhile Kate, apprenticed to Madame Mantalini, dressmaker, is exposed to the lecherous designs of Sir Mulberry Hawk, one of Ralph's associates. She is rescued by Nicholas, who breaks Sir Mulberry's head and makes a home for his mother and sister. Nicholas himself falls in love with Madeline Bray, the support of a selfish father. Ralph intends to marry Madeline to Gride, a revolting old moneylender. Ralph, whose hatred for Nicholas is intensified by the failure of his plans, knowing Nicholas's affection for Smike, con-

spires to remove the boy; his plots are thwarted with the help of Newman Noggs, his eccentric clerk, but nevertheless Smike declines, and eventually dies in Nicholas's arms. Confronted with ruin and exposure, and shattered by the discovery that Smike was his own son, Ralph hangs himself. Nicholas, befriended by the Cheerybles, marries Madeline, and Kate marries the Cheerybles' nephew Frank. Squeers is transported, and Gride is murdered.

NICHOLS, Grace (1950–) Poet and children's writer, born in Guyana. Her first collection of poetry, *I Is a Long-Memoried Woman* (1983), established her reputation for wittily demonstrating the literary qualities of *Creole for exploring Caribbean history, folklore, and myth, including Amerindian, Aztec, and Inca civilizations. Other volumes include *The Fat Black Woman's Poems* (1984), *Lazy Thoughts of a Lazy Woman* (1989), *Sunrise* (1996), and *Startling the Flying Fish* (2006). She is also a prolific writer of children's stories and poems. She is the partner of John *Agard.

NICHOLS, John (1745–1826) Printer and antiquary, editor and manager of the *Gentleman's Magazine* from 1792 until his death. In that role Nichols built up an invaluable collection of letters and documents, later published in nine volumes as *Literary Anecdotes of the Eighteenth Century* (1812–16), with further instalments in the eight-volume *Illustrations of the Literary History of the Eighteenth Century* (1817–58), the project being completed by his son.

NICHOLS, Peter (1927–) Playwright, whose works include *A Day in the Death of Joe Egg* (1967), in which a schoolteacher and his wife struggle to share the burden of their handicapped daughter Joe; *The National Health* (1969), a satirical hospital comedy which contrasts reality with soap opera; *Forget-Me-Not-Lane* (1971), a family drama; and *Privates on Parade* (1977), set in Malaysia, whose hero reappears in the post-war setting of *Lingua Franca* (2010). *Feeling You're Behind* (1984) is an autobiography; many of his plays reflect his own experiences.

NICHOLS, Robert (1893–1944) Poet and playwright. His volumes of poems, *Invocation* (1915) and *Ardours and Endurances* (1917), were highly regarded and he appeared in *Georgian Poetry*. After *Aurelia* (1920) he turned unsuccessfully to writing plays.

NICHOLSON, Norman (1914–87) Poet, born in the working-class iron town of Millom, Cumberland, where he lived all his life (apart from a spell in a sanatorium, suffering from tuberculosis) and which became the theme of most of his work. He evokes its buildings, its dying industry, its people, its geology, and the surrounding rural landscape in several volumes of verse, including *Five Rivers* (1944), *The Pot Geranium* (1954), and *A Local Habitation* (1972), the title of which indicates the intense, precise rootedness of his poetry. His *Collected Poems* (ed. Neil Curry) appeared in 1994.

NÍ CHUILLEANÁIN, EILÉAN (1942–) Poet and translator; her austere, anecdotal, sometimes slyly humorous lyrics conjure an enigmatic world in which vividly rendered details assume the dimensions of parable or myth. Her volumes include *Acts and Monuments* (1972), *Site of Ambush* (1975), *The Rose Geranium* (1981), *The Magdalene Sermon* (1989), *The Brazen Serpent* (1994), *The Girl who Married the Reindeer* (2001), and *The Sun-fish* (2009).

Nicolette *See* AUCASSIN AND NICOLETTE.

NICOLSON, Sir Harold George (1886–1968) Biographer and critic; MP for the National Labour Party 1935–45. He published critical and biographical works on Paul *Verlaine (1921), Alfred *Tennyson (1923), A. C. *Swinburne (1926), and George V (1952). *Curzon* (1934) and *Some People* (1927) draw on his experiences of the diplomatic service. His marriage to Vita *Sackville-West, which allowed them both to have other, same-sex relationships, is described in *Portrait of a Marriage* (1973) by his son Nigel Nicolson.

NÍ DHOMHNAILL, Nuala (1952–) Irish-language poet. Her collections include *An Dealg Droighin* (1981), *Feis* (1991), and *Cead Aighnis* (1999). Though rooted in Gaelic tradition, her voice is stubbornly contemporary in its feminist awareness. *Pharaoh's Daughter* (1990) includes translations by, among others, Seamus *Heaney, Michael *Longley, and John *Montague. The title of *The Astrakhan Cloak* (1992), with English versions by Paul *Muldoon, plays on *aistriúchán*, Irish for 'translation'. Other bilingual collections include *The Water Horse* (1999, with Medbh *McGuckian), and *The Fifty Minute Mermaid* (2007, with Muldoon). Ní Dhomhnaill was Ireland professor of poetry from 2002 to 2004.

NIETZSCHE, Friedrich Wilhelm (1844–1900) German philosopher. In his first work, *Die Geburt der Tragödie* (1872: *The Birth of Tragedy*), he challenged accepted ideas about classical civilization, arguing that Greek tragedy was made possible only by the mingling of 'Apollonian' values of measure, reason, and harmony with irrational energies which he termed 'Dionysiac'. *Die fröhliche Wissenschaft* (1882: *The Gay Science*), with its famous assertion 'God is dead', was followed by *Also sprach Zarathustra* (1883–5: *Thus Spake Zarathustra*), *Jenseits von Gut und Böse* (1886: *Beyond Good and Evil*), *Zur Genealogie der Moral* (1887: *On the Genealogy of Morals*), and *Die Götzen-Dämmerung* (1889: *Twilight of the Idols*). Nietzsche is considered by many to be among the most influential thinkers of modern times, but his reputation has suffered unfairly from guilt by association with Nazism as some of his ideas—the 'Übermensch' (superman), 'the morality of the slave', 'the will to power', etc.—were seized upon by Nazi ideologues. Nietzsche's thought influenced diverse literary figures such as George Bernard *Shaw, D. H. *Lawrence, W. B. *Yeats, Thomas Mann, and Rainer Maria Rilke, and his method, with its sensitivity to the inescapably figurative nature of language, anticipates Jacques *Derrida and *deconstruction.

NIGHTINGALE, Florence (1820–1910) Health reformer and writer. She became famous for her campaign to improve conditions for the sick and wounded soldiers of the Crimean War (1853–6). Her *Suggestions for Thought to Searchers after Religious Truth among the Artizans of England* remained unpublished in her lifetime. *Suggestions* included 'Cassandra', an impassioned essay on the confinements imposed on the lives of middle-class women of her generation, which was published by the feminist Ray Strachey (1887–1940) in 1928. Virginia *Woolf described it as 'shrieking aloud in agony' in *A *Room of one's Own*.

Nightmare Abbey A satire by Thomas Love *Peacock, published 1818, in which S. T. *Coleridge's German transcendentalism, Lord *Byron's self-dramatizing and P. B. *Shelley's esotericism are mocked as examples of the modish gloom infecting contemporary literature. Imitating the opening of William *Godwin's novel *Mandeville* (1817), Mr Glowry's isolated house is staffed by servants with long faces and names like Diggory Deaths-head. He gives a house party attended by Mr Toobad, the millenarian pessimist, Mr Flosky (Coleridge), Mr Cypress (Byron), and Mr Listless, the common reader, who is currently immersed in depression. Two guests remain unfashionably cheerful, Mr Asterias the scientist and Mr Hilary, whose literary tastes come from the Greeks. Scythrop Glowry, the son of the house, a young writer who resembles P. B. Shelley, cannot decide between two women, and loses both in a classic comic denouement, in which the ladies are discovered to one another. He briefly contemplates suicide in Werther's manner (*see* WERTHERISM), but calls instead for a bottle of Madeira.

Night Thoughts on Life, Death, and Immortality, The Complaint, or A poem of some 10,000 lines of blank verse, in nine books, by Edward *Young, published 1742-5. Amid gloomy meditations on life's vicissitudes, the poet laments the deaths of Lucia, Narcissa, and Philander, loosely identified as his wife, his stepdaughter, and her husband; he also addresses much reproof and exhortation to a young atheist, Lorenzo. The poem includes lines which have become proverbial, such as 'Procrastination is the thief of time' (I. 393); it was enormously popular in Britain and had considerable influence in Europe. The poem's piety and grandeur were praised by Samuel *Johnson, and its pathos by James *Boswell; William *Blake produced over 500 designs for a projected edition of 1795, but only one volume was published. *See also* GRAVEYARD POETS.

NIMMO, Dorothy (1932-2001) Poet, who began writing in her fifties, after being 'an actress for ten years, a wife-and-mother for 25'. Her collections of sharp, witty, deceptively simple poems often unsettle myths of family (her mother was the children's writer Elfrida Vipont, and a prominent *Quaker). They include *Homewards* (1987), *Kill the Black Parrot* (1993), *A Testimony to the Grace of God in the Life of James Nayler 1618-1660* (1993), *The Underhill Experience* (1995), *The Children's Game* (1998), and *The Wig Box: New and Selected Poems* (2000).

NIN, Anaïs (Angela Antolina Rosa Edelmira Nin y Culmell) (1903-77) Novelist and diarist, who studied psychoanalysis and was a patient of *Jung. She wrote Surrealist novels, including *House of Incest* (1936), the five-volume *Cities of the Interior* (1947-54; published in one volume in 1959), and erotica, published posthumously (*Delta of Venus*, (1977, and *Little Birds*, 1979). Her major work was a seven-volume diary (1966-80) which she kept throughout her life, and which was republished in unexpurgated form after her death. It provides an account of the literary and artistic circle which she

frequented, but is mostly celebrated as an intimate, interior exploration of female subjectivity and sexuality.

Nineteen Eighty-Four A novel by George *Orwell, published 1949; a dystopian story of totalitarianism of the future and one man's hopeless struggle against it. Winston Smith, the hero, has no heroic qualities, only a wistful longing for truth and decency. But in a social system where there is no privacy and where having unorthodox ideas incurs the death penalty he knows he has no hope. His brief love affair ends in arrest by the Thought Police, and when, after months of torture and brainwashing, he is released, he makes his final submission of his own accord. The book is a warning of the possibilities of the police state brought to perfection, where power is the only thing that counts, where the past is constantly being modified to fit the present, where the official language, 'Newspeak', progressively narrows the range of ideas and independent thought, and where Doublethink becomes a necessary habit of mind. It is a society dominated by slogans— 'War is Peace, Freedom is Slavery, Ignorance is Strength'—and controlled by compulsory worship of the head of the Party, Big Brother. The novel had an extraordinary impact, and many of its phrases and coinages (including its title) passed into the common language.

Nineteenth Century A monthly review founded in 1877 by James Knowles, formerly editor of the *Contemporary Review*. It was more impartial in its attitude than the *Fortnightly Review*, bringing together the most eminent advocates of conflicting views. Contributors included William *Gladstone, T. H. *Huxley, John *Ruskin, Beatrice *Webb, William *Morris, *Ouida, and Oscar *Wilde. *Tennyson, a friend of Knowles, provided a prefatory sonnet for the first issue, welcoming contributions from the faithful and from 'wilder comrades' seeking a harbour 'In seas of Death and sunless Gulfs of Doubt'. When the century of the title ended, the review added to its old title 'And After', and changed the whole title to the *Twentieth Century* in 1951. It ceased publication in 1972.

Nine Worthies 'Three Paynims, three Jews, and three Christian men', namely Hector of Troy, *Alexander the Great, and Julius *Caesar; Joshua, *David, and Judas Maccabaeus; *Arthur, *Charlemagne, and Godefroi de Bouillon (Caxton, preface to *Le *Morte Darthur*). The list of worthies in Shakespeare's *Love's Labour's Lost,*

n

v. ii, is not quite the same, for it includes Pompey and *Hercules.

Niobe Mother of many children who boasted of her superiority to the goddess Leto, who had only two, Apollo and Artemis (Diana). To punish her Apollo and Artemis slew all her children, and she was then transformed into a weeping rock. Her story is told in Homer's *Iliad*, Book 24, and *Ovid's *Metamorphoses*, Book 6. She became a symbol of grief. *Hamlet ironically describes Gertrude as 'Like Niobe, all tears'.

Njáls saga A prose epic written c.1280 but set nearly 300 years previously. It is generally considered the most distinguished of the Icelandic *sagas.

Noah See BIBLE.

Nobel Prizes were established under the will of Alfred Bernhard Nobel (1833–96), a Swedish chemist distinguished in the development of explosives, by which the interest on the greater part of his large fortune is distributed in annual prizes for the most important discoveries in physics, chemistry, and physiology or medicine respectively, to the person who shall have most promoted 'the fraternity of nations' (the Nobel Peace Prize), and to the 'person who shall have produced in the field of literature the most outstanding work of an idealistic tendency'. The Bank of Sweden also awards (since 1969) an associated prize in economics. See Appendix 3(a) for a list of winners.

Noctes Ambrosianae A series of dialogues, devised by John *Lockhart, published in *Blackwood's Edinburgh Magazine* from 1822 to 1835. The speakers are largely based on real people, such as James *Hogg (the 'Shepherd') and John *Wilson ('Christopher North'). The wide-ranging conversations, mostly written by Wilson, with contributions from Lockhart, Hogg, and William *Maginn, present a romanticized and whimsical view of Scotland.

Nōh plays A form of ceremonial, ritualistic drama peculiar to Japan, slow, symbolical, and spiritual in character. The style originated in the 14th century, was perfected in the 15th, and flourished during the Edo or Tokugawa period (1603–1868). About 200 Nōh plays are extant. In various respects the Nōh plays are comparable with the early Greek drama. Both Ezra *Pound and W. B. *Yeats were much influenced by the Nōh theatre

noir French term ['black'] Used to describe American films and fiction of the 1940s and 1950s, which combine different genres and entrapping plot twists. The mode grows out of *hardboiled narratives.

No Name A novel by Wilkie *Collins, published 1862; it is remarkable for its sympathetic portrayal of Magdalen Vanstone, its energetic and unscrupulous heroine.

nonjurors The name given to Church of England clergy and laymen in the 17th and 18th centuries who supported the Stuart succession and refused to take the oaths of allegiance to William and Mary after 1688 and to the Hanoverian Georges after 1714, thus excluding themselves from holding office. Notable nonjuring writers include Thomas Ken, Charles Leslie (1650–1722), Jeremy *Collier, Robert *Nelson, Thomas Hearne, William *Law, Charles Jennens (1700–73), and John *Byrom.

nonsense Usually in verse; has been associated with children because of its roots in nursery rhymes and singing games based on sound rather than sense. However, deliberate nonsense has undercurrents that are personal (as with Edward *Lear), or political (Dr *Seuss), or which may be the vehicle for complex intellectual games (as in Lewis *Carroll's *The Hunting of the Snark*, 1876). Spike Milligan is a modern practitioner.

NORRIS, Frank (Benjamin Franklin) (1870–1902) American novelist. The influence of *Zola and *naturalism is seen in his best work, which includes *McTeague* (1899); and in his unfinished trilogy *The Epic of the Wheat*: the first two volumes, *The Octopus* (1901) and *The Pit* (1903), describe the raising of wheat in California and speculation on the Chicago wheat exchange. A projected third volume, *The Wolf*, to be set in famine-stricken Europe, was never written.

NORRIS, John (1657–1712) Poet, clergyman, and philosopher. He was the first to publish an account of John *Locke's *Essay Concerning Human Understanding*. Mary *Astell published her correspondence with Norris as *Letters Concerning the Love of God* (1695). In philosophy he was a follower of the French philosopher Nicolas Malebranche (1638–1715), whose work develops the theories of *Descartes; his most important philosophical works are *An Account of Reason and Faith* (1697) and *An Essay towards the Theory of the Ideal or Intelligible World* (1701–4).

NORTH, Christopher Pseudonym of John *Wilson (1785–1854).

NORTH, Sir Thomas (1535–?1603) Translator; he was knighted in 1591, and pensioned by *Elizabeth I in 1601. His famous translations include the *Dial of Princes* from Guevara's *El relox de principes* (1557), published with *The Famous Book of Marcus Aurelius*, *The Moral Philosophy of Doni*, from the Italian (1570), and *Plutarch's *Lives* from the French of Jacques Amyot (1579). His Plutarch, written in noble and vivid English, was William *Shakespeare's chief source for classical history and had a great influence on Elizabethan prose.

North American Review (1815–1939) A Boston quarterly, later monthly periodical. Its editors included Charles Eliot Norton, James Russell Lowell, and Henry *Adams. Its contributors ranged from Ralph Waldo *Emerson and Washington *Irving to Henry *James and Mark *Twain.

North and South A novel by Elizabeth *Gaskell, published serially in *Household Words* 1854–5, in volume form 1855. It contrasts the values of rural southern England and industrial northern England, and is more conciliatory in its approach than the provocative *Mary Barton*. Margaret Hale is the daughter of a clergyman whose religious doubts force him to resign his Hampshire living and to move with his family to a sooty cotton-spinning northern city. Here, at a moment of conflict between workers and employers, Margaret meets the grim Mrs Thornton and her son, a stubborn manufacturer, whose lack of sympathy for the workers Margaret finds unattractive. She endangers herself to protect him from a mob of strikers; he misunderstands her motives and offers marriage, which she refuses. But when he suspects her of an intrigue with another man (in fact her brother, whom she has to shield as he is in danger of arrest), and shows his suspicion, she realizes that she loves him. After a series of misfortunes, Margaret and Thornton are finally united. Margaret, at first repelled by 'trade' and its practitioners, comes to respect the ideas and the family life of northern mill-hands and mill-owners.

Northanger Abbey A novel by Jane *Austen, begun 1798, published posthumously (1818) with *Persuasion*. The novel satirizes popular tales of romance and terror, such as Ann *Radcliffe's *Mysteries of Udolpho*, and contrasts the improbabilities of *Gothic fiction with the normal realities of life. Catherine Morland,

daughter of a well-to-do clergyman, is taken to Bath for the season by her friends Mr and Mrs Allen. Here she makes the acquaintance of Henry Tilney (son of the eccentric General Tilney) and his pleasant sister Eleanor. Catherine falls in love with Henry, and gains his father's approval, which is founded upon the exaggerated report of her parents' wealth given him by the foolish young John Thorpe, brother of Catherine's friend Isabella. Catherine is invited to Northanger Abbey, the medieval seat of the Tilneys. Somewhat unbalanced by her eager reading of Radcliffe's novels, Catherine imagines a mystery in which General Tilney is criminally involved with the death of his wife, and is mortified when her suspicions are discovered. General Tilney, having received a second report from John Thorpe as misleading as the first, representing Catherine's parents as extremely humble, packs her off back to her family. Henry, disobeying his father, follows Catherine to her home, proposes, and is accepted. General Tilney's consent is obtained after his discovery of the true financial position of Catherine's family.

North Briton A weekly political periodical (1762–71), founded by John Wilkes, in opposition to the *Briton*, which Tobias *Smollett was conducting in the interests of the Scottish prime minister Lord Bute. Wilkes was assisted by Charles *Churchill. In no. 45 (23 Apr. 1763) Wilkes attacked the king's speech and was imprisoned for libel.

Northern Lass, The A comedy by Richard *Brome, printed 1632. This is the earliest of Brome's extant plays, and was very popular.

Northward Ho A comedy by John *Webster and Thomas *Dekker, written 1605, printed 1607. The play was a good-humoured answer to the *Eastward Ho* of Chapman, Ben *Jonson, and John *Marston. Like *Westward Ho* it gives a vivid picture of the manners of the day. The little old poet Bellamont is a genial caricature of George *Chapman.

NORTON, Andre (1912–2005) American *science fiction and *fantasy author; her numerous books, including *Storm over Warlock* (1960) and *Catseye* (1961), introduced young people in the 1950s and 1960s to the central concerns of the genres. Their quality ensured a loyal readership. Her 'Witch World' fantasies, beginning with *Witch World* (1963), attracted a somewhat older audience.

NORTON, Caroline (1808–77) Née Sheridan, poet, novelist, editor, and hostess: she was a granddaughter of Richard *Sheridan. She became involved in a notorious divorce action and later in spirited and influential battles for the custody of her children and a revision of the laws relating to married women's property. Norton successfully supported her family by writing, publishing several volumes of *Byronic verse, including *The Undying One, and Other Poems* (1830), and *A Voice from the Factories* (1836), a powerful poem on child labour. She also edited several best-selling *poetry annuals and produced stories, essays, and novels, including *Lost and Saved* (3 vols, 1863). She served as a model for the heroine of Meredith's *Diana of the Crossways.*

NORTON, Mary (1903–92) Author of the *'Borrowers' series, she also wrote *Bedknob and Broomstick* (1957), filmed by Disney in 1971, and *Are All the Giants Dead?* (1975).

Norval See DOUGLAS (by John Home).

NOSTRADAMUS (1503–66) French astrologer, whose enigmatic prophecies, cast in the form of rhymed quatrains grouped in sets of 100 and published under the title *Centuries* (1555, English trans. 1672), enjoyed widespread popularity during the Renaissance. Interest in his prophecies has proved persistent.

Nostromo A novel by Joseph *Conrad, published 1904. In an imaginary South American country, Costaguana, Charles Gould runs a silver mine of national importance in the province of Sulaco. He is married to Emilia, a woman of charm and intelligence. In a time of political unrest and revolution the dictator President Ribiera flees the country and the opposing factions struggle for control. When the silver from the mine is in danger of being seized by the rebel forces, Gould becomes obsessed with the idea of saving it. He enlists the help of Decoud, a cynical journalist, and of an older man, Dr Monygham, a fond admirer of Emilia; together they appeal to Nostromo, an Italian sailor, and a hero to all. With great daring Decoud and Nostromo sail off with the silver, which they bury on a nearby deserted island. Left alone to guard the treasure, Decoud loses his mind and, after shooting himself, drowns, his body weighted with silver. The common assumption is that the silver was lost at sea and the temptation proves too much for Nostromo, who decides to steal it. His old friend Viola is appointed lighthouse keeper on the island and, unwittingly, guard for the silver. Nostromo trifles with

Viola's two infatuated daughters, grows rich as he gradually pilfers the silver, and is finally shot when mistaken for an intruder. Mortally wounded, he sends for Emilia, and confesses his crime in the hope of absolution, but dies without revealing the whereabouts of the treasure.

Notes and Queries An ongoing periodical founded in 1849 by William Thoms, originally subtitled 'a medium of inter-communication for literary men, artists, antiquaries, genealogists, etc.' It was conceived as part academic journal, part correspondence column, where scholars could seek or exchange information. Its motto was (until 1923) Captain Cuttle's 'When found, make a note of' (*see* DOMBEY AND SON).

nouveau roman ('new novel') A term applied to the work of a wide range of modern French novelists, including Nathalie Sarraute, Claude Simon (1913–2005), Marguerite Duras, Robert Pinget (1919–97), Alain Robbe-Grillet, and Michel *Butor. They argue that the traditional novel creates an illusion of order and significance which is denied by the reality of experience. The aim of the new novel is to foster change by dispensing with any technique which imposes a particular interpretation on events, or which organizes events in such a way as to endow them with a collective significance.

Nouvelle Héloïse, La See ROUSSEAU, JEAN-JACQUES.

novel, rise of the The word 'novellae' was employed in the 16th century to describe the short tales of the *Decameron and the *Heptameron, and others. Used in a modern sense, the word 'novel' appears in England in the mid-17th century, chiefly associated with romances of illicit love. The word 'history' was favoured to describe the long prose fictions of the 18th century which were the precursors of the modern novel. The novel form developed slowly, through the *memoir-novel and the *epistolary novel of the 16th and 17th centuries to the novel of the omniscient third-person narrator, the dominant form from the late 18th century onwards. The novelists Daniel *Defoe, Samuel *Richardson, Henry *Fielding, Tobias *Smollett, and Laurence *Sterne developed the form so fully that by the early 19th century Jane *Austen could write (albeit with a hint of irony), in *Northanger Abbey, that in the novel 'the greatest powers of the mind are displayed'. By 1824 Walter *Scott could confidently define the novel as 'a fictitious narrative . . . accommodated to the ordinary train of human events', a definition which has proved durable.

See also FASHIONABLE NOVEL; HISTORICAL FICTION; ORIENTAL NOVEL; SENTIMENT.

Novum Organum A Latin treatise on scientific method, which Francis *Bacon included in his *Instauratio Magna* (1620). This 'great renewal' of natural philosophy (which Bacon never completed) involved a systematic methodology, starting with fresh observation of natural phenomena, followed by carefully controlled experiments, to provide data from which scientific laws could be formulated. The 'new instrument' outlined here (the title alludes to the corpus of Aristotelian philosophy, known as the *Organon*) abandoned the main tool of logic, the syllogism, which Bacon criticized as a self-contained verbal procedure starting from propositions which were not based on experience. Instead, he recommended inductive reasoning, moving from specific observations to broader generalizations and theories, tested by the use of 'negative instances' (if 100 white swans are observed, the discovery of a single black one is enough to falsify the thesis that all swans are white).

Book I of the *Novum Organum* restates in the form of detached aphorisms Bacon's fundamental criticisms of science and his plans for its renewal. Calling for the direct observation of nature (rather than recycling *Aristotle's texts), Bacon was nonetheless aware of the possible distortions involved, brilliantly analysing the four 'Idols' (from the Greek εἴδωλα, illusions) to which human beings are prone. These are the Idols of the Tribe, Cave, Market Place, and Theatre. In the more technical Book II Bacon gives a worked example of inductive method as applied to heat. Though Bacon's inductive method has been misrepresented as a purely mechanical procedure, it includes deductive elements arising from hypotheses, representing a substantial contribution to natural science.

NOYES, Alfred (1880–1958) Poet; violently anti-modernist in his view of literature. His books of verse include *Drake* (1908) and *Tales of the Mermaid Tavern* (1913). His poem 'The Highwayman' is still well known. *Two Worlds for Memory* (1953) is an autobiography.

nunc dimittis 'now lettest thou thy servant depart in peace', the Latin version of the Song of Simeon after he has seen the child Jesus (Luke 2: 29–32). It forms part of Evensong in the *Book of *Common Prayer*.

'Nun's Priest's Tale, The' *See* CANTERBURY TALES, 20.

nursery rhymes Obscure in origin; mostly appear to date from the 17th century as part of the oral tradition. They include riddles, street cries, parodies, political satires, and singing games. Many collections have been illustrated, notably by Arthur Rackham (1923), Quentin *Blake (1983), and Michael Foreman (1990). The earliest printed version appears in *A Little Book for Little Children* (c.1702–12) by 'T.W.'; *Tommy Thumb's Pretty Song Book* (1744) is the first collection. James Orchard *Halliwell's *The Nursery Rhymes of England* (1842) is a seminal study; the definitive collection is the *Opies' *The Oxford Dictionary of Nursery Rhymes* (1951).

NYE, Robert (1939–) Novelist, poet, playwright, and critic. His first novel, *Doubtfire* (1967), shows the influence of James *Joyce, but he is best known for a sequence of pastiche biographies of characters from literature, folklore, and history. *Falstaff*, (1976) was followed by *Merlin* (1978), *Faust* (1980), *The Memoirs of Lord Byron* (1989), *Mrs Shakespeare* (1993), and *The Late Mr Shakespeare* (1998). Other works include the short story collections *Tales I Told my Mother* (1969) and *The Facts of Life* (1983) and *Collected Poems* (1996).

nymphs In Greek mythology, beautiful female divinities who inhabited trees (dryads), fresh water (naiads), the sea (nereids), caves and mountains (oreads). Several of them figure in *Ovid's *Metamorphoses*. They were often pursued by gods, for example Arethusa by Alpheus, Daphne by *Apollo, or Syrinx by *Pan. Nymphs could be dangerous to human beings, for example Salmacis to Hermaphroditus, or Calypso to Odysseus.

OATES, Joyce Carol (1938–) American novelist, short story writer, poet, and critic; she was professor of English at the University of Detroit and the city provides the setting for much of her work. Her fiction often portrays intense individual experiences as neo-*Gothic expressions of the dark and violent heart of American society. Her many novels include *them* (1969); *Black Water* (1992); *Foxfire* (1993), a powerful portrayal of a teenage girl-gang in upstate New York during the 1950s; *Blonde* (2000), chronicling the life of Marilyn Monroe; *What I Lived for* (1994); and *A Fair Maiden* (2010). Her short story collections include *By the North Gate* (1963), *Marriages and Infidelities* (1972), and *The Museum of Dr Moses* (2007). She has also published poetry, selections of essays and critical writings.

objective correlative A term used by T. S. *Eliot in his essay 'Hamlet and his Problems' (1919; included in *The Sacred Wood*, 1920). Eliot ascribes the alleged 'artistic failure' of Shakespeare's play *Hamlet* to the fact that Hamlet himself is 'dominated by an emotion which is inexpressible, because it is in *excess* of the facts as they appear . . . The only way of expressing emotion in the form of art is by finding an "objective correlative"; in other words, a set of objects, a situation, a chain of events which shall be the formula of that *particular* emotion.' The phrase was much cited in mid-20th-century criticism.

O'BRIEN, Edna (1930–) Irish novelist and short story writer. Her first novel, *The Country Girls* (1960), describes the girlhood of Caithleen Brady (Kate) and Bridget Brennan (Baba), who escape from their rural homes and repressive convent education to the 'crowds and lights and noise' of Dublin. The book was banned in Ireland and burned in her birthplace, Tuamgraney. Kate and Baba continue their search for experience in *The Lonely Girl* (1962; repr. as *The Girl with Green Eyes*) and *Girls in their Married Bliss* (1963). O'Brien's subsequent novels include *A Pagan Place* (1971), *Night* (1972), *Johnny I*

Hardly Knew You (1977), *House of Splendid Isolation* (1994), and *The Light of Evening* (2006). *Down by the River* (1997) fictionalizes the plight of a teenage rape victim who fell foul of Ireland's draconian abortion laws in 1992; *In the Forest* (2002) recreates the events surrounding a notorious 1994 triple murder in the author's native east Clare. O'Brien's lyrical descriptive powers and lack of inhibition have led to comparisons with Colette. Her short story collections include *A Scandalous Woman* (1974), *Mrs Reinhardt* (1978), *Returning* (1982), and *Lantern Slides* (1990).

O'BRIEN, Flann (1911–66) Pseudonym of Brian Ó Nualláin, Irish novelist. He contributed a satirical column to the *Irish Times* under the name 'Myles na Gopaleen'. His exuberant first novel, *At Swim-Two-Birds* (1939), operates on several levels of invention: a naturalistic portrayal of student and lower-middle-class life; a 'novel-within-a-novel' dealing with the legendary hero *Finn Mac Cool; and a layer of Irish folklore. The effect is a multidimensional exploration of the nature of fiction, extending an Irish tradition that runs from Laurence *Sterne to James *Joyce. O'Brien's second novel, *An Béal Bocht* (1941), written in Irish, is a hilarious parody of autobiography from Irish-speaking regions (trans. *The Poor Mouth*, 1973). *The Third Policeman* (written 1940; pub. 1967) is darker and disturbing.

O'BRIEN, Kate (1897–1974) Irish novelist, first recognized for her successful play *Distinguished Villa* (1926). *Without my Cloak* (1931) is a saga of the emergent Catholic Irish middle class. *Mary Lavelle* (1936) is set in Spain, where O'Brien had worked as an au pair; she was barred from the country after the publication of her travelogue *Farewell Spain* (1937). *That Lady* (1946), a forensic exposition of the injustices of patriarchy in the 16th century, also draws on her Spanish experience. *The Land of Spices* (1942) delicately portrays relationships in an isolated Irish convent. Like *Mary Lavelle*, it was banned in Ireland. O'Brien's other work includes *My Ireland* (1962) and the memoir *Presentation Parlour* (1963).

O'BRIEN, Sean (1952–) Poet and critic. His volumes include *The Indoor Park* (1983), *HMS Glasshouse* (1991), *Downriver* (2001), *Cousin Coat: Selected Poems 1976–2001* (2002), a version of *Dante's *Inferno* (2006), and *Night Train* (2009). O'Brien's poetry, colloquial yet at times formal, and characteristically driven by an unusual rhythm (often employing the *dactyl), evokes contemporary urban landscapes and popular culture, reinforced by strong literary and painterly allusions. The effect, often with sardonic political point, is of a slightly surreal, displaced, offbeat portrait of contemporary Britain.

Observer, The A Sunday newspaper, first issued on 4 December 1791. It was bought by Alfred *Harmsworth in 1905, and edited from 1948 to 1975 by David Astor (1912–2001), who commissioned work from writers such as George *Orwell and Vita *Sackville-West. In 1993 the *Observer* was bought by the group owning the *Guardian*.

O'CASEY, Sean (John Casey) (1880–1964) Irish playwright, who initially published articles, songs, and broadsheets under the name of Seán Ó Cathasaigh. His first plays were rejected by the *Abbey Theatre, but he received encouragement from Lady *Gregory, and *The Shadow of a Gunman* was performed in 1923, followed by *Juno and the Paycock* in 1924; they were published together as *Two Plays* (1925). *The Plough and the Stars* provoked nationalist riots at the Abbey in 1926. All three tragicomedies deal with the rhetoric and dangers of Irish patriotism, with tenement life, self-deception, and survival. O'Casey moved to England in 1926; his alienation from Ireland was confirmed by a rift with W. B. *Yeats and the Abbey over its rejection of *The Silver Tassie* (1928), an experimental anti-war play about an injured footballer, which introduced the *Expressionist techniques employed in his later works. These include *Within the Gates* (1933), *Red Roses for Me* (1942), *Cock-a-Doodle Dandy* (1949), and *The Bishop's Bonfire* (1955). He also published a series of flamboyant autobiographies, in six volumes, beginning with *I Knock at the Door* (1939) and ending with *Sunset and Evening Star* (1954).

Oceana *See* COMMONWEALTH OF OCEANA.

Ocean to Cynthia, The A poem by Walter *Ralegh reflecting on his shifting relationship with *Elizabeth I.

OCKHAM, William of (*c.*1287–1347) Philosopher and theologian; he joined the Franciscans and studied at Oxford, where he wrote a Commentary (known as the *Ordinatio*) on the first book of the *Sentences* of Peter Lombard. In 1324 he was summoned by the pope to Avignon to answer charges of unorthodoxy. In 1328 he fled from Avignon along with the Franciscan general, Michael of Cesena, having taken the side of the Spiritual Franciscans in their dispute with Pope John XXII. He was excommunicated. Thereafter he remained with the emperor Louis of Bavaria, concerned with the question of papal power. Ockham was influential in the fields of theology, philosophy, and political theory. The logical axiom associated with him is 'Ockham's Razor', namely the principle that (in W. J. Courtenay's words) 'plurality ought not to be posited without necessity'. His argument that shared characteristics do not exist apart from individuals influenced the later medieval philosophical tradition known as nominalism.

O'CONNOR, Flannery (1925–64) American novelist and short story writer, born in Georgia, whose works, often dealing with fanaticism, offer examples of Southern *Gothic. *Wise Blood* (1952) and *The Violent Bear It Away* (1960) are novels; her short stories are collected as *The Complete Stories* (1971).

O'CONNOR, Frank (1903–66) Pseudonym of Michael Francis O'Donovan, versatile Irish writer best known for his short stories and his translations and interpretations of Gaelic literature. His collections include *Crab Apple Jelly* (1944), *Traveller's Samples* (1951), and *Domestic Relations* (1957). Realistic and closely observed, his stories offer a portrait of the middle and lower classes of Ireland, and of the 'warm dim odorous feckless evasive southern quality' of his native Cork. He also wrote two volumes of autobiography, *An Only Child* (1961) and *My Father's Son* (1969). His translation of Brian *Merriman's *Midnight Court* (1945), like much of his fiction, was banned in Ireland.

octosyllabics Verse lines of eight syllables, usually iambic tetrameters (*see* METRE) and often paired in rhyming couplets.

Odd Women, The A novel by George *Gissing, published 1893, a relentlessly grim look at the prospects of England's half a million more women than men, the 'Odd Women' of the title. *See* NEW WOMAN FICTION.

ode A lyric poem in an elevated style on a serious subject, often celebrating a special event or hymning the qualities of some person, deity, or abstract entity. Odes are generally classified as either Pindaric or Horatian, depending upon their stanzaic structure and tone. The Pindaric ode—which is typically passionate, visionary, and sonorous—is modelled on the lyrics of *Pindar. Designed to be sung and danced by the Greek chorus either at a public festival or in a theatre, these lyrics were written in complex *stanzas which mirror the pattern of the dance and have a three-part structure: dancing to the left, the chorus chanted the strophe; dancing to the right, they repeated the pattern in the antistrophe; standing still, they brought the intricate pattern to a close in the epode, which had a different length and arrangement.

The Horatian ode (named after *Horace) tends to be meditative, tranquil, and colloquial. Horatian odes almost always repeat a single stanzaic form, and are typically shorter than the more declamatory Pindaric ode. Among the best-known Horatian odes are *Marvell's 'An Horatian Ode upon Cromwell's Return from Ireland', Thomas *Gray's 'Ode on a Distant Prospect of Eton College', and Keats's *'To Autumn'.

The first outstanding imitation of Pindar was *Jonson's 'To the Immortal Memory . . . of . . . Sir Lucius Cary and Sir H. Morison' (1629), with the three parts renamed as 'turn', 'counter-turn', and 'stand'. This was a 'regular ode' in that it closely followed Pindar's scheme of all strophes and antistrophes conforming to one stanzaic pattern, and all epodes following another. Abraham *Cowley's *Pindarique Odes* (1656) attempted to capture the spirit of Pindar, rather than furnish an exact translation. In this work and in his original Pindaric compositions, beginning with the 'Ode, upon the Blessed Restoration and Return of His Sacred Majesty' (1660), Cowley developed the 'irregular ode', which abandoned Pindar's stanzaic rules, each stanza now developing its own pattern of rhythm, rhyme, and number of lines.

*Dryden's odes, 'To the Pious Memory . . . of Mrs. Anne Killigrew' (1686), 'Ode in Honour of St Cecilia's Day' (1687), and 'Alexander's Feast, or The Power of Musique' (1697), and William *Collins's 'Ode to Liberty' (1746) provide further examples. Writing regular Pindaric odes, *Congreve and Gray (for example in 'The *Progress of Poesy' and 'The *Bard') worked against the prevailing trend. From the mid-18th century on-

wards, it often becomes more difficult and less useful to distinguish between the Pindaric and Horatian styles.

The Romantic poets produced a remarkable number of outstanding odes, including S. T. *Coleridge's 'Dejection: An Ode'; William Wordsworth's 'Ode: *Intimations of Immortality . . . '; P. B. *Shelley's *'Ode to the West Wind' and 'To a Sky-Lark'; and Keats's *'Ode to a Nightingale' and *'Ode on a Grecian Urn'. With a few notable exceptions, such as Alfred *Tennyson's 'Ode on the Death of the Duke of Wellington' (1852), the Pindaric ode was not congenial to Victorian sensibilities. One of the most successful modern examples of the form is Allen *Tate's 'Ode to the Confederate Dead' (1927, 1937).

'Ode on a Grecian Urn' A poem by John *Keats, written 1819, published 1820. While he describes the pastoral scenes of love, beauty, and joy illustrated on the urn, the poet reflects on the eternal quality of art and the fleeting nature of human love and happiness. The last two lines are particularly well known and their meaning much debated: 'Beauty is truth, truth beauty,—that is all | Ye know on earth, and all ye need to know.'

'Ode to a Nightingale' A poem by John *Keats, written 1819, published 1820. Keats's friend Charles Armitage Brown (1787–1842) relates that a nightingale had nested near his house in Hampstead (now known as Keats House), and that one morning Keats sat under a plum tree in the garden composing his ode on 'some scraps of paper'. Briefly, the poem is a meditation on the immortal beauty of the nightingale's song and the sadness of the observer, who must finally—as the price of his humanity—accept sorrow and mortality.

'Ode to Autumn' *See* 'TO AUTUMN'.

'Ode to the West Wind' A poem by P. B. *Shelley, written in October 1819, published 1820. The ode is a passionate invocation to the spirit of the West Wind, both 'Destroyer and Preserver'. It is composed in five sweeping stanzaic movements, each taking the form of a sonnet, but with complex musical patterns of internal rhyme and run-on lines, culminating in a breathless series of cries or questions. Shelley's observations of wind, water, wood, cloud, and sky combine imagery which is simultaneously scientific, mythical, and even biblical. The effect is one of hope and energy, achieved through suffering and despair.

ODETS, Clifford (1906–63) American dramatist, a founder member in 1931 of the Group Theatre, which followed the naturalistic methods of the *Moscow Arts Theatre; his reputation was made when it performed his short play *Waiting for Lefty* (1935), about a taxidrivers' strike. This was followed in the same year by two other dramas of social conflict, *Till the Day I Die*, and *Awake and Sing!* Later works include *Clash by Night* (1941), *The Big Knife* (1948), and *The Country Girl* (1950, first known in Britain as *Winter Journey*), about an alcoholic actor's marriage.

O'DONOGHUE, Bernard (1945–) Irish poet and medievalist, a fellow of Wadham College, Oxford. Many of the poems in his collections *The Weakness* (1991), *Gunpowder* (1995), *Here Nor There* (1999), and *Outliving* (2003) are set in the north Cork landscape of his childhood and are haunted by a sense of the dignity, fragility, and unknowability of ordinary people. The more recent work confronts themes of ageing and exile. See *Selected Poems* (2008). He has also published a translation of *Sir *Gawain and the Green Knight* (2006).

Odyssey An epic poem traditionally ascribed to *Homer, which relates the adventures of Odysseus on his return home to Ithaca ten years after the Trojan War. The local youth, assuming his death, compete to marry his wife Penelope, infesting the house and exhausting the royal resources. His son Telemachus sets out to find him. Odysseus, meanwhile, has adventures in unknown seas and lands. He is freed by *Zeus from the nymph Calypso, shipwrecked, allured by the Sirens' deadly song, attacked by six-headed Scylla, and nearly drowned in the whirlpool Charybdis. The young Princess Nausicaa, finding him naked on the Phaeacian shore, takes him to her father. He relates his encounters since Troy, with the Lotus-Eaters, Polyphemus the Cyclops, Aeolus, ruler of the winds, the cannibal Laestrygonians, the enchantress Circe, and the land of the dead, where he met Achilles. The second half of the narrative, following Odysseus' return to Ithaca, is slower and more realistic; with Telemachus' help, he kills the suitors and reclaims wife and realm. The most ambitious reworking of the story, under Odysseus' Latin name of Ulysses, is by James *Joyce.

Oedipus See SOPHOCLES.

O'FAOLAIN, Julia (1932–) Novelist and historian, daughter of Sean *O'Faolain. Her fiction includes a collection of short stories and eight novels, among which are *Women in the Wall* (1975), set in 6th-century Gaul and examining the phenomenon of nuns voluntarily immuring themselves; *No Country for Young Men* (1980), about history's difficult legacy in contemporary Ireland's private and public life; *The Obedient Wife* (1982); *The Irish Signorina* (1984); *The Judas Cloth* (1992), on the controversial career of the 19th-century pope Pius IX; and *Adam Gould* (2009), set in a lunatic asylum.

O'FAOLAIN, Sean (1900–91) Irish novelist, and short story writer. He was a member of the Irish Republican Army during the War of Independence (1919–21). His first collection, *Midsummer Night Madness and Other Stories*, appeared in 1932. Early novels, such as *Bird Alone* (1936), deal with the parochialism of Irish society and the betrayal of nationalist hopes. He published biographies and an essayistic study, *The Irish* (1947). An autobiography, *Vive-moi!*, appeared in 1964, and *Collected Stories* in 1981. His best-known stories evoke frustrated lives, missed opportunities, characters limited by their environment; later stories (*The Heat of the Sun: Stories and Tales*, 1966; *The Talking Trees*, 1971), and his novel *And Again?* (1979), tend to be dryer, more amusing, and more resilient in tone.

Of Dramatick Poesy: An Essay By John *Dryden, published 1668, in the form of a dialogue between Eugenius (Charles Sackville), Crites (Sir Robert Howard, 1626–98), Lisideius (Sir Charles *Sedley), and Neander (Dryden himself), who take a boat on the Thames on the day of the battle between the English and Dutch navies in June 1665, and discuss English drama. Largely concerned with justifying Dryden's current practice as a playwright, the essay contains historically interesting appreciations of William *Shakespeare, John *Fletcher, and Ben *Jonson.

O'FLAHERTY, Liam (1896–1984) Irish novelist and story writer. His novels include *Thy Neighbour's Wife* (1923), published with the encouragement of Edward *Garnett, *The Informer* (1925, filmed 1935), *The Assassin* (1928), *Skerrett* (1932), *Famine* (1937), and *Insurrection* (1950). His short stories, including the volumes *Spring Sowing* (1924) and *Two Lovely Beasts* (1948), portray rural themes in elemental terms and are notable for their presentation of life, or more often death, as seen from an animal's point of view. *Dúil* (1953) is a collection of short stories in Irish. O'Flaherty published three volumes of flamboyant memoirs: *Two Years*

(1930), *I Went to Russia* (1931), and *Shame the Devil* (1934).

Ogier the Dane A hero of the *Charlemagne romances, identified with a Frankish warrior, Autgarius, who fought against Charlemagne and then submitted to him. He is linked with a number of legends, some of which include him among the *Paladins.

O'HAGAN, Andrew (1968–) Scottish novelist. *Our Fathers* (1999), which criticizes tropes of Scottish nationhood through its portrayal of a brutal and alcoholic Glaswegian father, was followed by *Personality* (2003) and *Be Near Me* (2006), also with Scottish settings and themes. His other work includes *The Missing* (1995) a speculative, partly autobiographical history of missing persons; *The Atlantic Ocean* (2008), a collection of essays on Britain and America; and *The Life and Opinions of Maf the Dog, and of His Friend Marilyn Monroe* (2010).

O'HARA, Frank (1926–66) American poet and art critic, who became one of the leading members of the *New York School. His volumes of poetry, including *A City Winter* (1951) and *Lunch Poems* (1966), incorporate painterly techniques. He also published prints and other graphic texts.

O'HARA, John (1905–70) American novelist. More than 200 of his sharp, satiric short stories, originally published in the *New Yorker*, were later collected in volumes, from *The Doctor's Son* (1935) onwards. His novels, which gained wide popularity with their toughness, frankness, and sophistication, include *Appointment in Samarra* (1934); *Butterfield 8* (1935); and *Pal Joey* (1940; later a musical), told in the form of letters from a nightclub singer.

Oisin (Oisín) [pron. Uh-sheen] Known also as Ossian (*see* MACPHERSON, JAMES; FINGAL), a legendary Gaelic warrior and bard, son of *Finn. He is said to have returned to Ireland after 300 years in Tír na nÓg (The Land of Youth) and found his countrymen diminished in stature and weakened, a myth usually interpreted in relation to the supplanting of paganism by Christianity.

OKARA, Gabriel (1921–) Nigerian poet and novelist. His belief that African ideas needed to be translated almost literally from their African language is expressed in his novel *The Voice* (1964), a challenging transliteration using Ijaw phrasing and syntax: 'Who are you people be?' In *The Fisherman's Invocation* (1978) and

The Dreamer, his Vision (2005) his poems are poised between Africa and Europe. Unpublished manuscripts were destroyed during the Nigerian Civil War (Biafran War) of 1967–70.

O'KEEFFE, John (1747–1833) Irish actor and dramatist, who produced about 50 farces and musical plays, often playing on his Irish background. His best-known works are *The Castle of Andalusia* (1782); *The Poor Soldier* (1783), which had great success in America; and *Wild Oats* (1791), which was successfully revived in 1976. William *Hazlitt described him as 'the English Molière'.

OKIGBO, Christopher (1932–67) Nigerian poet, killed when serving as a major in the Nigerian Civil War (Biafran War). His family was Roman Catholic, and his grandfather was a priest of the Ibo god Idoto; his verse represents a quest to ritualize and explore the complex strands of his own identity, evoking T. S. *Eliot's *The Waste Land*. The separately published *Heavensgate* (1962), *Limits* (1964), *Silences* (1965), and *Path of Thunder* (1968) are all included in the posthumously published *Labyrinths* (1971) and *Collected Poems* (1986).

OKRI, Ben (1959–) Nigerian novelist and poet. His first novel, *Flowers and Shadows* (1980), was followed by *The Landscapes Within* (1981), revised and reissued as *Dangerous Love* (1996). *The Famished Road* (*Booker Prize, 1991) is narrated by a 'spirit child', Azaro, and blends myth, harsh contemporary reality, and a strong sense of African place: *Songs of Enchantment* (1993) and *Infinite Riches* (1998) are sequels. Other prose works include *Astonishing the Gods* (1995), *Arcadia* (2002), and *Starbook* (2007). *Stars of the New Curfew* (1989) and *Tales of Freedom* (2009) are collections of short stories. *An African Elegy* (1992) is a collection of poems and *Mental Fight* (1999) is an epic poem. Okri is known for his political and social concerns as well as for his distinctively glowing prose, often composed of short, arresting sentences, which move from closely observed detail to the visionary and strange.

Old Bachelor, The The first comedy of William *Congreve, produced 1693. The 'Old Bachelor' is Heartwell, who is tricked into marrying Silvia, Vainlove's ex-mistress. To his relief the marriage proves invalid because the parson was Vainlove's friend Bellmour in disguise. In the end Bellmour marries Belinda, but Vainlove, who loves women only as long as they refuse him, finds that the wealthy Araminta will not yet agree to marry him.

Oldcastle, The First Part of Sir John A play first printed in 1600, reprinted in 1619 as *Shakespeare's, and included in the third and fourth *folios of his plays. It is certainly not by him, though the historical John Oldcastle seems to have been Shakespeare's original model for *Falstaff. It is a collaborative work in which Anthony *Munday and Michael *Drayton among others had a hand. The play deals with the proceedings in Henry V's reign against Oldcastle as the chief supporter of the Lollards.

Old Curiosity Shop, The A novel by Charles *Dickens, published as a separate volume 1841. It was originally intended to be fitted into the framework of *Master Humphrey's Clock* (1840–41), but this narrative was soon abandoned.

Nell Trent lives in the grotesque atmosphere of the old curiosity shop kept by her grandfather. Reduced to poverty, he has borrowed money from Daniel Quilp, a hideous dwarf and a monster of iniquity, and this money he secretly expends in gambling, in the vain hope of retrieving his fortunes. Quilp, who believes him a rich miser, discovers his mistake, and seizes the shop. The old man and the child flee and wander about the country, suffering great hardships and haunted by the fear of being discovered by Quilp, who relentlessly pursues them. They finally find a haven in a cottage by a country church. The grandfather's brother, returning from abroad and anxious to relieve their needs, has difficulty in tracing them. At last he succeeds, but Nell, worn out with her troubles, has just died, and the grandfather soon follows her.

The death of Little Nell, in its day one of the most celebrated scenes in fiction, later became the focus of much of the reaction against Dickens's use of pathos.

Oldenbarnavelt, Sir John van A historical tragedy, probably by John *Fletcher and Philip *Massinger, successively written, censored, rewritten, and acted in 1619, within three months of the execution of its real-life central character. It deals with contemporary events in the Netherlands.

Old Fortunatus A comedy by Thomas *Dekker, written 1599, published 1600, based on a story contained in a German 'Volksbuch' of 1509 and dramatized by Hans Sachs in 1553. The beggar Fortunatus, encountering Fortune, is offered the choice between wisdom, strength, health, beauty, long life, and riches, and chooses the last. He receives a purse from which he can at any time draw ten pieces of gold. He goes on his travels, in the course of which he secures the marvellous hat of the soldan of Turkey, which transports the wearer wherever he wishes to go. But at the height of his success Fortune steps in and puts an end to his life. His son Andelocia, refusing to learn from his father's fate and equipped with the purse and hat, has a series of adventures at the court of Athelstane, loses his talismans, and meets a miserable death.

OLDHAM, John (1653–83) Poet and translator. He published several Pindaric *odes, but is chiefly remembered for his ironical *Satire against Virtue* (1679) and *Satires upon the Jesuits* (1681). His *Poems and Translations* were collected in 1683. He died young of smallpox, and John *Dryden commemorated him and his verse in the lines beginning 'Farewell, too little and too lately known'.

OLD MOORE (Francis Moore) (1657–?1714) Astrologer, and licensed physician. His *Vox Stellarum, an Almanac for 1698 with Astrological Observations* appeared in 1697. *Old Moore's Almanack* long outlived its creator, and sold extremely well throughout the 18th and 19th centuries. It still survives, thanks to its reputation for sensationalism and prophecy. *See* ALMANACS.

Old Mortality A novel by Walter *Scott, published 1816 in *Tales of my Landlord*, 1st series. 'Old Mortality' is the nickname of Robert Paterson who, towards the end of the 18th century, travels through Scotland cleaning and repairing the tombs of the Cameronians, a sect of fanatical Covenanters who took up arms for their religion against Charles II. The novel tells the story of young Henry Morton of Milnwood, a moderate Presbyterian of courage and integrity. The action takes place in the period between the uprising of the Covenanters at Drumclog and their defeat at Bothwell Bridge three weeks later, with a final section several years after.

OLDS, Sharon (1942–) American poet. *The Father* (1992) focuses on her father's death from cancer. Her work has drawn comparison with Walt *Whitman in its celebration of the body. *Strike Sparks* (2004) is a selection of her poems 1980–2002. *One Secret Thing* was published in 2008. *See also* WICKS, SUSAN.

Old Vic Theatre (previously **the Royal Victoria**) A theatre in the Waterloo Road, London, long famous for its notable productions of

Shakespeare's plays under the management of Lilian Baylis (1874–1937), who took it over in 1912, and, from 1963, for over ten years the home of the National Theatre Company.

Old Wife's Tale, The A play largely in prose by George *Peele, published 1595. The play is a satire on the romantic dramas of the time, the first English work of this kind. The play is rich in songs and magical invocations.

OLIPHANT, Margaret (1828–97) Née Wilson, a prolific Scottish writer; early widowed, she was compelled to write for an income, both for her own and for her brother's families. In 1849 she published *Passages in the Life of Mrs Margaret Maitland*, a tale of Scotland which had an encouraging reception; *Caleb Field* (1851) is a historical novel and *The Athelings* (1857) one of her many domestic romances. She wrote biographies of the brilliant heretical preacher Edward Irving (1862) and a life of Laurence Oliphant (1891, no relation). Her 'Chronicles of Carlingford' proved her most lasting success; the most notable of this series of novels are *Salem Chapel*, 1863; *The Perpetual Curate*, 1864; *Miss Marjoribanks*, 1866; and *Phoebe Junior*, 1876. Religious themes predominate, but the books are sharp and humorous, and she became one of the most popular novelists of her generation. Her other most interesting group of books, *Stories of the Seen and Unseen*, all connected in some way with death and the experience of the soul, began with *A Beleaguered City* (1880) which was followed by *A Little Pilgrim* (1882) and others. Her astute *Literary History of England* (1882) earned much praise, and her long association with *Blackwood's* was commemorated in the posthumous *Annals of a Publishing House* (1897). Her autobiography (1899) describes the destructive necessity of having to write so much, and movingly records the domestic tragedies that haunted her life.

Olive A novel by Dinah *Craik, published in 1850. It tells the story of Olive Rothesay, a disabled girl, resented by her mother and slighted by her father, who struggles with adversity in order to become a successful artist. Like *Jane Eyre*, with which it shares many preoccupations, the novel describes a process of intellectual and emotional growth which allows a disadvantaged young woman to value herself, and then to be valued. It has recently attracted the attention of scholars interested in fictional representations of disability.

Oliver In the *Charlemagne cycle of legends, one of Charlemagne's *Paladins. He is the close friend of *Roland, with whom he has a prolonged and undecided single combat (the origin of their comradeship), and is his equal in bravery, but more prudent. At the battle of Roncesvalles he urges Roland to summon help by sounding his horn, but Roland postpones doing so till too late. Oliver's sister Aude is betrothed to Roland.

Oliver Twist A novel by Charles *Dickens, published 1837–8. Oliver Twist is the name given to a child of unknown parentage born in a workhouse and brought up under ruthless conditions. Bumble, the parish beadle, is especially callous. Here Dickens demonstrates his hostility to Benthamism, and to the provisions of the 1834 New Poor Law. Unhappily apprenticed to an undertaker, Oliver runs away, reaches London, and falls into the hands of a gang of thieves, ruled by the old Jew Fagin. The burglar Bill Sikes, his mistress Nancy, and 'the Artful Dodger', an impudent young pickpocket, are also members of the gang. He is temporarily rescued by the benevolent Mr Brownlow, but kidnapped by the gang, acting on behalf of the sinister Monks, who wants to ensure Oliver's degradation. Oliver is forced to accompany Bill Sikes on a burglary, is wounded, and encounters the kindly Mrs Maylie and her protégée Rose, who take him in. The good-hearted Nancy reveals to Rose that Monks knows about Oliver's parentage, and wishes all proof of it destroyed. Enquiry is set on foot. Nancy's action is discovered by the gang, and she is brutally murdered by Bill Sikes. A hue and cry is raised; Sikes, trying to escape, accidentally hangs himself. The rest of the gang are caught, and Fagin executed. Monks, discovered and threatened with exposure, confesses that he is the half-brother of Oliver, and has pursued his ruin, animated by hatred and the desire to retain the whole of his father's property. Rose is the sister of Oliver's unfortunate mother. Oliver is adopted by Mr Brownlow. Monks emigrates and dies in prison. Bumble ends his career in the workhouse over which he formerly ruled.

Dickens, in a preface to the third edition (April 1841) dissociated it from the popular *'Newgate novels' of the period, by Harrison *Ainsworth, Edward *Bulwer-Lytton, and others.

Olivia The only novel written by Dorothy *Bussy, which she published anonymously in 1949 with the *Hogarth Press. Set in a girls' school, it depicts a lesbian relationship between two teachers and its impact on the pupils.

OLIVIER, Edith (1872–1948) Novelist, biographer, and country writer. Her novels include *The Love Child* (1927), *Dwarf's Blood* (1931), and *The Seraphim Room* (1932). Her love of Wiltshire is recorded in a series of country books, and in her autobiography, *Without Knowing Mr Walkley* (1938). She was a central figure in the group known as the Bright Young Things, forming close friendships with Rex Whistler (1905–44) and Cecil Beaton (1904–80).

O'MALLEY, Ernie (1897–1957) Irish revolutionary whose laconic guerrilla war memoir *On Another Man's Wound* (1936) was praised by John *McGahern and others. O'Malley enclosed close literary friendships, notably with Hart *Crane and Louis *MacNeice, who portrayed him as Aidan in *Autumn Sequel*.

Omar Khayyám, The Rubáiyát of A 'translation' by Edward *FitzGerald of the *rubais* or quatrains attributed to a 12th-century Persian poet. The 'translation' was first published anonymously in 1859; FitzGerald produced further editions, revised and with added quatrains, in 1868, 1872, and 1879. The work is in fact part translation, part inspired by the originals, and part invention. Sceptical of divine providence, suspicious of human grandeur, and concentrating on the pleasures of the fleeting moment, the poem includes felicitously phrased aphorisms which are among the most frequently quoted lines in English poetry.

ONDAATJE, Michael (1943–) Canadian poet and novelist, born in Sri Lanka. He first came to critical notice as a poet with *The Dainty Monsters* (1967), later collections include *There's a Trick with a Knife I'm Learning to Do* (1979), *Handwriting* (1998), and *The Story* (2006). *The Collected Works of Billy the Kid* (1970), a collage of poetry and prose and visual devices, presents an amalgam of history, fiction, and autobiography. *Coming through Slaughter* (1976) is a fictionalized study of the jazz musician Charles 'Buddy' Bolden (1876–1931). In *Running in the Family* (1982), blurring the boundaries between autobiography and fiction, Ondaatje drew on his family's Sri Lankan past. *The English Patient* (1992, filmed 1996, dir. Anthony Minghella), set at the end of the Second World War, won the *Booker Prize. Subsequent novels include *Anil's Ghost* (2000), set amidst the conflicts of contemporary Sri Lanka, and *Divisadero* (2007).

One Flew over the Cuckoo's Nest (1962) Novel by Ken *Kesey, set in the mental ward of an American hospital presided over by Big Nurse. Its surreal presentation of resistance to authority by the inmate McMurphy made it a classic of the counter-culture of the sixties. Adaptations include a 1963 stage version, and a 1975 film, starring Jack Nicholson.

O'NEILL, Eugene (1888–1953) American dramatist. The experimental Provincetown Players staged several of his early one-act plays, including *Bound East for Cardiff* (1916) and *The Moon of the Caribbees* (1918). His full-length naturalistic drama *Beyond the Horizon* (1920) was followed by his expressionistic tragedy *The Emperor Jones* (1920), *Anna Christie* (1921), *The Hairy Ape* (1922), *All God's Chillun Got Wings* (1924), and *Desire under the Elms* (1924). O'Neill's criticism of contemporary materialistic values was powerfully and poetically expressed in *The Fountain* (1925), *The Great God Brown* (1926), *Lazarus Laughed* (1927), and *Marco Millions* (1927). He experimented with a *stream-of-consciousness technique in *Strange Interlude* (1928), and adapted the theme of the *Oresteia to the aftermath of the American Civil War in his trilogy *Mourning Becomes Electra* (1931). *Ah! Wilderness* (1932) and *Days without End* (1934) were followed by a long absence from the stage; his tragedy *The Iceman Cometh* appeared in 1946, and his masterpiece, *Long Day's Journey into Night*, written in 1940–41, was posthumously produced and published in 1956. It is a semi-autobiographical family tragedy, portraying the mutually destructive relationships of drug-addicted Mary Tyrone, her ex-actor husband James, and their two sons, hard-drinking Jamie and intellectual Edmund. O'Neill's plays remain powerfully theatrical and original; he transcends his debt to *Ibsen and *Strindberg, producing an oeuvre in which the struggle between self-destruction, self-deception, and redemption is presented as essentially dramatic in nature.

onomatopoeia The formation of a word by an imitation of the sound associated with the object or action designated: as 'hurlyburly', 'buzz', 'creak'. The term is also applied to the use of a combination of words to evoke by sound a certain image or mood, the most frequently quoted example being Alfred *Tennyson's 'murmuring of innumerable bees'.

OPIE, Amelia (1769–1853) Novelist and poet, and friend of Sydney *Smith, Richard Brinsley *Sheridan, Madame de Staël, and many other writers. She came to know William *Godwin and Mary *Wollstonecraft, though her politics lacked their overt radicalism. Her copious works include *The Father and Daughter* (1801); *Poems* (1802); *Simple Tales* (1806); a *Memoir* of her husband in 1809; *Valentine's Eve* (1816); *Madeline* (1822); and *Lays for the Dead* in 1833. Her most notable fiction is **Adeline Mowbray*, suggested by the story of Mary Wollstonecraft. She was satirized by Thomas Love. Peacock in **Headlong Hall* as Miss Poppyseed, 'an indefatigable compounder of novels'.

OPIE, Iona (1923–) and **Peter** (1918–82) Authors, folklorists, and collectors specializing in childhood who produced distinguished works including the *Oxford Dictionary of Nursery Rhymes* (1951), *The Lore and Language of Schoolchildren* (1959), and *Children's Games in Street and Playground* (1969). Edited anthologies include *The Oxford Book of Children's Verse* (1973). After Peter's death Iona published *The People in the Playground* (1993) and *Children's Games with Things* (1997).

Ó RATHAILLE, Aodhagán (Egan O'Rahilly) (*c.*1670–1729) Born in Kerry, central figure in the *aisling tradition. Ó Rathaille's impassioned, intricately musical lyrics lament the fate of the aristocratic Gaelic order of Munster in the aftermath of the Williamite wars. They have been translated by James Clarence *Mangan, Frank *O'Connor, Seamus *Heaney, and others, and are cited in a variety of ways in the poetry of W. B. *Yeats, Hugh *MacDiarmid, and Thomas *Kinsella.

ORCZY, Baroness (Mrs Montague Barstow) (1865–1947) Hungarian-born novelist. She achieved best-seller status with her romantic novel *The Scarlet Pimpernel* (1905), the story of the League of the Scarlet Pimpernel, a band of Englishmen pledged to rescue innocent victims of the reign of terror in Paris. The success of the novel followed its success in a dramatized version, written by Orczy in collaboration with her husband. It was performed first in Nottingham in 1903, then, to great acclaim, in London in 1905.

Ordeal of Richard Feverel, The A novel by George *Meredith, published 1859. Meredith's first mature work, written just after the painful collapse of his first marriage. Its treatment of sexual themes meant that it was boycotted by *Mudie's Lending Library, limiting its early sales, and damaging Meredith's reputation. Sir Austin Feverel's wife runs off with a poet, leaving him with their son Richard. The

obtuse Sir Austin devises a 'System' for Richard's education, which consists in keeping the boy at home (for schools are corrupting) and in trusting to authoritarian parental vigilance. The slow collapse of the 'System', and Richard's struggle for freedom and knowledge, form the underlying theme of the book. Richard and Lucy Desborough, a neighbouring farmer's niece, fall in love at first sight, and an idyllic courtship ends in the discovery of their attachment. Lucy lacks the birth Sir Austin requires for his son. His attempts to separate the young couple result in their secret marriage. Ordered to await his father in London, Richard becomes entangled with a courtesan, while the predatory Lord Mountfalcon attempts to ensnare Lucy. Overcome with shame at his treatment of his wife, Richard hears that he is a father and that Lucy and Sir Austin are reconciled. But on returning he learns of the designs of Lord Mountfalcon; he challenges him to a duel and is seriously wounded. In the succeeding fever his confusions are stripped away and he is finally freed of his devouring father. These events overwhelm Lucy, who loses her mind and dies.

Oresteia, The A trilogy of plays by *Aeschylus. *Agamemnon* describes the return to Argos after the Trojan War of the victorious Agamemnon, brother of Helen's husband Menelaus, and his murder by his wife Clytemnestra, foretold by his captive, the prophetess Cassandra, daughter of King Priam of Troy. *The Libation Bearers* (*Choephoroe*) portrays the vengeance of the son and daughter of Agamemnon, Orestes and Electra: Orestes murders Clytemnestra and her lover Aegisthus, and is himself pursued by the Furies (Erinyes). The *Eumenides* shows the Furies in pursuit of Orestes, who is protected by the younger god Apollo. Orestes is tried, Athena, goddess of wisdom, delivers her casting vote on his behalf, and he goes free, released from the ancient blood vengeance: Athena reconciles the Furies to the new Law, and they are transformed into the Kindly Ones (Eumenides), who bless the city of Athens.

Other versions of the story appear in the works of *Sophocles (who wrote *Electra*) and *Euripides, and there are notable 20th-century dramatic versions by *T. S. Eliot (*The Family Reunion*, 1939), Eugene *O'Neill (*Mourning Becomes Electra*, 1931), and Jean-Paul *Sartre (*Les Mouches*, 1943).

Orfeo, Sir A metrical romance of the early 14th century in about 600 lines, identified in its prologue as a *Breton lay. It represents the story of Orpheus and Eurydice (*see* ORPHEUS) in a

Celtic guise: Queen Heurodys is carried off to fairyland and pursued by King Orfeo whose melodious playing of his harp succeeds in bringing her back to the world of men. This version of the story (to which Francis Child's ballad 'King Orfeo' is related) ends happily.

oriental novel (oriental tale)   A class of story set in the Middle or Far East, especially popular in the 18th century. Public interest in the Orient (encompassing Egypt, India, and Japan) as a zone of powerful fantasy was stimulated by Richard Knolles's influential history of the Turks; by the translation into English in 1705–8 of the *Arabian Nights*; and by the translations of Sir William *Jones. Many of the tales (such as those of Alexander Dow, John *Hawkesworth, James Ridley (1736–65), and Frances *Sheridan, and William *Beckford's *Vathek*) relate the flamboyant adventures of well-defined heroes and villains, often with supernatural intervention. Johnson's *Rasselas* uses an oriental setting to promote a moral fable. Robert *Southey's *The Curse of Kehama* (1810), Thomas *Moore's *Lalla Rookh*, and Lord *Byron's *The *Corsair* and *The *Giaour* are poems which explore oriental settings with ambiguous relish.

Origin of Species, On the   The great work of Charles *Darwin, published in 1859. Its full title was *On the Origin of Species by Means of Natural Selection, or the Preservation of Favoured Races in the Struggle for Life*.

Orinda   *See* PHILIPS, KATHERINE.

Ó RÍORDÁIN, Seán   (1916–77) Irish poet, whose ground-breaking debut *Eireaball Spideoige* ('A Robin's Tail', 1952) is at once deeply attuned to the traditions of Gaelic Munster and responsive—in rhythm as well as idiom—to the example of Gerard Manley *Hopkins and T. S. *Eliot. The lyrics of *Brosna* ('Firewood', 1964) are generally shorter and less disjunctive in style. Ó Ríordáin has been translated by Ciaran *Carson, Patrick Crotty, Greg Delanty, and others.

Orlando furioso   A poem by *Ariosto, published in its complete form in 1532, designed to exalt the house of Este and to continue the story of Orlando's love for Angelica begun by Boiardo in *Orlando innamorato*.

Saracens and Christians, in the days of *Charlemagne, are at war. The Saracens under Agramant, king of Africa, are besieging Charlemagne in Paris with the help of Marsilio, the Moorish king of Spain, and two mighty warriors, Rodo-

mont and Mandricardo. Angelica, who at the end of Boiardo's poem had been left by Charlemagne to the care of Namo, escapes. Orlando, chief of the *Paladins, hopelessly infatuated with Angelica, forgets his duty and pursues her. Angelica meets with various adventures, finally coming upon the wounded Moorish youth Medoro, whom she tends, falls in love with, and marries. They honeymoon in the woods. Orlando, arriving there by chance and learning their story, is seized with a furious and grotesque madness, and runs naked through the country, destroying everything in his path. He is finally captured by his own companions and miraculously cured of his madness and his love. In a conclusive battle he kills Agramant.

Other notable episodes in the work are the voyage of Astolfo on the hippogriff to the moon, whence he brings back the lost wits of Orlando; and the self-immolation of Isabella, the widow of the Scottish prince Zerbino, to escape the attentions of the pagan king Rodomont.

Edmund Spenser, in *The *Faerie Queene*, aimed to 'overgo' Ariosto's epic, and owes much to it for his characters and form of narration. The first complete English version 'in English Heroical Verse' is that of Sir J. *Harington (1591).

Orlando innamorato   A poem by Matteo Maria *Boiardo (Bks I and II, 1484, and with the unfinished third book, 1495), on the subject of the falling in love of *Orlando (the Roland of the *Charlemagne cycle) with Angelica, daughter of Galafron, king of Cathay. She arrives at the court of Charlemagne, with her brother Argalia, under false pretences, to carry off the Christian knights to her father's country. Several knights attempt to win her, the chief among them being Astolfo, Ferrau, Rinaldo, and Orlando. Argalia is slain and Angelica flees, but, drinking from an enchanted fountain, she falls in love with Rinaldo, who, drinking from another enchanted fountain, conceives a violent aversion to her. He runs away, pursued by her, and they reach her father's country, where she is besieged in the capital, Albracca, by Agrican, king of Tartary, to whom her hand had been promised (an incident to which Milton refers in *Paradise Regained*, III. 337ff.). Orlando comes to Angelica's rescue, slays Agrican, and returns with Angelica to France whither he has been summoned to assist Charlemagne against Agramant, king of the Moors. Drinking once more from the same enchanted fountains, Rinaldo this time falls in love with Angelica, and Angelica into hatred of him. A fierce combat ensues between Orlando and Rinaldo, suppressed by Charlemagne, who entrusts Angelica to Namo, duke of Bavaria.

Orley Farm A novel by Anthony *Trollope, published 1862. It was the first of Trollope's novels to be published in shilling numbers (1861–2), and he was especially pleased with the illustrations provided by John Everett *Millais. The plot concerns the contested inheritance of Orley Farm, by the son of a second marriage, in a codicil discovered to have been forged by his mother.

Ormond A novel by Maria *Edgeworth, published 1817. Largely a tale of life in Ireland, it also describes fashionable Parisian society in the 18th century. The main characters are Harry Ormond, an orphan; his fascinating but unprincipled guardian Sir Ulick O'Shane; the kind-hearted eccentric Cornelius O'shane, the 'king of the Black Islands'; and his daughter Dora.

Ormulum, The A poem in Middle English, of which about 20,000 short lines survive, written in the late 12th century in the south Lincolnshire dialect by Orm, an Augustinian canon. The poem is a series of sermons arranged chronologically around the Gospel versions of the life of Christ. The single version that survives comprises just over an eighth (32) of the writer's ambitious original scheme of 242 sermons. It is of great linguistic interest, particularly for the semi-phonetic spelling system devised by the writer (largely a matter of doubling consonants after short vowels).

Oroonoko, or The History of the Royal Slave A novel by Aphra *Behn, published *c.*1688, adapted for the stage by Thomas *Southerne, 1695. Oroonoko, grandson and heir of an African king, loves and wins Imoinda, daughter of the king's general. The king, who also loves her, is enraged and orders her to be sold as a slave. Oroonoko himself is trapped by the captain of an English slave-trading ship and carried off to Surinam, then an English colony, where he is reunited with Imoinda and renamed Caesar by his owners. He rouses his fellow slaves to revolt, is deceived into surrender by deputy governor Byam (a historical figure), and brutally whipped. Oroonoko, determined on revenge but not hoping for victory, kills Imoinda, who dies willingly. He is discovered by her dead body and cruelly executed.

The novel is remarkable as an early protest against the slave trade. The author comments on the superior simplicity and morality of both African slaves and the indigenous Indians, whose Christian oppressors are shown as treacherous and hypocritical. Behn's memories of her own visit to Surinam in 1663 provide a vivid background, and much of the story is narrated as by a personal witness. Southerne's tragedy follows the broad lines of the novel, but with changes which make the story less violent, and less provocative.

OROSIUS (*fl.* early 5th century) A priest of Tarragona in Spain, disciple of St Augustine and friend of St *Jerome, author of the *History against the Pagans*, a universal history and geography which was translated by the circle of King *Alfred in the 890s.

Orphan, The A tragedy in blank verse by Thomas *Otway, produced 1680. Castalio and Polydore are the twin sons of Acasto. Monimia, the orphan daughter of a friend of Acasto's, has been brought up with them, and both have fallen in love with her. She loves Castalio, and they are secretly married. Polydore, ignorant of this and overhearing them arranging for a meeting in the night, takes Castalio's place in the darkness, and is not detected. Castalio, coming later, is shut out. The truth is discovered through Chamont, Monimia's brother. Castalio and Polydore kill themselves, and Monimia takes poison. The play was very successful, and was frequently revived.

Orpheus A legendary Greek poet, supposedly son of *Apollo by the *Muse Calliope, and renowned as a musician, religious leader, and seer. He was reputed to have made trees and rocks follow his singing, been one of the Argonauts, visited Egypt, and founded mystery cults in several parts of Greece. He was eventually torn to pieces by Maenads (frenzied votaresses of the god Dionysus), and his head and lyre, thrown into the river Hebrus, drifted to Lesbos where the head became an oracle, while *Apollo placed the lyre among the stars. Many writings ascribed to Orpheus and his son *Musaeus are quoted by ancient writers. The best-known story, told by *Virgil in *Georgics*, Book 4, *Ovid in *Metamorphoses*, Book 10, and *Boethius in *De Consolatione Philosophiae*, Book III, is of Orpheus going down into hell, persuading *Hades to let him have back his wife Eurydice, and then losing her because he disregarded the instruction not to look back before they reached the light of day. Orpheus was especially important to John *Milton, who refers to his skill and plight in *'L'Allegro' and *'Il Penseroso', *'Lycidas', and *Paradise Lost*, Book VII. Important modern treatments include Rainer Maria Rilke's *Die Sonnette an Orpheus* (*Sonnets to Orpheus*, 1923), and Jean Cocteau's film trilogy *Le Sang d'un poète* (*The Blood of a Poet*, 1930), *Orphée* (1950), and *Le Testament d'Orphée* (*The Testament of Orpheus*, 1960).

ORRERY, earls of *See* BOYLE, JOHN; BOYLE, ROGER.

ORTON, Joe (1933-67) Playwright and novelist. His comedies, which include *Entertaining Mr Sloane* (1964), *Loot* (1965), and the posthumously performed *What the Butler Saw* (1969), are black, stylish, satirical, farcical, and violent, and their emphasis on corruption and sexual perversion made them a *succès de scandale*. Orton was battered to death in his Islington home by his friend and companion Kenneth Halliwell, who then committed suicide. *Prick up your Ears* (1978), a biography by John Lahr, formed the basis of a film scripted (1987) by Alan *Bennett. Lahr also edited *The Orton *Diaries* (1986).

ORWELL, George (1903-50) Pseudonym of Eric Arthur Blair, novelist and political writer. His experiences serving with the Indian Imperial Police in Burma, 1922-7 are reflected in his first novel, *Burmese Days* (1934), and in his essays, 'A Hanging' and 'Shooting an Elephant'. He resigned 'to escape not merely from imperialism but from every form of man's dominion over man', as he later put it. He lived off and on among tramps (see *Down and Out in Paris and London*, 1933, his first published book). His later novels include *A Clergyman's Daughter* (1935), *Keep the Aspidistra Flying* (1936), and *Coming up for Air* (1939). A journey north in 1936, commissioned by Victor *Gollancz, produced *The Road to Wigan Pier* (1937, published by the *Left Book Club) and his involvement in the Spanish Civil War resulted in *Homage to Catalonia* (1938). By this stage Orwell saw himself primarily as a political writer, a democratic socialist who avoided party labels, hated totalitarianism, and was to become more and more disillusioned with the methods of communism. V. S. *Pritchett, reviewing Orwell's *The Lion and the Unicorn: Socialism and the English Genius* (1941), compared him to Daniel *Defoe and William *Cobbett for his 'subversive, nonconforming brand of patriotism'. His collections of essays include *Inside the Whale* (1940), *Critical Essays* (1946), and *Shooting an Elephant* (1950). But his most popular works remain his political satires *Animal Farm* (1945) and *Nineteen Eighty-Four* (1949).

OSBORNE, Dorothy (1627-95) Letter writer. She met William *Temple in 1648 and they married, after considerable family opposition, in 1654. Her letters to him during the period 1652-4, were partly published in a life of Temple in 1836; Thomas *Macaulay singled them out for praise and they were edited by Sir Edward Parry (1888) and G. C. Moore Smith (1928). The letters, lively and witty, provide an intimate picture of the life, manners, and reading habits of the times, of the relations between the sexes, and particularly of a woman's attitudes to marriage and filial duty.

OSBORNE, John (1929-94) Playwright; the first volume of his autobiography, *A Better Class of Person* (1981), describes his childhood in suburbia, and his years as an actor in provincial repertory. He made his name with *Look Back in Anger* (1956; pub. 1957), which was followed by *Epitaph for George Dillon* (1957; pub. 1958; written in collaboration with Anthony Creighton); *The Entertainer* (1957, which starred Laurence Olivier as Archie Rice, a faded survivor of the great days of music hall); *Luther* (1961, based on the life of Martin *Luther); *Inadmissible Evidence* (1964); and *A Patriot for Me* (1965, set in Vienna, based on the rise and fall of Redl, a homosexual officer in the Austro-Hungarian army, ruined by blackmail). His later works (which include *West of Suez*, 1971; *A Sense of Detachment*, 1972; *Watch It Come Down*, 1976) became increasingly vituperative in tone; his outbursts of rage against contemporary society are frequently exhilarating, for the anger that made him known as an *'Angry Young Man' remained one of his strongest theatrical weapons, but he also expressed an ambivalent nostalgia for the past that his own work did so much to alter. His last play, *Déjàvu* (1991), is a sequel to *Look Back in Anger*, presenting the same characters in middle age. *Almost a Gentleman* (1991) was a second volume of autobiography; *Damn You, England* (1994) a miscellany of reviews and letters to the press. *See* KITCHEN SINK DRAMA.

O'SHAUGHNESSY, Arthur William Edgar (1844-81) Poet, protégé of Edward *Bulwer-Lytton, and friend of D. G. *Rossetti. His best-known poem, 'Ode' ('We are the music-makers'), appeared in *Music and Moonlight* (1874) and was set to music by Edward *Elgar.

Ossian Variant of *Oisin, a legendary Gaelic warrior and bard. *See* MACPHERSON, JAMES; FINGAL.

OSWALD, Alice (1966–) Poet; her work as a gardener at Chelsea Physic Garden is reflected in *The Thing in the Gap-Stone-Stile* (1996). *Dart* (2002, T. S. Eliot Prize) is a book-length evocation of the river, which she has described as 'a songline from source to sea'. The poem mingles the voices of the people who live and work on the banks of the Dart with characters from history and myth. *Woods etc* (2005) is a more elliptical and mysterious exploration of subjectivity, focused through the natural world. Oswald has continued to probe the boundaries of mainstream poetry, although her work also shows the influence of poets such as Gerard Manley *Hopkins and Ted *Hughes. Oswald's explicit turn towards the visionary also shows an alliance with earlier writers of the New Apocalypse, particularly Dylan *Thomas. Later collections include *A Sleepwalk on the Severn* (2009).

OSWALD, St (d. 992) One of the leading figures (along with *Dunstan and *Æthelwold) in the 10th-century Benedictine Revival in England. On Dunstan's initiative he was appointed bishop of Worcester in 961, founding monasteries at Westbury, Worcester, Winchcombe, and on the Isle of Ramsey. In 971–2 he was made archbishop of York.

Othello, the Moor of Venice A tragedy by *Shakespeare, written between 1602 and 1604 when it was first performed before James I at Whitehall. It was first printed in quarto in 1622, and again in a different version in the *folio of 1623. The story is taken from Cinzio, which Shakespeare probably read in Italian, possibly also in French.

The first act is set in Venice. Desdemona, daughter of Brabanzio, a Venetian senator, has secretly married Othello, a Moor in the service of the state. Accused before the duke and senators of having stolen Brabanzio's daughter, Othello explains and justifies his conduct, and is asked by the Senate to lead the Venetian forces against the Turks who are about to attack Cyprus.

In the middle of a storm which disperses the Turkish fleet, Othello lands on Cyprus with Desdemona, Cassio, a young Florentine, who helped him court his wife and whom he has now promoted to be his lieutenant, and Iago, a soldier, bitterly resentful of being passed over for promotion, who now plans his revenge. Iago uses Roderigo, 'a gulled gentleman' in love with Desdemona, to fight with Cassio after he has got him drunk, so that Othello deprives him of his new rank. He then persuades Cassio to ask Desdemona to plead in his favour with Othello, which she warmly does. At the same time he suggests to Othello that Cassio is, and has been, Desdemona's lover, finally arranging through his wife Emilia, who is Desdemona's waiting-woman, that Othello should see Cassio in possession of a handkerchief which he had given to his bride. Othello is taken in by Iago's promptings and in frenzied jealousy smothers Desdemona in her bed. Iago sets Roderigo to murder Cassio, but when Roderigo fails to do this Iago kills him and Emilia as well, after she has proved Desdemona's innocence to Othello. Emilia's evidence and letters found on Roderigo prove Iago's guilt; he is arrested, and Othello, having tried to stab him, kills himself.

ottava rima An Italian stanza of eight eleven-syllable lines, rhyming *abababcc*, possibly invented by *Boccaccio, and later employed by *Ariosto, *Tasso, and others. It was introduced into England by Thomas *Wyatt, and used to great effect by Lord *Byron in *Don Juan*, with a ten-syllable iambic line.

Otterbourne, The Battle of One of the earliest of English ballads, included in Thomas *Percy's *Reliques*. It describes how the Scots, led by James, earl of Douglas, attacked the castle of Otterburn in Northumberland in 1388.

Otuel, Sir Pagan knight, miraculously converted, subsequently one of *Charlemagne's *Paladins.

OTWAY, Thomas (1652–85) Playwright. He failed as an actor, being given a part by the kindness of Aphra *Behn. He died destitute aged 33. Of his three great tragedies, *Don Carlos*, in rhymed verse, was produced in 1676; *The *Orphan*, in blank verse, in 1680; and *Venice Preserved*, also in blank verse, in 1682. Of his other plays *Alcibiades*, a tragedy, was produced in 1675; *Titus and Berenice*, adapted from a tragedy by *Racine, and *The Cheats of Scapin*, from a comedy by *Molière, in 1676; *The History and Fall of Caius Marius*, an adaptation of *Romeo and Juliet*, in 1679; *Friendship in Fashion*, a comedy, in 1681; and *The Atheist*, also a comedy, in 1683.

OUIDA (1839–1908) Pen-name of Marie Louise de la Ramée, novelist; her pseudonym is a childish mispronunciation of 'Louise'. She began her career contributing stories to *Bentley's Miscellany* (1859–60) encouraged by its editor Harrison *Ainsworth. Her first real success was *Held in Bondage* (1863), followed by *Strathmore* (1865). In 1874 she settled in Florence where she pursued her work as a novelist while living in lavish style. Her other popular novels included *Under Two Flags* (1867; filmed 1936), *Folle-Farine* (1871), which Edward *Bulwer-Lytton considered 'a triumph of modern English fiction', *Two Little Wooden Shoes* (1874), *Moths* (1880), *A Village Commune* (1881), and *In Maremma* (1882). Her 45 novels show a spirit of rebellion against the moral ideals reflected in much of the fiction of the time. She suffered frequent ridicule for her extravagantly portrayed heroes, often languid guardsmen, miracles of strength, courage, and beauty, and for her inaccuracies in matters of men's sports and occupations; but her faults were redeemed by her narrative power and emotional energy.

Our Mutual Friend Charles *Dickens's last completed novel, published in monthly parts (May 1864–November 1865). John Harmon returns from the exile to which he has been sent by a harsh father, a rich dust-contractor; he expects to receive the inheritance to which his father has attached the condition that he shall marry a certain girl, Bella Wilfer. Bella is unknown to him, and he confides to a mate of the ship which is bringing him home his intention of concealing his identity until he has formed some judgement of his allotted wife. The mate lures him to a riverside haunt, attempts to murder him, throws his body into the river, and is in turn murdered and his body likewise thrown into the river. Harmon recovers and escapes; the mate's body is found after some days, and, owing to Harmon's papers found upon it, it is taken to be that of Harmon. Harmon's intention of remaining unknown is thus facilitated; he assumes the name of John Rokesmith and becomes the secretary of the kindly, disinterested Mr Boffin, old Harmon's foreman, who, in default of young Harmon, inherits the property. He meets Bella, who is adopted by Boffin and whose wealth has made her a coldly disdainful young woman. Rokesmith nevertheless falls in love with her and is contemptuously rejected. Harmon's identity is now discovered by the amiable Mrs Boffin, and the Boffins, devoted to their old master's son and convinced of Bella's soundness of heart, contrive a plot to prove her. Boffin pretends to be transformed by his wealth into a hardhearted miser, and heaps indignities on Harmon, who is finally dismissed. Bella, awakened to the evils of wealth and to the merits of Rokesmith, flies from the Boffins and marries her suitor, whose identity presently comes to light.

Among the notable characters in the book are the Veneerings, types of social parvenus; the good Jew Riah; the blackmailing waterside villain Rogue Riderhood; Jenny Wren, the dolls' dressmaker; Bella Wilfer's grotesque father, mother, and sister; and the spirited Betty Higden, an old woman haunted by dread of the workhouse.

Our Village, *Sketches of Rural Life, Character, and Scenery* By Mary Russell *Mitford, published 1832. Before beginning the series, Mitford declared that it would describe 'country scenery and country manners', and that she abhorred sentimentality. Seasons, places, events, and people are described with precision and humour, the original idea having come from the *Sketch Book* of Washington *Irving.

OVERBURY, Sir Thomas (1581–1613) Poet and essayist. He opposed the marriage of his patron Robert Carr (*c.*1587–1645; afterwards earl of Somerset) with the divorced countess of Essex, and was consigned to the Tower, where he was poisoned by Lady Essex's agents. Four of these were hanged; Somerset and Lady Essex were convicted and pardoned. *James I was possibly implicated. The prosecution was conducted by Francis *Bacon. Overbury's poem *A Wife* appeared in 1614, and with its second edition his Theophrastian 'Characters'. Later editions added new characters, some by John *Webster and some by Thomas *Dekker; John Earle responded to their satirical tone with his *Microcosmography*. *See* CHARACTER-WRITING.

OVERTON, Richard (*fl.* 1646) One of the leaders of the Leveller movement. A prolific, forceful, and versatile pamphleteer, he published much of his work anonymously, and some under the pseudonym of Martin Marpriest, in the tradition of *Martin Marprelate. His *Man's Mortality* (1643), arguing that the soul dies with the body, to be raised on the last day, aroused controversy, and he was imprisoned many times for his religious and political views. His stance is rational, tolerant, egalitarian, and anti-monarchical, and his style colourful and often caustic.

OVID (Publius Ovidius Naso) (43 BC–AD 17) Latin poet. He became known for his *Amores* (loves) and the mock-didactic *Ars Amatoria* (art of love), poems in *elegiac couplets in which he subverts the serious conventions of the *Propertian elegy. The *Heroides* (heroines) are imaginary verse letters to their lovers from lovelorn women of mythology: Ariadne, abandoned by ungrateful *Theseus; Phaedra, trying to reveal just enough to Hippolytus; Dido, reproaching Aeneas for desertion. Ovid then took up the challenge of creating a long poem in *hexameters, a rival to the *Aeneid*. He settled on the theme of *Metamorphoses*, transformations of form, by which mythical thought explained natural phenomena. So the cypress tree had been a pretty boy, Cyparissus; the spider had been a girl, Arachne, who challenged Athene to a weaving contest and was hideously transmogrified by the insulted goddess. Most of the stories were of unhappy loves. *Fasti*, versifying the Roman calendar and its festivals, was an attempt to re-establish himself morally, in the puritanical last years of Augustus. He was sent into permanent exile in Tomis on the Black Sea in AD 8. The cause remains unclear: Ovid speaks of a poem (his *Ars*) and an unexplained 'mistake'. The collections of elegies entitled *Tristia* (sorrows) and *Epistulae ex Ponto* (letters from Pontus) express his grief, despair, and occasional hope. Ovid's posthumous influence was enormous. *Chaucer and *Gower both borrowed his stories. Thomas *Lodge, Christopher *Marlowe, Edmund *Spenser, *Shakespeare, George *Chapman, Michael *Drayton were all indebted to him directly or through Arthur *Golding's translation of the *Metamorphoses*. Other notable translators include Marlowe, George *Sandys, John *Dryden, and Ted *Hughes.

Ovide moralisé A French work in octosyllabic couplets, written by an anonymous author early in the 14th century. It moralizes fifteen books of Ovid's *Metamorphoses* and is highly significant in the development of late medieval and Renaissance literature by bringing secular literature into the official canon. It was particularly influential on *Chaucer. Compare John Ridewall's *Fulgentius metaforalis* (*c*.1330) for the practice of allegorizing the stories of classical authors.

OWEN, Alun (1925-94) Welsh-Liverpudlian playwright, actor, and television scriptwriter. He is principally remembered for his gritty, realist television dramas, which helped to shape the emerging style of TV drama in the 1960s: these include *No Trams to Lime Street* (1959), and *After the Funeral* (1960); *A Little Winter Love* (1964) was a stage play. He also wrote the screenplay for the *Beatles' film *A Hard Day's Night* (1964).

OWEN, Robert (1771-1858) Socialist and philanthropist. In 1799 he purchased the New Lanark mills in Scotland, where he established his model community and village, organized on principles of mutual cooperation. His example was instrumental in bringing about the Factory Act of 1819. He published *A New View of Society* in 1813 and *The Revolution in Mind and Practice of the Human Race* in 1849. Owen was notorious in later life for his atheism.

OWEN, Wilfred (1893-1918) Poet, who joined the army in 1915. After concussion and shell-shock he was invalided to Craiglockhart War Hospital in Edinburgh, where he was greatly encouraged in his writing by Siegfried *Sassoon. He returned to France in 1918, won the MC, and was killed a week before the Armistice. He found his own voice as a poet of the trenches. After the war, his reputation slowly grew, assisted by Edmund *Blunden's edition of his poems, with a memoir, in 1931. His bleak realism, his energy and indignation, his compassion, and his high technical skills (he was a master of metrical variety, *assonance, and *pararhyme) are evident in most of his work. His poems were chosen by Benjamin *Britten for his *War Requiem* (1961).

'O Westren winde' The opening words of an early 16th-century quatrain. As a carol, it inspired masses by Christopher Tye (*c*.1505-*c*.1572), John Sheppard (d. 1559?), and John Taverner (*c*.1490-1545). The lines are used to great effect by Virginia *Woolf (in *The *Waves*) and Ernest *Hemingway (in *A Farewell to Arms*).

Owl and the Nightingale, The An early Middle English poem of 1,794 lines of *octosyllabic couplets, from the beginning or middle of the 13th century. It is a debate between the birds concerning the benefits each confers on mankind. It touches with light, scholastic legalism on many matters of serious contemporary interest, including foreknowledge, music, confession, and papal missions. It is a virtuoso poem, highly accomplished in its style and in its humorous tone, which reaches no definite conclusion. The debate is to be submitted at the end to the judgement of 'Nicholas of Guildford', who has been thought to be the author.

OXFORD, Edward De Vere, seventeenth earl of (1550-1604) Poet and courtier. Oxford married Lord Burghley's daughter Anne, and he raised high hopes as a courtier and patron, but they were dissipated by his capricious and violent temper. His most famous quarrel was with Philip *Sidney. He had some reputation as a poet during his lifetime, but the idea, initiated by John Thomas Looney (1870-1944) in

1920 and subsequently promoted by 'Oxfordians', that he was the author of William *Shakespeare's plays is without foundation. *See* SHAKESPEARE: AUTHORSHIP OF THE WORKS.

Oxford and Cambridge Magazine A periodical of the year 1856, of which twelve monthly numbers appeared, financed mainly by William *Morris. Among its (anonymous) contributors were Morris and Edward Burne-Jones (of Oxford), Henry Lushington (of Cambridge), and by invitation D. G. *Rossetti.

Oxford English Dictionary, The The scheme of 'a completely new English Dictionary' was conceived in 1858, chiefly as the result of the reading of two papers 'On some Deficiencies in Our English Dictionaries' by Richard Trench to the Philological Society in 1857. Herbert Coleridge (1830–61), and after him Frederick Furnivall, were the first editors. Their work consisted mainly in the collection of materials, and it was not until James *Murray took over in 1878 that the preparation of the dictionary took shape. The first part (*A–Ant*) was published in 1884; it was finished in 1928, 70 years from its beginning. Murray, who planned the work, did not live to see it completed (at his death, T had been reached). His co-editors were Henry Bradley (from 1888), William Craigie (from 1901), and Charles Onions (from 1914).

The essential feature of the dictionary is its historical method, by which the meaning and form of the words are traced from their earliest appearance on the basis of an immense number of quotations, collected by more than 800 voluntary workers. The dictionary contains a record of 414,825 words, whose history is illustrated by 1,827,306 quotations. The original title of the main work was 'A New English Dictionary on Historical Principles' (abbreviated as *NED*). The title *The Oxford English Dictionary* first appeared in the reprint of 1933, with a supplement of 867 pages. In 1957 work began, under the editorship of Robert Burchfield (1923–2004), on a new supplement, superseding that of 1933, and treating all the vocabulary which came into use while the main dictionary was being published or after its completion. The outcome of this work, entitled *A Supplement to the Oxford English Dictionary*, contains a record of approximately 120,000 words. The second edition, by J. Simpson and E. Weiner, was published in 1989. It was published on CD-ROM in 1992, and online in 2000. A third edition, expected to double the length of the dictionary, is currently in preparation, and will represent a nearly complete overhaul of the work. The on-line database is updated quarterly with revisions that will be included in the third edition.

Oxford Gazette The first real newspaper, other than a newsletter, to be published in England. It appeared in November 1665, the court being then at Oxford owing to the great plague, and was started by Henry *Muddiman under the direction of his patron Sir Joseph Williamson (1633–1701). It became the *London Gazette* in 1666. It still survives, not now a newspaper, but a record of official appointments, notices of bankruptcy, and other public events, having passed in 1923 into the keeping of the Stationery Office. *See* NEWSPAPERS.

Oxford Movement (Tractarian Movement)   A movement of thought and doctrine within the Church of England, centred at Oxford, which began with the Assize Sermon on National Apostasy preached by John *Keble in 1833. The movement aimed to defend the Church of England as a divine institution with an independent spiritual status, and to revive the High Church traditions of the 17th century. The Reform Act of 1832, and the views of *Broad Church supporters such as Thomas Arnold, had led many to believe that the church was in danger of increasing subordination to civil control. Keble's sermon inspired John Henry *Newman, Richard Hurrell Froude, and others to launch their series *Tracts for the Times* in 1833 (which gave the Tractarian movement its name); the series gained the influential support of Edward Pusey. It was Newman's famous Tract XC (1841) on the compatibility of the Thirty-Nine Articles with Roman Catholic theology that brought the Tractarians under official ban, but hostility had already been aroused by the publication of the first volumes of Froude's *Literary Remains* in 1838, with its strictures on the Reformation. *The Ideal of a Christian Church* (1844), by William Ward (1812–82), with its praise of the Roman Catholic Church, intensified suspicions that the Tractarians (and principally Newman) were subversively leading their followers towards Rome.

The impact of the Tractarians was immense. In literary terms, the revival of interest in the medieval and 17th-century church influenced Alfred *Tennyson, William *Morris and the *Pre-Raphaelites, Christina *Rossetti, and Charlotte *Yonge, among others. See Newman's *Apologia pro Vita Sua* (1864); the autobiography of Isaac *Williams, and Mark *Pattison's *Memoirs*.

Oxford University Press A publishing and (formerly) printing business owned by the university and directed by its delegates of the press, of whom the vice-chancellor is *ex officio* chairman. Its aims are to produce books of religious, scholarly, and educational value: since its surplus profits are devoted to financing the editing and production of unremunerative works of this kind, and to supporting the university, it has charitable status.

Printing in Oxford by independent craftsmen began in 1478, and in 1584 one of these was appointed 'Printer to the University'. This title was borne by a succession of printers in the 17th century and was revived in 1925 for the head of the printing department of the press. One press at Oxford was excepted from the prohibition of printing outside London by a decree of the Star Chamber in 1586, and in 1632 a royal charter allowed the university three presses and to print and sell 'all manner of books'. William *Laud in 1634 bound the university to provide itself with a printing house; but a press under its immediate control did not come into being until 1690. In the meantime John Fell had won an international reputation for scholarly Oxford books by setting up a press (1669) in the Sheldonian Theatre.

Since then, under the delegates' management, the press has produced such famous books as the earl of Clarendon's *History* (1703–7), William Blackstone's *Commentaries* (1765–9), James Clerk Maxwell's *Treatise on Electricity and Magnetism* (1873), the Revised Version of the English Bible (1885), the *Oxford English Dictionary*, completed in 1928, and the *Oxford Dictionary of National Biography* (2004), and, in recent times, the celebrated World's Classics series.

The copyright in Clarendon's works, once very profitable, is secured to the university in perpetuity, and in his honour the Walton Street building to which the press moved in 1829 was named 'the Clarendon Press'. This was formerly the imprint given to learned books published under the supervision of the secretary to the delegates at Oxford.

oxymoron [from two Greek words meaning 'sharp', 'dull'] A rhetorical figure by which two incongruous or contradictory terms are united in an expression so as to give it point, for example 'Faith unfaithful kept him falsely true' (Tennyson, *Idylls of the King*).

OYEYEMI, Helen (1984–) Nigerian-born novelist and playwright; she moved to London when she was 4. She wrote her first novel, *The Icarus Girl* (2006), while she was still at school; her plays *Juniper's Whitening* and *Victimese* (2005) were written and staged in Cambridge. Her recent novels, *The Opposite House* (2007) and *White is for Witching* (2009), share an interest in women and madness.

OYONO, Ferdinand (1929–2010) Cameroonian novelist, diplomat, and politician. Of his novels, which offer satirical portraits of the colonial relationship, the best known is *Une vie de boy* (1956; *Houseboy*, 1966). He served as minister of culture in Cameroon from 1997 to 2007.

Oz An underground magazine started in Sydney, Australia (1963–6), by Richard Neville (1941–), and relaunched by him in London in 1966 with Jim Anderson and Felix Dennis. The 'Schoolkids' issue (no. 28) was the occasion of a notorious trial during which the editors were convicted of issuing a publication likely to 'corrupt public morals', but were freed on appeal. *Oz* faded away in the winter of 1973, having reached a peak print-run of 70,000 in 1971.

Pacchiarotto and How He Worked in Distemper: *With Other Poems* A collection of nineteen poems, in various metres, by Robert *Browning, published 1876. The title poem, the three which follow it, and the epilogue were directed at Browning's critics.

PADEL, Ruth (1946–) Poet and writer. Her poetry, from *Summer Snow* (1990), through *Angel* (1993), *Rembrandt Would Have Loved You* (1998), and *The Soho Leopard* (2004), combines classical allusion with a contemporary, often erotic idiom. *Darwin: A Life in Poems* (2009) is a poetic biography of her great-great-grandfather. Her scholarly works display an interest in various kinds of mythologizing, madness, and masculinity, both ancient and modern. She has also published close critical readings of contemporary poems, including *The Poem and the Journey* (2007); the environmentalist study *Tigers in Red Weather* (2005); and a novel, *Where the Serpent Lives* (2010).

PAGET, Violet *See* LEE, VERNON.

PAINE, Thomas (1737–1809) Revolutionary and author. He was dismissed as an exciseman in 1774 after agitating for an increase in pay. At the suggestion of Benjamin *Franklin he sailed for America, where he published *Common Sense* (1776) and *The Crisis* (1776–83), a series of pamphlets encouraging American resistance to England; he also wrote against slavery and in favour of the emancipation of women. Having returned to England, he published the first part of *The *Rights of Man* (1791) in reply to Edmund Burke's *Reflections on the Revolution in France*. The second part appeared in 1792, when, alerted by William *Blake of impending arrest, Paine left for France, where he was elected a member of the Convention. However, he opposed the execution of Louis XVI, and narrowly escaped the guillotine. *The Age of Reason* (1793), an attack on Christianity and the Bible, was answered by Richard Watson, bishop of Llandaff, and others, and his effigy was repeatedly burned in England. He returned to America

in 1802. Paine's writings became a textbook for radicals in England, thanks to his clear style and direct connection with the American struggle and the French Revolution.

PAINTER, William *See* PALACE OF PLEASURE.

Pair of Blue Eyes, A (1873) A novel by Thomas *Hardy, set in Cornwall. Stephen Smith, a young architect, comes to Endelstow to restore the church tower and falls in love with Elfride Swancourt, the blue-eyed daughter of the vicar. Her father is incensed that someone of Stephen's humble origin should claim his daughter. Elfride and Stephen elope, but Elfride vacillates over marriage, and Stephen leaves for India. Henry Knight, Stephen's friend and patron, meets Elfride, and after she saves his life on a cliff they become engaged. However, Knight learns of Elfride's affair with Stephen, and rejects her. Eventually he and Stephen meet; Stephen learns that Elfride remains unmarried and Knight learns the innocent facts of her escapade with Stephen. But the train which carries them both to Cornwall also carries Elfride's corpse. They learn when they arrive at Endelstow that she has died, after marrying Lord Luxellian.

Palace of Pleasure, The A collection of translations into English of 'pleasant histories and excellent novels . . . out of divers good and commendable Authors', made by William Painter (1540?–95), published in 1566, 1569, and 1575. Many of the translations are from *Boccaccio, *Bandello, and Marguerite of Navarre (1492–1549; *see* HEPTAMÉRON), but Painter also drew on *Herodotus, *Livy, and Gellius. The book provided a storehouse of plots for Elizabethan writers, especially dramatists.

Paladins In the cycle of *Charlemagne legends, the twelve peers who accompanied the king. The origin of the idea is seen in the *Chanson de Roland* (*see* ROLAND), where the twelve peers or champions are merely an association of particularly brave warriors, under the leadership of Roland and *Oliver. From the Spanish war the idea was transported by later writers to other parts of the cycle, and Charlemagne is found always surrounded by twelve peers. Their names are differently stated by different authors, most of the original names given by the *Chanson de Roland* having been forgotten; but Roland and Oliver always figure. Among the best known are *Otuel, Fierabras or *Ferumbras, and *Ogier the Dane. Since the 16th century the word has been applied to any great knightly champion.

Palamon and Arcite The two Theban princes whose love for Emelye is the subject of Chaucer's 'The Knight's Tale' (*see* CANTERBURY TALES, 1), following the *Teseida* of *Boccaccio. It is also the subject of *The *Two Noble Kinsmen*.

PALEY, Grace (1922–2007) American short story writer and poet, of Russian-Jewish parentage, the author of three acclaimed volumes of short stories: *The Little Disturbances of Man* (1959); *Enormous Changes at the Last Minute* (1974); and *Later the Same Day* (1985). Pungent and laconic, her tragicomic stories resound with the cadences of New York. Paley campaigned on behalf of anti-war movements, nuclear disarmament, and women's rights; her essays and articles are collected in *Just as I Thought* (1997). *Begin Again* (2000), her collected poems, was followed posthumously by *Fidelity* (2008).

PALEY, William (1743–1805) Anglican clergyman and theologian. He published three influential works: *Moral and Political Philosophy* (1785), *Evidences of Christianity* (1794), and *Natural Theology* (1802). Paley was the major exponent of theological utilitarianism (the doctrine, partly derived from John *Locke, that human happiness lies in obedience to the will of God), and was strongly opposed to contemporary Scottish philosophy, which based ethics on the 'moral sense'. He attempted to rebut David *Hume's scepticism, finding proof of the existence of God in the design apparent in natural phenomena, and particularly in the mechanisms of the human body.

PALGRAVE, Francis Turner (1824–97) Critic and poet, chiefly remembered for his anthology *The Golden Treasury of Best Songs and Lyrical Poems in the English Language* (1861, and much reprinted; 2nd series, 1897). In the selection for the first edition, Palgrave was advised by his close friend Alfred *Tennyson; it contained no work by living poets, and is a reflection of Palgrave's distinctive taste (e.g. no John *Donne and no William *Blake,

though work by these poets was added to subsequent editions; Pope only as a lyricist). New and enlarged editions with poems by later writers have since appeared.

PALIN, Michael (1943–) Actor, television presenter, scriptwriter, and author. He made his name in television with *Monty Python's Flying Circus* (1969–74, with John Cleese and others) and *Ripping Yarns* (1975–9, with Terry Jones). He has written film scripts (including *Time Bandits*, 1981; *The Missionary*, 1982), plays (including *East of Ipswich*, 1987; *The Weekend*, 1994), a novel (*Hemingway's Chair*, 1995), and books for children. He is well known for his *BBC TV travel documentaries and books based on them: *Around the World in 80 Days* (1989), *Pole to Pole* (1992), *Full Circle* (1997), *Hemingway Adventure* (1999), *Sahara* (2002), *Himalaya* (2004), and *New Europe* (2007).

palinode [Greek, παλινῳδία, 'song sung over again', 'recantation'] Usually a poem or work in which the author retracts what she or he has formerly said or written. 'Palinode' is the Catholic shepherd in the 'May' eclogue of Edmund *Spenser's *The *Shepheardes Calender*.

Palliser Novels Collective term for the political (or, 'parliamentary') novels of Anthony *Trollope; *Can You Forgive Her?*, *Phineas Finn*, The *Eustace Diamonds*, *Phineas Redux*, The *Prime Minister*, and *The *Duke's Children*.

Pall Mall Gazette An evening paper founded in 1865 by Frederick Greenwood (1830–1909) and George *Smith to combine the features of a newspaper with political and social articles. Its name was taken from Thackeray's *Pendennis*, where Captain Shandon in the Marshalsea prepares the prospectus of 'The Pall Mall Gazette', 'written by gentlemen for gentlemen'. Early contributors included Sir Henry Maine (1822–88), Anthony *Trollope, James Fitzjames Stephen, Leslie *Stephen, and Matthew *Arnold. John Morley took over as editor, to be succeeded (1883–9) by W. T. *Stead, whose sensational campaigning journalism altered its character. The paper was incorporated into the *Evening Standard* in 1923.

Palmerin of England (*Palmeirim de Inglaterra*) A chivalric romance attributed to the Portuguese writer Francisco de Moraes (*c.*1500–1572). The Palmerin cycle deals with the exploits and loves of Palmerin d'Oliva, emperor of Constantinople, and his various descendants—one of them, Palmerin of England, is the subject of the sixth tale in the cycle. Anthony *Munday translated the Palmerin cycle into English (through a French intermediary), 1581–95. It was highly popular with the Elizabethan middle classes, and there are many references to Palmerin in the plays of the time (e.g. *The *Knight of the Burning Pestle*, where the vogue for such chivalric fantasies is mocked). A revised translation by Robert *Southey appeared in 1807. *Palmerin of England* and *Amadis of Gaul* were two romances of chivalry spared from the holocaust of such works in *Don Quixote* (I. 6).

Pamela, or *Virtue Rewarded* Samuel *Richardson's first novel, published 1740–41. *Pamela* consists entirely of letters and journals, of which Richardson presents himself as the 'editor'. His 'new species of writing' built on the existing form of the *epistolary novel by giving the six correspondents in *Pamela* their own particular style and point of view. Pamela herself provides most of the letters and journals, with the 'hero', Mr B., having only two. Pamela Andrews is a handsome, intelligent girl of 15 when her employer, Lady B., dies. Without protection, Pamela is pursued by Mr B., Lady B.'s son, but she rejects him and remains determined to retain her chastity. Mr B. dispatches her to B—Hall, his remote house in Lincolnshire, where she is imprisoned and guarded, and Mr B. arrives at B—Hall and offers to make her his mistress and keep her in style. She refuses indignantly, and he later attempts to rape her. Gradually each becomes aware of the genuine nature of their affection. However, Pamela again retreats and refuses his proposal of marriage. She is sent away from B—Hall, but a message gives her a last chance. Eventually, she decides to trust Mr B., and they are married. The book was enormously successful and fashionable, generating sermons, poems, stage versions, sequences of paintings, and unauthorized continuations of the story, including Eliza *Haywood's *Anti-Pamela*. Richardson's own sequel, usually known as *Pamela in her Exalted Condition*, appeared in 1741. Pamela is exhibited as a domestic paragon, patiently leading her profligate husband to reform, breastfeeding her children, and bringing about the penitence of the wicked through her good example. Richardson's novel was a foundational text of a new realism in English fiction, giving primacy to a working-class woman and her direct self-expression, but *Pamela* also generated much controversy and opposition: *Shamela* (1741, anonymous but assumed to be by Henry *Fielding) lampooned what the author regarded as the novel's hypocritical morality; and Fielding's *Joseph Andrews* (1742) begins as a parody of *Pamela*.

pamphleteering, origins of The word 'pamphlet' appears to derive, curiously, from the generalized use of the title of a popular 12th-century French love poem in Latin called *Pamphilus, seu de Amore*, which was adapted to 'Pamphilet'. George *Orwell, in his introduction to *British Pamphleteers* (vol. i, 1948), describes a pamphlet as 'a short piece of polemical writing, printed in the form of a booklet and aimed at a large public', usually of 5,000–10,000 words, and unbound. It is especially associated with printed tracts of an ephemeral and polemical kind.

Pamphleteering may be said to have got fully under way with the Reformation, and during the 16th century became widespread. It was associated as much with low-life *jest book, *coney-catching, and plague literature as with religious and political tracts (*see* NASHE, THOMAS; DEKKER, THOMAS; GREENE, ROBERT; MARTIN MARPRELATE). John *Knox's *First Blast of the Trumpet against the Monstrous Regiment* [i.e. 'government'] *of Women* (1558) was, perhaps, the first British political pamphlet. The religious and political ferment of the 17th century, along with the attendant breakdown of licensing and censorship, produced many thousands of pamphlets, some of high literary quality; John *Milton's are perhaps the best known (but *see also* WINSTANLEY, GERRARD; OVERTON, RICHARD; CLARKSON, LAURENCE; COPPE, ABIEZER; LILBURNE, JOHN; NEDHAM, MARCHAMONT; BERKENHEAD, SIR JOHN). Many, such as *Tyranipocrit Discovered* and *Light Shining in Buckinghamshire* (1648), were anonymous. The renewal of press control at the Restoration revived the *manuscript circulation of libellous, seditious, and obscene works. In the 18th century, though important works in pamphlet form were produced by writers like Daniel *Defoe and Jonathan *Swift, the rise of weekly periodicals tended to reduce the demand for this type of publication. The form was effectively and extensively revived during the 19th century by the *Oxford Movement and later by the Fabian Society.

Pan In Greek and Roman mythology a hairy, goat-legged, lecherous god, who inhabited *Arcadia, where he pursued *nymphs unsuccessfully and was sacred to shepherds. As the inventor of the reed pipes, the syrinx, he was associated with both music and poetry. He became a key figure in classical *pastoral, and in Renaissance pastoral, for example in Spenser's

Shepheardes Calender, he sometimes represented not only the lover and the poet but also Christ, because he is the good shepherd and in Greek Pan signifies all. Late 19th-century and early 20th-century literature saw a revival of interest in Pan, as a figure representing the unruly powers of natural fertility. Those who wrote of him in this guise include *Saki, E. M. *Forster, Arthur *Machen, and D. H. *Lawrence.

Pandarus In Homer's *Iliad*, a son of Lycaon who assisted the Trojans in their war against the Greeks. The role that he plays in *Chaucer's and *Shakespeare's stories of Troilus and Criseyde/Cressida was the invention of *Boccaccio in his *Filostrato. In Boccaccio he is the cousin of Cressida; Chaucer strikingly changes him from her cousin to her uncle and guardian, the effect of which is to increase the sense of irresponsibility towards her in arranging their love affair. The word 'pander' (as Shakespeare says: III. ii. 197) derives from his role as go-between for Troilus and Criseyde.

Pandemonium A word coined by John *Milton, the abode of all the demons; a place represented by Milton (*Paradise Lost*, I. 756) as the capital of hell, containing the council chamber of the devils.

Pandosto, or The Triumph of Time A prose romance by Robert *Greene first published in 1588. It is now best known as the source for *The *Winter's Tale*.

Panopticon Jeremy *Bentham's term (1843) for a proposed type of prison, consisting of cells ranged round a central point from which a warder could observe the prisoners while they could see neither him nor their fellow prisoners in adjacent cells. Michel *Foucault took up the idea in *Surveiller et punir* (1975), his study of the change in the way power was exercised after the 16th century.

Pantagruel See RABELAIS, FRANÇOIS.

Pantisocracy A utopian scheme invented by S. T. *Coleridge and Robert *Southey in 1794–5, to establish an egalitarian commune of six families in America, based on a joint-stock farm. The scheme ended in acrimony when Southey, to Coleridge's horror, suggested that the Pantisocrats should keep servants.

pantomime (1) Originally a Roman actor, who performed in dumb show, representing by mimicry various characters and scenes. (2) An English dramatic performance, assimilating some of the traditions of the Italian *commedia

dell'arte*, originally consisting of action without speech, but in its further development consisting of a dramatized traditional fairy-tale, with singing, dancing, acrobatics, clowning, topical jokes, a transformation scene, and certain stock roles, especially the 'principal boy' (i.e. hero) acted by a woman and the 'dame' acted by a man.

Paolo and Francesca Francesca, daughter of Giovanni da Polenta, count of Ravenna, was given in marriage by him to Giovanni (Sciancato, the Lame) Malatesta, of Rimini. She fell in love with Paolo, her husband's brother, and, their relations being discovered, the two lovers were put to death in 1289. *Dante, at the end of the fifth canto of the *Inferno*, relates his conversation with Francesca. The story of Paolo and Francesca was the subject of the poem *The *Story of Rimini* by Leigh *Hunt.

Paper Money Lyrics Burlesque poems by Thomas Love *Peacock, ridiculing political economists and bankers, published 1837.

Pap with an Hatchet The title of a tract supporting the bishops contributed in 1589 by John *Lyly to the *Martin Marprelate controversy.

Paracelsus A dramatic poem in blank verse by Robert *Browning, published 1835. The career of the historical Paracelsus (1493–1541), the maverick physician, provides Browning, despite his claim to the contrary, with an opportunity for his own exploration of the processes of the creative imagination, in particular the conflict between 'Love' (self-forgetting) and 'Knowledge' (self-assertion) in the mind of the artist.

paradise The name often given to the biblical garden of *Eden, but also to heaven, the blessed state after death; it can have literal or physical and spiritual or allegorical meanings, and can apply to past, present, or future states, both earthly and heavenly. See DIVINA COMMEDIA; EARTHLY PARADISE; PARADISE LOST; PARADISE REGAINED.

Paradise Lost An epic poem by John *Milton, originally in ten books, first printed 1667. Milton added to later copies of the first edition an 'Argument', summarizing the contents of each book, and also a defence of his choice of blank verse.

Book I. The poet, invoking the 'Heavenly Muse', states his theme, the fall of man through disobedience, and his aim, which is to 'justify the ways of God to men'. He then presents the defeated archangel *Satan, with *Beelzebub, his second in command, and his rebellious angels, lying on the burning lake of hell. Satan awakens his legions, rouses their spirits, and summons a council. The palace of Satan, *Pandemonium (a word coined by Milton), is built.

Book II. The council debates whether another battle for the recovery of Heaven should be hazarded, *Moloch recommending open war, *Belial and Mammon recommending peace in order to avoid worse torments. Beelzebub announces the creation of 'another world, the happy seat ¦ Of some new race called Man', which may prove a means of revenge. Satan undertakes to visit it alone, and flies up through the realm of Chaos.

Book III. Milton invokes celestial light to illumine the 'ever-during dark' of his own blindness, then describes God, who sees Satan's flight towards our world, and foretells his success and the fall and punishment of man, emphasizing that man will fall not through predestination but through free will. The Son of God offers himself as a ransom, is accepted, and exalted as the Saviour. Satan alights on our universe. He finds the stairs leading up to heaven, descends to the sun, disguises himself as 'a stripling cherub', and is directed to earth by Uriel, where he alights on Mount Niphates in Armenia.

Book IV. Satan, at first tormented by doubts, resolves 'evil be thou my good' and journeys on towards the garden of *Eden, where he first sees Adam and Eve 'in naked majesty', and overhears their discourse about the forbidden Tree of Knowledge. He resolves to tempt them to disobey the prohibition but is discovered by the guardian angels Ithuriel and Zephon, and expelled from the garden by their commander, *Gabriel.

Book V. Eve relates to Adam the disquieting dream of temptation which Satan had inspired. He comforts her, and they set about their daily tasks. Raphael, sent by God, comes to paradise, warns Adam, and enjoins obedience. They discuss reason, free will, and predestination, and Raphael, at Adam's request, relates how Satan, inspired by hatred and envy of the newly anointed Messiah, inspired his legions to revolt.

Book VI. Raphael continues his narrative, telling how Michael and Gabriel were sent to fight against Satan. After indecisive battles the Son of God himself, alone, attacked the hosts of Satan, and, driving them to the verge of heaven, forced them to leap down through chaos into the deep.

Book VII. Milton evokes Urania (whom he identifies as the spirit who inspired Moses to write the Book of Genesis), then continues Raphael's narrative, with an account of God's decision to send his Son to create another world from the vast abyss. He describes the six days of creation, ending with the creation of man, and a renewed warning to Adam that death will be the penalty for eating of the fruit of the Tree of Knowledge.

Book VIII. Adam enquires concerning the motions of the heavenly bodies, and is answered 'doubtfully'. The controversy regarding the Ptolemaic and Copernican systems was at its height when *Paradise Lost* was written, and Milton declined to decide between them. Adam relates what he remembers since his own creation, notably his own need for rational fellowship, and his plea to his Maker for a companion, which is answered by the creation of Eve. Adam and Raphael talk of the relations between the sexes, then, with a final warning to 'take heed least passion sway ¦ Thy judgement', Raphael departs.

Book IX. Milton describes Satan's entry into the body of the serpent, in which form he finds Eve, she having insisted, despite Adam's warnings, on going gardening alone. He persuades her to eat of the Tree of Knowledge. Eve relates to Adam what has passed and brings him some of the fruit. Adam, recognizing that she is doomed, resolves to perish with her. He also eats the fruit, and after initial intoxication in their lost innocence, they cover their nakedness and fall to mutual accusation.

Book X. God sends his Son to judge the transgressors. They greet him with guilt and shame, and confess, and he pronounces his sentence. Sin and Death resolve to come to this world, and make a broad highway to it from hell. Satan returns to hell and announces his victory. Adam, recognizing that in him 'all posterity stands cursed', at first reproaches Eve and despairs, but she suggests they seek mercy from the Son of God.

Book XI. The Son of God, seeing their penitence, intercedes. God decrees that they must leave paradise, and sends down Michael to carry out his command. Eve laments; Adam pleads not to be banished, but Michael reassures him that God is omnipresent, then unfolds to him the future, revealing to him the consequences of his original sin in the death of Abel and the future miseries of mankind, ending with the Flood and the new Covenant.

Book XII. Michael relates the subsequent history of the Old Testament, then describes the coming of the Messiah, his incarnation, death, resurrection, and ascension, which leads Adam to rejoice over so much good sprung from his own sin. Michael also foretells the corrupt state of the Church until the Second Coming. Eve meanwhile, during these revelations, has been comforted by a dream presaging 'some great good'. Resolved on obedience and submission, and assured that they may possess 'a Paradise within', they are led out of the garden.

Illustrators of *Paradise Lost* include *Fuseli, 1802; *Blake, 1806; John Martin, 1827 onwards; Turner, 1835; and Doré, 1866.

Paradise of Dainty Devices, The A collection of works by minor poets of the 1560s and 1570s, including Lord *Vaux, the earl of *Oxford, Thomas Churchyard, and William Hunnis (d. 1597). It was compiled by Richard *Edwards and published posthumously in 1576.

Paradise Regained An epic poem in four books by John *Milton, published 1671. It is a sequel to *Paradise Lost, and deals exclusively with the temptation of Jesus in the wilderness. According to the poet's conception, whereas paradise was lost by the yielding of Adam and Eve to *Satan's temptation, it was regained by the resistance of the Son of God to his temptation. Satan is here represented as a cunning, smooth, and dissembling creature. The style, by comparison with *Paradise Lost, is bare, conveying the rigour of Jesus' astringent intelligence.

Book I relates the baptism of Jesus and the proclamation from heaven that he is the Son of God. Satan, alarmed, summons a council of devils, and undertakes his temptation. Jesus is led into the wilderness, not knowing why, but trusting that God will reveal all he needs to know. After 40 days, without food, he is approached by Satan in disguise, who suggests he should turn the stones around him into bread. Jesus penetrates his disguise and rebukes him for tempting him to distrust God. Night falls on the desert.

Books II and III. Meanwhile Andrew and Simon seek Jesus, and Mary is troubled at his absence. Satan confers again with his council. He once more tries the hunger temptation, conjuring up a sumptuous banquet with the added allure of beautiful female attendants, which Jesus contemptuously rejects. Satan next appeals to the higher appetites for wealth and power, and a disputation follows as to the real value of earthly glory. Satan, confuted, reminds Jesus that the kingdom of David is under the Roman yoke, and suggests that he should free it. He takes Jesus to a high mountain and shows

him the kingdoms of the earth. To the east, the powers of Rome and Parthia, displayed in a vision, are pitted against each other, and Satan offers Jesus an alliance with, or conquest of, the Parthians, and the liberation of the Jews then in captivity.

Book IV. Jesus remaining unmoved by Satan's 'politic maxims', the tempter, turning to the western side, draws his attention to Rome and proposes the expulsion of the wicked emperor Tiberius; and finally, pointing out Athens, urges the attractions of its poets, orators, and philosophers. Jesus scornfully rejects these, maintaining that Hebrew poetry far excels Greek. Satan returns Jesus to the wilderness, and assails him during the night, but Jesus is undaunted. On the third morning Satan carries him to the highest pinnacle of the temple and bids him cast himself down, only to receive the enigmatic answer, 'Tempt not the Lord thy God' (a quotation from Deuteronomy 6: 16). Satan falls 'smitten with amazement' and a 'fiery globe' of angels bears Jesus away.

Paradiso, of Dante *See* DIVINA COMMEDIA.

pararhyme *See* RHYME.

Parasitaster, The, or *The Fawn* A comedy by John *Marston, published 1606.

'Pardoner's Tale, The' *See* CANTERBURY TALES, 14.

PARETSKY, Sara (1947–) American novelist. Her series of narratives centring on a female private investigator called V. I. Warshawski include *Total Recall* (2001) and *Blacklist* (2003).

Paris *See* ILIAD.

PARIS, Matthew (*c*.1200–1259) Benedictine monk and historian, who entered the monastery of St Albans in 1217, succeeding Roger of Wendover (d. 1236) as chronicler, and compiling the *Chronica Majora*, his greatest work, there from 1235 to 1259. Among Paris's many other works are abbreviated versions of the *Chronica Majora*; the *Historia Anglorum*, a summary of events in England from 1200 to 1253; the *Vitae Duorum Offarum* ('Lives of the two Offas', the king of the Angles and the king of Mercia); saints' lives; and the *Gesta Abbatum Monasterii S. Albani*, the lives of the first 23 abbots up to 1255.

'Parish Register, The' A poem by George *Crabbe, published 1807. Developing the form of *The *Village, 'The Parish Register' relates the memories of a country parson as he looks through the entries in his registers of births, marriages, and deaths. The tales include the terrible account, written possibly under the effect of opium, in 'Sir Eustace Grey', of a patient in a madhouse.

PARK, Mungo (1771-1806) Scottish explorer. In 1794 the African Association appointed him to determine the course of the river Niger. His best-selling *Travels in the Interior Districts of Africa* (1799) also includes detailed accounts of Mandinka culture. Contemporary readers were impressed by its verisimilitude, but the text also draws on conceptions of the picturesque, the sentimental, and the heroic associated with *Romanticism.

PARKER, Dorothy (1893-1967) Née Rothschild, American humorist and journalist, legendary for her instant wit and for her satirical verses; she also wrote sketches and short stories, many of them published in the *New Yorker*. She worked as a screenwriter in Hollywood and was blacklisted in the McCarthy era.

PARKER, Henry See MORLEY, LORD.

PARKER, Matthew (1504-75) Archbishop of Canterbury and patron of scholarship. In 1544 he was elected master of the college, where he reformed the library, to which he was to bequeath his superb collections of manuscripts, printed books, and plate. Having lost his offices during Queen Mary's reign, he reluctantly accepted the archbishopric of Canterbury on the accession of *Elizabeth I. He identified himself with the party (afterwards known as the Anglican party) which sought to establish a *via media* between Roman Catholicism and Puritanism. From 1563 to 1568 he was occupied with the production of the Bishops' Bible (*see* BIBLE, THE ENGLISH). Often using his own manuscripts, he instigated editions of Asser, *Ælfric, *Gildas, the *Flores Historiarum* of Matthew of Westminster, Matthew *Paris, and other early chroniclers.

Parker Society Named after Matthew *Parker, founded in 1840 by Church of England evangelicals to combat the effects of the *Oxford Movement and the spread of *Roman Catholicism. The society published the works of the 16th-century reformers in 54 volumes (1841-55), including William *Tyndale, John *Bale, Thomas *Cranmer, Miles *Coverdale, Hugh Latimer, Nicholas Ridley, John Jewel (1522-71), and John Whitgift (1530-1604), and volumes on the Elizabethan *liturgy.

PARKMAN, Francis (1823-93) American historian, born in Boston, who journeyed to Wyoming to study Native American life, giving an account of his experiences in *The Oregon Trail* (1849), which was dictated, owing to his own ill health, to his cousin and companion Quincy A. Shaw. His history of the struggle of the English and French for dominion in North America was published in a series of studies, beginning with his *History of the Conspiracy of the Pontiac* (1851) and continuing through several volumes, concluding with *A Half-Century of Conflict* (1892). Donald *Davie pays tribute to Parkman's evocation of historical figures in *A Sequence for Francis Parkman* (1961).

Parleyings with Certain People of Importance in their Day A volume of poems in blank verse by Robert *Browning, published 1887. The phrase 'certain people of importance' derives from a passage in *Dante's *Vita nuova*. Browning refers to a number of obscure historical figures whose works he had studied in his youth. Each of these figures is matched by a contemporary of Browning's. The collection constitutes an oblique autobiography and self-dramatization.

Parliament of Fowls, The A dream-poem (*c.* late 1370s–early 1380s) by Geoffrey *Chaucer in 699 lines of *rhyme royal. It may (but need not) have been written in connection with the marriage of Richard II to Anne of Bohemia (1382). After a prologue interweaving the themes of love and reading, the narrator reads Cicero's *Dream of Scipio*, in which Africanus, Scipio's grandfather, explains the importance of 'commune profyt'. Having fallen asleep, he dreams that Africanus pushes him into a garden in which the goddess Nature presides over the choosing of mates on St Valentine's Day. Here the theme of common profit is put under severe pressure as three male eagles pay court to a 'formel' (female). There follows a long dispute about the criteria for success in a love suit, the argument centring on the opposition between the eagles' courtly approach and the pragmatism exemplified by the duck. The female is unable to decide which suitor to take, and Nature, while granting the other birds their mates, accedes to her request to wait a year before deciding. The political and philosophical issues that the poem suggests are left undefined and unresolved.

Parnassus Plays, The The name given to a group of three plays produced between 1598 and 1602 by students of St John's College,

Cambridge, consisting of *The Pilgrimage to Parnassus* and *The Return from Parnassus*, the latter in two parts. Authorship has not been established, but they seem to be the work of two dramatists, unusually writing academic drama in English rather than Latin (or even Greek), as was more common. They present the attempts of a group of young men (one apparently modelled on Thomas *Nashe) to resist temptation and to gain preferment or at least a livelihood, and are full of allusions to contemporary literature and drama. The second play contains the earliest known parody of Shakespearian verse, written in the *rhyme-royal stanza form of *Lucrece*. In the third, more satirical, section Richard *Burbage and Will *Kemp audition recent students for places in their company, using Richard III's opening soliloquy as a test piece, and the students are shown on their way to London, learning how to catch a patron or cheat a tradesman, and following menial occupations. Eventually, discouraged, they 'return' to Cambridge. The plays were first published together in 1886.

PARNELL, Thomas (1679–1718) Irish poet, a friend of Jonathan *Swift and Alexander *Pope. He was a member of the *Scriblerus Club. His 'Hymn to Contentment' was published in Richard *Steele's *Poetical Miscellanies* (1714) and his mock-heroic *Homer's Battle of the Frogs and Mice with the Remarks of Zoilus* appeared in 1717 (*see* BATRACHOMYOMACHIA), but most of his work was published posthumously by Pope in 1721. His poems include 'The Hermit' and 'Night-Piece on Death', a *graveyard poem, which in Oliver *Goldsmith's view inspired 'all those night-pieces and churchyard scenes that have since appeared' (Goldsmith's *Life of Parnell*, 1770).

parody A work written in mocking imitation of the style of another work, that style being exaggerated or applied to an incongruous subject, as in *burlesque and *mock-epic verse. It may be distinguished from *pastiche on the basis of its mocking intent, and from *satire on the basis of its focus upon style rather than upon people and their conduct. In some cases, parody incorporates an element of literary criticism: notable English examples of this include Henry Fielding's *Shamela Andrews* (1741), a parodic critique of Samuel Richardson's novel *Pamela*; Jane Austen's *Northanger Abbey* (1818), written in affectionate mockery of the *Gothic novels of Ann *Radcliffe; and Stella Gibbons's *Cold Comfort Farm* (1932), which sends up the oversexed primitivism of Mary *Webb and other rural

novelists. The tradition of English parody begins with Chaucer's *Canterbury Tales*, notably in its 'Tale of Sir Thopas'. It flourished in the 18th century in the mock-epic works of Alexander *Pope (who also wrote a bawdy parody of Chaucer) and others, and in the prose of Fielding and of Laurence *Sterne, whose *Tristram Shandy* involves continuous parodic play with the conventions of novelistic narration. The 19th century was a fertile period for verse parody, the distinctive styles of William *Wordsworth, Robert *Browning, and A. C. *Swinburne especially attracting numerous parodic imitations. The celebrated *Rejected Addresses* (1812) of James and Horatio *Smith provide one highlight of that tradition, another being the verses in the *Alice* books of 'Lewis Carroll' (*Dodgson) in absurd imitation of Wordsworth, Isaac *Watts, Robert *Southey, and others. In the early 20th century, Max *Beerbohm's prose parodies of Henry *James and others in *A Christmas Garland* (1912) were widely admired, but the most versatile and accomplished parodist of the age was James *Joyce in his *Ulysses*: among many other parodic feats here, the fourteenth ('Oxen of the Sun') chapter manages to parody every phase in the development of English prose from the earliest times up to the then contemporary. In the later 20th century, Wendy *Cope established a reputation for verse parody, while parody and pastiche were strong elements in the plays of Tom *Stoppard.

paronomasia A rhetorical term for a pun or play on words, in which the repeated words are similar but not identical; for example, Lady Macbeth: 'I'll gild the faces of the grooms withal, ¦ For it must seem their guilt.'

PARRY, Sir William Edward (1790–1855) Arctic explorer, whose expeditions are described in his three *Journals* of voyages for the discovery of a North-West Passage, undertaken between 1819 and 1825 (published 1821, 1824, 1826), and in his *Narrative of an Attempt to Reach the North Pole, 1827* (1828).

'Parson's Tale, The' *See* CANTERBURY TALES, 24.

Parthenophil and Parthenophe Published 1591, a collection of sonnets by Barnabe *Barnes, one of the first to appear after Philip *Sidney's *Astrophel and Stella*.

PARTRIDGE, Frances (Catherine) (1900–2004) Diarist and translator. Six volumes of her diaries (1985–2001), covering her experiences in and beyond the *Bloomsbury

Group between the late 1930s and mid-1970s, gained her a wide readership late in life.

Parzifal Middle High German epic poem by Wolfram von Eschenbach. Composed early in the 13th century, its subject is the legend of *Perceval and the Holy *Grail.

Pasquil (Pasquin) 'Pasquino' or 'Pasquillo' was the name popularly given to a mutilated statue disinterred at Rome in 1501, and set up by Cardinal Caraffa at the corner of his palace near the Piazza Navona. It became the custom to salute Pasquin on St Mark's Day in Latin verses. Over time these anonymous *pasquinate* or pasquinades tended to become satirical, and the term began to be applied, not only in Rome but in other countries, to satirical compositions and lampoons, political, ecclesiastical, or personal. Replies to the pasquinades used to be attached to the *Marforio*, an ancient statue of a river god, thought to be of Mars.

Passage to India, A Last-written novel by E. M. *Forster, published 1924. It portrays a restive India under the British Raj, the clash between East and West, tensions between Hindus and Muslims, and the disastrous consequences of prejudice and 'muddle'. The story is told in three parts and concerns Aziz, a young Muslim doctor, whose friendliness and enthusiasm for the British turn to bitterness and disillusionment. A sympathy springs up between him and the elderly Mrs Moore, who has come to visit her son the city magistrate. Accompanying her is Adela Quested, who longs to know the 'real' India and tries to disregard the taboos and snobberies of the British. Aziz organizes an expedition to the famous Marabar Caves, where an unforeseen development plunges him into disgrace and rouses deep antagonism between the British and the indigenous population. Adela accuses Aziz of sexually assaulting her in the Caves; he is committed to prison, and stands trial. Adela realizes she has made a terrible mistake and withdraws her charge, but Aziz turns furiously away from the British. In the third part of the book he has moved to a post in a native state, and is bringing up his family in peace, writing poetry and reading Persian. He is visited by his friend Cyril Fielding, the former principal of the Government College, an intelligent, hard-bitten man. They discuss the future of India and Aziz prophesies that only when the British are driven out can he and Fielding really be friends. Other characters include the saintly Brahman Professor Godbole, the innocent cause of the contretemps.

Passetyme of Pleasure, or The Historie of *Graunde Amoure and La Bel Pucel* An allegorical poem in *rhyme royal and decasyllabic couplets by Stephen *Hawes, written about 1506 and printed by Wynkyn de *Worde in 1509. It describes the education of a certain Graunde Amoure in the accomplishments required to make a knight perfect and worthy of the love of La Bel Pucel, and narrates his encounters with giants (representing the vices), his marriage, and his death; the whole constituting an allegory of life in the form of a romance of chivalry.

Passionate Pilgrim, The An unauthorized anthology of twenty poems by various authors, some still unidentified, published by Jaggard in 1599 in two editions, and attributed on the title page to William *Shakespeare, but containing only two sonnets and three extracts from *Love's Labour's Lost* by him. A third edition with additional poems by Thomas *Heywood appeared in 1612; Heywood protested on his own and on Shakespeare's behalf.

PASTERNAK, Boris Leonidovich (1890–1960) Russian poet and prose writer. His poetry collection *My Sister Life* (1922) was followed by *Second Birth* (1932), but after 1933 no original work by Pasternak could be published for ten years, after which two further collections, *On Early Trains* (1943) and *The Breadth of the Earth* (1945), appeared. Original work gave way to translation, and he translated the works of many English poets into Russian, including Walter *Ralegh, Ben *Jonson, P. B. *Shelley, Lord *Byron, John *Keats, and William *Shakespeare. Pasternak's novel *Doctor Zhivago* was intended to be his testament to the experience of the Russian intelligentsia before, during, and after the revolution. It was published in Italy in 1957, and in an English version in 1958, but was only published in 1988 in Russia. For translations of his poetry, see Jon *Stallworthy and Peter France, *Selected Poems* (1984).

pastiche A literary composition written in imitation of the style of another author or authors, or pieced together from fragments of other writings. T. S. *Eliot's poem *The Waste Land* (1922) is a celebrated example. Pastiche usually differs from parody in that its imitations involve affectionate or respectful tribute rather than mockery.

Paston Letters A collection of letters preserved by the Pastons, a well-to-do Norfolk family, written between *c.*1420 and 1504. They are of great value for the evidence they give of the language of their time. They concern three generations of the family, and most were written in the reigns of Henry VI, Edward IV, and Richard III. They are unique as historical material, showing the violence and other complexities of life in 15th-century England, and the domestic conditions in which a family of this class lived.

pastoral A form of literature that celebrates in conventionally idealized terms the innocent loves and musical pleasures of shepherds and shepherdesses, usually in a mythical Arcadian 'Golden Age' of ease and harmony. Despite its extreme artificiality, it is often capable of oblique or overt social criticism, in which rural harmony is contrasted with the corruptions of court or city. English pastoral writing derives from classical sources (the *Idylls* of *Theocritus and the more influential *Eclogues* of *Virgil, along with the prose romance *Daphnis and Chloe*) mediated through writers of the Italian Renaissance (notably *Petrarch, *Mantuan, and *Tasso). The most important early landmark in this tradition is Edmund *Spenser's *The *Shepheardes Calender* (1579), followed by Philip *Sidney's *Arcadia* (posthumously published in 1590). Several Elizabethan writers of pastoral poems include Christopher *Marlowe, Thomas *Lodge, and Michael *Drayton, and some attempted prose romances in this vein, notably Lodge's *Rosalyne* (1590). The most important pastoral plays are *Shakespeare's *As You Like It* and *The *Winter's Tale*, along with John *Fletcher's *The *Faithful Shepherdess*. Pastoral poetry remained an important category of 17th-century English verse (e.g. in the works of *Milton, Andrew *Marvell, and Robert *Herrick). In the 18th century, Alexander *Pope and others wrote pastoral poems, but the classical pastoral conventions increasingly gave way to more realistic forms of bucolic poetry, and eventually to a directly anti-pastoral realism in which the true poverty and hardship of contemporary rural life was stressed, notably by Oliver *Goldsmith, George *Crabbe, John *Clare, and William *Wordsworth.

pastor fido, Il See GUARINI, GIOVANNI BATTISTA.

PATER, Walter Horatio (1839–94) Writer, whose interests in Hellenism, pre-Socratic and German philosophy, European art, and literature were encouraged at Oxford by Benjamin Jowett and Matthew *Arnold. He became a fellow of Brasenose in 1864. *Studies in the History of the Renaissance*, later acclaimed by Oscar *Wilde and others as 'the holy writ of

beauty', traces the rebirth of Hellenism in medieval France, the art of Botticelli, *Leonardo da Vinci, and Michelangelo, and the classicism of Winckelmann.

In Pater's prose fiction, the quality of life is always measured against the fact of death; the 'aesthetics of pain' is paramount. *Marius the Epicurean* (1885) is set in the days of Marcus Aurelius; *Gaston de Latour* (published 'unfinished' in 1896 but reissued with new materials in 1995) in the era of *Montaigne. Narratives such as 'Apollo in Picardy' (*Harper's New Monthly*, 1893) exploit the rebirth/twilight of the gods motif. *Appreciations: With an Essay on Style* (1889) and *Essays from the Guardian* (1896) reflect his engagement with Victorian periodical journalism and belles-lettres. *Plato and Platonism* (1893), based on lectures and scholarly essays, represents an eclectic synthesis of ancient and then-contemporary philosophy, and justifies a homoerotic sensibility. 'Demeter and Persephone', an 1876 lecture later published in *Greek Studies* (1895), praises ancient matriarchal religious practices; modernists such as Hilda *Doolittle (H.D.) and Virginia *Woolf were influenced by its revisionary mythmaking and the story of female empowerment.

Pater's works have long been associated with the *'art for art's sake' movement, and the cultivation of decadence in the 1880s and 1890s. W. B. *Yeats insisted that Pater's writings are 'permanent in our literature' because of their 'revolutionary importance'.

PATERSON, Banjo (Andrew Barton) (1864–1941) Australian author of 'Waltzing Matilda'.

PATERSON, Don (1963–) OBE, Scottish poet and jazz musician. His first book, *Nil Nil* (1993), introduced a distinctive style which spliced together demotic and recondite vocabulary in tightly wrought poems about sex, families, and reading. In *God's Gift to Women* (1997, T. S. *Eliot Prize), a more supple and confident style, influenced by Paul *Muldoon, explores the possibilities of postmodern lyric in a variety of self-conscious forms. Poems about memory, childhood, and failed relationships are connected by the structuring device of a train journey. *The Eyes* (1999) and *Orpheus* (2006) are creative versions of poetry by Antonio *Machado and Rainer Maria Rilke (1875–1926). Other collections are. *The White Lie* (2001). *Landing Light* (2003), and *Rain* (2009, Forward Prize). Paterson has also published several volumes of aphorisms: *The Book of Shadows* (2005), *The Blind Eye* (2007), and *Best Thought,*

Worst Thought (2008); plays and radio dramas; and has edited popular anthologies, including *New British Poetry* (with Charles *Simic; 2004).

pathetic fallacy A phrase coined by John *Ruskin in 'Of the Pathetic Fallacy' (*Modern Painters*, iii (1856), ch. 12), indicating the tendency of writers and artists to ascribe human emotions and sympathies to nature. Ruskin himself prefers the 'very plain and leafy fact' of a primrose to those poets (e.g. Wordsworth in *Peter Bell*) 'to whom the primrose is anything else than a primrose'. The poetic convention by which, for example, clouds 'weep' or flowers 'smile' is found extensively in English verse, and especially in that of the late 18th and early 19th centuries. *See also* APOSTROPHE.

Patience (opera) Opera by *Gilbert and *Sullivan, produced in 1881, a deliberate satire on the pretensions of the *Aesthetic movement; Bunthorne, the central character, is said to be modelled on Oscar *Wilde and Grosvenor on A. C. *Swinburne.

Patience (poem) An alliterative poem in 531 lines from the late 14th century, preserved in Cotton Nero A. X, also the sole manuscript of *Pearl*, *Cleanness*, and *Sir *Gawain and the Green Knight*. It frames the story of Jonah with exhortations to patience. Modern critics usually treat the four poems in the manuscript as the work of a single author on the basis of stylistic and thematic affinities.

Patient Grissil A comedy by Thomas *Dekker in collaboration with Henry *Chettle and William Haughton (d. 1605), written 1600, printed 1603, which dramatizes Geoffrey *Chaucer's 'Clerk's Tale' (*see* CANTERBURY TALES, 9). It contains the well-known song 'Golden slumbers kiss your eyes'.

PATMORE, Coventry (1823–96) Poet; son of Peter George Patmore. He published his first volume of *Poems* (including 'The Woodman's Daughter', later the subject of a well-known painting by *Millais) in 1844. His work was much admired by the *Pre-Raphaelites, with whom he became acquainted, and he contributed to the *Germ. In 1847 he married his first wife Emily, who inspired his long and popular sequence of poems in praise of married love, The *Angel in the House* (1854–63). Emily died in 1862, leaving her husband with six children. In 1864 he travelled to Rome, where he met his second wife Marianne, a Roman Catholic, and was himself converted to Catholicism. *The Unknown Eros* (1877) contains odes marked by an erotic mysticism, but also some more autobiographical pieces (now the most anthologized), including 'The Azalea', 'Departure', 'A Farewell', directly inspired by Emily's illness and death, and 'The Toys', inspired by a moment of anger and grief aroused by one of his sons. Later works include *Amelia, Tamerton Church-Tower, etc.*, with a preface on English metrical law (1878) and *The Rod, the Root and the Flower* (1895).

PATRICK, St (*c.*389–*c.*461) The patron saint of Ireland. Taken captive to Ireland as an adolescent, he returned there voluntarily to preach the gospel in 432. He journeyed first through Ulster and then, it is said, through the whole of Ireland. Many stories, legends, and purported writings of his are current in Ireland.

patronage Traditionally, financial help, payment in kind, or more indirect assistance or influence, exercised by royalty, the aristocracy, and the wealthy, on behalf of writers, in return for dedications, entertainment, and prestige (as well as sometimes for more altruistic motives). Patronage was of particular importance before writers were able to support themselves through the literary market-place. Thus Geoffrey *Chaucer was assisted by John of Gaunt, William *Shakespeare by the earl of Southampton, John *Donne by Sir Robert Drury, and William *Wordsworth by Sir George Beaumont. Ben *Jonson's tribute to the *Sidneys in his 'country-house poem' 'To Penshurst' (*see* PENSHURST PLACE) is a product of the system. But the relationship was not always happy, particularly by the 18th century, as commercial sources of income (journalism, and especially the newly popular form of the novel) began to give authors a sense of themselves as more independent figures. Alexander *Pope had begun his career under the protection of several noblemen, but made himself financially secure through the publication by subscription of his *Iliad* translation (dedicated to a fellow writer, William *Congreve); he ridiculed the pitiful dependency of dedicators in the *Epistle to Dr Arbuthnot* and *The *Dunciad*. Samuel *Johnson, who had sought, and belatedly received, the patronage of the earl of Chesterfield for his *Dictionary*, defined a patron as 'a wretch who supports with insolence, and is paid with flattery'. His letter of defiance to Chesterfield has come to be regarded as the end of patronage. Patronage passed largely from men of individual wealth to men of professional power or commercial interest, such as literary editors and library owners and suppliers. Many authors were also

p

clergymen, and patronage was also sometimes exercised through the gift of clerical livings; George *Crabbe, befriended by the duke of Rutland, wrote of such arrangements in 'The Patron' (1812).

Institutional patronage began formally in 1790 when David Williams (1738–1816) founded the *Royal Literary Fund to support impoverished writers, and in 1837 the Civil List Act permitted the treasury to assist authors by the grant of pensions, provided they could demonstrate 'desert and distress'. Authors who have benefited include Wordsworth, Alfred Lord *Tennyson, Matthew *Arnold, W. H. *Hudson, W. B. *Yeats, and T. F. *Powys. Joseph *Conrad returned his pension; Dinah *Craik set hers aside for less fortunate authors, and Harriet *Martineau refused several offers. The pension is now worth on average only £600 p.a. It is awarded on the recommendation of the Royal Literary Fund, the *Society of Authors, the *Poetry Society, and other bodies.

SEE WEB LINKS

• Patrons and Performances website

PATTEN, Brian (1946–) Poet, born and educated (to the age of 15) in Liverpool, where he became one of the *Liverpool poets. He published with Roger *McGough and Adrian *Henri in *The Mersey Sound* (1967), and has many subsequent volumes of his own, including *Little Johnny's Confession* (1967), *Vanishing Trick* (1976), *Armada* (1996), and *Selected Poems* (2007). He is a prolific writer for children in both prose and verse: titles include *Mr Moon's Last Case* (1977), *Gangsters, Ghosts and Dragon Flies* (1981), and *The Story Giant* (2001). Patten's anthologies for children are admired.

PATTISON, Mark (1813–84) Supporter of John Henry *Newman and the *Oxford Movement until Newman's departure for Rome. He was ordained priest in 1843 and became successively fellow and tutor (1843–55) of Lincoln College, Oxford, and in 1861 he was finally elected rector of Lincoln, after an earlier rejection. An influential tutor, he was keenly interested in university reform, and travelled to Germany to study continental systems of education. His ideas on education can be found in *Oxford Studies* (1855) and *Suggestions on Academical Organisation* (1868); his life work—a history of European learning surrounding a biography of Joseph *Scaliger—was never completed. His best-known work was his classic biography *Isaac Casaubon 1559–1614* (1875). In 1861 he married Emilia Francis Strong (later Lady Dilke)

who was 27 years his junior; this and the fact that both parties remained apart as far as convention would allow gave rise to the famous theory that Mr and Mrs Pattison were the originals of Casaubon and Dorothea in George Eliot's *Middlemarch*. His *Memoirs* (1885) are an important study of 19th-century Oxford.

PAUL, St (d. c.65) Early Christian missionary leader and *Bible letter writer. A Jew and a Roman citizen born in Tarsus, Cilicia, Saul (his Hebrew name) was a leading persecutor of the earliest Christians, complicit in the first Christian martyrdom, that of Stephen. On the road to Damascus he had an archetypal conversion experience, a blinding vision of Jesus ('Saul, Saul, why persecutest thou me?', Acts 9: 4), and became, as Paul, the most active apostle of Christianity. His mission was particularly to the Gentiles, rather than the Jews; he travelled, preached, and established and supported churches from Jerusalem to Rome. He was several times imprisoned, once escaping by a miracle, eventually exercising his right as a Roman citizen of appealing to Caesar and being sent to Rome, where he was executed during a persecution of the Christians by Nero. Acts narrates his missionary work.

His principal legacy is fourteen New Testament epistles ascribed to him in the King James Bible (Romans to Hebrews). Romans, 1, 2 Corinthians, Galatians, Philippians, 1 Thessalonians, and Philemon are generally agreed to be authentic, while his authorship of Ephesians, Colossians, and 2 Thessalonians is sometimes questioned; his authorship of the 'pastoral epistles' (1, 2 Timothy, Titus) is more doubtful, and he did not write Hebrews. With his teaching in Acts, these make him the dominant figure in the latter part of the New Testament: his stamp on Christianity has been almost as influential as that of Jesus. His teaching was founded on his belief in Jesus as the risen Messiah rather than on his life and teaching. Inspirational passages such as 1 Corinthians 13 on charity or love, resonant sayings such as 'the wages of sin is death' (Romans 6: 23), and complex theology mix with a dogmatism that is often difficult for modern churches on subjects such as relationships with the Jews or 'the powers that be' (Romans 13: 1) and the status of women.

PAULIN, Tom (1949–) Poet and critic, brought up in Belfast, the most overtly 'political' of the leading Northern Irish poets. The stanzaic and metrical formality of early poetry collections like *The Strange Museum* (1980) gives way to an increasingly spiky and improvisatory colloquial mode in *Walking a Line* (1994) and *The Invasion Handbook* (2002), the latter an ambitious tableau of pre-Second World War Europe. Other works include *The Road to Inver* (2004), *The Camouflage School* (2007), and critical works on William *Hazlitt.

Pauline A poem in blank verse, the first poem to be published by Robert *Browning; it appeared anonymously in 1833. Subtitled 'A Fragment of a Confession', the 'confession' is addressed to Pauline by the first in a long series of 'fallen' speakers whose ambivalent rhetoric combines self-reproach and self-justification.

Paul's, Children of A company of boy actors, recruited from the choristers of St Paul's Cathedral, whose performances enjoyed great popularity from 1575 to 1590, when their tiny theatre within the cathedral was closed, and again from 1599 to 1608. They performed among others the plays of John *Lyly and, later, satirical comedies by John *Marston, George *Chapman, Thomas *Middleton, and others. The Children of the Chapel, recruited from the choristers of the Chapel Royal, was another company enjoying popular favour at the same time. Their rivalry with men actors is alluded to in *Hamlet* (II. ii).

PAVER, Michelle (1943–) Novelist and writer for children, author of the *Chronicles of Ancient Darkness* series set in the Stone Age (*Wolf Brother*, 2004; *Spirit Walker*, 2005; *Soul Eater*, 2006; *Outcast*, 2007; *Oath Breaker*, 2008; and *Ghost Hunter*, 2009) and the Bronze Age series *Gods and Warriors* (2012 onwards). The first series reached sales of more than one million copies before the publication of the final book. She has also written *historical novels, beginning with *Without Charity* (2000); *Dark Matter* (2010) is a powerful *ghost story.

P'Bitek, Okot (1931–82) Ugandan poet and anthropologist, who wanted to counter what he saw as the alienation of a new generation of Western-educated Africans. His dramatic monologues, written in an Acholi oral tradition, *Song of Lawino* (1966), *Song of Ocol* (1970), *Song of Prisoner* (1971), and *Song of Malaya* (1971), are scathingly witty indictments of the political corruption of the African middle class, and a celebration of traditional village life.

PEACOCK, Thomas Love (1785–1866) Satirist, essayist, and poet, a close friend of P. B. *Shelley. Peacock's prose satires, *Headlong Hall* (1816), *Melincourt* (1817), and *Nightmare Abbey* (1818), survey the contemporary political and cultural scene from a radical viewpoint. Formally they owe most to two classical genres: the 'Anatomy', or miscellaneous prose satire, and the Socratic dialogue, especially perhaps *Plato's *Symposium* which, like many of Peacock's convivial arguments, takes place over a dinner table. The debate is diversified by a romantic love-plot, increasingly important in *Crotchet Castle* (1831) and *Gryll Grange* (1860–61), and by songs. In *Maid Marian* (1822) and *The *Misfortunes of Elphin* (1829) he employs historical settings, 12th-century England and 6th-century Wales, but the topical satirical reference remains unmistakable. Of his satirical poems, *Paper Money Lyrics* (1837) attack the dogmas of political economists and the malpractices of bankers. Peacock's sceptical attitude to the fashionable cult of the arts is apparent in his critical essay, 'The *Four Ages of Poetry' (1820), to which Shelley replied in a *Defence of Poetry*. Peacock's favourite child was his eldest daughter Mary Ellen, who became the first wife of George *Meredith, and features in Meredith's sonnet sequence *Modern Love*.

PEAKE, Mervyn (1911–68) Novelist, poet, artist, and illustrator. He was commissioned as a war artist, and also visited Belsen in 1945 on a journalistic expedition for *The Leader*, an experience which profoundly affected him. His novel *Titus Groan* (1946) was followed by *Gormenghast* (1950) and *Titus Alone* (1959), which as a trilogy form the work for which Peake is best remembered, a creation of grotesque yet precise *Gothic fantasy, recounting the life of Titus, 77th earl of Groan, in his crumbling castle of Gormenghast, surrounded by a cast of characters which includes the colourful Fuchsia, Dr Prunesquallor, and the melancholy Muzzlehatch. Peake's poetry includes *The Glassblowers* (1950) and *The Rhyme of the Flying Bomb* (1962), a ballad of the Blitz; he illustrated most of his own work, *The Rime of the *Ancient Mariner* (1943), *Treasure Island* (1949), and other works. A lighter side of his prolific imagination is seen in his posthumous *A Book of Nonsense* (1972).

PEARCE, Philippa (1920–2007) Children's writer; her reputation was established with her first novel, *Minnow on the Say* (1955), but it is *Tom's Midnight Garden* (1958), about a boy who travels between the worlds of Victorian and 20th-century England when the clock strikes thirteen, for which she will be remembered. Her best books are sophisticated mixtures of realism and fantasy, past and present.

Pearl An alliterative poem in 1,212 lines of twelve-line *octosyllabic stanzas from the late 14th century, preserved in Cotton Nero A. X, also the sole manuscript of *Patience, *Cleanness,* and Sir *Gawain and the Green Knight.* The pearl whose loss is lamented by the poem's narrator is soon identified as a young girl, who died before she was 2 years old. He falls asleep in the garden where she is buried, and has a vision of a river, beyond which lies a paradisal garden. Here he sees a maiden whom he recognizes as the dead girl. She criticizes his excessive grief and describes her blessed state. He questions the justice that makes her queen of heaven when she died so young. Convinced by her, he is granted a vision of the New Jerusalem. He plunges into the river in an attempt to join her, but awakes with renewed commitment to participation in Christian worship, as exemplified by the sacrament of the Eucharist.

PEARSON, Hesketh (1887-1964) Actor and biographer. His first book, *Modern Men and Mummers* (1921), contained portraits of many of the theatre personalities of the time. *The Whispering Gallery* (1926), an anonymous work purporting to be 'leaves from the diary of an ex-diplomat', occasioned a scandal, a court case, and an acquittal for Pearson, who went on to write many lively and widely read biographies. He also wrote literary travel books in collaboration with Hugh Kingsmill, and his autobiography, *Hesketh Pearson by Himself,* appeared posthumously in 1965.

PECOCK, Reginald (c.1392-c.1459) Bishop successively of St Asaph and Chichester. His extant English writings not only confronted the appeal of the *Lollards, but were also intended to provide lay people with systematic orthodox theology in English. He addresses heresy most explicitly in *The Repressor of Over Much Blaming of the Clergy,* which exhibits considerable eloquence and lexical variety. In his *Donet* and the *Folewer to the Donet* he sought to define a body of faith, and the more demanding *Book of Faith* is markedly philosophical in character. He was arraigned before the archbishop of Canterbury, and obliged to resign his bishopric and recant his opinions (1458).

PEELE, George (1556-96) Poet and playwright. His works fall into three main categories: plays, pageants, and 'gratulatory' and miscellaneous verse. His surviving plays are *The Arraignment of Paris* (1584); *Edward I* (1593); *The Battle of Alcazar* (1594); *The Old Wife's Tale* (1595); and *David and Fair Beth-*

sabe (1599). His miscellaneous verse includes *Polyhymnia* (1590) and *The Honour of the Garter* (1593), a gratulatory poem to the earl of Northumberland. The *jest book *The Merry Conceited Jests of George Peele* (1607) apparently bears little relation to Peele's actual personality.

Pegasus *See* BELLEROPHON.

Peg Woffington Charles *Reade's first published novel (1853), based on an episode in the life of the 18th-century actress Peg Woffington, and adapted from his play *Masks and Faces.*

Pelham, or *The Adventures of a Gentleman* A novel by Edward *Bulwer-Lytton, published 1828. It describes the adventures of Henry Pelham, a young dandy and aspiring politician, who falls in love with Ellen, sister of an old school friend, Reginald Glanville. Reginald is falsely suspected of murder, and tells his story to Pelham, who discovers the real murderer, Thornton (based on the notorious murderer John Thurtell). Bulwer-Lytton mocks the conventions of the *fashionable novel while he exploits them, creating a tone of witty cynicism which pleased contemporary readers, and made the hero's name a catchphrase.

PEMBROKE, Mary Herbert, countess of (1561-1621) The younger sister of Philip *Sidney, whose first version of the *Arcadia was written for her at Wilton shortly after her marriage to Henry Herbert, second earl of Pembroke (1534-1601), in 1577. After her brother's death in 1586 she became in effect his literary executrix, overseeing the publication of *The Arcadia* and the rest of his works for editions in 1593 and 1598. She completed the *Psalms,* of which Sidney had translated only the first 42, rendering them in a very wide variety of English verse forms; they were not published as a whole until 1963. She translated the *Discourse of Life and Death* by Du Plessis Mornay (1549-1623) and *Antonius,* a Senecan tragedy by Robert Garnier (1544-90). Both were published in 1592; the latter was also published as *Antonie* in 1595. At an unknown date she translated *Petrarch's *Trionfo della morte.* Her reputation as a patroness rivalled her specific achievements. William *Browne's epitaph on her was popular throughout the 17th century.

PEN An association of Poets, Playwrights, Editors, Essayists, and Novelists founded in 1921 by Amy Dawson Scott (1865-1934) to promote understanding and cooperation between writers in the interests of literature, freedom of expression, and international goodwill. Its first international gathering was in 1923 and it now has branches in more than 100 countries.

Pendennis, The History of A novel by W. M. *Thackeray, serialized in numbers November 1848–December 1850, and illustrated by himself. It is a *Bildungsroman* in which the main character, Arthur Pendennis, is the spoiled son of an unworldly widow, Helen. He falls in love with an actress, Emily Costigan ('Miss Fotheringay'), and is only rescued from an unsuitable marriage by the intervention of his uncle. Pendennis then goes to university, where he runs up bills and is rescued by a loan from Helen's adopted daughter Laura Bell. Helen hopes that Laura and her son will marry, but Pendennis's next entanglement is with Blanche Amory, an affected and hard-hearted girl.

Pendennis goes to London, supposedly to read for the bar. He shares chambers with George Warrington (descended from the Warringtons in The *Virginians*), who starts him on a literary career by introducing him to Captain Shandon, a debt-ridden Irish journalist (based on William *Maginn) who is editing a new magazine, the 'Pall Mall Gazette', from prison. Pendennis has a mild flirtation with a working-class girl, Fanny Bolton, who nurses him through a dangerous illness. After the exposure of the existence of Blanche's villainous father, an escaped convict, Pendennis feels obliged to go through with an engagement to her. Fortunately Blanche decides in favour of Harry Foker, heir to a brewing fortune, and Pendennis and Laura finally marry, after Helen's death.

Pendragon A title given to an ancient British or Welsh chief holding or claiming supreme power. In English chiefly known as the title of Uther Pendragon, father of *Arthur. The word means 'chief dragon', the dragon being the war standard.

Penelope *See* ODYSSEY.

Penguin Books An innovative series of paperbacks launched by Allen *Lane in 1935 and established as an independent publishing company in 1936. The first ten titles—colour-coded orange for fiction, blue for biography, and green for crime—sold for sixpence each, and included works by Agatha *Christie, Ernest *Hemingway, and Dorothy *Sayers. The Penguin Shakespeare and the non-fiction Pelican series followed in 1937; Puffin Picture Books for children followed in 1940. Other notable ventures include the Penguin Classics (1946 onwards), edited for

many years by E. V. Rieu (1887–1972), whose own translation of the *Odyssey* (1946) was its first and best-selling volume. The first unexpurgated edition of *Lady Chatterley's Lover* (1960) led to a celebrated Old Bailey trial and acquittal. Penguin was acquired by the Pearson Group in 1970.

PENHALL, Joe (1967–) Playwright and screenwriter. His first play, *Some Voices* (1994; screenplay, 2000), about a young schizophrenic unsuccessfully attempting to adjust to life outside the hospital, produced at the *Royal Court Theatre, was followed by *Blue/Orange* (2000) and *Landscape with Weapon* (prod. *National Theatre, 2007). His screenplays include Ian McEwan's *Enduring Love* (2004) and Cormac McCarthy's *The Road* (2009).

PENN, William (1644–1718) Quaker and founder of Pennsylvania. Sent to the Tower in 1668 for publishing *The Sandy Foundation Shaken* (dismissing the doctrine of the Trinity), he wrote *No Cross, No Crown* (1669), a Quaker classic. He went to America to escape persecution, and drew up a democratic constitution for Pennsylvania, a forerunner of the United States Constitution.

PENNANT, Thomas (1726–98) Naturalist, antiquary, and traveller. His works include *A Tour in Scotland* (1771), *A Tour in Wales* (1778–81), *A Tour in Scotland and Voyage to the Hebrides* (1774–6), and *The Journey from Chester to London* (1782). His travel writings were admired by Samuel *Johnson. He was also a distinguished zoologist, author of *British Zoology* (1768–70) and *Arctic Zoology* (1784–7). *Literary Life of the Late Thomas Pennant, Esq., by Himself* appeared in 1793.

penny dreadfuls (*dime novels in the USA) Cheap, sensational texts produced in the 19th century featuring the lurid adventures of Sweeney Todd, Spring-Heeled Jack, and others. They were targeted at boys, but many girls also read them. Robert Louis *Stevenson was among those influenced by their style. Attempts to replace them with 'healthy fiction' included *Chatterbox* and *The Boy's Own Paper*.

Penshurst Place, in Kent The birthplace of Philip and Robert *Sidney. Many writers enjoyed its hospitality, including Ben *Jonson, who paid a graceful tribute in 'To Penshurst' (*The Forest*, 1616). *See also* PATRONAGE.

Pentameron, The A prose work by Walter Savage *Landor, published 1837, an expression of Landor's admiration of *Boccaccio. The book consists of imaginary conversations between *Petrarch and Boccaccio. They speak mainly of Dante's *Divina commedia; but Petrarch also reproves Boccaccio for the licentious character of some of his tales.

pentameter A verse line with five stressed syllables, almost always iambic in *metre and thus of ten syllables, the stressed normally alternating regularly with the unstressed: 'And never lifted up a single stone' (William *Wordsworth, 'Michael'). This iambic pentameter is the standard line of English verse from *Chaucer onwards, and the basis of several major English verse forms including *blank verse, *heroic couplets, *rhyme royal, and the *sonnet. It is open to flexible variation in syllable count (variant lines may be of eleven or nine syllables), in the use and position of the *caesura, in the number of stressed syllables (variant lines may employ four or six, thus speeding or slowing the movement), and in their placing (stressing the first rather than second syllable of a line is the most common variation).

PEPYS, Samuel [pron. Peeps] (1633–1703) Diarist. He entered the household of Sir Edward Montagu (afterwards first earl of Sandwich), his father's first cousin, in 1656; and his subsequent successful career was largely due to Montagu's patronage. His famous *Diary* opens on 1 January 1660, when Pepys was living in Axe Yard, Westminster, and was very poor. Soon after this he was appointed 'clerk of the King's ships' and clerk of the privy seal, with a salary of £350 (supplemented by fees). In 1665 he became surveyor-general of the victualling office, in which capacity he showed himself an energetic official and a zealous reformer of abuses. Owing to an unfounded fear of failing eyesight he closed his diary on 31 May 1669. At the revolution of 1688 he was deprived of his appointment of secretary to the admiralty and afterwards lived in retirement. His *Diary* remained in cipher (a system of shorthand) at Magdalene College, Cambridge, until 1825, when it was deciphered by the clergyman John Smith and edited by Lord Braybrooke. Later 19th-century editions were superseded by a new and unbowdlerized transcription by R. Latham and W. Matthews (11 vols, 1970–83). On Pepys's death his friend and fellow diarist John *Evelyn remembered him as 'a very worthy, industrious and curious person, none in England exceeding him in knowledge of the navy... universally beloved, hospitable, generous, learned in many things, skilled in music, a very great cherisher of learned men'. See Claire *Tomalin, *Samuel Pepys: The Unequalled Self* (2003). *See also* RESTORATION.

Perceforest A vast 14th-century French prose romance, in which the author seeks to link the legends of *Alexander the Great and *Arthur. Perceforest is a follower of Alexander, so called because he has killed a magician in an impenetrable forest.

Perceval, Sir Probably to be identified with *Peredur of the *Mabinogion. He first appears in European poetry in the 9,000-line, incomplete *Perceval, ou le conte del Graal* of *Chrétien de Troyes (c.1182) and the German *Parzival* (c.1205) of Wolfram von Eschenbach. In English he appears in *Sir Perceval of Galles*, a 2,288-line romance, in 16-line stanzas in *tail-rhyme from the 15th century, and in Sir Thomas *Malory. The former tells of the childhood of Perceval and his being knighted by Arthur, without any allusion to the Holy *Grail. Malory makes him a son of King Pellinore, describing his success in the quest for the Holy Grail with the knights *Galahad and Bors.

PERCY, Thomas (1729–1811) Clergyman and literary scholar. In 1761 he published a translation (from the Portuguese) of the first Chinese novel to appear in English, *Hau Kiou Choaan*; his *Five Pieces of Runic Poetry Translated from the Islandic Language* (1763), had a considerable influence on the study of Norse in England. Percy also published poetry, translated from the Hebrew and Spanish, and wrote a *Memoir of Goldsmith* (1801). His collection of *ballads, *Reliques of Ancient English Poetry* (3 vols, 1765), tastefully 'improved' from materials in the *Percy Folio, was attacked by Joseph *Ritson as unscholarly, but contributed to the revival of interest in older English poetry.

Percy Folio A manuscript in mid-17th-century handwriting, the basis of Francis Child's (1825–96) collection of *ballads, and the source of the ballads included in Thomas *Percy's *Reliques*. It also contains the 14th-century alliterative allegorical poem 'Death and Life' (modelled on *Piers Plowman*) and 'Scottish Field' (mainly on the battle of *Flodden).

Peredur The Arthurian subject of one of the seven tales added by Lady Charlotte Guest (1812–95; an early translator of the *Mabinogion*) to the *Mabinogion* proper and now normally included in it. The Welsh *Peredur* is found most completely in the White Book, rather than the Red Book used by Guest (see *Mabinogion*).

The story corresponds closely to the *Perceval* of *Chrétien de Troyes and to a number of other Arthurian texts.

Peregrine Pickle, The Adventures of

A satirical novel by Tobias *Smollett, published 1751. As a boy Peregrine shows 'a certain oddity of disposition' which manifests itself in practical jokes. He falls in love with Emilia, who remains through all his wanderings a fixed point to which he always returns. But she is beneath him in fortune and in rank, and pride forbids him to court her. He undertakes a disastrous *Grand Tour, suffering imprisonment in the Bastille and passionately attaching himself to one woman after another. Returning to England, he becomes obsessed with the seduction of Eilia, falling ill when he fails to accomplish this. At this point, the lengthy 'Memoirs of a Lady of Quality' are abruptly inserted as chapter 81, breaking the pell-mell flow of adventure but providing an oblique perspective on Peregrine's life of debauchery. The 'Memoirs' are based on the life story of Frances Anne Hawes, Viscountess Vane (1713–88). When the main story resumes, Peregrine loses money in an attempt to enter politics, and is eventually imprisoned for libel. In prison Peregrine becomes morose and withdrawn, and begins to long for death. But he is rescued by Emilia's brother Godfrey, Emilia returns to him, and he inherits his father's fortune. When he and Emilia marry they reject the fashionable urban world and retire to the country. The novel contained savage caricatures of Henry *Fielding as Mr Spondy, David *Garrick as Marmozet, and Mark *Akenside as the Doctor.

performance poetry

A term applied to poetry specifically written to be performed out loud. The work may sometimes transfer successfully to the printed page, but its true power usually lies in the moment of public performance.

Often with an anti-establishment edge, performance poetry (or 'Spoken Word') is usually performed from memory or improvised, rather than read; it can be accompanied by highly choreographed gestures and subtle voice techniques, leading to accusations (not always unjust) of style over substance.

'It is very important to get poetry out of the hands of the professors and out of the hands of the squares,' declared American jazz poet Kenneth *Rexroth (1905–82) in 1958. 'We simply want to make poetry a part of show business.' Performing poets may appear in music venues,

bars, comedy festivals, and on radio; they may issue a CD before a book.

Jazz (*see* JAZZ POETRY) has been a consistently dominant influence, from Langston *Hughes and Vachel Lindsay (1879–1931); to Rexroth's 1950s jazz-poetry collaborations with Lawrence *Ferlinghetti; and continuing since the 1970s, with Amiri *Baraka, Jayne Cortez (1936–), Gil Scott Heron (1949–), and the Last Poets, through to contemporary hip-hop.

In the 1960s, Allen *Ginsberg took oral poetry into coffee houses, pop festivals, and art happenings. In Britain, the spirit was spread by Michael *Horovitz, Adrian *Mitchell, and the *Liverpool poets. Maverick figures with a music-hall tilt followed, including Glaswegian absurdist Ivor Cutler (1923–2006); then, in the mid-1970s, punky quickfire monologuist John Cooper Clarke (1950–), and from the mid-1980s cabaret scene, John Hegley (1953–).

Performance poetry has become most closely identified with black writers such as Benjamin *Zephaniah, Linton Kwesi *Johnson, John *Agard, and James *Berry. The Caribbean tradition from which their work derives is closely associated with the musical forms of calypso, ska, reggae, and dancehall and can be roughly divided into two forms: *'dub poetry', which is performed from memory without accompaniment, and the more improvisational 'toastin', which is accompanied by music.

In 1987, a new wave of performance activity was sparked in the United States when Marc Smith (1950–) started the first Poetry Slam at Chicago's Green Mill Cocktail Bar. These raucous stand-up poetry contests came to worldwide attention after Bob Holman (1948–) introduced them to the Nuyorican Poets Café. The format is now well enough established for Harold *Bloom to have described it in the *Paris Review* (Spring 2000) as 'the death of art', an assessment which supporters have welcomed as an endorsement of its anti-elitist credentials. Leading exponents include Patricia Smith (1955–) and Saul Williams (1972–), who starred in the 1998 film, *Slam*.

Peri Bathous, or The Art of Sinking in Poetry

(1727) A mock-critical manual by Alexander *Pope on literary 'bathos', supposedly 'depth' or 'profundity' (by analogy with *Longinus' 'hypsos' or 'sublimity'), but actually a record of the failure of poets to achieve literary sublimity and their tendency to fall flat instead. Pope used as examples quotations from Richard Blackmore, John Dennis, Ambrose *Philips, and Lewis *Theobald, among others. Angry responses were shortly afterwards absorbed into the material for Pope's *Dunciad*.

Pericles and Aspasia A prose work by Walter Savage *Landor, published 1836. The book consists of imaginary letters, most of them between Aspasia and her friend Cleone. Others pass between Pericles and Aspasia, or other prominent figures of the time, including Anaxagoras and Alcibiades. The letters discuss artistic, literary, religious, philosophical, and political subjects, ending with the death of Pericles.

Pericles, Prince of Tyre A romantic drama ascribed to *Shakespeare on its first publication in 1609, but now generally agreed to have been written in collaboration with George *Wilkins, who seems to have been mainly responsible for the first two acts. The play is based on the story of Apollonius of Tyre (which Shakespeare also used in The *Comedy of Errors) in John *Gower's *Confessio Amantis* and a prose version (itself derived from the *Gesta Romanorum*), *The Pattern of Painful Adventures*, registered 1576 and reprinted 1607, by Laurence Twyne.

The play is presented by Gower, who acts as chorus throughout. It tells how Pericles, prince of Tyre, discovers the incestuous relation between King Antiochus and his daughter by solving a riddle, and then finds his life in danger. He leaves his government in the hands of his honest minister Helicanus, and sails from Tyre to Tarsus where he relieves a famine. Off the coast of Pentapolis Pericles alone survives the wreck of his ship, and in a tournament defeats the suitors for the hand of Thaisa, daughter of King Simonides, whom he marries.

Hearing that Antiochus has died, Pericles sets sail for Tyre, and during a storm on the voyage Thaisa gives birth to a daughter, Marina, and collapses. Apparently dead, Thaisa is buried at sea in a chest, which is cast ashore at Ephesus, where Cerimon, a physician, opens it and restores Thaisa to life. She, thinking her husband drowned, becomes a priestess in the temple of Diana. Pericles takes Marina to Tarsus, where he leaves her with its governor Cleon and his wife Dioniza.

When the child grows up Dioniza, jealous of her being more favoured than her own daughter, seeks to kill her; but Marina is carried off by pirates and sold in Mytilene to a brothel, where her purity and piety win the admiration of Lysimachus, the governor of the city, and the respect of the brothel-keeper's servant, Boult, and secure her release. In a vision Pericles sees Marina's tomb, deceivingly erected by Cleon and Dioniza. He puts to sea again and lands at Mytilene, where to his intense joy Pericles discovers his daughter. In a second vision, Diana directs him to go to her temple at Ephesus and there tell the story of his life. In doing this, the priestess Thaisa, his lost wife, recognizes him, and is reunited with her husband and daughter. At the end of the play the chorus tells how Cleon and Dionyza are burnt by the citizens of Tarsus as a penalty for their wickedness.

periodical, literary A repeating series of literary journal, magazine, or review. The literary periodical began to flourish in the early 18th century. The trade journal *Mercurius Librarius*, begun in 1668, was the first periodical to catalogue books, and the *Universal Historical Bibliotheque* of 1687 the first to invite contributions and include comments on essays and other recent writings. The *Gentleman's Journal* (begun 1692) included much literary material, and the general magazine with some literary content was popularized by the *Tatler* (1709–11) of Joseph *Addison and Richard *Steele and Edward Cave's influential *Gentleman's Magazine* (begun 1731); the tradition continued in the 19th century with *Blackwood's Magazine* (1817–1980) and *Bentley's Miscellany* (1837–69). The single-essay periodical, best represented by the *Spectator* (1711–12, 1714) and Samuel *Johnson's *Rambler* (1750–52), had huge contemporary influence and reputation, but the form did not last beyond the end of the 18th century. Henry *Fielding was associated with several journals, especially The *Champion* (1739–41) and the *Covent-Garden Journal* (1752), which held occasional 'trials' of current publications, including those of Tobias *Smollett. Formal book reviews began with the *Monthly Review* (1749–1844) and Smollett's *Critical Review* (1756–90). Several periodicals identified themselves with political positions, such as The *Anti-Jacobin* (1797–8), which opposed the liberal outlook of the *Monthly Review* and of S. T. *Coleridge's The *Watchman* (1796); the *New Monthly Magazine* (1814–84) expressly opposed the radical *Monthly Magazine* (founded 1796).

By the early 19th century the periodicals and their editors (such as Leigh *Hunt in the *Indicator* and John *Scott in the *London Magazine*) were becoming increasingly influential. The *Englishman's Magazine* (1831–3) published and defended William *Wordsworth, Alfred *Tennyson, Thomas *Hood, and others. S. T. Coleridge's *Friend* and P. B. Shelley's *Liberal* (1822–4) stood apart from the magisterial opinion-formers of the 19th century such as the *Edinburgh Review* (1802-1929), the *Quarterly Review* (1809-1967), the *Examiner* (1808-81), the *Westminster Review* (1824-1914), the *Athenaeum* (1828-1921), the *Cornhill Magazine* (1860-1975), and the *Fortnightly Review* (1865-1934). Later periodicals established by writers to break away from commercial journalism include the *Yellow Book* (1894-7), the *English Review*, *Blast* (*see* VORTICISM), T. S. *Eliot's *Criterion*, *Horizon* (1940-50), and *Encounter* (1953-). Some of the functions of the literary periodical have been assumed by the book sections of newspapers such as the *Guardian, The *Times*, and the *Observer*. In Britain the most eminent periodicals devoted to books are the *Times Literary Supplement* (1902-) and the *London Review of Books* (1979-).

peripeteia A sudden reversal of the *protagonist's fortunes within a dramatic plot, usually that of a *tragedy.

Perkin Warbeck A historical play by John *Ford, printed 1634: its source is an episode in Francis Bacon's *Henry VII*.

PERRAULT, Charles (1628-1703) French writer, lawyer, and civil servant. In his day he was known for his participation in the quarrel between the ancients and moderns (*see* CORNEILLE, PIERRE); however, he is remembered for his collection of *fairy stories published under the name (and possibly with the collaboration) of his son Pierre: *Histoires ou contes du temps passé* (1697), subtitled 'Contes de ma Mère l'Oye' (*see* MOTHER GOOSE). He began by producing ironic verse tales, popular in sophisticated court circles: 'Grisélidis' (the story of *Patient Griselda, 1691), 'Les Souhaits ridicules' ('Three Ridiculous Wishes', 1693), and 'Peau d'Asne' ('Donkeyskin', 1695).

The *Histoires* transformed popular folk tales into moralizing works concluded with ironic verse homilies; they were translated into English as 'Mother Goose Tales' by Robert Samber in 1729. The original tales consisted of those known in English as 'Hop o' my Thumb'; 'Cinderella'; 'Sleeping Beauty'; 'Blue Beard'; 'The Fairies, or Diamonds and Toads'; 'Puss in Boots'; 'Little Red Riding Hood'; and 'Ricky with the Tuft'.

Perseus Mythical Greek hero, son of Zeus (*Jupiter) and Danaë. Aided by divine gifts, including winged sandals, helmet of invisibility, and shield used as a mirror, he cut off the head of the monstrous Gorgon Medusa, whose gaze turned those who looked at her to stone. The winged horse Pegasus sprang up from her blood. *Ovid describes his adventures, including his rescue of Andromeda, in *Metamorphoses* Book 4. Shakespeare and other Renaissance writers assumed that Perseus, not *Bellerophon, was the rider of Pegasus.

PERSIUS (Aulus Persius Flaccus) (AD 34-62) Roman poet, author of six satires. Persius writes as a Stoic and assumes that his reader is familiar with *Horace. His satires were imitated by John *Donne and translated by John *Dryden.

Persuasion A novel by Jane *Austen, written 1815-16, her last completed work, published posthumously 1818. Sir Walter Elliot, a spendthrift baronet and widower, with a swollen sense of his social importance and personal elegance, is obliged to let the family seat, Kellynch Hall. His eldest daughter Elizabeth, haughty and unmarried, is now 29; the second, Anne, now 27, had previously been engaged to a young naval officer, Frederick Wentworth, but had been persuaded by her trusted friend Lady Russell to break off the engagement. The breach had brought great unhappiness to Anne, and caused angry indignation in Wentworth. When the story opens Captain Wentworth, now prosperous, is thrown again into Anne's company by the letting of Kellynch to Admiral and Mrs Croft, his sister and brother-in-law. Sir Walter's youngest daughter Mary is married to Charles Musgrove, the heir of a neighbouring landowner. Wentworth becomes involved with Charles's sister Louisa. During a visit of the party to Lyme Regis, Louisa, being 'jumped down' from the Cobb by Wentworth, falls and is badly injured. Wentworth's partial responsibility for the accident increases his obligation to Louisa at the very time that his feelings are being drawn back to Anne. However, during her convalescence Louisa becomes engaged to Captain Benwick. Wentworth goes to Bath, where Sir Walter now lives with his two elder daughters and Elizabeth's artful companion Mrs Clay. Another suitor for Anne's hand, her cousin William Elliot, the heir to the Kellynch estate, is also flirting with Mrs Clay, in order to detach her from Sir Walter. Anne remains unshaken in her love for Wentworth and learns about the duplicity of William Elliot. Accidentally made aware of Anne's constancy, Wentworth renews his offer of marriage and is accepted.

There is a tradition—poorly substantiated—that a love story of Jane Austen's own life is reflected in Anne Elliot's, although she wrote

p

to her niece Fanny, 'You may *perhaps* like the heroine, as she is almost too good for me.'

PESSOA, Fernando (1888–1935) Portuguese poet and writer of prose. Pessoa was profoundly influenced by English literature and, in 1918, published, in English, *35 Sonnets and Antinous*. In 1913–17, he composed poetry in many different styles, published under the name of his 'heteronyms', fictional alter egos, whose biographies—and horoscopes—he also compiled. He has come to be considered one of the leading European *modernists.

PETER, St *See* BIBLE.

PETER I, the Great (Emperor Petr Alekseevich) (1672–1725) Russian tsar. Peter was the first Russian ruler to travel abroad (1697–8), accompanying in transparent incognito, rather than leading, a Grand Embassy that visited European capitals seeking support for Russia's struggle against the Turks. After meeting William III in Utrecht, Peter, still incognito, visited England in January 1698. The months he spent in London provided the colourful anecdotes (including his managing to devastate John *Evelyn's house and garden at Sayes Court) that ensured Peter's place in British memory and imagination. Despite subsequent deterioration in Anglo-Russian diplomatic relations, Peter became a legendary hero of the *Enlightenment. During the tsar's lifetime Daniel *Defoe published his fake memoir *Impartial History* (1723), and Aaron *Hill's poetic effusion *The Northern Star* went into five editions between 1718 and 1739. Peter became the star of dramas, comic operas, and tragedies, beginning with the anonymous *Northern Heroes* (1748), including John *O'Keeffe's *The Czar Peter* (1790), and finishing with Laurence Irving's performed but unpublished five-act tragedy *Peter the Great* (1898).

Peter Bell A poem by William *Wordsworth, written 1798, published with a dedication to Robert *Southey 1819. Bell is a lawless potter, who sees a solitary ass and hopes to steal it. The ass is gazing into the water at some object, which turns out to be the dead body of its owner. After a series of supernatural events Peter mounts the ass, which leads him to the cottage of the drowned man's widow. Peter's spiritual and supernatural experiences on this ride make him a reformed man. The comic nature of part of the poem was seen by some as ludicrous and diverted attention from its merits, and it became the subject of several parodies, including one by P. B. *Shelley, *Peter Bell the Third*.

Peter Bell the Third A satirical poem by P. B. *Shelley published 1839. It parodies William *Wordsworth's poem *Peter Bell*. A second 'Peter Bell' had already been published by John *Keats's friend J. H. *Reynolds. Shelley uses inventive doggerel, outrageous rhymes, and effervescent social satire to mock Wordsworth's 'defection' from the radical cause. He follows Peter's progress through a black, comic underworld, described in seven sections: 'Death', 'The Devil', 'Hell', 'Sin', 'Grace', 'Damnation', and 'Double Damnation'. Part III begins with the celebrated 'Hell is a city much like London'; while Part V draws a sympathetic cartoon of Peter the poet.

Peterborough Chronicle, The The last part of the Laud manuscript of the *Anglo-Saxon Chronicles*, written in Peterborough at various times between 1121 and 1154. It is the only part of the chronicles to extend beyond 1080, and exemplifies the developments between Old and Middle English. The 12th-century entries, in particular, as they describe the disasters and hardships of Stephen's reign, have vigour and circumstantiality far beyond the earlier parts of the chronicles.

'Peter Grimes' A tale in George *Crabbe's *The *Borough*. Grimes is a fisherman who 'fish'd by water and who filch'd by land'. Forbidden to keep apprentices after several die under his ill treatment, he lives and works alone. Guilt maddens him, and he dies after enduring imagined terrors. He is the principal figure in Benjamin *Britten's opera *Peter Grimes*.

Peter Pan, or *The Boy Who Would Not Grow Up* A play by J. M. *Barrie, first performed in 1904, featuring Peter Pan, who lives in Neverland with fairies, pirates, and the Lost Boys, where he takes the Darling children. It has been adapted as a musical (1954), and filmed by Disney (1953), P. J. Hogan (2003), and, as *Hook*, by Steven Spielberg (1991). *See* MCCAUGHREAN, GERALDINE.

Peter Porcupine *See* COBBETT, WILLIAM.

PETERS, Ellis *See* DETECTIVE FICTION.

PETRARCH (Francesco Petrarca) (1304–74) Italian poet and humanist, and the most popular Italian poet of the English Renaissance. In Avignon in 1327 Petrarch first saw the woman who inspired his love poetry. He calls her Laura; her true identity is unknown. Until 1353

Petrarch's life was centred on Provence, but he made extended visits to Italy and resided there from 1353. Today Petrarch is best known for the collection of Italian lyrics variously known as the *Canzoniere* or the *Rerum vulgarium fragmenta*, which includes the long series of poems in praise of Laura, now regarded as the fountainhead of the European lyric. He wrote a large number of treatises in Latin, including *De Viris Illustribus* (*On Famous Men*), *De Vita Solitaria* (*On the Solitary Life*), *De Remediis Utriusque Fortunae* (*Remedies for Fortune Fair and Foul*); a Latin epic, *Africa*, on the struggle between Rome and Carthage; and the *Secretum* (*The Secret*), a self-analysis in the form of a dialogue between himself and St Augustine. Influenced by Cicero, Petrarch consciously collected his own letters for public circulation. See *Rerum Familiarum Libri* (*Letters on Familiar Matters*), *Seniles* (*Letters of Old Age*).

For English writers, Petrarch's chief inspiration was to the early sonneteers (*see* SONNET); he was imitated and translated by the earl of *Surrey, Thomas *Wyatt, Thomas *Watson, and, later, by *Drummond of Hawthornden. Philip *Sidney bears witness to his powerful and pervasive influence, and both Henry Parker, Lord Morley (1476–1556) and the countess of *Pembroke translated works by him. The Petrarchan vogue declined in the 17th century with the waning popularity of the sonnet sequence, but Thomas *Gray, in a note on the last stanza of his *Elegy*, credits Petrarch with his phrase 'trembling hope' (*paventosa speme*), indicating a renewal of interest in the later 18th century.

Petronius Arbiter (probably 1st century AD) Roman satirical novelist, author of the *Satyricon*; traditionally identified with Petronius, the witty favourite of Nero who was forced to commit suicide in AD 66. The novel relates the adventures of the disreputable Encolpius, and those of his glamorous boy-friend, Giton. At times, it is the wrath of Priapus, god of fertility, which pursues them—a burlesque of the angry Poseidon of the *Odyssey* and the angry *Juno of the *Aeneid*. Most celebrated, and longest, of the surviving episodes is the grotesque dinner party given by a wealthy and ignorant freedman, which burlesques the motif of the philosophical party, a recurrent theme from *Plato's *Symposium* onwards. The story of the Widow of Ephesus is a classic of ribald misogyny. The novel is punctuated by passages of verse, a feature of *Menippean satire*, including a lengthy poem on the Civil Wars covering the same ground as *Lucan. The first English translation was published in 1694 by William Burnaby (1673–1706).

Retellings of Petronius include Federico Fellini's film *Satyricon*.

PETTIE, George (*c.*1548–89) Writer of romances. His *A Petite Palace of Pettie his Pleasure*, first published in 1576, was often reprinted. This collection of twelve 'pretty histories', all but one deriving from classical sources, concerns lovers. They are mainly made up of long speeches with little action, and their style partially anticipates John *Lyly's euphuism. Pettie's work follows on from William Painter's *Palace of Pleasure* from which he derived his title; his translation of most of *Civil Conversation* (1581) by Stefano Guazzo (1530–93) contributed to the Elizabethan vogue for *courtesy literature.

Peveril of the Peak A novel by Walter *Scott, published 1823, set in the Restoration England of Titus Oates's 'Popish Plot'.

PEYTON, K. M. (1929-) (Kathleen—'M' is her husband, Michael, a collaborator on some early books.) Children's novelist, known for her stories about horses and hunting, especially the trilogy of books beginning with *Flambards* (1968; televised, 1979). The Pennington books (1970, 1971, 1980) feature a musically talented but difficult working-class boy.

PFEIFFER, Emily (1827–1890) Née Davis, poet and essayist. Her works include *The Wynnes of Wynhavod* (1881); *Flying Leaves from East and West* (1885); *Flowers of the Night* (1889); and various feminist articles which were collected in *Women and Work* (1887).

Phalaris, Epistles of Letters attributed to Phalaris, a tyrant of Acragas in Sicily (6th century BC), with a reputation for extreme cruelty. They were edited by Charles Boyle, fourth earl of Orrery (1674–1731), in 1695 Richard *Bentley proved that they were spurious and dated from perhaps the 2nd century AD. There is an echo of the controversy in Jonathan Swift's *The *Battle of the Books*.

Phaon (1) In Edmund *Spenser's *Faerie Queene* (II. iv), the unfortunate squire who, deceived by Philemon and under the influence of Furor (mad rage), slays Claribel and poisons Philemon. (2) In classical mythology, the boatman with whom *Sappho is said to have fallen in love. John *Lyly's play *Sapho and Phao* (1584) dramatizes the subject.

Pharsalia See LUCAN.

Philaster, *or Love Lies a-Bleeding* A romantic tragicomedy by Francis *Beaumont and John *Fletcher, written 1608–9, printed 1620. One of the most successful of the Beaumont and Fletcher collaborations, the play draws on the conventions of the prose romances, notably on *Montemayor's *Diana* and Sidney's *Arcadia*.

philippics *See* CICERO, MARCUS TULLIUS; DEMOSTHENES.

Philip Quarll, The Adventures of An adventure story originally published as *The Hermit* (1727) by 'Edward Dorrington', but probably by Peter Longueville. A derivative of *Robinson Crusoe*, it describes Quarll's 50 years of solitude and suffering on a South Sea island. It was much adapted for children.

PHILIPS, Ambrose (1674–1749) Poet, and MP in the Irish Parliament. In 1709 his *Pastorals* were printed in the same miscellany as those of Alexander *Pope; following Thomas *Tickell's praise (in the *Guardian*) of Philips's versions, Pope added an extra paper, no. 40, in which he commended with 'unexampled and unequalled artifice of irony' (Samuel *Johnson) Philips's most risible effects. Philips also wrote *The Distrest Mother* (1712), a successful adaptation of *Racine's *Andromaque*, and a series of infantile trochaics addressed to children which earned him the nickname of 'Namby Pamby'.

PHILIPS, John (1676–1709) Poet. In *The Splendid Shilling* (unauthorized 1701, authorized 1705), a burlesque in Miltonic blank verse, Philips contrasts the happy possessor of the shilling with the starving poet in his garret, beset by creditors. In 1705 he published *Blenheim*, written at the suggestion of Robert Harley and Viscount Bolingbroke, as a Tory counterpart to Joseph *Addison's *The Campaign*. *Cyder* (1708), a two-book poem in blank verse written in imitation of *Virgil's *Georgics*, celebrates the cultivation, manufacture, and virtues of cider. The poem influenced Alexander Pope's *Windsor-Forest* and James Thomson's *The *Seasons*.

PHILIPS, Katherine (1631–64) Poet and translator, known as the 'Matchless Orinda'. In 1648 she married Parliamentarian James Philips of Cardigan: he was 59, she 17. Her poems were widely circulated in manuscript, inspiring eulogies by Henry *Vaughan in *Olor Iscanus* and *Thalia Rediviva*; a commendatory poem by 'Orinda' was prefixed to the latter volume. Her translation of *Corneille's *Pompée* was acted in Dublin with great success in 1663, and

her version of *Horace*, completed by Sir John *Denham, in 1668. Her collected poems appeared unauthorized in 1664. She died of smallpox, and was mourned in elegies by Abraham *Cowley and Sir William *Temple; her collected poems were published in 1667. They memorialize a coterie, a Platonic Society of Friendship, whose members were known by poetic sobriquets, including Anne Owen (1633–92; Lucasia), Mary Aubrey (1631–1700; Rosania), John *Berkenhead (Cratander), and Sir Charles Cotterell (1615–1701; Poliarchus), her correspondence with whom was published as *Letters from Orinda to Poliarchus* in 1705. These letters show Philips's careful construction of the persona of 'Orinda'. She was pre-eminently a poet of female friendship.

PHILLIPS, Caryl (1958–) Novelist and playwright, born in St Kitts, West Indies. He came to England with his family as a child. Early plays include *Strange Fruit* (1980) and *The Shelter* (1983), but he is better known for his novels dealing with race, migration, colonial and postcolonial concerns. *The Final Passage* (1985), describes the experiences of the post-war immigrant generation from the Caribbean to Britain. In *A State of Independence* (1986), the protagonist experiences dislocation on returning to his West Indian home. *Higher Ground* (1989), *Cambridge* (1991), *Crossing the River* (1994), and *In The Nature of Blood* (1997) range widely in their geographical and historical settings, but share a concern with oppression and the legacy of the Atlantic slave trade, seeing analogies between black slavery and oppressed Jewish experience over the centuries. *Dancing in the Dark* (2005) subtly fictionalizes the life of the black American vaudeville performer Bert Williams. Non-fiction works include *The European Tribe* (essays, 1987) *Foreigners* (2007), a portrait of three black men in England in different eras, and the partly autobiographical *Colour Me English* (2011). *Extravagant Strangers: A Literature of Belonging* (1997), edited by Phillips, is a survey and anthology of non-British-born writers and the invigorating effects of 'mongrelization' on the native tradition. *See* POSTCOLONIAL LITERATURE.

PHILLIPS, John (1631–1706) Younger brother of Edward Phillips, and nephew of John *Milton, by whom he was educated. He wrote a scathing attack on Puritanism in his poem *A Satire against Hypocrites* (1655), supported Charles II and Titus Oates (1649–1705), and worked as translator and hack-writer.

PHILLIPS, Mike (195?–) Innovative crime writer and essayist, born in Guyana; he moved to Britain as a child. Four of his novels feature a black journalist, Sam Dean, whom Phillips describes as 'a moral outlaw'. *A Shadow of Myself* (2000) plays with the doppelgänger theme. *A Kind of Union* (2005) examines identity in 21st century Britain.

PHILLIPS, Tom (1937–) English painter, illustrator, and composer. Much of his work has explored the material presence of books and the possibility of reordering printed words to reveal latent stories. *A Humument* (1966–) is a 'treated book' based on W. H. *Mallock's 1892 novel *A Human Document*, parts of which are picked out and elaborately illuminated in a process of constant revision. It has also been made available as an app for iPad and iPhone.

Philomela In classical myth raped by Tereus, husband of her sister Procne; he cut out her tongue, but she revealed her fate to Procne in an embroidered tapestry. The sisters took their revenge by serving up Procne's and Tereus' son to his father in a stew. Procne, Tereus, and Philomela were changed into birds, with Philomela in some versions becoming a nightingale. The story is told in *Ovid's *Metamorphoses* Book 6, and echoed in William *Shakespeare's *Titus Andronicus* and *Cymbeline*. The name Philomela or Philomel is often used poetically to designate the nightingale without reference to her story. Elizabeth *Rowe published her poems under the name Philomela.

Philosophical View of Reform, A A political essay by P. B. *Shelley, written at Pisa 1820, not published until 1920. Intended as an 'instructive and readable' booklet, this was Shelley's most mature political statement about Liberty, Revolution, and Reform: it confirms his position as a radical (rather than a liberal)—but not a violent revolutionary. The essay illuminates the thinking behind Shelley's political poems of 1817–20, and provided much material for the *Defence of Poetry*, such as the concept of 'unacknowledged legislators'.

Philotas A Senecan tragedy in blank verse by Samuel *Daniel, published 1605. The boasts of Philotas, a brave and generous soldier who is much admired among the Macedonians, make Alexander suspicious. He is accused of concealing his knowledge of a conspiracy against the king, is tortured, and, having confessed, is stoned to death. The author had subsequently to defend himself against the charge that the play implied sympathy for the rebellion of Essex. Performance of the play was suppressed in 1604.

Phineas Finn, the Irish Member A novel by Anthony *Trollope, published 1869, the second in the *'Palliser' series. Phineas Finn, a young Irish barrister, is elected to Parliament for the family seat of Loughshane. In London Phineas falls in love with the politically minded Lady Laura Standish. Lady Laura's fortune is diminished after paying the debts of her brother Lord Chiltern, and she feels she must marry the chilly but wealthy Mr Kennedy. Phineas seeks consolation elsewhere. He pursues Violet Effingham, Lord Chiltern's childhood sweetheart, but after a quarrel between the two suitors Violet settles for Chiltern. Madame Max Goesler, the rich widow of a Viennese banker, is Phineas's next favourite. Phineas loses his government salary by sticking to his principles over the issue of Irish Tenant Right. Madame Max offers to marry him, and to finance a fresh political career. But Phineas honours his prior engagement to a pretty Irish girl, Mary Flood-Jones, and returns to Ireland.

Phineas Redux A novel by Anthony *Trollope, published 1874, fourth in the *'Palliser' series. Phineas Finn's young wife Mary dies, and he returns to politics. But his progress is blocked by a series of misfortunes. First Mr Kennedy, enraged by Phineas's visit to his wife Lady Laura in her Dresden exile, tries to shoot him. Then Phineas quarrels with the president of the Board of Trade, Mr Bonteen, and when, later that night, Bonteen is murdered, he becomes a suspect. He is tried, and only the spirited efforts of Madame Max in discovering the true culprit, and a brilliant courtroom performance by the lawyer Chaffanbrass, succeed in getting him off. Bonteen's murderer turns out to have been Mr Emilius, the converted Jew who married Lizzie Eustace. Emilius is convicted of bigamy and imprisoned, but there is insufficient evidence to hang him. Phineas marries Madame Max.

In this novel the old duke of Omnium dies, and Plantagenet and Lady Glencora become duke and duchess.

Phiz *See* BROWNE, HABLOT KNIGHT.

phoenix In classical myth a unique Arabian bird which periodically was consumed by fire and reborn from its own ashes. It became a symbol of resurrection in a Christian sense and also of many kinds of rebirth: in *Annus Mirabilis* John *Dryden portrays a newly deified

London rising from the Great Fire. The phoenix motif was of particular importance to D. H. *Lawrence, and the phoenix Fawkes is an important character in the Harry *Potter series.

Phoenix, The An Old English poem of 677 lines, found in the *Exeter Book. It is a beast allegory of the kind found in the *bestiaries. The descriptive part of the poem is closely based on *Carmen de Ave Phoenice*, probably by the early Christian writer Lactantius (*c*.250–*c*.325).

'Phoenix and the Turtle, The' Regarded by many as William *Shakespeare's greatest non-dramatic poem, an allegorical elegy lamenting the death of the phoenix and the turtle-dove, who are presented as models of ideal, chaste wedded love, and are mourned by other birds. It was first published in 1601 in *Love's Martyr* a collection of poems on the same subject by Ben *Jonson, George *Chapman, John *Marston, and Robert Chester (*fl. c.*1586–1604).

Phoenix Nest, The A poetical miscellany published in 1593. It includes poems by the earl of *Oxford, Walter *Ralegh, and Thomas *Lodge, and opens with three elegies on Philip *Sidney, the 'Phoenix' of the title.

Phyllyp Sparowe A poem by John *Skelton.

'Physician's Tale, The' See CANTERBURY TALES, 13.

picaresque [from the Spanish *pícaro*] A wily trickster or picaroon; the form of novel described as 'picaresque' first appeared in 16th-century Spain with the anonymous *Lazarillo de Tormes* (1554 or earlier) and *Guzmán de Alfarache* (Pt I: 1599; Pt II: 1604) by Mateo Alemán (1547–*c*.1614), the fictional autobiographies of ingenious roguish anti-heroes. Examples of their descendants in English are *Moll Flanders*, *Roderick Random*, and *Tom Jones*. The term was apparently first used in England in the 19th century. Nowadays the term is commonly, and loosely, applied to episodic novels, especially those of Henry *Fielding, Tobias *Smollett, and others of the 18th century which describe the adventures of a lively and resourceful hero on a journey. *The Golden Ass* of *Apuleius is regarded as a forerunner of the picaresque novel, while Thomas *Nashe's *The *Unfortunate Traveller* (1594) is commonly accepted as the first picaresque romance in English.

PICKARD, Tom (1946–) Poet. In 1963 he instigated a celebrated series of poetry readings at the Mordern Tower in Newcastle, including one by Basil *Bunting, whom he encouraged in the production of his late masterpiece, *Briggflatts*. Pickard's own poetry reveals American influences such as Robert *Creeley. His books include *High on the Walls* (1967), and *The Dark Months of May* (2004), and *Ballad of Jamie Allen* (2007).

Pickwick Papers (The Posthumous Papers of the Pickwick Club) A novel by Charles *Dickens, first issued in 20 monthly parts April 1836–November 1837, and as a volume in 1837. Samuel Pickwick, chairman of the Pickwick Club, together with Tracy Tupman, Augustus Snodgrass, and Nathaniel Winkle, become the Club's Corresponding Society, reporting their journeys and observations of characters and manners. The Club links a series of incidents, without elaborate plot. The principal elements in the story are: (1) the visit of Pickwick and his associates to Rochester and their falling in with the specious rascal Jingle. (2) The visit to Dingley Dell, the home of the hospitable Mr Wardle; followed by the engagement of the brisk young Sam Weller as Pickwick's servant. (3) The visit to Eatanswill, where a parliamentary election is in progress. (4) The visit to Bury St Edmunds, where Mr Pickwick and Sam Weller are fooled by Jingle and his servant Job Trotter. (5) The pursuit of Jingle to Ipswich, where Mr Pickwick inadvertently enters the bedroom of a middle-aged lady at night; is in consequence involved in a quarrel with Mr Peter Magnus, her admirer. (6) The Christmas festivities at Dingley Dell. (7) The misunderstanding of Mrs Bardell, Mr Pickwick's landlady, regarding her lodger's intentions. (8) The visit to Bath, in which Winkle figures prominently. (9) Mr Pickwick's imprisonment in the Fleet; the discovery of Jingle and Job Trotter in that prison, and their relief by Mr Pickwick. (10) The affairs of Tony Weller (Sam's father) and the second Mrs Weller, ending in the death of the latter and the discomfiture of the hypocritical drunkard Stiggins, deputy shepherd in the Ebenezer Temperance Association. (11) The affairs of Bob Sawyer and Benjamin Allen, medical students and subsequently struggling practitioners. The novel ends with the happy marriage of Emily Wardle and Augustus Snodgrass, and the prosperous retirement of Pickwick and Weller in Dulwich.

PICO DELLA MIRANDOLA, Giovanni (1463–94) Italian humanist and philosopher. He spent part of his short life at Florence in the circle of Lorenzo de Medici. In 1486 he published 900 theses, offering to defend them at Rome, but some of his propositions were pronounced heretical and the public debate did not take place. The famous oration *De Dignitate Hominis*, with which he intended to introduce the debate, is one of the most important philosophical works of the 15th century. Pico was a daring syncretist, who tried to make a synthesis of Christianity, Platonism, Aristotelianism, and the Jewish cabbala. His life and some of his writings were translated by Sir Thomas *More. John *Colet was influenced by Pico.

picturebooks The most distinctive, complex, and underestimated contribution of children's literature to literary and artistic culture. The potential of the form, rooted in the use of wood-blocks in the early history of book production, was demonstrated by the imaginative innovations of figures like William *Blake. It was further developed by the printer Edmund Evans (1826–1905) and his artists Randolph *Caldecott, Kate *Greenaway, and Walter Crane. Picturebook narratives, as distinct from books with pictures and illustrated texts, are created by the interaction between words and images. They blossomed with the development of offset lithography in the 1920s, with artists such as Edward Ardizzone and William Nicholson. Contemporary picturebooks commonly push at the boundaries between visual and verbal texts.

picturesque A term which came into fashion in the late 18th century, principally to describe a certain kind of scenery. Writers on the picturesque include William *Gilpin, William *Mason, William Payne Knight (1750–1824, who published *The Landscape* in 1794), Uvedale Price (1747–1829, who published *Essays on the Picturesque*, 1794), and the landscape gardener Humphry Repton (1752–1818;). The impact of these writers on the writers of the 19th century was considerable. The 'picturesque', as defined by Price, was a new aesthetic category, to be added to Edmund *Burke's recently established categories of the *Sublime and the Beautiful; its attributes were roughness and irregularity. Ann *Radcliffe's works dwell frequently on the picturesque, and Jane *Austen and many of her characters were familiar with the works of Gilpin. The entertaining aesthetic disputes of Price and Knight, are satirized in Thomas Love Peacock's *Headlong Hall*, and William *Combe's adventures of Dr Syntax are aimed at the movement in general and Gilpin in particular. Although the excesses of picturesque theory became a popular target for satire, writers as diverse as Charles *Dickens, George *Eliot, and Henry *James found the term useful. The development of the picturesque movement into *Romanticism has been much debated.

PIEŃKOWSKI, Jan (1936–) Born in Warsaw, primarily an illustrator/designer of popular series including the *Meg and Mog* books (1972–, text by Helen Nicoll). He is also the creator of innovative *movable books including *The Haunted House* (1979; CD version 1996), *ABC Dinosaurs* (1993), *Botticelli's Bed and Breakfast* (1996), and *The First Noel* (2004).

Pierce Penniless, his Supplication to the Devil A fantastic prose satire by Thomas *Nashe, published 1592. The author, in the form of a humorous complaint to the devil, comments on modern vices, throwing interesting light on contemporary customs and everyday life. One of the best passages is that relating to the recently developed practice of excessive drinking.

Pierce the Ploughman's Crede An alliterative poem dating from the last decade of the 14th century, mainly concerned with an attack on the four orders of friars. It was heavily influenced by *Piers Plowman*, to which it pays tribute by featuring a poor but charismatic ploughman, also named Piers, who alone has the spiritual authority to teach the poem's narrator not the Apostles' *Creed but a markedly polemical alternative.

PIERCY, Marge (1936–) American novelist, active in the civil rights movement of the 1960s. Her poetry collections include *The Moon is Always Female*, 1980. Her novels have engaged with feminist subjects: *Woman on the Edge of Time* (1976) combines time travel with investigating the politics of mental care, and *He, She and It* (1991: UK title *Body of Glass*) portrays a woman's relation with a cyborg in a postapocalyptic America. Her *historical novels include *Sex Wars* (2005), set in the post-Civil War USA.

Piers Plowman The greatest poem of the Middle English *Alliterative Revival, thought to be by William *Langland. It survives in about 50 manuscripts, in three principal versions known as the A, B, and C texts. The A-text, totalling 2,567 lines in its longest version, was probably written *c.*1367–70; the B-text, usually considered an extension of the A-text, has 7,277 lines (or more) and probably dates from *c.*1377–9; and the C-text is a substantial revision of the B-text, about the same length, dating from *c.*1385–6. The principal division of the poem has been into two parts, the 'Visio' (vision) and the 'Vita' (life), the 'Visio' comprising the prologue and the first seven *passus* ('step', or section division) in the B-text (prologue and the first eight in A; the first ten *passus* in C, which sometimes does not have a prologue). This 'Visio'–'Vita' distinction is not found in B manuscripts at all (see Schmidt's edition, 1978). It is also unclear whether B or C is to be taken as the more authoritative text. The revisions in C have changed the shape of the poem at some points so that it no longer divides into coherent visions, describing falling asleep—vision—awakening. B is complete and coherent in this way, at least according to modern tastes. Moreover, some of the obscurities that C irons out, such as the tearing of the pardon in B.VII, display great imaginative power. Though some claims have been made for its integrity as a poem, the A-text generally receives less critical attention than other versions. The following unified account of the poem follows the B-text (where there is any divergence in the narrative), in its division into eight separate visions.

Vision 1. While wandering on the Malvern Hills, the narrator (who, it transpires later, is called Will) falls asleep and has a vision of a Tower where Truth dwells, a deep Dungeon, and between them 'a fair feeld ful of folk' (prologue, 17) going about their business. The worldly values thus raised are expounded by Lady Holy Church in *Passus* I; the theme is sustained by the analytical trial of Lady Meed in *Passus* II–IV which considers whether Meed (Reward or payment) is to be given to Wrong or according to Conscience and Reason.

Vision 2. The narrator observes the Sermon (preached here by Reason); Confession (by the Seven Deadly Sins, colourfully personified in *Passus* V, the longest in the poem); Pilgrimage (to Truth, led by Piers the Plowman who first appears here); and Pardon (a paper pardon sent by Truth, but torn up by Piers when its validity is questioned by a priest). The conflict with the priest awakens the dreamer; this is the end of the 'Visio' as distinct from 'Vita', if such a distinction is indicated.

Vision 3 shows Will turning to the faculties and sources of knowledge and understanding, as the search for Truth (now referred to as 'Dowel') becomes individualized. In *Passus* VIII–XII Will progressively consults Thought, Wit, Study, Clergy, Scripture, Ymagynatyf, and Reason.

Visions 4 and 5. The theme is Charity, and *Passus* XIII–XVII attempt to show in action the ideas concerning doing well which were offered in Vision 3. Piers reappears in a transfigured form in which his action is indistinguishable from that of Christ.

Vision 6. The Passion of Christ is described as the culmination of doing well in *Passus* XVIII, where the death of Christ is evoked with great power (ll. 57–63), and after his death the *Harrowing of Hell.

Visions 7 and 8. These *Passus* (XIX and XX) continue with the liturgical cycle begun in Lent in *Passus* XVI (l. 172) and show the attempts to put into practice the lessons gained from observing the actions of Christ. But these attempts to perfect the church are still frustrated by evildoers, and the poem ends with Conscience setting out to find Piers.

The structure and argument of *Piers Plowman* may initially seem confusing to modern readers, but such effects, which result from the imagination being brought to bear on urgent theological questions, are part of the poem's radicalism. Passages of great imaginative power (such as in *Passus* XVIII) have a sublimity beyond the reach of any other medieval English writer.

PILATE, Pontius *See* BIBLE.

Pilgrim's Progress, The, from This World to That Which Is to Come A prose *allegory by John *Bunyan (Part I 1678, Part II 1684). It was written while he was imprisoned in Bedford Jail for conducting services outside the auspices of the Church of England.

The allegory takes the form of a dream by the author. In this he sees Christian, with a burden on his back (sin) and reading in a book (the *Bible), from which he learns that the city in which he and his family dwell will be burned. On the advice of Evangelist, Christian flees from the City of Destruction, having failed to persuade his wife and children to accompany him. He stuffs his fingers in his ears so that he cannot hear their cries. Part I describes his pilgrimage through the Slough of Despond, the Interpreter's House, the House Beautiful, the Valley of Humiliation, the Valley of the Shadow of Death, *Vanity Fair, Doubting Castle, the Delectable Mountains, the country of Beulah, to the Celestial City. On the way he encounters various allegorical personages, among them Mr Worldly Wiseman, Faithful (who accompanies Christian on his way but is put to death in Vanity Fair), Hopeful (who next joins Christian), Giant Despair, the foul fiend Apollyon, and many others.

Part II relates how Christian's wife Christiana, moved by a vision, sets out with her children on the same pilgrimage, accompanied by her neighbour Mercy. They are escorted by Greatheart, who overcomes Giant Despair and other monsters and brings them to their destination. The work is a development of the Puritan conversion narrative (*see* GRACE ABOUNDING), drawing on popular literature such as *emblem books and *chapbooks, as well as John *Foxe's *Book of Martyrs* and the Bible. Its powerful, resonant, simple and succinct style combines colloquial and biblical English. It has been rightly identified as (apart from the Authorized Version of the Bible) the most influential religious work ever published in English. Bunyan's humorously caustic development of the tradition of name symbolism influenced Charles *Dickens, Anthony *Trollope, and W. M. *Thackeray. A version for children by Geraldine *McCaughrean was published in 1999.

PILKINGTON, Laetitia (1708–50) Irish autobiographer and poet, successively a friend of Jonathan *Swift, Colley *Cibber, and Samuel *Richardson. She turned to verse, playwriting, autobiography, and miscellaneous ghostwriting when her husband, the Revd Matthew Pilkington, publicly disgraced and divorced her. Her three-volume *Memoirs* (1730–54) incorporate a fragmentary tragedy and almost all her known poems. Celebrated for their vignettes of Swift, the *Memoirs* exhibit a breezy conversational style and a mastery of dialogue uncommon in narrative in this period.

PINDAR (*c.*518–after 446 BC) Greek lyric poet, the majority of whose surviving works are odes celebrating victories in the games at Olympia and elsewhere. Antiquity's most notable exponent of the greater ode, he served as an inspiration to all subsequent poets attempting this difficult genre. His compositions were elevated and formal, distinguished by the boldness of their metaphors and a marked reliance on myth and gnomic utterance. He used a framework of strophe (the opening section), antistrophe (with the same number of lines and metrical arrangement), and epode (of differing length and structure), which his imitators sought to copy, but in Pindar this pattern rested on an elaborate prosodic structure that remained unknown until it was worked out by August Boeckh in his edition of the Odes (1811). The 17th- and 18th-century writers of Pindarics—Abraham *Cowley, John *Dryden, Alexander *Pope, Thomas *Gray—employed a much looser prosodic system, so that their odes, although elevated and rich in metaphor, lack Pindar's architectural quality. *See also* ODE.

Pindaric *See* ODE.

PINERO, Sir Arthur Wing (1855–1934) Playwright. His first one-act play, *Two Hundred a Year* was performed in 1877. The first of his *farces, *The Magistrate* (performed 1885), brought Pinero fame and wealth. *Sweet Lavender* (1888) was a popular sentimental comedy. His first serious play, on what was to be the recurrent theme of double standards for men and women, was *The Profligate* (1889); it was noted for its frankness and for eschewing the standard devices of soliloquy and aside. *Lady Bountiful* (1891) was the first of the 'social' plays in which Pinero was deemed to display his understanding of women. *The Second Mrs Tanqueray* (1893) was a lasting success. Knighted in 1909, he lived through many years of dwindling reputation and disillusion, eclipsed by the rising popularity of the new theatre of Henrik *Ibsen and George Bernard *Shaw.

PINTER, Harold (1930–2008) Poet and playwright. His first play, *The Room*, was performed in Bristol in 1957, followed in 1958 by a London production of *The Birthday Party*, in which Stanley, an out-of-work pianist in a seaside boarding house, is mysteriously threatened and taken over by two intruders, an Irishman and a Jew, who present him with a *Kafkaesque indictment of unexplained crimes. Other critical and commercial successes followed, including *The *Caretaker* (1960), *The Lover* (1963), *The *Homecoming* (1965), *Old Times* (1971), and *No Man's Land* (1975). *Betrayal* (1978; film, 1982) is an ironic tragedy. Later plays include *A Kind of Alaska* (1982), based on a work by Oliver Sacks, *One for the Road* (1984), *Mountain Language* (1988), *Party Time* (1991), and *Ashes to Ashes* (1996, a short drama of the *Holocaust). Pinter's gift for portraying, by means of dialogue which realistically produces the nuances of colloquial speech, the difficulties of communication and the many layers of meaning in language, pause, and silence created a style labelled by the popular imagination as 'Pinteresque'. Pinter also wrote extensively for radio and television, directed plays, and wrote several screenplays, which include versions of L. P. *Hartley's *The Go-Between* (1969), and John *Fowles's *The French Lieutenant's Woman* (1982). *Poems and Prose, 1947–1977* was published in 1978. In 2005 he was awarded the *Nobel Prize for Literature. His second wife was Lady Antonia *Fraser.

Pippa Passes By Robert *Browning, published 1841 as no. I of the series **Bells and*

p

Pomegranates. In its final version it consists of an 'Introduction' in verse, and four parts, entitled 'Morning', 'Noon', 'Evening', and 'Night'. Its combination of verse and prose was perhaps influenced by Browning's study of Elizabethan and Jacobean drama; *see* SOUL'S TRAGEDY.

The play is set in and around Asolo, a small town in the Veneto. The plot is a web of dramatic ironies. The Introduction shows Pippa, a young silk-worker, waking up on the morning of her annual holiday. She contrasts the life of 'Asolo's Four Happiest Ones' with her own. These four constitute an ascending scale of value, from carnal love, through married love, and filial love, reaching at last the love of God. Each life turns out to be different from Pippa's imagining of it, though she herself does not realize this. Pippa 'passes' by each of the four main scenes in turn, singing as she goes. Each song, ironically juxtaposed with the action, effects a moral revolution in the characters concerned. At the end of the drama we see Pippa back in her room at nightfall, unaware of the day's events.

PIRANDELLO, Luigi (1867–1936) Italian dramatist, short story writer, and novelist. His challenge to the conventions of *naturalism was an important influence on European drama. He is best known for *Sei personaggi in cerca di autore* (1921: *Six Characters in Search of an Author*), and *Enrico IV* (1922: *Henry IV*). His plays anticipated the anti-illusionist theatre of Bertolt *Brecht, Thornton *Wilder, and Peter *Weiss; and his work foreshadows Samuel *Beckett, Eugene *O'Neill, Jean Anouilh, Jean Giraudoux, and Jean Genet.

Pirate, The A novel by Walter *Scott, published 1821. Set in 17th-century Shetland, it deals with the tension between tradition and new ideas brought into a closed community by outsiders.

PIRSIG, Robert M. (Maynard) (1928–) American writer. His best-selling *Zen and the Art of Motorcycle Maintenance* (1974), a combination of travel narrative and meditation on human values, was followed in by *Lila: An Enquiry into Morals* (1991).

Pistyl of Susan (The Pistil of Swete Susan) 'The epistle of Susanna', a northern alliterative poem from the late 14th century, in 364 lines of thirteen-line *tail-rhyme stanzas. Similar in genre to *Patience*, it narrates the biblical story of Susanna and the Elders (Daniel 13).

PITT-KETHLEY, Fiona (1954–) Poet, travel writer, novelist, and journalist, best known for her outspoken writing about sex. Her satirical poetry collections include *Sky Ray Lolly* (1986), *Private Parts* (1987), *The Perfect Man* (1989), and *Selected Poems* (2008). Other works include *Journeys to the Underworld* (1988) and *The Pan Principle* (1994), both travel books; *The Misfortunes of Nigel* (1991) and *Baker's Dozen* (2000), novels; *The Literary Companion to Sex* (1992), essays on red light districts around the world; and an autobiography (2000).

PIX, Mary (*c.*1666–1709) Playwright and novelist. She published a novel, *The Inhumane Cardinal*, in 1696, and wrote some dozen plays, of which the comedy *The Spanish Wives* (1696) held the stage longest.

Plague Year, A Journal of the A historical fiction by Daniel *Defoe, published 1722. It purports to be the narrative of a resident in London during 1664–5, the year of the Great Plague. It tells of the gradual spread of the plague, the terror of the inhabitants, and the steps taken by the authorities, such as the shutting up of infected houses and the prohibition of public gatherings. The symptoms of the disease, the circulation of the dead-carts, and the burials in mass graves are described with extraordinary vividness. The *Journal* condensed information from various sources, including official documents; some scenes appear to have been borrowed from Thomas *Dekker's *The Wonderfull Yeare* (1603). Defoe's subject was suggested by fears of another outbreak, following the one in Marseilles in 1721 which occasioned Sir Robert *Walpole's unpopular Quarantine Act.

Plain-Dealer, The A comedy by William *Wycherley, loosely based on *Molière's *Le Misanthrope*, probably performed 1676, published 1677. It was criticized for obscenity, and performed in the 18th century in a version bowdlerized by Isaac *Bickerstaff. Manly, Wycherley's blunt, principled hero, returns from the Dutch wars to find his love Olivia treacherously wedded to his friend Vernish. Fidelia, who loves Manly, and has followed him to sea in man's clothes, intercedes with Olivia on his behalf, in a scene reminiscent of the Olivia–Viola scene in *Twelfth Night*. Manly forswears Olivia and pledges himself to Fidelia.

The *Plain Dealer* is also the name of a periodical established by Aaron *Hill.

Plain Speaker, The A volume of essays by William *Hazlitt, published in 1826, the last such collection to appear before his death. The title reflects his forthright assertion and invective. It includes several of his finest pieces, such as 'On Dreams' ('We are not hypocrites in our sleep') and 'On the Pleasures of Hating', which concludes with Hazlitt's self-description as 'the dupe of friendship, and the fool of love'.

PLANCHÉ, James Robinson (1796–1880) Prolific and popular dramatist of Huguenot descent. In addition to burlesques and extravaganzas, he made translations and adaptations, including *fairy-tales by the Countess d' *Aulnoy (1855) and by *Perrault (1858). His works include *The Vampire, or The Bride of the Isles* (1820), an adaptation of John *Polidori's 'The Vampyre', which introduced the 'vampire trap' to the English stage (involving two spring leaves that parted under pressure and immediately re-closed, giving the impression a figure was passing through solid matter), and *The Island of Jewels* (1849).

PLATER, Alan (1935–2010) Dramatist and screenwriter. After contributing many episodes to BBC TV's *Z Cars* and its sequel *Softly Softly* in the 1960s, several stage plays followed: *Close the Coalhouse Door* (1972, from a story by ex-miner and novelist Sid Chaplin) heralded the effects of pit closures upon regional communities. Life in the north-east, sport, and jazz often featured in his considerable television output, including *Seventeen Per Cent Said Push Off* (1972), *The Land of Green Ginger* (1974), *Trinity Tales* (1975, a 'Chaucerian' pilgrimage of supporters to a Rugby League cup final), *The Beiderbecke Affair* (1985), inspired by the recordings of cornet-player Bix Beiderbecke, *The Last of the Blonde Bombshells* (2000), and *Belonging* (2004). His adaptations for television include Anthony *Trollope's *Barchester Chronicles* (1982) and Olivia *Manning's *The Fortunes of War* (1987) (from her *Balkan Trilogy*).

PLATH, Sylvia (1932–63) American poet and novelist. She married the poet Ted *Hughes in 1956 and the two often compared drafts of their work. Her first volume of poetry, *The Colossus*, appeared in 1960, and in 1963 her only novel, *The *Bell Jar*, based on her experience of electroconvulsive therapy, appeared under the pseudonym Victoria Lucas. Less than a month after its publication she committed suicide in London. Her best-known collection, *Ariel*, (1965), established her reputation with its courageous and controlled treatment of extreme and painful states of mind. 'Lady Lazarus' is based on her two previous suicide attempts, 'Daddy' on the early loss of her father: in both

she uses powerful imagery drawn from the *Holocaust, though she was not herself Jewish. Other posthumous volumes include *Crossing the Water* and *Winter Trees* (both 1971); *Johnny Panic and the Bible of Dreams* (1977, collected prose pieces); and *Collected Poems* (1981, with an introduction by Ted Hughes). Hughes's *Birthday Letters* (1998) is a response to the complexities of his marriage and suicide. Her books for children include *The It-Doesn't-Matter-Suit* (1996). Anne *Stevenson's biography *Bitter Fame* (1989) was written with the approval of the Plath estate.

PLATO (*c.*424/3–*c.*348/7 BC) With *Socrates, who taught him, and *Aristotle, whom he taught, a dominant philosophical figure of classical antiquity, author of numerous dialogues and founder of the Athenian Academy, a school formally closed by Justinian in AD 529. The dialogues—'Socrates' mostly leads; Plato himself is permanently absent—fall stylistically into three chronological groups: (I) *Defence of Socrates* ('*Apology*': actually not a dialogue), *Charmides, Cratylus, Crito, Euthydemus, Euthyphro, Gorgias, Hippias Minor, Ion, Laches, Lysis, Menexenus, Meno, Phaedo, Protagoras, Symposium*; (II) *Parmenides, Phaedrus, Republic, Theaetetus*; (III) *Sophist, Statesman, Philebus, Timaeus, Critias, Laws*. Central to all periods of Plato's writing is the importance of *dialectic*, that is, philosophy in the form of conversation; in some works, especially those in Group I, the emphasis seems to be on the demolition by Socrates of others' ideas, but certain positive ideas are more or less constant. (1) Plato and his Socrates oppose relativism of all kinds, especially value-relativism: things like justice, beauty, and above all the good can be *investigated*, and in principle their natures *discovered* (where what is investigated becomes the 'Form' in each case, in contrast to its instantiations, i.e. the 'particulars' that 'share' in the Form). (2) Plato appears permanently committed to the idea that his fellow human beings radically misunderstand the way things are, which is why they need philosophy; for (3) they will, above all, misunderstand what is truly good—which is what they (we) all, always, desire. This thoroughly optimistic view of human nature to sit alongside (4) a more pessimistic view, according to which parts of our souls resemble brute beasts. ('Platonic love' develops the properly Platonic figure of the philosopher–pupil relationship as a passionate but asexual joint search for the truth.) Plato's influence on European philosophy and literature is largely indirect: through Augustine and above all through the

p

*Neoplatonists, especially *Plotinus, who for many was indistinguishable from Plato. Central, for English literature, was the neo-Platonizing Thomas Taylor. His English translation of the whole corpus (1804) was read by S. T. *Coleridge, John *Keats, William *Wordsworth, and W. B. *Yeats; the American 'transcendentalists' around Bronson Alcott (1799–1888) and Ralph Waldo *Emerson were also inspired by Taylor. Modern, direct study of Platonic texts begins seriously with figures like Friedrich von *Schlegel and Schleiermacher (1768–1834) in Germany.

Platonists *See* CAMBRIDGE PLATONISTS.

PLAUTUS, Titus Maccius (*c.*250–184 BC) Early Roman dramatist who adapted the Greek New Comedy for the Roman stage. The extent of his originality remains uncertain. Twenty of his plays have survived, and it was from him and from his successor *Terence that Renaissance Europe learned about ancient comedy. Reading and acting Plautus in Latin was a standard part of humanist education. *Shakespeare drew on his *Menaechmi* in *The *Comedy of Errors*, Ben *Jonson conflated the *Captivi* and the *Aulularia* in *The *Case Is Altered*, and John *Dryden adapted his *Amphitryon*. Stephen Sondheim's long-running musical *A Funny Thing Happened on the Way to the Forum* (1962) borrows exuberantly from Plautine situations.

Playboy of the Western World, The A comedy by J. M. *Synge, performed and published 1907. Christy Mahon, 'a slight young man, very tired and frightened', arrives at a village in Mayo. He gives out that he is a fugitive from justice, who in a quarrel has killed his bullying father. He is hospitably entertained, and his character as a dare-devil gives him a great advantage with the women (notably Pegeen Mike and Widow Quin). But admiration gives place to angry contempt when the father himself arrives in pursuit of his son, who has merely given him a crack on the head and run away. The implication that Irish peasants would condone a murder and the frankness of some of the language caused riots when the play was first performed at the *Abbey Theatre. In his preface, Synge compares the 'joyless and pallid' words of the naturalistic theatre of *Ibsen with the 'rich and living' language of 'the country people of Ireland'.

Pleasant Satyre of the Thrie Estaitis, Ane, in *Commendatioun of Vertew and Vituperatioun of Vyce* (1552–4) A morality play by Sir David *Lindsay. In Part I Rex Humanitas is tempted by Sensuality, Wantonness, Solace, and others, while Good Counsel is hustled away, Verity is put in the stocks, and Chastity is warned off. After interludes, Part II presents the Three Estates summoned before the king, and their misdeeds denounced by John the Common Weal. The Lords and Commons repent, but the clergy remain impenitent, are exposed, and the malefactors brought to the scaffold. The work is long and exists in three different versions. It is written in a variety of metres and is in advance of all contemporary English plays.

Pleasures of Hope, The A poem by Thomas *Campbell, published 1799. In Part I Campbell considers the inspiration of Hope and the hard fate of a people deprived of it, described in a passage on Poland's downfall. In Part II he reflects on Love combined with Hope, and on the belief in a future life.

Pleasures of Imagination, The A philosophical poem by Mark *Akenside, published 1744. The poem is influenced by the philosophical and aesthetic doctrines of Joseph *Addison, the third earl of Shaftesbury, and Francis *Hutcheson. It examines the primary and secondary pleasures of the imagination, the first connected with the *sublime, the wonderful, and the beautiful, the second with passion and sense. The poem was influential through the *Romantic period; Anna *Barbauld edited it, with a sympathetic 'critical essay', in 1794.

Pleasures of Memory, The *See* ROGERS, SAMUEL.

Pléiade A group of seven 16th-century French poets, led by *Ronsard. The name derives from the seven stars of the constellation of the Pleiades. The other members of the group were Joachim *Du Bellay, Pontus de Tyard (1521–1605), Jean-Antoine de Baïf (1532–89), Étienne Jodelle (1532–73), Rémy Belleau (*c.*1528–77), and either Jacques Peletier du Mans (1517–82) or, according to some, Jean Dorat (1508–88). The Pléiade were largely responsible for the acclimatization of the *sonnet in France, and for the establishment of the *alexandrine as the dominant metrical form for much later French poetry.

PLINY the Elder (Gaius Plinius Secundus) (AD 23/4–79) Roman compiler of a *Natural History*, which is an encyclopedic rag-bag of popular science. Widely read in the Middle Ages, it provided a cosmology for Du Bartas's *La Semaine, ou création du monde* (1578), which Josuah *Sylvester's translation established for the 17th century as an English classic. The *Natural History* was translated by Philemon *Holland in 1601.

PLINY the Younger (Gaius Plinius Caecilius Secundus) (AD *c*.61–*c*.112) Roman letter writer, nephew of *Pliny the elder. Pliny was a more formal writer than *Cicero, and is remembered mainly for his description of the eruption of Vesuvius (6. 16), and his official correspondence with Trajan, including an important letter on the early Christians (10. 96).

PLOMER, William (1903–73) Poet and novelist, born in South Africa. His first novel, the savagely satirical *Turbott Wolfe* (1926, *Hogarth Press) is a portrait of South African life. In 1926, with Roy *Campbell, he founded the magazine *Voorslag* ('Whiplash'). Plomer came to England in 1929 and settled in Bloomsbury, where he was befriended by Leonard and Virginia *Woolf. His volumes of poetry include *Notes for Poems* (1927), *The Dorking Thigh* (1945), and *Collected Poems* (1960, enl. edn 1973). His poems are largely satirical and urbane, with a sharp eye for character and social setting; many of them are modern ballads with a macabre touch. His celebrated edition of Francis *Kilvert's *Diary* appeared in three volumes, 1938–40. He wrote four libretti for Benjamin *Britten, including *Gloriana* (1952); his last novel, *Museum Pieces*, appeared in the same year.

PLOTINUS (AD 205–270/71) Greek philosopher/Platonist, the chief figure in the movement described by moderns as *Neoplatonism, and the dominant figure in Western philosophy between *Aristotle and Augustine. His *Enneads*, like much Platonism before him, downplay what seems sceptical in *Plato; they also create, from authentically Platonic ideas, a new kind of metaphysics, based on a single first principle, the transcendent One, from which everything including matter ultimately derived. Christian thinkers found much to attract them in Plotinus' brilliant but difficult constructions, which also, through Marsilio *Ficino's translation (1492), exercised a wide influence on Renaissance thought, as they did on English Platonism, especially on the *Cambridge Platonists, and on his first English translator, Thomas Taylor (1758–1835).

Plough and the Stars, The *See* O'CASEY, SEAN.

Plowman's Tale, The A late 14th- or early 15th-century poem in 1,380 lines of eight-line stanzas rhyming on alternate lines, sympathetic to John *Wyclif, and indebted to *Pierce the Ploughman's Crede*. A griffin and a pelican debate the merits of endowed and poor clergy.

PLUTARCH (before AD 50–after 120) Prolific Greek biographer and moralist. His philosophical position was *Platonist and anti-*Stoic, and for many years he was a priest at Delphi. Fifty lives and 78 miscellaneous works survive. His *Parallel Lives*, which pair illustrious Greeks and Romans such as Alcibiades and *Coriolanus, and *Alexander and Julius *Caesar, illustrate the moral character of his subjects through a series of anecdotes. The influential version by Thomas *North (1579) served as a source-book for Shakespeare's Roman plays. John *Dryden's 'Life of Plutarch' prefaced a very successful five-volume translation of the *Lives* by 42 contributors (1683–6), later revised by Arthur Hugh *Clough. The *Moralia* or *Moral Essays* provide a compendium of ancient wisdom on a variety of topics: moral philosophy, religious belief, education, health, literary criticism, and social customs. Several Renaissance authors, including Sir Thomas *Wyatt, Sir Thomas Elyot, and George *Chapman, translated or drew on individual pieces. The first complete version in English, by Philemon *Holland, appeared in 1603, when its popularity was enhanced by the almost simultaneous publication of John *Florio's translation of *Montaigne, for the latter cites Plutarch on nearly every page. *See* BIOGRAPHY.

Plymley, Letters of Peter By Sydney *Smith, published 1807-8. The letters purport to be written by Peter Plymley to his brother in the country, the Revd Abraham Plymley ('a bit of a goose'), in support of Catholic emancipation.

PN Review A British literary periodical, publishing six times a year. It originated as *Poetry Nation* in 1973, and has been edited by Michael Schmidt for thirty years. It has been controversial in both its advocacies and detractions.

POE, Edgar Allan (1809–49) American writer; he became an orphan in early childhood, and was taken into the household of John Allan, adopting his foster-father's name as his middle name from 1824 onwards. He came to London with the Allans (1815–20). He published his first volume of verse, *Tamerlane and Other Poems* (1827), anonymously and at his own expense. After a period in the US army, and in journalism, he married his 13-year-old cousin Virginia in 1836. His first collection of stories, *Tales of the Grotesque and Arabesque* (1839, for 1840), contains 'The Fall of the House of Usher', a *Gothic romance in which the narrator visits the crumbling mansion of his childhood companion Roderick Usher to find both Usher and his twin sister Madeline in the last stages of mental and physical weakness. His tales characteristically explore states of obsession and mania. In 1845 his poem 'The Raven' was published in a New York paper and then as the title poem of *The Raven and Other Poems* (1845). Poe's one attempt at novel writing was the unfinished *Narrative of Arthur Gordon Pym of Nantucket* (1837), which describes a surreal voyage to the Antarctic. *Eureka: A Prose Poem*, an extended meditation on cosmology, appeared in 1848. Poe was much admired by *Baudelaire, who translated many of his works, and in Britain by Oscar *Wilde, W. B. *Yeats, and others. Freudian critics (and *Freud himself) have been intrigued by the macabre and pathological elements in his work, ranging from hints of necrophilia in his poem 'Annabel Lee' (1849) to the indulgent sadism of 'The Pit and the Pendulum' (1843). Jorge Luis *Borges and many others have been impressed by the cryptograms and mysteries of the stories which feature Poe's detective Auguste Dupin ('The Murders in the Rue Morgue', 1841; 'The Purloined Letter', 1845) and the morbid metaphysical speculation of 'The Facts in the Case of M. Waldemar' (1845). His critical writings include 'The Philosophy of Composition' (on the process of composing 'The Raven').

Poema Morale ('The Moral Ode') A southern poem in early Middle English of about 400 lines, dating from *c*.1175. A vigorous work on the themes of transience and repentance, it is very early in the Middle English period after the transition from Old English.

Poems in Two Volumes A collection of poems by William *Wordsworth, published 1807, in which he continued his avant-garde attempt to set aside *'poetic diction' and to write in what the 'Preface' to the *Lyrical Ballads* describes as the 'real language of men'. The collection contains *'Intimations of Immortality from Recollections of Early Childhood' and 'I wandered lonely as a cloud'.

Poetaster A comedy by Ben *Jonson, performed 1601, printed 1602. The play, a contribution to the so-called War of the Theatres, is

Jonson's retaliation to John *Marston's satire of him in *What You Will*.

Set in the court of the emperor Augustus, the main plot concerns the conspiracy of the poetaster (i.e. a poor poet) Crispinus and his friend Demetrius (who represent Marston and Thomas *Dekker) to belittle Horace, who represents Jonson. The matter is tried before Augustus, with Virgil as judge. Horace is acquitted, the 'dresser of plays' Demetrius is made to wear a fool's coat and cap, and Crispinus is made to vomit up his windy rhetoric. Marston and Dekker replied to the attack in *Satiromastix*, where the main characters of this play reappear.

poetic diction A term used to mean vocabulary and usage peculiar to poetry, which came into prominence with William *Wordsworth's discussion in his preface (1800; supplemented by an appendix in the 1802 edition) to the *Lyrical Ballads*, in which he asserts that there is and should be no essential difference between the language of prose and the language of metrical composition. Wordsworth thus implies that there should be no such thing as 'language and usage peculiar to poetry', and illustrates his point by attacking a sonnet of Thomas *Gray, who himself had declared (1742, letter to Richard West) that 'the language of the age is never the language of poetry'. Wordsworth's attack on poetical archaisms, personifications, hackneyed epithets, circumlocutions, and so on was both forceful and revolutionary, but was repudiated by his collaborator S. T. *Coleridge in *Biographia Literaria* (1817). Although English poetry became less stilted in its language, its vocabulary remained on the whole distinctive throughout the Romantic and Victorian periods and as far as the 1920s. It was not until the 20th century and the advent of the *Georgian and *modernist poets, followed by W. H. *Auden and Philip *Larkin, that a thorough extension of poetic vocabulary towards ordinary speech was achieved.

Poetics, The A fragment of a treatise by *Aristotle which greatly influenced the theory of *neo-classicism. It is the source of the principles misinterpreted by later critics as the *unities, and it also introduced many much-discussed concepts related to the theory of tragedy, such as *mimesis* (imitation); *catharsis (purification or purgation of pity and fear); *peripeteia* (reversal); and *hamartia* ('error of judgement', sometimes interpreted as 'tragic flaw'). *Hubris* (overweening pride or confidence) was a form of *hamartia*.

poet laureate The title given to a poet who receives a stipend as an officer of the royal household, with the duty (no longer enforced) of writing court odes and so on. The title was sometimes conferred by certain universities. For a list of poets laureate *see* Appendix 2. The title of poet laureate in the USA was established in 1985 by the US Senate: the salaried post has been held by, among others, Richard *Wilbur (1987), Joseph *Brodsky (1991), and Rita Dove (1993).

Poetry: *A Magazine of Verse* (1912–) Founded at Chicago by the American poet and critic Harriet Monroe (1860–1936), who edited it until her death. In its early days it published work by Ezra *Pound, Amy *Lowell, T. S. *Eliot, Robert *Frost, H. D. (Hilda *Doolittle), Ford Madox *Ford, and others, and it has continued to flourish, publishing work by nearly every major American poet of the 20th century.

• Modernist Journals Project

poetry annuals Published as giftbooks, annuals flourished from the mid-1820s to the 1840s and were the most influential force in poetry publishing in this period. Well-known titles included *The Literary Souvenir*, *The Keepsake*, *Forget-Me-Not*, and *Fisher's Drawing-Room Scrapbook*. Their popularity stemmed from their engravings of famous paintings, fashionable people, and exotic locations: authors produced poems to fit these pictures. The annuals paid well in a disastrous market, and poets such as William *Wordsworth, S. T. *Coleridge, Walter *Scott, and Alfred *Tennyson were tempted into contributing. Annuals also offered employment to women writers, for instance Letitia *Landon and the countess of Blessington, as contributors and editors.

Poetry Archive Archive of sound recordings of poets reading their own work, established by Andrew *Motion and the recording producer Richard Carrington in 1999, when Motion was Poet Laureate. It includes historic recordings (for example, of *Tennyson, *Kipling, and *Browning), as well as creating contemporary ones, and has American and children's poetry as well as British poems. The archive can be searched by poet, title, form, or theme and there is a glossary of poetic terms.

• Archive of recorded poetry

Poetry London A bi-monthly which became the leading poetry magazine of the 1940s. It was conceived by a group of four, Dylan *Thomas, James Meary Tambimuttu (1915–83), Anthony Dickins, and Keidrych Rhys, and edited by Tambimuttu, who had arrived in 1938 from Ceylon, almost penniless. Tambimuttu produced fifteen numbers: the first issue appeared in February 1939. It published work by George *Barker, Vernon *Watkins, Gavin *Ewart, Harold *Pinter, Charles *Tomlinson, David *Gascoyne, Lawrence *Durrell, and many others.

Poetry Nation A twice-yearly poetry magazine edited by C. B. Cox and Michael Schmidt (6 issues, 1973–6). Contributors included Charles *Tomlinson, Peter *Porter, Elizabeth *Jennings, Geoffrey *Hill, and Douglas *Dunn; Donald *Davie and C. H. *Sisson became co-editors of its thrice-yearly successor, *PN Review* (1976–).

Poetry Society Founded in 1909 (as the Poetry Recital Society) for the promotion of poetry and the art of speaking verse, and sponsored by many literary figures, including Gilbert *Murray, Thomas Sturge *Moore, Edmund *Gosse, Henry Newbolt, Arnold *Bennett, and A. C. *Benson. Its many activities now include the organization of poetry competitions, workshops, and slams (open competitions where poets read or recite new work). Its journal, *Poetry Review*, was founded in 1912; its first editor was Harold *Munro.

Poets' Corner Part of the south transept of Westminster Abbey containing the tombs of Geoffrey *Chaucer, Edmund *Spenser, Ben *Jonson, Aphra *Behn, John *Dryden, John *Gay, Samuel *Johnson, Alfred *Tennyson, Robert *Browning, and Charles *Dickens. Writers buried elsewhere but commemorated here include William *Shakespeare, John *Milton, John *Keats, Lord *Byron, Jane *Austen, the *Brontë sisters, and Henry *James.

POHL, Frederik (1919–) American *science fiction writer and editor. *The Space Merchants* (1953), satirizing the advertising industry, was part of his collaborative partnership with Cyril M. Kornbluth (1923–58). Pohl's stories, including 'The Midas Plague' (1954), lampooning American consumerism, are collected in *Platinum Pohl* 2005. During the 1960s he edited the magazines *Galaxy* and *if*. His numerous novels include *All the Lives He Led* (2011).

POLIAKOFF, Stephen (1952–) CBE, playwright, and film-maker. Modern city life and the alienation of young people was an early theme, notably in the play *City Sugar* (1975), and the films *Bloody Kids* (1980) and *Runners* (1983), both given limited cinema release. Multi-part television drama has allowed him to explore the legacy of the past, especially its buried secrets and scandals, in *Caught on a Train* (1980), *Shooting the Past* (1999), and *The Lost Prince* (2003). Since *Hidden City* (1988), he has largely directed his own scripts, and has developed a distinctive televisual form in the overlapping pairs of *Friends and Crocodiles* and *Gideon's Daughter* (2005) and *Joe's Palace* and *Capturing Mary* (2007).

POLIDORI, John William (1795–1821) Physician and writer. In 1816 he was hired by Lord *Byron as personal physician and travelling companion for a few months; the journal he kept was published as his *Diary* (1911). He participated in the famous ghost story competition in June 1816 that gave rise to Mary *Shelley's *Frankenstein* and eventually to Polidori's only novel, *Ernestus Berchtold* (1819). Byron's incomplete tale 'Augustus Darvell' provided the basis for Polidori's story 'The Vampyre', written in 1816 and misleadingly published as Byron's in 1819 by the *New Monthly Magazine*, which laid the foundations of modern *vampire fiction. The aristocratic villain, Lord Ruthven, was evidently modelled upon Byron. Polidori established an unsuccessful medical practice in Norwich, and committed suicide in 1821.

Political House that Jack Built, The A satirical pamphlet by William *Hone, with engravings by George *Cruikshank, published 1819. Running into over 50 editions, it attacked the Tory government, the church, and the prince regent, who is portrayed as a spendthrift and gluttonous libertine.

Political Register (1802–35) A weekly newspaper founded by William *Cobbett. It began as a Tory paper but by 1809 was thoroughly Radical. Cobbett continued to issue it even when imprisoned for an article condemning military flogging. His new version of the paper, produced in 1816 at 2*d.*, achieved a remarkable weekly circulation of 40,000–50,000. In 1821 *Rural Rides* began to appear, but Cobbett continued the paper until his death.

Poliziano (in English **Politian**), **Angelo** (1454–94) The name assumed from his birthplace, Montepulciano, by Angelo

Ambrogini, Italian humanist, professor of Greek and Latin at the University of Florence. *Orfeo*, 1480 is the first pastoral drama in Italian. His editorial and philological studies (*Miscellanea*) established him as the greatest textual scholar of his time. Thomas *Linacre was one of his students, and George *Chapman translated and imitated his verse.

Polly A musical play by John *Gay, published 1729, the sequel to The *Beggar's Opera*. Its performance was prohibited by the Lord Chamberlain for political reasons. Macheath has been transported to the West Indies, and has escaped from the plantation; he is disguised as the pirate chief Morano. Polly, in search of him, disguises herself as a man, joins the loyal Indians, helps to beat off an attack by the pirates, and takes Morano prisoner, discovering his identity too late to save him from execution.

Pollyanna (1913) By Eleanor Porter (1868–1920). Pollyanna is an orphan who changes the lives of everyone around her with her 'glad' game; her name has become synonymous with unquenchable cheerfulness. There were twelve sequels by four authors, a vogue for 'Glad Clubs', and films in 1920 and 1960.

POLO, Marco (1254–1324) Merchant, who accompanied his father and uncle to the court of the Mongol ruler, Kublai Khan, in 1271 on an embassy from the pope. They travelled overland to China and returned home by sea to the Persian Gulf, reaching Venice after an absence of 24 years. Marco Polo's account of his travels was dictated to Rustichello, a writer of romances, whilst both were imprisoned by the Genoese. The original text was in French (English trans. 1579). The textual complications make it difficult to differentiate what Marco saw himself from his indirect reports.

Polyhymnia A poem by George *Peele written and published in 1590 commemorating the retirement of Sir Henry *Lee from the office of queen's champion, and describing the ceremonies that took place on the occasion at the accession day tilt. The final song 'His golden locks, time hath to silver turned', is quoted in part in W. M. *Thackeray's *The Newcomes*, ch. 76.

Poly-Olbion, The (the spelling of the first edition) The most ambitious work of Michael *Drayton. It was written between 1598 and 1622 and consists of 30 'Songs' each of 300–500 lines, in hexameter couplets, in which the author tries to awaken his readers to the beauties and glories of their country. Travelling from the south-west to Chester, down through the Midlands to London, up the eastern counties to Lincoln, and then through Lancashire and Yorkshire to Northumberland and Westmorland, he describes, or at least enumerates, the principal topographical features of the country, but chiefly the rivers and rivulets, interspersing in the appropriate places legends, fragments of history, catalogues of British saints and hermits, of great discoverers, of birds, fishes, and plants with their properties. The first part, published 1612-13, was annotated by John *Selden. The word 'poly-olbion' (from the Greek) means 'having many blessings'.

polysyndeton [from Greek, 'using many connectives'] The repetition of conjunctions in close succession for rhetorical effect, as in 'Since brass, nor stone, nor earth, nor boundless sea' (Shakespeare, Sonnet 65).

POMFRET, John (1667-1702) A Bedfordshire vicar whose poem *The Choice* (1700) describes the pleasures of a quiet country estate. It enjoyed considerable success, and secured its author inclusion in Samuel Johnson's *Lives of the English Poets*.

Pompey the Great *See* CORNELIA.

POPE, Alexander (1688-1744) Poet; his health was damaged and his growth stunted by a childhood illness. His *Essay on Criticism* (1711) made him known to Joseph *Addison's circle, and the first version of The *Rape of the Lock* appeared in Bernard *Lintot's *Miscellanies* in 1712 and enlarged and published separately in 1714. In 1713 he published *Windsor-Forest*, grafting support for the Tories' Peace of Utrecht on to a *topographic celebration of the mythic and historical landscape of the Thames valley. Pope became a member of the *Scriblerus Club, a Tory association that included Jonathan *Swift, John *Gay, Thomas *Parnell, John *Arbuthnot, and Robert Harley. He published in 1715 the first volume of his translation into heroic couplets of Homer's *Iliad, supplemented in 1725-6 by a translation of the *Odyssey. Published by subscription, the two translations brought him financial independence.

In 1717 Pope published a magnificent volume of his *Works*, including new pieces such as *'Eloisa to Abelard', in which Eloisa describes her inner turmoil. Pope had already become embroiled in several literary controversies: the 'Pastorals' had led to a quarrel with Ambrose *Philips, the *Essay on Criticism* had provoked the lifelong hostility of John Dennis, he had poisoned the bookseller Edmund *Curll in

1716, and his Homer translations were undermined by Addison and routinely abused as the work of a *Jacobite. In a 1727 volume of *Miscellanies* by Pope and his Scriblerian friends he published his prose treatise *Peri Bathous, ridiculing contemporary poets including Lewis *Theobald, who in *Shakespeare Restored* (1726) had pointed out some errors in Pope's edition of Shakespeare (1725). This led to Pope's selection of Theobald as hero of his *Dunciad (1728, anonymously; 1729, 'variorum' text). The poem provoked threats, reprisals, and parodies, which Pope skilfully incorporated into the supplementary material surrounding the poem in its later manifestations.

Influenced in part by the philosophy of his friend Viscount Bolingbroke, Pope published a series of moral and philosophical poems: *An *Essay on Man* (1733-4), in four Epistles; and four *Epistles to Several Persons* (1731-5). In 1733 Pope began publishing the series of poems later known as *Imitations of Horace*, beginning with a paraphrase of the first satire of Horace's second book. In 1735 appeared the *Epistle to Dr Arbuthnot*, later thought of as a prologue to the Horatian Satires, and a brilliant showcase of irony and invective. It contains notable portraits of Addison (ll. 193-214) and Lord *Hervey. Pope was also occupied with the publication of his letters; in 1735 he contrived to have Curll publish a volume of his *Literary Correspondence*, allowing him to promote his own 'authorized' text of the letters in 1737. In 1742 Pope added an additional book, *The New Dunciad*, to his earlier poem; the complete *Dunciad* in four books, with Colley *Cibber replacing Theobald as hero, appeared in 1743. In his later years Pope came under the influence of William *Warburton, whose edition of Pope appeared in 1751.

Pope's poetic dominance came under attack from William *Cowper and Joseph *Warton (although he was defended in Samuel Johnson's *Lives of the English Poets*), and later by William *Wordsworth and William *Blake, with Lord *Byron his major defender in the early 19th century. It was not until F. R. *Leavis and William *Empson that serious attempts were made to rediscover Pope's richness, variety, and complexity.

POPPER, Sir Karl (1902-94) Austrian-born philosopher of science. Originally associated with the Vienna circle, the source of logical positivism, he left for New Zealand on Hitler's rise to power. In 1946 he came to England, joining the London School of Economics, where he was appointed professor of logic and

p

scientific method in 1949. Popper rejected the traditional idea that a scientific hypothesis can be verified by experimental testing. Instead he proposed that a hypothesis is only scientific by virtue of the fact that it can be falsified. On these grounds he dismissed the claims of psychoanalysis to scientific status and challenged the empirical basis and determinist pretensions of some *Marxist historiography. His influential works include *The Logic of Scientific Discovery* (*Logik der Forschung*, 1934); *The Open Society and Its Enemies* (1945), and *The Poverty of Historicism* (1957).

PORTER, Anna Maria (1780–1832) Poet and novelist, younger sister of Jane *Porter. Her martial tale of the French Revolution, *The Hungarian Brothers* (1807), inspired by her sister's successful *Thaddeus of Warsaw*, went into several editions.

PORTER, Jane (1776–1850) Novelist and dramatist; elder sister of Anna Maria *Porter. Her historical romance *Thaddeus of Warsaw* (1803) was immensely successful, and led to friendship with one of its heroes, the Polish General Kosciuszko. *The Scottish Chiefs* (1810), which tells the story of William Wallace and Robert the Bruce, ending with the battle of Bannockburn, is a precursor of the *historical fiction of Walter *Scott. *The Pastor's Fireside* (1815) is a story of the later Stuarts. *Sir Edward Seaward's Narrative* (1831), on Caribbean exploration, purported to be a genuine diary but was almost certainly largely fictitious.

PORTER, Katherine Anne (1890–1980) American short story writer and novelist, whose collections of short stories include *Flowering Judas* (1930), *Pale Horse, Pale Rider* (1939), and *The Leaning Tower* (1944). Her novel *Ship of Fools* (1962) is a heavily allegorical treatment of a voyage from Mexico to Germany on the eve of Hitler's rise to power.

PORTER, Peter (1929–2010) Poet, born in Brisbane; he came to England in 1951. He was briefly associated with the *Group in the 1960s, and the work in earlier collections such as *Once Bitten, Twice Bitten* (1961) and *The Last of England* (1970) provides a satiric portrait of London in the 'swinging sixties'. In the 1970s, his poetry, always mentored by the achievement of W. H. *Auden, became more meditative and allusive. His technical command of complex stanza forms, sometimes used parodically, is striking. *The Cost of Seriousness* (1978) and *English Subtitles* (1981) introduce a new and sombre exploration of the poet's conflicting

responsibilities to his art and to others, the former examining emotions following the death of his first wife in 1974. Later volumes include *Fast Forward* (1984), *The Chair of Babel* (1992), *Afterburner* (2004), and *Better Than God* (2009). There is a two-volume *Collected Poems* (1999). His work, often inflected with an outsider's quizzically sceptical view of English culture and attitudes, maintains a view of poetry as conversation, civility, and decency.

Portrait of a Lady, The A novel by Henry *James, published 1881, which describes the marriage of an idealistic heiress, Isabel Archer, to an American dilettante expatriate, Gilbert Osmond. He marries her for her fortune and ruins her life, but she remains loyal in spite of her realization of his vileness.

Portrait of the Artist as a Young Man, A An autobiographical novel by James *Joyce, first published in *The *Egoist*, 1914–15. It describes the development of Stephen Dedalus (who reappears in *Ulysses*) from his early boyhood, through bullying at school and an adolescent crisis of faith inspired partly by the famous 'hellfire sermon' preached by the Jesuit Father Arnall (ch. 3) and partly by the guilt of his own precocious sexual adventures, to student days and a gradual sense of his own destiny as dedicated artist who must leave Ireland in order to 'encounter...the reality of experience and to forge in the smithy of my soul the uncreated conscience of my race'. The novel's prose style changes as the novel progresses to mirror the growth and development of Stephen's mind.

Poseidon See NEPTUNE.

positivist philosophy See COMTE, AUGUSTE.

postcolonial literature Literatures in English emerging from the anglophone world outside Britain, Ireland, and the United States constitute an important and growing body of writing, often referred to as postcolonial or world literature in English. Many of the regions and countries from which this literature emerges—the Caribbean, the Indian subcontinent, West Africa, in particular Nigeria and Ghana, East and southern Africa, and Australasia and the Pacific islands—were once colonies of Britain, and now form part of the Commonwealth, hence the term 'postcolonial'. It is, however, beset with contradictions, not least in respect of the chronological limits of the postcolonial: did empire end with Indian independence in 1947, or in 1956 with Suez, or was it later, when many of the African countries gained their independence?

Nevertheless, the term 'postcolonial literature' is considered to be the most convenient way of embracing the diverse body of literary responses to the challenges presented by decolonization and the transitions to independence and after. Postcolonial literature might be broadly defined as that which critically or subversively scrutinizes the colonial relationship, and offers a reshaping or rewriting of the dominant meanings pertaining to race, authority, space, and identity prevalent under colonial and decolonizing conditions.

Many assumptions that are central to postcolonial literary studies emanate from the influential work of the critic Edward *Said, in particular his *Orientalism* (1978), and *Culture and Imperialism* (1993). These include the critical perception that cultural representations (of 'savages' and 'cannibals'; or of primitive Africa or the exotic East) were fundamental first to the process of colonizing other lands, and then again to the process of obtaining independence (imaginative and otherwise) from the colonizer. As Joseph *Conrad was among the first to acknowledge, in his 'Heart of Darkness' (1899), assuming control over a territory or a nation meant not only exerting political or economic power but also having imaginative command. Overturning and replacing imperial systems of control therefore involved contesting these European imaginative and literary versions of the colonial experience, or as Indian-born writer Salman *Rushdie famously put it, it involved the empire 'writing back'.

Postcolonial literature, in seeking to awaken political and cultural nationalism, has dwelt on popular revolts against colonial rule, exposing the lie of the passive and indolent native; the Trinidadian C. L. R. *James has brought to the fore neglected black heroes like Toussaint Louverture, who led the greatest slave revolt in history to set up Haiti, the first free black republic in the West. The world-view of the cane-cutters of the sugar plantations and other such 'lowly' people, expressed in their myths and legends, is given space in postcolonial literature, with writers like the Guyanese Wilson *Harris arguing that Amerindian mythology reveals values and perspectives as complex and mysterious as any originating from the Graeco-Roman or Judaeo-Christian traditions. There is a corresponding reappraisal of oral expression, in riddles and proverbs and songs and stories.

Writers as diverse as Caryl *Phillips, Nadine *Gordimer, Peter *Carey, and Arundhati

*Roy acknowledge that making a postcolonial world means learning how to live in and represent that world in a profoundly different way.

Language is inextricably bound up with culture and identity, and as the colonizers attempted, with varying degrees of success, to impose the English language on subject peoples, the response from the formerly colonized has ranged from the outright rejection of English as a medium through which to exercise their art, to the appropriation of it with subversive intent. After first using English as the medium for his fiction, the Kenyan writer *Ngugi wa Thiong'o finally decided to reject it. For others, like the Nigerian writer Chinua *Achebe, or Indian novelists Upamanyu *Chatterjee and Amit *Chaudhuri, English has been a means of uniting peoples across continents and of reaching a wider audience than would have been possible in their mother tongues. Caribbeanists like Derek *Walcott and V. S. *Naipaul have used techniques such as switching in and out of standard English and local *Creoles to emphasize that their cultural worlds are irrevocably multicultural and hybridized. Some see English as having become detached from Britain or Britishness. They claim the language as their own property, for they have moulded and refashioned it to make it bear the weight of their own experience.

There has been celebratory and affirmative acknowledgement of women's experiences, following painful legacies of 'double' and in some cases 'triple colonization' (as women, black, lower class, lower caste, 'queer', etc.) under empire. The distinguished and burgeoning list of postcolonial women writers includes Jean *Rhys, Anita *Desai, Bessie *Head, Doris *Lessing, Olive *Senior, Nadine *Gordimer, and Tsitsi *Dangarembga.

Postcolonial literature worldwide has registered the impact of *modernist and also *postmodernist traditions of Anglo-American writing. The montage effects and mythic adaptations of Anglo-American modernist poetry, for example, were enthusiastically adopted but also extended and enriched from local sources by writers such as Christopher *Okigbo and Wole *Soyinka. The subversive, playful techniques of metropolitan postmodernism have been appropriated by postcolonial writers in order to dramatize the unstable, provisional, and ever-shifting constitution of identities in the aftermath of empire, as in the work of Michael *Ondaatje and Dambudzo *Marechera. Postcolonial literature, as writers like Rushdie and Derek Walcott recognize, has itself formed and

p

informed modernist and postmodernist techniques.

POSTGATE, Oliver (1925–2008) Writer of scripts for and book/annual versions of popular children's television programmes such as *Ivor the Engine* (1958–77), *Noggin the Nog* (1959–65), *The Clangers* (1965–74), and *Bagpuss* (1974). *Seeing Things* (2000) is an autobiography.

Post-Impressionism An art movement christened off-the-cuff by Roger *Fry in 1910 to designate the painters Paul Cézanne (1839–1906), Paul Gauguin (1848–1903), Vincent Van Gogh (1853–90), and others. The term created the appearance of a coordinated group of artists who, according to Fry, gave priority to form over content. Reactions to Fry's first Post-Impressionist exhibition in Britain in 1910 ranged from veneration to outrage. Writers influenced by the stress on formalism included Virginia *Woolf. *To The Lighthouse endorses many of Fry's ideas, particularly in the figure of Lily Briscoe. Wyndham *Lewis admired the *Futurist element in the movement, and D. H. *Lawrence in *Women in Love expressed an antipathy to what he saw as its cold and inhuman qualities.

postmodernism The term applied by some commentators since the early 1980s to the cultural features characteristic of Western societies in the aftermath of artistic *modernism. In this view, 'postmodernity' asserts itself from about 1956 with the exhaustion of the high modernist project, reflected in the work of Samuel *Beckett among others, and the huge cultural impact of television and popular music. Many critics maintain that artistic or literary works described as 'postmodernist' are really continuations of the modernist tradition. Nevertheless, some general literary features of the period have been identified, such as tendencies to *parody, *pastiche, scepticism, irony, fatalism, the mixing of 'high' and 'low' cultural allusions, and an indifference to the redemptive mission of Art as conceived by the modernist pioneers. Postmodernism thus favours random play rather than purposeful action, surface rather than depth, inconclusiveness rather than 'closure'. The kinds of literary work that have been described as postmodernist include the Theatre of the *Absurd, and the poetry of, among others, John *Ashbery and Paul *Muldoon and, notably, prose fiction by American novelists such as Vladimir *Nabokov, John *Barth, Thomas *Pynchon, Kurt *Vonnegut, and Paul *Auster, and by the British authors John *Fowles, Angela *Carter, Julian *Barnes, Peter *Ackroyd, Salman *Rushdie, and Jeanette *Winterson. Outside the English-speaking world, the fictions of Jorge Luis *Borges and the later work of Italo *Calvino show similar tendencies. Distinctive features of this school include switching between orders of reality and fantasy (*see* MAGIC REALISM), resort to *metafiction, and the playful undermining of supposedly objective kinds of knowledge such as biography and history.

post-structuralism *See* STRUCTURALISM.

'Pot of Basil, The' *See* 'ISABELLA'.

POTTER, Beatrix (1866–1943) Writer and illustrator of *animal stories for children. *The Tale of Peter Rabbit* started as a letter to the son of her former governess and was published at her own expense in 1901, followed by *The Tailor of Gloucester* (1902). Her books are notable for their interactions between images and text, appealing but pointed use of animals in clothes, elaborate vocabulary, and lack of sentimentality. *Squirrel Nutkin* (1903) was her first great success; this and later works were published by F. Warne & Co. In 1913 she married William Heelis, a Lakeland solicitor, and thereafter devoted herself almost entirely to farming and the new National Trust. *Johnny Town-Mouse* (1918) was the last of her books in the old style; later books written for the USA such as *The Fairy Caravan* (1928) are of less interest.

POTTER, Dennis (1935–94) Playwright, best known for his own television plays, which show an original and inventive use of the medium. These include two plays dealing with the career of an aspiring working-class, Oxford-educated politician, *Vote, Vote, Vote for Nigel Barton* (1965) and *Stand up, Nigel Barton* (1965); *Pennies from Heaven*, a six-part serial (1978); and *Blue Remembered Hills* (1979), a tragic evocation of childhood. Potter's experience of psoriatic arthropathy, a debilitating condition affecting skin and joints, is central to his six-part serial *The Singing Detective* (1986), widely held to be his finest work: this is a multi-layered narrative, moving between a moody 1940s thriller and incorporating songs of that period, and a present-day hospital ward. *Blackeyes* (1989) is a study of sexual exploitation and *Lipstick on your Collar* (1993) is a musical black comedy based on Potter's National Service experiences. His final work was a pair of linked serials completed weeks before his death from cancer: *Karaoke* and *Cold Lazarus* (1996).

Potter, Harry Orphan hero of J. K. *Rowling's seven-part fantasy series (1997–2007) set in Hogwarts School of Witchcraft and Wizardry. Harry's parents, James and Lily Potter, were killed by Lord Voldemort, the embodiment of evil, when he was an infant, leaving him in the charge of his nasty aunt and uncle who live in the non-magical 'Muggle' world. He was marked with a distinctive lightning-bolt scar in the encounter. On his eleventh birthday Harry is astonished to learn that he is a wizard, and is taken to Hogwarts, where he becomes friends with Ron Weasley and Hermione Granger, and the favourite of headmaster Albus Dumbledore; together they struggle with Voldemort with varying degrees of success. There he discovers that like his father he is a naturally brilliant wizard and skilled player of Quidditch, the school sport. There are film, adaptations, starring Daniel Radcliffe (Warner Brothers, 2001–11), of all seven books (the seventh as two films).

POUND, Ezra (1885–1972) American poet; he met Hilda *Doolittle (H.D.) at the University of Pennsylvania. *A Lume Spento* (1908) was published at his own expense in Italy; he then moved to London, and soon became prominent in literary circles. Together with F. S. Flint (1885–1960), Richard *Aldington, and Hilda Doolittle he founded the *imagist school of poets, advocating the use of free rhythms, concreteness, and concision of language and imagery; in 1914 he edited *Des Imagistes: An Anthology*. Pound also championed the *modernist work of avant-garde writers and artists like James *Joyce, Wyndham *Lewis, Henri *Gaudier-Brzeska, and T. S. *Eliot. Further volumes of poetry include *Quia Pauper Amavi* (1919, which contains 'Homage to Sextus Propertius') and *Hugh Selwyn Mauberley* (1920). Pound's early volumes contained adaptations from Provençal and early Italian, a version of the Old English The *Seafarer, and *Cathay* (1915), translations from the Chinese of Li Po, via a transliteration. Pound was thus moving towards the rich, grandly allusive, multicultural world of the *Cantos*, his most ambitious achievement. The first three Cantos appeared in 1917 in *Poetry*. In 1920 Pound left London for Paris and in 1925 he settled permanently in Rapallo. The Cantos appeared intermittently over the next decades until the appearance of the final *Drafts and Fragments of Cantos CX to CXVII* (1970).

In Italy Pound embraced Social Credit theories, his own interpretations of which led him into anti-Semitism and at least partial support for Mussolini's social programme. During the Second World War he broadcast on Italian radio: in 1945 he was arrested and sent to a US Army Disciplinary Training Centre near Pisa, a period which produced the *Pisan Cantos* (1948). He was then moved to Washington, found unfit to plead, and confined to a mental institution; he was released in 1958 and returned to Italy, where he died.

Inevitably, Pound's literary reputation was obscured by the tragedy of his last decades, and also by the difficulty of the work itself, which resides principally in its astonishingly wide range of reference and assimilation of cultures.

POWELL, Anthony (1905–2000) Novelist, whose initial reputation as a satirist and light comedian rests on five pre-war books, beginning with *Afternoon Men* (1931) which maps a characteristically seedy section of pleasure-loving, party-going London.

After the war he embarked on a more ambitious sequence of twelve novels, *A Dance to the Music of Time*. They are: *A Question of Upbringing* (1951), *A Buyer's Market* (1952), *The Acceptance World* (1955), *At Lady Molly's* (1957), *Casanova's Chinese Restaurant* (1960), *The Kindly Ones* (1962), *The Valley of Bones* (1964), *The Soldier's Art* (1966), *The Military Philosophers* (1968), *Books Do Furnish a Room* (1971), *Temporary Kings* (1973), and *Hearing Secret Harmonies* (1975). The whole cycle is framed and distanced through the eyes of a narrator, Nicholas Jenkins, whose generation grew up in the shadow of the First World War to find their lives dislocated by the Second. Jenkins's canvas is especially rich in literary and artistic hangers-on, stiffened by a solid contingent from society, politics, and the City, enlivened and sometimes convulsed by eccentrics, derelicts, and drop-outs of all classes and conditions. Against these looms Kenneth Widmerpool, one of the most memorable characters of 20th-century fiction, whose ruthless pursuit of power is the chief of many threads binding this panoramic view of England.

Powell's memoirs, which shed considerable light on the creation of the characters of his fictional world, were published in four volumes, 1976–82, under the general title *To Keep the Ball Rolling*. Later works include the novels *O, How the Wheel Becomes It!* (1983) and *The Fisher King* (1986).

POWERS, Tim (1952–) American *science fiction and *fantasy author. His fiction often counterpoints historical characters with fantastic plots. Lord *Byron, P. B. *Shelley, and John *Keats, for example, appear in *The Stress of her Regard* (1989) which exploits the Romantics' fascination with vampires. *Declare* (2001) is a similar 'secret history' drawing upon the Cold War.

POWYS, John Cowper (1872–1963) Writer, brother of Llewelyn and Theodore *Powys, he was brought up in the Dorset–Somerset countryside which was to become of great importance in his work. His output was prolific, including volumes of poetry and many books and essays on philosophy, religion, literature, and the arts of living, as well as a remarkable *Autobiography* (1934). It is, however, for his highly individual novels that he is chiefly remembered, *Wood and Stone* (1915, NY; 1917, London), *Rodmoor* (1916) and *Ducdame* (1925) were followed by *Wolf Solent* (1929), his first major success. It is a crowded work, set in the West Country, of many interweaving stories, but chiefly concerning Wolf and Gerda, and the destructive pull of opposites. *A Glastonbury Romance* (1932, NY; 1933, London) was also conceived on a huge scale; Glastonbury and its legends exert a supernatural influence on the life of the town and on the complex loves, both sacred and sexual, of the town's inhabitants. *Weymouth Sands* (1934, NY) had, because of a libel action, to be recast as *Jobber Skald* (1935), but was restored and republished as *Weymouth Sands* in 1963. In *Maiden Castle* (1936, NY; 1937, London) the lives of the protagonists move towards disillusion and endurance. Most of the later novels, written after Powys had settled in Wales in the late 1930s, share an extravagance of subject and style and strong elements of the supernatural. In *Morwyn* (1937), cast as a letter from the narrator to his son, the theme of man's cruelty, to his fellows and to animals, is carried through various meetings with characters from history. *Owen Glendower* (1940, NY; 1941, London) was the most successful of his historical novels; it was followed by *Porius* (1951), set in AD 499, which presents a fraught world of giants, Mithraic cults, and Arthurian legend filling the void the Romans have left; *The Inmates* (1952), on the theme of madness; *Atlantis* (1954), in which Odysseus, returned from Troy, sets out again through a world of giants, heroes, talking animals, and inanimate objects, to discover the continent of America, where he settles; and *The Brazen Head* (1956).

Powys's stature as a writer has been much debated.

POWYS, Llewelyn (1884–1939) Writer, brother of J. C. and T. F. *Powys. His prolific output includes *Black Laughter* (1924); *Skin for Skin* (1925), an account of his tuberculosis and the idyllic Dorset interludes when it seemed to be cured; *Impassioned Clay* (1931), an intense meditation on the human condition, the Epicurean ethic, and death; and *Love and Death* (1939), an eloquent 'imaginary autobiography', on the theme of lost love and his own approaching end. *Apples Be Ripe* (1930, novel), and two volumes of essays, *Earth Memories* (1934) and *Dorset Essays* (1935), are also noteworthy. *Damnable Opinions* (1935) offered further evidence of the iconoclastic outlook he shared with J. C. Powys.

POWYS, T. F. (Theodore Francis) (1875–1953) Writer, brother of J. C. and L. *Powys. He farmed in Suffolk for six years before returning to Dorset in 1901 where the local landscape formed the backdrop to almost all his novels and stories. His many volumes include *An Interpretation of Genesis* (1907); *The Soliloquy of a Hermit* (1916); *The Left Leg* (1923), a collection of three long stories; *Black Bryony* (1923), *Mark Only* (1924), and *Mr Tasker's Gods* (1925), three pessimistic novels of village life; and *Mockery Gap* (1923) and *Innocent Birds* (1926), which developed his religious concerns. *Mr Weston's Good Wine* (1927) is a vivid allegory in which Mr Weston (or God) comes to the worldly village of Folly Down, selling from his old van his vintages of Love and Death; after his departure he leaves no paradise, but the good are happier, and the evil are vanquished. *Fables* (1929) is a volume of short stories. In *Unclay* (1931, novel), John Death (or the archangel Michael) arrives in Dodder with instructions from God to 'unclay', or kill, various people; however, he loses his instructions, is unsettled by the mysterious Tinker Jar, and falls in love with a village girl.

practical criticism The term used in academic literary studies for an exercise in which students are required to comment upon a poem or short prose passage without knowledge of its authorship, date, or circumstances of composition. This procedure encourages attention to form, diction, and style rather than 'extraneous' associations. It was adopted by I. A. *Richards at the University of Cambridge in the 1920s as an experiment which he records and analyses in his book *Practical Criticism* (1929). Thereafter it became a standard exercise, especially under the influence of the *New Criticism in America. In a more general sense, the term has been used, by S. T. *Coleridge and others, to designate the applied uses of criticism as distinct from the purely theoretical.

Practice of Pietie, The A devotional work by Lewis Bayly (*c.*1575–1631), bishop of Bangor, first published *c.*1612. This extraordinarily popular book, regularly republished and translated into the 19th century, combined a compendium of *Reformation doctrine with guidance on daily life, meditation, prayer, and preparation for death. John *Bunyan had a copy.

PRAED, Winthrop Mackworth (1802–39) Poet, remembered principally as a humorous poet and composer of elegant *vers de société*; 'The County Ball', 'A Letter of Advice', 'Stanzas on Seeing the Speaker Asleep', and 'The Vicar' are characteristic examples of his light verse. Like Thomas *Hood, he sometimes uses humour to clothe a grim subject, as in 'The Red Fisherman'. His verse was published largely in periodicals and annuals, but his inoffensive satire, gentle wit, and fluent metrical variations assured him a more lasting readership; his *Poems*, with a memoir by his friend Derwent Coleridge, appeared in 1864.

Praeterita ['things past'] Unfinished autobiographical work by John *Ruskin, published in 28 parts and at intervals between 1885 and 1889. Ruskin had no interest in giving a complete account of his life, as he admits. Instead, he writes about 'what it gives me joy to remember, at any length I like' and 'passing in total silence things I have no pleasure in reviewing'. His last work, it is a lyrical and fragmentary evocation of the past, particularly the lost landscapes of his childhood and the growth of his intense visual imagination.

pragmatism In philosophy, the doctrine that the test of the value of any assertion lies in its practical consequences, that is, in its practical bearing upon human interests and purposes. This view is associated chiefly with William *James, but has been revived in literary studies by the American critic Stanley Fish (1938–).

Prague Circle *See* STRUCTURALISM.

PRATCHETT, Sir Terry (1948–) OBE, *Fantasy and *science fiction writer, author of the successful 'Discworld' series, beginning with *The Colour of Magic* (1983). Since then, Discworld has developed from parodying

*fantasy conventions to become a location for thoughtful, witty, and morally acute satire. Abstractions acquire personalities—jokes arise from Death's inability to understand humans— and 'narrative causality' affects events, as characters find themselves having to decide how they *should* behave, rather than behaving according to narrative stereotypes. Granny Weatherwax, in particular, is the conscience of many of the books in which she appears, while the 'Vimes' series beginning with *Guards! Guards!* (1989) increasingly considers the nature of civic society. The collaboration with Neil *Gaiman, *Good Omens* (1990) addresses similar themes. Pratchett's books for children include his first published novel, *The Carpet People* (1971; 1992), the Nome or Bromeliad (1988–90) and Johnny Maxwell (1992–6) trilogies, *The Amazing Maurice and his Educated Rodents* (2001), and *Nation* (2008). Discworld reached its 39th title with *Snuff* (2011). Pratchett was the best-selling British writer of the 1990s. In 2007 he announced his diagnosis with early-onset Alzheimer's disease. There are adaptations of Pratchett's work for stage, radio, television, and as graphic novels, role-playing, and video games.

Prelude, The, *Or Growth of a Poet's Mind* An autobiographical poem in blank verse by William *Wordsworth, addressed to S. T. *Coleridge, and begun in 1798–9; a complete draft in thirteen books was finished in 1805, but it was several times remodelled, and published posthumously in its final version, in fourteen books in 1850. The poem was originally intended as an introduction to 'The Recluse' (*see* EXCURSION).

Although profoundly autobiographical, the poem does not proceed in terms of strict chronology; it deals with infancy, schooldays, Cambridge, his walking tour through the Alps, his political awakening in France, and consequent horrors, but (for example) the passage describing the 'visionary dreariness' of a highly charged moment in his early boyhood is delayed until Book XI ('Imagination, How Impaired and Restored'). The landscape described there is linked in the immediate past with his sister Dorothy and Coleridge, who are both intermittently addressed throughout the work. The tone is flexible and variable; conversational in some passages, narrative in others, it sometimes rises to an impassioned loftiness. A constant theme is Wordsworth's sense of himself as a chosen being, with an overriding duty to his poetic vocation. Apart from its poetic quality, the work is remarkable for its psychological insight into the significance of childhood experience, a theme dear to *Romanticism, but rarely treated with such power and precision.

Pre-Raphaelite Brotherhood A group of artists, poets, and critics—John Everett *Millais, Dante Gabriel *Rossetti, William Holman *Hunt, William Michael *Rossetti, Thomas *Woolner, Frederic George Stephens (1828–1907), and James Collinson (1825–81)—who first met as a group, led by the first three, in 1848. The initials 'P.R.B.' first appeared on their work in the Royal Academy exhibition of 1849. As its periodical *The *Germ* (1850) suggests, the movement was strongly literary, and some of its most striking paintings were inspired by John *Keats (see Millais's *Isabella*), *Dante, William *Shakespeare, and Alfred *Tennyson. Common aspirations of the group included fidelity to nature (manifested in clarity, brightness, detailed first-hand observation of flora, etc.), and moral seriousness, in some expressed in religious themes or symbolic mystical iconography. Many of the subjects were medieval as well as literary, and the movement (much influenced by John *Ruskin, who became its champion) saw itself in part as a revolt against the ugliness of modern life and dress. Artists connected with the PRB include Ford Madox Brown (1821–93), William Bell *Scott, William Dyce (1806–64), Henry Wallis (1830–1916), Arthur Hughes (1831–1915), Simeon Solomon (1840–1905), and William *de Morgan. The first phase of the movement was brief, and the group broke up around 1853; a second phase led by Dante Gabriel Rossetti and involving Edward Burne-Jones, William *Morris, and A. C. *Swinburne was often labelled 'Pre-Raphaelite' but was more accurately linked to the *Aesthetic movement.

((⊕)) SEE WEB LINKS

• Pre-Raphaelite Society website

Presbyterianism A church system overseen by a governing hierarchy of four courts (parochial, local, regional, and national), championed by English Puritans. The term comes from the New Testament Greek word πρεσβύτερος, rendered *presbyter* or *elder* in Protestant English Bibles but *priest* in Roman Catholic translations. The Westminster Assembly of Divines, summoned by the Long Parliament in 1643, issued a set of enduring Presbyterian formularies: directories of *Church-Government* (1644) and *Public Worship* (1645), a *Confession of Faith* (1648), and *Larger and Shorter Catechism* (1648); but a

national Presbyterian church was never established in England as it had been in Scotland.

Priam See ILIAD.

PRICE, Richard (1723–91) Dissenting minister; from 1791 one of the original members of the Unitarian Society. In *A Review of the Principal Questions in Morals* (1756) he questions Francis *Hutcheson's doctrine of 'moral sense', and argues that the rightness and wrongness of an action belong to it intrinsically. As minister at Newington Green, he influenced Samuel *Rogers and Mary *Wollstonecraft. He supported American independence and the French Revolution; his address to the Revolution Society of 4 November 1789 provoked Edmund Burke to write *Reflections on the Revolution in France*.

PRICE, Susan (1955–) Novelist, whose numerous works combine fantasy, realism, and history. *The Sterkarm Handshake* (1998) and its sequel, *A Sterkarm Kiss* (2003), describe what happens when 21st-century technology allows travel through a Time Tube (not unlike the Channel Tunnel) between centuries, raising ethical questions and creating emotional dilemmas.

PRICE, Uvedale See PICTURESQUE.

Pride and Prejudice A novel by Jane *Austen, published 1813.

Mr and Mrs Bennet live with their five daughters at Longbourn in Hertfordshire. In the absence of a male heir, the property is due to pass by entail to a cousin, William Collins. Through the patronage of the haughty Lady Catherine de Bourgh, Collins has been presented with a living near Rosings, the Kentish seat of Lady Catherine. Charles Bingley, a rich young bachelor, takes Netherfield, a house near Longbourn, bringing with him his two sisters and his friend Fitzwilliam Darcy, nephew of Lady Catherine. Bingley and Jane, the eldest of the Bennet girls, soon fall in love. Darcy, though attracted to the next sister, the lively and spirited Elizabeth, offends her by his supercilious behaviour at a ball. This dislike is increased by the account given her by George Wickham, a dashing young militia officer (and son of the late steward of the Darcy property), of the unjust treatment he has met with at Darcy's hands, and when Darcy and Bingley's two sisters, disgusted with the vulgarity of Mrs Bennet and her two youngest daughters, effectively separate Bingley from Jane.

Meanwhile the fatuous and grovelling Mr Collins, urged to marry by Lady Catherine, and thinking to remedy the hardship caused to the Bennet girls by the entail, proposes to Elizabeth. When firmly rejected he promptly transfers his affections to Charlotte Lucas, a friend of Elizabeth's, who accepts him. Staying with the newly married couple in their parsonage, Elizabeth again encounters Darcy, who is visiting Lady Catherine. Darcy proposes to her in terms which reveal the violence the proposal does to his self-esteem. Elizabeth indignantly rejects him, on the grounds of his overweening pride, the part he has played in separating Jane from Bingley, and his alleged treatment of Wickham. Mortified, Darcy writes to justify the separation of his friend and Jane, and makes it clear that Wickham is, in fact, an unprincipled adventurer.

On an expedition to the north of England with her uncle and aunt, Mr and Mrs Gardiner, Elizabeth visits Pemberley, Darcy's seat in Derbyshire, believing Darcy to be absent. However, Darcy appears, welcomes the visitors, and introduces them to his sister. His manner, though still grave, is now gentle and attentive. At this point news reaches Elizabeth that her youngest sister Lydia has eloped with Wickham. With considerable help from Darcy, the fugitives are traced, their marriage is arranged, and (again through Darcy) they are provided for. Bingley and Jane are reunited and become engaged. Darcy and Elizabeth also become engaged. The story ends with their marriages, and an eventual reconciliation with Lady Catherine.

Jane Austen regarded Elizabeth Bennet as her favourite among all her heroines, and there have been many successful film and television adaptations of the novel.

PRIEST, Christopher (1943–) Novelist and short story writer. Like Geoff *Ryman, Priest was first published as a *science fiction writer, with *Indoctrinaire* (1970), *Fugue for a Darkening Island* (1972), and *The Inverted World* (1974). In *The Affirmation* (1981), he patrols the frontier between sanity and insanity, rendering his narrator's fantasy world more real than the 'real' world. *The Prestige* (1995) is a compelling tale of doppelgängers and magicians, while *The Extremes* (1998) is concerned with virtual reality, *The Separation* (2002) with *alternate history.

PRIESTLEY, J. B. (John Boynton) (1894–1984) Journalist, novelist, and playwright. *The Good Companions* (1929), an account of theatrical adventures on the road, and his first major popular success, was followed by the grimmer *'realist' novel of London life, *Angel Pavement* (1930); his many other novels include *Bright Day* (1946), *Festival at Farbridge* (1951), *Lost Empires* (1965), and *The Image Men* (1968). Priestley also wrote some 50 plays and dramatic adaptations; amongst the best known are his 'Time' plays, influenced by the theories of J. W. Dunne (1875–1949) (*Dangerous Corner*, 1932; *I Have Been Here Before*, 1937; *Time and the Conways*, 1937), his psychological mystery drama *An Inspector Calls* (1947), and his West Riding farce *When We Are Married* (1938). *Britain Speaks* (1940) and *All England Listened* (1968) are collections of his popular and influential wartime broadcasts; *Journey down a Rainbow* (1955), written with his wife Jacquetta Hawkes (1919–96), describes travels in New Mexico; his volumes of autobiography include *Margin Released* (1962) and *Instead of the Trees* (1977).

PRIESTLEY, Joseph (1733–1804) Presbyterian minister, one of the founders of the *Unitarian Society in 1791. He wrote on theology, grammar, education, government, psychology, and history; his *Essay on the First Principles of Government* (1768) influenced Jeremy *Bentham's development of utilitarianism. His scientific research identified seven gases, oxygen (or 'dephlogisticated air') amongst them. In politics he was a radical, and supporter of the French Revolution, labelled 'Gunpowder' Priestley for his remarks about laying gunpowder 'under the old building of error and superstition'. He emigrated to Pennsylvania in 1794.

Prime Minister, The A novel by Anthony *Trollope, published 1876, fifth in the *'Palliser' series. This austere novel was not among Trollope's popular successes.

primitivism The idea that civilization corrupts the virtues of simplicity and nobility, which can only be rediscovered in remote, undeveloped cultures. A predominantly 18th-century phenomenon, associated with the educational and philosophic theories of Jean-Jacques *Rousseau, it is descended from the classical concept of the Golden Age. Critics such as Richard *Hurd and poets like Thomas *Gray led a mid-century revaluation of medieval, Celtic, and Norse writing. James *Macpherson's 'Ossian' was an attempt to recover the supposed simplicity of ancient Highland life, while Thomas *Percy's researches into early *ballads fed a growing taste for pre-classical simplicity. The phenomenon of the feral child, brought up by animals, also emerged: Lord Monboddo wrote a preface to a French case history of a 'savage girl' in 1768. (Later versions of the idea appear in Rudyard *Kipling's

Mowgli, and Edgar Rice *Burroughs's *Tarzan.) There was also great enthusiasm for travel writings about the 'noble savages' of the South Seas and elsewhere. Omai, brought from the Society Islands by James *Cook, was warmly welcomed in London in 1774 by James *Boswell, and Sir Joshua *Reynolds, who painted a magnificent portrait of him. The idea of the noble savage had been useful for campaigners against *slavery since its ambivalent appearance in Aphra Behn's *Oroonoko, and it was taken up by writers such as William *Cowper and Thomas *Day. George Colman's *Inkle and Yarico, George Cumberland's The *West Indian, Elizabeth *Inchbald's The Child of Nature (1788), and Robert Bage's *Hermsprong all stress the superiority of 'natural' education and simple living, values which continued into the *Romantic period.

PRIMROSE, Diana (*fl.*1630) Author of a poem-sequence, A Chain of Pearl, or A Memorial of … Queen Elizabeth (1630), based on William Camden's Annals of Queen Elizabeth (1615), which celebrates Elizabeth as a Protestant queen, and obliquely criticizes Charles I's pro-Catholic policies.

PRINCE, F. T. (Frank Templeton) (1912–2003) Poet, born in South Africa. His collections include Poems (1938), Soldiers Bathing and Other Poems (1954), and Afterword on Rupert Brooke (1977). Collected Poems 1935–1992 was published in 1993. He has been highly celebrated by Geoffrey *Hill and John *Ashbery.

PRINCE, Mary (*c.*1788–?1834) Born into slavery in Bermuda. She escaped from one of her brutal Caribbean masters in London. She dictated her intimate and idiomatic autobiography, The History of Mary Prince, a West Indian Slave, which went into three editions in 1831. See SLAVERY.

Princess, The: A Medley A poem by Alfred *Tennyson, published 1847. Some of the well-known lyrics ('The splendour falls') were added in the third edition of 1850, but others, including 'Tears, idle tears' (composed in 1834 at Tintern) and 'Now sleeps the crimson petal, now the white', were included in the first. The poem opens with a description of a summer fete based on an event at Park House, near Maidstone, the home of his friend Edmund Lushington (1811–93). It purports to be a tale of fancy composed in turn by some young people, based on an old chronicle.

A prince has been betrothed since childhood to Princess Ida, daughter of neighbouring King Gama. She becomes a devotee of women's rights, rejects marriage, and founds a university. The prince and two companions, Cyril and Florian, gain admission to the university dressed as women. The deceit is eventually detected by Ida, but her determination is unshaken, and a combat ensues, during which the three comrades are wounded. The university is turned into a hospital, the prince urges his suit, and he wins Ida; the epilogue is a plea for gradual social reform. The work was well received on the whole, an important statement about the public reach of poetry and, in particular, on the topical subject of women's education. It formed the basis of the satirical Gilbert and Sullivan operetta Princess Ida (1884).

PRINGLE, Thomas (1789–1834) Poet, briefly editor of the Edinburgh Monthly Magazine (later *Blackwood's Magazine). In 1809 he published his first volume of poems, which included 'The Emigrant's Farewell', and emigrated to South Africa. He is chiefly remembered as a poet of that country. His Ephemerides (1828) and African Sketches (1834) reveal his sympathetic interest in the native peoples and wildlife of Africa.

PRIOR, Matthew (1664–1721) Poet and diplomat. He joined with Charles Montagu, later earl of Halifax (1661–1715), in The Hind and the Panther Transvers'd to the Story of the Country Mouse and the City Mouse (1687), a satire against John *Dryden. His Carmen Seculare (1700) celebrates the arrival of William III, but Prior later joined the Tories and in 1711 went to Paris as a secret agent during the negotiations leading to the Treaty of Utrecht (1713). He was recalled on Queen Anne's death and imprisoned for over a year. A magnificent folio edition of his poems, produced with the advice of Alexander *Pope, was published by Jacob *Tonson in 1719 after his release. Prior wrote many occasional verses, epigrams, and bawdy pieces, but also large-scale didactic poems such as Solomon, or The Vanity of the World (1718). 'Henry and Emma' (1709) is a sentimental burlesque of the old ballad 'The Nut-Brown Maid'.

'Prioress's Tale, The' See CANTERBURY TALES, 16.

Prisoner of Chillon, The A dramatic monologue principally in rhymed octosyllabics by Lord *Byron, written in 1816 after a visit with P. B. *Shelley to the castle of Chillon on Lake Geneva, and published in the same year. It deals with the imprisonment there of the Swiss patriot François de Bonnivard (1496–1570).

Prisoner of Zenda, The With its sequel *Rupert of Hentzau*, novels by Anthony Hope (*Hawkins), published 1894 and 1898. They deal with the perilous and romantic adventures of Rudolf Rassendyll, an English gentleman, in Ruritania. *The Prisoner of Zenda* has repeatedly been adapted for film and television, notably in the swashbuckling 1937 version.

PRITCHETT, Sir V. S. (Victor Sawdon) (1900–97) Novelist, critic, and short story writer. His first book, *Marching Spain* (1928), reflects his enthusiasm for travel, as do *The Spanish Temper* (1954) and *Foreign Faces* (1964). His first novel, *Clare Drummer* (1929), was followed by several others, including *Dead Man Leading* (1937) and *Mr Beluncle* (1951), but he is principally known for his short stories, which began to appear in magazines in the 1920s. *The Spanish Virgin and Other Stories* (1930) was the first of many collections, including *You Make your Own Life* (1938), *When my Girl Comes Home* (1961), and *The Camberwell Beauty* (1974). Two volumes of *Collected Stories* appeared (1982, 1983). His stories show the influence of Chekhov, whose work Pritchett greatly admired. Pritchett's other works include two volumes of much-praised autobiography, *The Cab at the Door: Early Years* (1968), an account of a peripatetic childhood spent flitting with his family from lodgings to lodgings as a result of his improvident father's frequent business failures, and *Midnight Oil* (1971), which takes the story of his life to the end of the Second World War.

Private Memoirs and Confessions of a Justified Sinner, The A novel by James *Hogg, published 1824; a powerful mixture of *Gothic and psychological fiction. In the first part of the book Colwan, believing himself to be 'saved' according to the Calvinist doctrine of predestination, and under the influence of a malign stranger, commits a series of horrifying crimes, including the murder of his half-brother. The second section of the book purports to be a memoir written by Colwan, discovered when his grave was opened a century after his suicide. This reveals that he also murdered his mother, a girl, and a preacher, all under the supposed auspices of divine justice, before coming to believe that the stranger who haunts him is in fact the devil. His skull, on exhumation, is found to have two horn-like protuberances.

problem play A term used in two distinct senses, to denote either a play about a social issue such as prison conditions or women's rights, or a *Shakespearian play that some critics have found hard to accept as a *comedy because of its dark or cynical mood (thus a synonym for *tragicomedy). In the latter sense, three plays written at the start of the 17th century were often grouped as 'problem' cases by commentators in the early 20th century: *Measure for Measure, *All's Well That Ends Well, and *Troilus and Cressida. The former sense is applied chiefly to dramas written under the influence of *Ibsen in the 1890s and early 20th century, by G. B. *Shaw, *Galsworthy, and others.

PROCTER, Adelaide Anne (1825–64) Poet, daughter of B. W. Procter ('Barry *Cornwall'). She was Charles *Dickens's most published poet in *Household Words. In addition to her widely admired devotional lyrics Procter wrote witty, ironic poems about women's position ('A Woman's Last Word' is a rewriting of Robert *Browning's poem of the same title) and some lyrical ballads which draw attention to the position of fallen and single women. She also wrote some humane lyrics about the Crimean War.

PROCTER, Brian Waller See CORNWALL, BARRY.

Prodigal Son The general subject of a group of plays written about 1540–75, showing the influence of the continental neo-classic writers of the period, particularly Gnaphaeus in his *Acolastus*, on early Tudor dramatists and novelists. The chief of these are *Misogonus*, dating from about 1560 (author unknown), *Jacke Jugeler* (?1562), and George *Gascoigne's *Glasse of Government* (1575). The parable of the Prodigal Son is in Luke 15: 11–32.

Professor, The A novel by Charlotte *Brontë, written in 1846 (before *Jane Eyre), but not published until 1857. The story is based, like *Villette, on the author's experiences in Brussels. William Crimsworth, an orphan, goes to seek his fortune in Brussels. At the girls' school where he teaches English he falls in love with Frances Henri, an Anglo-Swiss pupil-teacher and lace mender, whose Protestant honesty and modesty are contrasted with the manipulating duplicity of the Catholic headmistress, Zoraide Reuter. Crimsworth resists Mlle Reuter's overtures, resigns his post, and is able to marry the firm-minded Frances. They establish a school together, and eventually return to England.

Progress of Poesy, The A Pindaric *ode by Thomas *Gray, written 1751–4, published 1757, describing the different kinds of poetry, its primitive origins, and its connections with political liberty. He recounts its progress from Greece, to Italy, to Britain, celebrating particularly William *Shakespeare, John *Milton, and John *Dryden, but finding no 'daring spirit' to continue their line.

prolepsis An anticipation, either in rhetoric or in narrative: thus the use of a descriptive term prior to the circumstances that would make it truly applicable (Hamlet: 'I am dead, Horatio'); or a 'flashforward' in which a story is interrupted by an account of events that should come much later.

Prometheus (meaning 'Forethought') Appears in Greek myth as one of the *Titans, descended from the original union of Uranus and Gaia. In some stories he is the creator of mankind and he is always their champion. He is supposed to have stolen fire for them from heaven when they were denied it by Zeus, and to have been punished by being fastened to a cliff in the Caucasus where an eagle tore daily at his liver. In *Aeschylus' *Prometheus Bound* he is the bringer of civilization to mankind and he refuses, despite his sufferings, to submit to the tyrant Zeus. The modern popularity of the myth dates from the 1770s with *Goethe's *Prometheus*. P. B. *Shelley's *Prometheus Unbound* is a highly original sequel to Aeschylus' version; Mary *Shelley's *Frankenstein*, subtitled *The Modern Prometheus*, also reinterprets the myth. Modern retellings include William *Golding's *Pincher Martin* and Ted *Hughes's *Prometheus on his Crag*.

Prometheus Unbound A lyrical drama in four acts by P. B. *Shelley, written in Italy 1818–19, published 1820. It is partly mythical drama and partly political allegory. Shelley began with the idea of completing the Aeschylean story of *Prometheus. He combined this with his view of Satan as the hero of *Paradise Lost*, and of God as the Oppressor. Rewriting or updating these two myths, he presents a Prometheus-Lucifer figure of moral perfection and 'truest motives', who is liberated by 'alternative' and benign forces in the universe and triumphs over Tyranny in the name of all mankind.

Act I shows Prometheus chained in agony, comforted by his mother Earth, but tempted to yield to Jupiter's tyranny by Mercury and the Furies. Act II introduces Asia and Panthea, the lovely daughters of Ocean, who decide to release Prometheus by confronting the ultimate source of power, *Demogorgon, a volcanic force dwelling in a shadowy underworld. Act III abruptly presents Jupiter vanquished by the eruption of Demogorgon, and Prometheus released and united with his beloved Asia. Their child, the Spirit of the Hour, prophesies the liberation of mankind. Act IV is a cosmic coda, or *epithalamium, sung by a chorus of Hours, Spirits, Earth, and Moon.

The sexual, scientific, and political symbolism of the drama have been variously interpreted, but the concept of liberation is central. The work has an important preface on the role of poetry in reforming society, which links with the *Defence of Poetry.

PROPERTIUS, Sextus (55/47–15/2 BC) Roman poet, whose four books of elegies celebrate his passion for 'Cynthia'. His poetry includes allusively mythological pieces in the Hellenistic tradition to which he was deeply indebted, presenting himself as the Roman *Callimachus. He is the subject of Ezra *Pound's 'Homage to Sextus Propertius' (1919).

Prophetic books The name sometimes given to the symbolic and prophetic poems of William *Blake, including *The Book of *Urizen*, *The Book of Los*, *Milton*, and *Jerusalem*.

prose poetry A term usually applied to short, self-contained passages of lyrical prose. It is closely connected with Charles *Baudelaire, and with Arthur *Rimbaud. Baudelaire's *Petits Poèmes en prose* (1869) were translated by Arthur *Symons and appeared as *Poems in Prose* in 1905. In the same year, *Poems in Prose* by Oscar *Wilde was privately printed. In 1906, Edward *Thomas observed that the prose poem 'has never had a real vogue' but it has had some prominent 20th-century exponents, including Geoffrey *Hill. In literary criticism, it had long been widely held that poetry need not be in verse. *Wordsworth notes that 'much confusion has been introduced into criticism by this contradistinction of Poetry and Prose, instead of the more philosophical one of Poetry and Matter of Fact, or Science'. Prose poetry is sometimes distinguished from poetic prose, the latter term applying to passages within longer prose works. Extracts from George *Borrow, Sir Thomas *Browne, Thomas *De Quincey, Walter *Pater, and others could stand alone as prose poems. W. B. *Yeats took from Pater's *Studies in the History of the Renaissance* (1873) the famous description of the *Mona Lisa* and, without changing a word, set it out as poetry at the start of *The Oxford Book of Modern Verse* (1936).

prosody *See* METRE.

'Prosopopoia' The main title of Edmund *Spenser's *'Mother Hubberds Tale'.

protagonist The central or leading character in a story or drama, usually although not necessarily the hero or heroine of the piece. In popular usage, the term has come to mean advocate or champion, regardless of the original dramatic sense; and the commonly found phrase 'main protagonist' is a pleonasm.

Protestantism Summary term for the convictions and practices shared by the religious traditions deriving from the movements that constitute the *Reformation. The term originated in the *Protestatio issued by those princes and cities of the Holy Roman Empire who dissented from the prohibition of the teachings of Martin *Luther agreed at the Diet of Speyer in 1529.

Protestantism encompasses the beliefs and practices of the various churches established in northern and western Europe in the 16th and 17th centuries in both the Lutheran and the subsequent Reformed tradition deriving from John *Calvin. Its characteristics are: repudiation of the overarching authority of the pope and the development of separate church polities and ministerial orders; a homiletic and pastoral, rather than sacerdotal, conception of ministry; an emphasis on the importance of faith, rather than works, in the scheme of salvation; a stress on the individual commitment of believers rather than upon obedience to ecclesiastical authority, with a consequent fostering of individualism and introspection; a prioritizing of biblical authority (in the vernacular) over ecclesiastical tradition; a hostility to images; and a tendency towards democratic habits of thought. To disseminate these ideas Protestantism made active use of the printing press and it played a very significant part in encouraging literacy, the habit of reading, and the development of a general reading public in England in the early modern period. The English literary tradition was to remain overwhelmingly Protestant in sensibility until the late 19th century.

Prothalamion A 'Spousall Verse' written by Edmund *Spenser, published 1596, to celebrate the double marriage of Lady Elizabeth and Lady Katherine Somerset, the earl of Worcester's daughters. Each verse ends with 'Sweete *Themmes* runne softly, till I end my Song'. Spenser formed the title on the model of his *Epithalamion.

PROULX, E. A. (Annie) (1935–) American novelist; her first novel, *Postcards* (1991), made her the first woman to win the PEN/Faulkner prize. *The Shipping News* (1993), won her a large British readership. In both of these, in *Accordion Crimes* (1996), and in her collected short stories (*Heart Songs and Other Stories*, USA 1988; *Heart Songs*, UK 1995) she combines two powerful strands of American writing: a regionalist emphasis on particular places and an encyclopedic attempt to grasp the diversity of America. For her short story 'Brokeback Mountain' (1997; film 2005), she dropped the 'E' and published as Annie Proulx. *That Old Ace in the Hole* (2002) takes place in the Texas panhandle. *Bird Cloud* (2011) is a memoir.

PROUST, Marcel (1871–1922) French novelist, essayist, and critic, author of *À la recherche du temps perdu* (1913–27). In the 1890s Proust moved in the most fashionable Parisian circles, but in later years became a virtual recluse, dedicating himself to the completion of *À la recherche*, which occupied him until the end of his life. In the period *c.*1896–1900 he worked on an early version of *À la recherche* which was published posthumously, as *Jean Santeuil*, in 1952. He explored his own literary aesthetic in *Contre Sainte-Beuve* (1954: *By Way of Sainte-Beuve*), where he defines the artist's task as the releasing of the creative energies of past experience from the hidden store of the unconscious, an aesthetic which found its most developed literary expression in *À la recherche*.

PROUT, Father Pseudonym of Francis Mahony, (1804–66), poet, translator and journalist.

Provençal, *or langue d'oc* (as distinct from the *langue d'oïl*). The language of the southern part of France, and the literary medium of the *troubadours. The language is now generally called *occitan*, though the terms Provençal and *langue d'oc* are still in use.

Proverbs, Book of *See* BIBLE.

Proverbs of Alfred, The An early Middle English poem of 600 lines, surviving in four manuscripts from the 13th century, comprising a section of proverbial instructions concerning the government of society (written *c.*1150–65) and one of parental instruction (written *c.*1200). The attribution of the proverbs to Alfred is no more than traditional.

'Proverbs of Hell' *See* MARRIAGE OF HEAVEN AND HELL.

Provok'd Husband, The, *or A Journey to London* A comedy by Sir John *Vanbrugh, finished by Colley *Cibber, produced 1728. Lord Townly, 'provok'd' by the extravagance of his wife, decides to separate from her and to make his reasons public. In Cibber's ending, this brings Lady Townly to her senses, and a reconciliation is promoted by Manly, Lord Townly's sensible friend.

Provoked Wife, The A comedy by Sir John *Vanbrugh, produced 1697, but possibly written before *The *Relapse*. Its serious main plot centres on the unhappy marriage of Sir John and Lady Brute and incorporates quotation from John *Milton's divorce pamphlets. Flirtation and intrigue are supplied by the gallants Constant and Heartfree, Lady Brute's niece Belinda, and Lady Fanciful.

Provost, The A novel by John *Galt, published 1822. The provost, Mr Pawkie, reflects on the arts of authority and rule, and his own successful manipulation of them throughout his life.

PRUDENTIUS (Aurelius Prudentius Clemens) (348–after 405) A Christian Latin poet, the composer of many hymns and of the *Psychomachia*, an allegorical account of the battle for the soul of man which was a very important influence on the development of medieval and Renaissance allegorical works.

'Prufrock, The Love Song of J. Alfred' A poem which became a keystone of *modernism, by T. S. *Eliot, written 1910–11, published 1915, and collected in *Prufrock* (1917).

Pryderi *See* MABINOGION.

PRYNNE, J. H. (Jeremy Halvard) (1936–) Poet. His first collection, *Force of Circumstance and Other Poems* (1962; later suppressed), bore similarities to Donald *Davie's gently modernist *Movement poetry, but his subsequent involvement in the British Poetry Revival exposed his work to the legacy of American Objectivism, particularly Charles Olson, and shifted it in a more experimental direction. *Kitchen Poems* (1968), *Aristeas* (1968), *Brass* (1971), *Wound Response* (1974), *High Pink on Chrome* (1975), and *Down Where Changed* (1979)—were collected as *Poems* in 1982. The notorious difficulty of this work—its daunting erudition and syntactic innovation—has been seen as a means of encouraging new forms of linguistic engagement with an increasingly heterodox human experience. Later volumes include *The Oval Window* (1983), *Bands around the Throat* (1987), *Word Order* (1989), *Not-You* (1993), *Her Weasels Wild Returning* (1994), and *For the Monogram* (1997). Prynne has published in Chinese (as Pu Ling-en), and contemporary Chinese poetry is a dominant influence on recent work, including *Pearls That Were* (1999), *Triodes* (2000), *Acrylic Tips* (2002), *Biting the Air* (2003), and *To Pollen* (2006). The comprehensive *Poems* (2nd edn, 2005) has cemented his reputation as the pre-eminent English experimentalist. Subsequent volumes include *Sub Songs* (2010).

PRYNNE, William (1600–69) Puritan pamphleteer, who wrote against *Arminianism from 1627, and endeavoured to reform the manners of his age. He published *Histriomastix*, an enormous work attacking stage plays, in 1633. For a supposed aspersion on Charles I and his queen in it he was sentenced by the Star Chamber, in 1634, to be imprisoned during life, to be fined £5,000, and to lose both his ears in the pillory. He continued to write in the Tower of London, and was again fined, deprived of the remainder of his ears, and branded on the cheeks with the letters S. L. ('seditious libeller'), which Prynne humorously asserted to mean 'Stigmata Laudis' (i.e. of Archbishop *Laud). He was released by the Long Parliament, and his sentences declared illegal in November 1640. He continued an active paper warfare. In 1660 he asserted the rights of Charles II, and was thanked by him. He published *Brevia Parliamentaria Rediviva*, in 1662, the most significant of about 200 books and pamphlets written by him.

Psalms One of the books of the Old Testament, a collection of 150 poems traditionally ascribed to *David, king of Israel, though it is now assumed that they were written by several authors at different times, probably as a part of early Jewish *liturgy. They cover a variety of subjects, for example praise of God and his creation (95, 100), thanks for the salvation of Israel (46, 115), and laments on behalf of the individual (42) or of Israel in exile (137). There are significant allusions to psalms in the New Testament (e.g. Matthew 21: 9; Acts 2: 25); Jesus quotes Psalm 22 on the cross. Christian interpreters read the psalms as prefiguring the coming of Jesus and his relationship with the church. Miles *Coverdale's version in the *Book of *Common Prayer* has been far more influential than that in the Authorized Version (*see*

BIBLE, THE ENGLISH). The popular metrical version by *Sternhold, Hopkins, and others, known as the Old Version (1562), was longer lasting than the New Version (1692) by *Tate and Brady designed to replace it. The Psalms have been translated and imitated by many English poets, including Thomas *Wyatt, Philip *Sidney and the countess of *Pembroke, George *Herbert, John *Milton, Joseph *Addison, Isaac *Watts, and Christopher *Smart (whose *Jubilate Agno* displays many characteristics of antiphonal psalms).

Pseudodoxia Epidemica: *or Enquiries into Very Many Received Tenets, and Commonly Presumed Truths* Often referred to as *Vulgar Errors*; by Sir Thomas *Browne, first published 1646, revised and augmented 1650, 1658, and 1672. Fulfilling Francis *Bacon's desire in *The *Advancement of Learning* for a 'Calendar of Dubitations, or Problems' and a 'Calendar of Falsehoods, and of popular Errors', it comprises one general book, treating of the sources and propagation of error (original sin, popular gullibility, logical fallacy, learned credulity and laziness, reverence for antiquity and authority, influential authors, and Satan), and six particular books, three on natural history (mineralogy, botany, zoology, physiology) and three on civil, ecclesiastical, and literary history (iconography, magic and folklore, chronology, historical geography, and biblical, classical, and medieval history). Browne examines more than 100 problems in the light of his extensive learning, the verdicts of reasoned argument, and the results of his own experiments and observations.

psychoanalytic criticism A form of literary interpretation that employs the terms of psychoanalysis (like the unconscious, repression, the Oedipus complex) to illuminate aspects of literature in its connection with conflicting psychological states. The beginnings of this modern tradition are found in Sigmund *Freud's *The Interpretation of Dreams* (1900), which provides a method of interpreting apparently unimportant details of narratives as 'displacements' of repressed wishes or anxieties. Freud often acknowledged his debts to the poets, and his theory of the Oedipus complex is itself a sort of commentary upon *Sophocles' drama. He also attempted posthumous analyses of Michelangelo, *Shakespeare, Ernst *Hoffmann, and other artists. Ambitious interpretations of literary works as symptoms betraying the authors' neuroses are found in 'psychobiographies' of writers, such as Marie Bonaparte's *Edgar Poe* (1935), which diagnoses sadistic

necrophilia as the problem underlying *Poe's tales. A more sophisticated study in this vein is Edmund *Wilson's *The Wound and the Bow* (1941). As Lionel Trilling and others have objected, this approach risks reducing art to pathology. More profitable are analyses of fictional characters, beginning with Freud's own suggestions about Prince Hamlet's inability to kill his uncle being a perfect illustration of the Oedipus complex. A comparable exercise is Wilson's essay 'The Ambiguity of Henry James' (1934), which interprets the ghosts in *The *Turn of the Screw* as imaginary projections of the governess's repressed sexual desires. A third possible object of analysis, after the author and the fictional protagonist, is the readership. Here the question is why certain kinds of story have such a powerful appeal to us, and numerous answers have been given in Freudian terms, usually focusing on the overcoming of fears (as in *Gothic fiction) or the resolution of conflicting desires (as in comedy and romance). Although Freud's writings are the most influential, some interpretations employ the concepts of heretical psychoanalysts, notably Alfred Adler (1870-1937), Carl *Jung, and Melanie Klein (1882-1960); or evolve their own partly Freudian schemes, as with Harold *Bloom. Since the 1970s, the theories of Jacques *Lacan have inspired a new school of psychoanalytic critics who illustrate the laws of 'desire' through a focus upon the language of literary texts. The advent of post-*structuralism has tended to cast doubt upon the authority of the psychoanalytic critic who claims to unveil a true 'latent' meaning behind the disguises of a text's 'manifest' contents. The subtler forms of psychoanalytic criticism make allowance for ambiguous and contradictory significances.

PTOLEMY (Claudius Ptolemaeus) Lived at Alexandria in the 2nd century AD; a celebrated mathematician, astronomer, astrologer, and geographer. He devised a system of astronomy according to which the sun, planets, and stars revolved round the earth, generally accepted until displaced by that of Copernicus. Combined with *Aristotle's natural philosophy, which saw Nature as orderly, hierarchical, and teleological, Ptolemaic astronomy when suitably Christianized formed the core of the medieval world picture. Ptolemy's work on this subject is generally known by its Arabic name of *Almagest*. His great geographical treatise remained a textbook until superseded by the discoveries of the 15th century. *Chaucer's Wife of Bath appeals to the authority of the *Almagest*, and the lustful astrologer Nicholas in 'The Miller's Tale' owns a copy.

publishing, subscription A system by which the author collected a pre-publication list of buyers prepared to pay for a book in advance; it was sometimes used to support deserving but impoverished authors such as Stephen *Duck and Robert *Burns, but more often to facilitate large-scale or multi-volume publications with high production costs or high prestige. Subscription lists were normally printed at the front of the ensuing publication. The first book published by subscription was John Minsheu's *Guide into Tongues* of 1617, although William *Caxton, in the late 15th century, secured promises of sales before producing major works. The system flourished most widely in the 18th century.

Puck Originally an evil or malicious spirit or demon of popular superstition; from the 16th century the name of a mischievous, tricksy goblin or sprite, also called Robin Goodfellow and Hobgoblin. In this character he figures in William *Shakespeare's *A *Midsummer Night's Dream* (ii. i. 40) and Michael *Drayton's *Nimphidia* (xxxvi).

PUDNEY, John Sleigh (1909–77) Poet, novelist, and journalist, a contemporary and friend of W. H. *Auden and Benjamin *Britten. His first volume of verse, *Spring Encounter* (1933), was followed by ten works of fiction, but he is principally remembered for his poem lamenting pilots who died in the war, 'For Johnny' ('Do not despair ¦ For Johnny-head-in-air'), written while he was an intelligence officer with the RAF in 1941. It became one of the most quoted poems of the Second World War.

PUGH, Sheenagh (1950–) Poet, novelist, and translator. Her volumes include *Crowded by Shadows* (1977); *Earth Studies and Other Voyages* (1982); *Beware Falling Tortoises* (1987); *Sing for the Taxman* (1993); *Stonelight* (1999); and *The Movement of Bodies* (2005). Pugh's poetry is marked by an ecological sensitivity and a defiantly populist directness of address. Her other writings include *Folk Music* (1999), a novel, and *The Democratic Genre* (2005), a study of fan fiction.

PUGIN, Augustus Welby Northmore (1812–52) Architect. He was a protagonist and theorist of the *Gothic Revival, and developed his thesis that Gothic was the only proper Christian architecture in *Contrasts, or A Parallel between the Noble Edifices of the Fourteenth and Fifteenth Centuries and Similar Buildings of the Present Day, Shewing the Present Decay of Taste* (1836), an important work that foreshadowed John *Ruskin and Thomas *Carlyle's *Past and Present*.

PULLEIN-THOMPSON, Josephine (1924–), **Christine** (1925–2005), and **Diana** (1925–) The sisters began long and prolific careers as writers of pony stories by co-authoring *It Began with Picotee* (1946). See their autobiography, *Fair Girls and Grey Horses* (1996).

PULLMAN, Philip (1946–) Children's writer whose reputation was established with the trilogy *His Dark Materials* (1995–2000). Other works include an inventive quartet of novels (*The Ruby in the Smoke*, 1985; *The Shadow in the North*, first published as *The Shadow in the Plate*, 1986; *The Tiger in the Well*, 1990; *The Tin Princess*, 1994) set in the 19th century and featuring the female detective Sally Lockhart (played by Billie Piper in the 2006 television adaptation). Like all Pullman's fiction, they display an interest in storytelling, referencing the contents and conventions of Victorian melodrama while also deliberately including anachronistic elements: Sally conducts herself like a 20th-century feminist rather than a suffragette.

Pullman has written several innovative shorter books for younger readers that demonstrate his admiration for the *comic strips of his youth. *Spring-Heeled Jack* (1989) is a comic version of the story about the legendary character—in this case cast as a superhero—told through a combination of prose and graphics. The *metafictional and much darker *Clockwork* (1996, made into an opera in 2004) is about a wind-up prince whose mechanical heart is rusting away, Gretel, whose love saves him, the Faust-like Dr Kalmenius whose murderous wind-up model is on the loose, and the relationship between characters, stories, and their tellers. *I was a Rat!* (1999, televised 2001) follows one of the rats in the Cinderella story who is accidentally left as a page-boy when the clock strikes midnight. Although this story ends happily, many of Pullman's novels and tales for younger readers reject happy endings in favour of more realistic, emotionally challenging endings. *Lyra's Oxford* (2003) is what Pullman describes as a stepping-stone between the trilogy and a forthcoming sequel (*The Book of Dust*) that provides information about the Oxford in which Lyra, the central female character in *His Dark Materials*, lives. He has also written plays, including an adaptation of *Frankenstein*

(1990) and *Sherlock Holmes and the Limehouse Horror* (1992).

Pullman is a notable reteller and creator of *fairy stories including short *picture books such as *Aladdin* (1995) and the novel-length *The Scarecrow and his Servant* (2004).

Punch The principal character in the most famous of English puppet plays, distinguished by humped back, hooked nose, and a tendency to beat his wife Judy and other victims: he is accompanied by his faithful dog Toby. The name of Punch came into the language after the Restoration through Pulcinella, a similar character in the *commedia dell'arte*.

Punch, or *The London Charivari* An illustrated weekly comic periodical, founded in 1841; at first a strongly radical paper, gradually becoming blander and less political. It closed in 2002.

It appears that the idea of starting in London a comic paper along the lines of Philippon's Paris *Charivari* first occurred to Ebenezer Landells, draughtsman and wood-engraver, who submitted it to Henry *Mayhew. Mayhew took up the proposal and enlisted the support of Mark *Lemon and Joseph Stirling Coyne (1803–68), who became the first joint editors. The first number appeared on 17 July 1841. Gilbert Abbott À Beckett and Douglas *Jerrold were among the original staff, soon joined by W. M. *Thackeray, Thomas *Hood, John Leech, and John *Tenniel, among others. Later editors included Tom Taylor from 1874; Francis Burnand from 1880; Malcolm Muggeridge, 1953–7; and Alan Coren (who introduced full-colour cartoon covers) from 1978. Contributors included Melvyn *Bragg, Hunter Davies, Benny Green, and Alan Brien.

The magazine's draughtsmen include George *du Maurier, who drew for the magazine from 1860. Richard Doyle's famous cover drawing was used from 1849 to 1956. Punch and the dog Toby usually appeared on the cover until 1969.

puppet play See MOTION.

PURCELL, Henry (1659–95) English composer. Much of his output consists of anthems and other sacred works, with words by Abraham *Cowley, Nahum *Tate, Francis *Quarles, Thomas Flatman, and others. Many of his songs were written for the 50 or so stage works (by Nathaniel *Lee, John *Dryden, Thomas *Shadwell, Thomas D'Urfey, Thomas *Southerne, William *Congreve, and others) for which Purcell is known to have provided music; a theme from Purcell's music for Aphra *Behn's play *Abdelazer* was chosen by Benjamin *Britten for his set of variations, *The Young Person's Guide to the Orchestra* (1945). Purcell's opera *Dido and Aeneas* was written to a *libretto by Nahum Tate. Purcell provided music for five 'semi-operas' in the last five years of his life, including *King Arthur* (by Dryden, 1691). Purcell was the subject of a sonnet by Gerard Manley *Hopkins.

PURCHAS, Samuel (1577–1626) Editor and publisher of travel literature. *Purchas his Pilgrimage . . .* (1613), essentially a religious geography, was followed in 1619 by *Purchas his Pilgrim . . . the Historie of Man*. In 1624–5 came his major work incorporating materials left by *Hakluyt, *Hakluytus Posthumus, or Purchas his Pilgrimes, Contayning a History of the World in Sea Voyages and Land Travell*, ranging from the travels of the biblical patriarchs to the latest reports of English voyages. The first section, after an introductory book, contains accounts of voyages to India, China, Japan, Africa, and the Mediterranean. The second part deals with attempts to discover the North-West Passage, the Muscovy expeditions, and explorations of the West Indies and Florida. Among the best narratives are William Adams's description of his voyage to Japan and residence there and William Hawkins's account of the court of the great mogul at Agra. The collection became a source for later writers, notably *Dryden, *Milton in *Paradise Lost* and S. T. *Coleridge for *Kubla Khan*.

PURDY, James (1923–2009) American novelist, whose work explores homosexuality, family breakdown, and sexual experimentation. His novels include, *Malcolm* (1959) and *The Nephew* (1961); he has also published plays, short story collections, and poetry.

Purgatorio, of Dante See DIVINA COMMEDIA.

Puritan, The, or *The Widow of Watling-Street* A comedy published in 1607 as 'written by W.S.' and included in the third and fourth Shakespeare folios, but by some other hand, almost certainly Thomas *Middleton's. The play is a farcical comedy of London manners.

Puritanism The term 'Puritan' became current during the 1560s as a pejorative nickname for Protestants who wished to continue the process of *reformation beyond the compromise of the established Elizabethan Protestant church, which retained government by bishops and a liturgy modelled on that of Rome.

Puritanism desired to recover the purity of doctrine, simplicity of worship, commitment of ministry, and integrity of faith that was thought to characterize the first three Christian centuries, after which the ascendancy of the church of Rome had supposedly corrupted the Christian gospel. Its revolutionary politics, leading in the mid-17th century to Civil War, regicide, and the ensuing Republic and Protectorate of Oliver Cromwell, hoped to create a constitutional order that would return to the godly practice of the early (or 'primitive' in the sense of 'pristine') church. The prospect of 'paradise regained' haunts the Puritan imagination of John *Milton and John *Bunyan, as of George *Fox and Richard *Baxter. Such aspirations, however, were readily lampooned as hypocrisy in the comedies of Ben *Jonson and *Shakespeare and in the poetry of Samuel *Butler. *See* BAPTISTS; CONGREGATIONALISM; PRESBYTERIANISM; PROTESTANTISM; QUAKERS.

Purple Island, The See FLETCHER, PHINEAS.

PUSHKIN, Aleksandr Sergeevich (1799–1837) Russian poet. Pushkin was a prolific writer in a wide variety of genres, but he owed his initial popularity to his early narrative poems, including *Ruslan and Ludmilla* (1820), and the so-called southern or *Byronic poems, *The Prisoner of the Caucasus* (1820–21), *The Fountain of Bakhchisarai* (1822), and *The Gypsies* (1824); *The Bronze Horseman* (1833) is set during the great flood of 1824. Pushkin's novel in verse *Eugene Onegin* (1823–31) has been much translated into English, from Colonel Henry Spalding's 1881 version, through *Nabokov's idiosyncratic unrhymed iambics and extraordinary commentary (1964; rev. edn 1977), to Roger Clarke's prose version (2000). Charles Johnston's influential stanzaic version (1977) inspired Vikram *Seth's *The Golden Gate* (1986).

PUTTENHAM, George (1529–1590/91) Writer and critic; almost certainly the author of *The Art of English Poesie*, published anonymously in 1589. Both a critical treatise and a rhetorical manual, it is divided into three books, *Of Poets and Poesie*, *Of Proportion*, and *Of Ornament*, and is important as a record of early Elizabethan taste and theory. The author's tone is lively and personal. He condemns John *Gower for 'false orthography', finds John *Skelton 'a rude railing rhymer and all his doings ridiculous', and praises Sir Thomas

*Wyatt and the earl of *Surrey as the stars of a 'new company of courtly makers'. In the second book he discusses 'courtly trifles' such as anagrams, *emblems, and posies, showing a fondness for 'ocular representations'—in particular for poems shaped like eggs and pillars. The third book defines and illustrates various figures of speech, suggesting new common terms for Greek and Latin originals, like 'single supply, ringleader and middlemarcher' (zeugma, prozeugma, and mezozeugma), 'the dry mock' (irony), 'the bitter taunt' (sarcasm), and 'the over reacher' (hyperbole). Among the illustrative quotations in the *Art* are extracts from poems in manuscript by *Elizabeth I, Edward *Dyer, and Philip *Sidney and from printed works including Richard *Tottel's *Miscellany* and volumes by George *Turbervile and George *Gascoigne.

PUZO, Mario (1920–99) American novelist of Sicilian origins, best known for his novels dealing with the Mafia in the USA, particularly *The Godfather* (1969), which was filmed with two sequels by Francis Ford Coppola.

Pwyll In Welsh mythology, prince of Dyfed and 'head of Hades', the subject of the first story in *The *Mabinogion*. The stories of Sir Pelleas and King Pelles in *Malory are perhaps connected with his myth.

PYE, Henry James (1745–1813) He became *poet laureate in 1790, largely for political reasons, and was the constant butt of contemporary ridicule.

Pygmalion Legendary king who because of his disgust for real women made himself a beautiful statue with which he fell in love. *Venus, in answer to his prayer, then transformed her into a woman. *Ovid tells the story in *Metamorphoses*, Book 10, William *Shakespeare draws on it in *The *Winter's Tale*; George Bernard *Shaw clothes it in modern dress in *Pygmalion*.

Pylon School A nickname for the group of younger left-wing poets of the 1930s, chiefly the 'MacSpaunday' group, W. H. *Auden, Cecil *Day-Lewis, Louis *MacNeice, and Stephen *Spender. Cyril Connolly referred to them as the 'Pylon Boys', alluding to their rather self-conscious use of modern technology. Spender's poem 'The Pylons' was published in 1933, and pylons and skyscrapers appear in Day-Lewis's poem to Auden in *The Magnetic Mountain* (1933).

PYM, Barbara (1913–80) Novelist; she worked as an editor at the International African Institute in London from 1946 until 1974. The anthropological perspective this familiarized her with is apparent in the six novels, starting with *Some Tame Gazelle*, that she published between 1950 and 1961: wry comedies of manners that record the habits and habitats of predominantly celibate women and men, in a High Anglican milieu. After the rejection of her seventh novel, *An Unsuitable Attachment*, in 1963 (it eventually appeared in 1982), she remained unpublished until David Cecil and Philip *Larkin revived interest in her work. The novels she subsequently published—*Quartet in Autumn* (1977), *The Sweet Dove Died* (1978), and *A Few Green Leaves* (1980)—are her finest, adding elegiac resonances to the ironic wit with which she scrutinizes the comedy and pathos of people who lead lives of decorous stoicism.

PYNCHON, Thomas (1937–) American novelist, whose novels are less concerned with character than with the effects of historical and political processes on individual behaviour. Their fragmented *picaresque narratives are often based on outlandish quests, and blend paranoia, literary game-playing, bawdy humour, social satire, and fantasy. Science provides an important source of metaphor and subject matter. His first novel, *V.* (1963), is a long and complex allegorical fable interweaving the adventures of a group of contemporary Americans with the secret history of a shape-changing spy, 'V', who represents a series of female archetypes. *The Crying of Lot 49* (1966) is a paranoid mystery story mixing philosophical speculation with satirical observation of American culture in the 1960s. *Gravity's Rainbow* (1973) is a multi-layered black comedy set at the close of the Second World War: its convoluted plots and conspiracies reflect the socio-political processes threatening personal freedom. In *Vineland* (1990), a darkly humorous conspiracy thriller, participants in the 'counter-culture' of the 1960s face up to the conservative political scene of the 1980s. *Mason & Dixon* (1997) is a pastiche *historical novel, based on the two 18th-century British surveyors who established the Mason–Dixon line, drawing parallels between the political and scientific upheavals of the Age of Reason and those of the late 20th century. *Against the Day* (2006) describes the uncertainties of the period from the Chicago World's Fair (1893) up to the impending outbreak of the First World War. *Inherent Vice* (2009) is a pastiche of *noir detective fiction.

pyrrhic *See* METRE.

'Q' *See* JERROLD, DOUGLAS WILLIAM; QUILLER-COUCH, SIR ARTHUR.

Quakers Members of the Society of *Friends.

QUARLES, Francis (1592–1644) Poet; he made his reputation in the 1620s by a series of biblical paraphrases (e.g. *A Feast for Worms*, 1620), and in 1629 published a 'vain amatory poem', *Argalus and Parthenia*, based on an episode in Philip *Sidney's *Arcadia*. He is chiefly remembered for his extremely popular *Emblems* (1635) and *Hieroglyphics of the Life of Man* (1638). In 1639 he was appointed chronologer to the City of London. From 1640 he turned to prose, publishing pamphlets, some anonymous, holding a constitutionalist–Royalist position. *Eclogues* (1646) and a comedy, *The Virgin Widow* (1649), were published posthumously.

Quarterly Review (1809–1967) Founded by John *Murray as a Tory rival to the Whig *Edinburgh Review*. Walter *Scott, who had been harshly reviewed in the *Edinburgh*, became an ardent supporter of the venture but refused the editorship. The journal stood for the defence of the established order, church, and Crown; its unwavering adherence to the bishops and the Church was satirized by Thomas Love *Peacock in *Melincourt*. The first editor, William *Gifford, brought with him several writers from the *Anti-Jacobin*, including George Canning and John *Frere. Unlike the *Edinburgh*, the *Quarterly* supported the *'Lake School' and *Byron, although it fiercely condemned John *Keats, Leigh *Hunt, Hazlitt, Charles *Lamb, P. B. *Shelley, and later Alfred *Tennyson, Macaulay, Charles *Dickens, and Charlotte *Brontë. Two of its more famous early articles were those of Scott in praise of Jane Austen's *Emma*, and John *Croker's hostile review of Keats's *'Endymion'. Gifford was succeeded as editor in 1825 by John *Lockhart, who was followed by a distinguished line, including members of the Murray family. The journal ceased publication in 1967.

quatrain A *stanza of four lines, or a group of four rhyming lines within a *sonnet. Varieties of quatrain stanza are distinguished by *metre and *rhyme scheme. The quatrain of rhymed *pentameters is known as the 'heroic quatrain'. More often found are those employing four-stress lines only (known as 'long measure') or in combination with three-stress lines arranged 4343 ('common measure', as in many *ballads) or 3343 ('short measure', as in some *hymns). The principal rhyme schemes are *abcb* (especially in ballads), *abab*, *aabb*, and *abba*; the quatrain of *octosyllabic lines rhyming *abba* is sometimes called the *In Memoriam* stanza.

QUEEN, Ellery Pseudonym created in 1928 by two American cousins, Daniel Nathan (Frederic Dannay) (1905–82) and Manford Lepofsky (Manfred Bennington Lee) (1905–71), who co-wrote numerous detective novels and stories under that name. In 1941 they founded *Ellery Queen's Mystery Magazine*, which became a key outlet for *detective fiction.

Queen Mab A visionary and ideological poem by P. B. *Shelley, published privately 1813. The poem is in nine cantos, using 'didactic and descriptive' blank verse greatly indebted to *Milton and to Robert *Southey's *Thalaba*. Despite its lyrical opening, invoking 'Death and his brother Sleep' and Mab the Fairy Queen in her time-chariot, the poem largely consists of attacks on monarchy, war, commerce, and religion. In place of these Shelley celebrates a future of Republicanism, Free Love, Atheism, and Vegetarianism. The verse is furiously polemical in style, with occasional passages of grandiloquent beauty. Seventeen prose Notes are attached as appendices, many of them substantial essays, 'against Jesus Christ, & God the Father, & the King, & the Bishops, & Marriage, & the Devil knows what'. The work was extremely popular among working-class radicals, and ran to over a dozen cheap editions by 1840.

Queen's Maries (Marys), the The four ladies named Mary attendant on *Mary Queen of Scots. The list is variously given, including: Mary Seton, Mary Beaton, Mary Livingstone, Mary Fleming, Mary Hamilton, and Mary Carmichael. They are frequently mentioned in Scottish ballads.

Queen's Wake, The A poem by James *Hogg, published 1813. Seventeen bards hold a competition to welcome Mary Queen of Scots to Holyrood in 1561. Their 'songs' are verse tales in various styles.

QUENEAU, Raymond (1903–76) French poet, novelist, and essayist. His works experiment with literary form and explore the divergence between spoken and written language; the best known is *Zazie dans le métro* (1959: *Zazie in the Underground*; filmed 1960, dir. Louis Malle). He co-founded the OuLiPo movement in 1960.

QUENNELL, Sir Peter (1905–93) Poet, biographer, and editor of the *Cornhill Magazine* (1944–51). His own works include *Masques and Poems* (1922), *Four Portraits* (1945; studies of James *Boswell, Edward *Gibbon, Laurence *Sterne, and John Wilkes), and two volumes of autobiography, *The Marble Foot* (1976) and *Wanton Chase* (1980).

Quentin Durward A novel by Walter *Scott, published 1823, set in 15th-century France. Like many of Scott's novels, it deals with the breakdown of traditional chivalric values and the opposition (and here, the reconciliation) of romance and reality.

Quest for Corvo, The: *An Experiment in Biography* A life of Frederick *Rolfe by A. J. A. *Symons, published in 1934. This account dwells as much on the author's pursuit of his eccentric subject as on his findings, and established a new genre of biography, in which the biographer's difficulties are part of the story: see Ian *Hamilton's life of J. D. *Salinger, and Richard *Holmes, *Footsteps* (1985).

QUEVEDO Y VILLEGAS, Francisco de (1580–1645) Spanish satirist, courtier, and wit. His *picaresque novel *La vida del buscón* (1626: *The Life of the Scoundrel*) was translated into English (through a French intermediary) by John Davies of Kidwelly (1657). His *Sueños* (1627: *Dreams*), which are biting satirical portraits of all classes of society, were translated by Richard Croshawe of the Inner Temple (from

the French) as *Visions, or Hels Kingdome* (1640), and later by Roger *L'Estrange (1667).

QUILLER-COUCH, Sir Arthur (1863–1944) Prolific author and anthologist; he wrote under the pseudonym 'Q'. His novel of adventure, *Dead Man's Rock* (1887), was followed by a vast output of fiction, verse, anthologies, and literary journalism, including the first *Oxford Book of English Verse* (1900). Knighted in 1910, he became professor of English at Cambridge in 1912. Two influential volumes of lectures, *On the Art of Writing* and *On the Art of Reading*, appeared in 1916 and 1920, and his edition of the *New Cambridge Shakespeare* began to appear in 1921. In 1928 his collected novels and stories appeared in 30 volumes. *Memories and Opinions* (1944) is the first volume of his unfinished autobiography.

QUINTILIAN (Marcus Fabius Quintilianus) (AD c.35–c.100) Roman rhetorician, educationist, and literary critic. His monumental *De Institutione Oratoria* ('On the Education of an Orator') is not only a treatise on rhetoric, but also discusses the training of an ideal orator for whom Quintilian like *Cicero advocates a wide general education; Book 10 contains a critical history of Greek and Roman literature. The complete text of the *Institutio* became known only after Poggio Bracciolini unearthed a complete text in Saint-Gall in 1416, after which it served the humanists as a guide on all literary and educational matters.

Quinze Joyes de mariage, Les A French misogynistic satire, of unknown authorship, dating from the late 14th/early 15th century. Several English versions of the work appeared in the 17th and 18th centuries, including one by Thomas *Dekker, entitled *The Batchelars Banquet* (1603), and a 1682 version called *The Fifteen Comforts of Rash and Inconsiderate Marriage*.

Quo Vadis? (1896) A popular and widely translated novel by the Polish author Henryk Sienkiewicz (1846–1916). Taking its title from Peter's question to Jesus, 'Where are you going?', the story of love between a Christian woman, Lygia, and a Roman patrician, Marcus Vinicius, is set against the turbulent background of Nero's dissolute rule and the Great Fire of AD 64, with historical figures including St Peter and St Paul. It has been frequently filmed from 1911 onwards.

Qur'ān (Koran) The 'Recitation', the sacred Scripture of Islam. For Muslims it is the word of

God, revealed in Arabic by the archangel Gabriel to Muhammad and thence to mankind. The revelations were oral and in prose, most of them apparently consisting of a relatively short number of verses (*āyāt* 'signs'). These basic revelations were then drawn into *sūra*s (chapters), the working units of the Qur'ān. The processes of revelation and compilation started about 610 and ended with Muhammad's death in 632. There are 114 *sūra*s, of widely disparate length. The canonical *sūra* order avoids chronological questions by placing them in rough order of length. There is evidence that parts of the Qur'ān were committed to writing in Muhammad's lifetime, but written versions became important only after his death.

The central theme of the Qur'ān is belief in one God, whose omnipotence is to be seen everywhere. Disobedience will lead to an apocalypse, which will be the prelude to the Day of Judgement, when each individual will be judged and the righteous conveyed to heaven and the unrighteous to hell. The message is strengthened by stories of prophets and of peoples who have been destroyed for not heeding them. Some are Arabian, but many more echo the Old Testament (and sometimes later Midrashic stories). Moses, Abraham, and Noah are all prominent. A smaller amount of material recalls the New Testament and Christian apocryphal sources, mostly telling of Jesus and Mary. The Qur'ān rejects the doctrine of the Trinity and also denies the Crucifixion. After Muhammad's move to Medina in 622 there are numerous passages offering more specific guidance on religious and legal matters and others arguing against Judaism and Christianity.

In Britain the first translation direct from Arabic was that of George Sale (1734), which was extremely influential in the 18th and 19th centuries, followed by John Rodwell (1861), Edward Palmer (1880), Richard Bell (1937-9), Arthur Arberry (1955), and Alan Jones (2007). There have been nearly 40 translations into English from the Indian sub-continent, by far the best of which is that of Muhammed Marmaduke Pickthall (1930). The best of several translations by Arabs is that by Majid Fakhry (1997).

q

RABAN, Jonathan (1942-) Travel writer, novelist, and essayist, whose travel books skilfully blend novelistic plots and character sketches with autobiography, historical information, acute observations on individual and national character, and political commentary. *Coasting: A Private Voyage* (1986) combines an account of Raban's journey by boat round the British Isles with reflections on his post-war childhood, and on the national march to war over the Falklands. In *Old Glory* (1981) Raban travels on the Mississippi in the wake of *Huckleberry Finn. His other books include *Soft City* (1974), a study of London life; *Arabia through the Looking Glass* (1979), written as an antidote to romantic and nostalgic views of the desert; *Hunting Mister Heartbreak* (1990), a journey exploring US emigration and identity; and *Passage to Juneau: A Sea and its Meanings* (1999). In 1990 Raban settled in Seattle.

RABE, David (1940-) American playwright and screenwriter, who served in the Vietnam War. This experience was used in his trilogy of plays about Vietnam draftees: *Sticks and Stones* (1971), *The Basic Training of Pavlo Hummel* (1972), and *In the Boom Boom Room* (1973). His screenplays include *The Firm* (1993).

RABELAIS, François (d. 1553) French humanist, physician, and author of comic fictions. He is best remembered for his comic fictions in French, *Pantagruel* (1532), *Gargantua* (1534-5), *Le Tiers Livre* (1546: *Third Book*), *Le Quart Livre* (1548-52: *Fourth Book*) and *Le Cinquième Livre* (1562-4: *Fifth Book*), though the authenticity of the latter is disputed. These fictions are characterized by unparalleled linguistic inventiveness, and by an encyclopedic frame of reference. Although he was known to Gabriel *Harvey and Francis *Bacon, he was not translated into English until Sir Thomas *Urquhart's version of 1653 (*Pantagruel* and *Gargantua*) and 1693-4 (*Le Tiers Livre*, together with Peter Motteux's translation of *Le Quart Livre*, and *Le Cinquième Livre*. His influence on English literature has been widespread, and is particularly marked on Samuel *Butler, Jonathan *Swift, Laurence *Sterne, Thomas Love *Peacock, and James *Joyce.

RACINE, Jean (1639-99) French dramatist. His tragedies derive from various sources, including Greek and Roman literature (*Andromaque*, 1667; *Iphigénie*, 1674; *Phèdre*, 1677), Roman history (*Britannicus*, 1669; *Bérénice*, 1670; *Mithridate*, 1673), recent Turkish history (*Bajazet*, 1672), and the Bible (*Esther*, 1689; *Athalie*, 1691). His comedy *Les Plaideurs* (1668: *The Litigants*) is drawn from *Aristophanes. The plays were extensively translated into English from the 1660s by, amongst others, Thomas *Otway. The most famous of the early English versions was *The Distrest Mother*, an adaptation of *Andromaque* by Ambrose *Philips, which was still being published in the 1820s. There are important modern versions of *Phèdre* by Robert *Lowell (1961), Tony *Harrison (1975), Derek *Mahon (1996), and Ted *Hughes (1998).

RACKHAM, Arthur (1867-1939) Children's book illustrator. Amongst his most successful works are *Fairy Tales of the Brothers Grimm* (1900), *Rip Van Winkle* (1905), which established him as the fashionable illustrator of his time, and *Peter Pan in Kensington Gardens* (1906). Rackham's vein of fantasy is Nordic— he created a sinister world, full of the twisting roots and tendrils of gnarled trees with gnome-like faces, and peopled by goblins, birds, mice, and monsters. *See* FAIRY STORIES.

RADCLIFFE, Ann (1764-1823) *Gothic novelist. She published five novels, *The Castles of Athlin and Dunbayne* (1789), *A Sicilian Romance* (1790), *The Romance of the Forest* (1791), *The *Mysteries of Udolpho* (1794), and *The Italian* (1797), and a description of journeys to the Netherlands, Germany, and the Lake District. A further romance, *Gaston de Blondeville*, and her journals of travels in southern England were published after her death.

Her portrayals of the raptures and terrors of her characters' imagination in solitude are compelling, and she was one of the first novelists to include vivid descriptions of landscape, weather, and effects of light. Her plots were wild and improbable, but she was expert at maintaining suspense and devising striking incidents. Radcliffe's stories, unlike those of her contemporary Matthew *Lewis, contain no supernatural elements. A best-seller in her day, the £500 advance which Radcliffe received for *Udolpho* was then unprecedented for a novel.

radio Originally developed by Nikola Tesla (1856–1943), Guglielmo Marconi (1874–1937), and others as 'wireless telegraphy', and first demonstrated publicly in Oxford in 1894. Broadcast programmes began in many countries in the early 1920s. In Britain, the *BBC became an important commissioner of talks, by such writers as E. M. *Forster and J. B. *Priestley, and of original radio drama. Ezra *Pound's pioneering radio opera *The Testament of François Villon* was transmitted by the BBC in 1931, and W. H. *Auden and Christopher *Isherwood included radio bulletins and songs in their experimental verse play *The Ascent of F6* (1937). Working with Louis *MacNeice and other writers, Dallas Bower (1907–99) created a new form of epic radio drama in the 1940s, attuned to propaganda needs, leading to a post-war golden age of radio drama on the BBC's Third Programme, which broadcast Dylan *Thomas's *Under Milk Wood* (1954).

Raffles *See* HORNUNG, E. W.

Ragged Trousered Philanthropists, The *See* TRESSELL, ROBERT.

Rainbow, The A novel by D. H. *Lawrence, published 1915. Beginning as a family saga, it focuses first on the farmer Tom Brangwen and his marriage to a Polish widow; then on Anna, her daughter from her first marriage, who marries Tom's nephew Will. It gradually becomes a *Bildungsroman concerned with Anna and Will's daughter Ursula. It traces Ursula's relationships—with Anton Skrebensky, son of a Polish émigré, and with Winifred Inger, a schoolmistress—and her trials as a teacher and a student. The book is remarkable for the rhythms and stylistic range of Lawrence's prose, for its study of the 'recurrence of love and conflict' within each generation's relationships, and for its attempt to capture the flux of human personality. The novel evolved from a draft called 'The Sisters'; the story of Ursula and of her sister Gudrun is continued in Lawrence's *Women in Love* (1920).

RAINE, Craig (1944–) Poet and critic; founding editor of the literary magazine *Areté*. In 1981 he became poetry editor at Faber & Faber. His collections of poetry include *The Onion, Memory*, (1978) and *A Martian Sends a Postcard Home* (1979). He is credited with having initiated a 'Martian' school of poetry (a term coined by James *Fenton) with his inventive transformations of the everyday. *A Free Translation* (1981) and *Rich* (1984) were followed by *History: The Home Movie* (1994), a lengthy, ambitious 'novel' in verse, a chronicle of the Raine and Pasternak families set against the background of 20th-century European history; *Clay: Whereabouts Unknown* (1996), and *À la recherche du temps perdu* (2000), an elegy for a former lover written with unconsoled frankness. There is a *Collected Poems* (1999).

RAINE, Kathleen (1908–2003) Poet. She published many collections of poetry, from *Stone and Flower* (1943), illustrated by Barbara Hepworth, to her *Collected Poems* of 2002, also three volumes of autobiography, collected as *Autobiographies* in 1991: the final volume includes an account of her important relationship with Gavin *Maxwell. Later collections include *The Oracle in the Heart* (1980) and *Living with Mystery* (1992). Much of her poetry is inspired by the landscapes of Scotland, particularly of Wester Ross, and has what she described as 'a sense of the sacred', an intense and mystic vision of the vitality of the natural world which also informs her critical work on William *Blake and the *Neoplatonic tradition. In 1981 she founded the review *Temenos*, a journal exploring 'the intimate link between the arts and the sacred'.

RAINE, Nina (1975-) Theatre director and playwright, daughter of Craig *Raine. Her first two plays *Rabbit* (2006) and *Tribes* (2010) are both centred on fathers; the main character of *Tiger Country* (2011) is a female doctor who first appeared in *Rabbit*.

Rake's Progress, The A series of engravings by William *Hogarth which inspired an opera by Igor *Stravinsky of the same title with a libretto by W. H. *Auden in collaboration with Chester Kallman (1921–75).

RALEGH, Sir Walter (1554–1618) Explorer and author. In Ireland in 1580 he became acquainted with Edmund *Spenser. Throughout the 1580s he seems to have enjoyed royal favour, though Thomas *Fuller's story of his throwing a plush cloak over a puddle for *Elizabeth I to tread on is most unlikely to be true. The journey to Guiana (now Venezuela) in 1595 in search of gold was in part a bid for royal favour; by his leadership of the expedition to sack Cadiz harbour in June 1596 and by adroitly dissociating himself from the earl of *Essex he maintained a strong position until the queen's death. Ralegh's trial, on largely trumped-up charges of high treason, was one of the first events of James I's reign, and from 1603 to 1616 he was imprisoned in the Tower with his wife and family, a dead man in the eyes of the law. He was released to search out the gold mine he claimed to have discovered in Guiana twenty years before. On his return from this disastrous expedition a commission of inquiry set up under Spanish pressure determined that the gold mine was a fabrication, the old charge of treason was renewed, and on 29 October 1618 Ralegh was executed.

His poems are beset by uncertainties as to date and authenticity, though a few of them, including the fragmentary '21th: and last booke of the Ocean to Scinthia', survive in his own handwriting. Among the authentic poems are his 'An Epitaph upon Sir Philip Sidney' and the prefatory sonnet to The *Faerie Queene. There are numerous prose works. His *Report of the Truth of the Fight about the Isles of Açores* (1591) was a source of Alfred *Tennyson's 'The Revenge' (1878). His *Discovery of Guiana* (1596) includes a description of 'El Dorado'.

The History of the World (1614), written during Ralegh's long imprisonment, was originally intended for Henry, prince of Wales (d. 1612). It deals with Greek, Egyptian, and biblical history up to 168 BC. The preface summarizes modern European history, demonstrating the unchangeableness of God's judgement. The *History* contains many reflective passages, most characteristically elegiac in tone.

Ralph Roister Doister The earliest-known English comedy, by Nicholas *Udall, probably performed about 1552 and printed about 1566, and perhaps played by Westminster boys while Udall was headmaster there. The play, in short rhymed doggerel, represents the courting of the widow Christian Custance, who is betrothed to Gawin Goodlucke, an absent merchant, by Roister, a swaggering simpleton, prompted by the mischievous Mathewe Merygreeke. Roister is sent packing by Custance and her maids; and Goodlucke, after being deceived by false rumours, is reconciled to her. The play is similar to the comedies of *Plautus and *Terence.

Rambler A twice-weekly *periodical by Samuel *Johnson in 208 numbers, published 20 March 1750 to 14 March 1752. The essays treat a great variety of subjects: ethics; crime; marriage and family life; economics; education; prostitution; history; self-knowledge; and many others. They include character studies, allegories, Eastern fables, and literary criticism (including a series on John *Milton). Minor contributions came from Samuel *Richardson, Elizabeth *Carter, Hester *Chapone, and Catherine Talbot (1720–70). Despite initial protests against its 'solemn' tone, the *Rambler* was pirated and imitated, and went through ten numbered reprintings in Johnson's lifetime.

RAMSAY, Allan (1684–1758) Scottish poet; he opened the first *circulating library in Edinburgh in 1726. In 1718 he brought out anonymously several editions of *Christis Kirk on the Green*, with supplementary verses of his own in fake antique *Scots. A collection of his elegies and satires appeared in 1721. In 1724–37 he issued *The Ever Green*, which contained work by the great poets of late medieval Scotland, notably William *Dunbar and Robert *Henryson, though with revisions and additions of his own. These contributed much to the revival of vernacular Scottish poetry. Ramsay's pastoral comedy *The Gentle Shepherd* (1725), with its Scots songs, was very successful and much admired by James *Boswell.

RAMUS, Peter (Pierre de la Ramée) (1515–72) French philosopher and grammarian. A convert to Protestantism from *c.*1560, he perished in the massacre of St Bartholomew. His *Dialectique* (1555) systematically challenged Aristotelian and *scholastic logic. It was introduced into England in the late 16th century and obtained wide academic currency, especially at Cambridge. His followers were known as Ramists and his anti-scholastic system of logic as Ramism.

RANDOLPH, Thomas (1605–35) Poet, playwright, and wit, follower of Ben *Jonson. His principal plays are *Hey for Honesty*, based on Aristophanes' *Plutus*, perhaps his first play but not printed till 1651, *The *Muses Lookinge-Glasse* (?1630), printed 1638, and *Amyntas*, a pastoral comedy acted at court (?1631). He wrote an eclogue included in *Annalia Dubrensia*, verses in celebration of the Cotswold Games (an annual celebration of sports held in the Cotswolds).

RANKIN, Ian (1960–) OBE, Scottish crime novelist. His Rebus series of novels, set in a vividly evoked Edinburgh and featuring the working-class police inspector John Rebus, includes *Knots and Crosses* (1987), *Let It Bleed* (1995), *Black and Blue* (1997), *The Falls* (2001), *Fleshmarket Close* (2004), and *Exit Music* (2007). He has also published *Doors Open* (2008), *The Complaints* (2009), and the graphic novel *Dark Entries* (2009).

RANSOM, John Crowe (1888–1974) American poet and critic. Whilst a professor at Kenyon College, Ohio, 1937–58, he founded and edited the important *Kenyon Review*, a scholarly publication committed to the close textual analysis associated with the *New Criticism. He cofounded the Fugitives group, which included Allen *Tate and Robert Penn *Warren. His critical works include *The New Criticism* (1941), an independent survey of the works of I. A. *Richards, Yvor *Winters, and others. His poetry includes *Chills and Fever* (1924) and *Two Gentlemen in Bonds* (1927).

RANSOME, Arthur Michell (1884–1967) Journalist and author. He was a reporter, first for the *Daily News*, then (in 1919) for the *Manchester Guardian*. He went to Russia in 1913 to learn the language, and covered the revolution at first hand; his Russian legends and fairy stories, *Old Peter's Russian Tales* (1916), had considerable success. Ransome is best remembered for his sequence of novels for children, beginning with *Swallows and Amazons* (1930) and ending with *Great Northern?* (1947). The books describe the adventures of the Walker (Swallow) and Blackett (Amazon) families, and various of their friends, in the Lake District, the Norfolk Broads, and other vividly drawn locations. He was the first winner of the Carnegie Medal for *Children's Literature, awarded for *Pigeon Post* in 1936.

Rape of Lucrece, The (*Lucrece*)   A poem in the seven-line *rhyme royal by *Shakespeare, published 1594 and dedicated to Henry Wriothesley, earl of Southampton. It is presumably the 'graver labour' which he promised to the earl in the dedication of *Venus and Adonis* the previous year. It is a highly rhetorical expansion of the story as told by *Ovid (in the *Fasti*) and *Livy. *See* LUCRETIA.

Rape of the Lock, The A poem by Alexander *Pope. A two-canto version was published in Bernard *Lintot's *Miscellany* (1712); a much-enlarged version was published separately in 1714. The poem was prompted by an incident in which Robert, seventh Baron Petre (1690–1713), cut a lock of hair from Arabella Fermor (*c.*1689–1738), giving rise to a quarrel between the families. In an attempt to mollify the parties,

Pope treated the subject in a playful *mock-heroic poem, in which the great set pieces of epic are miniaturized into the coffee-drinking, card-playing rituals of fashionable metropolitan living. Belinda's use of cosmetics is modelled on the arming of Achilles; the cutting of the lock is likened to the fall of Troy; Belinda's depression recalls the underworld voyages of epic; in the final battle the belles and beaus use fans and snuff-boxes as if they were heroic weapons. The overall effect is more benign than *The *Dunciad*, and the poem has been enduringly popular. More recently the underlying sexual politics of the poem has been the focus of much *feminist criticism. The 1714 version appeared with six illustrations; Aubrey *Beardsley produced eleven designs for the poem (1896–7).

RAPHAEL (**Raffaello Sanzio**) (1483–1520) Italian painter, born in Urbino. Throughout the 17th, 18th, and 19th centuries Raphael was generally revered as the greatest of all painters; his supremacy was challenged by the romantic admirers of Michelangelo in the 18th century but endorsed by the first president of the Royal Academy, Sir Joshua *Reynolds. In the 19th century the High Renaissance tradition was powerfully attacked first by the young John *Ruskin in *Modern Painters* then by the *Pre-Raphaelites who idealistically romanticized the purity, simplicity, and naturalism of Gothic art.

RAPHAEL, Frederic (1931–) Novelist and screenwriter, born in Chicago, but long resident in England. His novels, many dealing with the dilemmas of educated middle-class life, include *Obbligato* (1956), *The Limits of Love* (1960, set partly in Jewish north London), and *The Graduate Wife* (1962). *Lindmann* (1963) is based on the break-up of the illegal Jewish immigrant ship SS *Broda* off the Turkish coast in 1942. Other novels include *Orchestra and Beginners* (1967), *Heaven and Earth* (1985), and *Coast to Coast* (1998). Raphael's screenplays include a mid-term report on the Swinging Sixties, *Darling* (1965, John Schlesinger), a six-part TV series, *The Glittering Prizes* (1976), with sequels *Fame and Fortune* (2007) and *Final Demands* (2010), and *Eyes Wide Shut* (1999), for Stanley Kubrick. Raphael also translated *Catullus (1978, with K. McLeish) and *Aeschylus (1991). A memoir series based on unpublished notebooks, *Personal Terms*, reached its fourth volume in 2008.

Rasselas A philosophical romance by Samuel *Johnson, published as *The Prince of Abissinia: A Tale* (1759). It is an essay on the 'choice of life', a phrase repeated throughout the work. Rasselas, a son of the emperor of Abyssinia, weary of the joys of the 'happy valley' where the inhabitants know only 'the soft vicissitudes of pleasure and repose', escapes to Egypt, accompanied by his sister Nekayah, her attendant Pekuah, and the much-travelled philosopher Imlac. Here they study the various conditions of men's lives. The story illustrates the themes of *The *Vanity of Human Wishes*, stressing that no single system produces happiness, and demonstrating that philosophers, scientists, hermits, and the wealthy all fail to achieve it. In a 'conclusion, in which nothing is concluded' the characters resolve to return to Abyssinia.

Rat, the Cat, and Lovel the dog, the

In the political rhyme

> The Rat, the Cat, and Lovel the dog
> Rule all England under the Hog,

refer to three adherents of Richard III: Sir Richard Ratcliffe (killed at Bosworth, 1485), Sir John Catesby (d. 1487), and Francis, first Viscount Lovell (1457–c.1488). The Hog is the boar that is featured as one of the supporters of the royal arms.

RATTIGAN, Sir Terence Mervyn (1911–77) Playwright, whose first West End success was a comedy, *French without Tears* (1936). *The Winslow Boy* (1946) was filmed in 1948, and again, directed and with a screenplay by David *Mamet, in 1999. *The Browning Version* (1948) depicts a repressed and unpopular schoolmaster with a faithless wife. The heroine of *The Deep Blue Sea* (1952) is a judge's wife suffering from passion for a test pilot. *Separate Tables* (1954) comprises two one-act plays set in a hotel, and *Ross* (1960) is based on the life of T. E. *Lawrence. He created the character of 'Aunt Edna', the average middle-brow matinée attender whom playwrights must take into account, whom critics were later to use as a focus for their complaints about the middle-class, middle-brow nature of his own plays. The so-called *kitchen sink dramatists of the 1950s and 1960s reacted against Rattigan (expressly, in the case of Shelagh *Delaney), but David Rudkin in a BBC Radio 3 programme in 1976 stressed his sense of 'existential bleakness and irresolvable carnal solitude'.

Rattle Bag, The Anthology of poetry, edited by Ted *Hughes and Seamus *Heaney, first published 1982. The poems, a selection of the editors' favourites, are arranged in alphabetical order of title (first line for untitled poems), creating unexpected juxtapositions. Initially aimed at younger readers, it has been much used in schools, but its broad definition of poetry makes it an accessible and entertaining collection for readers of any age.

RAVEN, Simon (1927–2001) Novelist, whose first novel, *The Feathers of Death* (1959), brought him instant recognition. His major work is a ten-volume series of novels, *Alms for Oblivion*, beginning with *The Rich Pay Late* (1964), and ending with *The Survivors* (1976). *Fielding Gray* (1967) is chronologically the first in the sequence, which presents an uncompromising panorama of post-war life from 1945 to 1973 through the lives and vicissitudes of the same group of characters. Some of these also appear in the seven-volume series *The First-Born of Egypt*, which began with *Morning Star* (1984) and concluded with *The Troubadour* (1992).

RAVENHILL, Mark (1966–) Playwright. He shot to prominence with the *Royal Court production of *Shopping and Fucking* (1996), a deliberately confrontational analysis of the interconnectedness of sex and consumerism in a surreally realized 'queer' world. *Mother Clap's Molly House* (2002) was a sexual romp that moved between the 18th century and the present. He wrote the first ever *pantomime, *Dick Whittington and his Cat*, for the Barbican in 2006.

RAVERAT, Gwen (Gwendolen Mary) (1885–1957) Née Darwin, wood-engraver and granddaughter of Charles *Darwin. Her childhood is described in her autobiographical *Period Piece: A Cambridge Childhood* (1952). She was a close friend of Rupert *Brooke and associate of the *Bloomsbury Group. Works illustrated by her include *Spring Morning* (1915) by her cousin Frances *Cornford, and various anthologies in association with Kenneth *Grahame.

READ, Sir Herbert (1893–1968) Poet, novelist, and critic; he served in France throughout the First World War. His poetry, influenced initially by *imagism, includes philosophical poetry, dialogues, and modernist lyrics; a *Collected Poems* appeared in 1966. His only novel, *The Green Child* (1935), is a philosophical fantasy about forms of utopia. He was prolific as a critic of art, society, and literature: important works include *Education through Art* (1943), *Collected Essays in Literary Criticism* (1951), *The Philosophy of Modern Art* (1952), and *Anarchy and Order* (1954).

READE, Charles (1814–84) Playwright and novelist. After publishing a stage version of Smollett's *Peregrine Pickle* in 1851, he entered on his long career as theatre manager and dramatist. *Masks and Faces*, successfully produced in that year, became his first novel, *Peg Woffington*, in 1853. In that year he also published *Christie Johnstone*, urging the reform of prisons and the treatment of criminals, which was followed by *It Is Never Too Late to Mend* (1856), a highly successful work, which was later dramatized, and *Gold!* (1856), a play converted in 1869 into the novel *Foul Play*. At the same time Reade was writing short stories, working as a journalist, and writing plays. In 1854 he met the actress Laura Seymour, with whom he lived until her death in 1879. *The Autobiography of a Thief* and *Jack of All Trades* (both 1858) was followed by *Love Me Little, Love Me Long* (1859), the work for which he is chiefly remembered, *The *Cloister and the Hearth* (1861), *Hard Cash* (1863), a *sensation novel exposing the scandal of lunatic asylums, and *Griffith Gaunt* (1866). Its sexual frankness provoked litigation, in which Reade pugnaciously defended himself against 'the Prurient Prudes'. A long collaboration with *Boucicault, a highly successful adapter of plays and novels, began in 1867, and the last of Reade's major novels, *Put Yourself in his Place*, attacking the trade union practice of 'rattening' or enforcing membership, appeared in 1870. By the time he published *A Woman Hater* (1877) he had lost his determination to present honestly the problems of sex in society, and meekly agreed to all *Blackwood's objections. After the death of Laura Seymour in 1879 he wrote little, turned to religion, and in 1882 gave up theatrical management.

Reade was very successful, and often seen as the natural successor of *Dickens; among critics, both the young Henry *James and *Swinburne were admirers, placing his work above that of George *Eliot (a view which at the time did not seem eccentric). But he is now largely remembered only for *The Cloister and the Hearth* and *Griffith Gaunt*. He wanted to impart an authentic reality to his work, but the accumulation of detail often threatens to overwhelm his narratives. His interest in sexual frustration and fantasy, and its place in religious feeling, was much stifled by the proprieties of the time.

READING, Peter (1946–2011) Poet, who studied and taught at Liverpool College of Art. A prolific, hugely original poet, his first volume was *Water and Waste* (1970); numerous further books, which are usually organized around particular themes or motifs, include *Nothing for Anyone* (1977), *C* (1984, a grim meditation on cancer), *Ukulele Music* (1985), a fantasia on Thatcherite Britain which many regard as his outstanding single volume, *Perduta Gente* (1989), *Last Poems* (1994), and *Faunal* (2002). A *Collected Poems* was published in 2003. Reading's work displays a fertile inventiveness and aggression in typography, verse form, and subject matter. Characteristically, he contrasts a reporter's unsparing evocation of the underside and underclass of contemporary Britain—pub life, domestic brutality, street violence—with a mocking command of classical metrics. *Vendange Tardive* (2010) revisits the ecological concerns of *-273.15* (2005).

realism A broad tendency in literature that emphasizes fidelity to the observable and complex facts of life, in contradistinction to the idealized or simplified representations of *romance or *melodrama. It is associated particularly with prose fiction and drama since the mid-19th century. Literary realism of the 19th century was a major international tendency (although not quite a 'movement', except in the French realism that evolved into the *naturalism of *Zola) in fiction under the influences of Honoré de *Balzac, Stendhal, and Gustave *Flaubert; and later in drama under the influence of *Ibsen. In English fiction, the most celebrated exemplars are the novels of George *Eliot, notably *Middlemarch*, and of Arnold *Bennett, especially *The Old Wives' Tale*. The novels of Henry *James extend realist methods with new technical sophistication towards a 'psychological realism' that was further developed by *modernism. The tradition of realism in English drama is less distinguished, and appears mostly in socially concerned plays by e.g. John *Galsworthy and the *kitchen sink dramatists of the 1950s.

Rebecca Novel by Daphne *du Maurier (1938; film dir. *Hitchcock, 1940). The unnamed narrator becomes the second wife of Maxim de Winter and mistress of Manderley, his Cornish estate. Insecure in the role created by Maxim's glamorous first wife Rebecca, she is tormented by her failure to match her predecessor's social confidence, especially by the servant Mrs Danvers, who remains obsessively loyal to Rebecca's memory. Having assumed that Maxim also adored his first wife, the narrator discovers that in fact he hated and murdered her, disguising her death as a boating accident. The de Winters go into exile after Mrs Danvers sets fire to Manderley. The novel has echoes of *Jane Eyre* and of the wider *Gothic tradition.

Rebecca and Rowena A humorous sequel by W. M. *Thackeray to Scott's *Ivanhoe*, published as a Christmas book in 1850, with illustrations by Richard Doyle. Ivanhoe tires of domestic life with Rowena, and after various comic vicissitudes is reunited with Rebecca.

RECHY, John (1934–) American novelist, whose writings explore the world of gay sexual hustlers. His first book, *City of Night* (1963), drew on his own experiences in New Orleans. *Rushes* (1979) collects the stories of patrons to an inner-city gay bar.

'Recluse, The' *See* EXCURSION, THE.

Records of Woman (1838) A volume of nineteen poems by Felicia *Hemans, recording the legacies of famous women from history and legend. The dedication is to the Scottish female poet and playwright Joanna *Baillie. Several poems address the female artist, notably the elegy 'The Grave of a Poetess', referring to the Irish poet Mary *Tighe, which has a poignant epigraph, taken from Madame de Staël's *Corinne*, and may be translated as: 'Don't pity me; if only you knew how much suffering this tomb has spared me.'

Recruiting Officer, The A comedy by George *Farquhar, produced 1706 and performed more than 500 times during the 18th century; it is said to be the first play performed in Australia (1789). It draws on Farquhar's own experience of military recruiting in country towns.

recusant A term applied to Roman Catholics who refused to attend Church of England services as required by an Elizabethan law of 1559. In the reigns of *Elizabeth I and *James I recusants were subject to fines and imprisonment, and many priests were executed, including Edmund Campion and Robert *Southwell. Catholics were still subject to fines in the 18th century, as described by Alexander *Pope in *Imitations of Horace*. *See* ROMAN CATHOLICISM.

Red Badge of Courage, The A novel by Stephen *Crane, published 1895, describing the experiences of a raw young recruit in the American Civil War, famous for its *impressionistic technique.

Red Book of Hergest *See* MABINOGION.

Red Cotton Night-Cap Country, *or Turf and Towers* A poem in blank verse by Robert *Browning, published 1873. The title refers ironically to the description by Browning's friend Anne Thackeray *Ritchie of a district in Normandy as 'white cotton night-cap country'; Browning undertakes to show that the 'red' of passion and violence should replace the 'white'.

Redgauntlet A novel by Walter *Scott, published 1824. The plot concerns an apocryphal attempt by Prince Charles Edward to regain the throne, twenty years after 1745. The novel's memorable characters include Hugh Redgauntlet, a fanatical Jacobite, the Quaker Joshua Geddes, the crazy litigant Peter Peebles (a parody of the situation of the Young Pretender) and particularly Saunders Fairford, an affectionate and probably accurate portrait of Scott's own father. Embedded in the novel and thematically linked to it, is Scott's fine short story 'Wandering Willie's Tale'.

REDGROVE, Peter (1932–2003) Poet and novelist. A founder member of the *Group, his first volume of poetry, *The Collector and Other Poems* (1960), was followed by many others, including *The Force and Other Poems* (1966), *The Weddings at Nether Powers* (1979), *Assembling a Ghost* (1996), and *From the Virgil Caverns* (2002). A *Selected Poems* appeared in 1999. His poetry is marked by a richness of visual imagery, a sense of physical immediacy, and a deep preoccupation with religious and sexual mysteries. His novels, which include *In the Country of the Skin* (1973) and *The Beekeepers* (1980), are written in a highly poetic prose. He wrote several works in collaboration with Penelope *Shuttle, including *The Wise Wound* (1978), a study of the mythology and reality of menstruation.

Red Lion Playhouse London's first playhouse, built in the garden of a farm in Stepney by John Brayne (*c.*1541–1586), brother-in-law of James *Burbage, in 1567. It was built without foundations, which may explain why it seems not to have lasted longer than a few months.

REED, Henry (1914–86) Poet, translator, and radio dramatist. *A Map of Verona* (1946) contains his much-anthologized poem, inspired by his wartime experiences, 'Naming of Parts'. His plays made a notable contribution to *BBC radio drama in the 1950s, and two collections have been published: *The Streets of Pompeii* (1971) and *Hilda Tablet and Others* (1971), four prose comedies of contemporary cultural life. Reed's *Collected Poems*, edited by Jon *Stallworthy, appeared in a new edition in 2007.

REED, Ishmael (Scott) (1938–) African American novelist, active within the *Black

Arts Movement from his move to New York in 1962, co-founding the *East Village Other*. His fiction tends to involve parodies of accepted genres: of the detective novel in *Mumbo Jumbo* (1972) and slave narratives in *Flight to Canada* (1976). He has courted controversy over feminism in his *Reckless Eyeballing* (1986). Reed has published volumes of poetry, and edited *From Totems to Hip-Hop* (2003) among other anthologies.

REED, Talbot Baines (1852–93) Writer, who helped establish the conventions of the boys' *school story. His novels were often serialized in the *Boy's Own Paper*: 'My First Football Match, by an Old Boy' appeared on the front page of its first number, and he effectively donated his copyrights to its publishers, the *Religious Tract Society. His books' ethos mingles athleticism, duty, religion, and nationalism.

REES-JONES, Deryn (1968–) Anglo-Welsh poet and critic, born in Liverpool. From her first collection, *The Memory Tray* (1994), shortlisted for the Forward Prize, her volumes of poetry have been critically well-received. Her later volumes are: *Signs Round a Dead Body* (1998); *Quiver: A Murder Mystery* (2004), a long narrative poem set in Liverpool; and *Burying the Wren* (2012). The poet Michael Murphy (1965–2009) was her husband. The pamphlet *Falls & Finds* (2008), the outcome of a residency at the Natural History Museum, reflects her interest in poetry and science. She received a Cholmondeley award for achievement in poetry in 2010.

REEVE, Clara (1729–1807) Novelist. *The Champion of Virtue: A Gothic Story*, published 1777, was reprinted in 1778 as *The Old English Baron*, and enjoyed great success. It was often published with Horace *Walpole's *The *Castle of Otranto*, of which it was confessedly a descendant. The virtuous and noble Edmund moves resolutely through many adventures of romantic horror in order to obtain his rightful heritage, but the ghost of the murdered baron provides the only element of the supernatural. The story concludes with a dramatic day of trial and retribution. Clara Reeve wrote poems and several other novels, and an important critical dialogue on *The Progress of Romance* (1785).

'Reeve's Tale, The' *See* CANTERBURY TALES, 3.

Reflections on the Revolution in France By Edmund *Burke, published 1790. The treatise was provoked by Richard *Price's *Discourse of the Love of our Country*, delivered November 1789, in which Price exulted in the French Revolution and asserted that the king of England owed his throne to the choice of the people, who are at liberty to remove him for misconduct. Burke repudiated this constitutional doctrine, and contrasted inherited rights, which the English hold dear, with the 'rights of man' of the French revolutionaries, based on 'extravagant and presumptuous speculations', inconsistent with an ordered society and leading to poverty and chaos.

Reformation Referring primarily to the religious history of Europe in the early 16th century, though it can include both John *Wyclif and the 15th-century *Lollards and the later period to 1700. In its primary sense, the initiating event was the challenge to the selling of indulgences issued by Martin *Luther in 1517. This attack on corrupt practices quickly developed into a repudiation of the primacy of the pope and the ecclesiastical authority of Rome, and, led by Jean *Calvin in Geneva, Ulrich Zwingli (1484–1581) in Zurich, and John *Knox in Scotland, to the development of a distinctively Protestant conception of the Christian life, and the establishment of separate national, regional, and local congregational churches in northern and western Europe.

Under *Henry VIII England separated from Rome in the 1530s for political, rather than religious, reasons. Nevertheless, through the liturgy of Thomas *Cranmer, the sermons of Hugh Latimer, and the biblical translations of William *Tyndale, the national Church of England became increasingly Protestant, adopting under *Elizabeth I a *via media* (middle way) between Rome and continental Reformed churches. The integrity of this course, and the distinctive piety associated with it (afterwards known as Anglicanism), was first enunciated and defended in the *Apologia Ecclesiae Anglicanae* (1562) of John Jewel (1522–71), and subsequently in the work of Richard *Hooker, Lancelot *Andrewes, John *Donne, Henry Hammond (1605–60), and Jeremy *Taylor. It was attacked by *Puritan writers (such as *Martin Marprelate and John *Milton) and Roman Catholics (such as Robert Parsons (1546–1610)).

Reformation, History of the *See* KNOX, JOHN.

regional novel A novel describing people and landscapes outside the metropolis. Early examples are set in Ireland (Maria *Edgeworth, *Castle Rackrent*) and Scotland (John *Galt, *The*

Provost) and are primarily studies of individual characters. Walter *Scott began to combine a historically informed feeling for local customs with an appreciation of natural scenery. By the mid-19th century the localities described are often smaller and more exact, the focus being partly sociological, as in Charlotte *Brontë's *Shirley* (Yorkshire) and in the fiction of Elizabeth *Gaskell (Cheshire) and George *Eliot (the Midlands). In the works of Thomas *Hardy, set in a fictional Wessex, sensitivity to landscape complements a concern with agricultural and economic issues. In the mid-19th century, industrial or urban novels set in a specific town or city include Gaskell's *Mary Barton*, *Dickens's *Hard Times*, and Eliot's *Middlemarch*, and the tradition continued in the 20th century in the work of James *Joyce. Following Emily *Brontë's *Wuthering Heights* and R. D. *Blackmore's portrayal of Exmoor in *Lorna Doone*, other novelists adopted remote locations as settings for romantic dramas (Samuel Rutherford *Crockett's Galloway, Eden Phillpotts's (1862–1960) Dartmoor, Hugh *Walpole's Cumberland). The popularity of regional novels is reflected in the invention of fictional counties (Anthony *Trollope's Barsetshire, Winifred *Holtby's South Riding) or towns (Margaret *Oliphant's Carlingford). The genuinely regional work of Richard *Jefferies (Wiltshire), Constance Holme (1880–1955; Westmorland), and Francis Brett *Young (Worcestershire) combines social analysis with a celebration of local loyalties, as do the domestic novels set in Radstowe (Bristol) of Emily Hilda Young (1880–1949). More didactically slanted accounts of particular regions are found in the Shropshire romances of Mary *Webb and the early work of Henry *Williamson (Devon), in which country life is contrasted favourably with that of towns. The divergence between romantic and realistic handling of regionalism in the 20th century was reflected in the enormous popularity enjoyed by the Cornish novels of Daphne *du Maurier, the Tyneside ones of Catherine *Cookson, and the *historical Cornish novels of Winston Graham (1909–2003), whose Poldark series appeared in 1945. Examples of regionalism of a naturalistic kind are Arnold *Bennett's tales of the Staffordshire 'Five Towns' and the accounts of farming life of Sheila *Kaye-Smith (Kent and Sussex) and Adrian Bell (1901–80; Suffolk). Emphasis on social realism becomes more pronounced in the 1920s in the work of Phyllis Bentley (1894–1977), born in Halifax, who wrote of the textile industry in the West Riding of Yorkshire, and H. E. *Bates (Northamptonshire). In D. H. *Lawrence's The *Rainbow (Nottinghamshire) and

A Glastonbury Romance by John Cowper *Powys the potential limitations of the genre are surmounted through the integration of particular landscapes and places with individual psychological, religious, and emotional experience. In the second half of the 20th century regional writers continued to favour a realist approach, as in the work of Leo Walmsley (1892–1966), whose works *Sally Lunn* (1937), a trilogy set on the north Yorkshire coast; or John Moore (1907–67) with works based in Gloucestershire, Tewkesbury, and the surrounding villages (see the 'Brensham trilogy', 1946–8). The regional novel has often become a sociologically attuned vehicle for working-class concerns, *A Scots Quair* by Lewis Grassic *Gibbon anticipating the novels of Durham-born ex-miner Sid Chaplin (1916–86), Alan *Sillitoe, and Stan *Barstow in replacing nostalgia with radical questioning and social realism.

Rehearsal, The A farcical comedy attributed to George Villiers, second duke of *Buckingham, but probably written by him in collaboration with others, among whom are mentioned Samuel *Butler and Martin Clifford (*c.*1624–1677), master of the Charterhouse; printed 1672. The play satirizes the heroic tragedies of the day, and consists of a series of parodies of passages from these, strung together in an absurd heroic plot. The author of the mock play is evidently a laureate (hence his name 'Bays'), and Sir William *D'Avenant was probably intended; but there are also hits at John *Dryden (particularly his *Conquest of Granada*). Bays takes two friends, Smith and Johnson, to see the rehearsal of his play, and the absurdity of this work remains highly entertaining. It was one of the earliest of English dramatic *burlesques.

REID, Christopher (1949–) Poet; he was poetry editor at Faber & Faber between 1991 and 1999. His first book, *Arcadia* (1979), was widely regarded as a contribution to the 'Martian' kind of poetry which James *Fenton identified in relation to Craig *Raine's volume *A Martian Sends a Postcard Home*; and Reid is adept with the *defamiliarizing metaphors characteristic of the style. *Pea Soup* (1982) was followed by *Katerina Brac* (1985), in which Reid writes in the persona of a woman poet, translated into English, from an unspecified Eastern European country under a communist regime. The volume is a sophisticated exploration of the potentials, paradoxes, pitfalls, and peculiarities of the acts of translation, ventriloquism, self-concealment, and self-revelation that constitute the making of all poems, not only translations. Later volumes include *In the Echoey Tunnel* (1991), *Expanded Universes* (1996), and *For and After* (2002), which includes many translations from *Leopardi, *Pushkin, *Verlaine, Antonio *Machado, and others. The *elegies in *A Scattering* (2009) commemorate his wife's death. *The Song of Lunch* (2009) was televised in 2010. Reid has also published children's books, including *All Sorts* (1999), with his own press, Ondt and Gracehoper.

REID, 'Captain' Thomas Mayne (1818–83) Irish writer of boys' adventure stories. *The Rifle Rangers* (1850) was based on his experience in the Mexican War (1846–8). His first 'juvenile' was *The Desert Home* (1852).

Rejected Addresses By James and Horatio *Smith, published 1812. A competition was held to find a suitable address to celebrate the opening of the new *Drury Lane Theatre in 1812. James and Horatio Smith produced a large batch of bogus entries, purporting to be by William *Wordsworth, Lord *Byron, Thomas *Moore, Robert *Southey, S. T. *Coleridge, George *Crabbe, Walter *Scott, William *Cobbett, and others.

Relapse, The, *or Virtue in Danger* Sir John *Vanbrugh's highly successful first play, produced 1696. A continuation of *Love's Last Shift* by Colley *Cibber, it has two plots. In the first, Loveless, a reformed libertine, living happily in the country with his wife Amanda, suffers a relapse, on a visit to London, under the temptation of Berinthia, an unscrupulous young widow. In the comic sub-plot the absurd Sir Novelty Fashion's plans to marry Miss Hoyden, daughter of a country squire, are foiled by his younger brother, Young Fashion. The play was adapted by Richard Brinsley *Sheridan as *A Trip to Scarborough*.

Religio Laici A poem by John *Dryden, published 1682. Written in defence of Anglicanism against Deist, Catholic, and Dissenting arguments, *Religio Laici* combines an exalted recognition of religious sublimity with a defence of a 'layman's' reasonable and straightforward religious attitudes.

Religio Medici ('The Religion of a Doctor') A personal account of his religious faith by Sir Thomas *Browne, composed about 1635, first published in an unauthorized edition 1642, reprinted 1643 with authorial corrections and additions. It is written in magnificently sonorous yet intimate prose, and in its humanity,

lack of prejudice, tolerance of other religious persuasions, self-revelation, and frank self-doubt, it resembles *Montaigne's *Essays*. Its wit and learning made it a European best-seller. Its unorthodox views were deplored by Sir Kenelm Digby in his *Observations* (1643) and it was placed on the papal index of prohibited books in 1645.

Religious Tract Society Founded in 1799 to distribute cheap religious literature in the same interdenominational group of evangelicals who had earlier set up the London Missionary Society and were later to found the British and Foreign Bible Society. Its methods were influenced by Hannah *More's *Cheap Repository Tracts*, and its productions were much more readable than those put out by the *SPCK. A famous example from the early 19th century was Legh *Richmond's *The Dairyman's Daughter*. It published a great deal of children's literature, by authors such as Favell Bevan (1802–78) and Talbot Baines *Reed, a popular contributor to the Society's widely read *Boy's Own Paper*.

Reliques of Ancient English Poetry A collection of *ballads, historical songs, and metrical romances published in 3 volumes (1765) by Thomas *Percy. With its introductory 'Essay on the Ancient English Minstrels', the collection was an important landmark in the recovery of folk poetry (*see* PRIMITIVISM). Most of the texts were extracted from the *Percy Folio and 're-stored' by Percy with advice from William *Shenstone and Samuel *Johnson. Some were from medieval times, others were as recent as the reign of Charles I. Ancient poems from other sources and a few relatively modern pieces (by e.g. George *Wither, John *Dryden, and Richard *Lovelace), were added by the editor. Joseph *Ritson was sharply critical of Percy's editorial method. The editions of 1767, 1775, and 1794 each contained new matter.

REMARQUE, Erich Maria (1898–1970) German novelist. *Im Westen nichts Neues* (1929: *All Quiet on the Western Front*); filmed 1930; stage adaptation perf. 2006) is a fictionalized account of his experiences in the First World War. The novel's anti-war stance, for which it was denounced and publicly burnt in Nazi Germany, helped shape the attitudes of an inter-war generation that included William *Golding.

Remorse A tragedy by S. T. *Coleridge, written in 1797 as *Osorio* and produced at Drury Lane 1813. The story, set in Granada at the time of the Spanish Inquisition, tells of the slow corruption of the character of Osorio, a man who supposed himself strong but who is gradually led by temptations and events into guilt and evil.

Renaissance The great flowering of art, architecture, politics, and the study of literature, usually seen as the end of the Middle Ages and the beginning of the modern world, which came about under the influence of Greek and Roman models. The Renaissance (some scholars prefer to use the term 'early modern period') is generally said to have begun in Italy in the late 14th century and to have culminated in the High Renaissance in the early 16th century (the period of Michelangelo and *Machiavelli), and spread to the rest of Europe in the 15th century and afterwards. Its emphasis was humanist: that is, regarding the human figure and reason without necessarily relating them to the superhuman; but much of its energy also came from the *Neoplatonic tradition in writers such as *Pico della Mirandola. The Italian Renaissance is seen as a watershed in the development of civilization, both because of its extent and because of its emphasis on the human, whether independent of or in association with the divine. There are accounts by Jacob Burckhardt, *The Civilization of the Renaissance in Italy* (1860); Walter *Pater, *Studies in the History of the Renaissance* (1873) and John Addington *Symonds, *History of the Renaissance in Italy* (1875–86).

((⊕)) SEE WEB LINKS
• Cambridge English Renaissance Electronic Service

RENAULT, Mary (1905–83) Pseudonym of Mary Challans, novelist, known principally for her *historical novels, most of which are lively first-person narratives set in ancient Greece or Asia Minor, incorporating the new anthropological and historical insights of the 20th century. They include *The King Must Die* (1958) and *The Bull from the Sea* (1962), both retelling the legend of Theseus, and *The Persian Boy* (1972), set in the time of Alexander the Great.

RENDELL, Ruth Barbara, Baroness Rendell of Babergh (1930–) CBE, writer of *detective fiction and psychological thrillers. Starting with her first book, *From Doon with Death* (1964), her novels featuring Detective Chief Inspector Reginald Wexford and his colleague Mike Burden in the fictional Sussex town of Kingsmarkham increasingly use the 'police procedural' genre to explore contemporary social

issues. Tense crime novels (among which *A Judgement in Stone*, 1977, and *The Keys to the Street*, 1996, are outstanding) portray and probe aberrant psychologies and personalities warped by phobias. Under the pseudonym Barbara Vine, she has also written fictional studies of crime and violence (from *A Dark-Adapted Eye*, 1986, to *The Birthday Present*, 2008).

'Resolution and Independence' A poem by William *Wordsworth, written 1802, published 1807, sometimes known as 'The Leech Gatherer'. The poet describes his elation as he walks over the moors on a fine spring morning after a storm, and his sudden descent into apprehension and dejection, as he ponders the fate of earlier poets, such as Thomas *Chatterton. At this point he meets the aged leech gatherer, and cross-questions him in characteristically Wordsworthian manner about his way of life; the old man responds with cheerful dignity, and the poet resolves to remember him as an admonishment. The poem was based on a meeting recorded in Dorothy *Wordsworth's *Journal*, 3 October 1800. Wordsworth comments on his use of imagery in the poem and 'the conferring, the abstracting, and the modifying powers of the Imagination' in his 1815 preface.

Restoration The re-establishment of monarchy in England, with the return of Charles II (1660); also the period marked by this event of which the chief literary figures are John *Dryden, John Wilmot, earl of *Rochester, John *Bunyan, Samuel *Pepys, John *Locke, and the Restoration dramatists. One of the characteristic genres of the period is Restoration comedy, or the comedy of manners, which developed upon the reopening of the theatres. Its principal writers were William *Congreve, Sir George *Etherege, George *Farquhar, Sir John *Vanbrugh, and William *Wycherley, and its predominant tone was witty, bawdy, cynical, and amoral. The plays were mainly in prose, with passages of verse for the more romantic moments; the plots were complex and usually double, sometimes triple, though repartee and discussions of marital behaviour provide much of the interest, reflecting the fashionable manners of the day. Playwrights came under heavy attack for frivolity, blasphemy, and immorality (*see* COLLIER, JEREMY): they and their subsequent admirers defended their works as serious social criticism, and mirrors to the age. During the 18th century the plays were presented in more 'genteel' versions, and in the

19th century hardly at all: the 20th century saw a considerable revival of interest.

Resurrection *See* BIBLE.

Retaliation An unfinished poem by Oliver *Goldsmith, published 1774, consisting of a string of humorous epitaphs on David *Garrick, Sir Joshua *Reynolds, Edmund *Burke, and other friends, in reply to Garrick's mock epitaph on him: 'Here lies Nolly Goldsmith, for shortness called Noll, | Who wrote like an angel, but talked like poor Poll.'

Retrospective Review (1820–8) Founded by Henry Southern (1799–1853), its first editor, as a 'Review of past literature'. Extracts from poetry, essays, drama, and other prose, chiefly drawn from the 16th and 17th centuries, included the work of Francis *Bacon, Sir Thomas *Browne, George *Chapman, George *Herbert, Ben *Jonson, and Henry *Vaughan.

Return of the Native, The A novel by Thomas *Hardy, published 1878. The scene is the sombre Egdon Heath, powerfully and symbolically present throughout the novel. Damon Wildeve, once an engineer but now a publican, dallies between the gentle Thomasin Yeobright and passionate Eustacia Vye. Thomasin rejects the humble Diggory Venn and is eventually married to Wildeve. Thomasin's cousin Clym Yeobright, a diamond merchant in Paris, returns to Egdon to become a schoolmaster. He falls in love with Eustacia, and she marries him, hoping to escape the Heath by moving to Paris. But to her despair he will not return; his sight fails and he becomes a furze-cutter on the heath. She divides Clym from his beloved mother, and unintentionally causes the mother's death. This, together with the discovery that Eustacia's relationship with Wildeve has continued, leads to a violent scene between Clym and his wife. Eustacia flees, and she and Wildeve are drowned. Clym, blaming himself for the deaths of his wife and mother, becomes an itinerant preacher, and the widowed Thomasin marries Diggory Venn.

Revelation, Book of *See* APOCALYPSE; BIBLE.

revels, master of the An officer appointed to superintend *masques and other entertainments at court. He is first mentioned in the reign of Henry VII. Holders of the office in William *Shakespeare's day were Edmund Tilney, 1579–1610, and Sir George Buc, 1610–22.

Revenge of Bussy D'Ambois, The A tragedy by George *Chapman, written 1610/11, printed 1613, a sequel to *Bussy D'Ambois. Clermont D'Ambois, brother of Bussy, is urged by his brother's ghost to avenge his murder, but will only do so by the honourable method of a duel. The hero's reluctance to exact revenge recalls certain aspects of *Hamlet. *See* also REVENGE TRAGEDY.

Revenger's Tragedy, The A tragedy published anonymously in 1607, and from 1656 ascribed to Cyril *Tourneur; its authorship has been much disputed but since the later part of the 20th century Thomas *Middleton's claims have prevailed.

The central character is Vendice (or Vindice), intent on revenging the death of his mistress, poisoned by the lecherous old duke. The play is marked by a tragic intensity of feeling, a powerfully satiric wit, and passages of great poetic richness. *See* also REVENGE TRAGEDY.

revenge tragedy A dramatic genre that flourished in the late Elizabethan and Jacobean period, sometimes known as 'the tragedy of blood'. Kyd's The *Spanish Tragedy (c.1587), a much-quoted prototype, helped to establish the popularity of the form; later examples are Christopher Marlowe's The *Jew of Malta, Shakespeare's *Titus Andronicus, Thomas *Middleton's The *Revenger's Tragedy, and, most notably, *Hamlet; there are also strong revenge elements in John *Webster. Common ingredients include: the hero's quest for vengeance, often at the prompting of the ghost of a murdered kinsman or loved one; scenes of real or feigned insanity; a play-within-a-play; scenes in graveyards, severed limbs, and scenes of carnage and mutilation. Many of these features were inherited from *Seneca, with the difference that in revenge tragedy violence was not reported but took place on stage. The revenge code also produced counter-attacks, as in The *Atheist's Tragedy, in Chapman's The *Revenge of Bussy D'Ambois, and again in Hamlet, in which the heroes refuse or hesitate to follow the convention.

Review (1) a *periodical started by Daniel *Defoe in 1704, originally under the title of A Weekly Review of the Affairs of France, signalling one of its key areas of interest. It became A Review of the State of the British Nation in 1707 and continued until 1713, when the war with France ended. (2) A quarterly magazine of poetry and criticism, founded in 1962 and edited by Ian *Hamilton. It ran for 30 issues, and was succeeded by the *New Review*, also edited by Hamilton, which ran from 1974 to 1979.

Revolt of Islam, The An epic political poem by P. B. *Shelley, written at Great Marlow in 1817 (under the title 'Laon and Cythna: or The Revolution in the Golden City, A Vision of the Nineteenth Century'), published 1818. The poem is Shelley's idealized and orientalized version of the French Revolution, and the prose preface considers reactions to the revolution. It is composed in Spenserian stanzas, forming twelve cantos. The revolt is organized by a brother and sister, Laon and Cythna, whose temporary success is celebrated in incestuous love-making. But the tyrants recover power, and Islam is subject to plague and famine, vividly described. Brother and sister are burnt at the stake, but sail together with an illegitimate child to a visionary Hesperides. Though cumbersome, diffuse, and obsessive (there is much-disguised autobiography), the poem contains powerful images of struggle and renewal which Shelley returns to in his poems of 1819. The figure of Cythna, the revolutionary feminist, is of historical interest.

reward books There is a long tradition of giving books to children as rewards and prizes; in the 19th century the creation of suitable books for this purpose became a distinct part of the publishing industry. Reward books combined attractive presentation with warnings against such social evils as intemperance and discontent and the promotion of virtuous behaviour.

REXROTH, Kenneth (1905–82) American writer. His poetry from *In What Hour* (1940) onwards continues the line of *modernism, although Rexroth wrote many polemical essays, in *With Eye and Ear* (1970) among other volumes, stressing the value of an indigenous tradition of American writing. He also edited anthologies and produced translations from Japanese and other languages.

Reynard the Fox The central character in the *Roman de Renart*, a series of popular satirical fables, related to the *bestiaries and in the tradition of *Aesop's Fables, written in France at various times *c.*1175–1250. The first known cycle is a Latin one by Nivard of Ghent, *Ysengrimus* (*c.*1148), and this was followed by the Middle High German *Reinhard Fuchs* (*c.*1180). There is a Flemish version from *c.*1250; another

Flemish version (now lost) was translated into English and printed by William *Caxton in 1481. In these anthropomorphic stories, the fox is the man who preys on society, is brought to justice, but escapes by his cunning. The popularity of the series was most marked in French (which took from it the German word *Regin-hart*, 'strong in counsel', to become 'renard', for 'fox'), but there are some derived and related English works. The most important of these is the Middle English 'The Fox and the Wolf'. The encounter between the fox and cockerel in this poem anticipates that in Chaucer's 'The Nun's Priest's Tale' (*see* CANTERBURY TALES, 20), while its satire on ecclesiastical practices (in this case confession) make it an early example of a tradition to which Robert *Henryson's 'Morall Fabillis of Esope' (where the fox is called Lowrence) also belong. Later examples of the Reynard tradition are J. C. *Harris's Uncle Remus stories (where the role of the fox is taken by Brer Rabbit).

REYNOLDS, John Hamilton (1796–1852) Poet, and a close friend and correspondent of John *Keats. In 1814 Reynolds published *Safie*, an *oriental novel reminiscent of Lord *Byron, and *The Eden of the Imagination*, which echoes late 18th-century verse. *The Garden of Florence* (1821) includes two verse tales from *Boccaccio, as part of a Boccaccio volume he and Keats intended to write together, and for which Keats originally produced 'Isabella'. He had great skill in parody and comic verse; his anticipatory parody of William *Wordsworth's *Peter Bell* appeared in 1819 even before the original was published, *The Fancy* in 1820, and *Odes and Addresses to Great People* (with Thomas *Hood) in 1825.

REYNOLDS, Sir Joshua (1723–92) The most successful portrait painter of his age. He suggested the idea of the Club to his friend Samuel *Johnson. He painted Johnson at least five times and wrote a memoir of him and two Johnsonian dialogues; he is the dedicatee of James *Boswell's *Life of Johnson*, and Oliver *Goldsmith's *The *Deserted Village*. Reynolds's first literary works were three essays published in *The *Idler* (1759). In 1768 he was made first president of the Royal Academy and his *Discourses*, delivered to the students (1769–90), are his most significant achievement as a writer. William *Hazlitt pointed out the contradictions in the *Discourses* and William *Blake attacked Reynolds for his lack of faith in the inspiration of genius.

r

REZNIKOFF, Charles (1894–1976) American poet, a leading member of the Objectivists group. His major work was *Testimony* (1978–9), an assembly (or 'recitative') of American stories 1855–1915, taken initially from court records. Reznikoff used a similar method for his volume on the Nazi concentration camps, *Holocaust* (1975). *See* also HOLOCAUST.

rhetoric The ancient art of speaking (or by extension, writing) persuasively, much cultivated in antiquity, and revived as a major element of the medieval and Renaissance school syllabus up to the 17th century. This tradition of learning ultimately laid the foundations for English literature as an academic discipline, notably in the lectures of Hugh *Blair at Edinburgh. Literary rhetoric is concerned chiefly with the conscious exploitation of the various figures of speech, which were extensively named and categorized in antiquity and are still mostly known under their Greek names (although George *Puttenham attempted to provide colourful English translations for them). These are commonly divided into three kinds: (i) major 'figures of thought', also called 'tropes', which transform the meanings of words and expressions, as with *metaphor, *metonymy, personification, *irony, and *hyperbole; (ii) lesser 'figures of speech' which arrange words in attractive or memorable ways, as with *anaphora, asyndeton, *chiasmus, epanalepsis, *syllepsis, and dozens of others; and (iii) 'figures of sound', such as *alliteration and *onomatopoeia. A growing number of English schoolboys in the 15th, 16th, and 17th centuries, including Shakespeare and Milton, were required to identify, memorize, and illustrate examples of more than a hundred such figures, thus encouraging a vibrant culture of linguistic exuberance in these periods.

rhyme Correspondence of vowel and consonantal sounds in pairs of stressed syllables or of syllable-groups beginning with a stressed syllable, most commonly found at the ends of verse lines. There are various kinds of rhyme, the most common distinction being between 'masculine' rhymes on single stressed syllables only (born/forlorn) and 'feminine' rhymes with a further unstressed syllable included in the rhymed element (together/weather). Triple rhymes are also sometimes found, with two unstressed syllables following the main stress (beautiful/dutiful). Where more than one word makes up one of the rhymed pair of sounds in a feminine or triple rhyme (dreamy/see me), this is called 'mosaic rhyme'. All the rhyming pairs

illustrated here are examples of 'full' or 'true' rhyme, a norm from which various other forms deviate. These include *rime riche*, in which the consonants preceding the stressed syllable also match (veil/vale); 'eye rhyme', in which spellings match but pronunciation does not (bough/through); half-rhyme, in which the stressed vowel sounds do not match but the consonants (and sometimes unstressed syllables) coming after them do (love/have, lover/never); and pararhyme, a 'rich' version of half-rhyme in which stressed vowel sounds again fail to correspond while the preceding consonants as well as those following do (grieve/grave).

The ordered pattern in which rhyming sounds recur at the line-endings of a *stanza or poem is called the rhyme scheme, this being conventionally represented by alphabetical notation whereby each line-ending is allotted a letter in order, the same letter being allotted to all the lines that rhyme with it: thus a quatrain with two alternate rhymes has the rhyme scheme *abab*, while the rhyme scheme of Shakespeare's *sonnets is *ababcdcdefefgg*.

Rhyme is not essential to English poetry, and in the Old English and much of the Middle English periods was either an incidental device in *alliterative verse or a minor tradition subordinate to it. Rhyming poems appear with greater frequency after the Norman Conquest, as with *The *Owl and the Nightingale*, but they become the standard only in *Chaucer's work and thereafter. Chaucer made rhyming easier for himself by concluding many lines with French-derived words ending in '-esse', '-age', '-aunce', etc. Rhyming is generally harder in English than in French, but nonetheless rhymes have been found for most English words apart from 'month', 'orange', and a handful of others. Non-standard forms of rhyming such as pararhyme and half-rhyme were unusual until the early 20th century, when W. B. *Yeats, Wilfred *Owen, W. H. *Auden, Dylan *Thomas, and many others adopted them regularly.

rhyme (rime) royal A seven-line *stanza form of iambic *pentameter, rhyming *ababbcc*, used for narrative poetry from Chaucer (*Troilus and Criseyde*) to William *Morris.

Rhymers Club A group of poets that met at the Cheshire Cheese in Fleet Street for several years, from 1890, to read and discuss each other's poetry. The group was augmented in 1891 through association with Herbert Horne's artists' community at Fitzroy Street. Members and associates included W. B. *Yeats, Ernest *Rhys, Richard *Le Gallienne, Ernest *Dowson,

Lionel *Johnson, and Arthur *Symons. It published two collections of verse, 1892 and 1894.

Rhyming Poem, The An Old English poem from the *Exeter Book, therefore no later than the 10th century. The two halves of its alliterating lines rhyme (an occasional feature in later Old English poetry). It contrasts the misfortunes of a fallen king with his past glory, a common Boethian, elegiac theme in Old English. It may be a paraphrase of Job 29 and 30.

Rhyming Weavers A loose generic term for the Ulster *Scots poets of the late 18th and early 19th centuries, some of whom worked in the linen industry. They often thought of themselves as simultaneously Irish and Scottish, referring to Ireland as 'Eirlan'. Verse in Scots reflecting the impact of Allan *Ramsay's anthologies was published in broadsheets, newspapers, and other media in Ulster from the 1750s but greatly increased in quantity towards the end of the century in response to the popularity of Robert *Burns. The work of Samuel Thomson (1766–1816) and James Orr (1770–1816) is individual and sophisticated.

RHYS, Ernest (1859–1946) Editor, journalist, and poet; he helped found the *Rhymers Club and supplied an important Welsh dimension to the early Celtic enthusiasms of W. B. *Yeats. Rhys is chiefly remembered for his role in setting up and sustaining the Everyman's Library. *Everyman Remembers* (1931) provides a lively portrait of literary London over five decades.

RHYS, Jean (Ella Gwendolen Rees Williams) (1890–1979) Novelist, born in Dominica, the daughter of a Welsh doctor. She came to England in 1907, but left in 1919 and remained abroad for many years, living mainly in Paris. *The Left Bank: Sketches and Studies of Present-Day Bohemian Paris* appeared in 1927 with an introduction by Ford Madox *Ford, who became her lover and whom she portrayed as the predatory H. J. Heidler in *Postures* (1928; repr. 1969 under its American title, *Quartet*). The figure who came to be known as 'the Jean Rhys Woman'—lonely, impoverished, drinking too much, a prey to untrustworthy men—recurs in *After Leaving Mr Mackenzie* (1930) and *Good Morning, Midnight* (1939). A long silence followed this last novel, during which Rhys returned to England, living quietly in the West Country, until a radio adaptation of *Good Morning, Midnight* in 1958 brought her back to public attention. In 1966 she produced a new novel, *Wide Sargasso Sea*. A poetic, dreamlike

narrative set in Dominica and Jamaica during the 1830s, it describes the early life and marriage of Antoinette Cosway, a Creole heiress who becomes the mad Mrs Rochester in *Jane Eyre*. She subsequently published two collections of short stories, *Tigers Are Better Looking* (1968) and *Sleep It Off, Lady* (1976), set largely among the desperate and dispossessed. *Smile Please* (1979) is an unfinished autobiography.

Rhythm (1911–13) Superseded in 1913 by the *Blue Review*, a periodical edited by J. M. *Murry, with Michael Sadleir and Katherine *Mansfield. Murry conceived it as '*The *Yellow Book* of the modern movement', and it published work by D. H. *Lawrence, Mansfield, Ford Madox *Ford, Pablo Picasso, Henri *Gaudier-Brzeska, and others.

(()) SEE WEB LINKS

• Modernist Journals Project

RICE, Anne (1941–) American novelist. Her 'Vampire Chronicles', beginning with *Interview with the Vampire* (1976), highlighted the sexual undercurrents of the vampire mythos. Following her return to the Roman Catholic faith of her youth, she began a fictionalized biography of Jesus with *Christ the Lord: Out of Egypt* (2005). *See also* VAMPIRES IN LITERATURE.

RICE, Elmer (1892–1967) American dramatist, born Elmer Reizenstein in New York. His first major play was the expressionist drama *The Adding Machine* (1923), which satirized increasing regimentation and mechanization through the posthumous adventures of Mr Zero, a book-keeper. His plays of the 1930s (*We, the People*, 1933; *Judgment Day*, 1934; *Between Two Worlds*, 1934) are a response to the Depression and international ideological conflict. Rice was a campaigner for social justice and an outspoken critic of censorship. *Minority Report* (1963) is a memoir.

RICH, Adrienne (1929–2012) American poet, essayist, and critic. Her third collection, *Snapshots of a Daughter in Law* (1956), shows her characteristic, fractured, free verse, frequently in lengthy sequences. Rich's volumes through the 1960s, 1970s, and 1980s keep pace with her own increasing politicization and involvement with first the anti-war movement, and then lesbian/feminist politics. *Diving into the Wreck* (1971) and *The Dream of a Common Language* (1978) are outstanding collections, while *The Fact of a Doorframe: Poems Selected and New, 1950–1984* presents much of her most achieved work. Rich's essays, particularly

Compulsory Heterosexuality and Lesbian Existence (1981), have been seminal for her generation of feminists. *Poetry and Commitment* (2007) examines the cultural status of poetry.

RICH, Barnaby (1542–1617) Soldier and writer. From 1574 he turned to literature, writing romances in the style of John *Lyly's *Euphues*, *pamphlets, and reminiscences. From 1587 he received a pension. His best-known romance is *Rich, his Farewell to Military Profession* (1581), which includes 'Apolonius and Silla', the source of *Shakespeare's *Twelfth Night*.

RICHARD I (1157–99) 'Cœur de Lion', king of England 1189–99, was one of the leaders of the Third Crusade and became a romantic figure in England (in the *Robin Hood legends, for instance, and in Walter Scott's The *Talisman and *Ivanhoe), in spite of the fact that only six months of his ten-year reign were spent in England. For the Middle English verse romance see *Richard Cœur de Lion*.

Richard II, King A historical tragedy by *Shakespeare, probably written and acted 1595, printed 1597. After the death of *Elizabeth I a fourth quarto was issued in 1608, which contained the first appearance in print of the deposition scene (IV. i. 154–318), probably previously suppressed because of the politically contentious subject of the queen's succession, upon which it could be taken to reflect. Shakespeare's main source was the *Chronicles* of *Holinshed, but he appears possibly to have known the anonymous play about Richard II called *Woodstock*, and to have drawn on Samuel *Daniel's narrative poem The *Civil Wars*.

The play begins with the quarrel between Henry Bolingbroke, son of John of Gaunt, and Thomas Mowbray, duke of Norfolk, which King Richard resolves arbitrarily by exiling Mowbray for life and Bolingbroke for ten years. When John of Gaunt dies Richard confiscates his property to pay for his Irish wars, for which he leaves the country. Bolingbroke returns to claim his inheritance and takes Berkeley Castle, which the duke of York has as regent to yield him. The king returns to Wales, hears that his Welsh supporters have deserted him and that Bolingbroke has executed the king's favourites Bushy and Green. Accompanied by York's son Aumerle, he withdraws to Flint Castle, where Bolingbroke accepts his surrender. The first half of the play ends with a discussion between a gardener and Richard's queen about the government of the garden-state and the possibility of the king's deposition (III. iv).

In London Richard relinquishes his crown to Bolingbroke, who sends him to the Tower. The earls of Carlisle and Aumerle plot to kill Bolingbroke, who has now proclaimed himself Henry IV, but are foiled by York. Richard is transferred to Pomfret Castle, where he hears of Henry's coronation and is murdered by Sir Piers Exton.

Richard II, like *1 *Henry VI* and *King John*, is written entirely in verse.

Richard III, King A historical tragedy by *Shakespeare, probably written and performed 1592–3. It was first published in a quarto in 1597. The play's chief sources are the chronicles of Raphael *Holinshed and Edward *Hall which contained material from Polydore *Vergil's *Anglicae Historiae* and Sir Thomas More's The *History of King *Richard the Third*.

The play completes the tetralogy whose first three parts are the *Henry VI* plays. It centres on the character of Richard of Gloucester, afterwards King Richard III, ambitious and bloody, bold and subtle, treacherous, yet brave in battle, a murderer, and usurper of the crown. The play begins with the deformed Richard's announcement: 'Now is the winter of our discontent | Made glorious summer by this son of York', that is the king, Edward IV, who is dying. Richard, determined to succeed to the throne, sets out to eliminate any opposition and secure his position. He has his brother the duke of Clarence, who has been imprisoned in the Tower, murdered. As she accompanies the corpse of her dead father-in-law Henry VI, Anne, the widow of Edward, prince of Wales, is wooed by Richard, and they are later married.

When the king dies Richard begins his attack on the queen's family and supporters, helped by the duke of Buckingham. Hastings, Rivers, and Gray are all executed, and Buckingham persuades the citizens of London to proclaim Richard king. After his coronation he murders his nephews, the princes in the Tower, and following the death of his wife Anne, which he hastens, tries to marry his niece, Elizabeth of York. However, Buckingham rebels and goes to join Henry Tudor, earl of Richmond, who has landed in Wales at Milford Haven to claim the crown. Buckingham is captured and Richard has him executed, but he must now face Richmond's army at Bosworth. On the night before the battle the ghosts of those murdered by Richard appear to him and foretell his defeat. In the battle the next day he loses his horse and is killed by Richmond, who is then proclaimed Henry VII, the first of the Tudor monarchs.

Richard Cœur de Lion A romance in 7,136 lines of short couplets dating from the early 14th century, which may be by the same writer as *Of *Arthour and of Merlin* and **King Alisaunder*. The writer says he is taking his poem from a French source, but it is marked by spirited English patriotism and contempt for the French King Philip. It is assumed that the source is Anglo-Norman, dating from about 1230–50. The poem describes the defeat of the Saracens in the course of the Third Crusade and breaks off, unfinished, when a three-year truce is arranged.

RICHARDS, Frank Pseudonym of Charles *Hamilton.

RICHARDS, I. A. (Ivor Armstrong) (1893–1979) Rhetorician, one of the first lecturers in English at Cambridge (1919–29), where he wrote his best-known work, *Principles of Literary Criticism* (1924), *Science and Poetry* (1926), and *Practical Criticism: A Study of Literary Judgement* (1929). The last of these helped to establish *practical criticism as a central feature of literary education; while the first two proposed that poetry promotes vital kinds of psychological flexibility, in part because it offers 'pseudo-statements' rather than true or false propositions. This decoupling of literature from 'belief' proved controversial, and was resisted by his friend T. S. *Eliot, among others. Richards's attacks on vagueness, sentimentality, and laziness in poets and readers, and his praise of irony ('a characteristic of poetry of the highest order'), ambiguity, complexity, and allusiveness, did much to create the climate which accepted *modernism, and greatly influenced William *Empson, F. R. *Leavis, and the American *New Critics. His last specifically literary book was *Coleridge on Imagination* (1934).

RICHARDSON, Dorothy Miller (1873–1957) Novelist; she became an intimate friend of H. G. *Wells and other avant-garde thinkers of the day, who encouraged her to write. *Pointed Roofs*, (1915) was the first of a sequence of thirteen highly autobiographical novels entitled *Pilgrimage*. She pioneered the *stream-of-consciousness technique—May *Sinclair imported the term from psychology to describe Richardson's work—narrating the action through the mind of her heroine Miriam. She argued for an unpunctuated 'feminine prose', and Virginia *Woolf, reviewing *Revolving Lights* in 1923, credited her with inventing 'the psychological sentence of the feminine gender'. *Pilgrimage* was also innovative in the open-endedness of its narrative; the final volume,

March Moonlight, did not appear in Richardson's lifetime, being published only in 1967. She also wrote on cinema for *Close-Up*, and wrote short fiction. *Pilgrimage* was reissued in 1979 in four volumes by the *Virago Press.

RICHARDSON, Henry Handel (1870–1946) Pen-name of Ethel Florence Lindesay Richardson, Australian novelist who lived her adult life in Germany then England. Her first novel, *Maurice Guest* (1908), is an unconventional tale of *grande passion* set in Leipzig, while her second and most economical, *The Getting of Wisdom* (1910) reflects her school experience. Richardson's most ambitious work is *The Fortunes of Richard Mahony* (1930), initially published in three volumes: *Australia Felix* (1917), *The Way Home* (1925), and *Ultima Thule* (1929). Clearly based on the biography of her own parents, the epic story traces the attempts of its protagonist to find a psychological home between Britain and Australia. Later works include *The End of a Childhood and Other Stories* (1934), *Young Cosima* (based on the life of Cosima Wagner), and the autobiography, *Myself When Young* (1948), unfinished at her death.

RICHARDSON, Jonathan, the elder (1665–1745) British portrait painter, who also wrote about art, and the science of connoisseurship. His *Theory of Painting* (1715) was the first significant work on aesthetic theory by an English author; in the second edition, 1725, he added an influential essay on the *sublime. He had a wide circle of literary friends, amongst them Alexander *Pope, John *Gay, and Matthew *Prior, and with his son wrote a book *Explanatory Notes on Paradise Lost* (1734).

RICHARDSON, Samuel (1689–1761) Printer and novelist. He set up in business on his own in 1721, combining printing and publishing, and producing books, journals, advertisement posters, and other miscellaneous work. The inspiration for his first novel, *Pamela*, came from a series of 'familiar letters' which fellow printers had encouraged him to write on the concerns of everyday life; these were published separately as *Letters . . . to and for Particular Friends* (1741). *Pamela* was written between November 1739 and January 1740, and was published later in that year. The morality and realism of the work were much praised, but complaints about its impropriety persuaded him to revise his second edition considerably. In 1741 there appeared a riotously irreverent but astute parody called *An Apology for the Life of Mrs *Shamela Andrews*, which Richardson believed, probably correctly, to be by Henry *Fielding and which he never forgave. Fielding's *Joseph Andrews*, also begun as a parody of *Pamela*, appeared in 1742.

Richardson's business continued to prosper, despite poor health and occasional accusations of *Jacobite involvement. In 1733 he had begun printing for the House of Commons and in 1742 he secured the lucrative post of printer of its journals. His circle of friends now included many members of the *Blue Stocking circle. The first two volumes of *Clarissa* appeared in 1747 and were very favourably received. A further five volumes appeared in 1748. *Clarissa* was an undoubted success (even Fielding admired it) but there were complaints about both its length and its sexual content, and it was not reprinted as often as *Pamela*.

*Sir Charles *Grandison*, his final novel, published in seven volumes 1753–4, sold well and rapidly became fashionable, but was assailed in various critical pamphlets for its prolixity, tedium, improbability, and dubious morality. He published in 1755 *A Collection of the Moral and Instructive Sentiments . . . in the Histories of Pamela, Clarissa, and Sir Charles Grandison*, which he considered contained the essence of all his work.

All Richardson's novels were *epistolary, a form which he appreciated for its immediacy ('writing to the moment' as he called it). Richardson was acutely aware of the problems of prolixity and worked hard but somewhat ineffectually to prune his drafts. In Johnson's view, 'if you were to read Richardson for the story, your impatience would be so much fretted that you would hang yourself. But you must read him for the sentiment, and consider the story as only giving occasion to the sentiment'.

Richard the Third, The History of King

A history of the King's life by Sir Thomas *More, written in English and Latin and included in his *Works* (1557) and his *Omnia Opera* (1565). It is distinguished from earlier English chronicles by its unity of form and dramatic effectiveness. William *Shakespeare probably used More's work only as filtered through Edward *Hall and Raphael *Holinshed; it was More, however, who was ultimately responsible for the image of Richard as a *Machiavellian tyrant which Shakespeare transmits in *Richard III*. See also BIOGRAPHY.

RICHLER, Mordecai (1931–2001) Canadian novelist and screenwriter. His first novel, *The Acrobats* (1954), was followed by *The Apprenticeship of Duddy Kravitz* (1959), describing a Jewish boyhood in Montreal, which he adapted as an Oscar-nominated screenplay, *The Incomparable Atuk* (1963), a satire on popular culture, and *Cocksure* (1968), a ribald extravaganza set in theatrical London. *St Urbain's Horseman* (1971) is also set in 1960s London. *Joshua Then and Now*, a semi-autobiographical novel set in Montreal, was filmed by Ted Kotcheff in 1985. His other witty and irreverent novels include *Solomon Gursky Was Here* (1989): an ambitious epic which interweaves Jewish themes and Inuit folklore. *Barney's Version* (1997) recounts the unreliable and outrageous memories of Barney Panofsky in Montreal, London, and Paris.

RICHMOND, Legh (1772–1827) An evangelical clergyman who lived in the Isle of Wight, and wrote highly successful pious tales, published between 1809 and 1814, including *The Dairyman's Daughter*, *The Young Cottager*, and *The Negro Slave*.

RICKETTS, Charles (1866–1931) English aesthete, illustrator, designer, and painter. His friends included Oscar *Wilde, John Gray, W. B. Yeats, G. B. *Shaw, 'Michael *Field' (Edith Cooper and Katherine Bradley), and Laurence *Binyon. Ricketts illustrated and designed many of Wilde's books; most beautiful are *A House of Pomegranates* (1891) and *The Sphinx* (1894). After Wilde's death he wrote a memoir of him, *Recollections of Oscar Wilde* (1932). With Charles Shannon (1865–1937), Ricketts edited *The *Dial* (1889–97). His Vale Press, founded in 1896, was one of the most important of the private presses. Later Ricketts worked as a stage designer; G. B. Shaw's *Saint Joan* (1924) was his most successful production. Ricketts designed and illustrated two of his own prose works, *Beyond the Threshold* (1929) and *Unrecorded Histories* (1933).

RICKS, Sir Christopher (1933–) Literary critic and scholar. His major scholarly achievement is the annotated *Poems of Tennyson* (1969). His critical writings, clearly influenced by William *Empson, have been notable for their close attention to the sounds, semantic nuances, and verbal echoes of poetry, often re-echoed in his own punning style of commentary. His principal critical works include *Milton's Grand Style* (1963), *Keats and Embarrassment* (1974), *The Force of Poetry* (1984), *T. S. Eliot and Prejudice* (1988), and *Beckett's Dying Words* (1993). He has frequently championed the merits of Bob *Dylan as a poet, notably in his book *Dylan's Visions of Sin* (2004).

RICKWORD, Edgell (1898–1982) Poet, critic, and radical. The literary periodical he edited from 1925 to 1927, the *Calendar of Modern Letters*, influenced the critical attitudes of F. R. *Leavis, as did the two volumes of criticism he edited under the title *Scrutinies* (1928, 1932). Rickword also edited the *Left Review* (1936–8), and *Our Time* (1944–7). *Essays and Opinions* (1921–51), edited by A. Young, appeared in 1974, and *Collected Poems* in 1976.

Riddle of the Sands, The *See* CHILDERS, ERSKINE.

RIDING, Laura (1901–91) American poet and critic, born Laura Reichenthal in New York, who lived and worked with Robert *Graves from 1927 until 1939. Her elliptical verses were brought together in *Collected Poems* (1938), but around 1941 she renounced poetry. Critical works include (with Graves) *A Survey of Modernist Poetry* (1927) and *Contemporaries and Snobs* (1928). A novel, *A Trojan Ending*, appeared in 1937, and *Lives of Wives*, on various marriages in history, in 1939.

RIDLEY, Philip (1967–) Playwright, novelist, artist, photographer, songwriter, poet, screenplay writer, and film director; he has been described as a 'one man cultural revolution'. Many of his novels are for children, including *Krindlekrax* (1991) and *Zip's Apollo* (2005), and he has also written stage work for young people. *The Pitchfork Disney* (1991), *The Fastest Clock in the Universe* (1992), and *Ghost from a Perfect Place* (1994) mix magic realism with the depiction of raw emotion. His screenplays include *The Krays* (1990) and *Heartless* (2010).

Rights of Man, The A political treatise by Thomas *Paine in two parts, published 1791 and 1792. Part I is a reply to Edmund *Burke's *Reflections on the Revolution in France*; Paine denies that one generation can bind another as regards the form of government, and argues that the constitution of a country is an act of the people constituting the government. He traces the incidents of the French Revolution up to the adoption of the Declaration of the Rights of Man by the National Assembly, and criticizes Burke's account of these incidents as over-emotional and inaccurate. Part II compares the new French and American constitutions with those of British institutions, to the disadvantage of the latter. The work also contains Paine's far-sighted proposals for family allowances, maternity grants, and tax reform.

RILEY, Denise (1948–) Poet, *Marxism for Infants* (1977) was followed by *Dry Air* (1985), *Stair Spirit* (1982), and *Mop Mop Georgette* (1993): all were small press publications. A *Selected Poems* was published in 2000. Riley's prose, ranging from *War in the Nursery: Theories of the Child and Mother* (1983) to *Impersonal Passion: Language as Affect* (2005), includes work in feminist, psychoanalytical, and linguistic theory. Her challenging poetry characteristically slips between matters of philosophical and linguistic moment, reworkings of mythology, sudden plangencies associated with desire and death, political inspection and reproach, and a warily feminist delight in popular culture, particularly the pop music of the early 1960s.

RILEY, Joan (1958–) Born in Jamaica, moving to Britain as an adolescent. Her novels *The Unbelonging* (1985), *Waiting in the Twilight* (1987), and *Romance* (1988) focus on girls' and women's experience of migration and exile. *A Kindness to the Children* (1992) is a collection of short stories.

RIMBAUD, Arthur (1854–91) French poet. By the age of 17 he had written his most famous poem, 'Le Bateau ivre' ('The Drunken Boat'), which Samuel *Beckett translated in 1932. Between 1871 and 1873—the period of his association with Paul *Verlaine and his sojourns in England—he undertook a programme of 'disorientation of the senses' in order to try to turn himself into a *voyant*, or seer. Two collections of prose poems, *Les Illuminations* and *Une saison en enfer* (*A Season in Hell*), explore the visionary possibilities of this experiment. By the time he was 19, his poetic career was over.

Rime of the Ancient Mariner, The *See* ANCIENT MARINER, THE RIME OF THE.

Rimini, The Story of *See* STORY OF RIMINI, THE.

RINEHART, Mary Roberts (1876–1958) American author of mystery fiction, who published her first novel, *The Circular Staircase*, in 1908. Her use of a country-house setting here and elsewhere in her numerous works spanning the period 1908–53 earned her the sobriquet of the 'American Agatha *Christie'.

Ring and the Book, The A poem in blank verse, in twelve books by Robert *Browning, published in four monthly instalments November 1868–February 1869. The poem established Browning's contemporary reputation. The 'Ring' of the title is a figure for the process by which the artist transmutes the 'pure crude fact' of historical events into living forms; the 'Book' is a collection of documents relating to the Italian murder trial of the late 17th century on which the poem is based.

The story in bare outline is as follows. Pietro and Violante Comparini were a middle-aged childless couple living in Rome. Their income could only be secured after Pietro's death if they had a child; so Violante bought the child of a prostitute and passed it off as her own. This child, Pompilia, was eventually married to Count Guido Franceschini, an impoverished nobleman from Arezzo. The marriage was unhappy, and the Comparini, disappointed by life in Arezzo, returned to Rome, where they sued Guido for the restoration of Pompilia's dowry on the grounds of her illegitimacy, which Violante now revealed. Pompilia herself eventually fled from Arezzo in the company of a young priest, Giuseppe Caponsacchi. Guido pursued them and had them arrested on the outskirts of Rome; as a result, Caponsacchi was exiled to Civita Vecchia for three years, and Pompilia was sent to a convent while the lawsuits were decided. But then, because she was pregnant, she was released into the custody of the Comparini. A fortnight after the birth of her child, Guido and four accomplices murdered her and her putative parents. They were arrested and tried for the murder.

In Browning's poem, the story is told by a succession of speakers—citizens of Rome, the participants themselves, the lawyers, and the pope—each of whose single, insufficient perceptions combines with the others to form, it may be, the 'ring' of the truth. This design represents Browning's response to a number of pressing concerns in his own creative life, and to John Stuart *Mill's liberal conviction that truth will be established by debate.

RIORDAN, Maurice (1953–) London-based Irish poet. His poems reflect an interest in science and anthropology and bring a detached tone and fastidious eye for detail to their presentations of domestic situations. He has published *A Word from the Loki* (1995) and *Floods* (2000), which opens with the bravura archaeological meditation 'The Sloe'. His third collection, *The Holy Land* (2007) is a wry memorial to Riordan's farmer father.

'Rip Van Winkle' A story by Washington *Irving published in *The Sketch Book* (1820). Rip Van Winkle, taking refuge from a nagging wife in a solitary ramble in the Catskill mountains, falls asleep, and wakes after twenty years, to find his wife dead, his house in ruins, and the world completely changed.

RITCHIE, Anne Isabella Thackeray, Lady (1837–1919) Novelist, memoir writer, and biographer of her father W. M. *Thackeray. She grew up in France; her mother suffered post-natal depression which became prolonged mental illness. Her younger sister Minny, who died in 1875, was the first wife of Leslie *Stephen, and she was thus aunt to Virginia *Woolf, as well as a good friend of Woolf's mother, Julia Stephen. Woolf drew a portrait of her in *Night and Day* as 'Mrs Hilbery'. Her novels include the impressionistic *Old Kensington* (1873) and *From an Island* (1877). *Five Old Friends and a Young Prince* (1868) and *Bluebeard's Keys* (1874) are collections of modern fairy stories. She also wrote reminiscences of the literary figures she had known in her youth: *Records of Tennyson, Ruskin and Robert and Elizabeth Browning* (1892) and *Chapters from Some Memoirs* (1894), among others.

RITSON, Joseph (1752–1803) Antiquary. An implacable advocate of textual fidelity in the editing of early texts, he challenged Thomas *Warton's *History of English Poetry* (1782) and also Samuel *Johnson's and George *Steevens's edition of Shakespeare. In 1783 he published *A Select Collection of English Songs*, in which he accused Thomas *Percy of falsifying the texts in his *Reliques. In 1795 appeared his *Robin Hood: A Collection of All the Ancient Poems, Songs and Ballads Now Extant Relative to That Outlaw*, with illustrations by Thomas *Bewick. Ritson's *Ancient English Metrical Romances* appeared in 1802. He also published collections of songs, children's verses, and *fairy stories, and advised Scott on his *Minstrelsy of the Scottish Border. In later life he became a fanatical vegetarian (his diet was originally inspired by reading Bernard *Mandeville), and finally insane.

Rival Queens, The, or *The Death of Alexander the Great* A tragedy by Nathaniel *Lee, founded on the *Cassandre* of La Calprenède, produced 1677.

Rivals, The A comedy by R. B. *Sheridan, produced 1775, his first play. Captain Absolute, son of Sir Anthony Absolute, is in love with Lydia Languish, the niece of Mrs Malaprop (whose comic verbal mistakes have given rise to the term 'malapropism'). As he knows the romantic Lydia prefers a poor half-pay lieutenant to the heir of a baronet, he has assumed the character of Ensign Beverley, and is favourably received. But Lydia will lose half her fortune if she marries without her aunt's consent, and Mrs Malaprop will not approve of a low-ranking soldier, especially after Sir Anthony arrives in Bath to propose a match between his son and Lydia, a proposal Mrs Malaprop welcomes. Captain Absolute is now afraid of revealing his deception to Lydia in case he loses her; while Bob Acres, who is also Lydia's suitor and has heard of Beverley's courtship, is provoked by the fiery Irishman Sir Lucius O'Trigger to ask Captain Absolute to carry a challenge to Beverley. Sir Lucius himself, who has been deluded into thinking that some love letters received by him from Mrs Malaprop are really from Lydia, likewise finds Captain Absolute in his path, and challenges him. But when Acres finds that Beverley is in fact his friend Absolute, he declines the duel and resigns all claim to Lydia: Sir Lucius' misapprehension is removed by the arrival of Mrs Malaprop, and Lydia, after a pretty quarrel with her lover for shattering her hopes of a romantic elopement, forgives him.

Road to Oxiana, The See BYRON, ROBERT.

Roaring Girl, The, or Moll Cut-Purse A comedy by Thomas *Middleton and Thomas *Dekker, written and acted about 1611. In this play Moll Cutpurse, a notorious thief in real life, is portrayed as an honest girl, who helps lovers and defends herself with her sword. Sebastian Wentgrave loves and is betrothed to Mary Fitzallard, but his grasping father forbids the match. Sebastian pretends he has fallen desperately in love with Moll Cutpurse and is about to marry her; Moll good-naturedly cooperates. Old Wentgrave, appalled, is only too glad to give his blessing when the real bride turns out to be Mary Fitzallard.

ROBBINS, Tom (1936–) American novelist, who devised his writing style while reporting on a Doors concert in 1967; his fiction, including the novels *Even Cowgirls Get the Blues* (1976), *Skinny Legs and All* (1990), and *B is for Beer* (2009), has been linked to the *Beats.

Robene and Makyne A pastoral by Robert *Henryson, on the model of the French *pastourelle*, included in Thomas Percy's *Reliques*. Robene, a shepherd, is loved by Makyne (a form of Malkin, diminutive of Matilda, which seems to have been a stereotypical name for an unattractive woman: see *Piers Plowman* B I. 184).

Robert Elsmere A novel by Mary Augusta *Ward (Mrs Humphry Ward), published in 1888. It tells the story of an idealistic young clergyman, Robert Elsmere, who loses his Anglican faith as a result of his encounters with the cynical squire Roger Wendover, and the rationalist works he recommends. Despite the distress of his devout wife Catherine, Robert abandons the supernatural elements of religion, resigns his orders, and adopts an ethical approach to his calling, emphasizing practical work among the poor and ignorant. His arduous labours bring his life to a premature end, after a reconciliation with his wife. The best-selling novel of ideas of the 19th century, it sold more than a million copies, and its ideas were widely debated.

ROBERTS, Lynette (1909–95) Poet, who wrote much of her work in the 1940s in the remote village of Llanybri, Carmarthenshire. *Poems* (1944) and the book-length sequence *Gods with Stainless Ears* (1951), a wartime meditation remarkable for its use of arcane, *defamiliarizing diction, were published with the encouragement of T. S. *Eliot. See *Collected Poems*, ed. P. McGuinness (2005); *Diaries, Letters and Recollections* (2007).

ROBERTS, Michael (1902–48) Poet, critic, and editor. His anthologies *New Signatures* (1932), *New Country* (1933), and *The *Faber Book of Modern Verse* (1936) helped shape the *modernist canon. His own poetry, influenced by T. S. *Eliot, Herbert *Read, and Hart *Crane, drew on his love of mountaineering and his knowledge of science. *The Estate of Man* (1951), written 1947–8, issued a then unfashionable warning about the devastation of the earth's resources.

ROBERTS, Michèle (1949–) Novelist and poet; she was poetry editor of the magazine *Spare Rib* from 1975 to 1977 and her first novel, *A Piece of the Night* (1978), was the first original fiction published by the Women's Press. Other novels include *The Wild Girl* (1984), *The Book of Mrs Noah* (1987), *Daughters of the House* (1992), *Impossible Saints* (1997), *Fair Exchange* (1999), which reworks episodes from the lives of William *Wordsworth and Mary *Wollstonecraft, *The Mistressclass* (2003), and *Reader, I Married Him* (2005). *During Mother's Absence* (1993) and *Playing Sardines* (2001) are volumes of short stories. Her poetry includes *The Mirror of the Mother* (1986), and *All the Selves I Was* (1995); *Paper Houses* (2007) is a memoir of the 1970s.

ROBERT THE DEVIL Sixth duke of Normandy and father of William the Conqueror, legendary for his violence and cruelty. In *The Life of Robert the Devil*, Robert is represented as having been devoted to Satan by his mother, but as repenting and marrying the emperor's daughter (he in fact died on a pilgrimage to Palestine). This verse tale, printed c.1500 by Wynkyn de *Worde, is a translation from French. Thomas *Lodge wrote a prose version.

Robin Hood A legendary outlaw. 'Robertus Hood fugitivus' is mentioned in the portion of the Pipe Roll of 1230 relating to Yorkshire. He is mentioned in *Piers Plowman. As a historical character he appears in The Orygynale Cronykil (c.1420) by the historian Andrew Wyntoun (c.1350–c.1422), and is referred to as a ballad hero by Abbot Bower (d. 1449), John Mair and John *Stow. The first detailed history, Lytell Geste of Robyn Hode (printed c.1500), locates him in south-west Yorkshire; later writers place him in Sherwood and Plumpton Park (Cumberland), and finally make him earl of Huntingdon. Joseph *Ritson, who collected the ancient songs and ballads about him, says that he was born at Locksley, Nottinghamshire, c.1160, that his name was Robert Fitz-Ooth, and that he was reputed to have been earl of Huntingdon. There is an account of the activities of his band in Michael *Drayton's *Poly-Olbion, song 26. According to Stow, there were c.1190 many robbers and outlaws, among whom were Robin Hood and Little John, who lived in the woods, robbed the rich, killed only in self-defence, allowed no woman to be molested, and spared poor men's goods. Martin Parker (True Tale, c.1632) and the antiquary Ralph Thoresby (1658–1725) dated his death as 18 November 1247 and William Stukeley supplied his pedigree. Legend claims that he was bled to death by a treacherous nun at Kirklees, Yorkshire. He is the centre of a cycle of ballads, one of the best of which is Robin Hood and Guy of Gisborne, printed in Thomas *Percy's *Reliques. Popular plays embodying the legend appear to have developed out of the village May Day Game, Robin and *Maid Marian replacing the king and queen of May. Works on this theme were written by Anthony *Munday, Henry *Chettle, Alfred *Tennyson, and others. The True Tale of Robbin Hood was published c.1632, Robin Hood's Garland in 1670, and a prose narrative in 1678.

ROBINSON, E. A. (Edwin Arlington) (1869–1935) American poet. His admiration for Thomas *Hardy, George *Crabbe, and Robert *Browning is manifest in his many volumes of poetry about New England life, beginning with The Torrent and the Night Before (1896) and The Children of the Night (1897). As well as New England character sketches, he also wrote several long blank verse narratives, including an Arthurian trilogy (Merlin, 1917; Lancelot, 1920; Tristram, 1927) and The Man Who Died Twice (1924), a tale of genius destroyed.

ROBINSON, Henry Crabb (1775–1867) Diarist and journalist. He became a barrister, but is chiefly remembered for his diaries (over 30 volumes), reading-lists, and letters, first collected in 1869, which provide valuable information about the writers and events of his time. He was the friend of William *Wordsworth, S. T. *Coleridge, Charles *Lamb, William *Hazlitt, and later Thomas *Carlyle, and because of his indefatigable attendance at public lectures was able to provide useful descriptions of the lecturing of Coleridge (with his 'immethodical rhapsody'), Hazlitt, and others. He was an admirer of *Goethe, and did much to popularize German culture in England.

ROBINSON, Marilynne (1943–) American novelist. Housekeeping (1981, filmed 1987 dir. Bill Forsyth), about an unconventional household of women in Robinson's native Idaho, is narrated by the orphaned Ruth and luminously describes the neighbourhood of Fingerbone, its great lake, and the railroad bridge which carries trains and several of the novel's main characters across or into its depths. It was followed after more than two decades by the companion novels Gilead (2004, Pulitzer Prize) and Home (2008). Their setting, in small-town Iowa, and subject matter, two neighbouring preachers and their families, reflect aspects of the author's life and theological concerns as a Congregationalist and occasional preacher. Her non-fiction includes Absence of Mind (2010) on the debate between religion and science.

ROBINSON, Mary (1757/8–1800) Née Darby, poet, novelist, and actress. In 1774 she married Thomas Robinson, who incurred debts and was committed to debtors' prison. There, still not yet 20, she published a volume of Poems (1775). After her husband's release from jail she became a principal at Drury Lane, notably in a famous 1779 production of The *Winter's Tale. In the same year she became mistress of the prince of Wales (later George IV) who styled himself Florizel to her Perdita. She was a key member of the *Della Cruscan poetic coterie and wrote Modern Manners (1793), *Sappho and Phaon (1796), and several novels, such as the popular *Vancenza (1792) and The Natural Daughter (1799). Her poetry was admired by S. T. *Coleridge and her Lyrical Tales (1800) were influenced by the *Lyrical Ballads. Her daughter edited her *Memoirs, with Some Post-humous Pieces* (1801) and her *Poetical Works* (1806).

ROBINSON, Mary (later **Darmesteter,** later **Duclaux**) (1857–1944) Poet, her literary circle included Vernon *Lee, John Addington *Symonds, and Dante Gabriel *Rossetti. She gathered her many volumes of verse into *Collected Poems* in 1901, but continued to write. Her last volume, *Images and Meditations* (1923), was a meditation on the First World War.

Robinson Crusoe, The Life and Strange and Surprizing Adventures of A novel by Daniel *Defoe, published 1719. The story was in part inspired by the adventures of Alexander *Selkirk, who had joined a privateering expedition under William *Dampier, and in 1704 was put ashore after a quarrel on one of the uninhabited islands of the Juan Fernández archipelago. He was rescued in 1709 by Woodes Rogers (1679–1732). The story was told by Richard *Steele in *The Englishman* (1713), and elsewhere. Defoe's novel (told, like all his novels, in the first person, and presented as a true story) is vastly more vivid, detailed, and psychologically powerful, giving an extraordinarily convincing account of the shipwrecked Crusoe's efforts to survive in isolation. With the help of a few stores and utensils saved from the wreck and the dedicated exercise of labour and ingenuity, Crusoe builds himself a refuge, maps the island, domesticates goats, sows crops, and constructs a boat. Suffering from dreams and illness, he struggles to accept the workings of Providence, and has disturbing encounters with cannibals from other islands, from whom he rescues the man he later names 'Friday'. After 28 years, an English ship with a mutinous crew arrives; by some delicate management Crusoe subdues the mutineers, and returns, finally prosperous, to Britain. In *The Farther Adventures of Robinson Crusoe* (1719), Crusoe revisits his island, is attacked by a fleet of canoes on his departure, and loses Friday in the encounter. *Serious Reflections . . . of Robinson Crusoe . . . with his Vision of the Angelick World*, offering a pious and allegorical interpretation of the adventures, appeared in 1720. The influence of the *Robinson Crusoe* story has been enormous. The book had immediate success; it was pirated, adapted, and abridged in *chapbooks, translated into many languages, and inspired many imitations, known generically as 'Robinsonnades', including *Philip Quarll*, *Peter Wilkins*, and *The *Swiss Family Robinson*. It has also inspired many artists and film-makers. More recently it has been seen as an apologia for, or an ironic critique of, economic individualism, capitalism, and imperialism; a study in alienation; and an allegorical spiritual autobiography.

Robinsonnades A group of primarily children's island adventure stories originating in Daniel Defoe's *Robinson Crusoe*. Best known are *The *Swiss Family Robinson* (1812–13), Frederick *Marryat's *Masterman Ready* (1841–2), Ballantyne's *The *Coral Island* (1857), Robert Louis *Stevenson's *Treasure Island* (1881), J. M. Barrie's *Peter Pan* (1904), and William *Golding's *The Lord of the Flies* (1954).

Rob Roy A novel by Walter *Scott, published 1817. The novel, set in the period preceding the first Jacobite rebellion (1715), portrays the rise of a prosperous Whig mercantile class, personified by Francis Osbaldistone and Bailie Nicol Jarvie, over the fox-hunting, Tory world of Osbaldistone Hall, ruled by Francis's elder brother Sir Hildebrand. Francis's son Frank, on refusing to enter his father's business, is exiled to Osbaldistone Hall; in exchange, his father decides to give his youngest nephew Rashleigh the place designed for his son. The plot is complicated by Frank's and Rashleigh's rival interest in their cousin Diana Vernon, one of Scott's most vivid heroines. Rashleigh is entangled in plans for the forthcoming rebellion and uses his place in the firm to rob and ruin Francis. Frank, attempting to save his father's credit, goes to Scotland to seek the help of the firm's Scottish correspondent, Bailie Nicol Jarvie, the real hero of the novel. They search for Rob Roy in the Highlands. Jarvie's defence of the practical benefits to Scotland of the Union is set against a portrayal of the ignorance, brutality, and squalor of the Highlands which Scott is sometimes thought to romanticize. Rob Roy Macgregor does not appear until late in the novel. A historical figure and member of a proscribed clan, he has been driven by injustice to outlawry but is still capable of generosity. He is involved in Rashleigh's plans for the rebellion, but Frank needs his help to frustrate his cousin's designs. The rebellion fails, Rashleigh is killed by Rob Roy, and Frank inherits Osbaldistone Hall and marries Diana.

ROCHESTER, John Wilmot second earl of (1647–80) Lyric poet, satirist, and a leading member of the group of 'court wits' surrounding Charles II. At the age of 18 he romantically abducted the sought-after heiress Elizabeth Malet in a coach-and-six. Despite the resistance of her family, and after a delay of eighteen months, she married him. Subsequently his time was divided between periods of domesticity with Elizabeth and fashionable life in London with, among several mistresses, the brilliant actress Elizabeth Barry, and his riotous male friends, who included the earl of Dorset (Charles Sackville) and George Villiers, the second duke of *Buckingham. The wit and emotional complexity of Rochester's lyrics give him some claim to be considered one of the last important *metaphysical poets of the 17th century, and he was one of the first of the *Augustans, with his social and literary verse satires. He wrote more frankly about sex than anyone in English before the 20th century, and is one of the wittiest poets in the language. Andrew *Marvell admired him, John *Dryden, Jonathan *Swift, and Alexander *Pope were all influenced by him, and he has made an impression on many subsequent poets—*Goethe and Alfred *Tennyson, for example, and in modern Britain, William *Empson and Peter *Porter.

Roderick Hudson The first novel of Henry *James, published in 1876. It is the story of a young man transplanted from a lawyer's office in a Massachusetts town to a sculptor's studio in Rome. Incapable of adjustment to his environment, he fails in both art and love, and meets a tragic end in Switzerland.

Roderick Random, The Adventures of A novel by Tobias *Smollett, published 1748. Smollett's first novel, it is strongly influenced by *Lesage's *Gil Blas*, which Smollett translated the following year. In his preface the author declares his wish to arouse 'generous indignation . . . against the vicious disposition of the world'. Roderick, a Scot, is combative, often violent, but essentially innocent and genuine, capable of great affection and generosity. His father, on being disinherited, has left Scotland, leaving his young son penniless. His subsequent adventures, narrated in the first person, take him to London, where he is pressed as a common sailor aboard a man-of-war; to France, kidnapped by smugglers, where he joins the French army; and back to sea as surgeon on a ship under his uncle Tom Bowling's command; in the course of the voyage he meets Don Roderigo, who turns out to be his long-lost father, now a wealthy merchant. In a digression, Smollett inserts the story of Melopoyn, partly based on his own experience in trying to get his *The Regicide* accepted for the stage, and containing a character widely assumed to be a caricature of David *Garrick.

RODKER, John (1894–1955) Poet and publisher. His earliest works were published in the *New Age* (in 1912) and the *Egoist* (in 1914), and Rodker had privately published his first collection of poems in 1914. A conscientious objector, he was arrested and imprisoned during the First World War: he described his experiences in *Memoirs of Other Fronts* (published anonymously in 1932), and in the poem 'A CO's Biography'. He married Mary *Butts in 1918. He established the brief-lived Ovid Press, publishers of T. S. *Eliot's *Ara Vus Prec* (1920), Ezra *Pound's *Hugh Selwyn Mauberley* (1920), volumes of drawing by Edward Wadsworth and Wyndham *Lewis, and of his second volume of poems, *Hymns* (1920). His poetry draws on *imagism, but interweaves impersonal images with a more subjective and personal vocabulary. His poems, marked by neither D. H. *Lawrence's sexualized vitalism nor James *Joyce's fastidious detachment, speak from the indistinct territory between emotion, thought, and bodily sensation. The dominant emotion is fear. *Adolphe 1920* (1929), a phantasmagoric prose narrative, conveys a vivid sense of embodied mental life. See *Poems & Adolphe 1920*, ed. Andrew Crozier (1996).

ROETHKE, Theodore (1908–63) American poet. His first book of poems, *Open House* (1941), already displays characteristic imagery of vegetable growth and decay, rooted in childhood memories of the greenhouses of his father, who was a keen horticulturalist. It was followed by various volumes including *The Lost Son* (1948), *Praise to the End* (1951), a book of light verse (divided into 'Nonsense' and 'Greenhouse' poems) called *I Am! Says the Lamb* (1961), and a posthumous collection, *The Far Field* (1964).

ROGERS, Samuel (1763–1855) The son of a banker and himself a banker for some years, in his lifetime a highly successful poet, and well known as an art collector and for the celebrated 'breakfasts' which he held for over 40 years. In 1792 he published *The Pleasures of Memory*, in which the author wanders reflectively round the villages of his childhood. The work went into four editions in its first year, and by 1816 over 23,000 copies had been sold. He also published a fragmentary epic, *Columbus* (1810); *Jacqueline* (1814); *Italy* (1822–8), a collection of verse tales; and *Poems* (1832). His work was admired by Lord *Byron, who came to believe that only Rogers and George *Crabbe were free from 'a wrong revolutionary system'.

Roget's Thesaurus, of English Words and Phrases By Dr Peter Mark Roget (1779–1879), English physician and scholar, is a compilation of words classified in groups according to the ideas they express, the purpose of which is to supply a word, or words, which most aptly express a given idea; conversely, a dictionary explains the meaning of words by supplying the ideas they are meant to convey. The volume, first published in 1852, has been followed by many successive revised editions: by Roget's son John Lewis Roget (from 1879), and his grandson Samuel Romilly Roget (from 1933). The family connection came to an end with the death of Samuel Roget in 1953.

rogue literature A very popular type of writing about the underworld in the 16th and 17th centuries. Its practitioners include the Kentish landowner Thomas Harman (*fl.* 1547–67), whose *Caveat for Common Cursitors* first appeared in 1566; Robert Copland (*see* HIGH WAY TO THE SPITTLE HOUSE); Robert *Greene, whose *pamphlets describe 'coney-catching', that is, the deception of innocents; and Thomas *Dekker. Rogue literature is generally vividly descriptive and often allegedly confessional, providing an important source for our knowledge of everyday common life and its language, as well as for the language of thieves and beggars. It can be related to stories about *Robin Hood, *jest book literature, and early attempts at writing fiction and autobiography.

Rokeby A poem in six cantos by Walter *Scott, published 1813. The scene is laid chiefly at Rokeby in Yorkshire, immediately after the battle of Marston Moor (1644).

Roland The most famous of the *Paladins of Charlemagne. According to the chronicler Einhard, his legend has a factual basis. In August 778 the rearguard of the French army of Charlemagne was surprised in the valley of Roncevaux by the Basque inhabitants of the mountains; the baggage was looted and all the rearguard killed. In later poetic versions, the Saracens were substituted for the Basques, and Roland becomes the commander of the rearguard, appointed to the post at the instance of the traitor Ganelon, who is in league with the Saracen king Marsile. Roland's companion Oliver is introduced, the brother of Aude, Roland's betrothed. Oliver thrice urges Roland to summon aid by sounding his horn, but pride prevents him from doing so until too late. Charlemagne returns and destroys the pagan army. Ganelon is tried and executed.

The legend has been handed down in three principal forms: in the fabricated Latin chronicle of the 12th century mistakenly attributed to Archbishop Turpin (d. *c.*800); in the *Carmen de Proditione Guenonis* of the same epoch; and in the *Chanson de Roland*, in medieval French, also of the early 12th century. Roland, as Orlando, is the hero of Boiardo's **Orlando innamorato* and Ariosto's **Orlando furioso*. Roland's sword was called 'Durandal' or 'Durindana', and his horn 'Olivant'. *See* OLIVER.

ROLFE, Frederick William (1860–1913) Writer who styled himself 'Baron Corvo', or, equally misleadingly, Fr Rolfe, by turns schoolmaster, painter, and writer. From a Dissenting background, he was a convert to Roman Catholicism and an unsuccessful candidate for the priesthood. His most outstanding novel, *Hadrian the Seventh* (1904), combines autobiographical elements with wish-fulfilment, in which Rolfe's protagonist, George Arthur Rose, is rescued from a life of literary poverty and elected pope. His other writings include *Stories Toto Told Me* (published in 1898, after first appearing in the **Yellow Book*), *Chronicles of the House of Borgia* (1901), and *Don Tarquinio: A Kataleptic Phantasmatic Romance* (1905). Rolfe moved to Venice in 1908, and in his last work, *The Desire and Pursuit of the Whole: A Romance of Modern Venice* (written 1909, pub. 1934), he describes his poverty, his homoerotic fantasies, and the beauties of Venice, as well as abusing in characteristic vein many of those who had previously befriended him, including R. H. Benson (1871–1914). Rolfe's style is highly ornate and idiosyncratic; his vocabulary is arcane, his allusions erudite, and although he had admirers during his lifetime, he alienated most of them by his persistent paranoia and requests for financial support. The story of his unhappy life is told by A. J. *Symons in *The Quest for Corvo: An Experiment in Biography* (1934).

ROLLE, Richard of Hampole (*c.*1305/10–1349) One of the principal 14th-century English writers of religious prose and poetry. He became a hermit and lived at various places in Yorkshire, finally at Hampole where he died, near a Cistercian nunnery to which he was religious adviser. Among his disciples was Margaret Kirkby (d. 1391/4), who became an anchoress (i.e. a woman who withdraws from the world for religious reasons) and to whom a number of his major English works (notably the vernacular anchoritic manual *The Form of Living*) are addressed. He wrote in the Yorkshire dialect, in a highly rhetorical language which makes much use of alliteration. The essential element in his mysticism is personal enthusiasm. Among his best-known vernacular works are *Ego Dormio*, *The Commandment of Love*, and his translation of *The English Psalter*.

Rolls Series Otherwise *Chronicles and Memorials of Great Britain and Ireland from the Invasion of the Romans to the Reign of Henry VIII*. Their publication was authorized in 1847 at the suggestion of Joseph Stevenson, the archivist, and the recommendation of Sir John Romilly, master of the rolls, and it produced texts of many of the most important literary and historical writings of the Middle Ages and Renaissance.

roman à clef i.e. a 'novel with a key', in which the reader (or some readers) is intended to identify real people disguised more or less obviously as fictional characters. The key is sometimes literal, sometimes figurative, and sometimes provided by the author, as in the case of Delarivier *Manley's *The New Atalantis*, sometimes published separately by others, as in the case of Benjamin Disraeli's *Coningsby*. A modern example is *The Ghost* by Robert *Harris (2007), a thinly veiled novel about Tony Blair.

Roman Actor, The A tragedy by Philip *Massinger, acted 1626, printed 1629. The play is based on the life of the emperor Domitian as told by *Suetonius and Dio Cassius.

Roman Catholicism The beliefs and practices of the Roman Catholic Church. The spread of Islam in the 7th century overran all but two of the five patriarchates of the early Christian church (Alexandria, Antioch, Constantinople, Jerusalem, and Rome). Political and doctrinal tensions between the surviving claimants to Christian primacy, Constantinople and Rome, led to an enduring schism between the (Eastern or Greek) Orthodox Church and the (Western or Latin) Roman Catholic Church in 1054. The Church of Rome, however, has always maintained that, with papal authority deriving in direct succession from St Peter (Matthew 16: 18), it alone is the true apostolic and catholic church.

The Synod of Whitby in 664 determined that Celtic Christianity, originating in conversions during the Roman occupation of Britain, would henceforth adopt the Roman Catholic practices introduced by the mission of St Augustine in 597. From *Bede onward, Medieval English literature was Roman Catholic in its context, apparatus, and emphases, not only in devotional and homiletic texts but in its romances, in the *mystery cycles and *morality plays, and in its poetry. Within a generation of *Henry VIII's *Reformation, however, a virulent strain of anti-popery marked texts such as *The *Faerie Queene*. This was fuelled by the excommunication of *Elizabeth I by Pope Pius V in 1570 which, by releasing English Catholics from their allegiance, appeared to foster sedition, and by the Armada and the Gunpowder Plot. Hailing England as an elect Protestant nation, writers such as John *Bale, John *Foxe, and John *Milton took the pope to be Antichrist. In *Jacobean drama, Roman Catholics are commonly scheming Machiavellians. With the exception of Robert *Southwell, Richard *Crashaw, John *Dryden, and Alexander *Pope, not until after the emancipation of Roman Catholics from civil disadvantage in 1829 was a Roman Catholic allegiance and sensibility once more confidently to be articulated in English (by, for example, John Henry *Newman and Gerard Manley *Hopkins). *See* PROTESTANTISM.

romance [from the medieval Latin *romanice*, 'in a Romance language'] The Old French *roman*, derived from the phrase 'mettre en romanz', 'to translate into French', became synonymous with the popular courtly stories in verse on three traditional subjects: legends about Arthur; Charlemagne and his knights; and classical heroes (*see* MATTER). English equivalents, almost always translations, are found from the 13th century onwards. The best known include *King Horn*, *Havelok*, *Sir *Gawain and the Green Knight*, *Sir Orfeo* (*see* BRETON LAYS). From the 15th century, English romances are mostly in prose, and some 16th-century examples were the inspiration for Edmund *Spenser and *Shakespeare. A new interest in medieval romance (in writers such as Walter *Scott and John *Keats) contributed to the naming of 19th-century *Romanticism, though the term was also applied to some sentimental novels from the 18th century onwards, as in the *Mills and Boon romances of the modern era.

Roman de la Rose, Le The first 4,058 lines of this allegorical romance were written in *c.*1225–40 by Guillaume de Lorris to expound 'the whole art of love'; the remaining 17,622 lines were composed in *c.*1270–78 by Jean de Meun (d. 1305). The story in Guillaume's part of the poem is an allegorical presentation of *courtly love; the allegorical figures mostly embody various aspects of the lady whom the lover-narrator meets in his endeavours to reach the rose which symbolizes the lady's love. The story is set in the walled garden of the god of love, the unpleasant realities of life being depicted on the walls outside. In the second part Jean de Meun shows love in a wider context of scholarship, philosophy, and morals, shifting the work from the courtly to the encyclopedic literary tradition, in line with the rationalist and compendious spirit of the 13th century. The poem remained an immense literary influence all through the later Middle Ages. About one-third of the whole (ll. 1–5,154 and 10,679–12,360) is translated in the Middle English *Romaunt of the Rose*, the first part of which may be by *Chaucer.

roman-fleuve [French, 'river novel'] The term for a series of novels which follow the fortunes of a character or family and which thus give an account of a social period. Inspired by *Balzac and *Zola, the form reached its high point in the first half of the 20th century. Its major exemplars were: Romain Rolland (1866–1944); Roger Martin du Gard (1881–1958); Georges Duhamel (1884–1966); and Jules Romains (1885–1972). Translations of these works have been popular in England, but the English version of the phenomenon, descending from Anthony *Trollope and including such novelists as John *Galsworthy and C. P. *Snow, did not have the same impact.

romantic comedy *See* COMEDY.

romantic fiction A broad category of story, in which the trials and eventual triumphs of heterosexual love constitute the focus of narrative interest. *'Romance' is often used to designate medieval tales of courtly love written in the 'popular' languages derived from Latin, as opposed to *epic, which denotes narratives of heroism in the classical languages. Seventeenth-century prose fiction contains many stories of illicit love generally now thought of as romances, though there was often no clear distinction between romance and the emergent form of the *novel; Samuel *Richardson's novels, especially *Pamela* and *Clarissa*, may be said to fuse high aristocratic romance with the realistic world of the novel, presenting respectively comic and tragic versions of love and marriage. In *The Progress of Romance* (1785), Clara *Reeve differentiated the novel, which deals in the realistic details of everyday life, from the romance, which she conceived of as a more elevated form concerned with high emotion, aristocratic life, and the past. By this time

romantic fiction had already become a scapegoated genre, as in Charlotte Lennox's The *Female Quixote*, with its deluded heroine comically adrift in the real world thanks to an excess of romance reading. As the size of the reading public (especially amongst women) was perceived to increase and create its own market demands, much anxiety, amongst both early feminists such as Mary *Wollstonecraft and reactionary commentators of both sexes, focused on the likelihood of female readers being led astray by unrealistic fantasy fiction. Popular Gothic romances of the 1790s, such as those of Ann *Radcliffe or Charlotte *Dacre, were widely denounced for their pernicious effects on female minds.

Much of what remains as canonical in the history of the novel was written in conscious reaction against the romance. In the early 19th century, Jane *Austen, having mocked the potential errors of female reading of romances in *Northanger Abbey* and elsewhere, strengthened the major model of romantic fiction, the 'Cinderella' narrative in which the worthy but disadvantaged heroine wins the noblest hero, with wit, irony, psychological depth, and a hard-nosed interest in property. Walter *Scott fused history with romance in an attempt to masculinize the genre. The *Brontë sisters inherited a set of Gothic fixtures, including wild landscapes, tormented heroes, and haunted houses, but Emily Brontë may be said to have established a standard for the romance of doomed love in *Wuthering Heights*, while Charlotte Brontë's *Jane Eyre* is a template for the romance of a young woman's climb towards moral independence and a love validated by intellectual equality. The much-read and much-castigated *sensation novelists of the end of the century, such as Wilkie *Collins and Mary *Braddon, draw on these models. Daphne du Maurier's *Rebecca* (1938), is a later debtor to the Gothic romance. Best-selling 20th-century writers of romantic fiction include Ethel M. Dell (1881–1939); Edith M. Hull (1880–1947), whose exotic sexual fantasy The Sheik (1919) shocked an avid public; Georgette Heyer (1902–74); Catherine *Cookson, who reinvented the rags-to-riches tale of the resourceful northern heroine; and Joanna Trollope (1943–), whose Aga sagas have a more middle-class appeal. The 1980s and 1990s saw the rise of blockbuster romances by Jackie Collins (1937–), Judith Krantz (1928–), Barbara Taylor Bradford (1933–), Jilly Cooper (1937–), and Danielle Steele (1947–), who explored a more sexually liberated version of female power. The novels of Anita *Brookner, Mary *Wesley, and Margaret *Drabble might be said to contain elements of romantic fiction, and in the hands of playful postmodernists, such as David *Lodge in *Small World: An Academic Romance* (1984) or A. S. *Byatt in *Possession* (1990), romance has once again been turned into literary fiction. The simplest brand of romance, the formulaic fictions of the *Mills and Boon series, continue to sell millions of books a year in the UK alone.

Romanticism A profound transformation in artistic styles, in cultural attitudes, and in the relations between artist and society evident in Western literature and other arts in the first half of the 19th century. In Britain, a stark contrast appears between representative works of the preceding *Augustan age and those of leading figures in what became known as the Romantic movement or 'Romantic Revival' in the period from about 1780 to about 1848: William *Blake, Robert *Burns, Charlotte *Smith, William *Wordsworth, S. T. *Coleridge, Mary *Robinson (1757/8–1800), Robert *Southey, Walter *Scott, Lord *Byron, P. B. *Shelley, John *Keats, William *Hazlitt, Thomas *De Quincey, Thomas *Carlyle, Emily *Brontë, and Charlotte *Brontë.

In the most abstract terms, Romanticism may be regarded as the triumph of the values of imaginative spontaneity, visionary originality, wonder, and emotional self-expression over the classical standards of balance, order, restraint, proportion, and objectivity. Its name derives from *romance, the literary form in which desires and dreams prevail over everyday realities.

Romanticism arose from a period of turbulence, euphoria, and uncertainty. Political and intellectual movements of the late 18th century encouraged the assertion of individual and national rights, denying legitimacy (forcibly in the American and French revolutions) to kings and courtiers. In Britain, the expansions of commerce, journalism, and literacy had loosened the dependency of artists and writers upon noble patrons, releasing them to discover their own audiences in an open cultural marketplace—as Scott and Byron did most successfully—or to toil in unrewarded obscurity, like Blake. Nourished by Protestant conceptions of intellectual liberty, the Romantic writers tended to cast themselves as prophetic voices crying in the wilderness. The Romantic author, unlike the more socially integrated Augustan writers, was often seen a sort of modern hermit or exile, who usually granted a special moral value to similar outcast figures in his or her own writing: the pedlars and vagrants in Wordsworth's poems, Coleridge's *Ancient Mariner, Mary *Shelley's man-made monster, and the many tormented

pariahs in the works of Byron and P. B. Shelley. Although some (notably Keats and Shelley) continued to employ elements of Greek mythology and to adapt the classical form of the *ode, they scorned the imitation of classical models as an affront to the autonomy of the all-important creative imagination. Well above *Horace or *Juvenal they revered *Shakespeare and *Milton as their principal models of the *sublime embodied in the poet's boundless imaginative genius. In this, they took the partly nationalistic direction followed by Romantic poets and composers in other countries, who likewise rediscovered and revalued their local vernacular traditions.

Although inheriting much of the humane and politically liberal spirit of the *Enlightenment, the Romantics largely rejected its analytic rationalism; Wordsworth warned against the destructive tendency of the 'meddling intellect' to intrude upon the sanctities of the human heart, and he argued that the opposite of poetry was not prose but science. The Romantic revolt against scientific empiricism is compatible with the prevailing trend of German philosophy, notably Immanuel *Kant's 'transcendental' idealism, of which Coleridge and Carlyle were dedicated students.

In reaction against the spiritual emptiness of the modern calculating age, Romanticism cultivated various forms of nostalgia and of *primitivism. The imaginative sovereignty of the child, in the works of Blake and Wordsworth, implicitly shames the inauthenticity of adulthood, while the dignified simplicity of rural life is more generally invoked in condemnation of urban civilization. The superior nobility of the past tends also to be, as we now say, 'romanticized' for its imaginative conceptions of the ideal and the heroic, as reflected in Shakespeare, in chivalric romance, and in balladry. Antiquaries of the 18th century, notably Thomas *Percy in his *Reliques* and James *Macpherson in his Ossianic poems, had won a new respect for the older forms of popular or 'folk' poetry and legend.

Romantic writing exhibits a new emotional intensity taken to unprecedented extremes of joy or dejection, rapture or horror, and an extravagance of apparently egotistic self-projection. As a whole, it is usually taken to represent a second renaissance of literature in Britain, especially in lyric and narrative poetry, which displaced the Augustan cultivation of satiric and didactic modes. The prose styles of Hazlitt, De Quincey, Charles *Lamb, and Leigh *Hunt also show a marked renewal of vitality, flexibility, subjective tone, and what Hazlitt called 'gusto'. The arts of prose fiction were extended by Scott's historical novels, by the sensational effects of *Gothic fiction, and by the emergence of the short story form in the Edinburgh and London magazines. Although Byron, Shelley, and others wrote important dramatic poems, drama written for the theatres is not seen as the strongest aspect of Romantic literature. On the other hand, alongside the often vituperative and partisan conduct of reviewing in *Blackwood's Magazine and other periodicals, this was a great age of literary criticism and theory, most notably in the writings of Coleridge and Hazlitt, and in major essays by Wordsworth and Shelley.

Simplified accounts of Romanticism in Britain date its arrival from the appearance in 1798 of the *Lyrical Ballads* or in 1800 of Wordsworth's preface (effectively a manifesto) to that collection. 'Pre-Romantic' currents have been recognized in the latter part of the 18th century, however, including *'graveyard poetry', the novel of *sentiment, the cult of the sublime, and the *Sturm und Drang* phase of German literature in the 1770s led by *Schiller and the young *Goethe.

Romanticism flourished in the United States somewhat later, between 1820 and 1860, with James Fenimore *Cooper's historical romances, Ralph Waldo *Emerson's essays, Herman *Melville's novels, Edgar Allan *Poe's tales and poetry, Henry Wadsworth *Longfellow, Walt *Whitman, and the nature writings of Henry *Thoreau.

The convenient and conventional divisions of literary history into distinct 'periods' may obscure the extent to which the Romantic tradition remains unbroken in the later 19th century and beyond. The work of John *Ruskin, the *Pre-Raphaelite Brotherhood, and the Victorian advocates of the *Gothic Revival, displays Romantic attitudes in its nostalgia and its opposition to an unpoetical modern civilization; and the same might be said of W. B. *Yeats and D. H. *Lawrence in the early 20th century.

Critical opposition to the Romantic inheritance, in the name of *'classical' ideals, was advanced by Matthew *Arnold in the 1850s, and by some later critics under his influence, including the American scholar Irving *Babbitt, whose book *Rousseau and Romanticism* (1919) condemned the Romantic movement as an irresponsible 'pilgrimage in the void' that had licensed self-indulgent escapism and nationalist aggression, and his student T. S. *Eliot.

Romany Rye, The A novel by George *Borrow, published 1857. 'Romany Rye' in Romany language means 'Gypsy Gentleman', a name applied to Borrow by Ambrose Smith, the Norfolk gypsy. This book is a sequel to *Lavengro*, and continues, in episodic fashion, the story of the author's wanderings and adventures.

Romaunt of the Rose, The A translation into Middle English octosyllabics of about one-third of the *Roman de la Rose*, lines 1–5,154 and 10,679–12,360, made in the time of Geoffrey *Chaucer and previously attributed to him.

In the Garden of Mirth, the dreamer-narrator falls in love with a rosebud. Parts A and B describe the dreamer's instructions by the god of love. Part C satirizes the various hypocrisies of religion, women, and society.

Romeo and Juliet *Shakespeare's first romantic tragedy, based on the poem *The Tragical History of Romeus and Juliet* (1562) by Arthur Brooke (d. 1563), a translation from the French of Boaistuau of one of Matteo *Bandello's *Novelle*. Shakespeare's play was probably written about 1595 and first printed in 1597.

The Montagues and Capulets, the two chief families of Verona, are bitter enemies; Escalus, the prince, threatens anyone who disturbs the peace with death. Romeo, son of old Lord Montague, is in love with Lord Capulet's niece Rosaline. But at a feast given by Capulet, which Romeo attends disguised by a mask, he sees and falls in love with Juliet, Capulet's daughter, and she with him. After the feast he overhears, under her window, Juliet's confession of her love for him, and wins her consent to a secret marriage. With the help of Friar Laurence, they are wedded next day. Mercutio, a friend of Romeo, meets Tybalt, of the Capulet family, who is infuriated by his discovery of Romeo's presence at the feast, and they quarrel. Romeo arrives, and tries to reason with Tybalt, but Tybalt and Mercutio fight, and Mercutio falls dead. Then Romeo draws his sword and Tybalt is killed. The prince, Montague, and Capulet appear, and Romeo is sentenced to banishment. After spending the night with Juliet, he leaves Verona for Mantua, counselled by the friar, who intends to reveal Romeo's marriage at the right moment. Capulet proposes to marry Juliet to Count Paris, despite her attempts to avoid the match. Juliet consults the friar, who advises her to consent, but on the night before the wedding to drink a potion which will render her apparently lifeless for 42 hours. He will warn Romeo, who will rescue her from the vault when she wakes and carry her to Mantua. The friar's message to Romeo goes astray, and Romeo hears that Juliet is dead. Buying poison, he comes to the vault to have a last sight of Juliet. He chances upon Count Paris outside the vault; they fight and Paris is killed. Then Romeo, after a last kiss on Juliet's lips, drinks the poison and dies. Juliet wakes to find Romeo dead by her side, the cup still in his hand. Guessing what has happened, she stabs herself and dies. The friar and Count Paris's page reveal the story, and Montague and Capulet, faced by the tragic results of their quarrel, are reconciled.

Romola A novel by George *Eliot, published 1863. The background of the novel (meticulously researched by Eliot) is Florence at the end of the 15th century, the troubled period, following the expulsion of the Medici, of the expedition of Charles VIII, distracted counsels in the city, the excitement caused by the preaching of *Savonarola, and acute division between the popular party and the supporters of the Medici. Various historical figures, including Charles VIII, *Machiavelli, and Savonarola himself, are drawn with great care. The story describes the trials of the noble Romola, devoted daughter of a blind scholar. Into their lives comes a clever, adaptable young Greek, Tito Melema, whose self-indulgence develops into utter perfidy. He robs and abandons in prison the benefactor of his childhood, Baldassare. He cruelly goes through a mock marriage ceremony with the innocent little contadina Tessa. After marrying Romola he wounds her deepest feelings by betraying her father's solemn trust. He plays a double game in the political intrigues of the day. He is eventually destroyed by Baldassare, who escapes from imprisonment crazed with sorrow and suffering. Romola, her love for her husband turned to contempt, and her trust in Savonarola destroyed by his falling away from his high prophetic mission, is left alone, until she discovers her duty in self-sacrifice. She devotes her life to the care of Tessa and her children.

rondeau A medieval French verse form revived in English by A. C. *Swinburne, Austin *Dobson, and others in the later 19th century. It normally consists of thirteen octosyllabic lines (in three stanzas, of five, three, and five lines), having only two rhymes throughout, and with the opening words used twice as a refrain. A related form, the rondel, also uses only two rhymes, but with repetition of the opening two lines as lines 7 and 8, and of the first line as line 13. The term 'roundel' may refer to either of these forms or to an eleven-line variant upon them invented by Swinburne in *A Century of Roundels* (1883).

RONSARD, Pierre de (1524–85) French poet, leader of the *Pléiade. He published his first four books of *Odes* in 1550, followed by a fifth in 1552, with which he also published *Les amours* (*Loves*), a cycle of 183 decasyllabic love sonnets. A second cycle of love poetry followed in two collections: the *Continuation des amours* (1555) and the *Nouvelle Continuation des amours* (1556). His last important love sequence, the *Sonnets pour Hélène* (1578), was dedicated to Hélène de Surgères, lady-in-waiting to Catherine de Médicis. Imitated by Alexander *Montgomerie and plagiarized by Thomas *Lodge, Ronsard exerted a considerable influence on 16th- and 17th-century English poets, notably *Shakespeare, Robert *Herrick, and Andrew *Marvell. John *Keats and Andrew *Lang both translated him in the 19th century.

Room at the Top See BRAINE, JOHN.

Room of one's Own, A By Virginia *Woolf, a key work of the feminist movement, published 1929 and based on two lectures on 'Women and Fiction' that Woolf delivered in Cambridge in 1928. It begins with the visit of the imaginary Mary Beton to an imaginary Oxbridge college where she feels a complete outsider. Woolf goes on to describe the educational, social, and financial disadvantages against which women have struggled throughout history, arguing that women will not be able to write well and freely until they have privacy and financial independence. She pays tribute to women writers of the past; to women's achievements in the form of the novel; and projects a future in which increasing equality would enable women to become not only novelists but poets. In the last chapter she discusses 'androgyny': 'Perhaps a mind that is purely masculine cannot create, any more than a mind that is purely feminine.'

Room with a View, A Novel by E. M. *Forster (1908, *Merchant-Ivory film, 1985). It opens in a Florence *pensione*, where Lucy Honeychurch and her chaperone Charlotte Bartlett reluctantly accept the room with a view that the socially inferior Mr Emerson and his son George offer to vacate for them. Lucy is disturbed by witnessing a murder, and by an embrace from George Emerson, and a scandalized Miss Bartlett returns her to Surrey, where Lucy becomes engaged to Cecil Vyse. The Emersons take a cottage nearby and Lucy comes to realize that she loves George, not Cecil; and the remainder of the novel is played out against a background of tennis and tea parties, piano recitals and muddle. It ends in the Pensione Bertolini, with George and Lucy on their honeymoon.

ROS, Amanda McKittrick (1860–1939) Née Anna Margaret McKittrick, Irish writer, known as 'the World's Worst Novelist'. Her fiction was remarkable for its extraordinary and unselfconsciously colourful prose, to which Aldous *Huxley devoted an essay, 'Euphues Redivivus' (1923). *Irene Iddesleigh* (1897), her first novel, provides many choice examples: 'Every sentence the able and beautiful girl uttered caused Sir John to shift his apparently uncomfortable person nearer and nearer, watching at the same time minutely the divine picture of innocence, until at last, when her reply was ended, he found himself, altogether unconsciously, clasping her to his bosom, whilst the ruby rims which so recently proclaimed accusations and innocence met with unearthly sweetness, chasing every fault over the hills of doubt, until hidden in the hollow of immediate hate.' She was also a ludicrous poet, publishing *Poems of Puncture* (1912) and *Fumes of Formation* (1933).

Rosalynde, Euphues' Golden Legacy (1590) A pastoral romance in the style of John *Lyly's *Euphues*, interspersed with sonnets and eclogues, written by Thomas *Lodge during his voyage to the Canaries.

The story is borrowed in part from *The Tale of *Gamelyn* and was dramatized by William *Shakespeare in *As You Like It*. Lodge's Rosader is Shakespeare's Orlando; Saladyne is Oliver; Alinda, Celia; and Rosalind is common to both. Jaques and Touchstone have no equivalents. The ill treatment of Rosader (Orlando) is more fully developed by Lodge, and the rightful duke has his dukedom returned through force of arms instead of persuasion.

ROSAMOND, Fair (Rosamond Clifford) (d. ?1176) Probably mistress of Henry II in 1174. A legend transmitted by John *Stow, following *Higden, declares that Henry kept her in a maze-like house in Woodstock where only he could find her, but the queen, *Eleanor of Aquitaine, traced her whereabouts by following a thread and 'so dealt with her that she lived not long after'. The story is told in a ballad by *Deloney included in Percy's *Reliques*; in Samuel *Daniel's 'The Complaint of Rosamund' (1592), a poem in *rhyme royal; and *Addison's opera, *Rosamond*, (1707).

Rosciad, The (1761) A *mock-heroic verse satire by Charles *Churchill, originally 730

lines, but greatly expanded in later editions. It describes the attempt to find a worthy successor to Roscius, the Roman actor who died *c.*62 BC, and provides satiric sketches of many famous theatrical personalities of the day. David *Garrick, the chosen successor, is praised highly, but the poem was controversial and a bad review in the *Critical Review* prompted Churchill's *Apology* (1761), attacking the editor, Tobias *Smollett.

ROSCOE, William (1753–1831) Lawyer and banker, book-collector, writer, scholar, and botanist. He published works of poetry, biography, jurisprudence, botany, and arguments against the slave trade (see *Wrongs of Africa*, 1788). His principal work was his *Life of Lorenzo de' Medici* (1795). In 1805 (having learned Greek) he published the *Life of Leo the Tenth* (the 16th-century pope), and in 1806 *The Butterfly's Ball and the Grasshopper's Feast*, which became a children's classic. He did much to stimulate an interest in Italy and Italian literature in England.

Rose and the Ring, The A *fairy story written and illustrated by W. M. *Thackeray, first published 1855. The magic rose and ring have the property of making those who have possession of them seem irresistibly attractive. Thackeray makes gentle fun both of fairy-story conventions, and of 'improving' children's books in this 'Fireside Pantomime for Great and Small Children'.

ROSEN, Michael (1946–) Broadcaster, poet, and polemicist specializing in childhood culture. Since his first book of verse, *Mind your Own Business* (1974), he has written around 140 books, including anthologies, retellings, and *picturebooks. After the sudden death of his son Eddie he wrote *Michael Rosen's Sad Book* (2004) and, for adults, *Carrying the Elephant* (2002). He was Children's Laureate 2007–9.

ROSENBERG, Isaac (1890–1918) Poet. His parents were émigrés of Lithuanian origin. In 1912 he published at his own expense a collection of poems, *Night and Day*, and was encouraged by Gordon Bottomley, Ezra *Pound, and others. In 1915 he defied his family's pacifist views and joined the army, arriving as a private in the trenches in 1916. He was killed in action. His poetry is forceful, rich in its vocabulary, and starkly realistic in its attitudes to war (Rosenberg greatly disliked Rupert *Brooke's 'begloried sonnets'). His poor Jewish urban background gives the poems a note not

r

found in the work of his fellow war poets. Bottomley edited a selection of his poems, but it was only after the publication of his *Collected Works* (1937), with a foreword by Siegfried *Sassoon, that his importance became generally accepted.

Rosencrantz and Guildenstern Are Dead

A comedy by Tom *Stoppard, performed and published 1966, which places the peripheral 'attendant lords' from *Hamlet* at the centre of a drama in which they appear as bewildered witnesses and predestined victims. This device is used to serious as well as to comic effect, for underlying the verbal wit and Shakespearian parody there is a pervasive sense of man's solitude and lack of mastery over his own life reminiscent of Samuel *Beckett, whom Stoppard greatly admires. Stoppard's two protagonists consciously echo Vladimir and Estragon, from Beckett's *Waiting for Godot*, in their existentialist *angst* and their attempts to pass the time while they wait for something to happen.

ROSENTHAL, Jack (1931–2004) Dramatist, best known for an unusually wide-ranging television output. He wrote 150 early episodes of Granada Television's *Coronation Street*, and introduced a more demotic speech into the sitcom genre in *The Dustbin Men*. *The Evacuees* (1975) and *Bar Mitzvah Boy* (1976) were single plays drawing on his Jewish background. *The Knowledge* (1979) portrayed London cabdrivers facing a malevolent invigilator. *London's Burning* (1986) dramatized the perils of the fire service, and *And a Nightingale Sang* (1989) evoked wartime nostalgia. His autobiography, *By Jack Rosenthal* (2006), was published posthumously; it was adapted in a four-part radio version, *Jack Rosenthal's Last Act*, by his daughter Amy and with his wife, the actress Maureen Lipman, played by herself.

Rose Theatre, the On Bankside, Southwark, built in 1587, and altered and enlarged in 1592, closing in 1602. Philip *Henslowe was its owner and Edward Alleyn its leading actor. Shakespeare is thought to have acted there.

Rosicrucian A member of a supposed society or order, 'the brethren of the Rosy Cross', reputedly founded by one Christian Rosenkreuz in 1484, but first mentioned in 1614. Its manifestos were the *Fama Fraternitatis* (1614) and the *Confessio Fraternitatis* (1615). Its members were said to claim various forms of secret and magic knowledge, such as the transmutation of metals, the prolongation of life, and power over the elements and elemental spirits, and to derive much of their alchemy and mystical preoccupations from *Paracelsus. The Rosicrucian movement seems to have been rooted in some kind of anti-Jesuit Protestant alliance, with deep religious interests, as well as interests in alchemy, medicine, and the Cabbala (a school of thought based on mystical interpretations of Judaism). Frances Yates, in her study *The Rosicrucian Enlightenment* (1972), names as major figures in the English Rosicrucian movement John *Dee, Robert *Fludd, and Elias Ashmole; she also discusses the Rosicrucian connections of Francis *Bacon, Comenius, Isaac *Newton, *Leibniz, and many others.

ROSS, Alan (1922–2001) Poet, travel writer, and editor. *Open Sea* (1975) collects poems about the Second World War from earlier works, and includes his compressed epic 'J.W.51B', a haunting, first-hand description of naval endurance on the Arctic convoy route. A posthumous collection of his work, *Poems*, appeared in 2005. He edited the *London Magazine* from 1961 until his death.

ROSS, Alexander (1699–1784) Scottish poet and schoolmaster, author of *The Fortunate Shepherdess* (1768), later called *Helenore*, a lengthy pastoral poem in north-eastern *Scots.

ROSS, Martin See SOMERVILLE AND ROSS.

ROSSETTI, Christina Georgina (1830–94) Poet, sister of Dante Gabriel and William Michael *Rossetti. Christina, like her mother and sister Maria, was a devout High Anglican, much influenced by the Tractarians (*see* OXFORD MOVEMENT). She contributed to *The *Germ* (1850), where five of her poems appeared under a pseudonym. In 1861 *Macmillan's Magazine* published 'Up-hill' and 'A Birthday'. *Goblin Market and Other Poems* appeared in 1862, *The Prince's Progress and Other Poems* in 1866, *Sing-Song, a Nursery Rhyme Book* (with illustrations by Arthur Hughes) in 1872, and *A Pageant and Other Poems* in 1881. She also wrote numerous prose works, including *Speaking Likenesses* (1874), a collection of fairy-tales; *Time Flies: A Reading Diary* (1885), which consists of short passages linked to each day of the year, and several devotional works. Rossetti's technical virtuosity was considerable and her poems are distinctive for their beautifully constructed forms. Much of her poetry reflects her strong religious beliefs: it is also fascinated by loss, melancholy, and death, secrets, and unhappy or frustrated love. Rossetti's reputation as a relatively minor poet underwent a seismic shift with the advent of feminist criticism, and since the late 20th century she has been regarded as a leading Victorian woman poet, a peer of Emily *Brontë, E. B. *Browning, and Emily *Dickinson, and as a major Victorian poet irrespective of gender.

ROSSETTI, Dante Gabriel (1828–82) Poet and painter (his full first names were Gabriel Charles Dante, but his form of these has become customary), and brother to Christina *Rossetti, and William Michael *Rossetti. He studied painting with John Everett *Millais and Holman *Hunt, and in 1848, with them and four others, founded the *Pre-Raphaelite Brotherhood. Several of his poems, including 'The *Blessed Damozel' and 'My Sister's Sleep', and a prose piece, 'Hand and Soul', were published in *The *Germ* (1850). In 1854 he met John *Ruskin, who did much to establish the reputation of the Pre-Raphaelite painters, and in 1856 William *Morris, whom he greatly influenced; Morris's wife Jane was to become Rossetti's muse and lover. In 1860 Rossetti and Elizabeth *Siddal married: she died of an overdose, probably self-administered, in 1862, and Rossetti buried with her a manuscript containing many of his poems. Sixteen sonnets, including the 'Willowwood' sequence, were published in March 1869 in the *Fortnightly Review* and that summer he arranged the exhumation of the poems buried with his wife. *Poems* (1870) contained, *'Jenny', and the first part of his sonnet sequence *The *House of Life*. In October 1871 Robert *Buchanan's notorious attack 'The Fleshly School of Poetry' appeared (under the pseudonym Thomas Maitland) in the *Contemporary Review*, accusing Rossetti and his associates of impurity and obscenity. Rossetti's reply, 'The Stealthy School of Criticism', appeared in the *Athenaeum*, December 1872. Rossetti's later years were overshadowed by ill health and the abuse of the drug chloral, though he was recognized by a new generation of aesthetes, including Walter *Pater and Oscar *Wilde, as a source of inspiration; the admiration was not wholly mutual. *Poems* and *Ballads and Sonnets* both appeared in 1881; the first was largely rearrangements of earlier works, and the second completed *The House of Life* with 47 new sonnets, and also contained other new work, including 'The King's Tragedy' and 'The White Ship', both historical 'ballads'.

Many of Rossetti's poems were written as commentaries on his own and other paintings, and his finest poems have a Pre-Raphaelite sharpness of detail and undeniable emotional and erotic power. Rossetti was also a gifted translator from the Italian (*The Early Italian Poets Together with Dante's Vita Nuova*, 1861, known later as *Dante and his Circle*, 1874), and of *Villon.

SEE WEB LINKS
• The Rossetti archive

ROSSETTI, William Michael (1829–1919) Man of letters, art critic, and editor, brother of Dante Gabriel *Rossetti and Christina *Rossetti. He was a member of the *Pre-Raphaelite Brotherhood, edited *The *Germ*, and wrote the sonnet that was printed on its cover. His reviews of art exhibitions for the *Spectator* were published as *Fine Art: Chiefly Contemporary* (1867). He edited fifteen volumes of *Moxon's Popular Poets, and was responsible for important editions of William *Blake and P. B. *Shelley. He edited Walt *Whitman in 1868, introducing him to a British public. He translated *Dante, and was responsible for encouraging James *Thomson (1834–82). He also edited many of his family's papers, letters, and diaries, and wrote memoirs of his brother and his sister. His *Some Reminiscences* (1906) is a valuable biographical source.

ROSZAK, Theodore (1933–2011) American social commentator and novelist, who produced a study of the underground in *The Making of a Counter Culture* (1969) and of computing in *The Cult of Information* (1994). His novels include *Bugs* (1981), a cybernetic fantasy, and *Flicker* (1991), a postmodern investigation of an experimental film-maker.

ROTH, Joseph (1894–1939) Austrian novelist and essayist. Acutely aware of the threat of Nazism, he moved to Paris in 1933. In his works, he is a sardonic and clear-sighted chronicler of his times as well as a nostalgic apologist for the pre-1914 empire of Hapsburg Austria. His family epic *Radetzkymarsch* (1932: *The Radetzky March*) has remained his best-known work in England, but recent translations of earlier writing including *The Spider's Web* (2004), as well as translations of essays and journalistic pieces by Michael Hofmann have enabled a fuller reception of his work.

ROTH, Philip (1933–) Jewish American novelist. His complex relationship with his Jewish background is reflected in most of his works, and his portrayal of contemporary Jewish life has aroused much controversy. His works include *Goodbye, Columbus* (1959), *Letting Go* (1962), and a sequence of novels featuring Nathan Zuckerman, a Jewish novelist who has to learn to contend with success: *My Life as a Man* (1974), *The Ghost Writer* (1979), *Zuckerman Unbound* (1981), *The Anatomy Lesson* (1983), *The Prague Orgy* (1985). *Portnoy's Complaint* (1969) records the intimate confessions of Alexander Portnoy to his psychiatrist. *The Breast* (1972) is a Kafkaesque fantasy. Later novels include *Patrimony: A True Story* (1991), about his father Herman Roth; *Operation Shylock: A Confession* (1993), in which the author meets his double, whose self-appointed task is to lead the Jews out of Israel and back to Europe; *American Pastoral* (1997); *The Plot against America* (2004), an *alternate history where Charles Lindbergh the aviator has become president; and *Exit Ghost* (2007), which records Zuckerman's final fictional appearance. *Nemesis* (2010) concluded a series of four short novels: *Everyman* (2006), a bleak study of mortality, *Indignation* (2008), set at the time of the Korean War, and *The Humbling* (2009). *The Facts* (1988) is an autobiography.

Round Table In the Arthurian legend, the symbol of the common purpose of Arthur's court and knights. According to *Malory (in Vinaver's Tale 1) it was made for *Uther Pendragon who gave it to King Lodegrean of Camelerde (Cornwall). The latter gave it as a wedding gift, with 100 knights, to Arthur when he married Guinevere, his daughter. It would seat 150 knights, and all places round it were equal. The 'Siege Perilous' was reserved for the knight who should achieve the quest of the *Grail. In *Laȝamon's *Brut*, however, the table was made for Arthur by a crafty workman. It is first mentioned by the poet *Wace.

ROUSSEAU, Jean-Jacques (1712–78) Swiss writer and philosopher, who made his name with the publication in 1751 of his *Discours sur les sciences et les arts*, in which he argues that the development and spread of knowledge and culture, far from improving human behaviour, has corrupted it by promoting inequality, idleness, and luxury. The *Discours sur l'origine et les fondements de l'inégalité* (1755), reviewed by Adam *Smith in the first *Edinburgh Review*, contrasts the innocence and contentment of primitive man in a 'state of nature'—his mode of existence determined by none but genuine needs—with the dissatisfaction and perpetual agitation of modern social man.

A return to primitive innocence being impossible, the ills of society were only to be remedied, Rousseau held, by reducing the gap separating modern man from his natural archetype and by modifying existing institutions in the interest of equality and happiness. Such is the theme of his two novels: in *Julie, ou la Nouvelle Héloïse* (1761), a critical account of contemporary manners and ideas is interwoven with the story of the passionate love of the tutor Saint Preux and his pupil Julie, their separation, Julie's marriage to the Baron Wolmar, and the dutiful, virtuous life shared by all three on the baron's country estate; and *Émile* (1762) lays down the principles for a new scheme of education in which the child is to be allowed full scope for individual development in natural surroundings. In *Du contrat social* (1762), Rousseau advocates universal justice through equality before the law, a more equitable distribution of wealth, and defines government as fundamentally a matter of contract providing for the exercise of power in accordance with the 'general will' and for the common good, by consent of the citizens as a whole, in whom sovereignty ultimately resides.

Rousseau's last works, his posthumously published autobiographical *Confessions* (1782–9) and *Rêveries du promeneur solitaire* (1782) are landmarks of the literature of personal revelation (*see* AUTOBIOGRAPHY).

ROWE, Elizabeth Singer (1674–1737) Poet, whose verses appeared under the pseudonym 'Philomela' and who is chiefly known for the fervently devotional pieces in *Divine Hymns and Poems on Several Occasions* (1704) and *A Collection of Divine Hymns and Poems* (1709). Her much-reprinted *Friendship in Death: or, Twenty Letters from the Dead to the Living* (1728), a volume of prose stories celebrating the afterlife, was dedicated to Edward *Young. Isaac *Watts edited her posthumous collection, *Devout Exercises of the Heart in Meditation and Soliloquy, Prayer and Praise* (1737).

ROWE, Nicholas (1674–1718) Playwright. Apart from one unsuccessful comedy (*The Biter*, 1704), Rowe concentrated on verse tragedy: *The Ambitious Stepmother* (1700), *Tamerlane* (1701), *The *Fair Penitent* (1703), *Ulysses* (1705), *The Royal Convert* (1707), *Jane Shore* (1714), and *Lady Jane Grey* (1715). His 'She-Tragedies' (his own phrase) stressed the suffering and penitence of victimized women, and attempted to arouse 'pity; a sort of regret proceeding from good-nature'. Rowe was editor of the first modern edition of *Shakespeare (1709), using his theatrical experience to supply stage directions and act and scene divisions, making the text more intelligible, and giving the earliest substantial biography of the author.

ROWLANDS, Samuel (?1565–1630) A writer of satirical tracts, epigrams, and jests, mainly in verse. His works include a satire on the manners of Londoners, *The Letting of Humour's Blood in the Head-Vein* (1600); *'Tis Merry When Gossips Meet* (1602), a vivid and dramatic character sketch of a widow, a wife, and a maid who meet in a tavern and converse; *Greene's Ghost* (1602), on the subject of 'coney-catchers' (*see* GREENE, ROBERT); *Democritus, or Doctor Merryman his Medicines against Melancholy Humours* (1607); and *The Melancholy Knight* (1615).

ROWLANDSON, Thomas (1756–1827) Painter, book illustrator, and caricaturist, famous for his comic depiction of scenes from social life. Among his most important productions were *The Loyal Volunteers of London and Environs* (1799); *The Microcosm of London* (1808–10), with A. C. Pugin (*c.*1768/9–1832); *The Three Tours of Doctor Syntax*, for William *Combe; *The English Dance of Death* (1815–16); and *The Dance of Life* (1816–17), also with Combe.

ROWLEY, William (?1585–1626) Dramatist and actor. That he was Samuel Rowley's brother is no more than a guess. Collaborations, in which he usually contributed a comic sub-plot, account for nearly all of his surviving dramatic work. His most notable partnership was with Thomas *Middleton with whom he wrote *Wit at Several Weapons* (1613; printed 1647), *A *Fair Quarrel* (1616; printed 1617), *The Old Law* (1618–29, printed 1656), *The World Tossed at Tennis* (acted and printed 1620), and *The *Changeling* (1622; printed 1653). He also assisted in *The *Witch of Edmonton* (1621; printed 1658), with Thomas *Dekker and John *Ford; *The Maid in the Mill* (1623; printed 1647), with John *Fletcher; *A Cure for a Cuckold* (1624–5; printed 1661), with John *Webster; and *A New Wonder, a Woman Never Vexed* (1624–6; printed 1632), with an unknown collaborator. His speciality as an actor was the role of a fat clown, and he took the part of Jacques in his own *All's Lost by Lust* (*c.*1619).

ROWLING, J. K. (Joanne Kathleen) (1965–) OBE. Her seven-part series of books about Harry *Potter, beginning with *Harry Potter and the Philosopher's Stone* (1997), has been phenomenally successful worldwide, as have the accompanying films, computer games, and merchandise. From the publication of book four, *The Goblet of Fire* (2000), sales of Rowling's *crossover books have broken all records.

In many ways the books, which largely take place at Hogwarts School of Witchcraft and Wizardry, are *school stories with a *fantasy twist; however, when Bloomsbury bought the series in 1996, Rowling had already decided that her characters would age by a year from book to book, so adjusting the convention which sees characters staying perpetually schoolchildren or being replaced by a new generation of pupils as series evolve. As a consequence, her original audience of child readers matured with her characters and gradually the books became *young adult novels and arguably, in the case of book six, *Harry Potter and the Half-Blood Prince* (2005), and book seven, *Harry Potter and the Deathly Hallows* (2007), largely for adults, though they continue to have crossover appeal.

The series begins with the orphan Harry living miserably with his abusive guardians, the Dursleys. On learning that he is a wizard and being inducted into the world of wizards, Harry discovers that his world comprises 'Muggles' (non-magical people presumably living in the world we know) and wizards. Rowling mixes genres and modes in her reworking of the battle between 'good', represented by Harry and his friends including Albus Dumbledore, headmaster of Hogwarts, and 'evil' in the form of Lord Voldemort and his followers. As an orphan, Harry is seeking knowledge about his parents, murdered by Voldemort when Harry was a baby. Voldemort's attack not only left Harry with his signature scar in the shape of a lighting bolt running down his forehead but also inextricably linked the two in various ways, interestingly complicating the battle between them. The ambiguities around this relationship characterize the books: with the exception of Harry's close friends Ron Weasley (and his family including his sister Ginny who becomes Harry's girlfriend in book six) and Hermione Granger, it is impossible to tell who is trustworthy. The mysteries around character become darker over time, possibly reflecting increasing uncertainties in global politics though also in line with Harry's adolescent perception of the world.

***Roxana,** or The Fortunate Mistress* A novel by Daniel *Defoe, published 1724. It is presented as the autobiography of Mademoiselle de Beleau, the daughter of French Protestant refugees, brought up in England and married to a London brewer, who, having squandered his property, deserts her and her five children. Like the heroine of **Moll Flanders*, Roxana supports herself as a kept mistress, passing from one protector to another; she receives the name 'Roxana' after performing a 'Turkish' dance at the court of Charles II. The disturbing conclusion of the novel does not resolve the exact sequence of events, but Roxana experiences a catastrophic descent into poverty and remorse.

ROXBURGHE, John Ker, third duke of (1740–1804) An ardent bibliophile, who formed an unrivalled collection of books from William *Caxton's press. His splendid library was sold in 1812. The chief bibliophiles inaugurated the Roxburghe Club, the first of the 'book-clubs', consisting of 25 members, with T. F. Dibdin as its first secretary. The Club's first publication from an original manuscript was the metrical romance of *Havelok the Dane* (1828). Each member is expected once in his or her career to present (and pay for a limited edition of) a volume of some rarity.

ROY, Arundhati (1961–) Novelist, scriptwriter, and anti-globalization essayist and campaigner, born in Bengal and brought up in southern India. Her semi-autobiographical novel set in Kerala and much influenced by Salman *Rushdie, *The God of Small Things*, won the 1997 *Booker Prize.

Royal Court Theatre Built in 1888; it has a historic association with new writing. Under the management of J. E. Vedrenne and Harley *Granville-Barker from 1904 to 1907, it staged premieres by George Bernard *Shaw, John *Galsworthy, W. B. *Yeats, and John *Masefield. But it was with the foundation of the *English Stage Company in 1956, under the direction of George Devine (1910–66), that it became a national centre of new writing. The initial intention was to encourage novelists to write for the stage but, although work by Angus *Wilson and Nigel Dennis was presented, it was the production of *Look Back in Anger* by John *Osborne (8 May 1956) that liberated other writers through its scalding rhetoric and social candour. The Court has subsequently championed many living dramatists including Arnold *Wesker, John *Arden, Edward *Bond, David *Storey, Brian *Friel, Athol *Fugard, Caryl *Churchill, Mustapha Matura (1939–), and Timberlake *Wertenbaker. From 1979 until the late 1990s, Max Stafford-Clark and Stephen Daldry successively encouraged a new generation of socially angry, anti-materialist young writers, including Sarah *Kane and Mark *Ravenhill, and the Royal Court acquired fresh impetus through its encouragement and its promotion of eloquent new Irish dramatists, notably Martin *McDonagh and Conor *McPherson.

Royal Geographical Society Founded in London in 1830; it became the most significant non-governmental promoter of travel and exploration and its resulting literature. Lord *Byron's friend John Cam *Hobhouse was a founder. Literary and historical concerns were evident in early years, but the concerns of the practical servicemen and administrators building up Britain's interests around the world soon became dominant. The Society's role in making heroes of explorers in inhospitable tropical or frozen environments created a demand for their published work. The impact on boys' adventure stories by writers such as R. M. *Ballantyne is important. In the middle years of the 19th century, the search for the remains of Sir John *Franklin's expedition in the Arctic and the quest for the sources of the Nile in the middle of Africa raised enormous public interest and sometimes controversy, as when Henry *Stanley 'found' Livingstone in 1871. Oddly, little work on Britain appeared. The tradition of fostering expeditions persisted in the 20th century, not least in support of attempts to conquer Everest.

Royal Literary Fund A benevolent society for authors and their dependants in distress, founded in 1790 as the Literary Fund Society at the instigation of the Revd David Williams (1738–1813), a Dissenting minister. In 1818 it was granted a royal charter, and was permitted to add 'Royal' to its title in 1845. Beneficiaries here included S. T. *Coleridge, Thomas Love *Peacock, James *Hogg, John *Clare, D. H. *Lawrence, Edith *Nesbit, James *Joyce, and Dylan *Thomas. It has also made grants to literary refugees, including *Chateaubriand. The Fund receives no government subsidy and depends on gifts, subscriptions, and legacies—including authors' royalties.

Royal Society More correctly the Royal Society of London for the Improving of Natural Knowledge; obtained its royal charters in 1662 and 1663. Francis *Bacon provided the major philosophical inspiration for the Society; Solomon's House in *New Atlantis* has been taken as its model. Its founders and early members included Robert Boyle, Robert Hooke (1635–1703), Sir William Petty, John Ray, John Wilkins (1614–72), and Christopher Wren. Among more literary figures, Elias Ashmole, John *Aubrey, Abraham *Cowley, John *Dryden, John *Evelyn, and Edmund *Waller were members. The Society features prominently in Dryden's *Annus Mirabilis*. Its *Philosophical Transactions* (1665–), first edited by Henry Oldenburg (c.1619–1677), is the first permanent scientific journal.

Royal Society of Edinburgh Established in 1783 for 'the cultivation of every branch of science, erudition, and taste'. The membership was originally divided into the Physical Class and a larger Literary Class, the latter including Archibald Alison, James *Beattie, Hugh *Blair, Edmund *Burke, Alexander Carlyle, Adam *Ferguson, Alexander Gerard, John *Home, John Jamieson, Henry *Mackenzie, Thomas Reid (1710–96), and William Robertson (1721–93). Walter *Scott was president 1820–32, and Alfred *Tennyson and Thomas *Carlyle had honorary membership. The Literary Class was revived in 1976, its fellows including Norman *MacCaig, Sorley *Maclean, and Muriel *Spark.

Royal Society of Literature Founded in 1820 at the suggestion of Thomas Burgess (1756–1837), bishop of St David's, and under the patronage of George IV, who assigned the sum of 1,100 guineas to be applied in pensions of 100 guineas to each of ten Royal Associates, and in a premium of 100 guineas for a prize dissertation. Associates were elected by the council of the Society (Thomas *Malthus and S. T. *Coleridge were among the first ten). The Society has members, fellows, and, since 1961, companions; recipients of the title of companion have included John *Betjeman, Arthur *Koestler, E. M. *Forster, Angus *Wilson, and many others. It sponsors readings and lectures, awards prizes, and campaigns on matters of interest to writers.

RÓŻEWICZ, Tadeusz (1921–) Polish poet and playwright. With his compatriots Zbigniew *Herbert and Czesław *Miłosz he is one of the most influential writers of post-war Eastern Europe. His stark, powerful poems provide an often disturbingly realistic account of his country's recent history. *They Came to See a Poet: Selected Poems* (trans. Adam Czerniawski) appeared in 1991. Much of his controversial political drama, including *The Trap* (1982; trans. 1997), has also been published in English.

Rubáiyát of Omar Khayyám, The See OMAR KHAYYÁM, THE RUBÁIYÁT OF.

RUBENS, Bernice Ruth (1923–2004) Prolific novelist, born into an immigrant Jewish family of musical prodigies in Cardiff. *Madame Sousatzka* (1962) describes the struggle of a piano teacher to keep possession of a preternaturally gifted pupil, while *Spring Sonata* (1979) depicts the development of a violinist quite literally *in utero*. Other novels include *The Elected Member* (1969, *Booker Prize 1970); *Brothers* (1983), a historical account of the persecution of four generations of a Russian Jewish

family; and *Kingdom Come* (1990), based on the life of a 17th-century Messiah in Turkey. Later works include *The Waiting Game* (1997) and *I, Dreyfus* (1999).

RUDKIN, David (1936–) Playwright, who made his name with a powerful drama set in a rural district of the Black Country, *Afore Night Come* (1962); subsequent works, informed by a dark and passionate surreal mysticism, include *Ashes* (1974), *Penda's Fen* (TV 1974), *Sons of Light* (1976), *The Triumph of Death* (1981), *Space Invaders* (1983), and *The Saxon Shore* (1986). In 2003, he returned to the theatre with the mythological *Red Sun*, published with *Merlin Unchained* (perf. 2009).

'Ruin, The' A 45-line poem in Old English in the *Exeter Book. The poem describes the result of the devastation of a city, which the references to hot springs may identify as Bath, which was a ruin in Anglo-Saxon times.

'Ruined Cottage, The' ('The Story of Margaret') A poem by William *Wordsworth, written in 1797, and subsequently embodied in Book I of *The *Excursion.

'Ruines of Time, The' A poem by Edmund *Spenser, included in the *Complaints* published in 1591. It is an allegorical elegy on the death of Sir Philip *Sidney, which had also been the occasion of his earlier elegy *'Astrophel'. The poet passes to a lament on the decline of patronage and the neglect of literature.

RUKEYSER, Muriel (1913–1980) American poet, who used her poetry as a medium for social protest, experimenting with documentary techniques in *U.S. 1* (1938) and other volumes.

'Rule, Britannia' Patriotic British song with words by James *Thomson and music by Thomas *Arne, composed for *Alfred* (1740), a masque by Thomson and David *Mallet. It became popular during the Jacobite rebellion of 1745.

RUMENS, Carol (1944–) British poet. *A Strange Girl in Bright Colours* (1973) combined an interest in gender with wider political commitments. Her later collections include *Direct Dialling* (1985); *The Greening of Snow Beach* (1988); *Best China Sky* (1995), written during her residency in Belfast; and *Hex* (2002). Her substantial *Poems 1964–2004* (2004) defines her as one of the most versatile and outward-looking poets of her generation.

RŪMĪ, Jalāl ad-Dīn Muhammad (1207–73) Born in Balkh (Afghanistan), a Persian *Sufi famous as the author of the *Masnavī-i ma `nawī* ('Spiritual Couplets'), a vast poem that muses in myriad ways on how to escape from material preoccupations. Rūmī was also the inspirer, and probably the founder, of the Mevlevi Sufi order, better known as the 'Whirling Dervishes'.

rune A letter or character of the earliest surviving Germanic script, most extensively used in inscriptions on wood or stone by the Scandinavians and Anglo-Saxons. The earliest runic alphabet seems to date from about the 3rd century AD, and is formed by modifying the letters of the Greek and Roman alphabets. Magical and mysterious powers were associated with runes from the Anglo-Saxon period, perhaps because of their employment in riddles, as in the *Rune Poem*, a 94-line piece illustrating the runes of the Anglo-Saxon runic alphabet, the *futhorc* (see ASPR 6, 28–30 for edition). The poems of *Cynewulf have a runic signature.

RUNYON, Damon (1884–1946) American writer, who became famous for his sketches of New York life, particularly the world of Broadway, from the Prohibition era and onwards, including *Guys and Dolls* (1932) and *My Old Man* (1939), and numerous subsequent collections.

Rupert Bear *Comic-strip character created by Mary Tortel (1920–35), Alfred Bestall (1935–73), and John Harrold (1973–). The young bear, with his distinctive white fur, check trousers, yellow jumper, and scarf, features in the *Daily Express* and many annuals. The limited comic-strip text is supplemented by verse narratives.

Rural Rides Essays by William *Cobbett, published 1830, after appearing in the *Political Register*. Sceptical of proposed remedies for agricultural distress, Cobbett 'made up his mind to see for himself, and to enforce, by actual observation of rural conditions, the statements he had made in answer to the arguments of the landlords before the Agricultural Committee'. The result was this series of lively, opinionated accounts of his travels on horseback between September 1822 and October 1826, largely in the south and east of England. Later journeys, in the Midlands and the north, were described in subsequent editions. He rails against tax collectors, 'tax-eaters', landlords, gamekeepers, stockjobbers, and excisemen, and against the monstrous swelling of the 'Great Wen' of London; but the work is animated by his knowledge and love of the land, and breaks occasionally into rapturous praise for a landscape, a hedgerow, a hanging wood.

Ruritania An imaginary kingdom in central Europe, the scene of *The *Prisoner of Zenda* by Anthony Hope (*Hawkins). The name connotes more generally a world of make-believe romance, chivalry, and intrigue.

RUSHDIE, Salman (1947–) Novelist and short story writer, born in Bombay (Mumbai) to a Muslim family. His first book, *Grimus* (1975), an abstruse fantasy based on a medieval Sūfī poem, was followed by *Midnight's Children* (1981, *Booker Prize), a swarming comic saga which won him literary prominence. In it Saleem Sinai, born as midnight strikes the dawn of India's Independence, symbolizes his nation's changing fortunes and its intractable divisions. *Shame* (1983), a savage satirical fable interspersed with chapters of authorial comment, depicts lethal splits in Pakistan, especially between military and civilian rule (represented by thinly disguised versions of General Zia and the Bhutto family). Migration and displacement (from countries, cultures, and ideologies) are the central themes in his phantasmagoric novel *The Satanic Verses* (1988), which was denounced as blasphemous by some Muslims and led to his being sentenced to death in a *fatwa* issued by the Ayatollah Khomeini in 1989. Forced to live in hiding, under police protection, for many years, he continued to write, and published works such as *Haroun and the Sea of Stories*, an engaging novel for children about the pleasures and perils of storytelling (1990, adapted for the stage at the *National Theatre, 1998). *The Moor's Last Sigh* (1995), Rushdie's first novel after the *fatwa*, is narrated by a hunted man who ages at twice the normal rate. Subsequent novels include *The Ground beneath her Feet* (1999) in which the myth of Orpheus and Eurydice is recast as the story of two rock musicians; *Fury* (2001); *Shalimar the Clown* (2005), about the ruination of Kashmir and the making of a terrorist; and *The Enchantress of Florence* (2008). Like all Rushdie's fiction, they proclaim the evils of ideological single-mindedness and the moral, social, and artistic benefits of pluralism and tolerance.

RUSKIN, John (1819–1900) Critic. The only child of John James and Margaret Ruskin, he was born in London, and grew up in Herne Hill, in south London. His father built up the wine business of which he was a founding partner, and was able to pass on to his son. To his parents Ruskin owed a large fortune (much of which Ruskin gave away), a close knowledge of the Bible, a strong affection for romantic literature, stern political views, and an early attraction to contemporary landscape painting. The family took regular tours in Britain, and, from 1833, on the Continent. These fixed Ruskin's lifelong preference for French cathedral towns, the Alps, and certain cities of northern Italy, and focused his main passion, the study of the facts of nature. His early publications included essays in London's *Magazine of Natural History* (1834 and 1836). He contributed regularly to Christmas annuals from 1835 to 1846, mainly to *Friendship's Offering*, whose editor, W. H. Harrison, acted as his personal literary adviser. He admired the art of Copley Fielding, J. D. Harding, Clarkson Stanfield, James Holland, David Roberts, Samuel Prout, and, above all, J. M. W. *Turner. He took lessons from two of these artists (Fielding and Harding), made friends of several, and bought the work of all. With the first of the five volumes of **Modern Painters* (1843), an immediate success, he became their public champion.

Seven months' work in Italy in preparation for *Modern Painters II* (1846) compelled him to write of the medieval buildings of Europe before they should be destroyed by neglect, restoration, industrialization, and revolutions. *Modern Painters III* and *IV* did not appear until 1856. The interval produced *The Seven Lamps of Architecture* (1849) and *The *Stones of Venice* (1851–3). In 1854, after six unhappy years, his marriage to Euphemia Chalmers Gray was annulled, and soon afterwards she married John Everett *Millais.

Ruskin's middle years were extraordinarily active, and he became a prominent public figure. He wrote for the Arundel Society (*Giotto and his Works in Padua*, 1853–4, 1860), taught at the Working Men's College, produced drawing manuals, helped with plans for the Oxford Museum of Natural History building, arranged for the National Gallery the drawings of the Turner bequest, and tried to guide the work of individual artists, including Dante Gabriel *Rossetti, John Inchbold (1830–88), and John Brett (1831–1902). He gave evidence before parliamentary committees, and lectured extensively throughout the country. In the final volume of *Modern Painters* (1860) he denounced greed as the deadly principle guiding English life. In attacking the 'pseudo-science' of John Stuart *Mill and David Ricardo (1772–1823) in *Unto this Last* (1860) and *Essays on Political Economy* (1862–3; later *Munera Pulveris*, 1872), Ruskin entered new territory and declared open warfare against the spirit and science of his times.

This fight, against competition and self-interest, for the recovery of heroic, feudal, and Christian social ideals was to occupy Ruskin for the rest of his life. In the serial letters of **Fors*

Clavigera (1871–8) he found a form well suited to his public teaching and to the diversity of his interests, which also expressed themselves in practical projects, many associated with the Guild of St George, a utopian society (still thriving) founded by Ruskin under his own mastership in 1871.

In 1870 Ruskin became the first Slade professor of art at Oxford. But, despite caution, Ruskin did not keep his 'own peculiar opinions' out of his lectures. Senior members of the university were alarmed, Ruskin offended: he resigned in 1878. Although Ruskin returned to Oxford in 1883 and gave two more courses of lectures, some of his statements were even more startling than before, and he resigned again in 1885.

The isolation of his later years was mitigated by the loyalty of his disciples, including J. W. Bunney and George Allen, both students of the Working Men's College, and W. G. Collingwood, who acted as Ruskin's secretary at Brantwood, the house in the Lake District which was his home after 1870. Older friends, such as Sir Henry Acland and Thomas *Carlyle, remained doubtful about the schemes, the vehemence, and the frequent obscurity of his later pronouncements. They were also disturbed by Ruskin's passion for Rose La Touche, an Anglo-Irish girl, who was 11 when Ruskin came across her in 1858, 18 when he proposed in 1866. But he could not share her evangelical religious views, her parents were also opposed, and she died, mad, in 1875. Ruskin often wrote for her and, indirectly, of her, in later life, and in *Praeterita*, the autobiography on which he worked sporadically between 1885 and 1889, he would have spoken of her directly; but he did not complete it. After 1889 Ruskin wrote nothing and spoke rarely, but was cared for by his cousin Joan Severn at Brantwood. The influence of his thought on art and politics was profound, and enduring.

RUSS, Joanna (1937–) American *science fiction author. *The Female Man* (1975) described both the utopian and the dystopic preoccupations of the American women's movement. *Alyx* (1976) incorporated earlier work about a female mercenary hero. *How to Suppress Women's Writing* (1983) is a collection of essays.

RUSSELL, Bertrand, third Earl Russell (1872–1970) Philosopher and social critic, who wrote voluminously on philosophy, logic, education, economics, and politics, and throughout his life was the champion of advanced political and social causes. He was the inventor of the Theory of Descriptions. *The Principles of Mathematics* (1903) and *Principia Mathematica* (the latter in collaboration with A. N. Whitehead (1861-1947), 1910) quickly became classics of mathematical logic. Other important philosophical works include *The Analysis of Mind* (1921), *An Inquiry into Meaning and Truth* (1940), and *Human Knowledge, Its Scope and Limits* (1948). Russell was awarded the *Nobel Prize for Literature in 1950. He published a three-volume *Autobiography* (1967-9).

RUSSELL, Eric Frank (1905-78) The first British *science fiction writer to receive a *Hugo award, for 'Allamagoosa' (1955), his cheerful lampoon of military bureaucracy. *Sinister Barrier* (1943) suggests we are property, harvested by aliens. His wisecracking style and iconoclastic speculations made him a popular writer.

RUSSELL, George William (Æ) (1867-1935) Irish poet, dramatist, novelist, mystic, painter, and social reformer. The ethereal lyrics of *Homeward* (1894) set the *Celtic Twilight signature of the poetry of the early years of the *Irish Revival. His poetic drama *Deirdre* was performed in 1902 at the Irish National Theatre (later the *Abbey). His later volumes include *The Divine Vision* (1904), *The Interpreters* (1922), and *Midsummer Eve* (1928). He did much to support young writers, from Padraic *Colum to Patrick *Kavanagh. His prophetic novel *The Avatars* aroused much interest in 1933, the year he left Ireland in disgust at the emerging character of the new state.

RUSSELL, Willy (1947-) Playwright, whose play about the Beatles, *John Paul George Ringo . . . and Bert* (1974), first brought him to public notice. *Breezeblock Park* (1975) deals with life on a Liverpool housing estate; *Stags and Hens* (1978, filmed 1990 as *Dancin' thru the Dark*) describes the parties held by a couple on the eve of their wedding; *Educating Rita* (1980; filmed 1983), is about the transformative relations between an Open University tutor and Rita, his working-class student. The successful musical *Blood Brothers* (1983) treats the lives of twins separated at birth and brought up very differently; *Shirley Valentine* (1986; filmed 1989), describes a Liverpool housewife's escape from her dull life after a holiday in Greece.

Russian film or more accurately Soviet film, made a dramatic cultural and political impact outside Soviet Russia in the late 1920s. *Battleship Potemkin* by Sergei Eisenstein (1898-1948) opened in Germany in 1926, causing a sensation and provoking censorship and bans in many countries. It was not seen in Britain until a private screening in 1929, organized by the *Film Society and attended by Eisenstein. The new Soviet films of Eisenstein, Vsevelod Pudovkin (1893-1953), and Dziga Vertov (1896-1954) quickly became fashionable, and were eagerly analysed in the magazine *Close Up*, funded by *Bryher, and including criticism by H. D. (Hilda *Doolittle) and Dorothy *Richardson.

Also inspired by the techniques and themes of Soviet 'montage' *cinema, with its emphasis on industrial transformation, the British *documentary film movement emerged under the leadership of John Grierson (1898-1972).

Soviet film made a fresh impact abroad in the 1960s, when *Hamlet* (1964), by the film-maker Grigori Kozintsev (1905-73), appeared, based on Boris *Pasternak's translation. It was widely shown and admired, and was followed by his *King Lear* in 1971.

Russian formalism A school of literary criticism which originated in pre-revolutionary Russia and was suppressed in the early 1930s. Most of its founders were young men under the age of 20 who held that literature should be studied not as a reflection of an author's life, nor as a mirror of the society in which it had been produced, but as an autonomous phenomenon governed by its own laws. Major figures associated with formalism include Roman *Jakobson, Viktor Shklovsky (1893-1984), Iurii Tynianov (1894-1943), and Boris Eikhenbaum (1886-1959). The formalists aimed to transform the discipline of literary studies by adopting scientific and objective methodology. After the 1917 Revolution several formalists occupied prominent academic positions, but their insistence on the autonomy of literature contradicted the Bolshevik view of literature as a servant of the state. They were attacked by orthodox *Marxist critics for their refusal to treat literature as a reflection of social structures, and for their 'irrelevant' and 'escapist' concern with the specifics of poetic language.

Early formalist studies concentrated on examining the specific formal properties of poetic language, and identifying the ways in which certain 'devices' worked in a text to produce the quality of 'literariness'. One such 'device' was identified as the process of 'making strange' or defamiliarization. More accessible to non-Russian readers are studies of narrative devices in prose fiction.

In the later 1920s the formalists, now on the defensive, attempted to develop their work in directions which might be less controversial, recognizing, to some extent, the influence of society on literature, and, in some cases, reverting to something resembling a more traditional 'life and works' approach to authors.

Russian novel The first Russian novels were adaptations of Western European 18th-century works such as the epistolary novel *The Letters of Ernest and Doravra* (1766) by Fedor Emin (c.1735–1770), based on *Rousseau's *La Nouvelle Heloïse*. Russia's first historical novel, *Iurii Miloslavskii* (1829) by Mikhail Zagoskin (1789–1852), owed its conception to Walter *Scott's example which continued to influence numerous emulators in the 1830s, culminating in Alexander *Pushkin's *The Captain's Daughter* (1836). Pushkin's novel in verse *Eugene Onegin* (1823–31), inspired by Lord *Byron's *Don Juan*, is the first truly Russian novel, initiating the period from 1830 to 1880 when the major Russian classics by Pushkin, *Lermontov, *Gogol, Goncharov, *Turgenev, *Tolstoy, and *Dostoevsky were published. In its Russian context the novel, while portraying typical Russian heroes and heroines, invariably reflected social and political issues, and engaged with moral questions. In this the Russians were prompted by their English counterparts, particularly Charles *Dickens and George *Eliot, who were greatly admired. Dostoevsky's legacy of the ideological novel was the crowning achievement of an unparalleled half-century of novel writing that ended with Tolstoy's renunciation of literature in 1880 and the deaths of Dostoevsky in 1881 and Turgenev in 1883. The *symbolist movement (1890–1910) reacted against their predecessors' commitment to civic and moral issues, celebrating instead the values of beauty, mysticism, and untrammelled individualism in stylistically experimental works. *Bely's *Silver Dove* (1909) and *Petersburg* (1916) are outstanding examples of symbolist novels. The inheritance of social engagement was, however, evident in Gorky's early novels. His *Mother* (1907) was later adopted as a pattern for the *Socialist Realist novels that dominated the Stalinist period 1932–53. After Stalin's death, previously unpublishable novels now passed the censorship; most notably *Bulgakov's *The Master and Margarita* (1966–7), written in 1928–40. Official interference, however, prevented the publication in their homeland of *Pasternak's *Doctor Zhivago* (1957) and *Solzhenitsyn's novels until 1989.

Ruth *See* BIBLE.

Ruth A novel by Elizabeth *Gaskell, published 1853. Ruth Hilton, a 15-year-old orphan apprenticed to a dressmaker, is seduced and then deserted by wealthy Henry Bellingham. She is rescued from suicide by Thurston Benson, a Dissenting minister, who with the help of his sister and his outspoken servant Sally takes her into his house under an assumed name as a widow. She bears Bellingham's son, and is redeemed by love for her child and by Benson's guidance. Later she becomes a governess in the home of tyrannical Mr Bradshaw, where she is discovered by Bellingham, whose offer of marriage she rejects. Bradshaw, learning of her past, brutally dismisses her. Ruth regains respect by becoming a heroic nurse during a cholera epidemic, and dies after nursing Bellingham to recovery. In arousing sympathy for 'fallen women' who had been victims of seduction, Gaskell shocked many contemporary readers.

RUTHERFORD, Mark *See* WHITE, WILLIAM HALE.

Ruthwell Cross A stone monument over five metres high, in the parish church at Ruthwell, Dumfriesshire, dating perhaps from the 8th century, on which are inscribed in *runes some alliterating phrases closely corresponding to parts of the Old English poem *Dream of the Rood*.

RYMAN, Geoff (1951–) Canadian-born author resident in the UK. His first novel, *The Warrior Who Carried Life* (1985) was an acclaimed *fantasy; much of his subsequent work, including *Air* (2005) is *science fiction. His work also includes the web-based 'hypertext novel' *253* (published as a book 1998), and *The King's Last Song* (2006), set in modern and 12th-century Cambodia; and as writer and editor Ryman constantly questions genre boundaries. *Was* (1992) uses the device of a 'real' Dorothy who is the model for the protagonist of L. Frank *Baum's *The Wonderful Wizard of Oz* to explore America's dreams and dark fantasies.

RYMER, Thomas (1642/3–1713) Historian and critic. In *The Tragedies of the Last Age Considered* (1678) and *A Short View of Tragedy* (1692) he brutally lambasted British dramatists (including William Shakespeare, whose *Othello* is particularly condemned) for failing to observe the practice of the ancients (*see* BATTLE OF THE BOOKS) and French *neo-classical principles. These works were treated with respect by John *Dryden, Alexander *Pope, and Samuel *Johnson.

Sabine farm *See* HORACE.

Sackville, Thomas, first earl of Dorset and
Baron Buckhurst (*c.*1536–1608) Writer and administrator; he entered Parliament in 1558, was
raised to the peerage in 1567, and held a number of high official positions. He wrote the
Induction and The **Complaint of Buckingham*
for *A *Mirror for Magistrates*, and collaborated
(probably writing only the last two acts) with
Thomas Norton (1532–84) in the tragedy of
*Gorboduc. He was an ancestor of Vita **Sackville-West and is discussed in her *Knole and the
Sackvilles* (1922).

SACKVILLE-WEST, 'Vita' (Victoria Mary)
(1892–1962) Writer, who wrote eight novels as a
child before publishing *Poems of East and West*
(1917). *Knole and the Sackvilles* (1922), her novels, *Heritage* (1919), *The Heir* (1922), and *The
Edwardians* (1930) all centre on her childhood
home Knole, in Kent. In 1913 she married
Harold **Nicolson, and travelled widely before
settling at Sissinghurst, Kent, in 1930. In 1922
she met Virginia **Woolf; Sackville-West wrote
Seducers in Ecuador (1924) for her and received
Orlando (1928) in return. Her other works include a pastoral poem, *The Land* (1926), *All
Passion Spent* (1931, novel), and many works
on travel, gardening, and biography. Her unorthodox but harmonious marriage was described
by her son Nigel Nicolson in *Portrait of a Marriage* (1973).

SA`DĪ of Shiraz (d. *c.*1290) Famous Persian
literary figure, whose adventurous life included
a spell as a prisoner of the Crusaders in Syria.
He was already well known as a poet when, back
in Shiraz, he wrote his two principal works, the
Bustān or 'Orchard' (1257), comprising ten sections of verse on moralistic topics, and the *Guli-
stān* or 'Rose Garden' (1258), a lighter, more
humorous prose work interspersed with passages of verse. Their freshness and sharp wit
brought them a popularity that they still retain.
They are often used as early reading for those
studying Persian, and Sir William **Jones and,

later, Edward **FitzGerald knew them well.
Ralph Waldo **Emerson's acquaintance with
Sa`dī, about whom he wrote, came through
a 19th-century German translation.

Sad Shepherd, The, *A Tale of Robin Hood*
The last and unfinished play of Ben **Jonson, a
pastoral tragicomedy written *c.*1635, printed
1641. **Robin Hood invites shepherds and shepherdesses to a feast in Sherwood Forest, but it is
marred by the arts of the witch Maudlin, aided
by her familiar, Puck-Hairy. Only three acts
exist; there are continuations by Francis Wal-
dron (1783) and Alan Porter (1935).

saga An Old Norse word meaning 'spoken
narrative', applied to narrative compositions
produced in Iceland and Norway in the 13th,
14th, and 15th centuries, but typically set
much earlier. There are three main types of
saga: family sagas, dealing with the first settlers
of Iceland and their descendants; kings' sagas,
historical works about the kings of Norway; and
legendary or heroic sagas, fantastic adventure
stories about legendary heroes. The family sagas
and the kings' sagas share an elegant, laconic
style. The family sagas, previously thought to
be based almost wholly on oral traditions, are
now considered literary fictions with some historical basis, for example **Njáls saga*, which
stands out because of its scope and breadth of
characterization. *Eyrbyggja saga* is concerned
with the emergence of a politically stable community, though it also presents some supernatural incidents. *Laxdaela saga* deals with a tragic
love-triangle and the fortunes of one of Iceland's most powerful families at that time. *Gret-
tis saga* tells the story of a famous Icelandic
outlaw. Grettir's fights with the monstrous walking corpse Glámr and with a troll woman are
analogous to Beowulf's fight with Grendel and
Grendel's mother (*see* BEOWULF). Snorri Sturluson's **Heimskringla* comprises a history of
the kings of Norway; **Völsunga saga* recounts
the legends of the Goths and Burgundians
which underlie Richard **Wagner's *Ring des
Nibelungen* cycle. *Sturlunga saga*, with its five

feuding families, is unique in being a compilation of sagas about figures almost contemporary with their 13th-century authors. William *Morris did much to popularize Icelandic literature in England (*see* SIGURD THE VOLSUNG).

SAID, Edward (1935–2003) American critic, born in Jerusalem to Christian Palestinian parents. His works of general literary theory, *Beginnings* (1975) and *The World, the Text and the Critic* (1983), show the influence of Michel *Foucault. *Orientalism* (1978), argues that Western writers and 'experts' have constructed a myth of the 'Orient'; it is a founding text of modern *postcolonial theory, complemented by the essays collected in *Culture and Imperialism* (1993). *Out of Place* (1999) is his memoir.

ST AUBYN, Edward (1960–) Novelist. The trilogy *Never Mind* (1992), *Bad News* (1992), and *Some Hope* (1994) describes with horrific conviction the indulged but appalling childhood of Patrick Melrose, sexually abused by his father in the 1960s, then follows him to New York and back to London, as he struggles to cope with his drug addiction and his terrible paternal legacy. *On the Edge* (1998) is a journey through the New Age cults of the 1990s. *A Clue to the Exit* (2000) and *Mother's Milk* (2006) continue his complex and often painful portrayal of family allegiances and betrayals.

SAINT-EXUPÉRY, Antoine de (1900–44) French novelist; his novels, all quickly translated into English, are intimately linked with his flying experiences. He also wrote a deceptively simple book for children, *Le Petit Prince* (1943: *The Little Prince*). He failed to return from a reconnaissance mission in North Africa: his unfinished collection of desert meditations, *Citadelle* (1948: *Wisdom of the Sands*) was published posthumously.

St Leon A novel by William *Godwin, published 1799. Godwin tells the story of Reginald St Leon who has discovered the philosopher's stone and the alchemical grails of immortality and the secret of turning base metal into gold. The story mixes *Gothic elements with the socio-political concerns of his earlier **Caleb Williams*. The story influenced his daughter Mary *Shelley's *Frankenstein*.

St Ronan's Well A novel by *Walter Scott, published 1823. One of only two set within Scott's lifetime, it is the only one in which he attempts contemporary social *satire. St Ronan's Well is a tawdry, third-rate spa, inhabited by meretricious, pretentious characters. The novel ends in unrelieved misery.

Saint's Everlasting Rest, The See BAXTER, RICHARD.

SAKI (1870–1916) Pseudonym of Hector Hugh Munro, short story writer, born in Burma. 'Saki' is the name of the 'cypress-slender Minister of Wine' in *The Rubáiyát of *Omar Khayyám*. His stories, which mix the satiric, the comic, the macabre, and the supernatural, were collected as *Reginald* (1904), followed by *Reginald in Russia* (1910), *The Chronicles of Clovis* (1911), *Beasts and Super-Beasts* (1914), *The Toys of Peace* (1919), and *The Square Egg* (1924). *The Unbearable Bassington* (1912) and *When William Came* (1913) are both novels. In 1914 he enlisted as a trooper and was killed in France.

SALA, George Augustus (1828–96) Journalist and illustrator. He became a regular contributor to *Household Words* (1851–6), and was sent by Charles *Dickens to Russia as correspondent at the end of the Crimean War. He pioneered first-hand reporting from overseas conflicts, including the American Civil War and the Franco-Prussian War. His racy fiction, includes *The Seven Sons of Mammon* (1862), a satirical account of ruthless capitalist practices.

SALINGER, J. D. (Jerome David) (1919–2010) American novelist and short story writer. *The Catcher in the Rye* (1951, novel) is the story of adolescent Holden Caulfield who runs away from boarding school in Pennsylvania to New York, where he preserves his innocence despite various attempts to lose it. The colloquial, lively, first-person narration, with its attacks on the 'phoniness' of the adult world and its clinging to family sentiment in the form of Holden's affection for his sister Phoebe, made the novel popular with a wide readership. A sequence of works about the eccentric Glass family began with *Nine Stories* (1953, published in Britain as *For Esmé—With Love and Squalor*) and was followed by *Franny and Zooey* (1961), *Raise High the Roof Beam, Carpenters*, and *Seymour: An Introduction* (published together, 1963). A notably reclusive character, he was the subject of Ian Hamilton's *In Search of J. D. Salinger* (1988).

SALKEY, Andrew (1928–95) Caribbean poet, short story writer, editor, and broadcaster. His novels include *Escape to an Autumn Pavement* (1960) and *A Quality of Violence* (1978). Other works include stories and fables for younger readers, such as *Anancy's Score* (1973),

S

which takes its name from the Jamaican trickster spider of creation myths, Ananse.

SALLUST (Gaius Sallustius Crispus) (probably 86–35 BC) Roman historian whose surviving works are two monographs, *Bellum Catilinae* (*The Conspiracy of Catiline*), a major source for Ben *Jonson's *Catiline, and *Belum Iugurthinum* (*The War against Jugurtha*). His practice of including speeches, gnomic sayings, and character sketches in his narrative was copied by the 12th-century *William of Malmesbury. The *Jugurtha* was translated by Alexander *Barclay early in the 16th century, and Thomas *Heywood translated both works (1608). Sallust's condemnations of corruption were much savoured by the architects of the American Revolution.

Samson *See* BIBLE.

Samson Agonistes A tragedy by John *Milton, published 1671, in the same volume as *Paradise Regained*. It is modelled on Greek tragedy, and has been frequently compared to *Prometheus Bound* by *Aeschylus or *Oedipus at Colonus* by *Sophocles. Predominantly in blank verse, it also contains passages of metrical freedom and originality, and some rhyme. In a preface, Milton says it was never intended for the stage. 'Agonistes' means in Greek a contestant in the games or a champion. Based loosely on the biblical Book of Judges, the tragedy deals with the last phase of Samson's life when he is blinded and captive, a phase many have likened to Milton's situation after the collapse of the Commonwealth. In the course of the drama Samson is visited successively by friends from his tribe (the chorus), his father Manoa, his wife Dalila, Harapha, a strong man of Gath, and a Philistine officer who summons him to perform feats of strength to entertain his masters in the temple of Dagon. After his exit, a messenger brings news of his final feat—pulling down the supporting pillars and destroying himself and the audience.

SANCHO, Ignatius (?1729–80) Afro-British letter writer, born on a slave ship during the Middle Passage from Africa to the Americas. Brought to England as a child, he eventually became valet to the duke of Montague. Sancho published letters in newspapers on public affairs, corresponded with Laurence *Sterne, and was the first Afro-British patron of white writers and artists. He called Phillis *Wheatley a 'genius in bondage'. A former correspondent published *Letters of the Late Ignatius Sancho, an African* (1782). *See also* SLAVERY.

SANDBURG, Carl August (1878–1967) American poet, who challenged contemporary taste by his use of colloquialism and free verse. He published *Chicago Poems* (1916), *Cornhuskers* (1918), *Smoke and Steel* (1920), *Slabs of the Sunburnt West* (1922), *Good Morning America* (1928), and *Complete Poems* (1950). His film reviews are collected in *Carl Sandburg at the Movies* (1988). He also compiled a collection of folk songs, *The American Songbag* (1927), wrote stories and poems for children, a six-volume life of Abraham Lincoln (1926–39), and *Always the Young Strangers* (1953), an autobiography. *Remembrance Rock* (1948), a novel on an epic scale, traces the growth of an American family from its English origins and its crossing on the *Mayflower* to the present.

SANDFORD, Jeremy (1930–2003) Television playwright, remembered for his powerful BBC television drama *Cathy Come Home* (1966), which focused attention on the plight of a young family trapped in a downward spiral of poverty and homelessness. One of the landmarks of the socially committed drama documentary of the 1960s, it was followed by *Edna the Inebriate Woman* (1971, BBC), a sympathetic portrayal of an elderly 'bag lady'.

Sanditon An unfinished novel by Jane *Austen, written 1817. Mr Parker is obsessed with the ambition to transform the small village of Sanditon, on the south coast, into a fashionable resort. Charlotte Heywood, an attractive, alert young woman, is invited to stay with the Parkers, where she catches the fancy of Lady Denham, the local great lady. Denham's nephew and niece, Sir Edward and Miss Denham, live nearby, and the second heroine of the novel, Clara Brereton, is staying with her. Edward plans (with a frankness of expression new to the author) to seduce Clara; but his aunt intends him to marry a West Indian heiress, under the care of a Mrs Griffiths. After a ludicrous series of complications, the excited inhabitants of Sanditon find the expected invasion of visitors consists merely of Mrs Griffiths and three young ladies.

This entertaining fragment was written in the first three months of 1817, when Jane Austen was already suffering from Addison's disease (of which she died on 18 July).

SANDYS, George (1578–1644) English poet, and colonist, who travelled, starting in 1610, to France, Italy, Constantinople, Egypt, Mount Sinai. Palestine, Cyprus, Sicily, Naples, and Rome, and published his fascinating

Relation of a Journey in 1615. In 1621 he went to America as treasurer of the Virginia Company, advocating a lenient policy towards the Indians. He published a verse translation of *Ovid's Metamorphoses* (1621–6), a verse *Paraphrase upon the Psalms* (1636), and *Christ's Passion: A Tragedy*, translated from the Latin of Hugo Grotius (1640).

SANSOM, William (1912–76) Short story writer, travel writer, and novelist. His first stories were published in literary periodicals (*Horizon*, *New Writing*, the *Cornhill Magazine*, and others) and his first volume, *Fireman Flower and Other Stories* (1944), reflects his experiences with the National Fire Service in wartime London. His most successful novel, *The Body* (1949), is set in London. A collection of stories, with an introduction by Elizabeth *Bowen, appeared in 1963.

SANTAYANA, George (1863–1952) Spanish-born writer and philosopher. He was a speculative philosopher, opposed to German idealism, whose views are embodied in his *The Life of Reason* (1905–6). He later modified his philosophy in a series of four books, *Realms of Being* (1927–40). Santayana also published poetry, criticism (see *Essays in Literary Criticism*, 1956), reviews, and memoirs; other works include *Soliloquies in England* (1922), essays on the English character; *Character and Opinion in the United States* (1920), one of several studies of American life; and his three-volume *Persons and Places* (1944–53). He strongly influenced Wallace *Stevens, whose poem 'To an Old Philosopher in Rome' is a tribute to him.

SAPPER (1888–1937) The pseudonym of Herman Cyril McNeile, taken from the nickname of the Royal Engineers with whom he served during the First World War; he created the character of Hugh 'Bulldog' Drummond, the hearty, charming, xenophobic British ex-army officer who foils the activities of Carl Peterson, the international crook. He appears in *Bull-dog Drummond* (1920), *The Female of the Species* (1928), and many other popular thrillers; after McNeile's death the series was continued by his friend and collaborator G. T. Fairlie.

Sapphics Verses written in imitation of a predominantly trochaic *metre used in Greek by *Sappho and in Latin by *Horace in stanzas of four lines in which the first three lines have eleven syllables, the last line five. Philip *Sidney, A. C. *Swinburne, Ezra *Pound and

Peter *Reading are among those who attempted English Sapphics.

SAPPHO (b. *c.* late 7th century BC) The most famous woman poet of antiquity, a native of Lesbos. Evidence for her life and career is scanty and controversial. She had a husband and a daughter, Cleis. She writes of female erotic feelings. Some poems are homosexual in colouring, but there are also *epithalamia, celebrating marriages. She figured posthumously in Attic comedies, and romantic fantasies and scandal grew up about her name: she was a priestess of Aphrodite; she was a Lesbian, in the modern sense; she threw herself into the sea, for love of a man, Phaon. *Ovid includes this last doomed affair among the *Heroides*, and Alexander *Pope translated it as *Sapho* [sic] *to Phaon*. *Catullus closely imitated her one complete surviving ode. Her poems were collected and arranged into nine books (*c.*300 BC). Sappho was praised for the directness, simplicity, and power of her poetry.

Sappho and Phaon A collection of sonnets by Mary *Robinson (1757/8–1800), published 1796. The sonnet sequence relates the story of *Sappho's doomed love for the boatman Phaon. Rather than the more common Shakespearian sonnet, the sequence uses a Petrarchan form in imitation of 'that sublime Bard' John *Milton.

SARAMAGO, José (1922–2010) Portuguese novelist who was first brought to the attention of English readers with the translation (1988) of his novel *Memorial do convento* (1982; trans. as *Baltasar and Blimunda*). This subversive historical novel treats the 18th century in Portugal from a left-wing perspective. In *O ano da morte de Ricardo Reis* (1984: *The Year of the Death of Ricardo Reis*), set in 1936, Dr Ricardo Reis returns to Lisbon after a sixteen-year absence, and roams the city with, among others, the recently dead poet Fernando *Pessoa. In *Ensaio sobre a cegueira* (1995: *Blindness*) the spread of an epidemic of white blindness brings about the collapse of a civilized society. It was followed by *Ensaio sobre a lucidez* (2004: *Seeing*). His final novel was *Caim* (2009: Cain).

Sardanapalus A poetic drama by Lord *Byron, published 1821. The subject was taken from the *Bibliotheca Historica* of *Diodorus Siculus.

Sartor Resartus: *The Life and Opinions of Herr Teufelsdröckh* By Thomas *Carlyle,

published in **Fraser's Magazine* (1833–4), and
as a separate volume (Boston, 1836), partly
through the intervention of Ralph Waldo *Emerson.

The work was influenced by German *Romanticism, particularly Richter. It consists of
two parts: a discourse on the philosophy of
clothes (*sartor resartus* means 'the tailor re-
patched') based on the speculations of an imaginary Professor Teufelsdröckh, and leading to
the conclusion that all symbols, forms, and
human institutions are properly clothes, and as
such temporary; and a biography of Teufelsdröckh himself, which is in part Carlyle's autobiography. The prose, dotted with capital
letters, exclamation marks, phrases in German,
compound words of the author's own invention,
wild appeals to the reader, and outbursts of
bitter satire, is a memorable early example of
what came to be known as 'Carlylese'.

SARTRE, Jean-Paul (1905–80) French philosopher, novelist, playwright, literary critic, and
political activist. He was the principal exponent
of *existentialism in France, and, together with
Simone de *Beauvoir, had a considerable influence on French intellectual life in the decades
following the Second World War. He made important contributions in many areas: existentialist and Marxist philosophy (*L'Être et le néant*,
1943: *Being and Nothingness*); the novel (*La
Nausée*, 1938: *Nausea*); drama (*Les Mouches*,
1943: *The Flies*; *Huis clos*, 1945: *In Camera*);
literary criticism (*Qu'est-ce que la littérature?*,
1948: *What is Literature?*); and biography, with
studies of Charles *Baudelaire (1947), Jean
Genet (1952), and Gustave *Flaubert (1971–2).

SASSOON, Siegfried (1886–1967) Poet. In
the trenches in the First World War he began to
write poetry which displays his bleak realism,
his contempt for war leaders and patriotic
cant, and his compassion for his comrades. Dispatched as 'shell-shocked' to Craiglockhart War
Hospital in Edinburgh, he encountered and encouraged Wilfred *Owen, and organized a public protest against the war. In 1917 he published
his war poems in *The Old Huntsman* and in
1918 further poems in *Counter-Attack*. From
the late 1920s Sassoon began to think of himself
as a religious poet, and converted to Roman
Catholicism in 1957.

His semi-autobiographical trilogy (*Memoirs
of a Fox-Hunting Man*, 1928; *Memoirs of an
Infantry Officer*, 1930; and *Sherston's Progress*,
1936; as *The Complete Memoirs of George Sher-*

ston, 1937) relates the life of George Sherston, a
lonely boy who eventually finds himself a junior
officer in the trenches, where he is brutally
thrust into adulthood. *The Old Century and
Seven More Years* (1938), *The Weald of Youth*
(1942), and *Siegfried's Journey* (1945) are autobiographies.

Satan The devil, God's primary antagonist,
the figure who tempts Job in the Old Testament
and Jesus in the New (Luke, ch. 4), and who is
identified with the serpent who tempts Eve
(Genesis, ch. 2) and the dragon who fights
St *Michael in the war in heaven and is cast
down into the lake of fire (Revelation, chs 12
and 20). Satan before his fall is known as Lucifer, the morning star; he is also associated with
Apollyon, the angel of the bottomless pit (Revelation 9: 11), with whom Christian fights in **Pilgrim's Progress*, and Beelzebub, the prince of
devils. He was popularly portrayed with horns
and cloven feet: *Othello looks down at Iago's
feet for evidence of his diabolic nature. In **Paradise Lost* by contrast Satan has the characteristics of an implacable hero of classical epic.
He was a popular subject for 19th-century apocalyptic painters like John Martin.

'Satanic school' The name under which
Robert *Southey attacks Lord *Byron and
the younger Romantics in the preface to his
A *Vision of Judgement.

satire A poem or prose composition in which
prevailing vices or follies are held up to ridicule
or scorn; or a vein of such mockery found incidentally in many kinds of literary work, especially comic drama and fiction. In English
literature, satire may be held to have begun
with *Chaucer in his General Prologue to the
*Canterbury Tales. Subsequent 15th- and 16th-
century writers include William *Dunbar, John
*Skelton, George *Gascoigne, Thomas *Lodge,
and John *Marston. The first important dramatic satires are the major plays of Ben *Jonson,
notably **Volpone*. The great age of English satire
began in the 1660s with the enormous popularity of Butler's **Hudibras*. John *Dryden perfected the epigrammatic and antithetical use of
the *heroic couplet for satirical purposes in
*Mac Flecknoe and other works. Major satirists
in the *Augustan period include Alexander
*Pope and Jonathan *Swift, along with John
*Gay and Matthew *Prior (*see* MOCK EPIC). The
same tradition was followed by Charles
*Churchill, and brilliantly revived by Lord

*Byron in *English Bards and Scotch Reviewers.* The Victorian novel proved an excellent vehicle for social satire with Charles *Dickens, W. M. *Thackeray, and others. In the early 20th century, Thomas *Hardy, T. S. *Eliot, Siegfried *Sassoon, and Louis *MacNeice contributed to a revival of verse satire, while prose satire flourished in the novels of E. M. *Forster, Evelyn *Waugh, Wyndham *Lewis, Aldous *Huxley, Christopher *Isherwood, and George *Orwell. A 'satire boom' in 1960s was launched in the stage revue *Beyond the Fringe* (1960) by Alan *Bennett, Jonathan Miller (1934–), Peter Cook (1937–95), and Dudley Moore (1935–2002), and continued in the fortnightly magazine *Private Eye* (1962–). Satire is strongly evident in the 21st century fiction of, for example, Malcolm *Bradbury, Jonathan *Coe, Alasdair *Gray, and Salman *Rushdie.

Satiromastix, or The Untrussing of the Humorous Poet A comedy by Thomas *Dekker, written 1601 as part of the 'war of the theatres' (with John *Marston?), printed 1602. Ben *Jonson in his *Poetaster* had satirized Dekker and Marston, under the names of Demetrius and Crispinus, while he himself figures as Horace. Dekker here replies, bringing the same Horace, Crispinus, and Demetrius on the stage once more. Horace is seen sitting in a study laboriously writing an *epithalamium, and stuck for a rhyme. Crispinus and Demetrius enter and reproach him for his bad temper. Presently Captain Tucca (of the *Poetaster*) enters, mocking and abusing Horace. Horace's peculiarities of dress and appearance, his vanity and bitterness, are ridiculed; he is finally crowned with nettles.

Saturday Review An influential weekly review founded in 1855, pungently conservative in its early days, which ran until 1938. In the mid-Victorian period, its anonymous fiction reviews were sometimes savage—Charles *Dickens, W. M. *Thackeray, and Anthony *Trollope were among those who suffered. It later became more literary in its interests (notably under the editorship of Frank *Harris, 1894–8), publishing work by Thomas *Hardy, H. G. *Wells, Max *Beerbohm, Arthur *Symons, and others. George Bernard *Shaw was dramatic critic from 1895 to 1898.

Saturn (Greek 'Cronos') God whose throne was usurped by his son *Jupiter (Greek 'Zeus'). Saturn's reign was identified with the Golden Age in classical mythology: *Virgil's fourth eclogue prophesies its restoration. Later literary depictions usually follow Virgil, but John

*Keats's *Hyperion* portrays Saturn and his brethren the *Titans helplessly recognizing the beauty and power of the young gods who replace them. See FOUR AGES.

satyr drama A humorous performance with a chorus of satyrs that ancient Athenian dramatists were expected to append to tragic trilogies offered for competition. This practice, which had the incidental virtue of providing light relief, may have been due to the belief mentioned by *Aristotle (*Poetics*, ch. 4) that tragedy had its origin in performances by actors dressed as satyrs. The surviving fragments of *Aeschylus' *Diktyoulkoi* (The Net-Drawers) and *Sophocles' *Ichneutai* (The Trackers) reveal sympathy for the promptings of animal impulse and a lyrical feeling for nature. Only one satyric drama has survived intact, the *Cyclops* of *Euripides. Tony *Harrison's *The Trackers of Oxyrhynchus* (1988) is an English satyr play adapted from the fragmentary *Ichneutai.*

Satyricon See PETRONIUS ARBITER.

Saul See BIBLE.

SAUSSURE, Ferdinand de (1857–1913) Swiss linguistician. His lectures delivered at Geneva were reconstructed from students' notes into the *Cours de linguistique générale* (1915: *Course in General Linguistics*), the basis of modern linguistics and of much modern literary criticism. His most important and influential idea was the conception of language as a system of signs, arbitrarily assigned and only intelligible in terms of the particular system as a whole. This idea was applied outside language in the new science called semiotics. Language is a structure whose parts can only be understood in relation to each other; this *'Structuralism' has been influential in literary criticism and in other fields, such as sociology. Saussure's emphasis was on the value of synchronic study (with which the term 'linguistics' is sometimes used synonymously, as distinct from 'philology' for historical study), rather than the diachronic philology with which he had previously been concerned.

SAVAGE, Richard (*c*.1698–1743) Poet; the account given by Samuel *Johnson, in his psychologically intense biography (1744), contains much unverifiable detail. Savage was convicted of murder in 1727, and subsequently pardoned; he then wrote verse tributes to Queen Caroline (1683–1737) in a self-appointed capacity as 'volunteer laureate', and produced longer poems such as 'The Bastard' (1728), and *The *Wanderer* (1729). Savage died penniless in a Bristol jail.

Saved A play by Edward *Bond, which caused much controversy when it was first seen (members only) at the *Royal Court in 1965, having been refused a licence for public performance. Bond evokes a bleak south London landscape of domestic and street violence and the somewhat caricatured impoverished pastimes of the working class. In the central episode Pam's baby, which has been neglected by her and which cries loudly through much of the preceding action, is tormented and stoned to death in its pram by a gang of youths and its putative father, Fred. The subsequent lack of response to the child's death adds to the sense of dramatic shock.

SAVILE, George *See* HALIFAX, GEORGE.

SAVONAROLA, Fra Girolamo (1452–98) Dominican friar; an eloquent and powerful preacher, he castigated the artistic licence, interest in paganism, and moral corruption of late 15th-century Italy. His political and moral invectives antagonized the pope, Alexander VI Borgia and he was burnt at the stake in 1498. There is a sympathetic portrayal of him in George Eliot's *Romola*.

Savoy A short-lived but important 'art and literature' magazine, edited by Arthur *Symons, of which eight issues appeared in 1896, with contributions by Aubrey *Beardsley, Joseph *Conrad, Ernest *Dowson, W. B. *Yeats, and others.

Sawles Warde A work of alliterative prose, found in three manuscripts with the saints' lives called 'The *Katherine Group', dating from the end of the 12th century and from the west Midlands (probably Herefordshire). It is a loose translation of part of *De Anima* by Hugh of St Victor. It has connections with the morality castle, an allegorical representation of body and soul, found from *Grosseteste's *Chasteau d'Amour* to The *Castle of Perseverance*.

SAXO GRAMMATICUS A 13th-century Danish historian, author of the *Gesta Danorum*, a partly mythical Latin history of the Danes (which contains the *Hamlet* story).

SAYERS, Dorothy L. (1893–1957) Crime writer and playwright. Her novels are outstanding for their literariness, well-researched backgrounds, observant characterization, and

ingenious plotting, as well as for their detective Lord Peter Wimsey (*see* DETECTIVE FICTION). *Whose Body?* (1923) was followed by *Murder Must Advertise* (1933), *The Nine Tailors* (1934), and *Gaudy Night* (1935). From the early 1940s she threw herself into translating Dante's *Divina commedia*.

SCALIGER, Joseph Justus (1540–1609) The son of Julius Caesar *Scaliger, one of the greatest scholars of the *Renaissance. His edition of the 1st-century AD Roman author Manilius (1579) and his *De Emendatione Temporum* (1583) revolutionized ancient chronology by insisting on the recognition of the historical material relating to the Jews, the Persians, the Babylonians, and the Egyptians. He also issued critical editions of many classical authors.

SCALIGER, Julius Caesar (1484–1558) Classical scholar and physician. In the Renaissance debate about the purity of Latin, he was an advocate of *Cicero. He wrote an important treatise on poetics (1561) which contained the earliest expression of the conventions of classical tragedy.

SCANNELL, Vernon (1922–2007) Poet. His volumes include *Graves and Resurrections* (1948), *The Masks of Love* (1960), *A Sense of Danger* (1962), *The Loving Game* (1975), and later collections such as *Funeral Games* (1987), *Dangerous Ones* (1991), *A Time for Fire* (1991), and *Views and Distances* (2000). *Collected Poems 1950–1993* appeared in 1998. Many of the poems combine informal colloquial language and domestic subjects with a sense of underlying violence in an essentially hostile world. His volumes of autobiography include *An Argument of Kings* (1987), an account of his wartime experiences in the British army.

Scarlet Letter, The A novel by Nathaniel *Hawthorne, published 1850. Set in the Puritan New England of the 17th century, the novel describes how Hester Prynne is punished for adultery by having to wear a scarlet letter A, whose significance shifts positively as the novel develops. Hester's defiance of the authorities and her protection of her love-child Pearl make a study in independence. Her husband, in disguise, torments her lover, a respected clergyman who is concealing his guilt until a final public confession.

SCARRY, Richard (1919–94) American author-illustrator, best known for *The Best Word Book Ever* (1963) which depicts and labels huge numbers of everyday objects, and his many books about Busytown featuring Lowly Worm and his friends.

Scenes of Clerical Life Three stories by George *Eliot, published in *Blackwood's Magazine* (1857), and in two volumes, 1858.

'The Sad Fortunes of the Rev. Amos Barton' is the sketch of a commonplace clergyman, curate of Shepperton, who earns the affection of his parishioners by his misfortune—the death from overwork and general wretchedness of his gentle wife Milly.

'Mr Gilfil's Love-Story' tells of a man whose nature has been warped by tragedy. Maynard Gilfil was parson at Shepperton before the days of Amos Barton. The domestic chaplain and ward of Sir Christopher Cheverel, he had fallen deeply in love with Caterina Sarti (Tina), the daughter of an Italian singer, adopted by the Cheverels. But Captain Wybrow, the selfish heir of Sir Christopher, had flirted with Tina and won her heart. At his uncle's bidding he had abandoned her for a wealthier rival. This brings Tina to the verge of lunacy, as Gilfil watches with helpless sorrow and unabated love. Tina rallies for a time under his devoted care and finally marries him, but soon dies.

'Janet's Repentance' describes the influence of a sympathetic human soul. The Revd Edgar Tryan, earnest and evangelical, comes to Milby, an industrial town sunk in religious apathy, unmoved by the scanty ministration of the old curate, Mr Crewe. Tryan's efforts are vigorously opposed by a group of inhabitants led by Dempster, a drunken lawyer, who bullies his long-suffering wife Janet and drives her to drink. She shares her husband's prejudices against Tryan, until she discovers in him a sympathetic fellow sufferer. Her husband's brutality causes her to appeal to Tryan, and with his help she turns away from drink. Eliot's account of her struggle amounts to the first sympathetic treatment of alcoholism in English fiction.

scepticism A philosophical stance which questions the possibility of attaining lasting knowledge about the reality, as distinct from the appearance, of things, and which rejects all dogmatism, fanaticism, and intolerance. Scepticism originated in the teaching of some of the Sophists in the 5th century BC. 'Pyrrhonian' scepticism, associated with Pyrrho in the following century, held that any argument supporting one side of a case could be balanced by a contrary argument of equal weight, so that the wise person suspends judgement and cultivates tranquillity and indifference to outward things.

'Academic' scepticism, associated with the Academy of Carneades, held that although the same evidence is always compatible with two contrary conclusions, some beliefs are more reasonable than others and we can act upon the balance of probabilities. *Montaigne and Pierre Bayle in France and Joseph *Glanvill in England could combine scepticism with a devout theism, and sceptical techniques have frequently been practised by both supporters and opponents of religion to show that it rests on faith rather than reason. David *Hume carried the study to new lengths in his *Treatise of Human Nature* in a detailed analysis of the rational factors which generate scepticism and the psychological factors which allay or moderate it. Since the time of *Descartes critics of scepticism, particularly in religion and morals, have tended to depict it as a form of negative dogmatism, i.e. as seeking actually to deny the existence of anything whose nature is in doubt.

SCHELLING, Friedrich Wilhelm Joseph von (1775-1854) German philosopher. Schelling's ideas on the relation of mind and nature were incorporated by S. T. *Coleridge, without acknowledgement, in his *Biographia Literaria* (1817).

SCHILLER, Johann Christoph Friedrich von (1759-1805) German dramatist and poet. The plays *Die Verschwörung des Fiesko zu Genua* (1783: *The Conspiracy of Fiesco at Genoa*), *Kabale und Liebe* (1784: *Cabal and Love*), and *Don Carlos* (1787) are regarded as his *Sturm und Drang* works. His 'classical' verse plays are the *Wallenstein* trilogy (1797-1800), *Maria Stuart* (1801), *Die Jungfrau von Orleans* (1801: *The Maid of Orleans*), *Die Braut von Messina* (1803: *The Bride of Messina*), and *Wilhelm Tell* (1804). Matthew *Lewis and Walter *Scott both produced translations of plays by Schiller, and his work was admired as a critique of tyranny and political oppression, attracting none of the moral opprobrium which affected Goethe's reputation. In 1825 Thomas *Carlyle's previously serialized Life of Schiller appeared in book form. There are modern versions of *Maria Stuart*, translated and adapted by Stephen *Spender (1959), and Peter Oswald, and of *Don Carlos* (adapted by Mike Poulton).

SCHLEGEL, August Wilhelm von (1767-1845) German scholar, critic, and translator. His fame was established chiefly by his verse translations—with Ludwig Tieck (1773-1853) and others—of *Shakespeare's plays and his series of lectures, translated by John Black

(1783-1855) as *Lectures on Dramatic Art and Literature* (1815). In his own lecture series of 1811 S. T. *Coleridge borrowed ideas and passages from Schlegel without acknowledgement.

SCHLEGEL, Friedrich von (1772-1829) German critic, essayist, and scholar; a leading figure in the German *Romantic movement. The younger brother of A. W. *Schlegel, notable for his *Geschichte der alten und neuen Literatur* (1815), trans. John *Lockhart as *Lectures on the History of Literature, Ancient and Modern* (1818) and his work on Sanskrit language and poetry, *Sprache und Weisheit der Inder* (1808: *Language and Wisdom of the Indians*) which was an important early contribution to oriental studies in the West.

SCHOENBAUM, Samuel (1927-96) American scholar. His *Shakespeare's Lives* (1970; rev. 1991) is a scintillating history of accounts of Shakespeare's life; his *William Shakespeare: A Documentary Life* (1975) reproduces and comments authoritatively on most of the relevant documents; it was revised as *William Shakespeare: A Compact Documentary Life* (1977). A supplementary volume is *William Shakespeare: Records and Images* (1981). *See also* SHA-KESPEARE: AUTHORSHIP OF THE WORKS.

'Scholar-Gipsy, The' A poem by Matthew *Arnold, published 1853. The poem, is loosely based on a tale narrated by Joseph *Glanvill in *The Vanity of Dogmatizing*. Arnold's version concerns an 'Oxford scholar poor', who, tired of seeking preferment, joined the gypsies to learn their lore, roamed with them, and still haunts the Oxford countryside. The tone, as in many of Arnold's best works, is elegiac though it hails nonetheless a figure who has avoided modern contamination.

scholasticism The doctrines of medieval schoolmen, and the theological and philosophical teachings of the period 1100-1500, mainly an attempt to reconcile *Aristotle with the Scriptures, and Reason with Faith. It is characterized by its dialectical method of argument, often associated with *Abelard. Its best-known monument is the *Summa Theologica* of Aquinas. Between the 14th and the 16th centuries, scholasticism gradually exhausted itself as an intellectual movement.

School for Scandal, The A comedy by R. B. *Sheridan, produced at Drury Lane in May 1777. The play contrasts two brothers: Joseph Surface, a sanctimonious hypocrite, and Charles, a good-natured, reckless spendthrift.

Schoolmaster, The *See* ASCHAM, ROGER.

School of Abuse, The *See* GOSSON, STEPHEN.

School of Night A name drawn from a line in William *Shakespeare's *Love's Labour's Lost* (IV. iii), and first ascribed by Arthur Acheson in *Shakespeare and the Rival Poet* (1903) to a supposed coterie, led by Thomas *Harriot and Walter *Ralegh, and including Christopher *Marlowe and George *Chapman, which engaged in freethinking philosophical debate and dabbled in hermeticism, alchemy, and the occult. The existence of such a secret society is now widely disbelieved.

school stories A genre associated with writing for children. The earliest examples—beginning with Sarah *Fielding's *The Governess, or Little Female Academy* (1749)—were essentially didactic. The basic elements of the modern school story (the new child, the bully, codes of behaviour) were established in Harriet *Martineau's 'The Crofton Boys' (1841) and Thomas Hughes's *Tom Brown's School Days* (1857). Despite being debunked by Rudyard *Kipling's neo-realistic *Stalky & Co.* (1899), school stories were hugely popular in the early 20th century with writers like Charles *Hamilton and Angela *Brazil. They survive in J. K. *Rowling's 'Harry Potter' books. *See also* BLYTON, ENID (Malory Towers); BRENT-DYER, ELINOR (Chalet School).

SCHOPENHAUER, Arthur (1788-1860) German philosopher. His principal work *Die Welt als Wille und Vorstellung* (1819: *The World as Will and Idea*), without attempting to construct a philosophical system, articulates a profoundly pessimistic view of existence, denying free will and the existence of god as illusions. His work, which influenced Richard *Wagner, Friedrich *Nietzsche, Thomas Mann, and Ludwig *Wittgenstein, is sometimes seen as anticipating Sigmund *Freud's psychology of the unconscious.

SCHREINER, Olive (1855-1920) South-African-born writer. Her best-known novel, *The *Story of an African Farm* (1883), set in the vividly evoked landscape of her childhood, won her the friendship of Havelock *Ellis. Her other novels, both with feminist themes, *From Man to Man* (1927) and *Undine* (1929), appeared posthumously. Works published during her lifetime include collections of allegories and stories, *Trooper Peter Halkett of Mashonaland* (1897; an attack on Cecil Rhodes's activities), and *Woman and Labour* (1911). Courageous and unconventional as a woman and public figure, Schreiner has been acknowledged as a pioneer both in her treatment of women and in her fictional use of the African landscape.

SCHULBERG, Budd (1914–2009) American novelist and screenwriter, best known for his novel about a cynical opportunist achieving success in Hollywood, *What Makes Sammy Run?* (1941). Schulberg fictionalized his collaboration with F. Scott *Fitzgerald in *The Disenchanted* (1950).

SCHUYLER, James (1923–1991) American poet, who became a leading figure in the *New York School. His early poetry, as in *Alfred and Guinevere* (1958), uses Dadaist techniques and his later work evokes day-to-day situations in concrete detail. Schuyler was a close friend of Frank *O'Hara and John *Ashbery, collaborating with the latter on a novel, *A Nest of Ninnies* (1969).

SCHWARTZ, Delmore (1913–68) American poet and short story writer. His family-dream story 'In Dreams Begin Responsibilities' was published in 1937 in the *Partisan Review*. *The World is a Wedding* (1948) is a collection of stories; *Shenandoah* (1941) is a verse drama. Volumes of verse include *Summer Knowledge* (1959) and *Last and Lost Poems* (1979). Schwartz's decline into drinking and loneliness and his death in a cheap hotel room created a 'doomed poet' legend, and inspired elegies from John *Berryman. Saul *Bellow depicted him in *Humboldt's Gift* (1975).

science fiction 'Science fiction' suggests a hybrid, not quite ordinary fiction, not quite science, yet partaking of both. Beneath the label, we might find utopianism/dystopianism, *fantasy, *horror, or books on UFOs. Differences between E. E. Smith's 'Lensman' series (1937–), and Margaret *Atwood's *Oryx and Crake* (2003) might be more numerous than similarities, yet readers recognize them as, in some way, belonging to the same category. One of the pleasures of reading this fiction is that it challenges readers to decide whether what they are reading is within the bounds of the possible. The machine of H. G. *Wells's *The Time Machine* (1895) is an impossibility as far as we know; but the book has been taken seriously as both sociological and cosmological speculation.

Another broad definition of science fiction is that it considers the mythologies of power: to travel through time or space, to enter the thoughts of another, to overcome death, or the process of evolutionary forces. The long-running TV series *Star Trek* utilizes all these elements.

There are science fiction-like speculations in many periods. Mary *Shelley's *Frankenstein* (1818) reflects on the levers of power and human control. Shelley was well versed in the science of her time, rejecting any kind of supernatural agency in Victor Frankenstein's creation of life. Only when Frankenstein has engaged in scientific research does he achieve the seemingly impossible, giving us an iconic thought-experiment whereby we may examine the workings of the mind and the consequences of 'ardent curiosity'. In Shelley's *The Last Man* (1826) a plague wipes out all humanity except for one man. Jane Louden Webb's *The Mummy!* (1827) drew on both texts. Science fiction became a genre, without yet having a name.

Jules *Verne's adventure writings, such as *Journey to the Centre of the Earth* (1864) achieved worldwide success. Yet Wells was the great innovator, perfecting many themes, such as invasion, invention, and time travel, which have since been extensively cultivated. His influence touched Olaf *Stapledon, who in *Star Maker* presents a vision of the cosmos, past, present, and to come. C. S. *Lewis's *Out of the Silent Planet* (1938) is written against Wells's secular, scientific progressivism. Through reprints in Hugo *Gernsback's magazines, Wells was introduced to a new generation of American readers.

The invention in the 1880s of linotype machines led to a proliferation of magazines, all avid for short stories. *Amazing Stories*, beginning publication in 1926, fostered a vigorous fandom. Science fiction's ability to generate strange and striking images made television an ideal medium for visual effects. Both the movies (with Georges Méliès (1861–1938)) and British television (with Nigel Kneale's Quatermass series and George Orwell's *Nineteen Eighty-Four*) first acquired their mass audiences with science-fictional themes. The computer has again diversified and diluted the original strain of ideas.

British science fiction was perhaps less cut off from the main vein of literary culture than its American cousin. Edward *Bulwer-Lytton, Rudyard *Kipling, E. M. *Forster, Aldous *Huxley, George *Orwell, Kingsley *Amis, Anthony *Burgess, and, most considerably, Doris *Lessing have all written in this mode. In the 1960s, the British magazine *New Worlds* was taken over and transformed by Michael *Moorcock, with writers such as J. G. *Ballard and Brian *Aldiss. Events, however, made the USA the centre of a science-fictional industry which encroaches not only on movies and television, but also on such institutions as NASA; it is no coincidence that the revival of science fiction in China coincides with its space programme. Among the most thought-provoking authors are Arthur C. *Clarke, who commanded a worldwide audience with *Childhood's End* (1953), and his collaboration with Stanley Kubrick (1928–99); Stephen *Baxter; and the idiosyncratic Iain M. *Banks. The creator of Discworld, Terry *Pratchett, has been an immensely popular and productive contributor to the field. Notable American names include A. E. Van Vogt, Robert *Heinlein, Philip K. *Dick, Frank *Herbert, Harry Harrison, Ursula K. *Le Guin, William *Burroughs, William *Gibson and the cyberpunks, Gregory Benford, and Greg Bear.

 SEE WEB LINKS

• Science Fiction and Fantasy Research Database

science fiction drama One of the first major works of 20th-century *science fiction was a play: Karel *Čapek's *R.U.R. (Rossum's Universal Robots)*. George Bernard *Shaw's *Back to Methuselah* (1931) and J. B. *Priestley's *Time and the Conways* (1937) treat classic science fiction themes, but little subsequent science fiction, with the exception of Ray *Bradbury's adaptation of his own work, has found its way into the theatre. Ken *Campbell's 'Science fiction theatre of Liverpool' in the late 1970s was humorous and imaginative. The concerns of some kinds of science fiction feature in Tom *Stoppard's explorations of science and knowledge, while Alan *Ayckbourn (*Henceforward*, 1987) has used straightforward science fiction tropes, including robots. Science fiction's sense of spectacle often sits uneasily in the theatre unless the audience's imagination can make amends for lack of special effects. In contrast, radio and television drama are fruitful areas.

science fiction poetry Science fiction's experiments with image and language make it fertile territory for poetry. Practitioners include Thomas M. Disch, Ursula K. *Le Guin, Brian *Aldiss, and Edwin *Morgan.

scientific romance A term taken from C. H. Hinton's collection *Scientific Romances* (1886) to describe the fiction and non-fiction which would draw upon scientific speculations to become what was later called *science fiction. It was particularly applied to the work of H. G. *Wells.

Scilla's Metamorphosis A poem by Thomas *Lodge, first published 1589, and later (1610) as *Glaucus and Scilla*. The earliest of many Ovidian epyllia, or minor epics, in the Elizabethan period, it bears a generic and a specific relationship to William *Shakespeare's *Venus and Adonis*, including a brief account of Adonis' death.

SCOT, Reginald *See* SCOTT, REGINALD.

Scots A historical offshoot of the Northumbrian dialect of Anglo-Saxon. Gaelic, French, and Dutch elements combined to enhance the distinctiveness of Lowland speech, to which the political independence of Scotland gave national significance. Scots became the vehicle of a considerable poetic literature in John *Barbour, Robert *Henryson, William *Dunbar, Gawin *Douglas, and Sir David *Lindsay. The Union of Crowns in 1603 and of Parliaments in 1707 served, along with the general acceptance of the Authorized Version (*see* BIBLE, THE ENGLISH), to extend the influence of English and prevent the evolution of an all-purpose Scots prose. The 18th-century literary revival of Scots by Allan *Ramsay, Robert *Fergusson, and Robert *Burns was confined to poetry. In fiction from Walter *Scott, through Robert Louis *Stevenson and the *'Kailyard school' to Nan *Shepherd, Scots has been used mainly to represent rural speech. Some 20th-century poets (e.g. Hugh *MacDiarmid and Sydney Goodsir *Smith) attempted to develop the range of Scots to include modern themes. In Northern Ireland since the 1990s there have been attempts to revive for literary purposes the Ulster Scots that flourished briefly in the work of the *Rhyming Weavers.

 SEE WEB LINKS

• *Dictionary of the Scots Language*

Scots Musical Museum, The (1787–1803) Song collection edited by James Johnson (*c*.1750–1811) in six volumes, each containing 100 songs, variously antique, refurbished, and new. One-third are by Robert *Burns, who acted as editorial adviser to the project.

'Scots wha hae' A battle song by Robert *Burns composed in 1793. It is the anthem of the Scottish National Party.

SCOTT, C. P. *See* MANCHESTER GUARDIAN.

SCOTT, John (1783–1821) The first editor, 1820–1, of the remarkable *London Magazine*; he based it on roughly the same plan as *Blackwood's Magazine*'s, but with a greater emphasis on original writing. He attracted a brilliant set of contributors; Thomas De Quincey's *Confessions of an English Opium Eater*, Charles *Lamb's earlier 'Elia' essays, and much of William *Hazlitt's *Table-Talk* first appeared in the *London Magazine*, as well as work by John *Keats, John *Clare, Thomas *Hood, George Darley, Thomas *Carlyle, Allan *Cunningham, and others. His reviewers aimed to praise rather than to condemn, and were permitted no political bias. Conflict with *Blackwood's* was inevitable; he came to detest what he saw as its 'duplicity and treachery', and he felt obliged to defend his *'Cockney School'. His attacks on *Blackwood's*, in particular on John *Lockhart, led to a series of confusions which culminated in a duel with J. H. Christie, a close friend of Lockhart, in which Scott was killed.

SCOTT (Scot), Michael (d. *c*.1235) A Scottish scholar, who was attached to the court of Frederick II at Palermo, probably in the capacity of official astrologer. He translated works of *Aristotle from Arabic to Latin (including *De Anima*, pre-1220), and perhaps *Averroës' great Aristotelian Commentary. Because the science he studied was astronomy, legends of his magical power grew up and served as a theme for many writers from the disapproving *Dante (*Inferno*, XX. 116) to Walter Scott in The *Lay of the Last Minstrel*.

SCOTT, Paul (1920–78) Novelist; best known for the four novels known as the *Raj Quartet*— *The Jewel in the Crown* (1966), *The Day of the Scorpion* (1968), *The Towers of Silence* (1971), and *A Division of the Spoils* (1975)—televised in fourteen parts in 1984 as *The Jewel in the Crown*. Set in India during and immediately after the Second World War, these interlinked narratives give a panoramic picture of political, personal, racial, and religious conflicts in the period leading up to Independence and Partition. Scott's last novel, *Staying On* (1977, adapted for television, 1980), looks at the new India through the eyes of the Smalleys, two minor characters from the Quartet, who have remained after Independence and attempted to adjust to changed conditions.

SCOTT (Scot), Reginald (d. 1599) Author of *A Perfect Platform of a Hop Garden* (1574) and *The Discovery of Witchcraft* (1584). Written with the aim of preventing the persecution of poor, aged, and simple people who were popularly believed to be witches, *The Discovery* exposed the impostures and credulity that supported the common belief in sorcery. Scott's

learned scepticism about witches was attacked by the future *James I.

SCOTT, Robert Falcon (1868–1912) Antarctic explorer. He described his first Antarctic expedition (1901–4), which sledged further south than anyone previously, in *The Voyage of the 'Discovery'* (1905). His second expedition (1910–12) ended in tragedy when his party, beaten by Amundsen in a race to the Pole, perished on the harrowing trek back. His final diaries, published as *Scott's Last Expedition* (1913), and other accounts, including Apsley *Cherry-Garrard's, told a heroic story of nobility and bravery sacrificed for empire, though some questioned his leadership. Literary versions of the tragedy include Douglas Stewart's verse drama *The Fire on the Snow* (1941), Ted Tally's play *Terra Nova* (1977), and Beryl Bainbridge's novel *The Birthday Boys* (1991).

SCOTT, Sarah (1723–95) Née Robinson, novelist, sister of Elizabeth *Montagu. After a brief marriage (1751–2), ending in legal separation, she lived in Bath with Lady Barbara Montagu (*c*.1722–1765). Between 1750 and 1772 she published, anonymously, five novels, a translation of a French novel, and three historical works. The hero of *Sir George Ellison* (1766), perhaps conceived in the wake of Samuel Richardson's *Sir Charles *Grandison, first appeared in her best-known novel, the utopian *Millenium Hall* (1762).

SCOTT, Thomas (1747–1821) Clergyman, autobiographer, and biblical scholar, strongly influenced by John *Newton. In his much-reprinted spiritual autobiography *The Force of Truth* (1779), which William *Cowper polished stylistically, he described his intellectual journey from fashionable Socinian or *unitarian views back to *Calvinist ones.

SCOTT, Sir Walter (1771–1832) Scottish author. His interest in the old Border tales and ballads was stimulated by Thomas Percy's *Reliques* and he published anonymously *The Chase and William and Helen*, a translation of Bürger's 'Der wilde Jäger' ('The Wild Huntsman') and 'Lenore' (both 1797), and in 1799 a translation of *Goethe's *Götz von Berlichingen*. Scott's three-volume *Minstrelsy of the Scottish Border* (1802–3) was followed by his first considerable original work, the romantic poem *The *Lay of the Last Minstrel* (1805). *Marmion* (1808) was followed by *The *Lady of the Lake* (1810), *Rokeby* and *The Bridal of Triermain* (1813), *The Lord of the Isles* (1815), and *Harold the Dauntless* (1817), his last long poem. Scott supported the foundation in 1809 of the Tory *Quarterly Review*, after ceasing his contributions to the *Edinburgh Review*, alienated by its Whig attitude. In 1813 he refused the offer of the *poet laureateship and recommended Robert *Southey. Eclipsed by Lord *Byron as a poet, in spite of the popularity of his verse romances, he turned his attention to the novel. His works appeared anonymously in the following order: *Waverley (1814); *Guy Mannering (1815); The *Antiquary (1816); The *Black Dwarf and *Old Mortality (1816), as the first series of *Tales of my Landlord; *Rob Roy (1817); The *Heart of Midlothian (1818), the second series of Tales of my Landlord; The *Bride of Lammermoor and A *Legend of Montrose (1819), the third series of Tales of my Landlord; *Ivanhoe (1819); The *Monastery (1820); The *Abbot (1820); *Kenilworth (1821); The *Pirate (1821); The *Fortunes of Nigel (1822); *Peveril of the Peak (1823); *Quentin Durward (1823); *St Ronan's Well (1823); *Redgauntlet (1824); The *Betrothed and The *Talisman (1825), together as Tales of the Crusaders; *Woodstock (1826); *Chronicles of the Canongate (1827, containing 'The Highland Widow', 'The *Two Drovers', and 'The *Surgeon's Daughter'); Chronicles of the Canongate (2nd series): Saint Valentine's Day, or The *Fair Maid of Perth (1828); Anne of Geierstein (1829); Tales of my Landlord (4th series): Count Robert of Paris and Castle Dangerous (1831). Scott was created a baronet in 1820, and claimed authorship of the novels in 1827. In 1826 James Ballantyne & Co. became involved in the bankruptcy of Constable & Co., and Scott, as partner of the former firm, found himself liable for a debt of about £114,000. He henceforth worked heroically, shortening his life by strenuous efforts to pay off the creditors, who received full payment after his death.

Scott also wrote plays and wrote or edited historical, literary, and antiquarian works, including an abstract of the 'Eyrbyggja Saga' in *Northern Antiquities* (1814); *The Tales of a Grandfather* (1827–30); *History of Scotland* (1829–30); *Letters on Demonology and Witchcraft* (1830); and the *Military Memoirs of Captain Carleton* (1808). Scott founded the Bannatyne Club in 1823.

The Life of Scott by John *Lockhart (1837–8) is one of the great biographies of the 19th century. Scott's *Journal* was published in 1890.

Scott established the form of the *historical novel, and, according to V. S. *Pritchett, the form of the short story (with 'The Two Drovers' and 'The Highland Widow'). He was read and imitated throughout the 19th century, and there was a revival of interest from European *Marxist critics in the 1930s, who interpreted his works in terms of historicism. The Scottish 'Waverley' novels (including *The Antiquary, Old Mortality*, and *The Heart of Midlothian*) are generally reckoned his masterpieces.

SCOTT, William Bell (1811–90) Poet, artist, and art critic. Scott was associated with the birth of the *Pre-Raphaelite Movement, and contributed to The *Germ. His poems and verses range from rambling Pindaric *odes to *sonnets and medieval-style *ballads. His *Autobiographical Notes* (1892) gave much offence to the Rossetti family.

Scottish Enlightenment Retrospective term for the flowering of intellectual enquiry, centred on Edinburgh but also involving the universities of Glasgow and Aberdeen, in 18th-century Scotland. Though the scientists, philosophers, and *literati associated with the movement differed widely in attitude and opinion, they shared a faith in the primacy of reason, a commitment to social and economic 'improvement' through the application of their findings, an insistence on the interconnectedness of human activities, and a quest for underlying philosophical principles. The main philosophers were Francis *Hutcheson, David *Hume, Adam *Smith, Adam *Ferguson; and Hume's 'common-sense' antagonists Thomas *Reid and Dugald Stewart. Some literary figures, like John Home and James *Macpherson, identified with the values of the Enlightenment, while others, such as James *Boswell, Robert *Fergusson, and Robert *Burns, were at times antagonistic towards them. Numerous learned societies and journals flourished during the period, and the *Encyclopaedia Britannica* was founded.

Scottish Renaissance A movement which had its origins in Montrose, Angus, in the 1920s, where Edwin and Willa *Muir, the composer Francis George Scott (1880–1958), and the future novelist Fionn McColla (1906–75) all either lived or holidayed in proximity to Hugh *MacDiarmid, then at the most energetic phase of his career as poet and propagandist. All shared a sense of the degraded condition of post-war Scotland and a desire to internationalize the country's intellectual life and reanimate aspects of national tradition diminished by Protestantism and unionism.

Scottish Text Society Founded in 1882 for the purpose of furnishing scholarly but popularly accessible editions of historically significant Scottish texts. It has published more than

150 volumes of poetry, drama, and prose, including John *Barbour's *Bruce*, *The Original Chronicle of Andrew of Wyntoun*, *The *Kingis Quair*, and the poems of Robert *Henryson, William *Dunbar, Sir David *Lindsay, and William *Drummond of Hawthornden, and later writers, including Allan *Ramsay and Robert *Fergusson, along with the 19th-century ballad collection *The Song Repertoire of Amelia and Jane Harris*.

SCOTUS Eriugena, John (John the Scot) (*fl. c.*845–70) Distinguished philosopher of Irish origin, employed as a teacher at the court of Charles the Bald *c.*847. *De Divisione Naturae* expounds his philosophy of the unity of nature; this proceeds from (1) God, the first and only real being (Nature which creates and is not created); through (2) the Creative Ideas (Nature which creates and is created); to (3) the sensible Universe (Nature which is created and does not create); everything is ultimately resolved into (4) its First Cause (immanent, unmoving God: Nature which is not created and does not create). He was one of the originators of medieval mysticism, as well as a precursor of *scholasticism. The *Neoplatonic element in medieval philosophy owes much to his influence.

Scriblerus Club An informal group which included the writers Jonathan *Swift, John *Arbuthnot, Thomas *Parnell, Alexander *Pope, John *Gay, and the politician Robert Harley. The group appears to have met regularly only from January to July 1714, with the object of burlesquing false science and scholarship through the figure of an educated fool, 'Martinus Scriblerus'. A number of short satires under this name were printed or reprinted in miscellanies by Pope and Swift from 1727, and works such as *Gulliver's Travels*, *Peri Bathous*, and *The *Dunciad* were in part inspired by the original idea. *Memoirs of *Martinus Scriblerus* appeared in 1741.

Scrutiny A quarterly periodical of literary criticism which ran for 19 volumes, 1932–53; F. R. *Leavis, the dominant critical voice and the most regular reviewer, contributed an important 'Retrospect' to a twentieth volume containing an index published in 1963. Inspired in part by the *Calendar of Modern Letters*, it became an important vehicle for the views of the new Cambridge school of criticism, and published many seminal essays, particularly in the pre-war years, on *Shakespeare, *Marvell, and the traditions of the English novel. Its critical strictures proved notoriously destructive when applied to contemporary writing: it mauled Graham *Greene and Dylan *Thomas, dismissed Ernest *Hemingway as second-rate, derided much of Virginia *Woolf's writing, and repeatedly lamented the aridity of T. S. *Eliot's later work and the 'immaturity' of Auden's. The journal's stance was one of embattled rearguard defence of standards against a general cultural debasement abetted by the 'London literary establishment' comprising the BBC, the *Times Literary Supplement*, the British Council, and reviewers influenced by the *Bloomsbury Group.

SCUDÉRY, Madeleine de (1608–1701) Author of French heroic romances, which had an immense vogue throughout Europe.

SEACOLE, Mary (1805–81) Born in Jamaica, the daughter of a Scottish officer and a free black businesswoman, 'an admirable doctress'. Seacole's autobiography *The Wonderful Adventures of Mrs Seacole in Many Lands* (1857) tells how she travelled as a humane entrepreneur and healer, most notably during the Crimean War.

Seafarer, The An Old English poem of *c.*124 lines in the *Exeter Book. The opening section (of which Ezra *Pound made a loose but highly evocative translation) is a powerful evocation of the miseries and attractions of life at sea, the speaker contrasting a compulsion to be at sea with the comforts of life on land. The later section is explicitly Christian, concluding with a prayer. Some critics regard the didactic second part as an appendage to an earlier secular poem; others see the whole as an allegorical representation of human exile from God on the sea of life.

Seasons, The A poem in blank verse, in four books, by James *Thomson, published 1726–30. 'Winter', gradually expanded to 1,069 lines by 1746, describes the power of the elements and the sufferings of men and animals. 'Summer' (1727) has scenes of hay-making and sheep-shearing, followed by a panegyric to Great Britain. The episode in which Damon beholds Musidora bathing was highly popular, according to William *Wordsworth, because of its sexual content. 'Spring' (1728) describes the influence of the season on all the natural world, and ends with a panegyric on nuptial love. 'Autumn' (1730) gives a vivid picture of hunting, harvesting, and wine-making. The whole was completed by a Hymn (1730) and illustrations by William Kent. The work went through many editions in the 18th and 19th centuries, and was at the centre of the crucial *copyright cases of the 1770s. The text of Joseph Haydn's oratorio (1801) was adapted from Thomson's poem.

SEBALD, W. G. (Winfried Georg Maximilian (Max)) (1944–2001) German novelist, poet, and critic; founding director of the British Centre for Literary Translation at the University of East Anglia in 1989. Unusual in the use they make of photographs, his novels have a unique narrative voice, through which 'characters' are remembered in the act of remembering. These include *The Emigrants* (1996), *The Rings of Saturn* (1999), *Vertigo* (1999), and *Austerlitz* (2001). Lectures delivered in Zurich challenging German literature for its failure to record the trauma of Allied fire-bombing of German cities also instance his concern with the ethics of memory; on publication in 1999 they aroused great controversy (*On the Natural History of Destruction*, 2003). In 2001 two volumes of poetry appeared, *After Nature* (trans. Michael *Hamburger) and *For Years Now* (with images by Tess Jaray). The fact that his works were written in England and often translated under the auspices of his own institute lends the translations a particular authority.

'Second Nun's Tale' See CANTERBURY TALES, 21.

Secret Agent, The Novel by Joseph *Conrad, published 1907. A seedy Soho shop provides cover for Verloc, the lazy secret agent in question; he moonlights lackadaisically as a spy for a foreign embassy and an informer for the police. Winnie has married him chiefly to provide security for her simple-minded younger brother, Stevie. Verloc's shop is a meeting place for a bunch of anarchist misfits, comprising the Russian *agent provocateur* Vladimir; 'The Professor', a terrorist; and Ossipon, Yundt, and Michaelis, who are happy to fit their principles to their material needs. The embassy is planning a series of outrages aimed at discrediting the revolutionary groups to which London has been so accommodating, with the first target being the Greenwich Observatory. Verloc exploits Stevie as an accomplice, but the boy, rather than the Observatory, is blown to pieces. An outraged Winnie kills Verloc, flees, and, in terror of being hanged, throws herself overboard from a ferry.

Secreta Secretorum A compendium of pronouncements on political and ethical matters, written in Syriac in the 8th century AD

and claiming to be advice from *Aristotle to *Alexander the Great. It reached Europe through Arabic and 12th-century Hispano-Arabic. The main version in Latin was translated in Spain *c.*1230 and was influential on poets from then until the 16th century. It influenced in particular the tradition of writing works of advice to kings; it was translated in part by John *Lydgate, and Egidio Colonna's *De Regimine Principum* (an important source for *Hoccleve's *Regiment of Princes*) drew on it.

Secret Garden, The (1911) By Frances Hodgson *Burnett, tells the romantic story of the regeneration of two sickly, spoiled children, Mary Lennox and her cousin Colin, through contact with nature. One of the most intricately symbolic books in the children's literature canon, it was filmed in 1919, 1949, and 1993.

SEDLEY (Sidley), Sir Charles (?1639–1701) Dramatist and poet, famous for his wit and urbanity and notorious for his profligate escapades. His tragedy *Antony and Cleopatra* (1677) was followed by two comedies, *Bellamira* (1687) and *The Mulberry Garden* (1668), which was based partly on *Molière's *L'École des maris*. His poems and songs were published in 1702, with his *Miscellaneous Works*. Edmond *Malone identified him as the Lisideius of Dryden's *Of Dramatick Poesy*, who defends the imitation of French drama in English.

SEGALEN, Victor (1878–1919) French explorer, archaeologist, ethnographer, and writer, born in Brest. During his lifetime he published *Les Immémoriaux* (1907, novel), based on his experiences in Tahiti, and two collections of poetry, *Stèles* (1912) and *Peintures* (1916), influenced by his time in China. His posthumous publications include *René Leys* (1922, novel); *Équipée* (1929), an account of an imaginary expedition based on his various journeys in China; *Lettres de Chine* (1967); and *Essai sur l'exotisme* (1978). Following Henry Bouillier's 1961 study *Victor Segalen*, there has been increasing scholarly interest in Segalen's reflections on cultural difference and exoticism.

Sejanus his Fall A Roman tragedy by Ben *Jonson, performed by the King's Men 1603, with *Shakespeare and Richard *Burbage in the cast, printed 1605. It was successfully revived by the Royal Shakespeare Company in 2005.

Based mainly on *Tacitus, the play deals with the rise of Sejanus during the reign of Tiberius, his destruction of the family of Germanicus, and his poisoning of Tiberius' son Drusus.

Suspicious of Sejanus, Tiberius leaves Rome, setting his agent Macro to spy on him. Tiberius denounces Sejanus in a letter to the Senate, which condemns him to death. The mob, stirred up by Macro, tears him to pieces.

SELBY, Hubert, Jr (1928–2004) American novelist; his first novel, *Last Exit to Brooklyn* (1964), was prosecuted in Britain for obscenity. Selby shared many of the concerns of the *Beats. His later novels include *Requiem for a Dream* (1978).

SELDEN, John (1584–1654) English jurist, orientalist, and legal historian. His *De Diis Syriis* (1617), a work of comparative religion far ahead of its time, won him European fame as an orientalist. John *Milton consulted it when writing of the pagan gods in his *Nativity Ode*. His *Mare Clausum* (1635) was an answer to the *Mare Liberum* of Hugo Grotius, which had denied that the seas were susceptible to sovereignty. He withdrew from public affairs in 1649 on the principle that 'The wisest way for men in these times is to say nothing.' His *Table Talk*, drawn from the last twenty years of his life, and composed by his secretary Richard Milward (bap. 1609, d. 1680), appeared in 1689.

SELF, Will (1961–) Novelist and journalist. A former cartoonist, he has published short stories, novellas, and novels—such as *The Book of Dave* (2006)—much indebted to Martin *Amis in their fascination with the scabrous and penchant for surreal satire, lurid caricature, and arcane vocabulary. Collections of his journalism include *Junk Mail* (1995), about his drug addiction, *Feeding Frenzy* (2001), and *Psychogeography* (2007).

SELKIRK, Alexander (1676–1721) Scottish seaman and castaway. He ran away to sea and joined the privateering expedition of William *Dampier in 1703. Having quarrelled with his captain, Thomas Stradling, he was put ashore on one of the uninhabited Pacific islands of Juan Fernández in 1704, and remained there until 1709 when he was rescued by Woodes Rogers (*c.*1679–1732). He returned to Britain in 1711 after further voyages. Rogers gave an account of him in *A Cruising Voyage round the World* (1712). Selkirk is often advanced as a likely model for *Robinson Crusoe* (1719) by Daniel *Defoe. He also inspired a poem by William *Cowper published in 1782.

SELVON, Sam (Samuel Dickson) (1923–94) Born in Trinidad; he wrote novels, plays, and short stories. He came to England in 1950,

travelling on the same boat as George *Lamming. His first novel, *A Brighter Sun* (1952), set in Trinidad during the war, was written in London: it describes the life and brightening prospects of Tiger, a young Indian peasant. Selvon's novels about London include *The Lonely Londoners* (1956), *Moses Ascending* (1975), and *Moses Migrating* (1983), which chart with comedy, sympathy, and a pioneering use of Caribbean idiom the experiences of black immigrants trying to find fame and fortune, or at least a bed, in the unknown terrain of Earls Court, Notting Hill, and Bayswater. *See also* BLACK BRITISH WRITING.

SEMBÈNE, Ousmane (1923–2007) Senegalese novelist and film-maker. His involvement with working-class movements in France and Africa led to a critical engagement with both the idea of Négritude articulated by Léopold *Senghor, and *postcolonial Senegalese society. His most famous novel, *Les Bouts de bois de Dieu* (1960; *God's Bits of Wood*), is about the Dakar–Nigeria railway strike of 1947–8. Films such as *Mandabi* (1968) and *Xala* (1975) offer a satirical portrait of the Senegalese political elite.

SENDAK, Maurice (1928–) American author-illustrator. *Where the Wild Things Are* (1963, *In the Night Kitchen* (1970), and *Outside Over There* (1981) established his reputation. More recent work includes *We Are All in the Dumps with Jack and Guy* (1993) depicting street children, and the Holocaust-inspired *Brundibar* (2003), an illustrated book based in the opera of the same name, with a text by Tony Kushner (1956–).

SENECA, Lucius Annaeus (4 BC/AD 1–65) Roman Stoic philosopher, tragic poet, and, like his father the elder Seneca, a noted rhetorician. He was appointed tutor to the young Nero and, when the latter became emperor, acted as one of his chief advisers, checking his crimes for a period; but, finding this position untenable, he withdrew from the court in 62. Three years later he was accused of being implicated in a conspiracy and was forced to commit suicide. His writings consist of tragedies in verse, dialogues, treatises, and letters in prose, which in their different ways all aim to teach *Stoicism. Most of his nine plays are on subjects drawn from Greek mythology and treated in extant Greek dramas, but his manner is very different from that of Greek tragedy. He uses an exaggerated rhetoric, dwells habitually on bloodthirsty details, and

S

introduces ghosts and magic; the plays were almost certainly not intended for performance but for reading aloud, probably by the author himself, to a select audience.

Senecan drama was familiar in the 16th century at a time when Greek tragedies were scarcely known; all the nine plays were translated and imitated by dramatists from the time of *Gorboduc* onwards. Shakespeare's *Titus Andronicus* is the best-known example. Seneca's prose writings consist of moral treatises, some in the form of dialogues, on such topics as anger, clemency, providence, consolation for loss, and tranquillity of mind, and letters supposedly addressed to Lucilius after the author's retirement, constituting a practical course in Stoicism. These moral writings were widely read and taken to heart in the 17th and 18th centuries, and Seneca's antithetical style, often contrasted with *Cicero's, was much imitated, for example by Ben *Jonson. *L'Estrange's digest, *Seneca's Morals* (1678), was much reprinted.

SENGHOR, Léopold Sédar (1906–2001) Senegalese poet, intellectual, and politician. He left Senegal in 1928 to pursue his education in Paris, where he met fellow colonial subjects Aimé *Césaire and Léon Damas (1912–78). Together, they founded the Négritude movement. Senghor's poetry, first translated in the 1960s, celebrates a black identity which has its roots in traditional African spirituality, while at the same time seeking out universal values which can cut across racial difference. Following Senegal's independence from France in 1960, Senghor served as its first president until 1980.

SENIOR, Olive (1941–) Poet and short story writer who was born and brought up in Jamaica, and educated at Carleton University, Ottawa. Her collections of poetry, *Talking of Trees* (1985), *Gardening in the Tropics* (1994), and *Over the Roofs of the World* (2005), employ a wide range of voices, from the colloquial and the conversational to the prophetic, to explore the struggles and history of her land and its people. The stories in *Summer Lightning* (1986), *Arrival of the Snake Woman* (1989), and *Discerner of Hearts* (1995), often give a child's view of the world, and are alert to the range of Jamaican ethnicities.

sensation, novel of An enormously popular genre of fiction that flourished from *c.*1860 onwards. It relocated the terrors of the *Newgate and *Gothic novel to a recognizably modern, middle-class England. Its high-impact narrative style employed cliffhanging conclusions to chapters, and its plots commonly involved guilty family secrets, bigamy, arson, adultery, insanity, forgery, and murder (especially poisoning), often taking inspiration from real criminal cases. This accounts for an intense interest in legal papers, telegrams, diary entries, and written testimony. Many of Wilkie *Collins's sensation novels represent themselves as bundles of documents authored by witnesses in the case. The genre was also noted for its energetic—and frequently criminal—heroines, and for its enervated, hypersensitive heroes. The 'sensation' label was a negative one. The most influential works in the genre are Wilkie Collins's The *Woman in White (1860) and The *Moonstone (1868); Ellen Wood's *East Lynne (1861); Mary Braddon's *Lady Audley's Secret (1862); Charles Reade's *Hard Cash (1863); and Sheridan Le Fanu's *Uncle Silas (1864). The novels of Rhoda *Broughton and *Ouida are usually considered to be on the margins of the genre. Most mid-Victorian novelists show some traces of its influence, including Thomas *Hardy, Charles *Dickens, George *Eliot, and Anthony *Trollope. *Detective fiction can trace its roots back to sensation fiction.

Sense and Sensibility A novel by Jane *Austen, which grew from a sketch entitled 'Elinor and Marianne'; revised 1797–8 and 1809; published 1811. The tale is about two sisters: Elinor, the eldest, is the embodiment of good sense while her younger sister Marianne suffers from a potentially fatal excess of romantic sensibility. *Sense and Sensibility* subtly explores the psychology of romantic love and the restrictions placed upon individual desire by social probity and family duty.

Mrs Henry Dashwood and her daughters Elinor and Marianne, together with the younger Margaret, are left with little money, because the estate of which Mrs Dashwood's husband had the life interest has passed to her stepson John Dashwood. Henry Dashwood, before his death, had appealed to John to look after his stepmother and sisters, but John and his grasping wife are too selfish to help them. Mrs Henry Dashwood and her daughters retire to a cottage in Devon, but not before Elinor and Edward Ferrers, brother of Mrs John Dashwood, have become attracted to each other. In Devon Marianne is thrown into the company of John Willoughby, an attractive but poor and unprincipled young man, with whom she falls desperately—and very obviously—in love. Willoughby seems to respond, and their engagement is expected daily. Willoughby suddenly departs for London, leaving Marianne in acute distress. Eventually Elinor and Marianne also go to London, on the invitation of their tactless and garrulous old friend Mrs Jennings. Here Willoughby shows complete indifference to Marianne, and finally, in a cruel and insolent letter, informs her of his approaching marriage to a rich heiress. Marianne makes no effort to hide her grief. Meanwhile Elinor has learned, under pledge of secrecy, from Lucy Steele (a sly, self-seeking young woman) that she and Edward Ferrers have been secretly engaged for four years. Elinor, whose self-control contrasts with Marianne's demonstrative emotions, silently conceals her distress. Edward's engagement, which had been kept secret from his mother, now becomes known to her. Infuriated by Edward's refusal to break his promise to Lucy, she settles on his younger brother Robert the property that would otherwise have gone to Edward. At this juncture a small living is offered to Edward, and the way seems open for his marriage with Lucy. But the shallow Robert falls in love with Lucy, who, seeing her best interest in a marriage with the wealthier brother, throws over Edward and marries Robert. Edward, immensely relieved to be released from an engagement he has painfully regretted, proposes to Elinor and is accepted. Marianne, slowly recovering from the despair that followed her abandonment by Willoughby, accepts the proposal of Colonel Brandon, an old family friend.

sentiment, novel of A form of fiction, popular in the 18th century, illustrating and promoting 'sensibility', a combination of virtue, ready sympathy, and charitable impulse, based on the ethics of philosophers such as Shaftesbury and on medical theories of the nervous system. The novels of Samuel *Richardson and Sarah *Fielding stressed the importance of sentiment in the 1740s, and Henry Brooke's The *Fool of Quality (1765–70), Laurence Sterne's A *Sentimental Journey (1768), and Henry Mackenzie's The *Man of Feeling (1771) concentrated almost exclusively, though sometimes with comic irony, on feeling. The *Gothic novel later incorporated many of the conventions of sentimental fiction, and its decline was hastened by Jane Austen's mockery of its weeping heroines, and her suggestion, in *Northanger Abbey and *Sense and Sensibility, of the self-indulgence and delusion underlying its moral claims.

Sentimental Journey, A, through France and Italy By Laurence *Sterne, published 1768. Sterne travelled abroad in 1762–5 and wrote when the vogue for the *Grand Tour was at its height, parodying the travel journal and the novel as well as travel itself when he commented 'I seldom go to the place I set out for.' The narrative only gets as far as Lyons. The narrator is the amiable Parson Yorick (from *Tristram Shandy), a 'sentimental' traveller who 'interests his heart in everything', is frequently moved to tears, and fights his susceptibility to women of all ranks met along the way. He contrasts his own pleasure in France with the condemnation of Smelfungus, a caricature of Tobias *Smollett. After Sterne's death in 1768, the narrative was continued by a 'Eugenius', Yorick's friend and correspondent, assumed wrongly to be Sterne's old friend John *Hall-Stevenson.

series books Are the staple of popular and children's literature, their *lack* of variation being their primary attraction. Famous examples include Enid *Blyton's 'Famous Five' and R. L. Stine's 'Point Horror'. Series can develop their own internal dynamics and subtleties of character and narrative, as in Arthur Ransome's *Swallows and Amazons.

Series of Plays, A Collection of dramas by the Scottish poet and dramatist Joanna *Baillie, first published anonymously in 1798, and thought initially to be written by a man. The full title is illuminating: A Series of Plays on the Passions: in which it is Attempted to Delineate the Stronger Passions of the Mind, Each Passion Being the Subject of a Tragedy and a Comedy. Each play examines the effects of a key passion on the psychology and actions of the leading character: Count Basil (a tragedy) on love, The Tryal (a comedy) also on love, and De Montfort (a tragedy) on hate. The whole is prefaced by a justificatory 72-page 'Introductory Discourse'. Baillie argues that it is characters in extraordinary situations that fascinate us most, although she also shares William *Wordsworth's and S. T. *Coleridge's preoccupation in *Lyrical Ballads with socially marginal figures.

Serious Money By Caryl *Churchill (1987). Inspired by the 1986 deregulation of the City, known as the Big Bang, the play, written largely in spirited rhyming verse, evokes the ruthless greed, buoyant materialism, changing culture, and cynicism of the financial world in the monetarist 1980s. The play opens with a short satirical extract on speculation from Thomas

*Shadwell's comedy *The Volunteers, or The Stockjobbers* (pub. 1693), and then introduces a noisy gallery of contemporary traders, dealers, jobbers, bankers, and stockbrokers. The plot involves a possible murder and insider dealing in the context of an attempted takeover bid of the symbolically named company Albion: Churchill's ear for the new jargon of the media, PR, and the City itself is acute and the play, launched at the *Royal Court, was also a West End success, much enjoyed by those it mocked. The play ends with a chorus singing in praise and hope of 'Five more Glorious Years'—'pissed and promiscuous, the money's ridiculous—five more glorious years', a reference to the possibility of the then prime minister Margaret Thatcher being re-elected.

Sermon on the Mount See BIBLE.

SERRAILLIER, Ian (1912–94) Children's writer; he wrote poetry and adventure stories and retold classic texts, and is remembered for *The Silver Sword* (1956), set in Poland about the journey of four refugee children to Switzerland to find their parents.

SERVICE, Robert (1874–1958) Poet. He emigrated to Canada in 1895 where he observed the gold rush in the Yukon; this inspired his ballads, published in *Songs of a Sourdough* (1907, Toronto; as *The Spell of the Yukon*, New York). Its sequel, *Ballads of a Cheechako*, followed in 1909. Other volumes include *Rhymes of a Rolling Stone* (1912) and *Rhymes of a Red Cross Man* (1916). *Ploughman of the Moon* (1945) and *Harper of Heaven* (1948) are both autobiographical.

sestina An unrhymed poem of six six-line stanzas with a final three-line 'envoy', composed according to a fixed formula of repeated line-endings: in place of rhymed endings it employs full repetition of six words which reappear as line-endings in a different order in each successive stanza, in the sequence *abcdef, faebdc, cfdabe, ecbfad, deacfb, bdfeca*. Stanzas are thus linked by recurrence of the same line-ending in the final line of one stanza and the first line of the next. In the envoy, all six words reappear, three of them as line-endings. There is no required metre. The form originated among French *troubadour poets and was brought into English by Philip *Sidney in the *Arcadia*. Later poets who wrote English sestinas include *Swinburne, W. H. *Auden ('Paysage moralisé', 1933), and John *Ashbery ('The Painter', 1970).

SETH, Vikram (1952–) Poet, novelist, librettist, and travel writer, born in India, acclaimed for the versatility of his style and the brilliance of his generic ventriloquism. Early works included the collections of poems, *Mappings* (1981) and *The Humble Administrator's Garden* (1985), and a travel book, *From Heaven Lake: Travels through Sinkiang and Tibet* (1983). Poetry has continued throughout to be his *métier* of choice. The internationally praised *The Golden Gate* (1986) is a verse-novel set in San Francisco written in rhyming *tetrameter sonnet-stanzas, drawn in part from *Pushkin's *Eugene Onegin*. *A Suitable Boy* (1993) is an intricately structured novel in the realist tradition of the British Victorian multi-decker about the Mehra family's search for a suitable husband for their younger daughter, the entirely ordinary Lata. Noticeably tracing a trajectory away from magical-exotic evocations of South Asia, the novel is set in India some years after Independence and Partition, and the domestic and the political are entwined in the interlocking lives of four families, the Mehras, Kapoors, and Chatterjis (all Hindu), and the Khans (Muslim). Other works by this multilingual author include *Beastly Tales* (1992), *Three Chinese Poets* (1992, translation), *Arion and the Dolphin* (1994), *Two Lives* (2005, a memoir), and *An Equal Music* (1999, novel). *See* ANGLO-INDIAN LITERATURE.

SETTLE, Elkanah (1648–1724) Poet and playwright, whose series of bombastic oriental melodramas threatened John *Dryden's popularity and aroused his hostility. He appears to have written *Cambyses* (1667) while still at Oxford, and his *The Empress of Morocco* (1673) had such a vogue that Dryden, with John *Crowne and Thomas *Shadwell, wrote a pamphlet of criticism of it. Settle retorted with an attack on Dryden's *Almanzor and Almahide*, and Dryden vented his resentment by satirizing Settle as Doeg in the second part of *Absalom and Achitophel*. Settle published *Absalom Senior, or Achitophel Transprosed* in 1682, and *Reflections on Several of Mr Dryden's Plays* in 1687. He was appointed city poet in 1691, and wrote *drolls for Bartholomew Fair. He also wrote two interesting rogue biographies (*see* ROGUE LITERATURE).

SEUSS, Dr (Theodor Seuss Geisel) (1904–1991) American writer of books for children, and political cartoonist for the New York newspaper *PM* (1941–3). *And to Think That I Saw it on Mulberry Street* (1937) introduced Seuss's anarchic visual and verbal style, used in the 'Beginner Book' series which commenced with

The Cat in the Hat (1957). These books used a limited vocabulary, although he later 'came to despise' the idea. Legend has it that he wrote the best-selling *Green Eggs and Ham* (1960) on a bet from Bennett Cerf that he could not write a children's book using only 50 different words. Perhaps paradoxically, his wild, fluid *'non-sense'* rhymes and surreal cartoon-drawings are designed to help children learn the discipline of reading. *The Lorax* (1971) can be read as an environmentalist tract, while *The Butter Battle Book* (1984) is a satire on the arms race. The many films made from his books include *How the Grinch Stole Christmas* (2000) and *The Cat in the Hat* (2003).

Seven Champions of Christendom, The Famous History of the *See* JOHNSON, RICHARD.

seven deadly sins Usually pride, envy, anger, sloth, covetousness, gluttony, and lust; frequently personified (e.g. *Piers Plowman*, B, *Passus V*; William *Dunbar's 'The Dance of the Sevin Deidly Synnis'; Edmund *Spenser's *Faerie Queene*) and used in *Chaucer's 'Parson's Tale' (*see* CANTERBURY TALES, 24).

Seven Sages of Rome, The A metrical romance of the early 14th century, varying in length in different versions from 2,500 to 4,300 lines. In form it is a framed collection of tales, derived through Latin and French from Eastern collections, the original of which is the Indian *Book of Sindibad*; it is one of the earliest English instances of the form of verse story used by Chaucer in *The *Canterbury Tales*.

   The Emperor Diocletian's son is educated by seven sages. Jealous of the boy, his stepmother accuses him to the emperor of attempting to seduce her; the boy is silent for seven days, under the influence of the stepmother's magic, and he is ordered to execution. On each of the seven nights a tale is told by the queen to illustrate the dangers of supplantation of the emperor by his son, and on each of the following mornings a tale is told by one of the sages on the theme of the danger of trusting women. When the seven days are passed, the boy speaks and exposes the stepmother, who is burnt.

SEWARD, Anna (1742–1809) Poet and letter writer, known as the 'Swan of Lichfield', where she lived from the age of 10. Her grandfather John Hunter (*c*.1674–1741) had taught Samuel *Johnson, and she furnished James *Boswell with many details of Johnson's early life. Her poems included *Elegy on Captain Cook* (1780), and *Llangollen Vale, with Other Poems* (1796),

the title poem recalling a visit to the Ladies of Llangollen, Lady Eleanor Butler (?1739–1829) and Miss Sarah Ponsonby (?1735–1831). Her friends included Erasmus *Darwin (of whom she wrote a memoir, 1804), Thomas *Day, and William *Hayley. In 1802 she wrote an admiring letter to Walter *Scott, who edited her works in three volumes, with a memoir, in 1810, at her suggestion. Her letters were published in 1811 (6 vols).

SEWELL, Anna *See* BLACK BEAUTY.

SEWELL, Elizabeth Missing (1815–1906) Novelist and educationalist, one of twelve siblings; the family was not wealthy, and Sewell's literary earnings were important to their continuing prosperity after her father died in 1842, leaving only debts. Her earliest novels, including the popular *Amy Herbert* (1844), were published as having been edited by her brother, William Sewell. But relations with the volatile William became troublesome as Sewell's success grew, and her later works, like the powerful *Ursula* (1858), warned young female readers of the dangers of idolizing brothers. Sewell combined her writing with work as a teacher, and she founded and ran two schools on the Isle of Wight. Her strongest novels, including *The Experience of Life* (1853) and *Katharine Ashton* (1854), address the need for young women to have the means to achieve independence and self-respect, whether or not they marry; a serious and disciplined education is therefore necessary for their well-being. See *The Autobiography of Elizabeth M. Sewell*, edited by Eleanor Sewell (Elizabeth Sewell's niece) in 1907.

SEXTON, Anne (1928–74) American poet. Following an early elopement, children, and a breakdown, she started to write poetry as therapy. She attended Robert *Lowell's classes with Sylvia *Plath, with whom she shares the use of a dramatic, *confessional 'I', and the thematic territory of family life, jealous passion, and mental illness. Her early work makes dynamic use of strict poetic form, but, from the Pulitzer Prize-winning *Live or Die* (1966), this is replaced by free verse which relies on dense, sometimes surreal, metaphors, wit, and rhythmic lists for impact. Her later work is increasingly haunted by a troubled relationship with God. Despite much success, especially with her adaptation of the *Grimm brothers' fairy-tales, *Transformations* (1971), Sexton took her own life in 1974.

SFORZA family Dukes of Milan from 1450 until the end of the independent duchy of Milan in the mid-16th century; notable patrons of the arts. The family came to prominence with **Francesco** (1401–66), who served as condottiere to the last Visconti duke and seized power shortly after the latter's death. Francesco's political acumen is celebrated by *Machiavelli in *The Prince*.

SHACKLETON, Sir Ernest (1874–1922) Antarctic explorer, born Kildare, Ireland. In 1901 he joined Robert *Scott's first Antarctic expedition, maintaining his literary interests by editing the first *South Polar Times*. He led his own expedition on the *Nimrod* from 1907–9. He sledged to within 100 miles of the South Pole, recounting the harrowing journey in *The Heart of the Antarctic* (1909). In 1914, during his attempt to cross the continent, his ship *Endurance* was crushed by pack ice. To seek help, Shackleton led an epic voyage in an open boat to South Georgia, and climbed the uncharted Allardyce Range. He published his account, *South*, in 1919. Shackleton died on board the *Quest* in 1922, during his fourth expedition to the Antarctic.

SHADWELL, Thomas (?1642–92) Dramatist, whose first play *The Sullen Lovers* (1668) was based on *Molière's *Les Fâcheux*; in its preface he proclaimed himself a follower of Ben *Jonson's comedy of humours. He wrote some fourteen comedies, including *The Squire of Alsatia* (1688), *The Virtuoso* (1676, a satire on the *Royal Society), *Epsom Wells* (1672), and *Bury Fair* (1689); the last two give an interesting if scurrilous picture of contemporary manners, watering places, and amusements. He also wrote operas, adapting William *Shakespeare's *The *Tempest* as *The Enchanted Island* (1674). He was probably the author of *The Medal of John Bays* (1682) and other anonymous attacks on John *Dryden; Dryden's counter-attacks include *Mac Flecknoe* and the second part of *Absalom and Achitophel*, where Shadwell appears as Og. Shadwell somewhat plaintively defends himself from the charge of dullness in his dedication to Sir Charles *Sedley of his translation of the *Tenth Satire of Juvenal* (1687).

SHAFFER, Peter (1926–) Playwright. His first play, *Five Finger Exercise* (1958), a drama of middle-class family life, was followed by many other successes, including *The Royal Hunt of the Sun* (1964), an epic about the conquest of Peru; *Black Comedy* (1965), a cleverly constructed *farce set in a London apartment which reverses dark and light, so that the cast, in full glare of the lights and view of the audience, stumbles around during the pitch darkness of a dramatic electricity failure; *Equus* (1973), a drama about an analyst's relationship with his horse-obsessed patient; *Amadeus* (1979), which deals with the nature of creativity through a portrayal of the composers Mozart and Salieri; *Lettice and Lovage* (1987); and *The Gift of the Gorgon* (1992). His twin brother Anthony Shaffer (d. 2001), author of *Sleuth* (1970), was also a successful playwright.

SHAFTESBURY, Anthony Ashley Cooper, third earl of (1671–1713) Moral philosopher. His principal writings were collected in *Characteristics of Men, Manners, Opinions, and Times*, published 1711 (rev. edn 1714). Shaftesbury was influenced by *Deism and opposed the self-interest theory of conduct advocated by Thomas *Hobbes. Man has 'affections', Shaftesbury held, not only for himself but for the creatures about him. Moreover, man has a capacity for distinguishing right and wrong, the beauty or ugliness of actions and affections, and this he calls the 'moral sense'. To be truly virtuous, a man must have a disinterested affection for what he perceives to be right. Such views are echoed in Alexander *Pope's *Essay on Man*, in the novels of Henry *Fielding, and in the philosophy of Francis *Hutcheson. Shaftesbury's aesthetic thought, which asserts a close connection between art and morality, influenced later writers such as James Arbuckle and Mark Akenside.

SHAKESPEARE, Nicholas (1957–) Novelist and biographer, chosen as one of *Granta's* 'Best of Young British Novelists' in 1993, on the strength of *The Vision of Elena Silves* (1989), a story of religious visions and revolutionary dreams in South America, and *The High Flyer* (1993). Subsequent novels include *The Dancer Upstairs* (1995; filmed 2002), *Snowleg* (2004), about a failed love affair in Cold War East Germany and its long-term consequences, and *Secrets of the Sea* (2007). His biography of the novelist and travel writer Bruce *Chatwin was published in 1999.

SHAKESPEARE, William (1564–1616) Dramatist, actor, man of the theatre, and poet. His birth is traditionally celebrated on 23 April, which is also known to have been the date of his death.

The standard and kind of education indicated by Shakespeare's writings are such as he might have received at the local grammar school, whose records for the period are lost. On 28 November 1582 a bond was issued permitting him to marry Anne Hathaway of Shottery, a village close to Stratford. She was eight years his senior. A daughter, Susanna, was baptized on 26 May 1583, and twins, Hamnet and Judith, on 2 February 1585. We do not know how - Shakespeare was employed in early manhood; the best-authenticated tradition is John *Aubrey's: 'he had been in his younger years a schoolmaster in the country.'

Nothing is known of his beginnings as a writer, nor when or in what capacity he entered the theatre. In 1587 an actor of the Queen's Men was killed shortly before the company visited Stratford. That Shakespeare may have filled the vacancy is an intriguing speculation. The first printed allusion to him is from 1592, in the pamphlet *Greene's Groat's-Worth of Wit, ostensibly by Robert *Greene but possibly by Henry *Chettle. Mention of 'an upstart Crow' who 'supposes he is as well able to bombast out a blank verse as the best of you' and who 'is in his own conceit the only Shake-scene in a country' suggests rivalry, and parody of a line from 3 *Henry VI shows that Shakespeare was established on the London literary scene. He was a leading member of the Lord Chamberlain's Men soon after their refoundation in 1594. With them he worked and grew prosperous for the rest of his career as they developed into London's leading company, occupying the *Globe Theatre from 1599, becoming the King's Men on James I's accession in 1603, and taking over the Blackfriars as a winter house in 1608. He is the only prominent playwright of his time to have had so stable a relationship with a single company.

London necessarily became Shakespeare's professional base. But his family remained in Stratford. In August 1596 William's son Hamnet died, and was buried in Holy Trinity churchyard. In October Shakespeare was lodging in Bishopsgate, London, and in May of the next year he bought a substantial Stratford house, New Place. His father died in 1601. In 1604 he lodged in London with a Huguenot family called Mountjoy. In June 1607 his daughter Susanna married a physician, John Hall. His only granddaughter, Elizabeth Hall, was christened the following February; in 1608 his mother died and was buried in Holy Trinity.

In March 1613, he and the actor/artist Richard *Burbage received 44 shillings each for providing an *impresa, a tilting shield for the earl of Rutland at a court tournament. This is Shakespeare's last known literary enterprise. In February 1616 his second daughter Judith married Thomas Quiney. He died, according to the inscription on his monument, on 23 April, and was buried in Holy Trinity. His widow

died in 1623 and his last surviving descendant, Elizabeth Hall, in 1670.

Shakespeare's only writings for the press are the narrative poems *Venus and Adonis and The *Rape of Lucrece, published 1593 and 1594 respectively, each with the author's dedication to Henry Wriothesley, earl of Southampton, and the short poem 'The *Phoenix and the Turtle', published in 1601 in Robert Chester's collection Love's Martyr. His *sonnets, mostly dating probably from the mid-1590s, appeared in 1609. Whether he authorized the publication is disputed. They bear a dedication to the mysterious 'Mr W.H.'. The volume includes the poem 'A *Lover's Complaint', whose authorship also is disputed.

Shakespeare's plays were published by being performed. Scripts of only half of them appeared in print in his lifetime, some in short, sometimes manifestly corrupt, texts, often known as 'bad quartos'. Records of performance are scanty and haphazard: as a result dates and order of composition, especially of the earlier plays, are often difficult to establish. The list that follows gives dates of first printing of all the plays other than those that first appeared in the 1623 *folio.

Probably Shakespeare began to write for the stage in the late 1580s. The ambitious trilogy on the reign of Henry VI, now known as *Henry VI Parts 1, 2, and 3, and its sequel *Richard III, are among his early works. Parts 2 and 3 were printed in variant texts as The First Part of the Contention betwixt the Two Famous Houses of York and Lancaster (1594) and The True Tragedy of Richard, Duke of York (1595). Henry VI Part 1 may have been written after these, perhaps with a collaborator. A variant quarto of Richard III appeared in 1597. Shakespeare's first Roman tragedy is *Titus Andronicus, printed in 1594, probably written with George *Peele; his earliest comedies are The *Two Gentlemen of Verona, The *Taming of the Shrew (a derivative play, The Taming of a Shrew, was printed 1594), The *Comedy of Errors (acted 1594), and *Love's Labour's Lost (printed 1598). All these plays are thought to have been written by 1595.

Particularly difficult to date is *King John. *Richard II, printed 1597, is usually dated 1595. For some years after this, Shakespeare concentrated on comedy, in A *Midsummer Night's Dream and The *Merchant of Venice (both printed 1600), The *Merry Wives of Windsor (related to the later history plays, and printed in a variant text 1602), *Much Ado About Nothing (printed 1600), *As You Like It (mentioned in 1600), and *Twelfth Night, probably written in

1600 or soon afterwards. *Romeo and Juliet* (ascribed to the mid-1590s) is a tragedy with strongly comic elements, and the tetralogy begun by *Richard II* is completed by three comical histories: *Henry IV* Parts 1 and 2, each printed a year or two after composition (Part 1 1598, Part 2 1600), and *Henry V*, almost certainly written 1599, printed, in a shortened, possibly corrupt, text, 1600.

In 1598 Francis *Meres, a minor writer, published praise of Shakespeare in *Palladis Tamia: Wit's Treasury*, mentioning twelve of the plays so far listed (assuming that by *Henry the 4* he means both Parts) along with another, *Love's Labour's Won*, apparently either a lost play or an alternative title for an extant one.

Late in the century Shakespeare turned again to tragedy. A Swiss traveller, Thomas Platter, saw *Julius Caesar* in London in September 1599. *Hamlet* apparently dates from the following year, but was only entered for publication in the register of the *Stationers' Company in July 1602; a short text probably reconstructed from memory by an actor appeared in 1603, and a good text printed from Shakespeare's manuscript in late 1604 (some copies bear the date 1605). A play that defies easy classification is *Troilus and Cressida*, probably written 1602, printed 1609. The comedy *All's Well That Ends Well*, too, is probably of this period, as is *Measure for Measure*, played at court in December 1604. The surviving text may have been lightly adapted by Thomas *Middleton. The tragedy *Othello*, played at court the previous month, did not reach print until 1622. *King Lear* probably dates, in its first version, from 1605; the quarto printed in 1608, once regarded as a corrupt text, is now thought to have been badly printed from Shakespeare's original manuscript. The text printed in the folio appears to represent a revision dating from a few years later. Much uncertainty surrounds *Timon of Athens*, printed in the folio from uncompleted papers, and probably written in collaboration with Middleton. *Macbeth*, probably adapted by Middleton, is generally dated 1606, *Antony and Cleopatra* 1606–7, and *Coriolanus* 1607–9.

Towards the end of his career, Shakespeare turned to romantic tragicomedy. *Pericles*, probably written with George *Wilkins and printed in a debased text in 1609, certainly existed in the previous year; it and The *Two Noble Kinsmen* are the only surviving plays generally believed to be largely by Shakespeare that were not included in the 1623 folio. Simon Forman, the astrologer, records seeing both *Cymbeline* and

The *Winter's Tale* in 1611. The *Tempest* was given at court in November 1611.

The last three plays associated with Shakespeare appear to have been written in collaboration with John *Fletcher. They are *All Is True*, retitled *Henry VIII* in the folio, which 'had been acted not passing 2 or 3 times' before the performance at the Globe during which the theatre burnt down on 29 June 1613; a lost play, *Cardenio*, acted by the King's Men in 1613 and attributed to the two dramatists in a Stationers' Register entry of 1653; and The *Two Noble Kinsmen*, which appears to incorporate elements from a 1613 masque by Francis *Beaumont, and which was first printed in 1634. No Shakespeare play survives in authorial manuscript, though three pages of revisions to a manuscript play, *Sir Thomas *More*, variously dated about 1593 or 1601, are often thought to be by Shakespeare and in his hand.

It may have been soon after Shakespeare died, in 1616, that his colleagues John *Heminges and Henry Condell (d. 1627) began to prepare *Mr William Shakespeare's Comedies, Histories, and Tragedies*, better known as the first folio, which appeared in 1623. Only once before, in the 1616 Ben *Jonson folio, had an English dramatist's plays appeared in collected form. Heminges and Condell, or their agents, worked with care, assembling manuscripts, providing reliable printed copy when it was available, but also causing quartos to be brought wholly or partially into line with prompt-books. Above all, the folio is important because it includes sixteen plays which in all probability would not otherwise have survived. Its titlepage engraving, by Droeshout, is, along with the half-length figure bust by Gheerart Janssen erected in Holy Trinity, Stratford, by 1623, the only image of Shakespeare with strong claims to authenticity. The folio was reprinted three times in the 17th century; the second issue (1664) of the third edition adds *Pericles* and six more plays. Few scholars would add anything to the accepted canon except part (or even all) of *Edward III*, printed anonymously 1596.

Over 200 years after Shakespeare died, doubts were raised about the authenticity of his works (*see* SHAKESPEARE: AUTHORSHIP OF THE WORKS). The documents committed to print between 1593 and 1634 have generated an enormous amount of varied kinds of human activity. The first editor to try to bring Shakespeare's works into order, reconcile their discrepancies, correct their errors, and present them for readers of his time was the dramatist Nicholas *Rowe, in 1709. His 18th-century successors include Alexander

*Pope (1723–5), Lewis *Theobald (1733), Samuel *Johnson (1765), Edward *Capell (1767–8), and Edmond *Malone (1790). Early in the 20th century advances in textual studies transformed attitudes to the text. Subsequent editions include *Quiller-Couch's and J. Dover *Wilson's New Shakespeare (Cambridge, 1921–66) and the Riverside (1974). The Arden edition appeared originally 1899–1924; it was revised and largely replaced 1951–81. A new series, Arden 3, started to appear in 1995. The Oxford single-volume edition, edited by S. Wells and G. Taylor, was published in 1986 with a second edition, including full texts of *Sir Thomas More* and *Edward III*, in 2005. A Royal Shakespeare Company edition appeared in 2007.

The standard biographical studies are E. K. *Chambers, *William Shakespeare: A Study of Facts and Problems* (2 vols, 1930) and S. *Schoenbaum, *William Shakespeare: A Documentary Life* (1975).

Shakespeare: authorship of the works

Shakespeare's authorship of the works commonly attributed to him is amply demonstrated by documentary evidence from his own time and beyond. His name first appears in print on the title pages of *Venus and Adonis* (1593) and The *Rape of Lucrece* (1594). As was customary, his earliest plays were published without ascription to their author, but his name appears on title pages of many plays from 1598 onwards and of the sonnets in 1609. Many writers refer to him by name as the author of plays and poems during his lifetime and later, most significantly in the private conversations of around Christmas 1618 between Ben *Jonson and William *Drummond of Hawthornden. There are numerous manuscript allusions. The first *folio of 1623 prints tributes including Jonson's 'To the Memory of my Beloved the Author Mr William Shakespeare and What He Hath Left Us', in which Shakespeare is described as the 'sweet swan of Avon'. The inscriptions on the memorial in Holy Trinity Church Stratford-upon-Avon compare him to great figures of antiquity and praise 'what he hath writ'.

No questions were raised until the late 18th century, when James Wilmot, a literary scholar and clergyman, came up with the idea that the true author of the works was Francis *Bacon. The idea resurfaced in *The Romance of Yachting* (1848) a book by an American lawyer, Colonel Joseph C. Hart, and gathered force with the work of Delia Bacon, a mad American who in 1856 sought to open the Stratford grave in the hope of finding evidence to support her case that the plays were the work of a committee including Francis Bacon, Edmund *Spenser, and Sir Walter *Ralegh. This resulted in the forming of both an American and an English Bacon Society, which still exist. At least 60 candidates, from *Elizabeth I downwards, have since been proposed. In recent times the most popular have been Bacon, Christopher *Marlowe, and the earl of *Oxford.

The commonest anti-Stratfordian arguments are that Shakespeare was of relatively humble origins, is not known to have travelled overseas, and came from a small provincial town where he could not have received a good enough education to have written the plays. The facts are that it is not necessary to be an aristocrat to be a great writer—Jonson, who like Shakespeare did not attend a university, was the son of a bricklayer, Marlowe's father was a cobbler—that the plays show no knowledge of foreign countries that could not have been obtained from books or from conversation, and that Stratford had a good grammar school whose pupils received a rigorous education in the classics which would more than account for the learning displayed in the works. Anti-Stratfordians too easily ignore the logical necessity to disprove the evidence that Shakespeare wrote the works before trying to argue that someone else did. See S. *Schoenbaum, *Shakespeare's Lives* (1970; rev. 1991).

((∰)) SEE WEB LINKS

• The Shakespeare Authorship Page

'Shalott, The Lady of' *See* 'LADY OF SHALOTT, THE'; LAUNCELOT OF THE LAKE, SIR.

Shamela Andrews, An Apology for the Life of Mrs

A lively travesty of Samuel Richardson's *Pamela*, published anonymously in 1741, almost certainly by Henry *Fielding. The gullible Parson Tickletext writes to his friend, Parson Oliver, commending the beauty and virtue of 'sweet, dear, pretty Pamela'; Oliver, however, has in his possession letters which reveal the true history of the heroine. The main events of Richardson's story are preserved, but Parson Williams now appears as a scheming hypocrite, Mr B. as the foolish Mr Booby, and Pamela as a calculating and promiscuous slut, already the mother of an illegitimate child, and determined to use her reputation for 'vartue' to capture her master. Richardson's prized device of 'writing to the moment' is also ridiculed. Richardson was convinced the work was Fielding's and never forgave him. The novel's title alludes ironically to *An Apology for the Life of Colley *Cibber* (1740).

S

SHANGE, Ntozake (1948–) Born Paulette Williams, African American playwright and novelist. Her first play, or rather 'choreopoem', was *For Coloured Girls Who Have Considered Suicide When the Rainbow is Enuf* (1975). She has also published a number of volumes of poetry and her novels include *Sassafrass, Cypress & Indigo* (1982), and *I Live in Music* (1994), a mixed-media portrait of a trumpet player, and *Some Sing, Some Cry* (2010, with her sister, Ifa Bayeza).

SHAPCOTT, Jo (1953–) Poet. Her first collection was *Electroplating the Baby* (1988), whose title poem explored a characteristic vein of scientific and medical fantasia. Later volumes include *Phrase Book* (1992), with its invigoratingly feminist sequence of 'Mad Cow' poems and its widely celebrated title poem, written during the Gulf War; *My Life Asleep* (1998); *Her Book: Poems 1988–1998* (2000); *Tender Taxes* (2002), versions of Rilke's poems in French; and *Of Mutability* (2010). Shapcott's poetry combines contemporary references (to film, cartoon, and news stories) with literary and historical allusions, and is distinguished by sharp word-play and a disturbing surreal animism.

SHARP, William ('Fiona Macleod') (1855–1905) Scottish novelist, mystic and biographer. He wrote under his own name essays, verse, minor novels, and lives of D. G. *Rossetti (1882), P. B. *Shelley (1887), Heinrich *Heine (1888), and Robert *Browning (1890). He is chiefly remembered for his mystic Celtic tales and romances of peasant life written by his feminized persona 'Fiona Macleod', in the spirit of *The *Celtic Twilight*. The first work by 'Fiona Macleod' was *Pharais* (1894), followed by *The Mountain Lovers* (1895), *The Sin Eater* (1895), and plays, including *The House of Usna* (1903) and *The Immortal Hour* (1900). Sharp successfully concealed the identity of 'Fiona Macleod' (including writing a bogus entry in *Who's Who) until his death.

SHARPE, Tom (1928–) Novelist. He spent some years in South Africa (1951–61) and his first two novels, *Riotous Assembly* (1971) and *Indecent Exposure* (1973), are political satires set in that country. On his return to England he taught for a decade in Cambridge, and *Porterhouse Blue* (1974) is a farcical *campus novel set in a fictitious college. Other works, all in a vein of fierce and sometimes grotesque satiric comedy, include *Blott on the Landscape* (1975), *Wilt* (1976), and *Ancestral Vices* (1980).

SHAW, George Bernard (1856–1950) Dramatist and critic, born in Dublin. In 1876 he moved to London, and began his literary career by ghosting music criticism and writing five unsuccessful novels (including *Cashel Byron's Profession*, 1886). From 1885 he contributed music, art, and literary criticism to the *Dramatic Review, Our Corner*, the *Pall Mall Gazette, The World*, and *The Star* (as 'Corno di Bassetto'). He was a drama critic for the *Saturday Review (1895–8) and produced a series of controversial articles pleading for the performance of plays dealing with contemporary social and moral problems. He campaigned for a theatre of ideas in Britain comparable to that of Henrik *Ibsen and August *Strindberg in Scandinavia. He was a freethinker, a supporter of women's rights, and an advocate of income equality, the abolition of private property, and a change in the voting system. He was already well known as a journalist and public speaker when his first play, *Widowers' Houses*, was produced, with little success, in 1892. There followed, among others, *Arms and the Man* (1894), *The Devil's Disciple* (1897), *You Never Can Tell* (1899), *Mrs Warren's Profession* (1902, though published earlier), and *John Bull's Other Island* (1904), a play originally intended for the *Abbey Theatre and his first popular success in London.

The huge dramatic output of Shaw's maturity included *Man and Superman* (1905), *Major Barbara* (1905), *The Doctor's Dilemma* (1906), *Androcles and the Lion* (1913), *Pygmalion (1913), *Heartbreak House* (1920), *Back to Methuselah* (1921), *Saint Joan* (1923), *Too True to be Good* (1932), *Village Wooing* (1934), *In Good King Charles's Golden Days* (1939), and *Buoyant Billions* (1948). These plays were published (some in collections: *Plays Pleasant and Unpleasant*, 1898; *Three Plays for Puritans*, 1901) with lengthy prefaces setting out Shaw's views. The conflict in the plays involves a clash of thought and belief rather than of will or temperament. The witty, paradoxical dialogue won audiences over to the idea that mental and moral passion could produce absorbing drama. His major non-dramatic works include *The Quintessence of Ibsenism* (1891; expanded 1913), *The Perfect Wagnerite* (1898); *Common Sense about the War* (1914); and *The Intelligent Woman's Guide to Socialism and Capitalism* (1928). He was a prolific letter writer and much of his correspondence has been published.

In 1898 Shaw married Charlotte Payne-Townshend, with whom he appears to have lived in celibate companionship until her death in 1943. He was a strict vegetarian and never drank spirits, coffee, or tea, and remained active as a playwright and controversialist until his death at 94.

SHEFFIELD, John, third earl of Mulgrave, first duke of Buckinghamshire, and marquess of Normanby (1647–1721) Courtier and poet; patron of John *Dryden. Sheffield was an early friend of Alexander *Pope, who drew on his *Essay upon Poetry* (1682) in the **Essay on Criticism* and later edited his works (1723).

SHELLEY, Mary Wollstonecraft (1797–1851) Novelist, editor, biographer and travel writer, only daughter of William *Godwin and Mary *Wollstonecraft. Her mother died a few days after her birth. In 1814 she eloped to Italy with P. B. *Shelley, and married him in 1816 on the death of his wife Harriet. She returned to England in 1823, after Shelley's death the previous year, and pursued a professional writing career. She is famous for *Frankenstein, or The Modern Prometheus* (1818), but she is the author also of six further novels. *Valperga* (1823) is a romance set in 14th-century Italy; *The *Last Man* (1826), a novel set in the future. *Perkin Warbeck* (1830), a historical romance bearing the influence of Walter *Scott, addresses the historically contentious theory that the duke of York (the younger of the two princes imprisoned in the tower and allegedly put to death by Richard III) was the same person as the rebel leader Perkin Warbeck. *Lodore* (1835) returns to the theme of primitivism evident in *Frankenstein*. Her sixth and last novel *Falkner* (1837) was composed during the year of her father's death. She also published several biographies and short stories, most of which were published in the *Keepsake*; some have *science fiction elements, others are Gothic (*see* GOTHIC FICTION) or historical (*see* HISTORICAL FICTION). She also wrote *Rambles in Germany and Italy, in 1840, 1842 and 1843* (1844), and edited her husband's *Poems* (1839) and his *Essays, Letters from Abroad, Translations and Fragments* (1840). Her children's story *Maurice* was published in 1998 with an introduction by Claire *Tomalin.

SHELLEY, Percy Bysshe (1792–1822) English poet and radical. The eldest son of an MP, and destined for a parliamentary career. At school he was bullied as 'Mad Shelley' and the 'Eton Atheist'.

Encouraged in his 'printing freaks', he privately published a series of *Gothic novels and verses in his teens: *Zastrozzi* (1810); *Original Poetry by Victor and Cazire* (1810, with his beloved sister Elizabeth); and *St Irvyne, or The Rosicrucian* (1811). At Oxford he read radical authors—William *Godwin, Thomas *Paine, Condorcet—and in March 1811 was expelled for circulating a pamphlet, 'The Necessity of *Atheism', written with his friend T. J. *Hogg. He quarrelled with his father, and eloped to Scotland with 16-year-old Harriet Westbrook. Three years of nomadic existence followed. He tried setting up a radical commune of 'like spirits' first at Lynmouth, Devon, and later at Tremadoc, north Wales. Much of his early philosophy, both in poetry and politics, is expressed in *Queen Mab* (1813), with its remarkable *Notes*.

In 1814 his marriage collapsed. Shelley eloped abroad with Mary Godwin (Mary *Shelley), together with her 15-year-old stepsister Jane Clairmont (she subsequently called herself 'Claire'). His unfinished novella *The Assassins* (1814) reflects their dreamy travels through post-war France, Switzerland, and Germany, as does their combined journal, *History of a Six Weeks' Tour* (1817). Returning to London, he wrote **Alastor* (1816), which first brought him general notice and reviews. The summer of 1816 was spent on Lake Geneva with Lord *Byron. Mary began *Frankenstein*, and Shelley composed two philosophic poems much influenced by William *Wordsworth, the 'Hymn to Intellectual Beauty' and 'Mont Blanc'.

In the autumn of 1816 Harriet drowned herself in the Serpentine. Shelley immediately married Mary and began a Chancery case for the custody of his first two children, which he lost. The experience shook him deeply, and is recalled in many verse fragments, such as the 'Invocation to Misery' and the cursing 'To the Lord Chancellor' (1817—a so-called *'flyting'). However, friendships developed with Leigh *Hunt, John *Keats, William *Hazlitt, and others of the liberal *Examiner* circle. In 1817 the family settled at Great Marlow, on the Thames, where Shelley slowly composed 'Laon and Cythna', published, with alterations to avoid prosecution, as *The *Revolt of Islam* in 1818.

Harried by creditors, ill health, and 'social hatred', Shelley took his household permanently abroad, to Italy in the spring of 1818. He stayed at Lucca, and then at Venice and Este, where he composed *'Julian and Maddalo', based on his friendship with Byron. He wintered in Naples, where he wrote the passionately unhappy 'Stanzas Written in Dejection'. In the spring of 1819 he was working on *Prometheus Unbound*.

His domestic situation was increasingly strained. His little daughter Clara had died at Venice; now his favourite 'Willmouse' died at Rome and Mary suffered a nervous breakdown.

Yet the twelve months from the summer of 1819 saw Shelley's most extraordinary and varied burst of major poetry. He completed the fourth act of *Prometheus* (pub. 1820); wrote *The *Mask of Anarchy* (September 1819); *'Ode to the West Wind' (October 1819); the satirical *Peter Bell the Third* (December 1819); his long political odes, 'To Liberty' and 'To Naples' (both spring 1820); the lively, intimate 'Letter to Maria Gisborne' (July 1820); and the *'Witch of Atlas' (August 1820). Much of this work was inspired by news of political events, which also produced a number of short, angry, propaganda poems. At the same time he dashed off several pure lyric pieces, including 'To a Skylark' and 'The Cloud' (both spring 1820), of dazzling metrical virtuosity; and completed a verse melodrama, *The *Cenci* (1819).

The quieter period at Pisa which followed (1820–1) saw him at work on a number of prose pieces: *A *Philosophical View of Reform* (1820); the impish 'Essay on the Devil'; and his famous *Defence of Poetry* (1821).

In the spring of 1821 news of the death of Keats in Rome produced *Adonais*. A platonic love affair with Emilia Viviani, a beautiful 17-year-old heiress, resulted in *Epipsychidion* (1821).

In the winter of 1821 Byron also moved to Pisa, and a raffish circle formed round the two poets, including Edward *Trelawny, Edward and Jane Williams, and eventually Leigh Hunt, who came from England to edit a monthly journal, *The *Liberal* (1822–4). Shelley's last completed verse drama, *Hellas* (1822) was inspired by the Greek War of Independence.

In April 1822 he moved his household to an isolated beach house on the bay of Lerici. Here he began his last major poem, *The *Triumph of Life*. His letters, still full of political hope and magically descriptive of the Italian seascape, are nonetheless shadowed with personal premonitions. Shelley was drowned in August 1822, together with Edward Williams and an English boatboy, on a return trip from visiting Byron and Hunt at Livorno.

His lyric powers and romantic biography have until recently obscured Shelley's most enduring qualities as a writer: his intellectual courage and originality; his hatred of oppression and injustice; and his mischievous, sometimes macabre, sense of humour. He was widely read in the classics, philosophy, and contemporary science; he translated from Greek (Plato and Homer), Latin (Spinoza), Spanish (Calderón), German (Goethe), Italian (Dante), and some Arabic fragments. His essays—very few published in his lifetime—are highly intelligent, his political pamphlets both angry and idealistic.

SHENSTONE, William (1714–63) Poet; he published at Oxford *Poems upon Various Occasions* (1737), which included an early version of *The Schoolmistress*, the mock-Spenserian poem for which he is best known and which he later revised substantially (1742, 1748). From 1743 he transformed the Leasowes, his estate near Halesowen, in the west Midlands of England, into a *ferme ornée* or 'natural' landscape garden. He helped to edit Robert *Dodsley's *Collection of Poems*, and worked with Thomas *Percy on the *Reliques of Ancient English Poetry*. He wrote many elegies, odes, songs, 'levities', and a 'Pastoral Ballad' which Thomas *Arne set to music. The poetry won moderate praise from Samuel *Johnson in his *Lives of the English Poets*, though Johnson gently mocked Shenstone's improvident gardening obsessions. *Essays on Men, Manners, and Things*, the second volume of Dodsley's edition of Shenstone's works (3 vols, 1764–9), contains his influential essay on 'landskip gardening'.

SHEPARD, E. H. (Ernest Howard) (1879–1976) Author-illustrator. He worked for *Punch* from 1907 but is remembered for his illustrations for A. A. *Milne's children's books and Kenneth Grahame's *The *Wind in the Willows* (1931). His own children's books include *Ben and Brock* (1965).

SHEPARD, Sam (1943–) American playwright and actor. Shepard spent four years (from 1971) living in London, where a number of his plays were produced at the *National Theatre and the *Royal Court. His work deals with American mythologies, the death of the American dream, and Americans' relationship to their land and history. In his most famous work, *True West* (1980), two brothers in southern California argue over the nature of the 'true' American West—where each character fights to maintain his own identity and destroy his brother's. Shepard's 40 other plays include *Buried Child* (1978), which links *True West* in a trilogy with *Curse of the Starving Class* (1976); and *Fool for Love* (1983). He is also the author of a number of screenplays, including *Zabriskie Point* (1970) and *Paris, Texas* (1984), and has appeared in some 40 films, notably as the test pilot Chuck Yeager in *The Right Stuff* (1983) and in a number of *westerns.

Shepheardes Calender, The The earliest important work of Edmund *Spenser, published anonymously in 1579, and dedicated to Philip *Sidney. It was illustrated by original woodcuts and had accompanying glosses by one 'E.K.', possibly Edward Kirke (1553–1613).

It consists of twelve *eclogues, one for each month of the calendar year, beginning with January, modelled on the eclogues of *Theocritus, *Virgil, and more modern writers, such as *Mantuan and Marot. The pastorals are written in deliberately archaic language and, except for the first and last, take the form of dialogues among shepherds. 'January' and 'December' are complaints by 'Colin Clout', the poet's persona. Each eclogue is supplied with an argument and a woodcut and ends with one or more emblems or mottoes, followed by E.K.'s glosses. The eclogues deal with moral, religious, and political, matters, as well as with the nature, practice, and patronage of poetry itself; they show off the new poet's virtuosity in using new genres, such as pastoral elegy or a singing-match, new verse forms, such as the *sestina, and new metres.

Spenser follows contemporary practice by using pastoral and complaint to talk about 'secrete and particular' people and matters. The extent to which the work shadows a specific allegorical meaning has been disputed: some individuals, such as Algrind (Grindal), Roffy (John Young, bishop of Rochester), Dido and Elisa (*Elizabeth I), Tityrus (Geoffrey *Chaucer), Hobbinol (Gabriel *Harvey), or Wrenock (Richard *Mulcaster), seem clearly meant to be recognizable. Although hugely influential in Spenser's time and up to Alexander *Pope (and beyond), Samuel *Johnson mocked the poems' quaint language and use of dialogue.

SHEPHERD, Nan (1893–1981) Scottish novelist and nature writer. *The Quarry Wood* (1928), a wryly realistic *Bildungsroman, and *The Weatherhouse* (1930), a complex, polyphonic variation on the novel of rural community, are distinguished by Shepherd's superb ear for Scottish speech and by an anti-romantic acknowledgement of the constriction of women's lives. Published belatedly in 1977, *The Living Mountain* combines lyricism and science in its meditation on the Grampians and how they have been perceived.

Shepherd's Calendar, The A volume of verse by John *Clare, published 1827. It

describes rural and agricultural life in and around Clare's home village of Helpstone in Northamptonshire. Like *Spenser's *Shepheardes Calender, it consists of twelve poems, one for each month of the year. Though not a commercial success on first publication, it has come to be seen as one of the poet's finest achievements.

Shepherd's Week, The A series of six pastorals by John *Gay, published 1714. They are in mock-classical style, based somewhat loosely on *Virgil, but presenting shepherds and milkmaids of naive bucolic modernity rather than of Golden Age innocence. They were in part designed to parody the pastorals of Ambrose *Philips, which had been praised for their 'modern' simplicity at the expense of Alexander *Pope's classical exercises in the genre. Gay portrays his comic rustics (Blouzelinda, Bowzybeus, Cloddipole, Grubbinol) at work as well as at play, and includes many references to folklore, games, and superstitions.

SHERIDAN, Frances (1724–66) Novelist, wife of Thomas *Sheridan and mother of R. B. Sheridan. She was encouraged in her writing by Samuel *Richardson, to whom she dedicated her novel of *sentiment *The Memoirs of Miss Sydney Biddulph* ('after the manner of *Pamela*') in 1761. The novel, which ends in despair, describes the terrible misfortunes and distress of conscience of Sydney, who feels she has not the first claim to her beloved Faulkland. An expanded version appeared in 1767. *The Discovery*, a comedy starring David *Garrick, was very successful in 1763; it was adapted by Aldous *Huxley in 1924. *The History of Nourjahad*, an *oriental tale, appeared posthumously in 1767.

SHERIDAN, Richard Brinsley (1751–1816) The son of Thomas *Sheridan (1719–88), an Irish actor-manager, and Frances *Sheridan. He wrote *The *Rivals*, which was produced with great success at Covent Garden in 1775. It was followed in a few months by a farce, *St Patrick's Day*, and in the autumn by an opera, *The *Duenna*, both also successful. In 1776 Sheridan, with partners, bought David *Garrick's half-share in the *Drury Lane Theatre and became its manager. Early in 1777 appeared a musical play, *A Trip to Scarborough*, loosely based on Sir John Vanbrugh's *The *Relapse. The *School for Scandal* was produced, with Garrick's help and with a brilliant cast, in May. The play was universally acclaimed; it had 73 performances between 1777 and 1789 and made a profit of

£15,000. *The Critic* (1779) was likewise a hit. In 1779 he became the sole proprietor of Drury Lane, and began to live far beyond his means. He turned to politics, became the friend and ally of Charles James Fox, and in 1780 won the seat at Stafford. After only two years as an MP he became the under-secretary for foreign affairs, but he neglected his work both as a politician and as theatrical manager. In 1783 he became secretary to the treasury and established a reputation as a brilliant orator in the House of Commons. In 1792 the Drury Lane Theatre was declared unsafe and had to be demolished. Sheridan raised £150,000 for a new theatre, but he was plunging himself yet deeper into debt. *Pizarro*, adapted by Sheridan from Kotzebue, was performed in 1799 and was successful enough to bring a brief reprieve, but in 1802 the theatre funds were impounded. In 1809 the new Drury Lane was destroyed by fire, the debts became crushing, and Sheridan was excluded from all aspects of management. In 1811 he lost his seat at Stafford, and in 1813 he was arrested for debt. He died in July 1816. He wished to be remembered as a man of politics and to be buried next to Fox, but he was, perhaps more appropriately, laid near Garrick instead.

SHERIDAN, Thomas (1719–88) Irish actor, educationalist, and elocutionist author of the farce *The Brave Irishman, or Captain O'Blunder* (1743) and of *British Education, or The Source of the Disorders of Great Britain* (1756). His lecturing career took him to Edinburgh to enlighten the *literati on pronunciation. He was the husband of Frances *Sheridan and the father of Richard Brinsley Sheridan.

SHERRIFF, R. C. (Robert Cedric) (1896–1975) Playwright. His best-known play was *Journey's End* (1928; pub. 1929), based on his experiences in the trenches as a captain during the First World War. It portrays the relationships under stress of Captain Stanhope, new lieutenant Raleigh (with whose sister Stanhope is in love), the reliable second-in-command Osborne, and Hibbert, who has lost his nerve, and ends in mid-battle after the deaths of Osborne and Raleigh. Other plays include *Badger's Green* (1930), a comedy of village politics and cricket; *St Helena* (1934), about Napoleon's last years; *Home at Seven* (1950), in which a banker suffering from amnesia fears he may have committed a crime; and *The White Carnation* (1953), a ghost story about a conscience-stricken stockbroker. Sherriff's other works include screenplays, most memorably *Good-bye Mr Chips* (1939; from James *Hilton's 1934 novella), and

The Four Feathers (1939; from A. E. W. *Mason's 1902 novel).

SHERWOOD, Mary Martha (1775–1851) Writer and educationalist, who wrote numerous books, stories, and tracts, many for children, teaching the rewards of virtue. *Susan Gray*, written for her Sunday School scholars, appeared in 1802; *Little Henry and his Bearer* (1814), drawing on time spent in India, was translated into French, German, Hindustani, Chinese, and Sinhalese. The tremendous success of *The History of the Fairchild Family* (1818) led to sequels 1842 and 1847.

She Stoops to Conquer, (*The Mistakes of a Night*) A comedy by Oliver *Goldsmith, produced 1773. The principal characters are Mr and Mrs Hardcastle, and Miss Hardcastle their daughter; Mrs Hardcastle's son by a former marriage, the idle but cunning Tony Lumpkin, doted on by his mother; and young Marlow, 'one of the most bashful and reserved young fellows in the world', except with barmaids and servant-girls. His father, Sir Charles Marlow, proposes a match between young Marlow and Miss Hardcastle, and he and his friend Hastings accordingly travel down to visit the Hardcastles. They arrive in the dark at an inn, the Three Jolly Pigeons, where Tony Lumpkin mischievously directs them to a neighbouring inn, which is in reality the Hardcastles' house. In the resulting misunderstanding, Marlow treats Hardcastle as a pub landlord, and attempts to seduce Miss Hardcastle, whom he takes for one of the servants. This contrasts with his bashful behaviour when presented to her in her real character. The arrival of Sir Charles Marlow clears up the misconception and all ends well. The play was an immense success, and is still regularly performed.

She Would if She Could Sir George *Etherege's second comedy produced in 1668. Sir Oliver and Lady Cockwood and Sir Joslin Jolley, with his young kinswomen Ariana and Gatty, come up from the country to London for pleasure. Lady Cockwood pursues Mr Courtal, a gentleman of the town, while he and his friend Mr Freeman strike up acquaintance with the young ladies. Various farcical scenes follow, one set in the Bear in Drury Lane. In the happy ending the young couples are united and Lady Cockwood resolves to confine herself in future to family matters.

SHIEL, Matthew Phipps (1865–1947) Montserrat-born British writer known for his baroque style. *The Yellow Danger* (1898)

expresses the invasion fears of contemporary Britain. *The Purple Cloud* (1901) is a 'last man' story reminiscent of Mary *Shelley's.

SHIELDS, Carol (1935–2003) American novelist and poet; she lived mainly in Canada after her marriage in 1957. Her first published books were volumes of poetry, *Others* (1972) and *Intersect* (1974). The title of her first novel, *Small Ceremonies* (1975), suggested the often domestic territory of the everyday that she would explore in her fiction and would illuminate and transform both by her use of language and by subverting traditional narrative forms. None of her work was published in the UK until 1990, when *Mary Swann* (originally published in Canada as *Swann*, 1987) established her as a major 'new' writer. Her international reputation was made by *The Stone Diaries* (1993), a novel which uses the conventions of biography (including photographs purporting to depict the book's characters) to tell the story of one woman's life in the 20th century. *Larry's Party* won the Orange Prize in 1998, the same year Shields was diagnosed with cancer. Defying the prognoses of her doctors, Shields survived to produce a new volume of stories, *Dressing Up for the Carnival* (2000), a brief life of Jane Austen (2001), and a final novel, *Unless* (2002).

'Shipman's Tale, The' *See* CANTERBURY TALES, 15.

Ship of Fools, The A translation of Sebastian Brant's famous *Narrenschiff* by Alexander *Barclay. The original *Narrenschiff*, written in Swabian dialect and first published in 1494, became extremely popular and was translated into several languages. Published in England in 1509, Barclay's translation is an adaptation which gives an interesting picture of contemporary English life. Its theme is the shipping of fools of all kinds from their home to the Land of Fools, and its popularity was enhanced by the humorous woodcut illustrations. The work is notable as an early collection of satirical types, and its influence is seen in *Cock Lorell's Boat*.

Shirley A novel by Charlotte *Brontë, published 1849. The story is set in Yorkshire, during the latter part of the Napoleonic Wars, the time of the Luddite riots, when the wool industry was suffering from the collapse of exports. In spite of these conditions, the forceful mill-owner Robert Gérard Moore, half English and half Belgian, persists in introducing the latest labour-saving machinery, undeterred by the opposition of the workers, which culminates in an attempt to destroy his mill and take his life. To overcome his financial difficulties he proposes to Shirley Keeldar, an heiress of independent spirit, while under the mistaken impression that she is in love with him; he himself loves his gentle cousin Caroline Helstone, who is pining away for love of him and through enforced idleness in the oppressive atmosphere of her uncle's rectory. Robert is indignantly rejected by Shirley, who is in fact in love with his brother Louis, a tutor in her family. The misunderstandings are resolved, and the two couples united.

Despite touches of melodrama, this is Charlotte Brontë's most social novel. One of its recurrent themes is its plea for useful occupations for women, condemned either to matrimony or, as old maids, to a life of self-denial and acts of private charity. Shirley herself is an attempt to portray a woman with the freedom and power to act. Charlotte told Elizabeth *Gaskell that she was intended to be what Emily *Brontë might have been 'had she been placed in health and prosperity'.

SHIRLEY, James (1596–1666) Clergyman, schoolmaster, and dramatist. His first recorded play, *Love Tricks* (1625), was followed by some forty tragedies, comedies, and tragicomedies. Among the best known are *The *Traitor* (1631), *Hyde Park* (1632), *The *Gamester* (1633), *The *Lady of Pleasure* (1635), and *The *Cardinal* (1641). During the plague closure of 1636–7 he went to Ireland, where he wrote a number of plays, including *St Patrick for Ireland* (*c*.1639), for the theatre in Werburgh Street, Dublin, the first theatre built in Ireland. In London, most of his plays were performed by Queen Henrietta's Men, and he attracted royal favour by a sarcastic reference to William *Prynne (then awaiting trial for writing *Histriomastix*) in the dedication to *The Bird in a Cage* (1632–3). As a further sign of royal allegiance he wrote the masque *The *Triumph of Peace* (1634). On his return from Ireland in 1640 he succeeded Philip *Massinger as principal dramatist for the King's Men, but the outbreak of the Civil War put an end to this career. He served in the Royalist army under the duke of *Newcastle, returned to London after the Royalist defeat, was patronized by Thomas Stanley, and assisted John Ogilby in his translations of Homer. He took up schoolmastering again and wrote some pieces for school performance, among them *The Contention of Ajax and Ulysses* (pub. 1659), a dramatic debate interspersed with songs. Shirley and his wife are said to have died as a result of terror and exposure when they were driven from their home by the Great Fire of London.

S

SHIRLEY, John (1954–) American *science fiction writer and musician. Linked to cyberpunk, he collaborated with William *Gibson: the 1989 collection *Heatseeker* brings together his influential stories. He has also written *horror fiction and screenplays. *Crawlers* (2003) combines science fiction nanotechnology with apocalyptic horror.

Shoemakers' Holiday, The, *or The Gentle Craft* A comedy by Thomas *Dekker, written 1599, published 1600. Rowland Lacy, a kinsman of the earl of Lincoln, loves Rose, the daughter of the lord mayor of London. To prevent the match the earl sends him to France in command of a company of men. Lacy gives his place to a friend and, disguised as a Dutch shoemaker, takes service with Simon Eyre, who supplies the family of the lord mayor with shoes. Here he successfully pursues his suit, is married in spite of the efforts of the earl and the lord mayor to prevent it, and is pardoned by the king. *See also* DELONEY, THOMAS.

SHOLOKHOV, Mikhail Aleksandrovich (1905–84) Russian novelist. He became well known in the West for *And Quiet Flows the Don* (4 vols, 1928–40), a novel about Cossack life in the early 20th century, *Virgin Soil Upturned* (vol. i 1932, vol ii 1960), a classic of *Socialist Realism, chronicles life during the early period of agricultural collectivization in southern Russia.

SHORE, Jane (d. 1526/7?) Mistress of Edward IV. Born Elizabeth Lambert, her marriage to William Shore was annulled in 1476. With her beauty and wit, she greatly influenced Edward IV. She was made to do public penance in 1483, and tradition holds that she died in poverty. Sir Thomas *More's *History of Richard the Third*, provides a remarkable account of her. She is the subject of a ballad included in Thomas *Percy's *Reliques*, appears in Thomas Churchyard's *Shore's Wife* in A *Mirror for Magistrates, and is the subject of a descriptive note by Michael *Drayton in *England's Heroical Epistles*. She was first called Jane Shore in Thomas *Heywood's plays on Edward IV (1599) and is the *eponymous heroine of Nicholas *Rowe's tragedy (1714).

SHORTHOUSE, Joseph Henry (1834–1903) Novelist; the historical novel by which he is remembered, *John Inglesant* (1881, privately printed 1880), is an evocation of 17th-century religious intrigue and faith. Inglesant becomes a tool of the Jesuit faction, joins the court of Charles I, and after the king's death

visits Italy to seek vengeance for his brother's murder; the book includes a vivid account of Nicholas Ferrar's religious community at *Little Gidding. The novel was immensely successful, and something of a cult formed around it. It bears witness to the religious and historical interests revived by the *Oxford Movement and the *Pre-Raphaelites.

Short View *See* COLLIER, JEREMY.

Shropshire Lad, A *See* HOUSMAN, A. E.

SHUTE, Nevil (1899–1960) The pen-name of Nevil Shute Norway, popular novelist, who later (1950) settled in Australia. His many readable, fast-moving novels, several based on his involvement with the aircraft industry and his own wartime experiences, include *Pied Piper* (1942); *No Highway* (1948); *A Town Like Alice* (1950), in which an English girl is captured by the Japanese and survives the war to settle in Australia; and *On the Beach* (1957), which describes events after a nuclear holocaust.

SHUTTLE, Penelope (1947–) Poet and novelist. Her first volume of poetry was *The Orchard Upstairs* (1980); later volumes include *Adventures with my Horse* (1988), *A Leaf out of his Book* (1999), and *Selected Poems 1980–1996* (1998). Her poetry is distinguished by a rich, sensuous awareness of sexuality and the natural and animal worlds: her use of female imagery is arresting and celebratory. Her novels include *Wailing Monkey Embracing a Tree* (1973). She was married to Peter *Redgrove, with whom she collaborated on several works, including *The Wise Wound* (1978), a study of the reality and mythology of menstruation. Her volume *Redgrove's Wife* (2006) movingly celebrates and elegizes their life together.

Shylock The Jewish moneylender in *Shakespeare's *The *Merchant of Venice.

Sibylline Leaves A volume of poems by S. T. *Coleridge, published 1817. It is most notable for the publication of the revised and expanded version of the *The Rime of the *Ancient Mariner* with marginal notes, here acknowledged for the first time as Coleridge's poem.

SIDDAL (Siddall), **Elizabeth** ('Lizzie') (1829–62) Painter, poet, and model to the *Pre-Raphaelites. Siddal met D. G. *Rossetti in 1850, and in 1852 modelled for John Everett *Millais as the drowning Ophelia. She attended art school at Sheffield, drawing subjects from medieval lore and works by John *Keats, Alfred *Tennyson, and Robert *Browning; John

*Ruskin praised her later watercolours. Her poems reflect the unhappiness of her relationship with Rossetti. The two married in 1860, and, having long suffered ill health, Siddal gave birth in 1861 to a stillborn child. In 1862 she died, after taking an overdose of laudanum, and was buried in Highgate Cemetery. In 1869 Rossetti exhumed the manuscript notebook of his poems with which Siddal had been buried.

SIDGWICK, Henry (1838-1900) Philosopher; from 1883 professor of moral philosophy at Cambridge. A follower of John Stuart *Mill, his reputation rests on *The Methods of Ethics* (1874), where he considered ways of determining the right courses of action, and the practical obstacles which hinder our following them. In 1876 Sidgwick married Eleanor Balfour (1845-1936), who was from 1892 to 1910 principal of Newnham College, Cambridge; it was partly through their efforts on behalf of women's higher education that the college was founded.

SIDNEY, Algernon (1622-83) Grandnephew of Sir Philip *Sidney. He took up arms against Charles I and was wounded at Marston Moor. Employed on government service until the *Restoration, he aroused Oliver Cromwell's hostility by his implacable republicanism. At the Restoration he refused to give pledges to Charles II, and lived abroad in poverty and exile until 1677. On his return he joined the opposition to Stuart absolutism, was imprisoned in the Tower after the discovery of the Rye House Plot, tried before the notorious judge George Jeffreys (1645-89), condemned without adequate evidence, and executed. His *Discourses Concerning Government* (1698) were widely read in the American colonies. Thomas Jefferson regarded them as a philosophical basis for liberty and human rights.

SIDNEY, Sir Philip (1554-86) Writer and courtier, born at *Penshurst Place, nephew of Robert Dudley, earl of Leicester. His contemporaries at Oxford included William Camden, Richard *Hakluyt, and Walter *Ralegh. Between 1572 and 1575 he travelled in France, witnessing the massacre of St Bartholomew's Day in Paris, and in Germany, Austria, and Italy. After his return to England, Sidney did not achieve any official post which matched his ambitions until his appointment as governor of Flushing (Vlissingen, in the Netherlands) in 1585. His knighthood was awarded for reasons of court protocol in 1583.

Years of comparative idleness enabled him to write and revise the *Arcadia, and to complete *A Defence of Poetry*, *The Lady of May*, and *Astrophel and Stella*. The first *Arcadia*, and probably other works, were composed while he was staying with his younger sister Mary, countess of *Pembroke, at Wilton. The exact nature of his relations with Penelope Devereux (later Rich, the 'Stella' of Sidney's sonnet sequence) are not known. During these years Sidney also became a notable literary patron; he was the dedicatee of Edmund *Spenser's *The *Shepheardes Calender* (1579). Sidney was interested in experimenting with English verse in classical metres along the lines prescribed by Thomas Drant (*c.*1540-1578), and had discussions of this and other matters with Greville, Edward *Dyer, and Spenser (the 'Areopagus'). His last year was spent in the Netherlands. On 22 September 1586 he led an attack on a Spanish convoy bringing supplies to the fortified city of Zutphen; he received a musket shot in his thigh and died of infection three weeks later. Greville was not present, but subsequently told the story of the death with two famous embellishments, claiming that Sidney left off his thigh-armour deliberately, so as not to be better armed than a fellow soldier, and that as he was being carried wounded from the field he saw a dying soldier gazing at his water bottle, and gave it to him with the words 'Thy necessity is yet greater than mine.'

Sidney was buried in St Paul's Cathedral. Among many English elegies on him the best known, Spenser's *'Astrophel', was not printed until 1595, among his *Complaints*. This included elegies by Lodowick Bryskett (1546-1609/12), Matthew Roydon (*fl.* 1583-1622), Ralegh, and Dyer. Roydon's is unusual in evoking the hero's presence, his 'sweet attractive kind of grace'. Sidney's posthumous reputation, as the perfect Renaissance patron, soldier, lover, and courtier, far outstripped his documented achievements.

None of Sidney's works was published during his lifetime. The revised *Arcadia* was published under Greville's editorship in 1590; in 1593 the countess of Pembroke printed that version with the last three books of the earlier one appended; *Astrophel and Stella* was published in 1591; and *A Defence of Poetry* in 1595. Editions of the *Arcadia* from 1598 onwards included all the literary works except his version of the Psalms. These were completed posthumously by his sister, and not printed until 1823.

SIDNEY, Sir Robert (1563-1626) Poet and courtier, the younger brother of Sir Philip *Sidney. His early career closely followed that of his brother, whom he succeeded as governor of Flushing (Vlissingen, in the Netherlands) in 1589. He was created Baron Sidney by James I in 1603, Viscount Lisle in 1605, and earl of Leicester in 1618. Robert Dowland (1591–1641), who was his godson, dedicated *A Musical Banquet* (1610) to him. Sidney's estate and generous hospitality at *Penshurst Place were warmly praised by Ben *Jonson. An autograph manuscript of Sidney's poems, consisting of sonnets, pastorals, songs, and epigrams, apparently written in the later 1590s, was identified by P. J. Croft in 1973; he edited them in 1984.

Siege of Corinth, The A poem by Lord *Byron, published 1816. The poem is founded on the story of the Turkish siege of Corinth, then held by the Venetians, and it was the last of Byron's Eastern tales.

Siege of Rhodes, The One of the earliest attempts at English opera, by Sir William D'Avenant, performed 1656. Dramatic performances having been suppressed by the Commonwealth government, D'Avenant obtained permission in 1656 to produce at Rutland House an 'Entertainment after the manner of the ancients', in which Diogenes and *Aristophanes argue against and for public amusements; this was accompanied by vocal and instrumental music, composed by Henry *Lawes. Immediately after this prologue was given *The Siege of Rhodes* (at first in one, but in 1662 in two parts), a heroic play, the 'story sung in recitative music', which was composed by Dr Charles Coleman (d. 1664) and George Hudson (d. 1672/3). The play deals with the siege of Rhodes by Solyman the Magnificent.

SIGAL, Clancy (1926–) American novelist and screenwriter. He worked in Hollywood in the 1950s and came to England in 1957, where he wrote *Weekend in Dinlock* (1960), a fictionalized exploration of life in a mining community in Yorkshire. *Going Away* (1963) is a first-person 'road' novel. *Zone of the Interior* (USA 1976) is set in England where he lived for some 30 years before returning to live in California.

Sigurd the Volsung and the Fall of the Niblungs, The Story of An epic in *anapaestic couplets by William *Morris, founded on the *Völsunga Saga*, and published 1876; it did much to awaken popular interest in Icelandic literature. Morris described its subject as 'the Great Story of the North which should be to all our race what the Tale of Troy was to the Greeks'. It is in four books; the first, 'Sigmund',

is the story of Volsung's son Sigmund and of the fatal marriage of his sister Signy to the king of the Goths; the second and third, 'Regin' and 'Brynhild', deal with Sigmund's son Sigurd, his betrothal to Brynhild, his subsequent marriage (under the influence of a magic potion) to Gudrun, the Niblung king's daughter, and the deaths of Sigurd and Brynhild; the last, 'Gudrun', tells of Gudrun's own death and the fall of the Niblungs. *See* SAGA.

Silas Marner A pastoral novel by George *Eliot, published 1861. Silas Marner, a linen-weaver, is driven out of his religious community by a false charge of theft, and takes refuge in the agricultural village of Raveloe. He consoles himself with a growing pile of gold, which is stolen by the squire's reprobate son Dunstan Cass, who disappears. Dunstan's elder brother Godfrey loves Nancy Lammeter, but is secretly married to a working-class woman in a neighbouring town. Enraged by Godfrey's refusal to acknowledge her, this woman carries her child one New Year's Eve to Raveloe, intending to force her way into his house; but dies in the snow. Her golden-haired child, Eppie, toddles into Silas's cottage and is adopted by him, giving his life new meaning. After many years, a drained pond near Silas's door reveals the body of Dunstan with the gold. Moved by this revelation, Godfrey, now married to Nancy, acknowledges Eppie as his daughter, but she refuses to leave Silas. The serious tone of the story is varied by the humour of the rustic Rainbow Inn, and the genial motherliness of Silas's friend Dolly Winthrop.

Silent Woman, The *See* EPICENE.

SILKIN, Jon (1930–97) Poet. His volumes include *The Peaceable Kingdom* (1954), *Nature with Man* (1965, which contains many of his piercingly observed 'flower poems'), *Amana Grass* (1971, with work inspired by visits to Israel and America), *The Principle of Water* (1974); *Selected Poems* (1980). *The Psalms with their Spoils* (1980), *Autobiographical Stanzas* (1984), and *The Lens-Breakers* (1992). He founded the literary quarterly *Stand in 1952; his wife Lorna Tracy, short story writer, was his co-editor.

SILLITOE, Alan (1928–2010) Writer, brought up in Nottingham, son of an illiterate and often unemployed labourer; he married the American poet Ruth *Fainlight. His first volume of verse, *Without Beer or Bread* (1957), was followed by his much-praised first novel, *Saturday Night and Sunday Morning* (1958), which describes the life of Arthur Seaton, a dissatisfied young

Nottingham factory worker. It differed from other provincial novels of the 1950s (*see* COOPER, WILLIAM; AMIS, KINGSLEY; LARKIN, PHILIP; BRAINE, JOHN; WAIN, JOHN) in that its hero is a working man, not a rising member of the lower middle class. The title story of *The Loneliness of the Long Distance Runner* (1959) is a first-person portrait of a rebellious and anarchic Borstal boy. Many other books followed, including the novels *The Death of William Posters* (1965) and *A Start in Life* (1970); the semi-autobiographical *Raw Material* (1972); a collection of short stories, *Men, Women and Children* (1973); and a collection of autobiographical and critical essays, *Mountains and Caverns* (1975). His *Collected Poems* appeared in 1993. *A Man of his Time* (2004) is a sequel to *Saturday Night and Sunday Morning*.

silver-fork school *See* FASHIONABLE NOVEL.

SIMIC, Charles (1938–) Serbian-born poet, who moved to America at the age of 15. His portrayal of the familiar in startling, often unsettling ways runs through his later collections, most notably *Charon's Cosmology* (1977), *Classic Ballroom Dances* (1980), and *Austerities* (1982), and betrays the influence of the *Surrealists, as well as of Serbian poetry, which he has done much to promote.

simile An explicit likening of one object, scene, or action with another, e.g. 'as weak as a kitten', inviting imaginative comparison between the two terms rather than the more forceful identification suggested by *metaphor. A more elaborately extended variety is the *epic simile.

SIMMONS, Dan (1948–) American *science fiction author. His epic *Hyperion* (1989) employs literary echoes—including the life of John *Keats—to begin a metaphysical space opera. *Ilium* (2003) likewise draws upon *Homer, with post-humans observing events from the *Iliad*.

SIMMS, William Gilmore (1806–70) American novelist, who produced a series of romances, including *The Yemassee* (1835), depicting early phases of Southern history. He supported slavery and attacked *Uncle Tom's Cabin* through a rejoinder novel, *The Sword and the Distaff* (1852).

SIMON, Neil (1927–) Prolific Jewish American playwright and screenwriter, born in New York, whose plays include *Come Blow your Horn* (1961) and *The Odd Couple* (1965).

Simple Story, A A novel by Elizabeth *Inchbald, published 1791, with the avowed purpose of showing the value of 'a proper education'. Miss Milner, a clever but headstrong heiress, falls in love with her attractive and sensitive guardian Dorriforth, a Roman Catholic priest: when he inherits the title of Lord Elmwood he renounces his vows and marries her, but later becomes violently autocratic. During his prolonged absence overseas she is unfaithful to him, and dies. Their daughter Matilda, forbidden her father's presence, and brought up under many restrictions, is finally reconciled with him, and marries her father's favourite, Rushbrook. The novel's blend of *melodrama, *Gothic sexual intensity, and psychological observation has provoked much commentary. The expiation of jealousy and guilt over two generations has been compared to *The *Winter's Tale*, in which Inchbald may have acted.

SIMPSON, Habbie (1550–1620) Subject of 'The Life and Death of the Piper of Kilbarchan', a comic elegy by Robert Sempill of Beltrees (*c.*1595–1659) which circulated in broadsheet before its inclusion in *A Choice Collection of Comic and Serious Scots Poems both Ancient and Modern* (1706–11), published by the printer and bookseller James Watson (?1664–1722). Sempill's six-line stanza was adopted by Allan *Ramsay, who called it 'Standart Habbie', and further developed by Robert *Fergusson and Robert *Burns. Sometimes called 'the Burns stanza', it has been used by Douglas *Dunn, Seamus *Heaney (in his uncollected 'Open Letter', 1983), and Iain Crichton *Smith.

SIMPSON, Helen (1959–) Short story writer. Her first collection of stories, *Four Bare Legs in a Bed* (1990), established her reputation as a wry and elegant chronicler of modern life. A novella, 'Flesh and Grass', appeared with one by Ruth *Rendell in *Unguarded Hours* (1990), and although she has otherwise published only short stories, in 1993 she was chosen as one of *Granta*'s 'Best of Young British Novelists'. Subsequent volumes include *Dear George* (1995), *Hey Yeah Right Get a Life* (2000), which drew upon her experiences of motherhood, *Constitutional* (2005), and *In-Flight Entertainment* (2010).

SIMPSON, Matt (1936–2009) Poet, born in Bootle, Liverpool. Although of the same generation as his better-known contemporaries, the *Liverpool poets, Simpson's haunted, uneasy lyricism and his exploration of the vernacular mark an altogether more literary aesthetic. His main subject matters—his working-class upbringing, his relationship with his seafaring father, and his negotiations with Liverpool's imperial past—connect him to poets such as Tony *Harrison, Seamus *Heaney, and Douglas *Dunn. Collections include *Making Arrangements* (1982), *An Elegy for the Galosherman: New and Selected Poems* (1990), *Catching up with History* (1995), *Cutting the Clouds Towards* (1998), *Getting There* (2001), and *In Deep* (2006).

SIMPSON, N. F. (Norman Frederick) (1919–2011) Playwright, whose surreal comedies *A Resounding Tinkle* (1957) and *One-Way Pendulum* (1959) established him as a writer of the Theatre of the *Absurd. His work shows an affinity with that of Eugène Ionesco (1909–94), which enjoyed a considerable vogue in Britain in the late 1950s. Other works include *The Cresta Run* (1965) and a novel, *Harry Bleachbaker* (1976).

SINCLAIR, Catherine (1800–64) Philanthropist and prolific Scottish writer of travel, biography, children's books, novels, essays, and reflections. In *Holiday House* (1839) she produced a classic children's book that consciously resisted the prevailing fashion for moralizing tales for the young; her popular *Picture Letters* (1861–4) sold up to 100,000 copies each.

SINCLAIR, Clive (1948–) Novelist and short story writer. The title of his first novel, *Bibliosexuality* (1973), indicates an idiosyncratic strain of verbal play and erotic bravura that characterizes much of his work. It was followed by two volumes of short stories, *Hearts of Gold* (1979) and *Bedbugs* (1982). Sinclair was chosen as one of *Granta*'s original 'Best of Young British Novelists' in 1983. His other novels include *Cosmetic Effects* (1989), set in England and Israel, *Augustus Rex* (1992), and *Meet the Wife* (2002). He has also written *The Lady with the Laptop* (1996, short stories), *A Soap Opera from Hell* (1998, non-fiction), and a study of the brothers *Singer (1983).

SINCLAIR, Iain (1943–) British poet, novelist, London chronicler, and film-maker. Early poetry collections *Lud Heat* (1975) and *Suicide Bridge* (1979) were followed by his first novel, *White Chappell* (1987), which established his recurrent themes: the mythology of Jack the Ripper and the 'psychogeography' of east London. *Downriver* (1991) views the changing face of London from its rail and waterways. *Slow Chocolate Autopsy* (1997) is a collection of short stories and graphic tales (with artist Dave McKean) and *Lights out for the Territory* (1997), based on a series of London walks, explores such enthusiasms as the churches of Nicholas Hawksmoor, the secret state, and the films of Patrick Keiller (1950–). He has since collaborated on a film about the M25, *London Orbital* (screened in 2002), with Chris Pettit. *The Firewall* (2006) is a selection of his poetry.

SINCLAIR, May (Mary Amelia St Clair) (1863–1946) Novelist. Sinclair never married, and supported herself by reviewing, translating, and writing fiction. She was a supporter of women's suffrage, and deeply interested in psychoanalysis; her reviews and novels show considerable knowledge of both *Jung and *Freud. Among the most notable of her 24 novels are *The Divine Fire* (1904); *The Three Sisters* (1914), a study in female frustration with echoes of the lives of the *Brontë sisters; *The Tree of Heaven* (1917); *Mary Olivier: A Life* (1919); and *Life and Death of Harriett Frean* (1922). The last two are *stream-of-consciousness novels, taking a woman from girlhood to unmarried middle age. The plots of both are informed by ideas of degeneration, and both are keenly aware of the tendency towards self-denial in women's lives.

SINCLAIR, Upton (1878–1968) American novelist and journalist, best known for his novel *The Jungle* (1906), an exposé of the Chicago meat-packing industry, which resulted in a government investigation of the yards. Other novels include *The Metropolis* (1908), *King Coal* (1917), *Oil!* (1927), and *Boston* (1928). His Lanny Budd series, focusing on the illegitimate son of a munitions manufacturer, was designed as a panorama of modern history, including *World's End* (1940), *Dragon's Teeth* (1942), *The Return of Lanny Budd* (1953), and other works. Sinclair ran unsuccessfully for the governorship of California in 1934 and wrote studies of economics, extra-sensory perception, the Soviet Union and other subjects.

SINGER, Isaac Bashevis (1904–91) Polish-born American writer, the son and grandson of rabbis. In 1935 he emigrated to New York, and became a journalist, writing in Yiddish for the *Jewish Daily Forward*, which published most of his short stories. The first of his works to be translated into English was *The Family Moskat* (1950). His many other works include *Satan in Goray* (Yiddish, 1935; English, 1955); *The Magician of Lublin* (1960); *The Slave* (1962); *The Manor* (1967) and its sequel *The Estate* (1969).

His collections of stories include *Gimpel the Fool* (1957); *The Spinoza of Market Street* (1961); *Zlateh the Goat* (1966); and *A Friend of Kafka* (1970). Singer's work portrays the lives of Polish Jews in many periods of Polish history, coloured by hints of the mystical and supernatural. Many of his novels and stories describe the conflicts between traditional religion and rising scepticism, between varying forms of nationalism, and between the primitive, the exotic, and the intellectually progressive.

Singleton, The Life, Adventures and Piracies of the Famous Captain A novel by Daniel *Defoe, published 1720. Singleton tells how he was kidnapped in infancy and sent to sea. After a mutiny he is put ashore in Madagascar with his comrades; he crosses the continent of Africa from east to west, encountering many adventures and obtaining much gold, which he dissipates in England. He then becomes a pirate, acquiring great wealth from depredations in the West Indies, Indian Ocean, and China Seas; he returns home, unpunished but vaguely repentant, and marries the sister of his shipmate, William, a colourful Quaker pirate.

Sir Courtly Nice, or It Cannot Be A comedy by John *Crowne, produced 1685, based on *No puede ser el guardar una mujer*, by the Spanish dramatist Moreto (1618–69).

Sir Launfal By Thomas Chestre (*fl.* late 14th–early 15th century), a late 14th-century *Breton lay, in 1,044 lines in twelve-line, *tail-rhyme stanzas. It is one of the two English versions of *Marie de France's *Lanval*. Launfal is a knight of the *Round Table who leaves the court, affronted by tales of *Guinevere's misconduct. He falls in love with a fairy lady, Tryamour. When he returns to Arthur's court Guinevere declares her love for him, but he rejects her, declaring that his beloved's maids are more beautiful. The queen accuses him of trying to seduce her and at his trial he is asked to produce the beautiful lady he has boasted of. Tryamour appears, breathes on Guinevere's eyes, blinding her, and the lovers depart.

Sir Patrick Spens An early Scottish ballad, included in Thomas *Percy's *Reliques*. Sir Patrick goes to sea on a mission, has a premonition of disaster, and is lost with his ship's company. In Walter *Scott's version, the mission was to bring to Scotland the Maid of Norway (1283–90), who died on her voyage to marry Edward, prince of Wales.

Sir Thomas More See MORE, SIR THOMAS.

SISSAY, Lemn (?1967–) Dramatist, scriptwriter, and poet, born in Ethiopia but fostered by a British couple; he lost touch with his birth family. His work focuses on his search for them: poetry collections include *Tender Fingers in a Clenched Fist* (1988) and *The Emperor's Watchmaker* (2000); *Something Dark* (2004, radio adaptation, 2005) is an autobiographical play.

SISSON, C. H. (Charles Hubert) (1914–2003) Poet, translator, and essayist. Exposure to the febrile political rhetoric of 1930s Germany was a formative experience, as was his conversion from *Methodism to High Anglicanism. He joined the Civil Service in 1936. Inviting comparisons with Andrew *Marvell, Jonathan *Swift, and Barnabe *Barnes, he sought to integrate poetry and politics: not simply in his 'political poetry' (Tory reaction to the *Pylon School) but also his 'poetic politics'. His constitutional study *The Spirit of British Administration* (1959) appeals to an ancient and mystical bond between God, Crown, and nation. Volumes published include *The London Zoo* (1961), *Numbers* (1965), *Metamorphoses* (1968), *Anchises* (1976), *In the Trojan Ditch* (1974), *God Bless Karl Marx!* (1988), and *Antidotes* (1991). Biblical and classical themes are mingled with *Arthurian references and juxtaposed with portrayals of contemporary society. The result is often caustic satire, combining a Christian preoccupation with man's fallen nature and a classical view of his limitations. Sisson is sometimes seen as the antithesis to the *Movement in conservative post-war English poetry. He has translated Heinrich *Heine, Jean *Racine, *Catullus, *Horace, *Lucretius, *Virgil, Dante's *Divina commedia* (1980), and others. He published two novels: *An Asiatic Romance* (1953), which calls upon wartime experiences in India, and *Christopher Homm* (1965), which pre-empts Martin *Amis's *Time's Arrow* in recounting a life backwards from death to birth. A partial autobiography, *On the Look Out*, appeared in 1989.

SITWELL, Dame Edith (1887–1964) Poet and writer; her first published poem, 'Drowned Suns', appeared in the *Daily Mirror* in 1913. She despised much of the work published in *Georgian Poetry*, and from 1916 to 1921 edited *Wheels*, an anti-Georgian magazine. Her volumes include *The Mother and Other Poems* (1915) and *Gold Coast Customs* (1929), and she quickly acquired a reputation as an eccentric and controversial figure, confirmed by the first public performance, in 1923, of *Façade* (1922), with verses in syncopated rhythms and music by William *Walton. Her only novel, *I Live under a Black Sun* (1937), was poorly received, but she was acclaimed for her poems of the Blitz and the atom bomb (*Street Songs*, 1942; *Green Song*, 1944; *The Song of the Cold*, 1945; *The Shadow of Cain*, 1947). F. R. *Leavis had claimed in 1932 that 'the Sitwells belong to the history of publicity, rather than that of poetry', but Edith's status as a poet survived this dismissal. She was made a DBE in 1954. An autobiography, *Taken Care Of* (1965) appeared posthumously. Osbert and Sacheverell *Sitwell were her younger brothers.

SITWELL, Sir Osbert (1892–1969) Poet and writer; brother of Edith and Sacheverell *Sitwell. He served reluctantly in the First World War; his early poetry (e.g. *The Winstonburg Line*, 1919) is sharply satirical and pacifist in tone. He went on to produce further volumes of poetry (including *Argonaut and Juggernaut*, 1919, and *At the House of Mrs Kinfoot*, 1921), fiction, and autobiography, and was, with his brother and sister, an outspoken enemy of the *Georgian poets (whom he regarded as philistine) and an ardent supporter of their *modernist counterparts. His prose works include *Triple Fugue* (1924, stories); *Before the Bombardment* (1926, novel), describing the shock German naval shelling of Scarborough in 1914; *Winters of Content* (1932), describing travels in Italy; and *Escape with Me!* (1939), describing travels in China and the Far East. His most sustained achievement remains his autobiography, in five volumes (*Left Hand! Right Hand!*, 1945; *The Scarlet Tree*, 1946; *Great Morning!*, 1948; *Laughter in the Next Room*, 1949; *Noble Essences*, 1950: with a later addition, *Tales my Father Taught Me*, 1962).

SITWELL, Sir Sacheverell (1897–1988) Poet and writer; brother of Osbert and Edith *Sitwell. His first volume of verse, *The People's Palace*, was published in 1918, his last, *An Indian Summer*, in 1982. His prose works include the monumental *British Architects and Craftsmen* (1945); and *Bridge of the Brocade Sash* (1959), on the arts of Japan. His imaginative prose includes *The Dance of the Quick and the Dead* (1936), a series of interlocked reflections on literature, art, travel, etc.; *Valse des fleurs* (1941), a recreation of a day in St Petersburg in 1868; and *Journey to the Ends of Time* (1959).

Six Characters in Search of an Author
See PIRANDELLO, LUIGI.

skaldic (scaldic) verse A form of Old Norse poetry distinguished by elaborate *metre, *alliteration, consonance, and resourceful diction that includes the *kenning. The most usual metre is 'dróttkvætt', eight six-syllable lines, all ending in trochees. Usually each odd line contains two alliterating syllables in stressed positions; alliteration is continued on one stressed syllable in each following even line. Odd lines contain two internal half-rhymes, even lines two full rhymes. Skaldic verse flourished in the 10th and 11th centuries and much was composed to commemorate the deeds of chieftains then ruling in Norway. Such verses are preserved mainly in the kings' sagas; occasional verses, and some love poetry are included in the family sagas (*see* SAGA).

SKEAT, W. W. (1835–1912) 19th-century editor of Old and Middle English literature. His edition of *Lancelot of the Laik* (1865) was among the first publications of the Early English Text Society. He edited *Ælfric, John *Barbour's *Bruce*, Thomas *Chatterton, and the Anglo-Saxon Gospels. He also edited *Piers Plowman* (1886), setting out in parallel the three manuscript versions, the existence of which he discovered, and *Chaucer (7 vols, 1894–7, largely establishing the canon, with non-canonical works in vol. vii). He founded the English Dialect Society (1873). His *Etymological Dictionary* (1879–82; rev. and enl. 1910) was begun in order to collect material for the *New English Dictionary* (*see* MURRAY, SIR JAMES).

SKELTON, John (?1460–1529) Poet, created 'laureate' by the universities of Oxford, Louvain, and Cambridge, an academical distinction. He became tutor to Prince Henry (later Henry VIII). Skelton's extraordinary poetry is marked by its unrivalled linguistic and metrical inventiveness. He pioneered the verse form now known as 'Skeltonic verse', consisting of short lines grouped by end-rhymes. His principal works include: *The *Bowge of Courte* (the title refers to free board at the king's table), a satire on the court of Henry VII, printed by Wynkyn de *Worde; *A Garlande of Laurell* (a self-laudatory allegory, describing the crowning of the author among the great poets of the world); *Phyllyp Sparowe* (a lamentation put into the mouth of Jane Scrope, a young lady whose sparrow has been killed by a cat, followed by a eulogy of her by Skelton, and a defence of himself and the poem); and *Collyn Clout* (a complaint by a vagabond of the misdeeds of ecclesiastics), which influenced Edmund *Spenser. This poem and his satires *Speke Parrot* and *Why come ye nat to Courte* contained attacks on Cardinal Wolsey, but *A Garlande of Laurell* and his poem on the duke of Albany, both of 1523, are dedicated to Wolsey. *The Tunnyng of Elynour Rummyng* is a vigorous satire. His play **Magnificence* is an example of the **morality, although it may have been intended to satirize the expulsion from the privy chamber of some of Henry VIII's associates. Skelton's *Ballade of the Scottysshe Kynge* is a spirited celebration of the defeat of the Scots at the battle of **Flodden Field (1513).

Sketches by Boz A collection of vivid sketches of life and manners, by Charles **Dickens, first published in various periodicals, and in book form 1836–7 (in one volume, 1839). They represent some of Dickens's earliest literary work. *See* BOZ.

SLADEK, John T. (1937–2000) American **science fiction writer, who became involved with the **New Wave of science fiction. With Thomas M. Disch, he also wrote pseudonymous **Gothics like *The House that Fear Built* (1966). Much of his work draws on the absurdity of the human–robot contrast. *Roderick* (1980) described the **Candide*-like moral education of a young robot. *Maps* (2002) is a posthumous collection showing his surreal gifts as a short story writer.

slavery, literature of Literature written during or about the period between the 16th and 19th centuries when Europeans colonized the Americas and the Caribbean using slave labour from Africa. Slavery is treated ambivalently in Aphra Behn's **Oroonoko* (1688) and Thomas **Southerne's play of the same name (1696), and in Daniel Defoe's **Robinson Crusoe* and **Colonel Jack*. Later in the 18th century the anti-slavery movement began to attract writers; Thomas **Day's narrative poem about a runaway slave, *The Dying Negro* (1773), became one of the best-known abolitionist poems of the period, but other poets such as William **Cowper, William **Blake, Robert **Southey, and William **Wordsworth contributed notably to the cause. George **Colman the younger's popular play **Inkle and Yarico* (1787) was only the most sentimental of dozens of versions of the tale (from Richard Steele's **Spectator, 13 Mar. 1711) of the betrayal and abandonment of a 'noble savage' by a supposedly cultivated European. Such critiques of civilization and commerce link anti-slavery with **primitivism. **Sentimental novels such as Henry **Mackenzie's *Julia de Roubigné* (1777) and Sarah **Scott's *The History of Sir George Ellison* (1766) also used slavery as a focus for pathos. Even sympathetic observers such as John **Stedman, whose *Narrative* (1796), illustrated by Blake, catalogued the horrors of slavery in Surinam, argued for amelioration of the slaves' conditions rather than their freedom. Anti-slavery politics did not usually transcend the belief in the superiority of European culture and rarely provided insights into the experiences of slaves as individuals. However, literature produced by ex-slaves, such as the *Interesting Narrative of the Life . . . of Olaudah **Equiano* (1789) and the *Letters* (1782) of Ignatius **Sancho, played an important role in the abolition movement because writing and art were valued as expressions of humanity and civilization. The most famous of the 19th century American slave narratives are by Frederick **Douglass and Harriet **Jacobs. Such writings have formed the basis of newly constructed **African American canons (*see also* BLACK BRITISH WRITING). Toni Morrison's **Beloved* (1987) was written 'to fill in the blanks that the slave narratives left, to part the veil that was so frequently drawn'. In Britain, Fred **D'Aguiar, David **Dabydeen, Caryl **Phillips, and Beryl Gilroy (1924–2001) have written literature that reimagines the history of slavery, and novels by Phillipa Gregory (1954–), Barry **Unsworth, and Marina **Warner have explored the role slavery played in British society. In the Caribbean, the need to develop a postcolonial identity has encouraged writers such as George **Lamming, Derek **Walcott, and Earl Lovelace (1935–) to reinterpret the slave past.

'Sleepy Hollow, The Legend of' A popular story by Washington **Irving, included in *The Sketch Book* (1820). Ichabod Crane is a schoolmaster and suitor for the hand of Katrina van Tassel. He meets his death, or, according to another report, leaves the neighbourhood, in consequence of being pursued at night by a headless horseman, an incident for which his rival Brom Bones is suspected of having been responsible. The story forms the basis of a film starring Johnny Depp (1999).

Slough of Despond In John **Bunyan's **Pilgrim's Progress*, a bog into which Christian and Pliable fall shortly after quitting the City of Destruction. Calvinist horror of sin accompanying conversion is symbolized as a rank fen which the king's surveyors have been attempting to drain 'for this sixteen hundred years' (i.e. since Christ's crucifixion). As fen drainage was a preoccupation of the age, the image had immediacy, and has since become proverbial.

Small House at Allington, The A novel by Anthony *Trollope, published 1864, fifth in the *'Barsetshire' series, and one of the most enduringly popular. Lily Dale is engaged to the ambitious Adolphus Crosbie, but Crosbie is invited to a house party at Courcy Castle where he proposes to Lady Alexandrina de Courcy. Learning that Crosbie has jilted her, Lily accepts his perfidy stoically, but Johnny Eames, who loves her, assaults Crosbie at Paddington station. Crosbie's marriage fails; Lady Alexandrina returns to her family and Crosbie takes refuge in bachelordom. Meanwhile Eames grows out of his juvenile dissipations, clears up an unfortunate entanglement with the daughter of his London boarding-house keeper, and begins to spend much time at Allington. He becomes the protégé of Lord de Guest, and renews his suit to Lily. Lily, however, is stubbornly loyal to Crosbie. Meanwhile, Lily's sister Bell is expected to marry the heir of Squire Dale of the Great House at Allington, but instead chooses the worthy Dr Crofts.

SMART, Christopher (1722–71) Poet, educated at Pembroke Hall, Cambridge, where he won the Seatonian Prize for sacred poetry five times. In 1749 he came to London and began to write poems and reviews under various pseudonyms, including 'Mrs Midnight', for John *Newbery, whose stepdaughter he married in 1752. Newbery published his first collection of verse, *Poems on Several Occasions* (1752). *The Hilliad*, a *mock-heroic satire on the quack doctor John Hill (1714–75), written with Arthur *Murphy and modelled on *The *Dunciad*, appeared in 1753. In 1756 Smart was dangerously ill, and a year later he was admitted to a hospital for the insane; he spent the years 1759–63 in a private home for the mentally ill in Bethnal Green. His derangement took the form of a compulsion to public prayer, which occasioned the famous comment of Samuel *Johnson: 'I'd as lief pray with Kit Smart as anyone else.' After being rescued from the asylum he published *A Song to David* (1763), a hymn of praise to David as author of the Psalms; the poem is built on a mathematical and mystical ordering of stanzas grouped in threes, fives, and sevens, and was likened by Robert *Browning to a great cathedral. Smart also published translations of the Psalms, of the fables of Phaedrus, and of *Horace, two oratorios, and *Hymns for the Amusement of Children* (1770; ed. Edmund *Blunden, 1947). William *Mason, who on reading the *Song to David* declared Smart 'as mad as ever', was, with Charles Burney, a supportive friend. Smart died within the 'Rules' of

the King's Bench Prison, confined for debt. His work was little known until the publication of his extraordinary work *Jubilate Agno* in 1939. This unfinished work had been composed between 1758/9 and 1763, largely at Bethnal Green; Smart described it as 'my Magnificat', and it celebrates the Creation in a verse form based on the antiphonal principles of Hebrew poetry. It was to consist of parallel sets of verses, one beginning 'Let . . .', with a response beginning 'For . . .'. The arrangement of the lines intended by Smart himself was demonstrated in W. H. Bond's 1954 edition, based on the autograph manuscript in the Houghton Library at Harvard. The most celebrated passage is the one beginning 'For I will consider my cat Jeoffry . . .'. Benjamin *Britten set parts of the poem to music in 1943.

SMART, Elizabeth (1913–86) Canadian-born writer, who settled in England after the Second World War. She is remembered for her prose poem *By Grand Central Station I Sat Down and Wept* (1945), an account of her love for George *Barker. It is passionate and lyrical, with biblical echoes from the Song of Songs, and was described by Brigid *Brophy as 'shelled, skinned, nerve-exposed'. *A Bonus* (1977) and *In the Meantime* (1984) are volumes of poetry.

Smectymnuus The name under which five Presbyterian clergymen, Stephen Marshall (? 1594/5–1655), Edmund Calamy (1600–66), Thomas Young (c.1587–1655), Matthew Newcomen (d. 1669), and William Spurstowe (d. 1666), published a pamphlet in 1641 attacking episcopacy and Bishop Joseph *Hall. It was answered by Hall, and defended by John *Milton (who had been a pupil of Young) in his *Animadversions upon the Remonstrant's Defence against Smectymnuus* (1641) and his *An Apology against a Pamphlet Call'd A Modest Confutation of the Animadversions upon the Remonstrant against Smectymnuus* (1642). From 'Smectymnuus' is derived the 'Legion Smec' in Samuel *Butler's *Hudibras* (II. ii) (where the Presbyterians: 'New modell'd the army and cashier'd ¦ ¦ All that to Legion Smec adher'd').

SMEDLEY, Agnes (1892–1950) American political activist and writer; she spent much of the 1930s in China, becoming closely involved with the Communist cause. Her books include the autobiographical novel *Daughter of Earth* (1929) and the extraordinary works of reportage *China Fights Back* (1938) and *Battle Hymn of China* (1943).

SMEDLEY, Francis Edward (1818–64) Editor and novelist, disabled from childhood. He was for three years editor of *Cruikshank's Magazine* and author of high-spirited novels of sport, romance, and adventure, including the popular *Frank Fairleigh* (1850), illustrated by George *Cruikshank, *Lewis Arundel* (1852), and *Harry Coverdale's Courtship* (1855).

SMILES, Samuel (1812–1904) Scottish writer and reformer, he had a varied career as surgeon, newspaper editor, and secretary for a railway company. He devoted his leisure to the advocacy of political and social reform, on the lines of the *Manchester school, and to the biography of industrial leaders and humble self-taught students. His works include a *Life of George Stephenson* (1875), *Lives of the Engineers* (1861–2), *Josiah Wedgwood* (1894), and the immensely successful *Self-Help* (1859), which was translated into many languages. Advocating industry, thrift, and self-improvement, and attacking 'over-government'; it has been seen as a work symbolizing the ethics and aspirations of mid-19th-century bourgeois individualism. The titles of other works on similar themes (*Character*, 1871; *Thrift*, 1875; *Duty*, 1880) are self-explanatory. His *Autobiography* was published posthumously (1905).

SMILEY, Jane (1951–) American novelist, best known for her novel *A Thousand Acres* (1991). In this grim retelling of the *King Lear* story, set like much of Smiley's work in the American Midwest, Smiley describes the tragic consequences of a farm-owner's decision to retire and pass his farm down to his three daughters. Other novels include the thriller *Duplicate Keys* (1984) and *Moo* (1995), a wryly satirical look at university campus life in Midwestern America. *Ten Days in the Hills* (2007) describes a Hollywood house party. She has also published a collection of short stories, *The Age of Grief* (1988).

SMITH, Adam (1723–90) Scottish moral philosopher and political economist. His public lectures on rhetoric and belles-lettres in Edinburgh from 1748 to 1751 won him the friendship of Hugh *Blair, Adam *Ferguson, and David *Hume. He was appointed professor of logic at Glasgow in 1751, moving to the chair of moral philosophy the following year. In 1759 he published *The *Theory of Moral Sentiments*, and five years later resigned his professorship to accompany the young duke of Buccleuch as tutor to France, Switzerland, and Germany. While in Europe he met *Voltaire and other *Philosophes*, and renewed an existing acquaintance with Benjamin *Franklin. In 1766 he returned to Kirkcaldy to devote himself to the preparation of *An Inquiry into the Nature and Causes of the Wealth of Nations*, published in 1776. The argument of *The Wealth of Nations* that conventional 'mercantilist' policies restricted growth and perpetuated poverty revolutionized economic theory and (in due course) governmental practice. Most of Smith's voluminous and various manuscript writings were destroyed, in accordance with his instructions, on his death. *Essays on Philosophical Subjects* (1795) collected what was left.

SMITH, Alexander (1829–67) Scottish poet, who left school at the age of 11. *Poems* (1853), which included the already well-known 'A Life Drama', was greeted with enthusiasm. *Sonnets on the War* (1855), a patriotic sequence written in collaboration with Sydney *Dobell, was satirized, along with other works of the vehemently intense *Spasmodic school, in William *Aytoun's *Firmilian*. *City Poems* (1857) was followed by *A Summer in Skye* (1865), a vividly individual evocation of the island where Smith spent his annual vacation from 1858.

SMITH, Ali (1962–) Scottish novelist and short story writer. Her first volume of stories, *Free Love* (1995) was followed by her acclaimed first novel, *Like* (1997). She uses language and structure inventively and often experimentally, while always remaining highly readable and often very funny. *Hotel World* (2001) devotes five interlinking sections to five different women (including a ghost). Similarly, *The Accidental* (2004) gives a distinctive voice to each of the four very different members of a family whose holiday is invaded by a disruptive young woman. *Girl Meets Boy* (2007) retells the gender-swapping story of Iphis from *Ovid's *Metamorphoses*. *There but for the* (2011) satirizes contemporary society.

SMITH, Charlotte (1749–1806) Née Turner, poet and novelist, who also wrote many stories and sketches, and enjoyed considerable success. She was married at 15 to Benjamin Smith, the son of a London merchant (a circumstance she likened to being sold to 'slavery'). Abandoned by her spendthrift husband, she turned to writing to support her large family, beginning her literary career with *Elegiac Sonnets* in 1784. A second volume of sonnets followed in 1797. Like William *Wordsworth and S. T. *Coleridge, who admired her work, Smith's poetry is concerned with the notion of the solitary poet meditating on the beauty and sublimity of the landscape. She initially welcomed the French Revolution but renounced it as it progressed into the Terror. Her political position is articulated in *The Emigrants*. The melancholy of much of her poetry sprang in part from intense marital, family, and financial difficulties. *Beachy Head: With Other Poems* was published posthumously in 1807. Her eleven novels include *Emmeline* (1788) and *The Old Manor House* (1793). Her novels mix aspects of the *Gothic, sentimental, and domestic literary modes.

SMITH, Clark Ashton (1893–1961) American *fantasy author, painter, poet, and sculptor. His stories of far futures (Zothique) or distant pasts (Hyperborea) were frequently, like those of his correspondents H. P. *Lovecraft and Robert E. *Howard, published in *Weird Tales* and reprinted in numerous collections.

SMITH, Dodie (Dorothy Gladys) (1896–1990) Playwright and novelist. Her output comprises ten plays, among them *Dear Octopus* (1938), and six adult novels, including the romantic minor classic *I Capture the Castle* (1949; filmed 2003). Her children's book *One Hundred and One Dalmatians* (1956) was adapted by Disney in 1961 and 1996, with a sequel in 2000.

SMITH, George (1824–1901) Publisher, he joined in 1838 the firm of Smith & Elder, publishers and East India agents, which his father had founded in partnership with Alexander Elder in 1816. On his father's death in 1846 he became head of the firm. The chief authors whose works he published in his early career were John *Ruskin, his friend Charlotte *Brontë, whose *Jane Eyre* he issued in 1847, and W. M. *Thackeray, whose *The *History of Henry Esmond* he brought out in 1852.

In 1853 he took a business partner, H. S. King, and after weathering the storm of the Indian Mutiny, founded in 1859 the *Cornhill Magazine*, with Thackeray as editor and numerous leading authors and artists as contributors. In 1865 Smith (with Frederick Greenwood) founded the *Pall Mall Gazette*. In 1868 he dissolved partnership with King; his chief authors now included Robert *Browning, Matthew *Arnold, Leslie *Stephen, and Anne Thackeray *Ritchie, all of whom were personal friends. He was founder (1882) and proprietor of the *Dictionary of National Biography*.

SMITH, Horatio (Horace) (1779–1849) Brother of James Smith. He became famous overnight as the author, with his brother, of

Rejected Addresses in 1812, and of *Horace in London* (1813), imitations of odes of *Horace, chiefly written by his brother. In 1826 his *Brambletye House*, the story of a young Cavalier and a pale shadow of *Scott's *Woodstock* (published in the same year), went through many editions. *The Tor Hill* (1826) and many further novels followed, as well as plays, poems, and work for the *New Monthly Magazine*.

SMITH, Iain Crichton (Iain Mac a'Ghobhainn) (1928–98) Scottish poet, novelist, and short story writer, brought up in Lewis. Smith was a prolific writer who used both English and (to a diminishing degree) his native Gaelic. In volumes such as *Thistles and Roses* (1961), *The Law and the Grace* (1965), and *The Leaf and the Marble* (1998), Smith's poetry juxtaposes the spontaneous and creative with the authoritarian and dogmatic, associating the latter categories with the Roman Empire, the abstractions of ideology, and (persistently) the Scottish Free Church in which the poet was brought up. *Consider the Lilies* (1962) is an austere psychological novel of the Clearances, and *Murdo* (1981) a series of surreal, darkly hilarious sketches of Highland life.

SMITH, John (1618–52) *See* CAMBRIDGE PLATONISTS.

SMITH, Ken (1938–2003) Poet. *The Pity* (1967) introduced a nature poet with a strong human focus too. His work then appeared fugitively until *Bloodaxe Books published *Burned Books* (1981) and *The Poet Reclining: Selected Poems 1962–1980* (1982), which showed Smith's kinship with American speech-based poetry rather than the image-driven practice of English contemporaries. *Fox Running* (1980), his most celebrated work, concerns a period of breakdown in London. *Terra* (1986) is Smith's reading of the Thatcher–Reagan years 'from below', while *Wormwood* (1987) draws on experience as writer in residence at HM Prison Wormwood Scrubs. *Shed* appeared in 2002. From 1963 to 1972 he co-edited *Stand*.

SMITH, Stevie (1902–71) Poet. She wrote three novels, *Novel on Yellow Paper* (1936), *Over the Frontier* (1938), and *The Holiday* (1949), but has been more widely recognized for her caustic and enigmatic verse, much of it illustrated by her own drawings. Her first volume, *A Good Time Was Had by All* (1937), was followed by seven others, including *Not Waving but Drowning* (1957). Her *Collected Poems*, edited by James MacGibbon, appeared in 1975. She was an extraordinary reader of her own verse: Seamus *Heaney brilliantly characterizes her performances as 'pitching between querulousness and keening', both cajoling and forbidding. Her slyly subversive narratives and rewritings of legend and myth have been particularly influential, and so too have her treatments of solitude, death, loneliness, and conventionality. What was once seen as levity has been newly appreciated as an oblique, stoical manner of exploring some of the darkest, most disintegrative emotions and experiences. The poems rehearse a sceptical mistrust of marriage, painful feeling connected with relationships between mothers and daughters, and frustrated libidinous desire; and they are frequently drawn to molestation and murder. Her use of experimental forms, and her interest in oral modes such as *ballad, *folksong, *hymn and carol, are sometimes read as undermining certain masculinist assumptions about the literary, and about the authority or primacy of the textual.

SMITH, Sydney (1771–1845) Author, clergyman, and wit. He became a friend of Francis *Jeffrey and Henry *Brougham with whom he founded the *Edinburgh Review in 1802. He was himself the original 'projector' of the Review, the object of which was to provide a voice for liberal and Whig opinion to balance the Tory *Quarterly Review. Smith tried for a time to restrain what he saw as Jeffrey's tendency, as editor of the Review, to 'analyse and destroy'; but his own contributions ceased, as he came to feel that Jeffrey was making it 'perilous' for a cleric to be connected with the Review. In 1807 he published The Letters of Peter *Plymley in defence of Catholic emancipation. He was made a canon of St Paul's, London in 1831. His remarkable wit was chiefly evident in his conversation, but may also be found in his letters, reviews, and essays.

SMITH, Sydney Goodsir (1915–75) Poet, born in Wellington, New Zealand, who moved to Edinburgh in 1928. His first collection, Skail Wind (1941), included 'Epistle to John Guthrie', a wittily defiant apologia for his decision to write in *Scots. His most ambitious work is Under the Eildon Tree (1948), a sequence of 24 elegiac meditations on love, with a cast of characters ranging from *Dido and *Cuchulain to the poet's friend and mentor Hugh *MacDiarmid. The 'novel' Carotid Cornucopius (1947; rev. and extended, 1964) deploys flamboyantly erudite cross-linguistic puns to celebrate pub life and debauchery in Edinburgh. Smith's play The

Wallace (1960) was revived at the 1985 Edinburgh Festival.

SMITH, Zadie (1975–) Novelist, born in London to an English father and a Jamaican mother. Her first novel, White Teeth (2000), tells its story through three ethnically varied families. Though the novel is not autobiographical, Smith notes that when 'you come from a mixed-race family, it makes you think a bit harder about inheritance'. Her second novel, The Autograph Man (2002), is concerned with celebrity; the third, On Beauty (2005), pays homage to E. M. Forster's *Howards End. Set mainly in Boston, it wittily domesticates the fashionable academic posturing that humiliates student enthusiasm with the use of arcane jargon.

SMOLLETT, Tobias (1721–71) Novelist and critic, apprenticed to a surgeon. In 1739 he brought his play, The Regicide, to London, but he could not get it accepted. He joined the navy, became surgeon's mate, and sailed in 1741 for the West Indies. In 1744 he set himself up as a surgeon in Downing Street. Smollett's first publication, in 1746, was a poem, 'The Tears of Scotland', elicited by the duke of Cumberland's treatment of the Scots after 1745. Two verse satires on London life followed: Advice (1746) and Reproof (1747). The Adventures of *Roderick Random, drawing in part on Smollett's own naval experience, was published in 1748. In 1750 he moved to Chelsea. The Adventures of *Peregrine Pickle (1751) draws on his travels to Paris. He may have been the author, in 1752, of the scurrilous pamphlet The Faithful Narrative of Habbakkuk Hilding, attacking Henry *Fielding for plagiarism. Neither The Adventures of *Ferdinand Count Fathom (1753) nor his translation of *Cervantes, The History and Adventures of the Renowned Don Quixote (1755) was popular. His Complete History of England (1757–8) engendered much controversy, but sold well enough for Smollett to feel financially secure at last. Also in 1757 his naval farce The Reprisal was staged successfully at Drury Lane by David *Garrick. In 1760 The Life and Adventures of Sir Launcelot *Greaves began to appear in instalments in the British Magazine, Smollett's new venture, which ran until 1767. In 1762–3 Smollett wrote and edited the Tory journal the Briton, which was successfully opposed by Wilkes's *North Briton. A two-year tour in France and Italy produced Travels through France and Italy (1766), a caustic work which earned him from Laurence *Sterne the nickname of Smelfungus. The Adventures of an Atom (1769) was a rancorous satire on public men and affairs. *The Expedition of *Humphry Clinker* (1771), an *epistolary novel generally agreed to be Smollett's crowning achievement, was his last work.

SMYTH, Dame Ethel Mary (1858–1944) Composer and autobiographer. She became a supporter of the women's suffrage movement in 1910 and her *March of Women* became the anthem of the movement. Virginia *Woolf read her autobiographical writing, and admired her struggles and resistance, her 'great rush at life'. Smyth became the model for Rose Pargiter in Woolf's novel *The Years* (1937) and Miss La Trobe in *Between the Acts* (1941). Smyth's memoirs, which she began to write in her fifties, include *Impressions that Remained* (1919), *Streaks of Life* (1924), and *Female Pipings in Eden* (1934).

Snobs of England, The A very successful series of comic papers by W. M. *Thackeray which originally appeared in *Punch* (1846–7); published in one volume in 1848. A satirical investigation of 'thinking meanly of mean things', the work introduced the word 'snob' in its modern meaning to the English language.

SNORRI Sturluson (1178/9–1241) Icelandic historian and literary antiquary, distinguished author of *Heimskringla*, the Prose *Edda*, and perhaps *Egils saga*, the biography of a Viking poet. Snorri is the most important figure in Old Icelandic literature; our knowledge of Norse myth and understanding of Old Norse poetry is due largely to him.

SNOW, C. P. (Charles Percy) Baron Snow of Leicester (1905–80) Novelist. *Death under Sail* (1932), his first novel, was a detective story, but his major work is the *roman-fleuve Strangers and Brothers*. Published between 1940 and 1970, this traces the life of its narrator, Lewis Eliot, a barrister who, like Snow himself, rises from lower-middle-class provincial origins to enjoy worldly success and influence in academic and public life. *The Masters* (1951), a study of the internal politics of a Cambridge college, is the best known of the sequence but another, *The Corridors of Power* (1964), added a phrase to the language of the day. So too did his Rede Lecture on *The *Two Cultures and the Scientific Revolution* (1959). Snow was married to the novelist Pamela Hansford *Johnson.

Snowman, The (1978) Raymond *Briggs's wordless *picturebook uses *comic-strip techniques to depict the relationship between a boy and a snowman who comes alive in the night but melts the next day. It has been made into an animated film (1982), a musical (1998), and is frequently reformatted.

SNYDER, Gary (1930–) American poet, whose interest in mountaineering fed into his early poetry. Snyder was associated with the *Beats, and the poet Philip Whalen (1923–2002) was a close friend. He became a serious student of Zen Buddhism, living in Japan from 1956 to 1968. His environmental concerns are reflected in the sequence *Mountains and Rivers without End* (1996) and his essays began appearing with *Earth House Hold* (1969), continuing with *Back on the Fire* (2007).

soap opera Named after the detergent manufacturers who first sponsored popular serial drama on American radio in the 1930s. It began with *Clara, Lu and Em*, about the lives of three women in the small-town Midwest, initially on WGN Chicago then networked. The first British *radio soap (as such series are conventionally known) was *Mrs Dale's Diary*, which ran from 1948 to 1969, but *The Archers* has run continuously since 1951, and remains a mainstay of BBC Radio 4. The play *The Killing of Sister George* by Frank Marcus (1928–96), staged in 1964, explored the gulf between a soap's benign fictional world and the emotional turmoil among its cast. It was filmed by Robert Aldrich (1918–83) in 1968. The film *The Truman Show* (1998) portrayed its hero's life as an elaborate fake, broadcast as a soap. British *television's major soaps, ITV's *Coronation Street* (1960–) and BBC's *EastEnders* (1985–), regularly promote behind the scenes stories about their stars and guest appearances.

Socialist Realism A style of realistic art adopted as the official artistic and literary doctrine of the Soviet Union in 1934 at the First Congress of Soviet Writers, and subsequently adopted by its satellite Communist Parties. Party official Andrei Zhdanov's statements about the nature of Socialist Realism as a 'method' at the 1934 Congress emphasized the truthful depiction of everyday reality 'in its revolutionary development', and the writer's task of educating readers 'in the spirit of socialism'. The conventions governing matters of style and content were provided by a retrospectively constructed canon of model texts, including an early novel by Maxim Gorky, *The Mother* (1906–7). *Modernist works such as those of James *Joyce or Franz *Kafka were condemned as symptoms of decadent bourgeois pessimism. Soviet writers were required instead to affirm the struggle for socialism by portraying positive heroic actions in texts that were accessible to a mass readership. These principles were condemned by major *Marxist critics and writers like Bertolt *Brecht, Georg Lukács (1885–1971), or Leon Trotsky (1879–1940). Socialist Realism entailed a significant shift in the relationship between the state and writers; now cast as 'engineers of the soul' who were expected to educate their readers through works which addressed themes considered by the state to be of contemporary political importance. Under Stalin's tyranny, the doctrine was employed as a pretext for the persecution and silencing of nonconformist writers (*see* AKHMATOVA, ANNA; MANDELSHTAM, OSIP; PASTERNAK, BORIS), as well as a means of controlling published writers through censorship and critical attacks in the press. Both plot and characters in Socialist Realist texts are formulaic. Canonical titles include Nikolai Ostrovsky's *How the Steel was Tempered* (1934) and Mikhail *Sholokhov's *Virgin Soil Upturned* (1932). The most accessible legacy of Socialist Realism is in painting and statuary of the Soviet period, typified by the omnipresent image of the muscular and smiling tractor-driver.

social problem novel A phrase used (alongside terms such as 'the industrial novel', or the *'condition of England' novel) to describe mid-19th-century fiction which examines abuses and hardships affecting the working classes. These included many of the topics which were simultaneously being exposed by non-fictional writers. It sometimes sought to stimulate legislation, or (as in Elizabeth Gaskell's *North and South*, 1854–5) to promote understanding between masters and men on the basis of shared humanity, and shared material interests, as a way forward. Other notable examples include Harriet *Martineau's 'A Manchester Strike', in her *Illustrations of Political Economy* (1835; an early example of the genre); Charles Kingsley's *Yeast* (1848) and *Alton Locke* (1850), Benjamin Disraeli's *Sybil* (1845), Frances *Trollope's *Michael Armstrong, the Factory Boy* (1840) and *Jessie Phillips* (1842–3), and Charlotte Elizabeth Tonna's *Helen Fleetwood* (1841). Whilst Charles *Dickens's fiction is usually regarded as more complex in its focus than many of these novels, much of his writing, especially *Oliver Twist* (1838), The *Chimes* (1845), *Bleak House* (1852), and *Hard Times* (1854), deals very directly with poverty, inequality, and their consequences. The term can be extended to include writing about 'fallen women' and prostitution (as in Gaskell's *Ruth*,

1853; Felicia Skene's *Hidden Depths*, 1866). In its search for resolution, whether practical or emotional, the social problem novel differs from later realist fiction by writers like George *Gissing and Arthur *Morrison. *See also* CONDITION OF ENGLAND.

Society for Psychical Research A body founded in 1882 by Frederic *Myers, Henry *Sidgwick, and others 'to examine without prejudice...those faculties of man, real or supposed, which appear to be inexplicable in terms of any recognised hypothesis'. The Society, in a period of intense interest in spiritualism and the supernatural, investigated with high standards of scientific detachment such matters as telepathy, apparitions, etc., and was instrumental in exposing the fraudulent claims of, for example, Madame Blavatsky. Its presidents included Arthur Balfour, William James, and Sir Oliver Lodge (1851–1940); members and associates have included John *Ruskin, Alfred *Tennyson, William *Gladstone, and Alfred Russel *Wallace.

Society of Authors An organization founded in 1884 by Walter *Besant to promote the business interests of authors and fight for their rights, especially in *copyright. Besant's example was followed by George Bernard *Shaw, who fought arduously for playwrights *vis-à-vis* theatre managers, and to liberalize stage censorship; the League of Dramatists was founded in 1931 as an autonomous section of the Society. It conducted a successful 28-year campaign for Public Lending Right, and has helped to set up the Authors' Lending and Copyright Society, in order to secure income in respect of rights (e.g. photocopying) only possible on a collective basis. Its quarterly publication is the *Author*.

Society of Friends, the See FRIENDS, SOCIETY OF.

Socinianism *See* UNITARIANISM.

SOCRATES (469–399 BC) Athenian who dominated classical Greek philosophy in company with *Plato and *Aristotle. He wrote nothing, but his ideas and methods provided the foundations not only for Platonic philosophy but for many of what we call the 'Hellenistic' philosophical 'schools', notably Cynicism and *Stoicism. Plato uses a 'Socrates' as main speaker in most of his dialogues; other, rather different portraits are offered by *Aristophanes and *Xenophon. We may say with some probability that while claiming to know nothing, he was a master of argument, and that he thought argument (philosophy) essential to life—because (he claimed) our desires are, universally, for what is really good, and we go wrong only because of our mistaken *beliefs* about what our good really is. His execution by his fellow citizens (for impiety), despite an exemplary courage and incorruptibility, later evoked comparisons with Christ; admirers included *Erasmus and the third earl of *Shaftesbury.

'Sohrab and Rustum' A poem by Matthew *Arnold, published 1853. The story is taken from *Firdausī's Persian *epic. It recounts the fatal outcome of Sohrab's search for his father Rustum, the leader of the Persian forces. Rustum (who believes his own child to be a girl) accepts the challenge of Sohrab, now leader of the Tartars: the two meet in single combat, at first unaware of one another's identity, which is confirmed only when Sohrab has been mortally wounded.

Solomon, Song of (Song of Songs) *See* BIBLE.

SOLZHENITSYN, Aleksandr Isaievich (1918–2008) Russian prose writer. Arrested in 1945 for criticism of Stalin in a letter, he was sent first to labour camps, then in 1953 into exile in Kazakhstan. He received treatment for cancer in Tashkent 1954–5. 'Rehabilitated' in 1956, he returned to Riazan to work as a teacher. His first published story, *One Day in the Life of Ivan Denisovich* (1962), based on his labour camp experiences, brought immediate recognition. He was expelled from the Soviet Writers' Union in 1969 following the publication abroad of his major novels *Cancer Ward* (1968) and *The First Circle* (1969) which had been confiscated by the KGB in 1965. He was awarded the 1970 *Nobel Prize for Literature. Publication in the West of *August 1914* (1971) and *The Gulag Archipelago* (1974), an epic 'history and geography' of the labour camps, led to his deportation to West Germany in 1971. He lived in Zurich 1974–6, then in America 1976–94, where he continued a series of novels begun with *August 1914*, offering an alternative picture of Soviet history: an English version, *The Red Wheel: A Narrative in Discrete Periods of Time*, appeared in 1989. Meanwhile, with perestroika, his works were published in Russia and he was readmitted to the Writers' Union in 1989. His memoirs were translated by H. T. Willets as *The Oak and the Calf* (1980).

Some Experiences of an Irish R.M.
Published 1899, first and most famous of a series of three collections of stories by Edith *Somerville and Martin Ross. The others are *Further Experiences of an Irish R.M.*, 1908, and *In Mr Knox's Country*, 1915. The stories are narrated by Major Yeates, the resident magistrate, whose misfortune is to attract calamity. With his gallant wife Philippa, he lives at the centre of a vigorous and wily community as the tenant of a dilapidated County Cork demesne. Frequent rain, flowing drink, unruly hounds, and the eccentricities of the populace contribute to innumerable confusions involving collapsing carts, missed meals, sinking boats, shying horses, and outraged visitors.

SOMERVILE, William (1675–1742) Gentleman of Edstone, Warwickshire, whose *The Chace* (1735), a four-book poem in Miltonic *blank verse on hunting, had considerable success. *Hobbinol* (1740) a *mock-heroic account of rural games in Gloucestershire, was dedicated to William *Hogarth. *Field Sports*, a short poem on hawking, appeared in 1742.

SOMERVILLE (Edith) and **ROSS (Martin)** The pen-names of second cousins Edith Œnone Somerville (1858–1949, born in Corfu) and Violet Florence Martin (1862–1915, born in Co. Galway), who first met in 1886. Separately and together they wrote many books, mainly set in Ireland, as well as many articles, letters, diaries, and jottings. Their first collaboration was *An Irish Cousin* (1889). *The Real Charlotte* (1894) was their most sustained novel. In 1897 came *The Silver Fox*, their first book with hunting as a major theme, then *Some Experiences of an Irish R.M.* (1899). The international success of this book led in 1908 to *Further Experiences of an Irish R.M.* and in 1915 to the third of the series, *In Mr Knox's Country*. After Martin Ross's death Edith Somerville wrote another thirteen books, including *The Big House at Inver* (1925), a historical romance, but continued to name Ross as co-author.

'Somnium Scipionis' (Dream of Scipio) The fable with which *Cicero ends his *De Republica*, based on the myth of Er at the end of *Plato's *Republic*. The only extant manuscript of Cicero's treatise breaks off early in the last book, and the 'Somnium' has survived because in the 4th century it was reproduced by Macrobius, who furnished it with a Neoplatonist commentary that was of great importance for medieval thinkers. The fable relates how the younger Scipio saw his grandfather, the elder Scipio, in a dream and was shown the dwelling set aside in the Milky Way for those who follow virtue and especially for those who distinguish themselves in the service of their country. The 'Somnium' may have inspired *Petrarch's choice of Scipio Africanus as the hero of his epic *Africa*. Since the fable expressed to perfection the humanist ideal of combining a quest for personal distinction with tranquillity of mind and patriotic effort, it attracted numerous editors during the Renaissance. *Chaucer gives a poetical summary of it in *The *Parliament of Fowls*.

'Song of the Shirt, The' A poem by Thomas *Hood, originally published anonymously in *Punch* in 1843. One of Hood's best-known serious poems, it takes the form of a powerful protest by an overworked and underpaid seamstress—

> It is not linen you're wearing out
> But human creatures' lives.

The poem was a popular theme for illustration, and was treated by John Leech in *Punch* and by the painters Richard Redgrave (1844) and G. F. Watts (1850).

Songs of Experience *See* SONGS OF INNOCENCE.

Songs of Innocence A collection of poems written and etched by William *Blake, published 1789. Most of the poems are about childhood, some of them written, with apparent simplicity, as if by children (e.g. 'Little lamb, who made thee?' and 'The Chimney Sweeper'); others commenting on the state of infancy ('The Ecchoing Green'); and yet others introducing the prophetic tone and personal imagery of Blake's later work ('The Little Girl Lost', 'The Little Girl Found').

In 1795 Blake issued a further volume, entitled *Songs of Innocence and of Experience: Shewing the Two Contrary States of the Human Soul*, to which he added the 'Songs of Experience', some of them (e.g. 'The Chimney Sweeper' and 'Nurse's Song') bearing identical titles to poems in the first collection, but replying to them in a tone that questions and offsets their simplicities, and manifests with great poetic economy Blake's original vision of the interdependence of good and evil, of energy and restraint, of desire and frustration. They range from straightforward, if highly provocative, attacks on unnatural restraint ('The Garden of Love', 'London') to the extraordinary lyric intensity of 'Infant Sorrow', 'Ah! Sun-Flower', and 'Tyger! Tyger!'

sonnet A short rhyming lyric poem, usually of fourteen lines of iambic *pentameter. The term may be applied to poems of different lengths ranging from ten-and-a-half lines in some sonnets of Gerard Manley *Hopkins to sixteen in those of George *Meredith and Tony *Harrison, and some sonnets by Philip *Sidney and others have been composed in *alexandrines, but the widely accepted standard is fourteen pentameters. The *rhyme schemes of the sonnet have also varied, but fall into two basic patterns. (1) The Italian or Petrarchan sonnet begins with an octave using two rhymes (*abbaabba*), followed by a sestet with two or three further rhymes (either *cdcdcd* or *cdecde*), with a pause or redirection in the thought (called the 'turn' or *volta*) after the octave. English practitioners of this form, notably John *Milton and William *Wordsworth, have sometimes adapted it to allow a third rhyme in the octave (*abbaacca*) and a 'turn' in a later position around the tenth line. (2) The English sonnet comprising four *quatrains and a couplet has two major versions, the Spenserian form in which the quatrains are linked by rhyme, thus preserving the Italian restriction to five rhymes (*ababbcbccdcdee*), and the Shakespearian scheme of seven rhymes in which the quatrains remain unlinked (*ababcdcdefefgg*).

Italian in origin, and brought to prominence in the love poems of *Petrarch, the sonnet was introduced to England by *Wyatt, developed by *Surrey, and thereafter widely used, notably in the sonnet sequences of *Shakespeare (*see* SONNETS OF SHAKESPEARE), Sidney, Samuel *Daniel, Edmund *Spenser, and others. In the early 17th century, the major sonneteers were John *Donne and Milton, who both extended the subject-matter to religious, political, and philosophical themes. The sonnet underwent a significant revival from the late 18th century, in the verse of Charlotte *Smith and S. T. *Coleridge, then in the early 19th in the work of Wordsworth and John *Keats. Important Victorian sonneteers include Meredith, Hopkins, D. G. *Rossetti, and E. B. *Browning. Major early 20th-century practitioners include W. B. *Yeats and W. H. *Auden

(()) SEE WEB LINKS
• Sonnet Central: archive

Sonnets from the Portuguese A sonnet sequence by Elizabeth Barrett *Browning first published 1850; the so-called 'Reading Edition' of 1847 was a forgery by T. J. *Wise. The sequence reimagines the growth and development of her love for Robert *Browning, at first hesitating to involve him in her sorrowful invalid life, then yielding to gradual conviction of his love for her, and finally rapturous in late-born happiness. The title was chosen in part to disguise the personal nature of the poems by suggesting that they were a translation.

sonnets of Shakespeare Printed in 1609 and probably dating from the 1590s. In 1598 Francis *Meres referred to William *Shakespeare's 'sugred Sonnets among his private friends', but these are not necessarily identical with the ones we now have. Most of them trace the course of the writer's affection for a young man of rank and beauty: the first seventeen urge him to marry to reproduce his beauty, numbers 18 to 126 form a sequence of 108 sonnets, the same number as in Sidney's sequence *Astrophel and Stella*. The complete sequence of 154 sonnets was issued by the publisher Thomas Thorpe (1571/2–1625) in 1609, with a dedication 'To the onlie begetter of these insuing sonnets Mr W.H.' Mr W.H. has been identified as (among others) William, Lord Herbert (1580–1630), afterwards third earl of Pembroke, or Henry Wriothesley, earl of Southampton (1573–1624), and further as the young man addressed in the sonnets. Other views are that Mr W.H. was an unknown friend of Thorpe who may have procured the manuscript for him, or that W.H. is a printer's error for W.S., Shakespeare's initials. Other characters alluded to in the sequence include a mistress stolen by a friend (40–2), a rival poet (78–80 and 80–6), and a dark lady loved by the author (127–52). The dark lady has been variously identified as Mary Fitton (bap. 1578, d. 1641) or the poet Emilia *Lanier, and the rival poet as Christopher *Marlowe or George *Chapman. But all such identifications are purely speculative. For the form of these poems *see* SONNET.

Sons and Lovers By D. H. *Lawrence, published 1913, an autobiographical *Bildungsroman* set in the Nottinghamshire coal-mining village of Bestwood. Walter Morel has married Gertrude, 'delicate' but 'resolute', a high-minded woman better educated than himself. She shrinks from his lack of fine feeling; embittered, she turns their marriage into a battle. Walter, baffled and thwarted, is sometimes violent; Gertrude turns her love towards her four children, particularly her two eldest sons, William and Paul. She is determined that her boys will not become miners. William and Paul find clerical work in London and Nottingham respectively; William develops pneumonia and dies. Gertrude, numbed by despair, is roused only when Paul also falls ill. She nurses him back to health, and subsequently their attach-

ment deepens. Paul is friendly with the Leivers family of Willey Farm, and a tenderness grows between him and the daughter Miriam, a soulful, shy girl. Gertrude fears that Miriam will exclude her and tries to break up their relationship, while Paul, himself sickened at heart by Miriam's romantic love and fear of physical warmth, turns away. He becomes involved with Clara Dawes, a married woman and supporter of women's rights, separated from her husband Baxter. Paul is promoted at work, and begins to be noticed as a painter and designer. Clara returns to her husband. Meanwhile, Paul's mother falls ill with cancer. At last, unable to bear her suffering, he and his sister Annie give her an overdose of morphia. Paul resists the urge to follow her 'into the darkness' and, with a great effort, turns towards life. *Sons and Lovers* was perhaps the first English novel with a truly working-class background. The original text was heavily edited by Edward *Garnett.

SONTAG, Susan (1933–2004) American cultural critic, essayist, and novelist. Settling in New York as a teacher and an essayist for *Partisan Review* and other journals, she wrote two experimental novels, *The Benefactor* (1963) and *Death Kit* (1967), and collected her essays in two volumes, *Against Interpretation* (1966) and *Styles of Radical Will* (1969), in which she surveys a range of topics, from the 'camp' sensibility and pornographic writing to avant-garde music and painting. These early essays foreshadow many of the emphases of *postmodernism. While undergoing treatment for cancer in the 1970s, she wrote two provocative essays, *On Photography* (1977) and *Illness as Metaphor* (1978), and collected her short stories as *I, Etcetera* (1978). Later works include *AIDS and its Metaphors* (1989), a historical romance about Horatio Nelson and the Hamiltons, *The Volcano Lover* (1992) and the novel *In America* (1999).

SOPHOCLES (496/5–406 BC) Greek tragedian who wrote *c.*120 plays, of which seven survive, including *Ajax, The Women of Trachis, Electra*, and *Philoctetes*. The group known as the Theban plays, *Oedipus the King, Oedipus at Colonus*, and *Antigone*, have long been influential in English literature, either directly or in versions by *Seneca. Thomas *Watson's 16th-century translation of the *Antigone* into Latin was widely read, and both John Milton's *Samson Agonistes* and John *Dryden and Nathaniel *Lee's *Oedipus* draw on Sophocles. In the 19th century Edward *Bulwer-Lytton adapted *Oedipus the King*; Matthew *Arnold produced his Sophoclean play *Merope* and two Sophoclean fragments,

Antigone and *Dejaneira*; A. C. *Swinburne introduced Sophoclean touches into his *Erechtheus*. In the early 20th century Sigmund *Freud coined the phrase 'Oedipus complex', but it has little to do with the play. W. B. *Yeats produced a version of *Oedipus*, and Ezra *Pound adapted *Women of Trachis*. Recent adaptations include Seamus *Heaney's *Cure at Troy*, Steven *Berkoff's *Greek*, and Derek *Mahon's *Oedipus*. *See* AESCHYLUS; EURIPIDES; POETICS.

(⊕) SEE WEB LINKS

• Archive of Performances of Greek and Roman Drama

Sordello A narrative poem in iambic pentameter couplets by Robert *Browning, published 1840. The poem was received with incomprehension and derision by the critics and the public, and its notorious 'obscurity' caused prolonged damage to Browning's reputation. The *Pre-Raphaelites were *Sordello*'s first defenders, followed later by Ezra *Pound. Its genuine difficulty springs partly from the swiftness and compression of the language, the convoluted time-scheme of the narrative, and the fusion of intense specificity (of historical detail, landscape, etc.) with the abstract ideas which form the core of the argument.

The narrative is set in Italy during the period of the Guelf–Ghibelline wars of the late 12th and 13th centuries, and traces the 'development of a soul', that of the troubadour Sordello, along a path of self-realization where political, aesthetic, and metaphysical ideas reflect each other; all this in the framework of a plot strongly influenced by the elements of fairy-tale, including the lost heir, wicked stepmother, and unattainable princess.

SORLEY, Charles Hamilton (1895–1915) Poet. He served in the trenches in France in the First World War, where he was killed by a sniper. He left only 37 complete poems: his posthumous collection, *Marlborough and Other Poems* (1916), was a popular and critical success in the 1920s, but his verse was then long neglected, despite the efforts of Edmund *Blunden and Robert *Graves. Poems such as 'The Song of the Ungirt Runners', 'Barbury Camp', and the last, bitter, 'When you see millions of the mouthless dead' have become well known.

SORRENTINO, Gilbert (1929–2006) American writer, whose novels include the *postmodern meta-narrative *Mulligan Stew* (1979).

Soul's Tragedy, A A play by Robert *Browning, published 1846, together with

Luria, as no. VIII of *Bells and Pomegranates*. Its subtitle—'Act First, being what was called the Poetry of Chiappino's life: and Act Second, its Prose'—indicates both the play's genre, tragicomedy, and also its unusual form: the division (as opposed to mixture) of verse and prose represents Browning's idiosyncratic adaptation of Elizabethan and Jacobean models (*see also* PIPPA PASSES).

SOUTAR, William (1898–1943) Scottish poet. He served in the navy during the First World War, and contracted the ankylosing spondylitis which left him paralysed for the fourteen years before his death. Soutar wrote lyrics in *Scots and (less successfully) English. The Scots work is remarkable for its idiomatic purity and its dialogue with the *ballad and other elements of folk tradition. It includes epigrams, riddles, pieces for children ('bairn-rhymes'), and the extravagant miniatures the poet called 'whigmaleeries'. See Soutar, *The Diary of a Dying Man* (1991).

SOUTHERN, Terry (1924–95) American novelist and screenwriter, known for the grotesque dimension to his satires. His first novel (co-written with Mason Hoffenberg) was *Candy* (1957) followed in 1959 by *The Magic Christian*, a satire on national greed. His most famous screenplays were *Dr Strangelove* (1962, also published as a novel) and *The Loved One* (1965), which have become classics of *black humour.

SOUTHERNE (Southern), Thomas (1659–1746) Irish dramatist; he came to London 1678 and entered the Middle Temple. He wrote prologues and epilogues for several of his friend John *Dryden's plays, whose *Cleomenes* he revised and completed. His first tragedy, *The Persian Prince, or The Loyal Brother* (1682), was, like Thomas *Otway's *Venice Preserv'd*, its immediate contemporary, an attack on Shaftesbury and the Whigs. He is chiefly remembered for his two highly successful tragedies, *The *Fatal Marriage* (1694) and *Oroonoko* (1695), both based on novels by Aphra *Behn. He is regarded as a successor to Otway in the art of pathos, and as a link between *Restoration tragedy and the sentimental tragedies of the 18th century.

SOUTHEY, Robert (1774–1843) Poet. He went to Oxford with 'a heart full of poetry and feeling, a head full of Rousseau and Werther, and my religious principles shaken by Gibbon'. He became friendly with S. T. *Coleridge and together they planned their Pantisocratic society (*see* PANTISOCRACY). At Oxford he wrote a play, *Wat Tyler*, and another with Coleridge, *The *Fall of Robespierre*. From this time on his literary output was prodigious. In 1795 he married Edith Fricker (Coleridge married her sister Sara), and wrote *Joan of Arc* (1796). Between 1796 and 1798 he wrote many ballads, including 'The *Inchcape Rock' and 'The Battle of Blenheim' He settled in the Lake District, where he remained for the rest of his life as one of the *'Lake Poets'. A narrative *oriental verse romance, *Thalaba*, appeared in 1801, but sold poorly. In 1803 he published a translation of *Amadis of Gaul*; in 1805, *Madoc*; and in 1807 *Palmerin of England* and *Letters from England by Don Manuel Alvarez Espriella*, purporting to be from a young Spaniard and giving a lively account of life and manners in England. In 1809 began his long association with the *Quarterly Review*, which provided almost his only regular income for most of the rest of his life. He was appointed *poet laureate in 1813. In 1817 he produced an edition of *Malory and had to endure the publication, by his enemies, of his youthful and revolutionary *Wat Tyler*. In 1821, to commemorate the death of George III, he wrote *A *Vision of Judgement*, in the preface to which he vigorously attacked Lord *Byron as the leader of the *'satanic School of poetry'. Byron's parody in riposte, *The *Vision of Judgment*, appeared in 1822, and Southey is frequently mocked in *Don Juan*. His *Sir Thomas More*, in which he converses with the ghost of More, came out in 1829. Between 1832 and 1837 he worked on a life and an edition of William *Cowper. In 1835 he was granted a pension of £300 by Peel. His wife died in 1837, and in 1839 he married Caroline *Bowles. *The *Doctor* was begun in 1834, 7 vols (1834–47). Southey's last years were marked by an increasing mental decline.

Although an honest, generous man (who was particularly kind to Coleridge's abandoned family), he alienated many of his contemporaries, in particular William *Hazlitt and Byron, who felt that in accepting pensions and the laureateship, and in denying his youthful Jacobinism, he was betraying principles. In *Melincourt* Thomas Love Peacock caricatures him as Mr Feathernest.

SOUTHWELL, St Robert (1561–95) Poet and martyr; he became a Roman Catholic priest, coming to England in 1586. In 1589 he became domestic chaplain to the countess of Arundel, was captured in 1592, imprisoned, repeatedly tortured, and executed. In his poems, mainly written in prison, he sought to make spiritual love, instead of 'unworthy affections', the subject. His chief work was *St Peter's Complaint*, published 1595, a long narrative of the closing events of Christ's life in the mouth of the repentant Peter. He also wrote many fine shorter devotional poems (some of them collected under the title *Moeoniae*, 1595), Beatified in 1929, he was canonized in 1970.

SOYINKA, Wole (1934–) Nigerian novelist, poet, and playwright. He was play reader at the *Royal Court Theatre, London, where his *The Swamp Dwellers* (1958), *The Lion and the Jewel*, and *The Invention* (both 1959) were produced. These already demonstrated his development from simple village comedies to a more complex and individual drama incorporating mime and dance. After his return to Nigeria in 1960, he undertook further daring innovations, for instance in *A Dance of the Forests* (1960), a half-satirical, half-fantastic celebration of Nigerian independence. Soyinka's first novel, *The Interpreters* (1965), captures the idealism of young Nigerians regarding the development of a new Africa, possibly anticipating a new Biafra. In prison for pro-Biafran activity during 1967–9, he produced increasingly bleak verse and prose, *Madmen and Specialists* (1970), his second novel, *Season of Anomy* (1973), and *The Man Died* (1972), a prison memoir. His translation of the *Bacchae* of *Euripides was commissioned by and performed at the *National Theatre in 1973. *Death and the King's Horseman* (1975) embodied his post-Biafran cultural philosophy, enunciated in *Myth, Literature and the African World* (1976), of the need for the aesthetics of Africa and Europe to cross-fertilize each other. Later works include the drama *A Play of Giants* (1984), savagely portraying a group of African ex-dictators taking refuge in New York, and *The Open Sore of a Continent* (1996), denouncing the military regime in Nigeria, and the brutal execution in November 1995 of Nigerian writer and political activist Ken Saro-Wiwa. Soyinka himself had his Nigerian passport confiscated in 1994. His account of his childhood, *Aké* (1981), is witty and celebratory; he continues the story in *Isara* (1989) and published a long memoir in 2006, *You Must Set Forth at Dawn*.

Spanish Bawd, The See CELESTINA.

Spanish Curate, The A comedy by John *Fletcher, probably in collaboration with Philip *Massinger, written and performed 1622, and based on *Gerardo, the Unfortunate Spaniard* (1622), translated from the Spanish of Céspedes by Leonard Digges (1588-1635). It was very popular after the *Restoration.

Spanish Friar, The A tragicomedy by John *Dryden, produced and published 1681. The serious plot is characteristically about a usurpation. Torrismond, though he does not know it, is legitimate heir to the throne, and secretly marries the reigning but unlawful queen, who has allowed Torrismond's father, the true king, to be murdered in prison. The sub-plot is dominated by Father Dominic, a monstrous corrupt friar, who uses the jargon of Dissenters and who pimps for the dissolute and politically liberal Lorenzo. The play is like *Mr Limberham* in challenging comic as well as tragic convention, and in its deeply sceptical treatment of religious and political orthodoxies.

Spanish Gipsy, The (1) A romantic comedy by Thomas *Middleton and others (1623); (2) A dramatic poem by George *Eliot (1868).

Spanish Tragedy, The A tragedy, mostly in blank verse, by Thomas *Kyd, written c.1587, printed eleven times between 1592 and 1633. The political background of the play is loosely related to the victory of Spain over Portugal in 1580. Lorenzo and Bel-imperia are the children of Don Cyprian, duke of Castile (brother of the king of Spain); Hieronimo is marshal of Spain and Horatio his son. Balthazar, son of the viceroy of Portugal, has been captured in the war. He courts Bel-imperia, and Lorenzo and the king of Spain favour his suit for political reasons. Lorenzo and Balthazar discover that Bel-imperia loves Horatio; they surprise the couple by night in Hieronimo's garden and hang Horatio on a tree. Hieronimo discovers his son's body and runs mad with grief. He succeeds nevertheless in identifying the murderers, and revenges himself by means of a play, *Solyman and Perseda*, in which Lorenzo and Balthazar are killed, and Bel-imperia stabs herself. Hieronimo bites out his tongue before killing himself.

The play was the prototype of the English *revenge tragedy genre. It was seen by Samuel *Pepys as late as 1668. There have been successful modern revivals.

The play was one of *Shakespeare's minor sources for *Hamlet* and the alternative title given to it in 1615, *Hieronimo Is Mad Again*, provided T. S. *Eliot with the penultimate line of The *Waste Land.

SPARK, Dame Muriel (1918-2006) Née Camberg, novelist and poet; her Edinburgh school, James Gillespie's High School for Girls, was immortalized in her novel about the charismatic teacher of a group of schoolgirls in the 1930s, *The Prime of Miss Jean Brodie* (1961); the novel later became a play (1968), a film (1969), and a television series (1978). After six years in Rhodesia (recalled in stories in *The Go-Away Bird*, 1958, and *Voices At Play*, 1961), she returned to Britain in 1944. Editing *Poetry Review* from 1947 to 1949, she wrote studies of Mary *Shelley, Emily *Brontë, and John *Masefield, and published a book of poems, *The Fanfarlo and Other Verse*, in 1952. Her first novel, *The Comforters* (1957), begun after she converted to Roman Catholicism, was followed by a rapid succession of highly original and highly accomplished novels hallmarked by economy of style and structure, authorial omniscience, telling disruptions of normal chronology, ironic wit, and concentration on small worlds which are simultaneously satirized and given allegorical significance. Among them her sardonic survey of old age, *Memento Mori* (1959), and *The Girls of Slender Means* (1963), set in a Kensington hostel between VE and VJ days, particularly stand out. Her *Collected Poems* and *Collected Plays* (written for both stage and radio) were published in 1967; a collected edition of her stories, in 1986. A volume of autobiography, *Curriculum Vitae* (1992), gives an account of her early years, which two novels of reminiscence, *Loitering with Intent* (1981) and *A Far Cry from Kensington* (1988), imaginatively complement. A further volume of poetry, *Going up to Sotheby's*, was published in 1982. The last of her 22 novels, *The Finishing School*, appeared in 2004.

Spasmodic school A term applied by W. E. *Aytoun to a loosely affiliated group of poets which included P. J. *Bailey, J. W. *Marston, Sydney *Dobell, and Alexander *Smith. Their works briefly enjoyed great popularity, particularly in the case of Smith's *A Life-Drama* (1853) and Dobell's *Balder* (1854). Spasmodic poems tended to describe intense interior psychological drama, were violent and verbose, and were characterized by obscurity, *pathetic fallacy, and extravagant imagery. Their language and imagery is often highly derivative and much of it was drawn wholesale from poets they admired, including William *Shakespeare, John *Keats, and Alfred *Tennyson. Spasmodics generally focused on heroes (owing much to Lord *Byron and *Goethe) who were lonely, aspiring, disillusioned, and frequently poets themselves. Although spasmodism was rapidly discredited and became a laughing-stock after

S

the publication of Aytoun's parody of the genre, *Firmilian* (1854), it had a significant influence on Victorian poetry.

SPCK (Society for Promoting Christian Knowledge) Founded in 1698 by Dr Thomas Bray (1658–1730), it was a *Church of England society with an ambitious programme at home and in the American colonies for improving the education of the clergy through the establishment of libraries, teaching poor children to read and write and to understand the principles of the Christian religion, and distributing bibles and devotional and didactic works to poor families, servants, prisoners, soldiers, and sailors. In 1701 its overseas activities and missionary work were brought under a separate society, the Society for the Propagation of the Gospel in Foreign Parts (SPG). From the point of view of *Methodists and evangelicals it was objectionable because the devotional works it distributed—such as *The *Whole Duty of Man* and Robert *Nelson's *Companion for the Festivals and Fasts of the Church of England*—ignored what they regarded as the essential doctrines of the gospel.

Specimens of English Dramatic Poets Who Lived about the Time of Shakespeare By Charles *Lamb, published 1808; an anthology, with brief but cogent and illuminating critical comments, of extracts of scenes and speeches from Elizabethan and Jacobean dramatists, many of them little known or regarded in Lamb's day. His selections include extracts from Francis *Beaumont and John *Fletcher, Ben *Jonson, Christopher *Marlowe, John *Webster, and some dozen others.

Spectator (1) A periodical conducted by Richard *Steele and Joseph *Addison, from 1 March 1711 to 6 December 1712, succeeding the *Tatler*. It was revived by Addison in 1714, when 80 further numbers (556–635) were issued. It appeared daily, except Sundays, and was immensely popular with a middle-class and professional readership; it was strongly associated with London and its new meeting places, especially coffee houses. Addison and Steele were the principal contributors, in about equal proportions; other contributors included Alexander *Pope, Thomas *Tickell, Eustace Budgell (1686–1737), Ambrose *Philips, Laurence Eusden, and Lady Mary Wortley *Montagu. It centres on a small club of characters, including Sir Roger de Coverley, who represents the Tory-inclined country gentry, the Whig merchant Sir Andrew Freeport, Captain Sentry of the army, and Will Honeycomb, a man about town. Mr Spectator himself, who writes the papers, is a man of travel and learning, who frequents London as an observer. The most important literary papers are Addison's nineteen papers on *Paradise Lost* and his eleven essays on the 'pleasures of the imagination'. The tone is lightly satirical and the papers seek 'to enliven morality with wit, and to temper wit with morality'. The papers were collected and regularly reprinted in book form. (2) A weekly periodical started in 1828 by Robert Stephen Rintoul, with funds provided by Joseph Hume and others, as an organ of 'educated radicalism'. It supported Lord John Russell's Reform Bill of 1831 with a demand for 'the Bill, the whole Bill, and nothing but the Bill'. Lytton *Strachey was a frequent contributor. Other notable contributors include Peter *Fleming, Graham *Greene, Evelyn *Waugh, Peter *Quennell, Kingsley *Amis, Clive James (1939–), Bernard Levin (1928–2004), Peregrine Worsthorne (1923–), Katharine Whitehorn (1928–), and Auberon *Waugh.

speculative fiction A term used by Robert A. *Heinlein in 1947 to describe what *science fiction *did*, extrapolating from known facts; now used to suggest a broader range of exploratory genres (including *fantasy) or to establish a class distinction between so-called 'literary' fiction and science fiction.

SPEDDING, James (1808–81) Literary editor and biographer, a friend of Alfred *Tennyson, Edward *FitzGerald, and Thomas *Carlyle (who said of him that 'There is a grim strength in Spedding, quietly, very quietly, invincible'). He is now chiefly remembered for his pioneering edition of *The Works of Francis Bacon* (7 vols, 1857–9).

SPEGHT, Rachel (b. 1597, *fl.*1621) Daughter of a London Puritan minister, James Speght; she published at the age of 19 a spirited rebuttal of the misogynist *Arraignment of Lewd, Idle, Froward and Inconstant Women* by Joseph Swetnam (d. 1621). Her *A Mouzell for Melastomus* (1617: *A Muzzle for a Black Mouth*) objected to the 'excrement of your raving cogitations' as a slander on woman, who, as Eve's daughter, was fashioned from Adam's side, not his head or foot, 'near his heart, to be his equal'. In 1621 she published *Mortalities Memorandum, with a Dreame Prefixed*, the latter being an allegorical narrative poem urging the education of women, under guidance of tutelary female personifications (Thought, Experience, Industry, Desire, Truth).

SPEKE, John Hanning (1827-64) Explorer in Africa; he joined Sir Richard *Burton on expeditions to Somalia and then Lake Tanganyika in 1858. While Burton was ill, Speke diverted to Lake Victoria, claiming it was the Nile source. Although Speke solved the greatest of all geographical problems, his *Journal of the Discovery of the Source of the Nile* (1863), needed to be 'improved' by a publisher's reader.

SPENCE, Joseph (1699-1768) Clergyman, anecdotist, scholar. A man of much generosity, he befriended Robert *Dodsley in his early days, later helping him to edit his celebrated *Collection of Poems*, and also Stephen *Duck, whose life he wrote (1731, reprinted with Duck's poems, 1736). He also wrote a life of the blind poet Thomas Blacklock (1754). He was a close friend of Alexander *Pope, and from 1726 collected anecdotes and recorded conversations with Pope and other literary figures. These, although not published until 1820, were well known and widely quoted during the 18th century, and were made available to and used by William *Warburton and Samuel *Johnson. They are usually referred to under the title *Spence's Anecdotes*.

SPENCER, Herbert (1820-1903) Philosopher and social theorist. He published *Social Statics* (1850) and *Principles of Psychology* (1855). In 1860, after reading Charles *Darwin, he announced a systematic series of treatises, to the elaboration of which he devoted the remainder of his life: *First Principles* (1862), *Principles of Biology* (1864-7), *Principles of Sociology* (1876-96), and *Principles of Ethics* (1879-93). Among his other works were *Essays on Education* (1861), *The Classification of the Sciences* (1864), *The Study of Sociology* (1873), *Man versus the State* (1884), and *Factors of Organic Evolution* (1887).

Spencer was the founder of evolutionary philosophy, proposing the unification of all knowledge on the basis of the principle of evolution. He is the origin of the phrase 'survival of the fittest'. His philosophical writing was widely popular and achieved mass sales, though its reputation declined rapidly in the 1880s and 1890s.

Spencer's attempts to define an ethical system, based on the right to liberty of every individual, so long as others are not harmed, were less successful.

In a literary context Spencer is remembered for his friendship with George *Eliot, whom he met in 1851. She appears to have been more strongly attached to him, but transferred her affections to G. H. Lewes (*c.*1852-3).

SPENDER, Sir Stephen (1909-95) Poet and critic; he became friendly with W. H. *Auden and Isaiah Berlin (1909-97) at Oxford. A period of living in Germany sharpened his political consciousness. *Twenty Poems* (1930) was followed by *Poems* (1933), which was received with great acclaim. It contained both personal and political pieces, including 'The Landscape near an Aerodrome', and 'The Pylons', which gave the nickname of the *Pylon poets to himself and his friends. *The Destructive Element* (1935), a critical work mainly on Henry *James, ends with a section called 'In Defence of a Political Subject', in which he discusses the work of Auden and Edward *Upward, and argues the importance of treating 'politico-moral' subjects in literature. The poems in *The Still Centre* (1939) reflect his involvement with the Republicans during the Spanish Civil War. During the Second World War he was a member of the Auxiliary Fire Service. He retracts a number of his earlier positions in *The Creative Element* (1953), while he gives an account of his relationship with the Communist Party in his autobiography *World within World* (1951). The essentially personal and private nature of much of his own poetry is evident in his elegies for his sister-in-law, in *Poems of Dedication* (1947), and many of the poems in such later volumes as *Collected Poems 1928-1953* (1955). His other works include *Trial of a Judge* (1938), *The Thirties and after* (1978, a volume of memoirs), *Collected Poems 1982-85* (1985), and his *Journals 1939-83* (1985). *The Temple* (1989) is a novel inspired by an abandoned manuscript written in 1929, and rewritten as 'a complex of memory, fiction and hindsight'.

SPENSER, Edmund (?1552-1599) Poet; he claimed to be related to the Spencers of Althorp.

In 1569, while still at Cambridge, he contributed a number of 'Visions' and sonnets, translations from *Petrarch and *Du Bellay, to Jan van der Noodt's *Theatre for Voluptuous Worldlings*. His 'Hymne in Honour of Love' and that of 'Beautie' (first published 1596) reflect his study of *Neoplatonism. Through his college friend and tutor Gabriel *Harvey, he obtained a place in Robert Dudley, earl of Leicester's household. There he became acquainted with Philip *Sidney, to whom he dedicated his *Shepheardes Calender* (1579). He also began to write The *Faerie Queene. During the later 1580s he became one of the 'undertakers' for the settlement of Munster, having acquired Kilcolman Castle in

Co. Cork. Here he settled and occupied himself with literary work, writing his elegy *'Astrophel', on Sidney, and preparing The Faerie Queene for the press. The first three books of it were entrusted to the publisher during his visit to London with Walter *Ralegh in 1589. He returned reluctantly to Kilcolman, which he liked to regard as a place of exile, in 1591, recording his visit to London and return to Ireland in *Colin Clouts Come Home Againe (printed 1595). The success of The Faerie Queene led the publisher, Ponsonby, to issue his minor verse and juvenilia, in part rewritten, as Complaints, Containing Sundrie Small Poemes of the Worlds Vanitie (1591). This volume included 'The *Ruines of Time', which was a further elegy on Sidney, dedicated to Sidney's sister, the countess of *Pembroke, *'Mother Hubberds Tale', *'Muiopotmos', 'The *Teares of the Muses', and *'Virgils Gnat'.

Spenser married Elizabeth Boyle, whom he had wooed in his Amoretti, in 1594 and celebrated the marriage in his superb *Epithalamion: the works were printed together in 1595. He was probably in London for the publication of Books IV–VI of The Faerie Queene and his Fowre Hymnes in 1596, staying at the house of his friend the earl of Essex, where he may have written his *Prothalamion. He returned to Ireland, depressed both in mind and health, in 1596 or 1597. His castle of Kilcolman was burnt in October 1598, in a sudden insurrection of native rebels; Spenser was compelled to flee to Cork with his wife and three children. It is not known what works, if any, were lost at Kilcolman. He died in London and he was buried near his favourite Geoffrey *Chaucer in Westminster Abbey. His monument, set up some twenty years later by Lady Anne *Clifford, describes him as 'the prince of poets in his tyme': the poetry of both John *Milton and John *Keats had its origins in the reading of Spenser.

Spenserian stanza The stanza invented by Edmund *Spenser, in which he wrote The *Faerie Queene. It consists of eight five-foot iambic lines, followed by an iambic line of six feet (an alexandrine); it rhymes ababbcbcc (see METRE).

SPINOZA, Benedict de (Baruch de Spinoza) (1632–77) Amsterdam-born Jewish philosopher, expelled from the Jewish community for religious unorthodoxy. Spinoza's philosophy is pantheistic. He rejects René *Descartes's dualism of spirit and matter, acknowledging only 'one infinite substance, of which finite existences are modes or limitations'. God is synonymous with this infinite substance. Denial

of free will and of personal immortality are consequences of Spinoza's system. In his Ethics (finished about 1665, pub. 1677) he takes a relativist position (nothing is intrinsically good or bad). Reality is perfect: failure to see this comes from deficient perception. Emotion comes from inadequate understanding. Blessedness consists in being conscious of ourselves and Nature. The Ethics and the Tractatus Theologico-politicus (published 1670) have influenced modern philosophers including Gilles *Deleuze, and Ludwig *Wittgenstein.

Spirit of the Age, The Essays by William *Hazlitt, published 1825, presented as a portrait gallery of the eminent writers of his time: Jeremy *Bentham, William *Godwin, S. T. *Coleridge, William *Wordsworth, Walter *Scott, Lord *Byron, Robert *Southey, Thomas *Malthus, Charles *Lamb, and several others. The essays combine character sketches with lively critical assessments of the subjects' works and summaries of their reputations, placed in the context of the political and intellectual ferment of their times. They are strongly animated by Hazlitt's political loyalties, especially in the sustained assault upon the Tory critic William *Gifford for his 'ridiculous pedantry and vanity'.

spondee See METRE.

sprung (or 'abrupt') rhythm A term invented by G. M. *Hopkins to describe his own idiosyncratic poetic metre, as opposed to normal 'running' rhythm, the regular alternation of stressed and unstressed syllables. It was based partly on Greek and Latin quantitative metre and influenced by the rhythms of Welsh poetry and Old and Middle English *alliterative verse. Hopkins maintained that sprung rhythm existed, unrecognized, in Old English poetry and in *Shakespeare, *Dryden, and *Milton (notably in *Samson Agonistes). It is distinguished by a metrical foot consisting of a varying number of syllables. The extra, 'slack' syllables added to the established patterns are called 'outrides' or 'hangers'. Hopkins demonstrated the natural occurrence of this rhythm in English by pointing out that many nursery rhymes employed it, for instance 'Díng, Dóng, Béll, | Pússy's in the wéll'. Conventional metres may be varied by the use of 'counterpoint', by which Hopkins meant the reversal of two successive feet in an otherwise regular line of poetry; but sprung rhythm itself cannot be counterpointed because it is not regular enough for the pattern to be recognized under the variations. Hopkins, an amateur composer, often described his theory in terms of musical notation, speaking of rests, crotchets, and quavers. He felt strongly that his poetry should be read aloud, but seems to have felt that the words themselves were not enough to suggest the intended rhythms, and frequently added various diacritical markings to indicate where a sound was to be drawn out, and where syllables were to be spoken quickly. Some critics have suggested that sprung rhythm is not a poetic metre at all, properly speaking, merely Hopkins's attempt to force his own personal rhythm into an existing pattern, or recognizable variation of one, and that his sprung rhythm is in fact closer to some kinds of free verse or polyphonic prose. Variants of it are widely used in modern and contemporary verse.

SPURLING, Hilary Susan (1940–) CBE, journalist and biographer. Her two-volume biography of Ivy *Compton-Burnett (1974, 1984) has been followed by a biography of Paul *Scott (1990), a two-volume biography of the French painter Henri Matisse (1998, 2005), *The Girl from the Fiction Department* (2002), a biography of George *Orwell's wife Sonia (1918–80), and *Burying the Bones* (2010), a life of Pearl *Buck. She is the official biographer of Anthony *Powell.

spy fiction The British spy novel emerged during the international tensions of the years preceding the First World War. In the following century, two world wars, revolutions, the Cold War, and the war on terror continued to provide writers with material and subject matter for spy fiction.

Erskine *Childers's *The Riddle of the Sands* (1903), a suspenseful tale of two amateur British agents foiling a German invasion plot, is often described as the first spy novel. But the first spy writer to spring to public fame was William Le Queux (1864–1927), whose highly successful invasion novel *The Great War in England in 1897* (1894), featuring an enemy spy, heralded a cascade of best-sellers over the next three decades. Le Queux's great Edwardian rival was E. Phillips Oppenheim (1866–1946), whose novels, including *The Kingdom of the Blind* (1916) and *The Great Impersonation* (1920), featured glamorous seductresses and society high life. The year 1920 saw the creation by *Sapper (Herman Cyril McNeile) of the unabashed xenophobe and anti-Semite Bulldog Drummond, a muscular agent who robustly thwarted the plots of the communist arch-villain Carl Peterson in such titles as *The Black Gang* (1922), *The Final Count* (1926), and *The Return of Bulldog Drummond* (1932).

From this early period the writer who has best endured is John *Buchan, whose secret agent hero Richard Hannay first appeared in *The Thirty-Nine Steps* (1915), which defines much other spy fiction; there have been many adaptations. There followed such classics as *Greenmantle* (1916), *Mr Standfast* (1919), and *The Three Hostages* (1924).

The First World War, the Great Depression, and the rise of *Fascism created a sombre interwar climate that saw the emergence of a new generation of spy writers who broke sharply with the patriotic orthodoxies of their predecessors. Some, like Somerset *Maugham, had worked for British wartime intelligence and painted a far less glamorized picture of the secret agent's life. Maugham's *Ashenden* (1928) was an influential collection of short stories based closely on his personal experience.

In the 1930s, Eric *Ambler crafted plots of considerable technical skill and authenticity, combined with a leftist outlook, that featured innocent protagonists caught up in the machinations of 'merchants of death' and other capitalist villains. His best-known and most successful novel was *The Mask of Dimitrios* (1939). Ambler's ideological outlook was shared by Graham *Greene, whose *Stamboul Train* (1932), *The Confidential Agent* (1939), and *The Ministry of Fear* (1943) foreshadowed his post-Second World War novels, when he worked as a British intelligence officer for the Secret Intelligence Service (MI6): *The Quiet American* (1955), *Our Man in Havana* (1958), and *The Human Factor* (1978).

The dominating figure of the immediate postwar years was Ian *Fleming, whose *Casino Royale* (1953; filmed 2006) introduced the iconic figure of James *Bond. By 1964, the year of Fleming's death, his eleven Bond spy novels, including *From Russia with Love* (1957) and *Goldfinger* (1959), had sold over 40 million copies and his hero was beginning to appear in blockbuster movies.

The 1961 building of the Berlin Wall brought a serious chill to the Cold War climate, and in *The Spy Who Came in from the Cold* (1963) John *le Carré marked out the territory that was to dominate spy fiction until the end of the Cold War. Making an explicit and conscious break with Bond, he created the anti-heroic figure of George Smiley, the protagonist of *Smiley's People* (1980) and earlier novels, an eternally middle-aged and all too human intelligence officer who grapples with the moral ambiguities of real-life Cold War espionage. *The Looking-Glass War* (1965) is a particularly bleak dissection of a Cold War operation, while *Tinker, Tailor,*

S

Soldier, Spy (1974; filmed 2011), inspired by the infamous case of Kim Philby, explores the theme of the Soviet 'mole' within the service.

Len Deighton (1929–) made his name with *The Ipcress File* (1962) and *Funeral in Berlin* (1964), and went on to write three trilogies in the 1980s and 1990s featuring the Secret Service agent Bernard Samson; *A Choice of Enemies* (1973) was the first novel of the former intelligence officer Ted Allbeury (1917–2005); Anthony Price (1928–) created the historian and spy Dr David Audley. Yet even as le Carré and others explored the moral ambiguities of Cold War espionage, Frederick Forsyth (1938–) was marking another shift in mood. In best-sellers such as *The Day of the Jackal* (1971) and *The Odessa File* (1972), he returned to adventure stories on a global scale in which tough male heroes save the world from a variety of disasters, a trend also reflected in the novels of Ken Follett (1949–) such as *The Eye of the Needle* (1978) and *The Man from St Petersburg* (1982).

Since the ending of the Cold War, Le Carré has turned his attention to the iniquities of global capitalism in novels such as *The Constant Gardener* (2001). Forsyth's 2006 novel *The Afghan* features an undercover agent working to thwart an al-Qaeda terror plot. Younger writers in the genre include Henry Porter (1953–), author of *A Spy's Life* (2001), *Brandenburg* (2005), and *The Dying Light* (2009), which deals with the surveillance state in the internet age; and Charles Cumming (1971–), whose debut novel was *A Spy by Nature* (2001).

SQUIRE, Sir J. C. (John Collings) (1884–1958) *Georgian poet, literary journalist and editor, and a skilful parodist. He established the **London Mercury* in 1919, and exercised considerable power through his editorship; he and his friends formed a literary establishment—irreverently known as 'the Squirearchy'—which was vigorously opposed by the *Sitwells, the *Bloomsbury Group, and the *modernist avant-garde. His works include three widely popular volumes of *Selections from Modern Poets*, *Collected Parodies* (1921), and an autobiography, *The Honeysuckle and the Bee*, appeared in 1937. His *Collected Poems* (1959) were edited by John *Betjeman.

Squire of Low Degree, The A metrical romance, probably mid-15th century, opening with the distich: 'It was a squier of lowe degree | That loved the Kings doughter of Hungré.' The squire declares his love to the princess, who consents to marry him when he has proved himself a distinguished knight. But he is seen

in his tryst by a steward, whom he kills after the steward reports to the king. He is imprisoned but finally released because the princess is inconsolable, whereupon he sets out on his quest, proves his worth, and marries her. The romance is known from a printing *c.*1560 by W. Copland and fragments of a 1520 printing by Wynkyn de *Worde; de Worde's edition is dramatically entitled 'Undo youre Dore' from one of its episodes.

'Squire's Tale, The' *See* CANTERBURY TALES, 11.

STABLEFORD, Brian (1948–) *Science fiction author and critic, whose work ranges from routine space operas to erudite explorations of *Gothic/decadence. In the 'Hooded Swan' series from *The Halcyon Drift* (1972), he developed a sardonic voice which moved towards subverting the expectations of the form. The stories collected in *Sexual Chemistry* (1991), and the 'Emortality' series, beginning with *Inherit the Earth* (1998), exhibit science fiction's desire to examine the future.

STABLES, Gordon (*c.*1840–1910) Retired naval surgeon and children's writer; he produced numerous books and articles, usually for boys, though he contributed health advice to the *Girl's Own Paper*. Stables wrote adventure and animal stories and about health.

STACPOOLE, H. (Henry) de Vere (1863–1951) Novelist and sea captain. He achieved popularity with *The Crimson Azaleas* (1907), a sea adventure, but is chiefly remembered for his best-selling romance *The Blue Lagoon* (1908), the story of two cousins, Dick and Emmeline, marooned at the age of 8 on a tropical island where they grow up and produce a baby. It has been several times successfully filmed.

STAFFORD, Jean (1915–1979) American writer who began publishing with her novel *Boston Adventure* (1944). Her first marriage was to Robert *Lowell and her *Collected Stories* (1969) won the Pulitzer Prize.

STAFFORD-CLARK, Max (1941–) Theatre director; the single most important force in the introduction of new playwrights and plays into the modern British theatre. He ran the Traverse Theatre, Edinburgh, from 1968 and was director of its Theatre Workshop Company until 1974, the year that he co-founded the Joint Stock Theatre Company, an innovative workshop-based organization that nurtured the careers of many new writers. From 1979 to 1993 he was the longest-serving artistic director of the *Royal Court, where he actively supported new writing, including Caryl *Churchill's *Top Girls*. In 1993 he founded Out of Joint, with which he continues to promote the work of new writers. *Letters to George* (1997) is an account of his rehearsals for George *Etherege's *The Man of Mode*, and *Taking Stock: The Theatre of Max Stafford-Clark* (2007) was published with Philip Roberts.

STALLWORTHY, Jon (1935–) Poet and biographer. *The Astronomy of Love* (1961), was followed by *A Familiar Tree* (1978), a sequence which mixes family and local history with a story of migration, *The Guest from the Future* (1995), which celebrates female survival in the person of Anna *Akhmatova and others, and *Body Language* (2004). The title of *Rounding the Horn: Collected Poems* (1998) pays homage, as do many of his individual poems, to his New Zealand ancestry. With Peter France, he has translated Boris *Pasternak and Alexander *Blok, and he has published notable biographies of Wilfred *Owen (1974), and Louis *MacNeice (1995).

Stand A literary quarterly founded in 1952 by Jon *Silkin and published from 1965 in Newcastle-upon-Tyne. Political considerations have characterized its sense of the place of poetry, and a representative anthology in 1973 was entitled *Poetry of the Committed Individual*; it has also been warmly accommodating to work in translation. It publishes poetry, fiction, and criticism, and contributors have included Geoffrey *Hill, Seamus *Heaney, Simon *Armitage, Ken *Smith, a one-time editor, and, in translation, work by Miroslav Holub, Joseph *Brodsky, and Evgenii Evtushenko.

STANHOPE, Lady Hester (1776– 1839) Traveller, her father later the third Earl Stanhope, her mother the sister of William Pitt the younger, in whose house Hester gained a reputation as a formidable political hostess. In 1810 she left Europe for good with her wealthy young lover Michael Bruce (1787–1861), and travelled in style and without inhibition in Egypt and the Middle East, the first European woman to reach Palmyra. Bruce returned home and she stayed on in Lebanon, living in great magnificence among a semi-oriental retinue and wielding some political power. In later years her debts accumulated and her eccentricity increased. She claimed to be a prophetess and mistress of occult sciences. She was visited by distinguished European travellers, including Alphonse de Lamartine and Alexander *King-

lake. Her letters were edited posthumously by her physician and companion, Charles Meryon (1783–1877), and confirmed her as a legendary figure of female independence and unconventionality.

STANIHURST, Richard (1547–1618) Irish chronicler, literary theorist, translator, poet, and alchemist. He wrote most of the Irish materials in *Holinshed's *Chronicles*, drawing on researches he had conducted with Edmund Campion. *The First Four Books of Virgil's 'Aeneis' Translated into English Heroicall Verse* (1582) includes a dissertation on *prosody and the principles of spelling, and an appendix of poems embodying his somewhat eccentric views on these subjects.

STANLEY, Sir Henry Morton (1841– 1904) Explorer and journalist, born John Rowlands in Denbigh, Wales, where he spent his early years in a workhouse. In 1859 he went as a cabin boy to New Orleans, where, he claims, he was adopted by a merchant named Stanley. In 1869, as a reporter for the *New York Herald*, he was instructed by James Gordon Bennett Jr, a proponent of the 'new journalism', to find Dr David *Livingstone, whom he eventually encountered at Ujiji in 1871. The resulting book, *How I Found Livingstone* (1872), includes the famous, much-ridiculed greeting 'Dr Livingstone, I presume' Stanley's further explorations and discoveries in Africa are described in *Through the Dark Continent* (1878), and in *In Darkest Africa* (1890). He introduced a new journalistic and sensationalist style into writings of African exploration.

stanza A group of verse lines, popularly called a 'verse', of which the length, metrical scheme, and rhyming pattern correspond with those of at least one other such group of verse lines in a poem, often with those of all. Poems are described as stanzaic if they are composed of such matching groups, spatially separated when written or printed. In length, stanzas of English verse are most commonly of four lines (i.e. *quatrains), but various forms of five-line (quintain), six-line (sestet), seven-line (septet), eight-line (octave), and longer stanzas are also found. Possible permutations of *metre and *rhyme are numerous: metrically, stanzas divide between those in which lines are of uniform length and those combining longer with shorter lines. Stanzaic rhyme schemes are summarized by a customary alphabetic notation in which each rhymed or unrhymed line-ending is allotted a letter in sequence, recurrence of the same letter indicating rhymed lines: thus *abcb* for the standard quatrain 'ballad stanza' in which only the second and fourth lines rhyme, but *abab* for the quatrain of alternate rhymes often found in hymns. Most stanza forms are nameless, but exceptions among those longer than the quatrain include the six-line 'Burns stanza' of which the fourth and sixth are of two stresses while the remainder are four-stress lines, with the rhyme scheme *aaabab*; the *'rhyme-royal' stanza of seven iambic *pentameters rhyming *abbabcc*; the Italianate octave known as *ottava rima*; and the nine-line *Spenserian stanza.

Stanzaic Life of Christ, The A 14th-century compilation surviving in three 15th-century manuscripts in 10,840 lines of English quatrains, drawn from the *Polychronicon* of Ranulf *Higden and the *Legenda Aurea* of Jacobus de Voragine (*see* GOLDEN LEGEND). It was written by a monk of St Werburgh's, Chester, and it was an influence on the Chester *mystery plays.

Staple of News, The A comedy by Ben *Jonson, performed 1626, printed 1631. The play is watched throughout by four gossips, Mirth, Tattle, Expectation, and Censure, who sit on the stage and offer an undiscerning commentary at the end of each act.

STAPLEDON, Olaf (1886–1950) *Science fiction writer, philosopher, and activist. His novels *Last and First Men* (1930) and *Star Maker* (1937) have been widely cited as influences by Arthur C. *Clarke, Brian W. *Aldiss, Gregory Benford, Doris *Lessing, and Stephen *Baxter, among others, influencing several generations of science fiction authors. *Last and First Men* is a future history of epic proportions, with an astonishing range of biological and sociological speculation. *Star Maker* is a Dantesque vision of the universe evolving towards a cosmic mind. *Odd John* (1935) features a tragic mutant superman, and *Sirius* (1944) a dog with superhuman intelligence.

Star Trek American *science fiction television series, devised and produced by Gene Roddenberry (1921–99), which originally ran 1966–9 and was brought back after a campaign by fans. Its basic scenario, the voyages of the starship *Enterprise* headed by Captain Kirk and his half-alien first officer Spock, allowed for numerous adventures, often exploring moral dilemmas. Several well-known writers, such as Robert *Bloch, Harlan Ellison, and Theodore Sturgeon, contributed scripts. Since the first series, numerous motion pictures and spin-offs—*The Next Generation*, *Deep Space Nine*, *Voyager*,

Generations—have been produced, together with an industrial quantity of books, comics, and games.

Star Wars Originally a single American *science fiction film (1977, dir. George Lucas), *Star Wars* has become a popular-culture franchise rivalled only by *Star Trek*. Celebrated for astonishing special effects, it drew heavily on the American magazines of the 1930s; the first draft of the sequel *The Empire Strikes Back* (1980) was written by Leigh *Brackett. *The Return of the Jedi* followed in 1983. The series was completed by the prequels *The Phantom Menace* (1999), *Attack of the Clones* (2002), and *Revenge of the Sith* (2005).

STARK, Dame Freya (1893–1993) Travel writer and explorer. In 1927, having mastered Arabic, she began travelling in the Middle East, and in the next decade made adventurous solitary journeys in that region. She was appointed a fellow of the *Royal Geographical Society in 1936, and made a DBE in 1972. Among her many books on her travels in Iran, Iraq, southern Arabia, and Turkey, the most notable are *The Valleys of the Assassins* (1934), *The Southern Gates of Arabia* (1936), *A Winter in Arabia* (1940), *Iona: A Quest* (1954), and *The Lycian Shore* (1956). Stark was also an accomplished photographer, illustrating her books with striking portraits of the people and places she encountered. Four volumes of autobiography, including *Traveller's Prelude* (1950), appeared 1950–61.

STARKE, Mariana *See* MURRAY, JOHN.

Stationers' Company A London livery company concerned with the book trade and its related crafts. The Company existed from at least 1403 and was incorporated by royal charter in 1557. Under its provisions, only members of the Company might print anything for sale in the kingdom unless authorized by special privilege or patent. Since every member of the Company was required to enter in the register of the Company (the Stationers' Register) the name of any book that he desired to print, these registers furnish valuable information regarding printed matter during the latter part of the 16th century and well into the 17th century. The Company was not responsible for licensing or censorship: by payment of a small fee, the Register established the holder's right to the copy entered in the Register, but by no means all legitimately published works were entered in the Registers. Although the Company's regulatory control of the printing trade waned during the

17th century, it retained its right to print such works as psalters, almanacs, school- and law-books. The Stationers' Company merged with the Newspaper Makers' Company in 1937 and their extensive archives, including the original Registers, are kept at Stationers' Hall.

STATIUS, Publius Papinius (AD c.45–96) Roman poet. His *Silvae* ('trees' or 'materials'), in five books, is a collection of poems in various metres, some of considerable length, on various occasional topics such as thanks to patrons and descriptions of country houses. His epic *Thebais*, in twelve books, tells the story of the Theban War, from blinded *Oedipus' curse on his sons Eteocles and Polynices, to the expedition of the Seven against Thebes. The precedent of the *Aeneid*, in language and conception, is everywhere visible. He died before completing his second epic, *Achilleis*. Statius appears as a Christian convert in *Dante's *Purgatory*. Ben *Jonson's *Forest* owes a debt to *Silvae*; Alexander *Pope and Thomas *Gray tried their hands at translating the *Thebais*.

STEAD, Christina Ellen (1902–83) Australian novelist. She came to London in 1928 and subsequently worked and travelled in Europe and America; she returned to Australia on her husband's death in 1968. Her wandering life and her left-wing views (which also raised difficulties for her when she worked as a Hollywood scriptwriter) may have contributed to the neglect of her work, particularly in her native country. Her first collection of stories, *The Salzburg Tales*, and her first novel, *Seven Poor Men of Sydney*, were both published in 1934. Her best-known work, *The Man Who Loved Children* (1940), is a bitterly ironic view of family life and family conflict. Stead's other novels include *For Love Alone* (1945), *Letty Fox: Her Luck* (1946), and *Cotter's England* (1967; USA as *Dark Places of the Heart*, 1966), which presents a vivid portrait of post-war working-class Britain.

STEAD, C. K. (Christian Karlson) (1932–) New Zealand poet, critic, and novelist. In 1964 he published his first volume of poems, *Whether the Will Is Free*, and a well-received critical book, *The New Poetic: Yeats to Eliot*. His novels include *All Visitors Ashore* (1984), *The Death of the Body* (1986), and *The Singing Whakapapa* (1994), which characteristically mix New Zealand personal material with experimental techniques. *Mansfield* (2004) is a fictional portrait of the New Zealand short story writer Katherine *Mansfield. *My Name is Judas* (2006) fictionally recreates the life of Judas Iscariot (*see* BIBLE).

The Black River, a selection of poems, appeared in 2007.

STEAD, W. T. (William Thomas) (1849–1912) Journalist. In 1880 he became assistant editor of the *Pall Mall Gazette*. On becoming editor (1883–8) of the paper, he transformed it into a vigorous, modern, and campaigning journal. He achieved wide notoriety for his 'Maiden Tribute of Modern Babylon' (1885) exposing sexual vice, which prompted Parliament to raise the age of consent to 16 years. His role in the campaign led to a brief term of imprisonment. He founded the *Review of Reviews* in 1890 and continued his work for peace, friendship with Russia, and spiritualism (for which he was much ridiculed). He was drowned in the *Titanic* disaster.

STEDMAN, John Gabriel (1744–97) Army officer and author. He volunteered to help put down a slave rebellion (1772–7) and his subsequent *Narrative of a Five Years' Expedition against the Revolted Negroes of Surinam* (1796) provides a detailed portrait of plantation society as well as telling the story of the author's love affair with a young slave—fictionalized in Beryl Gilroy's *Stedman and Joanna* (1991). Stedman was not an abolitionist, but his blunt descriptions of the cruel treatment of slaves were seized on by anti-slavery campaigners. The book included engravings by William *Blake from Stedman's own drawings. *See also* SLAVERY, LITERATURE OF.

STEELE, Anne (1717–78) Baptist poet and *hymn-writer. In her lifetime she published *Poems on Subjects Chiefly Devotional* (1760) in two volumes under the name Theodosia; after her death the Baptist minister Caleb Evans (1737–91) republished these and added *Miscellaneous Pieces in Prose and Verse* (1780), again by Theodosia, but identifying her in the advertisement. Many of her hymns were included in *A Collection of Hymns Adapted to Public Worship* (1769), which went through seven editions.

STEELE, Sir Richard (1672–1729) Whig essayist, born in Dublin; he met Joseph *Addison at school at Charterhouse. *The Funeral* (1701) was the first and most successful of three early comedies. In 1707 he was appointed gazetteer. In 1709 he launched the *Tatler*, which he ran with the help of Addison until 1711 when it foundered in the new Tory hegemony, which also cost him the gazetteership. In April 1711 he and Addison set up the less political *Spectator*. This was followed by the *Guardian*. In 1713 Steele was elected MP for Stockbridge.

The publication of *The Crisis*, a pamphlet in favour of the Hanoverian succession, led to his expulsion from the House in 1714. In the same year he issued *Apology for Himself and his Writings* and edited the *Lover*, a paper in the manner of the *Spectator*. On the accession of George I he was appointed supervisor of Drury Lane Theatre, and was knighted in 1715. His last and most popular comedy, *The *Conscious Lovers*, was produced in 1722. Money difficulties forced him to leave London in 1724, and he died at Carmarthen. Steele's attacks on *Restoration drama; his approval of the 'sober and polite Mirth' of *Terence; his praise of tender affections and family life; and his own reformed and sentimental dramas did much to create an image of polite behaviour for the new century.

Steel Glass, The A satire in verse by George *Gascoigne, published 1576. The poet's 'steel glass' reveals abuses and how things should be, whereas the common looking-glass offers 'a seemly show', i.e. shows things much better than they really are. Looking into his 'steel glass', the author sees himself with his faults and then successively the faults of kings; covetous lords and knights; greedy, braggart, and drunken soldiers; false judges; merchants; and priests. Finally, the ploughman is held up as a model:

> Behold him (priests) and though he stink of
>   sweat
> Disdain him not: for shall I tell you what?
> Such climb to heaven, before the shaven
>   crowns.

STEEVENS, George (1736–1800) Shakespearian commentator. In 1766 he issued in four volumes *Twenty of the Plays of Shakespeare* from the earliest quarto texts (*see* FOLIOS AND QUARTOS), and in 1773 a ten-volume annotated edition, a revision of Samuel *Johnson's edition, further revised in 1778. He helped Edmond *Malone produce two supplementary volumes in 1780, but their increasing rivalry led Steevens to produce a further edition (1793), with materials for still another left in the hands of Isaac Reed. Steevens supplied to his editions a vast range of illustrative quotations from Elizabethan writings, but is also thought to have planted various hoax documents to mislead other scholars.

STEIN, Gertrude (1874–1946) American author. She studied psychology under William James, who introduced her to automatic writing. In 1902 she went with her brother Leo to Paris, where her home became a literary salon and art gallery. Visitors included Picasso, Ford Madox *Ford, and Ernest *Hemingway. Her friend, secretary, and companion from 1907 was San Francisco-born Alice B. Toklas (1877–1967), whom she made the ostensible author of her own memoir, *The Autobiography of Alice B. Toklas* (1933). Her fiction includes *Three Lives* (1909), of which the second portrait, 'Melanctha', was described by Richard *Wright as 'the first long serious literary treatment of Negro life in the United States'; *The Making of Americans* (1925); and *A Long Gay Book* (1932). *Tender Buttons* (1914) presents lexical experiments and an attempt at Cubist prose. Her style owes much to William James and to Henri *Bergson's concept of time, and represents a highly personal but nevertheless influential version of the *stream-of-consciousness technique. Her many varied published works include essays, sketches of life in France, works of literary theory, short stories, portraits of her friends, a lyric drama called *Four Saints in Three Acts*, and *Wars I Have Seen* (1945), a personal account of occupied Paris.

STEINBECK, John (1902–68) American novelist, born in California. He took his native state as the background for his early short stories and novels and described the lives of those working on the land. *Tortilla Flat* (1935) was followed by *In Dubious Battle* (1936) and *Of Mice and Men* (1937), the story of two itinerant farm labourers, one of huge strength and weak mind, exploited and protected by the other. *The Grapes of Wrath* (1939), is an epic account of the efforts of an emigrant farming family from the dust bowl of Oklahoma to reach the 'promised land' of California. Among his later novels are *East of Eden* (1952), a family saga, and *The Winter of our Discontent* (1961). His screenplays include *The Forgotten Village* (1941), a documentary, and *Viva Zapata!* (1952). *America and Americans* (2003) collects important non-fiction.

STEINER, George (Francis George Steiner) (1929–) American critic and author, born in Paris of émigré Austrian parents who took him to the USA in 1940. His critical works include *Tolstoy or Dostoevsky* (1959); *The Death of Tragedy* (1961); *Language and Silence* (1967); *In Bluebeard's Castle* (1971); and *After Babel: Aspects of Language and Translation* (1975). Steiner's criticism is wide-ranging and multilingual in its references and controversial in its content: one of his recurrent themes is the way in which the 20th-century experiences of the Holocaust, world wars, and totalitarianism have destroyed the assumption that literature is a humanizing influence. The Holocaust is also the subject of his novella *The Portage to San Cristobal of A.H.* (1979). Other works include *Real Presences* (1989), a response to *deconstruction, and *Proofs and Three Parables* (fiction, 1992). *Errata: An Examined Life* (1997) is a memoir, *Lessons of the Masters* (2003) a study of mentors and protégés. *See also* HOLOCAUST, LITERATURE OF THE.

Stella (1) The chaste lady, based on Penelope Rich, loved by Astrophel in Philip *Sidney's sonnet sequence *Astrophel and Stella*; (2) Jonathan *Swift's name for Esther Johnson, employed particularly in his *Journal to Stella*.

STEPHEN, Sir Leslie (1832-1904) Biographer and critic. From his family he inherited a strong tradition of evangelicalism and muscular Christianity, and he became a noted mountaineer: the best of his Alpine essays were collected in 1871 as *The Playground of Europe*. Stephen's reading of John Stuart *Mill, *Comte, and *Kant inclined him to scepticism, and he was increasingly influenced by Darwinism; by 1864, having abandoned his religious vocation, he had embarked on a literary career. From 1871 to 1882 he edited the *Cornhill Magazine*, then undertook the editorship of the *Dictionary of National Biography* (*DNB*). *History of English Thought in the 18th Century* (1876) reviews the *Deist controversy, and the intuitional and utilitarian schools of philosophy. His last important volume was *English Literature and Society in the Eighteenth Century* (1904). Stephen's first wife was W. M. *Thackeray's daughter 'Minny', who died in 1875. He then married Julia Duckworth, with whom he had four children, including Virginia *Woolf; after Julia's death in 1895, he wrote *The Mausoleum Book*, ostensibly as a record of their mother for his children and stepchildren, but it is also a form of autobiography. Woolf portrays some aspects of her conflictual relationship with her father in her portrait of Mr Ramsay in *To the Lighthouse* (1927).

STEPHENS, James (1880/82-1950) Irish poet and story writer. The sharp proletarian portraiture of *Insurrections* (1909), Stephens's first collection of poems, and the angry, grotesque variations on Ó Bruadair and other Gaelic poets in *Reincarnations* (1918) have their counterparts in the psychological realism and concern for social privation that offset the fairytale extravagance of his novels *The Charwoman's Daughter* (1912) and *The Demi-Gods* (1914). *The Insurrection in Dublin* (1916) offers a vivid first-hand account of the Easter Rising.

STEPHENSON, Neal (1959-) American *science fiction writer. His novels developed cyberpunk preoccupations with the social effects of computers and nanotechnology. *Cryptonomicon* (1999) explored the history of computing; much of it is set during the Second World War, with Alan Turing (1912-54) at the Bletchley Park code-breaking centre a major character. *Quicksilver* (2003) speculates about 17th-century systems of knowledge, and is as much *historical novel as science fiction. *Anathem* (2008) is a vast *alternate world philosophical fiction.

STERLING, Bruce (1954-) American author and journalist, instrumental in defining and promoting cyberpunk. With William *Gibson, he co-wrote *The Difference Engine* (1990). Climate change and longevity are the themes of *Heavy Weather* (1994) and *Holy Fire* (1996).

STERLING, John (1806-44) Writer, a leading member of the *Apostles and a disciple of S. T. *Coleridge. With F. D. Maurice he was briefly proprietor of the *Athenaeum* (1828). Thomas *Carlyle's vivid *Life of Sterling* (1851) reveals his friend's tragic history, dogged by persistent ill health. His monthly meetings of literary friends, from 1838, became known as the Sterling Club; among its members were Carlyle, Julius Hare, John Stuart *Mill, and Alfred *Tennyson. His published works include a novel, *Arthur Coningsby* (1833), *Poems* (1839), and *Essays and Tales* (1848).

STERNE, Laurence (1713-68) Novelist, the son of an impoverished infantry officer. He spent his early childhood in various barracks in Ireland and England. He met John *Hall-Stevenson at Jesus College, Cambridge. In 1741 he became a prebendary of York Cathedral, and married Elizabeth Lumley, a cousin of Elizabeth *Montagu. They had one surviving daughter, Lydia, who edited Sterne's letters and sermons after his death. Sterne earned a good reputation as a country pastor and led a very sociable life. In 1759, he wrote *A Political Romance* (later entitled *The History of a Good Warm Watch Coat*), a satire offensive enough to be suppressed by the authorities, and began *Tristram Shandy*. The first version of vols i and ii was rejected by the London publisher Robert *Dodsley. The next version of vols i and ii, was published in York in 1759, with Dodsley agreeing to take half the printing for sale in London. Early in 1760 Sterne found himself famous. He went to London and was fêted by society, had his portrait painted by Sir Joshua *Reynolds, and was invited to court. He was also presented with a third Yorkshire living, that of Coxwold, where he settled himself into 'Shandy Hall'. He published *The Sermons of Mr Yorick* and continued with *Tristram Shandy*, four further volumes appearing in 1761. Sterne had contracted tuberculosis at college and his health now deteriorated steadily. In 1762 his voice was badly affected, and the family left for France, where they lived at Toulouse and Montpellier until 1764, when Sterne returned to England to publish vols vii and viii of *Tristram Shandy* (1765). Back in France, he visited his wife and daughter, and undertook an eight-month tour of France and Italy, which provided him with material for *A *Sentimental Journey through France and Italy*. The ninth and last volume of *Tristram Shandy* and *A Sentimental Journey* both appeared in 1767. Sterne also met Elizabeth Draper (1744–78), the young wife of an official of the East India Company, and began his *Journal to *Eliza* after her enforced departure for India. He died in London in March 1768. His body was stolen by grave-robbers, and is said to have been recognized at an anatomy lecture in Cambridge, and secretly reburied; a skull believed to be that of Sterne was recovered in 1969 and buried in Coxwold.

Sterne's work has some links with the *Renaissance tradition of 'learned fooling' and the unflinching self-examination of essayists such as *Montaigne. His attention to the nuances and misunderstandings of mental processes makes him a progenitor of the *stream-of-consciousness novel. He acknowledges in *Tristram Shandy* his own debt in this respect to John *Locke, whose *Essay Concerning Human Understanding* seemed to Sterne 'a history-book . . . of what passes in man's own mind'. Throughout his work he plays with the developing conventions of the still-new 'novel', and its problems in presenting in language the realities of consciousness, space, and time.

STERNHOLD, Thomas (d. 1549) and **Hopkins, John** (1520/1–1570) Joint versifiers of the *Psalms. A collection of 44 metrical Psalms appeared in 1549; music was first supplied in the Geneva edition of 1556, and by 1640 about 300 editions had been published. In 1562 *The Whole Book of Psalms*, by Sternhold, Hopkins, Thomas Norton (1530/32–1584), and others, was added to the Prayer Book. John *Dryden ridiculed this version in *Absalom and Achitophel* (II. 403).

STEVENS, Wallace (1879–1955) Major American poet, and lawyer. His first volume, *Harmonium* (1923) contains 'Thirteen Ways of Looking at a Blackbird'. Later collections include *Ideas of Order* (1935) and *Notes towards a Supreme Fiction* (1942). The 'supreme fiction' in the latter denotes a satisfactory conceptualization of reality, more often an aim in his poetry rather than an achieved end. His enigmatic, elegant, intellectual, and occasionally startling meditations on order and the imagination and on the function of poetry can also be seen in his volume of essays *The Necessary Angel* (1951).

STEVENSON, Anne (1933–) Poet, critic, and biographer. Her collections include *Living in America* (1965), *Correspondences* (1973), which is a historical and contemporary saga of a New England family written in letters, prose, verse, and perhaps her most admired work, *The Fiction Makers* (1985), *The Other House* (1990), *A Report from the Border* (2003), and *Poems 1955–2005* (2005). Many of Stevenson's poems celebrate the landscapes and cultures of her two nations, America and Britain, and their interconnections: her tone is at times conversational, at times lyrical, at times wry. Her controversial biography of Sylvia *Plath, *Bitter Fame*, appeared in 1989, and her critical writing includes *Five Looks at Elizabeth Bishop* (1998), who is an important influence (*see* BISHOP, ELIZABETH), and *Between the Iceberg and the Ship: Selected Essays* (1998).

STEVENSON, Robert Louis (originally Lewis) (1850–94) Scottish novelist, essayist, and poet. He qualified as a lawyer, but had already begun publishing essays in the *Cornhill Magazine* and elsewhere when admitted advocate in 1875. He collaborated with W. E. *Henley on four plays, performed with little success 1880–5. Stevenson suffered from a chronic bronchial condition, and much of his life was spent going from country to country in search of health; travelling in due course emerged as a defining trope of his writing. In France in 1876 he met Mrs Fanny Osbourne, ten years his senior, recording his feelings for her in the essay 'On Falling in Love' (1877). In 1879, after the publication of *Travels with a Donkey in the Cevennes*, he set off for California in response to a telegram from Fanny, whom he married in March 1880, four months after her divorce. The couple stayed at an abandoned mine in Calistoga, as described in *The Silverado Squatters* (1883), before returning to settle for three years in Bournemouth, where Stevenson consolidated a friendship with Henry *James. By this time many of his stories, essays, and travel pieces had been collected in volume form (*Virginibus Puerisque*, 1881; *Familiar Studies of Men and Books*, 1882; *New Arabian Nights*, 1882). His first full-length work of fiction, **Treasure Island* (1883), brought him fame, consolidated by *The Strange Case of *Dr Jekyll and Mr Hyde* (1886). **Kidnapped* (1886), a bravura recasting of the historical novel as coming-of-age romance, and *The *Master of Ballantrae* (1889), at once a tale of high adventure and an acute analysis of sibling rivalry, have Scottish settings.

In 1888 Stevenson set out from San Francisco with his family entourage for the South Seas. He settled in Samoa at Vailima, where he temporarily regained his health, and became known as 'Tusitala' or 'The Story Teller'. He died there from a brain haemorrhage while working on **Weir of Hermiston* (1896), a final Scottish novel, following *Catriona*, a sequel to *Kidnapped* (1893).

Stevenson also wrote *The Merry Men* (1887, stories, including, the supernatural **Scots tale 'Thrawn Janet'* and, the **Gothic pastiche 'Olalla'*); *The Black Arrow* (1888), a historical romance; and *St Ives* (1897, unfinished, completed by Sir Arthur **Quiller-Couch), an episodic novel of the Napoleonic Wars. With his stepson Lloyd Osbourne he wrote the mischievous comedy *The Wrong Box* (1889) and *The Wrecker* (1892). He published three volumes of poetry, *A Child's Garden of Verses* (1885), a classic of children's literature; *Underwoods* (1887), a collection of **lyrics in English and Scots and of **ballads in English; and *Songs of Travel* (1896). The poetry shares the combination of surface delicacy with subterranean disturbance that characterizes Stevenson's fiction. The theme of dualism recurs in his work, as does a fascination with morally ambiguous heroes or anti-heroes. The concern with patrimony implicit in *Treasure Island* and *Kidnapped* emerges in the fierce father–son conflict of *Weir of Hermiston*. Stevenson's work was admired by Henry James, G. M. *Hopkins, *Nabokov, *Borges, and Graham *Greene.

STEWART, George Rippey (1895–1980) American *science fiction author. His influential *Earth Abides* (1949) is an elegiac chronicle of the attempts of a few survivors of a worldwide plague to rebuild civilization, set mostly in California.

STEWART, J. I. M. (John Innes Mackintosh) (1906–94) Novelist and critic. Under the pseudonym Michael Innes he wrote donnish *detective fiction, rich in literary allusions and quotations, featuring Inspector John Appleby. Published over a 50-year period, the Appleby books include *Death at the President's Lodging* (1936), *Hamlet, Revenge!* (1937), *Appleby on Ararat* (1941), *The Long Farewell* (1958), *Appleby at Allington* (1968), *Appleby's Answer* (1973), and *Appleby and the Ospreys* (1986). Under his own name he wrote literary criticism and a quintet of novels (1974–8) about life in Oxford with the collective title *A Staircase in Surrey*.

stichomythia In classical Greek drama, dialogue in alternate lines of verse, employed in sharp disputation. The form is sometimes imitated in English drama, e.g. in the dialogue between Richard III and Elizabeth in **Shakespeare's **Richard III* (IV. iv).

Stoicism A system of thought which originated in Athens during the 3rd century BC, flourished in Rome *c.*100 BC–*c.* AD 200, and enjoyed a vigorous revival at the time of the Renaissance. The Stoics' prime concern was ethics, but they held that right behaviour must be grounded on a general understanding of the universe, and their theories extended to cover the nature of the physical world, logic, rhetoric, epistemology, and politics. The founders, notably Zeno of Citium (*c.*334–*c.*262 BC) and Chrysippus of Soli (*c.*280–*c.*207 BC), held that 'virtue' or excellence was the only good, and that 'virtue' consisted in following reason, unaffected by the passions, passions being caused by false judgements. Echoing *Socrates, they said that ordinary 'goods' such as health or money were merely 'preferred', not good. Only fragments of these founders remain; the Stoics whose writings survive whole are those who lived under the Roman Empire, especially *Seneca, *Epictetus, and *Marcus Aurelius. The development of Christian thinking is often closely involved with Stoic ideas. *Petrarch in the 14th century expounded a Christian Stoicism in his *De Remediis Fortunae*, and in the 16th century a manufactured version of Marcus Aurelius' ideas, *Libro Aureo del Emperador Marco Aurelio* (translated into French and English in the 1530s, well before the *Meditations* became widely available, by Antonio de Guevara (*c.*1480–1545)) may have served to promote the Stoic revival ('neo-Stoicism') which came at the end of the century with *Montaigne's *Essais* (1580) and Lipsius' *De Constantia* (1585). In England the years 1595–1615 saw translations of Lipsius, Montaigne, his disciple Charron (1541–1603), Epictetus, and Seneca,

S

and the influence of Stoicism can be traced in a great number of writers from George *Chapman and Ben *Jonson to the third earl of *Shaftesbury and Francis *Hutcheson.

STOKER, Bram (Abraham) (1847–1912) Irish writer, who gave up his career as a civil servant in 1878 to become Sir Henry *Irving's secretary and business manager for the next 27 years, an experience that produced his two-volume tribute, *Personal Reminiscences of Henry Irving* (1906). Stoker is remembered for his vampire novel *Dracula* (1897), influenced by 'Carmilla', one of the tales in Sheridan Le Fanu's *In a Glass Darkly* (1872) *See* VAMPIRES IN LITERATURE.

Stones of Venice, The By John *Ruskin, published in three volumes (1851, 1853). A study of the architecture of Venice, it combines extensive and painstaking scholarship with an eloquent account of the moral, political, and religious significance of the city's rise and fall. The work confirmed Ruskin's reputation as one of the leading cultural critics of his generation. Ruskin's celebration of Byzantine and *Gothic architecture had a widespread influence on Victorian architects.

The first volume sets out first principles for discrimination between good and bad architecture, followed, in the second and third volumes, with a cultural and architectural history of the city. Ruskin describes the rise of medieval Venice, whose power he attributes to creativity, discipline, and religious faith, and its subsequent decline into what Ruskin saw as the pride, infidelity, and hedonism of the Renaissance. Ruskin's *Protestant and conservative sympathies shape this analysis. The famous chapter 'The Nature of Gothic' contrasts the imaginative freedom possible for the workmen who constructed the great Gothic buildings of Venice with the rigid confinement resulting from the division of labour and mechanical mass production in English manufacturing industries of the 19th century.

STOPPARD, Sir Tom (1937–) OM, CBE, dramatist. His play *Rosencrantz and Guildenstern Are Dead* (1966) created an overnight sensation. It was followed by many witty and inventive plays, including *The Real Inspector Hound* (1968, a play-within-a-play that parodies the conventions of the stage thriller); *Jumpers* (1972); *Travesties* (1974); *Dirty Linen* (1976, a satire of political life and parliamentary misdemeanours); *Every Good Boy Deserves Favour* (1977, about a political dissident in a Soviet

psychiatric hospital); *Night and Day* (1978, about the dangers of the 'closed shop' in journalism); *The Real Thing* (1982, a marital tragicomedy); *Arcadia* (1993, with a parallel setting in the present day and in 1809); and *Indian Ink* (1995, an exploration of cultural identity). *The Invention of Love* (1997) presents, through the contrasted fates of A. E. *Housman and Oscar *Wilde, the sexual complexities of the *Aesthetic movement, and the conflicts between art and scholarship. Stoppard has also written many works for film, radio, and television, including *Professional Foul* (TV, 1977), set in Prague, which portrays the concurrent visits of an English philosopher and an English football team. Stoppard's work displays a metaphysical wit, a strong theatrical sense, and a talent for pastiche. *The Coast of Utopia* (2002) is a trilogy about political radicalism in Russia. His sympathy for, and work on behalf of, dissident voices stifled in the Soviet Empire is evident in much of his work, and his *Rock 'n' Roll* (2006) looked at the dual history of his homeland, Czechoslovakia, from the Prague Spring of 1968 to the Velvet Revolution, and that of the British left seen from a right-wing perspective.

STOREY, David Malcolm (1933–) Novelist and playwright. His first novel, *This Sporting Life* (1960), describes the ambitions and passions of a young working man, Arthur Machin, a Rugby League player who becomes emotionally involved with his landlady. This was followed by *Flight into Camden* (1960), about the unhappy affair of a miner's daughter with a married teacher, and the highly ambitious *Radcliffe* (1963), a sombre, violent, Lawrentian novel about class conflict, the Puritan legacy, and destructive homosexual passion. Later novels include *Pasmore* (1972, an account of a young lecturer in a state of mental breakdown) and *Saville* (1976, *Booker Prize), an epic set in a south Yorkshire mining village. His plays include *In Celebration* (1969), in which two educated sons return north to visit their miner father; *The Contractor* (1970), in which the construction, then the dismantling, of a wedding marquee, forms the background for the presentation of the relationship of the contractor Ewbank (who had appeared in *Radcliffe*) with university-educated son; *Home* (1970), set in a mental home; *The Changing Room* (1971), again using Rugby League as a setting; *Life Class* (1974), set in an art college; and *Mother's Day* (1976), a violent black comedy set on a housing estate. Both plays and novels show a preoccupation with social mobility and the disturbance it may cause. Later works include the plays

Sister (1978), *Early Days* (1980), and *The March on Russia* (1989) and the novels *A Prodigal Child* (1982) and *Present Times* (1984). A collection of poems, *Storey's Lives: Poems 1951–1991*, appeared in 1992.

STORR, Catherine (1913–2001) Children's writer and psychiatrist. Her stories display her understanding of the juvenile psyche as in *Marianne Dreams* (1958, filmed as *Paper House*, 1988; Storr also wrote it as an opera libretto) in which two ill, prepubescent children meet in a dreamscape where, by overcoming various threats and anxieties, they heal each other. Her stories strike a balance between fear and reassurance, reality and fantasy; the popular tales about Clever Polly, beginning with *Clever Polly and the Stupid Wolf* (1955), have an everyday setting into which the wolf from fairy-tales regularly intrudes and tries to capture and eat Polly. Time and again Polly outwits him, making her a strong girl character at a time when these were rare in children's books.

Story of an African Farm, The A novel by the South African writer Olive *Schreiner (1883), published under the pseudonym 'Ralph Iron'. It was largely completed before Schreiner left Africa for England in 1881, and it is set in the landscape of the Karoo, where she had spent her childhood. It tells the stories of two orphaned cousins, stay-at-home Em and unconventional Lyndall, who was greeted by feminists as one of the first *'New Women'. Lyndall rejects her early religious training, becomes pregnant by a lover whom she refuses to marry, and dies, exhausted, after the death of her baby. She is devotedly tended in her final illness by the English farmer Gregory Rose, who disguises himself as a woman in order to act as a nurse. Gregory later proposes marriage to Em, and is accepted. The novel also describes the intellectual and spiritual development of the sceptic Waldo, son of the farm's German overseer, whose rebellious spirit is aroused (as was Schreiner's) by reading Herbert *Spencer's *First Principles*.

Story of Rimini, The A poem by Leigh *Hunt, published 1816 and in a heavily revised version in 1844. The work is based on *Dante's story of Paolo and Francesca. The work, with its flexible couplets, its use of both common speech and new words, and its luxuriant southern imagery, suggested new possibilities to the younger Romantic poets. *Blackwood's Magazine*, in attacking 'the Cockney School', derided Hunt's 'glittering and rancid obscenities'.

STOW, John (1524/5–1605) Chronicler and antiquary. At first Stow's interest was English poetry; then from about 1564 he began to collect and transcribe manuscripts and to compose historical works, the first to be based on systematic study of public records. He was suspected of being a *recusant, and in 1569 and 1570 was accused of possessing popish and dangerous writings; the charge was dropped. He is said to have spent as much as £200 a year on books and manuscripts.

As well as assisting Matthew *Parker with editing historical texts, his chief publications were: editions of the works of *Chaucer (1561) and of John *Skelton (1568); *Summary of English Chronicles* (1565), an original historical work; *The Chronicles of England* (1580), later entitled *The Annals of England* (1592); the second edition of Raphael *Holinshed's *Chronicles* (1585–7); and lastly *A Survey of London* (1598 and 1603), invaluable for the detailed information it gives about the ancient city and its customs. It was brought down to his day by John Strype in 1720.

STOW, Randolph (1935–) Australian novelist and poet. His first book was *Act One: Poems* (1957). His innovative novels *To the Islands* (1958), *Tourmaline* (1963), and *Visitants* (1979) respond to dilemmas of spirituality and colonial relations, particularly in Australia and its near north. *The Merry-Go-Round in the Sea* (1965) is semi-autobiographical.

STOWE, Harriet Beecher (1811–96) Née Beecher. Her anti-slavery novel *Uncle Tom's Cabin*, was her first book; it was serialized in the *National Era* in 1851-2 and published as a volume in 1852. A powerful tale, it describes the sufferings of pious Uncle Tom, who is sold by his well-intentioned Kentucky owner, Mr Shelby, to meet his debts. He is taken first to a New Orleans household and eventually beaten to death by a brutal cotton plantation owner. This action is counterpointed against a parallel plot describing the escape to freedom in Canada of Shelby's slave Eliza, her child, and her husband George. Stowe's stress on the anguish of parted families formed part of the novel's overt polemic, although this was offset by generalizations applying the period's race theory. The phrase 'Uncle Tom' came to indicate a supine collaboration with the oppressor. *A Key to Uncle Tom's Cabin* (1853) documents many of Stowe's sources for the novel. The latter's success brought Stowe to England in 1853, 1856, and 1859, where she was rapturously received, and honoured by Queen *Victoria.

Her other works include *Dred: A Tale of the Dismal Swamp* (1856), which also deals with slavery; *The Minister's Wooing* (1859), a protest against the doctrines of Calvinism; and *Old Town Folks* (1869) and *Poganuc People* (1878), tales of New England family life.

STRACHEY, Lytton (1880–1932) Biographer and essayist, named after his godfather, the first earl of *Lytton, viceroy of India. At Trinity College, Cambridge, he became a member of the *Apostles and a friend of the philosopher George Edward Moore (1873–1958), the economist John Maynard Keynes (1883–1946), and Leonard *Woolf. He was thereafter a prominent member of the *Bloomsbury Group; he spent the last sixteen years of his life in a *ménage à trois* with Dora *Carrington and her husband Ralph Partridge. He was also, in the First World War, a conspicuous conscientious objector. Strachey did not achieve fame until 1918, with the publication of *Eminent Victorians*, a landmark in the history of *biography. This was a collection of four biographical essays, on Cardinal Manning, Florence *Nightingale, Thomas Arnold, and General Gordon; Strachey's wit and narrative powers captured a large (though at times hostile) readership. However this important debunking of the moral pretensions of the Victorian age meant, as Edmund *Wilson wrote in 1932, that no one was 'able to feel quite the same about the legends that had dominated their pasts'; he equally brought a new literary inventiveness to the genre of biography. His irreverent but affectionate life of Queen *Victoria (1921), was also highly successful. His last full-body work, *Elizabeth and Essex: A Tragic History* (1928), with its emphasis on *Elizabeth I's relationship with her father and its effect on her treatment of Essex, shows a clear (and early) debt to Sigmund *Freud.

Strafford A tragedy in blank verse by Robert *Browning, published 1837. It was written at the instigation of William *Macready, who produced it at Covent Garden on the day of publication, with himself in the title role. The play received mixed notices and had only a brief run; it has never been professionally revived. Browning's prose life of Strafford (Sir Thomas Wentworth, 1593–1641) was originally written for John *Forster and published in his 'Lives of Eminent British Statesmen' series. As with his other historical works, Browning's speculations about the characters' motives are searching and inventive. The action of the play is not closely related to the actual course of events.

STRAPAROLA, Gianfrancesco (d. 1557) Italian author of *novelle* entitled *Piacevoli Notti* (*Pleasant Nights*), published in two parts, 1550 and 1553. It introduced various folk tales to European literature, including the stories of 'Puss in Boots' and 'Beauty and the Beast'. William Painter, in his *Palace of Pleasure*, drew on Straparola among others.

STRAUSS, David Friedrich (1808–74) German biblical scholar. His *Das Leben Jesu, kritisch bearbeitet* (1835–6: *The Life of Jesus, Critically Examined*), was a notorious example of German 'Higher Criticism' which scandalized Europe. In it Strauss subjected the Gospel accounts to close historical scrutiny, judging them based on myth rather than fact, and denied the divinity of Jesus. George *Eliot translated the work into English in 1846, and her study of it helped confirm her break with Christianity.

STRAVINSKY, Igor Fyodorovich (1882–1971) Russian composer; he took American citizenship in 1945. The *libretto for his opera *The Rake's Progress* (1951) is by W. H. *Auden, assisted by Chester Kallman, based on the famous series of *Hogarth engravings.

stream of consciousness A term used variously to describe either the continuity of impressions and thoughts in the human mind, or a special literary method for representing this psychological principle in unpunctuated or fragmentary forms of *interior monologue. The term was coined in William James's *Principles of Psychology* (1890), in the first sense. The literary sense of the term was introduced in 1918 by May *Sinclair in a review of early volumes in Dorothy *Richardson's novel sequence *Pilgrimage* (1915–38), which include the first notable English uses of the technique. As used by Richardson, and more famously by James *Joyce in his novel *Ulysses* (1922), the stream-of-consciousness style represents the 'flow' of impressions, memories, and sense-impressions through the mind by abandoning accepted forms of syntax, punctuation, and logical connection. Joyce himself attributed the origin of the technique to the little-known French novel *Les Lauriers sont coupés* (1888) by Édouard Dujardin (1861–1949). After Joyce's virtuoso demonstration of its possibilities in the unpunctuated final chapter of *Ulysses*, the stream-of-consciousness method of rendering characters' thought processes became an accepted part of the modern novelist's repertoire, used by Virginia *Woolf, William *Faulkner, and others.

STREATFEILD, Noel (1895–1983) OBE; she wrote children's books featuring creative, hard-working, middle-class children. *Ballet Shoes* (1936) was her first success; *The Circus is Coming* won the Carnegie Medal (1939). *The Painted Garden* (1949) is based on filming *The *Secret Garden*. *A Vicarage Family* (1963) commences a semi-autobiographical sequence.

Strephon The shepherd whose lament for his lost love Urania forms the opening of Philip *Sidney's revised *Arcadia*. 'Strephon' has been adopted as a conventional name for a rustic lover.

STRETTON, Hesba (1832–1911) The pen-name of Sarah Smith, novelist and short story writer. She began a career as a writer in 1858, publishing stories in periodicals including Charles *Dickens's *All the Year Round*. She wrote prolifically for children, and had a long publishing career with the *Religious Tract Society. *Jessica's First Prayer* (1867), a powerful account of a neglected child, was extraordinarily successful, and sold two million copies in her lifetime. It was in part an attack on the hypocrisy of prosperous church and chapel congregations who ignored the plight of the poor. But it was also motivated by Stretton's campaigning concern for the welfare of children. It was widely translated, and was for a while (by order of Tsar Alexander II) compulsory reading in all Russian schools.She also wrote well-received novels for adults, including *The Doctor's Dilemma* (1872) and *Through a Needle's Eye* (1879).

Strindberg, (Johan) August (1849–1912) Swedish author and playwright. His works are marked by a deeply neurotic response to religion, social class, and sexuality; he married three times, gained a reputation for anti-feminism and misogyny, and was tried for blasphemy, though acquitted. His first important play, *Master Olof* (written 1872–7; performed 1881), was followed by *The Father* (1887), *Miss Julie* (1888), and *Creditors* (1889), which combine a highly aggressive and original version of *naturalism with a sense of the extreme and pathological. His later works include *To Damascus* (1898–1901; 3 parts), *The Dance of Death* (1901), *A Dream Play* (1902), and *The Ghost Sonata* (1907), all distinctive, experimental plays which anticipate *Expressionism and which influenced the psychological and symbolic dramas of Eugene *O'Neill and the writers of the Theatre of the *Absurd.

Strindberg's non-dramatic works include a novel, *The Red Room* (1879), *Getting Married* (1884, 1885; 2 vols of short stories), which he wrote in response to *Ibsen's *A Doll's House*, and *Inferno* (written and published in French, 1898), an extraordinary account of his life in Paris after the collapse of his second marriage.

structuralism and post-structuralism
Broad schools of thought that arose in Paris from the 1950s to the 1970s. Structuralism aimed to create a single general 'science of signs' called semiotics or semiology and so to uncover the basic codes or systems of meaning underlying all human cultural activity. Post-structuralism abandons such grand scientific ambitions, while still roving freely among different cultural forms. Both share the same founding principle, which is the primacy of 'Language', conceived as an abstract system of differences, over the human mind, hitherto assumed to be the autonomous maker of all meanings, which is demoted to a subordinate position as 'the subject' generated by Language. This agreed, structuralism and post-structuralism disagree on whether Language is knowably fixed as an object of science, or unstably indeterminate and slippery. Opposed conclusions about the relations between literature and science follow: for structuralism, fictional texts are to be seen as instances of scientific laws, while post-structuralism often regards scientific laws as instances of textual fictions.

The origins of these movements lie in the foundation of modern linguistics by Ferdinand de Saussure, who redirected the study of languages away from 'diachronic' questions of their historical development and towards 'synchronic' study of their workings at a given time. Structuralism and post-structuralism avoid historical enquiry into the origins of phenomena. Saussure's second condition for the reconstruction of linguistics as a science was that its object of study should be, not individual utterances and their meanings (*parole*), but the system of rules and distinctions (the *langue*) that underlies them in a given language. So structuralism shows less interest in what a cultural product (a poem, an advertisement, a culinary ritual) may mean than in the implicit rules that allow it to mean something. The key principle of Saussure's linguistic theory is that a word is an 'arbitrary sign': that is, its form and meaning derive not from any natural quality of its referent in the world outside language, but solely from its differences from other words. Meanings are not to be found 'in' words but only through the differential relations between them, as conventionally established within a given language. Structuralism and post-structuralism alike are founded upon this principle of the 'relational' nature of signification. Abstracting from Saussure's work, which applies to the analysis of a given language such as English, they often invoke 'Language' as such, as a self-contained realm or general principle of differentiation. This permits the discovery of 'Language' in realms not usually regarded as properly linguistic: cuisine, costume, dance, and structures of kinship, for example, may all be read as 'sign-systems'. For the influential structuralist psychoanalyst Jacques *Lacan, it is Language that turns infants into human 'subjects', splitting their minds into conscious and unconscious levels as they enter its system of interchangeable pronouns.

After Saussure, the second founding father was the Russian linguist Roman Jakobson (1896–1982), initially of the Russian *formalist school. Jakobson helped to shape the ideas of the leading French structuralists of the 1960s—Claude *Lévi-Strauss, Roland *Barthes, Lacan, and the Marxist philosopher Louis Althusser (1918–90)—with his claim that the basic principles by which all sign-systems combine their elements into meaningful compounds are those of *metaphor and *metonymy.

As applied to the analysis of particular literary works, the structuralist method is not concerned with critical evaluation, but with uncovering the basic 'binary oppositions' (nature/culture, male/female, active/passive, etc.) that govern the text. It rejects traditional conceptions in which literature is held to express an author's meaning or to reflect the real world; instead, it regards the 'text' as a self-contained structure in which conventional codes of meaning are activated. In the English-speaking world, some critics such as Frank *Kermode, David *Lodge, and Jonathan Culler adopted elements of structuralist analysis.

Post-structuralism cannot be disentangled fully from structuralism: some of its leading figures, notably Barthes, move from one to the other. In general, post-structuralism pursues structuralist arguments about the autonomy of Language from the world, to the point at which structuralism's own authority is undermined. The philosophical pioneer in this new phase was Jacques *Derrida, who began to unpick the logic of structuralism in 1966, questioning the founding concepts of 'structure' and 'binary opposition'. Under his re-examination, fixed structures appear to dissolve, binary opposites appear to contaminate one another, and determinate meanings become indeterminate. Post-structuralism challenges the 'scientific' pretensions, not only of structuralism but of other explanatory systems, by appealing to the inherent uncertainty of Language. In particular, it discredits all 'metalanguages' (that is, uses of language that purport to explain other uses: linguistics, philosophy, criticism, etc.) by pointing out that they are just as unreliable as the kinds of language they claim to comprehend. Post-structuralism usually allows no appeal to a reality outside Language; instead, it sees every kind of 'discourse' as circularly self-confirming. This is not the same as denying the existence of a real world outside Language, although Derrida's notorious declaration that 'il n'y a pas d'hors-texte' gave that impression. The radical scepticism of this movement reflected in part the libertarian politics of the 1960s and in part the influence of Friedrich *Nietzsche, in its rejection of 'hierarchical' and 'totalitarian' systems of thought, its denial of objectivity, and its hostility to the 'grand narratives' of historical explanation associated with the *Enlightenment.

In terms of linguistic theory, the distinctive view of post-structuralism is that the 'signifier' (a written word, for example) is not fixed to a particular 'signified' (a concept), and so all meanings are provisional. Derrida's philosophical account of this idea found support in the psychoanalytic teachings of Lacan. Lacan's writings created an intersection of psychological, linguistic, and political concerns in which much post-structuralist theory operates, notably the work of Julia *Kristeva, Gilles *Deleuze, and Jean-François *Lyotard. A similar conjunction characterizes the work of Michel *Foucault. In the social sciences and beyond, this body of post-structuralist theory encouraged cultural relativism and the associated view that our models of reality are 'constructed' in Language or discourse. It also shaped the concept of *postmodernism.

In academic literary criticism, post-structuralism has won a greater influence than the more narrowly scientific propositions of structuralism, partly because it respects such literary values as verbal complexity and paradox. Post-structuralist literary theory and criticism have assumed varied forms, from the kind of linguistic and rhetorical analysis inspired by Derrida and known as *deconstruction, to the *New Historicism inspired by Foucault. They include a version of *feminist criticism associated with the work of Kristeva. Barthes's writings of the 1970s present the process of reading less as a decoding of structures than as a kind of erotic sport. Both Barthes and Kristeva championed *modernist literary experiment, in which they detected a politically liberating value opposed to the conservative implications of literary *realism.

STUBBES (Stubbs), Philip (*c.*1555–*c.*1610) A *Puritan pamphleteer, author of *The Anatomy of Abuses* (1583), a denunciation of contemporary evil customs which, in the author's opinion, needed abolition. It contains a section on stage plays and is one of the principal sources of information on the social and economic conditions of the period. His account of his wife Katherine, who died aged 19, *A Chrystal Glass for Christian Women* (1591), was very popular.

STUBBS, William (1825–1901) Historian and bishop of Oxford. Appointed Regius professor of modern history at Oxford in 1866. He may be said to have created the discipline of English medieval history single-handed. His great *Constitutional History of [Medieval] England*, 3 vols (1874–8), has been described as 'one of the most astonishing achievements of the Victorian mind', fit to rank with Charles Darwin's **Origin of Species*.

Stukeley A character in George Peele's **Battle of Alcazar*. The real Thomas Stucley (*c.*1520–1578) was said to be a natural son of *Henry VIII. An adventurer, spy, soldier, and pirate, he was killed at the battle of Alacazar.

Sturm und Drang [Storm and Stress] The term applied to a period of cultural ferment prevailing in Germany during the latter part of the 18th century and to the associated movements in literature and music. The name itself derives from the title of a play by F. M. Klinger (1752–1831) of 1776 about the American Revolution. The literary movement, which was greatly influenced by Jean-Jacques *Rousseau, was characterized by a revolt against highly sophisticated literary conventions and a preference for folk poetry, the cult of genius and veneration of *Shakespeare, a 'return to nature', and the expression of extreme emotion. It is generally represented as a challenge to *Enlightenment values and a precursor of *Romanticism. The principal figures of the movement were J. G. Hamann (1730–88), the young Johann Wolfgang von *Goethe, Johann Gottfried *Herder, J. M. R. Lenz (1751–92), and Friedrich von *Schiller.

STYRON, William, Jr (1925–2006) American novelist, who created controversy with *The Confessions of Nat Turner* (1967), about the 1831 slave revolt. *Sophie's Choice* (1979) describes a survivor of the Holocaust. *This Quiet Dust* (1982) collects Styron's non-fiction and *Darkness Visible* (1990) is a memoir of depression.

sublime A concept associated with awe, vastness, natural magnificence, and strong emotion, which fascinated 18th-century literary critics and aestheticians. Its development marks a movement away from *neo-classicism towards *Romanticism; it was connected with the idea of original genius which soars powerfully above rules and constraints. Sublimity was first analysed in an anonymous Greek work, *On the Sublime*, attributed to *Longinus, which was widely admired in England after Nicholas *Boileau's French translation of 1674. The concept was elaborated by many writers, including Alexander *Pope, Joseph *Addison, John Dennis, David *Hume, and Hugh *Blair. The most widely read work on the subject was Burke's *Philosophical Enquiry into the Origin of our Ideas of the *Sublime and Beautiful* (1757), which put a new emphasis on terror as 'productive of the strongest emotion which the mind is capable of feeling'. Longinus had described the immensity of objects in the natural world, such as stars, mountains, volcanoes, and the ocean, as a source of the sublime, and this idea was of profound importance to a growing appreciation of the grandeur and violence of nature. Enthusiasm for wild scenery and cosmic grandeur was already apparent in the writings of Edward *Young and James *Thomson; the poems of Thomas *Gray, the Ossianic writings of James *Macpherson, and the *Gothic novels of Ann *Radcliffe also promoted sublime landscapes. Many 18th-century writers making the *Grand Tour dwelt on the sublimity of the Alps, comparing them with the pictures of Salvator Rosa, whose stormy landscapes provided a pattern for 18th-century depictions of savage nature. From the 1760s travellers began to seek out the exhilarating perils of the remote mountain peak and the gloomy forest; sublimity became a fashion. The *Romantic poets rejected the categories of the 18th-century theorists, but the works of William *Blake, P. B. *Shelley, and William *Wordsworth in particular reflect the development of sublime aesthetics.

Sublime and Beautiful, *A Philosophical Enquiry into the Origin of our Ideas of the* A treatise by Edmund *Burke, published anonymously in 1757, with an 'Introduction on Taste' added in 1759. Burke distinguishes between the *sublime, which suggests infinity, vastness, darkness, solitude, and terror, and inspires a drive to self-preservation, and the beautiful, which consists in relative smallness, smoothness, and brightness of colour, and promotes an instinct for sociability. The treatise coincided with a renewed interest in wild landscapes, pre-civilized writing (*see* PRIMITIVISM), and the imagination. Burke's new emphasis on the power of the emotions, and of terror in particular, gave the *Gothic novel some legitimacy, but the treatise also had a strong influence on continental aestheticians such as G. E. Lessing and Immanuel *Kant.

SUCKLING, Sir John (1609–42) Poet and dramatist. From 1632 he lived at court in great splendour. He became a leader of the Royalist party in the early troubles, then fled to France and is said by John *Aubrey to have committed suicide in Paris. His chief works are included in *Fragmenta Aurea* (1646) and consist of poems, plays, letters, and tracts. His 'Sessions of the Poets', in which various writers of the day, including Ben *Jonson, Thomas *Carew, and Sir William *D'Avenant, contend for the laurel, was written in 1637, and is interesting as an expression of contemporary opinion on these writers. Suckling's play *Aglaura* (with two fifth acts, one tragic, the other not) was lavishly staged and printed in 1638 at his own expense. Later plays include *The Goblins* (1646), a romantic drama said by John *Dryden to illustrate Suckling's professed admiration for William *Shakespeare; and *Brennoralt* (1646), an expansion of the *Discontented Colonel* (1640), a tragedy. The plays are, however, chiefly valuable for their lyrics, and Suckling has enjoyed a steady reputation as one of the most elegant and brilliant of the *Cavalier poets. According to Aubrey, he invented the game of cribbage. *See* FALKLAND, LUCIUS.

SUETONIUS (Gaius Suetonius Tranquillus) (*c.* AD 70–*c.*130) Roman biographer whose major surviving work, the *Lives of the Caesars*, was composed in part while he was in charge of the imperial archives. Suetonius, writing about the Julio-Claudian and Flavian emperors under a new dynasty, saw no reason to treat them as heroes. His aim was to bring out the moral (or immoral) character of his subjects, and he paid attention to their private habits as well as to their imperial policy. His method was adopted by later Roman biographers. Philemon *Holland translated *Twelve Caesars* (1605), and Thomas *De Quincey imitated and expanded Suetonius in *The Caesars* (1853). The flavour of his writing has been best caught by Robert *Graves in *I, Claudius* and *Claudius the God*.

Sūfī A follower of Sūfism, Islamic mysticism, which originated in the 8th century. Sūfism has always attracted many devotees, including important authors in all the major Islamic languages. Its influence was particularly pervasive in Persian poetry, and it was translations from Persian by Sir William *Jones and Edward *FitzGerald that first brought it to the notice of English readers. Another channel was the German translations of Persian poetry taken up by Ralph Waldo *Emerson.

SUKENICK, Ronald (1932–2004) America writer, whose writer whose novels are usually meta-narratives exploiting different aspects of language and narrative construction, as in *Out* (1973) and *Blown Away* (1986). He founded the *Fiction Collective and his essays on fiction are collected in *In Form* (1985). *Down and In* (1987) is a memoir of the counter-culture.

SULLIVAN, Sir Arthur (1842–1900) English composer. Best known for his collaborations on the Gilbert and Sullivan operas, Sullivan had a distinguished career as a composer in his own right. His Opus 1 was a group of twelve pieces of incidental music for *The *Tempest*: their first performance in London (1862) made Sullivan famous, winning the approval of Charles *Dickens. His *Five Shakespeare Songs* (1866) were among the earliest of an enormous number of songs and ballads for the Victorian drawing room, of which 'The Lost Chord', to a poem by Adelaide *Procter, is the most famous. Sullivan also composed hymn tunes, including the melody for 'Onward, Christian soldiers'.

'Sumer is icumen in' One of the earliest known English lyrics, found in British Library MS Harley 978, a miscellany of Reading Abbey from the first half of the 13th century. The music, and Latin instructions for singing it, are also in the manuscript.

Summer's Last Will and Testament A play by Thomas *Nashe, published 1600, but written in the autumn of 1592 or 1593. It is framed by the playful comments of Will Summers, *Henry VIII's* jester (who died *c.*1560), and is an allegorical pageant in which Summer, seen as a dying old man, decides who should inherit his riches. The play reflects fear of the plague, of which there was a prolonged outbreak in 1592–3.

'Summoner's Tale, The' *See* CANTERBURY TALES, 8.

Supposes A comedy in prose, one of the earliest in English, by George *Gascoigne, translated from *Ariosto's *I suppositi*, and performed at Gray's Inn in 1566. It concerns a series of disguises and confused identities; the scenes with servants are effectively comic, especially those with the old nurse Balia. It influenced *Shakespeare's *The *Taming of the Shrew*.

'Surgeon's Daughter, The' A tale by Walter *Scott, set in India, published 1827 as one of the stories in the *Chronicles of the Canongate*. The orphaned Richard Middlemas is reared with Dr Gideon Grey's daughter Menie, whom he later lures to India to be sold as a concubine to Tippoo Sahib. Menie is rescued but dies single; Richard is killed on the order of Hyder Ali, a local potentate and Tippoo's father, by being trampled to death by an elephant.

'Surprised by joy—impatient as the wind' A sonnet by William *Wordsworth, first published in 1815, suggested by the death of his daughter Catherine in 1812, but written, by his own account, 'long after'.

Surrealism An artistic and literary movement founded in Paris as a breakaway from the Dada group by André Breton with his first *Manifeste du Surréalisme* (1924). It was conceived as a revolutionary mode of thought and action in politics, philosophy, and psychology as well as literature and art. The *Manifeste* attacked rationalism and 'bourgeois' logic: drawing on Sigmund *Freud's theories of the unconscious and its relation to dreams, it called for the exploration of hidden and neglected areas of the human psyche, and the resolution 'of the apparently contradictory states of dream and reality'. Breton's group of writers, painters, and film-makers, mostly French and Spanish, experimented with automatic processes, which were considered the best means of producing the surreal poetic image: the spontaneous coupling of unrelated objects. The principal literary works of the group were Louis *Aragon's *Le Paysan de Paris* (1926), Breton's *Nadja* (1928), and the poems of Paul Éluard. In the 1930s several Surrealists joined the Communist Party. Surrealism was a significant intellectual current between the wars. In England the movement attracted some attention among literary circles, but it was only after the appearance of the youthful David *Gascoigne's *Short Survey of Surrealism* (1935) and the International Surrealist Exhibition of June 1936 in London that a Surrealist group was formed, its members including Gascoyne, Herbert *Read, Roland Penrose (1900–84), Humphrey *Jennings, Roger Roughton (1916–41), and Hugh Sykes Davies (1909–84). The impact of Surrealism can be felt in the early stories of Dylan *Thomas, in Lawrence *Durrell's *The Black Book* (1938), and in the poems of Gascoyne, Charles *Madge, and Sykes Davies, among others. The legacy of Surrealism was repeatedly drawn upon by postwar writers in English, notably by the American poets Frank *O'Hara, John *Ashbery, and Robert Bly.

(((⊕))) SEE WEB LINKS
• Tate Gallery Surrealism Centre

SURREY, Henry Howard, earl of (by courtesy) (1516/17–1547) Poet, the son of Thomas Howard (1473–1554; afterwards third duke of Norfolk). He was with the army during the war with France (1544–6). Accused of various minor offences, he was, tried and executed on the charge of treasonably quartering the royal arms. His works consist of sonnets, poems, and translations in various metres notable for their elegance of construction. Like Sir Thomas *Wyatt he studied Italian models, especially *Petrarch, but his sonnets were predominantly in the 'English' form (*ababcdcdefefgg*), later to be used by *Shakespeare, which appears to have been his invention (*see* SONNET). A still more durable innovation was his use of blank verse in his translation of the *Aeneid*, Books 2 and 4. Forty of his poems were printed by Richard *Tottel in his *Miscellany* (1557).

SURTEES, Robert Smith (1805–64) Journalist and novelist. From 1830 he built up a reputation as a sporting journalist, and in 1831 founded (with Rudolph Ackermann) and edited the *New Sporting Magazine* to which he contributed his comic sketches of Mr Jorrocks, sporting cockney grocer, later collected as *Jorrocks's Jaunts and Jollities* (1838, initially illustrated by 'Phiz', the pseudonym of Hablot Knight *Browne). Jorrocks, whose adventures to some extent suggested the original idea of *Pickwick Papers*, reappears in *Handley Cross* (1843; expanded and illustrated by John Leech, 1854), one of Surtees's most successful novels, and in *Hillingdon Hall* (1845). Mr Soapey Sponge appears in the popular *Mr Sponge's Sporting Tour* (1853, illustrated by Leech), and Mr Facey Romford appears in his last novel, *Mr Facey Romford's Hounds* (1865). Surtees's eight long novels deal mainly with characteristic aspects of English fox-hunting society, but his vivid caricatures and the absurd scenes he describes, together with his convincing dialect, frequent catchphrases, and perceptive social observation distinguish him from other writers of this genre and won praise from W. M. *Thackeray and others.

Survey of London, A See STOW, JOHN.

'Suspiria de Profundis' Visionary prose by Thomas *De Quincey, published 1846 in *Blackwood's Magazine*, and a companion piece to his *Confessions of an English Opium Eater*. It contains the remarkable 'Levana and our Ladies of Sorrow', a description of the author's dreams of the goddess Levana.

SUTCLIFF, Rosemary (1920–92) CBE, novelist; she suffered from Still's disease and was confined to a wheelchair for much of her life; disability features in many of her books. Sutcliff remains the foremost writer of historical novels for children (although her books are essentially *crossover books); her major theme is reconciliation. She wrote about many historical periods, from the prehistoric (*Warrior Scarlet*, 1958) through the Roman (*The Eagle of the Ninth*, 1954) and Arthurian (*Sword at Sunset*, 1963) to the Saxon invasions of England (*Dawn Wind*, 1961). She is noted for her sense of historical continuity (symbolized by a signet ring that passes from generation to generation of her characters), and of developing appropriate argots for each period. She won the Carnegie Medal for *The Lantern Bearers* (1959). Her final published book was *Sword Song* (1997). *Blue Remembered Hills* (1983) is autobiographical.

SVEVO, Italo (1861–1928) Pseudonym of Ettore Schmitz, Italian novelist, born in Trieste from a Jewish Italo-German background (indicated by his pen-name). His novels are: *Una vita* (1892: *A Life*), *Senilità* (1898: a title translated by James *Joyce as *As a Man Grows Older*), *La coscienza del Zeno* (1923: *Confessions of Zeno*), *La novella del buon vecchio e della bella fanciulla* (1926: *The Tale of the Good Old Man and of the Lovely Young Girl*). He was working on a fifth novel, *Il vecchione* (1967: *The Grand Old Man*), when he died in a car crash. Svevo's work was unknown until Joyce helped him to publish his masterpiece, *Confessions of Zeno*, a complex novel in which time and point of view are relative. Arguing with his psychoanalyst, Zeno struggles with chance, time, marriage, and tobacco, disclosing the source of his malady as the Oedipus complex.

Swallows and Amazons (1930) Arthur *Ransome's novel about children sailing and camping in the Lake District, noted for its egalitarian tone, slow pace, circular construction, and adherence to family codes. The first in a sequence of twelve, it was adapted for television in 1963 and filmed in 1985.

Swan Theatre Built by Frances Langley on the Bankside in London in 1595, and closed down temporarily in 1597, following a performance by Lord Pembroke's Company of Ben *Jonson and Thomas *Nashe's controversial play *The Isle of Dogs*. The Lady Elizabeth's Company is believed to have performed *A *Chaste Maid in Cheapside* there around 1613. Johannes de Witt's sketch (*c*.1596) of the theatre is believed to be the only surviving representation of the interior of an Elizabethan playhouse. The name was adopted by the Royal Shakespeare Company for its galleried playhouse, which opened in Stratford in 1986.

SWANWICK, Michael (1950–) American *science fiction writer. *Stations of the Tide* (1991) and *Jack Faust* (1997) are convincing multi-layered revoicings of The *Tempest and *Faust.

SWEDENBORG, Emanuel (1688–1772) Swedish philosopher, scientist, and mystic. Towards the end of his long career as a scientist he became concerned with uncovering the spiritual structure of the universe, and he began to experience visions and to converse with angels, not only in his dreams, but, he claimed, in his waking life. His prolific writings, mostly in Latin, were designed to promote his peculiar interpretation of the Bible. Swedenborg died in London, and his followers there organized themselves into the New Jerusalem Church, of which William *Blake was for a while an active member. Blake was initially deeply influenced by Swedenborg's writings, which began to appear in English from the 1760s, but he then parodied them mercilessly. Ralph *Emerson, Henry James, Sr, and W. B. *Yeats were also devotees of Swedenborg.

SWEENEY, Matthew (1952–) Irish poet and children's writer. His collections include *A Round House* (1983), *Blue Shoes* (1989), *A Smell of Fish* (2000), and *Black Moon* (2007). Influences from Franz *Kafka and Charles *Simic as well as from oral tradition are detectable in Sweeney's strange, often sinister, verse narratives. His work for children includes fiction (*The Snow Vulture*, 1992; *Fox*, 2003) and poetry (*Up on the Roof: New and Selected Poems*, 2001).

Sweeney, the Frenzy of (*Buile Shuibhne*) 12th-century Irish text surviving in one 17th- and one 18th-century manuscript. Mixing prose and verse, it tells of the madness that overtook Sweeney, an Ulster king, at the 7th-century battle of Mag Rath (Moira, Co. Down) as a result of the curse of St Ronan, whose psalter he had cast into a lake. Sweeney flies from perch to perch in Ireland and Scotland, living off berries and alternately cursing his condition and praising the landscape in a series of impassioned lyrics. In *The White Goddess* Robert *Graves describes *Buile Shuibhne* as 'the most ruthless and bitter description in all European literature of an obsessed poet's predicament'. Sweeney features as an alter ego of Seamus *Heaney in 'Sweeney Redivivus' (1984) and as a character in Flann *O'Brien's *At Swim-Two-Birds* and Neil *Gaiman's *American Gods*. Heaney has translated the 18th-century manuscript version as *Sweeney Astray* (1983).

SWEET, Henry (1845–1912) A great phonetician and, after A. J. Ellis (1814–90) one of the founders of that study in England. He is said to have been the inspiration for George Bernard *Shaw's Henry Higgins in *Pygmalion*. His works are still a staple of the study of Old English and the philology of English; the most celebrated are *History of English Sounds* (1874, 1888); *Anglo-Saxon Reader* (1876); *Anglo-Saxon Primer* (1882); *A New English Grammar* (1892, 1898); *The History of Language* (1900); and *The Sounds of English: An Introduction to Phonetics* (1908).

SWIFT, Graham (1949–) Novelist and short story writer. *Shuttlecock* (1981) features an archivist who unearths wartime secrets which question his father's integrity. *Learning to Swim* (1982) and *Chemistry* (2008) are collections of short stories. Focusing on a history teacher, *Waterland* (1984) intertwines a story of family disorder with a retrospective panorama of the English fen country. *Out of This World* (1988) about a troubled photo-journalist, and *Ever After* (1992), in which a professor who has attempted suicide turns to ancestral research, likewise delve into the past. *Last Orders* (1996, *Booker Prize-winner) is a poignant and funny novel in which four south Londoners journey to the coast to scatter a friend's ashes. Later novels include *The Light of Day* (2003), *Tomorrow* (2007), and *Wish You Were Here* (2011).

SWIFT, Jonathan (1667–1745) Clergyman and writer. In 1689 he became secretary to Sir William *Temple. In 1695 Swift was ordained in the Church of Ireland and in 1697 wrote *The *Battle of the Books*, which was published in 1704 with *A *Tale of a Tub*. On the death of Temple in 1699, Swift went again to Ireland. In the course of frequent visits to London he became acquainted with Joseph *Addison, Richard *Steele, and Congreve. He was entrusted in 1707 with a mission to obtain the grant of Queen Anne's Bounty for Ireland. His poems of London life, 'Description of a City Shower' and 'Description of the Morning', appeared in the *Tatler* (1709).

From 1710 Swift aligned himself with the Tory ministry of Robert Harley and Viscount Bolingbroke; he attacked the Whig ministers in *The Virtues of Sid Hamet the Magician's Rod* (1710), and in the *Examiner*. Swift's *Proposal for Correcting, Improving and Ascertaining the English Tongue* (1712) was one of the few works to bear his name. He was appointed dean of St Patrick's in 1713, Queen Anne having apparently vetoed any high preferment in England. In 1714 he became friendly with like-minded wits such as Alexander *Pope, John *Arbuthnot, John *Gay, meeting at the short-lived *Scriblerus Club, but in August that year he returned to Ireland. During his time in London Swift had written the so-called *Journal to Stella* (1766), a series of intimate, teasing letters (1710–13) to Esther Johnson, giving a vivid account of Swift's daily life in London in the company of the Tory ministers. Stella was Swift's closest female companion; the *Journal* mentions his meeting with another woman, Esther Vanhomrigh (pron. 'Vanummery'; d. 1723); his relationship with her is playfully portrayed in the poem *Cadenus and Vanessa*.

Swift now occupied himself with Irish affairs. His *Drapier's Letters* (1724) prevented the introduction of 'Wood's half-pence' into Ireland. He came to England in 1726 and published *Gulliver's Travels*, with its bitter allegory of Irish independence, in the same year. He paid a last visit to England in 1727, returning to Ireland in time to witness the death of Stella (28 January 1728). Swift continued to publicize the problems faced by Ireland in *A Short View of the State of Ireland* (1728) and *A *Modest Proposal* (1729). His more important poems include *Verses on the Death of Dr Swift* (1731; pub. 1739), in which he reviews his life and work with ironic detachment, and the satirical *On Poetry, a Rhapsody* (1733). Poems such as *The Lady's Dressing-Room, A Beautiful Young Nymph Going to Bed*, and *Strephon and Chloe*, once considered obscene or misogynistic, are now seen as refusing to adopt patronizingly 'polite' attitudes towards women. His last prose works were the ironic *Directions to Servants* (written about 1731 and published after his death) and his *Complete Collection of Polite and Ingenious Conversation* (1738). The *Memoirs* of Laetitia *Pilkington contain much material relating to Swift's personality and behaviour. In 1735 the Dublin printer George Faulkner (1699–1755) published the first major collected edition of his work. He was buried by the side of Stella, in St Patrick's, Dublin, his own famous epitaph 'ubi saeva indignatio ulterius cor lacerare nequit' (where fierce indignation cannot further tear apart the heart) being inscribed on his tomb.

SWINBURNE, Algernon Charles (1837–1909) Poet and critic. He was associated at Oxford with Dante Gabriel *Rossetti, and the *Pre-Raphaelite circle. His first published volume, *The Queen-Mother and Rosamond* (1860), echoes Elizabethan dramatists, notably George *Chapman. *Atalanta in Calydon* (1865), a drama in classical Greek form, with choruses that revealed his exceptional metrical skills, brought him celebrity; *Chastelard* (1865), the first of three dramas on the subject of *Mary Queen of Scots, raised some doubts about the morality of Swinburne's verse, doubts reinforced by the first series of *Poems and Ballads* (1866). The volume contains many of his best poems (*'Dolores', 'Itylus', 'Hymn to Proserpine', 'The Triumph of Time', 'Faustine', 'Laus Veneris', etc.) which clearly demonstrate preoccupations with non-Christian belief structures, moral conundrums, distracting beauties, the links between sex and pain. Swinburne had a complicated regard for Christianity. Thomas *Hardy makes his heroine Sue Bridehead (in *Jude the Obscure*) an admirer of his rejection of Christian belief. *A Song of Italy* (1867) and *Songs before Sunrise* (1871) express his support for Mazzini in the struggle for Italian independence, and an impatience with authority which connects him to William *Blake, of whom Swinburne was an early and important admirer. *Poems and Ballads: Second Series* (1878) contains 'A Forsaken Garden', richly imbued with resistance to Christianity. Swinburne's health was seriously undermined by heavy drinking. In 1879 he moved to Putney with his friend Theodore *Watts-Dunton, who gradually weaned him from alcoholism. Later volumes include *Mary Stuart* (1881), *Tristram of Lyonesse and Other Poems* (1882), *Marino Faliero* (1885, a tragedy on the same subject as Lord *Byron's), and the elegiac *Poems and Ballads: Third Series* (1889).

Swinburne wrote extensively in classical metres, and commanded an exceptional variety of verse forms, including burlesques, modern and mock-antique ballads, and roundels. His prose works include two novels, *A Year's Letters* (serialized pseudonymously 1877; republished 1905 as *Love's Cross Currents*) and the sado-masochistic 'flogging novel' *Lesbia Brandon* (ed. R. Hughes, 1952). He was an important channel through which elements from contemporary French verse, including Charles *Baudelaire's, entered British culture. Swinburne was a critic of originality and brilliance; his studies of Chapman (1875), Christopher *Marlowe (1883, *Encyclopaedia Britannica*), Thomas *Middleton (1887), Cyril *Tourneur (1889, *EB*), and others were the first important successors to Charles *Lamb in the revival of interest in Elizabethan and Jacobean drama.

SWINDELLS, Robert (1939–) Writer; he had little formal education before becoming a teacher. His *young adult novels move between social critique and the supernatural: *Brother in the Land* (1984) is about a nuclear holocaust; *Stone Cold* (1993), murdered homeless teenagers; *Abomination* (1998), abusive Christian parents.

SWINNERTON, Frank (1884–1982) Critic and prolific novelist. His novels, often set in contemporary London, include *Nocturne* (1917, his greatest success) and *Harvest Comedy* (1937). He was literary critic of *Truth and Nation*, the *Evening News*, and the *Observer*. His knowledge of the period provided material for his literary reminiscences, notably *The Georgian Literary Scene* (1935), and two autobiographical works, *Swinnerton: An Autobiography* (1937) and *Reflections from a Village* (1969). *Arnold Bennett: A Last Word* (1978) appeared in his 94th year.

Swiss Family Robinson, The The story of a family wrecked on a desert island, written in German by Johann David Wyss (1743–1818), a Swiss pastor. Firmly Christian and moral in tone, it was published in two parts in Zurich in 1812–13. The first English translation came a year later. 'Robinson' refers to Daniel *Defoe's *Robinson Crusoe*; it is not the name of the family. The tale survives, usually expanded and changed, in many different forms, including numerous film and television adaptations.

sword and sorcery Term used to describe the heroic *fantasy exemplified (though not originated) by Robert E. *Howard's 'Conan the Barbarian' stories, published in *Weird Tales* in the 1930s. Conan gained a new lease of life in the 1970s with reprints and 'new' stories composed by L. Sprague *de Camp, Lin *Carter, and others. The term was coined by Fritz Leiber whose 'Newhon' series added irony and character interplay to the simple 'barbarian fights supernatural monster' format. The surprising flexibility of the form was further exploited by writers including C. L. Moore, Samuel R. Delany, and Michael *Moorcock.

SYAL, Meera (1963–) British-born writer, actor, and comedian. She wrote the script for Gurinder Chadha's film *Bhaji on the Beach* (1994) and is well known as a writer and actor in the television series *Goodness Gracious Me* and *The Kumars at No. 42*. Her novels *Anita and Me* (1996) and *Life Isn't All Ha Ha Hee Hee* (1999) explore satirically and sympathetically the position of British Asian girls and women.

Sybil, *or The Two Nations* A novel by Benjamin *Disraeli, published 1845; the second book of the trilogy *Coningsby—Sybil—*Tancred*. Like *Coningsby*, it celebrates the ideas of the 'Young England' Tories and was designed to describe 'the Condition of the People' and of the 'Two Nations of England, the Rich and the Poor' (*see* SOCIAL PROBLEM NOVEL). In this ambitious book, Disraeli suggests reforms a generation before his government was able to introduce them. Poverty and oppression are described with feeling, and the radical *Chartist spirit is sympathetically shown in Gerard, Morley, and others; aspects of the wealthy social and political world are described with ironic contempt.

Charles Egremont, younger brother of the pitiless landowner Lord Marney, falls in love with the beautiful Sybil, the daughter of the Chartist Walter Gerard, who is loved by Stephen Morley, a radical and atheist. When Sybil refuses Egremont because of his rank, he sets out to discover the true condition of the poor in Mowbray and to understand the feelings of the Chartists and incendiaries. Much of the narrative is concerned with the development of the Chartist rising. Five years of increasing poverty culminate in violent riots, in which Gerard is killed, Lord Marney stoned to death, and Morley shot. Egremont rescues Sybil, and the pair are later married.

syllabics Lines of verse composed according to a regular counting of the number of syllables to a line, regardless of stress patterns (*see* METRE). Syllabic verse is the standard metrical principle of modern Romance languages such as French, as it is in Chinese and Japanese; but in English poetry it is a minor tradition of modern experiment inaugurated by Robert *Bridges

in 'Poor Poll' (1921), and adapted later in some poems by W. H. *Auden, Dylan *Thomas, Marianne *Moore, Thom *Gunn, and Sylvia *Plath, among others. Uniform length of lines is favoured by some practitioners, as for instance in the twelve-syllable line of Bridges's long poem *The Testament of Beauty* (1929); but Moore and others favoured *stanza forms combining lines of different lengths. The *haiku, imported from the Japanese, is the most widely practised syllabic form.

syllepsis A figure of speech by which a word, or a particular form or inflection of a word, is made to refer to two or more words in the same sentence, while properly applying to them in different senses: e.g. 'Miss Bolo . . . went home in a flood of tears and a sedan chair' (Dickens, *Pickwick Papers*, ch. 35). *See also* ZEUGMA.

SYLVESTER, Josuah (*c*.1563–1618) A London merchant, whose translation into rhyming couplets of *The Divine Weeks and Works* of Du Bartas was, according to John *Davies of Hereford, 'admir'd of all'. The first instalment appeared in 1592, more in 1598, further parts in 1605-7, and a complete translation in 1608, which was reprinted for the fifth time in 1641. Sylvester's other works include poems in the important collection *Lachrymae Lachrymarum* (1613). This contained elegies by Joseph *Hall and John *Donne, among others, on Prince Henry.

Sylvia's Lovers A novel by Elizabeth *Gaskell, published 1863; her only historical novel. The scene is the whaling port of Monkshaven (based on Whitby in Yorkshire) during the Napoleonic Wars, and the plot hinges on the activities of the press-gangs, whose seizure of Monkshaven men to man naval warships provokes bitter resentment. The book is particularly notable for its early chapters, with their vivid reconstruction of life in the little town dominated by the whaling industry (which Gaskell carefully researched) and at the farm where noisy, unreasonable Daniel Robson, his quiet, devoted wife, and their sturdy old servant Kester combine to cherish the lovely but hapless Sylvia. Gaskell felt that this tale of betrayal and irremediable loss was 'the saddest story I ever wrote'.

Symbolism, symbolists A group of French writers of the 19th century. The term is widely applied, but in its most useful and restricted sense refers to the period *c*.1880-95. The movement may be seen as a reaction against dominant *realist and *naturalist tendencies in literature generally and, in the case of poetry, against the descriptive precision and 'objectivity' of the Parnassians. The symbolists stressed the priority of suggestion and evocation over direct description and explicit analogy, and the symbol was identified as an important means of distilling a private mood, or evoking subtle affinities between the material and spiritual worlds. Symbolist writers were particularly concerned to explore the musical properties of language, through the interplay of suggestive sound relationships, and were influenced by Richard *Wagner's music dramas. Other influences on the movement were the mystical writings of *Swedenborg, and the poetry of Gérard de Nerval, Charles *Baudelaire, and Edgar Allan *Poe. Generally associated with the symbolist movement are: the poets Mallarmé, Paul *Verlaine, Arthur *Rimbaud, and Jules *Laforgue; the dramatists Auguste *Villiers de l'Isle-Adam and Maurice Maeterlinck; and the novelists Joris-Karl Huysmans and Édouard Dujardin (1861–1949), whose *Les Lauriers sont coupés* (1888: *The Laurels Are Cut*) influenced James *Joyce. The movement exercised an influence on a wide range of 20th-century writers, including Ezra *Pound, T. S. *Eliot, Wallace *Stevens, W. B. *Yeats, Joyce, Virginia *Woolf, Paul Claudel, Paul *Valéry, Stefan George (1868–1933), and Rainer Maria Rilke.

SYMONDS, John Addington (1840–93) Poet and critic. He was attracted by the Hellenism of the Renaissance, and both his prose and poetry reveal his interest in *Platonic love and his admiration for male beauty. His largest work, *Renaissance in Italy* (1875–86), is more picturesque than scholarly. His works include volumes on Ben *Jonson, Philip *Sidney, P. B. *Shelley, Walt *Whitman, and Michelangelo; collections of travel sketches and impressions; volumes of verse; a translation of the autobiography of Cellini (1888); and translations of Greek and Italian poetry. He increasingly acknowledged his own homosexuality, and discreetly campaigned for legal reform. His privately printed pamphlets *A Problem in Greek Ethics* (1883) and *A Problem in Modern Ethics* (1891) were reproduced in part by Havelock *Ellis in *Sexual Inversion* (1897).

SYMONS, A. J. A. (Alphonse James Albert) (1900–41) Writer and bibliographer; he became an authority on the literature of the 1890s and published *An Anthology of 'Nineties' Verse* (1928). He wrote several biographies, but is best remembered for *The *Quest for Corvo: An Experiment in Biography* (1934), a life of F. W. *Rolfe. *A. J. A. Symons: His Life and Speculations*

(1950), by his brother Julian *Symons, is a vivid evocation of his paradoxical personality and diverse interests as book-collector, dandy, and epicure.

SYMONS, Arthur William (1865–1945) Literary scholar and author. Symons was fascinated by French decadent poetry, which influenced the poems of his *Days and Nights* (1889) and *London Nights* (1895). In 1890 he joined the *Rhymers Club where he befriended W. B. *Yeats. Throughout the 1890s he was a proponent of *'art for art's sake', publishing an influential article, 'The Decadent Movement in Literature' (1892) and *The Symbolist Movement in England* (1899). He was editor of the *Savoy* (1896), which published, among others, Aubrey *Beardsley, Joseph *Conrad, and Ernest *Dowson; and wrote critical studies of writers including William *Blake, Charles *Baudelaire, Walter *Pater, and Oscar *Wilde.

SYMONS, Julian Gustave (1921–94) Crime writer, critic, biographer, and scholar of crime fiction, brother of A. J. A. *Symons. His many novels, which include *Bland Beginning* (1949) and *The Belting Inheritance* (1965), showed interests in anarchy, forgery, and bibliography. His survey of the genre, *Bloody Murder: From the Detective Story to the Crime Novel*, appeared in 1972. *See also* DETECTIVE FICTION.

synecdoche [pron. 'sinekdoki'] A figure of speech which substitutes a whole for a part or a part for a whole, e.g. 'the police are coming' to refer to one police officer, or 'Australia' in reference to its cricket team; conversely 'the Press' in reference to the world of newspapers, or 'per head' meaning per person. A special form of *metonymy, it is found especially in politics ('Westminster' for the British government, etc.) and sport. In literary uses it commonly takes the form of reference to a bodily part in place of a whole person (Blake: 'And did those feet in ancient time . . . ').

SYNGE, John Millington (1871–1909) Irish playwright and poet. He met W. B. *Yeats in 1896. Following a suggestion from Yeats, he went to the Aran Islands, and stayed there annually from 1898 to 1902, perfecting his Irish and collecting material that would form the basis of much of his drama. His six mature plays fuse Gaelic syntax and idioms with the rhythms of Hiberno-English to create a dramatic language simultaneously brutal and lyrical, realist and ironic. *In the Shadow of the Glen* (1903), *Riders to the Sea* (1904), *The Well of the Saints* (1905), and the extravagant comedy *The *Playboy of the Western World* were all produced at the *Abbey Theatre, of which Synge became a director in 1906. *The Tinker's Wedding* (written 1902) was first performed in London in 1908, as Yeats judged that its disrespectful portrayal of a priest would further inflame sentiment if staged in Dublin. Synge's sinewy, compact lyrics, many of them shadowed by his impending death, were published in *Poems and Translations* (1909). From 1897 Synge had suffered from Hodgkin's disease, and he brought his last play, *Deirdre of the Sorrows* (1910), close to completion as he was dying. It was finished by Yeats and Synge's fiancée Molly Allgood.

Syntax, Dr *See* COMBE, WILLIAM.

SZIRTES, George (1948–) Poet and translator, born in Budapest into a family of Jewish origin, who entered Britain as refugees in 1956. His first collection, *The Slant Door* (1979), was followed by *November and May* (1982). His return to Budapest in 1984 energized his writing and precipitated a string of acclaimed translations. His poetry, formally precise and subtly shaded with emotional and cultural complexities, explores themes of exile, identity, and the interdependent structures of personal and political experience. It has appeared in numerous volumes, including *Reel* (2004), which won the T. S. *Eliot Prize. He maintains a strong public profile and runs his own website and blog.

((⊕)) SEE WEB LINKS
• George Szirtes website

SZYMBORSKA, Wislawa (1923–) Polish poet. *People on a Bridge* (1986, trans. 1990) is among the most widely admired of her collections; recent volumes include *Moment* (2002); *Rhymes for Big Kids* (2003); and *Colon* (2005).

S

TACITUS, Cornelius (c. AD 56–after 117) The greatest historian of imperial Rome. His first work was a biography of his father-in-law Julius Agricola (98), followed by an ethnographical account of the German tribes. The former provides a useful description of Roman Britain, the latter contains one of the earliest representations of the Noble Savage (*see* PRIMITIVISM). He also wrote a dialogue on the shortcomings of contemporary oratory. His fame rests on his *Annals* and his *Histories*, which related events from the death of Augustus to the Flavian period. About a third of the *Histories* and over half of the *Annals* survive. Tacitus' aim was to keep alive the memory of virtuous and vicious actions so that posterity could judge them, and his great achievement was to have drawn a picture of how men must live under tyranny. Little known in the Middle Ages, Tacitus was rediscovered by *Boccaccio in the 14th century. The *Agricola* and the *Histories* were translated into English by Sir Henry Savile (1591), the *Germania* and *Annals* by Richard Grenewey (1598); after this Tacitus became in John *Donne's phrase the 'Oracle of Statesmen' or at least the model for historians such as Sir John Hayward and Francis *Bacon. He was also influential as a stylist in the 17th century, when attempts were made to imitate his concision and trenchancy.

TAGORE, Rabindranath (1861–1941) Most eminent modern Bengali poet. He was also critic, essayist, composer, and author of short fiction of a kind that was new to Bengali literature. He is known outside India principally in English translation. *Gitanjali: Song Offering* (1912), his free verse re-creations of his Bengali poems modelled on medieval Indian devotional lyrics, won him the *Nobel Prize for Literature in 1913, its first award to an Asian. Tagore had an excellent command of English, but he wrote primarily in Bengali and tirelessly encouraged writers of the Indian vernaculars.

tail-rhyme [translated from the Latin *rhythmus caudatus*] The measure associated in particular with a group of Middle English *romances in which a pair of rhyming lines is followed by a single line of different length and the three-line pattern is repeated to make up a six-line stanza. *Chaucer's 'Sir Thopas' (*see* CANTERBURY TALES, 17) is an example; six are edited by M. Mills in *Six Middle English Romances* (1973).

Táin-Bó-Cuailnge The chief epic of the Ulster cycle of Irish mythology, an account in prose and verse of the raid by Queen *Maeve of Connaught to secure the Brown Bull of Cooley, and her defeat by *Cuchulain. There are modern translations by Thomas *Kinsella (1969) and Ciaran *Carson (2007).

Tale of a Tub, A A comedy by Ben *Jonson, performed 1633, printed 1640. Various suitors, including John Clay the tile-maker, Squire Tub, and Justice Preamble, try to marry Audrey, the daughter of Toby Turf, high constable of Kentish Town. This was Jonson's last completed play.

Tale of a Tub, A A satire in prose by Jonathan *Swift, written, according to his own statement, about 1696, published anonymously in 1704. The main story tells of a father who leaves as a legacy to his three sons a coat apiece, with directions that on no account are the coats (which represent religion) to be altered. The sons are named Peter, to symbolize the *Roman Catholic Church, Martin (from Martin *Luther) to represent the *Church of England, and Jack (from John *Calvin), as the *Protestant Dissenter. The sons gradually disobey the terms of the will (that is, the *Bible). Martin and Jack quarrel with Peter (the Reformation), then with each other, and separate. The narrative is interspersed with digressions, on critics, on learning, 'in praise of digressions', and on madness. The *Tale* was one of Swift's own favourite works; its dizzying paradoxes, brilliant scientific parodies, and unsparing ironies have inspired much controversy since its publication.

Tale of Two Cities, A A novel by Charles *Dickens, published 1859. The 'two cities' are

Paris, at the time of the French Revolution, and London. Dr Manette, a French doctor, has been imprisoned in the Bastille for eighteen years, to secure his silence about the vicious crimes of the marquis de St Évremonde and his brother. He maintains a precarious sanity by cobbling shoes. When the story opens he is brought to England, where he gradually recovers his balance of mind. Charles Darnay, who conceals the fact that he is a nephew of the marquis, has left France and renounced his heritage from detestation of the cruelty of the old French nobility; he falls in love with Lucie, Dr Manette's daughter, and they are happily married. During the Terror he goes to Paris to try to save a faithful servant, who is accused of having served the nobility. He is arrested, condemned to death, and saved only at the last moment by Sydney Carton, a reckless wastrel of an English barrister, whose character is redeemed by his generous devotion to Lucie. Carton, who strikingly resembles Darnay in appearance, smuggles the latter out of prison, and takes his place on the scaffold. The book's vivid picture of Paris at this period was modelled on Thomas *Carlyle's *The *French Revolution*. Carton's words as he goes to his death—'It is a far, far better thing that I do, than I have ever done'—became a celebrated moment in Dickens's fiction.

Tales of my Landlord Four series of novels by Walter *Scott: *The *Black Dwarf*, *Old Mortality* (1st series); *The *Heart of Midlothian* (2nd series); *The *Bride of Lammermoor*, *A *Legend of Montrose* (3rd series); *Count Robert of Paris*, *Castle Dangerous* (4th series). As Scott admitted, the title is misleading, for the tales were not told by any fictional landlord.

TALIESIN (*fl.*550) A British bard first mentioned in the *Saxon Genealogies* appended to the *Historia Britonum* (*c.*690). A mass of poetry, probably of later date, has been ascribed to him, and the *Book of Taliesin* (14th century) is a collection of poems by different authors and different dates. Taliesin features prominently in Peacock's *The *Misfortunes of Elphin*, and he is mentioned in Tennyson's *Idylls of the King* as one of the Round Table.

Talisman, The A novel by Walter *Scott, published 1825. The novel describes the adventures of a poor but brave Scottish knight, Sir Kenneth, who is caught up in the intrigues between Richard I of England, the king of France, the duke of Austria, and the Knights Templars. He is eventually discovered to be Prince David of Scotland. The most striking portrait in

the novel is that of Saladin, sultan of Egypt, whose wisdom and chivalry is contrasted throughout with the scheming and corruption of the Christian leaders.

TAMBIMUTTU, James Meary *See* POETRY LONDON.

Tamburlaine the Great A drama in blank verse by Christopher *Marlowe, written not later than 1587, published 1590. Its blank verse was livelier and more sophisticated that that of *Gorboduc*, and it was immediately popular. The material for it was taken by the author from Pedro Mexia's *Spanish Life of Timur*, translated into English in 1571.

Part I of the drama deals with the rise to power of the Scythian shepherd-robber Tamburlaine; he supports Cosroe's rebellion against his brother, the king of Persia, then challenges him for the crown and defeats him. Tamburlaine's ambition and cruelty carry all before him. He conquers the Turkish emperor Bajazet and leads him about, a prisoner in a cage, taunting him and his empress Zabina until they dash out their brains against the bars of the cage. His ferocity is softened only by his love for his captive Zenocrate, daughter of the sultan of Egypt, and when he takes Damascus she persuades him to spare the sultan's life.

Part II deals with his further conquests, which extend to Babylon, where he is drawn in a chariot dragged by the kings of Trebizond, Soria, Anatolia, and Jerusalem, 'pampered Jades of Asia' (a phrase quoted by Pistol in Shakespeare, *2 *Henry IV*, II. iv), The play ends with Tamburlaine's death.

Tamerlane A tragedy by Nicholas *Rowe, produced 1701, with the professed intention of celebrating William III as the high-minded conqueror of the title, and of vilifying Louis XIV under the character of the defeated Bajazet. The play was, until about 1815, revived annually on 5 November, the date of William's landing in England.

Taming of the Shrew, The A comedy by *Shakespeare, first printed in the *folio of 1623, probably written *c.*1592 or earlier and based in part on the *Supposes* adapted by George *Gascoigne from *Ariosto.

The play begins with an induction in which Christopher Sly, a drunken Warwickshire tinker, picked up by a lord and his huntsmen on a heath, is brought to a castle, sumptuously treated, and in spite of his protestations is assured that he is a lord who has been out of his mind. He is set down to watch the play that follows, performed solely for his benefit by strolling players.

Baptista Minola of Padua has two daughters, Katherina the Shrew, who is the elder of the two, and Bianca, who may not marry until a husband has been found for Katherina. Petruccio, a gentleman from Verona, undertakes to woo the shrew to gain her dowry and to help his friend Hortensio win Bianca. To tame her he pretends to find her rude behaviour courteous and gentle and humiliates her by being late for their wedding and appearing badly dressed. He takes her off to his country house and, under the pretext that nothing there is good enough for her, prevents her from eating or sleeping. By the time they return to Baptista's house, Katherina has been successfully tamed, and Lucentio, a Pisan, has won Bianca by disguising himself as her schoolmaster, while the disappointed Hortensio has to console himself with marriage to a rich widow. At the feast which follows the three bridegrooms wager on whose wife is the most docile and submissive. Katherina argues that 'Thy husband is thy lord, thy life, thy keeper, | Thy head, thy sovereign' and Petruccio wins the bet.

A play by John *Fletcher, The *Woman's Prize, shows Petruccio tamed in a second marriage after Kate's death. Petruccio's three times repeated request 'kiss me, Kate' supplied the title for Cole Porter's popular musical of 1948.

'Tam o' Shanter' A narrative poem by Robert *Burns, published in the *Edinburgh Herald* and the *Edinburgh Magazine* in March 1791. A mock moral tale, the poem is characterized by swift changes of perspective as it recounts the homeward progress of Tam from a snug Ayr alehouse, past 'Alloway's auld haunted kirk', to the brig o' Doon. Though terrifying witches pursue him after his drunken, licentious shout interrupts their Sabbath in the mysteriously lit kirk, he escapes with his life but without the tail of his faithful mare, Meg. The poem brilliantly reconciles the vernacular tradition with the neo-classical aesthetics Burns had been vainly trying to serve in his English verses since 1787.

TAN, Amy (1952–) Chinese American novelist. *The Joy Luck Club* (1989), describes the experiences of Chinese American immigrants. Tan collaborated over its 1993 movie adaptation. Her 2001 novel *The Bonesetter's Daughter* is typical of Tan's work in exploring the relation between daughters and mothers. *The Opposite of Fate* (2003) is a non-fiction volume of reflections.

Tancred *or The New Crusade* A novel by Benjamin *Disraeli, published 1847; the last of the trilogy *Coningsby—*Sybil—Tancred*. More mystical than its predecessors, and less directly concerned with social and political reform, the novel attempts to resolve the antagonism between Judaism and Christianity and to establish a role for a reforming faith and revitalized church in a progressive society.

Tancred and Gismund, The Tragedy of *or Gismond of Salerne* A rhetorical love tragedy by Robert Wilmot (*c.*1550–*c.*1608) and others, published 1591 but dating from 1566 or 1568. Act II is possibly by Henry Noel (d. 1597), Act IV by Sir Christopher Hatton. The play is the first of many to use an Italian tale as source material—in this case a story by *Boccaccio.

TANNAHILL, Robert (1774–1810) Scottish poet. At 17 he walked to Alloway to see the setting of *'Tam o' Shanter' and began writing songs. From 1805 his work began to appear in newspapers and journals and in 1807 he published *Poems and Songs*, which included a harshly criticized dramatic 'interlude', 'The Soldier's Return'. Embittered by having a revised edition declined by two publishers, he burnt his manuscripts and drowned himself.

Tarzan *See* BURROUGHS, EDGAR RICE.

Task, The A poem in six books by William *Cowper, published 1785. When Cowper's friend Lady Austen suggested to him the sofa in his room as the subject of a poem, the poet set about 'the task'. Its six books are entitled 'The Sofa', 'The Time-Piece', 'The Garden', 'The Winter Evening', 'The Winter Morning Walk', and 'The Winter Walk at Noon'. Cowper opens with a mock-heroic account of the evolution of the sofa ('I sing the sofa') but thereafter addresses a wide range of topics, from cucumbers to salvation, in an accessible, emotionally fluent style of blank verse. The poem stresses the delights of a retired life; describes the poet's own search for peace; and evokes the consolations of religious faith, the pleasures of gardening, and the comforts of evenings by the fireside. It condemns aristocratic diversions, French fashions, *slavery, and cruelty to animals; the poet shows tenderness not only for his pet hare, but even for worms and snails.

TASSO, Torquato (1544–95) Italian poet and playwright. He was from early life in constant terror of persecution and adverse criticism, and his conduct at Ferrara was such as to make it necessary for the duke, Alphonso II of Este, to lock him up as mad from 1579 to 1586. The legend of his passion for Leonora d'Este, the duke's discovery of it, and his consequent imprisonment was for long widely believed; John *Milton refers to it (in a Latin poem), Lord *Byron's *The Lament of Tasso* is based on it, and *Goethe's play *Torquato Tasso* (1790) supports it. Tasso was released on condition that he would leave Ferrara, and he spent the rest of his life wandering from court to court, unhappy, poverty-stricken, and paranoid.

His chief works were *Rinaldo*, a romance epic (1562); a pastoral play, *Aminta* (1573; English translation 1591); **Jerusalem Delivered* (1580–1); and a less successful tragedy, *Torrismondo* (1586–7). He was also a prolific and brilliant lyric poet, and Edmund *Spenser used his sonnets in many of his **Amoretti*. Tasso's epics and his critical works (*Discorsi dell'arte poetica*, *Discorsi del poema eroico*) had a great influence on English literature, displayed in the works of Samuel *Daniel, Milton, Giles and Phineas *Fletcher, Abraham *Cowley, John *Dryden, and others; Edward Fairfax's translation of *Jerusalem Delivered* (1600) also had an influence in its own right.

TATE, Allen (1899–1979) American poet and critic. He began his literary career as editor of the *little magazine the Tennessee *Fugitive* (1922–5), which published work by John Crowe *Ransom and others, and supported a sense of Southern regionalism. His poetry collections include *Mr Pope and Other Poems* (1928) and *Poems 1928–1931* (1932). His essays are collected in *On the Limits of Poetry* (1948) and other volumes.

TATE, Nahum (1652–1715) Playwright, most of whose dramatic works were adaptations from earlier writers; his highly popular 1681 version of **King Lear* omits the Fool, makes Edgar and Cordelia fall in love, and ends happily. Tate also wrote, with John *Dryden, the second part of **Absalom and Achitophel*; and the libretto of Henry *Purcell's *Dido and Aeneas*. In 1696 he published with Nicholas Brady (1659–1726) the well-known metrical version of the Psalms that bears their name. He was appointed *poet laureate in 1692, and was mocked by Alexander *Pope in *The *Dunciad*.

Tatler A *periodical founded by Richard *Steele, of which the first issue appeared on 12 April 1709; it appeared three times a week until 2 January 1711, numbering 271 issues in all. The author assumes the character of Isaac Bickerstaff, a name borrowed from Jonathan *Swift. According to no. 1, the *Tatler* was to include 'Accounts of Gallantry, Pleasure and Entertainment... under the Article of White's Chocolate House'; poetry under that of Will's Coffee House; foreign and domestic news from St James's Coffee house; learning from the Grecian; and so on. Gradually it adopted a loftier moral tone, attacking the evils of duelling and gambling, and discussing all questions of good manners from the standpoint of humane civilization and gentlemanly taste. The *Tatler* was republished in book form and was very widely read. Its vein of light satire was much imitated: Alexander Pope's **Rape of the Lock*, for example, borrows freely from the periodical's account of contemporary fashions. From an early stage in the history of the *Tatler* Steele had the collaboration of Joseph *Addison, who contributed notes, suggestions, and a number of complete papers. It was succeeded by the **Spectator*, which they edited jointly.

TAYLOR, Edward (*c*.1642–1729) American poet and pastor, born in England. He emigrated to Boston in 1668. His devotional poems, including *God's Determinations* and the *Preparatory Meditations*, remained in manuscript, at his own request, and were not published until 1937. His poetry belongs in the metaphysical tradition of George *Herbert and Francis *Quarles.

TAYLOR, Elizabeth (1912–75) Novelist and short story writer. Many of her books are set in provincial towns and villages amongst the middle classes, a circumstance which has sometimes led to this shrewd, witty, but compassionate observer of snobbery and the deceits and disappointments of everyday life being underrated. Taylor was in fact an atheist who joined the Communist Party in her early twenties and remained an active supporter of the Labour Party throughout her life, and there is nothing in the least bit cosy about her books. Her twelve novels, from *At Mrs Lippincote's* (1945), are written with an elegant and often deadly precision. *Angel* (1957), for example, describes the appalling and destructive self-deception of a popular novelist who genuinely believes in the ludicrous fantasy world she purveys in her books. Taylor was often compared with Jane *Austen, and *Palladian* (1946) knowingly brings the conventions of the Romantic novel up against the stark realities of the present day. Her equally fine short stories were collected in several volumes, including *The Blush* (1958), *A Dedicated Man* (1965), and *The Devastating Boys* (1972). The title novella of the collection

Hester Lily (1954) describes the havoc wreaked on a marriage by the husband's much younger cousin, while the childhood bond between two cousins in another of Taylor's best books, *A Game of Hide and Seek* (1951), persists catastrophically into adulthood. Her later novels include *Mrs Palfrey at the Claremont* (1971), a funny but unsparing portrait of impoverished but genteel old age, and the posthumously published *Blaming* (1976).

TAYLOR, Jane (1783–1824) and **Ann** (1782–1866) Probably the most imitated poets for children of the 19th century. *Original Poems for Infant Minds* (1804–5), which also contained poems by Adelaide O'Keefe (1776–1855), ran to 50 editions. It contains one of the most popular poems of the century, 'My Mother', and was part of the 'awful warning' school of poetry. *Rhymes from the Nursery* (1806) contained the classic 'The Star' ('Twinkle, twinkle, little star'), famously parodied by Lewis *Carroll, and rhymes with a republican flavour.

TAYLOR, Jeremy (1613–67) Clergyman and religious writer, chaplain to Laud and Charles I, and rector of Uppingham from 1638. He was taken prisoner in the Royalist defeat before Cardigan Castle in 1645, and retired to Golden Grove, Carmarthenshire. After the *Restoration he was made bishop of Down and Connor, Ireland, and subsequently of Dromore. He died at Lisburn and was buried in his cathedral of Dromore. His fame rests on the combined simplicity and splendour of his style, of which *The Rule and Exercises of Holy Living* (1650) and *The Rule and Exercises of Holy Dying* (1651) are perhaps the best examples. Among his other works, *The Liberty of Prophesying*, an argument for toleration, appeared in 1647; his *Eniautos*, or series of sermons for the Christian year, in 1653; *The Golden Grove*, a manual of daily prayers, in 1655; his *Ductor Dubitantium*, 'a general instrument of moral theology' for determining cases of conscience, in 1660; and *The Worthy Communicant* in the same year.

TAYLOR, John (1580–1653) The 'water poet'; he became a Thames waterman, and increased his earnings by writing rollicking verse and prose, obtaining the patronage of Ben *Jonson and others, and diverting both court and City. He went on foot from London to Braemar, visited the Continent, started from London to Queenborough in a brown-paper boat and narrowly escaped drowning, and accomplished other journeys, each one resulting in a booklet with an odd title. He published in 1630 a collected edition of his works, *All the Works of John Taylor, the Water-Poet*, but continued to write after this, notably Royalist ballads and news-sheets.

TAYLOR, Philip Meadows (1808–76) Anglo-Indian novelist and historian. He wrote the successful *Confessions of a Thug* (1839), a result of his investigation into Thuggism, the secret terrorist movement in India. His reputation rests mainly on stories written after his retirement to England in 1860, notably the trilogy *Tara: A Mahratta Tale* (1843), *Ralph Darnell* (1865), and *Seeta* (1872). His autobiography, ed. A. M. Taylor (his daughter), appeared in 1877.

TAYLOR, William (1765–1836) Critic and translator. He was significant for his role as an early advocate of German literature in England although his translations, which included Bürger's ballads, Gotthold Ephraim Lessing's *Nathan der Weise* in 1791, and Johann Wolfgang von *Goethe's *Iphigenia auf Tauris* in 1793, never became widely known. Like Henry Crabb *Robinson, Taylor's influence as a popularizer of German writers was chiefly personal. He encouraged Walter *Scott's interest in German and was a friend of Robert *Southey.

'Teares of the Muses, The' A poem by Edmund *Spenser, included in the *Complaints*, published 1591. In this the poet deplores, through the mouth of several *Muses, the decay of literature and learning.

TEATE, Faithfull (*fl.* 1650s) Irish poet and clergyman, father of Nahum *Tate. Teate went to England after the rebellion of 1641, in which three of his children were killed. His *Ter Tria* (1658) is a long, 'metaphysical' Trinitarian poem remarkable for its figurative vigour.

Telemachus *See* ODYSSEY.

television Grew out of *radio broadcasting and initially followed a similar programming pattern, with the BBC transmitting a limited service of music, news, and drama from 1936 until the outbreak of war in 1939. Programmes resumed in 1946 and interest was boosted by Elizabeth II's coronation in 1953, watched by an estimated 20 million viewers. After the single BBC channel was joined by a commercial channel in 1956 and BBC2 in 1964, British television drama became a highly competitive arena, with writers such as Harold *Pinter and Alun *Owen contributing to ABC's Armchair Theatre in the late 1950s, before BBC's Wednesday Play and

Play for Today series took the lead in the mid-1960s with challenging naturalistic work by two early specialists in television drama, David *Mercer and John Hopkins (1931–98), as well as original scripts by Dennis *Potter and Jim Allen (1926–99), and improvised drama by Mike *Leigh. Channel 4 supported films rather than television drama from 1982, and the 'single play' has largely disappeared from British television, replaced by drama series.

Tempest, The A romantic drama by *Shakespeare probably written in 1611, not printed until 1623 when it appeared as the first play in the first *folio. It is usually taken to be his last play written without a collaborator. Contemporary accounts of the shipwreck of the *Sea-Venture* in 1609 on the Bermudas and passages from Arthur *Golding's Ovid and John *Florio's Montaigne contribute details to the play, but no single source for it is known.

Prospero, duke of Milan, ousted by his brother Antonio and turned adrift with his child Miranda, is a castaway on a lonely island, once the place of banishment of the witch Sycorax. Prospero uses his knowledge of magic to release various spirits (including *Ariel) imprisoned by the witch, and these now obey his orders. He also keeps in service the witch's son Caliban, a misshapen monster, formerly the sole inhabitant of the island. Prospero and Miranda have lived in this way for twelve years. When the play begins a ship carrying the usurper, his confederate Alonso, king of Naples, Alonso's brother Sebastian and son Ferdinand, is by Prospero's art wrecked on the island. The passengers are saved, but Ferdinand is thought by the rest to be drowned, and he thinks this is their fate. According to Prospero's plan Ferdinand and Miranda are thrown together, and fall in love. Prospero appears to distrust Ferdinand and sets him to carrying logs. On another part of the island Sebastian and Antonio plot to kill Alonso and Gonzalo, an old councillor who had helped Prospero in his banishment. Caliban offers his services to Stefano, a drunken butler, and Trinculo, a jester, and persuades them to try to murder Prospero. As the conspirators approach, Prospero breaks off the masque of Iris, Juno, and Ceres, which Ariel has presented to Ferdinand and Miranda. Caliban, Stefano, and Trinculo are driven off and Ariel brings the king and his courtiers to Prospero's cell. There he greets 'My true preserver' Gonzalo, forgives his brother Antonio, on the condition that he restores his dukedom to him, and reunites Alonso with his son Ferdinand, who is discovered playing chess with Miranda.

While Alonso repents for what he has done, Antonio and Sebastian do not speak directly to Prospero, but exchange ironic and cynical comments with each other. The boatswain and master of the ship appear to say that it has been magically repaired and that the crew is safe. Before all embark for Italy Prospero frees Ariel from his service, renounces his magic, and leaves Caliban once more alone on the island.

Templars, Knights An order founded after the First Crusade and endorsed by the church in 1129. It consisted originally of nine knights whose profession was to safeguard pilgrims to Jerusalem. They became a source of weakness to the Christian king of Jerusalem because of their dependence on the pope and violation of treaties with Muslim powers. After the battle of the Horns of Hattin (1187) Saladin beheaded them all, about 200 in number. The order lost support and was suppressed by the kings of Europe under circumstances, especially in France, of great cruelty. It was suppressed by the pope and the Council of Vienne (1312).

TEMPLE, Sir William (1628–99) Diplomat and writer. He was envoy at Brussels in 1666, and visited The Hague, where he negotiated the triple alliance between England, the Netherlands, and Sweden. In 1654 he married Dorothy *Osborne, whose letters to him give a vivid picture of the times. Jonathan *Swift was a member of his household at Moor Park, near Farnham, Surrey. His principal works include three volumes of *Miscellanea* (1680, 1692, 1701). The second of these contains 'Of Ancient and Modern Learning', an essay which, by its uncritical praise of the spurious epistles of *Phalaris, exposed Temple to the censure of Richard *Bentley and led to a vigorous controversy. The *Miscellanea* also include 'Upon the Gardens of Epicurus', 'Of Health and Long Life', 'Of Heroic Virtue', and 'Of Poetry'. Temple's letters were published by Jonathan Swift, 1700–3, after Temple's death. His *Memoirs*, relating to the period 1672–9 were published in 1692.

Temptation of Christ *See* BIBLE.

Tenant of Wildfell Hall, The The second and last of Anne *Brontë's novels, published 1848. Written in the first person with a male narrator, Gilbert Markham, it has a complex epistolary and diary structure. Markham, a young farmer, falls in love with Helen Graham, a young widow and talented painter newly arrived in the neighbourhood with her son Arthur. She is the tenant of the title. Her youth, beauty, and seclusion, and her mysterious relationship with her landlord Lawrence, give rise to local gossip, which Markham refuses to credit until he himself overhears Helen and Lawrence in intimate conversation. He violently assaults Lawrence, and Helen reveals to him that she had married Arthur Huntingdon, who had lapsed into a dissolute life. She had fled, to protect her child, to Wildfell Hall, provided for her by Lawrence, who is her brother. Shortly after the revelation of this secret, Helen returns to nurse her husband through a fatal illness, and the way is left clear for Markham successfully to renew his suit. In her 'Biographical Notice' (1850) Charlotte *Brontë suggested that the portrait of Huntingdon was based on their brother Branwell.

Ten Commandments See MOSES.

TENN, William (1920–2010) Pseudonym of American *science fiction writer Philip Klass, noted for the darkly comic anti-war story 'The Liberation of Earth' (1953). *Of Men and Monsters* (1968), his only novel, imagines humanity as vermin scavenging among conquering aliens.

TENNANT, Emma (1937–) Novelist. She founded and edited the literary review *Bananas*. Her novels include early neo-*Gothic and *magic realist works such as *Hotel de Dream* (1976) and *The Bad Sister* (1978), and later revisionist versions of classic texts, among them *Pemberley* (1993), a sequel to *Pride and Prejudice*, and *The French Dancer's Bastard* (2006), a continuation of *Jane Eyre*.

TENNANT, William (1784–1848) Scottish clergyman and scholar, remembered for his poem *Anster Fair* (1812), a mock-heroic description of the fair in James V's reign, and of the courting, with fairy intervention, of Maggie Lauder by Rob the Ranter.

TENNIEL, Sir John (1820–1914) Illustrator. He worked for *Punch* from 1850; 'Dropping the Pilot' (1890), referring to Bismarck's resignation, is one of his best-known cartoons. His illustrations for *Alice's Adventures in Wonderland* (1865) and *Through the Looking-Glass* (1871) by Lewis Carroll (Charles *Dodgson) are perfect examples of the integration of illustration with text.

TENNYSON, Alfred first Baron Tennyson (1809–92) Poet. He joined the *Apostles at Trinity College, Cambridge, and became friends with Arthur Henry Hallam. *Poems by Two Brothers* (1827), which contains some early work that he chose not to reprint even in his juvenilia and poems by his brothers Charles and Frederick, was followed by *Poems Chiefly Lyrical* (1830, including *'Mariana'). In 1832 he travelled with Hallam on the Continent. Hallam, who had done much to encourage and promote Tennyson's work, died in Vienna in 1833. Tennyson's *In Memoriam*, a long elegy that he published seventeen years later, is written in what has become known as the Tennysonian stanza.

Poems (1832, dated 1833) included 'The *Lady of Shalott', 'The Two Voices', 'Oenone', 'The Lotos-Eaters', and 'A Dream of Fair Women'. In 1842 a much revised selection from the previous two volumes appeared, with new poems, including *'Morte d'Arthur' (the germ of *Idylls of the King*), *'Locksley Hall', *'Ulysses', and 'St Simeon Stylites'. The *Princess* (1847) followed, and in 1850 he published *In Memoriam*; was appointed *poet laureate; and married Emily Sellwood (1813–96). He wrote his 'Ode' on the death of Wellington in 1852 and 'The *Charge of the Light Brigade' in 1854.

Tennyson's fame was now firmly established, and *Maud, and Other Poems* (1855) and the first four *Idylls of the King* (1859) sold extremely well. Prince Albert called on Tennyson on the Isle of Wight in 1856, but despite the high esteem in which she held him, Queen *Victoria never visited, preferring to summon him to Osborne or Windsor. In London he frequented the literary and artistic salon of Sarah Prinsep (1816–87); her sister, the photographer Julia Margaret Cameron, moved to the Isle of Wight in 1860, where she was later commissioned by Tennyson to produce photographic illustrations for some of his poems. Later works include *Enoch Arden Etc.* (1864); *The Holy Grail and Other Poems* (including 'Lucretius') (1869 dated 1870); *Gareth and Lynette, etc.* (1872); *Tiresias, and Other Poems* (1885); and *The Foresters* (1892). He was buried in Westminster Abbey.

In 1870, Alfred *Austin described Tennyson's work as 'poetry of the drawing room', and many shared W. H. *Auden's view that 'his genius was lyrical', rather than narrative, epic, or dramatic. T. S. *Eliot called him 'the great master of metric as well as of melancholia', who has 'the finest ear of any English poet since Milton'.

TENNYSON, Frederick (1807–98) Poet, eldest brother of Alfred *Tennyson. He contributed (with Charles *Tennyson Turner) to *Poems by Two Brothers* (1827); other volumes include *Days and Hours* (1854) and *The Isles of Greece* (1890).

TENNYSON TURNER, Charles (1808–79) Poet, elder brother of Alfred *Tennyson. He contributed (with Frederick *Tennyson) to *Poems by Two Brothers* (1827) and published several volumes of sonnets (1830–80), some of them depicting life in the Lincolnshire wolds.

TERENCE (Publius Terentius Afer) (d. *c*.159 BC) Roman comic poet, allegedly born in Carthage and a slave at Rome. Four of his plays, *Andria, Adelphi, Eunuchus,* and *Heauton-timorumenos,* are adaptations of *Menander; his other two plays, *Hecyra* and *Phormio,* are also imitations of Greek originals. Although he employs the same limited range of characters that is found in *Plautus, he gives them greater depth and presents a world of genuine relationships. He was famed in antiquity for the elegance and colloquial character of his Latin. It was as a stylist that he was studied in the Middle Ages and figured in the curriculum of most Tudor schools: there is an early translation of the *Andria* (*c*.1520), a later one specifically for schools by Maurice Kyffin (1588), and a much-reprinted English version of all the six comedies by Richard Bernard (1598). But Terence was known more through imitations than through translations. Along with Plautus, he contributed plots, characters, and tone to comedy in 16th-century Italy, and in the France of *Corneille and *Molière, from where it spread to Restoration London.

Teresa (or **Theresa**), **St** (**Teresa of Ávila**) (1515–82) A Spanish saint, famous for her mystical writings. Her *Libro de la vida: Life* (written ?1561–6, pub. 1588) and *Libro de las fundaciones* (*The Book of the Foundations,* written 1573–82, pub. 1610) narrate her spiritual growth, evolving commitment to reforming the Carmelite order, and ceaseless journeys founding new convents. *Camino de perfección* (*The Way of Perfection,* written ?1562–79, pub. 1583), and *Moradas del castillo interior* (*The Interior Castle,* written 1577, pub. 1588) are further penetrating accounts of the inner life. She is the subject of Richard *Crashaw's 'Hymne to Sainte Teresa'. George *Eliot refers to her inspiring example in the 'Prelude' to *Middlemarch*.

TERKEL, Studs (1912–2008) American writer and radio broadcaster, active during the 1930s in the Federal Writers' Project, a government scheme to support writers during the Depression. His oral histories, including *Division Street: America* (1967) and *Hard Times* (1970), which collect accounts of the Depression, and *Working* (1974). *Touch and Go* (2007) is an autobiographical memoir.

TERSON, Peter (1932–) The pseudonym of Peter Patterson, playwright; he was associated with the Victoria Theatre, Stoke-on-Trent, with its tradition of social documentary and theatre-in-the-round, then with the National Youth Theatre. His works include *Mooney and his Caravans* (TV 1966), about a young and inadequate couple victimized by the owner of a caravan site; *Zigger Zagger* (1967), about a football fan; and *Good Lads at Heart* (1971), set in a Borstal. Later works include *Geordie's March* (1979) and *Strippers* (1984).

terza rima The measure adopted by *Dante in the *Divina commedia,* consisting of eleven-syllable lines in sets of three, the middle line of each rhyming with the first and third lines of the next set (*aba, bcb, cdc,* etc.). It was also used by *Petrarch for his *Trionfi* and by *Boccaccio in the *Caccia di Diana* (*Diana's Hunt*).

TESSIMOND, A. S. J. (Arthur Seymour John) (1902–62) Poet. He published three volumes of verse in his lifetime (*The Walls of Glass,* 1934; *Voices in a Giant City,* 1947; *Selection,* 1958), and his *Collected Poems* (ed. Hubert Nicholson) appeared in 1985. He is remembered for his wry, low-key, urban pieces.

Tess of the D'Urbervilles *A Pure Woman* A novel by Thomas *Hardy, published 1891. The sub-title was important to Hardy's purpose. Tess Durbeyfield's father, a poor villager of Blackmoor Vale, is told that they are descended from the ancient family of D'Urberville. Tess is cunningly seduced (perhaps raped) by Alec, a wealthy young man, whose family has bought the name of D'Urberville. Tess gives birth to a child, which dies after an improvised midnight baptism by its mother. Later, while working as a dairymaid, she becomes blissfully engaged to Angel Clare, a clergyman's son. On their wedding night she confesses to him the seduction by Alec; and Angel hypocritically abandons her. Misfortunes come upon her and her family, and accident throws her once more in the path of Alec D'Urberville. He has become an itinerant preacher, but his temporary religious conversion does not prevent him from persistently pursuing her. When her appeals to her husband, now in Brazil, remain unanswered, she is driven for the sake of her family to become the mistress of Alec. Clare, returning from Brazil and repenting of his harshness, finds her living with Alec. Maddened by this second wrong that has been done her by Alec, Tess stabs and kills

him. After a brief and happy period of conceal-
ment with Clare in the New Forest, Tess is
arrested at Stonehenge, tried, and hanged.

The publication of the novel, like that of *Jude
the Obscure*, created a violent sensation.

Testament, Old and New See BIBLE.

Testament of Cresseid, The A poem in
616 lines of *rhyme royal by Robert *Henryson.
Henryson circumvents the authority of Chaucer's *Troilus and Criseyde* by having his narrator take up another (fictional) source that
enables him to tell a different version. Diomede
leaves Cresseid, for which she reproaches
Venus and Cupid. A council of the gods discusses the punishment for her blasphemy;
Saturn deprives her of joy and beauty, and she
is struck with leprosy. As she sits by the roadside, Troilus passes and, though the leper brings
Cresseid to his mind, he does not recognize her,
nor she him. She receives alms from him and
then learns who he is. She dies after sending
him a ring he had once given her.

Testament of Love, The See USK,
THOMAS.

tetrameter A verse line with four stressed
syllables, the most common kind in English.
See METRE.

TEVIS, Walter Stone (1928–84) American
novelist and short story writer. His works include *The Hustler* (1959; filmed 1961) and *The
Man Who Fell to Earth* (1963; filmed 1976), a
*science fiction novel of the gradual corruption
of an alien by human society.

THACKERAY, Anne Isabella See
RITCHIE, ANNE THACKERAY.

THACKERAY, William Makepeace
(1811–63) Novelist. He entered the Middle
Temple, but never practised as a barrister.
From 1834 until 1837 he lived in Paris, making
a meagre living from journalism. He married
Isabella Shawe in 1836 their first child Anne
(Anne Thackeray *Ritchie) was born in 1837.
Thackeray began to contribute regularly to *Fraser's Magazine*, and also wrote for many other
periodicals, including the *Morning Chronicle,
the *New Monthly Magazine*, and The *Times.
After the birth of their third child, Harriet
Marian (later the first wife of Leslie *Stephen),
in 1840 Isabella Thackeray suffered a mental
breakdown which proved permanent. Thackeray made arrangements for her care, and sent
his children to live with his mother in Paris.

During the 1840s Thackeray began to make a
name for himself as a writer. *The Yellowplush
Papers*, a critique of what Thomas *Carlyle
called 'flunkeyism', appeared in *Fraser's Magazine* in 1837–8. These were followed by *Catherine*, and 'A Shabby Genteel Story' (1840). *The
Great Hoggarty Diamond* is a mock-heroic tale
narrated by Sam's cousin, Michael Angelo Titmarsh, Thackeray's most familiar pseudonym.
Other pseudonyms included 'George Savage
FitzBoodle', a bachelor clubman, 'author'
of *The FitzBoodle Papers* (1842–3), narrator
of *Men's Wives* (1843) and 'editor' of The *Luck
of Barry Lyndon* (1844). *The Irish Sketch Book*
of 1843 has a preface signed, for the first time,
with Thackeray's own name.

Thackeray began his association with *Punch
in 1842. *The Snobs of England, by One of Themselves* (1846–7; published as *The Book of Snobs*,
1848), introduced the term. *Mr Punch's Prize
Novelists* (1847) parodies the leading writers of
the day. In 1847 his first major novel, *Vanity
Fair*, began to appear in monthly numbers, with
illustrations by the author. *Pendennis followed
in 1848–50. The *History of Henry Esmond*,
(1852), was followed by The *Newcomes*, published in numbers in 1853–5.

The *Rose and the Ring* (by 'Mr M. A. Titmarsh'), a high-spirited children's story, was
published in 1855. The *Virginians*, set partly
in America, appeared in numbers in 1857–9.
In 1860 he became the first editor of the *Cornhill Magazine*, the *Roundabout Papers*. *Lovel
the Widower*, The Adventures of Philip*, and the
unfinished *Denis Duval* all first appeared in
the *Cornhill*. Thackeray died suddenly on
Christmas Eve 1863.

Anne Thackeray Ritchie published *Chapters
from Some Memoirs* in 1894, and her introductions to the *Biographical Edition* (1899) of her
father's works contain many anecdotes about
his life.

theatre criticism In the journalistic sense,
began in Britain in the early 18th century. Despite earlier attempts by John *Dryden in his
prefaces and Thomas *Rymer in *A Short View
of Tragedy* to uphold French *neo-classical principles, it was not governed by a continental
adherence to aesthetic rules. Its emergence
was determined by pragmatic factors: the
rise of the opinionated essayist, the strength of
Restoration acting, and the need to protect the
stage from moral censure. All three converge
in Richard *Steele who, writing on the death
of Thomas *Betterton in 1710, claims, 'There
is no human invention so aptly calculated for
the forming a free-born people as that of the

theatre.' Aaron *Hill and William Popple (1701–64) in *The Prompter* (1734–6) became the first professional theatre critics, pursuing a campaign for realistic acting that paved the way for David *Garrick. But it was Leigh *Hunt and William *Hazlitt who transformed dramatic criticism despite writing, between 1805 and 1830, in the period William *Archer called 'the winter solstice of English drama'. Hunt was often at his best writing about comic actors, whilst Hazlitt was inspired by the demonic genius of Edmund Kean. His reviews of Kean's Shakespearian performances combine astute technical analysis with vivid impressionistic images and he argued that Shakespeare's actors were his actors. George Bernard *Shaw used his coruscating columns in the *Saturday Review* in the 1890s to attack the reigning actor-manager Henry *Irving, and to endorse a drama that addressed social and moral issues. But the separate traditions of graphic reporter and militant enthusiast converged in Kenneth *Tynan, who both enshrined legendary performances, particularly those of Olivier, and used his *Observer* columns to champion Bertolt *Brecht and John *Osborne. Harold Hobson, in the *Sunday Times*, championed Samuel *Beckett, Harold *Pinter, and Marguerite Duras. The development of an alternative theatre movement in Britain from the mid-1960s and, in particular, the publication of the London magazine *Time Out* (together with its regional counterparts) has diminished the dominance of a small group of critics, although the work of Michael Billington for the *Guardian* is an occasional exception.

Théâtre de Complicité Influential physical theatre group founded in 1983. Their early work fed on European mime traditions and surreal British humour. Their productions include versions of John *Berger's *The Three Lives of Lucie Cabrol* (1994), Eugène Ionesco's *The Chairs* (1997), and Haruki Murakami's short stories, *The Elephant Vanishes* (2003).

Theatre of the Absurd *See* ABSURD, THEATRE OF THE.

Thel, The Book of *See* BLAKE, WILLIAM.

THELWALL, John (1764–1834) English radical and poet who in 1794 was arrested with John Horne Tooke for his revolutionary views, *The Peripatetic, or Sketches of the Heart, of Nature and Society; in a Series of Politico-Sentimental Journals* (1793), is part fictional travelogue in the manner of Laurence *Sterne, part radical call to arms.

THEOBALD, Lewis (1688–1744) Poet, critic, and Shakespearian scholar. His *Shakespeare Restored* (1726) exposed *Pope's faults as an editor of *Shakespeare; Pope retaliated with a devastating portrait of Theobald (or 'Tibbald') as hero of his *The *Dunciad*. Pope did incorporate some of Theobald's corrections in the second edition of his Shakespeare, but Theobald's own edition of 1733–4 superseded Pope's, and some 300 emendations made to the texts by Theobald are still given credence by modern editors. Theobald was a pioneer in the study of Shakespeare's sources and the writings of his contemporaries. *Double Falsehood* (1727) was announced by Theobald as his adaptation of *Cardenio*, but satirists including Pope and Henry *Fielding regarded the play as spurious.

THEOCRITUS (early 3rd century BC) Author of the *Idylls*, a collection of poems in the Doric dialect of Greek. His most famous poems evoke the life and rustic arts of Sicilian shepherds, maintaining a successful balance between idealization and realism; they were imitated by *Virgil in the *Eclogues*, and established the formal characteristics and setting that *pastoral poetry was to retain for centuries. Six of the *Idylls* were translated anonymously in 1588, and in 1684 Thomas Creech translated them into English. Many English elegies, notably John Milton's *Lycidas*, ultimately derive from Theocritus' lament for Daphnis. *See* ECLOGUE.

THEOPHRASTUS (*c*.371–287 BC) Greek philosopher, head of the Peripatetic school after *Aristotle. His influence on English literature stems from his *Characters*, thirty brief sketches of human types embodying particular faults: the flatterer, the overproud, the bad-mannered. The popularity of Theophrastus in modern times dates from the edition of the 23 *Characters* then known with Latin translations by Isaac *Casaubon (1592). An English version by John Healey (*c*.1585–*c*.1616) appeared in 1616, but before then Joseph *Hall enlarged Theophrastus' scope, adding good qualities to bad in his *Characters of Vertues and Vices* (1608). *See* CHARACTER-WRITING; OVERBURY, SIR THOMAS.

Theory of Moral Sentiments, The A philosophical work by Adam *Smith, published 1759, and originally delivered in the form of lectures at Glasgow. The author advances the view that all moral sentiments arise from sympathy, the principle which gives rise to our notions of the merit or demerit of the agent. The basis of morality is pleasure in mutual sympathy, which moderates our natural egocentricity. The desire for such pleasure requires us to see ourselves 'in the light in which others see us'. Smith's account of the role of the imagination in the operation of sympathy influenced Laurence *Sterne, in *A Sentimental Journey*, and other contemporary writers.

THERESA, St *See* TERESA, ST.

THEROUX, Paul Edward (1941–) American travel writer, novelist, short story writer, and journalist. He made his reputation with a series of vivid travel books about epic railway journeys: *The Great Railway Bazaar* (1975), describing a journey across Europe and Russia to Japan; *The Old Patagonian Express* (1979), depicting travels in South America; and *Riding the Iron Rooster* (1988), an account of a journey through China. In *The Kingdom by the Sea* (1983) Theroux turned his attention to the coastline of Britain, his adopted home for many years. *The Happy Isles of Oceania* (1992) describes a voyage in the South Pacific and *The Pillars of Hercules* (1995) a tour of the Mediterranean. Theroux's first novel, *Waldo* (1967), was followed by many others, of which *The Mosquito Coast* (1982) is probably the best known. *My Other Life* (1996) is an 'imaginary memoir' which disconcertingly mixes fact and fiction. *Sir Vidia's Shadow: A Friendship across Five Continents* (1998) charts the decline of Theroux's long-standing friendship with V. S. *Naipaul. *Dark Star Safari* (2002) recounts an overland trip from Cairo to Cape Town. In *Ghost Train to the Eastern Star: On the Tracks of The Great Railway Bazaar* (2008), Theroux revisits Eastern Europe and Asia thirty years after the journey recounted in *The Great Railway Bazaar*.

Thersites The most irritable and repellent member of the Greek army in the Trojan War. He laughs at Achilles' grief over the death of Penthesilea, the queen of the Amazons, and Achilles kills him for it. He appears in Shakespeare's **Troilus and Cressida* as a harsh cynic. See Alexander *Pope's translation of the **Iliad* (2. 255–74).

Theseus A son of the Greek god Poseidon, or, according to later legend, of Aegeus, king of Athens. His exploits (in association with Medea, the Minotaur, Ariadne, and Phaedra) figure in many literary works, including *Sophocles' *Oedipus at Colonus* and *Euripides' *Hippolytus*. He appears as the duke of Athens in *Shakespeare's *A *Midsummer Night's Dream*, with his newly won bride *Hippolyta, and also in Shakespeare and John Fletcher's *The *Two Noble Kinsmen*.

THESIGER, Sir Wilfred (1910–2003) Travel writer, explorer, and photographer, born in Addis Ababa, Abyssinia (now Ethiopia), where his father was a British diplomat. In 1933–4 he explored the little-known territories of the Danakil people in eastern Ethiopia (see his *Danakil Diary*, pub. 1998) and became increasingly taken with a desire to escape modern civilization. His experiences of living in the Empty Quarter of Arabia with the Bedu, and then in the marshes of southern Iraq, are recorded in *Arabian Sands* (1959) and *The Marsh Arabs* (1964). He lived in Kenya from 1960 to the mid-1990s. Later works include *Desert, Marsh and Mountain* (1979, an account of travels in Persia and Iraqi Kurdistan); *The Life of my Choice* (1987); *My Kenya Days* (1994); *Among the Mountains: Travels in Asia* (1998); *A Vanished World* (2001); and an extensive collection of photographs, left to the Pitt-Rivers Museum in Oxford.

Thierry King of France, and his Brother Theodoret, The Tragedy of A play by John *Fletcher, with the collaboration probably of Philip *Massinger and possibly of Francis *Beaumont, written *c*.1613, published 1621.

Thiong'o *See* NGUGI WA THIONG'O.

THIRKELL, Angela (1890–1961) Novelist and journalist. She was a granddaughter of Edward Burne-Jones, a cousin of Rudyard *Kipling, and the god-daughter of J. M. *Barrie; her son (by her first husband) was Colin *McInnes. After the failure of her second marriage, she earned her living (very successfully in the 1930s but less so after the war) as a writer of idealized English country life. Many of her novels are set in a Barsetshire borrowed from Anthony *Trollope, such as *Ankle Deep* (1933), *August Folly* (1936), and *The Brandons* (1939).

THOMAS À KEMPIS (Thomas Hämmerlein; Thomas Hämmerken) (*c*.1380–1471) Born at Kempen near Cologne. He became an Augustinian monk and wrote Christian mystical works, including the famous *De Imitatione Christi* (*The Imitation of Christ*), which has been translated from the Latin into many languages (into English in the middle of the 15th century). The work traces in four books the gradual progress of the soul to Christian perfection, its detachment from the world, and union with God; its simplicity and sincerity and the universal quality of its religious teaching gave it lasting influence. Maggie Tulliver draws comfort and support from it in George *Eliot's *The *Mill on the Floss*.

THOMAS, D. M. (Donald Michael) (1935–)
Poet, novelist, and translator, whose work is
much influenced by his familiarity with Russian
literature. He has published translations of the
poetry of Alexander *Pushkin, Anna *Akhmatova, and Evgenii Evtushenko, and volumes of
his own poetry such as *Two Voices* (1968) and
Love and Other Deaths (1975). His first novel,
The Flute-Player (1979), pays tribute to the persecuted creative spirit of 20th-century Russian
poets. *The White Hotel* (1981) combines an invented case history of one of *Freud's patients,
and the steps that lead her and her stepson to
death in the 1941 massacre at Babi Yar. *Ararat*
(1983) shows a similar brooding on the theme of
*holocaust (this time of the Armenians) and on
the relationship between sex and death. Other
works include the novels *Sphinx* (1986), *Lying
Together* (1990), and *Eating Pavlova* (1994); a
volume of autobiography, *Memories and Hallu-
cinations* (1988); and a biography of Alexander
*Solzhenitsyn (1997).

THOMAS, Dylan (1914–53) Welsh poet. He
knew very little Welsh, and moved to London in
1934. His first volume of verse, *18 Poems*, appeared in the same year. He then embarked on
a *Grub Street career of journalism, broadcasting, and film-making, and rapidly acquired a
reputation for exuberance and flamboyance.
He settled in Laugharne in Wales with his wife,
after many wanderings, in 1949. Thomas's romantic, affirmative, rhetorical style was both
new and influential (and much imitated by his
contemporaries of the New Apocalypse Movement). The publication of *Deaths and Entrances*
(1946) established him with a wide public:
his *Collected Poems 1934–1952* (1952) sold extremely well.

Thomas also wrote a substantial quantity of
prose, including *The Map of Love* (1939), a collection of prose and verse; *Portrait of the Artist
as a Young Dog* (1940), a collection of largely
autobiographical short stories; *Adventures in the
Skin Trade* (1955) a collection of stories; and *A
Prospect of the Sea* (1955), stories and essays. In
1950, he undertook the first of his lecture tours
to the United States, and he died there on his
fourth visit, as legend grew about his wild living
and hard drinking. Shortly before his death he
took part in a reading in New York of *Under
Milk Wood*.

THOMAS, Edward (1878–1917) Poet. He
married young and supported his family
by producing many volumes of prose, much
of it topographical and biographical, including
a biography of Richard *Jefferies (1909), who

profoundly influenced him. With the encouragement of Robert *Frost, he turned to poetry
soon after the start of the war. In 1915, Thomas
joined the army, and he was killed at Arras.
Most of his poetry was published posthumously,
though a few pieces appeared under the pseudonym 'Edward Eastaway' between 1915 and
1917. Both he and Frost advocated the use of
natural diction, and of colloquial speech
rhythms in metrical verse. There are memoirs
by his widow, Helen (*As It Was*, 1926; and *World
without End*, 1931), and by Eleanor *Farjeon.

THOMAS, R. S. (Ronald Stuart) (1913–
2000) Welsh poet and clergyman. Ordained in
1936, Thomas was successively rector of Mana-
fon, Montgomeryshire; vicar of Eglwysfach, Ceredigion; and vicar of Aberdaron, on the Llŷn
peninsula. Reviewers of *Song at the Year's Turning* (1955), *Tares* (1961), and other early collections up to *Not that He Brought Flowers* (1968)
dwelt mainly on Thomas's anti-pastoral portraits of Welsh rural life. His later work, including *H'm* (1972), *Laboratories of the Spirit* (1975),
and *Frequencies* (1978), has been described as
characterized by irony and allusiveness, and
haunted by a sense of the absence of God. Thomas's poetry progressively abandons stanzaic
and metrical formality in favour of a low-key,
disenchanted idiom which displays immense
technical cunning in its repudiation of the customary charms of lyricism. *Ingrowing Thoughts*
(1985) contains poetic responses to famous
paintings; *The Echoes Return Slow* (1988) plays
off quizzical verse commentaries against autobiographical prose fragments; *No Truce with the
Furies* (1995) and the posthumously published
Residues (2002) bring renewed figurative stami-
na to their treatment of old age and memory
(and its loss). *Neb* ('No one', 1985), a laconic
third-person prose autobiography in Welsh, has
been translated by Jason Walford Davies along
with three shorter texts as *Autobiographies*
(1997).

THOMPSON, E. P. (Edward Palmer) (1924–
93) Historian. His works include *The Making of
the English Working Class* (1963), in which he
sought 'to rescue the poor stockinger, the Luddite cropper, the "obsolete" hand-loom weaver,
the "utopian" artisan, and even the deluded
follower of Joanna Southcott, from the enormous condescension of posterity'.

THOMPSON, Flora (1876–1947) Author.
She began writing nature essays for national
magazines and newspapers to supplement a
meagre income. She published a volume of

verse called *Bog-Myrtle and Peat*, in 1921, but is chiefly remembered for her semi-autobiographical trilogy *Lark Rise to Candleford* (1945), published originally as *Lark Rise* (1939), *Over to Candleford* (1941), and *Candleford Green* (1943), works which evoke through the childhood memories and youth of 'Laura' a vanished world of agricultural customs, rustic culture, and rural decline. The trilogy was adapted for television in 2008. *Still Glides the Stream* appeared posthumously in 1948.

THOMPSON, Francis (1859–1907) Poet. He was intended for the Roman Catholic priesthood, but was judged not to have a vocation. He also failed to qualify as a doctor, and in 1885 left home to spend three years of homeless and opium-addicted destitution in London, till he was rescued by Wilfrid and Alice *Meynell. He never married, and never for long freed himself from opium. He published three volumes of verse, in 1893, 1895, and 1897, and much literary criticism. His best-known poems are 'The Hound of Heaven' and 'The Kingdom of God'. His finest work conveys intense religious experience in imagery of power, he admired especially P. B. *Shelley, Thomas *De Quincey, and Richard *Crashaw.

THOMPSON, Hunter S. (1937–2005) American journalist and writer. He spent many years writing for *Rolling Stone* magazine, in which the two works for which he is best known first appeared. *Fear and Loathing in Las Vegas* (1972), subtitled 'a savage journey to the heart of the American Dream', is an account of a heavily drugged visit to Las Vegas, offering a dissection of American culture. *Fear and Loathing on the Campaign Trail '72* (1973) covers the 1972 American presidential campaign. He spent a year riding with the Hell's Angels (his book about them appeared in 1966), ran for sheriff of Aspen, Colorado, in 1970, and subsequently awarded himself a doctorate. With Tom *Wolfe and Joan *Didion, he was a pioneer of *New (or *gonzo) Journalism, a mode blurring the border between reportage and fiction. His own irreverent political and cultural writing has been collected in four volumes as *The Gonzo Papers* (1979–94). *See* GONZO JOURNALISM.

THOMSON, James (1700–48) Scottish poet. Encouraged by his friend David *Mallet, he came to London in 1725, and wrote 'Winter', the first of The *Seasons. Thomson made the acquaintance of Alexander *Pope, Richard *Savage, and Aaron *Hill, and found patrons, including George Bubb Dodington and Lord

*Lyttelton. He travelled in France and Italy as tutor to Charles Talbot, son of the solicitor-general, and in 1735–6 published a long patriotic poem *Liberty*. Thomson wrote a series of declamatory and high-minded tragedies, beginning with *Sophonisba* (1730), followed by *Agamemnon* (1738) and *Edward and Eleanora* (1739), which was banned by the Lord Chamberlain on the eve of performance. *Tancred and Sigismunda* was acted in 1745 with David *Garrick as Tancred. *Coriolanus* (1749) was performed posthumously. The plays were conspicuously aligned with political opposition to Sir Robert Walpole (1676–1745). In 1740 the masque of *Alfred*, by Thomson and Mallet, was performed; it contains Thomson's *'Rule, Britannia'. In 1748, a few weeks before his death, appeared The *Castle of Indolence*, including a portrait of himself, which affectionately mocks the poet's notorious love of idleness. *The Seasons*, one of the most frequently reprinted and illustrated of English poems, developed in a highly distinctive manner the range of *topographical poetry. Thomson's landscapes were influenced by those of *Claude, Poussin, and Rosa, and were in turn greatly admired by J. M. W. *Turner.

THOMSON, James (1834–82) Scottish poet. He was sent in 1851–2 to Ireland as an army schoolmaster, where he met Charles Bradlaugh, and a young girl, Matilda Weller, who died in 1853 but who became an important symbolic figure in Thomson's later poetry. For his early poetry he used the pseudonym 'B.V.', representing his admiration for P. B. *Shelley with 'Bysshe' and for the German poet Hardenberg ('Novalis') with 'Vanolis'. In 1862 Thomson was discharged from the army, probably for drunkenness. He came to London, and until 1868 lodged with the Bradlaughs. He took various jobs and wrote poems, essays, and translations for several magazines. 'Weddah', a long poem relating a tragic Arabian love story, appeared in 1871, and led to friendship with W. M. *Rossetti. His best-known poem, 'The City of Dreadful Night' appeared in the *National Reformer* in 1874. This long poem, which much influenced the mood of *fin-de-siècle* poetic pessimism, is a powerful evocation of a half-ruined city, a 'Venice of the Black Sea', through which flows the River of the Suicides; the narrator, in vain search of 'dead Faith, dead Love, dead Hope', encounters tormented shades wandering in a Dantesque vision of a living hell, over which presides the sombre and sublime figure of Melancolia (based on Albrecht Dürer's engraving of 1514). In 1880 his first volume of verse, *The City of Dreadful Night and Other Poems*, and a second volume later in the same year, were well received. *Essays and Phantasies* appeared in 1881. But his alcoholism was by now out of control; *Satires and Profanities* was published posthumously in 1884. There is a life by Henry S. Salt, 1889.

THOMSON, Sir William first Baron Kelvin (1824–1907) Physicist and mathematician. His formulation of the second law of thermodynamics, predicting that the world would sooner or later suffer a heat death as a result of entropy, contributed significantly to late 19th-century pessimism. The ignorance of this law displayed by most 20th-century literary intellectuals was used as an illustration of the gap between the *'two cultures' by C. P. *Snow.

'Thopas, The Tale of Sir' *See* CANTERBURY TALES, 17.

THOREAU, Henry David (1817–62) American author. He became a follower and friend of Ralph Waldo *Emerson, and was, in his own words, 'a mystic, a transcendentalist, and a natural philosopher to boot'. A few of his poems were published in *The *Dial*, but he made no money from literature, and published only two books in his lifetime. The first, *A Week on the Concord and Merrimack River* (1849), described a journey undertaken in 1839 with his brother; the second, *Walden, or Life in the Woods* (1854), attracted little attention, but has since been recognized as one of the seminal books of the century. It describes his two-year experiment in self-sufficiency (1845–7) when he built himself a wooden hut on the edge of Walden Pond, near Concord; he describes his domestic economy, his agricultural experiments, his visitors and neighbours, the plants and wildlife, and his sense of the Indian past, with a challenging directness that questions the materialism and the prevailing work ethic of the age. Equally influential in future years was his essay on 'Civil Disobedience' (1849; originally entitled 'Resistance to Civil Government'), in which he argues the right of the individual to refuse to pay taxes when conscience dictates, and describes his technique of passive resistance, later adopted by Gandhi. Thoreau's reputation as philosopher and political thinker, as well as naturalist, was strengthened by a biography (1890) by the British socialist Henry S. Salt (1851–1939), and by the admiration of Edward *Carpenter and Havelock *Ellis in Britain. He has also been hailed as a pioneer ecologist.

THORPE, Adam (1956–) Poet and novelist. He left England in 1990 to live in France. His first volume of poetry was *Mornings in the Baltic* (1988); others include *Meeting Montaigne* (1990) and *Nine Lessons from the Dark* (2003). His first novel was *Ulverton* (1992), a tour de force which places a fictional Wessex village at the centre of three centuries of social, linguistic, and historical flux, with each chapter narrated in an appropriate style. Others include *Still* (1995), *Pieces of Light* (1998), and *The Rules of Perspective* (2005). His poems, like his novels, are much preoccupied with people in particular landscapes, pitted against historical forces. His work meditates on the continuum of history and explores ideas of Englishness.

Thousand and One Nights, The *See* ARABIAN NIGHTS ENTERTAINMENTS.

THRALE, Hester Lynch (1741–1821) Née Salusbury. In 1763 she married Henry Thrale, a wealthy brewer. In 1765 they met, through Arthur *Murphy, Samuel *Johnson, who at one period became almost domesticated at their house in Streatham Place. Henry Thrale died in 1781, and three years later, against opposition from her daughters and friends (including Fanny *Burney), she married Gabriel Piozzi (1740–1809), an Italian musician. Johnson sent her a letter of violent, anguished protest; their friendship, already under strain, was ruined. She published *Anecdotes of the Late Samuel Johnson*, an intimate portrait, in 1786, and a selection of her correspondence with Johnson in 1788. *Thraliana*, a mixture of diary, anecdotes, poems, and jests, covering the period 1776–1809, begun at the suggestion of Johnson, was edited in 1942 (rev. 1951), 2 vols, by K. C. Balderston.

Three Clerks, The A novel by Anthony *Trollope, published 1858. The three clerks are Harry Norman, Alaric Tudor, and Alaric's gauche cousin Charley. In the course of the novel each marries one of the daughters of Mrs Woodward. Charley's experiences reflect Trollope's own early days as a clerk at the Post Office.

THUBRON, Colin (1939–) Novelist and travel writer. His travel writings began in the eastern Mediterranean and include *Mirror to Damascus* (1967), *The Hills of Adonis* (1968), and *Journey into Cyprus* (1975), which provided the setting for his first novel, *The God in the Mountain* (1977). Later travel books took on increasingly difficult terrain and reflect Thubron's curiosity about societies that his generation found threatening. They include *Among the Russians* (1983), *Behind the Wall* (1987), *The Lost Heart of Asia* (1994), *In Siberia* (1999), and *Shadows of the Silk Road* (2006). Thubron's travel writing is characterized by historical detail, careful prose, conscientious character observation, and a self-effacing narrator. Many of Thubron's novels, which include *Emperor* (1978), *A Cruel Madness* (1984), *Distance* (1996), and *To the Last City* (2002), feature enclosed spaces and interior worlds; Thubron himself has remarked on the contrast with his travel books.

THUCYDIDES (*c.*460/455–*c.*400 BC) Athenian historian who left a brilliant account in eight books of the Peloponnesian War, waged disastrously by Athens against Sparta. Giving the story the inexorable dignity of a tragedy, he traced effects to natural human causes and emphasized the scientific value of eyewitness accounts, while creating powerful speeches for the leading figures in his narrative, of which Pericles' funeral oration (Bk 2) is the most famous. The first English translation from the Greek was by Thomas *Hobbes (1629). In 1830–5 Thomas Arnold published a commentary in which he tried to derive lessons for his own time from Thucydides' text, and Benjamin Jowett's elegant translation followed in 1881.

THURBER, James (1894–1961) American humorist, many of whose essays, stories, and sketches appeared in the *New Yorker*, including one of his best-known short stories, 'The Secret Life of Walter Mitty' (1932), which describes the colourful escapist fantasies of a docile husband. Many of his sketches ridicule contemporary fads like *Let your Mind Alone!* (1937).

THWAITE, Anthony (1930–) Poet, whose volumes of poetry include *Home Truths* (1957), *The Stones of Emptiness* (1967), *New Confessions* (1974), a meditation on St Augustine, and one of his most highly regarded volumes, and *A Move in the Weather* (2003). An early allegiance to Philip *Larkin has expanded into a wide variety of theme and subject matter, ranging from the domestic to the exotic, and prominently figuring historical material. *Victorian Voices* (1980) is a collection of fourteen *dramatic monologues which takes as subjects Victorian figures such as Philip Henry Gosse, John Churton Collins (1848–1908), and Lawrence Alma-Tadema. *Selected Poems 1956–1996* appeared in 1997. Thwaite is editor of two collected editions of

Larkin's poems, and of his *Selected Letters* (1992).

'Thyrsis, A Monody *to commemorate the author's friend, Arthur Hugh Clough, who died at Florence, 1861'* A poem by Matthew *Arnold, first published in *Macmillan's Magazine*, 1866. The poem is a pastoral elegy lamenting *Clough as Thyrsis. It invokes the *Scholar-Gipsy as a fragile image of hope and perpetual quest.

Tibert The cat in the *Roman de Renart* (*see* REYNARD THE FOX). The name is the same as Tybalt (see the exchange between Mercutio and Tybalt in *Romeo and Juliet*, III. i. 74–7: 'Tybalt, you rat-catcher... Good King of Cats, nothing but one of your nine lives').

TIBULLUS, Albius (55/48–19 BC) Roman elegiac poet, noted for his refined and simple style and his idealization of the countryside. Of the three books bearing his name, the first celebrates his love for a mistress (Delia) and a boy (Marathus), the second describes his love for a woman whom he calls Nemesis, and the third is a collection of poems by members of his literary circle. John *Dryden called Charles *Sedley 'a more elegant Tibullus'.

TICKELL, Thomas (1685–1740) Poet. His poem *On the Prospect of Peace* (1712) drew Pope's admiration, though he considered it a potential rival to his own *Windsor-Forest*. Tickell was a friend of Joseph *Addison, whose posthumous *Works* he later edited (1721); in 1715 he published, with Addison's approval, a translation of the first book of the *Iliad*, which Pope took as a direct challenge to his own translation. His sentimental *ballad *Lucy and Colin* (1725) was much admired by Thomas *Gray and Oliver *Goldsmith.

TIGHE, Mary (1772–1810) Irish poet; she later moved to London, which she experienced as displacement. She is best known for *Psyche, or The Legend of Love* (1805). Written in *Spenserian stanzas, it recounts in richly erotic language Cupid's forbidden love for Psyche.

Till Eulenspiegel *See* EULENSPIEGEL, TILL.

TILLOTSON, John (1630–94) Clergyman and preacher; a latitudinarian (i.e. conforming to the government and ritual of the *Church of England, but denying its divine origin and authority), he became archbishop of Canterbury. His sermons, which show a marked difference from the earlier *metaphysical style of John *Donne and Lancelot *Andrewes, were praised as models of lucidity and good sense through most of the 18th century.

Time and Tide *An Independent Non-Party Weekly Review* A periodical founded in 1920 by Viscountess Rhondda (Margaret Haig Thomas, 1883–1958), with the support of Rebecca *West, Cicely Hamilton (1872–1952), and others. Originally a strongly left-wing and feminist publication, it went through many shades of political opinion before its disappearance in 1977. Its contributors included D. H. *Lawrence, Virginia *Woolf, Aldous *Huxley, Storm *Jameson, George Bernard *Shaw, and Robert *Graves; in 1929 it serialized E. M. *Delafield's *Diary of a Provincial Lady*.

Times, The Founded under the name of *The Daily Universal Register* on 1 January 1785; it became *The Times* in 1788. *The Times* was one of the first papers to employ special foreign correspondents: H. C. *Robinson was sent to north Germany in this capacity in 1807, and W. H. Russell (1821–1907) was an important war correspondent, reporting from the Crimea. Notable writers who contributed to *The Times* in the 19th century include George *Borrow (from Spain), Leigh *Hunt, and Benjamin *Disraeli. The 'Times New Roman' font was designed for the newspaper by Stanley Morrison (1889–1967) in 1932. There are three weekly supplements: the *Times Literary Supplement* (founded 1901), the *Times Educational Supplement* (founded 1910), and the *Times Higher Educational Supplement* (founded 1971, as *THE* 2008–). In 1967 both *The Times* and the *Sunday Times* came under the umbrella of Times Newspapers Limited, a company set up by Lord Thomson of Fleet (1894–1976); in 1981 all the titles were acquired by News Corporation. The TES and THES were sold in 2005.

Times Literary Supplement (1902–) A weekly literary periodical of high international standing which first appeared with *The *Times* in 1902, then in 1914 became a separate publication. The first editor, Bruce Richmond, supported and encouraged many writers of his time, including Virginia *Woolf, T. S. *Eliot, J. M. *Murry, and Edmund *Blunden, both by commissioning reviews from them and by covering their own works. Contributions were anonymous until 1974 when under the editorship of John Gross they began to be signed.

Timon Athenian misanthrope described by *Plutarch, the subject of one of *Lucian's Dialogues and *Shakespeare's *Timon of Athens*. Alexander *Pope's Timon, in *An Epistle to Burlington*, ll. 98–168, is an example of ostentatious wealth without sense or taste.

Timon of Athens A drama by *Shakespeare, now generally acknowledged to be a collaboration with Thomas *Middleton, written probably about 1607 and apparently left unfinished; it was not printed until the first *folio of 1623. The material for the play is in *Plutarch's *Life of Antony*, William Painter's *Palace of Pleasure*, *Lucian's *Timon, or The Misanthrope*, and possibly an anonymous play *Timon* among the Dyce MSS in the Victoria and Albert Museum.

Timon, a noble and good-natured Athenian, ruins himself by his generosity to flatterers and parasites. He turns to the richest of his friends for help, and finds himself abandoned by those who had previously kept company with him. He surprises them by inviting them to another banquet; but when the covers are removed from the dishes (Timon crying, 'Uncover, dogs, and lap', III. vii. 84), they contain only warm water, which he throws in his guests' faces. Cursing the city, he retires to a cave, where he lives in disillusioned solitude. While digging for roots he finds a hoard of gold, which has now no value for him. His embittered spirit is revealed in his talk with the exiled Alcibiades, the churlish philosopher Apemantus, the thieves and flatterers attracted by the gold, and his faithful steward Flavius. When the senators of Athens, pressed by Alcibiades' attack, come to ask him to return to the city and help them, he offers them his fig tree, on which to hang themselves as a refuge from trouble. Soon his tomb is found by the seashore, with an epitaph expressing his hatred of mankind.

TINDALL, Gillian (1938–) Novelist, critic, and historian. Her novels, which show a sensitive interest in contemporary social and moral issues, and frequently feature the dilemmas of the liberal conscience, include *The Youngest* (1967), *Fly Away Home* (1971), *The Traveller and his Child* (1975), *Give Them All my Love* (1989), and *Spirit Weddings* (1992). Her work, both fiction and non-fiction, reflects her appreciation of the importance of place; *Countries of the Mind* (1991), is subtitled 'The Meaning of Place to Writers'. *The Fields Beneath* (1977) is a study of Kentish Town in north London, *Célestine* (1995) recreates the vanished world of a 19th-century French village, and *The House by the Thames* (2006) is an exploration of one old house and its role in London history.

'Tintern Abbey, Lines Composed a Few Miles above, On Revisiting the Banks of the Wye during a Tour' A poem by William *Wordsworth published in the first edition of the *Lyrical Ballads* (1798). Wordsworth had visited Tintern in 1793; the second visit recorded in this work was with his sister Dorothy, who is addressed in its closing passage. Written in *blank verse, its style is very different from the deliberately 'low' manner of the ballads, and Wordsworth himself referred to 'the impassioned music of the versification', which resembled the elevation of an ode. It is a central statement of Wordsworth's faith in the restorative and associative power of nature; he describes the development of his own love of nature from boyhood to the more reflective, moral, philosophic pleasures of maturity, informed by 'the still, sad music of humanity'.

TIPPER, Elizabeth (*fl.* 1693–8) Poet, author of *The Pilgrim's Viaticum, or The Destitute but not Forlorn* (1698), a book of pious reflections on personal struggles; Tipper also draws humour from her alternate situations as governess, teacher, servant, and book-keeper.

TIPTREE, James, Jr (1915–87) Pseudonym of Alice Bradley Sheldon, American *science fiction writer. She began publishing in 1968 as 'Tiptree', including 'The Women Men Don't See' (1973). Its rejection of the masculine world observed by a male 'unreliable narrator' invented by a woman writing as a pseudonymous man is fascinatingly recursive. She also published as Racoona Sheldon. Her female identity was revealed in 1977. *Her Smoke Rose up Forever* (1990) collects the best of her short fiction.

Tiresias Seer of Thebes, whose divinely inflicted blindness was compensated with the gift of prophecy. In the underworld in *Homer's *Odyssey* Book 11 he foretells Odysseus' final voyage, and he is a key figure in *Sophocles' *Oedipus* and *Antigone*. The blind John *Milton associates himself with Tiresias and other blind seers in *Paradise Lost* Book III. In one tradition, drawn on by *Ovid in *Metamorphoses* Book 3, he changed sex. T. S. *Eliot described his explicitly bisexual Tiresias as 'the most important personage' in The *Waste Land*.

'Tiresias' A dramatic monologue in blank verse by Alfred *Tennyson, published 1885, but mostly composed in 1833. The prophet Tiresias, blinded and doomed to 'speak the truth that no man may believe' as a consequence of glimpsing Athene naked, urges Menoeceus, son of Creon, to sacrifice himself for Thebes.

'Tis Pity She's a Whore A tragedy by John *Ford, printed 1633. The play deals with the guilty passion between Giovanni and his

sister Annabella. Pregnant, Annabella marries Soranzo, who discovers her condition. She refuses to name her lover, though threatened with death by Soranzo. On the advice of Vasques, his faithful servant, Soranzo pretends forgiveness, while Vasques succeeds in discovering the truth. Soranzo invites Annabella's father and the dignitaries of the city, with Giovanni, to a grand feast, intending to exact vengeance. Although warned of Soranzo's plans, Giovanni boldly comes. He has a last meeting with Annabella just before the feast and, to forestall Soranzo's vengeance, stabs her himself. He enters the banqueting room with her heart on his dagger, defiantly tells what he has done, kills Soranzo, and is killed by Vasques.

'Tis Pity is an obsessive play, focusing on the incest taboo, but treating it seriously and with penetrating honesty (see Act I sc. ii).

Titans According to *Hesiod's *Theogony*, the twelve children of Uranus and Gaia, the original gods of heaven and earth, including Oceanus, Hyperion, Cronos (Roman *Saturn), and their descendants, including *Prometheus, grandson of Oceanus. Intergenerational warfare is an essential part of the myth: Cronos defeated Uranus; the Olympian gods Zeus (Roman *Jupiter), son of Cronos, and his siblings waged war against the first generation of Titans, who were cast down to Tartarus (*see* HADES).

Titmarsh, Michael Angelo A pseudonym used by W. M. *Thackeray for much of his early journalism. 'Michael Angelo' is a comic reference to his broken nose and to his aspirations to be an artist. Samuel Titmarsh appears as a character in Thackeray's *The Great Hoggarty Diamond*.

Titus Andronicus A tragedy by *Shakespeare with, probably, George *Peele. It is probably his earliest tragedy and may date from 1590; it was published in a quarto in 1594, and included in the first *folio of 1623, with an added scene (III. ii). Various sources have been put forward, including the *Hecuba* of *Euripides. *Seneca's *Thyestes* and *Troades* contributed to the plot, as did *Ovid's version of 'the tragic tale of Philomel', in *Metamorphoses* Book 13, and *Plutarch.

The first half of the play deals with the return of Titus Andronicus to Rome after his sixth victory over the Goths. He brings with him their Queen Tamora and her three sons, the eldest of whom, Alarbus, is sacrificed to avenge his own sons' deaths. Titus is offered the imperial throne, but gives it instead to the late emperor's eldest son Saturninus, offering his daughter Lavinia as Saturninus' bride. But Lavinia is already promised to Saturninus' brother Bassianus, who steals her away, with the help of her brothers. Titus kills his son Mutius, who had tried to prevent his pursuit of the lovers. Saturninus renounces Lavinia, and marries Tamora, who engineers a false reconciliation between the emperor and Titus, whom she plans to destroy. With the encouragement of her lover Aaron, the Moor, Tamora's sons Chiron and Demetrius murder Bassianus, whose body is thrown into a pit, rape Lavinia, and cut off her tongue and hands. Titus' sons Quintus and Martius are then lured by Aaron to fall into the pit, where they are found and accused of Bassianus' murder. Aaron tells Titus that his sons will not be executed if he sacrifices his hand and sends it to the emperor. Titus does so, but gets it back again with the heads of his two sons.

In the second half of the play Titus discovers who raped and mutilated his daughter, and with his brother Marcus, and last remaining son Lucius, vows revenge. Lucius leaves Rome, but returns with an army of Goths, which captures Aaron and his child by Tamora. Tamora and her sons Demetrius and Chiron visit Titus disguised as Revenge, Rapine, and Murder and ask him to have Lucius' banquet at his house, where the emperor and the empress and her sons will be brought. Titus recognizes his enemies and with the help of Lavinia slits the throats of Chiron and Demetrius and uses their flesh in a pie, some of which Tamora eats at the banquet before Titus kills her. He also stabs Lavinia, but is killed by Saturninus, who is in turn killed by Lucius. Lucius is elected emperor and sentences Aaron to be buried breast-deep in the ground and starved to death.

The play was dismissed by its *Restoration adapter Edward Ravenscroft (*fl.* 1659–97) as 'rather a heap of Rubbish than a Structure.' More recent critics have related the play to *revenge tragedy. And*ron*icus in the play is accentuated on the second syllable; in Latin it is Andron*i*cus.

'To Autumn' A poem by John *Keats, written September 1819, published 1820. It was his last major poem, and although usually included in a discussion of the Odes (*see* ODE), Keats himself did not call it an ode. The poem, in three stanzas, is at once a celebration of the fruitfulness of autumn (lightly personified as a figure in various autumnal landscapes) and an elegy for the passing of summer and the tran-

sience of life, and its mood has been generally taken to be one of acceptance.

TODHUNTER, John (1839–1916) Poet, and pioneer of the Irish literary movement. His works include *The Banshee* (1888) and *Three Irish Bardic Tales* (1896).

TÓIBÍN, Colm (1955–) Irish novelist, journalist, and travel writer. Three years spent in Barcelona led to *Homage to Barcelona* (1990) and his first novel, *The South* (1990), about an Irish woman artist living in Spain in the 1950s. Tóibín's lyrical style and political concerns are displayed in *The Heather Blazing* (1992). Travels in South America resulted in *The Story of the Night* (1996), about a gay man in Argentina during the Falklands War. *The Blackwater Lighthouse* (1999) describes a family reunion at the sickbed of a man with Aids and is complemented by the collection of essays *Love in a Dark Time* (2002). is *The Master* (2004), is a novel about Henry *James. Tóibín's stories were collected in *Mothers and Sons* (2006).

TOKLAS, Alice B. *See* STEIN, GERTRUDE.

TOLAND, John (1670–1722) Irish freethinker and controversialist. 'Educated from the cradle in the grossest superstition', as he says in his *Apology* (1697), he repudiated *Roman Catholicism at the age of 15. *Christianity not Mysterious* (1696) made him notorious; it also began the *Deist controversy and initiated the greatest epoch of Irish philosophy. Toland's materialistic pantheism—he coined the word 'pantheist' in 1705—is flamboyantly expressed in *Pantheisticon* (1720). *Tetradymus* (1720) contains perhaps the first essay on the esoteric/exoteric distinction, or the difference between specialized or obscure knowledge and knowledge that is publicly available to all. Alexander *Pope ridiculed Toland; Jonathan *Swift called him 'the great Oracle of the Anti-Christians'.

TOLKIEN, J. R. R. (John Ronald Reuel) (1892–1973) Scholar and novelist. A member of the *'Inklings' group, he was Merton professor of English language and literature at Oxford University, 1945–59, and published a number of philological and critical studies, including 'Beowulf: The Monsters and the Critics' (in *Proceedings of the British Academy*, 1936). Alongside his scholarly career, he became internationally known for two books based on a complex mythology of his own devising: *The Hobbit* (1937) and its sequel *The *Lord of the Rings* (3 vols, 1954–5; filmed 2001–3). *The Silmarillion* (1977), which occupies an earlier place in this sequence of stories, was published posthumously. When *The Lord of the Rings* became a best-seller in the United States during the 1960s, Tolkien was unimpressed, referring ruefully to his 'deplorable cultus'. After Tolkien's death, his son Christopher supervised publication of a series of posthumous works and the negotiation of adaptation rights. *See also* FANTASY FICTION.

TOLLER, Ernst (1893–1939) German Jewish poet and dramatist. The experience of war made him a radical pacifist. He wrote *Expressionist plays such as *Die Maschinenstürmer* (1922: *The Machine Wreckers*). After the rise of Hitler he moved to New York, where he committed suicide, an act commemorated in an elegy by W. H. *Auden, who also translated the lyrics for Toller's satirical musical play *Nie wieder Friede!* (1937: *No More Peace!*).

TOLLET, Elizabeth (1694–1754) Poet. Her anonymous *Poems on Several Occasions: With Anne Boleyn to King Henry VIII. An Epistle* (1724) was reissued posthumously (1755), bearing her name and including much additional work. Her poem 'To my Brother at St John's College in Cambridge' deftly explores male and female patterns of reading; her most substantial poem, 'Hypatia', has a strongly *feminist argument.

TOLSTOY, Count Lev Nikolaevich (1828–1910) Russian prose writer, He served in the army 1852–6, seeing action during the Crimean War. He read widely, admiring *Plato, *Rousseau, Laurence *Sterne, W. M. *Thackeray, George *Eliot, and Charles *Dickens. The influence of *David Copperfield* was apparent in *Childhood* (1852), the opening part of a trilogy completed by *Boyhood* (1854) and *Youth* (1857). His first visit to the West in 1857 led to 'Lucerne', a lyrical short story attacking English behaviour. After publishing *Family Happiness* (1859) and *The Cossacks* (1863), he embarked on *War and Peace*, an epic historical novel of the Napoleonic campaigns and the lives of two aristocratic families, followed by *Anna Karenina* (1875–8), the story of a married woman's passion for a young officer and her tragic fate. Tolstoy subsequently renounced literature as art, and his later writing was to display a purely moral purpose, apparent in *A Confession* (1879–82), *What Men Live By* (1882), *What I Believe* (1883), and *What is Art?* (1898). His major late fictional works are *The Death of Ivan Ilyich* (1886), *The Kreutzer Sonata* (1891), *Master and Man* (1895), *Resurrection* (1899–1900), and

Hadji Murad (1904, published posthumously in 1912). Tolstoy's moral positions, involving non-resistance to evil, the renunciation of property, and the abolition of governments and churches, led to the banning of many of his works and to his excommunication by the Orthodox Church in 1901. Tolstoy's few plays, influenced George Bernard *Shaw, whose own play *The Shewing-up of Blanco Posnet* (1910) reworked Tolstoy's *The Power of Darkness*.

TOMALIN, Claire (1933–) Biographer. Her works, which have been notable for their scholarly and sensitive reclamation of women's lives from historical neglect or misunderstanding, include *The Life and Death of Mary Wollstonecraft* (1974), *Katherine Mansfield: A Secret Life* (1987), *The Invisible Woman: The Story of Nelly Ternan and Charles Dickens* (1990), *Mrs Jordan's Profession* (1994, a study of the actress Dorothy Jordan), and *Jane Austen: A Life* (1997). She also published biographies of Samuel *Pepys (2002) and *Thomas Hardy* (2006).

Tom and **Jerry** The two chief characters in Pierce *Egan's *Life in London*; hence used in various allusive ways, for instance to suggest riotous behaviour: they gave their names to the well-known cartoon characters.

Tom Brown's Schooldays (1857; filmed 1951, TV 2005) Seminal *school story by Thomas *Hughes, set in Rugby School in the 1830s. It helped establish staples of the genre with a God-like headmaster (Thomas Arnold) and the ultimate bully, *Flashman.

Tom Jones, The History of A novel by Henry *Fielding, published 1749. The kindly, prosperous widower Mr Allworthy (based on Ralph Allen and the dedicatee, Lord *Lyttelton) lives at 'Paradise Hall' in Somerset with his ill-humoured sister Bridget. Late one evening Allworthy finds a baby boy on his bed. He is charmed, names the baby Tom, and adopts him, adding the surname Jones on the assumption that the mother is Jenny Jones, a maidservant to the wife of the schoolmaster Partridge, who is accused of being the father and dismissed his post. Bridget marries the obnoxious Captain Blifil and they have a son, Master Blifil, who is taught, with Tom, by the sadistic chaplain Thwackum and the philosopher Square. When Tom is 19, his childhood affection for the beautiful and sweet-natured Sophia, daughter of the neighbouring fox-hunting Squire Western, matures into love. However, Sophia is destined by her father for Master Blifil, whose scheming gradually poisons Allworthy's affection for the good-natured but unruly Tom, and succeeds in having Tom expelled from the house. Filled with despair at alienating his beloved foster-father, Tom sets off for Bristol intending to go to sea. Meanwhile Sophia, disgusted by Blifil's courtship, runs away with her maid Honour. Amid numerous adventures on the road, Tom encounters Partridge, who is now travelling the country as a barber-surgeon. Tom and Sophia both arrive at an inn at Upton, but because of Partridge's malicious stupidity Sophia believes that Tom, then in bed with a woman known as Mrs Waters, no longer loves her, and flees on towards London. Tom follows, and in London is ensnared by Lady Bellaston, Sophia's kinswoman. Lady Bellaston and her friend Lord Fellamar keep Tom away from Sophia, on whom Lord Fellamar has designs, but the abrupt eruption of Squire Western into the picture is sufficient to save Sophia from the artistocrat's schemes of seduction. Partridge now reveals that Mrs Waters is Jenny Jones, and Tom briefly believes he has committed incest, but Jenny reveals that Tom's mother was really Bridget Allworthy, who has confessed to her brother on her deathbed. Tom's enemies arrange for him to be press-ganged, but instead a fight develops in which it at first appears that Tom has killed his assailant; he is in consequence arrested. Blifil arranges for the gang to give evidence against Tom, who despairs of obtaining Sophia's forgiveness; but with the help of a letter of confession and repentance from Square to Allworthy, Blifil's long-running envious machinations are finally revealed, and Tom is reinstated in his uncle's affection. He meets Sophia again, learns that she loves him, and receives the hearty blessing of her father. In the generosity of his heart, Tom forgives all who have wronged him.

The book's robust characterization, occasional exercises in *mock-heroic diction, and magisterial narrative voice defined a widely influential compromise between the new world of the 'realistic' novel and the more timeless genres of comedy and epic, and the book was an immediate success, selling some 10,000 copies in its first year.

TOMKIS, Thomas (?1580–?1634) Author of two university comedies, *Lingua, or The Combat of the Tongue and the Five Senses for Superiority* (1607) and *Albumazar* (1615). The latter was acted before *James I at Cambridge. Albumazar (historically an Arabian astronomer, 805–85) is a rascally wizard who transforms the rustic Trincalo into the person of his master, with absurd consequences. It was revived (1668) with a prologue by John *Dryden, and (1747) by David *Garrick.

TOMLINSON, Charles (1927–) Poet and artist. His qualities as a graphic artist (*Eden: Graphics and Poems* was published in 1989) are reflected in the visual qualities of his verse, which frequently figures paintings among its subjects. It also shows strong American influences, including Wallace *Stevens, William Carlos *Williams, and Marianne *Moore. *Some Americans* (1981) commemorates his relationships with such poets and painters as George Oppen and Georgia O'Keeffe (1887–1986). American landscapes, notably those of New Mexico, also figure prominently in the poems, along with those of rural Gloucestershire. Tomlinson is both a poet of place and a poet between places, and his poems maintain a dialogue between rootedness and instability, celebration and wry rumination. The natural world is characteristically scrutinized into a human significance while also remaining instructively, even caustically, other. Tomlinson's volumes of poetry include *Relations and Contraries* (1951), *Seeing is Believing* (USA 1958; London 1960), *The Way of the World* (1969), *Written on Water* (1972), *The Way in and Other Poems* (1974), which uncharacteristically explores his working-class childhood in Stoke, *Notes from New York* (1984), *Jubilation* (1995), and *Cracks in the Universe* (2006). A volume of *Collected Poems* was published in 1985. Tomlinson has also been prominent as a translator, producing versions of such poets as Fyodor Tyutchev (1803–73), Antonio *Machado, Cesar Vallejo (1892–1938), Octavio Paz, and Attilio Bertolucci (1911–2000).

TOMLINSON, H. M. (Henry Major) (1873–1958) Journalist and novelist. His early love of ships and the sea is reflected in his life and works, including his first book, *The Sea and the Jungle* (1912, an account of a voyage to Brazil and some 2,000 miles up the Amazon and the Madeira, its longest tributary), *London River* (1921, essays and reflections), and his first novel, *Gallions Reach* (1927). *All our Yesterdays* (1930) is an anti-war novel born of his experiences as an official war correspondent (1914–17).

Tommy Thumb's Song Book A collection of *nursery rhymes presumably printed and distributed by Mary *Cooper. Although no copy of this work has been located, Cooper advertised it in 1744 and copies of *Tommy*

Thumb's Pretty Song Book (vol. ii, 1744), containing many well-known verses, survive.

Tom o' Bedlam A wandering beggar. After the dissolution of the religious houses, where before the Reformation the poor used to be provided for, they wandered over the country, many assuming disguises designed to promote charitable giving. Some pretended to be mad and were called Bedlam beggars (like 'Diccon the Bedlam' in **Gammer Gurton's Needle* and Edgar, in **King Lear*, II. iii).

In Thomas *Dekker's *Bellman of London* (1608) 'Tom of Bedlam's band of madcaps' are listed among types of beggars. Some of these Bedlam beggars sang mad songs, examples of which are given in Thomas *Percy's **Reliques*. They were also called 'Abraham-men', possibly from the parable of the beggar Lazarus in Luke 18.

Tom Sawyer, The Adventures of A novel by Mark *Twain, published 1876, which describes a series of escapades centring on Tom, a lively and adventurous lad, and his companion Huckleberry Finn. At the close of the novel, they divide the treasure they discover between them, which marks the starting point for the classic sequel *The Adventures of *Huckleberry Finn*. Tom also features in *Tom Sawyer Abroad* (1894) and *Tom Sawyer, Detective* (1896).

Tom Thumb, a Tragedy A *mock-heroic farce by Henry *Fielding, performed and published in 1730, and republished in 1731 in an extended version as *The Tragedy of Tragedies, or The Life and Death of Tom Thumb the Great*, with an apparatus of mock-scholarly notes in the manner of Alexander *Pope's **Dunciad Variorum*. William *Hogarth supplied the frontispiece. The play burlesqued the 'Bombastic Greatness' of heroic tragedies by James *Thomson and others. Jonathan *Swift claimed that he had laughed only twice in his life, once at a Merry-Andrew, or clown, and once at *Tom Thumb*.

TONKS, Rosemary (1932–?) British novelist and poet. Since the 1990s there has been an increasing interest in her work, and poems have appeared in a wide range of 20th-century poetry anthologies. Her surreally inflected poetics of modern urban life—what she has described as its 'enraged excitement, its great lonely joys'—harness huge lyrical and colloquial energies. Tonks stopped publishing in the 1970s due to strong religious convictions, and her whereabouts is not currently publicly known. Poems include *Notes on Cafés and Bedrooms* (1963) and *Iliad of Broken Sentences* (1967) and novels include *Opium Fogs* (1963), *The Bloater* (1968), and *The Halt during the Chase* (1972).

TONSON, Jacob (1655–1736) Publisher and bookseller; the major literary publisher of his age. His long association with John *Dryden began in 1679; he also published Aphra *Behn, the earl of *Rochester, Thomas *Otway, Abraham *Cowley, Nicholas *Rowe, Matthew *Prior, William *Congreve, Joseph *Addison, and Richard *Steele, among many others. He bought up several lucrative copyrights, and published major editions of **Paradise Lost*, of the plays of William *Shakespeare (1709) and of the works of Edmund *Spenser (1715). His series of *Miscellanies*, appeared 1684–1709, and contained translations from *Horace, *Ovid, *Virgil, among other Latin poets, as well as work by Alexander *Pope, Ambrose *Philips, and Jonathan *Swift. The firm was continued by a nephew from 1718, and by a great-nephew of the same name.

TOOLE, John Kennedy (1937–69) American novelist. His comic novel *A Confederacy of Dunces* (1980) and *The Neon Bible* (1989) were published after his suicide at the age of 32.

TOOMER, Jean (1894–1967) African American writer, born Nathan Pinchback, who is primarily remembered for his mixed-media volume *Cane* (1923), which uses *modernist techniques to explore the gathering of sugar in Georgia. Toomer was an important figure in the *Harlem Renaissance but from the 1930s he withdrew from society.

TOPLADY, Augustus Montague (1740–78) Clergyman and *hymns-writer. His best-known hymn is 'Rock of Ages', published in the *Gospel Magazine* in 1776. Initially influenced by John *Wesley, he soon became his bitter opponent, and an extreme *Calvinist.

topographical poetry Described by Samuel *Johnson as 'local poetry, of which the fundamental object is some particular landscape . . . with the addition of . . . historical retrospection or incidental meditation', normally distinguished from poems praising country estates, such as Ben *Jonson's 'To Penshurst' or Andrew *Marvell's 'Upon Appleton House'. *Cooper's Hill* (1642), by Sir John *Denham, is regarded as the model for the genre, which includes poems by John *Dyer, Sir Samuel *Garth, Alexander *Pope, James *Thomson (1700–48), Richard *Jago, and Oliver *Goldsmith. 'Prospect poems' survey a large landscape from a high point; William *Wordsworth's 'Lines Composed a Few Miles above *Tintern Abbey' is a late example. *Remains of Elmet* (1979) and the less precisely located *River* (1983), poetic sequences by Ted *Hughes, lie partially within the topographical tradition, as does Alice *Oswald's *Dart* (2002).

To the Lighthouse Fifth novel by Virginia *Woolf, published 1927. It draws powerfully on her memories of family holidays at St Ives, Cornwall, although the setting is ostensibly the Isle of Skye. Woolf's parents were the inspiration for the maternal, gracious, managing, but manipulative Mrs Ramsay, and the self-centred, self-pitying, absurd, yet tragic Mr Ramsay, who together provide the focus for Woolf's most profound exploration of the conflicts between men and women and the dynamics of marriage. The novel is in three sections, of which the first and longest, 'The Window', describes the late afternoon and evening of an Edwardian September day, with the Ramsays on holiday with their eight children and assorted guests, including the lethargic elderly poet Augustus Carmichael; the painter Lily Briscoe; and the awkward young academic Charles Tansley. Family tension centres on the desire of the youngest child, James, to visit the lighthouse, and his father's apparent desire to thwart him; the frictions of the day are momentarily resolved around the dinner table. The second section, 'Time Passes', is a comparatively brief, lyrical treatment of the 1914–18 period and records, parenthetically, the deaths of Mrs Ramsay, her son Andrew (killed in the war), and daughter Prue, who dies in childbirth. It dwells with a desolate lyricism on the abandonment of the family summer home and its gradual post-war revival, and ends with the arrival of the Ramsays, Lily Briscoe, Carmichael, and others in September 1919. The last section, 'The Lighthouse', describes the finally successful efforts of Lily to complete the painting which she had abandoned ten years earlier and the parallel but equally successful efforts of Mr Ramsay, and two of his surviving children, Cam and James, to reach the lighthouse, despite the undercurrents of rivalry, loss, and rebellion that torment them.

TOTTEL, Richard (*c.*1528–1593) A publisher who is chiefly known as the compiler (with Nicholas Grimald) of *Songs and Sonnets*, known as *Tottel's Miscellany* (1557), in which many of Sir Thomas *Wyatt's and the earl of *Surrey's poems were printed for the first time. Besides lawbooks, he also published Sir Thomas

*More's *Dialogue of Comfort* (1553) and Surrey's *Aeneid* (1557).

TOURNEUR, Cyril (?1575–1626) Dramatist. Practically nothing is known of his life. He died at Kinsale in Ireland after accompanying Sir Edward Cecil to Cadiz in 1625 on an unsuccessful raid of Spanish treasure ships. His small known output includes an allegorical poem, *The Transformed Metamorphosis* (1600), a lost play, *The Nobleman* (1612), *The *Atheist's Tragedy* (1611), and an elegy on the death of Prince Henry (1613). *The *Revenger's Tragedy*, printed anonymously in 1607, was first ascribed to him in 1656 by Edward Archer in a play list, and was generally accepted as his until the end of the 19th century, when Thomas *Middleton was proposed as the author; Middleton is now generally accepted as the most likely candidate. *See also* REVENGE TRAGEDY.

TOURNIER, Michel (1924–) French novelist and short story writer, known for his reworkings of stories, myths, and legends. His first novel, *Vendredi, ou Les Limbes du Pacifique* (1967; trans. as *Friday*, 1969), restaged Daniel Defoe's *Robinson Crusoe* by having Man Friday rather than Crusoe leave the island for civilization. *Le Coq de Bruyère* (1978; trans. as *The Fetishist*, 1984) includes retellings of the Adam and Eve story and Charles *Perrault's 'Le Petit Poucet' (Tom Thumb).

TOWNSEND, John Rowe (1922–) Children's writer, historian, and critic. While Children's Books Editor for the *Guardian* in the 1970s he became concerned with the way children's books helped shape attitudes to social issues including class, gender, and the environment. *Gumble's Yard* (1961) and its sequels include working-class characters; *The Intruder* (1969) is about identity theft. Later works explore fantasy and future worlds and teenage romance.

TOWNSEND, Sue (1946–) Author of *The Secret Diary of Adrian Mole Aged 13¾* (1982) and its four sequels (televised 1985). Adrian reports on his own and others' behaviour, revealing concerns about his adolescent desires and body in an inadvertently comic way. The books comment on the politics, attitudes, and events of Britain in the 1980s and 1990s.

TOWNSHEND, Aurelian (?1583–?1643) Poet, a writer of court *masques. He seems to have collaborated with Inigo *Jones in *Albion's Triumph* and to have contributed verses for the queen's masque of *Tempe Restored*. He enjoyed favour at the court of Charles I, as his lyric 'On his Hearing Her Majesty Sing' records. His poems are collected in *Poems and Masks* (1912), edited by E. K. *Chambers.

Toxophilus See ASCHAM, ROGER.

toy books Books designed to stimulate play and so which function as toys have existed since the 18th century, but the term is usually applied to the large colourful picture books, based on traditional tales and nursery rhymes, published in the 19th century in tandem with—and possibly stimulating—developments in colour printing. They are particularly associated with the printer-engraver Edmund Evans (1826–1905) and his stable of artists including Walter Crane, Randolph *Caldecott, and Kate *Greenaway. Together they set the standard for the modern *picturebook, with its sophisticated interplay of word and image. They were sold inexpensively in vast print runs; a first printing usually started at 10,000 copies.

Tractarian Movement, *Tracts for the Times* See OXFORD MOVEMENT.

tragedy A dramatic (or, by extension, narrative) work in which events move to a fatal or disastrous conclusion for the *protagonist, whose potential greatness is cruelly wasted through error or the mysterious workings of fate. Aristotle's *Poetics was the first attempt to define the characteristics of tragedy as practised by *Sophocles and others, presenting its effect upon spectators in terms of pity, terror, and purification ('catharsis'). Roman tragedies, especially those of *Seneca, exerted a stronger influence upon the emergence of English tragic drama than did Greek practice or precept. A distinct contributory tradition was that of late medieval verse narratives recounting the fall of great men: for example *Boccaccio, *Chaucer's 'Monk's Tale' (*see* CANTERBURY TALES, 19), John *Lydgate's *Fall of Princes, and eventually the collaborative *Mirror for Magistrates. After Norton and Sackville's *Gorboduc (1561), tragic stage plays flourished in the late Elizabethan and Jacobean periods (*c.*1590–1625), notably in the form of *revenge tragedy. Thomas *Kyd, Christopher *Marlowe, and *Shakespeare developed new tragic conventions including the presentation of deaths onstage and an often rapid succession of scenes, in Kyd's *The *Spanish Tragedy, Marlowe's *Tamburlaine the Great and *Dr Faustus, and Shakespeare's *Romeo and Juliet, *Julius Caesar, and *Hamlet. Tragedies in the Jacobean period include the mature work of Shakespeare in *Macbeth,

*King Lear, *Othello, and *Antony and Cleopatra, along with Thomas Middleton and William Rowley's *The *Changeling and John Webster's *The *Duchess of Malfi. The rediscovery and codification of Aristotle's theory of tragedy in the rules of *neo-classicism gave rise to a purer form of tragic drama in France, of which *Racine's work is the great exemplar, but in England after the closure of the theatres in the mid-17th century the tragic tradition withered: some imitative neo-classical tragedies were attempted, notably John Dryden's *All for Love (1678), while John *Milton's *Samson Agonistes (1671) was a dramatic poem not intended for the stage (a *'closet drama', like some later tragic poems, e.g. Lord *Byron's *Manfred). There were recurrent unsuccessful attempts at tragedy in the Shakespearian manner, notably P. B. *Shelley's The *Cenci. Novels aiming at traditional tragic effects appeared in the 19th century, notably Thomas *Hardy's The *Mayor of Casterbridge, but the dramatic tradition, although revived by Henrik *Ibsen, has survived only fitfully in English, most clearly in the plays of Arthur *Miller.

tragicomedy A play that combines elements of *tragedy and *comedy moods, or that cannot be placed clearly in either category. This mixed form was first practised in the 16th century by the Italian dramatists Cinzio and Guarini, especially in *pastoral plays combining 'high' and 'low' styles and characters. English dramatists of the early 17th century, notably Francis *Beaumont and John *Fletcher in *Philaster and other works, developed both this mixture and the associated plot structure of surprising reversals that pluck happy endings from seemingly tragic stories. *Shakespeare had independently exploited similar reversals in such 'dark' comedies as The *Merchant of Venice and *Measure for Measure (*see* PROBLEM PLAY) and continued with the device in his late 'romance' plays, notably The *Winter's Tale. Many kinds of later drama may be regarded as tragicomedy: the sentimental comedy of the 18th century, the *melodrama of the 19th, and many plays by *Ibsen, *Chekhov, G. B. *Shaw, and *Brecht. In particular, *Beckett's designation of his *Waiting for Godot as a tragicomedy revived interest in the term in the 1950s and 1960s, in part as a clue to the enigmas of *Pinter's plays and of the Theatre of the *Absurd more generally.

TRAHERNE, Thomas (1637–74) Poet and visionary. In 1657 he was appointed rector of Credenhill, Herefordshire, where he may have joined a religious circle centring on the religious polemicist Susanna Hopton (1627–1709) at Kington, for whom he perhaps wrote the *Centuries*, a series of short meditations. He led a 'single and devout life', according to Anthony *Wood. He told John *Aubrey that he had visions. Traherne's *Centuries* and many of his poems were discovered in a notebook (now in the Bodleian) bought on a London bookstall in the winter of 1896–7. Bertram Dobell (1842–1914) identified Traherne as the author, and edited the *Poetical Works* (1903) and the *Centuries of Meditations* (1908). More poems, prepared for publication by Traherne's brother Philip as 'Poems of Felicity', were discovered in a British Museum manuscript and published in 1910. Traherne's other published works are *Roman Forgeries* (1673), *Christian Ethics* (1675), prepared for the press before he died, and *Thanksgivings* (1699). His memories, in the *Centuries*, of his own early intuitions are the first convincing depiction of childhood experience in English literature. He is also among the first English writers to respond imaginatively to new ideas about infinite space, which he at times virtually equates with God.

Traitor, The A tragedy by James *Shirley, acted 1631, printed 1635. This play was highly successful both before and after the Civil War. It is based on the assassination of the Florentine Duke Alessandro de' Medici by his kinsman Lorenzo.

Transcendental Club A group of American intellectuals who met informally for philosophical discussion at Ralph Waldo *Emerson's house and elsewhere. They represent a movement of thought, philosophical, religious, social, and economic, produced in New England between 1830 and 1850 by the spirit of revolutionary Europe, German philosophy, and William *Wordsworth, S. T. *Coleridge, and Thomas *Carlyle. Transcendentalism's literary organ was *The *Dial*. Its utopian aspect was reflected in the Brook Farm community (1841–7) of George Ripley (1802–80), unflatteringly portrayed in Nathaniel *Hawthorne's *The *Blithedale Romance*.

transition: *an international quarterly for creative experiment* A periodical founded in 1927 in Paris by Eugène and Maria Jolas. Central to the experimental work it published, and exemplary of its 'revolution of the word', was James *Joyce's 'Work in Progress' (*Finnegans Wake*); other authors included Gertrude *Stein, Hart *Crane, Dylan *Thomas, and Samuel *Beckett.

translation A vital dimension of English literary culture since the time of King *Alfred. From *Ælfric in the 10th century until 1611 the most important translations into English were biblical (*see* BIBLE, THE ENGLISH). Otherwise medieval translation was dominated by devotional texts from Latin sources, interspersed by secular romances from the French, as with the *Romaunt of the Rose* attributed in part to *Chaucer. The most prolific translator of the 15th century was John *Lydgate. William *Caxton printed his own translations of French works.

Gawin *Douglas's Scots version of *Virgil's *Aeneid* (1553) and *Surrey's version of the same poem's fourth book (1554) heralded the great humanistic programme of rendering the classics of antiquity into the vernaculars. Over the following 100 years appeared Arthur *Golding's version of *Ovid's *Metamorphoses* (1565–7); George *Gascoigne's *Jocasta* (1575, from an Italian version of Euripides); the tragedies of *Seneca, Englished by Jasper Heywood and others from 1559; Sir Thomas *North's translation of Plutarch's *Lives* (1579, from a French version); Christopher *Marlowe's translation of Ovid's *Amores* (c.1599); Philemon *Holland's versions of Livy (1600), Pliny (1601), and Suetonius (1606); and George *Chapman's *Works of Homer* (1616).

Meanwhile other works had come into English from Italian and French, notably in Thomas *Wyatt's versions of *Petrarch's lyrics, Geoffrey Fenton's tales from *Bandello (1567), Sir John *Harington's translation of *Ariosto (1591), Edward Fairfax's rendering of *Tasso's *Gerusalemme liberata* (as *Godfrey of Bulloigne*, 1600), Florio's translation of *Montaigne's *Essays* (1603), the unattributed English *Decameron* of 1620 (possibly also by John *Florio), and Sir Thomas *Urquhart's first two books of *Rabelais (1653). William Painter's *Palace of Pleasure* (1566–7) was a two-volume anthology of tales translated from Boccaccio, Bandello, Cinzio, and others, later raided by Shakespeare and John *Webster for the plots of their plays.

The 18th century landmarks are, Peter Motteux's *Don Quixote* (1700–03), Tobias *Smollett's *Gil Blas* (1749, from the French of *Lesage), John *Dryden's Virgil (1697), and Alexander *Pope's Homer: *Iliad* (1715–20) and *Odyssey* (1725–6).

The early 19th century produced translations of modern German literature, in S. T. *Coleridge's translation of the last two parts of *Schiller's *Wallenstein* (1800), and in Thomas *Carlyle's version of *Goethe's novel *Wilhelm

Meister's Apprenticeship (1824, 1827); and Henry Cary's blank verse translation of Dante's *Divina commedia* (1805, 1814). Victorian disagreements over principles of translation from the ancient Greek led to Matthew *Arnold's *On Translating Homer* (1861) and Robert *Browning's defiantly literal *Agamemnon of Aeschylus* (1877). Other significant Victorian and later translators include Edward *FitzGerald, for his free interpretation of the Persian poet *The Rubáiyát of *Omar Khayyám* (1859); William *Archer, who introduced the major works of Henrik *Ibsen to English audiences; Constance *Garnett, whose translations of modern Russian prose writers included as many as 70 volumes of Turgenev, Tolstoy, Dostoevsky, Gogol, and Chekhov; Ezra *Pound, for his verse translations from the Chinese in *Cathay* (1915); and Arthur *Waley, for his versions of Japanese and Chinese classics in *A Hundred and Seventy Chinese Poems* (1918), *Tale of Genji* (1925–33), and *Monkey* (1942).

Among the more notable 20th-century translations are the legendary translation of Marcel *Proust's *À la recherche du temps perdu* by C. K. Scott-Moncrieff (1889–1930) under the fanciful title *Remembrance of Things Past* (1922–30), Edwin and Willa *Muir's versions of Franz *Kafka's works (1930–49), Stephen *Spender's translation with J. B. Leishman of Rainer Maria Rilke's *Duino Elegies* (1939), Louis *MacNeice's *Agamemnon* (1936) and Cecil *Day-Lewis's Virgil (*Georgics*, 1940; *Aeneid*, 1952). Modern poets notable for their translations include Christopher *Logue (*Logue's Homer*, 2001), Tony *Harrison (*Oresteia*, 1981), Ted *Hughes (*Tales from Ovid*, 1997), Seamus *Heaney (*Beowulf*, 1999), Thomas *Kinsella, *The Táin* (1968), and Charles *Tomlinson, who edited *The Oxford Book of Verse in English Translation* (1983).

translation for children The earliest translated children's book is generally agreed to be John Amos Comenius' (Czech) *Orbis Sensualiam Pictus* (1658; *A World of Things Obvious to the Senses*, 1659). In the 18th century, translations specifically for children often lagged behind their adult counterparts; *The Oriental Moralist*, published by Elizabeth Newbery, *c*.1791 was an adaptation for children of the *Arabian Nights Entertainments* and Frances Newbery's *Mother Bunch's Fairy Tales* (1773) adapted Madame d'Aulnoy's *Contes des fées* (first translated into English in 1699). Charles *Perrault's *Histoires ou contes du temps passé* was translated in 1729, and the *Grimm brothers' *Kinder- und Hausmärchen* (1812–14)

was translated by Edgar Taylor as *German Popular Stories* (1823). There were many retellings of folk and fairy tales associated with other cultures in the 19th century, for example, Annie and Eliza Keary's *The Heroes of Asgard* (1857) and Charles *Kingsley's version of the Greek myths, *The Heroes* (1856), which has the curious distinction of having been translated *into* Greek. Hans Christian *Andersen's work was translated in five different versions in 1846. The translation of folk-tale materials continued into the 20th century with Arthur *Ransome's *Old Peter's Russian Tales* (1916).

Several 19th-century translated works have now been virtually naturalized into English culture, including *Der schweizerische Robinson* (1812–13); *The Family Robinson Crusoe*, 1814, possibly by William *Godwin); Johanna Spyri's *Heidi's Lehr- und Wanderjahre* (1881; *Heidi's Early Experiences* and *Heidi's Further Experiences*, 1884), Carlo Collodi's *Pinocchio* (1883), and Heinrich Hoffmann's satire on the moral tale *Lustiges Geschichten und drollige Bilder* (1845; *The English Struwwelpeter*, 1848).

Perhaps the most influential 20th-century children's book in translation was Erich Kästner's *Emile und die Detektive* (1929; *Emile and the Detectives*, 1930), a precursor of child-detective *series such as Enid *Blyton's 'Famous Five'. Scandinavia has contributed Tove Jansson's eco-fable about the Moomins, beginning with *Kometjakten* (1946; *Comet in Moominland*, 1951), Astrid Lindgren's books about Pippi Longstocking (*Pippi Långstrump*, 1945; *Pippi Longstocking*, 1954), and Alf Proysen's *Kjerringa som ble så lita some ei teskje* (1957; *Little Old Mrs Pepperpot*, 1959). The French have contributed Babar the elephant by Jean de Brunhoff (1932–93) and the graphic/comic books of René Goscinny and Albert Uderzo ('Astérix'); Belgium has contributed the graphic/comic 'Tintin' series by Georges Remi (Hergé). In recent years, despite the efforts of publishers such as Klaus Flugge (Andersen Press) and Aidan *Chambers, and the establishment of the biennial Marsh Award for Children's Literature in Translation (1996), the traffic of translation has remained almost entirely one-way.

TRAPIDO, Barbara (1941–) South African-born novelist. Her novels include *Brother of the More Famous Jack* (1982), the story of a timid student's involvement with a bohemian family, *The Travelling Hornplayer* (1998), and *Frankie and Stankie* (2003).

TRAPNEL, Anna (*fl.* 1642–60) Prophetess, She joined the radical dissenting Fifth

Monarchist movement in 1652, and was associated with the revolutionary church of John Simpson (1614/5-1662) at All Hallows the Great in London. Her spiritual and political extemporizations flowed forth in trances and were transcribed in shorthand. She achieved notoriety by a twelve-day ecstasy at Whitehall attacking Oliver Cromwell's Protectorate, after which she travelled to Cornwall, was arrested on suspicion of sedition, and committed to Bridewell, a journey she vividly recorded in *Anna Trapnel's Report and Plea*. Other accounts of her activities appeared in *Strange and Wonderful News from Whitehall*, *The Cry of a Stone*, and *A Legacy for Saints*, all published in 1654.

Traveller, The, or *A Prospect of Society* A *topographical poem by Oliver *Goldsmith, published 1764. From a vantage point in the Alps, the poet compares the national characteristics and social conditions of the surrounding countries, showing that the best aspects of each nation are balanced by some opposite demerit: even in Britain, the love of 'Liberty' leads to a loss of social interaction. Many of the landscapes (Italy, the Loire valley, the Netherlands) are vividly recalled from Goldsmith's own continental tour of 1755-6.

travel writing A genre that can be described as first-person accounts of travels by authors who have experienced the events they describe. However, questions about the authenticity and truthfulness of many works that are broadly accepted as travel writing, including the 14th-century travel book ascribed to Sir John *Mandeville, and the versions of Marco *Polo's journey to China, challenge any simple definition. Travels may be related in letters, journals, diaries, memoir, essays, reportage, verse, or other literary forms, sometimes, as in W. H. *Auden and Louis *MacNeice's *Letters from Iceland* (1937), within a single volume. Furthermore, certain types of novel, such as the *picaresque and the *Bildungsroman*, are structured around journey motifs. Jonathan *Swift's *Gulliver's Travels* (1726) and Laurence *Sterne's *A *Sentimental Journey* (1768), were presented as travel writing, while John *Bunyan's *The *Pilgrim's Progress* (1678) and Mark *Twain's *The Adventures of *Huckleberry Finn* (1884), depend upon journeys for their plot and themes. *Gothic novels turned to European travel accounts for their scene-setting. Poems of the *Romantic period, too, particularly those of S. T. *Coleridge and Lord *Byron, were informed, even inspired, by travel books; the narratives of explorers James *Bruce and Mungo *Park exhibit qualities associated with *Romanticism.

Under the influence of Edward *Said's *Orientalism* (1978), travel writing has been examined for its associations with imperialism and colonialism. Certainly, the major periods of global British expansion produced some of the most notable narratives of travel and exploration, including Richard *Hakluyt's monumental anthology *The Principall Navigations* (1589, 1598–1600). Later, tourist accounts, especially those of the *Grand Tour and of the Middle East, helped Britons exercise cultural and political authority. There is also a long tradition of travel and social exploration within Britain takes in books by Samuel *Johnson, William *Cobbett, and George *Orwell, while post-Freudian travel writing, such as Graham *Greene's *Journey without Maps* (1936), has explicitly drawn parallels between physical and psychological journeys. E. E. *Cummings, D. H. *Lawrence, and Wyndham *Lewis wrote important travel books in the 1920s and 1930s. Paul *Theroux, Bruce *Chatwin, Jonathan *Raban, and Bill *Bryson contributed to a resurgence in travel writing in the 1970s, despite Chatwin's and Raban's detestation of the term. In *Tracks* (1980), Australian Robyn *Davidson scorned the sexism and racism of her white compatriots, and reflected on her experience of being marketed as a woman celebrity. Simon *Armitage and Glynn *Maxwell in *Moon Country* (1996) recount their travels in the footsteps of Auden and MacNeice; similar accounts include Theroux's *Ghost Train to the Eastern Star: On the Tracks of The Great Railway Bazaar* (2008).

TRAVERS, Ben *See* FARCE.

TRAVERS, P. L. (Pamela Lyndon) (1906-96) Australian-born novelist and journalist, she came to England in 1924. Her accounts of her life involved some myth-making: she was allegedly influenced by W. B. *Yeats and Æ (George *Russell), and later by the Russian mystic G. I. *Gurdjieff. She disapproved of the Disney version of her *Mary Poppins series. Her other notable works include a refugee story, *I Go by Sea, I Go by Land* (1941) and *Friend Monkey* (1971).

Travesties A comedy by Tom *Stoppard, performed 1974, published 1975. The play is largely set, with various time shifts, in Zurich during the First World War, where Lenin, James *Joyce, and the Romanian Dadaist poet Tristan Tzara (1896-1963) happened to be residing; they appear as characters, as does the marginally historical figure of Henry Carr (1894–1962). Stoppard takes a minor incident from Richard *Ellmann's life of Joyce, describing a semi-amateur performance in Zurich in 1918 of The *Importance of Being Earnest, in which Joyce and Carr were involved, and builds from it an extravaganza which plays on Oscar *Wilde's original to produce a theatrical, informative, and witty commentary on the birth of Dada, the writing of *Ulysses, and the genesis of the doctrine of *Socialist Realism, and the nature of the artist as revolutionary or conformist.

TREASE, Geoffrey (1909–98) Children's writer. He became a teacher and, inspired by a Soviet project to develop young readers, began to write children's fiction which challenged dated ideas about empire, class, and gender characteristic of writing for the young. Bows against the Barons (1934) features a Robin Hood who supports peasants against an oppressive ruling class, told without the mock-historical language then typical of historical fiction. Cue for Treason (1940) features a theatre troupe who work with *Shakespeare, and two children who foil a plot against *Elizabeth I. It is notable for including a bold and intelligent girl at the centre of the action. Shadow under the Sea (1990) takes place during the Gorbachev years. There is a three-part autobiography (1971, 1974, 1998).

Treasure Island A novel by Robert Louis *Stevenson, published 1883. The flamboyant anti-hero Long John Silver was suggested by Stevenson's friend W. E. *Henley.

The narrator is Jim Hawkins, whose mother keeps the Admiral Benbow inn on the west coast of England in the 18th century. An old seaman comes to stay, with a map marking the whereabouts of Captain Flint's treasure hidden in his chest. His former confederates, led by the sinister blind pirate Pew, descend on the inn in a bid to steal it. But Jim Hawkins secures the map, and gives it to Squire Trelawney. The squire and his friend Dr Livesey set off for Treasure Island in the schooner Hispaniola taking Jim with them. Some of the crew are the squire's faithful dependants, but most are old buccaneers recruited by Long John Silver. Their design to seize the ship and kill the squire's party is discovered by Jim, and after a series of thrilling fights and adventures is defeated. The squire, with the help of the marooned pirate Ben Gunn, secures the treasure.

Treatise of Human Nature, A A philosophical work by David *Hume, published in three volumes 1739–40, rewritten as three separate works published between 1748 and 1757: An Enquiry (originally Philosophical Essays) Concerning Human Understanding, An Enquiry Concerning the Principles of Morals, and A Dissertation on the Passions. Hume's work is sometimes treated as the culmination of the empiricist understanding of mind attributed to John *Locke; equally influential is the view that Hume sought to extend and redirect the philosophy of Francis *Hutcheson. Other influences include Bernard *Mandeville, *Cicero, *Descartes, and Pierre Bayle.

In the first part, 'Of the Understanding', Hume agreed with Locke that there are no innate ideas, and that all the data of reason stem from experience. But he argued that reason has insufficient data in experience to form adequate ideas of the external world, bodily identity, causality, the self, and other minds, and that any beliefs we form about these must fall short of the full rational knowledge represented by abstract mathematics. We use the experience of acquired associations to identify causes and effects, past events and future contingencies; but this process cannot be independently justified. It ceases to be rational altogether when it involves inferences beyond the bounds of familiar experience (as with religion). Compensating for such inadequacies are certain 'natural instincts' by which the imagination forges its own links between distinct ideas according to principles of association and habituation. Through these associations, which Hume called 'fictions' (that is, they are not given directly by experience), and which he assumed were explicable in terms of the brain science of the day, we project onto the world a sense of the continuity of bodies, and the predictable sequencing of cause and effect. Hume's account of the self as a somewhat confused 'bundle or collection of different perceptions' was a striking departure from Locke. Hume characterized his general standpoint as 'mitigated scepticism', arguing that 'philosophical decisions are nothing but the reflections of common life, methodized and corrected' by the balanced interplay of reason, sense, and natural instinct. The second part of the Treatise dealt with 'passions' (emotions), and Part III with morals. Hume accepted Hutcheson's belief in a moral sense, but not his theological framework or psychological model. Insofar as there is a common structure of human nature, which approves whatever gives happiness to the parties affected without giving unhappiness to others, and enables us by the mechanisms of association to share the sentiments of others, there can be general consensus as to the motives and acts that are judged virtuous or vicious. Hume's distinction between natural virtues (such as benevolence) and artificial virtues (such as justice, which involves the application of appropriate conventions in circumstances of need) was widely misconstrued in his lifetime; the book was attacked by James *Beattie and Thomas Reid (1710–96), but was acknowledged as a prime stimulus by philosophers as various as Immanuel *Kant and Jeremy *Bentham.

TREECE, Henry (1911–66) Writer and teacher. He was associated with the *New Apocalypse movement, and co-edited, with James Findlay Henry (1912–86), *The White Horseman: Prose and Verse of the New Apocalypse* (1941). He is best known for his *historical novels for young people, such as *Viking's Dawn* (1955), the first in a trilogy about Harald Sigurdson. *The Horned Helmet* (1963) begins a trilogy for younger readers tracing the development of Beorn, an Icelandic boy who is adopted by a Viking warrior and participates in raids on the Scottish coast. His last book, *The Dream-time* (1967), about a Stone Age boy's desire not to become a warrior, was published posthumously.

TRELAWNY, Edward John (1792–1881) Novelist and memoirist, remembered principally for his connection with and records of P. B. *Shelley and Lord *Byron. He met Shelley in Pisa in January 1822 and attached himself first to Shelley (he was present at Livorno when Shelley was drowned) and later to Byron, whom he accompanied to Greece in July 1823. He was the author of the notable *Adventures of a Younger Son* (1831), an autobiographical novel published with the encouragement of Mary *Shelley. It is highly unreliable as autobiography. He also wrote *Recollections of the Last Days of Shelley and Byron* (1858), again unreliable, but again written with great poetry and panache; it was later expanded to *Records of Shelley, Byron, and the Author* (1878).

TREMAIN, Rose (1943–) Novelist, short story writer, and playwright. Her first novel, *Sadler's Birthday* (1976), was followed by *Letter to Sister Benedicta* (1978), *The Cupboard* (1981), and *The Swimming Pool Season* (1985). *Restoration* (1989; screenplay for film, 1996) is a first-person historical novel in which the central character is taken up by Charles II but suffers the king's disfavour after he marries Charles's former mistress. *Sacred Country* (1992) moves from Suffolk to Tennessee in its exploration of gender and identity. *The Way I Found Her* (1997) describes a summer in Paris, seen through the eyes of a 13-year-old boy. *Music & Silence* (1999) returns to the 17th century and tells the story of a lutenist at the court of the melancholy Christian IV of Denmark. *The Colour* (2003) takes place in New Zealand in the mid-19th century; *The Road Home* (2007) examines Britain from the perspective of an economic migrant from Eastern Europe; *Trespass* (2010) is set in the French countryside of the Cévennes. *The Colonel's Daughter* (1984), *The Garden of the Villa Mollini* (1987), *Evangelista's Fan* (1994), and *The Darkness of Wallis Simpson* (2005) are collections of Tremain's short stories. She has also written plays for radio and TV.

TRESSELL, Robert (1870–1911) The pen-name of the Irish author Robert Noonan. He is remembered for his posthumously published novel *The Ragged Trousered Philanthropists* (1914), edited from a manuscript left in the care of his daughter. It draws on his experiences while working for a builder in Hastings, where he settled in 1901 after various wanderings. He died of tuberculosis in Liverpool en route to Canada. An abridged edition of his novel appeared in 1918, but on the discovery of the original handwritten manuscript in 1946 it became clear that the author's intentions had been widely altered, and it was republished in 1955.

The action centres on the lives of a group of working men in the town of Mugsborough, and the novel is a bitter exposure of the greed, dishonesty, and gullibility of employers and workers alike. Debates on socialism, competition, employment, and capitalism are skilfully interwoven with a realistic and knowledgeable portrayal of the decorating and undertaking business, and with the human stories of the families of the workers. Principal characters include Frank Owen, socialist craftsman and atheist; Barrington, socialist son of a wealthy father, who wants first-hand experience of labour; and Slyme, a canting and unprincipled teetotaller. The book has become a classic text of the Labour movement. The ironically named 'philanthropists' of the title are the workers who for pitiful wages 'toil and sweat at their noble and unselfish task of making money' for their employers, while doing nothing to improve their lot.

TREVISA, John of (*c.*1342–*c.*1402) He translated the *Polychronicon* of Ranulf *Higden (1397), one of his most famous additions to which is the prefatory *Dialogue between a Lord* *and a Clerk* which contains important reflections on the cultural politics of translation into the vernacular. The *Polychronicon* translation is written in a vigorous and colloquial style, though he also has claims to a more elaborate manner. A translation of Giles of Rome's *De Regimine Principum* is attributed to him and by 1399 he had translated the *De Proprietatibus Rerum* of Bartholomaeus Anglicus. He also translated Richard Fitzralph's *Defensio Curatorum* and William of *Ockham's *Dialogus Inter Militem et Clericum*.

TREVOR, William (1928–) Irish novelist, short story writer, and sculptor. His novels include *The Old Boys* (1964), *Mrs Eckdorf in O'Neill's Hotel* (1969), *Elizabeth Alone* (1973), *The Children of Dynmouth* (1976), *Fools of Fortune* (1983), *Felicia's Journey* (1994), *The Story of Lucy Gault* (2002), and *Love and Summer* (2009); collections of short stories include *The Day We Got Drunk on Cake* (1969), *The Ballroom of Romance* (1972), *Beyond the Pale* (1981), *Family Sins* (1989), *The Hill Bachelors* (2000), and *Cheating at Canasta* (2007). There is a two-volume *Collected Stories* (2009). *Two Lives*, (1991) is made up of the novellas 'Reading Turgenev' and 'My House in Umbria'. Trevor's low-key, evocative prose covers a remarkably wide social range, from Catholic Irish small farmers to representatives of the declining Anglo-Irish ascendancy, from Dublin and London professionals to lower-middle-class characters in the Irish provinces and English Midlands. His later work addresses the complexities of communication across the Catholic–Protestant divide in Ireland and between Irish and English perspectives. *Excursions in the Real World* (1994) gathers personal essays on childhood, people, and places.

Trilby A novel written and illustrated by George *du Maurier, published 1894. The story's setting reflects the writer's years studying art in Paris, and the student friends of Trilby O'Ferrall (the Laird, *Little Billee, and Taffy) are portraits of friends. Trilby, an artist's model, slowly falls under the mesmeric spell of Svengali, a German-Polish musician, who trains her voice and establishes her fame as a singer. His power over her is so complete that when he dies her voice collapses, and she languishes and dies herself. Trilby's hat, a soft felt with an indented crown, is the origin of the 'trilby'.

trilogy In Greek antiquity, a series of three tragedies (originally connected in subject) performed at Athens at the festival of Dionysus.

Hence any series of three related dramatic or other literary works.

trimeter A verse line of three stresses. *See* METRE.

TRIMMER, Sarah (1741–1810) One of the foremost educationalists of the late 18th century, she ran her own Sunday Schools from 1772. Trimmer wrote educational texts for charity schools and edited *The Family Magazine* (1778–89) 'to counteract the pernicious tendency of immoral books', and *The Guardian of Education* (1802–6). Her first book was *Easy Introduction to the Knowledge of Nature* (1780); her most famous book, *Fabulous Histories* (1786; known from *c*.1820 as *The History of the Robins*), was an antidote to fairy stories.

Trimmer, Character of a See HALIFAX, GEORGE.

triolet A poem of eight lines, with two rhymes, in which the first line is repeated as the fourth and seventh, and the second as the eighth.

triplet A set of three successive verse lines rhyming together, occasionally introduced among *heroic couplets, e.g. by John *Dryden. The term is sometimes applied to a three-line stanza, more commonly called a tercet.

'Tristram and Iseult' A poem in three parts by Matthew *Arnold, published 1852. This is the first modern version of the story that was made familiar by Richard *Wagner, Alfred *Tennyson, and A. C. *Swinburne. In Part III Iseult of Brittany tells her children the story of *Merlin, entranced by Vivian.

Tristram and Isoud (*Tristan and Isolde*) The story of Tristram de Lyones is the fifth of Vinaver's eight *Works* of Sir Thomas *Malory. The love of Tristram and Isoud is much older than the corresponding Arthurian story of Launcelot and Guinevere, and it was incorporated into the Arthurian legends only at a late stage. There are three versions of Tristram romances surviving from the 12th century. The first English version is *Sir Tristrem*, a northern 3,344-line romance in eleven-line stanzas, dating from *c*.1300. In Malory's version, which draws on the 13th-century French prose *Tristan*, Tristram is the child of Meliodas, king of Lyonesse, and Elizabeth, the sister of King Mark of Cornwall, whose attitude to him varies in different versions from great affection to jealousy. Tristram defeats and kills Sir Marhalt, the brother of the queen of Ireland. Sent to Ireland to be cured of his wounds, Tristram falls in love with the queen's daughter, Isoud; when the queen discovers that he killed her brother, Tristram returns to Cornwall. King Mark sends Tristram to seek for him the hand of Isoud. The princess and her maid Brangwayn travel by ship to Cornwall; Brangwayn has been given a love potion to be given on their wedding night to Isoud and King Mark, which will bind them in unending love. By mistake Tristram and Isoud drink the potion and are bound in endless passion, although Isoud has to marry Mark. The rest of the story concerns the fated love of Tristram and Isoud and their subterfuges: as in the Lancelot romances, love is represented as a value that transcends morality. While fighting for Howell of Brittany, Tristram agrees to marry his daughter, Isoud of the White Hands, although the marriage is unconsummated. On the invitation of Isoud of Ireland, he returns to Cornwall, where he is killed by Mark while playing his harp before Isoud. In the version adopted by Richard *Wagner, Tristram sends for Isoud while he lies dying in Brittany. If she is on the ship when it returns, a white flag is to be flown; if not, a black one. The flag is white, but Isoud of the White Hands tells Tristram it is black, whereupon he dies. When Isoud comes to his bedside, she dies too.

Tristram of Lyonesse A poem in heroic couplets by A. C. *Swinburne, published 1882, which challenged Alfred *Tennyson's handling of the same story in *Idylls of the King.

Tristram Shandy, Gentleman, The Life and Opinions of A novel by Laurence *Sterne, published 1759–67. 'Shandy', a Yorkshire dialect word, means 'crack-brained, half-crazy'; Tristram declares his story a 'civil, nonsensical, good humoured Shandean book'. The slim story is constantly interrupted by digressions on a huge variety of scientific and philosophical matters, deliberately disordering the sequence of events; Tristram mocks the conventional linear development of narrative: he can never write fast enough to catch up with the life that he is living. The normal illusions of novelistic prose are further disrupted by wayward typography, including asterisks, dashes, diagrams, blank pages, multiple typefaces, and other devices. Volume i opens with Tristram's risibly inefficient conception, after which the other main characters are introduced: Tristram's excitable father Walter, a sort of benign *Scriblerus; the bewildered Mrs Shandy; Uncle Toby, Walter's innocent soldier brother, inter-

ested only in the problems of military fortifications; Corporal Trim, Toby's devoted, talkative servant; and the impulsive parson Yorick. Volume ii concentrates on the past military experiences of Toby and Corporal Trim. Tristram's birth is described in volume iii, after many diversions, including the comically overdue Preface. Volume iv includes an account of the misnaming of the infant 'Tristram' instead of 'Trismegistus'. Volume v covers the death of Tristram's brother Bobby, and the devising of the ill-fated *Tristapaedia* for Tristram's education. Volume vi includes the *sentimental tale of Lieutenant Le Fever and his son, a ludicrous discussion on the putting of Tristram into breeches, and Toby's tentative courtship of the amorous widow Wadman. In volume vii the family narrative is broken by a description of Tristram's travels in France, with Death in pursuit. Volume viii follows Toby's amour and Trim's attempt to tell his story of the king of Bohemia. Volume ix includes the pathetic tale of mad Maria (who reappears in A *Sentimental Journey). At the end, a conversation about Walter's bull gives rise to the famous inconclusive conclusion: 'L—d! said my mother, what is all this story about?—A COCK and a BULL, said Yorick—And one of the best of its kind, I ever heard.' The work made Sterne famous, although Samuel *Richardson, Oliver *Goldsmith, and others disliked its literary manner, and its insistent innuendo and tolerant bawdiness. In the 20th century the novel was celebrated as a humane comedy in the tradition of *Rabelais, *Cervantes, and Richard *Burton, and as a brilliantly ironic meditation on the new science of psychology, as found in John *Locke's *Essay Concerning Human Understanding.

Triumph of Life, The An unfinished visionary poem by P. B. *Shelley, published from rough drafts 1824. Composed in *terza rima, the poem is strongly influenced by *Dante's *Inferno, *Petrarch's *Trionfi, and the carvings of Roman triumphal processions Shelley had seen in the Forum. The 'triumph' or masquerade (as in The *Mask of Anarchy) belongs to the cruel Chariot of Life, dragging in its train even the greatest, like *Plato, *Alexander, or Napoleon. Only the 'sacred few', like Jesus and *Socrates escape compromise and captivity. The poetry has a bitter, lucid directness that is new to Shelley, with a grim passage about growing old and sexually disillusioned (ll. 137–69).

Triumph of Peace, The A *masque by John Shirley, acted and printed 1634; a spectacular torchlight procession (or 'triumph') of the masquers, from Holborn to Whitehall, preceded the masque proper. It was an expression of loyalty to the Crown on the part of the four Inns of Court, after William *Prynne—a member of Lincoln's Inn—had published his *Histriomastix* (1633) with a dedication to his fellow benchers at the Inn. Shirley's plot is simple: the chief anti-masquer, Fancy, presents a series of interludes showing the benefit and abuses of Peace; these are finally driven away by the entry of Peace, Law, and Justice. The masque was designed by Inigo *Jones, and its score (by William *Lawes and Simon Ives (bap. 1600, d. 1662) is among the few examples of masque music to have survived.

TRIVET, Nicholas (1257/65–?1334) Dominican known as the writer of three histories in the 1320s: his Anglo-Norman Chronicle, extending from the Creation to 1285, surviving in eight manuscripts and containing the tale of Constance, told by John *Gower in *Confessio Amantis* and by *Chaucer's Man of Law (*see* CANTERBURY TALES, 5); secondly, *Annals of Six Kings of England 1136–1307*, pro-Angevin and particularly useful for the reign of Edward I; and the *Historia ab Orbe Condito* (1327–9), an encyclopedic history influenced by *Vincent of Beauvais.

Trivia, or *The Art of Walking the Streets of London* A poem in three books by John *Gay, published 1716. Drawing on the 'town eclogue' as exemplified by Jonathan *Swift's 'Description of a City Shower' (1710), Gay adds mock-didactic elements akin to the *Georgics* of *Virgil. The poem is an imaginary perambulation of the streets of London with much jovially satirical comment. 'Trivia' is one of the titles of Hecate as goddess of the crossroads, and the humour is often dark. In its mock-heroic coupling of ancient myth with insalubrious modern reality (as in the comic passage on Cloacina, goddess of the sewers) the poem is an important source for Alexander Pope's *The *Dunciad*.

trochee, trochaic *See* METRE.

Troilus and Cressida A drama by *Shakespeare probably written 1602, printed in 1609, and in the first *folio, as the first play in the section of tragedies. As well as *Homer's and *Chaucer's handling of material concerning the lovers and the siege of Troy, Shakespeare knew of Robert Henryson's *Testament of Cresseid*, William *Caxton's *Recuyell of the Historyes of Troye*, and John *Lydgate's *Troy Book*, and drew on *Ovid's *Metamorphoses* Books 11 and

12, Robert *Greene's *Euphues his Censure to Philautus* (1587), and George *Chapman's *Seven Books of the Iliads* (1598).

Shakespeare's treatment of the love of Troilus and Cressida and its betrayal, against the setting of the siege of Troy by the Greeks, is conventional. The play contains much formal debate, and takes the story up to the death of Hector at the hands of Achilles: Troilus fails to kill his rival Diomedes, and the cynically railing Thersites escapes death. According to S. T. *Coleridge, 'there is none of Shakespeare's plays harder to characterize'.

Troilus and Criseyde Geoffrey *Chaucer's longest complete poem, in 8,239 lines of *rhyme royal, probably written during the first half of the 1380s. Chaucer takes the narrative from *Boccaccio's *Il filostrato*, adapting its eight books to five and changing the characters of Criseyde and *Pandarus. In Boccaccio Troilo falls in love with Criseida whose cousin, Troilo's friend Pandaro, persuades her, not unwillingly, to become Troilo's lover. In the end Criseida has to leave the Trojan camp to join her father who had defected to the Greeks; in the Greek camp she betrays Troilo by falling in love with Diomede. While following the same story in outline, Chaucer layers the narrative in several ways: by making Pandaro Criseida's voyeuristic uncle; by showing her deliberating at more length, and by having his narrator explicitly call into question the conventionally harsh judgement passed on her throughout the course of literary history; by introducing philosophical material, principally from *Boethius, calling into question the lovers' freedom of action and foregrounding their respective insights into their situation; and by complicating the texture of the narrative through the interpolation of *Ovidian and other classical references. The poem ends with an exhortation to the young to turn away from worldly vanity and to place their trust, not in unstable fortune as Troilus did, but in God. The love story has no basis in classical antiquity but is the invention of *Benoît de Sainte-Maure in his *Roman de Troie*, which was based on the pretended histories of Troy by *Dares Phrygius and *Dictys Cretensis. After Chaucer, the story was treated by Robert *Henryson in *The *Testament of Cresseid* and by William *Shakespeare in *Troilus and Cressida*.

Trojan War *See* AENEID; ILIAD.

TROLLOPE, Anthony (1815–82) Novelist, born in London. His father failed both as a lawyer and as a farmer and Frances *Trollope,

Trollope's mother, supported the family by her writing. Trollope, who introduced the pillar-box for letters, worked for the General Post Office in London from 1834, and was in Ireland in 1841–59. He stood unsuccessfully for Parliament as a Liberal in 1868, a painful experience often recalled in his fiction.

Trollope's fourth novel, The *Warden (1855) was the first of the 'Barsetshire' series, followed by *Barchester Towers (1857), *Doctor Thorne (1858), *Framley Parsonage (1861), The *Small House at Allington (1864), and The *Last Chronicle of Barset (1867). The action of these novels is for the most part set in the imaginary West Country county of Barset and its chief town, Barchester. The Barset novels are connected by characters who appear repeatedly, and Trollope developed this technique in his second series, known as the 'political', 'parliamentary', or 'Palliser' novels, which began with *Can You Forgive Her? (1864) and continued with *Phineas Finn (1869), The *Eustace Diamonds (1873), *Phineas Redux (1876), The *Prime Minister (1876), and The *Duke's Children (1880). Trollope established the novel sequence in English fiction; the form (known as *roman-fleuve) was used earlier and independently by *Balzac.

Trollope attributed his remarkable output to a disciplined regularity of composition. He produced a given number of words in the early morning before leaving for his post office duties (which he combined with an almost fanatical devotion to hunting). In his Autobiography (published posthumously 1883) Trollope writes of the novelist's need to live with his characters 'in the full reality of established intimacy. They must be with him as he lies down to sleep, and as he wakes from dreams' and stresses the importance of recording the effects of time: 'On the last day of each month recorded, every person in his novel should be a month older than on the first.'

Trollope's other principal novels include: The *Three Clerks (1857), The Bertrams (1859), *Orley Farm (1862), The *Belton Estate (1866), The *Claverings (1867), *He Knew He Was Right (1869), The *Vicar of Bullhampton (1870), The *Way We Live Now (1875), The *American Senator (1877), Doctor Wortle's School (1881), Ayala's Angel (1881), *Mr Scarborough's Family (1883). The Autobiography records that, down to 1879, his publications had brought him some £70,000. Writing in 1883, Henry *James summed up his achievement by saying that 'Trollope's great apprehension of the real . . . , came to him through his desire to satisfy us on this point—to tell us what certain people were and what they did in consequence of being so.'

TROLLOPE, Frances (1780–1863) Travel writer and novelist. A woman of tireless energy, who made an unfortunate marriage, and when she was past 50 wrote the first of over 40 books, by which she proceeded to support her large family, and eventually achieved wealth and fame. After the failure of the family's farm at Harrow (later to appear in her son Anthony *Trollope's Orley Farm) she sailed to New Orleans in 1827 with utopian aspirations and three of her children, and opened an exotic bazaar in Cincinnati. This venture failing, she travelled for fifteen months in America. Her caustic Domestic Manners of the Americans (1832) was published in England. Its resounding success brought contracts to write on the Belgians, the French, the Austrians, and others, and she lived for the next few years on the Continent. She published Paris and the Parisians (1835), Vienna and the Austrians (1838), and A Visit to Italy (where she became the friend of the *Brownings, Charles *Dickens, and W. S. *Landor) in 1842. She was also writing a long sequence of vivid popular novels, some of which, like Michael Armstrong, the Factory Boy (1840), dealt with social issues, and by the early 1840s was earning a considerable income. See also SOCIAL PROBLEM NOVEL.

troubadours Poets composing in Occitan (a Romance language spoken in southern France and parts of Italy and Spain) during the 12th and early 13th centuries. They were famous for the complexity of their verse forms, and for the conception of *courtly love which their poems to a great extent founded. Guilhem IX (1071–1126), count of Poitou and duke of Aquitaine, is the first known troubadour; Jaufre Rudel (fl. 1125–48) developed the theme of 'amor de lonh', love from afar. The most celebrated troubadour love poets are Bernart de Ventadorn (fl. 1147–70), Raimbaut d'Aurenga (c.1143–1173), Guiraut de Bornelh (c.1165–1212), and Arnaut Daniel (fl. 1180–1200), later admired by *Dante and *Petrarch, and Ezra *Pound. The troubadours flourished in the courts of Spain, Italy, and northern France, as well as in the south of France, and courtly poetry was being written and cultivated in Italy in the later 13th century (see Robert *Browning's *Sordello) when it was disappearing in the Midi. Through their influence on the northern French poets (such as *Chrétien de Troyes, and the writers of the *Roman de la Rose) and on the German poets (notably the *Minnesänger) they had a major effect on the development of European lyric poetry.

Troubles, literature of the The term 'the Troubles' is used to refer both to the years of the war for Irish independence (1919–21) and subsequent civil war (1922–3), and to the later (not unconnected) post-1968 period of Northern Irish violence which culminated in the ceasefires of 1994. In the first sense, the Troubles inspired work by W. B. *Yeats, Sean *O'Casey, Liam *O'Flaherty, Frank *O'Connor, and other writers, many of whom had participated in the turbulent politics of the time, and gave a title to J. G. *Farrell's *historical novel *Troubles* (1970). The discord in Northern Ireland, the second Troubles, also produced an important body of writing. It informs to a more or less direct degree much of the poetry of Seamus *Heaney, Michael *Longley, Ciaran *Carson, Paul *Muldoon, and other poets who came to prominence just before or in the early years of the conflict, and has given rise to a sub-genre, 'the Troubles novel', which includes Glenn Patterson's *Burning your Own* (1988), Robert McLiam Wilson's *Eureka Street* (1996), and Eoin McNamee's *Resurrection Man* (1994) and *The Ultras* (2004). Other historically focused novels include Naomi May's *Troubles* (1976); Maurice Leitch's *Silver's City* (1981); John Morrow's blackly comic *The Essex Factor* (1982); and Eugene McEldowney's thriller *A Kind of Homecoming* (1994). Many of the most celebrated Irish works of fiction from the later decades of the 20th century, from Jennifer *Johnston's *Shadows on our Skin* (1977) and Benedict Kiely's *Proxopera* (1977), through William *Trevor's 'Beyond the Pale' (1981) and Bernard *MacLaverty's *Cal* (1983), to Brian *Moore's *Lies of Silence* (1990) and Seamus *Deane's *Reading in the Dark* (1996), take a more indirect approach to the Troubles, exploring the moral ambiguities thrown up by sectarian conflict and by the struggle between paramilitary organizations and a state which fails to command the loyalty of considerable numbers of its citizens.

trouvères Poets composing narrative, dramatic, satiric, comic, and especially lyric verse in the north of France during the late 12th and 13th centuries. They were either professional entertainers, overlapping with *jongleurs* (or public entertainers), *clercs* (or scholars), or feudal lords composing fashionable verse. *Chrétien de Troyes was a *clerc*; other prominent trouvères were Conon de Béthune (d. *c.*1224), a Picard nobleman who composed crusading songs, Gâce Brulé (d. *c.*1220), *Blondel de Nesle, and Thibaut de Champagne (1201–53), count of Champagne and king of Navarre. Their poetry was much influenced by that of the Provençal *troubadours.

True Tragedy of Richard, Duke of York and the Good King Henry the Sixth, The *See* HENRY VI.

Trumpet Major, The A novel by Thomas *Hardy, published 1880; his only historical fiction. The story is set during the Napoleonic Wars, against a backdrop of preparations for invasion. It describes the courtship of Anne Garland, whose mother is tenant of a part of Overcombe Mill, where the dragoons come down from the nearby camp to water their horses. Among them is John Loveday, the trumpet major, the gentle, unassuming son of the miller. He loves Anne, but has a rival in his brother Bob, a cheerful, light-hearted sailor. Her third suitor is the boorish yeoman Festus Derriman. The story ends with the defeat of Festus and the success of Bob's courtship, while John marches away, to die on a battlefield in Spain.

TRUSS, Lynne (1955–) Novelist, journalist, and playwright. She has written many plays, dramatic monologues, short stories, and talks for BBC Radio, some of them collected in *A Certain Age* (2007). She has published three novels: *With One Lousy Free Packet of Seed* (1994), *Tennyson's Gift* (1996), a comic recreation of the poet *Tennyson's circle of friends and fellow artists on the Isle of Wight in the 1860s, and *Going Loco* (1999). *Eats, Shoots and Leaves* (2003) is an idiosyncratic plea for attention to the importance of punctuation. *Talk to the Hand* (2005) is a complementary attack on contemporary forms of rudeness.

TRUTH, Sojourner (Isabella Baumfree) (1797–1883) American preacher and autobiographer. She lived as a slave until 1827; thereafter she became a travelling preacher, speaking on behalf of abolition and women's rights. *The Narrative of Sojourner Truth* was published in 1850. Her legendary phrase 'Ain't I a Woman?' was part of a speech in Ohio in 1854. *See* SLAVERY.

Tuatha Dé Danann (Tuath Dé) In Gaelic mythology, the gods, the 'Folk of the goddess Danu', enemies of the *Fomorians. They are represented as invaders of Ireland, subsequent to the Fomorians and the *Fir Bolgs. They rout the Fomorians at the battle of Moytura, and are ousted in their turn by the Milesians. Conspicuous among the Tuatha Dé Danann are Lugh, the Gaelic sun god, their leader; and *Lêr, the god of the sea.

TUBMAN, Harriet (*c.*1820–1913) Abolitionist, née Araminta Ross. Born a slave in Maryland, she escaped in 1849, and began escorting many other slaves to freedom, using the network known as the Underground Railroad. Herself illiterate, she was the subject of an influential biography by an admirer, Sarah H. Bradford, *Scenes in the Life of Harriet Tubman* (1869). *See* SLAVERY.

TULLY *See* CICERO.

TUOHY, Frank (John Francis) (1925–99) Novelist. His novels—*The Animal Game* (1957), *The Warm Nights of January* (1960), and *The Ice Saints* (1964)—and short stories (collected edition, 1984) display his ironic wit, stylistic elegance, and powers of cultural evocation and analysis.

TUPPER, Martin Farquhar (1810–89) Prolific writer of verse and prose. His *Proverbial Philosophy* (1838–76, four series), presenting maxims and reflections couched in vaguely rhythmical form, remained a best-seller in Britain and America for more than a generation. Among his numerous other published works were two novels, *The Crock of Gold* (1844) and *Stephan Langton* (1858).

TURBERVILE, George (1543/4–*c.*1597) Poet and translator. He published *Epitaphs, Epigrams, Songs and Sonnets* (1567), various translations from *Ovid and *Mantuan, including Mantuan's eclogues (1567); and a verse account of the state of 'Moscovia', later reprinted by Richard *Hakluyt. Turbervile's *The Book of Falconry* (1575) is usually found bound with *The Noble Art of Venery or Hunting* (1575; repr. 1908): adapted from an unidentified French manual, the latter may be the work of George *Gascoigne. Turbervile's poems show the influence of Sir Thomas *Wyatt and the earl of *Surrey.

TURGENEV, Ivan Sergeevich (1818–83) Russian novelist and playwright, the first major Russian writer to find success in Europe. His novels include *Rudin* (1856), *A Nest of Gentlefolk* (1859), *On the Eve* (1860), *Fathers and Sons* (1862), in which, in Bazarov, he created a nihilist hero, *Smoke* (1867), and *Virgin Soil* (1877). His greatest short stories are 'Asia' (1858), 'First Love' (1860), and 'Torrents of Spring' (1870). The best of his ten plays is *A Month in the Country* (first version 1850;

perf. 1872), a psychological comedy which anticipated the drama of *Chekhov. He was closer than his contemporaries *Tolstoy and *Dostoevsky in both sensibility and literary practice to Western Europe. From 1847 up to 1881, Turgenev often visited England; he knew Charles *Dickens and George *Eliot, and was acquainted with many other writers. He was one of the earliest admirers of Henry *James, on whom he had a substantial influence. Perhaps the greatest English debt to him is owed by G. A. *Moore. By 1890 most of Turgenev's major work had appeared in English and exerted its influence on such writers as John *Galsworthy, Joseph *Conrad, and Virginia *Woolf. The most complete early translation is Constance *Garnett's *The Novels of Turgenev* (1894–9).

TURNER, J. M. W. (Joseph Mallord William) (1775–1851) English landscape painter, whose mature works convey a *Romantic vision of the violence of the elements. From 1798 many of his pictures exhibited at the Royal Academy were accompanied by verses printed in the catalogue; from 1800 he added lines composed by himself. His quotations are frequently from James *Thomson (1700–48). Between 1806 and 1815 Turner frequently wrote poems beside the drawings in his sketchbooks; they have been transcribed by Jack Lindsay in *The Sunset Ship* (1968). In the 1830s Turner did many designs for book illustrations, including vignettes for Samuel *Rogers's *Italy* (1830) and *Poems* (1834). He also illustrated works by John *Milton, Lord *Byron, Walter *Scott, and Thomas *Campbell. Turner endured much ridicule, including William *Hazlitt's famous description of his work as 'pictures of nothing and very like', but the first volume of John *Ruskin's *Modern Painters* (1843) was written in his defence.

Turn of the Screw, The A novella by Henry *James, published 1898. The narrator is a young governess, sent off to a country house, Bly, to take charge of two orphaned children, Miles and Flora. She gradually becomes convinced that the children are communicating with the spirits of an ex-valet and former governess, both dead. The narrative is a classic example of James's ambiguity and incorporates his interest in psychical research. Benjamin *Britten wrote a chamber opera (1954) based on this tale.

TUSSER, Thomas (*c.*1524–1580) Agricultural writer and poet. In 1557, he published his *Hundreth Good Points of Husbandry* (amplified to *Five Hundreth Points* in 1573) in quaint and pointed verse. The immensely popular work comprises a collection of instructions on farming, gardening, and housekeeping, together with humorous and wise maxims on conduct in general: many proverbs can be traced to it.

TUTUOLA, Amos (1920–97) Nigerian novelist. His inventive novel *The Palm-Wine Drinkard* (1952) polarized opinion; Dylan *Thomas's review praised it as bewitching but African critics disapproved of its mythological idiosyncrasy as it traces a drunk's excursion into the ghost world. Other works include *My Life in the Bush of Ghosts* (1952), *Simbi and the Satyr of the Dark Jungle* (1955), *The Brave African Huntress* (1958), *Feather Woman of the Jungle* (1962), *Ajaiyi and his Inherited Poverty* (1968), and *The Witch Herbalist of the Remote Town* (1981); they often draw on elements of myth and folklore.

TWAIN, Mark (1835–1910) Pseudonym of Samuel Langhorne Clemens, American writer. From 1857 to 1861 he was a river pilot on the Mississippi, and from 1862 worked as a newspaper correspondent for various Nevada and Californian magazines, coming under the influence of the humorist Artemus *Ward. He adopted the pseudonym 'Mark Twain', familiar to him from the call of crewmen testing the depth of the water on the Mississippi riverboats. His comic version of an old folk tale became the title story of *The Celebrated Jumping Frog of Calaveras County, and Other Sketches* (1867), which established him as a leading humorist, a reputation consolidated by *The *Innocents Abroad* (1869), an account of a voyage through the Mediterranean. *Roughing It* (1872), an account of his adventures as miner and journalist in Nevada, appeared in the year of his first English lecture tour; England provided the background for his democratic historical fantasy *The Prince and the Pauper* (1882), and for *A Connecticut Yankee in King Arthur's Court* (1889). He drew on his own childhood, in *The Adventures of *Tom Sawyer* (1876) and its sequel *The Adventures of *Huckleberry Finn* (1884), the latter combining satire with vernacular narration. *Life on the Mississippi* (1883), an autobiographical account of his life as a river pilot, contains a notable attack on the influence of Walter *Scott, whose romanticism did 'measureless harm' to progressive ideas and progressive works, creating, Twain alleges, the myth of the southern gentleman that did much to precipitate the Civil War. In his troubled last years

Clemens wrote some memorable if sombre works, including *The Man that Corrupted Hadleyburg* (1900), a fable about the venality of a smug small town, and *The Mysterious Stranger* (published posthumously in 1916, in a much-edited version), an extraordinary tale set in 16th-century Austria, in which Satan appears as a morally indifferent but life-enhancing visitor, to reveal the hypocrisies and stupidities of the village of Eseldorf. The unexpurgated version of his autobiography began to appear in 2010.

Twelfth Night or *What You Will* A comedy by *Shakespeare probably written 1601; it was first printed in the *folio of 1623. Shakespeare's immediate source for the main plot was 'The History of Apolonius and Silla' in Barnaby *Rich's *Riche his Farewell to Military Profession* (1581).

Sebastian and Viola, twin brother and sister, are separated in a shipwreck off the coast of Illyria. Viola, brought to shore in a boat, disguises herself as a youth, Cesario, and takes service as page with Duke Orsino, who is in love with the lady Olivia. Olivia rejects the duke's suit and will not meet him. Orsino makes a confidant of Cesario and sends her to press his suit on Olivia, much to Cesario's distress, for she has fallen in love with Orsino. Olivia in turn falls in love with Cesario. Sebastian and Antonio, captain of the ship that had rescued Sebastian, now arrive in Illyria. Cesario, challenged to a duel by Sir Andrew Aguecheek, a rejected suitor of Olivia, is rescued from her predicament by Antonio, who takes her for Sebastian. Antonio, being arrested at that moment for an old offence, claims from Cesario a purse that he had entrusted to Sebastian, is denied it, and hauled off to prison. Olivia, coming upon the true Sebastian, takes him for Cesario, invites him to her house, and promptly marries him. Orsino comes to visit Olivia. Antonio, brought before him, claims Cesario as the youth he has rescued from the sea; while Olivia claims Cesario as her husband. The duke, deeply wounded, is bidding farewell to Olivia and the 'dissembling cub' Cesario, when the arrival of the true Sebastian clears up the confusion. The duke, having lost Olivia, and becoming conscious of the love that Viola has revealed, turns his affection to her, and they are married.

Much of the play's comedy comes from the sub-plot dealing with the members of Olivia's household: Sir Toby Belch, her uncle, Sir Andrew Aguecheek, his friend, Malvolio, her pompous steward, Maria, her waiting-gentlewoman, and her clown Feste.

The play's gentle melancholy and lyrical atmosphere is captured in two of Feste's songs 'Come away, come away, death' and

> When that I was and a little tiny boy,
> With hey, ho, the wind and the rain.

Twentieth Century See NINETEENTH CENTURY.

Two Cultures and the Scientific Revolution, The 'The Two Cultures' is a phrase coined by C. P. *Snow in the Rede Lecture delivered at Cambridge in 1959 and published the same year. In it, he contrasts the culture of 'literary intellectuals' and that of 'scientists, and as the most representative, physical scientists'. He describes the increasing gulf between them, claiming that 30 years earlier the two sides could at least manage 'a frozen smile' but are now incapable of communication. His analysis of the educational attitudes that produced this situation and his recommendations for change were strongly attacked by F. R. *Leavis in his Richmond Lecture *Two Cultures? The Significance of C. P. Snow* (1962).

See THOMSON, SIR WILLIAM.

'Two Drovers, The' A short story by Walter *Scott, one of the *Chronicles of the Canongate*, published 1827, in which the tragedy turns on the conflict between Highland and Lowland views of life.

Two Foscari, The A poetic melodrama by Lord *Byron, published 1821. The son of Francesco Foscari, the doge of Venice, Jacopo, twice banished, once for corruption and once for complicity in murder, has been brought back from exile on a charge of treason, and the play opens with his interrogation on the rack. His broken-hearted father signs the sentence for his third, perpetual exile. But Jacopo's love for Venice is so intense that he dies in horror at the prospect. The Council of Ten decides to require the abdication of the old doge. He immediately leaves the palace, and as he descends the steps he falls and dies.

Two Gentlemen of Verona, The A comedy by *Shakespeare, probably written about 1590, often regarded as Shakespeare's first play. It was first printed in the *folio of 1623, where it is the second play in the section of comedies. Its main source is the story of Felix and Felismena in the *Diana* of Jorge de *Montemayor.

The two gentlemen of Verona are the friends Valentine and Proteus. Proteus loves Julia, who returns his affection. Valentine leaves Verona

for Milan, and there falls in love with Silvia, the duke of Milan's daughter. Presently Proteus also sets off on his travels, exchanging vows of constancy with Julia before starting. But arriving at Milan, Proteus is at once captivated by Silvia, and, betraying both his friend and his former love, reveals to the duke Valentine's plan to carry off Silvia. Valentine is banished and becomes a captain of outlaws, while Proteus continues to court Silvia. Meanwhile Julia, pining for Proteus, comes to Milan dressed as a boy and takes service as Proteus' page, unrecognized by him. Silvia, to escape marriage with Thurio, her father's choice, leaves Milan to rejoin Valentine, is captured by outlaws and rescued from them by Proteus. Proteus is violently pressing his suit on Silvia when Valentine comes on the scene. Proteus is struck with such remorse that Valentine surrenders Silvia to him, to the dismay of Proteus' page, the disguised Julia. She faints, and is recognized by Proteus. Her faithfulness wins back his love. The duke and Thurio arrive. Thurio shows cowardice in face of Valentine's determination, and the duke approves the match with Silvia, and pardons the outlaws.

Two Nations, The Subtitle of the novel *Sybil, by Benjamin *Disraeli.

Two Noble Kinsmen, The A tragicomedy attributed to John *Fletcher and *Shakespeare on its publication in 1634. In spite of its absence from the first *folio (1623), recent studies suggest that it is probably a genuine work of collaboration between Fletcher and Shakespeare, written for the King's Men in about 1613.

The play is closely based on *Chaucer's 'Knight's Tale' (see CANTERBURY TALES, 1), which Shakespeare had previously drawn on in *A *Midsummer Night's Dream*. The main addition to the plot is the unnamed Jailer's Daughter who is crazed by unrequited love for Palamon, and is cured by a lower-class wooer pretending to be Palamon. The overall tone is lighter than in Chaucer's poem. Theseus is a much less ominous figure than in Chaucer, and Arcite's death is rapid and dignified. The play is rarely performed.

Two on a Tower A novel by Thomas *Hardy, published 1882. Lady Constantine, whose disagreeable husband is away, falls in love with Swithin St Cleeve, a young astronomer who works at the top of a tower, where many of the scenes of the novel occur. Believing her husband dead, Lady Constantine secretly marries Swithin, but learns that marriage would deprive him of a legacy; and that her husband, though now dead, was alive when she married Swithin. The union is therefore void, and she insists on his seeking employment abroad. She discovers that she is pregnant, and accepts an offer of marriage from Bishop Helmsdale. A son is born. Swithin returns after the bishop's death, and proposes marriage, but she falls dead in his arms, overcome with joy.

2001: A Space Odyssey Film (1968) directed by Stanley Kubrick and scripted by Arthur C. *Clarke.

Two Years Ago The last of Charles *Kingsley's reforming novels, published 1857. Kingsley describes the arrival of cholera in the fishing village of Aberalva, attacks the sanitary conditions and public apathy that allowed it to take hold, and praises the heroism of various inhabitants. A secondary plot involves a denunciation of slavery in America, influenced by Harriet Beecher *Stowe's *Uncle Tom's Cabin*, and there are also references to the Crimean War. Elsley Vavasour is an opium-taking poet evidently of the *Spasmodic school, who prefers Art to Action and demonstrates the dangers of unleashed emotion by running wild on Snowdon, before a deathbed scene in which he desires that his poetry be burned and his children dissuaded from writing verse. This caused a quarrel with Alfred *Tennyson, who wrongly supposed Vavasour to be modelled on him.

TYLER, Anne (1941–) American novelist, born in Minneapolis, who began publishing with *If Morning Ever Comes* (1964). *Breathing Lessons* (1988) won the Pulitzer Prize. Most of her fiction has been set in Baltimore and she has been praised as a chronicler of the day-to-day.

TYLER, Wat (d. 1381) The leader of the Peasants' Revolt of 1381, who led the peasants of Kent and Essex to London. He was killed by William Walworth, the lord mayor of London, in the course of a discussion with Richard II at Smithfield. He is the subject of a drama by Robert *Southey.

TYNAN, Katharine (1861–1931) Poet and novelist, early confidante of W. B. *Yeats. Her many volumes of verse, from *Louise de La Vallière and Other Poems* (1885), fuse feminism, Catholicism, and an ethic of service increasingly at odds with the separatist enthusiasm of her compatriots. In addition to scores of novels and twelve collections of short stories, she published four volumes of memoirs.

TYNAN, Kenneth Peacock (1927–80) Dramatic critic, who championed the plays of John *Osborne, Arnold *Wesker, Shelagh *Delaney, N. F. *Simpson, Samuel *Beckett, and others, playing a leading role in the shift of taste from drawing-room comedy and the poetic drama of T. S. *Eliot and Christopher *Fry (which he disliked) to naturalism and 'working-class drama' (*see* KITCHEN SINK DRAMA). He also vigorously attacked theatre censorship. His various collections of reviews and essays include *Curtains* (1967), *The Sound of Two Hands Clapping* (1975), and *A View of the English Stage* (1976), which pay tribute to the role of the *English Stage Company in the development of British theatre. Tynan was also a moving force in the creation of the *National Theatre. *See also* THEATRE CRITICISM.

TYNDALE, William (c.1494–1536) Translator of the *Bible. About 1522 he formed the project of translating the Scriptures into the vernacular, but finding difficulties in England emigrated to Germany. An incomplete edition of Tyndale's translation of the New Testament was printed at Cologne in 1525; an edition of the whole translation was produced at Worms in 1526; when copies of this and the Cologne fragment were introduced into England, they were denounced by the bishops and destroyed. Tyndale eventually settled at Antwerp, becoming an active pamphleteer, and writing *An Answer* to Sir Thomas *More's *Dialogue* (1531). He was betrayed, arrested for heresy, imprisoned at Vilvorde in 1535, and strangled and burnt at the stake there, in spite of the intercession of Thomas Cromwell (c.1485–1540). Tyndale was one of the most remarkable leaders of the *Reformation, and the accuracy, straightforward style, and vivid language of his translation of the Bible—the New Testament (1525), Pentateuch (1530), and Jonah (1531?)—were endorsed by the translators of the Authorized Version.

Typee, or *A Peep at Polynesian Life* A novel by Herman *Melville, published 1846, first in Britain under the title *Narrative of a Four Months Residence among the Natives of a Valley of the Marquesas Islands*. Like Melville himself, *Typee's* hero Tommo and his friend Toby jump ship in the Marquesas, but their perception of the island paradise is darkened by fears of cannibalism. *Omoo* (1847) continues the narrative.

Tyranipocrit Discovered An anonymous radical pamphlet, published in Rotterdam in 1649. A plea for social equality, it attacks the 'White Devil' of tyrannical power, idleness, and greed disguised as Christian piety. There are extracts in George *Orwell and Reginald Reynolds, *British Pamphleteers* (1948).

Tyrannic Love *The Royal Martyr* A heroic play by John *Dryden, produced and published 1669. Based on the legend of the martyrdom of St Catherine by the Roman emperor Maximin, it contains some of Dryden's most extravagant heroic verse. It was ridiculed in *The *Rehearsal*, and by Thomas *Shadwell, and by Dryden himself in *Mac Flecknoe.

ubi sunt Derived from the opening words of a type of Medieval Latin poem ('Where are they?'), taken up in Old English poems such as *The *Wanderer* (ll. 92-3) and in many Middle English lyrics (especially the one beginning 'Where beth they, beforen us weren', *c.*1300).

Udall (Uvedale), Nicholas (1504–56) Dramatist and scholarly translator; he was author of *Ralph Roister Doister*, the earliest known English comedy, translated selections from *Terence and other works, and wrote Latin plays on sacred subjects. He figures in Ford Madox *Ford's novel *The Fifth Queen* (1906).

Udolpho, The Mysteries of See MYSTERIES OF UDOLPHO.

UGLOW, Jenny (1947–) Biographer and critic; her *Dictionary of Women's Biography* (1982) was followed by full-length biographies of George *Eliot (1987) and Elizabeth *Gaskell (1993). Her later work includes a biography of Henry *Fielding (1995), *Hogarth: A Life and a World* (1997), *Thomas Bewick* (2006), and *The Lunar Men* (2003), a study of the Lunar Society which included Erasmus *Darwin, Matthew Boulton, James Watt, Joseph *Priestley, and Josiah Wedgwood.

Ulysses Novel by James *Joyce, begun in 1914 and partly serialized in the *Little Review* (Chicago), 1918–20, and the *Egoist*. The editors of the *Little Review* were found guilty of publishing an obscenity, which is why the entire novel was first published by Sylvia *Beach in Paris in 1922. Copies of the first English edition were burned by the New York post office authorities and Folkestone customs officials seized the second edition in 1923. Various later editions appeared abroad, and it was not freely published in the USA until 1934 and the UK in 1936. The novel deals with the events of one day in Dublin, 16 June 1904 (the anniversary of Joyce's first walk with Nora Barnacle, who became his wife), now known as 'Bloomsday'. The principal characters are Stephen Dedalus (the hero of Joyce's earlier, largely autobiographical, *A *Portrait of the Artist as a Young Man*); Leopold Bloom, a part-Jewish advertisement canvasser; and his wife Molly. The plot follows the wanderings of Stephen and Bloom through Dublin, and their eventual meeting; the last chapter is an extended monologue by Molly Bloom. The eighteen chapters roughly correspond to the episodes of Homer's *Odyssey (Stephen representing Telemachus, Bloom Odysseus, and Molly Penelope), and are, in order: 'Telemachus', 'Nestor', 'Proteus', 'Calypso', 'Lotus Eaters', 'Hades', 'Aeolus', 'Lestrygonians', 'Scylla and Charybdis', 'Wandering Rocks', 'Sirens', 'Cyclops', 'Nausicaa', 'Oxen of the Sun', 'Circe', 'Eumaeus', 'Ithaca' and 'Penelope'. The style is highly allusive and employs a variety of techniques, especially those of *interior monologue and of *parody, and ranges from extreme realism to fantasy.

'Ulysses' A poem by Alfred *Tennyson, composed 1833, published 1842. In a dramatic monologue Ulysses describes how he plans to set forth again from Ithaca after his safe return from his wanderings after the Trojan War. The episode is based on *Dante (*Inferno*, XXVI). The poem took some of its energy from 'the need of going forward and braving the struggle of life' after the death of A. H. Hallam.

Uncle Remus See HARRIS, JOEL.

Uncle Silas A *sensation novel by Sheridan *Le Fanu, published 1864. Silas Ruthyn is suspected by many of the murder of a wealthy gambler at Bartram-Haugh, Silas's Derbyshire home. Believing in Silas's innocence, his elderly brother Austin at his death makes Silas his daughter Maud's guardian. Silas will inherit her fortune if she dies under age. Silas summons Maud to Bartram-Haugh, where he attempts to marry her to his boorish son Dudley, who is in fact already secretly married. When she refuses, he imprisons her at Bartram-Haugh, where Silas and Dudley, aided by a grotesque and sinister French governess, Madame de la Rougierre, try to kill her. The plot miscarries and the governess is horribly murdered by Dudley in mistake for Maud, who escapes.

Uncle Tom's Cabin, or *Life among the Lowly* Best-selling 1852 novel by Harriet Beecher *Stowe, which was triggered by the passage of the Fugitive Slave Act in 1850. It mounted a powerful attack on slavery, which led President Lincoln to attribute the American Civil War partly to its effectiveness. In *A Key to Uncle Tom's Cabin* (1853) Stowe assembled much of her source material.

Under Milk Wood A radio drama by Dylan *Thomas, first broadcast by the *BBC on 25 January 1954 and subsequently adapted for the stage; the published version was completed shortly before his death. Set in the small Welsh seaside town of Llareggub (Thomas had a backwards reading in mind: censoring editors used the title 'Llaregyb', from an earlier partial version in *Botteghe oscure*, 1952) it evokes the lives of the inhabitants—Myfanwy Price the dressmaker, and her lover Mog Edwards the draper; twice-widowed Mrs Ogmore-Pritchard; Butcher Beynon and his daughter Gossamer; the Reverend Eli Jenkins; the romantic and prolific Polly Garter; nostalgic Captain Cat, dreaming of lost loves; and many others. The poetic, alliterative prose is interspersed with songs and ballads.

Under the Greenwood Tree A novel by Thomas *Hardy, published 1872. Gentle and humorous, this short novel skilfully interweaves the love story of Dick Dewy and Fancy Day with the fortunes and misfortunes of a group of villagers, many of whom are musicians and singers in Mellstock church, ousted by the new-fangled organ. The novel marks the first appearance of Hardy's village rustics, who drew much critical comment, both favourable and unfavourable, and who were to reappear frequently in later novels.

Unfortunate Traveller, The, or *The Life of Jack Wilton* A prose tale by Thomas *Nashe, published 1594, the earliest *picaresque romance in English, and the most remarkable work of the kind before Daniel *Defoe.

Jack Wilton is 'a certain kind of an appendix or page' at the court of Henry VIII during the siege of Tournai. He lives by his wits, playing tricks on a mean old supplier of provisions and other naive occupants of the camp, and gets whipped for his pains. He later travels to Münster, and sees John of Leyden hanged; to Italy as the page of the earl of *Surrey; to Wittenberg where he hears Martin *Luther's disputations; and to Rome during an outbreak of the plague. He is last seen at the Field of the Cloth of Gold, in the English king's camp. The book includes much literary parody and pastiche, including Philip *Sidney's *Arcadia*.

UNGARETTI, Giuseppe (1888–1970) Italian poet. He founded hermeticism with his first two collections of poems *L'allegria di naufragi* (written 1914–19: *Gaiety of Shipwrecks*) and *Il porto sepolto* (1916: *The Buried Port*), in which he used neither rhyme nor punctuation. He translated William *Blake's visionary poems (*Visioni di William Blake*, 1965) and from *Shakespeare, and was himself translated by Robert *Lowell.

Unitarianism A system of Christian belief which rejects the Trinity and the divinity of Christ in favour of the single personality of the Godhead. Unitarianism is more radical in its anti-Trinitarianism than *Arianism. Though the term was not used in English until the 1680s, and Unitarianism was not legally tolerated as a religious denomination until the early 19th century, it had its origins in 16th- and 17th-century Polish Socinianism, from Fausto Sozzini (1539–1604), known as Socinus. John Biddle (1615/16–62) is regarded as the father of English Unitarianism. In the 18th century Dissenting congregations, particularly the English Presbyterians, turned first to Arian and then to Unitarian views. Joseph *Priestley in his *Appeal to the Serious and Candid Professors of Christianity* (1770) defended Unitarian principles, and in 1774 Theophilus Lindsey (1723–1808) formed the first Unitarian denomination. Both Priestley and his friend Richard *Price became original members of the Unitarian Society in 1791. S. T. *Coleridge briefly contemplated becoming a Unitarian minister. In the 19th century James Martineau led the development of rational Unitarianism. Elizabeth *Gaskell's fiction is imbued with Unitarian values.

unities Principles of dramatic composition derived questionably from Aristotle's *Poetics*. Recording the practice of the tragedians whose works he knew, Aristotle states that a play should have the unity of a living organism, the action it represents lasting, if possible, no longer than a single revolution of the sun. From these hints, Ludovico *Castelvetro and other 16th-century critics developed the rule of the three unities: action, time, and place, in the belief that audiences would be confused by the time of the action lasting longer than the time of its performance and that they would not accept changes of scene. The exclusion of sub-plots became the rule in France only after the controversy over *Corneille's *Le Cid* (1637). The time allowed for the action of a tragedy was extended by common consent to 24 hours; and the place the stage represented was allowed to shift from one point to another within a palace or even a city. Some dramatists circumvented the limitations of the unities by avoiding the mention of specific times and places. The later impact of this *neo-classicism on English tragedy was weakened by the taste for exciting action that was a legacy from the Jacobean stage, and especially by the example of *Shakespeare's irregular dramatic structures (only The *Two Gentlemen of Verona* and *The *Tempest*, conform to the unities). John Dryden's essay *Of Dramatick Poesy* (1668) offers the unities only half-hearted support, and neo-classical drama never took firm root in England. Samuel *Beckett's *Endgame* (*Fin de partie*, 1957) abides by the unities with self-conscious irony.

unreason, abbot of See MISRULE, KING, LORD, OR ABBOT OF.

UNSWORTH, Barry (1930–) Novelist; his travels in Greece and Turkey and his fascination with history are vividly reflected in his work. *Pascali's Island* (1980) takes place on the fringe of the decaying Ottoman Empire; *Stone Virgin* (1985) recreates different periods of Venice's history; *Morality Play* (1995) is a chillingly atmospheric tale of travelling players in 14th-century Northumbria; and *Sacred Hunger* (*Booker Prize, 1992), unrolls a grim panorama of the 18th-century slave trade. In his autobiographical black comedy *After Hannibal* (1996), the themes of greed, exploitation, and clashes between cultures are transposed to the contemporary Umbria of expatriate homes, where he now lives. His most recent novels are *The Songs of the Kings* (2002), *The Ruby in her Navel* (2006), and *Land of Marvels* (2009).

UPDIKE, John (1932–2009) American novelist, short story writer, and poet. His novels include the tetralogy *Rabbit, Run* (1960), *Rabbit Redux* (1971), *Rabbit is Rich* (1981), and *Rabbit at Rest* (1990), a small-town domestic tragicomedy which traces the career of ex-basketball champion Harry Angstrom. *The Centaur* (1963) uses a mythological framework to explore the relationship of a schoolmaster father and his teenage son and *Couples* (1968) is a portrait of sexual passion and realignment amongst a group of young married couples in a small Massachusetts town. Updike's characteristic preoccupations with the erotic, with the pain

and striving implicit in human relationships, and with the sacred in daily life are conveyed in an ornate, highly charged prose which reaches its most flamboyant in an atypical work, *The Coup* (1979), an exotic first-person narration by the ex-dictator of a fictitious African state. Other novels include *The Witches of Eastwick* (1984, filmed 1987) and *Toward the End of Time* (1997), an excursion into science fiction. *A Month of Sundays* (1975), *Roger's Version* (1986), and *S* (1988) form a linked sequence based on reworkings of Nathaniel *Hawthorne's *The *Scarlet Letter*. His volumes of short stories include *Pigeon Feathers and Other Stories* (1962), *Museums and Women* (1972), *Problems and Other Stories* (1979), *Trust Me* (1987), *The Afterlife* (1995), and *My Father's Tears and Other Stories* (2009). *Self-Consciousness* (1989) is an autobiographical memoir. His *Collected Poems 1953–1992* were published in 1993. *Due Considerations*, a volume of essays and criticism, appeared in 2007.

UPTON, Florence (1873–1922) Artist and illustrator, famous for illustrating a series of thirteen texts written by her mother, Bertha Upton (1849–1912), from *The Adventures of Two Dutch Dolls and a 'Golliwogg'* (1895) to *Golliwogg in the African Jungle* (1909). The Golliwogg, a gentlemanly and heroic figure in the books, became a highly popular toy, especially in Europe, where it was second only to the teddy bear. It was adopted as a brand image by the English makers of preserves James Robertson, 1910–2001, and used, negatively, as a character by Enid *Blyton. From the 1960s the golliwog has been regarded as a racist creation and widely censored.

UPWARD, Edward (1903–2009) Novelist, lifelong friend of Christopher *Isherwood; at Cambridge they both wrote *Barbellion-inspired diaries, and invented the surreal imaginary world of 'Mortmere'. A long Mortmere fragment appeared in Upward's *The Railway Accident and Other Stories* (1969) and its fantasies are described in Isherwood's *Lions and Shadows* (1938). Upward's *Journey to the Border* (1938) describes the progress of a neurotic tutor in an upper-middle-class household towards commitment to the workers' movement (Upward was for some years a member of the Communist Party); his trilogy *In the Thirties* (1962), *The Rotten Elements* (1969), and *No Home but the Struggle* (1977), published together in 1977 as *The Spiral Ascent*, describes the alternating political and artistic conflicts, over some decades, in the life of Marxist poet and school-master Alan Sebrill.

Urizen A principal character in the symbolic books of William *Blake, represented as god of reason and law-maker, to some extent to be identified with the Hebrew Jehovah. *The Book of Urizen* (1794) is Blake's version of the myth of Genesis, describing the creation of the material world by Urizen from the 'abominable void', from which is engendered Urizen's opponent, Los, and Pity, the first female form, who is named Enitharmon. The spirit of the book is of anguish, revolt, and suffering. Urizen, after long struggles with Los, surveys his creation with a sorrow that creates a web, 'The Net of Religion'. In the first plate of *Europe*, Urizen is portrayed majestically as an aged, Newtonian figure leaning down from the sun with a great pair of compasses to create the world.

Urn Burial *See* HYDRIOTAPHIA.

URQUHART, Sir Thomas (1611–60) Scottish writer and translator. He fought against the Covenanters, and was knighted in 1641. At the Royalist defeat at Worcester he lost many of his manuscripts, was imprisoned 1651–2, and died abroad. His best-known work is a translation of the first three books of *Rabelais, the first two 1653, the third 1693 (completed by Peter Motteux), and he wrote a plan for a universal language, and curious treatises on mathematics and other subjects, with strange Greek titles, collected in 1774 and 1834, among them *Ekskubalauron* (1651, known as 'The Jewel'), which contains in his 'Vindication of the Honour of Scotland' the story of the 'Admirable' *Crichton. He is said to have died laughing at news of the *Restoration.

USK, Thomas (c.1354–1388) The author of *The Testament of Love*. He was a professional scribe who became under-sheriff of London in 1387, by the mandate of Richard II. Eventually accused of involvement in a plot against the duke of Gloucester, he was proceeded against and executed by the 'Merciless Parliament' in 1388. *The Testament of Love* is an allegorical and philosophical prose work with some autobiographical elements, written as a dialogue between a prisoner and a Lady in the tradition of *Boethius' *Consolation of Philosophy*. It was written after 1384, as is clear from its borrowings from *Troilus and Criseyde* and *Piers Plowman*. The first letters of the sections form an acrostic reading 'Margaret of virtu have merci on THINUSK', i.e. 'thine Usk'.

Usnach, the Sons of *See* DEIRDRE.

USSHER, James (1581–1656) Irish theologian and historian, appointed archbishop of Armagh in 1625. Ussher was the nephew of Richard *Stanihurst, with whom he maintained correspondence across the Reformation divide. His *Annales Veteris et Novi Testamenti* (1650, 1654), a chronology of world history from the Creation to the dispersal of the Jews, was the source of the dates later inserted in the margins of the Authorized Version of the Bible. Ussher fixes the time of Creation as 23 October 4004 BC.

Uther Pendragon In the Arthurian legend, king of the Britons and father of *Arthur. Pendragon means 'chief dragon'. The narrative outline of Uther's life was established in *Geoffrey of Monmouth's *History of the Kings of Britain*. After he became king of the Britons, he lusted after *Igraine, wife of Gorlois, duke of Cornwall. He picked a quarrel with Gorlois and was transformed by Merlin's magic into his shape, whereupon he slept with Igraine three hours after Gorlois's death. In Sir Thomas *Malory's version, Arthur was conceived that night and Uther subsequently married Igraine.

'Utilitarianism' An influential essay by John Stuart *Mill, first published in a series of articles in *Fraser's Magazine* in 1861, in book form 1863. The term 'utilitarian' was first adopted by Mill in 1823, from John Galt's *Annals of the Parish*. In this work, Mill, while accepting the Benthamite principle (*see* BENTHAM, JEREMY) that Utility, or the greatest happiness of the greatest number, is the foundation of morals, departs from it by maintaining that pleasures differ in kind or quality as well as in quantity, 'that some *kinds* of pleasure are more desirable and more valuable than others'; also by recognizing in 'the conscientious feelings of mankind' an 'internal sanction' to be added to Bentham's 'external sanctions'. 'The social feelings of mankind, the desire to be in unity with our fellow creatures' constitute 'the ultimate sanction of the greatest happiness, morality'.

Utopia The principal literary work of Sir Thomas *More, an essay in two books, originally written in Latin and published in 1516 at Louvain: *Erasmus supervised its printing. The first book describes the current condition of England, implicitly contrasting it in Book II with the account of 'Utopia', 'Nowhere land', described by Raphael Hythloday, whom More says he met at Antwerp. The Utopians practise a form of communism, extending a national system of education to men and women alike,

u

and allowing the freest toleration of religion: they have only recently been introduced to Christianity and to printing. The work at once became popular, and was translated by Ralph Robinson (1520–77) into English in 1551, and into French, German, Italian, and Spanish.

The name 'Utopia', coined by More, passed into general usage, and has been adopted to describe, retrospectively, *Plato's *Republic*, and many subsequent works, including Francis *Bacon's *New Atlantis*, James *Harrington's *The *Commonwealth of Oceana*, William *Morris's *News from Nowhere*, and Edward *Bellamy's *Looking Backward*. Satirical utopias include Jonathan *Swift's *Gulliver's Travels* and Samuel *Butler's *Erewhon*.

The word *'dystopia' ('bad place') has been coined to describe nightmare visions of the future, such as Aldous *Huxley's *Brave New World*, Evgenii Ivanovich Zamiatin's *We*, and George *Orwell's *Nineteen Eighty-Four*. Many works of *science fiction use the utopian and dystopian forms.

UTTLEY, Alison (1884–1976) Author of series about 'Little Grey Rabbit' and 'Sam Pig', she wrote over 100 books, including the distinguished historical fantasy *A Traveller in Time* (1940) and many country books, notably the largely autobiographical *The Country Child* (1931).

Vala *See* FOUR ZOAS, THE.

Valentine and Orson The subject of an early French romance. Bellisant, King Pepin's sister, is married to Alexander, emperor of Constantinople. Accused of adultery, she is banished. Orson, one of her children, is carried away by a bear and reared as a wild man. The other (Valentine) is found by Pepin and brought up as a knight. Valentine meets Orson, conquers him, brings him to court, and tames him. There are many subsequent adventures.

The story appeared in English *c.*1510 translated by Henry Watson, and again *c.*1555 as *The History of the Two Valiant Brethren, Valentine and Orson*.

Valentinian, The Tragedy of A play by John *Fletcher, performed between 1610 and 1612, published 1647. A sensational drama with elements of *revenge tragedy.

VALÉRY, Paul (1871–1945) French poet, essayist, and critic, influenced by the *symbolists, particularly Stéphane *Mallarmé. His collection *Charmes* (1922: *Charms*) contains 'Le Cimetière marin' ('The Graveyard by the Sea'), memorably translated by Cecil *Day-Lewis (1946), by Graham D. Martin (1971), and (into Scots) by Douglas Young (1989).

Valperga, *or The Life and Adventures of Castruccio, Prince of Lucca* A novel by Mary *Shelley, published 1823. The successor to *Frankenstein*, it is a *historical fiction about the 14th-century Italian warrior Castruccio as he seeks to reclaim the land from which his family had been exiled by the Guelfs.

vampires in literature The word vampire, from the Hungarian, first appears in English in 1734 (*Oxford English Dictionary*). Robert *Southey's *oriental verse romance, *Thalaba the Destroyer* (1801) is credited with being the first appearance of the vampire in English literature. Vampires subsequently became one of the stock figures of *Gothic

fiction, following the model of Lord Ruthven (based on Lord *Byron) in *Polidori's *The Vampyre* (1819). James Robinson *Planché's *The Vampire* (1820) adapted Polidori for the stage. Later works include the Victorian *penny dreadful *Varney the Vampire* (1847) by James Malcolm Rymer (1814–84); Sheridan Sheridan *Le Fanu's *Carmilla* (1872, collected in *In a Glass Darkly*) and Bram Stoker's *Dracula* (1897).

In the 20th century, the vampire appears in the work of the American contemporaries Suzy McKee *Charnas, Anne *Rice, Chelsea Quin *Yarbro, and Octavia *Butler (*Fledgling*, 2005); in the *horror stories of Poppy Z. Brite and Stephen *King (notably *Salem's Lot*, 1975), and in the *science fiction of Josef Nesvadba (1926–2005), Colin Henry *Wilson, Richard *Matheson (*I Am Legend*, 1954; filmed, 1964, 1971, 2007), Brian Stableford (*The Empire of Fear*, 1988), Kim Newman (*Anno Dracula* series, 1992–), Brian Aldiss (*Dracula Unbound*, 1992), and Tim *Powers, whose work evokes the *Romantic era. Rice's *Vampire Chronicles* (1976–2003) introduced the multi-volume vampire sagas, now a staple of *young adult literature, including the *Twilight* series by Stephanie Meyer. Nalo *Hopkinson's *Brown Girl In The Ring* (1998) features a soucouyant, a Caribbean version of the vampire. Marcus Sedgwick's *My Swordhand is Singing* (2006) is a *historical novel which returns to the Eastern European origins of the vampire myth. J. K *Rowling's Harry *Potter series, and Terry *Pratchett's Discworld series both include vampire figures: the Discworld's Uberwald is based on cinematic stereotypes of Count Dracula's Transylvania.

The many screen vampires include, notably, the *expressionist *Nosferatu* (1922), reworked by Werner Herzog as *Nosferatu, the Vampyre* (1979), Hammer horror versions of *Dracula* (1958–74), and John Ajvide Lindqvist's *Let the Right One In* (2008). The popular *Buffy the Vampire-Slayer* (television series, 1997–2003) has been followed by Charlaine Harris's *The Southern Vampire Mysteries* from *Dead Until*

Dark (2001) up to *Deadlocked* (2012), televised as *True Blood*.

VANBRUGH, Sir John (1664–1726) Dramatist and architect. In 1696 he produced *The *Relapse, or Virtue in Danger*, with immense success, and *The *Provoked Wife* in 1697. His other principal comedies are *The Confederacy* (1705) and *The *Provok'd Husband*. His collected dramatic works appeared in 1730. He, together with William *Congreve, was specially attacked by Jeremy *Collier in his **Short View*.

Vanbrugh was the architect of Castle Howard and Blenheim Palace. *See* RESTORATION.

Vancenza By Mary *Robinson (1757/8–1800), published 1792, subtitled 'the Dangers of Credulity: A Moral Tale'. Set in 15th-century Spain, it portrays a virtuous but doomed heroine, Elvira, and is a plea for the improvement of female education. The novel sold out on publication, due, in part, to Robinson's personal celebrity.

Vanity Fair A novel by W. M. *Thackeray, published in numbers 1847–8, illustrated by the author. Set at the time of the Napoleonic Wars, the novel follows the fortunes of Rebecca (Becky) Sharp, the penniless orphaned daughter of an artist and a French opera dancer, and Amelia Sedley, the sheltered child of a rich City merchant. The two girls had been educated at Miss Pinkerton's Academy. Becky fails to force a proposal of marriage from Amelia's elephantine brother Jos, and becomes governess to the children of Sir Pitt Crawley, a brutal old man. She charms the Crawley family, becoming a favourite of Miss Crawley, Sir Pitt's rich sister. When his wife dies Sir Pitt proposes to Becky, but she has to confess that she is already married, to his younger son Rawdon. The young couple abruptly fall from favour with Miss Crawley, and have to live on Becky's wits.

Meanwhile Amelia's father has lost his money, and her engagement to George Osborne, the handsome but shallow son of another City magnate, has been broken off. William Dobbin, George's awkward, loyal friend, who secretly loves Amelia, persuades George to defy his father and marry Amelia, and Mr Osborne disinherits his son.

George, Rawdon, and Dobbin are all in the army, and Amelia and Becky accompany their husbands to Belgium, where Becky carries on an intrigue with George Osborne. George is killed at Waterloo, and Amelia, with her baby son Georgy, goes to live in poverty with her parents, while Becky and Rawdon manage to make a brilliant display in London society on 'nothing a year'. Amelia is finally forced by poverty to part with Georgy to his grandfather. Dobbin, despairing of winning Amelia's love, has spent ten years in India. Becky and Rawdon part, after Rawdon has discovered his wife in a compromising situation with Lord Steyne, who has, it turns out, been paying for Becky's extravagances. Becky leads an increasingly disreputable life on the Continent. Rawdon becomes governor of Coventry Island, and dies of fever. Amelia steadfastly refuses to marry Dobbin, until a chance meeting with Becky, who tells her of George Osborne's infidelity. Disillusioned, she marries Dobbin, but by then his love for her has cooled.

Vanity of Human Wishes, The A poem in heroic couplets by Samuel *Johnson, published 1749, in imitation of the Tenth Satire of *Juvenal. It was the first complete work to which Johnson put his name. Johnson illustrates the doomed futility of various ambitions—for power, learning, and military glory—citing the examples of Cardinal Wolsey (1470/1–1530), the earl of Clarendon, Archbishop *Laud, Jonathan *Swift and others. The bleak *Stoicism of Juvenal's conclusion is modulated by Johnson's hard-won Christian perspective.

VARGAS LLOSA, Mario (1936–) Novelist, playwright, essayist, journalist, and critic, born in Arequipa (Peru). *La ciudad y los perros* (1963: *The Time of the Hero*) is a key novel of the *Boom. This and later works show the influence of William *Faulkner's manipulation of time, narrative viewpoint, and structure. His *La casa verde* (1966: *The Green House*) and *Conversación en la catedral* (1969: *Conversation in the Cathedral*) are experimentally realist novels; *La tía Julia y el escribidor* (1977: *Aunt Julia and the Script Writer*) is a comic, semi-autobiographical novel.

VASSILTCHIKOV, Princess Marie Illarionovna (1917–78) Diarist, born in St Petersburg, Russia, to aristocratic parents who left Russia after the 1917 Revolution, and lived in Germany, France, and Lithuania. She worked in Germany during the Second World War and kept a diary which described the plot to kill Hitler and the bombing of Berlin, later published as *Berlin Diaries 1940–45* (1988).

Vathek, an Arabian Tale By William *Beckford, written in French and published in English 1786. It was one of the most successful of the *oriental tales then in fashion.

V

The cruel and sensual Caliph Vathek, whose eye can kill with a glance, is compelled, by the influence of his sorceress mother and the unbridled pride of his own nature, to serve Eblis, the Devil. He makes a sacrifice of 50 children, and sets off from his capital, Samarah, to the ruined city of Istakar, where he is to be shown the treasure of the pre-Adamite sultans. On the way he falls in love with Nouronihar, the exquisite daughter of one of his emirs, who accompanies him on his journey. Because of its supernatural elements, the novel has sometimes, perhaps mistakenly, been associated with the *Gothic novel.

'Vaudracour and Julia' *See* WORDSWORTH, WILLIAM.

VAUGHAN, Henry (1621–95) Poet, twin brother of Thomas Vaughan, a 'natural magician'. His wooing of his wife Catherine Wise is apparently recalled in the poem 'Upon the Priory Grove' printed in *Poems with the Tenth Satire of Juvenal Englished* (1646), his first collection. His second, *Olor Iscanus* (The Swan of Usk), has a dedication bearing the date 1647, but was not published till 1651. The poems in these two volumes are almost wholly secular, including fashionable love verses and translations from *Ovid and *Boethius. The great religious poetry of Vaughan's next volume, *Silex Scintillans* (1650: *Flashing Flint*), suggests a profound spiritual experience. Further devotional works followed: *The Mount of Olives, or Solitary Devotions* (1652) and *Flores Solitudinis* (1654). In 1655 the second edition of *Silex Scintillans* had an added second part with a translation of the *Hermetical Physic* of Heinrich Nolle (*fl.*1612–19). A translation of Nolle's *The Chemist's Key* followed in 1657. *Thalia Rediviva* (1678) contained poems by both Henry and Thomas. Vaughan acknowledged his great debt to George *Herbert, but his own religious poetry is unique and his beliefs are unusual. He was seized with the idea of the child's recollections of prenatal glory. He was fascinated by Hermeticism (*see* HERMES TRISMEGISTUS), and the idea of sympathetic bonds uniting microcosm and macrocosm. Many of his poems share ideas and even phrases with his brother Thomas's alchemical treatises.

VAUGHAN WILLIAMS, Ralph (1872–1958) Composer. His interest in *folk song and early English composers (signalled in the orchestral *Fantasia on a Theme of Thomas Tallis*, 1910) enabled him to break the dominance of *Romanticism. He profoundly reshaped English hymnody with his *English Hymnal* (1906). His first published work was the song 'Linden Lea' (1902, words by William *Barnes); other English settings include poems from D. G. Rossetti's 'The *House of Life' (1903), *Songs of Travel* (Robert Louis *Stevenson, 1904), the A. E. *Housman cycle *On Wenlock Edge* (1909), and *Five Mystical Songs* (George *Herbert, 1911). Later came settings of *Chaucer, John *Skelton, *Ten Blake Songs* (1957), and many choral settings of Walt *Whitman. *Riders to the Sea* (1937) is an intense setting of John Millington *Synge's tragedy.

VAUX, Thomas, second Baron Vaux (1509–56) Poet. A contributor to Richard *Tottel's *Miscellany* and *The *Paradise of Dainty Devices*, he is chiefly remembered now as the author of 'The Aged Lover Renounceth Love', the poem sung by the grave-digger in *Hamlet*.

VEGA CARPIO, Lope Félix de (1562–1635) Spanish poet and playwright. He sailed with the Armada in 1588. Immensely prolific and versatile in many genres, he is regarded as the founder of Spanish Golden Age drama; he claimed to have written 1,500 plays, of which several hundred survive.

Venice Preserv'd, *or A Plot Discovered* A tragedy in blank verse by Thomas *Otway, produced 1682. The play was well received and remained popular throughout the 18th and early 19th centuries. The bawdy comic scenes featuring the masochistic senator Antonio (a caricature of the first earl of Shaftesbury) were often cut.

Venus In Roman mythology the goddess of love (Greek 'Aphrodite'), daughter of *Jupiter, wife of Vulcan, mother of *Cupid, and lover of Mars. In the *Aeneid* she is the hero's mother by the mortal Anchises and tries to protect her son from *Juno. *Lucretius' *De Rerum Natura* 1 opens with an invocation to her, as does Chaucer's *Troilus and Criseyde*, III. She is also a major force in *The *Faerie Queene*, IV. x, and Edmund *Spenser' telling of the story of Venus and Adonis in III. vi (derived from *Ovid's *Metamorphoses*, 10) is very different from *Shakespeare's.

Venus and Adonis A narrative poem by *Shakespeare, published in 1593 and dedicated, like *The *Rape of Lucrece* (1594), to Henry Wriothesley, earl of Southampton, who has been connected with the *sonnets. Based on a short episode in *Ovid's *Metamorphoses*, the poem is written in the six-line stanza form known as *sesta rima*, a quatrain followed by a couplet. Shakespeare's poem was probably his first publication: it was extremely popular, being reprinted at least fifteen times before 1640.

Venus, in love with the youth Adonis, keeps him from hunting but cannot win his love. She begs him to meet her the next day, but he is then to hunt the boar. She tries in vain to dissuade him. When the morning comes she hears his hounds at bay; terrified, she searches for him and finds him killed by the boar.

VERA, Yvonne (1964–2005) Zimbabwean novelist and short story writer. Her work, alongside that of Bessie *Head, broke the mould of African women's writing, incorporating in a distinctive narrative voice violent revelations, lyrical evocations of place, and the vitality of orality. Her first book was a collection of short stories, *Why Don't You Carve Other Animals?* (1992); *Nehanda* (1993) is set in the 1890s during the African rebellion against colonialism in Rhodesia but told in the present tense; in *Without a Name* (1994), which can be read allegorically, Mazvita is raped during the war of liberation and kills her son, betrayed as she is by African patriarchal domination. Three more novels followed. Later books include *Under the Tongue* (1996), *Butterfly Burning* (1998), and *The Stone Virgins* (2002); *Obedience* was left unfinished at her death from AIDS.

Vercelli Book An Old English manuscript, made in England before the year 1000. It contains prose sermons and about 3,500 lines of Old English poetry; its most distinguished contents are the poems **Dream of the Rood* and **Andreas*, and two of the four signed poems of **Cynewulf: Elene* and *The Fates of the Apostles*.

Verdant Green, The Adventures of Mr
see BRADLEY, EDWARD.

VERDI, Giuseppe (1813–1901) Italian composer of operas, of which two, *I due foscari* (1844) and *Il corsaro* (*The Corsair*, 1848), are based on texts by Lord *Byron. Three more are based on William *Shakespeare, beginning with *Macbeth* (1847). He found in Arrigo Boito a librettist of inspiring skill and imagination. Their collaboration produced the two greatest of all Shakespeare operas: *Otello* (1887) and *Falstaff* (1893).

VERGIL, Polydore (*c.*1470–1555) Italian historian; he arrived in England in 1502 and was a friend of Sir Thomas *More and other English humanists. His *Anglica Historia* was published in 1534 and in revised and extended

editions in 1546 and 1555. He was also author of a *Proverbiorum Libellus* (Venice, 1498) which anticipated *Erasmus' *Adagia*.

verismo A movement in 19th-century Italian literature akin to *naturalism, associated particularly with Giovanni Verga (1840–1922). The literature of *verismo* sought to document social conditions—particularly of the lower classes. *Verismo* influenced the early works of Gabriele d'Annunzio and Luigi *Pirandello, and subsequently post-war neo-realism.

VERLAINE, Paul (1844–96) French poet. Perhaps his most significant work, characterized by an intense musicality and metrical inventiveness, appeared in *Romances sans paroles* (1874: *Songs without Words*). In 1884 he published a number of short studies of contemporary poets (including *Mallarmé and Arthur *Rimbaud) under the title *Les Poètes maudits* (*The Outcast Poets*). Verlaine's relationship with Rimbaud is the subject of a play by Christopher *Hampton, *Total Eclipse* (1968). *See* SYMBOLISM.

VERNE, Jules (1828–1905) French novelist. Among his most successful adventure novels are *Voyage au centre de la terre* (1864: *Voyage to the Centre of the Earth*), *Vingt mille lieues sous les mers* (1870: *Twenty Thousand Leagues under the Sea*), and *Le Tour du monde en quatre-vingts jours* (1873: *Round the World in Eighty Days*), recounting the travels of the Englishman Phileas Fogg. Three popular series of Verne's works in English appeared in the 1860s and 1870s translated by, amongst others, W. H. G. Kingston.

Vernon Manuscript The most substantial surviving collection of important Middle English writings. It was compiled in the Midlands in the later 1380s. The Simeon Manuscript, kept in the British Library (BL MS Add. 22283), provides a close parallel.

vers de société A term applied to a form of light verse dealing with events in polite society, usually in a satiric or playful tone, sometimes conversational, sometimes employing intricate forms such as the *villanelle or the *rondeau. English writers noted for their *vers de société* include Matthew *Prior, Oliver *Goldsmith, W. M. *Praed, C. S. *Calverley, Austin *Dobson, and Frederick *Locker-Lampson.

verse for children Isaac *Watts, in the Introduction to *Divine Songs* (1715), argued that verse was particularly suitable for the religious education of children; his advice was followed into the 19th century by versifiers such as Ann and Jane *Taylor, many of whom were parodied by Lewis *Carroll. Robert Louis *Stevenson's *A Child's Garden of Verses* (1885) was imitated by writers such as A. A. *Milne. Rudyard *Kipling and Ted *Hughes have written notable verse for children. In the late 20th century there has been a revival, with light, humorous, 'urchin verse', used to serious effect by, for example, Michael *Rosen and Roger *McGough; and *performance poetry, particularly by West Indian poets including Grace *Nichols and Benjamin *Zephaniah.

vers libre The French term often used in the early 20th century to denote many forms of metrically irregular verse, now more commonly referred to as *free verse.

Very Hungry Caterpillar, The See CARLE, ERIC.

VESEY, Elizabeth (*c.*1715–1791) An Irishwoman, the first of the *Blue Stocking hostesses. In the early 1750s she decided, with the support of her husband, who was an Irish MP, to open her doors to literary and fashionable society for an entirely new kind of evening party. According to Hannah *More in her poem *Bas Bleu*, she shared with Elizabeth *Montagu and Frances Boscawen (1719–1805) 'the triple crown' among Blue Stocking hostesses.

'Vicar of Bray, The' A satirical song, dating from the early 18th century, in which a clergyman boasts of keeping his position by adapting to the various religious policies in force from Charles II to George I. The idea is much older.

Vicar of Bullhampton, The A novel by Anthony *Trollope, published 1870, concerned with the ideal of English manliness in action.

Vicar of Wakefield, The A novel by Oliver *Goldsmith, published 1766. The manuscript was sold to John *Newbery for £60 by Samuel *Johnson on Goldsmith's behalf, to prevent the author's arrest for debt. The story contains many of the plot devices of *sentimental fiction. Dr Primrose and his wife Deborah live an idyllic life in a country parish with their children, George and Moses, Olivia and Sophia. On the eve of George's wedding to Arabella Wilmot, the vicar loses all his money through the bankruptcy of a merchant, preventing the marriage. The family move to a meagre living on the land of Squire Thornhill. An eccentric friend, Burchell, rescues Sophia from drowning. The dashing squire captivates Olivia then disappears. Thornhill reappears, now seriously courting Arabella;

he obtains a commission in the army for his rival, George. Primrose discovers his daughter Olivia being ejected from an inn; she has been seduced by Thornhill under pretence of marriage and cast off. The vicar receives her with joy, and they proceed home, only to find a terrible fire destroying his house. Thornhill has him removed to the debtors' prison where he encounters every mortification: he hears of Olivia's death, is told that Sophia has been abducted, and finds that George has been brought half-dead into the prison, having been set upon by Thornhill's servants. At this point Sophia appears with Burchell, whom George recognizes as Sir William Thornhill, Squire Thornhill's noble uncle. The nephew is denounced, and Arabella is united with George. It transpires that Olivia is not, after all, dead, and was in fact actually married to Thornhill. All proceed home, where Sophia and Sir William, with Arabella and George, are married at a double ceremony.

Vice A *fool or buffoon introduced into some of the *interludes and later moralities as a figure of evil. The descent of the figure from characters in *mystery cycles and *morality plays (such as 'The Vices', the *Seven Deadly Sins) is likely.

VICTORIA (1819–1901) Queen of England from 1837. She wrote innumerable letters and accumulated over 100 volumes of diaries and journals, kept from the age of 13 until shortly before her death; many selections have been published. Her only writings published in her lifetime were *Leaves from a Journal of our Life in the Highlands 1848–61* (1868). *More Leaves* (1883) covered the years 1862–3. Her lively letters to her eldest daughter Vicky have also been published.

In her diaries the queen notes her reading, which included sermons, *Shakespeare, Thomas *Macaulay, Frances Burney, and Jane *Austen. Though she took an interest in the novelists of her own reign, including Walter *Scott, Charles *Dickens, the *Brontës, Elizabeth *Gaskell, George *Eliot, and Benjamin *Disraeli, she preferred poetry ('in all shapes'), an enthusiasm which led to her friendship with Alfred *Tennyson. Their correspondence has been published.

( ) SEE WEB LINKS
• Victorian web

VIDAL, Gore (1925–) American novelist and essayist. He saw army service during the Second World War, and drew on the experience for his first novel, *Williwaw* (1946). Novels with historical settings include *A Search for the King* (1950), set in the time of Richard the Lionheart; *Julian* (1964) and *Two Sisters* (1970), set in the Roman world; and *Creation* (1981), set in the 5th century BC, the period of Darius, Xerxes, and Confucius. A sequence of 'Narratives of a Golden Age', chronicling the history of America from the mid-19th century, includes *Washington, D.C.* (1967), *1876* (1976), *Lincoln* (1984), *Empire* (1987), *Burr* (1973), and *Hollywood* (1990). *Myra Breckenridge* (1968), and its sequel, *Myron* (1974) wittily chronicle the adventures of a transsexual. Other works include *The Judgement of Paris* (1952), *Kalki* (1978), and *Live from Golgotha* (1992); collections of essays; plays for television and the stage; and detective stories under the pseudonym Edgar Box. *Palimpsest* (1995) is a candid memoir, followed by *Point to Point Navigation* (2006).

VIGNY, Alfred de (1797–1863) French Romantic poet, dramatist, and novelist. *Poèmes antiques et modernes* (*Poems Ancient and Modern*) and his historical novel *Cinq-Mars*, based on a conspiracy against Richelieu, appeared in 1826. This novel, together with his three tales *Servitude et grandeur militaires* (1835: *Military Servitude and Grandeur*) and his Romantic drama *Chatterton* (1835), which uses Thomas *Chatterton as a symbol of the solitary poet in the world, forms part of what he called his 'epic of disillusionment'.

Village, The A poem in two books by George *Crabbe, published 1783. The poem contrasts the dispiriting realities of country life with the idealized pastoral favoured by poets such as Oliver *Goldsmith. Samuel *Johnson and Edmund *Burke, Crabbe's patron, both assisted him with the poem, which established Crabbe's reputation as a writer.

villanelle A poem consisting of an uneven number (normally five) of three-lined stanzas (tercets) rhyming *aba* and a final *quatrain rhyming *abaa*, with only two rhymes throughout. The first and third lines of the first tercet are repeated alternately as final lines in the succeeding tercets, and form a final couplet in the quatrain. The form originated in 16th-century France, and was employed for *pastoral song. In English it appeared in light verse of the 19th century, but in the 20th century was used to more serious purpose by W. H. *Auden, William *Empson, Derek *Mahon, and in the best-known such poem, Dylan *Thomas's 'Do not go gentle into that good night' (1951).

Villette Charlotte *Brontë's last completed novel, published 1853. Like its predecessor *The *Professor (then unpublished), it is based on Brontë's experiences in Brussels, here renamed Villette, and centres on a pupil-teacher relationship. The narrator, Lucy Snowe, poor and plain, finds herself a post as teacher in a girls' school in Villette, where she wins the respect of the capable, if unscrupulous, headmistress, Madame Beck. She becomes deeply attached to the handsome John Bretton, the school's English doctor, in whom she recognizes an acquaintance from her childhood, but represses her own strong feelings for him. These feelings gradually attach themselves to the waspish, despotic, but good-hearted little professor Monsieur Paul Emanuel. His generosity leaves her mistress of her own school when he is called away on business to the West Indies. The ending is ambiguous, implying but not confirming that he is drowned on his way home. The novel gives a vivid portrayal of Belgian daily life, and makes use of elements of *Gothic fiction. In Paul Emanuel she successfully creates an unromantic hero very far removed from the *Byronic Rochester of *Jane Eyre.

VILLIERS DE L'ISLE-ADAM, Auguste (Jean-Marie-Mathias-Philippe-Auguste), comte de (1838–89) French novelist and dramatist. His visionary drama *Axël* (1890; trans. 1925), which first appeared in symbolist reviews, is a Wagnerian narrative of love and death set in an isolated German castle, which enshrines *Rosicrucian mysteries. It provided a title for Edmund *Wilson's study of symbolist writers, *Axel's Castle* (1931).

VILLON, François (c.1431–after 1463) French poet. His two major poems are the *Lais* (or *Petit Testament*), written in 1456, and the *Testament* (or *Grand Testament*), written in 1461–2 and published posthumously in 1489. His poetry was popular in England in the late 19th century, with translations of individual poems by D. G. *Rossetti, A. C. *Swinburne, and W. E. *Henley, and prose adaptations by John *Synge; of more recent versions, those by Basil *Bunting and Robert *Lowell stand out.

VINCENT of Beauvais (c.1190–c.1264) The Dominican author of the *Speculum Maius*, of which three parts were completed: *Speculum Naturale, Historiale, Doctrinale* (mid-13th century). A compilation of all received knowledge at the time, it was widely circulated, translated into some vernaculars, and was cited as an authority.

Vindication of the Rights of Woman,

A By Mary *Wollstonecraft, published 1792. Wollstonecraft attacks the educational restrictions and 'mistaken notions of female excellence' that keep women in a state of 'ignorance and slavish dependence'. The work was much acclaimed and is now seen as a founding document in modern feminism, but it also inevitably attracted contemporary hostility; Horace *Walpole referred to Wollstonecraft as 'a hyena in petticoats'.

VINGE, Joan D. (1948–) American *science fiction writer, born in Baltimore; author of the *Hugo award-winning *The Snow Queen* (1980), which echoes Robert *Graves and Hans Christian *Andersen.

Virago Press British publishing house founded by Carmen Callil in 1972. For more than three decades, Virago was one of the leading publishers of feminist writing in the English-speaking world. Its Virago Modern Classics series, launched in 1978, republished and championed neglected classics by Antonia *White, Willa *Cather, Christina *Stead, Elizabeth *Taylor, and others. Despite changes of ownership (since 2006 it has been part of the Hachette Publishing empire), Virago has largely succeeded in maintaining its reputation as an independent and innovative publisher.

Virgidemiarum, Sex Libri

By Joseph *Hall, two volumes of English satires, 1597 and 1598. The first volume, called 'Toothless', satirizes literary conventions in the spirit of *Martial and *Horace; the second, imitating *Juvenal, 'bites' such evils as sexual promiscuity, ostentatious piety, economic injustice, and impostures in astrology and genealogy. The title means 'sheaves of rods' (for corporal punishment). In a crackdown on satire in 1599 Hall's books were condemned to be burnt, along with satires by John *Marston, Thomas *Nashe, and others, but then reprieved.

VIRGIL (Publius Vergilius Maro) (70–19 BC) The greatest of Roman poets. His first publication was the *pastoral *Eclogues* (c.39–38), indebted to the *Idylls* of *Theocritus. Virgil's *Georgics* (published 29), a didactic and celebratory poem in four books about the life of the farmer which partly imitates the *Works and Days* of *Hesiod, is dedicated to his patron *Maecenas. The *Aeneid*, Virgil's *epic in twelve books about the remote legendary origins of what eventually became the Roman Empire, was composed during the last ten years of his life and was not quite finished at his death. It

seems to have grown out of his response to pressure placed on the poets of the day to produce a poem in praise of Augustus' martial exploits. Virgil's narrative of adventure and conquest, and keenly felt human suffering and loss, builds on the achievement of earlier Latin epic poets such as *Ennius. It deliberately invites comparison with *Homer, announcing its theme as both arms, as in the *Iliad*, and a man, an individual hero, as in the *Odyssey*. The poem contrives to bring together the legendary past and the moral, political, and religious concerns of Virgil's own times, most notably at the centre of the poem, in the sixth book, where Aeneas descends into the underworld, the place of the dead, and the future imperial destiny of Rome is revealed to him. This episode influenced John *Milton's hell in *Paradise Lost* and *Dante's *Inferno*. Virgil is Dante's guide through both hell and purgatory. The melancholy as well as the heroism of the *Aeneid* commended itself to Alfred *Tennyson and the poem has been much translated by other poets from Gawin *Douglas and John *Dryden to Cecil *Day-Lewis.

'Virgils Gnat'

A poem by Edmund *Spenser, published in the *Complaints* of 1591, and adapted from the *Culex* (or 'Gnat') attributed to *Virgil.

Virginians, The

A *historical novel of the American Revolution by W. M. *Thackeray, published in numbers, November 1857–October 1859. The prominent part played by George Washington offended some American readers. The novel traces the fortunes of George and Harry Warrington, grandsons of the Henry in *The *History of Henry Esmond*. George is thought to be killed in action against the French. Harry, now the heir, visits England, is corrupted by his dissipated Castlewood relations, and is trapped into an engagement to his much older cousin Maria. Imprisoned for debt, he is rescued by the reappearance of George, who has escaped from the French and come to England. Maria releases Harry from his engagement, since he is no longer the heir. George marries Theo, the daughter of a poor soldier, and is only saved from penury by becoming the heir of Sir Miles Warrington, of the English branch of the family. Harry joins the army, and is with Wolfe at the capture of Quebec. When the War of Independence breaks out, Harry joins Washington, and George, who is in the British army, resigns his commission rather than run the risk of fighting against his brother. He settles in England, and gives up the Virginian property to Harry.

Virgin Martyr, The A tragedy by Philip *Massinger and Thomas *Dekker, printed 1622. Set in the reign of the emperor Diocletian, the plot is based on the story of the Christian martyr, St Dorothea. She is denounced with her lover Antoninus by Theophilus, a zealous persecutor, who sends his daughters to Dorothea to convert her to paganism. The daughters are instead converted by Dorothea to Christianity, and are killed by their own father. Dorothea is tortured and executed, Antoninus dying by her side. Theophilus, summoned before Diocletian, proclaims his conversion to Christianity, courageously suffers torture, and dies. The same story has been treated in poems by A. C. *Swinburne and Gerard Manley *Hopkins.

Vision of Judgement, A A poem in hexameters by Robert *Southey, published 1821, when he was *poet laureate. The preface, written in defence of the poem's metrical innovation, also contains a violent attack on the works of Lord *Byron, 'those monstrous combinations of horrors and mockery, lewdness and impiety'. Byron responded with his parody The *Vision of Judgment.

Vision of Judgment, The A satirical poem in *ottava rima by Lord *Byron, published in the *Liberal, 1822. In 1821 Robert *Southey published A *Vision of Judgement, which described Byron as the leader of the *'Satanic school' of poetry. Byron's reply is an exuberant parody of Southey's poem. George III, at the celestial gate, is claimed by Satan, who then calls a crowd of witnesses, including John Wilkes and *Junius, to testify to the king's disastrous reign. Southey is swept up from the Lake District by a devil, and demonstrates his corruption by offering to add Satan's biography to his life of John *Wesley. The poem ends as Southey is knocked back down to his own lake by St Peter, and in the confusion King George slips into heaven.

Vita nuova See DANTE, ALIGHIERI.

Vivian Grey The first of Benjamin *Disraeli's novels, anonymously published 1826, with a continuation in 1827. It began a group of three novels (the others were Alroy and Contarini Fleming). Vivian, brilliant and difficult, is expelled from school, and discovers that charm can secure political advancement. By playing on the follies of discontented peers and MPs, he builds a faction round the powerful but disappointed marquis of Carabas. His secret efforts to create a new party are exposed by the tempestuous Mrs Lorraine (a reminiscence of Lady Caroline *Lamb). Challenged to a duel by the outraged Cleveland, leader-designate of the party, Vivian kills him. Ruined, he leaves England and begins a desultory life of intrigue and adventure among German princelings. The last four books were added by popular demand in 1827.

Disraeli came to dislike the novel, and in 1853 he drastically revised the work.

VIZENOR, Gerald (1934–) Native American novelist, poet, and ethnologist. His first novel, Darkness in Saint Louis Bearheart (1978), was followed by works drawing on traditional trickster tales, and on the writings of the Native American writer Navarre Scott *Momaday. Vizenor uses *postmodern strategies to question the cultural construction of 'Indian'. Interior Landscapes (1990) is an autobiography.

VIZETELLY, Henry (1820–94) Engraver, printer, publisher, journalist, and editor, whose defiance of censorship and policy of issuing cheap reprints had a considerable impact on the literary scene. In 1885, with George *Moore, he published a cheap one-volume edition of A Mummer's Wife, an act which did much to break the power of the *circulating libraries and the three-decker novel. In 1886, with Havelock *Ellis he founded the Mermaid Series of unexpurgated reprints of 'The Best Plays of the Old Dramatists'. He also published translations of *Flaubert, *Gogol, *Tolstoy, the Goncourts, and others, and seventeen novels by *Zola; it was his publication of Zola's La Terre that led to his three-month imprisonment in 1888 on an obscenity charge. This bankrupted his publishing company. Vizetelly's memoirs, Glances Back through Seventy Years (1893), give a lively portrait of bohemian society.

Volpone, or The Fox A comedy by Ben *Jonson, performed by the King's Men in 1605–6, printed 1607. Volpone, a rich and childless Venetian, pretends to be dying in order to draw gifts from his would-be heirs. Mosca, his accomplice, persuades each of these in turn that he is to be the heir, extracting costly presents from them. One of them, Corvino, even attempts to offer his wife to Volpone in hope of the inheritance. Finally Volpone overreaches himself. To enjoy the mortification of the vultures awaiting his death, he bequeaths his property to Mosca and pretends to be dead. Mosca then blackmails Volpone, but rather than be defeated Volpone chooses to reveal all to the authorities. They direct that Volpone shall be cast in irons until he is as infirm as he pretended to be, Mosca whipped and confined to the galleys, Corvino made to parade in ass's ears, and his wife be returned to her family with a trebled dowry.

Völsunga saga A prose version of a lost cycle of heroic songs of which fragments survive in the poetic *Edda, dealing with the families of the Volsungs and the Niblungs. It has been translated by William *Morris and Eirikr Magnusson (1888). See SIGURD THE VOLSUNG.

VOLTAIRE (1694–1778) Pseudonym of François-Marie Arouet, prolific French poet, dramatist, historian, satirist, fiction writer, polemicist, thinker, critic, and correspondent. He was the universal genius of the *Enlightenment. He made his name as a tragic dramatist, writing some 30 tragedies, from *Œdipe* (1718: *Oedipus*) to *Irène* (1778), and as a poet, publishing *La Ligue* (1723: *The League*; later retitled *La Henriade*, 1728). A period in exile in England (1726–8) inspired his first great prose work, the controversial *Lettres philosophiques* (1734: *Philosophical Letters*). First published in English (1733), it creates a satirical contrast between the liberty and tolerance of England and the abuses of the French *ancien régime*. His other prose works include his histories, notably *Le Siècle de Louis XIV* (1751: *The Century of Louis XIV*), which disregards providence as an explanatory principle, seeking instead evidence of social and moral progress, and his philosophical tales, most famously **Candide* (1759). His championing of justice and tolerance and his mockery of the cruelty and obscurantism of the civil and ecclesiastical establishments were relentless from the late 1750s onwards. A 35-volume edition of his collected works in English, masterminded by Tobias *Smollett and Thomas Francklin (1721–84), began to appear in 1761.

VON ARNIM, Elizabeth (1866–1941) Novelist and cousin of Katherine *Mansfield. In 1890 she married Count Henning August von Arnim-Schlagenthin, the 'Man of Wrath' in her best-known work, *Elizabeth and her German Garden*, published anonymously in 1898; part satire, part idyll, it describes her life at Nassenheide in Pomerania. E. M. *Forster and Hugh *Walpole were tutors to her children there. Her many novels include *The Pastor's Wife* (1914), *Vera* (1921), *The Enchanted April* (1922; adapted for film in 1992), *Love* (1925), and a quirky autobiography, *All the Dogs of my Life* (1936). Her work reveals a keen sense of women's struggle for autonomy within marriage.

VON HARBOU, Thea (1888–1954) German novelist, co-scriptwriter with her husband (until 1932) the director Fritz Lang. Her novel of the script for **Metropolis* (1927) illuminates the film. Other *science fiction includes *Frau im Mond* (1928: *The Girl in the Moon*).

VONNEGUT, Kurt (1922–2007) American novelist and short story writer. He served in the air force in the Second World War, was captured by the Germans, and survived the bombing of Dresden in 1945, an experience that he would later use in his most famous novel, *Slaughterhouse-Five, or The Children's Crusade* (1969). His earlier works drew on *science fiction and *fantasy to satirize the increasing mechanization and dehumanization of the post-war world. His first novel, *Player Piano* (1952), envisages a New York factory town whose automated structure turns its workers and scientists into virtual robots.

Other novels include *Cat's Cradle* (1963), *Breakfast of Champions* (1973), *Slapstick* (1976), *Jailbird* (1979), and *Deadeye Dick* (1983). Vonnegut shared *black humour techniques with Joseph *Heller and illustrated some of his own works.

Vorticism A literary and artistic movement that flourished 1912–15, dominated by Wyndham *Lewis and Ezra *Pound, and including Henri *Gaudier-Brzeska, the painters C. R. Nevinson (1889–1946) and Edward Wadsworth (1889–1949), and the photographer Alvin Langdon Coburn (1882–1966). It defined itself in opposition to *Futurism, an Italian-dominated movement. At its heart was a concern to reconcile the dynamism of modernity with form in art. The vortex, being both energetic and well shaped, served as a model of good aesthetic form. In the visual arts its revolutionary fervour was expressed in abstract compositions of bold lines, sharp angles, and planes. *Blast*, the vorticist periodical, attempted to draw together artists and writers of the English avant-garde.

Vortigern A legendary 5th-century British king reputed to have enlisted *Hengist and Horsa against the Picts, thus causing the transfer of Britain to the Anglo-Saxons. After a lifetime of feuds and alliances with the Germanic invaders, in the course of which he meets Merlin and is astonished by his prophecies, he is burnt alive in the Welsh tower to which he had retired. His story is told by *Nennius, *Bede, *Geoffrey of Monmouth, and *Laȝamon.

Vortigern and Rowena See IRELAND, WILLIAM.

VOYNICH, Ethel Lillian (1864–1960) Née Boole, Irish novelist, remembered for her revolutionary novel *The Gadfly* (1897), set in pre-1848 Italy, which sold in vast quantities in translation in the Soviet Union. She published two sequels, *An Interrupted Friendship* (1910) and *Put off thy Shoes* (1945).

Vulgar Errors See PSEUDODOXIA EPIDEMICA.

Vulgate [from the Latin *versio vulgata*, 'common translation'] The name given to the Latin version of the Bible collected together in the 6th century. St *Jerome's translation of the Old Testament from the Hebrew, completed 405, forms the greater part. The Clementine edition (1592) was until 1979 the authorized Latin text of the *Roman Catholic Church. *See* BIBLE.

Vulgate cycle An important group of Arthurian romances in French prose, dating from *c.*1215–35; the most influential version of the Arthurian legends between *Geoffrey of Monmouth and *Malory. It comprises the *Estoire del Saint Graal*, a version of Robert de *Boron's partially surviving *Merlin*, and the three romances which make up the Prose *Lancelot*, namely the *Lancelot propre*, the *Queste del Saint Graal*, and *Mort Artu*.

V

WACE (*fl.* 12th century) Author, in French verse of 15,000 short couplets, of the *Roman de Brut*, completed in 1155 and dedicated to *Eleanor of Aquitaine, a highly popular adaptation of *Geoffrey of Monmouth's *Historia Regum Britanniae* (*The History of the Kings of Britain*). It was the principal source of *Laȝamon's *Brut* in the early 13th century, and it retained considerable influence up to the 14th century.

Wade's boat In Geoffrey *Chaucer's 'The Merchant's Tale' (*see* CANTERBURY TALES, 10): widows 'konne so muchel craft on Wades boot' (IV. 1424). Wade was also mentioned in Sir Thomas *Malory (Caxton VII. ix: possibly Caxton's addition; not in Vinaver's *Sir Gareth: Works*, 188). The 'tale of Wade' is also mentioned in *Troilus and Criseyde*, III. 614. In the 13th-century German *epic *Kudrun*, Hettel, king of the Hegelings, wishes to marry Hilde, daughter of Hagen, king of Ireland. Hettel's servant Wade sails to Ireland, his fleet including a boat with a removable deck, beneath which he conceals an army. He and his men distract King Hagen while his daughter is lured onto the boat. The army emerges, kills her protectors, and abducts her so that she may marry Hettel.

'Waggoner, The' A comic narrative poem by William *Wordsworth, composed 1805, published 1819 with a dedication to Charles *Lamb.

WAGNER, Richard (1813–83) German composer, dramatist, and writer. His theoretical writings reached beyond the musical field: a revolutionary in 1848–9, he later came under the influence of Arthur *Schopenhauer. As a composer, Wagner attempted to create a new synthesis of music and drama, writing both words and music. His ideas were on the grandest scale: *Der Ring des Nibelungen* (based on the *Nibelungenlied*), planned as a single drama, developed backwards (each episode requiring previous explanation for its proper understanding) until the finished work required four separate evenings and eventually the construction of a new type of theatre. Wagner's first critical champion in Britain was G. B. *Shaw. D. H. *Lawrence's *The Trespasser* (originally entitled *The Saga of Siegmund*) contains much Wagnerian symbolism, and three deeply influential works of the 20th century, *The *Waste Land*, *Ulysses*, and *Finnegans Wake*, all quote directly from Wagner's operas. Amongst Wagner's early works, *Das Liebesverbot* (1836) is an adaptation of *Measure for Measure*, and *Rienzi* (1842), is partly based on Edward *Bulwer-Lytton's novel.

waif stories Socially conscious novels with great melodramatic potential, especially when concerned with deprived and abused children, popular in the 19th century. Best-sellers included Maria Louisa Charlesworth (1819–80) with *Ministering Children* (1854) and Hesba *Stretton's (Sarah Smith) *Jessica's First Prayer* (1867), which sold over 1.5 million copies. *Froggy's Little Brother* (1875) by Brenda (Georgina Castle Smith, née Meyrick, 1845–1933) was a hugely popular and influential tear-jerker. Notable episodes in the same tradition include the opening of *The *Water-Babies* and the scenes about *Dickens's crossing-sweeper, Jo, in *Bleak House* (1852–3). In the USA, waif stories overlapped the genre of self-help books such as Horatio *Alger Jr's *Ragged Dick* (1868), stressing social mobility and individual effort rather than religion or philanthropy. Vestiges of the genre survived into the 20th century in Frances Hodgson *Burnett's *A Little Princess* (1905).

WAIN, John Barrington (1925–94) Poet, critic, and novelist. His first novel, *Hurry on Down* (1953), a *picaresque account of a university graduate rebelling against the middle-class career that beckons him, has been linked with the work of the so-called *'Angry Young Men' of the 1950s, although Wain himself disliked the term. Other novels include *The Contenders* (1958), *Strike the Father Dead* (1962), *Young Shoulders* (1982), and a trilogy set in Oxford (*Where the Rivers Meet*, 1988; *Comedies*, 1990; and *Hungry Generations*, 1994). As a poet Wain was associated with the *Movement and contributed to *New Lines*; he published several volumes of verse, collected in *Poems 1949-79* (1981).

Waiting for Godot The first stage play of Samuel *Beckett, published in French as *En attendant Godot*, 1952, staged in French in Paris, 1953, first staged in English at the Arts Theatre, London, 1955. One of the most influential plays of the post-war period, it portrays two tramps, Estragon and Vladimir, trapped in an endless waiting for the arrival of the mysterious Godot, while disputing the appointed place and hour of his coming. They amuse themselves meanwhile with bouts of repartee and word-play, and are for a while diverted by the arrival of whip-cracking Pozzo, driving the oppressed and burdened Lucky on the end of a rope. Towards the end of each of the two acts, a boy arrives, heralding Godot's appearance, but he does not come; each act ends with the interchange between the two tramps, 'Well, shall we go?' 'Yes, let's go', and the stage direction, 'They do not move.' There are strong biblical references throughout, but Beckett's powerfully symbolic portrayal of the human condition as one of ignorance, delusion, paralysis, and intermittent flashes of human sympathy, hope, and wit has been subjected to varying interpretations. *See* ABSURD, THEATRE OF THE.

WALCOTT, Derek (1930-) OBE, poet and playwright, born in St Lucia, in the West Indies. He founded the Trinidad Theatre Workshop in 1959, and many of his own plays had their first performances there. These include *Dream on Monkey Mountain* (1967; pub. 1970), *The Joker of Seville* (1974; pub. 1978; based on Tirso de Molina's *El burlador de Sevilla*), *O Babylon!* (1976; pub. 1978), and *The Haitian Trilogy* (2002). His collections of poetry include *In a Green Night: Poems 1948-60* (1962), *The Castaway and Other Poems* (1965), *Sea Grapes* (1976), *The Fortunate Traveller* (1982), *Midsummer* (1984), *The Arkansas Testament* (1987), *Tiepolo's Hound* (2001), *The Prodigal* (2004), *White Egrets* (2010), and his epic Caribbean Odyssey *Omeros* (1990). Both plays and poetry show a preoccupation with the national identity of the West Indies and their literature, and with the conflict between the heritage of European and West Indian culture. Walcott's plays mingle verse and prose, *Creole vocabulary and the rhythms of calypso, and his poems, many of which are confessional and self-questioning, are rich in classical allusion and evoke with equal vividness both Caribbean and European landscapes. A wry wit enlivens his essays as well as plays and poems. He was awarded the *Nobel Prize for Literature in 1992. *See also* POSTCOLONIAL LITERATURE.

Walden, or Life in the Woods *See* THOREAU, HENRY.

'Waldhere' The name given to two fragments of an Old English poem in a manuscript from the Royal Library, Copenhagen, of the late 10th century, totalling 63 lines. Waldhere was the son of a king of Aquitaine, who became one of Attila the Hun's generals. He escaped with Hiltgund, a Burgundian princess. They were attacked, and Waldhere, after slaying his assailants in a fist fight, was ambushed and wounded the next day. But they were finally married.

WALEY, Arthur (1889-1966) Poet and authority on Chinese and Japanese literature, which he introduced to a wide public through his well-known translations. He taught himself the languages while working in the Print Room at the British Museum, and in 1918 published *A Hundred and Seventy Chinese Poems*. His translations are unrhymed, elegant, and lucid; his rhythms had, he believed, something in common with G. M. Hopkins's *sprung rhythm. His other translations in prose and verse include *The Tale of Genji* (1925-33), *The Pillow-Book of Sei Shonagon* (1928), and *Monkey* (1942). He spent most of his life in Bloomsbury, where he was on friendly terms with many of the *Bloomsbury Group and the *vorticists.

WALKER, Alice (1944-) African American novelist, poet, and short story writer, best known as the writer of *The Color Purple* (1982), which provoked controversy for its hostile depiction of African American men. This novel tells the story of Celie, a young black woman in the South, raped by the man she believes to be her father and then forced to marry an older man she despises. It is narrated through letters from Celie to God, and to and from her missionary sister Nettie. Walker has published collections of poetry, including *Once: Poems* (1968) and *Revolutionary Petunias and Other Poems* (1973). Her other work includes short stories and a collection of essays, *In Search of my Mother's Garden: Womanist Prose* (1983). Her novel *Possessing the Secret of Joy* (1992) examines female circumcision, and *The Same River Twice* (1996) is a memoir.

WALLACE, Alfred Russel (1823-1913) Naturalist and traveller. A self-taught botany enthusiast, he joined a collecting expedition to the Amazon in 1848. His 1853 account of the expedition was a best-seller. During an eight-year journey described in *The Malay Archipelago* (1869) he, independently of *Darwin, developed the theory of natural selection. Darwin presented their joint findings to the Linnean Society in 1858. Wallace coined the term 'survival of the fittest' and mapped 'Wallace's line' demarcating the Asian and Australasian faunal regions. He was overshadowed by the more established Darwin and marginalized by his interests in spiritualism, socialism, and women's suffrage.

WALLACE, Edgar (1875–1932) Writer and playwright. He published his first book, a collection of ballads, in 1898. He became an extremely successful and remarkably prolific writer of thrillers, including *The Four Just Men* (1905), *The Crimson Circle* (1922), and *The Green Archer* (1923). He also wrote successful plays, and died in Hollywood, where he had been working on the screenplay of *King Kong* (1933).

WALLACE, Sir William (d. 1305) A Scottish patriot of the time of Edward I, who devoted his life to resistance to the English and was finally captured by treachery and executed in London. He is the subject of a long poem (*see* HARY'S WALLACE). *Braveheart* (1995), Mel Gibson's stirring film about his life, greatly enhanced his status as national hero.

WALLER, Edmund (1606–87) Poet and politician. He is said to have entered Parliament at 16. In 1643 he plotted to seize London for Charles I, and was banished. He made his peace with Oliver Cromwell in 1651, and returned to England. His use of the heroic couplet led John *Dryden to praise him as 'the father of our English numbers'. 'Go, lovely rose' (from *Poems*, 1645) is his best-known lyric.

WALMSLEY, Leo *See* REGIONAL NOVEL.

WALPOLE, Horace, fourth earl of Orford (1717–97) Author and politician; at Eton College he formed a 'Quadruple Alliance' with Thomas *Gray, Richard West (1716–42) and Thomas Ashton (1715–75). Walpole was MP successively for Callington, Castle Rising, and Lynn, 1741–67. In 1747 Walpole settled in Twickenham in the house he made known as Strawberry Hill, rebuilding it as 'a little Gothic castle'. In 1757 he established his own printing press here; his first publication was Gray's Pindaric *Odes. In 1758 he printed *Fugitive Pieces in Verse and Prose*, and in 1762 his *Anecdotes of Painting in England*. His *Gothic novel *The *Castle of Otranto* appeared late in 1764. In 1765 Walpole met Madame du Deffand in Paris and they formed a lasting friendship. In 1768 he published *Historic Doubts on the Life and Reign of King Richard the Third* and printed but did not publish his tragedy *The *Mysterious Mother*. He was accused of hastening Chatterton's apparent suicide by his neglect and defended himself in a pamphlet of 1782. Walpole left his Memoirs ready for publication in a sealed chest, which was opened in 1818. *Memoirs of the Last Ten Years of the Reign of George II* was first edited in 1822; *Memoirs of the Reign of King George the Third* first appeared in 1845. Some of Walpole's letters appeared with his *Works* in 1798: the monumental Yale edition of the *Correspondence*, ed. W. S. Lewis *et al.* (48 vols, 1937–83) has established Walpole's reputation as an assiduous, stylish, and witty observer of his age.

WALPOLE, Sir Hugh (1884–1941) Novelist, born in New Zealand. The first of his 36 novels was *The Wooden Horse* (1909). *The Dark Forest* (1915) is based on his wartime service with the Russian Red Cross. Other works include *Jeremy* (1919) and the *Herries Chronicle*, a historical sequence set in Cumberland (where Walpole lived from 1924), consisting of *Rogue Herries* (1930), *Judith Paris* (1931), *The Fortress* (1932), *Vanessa* (1933), and two further novels. He was deeply offended by Somerset *Maugham's portrait of him as Alroy Kear, a hypocritical literary opportunist, in *Cakes and Ale* (1930).

WALSH, Jill (Gillian) Paton (1937–) CBE, novelist and children's writer. Her novels include *Lapsing* (1986), set in Oxford of the 1950s; *A School for Lovers* (1989), a country-house romance, and *Knowledge of Angels* (1994), a medieval romance which discusses the nature and grounds of belief. Her reputation as a children's writer was established with *Goldengrove* (1972) and its sequel *Unleaving* (1976) about the end of childhood; *The Emperor's Winding-Sheet* (1974), set during the fall of Constantinople, the time-slip fantasy *A Chance Child* (1978), and the plague story *A Parcel of Patterns* (1984). Walsh also writes detective stories featuring Imogen Quy. *Thrones, Dominations* (1998), a continuation of an unfinished work by Dorothy *Sayers, has been followed by two further Lord Peter Wimsey novels, *A Presumption of Death* (2002) and *The Attenbury Emeralds* (2010).

WALTON, Izaak (1593–1683) He was a friend of John *Donne and Sir Henry *Wotton and of Bishops Morley (?1598–1684), Sanderson (1587–1663), and Henry *King, and wrote biographies of Donne (1640), Wotton (1651), Richard *Hooker (1665), George *Herbert (1670), and Sanderson (1678). He is chiefly known for *The *Compleat Angler*, first published 1653, and largely rewritten for the second edition (1655). Often reprinted, this work combines practical information about angling with folklore, quotations from writers as diverse as *Pliny, Guillaume de Saluste Du Bartas, and Herbert, pastoral interludes of songs and ballads, and glimpses of an idyllic rural life of well-kept inns and tuneful milkmaids. *See* COTTON, CHARLES.

WALTON, Sir William (1902–83) English composer. Walton's innovative *Façade* (1922), for voice and six instruments, was based on 21 poems by Edith *Sitwell (recited at early performances by the poet herself). He also set texts by William *Dunbar, A. C. *Swinburne, and Louis *MacNeice, and wrote scores for Laurence Olivier's Shakespeare films *Henry V* (1944), *Hamlet* (1947), and *Richard III* (1955).

Wanderer, The An Old English poem of 115 lines in the *Exeter Book, one of the group known as 'elegies'. Beginning with the hardships of a man who has lost his lord, it becomes a plangent lament for the transience of life, culminating towards its end in a powerful *ubi sunt* passage. It begins and ends with a brief and bald statement of Christian consolation, but that is not the prevailing sentiment of the poem. It is paralleled in spirit and structure by *The *Seafarer*, particularly in the latter's first half, and similar arguments have been advanced for and against the coherence of organization in both poems. The poem was admired by W. H. *Auden and he translated it loosely.

Wanderer, The A poem in five cantos by Richard *Savage, published 1729. The suffering wanderer is taught to interpret the landscapes and figures of a 'strange visionary land' by an angelic hermit. The poem has several narrative episodes, advice on the life of the poet, passages of vivid natural description and dark reflections on murder, death, and suicide. Samuel *Johnson called it 'a heap of shining materials thrown together by accident, which strikes . . . with the solemn magnificence of a stupendous ruin'.

Wanderer, The, or Female Difficulties The last novel of Fanny *Burney, published in 1814. Less successful than her earlier works, it was criticized for its improbabilities and its convoluted style. It describes the adventures of its mysterious and, for much of the novel, nameless heroine, Juliet, escaped from revolutionary France and hard pressed by poverty, unwanted male attention, and the social conventions which prevent her from earning her own living. Her friend and foil, the passionate Elinor Joddrel, who loves Juliet's admirer Harleigh, provides an interesting portrait of the emancipated woman of the period, possibly based in part on Madame de Staël, whom Burney had met in 1793.

WANDOR, Michelene (1940–) Née Samuels, playwright, poet, and critic; she was involved in the Women's Liberation movement from 1969, and edited *The Body Politic*, a collection of feminist essays, in 1972. *The Wandering Jew* (1987) was the first play by a woman put on at the *National Theatre. She edited the first four volumes of the ground-breaking *Plays by Women*, and worked with the Women's Theatre Group and Monstrous Regiment. Her *Music of the Prophets* (2007) commemorates the 350th anniversary of the Jews' return to England in 1657.

WANLEY, Nathaniel (1632/3–80) Clergyman and poet. He published *The Wonders of the Little World* (1678), a collection of tales and superstitions in which Robert *Browning found the story of the 'Pied Piper of Hamelin' and other oddities. His poems, some in the vein of Henry *Vaughan, were edited by L. C. Martin (1928).

WARBURTON, John (1682–1759) Antiquary and manuscript collector. His manuscripts of Elizabethan and Jacobean plays, some of them unique, were mostly destroyed by Betsy Baker, his cook, who burned them or put them 'under pye bottoms'. Warburton's list of 55 destroyed plays (three more, with one fragment, were saved) is in the British Library, with other surviving manuscripts.

WARBURTON, William (1698–1779) Clergyman and writer, vigorously engaged in theological debate. His most famous work was *The Divine Legation of Moses* (1738–41), a controversial attack on *Deism. He defended the orthodoxy of Alexander *Pope's *Essay on Man*. His combative edition of *Shakespeare (1747) attacked Lewis *Theobald, a former friend. Warburton denounced the 'natural religion' of Pope's friend Viscount Bolingbroke in *A View of Lord Bolingbroke's Philosophy* (1754), and opposed the 'enthusiasm' of John *Wesley and David *Hume's views on miracles.

WARD, Artemus (1834–67) The pen-name of Charles Farrar Browne, American humorist, who purported to describe the experiences of a travelling showman, using, like 'Josh Billings' (Henry Wheeler Shaw, 1818–85), his own comic phonetic spelling. He helped shape the career of Mark *Twain.

WARD, Edward ('Ned') (1667–1731) Tavern-keeper and writer (under various pseudonyms) of *Hudibrastic verse, travel stories, and satires. *The London Spy*, issued in 18 monthly parts (1698–1700) recounts the sights, sounds, smells, and characters encountered in a series of walks through the capital. Ward was fined and pilloried for *Hudibras Redivivus*, a burlesque poem, published in 24 monthly parts (1705–7).

WARD, Mary Augusta Novelist and philanthropist, commonly known as Mrs Humphry Ward (1851–1920). Born in Hobart, Tasmania, she was partly educated at a boarding school in Ambleside run by Anne Jemima Clough (1820–92), first principal of Newnham College, Cambridge. Her father's reconversion to Anglicanism allowed him to teach in Oxford, where she joined the family, and met and married Thomas Humphry Ward. *Robert Elsmere* (1888, novel) is in part a vivid evocation of the Oxford of Walter *Pater, Mark *Pattison, and T. H. *Green, and of the many varieties of religious faith and doubt which succeeded the ferment of the *Oxford Movement. Its success was initially stimulated by a long and thoughtful review from W. E. *Gladstone; the author herself compared it to J. A. *Froude's *The Nemesis of Faith* and J. H. *Newman's *Loss and Gain*, novels which also dealt with the crisis of mid-Victorian faith. Most of her other novels deal with social, political, and religious themes, frequently contrasting traditional belief with the values of progress and intellectual freedom. They include *The History of David Grieve* (1892), *Marcella* (1894), *Helbeck of Bannisdale* (1898), *Lady Rose's Daughter* (1903), and *The Marriage of William Ashe* (1905). She supported the movement for higher education for women, but opposed women's suffrage, on the grounds that women's influence was stronger in the home than in public life. Her *A Writer's Recollections* (1918) draws a striking picture of Oxford life and of the domestic influence of William *Morris, Edward Burne-Jones, and Liberty prints; it also contains portraits of Benjamin Jowett, Pater, Henry *James, and other friends.

WARD, Plumer Robert (1765–1846) A lawyer and MP who, aged 60, unexpectedly published *Tremaine, or A Man of Refinement* (1825), a *fashionable novel, followed by *De Vere, or The Man of Independence* (1827) and *De Clifford, or The Constant Man* (1841). His motives were didactic, and he hoped that his works of fiction (which he did not care to call 'novels') would demonstrate how the standards of public and private morality could be upheld amid the dissipation of the times.

Warden, The A short novel by Anthony *Trollope, published 1855, the first in the *'Barsetshire' series. It represents a turning point in Trollope's career. The income of Hiram's Hospital, a charitable institution, has grown down the centuries, but the twelve bedesmen have not benefited. The surplus has created a pleasant sinecure for the gentle warden, Septimus Harding, a fact which John Bold, a local surgeon with a passion for reform, makes known to the national press. His son-in-law, the conservative Archdeacon Grantly, bullies him to dispute the case along party lines, but Harding sees the anomaly in his position, and with considerable personal courage resigns. The novel ends in an atmosphere of quiet goodwill.

WARNER, Alan (1964–) Scottish novelist and short story writer. His acclaimed first novel, *Morvern Callar* (1995), is written in the voice of a semi-literate young woman living in the West Highlands of Scotland in the early 1990s. The novel's style combines banal colloquialism with sophisticated lyricism. Warner's more experimental novel, *These Demented Lands* (1997), continues the story of Morvern to evoke a New Age nightmare of shipwreck, with echoes of William *Golding and Joseph *Conrad. *The Man Who Walks* (2002) presents a darkly comic, partly fantastical narrative of the interactions of a group of Scottish misfits, while the widely admired *The Worms Can Carry Me to Heaven* (2006) recounts the self-deluding life of Manolo, a Spanish playboy who learns that he is HIV-positive. Warner has sometimes been seen as a leader of the so-called *'Chemical Generation'

WARNER, Marina (1946–) CBE, novelist, critic, and cultural historian. Her novels include *The Skating Party* (1983), *The Lost Father* (1988), *Indigo, or Mapping the Waters* (1992), an exploration of colonialism and displacement, set on an imaginary Caribbean island, and *The Leto Bundle* (2001). Her scholarly works include

Alone of All her Sex (1976), a study of the myth and cult of the Virgin Mary, *Joan of Arc: The Image of Female Heroism* (1981) and *From the Beast to the Blonde* (1994), a study of *fairy-tales. *No Go the Bogeyman* (1998) investigates what scares us and how we master our fears by translating them into art and narrative; *Phantas-magoria* (2006) explores ideas of spirit and soul since the Enlightenment.

WARNER, Rex (1905–86) Poet, novelist, and translator. He met Cecil *Day-Lewis, W. H. *Auden and Stephen *Spender at Oxford. His *Poems* and his first novel, *The Wild Goose Chase*, both appeared in 1937. *The Professor* (1938) and *The Aerodrome* (1941; ironically sub-titled 'A Love Story'), which followed in quick succession are more sombre political parables which reflect the gathering gloom of the 1930s. His later fiction is based largely on Greek and Roman historical subjects, and he also translat-ed works by *Euripides and *Aeschylus.

WARNER, Sylvia Townsend (1893–1978) Novelist and poet, whose love of early music is reflected in her later fiction. Her vo-lumes of poems include *The Espalier* (1925) and *Opus 7* (1931), a novel in verse. Her *Collected Poems* appeared in 1982. Her original voice is heard more strongly in her novels, which often draw on folklore and include *Lolly Willowes* (1926), the story of a maiden aunt who realizes her vocation as a witch; *Mr Fortune's Maggot* (1927), which describes the eponymous mis-sionary's sojourn on a remote South Sea island; and *The True Heart* (1929), which retells the story of *Cupid and Psyche through the medium of a Victorian orphan. *After the Death of Don Juan* (1938) is an allegorical novel of the Spanish Civil War. *The Corner That Held Them* (1948) is set in a closed community of nuns in fourteenth-century East Anglia. Her *Letters* (1982) and *Diaries* (1994) describe her many friendships, notably with T. F. *Powys, and her love for the poet Valentine Ackland.

WARNER, William (1558/9–1609) Poet and author; also an attorney in London. He pub-lished *Pan his Syrinx*, seven prose tales (1584), but his chief work was *Albion's England*, a met-rical British history, written in *fourteeners, with mythical and fictitious episodes, extending in the first edition (1586) from Noah to the Nor-man Conquest. It was brought up to *Elizabeth I's reign in 1592; and a continuation, reaching *James I, was published in 1606.

War of the Worlds, The A *scientific romance by H. G. *Wells, published 1898. It describes the arrival of the Martians in Woking, driven from their own planet by its progressive cooling to take refuge in a warmer world. In a letter Wells described his plan for the work, in which: 'I completely wreck and sack Woking—killing my neighbours in painful and eccentric ways—then proceed via Kingston and Rich-mond to London, selecting South Kensington for feats of peculiar atrocity'; much of the no-vel's power depends on the contrast between the familiar complacent reactions of the hu-mans and the terrifying destructive intelligence of the Martians. They live by the injection into themselves of the fresh living blood of other creatures, mostly of human beings, and they devastate the country before eventually falling victims to terrestrial bacteria. A radio broadcast by Orson *Welles of a dramatization of the novel in the USA on 30 October 1938 caused a furore, many of its millions of listeners taking it for a factual report of the invasion of New Jersey by Martians.

war poetry, 20th-century It is generally agreed that the First World War (1914–18) inspired poetry of the highest order, some of it ground-breaking in both treatment of subject and technique: combatants included Wilfred *Owen, Siegfried *Sassoon, Isaac *Rosenberg, Robert *Graves, Charles Hamilton *Sorley, Ed-ward *Thomas, and Rupert *Brooke (the last of whom died before seeing active service). Mem-orable poems and elegies on the theme were contributed by Thomas *Hardy, Laurence *Bin-yon, A. E *Housman, and others. Rudyard *Ki-pling's poetry struck a different and more patriotic note from that of most of his contem-poraries, but the anguish of losing his son to the conflict left a deep mark on him and his work. The Spanish Civil War (1936–9), very much a writers' war, attracted some important British poets, including John *Cornford, Stephen *Spender, W. H *Auden, and Louis *MacNeice, as well as less well-remembered names like those of Clive Branson (1907–44), Bernard Gut-teridge (1916–85), and H. B. Mallalieu (1914–88). The Second World War produced a more disparate response: the poets most commonly associated with it are Keith *Douglas, Alun *Owen, and Sidney *Keyes, all of whom died in the conflict. However, F. T. *Prince, John *Pud-ney, and Henry *Reed are widely remembered for single, much-anthologized war poems, as well as other work, and later anthologies have revealed a considerable wealth and diversity of responses, some by writers like Alan *Ross and Charles *Causley who moved on to other subjects, some by writers who moved on to other careers. *See also* HOLOCAUST; HARSENT, DAVID.

WARREN, Robert Penn (1905–89) American poet, novelist, and critic. In the 1930s he was a member of the Southern Agrarians (a group of twelve traditionalist and conservative populist writers, including John Crowe *Ransom and Allen *Tate). His novels include *All the King's Men* (1946), *Band of Angels* (1955), *The Cave* (1959), and *Meet Me in the Green Glen* (1971); his volumes of poetry include *Promises* (1957), *Now and Then* (1978), and *Portrait of a Father* (1988). His critical works are associated with the *New Criticism, and include compilations in collaboration with Cleanth *Brooks.

WARREN, Samuel (1807–77) Lawyer and novelist. His first publication was the morbidly melodramatic *Passages from the Diary of a Late Physician* (1830–7). Warren is best remembered for the sensationally popular comic novel *Ten Thousand a-Year* (1840–1).

Wars of the Roses, The The collective title given to John Barton and Peter *Hall's three-part adaptation of Shakespeare's history cycle of *Henry VI*, Parts 1, 2, and 3, and *Richard III*, first performed at Stratford in 1963, directed by Peter Hall. Barton composed about 1,400 lines of it.

war stories for children *Children's literature has included stories about war almost since its inception. Some books have depicted the hardships, injustices, and tragedies of war, not least for children—this is particularly true of more recent events such as the First World War, the Holocaust, and other genocidal conflicts. Many writers, however, treat war as romantic and dramatic; a time when children can be valiant and have adventures as in the stories of G. A. *Henty and Robert *Westall. There are sub-genres about Second World War evacuees, typified by Nina *Bawden's *Carrie's War* (1975), and refugees: Alem in Benjamin *Zephaniah's *Refugee Boy* (2001) has fled civil war in Africa. *Series books, magazines, and *comics have all included war stories. Futuristic wars often raise ethical questions as in Orson Scott Card's *Ender's Game* (1994), in which adults use children, who think they are playing computer games, to exterminate an alien race.

WARTON, Joseph (1722–1800) Clergyman, poet, and critic, the son of Thomas *Warton (1688–1745). His own early poems, such as *The Enthusiast, or The Lover of Nature* (1744), *Odes on Various Subjects* (1746), and *An Ode to Evening* (1749), reacted against the poetic dominance of Alexander *Pope. Warton's *An Essay on the Writings and Genius of Pope* (1756, 1782) ranks poets of the *sublime, such as William *Shakespeare, Edmund *Spenser, and John *Milton, above poets of ethical reasoning, such as Pope.

WARTON, Thomas (1688–1745) Clergyman and poet. A collection of his odes, light satires, and 'runic' verse, with an imitation of Edmund *Spenser, was edited (and in part fabricated) by his sons Joseph and Thomas *Warton as *Poems on Several Occasions* (1748).

WARTON, Thomas (1728–90) Scholar and literary historian, the son of Thomas *Warton (1688–1745). He made his mark with *Observations on the Faery Queen of Spenser* (1754). He wrote much satiric verse and edited *The Oxford Sausage* (1764), an anthology of university poems; his serious verse includes many *sonnets, a form he helped to revive. He was a friend of Samuel *Johnson, and contributed three numbers to the *Idler. His *History of English Poetry* (3 vols, 1774–81), the first substantial literary history of England, showed unusual admiration for Geoffrey *Chaucer and other medieval authors. In 1782 Warton demonstrated that the poems produced by Thomas *Chatterton could not be medieval.

WASHINGTON, Booker T. **(Taliaferro)** (1856–1915) African American writer, born into slavery on a Virginia plantation. Freed, he taught himself to read, and became the founder and head of the Tuskegee Institute, Alabama, a school for African Americans. His works include an autobiography, *Up from Slavery* (1901), and *Working with the Hands* (1904). *See also* SLAVERY.

Washington Square A novel by Henry *James, published 1881. Catherine Sloper lives in Washington Square, New York, with her widowed father, a rich physician. She is plain and shy, and is approached by a handsome fortune-hunter, who drops his suit when her father threatens disinheritance. After the latter's death, he tries again, but is turned down by Catherine.

Waste Land, The A poem by T. S. *Eliot, first published 1922 in *Criterion* and a few days later in *The *Dial*. It consists of five sections, 'The Burial of the Dead', 'A Game of Chess', 'The Fire Sermon', 'Death by Water', and 'What the Thunder Said'. Eliot's own 'Notes' source his many allusions, quotations, and half-quotations (from John *Webster, *Dante, Paul *Verlaine, Thomas *Kyd, etc.), and indicate his general indebtedness to the *Grail legend and to the vegetation ceremonies in *Frazer's *The Golden Bough*. The poem was rapidly acclaimed as a statement of the post-war sense of futility; and hailed as a kind of protest against the older generation by the undergraduates of the day. Complex, erudite, cryptic, satiric, spiritually earnest, and occasionally lyrical, it became one of the most recognizable landmarks of *modernism. Eliot himself found the poem's reputation a burden, and described it as 'just a piece of rhythmical grumbling.' Valerie Eliot's edition, *The Waste Land: A Facsimile and Transcript of the Original Drafts* (1971), showed the detailed textual advice offered by Ezra *Pound (through which the poem's length was very considerably reduced).

Watchman, The (1796) A political and literary journal, of ten issues only, produced by S. T. *Coleridge. The journal was pacifist and opposed the Tory government of William Pitt, and included literary contributions from, among others, Thomas Lovell *Beddoes and Thomas Poole (1765–1837).

Water-Babies, The: *A Fairy Tale for a Land-Baby* By Charles *Kingsley, published in 1863 with illustrations by Sir (Joseph) Noël Paton (1821–1901). Supposedly written for Kingsley's son Grenville, the book is a Rabelaisian collection of fantasy episodes punctuated by authorial digressions on a wide range of the author's religious, philosophical, sexual, and social preoccupations. Its status as children's literature is ambiguous. It begins with a realistic picture of chimney-sweep Tom's Godless life in London with his drunken master Mr Grimes. While sweeping the chimneys of a large house, Tom gets lost, emerging into the symbolically white bedroom of the little girl Ellie, and is hounded by the household to his death (by drowning). He is then transformed into a water-baby, and the story effectively becomes a redemption allegory with the figures of Mrs Doasyouwouldbedoneby and Mrs Bedonebyasyoudid helping to develop Tom from a mindless slave to a moral being who appreciates the living world. This redemption extends to Grimes, after which Tom is reunited with Ellie. The book has survived into the 21st century largely in abridgements and adaptations; it was filmed in 1988.

WATERHOUSE, Keith Spencer (1929–2009) Journalist, novelist, and dramatist. His novels include *Billy Liar on the Moon* (1976), *Office Life* (1978), *Maggie Muggins* (1981), and *Unsweet Charity* (1992), following the success of *Billy Liar* (1959). He adapted this regional comedy, about a youth who attempts to escape his dull family life through fantasy, for the stage in 1960, with his long-standing friend and collaborator Willis Hall (1925–2005). Their other collaborations on stage, screen, and television plays, adaptations, and musicals include the film *Whistle down the Wind* (1961). Waterhouse wrote the screenplay of Stan *Barstow's *A Kind of Loving* (1960) and *Jeffrey Bernard Is Unwell* (1989) was his stage adaptation of Bernard's *Spectator columns. *City Lights* (1994) and *Streets Ahead* (1995) are autobiographies.

water poet, the *See* TAYLOR, JOHN.

WATERS, Sarah (1966–) Novelist. *Tipping the Velvet* (1998) brings a music-hall swagger to its accounts of a young lesbian's escapades in the 1880s. *Affinity* (1999) gives resonances reminiscent of Emily *Dickinson or Henry *James to a haunting tale of spinsters and spiritualists in the 1870s. *Fingersmith* (2002) plunges into the lurid world of the 1860s *sensation novel. Her thesis, uncovering lesbian existences scarcely glimpsed in 19th-century fiction motivated the writing of these books. *The Night Watch* (2006) spotlights covert, mainly homosexual, lives in the 1940s, portraying the impact on them of the Second World War and its aftermath. All four novels have been adapted for television. *The Little Stranger* (2009) is a *ghost story.

WATKINS, Vernon (1906–67) Poet, born in Wales of Welsh-speaking parents; he was a long-standing friend of Dylan *Thomas. Although sometimes associated with the *New Apocalypse, his poetry was, as Philip *Larkin—a perhaps unlikely admirer—was to record, 'much more controlled than theirs and reached further back to the symbolist poets of Europe'. The title poem of his first volume *Ballad of the Mari Lwyd* (1941) is rooted in Welsh folklore and mythology. Watkins's lyric gift was developed in many subsequent volumes, including *The Lamp and the Veil* (1945) and *Fidelities* (1968). His work was influenced by German and French poetry, and he translated Heinrich *Heine. *New Selected Poems* was published in 2006.

WATSON, John *See* KAILYARD SCHOOL.

WATSON, Thomas (1556/7–92) Poet and translator. He published a Latin version of *Sophocles' Antigone*, with an appendix of Latin allegorical poems and experiments in classical metres (1581). His major work was *The* Ἑκατομπαθια *or Passionate Century of Love* (1582), eighteen-line poems, called sonnets, often based on classical, French, and Italian sources, and accompanied by learned explanatory notes. His Latin-verse lamentations, *Amyntas* (1585), were translated without authority by Abraham Fraunce (1587). Watson published *The First Set of Italian Madrigals Englished* (1590) with music by Luca Marenzio and William *Byrd in the same year an *Eglogue*, in Latin and English versions, on the death of Sir Francis Walsingham (*c.*1532–1590). His Latin *pastoral *Amintae Gaudia* appeared posthumously (1592), and he may have written the *sonnet sequence *The Tears of Fancy* (1593). He was a close friend of Christopher *Marlowe, and was mentioned as 'Amyntas' in Edmund *Spenser's *Colin Clouts Come Home Againe*.

Watsons, The An unfinished novel by Jane *Austen, written some time between 1804 and 1807. The story is set at a social level below that of the other novels, and largely concerns the efforts of Emma Watson's three sisters, the good-natured Elizabeth and the unpleasant Margaret and Penelope, to get themselves married. Emma, who has been brought up by a well-to-do aunt, returns to her family, who live unfashionably in genteel poverty in a Surrey village. A pretty, sensible girl, Emma is here surrounded by people in every way inferior to herself. The other principal characters are Lady Osborne, and her son, Lord Osborne, a fine but cold young man; Mr Howard, a gentlemanly clergyman; and Tom Musgrave, a cruel and hardened flirt. The intention appears to have been that the heroine should marry Mr Howard, but Austen left no hint as to the future course of events.

WATT, Robert (1774–1819) Scottish bibliographer and doctor, who in his boyhood met Robert *Burns—'an extraordinary character'. His remarkable bibliographical compilation, which occupied him for some twenty years, *Bibliotheca Britannica, or A General Index to British and Foreign Literature*, provides lists of both authors and subjects, arranged alphabetically and then chronologically; it was published 1819–24.

WATTS, Isaac (1674–1748) *Congregational minister, hymn-writer, educator, philosopher,

and theologian. He was the leading Dissenting writer in the first half of the 18th century. He published four collections of verse, *Horae Lyricae* (1706; enl. 1709), *Hymns and Spiritual Songs* (1707; enl. 1709), *Divine Songs for the Use of Children* (1715), and *The Psalms of David Imitated* (1719). His *hymns had phenomenal sales and influence, and his *Divine Songs* were imitated and parodied by William *Blake and Lewis Carroll (C. L. *Dodgson). With his *Humble Attempt towards the Revival of Practical Religion* (1731) he was an early instigator of the *Evangelical Revival, and he published the first edition of Jonathan *Edwards's *Faithful Narrative* (1737).

WATTS-DUNTON, Theodore (1832–1914) Novelist and poet, born Watts. From 1876 to 1902 he was one of the most influential writers for the *Athenaeum*; as its chief poetry reviewer, he supported the work of his friends in the *Pre-Raphaelite movement. Like George *Borrow, whom he met in 1872, he was interested in the Gypsies; his collection of poetry *The Coming of Love* (1898) features the gypsy girls Rhona Boswell and Sinfi Lovell. They reappear in his successful novel *Aylwin* (1898), which recounts the love of Henry Aylwin for a Welsh girl, his separation from her through a Gnostic curse, and his pursuit of her until their final reunion (with Sinfi Lovell's aid) on Snowdon. His other works include introductions to Borrow's *Lavengro* (1893) and *The *Romany Rye* (1900), sketches of D. G. *Rossetti, Alfred *Tennyson, etc., collected as *Old Familiar Faces* (1916), and an essay, 'The Renascence of Wonder in English Poetry' (in Chambers's *Cyclopaedia of English Literature*, vol. iii, 1901), in which he strongly defends the Romantic movement. He loyally supported A. C. *Swinburne, whom he rescued from declining health in 1879, and who lived with him until his death in 1909.

WAUGH, Alec (1898–1981) Novelist and travel writer. His first novel, *The Loom of Youth* (1917), became a notorious success through its frank treatment of public-school homosexuality. Others include the late success *Island in the Sun* (1956), and several autobiographical volumes, such as *The Early Years of Alec Waugh* (1962) and *My Brother Evelyn and Other Profiles* (1967).

WAUGH, Auberon (1939–2001) Novelist, journalist, diarist, and editor; son of Evelyn *Waugh. *The Foxglove Saga* (1960) is based on his experiences of illness, school, and military life. Other novels include *The Path of Dalliance

(1963) and *A Bed of Flowers* (1972), but Waugh abandoned fiction because, he claimed, it was impossible to make a living from it. He published collected articles from his columns in the *Spectator and the *Daily Telegraph*, two volumes of diaries, originally published in the satirical magazine *Private Eye* (1976, 1985), and an autobiography (*Will This Do?*, 1991).

WAUGH, Evelyn (1903–66) Novelist, journalist, and travel writer; his unhappy years as a schoolmaster provided material for *Decline and Fall (1928), his immensely successful first novel. In 1928 he married Evelyn Gardner; in 1930 he was divorced, and was received into the Roman Catholic Church. *Vile Bodies* (1930), *Black Mischief* (1932, set in Africa), *A Handful of Dust* (1934), and *Scoop* (1938) are comic, satirical novels, which capture the brittle, cynical, determined frivolity of the inter-war generation. He also wrote accounts of a journey through Africa (*Remote People*, 1931), a journey through South America (*Ninety-Two Days*, 1934), and Mussolini's invasion of Abyssinia (*Waugh in Abyssinia*, 1936). In 1937 he married Laura Herbert, a cousin of his first wife. *Put out More Flags* (1942), written while he was serving in the army, was followed by *Brideshead Revisited* (1945) and a macabre comedy about Californian funeral practices, *The Loved One* (1948). His wartime experiences in Crete and Yugoslavia provided the material for his trilogy *Sword of Honour* (1965), originally published as *Men at Arms* (1952), *Officers and Gentlemen* (1955), and *Unconditional Surrender* (1961). *The Ordeal of Gilbert Pinfold*, a bizarre novel about a famous 50-year-old Roman Catholic novelist, corpulent, heavy-drinking, insomniac, out of tune with modern life, plagued by disgust and boredom, appeared in 1957. Waugh's other works include a biography of *Edmund Campion* (1935) and a volume of autobiography, *A Little Learning* (1964).

Waverley The first of the novels of Walter *Scott, published 1814. Edward Waverley, a romantic young man, has been brought up partly by a Hanoverian father, partly by his uncle Sir Everard Waverley, a rich landowner of *Jacobite leanings. Ambivalent in politics, he is commissioned in the army in 1745 and joins his regiment in Scotland. He visits his uncle's friend the Baron Bradwardine, a kind-hearted but pedantic old Jacobite, and attracts the interest of his daughter Rose. Curious, he visits Donald Bean Lean, a Highland freebooter, and Fergus MacIvor (Vich Ian Vohr) of Glennaquoich, a young Highland Jacobite chieftain. At Glennaquoich,

he falls in love with Fergus's sister Flora. These visits, unwise in a British officer at a time of political tension, compromise Edward with his colonel. Through the intrigues of Donald Bean Lean, he is accused of encouraging mutiny in his regiment and is arrested. He is rescued by the action of Rose Bradwardine and, influenced by a sense of unjust treatment, by Flora's enthusiasm, and by a kind reception by Prince Charles Edward, he joins the Jacobite forces. At the battle of Prestonpans he saves from death Colonel Talbot, a distinguished English officer and friend of his family, and Talbot's influence, after the eventual defeat of the Pretender's army, secures his pardon and the rehabilitation of Baron Bradwardine. Decisively rejected by the spirited Flora, Edward turns his affections to Rose, whom he marries. Fergus, convicted of treason, meets his end bravely; Flora retires to a convent.

Waverley is one of the best plotted of Scott's novels, and the opposition of romance and realism reappears in many of his later works.

Waves, The A novel by Virginia *Woolf, published in 1931 and commonly regarded as the most experimental of her works. It traces the lives of a group of friends (Bernard, Susan, Louis, Rhoda, Neville, and Jinny) from infancy to late middle age, evoking their personalities through their reflections on themselves, on one another, and on their friend Percival, a largely absent colonial administrator. The characters are presented through successive brief monologues: though the friends gather together on several occasions, they rarely respond directly to each other's words; Louis and Rhoda are the exceptions. Their individuality as characters emerges through their divergent lives and through recurring concerns, phrases, and images. There are lyrical prose 'interludes' between episodes which describe the rise and fall of the sun over a seascape. Though the characters' lives are uneventful, the death of Percival, and the rhythms of separation and reunion throughout provide the occasion for reflections on the mortality both of individuals and of the group as a unit, and on the forms taken by friendship and love.

Way of All Flesh, The A novel by Samuel *Butler (1835–1902), published posthumously 1903. This celebrated dissection of the stultifying effects of family life reflects many of Butler's own experiences. The story (narrated by a family friend, Overton) was originally called *Ernest Pontifex*; Ernest is the awkward and unhappy great-grandson of John Pontifex, a village carpenter, whose instinctive character he comes to revere. His own father, Theo, is tyrannical, repeating the attitudes of Ernest's grandfather George. After his ordination the inept Ernest mistakes a respectable woman for a prostitute and is sentenced to prison, where he tries to return to the simplicity of Old Pontifex. On his release he plunges into a disastrous union with Ellen, a drunken maidservant. Fortunately she turns out to be already married, and Ernest's beloved aunt Alethea leaves him sufficient money to devote himself to literature.

Way of the World, The A comedy by William *Congreve, produced 1700, in which Mirabell eventually wins the hand of Millamant, niece of the wealthy Lady Wishfort, who had wanted Millamant to marry her boisterous and good-natured country nephew Sir Wilful Witwoud. The plot is extremely complicated. The dialogue is brilliant, and Mirabell's undisguised materialism together with Millamant's insistence on retaining her freedom after marriage give the play exceptional sophistication.

Way We Live Now, The A novel by Anthony *Trollope, published 1875. Augustus Melmotte is supposedly a great financier, but no one thinks to examine the nature of his fortune until he is caught forging the deeds to an estate. His prize speculation, a Central American railway, is revealed as a gigantic confidence trick, and when it becomes clear that he has tampered with his daughter's trust fund, his disgrace is complete. After a drunken appearance in the House of Commons he commits suicide. Melmotte's worthless career is matched by his daughter Marie's experiences in the marriage market. She is treated as a commodity by the cautious Lord Nidderdale, and as a diversion by the dissipated Sir Felix Carbury. Carbury entices her to elope, but lets her down. She finally marries the devious Hamilton K. Fisker. Meanwhile, Lady Carbury's shifts as a glib authoress expose the shabbiness of literary life. Trollope conceived this bleak and powerful novel as an attack on 'the commercial profligacy of the age', dishonest at all levels.

weak ending The occurrence of an unstressed monosyllable (such as a preposition, conjunction, or auxiliary verb) in the normally stressed position at the end of an iambic verse line.

WEAVER, Harriet Shaw (1876–1961) Editor, publisher, and benefactor of James *Joyce. Business manager and later (1914) editor of the *Egoist*, she saw Joyce's A *Portrait of the Artist as a Young Man* through serial publication (1914–15), changing the journal's printers to do so. When Joyce could find no British publisher for the book, Weaver brought it out under the imprint of the Egoist Press; the Press also published work by T. S. *Eliot, Hilda *Dolittle, Marianne *Moore, and others. The *Egoist* published work by Ezra *Pound, T. S. Eliot, Wyndham *Lewis, William Carlos *Williams, and others, as well as early instalments of *Ulysses*. It ceased publication in December 1919 and the press closed in 1923.

WEBB, Beatrice (1858–1943) Writer, diarist, and social reformer, who shared with her husband Sidney Webb (1859–1947) an interest in both the theoretical and practical aspects of social reform, political economy, and sociology. From 1891, both were leading spirits in the Fabian Society, and they produced jointly numerous works on social history, served on many royal commissions, and helped to found the London School of Economics. Beatrice Webb also wrote two autobiographical works (*My Apprenticeship*, 1926; *Our Partnership*, 1948), and kept a remarkable diary, of which a four-volume edition, appeared between 1982 and 1985. It is a valuable record of the period's social life and progressive thought. Sidney and Beatrice Webb are lampooned in H. G. *Wells's novel *The New Machiavelli* (1911) as the Baileys, 'two active, self-centred people, excessively devoted to the public service . . . the most formidable and distinguished couple conceivable'.

WEBB, Jane Loudon (1807–58) Writer; she published the pre-*science fiction *The Mummy!* (1827), borrowing the image of a future England with balloon transportation from Mary *Shelley's *The *Last Man* (1826), together with ideas from *Frankenstein*.

WEBB, Mary (1881–1927) Novelist. She had contracted Graves' disease in 1901, an affliction which found its fictional counterpart in the harelip of Prudence Sarn, the narrator of her fifth and most famous novel, *Precious Bane* (1924). Her five other novels are *The Golden Arrow* (1916), *Gone to Earth* (1917), *The House in Dormer Forest* (1920), *Seven for a Secret* (1922), and *Armour Wherein he Trusted*, which appeared posthumously in 1929. They are tales of rustic life, written in a fervid prose easily ridiculed by Stella *Gibbons in *Cold Comfort Farm*. They were immensely popular in the 1930s and 1940s; Stanley Baldwin, in an introduction to a 1928 reprint of *Precious Bane*, praised her lyrical intensity, her evocation of the Shropshire landscape, and her 'blending of human passion with the fields and skies'.

WEBSTER, Augusta (1837–94) Née Davies, poet and feminist writer. She was expelled from South Kensington Art School for whistling. Her earliest works were published under the pseudonym 'Cecil Home': under her own name appeared *Dramatic Studies* (1866), *A Woman Sold and Other Poems* (1867), and *Portraits* (1870). Her inventive use of the *dramatic monologue, partly in admiring imitation of Robert *Browning, is particularly evident in the presentation of female character and predicament. 'The Castaway' (1870) is a lively challenge to conventional notions of prostitution. Her incomplete sonnet sequence *Mother and Daughter*, appeared in 1895 with a preface by W. M. *Rossetti.

WEBSTER, John (c.1578–c.1638) Playwright. He wrote several plays in collaboration with other dramatists; these include *Westward Ho* and *Northward Ho*, with Thomas *Dekker, both printed 1607; *A Cure for a Cuckold* (1661), probably with William *Rowley (and possibly Thomas *Heywood); and a lost play with John *Ford, Dekker, and Rowley, *Keep the Widow Waking* (1624). It has also been suggested that he had a hand in Thomas *Middleton's *Anything for a Quiet Life* (1661) and John *Fletcher's *The Fair Maid of the Inn* (1623). He expanded John *Marston's *The *Malcontent* in 1604, and published elegies on Prince Henry in 1613 with Heywood and Cyril *Tourneur. *The Devil's Law Case* (1623), a tragicomedy, mentions in its dedication a lost play, *Guise*. His two major works are *The *White Devil* (1612) and *The *Duchess of Malfi* (1623). Attempts by Nahum *Tate and Lewis *Theobald to accommodate the plays to 18th-century taste were followed in 1808 by Charles *Lamb's influential *Specimens*, which singled out the 'beauties'. The 20th century, when the plays were revived more frequently than those of any other of *Shakespeare's contemporaries, saw a strong revival of interest in the plays as drama, and in Webster as satirist and moralist.

WEBSTER, Noah (1758–1843) American lexicographer. In his great and scholarly *An American Dictionary of the English Language*, 2 vols (1828), he challenged the parochialism of British dictionaries and, with a strong national pride and spirit, established Americanisms and American usages. *See* DICTIONARY.

WEDDERBURN, James (c.1495–1553) Scottish reformer and poet, who with his brothers John (c.1505–1556) and Robert (c.1510–1555/60) produced a collection of verse *Ane Compendeous Buke, of Godlye Psalmes and Spirituall Sangis* (1565). Possibly dating from c.1540, it contains psalm translations as well as versions of popular songs designed to promote *Protestant doctrine.

WEELKES, Thomas (?1576–1623) English composer. With John *Wilbye, he was the most important of the English *madrigal composers after Thomas *Morley's introduction of the form. He published several collections and contributed one madrigal to *The Triumphes of Oriana* in 1601 (*see* MORLEY, THOMAS). Weelkes developed Morley's Italianate manner into a more characteristically English style.

WEEVER, John (1575/6–1632) Poet and antiquary. *Epigrams in the Oldest Cut, and Newest Fashion* (1599), is a collection of verse reflecting his Cambridge friendships and his knowledge of the London literary scene: a Shakespearian sonnet is addressed 'Ad Gulielmum Shakespear'. The Ovidian epyllion, or minor *epic, *Faunus and Melliflora* (1600) shows a knowledge of *Shakespeare's works, especially of *Venus and Adonis*.

WEIL, Simone (1909–43) French philosopher. Her moral and intellectual authority became generally apparent only posthumously. *La Pesanteur et la grâce* (1947: *Gravity and Grace*), *L'Attente de Dieu* (1950: *Waiting for God*), and *Cahiers* (1951–6: *Notebooks*) have earned her a unique respect for their intensity of thought, their moral commitment, and their religious inwardness.

WEINBAUM, Stanley (1902–35) American *science fiction writer. With the publication of 'A Martian Odyssey' (1934) in *Wonder Stories* he transformed the way alien beings were depicted in science fiction. *The New Adam* (1939) is a tragic story of a mutant 'superman'.

Weird Tales One of the most influential magazines in supernatural and *science fiction during its original incarnation (1923–54). The magazine, with its striking, sometimes lurid covers, published H. P. *Lovecraft, Robert E. *Howard, C. L. Moore, and Ray *Bradbury, together with early stories from a wider range of writers such as Tennessee *Williams.

Weir of Hermiston An unfinished novel by Robert Louis *Stevenson, published 1896.

Archie Weir is the only child of Adam Weir, Lord Hermiston, the lord justice clerk, a formidable 'hanging judge', based on the character of Robert Macqueen, Lord Braxfield (1722–99). His mother is an ineffectually religious woman who dies young, leaving Archie to the care of a father he dreads. The conflict comes to a head when Archie witnesses his father hounding a wretched criminal to death at a trial; he speaks out against capital punishment, and is banished to Hermiston, a remote Lowland village. There he lives with Kirstie, his devoted housekeeper and distant relative, who is aunt to the four 'Black Elliotts', brothers famed for hunting down their father's murderer. Archie falls in love with their sister Christina. The novel ends as Archie, warned by Kirstie, tells Christina that their secret meetings must end. We know from Stevenson's notes that the story was to conclude with another confrontation between father and son, in which Archie is on trial for his life for the murder of Christina's seducer Frank Innes. Archie and Christina are rescued by the Black Elliotts and escape to America, but the old man dies of shock.

WEISS, Peter (1916–82) Swedish-German playwright and novelist. *Marat/Sade* was first performed in London in 1964 in an adaptation by Geoffrey Skelton and Adrian *Mitchell, directed by Peter *Brook (filmed 1967). A landmark in the theatre of the 1960s, the work explores the clash of antithetical philosophies, revolutionary *Marxism (voiced by Marat), and a nihilistic individualism (voiced by de Sade). *Die Ermittlung* (1965: *The Investigation*), in which testimony about Auschwitz given at the Frankfurt war crimes trial is rendered in serene verse, is a harrowing example of literature of the *Holocaust. It was performed as a stage reading under Peter Brook's direction by the Royal Shakespeare Company, and adapted for radio and television.

WELDON, Fay (1933–) CBE, novelist, dramatist, and screenwriter. From *The Fat Woman's Joke* (1967) onwards, she has kept up a copious fictional output in which feminist polemic and hostility to such concerns as psychotherapy and genetic research have found didactic and whimsical expression. *The Life and Loves of a She-Devil* (1983), and other works have been adapted for film and television. *Big Women* (1998) is a fictionalized account of the founding of the feminist publishing company the *Virago Press. There is a memoir, *Auto Da Fay* (2002), which is partially continued in her hybrid novel *Mantrapped* (2004).

Well-Beloved, The A novel by Thomas *Hardy, published serially 1892, revised and reissued 1897. The story is set on the Isle of Slingers (i.e. Portland), and the central figure is Jocelyn Pierston, a sculptor, who falls in love successively with three generations of island women: Avice Caro, her daughter, and her granddaughter, all of the same name. He seeks the perfect form in woman, the 'well-beloved', as he seeks it in stone.

WELLES, Orson (1915–84) American actor and director, best remembered for his work in the cinema, notably *Citizen Kane* (1941), widely regarded as the greatest of all films; and *The Magnificent Ambersons* (1942), both of which he directed, and for his role in *The Third Man* (1949), directed by Carol Reed from a script by Graham *Greene. His radio version of H. G. *Wells's *The *War of the Worlds* (1938) created an early sensation. He also directed himself in three *Shakespeare films: as *Macbeth* (1948), *Othello* (1952), and as *Falstaff in his own adaptation, *Chimes at Midnight* (1966).

Well of Loneliness, The See HALL, RADCLYFFE.

WELLS, H. G. (Herbert George) (1866–1946) Writer. He won a scholarship in 1884 to the Normal School of Science in South Kensington, where he came under the lasting influence of T. H. *Huxley. His marriage in 1891 proved unhappy, and he eloped with his student Amy Catherine ('Jane') Robbins, whom he married in 1895 (though he continued to criticize conventional marriage). In 1903 he joined the Fabian Society, but was soon at odds with it, his sponsor George Bernard *Shaw, and Sidney and Beatrice *Webb.

His literary output was vast and extremely varied. His scientific romances were among the earliest products of the new genre of *science fiction. The first, *The Time Machine* (1895), is a social allegory set in the year 802701, describing a society divided into two classes, the subterranean workers, called Morlocks, and the decadent Eloi. This was followed by *The Wonderful Visit* (1895), *The *Island of Doctor Moreau* (1896), *The *Invisible Man* (1897), *The *War of the Worlds* (1898), *When the Sleeper Wakes* (1899), *The First Men in the Moon* (1901), *Men Like Gods* (1923), and others. Wells's preoccupation with social as well as scientific progress distinguishes them from the fantasies of Jules *Verne.

Another group of comic novels evokes the lower-middle-class world of his youth. *Love and Mr Lewisham* (1900) tells the story of a struggling teacher; *Kipps* (1905) that of an aspiring draper's assistant; *The History of Mr Polly* (1910) recounts the adventures of Alfred Polly, an inefficient shopkeeper who liberates himself by burning down his own shop and bolting for freedom, which he discovers as man-of-all-work at the Potwell Inn.

Ann Veronica (1909) is a feminist tract about a girl who, fortified by the concept of the *'New Woman', defies her father and conventional morality. *Tono-Bungay* (1909) is a picture of English society in dissolution, and of the advent of a new class of rich entrepreneurs. *The Country of the Blind, and Other Stories* (1911), his fifth collection of short stories, contains the memorable 'The Door in the Wall' (originally published 1906). He continued to reach a huge audience with *A Short History of the World* (1922), and with many works of scientific and political speculation (including *The Shape of Things to Come*, 1933) which confirmed his position as one of the great popularizers and one of the most influential voices of his age; his last prediction, *Mind at the End of its Tether* (1945), is darkly pessimistic.

His *Experiment in Autobiography* (1934) is a striking portrait of himself, his contemporaries (including Arnold *Bennett, George *Gissing, and the Fabians) and their times. Aspects of a Life (1984) is a memoir by Anthony West (1914–87), his son by Rebecca *West.

WELSH, Irvine (1957–) Scottish writer, the first of the so-called *'Chemical Generation' of 1990s British writers. The best-selling *Trainspotting* (1993, adapted for stage, and film, 1996), about a group of young heroin addicts in 1980s Edinburgh, was sexually and scatologically explicit, written in a pungent Edinburgh vernacular, and distinguished by great comic verve. *Porno* (2002) is a sequel and *Skagboy* (2012) a prequel. In further novels—*Marabou Stork Nightmares* (1995) and *Filth* (1998)—and short story collections—*The Acid House* (1994) and *Ecstasy: Three Tales of Chemical Romance* (1996)—the language is progressively explicit, and often extreme in its use of obscenity and violence: *Filth*, the story of a corrupt Edinburgh policeman, includes the narrative 'voice' of the protagonist's own excrement. *Glue* (2001) tells of the bonds uniting four characters over several decades. *The Bedroom Secrets of the Master Chefs* (2006) describes a civil servant who unwittingly curses a fellow worker. Recent works include *If You Liked School You'll Love Work*

(2007) and *Reheated Cabbage* (2009), short stories, and *Crime* (2008, novel).

WELSH, Jane *See* CARLYLE, JANE.

WELTY, Eudora (1909–2001) American short story writer, novelist, and photographer. The stories of *A Curtain of Green* (1941) derive from her experiences with the New Deal's Works Progress Administration in the 1930s, for which she travelled through her native state photographing inhabitants. *The Robber Bridegroom* (1942, novel), is an elaborately worked fairy-tale set in the Natchez Trace country *c.*1798. *Losing Battles* (1970) returns to the Depression for its subject. *The Optimist's Daughter* (1972) centres on the antagonism after a judge's death between his middle-aged daughter and insensitive young widow. *The Golden Apples* (1949) is a series of linked stories and *The Eye of the Story* (1978) collects essays.

WERTENBAKER, Timberlake (1951–) Dramatist, best known for *Our Country's Good* (1987), based on Thomas *Keneally's novel *The Playmaker*, which dealt with the first play (George *Farquhar's *The *Recruiting Officer*) performed by penal settlers in Australia. Other plays include *The Grace of Mary Travers* (1985), which dealt with a woman coming to personal and political awareness during the Gordon riots of the 1780s, and *Three Birds Alighting on a Field* (1992), which dealt with the commercial art market at the height of the Thatcher economic boom. *After Darwin* (1998) uses the historical figure of Charles *Darwin and mixes past and present in an examination of evolution and extinction. She has also written frequent stage, radio, and TV adaptations, including Edith *Wharton's *The Children*; *Sophocles' *Theban Plays* (for the RSC); and *Euripides' *Hecuba*. Recent productions include a modern reworking of the Cinderella story, *The Ash Girl* (2000), *A Credible Witness* (2001), about the struggle for identity in the contemporary world, *Galileo's Daughter* (2004), *Divine Intervention* (2006), and *The Line* (2009).

Wertherism A cultural phenomenon resulting from the fame throughout Europe of Johann Wolfgang von *Goethe's early work *Die Leiden des jungen Werthers* (1774: *The Sorrows of Young Werther*). An *epistolary novel of *sensibility, it owed its notoriety chiefly to its supposed defence of the hero's suicide. There followed a vogue for things to do with Werther, imitations, illustrations, supposed discoveries of 'new' letters, etc. Though it was still admired by P. B. *Shelley, Thomas *Carlyle disapproved of

Werther, and by the mid-19th century the term had come to stand for a self-indulgent melancholy or lachrymose sensitivity.

WESKER, Sir Arnold (1932–) Playwright. His early work was closely associated with the *English Stage Company, although *Chicken Soup with Barley* (1958) transferred there from the Belgrade Theatre, Coventry, which also put on the first productions of *Roots* (1959) and *I'm Talking about Jerusalem* (1960), three plays now grouped together as the Wesker Trilogy. *The Kitchen* (1959), which first appeared at the *Royal Court, shows the stresses and conflicts of life behind the scenes in a restaurant; its innovative use of the rhythms of working life did much to stimulate the growth of what was to be known (though in a slightly different sense) as *kitchen sink drama. Wesker's subsequent plays include *Chips with Everything* (1962), a study of class attitudes in the RAF during National Service; *The Four Seasons* (1965); *Their Very Own and Golden City* (1966) and *The Friends* (1970); *The Merchant* (1977; subsequently retitled *Shylock*), which attacks anti-Semitism through the story of *Shylock; *Caritas* (1981), which shows the spiritual anguish of a 14th-century anchoress who realizes she has mistaken her vocation; *Annie Wobbler* (1984), a one-woman play; and *Denial* (2000), about false memory syndrome. The title story of *Love Letters on Blue Paper* (1974), about the relationship of a dying trade unionist and his wife, was televised and adapted (1978) for the stage. *The Birth of Shylock and the Death of Zero Mostel* (1997) is a gripping account of the disastrous events attending the New York production of *Shylock*. *As Much as I Dare* (1994) is a volume of autobiography.

WESLEY, Charles (1707–88) Church of England clergyman and hymn-writer, one of the founders of *Methodism. He was a lifelong associate of his brother John *Wesley, though they had significant disagreements. His hymns, which resonate with allusions to the *Bible, *The Book of *Common Prayer*, and John *Milton, are his great contribution to Methodism and to poetry. They began appearing in *Hymns and Sacred Poems* (1739), and dominate John's standard edition, *A Collection of Hymns for the Use of the People called Methodists* (1780).

WESLEY, John (1703–91) Church of England clergyman, one of the founders of *Methodism. In Oxford from 1729 to 1735 he was one of a loose association (including his brother Charles *Wesley, and George *Whitefield)

nicknamed the 'Holy Club' or 'Methodists' for their religious practices. He quarrelled with Whitefield over predestination, always emphasizing Christian perfection and social holiness as the key teachings of Methodism. For over 50 years he conducted his ministry with extraordinary energy, travelling thousands of miles through the British Isles. Wesley's importance for popular publishing cannot be overestimated: he was editor and author of more publications than any other single figure in 18th-century Britain, with his own distribution system for his societies and from 1778 his own printing press in London. Of the over 400 titles he published, the majority are books he edited and abridged, chosen from a wide range of authors of different denominations, such as *Thomas à Kempis, Jonathan *Edwards, and William *Law. His most important original work is his *Journal* (1740–91).

WESLEY, Mary (1912–2002) Novelist and children's writer. Her first book for adults, *Jumping the Queue* (1983), published when she was 71, established her reputation for dark comedy. *The Camomile Lawn* (1984) is a family saga in which five cousins shuttle between a blacked-out London and a large house on the Cornish coast during the Second World War, discovering the delights and complications of sex. Drawing on her own aristocratic-bohemian (and often unhappy) background, she published eight further novels in which characters sometimes recurred and in which she explored such favourite themes as 'the ideal house', death, unorthodox sexual relationships, illegitimacy, and other uncertainties about identity.

WESLEY, Mehitabel (Hetty) (1697–1750) Poet, sister of John and Charles *Wesley. In 1725, after eloping and becoming pregnant, she was forcibly married to William Wright, a plumber and glazier. She bitterly attacked marriage in 'Wedlock: A Satire' (written *c.*1730; pub. 1862) and other poems. Only a few of her poems were published during her life: the *Gentleman's Magazine* printed 'To an Infant Expiring the Second Day of its Birth' in 1733 and an elegy on one of her sisters in 1736.

Wessex The name used by Thomas *Hardy to designate the south-west counties, principally Dorset, which form the setting of many of his works.

WEST, Jane (1758–1852) Novelist, poet, and moralist. Her anti-*Jacobin politics are evident in such works as *A Tale of the Times* (1799) and *The Infidel Father* (1802). She supported women's education, but disliked the feminism of Wollstonecraft's *Vindication of the Rights of Woman* (1792). She wrote two works of conduct literature, *Letters to a Young Man* (1801) and *Letters to a Young Lady* (1806).

WEST, Nathanael (1903–40) The pseudonym of Nathan Wallenstein Weinstein, American novelist. He is known principally for two novels, *Miss Lonelyhearts* (1933), the story of a heavy-drinking agony columnist who becomes involved in the life of one of his correspondents, and *The Day of the Locust* (1939), a satire of Hollywood life based on West's own experiences as a scriptwriter. He was killed in a car crash.

WEST, Dame Rebecca The adopted name of Cecily Isabel Fairfield (1892–1983). Rebecca (who adopted this name, after Henrik *Ibsen's heroine in *Rosmersholm*, at 19) became a feminist and journalist, much influenced at this stage by the Pankhursts and the movement to gain votes for women; from 1911 she wrote for *The Freewoman*, the *New Freewoman*, and *The Clarion*. *The Young Rebecca* (1982) collects many of her shrewd, witty, and combative pieces, including her outspoken review of H. G. *Wells's *Marriage* (1912), which led to a ten-year love affair and the birth of a son, Anthony West (1914–87). Her first novel, *The Return of the Soldier* (1918), which describes the return home of a shell-shocked soldier, was followed by *The Judge* (1922), *The Strange Necessity* (1928), *Harriet Hume* (1929), *The Thinking Reed* (1936), *The Fountain Overflows* (1956), and *The Birds Fall down* (1966). She was present at the Nuremberg trials, and *The Meaning of Treason* (1949) grew out of articles originally commissioned by the *New Yorker*. She continued to write and to review almost until her death, at 90.

WESTALL, Robert (1929–93) Prolific author of *war stories, realistic *young adult fiction, and supernatural tales. *The Machine-Gunners* (1975) established him as a writer prepared to use language and explore topics previously considered unsuitable for young readers.

western The name given to American novels and stories set in the Old West, usually in the period 1850–1900. The earliest examples were *dime novels, but the first western novel is usually taken to be Owen *Wister's *The Virginian* (1902). The genre was consolidated by the fiction of Zane Grey and Max Brand (1892–1944); and has continued to evolve, as in the novels of Cormac *McCarthy and Larry *McMurtry. In film and fiction alike traditional western subjects have included the conflict between settlers and Native Americans, and between law officers and 'gunslingers'.

West Indian, The A comedy by Richard *Cumberland, successfully produced by David *Garrick in 1771. The play's central character is a *Rousseauesque child of nature and the action explores the comic potential of *primitivism.

Westminster Review (1824–1914) Established by James Mill, an ardent supporter of Jeremy *Bentham, as the journal of the 'philosophical radicals', in opposition to the *Edinburgh Review* and the *Quarterly Review*. The conservatism of the *Quarterly* and the quality of the *Edinburgh* reviewers both came under attack. Lord *Byron, S. T. *Coleridge, Alfred *Tennyson, and Thomas *Carlyle were among the literary figures it supported. Under the editorship of John *Chapman from 1851 (when George *Eliot played a defining role in running the magazine) it published Herbert *Spencer, J. A. *Froude, Mark *Pattison, Walter *Pater, and George Eliot herself.

Westward Ho A comedy by John *Webster and Thomas *Dekker, printed 1607. The main plot deals with the escapades of three merry wives, whose innocence is eventually established.

Westward Ho! *See* KINGSLEY, CHARLES.

WEYMAN, Stanley John (1855–1928) Historical novelist. Born in Ludlow, and educated at Shrewsbury School and Christ Church, Oxford, he established his reputation with *A Gentleman of France* (1893, dealing with the period of Henry of Navarre), followed by other comparably vigorous romances, including *The Red Cockade* (1895), *Under the Red Robe* (1896), *Count Hannibal* (1901, based on the massacre of St Bartholomew), and *Chipping* (1906, in an English setting, at the time of the Reform Bill).

WHARTON, Edith (1862–1937) Née Newbold Jones, American novelist and short story writer, born of a distinguished and wealthy New York family. She married Edward Robbins Wharton in 1885; the marriage was not happy, and they were divorced in 1913. Henry *James was a close friend. *The House of Mirth* (1905), the tragedy of failed social climber Lily Bart, established her as a leading novelist. Many other works followed, including *Ethan Frome* (1911), a grim and ironic tale of passion and vengeance on a poor New England farm; *The

Custom of the Country (1913), in which the social ambitions of Undine Spragg propel her from the provinces to New York, and through a succession of marriages; *The Age of Innocence* (1920) describes the frustrated love of a New York lawyer, Newland Archer, for the unconventional and artistic Ellen Olenska; *The Mother's Recompense* (1925) concerns the struggle between runaway mother Kate Clephane and her daughter Anne for the hand of the same young man; and *Hudson River Bracketed* (1929) contrasts Midwest with New York society. She also published short stories, travel books, and an autobiography, *A Backward Glance* (1934). Her observant, satiric, witty portrayal of social nuance, both in America and Europe, shows her keen interest in what she called the 'tribal behaviour' of various groups.

What Maisie Knew A novel by Henry *James, published 1897. Maisie, the child of divorced parents, is used as a pawn in the power games of the adults who surround her; her perception of their corrupt lives leads her to a disconcerting maturity, yet she retains a fundamental honesty and innocence.

What You Will The subtitle of Shakespeare's *Twelfth Night*; it is his only play (with the possible exception of *Henry VIII*) with an alternative title—its meaning is 'whatever you want to call it'. It is clearly connected, in some way, with John *Marston's What You Will which probably appeared in 1601.

WHEATLEY, Dennis (1897–1977) British writer of thrillers covering historicals (*The Launching of Roger Brook*, 1947), espionage (*V for Vengeance*, 1942), and occasional *science fiction (*Star of Ill-Omen*, 1952), and of novels of the occult, including *The Devil Rides Out* (1935).

WHEATLEY, Phillis (?1753–84) African American poet, born in Gambia, Africa, and shipped as a child to the slave market of Boston, where she was purchased by John Wheatley, who encouraged her literary talent. Her *Poems on Various Subjects, Religious and Moral* were first published in London in 1773. *See* SLAVERY.

WHEELER, Sara (1961–) Travel writer, biographer, and journalist. In *Terra Incognita: Travels in Antarctica* (1996) and *The Magnetic North: Notes from the Arctic Circle* (2011), she provides a woman's perspective on regions more often associated with tales of masculine adventure, and portrays 'the pared-down

existence of polar lands and the grace of their peoples under pressure'.

Where the Wild Things Are (1963) *Picturebook by Maurice *Sendak, in which he experiments with frames, pace, and viewpoint. Max is sent to bed and fantasizes about sailing to an island inhabited by Wild Things. There is an opera (Oliver Knussen, 1980; libretto by Sendak); and film (dir. Spike Jonze, 2009).

WHETSTONE, George (1550–87) Poet and playwright. His verse play *Promos and Cassandra* (1578) (based on a tale in Cinzio's *Hecatommithi*) provided the plot for William *Shakespeare's *Measure for Measure* and is an early example of English romantic comedy.

WHICHCOTE, Benjamin *See* CAMBRIDGE PLATONISTS.

WHISTLER, James Abbott McNeill (1834–1903) American painter. His most famous works are the *Nocturnes*, paintings of the Thames at dusk. George du *Maurier's *Trilby* describes his bohemian life as a student in Paris (1855–9). Whistler moved to London in 1859; as a neighbour of Dante Gabriel *Rossetti, he mixed in *Pre-Raphaelite circles, and discussed his ideas on art with A. C. *Swinburne; he was at the centre of the *Aesthetic movement. In 1877 John *Ruskin attacked him for 'flinging a pot of paint into the public's face'; Whistler sued him, won, and was awarded a farthing damages. The trial stimulated Whistler's gifts as a polemicist; he wrote a series of pamphlets and vituperative letters to the press, later published together in *The Gentle Art of Making Enemies* (1890). His most serious and elegant attack on Ruskin's belief in the moral purpose of art was his *Ten O'Clock Lecture*. He had discussed many of his ideas with Oscar *Wilde, whom he later accused of plagiarism.

WHITAKER, Joseph (1820–95) Publisher and editor. As editor of the *Gentleman's Magazine* (1856–9), he became interested in readers' questions. He founded the *Bookseller* (1858), and *Whitaker's Almanack* (1868), a compendium of general information regarding the government, finances, population, and commerce of the world, with special reference to the British Commonwealth and the United States. *See* ALMANACS.

WHITE, Antonia (1899–1979) Novelist and translator. Her convent childhood is described in her first autobiographical novel, *Frost in May* (1933). Three subsequent novels, *The Lost*

Traveller (1950), *The Sugar House* (1952), and *Beyond the Glass* (1954), provide a fictionalized account of her own experiences as a struggling writer, her complex relationships with her father and with other men, and the mental illness which led to her confinement in an asylum. *The Hound and the Falcon* (1966) describes her reconversion to Catholicism. Antonia White also translated many of the novels of Colette (1873–1954).

WHITE, E. B. (Elwyn Brooks) (1899–1985) American author and critic. *Charlotte's Web* (1952; filmed 1973, 2006) mixes realism and fantasy: farmer's daughter Fern Zuckerman saves Wilbur, a runt piglet, from slaughter, helped by a literate spider, Charlotte, who weaves words in her web over Wilbur's head, and by Templeton the rat. *Stuart Little* (1945; filmed 1999 and 2002) has an uneasy premiss—a mouse born to humans. *See* ANIMAL STORIES.

WHITE, Edmund (1940–) American novelist and essayist. *Nocturnes for the King of Naples* (1978) is a non-realistic novel dealing with homosexual themes which were pursued more realistically in *A Boy's Own Story* (1982), a semi-autobiographical description of the gay adolescence of a child of divorced parents. *The Beautiful Room Is Empty* (1988) and *The Farewell Symphony* (1997), which moves into the AIDS era, are sequels. Other works include *States of Desire: Travels in Gay America* (1980) and the autobiographical *My Lives* (2006).

WHITE, Gilbert (1720–93) Clergyman and naturalist, who chose to spend most of his life as curate of Selborne. He sent detailed local observations on birds, bats, plants, weather conditions, and other natural phenomena to Thomas *Pennant and Daines Barrington (1727–1800), the correspondence forming the basis of his *Natural History and Antiquities of Selborne* (published 1788, dated 1789), a work read with appreciation by figures as various as S. T. *Coleridge, William *Cobbett, Charles *Darwin, and Richard *Jefferies. It has been continuously in print since its first publication.

WHITE, Patrick (1912–90) Australian novelist and playwright, educated in England. His first published novels were *Happy Valley* (1939) and *The Living and the Dead* (1941). He joined the RAF in 1941. He returned to Australia in 1948. White's first major novel, *The Aunt's Story* (1948), was followed by a series of *epic novels which collectively attempt to reconfigure the values of Australian society, rejecting equally the tenets of realist writing, and suburban

cant: *The Tree of Man* (1955), *Voss* (1957), *Riders in the Chariot* (1961), *The Solid Mandala* (1966), and *The Vivisector* (1970). His most studied novel, *Voss*, tells the story of the doomed attempt of Johann Voss to cross the Australian continent, describing the mystic communion that binds him to Laura Trevelyan, who, at home in Sydney, suffers with him and is released from fever at the moment of his death. *The Eye of the Storm* (1973) and *A Fringe of Leaves* (1976) create powerful female characters, a White signature, while *The Twyborn Affair* (1979) in some respects echoes Virginia *Woolf's *Orlando* with its gender-switching protagonist. *Flaws in the Glass* (1981) is an autobiography.

WHITE, T. H. (Terence Hanbury) (1906–64) Writer of the *crossover novels comprising *The Once and Future King* (1958) based on Arthurian legends, beginning with *The Sword in the Stone* (1938; filmed for Disney 1963). *Mistress Masham's Repose* (1947), featuring a girl who becomes involved with some Lilliputians, is a children's classic. Other books include *The Book of Beasts* (1954), translated from a Latin *bestiary.

WHITE, William Hale (1831–1913) Known as a writer under the pseudonym of 'Mark Rutherford'. Hale White was educated to become an independent minister, but became disillusioned with his training, and in 1854 he entered the Civil Service. *The Autobiography of Mark Rutherford, Dissenting Minister* (1881) describes the spiritual development of a young Dissenter, supposedly edited after his death by his friend Reuben Shapcott. Rutherford attends a Dissenting college and becomes a minister, but is beset by theological doubts and distressed by the narrow views of his colleagues and congregations. He loses his faith, becoming as disillusioned by the Unitarians as he was by his own church. It is a powerful account of the progress of 19th-century doubt. It was followed by *Mark Rutherford's Deliverance* (1885), *The Revolution in Tanner's Lane* (1887, a sympathetic portrait of Dissent, radical politics, and working men's lives), *Miriam's Schooling and Other Papers* (1893), *Catherine Furze* (1893), and *Clara Hopgood* (1896). He published under his own name a life of John *Bunyan (1905).

White Devil, The A tragedy by John *Webster, written between 1609 and 1612, when it was published. The duke of Brachiano, husband of Isabella, the sister of Francisco, duke of Florence, is weary of her and in love with Vittoria, wife of Camillo. The *Machiavellian Flamineo, Vittoria's brother, helps Brachiano to seduce her, and contrives (at her suggestion, delivered indirectly in a dream) the death of Camillo. Brachiano causes Isabella to be poisoned. Vittoria is tried for adultery and murder in the celebrated central arraignment scene (III. ii), and defends herself with great spirit. She is sentenced to confinement in 'a house of penitent whores', whence she is carried off by Brachiano, who marries her. Flamineo quarrels with his younger brother, the virtuous Marcello, and kills him; he dies in the arms of their mother Cornelia, who later, driven out of her wits by grief, sings the dirge 'Call for the robin redbreast, and the wren', a scene which elicits from Flamineo a speech of remorse.

Meanwhile Francisco, at the prompting of Isabella's ghost (*see* REVENGE TRAGEDY), avenges her death by poisoning Brachiano. Vittoria and Flamineo, both of whom die Stoic deaths, are murdered by Brachiano's dependants. The play has been one of the most frequently revived of *Jacobean tragedies.

WHITEFIELD, George (1714–70) Popular evangelical preacher, journal writer, and leader of the Calvinistic *Methodists. Whitefield encouraged John *Wesley to imitate him by preaching out of doors, but his own increasingly Calvinistic views resulted in a rift between them. He became the focus of the transatlantic *Evangelical Revival. He was widely ridiculed in novels, plays, prints, and poems, for example by Samuel *Foote in *The Minor*, Richard *Graves in *The Spiritual Quixote*, and William *Hogarth.

WHITEHEAD, William (1715–85) Poet and playwright. His tragedy *The Roman Father*, based on *Corneille's *Horace*, was successfully staged in 1750 with David *Garrick in the leading role. In 1757 he was appointed *poet laureate after Thomas *Gray declined the office. His *Poems and Plays* (2 vols, 1774) was supplemented by a third volume, containing a 'Memoir' by William *Mason, in 1788.

WHITING, John (1917–63) Playwright, whose plays, at first ill received, marked a historic break from the vogue for drawing-room comedy. His first popular success was *The Devils* (perf. 1961), adapted from *The Devils of Loudun* by Aldous *Huxley. A highly theatrical piece, influenced by Bertolt *Brecht, it deals with a case of hysterical demonic possession in a French nunnery.

WHITMAN, Walt (1819–92) American poet. He travelled in 1848 to New Orleans, returning to New York via St Louis and Chicago, and the experience of the frontier merged with his admiration for Ralph Waldo *Emerson to produce the first, self-published edition of *Leaves of Grass* in 1855, a sequence celebrating America through free verse, avoiding European models. When Emerson was sent a copy he replied hailing the work as 'the most extraordinary piece of wit and wisdom that America has yet contributed'. The second edition (1856) added 21 poems, and the third edition (1860) 122, including the group entitled 'Calamus', which has been taken as a reflection of the poet's homosexuality. There were six further editions in Whitman's lifetime, the work enlarging as the poet developed. During the Civil War Whitman worked as a volunteer hospital visitor among the wounded, an experience which affected him deeply, as can be seen in his prose *Memoranda during the War* (1875) and in the poems of *Drum-Taps* (1865). The *Sequel* to these poems (1865–6) contains an elegy on Abraham Lincoln, 'When Lilacs Last in the Dooryard Bloom'd'. Whitman's reputation began to rise after recognition in England by D. G. *Rossetti, A. C. *Swinburne, and others. The free, vigorous sweep of his verse conveys subjects at once national ('Pioneers! O Pioneers!', 1865), mystically sexual ('I sing the body electric', 1855), and deeply personal ('Out of the Cradle Endlessly Rocking', 1860), and his work proved a liberating force for many of his successors, including Henry *Miller and the poets of the *Beat Generation.

(⊕) SEE WEB LINKS
• The Walt Whitman Archive

WHITNEY, Geoffrey *See* EMBLEM BOOK.

WHITNEY, Isabella (*fl.*1566–73) The first English female poet to acknowledge her authorship of a volume of secular verse. She may have been the sister of the *emblem book writer Geoffrey Whitney. Her collections *The Copy of a Letter* (1566–7) and *A Sweet Nosegay* (1573) both survive only in single copies. In the second the poet (or her persona) describes her social and domestic circumstances and the reasons for her deciding to leave London. The final piece in the volume is a poetical last 'Will and Testament' which provides a striking picture of contemporary London, especially of its low life.

WHITTIER, John Greenleaf (1807–92) American poet, born of Quaker parents. A prolific and popular poet and hymn-writer (his hymns include 'Dear Lord and Father of mankind'), his first book was *Legends of*

New-England in Prose and Verse (1831). He became an ardent Abolitionist, and his poems on the subject of slavery were collected as *Voices of Freedom* (1846). He was a regular contributor to the *Atlantic Monthly*.

Whole Duty of Man, The A devotional work published 1658, in which man's duties to God and his fellow men are analysed and discussed in detail. The book was at one time attributed to Lady Dorothy Pakington (d. 1679). The book is probably by Richard Allestree (1619–81), chaplain in ordinary to the king, Regius professor of divinity, and provost of Eton College. For enduring contemporary appeal, it is comparable to *Thomas à Kempis's *De Imitatio Christi* and William *Law's *Serious Call*.

Who's Who An annual biographical dictionary of contemporary men and women published by A. & C. Black. It was first issued in 1849 but took its present form in 1897, when it incorporated material from *Men and Women of the Time*. Inclusion is regarded as a mark of prominence in public life. Members of the peerage are automatically included, while sports people or celebrities may not be. The entries are compiled with the assistance of the subjects themselves and updated annually. Once included in *Who's Who*, no subject is removed until death. The first *Who Was Who* volume, covering 1897–1916, appeared in 1920: these volumes (now added every five years) contain entries for subjects who have died, with final details and date of death added. An online edition of *Who's Who* was launched in 2005.

WHYTE-MELVILLE, George John (1821–78) Novelist; he is celebrated (with Anthony *Trollope and Robert Surtees) as a hunting novelist. His first novel was *Digby Grand* (1853); John *Galsworthy, at Oxford, fell under the spell of the 'Bright Things' in Whyte-Melville's novels, and Digby Grand was idolized by Jolyon (in *The *Forsyte Saga*). *Holmby House* (1859), a historical romance describing the Civil War, was followed by the equally popular *Market Harborough* (1861) and *The Gladiators* (1863). He was killed in a hunting accident.

WHYTHORNE, Thomas (1528–96) Poet and musician; after three years as 'servant and scholar' in the household of John *Heywood he became a music tutor. His *Songes for Three, Fower and Five Voyces* (1571) was one of the first English *madrigal books;. Whythorne's pioneering autobiography, *A Book of Songs and Sonetts*, written *c*.1576, was edited by James M. Osborn (1961). A revealing document of Tudor social life, it is written in phonetic spelling and thus offers a key to contemporary pronunciation.

WICKHAM, Anna (1883–1947) Pseudonym of Edith Harper, poet; she studied singing in London in 1905, and went to Paris to be coached for opera. She was an original and prolific poet, who charted the struggle of a woman artist to achieve freedom to work as well as to fulfil herself as wife and mother. Her friends included D. H. *Lawrence, Malcolm *Lowry, Kate *O'Brien, and Dylan *Thomas. Her publications include *The Contemplative Quarry* (1915), *The Little Old House* (1921), and *Thirty-Six New Poems* (1936).

WICKS, Susan (1947–) British poet and novelist. Her poetry collections include *Singing Underwater* (1992); *Open Diagnosis* (1994), her coming to terms with multiple sclerosis; *The Clever Daughter* (1996), which details the after effects of her mother's death and her relationship with her father; *The Night Toad: New and Selected Poems* (2003); *De-Iced* (2007) and *House of Tongues* (2011). Influenced by the American poet Sharon *Olds, Wicks also combines a strong interest in narrative with a restrained and acutely judged bareness of language.

Widsith A poem of 143 lines in Old English in the *Exeter Book. 'Widsith', its opening word, is the poet who unlocks the 'word-hoard' that constitutes the poem. It contains three 'thulas' (i.e. mnemonic name-lists), connected by his ostensible experience: the first names great rulers; the second lists the tribes among whom he claims to have travelled; the third names people whom he sought out.

'Wife of Bath's Tale, The' *See* CANTERBURY TALES, 6.

Wife's Lament, The An Old English poem of 53 lines in the *Exeter Book, one of the group usually called 'elegies'. Like *'Wulf and Eadwacer' it is a rare early English example of a *Frauenlied*.

WIGGIN, Kate Douglas (1856–1923) American children's writer and educationalist, the author of sentimental but popular books; notably *The Birds' Christmas Carol* (1887), *Rebecca of Sunnybrook Farm* (1903), and *Mother Carey* (1911).

WILBERFORCE, William (1759–1833) Politician, leading evangelical, and philanthropist, who devoted himself to the abolition of the slave trade. His *A Practical View of the Prevailing*

Religious System of Professed Christians (1797) was an influential and widely read work. A close friend of Hannah *More, he was the leading layman of the evangelical 'Clapham Sect', and lived just long enough to see carried the second reading of the Bill abolishing slavery.

WILBUR, Richard (1921-) American poet. His elegant, urbane, and witty poetry appears in several collections, starting with *Ceremony* (1950), and he has also translated plays by *Molière and *Racine.

WILBYE, John (1574–1638) English composer, one of the most important of the *madrigal composers following the lead of Thomas *Morley. He published *The First Set of English Madrigals* (1598), and *The Second Set of Madrigals* (1609), and contributed one madrigal to *The Triumphes of Oriana* (1601). The second set is often regarded as the finest English madrigal collection of all, for its subtle poetic understanding, musical expressiveness, purity of style, and variety of texture; it includes the melancholy six part 'Draw on sweet night'.

WILCOX, Ella Wheeler (1850–1919) American writer, whose many volumes of romantic, sentimental, and mildly erotic verse, especially *Poems of Passion* (1883), brought her a vast readership. She had long-standing interests in *Rosicrucianism, the New Thought Movement and the Theosophy of Madame Blavatsky.

WILDE, Jane Francesca ('Speranza') (1821–96) Poet, Irish nationalist, translator, and mother of Oscar *Wilde. 'Speranza' was a pseudonym used to avoid identification with her nationalistic writing. An advocate of women's rights, she campaigned for better education for women and fought against differing legal and moral codes for the sexes. Her first collection of *Poems* appeared in 1864.

WILDE, Oscar (1854–1900) Irish dramatist and wit; his mother was the nationalist poet 'Speranza' (*see* WILDE, JANE). He attracted attention, much of it hostile, for his flamboyant aestheticism; he proclaimed himself a disciple of Walter *Pater and the cult of *'Art for art's sake' mocked in Gilbert and Sullivan's *Patience* (1881). He made a lecture tour of the United States in 1882, after the publication of *Poems* (1881). In 1884 he married, and in 1888 published a volume of fairy stories, *The Happy Prince and Other Tales*. In 1891 followed a further volume of fairy stories, *A House of Pomegranates, Lord Arthur Savile's Crime, and Other*

Stories and his only novel, *The Picture of Dorian Gray*, a *Gothic melodrama. Wilde claimed in his preface, 'There is no such thing as a moral or an immoral book. Books are well written or badly written. That is all.' Theatrical success came with the London production of *Lady Windermere's Fan*, followed by *A Woman of No Importance* (1893) and *An Ideal Husband* (1895). All three are witty, moralizing social comedies displaying shrewd observation of upper-middle-class English manners. *The *Importance of Being Earnest* (1895) is a more enigmatic commentary on social and sexual identity. *Salomé* (now known chiefly by way of Richard Strauss's opera), written in French, was refused a licence, but was performed in Paris in 1896 and published in 1894 in an English translation by Lord Alfred *Douglas with illustrations by Aubrey *Beardsley. Lord Alfred's father, the marquess of Queensberry, disapproved of his son's association with Wilde and publicly insulted the playwright. After the failure of a libel action against Queensberry, Wilde was prosecuted for homosexual offences. He was declared bankrupt while in prison and wrote a letter of bitter reproach to Lord Alfred, published in part in 1905 as *De Profundis*. He was released in 1897 and went to France where he wrote *The Ballad of Reading Gaol* (1898). In exile he adopted the name Sebastian Melmoth, after the romance by Charles *Maturin (his great-uncle). He died in Paris. His other works include 'The Decay of Lying' and 'The Critic as Artist', in *Intentions*, 1891, his anarchistic political meditation *The Soul of Man under Socialism* (written after hearing G. B. *Shaw speak, and first published in the *Fortnightly Review* in 1891), and his fictionalized homoerotic meditation on *Shakespeare's sonnets, *The Portrait of Mr W.H.* (published as an article in *Blackwood's Magazine* in 1899. (Terry *Eagleton's play *St Oscar* (1989) foregrounds Wilde's Irishness and his homosexuality.

WILDER, Laura Ingalls (1867–1957) American author; her 'Little House' books, from *Little House in the Big Woods* (USA, 1932/UK, 1956) to *These Happy Golden Years* (1943/64), are edited versions of the Ingalls family's travels from Wisconsin to Kansas, Minnesota, and South Dakota between 1871 and 1889. Written in collaboration with Wilder's journalist daughter, Rose, they idealize Pa Ingalls and incorporate an anti-New Deal political agenda.

WILDER, Thornton (1897–1975) American novelist and dramatist. *The Bridge of San Luis*

Rey (1927, novel), describes the convergence of fortunes of those involved in the collapse of a bridge, and *The Ides of March* (1948) deals with the assassination of Julius *Caesar. His successful plays include *Our Town* (1938), *The Skin of our Teeth* (1942), and *The Merchant of Yonkers* (1938), a comedy which was revised as *The Matchmaker* (1954) and adapted as the musical comedy *Hello, Dolly!* (1963).

Wild-Goose Chase, The A comedy by John *Fletcher, acted with great success in 1621, printed 1652; it was very popular on the *Restoration stage. George *Farquhar's comedy *The Inconstant* is based on this play.

Wild Swans See CHANG, JUNG.

WILKIE, William (1721–72) Scottish poet, academic, and Presbyterian clergyman. He was author of *The Epigoniad* (1757), an epic poem in heroic couplets, in nine books, on the theme of the siege of Thebes: it was modelled on *Homer and inspired by the 'heroic Tragedy' of *Sophocles. It was highly regarded by David *Hume and by Adam *Smith. Wilkie was a member with Hume of the Select Society.

WILKINS, George (d. 1618) Pamphleteer, playwright, and innkeeper. *The Miseries of Enforced Marriage*, acted by the King's Men, published and probably acted in 1607; is based on the events that lie behind another King's Men play, *A *Yorkshire Tragedy*. He was almost certainly joint author, with *Shakespeare, of *Pericles*, and the novel of the play, *The Painful Adventures of Pericles Prince of Tyre*, in 1608. A disreputable and violent character, from no later than 1610 he had opened an inn that doubled as brothel.

WILLARD, Barbara (1909–94) Prolific, reclusive children's writer. The eight-book Mantlemass series (1970–80) is set in the Sussex house where Willard lived, it tells the interconnecting stories of the Mallory and Medley families over 250 years, beginning with *The Lark and the Laurel* about the end of the Wars of the Roses. Willard's female characters are usually strong women typified by Lilias Forstal (*The Iron Lily*, 1974).

William The character created by Richmal *Crompton as an ironic response to the early 20th-century 'beautiful child' cult. With his companions, 'the Outlaws', Ginger, Henry, and Douglas, long-suffering elder siblings Robert and Ethel, confederate Violet Elizabeth Bott, and rival gang led by Hubert Lane, William

Brown became part of English culture through 37 collections of short stories and one novel (*Just William's Luck*, 1948) between 1919 and 1970.

WILLIAM OF MALMESBURY (*c.*1090–*c.*1142) The first full-scale writer of history in England after *Bede. His major works were the *Gesta Regum Anglorum*, a history of England from 449 to 1120; the *Gesta Pontificum Anglorum*, an ecclesiastical history of England from 597 to 1125; the *Historia Novella*, the sequel to the *Gesta Regum*, dealing with 1128 to 1142 and left unfinished at his death; *De Antiquitate Glastoniensis Ecclesiae*; a treatise on miracles associated with the Virgin Mary; and *hagiographical works including lives of St Patrick, St Dunstan, and St Wulfstan. The *Gesta Regum* includes two stories about *Arthur whom William regards as a great warrior while discrediting many of the stories about him.

William of Palerne One of the earliest of the 14th-century English romances of the *Alliterative Revival, of 5,540 lines in a west Midland dialect. It was written for Humphrey de Bohun, based on the late 12th-century French *Roman de Guillaume de Palerne*. William is a prince of Apulia who is saved from his uncle's attempts to poison him by a werewolf who is really a prince of Spain turned into that shape by his wicked stepmother.

WILLIAMS, Anna (1706–83) Poet. She became completely blind in 1752, living in Samuel *Johnson's household for much of the rest of her life. Her *Miscellanies in Prose and Verse* (1766) included verses in praise of Samuel Richardson's *Sir Charles *Grandison*, 'Rasselas to Imlac', and a sonnet in imitation of Edmund *Spenser. Williams also received assistance from Elizabeth *Montagu. She features prominently in James Boswell's *Life of *Johnson*.

WILLIAMS, Charles (1886–1945) Poet, novelist, and theological writer. He is best known for his novels, which have been described as supernatural thrillers, and include *War in Heaven* (1930), *Descent into Hell* (1937), and *All Hallows Eve* (1944). His most original poetic achievement is his cycle on the Arthurian legend, *Taliessin through Logres* (1938) and *The Region of the Summer Stars* (1944), afterwards reissued in one volume (1974) together with *Arthurian Torso*, a study of Williams's poetry by his friend C. S. *Lewis. He was a member of the literary group known as the *Inklings.

WILLIAMS, Edward ('Iolo Marganwg') (1747–1826) Welsh stonemason, antiquarian, and poet, who collected a vast store of manuscripts and, under his 'bardic' pseudonym, made extravagant claims about the antiquity and continuity of Welsh tradition.

WILLIAMS, Helen Maria (?1761–1827) Poet and translator. In 1788, she travelled to Paris, where she became friendly with the leading Girondists, and made the acquaintance of Mary *Wollstonecraft; her *Letters from France* (1790–5) contain interesting information on the state of Paris and France just before and during the revolution. William *Wordsworth's first printed poem was 'Sonnet on Seeing Miss Helen Maria Williams Weep at a Tale of Distress' (1787), but he appears not to have met her until 1820 in Paris.

WILLIAMS, Hugo (1942–) Poet and travel writer. His first volume, *Symptoms of Loss* (1965) was followed by *Sugar Daddy* (1970), *Dock Leaves* (1994), *Billy's Rain* (1999), and *Dear Room* (2006). Williams's poems characteristically offer the potent combination of an insouciant flaneur's self-deprecation with sudden chasms of loss, grief, and yearning. His travel books include *No Particular Place to Go* (1981); *Freelancing: Adventures of a Poet* (1995) is a collection of his much-admired columns in the *Times Literary Supplement*.

WILLIAMS, Isaac (1802–65) Poet and theologian, influenced by John *Keble. His poems appeared in *Lyra Apostolica*, *The Cathedral* (1838), and *The Baptistery* (1842). His autobiography (edited by Sir G. Prevost, 1892) is a significant record of the history of the *Oxford Movement.

WILLIAMS, Raymond (1921–88) Critic and novelist. His best-known book, *Culture and Society, 1780–1950* (1958), surveys the history of the idea of 'culture' in British thought; and his later works, beginning with *The Long Revolution* (1961) and *Modern Tragedy* (1966), attempt to extend this concept in more democratic directions than those envisaged by T. S. *Eliot and others. His critical investigations included television as well as the history and sociology of drama and fiction. His more traditional literary studies challenged the view of English literature and society presented by F. R. *Leavis. A leading figure of the British 'New Left', he tried to move beyond the limits of orthodox *Marxist literary criticism into a more dynamic materialist view of cultural changes, explored in *Marxism and Literature* (1977). His early novels,

including *Border Country* (1960) and *Second Generation* (1964), are semi-autobiographical.

WILLIAMS, Roy (1968–) OBE. *Fallout* (2003), loosely based on the murders of Damilola Taylor and Stephen Lawrence, *Clubland* (2001), and *Sucker Punch* (2010) were staged at the *Royal Court Theatre, and *Sing yer Heart out for the Lads* (2002) at the *National Theatre.

WILLIAMS, Tad (1957–) American author of *science fiction and *fantasy novels. *The Dragonbone Chair* (1988) begins the 'Memory, Sorrow and Thorn' series, which subtly engages with *Tolkien's moral framework. The 'Otherland' sequence (1996–2001) shows virtual realities copying literary 'worlds'.

WILLIAMS, Tennessee (Thomas Lanier Williams III) (1911–83) American dramatist. He achieved success with the semi-autobiographical *The Glass Menagerie* (1944; pub. 1945), a poignant and painful family drama set in St Louis, in which a frustrated mother persuades her rebellious son to provide a 'gentleman caller' for her crippled daughter Laura, and *A Streetcar Named Desire* (1947), a study of sexual repression, violence, and aberration, set in New Orleans, in which Blanche Dubois's fantasies of refinement and grandeur are brutally destroyed by her brother-in-law Stanley Kowalski. Williams' prolific output, largely in a *Gothic and macabre vein, shows insight into human passion and its perversions, and a considerable warmth and compassion. Other works include *The Rose Tattoo* (1950); the symbolic and anti-naturalistic *Camino Real* (1953); *Cat on a Hot Tin Roof* (1955); *Suddenly Last Summer* (1958); *Sweet Bird of Youth* (1959); *The Night of the Iguana* (1962); and a novella, *The Roman Spring of Mrs Stone* (1950).

WILLIAMS, Ursula Moray (1911–2006) Author-illustrator, remembered for *Adventures of the Little Wooden Horse* (1938), about a courageous toy, and *Gobbolino the Witch's Cat* (1942), describing the exploits of a witch's kitten who wants an ordinary home.

WILLIAMS, William ('Pantycelin') (1718–91) Methodist hymn-writer, poet, and theologian, whose hymns, combining classical with dialect Welsh, and biblical allusion with force of individual personality, have been seen as the earliest and perhaps greatest achievement of Welsh romanticism.

WILLIAMS, William Carlos (1883–1963) American poet, novelist, short story writer, and, for many years, a paediatrician. His profession as doctor deeply affected his literary life. In his student days he was a friend of Ezra *Pound and Hilda *Doolittle (known as H.D.), and some early poems are *imagist, although he soon moved on to what he called Objectivism (a literary approach which presented the poem as an object, comprising a clear, intelligent reflection of the world). *Kora in Hell* (1920) is a volume of improvisations from this period. His poems range from the minimal, eight-line, sixteen-word 'The Red Wheelbarrow' (1923) to *Paterson* (1946–58), a long, five-part, free verse, collage evocation of the New Jersey industrial city. The title of his last collection, *Pictures from Brueghel* (1963), suggests the plain, poverty-stricken subjects of some of his verse and prose. His short stories were collected as *The Farmers' Daughters* (1961). Other prose works include *In the American Grain* (1925), essays exploring the nature of American literature and the influence of *Puritanism in American culture; novels: *White Mule* (1937), *In the Money* (1940), and *The Build-Up* (1952); and his *Autobiography* (1951).

WILLIAMSON, David (1942–) Australian playwright. Initially associated with the counter-cultural 'New Wave' drama of the late 1960s and 1970s, with works such as *Don's Party* (1971), *The Removalists* (1972), and *The Club* (1976), Williamson has over the course of writing nearly 40 plays increasingly become the leading dramatic chronicler and critic of the experiences and attitudes of his own generation of well-educated middle-class Australians. *After the Ball* (1997) reflects on Australia's social changes. The satire and social criticism often seem blunted by Williamson's many brilliant one-liners and sheer comic verve.

WILLIAMSON, Henry (1895–1977) Writer of *Tarka the Otter* (1927), the vivid, unsentimental account of the life of a wild animal. Williamson's most ambitious work was a series of fifteen novels known under the collective title *A Chronicle of Ancient Sunlight*, which trace the life, from childhood in the 1890s to the 1950s, of a writer whose experiences in the First World War, and with the Oswald Mosley-like character Sir Hereward Birkin, echo Williamson's own.

Willobie his Avisa One of the books which, with Gabriel *Harvey's and Thomas *Nashe's satirical works, was censored in 1599. The poem, first published in 1594, consists of 74 songs and a few other poems by Henry Willoughby (1574/5–1597/1605). They narrate the unsuccessful courting of Avisa, a country innkeeper's wife, by a nobleman before her marriage, and by four foreign suitors after it. The last of these has a 'familiar friend W.S.' as a companion; he has been identified with Shakespeare, who is also mentioned as author of *The Rape of Lucrece* in prefatory verses. The enigmatic and apparently allusive nature of the work has never been satisfactorily explained.

WILLS, W. G. (William Gorman) (1828–91) Irish dramatist, novelist and portrait painter, whose plays revived the popularity of verse drama in Victorian London. Successes such as *A Man and his Shadow* (1865) and *Man o' Airlie* (1867) led to his appointment as 'Dramatist to the Lyceum' and the composition of many historical dramas. In 1885 he produced a version of *Faust, and a long poem, *Melchior*, dedicated to Robert *Browning.

WILMOT, John See ROCHESTER, JOHN.

WILMOT, Robert See TANCRED AND GISMUND.

WILSON, A. N. (Andrew Norman) (1950–) Novelist, biographer, and reviewer.His first novels, *The Sweets of Pimlico* (1977) and *Unguarded Hours* (1978), are acid social comedies influenced by Evelyn *Waugh. Satire is blended with more complex exploration of character in *The Healing Art* (1980) and *Wise Virgin* (1982). *Incline our Hearts* (1989), *A Bottle in the Smoke* (1990), *Daughters of Albion* (1991), *Hearing Voices* (1995), and *A Watch in the Night* (1996) comprise the Lampitt Papers quintet, about a rogue biographer. Wilson has published many biographies, and a controversial memoir, *Iris Murdoch as I Knew Her*, (2003). *Winnie and Wolf* (2007) fictionalizes the relationship between Winifred Wagner and Adolf Hitler.

WILSON, Sir Angus (Frank Johnstone) (1913–91) Novelist. His volumes of short stories, *The Wrong Set* (1949) and *Such Darling Dodos* (1950), revealed an outstanding talent for satiric mimicry and sharp social observation. His first novel, *Hemlock and After* (1952), about an attempt to establish a writers' centre in a country house, was followed by *Anglo-Saxon Attitudes* (1956), whose plot revolves around an archaeological forgery reminiscent of the Piltdown case. *The Middle Age of Mrs Eliot* (1958), *The Old Men at the Zoo* (1961). *Late Call* (1964), and *No Laughing Matter* (1967), Wilson's most ambitious and masterly novel, which chronicles the fortunes of a large middle-class family, and, making brilliant use of parody and pastiche, opens up a vivid panorama of more than half a century of English cultural, political, social, and sexual life. Later works include the *picaresque novel *As if by Magic* (1973) and *Setting the World on Fire* (1980). Wilson explored his own creative processes in *The Wild Garden* (1963). There is a biography by Margaret *Drabble (1995).

WILSON, Colin Henry (1931–) Writer; he gained instant fame with *The Outsider* (1956), a study of alienated genius. Wilson has since written many works on mysticism, crime, and the occult; his novels include *Ritual in the Dark* (1960), *The Mind Parasites* (1967), and *The Space Vampires* (1976). *Dreaming to Some Purpose* (2004) is an autobiography.

WILSON, Edmund (1895–1972) American author. He served with the US army in France during the First World War, an experience which inspired his work in a lively and eccentric little anthology about death, *The Undertaker's Garland* (1922, with his friend J. P. *Bishop). His novel *I Thought of Daisy* (1929; rev. 1967), and his short stories, *Memoirs of Hecate Country* (1946), are set in New York. He is principally known for literary and social criticism, including *Axel's Castle* (1931), a study of *modernist writing as a continuation of *Symbolism (discussing W. B. *Yeats, *Valéry, James *Joyce, *Stein, and others); *The Triple Thinkers* (1938); *To the Finland Station* (1940), which traces socialist and revolutionary theory from Jules Michelet and Robert *Owen through *Marx to Lenin; *The Wound and the Bow* (1941), a series of essays employing *psychoanalytic approaches to Charles *Dickens and others; and *Patriotic Gore: Studies in the Literature of the American Civil War* (1962). His other works include experimental plays, collections of articles and reviews, and memoirs. He was associated with the *Partisan Review* and the New York Intellectuals: among these was his third wife, the novelist Mary *McCarthy. He was a friend from college days of Scott *Fitzgerald.

WILSON, Harriette (1786–1846) Née Dubochet, courtesan. She wrote a spirited account of her adventures and amours in the fashionable Regency world in *Memoirs of Harriette Wilson, Written by Herself* (1825), which went through many editions.

WILSON, Dame Jacqueline (1945–) Children's writer.From *Ricky's Birthday* (1973) she has appealed to young readers as a writer who acknowledges their problems and resourcefulness. A champion of literacy initiatives

and reading aloud, Wilson is known for her books for pre-teenagers which deal with the challenges of growing up in contemporary Britain. *The Story of Tracy Beaker* (1991; four television series 2001–8) purports to be written by a 10-year-old girl living in a children's home; *The Suitcase Kid* (1992) is the first of several to explore the impact of divorce on families; the 'Girls' books, from *Girls in Love* (1997) to *Girls in Tears* (2002), deal with issues such as anorexia and boyfriends. Wilson has campaigned to revive classic texts including stories by Noel *Streatfeild and Eve *Garnett.

WILSON, John (?1627–96) Playwright. His two principal plays are *The Cheats* (1663) and *The Projectors* (printed 1665, no recorded performance); they are Jonsonian satires in which sharks, gulls, usurers, and astrologers are vigorously and effectively displayed.

WILSON, John (1785–1854) Tory satirist, journalist, and poet. He joined the editorial staff of *Blackwood's Magazine*, and provided more than half of the series *Noctes Ambrosianae*, in which he appears as 'Christopher North'; he was part-author of the notorious 'Chaldee MS'; he wrote a ferocious attack on Coleridge's *Biographia Literaria*; and joined in John *Lockhart's prolonged onslaught on the *Cockney School. He admired P. B *Shelley's poetry though not his politics, and dubbed *Wordsworth, Walter *Scott, and Lord *Byron, as poets, 'the three great master-spirits of our day'. Wilson's praise alternated bewilderingly with derision and he declared, 'I like to abuse my friends.' He wrote several volumes of verse, notably *The Isle of Palms* (1812).

WILSON, John Dover (1881–1969) Shakespearian scholar and editor. Using the methods of the 'new bibliography', scientifically rigorous in examining every aspect of a text's transmission, he was responsible for editing most of the plays in the New Cambridge Shakespeare series which was begun in 1921.

WILSON, Thomas (1523/4–81) Humanist; he was made a privy counsellor and a secretary of state in 1577. He published *The Rule of Reason*, a work on logic (1551), and the *Art of Rhetoric* (1553; rev. and improved, 1560). The *Art* is a notable landmark in the history of English prose. Wilson provides interesting and useful models for letters and speeches in a variety of English styles.

Wilton, Jack *See* UNFORTUNATE TRAVELLER, THE.

WINCHILSEA, Anne Finch, countess of
(1661–1720) Née Kingsmill. In 1684 she
married Colonel Heneage Finch, who inherited
the Winchilsea earldom in 1712 and is addressed as 'Daphnis' in many of the lyrics she
wrote as 'Ardelia'. Her influential 'The Spleen:
A Pindaric Poem' was published in *A New Collection of Poems on Several Occasions* (1701).
Her *Miscellany Poems, on Several Occasions*
(1713) 'Written by a Lady' included 'The Petition for an Absolute Retreat' and 'A Nocturnal
Reverie', each celebrating the virtues of retirement, privacy, and contentment. She exchanged
verses with Alexander *Pope and he included
eight of her poems in *Poems on Several Occasions* (1717). Virginia *Woolf wrote of Finch's
melancholy in *A *Room of one's Own* (1928),
and John Middleton *Murry edited a selection
of her verse in 1928.

Wind in the Willows, The (1908) Kenneth *Grahame's account of riverbank society.
The Toad sections are based on stories and
letters for Grahame's son Alistair. Alan *Bennett
adapted it for the National Theatre (1990).

Windsor-Forest A *topographical poem by
Alexander *Pope, published in 1713 to celebrate
the Treaty of Utrecht. Partly modelled on Sir
John *Denham's *Cooper's Hill*, it also draws on
the *Georgics* of *Virgil, Jacobean court *masques
and William Camden's *Britannia*.

Wings of the Dove, The A novel by Henry
*James, published 1902, which explores the tri-
angular relationship between the impoverished
Kate Croy, the journalist Merton Densher, and
the rich heiress Milly Theale, who sickens and
dies prematurely.

Winnie-the-Pooh The bear of very little
brain in A. A. *Milne's children's stories. The
archetypal amiable teddy bear, he has become
something of a new-age shaman in books such
as Benjamin Hoff's *The Tao of Pooh* (1982).

WINSTANLEY, Gerrard (*c.*1609–1676)
Pamphleteer and leader of the Diggers, or True
Levellers. In 1649 with a group of comrades he
started cultivating the common land on St
George's Hill, Surrey, in a short-lived attempt
to claim it for 'the common people of England'.
His first Digger manifesto, *The True Levellers'
Standard Advanced*, dated 20 April 1649, was
followed by *A Watchword to the City of London,
and the Army* (1649), *Fire in the Bush* (1650),
and *The Law of Freedom, in a Platform* (1652).
His work expresses compassion for the poor and
ardour for social justice. See *The Law of Free-

dom and Other Writings, ed. Christopher *Hill
(1973).

WINTERS, Yvor (1900–68) American
poet and critic, whose own poems exemplify
his critical doctrine of classicism, restraint,
moral judgement, and 'cold certitude' (*see*
NEW CRITICISM). His *In Defense of Reason*
(1947) collects earlier work attacking obscurantism and *Romanticism, and an essay on his
friend, the highly dissimilar Hart *Crane, for
whom he also wrote an elegy, 'Orpheus'.

WINTERSON, Jeanette (1959–) OBE,
novelist, adopted by Pentecostal evangelists.
Her training for evangelical service and her recognition that she was lesbian inspired *Oranges
Are Not the Only Fruit* (1985; televised 1990).
The Passion (1987) and *Sexing the Cherry*
(1989) followed. Winterson's novels are noted
for formal experimentation: *Written on the Body*
(1992) explores gender within a triangular relationship; *Art & Lies* (1994) deploys three narrative voices from different historical periods; and
Gut Symmetries (1997) draws on quantum physics and the nature of time. Later novels include
The Powerbook (2000; adapted for the *National
Theatre 2002); *Lighthousekeeping* (2004); and
The Stone Gods (2007).

Winter's Tale, The A play by *Shakespeare
written 1610 or 1611, in which year it was performed at the *Globe (recorded by Simon Forman), printed 1623. Its main source is Robert
*Greene's *Pandosto*, and it also draws on
his coney-catching pamphlets (*see* ROGUE LIT-
ERATURE).

Leontes, king of Sicily, and Hermione, his
virtuous wife, are visited by Leontes' childhood
friend Polixenes, king of Bohemia. Leontes convinces himself that Hermione and Polixenes are
lovers, tries to poison Polixenes, and on his
escape imprisons Hermione, who in prison
gives birth to a daughter. Paulina, wife of Antigonus, a Sicilian lord, tries to move the king's
compassion by bringing the baby to him, but in
vain. He orders Antigonus to abandon the child
on a desert shore to die. He ignores a Delphian
oracle declaring Hermione innocent. He soon
learns that his son Mamillius has died of sorrow
for Hermione's treatment, and then he is told
that Hermione herself is dead, and is filled with
remorse. Meanwhile Antigonus leaves the baby
girl, Perdita, on the shore of Bohemia (in fact
Bohemia is landlocked), and is himself pursued
and eaten by a bear. Perdita is found and
brought up by a shepherd. Sixteen years pass.
When she grows up, Florizel, son of King

Polixenes, falls in love with her, and his love is returned. This is discovered by Polixenes, to avoid whose anger Florizel, Perdita, and the old shepherd flee from Bohemia to the court of Leontes, where the identity of Perdita is discovered, to Leontes' great joy, and the revival of his grief for the loss of Hermione. Paulina offers to show him a statue that perfectly resembles Hermione, and when the king's grief is intensified at the sight, the statue comes to life and reveals itself as the living Hermione, whose death Paulina had falsely reported in order to save her life. Polixenes is reconciled to the marriage of his son with Perdita, on finding that the shepherd-girl is really the daughter of his former friend Leontes.

WINTON, Tim (1960–) Australian novelist and short story writer. Damage, to people and to the environment, is the central preoccupation in his work—usually set in his native Western Australia—and the repercussions of physical and emotional injuries are explored with a tough sensitivity reminiscent of Raymond *Carver. His breakthrough novel, *Cloudstreet* (1991) begins with one character losing four fingers and another suffering brain injury. *Shallows* (1984) depicts clashes between conservationists and whalers in an Australian harbour town. *The Turning* (2005), a collection of stories which returns to this setting two decades later, and *Breath* (2008), set in the world of surfing, display his keenly sensuous response to his environment, psychological and social acuteness, skill at conveying intense physical experience, narrative power, vivid prose, lively dialogue, and deadpan humour.

WIREKER, Nigel (1135–1198) Benedictine monk of Christ Church, Canterbury, and author of *Burnellus* or *Speculum Stultorum*, a satire on monks featuring Burnell the ass.

Wisdom (also ***Mind, Will and Understanding*** or ***Wisdom, Who Is Christ***) A *morality play from c.1460, one of the group called *Macro plays, describing the seduction by Lucifer of Mind, Will, and Understanding in a series of dances.

WISE, Thomas James (1859–1937) Bibliographer, collector, and editor notorious for his forgeries of rare *pamphlets, notably an edition of E. B. *Browning's *Sonnets from the Portuguese* said to have been published in Reading in 1847, exposed in John Carter and Graham Pollard's *An Enquiry into the Nature of Certain 19th-Century Pamphlets*.

WISTER, Owen (1860–1938) American author of *westerns. *The Virginian* (1902), describing a cowboy caught up in the Wyoming range war, is a prototype of the genre.

Witch, The A play by Thomas *Middleton, written before 1616, printed 1778. The principal part of the plot is based on the story of the revenge exacted by Rosamond in 572 on her husband Alboin, ruler of Lombardy. The same subject is treated in William *D'Avenant's *Albovine*, and in A. C. *Swinburne's *Rosamund, Queen of the Lombards*. Middleton's play includes the witch Hecate, and Charles *Lamb in his *Specimens* indicated the difference between this figure and the witches in Shakespeare's *Macbeth*.

'Witch of Atlas, The' A poem of 78 stanzas in *ottava rima* by P. B. *Shelley, published 1824. The beautiful Witch is the daughter of *Apollo, and the spirit of mischief and poetry. Together with her mysterious companion, the Hermaphrodite, she circles the globe, weaving spells over stubborn kings, priests, soldiers, and young lovers (whose inhibitions are blissfully dissolved).

Witch of Edmonton, The A tragicomedy by Thomas *Dekker, John *Ford, William *Rowley, 'etc.' (possibly John *Webster), first performed probably 1621, published 1658. It is partly based on the story of Elizabeth Sawyer, who was hanged as a witch in April 1621. Her character is notable for the characteristic sympathy shown by Dekker for the poor outcast, and the tone of the play is markedly humane. Its two plots are engaged with the theme of revenge, but are otherwise little connected.

WITHER, George (1588–1667) Poet and *pamphleteer. His satires *Abuses Stripped and Whipped* (1613) earned him imprisonment in the Marshalsea, where he wrote the pastorals *The Shepherd's Hunting*, a continuation of his friend William *Browne's *The Shepherd's Pipe*. *Fidelia* (1615), was reprinted in 1619 with the song 'Shall I, wasting in despair', included by Thomas *Percy in his *Reliques. Wither was again briefly imprisoned for his satire *Wither's Motto* (1621). Other works include *Fair-Virtue, the Mistress of Phil'Arete* (1622) *Hymns and Songs of the Church* (1623), a book of *emblems (1634–5), and *Halleluiah* (1641). He was satirized (as 'Chronomastix') in Ben *Jonson's masque *Time Vindicated* (1623).

Wits, The A comedy by Sir William *D'Avenant, published 1636, revised by him after the

*Restoration, and generally considered his best comedy. Young Pallatine, a spendthrift wit, is in love with Lucy, who sells her jewels to provide him with money and is thrown out by her cruel aunt. Pallatine's wealthy elder brother comes to town, where he is involved in a series of adventures, and fooled into making liberal provision for his brother and Lucy.

WITTGENSTEIN, Ludwig Josef Johann

(1889–1951) Anglo-Austrian philosopher, who came to England in 1908 to pursue a doctorate in aeronautics at Manchester. Through the study of the logical foundations of mathematics with Bertrand *Russell he became interested in philosophy. He acquired British citizenship in 1939, having served in the Austrian army during the First World War. In his *Tractatus Logico-Philosophicus* (1921) he claimed to have solved the problems of philosophy by defining those areas in which the meaningful use of language was possible and in which it was not. Later doubting his conclusions, his new approach stressed that language had a multiplicity of uses and that the traditional problems of philosophy arose from a misunderstanding of the use of those concepts in terms of which the problems arose; thus, by carefully bringing out the true character of the language in which they were framed, the problems of philosophy were to be 'dissolved' rather than solved. The *Philosophical Investigations* (1953) contain a full account of this later position. His later ideas on language have been variously seen as representing a serious challenge to, or as support for *deconstructionism.

Wives and Daughters The last and unfinished novel of Elizabeth *Gaskell, published 1864–6, and in volume form 1866. The novel centres on two families, the Gibsons and the Hamleys. Mr Gibson is a widower with one daughter, Molly. As she grows up her father proposes to a widow, Mrs Kirkpatrick, formerly governess in the family of Lord Cumnor, the local magnate. Molly is made unhappy by her graceful stepmother's selfishness, but her lot is improved when her stepmother's daughter by her previous marriage joins the household. Cynthia is beautiful, and more sincere than her mother, but has few moral principles.

The Hamleys are a county family—the proud and hot-tempered squire, his invalid wife, their elder son Osborne who is handsome and clever, and a younger son, Roger, sturdy, honest, and a late developer. Staying with the Hamleys, Molly discovers that Osborne is secretly married to a French nursery-maid. Molly begins to love and

admire Roger, but he becomes engaged to Cynthia, and, now a successful scientist, leaves on an expedition to Africa. Cynthia is in fact already secretly engaged to Preston, Lord Cumnor's clever but ill-bred agent, and she enlists Molly's help in extricating herself from this entanglement, compromising Molly's reputation. Osborne Hamley is bitterly estranged from his father, but when Osborne dies and the secret of his marriage is revealed, Squire Hamley adopts Osborne's baby son. Cynthia throws over Roger Hamley and when he returns he has realized that it is Molly whom he really loves.

Wizard of Oz, The Wonderful (1900; filmed 1939) L. Frank *Baum's fantasy (named after the O–Z drawer in his filing cabinet). Dorothy and her dog Toto are transported to bright, colourful Oz, where Dorothy accidentally defeats the Wicked Witch of the West, and with her companions, a Tin Man, a Scarecrow, and a Cowardly Lion, is tricked by the 'Wizard' (a 'Great Humbug') into finding their missing desires (heart, brain, courage, and Dorothy's Kansas home). *Wicked* is a musical companion, told from the Witch's perspective. The book can be read as a satirical or utopian metaphor for the USA.

WODEHOUSE, Sir P. G. (Pelham Grenville) (1881–1975) Prolific novelist and short story writer. He published extensively in the *Strand Magazine*, *Punch*, etc., establishing himself as one of the most widely read humorists of his day. His first novel, *The Pothunters* (1902), was a *school story. *The Man with Two Left Feet* (1917) introduced the amiably dim-witted Bertie Wooster and his wily manservant, Jeeves, whose joint antics continued in *My Man Jeeves* (1919), *The Inimitable Jeeves* (1923), *Carry On, Jeeves* (1925), etc. Wodehouse spent much of his life in America, where he wrote plays, worked in Hollywood, and had a notable career in musical theatre, working with Jerome Kern, George Gershwin, and others. From 1934 he lived in France, where he was captured by the invading Germans in 1940. Taken to Berlin, he was persuaded to make some radio broadcasts which led to British accusations of collaboration and even treason. He returned to America after the war, taking American citizenship in 1955. His last novel, *Sunset at Blandings* (1977), was completed by Richard Usborne.

WOLCOT, John (1738–1819) Satirist, who wrote under the pseudonym 'Peter Pindar'. He began his career as a physician, was ordained, then began writing vigorous and witty satirical

verses, including *Lyric Odes to the Royal Academicians* (1782-5), mocking their painting; a *mock-heroic poem, The Lousiad* (1785-95), and various other satires on George III. *Bozzy and Piozzi*, in which James *Boswell and Hester *Thrale set forth their reminiscences of Samuel *Johnson, appeared in 1786, as did his *Poetical and Congratulatory Epistle to James Boswell. Instructions to a Celebrated Laureate* (1787) professes to teach Thomas *Warton (1728-90) how he should celebrate the visit of George III to Whitbread's brewery.

WOLFE, Charles (1791-1823) Irish poet. 'The Burial of Sir John Moore' was apparently based on Robert *Southey's narrative in the *Annual Register*, and first published in the *Newry Telegraph* in 1817.

WOLFE, Gene (1931-) American author of *fantasy and *science fiction, described as a North American *Borges. *The Book of the New Sun* (1980-3), has been published both as fantasy and science fiction. *The Fifth Head of Cerberus* (1972) contains three related stories which require a close concentration upon the questions of identity to be fully understood as a whole. Wolfe's technique frequently involves unreliable narrators, including the forgetful Latro in *Soldier of the Mist* (1986), or the paraphrasing narrator of *Pirate Freedom* (2007).

WOLFE, Humbert (1886-1940) Writer and civil servant. His many volumes of serious light verse, more urbane than *Georgian in tone, include *London Sonnets* (1920). *The Unknown Goddess* (1925), *Requiem* (1927), and *Kensington Gardens in Wartime* (1940).

WOLFE, Reyner (Reginald Wolfe) (c.1530-1573) Bookseller, and printer of the first Greek book printed in England: the *Homilies* of Chrysostom, edited by Sir John Cheke, with Greek and Latin text (1543). He enjoyed the patronage of Archbishop *Cranmer.

WOLFE, Thomas Clayton (1900-38) American novelist. His autobiographical novel *Look Homeward, Angel* (1929) describes at length and with much intensity the adolescence of Eugene Gant. The original version was reconstructed and published as *O Lost* (2000). *Of Time and the River* (1935) was a sequel.

WOLFE, Tom (1931-) American novelist and journalist. With his contemporaries Joan *Didion and Hunter S. *Thompson, he was a pioneer of *New Journalism. His satirical first novel. *The Bonfire of the Vanities* (1987), a

sharply critical look at Ronald Reagan's America, traces the downfall of an ambitious Wall Street dealer. His 2004 novel *I Am Charlotte Simmons* deals with sexual promiscuity in a small American university.

WOLFF, Tobias (1945-) American writer. His first collection of stories, *Hunters in the Snow* (1982) established his characteristic subject of alienation in small-town America. *The Barracks Thief* (1984, novel) is set during the Vietnam War. His two volumes of autobiography are *This Boy's Life* (1989), describing his early adolescence, and *In Pharaoh's Army* (1994), an account of his experiences of service in Vietnam.

WOLLSTONECRAFT, Mary (1759-97) Writer and feminist, largely self-taught. She opened a school at Newington Green in 1784 with her sister Eliza and a friend, where she made the acquaintance of Richard *Price and other eminent Dissenters. After writing *Thoughts on the Education of Daughters* (1787), she spent some years writing reviews and translations for the radical publisher Joseph *Johnson, who published her fiction *Mary* (1788), her *A Vindication of the Rights of Men* (1790, an early reply to Edmund *Burke), and her *Vindication of the Rights of Woman* (1792). During these years she encountered leading members of Johnson's circle, including William *Godwin, Thomas *Holcroft, and Henry *Fuseli. In 1792 she went to Paris, where she met Gilbert *Imlay, an American writer, by whom she had a daughter. Wollstonecraft's 'View' of the French Revolution (1794) was followed by *Letters Written during a Short Residence in Sweden, Norway and Denmark* (1796). Imlay's neglect drove her to two suicide attempts; she reintroduced herself in 1796 to Godwin, and in 1797 she married him. She died shortly after the birth of her daughter, the future Mary *Shelley. Godwin published a memoir in 1798, edited her *Posthumous Works* (which included her unfinished novel *The *Wrongs of Woman*), and portrayed her in his novel *St Leon* (1799).

Wolsey, The Life and Death of Cardinal See CAVENDISH, GEORGE.

Woman in the Moon, The A prose play by John *Lyly, published 1597.

Woman in White, The A novel by Wilkie *Collins, published 1860, an early and influential example of the novel of *sensation. The novel's complex narrative strategy was among its innovations, combining diaries, documentary testimony, and legal evidence to give the dramatic twists of the story an air of solid reality. Walter Hartright encounters a mysterious woman dressed in white on a lonely road at midnight, and helps her to escape from pursuers. Working as a drawing master in the family of Mr Fairlie, a selfish hypochondriac, he falls in love with his niece Laura, who strikingly resembles the woman in white. She returns his love, but is engaged to Sir Percival Glyde, whom she marries. It comes to light that Sir Percival was responsible for the confinement of the woman in white, Anne Catherick, in an asylum, as she and her mother know a secret concerning Sir Percival, the revelation of which he is determined to prevent. Unable to obtain Laura's signature to the surrender of her money, Sir Percival and his friend Count Fosco contrive to get Laura confined in an asylum as Anne Catherick, while Anne Catherick, who dies, is buried as Laura Glyde. The scheme is uncovered by Marian Halcombe, Laura's half-sister, and Laura is rescued. Hartright takes Laura and Marian under his care, and discovers Sir Percival's secret (that he was born out of wedlock and has no right to the title). Sir Percival is burnt to death while tampering with a parish register. Fosco is forced to supply the information which restores Laura to her identity, and is killed by a member of an Italian secret society which he has betrayed.

Woman Killed with Kindness, A A domestic *tragedy by Thomas *Heywood, acted about 1603, printed 1607. Frankford, a country gentleman, is the husband of Anne, a 'perfect' wife. Frankford discovers the adultery of Anne and Wendoll, a guest to whom he has shown every kindness and hospitality, but instead of taking immediate vengeance on her, he determines to 'kill her even with kindness'. He sends her to live in comfort in a lonely manor house, only prohibiting her from seeing him or her children again. She dies from remorse, after having sent for Frankford to ask forgiveness on her deathbed and received it.

Woman's Prize, The, or *The Tamer Tamed* A *comedy by John *Fletcher, written 1609–11, printed 1647. It was expurgated for performance before Charles I and his queen in 1633, when it was given back to back with *Shakespeare's play, as also by the Royal Shakespeare Company in 2003. It shows the second marriage of Petruccio, from Shakespeare's The *Taming of the Shrew.

Woman Who Did, The *See* ALLEN, GRANT.

Women Beware Women A *tragedy by Thomas *Middleton, written c.1621, published 1657. Set in Florence, the action involves two interwoven plots. The sub-plot is concerned with the guilty love of Hippolito for his niece Isabella. Hippolito's sister Livia acts as go-between. The main plot is loosely based on the life of the historical Bianca Cappello, who became the mistress, and then the consort, of Francesco de' Medici (1541–87). In Middleton's version, she is at the opening of the play innocently but secretly married to the poor but honest young Leantio. The duke sees her at a window and falls in love with her. While Livia outwits Leantio's mother at chess (a scene invoked by T. S. *Eliot in The *Waste Land), the duke gains access to Bianca and seduces her. Both she and Leantio are consumed by the corruption of the court. Bianca becomes the duke's mistress: the duke, reproved by the cardinal, his brother, for his sin, contrives the death of Leantio. These crimes finally meet with retribution in a wholesale massacre of the characters, through the theatrical medium of a masque accompanied by poisoned incense. Bianca destroys herself by drinking from a poisoned cup.

Women in Love Novel by D. H. *Lawrence, published in New York, 1920, and London, 1921. The sisters Ursula and Gudrun Brangwen (who first appear in The *Rainbow, 1915) live in a small Midlands colliery town. Ursula is a teacher at the local school and Gudrun has just returned from art school in London. Ursula is in love with Rupert Birkin (a self-portrait of Lawrence), a school inspector involved in an unsatisfactory affair with Hermione Roddice, a literary hostess based on Lady Ottoline *Morrell). Gudrun meets Gerald Crich, son of the local colliery owner, and the two are drawn together as if by a powerful electrical force. His father is dying and he takes over management of the mine. Birkin breaks free from Hermione and hopes to find with Ursula the complete union between man and woman. Gerald suffers in his relationship with Gudrun, his mixture of violence and weakness arousing a destructive demon in her. Birkin offers him love and friendship to be based on a new intimacy between men, but Gerald is unable to accept. Ursula and Birkin are married and together with Gudrun and Gerald they take a trip to the Alps where they meet the sculptor Loerke, with whom Gudrun flirts. The relationship between Gudrun and Gerald becomes increasingly destructive until Gerald wanders off into the snow and dies.

WOOD, Anthony (1632–95) or, as he later called himself, Anthony à Wood. His treatise on the history of the University of Oxford was translated into Latin and edited (with alterations) by Dr John Fell and published as *Historia et Antiquitates Univ. Oxon.* (1674). Wood received much ill-acknowledged help from John *Aubrey. Wood published *Athenae Oxonienses* (1691–2), a biographical dictionary of Oxford writers and bishops, and was expelled from the university at the instance of Henry Hyde (1638–1709), for a libel which the work contained on his father Edward Hyde, the first earl of Clarendon (1609–74).

WOOD, Ellen (Mrs Henry Wood) (1814–87) Née Price, novelist and journalist. She was disabled as a girl by a spinal disorder that left her in poor health for the rest of her life. In 1836 she married Henry Wood, an unsuccessful banker, and she began to write fiction to help support her family. **East Lynne* (1861), her second novel, was a best-seller. Wood subsequently owned and edited the magazine the *Argosy*, and wrote nearly 40 novels, including *Mrs Halliburton's Troubles* (1862), *The Channings* (1862), and *The Shadow of Ashlydyat* (1863). *Lord Oakburn's Daughters* (1864), *Elster's Folly* (1866), and *Roland Yorke* (1869), with their ingenious plots about murders, thefts, and forgeries, numerous court scenes and well-planted clues, are forerunners of the modern *detective story. Conservative and Christian, Wood grounds her thrilling narratives in a firmly moral view of the world, in which vice is punished and character strengthened by adversities courageously endured. She is consistently sympathetic to the situation of women trapped in unsatisfactory marriages, without financial resources of their own, and she often used industrial and trade union problems—slumps, unemployment, strikes—in her novels. Many of her books were world best-sellers, widely read in America, and outstripping even Charles *Dickens in Australian sales.

WOODFORDE, Revd James (1740–1803) Diarist, rector of Weston Longeville, Norfolk, from 1774 until his death. He kept a daily diary, plain but vivid in style, for 43 years, from which large selections were eventually published as *The Diary of a Country Parson* (ed. J. Beresford, 5 vols, 1924–31). It covers the period of the American War of Independence and the French Revolution, but the life Woodforde describes is more concerned with local tradesmen, agriculture, squires, friends, sporting events, travels, prices, gossip, and crime.

Woodlanders, The A novel by Thomas *Hardy, published 1887. In Little Hintock, a Dorset village, live the native woodlanders, whose living depends upon trees, and a group of outsiders with whom their lives become entwined. Giles Winterbourne, who tends trees and travels in the autumn with his cider-press, loves and is betrothed to Grace Melbury, daughter of a well-to-do Hintock timber merchant. Giles suffers financial misfortune, and Grace's father brings the engagement to an end, and persuades his daughter to marry Edred Fitzpiers, an attractive young doctor. Meanwhile Marty South, a village girl who had always loved Giles, has to sell her splendid hair to provide for herself and her sick father. Fitzpiers is lured away from Grace by a wealthy widow, Felice Charmond. The hope of divorce brings Grace and the faithful Giles together again. But the hope is illusory, and when Fitzpiers returns from his travels with Mrs Charmond Grace flies to Giles's cottage in the woods. To protect her honour Giles, although ill, leaves his cottage and sleeps outside. Grace discovers his condition, drags him back into his hut, and fetches Fitzpiers to help, but despite their efforts Giles dies. The loving, faithful Marty meets Grace by Giles's deathbed, and together they regularly visit his burial-place. With Mrs Charmond's death Grace and Fitzpiers are reconciled, and Marty is left alone to tend Giles's grave.

Woodstock, or The Cavalier A novel by Walter *Scott, published 1826; set in the Civil War, it describes the escape from England of Charles II after the battle of Worcester. The work was written when Scott was oppressed by financial difficulty, his wife's death, and the serious illness of his beloved grandson. There are clear parallels between the situation of Sir Henry Lee, an old Cavalier, and himself.

WOOLER, T. J. (*c.*1796–1853) Publisher, editor, and radical reformer. He became the publisher of a number of radical and freethinking periodicals: *The Reasoner*, *The Republican*, and, most notably, the *Black Dwarf* (1817–24), a mixture of incendiary polemic and sharp satire. He was twice prosecuted for seditious libel.

WOOLF, Leonard (1880–1969) Writer, political commentator, and publisher. At Trinity College, Cambridge, he became a member of the *Apostles, a friend of Lytton *Strachey and E. M. *Forster, and was much influenced by the philosopher G. E. Moore (1873–1958). He entered the colonial Civil Service and in 1904 went to Ceylon (Sri Lanka). His novel, *The Village in* *the Jungle* (1913), reflects his profound anti-imperialist disquiet. Woolf returned to England on leave in 1911, and in 1912 resigned from his post to marry Virginia Stephen (*see* WOOLF, VIRGINIA). *The Wise Virgins* (1914) was his second and last novel. The Woolfs shared a close intellectual comradeship and a commitment to fiction in the form of the *Hogarth Press. He wrote on the Cooperative movement, socialism, imperialism, the League of Nations, and international affairs; the five volumes of his autobiography: *Sowing* (1960), *Growing* (1961), *Beginning Again* (1964), *Downhill All the Way* (1967), and *The Journey Not the Arrival Matters* (1969) together constitute a clear-sighted view of a life devoted to social progress and international understanding, and rich in intellectual and literary friendships.

WOOLF, Virginia (1882–1941) Writer and publisher, daughter of Sir Leslie *Stephen and his second wife Julia Duckworth (1846–95), born at Hyde Park Gate, Kensington, London, where she lived with her sister Vanessa (later the artist Vanessa *Bell) and her brothers until her father's death in 1904. The four Stephen children then moved to Bloomsbury, where they formed the nucleus of the *Bloomsbury Group. In 1905 Woolf began to write for the *Times Literary Supplement. In 1912 she married Leonard *Woolf; she had been working on her first novel, *The Voyage Out*, since 1908 and it was published in 1915. Woolf herself had meanwhile experienced several bouts of acute mental disturbance, brought on in part by her mother's death in 1895, and it was partly as therapy for her that she and Leonard founded, in 1917, the *Hogarth Press. Her second novel, *Night and Day* (1919), set in London, centres on Katharine Hilbery, granddaughter of a famous Victorian poet, whose restricted pursuits are contrasted with her friend Mary Datchet's involvement in the women's suffrage movement. *Jacob's Room* (1922), a novel which spasmodically evokes the life and death (in the First World War) of Jacob Flanders (clearly related to the death from typhoid of Woolf's elder brother Thoby in 1906), was recognized as a new development in the art of fiction; it was hailed by friends such as T. S. *Eliot and attacked by, John Middleton *Murry for its lack of plot. Shortly afterwards she published one of her important statements on modern fiction, 'Mr Bennett and Mrs Brown', which attacked the realism of Arnold *Bennett and advocated a more fluid and impressionistic approach to the problem of characterization and the representation of reality. From this time onwards

Woolf was regarded as one of the principal exponents of *modernism, and her subsequent major novels, *Mrs Dalloway* (1925), *To the Lighthouse* (1927), and *The *Waves* (1931), established her reputation. She also wrote *Orlando* (1928; filmed 1993), a fantastic biography inspired by her friend Vita *Sackville-West, which traces the history of the youthful, beautiful, and aristocratic Orlando through four centuries and both male and female manifestations; *Flush* (1933), a biography of Elizabeth Barrett *Browning's spaniel; *The Years* (1937); and her last work, *Between the Acts* (1941). It was shortly after finishing it, and before its publication, that Woolf drowned herself in the river Ouse, near her home at Rodmell, Sussex. Virginia Woolf is now acclaimed as one of the greatest novelists in the literary canon; many of her experimental techniques (such as the use of *free indirect discourse and *interior monologue) have been absorbed into mainstream fiction. She was also a literary critic, essayist, and journalist of distinction. *A *Room of one's Own* (1929) is a classic of the feminist movement; a sequel, *Three Guineas* (1938), articulates Woolf's view that patriarchal tyranny at home is intimately connected with tyranny abroad. Her critical essays were published in several collections, including *The Common Reader* (1925; 2nd series, 1932), and the posthumous *The Death of the Moth* (1942), *The Captain's Death Bed* (1950), and *Granite and Rainbow* (1958). Woolf was also a tireless letter writer and diarist. Her *Letters* (6 vols, 1975–80) are a dazzling evocation of a world of literary and social friendships and intrigues; her *Diary* (5 vols, 1977–84) is a unique record of the joys and pains of the creative process.

WOOLMAN, John (1720–72) American Quaker, itinerant preacher, and anti-slavery campaigner. His *Journal* (1774) records his spiritual life and humanitarian and social concerns. Charles *Lamb declared, 'Get the writings of John Woolman by heart, and love the early Quakers.'

WOOLNER, Thomas (1825–92) Poet and sculptor, one of the original *Pre-Raphaelite Brotherhood, who contributed to *The *Germ* two cantos of what was to become *My Beautiful Lady* (1863). He became a prosperous portrait sculptor, particularly with busts and statues of (among many others) Alfred *Tennyson, John Henry *Newman, Charles *Kingsley, and John Stuart *Mill. His other poems include the blank verse *Pygmalion* (1881). 'The Piping Shepherd', which appears as a frontispiece to Francis Turner *Palgrave's *Golden Treasury*, is by him.

WORDE, Wynkyn de (*fl.*1479–1535) Printer at Westminster and in London. He was probably William *Caxton's principal assistant until his death in 1492, whereupon de Worde succeeded to the printing business, moving it to Fleet Street in 1500. He printed large numbers of important vernacular works, including poems by *Chaucer, religious books, and grammars, which were highly in demand.

WORDSWORTH, Dorothy (1771–1855) Poet and diarist,the sister of William *Wordsworth. Dorothy settled with William in 1795, and from that time they lived together, through William's marriage until his death. They moved to Alfoxden in Somerset, to be near S. T. *Coleridge at Nether Stowey. Here in 1798, when she, William, and Coleridge walked and talked, as Coleridge wrote, 'as three persons with one soul', she began the *Alfoxden Journal*, of which only January–April 1798 remain. The *Grasmere Journal* covers the years 1800–3; her skill with words is evident in the precise descriptions both of the world about them and of the daily events of life in Dove Cottage.

Dorothy kept several other journals of travels and expeditions. In 1805 she finished *Recollections of a Tour Made in Scotland*. Her spirited accounts of an 'Excursion on the Banks of Ullswater' (1805) and 'An Excursion up Scawfell Pike' (1818) were both used by Wordsworth in his *Guide to the Lakes* (1823). A long *Journal of a Tour on the Continent 1820* was followed by a sprightly *Journal of a Second Tour in Scotland* (1822), and a *Journal of a Tour in the Isle of Man* (1828).

It is clear from passages in his notes and from certain of his poems (most notably, 'I wandered lonely as a cloud') that Wordsworth made use of his sister's journals. Coleridge seems to have used the Alfoxden journal for certain passages in *'Christabel'. In his 1933 biography, Dorothy's editor Ernest de Selincourt calls her 'probably . . . the most distinguished of English writers who never wrote a line for the general public'.

WORDSWORTH, William (1770–1850) English poet, born at Cockermouth, Cumbria. His mother died in 1778, his father in 1783, losses recorded in The *Prelude*, which describes the mixed joys and terrors of his boyhood with a peculiar intensity. In 1790 he went on a walking tour of France, the Alps, and Italy, and returned to France late in 1791, to spend a year there.

During this period he fell in love with the daughter of a surgeon at Blois, Annette Vallon, who bore him a daughter. This love affair is reflected in 'Vaudracour and Julia' (1820). After his return to England he published in 1793 two poems in heroic couplets, *An Evening Walk* and *Descriptive Sketches*, both conventional attempts at the *picturesque and the *sublime. In this year he also wrote (but did not publish) a *Letter to the Bishop of Llandaff* (Richard Watson) in support of the French Republic. England's declaration of war against France shocked him deeply, but the institution of the Terror marked the beginning of his disillusion with the French Revolution, a period of depression reflected in his verse drama *The Borderers* (1842). In 1795 he received a legacy of £900 from his friend Raisley Calvert to enable him to pursue his vocation as a poet; it also allowed him to be reunited with his sister Dorothy (*see* WORDSWORTH, DOROTHY); they settled first at Racedown in Dorset, then at Alfoxden in Somerset, to be near S. T. *Coleridge, whom Wordsworth had met in 1795. This was a period of intense creativity for both poets, which produced the *Lyrical Ballads* (1798), a landmark in the history of English *Romanticism (*see* ANCIENT MARINER; 'IDIOT BOY'; 'TINTERN ABBEY').

The winter of 1798-9 was spent in Goslar in Germany, where Wordsworth wrote the enigmatic *'Lucy' poems. In 1799 he and Dorothy settled in Dove Cottage, Grasmere; to the next year belong 'The Recluse', Book I (later *The *Excursion*), 'The Brothers', *'Michael', and many of the poems included in the 1800 edition of the *Lyrical Ballads* (which, with its provocative preface on *poetic diction, aroused much criticism). In 1802 Wordsworth and Dorothy visited Annette Vallon in France, and later that year William married Mary Hutchinson. In the same year he composed *'Resolution and Independence', and began his ode on *'Intimations of Immortality from Recollections of Early Childhood', both of which appeared in *Poems in Two Volumes* (1807), along with many of his most celebrated lyrics. To the same period belong the birth of five children, travels with Dorothy and Coleridge, and new friendships, notably with Walter *Scott, George Beaumont, and Thomas *De Quincey. Wordsworth's domestic happiness was overcast by the shipwreck and death of his sailor brother John in 1805 (which inspired several poems, including 'Elegiac Stanzas Suggested by a Picture of Peele Castle', 1807), the early deaths of two of his children (one of which inspired his sonnet *'Surprised by joy', 1815), and the physical deterioration of Coleridge, from whom he was for some time estranged, and with whom he was never entirely reconciled. But his productivity continued, and his popularity gradually increased. *The Excursion* was published in 1814, *The White Doe of Rylstone* and two volumes of *Miscellaneous Poems* in 1815, and **Peter Bell* and *The *Waggoner* in 1819. Wordsworth slowly settled into the role of patriotic, conservative public man, abandoning the radical politics and idealism of his youth. Much of the best of his later work was topographical, inspired by his love of travel. In 1843 he succeeded Robert *Southey as *poet laureate. He died at Rydal Mount, after the publication of a finally revised text of his works, 6 vols (1849–50), and *The Prelude* was published posthumously in 1850.

De Quincey wrote of Wordsworth in 1835, 'Up to 1820 the name of Wordsworth was trampled underfoot; from 1820 to 1830 it was militant; from 1830 to 1835 it has been triumphant.' Early attacks in the **Edinburgh Review* were followed by criticism and satire by the second generation of Romantics; Lord *Byron and P. B. *Shelley mocked him as 'simple' and 'dull', John *Keats distrusted what he called the *'egotistical sublime', and William *Hazlitt, and later Robert *Browning, deplored him as 'The Lost Leader', who had abandoned his early radical faith. But these doubts were counterbalanced by the enormous and lasting popularity of much of his work, which was regarded by writers such as Matthew *Arnold and John Stuart *Mill with almost religious veneration, as an expression in an age of doubt of the transcendent in nature and the good in man. A great innovator, his notions of the creative imagination and of the centrality of poetic selfhood were essential to the development of English *Romanticism.

world literature in English *See* POSTCO-LONIAL LITERATURE.

WOTTON, Sir Henry (1568–1639) Author and ambassador. *James I appointed him ambassador to Venice (1604–21), a role he defined as 'an honest man, sent to lie abroad for the good of his country'. *Reliquiae Wottonianae* (1651; enlarged edns 1672, 1685) collects his poetical and other writings including the 'Character of a Happy Life' and 'You meaner beauties of the night' (honouring James I's daughter Elizabeth). His life was written by his friend Izaak *Walton (1651).

'Wreck of the Deutschland, The' A poem by Gerard Manley *Hopkins, occasioned

by the shipwreck in December 1875 of a German transatlantic steamer off the Kentish coast. Among the dead were five Franciscan sisters from Westphalia; the poem identifies them as victims of Bismarck's anti-Catholic 'Falk' laws, which forced many into exile. The text experiments with a new metric Hopkins 'long had haunting [his] ear', *sprung rhythm. *The Month*, a Jesuit journal, declined to publish the poem in 1876; Robert *Bridges included it in the 1918 edition of Hopkins's poetry, and it is now recognized as central in Hopkins's work.

WREN, P. C. (Percival Christopher) (1875–1941) Novelist. *Beau Geste* (1924; filmed 1926, 1939, and 1966), one of his many Foreign Legion novels, is a romantic adventure story which became a best-seller. *Beau Sabreur* (1926), *Beau Ideal* (1928), and others followed.

WRIGHT, David (1920–94) Poet, born in Johannesburg, who lost his hearing at the age of 7. His volumes of poetry include *Poems* (1949), which appeared in James Meary Tambimuttu's **Poetry London* imprint. He also published translations of **Beowulf* (1957) and *The *Canterbury Tales* (1964), and *Deafness: A Personal Account* (1969).

WRIGHT, Judith (1915–2000) Australian poet, born in Armidale, New South Wales, to a wealthy pastoral family. Her first book, *The Moving Image* (1946) was followed by more than a dozen volumes (see *Collected Poems*, 1994). Wright's poems are intensely imagined and beautifully crafted, concerned with human relationships (as in 'Woman to Man'), rural and wild landscapes ('South of my Days'), and the violence of colonial history ('Nigger's Leap'). An original and impassioned thinker, from the 1960s Wright immersed herself in struggles for conservation and for a treaty with Indigenous Australians, chronicled in Veronica Brady's biography, *South of my Days* (1998).

WRIGHT, Kit (1944–) Poet and children's writer, praised as a master of light verse, for his comic observations of human behaviour, and his offbeat wit. His poems reveal a fascination with English eccentricity, and include compassionate portraits of characters who are often lost, failed, or doubting their sanity. *The Bear Looked over the Mountain* (1977) was followed by *Bump-Starting the Hearse* (1983), which includes 'The Day Room', a moving sequence on life in a psychiatric ward, and *Short Afternoons* (1989). *Hoping It Might Be So: Poems 1974–2000* was published in 2000. Wright's children's books include *Hot Dogs and Other Poems* (1982) and *Cat among the Pigeons* (1987).

WRIGHT, Richard (1908–60) African American writer. He joined the Communist Party in the 1930s, but left in the 1940s, as he records in *American Hunger* (1977). *Uncle Tom's Children* (1938) brought him recognition with stories of Southern racism. His first novel *Native Son* (1940), based on an actual case, describes the killing of a white girl in Chicago by her African American driver and the subsequent trial. Estranged from American society by its racism and by being dogged by the FBI, Wright moved to Paris in 1947, where he met James *Baldwin. He continued writing with his *existential novel *The Outsider* (1953). *The Colour Curtain* (1956) and *White Man, Listen!* (1957) both reported on third-world politics and racism in the post-war world.

WRIGHT, Sydney Fowler (1874–1965) British writer of *scientific romances comparable with, and often written in antagonism to, those of H. G. *Wells. *Deluge* (1928) describes a flooded England. *The New Gods Lead* (1932) collected some of his *dystopian stories.

Wrongs of Woman, The, or *Maria* A fiction by Mary *Wollstonecraft, published posthumously in 1798. The (semi-autobiographical) narrative tells of Maria, who flees to France with her infant daughter to escape her dissolute husband, but is intercepted en route and confined on his instruction in a madhouse. Here she falls in love with fellow prisoner Darnford, and bonds with her female janitor, also a victim of patriarchy. The fiction is a revolutionary defence of a woman's right to assert her sexuality.

'Wulf and Eadwacer' An Old English poem from the *Exeter Book. Its theme is thought to be the separation of lovers. Modern translations include a version by Craig *Raine in *Rich* (1984).

WULFSTAN (d. 1023) Archbishop of York, author of homilies in English including the famous 'Address of the Wolf to the English', *Sermo Lupi ad Anglos*, in which he describes the desolation brought about by the Danish raids and castigates the demoralization of the people. He had contacts with *Ælfric, with whom he shares a distinction as a writer of rhythmical, *alliterative prose.

Wuthering Heights Emily *Brontë's only novel, published 1847. The story begins with the journal of Lockwood, temporary tenant of Thrushcross Grange, who stumbles unsuspecting into the violent world of Wuthering Heights, home of his landlord Heathcliff. The narration is taken up by the housekeeper, Nelly Dean, who had witnessed the interlocked destinies of the original owners of the Heights, the Earnshaw family, and of the Grange, the Linton family. Events are set in motion by the arrival at the Heights of Heathcliff, picked up as a waif in the streets of Liverpool by the elder Earnshaw, who brings him home to rear as one of his own children. Bullied and humiliated after Earnshaw's death by his son Hindley, Heathcliff's passionate nature finds its complement in Earnshaw's daughter Catherine. Their childhood collusions develop into an increasingly intense though vexed attachment, but Heathcliff, overhearing Catherine tell Nelly that she cannot marry him because it would degrade her, and failing to stay to hear her declare her passion for him, leaves the house. He returns three years later, mysteriously enriched, to find Catherine married to the gentlemanly Edgar Linton. Heathcliff is welcomed by Hindley, now widowed with a son, Hareton, and a hardened drinker and gambler. Heathcliff marries Edgar's sister Isabella and cruelly ill-treats her, hastens Catherine's death by his passion as she is about to give birth to a daughter, Cathy, and brings Hindley and his son Hareton under his power, brutalizing Hareton in revenge for Hindley's treatment of himself as a child. Edgar Linton dies, after trying to prevent a friendship between Cathy and Heathcliff's feeble son Linton; Heathcliff forces a marriage between them in order to secure the Linton property. Linton also dies, and an affection springs up between Cathy, an unwilling prisoner at the Heights, and the ignorant Hareton, whom she attempts to educate. Heathcliff now longs for the death that will reunite him with Catherine; it is implied that the contrasting worlds represented by the Heights and the Grange will be united in the marriage of Cathy and Hareton.

The story is told in a series of brilliantly handled flashbacks and time shifts, with acute evocation of place, and a highly original handling of *Gothic and Romantic elements.

WYATT, Sir Thomas (*c.*1503–1542) Poet. He held various diplomatic posts in the service of *Henry VIII. His first visit to Italy in 1527 probably stimulated him to translate and imitate the poems of *Petrarch. In the same year he made a version of a *Plutarch essay, based on the Latin translation of Guillaume Budé (1467-1540), *The Quiet of Mind*, which he dedicated to the queen (Catherine of Aragon) whom the king was in process of divorcing. Wyatt was certainly closely acquainted with Henry VIII's next bride, Anne Boleyn before her marriage and, according to three 16th-century accounts, confessed to the king that she had been his mistress and was not fit to be a royal consort. If true, this frankness may explain why Wyatt was not executed, along with Anne's alleged lovers, in 1536, suffering only a period of imprisonment in the Tower. In 1537-9 he held the important post of ambassador to Charles V's court in Spain. He celebrated his departure from Spain, June 1539, in the epigram 'Tagus, farewell'. In 1540 the tide of Wyatt's fortunes turned, with the execution of his friend and patron Thomas Cromwell (c.1485-1540), which is probably referred to in the sonnet (based on Petrarch) 'The pillar perished is whereto I lent'. Wyatt himself was arrested, on charges of treason, in January 1541; though released two months later he never fully regained favour.

Wyatt's poetry is beset by problems in three main areas; authorship, biographical relevance, and artistic aims. Though the canon of his poems is generally taken to include all the poems in the Egerton Manuscript, even this cannot be proved with certainty. The authenticated poems and translations include *sonnets, *rondeaux, *epigrams, epistolary satires, lute songs, and a version in *terza rima* of the seven Penitential *Psalms. Richard *Tottel in his *Songs and Sonnets* (1557) adapted many of Wyatt's poems to conventional iambic stress, including 'They flee from me that sometime did me seek'. Modern critical estimates of Wyatt's poetry have varied widely. C. S. *Lewis called him 'the father of the Drab Age', but others have viewed him as a complex and original writer whose love poems anticipate those of *Donne.

WYCHERLEY, William (1641-1715) Playwright. His first play, *Love in a Wood, or St James's Park*, a comedy of intrigue set in St James's Park, was probably acted in 1671, and published in 1672; it was followed by *The *Gentleman Dancing-Master*, probably acted 1671, published 1673; *The *Country Wife* published and probably acted 1675; and *The *Plain-Dealer*, probably acted 1676, published 1677. His *Miscellany Poems* (1704) led to a friendship with Alexander *Pope, who revised many of his writings. His *Posthumous Works* appeared in 1728.

Wycherley's plays are admired for their acute social criticism, particularly of sexual morality and the marriage conventions. *See* RESTORATION.

WYCLIF, John (d. 1384) Theologian and controversialist. He was studying theology by c.1362-3 and became rector of Lutterworth, Leicestershire, in 1374. Wyclif's views regarding the authority of the pope and the temporal possessions of the church aroused suspicion in 1377, when Gregory XI issued five bulls condemning his views. At the Blackfriars Council of 1382, ten arguments were condemned as heretical, and fourteen as erroneous, the issues concerned ranging from the church's temporalities and the powers of the pope to the sacraments of confession and the Eucharist. Wyclif was not named in these proceedings, but the growing controversy had already led to his retirement to Lutterworth in 1381, where he remained until his death. Wyclif's influence on English religious thought of this period is partly reflected in a significant body of writings in English directly influenced or at least inspired by his ideas. This includes two versions of the *Bible in English, a substantial sermon cycle, many polemical works and the *Testimony of William Thorpe*, which depicts the interrogation of a suspected Wycliffite by Thomas Arundel, archbishop of Canterbury. *See also* LOLLARDS.

WYLIE, Elinor (1885-1928) Née Hoyt, American writer and painter. Her works include *The Orphan Angel* (1926, UK title *Mortal Image*), a fantasy-continuation of the life of P. B. *Shelley

WYNDHAM, John (1903-69) The best-known pseudonym of John Wyndham Parkes Lucas Beynon Harris, *science fiction writer, adopted for *The Day of the Triffids* (1951), which introduced science fiction to a mass British audience. He preferred the description 'logical fantasy' for his own works, which also included *The Kraken Wakes* (1953), *The Chrysalids* (1955), *The Midwich Cuckoos* (1957), and *Chocky* (1968). Several of his works were filmed; most are distinguished by the contrast between a comfortable English background and the sudden invasion of catastrophe. The blindness which strikes in *Triffids*, for instance, lays humanity open to predatory mobile carnivorous plants until then safely domesticated for their oil. The novella 'Consider her Ways' (1956) postulates a plague which wipes out men, leaving

w

women to develop a social structure based upon ant-like 'castes'.

Wynnere and Wastour An alliterative dream-poem of *c*.500 lines in a north-west Midland dialect, certainly written after 1352, discussing contemporary economic problems. The narrator sees in a dream two armies drawn up on the plain: with Winner (the gainer of wealth in society) are the pope and the traditionally avaricious friars; with Waster (the prodigal spender) are the nobility and the soldiery. The poem has often been compared to *Piers Plowman*.

Xanadu In S. T. *Coleridge's *'Kubla Khan', the place where the khan decreed 'a stately pleasure-dome'.

XAVIER, St Francis (1506–52) A Spaniard, one of the founders of the Society of Jesus, and a famous missionary in the Far East.

XENOPHON (*c.*428–354 BC) Athenian writer and associate of *Socrates. His many works include *Anabasis* (the march up country), the first-hand story of Greek mercenaries in a failed rebellion; *Hellenica*, a continuation of *Thucy-dides' history; *Cyropaedia* (the education of Cyrus), a work of edifying fiction, describing the formation of a perfect ruler, the Persian King Cyrus the Great; and a group of Socratic memoirs: *Apology*, supposed to have been spoken by Socrates at his trial, *Memorabilia*, which relates anecdotes of Socrates' conversation, and *Symposium*, which unlike *Plato's text of that name shows Socrates giving practical advice. An English translation of *Cyropaedia* was published in 1554 by William Barker (*fl.*1540–76), and *Memoirs of Socrates* by Sarah *Fielding (1762).

YARBRO, Chelsea Quin (1942-) American writer, born in Berkeley, California; author of *Hotel Transylvania* (1978), first of a series featuring Saint-Germain, an immortal vampire, ranging from ancient Rome to modern America. *Time of the Fourth Horseman* (1976) is a *science fiction novel about a macabre experiment in population control.

YATES, Dornford (1885-1960) Pseudonym of Cecil William Mercer, novelist and short story writer. His books featuring Berry Pleydell and his family include *The Brother of Daphne* (1914), *Berry and Co.* (1920), and *The House that Berry Built* (1945). Both these and his nine Chandos thrillers (including *Blind Corner*, 1927) reflect a world of wealth and idleness and were immensely popular between the wars.

YEARSLEY, Ann (1752-1806) Née Cromartie, poet, who began writing while working as a dairywoman. In 1784 Hannah *More, with Elizabeth *Montagu, arranged the publication of Yearsley's *Poems, on Several Occasions* (1785). As a supposed curiosity of literary *primitivism, 'Lactilla' provoked much interest, and the book's profits were invested by More on Yearsley's behalf. Yearsley furiously rejected this arrangement, denouncing More in an 'Autobiographical Narrative' attached to the fourth edition of the *Poems*. Under different *patronage Yearsley produced *Poems on Various Subjects* (1787); a *Poem on the Inhumanity of the Slave Trade* (1788); a tragedy, *Earl Goodwin* (1791), a novel, *The Royal Captives* (1795), and some final poems, *The Rural Lyre* (1796). From 1793 she ran a *circulating library.

Yeast: A Problem A novel by Charles *Kingsley, published in **Fraser's Magazine* 1848, in volume form in 1851. The first of Kingsley's novels, *Yeast* deals with social and religious problems of the day (the miserable conditions of the rustic labourer, the Game Laws, and Tractarianism: *see* OXFORD MOVEMENT), largely by means of dialogues between the hero and other characters.

YEATS, William Butler (1865-1939) Poet, dramatist, essayist, autobiographer, and dominating figure of the *Irish Revival. The eldest son of J. B. Yeats and brother of Jack Yeats, both painters, he studied at the Dublin Metropolitan School of Art, where with his fellow student G. W. *Russell (Æ) he developed an interest in mystical religion and the supernatural. At 21 he abandoned art in favour of literature, writing the novels *John Sherman and Dhoya* (published pseudonymously in 1891) and editing *The Poems of William Blake* (1893), *The Works of William Blake* (with F. J. Ellis, 3 vols, 1893), and *Poems of ' Spenser* (1906). Founding an Irish Literary Society in London in 1891 and another in Dublin in 1892, he applied himself to the creation of an Irish national theatre, an objective which, with the help of Lady *Gregory and others, was partly realized in 1899 when his play *The Countess Cathleen* (1892) was acted in Dublin. The English actors engaged by the *Irish Literary Theatre gave way to an Irish amateur company, which produced his and Gregory's incendiary nationalist prose play *Cathleen ni Houlihan* in 1902. This Irish National Theatre Company then acquired the Dublin building which became the *Abbey Theatre in 1904. Yeats's early interest in the lore of the countryside resulted in the anthology *Fairy and Folk Tales of the Irish Peasantry* (1888) and *The Celtic Twilight* (1893). Associated mystical concerns are explored in the short fictions of *The Secret Rose* (1897). Mythological and faery themes, along with delicate evocations of the weather, topography, and place-names of the west of Ireland, characterize *The Wanderings of Oisin and Other Poems* (1889), *The Countess Kathleen and Various Legends and Lyrics* (1892), and *The Wind among the Reeds* (1899). Yeats's 19th-century poems at once dramatize and ironize the appeal of escape from the burdens of modern living, many of them exploring his hopeless love for the beautiful nationalist activist Maud Gonne. Subsequent collections use an increasingly colloquial and socialized idiom: *In the Seven Woods* (1903), *The Green Helmet and Other Poems* (1910) and the laconic and disenchanted *Responsibilities* (1914). The Easter Rising of 1916 restored his faith in the heroic character of his country and produced 'Easter 1916', his first fully modern lyric masterpiece. In 1917 he published *The Wild Swans at Coole* and married George Hyde-Lees (1892–1968), a young Englishwoman who on their honeymoon attempted automatic writing, an event that exercised a profound effect on his life and work. His wife's 'communicators' provided him with the philosophical 'system' set out in *A Vision* (1925) and exploited in some of the poems in *Michael Robartes and the Dancer* (1921), and in *The Tower* (1928) and *The Winding Stair and Other Poems* (1933), notable for their symbolically freighted meditative style. *Parnell's Funeral and Other Poems* (1935), *New Poems* (1938), and the posthumously published *Last Poems* (1939) explore a variety of modes. Yeats served as a senator of the Irish Free State from 1922 to 1928, and in 1923 received the *Nobel Prize for Literature. He developed an increasingly adversarial relationship with Ireland as the country grew more theocratic in the 1930s. Yeats's dramatic output, which includes five plays in which he develops the character of *Cuchulain as a tragic alter ego, has slowly grown in critical stature. One of the Cuchulain cycle, *At the Hawk's Well* (performed 1916; pub. 1917), is the first example of *Nōh drama in English. Some of Yeats's major critical writings are collected in *Essays and Introductions* (1961), while the memoirs he published in his lifetime were brought together as *Autobiographies* in 1955.

yellowbacks Cheap (usually costing 2*s*, or 2*s*. 6*d*.) editions of novels, so called from being bound in yellow boards. First produced in the 1850s, they were the ordinary 'railway novels' of the 1870s and 1880s.

Yellow Book (1894–7) An illustrated journal devoted to literature and art, startling in its time for being bound as a book with bright yellow covers. Published and promoted by John *Lane and edited by Henry Harland, with Aubrey *Beardsley initially as art editor, it was controversial from its first issue (which included Max *Beerbohm's essay 'A Defence of Cosmetics'). Writers and artists published included Henry *James, Robert *Gissing, John *Davidson, Ernest *Dowson, Ella *Dixon, Arnold *Bennett, Aubrey

*Beardsley, Walter Sickert (1860–1942), and Wilson Steer (1860–1942).

YOLEN, Jane (1939–) American author and editor of numerous books of *fantasy and *science fiction for children and adults; she often draws on folklore and fairy-tales. *Briar Rose* (1992) uses the traditional tale to reflect the narrator's experiences during the Second World War.

YONGE, Charlotte M. (Mary) (1823–1901) Novelist, whose writing is markedly influenced by her mentor John *Keble, one of the founders of the *Oxford Movement. Yonge published over 150 works, including novels, historical, educational, and religious textbooks, short stories of village life, a life of the prince consort (1890), and many children's books, and edited magazines including the *Monthly Packet* (1851–99). Her novels, which include the *Tractarian *The *Heir of Redclyffe* (1853), *Countess Kate* (1852), and *Hopes and Fears* (1860), were often interlinked family sagas advocating a life of submission and duty, primarily designed for young female readers. Some, notably *The Daisy Chain, or Aspirations* (1856), are *crossover books, appealing to both adult and young readers. Her historical novel for children *The Little Duke* (1854) inspired Mark *Twain's *The Prince and the Pauper* (1881). She edited magazines including the *Monthly Packet* (1851–99) and *The Monthly Paper of Sunday Teaching* (1860–75). Her pamphlet *What Books to Lend and What to Give* (1887) is one of the earliest critical works on children's literature. The Charlotte Mary Yonge Fellowship has an exhaustive website including an annotated bibliography.

(⊕) SEE WEB LINKS
• The Charlotte Mary Yonge Fellowship

Yorick (1) in Shakespeare's *Hamlet* (V. i), the king's jester, whose skull the grave-diggers throw up when digging Ophelia's grave; (2) in Laurence Sterne's *Tristram Shandy*, 'the lively, witty, sensible, and heedless parson', of Danish extraction, and probably a descendant of Hamlet's Yorick. Sterne adopted 'Yorick' as a pseudonym in his *Sentimental Journey* and entitled his own homilies *The Sermons of Mr Yorick*, first published in 1760.

Yorkshire Tragedy, A A brief but powerful play published in 1608, stated in the title to be by *Shakespeare and to have been acted by the King's Men as part of an otherwise unknown *Four Plays in One*, but internal evidence makes it extremely improbable that Shakespeare had any part in its authorship. It is probably by

Thomas *Middleton. The play is based on a pamphlet, *Two Most Unnatural and Bloody Murders* (1605) describing actual murders committed in that year. George *Wilkins's play *The Miseries of Enforced Marriage* (1607) is also based on the case.

YOUNG, Andrew (1885–1971) Scottish poet and clergyman. In 1910 his father paid for the publication of his *Songs of Night*, the first of many slim volumes of poetry. The first *Collected Poems* appeared in 1936 and the verse play *Nicodemus* in 1937. *The Green Man* (1947) is sometimes considered his best collection. In 1952 he published a long, disturbing poem, 'Into Hades', which was later combined with the visionary 'A Traveller in Time' to create *Out of the World and Back* (1958). His spare line, sharp specific imagery, quiet concision, and skill with conceit have been much admired; he acknowledged a particular debt to Thomas *Hardy, and to George *Crabbe and George *Herbert. *The Poetical Works* (1985) is edited by his daughter.

YOUNG, Edward (1683–1765) Poet and clergyman, whose early works include the tragedies *Busiris* (1719) and *The Revenge* (1721), both produced at Drury Lane. In 1725–8 he published a series of verse satires on the 'Love of Fame' under the title *The Universal Passion*. His most celebrated poem was *The Complaint, or *Night Thoughts on Life, Death and Immortality* (1742–5). *The Brothers*, a tragedy written decades earlier, was performed in 1753. Young's essay *Conjectures on Original Composition* (1759), addressed to his close friend Samuel *Richardson, marked an important cultural shift towards an emphasis on originality and genius.

YOUNG, Francis Brett (1884–1954) Novelist, short story writer, and poet; he served during the First World War in East Africa. He is remembered largely for his best-selling novels of the West Midlands, which include *Portrait of Clare* (1927) and *My Brother Jonathan* (1928), but he also wrote novels based on his African experiences, including *Jim Redlake* (1930) and *They Seek a Country* (1937). *Poems 1916–1918* (1919) was written during convalescence in Africa, and *The Island* (1944) is a verse history of England, employing the verse forms of succeeding periods in strict chronological sequence.

YOUNG, Gavin (1928–2001) Welsh travel writer. He met Wilfred *Thesiger in Iraq, who took him to visit the Marsh Arabs, with whom he stayed for two years. He then spent two years in south-western Arabia, before moving in 1956 to North Africa, where he worked for Radio Maroc. Young became foreign correspondent of the *Observer* in 1960. His books include *Slow Boats to China* (1981), and *In Search of Conrad* (1991; *see* CONRAD, JOSEPH). *A Wavering Grace* (1997) follows the fortunes of a Vietnamese family whom he befriended during the war.

young adult literature An area of 'children's' literature addressed to the adolescent/ teenage market. Originating in the USA, they were originally greeted sceptically in the UK; however, since the 1970s, books for the 13–18 age-range have dominated the juvenile market. Initially restricted by a supposed need for balance and resolution, and caution about content, young adult (YA) novels have pushed back the boundaries of what is acceptable in technique (Aidan *Chambers) and content (Judy *Blume, Robert *Cormier, and Melvin *Burgess). *Salinger's *The Catcher in the Rye* (1951) inspired thousands of 'problem' novels: notable exponents have been Paul Zindel (*The Pigman*, 1968), Cynthia Voight (*Homecoming*, 1981), and Jacqueline *Wilson. While many commercial *series such as 'Point Horror' are designed for the YA market, many strong *crossover novels, including those by Philip *Pullman, have also originated there.

Ywain and Gawain A northern *romance from the first half of the 14th century of 4,032 lines in short couplets, surviving in a single manuscript. The poem is a translation (with variations) from the 6,818 lines of *Yvain* by *Chrétien de Troyes. The translation has elements in common with other versions of the story (such as the Welsh *Owein*). Ywain kills the knight of a castle and, aided by her serving-lady Lunet, marries his widow Alundyne. Gawain persuades him to abandon his lady and go in search of adventure, assisted by a lion. The two knights have many adventures, eventually fighting each other incognito; but they recognize each other and are reconciled. Ywain is reconciled to Alundyne, again by the skills of Lunet.

y

Z

ZAMIATIN, Evgenii Ivanovich (1884–1937) Russian writer, who joined the Bolshevik Party in 1905 and was almost immediately arrested and exiled. After the October Revolution of 1917, Zamiatin produced a steady flow of stories, among the best of which are 'The North' (1918), 'The Cave' (1920), 'Mamai' (1920), 'The Yawl' (1928), and 'The Flood' (1929), in which his major themes, the cult of the primitive and condemnation of the city, appear. He also edited collections by H. G. *Wells, George Bernard *Shaw, Jack *London, and O. *Henry. He greatly admired Wells and his 'social-fantastic novels', especially *The Time Machine*, which influenced his dystopian satire *We* (1920). Suppressed in Russia (until 1988), it appeared first in English translation in 1924. Its influence on *Nineteen Eighty-Four* was acknowledged by George *Orwell. Vilified for the novel in his homeland, Zamiatin was allowed to leave in November 1931, settling and dying in Paris.

ZANGWILL, Israel (1864–1926) Novelist, born in London of Russian and Polish immigrant parents. The popular novel *Children of the Ghetto* (1892) established his reputation through its realistic and sympathetically critical portrayal of London's poor Jews. *Ghetto Tragedies* (1893), *Ghetto Comedies* (1907), and *The King of Schnorrers* (1894), a *jeu d'esprit*, contain vignettes of Jewish life. The historical *Dreamers of the Ghetto* (1898) testifies both to Judaism's inner strength and to its role in civilization. *The War for the World* (1916) and *The Voice of Jerusalem* (1920) combine apologia with polemic. His plays are vehicles for ideas, notably *The Melting Pot* (1909), which coined the phrase.

Zastrozzi *See* SHELLEY, PERCY.

Zeitgeist [German, 'time-spirit'] The word signifies the prevailing or defining intellectual or cultural climate of an era. Its first recorded use in English was by Matthew *Arnold.

Zeluco A novel by John *Moore, published 1786, which 'traces the windings of vice' through the life of a wholly wicked man.

ZEPHANIAH, Benjamin (1958–) Poet and playwright; he came to public attention as a *performance poet with the anti-racist demonstrations of the late 1970s and early 1980s. *Job Rocking* (pub. 1989) is recognized as Britain's first rap play. In 1991 he co-wrote *Dread Poets Society*, a BBC-TV play, in which he played himself in a fictional encounter with P. B. *Shelley, Mary *Shelley, and Lord *Byron. After *Streetwise* (1990), he stopped writing for the stage on the grounds that most theatre did not reach ethnic minorities or the most disadvantaged communities. Collections of poetry include *City Psalms* (1992) *Too Black, Too Strong* (2001); and collections for children. Novels for teenagers include *Face* (1999) and *Teacher's Dead* (2007).

zeugma A figure of speech by which a single word is made to refer to two or more words in a sentence, when properly applying literally to only one of them; e.g. 'See Pan with flocks, with fruits Pomona crowned'. *See also* SYLLEPSIS.

Zeus *See* JUPITER.

Zofloya A novel by Charlotte *Dacre, published 1806. A *Gothic tale of criminality and sexual misconduct depicting the liaison between the callous *femme fatale* Victoria, set a bad example by her flighty mother, and the sexually magnetic and diabolical Moor, Zofloya, to whom she willingly surrenders her soul.

ZOLA, Émile (1840–1902) French novelist and leading figure of the *naturalist movement. Zola was influenced by *realist writers such as *Balzac, and by the scientific doctrines of positivism and determinism formulated by Hippolyte Taine. He saw the novel as a laboratory in which the ingredients dictating human behaviour—Taine's famous trilogy of race, milieu, and moment—could be combined and tested. His first naturalist novel, *Thérèse Raquin* (1867), was followed by *La Fortune des Rougon* (*The Fortune of the Rougons*) (1871) beginning a twenty-novel cycle. *Les Rougon–Macquart* chronicles the activities of the Rougons and the Macquarts, two branches of a family whose conduct is conditioned through several generations by environment and inherited characteristics; it includes. *Germinal* (1885); *La Terre* (1887: *The Earth*); *La Bête humaine* (1890: *The Human Beast*); *La Débâcle* (1892), on the catastrophe of the Franco-Prussian War; and concludes with *Le Docteur Pascal* (1893). The later trilogy *Les Trois Villes* (*The Three Cities*)—*Lourdes* (1894), *Rome* (1896), *Paris* (1898)—examines the claims of the religious and social organizations of the day to minister to human needs. The novels of his final work, *Les Quatre Évangiles* (*The Four Gospels*)—*Fécondité* (1899: *Fertility*), *Travail* (1901: *Work*), *Vérité* (1903: *Truth*), and the unfinished *Justice*—are optimistic presentations of social ideals. *Vérité* refers to the Dreyfus case in which Zola intervened, notably in 'J'accuse' ('I Accuse'), his letter to the newspaper *L'Aurore*. To avoid the sentence of imprisonment for libel that followed its publication, he spent eleven months in exile in England (1898-9), where, a decade earlier, Henry *Vizetelly had been found guilty of charges of obscenity for publishing his large-scale translation of Zola, totalling eighteen volumes between 1884 and 1888.

ZUKOFSKY, Louis (1904–78) American poet. In 1931 with Ezra *Pound's sponsorship he edited the 'Objectivists' issue of *Poetry*, Chicago, followed in 1932 by *An 'Objectivists' Anthology*, featuring among others Carl Rakosi (1903–2004), George Oppen, and Basil *Bunting. Zukofsky's lyrics, collected in the *Complete Short Poetry* (1991), are vividly textual, often witty, always stylish. The interpretative drive within Objectivism, a movement which presented poems as objects, differentiated it from *imagism's lyric base. It is fully explored in Zukofsky's *modernist long poem *A*, written over 45 years in 24 categorical parts. *Bottom: On Shakespeare* (1963) combines Zukofsky's tribute to *Shakespeare with a running meditation on Western culture. *See also* WILLIAMS, W. C.

Zuleika Dobson Max *Beerbohm's only novel, published in 1911. Zuleika is a mesmerizing *femme fatale* who pays a fatal visit to her grandfather, the warden of Judas College, Oxford, during the Eights Week regatta. All the young men fall madly in love with her and, when rejected, they rush 'like lemmings' into the river and drown themselves.

Z

Appendix 1. Chronology

Date	Literary works	Historical events
*c.*1000	Four surviving MSS of Anglo-Saxon poetry: Vercelli, Exeter, Cædmon, and *Beowulf*	
		Norman Conquest 1066
		Doomsday survey 1086
*c.*1155	Wace, *Roman de Brut*	
		Thomas Becket murdered 1170
*c.*1200	*The Owl and the Nightingale*	
*c.*1205?	Laȝamon, *Brut*	
		Magna Carta signed 1215
*c.*1230	*Ancrene Wisse* (*Ancrene Riwle*)	
		Jews expelled from England 1290
*c.*1307–21	Dante, *Divina commedia*	
1314	*King Alisaunder; Sir Orfeo*	
		Hundred Years War begins 1337
		First outbreak of plague in Britain 1348
*c.*1350–2	Boccaccio, *Decameron*	
*c.*1367–70	Langland, *Piers Plowman* (A-text; B-text *c.*1377–9; C-text *c.*1385–6)	
		Peasants' Revolt 1381
*c.*1385	Chaucer, *Troilus and Criseyde*	
*c.*1387–1400	Chaucer, *The Canterbury Tales*	
*c.*1400	Sole surviving MS (Cotton Nero A x) of *Sir Gawain and the Green Knight, Pearl, Cleanness,* and *Patience*	
		Henry V 1413
		Battle of Agincourt 1415
		Wars of the Roses 1455–85
1473–4	Caxton, *Recuyell of the Historyes of Troye*	
		Luther's 1517 Wittenberg theses
		Henry VIII marries Anne Boleyn and breaks from Rome 1533
1535	Coverdale's Bible (first pub. probably Zürich)	
		Dissolution of the monasteries (1536–9)
1539	The Great Bible	
		Copernicus (d. 1543), *De Revolutionibus*

Date	Literary works	Historical events
1549	Cranmer, *Book of Common Prayer*	
		Mary I (–1558)1553
1557	Tottel and Grimald, *Songs and Sonnets* (*Tottel's Miscellany*)	
		English lose Calais; **Elizabeth I** (–1603)1558
1563	Foxe, *Acts and Monuments* ('Book of Martyrs')	
		William Shakespeare b.; Hawkins's first voyage opens slave trade 1564
1577	Holinshed, *Chronicles*	Drake's circumnavigation of the globe (1577–1580)
		Virginia colonized by W. Ralegh 1585
		Mary Queen of Scots executed 1587
c.1587	Kyd, *The Spanish Tragedy*	
		Defeat of Spanish Armada 1588
1590	Marlowe, *Tamburlaine*; Sidney (d. 1586), *Arcadia* (revised version); Spenser, *Faerie Queene*, i–iii (iv–vi, 1596)	Plague closes theatres for two years 1592–4.
1593	Shakespeare, *Venus and Adonis*	
c.1595	Shakespeare, *Romeo and Juliet* written (pub. 1597, 1599)	
1595–6	Shakespeare, *A Midsummer Night's Dream* written (pub. 1600)	
c.1596–8	Shakespeare, *The Merchant of Venice* written (pub. 1600)	
c.1599	Shakespeare, *Julius Caesar* written (pub. 1623); *As You Like It* registered (pub. 1623)	
1599–1601	Shakespeare, *Hamlet* written (pub. 1603; short text)	
1601	Shakespeare, *Twelfth Night* written (pub. 1623)	
c.1602–4	Shakespeare, *Othello* written (pub. 1622)	
		James I (1603–1625)
1604	Marlowe (d. 1593), *Dr Faustus*	
1604–5	Shakespeare, *King Lear* written (pub. 1608); Cervantes, *Don Quixote*, I (ii, 1615)	Gunpowder Plot 1605
c.1606	Shakespeare, *Macbeth* written (pub. 1623)	
c.1606–7	Shakespeare, *Antony and Cleopatra* written (pub. 1623)	
1609	Shakespeare, *Sonnets*	

Date	Literary works	Historical events
1610–11	Shakespeare, *The Winter's Tale* written (pub. 1623);	
1611	Authorized Version of the Bible	
c.1611	Shakespeare, *The Tempest* written (pub. 1623) Jonson, *The Alchemist* (perf. 1610); Webster, *The White Devil*	
		Pilgrim Fathers emigrate to New World 1620
1623	Webster, *The Duchess of Malfi*; Shakespeare (d. 1616), 'First Folio'	
		Charles I (–1649) 1625
1631	Jonson, *Bartholomew Fair* (perf. 1614)	
1633	Donne (d. 1631), *Poems*	
1638	Milton, *Lycidas*	
		Civil War begins (–1649); public theatres closed (–1660) 1642 Execution of **Charles I**; **The Commonwealth** (–1660) 1649 massacres of Drogheda and Wexford 1650
1651	Hobbes, *Leviathan* (definitive Latin text 1668)	
		Act of Settlement (Ireland); Quakerism founded 1652 Oliver Cromwell becomes Protector 1653 The Restoration; **Charles II** (–1685); Samuel Pepys begins his diary (–1669); Anne Marshall first woman on English stage 1660
1662	Prayer Book (final version)	
		The Great Plague 1665 Great Fire of London 1666
1667	Milton, *Paradise Lost* (10 books)	
1674	Milton (d. 1674), *Paradise Lost* (2nd edn, 12 books)	
1677	Aphra Behn, *The Rover*, i (ii, 1681)	
1678	Bunyan, *Pilgrim's Progress*, i (ii pub. 1684)	
1681	Dryden, *Absalom and Achitophel*, i	
		Glorious Revolution 1688
1690	Locke, *Essay Concerning Human Understanding*	Battle of the Boyne 1690
1707	Watts, *Hymns*	Union of England and Scotland 1707 first Copyright Act 1709
1712	Pope, *The Rape of the Lock* (in Lintot's *Miscellanies*)	

Date	*Literary works*	*Historical events*
1719	Defoe, *Robinson Crusoe*	
1726	Swift, *Gulliver's Travels*	
1734	George Sale, first English translation of the Qur'ān	
1739	Hume, *Treatise of Human Nature* (completed 1740); John and Charles Wesley, *Hymns and Sacred Poems*	
1740	Thomson, *Alfred* (containing 'Rule Britannia'); Richardson, *Pamela*	
1743	Blair, *The Grave*	
		Second Jacobite Rebellion 1745
1747	Richardson, *Clarissa* (8 vols, 1747–9)	
1749	Fielding, *The History of Tom Jones*	
1751	Gray, *Elegy Written in a Country Church-Yard*	
		Gregorian Calendar adopted: eleven days 'lost' 1752
1755	Johnson, *A Dictionary of the English Language*	
1757	Burke, *Philosophical Enquiry into . . . the Sublime and the Beautiful*	
1759	Johnson, *Rasselas;* Voltaire, *Candide*	British Museum opens 1759
1760	Sterne, *The Life and Opinions of Tristram Shandy*, i–ii (iii–vi: 1761–2; vii and viii: 1765; ix: 1767)	
1762	Macpherson, *Fingal, an Ancient Epic Poem*	
1765	Percy, *Reliques of Ancient English Poetry;* Walpole, *The Castle of Otranto*	
1773	Goldsmith, *She Stoops to Conquer*	Boston Tea Party 1773
1774	Goethe, *Die Leiden des jungen Werthers* (The Sorrows of Young Werther)	War of American Independence 1775
1776	Gibbon, *Decline and Fall of the Roman Empire*, i (ii and iii: 1781; iv–vi: 1788); Smith, *The Wealth of Nations*	American Declaration of Independence 1776
1783	Crabbe, *The Village*	
1786	Burns, *Poems Chiefly in the Scottish Dialect*	
		American Constitution signed 1787
1789	Blake, *Songs of Innocence*; Equiano, *Interesting Narrative*; G. White, *The Natural History of Selborne*	French Revolution 1789

Date	Literary works	Historical events
1791	Blake, *The French Revolution*; Boswell, *The Life of Samuel Johnson*; Paine, *The Rights of Man*, i (ii: 1792)	
1792	Mary Wollstonecraft, *A Vindication of the Rights of Woman*	Monarchy abolished in France 1792
		Execution of Louis XVI (Jan.1793) French reign of terror 1793–4)
1794	Blake, *Songs of Experience*; Radcliffe, *The Mysteries of Udolpho*	
1795	Blake, *Songs of Innocence and Experience*	
1798	Malthus, *An Essay on the Principles of Population*; Wordsworth and Coleridge, *Lyrical Ballads* (1st edn; 2nd edn 1800, rev 1802)	
1799	Mungo Park, *Travels in the Interior of Africa*	
1801	Edgeworth, *Moral Tales for Young People*	Union with Ireland 1801
1802	Paley, *Natural Theology*	
		Napoleonic wars 1803–15 Battle of Trafalgar 1805 Abolition of slave trade 1807 Peninsular War begins 1808
1812	Byron, *Childe Harold*, i and ii (iii–iv, 1816–18)	
1813	Austen, *Pride and Prejudice*	
1814	Austen, *Mansfield Park*; W. Scott, *Waverley*	
		Defeat of Napoleon at Battle of Waterloo, 18 June 1815
1816	Austen, *Emma*; Coleridge, *Christabel and Other Poems*	
1818	M. Shelley, *Frankenstein*	
1819	Byron, *Don Juan*, i and ii (iii–xvi, 1821–4)	Peterloo massacre 1819
1820	Clare, *Poems, Descriptive of Rural Life*; Keats, *Lamia*; P. B. Shelley, *Prometheus Unbound*	
		Famine in Ireland (1821–3) Stockton and Darlington passenger railway opened 1825 Catholic Emancipation 1829
1825	Hazlitt, *The Spirit of the Age*	
1830	Cobbett, *Rural Rides*	
1832	Tennyson, *Poems* (inc. 'The Lady of Shalott')	First [Parliamentary] Reform Bill 1832

Date	*Literary works*	*Historical events*
1833	Newman, Pusey et al., *Tracts for the Times* (90 numbers, 1833–41)	Slavery Abolition Act 1833
1837	Dickens, *The Pickwick Papers*	Accession of **Victoria** (d. 1901) Sir Charles Lyell, *Elements of Geology* 1838
1842	Tennyson, *Poems* (inc. 'Morte d'Arthur')	
1843	Dickens, *A Christmas Carol*; Ruskin, *Modern Painters*, i (ii: 1846; iii and iv 1856; v: 1860)	
1844	Disraeli, *Coningsby*	
1845	Poe, *Tales of Mystery and Imagination*	
1846	G. Eliot, tr. Strauss's *The Life of Jesus Critically Examined*	
1847	A. Brontë, *Agnes Grey* (by 'Acton Bell'); C. Brontë, *Jane Eyre* (by 'Currer Bell'); E. Brontë, *Wuthering Heights* (by 'Ellis Bell')	
1848	Gaskell, *Mary Barton*; Thackeray, *Vanity Fair* (vol. pub.)	European revolutions; Marx and Engels, *Communist Manifesto* 1848
1850	Dickens, *David Copperfield* (vol. pub.); Hawthorne, *The Scarlet Letter*; Tennyson, *In Memoriam*; Wordsworth, *The Prelude*	Public Libraries Act 1850

The Great Exhibition 1851 |
1852	Stowe, *Uncle Tom's Cabin*	
1853	Dickens, *Bleak House* (vol. pub.); Gaskell, *Ruth*; *Cranford* (vol. pub.)	
1854	Dickens, *Hard Times* (vol. pub.); Thoreau, *Walden*	Crimean War 1853–6.
1855	R. Browning, *Men and Women*; Whitman, *Leaves of Grass*	National Portrait Gallery founded 1856
1857	Trollope, *Barchester Towers*	Museum of Ornamental Art (Victoria and Albert Museum) founded; Baudelaire, *Les Fleurs du mal*

Indian Mutiny 1857–8 |
1859	C. Darwin, *On the Origin of Species by Means of Natural Selection*	
1860	Collins, *The Woman in White* (vol. pub.); G. Eliot, *The Mill on the Floss*	
1861	Dickens, *Great Expectations* (vol. pub.)	American Civil War (1861–5)
1862	C. Rossetti, *Goblin Market and Other Poems*	
1863–9	Tolstoy, *War and Peace*	

Date	Literary works	Historical events
1865	Carroll, *Alice in Wonderland*	Abraham Lincoln assassinated 1865
1866	Dostoevsky, *Crime and Punishment*	
1869	M. Arnold, *Culture and Anarchy*; J. S. Mill, *On the Subjection of Women*	
		First Married Women's Property Act 1870
1872	G. Eliot, *Middlemarch* (vol. pub.)	
1874	Hardy, *Far from the Madding Crowd*	
1881	H. James, *Portrait of a Lady*	
1888	Conan Doyle, *A Study in Scarlet*	
		Ibsen's *A Doll's House* perf. in England 1889
1891	Hardy, *Tess of the d'Urbervilles*; Wilde, *The Picture of Dorian Gray*	
1894	Kipling, *The Jungle Book*; Beardsley et al., *The Yellow Book* (-1897)	
1895	Hardy, *Jude the Obscure*; Wells, *The Time Machine*	Wilde convicted of gross indecency
1898	Wilde, *The Ballad of Reading Gaol*	
		Second Anglo-Boer War 1899-1902
1900	Sigmund Freud, *The Interpretation of Dreams*	
1901	Kipling, *Kim*; Chekhov, *Three Sisters*	
1902	Kipling, *Just So Stories*; Yeats, *Cathleen Ni Houlihan*	
1904	Barrie, *Peter Pan* (stage version); M. R. James, *Ghost Stories of an Antiquary*	Abbey Theatre, Dublin, founded 1904
1905	Wilde (d. 1900), *De Profundis*	Sinn Fein founded in Dublin 1905
1910	Buchan, *Prester John*; Forster, *Howards End*	
1912	Shaw, *Pygmalion*	*Titanic* sinks 1912
1913	D. H. Lawrence, *Sons and Lovers*; Proust, *Du côté de chez Swann* (*Swann's Way*, vol. i of *À la recherche du temps perdu*, completed 1927)	
1914	Hardy, *Satires of Circumstance*; Joyce, *Dubliners*	Britain declares war on Germany (4 Aug.)-1918
1915	F. M. Ford, *The Good Soldier*; D. H. Lawrence, *The Rainbow*	
1916	Joyce, *A Portrait of the Artist as a Young Man*	Easter Rising, Dublin 1916
1917	T. S. Eliot, *Prufrock*	Russian Revolution 1917
1918	R. Brooke (d. 1915), *Collected Poems*; Hopkins (d. 1889), *Poems*	'Spanish flu' pandemic; Armistice (11 Nov.); women over 30 gain vote 1918
1919	Sassoon, *War Poems*	Lady Astor first woman MP 1919
1920	Pound, *Hugh Selwyn Mauberley*	
		Irish Free State established 1921

Date	*Literary works*	*Historical events*
1922	T. S. Eliot, *The Waste Land*; Joyce, *Ulysses*	
1924	Forster, *A Passage to India*	First Labour government 1924
1925	F. Scott Fitzgerald, *The Great Gatsby*; V. Woolf, *Mrs Dalloway*	
1926	Christie, *The Murder of Roger Ackroyd*	General Strike 3–12 May 1926
1927	V. Woolf, *To the Lighthouse*	
1928	R. Hall, *The Well of Loneliness*; D. H. Lawrence, *Lady Chatterley's Lover* (privately printed, Florence); V. Woolf, *Orlando*; Yeats, *The Tower*	Women's Suffrage extended to women over 21 1928
1929	Faulkner, *The Sound and the Fury*; V. Woolf, *A Room of one's Own*	
1932	A. Huxley, *Brave New World*	
1936	Auden and Isherwood, *The Ascent of F6* (perf. 1937)	Edward VIII abdicates (11 Dec.) 1936; BBC Television Service begins (Nov. 1936); Spanish Civil War 1936–9
1937	Orwell, *The Road to Wigan Pier*	
1939	Steinbeck, *The Grapes of Wrath*	Second World War begins (3 Sept.) 1939
1940	Auden, *Another Time*; Greene, *The Power and the Glory*	Fall of France; Battle of Britain 1940
		Japanese attack Pearl Harbor; USA, and Soviet Union enter war 1941
1944	T. S. Eliot, *Four Quartets*	Normandy landings (6 June); Education Act 1944
1945	Orwell, *Animal Farm*; E. Waugh, *Brideshead Revisited*	Second World War ends; Labour election landslide 1945
		Partition of India, Pakistan established 1947
1948	Pound, *Pisan Cantos*	Gandhi assassinated; the *SS Empire Windrush* brings first large group of West Indian immigrants to Britain 1948
1949	Orwell, *Nineteen Eighty-Four*	
1951	Salinger, *The Catcher in the Rye*; Wyndham, *The Day of the Triffids*	Defection of Burgess and Maclean, Russian spies 1951
1952	Christie, *The Mousetrap*	
1953	Baldwin, *Go Tell It on the Mountain*; R. Bradbury, *Fahrenheit 451*; I. Fleming, *Casino Royale*; A. Miller, *The Crucible*	Conquest of Everest; execution of Rosenbergs in USA 1953
1954	Golding, *Lord of the Flies*; Tolkien, *The Lord of the Rings*(–1955)	
1955	Beckett, *Waiting for Godot*; Larkin, *The Less Deceived*; Nabokov, *Lolita*	

Date	*Literary works*	*Historical events*
1956	J. Osborne, *Look Back in Anger*	Suez crisis; first Aldermaston CND march; Hungarian uprising 1956
1957	Ted Hughes, *The Hawk in the Rain*	
1958	Achebe, *Things Fall Apart*; Sillitoe, *Saturday Night and Sunday Morning*	
		Leavis and Snow 'Two Cultures' debate 1959
1960	D. H. Lawrence (d. 1930), *Lady Chatterley's Lover* (full text); Harper Lee, *To Kill a Mockingbird;* Pinter, *The Caretaker*	
1961	Heller, *Catch-22*	Berlin Wall built 1961
1962	D. Lessing, *The Golden Notebook*	
1963	Plath, *The Bell Jar*	
		Vietnam War 1964–75; Nelson Mandela imprisoned 1964–90
1965	Plath, *Ariel*	Malcolm X assassinated 1965
1966	Bunting, *Briggflatts;* Drabble, *The Millstone;* Heaney, *Death of a Naturalist*	
1967	A. Carter, *The Magic Toyshop*	Sexual Offences Act partially decriminalizes homosexual acts 1967; Nigerian Civil War 1967–70 Martin Luther King assassinated; Theatres Act abolishes power of lord chamberlain 1968
1969	Roth, *Portnoy's Complaint*	Manned landing on the moon 1969
1970	Hare, *Slag*; Ted Hughes, *Crow*	
1971	G. Hill, *Mercian Hymns*	
1972	Heaney, *Wintering Out*; Stoppard, *Jumpers*	'Bloody Sunday' (Belfast) 30 October 1972
		Britain enters Common Market 1973
1974	Larkin, *High Windows*; le Carré, *Tinker, Tailor, Soldier, Spy*	
1978	Potter, *Brimstone and Treacle*	
1979	A. Carter, *The Bloody Chamber and Other Stories*; Naipaul, *A Bend in the River*	Conservative government elected in Britain (Thatcher) 1979–90
1981	Rushdie, *Midnight's Children*	
1983	Weldon, *The Life and Loves of a She-Devil*	
1984	M. Amis, *Money*; I. Banks, *The Wasp Factory*; A. Carter, *Nights at the Circus*	
1985	Atwood, *The Handmaid's Tale*	
1986	Seth, *The Golden Gate*	
1987	C. Churchill, *Serious Money*; T. Morrison, *Beloved*	
1988	Rushdie, *The Satanic Verses*	
1989	M. Amis, *London Fields*	*Fatwa* issued against Salman Rushdie 1989

Date	Literary works	Historical events
		Sir Tim Berners-Lee initiates the World Wide Web; reunification of Germany; Nelson Mandela released 1990
1993	Stoppard, *Arcadia*; Welsh, *Trainspotting*	
1994	Jonathan Coe, *What a Carve Up!*	Mandela becomes president of South Africa; IRA ceasefire 1994
1995	Barker, *The Ghost Road*; Pullman, *His Dark Materials* (–2000)	Ken Saro-Wiwa hanged in Nigeria 1995
1997	D'Aguiar, *Feeding the Ghosts*; J. K. Rowling, *Harry Potter and the Philosopher's Stone*	Labour government elected in Britain; Diana, princess of Wales d. 1997
1998	Ted Hughes, *Birthday Letters*	
		Scottish parliament restored 1999
2001	McEwan, *Atonement*	9/11 terrorist attack in New York; USA invades Afghanistan 2001
2004	Alan Hollinghurst, *The Line of Beauty*	Boxing Day tsunami in Indian Ocean 2004
		Hurricane Katrina floods New Orleans 2005
2006	Seamus Heaney, *District and Circle*	
2007	J. K. Rowling, *Harry Potter and the Deathly Hallows*	
		Financial crisis threatens global economy; Barack Obama elected president of the United States of America 2008
2009	Colm Tóibín, *Brooklyn*; Hilary Mantel, *Wolf Hall*	
2010	Yiyun Li, *Gold Boy, Emerald Girl*	
2011	Julian Barnes, *The Sense of an Ending*	'Arab Spring' pro-democracy uprisings 2011

Appendix 2. Poets Laureate

1616–37	Ben *Jonson
1638–?	Sir William *D'Avenant

Official Holders

1668–89	John *Dryden
1689–92	Thomas *Shadwell
1692–1715	Nahum *Tate
1715–18	Nicholas *Rowe
1718–30	Laurence Eusden
1730–57	Colley *Cibber
1757–85	William *Whitehead
1785–90	Thomas *Warton
1790–1813	Henry James *Pye
1813–43	Robert *Southey
1843–50	William *Wordsworth
1850–92	Alfred *Tennyson
1896–1913	Alfred *Austin
1913–30	Robert *Bridges
1930–67	John *Masefield
1968–72	Cecil *Day-Lewis
1972–84	Sir John *Betjeman
1984–98	Ted *Hughes
1999–2009	Andrew *Motion
2009–2019	Carol Ann *Duffy

Appendix 3. Children's Laureates

Appendix 4. Literary Awards

(A) Nobel Prize for Literature

1901	René-François-Armand-Sully Prudhomme	1946	Hermann *Hesse
1902	Theodor Mommsen	1947	André Gide
1903	Björnstjerne Björnson	1948	T. S. *Eliot
1904	José Echegaray/Frédéric Mistral	1949	William *Faulkner
1905	Henryk Sienkiewicz	1950	Bertrand *Russell
1906	Giosuè Carducci	1951	Pär Lagerkvist
1907	Rudyard *Kipling	1952	François Mauriac
1908	Rudolf Eucken	1953	Winston S. Churchill
1909	Selma Lagerlöf	1954	Ernest *Hemingway
1910	Paul Heyse	1955	Halldór Laxness
1911	Maurice Maeterlinck	1956	Juan Ramón Jiménez
1912	Gerhart Hauptmann	1957	Albert *Camus
1913	Rabindranath *Tagore	1958	Boris *Pasternak
1914	No award	1959	Salvatore Quasimodo
1915	Romain Rolland	1960	Saint-John Perse
1916	Verner von Heidenstam	1961	Ivo Andrić
1917	Karl Gjellerup/Henrik Pontoppidan	1962	John *Steinbeck
1918	No award	1963	George Seferis
1919	Carl Spitteler	1964	Jean-Paul *Sartre
1920	Knut Hamsun	1965	Mikhail *Sholokhov
1921	Anatole France	1966	S. Y. Agnon/Nelly Sachs
1922	Jacinto Benavente y Martínez	1967	Miguel Angel Asturias
1923	W. B. *Yeats	1968	Yasunari Kawabata
1924	Władysław Reymont	1969	Samuel *Beckett
1925	G. B. *Shaw	1970	Alexander *Solzhenitsyn
1926	Grazia Deledda	1971	Pablo *Neruda
1927	Henri *Bergson	1972	Heinrich Böll
1928	Sigrid Undset	1973	Patrick *White
1929	Thomas Mann	1974	Eyvind Johnson/Harry Martinson
1930	Sinclair *Lewis	1975	Eugenio Montale
1931	Erik Axel Karlfeldt	1976	Saul *Bellow
1932	John *Galsworthy	1977	Vicente Aleixandre
1933	Ivan *Bunin	1978	Isaac Bashevis *Singer
1934	Luigi *Pirandello	1979	Odysseus *Elytis
1935	No award	1980	Czesław *Miłosz
1936	Eugene *O'Neill	1981	Elias Canetti
1937	Roger Martin du Gard	1982	Gabriel *García Márquez
1938	Pearl S. *Buck	1983	William *Golding
1939	F. E. Sillanpää	1984	Jaroslav Seifert
1940–3	No awards	1985	Claude Simon
1944	Johannes V. Jensen	1986	Wole *Soyinka
1945	Gabriela Mistral	1987	Joseph *Brodsky
		1988	Naguib *Mahfouz

1989	Camilo José Cela	2001	V. S. *Naipaul
1990	Octavio Paz	2002	Imre Kertesz
1991	Nadine *Gordimer	2003	J. M. *Coetzee
1992	Derek *Walcott	2004	Elfriede Jelinek
1993	Toni *Morrison	2005	Harold *Pinter
1994	Kenzaburo Oë	2006	Orhan Pamuk
1995	Seamus *Heaney	2007	Doris *Lessing
1996	Wisława *Szymborska	2008	Jean-Marie *Le Clézio
1997	Dario Fo	2009	Herta Müller
1998	José *Saramago	2010	Mario Vargas Llosa
1999	Günter *Grass	2011	Tomas Tranströmer
2000	Gao Xingjian		

(B) Pulitzer Prize for Fiction

1918	Ernest Poole, *His Family*
1919	Booth Tarkington, *The Magnificent Ambersons*
1920	No award
1921	Edith *Wharton, *The Age of Innocence*
1922	Booth Tarkington, *Alice Adams*
1923	Willa *Cather, *One of Ours*
1924	Margaret Wilson, *The Able McLaughlins*
1925	Edna *Ferber, *So Big*
1926	Sinclair *Lewis, *Arrowsmith*
1927	Louis Bromfield, *Early Autumn*
1928	Thornton *Wilder, *The Bridge of San Luis Rey*
1929	Julia Peterkin, *Scarlet Sister Mary*
1930	Oliver La Farge, *Laughing Boy*
1931	Margaret Ayer Barnes, *Years of Grace*
1932	Pearl S. *Buck, *The Good Earth*
1933	T. S. Stribling, *The Store*
1934	Caroline Miller, *Lamb in his Bosom*
1935	Josephine Winslow Johnson, *Now in November*
1936	Harold L. Davis, *Honey in the Horn*
1937	Margaret *Mitchell, *Gone with the Wind*
1938	John Phillips Marquand, *The Late George Apley*
1939	Marjorie Kinnan Rawlings, *The Yearling*
1940	John *Steinbeck, *The Grapes of Wrath*
1941	No award
1942	Ellen Glasgow, *In This our Life*
1943	Upton *Sinclair, *Dragon's Teeth*
1944	Martin Flavin, *Journey in the Dark*
1945	John *Hersey, *A Bell for Adano*
1946	No award
1947	Robert Penn *Warren, *All the King's Men*
1948	James A. *Michener, *Tales of the South Pacific*
1949	James Gould Cozzens, *Guard of Honour*
1950	A. B. Guthrie Jr, *The Way West*
1951	Conrad Richter, *The Town*

1952	Herman Wouk, *The Caine Mutiny*
1953	Ernest *Hemingway, *The Old Man and the Sea*
1954	No award
1955	William *Faulkner, *A Fable*
1956	Mackinley Kanter, *Andersonville*
1957	No award
1958	James Agee, *A Death in the Family*
1959	Robert Lewis Taylor, *The Travels of Jamie McPheeters*
1960	Allen Drury, *Advise and Consent*
1961	Harper *Lee, *To Kill a Mockingbird*
1962	Edwin O'Connor, *The Edge of Sadness*
1963	William *Faulkner, *The Reivers*
1964	No award
1965	Shirley Ann Grau, *The Keepers of the House*
1966	Katherine Anne *Porter, *The Collected Stories of Katherine Anne Porter*
1967	Bernard *Malamud, *The Fixer*
1968	William *Styron, *The Confessions of Nat Turner*
1969	N. Scott *Momaday, *House Made of Dawn*
1970	Jean *Stafford, *Collected Stories*
1971	No award
1972	Wallace Stegner, *Angle of Repose*
1973	Eudora *Welty, *The Optimist's Daughter*
1974	No award
1975	Michael Shaara, *The Killer Angels*
1976	Saul *Bellow, *Humboldt's Gift*
1977	No award
1978	James Alan McPherson, *Elbow Room*
1979	John *Cheever, *The Stories of John Cheever*
1980	Norman *Mailer, *The Executioner's Song*
1981	John Kennedy *Toole, *A Confederacy of Dunces*
1982	John *Updike, *Rabbit is Rich*
1983	Alice *Walker, *The Color Purple*
1984	William Kennedy, *Ironweed*
1985	Alison *Lurie, *Foreign Affairs*
1986	Larry *McMurtry, *Lonesome Dove*
1987	Peter Taylor, *A Summons to Memphis*
1988	Toni *Morrison, *Beloved*
1989	Anne *Tyler, *Breathing Lessons*
1990	Oscar Hijuelos, *The Mambo Kings Play Songs of Love*
1991	John *Updike, *Rabbit at Rest*
1992	Jane *Smiley, *A Thousand Acres*
1993	Robert Olen Butler, *A Good Scent from a Strange Mountain*
1994	E. A. *Proulx, *The Shipping News*
1995	Carol *Shields, *The Stone Diaries*
1996	Richard Ford, *Independence Day*
1997	Steven Millhauser, *Martin Dressler: The Tale of an American Dreamer*
1998	Philip *Roth, *American Pastoral*
1999	Michael Cunningham, *The Hours*
2000	Jhumpa Lahiri, *Interpreter of Maladies*
2001	Michael Chabon, *The Amazing Adventures of Kavalier & Clay*
2002	Richard Russo, *Empire Falls*

2003	Jeffrey Eugenides, *Middlesex*
2004	Edward P. Jones, *The Known World*
2005	Marilynne *Robinson, *Gilead*
2006	Geraldine Brooks, *March*
2007	Cormac *McCarthy, *The Road*
2008	Junot Diaz, *The Brief Wondrous Life of Oscar Wao*
2009	Elizabeth Strout, *Olive Kitteridge*
2010	Paul Harding, *Tinkers*
2011	Jennifer Egan, *A Visit From the Goon Squad*

(C) CILIP (Library Association) Carnegie Medallists

Instituted in 1936 to mark the centenary of the birth of Andrew Carnegie, philanthropist and benefactor of libraries, the CILIP (Library Association) Carnegie Medal is awarded annually for an outstanding book for children written in English and receiving its first publication in the United Kingdom during the preceding year. Before 2007 the year refers to when the book was published rather than when the medal was awarded i.e. the 2005 winner was announced and the medal presented in July 2006.

1936	Arthur *Ransome, *Pigeon Post*
1937	Eve *Garnett, *The Family from One End Street*
1938	Noel *Streatfeild, *The Circus is Coming*
1939	Eleanor Doorly, *The Radium Woman* (children's biography of Marie Curie)
1940	Kitty Barne, *Visitors from London*
1941	Mary Treadgold, *We Couldn't Leave Dinah*
1942	'B. B.' (D. J. Watkins-Pitchford), *The Little Grey Men*
1943	No award
1944	Eric *Linklater, *The Wind on the Moon*
1945	No award
1946	Elizabeth *Goudge, *The Little White Horse*
1947	Walter *de la Mare, *Collected Stories for Children*
1948	Richard Armstrong, *Sea Change*
1949	Agnes Allen, *The Story of your Home* (non-fiction)
1950	Elfrida Vipont, *The Lark on the Wing*
1951	Cynthia *Harnett, *The Wool-Pack*
1952	Mary *Norton, *The Borrowers*
1953	Edward Osmond, *A Valley Grows Up* (non-fiction)
1954	Ronald Welch, *Knight Crusaders*
1955	Eleanor *Farjeon, *The Little Bookroom*
1956	C. S. *Lewis, *The Last Battle*
1957	William *Mayne, *A Grass Rope*
1958	Philippa *Pearce, *Tom's Midnight Garden*
1959	Rosemary *Sutcliff, *The Lantern Bearers*
1960	Ian W. Cornwall and Howard M. Maitland, *The Making of Man* (non-fiction)
1961	Lucy M. *Boston, *A Stranger at Green Knowe*
1962	Pauline Clarke, *The Twelve and the Genii*
1963	Hester Burton, *Time of Trial*
1964	Sheena Porter, *Nordy Bank*
1965	Philip Turner, *The Grange at High Force*
1966	No award
1967	Alan *Garner, *The Owl Service*
1968	Rosemary Harris, *The Moon in the Cloud*

a	1969	K. M. *Peyton, *The Edge of the Cloud*
	1970	Edward Blishen and Leon *Garfield, *The God Beneath the Sea*
	1971	Ivan Southall, *Josh*
	1972	Richard *Adams, *Watership Down*
	1973	Penelope *Lively, *The Ghost of Thomas Kempe*
	1974	Mollie Hunter, *The Stronghold*
	1975	Robert *Westall, *The Machine-Gunners*
	1976	Jan *Mark, *Thunder and Lightnings*
	1977	Gene Kemp, *The Turbulent Term of Tyke Tyler*
	1978	David Rees, *The Exeter Blitz*
	1979	Peter *Dickinson, *Tulku*
	1980	Peter *Dickinson, *City of Gold*
	1981	Robert *Westall, *The Scarecrows*
	1982	Margaret *Mahy, *The Haunting*
	1983	Jan *Mark, *Handles*
	1984	Margaret *Mahy, *The Changeover*
	1985	Kevin *Crossley-Holland, *Storm*
	1986	Berlie Doherty, *Granny Was a Buffer Girl*
	1987	Susan *Price, *The Ghost Drum*
	1988	Geraldine *McCaughrean, *A Pack of Lies*
	1989	Anne *Fine, *Goggle-Eyes*
	1990	Gillian *Cross, *Wolf*
	1991	Berlie Doherty, *Dear Nobody*
	1992	Anne *Fine, *Flour Babies*
	1993	Robert *Swindells, *Stone Cold*
	1994	Theresa Breslin, *Whispers in the Graveyard*
	1995	Philip *Pullman, *Northern Lights*
	1996	Melvin *Burgess, *Junk*
	1997	Tim Bowler, *River Boy*
	1998	David *Almond, *Skellig*
	1999	Aidan *Chambers, *Postcards from No Man's Land*
	2000	Beverley Naidoo, *The Other Side of Truth*
	2001	Terry *Pratchett, *The Amazing Maurice and his Educated Rodents*
	2002	Sharon Creech, *Ruby Holler*
	2003	Jennifer Donnelly, *A Gathering Light*
	2004	Frank Cottrell Boyce, *Millions*
	2005	Mal Peet, *Tamar*
	2007	Meg Rosoff, *Just in Case*
	2008	Philip Reeve, *Here Lies Arthur*
	2009	Siobhan Dowd, *Bog Child*
	2010	Neil Gaiman, *The Graveyard Book*
	2011	Patrick Ness, *Monsters of Men*

(D) Man Booker Prize for Fiction (Booker Prize until 2002)

1969	P. H. *Newby, *Something to Answer for*
1970	Bernice *Rubens, *The Elected Member*
1971	V. S. *Naipaul, *In a Free State*
1972	John *Berger, *G*
1973	J. G. *Farrell, *The Siege of Krishnapur*
1974	Nadine *Gordimer, *The Conservationist*; Stanley *Middleton, *Holiday*
1975	Ruth Prawer *Jhabvala, *Heat and Dust*
1976	David *Storey, *Saville*
1977	Paul *Scott, *Staying On*
1978	Iris *Murdoch, *The Sea, the Sea*
1979	Penelope *Fitzgerald, *Offshore*
1980	William *Golding, *Rites of Passage*
1981	Salman *Rushdie, *Midnight's Children*
1982	Thomas *Keneally, *Schindler's Ark*
1983	J. M. *Coetzee, *Life and Times of Michael K*
1984	Anita *Brookner, *Hotel du Lac*
1985	Keri Hulme, *The Bone People*
1986	Kingsley *Amis, *The Old Devils*
1987	Penelope *Lively, *Moon Tiger*
1988	Peter *Carey, *Oscar and Lucinda*
1989	Kazuo *Ishiguro, *The Remains of the Day*
1990	A. S. *Byatt, *Possession*
1991	Ben *Okri, *The Famished Road*
1992	Michael *Ondaatje, *The English Patient*; Barry *Unsworth, *Sacred Hunger*
1993	Roddy *Doyle, *Paddy Clarke Ha Ha Ha*
1994	James *Kelman, *How Late It Was, How Late*
1995	Pat *Barker, *The Ghost Road*
1996	Graham *Swift, *Last Orders*
1997	Arundhati *Roy, *The God of Small Things*
1998	Ian *McEwan, *Amsterdam*
1999	J. M. *Coetzee, *Disgrace*
2000	Margaret *Atwood, *The Blind Assassin*
2001	Peter *Carey, *True History of the Kelly Gang*
2002	Yann *Martel, *Life of Pi*
2003	DBC Pierre, *Vernon God Little*
2004	Alan *Hollinghurst, *The Line of Beauty*
2005	John *Banville, *The Sea*
2006	Kiran *Desai, *The Inheritance of Loss*
2007	Anne *Enright, *The Gathering*
2008	Aravind Adiga, *The White Tiger*
2009	Hilary Mantel, *Wolf Hall*
2010	Howard Jacobson, *The Finkler Question*
2011	Julian Barnes, *The Sense of an Ending*

(E) King's and Queen's Gold Medal for Poetry

The Gold Medal for Poetry was instituted by George V in 1933 at the suggestion of the poet laureate, John Masefield. The medal is awarded for an outstanding book of verse published by an author from the United Kingdom or (from 1985) the Commonwealth. The nominating committee is chaired by the poet laureate. Until 2009 the announcement of the award was made on the birthday of William Shakespeare; the medal is now presented with the New Year's Honours, following an announcement in late December.

1934	Laurence Whistler	1974	Ted *Hughes
1937	W. H. *Auden	1977	Norman *Nicholson
1940	Michael Thwaites	1981	D. J. *Enright
1952	Andrew *Young	1986	Norman *MacCaig
1953	Arthur *Waley	1988	Derek *Walcott
1954	Ralph *Hodgson	1989	Allen *Curnow
1955	Ruth Pitter	1990	Sorley *Maclean
1956	Edmund *Blunden	1991	Judith *Wright
1957	Siegfried *Sassoon	1992	Kathleen *Raine
1959	Frances *Cornford	1996	Peter *Redgrove
1960	John *Betjeman	1998	Les *Murray
1962	Christopher *Fry	2000	Edwin *Morgan
1963	William *Plomer	2001	Michael *Longley
1964	R. S. *Thomas	2002	Peter *Porter
1965	Philip *Larkin	2003	U. A. *Fanthorpe
1967	Charles *Causley	2004	Hugo *Williams
1968	Robert *Graves	2006	Fleur *Adcock
1969	Stevie *Smith	2007	James *Fenton
1970	Roy *Fuller	2009	Don *Paterson
1971	Stephen *Spender	2010	Gillian Clarke
1973	John *Heath-Stubbs	2011	Jo Shapcott

(F) T. S. Eliot Prize for Poetry

The T. S. Eliot Poetry Prize is awarded by the Poetry Book Society annually to the best collection of new poetry in English published in the UK or the Republic of Ireland. It was inaugurated in 1993, to celebrate the Poetry Book Society's 40th birthday and honour its founding poet, T. S. Eliot. The prize money is donated by his widow, Valerie Eliot.

1993	Ciaran *Carson, *First Language: Poems*
1994	Paul *Muldoon, *The Annals of Chile*
1995	Mark Doty, *My Alexandria*
1996	Les *Murray, *Subhuman Redneck Poems*
1997	Don *Paterson, *God's Gift to Women*
1998	Ted *Hughes, *Birthday Letters*
1999	Hugo *Williams, *Billy's Rain*
2000	Michael *Longley, *The Weather in Japan*
2001	Anne Carson, *The Beauty of the Husband*
2002	Alice *Oswald, *Dart*
2003	Don *Paterson, *Landing Light*
2004	George *Szirtes, *Reel*
2005	Carol Ann *Duffy, *Rapture*
2006	Seamus *Heaney, *District and Circle*
2007	Sean *O'Brien, *The Drowned Book*
2008	Jen *Hadfield, *Nigh-No-Place*
2009	Phillip *Gross, *The Water Table*
2010	Derek Walcott, *White Egrets*
2011	John *Burnside, *Black Cat Bone*

Oxford Paperback Reference

The Concise Oxford Companion to English Literature
Dinah Birch and Katy Hooper

Based on the best-selling *Oxford Companion to English Literature*, this is an indispensable guide to all aspects of English literature.

Review of the parent volume
'the foremost work of reference in its field'

Literary Review

A Dictionary of Shakespeare
Stanley Wells

Compiled by one of the best-known international authorities on the playwright's works, this dictionary offers up-to-date information on all aspects of Shakespeare, both in his own time and in later ages.

The Oxford Dictionary of Literary Terms
Chris Baldick

A best-selling dictionary, covering all aspects of literature, this is an essential reference work for students of literature in any language.

A Dictionary of Critical Theory
Ian Buchanan

The invaluable multidisciplinary guide to theory, covering movements, theories, and events.

'an excellent gateway into critical theory' *Literature and Theology*

Oxford Paperback Reference

The Concise Oxford Dictionary of English Etymology
T. F. Hoad

A wealth of information about our language and its history, this
reference source provides over 17,000 entries on word origins.

'A model of its kind'

Daily Telegraph

A Dictionary of Euphemisms
R. W. Holder

This hugely entertaining collection draws together euphemisms from all
aspects of life: work, sexuality, age, money, and politics.

Review of the previous edition
'This ingenious collection is not only very funny but extremely
instructive too'

Iris Murdoch

The Oxford Dictionary of Slang
John Ayto

Containing over 10,000 words and phrases, this is the ideal reference for
those interested in the more quirky and unofficial words used in the
English language.

'hours of happy browsing for language lovers'

Observer

OXFORD

Oxford Paperback Reference

The Kings and Queens of Britain
John Cannon and Anne Hargreaves

A detailed, fully-illustrated history ranging from mythical and pre-conquest rulers to the present House of Windsor, featuring regional maps and genealogies.

A Dictionary of World History

Over 4,000 entries on everything from prehistory to recent changes in world affairs. An excellent overview of world history.

A Dictionary of British History
Edited by John Cannon

An invaluable source of information covering the history of Britain over the past two millennia. Over 3,000 entries written by more than 100 specialist contributors.

Review of the parent volume
'the range is impressive ... truly (almost) all of human life is here'
Kenneth Morgan, *Observer*

The Oxford Companion to Irish History
Edited by S. J. Connolly

A wide-ranging and authoritative guide to all aspects of Ireland's past from prehistoric times to the present day.

'packed with small nuggets of knowledge' *Daily Telegraph*

The Oxford Companion to Scottish History
Edited by Michael Lynch

The definitive guide to twenty centuries of life in Scotland.
'exemplary and wonderfully readable'

Financial Times

OXFORD

Oxford Paperback Reference

The Concise Oxford Dictionary of Art & Artists
Ian Chilvers

Based on the highly praised *Oxford Dictionary of Art*, over 2,000 up-to-date entries on painting, sculpture, and the graphic arts.

'the best and most inclusive single volume available, immensely useful and very well written'

Marina Vaizey, *Sunday Times*

The Concise Oxford Dictionary of Art Terms
Michael Clarke

Written by the Director of the National Gallery of Scotland, over 1,800 entries cover periods, styles, materials, techniques, and foreign terms.

A Dictionary of Architecture and Landscape Architecture
James Stevens Curl

Over 5,000 entries and 250 illustrations cover all periods of Western architectural history.

'splendid ... you can't have a more concise, entertaining, and informative guide to the words of architecture.'

Architectural Review

'excellent, and amazing value for money ... by far the best thing of its kind.'

Professor David Walker

Oxford Paperback Reference

The Concise Oxford Dictionary of Quotations
SIXTH EDITION
Edited by Susan Ratcliffe

Now based on the highly acclaimed seventh edition of *The Oxford Dictionary of Quotations*, this new edition maintains its extensive coverage of literary and historical quotations, and contains completely up-to-date material. A fascinating read and an essential reference tool.

Oxford Dictionary of Quotations by Subject
Edited by Susan Ratcliffe

The ideal place to discover what's been said about what, the dictionary presents quotations on nearly 600 areas of special interest and concern in today's world.

The Oxford Dictionary of Humorous Quotations
Edited by Ned Sherrin

From the sharply witty to the downright hilarious, this sparkling collection will appeal to all senses of humour.

The Oxford Dictionary of Political Quotations
Edited by Antony Jay

This lively and illuminating dictionary from the writer of 'Yes Minister' presents a vintage crop of over 4,000 political quotations. Ranging from the pivotal and momentous to the rhetorical, the sincere, the bemused, the tongue-in-cheek, and the downright rude, examples include memorable words from the old hands as well as from contemporary politicians.

'funny, striking, thought-provoking and incisive ... will appeal to those browsing through it as least as much as to those who wish to use it as a work of reference'
Observer

Oxford Dictionary of Modern Quotations
Edited by Elizabeth Knowles

The answers to all your quotation questions lie in this delightful collection of over 5,000 of the twentieth century's most famous quotations.

'Hard to sum up a book so useful, wayward and enjoyable'
Spectator

OXFORD